THE ROUGH GUIDE TO

Mexico

This tenth edition updated by

Alasdair Baverstock, Sarah Hull, Stephen Keeling
and Shafik Meghji

ROUGH
GUIDES

roughguides.com

Contents

3 3113 03298 9354

Introduction to
Mexico

The home of tacos, Aztecs, sombreros and tequila – not to mention Pancho Villa, Salma Hayek and Frida Kahlo – almost everyone on the planet knows something about Mexico. Yet there's a lot more to this country beyond the stereotypes. One of the world's great civilizations, Mexico offers a tantalizing blend of Mesoamerican cultures, Spanish traditions and contemporary arts. Its landscapes range from the shimmering blue coastline of Baja California and the iconic cactus-strewn deserts of the north, to the Maya villages and gorgeous palm-smothered beaches of the south. You can climb volcanoes, watch whales and tour agave farms. And sprinkled throughout you'll find richly adorned colonial churches, giant pyramids and a sophisticated cuisine.

The 122 million people of Mexico reflect this variety, too. Communities of full-blooded **indígenas** represent around ten percent of the population, with the Nahua, Maya, Zapotec, Mixtec, Otomí and Totonac the largest groups. There are also a few Mexicans of pure **Spanish** or European descent, invariably forming the ranks of the mega rich, even if billionaire Carlos Slim (see p.8) is actually of Lebanese ancestry. The great majority of the population (over eighty percent), though, is **mestizo**, combining in themselves European and indigenous traditions with, to a greater or lesser extent, a veneer of urban sophistication. Add in a multitude of distinct regional identities, from the cowboy culture of the northern deserts to the Mesoamerican traditions of the south, and you have a thrilling, constantly surprising place to travel.

Despite the inevitable influence of the US, looming to the north, and close links with the rest of the Spanish-speaking world (an avid audience for Mexican pop and soap operas), the country remains resolutely individual. The music that fills the plazas in the evenings, the buildings that circle around them, even the smells emanating from a row of taco carts: they all leave you without any doubt about where you are.

Many first-time visitors are surprised to find that Mexico is far from being a "developing" nation: the country has a robust economy, the world's fifteenth largest, a

ABOVE PYRAMID OF KUKULCÁN, CHICHÉN NUEVO **OPPOSITE** QUETZAL DANCERS IN AZTEC COSTUMES, PUEBLA remarkably thorough and efficient internal transport system and a vibrant contemporary arts and music scene. Indeed, in the last twenty years or so Mexico has finally become a **middle-class society**, perhaps the country's greatest achievement since Independence. Mexico has the highest GDP in Latin America after Brazil, reduced inflation, interest rates at record lows and increased per capita income, despite huge inequalities of wealth.

It's certainly not all suburbs and SUVs quite yet, though; adventure can still be found through happening upon a **village fiesta**, complete with a muddy bullfight and rowdy dancing, or hopping on a rural bus, packed with farmers all carrying machetes half their height and curious about how you've wound up going their way. It's also true that Mexico is not always an easy place to travel around. The power may go off, the water may not be drinkable. Occasionally it can seem that there's incessant, inescapable noise and dirt. And although the *mañana* mentality is largely an outsiders' myth, rural Mexico is still a land where timetables are not always to be entirely trusted, where anything that can break down will break down (when it's most needed) and where any attempt to do things in a hurry is liable to be frustrated.

More deeply disturbing are the extremes of ostentatious wealth and grim poverty that still exist, most poignantly in the big cities, where unemployment is high and living conditions beyond crowded, as well as the ongoing **drug wars** that provide a seemingly non-stop stream of sensational, often gruesome, headlines. While the violence is very real in some parts of the country, the danger for tourists is minimal – for the most part, you'll find this is a friendly, varied and enormously enjoyable place in which to travel.

San Diego
Tijuana
Ensenada
Mexicali
Phoenix
8
Sonoita
Tucson
10
25
USA
Nogales
Agua Prieta
El Paso
Ciudad Juárez
HWY 1
HWY 45
Río Bravo
10
10
Río Grande
Hermosillo
Guerrero Negro
Guaymas
Ciudad Obregón
Alamos
Creel
Barranca del Cobre
Chihuahua
Santa Rosalía
Hidalgo del Parral
Jiménez
Sea of Cortez
Los Mochis
Culiacán
Torreón
HWY 40
Tropic of Cancer
La Paz
Durango
Cabo San Lucas
San José del Cabo
Mazatlán
Zacatecas
Aguascalientes
Leó
Guanajuat
San Blas
Tepic
Guadalajara
PACIFIC
OCEAN
Puerto Vallarta
HWY 200
Laguna de Chapala
Morel
Pátzcuaro
Uruapan
Barra de Navidad
Colima
Manzanillo
Lázaro Cárdenas
Ixta
Zihuataneju

Metres
2000
1500
1000
500
200
0

MEXICO

Where to go

Mexico City, though a nightmare of urban sprawl, is totally fascinating, and in every way – artistic, political, cultural – the capital of the nation. Around the city lie the chief relics of the pre-Hispanic cultures of central Mexico: the massive pyramids of **Teotihuacán** and the main Toltec site at **Tula**. **Guadalajara**, to the west, is a city on a more human scale, capital of the state of **Jalisco** and in easy reach of **Michoacán**: between them, these states share some of the most gently scenic country in Mexico, where the thickly forested hills are studded with lakes and ancient villages.

South of the capital, the states of Oaxaca and Chiapas, home to some of the largest populations of pure indigenous groups, are mountainous and beautiful, too, but in a far wilder way. The city of **Oaxaca** is especially enticing, with an extraordinary mix of colonial and indigenous life, superb markets and fascinating archeological sites. Likewise, the strength of indigenous traditions in and around the market town of **San Cristóbal de las Casas** in Chiapas continues to make it a big travellers' centre. It's typically the stop before the picturesque Maya ruins of **Palenque**. East into the **Yucatán** there is also traditional indigenous life, side by side with a tourist industry based around truly magnificent Maya cities – **Chichén Itzá** and **Uxmal** above all – and the burgeoning Caribbean resorts that stretch down the coast from **Cancún**.

On the Pacific coast, where the surf is wilder and the scenery more rugged than in the Caribbean, **Acapulco** is the best known of the beach destinations. Along the ocean to the north, hundreds of kilometres of relatively empty sand are broken up only by resort cities like **Mazatlán** and **Puerto Vallarta**. Few tourists venture over to the Gulf coast, despite the attractions of **Veracruz** and its mysterious ruins. A pity, as for music and general bonhomie, the city's central plaza is one of the country's finest destinations.

Coming through the **Bajío**, the heart of the country, you'll pass the beautiful silver-mining towns of **Zacatecas** and **Guanajuato**, the historic centres of **San Miguel de**

Allende and **Querétaro**, and many smaller places with a legacy of superb colonial architecture. Between here and the US border lie vast deserts and mountain ranges, home to the **Copper Canyon**, with its spectacular rail journey, the mysterious ruins at **Paquimé** and the dynamic industrial city of **Monterrey**. **Baja California** in the far northwest of Mexico is a major destination in its own right, with world-class whale watching, untrammelled beaches and crumbling Spanish ruins.

MEXICO'S MAGNIFICENT MARKETS

The colour and bustle of Mexico's **markets** is hard to beat. Even if you have no intention of buying, half an hour is always well spent meandering through narrow aisles surrounded by heaps of perfectly ripe fruit and stacks of *nopal* cactus leaves (though stay away from the meat sections if you're at all squeamish). In small villages, like those around Oaxaca (see p.610), inhabitants still recognize one day of the week as the traditional market day.

Towns of any size will have a market, usually daily, an important centre of local life and source of cheap eats (San Cristóbal de las Casas and Papantla are good examples), while in the cities, each *barrio* has its own vibrant mercado: among the best are Mexico City's **La Merced** (see p.135) and the arts and crafts-oriented Ciudadela (see p.135). Markets in San Miguel Allende are also better known for arts and crafts (see p.333), as are Oaxaca's city **mercados** (see p.596). Toluca (see p.191) is the mother of them all, Mexico's largest market held every Friday.

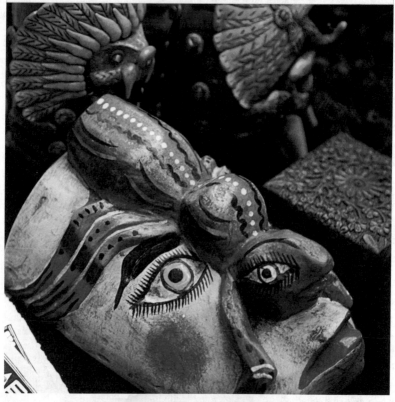

ABOVE TRADITIONAL MASKS **OPPOSITE FROM TOP** IGLESIA DE SAN JUAN BAUTISTA, SAN JUAN CHAMULA; CENOTE X'KEKEN, YUCATÁN

Author picks

Surviving 42-degree desert heat, tramping hurricane-battered Pacific beaches and scaling lofty volcanoes, our hard-travelling authors have visited every corner of this vast, magnificent country – from the ancient caves of Baja California to the dense rainforest of the Lacandón Jungle. Here are a few of their favourite things:

Dawn by kayak Paddling through the glassy, desert-backed waters of Bahía Concepción as the sun rises, surrounded by marine life, is an otherworldly experience (p.558).

Hit the Road Driving Hwy-1, from the US border to the southern tip of Baja California through deserts, isolated mountain ranges and tropical beach towns, rates as one of the world's greatest road journeys (p.529).

Get retro chic The 1950s meets modern cool at the *Boca Chica* hotel (p.207) in Acapulco, where fashionable *chilangos* sip cocktails at the pool above the madness at Playa Caleta.

Subterranean swimming The *cenotes* of northern Yucatán – vast sun-lit caverns filled with water – are magical places for a refreshing dip; X'keken and Samula are two of the best (p.756).

A window onto the Aztec world Rent a boat and soak up the carnival atmosphere, flowers and traditional floating gardens at the Mexico City suburb of Xochimilco (p.112).

Go syncretic The Iglesia de San Juan Bautista (p.674), in the village of San Juan Chamula, Chiapas, is an incredibly vibrant blend of Catholicism and animist tradition, with the local Maya praying on a floor of pine needles.

Best underground club You can't get more underground than *La Mina Club* (p.374) in Zacatecas – it's inside the old El Edén mine shafts.

Microbreweries Baja California's expanding craft beer scene can be sampled at *Plaza Fiesta* (p.535) and *La Taberna* (p.535) in Tijuana, *Cervecería Wendlandt* (p.543) in Ensenada and *Baja Brewing Co* in San José del Cabo (p.578).

Our author recommendations don't end here. We've flagged up our favourite places – a perfectly sited hotel, an atmospheric café, a special restaurant – throughout the guide, highlighted with the ★ symbol.

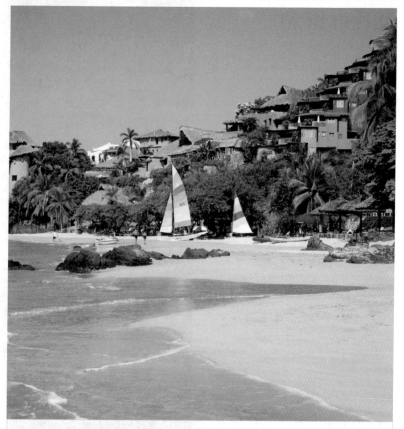

MEXICO'S BEST BEACHES

Mexico boasts a mesmerizing **coastline** of around 9330km, with millions of tourists coming here solely for the country's exceptional **beaches**. The following have been selected as much for the scene – whether backpacker or spring-breaker – as for sand quality, water and scenery.

Playa Cacaluta Wonderfully isolated Huatulco beach, accessible only by boat. See p.639

Mahahual A real castaway, end-of-the-world beach. See p.802

Playa La Audiencia, Manzanillo Bay Perfect cove of honey-coloured sands. See p.223

Playa de Balandra, La Paz Family friendly, shallow lagoons of crystal-clear water. See p.564

Playa Maruata, Michoacán Long, wild and mostly empty. See p.220

Playa El Requesón Gorgeous spit of sand jutting into the Sea of Cortez and surrounded by cactus-spiked mountains. See p.558

Playa La Ropa, Zihuatanejo Classic Pacific resort beach, hemmed in by palm trees (pictured above). See p.212

Tulum Maya ruins, pristine Caribbean waters and silky sands. See p.793

Yelapa, Puerto Vallarta Another beach only accessible by boat, lined with fun bars and palapa restaurants. See p.242

Zipolite This laid-back beach is a great place just to chill out. See p.634

CLIMATE

To convert °C to °F, multiply by 9, then divide by 5, then add 32.

	Jan	Mar	May	Jul	Sep	Nov
ACAPULCO						
Max/Min (°C)	31/22	31/22	32/25	33/25	32/25	32/24
Rainfall (mm)	13	5	0	203	279	15
MÉRIDA						
Max/Min (°C)	28/18	32/20	34/21	33/23	32/23	29/19
Rainfall (mm)	25	13	76	127	178	25
MEXICO CITY						
Max/Min (°C)	22/6	27/10	27/13	24/13	23/13	23/9
Rainfall (mm)	13	13	76	152	127	13
OAXACA						
Max/Min (°C)	28/8	32/12	32/15	28/15	27/15	28/10
Rainfall (mm)	51	25	127	203	279	51
TIJUANA						
Max/Min (°C)	20/6	21/8	23/12	27/16	27/16	23/10
Rainfall (mm)	51	25	5	0	13	25

When to go

Summer, from June to October, is in theory the **rainy season** in Mexico, but just how wet it is varies wildly from place to place. In the heart of the country you can expect a heavy but short-lived downpour virtually every afternoon; in the north hardly any rain falls, ever. Chiapas is the wettest state, with many minor roads washed out in the autumn, and in the south and low-lying coastal areas summer is stickily humid too. Along the beaches, September to mid-October is **hurricane season** – you'll usually get wet weather, choppy seas and mosquitoes, if not a full-on tropical storm. Late **winter** is the traditional tourist season, and in the big resorts like Acapulco and Cancún, the months from December through to April are the busiest. Mountain areas, though, can get very cold then; in fact, nights in the mountains can be extremely cold at any time of year.

Visitors come all year round – sticking on the whole to the highlands in summer and the coasts in winter. November is probably the ideal time to visit, with the rains over, the land still fresh and the peak season not yet begun.

30

things not to miss

It's not possible to see everything Mexico has to offer in one trip – and we don't suggest you try. What follows, in no particular order, is a selective taste of the country's highlights: ancient ruins, vibrant cities and spectacular landscapes. All highlights are colour-coded by chapter and have a page reference to take you straight into the Guide, where you can find out more.

1 GUANAJUATO
Page 345

This gorgeous colonial town, sandwiched into a narrow ravine, is home to one of the country's finest Baroque churches, a thriving student scene and a relaxed café and bar culture.

2 SILVER JEWELLERY FROM TAXCO
Page 184

The town of Taxco, an interesting place in itself, offers the most exquisite silver products in the country.

3 SIAN KA'AN BIOSPHERE RESERVE
Page 798

A huge, stunning coastal nature reserve with ecosystems ranging from tropical forest through fresh- and saltwater marshes to barrier reef. Wildlife of every sort lives here, but it's especially good for bird watching.

4 TEQUILA
Page 276

Visit the town that gave birth to Mexico's favourite tipple, surrounded by fields of blue agave, and enjoy tours of local distilleries.

5 THE BONAMPAK MURALS
Page 693

The ancient temples at Bonampak depict vivid scenes of Maya life.

6 BAJA BEACHES
Page 558

Tour the Sea of Cortez beaches along Bahía Concepción, with pristine azure waters contrasting with desert-fringed mountains.

7 EL TAJÍN
Page 420

Once the most important city on the Gulf coast but only rediscovered in 1785.

8 DIVING COZUMEL
Page 787

Mexico has fantastic diving opportunities: the coral reefs off Isla Cozumel provide some of the best.

9 BAJA WHALE WATCHING
Pages 551 & 553

From December to April, thousands of grey whales come to mate in the lagoons of Guerrero Negro and San Ignacio.

10 REAL DE CATORCE
Page 384

This picturesque ghost-town once thrived on the wealth of its silver mines. Huichol pilgrims visit the nearby desert in search of peyote.

11 THE ZÓCALO, MEXICO CITY
Page 69

The eternal heart of the city, the capital's main plaza is surrounded by its cathedral and the ruins of Aztec Tenochtitlán.

12 VOLADORES DE PAPANTLA
An ancient religious ritual, this gravity-defying spectacle is still mesmerizing.

13 CALAKMUL
Deep in the heart of the jungle, this is the largest-known archeological zone in Mesoamerica.

14 TULUM
This important Maya spiritual and cultural centre is one of the most picturesque, with a spectacular beach.

15 CENOTES, VALLADOLID
Take a refreshing dip in crystal-clear sinkholes, one with the roots of a huge alamo tree stretching down into it.

16 MUSEO FRIDA KAHLO
Politics, art and national identity combine at the home of Frida Kahlo and Diego Rivera.

17 THE RIVERA MURALS
Diego Rivera's murals at the Palacio Nacional in Mexico City.

18 PALENQUE
This Maya site is remarkable for its distinctive architectural style and its setting in jungle-smothered hills.

12

13

14

15

16

17

18

25 LAGO DE PÁTZCUARO
Page 294

Most famous for its Day of the Dead celebrations, this enchanting lake is a worthy destination year-round.

26 OAXACA MARKETS
Page 596

Any market in Mexico is a feast for the senses, but Oaxaca's are especially vibrant, with everything from fresh produce to some of the country's most imaginative textiles.

27 ACAPULCO'S CLIFF DIVERS
Page 211

Watch the *clavadistas* plunge into the sea from precipitous cliffs.

28 ZACATECAS
Page 366

Ancient silver mines, thrilling ziplines and one of Mexico's most opulent cathedrals.

29 CHARREADA
Page 52

If bullfights aren't for you, head to a *charreada* (rodeo) instead; the ultimate *charro* (cowboy) event, traditional *charreadas* make a brilliant spectator sport.

30 THE COPPER CANYON
Page 500

Whether you take the awe-inspiring train ride or hike along the canyon floor, a visit to this vast system of chasms is a definite highlight.

25

26

27

28

29

30

Itineraries

The following itineraries span the entire length of this incredibly diverse country, from the deserts and jaw-dropping canyons of the north to the grand colonial cities of the centre and the Maya ruins, beaches and jungles of the south. Given the vast distances involved, you may not be able to cover everything, but even picking a few highlights will give you a deeper insight into Mexico's natural and historic wonders.

CLASSIC MEXICO

This three-week tour focuses on the southern and central parts of the country, traditionally the most popular targets for independent travellers.

❶ **Mexico City** Soak up the museums, murals and markets of the nation's crazy, high-octane capital, leaving a couple of days for Cholula and Teotihuacán. **See p.64**

❷ **Oaxaca** Head to Mexico's most enticing state, its capital the best place to sample *mole*, mescal and indigenous crafts. **See p.586**

❸ **Zapotec and Mixtec heartland** After the obligatory visit to Monte Albán, spend two to three days exploring the indigenous markets and lesser-known ruins around Oaxaca. **See p.608**

❹ **San Cristóbal de las Casas** Heading east into Chiapas this colonial city is worth at least two days, plus a day or two to take in the remarkable Maya villages nearby. **See p.665**

❺ **Palenque** Heading north, these are some of the grandest jungle-smothered Maya ruins in the country, all easily accessible. **See p.684**

❻ **Yaxchilan and Bonampak** From Palenque you can strike out into the Lacandón Maya heartland and these more isolated, romantic ruins. **See p.695 & p.692**

❼ **Cozumel** Hit the Caribbean coast for the spectacular diving from this offshore island. **See p.787**

❽ **Playa del Carmen and Tulum** Back on the Yucatán mainland enjoy the balmy beaches and nightlife of the Riviera Maya. **See p.778 & p.790**

❾ **Chichén Itzá and cenotes** End your trip by soaking up Mexico's most magical Maya ruins followed by a dip in the cooling waters of a giant sinkhole. **See p.749 & p.752**

THE GREAT OUTDOORS

Mexico is home to exceptionally varied landscapes and ecosystems, but you can get a decent taster in two to three weeks. This tour starts at the US border and works south.

❶ **Whale watching in Baja** Witness the annual grey whale migration from the central Baja towns of Guerrero Negro and San Ignacio. **See p.551 & p.553**

❷ **Cave paintings** Arrange guides in San Ignacio or Mulegé to visit the enigmatic prehistoric cave art of the Sierra de San Francisco. **See p.553 & p.557**

❸ **Bahía Concepción** South of Mulegé lie the finest beaches in Baja, perfect for kayaking or just lounging on the sands. **See p.558**

ABOVE DRIVING AROUND REAL DE CATORCE

❹ Isla Espíritu Santo Take a day trip from La Paz to see sea lions, dolphins, manta rays and whale sharks frolicking. **See p.564**

❺ Copper Canyon Railway Take the ferry from La Paz to Los Mochis and the terminus for this thrilling train ride into the mountains. **See p.501**

❻ Hiking in the Sierra Tarahumara Jump off the Copper Canyon railway to explore remote trails, ruins and Rarámuri settlements. **See p.512**

❼ Costalegre Continue south along the Pacific to the wildest, least developed stretch of Mexican coast. **See p.229**

❽ Climbing volcanoes Head inland to conquer the majestic peak of the Nevado de Colima, or bypass Mexico City to check out volcanic activity at Popocatépetl. **See p.227 & p.171**

❾ Rafting at Jalcomulco End up on Mexico's Gulf coast near Xalapa for whitewater rafting, kayaking, climbing and canyoning. **See p.399**

RUTA DE LA PLATA (THE SILVER ROUTE)

Spanish Mexico was fuelled by silver, leaving a rich architectural and cultural legacy in the heart of the country. Take at least two weeks to travel this route between Mexico City and Monterrey.

❶ Taxco Start by loading up on jewellery at Mexico's silver capital, just south of Mexico City,

a confection of cobbled alleys and colonial, whitewashed homes. **See p.182**

❷ Real del Monte, Hidalgo Head north of Mexico City to this charming mountain retreat, an old mining town with a curious Cornish connection. **See p.155**

❸ Guanajuato Continue into the Bajío to enjoy the cafés, bars, restored mining shafts and creepy nineteenth-century mummies of this grand colonial silver town. **See p.345**

❹ San Miguel Allende Take the short bus ride to the most beautifully preserved and cosmopolitan town in the Bajío, crammed with art galleries and craft stalls. **See p.329**

❺ Pozos This crumbling mining community is a less developed, more romantic version of San Miguel, home to vast, abandoned mine workings. **See p.343**

❻ San Luis Potosí Dynamic, booming city with elegant Baroque buildings and museums dedicated to sculptor Federico Silva. **See p.377**

❼ Zacatecas The capital of the northern Bajío is rich in silver history, with the restored El Edén mine, silversmith school and spectacular art collections. **See p.366**

❽ Real de Catorce End with an extended stay among the colonial hotels, ruined mines and haunting desert scenery of this semi-ghost-town, halfway to Monterrey. **See p.384**

DELIVERING BREAD, MEXICO CITY

Basics

Getting there

The quickest and easiest way to get to Mexico is to fly. If you're willing to have your journey take a little longer, it is also possible to travel overland from the US via train, bus or car, or by water – several cruise lines stop along the country's Pacific and (to a lesser extent) Caribbean coasts.

To some extent, airfares to Mexico depend on the **season**. Ticket prices to Mexico City and other non-resort destinations show little, if any, fluctuation. Some fares though, especially to resort areas, do vary; they tend to be highest around Easter, from early June to mid-September and at Christmas and New Year. Prices may drop during the "shoulder" seasons – mid-September to early November and mid-April to early June – and the best deals are usually available during the low season (November to April, excluding Christmas and New Year). Flying at weekends can also sometimes add to round-trip fares; the round-trip prices quoted here assume mid-week travel and include tax.

Flights from the US and Canada

From most places in North America, flying is the most convenient way to reach Mexico. There are **flights** from just about every major **US** city, with the least expensive and most frequent leaving from "gateway" cities in the south and west, especially Dallas, Houston, Los Angeles and Miami. If you live close to the border, it's usually cheaper to cross into Mexico and take an **internal flight**. If it's a resort that you want, you may well find that one of the airlines offers an attractive deal including a few nights' accommodation.

Aeroméxico (**W**aeromexico.com) flies direct to dozens of destinations in Mexico, and can make connections to many others. The bigger US airlines – especially American Airlines (**W**aa.com), Delta (**W**delta.com), United (**W**united.com) and US Airways (**W**usairways.com) – have connections to Mexico City and the more popular resorts from all over the US. Budget Mexican airlines, such as Viva Aerobus (**W**vivaaerobus.com), Volaris (**W**volaris.mx) and Interjet (**W**interjet.com), also run flights into Mexico from a handful of American cities.

For the lowest-priced round trip to Mexico City or Cancún in high season, expect to pay around US$420–450 out of Dallas, US$450–500 from Miami, US$400–500 from Houston, US$550–650 from New

York or US$400–500 from LA. There are direct flights to many parts of Mexico from numerous other US airports, but adding a feeder flight from any US or Canadian city to one of the main gateways should be straightforward.

There are fewer direct scheduled flights from **Canada** to Mexico, although Air Canada (**W**aircanada.com) flies to Mexico City from Toronto and Vancouver, and Aeroméxico flies there from Montréal. Air Canada also serves Cancún from Toronto and Montréal. However, the biggest choice of direct flights is offered by WestJet (**W**westjet.com), which does not serve Mexico City, but does have flights to Cancún and several other beach resorts from a number of Canadian airports, supplemented in some cases by Sunwing (**W**flysunwing.com), Air Transat (**W**airtransat.ca), and winter charter flights. Flying via the US expands your options further.

Typical lowest high-season round-trip fares to Mexico City or Cancún cost around Can$530–600 from Toronto, Can$550–620 from Montreal or Can$700–800 from Vancouver.

Flights from the UK and Ireland

BA (**W**britishairways.com) has direct scheduled flights from London to Mexico City and Cancún; Virgin (**W**virgin-atlantic.com) has direct flights to Cancún. There are also (generally cheaper) charter flights to Cancún from Gatwick, Birmingham and Manchester with Thomson (**W**thomson.co.uk) and Thomas Cook (**W**thomascook.com). Flying from anywhere else in the UK or Ireland, or to any other destination in Mexico, you will have to change planes somewhere.

Even from London, although a direct flight is easiest, it can be cheaper to take an indirect flight with a European or US carrier. From other British and Irish airports, you can either fly via London with BA, or use a European or North American airline, changing planes at their hub cities (Air Europa, for example, codeshares with Aeroméxico via Madrid;

waireuropa.com). Another possibility is to fly via the US and either continue overland or buy an onward flight once in the country. LA and Houston are logical points from which to set off overland, and, along with Miami, have reasonably priced onward flights to several Mexican destinations. **Prices** for scheduled return flights from London to Mexico City start at around £550 off-season, but can cost around £900 in August. A charter flight to Cancún can cost as little as £450 in low season, but up to £800 in August, and your stay will probably be limited to one or two weeks.

If flying via the US, it's worth checking if your transatlantic carrier has an **airpass** deal for non-US residents – most major US airlines do – by which you purchase coupons at a flat rate for a certain number of flights in North America (with a usual minimum of three). Depending on the airline, the pass will usually also include one or more destinations in Mexico and Canada.

From Australia, New Zealand and South Africa

The **high season** for flights to Mexico from the southern hemisphere is mid-June to mid-July and mid-December to mid-January, though prices do not vary vastly between seasons. There are no direct flights to Mexico from Australia, New Zealand or South Africa, so you will have to change planes somewhere en route.

From **Australia**, your widest choice of airlines is out of Sydney, where there are flights to Mexico with Delta (**w**delta.com) via LA or Houston, with United (**w**united.com) via LA, with Air Canada (**w**aircanada.com) via Vancouver, or with LAN (**w**lan.com) via Santiago de Chile. United also serve Melbourne. Otherwise, you can fly with Qantas (**w**qantas.com.au) from almost any Australian airport to LA, continuing to Mexico with an American or Mexican airline. Prices start at around Aus$1500 for the round trip.

From **New Zealand**, your choice is very similar: Air Canada via Vancouver, an American airline via LA or Auckland to LA with Air New Zealand

(**w**airnewzealand.com), continuing with a Mexican or American airline. From other New Zealand airports, you will probably need to change planes additionally at Auckland or Sydney. Prices start from around NZ$1700 return.

From **South Africa**, your most direct route is with Delta or United from Johannesburg via the US, or on SAA (**w**flysaa.com) in combination with an American or Mexican airline. You can also fly with a European airline such as KLM (**w**klm.com), Lufthansa (**w**lufthansa.com) or British Airways (**w**britishairways.com) via their hubs in Europe. From other South African airports, you'll usually have to fly via Johannesburg. Fares start at around R14,000 return.

Trains

US passenger **train** services reach the border at El Paso, on the LA–Dallas line. El Paso is served by Amtrak's *Sunset Limited* service three times weekly from New Orleans, Houston, Tucson and LA. The *Sunset Limited* also picks up Amtrak's *Texas Eagle* (from Chicago, St Louis, Little Rock and Dallas) overnight at San Antonio. The journey takes just over sixteen hours from LA, nineteen and a half from Houston, or – including an eight-hour layover in San Antonio – 26.5 hours from Dallas and 48.5 hours from Chicago.

Arrivals on these services (around 8am from LA, 4.15pm from Chicago and New Orleans) give you time to cross the border, have something to eat in Ciudad Juárez and catch a bus on to Mexico City.

Check current timetables with Amtrak (**T**1 800 872 7245, **w**amtrak.com).

Buses

US **bus** travel is pretty grim compared to the relative comfort of Amtrak, but you have a wider range of US border posts to choose from. Count on at least 52 hours' journey time from New York to El Paso or twelve hours from San Francisco to Tijuana – and at least a further day's travel from either point to Mexico City.

A BETTER KIND OF TRAVEL

At Rough Guides we are passionately committed to travel. We believe it helps us understand the world we live in and the people we share it with – and of course tourism is vital to many developing economies. But the scale of modern tourism has also damaged some places irreparably, and climate change is accelerated by most forms of transport, especially flying. All Rough Guides' flights are carbon-offset, and every year we donate money to a variety of environmental charities.

BORDER CROSSINGS

There are some forty **frontier posts** along the US–Mexico border. Many of them are only open during the day, and are more or less inaccessible without your own transport. For a full list, see ⓦapps.cbp.gov/bwt. The main ones, open 24 hours a day, seven days a week, are, from west to east:

San Diego, California (San Ysidro)–**Tijuana**, Baja California.
Calexico, California–**Mexicali**, Baja California.
Nogales, Arizona–**Nogales**, Sonora.
Douglas, Arizona–**Agua Prieta**, Sonora.
El Paso, Texas–**Ciudad Juárez**, Chihuahua.
Laredo, Texas–**Nuevo Laredo**, Tamaulipas.
Brownsville, Texas–**Matamoros**, Tamaulipas.

BORDER PRACTICALITIES

Crossing the border, especially on foot, it's easy to go straight past the immigration and customs checks. There's a **free zone** south of the frontier, and you can cross at will and stay for up to three days. If, as likely, you're heading further south, however, be sure to stop at the Mexican immigration office, pay the M$295 entry fee (*derecho de no inmigrante*), pick up a **tourist card (FMM)**, and get it stamped and your bags checked. Otherwise, you'll be stopped after some 20km and sent back to complete the formalities. See "Entry requirements", p.31, for more information.

TROUBLED AREAS

The area bordering the US, particularly **Ciudad Juárez**, and also Tijuana, are some of the biggest hot spots in Mexico's **drugs war** (see p.39). Extra caution should be exercised when crossing this area, especially by car.

Greyhound (☎1 800 231 2222 or ☎1 214 849 8100, ⓦgreyhound.com) runs regularly to all the major border crossings. Some of their buses will also take you over the frontier to a Mexican bus station, which saves a lot of hassle. Greyhound agents abroad should be able to reserve your through tickets with their Mexican counterparts, which is even more convenient but involves pre-planning. Additionally, many Mexican bus companies cross the border into the US, so that you can pick up a bus to Mexico City as far north as Houston or LA.

More countercultural, and arguably better value, are overland tours from San Francisco with Green Tortoise Adventure Travel (☎1 800 867 8647, ⓦgreentortoise.com). Converted school buses provide reasonably comfortable transport and sleeping space for up to 35 people; the clientele comes from all over the world, and communal alfresco cooking is the rule.

Driving

Taking your own **car** into Mexico will obviously give you a great deal more freedom, but it's an option fraught with complications. Aside from border formalities, you'll also have to contend with the state of the roads, the style of driving and the quality of the fuel.

Licences and permits

Driving licences from the US, Canada, the UK, Ireland, Australia, New Zealand and most European countries are valid in Mexico, but it's a good idea to arm yourself with an **International Driving Licence** – available from motoring organizations such as the AAA in the US, the CAA in Canada or the AA in Britain. If you fall foul of a Mexican traffic cop for any reason, show that first; if they abscond with it you at least still have your own licence.

As a rule, you can drive in Baja California, western Sonora and the Zona Libre (the border area extending roughly 25km into Mexico) without any special formalities. To drive elsewhere in Mexico, however, you must obtain a temporary **importation permit** (currently US$48.84) at the border, or online at ⓦbanjercito.com.mx (click on "Application for Temporary Import Permit for vehicles, boats and RVs").

To make sure you don't sell the car in Mexico or a neighbouring country, you'll also be required to post a cash bond, the amount of which will depend on the make and age of your vehicle, though it will be at least US$400 for a car less than five years old. This can be done in cash (US dollars only), or with the credit or debit card of the owner of the vehicle (who must be present), at Banjército, the Mexican army bank, which has offices at border

TOP 5 ARCHEOLOGICAL SITES
Chichén Itzá. See p.749.
Teotihuacán. See p.192.
Palenque. See p.684.
Calakmul p.811.
Monte Albán. See p.605.

posts specifically for the purpose. You'll need to show registration and title documents for the car, plus your driver's licence and passport, and you'll probably be asked to supply two photocopies of these as well as your tourist card.

The permits are good for 180 days, during which time you can drive your car out of Mexico and return, but there are penalties in force if you exceed the limit, including forfeiture of your vehicle, and you must be sure to have your importation permit terminated when you finally do leave, or the authorities may assume your vehicle is still in the country; if you write it off while you are in Mexico, you need to inform Mexican customs and obtain permission to leave without it.

Insurance

US and Canadian **auto insurance** policies don't cover Mexico, so you will need to take out a Mexican policy, available from numerous agencies on either side of every border post. Rates depend on the value of the vehicle and what kind of coverage you want, but figure on US$10–20 or so a day for basic liability on a short trip. To arrange a policy before leaving the US, call Instant Mexico Insurance Services (☎1 800 345 4701, ⓦinstant -mex-auto-insur.com), International Gateway (☎1 619 271 0572, ⓦigib.com), Oscar Padilla Mexican Insurance (☎1 800 466 7227, ⓦmexicaninsurance .com), or the acknowledged leader in the field, Sanborn's Insurance (☎1 800 222 0158, ⓦsanborns insurance.com).

To get discounts on insurance, it might be worth joining a travel club, such as Discover Baja Travel Club (☎1 800 727 2252, ⓦdiscoverbaja.com) or Sanborn's Sombrero Club (☎1 800 222 0158). These clubs typically also offer discounts on accommodation and free travel advice.

The American and Canadian AAs produce road maps and route planners for travel to Mexico, and members may qualify for discounted insurance at affiliated border agencies, but their emergency/breakdown services do not cover you once you are inside Mexico.

Boats

If you want to **sail** to Mexico in your own boat, similar conditions apply to those in effect for motor vehicles (see p.29).

Alternatively, you could take a **cruise**. Several lines offer cruises on the Pacific coast, most popularly between LA and Acapulco, stopping at Los Cabos, Mazatlán, Puerto Vallarta and Zihuatanejo. Others ply the Caribbean side out of Miami, taking in Cozumel, Playa del Carmen and other Mexican destinations. Prices start at around US$500 per person for a week-long cruise, plus airfare to the starting point, and go (way) up from there. Agencies specializing in cruises include those listed below.

AGENTS AND OPERATORS

Cathy Matos Mexican Tours UK ☎020 3592 6917, ⓦmextours .co.uk. A wide variety of tailor-made tours, including colonial cities, beaches, sightseeing and archeology, whale watching and destination weddings.

Journey Latin America UK ☎020 3432 6049, ⓦjourney latinamerica.co.uk. Well-established Latin America specialists offering a range of itineraries throughout the country, including ones focusing on the country's Maya and Aztec heritage.

My Mexico Tours US ☎1 831 476 9693, ⓦmymexicotours.com. A range of interesting small-group tours, on and off the beaten track, with an emphasis on getting to know the country.

North South Travel UK ☎01245 608 291, ⓦnorthsouthtravel .co.uk. Friendly, competitive travel agency, offering discounted fares. Profits are used to support projects in the developing world, especially promoting sustainable tourism.

STA Travel UK ☎0871 230 0040; US ☎1 800 781 4040; Australia ☎134 782; New Zealand ☎0800 474 400; South Africa ☎0861 781 781, ⓦstatravel.co.uk. Independent travel specialists, offering good discounts for students and under-26s.

Trailfinders UK ☎020 7368 1200, Ireland ☎01 677 7888, Australia ☎1300 780 212, ⓦtrailfinders.com. One of the best-informed and most efficient agents for independent travellers.

Travel Cuts Canada ☎1 800 667 2887, US ☎1 800 592 2887, ⓦtravelcuts.com. Canadian youth and student travel firm.

USIT Ireland ☎01 602 1906, Northern Ireland ☎028 9032 7111, ⓦusit.ie. Ireland's main youth and student travel specialists.

CRUISE LINE CONTACTS

Carnival Cruise Lines US & Canada ☎1 800 764 7419, UK ☎0843 374 2272, Australia ☎1 300 385 624 ⓦcarnival.com.

Holland America US & Canada ☎1 877 932 4259, UK ☎0845 351 0557, ⓦhollandamerica.com.

Royal Caribbean Cruises US & Canada ☎1 866 562 7625, UK ☎0844 493 4005, Australia ☎1 800 754 500, ⓦroyalcaribbean .com.

Entry requirements

Citizens of the US, Canada, the UK, Ireland, Australia, New Zealand, Japan and most EU countries do not need visas to enter Mexico as tourists for less than 180 days. Other Europeans can stay for ninety days. Non-US citizens travelling via the US, however, may need a US visa (see box below).

Visas, obtainable only through a consulate (in person or by mail), are required by nationals of South Africa and many developing countries, as well as by anyone entering Mexico to work, to study or for stays longer than six months. Business visitors usually need a Business Authorization Card available from consulates, but nationals of countries exempt from a tourist visa can enter on business for up to thirty days on a tourist card (see below). For more detailed information on who needs a visa, visit the website of the Instituto Nacional de Migración at ⓦinm.gob.mx (click on "English" top right).

Tourist cards and the derecho do no inmigrante

All visitors, regardless of nationality, need a valid **passport** and a **tourist card** (or FMM – *Forma Migratoria Múltiple*). The only exception applies to visits of less than three days to the 20km, duty-free strip adjoining the US border, into which you can come and go more or less as you please (though you still need a passport or photo ID). Visitors entering by land and passing beyond this Zona Libre (you'll be sent back at a checkpoint if you haven't been through customs and immigration) are also required to pay a M$295 *derecho de no inmigrante* entry fee, payable at a bank. Some land crossings have a bank at the border post, otherwise you'll need to go to a bank to pay it before you leave Mexico.

Tourist cards are otherwise free, and if you're flying direct, you should get one on the plane or from the airline before leaving. A good travel agent should be able to arrange one for you, too, and they're also issued by Mexican consulates (every major US city and most border towns have one), in person or by post. Finally, failing all these options, you should be able to get tourist cards at airports or border crossings on arrival. However, if they've run out, you'll have to twiddle your thumbs until the next batch comes in, and if your passport is not issued by a rich Western country, you may encounter difficulty in persuading border officials to give you a card at all; it's therefore preferable to get one in advance. Entering from Belize or Guatemala, it's not unknown for border posts to run out of tourist cards, or for officials to (illegally) demand a fee for issuing them. To find the address of an embassy or consulate not listed below, see under "Representaciones" at ⓦ sre.gob.mx.

Most people officially need a **passport** to pick up their tourist card, but for US and Canadian citizens entering by land, all that's required is proof of citizenship (an original birth certificate or notarized copy, for instance, or naturalization papers), along with some form of photo ID (such as a driver's licence). Passports are still best, however.

A tourist card is valid for a **single entry** only, so if you intend to enter and leave Mexico more than once you should pick up two or three. On the card, you are asked how long you intend to stay. Always apply for longer than you need, since getting an extension is a frustrating and time-consuming business. You don't always get the time you've asked for, and at land borders with Belize and Guatemala they sometimes only give fifteen or thirty days (though they may give you more if you specifically ask). Immigration officers sometimes ask to see bank statements or other proof of sufficient funds for your stay, especially if they judge that you do not look sufficiently wealthy (or are from a developing country).

Don't lose the tourist card stub that is given back to you after immigration inspection. You are legally required to carry it at all times, and if you have to show your papers, it's more important than your passport. It also has to be handed in on leaving the country – without it, you may encounter problems and delays. Note that, contrary to what crooked border officials may tell you, there is no exit fee when leaving Mexico.

> ## US VISAS
>
> Non-US citizens travelling via the US may need a **US visa**, even if they will only be In the country in transit. Citizens of the UK, Ireland, Australia, New Zealand and most Western European countries can enter under the Visa Waiver Program. Apply well in advance at ⓦesta.cbp.dhs .gov/esta. South African citizens need to obtain a visa. Visit the website of the US embassy in your country of residence for further details.

Should you lose your tourist card, or need to have it renewed, head for the nearest **immigration department office** (Departamento de Migración); there are branches in the biggest cities. In the case of renewal, it's far simpler to cross any of Mexico's borders (or even fly to Cuba or Jamaica) for a day and get a new card on re-entry than to apply for an extension; if you do apply to the immigration department, it's wise to do so a couple of weeks in advance, though you may be told to come back nearer the actual expiration date. Whatever else you may be told, branches of SECTUR (the tourist office) cannot renew expired tourist cards or replace lost ones – they will only direct you to the nearest immigration office.

MEXICAN CONSULATES AND EMBASSIES ABROAD

Australia 14 Perth Ave, Yarralumla, Canberra, ACT 2600 ☎ 02 6273 3963, ⓦ mexico.org.au.

Belize Corner of Wilson St and Newtown Barracks, Belize City ☎ 223 0193, ⓦ embamex.sre.gob.mx/belice.

Canada 45 O'Connor St, Suite 1000, Ottawa, ON K1P 1A4 ☎ 1 613 233 8988, ⓦ embamex.sre.gob.mx/canada; 2055 Peel, Suite 1000, Montreal, PQ H3A 1V4 ☎ 1 514 288 2502, ⓦ consulmex.sre.gob. mx/montreal; 11 King St W, Suite 350, Commerce Court W, Toronto, ON M5H 4C7 ☎ 1 416 368 2875, ⓦ consulmex.sre.gob.mx/toronto; 1177 W Hastings St, Suite 411, Vancouver, BC V6E 2K3 ☎ 1 604 684 3547, ⓦ consulmex.sre.gob.mx/vancouver; 833 4th Ave SW, Suite 1100, Calgary, AL T2P 3T5 ☎ 1 403 264 4819, ⓦ consulmex.sre .gob.mx/calgary.

Cuba 518 C 12 (at the corner of Ave 7ma), Reparto Miramar, Municipio Playa, Havana ☎ 204 7722, ⓦ embamex.sre.gob.mx /cuba.

Guatemala 7–57 2ª Av, Zona 10, Apartado Postal 01010, Guatemala City ☎ 2420 3400, ⓦ embamex.sre.gob.mx/ guatemala; 5 C 17–24, Zona 3, Quetzaltenango ☎ 7767 5542 to 4, ⓦ consulmex.sre.gob.mx/quetzaltenango; 3-A Av 4-74, Zona 1, Tecún Umán ☎ 7776 8114, ⓦ consulmex.sre.gob.mx/tecunuman.

Ireland 19 Raglan Rd, Ballsbridge, Dublin 4 ☎ 01 667 3105, ⓦ embamex.sre.gob.mx/irlanda.

New Zealand 185–187 Featherston St, Level 2 (AMP Chambers), Wellington ☎ 04 472 0555, ⓦ embamex.sre.gob.mx/ nuevazelandia.

South Africa Parkdev Building, Brooklyn Bridge, 570 Fehrsen St, Brooklyn, Pretoria 0181 ☎ 012 460 1004, ⓦ embamex.sre.gob.mx /sudafrica.

UK 16 St George St, London W1S 1FD ☎ 020 7499 8586, ⓦ embamex.sre.gob.mx/reinounido.

USA 1911 Pennsylvania Ave NW, Washington, DC 20006 ☎ 1 202 728 1600, ⓦ embamex.sre.gob.mx/eua; and in nearly fifty other US towns and cities, including these near the border:

Arizona 1201 F Ave, Douglas, AZ 85607 ☎ 1 520 364 3107, ⓦ consulmex.sre.gob.mx/douglas; 135 W Cardwell St, Nogales, AZ 85621 ☎ 1 602 287 2521, ⓦ consulmex.sre.gob.mx/nogales.

California 408 Heber Ave, Calexico, CA 92231–2811 ☎ 1 760 357 3863, ⓦ consulmex.sre.gob.mx/calexico; 1549 India St, San Diego, CA 92101 ☎ 1 619 231 8414, ⓦ consulmex.sre.gob.mx/sandiego.

Texas 301 Mexico Bvd, Suite F-2, Brownsville, TX 78520 ☎ 1 956 542 4431, ⓦ consulmex.sre.gob.mx/brownsville; 2398 Texas Spur 239, Del Rio, TX 78840–8980 ☎ 1 830 775 2352 or ☎ 1 866 701 7777, ⓦ consulmex.sre.gob.mx/delrio; 2252 E Garrison St, Eagle Pass, TX 78852 ☎ 1 830 773 9255 or 6, ⓦ consulmex.sre.gob.mx/ eaglepass; 910 E San Antonio Ave, El Paso, TX 79901 ☎ 1 915 549 0003, ⓦ consulmex.sre.gob.mx/elpaso; 1612 Farragut St, Laredo, TX 78040 ☎ 1 956 723 6369, ⓦ consulmex.sre.gob.mx/laredo; 600 S Broadway St, McAllen, TX 78501 ☎ 1 956 686 0243, ⓦ consulmex .sre.gob.mx/mcallen; 127 Navarro St, San Antonio, TX 78205 ☎ 1210 227 9145 or 6, ⓦ consulmex.sre.gob.mx/sanantonio.

Customs

Duty-free allowances into Mexico include: 20 packets of cigarettes, 25 cigars or 300g of tobacco; three litres of alcoholic drinks or six litres of wine; two cameras; one laptop; and three mobile phones. If you are carrying more than US\$10,000 with you, you must declare it. For full details, see ⓦ aduanas .gob.mx (click on "English" top right). Leaving Mexico, note that it is illegal to take antiquities (including Aztec and Maya artefacts) out of the country, and penalties are serious.

Getting around

Distances in Mexico can be huge, and if you're intending to travel on public transport, you should be prepared for some very long journeys. Getting from Tijuana to Mexico City, for example, can take nearly two days nonstop by bus. Although public transport at ground level is frequent and reasonably efficient everywhere, taking an internal flight at least once may be worthwhile for the time it saves.

By bus

Within Mexico, **buses** (long-distance buses are called *camiones* rather than *autobuses* in Mexican Spanish) are by far the most common and efficient form of public transport. The legendary craziness of Mexican bus drivers is largely a thing of the past, and many bus companies have installed warning lights and buzzers to indicate when the driver is exceeding the speed limit (though these are often ignored by the driver). In recent years the government has been trying to improve the safety record through regular mechanical checks and also with random alcohol and drug tests on the drivers.

Classes

There are basically two **classes** of bus, first (*primera*) and second (*segunda*), though on major long-distance routes there's often little to differentiate them. First-class vehicles have reserved seats, videos and air-conditioning (which can be fierce – you may want a jumper), though an increasing number of second-class lines have the same comforts. The main differences will be in the number of stops – second-class buses call at more places, and consequently take longer to get where they're going – and the fare, which is about ten percent higher on first-class services (sometimes a lot more). On important routes there are also **deluxe**, or **pullman**, buses, with names like *Primera Plus* or *Turistar Plus* and fares around thirty percent higher than those of first-class buses.

Stations

Most towns of any size have a modern **bus station**, known as the **Central Camionera** or **Central de Autobuses**. Don't let the word "central" fool you, as they are usually located a long way from the town centre. Where there is no unified terminus you may find separate first- and second-class terminals, or individual ones for each company, sometimes little more than bus stops at the side of the road. There is some form of baggage deposit (left luggage) office in most bus stations – usually known as a *guardería*, *consigna* or simply *equipaje*. Before leaving anything, make sure that the place will be open when you come to collect your bags. If there's no formal facility, staff at the bus companies' baggage dispatching offices can often be persuaded to look after your things for a short while.

Tickets

Always check your route and arrival time, and whenever possible buy **tickets** from the bus station in advance to get the best (or any) seats. Alternatively, try the operator's website or an agent such as Ticketbus (W ticketbus.com.mx). Prices are reasonable: a first-class ticket on the Cancún–Mérida route costs from M$370, for example. While there are very rarely problems getting a place on a bus from its point of origin or from really big towns, in smaller, mid-route places, you may have to wait for the bus to arrive (or at least to leave the previous stop) before discovering if there are any seats – the increased prevalence of computerized ticketing is easing the problem.

Timetables

Terms to look out for on the timetable, besides *local* and *de paso* (buses that originate in another destination), include *vía corta* (by the short route) and *directo* or *expreso* (direct/nonstop – in theory at least). *Salida* is departure, *llegada* arrival. A decent road map will be extremely helpful in working out which buses are going to pass through your destination. W ticketbus.com.mx is a useful site for checking schedules.

By air

There are more than fifty airports in Mexico with regular passenger **flights** run by local airlines, plus several smaller airports with feeder services. The big company – formerly state-owned and with international as well as domestic flights – is Aeroméxico

---

BANDITRY: A WARNING

You should be aware when driving in Mexico, especially in a foreign vehicle, of the danger of **bandits**. Robberies and even more serious assaults on motorists do occur, above all in the northwest and especially in the state of Sinaloa. This was something tragically highlighted in late 2015 when two Australian travellers driving through Sinaloa were stopped, robbed and shot dead by a gang. Robbers may try to make you stop by indicating that there is something wrong with your vehicle; they've also been known to pose as policemen, hitchhikers and motorists in distress, so think twice about offering a lift or a helping hand. On the other hand, there are plenty of legitimate police checkpoints along the main roads, where you must stop, and increased security (to combat the drug cartels) has very much reduced hold-ups of buses. Robbers mainly target cargo trucks rather than private cars, but it is nonetheless best to avoid driving at night, particularly in the north of the country, but also in Michoacán and Guerrero, on Hwy-200 along the Pacific coast from Jalisco to Oaxaca, and on Hwy-57 (Mexico City–San Luis Potosí–Matahuela). It's always safer to use a toll (*cuota*) highway than a free one. The US State Department currently advises its citizens to avoid travelling at night on highways anywhere in the country.

(@aeromexico.com), which connects most places to Mexico City, usually several times a day. There are numerous other smaller and no-frills airlines such as Aeromar (@aeromar.com.mx), Interjet (@interjet .com.mx), Volaris (@volaris.com), Mayair (@mayair .com.mx), Viva Aerobus (@vivaaerobus.com) and AeroServicio Guerrero (@asg.com.mx), which also cover most major destinations. Competition between the companies keeps prices steady and relatively low: a one-way trip between Mexico City and Cancún, for example, can cost as little as US$40.

Internal **airfares** reflect the popularity of the route: the more popular the trip, the lower the price. Thus the flight from Tijuana to Mexico City costs much the same as the much shorter but less popular flight from Tijuana to Chihuahua, but even the more expensive routes can be worthwhile for the time they save. While the smaller airlines might be cheaper, there are few discounts and the price of a ticket on a particular flight doesn't normally vary from agent to agent.

By rail

Since Mexico's railways were privatized in 1995, all passenger services have been withdrawn bar one suburban service out of Mexico City and a couple of tourist lines: the **Copper Canyon railway** in Chihuahua, an amazing scenic journey and one of the country's top tourist attractions (see p.501), and the **Tequila Express** from Guadalajara (see p.278).

By boat

Ferries connect Baja California with a trio of ports on the Pacific mainland: Santa Rosalía to Guaymas, and La Paz to Mazatlán and Topolobampo (for Los Mochis). For information on schedules and fares see @mexbound.com/mexico-ferry.php. There are also smaller boats to islands off the Caribbean and Gulf coasts: from Chiquilá to Isla Holbox, from Cancún to Isla Mujeres and from Playa del Carmen to Cozumel. Though more expensive than they once were, all these services are still pretty reasonable.

By car

Driving in Mexico requires care and concentration, and almost inevitably involves at least one brush with bureaucracy or the law (for details on licences and insurance, see p.55). Hitchhiking is possible, but due to safety concerns, the scarcity of lifts and the vast distances involved, it's not recommended.

DISTANCE CHART (IN KM)

	Acapulco	Aguas-calientes	Cancún	Chihuahua	Ciudad Juárez	Durango	Guadalajara	Matamoros
Acapulco	–	889	1951	1732	2109	1281	859	1361
Aguascalientes	889	–	2144	979	1356	417	250	819
Cancún	1951	2144	–	3086	3463	2524	2174	2331
Chihuahua	1732	979	3086	–	377	632	1188	1097
Ciudad Juárez	2109	1356	3463	377	–	1009	1565	1474
Durango	1281	417	2524	632	1009	–	556	880
Guadalajara	859	250	2174	1188	1565	556	–	995
Matamoros	1361	819	2331	1097	1474	880	995	–
Mérida	1647	1840	304	2782	3159	2220	1870	2027
Mexico City	390	514	1630	1456	1833	894	544	971
Monterrey	1341	582	2349	790	1167	573	771	307
Nogales	2572	1748	3855	769	635	1508	1698	2050
Oaxaca	653	984	1702	1938	2315	1376	1026	1368
San Luis Potosí	800	168	2043	1043	1420	481	344	651
Tampico	863	575	1833	1307	1684	888	751	498
Tijuana	3151	2504	4597	1532	1294	2087	2777	2629
Tuxtla Gutiérrez	967	1389	1155	2331	2708	1769	1419	1764
Veracruz	711	898	1332	1808	2185	1279	929	999
Villahermosa	1090	1283	861	2225	2602	1663	1313	1470

Car rental

Renting a car in Mexico is often an extremely good way of quickly seeing a small area that would take days to explore using public transport. Always check **rates** carefully to make sure they include insurance, tax and the mileage you need. Daily rates with unlimited mileage start at around US$50/£32; weekly rates usually cost around the same as six days. In some resorts **mopeds**, **motorbikes** and even **golf carts** are also available for short distances, but most of the large, international companies don't deal with them because of the high frequency of accidents.

Fuel

The government oil company, PEMEX, has a monopoly and sells two types of **petrol**: Magna Sin (regular unleaded), and Premium (high-octane unleaded). Both of these cost slightly more than regular unleaded north of the border, at about M$13.50–15 per US gallon.

Roads and traffic

Traffic circulates on the right, and the normal speed limit is 40km/h (25mph) in built-up areas, 70km/h (43mph) in open country and 110km/h (68mph) on the freeway. Some of the new highways are excellent, and the toll (*cuota*) superhighways are better still, though extremely expensive (check prices online at ⓦsct.gob.mx, clicking on "Tarifas vigentes de carreteras"). Away from the major population centres, however, roads are often narrow, winding and potholed, with livestock wandering across at unexpected moments. Get out of the way of Mexican bus and truck drivers – if you signal left to them on a stretch of open road, it means it's clear for them to overtake.

Every town and village limits the speed of through traffic with a series of *topes* (speed bumps) across the road. Look out for the warning signs and take them seriously; the bumps are often huge. It's wise to avoid driving at night, not only for road safety reasons, but also because of the threat of hold-ups (see box, p.33). Any good road map should provide details of the more common symbols used on Mexican **road signs**. One convention of note: the first driver to flash their lights at a junction, or where only one vehicle can pass, has the right of way – you're not being invited to go first.

Most large towns have extensive **one-way systems**. Traffic direction is often poorly marked (look for small arrows affixed to lampposts), though this is less of a problem than it sounds: simply note

Mérida	Mexico City	Monterrey	Nogales	Oaxaca	San Luis Potosí	Tampico	Tijuana	Tuxtla Gutiérrez	Veracruz	Villa-hermosa
1647	390	1341	2572	653	800	863	3151	967	711	1090
1840	514	582	1748	984	168	575	2504	1389	898	1283
304	1630	2349	3855	1702	2043	1833	4597	1155	1332	861
2782	1456	790	769	1938	1043	1307	1532	2331	1808	2225
3159	1833	1167	635	2315	1420	1684	1294	2708	2185	2602
2220	894	573	1508	1376	481	888	2087	1769	1279	1663
1870	544	771	1698	1026	344	751	2777	1419	929	1313
2027	971	307	2050	1368	651	498	2629	1764	999	1470
–	1326	2046	3551	1398	1739	1529	4293	851	1028	557
1326	–	954	2242	482	413	473	2821	875	385	769
2046	954	–	1743	1387	541	517	2322	1783	1018	1489
3551	2242	1743	–	2707	1812	2076	817	3100	2577	2994
1398	482	1387	2707	–	895	870	3303	547	369	841
1739	413	541	1812	895	–	407	2568	1288	798	1182
1529	473	517	2076	870	407	–	2839	1266	501	972
4293	2821	2322	817	3303	2568	2839	–	1070	305	776
851	875	1783	3100	547	1288	1266	1070	–	765	294
1028	385	1018	2577	369	798	501	305	765	–	471
557	769	1489	2994	841	1182	972	776	294	471	–

ADDRESSES

In Mexico **addresses** are frequently written with just the street name and number (thus: Madero 125), which can lead to confusion as many streets are known only as numbers (C 17). Calle (C) means "street"; Avenida (Av), Bulevar (Blv), Calzada and Paseo are other common terms – most are named after historical figures or dates. An address such as Hidalgo 39 8° 120, means Hidalgo no. 39, 8th floor, room 120 (a ground-floor address would be denoted PB for *planta baja*). Many towns have all their streets laid out in a **numbered grid** fanning out from a central point – often with odd-numbered streets running east–west, even ones north–south. In such places a suffix – Ote (for *Oriente*, East), Pte (for *Poniente*, West), Nte (for *Norte*, North) or Sur (South) – may be added to the street number to tell you which side of the two central dividing streets it is.

Note that "s/n" is used in an address to indicate "sin número", meaning that the building in question does not have a street number.

the direction in which the parked cars, if not the moving cars, are facing.

Parking

Parking restrictions are complicated and foreigners are easy pickings for traffic police, who usually remove one or both plates in lieu of a ticket (retrieving them can be an expensive and time-consuming business). Since **theft** is also a real threat, you should use a hotel with secure parking. In Mexico City, residents' cars are banned from driving on one day of every week, determined by their licence number (see p.70): the ban also applies to foreign cars, but rented vehicles are exempt.

Breakdowns and accidents

Unless your car is a basic-model VW, Ford or Dodge (all manufactured in Mexico), **spare parts** are expensive and hard to come by – bring a basic spares kit. Tyres in particular suffer on burning-hot Mexican roads, so you should carry at least one good spare. Roadside *vulcanizadoras* and *llanteros* can do temporary repairs; new tyres are expensive, but remoulds aren't a good idea on hot roads at high speed. If you have a breakdown on any highway between 8am and 8pm, there is a free mechanic service known as the **Ángeles Verdes** (Green Angels; ⓦav.sectur.gob.mx). As well as patrolling major routes looking for beleaguered motorists, they can be reached by phone on ☎078 or on local state hotlines, or by email at ✉angelesverdes@sectur.gob.mx, and they speak English.

Should you have a minor **accident**, try to come to some arrangement with the other party – involving the police will only make matters worse, and Mexican drivers will be just as anxious to avoid doing so. If you witness an accident, you may want to consider the gravity of the situation before getting involved. Witnesses can be locked up along

with those directly implicated to prevent them from leaving before the case comes up – so consider if your involvement is necessary to serve justice. In a serious incident, contact your consulate and your Mexican insurance company as soon as possible.

By bike

Mexico is not big on **cycling**, and with its vast size and the heavy and inconsiderate traffic in big cities, not to mention the danger of banditry, few tourists travel the country by bicycle. The Yucatán Peninsula, being quite flat, lends itself to cycling, and bicycles can be rented in Campeche, Isla Mujeres, Playa del Carmen, Isla Cozumel and Tulum (see p.722, p.774, p.780, p.787 & p.793). So does the area around Oaxaca, where you can also rent bikes (see p.598). Bicycle tour firms in Mexico include Bicicletas Pedro Martinez (ⓦbicicletas pedromartinez.com), ¡El Tour (ⓦbikemexico.com) and Backroads (ⓦbackroads.com).

Local transport

Public transport within Mexican towns and cities is always plentiful and inexpensive, though crowded and not particularly user-friendly. Mexico City has an excellent **metro** system and there are smaller metros in both Guadalajara and Monterrey. Elsewhere, however, you'll be reliant on buses (often a flat fare, though this varies from place to place). Wherever possible we've indicated which bus to take and where to catch it, but often only local people will fully understand the intricacies of the system and you may well have to ask: the main destinations of the bus are usually marked on the windscreen, which helps.

In bigger places *combis* or **colectivos** offer a faster and perhaps less crowded alternative for only a little more money. These are minibuses, vans or large sport utility vehicles that run along fixed routes to set destinations; they'll pick you up and drop you off wherever you like along the way, and you simply pay the driver for the distance travelled. In Mexico City, *combis* are known as **peseros**.

Taxis

Regular **taxis** can also be good value, but be aware of rip-offs – unless you're confident that the meter is working, fix a price before you get in. In the big cities, there are often tables of fixed prices posted at prominent spots. At almost every airport and at some of the biggest bus stations you'll find a booth selling vouchers for taxis into town at a fixed price depending on the part of town you want to go to – sometimes there's a choice of paying more for a private car or less to share. This will invariably cost less than just hailing a cab outside the terminal, and will certainly offer extra security. In every case you should know the name of a hotel to head for, or they'll take you to the one that pays the biggest commission. Never accept a ride in any kind of unofficial or unmarked taxi, and in Mexico City be especially cautious (see p.117).

Accommodation

Finding a room is rarely difficult – in areas that are not overly touristy the inexpensive places to stay are usually concentrated around the main plaza (the zócalo), with others near the market, train station or bus station (or where the bus station used to be, before it moved to the outskirts of town). In bigger cities, there's usually a relatively small area in which you'll find the bulk of the less expensive possibilities. The more modern and expensive places often lie on the outskirts of towns, accessible only by car or taxi. The only times you're likely to have big problems finding somewhere to stay are in coastal resorts over the peak Christmas season, **at Easter, on Mexican holidays and almost anywhere during a local fiesta, when it's well worth trying to reserve ahead.**

Hotels

Mexican hotels may describe themselves as anything from *paradores*, *posadas* and *casas de huéspedes* to plain *hoteles*, all terms that are used more or less interchangeably. A *parador* is totally unrelated to its top-end Spanish namesake, for example, and although in theory a *casa de huéspedes* means a small cheap place like a guesthouse, you won't necessarily find this to be the case.

All rooms should have an official **price** displayed. A room with one double bed (*cama matrimonial*) is almost always cheaper than a room with two singles (*doble* or *con dos camas*), and most hotels have large "family" rooms with several beds, which are tremendous value for groups. In the big resorts, there are lots of apartments that sleep six or more and include cooking facilities, for yet more savings. A little gentle haggling rarely goes amiss, and many places will have some rooms that cost less, so just ask ("*Tiene un cuarto mas barato?*").

A/c (*aire acondicionado*) is a feature that inflates prices – it is frequently optional. Unless it's very hot and humid, a room with a simple ceiling fan (*ventilador*) is generally fine. In winter, especially at altitude or in the desert, it will of course be **heating** rather than cooling that you want – if there isn't any, make sure there's enough bedding and ask for extra blankets if necessary.

When looking at a room, you should always check its **insect proofing**. Cockroaches and ants are common, and there's not much you can do about them, but decent netting will keep mosquitoes out.

Campsites, hammocks and cabañas

Camping is easy enough if you are hiking in the backcountry, or happy simply to crash on a beach, but **robberies** are common, especially in places

---

PRICES QUOTED IN THIS BOOK

The hotel prices we quote in this book are for the least expensive room for two people in high season, at the time the book was researched. Obviously the price may well have changed since then, and other options are usually available, including rooms with two beds, single rooms, dormitory accommodation in hostels and so on. Where appropriate, we also give prices for some of these. In instances where hotels quote in US dollars (particularly common on the Caribbean Coast; see box, p.675), this price is given first with the peso equivalent (at the time of research) following in brackets.

ACCOMMODATION ALTERNATIVES

Useful websites that provide alternatives to standard hotel and hostel accommodation:

Airbnb ⓦ airbnb.com.
CouchSurfing ⓦ couchsurfing.org.
Homestay ⓦ homestay.com.
Tripping ⓦ tripping.com.
Vacation Rentals by Owner ⓦ vrbo.com.

with a lot of tourists. There are very few organized campsites, and those that do exist are first and foremost trailer parks, not particularly pleasant to pitch tents in. Of course, if you have a van or **RV** you can use these or park just about anywhere else – there are a good number of facilities in the well-travelled areas, especially down the Pacific coast and Baja.

If you're planning to do a lot of camping, an **international camping card** is a good investment, serving as useful ID and getting you discounts at member sites. A range is available online.

In a lot of less official campsites, you will be able to rent a hammock and a place to sling it for the same price as pitching a tent (around US$5–10/£6.25–6.50), maybe less, especially if you're packing your own hammock (Mexico is a good place to buy these, especially in and around Mérida in the Yucatán).

Beach huts, or **cabañas**, are found at the more rustic, backpacker-oriented beach resorts, and sometimes inland. Usually just a wooden or palm-frond shack with a hammock slung up inside (or a place to sling your own), they are frequently without electricity, though as a resort gets more popular, they tend to transform into sturdier beach bungalows with modern conveniences and higher prices. At backwaters and beaches too untouristed even for cabañas, you should still be able to sling a hammock somewhere (probably the local bar or restaurant, where the palapa serves as shelter and shade).

TOP 5 PLACES TO STAY

Luz en Yucatán Mérida. See p.731.
Tribu Isla Holbox. See p.763.
Playa Frambes Lighthouse Resort Mulegé. See p.559.
Las Golondrinas Oaxaca. See p.601.
Quinta Chanabnal Palenque. See p.687.

Hostels

There are numerous hostels in Mexico, mainly concentrated in the more touristy areas. Some eighteen are affiliated to Hostelling International (ⓦ hihostels.com); an HI card gets you a small discount, but is not essential. HI-affiliated hostels, however, are not necessarily better than non-affiliated ones, of which there are many.

Crime and personal safety

Despite soaring crime rates and dismal-sounding statistics, you are unlikely to run into trouble in Mexico if you stick to well-travelled paths. Even in Mexico City, which has a dangerous reputation, the threat is not that much greater than in many large North American and European cities. Obviously there are areas in cities where you wander alone, or at night, at your peril; but the best precaution is common sense. The narco war (see box opposite) and the still-simmering conflict in Chiapas do not generally affect tourists.

Avoiding theft

Petty theft and **pickpockets** are your biggest worry in Mexico, so don't wave money around, try not to look too obviously affluent, don't leave cash or cameras in hotel rooms, and deposit your valuables in your hotel's safe if it has one (make a note of what you've deposited and ask the hotelier to sign it if you're worried). Crowds, especially on public city transport, are obvious hot spots: thieves tend to work in groups and target tourists. Distracting your attention, especially by pretending to look for something (always be suspicious of anyone who appears to be searching for something near you), or having one or two people pin you down while another goes through your pockets, are common ploys. Razoring of bags and pockets is another gambit, as is the more brutish grabbing of handbags, or anything left unattended even for a split second. **Mugging** is less common than pickpocketing, but you should steer clear of obvious danger spots, such as deserted pedestrian underpasses in big cities – indeed, avoid all deserted areas in big cities. Use ATMs in shopping malls or enclosed premises, and only in daylight when there are plenty of people around.

Robbery and sexual assault on tourists by cab drivers are not unknown, and it is not a good idea to hail a cab in the street in Mexico City (see p.117). Instead, phone for a radio cab or, failing that, take the next best option and get a cab from an official *sitio*. At night the beaches in tourist areas are also potentially dangerous.

When travelling, keep an eye on your bags (which are safe enough in the luggage compartments underneath most buses). Hold-ups of buses happen from time to time, and you may well be frisked on boarding to check for arms, since the bandits are most often passengers on the bus.

Drivers are likely to encounter problems if they leave anything in their car. The **vehicle** itself is less likely to be stolen than broken into for the valuables inside. To avoid the worst, always park legally (and preferably off the street) and never leave anything visible inside the car.

Police

Mexican **police** are poorly paid and **graft** is an accepted part of the job, though often difficult for foreign visitors to accept. If a policeman accuses you of some violation (this is almost bound to happen to drivers at some stage), explain that you're a tourist, not used to the ways of the country – you may get off scot-free, but more likely the subject of a "**fine**" will come up. Such on-the-spot fines are open to negotiation, but only if you're confident you've done nothing seriously wrong and have a reasonable command of Spanish. Otherwise pay up and get out.

These small bribes, known as *mordidas* (bites), may also be extracted by border officials or bureaucrats (in which case, you could get out of paying by asking for a receipt, but it won't make life easier). In general, it is always wise to back off from any sort of confrontation with the police and to be extremely polite to them at all times.

Far more common than the *mordida* is the **propina**, or tip, a payment made entirely on your initiative. There's no need to do this, but it's remarkable how often a few pesos complete paperwork that would otherwise take weeks, open firmly locked doors or even find a seat on a previously full bus. All such transactions are quite

THE DRUGS WAR

Mexico is a major staging post on the **cocaine-smuggling** route from South America to the US, and use of cocaine is widespread and growing, with **crack** a blight in parts of the capital and some northern cities. Also growing is the use of **methamphetamine** ("hielo"), which is manufactured in Mexico, especially in areas close to the US border. **Heroin** is also manufactured in some northern states. In this ever-growing and increasingly lucrative trade, powerful, well-connected cocaine- and methamphetamine-smuggling cartels, known as "**narcos**" have long fought over territory, with each gang having its own pet politicians and police in the states it controls.

The situation changed radically in 2007 when President Felipe Calderón declared war on the *narcos*, who turned their guns on the police and army as well as each other. Innocent civilians often got caught in the crossfire, and thousands of people a year were killed in incidents related to the drugs war, with the biggest hot spots in areas bordering the US, and in major drug-producing states such as Sinaloa, though nowhere was safe.

Calderón's successor, **Enrique Peña Nieto**, initially changed tack, setting up a national police force, the *gendarmerie*, to tackle the problem. However, a surge in violence in Michoacán soon forced him to send in the army again.

Civicus, an international civil society NGO, stated in 2015: "Successive Mexican governments have ramped up the rhetoric about getting tough on drug trafficking. The result has been an egregious and sustained assault on human rights: it is estimated that 100,000 people have been killed in the drug war, and a further 25,000 'disappeared'."

THE DRUGS WAR AND TOURISM

Tourists are not usually affected, but June 2009 saw tourist hotels hurriedly evacuated as a two-hour gun battle engulfed a section of Acapulco. At the time of writing, in 2015, drug-related violence was a particular problem in the northern states of Sonora, Chihuahua, Coahuila, Nuevo Leon, Tamaulipas, Sinaloa and Durango, and also in Guerrero, Jalisco, Michoacán and Nayarit. Armed clashes between security forces and drug groups may break out without warning, and you should exercise extreme caution outside of tourist areas in all of these states.

open, and it's up to you literally to put your money on the table.

Should a crime be committed against you – in particular if you're robbed – your relationship with the police will obviously be different, although even in this eventuality it's worth considering whether the lengthy hassles you'll go through make it worth reporting. Some insurance companies will insist on a police report if you're to get any refund – in which case you may practically have to dictate it to the officer and can expect little action. Other firms may be prepared to accept that you were robbed and the theft was not reported to the police, but they are quite within their rights to demand that you do report it, and you will need to check with them. The department you need in order to *presentar una denuncia* (report the theft officially) is the Procuraduría General de Justicia.

The Mexican **legal system** is based on the Napoleonic code, which assumes your guilt until you can prove otherwise. Should you be jailed, your one phone call should be to your **consulate** – if nothing else, they'll arrange an English-speaking lawyer. You can be held for up to 72 hours on suspicion before charges have to be brought. Mexican jails are grim, although lots of money and friends on the outside can ameliorate matters slightly.

Drugs

Drug offences are the most common cause of serious trouble between tourists and the authorities. Under heavy pressure from the US to clamp down on the trade, local authorities are particularly happy to throw the book at foreign offenders. While the law has decriminalized small quantities of cannabis (up to 5g), cocaine (up to 0.5g) and heroin (up to 0.05g), if you're caught with quantities reckoned to be for distribution you can wave goodbye to daylight for a long time, and don't expect much help or sympathy from your consulate.

Other naturally occurring drugs – Mexico has more species of psychoactive plants than anywhere else in the world – still form an important part of many indigenous rituals, most notably the **peyote cactus** (used primarily by the Huichols in the northern deserts). Though the authorities turn a blind eye to indigenous use, use by non-indigenous Mexicans and tourists is as strongly prohibited as that of any other illegal drug, and heavily penalized. Expect searches and even occasionally hotel raids by police if staying in areas known for peyote.

Health

Most travellers visit Mexico without catching anything more serious than a dose of "Montezuma's Revenge". You will still want the security of health insurance (see p.55), but the important thing is to keep your resistance high and to be aware of the health risks linked to poor hygiene, untreated water, mosquito bites, and undressed open cuts.

Lack of sanitation in Mexico is much exaggerated, but a degree of caution is wise. Avoid food that looks like it has been on display for a while or not freshly cooked, and always peel fruit before eating it. Avoid raw shellfish, and don't eat anywhere that is obviously dirty (easily spotted, since most Mexican restaurants are scrupulously clean). Salads are healthy, but think twice before eating them if you have a sensitive stomach. In general, keep an eye out for cleanliness of street stalls – beware of food that has been left out to breed germs rather than food that has been freshly cooked. For advice on water, see box opposite.

There are no required vaccinations for Mexico, but it's worth visiting your doctor at least four weeks before you leave to check that you are up to date with **tetanus**, **typhoid** and **hepatitis A** shots, as well as a **rabies** shot and **anti-malarial** pills if you're going to be in areas where they are recommended (see opposite).

For comprehensive coverage of the sort of health problems encountered by travellers, try the *Rough Guide to Travel Health* by Dr Nick Jones – unfortunately now out of print, but still obtainable from some suppliers.

Diarrhoea

Diarrhoea (Montezuma's Revenge, or simply *turista* as it's also known in Mexico) is the medical problem you're most likely to encounter, and no one, however cautious, seems to avoid it altogether. If you go down with a mild dose unaccompanied by other symptoms, it may simply be due to your body being unfamiliar with the local bacteria, but if your diarrhoea is accompanied by cramps and vomiting, it could be **food poisoning** of some sort. Either way, it will probably pass of its own accord in 24 to 48 hours without treatment. In the meantime, it's essential to replace the fluid and salts you're losing, so drink lots of water. If you have severe diarrhoea, and whenever young children have it, add **oral rehydration salts** – *suero oral* (brand names:

Dioralyte, Electrosol, Rehidrat). If you can't get these, dissolve half a teaspoon of salt and three of sugar in a litre of water.

Avoid greasy food, heavy spices, caffeine and most fruit and dairy products; some say bananas, papayas, guavas and prickly pears (*tunas*) help, while plain yogurt or a broth made from yeast extract (such as Marmite or Vegemite, if you happen to have some with you) can be easily absorbed by your body when you have diarrhoea. Drugs like Lomotil or Imodium plug you up – and thus undermine the body's efforts to rid itself of infection – but they can be a temporary stop-gap if you have to travel. If symptoms persist for more than three days, or if you have a fever or blood in your stool, seek medical advice (see "Getting medical help", p.43).

Malaria and dengue fever

Malaria, caused by a parasite that lives in the saliva of female *Anopheles* mosquitoes, is endemic in some parts of Mexico. Areas above 1000m (such as the capital) are malaria-free, as are Cancún, Cozumel, Isla Mujeres and all the beach resorts of the Baja and the Pacific coasts. Daytime visits to archeological sites are risk-free, too, but low-lying inland areas can be risky, especially at night. According to the US-based Centers for Disease Control and Prevention (CDC) the main risk areas are Chihuahua, Chiapas, Durango, Nayarit and Sinaloa, with rare cases in Campeche, Jalisco, Oaxaca, Sonora, Tabasco and the municipality of Othon P. Blanco in the southern part of Quintana Roo, bordering Belize. Chloroquine (brand names: Nivaquin, Resochin, Avloclor, Aralen) is the recommended malaria prophylactic for travellers to Mexico; you need to start taking the pills one week before you arrive and continue for one month after you depart. Chloroquine is unsuitable for sufferers from various complaints such as epilepsy and psoriasis but daily proguanil (brand name Paludrine) can be used in its place. Consult a physician before beginning any course of medication; see Ⓦ wwwnc.cdc.gov/travel for more information on malaria in Mexico.

WHAT ABOUT THE WATER?

In a hot climate and at high altitudes, it's essential to increase **water** intake to prevent dehydration. Most travellers, and most Mexicans if they can, stay off the tap water. A lot of the time it is in fact drinkable, and in practice it may be impossible to avoid completely: ice made with it, unasked for, may appear in drinks, utensils are washed in it, and so on.

Most restaurants and *licuaderías* use **purified water** (*agua purificada*), but always check; most hotels have a supply and will often provide bottles of water in your room. Bottled water (generally purified with ozone or ultraviolet) is widely available, but stick with known brands, and always check that the seal on the bottle is intact since refilling empties with tap water for resale is common (carbonated water is generally a safer bet in that respect).

There are various methods of **treating water** while you are travelling, whether your source is from a tap or a river or stream. Boiling it for a minimum of five minutes is the time-honoured method, but it is not always practical, will not remove unpleasant tastes and is a lot less effective at higher altitudes – including much of central Mexico – where you have to boil it for much longer.

STERILIZATION AND PURIFICATION

Chemical sterilization, using either chlorine or iodine tablets or a tincture of iodine liquid, is more convenient, but leaves a nasty aftertaste (which can to some extent be masked with lime juice). Chlorine kills bacteria but, unlike iodine, is not effective against amoebic dysentery and giardiasis. Pregnant women or people with thyroid problems should consult their doctor before using iodine sterilizing tablets or iodine-based purifiers. Too many iodine tablets can cause gastrointestinal discomfort. Inexpensive iodine removal filters are available and are recommended if treated water is being used continuously for more than a month or is being given to babies.

Purification, involving both filtration and sterilization, gives the most complete treatment. Portable water purifiers range in size from units weighing as little as 60g, which can be slipped into a pocket, up to 800g for carrying in a backpack.

Another user-friendly alternative is a handheld ultraviolet (UV) water purifier such as Steripen (Ⓦ steripen.com).

If you go down with malaria, you'll probably know. The fever, shivering and headaches are like severe flu and come in waves, usually beginning in the early evening. Malaria is not infectious, but can be dangerous and sometimes even fatal if not treated quickly, so you should seek medical help immediately.

The most important thing, obviously, is to avoid **mosquito** bites altogether. Though active from dusk till dawn, female *Anopheles* mosquitoes prefer to bite in the evening. Wear long sleeves, skirts or trousers, avoid dark colours, which attract mosquitoes, and put **repellent** on all exposed skin, especially feet and ankles, which are their favourite targets. Plenty of good brands are sold locally, though health departments recommend carrying high-DEET brands available from travel clinics at home. An alternative is to burn coils of **pyrethrum** incense such as Raidolitos (these are readily available and burn all night if whole, but break easily). Sleep under a **net** if you can – one that hangs from a single point is best if you're going to buy one (you can usually find a way to tie a string across your room to hang it from). Special mosquito nets for hammocks are available in Mexico.

Another illness spread by mosquito bites is **dengue fever**, whose symptoms are similar to those of malaria, plus a headache and aching bones. Dengue-carrying mosquitoes are particularly prevalent in urban areas during the rainy season and fly during the day, so wear insect repellent in the daytime if mosquitoes are around. The only treatment is complete rest, with drugs to assuage the fever – and take note that a second infection can be fatal.

Other bites and stings

Other biting insects can also be a nuisance. These include bed bugs, sometimes found in cheap (and, occasionally, in not so cheap) hotels – look for squashed ones around the bed. Sandflies, often present on beaches, are quite small, but their bites, usually on feet and ankles, itch like hell and last for days. Head or body lice can be picked up from people or bedding, and are best treated with medicated soap or shampoo.

Scorpions are mostly nocturnal and hide during the day under rocks and in crevices, so poking around in such places when in the countryside is generally ill-advised. If sleeping in a place where they might enter (such as a beach cabaña), shake your shoes out before putting them on in the morning, and try not to wander round barefoot.

Some scorpion stings are dangerous and medical treatment should always be sought – cold-pack the sting in the meantime. **Snakes** are unlikely to bite unless accidentally disturbed – walk heavily and they will usually slither away. A fifth or so of Mexico's snake species are venomous, the most dangerous being rattlesnakes (cascabel, found in the north), coral snakes (corallilo, found particularly in Guerrero, Oaxaca, Veracruz and Chiapas) and the nauyacas (found mainly in the south and the Yucatán). If you do get bitten or stung, remember what the snake or scorpion looked like (kill it if you can do so without receiving more bites), try not to move the affected part (tourniquets are not recommended due to dangerous risk of gangrene – if you do use one, it is vital to relieve it for at least ninety seconds every fifteen minutes), and seek medical help: antivenins are available in most hospitals. Black widow spiders also exist in Mexico; tarantulas are more fearsome-looking, but a lot less dangerous.

Altitude and heat problems

Two other common causes of health problems in Mexico are altitude and the sun. The solution in both cases is to take it easy. Arriving in Mexico City (2240m), in particular, you may find any activity strenuous, and the thin air is made worse by the high concentration of pollutants. Allow yourself time to acclimatize. If going to higher altitudes (mountain climbing, for example), you may develop symptoms of **Acute Mountain Sickness (AMS)**, such as breathlessness, headaches, dizziness, nausea and appetite loss. More extreme cases may include vomiting, disorientation, loss of balance and coughing up of pink frothy phlegm. A slow descent almost always brings immediate recovery.

Tolerance to the sun, too, takes a while to build up: use a strong **sunscreen** and, if you're walking during the day, wear a hat or keep to the shade. Be sure to avoid dehydration by drinking enough (water or fruit juice rather than beer or coffee, and aim to drink at least three litres a day), and don't exert yourself for long periods in the hot sun. Be aware that overheating can cause **heatstroke**, which is potentially fatal. Signs are a very high body temperature without a feeling of fever, accompanied by headaches, disorientation and even irrational behaviour. Lowering body temperature (a tepid shower, for example) is the first step in treatment.

Less serious is **prickly heat**, an itchy rash that is in fact an infection of the sweat ducts caused by excessive perspiration that doesn't dry off. A cool shower, zinc oxide powder and loose cotton clothes should help.

Hepatitis

Hepatitis A is transmitted through contaminated food and water, or through saliva, and thrives in conditions of poor hygiene. It can lay a victim low for several months with exhaustion, fever and diarrhoea, and can even cause liver damage. The Havrix vaccine has been shown to be extremely effective; with a booster after six months, protection lasts for ten years.

Hepatitis symptoms include a yellowing of the whites of the eyes, general malaise, orange urine (though dehydration can also cause this) and light-coloured stools. If you think you have it and are unable immediately to see a doctor, it is important to get lots of rest, avoid alcohol and do your best not to spread the disease. If medical insurance coverage is an issue, you can go to a pathology lab (most towns have them) to get blood tests before paying a greater amount to see a doctor.

More serious is **hepatitis B**, which is passed through blood or sexual contact, in the same way as HIV, but more easily. A hepatitis B jab is recommended if you will be in contact with those with weaker immune systems, for example, working around medical patients or with children. Ideally three doses are given over six months, but, if time is short, there are other options that take one to two months, with a booster given after a year.

Other diseases

Typhoid and cholera are spread in the same way as hepatitis A. **Typhoid** produces a persistent high fever with malaise, headaches and abdominal pains, followed by diarrhoea. Vaccination can be by injection or orally, though the oral alternative is less effective, more expensive and only lasts a year, as opposed to three for a shot in the arm. **Cholera** appears in epidemics rather than isolated cases – if it's about, you will probably hear about it. Cholera is characterized by sudden attacks of watery diarrhoea with severe cramps and debilitation.

Immunizations against **mumps, measles, TB** and **rubella** are a good idea for anyone who wasn't vaccinated as a child and hasn't had the diseases, and it's worth making sure you are covered for **tetanus.** You don't need a shot for **yellow fever** unless you're coming from a country where it's endemic (in which case you need to carry your vaccination certificate).

Rabies exists in Mexico and the rabies vaccine is advised for anyone who will be more than 24 hours away from medical help, for example if going trekking in remote areas. The best advice is simply to give dogs a wide berth, and not to play with animals at all, no matter how cuddly they may look. A bite, a scratch or even a lick from an infected animal could spread the disease – rabies can be fatal, so if you are bitten, assume the worst and get medical help as quickly as possible. While waiting, wash any such wound immediately but gently with soap or detergent and apply alcohol or iodine if possible. If you decide to get the vaccination, you'll need three shots spread over a four-week period prior to travel.

Getting medical help

For minor medical problems, head for a **farmacia** – look for a green cross and the *Farmacia* sign. Pharmacists are knowledgeable and helpful, and many speak some English. One word of warning, however: in many Mexican pharmacies you can still buy drugs such as Entero-Vioform and Mexaform (both used to treat diarrhoea), which can cause optic nerve damage and have been banned elsewhere; it is not a good idea, therefore, to use local brands unless you know what they are. Note that the purchase of prescription drugs without a Mexican prescription is illegal; a US prescription will not suffice.

For more serious complaints you can get a list of English-speaking **doctors** from your government's nearest consulate. Big hotels and tourist offices may also be able to recommend medical services. Every Mexican border town has hundreds of doctors (dentists, too) experienced in treating gringos, since they charge less than their colleagues across the border. Every reasonably sized town should also have a state- or Red Cross-run **health centre** (*centro de salud*), where treatment is free. Treatment at health centres should be adequate for minor problems, but for anything involving an overnight stay, go to a private hospital (for which your travel insurance should cover you).

MEDICAL RESOURCES

Canadian Society for International Health ☎ 613 241 5785, ⓦ csih.org. Has an extensive list of travel health centres.
CDC ☎ 1 800 232 4636, ⓦ cdc.gov/travel. Official US government travel health site.
International Society for Travel Medicine US ☎ 1 404 373 8282, ⓦ istm.org. Has a full list of travel health clinics.

Hospital for Tropical Diseases Travel Clinic UK ☎ 020 3447 5999, ⓦ www.thehtd.org/travelclinic.aspx.
MASTA (Medical Advisory Service for Travellers Abroad) UK ☎ 0330 100 4200, ⓦ masta-travel-health.com for the nearest clinic.
Tropical Medical Bureau Ireland ☎ 1850 487 674, ⓦ tmb.ie.
The Travel Doctor Aus ☎ 1 300 658 844, ⓦ traveldoctor.com.au.
Lists travel clinics in Australia, New Zealand and South Africa.

Food and drink

Whatever your preconceptions about Mexican food, if you've never eaten in Mexico, they will almost certainly be wrong. Food here bears very little resemblance to the concoctions served in "Mexican" restaurants or fast-food joints in other parts of the world – you certainly won't find chile con carne outside the tourist spots. Nor, as a rule, is it especially spicy.

Where to eat

Basic meals are served at **restaurantes**, but you can get breakfast, snacks and often full meals at cafés too; there are **takeaway** and **fast-food** places serving sandwiches, tortas (filled rolls) and tacos (tortillas folded over with a filling), as well as more international-style restaurants; there are establishments called **jugerías** (look for signs saying "Jugos y Licuados") serving nothing but wonderful *jugos* (juices), *licuados* (fruit blended with water or milk) and fruit salads; and there are **street stalls** dishing out everything from tacos to orange juice to ready-made vegetable salads sprinkled with chile-salt and lime. Just about every **market** in the country has a cooked-food section, too, and these are invariably the cheapest places to eat, if not always the most enticing surroundings. Big cities and resorts have international restaurants – **pizza**, **burgers** and **Chinese** food are ubiquitous, and **Argentine** restaurants are the places to go for well-cooked, quality steaks.

On buses (especially second-class ones), people clamber on at stops with home-made foods, local specialities, cold drinks or coffee. You'll find wonderful things this way that you won't come across in restaurants, but they should be treated with caution, and with an eye to hygiene.

What to eat

The basic Mexican diet is essentially one of **corn** (*maíz* as a crop, *elote* when eaten), supplemented by **beans** and **chiles**. These three things appear in an almost infinite variety of guises.

Beans and vegetables

Beans (*frijoles*), an invariable accompaniment to egg dishes – and pretty much everything else too – are usually of the pinto or kidney variety and are almost always served **refritos**, ie boiled up, mashed and "refried" (though actually it is the first time they're fried). They're even better if you can get them whole in some kind of country-style soup or stew, often with pork or bacon, as in **frijoles charros**. You'll find **corn** in soups and stews such as **pozole** (with meat), or roasted on the cob at street stalls. Mexican **vegetables** include the green tomatillo (*tomate*, as opposed to *jitomate*, which is

---

SALSA

Most Mexican food is not in itself terribly spicy – the fire comes from the red and green salsa supplied as condiments on the table, and the salsa can be a good guide to the quality of a restaurant. A place with a superior salsa on the table will probably serve up some decent food, whereas a place that takes no pride in its salsa is likely to treat its food in the same manner. To a certain extent you can tell from the presentation: a place that has grubby, rarely changed salsa dishes probably just refills them from a supermarket-bought can, and will not take the same pride in its food as a *casero* (home-cooking) restaurant that proudly puts its own salsa on the table in a nice bowl. Usually you get a red salsa and a green one, and sometimes bottled hot-sauce condiments too.

Nowadays, the red bowl may contain a **raw**, California-style salsa: tomato, onion, chile and coriander (cilantro) finely chopped together. More common, though, are the traditional **cooked** salsas: either green or red, and relatively mild (though start eating with caution, just in case). The recipes are – of course – closely guarded secrets, but the basic ingredients are tomato (the verdant Mexican tomatillo in green versions), onion and one or more of the hundreds of varieties of chile.

REGIONAL CUISINE

It's easy to think of Mexican food as one cuisine. In reality, while there are common themes, each region has its own excellent specialities. Here are a few regional highlights.

BAJA CALIFORNIA

In Baja, the sea is all around, so it makes sense that *mariscos* (seafood) and *pescado* (fish) dominate menus – the fish taco is an eternal favourite. Northern Baja is home to Mexico's wine industry, and drinking wine with your meal is far more common here than elsewhere in the country.

THE NORTH

Dining in the north, where the land is too dry to grow produce, tends to revolve around grilled meat: the *asado* (barbecue) is king. *Cabrito asado* (roast kid) is the classic dish, often served in gargantuan portions and accompanied only by tortillas and salsa. These basic ingredients combine into burritos and fajitas, dishes that have travelled north of the border to become what most of the world thinks of as "Mexican food".

CENTRAL MEXICO

With fertile valleys and highlands that receive enough rain to sustain agriculture, central Mexico has the widest range of local ingredients. This is the land of the avocado (and therefore guacamole) and the birthplace of tequila. Mexico's second city, Guadalajara, excels with its *birria*, a soupy stew, while coastal towns dish up tasty *camarones* (prawns). Further south, Oaxaca claims the country's finest tamales, stuffed cornmeal dough cooked in banana leaves.

THE YUCATÁN

Influenced by the flavours of the Caribbean, an abundance of tropical fruits and the all-powerful burn of the *habanero chile*, Yucatecan cuisine is a world apart from that of central Mexico. The most celebrated dish is *cochinita pibil*, pork marinated in a *recado* made from garlic, chiles, black pepper, cumin, cinnamon, oregano and vinegar, then wrapped in plantain leaves and grilled. For more on Yucatecan cuisine, see p.732.

---

an ordinary tomato), *nopales*, which are prickly pear fronds (the fruit being a *tuna*), and *huitlacoche*, a fungus that grows on corn. You may also get to eat courgette flowers (*flor de calabaza*), which are especially popular in quesadillas.

Tortillas and tamales

As well as being eaten as a vegetable in its own right, corn is ground into flour for **tortillas**, basically flat maize pancakes (tortillas made of wheat flour, or *de harina*, are rare except in the north). The ground maize is combined with salt and water in a paste (*masa*) which is pressed or patted flat by hand, then heated on a *comal*, a flat steel sheet. While smarter restaurants serve bread rolls (*bolillos*), a stack of tortillas is a common accompaniment in cheaper places, and they also form the basis of most **antojitos** (appetizers or light courses). Simplest of these are **tacos**, tortillas filled with almost anything, from beef and chicken to green vegetables, and then fried (they're usually still soft, not at all like the baked taco shells you may have had at home). With cheese, either alone or in addition to other fillings, they are called

quesadillas. **Enchiladas** are rolled, filled tortillas covered in salsa and baked; **enchiladas suizas** are filled with chicken and have sour cream over them. **Tostadas** are flat tortillas toasted crisp and piled with ingredients – usually meat, salad vegetables and cheese (smaller bite-size versions are known as *sopes*). Tortillas torn up and cooked together with meat and (usually hot) sauce are called **chilaquiles**; this is a traditional way of using up leftovers. In the north, especially, you'll also come across **burritos** (large wheat-flour tortillas, stuffed with anything, but usually beef and potatoes or beans) and **gorditas** (delicious fat corn tortillas, sliced open, stuffed and baked or fried). Also short and fat are **tlacoyos**, tortillas made with a stuffing of mashed beans, often using blue-corn flour, which gives them a rather bizarre colour.

Corn flour, too, is the basis of **tamales** – found predominantly in central and southern Mexico – which are a sort of cornmeal pudding, stuffed, flavoured and steamed in corn or banana leaves. They can be either savoury, with additions like shrimp or corn kernels, or sweet when made with something like coconut.

Meat, seafood and eggs

Except in the north, **meat** is not especially good – beef in particular is usually thin and tough; pork, goat and occasionally lamb are better. If the menu doesn't specify what kind of meat it is, it's usually pork – even steak (*bistec*) can be pork unless it specifies *bistec de res*. For thick American-style steaks, look for a sign saying "Carnes Hereford" or for a "New York Cut" description (only in expensive places or in the north or at fancier resorts). **Seafood** is almost always fresh and delicious, especially the spicy shrimp or octopus cocktails which you find in most coastal areas (**coctél/campechana de camarón** or **pulpo**), but beware of eating uncooked shellfish, even *ceviche* (though the lime juice it is marinaded in does kill off most of the nasties). **Eggs** in country areas are genuinely free range and flavoursome. They feature on every menu as the most basic of meals, and at some time you must try the classic Mexican combinations of **huevos rancheros** (fried eggs on a tortilla with red salsa) or **huevos a la mexicana** (scrambled with onion, tomato and chile).

Vegetarian food

Vegetarians can eat well in Mexico, although it does take caution to avoid meat altogether. Many Mexican dishes are naturally meat-free and there are always fabulous fruits and vegetables available. Most restaurants serve vegetable soups and rice, and items like quesadillas, *chiles rellenos* and even tacos and enchiladas often come with non-meat fillings. Another possibility is **queso fundido**, simply (and literally) melted cheese, served with tortillas and salsa. Eggs, too, are served anywhere at any time, and many *jugerías* serve huge mixed **salads** to which grains and nuts can be added.

However, vegetarianism, though growing, is not particularly common, and a simple cheese and chile dish may have some meat added to "improve" it. Worse, most of the fat used for frying is animal fat (usually lard), so that even something as unadorned as refried beans may not be strictly vegetarian (especially as a bone or some stock may have been added to the water the beans were originally boiled in). Even "vegetarian" restaurants, which can be found in all the big cities, often include chicken on the menu. You may well have better luck in pizza places and Chinese or other ethnic restaurants.

Meals

Traditionally, Mexicans eat a light breakfast very early, a snack of tacos or eggs in mid-morning, lunch (the main meal of the day) around 2pm or later – in theory followed by a siesta, but decreasingly so, it seems – and a late, light supper. Eating a large meal at lunch time can be a great way to save money – almost every restaurant serves a cut-price **comida corrida** (a set meal, changing daily).

Breakfast (*desayuno*) in Mexico can consist simply of coffee (see opposite) and *pan dulce* – sweet rolls and pastries that usually come in a basket; you pay for as many as you eat. More substantial breakfasts consist of eggs in any number of forms (many set breakfasts include *huevos al gusto*: eggs any way you like them), and at

---

SOME LIKE IT NOT SO HOT: THE MEXICAN CHILE

Mexican cooks use at least a hundred different types of **chiles**, fresh or dried, in colours ranging from pale green to almost black, and all sorts of different sizes (large, mild ones are often stuffed with meat or cheese and rice to make **chiles rellenos**). Each has a distinct flavour and by no means all are hot (which is why we don't use the English term "chilli" for them), although the most common, **chiles jalapeños** – which can be green or red, and are traditionally grown around the city of Xalapa – certainly are. The hottest is the **habanero**, 25 times hotter than the **jalapeño**. Far less intimidating is the **chile poblano**, a large, mild chile used in dishes such as **chiles rellenos** and **chiles en nogada**, a seasonal dish of stuffed poblano chiles in a white sauce made of walnuts and cream cheese or sour cream, topped with red pomegranate: the colours of the national flag.

MOLE

Chile is also the basic ingredient of more complex cooked sauces, notably **mole**, which is Mexico's version of a curry, traditionally served with turkey or chicken, but also sometimes with enchiladas (rolled, filled tortillas). There are several types of *mole*, the two most common being the rather bland *mole verde*, and the far richer and more exciting **mole poblano**, a speciality of Puebla. Half of the fifty or so ingredients in this extraordinary mixture are different types of chile, but the most notable ingredient is chocolate.

CHOCOLATE

The Olmecs of the Gulf coast began mixing cacao beans into a bitter **chocolate** drink around three thousand years ago. By the time Cortés and the conquistadors reached New Spain in the early sixteenth century, the use of cacao had spread to the Aztecs, who consumed *chocoatl* cold and mixed with spices – this "drink of the gods" was said to be a favourite of Aztec emperor Moctezuma. Chocolate remains a popular drink in Mexico today (now with lots of added sugar), but its most distinctive use is in **mole poblano**, a thick sauce of chocolate and chiles that accompanies otherwise savoury dishes – particularly chicken. Though found all over the country, *mole* remains a speciality of Puebla in central Mexico, where the dish originated in the colonial era.

fruit-juice places you can have a simple *licuado* (see opposite) fortified with raw egg (*blanquillo*). Freshly squeezed orange juice (*jugo de naranja*) is always available from street stalls in the early morning.

Snacks mostly consist of some variation on the taco/enchilada theme (stalls selling them are called *taquerías*), but tortas – rolls heavily filled with meat or cheese or both, garnished with avocado and chile and toasted on request – are also wonderful, and you'll see takeout torta stands everywhere. Failing that, you can of course always make your own snacks with bread or tortillas, along with fillings such as avocado or cheese, from shops or markets.

At **lunch time** (around 1–5pm) many restaurants serve a comida corrida (known in smarter places as the *menu del día* or *menu turístico*), usually consisting of three or four courses for US$5–8/£3.25–5.20 or less – sometimes even half that price. A typical *comida* will consist of "wet" soup, probably vegetable, followed by "dry" soup – most commonly *sopa de arroz* (rice seasoned with tomato or chile), or perhaps a plate of vegetables, pasta, beans or guacamole (avocado mashed with onion, and maybe tomato, lime juice and chile). Then comes the main course (usually meat or fish), followed by pudding, usually fruit, *flan* or *pudin* (crème caramel-like concoctions), or rice pudding. Other Mexican desserts worth looking out for include meringue made with *pulque* (see p.48), and *capirotada* (bread pudding, especially popular during Lent).

Some restaurants also offer set meals in the evening, but this is rare, and on the whole going out to **eat at night** is much more expensive.

Drinks

The basic drinks to accompany food are water or beer. If you're drinking **water**, stick to bottled stuff (*agua mineral* or *agua de Tehuacán*) – it comes either plain (*sin gas*) or carbonated (*con gas*).

Jugos, licuados and refrescos

Soft drinks (*refrescos*) – including Coke, Pepsi, Squirt (fun to pronounce in Spanish), and Mexican brands like apple-flavoured Sidral (which are usually extremely sweet) – are on sale everywhere. Far more tempting are the real **fruit juices** and *licuados* sold at shops and stalls displaying the "Jugos y Licuados" sign and known as *jugerías* or *licuaderías*. Juices (**jugos**) can be squeezed from anything that will go through the extractor. Orange (naranja) and carrot (zanahoria) are the staples, but you should also experiment with some of the more obscure tropical fruits such as soursop or mamey. *Licuados* are made of fruit mixed with water (**licuado de agua** or simply **agua de...**) or milk (**licuado de leche**) in a blender, usually with sugar added, and are always fantastic. **Limonada** (fresh lemonade) is also sold in many of these places, as are **aguas frescas** – flavoured cold drinks, of which the most common are **horchata** (rice milk flavoured with cinnamon) and **agua de arroz** (like an iced rice-pudding drink – delicious), **de jamaica** (hibiscus) or **de tamarindo** (tamarind). These are also often served in restaurants or sold in the streets from great glass jars. Make sure that any water and ice used is purified – street stalls are especially suspect in this regard. Juices and *licuados* are also sold at many ice-cream parlours – *neverías* or *paleterías*. The ice cream, more like Italian *gelato* than the heavy-cream US varieties, can also be fabulous and comes in a huge range of flavours.

Coffee and tea

A great deal of **coffee** is produced in Mexico, and in the growing areas, especially the state of Veracruz, as well as in the traditional coffeehouses in the capital, you will be served superb coffee. In its basic form, **café solo** or **negro**, it is strong, black, often sweet (ask for it *sin azúcar* for no sugar), and comes in small cups. For weaker black coffee ask for **café americano**, though this may mean instant (if you do want instant, ask for "Nescafé"). White is **café**

TOP 5 PLACES TO EAT

Cetli Tulum. See p.796.
Ceviche de Guerrerense Ensenada. See p.542.
Taquería Hermanos González La Paz. See p.567.
Oaxaca's markets Oaxaca. See p.596.
La Viña de Bacco San Cristóbal de las Casas. See p.672.

cortado or **con un pocito de leche**; **café con leche** can be delicious, made with all milk and no water (ask if it's "hecho de leche" – made of milk). **Espresso** and **cappuccino** are often available too, or you may be offered **café de olla** – stewed in the pot for hours with cinnamon and sugar, it's thick, sweet and tasty. Outside traditional coffee areas like Chiapas, however, the coffee is often terrible, with instant common.

Tea (té) is often available too, and you may well be offered a cup at the end of a *comida*. You may also be offered herb teas such as **manzanillo** (camomile) or **yerbabuena** (mint). If you get the chance to try traditional **hot chocolate** ("the drink of the Aztecs"), then do so – it's an extraordinary, spicy, semi-bitter concoction, quite unlike the milky bedtime drink of your childhood. Artisan chocolate shops sell the chocolate for this (you just add boiling water), and occasionally sell it as a drink too.

Alcohol

You'll normally be drinking in **bars**, the least heavy atmosphere among which is in **hotel bars**, tourist areas or anything that describes itself as a "ladies' bar". **Cantinas** are for serious drinking, traditionally macho places that were closed to women (they typically had a sign above the door prohibiting entry to "women, members of the armed forces and anyone in uniform"). Especially in big cities they are now more liberal, but in small, conservative places they remain exclusively male preserves with an atmosphere of drunken bonhomie and an undercurrent of readiness for a fight, where women may not be welcome and are sometimes still even banned.

If you don't feel comfortable in bars, you can buy alcohol from most shops, supermarkets and, cheapest of all, *agencias*, which are normally agents for just one brand. For bottles you pay a deposit: to get it back, keep your receipt and return your bottles to the same store. Bigger, 940ml bottles are known as *caguamas* (turtles), or in the case of Pacífico, *ballenas* (whales).

Beer and wine

Mexican beer (*cerveza*) is mostly light lager (*cerveza clara*) – usually light in flavour as well as colour. Sol, Tecate and Dos Equis are typical brands; if you want something more flavoursome try Modelo, Bohémia or Corona, or a dark (*oscura*) beer, of which the best are Negra Modelo, Indio and Bohémia Obscura. Microbreweries are increasingly springing up. Try a *michelada*, a beer cocktail made by adding ice, lime and Worcestershire and Tabasco sauces to dark beer and rimming the glass with salt. The milder *chelada* is a light beer mixed with plenty of lime and salt, and both are refreshing on a sunny day.

Wine (*vino* – *tinto* is red, *blanco* is white) is not seen a great deal, although Mexico does produce a fair number of perfectly good vintages. You're safest sticking to brand names like Hidalgo or Domecq, although it may also be worth experimenting with some of the new labels, especially those from Baja California, such as L. A. Cetto, which are attempting to emulate the success of their neighbours across the border and in many cases have borrowed American techniques and wine-makers.

Tequila, mescal and pulque

Tequila, distilled from the cactus-like agave plant and produced mainly in the state of Jalisco, is the most famous Mexican spirit, usually taken with lime and salt, or a chile and tomato chaser called *sangrita*, but *añejo* or *reposado* tequila (aged in the vat) should be sipped straight, and not wasted in cocktails such as margarita (tequila, lime juice and triple sec – considered a ladies' drink). Mexican law allows up to 49 percent cane or corn to be added to the agave from which tequila is made, so unless the label says "100% de agave", it won't be. The proprietary brands, José Cuervo and Sauza, make bog-standard white tequilas as well as smoother, aged versions (Cuervo Tradicional and Sauza Hornitos), but connoisseurs prefer posher makes such as Herradura or Don Julio. "Gold" tequila contains extraneous colourings and is worth avoiding. For more on tequila, see box, p.279.

Mescal (often spelled mezcal) is basically the same thing as tequila, but is made from a slightly different variety of plant, the maguey, and is younger and less refined. In fact, tequila was originally just a variety of mescal. The spurious belief that the worm in the mescal bottle is hallucinogenic is based on confusion between the drink and the peyote cactus, which is also called mescal, but by the time you've got down as far as the worm, you'll be too far gone to notice anyway.

THE SODA TAX

Mexicans have dangerously sweet teeth: more than thirty percent of the population is obese, many more are overweight, and diseases like diabetes are rife. **Sugary drinks** are one of the key causes: each Mexican drinks the equivalent of 163 litres of Coca-Cola a year – the highest rate in the world.

In an attempt to tackle this expanding problem, the Mexican government introduced a ten percent **"soda tax"** in January 2014, plus additional taxes on high-calorie snacks like crisps and biscuits. Six months later these policies were followed by wide-ranging restrictions on TV and cinema advertising of sugary soft drinks and high calorie foods.

Early signs suggested that these steps were having a positive impact: sugary drink purchases had fallen six percent by the end of 2014, and the "soda tax" had raised more than M$18 billion in revenue. Inevitably, however, there has been a **backlash**. In late 2015, following fierce lobbying from multinational fizzy drinks manufacturers, the government agreed to halve the tax for sweetened drinks with a "lower sugar content".

Campaigners and public health experts, by contrast, are urging the government to go further and instead increase the tax, abolish VAT on bottled water to make it cheaper than sugary drinks, and to provide free drinking water in schools, among other measures.

Pulque, a mildly alcoholic milky beer made from the same maguey cactus, is the traditional drink of the poor and sold in special bars called *pulquerías*. The best comes from the State of Mexico, and is thick and viscous – it's a little like palm wine, and definitely an acquired taste. Unfermented *pulque*, called *aguamiel*, is sweet and non-alcoholic.

Other spirits and cocktails

Drinking other spirits, you should always ask for **nacional**, as anything imported is fabulously expensive. **Rum** (*ron*), **gin** (*ginebra*) and **vodka** are made in Mexico, as are some very palatable **brandies** (brandy or coñac – try San Marcos or Presidente). Most of the **cocktails** for which Mexico is known – margaritas, piñas coladas and so on – are available only in tourist areas or hotel bars, and are generally pretty strong.

The media

The Mexican media can be very sensationalist, and news is mostly local, and often heavily slanted towards the government, but for Spanish-speakers there is an independent press, as well as some interesting programmes on TV.

Newspapers

Few domestic **newspapers** carry much foreign news, and the majority of international coverage does not extend beyond Latin America. Most papers are lurid scandal sheets, brimming with violent crime depicted in full colour. Each state has its own press, however, and they do vary: while most are little more than government mouthpieces, others are surprisingly independent.

If you read Spanish you could try *Reforma* (Ⓦreforma.com), which has a good reputation for independence and political objectivity, while the more left-wing *La Jornada* (Ⓦjornada.unam.mx) is quite daringly critical of government and organized crime, and its journalists regularly face death threats as a result. The press has gradually been asserting its independence since the mid-1990s, tackling such subjects as human rights, corruption and drug trafficking, though journalists still face danger if they speak out, not only from shady government groups but also from drug traffickers. Reporting on links between the two is particularly dangerous. At least 26 journalists have been killed in Mexico since 2009, according to press freedom NGO Reporters Without Borders, who rate it as one of the most dangerous countries in the world for journalists.

Television

You can usually pick up a dozen channels in Mexico without cable or satellite. Four are run by the main **TV** company, Televisa, and another couple by TV Azteca. Canal 22 tends to show cultural programmes, though they are often rather dry. Canal Once is the most original and independent channel, and frequently has something quite interesting on, especially late in the evening. **Cable** and **satellite** are widespread, and even quite budget hotels offer numerous channels, many of them American.

On Mexican TV you can watch any number of US shows dubbed into Spanish, but far and away the most popular programmes are the *telenovelas* – soap operas that dominate the screens from 6pm to 10pm and pull in millions of viewers. Each episode takes melodrama to new heights, with nonstop action and emotions hammed up to the maximum for riveted fans. Plot lines make national news, and *telenovela* stars are major celebrities, despite their ludicrously over-the-top acting styles.

Radio

Radio stations in the capital and Guadalajara (among others) have programmes in English for a couple of hours each day, and in many places US broadcasts can also be picked up. Reactor (in Mexico City on 105.7MHz FM, and online at Ⓦreactor.imer.com.mx) plays a mix of music including modern Mexican sounds, and from México state, Radio Chapingo (1610kHz AM, Ⓦchapingo.mx/radiochapingo/live) plays the traditional music of indigenous ethnic groups as well as modern Mexican music of various genres. If you have a short-wave radio, you can get the Voice of America (Ⓦvoanews.com) and, at certain times, Radio Canada (Ⓦici.radio-canada.ca).

Festivals

Stumbling, perhaps accidentally, onto some Mexican village fiesta may prove to be the highlight of your travels. Everywhere, from the remotest indigenous village to the most sophisticated city suburb, devotes at least one day annually to partying. Usually it's in honour of the local saint's day, but many fiestas have pre-Christian origins, and any excuse – from harvest celebrations to the coming of the rains – will do.

Even the tiniest village in Mexico has an annual fiesta. They usually last at least a couple of days and often involve some blend of rodeos, bullfights, dancing, fried snacks, carnival rides, fireworks and processions around the church. They offer a great opportunity to see indigenous dances – such as the **Danza de los Viejitos** (Dance of the Little Old Men) in Michoacán, or the feather-bedecked **quetzales** in Cuetzalan, Puebla. Details of the most important local fiestas can be found at the end of each chapter, while the most important nationwide are listed below.

In addition to these, there are plenty of lesser local festivals, as well as certain major festivals celebrated throughout the country. Traditional dances and music form an essential part of almost every fiesta, and most include a procession behind some revered holy image or a more celebratory secular parade with fireworks. No two fiestas will be quite the same. The Catholic saints' calendar provides countless opportunities for celebrating, with many of the biggest events observed with a combination of religious fervour and all-out partying.

A festival calendar

JANUARY

New Year Jan 1. Still largely an occasion to spend with family, the actual hour being celebrated with the eating of grapes.

Twelfth Night (Epiphany, Reyes) Jan 6. Presents are traditionally given on this, the last day of Christmas, when the biblical Magi are believed to have arrived bearing gifts. Nowadays, things are shifting into

DÍA DE LOS MUERTOS

If visitors know just one Mexican holiday, it's probably the **Day of the Dead**, when families honour and remember those who have died. Actually taking place over two days, November 1 and 2, it's an indigenous tradition unique to Mexico. With a few exceptions (such as the beautiful torch-lighting ceremony and festive dances around Lago de Pátzcuaro), it's usually a private rite. In every home, and in many businesses, people set up *ofrendas* (altars) for the deceased: the centrepiece is always a photograph, lit by candles. In addition to the photo, the person's favourite foods are also placed on the altar, as a way of luring the soul back to this world. For the same reason, strong-scented, bright orange marigolds are often laid in a path leading to the altar, and resinous *copal* incense is lit.

On the streets, market stalls brim with eggy, orange-scented *pan de muertos* and colourfully iced sugar skulls. Families usually gather to eat dinner on the night of November 1, then visit gravesites, which are also cleaned and decorated. Far from being a sad time, the Day of the Dead is an occasion for telling funny stories, bonding with family and generally celebrating life.

line with American custom, and more and more people are exchanging gifts on December 25 instead.

Ortiz Tirado Music Festival late Jan. A festival of classical music held annually in Alamos, Sonora, in honour of opera singer Alfonso Ortiz Tirado (who died in 1960), draws leading classical musicians and singers from across the world.

FEBRUARY

Carnaval moveable. The last week of taking one's pleasures before the forty-day abstinence of Lent, celebrated throughout the Roman Catholic world, but is at its most exuberant in Latin America. Like Easter, its date is not fixed, but generally falls in February or early March, celebrated with costumes, parades, eating and dancing, most spectacularly in Veracruz and Mazatlán, working its way up to a climax on the last day, Mardi Gras (Shrove Tues). Carnaval is celebrated most vigorously in the coastal cities, including Veracruz and San Miguel on Cozumel. The city of Mazatlán claims to have the world's third-largest Mardi Gras party, after Rio and New Orleans.

MARCH

Festival Internacional de Guitarra late March or early April. A celebration of guitar music held annually in Morelia, and attended by musicians from around the world.

APRIL

Semana Santa (Holy Week) moveable. The country's biggest holiday, beginning on Palm Sunday and finishing a week later on Easter Sunday. Still a deeply religious festival in Mexico, it celebrates the resurrection of Christ, and is also an occasion to venerate the Virgin Mary, with processions bearing her image now a hallmark of the celebrations. Pilgrims converge on churches, and people re-enact the Passion of Christ. The most famous staging is in Iztapalapa, outside Mexico City, where the event involves a cast of thousands, buckets of fake blood and more than a million spectators. Transport is disrupted everywhere as virtually the whole country is on the move, and you will definitely need to plan ahead if travelling. Many places close for the whole of Holy Week, and certainly from Thursday to Sunday.

MAY

Cinco de Mayo May 5. Commemorating the 1862 Battle of Puebla, it's a public holiday in Mexico, but is actually celebrated more enthusiastically in the US, where many Gringos (who see the date as a chance to have a theme party involving sombreros, nachos and tequila) have come to believe that it's Mexico's equivalent of the US's July 4. In Mexico it's not such a big deal, except in Puebla, where it is celebrated with an exuberant fiesta.

JUNE

Día de San Juan (St John's Day) June 24. Celebrating the birth of the biblical St John the Baptist, but also handily close to the summer solstice, this is celebrated with bonfires, fairs, *charreadas* (rodeos) and sometimes water throwing in towns and villages nationwide.

JULY

Día de Santiago (St James's Day) July 25. An opportunity for a fiesta in many parts of the country, most notably in Chiapas, where big celebrations are held at San Cristóbal de las Casas.

AUGUST

Día de la Asunción (Assumption Day) Aug 15. This is the day when the Virgin Mary is believed to have ascended to heaven, and although it isn't a public holiday, it's celebrated around the country, most notably at Oxkutzcab and Izamal in Yucatán, and Cholula in Puebla State.

SEPTEMBER

Independence Day Sept 16. While Easter and Carnaval are popular, this one is more official, marking the historic day in 1810 when Manuel Hidalgo y Costilla issued the Grito (Cry of Independence) from his parish church in Dolores, now Dolores Hidalgo, Guanajuato, which is still the centre of commemoration. You'll also find the day marked in the capital with mass recitation of the Grito in the Zócalo, followed by fireworks, music and dancing. Nevertheless, in some ways it's more solemn than the religious festivals.

Festival Internacional de Santa Lucía end of Sept and beginning of Oct. Formerly the Festival Cultural of Monterrey's Barrio Antiguo, showcasing local rock bands and other eclectic musicians, this festival has been reborn, having outgrown the confines of the Barrio Antiguo to become a citywide event. It's now Mexico's third-biggest music festival after Guanajuato's Festival Cervantino and Alamos' Festival Ortiz Tirado.

OCTOBER

Festival Internacional Cervantino mid-Oct. Guanajuato's big, two-and-a-half-week music fest, dating back to the 1970s. Every October, it brings together Mexican marimba legends, French jazz artists, choral music from England and international dance troupes. For more details, see box, p.355.

NOVEMBER

The Day of the Dead (All Saints'/Souls' Day, and its eve) Nov 1–2. Offerings are made to ancestors' souls, frequently with picnics and all-night vigils at their graves, and people build shrines in their homes to honour their departed relatives. Sweetmeats and papier-mâché statues of dressed-up skeletons give proceedings a rather gothic air. Head for cemeteries to see the really spectacular stuff, or to Pátzcuaro (see p.289). For more details, see box, p.296.

DECEMBER

Día de la Virgen de Guadalupe Dec 12. Celebrations everywhere, and a huge day for pilgrims at the Basílica de Nuestra Señora de Guadalupe in Mexico City, home of Mexico's most important Virgin (a manifestation, that is, of the biblical Virgin Mary), who appeared on this day in 1551 (see box, p.116).

Christmas Dec 25. A major holiday, with loads of people on the move and transport booked solid for weeks ahead. Gringo influence is heavy nowadays, with Santa Claus and Christmas trees, but the Mexican festival remains distinct in many ways, with a much stronger religious element (virtually every home has a Nativity crib). One of the more bizarre Christmas events takes place in Oaxaca, where there is a public display of Nativity cribs and other sculptures made of radishes.

Sports and outdoor activities

You'll find facilities for golf, tennis, sailing, surfing, scuba diving and deep-sea fishing – even horseriding and hunting – at all the big resorts.

Sport fishing is enormously popular in Baja California and the big Pacific coast resorts, while freshwater bass fishing is growing in popularity too, especially behind the large dams in the north of the country. **Diving** and **snorkelling** are big on the Caribbean coast, with world-famous dive sites at Cozumel and on the reefs further south. The Pacific coast has become something of a centre for **surfing**, with few facilities as yet (though you can rent surfboards in major tourist centres such as Acapulco and Mazatlán) but with plenty of Californian surfers who follow the weather south over the winter. The most popular places are in Baja California and on the Oaxaca coast, but the biggest waves are to be found around Lázaro Cárdenas in Michoacán. A more minority-interest activity for which Mexico has become a major centre is **caving**. With a third of the country built on limestone, there are caverns in most states that can be explored by experienced potholers or spelunkers.

The Ministry of Tourism publishes a leaflet on participatory sports in Mexico, and can also advise on licences and seasons.

Spectator sports

Mexico's chief spectator sport is soccer (*fútbol*; see box, p.156). Mexican teams have not been notably successful on the international stage, but going to a game can still be a thrilling experience. The capital and Guadalajara are the best places to see a match, and the biggest game in the domestic league, "El Clásico", between Chivas from Guadalajara and América from Mexico City, fills the city's 150,000-seater Aztec stadium to capacity. **Baseball** (*béisbol*) is also popular, as is **American football** (especially on TV). **Jai alai** (also known as **frontón**, or **pelota vasca**) is Basque handball, common in big cities and played at a very high speed with a small hard ball and curved scoop attached to the hand; it's a big gambling game.

Mexican rodeos (*charreadas*), mainly seen in the north of the country, are as spectacular for their style and costume as they are for the events, while **bullfights** remain an obsession: every city has a bullring – Mexico City's Plaza México is the world's largest – and the country's *toreros* are said to be the world's most reckless, much in demand in Spain. Another popular blood sport, usually at village level, is **cock fighting**, still legal in Mexico and mainly attended for the opportunity to bet on the outcome.

Masked **wrestling** (*lucha libre*) is very popular in Mexico, too, with the participants, Batman-like, out of the game for good should their mask be removed and their secret identity revealed. Nor does the resemblance to comic-book superheroes end in the ring: certain masked wrestlers have become popular social campaigners out of the ring, always ready to turn up just in the nick of time to rescue the beleaguered poor from eviction by various landlords or persecution by corrupt politicians. For more on wrestling, see box, p.136.

Culture and etiquette

Mexicans are generally very courteous, and in some ways quite formal. It is common, for example, to address people as señor or señora, while being too brusque can give quite a bad impression.

Most Mexicans are also quite religious, and about three-quarters are **Roman Catholic**; you will often see little altars by the roadside, and many people cross themselves whenever they pass a church. It is wise to avoid open disrespect for religion unless you are sure of your company. While male travellers will find the country very easy-going, women may encounter a few difficulties arising from traditional Latin machismo.

Sexual harassment and discrimination

Machismo is engrained in the Mexican mentality and, although it's softened to some extent by the gentler mores of indigenous culture, most women will find that a degree of harassment is inevitable.

On the whole, most hassles will be limited to **comments** (*piropos*, supposedly compliments) in the street, but situations that might be quite routine at home can seem threatening without a clear understanding of the nuances of Mexican Spanish. Avoid eye contact – wearing sunglasses helps. Any provocation is best ignored – Mexican women are rarely slow with a stream of retaliatory abuse, but it's a dangerous strategy unless you're very sure of your ground, and coming from a foreigner, it may be taken as racism.

Public transport can be one of the worst places for harassment, especially groping in crowded situations. On the Mexico City Metro, there are separate women's carriages and passages during rush hours. Otherwise, if you get a seat, you can hide behind a newspaper.

Problems are aggravated in the big tourist spots, where legendarily "easy" tourists attract droves of would-be gigolos. Away from resorts and big cities, though, and especially in indigenous areas, there is rarely any problem – you may as an outsider be treated as an object of curiosity, and usually such curiosity can also extend to friendliness and hospitality. On the whole, the further from the US border you get, the easier things will become.

The restrictions imposed on drinking are without a doubt irksome: women can now drink in cantinas, but even in so-called "ladies' bars", "unescorted" women may be looked at with suspicion. Even in the roughest places, you are unlikely to be refused service nowadays, but whether or not you would feel comfortable drinking there is a different matter.

Tipping

At expensive restaurants in tourist resorts, waiters and waitresses are used to American tipping levels (15–20 percent), but elsewhere levels are more like those in Europe (10–15 percent). In mid-range and upmarket hotels, you will be expected to tip chambermaids (a few dollars, depending on the standard of the hotel and the length of your stay) and porters (10–20 pesos or a dollar is fine). It is not usual to tip taxi drivers, but small tips are expected by petrol-station and car-park attendants and the bagboys at supermarkets (all of these will be happy with a few pesos of small change).

Shopping

The craft tradition of Mexico, much of it descended directly from arts practised long before the Spanish arrived, is still extremely strong. Regional and highly localized specialities survive, with villages throughout the republic jealously guarding their reputations – especially in the states of Michoacán, Oaxaca and Chiapas, as well as the Yucatán Peninsula. There's a considerable amount of Guatemalan textiles and embroidery about, too.

Crafts

To buy crafts, there is no need to visit the place of origin – **shops** in Mexico City and all the big resorts gather the best and most popular items from around the country. On the other hand, it's a great deal more enjoyable to see where the articles come from, and certainly the only way to get any real bargains. The good stuff is rarely inexpensive wherever you buy it, however, and there is an enormous amount of dross produced specifically for tourists.

FONART shops, in major centres throughout Mexico, are run by a government agency (Ⓦ fonart .gob.mx) devoted to the promotion and preservation of crafts; their wares are always excellent, if expensive, and the shops should be visited to get an idea of what is available. Where no such store exists, you can get a similar idea by looking at the best of the tourist shops.

Among the most popular items are: **silver**, the best of which is wrought in Taxco, although rarely mined there; **pottery**, made almost everywhere, with different techniques, designs and patterns in each region; **woollen goods**, especially blankets, which are again made everywhere, and *sarapes* from Oaxaca – always check the fibres and go for more expensive natural dyes; **leather**, especially tyre-tread-soled *huaraches* (sandals), sold cheaply wherever you go; **glass** from Jalisco; **lacquerware**, particularly from Uruapán; and **hammocks**, the best of which are sold in Mérida.

It is illegal to buy or sell antiquities, and even more criminal to try taking them out of the country (moreover, many items sold as valuable antiquities are little more than worthless fakes) – best just to look.

Markets

For bargain hunters, the **mercado** (market) is the place to head. There's one in every Mexican town which, on the traditional market day, will be at its busiest with villagers from the surrounding area bringing their produce for sale or barter. Mercados are mainly dedicated to food and everyday necessities, but most have a section devoted to crafts, and in larger towns you may find a separate crafts bazaar.

Unless you're completely hopeless at bargaining, prices will always be lower in the market than in shops, but shops do have a couple of advantages. First, they exercise a degree of quality control, whereas any old junk can be sold in the market; and second, many established shops will be able to ship purchases home for you, which saves an enormous amount of frustrating bureaucracy.

Bargaining and haggling are very much a matter of personal style, highly dependent on your command of Spanish, aggressiveness and, to some extent, experience. The old tricks (never showing the least sign of interest – let alone enthusiasm – and walking away will always cut the price dramatically) do still hold true; but make sure you know what you want, its approximate value and how much you are prepared to pay. Never start to haggle for something you definitely don't intend to buy – it'll end in bad feelings on both sides. In shops there's little chance of significantly altering the official price unless you're buying in bulk, and even in markets most food and simple household goods have a set price (though it may be doubled at the sight of an approaching gringo).

Travelling with children

Children under the age of 18 can enter the country either with their own passport or on the passport of a parent with whom they are travelling, but if they are not accompanied by both parents, they will need written consent from whichever parent is not with them (or from both if they are on their own).

Travelling with younger kids is not uncommon – most Mexicans dote on children and they often help to break the ice with strangers. The main problem, especially with small children, is their extra vulnerability. They need protecting from the sun, unsafe drinking water, heat and unfamiliar food. Chile peppers in particular may be a problem for kids who are not used to them. Diarrhoea can also be dangerous for younger children: rehydration salts (see p.40) are vital. Ensure that your child is aware of the dangers of rabies and other animal-borne illnesses; keep children away from all animals and consider a rabies shot.

For touring, hiking or walking, child-carrier backpacks are ideal: they can weigh less than 2kg. If the child is small enough, a fold-up buggy is also well worth packing – especially if they will sleep in it while you have a meal or a drink.

Travel essentials

Costs

The developed tourist resorts and big cities are invariably more expensive than more remote towns, and certain other areas also have noticeably higher prices – among them the industrialized north. Prices can also be affected by **season** and many hotels raise their prices during busy times of the year. Summer, Christmas and Easter are the peak times for Mexican tourists, and areas like Acapulco and Cancún, which attract large numbers of overseas visitors, put their prices up during the high season. Special events are also likely to be marked by price hikes.

Nonetheless, wherever you go you can probably get by on US$450/£290/€403 a week (you could reduce that if you hardly travel around, stay on campsites or in hostels, live on basic food and don't buy any souvenirs, though this requires a lot of discipline); you'd be living well on US$650/£418/€582.

As always, if you're **travelling alone** you'll end up spending more – sharing rooms and food saves a substantial amount. In the larger resorts, you can get apartments for up to six people for even greater savings. If you have an **International Student** or **Youth Card**, you might find the occasional reduction on a museum admission price, but don't go out of your way to obtain one, since most concessions are, at least in theory, only for Mexican students. Cards available include the ISIC card for full-time students and the International Youth Travel Card (IYTC) for under-31s, both of which are available from youth travel firms such as STA Travel

---

ROUGH GUIDES TRAVEL INSURANCE

Rough Guides has teamed up with WorldNomads.com to offer great travel insurance deals. Policies are available to residents of over 150 countries, with cover for a wide range of adventure sports, 24hr emergency assistance, high levels of medical and evacuation cover and a stream of travel safety information. Roughguides.com users can take advantage of their policies online 24/7, from anywhere in the world – even if you're already travelling. And since plans often change when you're on the road, you can extend your policy and even claim online. Roughguides.com users who buy travel insurance with WorldNomads.com can also leave a positive footprint and donate to a community development project. For more information, go to ⓦ roughguides.com/travel-insurance.

(@statravel.com). A university or college photo ID card might even work in some places.

Most restaurant bills come with fifteen **percent IVA** (Impuesto de Valor Añadido, or Valued Added Sales Tax) added; this may not always be included in prices quoted on the menu. **Service** is sometimes added to bills; if not, the amount you tip is entirely up to you – in cheap places, it's typically 10–15 percent, but more like 15–20 percent in smarter venues. See p.53 for more on tipping.

Electricity

Theoretically 110 volts AC, with simple two-flat-pin rectangular plugs – most North American appliances can be used as they are. Travellers from the UK, Ireland, Europe, Australasia and South Africa should bring along a converter and a plug adaptor. Cuts in service and fluctuations in current sometimes occur.

Insurance

There are no reciprocal health arrangements between Mexico and any other country, so travel **insurance** is essential. Credit cards (particularly American Express) often have certain levels of medical or other insurance included, and travel insurance may also be included if you use a major credit card to pay for your trip. Some package tours, too, may include insurance.

Before paying for a new policy, it's worth checking whether you are already covered: some all-risks home insurance policies may cover your possessions when overseas, and many private medical schemes include cover when abroad. In Canada, provincial health plans usually provide partial cover for medical mishaps overseas, while holders of official student/teacher/youth cards in Canada and the US are entitled to meagre accident coverage and hospital in-patient benefits. Students in Canada and the US will often find that their health insurance policies extend over the holidays and for one term beyond the date of last enrolment.

After exhausting the possibilities above, you might want to contact a specialist travel insurance company, or consider the travel insurance deal offered by Rough Guides (see box opposite). A typical travel insurance policy usually provides cover for the loss of baggage, tickets and – up to a certain limit – cash or cheques, as well as cancellation or curtailment of your journey. Most of them exclude so-called **dangerous sports** unless an extra premium is paid: in Mexico

this can mean scuba diving, whitewater rafting, windsurfing and trekking, though probably not kayaking or jeep safaris. Many policies can be chopped and changed to exclude coverage you don't need – for example, sickness and accident benefits can often be excluded or included at will. If you do take medical coverage, ascertain whether benefits will be paid as treatment proceeds or only after your return home, and whether there is a 24-hour medical emergency number. When securing **baggage cover**, make sure that the per-article limit – typically under US$1000/£640 – will cover your most valuable possession. If you need to make a claim, you should keep receipts for medicines and medical treatment, and in the event you have anything stolen, you must make an official statement to the police and obtain a copy of the declaration (*copia de la declaración*) for your insurance company.

Internet

Internet cafés are easy to find in all the larger cities and resort destinations, and the level of service is usually excellent. One or two offer cheap VOIP phone calls too. In smaller towns and villages, such facilities are still rare. Depending on where you are, internet access can cost anything from M$8 to M$25 an hour. Major tourist resorts can be the most expensive places, and in these areas it's best to look for cheaper internet cafés around the town centre and avoid those in the luxury hotel zones. Internet facilities in large cities are usually open from early morning until late at night, but in smaller towns they have shorter opening hours and may not open on Sundays. Wi-fi (generally free) is widespread in hotels, hostels, restaurants, cafés and even town plazas.

Laundry

Lavanderías (laundries) are ubiquitous in Mexico, as the majority of households don't own a washing machine. Most *lavanderías* charge by the kilo, and for a few dollars you'll get your clothes back clean, pressed and perfectly folded in less than 24 hours. Many hotels also offer laundry services that, although convenient, tend to charge by the item, adding up to a considerably greater cost.

LGBT travellers

There are no federal laws governing **homosexuality** in Mexico, and hence it's **legal**. There are, however, laws enforcing "public morality", which, although they are supposed only to apply to prostitution, are often used against gays. 1997 saw the election of Mexico's first "out" congresswoman, the left-wing PRD's Patria Jiménez, and in 2003 the federal parliament passed a law against discrimination on various grounds including sexual preference. In 2005, however, a gay man from Tampico successfully claimed political asylum in the US after demonstrating the extent of persecution he faced in his hometown. There have been more positive moves recently, though: in June 2015 the Supreme Court issued a "jurisprudential thesis" that changed the legal definition of marriage to include same-sex couples.

There are a large number of **gay groups** and **publications** in Mexico. The **lesbian** scene is not as visible or as large as the gay scene for men, but it's there and growing. There are gay bars and clubs in the major resorts and US border towns, and in large cities such as the capital, and also Monterrey, Guadalajara, Veracruz and Oaxaca; elsewhere, private parties are where it all happens, and you'll need a contact to find them.

As far as popular **attitudes** are concerned, religion and machismo are the order of the day, and prejudice is rife, but attitudes are changing. Soft-core porn magazines for gay men are sold openly on street stalls and, while you should be careful to avoid upsetting macho sensibilities, you should have few problems if you are discreet. In Juchitán, Oaxaca, on the other hand, gay male transvestites, known as *muxes*, are accepted as a kind of third sex, and the town even has a transvestite basketball team.

You can check the latest gay rights situation in Mexico on the International Gay and Lesbian Human Rights Commission website at ⓦ iglhrc.org,

and information on the male gay scene in Mexico (gay bars, meeting places and cruising spots) can be found in the annual *Spartacus Gay Guide*, available in specialist bookshops at home, or online at ⓦ spartacusworld.com.

Living in Mexico

There's virtually no chance of finding temporary **work** in Mexico unless you have some very specialized skill and have arranged the position beforehand. Work **permits** are almost impossible to obtain. The few foreigners who manage to find work do so mostly in language schools. It may be possible, though not legal, to earn money as a private English tutor by advertising in a local newspaper or at a university.

The best way to extend your time in Mexico is on a **study programme** or **volunteer project**. A US organization called AmeriSpan selects language schools in countries worldwide, including Mexico, to match the needs and requirements of students, and provides advice and support. For further information, call (US or Canada) ☏ 1 800 879 6640 or ☏ 1 215 531 8001, or see ⓦ amerispan.com.

Volunteers need to apply for a voluntary work visa (FM3), for which you will need to present a letter of invitation from the organization for which you are volunteering.

STUDY AND WORK PROGRAMMES

AFS Intercultural Programs ⓦ afs.org; US ☏ 1 800 237 4636, ⓦ afsusa.org; Canada ☏ 1 800 361 7248 or ☏ 1 514 288 3282, ⓦ en.afscanada.org; Australia ☏ 1 300 131 736, afs.org.au; New Zealand ☏ 0800 600 300 or ☏ 04 494 6020, ⓦ afs.org.nz; South Africa ☏ 0861 237 468 or ☏ 011 431 0113, ⓦ afs.org.za; international enquiries ☏ +1 212 807 8686. Intercultural exchange organization with programmes in over fifty countries, including Mexico (but there's no branch in the UK).

Casa Hoy Río Mexapa 130, Colonia Hacienda Tetela, 62160 Cuernavaca, Morelos, Mexico ☏ 777 176 7868, ⓦ hoycommunity -online.net. A volunteers' hostel which can organize short-term community service activities as well as contacts with local activists and cultural immersion.

Council on International Educational Exchange (CIEE) US ☏ 1 207 553 4000, ⓦ ciee.org. Leading NGO offering study programmes around the world including Mexico.

Earthwatch Institute UK ☏ 01865 318 838, US & Canada ☏ 1 978 461 0081, Australia ☏ 03 9682 6828; ⓦ earthwatch.org. Matches volunteers with scientists working on particular projects, sometimes in Mexico, but it's not cheap: volunteers must raise a minimum contribution (average about US$3000) to the cost of research for each one- to two-week stint.

Studyabroad.com UK ☎ 01865 318 838, US ☎ 1 484 766 2920, ⓦ studyabroad.com. Language programmes, semester-long and year-long courses and internships in Guadalajara, Cuernavaca, Puebla and Mexico City.
Volunteer South America ⓦ volunteersouthamerica.net. A useful site with links to free and low-cost volunteering opportunities across Latin America, including Mexico.

Mail

Mexican **postal services** (*correos*) can be quite slow and unreliable. Airmail to the capital should arrive within a few days, but it may take a couple of weeks to get anywhere at all remote. Packages frequently go astray. **Post offices** (generally open Mon–Fri 8am–4.30pm, Sat 8am–noon, sometimes longer at the central office in big cities) usually offer a **poste restante/general delivery** service: letters should be addressed to "Lista de Correos". Mail is held for two weeks, though you may get around that by sending it to "Poste Restante" with "Favor de retener hasta la llegada" (please hold until arrival) on the envelope. Letters are often filed incorrectly, so you should have staff check under all your initials. To collect, you will need your passport or some other official ID with a photograph. There is no fee.

For personal mail, Mexican **addresses** begin with the street and house number. The number goes after the street name (Juárez 123 rather than 123 Juárez), and is followed if appropriate by the floor or apartment number (*planta baja* means ground floor). After that comes the *cólonia* (the immediate neighbourhood), then the town, then finally the zip code and the state (on one line in that order – in the case of Mexico City, "México DF" is the equivalent of the state).

Sending letters and cards home is also easy enough, if slow. Anything sent **abroad** by air should have an airmail (*por avión*) stamp on it or it is liable to go by surface mail. Letters should take around a week to North America, two to Europe or Australasia, but can take much longer (postcards in particular are likely to be slow). Anything at all important should be taken to the post office and preferably registered rather than dropped in a mailbox, although the dedicated airmail boxes in resorts and big cities are supposed to be more reliable than ordinary ones. Postcards or letters up to 20g cost M$11.50 to North America or the Caribbean, M$13.50 to the British Isles, Europe or South America and M$15 to Australasia, Asia, Africa or the Pacific.

The process of sending **packages** out of the country is drowned in bureaucracy. Regulations about the thickness of brown paper wrapping and the amount of string used vary from state to state, but any package must be checked by customs and have its paperwork stamped by at least three other departments. Take your package (unsealed) to any post office and they'll set you on your way. Many stores will send your purchases home for you, which is much easier. Within the country, you can send a package by bus if there is someone to collect it at the other end.

Maps

Reliable options available outside of Mexico include Mexico road maps published by Globetrotter (1:3,500,000), GeoCenter (1:2,500,000), Hallwag (1:2,500,000) and Freytag & Berndt (1:2,000,000). In Mexico itself, the best maps are those produced by Guía Roji, who also publish a Mexican road atlas and a Mexico City street guide. Guía Roji maps are widely available – try branches of Sanborn's or large Pemex stations – and can also be ordered online at ⓦ tienda.guiaroji.com.mx.

More detailed, large-scale maps – for hiking or climbing – are harder to come by. The most detailed, easily available area maps are produced by International Travel Map Productions (ⓦ itmb.ca), whose Travellers' Reference Map series covers various regions of the country. INEGI, the Mexican office of statistics, also produce very good topographic maps on various scales. They have an office in every state capital (addresses on their website at ⓦ inegi.org.mx – click on "Productos y Servicios", then on "Atención a Usuarios" and finally select "Centros de Información INEGI"). Unfortunately, stocks can run rather low, so don't count on being able to buy the ones that you want.

Money

The Mexican **peso**, usually written $, is made up of 100 centavos (¢, like a US cent). Bills come in denominations of $20, $50, $100, $200, $500 and $1000, with coins of 10¢, 20¢, 50¢, $1, $2, $5 and $10. The use of the dollar symbol for the peso is occasionally confusing; the initials MN (*moneda nacional* or national coin) are occasionally used to indicate that it's Mexican, not American, money that is being referred to. Prices in this book are generally quoted in Mexican pesos (M$). Note, however, that these will be affected by factors such as inflation and exchange rates. Check an online currency converter such as XE (Ⓦxe.com) or OANDA (Ⓦoanda.com) for up-to-date rates. At the time of writing, US$1 was worth approximately M$17, CAN$1 approximately M$12, £1 sterling approximately M$25 and €1 approximately M$19. Some tour operators and large hotels quote prices in US dollars, and accept payment in that currency.

ATMs

The easiest way to access your money in Mexico is in the form of **plastic**, though it's a good idea to also have some cash back-up. Using a Visa, MasterCard, Plus or Cirrus card, you can withdraw cash from **ATMs** in most towns and tourist resorts. By using these you get trade exchange rates, which are somewhat better than those charged by banks for changing cash, though your card issuer may well add a foreign transaction fee, and these can be as much as five percent, so check with your issuer before leaving home. Local ATM providers may also charge a transaction fee, typically around M$30; generally speaking, rates and fees make it cheaper to use an ATM for more than around US$100/£65, but to change cash in a *casa de cambio* (see below) for anything much less than that. If you use a credit card rather than a debit card, note all cash advances and ATM withdrawals obtained are treated as loans, with interest accruing daily from the date of withdrawal. Travellers' cheques are increasingly difficult to change in Mexico, but it is possible to get a **prepaid card**, like a form of travellers' cheques in plastic, which you charge up with funds at home and then use to withdraw money from ATMs – MasterCard, Visa and American Express all issue them. Some ATMs in big city centres and resorts can issue US dollars as well as – or instead of – pesos.

Banks and exchange

Banks are generally open Monday to Friday from 9.30am to 5pm, often with shorter hours for **exchange**. Commission on currency exchange varies but the exchange rate is fixed daily by the government. Not all banks can change money, and only larger branches of the big banks, plus some in tourist resorts, will change currencies other than dollars – and even then at worse rates than you would get for the dollar equivalent.

Casas de cambio (*forex bureaux* aka *bureaux de change*) have varying exchange rates and commis-

sion charges, and tend to have shorter queues, less bureaucratic procedures and longer opening hours. The exchange rates are generally better than at banks, but always worth checking, especially for travellers' cheques. Some *casas de cambio* will change only US dollars, but others take euros, Canadian dollars, pounds sterling and other currencies. $100 bills usually attract a better rate than small bills. Again, it's worth shopping around, especially if you intend to change a large sum. Even in a *casa de cambio*, you'll need your passport to change money.

Guatemalan quetzales and Belizean dollars are best got rid of before entering Mexico; otherwise, your best bet for changing them is with tourists heading the other way – try Ⓦweswap.com, a useful website that allows travellers to swap foreign currency with each other. It is a good idea to change other currencies into US dollars at home before coming to Mexico, since the difference in the exchange rate more than outweighs the amount you lose in changing your money twice. In some touristy places, such as Acapulco and Tijuana, US dollar bills are almost as easy to spend as pesos. If you're desperate, hotels, shops and restaurants that are used to tourists may change dollars or accept them as payment, but rates will be very low.

Opening hours

It's almost impossible to generalize about **opening hours** in Mexico; even when times are posted at museums, tourist offices and shops, they're not always adhered to.

The **siesta** is still around, and many places will close for a couple of hours in the early afternoon, usually from 1pm to 3pm. Where it's hot – especially on the Gulf coast and in the Yucatán – everything may close for up to four hours in the middle of the

---

USEFUL AND EMERGENCY NUMBERS

General emergency number ☎066
Police ☎060
Fire ☎068
Ambulance ☎065
Green Angels (tourist highway breakdown) ☎078
National operator ☎020
International operator ☎090
Directory enquiries ☎040
Tourist information ☎078

DIALLING CODES

Mexico long-distance ☎01 + area code + number
US & Canada ☎001 + area code + number
UK ☎00 44 + area code (minus initial zero) + number
Ireland ☎00 353 + area code (minus initial zero) + number
Australia ☎00 61 + area code (minus initial zero) + number
New Zealand ☎00 64 + area code (minus initial zero) + number
South Africa ☎00 27 + area code (minus initial zero) + number

day, and then reopen until 8pm or 9pm. In central Mexico, the industrial north and highland areas, hours are more like the standard nine-to-five, and shops do not close for lunch.

Shops tend to keep long hours, say from 9am to 8pm. Museums and galleries open from about 9am or 10am to 5pm or 6pm. Many have reduced entry fees – or are free – on Sunday, and most are closed on Monday. Some museums close for lunch, but archeological sites are open all day. For opening of post offices see p.57; for banks see opposite.

Phones

Local **phone** calls in Mexico are cheap, and some hotels will let you call locally for free. Coin-operated **public phones** exist, but internal long-distance calls are best made with a **phonecard** (sold at newsstands and usable in public phones on almost every street corner). Slightly more expensive, but often more convenient, are *casetas de teléfono* (phone offices), mainly found at bus stations and airports. Calling abroad with a phonecard or from a *caseta* is expensive. Some internet offices offer **VOIP international calls**, which may be cheaper, but the line will not be as good. Skype is generally the best option.

It is also possible to **call collect** (*por cobrar*). In theory, you should be able to make an international collect call from any public phone, by dialling the international operator (☎090). If you have a calling card from your home phone company, you can use the company's toll-free number and have the call billed to you at home.

Calling Mexico from abroad, dial the international access code (☎011 from the US or Canada, ☎00 from Britain, Ireland or New Zealand, ☎0011 from

Australia, ☎09 from South Africa), followed by the **country code** for Mexico, which is 52. Mexican **numbers** are ten-digit including the area code (*lada*), which is usually three digits, although Mexico City (☎55), Guadalajara (☎33) and Monterrey (☎81) have two-digit area codes. The number itself is usually seven digits, again excepting Mexico City, Guadalajara and Monterrey, where phone numbers have eight digits. If dialling from abroad, you dial the area code immediately after the 52 for Mexico. If dialling long-distance within Mexico, or from a mobile, you need to dial ☎01, then the area code and the number. If dialling from a landline with the same area code, you omit it. The area code for toll-free numbers is ☎800, always preceded by the ☎01.

Mobile phones

To use a **mobile phone** in Mexico is expensive if you simply take your own phone and use it under a roaming agreement. If you are there for any length of time, buy a prepaid phone (around M$500–800, including a varying amount of call credit). You can buy a Mexican SIM-card (around M$100–200) to get a Mexican number for your own handset, but this involves registering your identity (so you'll need a passport, and you may need to go to the phone company's main office), something that doesn't always work for a foreigner, so make sure your mobile works before you leave the store. Your phone charger will not work in Mexico if it is designed for a 220–240v electricity supply. Calls from mobiles are pricey, and with a SIM-card from abroad you pay to receive as well as make international calls.

Like landlines, Mexican mobile phones have ten-digit numbers, of which the first two or three are the area code. Generally speaking, to call a mobile from a landline, first dial ☎044 if it has the same area code, ☎045 if not, or the international access code plus ☎52-1 if calling from abroad, and then the ten-digit number; note, however, that some mobile numbers work in the same way as dialling landline numbers – unfortunately, you cannot tell from the number alone how it will work.

Photography

It's easy enough to get prints made from a **USB** stick in Mexico. **Film** is also manufactured in the country and, if you buy it from a chain store like Sanborn's rather than at a tourist store, costs no more than at home. Slide film is hard to come by, and any sort of camera hardware will be expensive.

Senior travellers

Mexico is not a country that offers any special difficulties – or any special advantages – to **older travellers**, but the same considerations apply here as to anywhere else in the world. If choosing a package tour, consider one run by firms such as Road Scholar (**W** roadscholar.org) or Saga (**W** saga .co.uk), which specialize in holidays for the over-50s.

Do remember that Mexico's high altitude, desert heat and tropical humidity can tire you out a lot faster than you might otherwise expect. As far as comfort is concerned, first-class buses are generally pretty pleasant, with plenty of legroom. Second-class buses can be rather more boneshaking, and you may not want to take them for too long a journey.

Senior citizens are often entitled to **discounts** at tourist sights, and on occasion for accommodation and transport, something which it's always worth asking about.

Time

Five **time zones** exist in Mexico. Most of the country is on GMT−6 in winter, GMT−5 in summer (first Sun in April till last Sun in Oct), the same as US Central Time. Baja California Sur, Sinaloa, Nayarit and Chihuahua are on GMT−7 in winter, GMT−6 in summer (the same as US Mountain Time). Baja California is on GMT−8 in winter, GMT−7 in summer, the same as the US West Coast (Pacific Time); and finally, Sonora is on GMT−7 all year round, and does not observe daylight saving time. The state of Quintana Roo changed time zones in early 2015, moving to GMT−5 in winter and GMT−4 in summer, bringing it into line with Eastern Standard Time.

Toilets

Public toilets in Mexico are usually decent enough, but in bars or hole-in-the-wall restaurants, they can be quite basic, and may not have paper. It's therefore wise to carry toilet paper with you. In bus stations, you usually have to pay to use them. Paper should usually be placed in a bin after use, rather than flushed, as it may otherwise block the plumbing.

Toilets are usually known as *baños* (literally bathrooms) or as *excusados* or *sanitarios*. The most common signs are "Damas" (Ladies) and "Caballeros" (Gentlemen), though you may find the more confusing "Señoras" (Women) and "Señores" (Men) or even symbols of the moon (women) and sun (men).

Tourist information

The first place to head for **information**, and for free maps of the country and many towns, is the Mexican Government Ministry of Tourism (**Secretaría de Turismo**, abbreviated to **SECTUR**; **W** sectur.gob.mx, with travel information at **W** visitmexico.com), which has offices throughout Mexico and abroad.

Once you're in Mexico, you'll find tourist offices (sometimes called *turismos*) in most towns. Each state capital will have one run by SECTUR, but most are run by state and municipal authorities; sometimes there'll be two or three rival ones in the same town. Many tourist offices are extremely friendly and helpful, with informed staff and free information and leaflets by the cart-load, but others are barely capable of answering the simplest enquiry. We have listed the most useful ones in the relevant city and regional sections throughout the Guide. You can also call SECTUR toll-free round the clock in Mexico at ☎078 or ☎800 006 8839, or toll-free from the US or Canada on ☎1 866 640 0597, or from the UK ☎00 800 1111 2266.

GOVERNMENT TRAVEL ADVICE

Australian Department of Foreign Affairs **W** smartraveller .gov.au.
British Foreign & Commonwealth Office **W** gov.uk/ government/organisations/foreign-commonwealth-office.
Canadian Department of Foreign Affairs **W** voyage.gc.ca.
US State Department **W** travel.state.gov.

Travellers with disabilities

An estimated five percent of Mexicans have some kind of significant disability, and Mexico has made massive advances in accessibility in recent years, although problems still remain. Ramps and wheelchair accessibility are now the norm in public buildings, and braille is increasingly common on public notices too. The real scandal so far as people with disabilities are concerned is the continued abuse of those confined to residential institutions or living on the street.

Hotels vary, but, especially at the top end of the market, it shouldn't be too difficult to find accommodation and tour operators who can cater for your particular needs. If you stick to **beach resorts** – Cancún and Acapulco in particular – and top-end hotels, you should be able to find places that are wheelchair-friendly and used to disabled guests. US chains are very good for this, with Choice, Days Inn, Holiday Inn, Leading Hotels of the World, Marriott, Radisson, Ramada, Sheraton and Westin claiming to have the necessary facilities for at least some disabilities in some of their hotels. Check in advance with tour companies, hotels and airlines that they can accommodate you specifically.

Unless you have your own **transport**, the best way to travel in Mexico may be by air; buses still rarely cater for disabled people and wheelchairs. Kerb ramps are increasingly common, especially in big cities, but less so in smaller places, where streets and pavements may not be in great nick, and

people are not especially more likely to volunteer help than at home. Depending on your disability, you may want to find an able-bodied helper to accompany you.

RESOURCES

Disabled Holidays UK ☎ 01457 833 444,
ⓦ disabledholidaydirectory.co.uk. UK travel agency specializing in holidays for people with disabilities. Their website has a page on Mexico, with information on accessible hotels across the country.

Mexico Accesible Mexico ☎ 322 225 0989, US ☎ 1 866 519 6165, Canada ☎ 1 877 839 3484, ⓦ accesiblemexico.com. A Puerto Vallarta firm offering a range of services, from mobility equipment to wheelchair-friendly timeshares.

Mexico City

DIEGO RIVERA MURAL, TEATRO DE LOS INSURGENTES

1

Mexico City

One of the world's mega-cities, with over 25 million people occupying a shallow mountain bowl at over 2400m above sea level, Mexico City has to be seen to be believed. Spreading out beyond the federal district (Distrito Federal) which is supposed to contain it, the city has a vibe which is at once both edgy and yet laid-back and cosmopolitan at the same time. Despite its terrible pollution (see p.70), the capital is a fun place to be, and nowhere near as intimidating as you might expect. It's also very easy to find your way around, with an efficient metro system, and generally easy-to-navigate grid of streets.

On arrival you may brace yourself for the city's hard edge, but be prepared to be lulled by it. Mexico's capital may initially seem to lack the colour and charm of some of the country's smaller towns, but it can be pretty too, and there's certainly no denying its dynamism. The city centre still retains its colonial feel, its streets bustling with the comings and goings of daily commerce. The fact that different products are sold in specific areas – stationery here, electrical fittings there – sometimes makes it seem like a giant market. To the west, steel and glass take over from brick and stone as tradition gives way to modernity, but in the suburbs, in laid-back *barrios* like San Ángel and Coyoacán, there's as much charm as in any small Mexican town, and a surprising number of little squares overlooked by old churches amid leafy residential backstreets. For many Mexicans, in fact, the city's most important site is the **Basílica de Guadalupe**, sited in the suburbs to the north of town. To the southwest, meanwhile, is Chapultepec Park and some of the biggest attractions you'll want to see, notably the outstanding **Museo Nacional de Antropología**. Even in the centre, around the garden known as the **Alameda** in particular, there's music, art (**Diego Rivera** and **Frida Kahlo**, as well as their contemporaries) and colour enough to seduce you, and the hustle and bustle only seem to amplify it. While the outer edges of the city are largely shantytowns, built piecemeal by migrants from elsewhere in the country, hidden among them are a number of gems, such as the **pyramids** of Tenayuca, Santa Cecilia Acatitlán and Cuicuilco, and the canals of **Xochimilco**.

As much the heart of the modern capital as it was of the Aztec civilization that once thrived here, the **Zócalo**, or main square, is the place to get your bearings. Immediately to its west, in the streets between the Zócalo and the Alameda, is the main **commercial area**. Beyond that, the city stretches northward and southward, its urban area now extending beyond the political boundaries of the **Distrito Federal** which is supposed to contain it (in

TRAJINERAS BOATS, XOCHIMILCO GARDENS

Highlights

❶ The Zócalo Mexico City's huge central square, surrounded by the cathedral, Aztec ruins and the Palacio Nacional. **See p.69**

❷ Palacio de Bellas Artes Not only an architectural masterpiece in its own right, with a smashing Art Deco interior, but also home to some of the city's most impressive murals. **See p.84**

❸ Museo Mural Diego Rivera Rivera's most Mexican mural, depicting just about everybody from Mexican history, all out on a Sunday afternoon stroll in the Alameda. **See p.87**

❹ Museo Nacional de Antropología The country's finest museum, with displays on all of Mexico's major pre-Columbian cultures. **See p.95**

❺ Coyoacán Visit the houses where Frida Kahlo and León Trotsky lived, spend an evening checking out the local bars, then come back for the colourful Sunday market. **See p.105**

❻ Museo Dolores Olmedo Patiño A huge collection of works by Diego Rivera and Frida Kahlo. **See p.112**

❼ Xochimilco Ride the ancient waterways on flower-festooned boats. **See p.112**

❽ Plaza Garibaldi The frenetic site of massed mariachi bands. **See p.134**

❾ La Merced Explore Mexico City's largest and most vibrant market. **See p.135**

HIGHLIGHTS ARE MARKED ON THE MAPS ON P.66 & PP.72–73

1

Tula & Querétaro   Tula & Querétaro   Teotihuacán & Pachuca

HIGHLIGHTS

4 Museo Nacional de Antropología

5 Coyoacán

6 Museo Dolores Olmedo Patiño

7 Xochimilco

Freight Only

0   2
kilometres

San Rafael

Santa Cecilia Acatitlán

Tenayuca

Tlalnepantla

ANILLO PERIFÉRICO

Fortuna

INDIOS VERDES

Basílica de Nuestra Señora de Guadalupe

GUADALUPE

Terminal del Norte (Bus Station)

CALZ VALLEJO

CALZ DE GUADALUPE

BOSQUE DE ARAGÓN

AV M A CAMACHO

Toluca

CALZ CUITLÁHUAC

TACUBA

La Raza

AV RÍO CONSULADO

CALZ SAN JOAQUIN

Buenavista

Plaza de las Tres Culturas

Instituto de Migración

SEE "CHAPULTEPEC & POLANCO" MAP

SEE "CENTRAL MEXICO CITY" MAP

Alameda

Cathedral

Hipódromo de las Américas

POLANCO

MUSCAMPO

Cathedral

TAPO (Bus Station)

Airport

Museo Nacional de Antropología

PASEO DE LA REFORMA

ZÓCALO

Palacio National

DEPORTIVA VENUSTIANO CARRANZA

BLVD PUERTO AÉREO

CALZ ZARAGOZA

CHAPULTEPEC

CHAPULTEPEC PARK

INSURGENTES

Puebla

SEE "ZONA ROSA, ROMA & CONDESA" MAP

LÁZARO CÁRDENAS

CALZ SAN ANTONIO ABAD

CIUDAD DEPORTIVA MAGDALENA MIXHUCA

AV CONSTITUYENTES

World Trade Center

CIUDAD DEPORTIVA

Toluca

ABC Hospital

Polyforum Siqueiros

CALZ DE TLALPAN

RÍO CHURUBUSCO

Terminal Poniente (Bus Station)

Estacho Azul Plaza México

Museo Frida Kahlo

Teatro de los Insurgentes

AV UNIVERSIDAD

Museo Nacional de las Intervenciones

SAN ÁNGEL

5 COYOACÁN

EL PEDREGAL

SEE "COYOACÁN & SAN ÁNGEL" MAP

DIVISIÓN DEL NORTE

Central de Autobuses del Sur (Bus Station)

Puebla

CIUDAD UNIVERSITARIA

ANILLO PERIFÉRICO

ANILLO PERIFÉRICO

Estadio Olímpico

University Library

Museo Diego River Anahuacalli

Estadio Azteca

CALZ DE TLALPAN

Cuicuilco

TLALPAN

6 Museo Dolores Olmedo Patiño

7 XOCHIMILCO

N

MEXICO CITY

Cuernavaca

1

FINDING YOUR STREET

Many **street names** are repeated over and over in different parts of Mexico City – there must be dozens of thoroughfares called Morelos, Juárez or Hidalgo, and a good score of 5 de Mayos. If you're taking a cab, or looking at a map, be clear which area you are talking about – it's fairly obvious in the centre, but searching out an address in the suburbs can lead to a series of false starts unless you know the name of the official **colonia**, or urban district (abbreviated "Col" in addresses outside the centre), that you're looking for. If you're going to be spending much time in the city, and are likely to be visiting places out of the centre, consider investing in Guia Roji's *Ciudad de México* street atlas, which is available at bookshops and street stalls all over town, and covers every street of the city and its suburbs, with an index.

the same way that the DC is supposed to contain the city of Washington). It's crisscrossed by a series of axes (*ejes* in Spanish), of which the north–south *eje central* (central axis, aka Lázaro Cárdenas) is plied by a very useful trolleybus linking the northern and southern bus terminals. Roughly parallel with it, 1km or so over to the west, **Avenida de los Insurgentes** also bisects the city more or less from north to south, and is said to be the longest continuous city street in the world, linking the centre to **San Ángel** and **Coyoacán**, and the **University City**, all at the southern end of town. Even more important from a tourist perspective is **Paseo de la Reforma**, which runs diagonally across the city, northeast to southwest, connecting the centre with **Chapultepec Park**.

Brief history

The **Aztecs** (or, to use their own name, the Mexica), an ambitious and flourishing culture, founded their capital of **Tenochtitlán** in 1325 on an island in the middle of a lake, at a spot where their god Huitzilopochtli told them they would find an eagle devouring a snake atop a nopal cactus. It was from here that their empire grew to cover the whole of central Mexico. This empire was already firmly established when **Hernán Cortés** and his troops arrived in November 1519. The Aztec emperor, **Moctezuma II** (Montezuma), a broodingly religious man, apparently believed Cortés to be a reincarnation of the pale-skinned, bearded god Quetzalcoatl. Accordingly, he admitted him to the city – fearfully, but with a show of ceremonious welcome. The Spanish repaid this hospitality by taking Moctezuma prisoner. They then attacked the great Aztec temples, killing priests and placing Christian chapels alongside their altars.

Growing unrest in the city at the emperor's passivity, and at the rapacious behaviour of his guests, led to **rebellion**. In June 1520, Moctezuma was killed – according to the Spanish, stoned to death by his own people while trying to quell a riot – and the Spaniards fled the city with heavy losses on what they called **Noche Triste** (Sad Night; see p.820). Cortés and his surviving followers escaped to Tlaxcala to regroup. In May 1521, with numbers swelled by indigenous allies, and ships built in secret to attack by water, the Spaniards laid **siege** to Tenochtitlán, landing on the south of the island and fighting their way north through the city, street by bloody street. The Aztec emperor **Cuauhtémoc** was finally captured on August 13, 1521, and subsequently tortured to try to find out where his supposed treasure was hidden. He was finally executed four years later in Honduras.

Spanish and post-colonial Mexico City

The Spanish systematically smashed every visible aspect of Aztec culture, as often as not using the very stones of the old city to construct the new. The **new city** developed slowly in its early years. It spread far wider, however, as the lake was drained, filled and built over. Pestilent from the earliest days, the inadequately drained waters harboured fevers, and the native population was constantly swept by epidemics of European diseases. Many of the buildings, too, simply began to sink into the soft lake bed, a process probably accelerated by regular earthquakes.

1

TENOCHTITLÁN – THE CITY THAT WALKED ON WATER

And when we saw all those cities and villages built in the water, and other great towns on dry land, and that straight and level causeway leading to Mexico, we were astounded. These great towns and cities and buildings rising from the water, all made of stone, seemed like an enchanted vision from the tales of Amadis. Indeed, some of our soldiers asked whether it was not all a dream.

Bernal Díaz, The Conquest of New Spain

The Aztec capital of **Tenochtitlán** was built on an island in the middle of a lake traversed by great causeways, a beautiful, strictly regulated, stone-built city of three hundred thousand residents. The Aztecs had arrived at the lake around 1325, after years of wandering and living off what they could scavenge or pillage from settled communities. According to legend, their patron god Huitzilopochtli had ordered them to build a city where they found an eagle perched on a nopal cactus, and devouring a snake. It is this legend that is the basis of the nopal, eagle and snake motif that forms the centrepiece of the modern Mexican flag.

The lake proved an ideal site: well stocked with fish, it was also fertile, once the Aztecs had constructed **chinampas**, or floating gardens of reeds. These enabled them to grow crops on the lake, as a result of which they were self-sufficient in food. The lake also made the city virtually impregnable: the **causeways**, when they were completed, could be flooded and the bridges raised to thwart attacks (or escape, as the Spanish found on the Noche Triste; see p.820).

The island city eventually grew to cover an area of some thirteen square kilometres, much of it reclaimed from the lake, and from this base the Aztecs were able to begin their programme of **expansion**: initially dominating the valley by a series of strategic alliances, war and treachery, and finally, in a period of less than a hundred years before the brutal Spanish Conquest of 1521, establishing an empire that demanded tribute from, and traded with, the most distant parts of the country. Yet almost nothing of this amazing city survived the Conquest. "All that I saw then," Bernal Díaz later wrote of his account of Tenochtitlán, "is overthrown and destroyed; nothing is left standing." It is only relatively recently – particularly during construction of the Metro, and with the 1978 discovery of remains of the Templo Mayor beneath the colonial Zócalo – that a few remains of Tenochtitlán have been brought to light.

The city's defeat, moreover, is still a harsh memory: Cortés himself is hardly revered, but the natives who assisted him, in particular La Malinche, the Veracruz woman who acted as Cortés' interpreter, are non-people. Tributes to Moctezuma are rare, though **Cuauhtémoc**, his successor who led the fierce resistance, is commemorated everywhere; Malinche is represented, acidly, in some of Diego Rivera's more outspoken murals.

By the third quarter of the nineteenth century, the city comprised little more than the area around the Zócalo and Alameda. Chapultepec Castle, Coyoacán, San Ángel and the Basilica of Guadalupe were still surrounded by fields and the last of the basin's former lakes. From late 1870 through to 1911, however, the dictator Porfirio Díaz presided over an unprecedented, and self-aggrandizing, **building programme** that saw the installation of trams, the expansion of public transport and the draining of some of the last sections of the Lago de Texcoco, which had previously hemmed the city in. These all fuelled further growth, and by the outbreak of the Revolution in 1910, Mexico City's residents numbered over four hundred thousand, regaining for the first time in four centuries the population level it had held before the Conquest.

The modern city

During the Revolution, thousands fled to rapidly industrializing Mexico City in search of jobs and a better life. Between 1910 and the mid-1940s the city's population quadrupled and the cracks in the infrastructure quickly became gaping holes. Houses couldn't be built quickly enough to cope with the seven-percent annual growth, and many people couldn't afford them anyway, so **shantytowns** of scrap metal and cardboard sprang up. Most neighbourhoods had little or no water supply and sanitation was an afterthought. Gradually, civic leaders tried to address the lot of citizens by improving the services and housing in shantytowns, but even as they worked, a new ring of slums mushroomed just a little further out. This expansion badly strained the transport system, necessitating the construction of a **Metro** system in the late 1960s.

Urban growth continues today: some statisticians estimate that there are a thousand new arrivals each day, mainly from high-unemployment rural areas, and the urban area now extends beyond the limits of the Distrito Federal and into the surrounding states. Despite the spread, Mexico City remains one of the world's most densely and heavily populated cities, with an unenviable list of major social and physical problems, including an extreme vulnerability to earthquakes – the last big one, in 1985, killed over nine thousand people, made one hundred thousand homeless and left many of the city's buildings decidedly skewed.

Central Mexico City

The heart of Mexico City is the **Zócalo**, built by the Spanish right over the devastated ceremonial centre of the Aztec city of Tenochtitlán. Extraordinary uncovered ruins – chief of which is the **Templo Mayor** – provide the Zócalo's most compelling attraction, but there's also a wealth of great colonial buildings, among them the huge **cathedral** and the **Palacio Nacional** with its striking **Diego Rivera murals**. You could easily spend a couple of days in the tightly packed blocks hereabouts, investigating their dense concentration of museums and galleries, especially notable for works by Rivera and his "Big Three" companions, David Siqueiros and José Clemente Orozco.

West of the Zócalo the *centro histórico* stretches through the main commercial district past the **Museo Nacional de Arte** to the sky-scraping **Torre Latinoamericana** and the **Palacio de Bellas Artes** with its gorgeous Art Deco interior. Both overlook the formal parkland of the **Alameda**, next to which you'll find a number of museums, including **Museo de Tequila y Mezcal**, which tells the story of Mexico's best-known liquors, and the **Museo Mural Diego Rivera**, with the artist's famed *Sueño de una Tarde Dominical en la Alameda*. Further west, the **Monumento a la Revolución** heralds the more upmarket central suburbs, chiefly the **Zona Rosa**, long known as the spot for plush shops and restaurants, though that title has largely been usurped by swanky **Polanco** and hipper **Condesa**.

The Zócalo

Metro Zócalo

The vast paved open space of the **Zócalo** – properly known as the Plaza de la Constitución – was once the heart of **Aztec Tenochtitlán**, and is today one of the largest city squares in the world after Beijing's Tiananmen Square and Moscow's Red Square. The city's political and religious centre, it takes its name from part of a monument to

---

MÉXICO, MEXICO CITY AND EL DF

For clarity, we've referred to Mexico's capital as **Mexico City** throughout this Guide, though Mexicans frequently refer to it simply as **México**, in the same way that Americans refer to New York City as New York. It's a source of infinite confusion to visitors, but the country took its name from the city, so "México" can mean either, and in conversation it most often means the latter. The capital is also referred to as **El DF** ("El Day Effay"), short for "Distrito Federal". The title **Ciudad de México** is used much less commonly, usually in an official context. The country as a whole is generally called 'La República', while any area that lies outside Mexico City and Mexico State that envelops it can be referred to as "La Provincia" (The Province), although this is not a term which is appreciated by those who live there.

1

COUGHS AND ROBBERS – SELF-PRESERVATION IN MEXICO CITY

Mexico City comes with an unenviable reputation for overcrowding, grime and crime, and to some extent this is deserved. Certainly there is **pollution**. The whole urban area sits in a low mountain bowl that deflects smog-clearing winds away from the city, allowing a thick blanket of haze to build up throughout the day. Conditions are particularly bad in winter, when there is no rain, and pollution levels (reported daily in the English-language newspaper, *The News*, ⓦ thenews.com.mx) tend to peak in the early afternoon. In response, the **Hoy No Circula** ("Don't drive today") law prohibits car use from 5am to 10pm for one day in the working week for vehicles over six years old, the day depending on the car's numberplate. Nonetheless, those prone to **respiratory problems** may have some difficulty on arrival, due to the city's air quality and altitude.

The capital is where the Mexican extremes of **wealth** and **poverty** are most apparent, with shiny, valet-parked SUVs vying for space with pavement vendors and beggars. Such financial disparity fuels **theft**, but just take the same precautions you would in any large city; there is no need to feel particularly paranoid. Keep your valuables – especially credit or debit cards – in the hotel safe (even cheap hotels often have somewhere secure; muggers who catch you with an ATM card may keep hold of you till they have extracted enough cash with it), don't flash large wads of money around and keep an eye on your camera and other valuables in busy market areas. At night, avoid the *barrio* known as **Doctores** (around the Metro station of the same name, so-called because the streets are named after doctors), and the area around Lagunilla market, both centres of the street drug trade, and therefore opportunist crime. Note that mugging is not the only danger – abduction for ransom is increasingly common too.

Taxis have a bad reputation and, though drivers are mostly helpful and courteous, there are reports of people being robbed or abducted (often in stolen taxis). If possible, get your hotel to call you a cab (more expensive), or call one yourself, for example from one of the firms mentioned on p.117. If you do have to hail a cab in the street, always take one whose registration, on both the numberplate and the side of the vehicle, begins with an L (for "libre" – to be hailed while driving around), and which has the driver's identification prominently displayed. Better still, find a taxi rank and take a *sitio* taxi that can be traced to that rank (with a number beginning in R, S or T, and again with the driver's ID prominently displayed). Do not take taxis from the airport or bus terminals other than prepaid ones, and avoid taking those waiting outside tourist spots.

Independence that was planned in the 1840s for the square by General Santa Anna. Like most of his other plans, this went astray, and only the statue's base (now gone) was ever erected: *el zócalo* literally means "the plinth". By extension, every other town square in Mexico has adopted the same name. It's constantly animated, with pre-Hispanic revivalist groups dancing and pounding drums throughout the day and street stalls and buskers in the evening. Stages are set up here for major national holidays, and, of course, this is the place to hold demonstrations. Over one hundred thousand people massed here in March 2001 to support the Zapatistas after their march from Chiapas in support of indigenous people's rights; in July 2006 the square proved too small to contain the millions of demonstrators who gathered to challenge the result of that year's presidential election, a contest widely believed – especially in the left-leaning DF – to have been fixed. Spreading out from the Zócalo, the crowds reached as far as Paseo de la Reforma.

Though you're not guaranteed to see any protests, among the Zócalo's more certain entertainments is the ceremonial **lowering of the national flag** from its giant pole in the centre of the plaza each evening at sundown (typically 6pm). A troop of presidential guards march out from the palace, strike the enormous flag and perform a complex routine, at the end of which the flag is left, neatly folded, in the hands of one of their number. With far less pomp, the flag is quietly raised again around half an hour later. You get a great view of this, and of everything else happening in the Zócalo, from the rooftop terrace restaurants (see p.123) in the *Hotel Majestic* and *Gran Hotel Ciudad de México* on the west side of the square.

Weekends in the Zócalo see a small tourist market on the west side of the cathedral, offering the same knick-knacks you'll see at most tourist sites around the country. Witch doctors also patrol the area offering pre-Hispanic cleansing rituals. During the week tradesmen offering freelance work occupy this bit of pavement; they don't appreciate having their photos taken.

Catedral Metropolitana

North side of Zócalo • Daily 8am–8pm (discretion is required during services); guided tours hourly • Free; tours M$20 • Metro Zócalo

Mexico City's cathedral holds the distinction of being the largest church in Latin America. Like so many of the city's older, weightier structures, it has settled over the years into the soft, wet ground beneath – the tilt is quite plain to see, despite extensive work to stabilize the building. The first church on this site was constructed only a couple of years after the Conquest, using stones torn from the Temple of Huitzilopochtli, but the present structure was begun in 1573 to provide Mexico City with a cathedral more suited to its wealth and status as the jewel of the Spanish empire. The towers weren't completed until 1813, though, and the building incorporates a plethora of architectural styles. Even the frontage demonstrates this: relatively austere at the bottom where work began soon after the Conquest, it flowers into full Baroque as you look up, and is topped by Neoclassical cornices and a clock tower. If you want to climb the clock tower, join one of the guided tours that start from the information desk to the right as you enter.

Inside, although the size of the cathedral is striking, the chief impression is that it's a rather gloomy space, with rows of dimly lit side chapels. It is enlivened mostly by the **Altar de los Reyes**, a vast gilt *reredos* built of wood between 1718 and 1737. It's located behind a main altar that features effigies of European kings and queens as well as two early eighteenth-century oil paintings, the *Asunción de la Virgen* and *Adoración de los Reyes* by Juan Rodríguez Juárez. Fans of ornate handiwork will also appreciate the detailed work in gold and wood on the central *coro* (choir).

Sagrario

Next door to the cathedral • Daily 8am–8pm (no entry wearing caps, shorts, miniskirts or dark glasses) • Free

The **Sagrario**, despite its heavy, grey Baroque facade and squat, bell-topped towers, feels both lighter and richer inside, with exuberant churrigueresque decoration and liberal use of gold paint. It was originally built as the parish church, and performs most of the day-to-day functions of a local church, such as baptisms and marriages.

Templo Mayor

Seminario 8 • Tues–Sun 9am–5pm • M$64; video M$45 • ⓦ templomayor.inah.gob.mx • Metro Zócalo

Just off the Zócalo, down beside the cathedral, lies the entrance to the site where the **Templo Mayor** has been excavated. Although it had been worked out by the beginning of the twentieth century that Tenochtitlán's ceremonial area lay under this part of the city, it was generally believed that the chief temple, or Teocalli, lay directly beneath the cathedral. Archeological work only began in earnest in 1978 after workmen uncovered a huge stone disc, weighing over eight tonnes, which depicted the fall of **Coyolxauhqui**, goddess of the moon. The disc's symbolism (see box, p.74) indicated that it must have lain at the foot of the city's Teocalli, which would have been topped by a double shrine, dedicated to the sun god **Huitzilopochtli** and the rain god **Tlaloc**. The nineteenth- and twentieth-century buildings on the site were therefore cleared away, and excavation began.

The temple remains

Entering the site, you'll be able to see the bare ruins of the foundations of the great temple and one or two buildings immediately around it. The excavations are highly confusing since, as was normal practice, a new temple was built over the old at the end of every 52-year calendar cycle (and apparently even more frequently here), resulting in a whole series of temples stacked inside each other like Russian dolls – there are seven

1

CENTRAL MEXICO CITY

HIGHLIGHTS

1 The Zócalo

2 Palacio de Bellas Artes

3 Museo Mural Diego Rivera

8 Plaza Garibaldi

9 La Merced

ACCOMMODATION

Azores	5	Isabel	22
Casa Blanca	12	Juárez	9
Casa de los Amigos	2	Majestic	16
Catedral	7	Managua	1
Fleming	18	Mexico City Hostel	6
Gillow	13	Montecarlo	21
Gran Hotel Ciudad		Pánuco	19
de México	17	República	4
Hostal Amigo	20	San Antonio	14
Hostal Moneda	15	Washington	11
Hostel Catedral	8	Zamora	10
Hotel de Cortés	3		

here. Look at the models and maps in the museum first (see opposite) and it all makes more sense.

Of the seven reconstructions of the temple, layers as far down as the second have been uncovered, though you can only see the top of the structure as the bottom is now well below the water table. Confusing as it is trying to work out what's what, it's a fascinating site, scattered with odd sculptures, including some great serpents, and traces of its original bright paintwork in red, blue and yellow. Seeing it here, at the heart of

DRINKING & NIGHTLIFE		SHOPPING		EATING			
Los Duellistas	6	American Book Store	5	Café Emir	18	Hostería de Santo	
La Hermosa Hortensia	1	Centro Artesanal		Café del Palacio	5	Domingo	1
El Marrakech	3	Buenavista	1	Café el Popular	8	Jugos Canada	11
La Opera	2	Centro Artesanal		Café de Tacuba	3	Kam Ling	6
La Risa	7	de San Juan	9	Cafetería el Cuadrilatero	19	Oriental	15
Tio Pepe	5	Ciudadela	8	Casa de los Azulejos	9	Pastelería Ideal	17
Zinco Jazz Club	4	FONART	3	La Cocinita de San Juan	20	Restaurant Bar Chon	21
		Liverpool	7	Danubio	16	La Terraza	13
		El Palacio de Hierro	6	Dulcería de Celaya	10	Terraza	14
		Sanborns	4	Gili Pollos	7	La Vasconia	4
		La Torre del Papel	2	Los Girasoles	2	Los Vegetarianos	12

the modern city, brings the ceremonies and sacrifices that took place rather close to home. It's also worth walking past here in the evening when the **floodlit pyramid ruins** can be seen from the surrounding streets.

Museo del Templo Mayor
The **museum** of the Templo Mayor, entered through the site on the same ticket, helps set the temples in context, with some welcome reconstructions and models of how

1

Tenochtitlán would have looked at its height. There are some wonderful pieces retrieved from the site, especially the replica **tzompantli** (wall of skulls) as you enter, the eagle in Room 1 with a cavity in its back for the hearts of sacrificial victims, a particularly beautiful *pulque* god statue and, of course, the huge **Coyolxauhqui stone** (see p.71), displayed so as to be visible from points throughout the museum. The museum's design is meant to simulate the temple, so you climb through it to reach two rooms at the top, one devoted to Huitzilopochtli, the other to Tlaloc, in the same way that the temple was originally topped by two shrines, one for each god.

The best items are towards the top of the museum, including some superb stone masks such as the one from Teotihuacán, black with inset eyes and a huge earring, typical of the objects paid in tribute by subject peoples from all over the country. On the highest level are two magnificent, full-size terracotta eagle warriors and numerous large stone pieces from the site. The descent back to the ground level concentrates on everyday life in Aztec times – with some rather mangy stuffed animals to demonstrate the species known to the Aztecs – along with a jumble of later items found while the site was being excavated. There are some good pieces here: look for the superb turquoise mosaic, little more than a handspan across, but intricately set with tiny pieces forming seven god-like figures; and the two large ceramic sculptures of **Mictlantecihtli**, the god of death, unearthed in 1994 from tunnels excavated below the nearby Casa de las Águilas.

Palacio Nacional

East side of Zócalo, but public entrance from Moneda • Tues–Sun 9am–5pm • Free, but ID required to enter; locker for bags M$20 in coins • Metro Zócalo

The east side of the Zócalo is entirely taken up by the more than 200m-long facade of the **Palacio Nacional**. The so-called New Palace of Moctezuma stood here and Cortés made it his first residence. From 1562 the building was the official residence of the Spanish viceroy, and later of presidents of the republic. The present building, for all its apparent unity, is the result of centuries of agglomeration and rebuilding – the most recent addition was the third storey, in 1927. It still holds the office of the president, who makes his most important pronouncements from the balcony – especially on September 15, when the **Grito de la Independencia** (see box, p.139) signals the start of the country's Independence celebrations.

Diego Rivera's murals

The chief attraction in the Palacio Nacional is the series of **Diego Rivera murals** that decorate the stairwell and middle storey of the main courtyard. Begun in 1929, the murals are classic Rivera, ranking with the best of his work. The great panorama of Mexican history, *México a Través de los Siglos*, around the **main staircase**, combines an unbelievable wealth of detail with savage imagery and a masterly use of space. On the right-hand wall Quetzalcoatl sits in majesty amid the golden age of the Valley of

---

COYOLXAUHQUI AND HUITZILOPOCHTLI

Coyolxauhqui was the daughter of Coatlicue, the mother goddess who controlled life and death; on discovering that her mother was miraculously pregnant, Coyolxauhqui vowed to wipe out the dishonour by killing her. Before she could do so, however, **Huitzilopochtli** sprang fully armed from Coatlicue's womb, and proceeded to decapitate and dismember his sister (who is therefore always portrayed with her head and limbs cut off) and threw her body down a mountain. He then drove off the four hundred other brothers who had gathered to help her: they scattered to become the stars. The human sacrifices carried out in the temple – meant to feed Huitzilopochtli, the sun god, with the blood he needed to win his nightly battle against darkness – were in part a re-enactment of this, with the victims being thrown down the steps afterwards.

1

México, surrounded by an idealized vision of life in Teotihuacán, Tula and Tenochtitlán. The main section depicts the Conquest, oppression, war, Inquisition, invasion, Independence and eventually Revolution. Almost every major personage and event of Mexican history is here, from the grotesquely twisted features of the conquistadors to the national heroes: balding, white-haired Hidalgo with the banner of Independence; squat, dark Benito Juárez with his Constitution and laws for the reform of the Church; Zapata, with a placard proclaiming his cry of "*Tierra y Libertad*"; and Pancho Villa, moustachioed and swaggering. On the left are post-Revolutionary Mexico and the future (as Rivera envisaged it), with Karl Marx pointing the way to adoring workers. Businessmen stand clustered over their tickertape in front of a somewhat ironic depiction of the metropolis with its skyscrapers and grim industrial wastes. Rivera's wife, the artist Frida Kahlo, is depicted, too, behind her sister Cristina (with whom Rivera was having an affair at the time) in a red blouse with an open copy of the Communist Manifesto.

A series of smaller panels was intended to go all the way round the upper (now middle) storey, an over-ambitious and unfinished project. The uncoloured first panel lists the products that the world owes to Mexico, including maize, beans, chocolate, tobacco, cotton, tomatoes, peanuts, prickly pears and *chicle* (the source of chewing gum). The remainder of the completed paintings reach halfway around and mostly depict the idyll of aspects of life before the Conquest – market day, dyeing cloth, hunting scenes and so on. The last (completed in 1951) shows the arrival of the Spanish, complete with an image of La Malinche (the Maya woman widely perceived to have betrayed native Mexicans by shacking up with Cortés) bearing Cortés' blue-eyed baby – the first Mexican *mestizo*.

Other attractions

Also on the Palacio's middle storey is the chamber used by the Mexican Legislature from 1845 to 1872, when it was presided over by Benito Juárez, who lived in the palace until his death. The room houses the original copy of the 1857 Constitution, which was drawn up there, but is frequently closed for renovations.

Before leaving the building, it's worth taking a moment to wander around some of the other **courtyards** (there are fourteen in all), and through the small floral and cactus **gardens**.

Gran Hotel Ciudad de México

16 de Septiembre 82 • Ⓦ granhoteldelaciudaddemexico.com.mx • Metro Zócalo

Located at the southwest corner of the Zócalo, the **Gran Hotel Ciudad de México** (see p.123) is well worth a visit to admire the opulent lobby with its intricate ironwork, cage-lifts and wonderful Tiffany stained-glass dome. Indeed, it's worth going up to the third and fourth floors for a closer look at the ceiling. Like the *Majestic* (see p.123) in the same block, the *Gran Hotel* has a terrace restaurant with great views over the Zócalo.

Nacional Monte de Piedad

Monte de Piedad 1, at corner of the Zócalo and 5 de Mayo • Mon–Fri 10am–5pm, Sat 10am–3pm • Metro Zócalo

On the west side of the Zócalo, arcades shelter a series of shops, almost all of which sell hats or jewellery. For an unusual shopping experience, though, you can't beat the **Nacional Monte de Piedad**, just to the north. This huge building, supposedly on the site of the palace in which Cortés and his followers stayed as guests of Moctezuma, is now the National Pawn Shop, an institution founded as far back as 1775. Much of what is pawned here is jewellery, but there's also a wide variety of fine art and sculptures, and just about anything that will command a reasonable price. From time to time they hold major auctions to clear the place out, but it's worth coming here just to take in the atmosphere and watch the milling crowds.

1

North of the Zócalo

Just a couple of blocks north of the centre the vast openness of the Zócalo gives way to a much more intimate section of small colonial plazas and mostly eighteenth-century buildings. It is still an active commercial area, and is packed with a variety of interesting sights, including ornate churches, small museums and some very fine Rivera and Siqueiros **murals**, all of which can be seen in a few hours.

Plaza Santo Domingo

Metro Zócalo

Beside the cathedral, Calle Monte de Piedad runs three blocks north (becoming República de Brasil) to the little colonial plaza of **Santo Domingo**. In the middle of the square, a small fountain plays on a statue honouring La Corregidora, a heroine of Mexico's Independence struggle (see p.316). Eighteenth-century mansions line the sides of the plaza along with the fine Baroque church of Santo Domingo, built on the site of the country's first Dominican monastery. Under the arcades you'll still find clerks sitting at little desks with ageing electric typewriters, as you will in most large

---

DIEGO RIVERA

Diego Rivera (c.1886–1957), husband of **Frida Kahlo** (see box, p.109), was the greatest of *Los Tres Grandes*, the "Big Three" Mexican artists – the other two being **José Clemente Orozco** and **David Siqueiros** – who interpreted the Revolution and Mexican history through the medium of enormous murals, and put the nation's art onto an international footing in the first half of the twentieth century. His works remain among the country's most striking sights.

Rivera studied from the age of 10 at the **San Carlos Academy** in the capital, immediately showing immense ability. He later moved to Paris, where he flirted with many of the new artistic trends, in particular Cubism. More importantly, though, he and Siqueiros planned, in exile, a popular, native art to express the new society in Mexico. In 1921 Rivera returned from Europe to the aftermath of the Revolution, and right away began work for the Ministry of Education at the behest of the socialist Education Minister, poet and presidential hopeful José Vasconcelos. Informed by his own Communist beliefs, and encouraged by the leftist sympathies of the times, Rivera embarked on the first of his massive, consciousness-raising **murals**, whose themes – Mexican history, the oppression of the natives, post-Revolutionary resurgence – were initially more important than their techniques. Many of his early murals are deceptively simple, naive even, but in fact Rivera's style remained close to major trends and, following the lead of Siqueiros, he took a scientific approach to his work, looking to industrial advances for new techniques, better materials and fresh inspiration. The view of industrial growth as a panacea (particularly in the earlier works of both Rivera and Siqueiros) may have been simplistic, but the artists' use of technology and experimentation with new methods and original approaches often had startling results.

RIVERA AND TROTSKY

Communism continued to be a major source of motivation and inspiration for Rivera, who was a long-standing member of the Mexican Communist Party. When ideological differences caused a rift in Soviet politics, he came down on the side of **Leon Trotsky**'s "revolutionary internationalism". In 1936, with Trotsky running out of countries that would accept him after seven years on the run from Stalin's henchmen, Rivera used his influence over Mexican President Lázaro Cárdenas to get permission for Trotsky and his wife Natalia to enter the country. They stayed with Diego and Frida rent-free at their Coyoacán house before Trotsky moved down the road to what is now the **Museo Casa de León Trotsky**. The passionate and often violent differences between orthodox Stalinists and Trotskyites spilled over into the art world, creating a great rift between Rivera and ardent Stalinist Siqueiros, who was later jailed for his involvement in an assassination attempt on Trotsky (see box, p.110). Though Rivera later broke with Trotsky and was eventually readmitted to the Communist Party, Trotsky continued to admire Rivera's murals, finding them "not simply a 'painting', an object of passive contemplation, but a living part of the class struggle".

Mexican cities – carrying on the ancient tradition of public scribes, their main function is to translate simple messages into the flowery, sycophantic language essential for any business letter in Spanish, but they'll type anything from student theses to love letters. Alongside them are street printers working with antiquated hand presses, churning out business cards, forged documents and invitations on the spot.

Museo de la Medicina

Brasil 33, on northeast corner of Plaza Santo Domingo • Daily 9am–6pm • Free • ☎ 55 5623 3123 • Metro Zócalo

The **Museo de la Medicina** occupies grand rooms around a courtyard that was once the headquarters of the Inquisition in New Spain. It was here that heretics were punished, and although the cruelty of the Inquisition is often exaggerated, it was undoubtedly the site of some gruesome scenes. The extensive museum kicks off with interesting displays on indigenous medicine, religion and herbalism, often with reference to infirmity, in sculpture. It is surprising how often skin diseases, humped backs and malformed limbs crop up in pre-Columbian art: note the terracotta sculpture bent double from osteoporosis. The progress of Western medicine from colonial times to the present is

---

FOLLOWING THE RIVERA TRAIL

There is a huge amount of Rivera's work accessible to the public, much of it in Mexico City, but also elsewhere around the country. The following is a rundown of the major Rivera sites, approximately ordered in accordance with their importance within each area.

NEAR THE ZÓCALO, THE ALAMEDA AND CHAPULTEPEC

Palacio National (see p.74). Major murals right in the heart of the capital.
SEP (see p.78). There are many of Rivera's early murals around the courtyards of the Ministry of Education.
Palacio de Bellas Artes (see p.84). Rivera's monumental *El Hombre en Control del Universo* (and others), as well as murals by his contemporaries.
Museo Mural Diego Rivera (see p.87). One of Rivera's most famous murals, *Sueño de una Tarde Dominical en la Alameda*, is on display here.
Museo de Arte Moderno (see p.99). Several quality canvases by Rivera and his contemporaries.
Antiguo Colegio de San Ildefonso (ENP) (see p.78). One relatively minor Rivera mural.
Museo Nacional de Arte (see p.85). A handful of minor canvases.

THE SUBURBS

Cárcomo de Dolores (see p.101). Two murals on water-related subjects by a lake in the Bosque de Chapultepec.
Estadio Olímpico (see p.110). Mosaic relief depicting the relationship between sport and the family.
Museo Dolores Olmedo Patiño (see p.112). A massive collection of Rivera works from almost every artistic period.
Museo Frida Kahlo (see p.106). Just a couple of Diego's works displayed in the house where he and Frida spent some of their married life.
Museo Casa Estudio Diego Rivera y Frida Kahlo (see p.105). Diego's and Frida's pair of houses designed by Juan O'Gorman.
Museo Diego Rivera Anahuacalli (see p.111). Large Maya-style house built by Rivera and housing his collection of pre-Columbian sculpture.
Teatro de los Insurgentes (see p.102). Mosaic depicting the history of Mexican theatre.

OUTSIDE THE CAPITAL

Palacio de Cortés, Cuernavaca (see p.174). Early murals on a grand scale.
Museo Robert Brady, Cuernavaca (see p.175). A few paintings by both Frida and Diego.
Museo Casa Diego Rivera, Guanajuato (see p.350). Relatively minor works and sketches in the house where Diego was born.

1

also well covered, with an intact nineteenth-century pharmacy, a complete radiology room from 1939 and an obstetrics and gynaecology room filled with human embryos in bottles. A "wax room" upstairs shows full-colour casts of various skin ailments, injuries and infections – the diseased genitalia are always a hit with local schoolkids. As you leave, don't forget the "exhibit of the week" room by the entrance.

SEP

Brasil 31 (with another entrance at Argentina 28) • Mon–Fri 9am–6pm • Free • Metro Zócalo

From the Plaza de Santo Domingo, República de Cuba runs a block east to the **Secretaría de Educación Pública (SEP)**, the Ministry of Education building, where, in 1923 and 1924, Rivera painted his first **murals** on returning from Paris. Don't be put off by the tight security – simply proclaim the word "murales" and you'll be shown straight through.

The driving force behind the murals was **José Vasconcelos**, a revolutionary Minister of Public Education in the 1920s but better known as a poet and philosopher, who promoted educational art as a means of instilling a sense of history and cultural pride in a widely illiterate population. He is the man most directly responsible for the murals in public buildings throughout the country. Here, three floors of an enormous double patio are entirely covered with frescoes, as are many of the stairwells and almost any other flat surface. Compared with what he later achieved, Rivera's work is very simple, but the style is already recognizable: panels crowded with figures, drawing inspiration mainly from rural Mexico, though also from an idealized view of science and industry.

The most famous panel on the ground floor is the relatively apolitical *Día de los Muertos*, which is rather hidden away in a dark corner at the back. Continuing clockwise, there are equally striking images: *Quema de Judas* and *La Asamblea Primero de Mayo*, for example, and the lovely *El Canal de Santa Anita*. On the first floor the work is quite plain, mostly in tones of grey – here you'll find the shields of the states of Mexico and such general educational themes as *Chemistry* or *Physics*, mostly the work of Rivera's assistants. On the second floor are heroic themes from the Revolution. At the back, clockwise from the left-hand side, the triumphant progress of the Revolution is traced, culminating in the happy scenes of a Mexico ruled by its workers and peasants.

Museo de la Caricatura

Donceles 99 • Daily 10am–6pm • M$20 • Metro Zócalo

The **Museo de la Caricatura** is a museum of Mexican cartoons and caricatures. Located in a particularly fine example of an eighteenth-century nobleman's dwelling, complete with central courtyard, it exhibits a selection of work from Mexico's most famous caricaturists, but without a strong sense of Mexican history and a comprehensive grasp of Spanish much of the impact is lost. It's still worth nipping in to see a small selection of bizarre nineteenth-century prints of skeletal mariachis by **José Guadalupe Posada**, a great influence on the later Muralist movement, and to take a break in the museum coffee shop in the central patio.

ENP (Antiguo Colegio de San Ildefonso)

Justo Serra 16 • Tues 10am–7.30pm, Wed–Sun 10am–5.30pm • M$45, free Tues • Metro Zócalo

As in the SEP (see above), José Vasconcelos was largely responsible for the murals which adorn the interior of the eighteenth-century **Antiguo Colegio de San Ildefonso** (also called the Escuela Nacional Preparatoria, or **ENP**), a building also notable for its imposing colonial facade on Justo Serra, facing the north side of the Templo Mayor. Many artists are represented here, including Rivera and Siqueiros, but the most famous works are those of **José Clemente Orozco**, which you'll find on the main staircase and around the first floor of the main patio.

Museo de la Luz
San Ildefonso 43 • Mon–Fri 9am–4.30pm, Sat & Sun 10am–4.30pm • M$35 • Metro Zócalo

Housed in part of the northern wing of the Antiguo Colegio de San Ildefonso, with its entrance on San Ildefonso, the **Museo de la Luz** is a kind of hands-on celebration of all facets of reflection, refraction, iridescence and luminescence, spread over three floors. Good Spanish is essential if you want to learn anything, but it's fun just playing with the optical tricks and effects, and exploring the use of light in art.

Museo de las Constituciones
San Ildefonso (cnr Aztecas), almost diagonally opposite the Museo de la Luz • Tues–Sun 10am–6pm • Free • Metro Zócalo

The former Templo de San Pedro y San Pablo, built for the Company of Jesus between 1576 and 1603, was later used as a library, military college and correctional school, and was eventually taken over by the university. The interior decoration – plain white, with the arches and pilasters painted in floral designs by Jorge Enciso and Roberto Montenegro – was, like those in SEP (see opposite) and the ENP (see opposite), influenced by Vasconcelos. The church has since been turned into the **Museo de las Constituciones**, with exhibits and explanations in Spanish on the string of constitutions which Mexico has had since Independence, but the murals will be of far more interest to most visitors, particularly Montenegro's almost pre-Raphaelite 1922 *Tree of Life*, at the far end of the building as you enter.

Plaza de Loreto and around
Three blocks northeast of the Zócalo • Metro Zócalo

The **Plaza de Loreto** feels a world apart. It is a truly elegant old square, entirely unmodernized and flanked by a couple of churches. On one side is the **Templo de Loreto**, with its huge dome leaning at a crazy angle: inside, you'll find yourself staggering across the tilted floor. **Santa Teresa**, across the plaza, has a bizarre cave-like chapel at the back, entirely artificial. North of the Templo Loreto is a large and not especially exciting covered market, the **Mercado Presidente Abelardo Rodriguez**, inside most entrances of which is a series of large murals dating from the 1930s by an assortment of artists including Antonio Pujol and Pablo O'Higgins.

East of the Zócalo: along Calle Moneda

Calle Moneda, running east from the centre, is one of the oldest streets in the city, and it's fascinating to wander up here and see the rapid change as you leave the immediate environs of the Zócalo. The buildings remain almost wholly colonial, prim and refurbished around the museums, then gradually become shabbier and shabbier. Within four or five blocks you're into a very depressed residential area, with street stalls spreading up from the giant market of La Merced, to the south.

Museo de la SHCP
Moneda 4 • Tues–Sun 10am–5pm • Free • Metro Zócalo

Just a few steps from the Zócalo, the **Museo de la SHCP** occupies the former archbishop's palace and presents Mexican fine art from the last three centuries in rooms surrounding two lovely open courtyards. The building was constructed over part of Tenochtitlán's ceremonial centre, the Teocalli, and excavations have revealed a few foundation sections for the Templo de Tezcatlipoca pyramid that once stood here. Notice the short flight of stairs, a jaguar carved in high relief and a series of anthropomorphic sculptures.

Casa de la Primera Imprenta
Licenciado Primo Verdad 10 (at Moneda) • Mon–Fri 10am–6pm, Sat 10am–3pm • Free • Metro Zócalo

The **Casa de la Primera Imprenta** occupies the house where the first printing press in the Americas was set up in 1535, though the only indication of this is the

1

model of the press that sits close to the entrance. Archeological finds unearthed during restoration work are displayed in one room; other rooms house temporary exhibits.

Centro Cultural Ex-Teresa Arte
Licenciado Primo Verdad 8 • Daily 10am–6pm • Free • Metro Zócalo

You'll feel as if you aren't on solid ground the moment you step into the **Centro Cultural Ex-Teresa Arte**, one of the city's most subsided buildings which exhibits art and photography inside a Spanish imperial stone church. The exhibitions are put on by a non-profit organization funded by the National Institute of Fine Arts, which are usually interesting but make rather poor use of the dizzying space.

Museo Nacional de las Culturas
Moneda 13 • Tues–Sun 10am–5pm • Free • Metro Zócalo

The **Museo Nacional de las Culturas** occupies the sixteenth-century Casa de la Moneda, the official mint until 1848 and later the National Museum, where the best of the Aztec artefacts were displayed until the construction of the Museo Nacional de Antropología (see p.95). Now immaculately restored, it houses a collection devoted to the archeology and anthropology of other countries. With rooms of exhibits set around a quiet patio, it is more interesting than you might guess, though still somewhat overshadowed by so many other high-class museums in the city.

Santa Inés
Moneda 26 • Daily 9am–6pm • Free • Metro Zócalo

The eye-catching blue and gold **dome** of the church of **Santa Inés** is the church's only striking feature, and there's little else to admire apart from the delicately carved wooden doors. Painters Miguel Cabrera and José Ibarra are both buried somewhere inside, but neither is commemorated in any way.

Museo José Luis Cuevas
Academia 13 • Tues–Sun 10am–6pm • M$20, free Sun • Metro Zócalo

The church of Santa Inés' former convent buildings have been transformed into the **Museo José Luis Cuevas**, an art gallery with changing displays centred on the 8m-high bronze, *La Giganta*, designed by Cuevas. The only permanent collection is one room full of erotica ranging from pre-Hispanic sculpture to line drawings, some by Cuevas.

Academia de San Carlos
Academia 22, on the corner of Moneda and Academia • Mon–Fri 9am–7pm • Free • Metro Zócalo

The **Academia de San Carlos** still operates as an art school, though on a considerably reduced scale from its nineteenth-century heyday; inside are galleries for temporary exhibitions and, in the patio, copies of classical sculptures.

Templo de la Santísima Trinidad
Santísima 12 • Metro Zócalo

The **Templo de la Santísima Trinidad**, from which the street takes its name, boasts one of the city's finest Baroque facades, floridly decorated with saints and cherubs. As with many old colonial churches in the city centre, its soft footing has caused it to slump, and its sideways list has become so serious that it is now closed for strengthening work, though you can still admire the exterior.

CLOCKWISE FROM TOP PALACIO DE BELLAS ARTES (P.84); MARIACHI IN PLAZA GARIBALDI (P.134); DRIED CHILE PEPPERS FOR SALE AT LA MERCED (P.135)>

1

South of the Zócalo

South of the Zócalo, Pino Suárez leads down to meet Izázaga, which marks the southern edge of the city centre proper. The area to the east of Pino Suárez is largely a market area, and leads over to the wonderful **La Merced** market, while both Pino Suárez and Izázaga have a couple of sights that are worth a brief foray.

Suprema Corte de Justicia

On the corner of the Zócalo • Mon–Thurs 9am–2pm, Fri 9am–1.30pm • Free, but ID required to enter • Metro Zócalo

A colonial-style modern building houses the **Suprema Corte de Justicia**. Inside are three superb, bitter murals by Orozco named *Luchas Proletarias* (*Proletarian Struggles*), *Las Riquezas Nacionales* (*The Nation's Riches*) and *La Justicia* (*Justice*). The last, depicting Justice slumped asleep on her pedestal while bandits rob the people of their rights, was, not surprisingly, unpopular with the judges and powers that be, and Orozco never completed his commission here.

Museo de la Ciudad de México

Pino Suárez 30 • Tues–Sun 10am–5.30pm • M$24, free Wed • ⓦ cultura.df.gob.mx • Metro Zócalo

A couple of blocks south of the Zócalo, the **Museo de la Ciudad de México** is housed in the colonial palace of the Condes de Santiago de Calimaya. This is a fabulous building, with carved stone cannons thrusting out from the cornice, magnificent heavy wooden doors and, on the far side, a hefty plumed serpent obviously dragged from the ruins of some Aztec temple to be employed as a cornerstone. The rooms are mostly given over to temporary exhibits on all manner of themes, but on the top storey is the preserved studio of the landscape artist **Joaquín Clausell**, its walls plastered with portraits and little sketches that he scribbled between working on his paintings.

The church and hospital of Jesús Nazareno

On the west side of Pino Suárez • Daily 9am–5pm • Metro Pino Suárez

A memorial marking the spot where, according to legend, Cortés first met Moctezuma, is where you'll find the church and hospital of **Jesús Nazareno**. The **hospital**, still in use, was founded by Cortés in 1528. As such, it's one of the oldest buildings in the city, and exemplifies the severe, fortress-like construction of the immediate post-Conquest years. The **church**, which contains the remains of Cortés and a bronze plaque to the left of the altar with the simple inscription "H.C. (1485–1547)", has been substantially remodelled over the years, its vaulting decorated with a fresco of the Apocalypse by Orozco.

Pino Suárez and Zócalo Metro stations

More or less opposite Jesús Nazareno (see above) is a small open space and an entrance to a bookshop-lined subterranean walkway, the **Tunel del Libro**, between Zócalo and Pino Suárez Metro stations, where there's a café and a space for silent reading. **Zócalo station** has models of the Zócalo at different times in the past in its main concourse, and old pictures of the famous square reproduced on its platforms. **Pino Suárez station**, meanwhile, has a whole **Aztec shrine** in the middle of it. Uncovered during the station's construction, it has been preserved as an integral part of the concourse, and you'll pass right by it if changing lines here. Dating from around the end of the fourteenth century, the shrine was dedicated to Quetzalcoatl in his guise of Ehecatl, god of the wind.

Claustro de la Merced

Uruguay 168 • Metro Merced or Pino Suárez

Heading east from Pino Suárez along Salvador or Uruguay takes you to the giant **market** area of La Merced (see p.135). If you walk on Uruguay you'll pass a beautiful cloister (claustro), all that remains of the seventeenth-century **Convento de la Merced**, the subject of extensive recent restoration work.

Museo de la Charrería

Isabel la Católica 108 • Mon–Fri 11am–5pm • Free • Metro Isabel la Católica

On the south side of Izázaga, at Isabel la Católica, a handsome colonial building holds the **Museo de la Charrería**, dedicated to all things cowboy, with a collection that includes old photographs, some of them inevitably rather camp, as well as sketches, watercolours, costumes, spurs and brands.

West to the Alameda

The streets that lead down from the Zócalo towards the Alameda – **Tacuba**, **5 de Mayo**, **Madero**, **16 de Septiembre** and the lanes that cross them – are the most elegant and least affected by modern development in the city, lined with ancient buildings, traditional cafés, and shops and mansions converted into offices, banks or restaurants. At the end of Madero, you come to the outer edge of the colonial city centre, and should find yourself, by contrast, standing between two of the most striking modern buildings in the capital: the **Torre Latinoamericana** and the **Palacio de Bellas Artes**. Though it seems incredible when you compare them, they were completed within barely 25 years of each other.

Along Madero

On **Madero** you'll pass several former aristocratic palaces now given over to a variety of uses. At no. 27 stands a slightly dilapidated mansion built in 1775 by mining magnate José de la Borda (see p.182) for his wife and presided over, on the corner of Bolívar, by a statue of the Virgin of Guadalupe. Still further down Madero, at no. 17, you'll find the **Palacio de Iturbide** (Metro Allende), currently occupied by Banamex and thoroughly restored. Originally the home of the Condes de Valparaíso in the eighteenth century, it was, from 1821 to 1823, the residence of the ill-fated "emperor" Agustín de Iturbide. Nowadays it periodically houses free art exhibitions laid on by the bank. In the next block, the last before you emerge at Bellas Artes and the Alameda, the churrigueresque church of **San Francisco** (Metro Bellas Artes) stands on the site of the first Franciscan mission to Mexico.

Casa de los Azulejos

Madero 4 • Metro Bellas Artes

The sixteenth-century **Casa de los Azulejos** (House of Tiles), now a branch of the Sanborns department store chain, is so-called for its exterior, swathed entirely in blue and white tiles from Puebla that were added during remodelling in 1737. The building survived a gas explosion in 1994 – though there was quite a bit of structural damage, luckily no one was hurt, and one of the most famous features of the building, the giant Orozco mural on the staircase, suffered few ill effects. Inside you'll find a restaurant (see p.128) in the glassed-over patio, as well as all the usual shopping (see p.135).

Torre Latinoamericana

Lázaro Cárdenas 2 • Daily 9am–10pm • M$60 • ⓦ torrelatino.com • Metro Bellas Artes

The distinctly dated steel-and-glass skyscraper of the **Torre Latinoamericana** was completed in 1956 and, until a few years ago, was the tallest building in Mexico and, indeed, the whole of Latin America. It has now been outdone by the World Trade Center (formerly the *Hotel de México*, on Insurgentes) and doubtless by others in South America, but it remains the city's outstanding landmark and a point of reference no matter where you are. By world standards it is not especially tall, but on a clear day the views from the 139m observation deck are outstanding; if it's smoggy you're better off going up around dusk, catching the city as the sun sets, then watching as the lights delineate it far more clearly. Having paid the fee, you're whisked up to the 36th floor where another lift takes you to "El Mirador", a glassed-in **observation area** with coin-operated telescopes on the 42nd and 43rd floors, and an outdoor terrace on the 44th floor.

1 Palacio de Bellas Artes

Av Juárez (at Lázaro Cárdenas) • Museum Tues–Sun 10am–6pm; main theatre tours Mon–Fri 1pm & 1.30pm • Museum M\$49, free Sun or when there is no special exhibition on; main theatre tours free; M\$30 to take photos, even with a phone • ⓦ palacio.bellasartes.gob.mx • Metro Bellas Artes

Facing the Torre Latinoamericano across Avenida Juárez, there's an equally impressive and substantially more beautiful engineering achievement in the form of the **Palacio de Bellas Artes**. It was designed in 1901, at the height of the Díaz dictatorship, by the Italian architect Adamo Boari and built, in a grandiose Art Nouveau style, of white marble imported from Italy. The construction wasn't actually completed, however, until 1934, with the Revolution and several new planners come and gone. Some find the whole exterior overblown, but whatever your initial impressions, nothing will prepare you for the magnificent interior – an Art Deco extravaganza incorporating spectacular lighting, chevron friezes and stylized masks of the rain god, Tlaloc.

Much of the interior splendour can be seen any time by wandering into the amazing Art Deco **foyer** (free) and simply gazing around the lower floor, where there is a good arts bookshop and the *Café del Palacio* restaurant (see p.127). Some of the finest interior decor in the building is generally hidden from view in the **main theatre**, an important venue for classical music, opera and dance, but it can be seen, without attending a concert, if you join a tour, on which you'll be shown the amazing Tiffany glass curtain depicting the Valley of México and volcanoes, as well as the detailed proscenium mosaic and stained-glass ceiling.

Museo del Palacio de Bellas Artes

If you want to see more of the building, you might consider visiting the art museum on the middle two floors, the **Museo del Palacio de Bellas Artes**. In the galleries here you'll find a series of exhibitions, permanent displays of Mexican art and temporary shows of anything from local art-school graduates' work to that of major international names. Of constant and abiding interest, however, are the great murals surrounding the museum's central space. On the first floor are *Nacimiento de la Nacionalidad* (*Birth of Our Nationality*) and *México de Hoy* (*Mexico Today*) – dreamy, almost abstract works by **Rufino Tamayo**. Going up a level you're confronted by the unique sight of murals by **Rivera**, **Orozco** and **Siqueiros** gathered in the same place. Rivera's *El Hombre en Control del Universo* (*Man in Control of the Universe*), celebrating the liberating power of technology, was originally painted for Rockefeller Center in New York City, but destroyed for being too leftist – arch-capitalist Nelson Rockefeller objected to Rivera's inclusion of Karl Marx, even though he was well aware of Rivera's views when he commissioned the work. This is Rivera's own copy, painted in 1934, just a year after the original. It's worth studying the explanatory panel, which reveals some of the theory behind this complex work.

Several smaller panels by Rivera are also displayed; these, too, were intended to be seen elsewhere (in this case on the walls of the *Hotel Reforma*, downtown) but for years were covered up, presumably because of their unflattering depiction of tourists. The works include *México Folklórico y Turístico*, *La Dictadura*, *La Danza de los Huichilobos* and, perhaps the best of them, *Agustín Lorenzo*, a portrayal of a guerrilla fighter against the French. None of them was designed to be seen so close up, and you'll find yourself wanting to step back to get the big picture. *Catarsis*, a huge, vicious work by Orozco, occupies almost an entire wall, and there are also some particularly fine examples of Siqueiros' work: three powerful and original panels on the theme of *Democracía* and a bloody depiction of the torture of Cuauhtémoc in *El Tormento de Cuauhtémoc*, and of the same Aztec ruler's heroism in *Apoteosis de Cuauhtémoc* (*Cuauhtémoc Reborn*). The uppermost floor is devoted to the **Museo de la Arquitectura** (same ticket and hours), which has no permanent collection, but frequently has interesting exhibits.

Correo Central

Corner of Tacuba and Lázaro Cárdenas • Mon–Fri 8am–5.30pm, Sat 8am–1.30pm • Metro Bellas Artes

The **Correo Central** is the city's main post office. Completed in 1908, it was, like the Palacio de Bellas Artes, designed by Adamo Boari, but in a style much more consistent with the buildings around it. Look closely and you'll find a wealth of intricate detail on the facade, while inside it's full of richly carved wood.

Museum of Naval History

On the fourth floor of the Correo Central • Tues–Fri 10am–4.30pm, Sat 10am–1.30pm • Free • Explanations in Spanish only

Naval buffs will enjoy the **Museum of Naval History**, featuring models of old ships, a reconstruction in miniature of Cortés' waterborne battle against the Aztecs on the Lake of Texcoco, plus photos and artefacts of the 1914 US occupation of Veracruz.

Palacio de Minería

Tacuba 5 • Museo Manuel Tolsá Wed–Sun 10am–6pm; guided tours Sat & Sun 11am & 1pm • M$15 • ⓦ palaciomineria.unam.mx

The **Palacio de Minería** is a Neoclassical building which was built right at the end of the eighteenth century. It was designed by Spanish-born Manuel Tolsá, who is the subject of the devotional **Museo Manuel Tolsá** (accessed from a door to the east of the main entrance) – a couple of rooms of paintings and architectural drawings, strictly for fans only. The exterior of the palacio makes an interesting contrast with the post office and with the Museo Nacional de Arte directly opposite (see below), and the main entrance has some impressively large meteorites on display.

Museo del Ejército y Fuerza

Filomeno Mata 6 • Tues–Sat 10am–6pm, Sun 10am–4pm • Free

The Convento de las Betlemitas, a small seventeenth-century convent, now houses the **Museo del Ejército y Fuerza** (Army Museum). Its exhibits are a mix of vintage weapons, flags, uniforms and paintings (plus a few photos) of battles and patriotic heroes, notably the Niños Héroes (see p.94). Aside from diehard Mexican patriots, the museum will mostly appeal to weapons buffs.

Torture and Capital Punishment Exhibition

Tacuba 15 • Daily 10am–6pm • M$60 • Metro Bellas Artes

The macabre **Exposición de Instrumentos de Tortura y Pena Capital** exhibits instruments of torture and execution from the time of the Inquisition onwards. Kicking off with instruments of public humiliation, such as an old pillory, it swiftly moves on to fiendish implements of torture, methods of applying the death penalty and instruments used specifically on women. Skeletons and dummies of the victims add to the gruesomeness.

Museo Nacional de Arte

Tacuba 8 • Tues–Sun 10.30am–5.30pm • M$37, free Sun, photo permit M$5 • ⓦ munal.com.mx • Metro Bellas Artes

The **Museo Nacional de Arte** is set back from the street on a tiny plaza in which stands one of the city's most famous sculptures, **El Caballito**, portraying Carlos IV of Spain. This enormous bronze, the work of Manuel Tolsá, was originally erected in the Zócalo in 1803. In the intervening years it has graced a variety of sites and, despite the unpopularity of the Spanish monarchy (and of the effete Carlos IV in particular), is still regarded affectionately. The latest setting is appropriate, since Tolsá also designed the nearby Palacio de Minería (see above). The open plaza around the sculpture is now often the scene of intense pre-Columbian drumming and dancing, which usually draws an appreciative crowd.

Though the museum is the foremost showcase of Mexican art from the 1550s to the 1950s, with a collection of over a thousand pieces, its interest is mainly historical. Most of the major Mexican artists are represented, but with essentially mediocre examples spiced only occasionally with a more striking work. It's worth coming here to see

1

something of the dress and landscape of old Mexico, and also some of the curiosities, but don't expect masterpieces.

Temporary displays take up the ground floor (along with a good bookshop and café), leaving the two floors above for the permanent collection.

The top floor

To follow the displays in chronological order, start on the **top floor**, where rooms 1 to 14 cover **pre-Independence art**, the earliest works indistinguishable from those of Inquisition Spain – lots of saints, virgins and gory martyrdoms. José de Mora's 1719 *Señor de Chalma* in room 10 – a crucifixion scene apparently copied from a painting in Chalma that was later destroyed by fire – seems to give the first hint of an emerging Mexican style. **Nineteenth-century art** starts in rooms 15 to 19 – **José Maria Obregón**'s depiction of the medieval Italian painters Giotto and Cimabue in room 17 may interest art historians – and continues on the middle floor.

The middle floor

As the nineteenth century progresses, Mexican themes take hold, with paintings like Obregón's *El Descubrimiento del Pulque* (*The Discovery of Pulque*) and *La Fundación de México* in room 20. **José Maria Velasco**'s landscapes of the Valley of México in room 22 abandon the history in favour of contemporary Mexico, and in the same room, an illustration of the Zócalo in the early nineteenth century by the British artist and traveller John Phillips is interesting more for historical than artistic reasons.

Room 27 heralds the **twentieth century**, with paintings like the macabre 1914 *Paisaje de Zacatecas con Ahorcados II* (*Zacatecas Landscape with Hanged Men II*) by Francisco Goitia. That room, and the next, also have a handful of minor works by **Diego Rivera**, but the cubist works by him in room 31 are a lot more interesting. Indeed, room 31 marks the climax of the collection, with strking works by Rivera's fellow muralists **David Siqueiros** (such as *Accidente en la Mina*), **José Clemente Orozco** (*Cabeza Flechada* or *Head Shot Through with Arrows*) and a self-portrait by **Juan O'Gorman**, as well as Rivera's excellent portrait of Adolfo Best Maugard. Siqueiros' full-length portrait of art patron Maria Asúnsolo coming downstairs, in room 30, is also not to be missed.

The Alameda and beyond

From behind Bellas Artes, Lázaro Cárdenas runs north towards the **Plaza Garibaldi** (see p.134) through an area crowded with seedy cantinas and eating places, theatres and burlesque shows. West of the Palacio de Bellas Artes lies the **Alameda**, first laid out as a park in 1592, and taking its name from the *alamos* (poplars) then planted. The Alameda had originally been an Aztec market and later became the site where the Inquisition burned its victims at the stake. Most of what you see now – formally laid-out paths and flowerbeds, ornamental statuary and fountains – dates from the nineteenth century, when it was the fashionable place to stroll. It's still popular, always full of people, particularly at weekends, but it's mostly a transient population – office workers taking lunch, shoppers resting their feet, messengers taking a short cut and street vendors selling T-shirts.

Museo de Tequila y Mezcal

Plaza Garibaldi • Mon–Wed & Sun 1–10pm; Thurs–Sat 1pm–midnight • M$50 • ⓦ mutemgaribaldi.mx • Metro Garibaldi or Bellas Artes

The Museum of Tequila and Mezcal (MUTEM) tells the story of Mexico's best-known liquors, as well as that of Plaza Garibaldi and its mariachis. Explanations are in Spanish and English, with lots of old photos. It's one of those museums that would be equally good as a book – there aren't any exhibits as such, apart from a large variety of agave plants – and the very limited free samples aren't worth getting excited about

1

either, although the rooftop bar is good. It nevertheless makes for a fun half-hour's worth of information, and if you come here on a Friday or Saturday night, you can spill out into the square afterwards to sample the liquors in question to the sound of mariachi musicians.

Museo de la Estampa
Hidalgo 39 • Tues–Sun 10am–5.45pm • M$10; free Sun • Metro Bellas Artes

On the north side of the Alameda, Avenida Hidalgo traces the line of an ancient thoroughfare, starting from the Teatro Hidalgo, right opposite Bellas Artes. To the west, a little sunken square by the church of Santa Vera Cruz, the **Museo de la Estampa**, is dedicated to engraving, an art form taken seriously in Mexico, where the legacy of José Guadalupe Posada (see p.362) is still revered. There is no permanent collection, but you may expect anything from engravings and printing plates from pre-Columbian times to the modern age, including works by Posada.

Laboratorio Arte Alameda
Dr Mora 7 • Tues–Sun 9am–5pm • M$19; free Sun • ⓦ artealameda.bellasartes.gob.mx • Metro Hidalgo

The **Laboratorio Arte Alameda** is an art museum built into the glorious seventeenth-century monastery of San Diego. The cool, white interior is filled with temporary exhibitions of challenging contemporary art. They're all superbly displayed around the church, chapel and cloister of the old monastery.

Museo Mural Diego Rivera
Corner of Balderas and Colón • Tues–Sun 10am–6pm • M$21; free Sun; photo permit M$5 • ⓦ museomuraldiegorivera.bellasartes .gob.mx • Metro Hidalgo

One of the buildings worst hit by the 1985 earthquake was the *Hotel del Prado*, which contained the Rivera mural *Sueño de una Tarde Dominical en la Alameda* (*Dream of a Sunday Afternoon in the Alameda*). The mural survived the quake, and was subsequently picked up in its entirety and transported around the Alameda – it can now be seen in the **Museo Mural Diego Rivera**, at the western end of the park. It's an impressive work – showing almost every famous Mexican character out for a stroll – but one suspects that its popularity with tour groups is as much to do with its relatively apolitical nature as with any superiority to Rivera's other works. Originally it included a placard with the words "God does not exist", which caused a huge furore, and Rivera was forced to paint it out before the mural was first displayed to the public.

Panels at the back of the sala housing the mural (Spanish on one side, English on the other), and also a leaflet available at the entrance (M$10), explain every character in the scene: Cortés is depicted with his hands stained red with blood; José Guadalupe Posada stands bowler-hatted next to his trademark skeleton, *La Calavera Catrina*, who holds the hand of Rivera himself, portrayed as a 9-year-old boy; Frida Kahlo stands in motherly fashion, just behind him.

Paseo de la Reforma and around

Paseo de la Reforma is the most impressive street in Mexico City, lined by tall, modern buildings. It was originally laid out in the 1860s by Emperor Maximilian to provide the city with a boulevard to rival the great European capitals, and doubled as a ceremonial drive from his palace in Chapultepec to the centre. It also provided a new impetus, and direction, for the growing metropolis. The original length of the broad avenue ran simply from the Bosque de Chapultepec to the junction of Juárez – at 5km a very long walk, but there are plenty of buses and *peseros* – and although it has been extended in both directions, this stretch is still what everyone thinks of as Reforma.

"**Reforma Norte**", as the extension towards Guadalupe is known, is just as wide (and the traffic just as dense), but is almost a term of disparagement. **Real Reforma**,

1

however, remains imposing – ten lanes of traffic, lines of trees, grand statues at every intersection and perhaps three or four of the original French-style, nineteenth-century houses still surviving. Twenty or thirty years ago it was the dynamic heart of the growing city, with even relatively new buildings being torn down to make way for yet newer, taller, more prestigious towers of steel and glass. The pulse has since moved elsewhere, and the fancy shops have relocated, leaving an avenue now mostly lined with airline offices, car rental agencies and banks, and somewhat diminishing the pleasure of a stroll.

Church of San Hipólito

Corner of Reforma and Puente de Alvarado • Mon–Sat 9am–5pm, Sun 6am–5pm • Free • Metro Hidalgo

The church of **San Hipólito** was founded by the Spanish soon after their eventual victory, both as a celebration and to commemorate the events of the Noche Triste (see p.820). The present building dates from 1602, though over the years it has been damaged by earthquakes and rebuilt. It now lists very visibly to one side.

Panteón de San Fernando

Plaza San Fernando • Tues–Sun 9am–7pm • Free • Metro Hidalgo

The Baroque eighteenth-century church of **San Fernando**, by the plaza of the same name, was once one of the richest churches in the city. Stripped over the years, it is now mostly of interest for its *panteón* (graveyard), last resting place of **Benito Juárez** and many of his colleagues in the reform movement, whose names will be familiar from the streets which now bear them: Ignacio Zaragoza, Guillermo Prieto, Miguel Lerdo de Tejada, Melchor Ocampo, Ignacio Comonfort.

Museo Nacional de San Carlos

Puente de Alvarado 50 • Daily except Tues 10am–6pm • M$31, free Sun • Ⓦ mnsancarlos.com • Metro Revolución

Where Puente de Alvarado meets Ramos Ariza, the **Museo Nacional de San Carlos** houses the country's oldest art collection, begun in 1783 by Carlos III of Spain, and comprising largely European work of the seventeenth and eighteenth centuries with some notable earlier and later additions. Major names are largely absent, but look for the delicate *San Pedro, San Andrés y San Mateo* by fifteenth-century Spanish painter Maestro de Palaquinos, portraits by Reynolds, Rubens and Hals and a luminous canvas of Breton women by the sea (*Mujeres Bretones a la Orilla del Mar*) by another Spaniard, Manuel Benedito y Vives. Travelling exhibitions are also frequently based here.

PUENTE DE ALVARADO

West of Reforma, Calle Hidalgo becomes the **Puente de Alvarado**. This was once one of the main causeways leading out of Tenochtitlán, across the lake which surrounded it, and was the route by which the Spanish attempted to flee the city on **Noche Triste** (Sad Night), July 10, 1520. Following the death of Moctezuma, and with his men virtually under siege in their quarters, Cortés decided to escape the city under cover of darkness. It was a disaster: the Aztecs cut the bridges and, attacking the bogged-down invaders from their canoes, killed all but 440 of the 1300 Spanish soldiers who set out, and more than half their native allies. **Greed**, as much as anything, cost the Spanish troops their lives, for in trying to take their gold booty with them they were, in the words of Bernal Díaz, "so weighed down by the stuff that they could neither run nor swim".

The street takes its name from **Pedro de Alvarado**, one of the last conquistadors to escape, crossing the broken bridge "in great peril after their horses had been killed, treading on the dead men, horses and boxes". In 1976, a **gold bar** like those made by Cortés from melted-down Aztec treasures was dug up in Calle Tacuba. It's now in the Museo Nacional de Antropología (see p.95). Without doubt, it was part of the treasure being carried by one of the conquistadors attempting to flee the city – a treasure which, as in all good treasure stories, ended up putting a curse on its robbers.

Monumento a la Revolución

Plaza de la República; mirador entrance from west side • Mon–Thurs 10am–6pm, Fri & Sat 10am–10pm, Sun 10am–8pm • M$40; free Wed • Metro Revolución

The vast **Monumento a la Revolución** was originally intended to be the central dome of a new home for the Cortes (parliament), though its construction was interrupted by the Revolution and never resumed – in the end they buried a few heroes of the Revolution under the mighty columns (including Pancho Villa and presidents Madero, Carranza and Cárdenas) and turned the whole thing into a memorial. An **elevator** has now been added to take you up to the **mirador** at the top. The views aren't as good as from the Torre Latinoamericano (see p.83), but you can see out to the edge of the city, especially to the north and west.

Museo Nacional de la Revolución

Tues–Sun 9am–5pm • M$24, free Sun

Underneath the monument, the **Museo Nacional de la Revolución** tells the history of the Revolution through archive pictures, old newspapers, films and life-size tableaux. Part of the museum is devoted to the construction of the monument itself. Other sections cover the Porfirio Díaz dictatorship, the various stages of the revolution, and how it broke down into civil war, resulting in the emergence of a new constitution and republic.

Zona Rosa

To the south of Reforma lies the **Zona Rosa** (Metro Insurgentes), a triangular area bordered by Reforma, Avenida Chapultepec and, to the west, Chapultepec Park. You'll know you're there as the streets are all named after famous cities. Packed into this tiny area are hundreds of bars, restaurants, hotels and shops, all teeming with a vast number of tourists and a cross section of Mexico City's aspiring middle classes. Until the 1980s this was the city's swankiest commercial neighbourhood, but the classiest shops have moved to Polanco (see p.92) and many of the big international chains have relocated to the out-of-town shopping centres that have sprung up around the Periférico. Though there's no shortage of good shops, and the selection of restaurants, cafés, clubs and bars in the Zona Rosa is respectable (see p.129, p.127 & p.132), it has lost its exclusive feel. It does however claim to have an *ambiente joven* (young vibe), and it's certainly popular with young people, as well as hosting Mexico City's **gay village**, which is located around the northern end of Amberes. Otherwise, there isn't much you'd come here especially to see. One historical figure who stayed here was **Pancho Villa**, quartered, when his troops were in town, at Liverpool 76.

El Ángel

Paseo de la Reforma at Florencia and Rio Tiber • Mon–Fri 10am–6pm, Sat & Sun 10am–3pm; elevator Mon–Fri 10am–6pm; Sat & Sun 10am–1pm • Free, but ID needed for the lift • Metro Insurgentes or Sevilla

The column of **El Ángel**, officially known as the **Monumento a la Independencia**, was built in 1910. In its base you can visit a room containing the skulls of Independence heroes Hidalgo, Aldama, Allende and Jiménez, and at weekends you can take a lift to the top of the monument, but it's a popular ride, so expect queues (the line snakes around from the door in the plinth). You can go up on weekdays, but you'll need to request permission from the *delegacion's* offices beforehand: a tedious exercise that requires around an hour and your passport.

Museo de Cera and ¡Aunque Ud. No lo Crea!

Londres 6 • Daily 11am–7pm • One museum M$70, joint ticket for two museums M$130 • Metro Cuauhtémoc

The Zona Rosa's only real attraction is the **Museo de Cera** (Wax Museum), located on its eastern fringes. Thoroughly tacky, with a basement chamber of horrors that includes Aztec human sacrifices, it shares its site with the Mexican branch of **Ripley's Believe It**

1

GLORIETAS

The length of Reforma is punctuated by **glorietas** – roundabouts at the major intersections – each with a distinctive statue, providing easy landmarks along the way. The first, if heading southwest from the Alameda, is the **Glorieta Colón**, with a statue of Christopher Columbus. Around the base of the plinth are carved various friars and monks who assisted Columbus in his enterprise or brought the Catholic faith to the Mexicans.

The Plaza de la República is just off to the north. Next comes the crossing of Insurgentes, nodal point of all the city's traffic, with **Cuauhtémoc**, last emperor of the Aztecs and leader of their resistance, poised aloof above it all in a plumed robe, clutching his spear, surrounded by warriors. Bas-relief engravings on the pedestal depict his torture and execution at the hands of the Spanish, desperate to discover where the Aztec treasures lay hidden. **El Ángel**, a golden winged victory atop a 40m column (see p.89), is the third to look out for, and the place to alight for the centre of the Zona Rosa.

or Not Museum (called in Spanish "¡Aunque Ud. No lo Crea!"), which displays such marvels as flea costumes and hair sculpture.

Colonia Cuauhtémoc

The northern side of Reforma, where the streets are named after rivers (Tiber, Danubio and the like), is a much quieter, posh residential area officially known as **Colonia Cuauhtémoc**, though it's usually just bundled in with the Zona Rosa. Here you'll find some of the older embassies, notably the US embassy, on Reforma, bristling with razor wire and security cameras.

Museo Venustiano Carranza

Río Lerma 35 • Tues–Sat 9am–6pm, Sun 9am–5pm • M$42, free Sun, video permit M$45 • Metro Insurgentes

Near the British embassy in Cuauhtémoc is the **Museo Venustiano Carranza**. Carranza was a Revolutionary leader and president of the Republic who was shot in 1920. The building was his home in Mexico City and contains exhibits relating to his life and to the Revolution.

Parque Sullivan

Just north of the junction of Reforma and Insurgentes

Parque Sullivan hosts free open-air exhibitions and sales of paintings, ceramics and other works of art every Sunday (roughly 10am–4pm); some of them are very good, and a pleasant holiday atmosphere prevails.

Roma and Condesa

South of the Zona Rosa lie the residential districts of **Roma** and **Condesa**, full of quiet leafy streets once you get away from the main avenues that cut through. Both suburbs were developed in the 1930s and 1940s, but as the city expanded they became unfashionable and run-down. That all changed in the 1990s when artists and the bohemian fringe were drawn here by low rents, decent housing and proximity to the centre of the city. Small-time galleries sprang up and the first of the bars and cafés opened.

Condesa, in particular, is now one of the best areas for good eating in the city, and definitely the place to come for lounging in pavement cafés or dining in bistro-style restaurants (see p.129). The greatest concentration is around the junction of Michoacán, and Tamaulipas, but establishments spread out into the surrounding streets, where you'll often find quiet neighbourhood places with tables spilling out onto the pavement. Sights in the usual sense are virtually nonexistent, but you can pass a few hours just walking the streets keeping an eye out for interesting art galleries, which seem to spring up all the time. The leafy thoroughfare of Nuevo Leon bisects the *colonia*, with the leafy Parque México to the east, which is a popular haven from the raucous city outside the limits of the circular Avenida Amsterdam, where jogging and café culture are the main order of business.

Parque México and around

Parque México, officially Parque San Martín, is a large green space virtually in the heart of Condesa that was set aside when the owners of the horse track sold it to developers

1

back in 1924. The streets around the park, especially Avenida México, are rich in 1930s architecture, showcasing Mexico's own distinctive version of Art Deco.

GETTING TO ROMA AND CONDESA

By Metro The Metro system gives Condesa a wide berth, with line 1 skirting the north and west while line 9 runs along the south side. For more direct access to Condesa's main restaurant district take line 1 to Juanacatlán, and cross the Circuito Interior using the nearby footbridge. This brings you onto Francisco Marquez, which leads to the restaurants – a 10min walk in all. Alternatively, take line 9 to Chilpancingo.

By Metrobús Take line 1 to Sonora or Campeche.

On foot It is easy enough to walk to Condesa south from the Zona Rosa (Metro Insurgentes, Sevilla or Chapultepec).

Polanco

High-priced high-rise hotels line the northern edge of Chapultepec Park, casting their shadow over the smart suburb of **Colonia Polanco**. Along the *colonia's* main drag, **Presidente Masaryk**, the beautiful people drive by in their Porsches and Lexus SUVs on their way to the Fendi or Ferragamo stores, and Polanco also has great dining, but otherwise, unless you've got brand-name shopping in mind or need to visit one of the district's embassies, there's not much reason to come out this way. In recent years something of a culinary renaissance has occurred to the north of **Parque Lincoln**, where three blocks of restaurants serve up varying qualities of world cuisine to a predominantly expat community.

Sala de Arte Público David Siqueiros

Tres Picos 29 • Tues–Sun 10am–6pm • M$12, free Sun • Metro Polanco

The only tourist sight in Polanco is the **Sala de Arte Público David Siqueiros**, a small but interesting collection of the great muralist's later work, including sketches he made for the Polyforum murals (see p.102). They're all displayed in his former residence and studio, donated (along with everything in it) to the people of Mexico just 25 days before his death in 1973.

If it is not already playing, ask to see the hour-long **video** (in English) on his life and work made just before his death, and watch it surrounded by his murals, which cover just about every piece of wall space.

Bosque de Chapultepec

The **Bosque de Chapultepec** (🌐 chapultepec.org.mx) is a vast green area, about a thousand acres in all, dotted with trees, museums, boating lakes, gardens, playing fields and a zoo. It provides an escape from the pressures of the city for seemingly millions of Mexicans, with the result that the most visited areas get a heavy pounding and some areas are occasionally fenced off to allow the plants to recover.

Most of the Bosque is taken up by **Chapultepec Park**, which is divided into three sections: the easternmost **Primera Sección**, or First Section, is home to the points of greatest interest, including the zoo; the **Segunda Sección**, or Second Section, is mostly aimed at kids, with an amusement park, technology museum and natural history museum; and the **Tercera Sección**, or Third Section, is currently being re-landscaped.

Brief history

The rocky outcrop of **Chapultepec** (Náhuatl for "hill of the locust"), from which the entire area has taken its name, is mentioned in **Toltec** mythology, but first gained historical significance in the thirteenth century when it was no more than an anonymous island among the lakes and salt marshes of the valley. Here the **Aztecs**, still a wandering, savage tribe, made their first home, though it proved to be temporary

■ ACCOMMODATION		● EATING		La Ciudad de Colima	1	■ DRINKING & NIGHTLIFE	
Busue	1	Bistro Charlotte	3	Denominación de Origen	4	Love	1
Hyatt Regency	2	Butcher & Sons	5	Eltuca's	2		

when they were defeated and driven off by neighbouring cities. Once **Tenochtitlán**'s power was established they returned here, channelling water from the springs into the city, and turning Chapultepec into a summer resort for the emperor, with plentiful hunting and fishing around a fortified palace. Several Aztec rulers had their portraits carved into the rock of the hill, though most of these images were destroyed by the Spaniards soon after the Conquest.

ESSENTIALS

BOSQUE DE CHAPULTEPEC

OPENING HOURS

Chapultepec is a big place with a lot to do. You could easily spend a couple of days here and still not see everything, but if you are selective you can cover the best of it in one tiring day. It can be tempting to visit on Sun, when some of the museums are free, and the park is at its vibrant best. However, if you want to be able to move freely it's worth coming during the week.

1

The Primera Sección The Primera Sección and its museums are only open during the daytime, and are closed on Mon. The Museo de Arte Moderno and Rufino Tamayo museums are free on Sun; the Museo Nacional de Antropología used to be, but no longer is. The entrances to these museums are grouped together along Paseo de la Reforma, less than a 15min walk from Chapultepec Metro station, but you may prefer to catch a *pesero* ("Auditorio", "Reforma km 13" and others) along Reforma.

The Segunda and Tercera Secciónes These secciónes – though not the attractions inside them – are open all the time.

ACCESS

How you approach the Bosque depends on what you want to see first.

The Primera Sección The easiest access to the First Section of the park is via the Metro Chapultepec station, from where you follow the crowds over a bridge across the Circuito Interior (inner ring road). Straight ahead you'll see the Niños Héroes monument and the castle containing the Museo Nacional de Historia. What you may be more interested in taking in along with Section One are the Museo Nacional de Antropología, the Museo de Arte Moderno and the Museo Rufino Tamayo, all officially outside of the Primera Sección yet still surrounded by parkland. You're unlikley, however, to fit all of these into one day.

The Segunda Sección Visitors with kids may want to head straight for the Second Section, either picking up a *pesero* along Constituyentes (routes 2, 24 and others) from Metro Chapultepec, or going direct to Metro Constituyentes and walking from there.

Primera Sección and around

Tues–Sun: summer 5am–6pm; winter 5am–7pm • Free • Metro Chapultepec

The **First Section** of the park is dominated by **Chapultepec Hill**, crowned by Emperor Maximilian's very peaceful-looking "castle". Also in the First Section is the **zoo** and the nearby **boating lake**, All week, but especially on Sundays, the area around these attractions is full of vendors selling souvenirs, snacks and sweets.

Monumento a los Niños Héroes

Directly opposite the park's main entrance, coming in from Chapultepec metro station

This strange, six-columned monument is dedicated to the **Niños Héroes**: cadets who attempted to defend the castle (then a military academy) against American invaders in 1847. According to the story, probably apocryphal, the last six flung themselves off the cliff wrapped in Mexican flags rather than surrender.

Museo de Caracol

Near the top of Chapultepec Hill • Tues–Sun 9am–4.15pm • M$39, free Sun

The modern **Museo de Caracol** is devoted to "the Mexican people's struggle for Liberty". Its full name is the Museo Galería de la Lucha del Pueblo Mexicano por su Libertad, but it's colloquially known as the "shell museum" for the snail-like spiralling route through the displays. These trace the history of the constant wars that have beset the country – from Independence, through the American and French interventions to the Revolution.

Museo Nacional de Historia

At the top of Chapultepec Hill • Tues–Sun 9am–5pm • M$51, free Sun • Ⓜ mnh.inah.gob.mx • Land trains from the bottom of the hill run every 15min, costing M$13 for the round trip

The castle which today houses the **Museo Nacional de Historia** was built in 1785 as a summer retreat for the Spanish viceroy. Until then it had been the site of a hermitage established on the departure of the Aztec rulers. Following Independence it served as a military school, but the present design was dictated by Emperor Maximilian, who remodelled it in the image of his Italian villa.

The setting is very much part of the attraction, with many rooms retaining the opulent furnishings left behind by Maximilian and Carlota, or by later inhabitants with equally expensive tastes, notably Porfirio Díaz. Rivalling the decor is a small group of carriages, including the fabulously pompous Cinderella-goes-to-the-ball state coaches favoured by Maximilian. A collection of furniture, glassware and medals leads on to the main attraction of the lower floor, a series of ornate rooms viewed from a black-and-white tiled terrace that affords great views over the park and city. Peer into Maximilian's office, games room and drawing room, all gilt and dark wood, then move on to Carlota's bedroom and a gorgeous tiled bathroom.

There are several murals here as well, including a number of works by **Orozco** and **Siqueiros**, but the ones by **Juan O'Gorman** most directly attract attention for their single-minded political message.

Lago Chapultepec

On the south side of Reforma, opposite the Museo de Antropología • Boat rental M$60–100/hr for 1–5 people, depending on the size of the boat

If you like messing about in **boats**, you'll probably enjoy **Lago Chapultepec**, a boating lake where you can rent vessels of various sizes and while away a leisurely afternoon. A smaller lake, just across the path from the Monument to the Niños Héroes, is used for radio-controlled boats.

Parque Zoológico de Chapultepec

At the western side of Lago Chapultepec • Tues–Sun 9am–4.30pm • Free • Ⓦ sedema.df.gob.mx/zoo_chapultepec

The **Parque Zoológico de Chapultepec** occupies a large area in the centre of the park and is divided up into climatic zones (desert, tropical, temperate forests, etc), some of which work better than others. Enclosures are mostly open air and tolerably large, though the animals still look bored and confined, and you wonder about their sanity on a Sunday afternoon when half of Mexico City's children seem to be vying for their attention. Probably the most satisfying sections are the most archetypally Mexican: the desert zone, and the enclosure of **xoloitzcuintles**, the hairless dogs that represent the last surviving of four pre-Columbian breeds.

All the big beasts make an appearance, too: tigers, bears, lions, bison, camels, giraffes, hippos, elephants and the ever-popular **giant pandas**. The zoo is inordinately proud of these, evidenced by the posters around town that advertise new baby bears when they are born – in fact, this was the first place in the world to breed giant pandas in captivity.

Los Pinos and around

The street which heads south from Metro Auditorio, Calzada Chivatito, changes its name about halfway to Molino del Rey, after the major battle fought here during the Mexican–American War. Near its southern end is **Los Pinos**, the president's official residence, which is strictly off-limits. A couple of footbridges lead across the *periférico* (Blv López Mateos) to the park's Second Section.

Casa Luis Barragán

Francisco Ramírez 14 • Appointment only Mon–Fri 10.30am, 11.30am, 12.30pm, 3pm & 4pm, Sat 10.30am & 12.30pm • M$150 • ☏ 55 5515 4908, Ⓦ casaluisbarragan.org • Metro Constituyentes

Outside the park limits, south of Avenida Constituyentes, the **Casa Luis Barragán** is a 1948 modernist house designed by Mexican architect Luis Barragán, all whitewash and right angles. Nowadays, it's used for modern art exhibitions.

Museo Nacional de Antropología

Tues–Sun 9am–7pm • M$64, video M$45 • Ⓦ mna.inah.gob.mx

The park's outstanding attraction – for many people the main justification for visiting the city at all – is the **Museo Nacional de Antropología**, one of the world's great museums, not only for its collection, which is vast, rich and diverse, but also for the originality and practicality of its design. Opened in 1964, the exhibition halls surround a patio with a small pond and a vast, square concrete umbrella supported by a single slender pillar around which splashes an artificial cascade. The halls are ringed by gardens, many of which contain outdoor exhibits.

1

The entrance from Reforma is marked by a colossal statue of the rain god Tlaloc – the story goes that its move here from its original home in the east of the city was accompanied by furious downpours in the midst of a drought. Just east of the museum is a large open plaza, at one end of which is a small clearing pierced by a 20m pole from which **voladores** "fly". This Totonac ceremony (see box, p.419) is performed several times a day, and loses a lot of its appeal through its commercial nature – an assistant canvasses the crowd for donations as they perform – but it is still an impressive spectacle.

Pre-Classic

The **Pre-Classic** room covers the development of the first cultures in the Valley of México and surrounding highlands – pottery and clay figurines from these early agricultural communities predominate. Notice especially the **small female figures** dated 1700–1300 BC from Tlatilco (a site in the suburbs), which are probably related to some form of fertility or harvest rites. The influence of the growing Olmec culture begins to be seen in later artefacts, including the amazing **acrobat** vase, also from Tlatilco. With the development of more formal religion, recognizable images of gods also appear: several of these, from Cuicuilco in the south of the city, depict **Huehueteotl**, the old god or god of fire, as an old man with flames on his back.

Teotihuacán

The next hall is devoted to **Teotihuacán** (see p.142), the first great city in the Valley of México. A growing sophistication is immediately apparent in the more elaborate nature of the pottery vessels and the use of new materials, shells, stone and jewels. There's a full-scale reproduction of part of the **Temple of Quetzalcoatl** at Teotihuacán, brightly polychromatic as it would originally have been. It contains the remains of nine sacrificial victims dressed as warriors, complete with their funerary necklaces: a relatively recent confirmation of human sacrifice and militarism at Teotihuacán. Nearby is a reconstruction of the inside courtyard and central temple of an apartment complex bedecked in vibrant murals representing ritual life in the city, including *El Paraíso de Tlaloc*, a depiction of the heaven reserved for warriors and ball-players who died in action.

Toltec

The **Toltec** room begins with reproductions of vibrant red and blue murals from Cacaxtla near Tlaxcala (see p.161) and then objects from Xochicalco, a city near modern Cuernavaca (see p.172), which flourished between the fall of Teotihuacán and the heyday of Tula. The large stone carvings and pottery show a distinct Maya influence: particularly lovely is the stylized stone **head of a macaw**, similar to ones found on Maya ball-courts in Honduras. Highlights of the section devoted to Tula are the weighty stone carvings, including one of the Atlantean columns from the main temple there, representing a warrior. Also of note are the **Chac-mool**, a reclining figure with a receptacle on his stomach in which sacrificial offerings were placed, and high up, above a large frieze, the **standard bearer**, a small human figure that acted as a flagpole when a standard was inserted into the hole between its clasped hands. Overlooking some human remains, there's an exquisite little mother-of-pearl-encrusted sculpture of a **coyote's head** with teeth made of bone and a bearded man (possibly a warrior in a headdress) emerging from its mouth.

Mexica (Aztec)

Next comes the biggest and richest room of all, the **Mexica Gallery**, characterized by massive yet intricate stone sculpture, but also displaying pottery, small stone objects, even wooden musical instruments. Facing you as you enter is the **Ocelotl-Cuauhxicalli**, a jaguar with a hollow in its back in which the hearts of human sacrifices were placed (it may have been the companion of the eagle in the Templo Mayor museum; the two

NAVIGATING THE MUSEO NACIONAL DE ANTROPOLOGÍA

The museum's rooms, each devoted to a separate period or culture, are arranged chronologically in an anticlockwise pattern around the central courtyard. As you come into the **entrance hall** there's a small circular space with temporary exhibitions, usually very interesting and devoted to the latest developments in archeology; here too is the small **Sala de Orientación**, which presents an audio-visual overview of the major ancient cultures. Off to the left you'll find the **library** and a **shop** selling postcards, souvenirs, books in several languages on Mexican culture, archeology and history, and **guidebooks** (two sizes, in Spanish, English, French or German; M\$78 and M\$299), which provide photographs and descriptions of most of the important pieces. **The ticket office**, and the **entrance** to the museum proper, is by the huge glass doors to the right, where you can also rent headsets, which effectively take you on a **tour** of the museum's highlights in Spanish, English or French for M\$75 (and you have to deposit a piece of ID as security); they're very cursory, but you do get around the whole museum with some form of explanation. Labelling of individual items is mostly in Spanish, though the general introduction to each room is accompanied by an English translation.

THE COLLECTION

A complete tour of the museum starts on the right-hand side with three **introductory rooms** giving an overview of indigenous culture, an introduction to anthropology and a history of the peopling of the Americas. These rooms are followed on the right-hand side by halls devoted to the **Pre-Classic**, **Teotihuacán** and **Toltec** cultures. At the far end is the vast **Mexica** (Aztec) room, followed around the left wing by **Oaxaca** (Mixtec and Zapotec), **Gulf of Mexico** (Olmec), **Maya** and the cultures of the **north** and **west**. Every hall has at least one outstanding feature, but if you have limited time, the Aztec and the Maya rooms are the **highlights**; what else you see might depend on what area of the country you plan to head on to. The upper floor is given over to **ethnography collections**, which are devoted to the life and culture of the various indigenous groups today; stairs lead up from each side. Downstairs, behind the hall given over to the cultures of the north and west, is a very welcome **restaurant**.

were found very close to each other, though over eighty years apart). Among the hundreds of other powerful pieces – most of the vast Aztec pantheon is represented – snakes, eagles and human hearts and skulls are prominent. Among the statues is a vast image of **Coatlicue**, goddess of the earth, life and death, and mother of the gods. She is shown with two serpents above her shoulders, representing the flow of blood; her necklace of hands and hearts and pendant of a skull represent life and death respectively; her dress is made of snakes; her feet are eagles' claws. As a counterpoint to the viciousness of most of this, be sure to notice **Xochipilli**, the god of love, flowers, dance and poetry. You'll come across him, wearing a mask and sitting cross-legged on a throne strewn with flowers and butterflies, in the section to the left of the entrance as you come in. Also impressive is a reconstructed version of **Moctezuma's headdress**, resplendent in bright blue quetzal feathers, and a **gold bar** lost by one of Cortés' troops during their attempted escape on "Noche Triste" (see p.820).

Piedra del Sol

The room's undoubted highlight, directly opposite the entrance, is the enormous 24-tonne **Piedra del Sol**, the Stone of the Sun or Aztec Calendar Stone. The latter, popular name is not strictly accurate, for this is much more a vision of the Aztec cosmos, completed under Moctezuma only a few years before the Spanish arrived. The stone was found by early colonists, and deliberately reburied for fear that it would spread unrest among the population. After being dug up again in the Zócalo in 1790, it spent years propped up against the walls of the cathedral. In the centre is the sun god and personification of the fifth sun, Tonatiuh, with a tongue in the form of a sacrificial knife and claws holding human hearts on each side, representing the need for human sacrifice to nourish the sun; around him are symbols for the four previous incarnations

1

of the sun – a jaguar, wind, water and fiery rain; this whole central conglomeration forms the sign for the date on which the fifth world would end (as indeed, with the Spanish Conquest, it fairly accurately did). Encircling all this are hieroglyphs representing the twenty days of the Aztec month and other symbols of cosmic importance, and the whole thing is surrounded by two serpents.

Oaxaca

Moving round to the third side of the museum, you reach the halls devoted to cultures based away from the highlands, starting, in the corner of the museum, with the **Zapotec** and **Mixtec** people of **Oaxaca**. Although the two cultures evolved side by side, the Zapotecs flourished earlier (from around 900 BC to 800 AD) as accomplished architects with an advanced scientific knowledge, and also as makers of magnificent pottery with a pronounced Olmec influence. From around 800 AD many of their sites were taken over by the Mixtecs, whose overriding talents were as craftsmen and artists, working in metal, precious stone and clay. The best site in the country for both these cultures is Monte Albán (see p.605).

The Zapotec collection demonstrates a fine sense of movement in the human figures: a reproduction of part of the carved facade of the Temple of the Dancers at Monte Albán; a model of a temple with a parrot sitting in it (in the "Monte Albán II" section); vases and urns in the form of various gods; and a superb jade mask representing the bat god Piquete Ziña.

Gulf of Mexico

Next is the **Gulf of Mexico** room, in which are displayed some of the treasures of **Olmec** art as well as objects produced in this region during the Classic period. The Olmec civilization is considered the mother culture of Mexico for its advanced development as early as 1500 BC, which provided much of the basis for the later Teotihuacán and Maya cultures. Olmec figures are delightful, but have many puzzling aspects, in particular their apparently African features, nowhere better displayed than in some of the famed **colossal heads** dating from 1200–200 BC, long before Africa is supposed to have had any connection with the Americas. Many of the smaller pieces show evidence of deliberate deformation of the skull and teeth. The statue known as "the wrestler" (though labelled in Spanish only as "*hombre barbado*"), with arms akimbo as if at the point of starting a bout, and the many tiny objects in jade and other polished stones are all outstanding. The later cultures are substantially represented, with fine figures and excellent pottery above all. The two most celebrated pieces are a statue of **Huehueteotl** (though labelled only as a "*dios viejo*") looking thoroughly grouchy with a brazier perched on his head, and the so-called **Huastec Adolescent**, a young Huastec Indian priest of Quetzalcoatl (perhaps the god himself) with an elaborately decorated naked body and a child on his back.

Maya

The hall devoted to the **Maya** is the most varied, reflecting the longest-lived and widest-spread of the Mesoamerican cultures. In some ways it's a disappointment, since their greatest achievements were in architecture and in the decoration of their temples – many of which, unlike those of the Aztecs, are still standing – so that the objects here seem relatively unimpressive. Nevertheless, there are reproductions of several buildings, or parts of them, friezes and columns taken from them and extensive collections of jewellery, pottery and minor sculpture. Steps lead down into a section devoted to burial practices, including a reproduction of the Royal Tomb at **Palenque** (see p.684) with many of the objects found there – notably the prince's jade death mask.

Temple of Paintings

Outside, a trio of small temples from relatively obscure sites is reproduced, the Temple of Paintings from **Bonampak** (see p.692) among them. The three rooms of the temple are entirely covered in frescoes representing the coronation of a new prince, a great battle and the subsequent punishments and celebrations. They are much easier to visit than the originals and in far better condition.

Northern and western societies

As a finale to the archeological collections on the ground floor, there's a large room devoted to the north and the west of the country. **Northern** societies on the whole developed few large centres, remaining isolated nomadic or agricultural communities. The small quantities of pottery, weapons and jewellery that have survived show a close affinity with native peoples of the southwestern USA. The **west** was far more developed, but it, too, has left relatively few traces, and many of the best examples of **Tarascan culture** (see p.297) remain in Guadalajara. Among the highlights here are some delightful small human and animal figurines in stone and clay, a Tarascan Chac-mool, a jade mask of Malinaltepec inlaid with a turquoise and red-shell mosaic, and a two-storey reconstruction of the houses at Paquimé in the Chihuahua desert.

The Ethnography Section

The **Ethnography Section** is on the upper floor. You must cross the courtyard back towards the beginning of the museum before climbing the stairs – otherwise you'll go round in reverse order. The rooms relate as closely as possible to those below them, showing the lifestyle of surviving indigenous groups today through photographs, models, maps and examples of local crafts. Regional dress and reproductions of various types of huts and cabins form a major part of this inevitably rather sanitized look at the poorest (and most oppressed) people in Mexico, and there are also objects relating to their more important cults and ceremonies.

Museo de Arte Moderno

Paseo de la Reforma, some 300m east of the Museo Nacional de Antropología • Tues–Sun 10.15am–5.30pm • M$25, free Sun

The **Museo de Arte Moderno** consists of two low circular buildings dedicated to twentieth-century Mexican and Latin American art. The majority of the galleries, along with a separate gallery reached through the **sculpture garden**, are devoted to temporary and touring exhibitions, which are usually well worth inspection.

Permanent collection

The **permanent collection** is exhibited only in Sala D, which does not hold all of it, so the works are rotated regularly. Among them, all the major Mexican artists of the twentieth century are represented. Of works by Siqueiros, the most powerful is *Madre Campesina*, in which a peasant woman carries her child barefoot through an unforgiving desert of cacti. Diego Rivera's portrait of his second wife, Lupe Marín, was painted in 1938, long after their divorce. The eponymous fruit-seller in Olga Costa's *Vendedora de Frutas* is surrounded by bananas, sugar cane, watermelons, pumpkins, pawpaws, soursops and *mameyes*, all painted in vibrant reds and yellows – about as Mexican a subject as you could want.

Las Dos Fridas

The museum's star attraction must be Frida Kahlo's *Las Dos Fridas*, which stands out even among the museum's fine representative selection of haunting and disturbing canvases by Kahlo. One of her earliest full-scale paintings, it depicts her on the left in a white traditional dress, her heart torn and wounded, and her hand being held by a stronger Frida on the right, dressed in modern clothes and holding a locket with a picture of her husband Diego Rivera as a boy. As the works are rotated, not all of these will necessarily be on display at any one time.

1 ## Museo Rufino Tamayo

Paseo de la Reforma • Tues–Sun 10am–6pm • M$25, free Sun • ⓦ museotamayo.org

Hidden among trees across the street from the Museum of Modern Art is the **Museo Rufino Tamayo**, another fine collection of modern art – this one with an international focus. The modernist structure was built by the artist Rufino Tamayo, whose work in murals and on smaller projects was far more abstract and less political than the Big Three, though he was their approximate contemporary and enjoys a reasonable amount of international fame. There is much of his own work here, and exhibits of his techniques and theories, but also a fairly impressive collection of European and American twentieth-century art – most of it from Tamayo's private collection. Artists represented may include Picasso, Miró, Magritte, Francis Bacon and Henry Moore, though not all of these are on permanent display. First-rate contemporary international exhibits usually find their way here and sometimes take over the space of parts of the permanent collection.

Segunda and Tercera secciónes and around

Over the years, new sections of parkland have been added to the west of the original Bosque de Chapultepec. These are occasionally still referred to as the **Nuevo Bosque de Chapultepec**, but are more commonly known as the **Segunda Sección** and **Tercera Sección**. With very few places to cross the *periférico*, it is difficult to reach the newer parts of the park from the old. It is far better to make a separate visit to these sections, especially if you've got kids.

Segunda Sección

There are few compelling reasons to visit either section for adults, though the Second Section is an enjoyable area to stroll about, and a good deal quieter than the main section of the park. Approaching the Second Section from Metro Constituyentes, follow Avenida Constituyentes west for a few metres and then cross it on a footbridge.

Mexico en Miniatura

Just inside the Segunda Sección's main entrance on Constituyentes • Daily 10am–5pm • M$10

All that's now left of the rather tacky Mexico Magic fun park is **Mexico en Miniatura**, a collection of 150 models of "the most emblematic monuments of the republic" created by artist Pedro Ramírez Vásquez. Sights represented here include all the famous pre-Hispanic ruins, plus colonial and modern attractions from around the country, including Mexico City's Zócalo, the Palacio de Bellas Artes and archeological sites from Teotihuacán to Chitchén Itzá.

Papalote Museo del Niño

Constituyentes 268 • Mon–Wed & Fri 9am–6pm, Thurs 9am–11pm, Sat & Sun 10am–7pm • Museum M$120; cinema M$99; museum and cinema combination ticket M$175; music-and-visuals dome M$99; museum and music-and-visuals dome combination ticket M$175; museum, cinema and music-and-visuals dome combination ticket M$189 • ⓦ papalote.org.mx

If you turn right after coming in through the Segunda Sección's main entrance on Constituyentes, you'll come to the **Papalote Museo del Niño**, a kind of cross between an adventure playground and a science experiment, with loads of fascinating hands-on experiments, plus an IMAX cinema and a music-and-visuals dome. Adults may feel as if they have entered some sort of psychotic kindergarten, but if you have kids, it will keep them entertained.

La Feria

Tues–Sun 10am–8pm • Entry packages M$90–190; all packages include some but not all rides

La Feria is the city's premier fun park. Here you'll find assorted rides and sideshows, easily the best of which is the old-fashioned wooden roller coaster (*montaña rusa*).

For adrenaline-fiends, there's also a newer and more exciting roller coaster, right by the entrance. The cheaper entry packages mostly include children's rides (with 1.40m height restrictions), but fewer adult ones.

Museo de Historia Natural and Cárcomo de Dolores

Tues–Sun 10am–5pm • M$45; free Tues; M$12.50 to bring in a camera

The **Museo de Historia Natural** consists of ten interconnecting domes filled with displays on nature and conservation, biology and geology, including rundowns on Mexico's mineral wealth, flora and fauna. Modern and well presented – and with the obligatory dinosaurs – it is again particularly popular with children, but the educational value of the explanations will be lost if you don't speak Spanish.

The ticket for the Museo de Historia Natural also entitles you to visit the **Cárcomo de Dolores**, near the Lago Menor lake, a gazebo containing two murals by Diego Rivera: *El Agua, Origen de la Vida* and *El Fuente de Tlaloc*.

Panteón Civil de Dolores

On Constituyentes, between the second and third sections of Chapultepec Park • Daily 7am–5pm • Free • Pesero (route #24 to "Panteón Dolores") from Metro Chapultepec or along Av Constituyentes

The **Panteón Civil de Dolores** is a huge cemetery, Mexico City's answer to Père Lachaise or Highgate. Among those buried here are Diego Rivera, José Clemente Orozco and other illustrious Mexicans. There's an information office at the main gate (closed at weekends) where you can ask for directions to specific graves.

Tercera Sección

The **Tercera Sección** of Chapultepec Park lies 1km west of the Second Section, beyond the Panteón Civil de Dolores cemetery. It formerly hosted a number of weekend amusement park-type attractions, but those are all now closed, and the space is now used mainly by joggers who live in the surrounding neighbourhoods.

South of the centre

Mexico City spreads itself furthest to the south, where a series of old villages has been swallowed up by the urban sprawl. These harbour some of the most enticing destinations outside the centre, including the colonial suburbs of **Coyoacán** and **San Ángel**, the archeological site of **Cuicuilco** and the canals of **Xochimilco**.

GETTING TO THE SOUTHERN SUBURBS

It's not at all difficult to get out to any of the sights outside the city centre on public transport, but getting from one to the other can be tricky if you're cutting across the main north–south routes. In fact, there is easily enough to see out this way to justify a couple of separate trips, thereby avoiding the slightly complicated matter of traversing the area. And while none of the connections you have to make are impossible, it's worth taking a few short taxi rides between them, from San Ángel to Coyoacán, for example, or from Coyoacán to Rivera's Anahuacalli Museum. If you want to see as much as possible in a day or even an afternoon, you might consider hiring a taxi to take you round the lot; if you bargain, this may not be as expensive as it sounds.

To San Ángel and the University City The best approach is along Insurgentes Sur, plied by the Metrobús (see p.120). There are also plenty of *peseros* from the bus stands by Metro Chapultepec or Tasqueña for services along the Calzada de Tlalpan and to the southwest of the city, above all to Xochimilco. If you'd rather stick to the Metro, take line 3 to Miguel Ángel de Quevedo, between San Ángel and Coyoacán.

To Coyoacán If you don't fancy walking from San Ángel (see box, p.104), buses head down Altavista by the *San Ángel Inn*; from the centre, buses leave from Metros Chapultepec, Insurgentes or Cuauhtémoc. In each case look for "Coyoacán" or "Colonia del Valle/Coyoacán". There's also a trolleybus which runs in both directions along Lázaro Cárdenas. Metro line 3, too, passes close by, though note that Viveros station is considerably closer to the action than

1

Coyoacán station: from Viveros, walk south on Av Universidad, then turn left (east) to reach the centre. If you're coming straight from the centre of town down Cuauhtémoc or Lázaro Cárdenas, it makes sense to visit the Kahlo and Trotsky museums (see p.106 & p.108) first, in which case you'll want to get off the bus immediately after passing under Av Río Churubusco. The Metro stops are slightly more distant, but a good approach is to take line 2 to General Anaya and walk west past the Museo de las Intervenciones and the Trotsky and Frida Kahlo houses.

Insurgentes

Insurgentes, the most direct approach to the suburbs, is interesting in its own right: leaving behind the Glorieta de Insurgentes (the roundabout at Insurgentes Metro station), it runs almost perfectly straight all the way out to the university, lined the whole way with huge department stores and malls, cinemas, restaurants and office buildings. A little under halfway to San Ángel, you pass on the right the enormous **World Trade Center**, crowned by *Bellini*, an expensive revolving restaurant (see p.129).

Polyforum Siqueiros

Insurgentes Sur 701 (cnr Filadelfia) • Daily 10am–6pm; sound-and-light show Sat & Sun noon & 2pm • M$15; sound-and-light show M$30 • ☎ 55 5536 4520 to 24, ⓦ polyforumsiqueiros.com.mx • Metrobús Poliforum

The exterior of the garish **Polyforum Siqueiros** is plastered in brash paintings by David Siqueiros and some thirty other artists. Inside, it contains what is allegedly the world's largest mural (about 4500 square metres), painted by Siqueiros alone, entitled *La Marcha de la Humanidad en la Tierra y hacia el Cosmos* (*The March of Humanity on Earth and Towards the Cosmos*). For the full impact of the changing perspectives and use of sculptural techniques, try to see the **sound-and-light show** with taped narration (in Spanish) by Siqueiros. Elsewhere, the building houses visiting art exhibitions and a sizeable display of expensive crafts for sale.

Plaza México and around

Off Insurgentes to the west • Metro San Antonio or Metrobús Ciudad de los Deportes

Plaza México is the largest bullring in the world, with a capacity of 48,000. You can't actually see it from Insurgentes, but it's only a ten-minute walk along San Antonio. Hard by is the **Estadio Azul**, a 65,000-seat football stadium that is Cruz Azul's home ground.

Teatro de los Insurgentes

Just before San Ángel • Metrobús Teatro Insurgentes

The facade of **Teatro de los Insurgentes** is covered in a huge mosaic designed by Diego Rivera depicting the history of Mexican theatre, and assorted historical figures. At the top are the insurgents (*los Insurgentes*) of Mexico's War of Independence: Hidalgo, Morelos and Benito Juárez on the left, and Zapata on the right.

San Ángel

The upmarket colonial suburb of **San Ángel** lies 12km southwest of central Mexico City, clustered around the point where Insurgentes Sur and Revolución almost meet, linked by the 200m-long Avenida La Paz. With its markets, ancient mansions and high-priced shops – Cartier, Italian designer furniture and the like – around flower-draped patios, San Ángel is a very exclusive place to live. It also makes an inviting place to visit, packed with little restaurants and cafés where you can sit outside and watch the crowds go by. Whether you choose to visit on Saturday (market day – see p.135) or one of the quieter days of the week, consider sticking around until evening to blow an appreciable wad of cash on some of the finest dining in the city (see p.130).

1

Plaza San Jacinto

San Ángel is especially appealing on Saturdays when the delightful **Plaza San Jacinto** is taken over by **Bazar Sábado**, a lively outdoor art market. Initially, the Saturday market was based in one of the mansions on the square, which still opens every weekend selling upmarket crafts and artworks, but nowadays there are stalls in all the surrounding streets, complete with fairground rides.

Casa del Risco

Plaza San Jacinto 15 • Tues–Sun 10am–5pm • Free • ⓦ isidrofabela.com • Metrobús Dr Galvez

Plaza San Jacinto is surrounded by San Ángel's oldest mansions, notably the eighteenth-century **Casa del Risco**, housing a collection of mostly European antique furniture and paintings put together by twentieth-century diplomat Isidro Fabela. There's an extraordinary fountain in the central patio made from seashells and old porcelain plates and cups, broken and whole.

Museo del Carmen

On Revolución just south of its junction with La Paz • Tues–Sun 10am–4.45pm • M$46, free Sun • Metrobús Dr Galvez

San Ángel takes its name from the former Carmelite Convent of San Angelo Mártir, which is now run as the **Museo del Carmen**. Its three brightly coloured, tiled domes preside over this part of town and add the final touch of grace to what is a lovely example of early seventeenth-century architecture. The church is still used but the rest of the convent has become a museum where just walking through the maze of monks' cells, rooms and courtyards is pleasurable enough, though there's also an extensive collection of colonial religious paintings and furniture. Just about everyone wants to make their way to the crypt to see the dozen **mummies**, found here by troops during

---

A WALK FROM SAN ÁNGEL TO COYOACÁN

The most enjoyable way to take in San Ángel and Coyoacán on the same day is to put an hour or so aside and **walk** between the two. The most pleasant route (see map, p.107), through quiet streets past some of the city's prime real estate, starts at the main junction in the centre of San Ángel where Revolución passes the Museo del Carmen (see above). From here, follow La Paz northeast and cross Insurgentes to reach the **Jardín de la Bombilla**, a small park centred on a blockish concrete **monument** to General Alvaro Obregón, who was assassinated here in 1928, soon after being re-elected as president. Revolutionary workers (holding a corn cob, oak leaves, a hammer and a sickle) flank the monument, and you can duck inside to see the bronze statue of Obregón.

On the east side of the park, cross Chimalistac and walk through the tiny Plaza Frederico Gamboa, overlooked by the sixteenth-century **Capilla de San Sebastián Martir**, with a statue of the Virgin of Guadalupe above the door. When you reach the other side of the square, take a left (you're now headed north) and cross Miguel Ángel de Quevedo, passing **Parque Tagle** on your left, then turn right into Arenal. This leads you across Universidad to the **Capilla de San Antonio de Padua**, a little red chapel sited attractively next to a small stone bridge.

Continue east on the peaceful, cobbled Francisco Sosa, one of the most beautiful streets in the city, and also one of the oldest. Peer over the high walls lining the street to catch a glimpse of some gorgeous residences – the only way to get any closer to these houses is to visit the **Museo Nacional de la Acuarela**, Salvador Novo 88 (daily 10am–6pm; free; ⓦ acuarela.org.mx), a small museum inside one. Devoted to watercolour painting, the collection includes some architectural and graphic art as well. Look for work by early twentieth-century painter Saturnino Herrán, and don't miss the temporary exhibits in a separate gallery reached through a small sculpture garden.

Ten minutes' walk further along Francisco Sosa brings you to the **Plaza Santa Catarina**, a tranquil square overlooked by a mustard-yellow church and with a couple of restaurants. From here it is a short walk to Coyoacán's Plaza Central, reached through a twin-arched gateway.

If you're still in a walking mood, you could continue along Avenida Hidalgo to the Museo Nacional de las Intervenciones (see p.111) and General Anaya metro station.

the Revolution and thought to be eighteenth-century nuns and monks, now displayed behind glass. Elsewhere, check out the extensive displays on daily life in New Spain and a collection of eighteenth-century oils by Cristóbal de Vallalpando.

Museo Casa Estudio Diego Rivera y Frida Kahlo and the San Ángel Inn

Diego Rivera 2 • Tues–Sun 10am–6pm • M$20, free Sun

From central San Ángel, it's just over half a kilometre along Altavista to the **Museo Casa Estudio Diego Rivera y Frida Kahlo**, a pair of modernist houses built for Diego Rivera and Frida Kahlo in 1931–32 by the leading contemporary architect, Juan O'Gorman. Tucked behind an organ cactus fence opposite the prestigious *San Ángel Inn* restaurant (see p.131) sits a small compound with a large maroon-coloured house (Diego's) and a much smaller blue abode (Frida's), connected by a rooftop causeway. From 1933 to 1941 they both stayed here, living and working apart yet still near enough to visit each other and for Frida to deliver Diego's meals. In both buildings the walls are concrete, the floors are wooden and many of the windows go from floor to ceiling – very advanced for the early 1930s and especially for Mexico. Indeed, the whole set-up is in such contrast to the Blue House in Coyoacán (see p.106) that it is hard to imagine that the houses were inhabited by the same people.

Diego's studio contains some of his painting materials, along with personal items, reproductions of some of his work and some large papier-mâché skeletons. Temporary exhibits take up much of Frida's house, though there are a couple of fine portraits of her taken by photographer Nikolas Muray, with whom Frida had an affair in the late 1930s, and some of Frida's own *ex voto* paintings of her debilitating accident.

Coyoacán

Around 3km east of San Ángel lies **COYOACÁN**, another colonial township that has been absorbed by the city. Even before the Conquest it was a sizeable place. Originally the capital of a small lakeshore kingdom, it was subjugated by the Aztecs in the mid-fifteenth century. Cortés based himself in Coyoacán during the siege of Tenochtitlán, and continued to live here while the old city was torn down and construction began on the capital of Nueva España. The focus of the area is the spacious **Plaza Central**, but no visit to Coyoacán is complete without strolling out to the northern reaches of the suburb to the two main sights, the **Frida Kahlo** and **Leon Trotsky museums**.

Plaza Central

Coyoacán's **Plaza Central** is one of the city's main stomping grounds for artists, artisans and musicians. It is actually made up of two adjoining plazas – **Plaza Hidalgo** and the **Jardín del Centenario**. Bars and cafés ring the plaza, and on the south side of Plaza Hidalgo is the sixteenth-century **Church of San Juan**. On Sunday, there's a market in the Plaza Central, and the area is taken up by stalls and various rock, folk and reggae bands. It's far and away the most fun place in the city to buy your souvenirs (T-shirts make good buys here, some of them hand-painted), though a lot of things can be found cheaper elsewhere.

Palacio Municipal

On the north side of Plaza Hidalgo • Palacio Municipal daily 9am–8pm; tourist office daily 9am–8pm • ☎ 55 5658 0221

The small **Palacio Municipal** (also known as the Casa de Cortés) is said to have been commissioned by Hernán Cortés himself. Inside the *palacio* are two **murals** by pupils of Rivera's – one by Aurora Reyes depicting the Conquest, and one by Diego Rosales showing the torture of Cuauhtémoc. The latter is particularly apposite since it was in Coyoacán that the Aztec leader was tortured and finally killed. The murals aren't usually open to the public, but if you ask at the **tourist office** in the same building they might let you take a peek at Reyes's mural, in the Sala de Cabildos, a municipal office. The other mural is in the

1

capilla (registry office), which is generally only open if there's a wedding on – should you stumble upon one you can discreetly put your head round the door for a quick look.

Plaza la Conchita

Southeast of Coyoacán's main square, Calle Higuera leads down to the small but pretty Plaza la Conchita. On the east side of the plaza, the **Capilla de la Concepción** still has traces of the original red paint on its facade, and is currently undergoing much-needed restoration work. Overlooking the square from the other side, on the corner with Higuera, the distinctive red **Casa de la Malinche** at Vallarta 47 (not open to the public) is the house in which Hernán Cortés installed his Maya mistress – and where he allegedly later murdered his wife shortly after her arrival from Spain.

Museo de Culturas Populares and around

Av Hidalgo 289, just off Plaza Hidalgo • Tues–Thurs 10am–6pm, Fri–Sun 10am–8pm • M$11, free Sun

The **Museo de Culturas Populares** has colourful displays on popular cultural forms, mostly dolls, masks and costumes. Avenida Hidalgo also leads to the Museo Nacional de las Intervenciones (see p.111) – to find it, continue down Avenida Hidalgo for about 300m, and bear left down General Anaya, which leads directly to the museum (crossing División del Norte on the way), a fifteen- to twenty-minute walk.

Museo Frida Kahlo

Londres 247, at Allende • Tues 10am–5.45pm, Wed 11am–5.45pm, Thurs–Sun 10am–5.45pm • Mon–Fri M$120, Sat & Sun M$140; ticket also valid for Museo Anahuacalli (see p.111); audio guide M$35 • ⓦ museofridakahlo.org.mx • Metro Coyoacán

The **Museo Frida Kahlo** is just a few minutes' walk from the centre of Coyoacán. The appropriately named Blue House was the Kahlos' family home and this is where Frida was born and spent most of her life, sporadically with husband Diego Rivera, who donated the house to the nation shortly after her death. It was during Frida and Diego's tenure here in the late 1930s that they played host to the newly arrived **Leon Trotsky** and his wife. Trotsky, ever fearful of assassins, apparently expressed his concern about the ease of access from a neighbouring property, and in a typically expansive gesture Diego simply bought the other house and combined the two. Continually at the centre of the capital's leftist bohemian life, Diego and Frida hosted a coterie of artists and intellectuals at this house; D.H. Lawrence was a frequent visitor, though he had little political or artistic sympathy with Kahlo, let alone Trotsky.

Galleries

Several rooms have been set aside as **galleries**. The first features around twenty relatively minor (and less tortured) examples of Frida's work, from some of her early portraits through to her final work, *Viva la Vida*, a still life of sliced watermelons. She painted it in 1954, when the pain and trauma of her recent leg amputation had taken their toll on her painterly control, if not her spirit. Look too for a beautiful charcoal self-portrait from 1932 and the more political *El Marxismo Dará la Salud a los Enfermos* (*Marxism Will Give Health to the Sick*) from 1954. A room full of Frida's signature **tehuana dresses** leads to more paintings, including over a dozen by Rivera, such as *Paisaje de la Quebrada*, which shows a rock face at Acapulco into which Diego painted his own face in purple. Alongside are several works by Velasco and Orozco, as well as a Klee and a Tanguy.

Interior and artefacts

Other sections of the house faithfully show the artesanía style that Frida favoured. Witness the blue and yellow kitchen with "Diego" and "Frida" picked out in tiny ceramic mugs on the wall. Its extraordinary decoration continues with bizarre papier-mâché animals and figures, and an impressive collection of *retablos* around the stairway. This leads up to Frida's airy studio where her wheelchair is artfully set next to

1

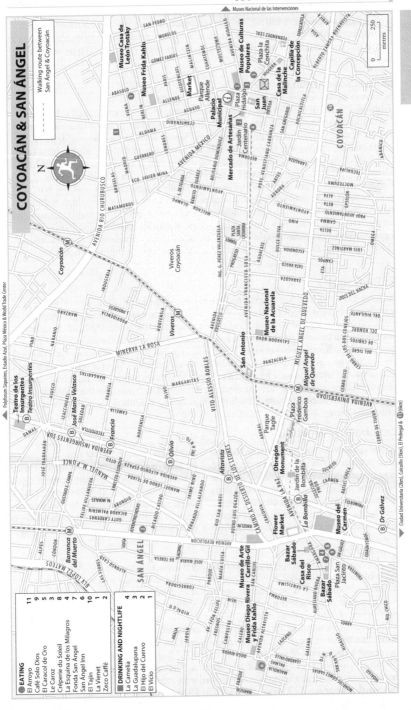

COYOACÁN & SAN ÁNGEL

Walking route between
San Ángel & Coyoacán

N

0   250
metres

EATING

El Arroyo   11
Café Solo Dios   9
El Caracol de Oro   5
Le Caroz   3
Crêperie du Soleil   8
La Esquina de los Milagros   4
Fonda San Ángel   7
San Ángel Inn   6
El Tajín   10
La Vienet   1
Zeco Caffé   2

DRINKING AND NIGHTLIFE

La Camelia   4
La Guadalupana   3
El Hijo del Cuervo   2
El Vicio   1

1

an easel and, of course, a mirror. Diego's influence in the house is seen more through his interest in Mexico's pre-Hispanic culture. Artefacts are scattered throughout the house and a small collection is displayed in the courtyard on a two-step pyramid he had constructed there.

Museo Casa de León Trotsky

Río Churabasco 410 • Tues–Sun 10am–5pm • M$40, camera M$15 • Metro Coyoacán

Trotsky's House, or the **Museo Casa de León Trotsky**, where the genius of the Russian Revolution and organizer of the Red Army lived and worked, is about four blocks away and represents virtually the only memorial to Trotsky anywhere in the world. After Lenin's death, Trotsky was forced into exile and condemned to death, and as increasing numbers of countries refused him asylum he sought refuge in Mexico in 1937, aided by Diego Rivera (at the time an ardent Trotskyite), who petitioned President Lázaro Cárdenas on his behalf. Here Stalin's long arm finally caught up with him (see box, p.110), despite the house being reinforced with steel gates and shutters, high walls and watchtowers. Today the fortified building seems at first a little incongruous, surrounded by the bourgeois homes of a prosperous suburb, but inside it's a human place, set up as he left it, if rather dustier: books on the shelves, his glasses smashed on the desk and all the trappings of a fairly comfortable ordinary life – except for the bullet holes.

El Pedregal

Around 2km south of San Ángel, Insurgentes enters the great lava field of **El Pedregal**, which gets its name from the vast lava flow that spreads south of San Ángel through the University City and beyond. Craggy and dramatic, it was regarded as a completely useless stretch of land, the haunt of bandits and brigands, until the early 1950s, when architect Luis Barragán began to build extraordinarily imaginative houses here, using the uneven lava as a feature. Now it's filled with an amazing collection of luxury homes, though you'll unfortunately be able to see little of what is behind the high walls and security fences even if you drive around. El Pedregal is also home to the **university campus**, the **Olympic Stadium** (Estadio Olímpico) and **Cuicuilco**, the oldest pyramid in central Mexico.

GETTING TO EL PEDREGAL

By bus/pesero/Metrobús Getting to the Pedregal area is easy, as it's reached from San Ángel by just about any bus or *pesero* heading south along Insurgentes. All stop outside the Olympic Stadium, right opposite the university library, and many (try those marked "Villa Olímpica", "Cuicuilco" and "Tlalpan") continue on to the pyramid at Cuicuilco, visible on the left just after you pass under the *periférico*.

Metrobús line 1 also plies the same route.

By Metro The university can also be reached on Metro line 3, but note that Copilco is the most convenient station, Universidad much less so as it brings you out at the back of the campus, from where you have to walk all the way through – past the *frontón* courts and medical faculty – to reach the library.

University City

To the east of Insurgentes is the **University City** (Ciudad Universitaria). After over fifty years of use, the campus is beginning to show its age, and while it's no longer the avant-garde sensation it was when it opened, it remains a remarkable architectural achievement. The whole thing was built in just five years (1950–55) during the presidency of Miguel Alemán, and is now one of the largest universities in the world, with some three hundred thousand students and staff. It's also the oldest on the American continent: granted a charter by Philip II in 1551, the University of Mexico occupied a succession of sites in the city centre (including the Hospital de Jesús Nazareno and what is now the Escuela Nacional Preparatoria), was closed down several times in the nineteenth century and was finally awarded its status as the Universidad Nacional Autónoma de México (UNAM) in 1929.

FRIDA KAHLO

Since the 1970s, **Frida Kahlo** (1907–54) has been considered Mexico's most internationally renowned artist, outshining even her husband, Diego Rivera (see p.76), who recognized her as "the first woman in the history of art to treat, with absolute and uncompromising honesty, one might even say with impassive cruelty, those general and specific themes which exclusively affect women". Julie Taymor's 2002 biopic *Frida*, starring Salma Hayek, further consolidated her role as a **feminist icon**. Her work is deeply personal, centred on her insecurities and her relations with her family, her country and her politics. "I paint myself," she said, "because I am so often alone, and because I am the subject I know best." Her relatively short painting career was never prolific and the largest collection of her work is at the **Museo Dolores Olmedo Patiño** (see p.112).

EARLY LIFE

The daughter of a *mestizo* Mexican mother and Hungarian Jewish father, Frida was born in the Blue House in Coyoacán (now the **Museo Frida Kahlo**, see p.106). When she was 6, she battled a bout of polio that left her right leg withered. She rebounded and, as a precocious 14-year-old at Mexico City's top school, first met **Diego Rivera** (twenty years her senior) who was painting a mural there. She shocked her friends by declaring that she wished to conceive his child "just as soon as I convince him to cooperate", but they didn't meet again for many years.

MARRIAGE TO RIVERA

At 18, and already breaking free of the roles then ordained for women in Mexico, Frida had begun to pursue a career in medicine when she suffered a gruesome **accident**. The bus she was riding in was struck by a tram, leaving her with multiple fractures and a pelvis skewered by a steel handrail. It was during the months she spent bedridden, recovering, that she first took up a paintbrush. Later in life, she reflected "I had two accidents in my life. One was the bus, the other Diego." After her recovery she fell in with a left-leaning bunch of artists, free-thinkers and Communists where she again met Rivera. Within a year they were married: she a striking, slender woman of 21; he a massively overweight man twice her age with a frog-like face and an unparalleled reputation for womanizing. Diego went about his affairs quite publicly (including briefly with Frida's sister, Cristina). He was furious when Frida took up with other men, but her several affairs with women seemed to delight him. After her death he wrote, "Too late now, I realized that the most wonderful part of my life had been my love for Frida."

ARTISTIC CAREER

Encouraged by Diego, Frida pursued her **painting** career. Over half of her canvases are **self-portraits**: imbued with sophisticated personal symbolism, with themes of abortion, broken bones and betrayed love explored through the body set in an unlikely juxtaposition of elements.

In 1932 Frida miscarried and was hospitalized in Detroit where she painted *Henry Ford Hospital*. This disturbing depiction of her grief shows her naked body lying on a bed in an industrial wasteland, surrounded by a foetus, pelvic bones and surgical implements all umbilically tied back to her. After returning to Mexico, her circle of friends expanded to include Trotsky (with whom she had a brief affair), Cuban Communist Julio Antonio Mella and muralist David Siqueiros (later implicated in an attempt to kill Trotsky, see box, p.110). By now Frida and Diego were living in paired houses in San Ángel (see p.105), which allowed them to maintain relatively separate lives. In 1939 they **divorced**, a devastating event Frida recorded in *Autoretrato con el Pelo Cortado* (*Self-Portrait with Cropped Hair*), in which her trademark long tresses and indigenous *tehuana* dresses (both much loved by Diego) are replaced by Diego's oversized suit and cropped hair. They **remarried** a year later, with Frida insisting on financial independence and a celibate relationship.

The injuries from her accident dogged her throughout her life, and as her physical condition worsened she found solace in her work (as well as in drink and painkilling drugs), painting *La Columna Rota* (*The Broken Column*) in 1944, with her crushed spine depicted as an Ionic column. Despite increasing commercial and critical success, Frida had only one **solo exhibition** of her work during her lifetime, in Mexico City just a year before she died. In her later years she was wheelchair-bound, but continued the **political activism** she had always pursued, and died after defying medical advice and taking part in a demonstration against American intervention in Guatemala while she was convalescing from pneumonia in July 1954. By this stage, she knew she was dying; defiantly, on her last work, she daubed the words "Viva la Vida" – "Long Live Life".

1

The Library

Ciudad Universitaria • Daily 8.30am–9.30pm • Metro Copilco (south down Cerro del Agua from the station, bearing right after the campus entrance gate, and it's over to the left after 500m)

The campus is dominated by the astonishing, rectangular twelve-storey university **library**, each face of which is covered in a mosaic designed by **Juan O'Gorman** – mostly natural stone with a few tiles or glass to supply colours that would otherwise have been unavailable. Representing the artist's vision of the country's progression through history, the focus of the larger north and south faces is on pre-Hispanic and colonial Mexico; on the west wall are the present and the university coat of arms; on the east, the future is ranged around a giant atom. It's remarkable how these have been incorporated as an essential feature of the building – at first it appears that there are no windows at all, but look closely and you'll see that in fact they're an integral part of the design, appearing as eyes, mouths or as windows of the buildings in the mosaic.

The rest of the campus

More or less opposite the library are the long, low **administration buildings** (*rectoría*), with a **giant mural** in high relief by Siqueiros (or a "sculptural painting", as he called it), intended to provide a changing perspective as you walk past. At the front of the *rectoría* are the university theatre and the **Museo Universitario de Ciencias y Artes** (MUCA; Mon–Sat 10am–6pm; free), the latter a wide-ranging general collection, with interactive scientific exhibits, plus displays on contemporary art and culture. Behind them spread out the enormous grounds of the main campus, starting with a large esplanade known as the Plaza Mayor, with sculptural groups dotted around a shallow artificial pond. Towards the back of the *rectoría* are more murals, adorning the **Faculties of Science and Medicine**; continue past these to reach another grassy area with the **Botanical Gardens** and several large walls against which the students play *frontón*.

Estadio Olímpico

Directly across Insurgentes from the university library

The sculptural oval of the one-hundred-thousand-seat **Estadio Olímpico** was built in 1952. Its main facade is decorated with a mosaic relief by Diego Rivera designed to represent the development of human potential through sport. Most taxi drivers will tell you that the stadium was deliberately designed to look like a giant sombrero, but this, sadly, is not the case; it's undeniably odd, though, half sunk into the ground as if dropped here from a great height and slightly warped in the process.

THE ASSASSINATION OF TROTSKY

The first attempt on Trotsky's life, in his house at Coyoacán (see p.108), left more than seventy scars in the plaster of the bedroom walls. At 4am on May 24, 1940, a heavily armed group led by painter David Siqueiros (who had been a commander in the Spanish Civil War and was working under the orders of the Stalinist Mexican Communist Party) overcame the guards and pumped more than two hundred shots into the house. Trotsky, his wife and son survived only by hiding under their beds. After this, the house, already heavily guarded, was further fortified. Unknown to all, though, the eventual assassin had already inveigled his way into the household, posing as a businessman being converted to the cause. Although he was never fully trusted, his arrival at the house on the afternoon of **August 20**, with an article that he wanted Trotsky to look over, seemed innocuous enough. Trotsky invited him into the study and moments later the notorious **ice pick** (the blunt end), which had been concealed under the killer's coat, smashed into Trotsky's skull. He died some 24 hours later, in the hospital after an operation failed to save his life. The killer, who called himself Frank Jackson and claimed to be Belgian, served twenty years in jail, though he never explained his actions or even confessed to his true identity, **Jaime Ramón Mercader del Río**.

Calzada de Tlalpan

1

Along with Insurgentes, the other main approach to the south is the **Calzada de Tlalpan**, which runs south from the Zócalo more or less in parallel with Metro line 2 (initially underground, then running down the middle of the road) and subsequently the Tren Ligero, almost all the way to Xochimilco.

The two train lines provide the easiest access to some fine museums – including Diego Rivera's Anahuacalli and the wonderful Museo Dolores Olmedo Patiño. The Tren Ligero passes the giant **Estadio Azteca** football stadium on its way to the canals of Xochimilco, and Metro line 2 also provides alternative access to the eastern end of Coyoacán.

Museo Nacional de las Intervenciones

20 de Agosto and General Anaya • Tues–Sun 9am–6pm • M$46, free Sun • Metro General Anaya (exit to the west of the Calzada de Tlalpan and 5min walk along 20 de Agosto); for the Trotsky and Frida Kahlo museums (see p.108 & p.106), take General Anaya, cross División del Norte and go straight ahead for about 500m, by which time Anaya has merged into Hidalgo; for central Coyoacán, continue straight on (see map, p.107); for the Trotsky Museum, take a right down Morelos (not signposted) opposite Hidalgo 62

The **Museo Nacional de las Intervenciones** occupies the old Franciscan **Convento de Churubusco**, which owes its present incarnation to the 1847 battle in which the invading Americans, led by General Winfield Scott, defeated a Mexican force under General Anaya – another heroic Mexican effort in which the outnumbered defenders fought to their last bullet.

The building itself is a stunner, especially if you arrive at the darkening of day as the lights are coming on in the gardens. The exhibits, all on the upper floor, may not mean a great deal unless you have a reasonable grasp of Mexican history. They're labelled only in Spanish – and not very fully at that – and are dedicated to the history of foreign military adventures in Mexico: skeletons in the cupboards of Britain, Spain, France and the US are all rattled loudly. One section is devoted largely to the Mexican–American wars – with a very different perspective from that of the Alamo. Much of what's on show, however, comprises paintings of generals and flags, and unless you're a history buff you might better spend your time in the pleasant surrounding gardens. Apart from the Metro, the museum is also accessible by *pesero* ("Gral Anaya") from Coyoacán: pick it up by the market at the junction of Allende and Xicoténcatl.

Museo Diego Rivera Anahuacalli

Museo 150 • Wed–Sun 11am–5pm; guided tours only, every 30min until 4.30pm, except on Fri, when the last is at 4.15pm • M$80 or free with ticket from Museo Frida Kahlo (see p.106) • ⓦ museoanahuacalli.org.mx • Tren Ligero Xotepingo; from the station, follow the signs to the Calle Museo exit, double back at the bottom of the steps and take the first left down Museo; after 100m, cross División del Norte, and it's about 500m ahead on your right

It's a ten-minute walk from the Tren Ligero station at Xotepingo to the bizarre **Museo Diego Rivera Anahuacalli**, designed and commissioned by Diego Rivera to house his huge collection of pre-Hispanic artefacts. It's an extraordinary blockish structure, started in 1933 and worked on sporadically until Rivera's death, then finished off by Juan O'Gorman and opened in 1963. Inspired by Maya and Aztec architecture, this sombre mass of black volcanic stone is approached through a courtyard reminiscent of a Maya ball-court. The exquisite objects in the collection form part of a thoroughly imaginative exhibit: one small chamber contains nothing but a series of **Huehueteotls**, all squatting grumpily under the weight of their braziers, and the studio has ball-player and animal displays.

The **ground floor** is devoted to objects from the main cultures of the Valley of México – Teotihuacán, Toltec and Aztec – which provided Rivera with an important part of his inspiration. On the **middle floor**, rooms devoted to the west of Mexico (arguably the best such collection in the country) surround the huge airy space that Rivera planned to use as a studio. It's been fitted out with portraits and sketches, including preliminary studies for *El Hombre en Control del Universo*, his massive mural in the Palacio de Bellas Artes (see p.84). On the **top floor** are more Aztec objects, along with pottery and small figures from Oaxaca and the Gulf coast. Up here you can also get out onto the **rooftop**

1

terrace, from where there are magical views of Popocatépetl and Ixtaccíhuatl, both of which seem really close here, their snowy peaks glistening on less smoggy days.

Walking through the dark recesses of the museum, note the ceilings, each with individual mosaic designs, and even the floor of the rooftop terrace, which is inlaid with snake, dog and frog forms, distinct but barely noticeable if you're not looking for them. As you leave the main museum, you'll see a low building diagonally to the left, which houses temporary exhibitions and is worth a visit if only to get a sense of the underlying volcanic rock – part of El Pedregal (see p.108) – which was hewn away to provide building materials for the museum.

Museo Dolores Olmedo Patiño

Av México 5843 • Tues–Sun 10am–6pm • M$75, free Tues • ⓦ museodoloresolmedo.org.mx • Tren Ligero La Noria; from the station, go straight ahead from the exit and take the first left – the museum is a 2min walk on your left

Just round the corner from La Noria Tren Ligero station, the **Museo Dolores Olmedo Patiño** sits amid peaceful and beautifully tended grounds where peacocks strut, oblivious of the busy streets outside, and houses the largest private collection of Diego Rivera's work. It's built into a seventeenth-century mansion, donated in 1994 by the elderly Dolores Olmedo, a wealthy collector and longtime friend and patron of Rivera's. Over the years she amassed over 130 of his works, all of which are on display here. They span his career, from his Cubist period in the early twentieth century through self-portraits (exhibiting varying degrees of flattery) to 25 sunsets painted in Acapulco from the balcony of his patron's house. The collection is immensely varied, making this perhaps the best place to get a true sense of just how versatile a master he was. Look particularly for three large and striking nudes from the early 1940s, and sketches for his famous paintings of calla lilies.

Rivera's work is reason enough to come here, but the museum also has an outstanding collection of two dozen paintings by **Frida Kahlo**. With the works arranged in approximate chronological order, it is easy to see her development as an artist, from the Riveraesque approach of early works such as 1929's *The Bus*, to her infinitely more powerful self-portraits. Many of her finest works are here, including *Henry Ford Hospital*, *A Few Small Pricks*, *La Columna Rota* and *Autorretrato con Mono* (Self-Portrait with Monkey), the latter featuring Mexico's most distinctive canine breed, the grey-skinned Xoloitzcuintle, of which Kahlo kept several as pets. To see these hairless pre-Columbian dogs in the flesh, wander out into the garden where a few are still kept. There's also a portrait of Kahlo by Rivera elsewhere in the museum, in a pastiche of her own style.

Though easily overshadowed by the Rivera and Kahlo pieces, there is also a worthwhile collection of wood-block prints done by **Angelina Beloff**, Diego's first wife, featuring scenes from Mexico and her native Russia.

Xochimilco

Tren Ligero Xochimilco

The **floating gardens** adjoining the suburb of **Xochimilco** offer an intense carnival atmosphere every weekend and are likely to be one of your most memorable experiences of the city. Considerable effort has been expended in recent years to clean up the canals and maintain the water levels that had been dropping here, so Xochimilco ("place of the flower fields" in Náhuatl) looks set to remain the most popular Sunday outing for thousands of Mexicans. It's also the one place where you get some feel for the ancient city and its waterborne commerce, thriving markets and dazzling colour – or at least an idealized view of it. Rent any of the colourful boats and you'll be ferried around many kilometres of canals, continually harangued by women selling flowers, fruit and hot food from tiny canoes, or even by larger vessels bearing marimba players and entire mariachi bands who, for a small fee, will grapple alongside you and blast out a couple of numbers. The floating gardens themselves are no more floating than the *Titanic*: following the old Aztec methods of making the lake fertile, these *chinampas* are formed by a raft of mud and reeds, firmly rooted to the

1

bottom by the plants. The scene now appears like a series of canals cut through dry land, but the area is still a very important gardening and flower-producing centre for the city. If you wander the streets of Xochimilco town you'll find garden centres everywhere, with wonderful flowers and fruit in the **market** that enlivens the town centre for much of Saturday (though whether it's healthy to eat food raised on these dirty waters is open to question).

Off the huge central plaza is the lovely sixteenth-century church of **San Bernardino**, full on Sundays with a succession of people paying homage and leaving offerings at one of its many chapels; in the plaza itself there are usually bands playing or mime artists entertaining the crowds.

ESSENTIALS   **XOCHIMILCO**

GETTING THERE

For the easiest approach to Xochimilco, take the Metro to Tasqueña station (line 2) and the Tren Ligero (light rail, identifiable by a separate icon) from there to Xochimilco (end of the line); there are also buses and *peseros* from Tasqueña as well as buses direct from the city centre, down Insurgentes and around the *periférico* or straight down the Calzada de Tlalpan. On Sun many extra services are laid on. To get a boat, go straight ahead from the Tren Ligero station exit and follow the "embarcaderos" signs (about a 10min walk).

BOAT HIRE

CostLanchas (launches) currently cost M$350 for up to twenty people – the official price should be posted up at the *embarcadero* (dock), and it's probably best to avoid *embarcaderos* where it isn't. There's a long tradition of

milking tourists here, so be certain of what you've agreed on before parting with any money. Remember that there are likely to be sundry extras, including the cold beers thoughtfully provided by the boatman, and any flowers, food or music you find yourself accepting on your way.

Trips You'll be encouraged to go for two hours, but try to avoid paying upfront or you're likely to get only an hour and a half, which will include a visit to the garden centre of their choice. The boatman won't like it, but you can always take your business elsewhere. Also, be clear which boat you are getting or you are liable to be shuffled to an inferior and less attractive model.

When to go You can rent a boat on any weekday for a little less-crowded cruising, but Sun is by far the most popular and animated day; Sat is lively, too, partly because of the produce market.

North of the centre

Compared to the southern suburbs, the area north of the city centre has less to offer, but two sites of compelling interest – the emotive **Plaza de las Tres Culturas** and the great **Basílica de Guadalupe** – are worth an afternoon of your attention. Further out, and harder to get to, you'll find the pyramids of **Tenayuca** and **Santa Cecilia Acatitlán**, the city's two most dramatically preserved remains of Aztec architecture (though strictly speaking outside of the Distrito Federal).

Plaza de las Tres Culturas

Eje Central trolleybus (get off at Flores Magón), or Metro Garibaldi (cross Reforma then 400m north up Lázaro Cárdenas), or take a northbound bus or *pesero* along Reforma Norte to Glorieta Cuitlahuac

The **Plaza de las Tres Culturas** is the site of the ancient city of Tlatelolco, located to the north of Tenochtitlán. Today, a lovely **colonial church** rises in the midst of the city's **excavated ruins**, exemplifying the second of the three cultures from which the plaza takes its name. The **modern buildings** that surround it – mostly a rather ugly 1960s housing project but including the Ministry of Foreign Affairs – represent the third culture. The area's most striking modern building, 1km west of the plaza at the junction of Flores Magón with Insurgentes Norte, is the triangular **Torre Insignia**, which dates from 1962.

The ruins of Tlatelolco

Daily 8am–6pm; guided tours Mon–Fri 9am–2pm, in English by arrangement in advance • Free • ☎ 55 5583 0295

The ancient ruins of **Tlatelolco** were once the core of a city considerably more ancient than Tenochtitlán, based on a separate but nearby island in the lake. For a long time,

1

its people existed under independent rule in close alliance with the Aztecs of Tenochtitlán, but it was by far the most important commercial and market centre in the valley; even after its annexation to the Aztec empire in 1473, Tlatelolco retained this role. When **Cortés** and his troops arrived, they marvelled at the size and order of the Tlatelolco market. Cortés himself estimated that some sixty thousand people – buyers and sellers – came and went each day, and Bernal Díaz wrote:

We were astounded at the great number of people and the quantities of merchandise, and at the orderliness and good arrangements that prevailed…every kind of goods was kept separate and had its fixed place marked for it… Some of the soldiers among us who had been in many parts of the world, in Constantinople, in Rome, and all over Italy, said that they had never seen a market so well laid out, so large, so orderly, and so full of people.

In 1521 the besieged **Aztecs** made their final stand here, and a plaque in the middle of the plaza recalls that struggle: "On the 13th of August 1521", it reads, "defended by the heroic Cuauhtémoc, Tlatelolco fell under the power of Hernan Cortés. It was neither a triumph nor a defeat, but the painful birth of the mixed race that is the Mexico of today." The ruins are a pale reflection of the ancient city – the original temples, whose scale can be inferred from the size of the bases, rivalled those in Tenochtitlán. The chief temple, for example, had reached its eleventh rebuilding by the time of the Conquest – what you see now corresponds to the second stage, and by the time nine more had been superimposed it would certainly have risen much higher than the church that was built from its stones. On top was likely a double sanctuary similar to that on the Templo Mayor of Tenochtitlán. The smaller structures include a square **tzompantli**, or wall of skulls, near which nearly two hundred human skulls were discovered, all with holes through the temples – presumably the result of having been displayed side by side on long poles around the sides of the building.

Church of Santiago Tlatelolco

Adjacent to the Tlatelolco ruins – though still in use and not considered part of them – is the **Church of Santiago Tlatelolco**. Erected in 1609, it replaced an earlier Franciscan monastery, parts of which survive, arranged about the cloister. In the early years after the Conquest, the friars established a college at which they instructed the sons of the Aztec nobility in European ways, teaching them Spanish, Latin and Christianity. Bernardino de Sahagún was one of the teachers, and it was here that he wrote down many of the customs and traditions of the natives, compiling the most important existing record of daily Aztec life in his famous *Historia General de las Cosas de Nueva España*.

Basílica de Nuestra Señora de Guadalupe

Half a kilometre east of Insurgentes on the Eje 5 Norte • Museum Tues–Sun 10am–6pm • M$10 • Metro La Villa Basilica; also accessible by bus or *pesero* north along Reforma, or by trolleybus along Reforma from Metro Hidalgo (direction "Indios Verdes")

The **Basílica de Nuestra Señora de Guadalupe** is in fact a whole series of churches, chapels and shrines set around an enormous stone-flagged **plaza** and climbing up the rocky hillock where the miracles that led to its foundation occurred. It is Mexico's most important religious site, and is visited by millions of pilgrims from all across Latin America every year. Indeed, its religious significance predates the arrival of Christianity, as it was previously a shrine to the Aztec mother goddess Tonantzin. The first church here was built in 1533, but the large (and massively subsided) Baroque basilica you see straight ahead of you as you come through the main entrance to the plaza was completely reconstructed in the eighteenth century and again remodelled in the nineteenth and twentieth.

Around the site, there swirls a stream of humanity – pilgrims, sightseers, priests and salesmen offering candles, souvenirs, pictures of the Virgin, snacks and any number of mementos. On **December 12**, the anniversary of the second apparition, their numbers swell to hundreds of thousands (newspaper reports claim millions). You'll see the

THE TLATELOLCO MASSACRE

The Mexican state showed its most brutal side in the Plaza de las Tres Culturas on October 2, 1968, when troops and tanks were **ordered to fire** on an almost 250,000-strong **student demonstration**. It was the culmination of several months of student protests over the government's social and educational policies, which the authorities were determined to subdue, with only ten days left before the Olympic Games opened in the city. Records of the death toll vary from an official figure at the time of thirty to student estimates of more than five hundred, but it seems clear today that hundreds is more accurate than tens. Mexican philosopher Octavio Paz saw the violence as part of the cycle of history – a ritual slaughter to recall the Aztec sacrifices here – but it's perhaps better seen as an example of at least one thread of continuity between all Mexico's civilizations: the cheapness of life and the harsh brutality of their rulers. Paco Ignacio Taibo II's book, *68*, which is available in English translation, analyzes the incident in detail.

pilgrims on the approach roads to the capital for several days beforehand, many covering the last kilometres on their knees in an act of penance or devotion. For others, though, the day is more of a vast fiesta, with dancing, singing and drinking.

The main church

To the left of the great plaza as you come in from Calzada de Guadalupe is the modern home of Juan Diego's cloak with the image of the Virgin on it. This huge, round modern **church** was built in 1976, with space inside for ten thousand worshippers and for around four times that when the great doors all round are thrown open to the crowds, as they are pretty much every Sunday. You'll find it crowded whenever you visit, and there seems to be a service permanently in progress. The famous **cloak**, framed in gold and silver, hangs above the main altar. To prevent anyone lingering too long at the spot right underneath, you must board a travelling walkway and admire the image as you glide respectfully by.

The church museum

Around the back of the Baroque basilica, the **Museo de la Basílica de Guadalupe** contains a large collection of *ex voto* offerings, and some of the church's religious art treasures, including a series of slightly insipid early eighteenth-century canvases by José de Ibarra and more powerful oils by Miguel Cabrera and Cristóbal de Villalpando.

Capillas on the hill

From the plaza you can walk round to the right and up the hill past a series of little chapels associated with the Virgin's appearance. Loveliest is the **Capilla del Pocito**, in which there is a well said to have sprung forth during one of the apparitions. Built in the eighteenth century, it consists of two linked elliptical chapels, one smaller and one larger, both with colourful tiled domes and magnificently decorated interiors. On the very top of the hill, the **Capilla de las Rosas** marks the spot where the miraculous roses grew.

Museo de los Ferrocarrileros

Alberto Herrera • Daily 10am–5pm • Free • Metro La Villa Basilica

If heading to the Basilica from La Villa Basilica Metro station, train buffs will want to stop off first at the **Museo de los Ferrocarrileros**, a small railway museum in the former train station of La Villa, just outside the Metro station to the east of Calzada de Guadalupe. Inside are exhibits in Spanish on the trade in *pulque* (the station was on the Mexico City–Veracruz railway, an important route for transporting it), but of most interest are the old locomotives standing outside, which enthusiasts will definitely want to see, although you can't climb onto them.

THE VIRGIN OF GUADALUPE

The **Virgin of Guadalupe**, Mexico's first indigenous saint, is still the nation's most popular – you'll see her image in churches throughout the country. The Virgin's banner has been fought under by both sides of almost every conflict the nation has ever seen, most famously when Hidalgo seized on it as the flag of Mexican Independence. According to the legend, an Aztec Christian convert, **Juan Diego**, was walking over the hill here (formerly dedicated to the Aztec earth goddess Tonantzin) on his way to the monastery at Tlatelolco one morning in December 1531, when he was stopped by a brilliant vision of the Virgin, who ordered him, in Náhuatl, to go to the bishop and tell him to build a church on the hill. Bishop Juan de Zumarraga was unimpressed until, on December 12, the Virgin reappeared, ordering Diego to gather roses from the top of the hill and take them to the bishop. Doing so, he bundled the flowers in his **cloak**, and when he opened it before the bishop he found the image of the dark-skinned Virgin imprinted into the cloth. Today Diego's cloak hangs above the altar in the gigantic modern basilica, which takes its name from the celebrated (and equally swarthy) Virgin in the monastery of Guadalupe in Spain.

Tenayuca

Just off Av de los Cien Metros • Tues–Sun 10am–5pm • M$50, video permit M$45 • "Ruta 88" *pesero* northbound from Metro Deportivo 18 de Marzo (5 blocks west of the Basílica de Nuestra Señora de Guadalupe) or La Raza (40min, but not all go to the *pirámide* of Tenayuca, so check first) or "Tenayuca" *pesero* northbound from Lázaro Cárdenas; some bus tours visit Tenayuca and Santa Cecilia on their way to Tula and Tepotzotlán

The 20m-high pyramid in the main square at **Tenayuca**, a suburb just outside the city limits, is another site that predates Tenochtitlán by a long chalk. Indeed, there are those who claim it was the capital of the tribe that destroyed Tula. In this, its history closely mirrors almost all other valley settlements: a barbarian tribe from the north invades, conquers all before it, settles in a city and becomes civilized, borrowing much of its culture from its predecessors, before being overcome by the next wave of migrants. There's little evidence that Tenayuca ever controlled a large empire, but it was a powerful city and provides one of the most concrete links between the Toltecs and the Aztecs.

The site

The pyramid that survives dates from the period of Aztec dominance and is an almost perfect miniature replica of the great temples of Tlatelolco and Tenochtitlán. Here the structure and the monumental double stairway are intact – only the twin sanctuaries at the top and the brightly painted decorations would be needed for it to open for sacrifices again tomorrow. This is the sixth superimposition; five earlier pyramids (the first dating from the early thirteenth century) are contained within it and are revealed in places by excavations which took place in the 1920s. Originally there was a seventh layer built on top, of which some traces remain.

The most unusual and striking feature of Tenayuca's pyramid is the border of interlocking stone **snakes** that must originally have surrounded the entire building – well over a hundred of them survive. Notice also the two coiled snakes (one a little way up the north face, the other at the foot of the south face) known as the "turquoise serpents". Their crests are crowned with stars and aligned with the sun's position at the solstice.

Santa Cecilia Acatitlán

Tues–Sun 10am–5pm • M$60, video permit M$45 • *Pesero* route #88 (see p.122), and also #79, continues from Tenayuca to Santa Cecilia Acatitlán; alternatively, it's a 20min walk, or short taxi ride, from Tenayuca, or a short ride on feeder bus #R10 from San Rafael station on the suburban train line from Buenavista; to return to the city, catch a *pesero* to Metro Deportivo 18 de Marzo (lines 3 & 6)

The pyramid at **Santa Cecilia Acatitlán** is much smaller and simpler than that at Tenayuca, but it's been wholly restored and is remarkably beautiful with its clean lines. When first encountered by the Spanish, this was a temple with a double staircase very similar to the others, but the outer structure was stripped away during excavation to reveal an earlier, well-preserved building inside. It's a very plain structure, rising in four steps to a single-roofed shrine approached by a ramped stairway. The studded decorations around the roof represent either skulls or stars. You approach the pyramid through a small museum in a colonial house, whose displays of finds from the site and elsewhere include an Aztec incense burner and a reconstructed nineteenth-century kitchen; in the garden just outside, you are greeted by a large, inanely grinning stone skull.

ARRIVAL AND DEPARTURE   MEXICO CITY

Being dropped unprepared into the vastness of Mexico City may seem daunting, but it's not hard to get into the centre, or to a hotel, from any of the major points of arrival. The only problem is likely to be hauling large items of luggage through the invariable crowds – take a cab if you are at all heavily laden, but make sure it's a prepaid "authorized" taxi (see box below).

BY PLANE

Mexico City's airport (Terminal 1 ☎ 55 2482 2424, Terminal 2 ☎ 55 2598 7000, ⟨w⟩ aicm.com.mx) is surprisingly central, just 6km east of the Zócalo (if you're sitting on the left-hand side of the plane the views as you come in to land are amazing). Most hotels are used to late arrivals, so don't be overly concerned if your flight gets in late at night, though it is wise to have somewhere booked in advance for your first night. There are two terminals, on opposite sides of the airport, and quite a long way from each other by land; most airlines use Terminal 1, which is rather more convenient than the new Terminal 2.

Facilities Wherever you come in, you'll find several ATMs and numerous *casas de cambio*, open 24hr and with reasonable rates for US dollars (rates vary, so shop around), though not always such good rates for travellers' cheques or other currencies (they'll usually take Canadian dollars, pounds sterling, euros, and sometimes Swiss francs, Japanese yen and some Latin American currencies). There are also plenty of pricey restaurants and snack bars, car rental agencies (see p.122), a post office, internet cafés and 24hr left luggage lockers.

Information There are several airport enquiry desks dotted around, and tourist information kiosks in Terminal 1, Sala A (daily 9am–6pm; ☎ 55 5786 9002), and Terminal 2 near exit gate 2 (daily 9am–9pm; ☎ 55 2598 3532), which are helpful but have a limited range of information, and only cover Mexico City.

Transfers between terminals To get from one terminal to the other, there's a monorail service called Aerotrén (upstairs from Sala D in Terminal 1, upstairs in Sala M in Terminal 2), but only passengers with boarding passes are allowed to use this.

Otherwise there are red buses (daily 4am–1am; M$15) from exit gate 6 (Sala D) in Terminal 1 and exit gate 4 in Terminal 2.

Taxis The only way to get into town is by prepaid authorized taxi, and there are desks for these in both terminals. Prices vary slightly from firm to firm, so it's worth comparing rates before choosing; current rates are around M$290 to the Zócalo and Zona Rosa, M$270 to Condesa/Roma and M$319 to Polanco. The authorized airport taxis have a monopoly on arrivals and it's illegal for regular taxi drivers to pick up passengers at the airport, so don't bother trying to flag one down. Getting from town back to the airport is simpler. Any taxi driver will make the trip, and you can expect to pay around M$100.

Metro Metro Terminal Aérea, line 5, calls at Terminal 1. Come out of the doors at the end of Sala A, then follow the covered walkway for 200m. Note that large bags are banned on the Metro (see p.120). From Terminal 2 (but not in the other direction), the inter-terminal bus (see below) stops at Hangares metro station, but in fact the nearest metro station is Pantitlan (out of the airport precincts and then take a left along the main road for 500m, or hop on a *pesero*), far more convenient than Hangares because it is on four different lines, but not a good area to be with your baggage at night.

Metrobús Line 4 of the Metrobús, which takes two east–west routes through the city centre to TAPO (see p.120), serves both airport terminals, charging M$30 for the journey, and without baggage restrictions. At the airport you can pick it up from exit gate 6 (Sala D) in Terminal 1 and exit gate 4 in Terminal 2.

Pesero The main road outside Terminal 2 can be reached by *peseros* bound for Pantitlan from Rayón at Reforma

---

AUTHORIZED TAXIS

The airport and all four bus terminals have a system of **authorized taxis** which **guarantee the clients' safety**, and all have booths selling rides inside the terminal buildings. The authorized system is the same wherever it operates from – you'll find a large map of the city marked out in zones, with a standard, set fare for each; you pick where you're going, buy a ticket at the booth, then walk outside and present the ticket to one of the waiting cabs. One ticket is good for up to four people to one destination. The driver may drop you a block or two from your hotel rather than take a major detour through the one-way systems (best to accept this unless it's very late at night), and may occasionally demand a large tip, which you're in no way obliged to pay.

1

(Metro Garibaldi, lines B & 8). From the terminal, head out to the main road to pick up a *pesero* to Metro Garibaldi.

Intercity buses If you don't want to stop in Mexico City, there are first-class buses from the airport straight to Cuernavaca, Pachuca, Puebla, Toluca and Querétaro. The bus stops are upstairs from Sala E1 in Terminal 1 and at exit gate 4 in Terminal 2.

Car rental Desks are located in zones E1 and E2 of Terminal 1, and on the main concourse of Terminal 2. The cheapest deals are with local firm Gold Car Rental (located in Terminal 1, zone E1, ☏55 2599 0090, ✉intgold @avantel.net). International franchise chains represented at the airport include Avis (☏55 5762 3688 or ☏01 800 288 8888, ⓦavis.com.mx), Budget (☏01 800 700 1700, ⓦbudget.com.mx), Europcar (☏55 5786 8264 or ☏800 201 2084, ⓦeuropcar.com.mx), Hertz (☏01 800 709 5000, ⓦavasa.com.mx), National (☏55 5703 2222 or ☏01 800 716 6625, ⓦnationalcar.com.mx) and Sixt (☏55 5784 3011, ⓦsixt.com.mx). Rental cars are exempt from the Hoy No Circula one-day-a-week driving restriction (see p.70). For cheaper rentals head to Av Baja California, where Royal Rent a Car (C Medellín 350, ☏55 5574 4080, ⓦroyalrent .com.mx) and Eclipse (Baja California 111, ☏ 55 5564 6489, ⓦeclipserent.com) have more competitive deals than the international companies.

Airlines Aeromar, Reforma 505 (ground floor) ☏55 5256 0877 or ☏01 800 237 6627; Aeroméxico, Juárez 76, ☏55 5512 4000 or ☏01 800 021 4000; Air Canada, Manuel Avila Camacho 1 8°, Lomas de Chapultepec ☏55 9138 0280 or ☏800 719 2827; Delta, Masaryk 513, Polanco ☏55 5279 0909; Iberia, Ejercito Nacional 436 9°, Polanco ☏55 1101 1515; Lufthansa, Paseo de las Palmas 239, Lomas de Chapultepec ☏55 4738 6561; United, Andres Bello 45, Polanco ☏55 5283 5500 or ☏01 800 900 5000; VivaAerobus, Mesones 47 and other locations including Central de Autobuses del Norte ☏55 4777 5050.

Destinations The further the destination is from Mexico City, the more sense it makes to fly there; you won't gain much flying to cities that are only a few hours away by road, and much more expensive by air, but if you're heading to places like Tijuana or Cancún, the plane will not only be faster, but much cheaper too. Flights are likely to be cheapest if you can book them a few weeks ahead. The following domestic airports are served by direct flights from Mexico City: Acapulco (6–10 daily; 55min); Aguascalientes (5–9 daily; 1hr 5min); Bajío/León (6–8 daily; 55min); Cabo San Lucas (4–7 daily; 2hr); Campeche (3–4 daily; 1hr 40min); Cancún (30–37 daily; 1hr 30min–2hr 10min); Chetumal (1–2 daily; 1hr 50min); Chihuahua (6–8 daily; 2hr 10min); Ciudad Carmen (3–6 daily; 1hr 30min); Ciudad Juárez (3–6 daily; 2hr 20min); Ciudad Obregón (2–3 daily; 2hr 25min); Ciudad Victoria (3–5 daily; 1hr 30min); Colima (2–5 daily; 1hr 25min); Cozumel (4 weekly; 2hr); Culiacán (10 daily; 2hr); Durango (3–4

daily; 1hr 40min); Guadalajara (26–33 daily; 1hr 10min); Hermosillo (7–9 daily; 2hr 40min); Huatulco (3–7 daily; 1hr 10min); Ixtapa/Zihuatanejo (4–7 daily; 1hr); La Paz, Baja California Sur (4 daily; 2hr 20min); Lázaro Cárdenas (1–2 daily; 1hr 15min); Los Mochis (1–2 daily; 2hr 15min); Manzanillo (4–6 daily; 1hr 40min); Matamoros (1–2 daily; 1hr 25min); Mazatlán (3–4 daily; 1hr 40min); Mérida (12–14 daily; 1hr 40min); Mexicali (2–3 daily; 3hr 35min); Monterrey (23–37 daily; 1hr 30min); Morelia (4–6 daily; 50min); Nuevo Laredo (1–3 daily; 1hr 40min); Oaxaca (7–10 daily; 1hr); Puerto Escondido (1–2 daily; 1hr 30min); Puerto Vallarta (6–10 daily; 1hr 30min); Reynosa (4–6 daily; 1hr 35min); Saltillo (2–7 daily; 2hr); San Luis Potosí (5–9 daily; 1hr 10min); Tampico (5–9 daily; 1hr); Tapachula (3 daily; 1hr 40min); Tepic (1–2 daily; 1hr 25min); Tijuana (12–15 daily; 3hr 35min); Torreón (4–5 daily; 1hr 40min); Tuxtla Gutiérrez (8–11 daily; 1hr 25min); Veracruz (6–12 daily; 50min); Villahermosa (5–12 daily; 1hr 20min); Zacatecas (3–4 daily; 1hr 20min).

BY BUS

There are four principal long-distance bus stations in Mexico City, one for each point of the compass, though in practice the northbound terminal handles far more than its share, while the westbound one is tiny. All have Metro stations pretty much right outside, as well as authorized taxis (see box, p.117).

Destinations The list opposite indicates which destination is served from which station, but if you're uncertain which bus station you should be leaving from, any taxi driver should know which terminal to take you to. The further a destination is from Mexico City, the more likely it is that the long and arduous bus ride will cost you more than the plane fare, so it's worth checking the price of a flight before you book that *camión*.

Facilities The terminals have guarderías (left luggage offices, often expensive, especially at TAPO and Taxqueña), post and telephone offices, ATMs and a tourist information kiosk.

Tickets It's rare not to be able to get onto a bus at short notice, but it can be worth booking in advance for long-distance journeys or for express services to popular destinations at busy times – that way you'll have a choice of seat and be sure of getting the fastest service. Ticket Bus (☏55 5133 5133 or toll-free on ☏01 800 009 9090, ⓦticketbus.com.mx) – with offices at TAPO bus station (Tunnel 1), Isabel la Católica 83 in the centre, Hamburgo 254 (at Sevilla) in the Zona Rosa and Masaryk with Hegel in Polanco, among other places – can book tickets for a small fee with many but not all bus lines.

TERMINAL DEL NORTE

From anywhere north of Mexico City, you'll probably arrive at the Terminal del Norte, Av de los Cien Metros 4907. The largest of the city's four stations, it handles direct routes to and from the US border, and services to every major city north of Mexico City, including the fastest services to Guadalajara and Morelia. There's a Metro station right outside the entrance (Metro Autobuses del Norte; line 5), and trolleybuses just outside, which head down the Eje Central (Lázaro Cárdenas) to Bellas Artes and on to the Central de Autobuses del Sur. Alternatively, if you head four blocks east, you come to Insurgentes, where you can catch the Metrobús Line 1 (see p.120). If you want to get a taxi, go to the kiosk selling tickets for authorized taxis (see box, p.117), which cost about M$160 to the Zócalo and Alameda, M$120 to the Zona Rosa and M$200 to Polanco (all plus M$40 surcharge 10.30pm–6.30am). If you arrive late at night and don't want to search for a hotel in town, there are places nearby (see p.125).

TERMINAL DE AUTOBUSES DE PASAJEROS DE ORIENTE (TAPO)

Buses from points east (including a number of places that you may think of as south, such as Chiapas or the Yucatán), will usually drop you at the Terminal de Autobuses de Pasajeros de Oriente, known as TAPO, which is located on Av Ignacio Zaragoza. It has a Metro station (Metro San Lázaro; lines 1 and B) just down a connecting tunnel, which also leads you to the stops for city buses and *colectivos* plying Zaragoza towards the Zócalo and the Alameda, as well as Metrobús line 4 (see p.120). In the same tunnel, opposite the Metro entrance, is a sales desk for the authorized taxis (see box, p.117), which cost M$150 to the Zócalo and Alameda, M$160 to the Zona Rosa and M$180 to Polanco (all plus M$20 10.30pm–6.30am).

CENTRAL DE AUTOBUSES DEL SUR (TAXQUEÑA)

Buses from the Pacific coast (Cuernavaca, Taxco and Acapulco in particular) generally arrive at the Central de Autobuses del Sur (Tasqueña or Taxqeña), Av Tasqueña 1320, outside which is a big terminus for local buses and *peseros* (*combis*) to the centre and points south of town, and a Metro station (Metro Tasqueña; line 2). To find the Metro, head right as you leave the terminal, and you'll see the sign. Alternatively, to your left, on Av Tasqueña, trolleybuses head up the Eje Central (Lázaro Cárdenas) to Bellas Artes, and on to the Terminal del Norte. Authorized taxis (see box, p.117) cost M$140 (M$180 9pm–6am) to the Zócalo, Alameda or Zona Rosa, and M$200 (M$240) to Polanco.

TERMINAL PONIENTE (OBSERVATORIO)

Buses from places west of Mexico City, especially services passing through Toluca, but also Jalisco, Michoacán and the western part of the State of Mexico, terminate at the Terminal Poniente (Observatorio), at the junction of calles Sur and Tacubaya. To get the Metro (Metro Observatorio; line 1), leave from the exit in the middle of the terminal, where it makes a bend (next to the authorized taxi kiosk), and the entrance is

straight ahead, hidden behind the market stalls. Authorized taxis (see box, p.117) cost M$120 to Polanco, M$140 to the Zona Rosa and M$150 to the Alameda and Zócalo (M$40 surcharge 9pm–6am). Buses (signed "Metro Observatorio") head south on Reforma to the terminal, or pick up from the stands by the entrance to Chapultepec Park.

OTHER STOPS

Apart from the major terminals listed above, there are large open-air bus stops at the end of all the Metro lines such as Indios Verdes (line 3) or El Rosario (lines 6 and 7), with slow services to places up to an hour or so outside the city limits. For destinations in the capital's hinterland it can sometimes be quicker to leave from these. Obviously, the best way into town from these places is by Metro.

DESTINATIONS

(N = Terminal del Norte; S = Central de Autobuses del Sur/ Taxqueña; E = TAPO; W = Terminal Pte/Observatorio) Acapulco (S, 55 daily; 6hr); Aguascalientes (N, 29 daily; 6hr); Amecameca (E, every 15min; 1hr 15min); Campeche (E, 7 daily; 17hr); Cancún (E, 7 daily; 24hr); Chalma (W, every 20min; 2hr 30min); Chetumal (E, 2 daily; 18hr); Chihuahua (N, 22 daily; 18hr); Chilpancingo (S, 28 daily; 3hr 30min); Ciudad Juárez (N, 16 daily; 24hr); Ciudad Obregón (N, at least hourly; 26hr); Colima (N, 6 daily; 11hr); Córdoba (E, at least hourly, more at weekends; 4hr); Cuautla (S, every 10min; 2hr; E, every 10min; 3hr); Cuernavaca (S, every 15min; 1hr 30min); Dolores Hidalgo (N, every 40min; 4hr); Durango (N, 9 daily; 12hr); Guadalajara (N, hourly; 6hr; W, 14 daily; 7hr); Guanajuato (N, 11 daily; 5hr); Guaymas (N, 12 daily; 27hr); Hermosillo (N, hourly; 32hr); Ixtapa (S, 5 daily; 10hr); Ixtapan de la Sal (W, hourly; 2hr); León (N, 1–2 hourly; 5hr); Los Mochis (N, at least hourly; 21hr); Malinalco (W, 2 daily 10am & 3pm; 2hr 30min, or via Chalma); Manzanillo (N, 4 daily; 12hr); Matamoros (N, 10 daily; 14hr); Matehuala (N, 13 daily; 7hr); Mazatlán (N, hourly; 15hr); Mérida (E, 5 daily; 28hr); Mexicali (N, 22 daily; 30hr); Monterrey (N, 17 daily; 12hr); Morelia (W, every 30min; N, hourly; 4hr 30min); Nuevo Laredo (N, hourly; 15hr); Oaxaca (E, 22 daily; 6hr); Orizaba (E, at least hourly, more at weekends; 4hr); Pachuca (N, every 10min; 2hr); Palenque (E, 1 daily; 13hr); Pátzcuaro (W, 10 daily; N, 8 daily; 7hr); Playa del Carmen (E, 4 daily; 22hr); Puebla (E, every 20min; N, hourly; 2hr); Puerto Escondido (S, 6 daily; E, 1 daily; 15hr); Puerto Vallarta (N, 7 daily; 12hr); Querétaro (N, every 15min; 2hr 40min); Saltillo (N, 10 daily; 10hr); San Cristóbal de las Casas (E, 8 daily; 17hr); San Luis Potosí (N, hourly; 5hr); San Miguel Allende (N, every 40min; 4hr); Taxco (S, 13 daily; 2hr 30min); Tehuacán (E, hourly; 4hr); Tehuantepec (E, 6 daily; 10hr); Teotihuácan (N, every 15min; 1hr); Tepic (N, hourly; 12hr); Tepoztlán (S, every 40min; 1hr 15min); Tijuana (N, hourly; 42hr); Tlaxcala (E, every 20min; 1hr 40min); Toluca (W, every 5min; 1hr 30min); Tula (N, every

1

40min; 1hr 30min); Tuxpan (N, hourly; 4hr); Tuxtla Gutiérrez (E, 14 daily; 14hr); Uruapan (W, 16 daily; N, 8 daily; 6hr 30min); Valle de Bravo (W, every 20min; 3hr); Veracruz (E, at least hourly, more at weekends; 7hr); Villahermosa (E, 20 daily; 11hr); Xalapa (E, at least hourly; 5hr); Zacatecas (N, 14 daily; 8hr).

GETTING AROUND

For all its size and frantic pace, once you're used to the city, it is surprisingly easy to get around, with an efficient and very cheap public transport system as well as reasonably priced taxis. You'll probably want to **walk** around the cramped streets of the centre, but remember the altitude – walking gets tiring quickly, especially for the first day or so. If you're heading for Chapultepec or the Zona Rosa, you're better off taking the **bus** or **Metro** – it's an interesting walk all the way down Reforma, but a very long one. As for the outer suburbs, you've got no choice but to rely on public transport. You'll save a lot of hassle if you avoid travelling during **rush hour** (about 7–9am & 6–8pm).

BY METRO

Mexico City's Metro system (☎ 55 5709 1133 ext 5051 or 5009, ⓦ www.metro.df.gob.mx) is French-built, fast, quiet and efficient, though in some respects not tremendously well designed: interchanges can be very long, and the system seems to be configured so that journeys often require two legs. It can also get pretty crowded, and at peak hours stations designate separate entries for women and children (look for the "Mujeres" signs), who have exclusive use of the front two cars.

Tickets Tickets cost M\$3 and are sold individually. There's no discount for bulk purchases, though to save time queuing and messing about with tiny quantities of change it makes sense to buy several at a time.

Luggage In theory you're not allowed luggage of any size on the Metro (the official limit is 80cm x 50cm x 30cm), but in practice you can get away with carrying a big bag if you board at a quiet station at a calm time, and these days even a backpack seems to be tolerated at busy times. The first train leaves from each end of the line at 5am on weekdays (6am Sat and 7am Sun), with the last train at midnight.

Orientation There aren't always maps of the system on platforms, and certainly not on the trains, where you'll just find pictographic representations of the line you are on, along with the stations where you can transfer to other lines. The map opposite details the system, but it's wise to work out before you set off which way you'll be travelling on each line, and where to change. Direction is indicated by the last station at either end of the line (thus on line 2 you'll want either "Dirección Cuatro Caminos" or "Dirección Tasqueña"). To find your connection at interchange stations, follow the "Correspondencia" signs.

BY TREN LIGERO

Tren Ligero (light rail) runs south from Tasqueña (the southern terminus of line 2) as far as Xochimilco, entirely above ground. It requires a different ticket from the Metro system – when you change at Tasqueña you'll need to buy

BY TRAIN

Following privatization, intercity passenger train services ceased to run, and the only service now running out of Buenavista station (on Mosqueta by Insurgentes Nte; metro or metrobús Buenavista) is a suburban train (ⓦ fsuburbanos.com) to Cuautitlán in México state.

a Tren Ligero ticket (good for any one-way journey) from the ticket window or the machines on the concourse (M\$5).

BY BUS

Buses in Mexico City are very efficient, if you know where you're going. Fares are M\$3–6, depending on the route and the length of your journey. Destinations are displayed in the front window, which is somewhat more helpful than looking for route numbers, since the latter are not posted up and rarely used, and some buses terminate before the end of the route. One of the most useful routes is along Reforma, and the area just by Chapultepec Metro station at the entrance to the park is also a major bus terminus, from where you can get to almost any part of the city. Note that during rush hour it can be almost impossible to get a bus: once they're full, they simply don't stop to let passengers on. In 2008, the city government introduced pink buses for women only, mostly to tackle the problem of groping on public transport; the women-only buses are easily recognizable from their colour, and say "Servicio Exclusivo Mujeres" on the front, but most women of course just take whatever bus turns up first.

BY TROLLEYBUS

There are also trolleybuses running in both directions along Lázaro Cárdenas (the "Eje Central", or Central Axis) between Terminal del Norte and Central del Sur (Tasqueña), as well as on some other major routes. There's a flat fare of M\$4, and they don't give change.

BY METROBÚS

On four routes, there is a service called Metrobús (ⓦ metrobus.df.gob.mx), an articulated bus with its own dedicated lane, and fancy bus stops that look more like stations. The most useful route is line 1, which plies Insurgentes from pretty much one end to the other. Also useful is line 4, which runs east–west and serves the airport. Except for the airport service (which costs M\$30), there's a flat fare of M\$5, but in order to use the metrobús,

MEXICO CITY METRO

Ciudad Azteca
Plaza Aragón
Olímpica
Ecatepec
Músquiz
Río de los Remedios
Impulsora
Nezahualcóyotl
Villa de Aragón
Bosque de Aragón
Deportivo Oceanía

Politécnico · Indios Verdes

EL ROSARIO · Tezozomoc · Azcapotzalco · Ferrería · Norte 45 · Lindavista

DEPORTIVO 18 DE MARZO

MARTÍN CARRERA

Aquiles Serdán · Vallejo · La Villa Basílica · Talismán

Camarones · Potrero · LA RAZA · Bondojito · CONSULADO

Refinería · Misterios · Valle Gómez · E. Molina

INSTITUTO DEL PETRÓLEO · Autobuses del Norte · Tlatelolco · Aragón

Cuatro Caminos · TACUBA · Cuitláhuac · Buenavista · GUERRERO · Lagunilla · Tepito · Canal del Norte · OCEANÍA

Panteones · Popotla · GARIBALDI · MORELOS · SAN LÁZARO · Romero Rubio

San Joaquín · Colegio Militar · Normal · San Cosme · Revolución · HIDALGO · BELLAS ARTES · Allende · CANDELARIA · R. Flores Magón

Polanco · Juárez · San Juan de Letrán · Zócalo · Terminal Aérea

Auditorio · Cuauhtémoc · SALTO DEL AGUA · Isabel la Católica · Moctezuma · Hangares

Insurgentes · BALDERAS · Merced · Balbuena

Sevilla · Niños Heroes · PINO SUÁREZ · Fray Servando · Boulevard Puerto Aereo

Constituyentes · Chapultepec · Hospital General · Doctores · San Antonio Abad · Gómez Farías · PANTITLÁN

TACUBAYA · Juanacatlán · CENTRO MÉDICO · Obrera · CHABACANO · JAMAICA · Zaragoza · Puebla · Agrícola Oriental

Observatorio · Patriotismo · Chilpancingo · Lázaro Cárdenas · La Viga · Mixiuhca · Velódromo · Ciudad Deportiva · Canal de San Juan

San Pedro de los Pinos · Etiopía · Viaducto · SANTA ANITA · Coyuya · Tepalcates

San Antonio · Eugenia · Xola · Iztacalco · Guelatao

MIXCOAC · División del Norte · Parque de los Venados · Villa de Cortés · Apatlaco · Peñón Viejo

Barranca del Muerto · ZAPATA · Nativitas · Aculco · Acatitla

Coyoacán · Eje Central · Portales · Mexicaltzingo · Santa Martha

Viveros · ERMITA · Escuadrón 201 · ATLALILCO · Los Reyes

M. A. de Quevedo · General Anaya · Iztapalapa · Cerro de la Estrella · UAM-1 · Constitución de 1917 · La Paz

Copilco · TASQUEÑA

Universidad · Las Torres

Ciudad Jardín

La Virgen

Xotepingo
Nezahualpilli
Registro Federal
Textitlán
El Vergel
Estadio Azteca
Huipulco
Xomali
Periférico · Tepepan · La Noria · Huichapan · Francisco Goitia · Xochimilco

LINE 1		LINE 8	
LINE 2		LINE 9	
LINE 3		LINE 12	
LINE 4		LINE A	
LINE 5		LINE B	
LINE 6		TREN LIGERO	
LINE 7			

you have to buy a card (M$15 including one journey) from a machine at one of the stations on lines 1, 2 or 3. You charge up the card with credit at the same machines. Stations on line 4 don't have machines, but there should be attendants on hand who will sell you a card. You can also obtain and charge cards in branches of 7-Eleven or the similar chain Extra. The system is rather inconvenient if you just want to take the odd journey (especially as the machines don't give change, like rejecting coins and often have a queue, and credit has been known to mysteriously vanish from the cards), but there's no other way to pay the fare.

1

BY PESERO

Running down the major through routes, especially on Reforma and Insurgentes, you'll find *peseros* (*colectivos*), which are smaller and faster but charge more than the bus (if less than a regular taxi) and will let you on and off anywhere along their set route. They're mostly thirty-seater buses or VW vans, usually green with a white roof, and with their destination displayed on the windscreen – drivers of the smaller vehicles may sometimes hold up a number of fingers to indicate how many free seats they have. Like buses, *peseros* have route numbers, but routes often have branches, and a vehicle may start or finish in the middle of a route rather than at the end, so again it's more helpful to check the destination in the window. One of the most useful routes runs from Chapultepec Park via Av Chapultepec to the Zócalo.

BY TAXI

Ordinary taxis (usually red and gold) come in a variety of forms (some are still VW beetles, though these are fast disappearing) and there have been robberies at the hands of the drivers (see p.70), so you should think twice before taking one, especially if you are on your own. If you do decide to, it's best to take one from a taxi rank (*sitio*) rather than hail one in the street. From the airport or bus terminals, always use a prepaid authorized taxi, and never go with a driver who accosts you on arrival with the offer of a cab. Legitimate taxis other than authorized prepaid ones should have a meter – make sure it's switched on. Red-and-white radio taxis, which you have to call by phone, charge slightly more, but in general work the same way. *Taxis de turismo* lie in wait outside hotels and charge rates at least triple those of ordinary taxis; in the normal course of events you should avoid them, but they do have a couple of advantages, namely that the drivers know the tourist

sights, and should speak English – they can be worth it if, for example, you want to go on a tour for a few hours, in which case, with some ferocious haggling, you might even get a bargain. If you need to phone a taxi, try Servitaxis (☎ 55 5272 1123) or Taxi-Mex (☎ 55 5634 9912) or, to the airport, one of the firms listed on p.117. It can be difficult to get a taxi in the rush hour.

BY CAR

Rental cars (see p.118) are available from the airport and elsewhere, but it is generally better to wait until you are ready to leave the city before renting. There are thousands of agencies throughout the city, and the small local operations are often cheaper than the big chains. Either way, renting a car isn't going to be cheap, and a car can be a liability while you're in the city. Expect to pay M$400–800 a day for the cheapest car with tax, insurance and unlimited mileage, more in July and Aug; the usual deal for a week is that you pay for six days and get the seventh free. The major operators have offices at the airport and in the Zona Rosa, and some of the smaller companies do too.

If you already have a car, choose a hotel with secure parking and leave it there for the duration of your stay, except possibly to do a tour of the south of the city. Driving in the city is a nightmare, compounded by confusing one-way and through-route systems and by the near-impossibility of finding anywhere to park. Also note that the "Green Angels" who operate on highways (see p.36) do not operate within Mexico City.

BY BICYCLE

On Sun mornings, many streets in the city centre are closed to motorized traffic so that cyclists have exclusive use of the roadways.

INFORMATION AND TOURS

TOURIST OFFICES

Mexico City tourist office The DF government's tourist authority maintains a useful website (ⓦ www.mexicocity .gob.mx), in Spanish and English, with excellent background information, advice, tips and patchy listings, and you can call them on ☎ 55 5212 0259, or toll-free from outside the city on ☎ 800 008 9090. They also maintain tourist information booths at the airport (see p.117), at all four bus terminals, and dotted around town. None have much printed material to take away, but the staff are usually very helpful and well versed in the ways of the city. The most central is in the Zócalo between the cathedral and Monte de Piedad (daily 9am–6pm; ☎ 55 5518 1003; Metro Zócalo).

SECTUR The Mexico City branch of SECTUR (Mexican federal government's tourist office) is at Presidente Mazaryk 172, Polanco (Mon–Fri 8am–6pm; call 24hr on ☎ 55 3002 6300 or ☎ 078; Metro Polanco). It's flush with handouts about Mexico City and the country as a whole,

but inconveniently sited a long way from where you're likely to be spending your time.

CITY TOURS

Sightseeing tours that take in the city and often include the surrounding area are available from most of the more expensive hotels, while the DF government runs an hour-long city-centre tour on buses in the style of old trams leaving from Juárez by Bellas Artes (Mon–Sat 10am–5pm, Sun 2–5pm; M$50), though the commentary is in Spanish only.

Turibus ☎ 55 5141 1360 ext 2000, ⓦ turibus.com.mx. One of the best independent tour operators, running open-top double-deckers on two routes: a northern route taking in the city centre, and a southern route that heads down Insurgentes Sur to Coyoacán and the University. You can get on and off the bus at any stage en route; stops for the northern route include the Zócalo (República de Brasil, on the west side of the cathedral), the Benito Juárez Monument on the south side of the Alameda and El Ángel on Reforma; at Las Cibeles (Plaza Madrid) in Roma, you can change from the northern to the southern route. Both run daily (every 30–40min, 9am–9pm) and tickets cost M$140 weekdays, M$165 weekends (M$210/245 for a two-day ticket). Each circuit takes around 3hr, and the commentary comes in a choice of languages including English.

ACCOMMODATION

Accommodation in Mexico City ranges from budget **hostels** to some of the swankiest **hotels** in the country, but the best-value places can fill up quickly, so **booking ahead** is always a good idea. Most places have 24hr reception desks and are geared for late arrivals and early departures, and, with reasonably cheap taxi fares into the Zócalo or Zona Rosa, it seldom makes financial sense to stay near the bus stations or airport. However, if you arrive especially late or are just in transit and need a place to rest up for a while, there are places to stay that are very handy for the **airport** and **Terminal del Norte**.

HOTELS
AROUND THE ZÓCALO

Azores Brasil 25 ☎ 55 5521 5220, ⓦ hotelazores.com; Metro Allende or Zócalo; map pp.72–73. Well-situated modern hotel with small but clean and comfy rooms around a central atrium, each en suite and with TV, though only one room on each floor has an outside window. M$420

Catedral Donceles 95 ☎ 55 5518 5232, toll-free from US or Canada ☎ 1 866 291 2312, ⓦ hotelcatedral.com; Metro Zócalo; map pp.72–73. Very presentable mid-range place. All rooms have TV and telephone, and some even have a jacuzzi. Internet access is available, and there's a good restaurant and a terrace overlooking the cathedral. M$875

★**Gillow** Isabel la Católica 17 ☎ 55 5518 1440, ⓦ hotelgillow.com; Metro Allende; map pp.72–73. Friendly and good-value mid-priced hotel with carpeted rooms, in-house travel agency and leather sofas in the public areas. Cable TV, wi-fi and the expected amenities in rooms (it's worth paying a little extra for a larger room with a small patio or seating area). Ten percent discount for cash payment. M$820

Gran Hotel Ciudad de México 16 de Septiembre 82 ☎ 55 1083 7700, ⓦ granhoteldelaciudaddemexico .com.mx; Metro Zócalo; map pp.72–73. The city's most famous hotel, situated right on the Zócalo with sumptuous public areas (see p.75), and a selection of rooms and suites, some of which are gorgeously deluxe. Breakfast included and does significant discounts if you book in advance, particularly via the website. M$3770

Isabel Isabel la Católica 63 ☎ 55 5518 1213 to 7, ⓦ hotel -isabel.com.mx; Metro Isabel la Católica; map pp.72–73. Good-value hotel offering services such as taxis and laundry, plus a restaurant and bar. Rooms (with or without bathroom, the latter on the roof), though a little bit sombre, are quite spacious with TV and safe. Rooms at the back are quieter. It's worth booking a few days ahead. M$350

Juárez Callejón de 5 de Mayo 17 1° ☎ 55 5512 6929, ⓔ hoteljuarez@prodigy.net.mx; Metro Allende or Zócalo; map pp.72–73. Very central, clean and good-value budget tourist hotel, but not recommended for lone women travellers. Avoid room no. 4, which is next to the

hotel's main water pump. M$270

Majestic Madero 73 ☎ 55 5521 8600, ⓦ hotelmajestic .com.mx. Metro Zócalo; map pp.72–73. This luxury Best Western hotel on the Zócalo is rather stately and has bags of character. It's considerably cheaper than many of the places in the Zona Rosa and has many of the same facilities. Some rooms have Zócalo views, as does the *La Terraza* restaurant on the top floor (see p.128). Breakfast included. M$1620

Montecarlo Uruguay 69 ☎ 55 5518 1418; Metro Zócalo; map pp.72–73. Good-value cheapie with a touch of faded glory, and once briefly inhabited by D.H. Lawrence. Quiet and comfortable with a garage and a beautiful inner courtyard that is a little out of keeping with the rather small and dark en-suite rooms. M$350

República Cuba 57 ☎ 55 5512 9517; Metro Allende; map pp.72–73. Old and fairly dingy but also very cheap hotel (especially for two people sharing a double bed) on a quiet street. All rooms are en suite and some have TV. M$170

San Antonio Callejón de 5 de Mayo 29 2° ☎ 55 5518 1625; Metro Allende or Zócalo; map pp.72–73. Quiet, friendly place hidden away in a side street between 5 de Mayo and La Palma. Standards are high considering the price, with light, airy, spotless rooms, good firm beds, decent sheets and free bottled water. It's worth paying the M$30 difference for an en suite. M$350

Washington 5 de Mayo 54 ☎ & ☎ 55 5512 3502; Metro Allende or Zócalo; map pp.72–73. Good-value hotel very near the Zócalo. The cheapest rooms are pretty poky, but they're all decent, and come with a nicely tiled bathroom, cable TV, phone and wi-fi. It's worth asking for a corner room, which is bigger and better, with outside windows, for only M$20 more. M$380

Zamora 5 de Mayo 50 ☎ 55 5512 8245, ⓔ hotelzamora1 @gmail.com; Metro Allende or Zócalo; map pp.72–73. One of the more basic downtown hotels. The low prices, excellent location, free wi-fi and friendly management make the occasional noise, threadbare towels and variable cleanliness acceptable. You'll pay M$50 extra for a private bathroom. It's very popular so you may have to book ahead at busy times. M$180

1

AROUND THE ALAMEDA

Fleming Revillagigedo 35 ☎ 55 5510 4530, ⓦ hotelfleming.com.mx; Metro Juárez; map pp.72–73. A charcoal, grey cube on the outside, with salmon-pink, carpeted rooms on the inside: the decor at this business-style hotel is a little bit stuck in the 1980s, but it's comfortable enough and there's room service, wi-fi and a bar and restaurant. M$525

★**Hotel de Cortés** Hidalgo 85 ☎ 55 5518 2181, ⓦ boutiquehoteldecortes.com; Metro Hidalgo; map pp.72–73. Very classy boutique hotel in a building dating from 1620, but with rooms that are super-modern and stylish, with wooden deck floors throughout (even in the shower). The hotel also has a spa and fitness centre, a Spanish–Mexican restaurant, two bars and free wi-fi. M$2150

Managua Plaza de San Fernando 11 ☎ 55 5512 1312; Metro Hidalgo; map pp.72–73. Good-value if functional place with a cafeteria that does room service, and rooms with TV, bathroom and free bottled water, all in a quiet location facing the Jardín de San Fernando. M$200

Pánuco Ayuntamiento 148 ☎ 55 5521 2916; Metro Juárez; map pp.72–73. Clean and good value. Located in a drab part of town a little distance from the most popular tourist areas, though tolerably close to the Zona Rosa. The carpeted rooms each have a writing desk and TV – and a lot of fake marble. Parking and a restaurant on site. Often full Fri and Sat. M$280

AROUND THE REVOLUTION MONUMENT

Casa Blanca Lafragua 7 ☎ 55 5096 4500 or ☎ 800 200 2252, in the US & Canada ☎ 1 800 905 2905, ⓦ hotel-casablanca.com.mx; Metro Revolución; map pp.72–73. Attractive but rather impersonal modern high-rise hotel with perfectly decent rooms at prices a good deal lower than a lot of the Zona Rosa places. There's even a rooftop pool, a gym, business facilities and a restaurant. Wheelchair-friendly with an adapted room. Breakfast included. M$1160

Manalba Antonio Caso 23 ☎ 55 5566 6066, ⓔ hotelmanalba@hotmail.com; Metro Revolución; map p.91. Squat and ugly from outside but tastefully decorated within. Good-value rooms all come with cable TV and purified water, though you might want to spend M$120 extra for a more spacious double (with the standard two double beds) or for twin beds and a jacuzzi. M$695

THE ZONA ROSA, ROMA AND CONDESA

★**La Casona** Durango 280, at Cozumel ☎ 55 5286 3001, ⓦ hotellacasona.com.mx; Metro Sevilla; map p.91. In an early twentieth-century building at the northern end of Condesa, *La Casona* has an understated, if slightly quirky, European-style elegance, with polished wooden floors, antique furniture, a piano in its lounge and

quite a collection of art – including masks, original cartoons and paintings. The rooms are all different, with an aesthete's attention to detail, and it has a good restaurant. Breakfast included. M$2450

Geneve Londres 130 ☎ 55 5080 0841 or ☎ 800 900 0000, from the US & Canada ☎ 1 800 714 6549, ⓦ hotelgeneve.com.mx; Metro Insurgentes; map p.91. A large, century-old, but thoroughly modern hotel right in the heart of the Zona Rosa with an understated, elegant feel. Rooms are comfortable if unspectacular, with cable TV and mini-bars, but the facilities are excellent, and include the lovely Salon Jardín with its stained glass and iron roof, a restaurant, gym, spa and on-site *Sanborns* restaurant. The lobby has interesting exhibits on the hotel's history and past clients, who have included Marlon Brando, William Randolph Hearst and Charles Lindbergh. Breakfast included. M$1580

Hotel Del Principado Londres 42 ☎ 55 5533 2944 or ☎ 800 830 6040, ⓦ hoteldelprincipado.com.mx; Metro Insurgentes; map p.91. The double rooms (with two double beds) are rather more spacious and get rather more light than the one-bed rooms (in which it's worth asking for a king-size bed, as these cost no extra), but all have a TV and phone, and there's free wi-fi, parking facilities and a laundry service. Breakfast included. M$890

★**Maria Cristina** Rio Lerma 31, Cuauhtémoc ☎ 55 5703 1212, ⓦ hotelmariacristina.com.mx; Metro Insurgentes; map p.91. A lovely little colonial-style hotel near the Museo Venustiano Carranza. Popular with European visitors, the rooms are bright and quiet, though without the wood panelling and blue tiles of the public areas. Standard rooms have fans, deluxe rooms have a/c. M$850

Posada Viena Marsella 28, at Dinamarca ☎ 55 5592 7312 or ☎ 800 849 8402, in the US ☎ 1 888 698 0690, ⓦ posadavienahotel.com; Metro Cuauhtémoc or Insurgentes; map p.91. Lovely fresh and bright rooms decorated in rustic Mexican style, with ceiling fans though no a/c, at this comfortable but unpretentious four-star. The room price is the same for double, king-size or twin beds. M$685

Roosevelt Insurgentes Sur 287 ☎ 55 5208 6813, ⓦ hotelroosevelt.com.mx; Metro Insurgentes; map p.91. The 1938 Art Deco exterior of this mid-range hotel on the edge of Condesa has been spruced up, and the interior and rooms have been intelligently and stylishly modernized with tasteful use of grey, pink and brick-red. There's also satellite TV, wi-fi and a decent downstairs restaurant. M$730

Segovia Regency Chapultepec 328 ☎ 55 5525 0388 or ☎ 800 007 3845, ⓦ hotelsegovia.com.mx; Metro Insurgentes; map p.91. Reliable high-rise hotel with parking facilities. The carpeted rooms aren't huge, though they're certainly not spartan either, and all have a/c and wi-fi. It's often fully booked with business regulars, so reserve ahead, especially during the week. M$625

POLANCO

Busue Eugenio Sué 45 ☎ 55 6650 5916, ✆ busue.mx; Metro Polanco; map p.93. Very stylish boutique hotel a short walk from Mexico City's hottest shopping district. Mega-bathrooms and king-size beds throughout; even a deluxe room (the most basic option) comes with butler service. Supremely comfortable beds, jacuzzi, high-speed internet, fax machine, satellite TV, stereo, music library and free daily international paper. There's also a superb restaurant and bar on site. US$226 (M$3860)

Hyatt Regency Campos Elisos 204 ☎ 55 5083 1234, ✆ mexicocity.regency.hyatt.com; Metro Polanco; map p.93. Not the most expensive high-rise business hotel in the city but as luxurious as you could want, with an indoor pool, rooftop tennis courts, gym and acres of glass and marble. US$380 (M$6490)

THE AIRPORT AND AROUND

Hilton Mexico City Airport Airport Terminal 1 ☎ 55 5133 0507 or ☎ 800 003 1400, in the US ☎ 1 800 HILTONS, ✆ hilton.com; Metro Terminal Aérea. An elevator from Sala G (upstairs from Sala E3) takes you up to this efficient upmarket hotel which occupies much of the terminal's third floor with its restaurants, bars, gym and well-appointed, though not especially large, rooms (some with runway views). The multichannel TV even has in-house movies and flight information screens. The rack rate may apply when demand is high, but rates are usually substantially lower (sometimes by as much as half) at weekends in particular. US$174 (M$2975)

Hotel Aeropuerto Blv de Puerto Aéreo 380 ☎ 55 5785 5851, ☎ 55 5784 1329; Metro Terminal Aérea. The cheapest of the hotels near the airport, with well-maintained rooms (some with runway views); all have TV and phone, plus there's room service from the on-site restaurant. The hotel is a taxi ride from Terminal 2, but just a short walk from Terminal 1 (follow signs from Sala A to the Metro, and cross the busy road using the footbridge). M$640

NH Aeropuerto Airport Terminal 2 ☎ 55 5786 5750 or ☎ 800 903 3300, ✆ nh-hoteles.es; Metro Hangares. A very sleek, modern hotel, with extremely spacious public areas. The large rooms are equipped with either a king-size bed or two double beds, and the five-star facilities include a pool, gym and fitness centre. An elevator takes you from the ground floor of the terminal to the sixth floor, where the hotel is located. M$1699

Ramada Aeropuerto México Blv de Puerto Aéreo 390 ☎ 55 5133 3232 or ☎ 800 062 1218, ✆ ramadamexico .com; Metro Terminal Aérea. Attractive business hotel with lower prices than the big airport hotels but still with most of their features and facilities. It's located next to the *Hotel Aeropuerto* (see above), a short walk from Terminal 1, so it is barely worth using the hotel's free airport transfer, unless you're going to Terminal 2, or if you suffer from impaired mobility (the hotel is wheelchair-friendly with an adapted room). Breakfast included. M$1928

TERMINAL DEL NORTE AND AROUND

Brasilia Av de los Cien Metros 4823 ☎ 55 5587 8577 or ☎ 800 503 5212, ✆ hotel-brasilia.com.mx; Metro Autobuses del Norte. Good-value business-style hotel (though sometimes a bit snooty towards backpackers) just 150m southeast of the bus station (turn left as you exit and it's straight ahead of you), where you can get a peaceful sleep in comfortable, carpeted rooms with cable TV and phone. There's a decent if slightly pricey restaurant on site, parking facilities and even room service. You'll pay M$100 extra for a/c. M$600

Cartagena Av de los Cien Metros ☎ 55 5368 3527; Metro Autobuses del Norte. A hotel/motel a block from the terminal, this option is a secure and comfortable building which takes reservations a week in advance and offers discounts if you pay in cash. M$490

HOSTELS

AROUND THE ZÓCALO

Hostal Amigo Isabel la Católica 61 ☎ 800 746 7835 or ☎ 55 5512 3496, ✆ hostalamigo.com; Metro Isabel la Católica; map pp.72–73. Backpackers' hangout with eight- to ten-bed dorms, some with outside windows, but there are lockers (bring your own padlock), several private rooms (not cheap), free internet, a luggage deposit, a bar, a kitchen and communal areas. The hostel also runs tours, some of which are free to guests. Breakfast and dinner included. Dorms M$190, doubles M$490

Hostal Moneda Moneda 8 ☎ 55 5522 5803; Metro Zócalo; map pp.72–73. Convivial hostel with eight-bed dorms, a couple of lounges (one with TV), a decent kitchen, a bar and a panoramic rooftop terrace where the buffet breakfast is served. Private rooms are also available, but pricey. Make a reservation if you are to arrive after 11pm. Half board included in price. Dorms M$165, doubles M$465

Hostel Catedral Guatemala 4 ☎ 55 5518 1726; Metro Zócalo; map pp.72–73. Large, secure and efficiently run modern place behind the cathedral. Open 24hr, it has spotless six-bunk rooms, most with private bathroom, and some private rooms. There's an on-site travel agency, internet access, a café and bar, free coffee all day, Spanish classes available and a rooftop terrace with fabulous views. The only drawbacks are the small kitchen, limited communal areas and noise. Bring your own lock for the lockers, and consider bringing earplugs too. If you pay for four nights at once, the fifth is free. Discount with HI card. Breakfast included. Dorms M$190, doubles M$312

Mexico City Hostel Brasil 8 ☎ 55 5512 7731, ✆ mexicocityhostel.com; Metro Zócalo; map pp.72–73. Great location and decent enough eight- or twelve-bed dorms, as well as wi-fi and free internet access, but the

1

small, dark, private rooms are seriously overpriced, and you may have to go up or down a floor to find a bathroom. Breakfast included. Dorms M$200, doubles M$500

AROUND THE REVOLUTION MONUMENT

★**Casa de los Amigos** Ignacio Mariscal 132 ☎55 5705 0521, ⓦcasadelosamigos.org; Metro Revolución; map pp.72–73. The community-oriented, Quaker-run *Casa*, on a quiet street in the house where José Clemente Orozco spent the last decade of his life, pitches itself as a guesthouse, though it still has eight-and four-bed dorms as well as a few singles and doubles. Clean and comfortable with a good kitchen (breakfast available), a meditation room/library and occasional film screenings, it's popular with long-stay guests (minimum two-night stay). No alcohol and no smoking. Dorms M$100, doubles M$300

ROMA & CONDESA

Hostel Home Tabasco 303, Roma ☎55 5511 1683; Metro Sevilla; map p.91. This small twenty-bunk hostel in a quiet street is called "*Home*" because it was originally a family house. It's a little distant from the main sights, but has, as it advertises, a "chilled atmosphere", a kitchen and free internet, and is open 24hr. As well as the six- and eight-bunk dorms there's a sunny lounge and a small kitchen. Breakfast included. Dorms M$170, doubles M$450

Stayinn Barefoot Juan Escutia 125, Condesa ☎55 6286 3000; Metro Chapultepec; map p.91. This multi-storey building around a sunken courtyard is a good catch-all budget option for those wanting to stay close to the action in Condesa. Decor is modern and dorms and private rooms are simple and elegant. Also has a lively bar at the entrance which doubles up as a reception during the day. Dorms M$250, doubles M$500

EATING

There are reasonably priced restaurants, cafés, *taquerías* and juice stands on every block. The choice of where to eat ranges from traditional coffeehouses to fast-food lunch counters, taking in expensive **international** and rock-bottom **Mexican** cooking along the way, as well as food stalls in **markets** throughout the city: Merced is the biggest, but not a terribly pleasant place to eat. At the back of Plaza Garibaldi, there's a whole market hall given over to nothing but food stands, each vociferously competing with its neighbours. Mexico City also abounds in **rosticerías**, roast chicken shops, serving tasty set meals and crispy chicken with beer in a jolly atmosphere. More so than anywhere else in the country, Mexico City is flooded with **chain restaurants**, both American franchises and slightly classier Mexican chains such as *Sanborns* and *VIPS*; on the whole, you're much better off with a comida corrida. Top-class restaurants are mostly concentrated in **Polanco**.

CAFÉS, CHEAP EATS AND SNACKS
AROUND THE ZÓCALO

Café Emir Uruguay 45 ☎55 5521 2669; Metro Zócalo; map pp.72–73. Modernized café that's been operating since 1936 and serves good espresso, empanadas, cakes and even a range of baklava (*dulce árabe*; M$13 a piece). Mon–Fri 8am–9pm, Sat 10am–8pm, Sun noon–8pm.

Café el Popular 5 de Mayo ☎55 5518 6081; Metro Allende; map pp.72–73. A cheap place with an old-fashioned feel, serving simple food round the clock. It's almost always crowded, and the turnover is pretty fast, with great breakfasts, coffee and snacks. Meal deals include beef with fries, *refritos*, scrambled egg, coffee and a roll, all for M$60. Daily 24hr.

★**Café de Tacuba** Tacuba 28 ☎55 5521 2048; Metro Allende; map pp.72–73. There's good coffee and excellent food at moderate prices (*pollo al mole* M$205, chiles stuffed

with cheese M$172) at this famous cantina-style restaurant a world apart from the city life outside. The locals have been packing it out since 1912, often bringing in mariachi bands off the street who will play continuously if paid enough. Daily 8am–11.30pm.

Dulcería de Celaya 5 de Mayo 39 ☎55 5521 1787, ⓦdulceriadecelaya.com; Metro Allende; map pp.72–73. Founded in 1874, this is wonderland for sweet lovers, with real old-school fruit-based confectionery, including candied fruit, *dulce de membrillo* (quince jelly), *camotes* (sweet-potato candy), and limes stuffed with coconut. Daily 10.30am–7.30pm.

Jugos Canada 5 de Mayo 49 ☎55 5518 3717; Metro Allende; map pp.72–73. Very good torta and juice bar with decent prices, despite its central location. A *vampiro* (blood-like combination of orange, celery and beetroot juice) goes for M$28; *licuados* start at M$27. Mon–Sat 8am–10pm, Sun 9am–9pm.

Pastelería Ideal Uruguay 74 ☎55 5130 2170, ⓦpasteleriaideal.com.mx; Metro San Juan de Letrán; map pp.72–73. A cavernous bakery (made to look even larger by mirrors), with a huge range of cakes, biscuits and moulded gelatine confections, not to mention luscious chocolate cherries (M$20/100g). Daily 6.30am–9.30pm.

La Vasconia Tacuba 73 ☎55 5521 0659; Metro Allende; map pp.72–73. One of the best bread and cake shops in

---

TOP 5 PLACES TO EAT TRADITIONAL MEXICAN FOOD

Los Girasoles p.128
Restaurant Bar Chon p.128
El Arroyo p.130
Fonda San Ángel p.131
San Ángel Inn p.131

the centre, founded in 1870, with a huge range of rolls, biscuits, pastries and even lemon meringue "*pay*" (M$25). There's also an eating area where they serve breakfasts (M$50–90), snacks and main courses (a quarter of a roast chicken, for example, for M$30). Daily 7am–9.30pm (restaurant 7am–9pm).

AROUND THE ALAMEDA

Café del Palacio inside Bellas Artes ☎ 55 5518 5078; Metro Bellas Artes; map pp.72–73. An elegant café-restaurant in Art Deco surroundings. Enjoy limited views of Tamayo's murals as you eat amid business lunchers and pre-theatre diners. The list of what's available isn't huge, but they change it fortnightly. Typical dishes include *huachinango a la veracruzana* (snapper in red chile sauce; M$180), or roast beef in balsamic sauce (M$180). There's also a two-course *menu del Palacio* (M$280). Meals served daily 1–5pm, coffee served Mon noon–5pm, Tues–Sat 10am–7pm or later if there's a show.

Cafetería el Cuadrilatero Luis Moya 73 ☎ 55 5521 3060; Metro Balderas; map pp.72–73. Like Mexico City's other wrestling cafés, *El Cuadrilatero* ("the ring") is owned and run by Super Astro, an ex-wrestler, with wrestling masks framed on the walls along with photos of his glory days. The food's good, including standard Mexican mains, burgers and tortas big enough for a wrestler or for two mere mortals. The house speciality is a 1.3kg solid meat *gladiador* sandwich – if you can eat it in 15min, it's free, otherwise M$210 (or get a smaller version for M$128). Mon–Sat 7am–8pm.

ZONA ROSA

Barro-Barroco Londres 211 ☎ 55 5207 6433; Metro Insurgentes; map p.91. A small and peaceful café a little away from the main bustle of the Zona, serving coffee, breakfasts and meals at prices that are modest for the area. Mon–Fri 8am–4.30pm.

Blah Blah Café Florencia 44 (at Londres) ☎ 55 5514 6753; Metro Insurgentes; map p.91. Café, bar and Argentine grill, where an executive steak meal (12.30–8pm) will set you back around M$178, or you can have a lighter set meal for M$99, or a mixed grill for M$247. Mon–Fri 11am–midnight, Sat noon–midnight, Sun noon–11pm.

La Casa del Toño Londres 144 ☎ 55 5386 1125; Metro Sevilla; map p.91. The spot for *pozole*, an Aztec pork stew that many see as the ultimate hangover cure. This 24hr branch of the city-wide chain serves up piping-hot bowls (M$85) of the delicious stuff along with tacos and other staples. A very popular place for food following a party in the Zona Rosa. Daily 24hr.

El Trompito Londres 119-A ☎ 55 5511 1015; Metro Insurgentes; map p.91. If you're looking for a cheap snack amid the Zona's tourist traps, this modest little *taquería* could be the oasis you need, with tacos (*al pastor* M$26),

tortas (M$35–55) and *alambres* (small kebabs; M$51–93) at reasonable prices in clean surroundings. Mon–Sat 1pm–4am, Sun noon–9pm.

CONDESA

Neve Gelato Cuernavaca 124 (at Michoacán) ☎ 55 5256 3345, ⓦ nevegelato.mx; Metro Patriotismo or Juanacatlán; map p.91. They do crêpes and cakes here, but what draws the crowds is the luscious ice cream in flavours fruity (soursop, black cherry, *mamey*) or nutty (toasted almond, amaretto, hazelnut, tiramisú). One scoop for M$42, two scoops for M$61. Daily 7am–10pm.

Neveria Roxy Tamaulipas at Alfonso Reyes ☎ 55 5256 1854, Metro Patriotismo; map p.91. Located on a pretty corner, this classic of the Condesa has been serving up delicious ice cream and sorbet since 1946. Two scoops (M$40) served in a cone, waffle cup or bowl are a delight on a hot day. Also serves up big sundaes (M$38) and banana splits (M$75). Daily 11am–9pm.

POLANCO

La Ciudad de Colima Horacio 522, at Lamartine ☎ 55 5545 2719; Metro Polanco; map p.93. Good but overpriced *jugería* with some unusual *jugos* such as (depending on the season) starfruit (*carambola*), kiwi, sapodilla (*chicu*) and *mamey*. Prices start at M$35. Daily 7am–9pm.

SAN ÁNGEL AND SOUTH

Café Solo Dios Plaza San Jacinto 2 ☎ 55 5550 3302; Metrobús Dr Gálvez; map p.107. This popular hole-in-the-wall café and takeaway spot does great espressos, frappés and all the usual variations, all made from organic Chiapas beans. Daily 7am–9pm.

Crêperie du Soleil Madero 4-C ☎ 55 5550 2585, ⓦ creperiedusoleil.com; Metrobús Dr Gálvez; map p.107. Small and peaceful café that's good for an espresso, cakes and, of course, crêpes, both sweet (for example three berries, with blackberries, raspberries and strawberries for M$80) and savoury (try popeye, with creamed spinach and cheese for M$65). Daily 8am–7pm.

COYOACÁN

El Caracol de Oro Higuera 22 ☎ 55 5658 9054; map p.107. Laid-back restaurant and juice bar serving salads, pasta dishes (such as vegetarian lasagne for M$85), chiles stuffed with various fillings (chile stuffed with cheese in mango sauce is M$75), breakfasts, tea, coffee and excellent juices and energy drinks. There are always plenty of vegetarian options on the menu. Mon–Sat 10am–10.30pm, Sun 10am–10pm.

Le Caroz Allende 5, on Plaza Hidalgo ☎ 55 5554 6374, ⓦ lecaroz.com; map p.107. Coyoacán's excellent local bakery supplies a wide range of breads, luscious cakes, wobbly multicoloured jellies and a few savouries. Their

1

speciality is *pan dulce*. Mon–Sat 6.15am–10pm, Sun 6.15am–9.50pm.

La Vienet Viena 112, at Abasolo ☏ 55 5554 4623; map p.107. A good place for refreshments in between visits to the Kahlo and Trotsky houses, this small daytime café serves great coffee and cakes as well as breakfasts (until noon), lunch-time menus (M$140) and dishes such as *quesadillas sincronizadas* (M$70) and *enchiladas suizas* (M$85). Mon–Fri 8am–9pm, Sat & Sun 9am–6pm.

RESTAURANTS
AROUND THE ZÓCALO

Casa de los Azulejos Madero 4 ☏ 55 5512 1331; Metro Bellas Artes; map pp.72–73. Flagship *Sanborns* restaurant in a wonderful sixteenth-century building (see p.83), with prime seating around a fountain in an enclosed three-storey courtyard. The food is *Sanborns* stock in trade of well-prepared Mexican staples, though a little overpriced. Breakfasts are M$88–126, chicken fajitas M$125 and chicken tacos M$92. Daily 7am–midnight.

★**Danubio** Uruguay 3 ☏ 55 5512 0912, ⓦ danubio .com; Metro San Juan de Letrán; map pp.72–73. Established restaurant that has specialized in seafood since 1936. A hearty *bacalao a la Vizcaina* (Basque-style saltfish, in red pepper and tomato sauce) is M$280, or there's succulent seabass fillet stuffed with seafood for M$305. Mon–Sat 1–11pm.

Gili Pollos 5 de Mayo at Isabel la Católica 10 ☏ 55 5254 4078; Metro Allende; map pp.72–73. Is your Spanish up to the wordplay? Either way this is the best rotisserie chicken spot in the centre. With the sizzling birds seasoned a few different ways (roasted/BBQ/*ranchero*) behind the metal counter, take a seat ringside, upstairs or grab tacos, tortas and whole (M$86), half (M$49) and quarter (M$28) chickens to go. Daily 9am–9pm.

★**Los Girasoles** Tacuba 8-A (at Plaza Manuel Tolsá) ☏ 55 5510 0630; Metro Allende; map pp.72–73. One of the most appealing restaurants in the centre, with Mediterranean decor, a casual atmosphere and great food served at moderate prices, including burritos of *pibil* pork (M$98), which you might follow with chicken in *mole poblano* (M$156). Opens earlier for breakfast on Sun. Mon–Sat 1–11.30pm, Sun 10am–9pm.

Hostería de Santo Domingo Belisario Dominguez 72 ☏ 55 5526 5276; Metro Allende; map pp.72–73. Full of character, this moderately priced restaurant in part of a former convent looks great, with decorations hanging from the ceiling, artesanía all over the walls and, usually, a pianist and singer in the corner. But the food is not quite as good as they think it is; even their signature *chiles en nogada* (M$195) is better done elsewhere. There's a Sun buffet 9am–noon (including *chiles en nogada*) for M$130. Daily 9am–10pm.

Kam Ling Cerrada de 5 de Mayo 14 ☏ 55 5521 5661; Metro Allende; map pp.72–73. Straightforward Chinese

food in seriously large proportions to eat in or take away. There's a buffet for M$73, set menus (M$60–90) or individual dishes such as Cantonese-style squid with green pepper in black bean sauce (M$58), or chow mein of chicken, beef or pork (M$55), all washed down with huge pots of jasmine tea (M$20). Daily 11am–10pm.

Restaurant Bar Chon Regina 160 ☏ 55 5542 0873; Metro Merced; map pp.72–73. A veritable eating adventure, specializing in pre-Hispanic dishes, with starters such as *mescal* worms (M$260), *escamoles* (ant eggs; M$240) or *chapulines* (grasshoppers; M$100), served with or without guacamole. If you prefer a main course from outside the insect kingdom, there's frogs' legs (M$140), or crocodile steak in *mole verde* (M$230). Mon–Sat 11am–7pm.

La Terraza 4th floor of Majestic (see p.123) ☏ 55 5521 8600; Metro Zócalo; map pp.72–73. Restaurant with a terrace overlooking the Zócalo, although the view deteriorates significantly once you're seated. The buffet breakfast (7am–noon; M$140 weekdays, M$170 weekends) is good, and in the evening there's à la carte dining with well-prepared Mexican standards such as chicken with a choice of *moles* (M$140). Daily 7am–11pm.

Terraza 7th floor of Gran Hotel Ciudad de México (see p.123) ☏ 55 1083 7700 or ☏ 800 088 7700, ⓦ restauranteterrazaciudaddemexico.com.mx; Metro Zócalo; map pp.72–73. High-class eating and unbeatable views over the Zócalo at this top-notch renovated rooftop restaurant bar, and on the way up you can even snatch a peek at the *Gran Hotel*'s amazing Tiffany glass ceiling (see p.75). You could just pop up for one of their enormous cocktails (the house speciality is a gargantuan strawberry margarita for M$140), but then you'd be missing out on dishes like snapper steak in garlic with veg of the day (M$250) or *pollo en mole poblano* (M$115). Alternatively, drop by any time before 6pm at the weekend for a gluttonous M$290 buffet brunch. Mon–Fri 1–11pm, Sat & Sun 9am–11pm.

Los Vegetarianos (Vegetariano Madero) Upstairs at Madero 56 ☏ 55 3521 6880; Metro Zócalo; map pp.72–73. This sunny, spacious vegetarian restaurant lurks behind an unprepossessing stairway entrance but offers some of the best-value vegetarian food around, usually with piano accompaniment at lunch time. The four-course *menu del día* (M$75–110) is especially good value, though they also do great breakfasts. Daily 8am–8pm.

AROUND THE ALAMEDA

La Cocinita de San Juan Ernesto Pugibet 21 ☏ 55 5512 5237; Metro Pino Suarez; map pp.72–73. If you're after proper pre-Hispanic cuisine, including such delights as ant eggs (*escamoles*), spiders, wild boar or crocodile (a real treat), this place beside the exotic meats market gets them all in fresh daily. You can have your meat a number of different ways (tacos, tortas, myriad sauces), or opt for more traditional options like hamburgers or *mole*, but the truly brave will go for the "mixed insects" (M$400). Daily 10am–8pm.

Oriental Dolores 27 ☎ 55 5521 3093; Metro Bellas Artes; map pp.72–73. A reasonable choice among the chop-suey houses in Mexico City's mini-Chinatown, serving the usual standards (apart from chow mein, which is inexplicably absent from the menu), as well as its own specialities such as chicken Canton (M$85) or steamed fish with ginger (M$170). Daily noon–8.30pm.

ZONA ROSA

Bistrot Mosaico Reforma 316 ☎ 55 5525 8300; Metro Insurgentes; map p.91. A chain of French bakeries and restaurants, this Reforma-side locale serves up fresh bread and pastries out of the shop-front counter, while those looking for classic French cooking such as *bœuf bourguignon* (M$160) won't be disappointed in the restaurant. Also has a good selection of wines (around M$400 for a good bottle). Daily 8am–11pm.

Don Asado Rio Lerma 210, Cuauhtémoc ☎ 55 5533 9000, ⓦ donasado.com.mx; Metro Sevilla; map p.91. Uruguayan steak house serving wonderful chargrilled steaks, perfectly done to whatever turn you so desire. A *tira de asado* (a typical Uruguayan cut) will set you back M$140, or you can opt for a mixed grill for two at M$360. Mon & Sun 1–8pm, Tues–Thurs 1–11pm, Fri & Sat 1–11.30pm.

La Lanterna Reforma 458, at Toledo ☎ 55 5207 9969, ⓦ lalanterna.neositios.com; Metro Insurgentes; map p.91. Long-standing and convivial trattoria with an intimate and suitably Italian feel, enhanced by pasta freshly made in-house and combined with a choice of delicious sauces (M$151). The *segundi piatti* are equally wonderful, with *osso buco alla milanese* or *saltimbocca alla romana* for M$199. Mon–Sat 1–11pm.

Restaurante Vegetariano Yug Varsovia 3 ☎ 55 5525 5330; Metro Insurgentes; map p.91. A worthy contact point for vegetarians and vegans, with breakfasts, salads (house salad M$51) and *antojitos* in bright cheery surroundings. There's a particularly good buffet lunch upstairs (1–5pm; Mon–Fri M$90, Sat & Sun M$100). Mon–Fri 7am–9pm, Sat & Sun 8.30am–8pm.

CONDESA

For serious dining, especially in the mid-range, head to Condesa, about 20min walk south of the Zona Rosa. We've mentioned a few options in this area, but they are really just starting points, and the real pleasure is in simply wandering around and seeing what takes your fancy. The two principal streets for hungry visitors are Tamaulipas and Michoacán on the west side of Nuevo León, and Amsterdam to the east, the circular road that runs around Parque México.

Agapi Mu Alfonso Reyes 96 ☎ 55 5286 1384, ⓦ agapimu.com.mx; Metro Juanacatlán or Patriotismo; map p.91. The best Greek restaurant in the city, but very low-key and affordable as long as you don't go too mad on the *retsina* and Hungarian wines. It's especially fun from Thurs to Sat, when there's live music and Greek dancing. Moussaka (M$155) inevitably heads the list of main courses, followed by less well-known but equally delicious dishes such as *psári costas* (fish wrapped in vine leaves in an egg and lemon sauce; M$140). Mon & Sun 1.30–6pm, Tues–Sat 1.30–11pm.

Bellini 45th floor, World Trade Center, Av de las Naciones ☎ 55 9000 8305, ⓦ bellini.com.mx; Metrobús Poliforum; map p.91. A posh revolving restaurant at the top of the city's third-tallest building (see p.102), where business people come to impress their clients, and the romantically inclined enjoy candlelit dinners. Dishes from an international menu are prepared to the highest standards and service is impeccable. It's obviously not the cheapest place in town, but not stupidly expensive either: even at the top end of the menu, you can start with smoked salmon, caviar and avocado for M$215, followed by red snapper in lobster sauce for M$290. On Sun there's a M$350 brunch until 2pm. Mon–Sat 1pm–2am, Sun 9am–11pm.

Bottega Culinaria Sonora 180 ☎ 55 6434 9592; Metrobús Sonora; map p.91. A delicatessen with a kitchen offering some of the best food around Parque México, this relaxing spot is something of an oasis from the busier street a few metres beyond the chunky wooden tables. Serves up excellent cronuts (a croissant-doughnut hybrid), strong coffee and very tasty sandwiches. Mon–Sat 9am–midnight, Sun 9am–10pm.

Café la Gloria Vicente Suarez 43 ☎ 55 5211 4185; Metro Patriotismo or Juanacatlán; map p.91. Pleasant little bistro serving pasta dishes, salads or the likes of chicken with mushrooms, spinach and cream of *elote* (corn), or *filet mignon* (boh M$175). Desserts include profiteroles, chocolate mousse or blueberry cheesecake. Mon–Fri 1pm–midnight, Sat & Sun 10am–1am.

Daikoku Michoacán 25 ☎ 55 5584 9419; Metrobús Sonora; map p.91. The best sushi in Condesa, and possibly the city as a whole, Daikoku also serves up good ramen, sashimi, tempura and Japanese desserts for fair prices (around M$200/person). Also has a cookery school upstairs where you can spend anywhere from an afternoon to three months learning the mind-bogglingly precise art of sushi. Daily 1pm–12.30am.

Fonda Garufa Michoacán 93 ☎ 55 5286 8295, ⓦ garufa .com; Metro Patriotismo or Juanacatlán; map p.91. The original eatery of the colonia; the loyal regulars will tell you was here before Condesa was cool, and it's no wonder it has such longevity. Top-quality cuisine as well as pastries and excellent coffee. Grab a street-side table or head for the balony upstairs and watch peaceful Condesa life go by as you tuck into excellent steaks (house steak M$190) or dishes such as salmon mayonnaise (M$180). Daily 8am–1am.

El Jamil Amsterdam 306 (at Celaya) ☎ 55 5564 9486;

Metro Sevilla; map p.91. A good Lebanese restaurant with *mezze* such as hummus or *babaghanouj* (aka *moutabel* – eggplant and tahini dip) for M$60, and mains such as *shish tawouk* (charcoal-grilled chicken kebab) for M$155. You can round it off with coffee and baklava, or sit outside and smoke a *sheesha* (water-pipe). Mon–Wed 1.30–11pm, Thurs–Sat 1.30–11.30pm, Sun 9am–8pm.

Kitchen 6 Teotihuacan 14 at Amsterdam ☎55 5264 1748; Metrobús Sonora; map p.91. Build your own burger (around M$120) with the best ingredients, choosing everything from the bread onwards, at this stylish (although rather dark) restaurant with street-side tables and an extensive selection of craft beer. The six-sauce fries (M$70) are also a good sharing option as well as sandwiches and salads for those looking for something different. Daily 1pm–midnight.

★**Mercado Roma** Queretaro 225 ☎55 5564 1396 ⓦmercadoroma.com; Metrobús Sonora; map p.91. A big food hall with a collection of gourmet world cuisines ranging from fantastic shawarma to delectable tapas, with a friendly and attractive seating area at the back, ringed by various bars serving up craft beer, wines and the country's best mescal and tequila. There's a mezzanine offering desserts and a rooftop bar with microbrewed beers and signature cocktails. A very popular spot for the trendy crowd at weekends. Daily 9am–6pm (ground floor), 9am–midnight (mezzanine and rooftop).

Mibong Campeche 396 ☎55 5211 2078; Metro Juanacatlán; map p.91. Serving authentic Southeast Asian food from an open kitchen with fresh ingredients, this pleasant restaurant is a popular lunch-time destination for Condesa residents. The *phô* soup (M$165) is particularly good, although you do the majority of the seasoning yourself. Mon–Wed & Sun 1pm–12.30am, Thurs–Sat 1pm–1.30am.

Second Amsterdam 76 (at Parras) ☎55 5553 3902; Metro Juanacatlán; map p.91. Relaxed, low-lit corner restaurant and café, open on both sides to pavement seating. Salads, pasta dishes and mains such as chicken breast served with *al dente* vegetables (M$82) are all well prepared. Daily 11am–1am.

Tandoor Amsterdam 72 (at Parras) ☎55 5553 9592; Metro Juanacatlán; map p.91. The best curry in the area, thanks largely to the fact they use a real *tandoor* oven, is served up in this maharaja-style building with a pretty rooftop (the second-generation management have their roots in Pakistan). The spices are authentic and you can expect to eat well. Meals around M$300 per person, also does takeaway. Mon–Sat 1pm–10.30pm, Sun 1–7pm.

El Zorzal Cnr of Alfonso Reyes and Tamaulipas ☎55 5273 6023; Metro Patriotismo; map p.91. Argentine steakhouse serving up juicy slices of steer (a 300g churrasco, for example, for M$160), and *alfajor* pastries or crêpes filled with *dulce de leche* for dessert. There's also a

famous torta stand that operates on the same corner (look for the multicoloured umbrella and long queue) that serves up *chilaquiles* and chicken sandwiches. Mon–Sat 1pm–midnight, Sun 1–10pm.

POLANCO

Bistro Charlotte Lope de Vega 341, at Presidente Masaryk ☎55 5250 4180, Metro Polanco; map p.93. Great little lunch-time bistro where the menu changes every fortnight or so and always offers an interesting and international selection (roast beef and Yorkshire pudding is not unknown, at M$285, even bangers and mash for M$146, or prawns provençale for M$184). Mon–Fri & Sun 1–6pm.

★**Butcher & Sons** Virgilio 8, at Parque Lincoln ☎55 5280 4247; Metro Auditorio; map p.93. This chain, which also has a stand in Mercado Roma (see above), cooks up the best burgers (around M$140) in Mexico City, with fresh-baked buns, delicious patties and ingredient combinations named after rock stars. It's worth waiting for a street-side table since the interior gets a little cramped. Mon, Tues & Sun noon–11pm, Wed–Sat noon–1am.

Denominación de Origen Hegel 406, at Presidente Masaryk ☎55 5255 0612; Metro Polanco; map p.93. Classy modern Spanish restaurant with a long bar, lots of whole hams and dishes like *bacalao a la vizcaína* (saltfish Basque-style, in sweet pepper sauce; M$314), or a superb Andalusian *gazpacho* (M$77). Mon–Sat 1pm–midnight, Sun 1–5pm.

Eltuca's Newton 116, at Lamartine ☎55 5545 8388 or 9; Metro Polanco; map p.93. Forget the rubbish they sell at the international junk-food chains: what you get here are proper burgers, made from sirloin steak and grilled over charcoal. You don't get them flipped in an instant, but they're worth the wait. A straight burger is M$55, and for non-carnivores there are salads, salmon-burgers (M$75) and veggie-burgers (M$75). Home delivery available within Polanco. Daily noon–10pm.

SAN ÁNGEL AND SOUTH

The southern suburbs of San Ángel and Coyoacán are good hunting grounds and it is worth sticking around for your evening meal after a day's sightseeing.

El Arroyo Insurgentes Sur 4003, Tlalpan, 6km south of San Ángel ☎55 5573 4344, ⓦarroyorestaurante.com.mx; Metrobús Fuentes Brotantes; map p.107. Well off the beaten path, but worth the journey, this unusual restaurant has a small bullring (used by novice bullfighters in bloodless *corridas* April–Oct) and almost a dozen dining areas that can jointly seat over 2500. There's always a lively atmosphere, helped along by mariachis and other entertainment starting weekdays at 4pm, weekends at 5pm. The Mexican food is good too – barbecued meats are the speciality, ordered by the portion or by the kilo (pork barbecued in maguey leaves goes for M$510 per kilo or M$260 a portion, a kilo being around four portions) – and they usually keep at least four types of flavoured *pulque*. Daily 8am–8pm.

Fonda San Ángel Plaza San Jacinto 3 ⊕ 55 5550 1641, Metrobús Dr Gálvez; map p.107. Moderately priced restaurant specializing in contemporary Mexican cuisine. Start off with a "pre-Hispanic platter" of *escamoles* (ant eggs), mescal worms and *chipulines* (grasshoppers) for M$345, followed by *bacalao a la veracruzana* (saltfish with onions and tomatoes) for M$170, or *lengua a la veracruzana* (tongue prepared in a similar fashion) for M$150. Mon–Sat 9am–midnight, Sun 9am–7pm.

San Ángel Inn Diego Rivera 50, at Altavista ⊕ 55 5616 2222, ⓦ sanangelinn.com; Metrobús Dr Gálvez; map p.107. Popular with visiting dignitaries and tourists, this late seventeenth-century former Carmelite monastery has been an elegant restaurant with a sumptuous garden setting since 1915. The menu has European overtones, but is mainly Mexican, featuring starters such as *huitlacoche* crêpes (M$115), and mains such as chiles stuffed with meat and cheese (M$160), plus fine wine or margaritas to accompany it. Reservations required. Daily 1pm–1am.

Zeco Caffé Revolución 1382 ⊕ 55 5680 1092; Metro Barranca del Muerto; map p.107. Smart modern Italian establishment combining a café and spacious dining area. It is a little inconveniently sited, but worth the journey for excellent risotto and pasta dishes (such as risotto with prawns, *nopales* and green coriander for M$155) and a wide range of mains (such as roast goat for M$245). It also doubles as a bar and bakery. Mon–Sat 8am–midnight, Sun 8am–7pm.

COYOACÁN

La Esquina de los Milagros Plaza Jardín del Centenario 18-B ⊕ 55 5659 2454; map p.107. Elegant indoor dining with white tablecloths, or outdoors on decking on the main square, with dishes such as stuffed

---

PULQUE AND PULQUERÍAS

Pulque is the fermented sap of the maguey cactus, a species of agave that grows in the countryside north and east of Mexico City. A pre-Hispanic concoction traditionally considered to be a poor man's drink, *pulque* had its heyday in the first half of the twentieth century – but as beer, wine and spirits became more affordable, *pulque*'s stock went down. At one time there were over 1400 **pulquerías** in the capital, but today owners estimate that there are only around a hundred or so left. It's possible, however that Mexico City's *pulquerías* may yet see a revival, as the drink has seen a rise in popularity of late among young Mexicans, particularly students interested in their cultural roots. Regardless of demand, production continues much as it has done for centuries, with barrels being shipped daily to the capital.

Unless you are looking for them, *pulquerías* are hard to spot; they're concentrated in less salubrious areas of town mostly unvisited by tourists and often have no sign, just a pair of swinging doors guarding a dark interior. Like cantinas, they are traditionally macho territory, and women are more likely to receive a respectful welcome when accompanied by male friends.

These places are not set up for anything much more sophisticated than knocking back glasses of the slightly astringent, viscous green-white beverage, usually ladled out of barrels behind the bar. The emphasis is as much on socializing as drinking, which is a good thing since most *pulque* is only two to four percent alcohol and getting drunk requires considerable commitment, particularly since the thick liquid is extremely bloating. The task is made easier when *pulque* is blended with fresh fruit juices – pineapple, oats, guava and many others – *pulque* flavoured in this manner is known as *curado*. The most popular hunting ground is the **Plaza Garibaldi**, although there's a chance to try it on a night out in Condesa (see *Wichitos* below).

Los Duellistas Aranda 30; Metro Sam Juan Letrán; map pp.72–73. During the day you are best off exploring the district south of Bellas Artes, where choices include this place which attracts a young clientele. Mon–Sat 9am–9pm.

La Hermosa Hortensia Plaza Garibaldi; Metro Garibaldi; map pp.72–73. Always brightly lit and usually has several good flavours served up to a cross section of men and women, locals and foreigners. Daily noon–midnight.

La Risa Mesones 71, on the cnr of Callejón de Mesones; Metro Isabel La Católica; map pp.72–73. Like the nearby *Los Duellistas*, this *pulquería* is another good daytime option, dating back to 1903. Daily 11am–10pm.

Wichitos Tamaulipas 104 ⊕ 55 5211 7098; Metro Juanacatlán; map p.91. The only Condesa *pulquería*, serving up pure or *curado* flavours including pineapple, oats and guava by the quarter (M$45), half (M$60) and whole litre (M$100). Has a good food menu that tries to pack in the whole of Mexican rustic cuisine. You can also try a sampler of three different *pulques* for M$35. Gets very lively at the weekends when crowds come for the regular drinks they also serve. Mon & Sun noon–7pm, Tues & Wed noon–midnight, Thurs–Sat noon–2am.

1

chile poblano (M$120) or fish cooked in a banana leaf (M$135). There's a lunch-time menu (1–5pm) for M$95, and live jazz music Thurs–Sat 9–11pm, with jam sessions on Mon from 8pm. Daily 9am–midnight.

El Tajín Centro Veracruzano, Miguel Ángel de Quevedo 687 ☎ 55 5659 4447, ⬤ eltajin.com.mx; map p.107.

Veracruz specialities at medium to high prices; the fish dishes, such as *huachinango a la Veracruzana* (snapper in tomato, olive and caper sauce; M$200), and octopus in green herbs (M$185), are exquisite. Mon–Fri 1–6pm, Sat & Sun 1–7pm.

DRINKING AND NIGHTLIFE

Club-oriented nightlife starts late, with live acts often hitting the stage after 11pm and few places really getting going before midnight. Cuban music is particularly popular, and with Cuba just a short flight away, Mexico City provides a local but international proving ground for the island's talent.

BARS

Bars range from dirt-cheap *pulquerías* and cantinas to upscale lounges and hotel bars. As elsewhere in the country, cantinas and *pulquerías* are still largely a male preserve. More civilized bars, where you might sit around and chat, are relatively thin on the ground.

AROUND THE ZÓCALO AND THE ALAMEDA

La Ópera 5 de Mayo 10, near Bellas Artes ☎ 55 12 8959. Metro Bellas Artes; map pp.72–73. The best watering hole downtown, in the grand tradition of upmarket cantinas with magnificent *fin-de-siècle* decor – ornate mahogany panelling, a brass-railed bar, gilt-framed mirrors in the booths – and a bullet hole in the ceiling reputedly put there by Pancho Villa. You also can dine here, but most people come for a fairly pricey beer, tequila or cocktails in the booths or at the bar. Mon–Sat 1pm–midnight, Sun 1–6pm.

Tío Pepe Independencia 26, at Dolores ☎ 55 5521 9136; Metro Bellas Artes; map pp.72–73. Convivial cantina with moulded ceilings and wooden bar. Minstrels frequently drop in to bash out a few numbers, and women are nowadays welcome, but may feel more comfortable in the saloon (*La Mascota*) next door. Mon–Thurs noon–10pm, Fri noon–11pm, Sat noon–9.30pm.

ZONA ROSA, ROMA AND CONDESA

Wallace Tamaulipas 45, Condesa ☎ 55 5256 3534; Metro Chilpancingo; map p.91. A stylish whisky bar on a street with a number of cool options. The island bar here has over 100 brands of whisky and can make just about any cocktail you request. There's a chilled-out lounge upstairs, but reserve a street-side table ahead of time if you want to make the most of the street's party atmosphere. DJs Thurs–Sat. Daily 3pm–2.30am.

SAN ÁNGEL AND COYOACÁN

La Camelia Madero 3 (by Plaza San Jacinto), San Ángel ☎ 55 5616 5643; Metrobús Dr Gálvez; map p.107. Early-evening boozing to recent US and Latin pop hits, either inside or out on the street, at this vintage cantina dating from 1931. There's decent food and a traditional, if never raucous, cantina atmosphere. Daily noon–11pm.

La Guadalupana Caballo Calco 7, on Plaza Hidalgo, Coyoacán ☎ 55 5554 6253; map p.107. Rather a refined and classic cantina (established in 1932), and an excellent place to sink a few beers of an evening. Mon–Sat 1pm–midnight.

El Hijo del Cuervo Jardín Centenario 17, Coyoacán ☎ 55 5659 5196, ⬤ elhijodelcuervo.com.mx; map p.107. Dark and hip bar with seats overlooking the square and music that ranges from Latin rap to rock. There's no cover charge, and a lively evening atmosphere. Mon–Thurs 4pm–midnight, Fri & Sat 11am–2.30am, Sun 1–11.30pm.

LIVE MUSIC VENUES

The live music scene has broadened appreciably in recent years, and there are venues for all kinds of bands, offering anything from old-fashioned romantic ballads to cutting-edge alternative rock bands.

AROUND THE ZÓCALO AND THE ALAMEDA

Zinco Jazz Club Motolina 20, at 5 de Mayo ☎ 55 5512 3369, ⬤ zincojazz.com; Metro Allende; map pp.72–73. Small but congenial venue, really just a bar/restaurant with entertainment by local jazz bands, tucked away in the vaults beneath the Art Deco splendour of the Banco de México building. Entry M$80–250, depending on what's on. Wed–Sat (and sometimes Tues) 9pm–2am.

ZONA ROSA, ROMA AND CONDESA

Cantina Bicentenario Vicente Suarez 42, Condesa ☎ 55 5553 5451; Metro Juanacatlán; map p.91. The most authentic cantina in trendy Condesa, this is the place to come for a real Mexican drinking experience. Mariachi bands, micheladas and botanas are served up here with relish, no matter how messy you get. Mon–Wed noon–midnight, Thurs–Sat noon–2am.

Multiforo Alicia Cuauhtémoc 91, between Colima and Durango, Roma ☎ 55 5511 2100, ⬤ multiforoalicia.blogspot.mx; Metro Cuauhtémoc; map p.91. "Who hasn't been to Alicia doesn't know rock music", they claim, which may be an exaggeration, but this is still the place to catch Mexico's latest rock *ondas*. Most of the action is on Fri & Sat, from 8.30pm, but some shows start as early as 5pm.

1

TOQUES: SUPERCHARGED NIGHTLIFE

When out drinking in Mexico City, it's not unusual to witness Mexicans electrocuting themselves for fun. The traditional drinking game **Toques** sees individuals or groups forming a human chain, undergoing increasingly strong electrical currents until they can take no more. The aim is to withstand the current as high up the voltage meter as possible before **shouting for mercy**, or "Ya!" in Spanish. The voltage starts at 20 and reaches a rare maximum of 120. The difficult leap is from 95 volts to 110. The men who offer this bizarre game patrol a route around the popular drinking areas (particularly the centre, Condesa, Roma, Zona Rosa) and identify themselves by clicking together the metal handles of their apparatus. A game costs around M$20 and ends when you cry for mercy. Groups play by linking hands (or touching any other bare bit of skin) to form a chain which can be broken by releasing any link. Despite the screams it may elicit, the game is safe, although it should be avoided by anyone with a heart pacemaker.

Expect to pay M$70–150, depending who's on. Hours vary according to programme.

Pata Negra Tamaulipas 30, Condesa ☎55 5211 5563; Metro Patriotismo or Sevilla; map p.91. Music bar with an impressive selection of fine spirits and live acts, mainly rock, usually Mon, Tues & Sat, with DJs Fri and Sun. No cover charge for the upstairs bar which has salsa classes on Wed and Sat at 8pm. Main bar daily 1.30pm–2.30am (music from 8.30pm); upstairs bar Tues–Sat 9pm–3am.

Ruta 61 Baja California 281, Condesa ☎55 5211 7602; Metro Chilpancingo; map p.91. This cosy little blues club has jam sessions on Wed (free), and live music Thurs–Sat (M$60–120 entry), with tables to sit at while listening (reservation advised). Wed–Sat 8pm–2am; music starts at 10pm.

CLUBS

Entry can be expensive, as much as M$300 for men (women often get in for much less or sometimes for free), though this is likely to include a drink, or even *bar libre*, where your drinks are free for at least part of the evening. Be aware that dress restrictions are still very much the order of the day here, and a lot of clubs won't let you in wearing jeans or trainers.

Love Masaryk 169, Polanco ☎55 5254 3535; Metro Polanco; map p.93. A discotheque, like they used to make them, complete with dress-to-impress wardrobe rules, chic decor and lots of pretty young patrons shaking their booties to pop hits old and new, but unless you're a VIP, you'll need to reserve in advance (by phone or online) in order to get in. Entry usually M$250 for men, free for women. Wed–Sat 11pm–4.30am.

Mama Rumba Querétaro 230, at Medellín, Roma ☎55 5564 6920 or ☎55 5564 7823; Metro Insurgentes; map p.91. Reservations are advised for this dance bar. The Hispano-Afro-Caribbean rhythms pumped out by the Cuban house band get the small dancefloor packed, so come prepared to move your feet even if you don't know the steps. Bands come on at 11pm. Wheelchair access. Wed–Sat 9pm–3am.

El Vicio (formerly El Hábito) Madrid 13, Coyoacán ☎55 5659 1139, ⓦelvicio.com.mx; Metro Coyoacán (800m); map p.107. Small and quirky fringe theatre and music club, with plays and live jazz. Also on site are *Novo's* restaurant and the Teatro la Capilla. Hours vary according to what's on, but typically Wed–Sun 8.30am–2am.

GAY BARS

The Zona Rosa (pink zone) is Mexico City's gay zone, and in particular the northernmost section of Amberes between Hamburgo and Reforma, where you'll find a slew of gay and lesbian bars. The listings magazine *Tiempo Libre* also has a section on gay and lesbian events and locales.

El Marrakech Generalito Filomeno Mata 18-H ☎55 5518 3711; Metro Allende; map p.72–73. One of the city centre's most popular gay spots away from the Zona Rosa, although straight people are also welcome. There's a sweaty dancehall at the back which is definitely for those of rainbow flag persuasion, and lively karaoke on Sun. Also does decent food until around 7pm. Mon–Wed noon–11pm, Thurs–Sun noon–3am.

Gayta Amberes 18 ☎55 5207 7626; Metro Insurgentes; map p.91. Pumping house music, black lights and a generally garish ambience make this pretty loud all round for such a small venue. Lesbians supposedly have their own smoochy pink section called the *Pussy Bar*, although male-male and male-female couples can also be found there. Mon–Thurs & Sun 1pm–midnight, Fri & Sat 1pm–2am.

Papi Amberes 18 at Estrasburgo ☎55 5208 3755; Metro Insurgentes; map p.91. Billing itself as "the original fun bar", this is a place for kitsch pop music, drag acts, beer, cocktails and general hedonism, generally for boys rather than girls, but it's not as if they're fussy. Mon–Wed & Sun 4pm–2am, Thurs–Sat 3pm–3am.

Touch Amberes 11 at Reforma ☎55 3231 9728; Metro Insurgentes; map p.91. A multi-level club offering raucous karaoke on the ground floor, a disco playing classic hits in the middle and full-on rave/electro higher up. There's a quieter terrace for smoking and chat on the top. Tues–Sun 5pm–2.30am.

1

ENTERTAINMENT

Mainstream Hollywood **movies** make it to Mexico just a few weeks after their release in the US and often before they get a British or European release. One of the largest concentrations of cinemas is along Insurgentes, where half a dozen multiplexes total around fifty screens in all, with prices around M$40–60. While Mexican **theatre** tends to be rather turgid, there are often excellent **classical music** concerts and **opera** or **ballet** performances by touring companies. The Palacio de Bellas Artes (see p.84) and the Auditorio Nacional are the main venues, but other downtown theatres, as well as the Polyforum (see p.102) and the Teatro de los Insurgentes (see p.102), may have interesting shows. For listings, see the weekly magazine *Tiempo Libre* (ⓦ tiempolibre.com.mx).

Casa del Lago Bosque de Chapultepec (by the lake, near entrance on Reforma) ☎ 55 5553 6362, ⓦ www .casadellago.unam.mx; Metro Auditorio; map p.93. Music, dance and film all feature among the cultural activities organized by the University (UNAM) at this beautiful lakeside mansion in Chapultepec Park, but the most popular events are the Sat afternoon classical concerts, which are listed on the website, and almost always free. Sat afternoon concerts usually either noon–1pm or 1–2pm; times for other events vary.

SHOPPING AND MARKETS

The big advantage of **shopping** in the capital is that you can get goods from all over the country and, if you are flying out of here, you don't have to lug them around Mexico, though they will usually be more expensive than at the source. An odd hangover from Aztec times is the practice of devoting a whole street to one particular trade, which occurs to some extent throughout the city. There are blocks where you can buy nothing but stationery, while other areas are packed exclusively with shoe shops and still others only sell musical instruments. Every area of the city has its own **market** selling food and essentials, and many others set up stalls for just one day a week along a suburban street. Replica Mexican football shirts can be found in the *tianguis* (street markets) on San Juan Letrán between Bellas Artes and Salto del Agua, or those in the streets north and east of the Zócalo.

DEPARTMENT STORES

Liverpool Carranza 92 (across 20 de Noviembre from El Palacio de Hierro) ☎ 55 5133 2800, ⓦ liverpool.com .mx; Metro El Sagrario; map pp.72–73. The original branch of a nationwide chain founded in the nineteenth century, which originally imported much of its stock from the English port from which it takes its name. Mon–Fri 11am–8.30pm, Sat 11am–9pm, Sun 11am–7.30pm.

El Palacio de Hierro 20 de Noviembre 3 (just south of the Zócalo) ☎ 55 5728 9905, ⓦ elpalaciodehierro.com .mx; Metro El Sagrario; map pp.72–73. A department store whose original branch, established in 1891, is

---

MARIACHI IN PLAZA GARIBALDI

Plaza Garibaldi (Metros Bellas Artes and Garibaldi) is the traditional final call on a long night around the capital's bars, and as the night wears on and the drinking continues, it can get pretty rowdy. The plaza is on Lázaro Cárdenas, five blocks north of Bellas Artes in a thoroughly sleazy area of cheap bars, grimy hotels and several brightly lit theatres offering burlesque and strip shows. Despite a high-profile police presence, **pickpockets** are always a threat and it's best to avoid coming laden down with expensive camera equipment or an obviously bulging wallet.

Hundreds of competing **mariachi** bands gather here in the evenings, all in their tight, silver-spangled *charro* finery and vast sombreros, to play for anyone who'll pay them. A typical group consists of two or four violins, a brass section of three trumpeters standing some way back so as not to drown out the others, three or four men on guitars of varying sizes and a vocalist, though a truly macho man will rent the band and do the serenading himself. Mariachis take their name, supposedly, from the French *mariage*, it being traditional during the nineteenth-century French intervention to rent a group to play at weddings. You may also come across *norteño* bands from the border areas with their Tex-Mex brand of country music, or the softer sounds of **marimba** musicians from the south. Simply wander round the square and you'll get your fill – should you want to be individually serenaded, pick out a group and negotiate your price.

At the back of the square is a huge market hall in which a whole series of stalls serve simple food and vie furiously for customers. Alternatively, there is at least one prominent *pulquería* on the square (see box, p.131), and a number of fairly pricey restaurant/bars, which try to drown out the mariachi bands with their own canned music, and tempt customers with their no-cover entry. The last Metro leaves at midnight.

1

BALLET FOLKLÓRICO

The **Ballet Folklórico** (☎ 55 5529 9320 to 22, ⊛ balletamalia.com) is a long-running, internationally famed compilation of traditional dances from all over the country, elaborately choreographed and designed, and interspersed with Mexican music and singing. Despite the billing, it isn't really very traditional – although it does include several of the more famous native dances, they are very jazzed up and incorporated into what is, in effect, a regular musical that wouldn't be out of place on Broadway.

The Ballet Folklórico perform in the **Palacio de Bellas Artes** (see p.84), where the theatre is an attraction in itself. Performances are on Sunday at 9.30am and 8.30pm, and Wednesday at 8.30pm. You should try to book at least a couple of days in advance – **tickets** (M$300–800) are available either from the Palacio de Bellas Artes box office direct (Mon–Sat 11am–7pm, Sun 8.30am–7pm) or through Ticketmaster (☎ 55 5325 9000, ⊛ ticketmaster.com.mx) – or arrange to go with an organized tour, for which you'll pay a considerable premium.

actually in colonia Roma (at Durango 230). It's generally considered the most upmarket of Mexico City's department stores. Mon–Fri 11am–8.30pm, Sat 11am–9pm.

Sanborns Madero 4 (near the main post office) ☎ 55 5512 7882, ⊛ sanborns.com.mx; Metro Bellas Artes; map pp.72–73. Sells books, maps and quantities of tacky souvenirs, and also has a sizeable pharmacy, as well as a good restaurant (see p.128), all housed in the beautiful Casa de los Azulejos (see p.83). Daily 7am–1am.

CRAFTS

Central Artesanal Buenavista Aldama 187, just east of the former train station; Metro Buenavista; map pp.72–73. Handicrafts from around the country in what is claimed to be Mexico's largest shop. Rather pricey compared to the Ciudadela, and less characterful. Daily 9am–6pm.

Centro Artesanal de San Juan (Mercado de Curiosidades Mexicanas) About five blocks south of the Alameda along Dolores; Metro San Juan de Letrán; map pp.72–73. Modern tourist-oriented complex that's possibly the least appealing of the major artesanía markets, though there are still deals to be had (particularly in silver), provided you haggle. Mon–Sat 9am–7pm, Sun 9am–4pm.

Ciudadela cnr of Balderas and Emilio Donde; Metro Balderas; map pp.72–73. The best place in the capital to buy regional crafts and souvenirs from every part of the country. If you forgot to pick up a hammock in the Yucatán or some Olinalá lacquerwork in Guerrero, fear not: you can buy them here for not a great deal more. Bargaining has limited rewards. Mon–Sat 9am–7pm, Sun 9am–6pm.

FONART Juárez 89 (at Balderas) ☎ 55 5521 0171, ⊛ fonart.gob.mx; Metro Hidalgo; map pp.72–73. FONART is a government agency that promotes crafts and helps the artisans with materials and marketing. The fixed prices are usually higher than elsewhere, but it is worth visiting to check price and quality before venturing to the markets. FONART also has outlets at Reforma 116 (at Milán; Metro Cuauhtémoc) and the airport (Terminal 2). Mon–Fri 10am–7pm, Sat 10am–6am, Sun 10am–4pm.

MARKETS

Bazar Sábado Plaza San Jacinto, San Ángel; Metrobús Dr Gálvez; map p.107. Very popular open-air art and sculpture market that operates on Sat only, although pretty much the same market moves lock, stock and barrel the next day (Sun) to Parque Sullivan, just north of the Zona Rosa (see p.90). Sat 11am–5pm.

Coyoacán markets Metro Viveros; map p.107. There are two interesting markets in Coyoacán: the daily market, three blocks up from Plaza Hidalgo, on Allende between Malintzin/Xicoténcatl and Plaza Hidalgo, is mostly given over to food, although it also sells crafts, clothing and other things; the Mercado de Artesanías, at Carrillo Puerto 25, is a covered market for crafts and street fashion formerly held on Sun in the main square. Daily market 9am–7pm; Mercado de Artesanías daily (but biggest day Sat) 10am–9pm.

La Lagunilla Spreading along Rayon, a couple of blocks north of the Plaza Garibaldi; buses ("La Villa") heading north on Reforma, or Metro Garibaldi; map pp.72–73. Comes closest to rivalling La Merced in size and variety, but is best visited on a Sun when the *tianguis* expands into the surrounding streets, with more stalls selling stones, used books, crafts and bric-a-brac. Daily 10am–7pm.

Mercado de Sonora Three blocks south of La Merced on Fray Servando Teresa de Mier; Metro La Merced; map pp.72–73. This market is famous for its sale of herbal medicines, medicinal and magical plants, and the *curanderos* (indigenous herbalists) who go there. Nowadays you'll find anything from conjuring tricks and novelties to statues of underground religious figures such as La Santa Muerte and Jesús Malverde. Mon–Sat 8am–7pm, Sun 8am–5pm.

La Merced Corner of Izazaga San Pablo and Eje 1 Ote; Metro La Merced; map pp.72–73. The city's largest market, a collection of huge modern buildings, which still can't contain the vast number of traders who want to set up here. Almost anything you could conceive of finding in a Mexican market (and much more) is sold here, though fruit, vegetables and other foods dominate. Even if you're not buying you could easily spend half a day browsing

1

THE DEMISE OF HAGGLING

Haggling for a bargain is no longer the thrilling (or daunting) prospect it once was in Mexico City. The nation's increasing prosperity and sophistication means that most things have fixed prices. As a tourist (and especially if your Spanish is poor) you can expect people to try to bump up the price occasionally, but on the whole what you see is what you pay.

metre-diameter columns of *nopal* leaves as high as a man, stacks of dried chiles and all manner of hardware from juice presses to volcanic-stone mortars known as *molcajetes*. The Metro takes you right into the heart of things. Daily 6am–6pm.

Palacio de las Flores Corner of Luis Moya and Ernesto Pugibet; Metro Salto de Agua or Balderas; map pp.72–73. A small market selling nothing but flowers – loose, in vast arrangements and wreaths, growing in pots, even paper and plastic. Similar markets can be found in San Ángel and Xochimilco. Mon–Sat 8am–8pm, Sun 8am–2pm.

ENGLISH-LANGUAGE BOOKS AND NEWSPAPERS

International weeklies are available downtown from newspaper stands (especially along 5 de Mayo). Sanborns, dotted all over town, usually have a modest supply of English-language material, much of it business-oriented. Terminal 1 at the airport has numerous small shops partly stocked with English-language magazines and airport novels, plus a few foreign newspapers.

American Book Store Bolivar 23, Centro Histórico ☎ 55 5512 0306; Metro Allende; map pp.72–73. Despite the name, their stock of books in English is limited and mostly business or computer-oriented. OK for a few paperbacks, magazines and newspapers. Mon–Fri 10am–6.45pm, Sat 10am–5.45pm.

La Torre del Papel Callejón de Betlemitas 6a, beside the Museo del Ejército y Fuerza, near the central post office; Metro Bellas Artes; map pp.72–73. Stocks up-to-date newspapers from all over Mexico and Latin America as well as a good showing of US, British, Spanish and Italian newspapers, plus magazines such as *National Geographic*, *The Economist*, *Entertainment Weekly* and *Paris Match*. Mon–Fri 8am–6pm, Sat 9am–3pm.

LA LUCHA LIBRE

Though its popularity has waned in recent years, **lucha libre**, or wrestling, remains one of Mexico's most avidly followed spectator sports. Over a dozen venues in the capital alone host fights several nights a week for a fanatical public. Widely available magazines, comics, photonovels and films recount the real and imagined lives of the rings' heroes and villains, though the nightly telecasts are now a thing of the past.

Mexican wrestling is generally faster, with more complex moves, and more combatants in the ring at any one time than you would normally see in an American or British bout. This can make the action hard to follow for the uninitiated. More important, however, is the maintenance of stage personas, most of whom, heroes or villains, wear **masks**. The *rudos* tend to use brute force or indulge in sneaky, underhanded tactics to foil the opposition, while the *técnicos* use wit and guile to compensate for lack of brawn. This faux battle, not at all unlike WWE on-screen antics, requires a massive suspension of disbelief – crucial if you want to join in the fun.

One of the most bizarre features of wrestling was the emergence of wrestlers as political figures – typically still in costume. The most famous of these, **Superbarrio**, arose from the struggle of Mexico City's tenant associations for fair rents and decent housing (after the 1985 earthquake), to become part of mainstream political opposition, even challenging government officials to step into the ring with him, and acting as a sort of unofficial cheerleader at opposition rallies.

The most famous wrestler of all time, however, was without doubt **El Santo** ("the Saint"). Immortalized in more than twenty movies, with titles such as *El Santo vs the Vampire Women*, he would fight, eat, drink and play the romantic lead without ever removing his mask, and until after his retirement, he never revealed his identity. His reputation as a gentleman in and out of the ring was legendary, and his death in 1984 widely mourned. His funeral was allegedly the second best-attended in Mexican history after that of President Obregón.

In Mexico City, fights can usually be seen on Tuesdays at the **Arena Coliseo**, Peru 77 (Metro Allende), and on Fridays at the **Arena México**, Dr Lucio 197 at Dr Lavista, Colonia Doctores (two blocks south and one east of Metro Balderas, but not a good area to be in at night). Tickets are sold on the door.

SPORT

Sport is probably the city's biggest obsession, and while **football**, **wrestling** and **bullfighting** are the three leading lights, the sporting calendar doesn't stop there. One sport that's missing is **Frontón** (see p.52), which used to be played at Frontón México, on Plaza de la República, but it closed when the players went on strike in 1993, and has never reopened.

HORSE RACING AND RODEO

Hipodromo de las Americas Industria Militar, Lomas de Sotelo ☎55 5387 0600, ⓦhipodromo.com.mx; Metro Cuatro Caminos; map p.66. Horse racing throughout the year, particularly Sat afternoons; buses and *peseros* heading west on Reforma will take you there – look for "Hipodromo".

Rancho del Charro Constituyentes 500 (near the Third Section of Chapultepec Park) ☎55 5277 8706, ⓦasociacionnacionaldecharros.com; pesero (routes #2, #24 and others) along Constituyentes from Metro Chapultepec; map p.93. More exciting horse action in the *charreadas*, or rodeos, put on here by amateur but highly skilled aficionados most weekends (often free); call or check their website to find out what's going on.

FOOTBALL

Fútbol (football, meaning soccer) is undoubtedly Mexico's most popular sport. There are usually at least two games every Sun afternoon (Jan–June & Aug–Nov; check local papers for fixture details) and you can almost always get a ticket (M$100–1500) at the gate. The exceptions are the big games such as major local derbies, and "El Clásico", when América host Chivas from Guadalajara, the biggest team from the country's second-largest city; if you want to be sure of a ticket, they can be bought in advance from Ticketmaster (☎55 5325 9000, ⓦticketmaster.com.mx).

Estadio Azteca Tren Ligero or Ruta #26 ("Xochimilco") colectivo, both from Metro Tasqueña; map p.66. The big games are held at the 114,000-seat Estadio Azteca, which hosted the World Cup finals in 1970 and 1986, and is home to América (Las Águilas, or The Eagles), the nation's most

popular and consistently successful club side. Mexico City's other major team, Atlante (Los Potros, "the Colts"), shares the stadium with América.

Estadio Azul Metro San Antonio or from Metrobús station Ciudad de los Desportes on Insurgentes; map p.66. Cruz Azul (known as Los Cementeros for having been started and still owned by a cement company to the north of the city) pack out Estadio Azul right by the city's main bullring (see p.102).

Estadio Olímpico "Tlalpan" bus from Metro Chilpancingo; map p.66. Elsewhere in the city, the university side, UNAM (Las Pumas), have a strong following at the Estadio Olímpico across the road from the university (see p.110).

BULLFIGHTING

Plaza México Ciudad de los Deportes ⓦlamexico.com; Metrobús down Insurgentes to Ciudad de los Deportes, or walk 10min east from Metro San Antonio; map p.66. This giant 48,000-seat arena is the largest bullring in the world, with elaborate posters around town and most major newspapers advertising upcoming events. Look out too for the weekly coverage of the scene in the press during the season. Tickets can be bought at the gate and you can pay as little as M$70 for general admission to sunny concrete benches far from the action. Ten pesos more and you'll have the luxury of some shade, and from there prices rise rapidly the closer you get to the ring, reaching as much as M$700 for a front-row seat in the shade. During the season (the longer *temporada grande*, late Oct or early Nov to early April, or the shorter *temporada chica*, July to early Oct) fights take place every Sun at 4pm.

DIRECTORY

Banks and exchange ATMs are widespread. If using a bank, note that many will only change money in the morning, and may not change currencies other than US dollars; Banamex is generally your best bet. Most large hotels and shops will change dollar travellers' cheques and cash dollars, but the quickest and easiest places to change money are *casas de cambio*, scattered all over town. In the *centro histórico* try CI Banco, Madero 27, at Bolivar (Mon–Fri 9am–6pm, Sat 10am–4pm), or Cambios Exchange, at Madero 13, near Gante (Mon–Sat 9.30am–7pm, Sun 10am–6pm). You'll find several in the Zona Rosa, especially on Amberes, Londres and Liverpool, and a couple on the south side of Reforma, just south of the Monumento a la Revolución.

Courier services DHL, Madero 70-C, Centro Histórico

☎800 765 6345, ⓦdhl.com.mx; FedEx, Reforma 308, Zona Rosa (Mon–Fri 9am–7pm, Sat 9am–2pm), and other locations (☎800 900 1100, ⓦfedex.com/mx_english).

Cultural institutes Several countries maintain cultural institutes and libraries for their nationals within Mexico City, often allowing short-term visitors to use some of their facilities. They can also be useful places for contacts, and if you're looking for work, long-term accommodation or travelling companions, their notice boards are good places to start. The US has the Biblioteca Benjamín Franklin, Liverpool 31, at Berlin (Mon–Fri 10am–7pm; ☎55 5592 3483, ⓦusembassy-mexico.gov/biblioteca; Metro Cuauhtémoc); the UK has the British Council, Lope de Vega 316, Chapultepec (Mon–Fri 8am–7pm; ☎55 5263 1900; Metro Polanco).

1

Embassies and consulates Australia, Rubén Darío 55, Polanco (☎55 1101 2200, ⑩mexico.embassy.gov.au; Metro Auditorio); Belize, Bernardo de Gálves 215, Lomas de Chapultepec (☎55 5520 1274, ✉embelize@prodigy .net.mx); Canada, Schiller 529, Polanco (☎55 5724 7900, toll-free emergency number for Canadians ☎001 800 514 0129, ⑩canadainternational.gc.ca/mexico-mexique; Metro Polanco); Guatemala, Explanada 1025, Lomas de Chapultepec (☎55 5520 6680, ⑩embajadaguatemalamx .mex.tl); Ireland, Manuel Avila Camacho 76 3°, Lomas de Chapultepec (☎55 5520 5803, ⑩irishembassy.com.mx; Metro Polanco or Auditorio); New Zealand, Jaime Balmes 8 4°, Polanco (☎55 5283 9460, ⑩nzembassy.com/mexico; Metro Polanco); South Africa, Andrés Bello 10 9°, Polanco (☎55 1100 4970, ✉safrica@prodigy.net.mx; Metro Polanco); UK, Río Lerma 71, consular section at Rio Usumacinta 30, Cuauhtémoc (☎55 1670 3200, ⑩ukinmexico.fco.gov.uk/en; Metro Insurgentes); US, Reforma 305 at Danubio, Zona Rosa (☎55 5080 2000, ⑩mexico.usembassy.gov; Metro Insurgentes).

Emergencies All emergency services (police, fire, ambulance) ☎080; police ☎060; fire department ☎068; Red Cross ambulance ☎065; Locatel, which gives information on missing persons and vehicles, medical emergencies, emotional crises and public services ☎55 5658 1111, ⑩locatel.df.gob.mx; tourist helpline ☎55 5250 0123 or ☎55 5250 0151.

Hospitals The American-British Cowdray Hospital (ABC) is at the junction of Observatorio and Sur 136, Col Las Américas (☎55 5230 8000, ⑩abchospital.com; Metro Observatorio). Embassies should be able to provide a list of multilingual doctors if necessary. As for pharmacies, Sanborns offers a wide range of products at most branches, as well as dispensing some prescription drugs. Other options include El Fénix, Madero 41 (at Motolinia; ☎55 5527 0060), and Isabel la Católica 15 (at 5 de Mayo; ☎55 5527 0060). There are homeopathic pharmacies at Mesones 111-B (at 20 Noviembre; ☎55 5542 2755) and República Guatemala 16 (behind the cathedral; ☎55 5512 3527).

Internet Cybercafés generally charge around M$10–15/ hr. Those in the suburbs (there are several in Xochimilco, for example) tend to be slightly cheaper than those in town. In the centre, most places are closed at weekends; options include: Internet Express, ground floor, Centro

---

BULLFIGHTING

Soccer and wrestling may be more popular, but there is no event more quintessentially Mexican than the **bullfight**. Rooted in Spanish machismo and imbued with multiple layers of symbolism and interpretation, it transcends a mere battle of man against animal. If you don't mind the inherent cruelty of the spectacle (essentially you're watching an animal being artfully tortured to death), it's worth attending a *corrida de toros* to see this integral part of the Mexican experience. It is a sport that transcends class barriers; every Sunday afternoon during the winter season men and women from all walks of Mexican society file into the stadium – though some admittedly end up in plush *sombra* (shade) seats while the masses occupy concrete *sol* (sun) terraces.

Each *corrida* lasts around two hours and involves six bulls, all from one ranch, with each of three matadors taking two bulls. Typically there will be two Mexican matadors and one from Spain, which still produces the best performers. Each **fight** is divided into three *suertes* (acts) or *tercios* (thirds), each announced by a trumpet blast. During the first *tercio*, several *toreros* with large capes tire the bull in preparation for the *picadores* who, from their mounts atop heavily padded and blindfolded horses, attempt to force a lance between the bull's shoulder blades to further weaken him. The *toreros* then return for the second *tercio*, in which one of their number (and sometimes the matador himself) will try to stab six metal-tipped spikes (known as *bandilleras*) into the bull in as clean and elegant a manner as possible.

Exhausted and frustrated, but by no means docile, the bull is now considered ready for the third and final *tercio*, the *suerte de muleta*. The matador continues to tire the bull while pulling off as many graceful and daring moves as possible. By now the crowd will have sensed the bravery and finesse of the matador and the spirit of the bull he is up against, and shouts of "¡Olé!" will reverberate around the stadium with every pass. Eventually the matador will entice the bull to challenge him head-on, standing there with its hooves together. As it charges he will thrust his sword between its shoulder blades and, if it is well executed, the bull will crumple to the sand. However barbaric you might think it is, no one likes to see the bull suffer and even the finest performance will garner the matador little praise without a clean kill. Successful matadors may be awarded one of the bull's ears, rarely two, and perhaps two or three times a season the tail as well. An especially courageous bull may be spared and put out to stud, a cause for much celebration, but this is a rare spectacle.

FIESTAS IN MEXICO CITY

Día de los Santos Reyes (Jan 6). Celebrations include a fiesta with dancing at Nativitas, a suburb near Xochimilco.

Bendición de los Animales (Jan 17). Children's pets and peasants' farm animals are taken to the cathedral to be blessed.

Día de San Pedro (June 29). Marked by traditional dancing in San Pedro Actopan, on the southern outskirts of the DF.

Día de Santa Marta (July 25). Celebrated in Milpa Alta, near Xochimilco, with Aztec dances and mock fights between Moors and Christians.

Independence Day (Sept 15). The president of the republic proclaims the famous Grito at 11pm in the Zócalo, followed by the ringing of the Campana de Dolores and a huge firework display.

Día de Santa Cecilia (Nov 22). Santa Cecilia is the patron saint of musicians, and her fiesta attracts orchestras and mariachi bands from all over to Santa Cecilia Tepetlapa, near Xochimilco.

Día de la Señora de Guadalupe (Dec 12). The saint's day of Mexico's favourite Virgin heralds a massive pilgrimage to the Basílica of Guadalupe (see p.114), running for several days, with a more secular celebration of music and dancing.

Comercial Bialos, Donceles 87, on the corner of Brasil (Mon–Sat 10am–6pm; M$20/hr; Metro Zócalo or Allende); Lafoel Internet Service, Donceles 80, at Brasil (Mon–Fri 9am–9pm; M$25/hr; Metro Zócalo or Allende); Alegro, Tacuba 849 (Mon–Fri 9am–8pm; M$25/hr; Metro Allende). In the Zona Rosa, there are several inside the roundabout at Glorieta Insurgentes, all charging around M$20/hr.

Laundry Self-service launderettes are surprisingly rare in Mexico City, but most hotels should be able to point one out. Options include: La Maquina, 2nd floor, Centro Comercial Bialos, Donceles 87, on the corner of Brasil (Mon–Fri 8am–6pm, Sat 9am–2pm); and Lavandería Automática Edison, Edison 91, at Arriaga, near the Plaza de la República (Mon–Fri 9am–7pm, Sat 9am–6pm; Metro Revolución).

Left luggage Most hotels will hold your bags for the rest of the day after you've checked out, and some will allow you to leave excess luggage for several days, sometimes for a small charge. All four main bus terminals and both airport terminals have left-luggage facilities, though prices vary vastly (the Central del Norte is the cheapest).

Photographic supplies For specialist needs, head to C Donceles, between Republica de Argentina and Allende, or Foto Regis at Juárez 80, on the south side of the Alameda (fotoregis.com).

Post office The main post office is on Lázaro Cárdenas at Tacuba, across the street from Bellas Artes (Mon–Fri 8am–5.30pm, Sat 8am–1.30pm). Branch offices (Mon–Fri 8am–4.30pm, Sat 8.30am–noon) can be found at Ponciano Arriaga 11, near the Revolution Monument, and Higuera 23 in Coyoacán, among other places. For speedier and more reliable delivery (though a lot more expensive, of course), see "Courier services", p.137.

Spanish courses There are many Spanish courses in the city, though most people prefer to study in such places as Cuernavaca, San Miguel de Allende and Guanajuato. For those who prefer the metropolis, the most prestigious language school in town is the Universidad Autonomo's Centro de Enseñanza para Extranjeros, located at Universidad 3002 in the Ciudad Universitaria (☎55 5622 2470, cepe.unam.mx). Also worth checking out is planeta.com/mexico.html, which has good links to Mexican language schools.

Telephones Local, domestic long-distance and international phone calls can be made from any public phone with a phonecard. Cheaper international calls can be made via the internet, though very few internet locales offer this service – those which do include a couple inside the roundabout at Glorieta Insurgentes. Otherwise, a number of shops have public phones (for international services look for the blue "Larga Distancia" signs). You can dial direct from most big hotels, but it will cost much more. *Casetas de larga distancia* are closing down in the face of widespread use of cardphones.

Visas and tourist cards Should you lose your tourist card, or want an extension, apply, when your original length of stay is almost finished, to the Instituto de Migración, Ejército National 862, at the western end of Polanco (Mon–Fri 9am–1pm; ☎800 004 6264; *peseros* from Chapultepec to Toreo run along Ejército Nacional). Extensions are pretty much routine if the period is two weeks or less, and should take around half an hour; go to desk D23 – "Ampliación de Estancia". Longer extensions will require copies, form filling and possibly an onward ticket or proof of sufficient funds.

Travel agencies A particularly good firm for youth and student fares is Mundo Joven (mundojoven.com), with offices at Guatemala 4 behind the cathedral (☎55 5518 1755), Eugenio Sue 342, at Homero in Polanco (☎55 5250 7191), and Terminal 1, Sala E2 in the airport (☎55 2599 0155).

Around Mexico City

HOT-AIR BALLOON OVER THE PIRÁMIDE DEL SOL, TEOTIHUACÁN

Around Mexico City

Striking out from Mexico City, there are places worth visiting in every direction. Those covered in this chapter can all be taken in on day trips from the capital, but many are worth a longer stay. The heart of this region is the Valley of México, a mountain-ringed basin dominated by the vast snowcapped peaks of Popocatépetl and Ixtaccíhuatl. Since long before the Mexican nation existed, it has been the country's centre of gravity. Even in the days of the Aztecs, cities such as Texcoco (now in the State of México) and Tlaxcala (now capital of its own little state) vied with Tenochtitlán (Mexico City) for domination.

Much of the region around Mexico City belongs to the **State of México**, whose capital is **Toluca**, to the west, but the state actually reaches all the way round the northern edge of Mexico City and covers its eastern side as well. Also encrusted around the capital are the small states of **Hidalgo** (to the north), **Morelos** (to the south) and **Tlaxcala** (to the east). The city of Puebla, though its state sprawls eastward towards Veracruz, is tucked in tidily next to Tlaxcala, just as **Taxco** is next to Morelos, though actually it belongs to Guerrero, the same state as Acapulco. All around the region, but particularly to the north of Mexico City, you'll be able to see impressive pre-Hispanic sites.

North of Mexico City

The day trip that almost everyone takes from Mexico City is to the pyramids of **Teotihuacán**, about 50km northeast, easily the largest of Mexico's archeological sites, with enough to see to occupy a full day. Also among the destinations accessible as day trips from Mexico City's Terminal del Norte is **Tula**, the centre that succeeded Teotihuacán as the valley's great power. On the way you can stop at **Tepotzotlán**, which holds some of the finest Baroque and colonial art in the country. To the east, **Pachuca** is home to the national photography museum, and nearby is **Real del Monte**, where Cornish miners introduced soccer to Mexico in the nineteenth century.

Teotihuacán

Ruins Daily 7am–5pm; **Museo del Sitio** Daily 9am–4.30pm • M$57, video permit M$45

Most visitors to Mexico City head out at some stage to the pre-Columbian pyramids at **Teotihuacán**: there's a constant stream of tours, buses and cars heading this way, and the ruins can get quite busy, especially on a Sunday. As it's an extensive site that can easily take up most of a day, it's best, if possible, to head out here as early as you can manage and do most of your exploration in the cool of the morning, before the crowds arrive.

The ruins reveal a city planned and built on a massive scale, the great **pyramids** so huge that before their refurbishment one would have passed them by as hills without a

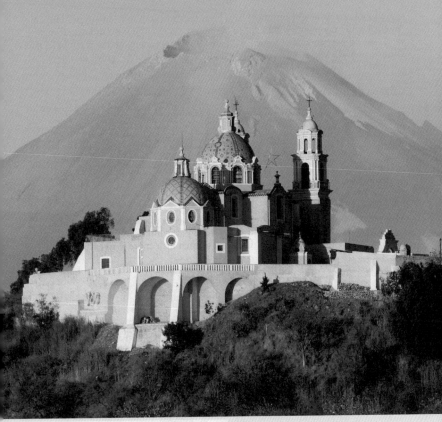

NUESTRA SEÑORA DE LOS REMEDIOS, CHOLULA

Highlights

❶ Teotihuacán The largest pre-Hispanic site in the country, dominated by the huge Pirámide del Sol and only slightly less huge Pirámide de la Luna. **See p.142**

❷ Real del Monte A lovely mountain town with fresh air, and an unexpected Cornish influence dating from the nineteenth century. **See p.155**

❸ Puebla Marvellous Spanish architecture and wonderful cuisine in the original home of *mole poblano*. **See p.161**

❹ Cuernavaca Charming colonial city that's a favourite place to study Spanish. **See p.172**

❺ Taxco Once a silver-mining centre, now a silver-buying centre, this whitewashed hillside town makes a welcome stop on the road to Acapulco. **See p.182**

❻ Malinalco This charmingly picturesque little village is overlooked by a small but breathtakingly scenic archeological site. **See p.187**

❼ Valle de Bravo A peaceful lake surrounded by lush green hills, this popular escape from Mexico City is a blissful world apart and perfect for a few days in the sun. **See p.193**

HIGHLIGHTS ARE MARKED ON THE MAP ON P.144

second look. At its height this must have been the most imposing city in pre-Hispanic America, with a population thought to have been around 150,000 (though estimates vary), spread over an area of some 23 square kilometres (as opposed to the four square kilometres of the ceremonial centre). Back then, every building – grey hulks now – would have been covered in bright polychrome murals.

Calzada de los Muertos

The main entrance, by Puerta 1, is at the southern end of the 2km-long **Calzada de los Muertos** (Causeway of the Dead), which originally extended 1.5km further south, and formed the axis around which the city developed. A broad roadway some 40m wide and linking all the most significant buildings, it was built to impress, with the low buildings that flank most of its length serving to heighten the impact of the two great pyramid temples at the northern end. Other streets, leading off to the rest of the city, originally intersected it at right angles, and even the Río San Juan was canalized so as not to disturb the symmetry (the bridge that then crossed it would have extended the full width of the street).

Its name is somewhat misleading, as it's more a series of open plazas linked by staircases than a simple street. Neither is it in any way linked with the dead, although the Aztecs believed the buildings that lined it, then little more than earth-covered

Querétaro (252km) & Monterrey (954km)

Tampico

Poza Rica (220km)

Guadalajara (544km)

Ixmiquilpan

HIDALGO

Real del Monte

Pachuca ❷

Tula

PUEBLA

MÉXICO

HWY 57

Tepotzotlán

Cuautitlán

❶ **Teotihuacán**

San Juan Teotihuacán

Tepexpan

Chiconcuac

TLAXCALA

Apizaco

Tlaxcala

❖ Cacaxtla

Morelia (303km)

HWY 15

Monumento

Calixtlahuaca

MEXICO CITY

Cerro Pelón

HWY 15

Toluca

Metepec

D.F.

Amecameca

Ixtaccíhuatl (5286m)

Cholula ❼ ❸ Puebla

Jalapa (300km)

Valle de Bravo

Los Saucos

Nevado de Toluca (4577m)

Tenango del Valle

HWY 55

Tenancingo

Malinalco

Chalma

❹

Tepoztlán

Popocatépetl (5452m)

Atlixco

Veracruz (385km)

HWY 134

Ixtapan de la Sal

❻

Cuernavaca

Xochicalco

Cuautla

PUEBLA

Izucar de Matamoros

Grutas de Cacahuamilpa

MORELOS

Taxco ❺

GUERRERO

0   50
kilometres

AROUND MEXICO CITY

Iguala

HWY 95

Acapulco (390km)

Oaxaca (653km)

HIGHLIGHTS

❶ Teotihuacán   ❹ Cuernavaca   ❻ Malinalco

❷ Real del Monte ❺ Taxco   ❼ Valle de Bravo

❸ Puebla

THE RISE AND FALL OF TEOTIHUACÁN

The rise and fall of **Teotihuacán** is almost exactly contemporary with imperial Rome. There is evidence of small agricultural communities in the vicinity dating to around 600 BC; by 200 BC a township had been established on the present site. From then until 1 AD (the period known as the **Patlachique** phase) the population increased, and the city assumed its most important characteristics: the great pyramids of the Sun and Moon were built, and the Calzada de los Muertos laid out. Development continued through the **Tzacualli** and **Miccaotli** phases (1–250 AD) with more construction and the blossoming of artistic expression. Then through the **Tlamimilolpa** phase (250–450 AD) there is evidence of the city's influence (in architecture, sculpture and pottery) occurring at sites throughout modern Mexico and into Guatemala and Honduras. From 450 to around 650 AD (**Xolalpan** phase) it reached its peak in both population and power, with much new building and addition to earlier structures.

By the end of this period, however, there were already signs of decline, and the final phase, the **Metepec**, lasted, at most, a century before the city was sacked, burnt and virtually abandoned. This may have been the result of invasion or internal strife, but the underlying reasons could have been as much ecological as military. Vast forests were cut down to build the city (for use in columns, roof supports and door lintels) and huge quantities of wood burnt to make the lime plaster that coated the buildings. The result was severe soil erosion that left the hillsides as barren as they appear today. In addition, the agricultural effort needed to feed so many people (with no form of artificial fertilizer or knowledge of crop rotation) gradually sapped what land remained of its ability to grow more.

Whatever the precise causes, the city was left, eventually, to a ruination that was advanced even by the time of the Aztecs. To them it represented a holy place from a previous age, and they gave it its present name, which translates as "the place where men became gods". Although Teotihuacán features frequently in Aztec mythology, there are no written records – what we know of the city is derived entirely from archeological and artistic evidence, so that even the original name remains unknown.

mounds, to be the burial places of kings. They are not, and although the exact function of most remains unclear, all obviously had some sacred significance. The design, seen in the many reconstructions, is fairly uniform: low three- or four-storey platforms consisting of vertical panels (*tableros*) supported by sloping walls. In many cases several are built on top of each other – clearly demonstrated in the **Edificios Superpuestos** (superimposed buildings) on the left-hand side shortly beyond the river. Here, excavated structures underneath the present level may have been the living quarters of Teotihuacán's priests.

La Ciudadela

Directly opposite the entrance at Puerta 1 lies **La Ciudadela**, the Citadel. This enormous sunken square, surrounded by stepped platforms and with a low square altar in the centre, was the city's administrative heart, with the houses of its chief priests and nobles arranged around a vast meeting place. Across the open space stands a tall pyramid construction inside which, during excavations, was found the **Temple of Quetzalcoatl**. With the back of the newer pyramid demolished, the elaborate (Miccaotli phase) temple structure stands revealed. Pyramids aside, this is one of the most impressive sections of the whole site, rising in four steps (of an original six), each sculpted in relief and punctuated at intervals by the stylized heads of Quetzalcoatl, the plumed serpent, and **Tlaloc**, the rain god. Traces of the original paint can be seen in places.

Pirámide del Sol

The great **Pirámide del Sol** (Pyramid of the Sun) is Teotihuacán's outstanding landmark, a massive structure 70m high and, of Mexico's ancient buildings, second in size only to Cholula (itself a total ruin). Its base is almost exactly the same size as that of the great

2

Pyramid of Cheops in Egypt, but the lower-angled sides and its stepped nature make it very much lower. There are wonderful views from the top nonetheless, and the bulk is all the more remarkable when you consider the accuracy of its alignment: on two days a year (May 19 and July 25), the sun is directly over the pyramid at noon, and the main west facade faces the point at which the sun sets on these days. This alignment just off the cardinal points determined the line of the Calzada de los Muertos and of the entire city. Equally remarkable is the fact that the 2.5 million tonnes of stone and earth used in its construction were brought here without benefit of the wheel or any beast of burden, and shaped without the use of metal tools. The pyramid you see was reconstructed by **Leopoldo Batres** in 1908, in a thoroughly cavalier fashion. He blasted, with dynamite, a structure that originally abutted the south face, and stripped much of the surface in a search for a more complete building under the present one. In fact, the Pirámide del Sol, almost uniquely, was built in one go at a very early stage of the city's development (about 100 AD), and there is only a very small older temple right at its heart.

TEOTIHUACÁN

The cave

You approach the pyramid by a short staircase leading to the right off the Calzada de los Muertos onto a broad esplanade, where stand the ruins of several small temples and priests' dwellings. The main structure consists of five sloping layers of wall divided by terraces – the large flat area at the top would originally have been surmounted by a sanctuary, long disappeared. Evidence of why this massive structure came to be raised here emerged in 1971 when archeologists stumbled on a tunnel (closed to the public) leading to a clover-leaf-shaped **cave** directly under the centre of the pyramid.

This, clearly, had been some kind of inner sanctuary, a holy of holies, and may even have been the reason for Teotihuacán's foundation and the basis of its influence. Theories abound as to its exact nature, and many fit remarkably with legends handed down through the Aztecs. It's most likely that the cave was formed by a subterranean spring, and came to be associated with Tlaloc, god of rain but also a bringer of fertility, as a sort of fountain of life. Alternatively, it could be associated with the legendary "seven grottoes", a symbol of creation from which all later Mexican peoples claimed to have emerged, or to have been the site of an oracle, or associated with a cult of sacrifice – in Aztec times the flayed skins of victims of Xipe Totec were stored in a cave under a pyramid.

2

Pirámide de la Luna

At the end of the Calzada de los Muertos rises the **Pirámide de la Luna** (Pyramid of the Moon), a smaller structure built slightly later (but still during the Tzacualli phase), whose top, thanks to the high ground on which it's built, is virtually on a level with that of the Pirámide del Sol. The structure is very similar, with four sloping levels approached by a monumental stairway, but for some reason this seems a very much more elegant building: perhaps because of the smaller scale, or perhaps as a result of the approach, through the formally laid-out **Plaza de la Luna**. The top of the pyramid offers the best overview of the site's layout, looking straight back down the length of the central thoroughfare. It is perfect for sunset, though as it is then close to closing time the guards will soon chase you down.

Palacio de Quetzalpapálotl

The **Palacio de Quetzalpapálotl** (Palace of the Quetzal-butterfly) lies to the left of the Plaza de la Luna, behind the low temples that surround it. Wholly restored, it's virtually the only example of a pre-Hispanic roofed building in central Mexico and preserves a unique view of how the elite lived at Teotihuacán. The rooms are arranged around a patio whose elaborately carved pillars give the palace its name – their stylized designs represent birds (the brightly coloured quetzals, though some may be owls) and butterflies. In the galleries around the patio several frescoes survive, all very formalized and symbolic. **Mural art** was clearly very important in Teotihuacán, and almost every building has some decoration, though much has been removed for restoration.

Palacio de los Jaguares and Templo de los Caracoles Emplumados

Two earlier buildings, half-buried under the palace, still have substantial remains. In the **Palacio de los Jaguares**, jaguars in feathered headdresses blow conch shells from which emerge curls of music, or perhaps speech or prayers to Tlaloc (who appears along the top of the mural); in the **Templo de los Caracoles Emplumados** (Temple of the Plumed Snail Shells), you see a motif of feathers and seashells along with bright green parrots. Other murals, of which only traces remain, were found in the temples along the Calzada de los Muertos between the two pyramids.

Tepantitla, Tetitla and Atetelco

Mural art was not reserved for the priests' quarters – indeed, some of the finest frescoes have been found in outlying apartment buildings. The famous *Paradise of Tlaloc* mural, reproduced in the Museo Nacional de Antropología (see p.95), was discovered at

2

Tepantitla, a residential quarter of the old city across the road from the back of the Pirámide del Sol. Only a part of it survives here, but there are others in the complex depicting a procession of priests and a ball-game. All have great vitality and an almost comic-strip quality, with speech bubbles emerging from the figures' mouths, but their themes always have a religious rather than a purely decorative intent. More can be seen at **Tetitla**, to the west of the main site, and **Atetelco**, a little further west, just off the map on p.144.

Museo del Sitio

Plan to spend at least some of your time in Teotihuacán's excellent **Museo del Sitio**, situated behind the Pirámide del Sol and surrounded by a lovely sculpture and botanical garden. In the **first room**, artefacts from the site are well laid out and effectively lit to highlight the key features of each item in the cool interior. There's just about everything you would expect of a ritual site and living city, from sharp-edged obsidian tools and everyday ceramics to some fine polychrome vessels decorated with animal and plant designs, and a series of five ceremonial braziers or censers ornamented with appliqué flowers, butterflies and shields.

Vast windows framing the Pirámide del Sol take up one entire wall of the **second room**, where you walk across a glass floor over a relief model of the entire city as it might once have been. The glass floor leads you to the **third room**, where burials from under the Temple of Quetzalcoatl have been relocated, along with statues of gods (often bottom-lit to accentuate the gruesome features), including a trio of braziers carried by the sun god Huitzilopochtli.

ARRIVAL AND DEPARTURE   TEOTIHUACÁN

By bus Buses leave (every 15min, 6am–9pm; 1hr) from Mexico City's Terminal del Norte (see p.118). Go to the second-class (left-hand) side of the bus station and look for the Autobuses Teotihuacán stand in Sala 8 (☎ 55 5781 1812); be aware that these buses have, from time to time, been targeted by bandits, so don't bring a lot of cash or your passport; carry a photocopy instead. A slightly quicker alternative is to catch the Metro to Indios Verdes (line 3) and head to the northern end of the parking area outside, from where buses leave frequently for "Las Pirámides". A road, the Carretera de Circunvalación, provides access to the main structures through one of six gates (each with parking and lines of souvenir stalls): buses might arrive at any *puerta* (gate), though Puerta 1 and Puerta 2 are the most common. These are also the best places to wait for buses back to Mexico City (the last at 9.45pm), but late in the day most return buses visit all the gates before departing the site.

EATING

Cinco Estrellas Outside Puerta 2 ☎ 594 956 2555. This is one of a little group of cheap eateries just outside Puerta 2 – all remarkably good value – whose representatives will be on your case as soon as you set foot outside the gate (you can leave the site and re-enter, so long as you hold on to your ticket). A comida corrida here will set you back the princely sum of M$49, and that includes a free glass of tequila or *pulque*, or you can get a portion of quesadillas for M$28, and they also do breakfasts. Daily 8am–8pm.

La Gruta 200m west of Puerta 5 ☎ 594 956 0104. A fancy and very impressive-looking restaurant, set deep in an open-sided cave, with white-jacketed waiters and a live show on Sat at 3.30pm, and Sun at 3.30pm and 5.30pm. The setting is wonderful, but the food and service don't always match the price, with offerings such as chicken with red and green *mole* (M$185) or Tampico-style tenderloin with Mexican trimmings (M$300). Daily 11am–7pm.

Las Pirámides main entrance, Puerta 1 ☎ 594 956 8877. The main restaurant and bar on the site itself offers a three-course tourist menu for M$145–182 and some basic à la carte dishes such as chicken in red or green *mole* (M$169). Prices are high considering the quality of the food, but the view of the site from the top-floor restaurant is great. Daily 10am–6pm.

Tepotzotlán

TEPOTZOTLÁN lies en route from the capital to Tula, and it's possible to visit the two on one long day from the metropolis. Tepotzotlán is also close enough to the city to be a morning's excursion, though once you're there, you may find the town's slow pace and colonial charm seduces you into staying longer. On Saturdays, with loads of Mexican visitors, the festive atmosphere is particularly enjoyable, while on Sundays a crafts market draws large crowds. In the week before Christmas, Tepotzotlán's renowned *pastorelas*, or **Nativity plays**, are staged here (with accommodation booked up far in advance). At other times of the year, you may catch a concert in the church or cloisters.

Museo Nacional del Virreinato

Beside the cathedral on the main plaza • Tues–Sun 9am–5.45pm • M$62 (M$40 for video permit); guides around M$50 • ⓦ virreinato.inah.gob.mx

Atmosphere apart, the reason most people come to Tepotzotlán is to see the magnificent Baroque **Church of San Francisco Javier** and the adjacent **Colegio**, now together forming the **Museo Nacional del Virreinato** (Viceroyalty Museum). The entire museum is in Spanish, but English-speaking guides can be found for hire at the museum's entrance. The church was founded by the Jesuits, who arrived in 1580 on a mission to convert the Otomí locals. Most of the huge complex you see today was established during the following century but constantly embellished right up to the expulsion of the Jesuits in 1767. The **facade** of the church – which looks onto the main square and is considered one of the finest examples of churrigueresque architecture in the country – was completed barely five years before. The wealth and scale of it all gives some idea of the power of the Jesuits prior to their ousting; after they left, it became a seminary for the training of regular priests until the late nineteenth century, when the Jesuits were briefly readmitted. The Revolution led to its final abandonment in 1914.

Iglesia de San Francisco Javier

The main entrance to the Colegio de San Francisco Javier leads into the **Claustro de los Aljibes**, with a well at the centre and pictures of the life of Ignatius Loyola (founder of the Jesuits) around the walls. Off the cloister is the entrance to the church, the **Iglesia de San Francisco Javier**. If the facade is spectacular, it's still barely preparation for the dazzling interior. Dripping with gold, and profusely carved with a bewilderment of saints and cherubim, it strikes you at first as some mystical cave of treasures. The main body of the church and its chapels house five huge gilded cedar-wood altarpieces, stretching from ceiling to floor and beautifully lit to bring out the fascinating detail from both the alabaster around the windows and discreetly placed lamps. Much of the painting on the main altar (dedicated to the church's patron saint) is attributed to **Miguel Cabrera**, sometimes considered to be Mexico's Michelangelo, whose talents are also on display towards the main church door, which is framed by two large oils, one depicting worshippers bathing in the blood from Jesus's crucifixion wounds.

Camarín and Capilla of the Virgen de Loreto

All this is still only the start, for hidden to one side is arguably the greatest achievement of Mexican Baroque, the octagonal **Camarín de la Virgen**. It's not a large room, but every centimetre is elaborately decorated and the hand of the native craftsmen is clearly evident in the exuberant carving – fruit and flowers, shells and abstract patterns crammed in between the angels. There's a mirror angled to allow visitors to appreciate the detail of the ceiling without straining their necks. The Camarín is reached through the **Capilla de la Virgen de Loreto**, inside which is a "house" tiled with eighteenth-century *azulejos* – supposedly a replica of Mary's house at Nazareth, in which Jesus grew up.

Around the central cloister

Directly off the **central cloister** of the Colegio are rooms packed with a treasure of beautiful silver reliquaries and crucifixes, censers, custodia, vestments and even a pair of

2

silver sandals; notice, too, the painted panel depicting the spiritual conquest of New Spain and showing the relative influence of the Franciscans, Augustinians and Dominicans in the sixteenth century, and above it the diagram of churches liberally dotted among the lakes of the Valley of México.

The **upper storey** around the cloister contains more religious paintings than anyone could take in on one visit, including portraits of the Society of Jesus and others of beatific eighteenth- and nineteenth-century nuns. Here too is the **Cristo del Árbol**, a crucifix carved towards the end of the seventeenth century from a single piece of wood.

Claustro de los Naranjos and Huerta

Stairs descend to the **Claustro de los Naranjos**, planted with orange and lemon trees and with a fountain in the middle. Around it are displays of wooden religious statuary – Balthazar and Caspar, two of the three Magi, are particularly fine. Other rooms contain more colonial miscellany – lacquerwork, furniture (notably an inlaid wooden desk) and clothes – and some temporary exhibition space. Outside extends the walled **Huerta**, or garden, some seven acres of lawns, shady trees and floral displays, as well as vegetables and medicinal herbs cultivated as they would have been by the monks. It is not as well tended as it could be, but makes a break from the museum and has a few architectural pieces and large sculptures dotted around, including, at the far end, the original eighteenth-century **Salto del Agua** that stood at the end of the aqueduct carrying water from Chapultepec into Mexico City (a replica of the fountain stands in the capital now, near Metro Salto del Agua).

The Botica and Capilla Doméstica

Returning to the main cloister, you find a mixed bag, with pre-Hispanic statuary leading on to details of Spanish exploration, suits of armour, exquisite marquetry boxes and a sequence of rooms, one filled with ivory statues, another laid out for Spanish nobles to dine, and then the **Botica**, or pharmacy, with bottles, jars, pestles and mortars, and all the other equipment of an eighteenth-century healer. The **Capilla Doméstica** also opens off the cloister, a whirl of painted and gilded Rococo excess, with a magnificent gilded *retablo* full of mirrors and little figures.

ARRIVAL AND DEPARTURE   TEPOTZOTLÁN

By bus Buses to Tepotzotlán from Metro Cuatro Caminos or Metro Rosario in Mexico City are slow, rattling their way round the suburbs for what feels like hours (though the total journey is actually little over 1hr) before finally leaving the city. Alternatively, take an indirect ("via Refinario") Tula bus or a second-class Querétaro bus from the Terminal del Norte to the Caseta de Tepotzotlán, a road junction about 200m before the first motorway tollbooths.

From there it's about a 15min walk (or 5min by local bus or taxi) west along Av Insurgentes into the centre of Tepotzotlán. The same road junction by the tollbooths is also the place to pick up buses on to Tula or back to Mexico City. Local buses and *peseros* serve Cautitlán and Lechería stations on the suburban train line to Buenavista in Mexico City (but not all those going to Cautitlán serve the station).

ACCOMMODATION

The town's most central hotel, the *Posada San José*, beside *Pepe's* on the central plaza (see opposite), was undergoing renovation at time of research and is Tepotzotlán's best sleeping option if it's ready when you visit.

Hotel Posada Los Angeles Av Insurgentes 10 ☎ 55 5876 0523. One of four pleasant hotels occupying a cul-de-sac at the southeast corner of the cathedral complex, this is well located, being a short stroll from the busier centre, and with various eating options nearby. All rooms are en suite and tastefully decorated. M$350

Hotel Principal Calle Eva Samano 17 (a block north of the plaza) ☎ 55 5876 9026. An inexpensive and very central option which offers significant discounts on weeknights, as well as for those who pay with cash. Two tiers of eighteen basic rooms, all en suite and clean, look out over a slim courtyard with a café above the entrance. M$250

EATING

Hostería del Convento Plaza Virreinal (east side) ☎ 55 5876 1646, ⓦ hosteriadelconvento.com.mx. Quite pricey but set beautifully in the grounds of the seminary, and serving excellent Mexican and international food (steak with chipotle M$147, filet mignon with fries and salad M$153). They also do a M$180 buffet. Daily 10am–8pm.

Municipal market On the west side of the plaza. Has multiple stands offering classic Mexican dishes such as *birria*, *pozole* and *huarache* in a classic Mexican setting. Pull up a stool at any of the informal eateries and enjoy the lively atmosphere. You'll be pestered by the stand owners for custom when you walk in, but the stands with the most customers are usually the safest bets, so don't let the hollering influence your decision, nor should you expect it to continue once you plump for a set stand. Daily 6am–6pm.

Pepe's Plaza Virreinal 13 ☎ 55 5876 0520. The *Hotel Posada San José's* restaurant, with a terrace directly opposite the Church of San Francisco Javier, which you can gaze at while enjoying their speciality, *cabrito Pepe* (slow-roasted goat; M$288). If you want to get pre-Hispanic, you can precede it with a plate of *escamoles* (ant eggs) as a starter (M$230). Daily 8am–9pm.

Los Virreyes Plaza Virreinal 32 ☎ 55 5876 0235. This relaxing and well-run restaurant on the north side of the square offers gourmet dining on its airy terrace overlooking the square and the smog you've just emerged from further to the south. Don't allow the waiters to lead you up here if you're only after a few drinks and a snack, though, as much of the local fare is available for less in the downstairs bar, including Mexican classics such as mescal worms (M$240) and rabbit *al pastor* (in an *adobe* of dried chiles; M$150). At weekends they do a M$110 buffet until 6pm, and from 1pm on Sun the dishes available in the buffet include paella. Daily 8am–8pm.

Tula

The modern city of **Tula de Allende** lies on the edge of the Valley of México, 50km north of Mexico City. A pleasant enough regional centre with an impressive, if fortress-like, mid-sixteenth-century **cathedral and Franciscan monastery**, Tula is most notable for its wonderful pre-Hispanic pyramid site.

Tula's archeological site

2km north of Tula's town centre • Daily 9am–5pm • M$52, free Sun, video permit M$45 • From the bus station (a 30min walk), turn right up Xicohténcatl to the main road (Ocampo), then turn right again, over the river and left before the train tracks (by the *Hotel Sharon*), following signs to "Zona Arqueológica" (or the pyramid symbol); on buses into town, ask to be dropped off beside the train tracks by the *Hotel Sharon*; a taxi from town is around M$30

TULA AND THE TOLTECS

In legend at least, the mantle of Teotihuacán fell on Tollan, or **Tula**, as the next great power to dominate Mexico. The **Aztecs** regarded the city they constructed as the successor to Tula and hence embellished its reputation – the streets, they said, had been paved with gold and the buildings constructed from precious metals and stones, while the **Toltecs**, who founded Tula, were regarded as the inventors of every science and art. In reality, it seems unlikely that Tula was ever as large or as powerful a city as Teotihuacán had been – or as Tenochtitlán was to become – and its period of dominance (about 950–1150 AD) was relatively short. Yet all sorts of **puzzles** remain about the Toltec era, and in particular their apparent connection with the Yucatán – much of the architecture at **Chichén Itzá**, for example, appears to have been influenced by the Toltecs. Few people believe that the Toltecs actually had an empire that stretched so far: however warlike (and the artistic evidence is that Tula was a grimly militaristic society, heavily into human sacrifice), they would have lacked the manpower, resources or any logical justification for such expansion.

One possible answer lies in the legends of **Quetzalcoatl**. Adopted from Teotihuacán, the plumed serpent attained far more importance here in Tula, where he is depicted everywhere. At some stage Tula apparently had a ruler identified with Quetzalcoatl who was driven from the city by the machinations of the evil god Texcatlipoca, and the theory goes that this ruler, defeated in factional struggles within Tula, fled with his followers, eventually reaching Maya territory, where they established a new Toltec regime at Chichén Itzá. Though popular for a long time, this hypothesis has now fallen out of fashion following finds at Chichén Itzá that seem to undermine it (see p.749).

Only a small part of Tula's **archeological site** itself is of interest: though the city spreads over some considerable area only some of it has been excavated, and the outlying digs are holes in the ground, meaningful only to the archeologists who created them. The ceremonial centre, however, has been partly restored. The significance of the site is made much clearer if your Spanish is up to translating all the information presented in the **museum** (same hours) by the entrance, and filled with fragments of Atlantes, Chac-mools and basalt heads, along with assorted bits of sculpture and frieze.

2

Templo de Tlahuizcalpantecuhtli and Atlantes

The site's centrepiece is the low, five-stepped pyramid of the **Templo de Tlahuizcalpantecuhtli** (Temple of the Morning Star, or Pyramid B), atop which stand the **Atlantes** – giant, 5m-tall basalt figures that originally supported the roof of the sanctuary and represent Quetzalcoatl in his guise as the morning star, dressed as a Toltec warrior. The figures wear elaborately embroidered loincloths, sandals and feathered helmets, and sport ornaments around their necks and legs – for protection, each bears a sun-shaped shield on his back and a chest piece in the form of a stylized butterfly. Each also carries an *atlatl*, or spear-thrower, in his right hand and arrows or javelins in his left.

Other pillars are carved with more warriors and gods. Reliefs such as these are a recurrent theme in Tula: the entire temple was originally faced in sculpted stone, and although it was pillaged long ago you can still see some remnants – prowling jaguars and eagles, symbols of the two great warrior groups, devouring human hearts. In front of the temple is a great L-shaped colonnade, where the partly reconstructed pillars originally supported a huge roof under which, perhaps, the priests and nobles would review their troops or take part in ceremonies in the shade. Part of a long bench survives, with its relief decoration of a procession of warriors and priests. More such benches survive in the **Palacio Quemado** (Burnt Palace – it was destroyed by fire), next to the temple on the western side. Its three rooms, each a square, were once covered with a small central patio to let light in. The middle one is the best preserved, still with much of its original paint and two Chac-mools.

The ball-courts and the Coatepantli

The main square of the city stood in front (south) of the temple and palace, with a low altar platform in the centre and the now ruinous pyramid of the Templo Mayor on the eastern side. The larger of two **ball-courts** in the central area is on the western side of the square: although also largely ruined, this marks one of the closest links between Tula and Chichén Itzá, as it is of identical shape and orientation to the great ball-court there. To the north of the temple stands the **Coatepantli** (Serpent Wall), elaborately carved in relief with images of human skeletons being eaten by giant snakes; beyond this, across an open space, there's a second ball-court, smaller but in better order.

Sala Histórica Quetzalcoatl

C Zaragoza, just off the main square • Tues–Sun 9am–5pm • Free

In Tula itself, a small local museum, the **Sala Histórica Quetzalcoatl**, hosts art exhibitions on the ground floor, and upstairs has a small display of archeological finds, including a mammoth tusk and some Toltec artefacts, which won't take you more than ten minutes to check out.

ARRIVAL AND DEPARTURE   **TULA**

By bus The bus station is on Xicohténcatl, close to the town centre. For the town centre, turn right as you leave, take the first left (Rojo del Rio) to the end, where a right turn into Hidalgo brings you to the cathedral and main square (Plaza de la Constitución). If you're coming from Mexico City's Terminal del Norte, note that tickets to Tula are sold by Autobuses del Valle de Mezquital – the desk furthest to your left when you enter the terminal. The second-class service can set you down at the Caseta de Tepozotlán (see p.150; 1hr).

Destinations Mexico City Nte (direct every 40min; 1hr 30min; second class "via Refinario" every 15min; 2hr); Pachuca (every 40min; 1hr 15min); Querétaro (9 daily; 2hr 30min).

ACCOMMODATION

Casablanca Pasaje Hidalgo 11 (off C Hidalgo by no. 129) ☎773 732 1186, ⓦcasablancatula.com. Friendly staff and sparkling rooms – all en suite – around a brightly painted tangerine and orange courtyard (with parking) make this a good choice. Windows face into the courtyard, so rooms at the top get the most light. M$400

Cuéllar 5 de Mayo 23, opposite the cathedral ☎773 732 0442, ⓦhotelcuellar.com. A modern hotel with cool, shaded rooms, a sunny courtyard, small pool and outdoor jacuzzi, plus parking space and wi-fi. M$600

Real Catedral Zaragoza 106, next to the museum ☎773 732 0813, ⓦhotelrealcatedral.com. A charming old colonial building on the outside, but less so within, especially in the cheapest rooms, which are small and dark with low ceilings. All stays include breakfast and they'll usually do you a deal on the price, especially if you're staying more than one night. M$650

EATING

Casablanca Hidalgo 114 ☎773 732 2274. A large, slightly old-fashioned hall where they serve breakfasts (M$54–159) and, from 1.30pm onwards, buffets with salad bar (M$149), and comidas corridas (M$99). Mon–Fri 7am–9pm, Sat 7.30am–9pm, Sun 7.30am–6pm.

Crepería D'Pilli North side of Plaza de la Constitución. A small café and crêperie on the main square serving crêpes both sweet (chocolate M$65) and savoury (ham and cream cheese M$59). Daily noon–10pm.

El Rey Juanelo Hidalgo at Morelos (at the back of a shopping arcade). If you're venturing no further into Hidalgo state, then this is the place to try out the region's famous pastes, Mexicanized Cornish Pasties brought here by English miners in the nineteenth century. Savoury and sweet fillings are various (around M$12), although be warned that they are a lot spicier than their European ancestors. Daily 8am–8pm.

Wings & Beer Southeast corner of the plaza ☎773 148 1080. A rooftop spot serving up exactly what the name suggests, this is one of the town's few bars and a good place to people-watch as the sun sets over the archeological site in the distance. Prepares a good *michelada*, and also offers more filling meals from its extensive menu. Daily noon–11pm.

Pachuca

In recent years, **Pachuca**, the capital of Hidalgo state, has burst out of the ring of hills that once hemmed it in, its expansion fuelled by the need to move industry away from Mexico City. It remains a fairly small city by Mexican standards, although the uncontrolled expansion is obvious on the hills surrounding its centre, which is easily walkable and full of colonial mansions built on the profits of the rich silver-mining country all about. If you have the time, it is worth venturing to nearby towns where the mining heritage is more apparent and the clean mountain air is refreshing.

The zócalo and around

Pachuca's centre boasts two main squares: **Plaza de la Constitución**, where *colectivos* from the bus station will drop you, and a block to its southeast (south down Hidalgo then east along Ocampo), the **zócalo**. The zócalo, all rather prim and proper, is dominated by the **Reloj Monumental**, a 40m Neoclassical clock tower whose construction was funded by the Cornish-born local mining magnate Francis Rule in 1910 to mark a hundred years of Mexican independence. There's further evidence of Pachuca's Cornish connection just a block north of the zócalo (or east of Plaza de la Constitución) at Allende 102, where the **Methodist Church** (daily 6.30am–7pm) was originally built for Cornish miners at the beginning of the twentieth century. For more on Pachuca's Cornish heritage, see p.155.

Museo de la Fotografía

Inside the Centro Cultural Hidalgo on Casasola (at Hidalgo), reached by walking three blocks south along Matamoros, then left for 300m along Revolución (which becomes Arista) • Tues–Sun 10am–6pm • Free

The late sixteenth-century ex-Convento de San Francisco now operates as the **Centro Cultural Hidalgo**, and contains Pachuca's most compelling museum, the **Museo de la Fotografía**. Drawing on over a million photographic works stored here as part of the national archive, the museum does a great job of showcasing both Mexican and foreign photographers. Early photographic techniques are illustrated before you move on to the gallery space, where displays change constantly but almost always include images from the Casasola Archive. The pre-eminent Mexican photojournalist of his day, **Agustín Casasola** chronicled both the Revolution and everyday life in its wake, forming an invaluable record of one of Mexico's more turbulent periods.

Museo de Minería

Mina 110, one block south and two blocks east of the zócalo • Tues–Sun 10am–6pm • M$30 • ⓦ distritominero.com.mx

Pachuca's **Museo de Minería** is of historical importance because it houses the state's mining archives, but from a visitor's point of view, unless you have a particular interest in the history of mining, its exhibition of mineral samples and old mining equipment (picks, helmets, lamps and the odd ore cart) is only mildly diverting.

ARRIVAL AND INFORMATION

PACHUCA

By bus The bus station is about 5km south of the centre. *Colectivos* outside run frequently to Plaza de la Constitución in the town centre.
Destinations Mexico City Nte (every 10min; 2hr); Mexico City airport (13 daily; 2hr); Puebla (20 daily; 2hr); Tula (second class every 15–20min; 2hr 30min; direct every 30–60min; 1hr 15min).

By colectivo *Colectivos* to the bus station ("Centro-Central"; 10min) depart from the northwest corner of Plaza de la Constitución. To Real del Monte (20min) and Mineral del Chico (45min), they depart from one block north of Plaza de la Constitución, at La Raza with Carranza. Note that there is no direct transport between Real del Monte and Mineral del Chico, so you have to come back to Pachuca to get from one to the other, and the last *colectivos* back to Pachuca from both of them leave at around 7pm.

Tourist information There's a small tourist office (daily 8am–6pm; ☎771 715 1411) in the base of the Reloj Monumental clock tower on the zócalo. The state tourist office has a website at ⓦ www.hidalgo.travel.

ACCOMMODATION

América Victoria 203, a block south of the zócalo ☎771 715 0055. A very basic option, but not bad for the price and its fairly central location, with rooms arranged around a very orange patio, with bath, TV and some with king-size beds. M$180

Ciro's Plaza de Independencia 100, north side of the zócalo ☎771 715 5351, ⓦ hotelciros.com. A very centrally located three-star with a bright orange facade, offering a slightly higher standard of comfort than most Pachuca hotels, but less character. Pleasantly furnished rooms have phone and TV; and those at the front have views over the zócalo. There are often promotional discounts available, and a junior suite doesn't cost much more than a standard room. Breakfast included. M$1279

Emily Plaza de Independencia, south side of the zócalo ☎771 715 0828, ⓦ hotelemily.com.mx. This four-star is run by the same firm as *Ciro's* across the zócalo, with the same orange facade, though it's slightly posher, with a restaurant. A junior suite here costs the same as a standard room, and also the same as a junior suite at *Ciro's*, and there are master suites as well. Breakfast included. M$1433

Gran Hotel Independencia Plaza independencia 116, west side of zócalo ☎771 715 0515 ⓦ granhotel independencia.com. Grand it ain't, but it is the cheapest option on the plaza, with clean and comfortable rooms, all en suite, as well as a colourful cantina-style bar in the downstairs courtyard. Staff can help with arranging trips in the surrounding area. M$550

★ Hotel de los Baños Matamoros 205, east side of the zócalo ☎771 713 0700. The most characterful place in town, just off the zócalo, with carpeted rooms, each with TV and bathroom, around a central, enclosed courtyard. For very little more than the standard room prices, you can opt for type "A" doubles with attractively carved wooden furniture, or type "B" where the craftsmanship is decidedly over the top. M$580

EATING

Pachuca is known in Mexico for **pastes**, which originated with the Cornish pasties once made by miners working in nearby Real del Monte (see opposite). They still come *tradicional* (or *tipo Inglés*), filled with ground meat, onion, potato and *jalapeños* (for that Mexican twist), as well as with fillings such as chicken *mole* or *refritos*. Though they differ in shape, they're closely related to typical Mexican empanadas, which are usually sold in the same shops and are stuffed with tuna, pineapple or even rice pudding. You'll find bakeries selling *pastes* all over the region.

Alex Steak Glorieta Revolución 102, about 500m south of the zócalo ☎771 713 0056. Enormous and beautifully prepared steaks are the speciality here, with most cuts available. The house steak (M$209) comes with mushroom sauce, and they do a barbecue brunch on Sun in summer (from 8am). Daily noon–midnight.

La Gran Titania Guerrero 1000. On the northeast corner of the food market where more delights can be found, this rustically styled eatery offers good *carnitas* (non-traditional meats) such as tongue, ribs and *surtido* to get your Mexican juices flowing. Hailed throughout the town as a good hangover-cure spot. Daily 9am–10pm.

Mi Antiguo Café Matamoros 115, east side of the zócalo ☎771 107 1837. Good for espressos, croissants, burgers and *antojitos* (such as chicken *fajitas* at M$72), with set breakfasts (M$57–76) and a lunch-time menu (M$62–66). Mon–Sat 8.30am–10.30pm, Sun 9am–9pm.

Mirage Guerrero 1210, a block west of the zócalo and 300m south ☎771 719 0909. Airy family-style restaurant, where you can try *tacos mineros* (chicken

tacos with salsa and cheese) for M$71, or *enchiladas suizas* for M$69. Mon–Fri 8am–10pm, Sat 8am–11.30pm, Sun 9am–10pm.

Pastes el Billar Ocampo 100, just off the east side of the zócalo ☎771 715 6060. This firm claims to have been the first to sell Cornish pasties in Mexico, and they still do Cornish-style meat and potato *pastes* (M$12), as well as chicken *pastes* with red or green *mole*, and rice pudding versions for afters. Daily 9am–7pm.

Reforma Matamoros 111, east side of the zócalo. An informal place on the plaza, offering a lunch-time menu (M$63) and *antojitos* including enchiladas and *chilaquiles* (both M$47, with red or green sauce). Mon–Sat 8am–10pm, Sun 9am–6pm.

Real del Monte

Fourteen kilometres north of Pachuca, draped across pine-clad hills, sits **REAL DEL MONTE** (aka Mineral del Monte), a once very wealthy silver-mining town, and, at over 2700m, a nice retreat from Mexico City. It's a quietly appealing place where you can wander around the well-tended streets, and carefully explore mining relics in the surrounding hills. The town's architecture is largely Spanish colonial, but is given an odd twist by the almost exclusive use of red corrugated-iron roofing, and the existence of Cornish-style cottages with their double-pitched rooflines.

Paste Museum

Av Juarez 114, at the town entrance • Mon & Wed–Sun 9am–6pm (last tour at 5.15pm) • M$35

Not content with selling the town's signature delicacy at every possible outlet, Real del Monte now boasts the world's only museum dedicated to *pastes*. The highlight of the tour is the making and subsequent consumption of your own creation, filled with either meat and potato, or refried beans for those of a Mexican persuasion. All explanations are in Spanish, including the baffling fifteen-minute video documenting the pasty's exodus from Cornwall to the mountains of central Mexico and the wider world. There's an interesting collection of ovens used to make the baked turnover through the ages. Don't miss the awkward photos of Prince Charles' visit during its 2012 inauguration.

The British cemetery

On the edge of town • Daily 10am–6pm

Many of Real del Monte's original Cornish tin miners (see box below), who were Methodist rather than Catholic, now rest in the British cemetery (**Panteón Inglés**), the visiting of which entails a bit of a climb. You'll need to find the caretaker to open it up, but he should, with luck, be somewhere nearby (and will appreciate a tip for his trouble).

HIDALGO'S CORNISH CONNECTION

In 1824, a British firm took over the old **silver mines** in Real del Monte, which had first been opened by the Spanish in the mid-sixteenth century. Needing some mining expertise, the British brought over some 350 **Cornish tin miners** to help run the pits, but pulled out in 1848, to be replaced by a Mexican successor firm. Most of the tin miners stayed on, however, and their legacy in Pachuca and Real del Monte lives on too, in the form of some surprisingly authentic **Cornish pasties**, and the introduction of **fútbol** (soccer), which was played for the first time on Mexican soil in Real del Monte. A plaque in the car park at the southern end of Hidalgo marks the spot where that first game was played, and it was this same Cornish community who went on to found Pachuca football club and the Mexican football league (see box, p.156).

Mina de Acosta

Guerrero, at the northeastern end of town • Wed–Sun: summer 10am–6pm; winter 9.30am–5pm • M$30, photo permit M$20, video permit M$50 • ⓦ distritominero.com.mx

This old silver mine, now converted into a museum, was in use from 1727 until 1985. The chimney and elevator date from the nineteenth century. Not only can you can see all the workings and ore bogeys, but you can even go inside one of the original mining tunnels, with a free guided tour.

2

FOOTBALL IN MEXICO

As in much of Latin America, **fútbol** in Mexico is a national addiction, if not an obsession. Turn on the TV and often as not you'll find a match. If you can get to see a live game, it's a different experience entirely. For **up-to-date information** on Mexican league teams, fixtures and tables, visit ⓦ futmex.com or ⓦ futbolmexicano.net.

ORIGINS

Football was introduced to Mexico in the nineteenth century by Cornish miners in Real del Monte, Hidalgo (see box, p.155), and it was in that state, by descendants of those same Cornishmen, that Mexico's first football club, Pachuca, was founded in 1901. The football **league** was created six years later.

THE LEAGUE TABLE

Mexico's football league follows a complicated ladder system: the first division is divided into three tables of six teams each, which are decided by the previous season's placings, with the league champions placed first in table one, second placed top of table two and so on. The top two teams of each table compete in a play-off for the league championship.

There are two **seasons** a year: Apertura (Aug–Nov) and Clausura (Jan–June). At the end of the Clausura season, the two seasons' winners (if they are different) compete to decide that year's champion of champions.

Relegation to a lower division is decided over a two-season (yearly) loss average, so it is, in fact, technically possible to come first in the league and be relegated in the same season. However, relegation need not be the disaster that it might seem. Take, for example, Puebla C.F., who, when relegated in 1999, simply bought the team promoted from Primera B (Curtodores), changed their name to Puebla and relocated them, which is perfectly legal under Mexican financial regulations. Similarly, there are no regulations preventing anyone from owning more than one team, which can lead to a clash of interests that are never more than speculated upon; suspicion of corruption is rife but rarely, if ever, investigated.

WATCHING A GAME

Matches are always exciting and enjoyed by even the most diehard "anti-futbolistas". Music, dancing and, of course, the ubiquitous **Mexican Wave** make for a carnival atmosphere, enhanced by spectators dressing up and wearing face paint. They're usually very much family affairs, with official salespeople bringing soft drinks, beer and various types of food at fixed prices to your seat. **Stadiums** tend to be mostly concrete, with sitting room only, and can sometimes be dangerously overcrowded, though accidents are thankfully rare.

The bigger clubs are those of Mexico City (América, Cruz Azul, Pumas – the national university side – Necaxa and Atlante) and Guadalajara (Chivas, Atlas and Tecos), and the games between any of these can draw crowds of up to eighty thousand, while smaller clubs like those of Puebla, Irapuato and Celaya may get no more than ten thousand or fifteen thousand spectators per game. The vast distances between clubs make travelling to away games impossible for many fans, one reason why smaller, more out-of-the-way clubs don't get as much support. Opposing fans aren't generally separated, but an atmosphere of self-policing prevails – making it an ideal family occasion. The greatest risk is often to the referee, who is frequently escorted from the pitch by armed riot police.

For **national games** the whole country is united, and football has many times been shown to rise above partisan politics. In 1999, despite being outlawed by the government, the EZLN football squad even played an exhibition match against the national side in Mexico City's Estadio Azteca.

ARRIVAL AND INFORMATION

By colectivos *Colectivos* from Pachuca will drop you on Hidalgo, which leads down to the main square in the centre of town. The last one back to Pachuca leaves around 7pm from the southern end of Hidalgo.

Tourist office Located in the town hall (Palacio Municipal)

just off the main square on Licona Ruiz (Mon–Fri 9am–3pm; ☎771 797 1216 or ☎01 800 718 2600), and at weekends there's a stall in the main square (10am–6pm). Online information can be found at ⊛realdelmonte.com.mx.

ACCOMMODATION

Los Portales Licona Ruiz 2, on the main square ☎771 797 0423. Polished wooden floorboards and wooden furniture add character to the rooms in this wonderful old mansion dating from 1855. The cheapest rooms have views over the main square, and Emperor Maximilan and Empress Carlota are supposed to have stayed here when they visited in 1865. **M$450**

Real del Monte Iturbide 5, off the main square, behind the church ☎771 712 0201, ⊜hotelreal delmonte@prodigy.net.mx. A small hotel with old-fashioned rooms, all different, but all with wooden floors, antique-style furniture and heaters to ward off the chilly nights. Some have views over the rooftops on the hillside below. M$50 extra Fri & Sat. **M$700**

EATING AND DRINKING

Bar La Especial Plaza Hidalgo ☎771 797 0322. Founded in 1967, this is one of the oldest bars in town, with a history you'll feel the second you stroll through the swinging saloon doors, a friendly cantina with a brass-topped bar and more tequila than you can wave a mescal worm at. Serves up lots of free snacks alongside the drinks and they stay open until the last client stumbles out of the door. Mon–Fri 3pm–late, Sat & Sun noon–late.

Real de Plateros Hidalgo 56 ☎771 797 0735. This chain, which you'll see throughout town and in other parts of Hidalgo state, is popular for a reason, producing the best *pastes* (meat and potato M$12), as well as empanadas

including cheese and chorizo, and sweet ones such as pineapple, blackcurrant jam or rice pudding (all M$12). Daily 9am–10pm.

Restaurante Real del Monte Av Hidalgo 55 ☎771 797 0966. One of the few places in town where you can escape the *paste* fever, this friendly and expansive restaurant has a balcony with fantastic views over the town and valley beneath. Does Mexican classics as well as traditional local food. The speciality Is the Molcajete Minero (M$171), a mix of steak, sausage, fried cheese and salsa verde served up in a bubbling mortar. Also has an extensive selection of tequilas. Mon–Sat 9am–10pm, Sun 9am–8pm.

Mineral del Chico

The scenic village of **Mineral del Chico** is the main base for exploring the **Parque Nacional El Chico** (⊛parqueelchico.gob.mx), which is known for its excellent hiking among beautiful pine forests and rugged rock formations, as well as wildlife including armadillos, grey foxes, eagles, falcons and rattlesnakes. Although there are campsites in the park, most people prefer to stay in the village, which is small (as its name suggests) and picturesque, spreading uphill from its church and main square.

ACCOMMODATION AND EATING

Gran Compaña Alfonso Corona del Rosal ☎771 715 4421. Mineral del Chico's main eating option, doubling up as a bar when the tourists are in town. New York strip (M$150) is among the various steak options on offer, along with chicken and fish dishes. Daily 8am–9.30pm.

El Paraíso 1km from the village centre on the road to Pachuca ☎771 715 5654, ⊛hotelesecoturisticos.com .mx. A beautiful location among verdant woodland, surrounded by mountains with well-kept gardens and fresh, modern rooms in chalet-style buildings. Fri & Sat M$100 extra. **M$850**

Posada del Amanecer Morelos 7 ☎771 715 0190, ⊜posadadelamanecer@hotmail.com. Welcoming

accommodation in the centre of the village. All rooms are carpeted and come with big TVs and fireplaces (no wi-fi as yet, but it's promised). There's also a good restaurant. **M$950**

★**La Trucha Grilla** Alfonso Corona del Rosal ☎771 7123 4394, ⊜lizkintanar@hotmail.com. The enormous metal trout suspended over the entrance and the fantastic smells coming out of the open kitchen as you walk in shouldn't leave you in much doubt as to what the house speciality is here. The fresh local fish are prepared a number of different ways, all using local herbs and spices. Also does steak, chicken and vegetarian options. The owners actually head up the local tourism board and are on hand with ready advice. Daily 11am–9pm.

East of Mexico City

East of Mexico City, and among the destinations reached from its TAPO bus terminal, is the region's second-largest city, the thriving and ultra-colonial **Puebla**. This city not only warrants a couple of days of your time in its own right, but makes an excellent base for forays north to more tranquil **Tlaxcala**, and west to **Cholula** with its enormous ruined pyramid. Both were important tributary states of the Aztecs when Cortés marched this way from the coast to pillage and conquer in the name of European civilization. Puebla and Cholula also offer excellent views of central Mexico's twin volcanoes, **Popocatépetl** and **Ixtaccíhuatl**, although the former is currently off-limits due to the continuing threat of eruption.

Tlaxcala

Allied to Cortés in his struggle against the Aztecs, as well as with colonial Spain in the War of Independence, **TLAXCALA**, the capital of a tiny state of the same name, has become a byword for treachery. Because of its alliance with Cortés, the town suffered a very different fate from that of nearby Cholula, which aligned itself with the Aztecs (see p.168), and in the long run this has led to the disappearance of its ancient culture. The Spaniards founded a colonial town here – now restored and very beautiful in much of its original colonial glory, but whether because of its traitorous reputation or simply its isolation, development in Tlaxcala has been limited.

The town lies 131km west of Mexico City and 30km north of Puebla in the middle of a fertile, prosperous-looking upland plain surrounded by rather bare mountains. It's an exceptionally pretty and much rehabilitated colonial town, comfortable enough but also fairly dull. Most of the interest lies very close to the zócalo, with its cluster of banks, post office and central bandstand, where the terracotta and ochre tones of the buildings lend the city its tag of "Ciudad Roja", the Red City.

Palacio de Gobierno

North side of the zócalo • Daily 7am–6pm (entry via easternmost door) • Free

The entire north side of the zócalo is taken up by the **Palacio de Gobierno**, whose patterned brick facade is broken by ornate windows and doorways. The building incorporates parts of a much earlier structure, erected soon after the Conquest, and inside boasts a series of brilliantly coloured **murals** by local artist Desiderio Hernandez Xochitiotzin, who took nearly fifty years to complete them. The panels depict the history of the Tlaxcalan people from their migration from the north to their alliance with Cortés. The two most spectacular are one on the stairs depicting the Spanish Conquest and another at the bottom showing the Great Market.

Parroquia de San José
1 de Mayo 4 • Daily 9am–6pm • Free

The tiled facade of the **Parroquia de San José** dominates a small square off the side of the zócalo. It's an attractive building, but except for two fonts beside the door depicting Camaxtli, the Tlaxcalan god of hunting and war, the inside is a disappointment. Note the seventeenth-century painting beside the altar that depicts the baptism of a Tlaxcalan chief, as overseen by Cortés and his mistress, La Malinche.

Museo de Artes y Tradiciones Populares
Sanchez 1 at cnr 1 de Mayo, three blocks west of the zócalo • Tues–Sun 10am–6pm • M$15

Tlaxcala's third museum is the **Museo de Artes y Tradiciones Populares**. It focuses on traditional crafts and customs, with sections on bell making (including an example cast on the site) and a fascinating room on the manufacture and consumption of *pulque*.

Museo de la Memoria
Independencia 3 (on Plaza Xicohténcatl) • Tues–Sun 10am–5pm • M$15

Directly south of the zócalo is a smaller square, Plaza Xicohténcatl, where you'll find the **Museo de la Memoria**, a modern museum devoted to the cultural history of the region. Its imaginative displays (some interactive) – illustrating pre-Hispanic *tianguis* (markets), Franciscan life under the Spaniards and the ruling hierarchy in Tlaxcala before and after Cortés – make up for the fact that it's light on artefacts.

Museo Regional de Tlaxcala
Calzada ex-Convento San Francisco • Daily 10am–6pm • M$46

At the southeastern corner of Plaza Xicohténcatl, a broad, tree-lined path leads up to a triple set of arches. Beyond them, an open area overlooking the city's pretty nineteenth-century bullring is flanked on one side by the ex-Convento de San Francisco, started in 1537. Wrapped around the convent's cloister, the **Museo Regional de Tlaxcala** covers local life from prehistoric times to the present day – an unexceptional collection, but well displayed, in a series of whitewashed rooms.

Catedral de Nuestra Señora de la Asunción
Calzada ex-Convento San Francisco, next door to the Museo Regional • Daily 7am–6pm • Free

The **Catedral de Nuestra Señora de la Asunción** is relatively plain, though it has a beautiful vaulted wooden ceiling decorated in Mudéjar style, with a strong Moorish influence, as was then common in southern Spain. The Moors were expelled from Spain in 1492, and though their influence continued for some decades, it is only apparent in Mexican churches started immediately after the Conquest. One large chapel, more richly decorated than the rest, contains the font in which Xicohténcatl and other Tlaxcalan leaders were baptized in the presence of Hernán Cortés in 1520.

The open chapel
At the end of Calle Capilla Abierta (a continuation of Guerrero) • Open access

Opposite Museo Regional and the Catedral de Nuestra Señora de la Asunción, steps lead down to the **open chapel** (*capilla abierta*). Open chapels – in the open air, that is, rather than inside a church – are a particularly Mexican religious structure, typical of the very early colonial period, and this one, built in 1537, is no exception. Like most open chapels, it has three arches, but the ones here are unusual for being pointed. The lower walls bear traces of ancient frescoes.

Santuario de Ocotlán

Hidalgo 1, Ocotlán, 1km east of the zócalo, walking one block north on Juárez, then right onto Guridi y Alcocer until it forks, bearing left onto the very steep Calzada de Agua Santa, past the Pocito chapel • Tues–Sun 8am–6pm • Free

The twin wedding-cake towers of the **Santuario de Ocotlán** overlook the town from a hill to the east, which gives great views over the surrounding countryside. The church's facade is a riot of churrigueresque excess that ranks it alongside those at Tepotzotlán and Taxco, and it's no less florid inside. The huge Baroque *retablo* seems to spread seamlessly to the dome and along the transept in a frenzy of gilt woodwork, an exuberance justified by the miraculous work of the church's Virgin.

According to legend, she appeared to a poor Indian in 1541 with instructions to cure an epidemic with waters from a stream that had miraculously sprung forth. Naturally everyone recovered. Then the Virgin asked the Indian to bring the local Franciscan monks to a forest. Once they were there, fire suddenly burst forth, but though the flames were fierce, they didn't burn the trees. The next day the monks returned, to find that one pine tree (*ocotlán*) contained a wooden image of the Virgin. Now installed on the altar, it is carved and painted very much in the style of the times. The life of Our Lady of Ocotlán is portrayed around the eight walls of the ornate **Camarín de la Virgen** (the Virgin's Dressing Room) behind the altar. In May, the church and surrounding streets host the procession of the Virgin, attended by thousands of pilgrims.

ARRIVAL AND DEPARTURE

TLAXCALA

By bus The bus station is southwest of the centre on Josefa Castelar. *Colectivos* parked outside the bus station run to nearby villages and the zócalo, though it's only a 10min walk: exit the bus station and turn right downhill to the next main junction, then take a right down Guerrero for five blocks and left down Juárez. To return to the bus station, go back the way you came, or, for a short cut, climb the stairs at the southern end of Mariano Sanchez (Escalinata de los Héroes), or take a *colectivo* from 20 Noviembre at Lardizábal. At the same spot, you'll also find frequent but slow second-class buses to Puebla (1hr).

Destinations Mexico City TAPO (every 20min; 1hr 45min); Pachuca (17 daily; 3hr); Puebla (every 15min; 40min).

INFORMATION

Banks Banorte, on the zócalo at Plaza de la Constitución 10, is the most central bank with exchange facilities and an ATM, but there are others along Independencia.

Internet Lorena, Porfirio Díaz 13 (Mon–Sat 8am–9pm, Sun 10am–6pm; M$12/hr).

Post office Plaza de la Constitución 20, east side of the zócalo (Mon–Fri 8am–4.30pm, Sat 8am–noon).

Tourist office Juárez and Lardizábal, behind the Palacio de Gobierno (Mon–Fri 8.30am–7pm, Sat & Sun 10am–7pm; 246 465 0960, toll-free from outside the state 01 800 509 6557). The state tourist office's website is at turismotlaxcala.com.

ACCOMMODATION

Hotel Alifer Morelos 11, near the junction with Xicohténcatl 246 466 0620, hotelalifer.com.mx. This is the nearest you'll get to low-cost accommodation in Tlaxcala, and it's pretty good value. The rooms are all carpeted, with TV, and there's parking, wi-fi and a bar-cum-restaurant. M$650

Hotel Misión San Francisco Plaza de la Constitución 17, southern side of the zócalo 246 462 6022, hotelesmision.com. A beautiful sixteenth-century building, with some original features, though largely rebuilt in the nineteenth century. The rooms are all modern, but if you want one with period features in the oldest part of the hotel, ask for one in the *zona antigua*. The lobby has an amazing stained-glass ceiling, and a cosy little bar just off it. Breakfast included. M$1399

Posada la Casona de Cortés Lardizábal 6 246 462 2042, lacasonadecortes.com.mx. A beautiful and very good-value little hotel, with a variety of rooms of different shapes and sizes around a pretty patio garden. M$750

EATING

Coffee Station Plaza de la Constitución 12, south side of the zócalo 246 462 5672. A little place with outdoor seating, just beyond the portales (arcade), offering "gourmet" coffee and a range of set breakfasts (until

1.30pm; M$32–68). Daily 9am–midnight.

Fabrik Plaza de la Constitución 10, east side of the zócalo ☎ 246 476 6405. Good coffee, and also crêpes, with fillings such as mushroom and three cheeses (M$45) or the house special, cream cheese and ice cream (M$48). Daily 8am–11pm.

Mesón del Rey Morelos at Xicohténcatl ☎ 246 108 4992. A pleasant eating space, with tiled floor and polished wooden tables, offering breakfasts (till noon; M$35–50) and good-value set menus (M$30 and M$40). Daily 8am–6pm.

Los Portales Plaza de la Constitución 8, east side of the zócalo ☎ 246 462 5419, ⓦ restaurantelosportales.com .mx. A broad range of *antojitos*, burgers, salads, pasta dishes and the delicious *sopa tlaxcalteca* (M$55), made from black beans, tortilla chips, cheese, avocado and *chicharrón* (pork crackling). Daily 7am–11pm.

DRINKING AND NIGHTLIFE

Pulquería la Tía Yola Plaza Xicohténcatl, southeast corner ☎ 246 462 7309. This jolly little *pulquería* was opened with the specific aim of reviving the art of *pulque*-making (not to mention *pulque*-drinking), and claims to have the state's best, available in several fruit flavours. Daily 11am–8pm.

Revolución Plaza de la Constitución 9 (upstairs) ☎ 246 466 1637. Overlooking the zócalo above *Los Portales*, this low-ceilinged, stone-walled music bar gets quite lively after 8pm, when there are live bands performing most nights. Daily 9am–2am.

Las Ventas Morelos 10-D, on the north side of Plaza Xicohténcatl ☎ 246 462 3030. A convivial saloon bar where you can sink a few *chelas* (beers) while admiring the paintings of naked women bullfighting which decorate the walls. Daily 4pm–midnight.

Cacaxtla, Xochitécatl and Tizatlán

Some 17km southwest of Tlaxcala **Cacaxtla and Xochitécatl** Daily 9am–5.30pm • M$55 **Tizatlán** Tues–Sun 10am–5pm • M$35 • Cacaxtla can be reached by frequent *colectivo* ("San Miguel del Milagro") from Mariano Sanchez and Lardizábal in Tlaxcala (40min); from Puebla, buses serve the village of Nativitas, 5km away

A particularly fine series of murals depicting battle scenes was discovered in 1975 at the ancient site of **Cacaxtla**. They are clearly Maya in style, which would seem to indicate trade or perhaps even a Maya settlement here. Two kilometres west of Cacaxtla, the ruins of **Xochitécatl** have three impressive pyramids and monolithic stones, but it isn't served by public transport. The rather less impressive archeological site of **Tizatlán**, 4km north of town, can be reached by *colectivo* from Lardizábal and 20 de Noviembre.

Puebla

The elegant colonial city of **PUEBLA**, the republic's fifth-largest city (after Mexico City, Guadalajara, Monterrey and Tijuana), is an easy forty-minute trip from Tlaxcala, or a couple of hours by bus from Mexico City – with glorious views of the snowy heights of Popocatépetl and Ixtaccíhuatl on the way. Known for its fine cuisine, Puebla has a remarkable concentration of sights – a fabulous **cathedral**, a "hidden" **convent**,

CINCO DE MAYO

Military defeat seems to play a larger part in Puebla's history than it does in most of Mexico – the city fell to the Americans in 1847 and to the French in 1863 – but that isn't what's remembered. Rather, what's remembered and commemorated here is the greatest victory in the country's history, the **Battle of Puebla** in 1862, when a force of some two thousand Mexicans defeated a French army three times its size. The French were trying to make the Austrian prince Maximilian emperor of Mexico, but when they tried to occupy Puebla, Mexican troops based in the two forts on the Cerro de Guadalupe (the Fuerte de Loreto and the Fuerte de Guadalupe; see p.165 & p.166) beat them off, forcing them to withdraw back towards their base at Veracruz and putting a serious dent into French plans. To this day, Puebla commemorates May 5 (**Cinco de Mayo**) with a massive fiesta, and there's a public holiday throughout the country.

CAPU Bus Station (5km), Tlaxcala, Airport (25km)

PUEBLA

EATING

Café Aguirre	5
Café Munich	4
Caldos Angelita	1
Fonda de Santa Clara	2/6
Italian Coffee Company	3/7/8
Sacristía de la Compañía	10
La Zanahoria	9

DRINKING & NIGHTLIFE

La Boveda	4
Librería Cafetería Teorema	1
Litrox	3
PKDO	2

ACCOMMODATION

Hostal de Santo Domingo	3
Colonial de Puebla	6
Palace	5
Reforma 2000	1
Regio	7
Sacristía de la Compañía	4
Virrey de Mendoza	4

museums and colonial **mansions** – while the mountainous surrounding country is in places startlingly beautiful. The city centre and Cerro de Guadalupe, where all these sights are to be found, form quite a compact area, easy to get around, and you can see the best of the city and nearby **Cholula** in a couple of leisurely days, or even – at a brisk trot – in one packed day.

Brief history

The city was founded by the Spaniards in 1531, preferring it to the ancient sites of Cholula and Tlaxcala possibly because the memories of indigenous power there remained too strong. It rapidly assumed great importance as a staging point on the journey from the capital to the port at Veracruz and for the shipment of goods from Spain's Far Eastern colonies, which were delivered to Acapulco and transported across Mexico from there. Wealth was brought, too, by the reputation of Puebla's ceramics, particularly its tiles. This industry – still very much in evidence – was helped by an abundance of good clays in the region, and by settlers from Talavera in Spain, who brought traditional ceramic skills with them. The city did well out of colonial rule, and, perhaps not surprisingly, it took the wrong side in the War of Independence. As a result, it preserves a reputation for conservatism and traditional values, not dispelled even by the fact that the start of the Revolution is generally dated from the assassination of Aquiles Serdán in his Puebla home.

The zócalo

Puebla's **zócalo** is one of the country's prettiest, with trees, grass, benches and a large fountain, lined on three sides with arcades, the perfect spot to imbibe a dose of fine caffeine while watching the comings and goings in the square. Beautiful colonial buildings, such as the **Palacio Municipal** (town hall) on the north side, give the square a lovely Baroque feel. The zócalo is also the centre for the numbering system of Puebla's ancient grid of streets, the lowest numbers indicating streets nearest to the square.

The cathedral

South side of zócalo • Mon–Fri 10–11.30am & 1–5.30pm, Sat 10–11am & 2–5pm, Sun 3–5.30pm • Free

The zócalo's south side is dominated by the great looming **cathedral**, the second largest in the republic. Built between 1562 and the middle of the following century, the exterior is ugly and grey, but the inside improves considerably, with amazing ornamentation in onyx, marble and gilt, and a wonderful altar designed by Manuel Tolsá in 1797. The cathedral, and particularly the tower, was partly funded by Bishop Juan de Palafox y Mendoza, an illegitimate son of a Spanish nobleman who grew up with his poor mother but inherited his father's fortune.

The Archbishop's Palace

5 Oriente 5, behind the cathedral • **Biblioteca Palafoxiana** Tues–Fri 10am–5pm, Sat & Sun 10am–4pm • M$30 **Casa de la Cultura** Mon–Sat 8am–8pm, Sun 10am–4pm • Free • ☏ 222 246 6922

The old **Archbishop's Palace** was converted to a library in the seventeenth century – the Biblioteca Palafoxiana, reputed to be the oldest library in the Americas – and houses the original collection of ancient books and manuscripts on its upper floor. Downstairs there's the **Casa de la Cultura**, which hosts regular exhibitions of local arts and crafts.

Museo Amparo

2 Sur 708 at 9 Ote • Daily except Tues 10am–6pm; guided tours (Spanish only) Sun 12.30pm • M$35, free Mon, camera M$50 • Ⓦ museoamparo.com

The undoubted star in Puebla's museum firmament is the modern **Museo Amparo**, which concentrates on art from pre-Hispanic Mesoamerica, with additional material from the colonial and more recent eras. Set in a pair of modernized colonial buildings with peaceful courtyards and piped classical music, the collection is the legacy of philanthropist Manuel Espinosa Iglesias, who set up the Amparo Foundation in honour of his wife. Everything in the museum is thoroughly documented at strategically located computer consoles.

The historical significance of the pieces isn't glossed over, but the focus is firmly on aesthetics, with well-presented cases displaying artefacts to their best advantage. To set the tone, the entrance features an impressive glass replica of a **tzompantli skull-wall** with alternating Olmec and Totonac heads in each of the glass blocks. A room decorated with reproduction **cave paintings** from Altamira in Spain, Arnhemland in Australia, Utah, Norway and Baja California puts Mexico's cultural development into some sort of context.

The main collection

Though far smaller than that in Mexico City's anthropology museum, the main collection is well chosen and a good deal more manageable. It is particularly strong on the Olmecs, a people who greatly influenced life around Puebla and left behind some strikingly beautiful pieces such as the half-metre-wide stone head on display here. Elsewhere notice the exquisite Colima jaguar, the beautiful carved conch shell from the Gulf coast and the sculpture of a kneeling woman from Nayarit with her distinctive face and body painting.

La Estrella de Puebla

Osa Mayor 2520 • Mon–Fri 4–9.30pm Sat & Sun 11am–9.30pm • M$30 (M$300 for VIP booth) • ☏ 01 800 326 8656

North America's largest Ferris wheel is Puebla's most modern attraction, and particularly worth the ride on clear days when the enormous masses of Popcatépetl and

2

Iztacchíhuatl are visible at the fringes of the city. The ride lasts around twenty minutes and takes you up to altitudes of 80m. For those less keen on heights the area is surrounded by various restaurants, bars and a brand-new shopping mall with original Botero artwork throughout.

Museo Regional de la Revolución Mexicana

6 Ote 206 • Tues–Sun 10am–5pm • M$30, free Tues

The devotional **Museo Regional de la Revolución Mexicana** records the struggles for Liberalism of the Serdán family against the dictatorship of Porfirio Díaz. The assassination of Aquiles Serdán in this house was one of the most important steps in the fall of Díaz: the date of Serdán's death, November 18, 1910, is – in the absence of any firmer indicators – generally recognized as marking the start of the Revolution. The bullet holes in the house have been lovingly preserved, and a huge smashed mirror still hangs on the wall where it appears in contemporary photos of the carnage. Revolution buffs will also enjoy the biographies of key figures in the struggle, photos of the ragtag bands of wide-hatted revolutionaries with their bandoleers, and the trap door in the floor under which Serdán spent several fruitless hours trying to avoid his eventual end.

Mercado Victoria and around

3 Nte between 4 and 8 Pte

The impressive glass-and-iron **Mercado Victoria** was once Puebla's main market, but is now a rather sanitized shopping centre. East of the market, candy stores along 6 Oriente sell **camotes**, gooey fingers of sweet potato and sugar flavoured with various fruits, which are a local speciality. If you're thinking of buying any to take home, however, note that they only last a couple of weeks.

Church of Santo Domingo

5 de Mayo between 4 and 8 Pte, and opposite 6 Ote • Mon–Sat 8am–12.50pm & 4–8.30pm, Sun 8am–2pm & 4–8.30pm • Free

Head north from the zócalo along 5 de Mayo and you'll reach the church of **Santo Domingo**, which is directly to the east of the Mercado Victoria. The church's main chapel, the **Capilla del Rosario**, is – even in comparison with the cathedral – a quite unbelievably lavish orgy of gold leaf and Baroque excess; a constant hushed, shuffling stream of devotees lights candles and prays to the image of the Virgin.

Museo José Luis Bello y Zetina

5 de Mayo 408, three doors north of the church of Santo Domingo • Tues–Sun 10am–4pm • Free

The **Museo José Luis Bello y Zetina** displays the paintings and furniture of the wealthy Bello family, who lived here during the nineteenth century – you'll see everything from seventeenth-century Flemish masters to a Napoleonic bedroom suite. It somehow seems too comfortless to be a home yet not formal enough for a museum, though the enthusiasm of your personal guide (whose services are free but not compulsory) may rub off.

Taller Uriarte

4 Pte 911 at 9 Nte • Mon–Fri 9.30am–7pm, Sat 9.30am–6pm, Sun 9.30am–5pm; tours every 30min, Mon–Fri 10am–1pm • Free; tours M$50 • ☎ 222 232 1598, 🌐 uriartetalavera.com.mx

The **Taller Uriarte** is about the best known of Puebla's pottery factories. It's a small-scale affair shoehorned into what appears to be just another urban house, but it's well set up for visitors. You can see every stage of the pottery-making process, from forming the plates and bowls to painting the intricate designs in paints whose colours are completely transformed during firing into distinctive blues and yellows. And of course you can buy examples of the pottery afterwards.

Ex-Convento de Santa Rosa

3 Nte 1203 • Tues–Sun 10am–5pm • M$30, free Tues

The **ex-Convento de Santa Rosa's** main claim to fame is that the great *mole poblano* was invented here in its wonderful yellow-tiled kitchens. The kitchens are the highlight of a guided tour that includes rooms full of crafts from around the state of Puebla.

Museo Religioso Santa Mónica

18 Pte 103 at 5 de Mayo, nine blocks north of the zócalo • Tues–Sun 9am–6pm • M$30, free Sun

The city's remarkable convent now operates as the **Museo Religioso Santa Mónica**. Here, from the suppression of the church in 1857 until their discovery in 1934, several generations of nuns lived hidden from the public gaze behind a smokescreen of secret doors and concealed passages. Just how secret they were is a matter of some debate – many claim that the authorities simply turned a blind eye – and certainly several lay families were actively supportive, providing supplies and new recruits. But it makes a good story, embellished by the conversion of the building into a museum that preserves the secret entrances along with many religious artworks and a beautiful seventeenth-century cloister. Several simple cells are also in evidence, and from the hidden chapel you can look down through a screen at the still-operating church next door.

Cerro de Guadalupe

2km northwest of the city centre • *Colectivo* #72 (sometimes marked "Centro Cívico") from Héroes del 5 de Mayo, three blocks east of the zócalo

Crowning the **Cerro de Guadalupe**, the site of numerous nineteenth-century battles and sieges, is the **Centro Cívico 5 de Mayo**, a collection of museums. Neither of the two forts nor any of the museums here is a match for sights downtown, but they are a decent place to spend a couple of hours away from the fumes and the noise of the centre.

Fuerte de Loreto

Tues–Sun 10am–5pm • M$42, free Sun

Your first stop on the Cerro de Guadalupe should be the **Fuerte de Loreto**, a fort whose moat and high walls protect a large empty parade ground and a small church containing the **Museo de la No Intervención**. This focuses on the events surrounding the 1862 Battle of Puebla, celebrated on 5 May (Cinco de Mayo; see box, p.161), and records 150 years of the defence of the republic through replicated battle scenes. The views of Popo and Ixta from the battlements are some of the best in Puebla.

Museo Regional de Puebla

Tues–Sun 9am–6pm • M$46, free Sun

The best of the rest of the sights on the Cerro de Guadalupe is the modern **Museo Regional de Puebla**, largely devoted to the state's archeology and ethnology. There's some exquisite Olmec jade sculpture and sculptural pieces along with a 4m-high polychrome statue of San Cristóbal from the seventeenth century and sections of wider relevance, such as a detailed explanation of native migration from east Asia through Alaska.

Museo Interactivo Imagina

Mon–Fri 9am–1pm & 2–6pm, Sat & Sun 10am–6pm • M$50, extra for some exhibits

Across the way from the Museo Regional, the modern **Museo Interactivo Imagina** is a collection of educational interactive games and exhibits aimed largely at children, its main theme being a scientific understanding of the world. It kicks off with a look at the human body and its place in evolution, followed by technology (with lots of machines to play with), the physical world, art and finally a taxidermic exhibition of animals from different parts of the world. Unfortunately, all explanations are in Spanish.

Planetarium

Shows Tues–Sun 12.30pm, 4pm & 6pm • M$55 • ⓦ planetariopuebla.com

Next door to the Museo Interactivo, Puebla's **planetarium** is state-of-the-art, with an IMAX screen and impressive explanatory films about the cosmos, with digital projection and three shows a day. Commentary is in Spanish, but that won't stop you being gobsmacked by the photography and special effects.

Fuerte de Guadalupe

Tues–Sun 9am–5.30pm • M$37, free Sun

The highest point on the hill is occupied by the **Fuerte de Guadalupe**, the meagre but well-tended remains of a nineteenth-century fort. Along with the Fuerte de Loreto, to which it was connected by a trench, the fort played a crucial part in the 5 May 1862 Battle of Puebla (see box, p.161). For all the sense of history, however, all that remains of the fort now are just a few arches and roofless rooms.

ARRIVAL AND DEPARTURE
PUEBLA

By plane Puebla's airport (officially Aeropuerto Hermanos Serdán, though of course nobody really calls it that) is near the village of Huejotzingo, 25km northwest of Puebla and 7km northwest of Cholula (ⓣ 227 102 5080). Buses, minibuses and authorized taxis connect it to CAPU and central Puebla and Cholula.

Destinations Cancún (1 daily; 2hr 5min); Guadalajara (3 weekly; 1hr 10min); Monterrey (6 weekly; 1hr 25min); Tijuana (1 daily; 3hr 55min).

By bus Puebla's bus station, known by the acronym CAPU (Central de Autobuses de Puebla ⓣ 222 231 6401, ⓦ capu .com.mx), is 5km northwest of the city centre. Buses into town run from outside the station; going the other way they can be picked up on 9 Sur or Nte. There are also authorized taxis to the centre for M$57 (or M$63 10pm–6am). CAPU has a guardería (baggage deposit), ATMs and a bureau de change. Tlaxcala is also served, more conveniently by buses from the Flecha Azul terminal on 10 Pte between 11 Nte and 13 Nte, by the railway museum (every 5–10min; 1hr).

Destinations Cholula (every 10–15min; 20min); Cuernavaca (hourly; 3hr 30min); Mexico City TAPO (12–16 hourly; 2hr); Mexico City Nte (hourly; 2hr), Mexico City airport (hourly; 2hr 15min); Oaxaca (18 daily; 4hr 30min); Pachuca (20 daily; 2hr); Tlaxcala (every 15min; 40min); Veracruz (28 daily; 4hr 30min).

By combi Cholula is served by frequent *combis* from 14 Pte at 11 Nte, saving you the need to trek out to CAPU.

INFORMATION AND TOURS

Municipal tourist office Palafox y Mendoza 14, on the north side of the zócalo (daily 9am–8pm; ⓣ 222 404 5047 or toll-free from outside the state ⓣ 800 087 1980, ⓦ turismopuebla.gob.mx). Has free maps and information about the city and runs a tourist information kiosk on the south side of the square (Mon–Fri 10am–5.30pm).

State tourist office 5 Ote 3, near the corner of 16 de Septiembre (Mon–Sat 8am–8pm, Sun 9am–2pm; ⓣ 222 777 1519, toll-free from outside the state ⓣ 01 800 326 8656), with information about Puebla and the region.

Banks and exchange Banamex, at Reforma 135 (between 3 Nte and 5 de Mayo), is among the banks near the zócalo which change money and have ATMs. There's a *casa de cambio* in the arcade between the north side of the zócalo and 2 Ote, and one at CAPU.

Internet CyberByte, 2 Sur 505 (daily 9am–midnight; M$6/hr); Cyber Space, 2 Sur 701 (Mon–Sat 9am–9.30pm, Sun 10am–8.30pm; M$10/hr).

Post office The main post office, at 16 de Septiembre and 5 Ote, has an efficient Lista de Correos; there's also a branch office at 2 Ote 411.

City tours Túribus (ⓣ 222 226 7289) runs a 90min sightseeing tour (hourly 10am–6pm; M$80) from the west side of the zócalo.

ACCOMMODATION

Hostal de Santo Domingo 4 Pte 312 ⓣ 222 232 1671, ⓔ hostalstodomingo@yahoo.com.mx. More like a budget hotel than a hostel, but still backpacker-oriented and very friendly. The ten-bed dorms (including one for women only, for M$20 extra) each have their own bathrooms, and the private rooms are spacious and mostly en suite. Breakfast included. Dorms M$150, doubles M$450

Colonial de Puebla 4 Sur 105 ⓣ 222 246 4612 or ⓣ 01 800 013 0000, ⓦ colonial.com.mx. Luxurious lodgings in a beautiful colonial building next to the Autonomous University of Puebla. All rooms have TV and phone, and many have beautifully tiled bathrooms. There's also a fine restaurant on site. M$825

Palace 2 Ote 13 ☎222 232 2430, ⊛hotelpalace.com.mx. Good-value, modern three-star hotel just one block off the zócalo. The lobby area and restaurant are pretty busy, and the rooms aren't huge, but they're clean and fresh, with TV, fan and good bathrooms. M$495

Reforma 2000 4 Pte 916, corner of 11 Nte ☎222 242 3363, ⊛hotelreforma2000.com. Handy for the bars in the Zona Esmeralda, as well as for transport to CAPU, Cholula and Tlaxcala, this well-priced little hotel has spacious, carpeted rooms with TV and phone, its own lively bar and restaurant, and parking facilities. M$250

Regio 5 Mayo 1004 ☎222 232 4774. Rock-bottom prices, and basic, yes, but very far from being the worst accommodation in town. The staff aren't always close to the phone so reserving ahead can be a hassle, although they nearly always have space for walk-ins. It's friendly,

decent, housed in a nice old colonial building, and has its own slightly shabby charm. It's worth paying M$25 extra for en suite. M$100

★**Sacristía de la Compañía** 6 Sur 304 ☎01 800 161 9985 or ☎222 232 4513, ⊛mesones-sacristia.com. Gorgeous hotel in a two-hundred-year-old house with just nine spacious junior and master suites, each one different, but all with wooden beams and elegantly decorated with antiques. The restaurant is excellent (see below), and they even offer cookery classes. Breakfast included. Junior suite M$1600, master suite M$2000

Virrey de Mendoza Reforma 538 ☎222 242 3903, ⊕virreydemendoza@hotmail.com. Good value and one of the best of the mid-range places, a small hotel with a verdant central courtyard done out in rather violent candy-pink. The big, carpeted rooms, set around it, are in a rather more tasteful pistachio green. M$350

EATING

While in town you should definitely check out the **local specialities**, particularly **mole poblano**, an extraordinary sauce made from chocolate, chiles and any number of herbs and spices. Typically served over chicken, turkey or enchiladas, Puebla's is the original, where it was supposedly invented in colonial times for the viceroy's visit to the Convento de Santa Rosa. Another taste sensation is **chiles en nogada**, a dish reputedly concocted in 1821 to celebrate Mexican Independence and made to resemble the colours of the Mexican flag; it's usually served July–Sept.

CAFÉS AND CHEAP EATS

Café Aguirre 5 de Mayo 4 ☎222 242 0997, ⊛cafeaguirre.com. Predictable and reliable café-restaurant that's a long-standing local favourite and is always popular with businesspeople. Their speciality is chilaquiles (M$115), but they also do a good-value lunch-time menu for M$85. Mon–Sat 7.30am–11pm.

Café Munich corner 3 Pte 304 and corner 5 Sur ☎222 242 3519. Basic but reliable café-restaurant serving a wide range of soups and mains, and a great comida corrida in a room decorated with photos of Bavarian scenes and drawings of Einstein, Beethoven, Goethe and Wagner. Cheap (M$39) and pricier (M$65) menus are available at lunch time. Daily 8am–6.30pm.

Caldos Angelita 9 Nte 607 and cnr 6 Pte ☎222 246 5414. A popular no-nonsense diner doling out hearty bowlfuls of wonderful chicken broth (M$28) and excellent mole poblano (M$30), but be warned that the food often runs out before closing time. Daily 10am–6.30pm.

Italian Coffee Company Reforma 121 ☎222 232 1859, ⊛italiancoffee.com. Teas, infusions, flavoured espresso coffees and cakes in convivial surroundings. Other branches around town include one at 4 Ote 202, one at 16 Septiembre opposite the cathedral and two more in the zócalo – in fact, they now have branches nationwide, and in the US too, but they started here in Puebla. Daily 8.30am–10pm.

La Zanahoria 5 Ote 206 ☎222 232 4813. A bustling vegetarian café and restaurant in Mexican style, with a vast array of wholesome herbivorous choices. Soya burgers (M$30) and salads are good value, though no match for the M$69 buffet (M$89 at weekends), or the M$65 menu del día (served 1–6pm). Daily 7am–8.30pm.

RESTAURANTS

Fonda de Santa Clara 3 Pte 307, a couple of blocks northwest of the zócalo ☎222 242 2659, ⊛fondadesantaclara.com. The best-known – and most touristy – restaurant in town, serving local food with an upmarket twist (pollo al mole poblano M$120, enchiladas in three different mole sauces M$95) in a pretty room decorated with Mexican art, but service is not very good, and the food can be hit or miss. There's a second branch at 3 Pte 920 (☎222 246 1952). Daily 8am–11pm.

Sacristía de la Compañía 6 Sur 304 ☎222 242 3554, ⊛mesones-sacristia.com. Come here for fine dining in this superb hotel's lovely enclosed courtyard. Efficient, friendly service and a good wine list make this one of Puebla's best dining experiences. Try the house mole (M$120), preceded by their special soup made with fried tortilla chips, chicharrón, cheese and chipotle (M$60). Also has a great bar at the back for a pre- or post-dinner drink. Mon–Sat 1–11.30pm, Sun 11am–6pm.

2

DRINKING AND NIGHTLIFE

Central Puebla is mostly quiet at night and to find any **bars** you'll have to head a few blocks south to the **Plazuela de los Sapos**, beside the enormous Estrella de Puebla Ferris wheel (see p.163) near 6 Sur and 5 Pte, where several lively drinking holes face each other across a small square. On Thurs, Fri and Sat nights in particular, you might also head around six long blocks west of the zócalo to the Zona Esmeralda, where there's a string of bars and clubs to keep you going. Otherwise, many people head out to **Cholula** to join the lively, student-heavy crowd there, though you'll have to be prepared for a fairly expensive taxi ride back: buses stop running at around 11pm, just when the clubs start warming up.

La Boveda 6 Sur 503 ☎222 246 7555. The most happening among a handful of bars on the Plazuela de los Sapos that pump out Latin and US pop hits. It has live music most nights from 8pm. Daily noon–4am.

Librería Cafetería Teorema 2 Pte 703 ☎222 298 0028. Combined bar, café and live music venue in an old colonial building with food, beer, tequila, coffee, a smoking area and a relaxed bohemian atmosphere. Gigs usually start around 9.30pm, with acoustic *trova* most days, Cuban music Fri. Reservations recommended. Mon–Sat noon–1am.

Litrox Juárez 1305 ☎222 224 4584. Lively sweatbox bar west of the town centre in the Zona Esmeralda (Juárez is a continuation of 7 Pte west of the Paseo Bravo) with music nightly from 8pm and no cover charge. Daily 9am–3pm & 6pm–3am.

PKDO Juárez 1308 ☎222 681 0402. Thurs, Fri and Sat nights are the best time to hit this music bar, when live bands play anything from salsa or reggaeton to *norteño* folk, and the crowd exhudes a boozy bonhomie. Tues–Sat 3pm–3am.

Cholula

Puebla's expansion in recent years has made **Cholula**, 15km to the west, virtually a suburb. Nonetheless, it retains its small-town charm and has one abiding reason to visit: the **ruins of Cholula**. A rival of Teotihuacán at its height, and the most powerful city in the country between the fall of Teotihuacán and the rise of Tula, Cholula was, at the time of the Conquest, a vast city of some four hundred temples, famed as a shrine to Quetzalcoatl and for the excellence of its pottery (a trade dominated by immigrant Mixtecs). But it paid dearly for an attempt, inspired by its Aztec allies, to ambush Cortés on his march to Tenochtitlán: the chieftains were slaughtered, their temples destroyed and churches built in their place. The Spaniards claimed to have constructed 365 churches here, one for each day of the year. Although there are a lot of churches, the true figure certainly doesn't live up to the claim. There may well be 365 chapels within the churches, though, which is already a few hundred more than the village population could reasonably need.

Pirámide Tepanapa

Between San Andrés, 6 Sur, 6 Pte and 5 Nte • **Nuestra Señora de los Remedios** Daily 7am–8pm • Free **Archeological site** Daily 9am–5.30pm • M$50 (including museum), M$70 to bring in a video camera

Arriving in Cholula, you can't miss the **Nuestra Señora de los Remedios**, picturesquely sited atop a hill with Popocatépetl in the background. If you climb up to it, you can buy snacks such as *chapulines* (fried grasshoppers) on the way. What's not immediately apparent is that the hill is in fact the remains of the **Great Pyramid of Cholula** – the Pirámide Tepanapa – the largest pyramid ever constructed, though it's now ruined, overgrown and really not much to look at. At 66m, it is lower than the largest of the Egyptian pyramids, but with each side measuring 350m it is also squatter and bulkier. As at other sites, the outer shell was built over a series of nested pyramids, constructed between 200 BC and 800 AD.

The archeological site

The **archeological site** around and underneath the pyramid is usually accessed from an entrance on San Andrés through a 400m-long series of tunnels dug by archeologists. Though undoubtedly fascinating, the ruins are a good deal less

OPPOSITE CHURCH OF SAN FRANCISCO, ACATEPEC (P.171)>

2

impressive than some of the more famed sites around the Valley of México. The ring of superimposed structures around the **Patio de los Altares** is certainly worth a look, and there are some fine **murals**, but these can be better appreciated in the site **museum** where replicas are kept.

The tunnels

Even when you can go inside, the section open to the public is just a fraction of the 8km of exploratory tunnels which honeycomb the pyramid. They're well lit and capacious enough for most people to walk upright, but there's still a palpable sense of adventure as you spur off down side tunnels, which reveal elements of earlier temples and steep ceremonial stairways that appear to go on forever into the gloom. Emerging at the end of one tunnel, you'll find an area of open-air excavations, where part of the great pyramid has been exposed alongside various lesser shrines with explanations in English of their importance.

The zócalo

Capilla Real Mon–Sat 9am–1pm & 4.30–6pm • Free

One side of Cholula's large zócalo – the Plaza de la Concordia – is taken up by the ecclesiastical buildings of the **Convento de San Gabriel**, built from 1529 on the site of the temple of Quetzalcoatl. The Gothic main church is of little interest, but behind it is the great mustard-yellow **Capilla Real**, topped by 49 tiled cupolas. Moorish in conception, the interior comes with a forest of columns supporting semicircular arches and immediately recalls the Mezquita in Córdoba, Spain.

ARRIVAL AND DEPARTURE

CHOLULA

By bus Buses for TAPO in Mexico City serve the Estrella Roja terminal at 12 Pte 108 (8 daily; 3hr). Buses for CAPU in Puebla can be picked up across the street at the corner of 3 Nte (every 15min until around 9pm; 30min). From the Estrella Roja terminal, head down 5 de Mayo to get to the zócalo; from there, follow Morelos past the old train tracks to reach the pyramid.

By colectivo There's a constant stream of *colectivos* from Puebla (14 Pte, between 9 and 11 Nte) that run from around 5am to 10pm, most of which run right by the archeological site. To get back to Puebla you can pick them up on 5 Pte.

ACCOMMODATION

Reforma 4 Sur 101 at Morelos ☎ 222 247 0149. Small rooms with tiny bathrooms, all round the ground-floor car park. Its relatively central location and low rates are the only thing that make this place stand out. **M$250**

Suites San Juan 5 Sur 103 at Hidalgo ☎ 222 178 0398. It looks like a car park but there are Tardis-like rooms tucked away in the corner, a lot bigger on the inside than they look on the outside. Some are even bigger than others, and as they're all the same price, it's worth asking for a large room. There's also a restaurant, where breakfast is included in the weekend price (M$410), but not in the weekday price. **M$351**

Trailer Park Las Américas 6 Nte at 30 Ote ☎ 222 247 8801. You may have a job finding anyone in attendance at this slightly ramshackle site, where you can camp or park an RV, so it's wise to call in advance. Camping **US$20** **(M$330)**

Villas Arqueológicas 2 Pte 601 ☎ 222 273 7900 or ☎ 01 800 557 7755, ⌂ villasmex.com. Fresh rooms with tiled floors set around a pool. The rooms aren't huge, but they're cool and relaxing, and "spa" services (massage, in other words) are available to help you relax even more. Prices rise at weekends (M$1250). **M$980**

EATING

Enamorada Portal Guerrero 1, west side of zócalo ☎ 222 247 0292. Eternally popular with coffee lovers, diners and those here to drink while listening to the occasional band (most nights from 8pm), this place also does a good Sun morning buffet brunch (8am–noon). Starters include *huitlacoche* (corn fungus; M$60), with mains such as steak in mustard sauce (M$85). Tues–Sun 8am–11pm.

Güero's Hidalgo 102, south side of zócalo ☎ 222 247 2188. A bright, modern restaurant where they'll do you a good set breakfast till noon, and solid Mexican food thereafter, including *tampiqueña* (sliced beef served with chile, relish, cheese, *refritos* and guacamole; M$99) and *pozole* (soup with meat and corn; M$36). Mon–Sat 7.30am–11pm, Sun 7.30am–8pm.

Los Jarrones Portal Guerrero 7, west side of zócalo ☎ 222 247 1098. Students swarm to this rustic-style café, which does a good M$60 comida corrida, as well as dishes such as roast *cecina* (cured beef) for M$95, or sirloin steak in roquefort sauce for M$165. Mon & Tues 8am–5pm, Wed–Sun 8am–midnight.

NIGHTLIFE

Cholula is generally regarded as the **nightlife** capital of the Puebla region, but aside from a few bars in town, most of the action has moved about 3km out to the Recta A Cholula, the main Cholula–Puebla highway, which is thoroughly inconvenient and makes taxi rides essential. Establishments also tend to be far apart from each other. The best bet is to ask locally for the current hot spot and commit yourself to just one place for the night – not a bad idea when entry can cost M$100 or more.

Around Cholula

Churches Variable opening hours; if closed just knock for access • "Chipilo" buses from the corner of 3 Nte and 6 Pte run to Acatepec and Tonatzintla

If you want to explore some of the churches around Cholula, head for **ACATEPEC**, easily reached by local bus. The spectacular village church here, San Francisco, has a superb Baroque facade entirely covered in glazed bricks and *azulejos* of local manufacture. It's not particularly large but it is beautifully proportioned and quite unexpected in this setting.

In the village of **TONATZINTLA**, a 1km walk to the northwest, the plain facade of the church of Santa María conceals a remarkably elaborate Baroque treasury. Here local craftsmen covered every available centimetre in ornament, interspersing bird, plant and native life with the more usual Christian elements.

Popocatépetl and Ixtaccíhuatl

"Popo" and "Ixta", as the snow-clad volcanic peaks of **Popocatépetl** (5452m) and **Ixtaccíhuatl** (5285m) are affectionately known, are the nation's second- and third-highest peaks (after the 5700m Pico de Orizaba). You get excellent views of them from almost anywhere west of the capital, and viewing from afar is all most people do these days. "Popo" has been rumbling and fuming away since September 1994, and for much of the time since then the region has been on Yellow Alert, with evacuation procedures posted throughout surrounding towns. Activity was renewed in December 2000, culminating in the largest eruption on record. Though there were no devastating lava flows, the crater spat out hot rocks, dust fell on the capital and, on several occasions, Mexico City's airport (over 60km away) was closed for a few hours. Local villagers, evacuated for weeks during the eruption, were forced to stand idly by while their livestock trampled their fields. In April 2012, renewed activity, including the expulsion of volcanic ash, led the authorities to step up the level of alert to "**Yellow Phase 3**", which means among other things that no access is allowed within 12km of the volcano until further notice.

Parque Nacional de Volcanes

Daily 7am–9pm • M$35 per day when operating; to enter the park you'll need to fill out and submit a formal request, using a form which can be found on the website – the link is on the "Acceso" page • Park office in Amecameca at Plaza de la Constitución 9 (☎ 597 978 3830, ⓦ iztapopo.conanp.gob.mx)

Given the unpredictable and intermittent explosions of Popocatépetl and Ixtaccíhuatl (particularly the former), much of the **Parque Nacional de Volcanes** and its 12km radius is often off limits to the public. A small section of the **park remains open**, where the **Cultural Conservation Centre** at the top opens from time to time and offers talks (all in Spanish) on the geography of the area and the cultural history of the peaks. For details on the latest situation, contact the park office.

A good option if you're after an eyeful of the huge peaks is the town of **Amecameca** (often just "Ameca"), an hour east of Mexico City, where dramatic views of the

2

THE LEGEND OF "POPO" AND "IXTA"

The full names of Mexico's ever-smoking **volcanoes** come from an **Aztec Romeo-and-Juliet-style legend**. Popocatépetl (Smoking Mountain) was a warrior, Ixtaccíhuatl (White Lady) his lover, the beautiful daughter of the emperor. Believing Popocatépetl killed in battle, "Ixta" died from grief, and when he returned alive he laid her body down on the mountain, where he eternally stands sentinel, holding a burning torch. From the west, Ixta does somewhat resemble a reclining female form and the various parts of the mountain are named accordingly – the feet, the knees, the belly, the breast and so on.

---

volcanoes can be enjoyed from the comfort of the palm-lined zócalo. From here you can drive, hitch or get a taxi (there are no buses), when the situation allows, to the Paso de Cortés, a 3800m-high pass between the volcanoes. It makes for a memorable experience, with the two giants rising high above you on either side. **Climbs** up Ixta also begin in Ameca; this is a challenging trek for serious mountaineers only, involving a night or two at very high altitude, and a technical 3km-long ridge traverse (often requiring ropes) to reach the summit.

ARRIVAL AND DEPARTURE
PARQUE NACIONAL DE VOLCANES

By bus The bus station in Amecameca, served by "Servicio Volcánes" (AV) buses from TAPO in Mexico City (every 20min, 5am–9pm; 1hr 30min;) and in the other direction from Cuautla, is on 20 de Noviembre, just off the zócalo's northwest corner.

ACCOMMODATION

El Marques 20 de Noviembre, at the beginning of town, three blocks northwest of bus station, Ameca ☎ 597 978 1192. Shades of jolly orange and sunny yellow deck out the bright, spacious rooms, where you can park your car right outside. Good views of the sierra from the front. M$290

San Carlos Constitución 10, southeast corner of the zócalo, by the church, Ameca ☎ 597 978 0746. An absolute bargain: the rooms are fresh and clean, all with bathrooms, and the place is as central as you could want. You do, however, pay M$40 extra to have a telly in your room. M$130

South of Mexico City

Heading south from Mexico City, you climb over the mountains and descend to **Cuernavaca**, which brims with colonial mansions and gardens, and draws visitors on account of its proximity to several important archeological sites, notably the hilltop pyramid sites of **Tepoztlán** and **Xochicalco**. An hour further south the silver town of **Taxco** straggles picturesquely up a hillside, making it one of the most appealing destinations hereabouts. From Mexico City, all of these places can be reached via the Central de Autobuses del Sur at Taxqueña.

Cuernavaca

With its refreshing spring-like climate, **CUERNAVACA** has always provided a place of escape from Mexico City, but it isn't always as refreshing as it claims to be. The state capital of Morelos is rapidly becoming industrialized, and the streets in the centre are permanently clogged with traffic and fumes. The gardens and villas that shelter the rich are almost all hidden away or in districts far from the centre, and many of them belong to narco-barons, whose rivalries brought a spate of **violence** in 2010. The spring of that year saw discotheques attacked and castrated corpses hung from bridges as deputies of a local kingpin fought for succession in the wake of his assassination by Mexican marines. The ensuing conflict left some fifty people dead, although the situation has calmed down somewhat since then.

2

▲ Mexico City

CUERNAVACA

0   100
metres

1 Cuautla & Pyramid of Tepanzolco

Pyramid of Teopanzolco ▶

◀ Salto de San Antón

DRINKING & NIGHTLIFE
Barecito	2
El Garage	3
Samanna	1
Tumbao	4

Estrella Blanca bus terminal

LINARES

GUERRERO

CUAGLIA

Pullman de Morelos Casino de la Selva bus terminal

AVENIDA DEL PARQUE

AVENIDA OBREGÓN

ARISTA

MATAMOROS

DEGULLADO

NO REELECCIÓN

Market

LÓPEZ MATEOS

GÁNDARA

ARAGÓN Y LEÓN

Laundry

MORROW

ARTEAGA

Market bus terminal

Jardín Borda

MORELOS

LERDO DE TEJEDA

COMONFORT

JARDÍN JUÁREZ

Catedral de la Asunción

RAYÓN

HIDALGO

PLAZA DE ARMAS

GUTENBERG

Museo Robert Brady

NETZHUALCOYOTL

PLAZUELA DEL ZACATE

CASAS

Museo Regional Cuauhnahuac

CUAUHTÉMOC

ATLACON

ABASOLO

BULEVAR JUÁREZ

FRANCISO LEYVA

Pullman de Morelos downtown terminal

GALEANA

MOTOLINIA

N

CUAUHTÉMOTZIN

Estrella Roja bus terminal

BOCANEGRA

HUMBOLDT

AVENIDA MORELOS

FRANCISCO LEYVA

HIMNO NACIONAL

EATING
Los Arcos	8
Casa Hidalgo	8
La Comuna	2
Emiliano's	6
La India Bonita	3
Las Mañanitas	1
Marco Polo	5
Pollo y Más	7
Vienes	4

ACCOMMODATION
América	4
Casa Colonial	7
Colonial	5
Hostería del Sol	6
Las Mañanitas	1
Roma	2
Royal	3

Estrella de Oro bus terminal

RUFINO TAMAYO

Jardín Etnobotánico

▼ Acapulco

2

Brief history

The Aztecs called the city Cuauhnahuac ("place by the woods"), and it became a favourite resort and hunting ground for their rulers; the Spaniards corrupted the name to Cuernavaca ("cow horn") simply because they couldn't pronounce Cuauhnahuac. Hernán Cortés seized and destroyed the city during the siege of Tenochtitlán, then built himself a palace here. The palace-building trend has continued over the centuries: Emperor Maximilian and the deposed Shah of Iran both had houses here, and the inner suburbs are packed with the high-walled mansions of wealthy Mexicans and expats.

The zócalo

Cuernavaca's **zócalo** has two parts: the Plaza de Armas and, to its northwest, the smaller Jardín Juárez, with its bandstand. Around the twin plazas you'll find a series of cafés where you can sit outdoors under the watchful eye of a huge, black, volcanic-rock **statue of Morelos** that faces the Palacio de Gobierno, across the plaza.

Museo Regional Cuauhnahuac

Eastern end of the Plaza de Armas • Tues–Sun 9am–6pm • M$46 • ☎ 777 312 6996

Located behind the Plaza's statue of Morelos, the **Museo Regional Cuauhnahuac** is housed in the sixteenth-century **Palacio de Cortés**. Work on this building began as early as 1522, when, although Tenochtitlán had fallen, much of the country had yet to come under Spanish control – the fortress-like aspect of the palace's older parts reflects this period. Over the centuries, though, it's been added to and modified substantially – first by Cortés himself and later by the state authorities to whom it passed – so that what you see today is every bit a palace. The museum is a good one, spacious and well laid out with a substantial section covering local archeology, including some fine examples of steles and a lovely seated figure from Xochicalco. In fact, the building is partly constructed over the ruins of a small pyramid, which can be seen in the courtyard and elsewhere. There's also a substantial collection of colonial art, weaponry and everyday artefacts – look for the sixteenth-century clock mechanism from the cathedral and a reproduction of a *cuexcomate*, a kind of thatched granary still found around the state.

Diego Rivera murals

The museum's highlight, though, is a series of **murals** around the gallery, painted by Diego Rivera in 1929 and 1930. Depicting Mexican history from the Conquest to the Revolution, they concentrate in particular on the atrocities committed by Cortés, and on the revolutionary Emiliano Zapata, who was born in the state of Morelos, raised most of his army from among its peasant farmers and remains a local hero. From the balcony, there are wonderful, though sometimes hazy, views to the east with Popocatépetl in the far distance.

The cathedral

Cnr of Morelos and Hidalgo • Daily 9am–7pm • Free • ⓦ catedraldecuernavaca.org

The **Catedral de la Asunción** is three blocks west of the zócalo on the south side of a grassy tree-shaded compound that also contains a couple of other small churches. Founded by Cortés in 1529, the cathedral looks bulky and threatening from the outside (at one stage there were even cannons mounted along the battlemented roof line), but it has been tastefully refurbished within and stripped almost bare, a modernist approach which can be an enormous relief if you've grown tired of the churrigueresque and Baroque flamboyance elsewhere. Most of the decor is understated, but traces of murals discovered during the redecoration have been uncovered in places – they have a remarkably East Asian look and are believed to have been painted by a Christian Chinese or Filipino artist in the days when the cathedral was the centre for

THE MARIACHI MASS

Until his death in 2000, Cuernavaca's bishop was **Luis Cervantes**, one of the country's most liberal and outspoken clergymen. Apart from doing up his cathedral (see above), he was renowned for instituting the "Mariachi Mass", which has been continued by his disciples. Every Sunday, this service is conducted to the accompaniment of traditional Mexican music and usually attracts large crowds.

2

missions to the Far East. At one time, the main Spanish trade route came through here, with goods brought across the Pacific to Acapulco, overland through central Mexico and on from Veracruz to Spain. If, after viewing the interior of the cathedral, you need your fix of golden exuberance, pop into the **Capilla del Santísimo**, where there's a small gilt *retablo* and Stations of the Cross in charcoal on paper.

Museo Robert Brady

Netzahualcoyotl 4 at cnr 20 de Noviembre • Tues–Sun 10am–6pm • M$35 • ☎ 777 318 8554

The **Museo Robert Brady** occupies a former sixteenth-century convent and holds the Iowa-born artist's private collection. Brady moved to Cuernavaca in the 1960s, and lived here until his death in 1986. Filled with art from around the world and decorated in an intensely colourful artesanía style, the museum is a fabulous place, with rooms arranged aesthetically, and without regard to history, geography or classification of artistic styles. As a result, what you see is more like a beautiful home than a typical museum, and is well worth a visit.

The rooms, arranged around a couple of outside patios complete with sculptures and a delightful pool, are filled with works by most of the greats of twentieth-century **Mexican art**. Even the bathrooms contain works by Diego Rivera and Rufino Tamayo, and there are also pieces by Frida Kahlo, Graham Sutherland, and some particularly good works by Rafael Coronel, including a portrait of Peggy Guggenheim. Everything is labelled in English.

Jardín Borda

Morelos 271, immediately west of the cathedral • Tues–Sun 10am–5.30pm • M$30 • ☎ 777 318 1050

A large formal garden adjacent to the mansion of Taxco mining magnate José de la Borda (see p.182), the **Jardín Borda** falls short of the grandeur Borda dreamed of when he commissioned the garden in the eighteenth century, yet both the garden and the mansion are a delightfully tranquil reminder of the haven Cuernavaca once was. Emperor Maximilian and Empress Carlota later adopted Borda's mansion as their weekend home.

Salto de San Antón

Bajada del Salto, Barrio de San Antón • Daily 8am–6pm • Free

About twenty minutes' walk into the suburbs beyond the Jardín Borda is the **Salto de San Antón**, a beautiful 36m cascade surrounded by vegetation and natural columns of crystallized basalt. Unfortunately, the site has been overdeveloped and is marred by concrete walkways, litter and a faint stench from the polluted water, but it's still pretty, and the road to the falls passes a number of flower shops and restaurants.

Jardín Etnobotánico

Matamoros 200, Col. Acapantzingo, 2km southeast of the centre • Daily 9am–5pm • Free • ☎ 777 312 5955

The pretty grounds and collection of medicinal plants at the **Jardín Etnobotánico** are just about worth taking a taxi (or a long walk) to see. As well as the labelled specimens – coffee, guavas, roses and medicinal herbs – there is a small museum of traditional medicine. This latter is housed in the **Casa de la India Bonita**, a retreat commissioned in 1866 by Emperor Maximilian for himself and the local girl he took for a mistress, who is known to history only as "La India Bonita".

2

Pyramid of Teopanzolco

Rio Balsas, 2km northeast of the city centre • Daily 10am–5pm • M$35 • City bus #4 or #10 from Degollado, but check with the driver because not all buses go as far as the pyramid

The **Pyramid of Teopanzolco** is the area's sole significant reminder of the pre-colonial period. So effectively buried was this site that it took an artillery bombardment during the Revolution to uncover it. Located to the northeast of the centre beyond the old train station (which is what the gunners were aiming at), it's a small temple containing two pyramids, one built over the other.

ARRIVAL AND DEPARTURE   CUERNAVACA

By bus Cuernavaca doesn't have a single main bus station. Instead, bus companies have their own depots in different parts of town. Pullman de Morelos operate very frequent buses from Mexico City's Central del Sur to their city-centre terminal on Netzahualcoyotl at Abalolo, but they also have a second, less convenient terminal at Casino de Selva, so when buying Pullman de Morelos tickets from Mexico City, take a bus to "Centro" rather than "Casino" if you want to end up downtown. Estrella Blanca's terminal is easy to find, on Morelos, just north of the centre, with services to and from Guerrero (Taxco and Acapulco) and the west of Mexico state (Ixtapan de la Sal and Toluca). Estrella Roja (Puebla and Cuautla) have a terminal three blocks south of the zócalo at Cuauhtémotzin and Galeana, and Estrella de Oro's terminal (the best for Acapulco) is even further south, on Morelos near its junction with Galeana. Finally, there's a terminal for second-class services within the state of Morelos (notably Tepoztlán and Cuautla) by the market.

From Puebla, although a few services use the Estrella Roja terminal, you'll more likely be dumped at the Autobuses Oro terminal, which is way out on Blv Cuauhnahuac, 5km southeast of the centre, from where you'll need to take a local bus or taxi into town.

Destinations Acapulco (Estrella de Oro terminal, 15–18 daily; Estrella Blanca terminal, 5 daily; 5hr from both); Cuautla (Estrella Roja terminal, every 20–30min; 1hr 20min; market terminal, every 30min; 1hr 40min); Ixtapan de la Sal (Estrella Blanca terminal, hourly; 2hr 30min); Mexico City (Pullman de Morelos terminal, every 15min; Casino terminal every 10min; roughly 1hr 30min from both); Mexico City airport (Casino terminal, hourly; 1hr 30min); Puebla (Estrella Roja terminal, 4 daily; Autobuses Oro terminal, hourly; 3hr 30min from both); Taxco (Estrella Blanca terminal, hourly; 1hr 40min); Tepoztlán (market terminal, every 30min; 45min); Toluca (Estrella Blanca terminal, every 30min; 2hr 30min).

INFORMATION

Tourist office The state tourist office, near the Estrella de Oro terminal, at Morelos 187 Sur (Mon–Fri 8.30am–5pm; ☎777 314 1880, ⓦmorelostravel.com), is generally helpful, with information on buses and excursions, but their branch office at Hidalgo 5 in the city centre (daily 9am–6pm; ☎777 314 3920) tends to be better informed about local tourist sights.

ACCOMMODATION

Cuernavaca has a reasonable range of **hotels** close to the centre but little that is particularly appealing in budget categories: many of the cheaper options are just north of the centre on Matamoros and the streets that connect it with Morelos. Visitors looking for mid-range and top-end places are well served, with some establishments occupying grand old mansions in the centre and others spread around pools and lush gardens in the suburbs. The tourist office has a list of contact addresses for families offering **private rooms**, a service aimed at students attending local language schools – the schools themselves and their notice boards are also good sources for such accommodation.

América Aragón y León 14 ☎777 318 6127. A simple but clean and respectable place in a street mostly full of dives; all rooms have bath, but only those at the front have outside windows (the others have windows onto the inner courtyard). M$310

Casa Colonial Netzahualcoyotl 37 ☎777 312 7033. Gorgeous rooms in a delightful eighteenth-century mansion close to the Museo Robert Brady (see p.175). With attractive colonial public areas and a pool, this is one of the most appealing places in the centre, and the price includes breakfast. TV on request, but no phones. Prices rise by some

M$370 on Fri & Sat. M$1215

Colonial Aragón y León 19 ☎777 318 6414, ⓔhotelcolonialcortes@hotmail.com. This is the most comfortable hotel on Aragón y León. Its rooms all have ceiling fans, bathroom and TV, and are arranged around a pleasant little patio garden. M$420

Hostería del Sol Callejón de la Bolsa del Diabolo, by Hidalgo 3 ☎777 318 3241, ⓔhosteríadelsol@hotmail .com. This well-kept little place has some quite charming rooms, nicely decorated with pretty tiles and paintwork. En-suite rooms cost M$200 extra. M$400

★ **Las Mañanitas** Linares 107 ☎ 777 362 0000, in the US ☎ 1 888 413 9199, ⓦ lasmananitas.com.mx. Beautiful luxury hotel, just a 10min walk from the zócalo. The streetfront entrance gives little clue of the oasis within, where peacocks, flamingoes and African cranes strut around a pool and lush gardens. The tiled-floor rooms come with heavy wooden furniture and all the fittings, and there's a superb restaurant on site (see below). Breakfast included. Prices rise to M$5135 on Fri & Sat. M$4190

Roma Matamoros 17 ☎ 777 318 8778. This little hotel has rooms set around a small atrium, all with bathroom, TV and overhead fans, plus suites with a/c. There's a small swimming pool and bar as well as a café-restaurant, wi-fi and parking facilities. Rates include breakfast for one person, and rise to M$695 on Fri & Sat. M$575

Royal Matamoros 11 ☎ 777 314 4018, ⓦ hoteles-royal .com. The rooms here are arranged around a tangerine-coloured central patio with parking space, and the ones on the top floor are the cheapest, though they're otherwise exactly the same as the rest. There's wi-fi throughout. M$400

EATING

CAFÉS, CHEAP EATS & SNACKS

★ **La Comuna** Morrow 6 ☎ 777 314 4132. Small and friendly cooperatively run café, serving comidas corridas for M$35, enchiladas of various sorts for M$45–59 and excellent breakfasts. The food is good but it's also a great place just to hang out with a coffee or a beer. Daily 10am–8pm.

Emiliano's Rayón 5–C ☎ 777 314 5756. This cheap and cheerful diner with three separate eating spaces is an excellent place for a filling budget meal, offering set breakfasts (M$30), comidas corridas (M$35) and *pozole* (M$55). Daily 8am–8pm.

Pollo y Más Galeana 4 ☎ 777 312 8915. This cheap snack bar opposite the zócalo churns out decent roast chicken, burgers, enchiladas and *antojitos*, M$38 for comidas corridas, posher set menus at M$65 and M$85, and set breakfasts at M$35–80. Daily 8am–8pm.

Vienes Lerdo de Tejada 302 ☎ 777 241 5223. Austro-Hungarian café, bar, patisserie and restaurant (set menu M$55), just a block from the zócalo; a great spot for continental-style coffee and pastries. The name is a pun on *vienés*, meaning "Viennese", and *vienes*, meaning "you come". Daily 7.30am–8pm.

RESTAURANTS

Los Arcos Jardín de los Héroes 4 ☎ 777 312 1510. Ever-popular restaurant and bar on the south side of the zócalo serving espresso coffee and a wide range of dishes from Cuernavaca-style enchiladas (stuffed with chorizo) at M$65 to steak in mustard sauce for M$125. There's also an M$85 set menu. In the evening most people are here to drink and listen to the live music, which comes in a variety of styles and abilities, and starts at 8pm. Daily 8am–midnight.

Casa Hidalgo Jardín de los Héroes 6 ☎ 777 312 2749. Next door to *Los Arcos* but rather posher, with white table linen, an outside terace, a roof terrace and various balconies with views over the zócalo. Dishes include stuffed chiles (M$125–139, depending on the filling), or fish with mango and green coriander (M$175). Mon–Thurs & Sun 1.30–11pm, Fri & Sat 1.30pm–midnight.

La India Bonita Morrow 15-B, just off Morelos ☎ 777 312 5021. This lovely restaurant with a pleasant outdoor patio has excellent food and impeccable service. House *mole* is M$149, you can get a grilled rib-eye for M$199 and a set breakfast costs M$70–154. There's live music from 8pm, which on Sat takes the form of a folk ballet. Daily 8am–10pm.

Las Mañanitas Ricardo Linares 107 ☎ 777 362 0000 or ☎ 01 800 221 5299. People drive hours to visit this well-known restaurant which serves fine Mexican and international cuisine in the sumptuous grounds of the hotel of the same name (see above). Traditional Mexican starters include red maguey worms (M$179), followed by mains such as rock-lobster tails thermidor (M$539) or entrecôte bourgignonne (M$564). Daily 1–11pm.

Marco Polo Hidalgo 30 ☎ 777 312 3484, ⓦ marco-polo .com.mx. Superior Italian restaurant serving up its own home-made pasta (M$95–165), or you can attempt to get through one of their huge pizzas (M$66–142). Mon–Thurs 1–10.30pm, Fri & Sat 1pm–midnight, Sun 1–10pm.

DRINKING AND NIGHTLIFE

There are two main centres of evening activity in Cuernavaca: in the centre, Plazuela del Zacate, south of the zócalo, is a lively square full of bars, while 2km to the east, in Lomas del Mirador, a block of Av Plan de Ayala just east of Av Tepanzolco has the city's biggest concentration of clubs. For something more sedate, there are free concerts from the bandstand in the Jardín Juárez every Thurs evening at 6pm, and live music at 8pm in *Los Arcos* and *La India Bonita* (see above). Be aware that when tensions between the narco-barons are high, nightspots are a prime target for violence, so keep your ear to the ground, and maybe avoid going out during times of trouble.

Barecito Comonfort 17 ☎ 777 314 1425. This place is a bit café-like for a nightlife bar, but it's lesbian-owned and gay-friendly, as well as being a generally laid-back venue, which is handy if you just want to hang out with a quiet

2

drink rather than go for it on the dancefloor. Mon–Fri 4–11pm, Sat & Sun 3pm–1am.

El Garage Casas 5 ☎ 777 240 0820. There's live music every night, with an eclectic mix of bands, at this bustling bar on the Plazuela del Zacate, which also does good cocktails, as well as *chelas* (beers) and shorts (largely mescal and tequila). Daily 6pm–late.

Samanna Plan de Ayala 708, Lomas del Mirador ☎ 777 100 0530. The city's longest-standing discotheque starts off the evening as a bar (happy hour till 10pm), often with live bands later on, and it's even been known to host the odd salsa festival. It's fun rather than sophisticated, and quite popular with local rich-kids, but not exclusively so. Daily 5pm–late.

Tumbao Casas 11. With fluorescent tropical decor, and DJs mixing everything from salsa to techno, this is the liveliest of the bars on Plazuela del Zacate, and definitely the one to go for if you want to give your booty a good old shake. Daily 6pm–around 2am.

DIRECTORY

Banks and exchange *Casas de cambio* include Gesta on the cnr of Galeana and Lerdo de Tejada, plus more at Morrow 9, Matamoros 10 and Hidalgo 7.

Internet All hotels have wi-fi, although internet cafés abound if you need a computer. Try Cyber Gasso, Hidalgo 22–D (Mon–Fri 8am–9pm, Sat & Sun 10am–9pm; M$15/hr).

Laundry Try the laundrette opposite *Hotel América* (Mon–Fri 8am–8pm, Sat 9am–7pm).

Pharmacy The handiest pharmacy is the 24hr Farmacia del Ahorro at the cnr of Hidalgo and Galeana, just south of the zócalo.

Post office At the southwest cnr of the zócalo (Mon–Fri 8am–7.30pm, Sat 9am–12.30pm).

Spanish courses The state tourist office website has a page on schools offering Spanish language courses in Cuernavaca. One that has been recommended is CETLALIC (☎ 777 313 2637, ⓦ cetlalic.org.mx).

Tepoztlán

An interesting side trip from Cuernavaca is to **TEPOZTLÁN**, just 21km to the northeast and dramatically sited in a narrow valley spectacularly ringed by volcanic mountains. Until recently this was an isolated agrarian community inhabited by Nahuatl-speaking people whose lives had changed little between the time of the Conquest and the beginning of the twentieth century. Given its history as an important stronghold of the original Zapatista movement, it was on Tepoztlán that anthropologist Oscar Lewis based his classic study *Life in a Mexican Village*, in which he traced the effects of the Revolution. In recent years, though, new roads and a couple of luxury hotels have begun to change things – Tepoztlán has become a popular weekend retreat from the capital, with its good selection of restaurants and quality arts and crafts shops, though midweek it is still a peaceful spot. For now, at least, the stunning setting also survives, as does a reputation for joyously boisterous **fiestas** (especially Sept 8, celebrating the conversion of the local ruler to Christianity in 1538). Note that accommodation is expensive in Tepoztlán, so you may decide to visit on a day trip.

Ex-Convento Dominico de la Natividad

Eastern side of the zócalo • Museo de Arte Prehispánico daily 10am–6pm • M$10

On Sundays and Wednesdays a **market** is held in the zócalo, where you'll also find the massive **ex-Convento Dominico de la Natividad**. It was a fortress for a while during the Revolution, but is now in a rather beautiful state of disrepair with some attractive murals still surviving in the cloister. Around the back and accessed off Gonzales, part of the church has been given over to the **Museo de Arte Prehispánico**, which holds a remarkably good archeological collection.

Santuario del Cerro Tepozteco

Daily 9am–5.30pm • M$42, free Sun, video permit M$45

Several pre-Hispanic temples have been found on the hilltops in the area, and you can see one to the north, perched high up in impossibly steep-looking terrain. This is the **Santuario del Cerro Tepozteco**, reached from the northern end of Tepozteco after an exhausting 5km walk of an hour or so up what is little more than an upgraded dry stream bed at times. If you're fit, the hike is worth it for the views from this artificially flattened hilltop, and for the chance to inspect the site at close quarters. The small, three-stepped, lime-washed pyramid here was dedicated to Tepoztecatl, a god of *pulque* and of fertility, represented by carvings of rabbits. There were so many *pulque* gods that they were known as the four hundred rabbits: the drink was supposedly discovered by rabbits nibbling at the agave plants from which it is made. This one gained particular kudos when the Spaniards flung the idol off the cliffs, only for his adherents to find that it had landed unharmed – the big September fiesta is in his honour. Follow the example of Mexicans and reward your efforts with a picnic lunch (water and soft drinks are available at a price), but do buck the litter-dropping trend and take your empty containers away with you.

2

ARRIVAL AND INFORMATION

TEPOZTLÁN

By bus Second-class bus services from Cuernavaca's market terminal (every 15min; 45min) use a terminal in Tepoztlán on the old Cuernavaca road, a continuation of 5 de Mayo about 0.5km south of the zócalo. The other bus terminal, used by Cristobal Colón's services between Cuautla (every 30min; 40min) and Mexico City Sur (every 30min; 1hr 15min), is by a *gasolinera* about 300m further out along the same road. Estrella Roja services (roughly every 30min) stop just round the corner. Some of the more frequent Mexico City–Cuautla *directo* services (every 10min) may set you down at the *caseta* on the *autopista* west of town (accessed from the western end of 22 de Febrero, which runs off 5 de Mayo a block south of the zócalo), but don't count on being able to board buses here.

ACCOMMODATION

Posada Ali Netzahualcoyotl 2, off Tepozteco three blocks north of the zócalo ☎ 739 395 1971. Out towards the ruins, this little hotel keeps its lower-cost rooms tucked under the eaves. Larger rooms have sunflower-carved headboards on the beds and wood-beamed ceilings, and everyone has access to the small pool and *frontón* court. Prices may be open to negotiation, especially midweek. M$800

★ **Posada del Tepozteco** Paraíso 3, parallel with 5 de Mayo, a block west of the zócalo ☎ 739 395 0010, ⊛ posadadeltepozteco.com. If your budget can manage it, *the* place to stay in Tepoztlán is this elegant but unpretentious *posada*, wonderfully sited above most of the town, with lovely views of the mountains from the terraces and outdoor pool. The rooms and suites are simple but well equipped, though you pay slightly more for a balcony and mountain view. For a weekend reservation there's a 2-night minimum (M$4720), although discounts are always available midweek. Breakfast included. M$1970

EATING

El Chinelo Tepozteco 15, half a block north of the zócalo ☎ 739 395 1112. Solid Mexican cuisine in simple surrounds with no messing about. Dishes on offer include enchiladas *suizas* (M$90), chicken *mole* (M$95) or chile stuffed with cheese (M$90). Daily 9am–7pm.

Los Colorines Tepozteco 13 (half a block north of the zócalo, next door to El Chinelo) ☎ 739 395 0198. As colourful as its name suggests, this jolly restaurant does a good line in superior Mexican cuisine, and is an excellent place to try *cecina de Yecapixtla* (M$140), Yecapixtla being a town near Cuautla which is known nationwide for its cured beef (*cecina*). And should you fancy a tasty Mexican vegetable for your starter, they'll do you a plate of *huauzontles* (the flowering heads of a quinoa-like plant, not dissimilar to broccoli) for M$75. Mon–Fri 9.30am–9pm, Sat & Sun 8.30am–midnight.

Teposnieves 5 de Mayo 21, half a block north of the zócalo ☎ 739 395 4839. The original branch of what is now a chain has ice creams and sorbets in more flavours than you can count; fig and mescal is a favourite, but if you want something more unusual, there's chile and cucumber, rose petal or beetroot sorbet. M$15 will get you two flavours, M$20 three, and they do tasters to help you decide what you want. There are several smaller branches around town too. Daily 8am–8pm.

Cuautla

Some 42km southeast of Cuernavaca, and an hour and a half by bus, lies **Cuautla**, a pleasant if unexciting little town, where Independence leader and local boy **José María Morelos** was besieged by a royalist army in 1812, and where the great revolutionary leader **Emiliano Zapata** is buried, a block south of the zócalo in the Plazuela de la

Revolución del Sur. Born in the adjoining village of Anenecuilco, he now lies under a huge bronze statue depicting him in heroic pose – moustached, with a broad-brimmed sombrero on his head and a bandoleer across his shoulder; in one hand he clutches a rifle, and in the other a proclamation demanding "Tierra y Libertad" ("land and freedom").

Casa de Morelos

West side of zócalo • Tues–Sun 9.30am–5pm • M$35, free Sun

The **Casa de Morelos** is a beautiful colonial mansion with gardens that was, for three months in 1812, home to José María Morelos (see p.303), and contains archeological finds and items of local historical interest, some of which were only discovered when the place was being done up in 1992, as well as information (in Spanish) on local history, indigenous peoples and local heroes, including Morelos, of course, and also Zapata.

Museo José María Morelos y Pavón

Batalla 19 de Febrero de 1812 (continuation of Galeana) • **Museum** Tues–Sun 10am–5pm • Free **Steam locomotive rides** every 15min, 4–8pm • M$20 • ☎ 735 352 5221

Cuautla's former train station is now home to the **Museo José María Morelos y Pavón**, which mainly traces the life and times of Morelos and the Independence movement of the state that bears his name. For train buffs, the 1904 **steam locomotive** and carriages once used by the town's other great native son, Emiliano Zapata, may be of interest. From time to time, you can take a very short (800m) ride on it, but the days on which it operates are sporadic.

Agua Hedionda

Av Progreso, Col. Otilio Montaño, 2km east of the town centre • Daily 6.30am–5.30pm • Mon–Fri M$50, Sat & Sun M$75 • ☎ 735 352 0044, ⊕ balnearioaguahedionda.com • Yellow-and-white #11 *combi* from Plazuela de la Revolución (15min)

Cuautla has something of a reputation for its thermal **spas**, and there are several large complexes a little way out from the centre, though the emphasis is more on swimming than luxuriating. The most renowned of the spas is **Agua Hedionda**, known for the high concentration of therapeutic minerals in its waters. It has a big pool for splashing about in at a warm 27°C, as well as private pools, jacuzzis and hydromassage services, and you could easily spend half a day luxuriating there, especially if you happen to have a skin condition that responds well to hot, sulphurous mineral waters (or any other excuse really).

ARRIVAL AND INFORMATION
CUAUTLA

By bus Cuautla has three bus stations, all close to each other a couple of blocks east of the zócalo, on or off 2 de Mayo.
Destinations Amecameca (Cristobal Colón terminal, every 10min; 1hr 30min); Cuernavaca (Estrella Roja terminal, every 30min; 1hr 20min); Mexico City Sur (Cristobal Colón terminal, every 10min; 2hr); Mexico City TAPO (Cristobal Colón terminal, every 10min; 3hr); Tepoztlán (Cristobal

Colón and Estrella Roja terminals, every 30min from each; 40min).
Tourist office There's a small and very helpful tourist office at the old train station, four blocks north of the zócalo on Galeana (daily 8am–8pm; ☎ 735 352 5221), but not all the staff speak English. Their website has some useful information, but is not kept very up to date.

ACCOMMODATION

Colón South side of zócalo at corner of Guerrero ☎ 735 352 2990. How good this hotel is depends on what room you get: the front rooms are bright and spacious, with panoramic views of the zócalo, and are an outstanding bargain, especially if you're coming here from tourist traps like Cuernavaca or Tepoztlán. The interior rooms, on the other hand, which cost exactly the same, are small and stuffy with

no outside windows (though still very cheap). It's first come, first served, so early birds stand the best chance of catching the worm. M$50 extra for a kingsize bed. **M$150**
Defensa del Agua Defensa del Agua 34, three blocks north and two east of the zócalo ☎ 735 352 1679. Spacious modern rooms with ceiling fans surround a patio shared between a small pool and a car park. There's also

wi-fi and a branch of the *Italian Coffee Company* (see p.167) on the premises. Rooms cost M$100 extra at weekends (Fri & Sat). **M$200**

España 2 de Mayo 22, one block south and half a block east of the zócalo ☎735 352 2186. A good budget bargain, very handy for the zócalo and the bus terminals, with rooms done out in cool peppermint green and white, and equipped with a TV and fan. **M$150**

EATING

Las Golondrinas Nicolás Catalán 19–A, one block north of the zócalo ☎735 354 1350. This restaurant may not be as elegant as it evidently once was, but the fountains still splash as you sink back in comfy chairs and tuck into corn and *cuitlacoche* soup (M$39), a fish *brochette* in *ranchera* sauce (M$116) or regional specialities such as barbecued rabbit *molcajete* (M$125). Daily 8am–11.30pm.

Tony y Tony's Southwest corner of zócalo ☎735 308 0098. An unassuming little bar-café with outside seating, bargain breakfasts (M$38 for enchiladas, coffee, fruit and juice), decent mains (steak and trimmings M$75) and karaoke nights, which can be fun if you're drunk enough. Daily 9am–midnight.

Xochicalco

Some 38km southwest of Cuernavaca • Daily 9am–6pm • M$48

While not much is known of the site's history, or the people who inhabited it, the impressive hilltop ruins of **Xochicalco** are regarded by archeologists as one of the most significant in central Mexico because of the connections it shows to both the ancient culture of Teotihuacán and the later Toltec peoples. Xochicalco flourished from around 700 to 900 AD – thus overlapping with both Teotihuacán and Tula – and also displays clear parallels with Maya and Zapotec sites of the era.

The setting, high on a bare mountaintop, is reminiscent of Monte Albán (see p.605), the great Zapotec site near Oaxaca. Like Monte Albán and the great Maya sites (but unlike Tula or Teotihuacán), Xochicalco was an exclusively religious and ceremonial centre rather than a true city. The style of many of the carvings, too, recalls Zapotec and Maya art. Their subjects, however, and the architecture of the temples, seem to form a transition between Teotihuacán and Tula. The appearance of **Quetzalcoatl** as a human is especially noteworthy, as he was to turn up in this form at Tula and almost every subsequent site, rather than simply as the feathered serpent of Teotihuacán.

The museum

Arriving at the site, your first stop is at the **museum**, on a neighbouring hilltop from the ruins themselves, where you can take a look at some of the more portable pieces unearthed here. A carved stele that once graced one of the lower courtyards (and has now been replaced by a concrete pillar) takes pride of place in the first room, and is followed by numerous slabs of carved stone, a delicate alabaster bowl and some fine jade masks. From here it is a ten-minute walk to the ruins themselves.

Pirámide de Quetzalcoatl

Much the most important surviving monument here is the **Pirámide de Quetzalcoatl**, on the highest part of the site. Around its base are carved extremely elaborate plumed serpents, coiling around various seated figures and symbols with astronomical significance – all clearly Maya in inspiration. On top, part of the wall of the sanctuary remains standing, though it now surrounds a large hole. In 1993 the centre of the pyramid was excavated to reveal the remains of an earlier pyramid inside.

The Solar Observatory

The other main point of interest is the **Solar Observatory**, located to the northwest of the main pyramid and down the hill a little, accessed through the northern ball-court. Here you'll find the entrance to some subterranean passages, a couple of natural **caves** augmented by steps and tunnels, one of which features a shaft in the roof that is oriented so as to allow the sun to shine directly in. At astronomical midday (midway

2

between sunrise and sunset) for around five weeks either side of the summer solstice – May 14/15 to July 28/29 – the shaft casts a hexagonal patch of light onto the cave floor. At any time, the custodian should point out the remains of frescoes on the walls.

ARRIVAL AND DEPARTURE	XOCHICALCO

By bus There's a very slow and circuitous second-class bus from Cuernavaca's market bus station (every 30min; 1hr). The alternative is to take the half-hourly Miacatlán bus from Cuernavaca's Pullman de Morelos terminal (every 30min; 30min), which will take you to the Crucero de Xochicalco, 4km from the site. There's often a taxi waiting here to run you to the site for about M$25; otherwise you'll either have to walk (uphill) or else wait for the second-class bus to come by.

By car If you're driving, or if you go with a tour, you can continue another thirty-odd kilometres down the road beyond Xochicalco to the caves of Cacahuamilpa (see p.186), from where Taxco (see below) is only a short distance.

Taxco

Silver has been mined in **TAXCO** since before the Conquest. Supplies of the metal have long been depleted, but it is still the basis of the town's fame, as well as its livelihood, in the form of jewellery, which is made in hundreds of workshops here, and sold in an array of shops (*platerías*) catering mainly to tourists. The city is an attractive place, like some Mexican version of a Tuscan village, with a mass of terracotta-tiled, whitewashed houses lining narrow, cobbled alleys that straggle steeply uphill. At intervals the pattern is broken by a larger mansion, or by a courtyard filled with flowers or by the tower of a church rearing up; the twin spires of **Santa Prisca**, a Baroque wedding cake of a church in the centre of town, stand out above all.

Brief history

Though it might seem a prosperous place now, Taxco's development has not been entirely straightforward – indeed, on more than one occasion the town has been all but abandoned. The Spaniards came running at the rumours of mineral wealth here (Cortés himself sent an expedition in 1522), but their success was short-lived, and it wasn't until the eighteenth century that French immigrant **José de la Borda** struck it fabulously rich by discovering the San Ignacio vein. It was during Borda's short lifetime that most of what you see originated – he spent an enormous sum on building the church of Santa Prisca, and more on other buildings and a royal lifestyle here and in Cuernavaca; by his death in 1778 the boom was already over. In 1929 however, the silver trade saw a revival, sparked by the arrival of American architect and writer **William Spratling**, who set up a jewellery workshop in Taxco, drawing on local traditional skills and pre-Hispanic designs. With the completion of a new road around the same time, a massive influx of tourists was inevitable – the town has handled it all fairly well, becoming rich at the expense of just a little charm.

The church of Santa Prisca

Plaza Borda • Daily 9am–6.30pm • Free

The heart of town is the diminutive **Plaza Borda** (zócalo), ringed by recently restored colonial buildings and dominated by Taxco's one outstanding sight, the church of **Santa Prisca**. Towering over the zócalo, its hyper-elaborate facade was built in a single stint between 1751 and 1759, and displays a rare unity. Inside there's a riot of gilded churrigueresque altarpieces and other treasures, including paintings by Miguel Cabrera, a Zapotec who became one of Mexico's greatest colonial religious artists.

Casa Borda

Plaza Borda 1 • Daily 10am–7pm • Free

It's worth popping in for a quick look at José de la Borda's house, the **Casa Borda**, in the northeast corner of the zócalo. Built to order in 1759, it had two sets of quarters, one for Borda himself, and another for his son, who was the priest at Santa Prisca.

TAXCO

Grutas de Cacahuamilpa (20km), Los Arcos, Mexico City, Tourist Information, Teleférico & Plazuela de los Mineros ▲

Mexico City ▲

Museo de Arte Virreinal

Casa Borda

Santa Prisca

Museo Guillermo Spratling

Market

Estrella Blanca terminal

Estrella de Oro terminal

●EATING	
El Adobe	2
Restaurant Bar Acerto	1
Restaurante Ethel	3
Santa Fe	4

■DRINKING & NIGHTLIFE	
Bar Berta	1
La Concha Nostra	2

■ACCOMMODATION	
Agua Escondida	3
Los Arcos	2
Casa de Huéspedes Arellano	5
Casa Grande	6
Emilia Castillo	4
Posada San Javier	1
Santa Prisca	7

0   100
metres

Nowadays it's used as a cultural centre, with theatrical workshops and the occasional exhibition, but it's open to the public and offers good views over the town from many of its windows. There are two storeys at the front, but four at the back.

Museo Guillermo Spratling

Porfirio Delgado 1 • Tues–Sat 9am–5pm, Sun 9am–3pm • M$35

William Spratling's personal collection of antiquities is contained in the **Museo Guillermo Spratling**, right behind Santa Prisca and reached down Calle del Arco at the right-hand side of the church. There are several good pieces, but overall it's disappointing, especially if you've already been to the Museo Nacional de Antropología in Mexico City (see p.95).

Museo de Arte Virreinal

Juan Ruíz de Alarcón 6 • Tues–Sun 10am–6pm • M$20

Taxco's most interesting museum, the **Museo de Arte Virreinal** is housed in the beautiful colonial Casa Humboldt, an old staging inn named after a German explorer-baron who

2

spent just one night here in 1803. Labels in Spanish and English provide detailed and diverting background on the town, its religious art and history, partly focusing on Taxco's importance on the Spanish trade routes between Acapulco and Veracruz.

The silver shops

Beyond the few sights, the way to enjoy Taxco is simply to wander the streets, nosing about in *platerías* and stopping occasionally for a drink. If you're in the market for **silver** you can be fairly sure that the stuff here is the real thing (check for the mark: ".925" or "sterling"), but prices are much the same as they would be anywhere and quality and workmanship can vary enormously: there's everything from mass-produced belt buckles and cheap rings to designer jewellery that will set you back thousands of dollars. The shops off the main streets will be cheaper and more open to bargaining. A section in the **market**, down the steps beside the zócalo, dedicated to silver-hawkers, is a good place to start. But the bulk of the market seems to specialize in tacky tourist goods.

The teleférico

At the northern edge of town • Daily 7am–7pm • M$75 return

There is little of interest in the immediate vicinity of Taxco, but to while away an afternoon you could catch the **teleférico** (cable car) to the hilltop *Hotel Monte Taxco*, where you'll be rewarded with great views. The stroll up to the *teleférico* is a pleasant one anyway: follow Benito Juárez to Plazuela el Minero, a small square with a statue of a miner, and then head left up Avenida de los Plateros to the northern end of town (around 2km), where the remains of the Los Arcos aqueduct cross the road. If you don't fancy the walk, take a "Los Arcos" *combi* from the zócalo.

ARRIVAL AND DEPARTURE   **TAXCO**

BY BUS

Taxco has two bus stations, about 1km apart on Av de los Plateros (formerly Av Kennedy), the main road that contours around the side of the valley at the bottom of town. Estrella Blanca has the most frequent services to Cuernavaca (17 daily; 1hr 40min); Mexico City Sur (9 daily; 2hr 15min); Ixtapan de la Sal (every 40min; 1hr 20min); Toluca (every 40min; 3hr 30min) and most other destinations, but for buses to destinations within Guerrero, you're better off heading for the Estrella de Oro terminal, where you'll find more buses to places like Acapulco (12 daily; 5hr) and Chilpancingo (20 daily; 3hr).

Getting to/from town From either terminal it's a very steep 10min walk, a M$5.50 *combi* or M$35 taxi ride to Plaza Borda (the zócalo). Ignore offers of a free taxi to a "silver mine" – in fact just a small tunnel (not a mine) with a tacky souvenir shop. To get into town on foot from the Estrella Blanca terminal, cross the road and turn right up the hill and then left to climb even more steeply past the church of Santa Veracruz to the centre. From Estrella de Oro, head straight up Calle de Pilita, the steep alley directly across from you, until you come to the Plazuela de San Juan, on your right; from there go down Cuauhtémoc to the zócalo.

INFORMATION

Banks and exchange There are several banks with ATMs on the streets surrounding the zócalo. *Casas de cambio* include Balsas, just off Plazuela de San Juan at Carlos Nibbi 2 (Mon–Fri 9.30am–3pm & 4.30–5.30pm, Sat & Sun 8am–3.30pm).
Internet Cyber Click, Hidalgo 8 (daily 10am–9pm; M$10/hr); unnamed internet station, Cuauhtémoc 14 (Mon–Sat

10am–9.30pm, Sun 4–9.30pm; M$10/hr).
Tourist office Av de los Plateros, opposite Plazuela el Minero, at the northern end of Juárez (daily 9.30am–7pm; 🕾 762 622 0798). A more conveniently located kiosk on the west side of the zócalo (daily 9.30am–7pm) dispenses much the same information.

ACCOMMODATION

Taxco has some excellent **hotels**, and when the day-trippers have left, the place settles into a calmer mode. There are inexpensive places near the zócalo, and at the higher end of the scale you're swamped with choices. Particularly nice are some lovely restored colonial buildings that now serve as comfortable hotels.

Agua Escondida Plaza Borda 4, north side of zócalo 🕾 762 622 1166, 🖳 aguaescondida.com. The deceptively small frontage gives little clue to the actual size of this rambling hotel. There are several cheaper, older rooms hidden away at the back (where there's also a pool), or slightly newer ones – some with good views – nearer the reception, but they aren't worth the price difference. Those at the front can be noisy at night. Up to fifty percent discounts if you book over the phone a few days in advance. M$1150

★ **Los Arcos** Juan Ruíz de Alarcón 2 ☎ 762 622 1836. A couple of blocks east of the zócalo, this beautiful hotel has wonderfully cool, large rooms in a seventeenth-century colonial building set around a lovely brick and stone courtyard with a big tree growing through it, as well as an excellent (and not particularly expensive) restaurant. Book ahead, particularly at weekends when the price goes up to M$950. M$800

Casa de Huéspedes Arellano Pajaritos 23 ☎ 762 622 0215. A good-value budget hotel right in the market, with three sun terraces. The higher up you get, the cheaper the rooms, though some only have shared bathroom facilities. M$350

Casa Grande Plazuela de San Juan 7 ☎ 762 622 0969, �🌐 hotelcasagrandetaxco.com.mx. A fun place to stay, friendly, with a slightly run-down charm, and cheerful rooms, some of which are en suite (M$140 extra). Those on

the top floor have direct access to the scenic rooftop terrace. M$515

Emilia Castillo Juan Ruíz de Alarcón 7 ☎ 762 622 1396, �🌐 hotelemiliacastillo.com. Beyond a glass mosaic sunsplash in reception and a big mural in the lounge area, this bright hotel in a colonial mansion near the zócalo has homely if smallish rooms with tiled floors and warm colours. Rooms cost M$850 on Fri and Sat. M$720

Posada San Javier Estacadas 32 ☎ 762 622 3177. Spacious hotel on a steep hill, with a pool and attractive gardens. Rooms are large and simply but tastefully decorated (and some have good views). Rate includes continental breakfast. M$850

Santa Prisca Cena Obscuras 1, just off Plazuela de San Juan ☎ 762 622 0080 or ☎ 762 622 0980, ✉ htl_staprisca@yahoo.com. Attractive converted colonial building just off the zócalo, with a pleasant flower-filled patio with banana trees and bougainvillea, and a variety of rooms. Don't get too excited about the "balconies" on offer with some rooms, however: the views are great and the rooms themselves are larger, but the "balconies" aren't big enough to sit out on (and cost M$150 extra). M$500

EATING

Finding somewhere to **eat** in Taxco is no problem: there are several enticing places around the zócalo that are wonderful for watching the world go by. They do tend to be expensive, though, and by sacrificing a little atmosphere you'll do better along some of the streets that lead away from the centre. All except the cheapest of the hotels have their own dining rooms, and, for rock-bottom prices, the market has a section of food stalls, which are better than they look.

El Adobe Plazuela de San Juan 13 ☎ 762 622 1416. Homely restaurant where excellent Mexican food is served for moderate prices either in the cosy interior or on a balcony overlooking the square. Try the house steak, with chile and *epazote* (a Mexican herb with a distinctive flavour) for M$120. There's live guitar music Fri & Sat from 8pm. Daily 8am–11pm.

Restaurant Bar Acerto Plaza Borda 12 ☎ 762 622 0064. Directly opposite Santa Prisca and with excellent views, especially if you can get one of the prized window seats. Formerly known as *Bar Paco*, it has been the place to come since 1937 and remains a nice spot for sipping a beer or dining on well-prepared dishes, including Mexican

classics such as *pollo al mole* (M$120). Daily 11am–midnight.

Restaurante Ethel Plazuela de San Juan 14 ☎ 762 622 0788. A small, family-run restaurant where you can tuck into good, homestyle Mexican cooking, in the form of a good-value breakfast (M$60–85), a comida corrida (M$80) or a hearty bowl of *pozole* (M$85). Daily 9am–7pm.

Santa Fe Hidalgo 2 ☎ 762 622 1170. Amid walls decked with photos of past patrons and old-time Taxco, this popular local restaurant has been serving up good, solid grub since 1954. If it's breakfast you're after, you can get one for M$48–68, and if not, they'll do you anything from a *pozole* (M$65) to a T-bone (M$120). Daily 8am–10pm.

DRINKING AND NIGHTLIFE

In the evening everyone gathers around the zócalo to see and be seen, to stroll or to sit outdoors with a coffee or a drink at one of the **bars**.

Bar Berta Plaza Borda 9 ☎ 762 622 0172. Traditional meeting place almost next to the church, and one of several places in Mexico claiming to be the original home of the margarita, though their version of it is unique: a mix of tequila, lime, mineral water and honey, known as a "Berta", invented by the bar's original *dueña* (the eponymous Berta) back in the 1930s. Daily 11am–11.30pm.

La Concha Nostra Upstairs at Plazuela de San Juan 7 (same building as the Casa Grande hotel) ☎ 762 622 7944. A lively bar overlooking Plazuela de San Juan, with live music weekends (rock Fri, *trova* guitar music Thurs & Sat), but also serving pasta, pizza and *antojitos*, especially during the day (spaghetti with octopus M$60, mushroom quesadillas M$38). Daily noon–2am.

2

Grutas de Cacahuamilpa

Daily 10am–5pm • M$65 with obligatory 90min guided tour • ⓦ cacahuamilpa.conanp.gob.mx • Buses between Taxco (Estrella Blanca terminal) and Ixtapan de la Sal pass within 1km of the entrance (ask to be dropped off at the junction and walk down the hill for 15min); there are also *combis* to the Grutas every hour or so from opposite Taxco's Estrella Blanca bus terminal

Just 20km north of Taxco on the highway to Ixtapan de la Sal and Toluca, you pass close to the vast complex of caves known as the **Grutas de Cacahuamilpa**. This network of caverns, hollowed out by two rivers, extends for some 70km. The ninety-minute obligatory tour (in Spanish only) obviously takes in only a fraction of these, passing evocative rock formations, all illuminated to better illustrate their names: "the hunchback", "the bottle of champagne" and others. Among the graffiti you're shown a rather prim note from the wife of Maximilian: "María Carlota reached this point". Alongside, Lerdo de Tejada, who became president in 1872, five years after Maximilian's execution, has scrawled "Sebastian Lerdo de Tejada went further". There's a restaurant and several food stalls by the entrance.

West of Mexico City

The southwest of the State of Mexico is dominated by the state capital, **Toluca**, which is served by extremely frequent buses from Mexico City's Terminal Poniente. The main artery through the region is Hwy-55, superseded in places by a modern *autopista* but still used by most of the buses to the small towns. Coming up from Acapulco or Taxco, Hwy-55 passes through the spa town of Ixtapan de la Sal on its way to Toluca, though you'll need to take a detour to see the charming – and increasingly upmarket – village of Malinalco, with its hilltop temple, and the nearby market town of Tenancingo. West of Toluca, on the way out to Michoacán, the main attraction is the beautiful lakeside town of Valle de Bravo, which is also a good base for visiting parts of the Monarch Butterfly Sanctuary.

Tenancingo

If you're heading north from Ixtapan de la Sal towards Toluca, the next town of any size along Hwy-55 is **TENANCINGO**. Although it's a friendly place with a bustling market, most tourists only come here to pick up a vehicle to or from Malinalco (see opposite). Tenancingo is worth at least a brief stop in its own right, however. The town's tiny zócalo stands at the top (northern, uphill end) of Juárez, its central street running past the **market** (four blocks south of the zócalo), which is at its height on Thursdays and Sundays, when you can hardly move in the surrounding streets. Liqueurs made from the fruits that grow in abundance on the plain surrounding the village and finely woven traditional *rebozos* (shawls) are sold here, many of them produced at the lovely monastery of **El Santo Desierto**. This is also a big flower-growing region, and as you pass through you'll see whole fields devoted to one bloom – such as roses and chrysanthemums – and acres of land protected by plastic greenhouses.

ARRIVAL AND DEPARTURE | TENANCINGO

By bus Many people will only be here to change buses, but this may involve a walk across the town centre. Buses between Toluca and Ixtapan de la Sal (every 20min; 45min to Ixtapan, 1hr to Toluca) run along Paseo de los Insurgentes (Hwy-55), which skirts the eastern edge of the town centre, and will drop you off at the junction with Hidalgo or Madero (follow these for five blocks west to reach Victoria). Some buses to Ixtapan may also run along Hidalgo,

however, stopping typically at Farmacia Morelos, near the junction with Victoria. On Thurs and Sun in particular, however, you will have to to pick them up at Insurgentes with Hidalgo or Madero. *Combis* and shared taxis for Malinalco (frequent; 30min) run from Victoria with Juárez (six blocks south of the zócalo). For Chalma (frequent; 45min), they run from a terminal at the southern end of Victoria (near its junction with Insurgentes).

ACCOMMODATION AND EATING

Hotel Lazo Victoria 100, two and a half blocks south of the zócalo ☎ 714 142 0083. Rooms are plain and functional, but they all have bathrooms with constant hot water, and they're set around a verdant courtyard with caged birds and lots of foliage. Several small cafés nearby serve cheap Mexican staples. M$200

Malinalco

The village of **Malinalco**, 20km east of Tenancingo, is a lovely little place nestled in a fertile, alluvial valley at 1800m and surrounded by rich villas – many of them, complete with swimming pools, the weekend homes of the capital's privileged few. The fact that it is noticeably warmer than most of the towns hereabouts makes it a popular retreat in winter. While the village centres on the huge Augustinian church of **Santa Mónica** and has a vibrant Wednesday morning **market**, the real reason to come here is to see the exemplary **Aztec ruins**.

The Malinalco archeological site

Guerrero • Tues–Sun 9am–5pm • M$52

The Aztec **site of Malinalco** sits high on a hill to the west of town (follow Guerrero west from the zócalo) and can be reached after a twenty- to thirty-minute walk up a very steep, stepped path. Having only been started in 1501, it was still incomplete at the time of the Conquest but it is undeniably one of the most evocative sites of its kind, carved in part from the raw rock hillside of the Cerro de los Idolos. Looking back over the village and valley, the ruins may be small, but they are undeniably impressive, the main structures and the stairways up to them partly cut out of the rock and partly constructed from great stone blocks.

The main temple

The most remarkable aspect is the circular inner sanctuary of the main temple or **Cuauhcalli** (House of the Eagle), hewn entirely from the face of the mountain. You approach up a broad staircase, on either side of which sit stone jaguars – in the centre an all but worn-away human statue would have held a flag. This was the setting for the sacred **initiation ceremonies** in which Aztec youths became members of the warrior elite, and there are images of warriors throughout: to one side of the entrance, a broken eagle warrior sits atop Quetzalcoatl, the feathered serpent; guarding the other side are the remains of a jaguar warrior, representative of the second Aztec warrior class.

The rest of the site

Other structures at the site include a small circular **platform** by the entrance, unfinished at the time of the Conquest, and a low **pyramid** directly in front of the main temple. Beyond this lie two larger temples. The first, **Edificio III**, again has a circular chamber at the centre, and it is believed that here Aztec warriors killed in battle were cremated, their souls rising to the heavens to become stars. **Edificio IV** was originally a temple of the sun; much of it was used to construct the church in the village. Below the pyramids, visible from about halfway up the steps to the ruins, you can see another **pre-Hispanic building** nestling among the mountains. It's still used by local residents as a place of pilgrimage each September 29: formerly a shrine to an Aztec altar-goddess, it is now dedicated to San Miguel.

Museo Universitario Schneider

Guerrero • Tues–Sun 10am–5.30pm • M$10, video permit M$40

On the way from the town centre to the archeological site, the **Museo Universitario Schneider** is a well-laid-out little museum of archeological finds from the area, many donated by local residents who unearthed them while gardening or working on their homes. There's also a suit of conquistador armour, and a reconstruction of the shrine of Cuauhcalli from the site.

ARRIVAL AND INFORMATION

By bus or shared taxi The easiest way to reach Malinalco is by bus or shared taxi from Tenancingo (see p.186). Most buses arrive in the zócalo in front of the church of Santa Mónica, but those through to Chalma sometimes hurtle straight down Morelos, which bypasses the centre: ask to be dropped at the end of Hidalgo, which runs 200m to the zócalo. From Mexico City Pte, there are two direct daily buses to Malinalco (10am & 3pm; 2hr 30min), though there are departures every 20min for Chalma, from where

2

there are frequent local services.

Tourist office There's a tourist office in the town hall at the uphill end of the zócalo (Mon–Sat 9am–3pm; ☎714 147 0111), with a kiosk under the bandstand at the lower end of the zócalo (daily 9am–4pm).

Banks There are ATMs by the town hall and just off the zócalo at Hidalgo 203.

Internet Cyber Mali, Hidalgo 207 (just off the zócalo; daily 9am–8pm; M$10/hr).

ACCOMMODATION

Casa Limón Rio Lerma 103, 1km south of the zócalo ☎714 147 0256, ⓦcasalimon.com, ⓔinfo@casalimon.com. If only the most exclusive place in town will do, this super-chic boutique hotel will fit the bill, though it isn't very conveniently located. With its elegant stone decor, modern, spacious rooms, a bar, restaurant and pool, it's very classy indeed, but – except by special arrangement (which you may be able to arrange) – it's only open for business Thurs–Sun, and lovely though it undeniably is, it isn't worth six times the price of the *Marmil* or *Santa Mónica*, which is what it will cost you. Breakfast included. **M$2950**

Marmil Progreso 67 ☎714 147 0916, ⓦhotelmarmil malinalco.mex.tl. It's a steep 10min walk uphill from

the zócalo to this pretty little hacienda-style hotel. With country-style rooms, off-street parking, ceiling fans, a pool and cable TV, it's very popular and is almost always full at weekends, so reserve ahead if you can. If coming by bus from Tenancingo, ask to be dropped near the hotel. **M$440**

Santa Mónica Hidalgo 109, near the zócalo on the way to the archeological site ☎714 147 0031, ⓔmail_gro@hotmail.com. A very homely, rustic, family-run little place. Its rooms, set around a pretty little garden, are small but have everything you'll need (bathroom, wi-fi, TV). Rooms cost $M100 extra Fri & Sat. **M$300**

EATING

Come in the middle of the week and you'll find some of the **restaurants** closed, but at weekends there are at least half a dozen places catering to the weekly influx from the capital and Cuernavaca. Everything is close by so you can walk around and take your pick. Cheap food stalls are found at the top end of Juárez, in the southeast corner of the main plaza. One thing that's really good to eat in Malinalco is trout, fresh from a local trout farm, and widely available in local restaurants.

Ehecatl Hidalgo 210, a block east of the main square ☎714 366 1297. A magical garden setting, done out in pretty colours but still very rustic, makes the perfect spot to lunch or dine on anything from a trout fillet (M$90) to a T-bone steak (M$140). Daily 9am–7pm.

Má-Li Hidalgo 22, by a bridge over a stream on the way from the zócalo to the archeological site ☎714 147 0129. The arrival of this wine bar, which also specializes in fondue and *pepitos* (steak sandwiches), signals just how upmarket tourism in Malinalco has become. For such a little village, it's mighty posh, but tasteful too, with a play area for kids, for example, and a

little library, including some books in English. A fondue for two here will set you back M$260, or try a trout stuffed with ham and wrapped in bacon for M$210. Mon–Sat 1–11pm, Sun 10am–6pm.

Los Placeres Plaza Principal 6-B, west side of zócalo ☎714 147 0855, ⓦlosplaceresmalinalco.com. The best of the bar-restaurants on the zócalo, with a great ambience and excellent food including vegetarian dishes, lots of healthy salads and delicious breakfasts. It's only open a few days a week, however. Thurs & Fri 2–11pm or later, Sat 9.30am–11pm or later, Sun 9.30am–5pm.

Chalma

7km east of Malinalco • *Colectivos* (every few min) and shared taxis from Malinalco's zócalo, buses from Mexico City Pte (every 20min; 2hr 30min), and *colectivos* from Tenancingo

Nestled among impressive craggy peaks, **Chalma** is an important place of pilgrimage, although the town itself is a complete dump. Its filthy, muddy streets are lined with stalls offering tacky souvenirs to the pilgrims who converge here every Sunday and at times of special religious significance (especially the first Fri in Lent, Semana Santa and Sept 29), camping out for many kilometres around. In fact, so many people come here that it's impossible to get anywhere near the church.

The Sanctuario

The pilgrims flock here to take part in rituals that are a fascinating blend of Christian and more ancient pagan rites. Originally, the deity Oztocteotl, god of caves, was venerated here in a natural cave. When the first missionaries arrived, he was "miraculously" replaced by a statue of Christ, which was moved in the seventeenth century to a new church, the **Sanctuario de Chalma**. It is this church that is now the focus of pilgrimage and the site of miraculous appearances by a Christ-like figure.

The sacred ahuehuete tree

There's another heavily visited wet shrine on the way into town (buses, taxis and *combis* will set you down on request), at Ocuilán de Arteaga, 6km to the north, where a miraculous spring issues from the roots of a huge old **ahuehuete tree**. Many people stop here first, and then proceed the last few kilometres to the Sanctuario on foot.

Teotenango

Accessible from Tenango del Valle, 15km north of Tenancingo • Tues–Sun 10am–5pm • M$10 • Regular combis to Tenango del Valle from Tenancingo (30min), and buses from Toluca (every 10min; 30min)

From **TENANGO DEL VALLE**, you can visit the nearby remains of the large fortified Malatzinca township of **Teotenango**. From Tenango, it's a fifteen-minute walk to the entrance, then a steep ten-minute hike up to the site: to get there from the centre of the village, head north along Porfirio Díaz Norte, then take a left up Roman Piña Chan Norte. There's a small museum on site.

Metepec

Some 25km north of Tenango de la Valle, and 10km south of Toluca • From Toluca, take a local bus from 5 de Mayo (off Inés de la Cruz a block east of Hotel San Francisco)

The village of **METEPEC** is famed as a **pottery**-making centre. Brightly coloured wares can be found at craft shops throughout the country; supposedly, the figures that characterize these pots were originally inspired by the saints on the facade of Metepec's sixteenth-century monastery, and in the twentieth century Diego Rivera taught the villagers new techniques of colouring and design. There's a market here on Mondays.

Toluca

The capital of the state of México, **TOLUCA DE LERDO** is today a large and modern industrial centre, sprawling across a wide plain. At an altitude of nearly 2700m, it is the highest city in the country, and is surrounded by beautiful mountain scenery, dominated by the white-capped **Nevado de Toluca**. It is probably not a place you'll want to linger, but on Fridays it is the site of what is allegedly the largest single **market** in the country.

Unusually for a Mexican city, Toluca's centre is marked not by an open plaza, but by a central block surrounded on three sides by the nation's longest series of arcades, built in the 1830s and known as **portales**, lined with shops, restaurants and cafés: Portal Madero is to the south along Hidalgo; Portal 20 de Noviembre is to the east along Allende; and Portal Reforma is to the west along Bravo. The fourth side is taken up by the nineteenth-century **cathedral** and, to its east, the mustard-yellow church of **Santa Cruz**. Most of the central sights are clustered north of the *portales* and the cathedral, close to the two massive open plazas: **Plaza de los Mártires**, north of the cathedral, which is dominated on its north side by the Palacio del Gobierno, and to its east, **Plaza Garibay**, which is rather prettier, with shrubbery and fountains.

Jardín Botánico Cosmovitral

Plaza Garibay (east side) • Tues–Sun 10am–6pm • M$10, photo permit M$20

The **Jardín Botánico Cosmovitral** is Toluca's botanical garden. It's housed in an enormous, 100m-long Art Nouveau greenhouse, which was built in 1909 and served as the main market until 1975. With predominantly semi-tropical displays, small pools and even a well-tended Japanese corner, the Jardín Botánico is extremely attractive in itself, but the highlight is undoubtedly the building's amazing Mexican-muralist-style stained-glass panels by local artist Leopoldo Flores. Come early or late to catch the low sun giving a coloured cast to the plants.

Museo de Bellas Artes

Santos Degollado 102, on northwestern corner of Plaza Garibay • Tues–Sat 10am–6pm, Sun 10am–3pm • M$10, free Wed & Sun

The **Museo de Bellas Artes** typically shows off some of the best fine arts in the state. The building it's located in – a Carmelite convent dating from 1697 – is no less interesting than the exhibits, which are mainly religious images, both paintings and sculptures, dating from the sixteenth to the twentieth centuries.

Museo José Maria Velasco

Lerdo de Tejada 400, at Nicolás Bravo • Tues–Sat 10am–6pm, Sun 10am–3pm • M$10, free Wed & Sun

The **Museo José Maria Velasco** occupies two floors of a colonial house and displays a good collection of nineteenth-century paintings, much of it by Velasco, who was born in the State of México in 1840, though he spent much of his life in Mexico City. There's a re-creation of his studio, along with busts, portraits and some delightful landscapes, including a delicate rendering of the volcanoes and the Valley of México.

Museo Felipe Santiago Gutiérrez and Museo Taller Nishizawa

Museo Felipe Santiago Gutiérrez Nicolás Bravo 303 • Tues–Sat 10am–6pm, Sun 10am–3pm • M$10, free Wed & Sun • **Museo Taller Nishizawa** Nicolás Bravo 305 • Tues–Sat 10am–6pm, Sun 10am–3pm • M$10, free Wed & Sun

The State of México makes a point of honouring its artistic sons, and adjoining the Velasco museum (entrance round the corner on Nicolás Bravo) are two more museums dedicated to local painters. The **Museo Felipe Santiago Gutiérrez** fills a colonial mansion with sketches, oils and portraits of prominent nineteenth-century Mexicans; but there is more interest next door at the **Museo Taller Nishizawa**, where large abstract landscape canvases by Japanese-Mexican artist Luis Nishizawa take pride of place alongside pen-and-ink drawings and some of his more recent portraiture.

The market

On and around Paseo Tollocan, 3km southeast of the centre, just east of the bus station • Every Fri (and to a lesser extent throughout the week)

For many people, the market constitutes the overriding reason to visit Toluca. It certainly attracts hordes of visitors from the capital, but is so vast that there can be no question of its being overwhelmed by tourists; quite the opposite, many outsiders find themselves overwhelmed by the scale of the place, lost among the thousands of stalls and crowds from the state's outlying villages. Though increasingly dominated by cheap imported goods and clothing, there is still a substantial selection of **local crafts** – woven goods and pottery above all. Many visitors stop over on a Thursday night (book accommodation in advance), or make an early start from Mexico City on Friday morning.

Centro Cultural Mexiquense

Some 8km west of the city centre at Bvd Jesús Reyes Hercoles 302, Delegación San Buenaventura • All museums Tues–Sat 10am–6pm, Sun 10am–3pm • M$10, free Wed & Sun

The **Centro Cultural Mexiquense** harbours several museums scattered in park-like grounds. Among them are the **Museo Regional**, devoted to the archeology and history of the state, a small **Museo de Arte Moderno** and, perhaps the most interesting, the **Museo de Artes Populares**, a collection of local crafts, ancient and modern, in a restored hacienda. Although local buses run out there (look for buses marked "Centro Cultural Las Palomas" running along Lerdo de Tejada), you really need your own transport to explore the place fully.

ARRIVAL AND DEPARTURE   **TOLUCA**

By plane The airport, 11km northwest of town, off Hwy-134, is connected to the city centre by taxi (M$180) and local bus (picked up in town on Santos Degollado). There are also direct buses from the airport to Mexico City's Terminal Poniente (Observatorio) bus station.

Destinations Acapulco (1–2 daily; 50min); Cancún (3–4 daily; 2hr 45min); Cabo San Lucas (1 daily; 1hr 55min); Guadalajara (1 daily; 1hr 10min); Ixtapa/Zihuatanejo (1 daily; 50min); Monterrey (1–2 daily; 1hr 25min); Puerto Vallarta (1 daily; 1hr 15min).

By bus Toluca's modern bus station (usually referred to as *la terminal* rather than *la central*) is right by the market,

3km southeast of the centre. To pick up a local bus to the centre, exit the bus station and head left down Felipe Berriázabal (the street in front of the terminal) to the junction with Paseo Tollocan; buses into the centre run along Rayón, and you should get off at Hidalgo. Coming back, pick up your bus (marked "Terminal") on Juárez (parallel with Rayón, one block to the west). Note that local buses stop running around 9.30pm and that *de paso* services from Zitácuaro (see p.307) and Valle de Bravo (see p.193) to Mexico City usually stop on the bypass (Av las Torres, with pylons running down the middle), 500m south of the bus station.

2

Destinations Cuernavaca (every 30min; 2hr 30min); Ixtapan de la Sal (every 20min; 1hr); Mexico City Pte (every 5min; 1hr 30min); Morelia (hourly; 4hr); Querétaro (hourly; 3hr 30min); Taxco (every 40min; 3hr); Tenancingo (every 10min; 1hr); Tenango del Valle (every 10min; 30min); Valle de Bravo (every 20min; 2hr).

ACCOMMODATION

In general, Toluca's **hotels** are at the low end of the scale, with very few places in the centre, and a number of fairly grotty ones clustered around the market. The ones near the market tend to fill up by Thurs nights when finding a room can be difficult, even in the city centre, so it's worth booking ahead then if possible.

Colonial Hidalgo Ote 103 ☎722 215 9700. One of the better city-centre options, quirky and eccentric with parquet floors and an old-fashioned feel. The large lobby area even has stained-glass windows, All rooms have cable TV, wi-fi and 24hr hot water. M$500

Rex Matamoros 101, opposite Portal Madero ☎722 215 9300, ✉hotelrex@prodigy.net.mx. A clean and relatively low-priced city-centre hotel, with simple but well-maintained rooms, all with bathroom and TV. You pay a bit more to have a carpeted room than for one with a wooden floor (otherwise there's no difference). M$350

San Francisco Rayón Sur 104 ☎722 213 4415. This was once quite a plush business hotel – it even had a pool (now out of commission) – but it's become rather worn around the edges over the years, although it still has an atrium with a panoramic elevator, and some quite impressive paintings on the walls. The rooms are spacious and comfortable, even if the carpet's getting a bit threadbare in places. It's still the most upmarket city-centre choice, and they usually offer a discount of about a third on the rack rate. M$730

Terminal Felipe Berriázabal 101 ☎722 217 4588. Right by the bus station, with direct access from the terminal, and as functional as you'd expect a bus terminal hotel to be, but it's clean and decent, the rooms are large and have a bathroom, 24hr hot water and TV, and those on the fifth floor upwards are carpeted (with slightly higher rates). M$300

EATING

Café Hidalgo Hidalgo 233 at Nicolás Bravo, opposite the southwest corner of the portales ☎722 215 2793. A great spot for coffee or breakfast in pleasantly old-fashioned surroundings, or for a comida corrida (M$75), or a steak M$90. The house speciality is *platillo Hidalgo*, which is basically just a mixed grill (M$190). Mon–Sat 7.30am–10pm, Sun 7.30am–8pm.

Hostería de las Ramblas Portal 20 de Noviembre 107-D, on the east side of the portales ☎722 215 5488, ✪lasramblas.mx. This large, popular dining hall serves an excellent range of *antojitos* (*chilaquiles* with chicken or chorizo M$65), main courses (*chamorro a la ranchera* M$130) and breakfasts (M$68–100). Daily 8am–9pm.

Las Ramblitas Portal Reforma 108, on the west side of the portales ☎722 215 5488. This cheap and cheerful diner is a good place for a budget city-centre meal, serving tasty set breakfasts (M$45–70), as well as *pozole* (M$65), dishes such as enchiladas or *mole poblano* and a M$60 lunch-time menu. Daily 8am–9pm.

La Vaquita Negra del Portal Portal Reforma 124, at the northeast corner of the portales ☎722 215 0647. An excellent deli and *tortería*, selling cheeses and cold cuts by weight or in tortas, which you can eat seated at the counter with big plates of chile pickles to spice them up. A torta *toluqueña* ("Tolucan torta"; M$28) contains local white cheese and chorizo. Daily 8am–9pm.

Calixtlahuaca

5km north of Toluca • Tues–Sun 10am–5pm • M$42 • From Toluca either by taxi (roughly M$180) or by circuitous local bus (roughly every 15min; 30min) from the stop on Santos Degollado, one block north of the main square at its junction with Nicolás Bravo

While in Toluca, put a couple of hours aside to visit the archeological site of **Calixtlahuaca**, located on a hillside just outside the village of Calixtlahuaca. This was the township of the Matlazinca people, inhabited from prehistoric times and later subjugated by the Aztecs, who established a garrison here in the fifteenth century. Calixtlahuaca was not a willing subject, and there were constant rebellions; after one, in 1475, the Aztecs allegedly sacrificed over eleven thousand Matlazinca prisoners on the **Temple of Quetzalcoatl**. This, several times built over, is the most important structure on the site. Dedicated to the god in his role as Ehecatl, god of wind, its circular design is typical, allowing the breezes to blow freely around the shrine.

Nevado de Toluca

If you've got your own vehicle – and a sturdy model at that – one trip you should make is to the crater of the extinct **Nevado de Toluca** (Xinantécatl; 4690m), which rises high enough above the surrounding plain for it to rank as Mexico's fourth-highest peak. A rough dirt road – impractical during the rainy season or midwinter – leads all the way to the crater rim, from where there are numerous trails leading down to the sandy crater floor and two small lakes, the **Lagos del Sol** and **de la Luna**, right in its heart. From its jagged lip the views are breathtaking: below you the lakes; eastwards a fabulous vista across the valleys of Toluca and México; and to the west a series of lower, greener hills ranging towards the peaks of the Sierra Madre Occidental. If you do hike down into the crater, remember to take it easy in this thin, high-altitude air.

Valle de Bravo

West from Toluca, the road towards Morelia and the state of Michoacán is truly spectacular. Much of this wooded, mountainous area – as far as Zitácuaro – is given over to villas inhabited at weekends by wealthy refugees from the capital, and nowhere more so than at the small lakeside town of **VALLE DE BRAVO**. Set in a deep, pine-clad valley, the town sits on the eastern shore of an artificial lake, **Lago Avandaro**. With terracotta-tiled roofs, iron balconies affixed to many of the older buildings and a mass of whitewashed houses all huddled together, it is an immediately appealing place, something that has drawn a coterie of artistic refugees from the big city. They mostly keep to themselves, leaving the water's edge for weekenders who descend for upmarket relaxation: boat trips, sailing, swimming, waterskiing, riding, paragliding, hiking and golf.

The zócalo, ringed with restaurants and centred on a twin-towered church, sits on a rise a fifteen-minute walk from the waterfront, where most of the action is centred, and sees spectacular sunsets. Here there's a wharf (*embarcadero*) from which you can take boat rides to the parts of the lake inaccessible by road: either rent one from M$500–600 an hour, or join a *lancha colectiva* for M$80 an hour.

ARRIVAL AND INFORMATION

VALLE DE BRAVO

By bus Second-class buses to Valle de Bravo run from Toluca (every 20min; 2hr) and Mexico City Pte (every 20min; 3hr). To travel to or from Morelia or Zitácuaro, you'll have to change at a junction called "Monumento", which has hourly buses to Valle, but don't leave it too late as buses won't stop there after dark. The bus station is on 16 de Septiembre (no guardería). Head downhill and take a right at the end (Juárez) to get to the centre.

Tourist office Auditorio Municipal on Porfirio Díaz, off Juárez between 16 de Septiembre and Independencia (daily 9am–5pm; ☎726 269 6200). There's also a tourist information kiosk by the *embarcadero* (daily 9am–5pm), and, at weekends, one in the zócalo too (Fri–Sun 9am–5pm).

BUTTERFLY SANCTUARIES IN THE STATE OF MEXICO

Valle de Bravo is a good base for visiting the **Monarch Butterfly Sanctuary** areas in the State of Mexico. The price and season are exactly the same as they are over the state line in Michoacán (see p.306; mid-Nov to end of March, daily 9am–4pm, M$55 including compulsory guide), but the sanctuary areas here receive fewer visitors and are more unspoilt, if less scenic. The easiest sanctuary area to visit from Valle de Bravo is at **Los Saucos**, whose gate is right on a main road and served by hourly buses between Valle de Bravo and Mexico City – make sure you get on a "por Saucos" bus. There are also organized tours every day in season, which can be booked through the tourist office or the tourist information kiosks in Valle de Bravo. **Cerro Pelón**, which is considered by many to be the prettiest of all the butterfly sanctuary areas, is slightly more remote, but can be reached on hourly Tepascelptepec-bound buses from Valle de Bravo.

2

ACCOMMODATION

Posada Casa Vieja Juárez 101 ☎ 726 262 0318, ⓔ posadacasavieja@yahoo.com.mx. A hacienda with iron gates, behind which a central patio (with fountain) doubles as a car park, and is surrounded by a sunny veranda with a variety of rooms. Some are bigger than others (so it may be worth checking a few), but all are cool and attractive. <u>M$636</u>

Posada los Girasoles Plaza Independencia 1 ☎ 726 262 2967, ⓔ posadafamiliarlosgirasoles@hotmail.com. Right on the main square, this charming little hotel has big, fresh rooms with red-tiled floors and firm beds, though

some of them are a bit dark. Rooms cost M$50 extra Fri and Sat. <u>M$350</u>

Puesta del Sol Santa Maria 119, just east of the lakefront plaza ☎ 726 262 2472 ⓦ puestadelsolhotel .net. A charming and recently refurbished hotel with stunning views across the lake and just a stone's throw from the jetty. The prices rise at the weekends, but during the week they're often willing to negotiate a discount, particularly if you book ahead. With restaurant, massage, spa and jacuzzi on site, you may not feel the need to leave. <u>M$720</u>

FIESTAS AROUND MEXICO CITY

Bendicíon de los Animales (Jan 17). Children's pets and peasants' farm animals are taken to church to be blessed – a particularly bizarre sight at the cathedral in Taxco (see p.182), where it coincides with the fiestas of Santa Prisca (Jan 18) and San Sebastián (Jan 20).

Carnaval (the week before Lent, variable Feb–March). Especially lively in Cuernavaca (see p.172) and nearby Tepoztlán; also in Chiconcuac on the way to Teotihuacán.

Palm Sunday (the Sun before Easter Sun). A procession with palms in Taxco (see p.182), where representations of the Passion continue through Holy Week.

Semana Santa (Holy Week). Observed everywhere. There are very famous Passion plays in the suburb of Itzapalapa, culminating on the Friday with a mock Crucifixion on the Cerro de la Estrella, and similar celebrations at Chalma and nearby Malinalco (see p.187).

May Day (May 1). In Cuautla marked by a fiesta commemorating an Independence battle.

Día de la Santa Cruz (May 3). Celebrated with fiestas and traditional dancing, in Xochimilco (see p.112), Tepotzotlán (see p.148) and Valle de Bravo (see p.193).

Cinco de Mayo (May 5). Public holiday for the Battle of Puebla – celebrated in Puebla (see p.161) itself with a grand procession and re-enactment of the fighting.

Día de San Isidro (May 15). Religious processions and fireworks in Tenancingo (see p.186), and a procession of farm animals through Cuernavaca (see p.172), on their way to be blessed at the church.

Religious festival in Tlaxcala (see p.158; third Mon in May). An image of the Virgin is processed around the town, followed by hundreds of pilgrims.

Día de Santiago (July 25). Particularly celebrated in Chalco, near Amecameca. The following Sunday sees a market and regional dances at the Plaza de las Tres Culturas (see p.113) and dances, too, in Xochimilco (see p.112).

Día de Santa Marta (July 29). In Milpa Alta, near Xochimilco, celebrated with Aztec dances and mock fights between Moors and Christians.

Día de la Asunción (Assumption; Aug 15). Honoured with pilgrimages from Cholula (see p.168) to a nearby village, and ancient dances in Milpa Alta.

Día de San Miguel (Sept 29). Provokes huge pilgrimages to both Taxco (see p.182) and Chalma.

Día de San Francisco (Oct 4). A *feria* in Tenancingo (see p.186), with much traditional music-making, and also celebrated in San Francisco Tecoxpa, a village on the southern fringes of the capital.

Fiesta del Santuario de la Defensa (Oct 12). A street party that centres around an ancient church just outside Tlaxcala (see p.158).

Día de Santa Cecilia (Nov 22). St Cecilia is the patron saint of musicians, and her fiesta attracts orchestras and mariachi bands from all over to Santa Cecilia Tepetlapa, not far from Xochimilco.

Feria de la Plata (Dec 1). The great silver fair in Taxco (see p.182) lasts about ten days from this date.

Christmas (Dec 25). In the week leading up to Christmas, Nativity plays – also known as *posadas* – can be seen in many places. Among the most famous are those at Taxco (see p.182) and Tepotzotlán (see p.148).

EATING

The four boat-like restaurants close to the jetty are some of the best places to watch the town's spectacular sunsets, although patrons should avoid *La Balsa*, where both service and product are shoddy.

El Portal Plaza Independencia 101 ☎726 262 0623. A good upmarket choice, right on the zócalo, where you can get salads, pizzas or *antojitos*, followed by dishes such as trout (M$95), steak (M$120) or a mixed grill for two (M$200). Daily 8am–11pm.

La Ranchita 16 de Septiembre 400. Low-priced eats on the way to the bus station, with a M$30 comida corrida, or a slice of beef, pork or chicken with *refritos* for M$40. Daily 7am–10pm.

Restaurante Paraíso C Atardecer at Plaza Estrella ☎726 262 4731. Grab the table at the very edge of this building as it tapers off to a point over the waterfront plaza and watch the action below. Serves up lots of different cuts of steak as well as good seafood. The perfect spot to watch day turn into night in this pretty little plaza. Daily 8am–10pm.

El Rincón Suizo C Atardecer, 100m up from plaza ☎726 262 1773. Genuine Swiss owner Jean-Paul moved here over fifteen years ago to serve up genuine Swiss delights from this waterfront establishment. The menu is divided into either fondue or roesti (large eastern-European hashbrown), accompanied by a wide range of extras. A safe bet for eating well in a town overrun with establishments serving up tourist slop, though a shame it's only open at the weekends. Mains around M$180. Fri & Sat noon–midnight, Sun noon–8pm.

2

Acapulco and the Pacific beaches

ACAPULCO BAY AT SUNSET

Acapulco and the Pacific beaches

The journey north from Acapulco to Puerto Vallarta, some 800km along the Pacific coast, is defined by languid, tropical beach life at its finest. There's history here, to be sure, but it's the buttery sands studded with palms, the makeshift bars on the beach, lagoons and torpid villages that dominate, topped off with heart-melting sunsets and a rich array of seafood. Separating these stretches of wild, untouched coastline – and in stark contrast – are some of the most popular and enjoyable resorts in Mexico.

3

Acapulco – the original, the biggest and, for many, the best of these resorts – is a steep-sided, tightly curving bay that, for all its excesses of high-rise development, remains breathtakingly beautiful. While tourists swarm the congested beaches, the city retains a local feel, with the coarse characteristics of a working port. Further north **Zihuatanejo** is an attractive, gentle resort where magnificent villas have popped up on the slopes overlooking inviting swathes of beach littered with palms, while the handsome colonial towns of **Colima** and **Comala** provide the allure (and dramatic volcanic scenery) inland. Further along the Pacific, the **Costalegre** contains some of the wildest and most beautiful stretches of coast anywhere, anchored by **Barra de Navidad** and its glorious sweep of sand surrounded by flatlands and lagoons. At the northern end of Jalisco state, international **Puerto Vallarta** feels altogether more manageable than Acapulco, with cobbled streets fanning out from a colonial plaza overlooking an oceanfront boulevard. With its party ambience and unbridled commercialism it's certainly a resort, but if you travel far enough from the downtown beaches you can still find cove after isolated cove backed by forested mountains.

Acapulco

Most people – even if they've not the remotest idea where it is – have heard of **ACAPULCO**. It's been the *grande dame* of the Mexican tourist industry since the 1950s, and today Mexico City-by-the-sea is a crazy, tropical party town where the rich and poor of the capital come to play; the swankiest clubs and restaurants nestle in the hills, while the masses pack the beaches, fiesta-style. But what makes Acapulco really special is its stunning **bay**: a sweeping scythe-stroke of yellow sand backed by the white towers of the high-rise hotels and, behind them, the jungly green foothills of the sierra. Even though the city itself has a population of over one and a half million and hundreds of thousands of visitors come through each year, it rarely seems overcrowded. There's

HUMPBACK WHALE, BAHÍA DE BANDERAS

Highlights

❶ Acapulco The king of Mexican resorts is a brash, exhilarating city with romantic dining, serious partying and death-defying cliff divers. **See p.198**

❷ Barra de Potosí An untouched beach where you can eat fresh fish and row through a mangrove lagoon. **See p.213**

❸ The Michoacán coast Explore one of the wildest sections of the Pacific coast, anchored by the gorgeous beaches at Playa Maruata. **See p.219**

❹ Nevado de Colima Hike the pine-smothered slopes of this awe-inspiring volcano. **See p.227**

❺ Comala Captivating colonial town, where you can sip a beer and feast on free snacks while mariachis compete for your attention in the plaza. **See p.229**

❻ Costalegre A tantalizing stretch of coastline punctuated by small, low-key resorts. **See p.229**

❼ Puerto Vallarta Luxury resorts, stylish B&Bs and a languid colonial centre make this an ideal base from which to explore the beaches of the Bahía de Banderas, and to watch humpback whales frolic offshore from December to April. **See p.233**

HIGHLIGHTS ARE MARKED ON THE MAP ON P.200

certainly always space to lie along the beach, partly because of its sheer size, and partly because of the number of rival attractions – everything from hotel pools to para sailing to romantic cruises. If you only do one thing in Acapulco, though, make sure you see its most celebrated spectacle, the leap of the daredevil **high divers** (see p.211).

Centro Histórico

Acapulco's scrappy **Centro Histórico** wraps around the western end of the bay, with Plaza Álvarez, better known simply as the **zócalo**, at its centre, a shady, languid square with kioscos and fountains. The plaza is packed with cheap gift stalls on Sundays, and is surrounded by budget places to eat and drink, but there's not much to see. The **Catedral de Nuestra Señora de la Soledad** is a modern construction completed in 1950, with a slightly bizarre blue dome that resembles a Russian Orthodox church. Walk down to the malecón for boat trips around the bay, fishing trips and the incongruous strip of sand known as **Playa de Tlacopanocha**, usually packed out on holidays, though it's a poor place to swim.

Museo Histórico de Acapulco

Hornitos s/n • Tues–Sun 9am–6pm • M$46, free Sun • ☎ 744 482 3828

About the only place in Acapulco that gives even the slightest sense of the historic role the city played in Mexico's past is the excellent **Museo Histórico de Acapulco**, a short

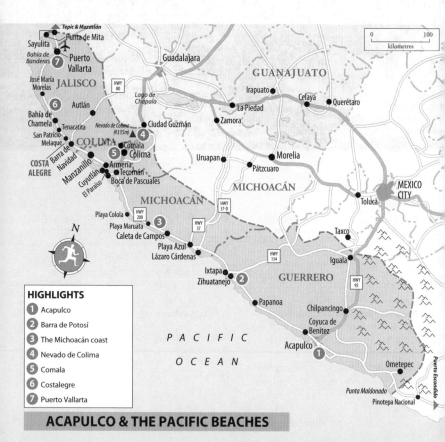

HIGHLIGHTS

1. Acapulco
2. Barra de Potosí
3. The Michoacán coast
4. Nevado de Colima
5. Comala
6. Costalegre
7. Puerto Vallarta

ACAPULCO & THE PACIFIC BEACHES

3

> **WHEN TO VISIT ACAPULCO**
>
> Like many of Mexico's top resorts, Acapulco now experiences two **high seasons**: late November or early December through to the end of April (when *norteamericanos* flock south), and the hurricane season of July and August, when Mexican families take their summer vacations. Indeed, unlike Cancún, Los Cabos and Puerto Vallarta, 75 percent of Acapulco's visitors are domestic tourists. If you can, it's best to avoid Christmas and Semana Santa (Easter) altogether, and remember that any US or Mexican public holiday will likely bring the crowds. Thursday to Sunday tends to be busy year-round. Low season in Acapulco is May and June (when the weather is still good), and September and October (when it's usually rainy).

walk away from the zócalo inside the **Fuerte de San Diego**. Soon after it was founded by the Spanish in the 1520s, the **shipping route** between the city and the Spanish colony of the Philippines, on the other side of the Pacific, became the most prized and preyed upon in the world. From Acapulco, goods were transported overland to Veracruz and then shipped onwards to Spain.

Galleries inside cover the history of the fort and the Acapulco region, beginning with the pre-Hispanic **Yopes** and **Tepozteco** cultures. The most interesting rooms chronicle Spain's exploration of the Pacific from Acapulco, beginning in the 1500s, with special focus on the Manila/Asian trade; the Philippines and Mexico still share much in common, from the Catholic Church and food and drink, to a love of telenovelas. **Pirates** are covered (Brits beware, Sir Francis Drake is definitely one of the pirates here), as is the role of **José María Morelos** in the fight for independence.

La Casa de los Vientos
Inalámbrica 6, Cerro de la Pinzona (off La Quebrada) • Interior closed to the public

The only other cultural diversion in the *centro histórico* is **La Casa de los Vientos** (aka "Exekatlkalli" or "House of the Winds"), the house where **Diego Rivera** spent the last two years of his life with his former model and partner, Dolores Olmedo Patiño. Rivera spent eighteen months working on five grand **murals** here between 1955 and 1957, several preserved in his studio on the grounds; sadly, the house has remained in private hands since Olmedo's death in 2002 and is off-limits. Instead, art fans traipse up here to see the stunning murals that cover the entire outside wall of the house, made of seashells and coloured tiles; the 20m snake on the right depicts **Tlaloc**, the Aztec god of rain, fertility and lightning, while the 12.7m feathered serpent on the left is **Quetzalcoatl**, another important Aztec god but worshipped by many Mesoamerican civilizations.

Playas Caleta and Caletilla
Playas Caleta and **Caletilla** (take any "Caleta" bus from Costera) have a quite different atmosphere from those in the main part of the bay. Both have almost legendary status in Mexico, but it's the party families come for, not tranquillity. The beaches are actually very small, divided by a small rocky outcrop – they tend to be jam-packed at weekends, with a boisterous, carnival-like atmosphere and every centimetre of sand covered with beach umbrellas and towels. You wouldn't come here for seclusion, but it's loads of fun, the water is almost always calm and the beach is reasonably clean. You can sit at shaded tables on the sand, surrounded by Mexican matrons whose kids are paddling in the shallows, and be brought cheap drinks from the cafés behind. From here you can take a water taxi across to Isla La Roqueta (see p.204), hang out at super-cool *Boca Chica* (see p.207), or rent kayaks (M$130–150/hr).

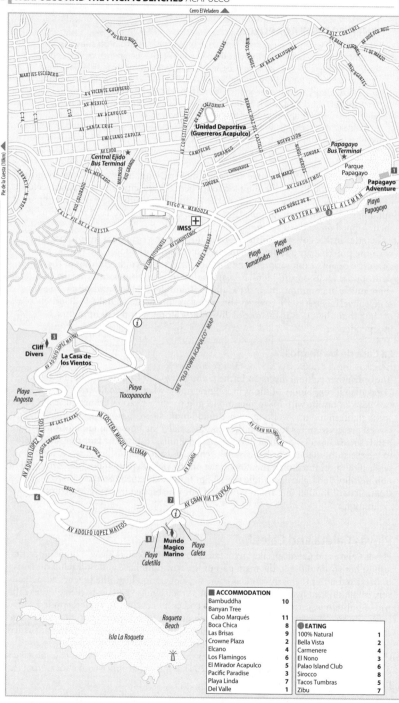

Cerro El Veladero

Pie de la Cuesta (10km)

3

AV PUEBLA NUEVA
MARTIES ESCUDERO
AV VICENTE GUERRERO
AV MEXICO
AV ACAPULCO
AV SANTA CRUZ
EMILIANO ZAPATA
DEL MERCADO
MALPASO
RIO GRANDE
RIO COLORADO
CALZ. PIE DE LA CUESTA

RIO BALSAS
NIÑOS HEROES
RIO BALSAS
AV BAJA CALIFORNIA
AV RUIZ CORTINES
AV BAJA CALIFORNIA
AV JOSE FCO. RUIZ
11 DE MARZO
INSURGENTES
AV BAJA CALIFORNIA
BERNAL DIAZ DEL CASTILLO
AV CONSTITUYENTES
AV BAJA CALIFORNIA

**Unidad Deportiva
(Guerreros Acapulco)**
CAMPECHE
DURANGO
CHIHUAHUA
SONORA
NUEVO LEON
18 DE MARZO
NIÑOS HEROES
SONORA

**Central Ejido
Bus Terminal** ★

**Papagayo
Bus Terminal** ★
Parque
Papagayo
**Papagayo
Adventure**
1

DIEGO H. MENDOZA
AV CUAUHTEMOC
VASCO NUÑEZ DE B.
AV COSTERA MIGUEL ALEMAN
3
Playa
Papagayo

IMSS ✚
AV CONSTITUYENTES
AV CUAUHTEMOC
VALDEZ ARETALO
Playa
Tamarindos
Playa
Hornos

SEE "OLD TOWN ACAPULCO" MAP

ⓘ

**Cliff
Divers** 5
AV ADOLFO LOPEZ MATEOS
**La Casa de
los Vientos**

Playa
Tlacopanocha

Playa
Angosta

AV LAS PLAYAS
AV COSTERA MIGUEL ALEMAN
AV GRAN VIA TROPICAL
AV ADOLFO LOPEZ MATEOS
AV COSTA GRANDE
AV LA SUIZA
AV AGUDA
OASIS
6
7
AV GRAN VIA TROPICAL
ⓘ
AV ADOLFO LOPEZ MATEOS
8 **Mundo
Magico
Marino**
Playa
Caletilla
Playa
Caleta

6
Roqueta
Beach

Isla La Roqueta

■ ACCOMMODATION

Bambuddha	10
Banyan Tree Cabo Marqués	11
Boca Chica	8
Las Brisas	9
Crowne Plaza	2
Elcano	4
Los Flamingos	6
El Mirador Acapulco	5
Pacific Paradise	3
Playa Linda	7
Del Valle	1

● EATING

100% Natural	1
Bella Vista	2
Carmenere	4
El Nono	3
Palao Island Club	6
Sirocco	8
Tacos Tumbras	5
Zibu	7

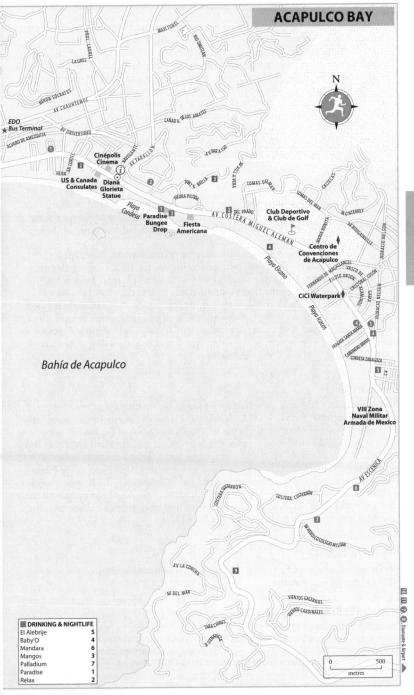

ACAPULCO BAY

N

EDO
★ Bus Terminal

Cinépolis
Cinema

US & Canada
Consulates

Diana
Glorieta
Statue

Playa
Condesa

Paradise
Bungee
Drop

Fiesta
Americana

Club Deportivo
& Club de Golf

Centro de
Convenciones
de Acapulco

CiCi Waterpark

Playa Icacos

Playa Elcano

Bahía de Acapulco

VIII Zona
Naval Militar
Armada de Mexico

3

💎 & Airport

DRINKING & NIGHTLIFE	
El Alebrije	5
Baby'O	4
Mandara	6
Mangos	3
Palladium	7
Paradise	1
Relax	2

0 — 500
metres

Isla La Roqueta

Water taxis to the island (daily 8.30am–5pm; every 30min) are M$40 (return) for a direct launch or M$70 for detours past the submerged bronze statue of the Virgin of Guadalupe in glass-bottomed boats • Fondo de Cristal ☎ 744 429 6823

From the entrance to Mágico Mundo Marino between the two beaches, small boats ply the channel to the **Isla La Roqueta**, where there is another small but cleaner beach with a palapa restaurant. From the beach you can hike up to the small **lighthouse** on top of the island for views of the city, or take another water taxi to the famous *Palao Island Club* restaurant (see p.209), further along the island shore. The other side of the island is prime scuba-diving and snorkelling territory (see box, p.207). If you take the glass-bottomed boat out here you'll see the underwater bronze statue of the **Virgen de Guadalupe**, said to have been created by local fishermen in 1956. The story goes that the metal was collected from locals donating old keys.

Zona Dorada

The **beaches** around **Acapulco Bay**, despite their various names – Tamarindo, Hornos, Hornitos, El Morro, Condesa and Icacos – are in effect a single sweep of sand along what's known as the **Zona Dorada** (roughly from where the old town ends at the big Mexican flag to the end of the bay).

From Caleta, a single seafront drive, the **Costera Miguel Alemán** – usually just "Costera" – stretches from the old town around the bay for 10km, linking almost everything of interest. For authentic Mexican seaside atmosphere it's hard to beat the stretch of Costera between the **Diana Glorieta statue** (traffic circle) and the **Fiesta Americana** hotel, lined with restaurants, bars blaring music and the **Paradise Bungee Drop** (M$650). Stroll along the malecón to soak it all up. The beaches around here are also the place to come if you want to indulge in such frolics as being towed around the bay on the end of a parachute, water-skiing or sailing. Outfits offering all of these are dotted at regular intervals along the beach.

Diamante

Beyond Acapulco Bay, across the hills to the south, lies another major resort zone known as **Diamante**, with deluxe hotels lining the coast all the way to the airport and the former village of **Barra Vieja**. On the way you'll pass some of the fanciest hotels and villas in Acapulco, as well as some mesmerizing views of the city. **Puerto Marqués** (buses marked "Puerto Marqués") is the first of the beaches, a sheltered, deeply indented cove with restaurants and beach chairs right down to the water's edge. Nearby, the **Punta Diamante** is occupied by the most expensive hotel in Acapulco – the *Banyan Tree Resort* – but you can continue by road to **Playa Revolcadero** (though only an occasional bus comes this far). This beach, a long, exposed stretch of sand, is beautiful but frequently lashed by heavy surf that makes swimming impossible.

Pie de la Cuesta

The public bus from Acapulco (marked "Pie de la Cuesta") runs every 10min or so down Escobeda then along Costera east of the zócalo (M$10); the last bus back leaves around 8pm

---

ADDRESSES ALONG COSTERA

Finding places along Costera can be tricky, as the numbering system is completely meaningless: 50 could be followed by 2010, which is next door to 403. The best **landmarks**, apart from the big hotels, are (moving east from the zócalo): **Parque Papagayo**, the roundabout with the **Diana Glorieta statue** and the **CiCi Waterpark**.

STAYING SAFE IN ACAPULCO

Since 2008 Acapulco has been adversely affected by what locals call "the media war on Mexico" (and you'll see why if you pick up a copy of state newspaper *Vértice*). Yet the idea that Acapulco is overrun by gangsters is simply not true, and it's extremely rare for tourists to be affected by the drug violence. Since 2011 the streets (and skies) have been patrolled by Federal police, making things especially safe. Like any big city, Acapulco suffers some petty crime and the usual rules apply: avoid empty backstreets at night, don't flash expensive equipment and only take official taxis.

Around 15km north along the coast from central Acapulco, **PIE DE LA CUESTA** is far more serene than the city and a good place to watch the sun sink into the Pacific, enjoy a day out at the **Laguna de Coyuca**, or to ride horseback along the shore where the thunderous waves are a multi-sensual spectacle. The sand extends for many kilometres up the coast, but at the Acapulco end, where the bus drops you, there are several rickety bars and some tranquil **places to stay** (see p.208).

3

Laguna de Coyuca

Behind the beach, and only separated from the ocean by the hundred-metre-wide sandbar on which Pie de la Cuesta is built, lies the **Laguna de Coyuca**, a vast freshwater lake said to be three times the size of Acapulco Bay. Fringed with palms and rich in bird and animal life, the lagoon is big enough to accommodate both the ubiquitous noisy jet skiers and the more sedate **boat trips** that visit the three lagoon islands (see box, p.207).

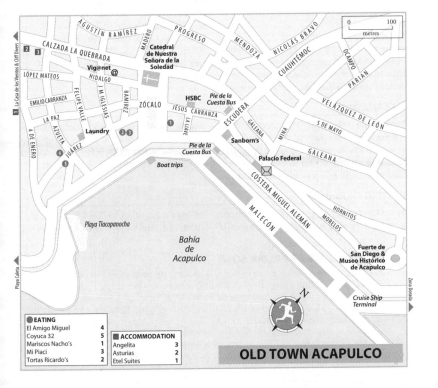

● EATING	
El Amigo Miguel	4
Coyuca 32	5
Mariscos Nacho's	1
Mi Piaci	3
Tortas Ricardo's	2

■ ACCOMMODATION	
Angelita	3
Asturias	2
Etel Suites	1

OLD TOWN ACAPULCO

ARRIVAL AND DEPARTURE

BY PLANE

Acapulco is connected to the US and Canada by numerous seasonal flights (typically Nov–April), but domestic choices are far smaller, and flying elsewhere in Mexico usually involves a change in Toluca (Interjet) or Mexico City. Arriving at Acapulco's General Juan N. Álvarez International Airport (☎744 435 2060), 23km southeast of the city, you'll find a couple of ATMs, Alamo, Europcar, Hertz and Thrifty car rental counters and basic information on the city. Transport prices are set according to an expensive zone system (buy tickets before you leave the baggage claim area): the cheapest option is a shared minibus ride, which will take you anywhere in the city for M$120 – you need to reserve this service in advance to get back (allow at least 40min for the journey (☎744 462 1095). You can also take taxis (which cost an exorbitant M$400–600 to most destinations in the city) or hire a whole van for M$500–700. Hotel taxis charge M$300–450 for the return journey, but you can get cheaper rates from taxis in the street (see opposite).

Destinations Mexico City (frequent; 50min); Monterrey (3 weekly; 1hr 55min); Tijuana (seasonal, 1 daily; 2hr 30min); Toluca (1 daily; 50min).

BY BUS

Most long-distance buses arrive at one of three terminals: the two main ones are the Estrella de Oro group terminal ("EDO"), 3km east of the zócalo at Cuauhtémoc 1490 (at the northeast corner of Parque Papagayo), connected to the centre by "Caleta" city buses (cross over Cuauhtémoc), or to

the hotels along Costera by "Río/Base" buses; and the Papagayo (Central de Lujo) terminal, further west at Cuauhtémoc 1605 at Caminos, facing Parque Papagayo (Estrella Blanca, Futura, Pacifico, Chihuahuenses, Costa Line and Turistar use this). To get to the zócalo, take a "Zócalo" bus. The Central Ejido terminal, at Ejido 47, 2km north of the zócalo, mostly serves buses along the coast. Buses (M$6) marked "Centro" or "Caleta" go to the zócalo. Taxis are always available at all terminals: from the EDO or Papagayo to the zócalo is M$70, to Caleta or Costera M$80; from Central Ejido to the zócalo is M$60; to Caleta and Costera M$80.

Destinations EDO Terminal: Chilpancingo (every 30min; 2hr; M$90–110); Lázaro Cárdenas (frequent; 6–7hr; M$225–260); Mexico City (hourly; 5–6hr; M$450); Taxco (7 daily; 5hr; M$230); Zihuatanejo (first class 6am, 2.30pm, 6.20pm; M$170–190; Económica at least hourly; 4–5hr; M$148).

Destinations Papagayo (Central de Lujo): Guadalajara (Turistar 7.15pm; 14hr; M$1260; first class 5 daily; 14hr; M$1295; Económica frequent; 14hr; M$1059); Mexico City every terminal served (frequent; 5–6hr; First Class Primera Plus to TAPO M$1950; local services M$455); Puerto Escondido (5 daily; 7hr; M$358); Puerto Vallarta (2 daily; 18–19hr; M$1326); Tijuana (2 daily; 49hr; M$2520).

Destinations Central Ejido: Manzanillo (1 daily; 13hr; M$686); Mazatlán (2 daily; 20hr 30min; M$1276–1502); Taxco (3 daily; 4hr; M$230); Zihuatanejo (10 daily; 4–5hr; M$182).

INFORMATION

Tourist office The Fideicomiso de Promoción Turística de Acapulco (Mon–Fri 9am–6pm, Sat 9am–2pm; ☎744 484 4159, ⓦvisitacapulco.com.mx or ⓦvisiteacapulco.com) is based at Costera 2408, in Plaza Comercial Arrecife (Fracc Club Deportivo), but you'll get more information from the

booths (usually daily 8am–2pm & 3–9pm) set along the waterfront: at Caleta Beach, at the pier in front of the zócalo, at the big Mexican flag in front of Papagayo Park and at the Diana Glorieta circle.

GETTING AROUND

By bus You can reach everywhere near the zócalo on foot, but to get further afield, you'll need to take taxis or one of

the frequent buses (look for "Caleta/Base", "Zócalo" or "Hornos") that run all the way along Costera. From the east,

---

THE MYSTERIES OF PALMA SOLA

High above the city, on the slopes of the Cerro El Veladero, lies Acapulco's most unexpected (and under-visited) sight, ancient carvings and enigmatic petrogylphs dating back to 800 BC. Protected within the **Zona Arqueológica de Palma Sola** (Wed–Sun 9am–5pm; free), the site is thought to have been a ceremonial and pilgrimage centre, though little else is known about who created the other-worldly images. You can wander the eighteen most important granite rocks (via some steep paths) and visit the small exhibition hall on site, but it can be awkward to find (it's at the end of Av Palma Sola, along a pedestrian-only lane called La Mona, in the colonia of Independencia) – taxis will charge around M$120 (ask the driver to wait). Be prepared for jaw-dropping views across the city.

ACAPULCO BOAT TRIPS AND THEME PARKS

Acapulco Bay has a multitude of watersports activities and tours on offer. Touristy **cruises** depart from the docks along the malecón in front of the zócalo, while kiosks offer everything from banana boats and jet skis, to snorkelling and parasailing. Additionally, various outfits along the hotel strip in Pie de la Cuesta offer tours to Laguna de Coyuca (see p.205) – prices hover around M$150 per person – but it's worth checking what's on offer and how long the cruise is, as times tend to differ. Most boats stop on one island for lunch (not included in the price) and swimming. You can also get picked up from Acapulco: contact Aca Tours (☎744 484 4875), which charges M$400 (pick-ups, tour in English, open bar and buffet).

Aca Rey Costera 100 (near zócalo) ☎744 484 7080. The best of the tour boats charges around M$280 for three hours around the bay (sunset cruises Oct–April 4.30–7pm; May–Sept 5.30–8pm; moonlight cruise year-round 10.30pm–1am).

Fish-R-Us Costera 100 ☎744 482 8282, ⊛fish-r-us .com. This professional outfit runs sea-fishing and scuba-diving (from M$850) tours as well as cruises around the bay. Night-time excursions (typical catch are sailfish, dorado and red snapper) are particularly appealing, illuminated by the lights of the town shining out from all around the coast.

AMUSEMENT PARKS

CiCi Waterpark Costera Miguel Alemán s/n, at the cnr of Cristóbal Colón ☎744 484 1970. Fun waterpark where you can splash around in swimming pools and on water slides, and watch or swim with performing dolphins – a welcome break from the beach. Tickets from M$250. Daily 10am–6pm.

Parque Papagayo Manuel Gómez Morín 1, at Costera. This fifty-acre public park at the edge of the *centro histórico* attracts picnicking families and joggers with its green spaces, swimming pool, aviary, roller-skating rink, boating lake and fairground rides (free). **Papagayo Adventure** (☎744 485 3795) is the newest pay to enter (M$75–125) section, featuring a ropeway, climbing wall and various activities for kids. Fairground rides daily 8am–8pm; Papagayo Adventure Tues–Thurs 1–8pm, Fri–Sun 1–10pm.

3

"C Río" buses travel past the big hotels, then turn inland onto Cuauhtémoc, where they pass the Estrella de Oro bus station and the market before rejoining Costera just before the zócalo. "Caleta" buses continue round to Playa Caleta – note that in bad traffic (which is most of the time), it can take almost an hour to ride the length of Costera. Buses cost M$6 (or M$10 with a/c); be prepared for blaring techno or Latino pop at all hours of the day.

By taxi Taxis are plentiful all over the city; at all the bus stations and major hotels, they operate on a zone system, which is more or less the same wherever you are (though some hotel taxis charge a little more), with rates usually displayed on boards. Between *centro histórico* and the bus stations it's M$60–70, Caleta is M$80, while locations along Costera cost M$70–100. You'll save money by flagging down the cheaper VW beetle taxis on the street, but even here you'll have to negotiate pretty hard to pay local rates, as these drivers are well aware of the tourist "zone" system; these taxis should charge fifty percent less (locals pay around M$25 for the first few km), but you'll likely only get a maximum M$10–20 discount on zone rates.

ACCOMMODATION

IN THE CENTRE

Angelita Calzada La Quebrada 37 ☎744 483 5734; map p.205. One of Acapulco's cheapest options. Spartan but sizeable rooms with private bath and fan lead off a courtyard. The eccentric management of Doña Angelita keeps life interesting. M$250

Asturias Calzada La Quebrada 45 ☎744 483 6548, ⊜gerardomancera@aol.com; map p.205. A welcoming budget option with clean, passable rooms around a courtyard. It is fractionally more expensive than the competition by virtue of its small pool. M$280

Etel Suites Pinzona 92 ☎744 482 2241, ⊛etelsuites .com; map p.205. This very hospitable, family-run hotel is extremely clean and well equipped, with 1950s-style three-bed rooms with kitchens, balconies and a/c in lovely gardens overlooking La Quebrada. Good for groups and long-stay guests. M$500

El Mirador Acapulco Plazoleta La Quebrada 74 ☎744 483 1155, ⊛miradoracapulco.com; map pp.202–203. The location of this classic 1930s hotel – right above La Quebrada (see box, p.211) – couldn't be better. Lodging is in clean, rather characterless, Alpine-style rooms with kitchenettes. There are three pools and a bar-restaurant on site, from which you won't have to pay to see the divers plummet. M$713

CALETA AND CALETILLA

★ **Boca Chica** Playa de Caletilla s/n ☎744 482 7879, ⊛hotel-bocachica.com; map pp.202–203. Beautifully renovated resort carved into the cliff-face at the end of Playa Caletilla, with all-white rooms featuring retro showers, flat-screen TVs, iPod docks and free wi-fi – Mexican artist Claudia Fernández has decorated the 1950s interior, with a luxurious spa, gym, massage cabañas, pool terrace and special sushi takeout menu adding to the allure. It's a bit like a Mediterranean beach club. M$3689

Los Flamingos López Mateos s/n ☎744 482 0690, ⓦ hotellosflamingos.com; map pp.202–203. An Acapulco retro classic, this landmark 1930s hotel was once owned by a Hollywood gang that included Tarzan (Johnny Weissmuller), Cary Grant and John Wayne. The "coco loco" cocktail was apparently invented here in 1935, and the lush gardens and sublime sunset views from Acapulco's highest cliffs are a perfect accompaniment. The rooms have seen better days but are still spacious, characterful and comfortable. M$600

Playa Linda Costera 1 ☎744 482 0814, ⓦ playa lindaacapulco.com; map pp.202–203. Modern budget hotel with nicely decorated rooms, some with sea-view balconies, a short walk from the beaches. All rooms (sleeping up to four) have a/c, TV and fully equipped kitchenettes. M$450

ZONA DORADA

★ **Las Brisas** Carretera Escénica 5255 ☎744 469 6900, ⓦ brisashotelonline.com; map pp.202–203. Over-looking the eastern end of the bay, high above the ocean amid blossom-smothered gardens, this luxury resort – established in 1957 with a unique all-pink-and-white colour scheme – is the most exclusive in the city. More like a small village, its individual villas offer private swimming pools, jacuzzis and delivered breakfasts, and they also rent out pink jeeps to any occupant. You access the water via the La Concha beach club below, and every room has a sea-view terrace with mesmerizing vistas. The hotel was immortalized in a Ringo Starr song, and famous guests have left hand prints in pink plaster (Sophia Loren, Neil Armstrong, JFK, Denzel Washington and Morgan Freeman among them). M$3628

Crowne Plaza Costera 123 ☎744 440 5555, ⓦ ichotels group.com; map pp.202–203. Certainly the most memorable building on the beach (it's like a curved pyramid), with clean, bright modern rooms with cable TV and an attractive pool. Free wi-fi. M$875

Elcano Costera 75 (at Del Parque and Las Palmas) ☎744 435 1500, ⓦ hotelelcano.com.mx; map pp.202–203. This renovated 1950s monolith with an all-pervasive nautical theme feels fresh: spic-and-span blue-and-white rooms have tiled floors, cable TV, comfortable beds and well-proportioned bathrooms, though the a/c can be weak. The best rooms have terraces overlooking the ocean,

but all rooms have ocean views. There's a beachside pool, jacuzzi, gym and two bars. M$1200

Pacific Paradise Punta Bruja 1, near Playa Condesa ☎744 481 1413; map pp.202–203. Mediterranean-style budget resort with spotless, attractive rooms on three floors. Situated a few blocks back from Costera, so nights are quieter and it's better value than many of the beachside establishments. M$850

Del Valle Manuel Gómez Morín 150, opposite the eastern entrance to Parque Papagayo ☎744 485 8336; map pp.202–203. *Del Valle* has a convenient location, spacious, well-maintained rooms (some with a/c), a pool and private kitchens (outside the rooms) that can be rented for M$100 a day. M$300

DIAMANTE

★ **Bambuddha** Carretera Barra Vieja km 37 ☎744 444 6406; map pp.202–203. This gorgeous Asian-themed boutique hotel, with bamboo palapas right on the beach, is a wonderfully languid retreat, specializing in yoga, meditation and detox programmes. M$1500

Banyan Tree Cabo Marqués Cabo Marqués, Lote 1, Col Punta Diamente ☎744 434 0100, ⓦ banyantree .com/en/em-mexico-cabo-marques; map pp.202–203. This resort is the new gold standard in Acapulco luxury, though if you stay here you may not leave; it's a self-contained, all-inclusive resort with villas set into the cliffs. The jaw-dropping infinity pool comes with a stunning view of the Pacific, but all the facilities are first class (spa, restaurant, bar). Travelling into the city can be time-consuming and expensive from here – most guests hire drivers. M$7500

PIE DE LA CUESTA

Acapulco Trailer Park ☎744 460 0010. Some 15km north of central Acapulco lies the only place with official year-round camping, with sixty full hook-ups and spaces for tents as well as RVs; it's relatively pricey but includes free wi-fi and water. M$250

Baxar Hotel Fuerza Aérea Militar 356 ☎744 460 2502, ⓦ baxar.com.mx. Rustic chic epitomized, this intimate beachside enclave has colourful, breezy rooms with tiled private bath and mosquito nets (some have a/c). The restaurant serves great fresh fish and there's a pool and guaranteed relaxation. M$850

★ **Villa Nirvana** Fuerza Aerea 302 ☎744 460 1631, ⓦ lavillanirvana.com. American expats Pamela and Daniel built this wonderful expansive villa right on the beach, with chilled-out pool, wi-fi and hammocks slung throughout, as well as a fridge full of ice-cold beer. Thunderous breaking waves on one of the area's wildest stretches of coastline make for a wonderful backdrop. Ask for room 16. M$1050

EATING

To eat cheaply in Acapulco you're confined to the area around the **zócalo** where no-frills joints serve unmemorable but filling comidas corridas. Eating by the **beach** – where there's some kind of restaurant at every turn – is of course more expensive, and increasingly so as you head east. Throughout the tourist zone, especially along Costera, you'll find the usual US and Mexican chains such as *Señor Frog's* and *Hard Rock Café*. Heading into the hills of **Diamante**, the Avenida Escénica has world-class restaurants where delectable food, flawless service and goose-bump-inducing views are likely to be the highlight of your stay. Prices are, of course, on a par with upscale New York and London, but well worth the splurge. *Ceviche Acapulco* is the city's signature dish, served in numerous restaurants; the other local speciality, *Pescado a la Talla* (whole, charred-grilled red snapper), is best experienced in Barra Vieja.

CENTRO HISTÓRICO

El Amigo Miguel Juárez 31 ☎ 744 483 6981; map p.205. The original of an Acapulco chain (the most popular is on the malecón) serving good soups, *antojitos* and seafood – sea bass, garlic shrimp and broiled Pacific lobster – at reasonable prices in clean, if institutional, surroundings with a pleasant second-floor dining room (mains M$80–250). Daily 10am–9pm.

Coyuca 32 Juárez 5 (one block from the zócalo) ☎ 744 482 6459; map p.205. Another no-frills budget restaurant in the centre that's been here for years, with the added allure of a breezy patio, serving good *pozole* and comidas corridas all day for M$60; soups, pastas, fried fish and steaks, all for less than M$100. Great for soaking up the local atmosphere. Daily 8am–9pm.

Mariscos Nacho's Azueta 7 ☎ 744 822 8910; map p.205. Multi-storey seafood place with fresh daily produce from the local markets. Does a good pasta marinera (M$110) and shrimp done however you like (M$150). Daily 9am–10pm.

Mi Piaci Plaza Alvarez 6 (zócalo) ☎ 744 482 5555; map p.205. Probably the most modern place on the plaza, a respectable Italian restaurant serving all the usual pizzas, pastas and calzones for around M$60–80. Daily 8.30am–11pm.

Tortas Ricardo's Juarez 9 ☎ 744 482 1140; map p.205. Huge variety of generously stuffed tortas (rolls) for around M$48, just off the zócalo, with some seating in the no-frills but clean interior. Daily 7am–11pm.

ISLA DE LA ROQUETA

Palao Island Club Isla de la Roqueta ☎ 744 482 4313; map pp.202–203. Fun place to spend the afternoon, with a small beach, walking trails over the island and heaps of seafood and cold beers. The buffet lunch is M$120 (with floor show and boat ride). Ferries depart daily from Muelle Palao, Costera 100 (11am–1.30pm; return 3.30–5.30pm). Daily 10am–6pm.

ZONA DORADA AND DIAMANTE

100% Natural Costera 200 (plus several other branches) ☎ 744 485 3982, ⓦ 100natural.com; map pp.202–203. One of a chain of "healthy" eating places

which serves good salads, fruit shakes and burgers (breakfasts M$65–100; sandwiches M$70–100). Open 24hr.

★**Bella Vista** Inside Hotel Las Brisas, Carretera Escénica 5255 ☎ 744 469 6900, ⓦ brisas.com.mx; map pp.202–203. Try to visit this stunning resort for a drink or meal even if you're not staying here – the views are utterly mind-blowing. Right on the top of the cliff, the efficient staff serve breakfast and dinner, while *Sunset Bar* (from 5.30–8.30pm) mixes up their house margaritas to enjoy over the stunning sunsets. Daily 7.30am–noon, 7–11pm.

Carmenere Costera, next to Oceanic 2000 ☎ 744 484 2561; map pp.202–203. Newish Mediterranean cuisine in a small, beautiful space just off Costera; the romantic ambience enhances the subtle flavours, al dente pastas (M$120) and delectable mains such as nut-coated Pacific sea bass (M$195), or rib-eye steaks (M$299). Daily 2pm–midnight.

El Nono Costera 179 ☎ 744 485 1672; map pp.202–203. This no-frills, open-air restaurant is the perfect place to soak up the Costera beach scene, with fresh seafood (M$75–150), not far from the old town. Daily 11am–10pm.

★**Sirocco** Escénica 120 ☎ 744 433 3055, ⓦ sirocco .com.mx; map pp.202–203. Classic Spanish restaurant, with especially good paellas (M$250–285), seafood (M$200–400) and tapas (from M$99). The views over Puerto Marqués add to the wow factor, especially after a few mojitos. Reservations essential. Daily 1pm–midnight.

★**Tacos Tumbras** Costera, 62 opposite Oceanic 2000 ☎ 744 484 1100; map pp.202–203. Cheap local chain with a couple of outdoor restaurants on Costera, with plastic furniture, and meat roasted at the counter. The clubbers' and taxi drivers' late-night favourite for its very succulent tacos *carne asada*. Daily 7pm–5am.

★**Zibu** Escénica s/n ☎ 744 433 3058, ⓦ zibu.com.mx; map pp.202–203. High above Puerto Marqués, the views from this Mex-Thai fusion restaurant are phenomenal (with hummingbirds flitting between flowers), but the food is the real star. Asian and Mexican flavours are delicately balanced; jalapeño sauces replace wasabi on tuna sashimi, shrimps come with sweet tamarind and mango dressing, and while ribs and steaks are only lightly spiced, the lamb is served with an incredible mint sauce puree. Owner Eduardo Wichtendahl is the son of celebrity Mexican chef Susanna Palazuelos. Daily 7pm–midnight.

BARRA VIEJA

★**Esmirna del Mar** Carretera Barra Vieja 1 ☎744 444 6069. Chilled-out beach restaurant lauded for its interpretation of the local speciality, *Pescado a la Talla*. Fresh fish is served with adobo or garlic seasoning, rice, salads, *pico de gallo* and corn tortillas. Daily 11am–11pm.

PIE DE LA CUESTA

Ricarda Yopes Seafront, 100m west of Villa Nirvana (see p.208); no phone but look for yellow sign. The best place to eat on the beach at Pie de la Cuesta is justifiably popular. Friendly Ricarda serves up filling breakfasts and delicious dinners of fresh fish and shrimp from the local market. Grab a table on the sand and enjoy the thunderous waves as you eat. She also has a great michelada mix, and offers tours of the lagoon behind the town for M$100. Daily 8am–11pm.

DRINKING AND NIGHTLIFE

When it comes to nightlife, Acapulco firmly adheres to the Madrid school of partying; many people don't even think about eating dinner until 10pm, and clubs won't get going till long after midnight. Indeed, you could spend several weeks in Acapulco simply trawling its scores of **nightclubs** and **bars**, discos and dinner-dances – there are people who claim never to have seen the town during daylight hours. Anywhere with music or dancing will demand a hefty **cover charge** – in high season usually not less than M$300 for men and M$250 for women.

El Alebrije Costera 3308 ☎744 484 5902, ⊛acapulco.com/es/nightlife/alebrije; map pp.202–203. Opposite the *Grand Hotel*, this cavernous mega-club with light shows is popular with a youngish local crowd post-1am and couples earlier in the evening (it's not as exclusive as some of the other city clubs). The music runs the gamut of mainstream dance, pop and Latin tropicana. Cover at the weekend is around M$360 for men, M$260 for women, and includes all drinks (usually watered down). Daily 10.30pm–5am.

Baby'O Costera 22, east of CiCi Waterpark ☎744 484 7474, ⊛babyo.com.mx; map pp.202–203. Set in an imitation cave, this is one of the more consistently popular clubs as well as one of the most expensive (cover M$300–600) – drinks are not included. The well-dressed, well-heeled crowd is usually high on attitude if they have managed to get in – *Baby'O* tries to maintain a spurious exclusivity by turning people away at the door (it can only accommodate 250). All in all a mainstream affair, with cheesy 1980s music mixed with house and Latin. Daily 10pm–5am.

Mandara Escénica, north of Las Brisas hotel ☎744 446 5711, ⊛acapulcomandara.com; map pp.202–203. Elegant club complete with terraced levels designed to see and be seen ("Philippe Starck-style"), as well as large windows overlooking the bay. Exclusive and luxurious, cover around M$400. Daily 10.30pm–4am.

Mangos Costera (near bungee jump) ☎744 484 4762; map pp.202–203. Great place for a cold beer, cocktail, or to watch the latest sports events, with plenty of decent bar food and a fun English/Latino music selection from the 1980s on. No cover – this is more bar than club. Daily noon–4am.

★**Palladium** Escénica, Playa Guitarrón ☎744 446 5490, ⊛palladium.com.mx; map pp.202–203. It's all about the glorious bay view at this justifiably hyped club with the best music selection – techno, house and hip-hop – in the city. A slightly older and dressier crowd adds to the friendly, gregarious atmosphere. Considered the best disco in the city, and long queues testify to its kudos. Cover around M$350, but open bar. Daily 10pm–5am.

Paradise Costera 107 ☎744 484 5988; map pp.202–203. Popular restaurant-bar just off Condesa beach, near the bungee tower and on the busiest section of Costera – a good place to start your evening. The restaurant section fades away as the evening wears on, replaced by a boisterous club-like atmosphere replete with local entertainers, wet T-shirt contests and plenty of cheap booze. Daily 6pm–5am.

Relax Lomas del Mar 4, opposite El Presidente hotel ☎744 484 0421; map pp.202–203. While not as gay-friendly as Puerto Vallarta (see p.233), Acapulco does have a thriving gay scene: this is one of the more reliable clubs – small and a little claustrophobic, but featuring strippers and other live shows. Thurs–Sat 11pm–5am.

DIRECTORY

Banks Banks (particularly Banamex) and *casas de cambio* (slightly poorer rates) are numerous along Costera. Bancomer is on the zócalo; HSBC is not far away at Carranza 7.

Consulates Canada, Pasaje Diana, Costera 121, Fracc Magallanes ☎744 484 1305 (Mon–Fri 9.30am–12.30pm);

UK, Plaza Arrecife, Suite 105, Costera 2408, Fracc Club Deportivo ☎744 484 3331 (Mon–Fri 10am–2.30pm); US, Pasaje Diana (next to *Hotel Continental Emporio*), Costera 121, Office 14, Fracc Magallanes ☎744 481 0100 (Mon–Fri 10am–2pm).

Emergencies ☎066.

ACAPULCO'S DIVERS

Acapulco's famed **clavadistas** (cliff divers) have been plunging some 35m from the heights of La Quebrada into a rocky channel since the early 1920s (organized officially since 1934), timing their leap to coincide with an incoming wave. Mistimed, there's not enough water to stop them hitting the bottom, though the chief danger these experts seem to face is getting back out of the water without being dashed against the rocks. It could easily be corny, but it's undeniably impressive, especially when floodlit at night. The **dive times** – 1pm, 7.30pm, 8.30pm, 9.30pm and 10.30pm – are rigidly adhered to. A typical display involves several exponents, most taking the lower (25m) platform with some diving simultaneously, and a final dive from the upper level after first asking for the Virgin's intervention at the clifftop shrine. The final diver at the 10.30pm show leaps into the darkness (they turn off the floodlights) with two flaming torches. From the road you can see the spectacle for nothing (get there early), but you'll get a much better view if you go down the steps from the Plazuela de Quebrada to a **viewing platform** (M$40) more or less opposite the divers. Get here early for a good position. Alternatively, you can sit in the lobby bar at *El Mirador Acapulco* hotel (M$200 cover includes two drinks); watching from their overpriced *La Perla* restaurant is not worth it, however. To get there, simply climb the Calzada La Quebrada from the town centre, about fifteen minutes' walk from the zócalo. Heading back, hotel taxis will charge M$50 into the centre, M$80 to the bus terminals and M$100–140 along Costera.

Hospital Cruz Roja ☎ 065 or ☎ 744 445 5912; Emergency IMSS Hospital, Cuauhtémoc 95 ☎ 744 445 5353.

Internet Try Vig@net at Hidalgo 8, just west of the zócalo (daily 8am–midnight; M$20/hr).

Laundry Lavandería Coral, Juárez, at Felipe Valle (Mon–Fri 9am–2pm & 4–7pm, Sat 9am–5pm; M$13/kg; ☎ 744 480 0735).

Pharmacy Plenty of 24hr places in the hotel zone along Costera, and Botica Acapulco near the zócalo at Carranza 3 (also 24hr).

Police ☎ 744 486 8220; tourist complaints ☎ 744 484 4416.

Post office At Costera 315, three blocks east of the zócalo (Mon–Fri 8am–5.30pm, Sat 9am–1pm).

Zihuatanejo

Around 240km along the coast from Acapulco, **ZIHUATANEJO** ("zee-watt-a-NEH-ho"), for all its growth in recent years, has retained something of the look and feel of the traditional fishing village it once was. In stark contrast to neighbour Ixtapa, what building there has been is small-scale, low-key and low-rise, and the town looks over an attractive bay, ringed by broad, sandy beaches excellent for swimming and snorkelling. This said, it is definitely a **resort**: taxi drivers are forever advertising for customers, trinket and tacky T-shirt shops are abundant and as likely as not there'll be a cruise ship moored out in the bay. Despite the proliferation of luxury hotels, though, there are at least a fair number of small, reasonably priced places to stay as well as some inexpensive restaurants. For some, Zihuatanejo is the ideal compromise – quiet by night, yet with the more commercial excitements of Ixtapa nearby.

Museo Arqueológico de la Costa Grande

Paseo del Pescador 7, at Plaza Olof Palme • Tues–Sun 10am–6pm • M$10 • ☎ 755 554 7552

The pedestrianized Paseo del Pescador (or just malecón) runs behind the beach, and at the southern end you'll find the **Museo Arqueológico de la Costa Grande**, a small and straightforward look at the early history of the region. Inside you'll find pre-Columbian archeological finds such as pottery, tools, simple jewellery and rock engravings from important sites such as Cerro de la Madera and Tierras Prietas, with exhibits beginning with the first settlements in the region and ending with the arrival of the Spaniards. Most labelling is Spanish only. From the museum a path cuts through the rocks to Playa La Madera.

Playa La Madera

Four main beaches surround the Bahía de Zihuatanejo, but the **Playa Principal**, the main town beach, is best avoided – with muddy water, brown sand and persistent hawkers, it is an interesting place to people-watch, but with the port nearby it's a bad idea to swim here. Instead follow the footpath east from the end of the beach across the normally dry outlet of a drainage canal, then around a rocky point to the calm waters of **Playa La Madera**, a broad, moderately clean 400m strand of sand that shelves softly into the ocean, making it a good option for kids. There's a handful of restaurants and hotels on the hill behind, as well as some expensive condos.

Playa La Ropa

A kilometre or so over the headland from Playa La Madera, past the *mirador* with great views across the bay, lies **Playa La Ropa** (bus M$6), which takes its name – "Clothes Beach" – from silks washed up here when one of the *nao de China* (trading ships from China) was wrecked offshore. This is Zihuatanejo's finest road-accessible beach, perfect for swimming and palm-fringed for more than a kilometre, with a variety of beachfront restaurants and hotels.

Playa Las Gatas

You can walk fifteen minutes beyond the end of Playa La Ropa to gorgeous **Playa Las Gatas**, named after the nurse sharks that used to populate the waters, but the path is

ACCOMMODATION			
Amuleto	12	Casa Kau Kan	10
Arrecife	13	Catalina Beach Resort	14
Brisas del Mar	6	La Casa Que Canta	9
Bungalows Adelamar	7	Hostel Rincón del Viajero	1
Bungalows Sotelo	5	R3 Marias	4
Casa Cuitlateca	8	Tentaciones Hotel & Lounge Pool	11
Casa de Huéspedes Elvira	3	Villas-Tuparaiso	15
		Zihuatanejo	2

EATING		
La Bocana	8	Tamales y Atoles 2
Cenaduría Antelia	5	Any
Coconuts	4	
Doña Licha	3	**DRINKING &**
El Mediterráneo	6	**NIGHTLIFE**
La Papa Loca	1	Kokomo Bar 1
La Sirena Gorda	7	

THE VIRGIN OF THE TREE

The car park at Playa La Ropa might seem an unlikely place for a miracle, but according to locals, on November 27, 2006 an image of the **Virgin of Guadalupe** – Mexico's patron saint and most revered apparition of Mary – suddenly appeared carved into the trunk of a plum tree right here. The image was quickly deemed a miracle, and though officially unsanctioned by the Church, it is now a mini-pilgrimage site, with candles, offerings and bright flowers enveloping the tree.

---

difficult to follow: as there are no roads, most people take boats from the main pier in Zihuatanejo (daily 8am–5pm, last return 5.30pm; 10min; M$40 return). Las Gatas is the last of the bay's beaches, its crystalline blue water hemmed in by jungle-smothered hills and surrounded by a reef, giving it the enclosed feel of a South Pacific swimming pool. It's safe for kids, though the sea bottom is mostly rocky and tough on feet. The clear waters are great for **snorkelling** – you can rent gear (around M$100/day) from vendors among the rather pricey palapa restaurants.

3

Barra de Potosí

For absolute peace and quiet, the best thing you can do is to take a day trip out of Zihuatanejo to **Barra de Potosí**, a tiny community situated at the southern end of the expansive, postcard-perfect, golden sandy beaches of Playa Larga and Playa Blanca, which curve steeply round the bay and keep going as far as the eye can see. There are plenty of *enramadas* (beach restaurants) here that sell delicious seafood for half the price of the restaurants in town, and boat trips into the **Laguna de Potosí**, a large mangrove estuary teeming with birdlife. It's possible to travel to Barra de Potosí by public transport (see below).

El Refugio de Potosí

Mon, Thurs & Sun 10am–5pm • M$60 • ☎ 755 100 0743, ⓦ elrefugiodepotosi.org

Halfway along the Los Achotes–Barra de Potosí road you'll pass family-friendly **El Refugio de Potosí**, a small ecological park dedicated to preserving local ecosystems, containing botanical displays, insect, spider and snake exhibits, an iguana habitat, macaw roosts, hummingbird feeding stations, a butterfly house and a 15m observation tower.

ARRIVAL AND DEPARTURE	**ZIHUATANEJO**

ZIHUATANEJO

By plane From the Ixtapa-Zihuatanejo International Airport, 20km south of the centre (only 2km off the highway to Acapulco), ignore the crowds of time-share sellers offering lifts and buy transport tickets from the official counters: *colectivo* (shared) taxis charge M$120, while regular taxis will be at least M$400; in the other direction the taxi fare is just M$120. Almost all the flights here are from the US and Canada (seasonal); Aeroméxico and Interjet fly once or twice daily to Mexico City depending on the season, where you must change for all other domestic destinations.

By bus Buses arrive at Zihuatanejo's Central de Autobuses (and the adjacent Estrella de Oro terminal), about 2km and a 25min walk from the centre of town on the road to Acapulco (Hwy-200). There are plenty of taxis (M$30) outside the station, and if you cross Hwy-200 via the

overpass, you can pick up passing "Zihuatanejo" buses (10min; M$6), which will generally drop you off at the top of Juárez (heading back, catch "La Correa" buses).

Destinations Acapulco (hourly; 4–5hr); Ixtapa (continuously; 15min); Lázaro Cárdenas (hourly; 2hr); Manzanillo (3 daily; 7–8hr); Mexico City (frequently; 9hr); Morelia (6 daily; 5–6hr); Puerto Vallarta (2 daily; 12–13hr); Tijuana (2 daily; 40hr).

BARRA DE POTOSÍ

By bus/truck To get to Barra de Potosí, board a Petatlán-bound bus from the main bus station or bus stop on Las Palmas and Cocos in downtown Zihuatanejo and ask the driver to drop you off at the village of Los Achotes (M$13). From here, pick-up trucks (*colectivos*) leave when full to run the final bone-rattling 20min to the beach (around M$12).

GETTING AROUND

By bus Once in town, local "microbuses" cost M$8 to M$14 depending on the destination: Zihuatanejo to Ixtapa is M$12. Pick them up on Juárez.

By taxi Taxis charge according to a schedule of fixed fares; rides between downtown Zihuatanejo and Ixtapa should be M$60–70; Zihuatanejo to Playa La Ropa M$35–40; to Playa Madera M$20; trips within downtown (including the bus station) M$20–30; to Playa Larga M$70; and to Playa Linda M$115. Add forty percent between midnight and 5am.

INFORMATION

Tourist office The municipal tourist office (Mon–Fri 8am–4pm; ☎755 554 2001, ⓦtravelixtapazihuatanejo .com) is inconveniently located about 2km out of town in the Palacio Municipal, Paseo Zihuatanejo 21, near the Fuente del Sol fountain. There is a smaller office on Paseo de la Bahía s/n, close to Playa La Ropa and, in high season only, a tourist booth in the centre at Álvarez s/n.

State tourism office The helpful state tourism office is at Galo 3, near Plaza Kioto (Mon–Fri 8am–3.30pm & 5–7pm, Sat 8am–1pm; ☎755 544 8361). Useful websites include ⓦixtapa-zihuatanejo.com and ⓦzihuatanejo.net/blog.

ACTIVITIES

Zihuatanejo offers various activities to distract you from lounging on the beach. Quite apart from jet skiing, parasailing and getting dragged around on a huge inflatable banana, you could arrange to go **fishing** for dorado, yellowtail, bonito or big game; numerous fishermen offer this service along the main beach and around the pier. Options are small game along the coast (think bonito and dorado) and big game further out in open ocean (sailfish, mahi-mahi and marlin). Prices vary, but aim for around M$1200 for five hours of small game, M$1500 for big game, don't pay more than thirty percent up front and be prepared to argue over the final cost if you come back empty-handed. **Diving** is also popular in the area.

Carlo Scuba Playa Las Gatas ☎755 554 6003, ⓦcarloscuba.com. Carlo's runs PADI-certified dives (from US$65/M$1085) from its base at Playa Las Gatas (all trips include transport from Zihuatanejo pier). Other options include Discover Scuba Dive (US$90/M$1500) and PADI Open Water Course (4 days; US$450/M$7500).

Ixtapa Sportfishing Charters US ☎570 688 9466, ⓦixtapasportfishing.com. Zihuatanejo is a sailfish angling paradise. Trips start at around M$1500/day in a small super-*panga*.

Zihuatanejo Dive Center Paseo Las Salinas, beside the footbridge ☎755 111 5457. Poto, as he likes to be called, offers PADI-certified dives to forty locations around the coast, including the particularly rewarding Morros del Potosi. US$90 (M$1500) for a day's diving, US$35 (M$585) for snorkelling.

ACCOMMODATION

Zihuatanejo's **high season** is fairly long, from around mid-Nov to the end of April. Outside those times some of the marginally more expensive hotels drop their **rates** to those of the budget places – which tend to vary their prices less. **Playa La Madera**, while part of Zihuatanejo, has a different feel, slightly removed and a touch exclusive – though not necessarily more expensive. **Playa La Ropa**, more than 1km from the centre, feels a world apart and is home to the most luxurious options.

CENTRAL ZIHUATANEJO

Casa de Huéspedes Elvira Paseo del Pescador 9 ☎755 554 2061. The oldest hotel in town is a long-standing favourite budget option with a friendly owner, who is probably the oldest man in town. There's a communal kitchen and very good restaurant on site. The six rooms with shared bath (no hot water) are unadorned but perfectly adequate (M$100 extra for a/c). M$200

Hostel Rincón del Viajero Paseo Las Salinas 50, La Noria ☎755 105 4398, ⓦrinconviajerozihua.4t.com. The town's only hostel is unfortunately rather a shambles. While hippy art graces the walls, little of the implied spirit is evident in the management, who charge extra for everything. It's the go-to backpacker spot in town, but few leave smitten with Zihuatanejo. Dorms M$170, doubles M$360

R3 Marias Paseo Las Salinas, right beside the pedestrian bridge ☎755 554 6706, ⓦ3marias.net. Good strong a/c and a friendly family are the bedrock of this hotel at the town's lagoon inlet. Stunning views over the bay beyond (ask for room "Zihua"), a chilled-out vibe and a 2min stroll from the action make this one of the most appealing options in town. M$400

Zihuatanejo Centro Ramírez 2 ☎755 554 5330, ⓦzihuacentro.com. One of the most comfortable options in the centre, a couple of blocks from the waterfront. Its a/c rooms are equipped with decent cable TV, and there's access to a small pool and bar. M$850

PLAYA LA MADERA

Brisas del Mar López Mateos, Playa La Madera ☎755 554 2142. Not quite as astronomically priced as many places in these parts, this charming hotel has comfortable, artistically decorated suites with tasteful wooden furnishings. Large private terraces have hammocks from which to enjoy the sea views. Other facilities include a swimming pool, volleyball court, library, fitness centre with sauna, steam room and massages. M$1370

Bungalows Adelamar Adelita 40, Playa La Madera ☎755 554 9190, ⓦixtapasportfishing.com/adelamar. Eight immaculately clean, modern apartments (holding up to four people) in a tranquil location close to the beach, all with well-equipped kitchens and some with small gardens. There's also an excellent communal pool. M$1150

Bungalows Sotelo López Mateos, Playa La Madera ☎755 554 6307, ⓦbungalowssotelo.com. Comfortable apartments with a/c, internet, satellite TV, balconies, kitchens and great sea views. The most luxurious rooms have jacuzzis on the balcony. M$1000

★**Casa Cuitlateca** Camino Escénico, Playa La Madera s/n ☎755 554 2448, ⓦcasacuitlateca.com. Spectacular five-room boutique hotel reached by a swaying suspension bridge (in between La Ropa and La Madera), with an indigenous Mexican theme (each room is decorated with art from a different region), infinity pool and rooftop sun deck. Adults only. M$1600

PLAYA LA ROPA

Amuleto Camino Escéncio 9, Playa La Ropa s/n ☎755 544 6222, ⓦamuleto.net. *The* place to splurge, and one of the most opulent hotels on the coast, this six-suite boutique is a justly popular romantic getaway, with jaw-dropping views at every turn, elegant four-posters and impeccable service (internet but no TVs or alarm clocks). M$4420

★**Arrecife** Playa La Ropa, next door to Catalina Beach Resort (see opposite) ☎755 111 1089 or ☎755 113 9533. This hidden gem is an entire villa overlooking the sea which Doña Bucio, a local businesswoman, rents out to friends and tourists alike. The house has a/c throughout, two bedrooms and a stunning terrace overlooking the sea. It's on this same terrace that the inclusive breakfast is served. A fantastic option for those looking for a slice of private paradise. Make sure you reserve ahead, and explain your travel arrangements as they'll collect you from the bus station. M$500

★**La Casa Que Canta** Camino Escéncio, Playa La Ropa ☎755 555 7030, ⓦlacasaquecanta.com. Guests rave about this beautifully designed, thatched-roof hotel draped over the hillside. The breezy rooms are luxuriously decorated with traditional artesanía, and the secluded, romantic gardens are composed of labyrinthine pathways that lead to intimate hideaways. There's also a stellar restaurant and a spa and fitness centre. US$395 (M$6585)

Catalina Beach Resort Playa la Ropa s/n ☎755 554 2137, ⓦcatalina-beach-resort.com. A good-value beachfront option, *Catalina* is one of the oldest and friendliest hotels in town with great facilities for the price. The rooms do vary – some betray their age more than others, and the new suites are well worth the extra – but the large terraces with hammocks and glorious views are the attraction here. Tropical gardens, a pool and an oceanfront restaurant (complimentary breakfast) are perfect for relaxing. M$1390

Tentaciones Hotel & Lounge Pool Camino Escéncio, Playa La Ropa ☎755 544 8383, ⓦhoteltentaciones.com. Another gorgeous luxury hideaway, hidden among lush cliffs and ponds above the beach, and consisting of four one-bedroom palapa suites with verandas overlooking the bay. All come with satellite TV, marble-clad bathrooms and the usual plush amenities. M$3670

PLAYA LARGA

Casa Kau Kan Domicilio Conocido s/n, Playa Larga ☎755 554 6226. The essence of good taste and discretion, this small, beachside boutique hotel has spacious, artful suites with separate living areas and plush bathrooms. Gourmet food, tranquil pool and gorgeous gardens create an aura of refined pampering in an isolated natural setting with many kilometres of deserted beach (no phones or TVs). M$1225

BARRA DE POTOSÍ

★**Villas-Tuparaiso** Ing Javier Rodriguez 58, Col Playa Blanca ☎755 556 2526, ⓦvillas-tuparaiso.com. Four cosy en-suite bungalows, all with two bedrooms, a kitchenette (kettle, mini-fridge, dishes etc) and iPod docks. Each also comes with a small screened veranda with table and chairs (there's also a communal full kitchen). M$550

EATING

CENTRAL ZIHUATANEJO

Cenaduría Antelia Nicolás Bravo 14 ☎755 554 3091. Open since 1975, this snug old-time joint is a great little spot to eat unadulterated Mexican staples for under M$50 – tacos, enchiladas and the like – until midnight. The rich desserts are also worth the havoc they'll wreak on your midriff. Low season daily 5pm–midnight; high season daily 8am–2pm & 5pm–midnight.

Coconuts Pasaje Agustín Ramírez 1 ☎755 554 2518. Set in a charming old house (the remains of a coconut factory built in 1865) with a stunning patio. The food is good, with a varied menu featuring healthy fish, fresh poultry and creative vegetarian dishes. The overall ambience is quite romantic, especially with low-key jazz in the evenings. Mains M$190–230. June–Oct daily noon–4pm & 6pm–midnight.

Doña Licha Los Cocos 8 ☎755 554 3933. A wide menu of excellent and inexpensive comidas corridas (ribs, tripe and pork chops), served with mountains of rice and beans, has earned this place a loyal following. With a lackadaisical, raw atmosphere, complete with blasting TV and erratic service, the copious platters of food are undoubtedly the main attraction – meals for less than M$75. Daily 8am–6pm.

El Mediterráneo 5 de Mayo 4 ☎755 115 4010. This Greek-themed Mexican/Mediterranean fusion restaurant is especially lauded for its pastas and fresh tuna – sit in the garden at the back to soak up the relaxed ambience. Tues–Sun 3–11pm.

La Papa Loca Colegio Militar at Palapas (all taxi drivers know it). A local institution serving up baked potatoes, smashed open and covered with all sorts of delights including cheese, carne al pastor, cream and sauce. Indeed the "Crazy Potato" (M$60), their signature dish, features all of them. Also does tacos, fish and big juices for cheap. The street-level tables and atmosphere make this unmissable. Daily 5pm–late.

La Sirena Gorda Paseo del Pescador 90 ☎755 554 2687. Fairly expensive (M$85–230) but well sited, right where evening strollers can watch you dine on succulent tuna steaks (which are particularly good) and seafood

cocktails, as well as a selection of American dishes, in the balmy night air. Creatively decorated with paintings of the eponymous chunky mermaid. Mon, Tues & Thurs–Sun 8.30am–10.30pm.

Tamales y Atoles Any Guerrero 38, at Ejido. No prizes for what is on the menu at this good-value, bustling, beach joint that packs in locals and tourists looking for its sixteen different kinds of tamales (from M$25), which range from chicken and chile to cheese and squash blossom. The signature dish is *pozole* (pork stew, traditionally eaten on Thurs). Mexican breakfasts served daily. Daily 8am–11pm.

PLAYA LA ROPA

La Bocana Blv Playa La Ropa 109 ☎755 554 1302, ⊕la-bocana.com. Set in the jungle, 5min walk from La Ropa beach, and with roots in the 1960s, this is one of the city's most popular restaurants, serving a range of superbly executed Mexican dishes such as *pozole* (only on Thurs), but also more playful items such as the Swiss enchilada topped with cheese. The freshly squeezed juices are another highlight. Daily 8am–5.30pm.

DRINKING AND NIGHTLIFE

Kokomo Bar Palapas at Los Cocos. Lively green-painted joint with a packed bar and tables further back. Very

popular with the locals and a sure-fire bet for a rowdy drink or two. Happy hour 5–7pm. Daily 6pm–midnight.

DIRECTORY

Emergencies ☎066; Cruz Roja (Red Cross) ☎065.

Internet There are numerous cafés in town and especially along Guerrero, most of which charge M$10–20/hr. Try Ciber Zihua at Bravo 12 (daily 8am–10pm; M$10/hr).

Money and exchange Banamex, on Ejido at Guerrero (Mon–Fri 9am–6pm; 24hr ATM), and Banorte, Ejido 8 at

Juárez (Mon–Fri 9am–5pm, Sat 9am–2pm).

Pharmacy Farmacia Principal, Ejido 34, at the corner of Cuauhtémoc in Zihuatanejo (Mon–Sat 9am–9pm).

Police Tourist police ☎060 or ☎755 554 2207.

Post office Edificio SCT, between Telegrafistas and Palmar (Mon–Fri 8am–6pm, Sat 9am–1pm).

Ixtapa

Just 7km north of Zihuatanejo, **IXTAPA** could hardly be more different. Ixtapa is a computer-planned "paradise" resort, established by Fonatur in the 1970s, and, even today, a fairly soulless place. Its single coastal drive (**Paseo Ixtapa**) runs past a series of concrete boxes of varying heights, making Zihuatanejo far more appealing.

The beaches

Hotels and condos completely cordon off Ixtapa's lovely 2.5km stretch of beach – **Playa de Palmar** – from the road, forcing those who can't afford the hotels' inflated prices to squeeze through a couple of access points or use the hotels' facilities for day rates of around M$100. The beach is fine for volleyball or long walks, but often too rough for easy swimming, and plagued by jet skis.

Playa Quieta

Powered watersports are also in evidence at the inappropriately named **Playa Quieta**, some 5km north of Ixtapa, which is dominated by *Club Med* and seemingly perpetual clans of inebriated spring-breakers. The water here is wonderfully clear and the

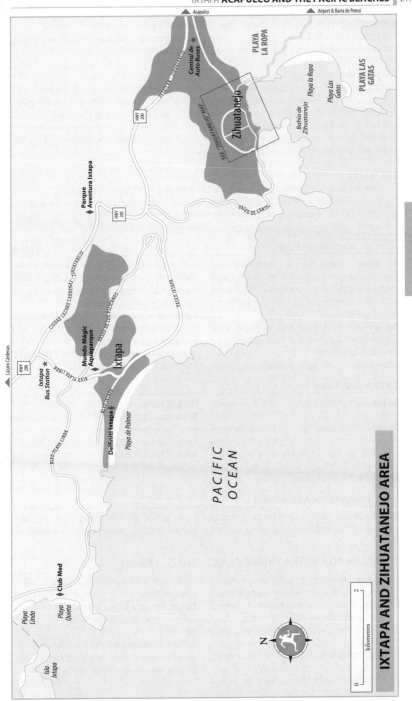

IXTAPA AND ZIHUATANEJO AREA

surrounding vegetation magnificent, but with the exception of a solitary seafood restaurant you won't get anything to eat or drink unless you pay handsomely to enter the confines of the three luxury resorts that dominate the beach.

Playa Linda

Playa Linda is a huge sweep of greyish sand, with a cluster of *enramadas* at the pier end where the local bus from the centre of town (M$10) drops you off. As well as the usual trinket vendors, you can hire horses or rent jet skis and surfboards at the shacks along the beach. To find all the space you need, keep walking away from the crowded pier end: the restaurants are supplanted by coconut groves, which in turn give way to small cliffs and an estuary with birdlife and reptiles.

Isla Ixtapa

Boats leave from the pier at Playa Linda for **Isla Ixtapa**, a small island a couple of kilometres offshore with two fine swimming beaches, a spot reserved for snorkelling (rent gear for M$120) and diving (you can easily walk between the three locations) and a few restaurants, but nowhere to stay.

ARRIVAL AND DEPARTURE   IXTAPA

By plane Transport from the Ixtapa-Zihuatanejo International Airport (see p.213) is the usual overpriced monopoly: *colectivo* taxis charge around M$150 per person, while taxis will be at least M$360; in the other direction the fare is just M$170.

By bus Some long-distance buses now serve Ixtapa directly via the bus terminal at Plaza Ixpamar, in the commercial area behind the seafront (Paseo Ixtapa), but otherwise you'll have to change at Zihuatanejo's Central de Autobuses (see p.213); you can catch a local bus (every 15min, 6am–11pm; M$8) along the seafront to Ixtapa across Hwy-200 from the bus station or from the top of Juárez at Morelos in downtown Zihua.

Tourist office For information, try online travel agencies such as ⓦ visitixtapazihuatanejo.com, or visit the Oficina de Convenciones y Visitantes, inside the Edificio Plaza Zocalo, Local 8 Altos, Andador Cerro La Puerta, Manzana 2, Lote 16 (Mon–Fri 8am–4pm; ☎ 755 553 1270).

GETTING AROUND

By bus Local "microbuses" M$8–12 (Ixtapa to Zihuatanejo M$8).

By taxi Taxis charge fixed fares; rides between downtown Zihuatanejo and Ixtapa M$60–70; Ixtapa to Playa La Ropa M$90–110; to Playa La Madera M$70; trips within downtown M$35; to Playa Larga M$125; to Playa Linda M$60–80. Add forty percent midnight–5am.

ISLA IXTAPA

By boat Boats depart when full from Playa Linda (usually every 30min, 9am–5pm; 20min; M$70 return). You can also get there on a daily launch from Zihuatanejo, which leaves at 11am and returns at 5pm (1hr; M$250 round trip).

ACCOMMODATION AND EATING

Casa Candiles 65 Paseo de Las Golondrinas (next to the Palma de Real golf course, and not far from the beach) ☎ 755 101 2744 US ☎ 1 717 207 8471, ⓦ casacandiles.com. Independent travellers usually skip

---

IXTAPA FOR KIDS – THEME PARKS AND DOLPHINS

Delfiniti Ixtapa Lote Anexo 6B, Zona Hotelera 1 ☎ 755 553 2736, ⓦ delfiniti.com. Meet the dolphins through six interactive programmes, from 45min swims (US$124/M$2070) to 20min encounters (US$82/ M$1365). There are packages for families and a special programme for kids 3–7 years of age.

Mundo Mágico Acuaparque Paseo de la Garzas, ☎ 1 800 917 5292, ⓦ mundomagicoixtapa.com. Every kid loves a water park, and though this is a small one, it delivers with fun slides and pools (entry M$100). Tues–Sun 10am–5pm.

Parque Aventura Ixtapa Carretera Zihuatanejo-Lázaro Cárdenas (Hwy-200) km 4.8 ☎ 755 115 1733. Rope ladders, Himalayan rope bridges and eleven zip lines (some 250m long and 30m high; US$45/M$750) provide the thrills at this popular theme park, though it's fairly tame by international zip standards. Daily 8.30am–6.30pm.

Ixtapa's resort hotels in favour of Zihuatanejo, but one appealing alternative here is this intimate American-run inn with just three comfy suites, garden and pool. **M$2500**
Ruben's Hamburgers Centro Comercial Flamboyant, Andador Punta San Esteban ☎755 553 0055. For something tasty and quick in town, head to *Ruben's* for juicy sirloin, cheese and chicken charbroiled burgers (from M$50), and huge baskets of fries. Mon–Thurs

11am–11pm, Fri–Sun 10am–1am.
Villa de la Selva Paseo de la Roca s/n ☎755 553 0362, ⌨villadelaselva.com.mx. South of Ixtapa in a wonderful cliff-side spot, this posh restaurant serves fabulous contemporary Mediterranean and Mexican dishes from M$150; think salmon glazed with chipotle and apricot, and smoked marlin spring rolls. Daily: June–Aug 7pm–midnight; Oct–May 6–11pm.

DRINKING AND NIGHTLIFE

Generals Sports Bar Plaza Kiosko ☎755 553 3672. Popular with tourists, expats and locals alike, with the coldest beer in town, TV screens for live events and excellent bar food – all presided over by the inimitable "general" himself. Daily 10am–11pm.

Señor Frog's Centro Comercial La Puerta, Paseo de Ixtapa s/n Mza, 11 Lote 5 ☎755 553 2282 ⌨senorfrogs .com. A typical night out starts at *Señor Frog's* opposite the *Presidente Inter-Continental* hotel, with dancing on tables and all the usual drunken revelry. Daily 6pm–3am.

The Michoacán coast

North of Ixtapa, Hwy-200 follows the coast for 100km or so before crossing the Guerrero border into **Michoacán** state and the industrial city of **Lázaro Cárdenas**. From here the highway continues for another 260km through a wilder, virtually uninhabited area: there are fabulous beaches, but for the most part the mountains of the **Sierra de Coalcomán** drop straight into the ocean – it's the most spectacular, best preserved and least developed section of the Pacific coast. You'll make the most of this region if you have your own transport, though experienced hikers often camp and walk large sections of the coast. If you do travel by bus, sit at the front and prepare for some severe hairpin bends. In all cases, avoid travel at night.

Playa Azul

Once a small-time, slow-moving beach surrounded by lagoons, **PLAYA AZUL** has been rather overrun by the growth of Lázaro Cárdenas, 24km away. However, there are still several reasonably priced hotels and a wide, often deserted strip of silky sand, backed by scores of palapa restaurants.

ARRIVAL AND DEPARTURE   PLAYA AZUL

By bus Long-distance buses don't pass directly through Playa Azul, so ask to be dropped off at La Mira, the nearest town on Hwy-200 – from here *colectivos* run the remaining 7km down to Playa Azul (M$7).

By colectivo *Colectivos* (M$15; 40min) run back and forth to Lázaro Cárdenas bus station from the centre, and you can also take taxis for around M$150. The road into town runs parallel to the beach down to the vast plaza at the southern end.

ACCOMMODATION AND EATING

María Isabel Madero s/n ☎753 536 0016. For somewhere cheap, try the basic but comfortable *María Isabel*, on the far side of the plaza, which has spotless motel-like rooms, very friendly staff and a pool of its own. You'll pay M$100 extra for a/c. **M$400**
María Teresa Independencia 626 (on the plaza) ☎753 536 0005. The best accommodation in town is *Hotel María Teresa*, on the plaza, which features attractive rooms, a decent pool and a garden bar-restaurant serving breakfast only (included in the price). **M$660**
El Pirata del Caribe Central Malecón ☎753 108 5399.

A friendly beachfront option with red snapper cooked however you want for M$100. Also has big and inexpensive *micheladas* for those hot days. Daily 8am–8pm.
Playa Azul Venustiano Carranza s/n ☎753 536 0088. Rooms here are clustered around a leafy courtyard and have a/c and a pool view. You can also camp here, though the site is little more than a patch of dirt behind the hotel. The pool is a better prospect (M$30 for non-guests). Charges M$250 extra for a/c. Doubles **M$350**, camping per person **M$70**

Caleta de Campos

As you move deeper into Michoacán, **CALETA DE CAMPOS**, some 56km from Playa Azul, is in many ways the best place to stop. A small village that acts as a service centre for the area, it's friendly and unassuming, with two lovely beaches and impressive ocean views. There is something of a Wild West feel to the place: the streets are unpaved, and horses stand tied to hitching posts alongside the camper vans of North American surfers and the fancy new cars belonging to visitors from the city. For much of the year the place is virtually deserted, but in winter, when Californian beach boys come down in pursuit of sun and surf (the waves are perfect for beginners), and at weekends, when families from Lázaro Cárdenas pile in, it can get crowded.

ARRIVAL AND DEPARTURE

CALETA DE CAMPOS

By bus Buses stop on Hwy-200 or at the small station on the plaza. It should be possible to pick up long-distance buses to Manzanillo (north) or Lázaro Cárdenas (south), but you won't be able to reserve seats. Minibuses (hourly; around M$55) also connect Caleta de Campos with Lázaro (1hr 20min), where you can more easily change to long-distance services.

ACCOMMODATION AND EATING

You'll find plenty of budget accommodation in Caleta, much of it close to the beach, and numerous places to grab a meal; there is a string of bars and restaurants down at the beach and a plethora of taco stands and mini-markets along the main street.

Parador Turistico North end of town ☎ 753 114 1111. Cliff-top complex at the northern extremity of town that offers everything from basic rooms with kingsize beds right up to entire villas with kitchens, decks and jacuzzis rentable by the night. All options have a/c. Doubles M$850, villas M$1800

Yuritzi Corregidora 10 ☎ 753 531 5010, ⓦ hotelyuritzi .mx. A modern, well-managed establishment that has its own generator and water supply. All rooms come with TV, but it's M$100 extra for a/c. M$500

Playa Maruata and Colola

Just over 100km from Caleta de Campos, **PLAYA MARUATA** is by far the most enticing beach on the coast, and the best one for camping. Once an isolated **Nahua** fishing village, it has developed into a laid-back backpacker and surfer resort, with locals providing cheap eats and accommodation, as well as leading the effort to protect the turtles that frequent their beaches.

The main beach is a 3km stretch of sand perfect for swimming and snorkelling, while the more intriguing middle section is riddled with boulders and caves, including an enigmatic finger of rock known as the **Dedo de Dios** ("God's finger"). The third section is known as Playa de los Muertos, dogged by dangerous currents and waves. From Maruata it's another 80km to the Colima border at Boca de Apiza – there are numerous surfer hangouts along the way (Playa La Ticla and San Juan de Alima among them).

A further 8km up the coast from Plata Maruata is Colola, another long stretch of sand much favoured by wildlife spotters, as it's far less known and tends to attracts more turtles than Maruata. During October and November both leatherback and green turtles make their way up the sandbar to lay their eggs, and hotel owners organize beach walks to see them.

ARRIVAL AND DEPARTURE

PLAYA MARUATA AND COLOLA

By bus To get to Playa Maruata by bus you'll need to take a Tecomán/Lázaro Cárdenas–Manzanillo bus and tell the driver you want to go to Maruata or Colola: he'll drop you on Hwy-200 where it's a 1.5km walk down to the beach and the main village. Heading back you'll just have to flag buses down (no reservations).

ACCOMMODATION

Cabañas Colola Colola Beach (no phone). A number of three-bedroom structures (given their balconies, the best rooms are the upstairs lofts) overlook the beach where turtles appear around dusk. There's a restaurant, which operates in the Aug–Jan high season (outside of which prices drop by M$100), as well as a swimming pool, which operates all year round. M$400

Parador Turístico Maruata ☎ 555 150 5110. You'll get the most out of Maruata by camping under their thatched stand on the beach, though these simple cabañas come with showers and bathrooms. You'll find them at the western end of the beaches. It can be hard to book in advance, but as long as it's not Easter or Christmas, you can be fairly sure of space. Cabañas M$500, camping per person M$50

The Colima coast

The relatively tiny state of **Colima** has just 139km of coastline, stretching from the Boca de Apiza to the Cerro de San Francisco in Jalisco, but there's plenty to tempt you off Hwy-200. The southern section boasts several laid-back villages worth exploring, from the surf magnet of **Boca de Pascuales** to **Cuyutlán**, with a long beach lined with palapa restaurants. In stark contrast, **Manzanillo** is a major resort and another Mexican fishing port claiming the title "sailfish capital of the world".

3

Boca de Pascuales

BOCA DE PASCUALES, 13km from the workday town of **Tecomán**, is little more than a bunch of palapa restaurants, but its beach is renowned for huge waves and challenging **surf**; this is a river-mouth beach break with some of the nastiest and fastest tubes in Mexico (breaking right and left) – it's definitely not for the inexperienced. Even swimming can be dangerous, but otherwise it's a fine place to hang out for a few days.

ARRIVAL AND DEPARTURE   BOCA DE PASCUALES

By bus To reach Boca de Pascuales, you'll first need to take a bus to Tecomán, 50km south of the city of Colima and 30km from the Michoacán border. Buses run to Tecomán from Colima, Lázaro Cárdenas and Manzanillo. Minibuses run to Boca from Tecomán's bus station (hourly, 7am–8pm; M$8; 20min).
By taxi Taxis charge M$80 from Tecomán to Boca.

ACCOMMODATION AND EATING

★**Las Hamacas del Mayor** ☎ 313 103 6903, ⓦ las hamacasdelmayor.webnode.es. The best restaurant in town has been serving top-notch seafood since 1953 and still draws a large crowd, in spite of its remote location. Mains M$80–225, lobster M$600/kg. Daily 10.30am–6.30pm.

Paco's Hotel Av de los Surfistas 113 ☎ 313 123 2027. The best accommodation option, easy to spot on the way in to the village, offering colourful and cosy rooms (some a/c; M$50 extra) with bathroom and free wi-fi. M$520

Cuyutlán

Some 25km west of Tecomán on Hwy-200, **CUYUTLÁN** is the most appealing of a series of tiny resorts that adorn the shoreline between the Michoacán border and Manzanillo, backed by an immense coconut grove that stretches along a narrow peninsula almost as far as the port city. Popular with Mexican holidaymakers, the old town around the main plaza is sleepy, its inhabitants idling away the day on wooden verandas under terracotta roofs. In spring, the **coast** both here and further south is subject to the **Ola Verde**: vast, dark-green waves up to 10m high that crash down on the fine grey sand. Theories to explain their green hue vary widely – though most experts think it is phosphorescence created by microscopic phytoplankton – but whatever the reason, the Ola Verde has been a part of Cuyutlán lore ever since a huge tsunami destroyed the town in 1932. At other times of the year the surf is impressive but easier to handle and it's OK to swim; surfers usually head south to **Paraíso** and Boca de Pascuales (see above).

Centro Ecológico de Cuyutlán "el Tortugario"

Around 4km on the road to Paraíso • Mon, Tues & Thurs–Sun 10am–5pm • M$25 • ☎ 313 107 4069

It's worth taking a trip out to the **Centro Ecológico de Cuyutlán "el Tortugario"** – catch a cab from the plaza (M$40–50) or stroll south down the beach for about 45 minutes. From July to December, three **turtle** species (the olive ridley, the black and the leatherback) visit the local beaches to lay their eggs, and a team from the centre goes out every night to collect them before they end up as someone's dinner. The newly hatched turtles are then kept in tanks for a couple of days before being released back into the sea (usually Aug–Dec Sat 3pm). Out of the egg-laying season, there's a resident turtle population, crocodiles, iguanas and lots of information on hand. The sanctuary also organizes 45-minute boat **tours** (M$40) through the mangrove tunnels of the idyllic, jungly **Estero Palo Verde**, part of the **Laguna Cuyutlán** and well known for its birdlife.

Museo de la Sal

Juárez, at Progreso, two blocks east of the plaza • Daily 9am–6pm • Donation M$10 • ☎ 313 322 16 87

Cuyutlán was once an important salt-producing centre under the Spanish, but salt was being made here way back in pre-Columbian times. This long history is celebrated at the **Museo de la Sal**, housed in an original, wooden salt *bodega*. If you're interested, the retired salt-workers who run the place will talk you through the compound's long history.

ARRIVAL AND DEPARTURE   CUYUTLÁN

By bus To get to Cuyutlán you must first catch a bus for the 12km journey northeast to the inland market town of Armería (40km southeast of Manzanillo, 20km west of Tecomán), which has a bank, a post office and a long-distance bus stop on the main street (Hwy-200). Here, walk two blocks north from the long-distance bus stop, then one block east to the market, where there are regular buses (every 30min, 6am–7.30pm; 20min; M$12).

ACCOMMODATION AND EATING

Fénix Hidalgo 201 ☎ 313 326 4082. The *grande dame* of the town since 1933 and the tsunami era, featuring some great old-fashioned rooms opening onto spacious communal verandas. The rooms on the second floor are bigger, and all go for half the price for solo travellers. Free wi-fi, satellite TV and restaurant/bar on site, and they'll also let you use the kitchen if you clean up after yourself. **M$620**

Mariscos Lupita Northern end of malecón. *Lupita's* signature dish is shrimp in tamarind sauce (M$120), and it's reason enough on its own to come to town; you'll get it nowhere else on the coast and it's absolutely delicious. They also mix up a good piña colada. Daily 9am–10pm.

Morelos Hidalgo 185 ☎ 313 326 4013. With clean, basic rooms (the renovated ones are the most comfortable), fans, hot water and the area's best swimming pool, this is one of the best deals in town. **M$280**

San Rafael Veracruz 46 ☎ 313 326 4015, ⊕ hotel sanrafael.com. Lovely rooms, some facing the beach, all with fans, hot water and access to an outdoor pool. Also boasts the decent *7-Seas Restaurant* on site. **M$600**

Manzanillo

Colima state's second city and the busiest cargo port in Mexico, **MANZANILLO** is clearly a working town: tourism – although highly developed – very definitely takes second place to trade. Downtown, crisscrossed by railway tracks, rumbles with heavy traffic and is surrounded by a bewildering array of inner harbours and shallow lagoons that seem to cut the city off from the land. It's this genuine, workaday character that makes Manzanillo stand out on this stretch of coast, its **centro histórico** making a pleasant contrast with the great scythe of beaches and resorts along Manzanillo and Santiago bays.

Centro histórico

Much of Manzanillo's old town, or **centro histórico**, has been spruced up in recent years, centring on its main plaza, the **Jardín Alvaro Obregón**, right on the harbour and embellished with rose gardens and exuberant topiary. The long **boardwalk**, dominated by a 25m-tall **sailfish memorial** and local favourite the **Fuentes Danzarinas** (dancing fountains), is best ambled along at sunset. That said, few tourists spend time in the centre – most head to the hotels and club resorts of the **Península de Santiago** around Manzanillo Bay to the northwest – even though old Manzanillo is a lot more interesting than this sanitized resort area, and cheaper, too.

Playa Las Brisas

While locals might go **swimming** from the tiny harbour beach of **Playa San Pedrito** and in the Laguna de Cuyutlán behind the town, both are polluted. You're far better off heading for the **beaches** further along Manzanillo Bay, along the Zona Hotelera. The nearest of these, at **Playa Las Brisas**, is closer to town than you would think – just across the entrance to the inner harbour – though it seems further away due to convoluted routes around the Laguna de San Pedrito. Frequent **buses** (20min; M$6) from the centre (from Juárez near the plaza and marked "Las Brisas") run all the way along the single seafront drive. The 6km beach (which is known as **Playa Azul** at the top end) shelves steeply to the ocean, causing the tide to crash upon the shore; consequently, the beach is not as conducive to swimming as those further around the bay.

Playa La Audiencia

Better and more sheltered swimming can be found along the coast 11km from downtown, where Manzanillo Bay is divided from Santiago Bay by the rocky **Península de Santiago**. If you're prepared to walk a little way, you can reach the calm and tranquil waters of the beautiful cove of **Playa La Audiencia**, on the west side of the Santiago peninsula (facing Santiago Bay).

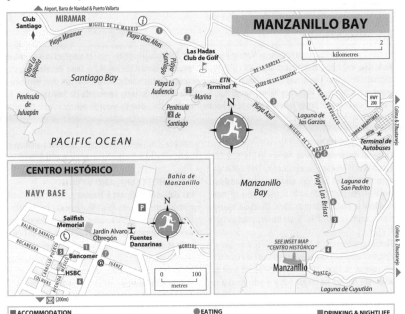

ACCOMMODATION				EATING				DRINKING & NIGHTLIFE	
Colonial	5	Pepe's Hideaway	2	Café Costeño	6	La Perlita	2	Bar Social	1
Flamingo's	6	La Posada	3	Chantilly	7	La Sonrisa	3		
Las Hadas Golf Resort & Marina	1	Zar Manzanillo	4	Dolphy	5	El Vaquero	4		
				Juanito's	1				

Santiago Bay beaches

Santiago Bay stretches for around 8km beyond the Península de Santiago, with "Miramar" **buses** (M$6) running all the way to the far side and passing a string of beaches. The main four, from east to west, are: Playa Santiago; Playa Olas Altas; Playa Miramar 3km further on, the best beach for **surfing** (shops rent boards on the beach); and Playa La Boquita, another 3km and a bit harder to reach, via Club Santiago.

ARRIVAL AND DEPARTURE

MANZANILLO

By plane The Aeropuerto Internacional Playa de Oro is 30km north of Manzanillo's Zona Hotelera (Hwy-200 km 42). There are no buses to the airport, so you have to take a fixed-price *colectivo* (M$155) or taxi (M$375–450), with rates set according to a zone system. Alamo (☎ 314 334 124), Budget (☎ 314 334 2270), Hertz (☎ 314 333 3191) and Thrifty (☎ 314 334 3282) have car-rental desks at the airport. The airport ATM is temperamental, so make sure you have pesos on arrival. Flights primarily connect Manzanillo with cities in the US and Canada: for domestic destinations you'll have to change in Mexico City via Aeromar or Aeroméxico.

By bus The Terminal de Autobuses is several km northeast of the centre, just off Hwy-200 near Playa Las Brisas. Buses (M$6–8) to the main plaza (marked "Jardín" or "Centro") and the beaches (marked "Santiago") leave from the station entrance. Taxis should be around M$40 to the centre and M$100 to Península de Santiago, but fix the price first. The ETN bus station is off Hwy-200 at km 13.5.

Destinations Acapulco (3 daily; 12hr); Barra de Navidad (frequently; 1hr 30min); Colima (frequently; 1hr 30min); Guadalajara (frequently; 5–6hr); Lázaro Cárdenas (7 daily; 6–7hr); Mexico City (4 daily; 12hr); Puerto Vallarta (hourly; 5–7hr); Tecomán (frequent; 1hr); Tijuana (2 daily; 38hr).

INFORMATION AND TOURS

Tourist office The helpful Oficina de Convenciones y Visitantes is north of Playa Azul several km out of town, at Miguel de la Madrid 14540 (Mon–Fri 9am–2pm & 4–7pm; ☎ 314 333 2277, ⓦ vivemanzanillo.com.mx).

Tours Given the steady flow of North American cruise and package tourists visiting Manzanillo, it's no surprise that local travel agents have developed a wide range of day trips taking in everything from tours of Colima, the volcanoes and Cuyutlán, to zip lines, iguana farms and ATV expeditions. Try Tlaloc Tours (ⓦ tlaloctours.com) or Manzanillo Adventures (ⓦ manzanilloadventures.com).

ACCOMMODATION

Finding a **place to stay** is no problem in Manzanillo, with most of the budget options close to the plaza in the **centro histórico**, and a host of mid-range and luxury resorts stretching north around the bay in the **Zona Hotelera**; as the original seaside strip, **Las Brisas** offers a number of dated, monolithic hotels which tend to be cheaper than elsewhere, except when the area is flooded by holidaymakers from Guadalajara, while the rocky **Península de Santiago**, further north, is smothered in luxury resorts. **Prices** at all but the cheapest hotels drop by about 25 percent outside the high season (roughly Dec–May) and Semana Santa.

CENTRO HISTÓRICO

Colonial Bocanegra 28, at México ☎ 314 332 1080 ⓔ hotelcolonialmanz@hotmail.com. This 1940s gem drips with faded colonial grandeur: an Andalucian mosaic-tiled courtyard with a fountain and heavy wooden furnishings add to its allure. The clean, spacious rooms, with a/c and cable TV, are perfectly comfortable. M$720

Flamingo's Mexico 28 ☎ 312 157 6226. A central and inexpensive option close to the malecón. It's in a crumbling old colonial building, but most of the rooms have a/c, which you can get for the price of a regular room if you negotiate. M$260

Zar Manzanillo Azueta 3 ☎ 314 332 6566. If you want to be by the sea, but still within walking distance of the main plaza, try this relatively new resort set around a pool, backing onto Playa San Pedro, about 1km east of the centre (a 20min walk from the plaza along the waterfront); rooms come with flat-screen TVs and free wi-fi. M$800

ZONA HOTELERA AND BEYOND

Las Hadas Golf Resort & Marina Av de los Riscos and Vista Hermosa, Península de Santiago ☎ 314 331 0101, ⓦ brisas.com.mx. This amazingly flashy wedding-cake-style hotel complex is where Dudley Moore and Bo Derek frolicked in the film *10*, with a vast range of amenities and Moorish-themed architecture; rooms are all white, with marble floors and bay views. M$1885

★**Pepe's Hideaway** Camino Don Diego 67, Península de Santiago ☎ 314 333 0616, ⓦ pepeshideaway.com. Glittering beachside resort of luxury palapas with mesmerizing views and sunsets, handmade chairs and tables, tiled bathrooms and ceiling fans; it feels very remote and tranquil, right on the tip of the peninsula. M$1700

La Posada Cárdenas 201, Playa Las Brisas ☎ 314 333 1899, ⓦhotel-la-posada.info. Bright, pink-washed B&B right on the beach, with tranquil gardens, a pool and rooms fitted with folksy Mexican rugs and blankets (some with a/c and kitchenette) exuding a retro 1950s vibe. There are excellent made-to-order breakfasts, internet access, an honour bar and a pool included in the price. M̲$̲6̲0̲0̲

EATING

Rather like the hotels, the cheapest **places to eat** are concentrated around Jardín Alvaro Obregón in Centro, while you'll find modern chains and posher places spread out along the bay on Hwy-200. If you head down México, Centro's main commercial and shopping street, you'll find a whole series of *taquerías*, while there are several very cheap places – grimy and raucous on the whole – in the market area three blocks down México and at the bottom end of Juárez by the railway tracks.

CENTRO HISTÓRICO
Chantilly Juárez at Madero ☎ 314 332 0194. This locally famous and bustling restaurant makes a substantial comida corrida, good *antojitos* and the best ice cream in town (mains M$80–150). Daily 8am–11pm.

Dolphy Morelos, at Jardín Alvaro Obregón ⓦdolphy.com.mx. Tempting ice-cream shop, strategically located on the main plaza (there are several branches dotted around the city). Try the "sundae yogurt" flavour, topped with chocolate sauce and gummie bears. Daily 11am–11pm.

ZONA HOTELERA AND BEYOND
Café Costeño Cárdenas 1613, Playa Las Brisas ☎ 314 333 9460. Excellent, relaxing place for a coffee – or a frozen cappuccino – inside or on a shady patio. Does tasty oversized American breakfasts or all the classic Mexican dishes from M$40 (cash only). Mon–Sat 8am–11pm, Sun 5–11pm.

Juanito's Miguel de la Madrid km 14, Playa Santiago ☎ 314 333 1388, ⓦjuanitos.com. Fun, family restaurant specializing in breakfasts, burgers, *chilaquiles*, tacos and refreshing drinks (fresh-fruit smoothies) since 1976. Daily 8am–11pm.

La Perlita Independencia 23, off Miguel de la Madrid, Playa Santiago ☎ 314 120 3753. Venerable seafood restaurant trading since 1968, now housed in plush modern premises dishing up all sorts of *antojitos*, *ceviche*, shellfish and pastas for around M$100. Daily 6am–midnight.

★ **La Sonrisa** Miguel de la Madrid, Playa Azul. The best tacos in the city, especially famous for their giant chorizo and *carne asada* quesadillas for M$35. Some tables inside and on the street. Any taxi driver will know it. Daily 11am–4am.

El Vaquero Crucero Las Brisas 19 ☎ 314 333 1654. Serves a hearty menu of grilled meats in a suitably cowboy-inspired palapa setting (now has three locations in the area). The fruity sangria is the perfect accompaniment to the mesquite-broiled steaks, sold by the kilo (1kg is enough for four people) or by the gram (350g is considered a regular steak). Daily noon–midnight.

DRINKING AND NIGHTLIFE

Bar Social Juárez and 21 de Marzo (on Jardín Alvaro Obregón). This classic cantina is a throwback to the 1950s, with crusty old regulars propping up the bar and even older staff. It's all very friendly though, and perfectly safe for women – an atmospheric place for a couple of M$30 beers with lots of free snacks. Mon–Sat noon–midnight.

DIRECTORY

Banks HSBC (at Bocanegra) and Bancomer (no. 122), with ATMs, are both on México.
Internet Try WWW.CAFE (daily 9am–11pm; M$20/hr) at Miguel de la Madrid 1161, or Members.com at Juárez 12, just off the plaza in downtown (Mon–Fri 9am–10pm, Sat & Sun noon–9pm; M$15/hr).
Post office The post office is at Galindo 30, in the *centro histórico* (Mon–Fri 9am–5pm, Sat 9am–1pm).

Colima and around

COLIMA, capital of the state and 98km inland from Manzanillo, is a distinctly colonial city, and a very beautiful one too, overlooked by the perfectly conical **Volcán de Colima** and, in the distance, the Nevado de Colima. With a handful of sights inside the city limits and interesting excursions nearby, it's a pleasant place to stop over for a night or two. Colima's Old World ambience, favourable climate – cooler than the coast, but never as cold as in the high mountains – and several good-value hotels and restaurants add to its appeal.

ACCOMMODATION

Best Western Hotel Ceballos	2
Buena Aventura	3
Los Flamingos	5
Hospedajes del Rey	1
La Merced	4

EATING

1800	2
Ah Qué Nanishe!	1
Los Naranjos	3
Pichichi Silvón	4
La Placita	6
El Trébol	5

The city's prettiest features are its chain of shady formal **plazas** or jardíns – Colima is known as the "City of Palms" – and a number of attractive **courtyards**, many of which are now used as restaurants and cafés and make wonderfully cool places to relax. The central **Plaza Principal** (known as Jardín Libertad) is where you'll find the government offices and the unimpressive Neoclassical cathedral, which dates from 1941.

Museo Regional de Historia

Portal Morelos 1, at Reforma • Tues–Sun 9am–6pm • M$52, free Sun 5–8pm • ☎ 312 312 9228

The **Museo Regional de Historia** stands across the street from the Palacio de Gobierno in a lovely nineteenth-century building that also houses the university art gallery. Move swiftly through the displays on **local crafts** – though the animal and diabolical masks used in traditional dances are interesting – and make for the later rooms, chock-full of **pre-Hispanic ceramics**: gorgeous figurines with superbly expressive faces, fat Izcuintli dogs and people working on mundane, everyday tasks. Though characteristic of western Mexican culture, these examples are specific to Colima, many of them found in *tumbas de tiro* – well-like tombs up to 16m deep, more commonly found in South America and the Pacific Islands. The cultural parallel isn't well understood, but explanatory panels (all in Spanish) show the different styles.

Museo Universitario de Artes Populares

Gabino Barreda and Manuel Gallardo Zamora, Universidad de Colima • Mon–Sat 10am–2pm & 5–8pm, Sun 10am–1pm • M$20 • ☎ 312 312 6869

If you've more time to spare, wander eight blocks north of the plaza to the **Museo Universitario de Artes Populares**, which has an eclectic but poorly explained collection of folk art, including masks, traditional textiles and costumes modelled by enormous papier-mâché figures, shoes, ceramics, images of the Virgin, toy aeroplanes and a small musical instrument collection – look for the violin made from scrap wood and a Modelo beer can.

La Campana

Av Periférico Norte, between Tecnológico de Colima and Arroyo Pereira, 3km northwest of the centre; head north out of town along Gabino Barreda and take a left onto Tecnológico • Daily 9am–6pm • M$42 • ☎ 312 313 4946

The source of some of the Museo Regional de Historia's treasures is the ruined Early Classic city at **La Campana**, which dates back to around 300 BC and is believed to have

---

CLIMBING THE NEVADO DE COLIMA

The **Parque Nacional Volcán Nevado de Colima** comprises two spellbinding volcanoes rising north of Colima. The **Volcán de Colima** (3860m), also known as Volcán de Fuego, is officially still active and smokes from time to time, though there seems little imminent danger. It is far less frequently climbed than its larger and more passive brother, the **Nevado de Colima** (4330m), which, with its pine- and oak-forested slopes, is popular with local mountaineers during the clear, dry winter months. Unless there's a lot of snow – in December and January crampons and an ice axe are essential – and provided you are fit and can get transport high enough, it's a relatively easy **hike** up to the summit. Joining an **organized tour** is the hassle-free alternative and recommended for less experienced hikers: Volcano Tours (☎ 312 310 7483) offers day trips from Colima and Manzanillo for around M$800.

Independently, you'll need to set three days aside for the climb, take a sleeping bag and waterproofs, enough food and water for the trip, and walk from the village of El Fresnito. First, take a bus from Terminal Foránea in Colima to Ciudad Guzmán (about 1hr 30min) and from there catch a bus from stall #21 to **El Fresnito** (M$15), where there are very limited supplies. Ask for the road to La Joya – on foot now, take this road and keep right until the route becomes obvious. This rough service road for the radio antennae leads up through cow pastures and goes right past the cabin at La Joya (3500m), about six to eight hours' walking (35km). You pay the **entry fee** (M$20) and can tank up from the supply of running water here, but don't expect to stay in the hut, which is often locked, and even if open may be full, as it only sleeps six – bring camping equipment. The usual route from here is via a steep climb to the radio antennae ("Las Antenas"), from where it's another stiff but non-technical walk to the summit. Plan on a day from La Joya to the summit and back, then another to get back to Colima, though a very fit walker starting before dawn could make the trip back to Colima, or at least Ciudad Guzmán, in a day. Note that **hitching** isn't an option as the logging roads up here are rough, requiring high clearance or 4WD vehicles, and see very little traffic. Check ⓦ nevadodecolimatours.blogspot.com for the latest information.

reached its zenith between 100 and 600 AD. Excavations have revealed some small pyramids, temple remains and one shaft tomb indicative of the Tehuchitlán tradition.

ARRIVAL AND DEPARTURE   COLIMA AND AROUND

By plane The Aeropuerto Nacional de Colima (☎ 312 313 1340) is 22km northeast of the centre of Colima, with daily flights from Mexico City on Aeromar and Aeroméxico, and flights to Tijuana via Volaris. Taxis charge around M$280 into the centre of Colima, and around M$800 to Manzanillo.

By bus Some 2km east of the centre, Colima's main bus station, the Terminal Foránea (or Central de Autobuses), handles frequent first- and second-class buses from Guadalajara and Manzanillo (M$110). Taxis (M$25) and city buses #2, #4 and #5 (M$5) run towards the central plaza from the station. Many second-class Manzanillo buses and all local services, including the one to Comala, operate from the Terminal Rojos, 7km west of the centre of town. If you arrive here, a #4 or #6 bus will take you to the centre of town; from the centre, take a #2 or buses marked "Rojos" from Madero, at Revolución, to get back.

Destinations Comala (every 10–15min; 20min); Guadalajara (at least hourly; 3hr); Lázaro Cárdenas (4 daily; 6–7hr); Manzanillo (frequent; 1hr 30min–2hr); Mexico City (8 daily; 10–11hr); Puerto Vallarta (3 daily; 6hr); Tecomán (every 15min; 45min); Tijuana (2 daily; 38hr).

INFORMATION

Tourist office Colima's extremely helpful tourist office, inside the Palacio de Gobierno, on Reforma and Hidalgo at the Plaza Principal (Mon–Fri 9am–3pm & 6–9pm, Sat 9am–1pm; ☎ 312 312 4360), has a variety of maps and pamphlets.

ACCOMMODATION

★**Best Western Hotel Ceballos** Portal Medellín 12 ☎ 312 312 4444, ⬥ hotelceballos.com. In a prime location, right on the Jardín Libertad, this characterful *Best Western*-owned hotel exudes Old World colonial grandeur (dating from 1880, it once housed the state governors). While all have a/c, rooms vary enormously; the best are the light and airy, newly refurbished deluxe ones (worth the extra M$100) with hand-painted furniture, French windows and wrought-iron balconies There's a great café next door. M$1225

★**Buena Aventura** Juárez 70 ☎ 312 136 1246. Fabulous mid-range option, with eleven simple but stylish rooms with tiled floors, a/c, satellite TV and bathroom. You also get free wi-fi, gym and tea and coffee – it's a real bargain. M$550

Los Flamingos Rey Colimán 18 ☎ 312 312 2525. One of the better budget options. The rooms are a little institutional, but have private bath, good beds, balconies and TV. M$280

Hospedajes del Rey Colima 125 ☎ 312 313 3683. A decent option with sixteen rooms and an off-licence on site. There's private parking and fast wi-fi which reaches even to the farthest rooms, all of which are en suite and some of which have a/c for M$100 extra. M$400

La Merced Juárez 82 ☎ 312 312 6969. Characterful old hotel with passable fan-ventilated rooms with bath around a central patio and some less attractive, newer rooms – the best rooms are at the back. TV and parking. M$360

EATING

1800 5 de Mayo 15, between Carranza and Constitución ☎ 312 312 9300. Fashionable café and bar attracting mostly local students to its comfy couches and billowing drapes. Serves tasty *antojitos* (from M$45) and decent cocktails (from around M$30). Daily 7pm–2am.

Ah Qué Nanishe! 5 de Mayo 267, west of Mariano Arista ☎ 312 314 2197. The name of this surprisingly inexpensive courtyard restaurant appropriately means "how delicious" in Zapotec. It specializes in dishes from the owner's native Oaxaca: *mole*, *chapulines* (baked grasshoppers) and *tlyaduas* (large flour tortillas). Well worth the walk from the centre. Wed–Mon 1–11pm.

★**Los Naranjos** Gabino Barreda 34, north of Madero ☎ 312 312 0029. Friendly dual restaurant, with one informal side serving up a comida corrida for M$60, while the other offers a buffet for M$120 that includes *chilaquiles*, quesadillas, eggs, fruit, tea and coffee, as well as à la carte options. Daily 8am–11.30pm.

Pichichi Silvón Portal Medellín. Hole in the wall opposite *Hotel Ceballos*, serving crispy *churros rellenos* (M$5) stuffed with chocolate. Daily noon–10pm.

La Placita South side of main square ☎ 312 313 2910. One of a series of places housed under the colonnades and arches of the main square, where an antique a/c system is a rumbling background accompaniment to the lunch specials (M$38) and cheap beers. Mon & Wed–Sun noon–2am.

El Trébol Degollado 59, at 16 de Septiembre ☎ 312 312 2900. Comfortable, cosy and inexpensive place just off the plaza for egg dishes, snacks and light meals (from M$30). Mon–Fri & Sun 8am–11pm.

DIRECTORY

Banks and exchange There's a Banamex with an ATM on Hidalgo, a few doors down from the tourist office, and several *casas de cambio* on Juárez, along the western side of Jardín Nuñez.

Pharmacy Farmacias Zapotlan, Francisco Madero at main plaza (daily 9am–7pm).

Post office The post office is at Nuñez 247, at Madero (Mon–Fri 8.30am–5.30pm).

Comala

You can get a closer look at the regal volcanoes north of Colima by spending an afternoon at **COMALA**, a tidy, picture-perfect Pueblo Mágico 10km north of the state capital. Here, in the central plaza or **Jardín Principal**, admire the church of **San Miguel del Espíritu Santo**, completed in 1832, or just sip a beer or margarita while enjoying a stellar view of the mountains and listening to mariachi bands. Friday and Saturday are the liveliest times, when you can mingle with day-tripping, predominantly middle-class Mexicans from Guadalajara; on Sundays and Mondays there are craft markets in the square.

ARRIVAL AND DEPARTURE   COMALA

By bus Buses run frequently to Comala from Colima's   Terminal Rojos (every 15min; M$7; 20min).

EATING

Los Portales Jardín Principal. Restaurants huddled together under the Jardín Principal's southern portal each try to outdo the others by producing better *botanas* – plates of snacks, dips and tacos – free with drinks from noon until about 6pm. There's little to choose between them – the drinks are uniformly priced (around M$35 for a beer or soft drink, including the local *ponche de frutas*, fruit punch), but you can still get a fairly economical lunch. Daily around 9am–9pm.

The Costalegre

Most of the Jalisco coast, between Manzanillo and Puerto Vallarta, has been dubbed the **Costalegre** (the "happy coast"; ⓦcostalegre.com), the wildest, most undeveloped stretch of Mexico's Pacific shore. Beyond the low-key resorts of Melaque and Barra de Navidad, Hwy-200 snakes north for around 225km past lonely beaches, small villages and vast swathes of jungle-smothered mountains.

Barra de Navidad

Some 60km north of Manzanillo, just across the border in Jalisco, the **Bahía de Navidad** is edged by fine, honey-coloured sands anchored by the twin towns of **San Patricio-Melaque** and **BARRA DE NAVIDAD** at the southern end of the bay – here the beach runs out into a sandbar, forming a lagoon behind the town.

The beaches

Barra de Navidad is a small, sleepy town, where the main activities revolve around **beaches**. A continuous arc of golden sand joins Barra with Melaque, running along the bay for some 8km – at Barra it's known as **Playa de Navidad**, a fairly narrow and steep section that is often washed away during hurricanes (the last bad one was Hurricane Patricia in 2015).

If you have time, it's worth taking a **panga** across the Laguna de Navidad to check out one of the bars or restaurants in the *Grand Bay Hotel* (see p.232) on the **Isla Navidad**, back in Colima state, or **Colimilla**, a small village a bit further along the lagoon. Colimilla is popular chiefly for its seafood restaurants (see p.232), and as a base for the 2–3km walk over to the rough Pacific beach of **Playa de los Cocos**.

BARRA DE NAVIDAD

ARRIVAL AND DEPARTURE

By plane The nearest airport is at Manzanillo (see p.224), just a 20min drive away. Taxis charge around M$350 to Barra (*colectivos* M$155).

By bus Buses arrive at the town's main terminals, which are on Veracruz, Barra's main drag: ETN is at Veracruz 275, Primera Plus is at Veracruz 269. The services you are likely to need – post office, phones and hotels – are all close by; in any case, it only takes 20min to walk around the whole town.

Destinations Guadalajara (every 30min; 4hr 15min via toll road); Manzanillo (every 30min; 1hr 30min); Puerto Vallarta (18 daily; 5hr).

GETTING AROUND

By bus Minibuses run along Veracruz (the local bus station is at Veracruz 228) and on to Melaque via Hwy-200 (M$6) every 15min.

By taxi Taxis line up at Veracruz and Michoacán, with prices to most places fixed: Melaque (M$50–60); Manzanillo airport (M$400–450); Manzanillo (M$400);

Playa de los Cocos (M$150); and Tenacatita (M$300).

By boat *Pangas* depart from the jetty at the end of Veracruz to Isla Navidad and the *Grand Bay Hotel*, and also to Colimilla (every 30min, 6am–6pm; M$15 by *panga*; M$50 return by private *lancha*).

INFORMATION AND TOURS

Tourist office The office at Jalisco 67 (Mon–Fri 9am–5pm, Sat & Sun during high season; ☎315 355 5100, ⍟ barradenavidad.com) serves both Barra de Navidad and San Patricio-Melaque.

Sea to Sierra Veracruz 204 ☎315 355 5790. Runs a variety of land and water tours, including a one-hour boat trip that winds through the mangroves of the Laguna de Navidad (from M$600), horseriding trips (M$250/hr), one-tank dives (M$850) and two- to four-hour mountain-bike tours (from M$500 for 2–4 people).

ACCOMMODATION

Barra de Navidad Legazpi 250 ☎338 244 4043, ✉hotel_barra@yahoo.com.mx. For unrivalled beach access, this is a good-value choice – it's right on the sand. Rooms are simple but comfortable, with big-screen TVs and a/c; the best have wonderful sea views. There's also a pool on site and a huge breakfast included. M$860

Caribe Sonora 15 ☎315 335 5952. The best of the budget options, with clean, if rather lacklustre, rooms and a pleasant rooftop terrace with rocking chairs. M$250

★**Coco Cabañas** Playa de los Cocos km 8.2 ☎335 004 2686. Barra's most enticing accommodation lies across the lagoon where these ecofriendly cabins overlook the beach. Each one can sleep up to four adults and six kids, with breakfast (the restaurant is excellent), hot water and solar-generated power but no phones or TVs. Taxis charge M$150 from Barra de Navidad. M$1250

Delfín Morelos 23 ☎315 355 5068, ⊛hoteldelfinmx .com. Bright, arcaded hotel 5min from the beach. Clean, very spacious rooms with fan lead off an attractive balcony with views of the bay. There is a great pool with sun deck, a restaurant where breakfast is served, and a small gym. M$495

Grand Bay Hotel-Isla Navidad Resort Circuitos de los Marinos, Isla Navidad (across the bay) ☎315 331 0500, ⊛wyndham.com/hotels/ZLOGB. Luxurious *Wyndham*-owned resort with a mountain backdrop, an idyllic location on the bay and a complete range of facilities for golfers and watersports enthusiasts as well as those in need of serious pampering. Rooms are the epitome of taste and style, dripping with marble and exotic woods, and with all the luxuries you'd expect. M$1800

EATING

Norma's Pasteles Veracruz and Legazpi. This popular stall (manned by the indomitable Norma Torres) sells irresistible M$25 slices of home-made cakes and desserts. Try the *pastel de tres leches* (sweet milk pudding). Daily 3–10pm.

Pancho's Legazpi 53 ☎315 355 5176. This earthy restaurant is one of Barra's original palapas, now managed by Pancho's son and serving great fresh seafood: specials include the shrimp "a la diabla" (spicy devilled shrimp) and zesty marlin *ceviche*. Daily 8am–8pm.

★**Ramón** Legazpi 260, opposite Hotel Barra de Navidad (see above) ☎315 355 6435. Open all day and with an extensive range of Mexican and international food, including some excellent fish and chips, and *chiles rellenos*, especially good with shrimp. Lots of free salsa and chips (crisps) to start. Daily 7am–11pm.

Restaurant Paty Jalisco 52, at Veracruz ☎315 355 5907. The best of a number of similar budget places, serving decent *ceviche*, fresh fish, *carne asada* and fantastic barbecue chicken, as well as all the Mexican staples. Daily 8am–11pm.

PLAYA DE LOS COCOS

Fortino's Southern end of main drag ☎314 337 9075. Family favourite since 1967, priding itself on serving only the freshest seafood. Bring insect repellent if dining after dark. Daily 10am–8pm.

Restaurante Colimilla 250m north of Fortino's ☎314 337 9105. Large beachside restaurant whose palapa extends into the lagoon. Huge range of fish and seafood, and as a plus you can pay by credit card (most restaurants here are cash only). Mains M$50–100. Daily 9am–7pm.

DRINKING AND NIGHTLIFE

★**Piper Lover Blues Bar** Legazpi 240-C ☎315 108 1406. Facing the beach on Legazpi, this is the best bar in town, with live rock, jazz and especially blues most nights. Dec–March daily 4pm–2am.

★**Sunset Bar** Jalisco 214. Rafael serves up what are

possible the best margaritas on the coast: strong, sweet and good for M$60. A great place to set up a table and watch the sun go down. He's apparently known all over the world, and after a couple of his concoctions you won't forget him easily either. Daily noon–2am.

DIRECTORY

Banks and exchange The town now has Bancomer and Banamex ATM machines on Veracruz (these often malfunction), but no actual bank branches.

Internet You should find internet cafés on Veracruz,

though owners come and go; try Cyber Spiaggia (daily 9am–10pm; M$15/hr).

Post office The post office is at Veracruz 179 (Mon–Fri 9am–2pm).

San Patricio-Melaque

Perched at the northern end of the Bahía de Navidad, **SAN PATRICIO-MELAQUE** seems much more typically Mexican than Barra de Navidad (5km south), with a central plaza, church and largish market. Though it remains popular with Mexican families and budget travellers, Melaque is also much scruffier than Barra, more commercial and has a more transitory feel – the main highlight, unsurprisingly, is its pristine beach, **Playa Melaque**, ending in a smattering of rustic palapa restaurants at the west end. There's no tourist office; the office in Barra de Navidad serves both towns (see p.230).

ARRIVAL AND DEPARTURE
SAN PATRICIO-MELAQUE

By bus The two long-distance bus stations (Primera Plus and Elite) face each other at the junction of Carranza and Gómez Farías and have frequent connections to Barra de Navidad (every 15min; M$6; 10min).

Destinations Guadalajara (every 2hr; 5hr); Manzanillo (hourly; 1hr 30min); Puerto Vallarta (4 daily; 4–5hr).
By taxi Taxis to Barra cost around M$50–60.

ACCOMMODATION

Accommodation in Melaque is generally very cheap, especially during the low season (Aug–Nov) when prices are negotiable down to a third of their cost, though little is open at this time.

Bahía Legazpi 5 ☎315 355 6894, ⓦmelaque hotelbahia.com. The friendly Moreno family runs this little bargain hotel, a short walk from the beach and one of the best deals in town. Its 23 compact rooms enclose a tranquil inner patio and a pool, and come with tiled floors, basic cable TV, free wi-fi and fan (some with a/c). M$450
La Paloma Ocean Front Retreat Las Cabañas 13 ☎315 355 5345, ⓦlapalomamexico.com. Luxurious resort right on the beach, hosted by an amicable bunch of Canadians and featuring spacious studios with kitchen, sun deck, ocean views and clean, cheerful decor. The on-site Paloma Art Center runs week-long workshops in watercolour painting. M$1560
Posada Pablo de Tarso Gómez Farías 408 ☎315 355 5117, ⓦposadapablodetarso.com. Pleasant, white-painted rooms with TV, fan, terracotta floor tiles around a

verdant colonial courtyard and a good pool. M$600
Santa María Abel Salgado Velazco 85 ☎315 355 5553. Great budget option not far from the beach with basic one-bedroom motel-style apartments equipped with kitchenettes, TV and fans – the second-floor rooms are generally nicer. The oceanfront pool terrace is a good place to chill and prices are very negotiable. M$300
★**Villas Camino del Mar** Francisco Villa 6, corner Abel Salgado Velazco ☎315 355 5207, ⓦvillascamino delmar.com.mx. Wonderful hideaway on the south side of town hosted by the lovely Gloria, and offering a range of apartments in a new building around an inviting pool overlooking the beach; all come with kitchenettes, wi-fi and fans, and some have a/c. There are also a few villas next door which Gloria can offer for the price of an apartment if no one is around and you're nice to her. M$670

EATING

Some of the best **eating** in Melaque can be had from street stalls around the central plaza, or enjoying the sunset from numerous identical palapa joints along the beachfront. During the quieter months many restaurants and stalls will be closed.

★**Flor Morena** Juárez 21, on the plaza (no phone). Cosy Mexican diner, knocking out fresh, home-made classics like enchiladas, tamales and tacos, though little seafood apart from their legendary shrimp *pozole*. Dishes for less than M$60 – this is probably Melaque's most popular restaurant, so expect a wait. Tues–Sun 5–11pm.
Taco Surf Juarez 16 ☎314 135 2410. A street-level taco kitchen with lots of tables to account for its popularity. Efrain serves up *gringas de camarón* (M$35), and plates of five fish tacos for M$50. All very delicious and served with a

smile. Daily 5pm–midnight.
La Terraza Gordiano Guzmán 4 ☎315 107 3499. Serves generous breakfasts of freshly baked bread, granola, fruit, cinnamon rolls and yogurt, as well as traditional Mexican fare for lunch on the cooling, second-floor patio. Daily 8am–4pm.
Scooby's North of main square ☎315 355 5313. A very popular place with the town's gringo expats, *Scooby's* serves up M$60 margaritas and cheap Mexican food from a clean kitchen. Occasionally does roast lamb. Mon–Wed & Fri–Sun 6.30pm–1am.

DIRECTORY

Banks and exchange Opposite the bus station, in the Pasaje Comercial, you'll find the *casa de cambio* Melaque (which changes travellers' cheques). Opposite on Gómez Farías is Banamex bank (Mon–Fri 9am–4pm, Sat 10am–2pm), with a 24hr ATM; you can also exchange travellers' cheques here.

Internet Try Cyber La Playita on López Mateos just south of the plaza (daily 9am–11pm; M$15/hr).
Post office The post office is at Orozco 13 (Mon–Fri 8am–4.30pm, Sat 9am–1pm), around the corner from *Hotel San Patricio*.

Playa Tenacatita

Some 27km north of Barra de Navidad and Melaque, a signed, paved road off Hwy-200 leads 9km to **PLAYA TENACATITA**, a gorgeous curve of bone-white sand on a coral-strewn cove, with the added attractions of a mangrove lagoon that teems with birdlife and still, clear waters perfect for snorkelling.

Costa Careyes

Some 25km north of Tenacatita (at Hwy-200 km 52) lies **Costa Careyes** (the "turtle coast"), another series of fine beaches with Playa Careyes itself gate-guarded and ringed by expensive villas, nestled in the hills. Even if you can't afford to stay here, Playa Careyes is a fun place to visit for the day: explain you want access to the beach and the guards will open the gates for you. On nearby protected **Playa Teopa**, endangered **olive ridley turtles** lay their eggs (Aug–Oct); biologists have recruited local activists and established a conservation programme to make sure the turtles' eggs are collected before they fall victim to predators (the babies are released after the eggs hatch in a laboratory).

Bahía de Chamela

A further 20km north from Careyes on Hwy-200, the **Bahía de Chamela** comprises a huge, sweeping arc of superb beaches and nine islands, which are popular dive spots. Although large hotels are also cropping up here with alarming frequency, you'll still find long sections of untouched beach where you can pitch a tent.

The focal point of the area is the junction known as "**El Super**" at Hwy-200 km 72, while the village of **Chamela** itself is at km 63. From El Super there's an unpaved road that leads to the honey-coloured sands of **Playa Chamela**, while **Playa Pérula**, at the northern end of the bay, is a 1km walk or drive down a dusty track from Hwy-200 km 76. Note that since 2010 beaches along the bay have been facing **legal disputes**, much like Tenacatita (see p.233), with the result that beach access has been limited in places – check before you go.

ARRIVAL AND DEPARTURE

BAHÍA DE CHAMELA

By bus Take a second-class bus from Barra de Navidad (see p.230) towards Vallarta, ask to get off at km 72 (El Super) and walk 1km down to the beach.

By car The easiest way to explore this section of the coast is by car (you can rent cars relatively easily in Puerto Vallarta; see p.238).

ACCOMMODATION AND EATING

Hotel Punta Pérula Tiburón 98, at Juárez (Hwy-200 km 76), Playa Pérula ☎315 333 9782. You can stay at the average, fourteen-room *Hotel Punta Pérula*, one block north of the main road at Juárez and Tiburón (inland from the beach); rooms come with fan and rustic furnishings. M$450

Bungalows Mayar Chamela Hwy-200 km 72, Playa Chamela ☎315 333 9711. These eighteen basic but spacious cabañas have palatable rooms with fan, kitchen and an on-site pool. Quality varies, so take a look first before accepting a room. M$500

Paraíso Costa Alegre Hwy-200 km 72, Playa Chamela ☎315 333 9778, ⓦparaisocostalegre.com.mx. Attractive oceanfront Polynesian-style cabañas ("Villas Tahitianas") surrounded by palm trees, with bathroom (hot water), fan and terrace (no TV). Larger cabins can accommodate groups. M$839

Puerto Vallarta and around

Thanks to its mesmerizing sunsets, kilometres of sandy beaches and a laid-back, colonial centre, **PUERTO VALLARTA** is a small city dependent almost entirely on tourism; it attracts a mixed bag of North American retirees, Mexican families, spring-breakers, cruise-ship day-trippers and gay visitors taking advantage of its

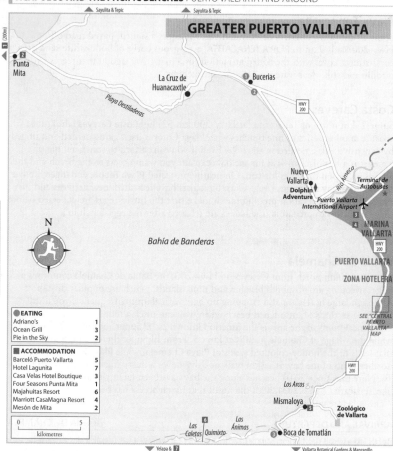

GREATER PUERTO VALLARTA

Sayulita & Tepic

Bucerías

La Cruz de Huanacaxtle

Playa Destiladeras

Punta Mita

HWY 200

Nuevo Vallarta

Dolphin Adventure

Río Ameca

Terminal de Autobuses

Puerto Vallarta International Airport

MARINA VALLARTA

HWY 200

PUERTO VALLARTA

ZONA HOTELERA

SEE "CENTRAL PUERTO VALLARTA" MAP

Bahía de Banderas

N

HWY 200

Los Arcos

Mismaloya

Zoológico de Vallarta

Las Caletas

Quimixto

Las Ánimas

Boca de Tomatlán

Yelapa & 7

Vallarta Botanical Gardens & Manzanillo

EATING

Adriano's	1
Ocean Grill	3
Pie in the Sky	2

ACCOMMODATION

Barceló Puerto Vallarta	5
Hotel Lagunita	7
Casa Velas Hotel Boutique	3
Four Seasons Punta Mita	1
Majahuitas Resort	6
Marriott CasaMagna Resort	4
Mesón de Mita	2

0   5
kilometres

emergence as one of the **gay** centres of Mexico. If you're looking for traditional Mexico you might find this wholly unappealing, but while it's true that PV (as it's known) can be more expensive and certainly more touristy than the average Mexican town, it can also be lots of fun. It's smaller and more relaxed than Cancún and Acapulco, and its location, surrounded by lofty mountains, is spectacular. Behind the beaches there's a vibrant Mexican city, largely undisturbed by the flow of visitors, which means that the choice of tasty, cheap **street food** – especially tacos – is some of the best on the coast, and in between the souvenir shops and chichi boutiques are some exceptionally good **art galleries**. The beach remains the primary attraction, however, with the less crowded resorts and villages of the **Bahía de Banderas** fringed by endless stretches of sand and backed by the jungle-covered slopes of the Sierra Madre.

Brief history

The town was officially founded in the 1850s (when it was known as Las Peñas – it was renamed in 1918, after Ignacio L. Vallarta, former governor of Jalisco), but there had been a small fishing and smuggling village located where the Río Cuale spills out into the bay for years. Initially developed by the Union en Cuale mining company, it remained a sleepy place until the 1950s, when Mexican airlines started promoting the town as a resort (the first hotel opened in 1948). Their efforts received a shot in the arm in 1963, when **John Huston** chose Mismaloya, 10km south, as the setting for his film of Tennessee Williams' play *The Night of the Iguana*, starring Richard Burton. Over the last decade, frantic development has mostly overwhelmed the tropical-village atmosphere, though the historic town centre at least retains its charming cobbled streets and white-walled, terracotta-roofed houses.

Centro Histórico

The **Plaza Principal**, official buildings, market and the bulk of the shops and upscale restaurants lie on the north side of the **Río Cuale**, Vallarta's busy downtown or **Centro Histórico**. The plaza lies at the heart of the old town, with its pleasant cobbled streets, colonial-style houses and breezy oceanfront boulevard. Here, families gather in the evenings among the balloon sellers and hot-dog stands, while tourists explore the city's restaurants, bars and clubs.

Templo de Nuestra Señora de Guadalupe

Hidalgo 370, between Zaragoza and Iturbide • Daily 7am–8pm • Free • ☎ 322 222 1326, ⓦ parroquiadeguadalupepv.com

The Plaza Principal is backed by the most memorable building in PV, the vaguely Art Nouveau **Templo de Nuestra Señora de Guadalupe**. Building started in 1918, with the famous crown that makes it so special completed in 1963; this collapsed in the earthquake of 1995, and what you see today is a giant fibreglass tiara replacement ("La Corona de Nuestra Señora") modelled on one that Emperor Maximilian's wife, Carlota, wore in the 1860s. The image of the Virgin of Guadalupe inside is said to have been painted by famed San Miguel Allende artist **Ignacio Ramírez** (aka "El Nigromante").

The malecón

Puerto Vallarta's wide **malecón** skirts the beaches in front of the old town, a pleasant promenade to admire the bay and those heavenly sunsets. The malecón meets the main plaza at the tiny **Plaza Aquiles Serdán**, with a strange little amphitheatre and **Los Arcos**, four arches looking out over the sea like a lost fragment of the Roman empire; with hawkers, mimes, musicians and food stands, it is one of the best places for people-watching in the city. A short stroll northwards along the malecón brings you past several statues, among them another Puerto Vallarta icon, the *Cabelleo del Mar* created by Rafael Zamarripas, a 3m-high bronze statue of a sea horse with a naked boy riding on its back. The malecón goes north as far as 31 de Octubre and *Hotel Rosita* on the edge of downtown; to the south it crosses the Río Cuale to run along the town beach and the cheaper hotels in what's optimistically labelled the **Zona Romántica**.

Museo Histórico Naval

Zaragoza 4, just off Plaza Principal and the malecón • Tues–Fri 9am–7.30pm, Sat & Sun 10am–2pm & 3–7.30pm • Free • ☎ 322 223 5357

The rather stuffy **Museo Histórico Naval** provides a fairly detailed history of the town and region from a nautical perspective, starting with the Spanish Conquest and ending with Mexico's modern navy. Some interesting episodes are covered, but there's not much to see beyond a few dioramas, paintings and photos, and everything is labelled in Spanish.

PV ARTWALK

Vallarta's art scene has boomed since the 1990s, with contemporary artists such as Xaime Ximénez, Michael Whitlow and Rodo Padilla among many with studios in the city. Get a taster on the weekly ArtWalk evenings (late Oct to April; ⓦ vallartaartwalk.com), when the best thirteen galleries downtown open their doors every Wednesday 6–10pm.

CENTRAL PUERTO VALLARTA

■ ACCOMMODATION		● EATING				■ DRINKING & NIGHTLIFE	
Azteca	3	Archie's Wok	24	Marisma Fish Taco	1	Apaches	8
Belmar	8	Café des Artistes	4	La Michoacana	17	La Bodeguita del Medio	1
Blue Chairs Resort	13	Café de Olla	19	Los Muertos Brewing	10	Cheeky Monkey	5
Casa Amorita	5	El Carbonito	7	El Palomar de los Gonzáles	2	Mandala	3
La Casa del Puente	9	Daiquiri Dicks	23	Panadería y Pastelería Yarita	14	Memories	4
Los Cuatro Vientos	2	Derby City Burger	21	Pepe's Taco	6	Paco's Ranch	7
Hacienda Alemana	6	La Dolce Vita	12	Planeta Vegetariano	9	Route 66	6
Hortencia	10	Fredy's Tucán	15	Rico Mac Taco	8	The Zoo	2
Oasis Downtown	7	La Hormiga Feliz	13	River Café	16		
Oasis Hostel	1	Joe Jack's Fish Shack	18	Tacos Memo Grill	3		
Playa Los Arcos	12	Kaiser Maximilian	22	Las Tres Huastecas	20		
Posada de Roger	11	Langostinos	25	Trio	11		
Villa del Mar	4	Mariscos El Jefe	5				

Mercado Municipal Rio Cuale

Rodríguez, at Insurgentes and the river • Tues–Fri 9am–7.30pm, Sat & Sun 10am–2pm & 3–7.30pm • Free

Near the river, the two-storey **Mercado Municipal del Cuale**, aka the Flea Market, dates back to the 1960s, and was extended in 1979. The market is crammed with local jewellery, papier-mâché, clothes and souvenir stalls, but remember never to accept the first price – bargain for everything.

Isla Río Cuale

The **Isla Río Cuale**, in the middle of the river that splits the old town and the Zona Romántica, is a lush, garden-like pedestrian-only space, containing a museum (see below), a clutch of souvenir shops and some good restaurants. On the north side, at Serdán 437, there is the **Centro Cultural Cuale** (Mon–Fri 10am–2pm & 4–8pm, Sat 8am–2pm, ☎322 223 0095), which holds all sort of arts classes and shows local art exhibits; on the way you'll pass **John Huston's statue** (with a rather odd quote, eulogizing Bogart).

Museo del Cuale

Isla Río Cuale • Tues–Sat 9am–2pm & 3–6pm • Free • ☎322 223 2424

At the seaward end of the island, the **Museo del Cuale** is a small but worthy attempt to document the pre-Columbian history of the region with plenty of rare artefacts and captions in English. Highlights include the symmetrical patterned ceramics of the **Chupícuaro** culture (400 BC–200 AD), shaft tombs dating from 0–500 AD and the sophisticated pottery of **Aztatlán** culture (900–1200 AD). Ceramic female images figure prominently, emphasizing the importance of women to West Mexico cultures.

The beaches

Puerto Vallarta's **beaches** vary in nature as you move round the bay: to the north, Vallarta's busy downtown eventually morphs into an area of good beaches and fancy hotels imaginatively dubbed **Zona Hotelera** by the local authorities. This ends at the upscale **Marina Vallarta** development and the airport. Further north, beyond the Río Ameca, lies **Nuevo Vallarta** (see p.245).

Playa de los Muertos

The main (and most fun) town beach lies in the Zona Romántica, south of the plaza and the river. **Playa de los Muertos** (Beach of the Dead), or "Playa del Sol" as the local tourist office would prefer it known, is not very large, and features coarse, brown sand and reasonably calm surf, despite facing apparently open water. It's also the most crowded of the city's beaches – locals, Mexican holidaymakers and foreign tourists are packed in cheek by jowl during the high season. With the omnipresent hawkers selling everything from fresh fruit and tacos to handicrafts and fake jade masks, it can be a far from relaxing experience, but it's always entertaining. The **gay** section of this beach is at its southern end, opposite the *Blue Chairs Resort* (see p.238) – look out for the blue chairs. Further south is a series of steep-sided coves, sheltering tiny, calm enclaves (see p.242).

ARRIVAL AND DEPARTURE   PUERTO VALLARTA

BY PLANE

Arrival Puerto Vallarta's airport (officially Aeropuerto Internacional Gustavo Diaz Ordaz; ☎ 322 221 1298) lies 10km north of the centre on the coastal highway (Hwy-200), with numerous flights connecting Puerto Vallarta with the US and Canada. Useful domestic links include Aéreo Calafia's daily service to Mazatlán (and on to Los Cabos). Pay for taxis at the booth before leaving the terminal: rates are tied to an expensive zone system which starts at M$200 (Marina Vallarta) and rises to M$300 for downtown, and M$320 for the Zona Romántica or Nuevo Vallarta. *Colectivos* start at M$75 and rise to M$110 for downtown, and M$120 for the Zona Romántica, but only go when full and when enough people are heading in the same direction. In all cases, ignore the hordes of time-share sellers. If luggage is not a problem, a far cheaper option is to walk out of the terminal onto the main road and catch a city bus (marked "Olas Altas" or "Centro") for M$8. Regular taxis charge around M$100 from here into downtown (see below). All the major car-rental firms (see p.238) have desks at the airport, and you'll find a few ATMs and places to change money.

Destinations Guadalajara (5–7 daily; 40min); Mazatlán (1 daily; 1hr); Mexico City (frequent; 1hr 30min); Monterrey (1 daily; 1hr 35min); Tijuana (4 weekly; 3hr 40min); Toluca (1 daily; 1hr 15min).

BY BUS

The Terminal de Autobuses is around 12km north of the city centre (beyond the airport), one long block off the main highway (Hwy-200). Local buses (M$6.50) pass along the road outside – buses heading south are usually marked "Olas Altas" or "Centro", while those in the other direction are marked "Hoteles", "Ixtapa" or "Juntas"; be sure to ask the driver if the bus is going to the city centre, just in case. Taxis follow a fixed-rate system (rates displayed at the exit): *Centro Histórico* M$100; Zona Romántica M$120; Marina M$70; Mismaloya M$250; Nuevo Vallarta M$135; Bucerías M$160; Punta Mita M$470; Sayulita M$400. Expect to pay the same coming back. ETN buses are the most expensive and luxurious, but infrequent. Sample fares: Acapulco (M$1310); Barra de Navidad (M$229); Guadalajara (Pacífico, TAP; M$445; ETN M$349); Los Mochis (TAP only; M$820); Manzanillo (M$304); Mazatlán (TAP only; M$400); Mexico City (M$929); Tijuana (TAP only; M$1340). Note that the buses to San Blas are second class only (no toilets).

Destinations Acapulco (2 daily; 18hr); Barra de Navidad (4 daily; 3hr 30min); Guadalajara (every 30min; 6hr); Los Mochis (3–4 daily; 14–15hr); Manzanillo (6 daily; 5–7hr); Mazatlán (7 daily, via Tepic; 8hr); Mexico City (9 daily; 14hr); San Blas (4 daily; 3–4hr); Tepic (frequently; 3hr 30min–4hr); Tijuana (3–4 daily; 34hr).

GETTING AROUND

By bus Destinations are marked on the front of public buses (daily 5am–11.30pm; M$8): downtown buses are marked "Centro" ("Tunel" means the bus bypasses the *Centro Histórico* and goes straight to the Zona Romántica). To get to the Terminal de Autobuses catch the Las Juntas or Ixtapa bus with "Central Camionera" on the front.

By taxi Always fix the price before you get in a taxi (no meters). Most drivers charge according to a vaguely set fixed-rate system (for foreigners at least): hops around the *Centro Histórico* and Zona Romántica will be M$50, with trips up to the airport and Marina area M$80 from Centro and M$120 from the Zona Romántica. From Centro to

3

Bucerías will be around M$260, and much more to Punta Mita – at least M$570. To Mismaloya should be M$150 (Boca de Tomatlán; M$180).

Car rental Alamo, Francisco Medina Ascencio s/n ☏ 322

221 3030 or the airport ☏ 322 221 1228; Avis, at the airport ☏ 322 221 1657 and *Villa del Palmar*, Francisco Medina Ascencio, km 3 ☏ 322 226 1400; and Hertz, also at *Villa del Palmar*, Francisco Medina Ascencio, km 3 ☏ 322 222 0024.

INFORMATION AND ACTIVITIES

Tourist office The Dirección de Turismo office (Mon–Sat 8am–7pm, Sun 10am–4pm; ☏ 322 224 1175, ⓦ visit apuertovallarta.com.mx) is on the corner of Independencia and Juárez, just off the Plaza Principal.

Newspapers For up-to-date, if somewhat promotional, information on what's going on in town, pick up the free English-language daily *Vallarta Today* (ⓦ vallartatoday .com), available in gringo hangouts.

Websites Puerto Vallarta is also well represented on various websites such as ⓦ puertovallarta.net, ⓦ vallarta-info.com (which has the best maps) and ⓦ vallartablog.com.

Chico's Dive Shop Díaz Ordaz 772 ☏ 322 222 1895, ⓦ chicos-diveshop.com. Runs diving (M$630) and snorkelling trips (M$200; two reefs) to nearby sites daily at 10am and 3pm. The best time to see manta rays is July–Nov.

Vallarta Under Sea Edificio Marina del Rey, Marina Vallarta ☏ 322 209 0025, ⓦ vallartaundersea.com. Runs daily dive trips at 9am to Los Arcos and Las Islas Marietas from M$1100, and also rents snorkelling and scuba gear.

ACCOMMODATION

Staying in Puerto Vallarta means opting for one of the resorts along the coast, or a hotel downtown, within easy walking distance of Playa de los Muertos and the Plaza Principal. Many **resorts** offer all-inclusive packages, and, with a few exceptions, are quite similar; you'll find good deals on the internet, but remember that meals (often you'll have little choice but to eat at the hotel), transport and extra charges can add up. The more affordable options mainly lie south of the Río Cuale in the Zona Romántica, close to the old town. **Camping** on any of the more popular beaches around the middle of the bay is prohibited, but if you're reasonably well equipped and protected against mosquitoes, you could try **Punta de Mita** at the northern end of the bay or **Boca de Tomatlán** to the south (where the main road turns inland), each of which from time to time sees small communities established on the sand.

CENTRO HISTÓRICO

★**Casa Amorita** Iturbide 309, at Matamoros ☏ 322 222 4926, ⓦ casaamorita.com; map p.236. One of the most enticing downtown hotels, with just five rooms three blocks from the malecón, all with balconies, ornate metalwork beds and cool tiled floors; there's a Venetian tile pool, roof bar and terrace, with spellbinding views of the ocean and cathedral, especially at night. M$1450

La Casa del Puente Libertad at Miramar, accessed via Restaurant La Fuente del Puente ☏ 322 222 0749, ⓦ casadelpuente.com; map p.236. A real home from home: spacious, bright, elegantly furnished apartments, a wonderful communal area with huge windows overlooking the river and an extremely friendly owner. Only two suites (with fully equipped kitchens) and one double room, so book early (rates drop by fifty percent in summer). M$600

Los Cuatro Vientos Matamoros 520 ☏ 322 222 0161, ⓦ cuatrovientos.com; map p.236. A PV institution, with many return guests. Artistic touches and local handicrafts give the spotless rooms a homely feel. There is a small pool and the terrace has wonderful views. Owner Gloria is a good resource when planning tours or dining out in the area. M$750

Oasis Downtown Juarez 386 ☏ 322 178 2352, ⓦ oasishostel.com; map p.236. Just off the main square, this comfortable hostel, owned by *Oasis Hostel* (see opposite), gives you a free beer on arrival to get you

through the 15min talk on how to stay there. It's Vallarta's best budget place, however, and it encourages a sociable clientele. Dorms M$200, doubles M$500

ZONA ROMÁNTICA

Azteca Madero 473, at Jacarandas ☏ 322 222 2750; map p.236. A long-standing, reliable choice with simple, surgically clean rooms with fans, hot water and free wi-fi overlooking a peaceful courtyard full of flourishing plants. There's no sign, but look for the sombrero over the porch; nor is there a bell, so you may have to shout. Street-facing rooms are brighter but noisier. Panoramic views from the rooftop terrace. M$400

Belmar Insurgentes 161 ☏ 322 222 0572, ⓦ belmar vallarta.com; map p.236. Well located and economical, this snug, friendly hotel has clean, pleasant rooms with TV, wi-fi, fans and closet-size bathrooms – it's M$200 extra for a kitchenette. Request a room with a balcony on the top floor. M$450

Blue Chairs Resort Malecón and Almendro 4, at Playa de los Muertos ☏ 322 222 5040, ⓦ hotelbluechairs .com; map p.236. Gay visitors, even if not staying here, will inevitably gravitate to this gay-owned and operated landmark on the town beach. The resort has suites with or without kitchens and ocean views, as well as a rooftop bar and pool. Straight guests are also welcome. M$1750

★**Hacienda Alemana** Basilio Badillo 378 ☎322 222 2071, ⊛haciendaalemana.com; map p.236. Top B&B with ten crisp, stylish rooms with flat-screen TVs and *sauerbraten*, *bratwurst* and German beer in *steins* – they even celebrate Oktoberfest here. Free wi-fi, sauna and gourmet breakfast included, all a short walk from the beach. M$1840

Hortencia Madero 336, at Insurgentes ☎322 113 0473, ⊛hotelhortencia.com; map p.236. A variety of whitewashed, clean, spacious quarters all with a/c, cable TV, free wi-fi and fan in a convenient location. M$450

Oasis Hostel Libramiento 222 ☎322 222 2636, ⊛oasishostel.com; map p.236. Clean and sociable hostel a 15min walk from the city centre. Dorm beds come with breakfast and internet access included, and there are also two en-suite doubles, as well as a TV room with cable and DVDs. Dorms M$200, doubles M$500

Playa Los Arcos Olas Altas 380, at Diéguez ☎322 226 7102, ⊛playalosarcos.com; map p.236. The best-equipped and most spacious of the beachfront hotels, with a lively social scene centred around the large pool and adjacent palapa restaurant, where live sports action and beer predominate. Well-appointed rooms with a/c, TV and safe, though they can smell very musty in the rainy season. M$1890

Posada de Roger Basilio Badillo 237 ☎322 222 0639, ⊛hotelposadaderoger.com; map p.236. Some of the sombre rooms here have seen better days,but they all have a/c, cable TV, safe and fan, and overlook a spacious, shady courtyard where excellent breakfasts are served – the on-site *El Tucan* restaurant is considered the best breakfast spot in town. Only a couple of blocks from the beach, and with a small rooftop pool. M$630

Villa del Mar Madero 440, at Jacarandas ☎322 222 0785, ⊛hvilladelmar.com; map p.236. Relaxed, long-time favourite of budget travellers. All motel-style rooms have bathrooms; the larger, more expensive "suites" also have small balconies, a/c, TV and kitchenettes. M$450

MARINA VALLARTA

★**Casa Velas Hotel Boutique** Pelícanos 311 ☎322 226 6688, ⊛hotelcasavelas.com; map p.234. Pick of the elegant new resorts along Vallarta's northern coast, ideal for some serious pampering (and spending). Ultra-stylish suites blend Mexican and contemporary decor, and there's plenty of massages, golf and swimming pools – the private beach club is a 15min walk (or free shuttle ride) away. If you ever decide to venture off the premises, remember it's quite a hike to the old town. M$2800

★**Marriott CasaMagna Resort** Paseo La Marina Norte 435 ☎322 226 0000, ⊛marriott.com; map p.234. Resort featuring luxurious rooms with huge flat-screen TVs, balconies and gasp-inducing views. Lounge at the huge pool, sample the best spa in town (see box, p.240) and dine in one of several excellent restaurants on site. The cute chile garden, kids' club and Huichol art throughout are nice touches. A daypass to the pool is M$350 (includes M$300 credit for food and drink). One of the best buffet breakfasts in the city (daily 6.30am–noon; M$276). Internet is M$120 for 24hr (1hr free at the Deli). M$2650

EATING

CENTRO HISTÓRICO

★**Café des Artistes** G. Sanchez 740 ☎322 222 3228, ⊛cafedesartistes.com; map p.236. The epitome of Pacific coast gourmet dining. The quality of chef Thierry Blouet's French cuisine matches the sophisticated surroundings – the intriguing menu features shots of foie gras with mango confit (M$280), roasted sea bass (M$245) and decadent desserts (from M$90). Eat in the garden or dining room decorated with vivid artwork. Live piano and flute music add to the refined atmosphere. Daily 6–11.30pm.

La Dolce Vita Díaz Ordez 674, at Dominguez ☎322 222 3852, ⊛dolcevita.com.mx; map p.236. Pizzas, pasta and other dishes, such as beef carpaccio and chicken *cacciatore*, at reasonable prices (mains average M$115–125). Live jazz Thurs–Sun. Mon–Sat noon–2am, Sun 6pm–midnight.

La Michoacana Plaza Principal, at Morelos and Zaragoza; map p.236. This place has been dishing up heavenly ice cream and fruity ice popsicles (think coconut, *mamey* and lemon pie) since 1957 (single scoop M$23, doubles M$41), and remains a firm favourite with the crowds milling around the plaza. Daily 11am–11pm.

Planeta Vegetariano Iturbide 270, at Hidalgo ☎322 222 3073; map p.236. Large menu and all-you-can-eat vegetarian buffet (8–11.30am M$60; noon–10pm M$85) with a choice of main courses, salads, soup, dessert and a soft drink. The walls are painted with fantastic frescoes, and the food is cheap and deliciously spiced. Mon–Sat 8am–10pm.

River Café Isla Río Cuale 4 ☎322 223 0788, ⊛rivercafe.com.mx; map p.236. High-quality dining in the middle of leafy Isla Río Cuale, with creations such as *chipotle* mussels, baked brie wheels and baked lamb lasagna. Daily 9am–11.30pm.

Trio Guerrero 264 ☎322 222 2196, ⊛triopv.com; map p.236. An elegant townhouse filled with original art and hanging plants provides the setting for Mediterranean-fusion cuisine prepared by a German-Swedish chef with Michelin credentials. In addition to dishes like rabbit with garlic sauce and braised veal with almond sauce, there are home-made pastas, Lebanese salads, sautéed calamari and an imaginatively prepared selection of seafood dishes. It's a fabulous treat, if you can afford it (mains M$175–300). Daily 6pm–midnight.

3

ZONA ROMÁNTICA

CAFÉS, CHEAP EATS & SNACKS

Café de Olla Basilio Badillo 168, between Olas Altas and Pino Suárez ☎322 223 1626, ⊛cafedeollavallarta .com; map p.236. Good traditional Mexican food – enchiladas, *carne asado*, *chile relleno* – served in a lively dining room adorned with local artwork, and delivered by cheerful, attentive waiters. Always popular and brimming with diners who come again and again (no reservations). Mains M$85–170. Mon & Wed–Sun 10am–11pm.

Daíquiri Dicks Olas Altas 314 ☎322 222 0566, ⊛ddpv .com; map p.236. Informal beachside dining (perfect for sunset drinks) and a varied menu of generous dishes draws a big gringo crowd. The signature dish, *pescado vallarta* – a whole grilled, seasoned fish served on a stick – is worth the 30min wait. Other crowd pleasers, including lobster tacos and chicken in masala sauce, are equally good (mains M$175–265). May–Oct Mon & Wed–Sun 9am–11pm; Nov–April daily 9am–11pm.

★**Panadería y Pastelería Yarita** Basilio Badillo 244; map p.236. Best traditional bakery in the city, with irresistible empanadas, banana bread, pastries, cake and M$7 mini custard éclairs. Mon–Sat 7am–9pm, Sun 10am–2pm.

Pepe's Taco Honduras 173, between Peru y México ☎322 223 1703; map p.236. This no-frills restaurant (plenty of seating) has been serving mouthwatering *tacos carne asada* (M$12) since 1987. Tues–Sun 1pm–6am.

RESTAURANTS

Archie's Wok Rodríguez 130 ☎322 222 0411, ⊛archieswok.com; map p.236. State-of-the-art Asian cooking served in a stylish setting by the wife and daughter of John Huston's former personal chef. Delicious, healthy fare with an emphasis on seafood in Filipino, Thai and Chinese sauces – think Thai garlic shrimps, almond chicken and sizzling fish in banana leaves. A little pricey (mains average M$150–175), but touted by fans as one of the best Asian restaurants on the Pacific coast. Live music at the weekend. Oct–July Mon–Sat 2–11pm.

Derby City Burger 365 Olas Atlas ☎322 223 3323; map p.236. Perhaps not the "tastiest burgers in Mexico", but close; gourmet beef burgers from M$95, ranging through the classic House Burger to Bluegrass BBQ Burgers and the "Mex-Cali" (pepper jack cheese, *jalapeños*, avocado

and sour cream). Cash only. Mon–Thurs noon–10pm, Fri & Sat noon–11pm.

Fredy's Tucán Basilio Badillo 245, at Vallarta ☎322 223 0778, ⊛fredystucan.com; map p.236. Bright, airy and with tropical decor, this is one of the best venues for Mexican, continental and American breakfasts: omelettes, pancakes, French toast, granola and yogurt, and fresh-baked bread are served until 2.30pm in a new dining room, adjacent to the *Posada de Roger* hotel. European football matches are screened in the hotel bar on evenings and at weekends. Daily 8am–2.30pm.

★**Joe Jack's Fish Shack** Basilio Badillo 212 ☎322 222 2099, ⊛joejacks-fishshack.com; map p.236. Fabulous seafood, but best known for its fish and chips (M$155) and chowders (M$95), which are renowned as tastiest in town; the M$125 "Tasty" burger is also excellent. Sit at the bar downstairs, or enjoy the views from the rooftop dining area. "Burger Wednesdays" offers any burger at M$85. Free wi-fi. Daily noon–11pm.

Kaiser Maximilian Olas Altas 380-B, next to Playa Los Arcos hotel (see p.239) ☎322 223 0760; map p.236. Upscale, expensive restaurant (mains M$190–300) with an old-European slant: traditional Austrian dishes like lamb with rosemary and sautéed squid, as well as more traditional Mexican and international offerings. The restaurant's pavement patio is a nice spot for a gourmet coffee and an exceedingly rich pastry. Mid-July to May Mon–Sat 8am–11pm.

Langostinos Diéguez 109 at Playa Los Muertos ☎322 222 0894; map p.236. Phenomenal sunset views, excellent lime margaritas and tasty surf and turf combos – the menu includes everything from burgers and snacks to fresh fish and lobster (mains average M$80). Happy hour 5–8pm; bring cash as they'll charge three percent extra on your card. Oct–Aug daily 8am–11pm.

★**Los Muertos Brewing** Constitucion at Lazaro Cardenas ⊛losmuertosbrewing.com; map p.236. For those who like craft and artisanal beer, this relaxed spot pours a range of seven house brews, ranging from blonde ale to stout and occasional seasonal specials. Happy hour (from 4–6pm) sees pints for M$25. Also serves fabulous seafood, though it's best known for its fish and chips (M$120) and chowders (M$80; sit at the bar downstairs, or enjoy the views from the rooftop dining area. Free wi-fi. Daily 11am–midnight.

SPA THERAPY

If the heat, crowds and traffic are getting you down, make for the *Marriott CasaMagna Resort*'s **Ohtli Spa** (see p.239), the most luxurious and soothing in town. The place was completely renovated in 2012, with single-sex plunge pools, steam rooms, saunas, an aqua therapy pool and themed treatment rooms, from Thai massage beds to a romantic couples/group room with jacuzzi. Guests pay US$15 (M$250) for the pools and steam rooms, non-guests US$25 (M$415) – treatments are extra. Daily 6am–11pm (pools 7am–9pm).

TACO TOUR

Numerous **tacos** stalls occupy the streets of Puerto Vallarta at night, offering a tasty introduction to this essential street food. The following tour starts a few blocks east of the malecón in the Zona Romántica and roughly heads north through downtown, though you'd have to be extremely hungry to visit every stall in one night.

La Hormiga Feliz ("The Happy Ant") Madero, at Vallarta; map p.236. This stall has been knocking out delicious *bírria*, tacos and quesadillas since the 1970s (from M$4). Usually open Mon & Wed–Sun 9am–2pm & 7pm–1am.

Tacos Memo Grill Badillo, at Aguacate; map p.236. Sumptuous *tacos asada, quesadillas con carne* (M$6), *hamburguesas* and burritos from M$25. Usually open daily 8pm–2am.

Marisma Fish Taco Naranjo 320, at Carranza (don't confuse it with the carne asada place opposite) ☎ 332 222 1395, ⓦ marismafishtaco.com; map p.236. The best fish tacos in town (M$10); shrimp tacos from around M$15. Daily 10am–6pm.

Rico Mac Taco México 1139 ☎ 332 222 4204; map p.236. Though this congenial sit-down place attracts a fair share of tourists, the tacos are excellent and there are lots of bars nearby. Daily 8am–midnight.

Mariscos El Jefe México and Chile; map p.236. Not strictly a taco place but equally beloved for its fresh, local seafood, delicious *ceviche* and prawn cocktails since 1970. Daily noon–8pm.

El Carbonito Across from Pepe's (see opposite); map p.236. End up at the connoisseurs' favourite – a small (usually unmarked) stall known for serving the finest *tacos el pastor* in the city. The secret: mesquite-infused charcoal and superb, tongue-singeing salsa. Mon–Thurs 8.30pm–1am, Fri–Sun 8.30pm–4am.

El Palomar de los Gonzáles Aguacate 425 ☎ 322 222 0795, ⓦ restauranteelpalomarpv.com; map p.236. Perfect for a romantic candlelit dinner, this elegant mansion, carved into the hillside south of the centre, has stunning views from its rooftop patio. The seafood dishes are the highlight of the menu (M$175–325), but the Mexican specialities (around M$150) are also well executed. A good wine list and exotic desserts ensure a long, indulgent evening. Daily 6–11pm.

Las Tres Huastecas Olas Altas 444, at Rodríguez ☎ 322 222 3017; map p.236. No-frills, cantina-style restaurant since 1965, a block from Playa de los Muertos, that specializes in classic Mexican dishes such as chicken in *mole* sauce and a creative ensemble of fish tacos and enchiladas. One of the cheapest places in this part of town (most dishes under M$85, breakfasts under M$45). Daily 7am–9pm.

DRINKING AND NIGHTLIFE

The **malecón** (Paseo Díaz Ordez) is the centre of Puerto Vallarta's night-time activity, lined with ornate, hangar-size places that specialize in creating a high-energy party atmosphere – pop, techno and 1980s rock compete for the airwaves with salsa, jazz and the more gentle strumming of marauding mariachis. Check ⓦ pvscene.com for the latest events and listings. The Zona Romántica also has its share of clubs, which are generally less pretentious and more varied in character. This is where you'll find most of the **gay nightlife** (see ⓦ gayguidevallarta.com).

CENTRO HISTÓRICO

La Bodeguita del Medio Paseo Díaz Ordez 858 (malecón) ☎ 322 223 1584, ⓦ labodeguitadelmedio .com.mx; map p.236. Write your name on the wall if you can find the space in this Cuban chain made famous by the original Hemingway Havana haunt. The *mojitos* are the signature tipple (ask for Havana Club seven-year-old rum), and the live salsa goes from open til close. There's quieter bit at the back where you can eat traditional Mexican food (main dishes up to M$240). Daily 11am–2am.

★**Cheeky Monkey** Paseo Díaz Ordez 556 (malecón), at Corona ☎ 322 222 8938; map p.236. Difficult to turn down another dollar-margarita, especially when they're as potent as these. This bar above the malecón is the perfect place to get your evening started – three levels, balcony views of the bay and stunning sunsets. The food isn't bad either. Daily 11.30am–10pm.

Mandala Paseo Díaz Ordez 640 (malecón), at Abasolo ☎ 322 121 5002, ⓦ mandalanightclub.com; map p.236. Huge, warehouse-like *discoteca* and video bar, attracting tourists and upscale locals with its Asian-themed interior (think *Buddha Bar*) and Latino pop and dance music. Cover M$100. Daily 9.30pm–6am.

Memories Mina 207, at Juárez ☎ 322 205 7906; map p.236. Sultry bar popular with dating couples who are delighted to be able to hold a conversation (a novelty in a PV bar) in between sips of coffee and speciality cocktails. Daily 7pm–midnight.

★**The Zoo** Paseo Díaz Ordez 630 (malecón) ☎ 322 222 4945; map p.236. Leopard- and zebra-skin chairs and plastic gorillas swinging from the rafters lend a kitsch element to this wildly popular club, where DJs play the latest dance tunes for a hip young clientele. Cover M$100 (free Tues). Daily: bar 10am–4am, club 10pm–6am.

ZONA ROMÁNTICA

Apaches Olas Altas 439 ☎ 322 222 5235; map p.236. Popular and welcoming lesbian-owned, gay-friendly joint where groups gather for martinis and cocktails at happy hour (6–8pm), filling the cosy, indoor bar and pavement tables. Daily 6pm–2am.

Paco's Ranch Vallarta 237 ☎ 322 222 8147; map p.236. An unmissable experience, this is the largest and most popular gay club in town. Also drawing a straight

contingent, it's a multifaceted venue with DJs playing the latest in techno, hip-hop and pop on the ground floor; Mexican music, a cantina and pool table on the first floor (open from 1pm); a rooftop bar on the second; and strippers in a smaller space connected to the main club by a passageway. There are crazy drag shows at 1.30am on Tues, and at 12.30pm & 3am on both Wed and Sun. Daily 10pm–6am.

Route 66 (ex-Club Roxy) Vallarta 217, at Madero ☎ 322 223 2404; map p.236. A popular bar-club with bands (10pm–2am) playing blues, reggae and rock in an uplifting, if at times raucous, atmosphere that attracts locals and tourists alike. Daily 6pm–4am.

DIRECTORY

Banks and exchange Banamex, on the Plaza Principal (Mon–Sat 9am–4pm) has an ATM. There are branches of Banorte downtown, at Díaz Ordaz 690 (Mon–Fri 9am–5pm, Sat 9am–2pm), and in Zona Hotelera, at Francisco Medina Ascensio 500 (same hours). Other ATMs are plentiful. You can change money at the numerous *casas de cambio* on the streets surrounding the plaza: rates vary, so shop around.

Consulates Canada, Plaza Peninsula, Francisco Medina Ascensio 2485, Zona Hotelera Norte ☎ 322 293 0098 (Mon–Fri 9am–1pm); US, Paseo de los Cocoteros 85 Sur, Paradise Plaza, Interior Local L-7, Nuevo Vallarta ☎ 322 222 0069 (Mon–Fri 8.30am–12.30pm; closed every third Wed) – in emergencies call US Consulate General in Guadalajara (☎ 333 268 2145).

Emergencies ☎ 060 (tourist police). Police ☎ 322 223 2500.

Hospitals English-speaking medics at CMQ Clinic, Basilio

Badillo 365, between Insurgentes and Aguacate ☎ 322 223 1919; and Cruz Roja, Río Balsas and Río Plata ☎ 322 222 1533.

Internet Many restaurants and bars have wi-fi, though actual internet cafés come and go: try Madero 265 (between Constitución and Vallarta), open daily 10am–midnight (M$20/hr).

Laundry There are facilities scattered throughout town, all charging around M$45 per load – try Lavandería El Jabon, Cardenas 258 (daily 9am–6pm; M$11/kg, minimum 3.2kg for M$45), or Lavandería Paola, Guerrero 317 (M$13/kg).

Pharmacy CMQ, Basilio Badillo 367 ☎ 322 222 2941, next to CMQ Clinic, is open 24hr; or try Farmacia Guadalajara at Zapata 232 (☎ 322 222 0101), also 24hr.

Post office The main post office is at Colombia 1014, at Argentina, north of the old town (Mon–Fri 9am–5pm, Sat 9am–1pm).

Bahía de Banderas

Puerto Vallarta lies at the centre of the **Bahía de Banderas**, prime beach territory easily explored via rental car, or, with more time, public bus and water taxi. Indeed, for the more peaceful and scenic **beaches** further south – **Playa Las Animas** and **Yelapa** are the most appealing – a boat is the only means of access.

To the north, over the state line in Nayarit, the bay arcs out to **Punta de Mita**, some 30km away. A summer preserve for Guadalajarans and a winter retreat for motorhome vacationers from the north, these gorgeous beaches offer facilities in just a few spots – **Nuevo Vallarta**, **Bucerías** and **Punta de Mita** – leaving many kilometres of secluded sand for camping and some excellent surf breaks.

Mismaloya

Some 10km south of Puerto Vallarta, the best-known and most accessible beach is **Mismaloya**. Here John Huston filmed *The Night of the Iguana*, building his set at the mouth of what was once a pristine, jungle-choked gorge on the southern side of the gorgeous bay; it's been endowed with a romantic mystique ever since. The beach itself remains pretty but quite small, with a handful of palapa restaurants and enthusiastic

> ## LOS ARCOS
>
> From the beach at Mismaloya boats are on hand to take you snorkelling at **Los Arcos**, a magical underwater park around a group of offshore islands, some creating the eponymous arched geological formations. A superb array of brightly coloured fish – parrot, angel, pencil, croaker and scores of others – negotiates the deep rock walls and the boulder-strewn ocean floor. In addition to ninety-minute trips from the beach, boats are rented to groups for unlimited periods. Operators usually charge M$250 for basic snorkelling trips.

vendors, selling everything from coconuts to sarongs, crammed into the southern end. Boats depart the beach for **Los Arcos** (see box above). Public access is via the Paseo del Rio along the river, just to the south of the hotel entrance; you can use the hotel facilities for M$440 per day (includes buffet lunch).

Zoológico de Vallarta

Camino El Edén, just under 1km (15–20min walk) from the *Barceló* entrance and the Mismaloya bus stop • Daily 10am–6pm • M$100 • ☎ 322 228 0955, ⓦ zoologicodevallarta.com

Baby tigers in Mexico? At the **Zoológico de Vallarta** you can feed and play with some of the resident animals, especially cute babies such as white tiger cubs, as well as the "ugliest dog in the world" aka the xoloescuincle or Mexican hairless dog, a bit like a cross between a piglet and a seal. Kids usually love the experience, but note that this is in many ways an old-fashioned zoo: cages are small, conditions are basic and some may find the condition of the animals distressing. Most of the animals were supposedly saved from the circus, which partly explains their poor state.

Boca de Tomatlán

If you're after peace and quiet, your best option is to continue along the highway for another 4km past Mismaloya until you reach the village of **Boca de Tomatlán**, the departure point for the *lanchas* that shuttle passengers to and from the southern beaches (see below). There's not much in Boca itself beyond a few convenience stores in the village, and the usual seafood palapas on a small beach dotted with fishing boats and water taxis, and surrounded by densely forested hills. The bus from Vallarta terminates at the top of the hill – it's a short walk down to the beach and *embarcadero* from here to catch a **water taxi** (see p.246). Look out for dolphins and rays as the boat speeds south.

Vallarta Botanical Gardens

Hwy-200 km 24 • Jan–March daily 10am–6pm; April–Dec Tues–Sun 10am–6pm • M$60 • ☎ 322 223 6182, ⓦ vbgardens.org • Take the El Tuito bus from Carranza and Aguacate in the Zona Romántica (every 20min)

In the hills high above Boca de Tomatlán lies the 20-acre **Vallarta Botanical Gardens**, a lush, tropical interlude from the beaches below. In addition to admiring the blossoms, Mexican orchids, blue agave and exotic plants, you can enjoy jungle river-swimming, visit the Hacienda de Oro Visitor Centre and eat at the restaurant.

Las Ánimas

Usually the first stop on the water-taxi route, around ten minutes from Boca, **Las Ánimas** is a large bay with a long, sandy beach. There are plenty of beach restaurants here, and watersports – jet skiing, banana boats and parasailing – so it tends to be the busiest stop, especially in the afternoons.

Quimixto and Las Caletas

Quimixto is the second stop on the water-taxi route, though it's become less popular in recent years and therefore much less crowded. The beach is similar to Las Ánimas, but with no activities and far fewer places to eat – there's also a small village at the southern end. The other main attraction is the hike or horse ride (M$150) to the local waterfall, a 30m cascade that plunges into a lagoon safe for swimming. A bit further south, the small cove and beach known as **Las Caletas** (John Huston's former home) has become a private watersports centre for Vallarta Adventures (ⓦvallarta-adventures.com), but water taxis will also stop here.

Yelapa

The old hippy hangout of **Yelapa** remains the most enticing target along this stretch of coast, some thirty minutes from Boca and the final water-taxi stop. Beautifully located on a gorgeous bay, hemmed in by tropical hills and coconut palms, it has managed to retain a rustic, laid-back vibe, despite the arrival of day-trippers, electricity and satellite dishes; locals still hook octopus and surgeonfish right off the pier, frigate birds glide over the water and turkey vultures skulk in the trees.

Yelapa is divided into two main sections: boats pull up first at **La Playa**, the white-sand beach lined with palapa restaurants, before heading across the bay to **El Pueblo**, the "town", a cluster of houses clinging to the cliffs (with a church and a few small stores).

The Falls

From the beach you can walk up the Rio del Tuito to the **Upper Cascadas** (aka "Cascada Catedral"), through the languid village of El Paso, past fields of maize, mango trees and sleepy dogs and cattle (around 1.5hr hike). Check directions before you go, as it's a bit tricky at the end. From El Pueblo, another cobblestone path leads up to the much closer and slightly more impressive lacy falls of **La Cascada Cola de Caballo**, where there's a small pool and drink stall. Horses and guide can be hired at the beach to take you up to either falls (M$300 and M$200 respectively), but you won't get lost walking – the friendly locals will point you in the right direction (and invariably speak some English).

Nuevo Vallarta

Just across the Nayarit state border, **NUEVO VALLARTA**, 12km north of PV airport, is a mega-resort, an ever-expanding cluster of astronomically expensive hotels. Although the creamy-white beach here is spectacular, it's backed by modern towers.

Dolphin Adventure

Paseo de la Palmas 39 • Daily 10am–4pm • US$69–169 (M$1150–2820) to swim with dolphins • ☎322 297 1212 ext 25, ⓦdolphin-adventure.com

There's nothing much for the day-tripper to do in Nuevo Vallarta save pay a visit to the **dolphins** at the professionally managed **Dolphin Adventure**. As well as swimming with dolphins (1hr 30min), you can also spend a day with a dolphin trainer (US$195/M$3250). The dolphins are well treated – they spend only a combined total of less than two hours each day interacting with the public, get daily health assessments and are never forced to participate in activities.

BAHÍA DE BANDERAS ZIP LINES

The region boasts two zip lines (aka "canopy tours") competing for your pesos. The oldest is **Los Veranos Canopy Tour** (Mon–Sat 8am–8pm, Sun 9am–5pm; 1.5hr–2hr; M$850 (minibus shuttle M$200); ☎322 223 6060, ⓦcanopytours-vallarta.com), in the small village of Las Juntas y Los Veranos, above Boca de Tomatlán. This is a series of fourteen exhilarating zip lines along cables up to 60m high and 335m long over the Río Orquídeas, whizzing past coffee trees, vanilla vines and agave plants. Competition is supplied by **Canopy River** (daily 9am–3pm; from M$650 ☎322 222 0560, ⓦcanopyriver.com), with twelve higher zip lines (200m) including the longest in Mexico (420m), a small river beach in the jungle and transportation to the site (they'll collect you at your hotel).

ZONA PACÍFICO TIME

If you travel north of Puerto Vallarta you need to put your watch back one hour: Nuevo Vallarta, Bucerías, Punta de Mita and Sayulita officially lie within the Zona Pacífico (Pacific Zone), the equivalent of Canadian and US Mountain Time, which starts at the Jalisco/Nayarit state border, just north of Puerto Vallarta's airport. However, because Nuevo Vallarta, Bucerías and Punta de Mita are so close to PV, most businesses work on Zona Central (US Central) times; Sayulita officially changed to Central time in 2011. If you are given a time followed by the word Jalisco, it means Zona Central; if followed by Nayarit, it is Zona Pacífico time.

Bucerías

For a more local beach experience, you're better off pushing on to laid-back **BUCERÍAS**, the last stop along the northern side of the bay before Hwy-200 cuts inland, which has wonderful views across the water to Puerto Vallarta from its seafront **restaurants** (see opposite). The village is a bit shabby, but the flea-market stalls make for good shopping, and the popular beach is a long swathe of chalk-white sand.

Punta de Mita

PUNTA DE MITA is more developed than Bucerías (19km away), with most of the bars, cafés and seafood restaurants along the handsome beach attached to hotels and resorts in the area known as **Playa Anclote**. The beach here is a wide, kilometre-long curve of silky coral sand, and the water is shallow with long wave breaks, making it perfect for beginner surfers. Note that, thanks to the new highway, you can continue north to **Sayulita** from here by taxi van (see below), without backtracking to Vallarta.

ARRIVAL AND DEPARTURE

By bus (north side) To get to the beaches north of Puerto Vallarta, catch any northbound Autotransportes Medina "Punta de Mita" bus (every 10min; Bucerías and Nuevo Vallarta M$12; Destiladeras M$16; Punta de Mita M$25). These buses originate in downtown Vallarta at 1410 Brasil, between Guatemala and Brasilia. Taxi vans will whisk you to Sayulita from Punta Mita for M$250 (20min); alternatively, take the bus back to Bucerías (M$10), and catch the local bus from Vallarta to Sayulita from there (M$12).

By bus (south side) Buses (M$7) to Mismaloya (20–25min) and Boca de Tomatlán (another 10min) every 10–15min. Water taxis depart from Boca (see below). Buses to El Tuito (M$20) via the Botanical Gardens depart Carranza and Aguacate in the Zona Romántica every 20–30min.

By taxi Taxis from downtown to Nuevo Vallarta are around M$180; to Bucerías is around M$260 and at least M$570 to

BAHÍA DE BANDERAS

Punta Mita; you can also get taxis to Mismaloya (M$150) and Boca de Tomatlán (M$180), though you might save some pesos starting in the Zona Romántica. From Bucerías, Nuevo Vallarta is M$85–130, Punta de Mita M$250 and Sayulita M$200. Taxis within each area charge M$50 for short rides.

By water taxi From Playa de los Muertos in the Zona Romántica, water taxis (M$300 return) depart 10am, 11am and 11.45am (usually hourly, 9am–6pm in high season, Nov–March) for Las Ánimas, Quimixto and Yelapa (25–45min). The last boat back departs 4pm. Water taxis from Boca de Tomatlán also run to Las Ánimas (M$50; 10min), Quimixto (M$50) and Yelapa (M$80; 30min), but always check current schedules at the dock: boats usually run every 90min or so from 7am, with the last boat back usually 4pm. If you get stuck, a private boat ride from Yelapa back to Boca will cost at least M$1000.

TOURS AND ACTIVITIES

Boat tours If you'd rather take an organized boat tour or "booze cruise" to the southern beaches, visit ⓦ puertovallartatours.net or ⓦ vallarta-adventures.com. Most day cruises cost M$400 to Los Arcos, Las Ánimas and Quimixto (M$600 to Yelapa), usually with food, soft drinks and snorkelling included.

Whale-watching tours Alternatively, book an organized whale-watching tour from Puerto Vallarta with an operator such as Open Air Expeditions, Guerrero 339 (US$95/M$1585; ☎322 222 3310, ⓦvallartawhales.com). Humpback whales appear in the bay from around Dec to April.

ACCOMMODATION

MISMALOYA

Barceló Puerto Vallarta Hwy-200 km 11.5 ☎322 226 0660, ⓦbarcelopuertovallarta.com; map p.234. This huge luxury hotel dominates the beach at Mismaloya, a full-scale all-inclusive resort with four pools, top restaurants and activities. Each suite comes with at least partial views of the sea, living room with sofa and two TVs. M$900

YELAPA

Accommodation here is primarily provided by rental apartments; just arriving on the beach and enquiring will usually get you a place (see ⓦyelapa.info).

Hotel Lagunita At the far end of Yelapa beach ☎322 209 5055, ⓦhotel-lagunita.com; map p.234. Beautiful open-air cabañas (holding up to six people) on a beach with its own pier. There's also a pool and beachfront restaurant serving Mexican and international food. M$1050

★**Majahuitas Resort** Between Quimixto and Yelapa ☎322 293 4506, ⓦmajahuitasresort.com; map p.234. Accessed by private boat from Boca de Tomatlán (though the water taxis will also stop here), this ecofriendly resort is a guaranteed love-it or leave-it experience: eight comfy but simple *casitas ecológicas*, each sleeping four. There's solar-powered lighting but no phones or internet, and communal meals are served by candlelight (rates include breakfast, lunch and dinner). June and July rates drop to M$2000. Oct–July. M$4200

PUNTA DE MITA

Four Seasons Punta Mita At the western end of the headland ☎329 291 6000, ⓦfourseasons.com/puntamita; map p.234. The luxury resort that sparked the current building boom at Punta Mita is still the most luxurious place to splash out, with spacious *casita*-style accommodation with beachfront or ocean views, gourmet restaurants, two Jack Nicklaus-designed golf courses, three pools and tennis courts. M$6000

Mesón de Mita Anclote 200 ☎329 291 6330, ⓦhotelmesondemita.com; map p.234. Staying in Punta de Mita doesn't have to break the bank; this lovely hotel faces the ocean with sixteen cosy rooms equipped with TVs, a/c and wi-fi. M$650

EATING

PLAYA COLOMITOS (BOCA DE TOMATLÁN)

★**Ocean Grill** ☎329 223 7315, ⓦoceangrillvallarta.com; map p.234. Quite simply the most spectacular place to eat on the bay, this gourmet restaurant overlooks Playa Colomitos, a short boat ride (M$20 or free restaurant shuttle) from Boca de Tomatlán. Pick the catch of the day, lobster, octopus (M$190) or luscious shrimp (M$320) smothered in a choice of six sauces (try the lemon ginger butter). Cash only. Mon & Wed–Sun 11am–5.30pm.

BUCERÍAS

Adriano's Del Pacífico 11 ☎329 298 0088; map p.234. With bright-orange walls and an extensive range of fresh fish, this is the best but also the most pricey restaurant on the strip, with superbly executed international (filet mignon with creamy mushroom sauce) and Mexican classics for M$100–120. Daily 11am–10pm.

Pie in the Sky Héroe de Nacozari 202 ☎329 298 0838, ⓦpieinthesky.com.mx; map p.234. For a tea-time treat, visit the locally renowned *Pie in the Sky* bakery, opposite the *De Camarón* hotel, for heavenly molten fudge chocolate brownies (*beso*), Belgian chocolate mousse, bagels and exotic cheesecakes. Free wi-fi. Daily 8am–10pm.

YELAPA

Yelapa's beach palapas offer a similar range of beers, cocktails and seafood such as lobster (M$250), shrimp (M$180) and fish tacos (M$95) – fresh, but not especially cheap. You'll get cheaper food in El Pueblo's cafés.

★**Café Bahia** ☎322 209 5192. This friendly restaurant acts as a de facto information centre, just off the water-taxi pier, selling excellent hand-drawn maps along with superb home-cooked food, everything from full American breakfasts to baked goods, Mexican classics, veggie dishes and some mean cocktails. Cash only. Oct–April Mon–Sat 9am–7pm, Sun 9am–3pm.

Café Shambhala Marlin 31–32 (main path between the beach and town areas) ☎322 138 0612. Delicious Mexican and Asian-influenced classics for breakfast or lunch (Sun is "*birria* special" day), from tender *arrachera* steak to spring rolls and sushi. Free internet. Mains M$50–80. Mon 9am–2.30pm, Tues–Sat 9am–2.30pm & 4–10pm, Sun 9am–late.

Sayulita

On the other side of the Punta de Mita, 22km north of Bucerías on Hwy-200, languorous **SAYULITA** is another popular gringo outpost with an enchanting, jungle-fringed beach, famous fish and shrimp tacos and some inviting places to stay. The calm was temporarily shattered in 2007 when the town served as backdrop for the cheesy (but commercially successful) Disney movie *Beverly Hills Chihuahua* – many locals were hired as extras.

Other than lounging on the sands and making jokes about the movie, the main activity here is **surfing**: the main (right) break in town is in front of *Papa's Palapas*, while you'll find a faster left break north of the river mouth (near the campsite).

The town has a noticeable presence of gangsters, who hang around the main square after dark. As a result, the town centre is not a place to linger at night.

ARRIVAL AND DEPARTURE SAYULITA

By bus Regular "Compestela" buses (usually white and green) connect Puerto Vallarta bus station with Sayulita every 30min (last bus 7pm; 1.5hr; M$25); these also stop at Bucerías (M$12) and pass by Puerto Vallarta airport on Hwy-200 (make sure it says "Sayulita" on the front). Buses to and from Puerto Vallarta terminate at Sayulita outside the Salud Clinic, located on the main road into town. The last bus back to PV usually leaves around 8.40pm. Vallarta Plus (ⓦ vallartaplus.com) operates

first-class buses between Sayulita and Guadalajara (departing Guadalajara at 7.30am and Sayulita at 3pm; 4hr 25min; M$330).

By taxi Taxis from downtown Vallarta cost anything between M$300 and M$700 depending on the group size and your negotiation skills (should be M$550 via airport taxi, or just M$300 outside the airport on Hwy-200). Figure on around M$250 from Punta de Mita and M$200 from Bucerías.

INFORMATION AND ACTIVITIES

Tourist information There's no tourist office; check ⓦ sayulita.com or ⓦ sayulitalife.com for the latest information.

Banks and exchange There are several ATMs in town.

Lunazul Surf School ☎ 329 291 2009, ⓦ lunazulsurfing .com. Rents boards (M$200–300/day) and offers lessons (M$450–550).

ACCOMMODATION

Amazing Hostel Sayulita Pelicanos 102 ☎ 329 291 3688, ⓦ theamazinghostelsayulita.com. As the name suggests, this HI-affiliated hostel two blocks from the beach, with its own pool, climbing wall, surfboards, kayaks

and bikes, is the best place to stay in town. The mixed and female-only dorms (M$220) are clean and come with lots of ceiling fans. There are also two private rooms (M$300/ person), communal kitchen, laundry and free wi-fi. **M$700**

PACIFIC COAST FIESTAS

Día de la Candelaria (Feb 2). Celebrated in Colima with dances, processions and fireworks.

Fiesta Brava (Feb 5). A day of bullfights and horse races in Colima.

Carnaval (the week before Lent; variable Feb–March). Acapulco and Manzanillo are both famous for the exuberance of their celebrations; rooms can be hard to find.

Semana Santa (Holy Week). Widely observed: the Palm Sunday celebrations in Petatlán, just south of Zihuatanejo, are particularly fervent.

Cinco de Mayo (May 5). Celebrations in commemoration of the victorious battle of Cinco de Mayo, especially in Acapulco.

Festival de las Lluvias (May 8). Celebrated in Mochitlán, near Chilpancingo, the festival has pre-Christian roots: pilgrims, peasants and local dance groups climb a nearby volcano at night, arriving at the summit at dawn to pray for rain.

Founder's Day (May 8). The city of Manzanillo celebrates the day it was founded.

Día de San Isidro (May 15). A week-long festival in Acapulco to celebrate St Isidore the Labourer, the patron saint of farmers, with dances and cockfights.

Día de la Marina (Navy Day; June 1). Celebrated in the ports, particularly Puerto Vallarta, Manzanillo and Acapulco.

Día de Santiago (Sept 28). Celebrated in several villages immediately around Acapulco.

Feria (first week of Nov). Colima's major festival runs from the last days of October until November 8.

Día de los Muertos (Day of the Dead; Nov 2). Widely observed, with picturesque traditions in Atoyac de Alvarez, just off the Acapulco–Zihuatanejo road.

Día de la Virgen de Guadalupe (Dec 12). In honour of the patroness of Mexico. Acapulco has fervent celebrations, while in Manzanillo the celebrations start at the beginning of the month. In Puerto Vallarta they continue until the end of it.

Petit Hotel Hafa Revolución 55 ☎ 329 291 3806, ⓦ hotel hafasayulita.com. For more of a boutique experience try this exceptionally stylish hotel, an artsy North African-themed gem two blocks from the beach. Free wi-fi and tranquil roof deck, but a/c is M$50 extra per night. M$750

Playa Escondida Playa Escondida 1 ☎ 329 291 3641, ⓦ playa-escondida.com. This luxurious, secluded beach resort, with four-to-eight-person cabañas facing a serene stretch of beach or tucked away in jungle and palms, is the most enticing place to stay in town. There's a minimum two-night stay and most rooms come with canopy beds, ocean views and free wi-fi. M$3605

EATING

Sayulita is well known for its **fish and shrimp tacos**, which come with optional pickled cabbage and the other regular accompaniments. They're found all over town, but you'll do well to avoid the rip-off merchants in the town centre, who can be very aggressive. *Restaurant Carmelita's* is a particular offender.

Aaleyah's Nachos & Wings Niños Héroes 2 ☎ 329 291 3353. Everything from tacos to addictive nachos, burgers, tortas and salads, as well as knockout margaritas (2 for 1 at M$60). Mon–Sat 8.30am–10pm.

ChocoBanana Plaza Mayor ☎ 329 291 3051, ⓦ la originalchocobanana.mx. Open-fronted and friendly, this bustling café serves up great breakfasts all day (M$45–95), while its blissfully powerful ceiling fans hum alongside the chatter. Don't leave without trying the eponymous "chocobanana" (M$30), a chilled banana dipped in molten chocolate and then rolled in granola. Daily 6am–6pm.

Don Pedro's Marlin 2 ☎ 329 291 3090, ⓦ donpedros .com. This huge beachfront palapa restaurant knocks out dependable Mexican-influenced Mediterranean-style cuisine, wood-fired-oven pizzas and tasty dishes such as beer-battered shrimp and *mahi-mahi ceviche*. Daily 8am–10pm.

Rollie's Revolución 58 ☎ 329 291 3347. Of the many institutions in town, everyone tries at least one breakfast at *Rollie's*, with a vast choice of filling egg, pancake and waffle plates from M$55. At night the place turns into a bar, *Rollie's At Night*. Café daily 8am–noon, bar daily 5.30–9pm.

3

Inland Jalisco and Michoacán

TEATRO DEGOLLADO, GUADALAJARA

Inland Jalisco and Michoacán

Separated from the country's colonial heartland by the craggy peaks of the Sierra Madre, the stretch of land from Guadalajara to Mexico City through the semitropical states of Jalisco and Michoacán has an unhurried ease that marks it out from the rest of the country. Containing a complex landscape of lofty plains and rugged sierras, the area is blessed with supremely fertile farms, fresh pine woods, cool pastures and lush tropical forest.

Something of a backwater until well into the eighteenth century, the high valleys of Michoacán and Jalisco were left to develop their own strong regional traditions and solid farming economy. Wherever you go, you'll find a wealth of local commercial goods, both agricultural and traditionally manufactured items, from avocados to tequila, glassware to guitars. Relative isolation has also made the region a bastion of conservatism – in the years following the Revolution, the Catholic *Cristero* counter-revolutionary guerrilla movement enjoyed its strongest support here.

Easy-going **Guadalajara**, Mexico's second city, is packed with elegant buildings and surrounded by scenic countryside. Outside the city, the land is spectacularly green and mountainous, studded with volcanoes and lakes, most famously **Laguna de Chapala**. There are also some superb colonial relics, especially in the forms of **Morelia** and **Pátzcuaro**, although it's the latter's majestic setting and well-preserved indigenous tradition that first call your attention.

The region has not been unaffected by the country's **drug wars**, however, as was gruesomely illustrated during Independence Day celebrations in 2008, when gangsters threw grenades into the crowd in Morelia's main square, killing eight people. The drug lords aren't interested in law-abiding tourists, so there's no cause for undue alarm, but you'll notice an increased presence of heavily armed soldiers and federal police, especially in smaller towns. What you won't see is the number of Michoacán's villages which are now under the control of armed gangs, whether drug producers or local vigilantes, but at any rate no force belonging to the state. Unless you go looking for trouble in the cities, you should be fine. If travelling along the state's byways, do so during the hours of daylight.

EVE OF THE DAY OF THE DEAD, LAGO DE PÁTZCUARO

Highlights

❶ Guadalajara Experience the drama of mariachi music in Mexico's second-largest city, the capital of Jalisco. **See p.255**

❷ Tequila Visit a tequila distillery and, more importantly, sample the legendary spirit in a café on the town's plaza. **See p.276**

❸ Uruapan Take in the cascading waterfalls and lush surroundings of the Parque Nacional Eduardo Ruíz. **See p.284**

❹ Paricutín Hike through an unearthly landscape of lava fields to climb up this still-active volcano. **See p.287**

❺ Lago de Pátzcuaro One of the best places in Mexico for seeing the spectacular and moving Day of the Dead celebrations on a stunning volcanic lake. **See p.294**

❻ Morelia Enjoy *pan dulces*, wine and classical music in one of the cafés overlooking the central plaza of this wonderful old colonial city. **See p.298**

❼ Monarch Butterfly Sanctuary See the millions of brightly coloured migratory butterflies which in winter blanket the fir trees around Angangueo. **See p.306**

HIGHLIGHTS ARE MARKED ON THE MAP ON P.254

INLAND JALISCO & MICHOACÁN

HIGHLIGHTS

1. Guadalajara
2. Tequila
3. Uruapan
4. Paricutín
5. Lago de Pátzcuaro
6. Morelia
7. Monarch Butterfly Sanctuary

MICHOACÁN

JALISCO

ZONA DE MONTAÑA

MEXICO CITY

Guadalajara

The second city of the Mexican Republic and capital of the state of Jalisco, **GUADALAJARA** is considered the most "Mexican" of the country's big cities. Being less frenetic than the capital, however, doesn't make it peaceful, and Guadalajara is huge and sprawling. Its conversion to a sleek metropolis has resulted in a hike in prices and some sacrifice of Mexican mellowness in favour of a US-style business ethic, but it's still an enjoyable place to visit, with the edge on Mexico's other big cities for trees, flowers, cleanliness and friendliness. Parks, little squares and open spaces are numerous, while downtown, around the cathedral, is a series of plazas unchanged since the days of the Spanish colonization. This small colonial heart of Guadalajara can still, especially at weekends, recall an old-world atmosphere and provincial elegance. The centre is further brightened by the **Plaza Tapatía**, which opens out the city's historical core to pedestrians, mariachi bands and street theatre.

Guadalajara's rapid expansion has swallowed up numerous communities: once-distinct villages are now barely distinguishable from the city all around. Heading **west**, the university area blends into chic suburbs and some of the city's most expensive real estate. **East**, Tlaquepaque and Tonalá are the source of some of the area's finest handicrafts. And finally to the **north**, Zapopan has a huge, much revered church and a museum of indigenous traditions, while the Barranca de Oblatos offers stunning canyon views and weekend picnic spots.

Brief history

Guadalajara was founded in 1532, one of the fruits of the vicious campaign of **Nuño de Guzmán** at the time of the Conquest – his cruelty and corruption were such that he appalled even the Spanish authorities, who threw him into prison in Madrid, where he died. The city, named after Guzmán's birthplace, thrived, was officially recognized by Charles V in 1542 and rapidly became one of the colony's most Spanish cities – in part because so much of the indigenous population had been killed or had fled during the Conquest. Isolated from the great mining industry of the Bajío, Guadalajara evolved into a regional centre for trade and agriculture. The tight reins of colonial rule restrained the city's development, and it wasn't until the end of the eighteenth century, as the colonial monopolies began to crumble, that things really took off. Between 1760 and 1803 the city's population tripled, reaching some 35,000; a new university was established; and the city became famous for the export of wheat, hides, cotton and wool.

When Spain's colonial empire finally fell apart, Guadalajara supported Hidalgo's independence movement and briefly served as the capital of the nation. By the beginning of the twentieth century it was already the second-largest city in the Republic, and in the 1920s the completion of the rail link with California provided a further spur for development. More recently, the exodus from Mexico City and attempts at industrial decentralization have continued to swell the urban area's population, which now tops four and a half million.

The centre of the old city is a relatively compact **grid** around the junction of Morelos and 16 de Septiembre. East of here Morelos leads to the Plaza Tapatía and the Mercado Libertad, while to the west are busy shopping streets. Juárez, a couple of blocks south, is actually the main east–west **thoroughfare** in the centre, heading out to the west past the university, where it becomes Vallarta. The main north–south arteries in the centre are the Calzada del Federalismo, along which the Tren Ligero, the city's metro, runs, and Calzada Independencia, off which Revolución leads southeast, to Tlaquepaque, the new bus station and Tonalá.

Plaza Guadalajara and around

Plaza Guadalajara, formerly known as the Plaza de los Laureles for its topiaried laurel trees, faces the main west entrance of the **cathedral**, which is where any tour of the city inevitably starts. The porticoed building on Plaza Guadalajara's north side, the **Presidencia Municipal**, was only built in 1952, though you wouldn't know it. In common with the other nearby plazas, crowds of people are entertained by an array of street performers and wandering musicians at weekends and on warm evenings; there are frequently bands playing during the day, too.

The cathedral

Alcalde (between Hidalgo and Morelos) • Daily 8am–8pm • Free

With the Sagrario, or sacristy, next door, the cathedral takes up an entire block at the very heart of the city's colonial centre, bordered by a further three plazas to form the shape of a Latin cross. With its pointed, tiled twin towers, the cathedral is a bizarre but successful mixture of styles. Building work began in 1561 and didn't finish for over a century – since then, extensive modifications, which effectively disguise the fact that there was probably never a plan behind the original design, have included a Neoclassical facade and new twin yellow-tiled towers (the originals collapsed in an 1818 earthquake). The richly decorated interior is best seen in the evening, when they turn on the lights. The picture of the Virgin in the sacristy is attributed to the Spanish Baroque artist Bartolomé Esteban **Murillo**.

Rotonda de los Jaliscienses Ilustres

On the north side of the cathedral

The **Rotonda de los Jaliscienses Ilustres** is a Neoclassical circle of seventeen Doric columns, the latest architectural expression of Jaliscan pride, and one which commemorates the state's heroes, 26 of whom surround it in the form of statues, although only a few occupy any of the 98 niches set aside for their ashes.

Plaza de la Liberación

The largest of the four squares surrounding the cathedral is the **Plaza de la Liberación**, to its east. The square is surrounded by interesting buildings, including the Museo

Regional (see below), the Palacio de Gobierno (see below), the Teatro Degollado (see below) and the church of San Agustín (see below).

Museo Regional

Liceo 60, east side of Rotonda de los Jaliscienses Ilustres and north side of the cathedral • Tues–Sat 9am–5.30pm, Sun 9am–4.30pm • M$52, free Sun; camera or video permit M$45

Housed in an eighteenth-century colonial mansion, the **Museo Regional** has, over time, been a religious seminary, a barracks and a school; it's now a supremely elegant setting for an extensive and diverse collection. Downstairs, exhibits start with a section devoted to regional **archeology** and range from stone tools and the skeleton of a mammoth to the finest achievements of western Mexican pottery and metalworking. The peoples of the west developed quite separately from those in southern and central Mexico, and there is considerable evidence that they had more contact with South and Central American cultures than with those who would now be regarded as their compatriots. The deep **shaft tombs** displayed here are unique in Mexico, but were common down the Pacific coast in Peru and Ecuador.

Upstairs, along with rooms devoted to the state's **modern history** and ethnography, is a sizeable gallery of colonial and modern art. Most remarkable here is the large collection of **nineteenth-century portraiture**, a local tradition that captures relatively ordinary Mexicans in a charmingly naive style.

Teatro Degollado

Degollado 53 (east side of Plaza de la Liberación) • Tues–Sun noon–2pm except when the theatre is in use • Free

The **Teatro Degollado** was modelled on La Scala in Milan. Built in the mid-nineteenth century and inaugurated in 1866 during the brief reign of Emperor Maximilian (see p.824), it's an imposing, domed Neoclassical building with a Corinthian portico; look on the portico's pediment for a frieze depicting the Greek Muses. A programme of drama and concerts is still staged here, mostly in October during the fiesta, though also sporadically throughout the rest of the year. The impressively restored **interior** is notable for its frescoed ceiling, which illustrates scenes from the fourth canto of Dante's *Divine Comedy*.

The churches of Santa María and San Agustín

On either side of the theatre, at Hidalgo 158 and Degollado 33 respectively

Two small churches, **Santa María** and **San Agustín**, are the only remains of a monastery that once stood here. San Agustín has a fine Baroque facade; relatively plain Santa María is one of the oldest churches in the city, built in the seventeenth century on the site of Guadalajara's first cathedral.

Plaza de Armas

Plaza de Armas, on the south side of the cathedral, is flanked by the Palacio de Gobierno and centres on an elaborate *belle époque* **rotunda**, which was a present from the people of France. With a canopy held up by topless Art Nouveau maidens bearing musical instruments, it's still in use as a bandstand, with music (often the state band) in the evenings (Tues–Fri & Sun 6.30pm).

Palacio de Gobierno

Plaza de Armas • **Palacio** Daily 9am–7.30pm • Free **Museum** Mon–Sat 10am–6pm, Sun 10am–3pm; guided tours Mon–Sat 11am, 1pm & 4pm, Sun 11am & 1pm • Free

Dominating the eastern side of the Plaza de Armas, the **Palacio de Gobierno** is recognizable by its Baroque facade with a clock surrounded by elements from the Aztec calendar. It was here that Padre Miguel Hidalgo y Costilla (the "father of Mexican Independence") proclaimed the abolition of slavery in 1810, and, in 1858, Benito

CENTRO HISTÓRICO

◼ ACCOMMODATION				● EATING				◼ DRINKING & NIGHTLIFE	
Ana-Isabel	5	Maya	6	Alta Fibra	14	La Fonda de San		Club Ye*Ye	5
Chapala	4	Posada Regis	8	Birriería Las		Miguel Arcangel	3	La Condesa	6
Don Quixote Hotel	12	Posada San Pablo	10	Nueve Esquinas	16	La Gorda	13	La Fuente	1
Fénix	7	Santiago de		Café Madoka	4	Pastelería Luvier	12	Green Light Eco-Bar	3
Francés	2	Compostela	11	Café Madrid	6	La Rinconada	7	Hotel Francés	2
Hamilton	9			Chai		El Tacazo	5	La Mutualista	4
Hospedarte				La Chata	10	Taquería Los Faroles	15	La Prisciliana	5
(Hostel Guadalajara)	3			Chong Wah	8/9	Villa Madrid	11		
Hotel de Mendoza	1			El Despertador	1			● SHOPPING	
León	13							Librería Gonvill	1

Juárez was saved from the firing squad by the cry of "*Los valientes no asesinan*" – "the brave don't murder". But the overwhelming reason to enter the arcaded courtyard is to see the first of the great **Orozco murals**.

The main mural dates from 1937 and is typical of Orozco's work (see box opposite) – Hidalgo blasts triumphantly through the middle, brandishing his sword against a background of red flags and the fires of battle. Curving around the sides of the staircase, scenes depict the Mexican struggle for liberty, from a pre-Conquest Eden to post-Revolutionary emancipation. Upstairs in the domed Congress Hall a smaller Orozco mural (painted just before his death in 1949) also depicts Hidalgo, this time as *El Cura de Dolores* (the priest from Dolores), legislator and liberator of slaves.

The Museum

The Palacio also contains a **museum**, covering the history of the city, the history of the Palacio de Gobierno itself and the manufacture of tequila. Aside from the guided tours, which are in Spanish and English, the explanations are in Spanish only. The most interesting thing in the museum is the chance to enter one of the Palacio's corner bastions to see how the round loopholes allowed soldiers to shoot directly along the sides of the building and down the adjoining streets.

Plaza Tapatía

Spanning Independencia, which passes underneath it, **Plaza Tapatía** is not so much a square as a very long and elegant pedestrian precinct. Though it looks thoroughly modern, the plaza was constructed in the late nineteenth century, demolishing some of the city's oldest neighbourhoods in the process. It takes its name from *tapatío* – an adjective used to describe anything typical of Guadalajara, supposedly derived from the capes worn by Spanish grandees; Guadalajarans themselves are often referred to as *Tapatíos*.

At its eastern end, the plaza opens out to a broad paved area full of wacky anthropomorphic **bronze sculptures**, the work of Guadalajara native **Alejandro Colunga**. Stretched, squashed and generally distorted human figures form chairs, their patinas rubbed shiny by thousands of tired shoppers and tourists.

Instituto Cultural–Hospicio Cabañas

Plaza Tapatía (eastern end) • Tues–Sun 10am–6pm • M$70, free Tues; M$30 to bring in a camera, M$45 for a video camera

Overlooking the eastern end of Plaza Tapatía, the **Instituto Cultural–Hospicio Cabañas** was founded as an orphanage by Bishop Juan Cabañas y Crespo in 1805 and took nearly fifty years to complete. Designed by Spanish architect Manuel Tolsá, the Hospicio is a huge, beautiful and tranquil building, with 23 separate patios surrounded by schools of art, music and dance; an art cinema/theatre; various government offices; and a small cafeteria. The chapel, the **Capilla Tolsá**, is a plain and ancient-looking structure in the form of a cross, situated in the central patio right at the heart of the building.

The Orozco murals

The Instituto also houses various Orozco **murals** which, in keeping with their setting, are more spiritual than those in the government palace, though you certainly couldn't call them Christian: the conquistadors are depicted as the Horsemen of the Apocalypse, trampling the native population beneath them. The Man of Fire – who leads the people

JOSÉ CLEMENTE OROZCO

José Clemente Orozco (1883–1949) was a member, along with Diego Rivera and David Siqueiros, of the triumvirate of brilliant artists who emerged from the Revolution and transformed Mexican painting into an enormously powerful and populist political statement, especially through the medium of the **giant mural**. Their chief patron was the state – hence the predominance of their work in official buildings and educational establishments – and their aim was to create a national art that drew on native traditions. Almost all their work is consciously educational, rewriting – or, perhaps better, rediscovering – Mexican history in the light of the Revolution, casting the imperialists as villains and drawing heavily on pre-Hispanic themes. Orozco, a native of Jalisco (he was born in Zapotlan, now Ciudad Guzmán), was perhaps the least overtly political of the three; certainly, his later work, the greatest of which is here in Guadalajara, cocentrates on his nuanced style.

As a child he moved to Guadalajara and then to Mexico City, where he was influenced by renowned engraver **José Guadalupe Posada** (see box, p.362) and where he painted murals from 1922 to 1927. His best works from this period are the series including *The Destruction of the Old Order* which he painted at the Antiguo Colegio de San Ildefonso in Mexico City (see p.78). Then followed seven years in the US, where works included his mammoth *The Epic of American Civilization* at Dartmouth College in Hanover, New Hampshire, where it's now displayed. It was in the years following his return, however, in the late 1930s and 1940s, that his powers as an artist reached their peak, above all in his works at Guadalajara's Hospicio Cabañas and the University of Guadalajara (see above & p.261).

from their dehumanizing, mechanized oppression – has a symbolic role as liberator, which is clearly the same as that of Hidalgo in the palace murals. In this case, he is a strange synthesis of Christian and Mexican deities, a Christ-Quetzalcoatl figure. There are benches on which you can lie back to appreciate the murals, and also a small museum dedicated to Orozco, with sketches, cartoons and details of the artist's life.

Mercado Libertad

Javier Mina

The vast **Mercado Libertad** is known locally as **Mercado San Juan de Dios**. Guadalajarans claim it's the largest indoor market in the world. Although the building is modern, much of what's inside is thoroughly traditional, and it's one of the few places in the city where you can still haggle over prices. Beyond the touristy souvenir stalls, you'll find *curanderas* offering herbal remedies, dried iguanas (for witches' brews) and the renowned Paracho guitars. There are also countless stalls selling regional food and colourful fruit, vegetables, chocolate, spices and traditional leather goods from saddles to clumpy working boots. The market is chaotic and engrossing, but before you buy crafts here, pay a visit to the **Instituto de la Artesanía** by the Parque Agua Azul (see below), or to the expensive boutiques in Tlaquepaque (see p.263), to get some idea of quality and value.

Immediately southwest of the Mercado is the **Plaza de los Mariachis**, a place to return after dark to hear Guadalajara's finest musicians (see p.274).

The churches of San Francisco and Nuestra Señora de Aranzazu

16 de Septiembre • Free

The churches of **San Francisco** and **Nuestra Señora de Aranzazu** face each other at the southern end of the city centre. San Francisco lies on the site of what was probably Guadalajara's first religious foundation, a Franciscan monastery established in the years just after the Conquest. The present church was begun in 1684 and has a beautiful Baroque facade. Aranzazu, by contrast, is entirely plain on the outside, but conceals a fabulously elaborate interior, with three wildly exuberant, heavily carved and gilded churrigueresque retables. The **Jardín de San Francisco**, which would be pleasantly peaceful were it not for the number of local buses rattling by, lies across from the two churches.

Parque Agua Azul

Independencia (entrance just south of the junction with Calzado González Gallo) • Tues–Sun 10am–6pm • M$5 • Buses ("Parque Agua Azul") from Jardín de San Francisco; *macrobús* Niños Héroes

Though it's an important area of green in the bustling city, you couldn't really describe **Parque Agua Azul** as peaceful: there's always some kind of activity going on and the green areas are permanently packed with kids enjoying the zoo and playgrounds. An outdoor concert stage, *la concha* (the shell), hosts popular free performances on Sundays, and weekends see football games and crowds. Nonetheless, by Guadalajara standards, it's a haven of calm, especially during the week, and the entrance fee includes attractions such as a dome full of butterflies; exotic caged birds, including magnificent toucans; a palm house, also full of tropical birds; and a strange, glass-pyramid orchid house.

Instituto de la Artesanía Jalisciense

Calzado González Gallo 20, just north of the entrance to the Parque Agua Azul • Mon–Sat 9am–5pm, Sun 9am–3pm • Free

The **Instituto de la Artesanía Jalisciense** is a showcase for regional crafts that is as much a museum as a shop. Its collection is ambitious, with examples of all sorts of local crafts – furniture, ceramics, toys, glassware, clothing – of the highest quality. Many of the items are expensive, but are worth it considering the fine quality of worksmanship.

Biblioteca IberoAmericana Octavio Paz

Colón 70, some four blocks north of San Francisco, and just west of the Plaza de Armas at the junction of Pedro Moreno and Colón • Mon–Fri 9am–3pm & 4–9pm, Sat 9am–5pm • Free

The "Ex-Templo de la Compañía", or the **Biblioteca IberoAmericana Octavio Paz**, was originally a church and later became a university lecture hall, during which time the nineteenth-century Neoclassical facade was added and it was decorated with **murals** by **David Siqueiros** and **Amado de la Cueva**. Currently a library, it has dramatic crimson-hued murals depicting workers, peasants and miners in a heroic-socialist style; they are open to visitors and make an interesting contrast to Orozco's work. Outside there's an attractive little plaza, and the pedestrianized streets make a pleasant escape from the traffic, if not the crowds.

The churches of Santa Monica, San Felípe and Las Capuchinas

Some six blocks north of the Biblioteca IberoAmericana Octavio Paz and very close to the junction of San Felipe and González Ortega • Free

Among these three good examples of the beautiful, little-known Baroque churches that stud Guadalajara, the oldest is the **Templo de Santa Monica**, on Santa Monica between San Felípe and Reforma, with fabulously rich doorways and an elegant stone interior. The nearby **Templo de San Felípe Neri**, on San Felípe at Contreras Medellin, is a few years younger – dating from the second half of the eighteenth century – and more sumptuously decorated, with a superb facade and lovely tower. Both of these churches have extravagant rain-spouts, which take the form of dragons on San Felípe. A block along González Ortega, at the corner of Garibaldi, the **Templo de las Capuchinas** is, conversely, plain and fortress-like; inside, though, it's more interesting, with paintings and a lovely vaulted brick roof.

4

Museo de la Ciudad

Independencia 684 • Tues–Sat 10am–5.30pm, Sun 10am–2.30pm • M$15.50, free Sun

The **Museo de la Ciudad**, housed in a former convent, showcases the city's history through photos and artefacts, with explanations in Spanish. The downstairs rooms illustrate the city's history from the sixteenth to the nineteenth centuries, with items such as a barbed scourging chain, which may interest S&M fetish enthusiasts, and some unusual statuettes of Jesus – one of him post-crucifixion, lying on his father's lap, and another of him as a child, maybe 7 or 8 years old, complete with stigmata, holding up a chalice. The twentieth-century section upstairs contains some interesting photos of the city as it was in bygone years.

Ex-Convento del Carmen

Juárez (at 8 de Julio)

Four blocks south of the Museo de la Ciudad, the **Ex-Convento del Carmen** was one of the city's richest monasteries, but its wealth has largely been stripped, leaving an austere, white building of elegant simplicity. Modern art exhibitions, dance events and concerts are regularly staged here, and a programme of forthcoming events is posted outside the entrance.

Universidad de Guadalajara

The Parque Revolución, on Federalismo (and the north–south Tren Ligero line), west of the Ex-Convento del Carmen, marks the eastern end of the campus of the **Universidad de Guadalajara**. A fifteen-minute walk west along Juárez from the centre, the university area is quieter, the streets broader and there's also a younger atmosphere, with plenty of good restaurants and cafés.

Rectoría General

Juárez 975 • Mon–Fri 9am–8pm, Sat 9am–noon • Free

The University's **Rectoría General** contains some of José Clemente Orozco's most important murals, which were among the first he painted in Guadalajara. To see them, head for the main hall (*paraninfo*) and check out the frescoed dome and front wall. As so often with Orozco, the theme of the works fits the setting: the dome shows the glories and benefits of learning, while the wall shows the oppressed masses crying out for books and education, which are being denied them by fat capitalists and the military.

Museo de las Artes and around

Museum López Cotilla 930 • Tues–Fri 10am–6pm, Sat & Sun 10am–4pm • Free

Round the back of the Rectoría General, the **Museo de las Artes** houses temporary exhibitions, usually of modern art, and usually worth popping in to see. Immediately south of the museum is the **Templo Expiatorio**, a modern neo-Gothic church modelled on Orvieto Cathedral in Italy and featuring some innovative stained glass and an attractive altarpiece.

San Pedro Tlaquepaque

5km southeast of the centre • #275 or TUR bus from the centre (16 de Septiembre) to Niños Héroes with Independencia (just after a brick pedestrian bridge and traffic circle), then walk down Independencia to El Parian

TLAQUEPAQUE (officially San Pedro Tlaquepaque) is famous for its artesanías and its **mariachi** bands. Once a separate town, it has long since been absorbed by urban sprawl, and most of its traditional crafts taken over by chichi designer-furniture and jewellery stores, but you can still find crafts such as ceramics, glass, jewellery and textiles. Prices are high, but so are standards, and there are usually some moderately priced ceramics and glassware.

Tlaquepaque centres around a pleasantly laid-back main square complete with bandstand, on whose north side is the blockish church of **San Pedro**. To the west of the square, the three-domed **Nuestra Virgen de la Soledad** is an almost equally distinctive landmark. To the east there's a small local Mercado Municipal; its entrance is on the north side of El Parian (see below). Nearby, several banks have ATMs in case you've been carried away by the shopping experience.

El Parian

At the plaza's southeast corner

El Parian, ostensibly an enclosed plaza, is, in effect, the biggest bar that you've ever seen – actually a dozen or so separate establishments, but since everyone sits outside, with the tables tending to overlap and strolling serenaders wandering around at random, it all feels like one enormous place. Food, drink and prices are good, but check the bill for added service charges. At the weekend, particularly Sunday afternoons, you'll see mariachi at its best here, and locals add their own vocal renditions to the musicians' backing. On weekdays it can be disappointingly quiet (or pleasantly peaceful, depending on your fondness for mariachi).

Museo Pantaleón Panduro

Princiliano Sánchez at Flórida • Daily 11am–8pm • M$65

For an insight into just how wonderful the local ceramics can be, visit the **Museo Pantaleón Panduro**, which was named after the father of Jaliscan ceramicists. Here you can see exemplary prizewinning pieces from the museum's annual ceramics competition (held each June).

Museo Regional de la Cerámica

Independencia 237 • Mon–Sat 10am–6pm, Sun 10am–3pm • Free

To learn something of the techniques used in making ceramics, visit the small **Museo Regional de la Cerámica**, which has displays of pottery not only from Tlaquepaque but

● **SHOPPING**

Agustín Parra	2
Antigua de México	3
Arte Indio	4
Galeria Sergio Bustamante	1

■ **ACCOMMODATION**

Casa Campos	3
La Casa del Retoño	4
Donde el Indio Duerme	2
La Villa del Ensueño	1

● **EATING**

Café San Pedro	2
Casa Fuerte	1

from all over the state, especially Tonalá (see below). Beyond the individual works of some of the finest craftsmen, there's a traditional kitchen on display, complete with all its plates, pots and pans, and the building is a fine old mansion in its own right. Of course, there is also a shop.

The shops

Tlaquepaque's fancier **shops** and galleries lie near the Museo Regional, many in lovely colonial-era houses along Independencia, itself closed to traffic and so a pleasant street along which to window-shop. The parallel Juárez is a little less exclusive and may be a better hunting ground for more moderately priced goods. For full details of all the area's recommended shops, see p.275.

Tonalá

8km southeast of Tlaquepaque • #275 or TUR bus southbound from 16 de Septiembre to Av Tonalá at Tonaltecas Sur

TONALÁ is a ceramics manufacturing centre, and, like Tlaquepaque, it was once an autonomous village, but that's where the similarities end. There's more of a workaday feel to Tonalá, with no pedestrian streets, and fewer designer home-furnishing stores. Here, the emphasis is more on the crafts themselves. Goods are cheaper, too, especially if you go (as you should) for the animated **street markets** (Thurs & Sun roughly 8am–4pm), when Tonaltecas Sur is clogged with stalls selling all sorts of ceramic goods, glassware and handicrafts. Some are pretty good value, some are factory seconds and others are just junk. Mostly, Tonalá is about strolling and browsing, but if you've more than a passing interest in ceramics, see p.275 for some specific **shops**.

Museo Nacional de la Cerámica
Constitución 104 • Tues–Sun 10am–6pm • Free

Specific sights are limited in Tonalá, but you might like to visit the **Museo Nacional de la Cerámica**. For those with an interest in Mexican ceramics, the museum has examples from every Mexican state, with both contemporary and antique pots to demonstrate the different styles.

Zapopan
7km northwest of the city centre • #275 and TUR buses from Tlaquepaque and northbound on 16 de Septiembre

ZAPOPAN is the site of the **Basílica de la Virgen de Zapopan**, one of the most important churches in the city, much revered by the Huichol people. Pope John Paul II gave a Mass in the giant **Plaza de las Américas** in front of the church during a visit to Mexico in 1979, and a statue commemorates the event. The Baroque temple houses a miraculous image of the Virgin: the 25cm-high figure was dedicated to the local Indians by a Franciscan missionary, Antonio de Segovia, after he had intervened in a battle between them and the conquistadors. Since then, it has been constantly venerated and is still the object of pilgrimages, especially on October 12, when several hundred thousand people gather early in the morning to march the Virgin back to the Basílica after an annual six-month tour of all the churches in Guadalajara.

Museo Huichol Wixarica de Zapopan
Eva Briseño 152 (Plaza de las Américas, north side) • Mon–Sat 10am–2pm & 3–6pm, Sun 10am–3pm • M$10

Beside the church, the small **Museo Huichol Wixarica de Zapopan**, an ethnographic museum, exhibits clothes and objects relating to Huichol traditions, as well as a photographic display of their modern way of life. They also sell Huichol crafts, including psychedelic yarn paintings (*cuadros de estambre*) and beadwork.

Museo de Arte de Zapopan
Andador 20 de Noviembre 166 • Tues–Sun 10am–6pm (open til 10pm Thurs) • Free • ⓦ mazmuseo.com

Just south of the Plaza de las Américas, the **Museo de Arte de Zapopan** is Guadalajara's best contemporary art gallery. Changing exhibitions cherry-pick the best talent from Mexico and abroad – painting, sculpture, photography, video installations, you name it.

Parque Mirador Independencia
About 8km north of the city, at the end of Calzada Independencia • Daily 7am–7pm • M$5 • *Macrobús* stop Mirador

The **Barranca de Oblatos** is a magnificent 600m-deep canyon, along the edge of which a series of parks offers superb views and a welcome break from the city. The

TONALÁ

0   100
metres

Museo Nacional de la Cerámica

Santuario del Sagrado Corazón

Market

Buses to central Guadalajara

● SHOPPING
La Casa de Salvador Vásquez Carmona	1	Galeria José Bernabe 2
		Mis Amores 3

Parque Mirador Independencia, a popular family spot with picnic areas, is located by the northern terminal of the Independencia *macrobús* route. Concrete paths wind down to the brink of the canyon, where you can gaze down past vegetated bluffs and cliffs to the river far below. Looking along the canyon, it becomes evident how the *barranca* limits the city's northward expansion, as buildings come right to the edge. Indeed, a new building at the adjacent design and architecture school is cantilevered right over the void. Several good cafés and restaurants near the entrance to the Parque Mirador cater to student budgets.

ARRIVAL AND DEPARTURE   GUADALAJARA

BY PLANE

Guadalajara's airport is some 17km southeast of the city on the road to Chapala, and has flights to US and Canadian as well as Mexican destinations. Airport facilities include money exchange and car rental, and there's also the usual system of fixed-price taxis and vans to take you downtown, with vouchers sold inside the terminal (around M$250 for a car with up to four people; 45min–1hr). The cheap way of getting into town (M$6–7) is to head out of the terminal and right, continue for about 200m to the next junction, and take a bus (every 20min, 5am–9pm) from the stop in front of the PEMEX station to the Central Vieja (see opposite). City bus #176 to the city centre also passes here, but does not usually stop to pick up passengers.

Destinations Cabo San Lucas (1–4 daily; 1hr 30min); Cancún (2–4 daily; 2hr 45min); Chihuahua (6 weekly; 1hr 45min); Ciudad Juárez (1–2 daily; 2hr 10min); Ciudad Obregón (1 daily; 1hr 45min); Hermosillo (2–3 daily; 2hr 5min); La Paz, Baja California Sur (1 daily; 1hr 40min); Mazatlán (2 daily; 55min); Mérida (2 weekly; 2hr 25min); Mexicali (1–2 daily; 2hr 50min); Mexico City (24–32 daily; 1hr 15min); Monterrey (7–13 daily; 1hr 40min); Puerto Vallarta (3–4 daily; 40min); Tijuana (8 daily; 3hr); Torreón (6 weekly; 1hr 15min); Tuxtla Gutierrez (3 weekly; 2hr); Veracruz (5 weekly; 1hr 30min); Villahermosa (3 weekly; 2hr).

Airlines Aeromexico, Vallarta 2440 (☎ 333 630 3271), and downtown at Corona 196; American, Vallarta 2440 (☎ 333 616 4090); Delta, Air France and KLM, López Cotilla 1701 (☎ 333 615 2850); InterJet, Vallarta 2440 (☎ 333 630 5203); United, Astral Plaza, Moctezuma 3515 (☎ 800 900 5000); VivaAerobus, Vallarta 1088 (☎ 334 777 0770).

BY TRAIN

The train station, 2km south of the centre at the bottom of Calzada Independencia, is used by both the Tequila Express and José Cuervo Express (see box, p.278), which can only be taken as part of a pre-booked tour.

BY BUS

Central Nueva Long-distance first-class buses use the Central Nueva (or Camionera Nueva), out in suburbia 10km southeast of the city centre (map p.256). It consists of seven buildings strung out in a wide arc, plus shops and two half-decent hotels (see p.269). The buildings are organized by bus company rather than route, so there are buses to Mexico City

from just about every building, for example, but staff are usually happy to tell you which company, and therefore which building, suits your needs. In general, *salas* 1 and 2 serve destinations in Jalisco, Colima and Michoacán, and many of the premium services to Mexico City, Morelia and many towns in the Bajío. *Salas* 3 and 4 have buses to the north and northwest, with services to Puerta Vallarta, the US border and up the Pacific coast, plus points en route. *Sala* 5 is for eastbound services towards San Luis Potosí and Tampico, as well as some more local services. *Sala* 6 serves the Bajío, the northeast and many local second-class buses. *Sala* 7 serves the north and northeast again, as well as Mexico City. **Transport into town** #616 ("Centro") and the slightly dearer (but faster) turquoise TUR bus stop outside each *sala*, while #644B or #275 go from Av Revolución, the main road behind *sala* 1 (which takes a more direct route than #616); all these take you to Av 16 de Septiembre. The last city buses between the terminal and the centre leave at around 10pm. An authorized taxi downtown costs M$200. Going the other way, take #616, #644B, #275, the faster TUR bus, or anything marked "Central Nueva" heading south along 16 de Septiembre. Note that the Central Neuva is connected to the Central Vieja by the #616 city bus.

Destinations Aguascalientes (every 30–60min; 3hr); Colima (approximately every 30min; 3hr); Guanajuato (9 daily; 4hr); Lagos de Moreno (28 daily; 2hr 30min); Manzanillo (38 daily; 5hr); Mazatlán (2–3 hourly; 6hr); Mexico City (every 20–30min, plus numerous overnight; 7hr); Morelia (48 daily; 3–5hr); Pátzcuaro (2 daily; 5hr); Puerto Vallarta (2–3 hourly; 5hr); Querétaro (every 30–60min; 5hr); San Juan de los Lagos (20 daily; 3hr); San Luis Potosí (hourly; 5hr); Tepic (1–2 hourly; 3hr); Tijuana (13 daily; 35hr); Toluca (16 daily; 6hr); Uruapan (25 daily; 4hr).

Central Vieja Second-class services for destinations within about 150km of Guadalajara use the Central Vieja (old bus station) between Los Angeles and 5 de Febrero, an easy walk from the city centre (map p.262). Alternatively, it's about M$35 by cab, M$6 by either #616 bus from 16 de Septiembre, or *macrobús* to Niños Héroes. There are two *salas*, each costing M$0.50 to enter.

Destinations Ajijic (*Sala* A; every 30min; 1hr 15min); Chapala (*Sala* A; every 30min; 1hr); Guadalajara airport (*Sala* A; every 20min, 5am–9pm; 20min); Jocotepec (*Sala* A; hourly; 1hr 15min); Tapalpa (*Sala* B; 13 daily; 3hr); Tequila (*Salas* A & B; every 20min from each; 2hr).

GETTING AROUND

Getting around town is not too difficult once you've got the hang of the transport system, but the best way to get around is usually **on foot** – Guadalajara's streets are even more pleasant if you appreciate them slowly, and most city-centre attractions are within walking distance of each other.

By bus Almost all buses are funnelled through the centre on a few main roads, with destinations on the windscreen. The sheer number of buses and the speed at which they move can make things slightly more difficult, however, especially at peak hours when you may have to fight to get on; if possible, get a local to show you exactly where your bus stops. Most bus rides cost M$6, but the turquoise, a/c TUR express buses cost M$15. For the most useful routes, see box below. Along Calzada Independencia, the *macrobús*, with its own dedicated lanes, and stations with platforms, costs M$6 per journey in exact coins (no change is given). If using the *macrobús* a lot, it may be more convenient to buy a card (M$20) from a machine at any stop, which you can charge up with credit at the same machine, thus saving the need for exact change.

By metro The Tren Ligero (metro system), with one north–south and one east–west line, is designed for local commuters. You may not use it at all, though it can be handy for quick east–west travel across the centre. To ride,

pay M$6 in exact coins into a machine on the platform or, as with *macrobús* (see above), buy a chargeable M$20 card from a machine in the station.

By taxi Taxis are reliable if you're in a hurry, and for a group they aren't usually too expensive as long as you establish a price at the outset; many downtown taxi ranks post a list of fixed prices. From the centre to the Plaza del Sol, Central Nueva or Zapopan should cost around M$100; it'll be around M$80 to Tlaquepaque and M$200 to the airport. Fares are generally 25 percent higher between 10pm and 6am.

Car rental Agents can be found at the airport, and there's a slew on Niños Héroes at Manzano (just west of 16 de Septiembre); firms include Budget, Niños Héroes 125 (☎333 613 0027); Europcar, Lázaro Cárdenas 2838 (☎333 122 6979); National, Niños Héroes 961-C (☎333 614 7175); Quick, Niños Héroes 954 (☎333 614 6052); and Alamo, Niños Héroes 982 (☎333 613 5560).

INFORMATION AND TOURS

Tourist office There's an office at Paseo Degollado 105 (daily 9am–5pm), and tourist information booths (opening times vary slightly, but all approximately Mon–Fri 9am–2pm & 3–7pm, Sat & Sun 9am–3pm) at the airport, Plaza de Guadalajara, Plaza de la Liberación, Morelos with Independencia, Plaza Tapatía and Jardín de San Francisco. Finally, there's also a booth at the corner of Juárez and Progresso, by El Parian in Tlaquepaque (Mon–Fri 10am–8pm, Sat & Sun 10am–7pm). Alternatively, you can call the state tourism office on ☎333 668 1600, or toll free from elsewhere in the country on ☎01 800 363 2200. Guadalajara's city council has a very good tourist information website, ⓦ vive.guadalajara.gob.mx.

Listings The best source of listings information is the *Ocio* magazine section that comes with the Friday edition of Guadalajara's main newspaper, *Milenio*. The cooler cafés often have a copy lying around, and tourist information booths sometimes keep one. In English, the weekly

Guadalajara Reporter (ⓦ guadalajarareporter.com) reflects the concerns of the expat community in town and around Laguna de Chapala.

City bus tours Tapatío Tour (☎333 613 0887 or ☎01 800 001 1827) run an hourly hop-on, hop-off bus tour on two central routes, and every 2hr on two outer routes (daily 10am–8pm), with tickets valid on all four routes during one day for M$120. Tickets can be bought on board or at major stops, or from their central stop on the south side of Rotonda de los Jaliscenses Ilustres.

Calandria tours A more leisurely alternative is by *calandria*, an elegant horse-drawn covered carriage. These can be picked up from Plaza Guadalajara (north side), Mercado de San Juan de Dios, or Jardín de San Francisco. Most drivers are knowledgeable (and entertaining) city guides and charge around M$250 (for 1–5 people) for a 35min tour, or M$400 for a longer (1hr) tour.

USEFUL BUS ROUTES IN GUADALAJARA

All of these also run in the opposite direction: the #600 numbers are minibuses.
#62 Calzada Independencia–soccer stadium and bullring–Central Vieja
#176 Centro (Ramón Corona at Degollado)–airport
#275 Tonalá–Central Nueva–Tlaquepaque–Centro (16 Septiembre)–Zapopan
#616 Centro (Jardín de San Francisco)–Central Vieja–Central Nueva
#629 Centro–Morelos (westbound)/Pedro Moreno (eastbound)–Minerva Circle
#702 TUR Tonalá–Central Nueva –Tlaquepaque–Centro (16 de Septiembre)–Zapopan

ACCOMMODATION

With a range of **hotels** to suit all budgets (as well as a couple of **hostels**) right in the *centro histórico*, there is little reason to stay elsewhere in the city. In this area you'll be able to walk to everything in the centre and have easy access to buses for the outlying suburbs. If you're looking for a budget option and the central places are all full, consider some of the **cheap hotels** around the old bus station or in the streets south of the Mercado Libertad. Both areas are noisy and none too appealing, though the hotels we've listed are fine. Most of the more **expensive** business hotels tend to be a long way out to the west of the city, though you're almost certainly better off in the **luxury B&B-style places** downtown or in Tlaquepaque. There's also Av López Mateos, 2km to the west of the centre, which is Guadalajara's **motel** row.

HOTELS AND B&BS
CENTRO HISTÓRICO

Ana-Isabel Javier Mina 164 ☎333 617 7920; map p.258. Simple but clean tiled rooms with TVs and parking nearby. Apart from one room, windows face inward, which can make them rather dark (those on the top floor less so). Go for the quieter rooms at the back if possible. M$400

Chapala José María Mercado 84 ☎333 617 7159; map p.258. Overlooking the market, but entered down a side street, this place doesn't look very inviting at first glance, but the rooms, though small, are neat and equipped with a TV and ceiling fan (though not wi-fi). M$280

Don Quixote Hotel Héroes 91 ☎333 658 1299, ⊛www.hoteldonquijoteplaza.com.mx; map p.258. This small, friendly hotel has a rather dark, colonial-style courtyard, with fish and turtles in its central fountain, but the rooms are fresh and modern, and it has a bit more character than most of the hotels in this price bracket. M$750

Fénix Corona 160 ☎333 614 5714 or ☎01 800 361 1100, ⊛fenixguadalajara.com.mx; map p.258. Large, modern, four-star hotel with impeccable rooms right in the centre. Go for one on the upper floors with views of the cathedral. Promotional rates are usually available. Wheelchair-accessible. Breakfast included. M$833

Francés Maestranza 35 (just off the plaza behind the cathedral) ☎333 613 1190, ⊛hotelfrances.com; map p.258. Guadalajara's most appealing upmarket hotel, in a beautiful colonial building, founded as an inn in 1610 (its elevator is said to be the second ever installed in the city). The rooms are a little drab, though, and you might want to upgrade to a suite, which doesn't cost much more. Even if you're not staying, it's worth dropping in for a superbly mixed margarita in the lobby bar. M$643

Hamilton Madero 381 ☎333 641 6726; map p.258. Clean and friendly, the *Hamilton*'s low rates (a double room here during the week costs about the same as a dorm bed in a hostel) make it a popular spot with backpackers and young Mexican couples. Rooms have private bath and wi-fi, but you pay M$40 more to have a TV. At weekends (Fri & Sat) rooms cost M$50 extra. M$190

Hotel de Mendoza Carranza 16 (at Hidalgo) ☎333 942 5151, ⊛demendoza.com.mx; map p.258. Attractive establishment in a refurbished colonial convent – the great location makes it an ideal base for sightseeing. Rooms come with all amenities (including a safe) and access to the nicest pool in the centre. Breakfast included. M$1178

Maya López Cotilla 39 ☎333 614 5454; map p.258. Verging on the kitsch, with a model of a Maya temple on the reception desk, this place offers vibrant pink decor in the public areas, and lilac and yellow in the rooms, which all have TVs, but don't all have fans. Rooms with fans cost no extra, so you may as well ask for one, and rooms on the top floors are brighter and quieter. The area's a bit noisy, but close to the centre. M$350

Posada Regis Corona 171 ☎333 614 8633, ⊛posadaregis.com; map p.258. Run by the same people as the *Posada San Pablo* (see below), this appealing old building, smack-bang in the centre of town, has high-ceilinged rooms around a peaceful, covered courtyard with great murals. Of the downstairs rooms, only #8, #9 and #10 have outside windows, but they also have small economy rooms on the roof (M$350) that are ideal for one person but acceptable for two. M$550

Posada San Pablo Madero 429 ☎333 614 2811, ✉posadasanpablo@prodigy.net.mx; map p.258. The rooms at this *pension*-style hotel are arranged around a slippery covered courtyard, and they're all immaculately

HACIENDA RETREATS

For a completely different perspective on Jalisco, consider staying at one of the numerous well-preserved **haciendas** within an hour's drive of Guadalajara. They are easy, if somewhat pricey, overnight escapes which offer a change of pace from the bustling city. Haciendas are ideal for those on shorter trips who want quickly and comfortably to experience a bit of the countryside, and learn a little about a different side of *Tapatío* lifestyle. Jalisco's state tourist office (☎333 668 1600 or ☎01 800 363 2200, ⊛visita.jalisco.gob.mx) can provide information on these and other rural homes and relaxing retreats. You can also go directly to ⊛haciendasycasonas.com, which has links to more than twenty such places.

kept. While the downstairs rooms mostly lack outside windows, most of those upstairs have balconies, so it's worth asking for one of the latter. Ring the bell at the front door for entrance. M$395

Santiago de Compostela Colón 272 ☎333 613 8880, ⊛www.hotelsantiagodecompostelagdl.com; map p.258. Attractive hotel set around an enclosed courtyard decorated with Turkish rugs. Rooms are well appointed with a/c, carpets and cable TV, though the streetside ones can be noisy. All have a deep tiled bath, but you may just prefer to use the lovely rooftop pool. M$825

AROUND THE CENTRAL VIEJA

Canada Estadio 77 ☎333 619 4014; map p.262. One of dozens of hotels surrounding the old bus station, this large place is pretty good value with the bonus of a restaurant and a range of rooms and "suites" (really just larger rooms), of different sizes and with different amenities. Don't confuse this place with the *Gran Hotel Canada* nearby. M$210

León Independencia 557 Sur ☎333 619 6141; map p.258. This place is very cheap and basic, but perfectly serviceable if you don't mind just the bare-bones essentials. Rooms have bathrooms and (just about tepid) "hot" water, with towels and soap provided, but no TV or wi-fi. Even so, it's still a budgeteers' bargain. M$120

WEST OF THE CENTRE

Consulado López Cotilla 1405 ☎333 563 6465, ⊜hotelconsulado@hotmail.com; map p.262. With its chic modern entrance and minimal leather sofas this place is unlike almost everywhere else in town, though the comfortable rooms don't quite follow the style. There's wi-fi in the lobby, off-street parking and several restaurants nearby. M$750

Quinta Real México 2727 ☎333 669 0600, ⊛quintareal.com; map p.262. Gorgeous luxury hotel that's also well set up for business guests. The grounds are spacious and immaculately tended, with a pool, and the suites (there are no plain rooms) come with neocolonial styling and every amenity. M$5117.70

Villa Ganz López Cotilla 1739 ☎333 120 1416, ⊛mexicoboutiquehotels.com/villaganz; map p.262. A gorgeous boutique hotel with nine impeccably decorated suites and most luxuries on hand; no pool but free use of a nearby gym. Common areas are so delightful you'll never want to step outside, though it is only a short walk to some great bars and restaurants. Promotional rates are often available. US$200 (M$3300)

TLAQUEPAQUE AND CENTRAL NUEVA

Casa Campos Miranda 30-A ☎333 838 5297, ⊛casacampos.mx; map p.264. One of the most charming places in town to lay your head, this beautifully remodelled colonial house comes with modern fittings, an understated elegance and a family of palm-size marmoset monkeys that have free range in the garden. Downstairs rooms have ceiling fans, upstairs rooms have a/c. Reserve well ahead, especially in winter. Breakfast included. M$850

★**La Casa del Retoño** Matamoros 182 ☎333 635 7636, ⊛lacasadelretono.com.mx; map p.264. Neatly set away from the commercial bustle of Tlaquepaque, this lovely little B&B has eight beautiful, artesanía-decorated rooms, a sunny terrace so full of plants it's almost a bit of jungle, and a garden where you can eat breakfast or just hang out. Breakfast included. M$850

Donde el Indio Duerme Independencia 74 ☎333 535 2189; map p.264. More basic than everything else hereabouts; simple, clean rooms at good prices. You have a choice of slightly older, cheaper rooms, or newer rooms with TV. M$250

La Villa del Ensueño Florida 305 ☎333 635 8792, ⊛villadelensueno.com; map p.264. This "Villa of Dreams" is a delightful boutique hotel with spacious rooms all tastefully decorated and with lovely tiled bathrooms. A pool and quiet little spaces to hang out in make it a great place to come back to between shopping forays. Breakfast included. M$1600

Vista Junior Revolución, beside Sala 1 ☎333 600 0910, ⊜veritas-st@vistajunior.com.mx; map p.264. Conveniently located by the Central Nueva, this hotel is modern and soulless, and not the cleanest place in town, but has two pools, a restaurant and 24hr room service, and the rooms are reasonably quiet. M$550

HOSTELS

★**Hospedarte** (**Hostel Guadalajara**) Maestranza 147 ☎333 562 7520, ⊛hospedartehostels.com; map p.258. Very central and modern hostel housed in an old building and still popularly known by its previous incarnation as *Hostel Guadalajara*. This place is full of backpackers and language students, with internet access, laundry and cooking facilities, free bicycle rental, private lockers and friendly staff who regularly organize nights out to interesting bars. A light breakfast is included and various packages including multi-day stays and tours are available. There's a discount available for card-carrying Hostelling International members. Dorms M$190, doubles M$500

EATING

Tapatíos take their food seriously. Guadalajara boasts hundreds of **places to eat**, ranging from elegant restaurants to unpretentious cafés, and from *loncherías* (cafés with an emphasis on short orders) to *neverías* (with ice cream and fresh-fruit drinks). Don't pass up the **street vendors** either – their fresh tacos and bags of spiced fruit are delicious and make a cheap, healthy snack. For basic meals, the mezzanine of the **Mercado Libertad** has seemingly hundreds of little stands, each displaying their own specialities. There's a more limited, if handier, selection at the **Mercado Corona**. In the centre, your best choice is west of the cathedral, where traditional cafés and restaurants line **Juárez**. The town's signature dish is the torta ahogada (drowned sandwich) – a pork roll with *pozole* broth poured all over it. Eaten with a spoon, accompanied by chopped onions and lime juice, it's absolutely delicious when done well.

CAFÉS
CENTRO HISTÓRICO AND AROUND

Café Madoka Gonzalez Martínez 78 ☏ 333 613 0649; map p.258. Big, traditional café, operating since 1959 and serving tasty breakfasts (especially the *chilaquiles al pollo*; M$66 with juice and coffee), soups and *antojitos* (*enchiladas suizas* M$69). You can also just play dominoes and sip a coffee; try the "Café Madoka Especial", served with a dollop of vanilla ice cream (M$35). Daily 7am–10pm.

Café Madrid Juárez 264 near Corona ☏ 333 614 9504; map p.258. A smallish 1950s-style diner and coffee bar, good for moderately priced breakfasts, comidas corridas (M$59), sandwiches and snacks such as chicken or beef *fajitas* (M$85). Daily 7.30am–10.30pm.

Chai Juárez 200, at Maestranza ☏ 333 613 0001; map p.258. A bright, trendy café serving, as its name suggests, Indian-style tea (M$22–29), as well as coffees, snacks, panini (M$36), deli-style sandwiches and even pizzas, not to mention weekend buffet brunches (9am–2pm; M$78). It's also a popular spot for an evening beer for the city's trendy crowd. Mon–Thurs & Sun 8am–midnight, Fri & Sat 8am–1am.

El Despertador Reforma 319 ☏ 333 350 2220; map p.258. For those who care about their coffee, this is the best in town: espresso, Americano or permutations thereof, served at the counter or in the small adjoining salon, decorated with an eclectic mix of pictures. They also do teas and infusions, a lunch-time dish of the day (M$53) and breakfast options such as *chilaquiles*, but it's the coffee that makes this place live up to its name (which translates as "the waker-upper"). There's also free wi-fi. Mon–Sat 9am–6pm.

TLAQUEPAQUE

Café San Pedro Juárez 81 ☏ 333 639 0616; map p.264. Tlaquepaque's best coffee, though a bit pricey (espresso M$19, Americano M$23), with seating under the *portales* and a great range of teas and cakes. Their speciality is frappuccino (M$29). Daily 8.30am–11pm.

CHEAP EATS AND SNACKS
CENTRO HISTÓRICO AND AROUND

Alta Fibra Sanchez 370, between Ocampo and Galeana ☏ 333 124 1510; map p.258. Very popular with *Tapatío* (Guadalajara native) families, *Alta Fibra* specializes in high-fibre foods; the menu isn't vegetarian, but it's low fat, with lots of salads. Excellent-value comidas corridas are M$42 for three courses or M$52 for four, and there's a wholemeal bakery next door. Mon–Sat 8am–6pm.

Chan Los Ángeles 131 ☏ 333 619 9446; map p.262. A handy cheap diner by the Central Vieja, offering fish and meat dishes, and reasonable M$45 comidas corridas (noon–6pm). They also offer breakfasts for the same price (7am–noon), but the coffee is instant only. Mon–Sat 7am–11pm.

Pastelería Luvier Colón 183 ☏ 333 613 0734; map p.258. One of the best of many *panaderías* and *pastelerías* in the centre, with lots of sweet breads, cakes, pastries and tarts, but not too much in the savoury department bar plain bread rolls. Mon–Sat 7am–9.15pm, Sun 8am–8.30pm.

El Tacazo Juárez 246 ☏ 333 614 7974; map p.258. A little hole-in-the-wall place serving fast, flavourful tacos, popular and cheap. Choices include *tacos al pastor* (with pork in *chimole* sauce; M$9), or, for the more adventurous, tacos with *lengua de res* (ox tongue; M$12) or *cabeza de res* (ox head; M$9). Daily 8am–1am.

Taquería Los Faroles Ramón Corona 250 ☏ 333 609 8165; map p.258. This popular taco and torta joint serves a wide range of tacos, and is a decent place to have your first taste of torta ahogada (plus 2 tacos dorados for M$30), washed down with *horchata*. Daily 8am–midnight.

Villa Madrid López Cotilla 551 at Gonzalez Martínez ☏ 331 592 5703; map p.258. A snack bar and *licuadería*, offering great *licuados* (M$20–30), juices and fruit salads, as well as sandwiches and burgers, and dishes such as chicken *mixiote* (M$80). There's also live music in the afternoons (3–6pm). Daily noon–8pm.

RESTAURANTS
CENTRO HISTÓRICO AND AROUND

Birriería Las Nueve Esquinas Colón 384 ☏ 333 613 6260; map p.258. Peacefully set on a quiet plaza, this little restaurant serves up traditional Mexican mutton dishes and does excellent *birria de chivo* (goat stew; M$74 for a small helping, or M$97 for a big one). Mon–Sat 8am–11pm, Sun 8am–9pm.

La Chata Corona 126 ☏ 333 613 1315; map p.258. Excellent medium-priced Mexican dishes, including

---

> ## TOP 5 GUADALAJARA EATING PLACES
>
> Birriería las Nueve Esquinas p.270
> La Fonda de San Miguel p.271
> Ahogadas Beto's p.271
> Pierrot p.271
> La Trattoria p.271

GASTRONOMÍA JALISCIENSE: TAPATÍO SPECIALITIES

While in Guadalajara, you shouldn't miss out on some of Jalisco's culinary specialities. The most celebrated is **birria**, stewed beef or mutton in a spicy, but not particularly hot, sauce, and served with tortillas or in tacos from street stalls, bars and in markets. **Roast goat** is another favourite, often seen in the markets along with a goat's skull (just in case you don't know what *chivo* means). **Pozole**, a stew of pork and hominy (ground maize), is also popular, and typically found as a restaurant special on Thursdays. Rarely seen much beyond the city limits, there's also **torta ahogada** (literally "drowned sandwich"), a bread roll stuffed with a filling of your choice (traditionally pork) then drenched with a thin, spicy salsa that soaks right through the bread. It's a bit messy, but extremely delicious. And then, of course, there's **tequila**, discussed more fully on p.279.

chicken *mole* (M$80) and *platillo jalisciense* (chicken with side snacks; M$80). Hugely popular with local families since 1942, so expect to queue, especially at mealtimes. Extensive breakfasts go for M$79–84. Daily 7.30am–midnight.

Chong Wah Juárez 558 ☎333 613 9950; map p.258. Moderately priced Cantonese food to eat in or take away. Though there are now a fair few Chinese restaurants around town, this remains the best, and their buffet lunch (M$65) is also one of the best. There's another branch literally just round the corner at Gonzalez Martínez 77. Daily 10am–9pm.

★**La Fonda de San Miguel Arcangel** Donata Guerra 25 ☎333 613 0809; map p.258. A delightful restaurant in the courtyard of a former convent in the *centro histórico*. The tinkling fountain and caged birds are replaced at night by a constellation of pinprick lampshades creatively imitating the night sky. Specialities include *chamorro* (leg of young pig) in tomato, chile and *chipotle* sauce (M$137), or *filete de res oro y negro* (black and gold steak) cooked in huitlacoche (M$164). Daily 8.30am–midnight.

La Gorda Corona 181 ☎333 827 5845; map p.258. A Guadalajara insutitution, "The Fat Girl" serves up exactly what made its patron so rotund: large helpings of classic Mexican *antojitos* such as enchiladas (M$69) and *sopa azteca* (M$45) at relatively cheap prices. There are various locations around town but this is the original. It's very popular with the locals, so be prepared to queue. Mon–Sat 8am–midnight, Sun 8am–11pm.

La Rinconada Morelos 86, at Callejón del Diable, Plaza Tapatía ☎333 613 9914; map p.258. In a glorious colonial setting, this moderately expensive restaurant serves seafood dishes (salmon with fine herbs or *pimiento verde* for M$130), US-style steaks (rib-eye M$230) and Mexican specialities. Their lunch buffet (M$80) is good value. Mon–Sat 9am–8pm.

WEST OF THE CENTRE

★**Ahogadas Beto's** Buzeta 757 ☎333 342 0529; map p.262. Guadalajara's best torta ahogada by popular

consent, this neighbourhood joint serves up their delicious drowned sandwiches from both the to-go stand out front and their simple restaurant inside. This hidden gem is a bit of a mission to get to (a taxi from the centre will charge M$50) but well worth the effort for the original scoff. Daily 8am–4.30pm.

La China Poblana Juárez 887 ☎338 825 6632; map p.262. This little place opens only very briefly in the afternoon for traditional Puebla dishes at reasonable prices, including favourites such as chicken *mole* (M$110) and *chiles en nogada* (M$130). Daily 2–6pm.

Goa López Cotilla 1520 ☎333 615 6173; map p.262. Guadalajara's only Indian restaurant, intimately lit and with Bollywood on the screen. Serves a range of excellent dishes, several straight out of the tandoor. Dishes include tamarind chicken (M$95) and fish vindaloo (M$130). You can also order a hookah pipe with fruit-flavoured tobacco (M$130). Mon 4–11pm, Tues–Sat 1pm–midnight, Sun 1–8pm.

Los Itacates Chapultepec Nte 110, at Sierra ☎333 825 1106; map p.262. Traditional Mexican food including their own *pollo itacate* (chicken in an *adobe* sauce with rice and potatoes; M$71), a wide range of tacos at M$15 apiece and a breakfast buffet for M$88. Mon–Sat 8am–11pm, Sun 8am–7pm.

Pierrot Justo Sierra 2355 ☎333 630 2087; map p.262. The city's finest French restaurant, in gracious surroundings and with attentive but never intrusive service. The filet mignon in mushroom sauce (M$195) and the chocolate mousse (M$75) are both spectacular. Mon–Sat 1.30pm–1am.

La Trattoria Niños Héroes 3051 ☎333 122 1817; map p.262. This spacious and lively Italian restaurant is one of Guadalajara's best. *Segundi piatti* include *saltimbocca* (M$141) and devilled prawns (M$141). Evening reservations recommended. Mon–Sat 1pm–midnight, Sun 1–9pm.

TLAQUEPAQUE

Casa Fuerte Independencia 224 ☎333 639 6481 or ☎01 800 024 6474, ⊛casafuerte.com; map p.264.

Pleasant courtyard restaurant in a majestic mansion. Enjoy the live accompaniment, often mariachi, while you sample the likes of tamarind shrimp or salmon in orange and paprika sauce. Daily 12.30–7.30pm.

★**Mariscos el Social** Calzada Delicias 117 (1km south to the end of Herrera y Cairo, then 400m east) ☎ 333 635 6876; map p.256. Locally – and deservedly – renowned seafood diner, where a big cup of juicy king prawns and octopus (M$94) is helped down by zingy, fresh, raw *habanero* salsa and ice-cold beer – or excellent tequilas accompanied by their own *sangrita*. They also do wonderful grilled snapper, *ceviche* and seafood soup with a whole crab and a pair of nutcrackers (M$99). Mon–Sat 10am–6pm.

DRINKING AND NIGHTLIFE

Traditionally the centre of town hasn't been that lively, but things are picking up, particularly southwest of the cathedral (along López Cotilla, Madero and Sanchez) and in the **Nueve Esquinas** quarter, three blocks further south, where Colon and Galeana meet. The best of the town's nightlife is concentrated along Av Chapultepec, a north–south thoroughfare 2km west of the centre, where the social street offers everything from chilled-out bars to electro clubs. Take time to stroll through the pedestrianized walkway in the middle where street performers and dancercise go until the early hours. **López Mateos** has a number of trendy pubs with live music and a younger crowd. Some have open bars on certain nights of the week with a cover charge of around M$100 for men, M$50 or less for women.

BARS

The Black Sheep Libertad 1872 ☎ 333 825 7000; map p.262. Lively multi-storey bar in what looks like a haunted mansion, but is actually a former brothel (and actually the club-like extension of the original business three doors down the road, under the same management, but which caters to a rockier crowd). Offers strong and cheap cocktails as well as a range of imported beers. Daily noon–1am.

El Callejón de los Rumberos Chapultepec Sur 287, at Lerdó de Tejeda ☎ 333 827 1262; map p.262. Cuban-style dance bar featuring salsa and other Latin sounds. They even have dance classes, but shorts and T-shirts are banned (though the bar features plenty of photos of visiting musicians wearing the latter). Mon–Sat 6.30pm–1am, Sun noon–1am.

Casa Bariachi Vallarta 2221 ☎ 333 616 9900; map p.262. Loud and colourful restaurant-bar decorated with giant *piñatas*, where the entertainment includes 2hr cabaret sessions featuring traditional dance and mariachi bands at 3.30pm and 9.30pm. Daily 1pm–3am.

La Condesa Colón 349, at Libertad; map p.258. A lively cantina, where there's music and dancing from 6pm nightly. The dancefloor isn't huge, but it's just the right size to keep this a cantina with dancing rather than a dance club with a bar. Daily noon–3am.

★**La Fuente** Pino Suarez 78; map p.258. A bare bones piano bar and cantina that looks like it's been around longer than Guadalajara itself. It's nevertheless the most authentic watering hole you'll find in the city, with cheap beers (M$23) and a lively atmosphere. Look out for the old bicycle above the bar. It was left by a client in the 50s who drank his weight in beer before announcing he had no money to pay his bill. He left his bike in lieu of payment, promising to return the following day with the money. He never came back, and his legacy has become the bar's symbol, as well as the fact that clients have to pay for each round immediately. Mon–Sat noon–midnight.

Green Light Eco-Bar Madero 494, at González Martínez ☎ 333 613 3276; map p.258. It isn't clear what exactly is ecological about this trendy bar-café, but the alfresco roof terrace, shaded with parasols, is a top place to relax with a beer, a coffee or a snack of an afternoon or evening. It's something of a gay hangout, but certainly not exclusively so. The downstairs area is a music video bar. Mon, Tues & Sun 4pm–1am, Wed–Sat 4pm–3am.

Hotel Francés Maestranza 35 ☎ 333 613 1190; map p.258. Piano-bar-style establishment in the courtyard of one of the centre's grander hotels. Come in the early evening (before 8pm) for 2x1 happy-hour drinks (margarita M$65). On Fri from 7.20pm there are mariachis, folk dancers and a *charreo* lassooist. Daily noon–10pm.

La Moresca López Cotilla 1835, at De Cervantes Savedra ☎ 333 616 8277; map p.262. An elegant restaurant downstairs, with an upmarket wine bar upstairs that makes a good spot for a bottle of house red (or white) and a bruschetta. Mon–Thurs 6pm–12.30am, Fri & Sat 6pm–1.30am.

LIVE MUSIC VENUE

La Mutualista Madero 553 ☎ 333 614 2176; map p.258. On Thurs, Fri and Sat nights from 8pm this cavernous venue (ordinarily just a large and friendly cantina) gets taken over by a band (usually Cuban, sometimes rock) and everyone hits the dancefloor. Ceiling fans and wide-open windows give a suitably Cuban dancehall feel. Mon–Wed 2pm–1am, Thurs–Sat 2pm–3am or later.

GUADALAJARA FIESTAS

Several entertaining **fiestas** take place throughout the year, including the highly animated Día de San Pedro in Tlaquepaque (June 29), with mariachi, dancing and processions; and the Día de la Virgen de Zapopan (Oct 12), an all-night fiesta capped with a massive early morning procession that starts before dawn at the cathedral and finishes in Zapopan. Crowds and assorted food vendors start arriving the evening before, with all sorts of music and the *portales* choked with people bedding down for the 4am start. In the autumn, everything cranks up to fever pitch for the Fiestas de Octubre (w fiestasdeoctubre.com.mx), a month-long celebration when downtown Guadalajara comes alive with all manner of outdoor performances and bands, often free. Daily events include *charreadas* (rodeos), processions and fireworks, as well as all kinds of free entertainment – modern Mexican music performances are put on from noon till 10pm in the fairgrounds of the Benito Juárez auditorium.

ENTERTAINMENT

There's an impressive range of traditional Mexican and classical concerts, contemporary gigs, classic and modern film, theatre and opera performances and art exhibitions in town – you can see some kind of performance most nights of the week. Anyone on a tight budget should check out the **Plaza de Armas**, where there's usually something free happening. One thing no visitor to Guadalajara should miss is hearing mariachi in its home town, specifically at the **Plaza de los Mariachis**. Going to the **cinema** in Guadalajara is not particularly convenient, as suburban multiplexes have killed downtown movies. The big shopping centres such as Centro Magno and Plaza del Sol have the latest blockbusters, and we've also listed a couple of more convenient alternatives.

LIVE MUSIC AND THEATRE

Instituto Cultural Mexicano Norteamericano de Jalisco (ICMNJ) Enrique Díaz de León 300 ☎ 333 825 5838, w institutocultural.com.mx; map p.262. This is a language school, offering lessons in English for locals and Spanish for foreigners, but it also puts on free cultural events, including, from time to time, classical music concerts and recitals.

Plaza de Armas map p.258. There are regular free performances of Jaliscan music in the rotunda just south of the cathedral, often featuring the State Band of Jalisco or Guadalajara's own Municipal Band. Times vary, but roughly Tues, Thurs & Sun 6.30–8.30pm.

Plaza de los Mariachis map p.258. Guadalajara is the home of mariachi, and you shouldn't leave town without experiencing it. It all happens in the Plaza de los Mariachis, a short pedestrianized street by the Mercado Libertad and the church of San Juan de Dios, where mariachi bands stroll between bars, playing to anyone prepared to cough up for a song. Musicians start arriving in the late afternoon, but it's best after dark, when there are usually several bands. Unless they play for you personally – in which case you'll have to negotiate a price before they start, reckon on M$100 per song – you needn't spend anything at all. You'll also find mariachi bands in Tlaquepaque. No fixed hours.

Teatro Degollado Degollado 53 ☎ 333 614 4773; map p.258. This magnificent theatre in central Guadalajara (see p.257) hosts a regular programme of theatre and dance. Pick up details of events from the tourist office or from Ticketmaster (☎ 33 3818 3800, desk in Fabricas de Francia department store at Juárez 272).

Teatro Diana 16 de Septiembre 710 ☎ 333 614 7072, w teatrodiana.com; map p.262. This large, modern theatre puts on everything from serious plays, opera and ballet to classical and folk music concerts and children's matinees, but all the performances are of course in Spanish.

CINEMA

Cineclub Alianza Alianza Francesa, López Cotilla 1199 ☎ 333 825 2140, w guadalajara.af.org.mx; map p.262. Attached to Guadalajara's French cultural institute, this cinema shows French films on Tues at 8.15pm, usually with Spanish subtitles.

Cinépolis Centro Magno Vallarta 2425 ☎ 333 630 3940, w cinepolis.com.mx; map p.262. A large chain multiplex in an upmarket shopping mall, around 3km west of downtown. Movies here are the latest Hollywood offerings, dubbed into Spanish.

Ex-Convento del Carmen Juárez 638 ☎ 333 030 1350; map p.258. This arthouse cinema attached to the former convent shows alternative and classic movies, and holds the occasional film festival. Foreign films are usually shown in their original language with Spanish subtitles. Tickets usually M$25.

GAY GUADALAJARA

Guadalajara has a reputation for being one of Mexico's gayest cities, and while that doesn't mean public displays of affection are widely accepted, there's greater freedom in the dozen or so bars and clubs that advertise their orientation with rainbow flags. Guadalajara's **gay quarter** is centred on the junction of Ocampo and Sanchez, about five blocks southwest of the cathedral. Spanish-speakers can check out what's going on at w gaygdl.com.

La Prisciliana Sanchez 396 ☎ 333 562 0725; map p.258. Dark and chilled-out upstairs gay bar (though non-gays are welcome too) with casual drinking to Latin dance beats. *Club Ye*Ye* downstairs, with minimal grey and black

decor and big video screens, is also very popular with both lesbians and gay men (and heterosexuals). La Prisciliana Mon–Thurs & Sun 5pm–1.30am, Fri & Sat 5pm–3am; Club Ye*Ye Daily 5pm–3am.

SHOPPING AND MARKETS

The giant Mercado Libertad (see p.260) may be the biggest of Guadalajara's markets, but every city *barrio* has its own. They include the very touristy Mercado Corona near the cathedral, and craft markets and upscale boutiques in Tlaquepaque and Tonalá. The flea market El Baratillo (Sun) is vast, sometimes stretching a kilometre or more along Javier Mina, starting a dozen blocks east of the Mercado Libertad. You're better off looking for English-language **books and magazines** in Chapala and Ajijic (see p.279 & p.281), but you will find limited supplies at the places listed below.

BOOKS
Librería Gonvill López Cotilla 501, at Donato Guerra ☎ 333 613 0123, w gonvill.com.mx; map p.258. A good city-centre bookshop, with a wide selection of books in Spanish, as well as a small section of books in English, mostly novels. Mon–Sat 10am–8.30pm.

Sandi Bookstore Tepeyac, 8km west of the centre in Colonia Chapalita 718 ☎ 333 121 0863, w sandibooks .com; map p.262. A store specializing in books in English, including travel guides. Mon–Fri 9.30am–7pm, Sat 9.30am–2pm.

CRAFTS
TLAQUEPAQUE
Agustín Parra Independencia 158 ☎ 333 684 1313, w agustinparra.com.mx; map p.264. Don't miss this fabulous array of Baroque-style furniture, doors and religious icons, some of them enormous. Two popes have visited the shop, as shown in photos above the counter. Tues–Sun 11am–8pm.

Antigua de México Independencia 255 ☎ 333 639 2997, w antiguademexico.com; map p.264. Comprises two lovely colonial houses that sell upmarket fabrics, furniture and antiques to a mainly Mexican clientele. Mon–Fri 10am–2pm & 3–7pm, Sat 10am–6pm.

Arte Indio Juárez 130 ☎ 333 635 6981; map p.264. Considerably cheaper than most of the galleries on Independencia, stocking goods such as crucifixes, mirrors and rustic furniture. Mon–Sat 10am–2.30pm & 4–7pm.

Galeria Sergio Bustamante Independencia 238

☎ 333 639 1272, w sergiobustamante.com.mx; map p.264. The showcase for world-famous painter and sculptor Bustamente's works – the gallery is full of his fantastical figures in papier-mâché, resin and bronze. They are worth looking at even if the price and size are such that you won't be buying. Don't miss the toilet, which has more sculpture in its own enclosed courtyard. Daily 11am–8pm.

TONALÁ
La Casa de Salvador Vásquez Carmona López Cotilla 328 ☎ 333 683 2896; map p.265. You may need to knock on the door to gain access – the place looks like a simple private residence, and gives no indication of being a shop or workshop. However, around the rear patio, Carmona shapes pots and bowls, hand-fires them, then paints the finished article. He'll show you his gallery complete with finished pots that have graced the covers of magazines and design glossies. Daily 8am–10pm.

Galeria José Bernabe Hidalgo 83 ☎ 333 683 0040; map p.265. Close to Tonalá's central plaza, this is the place to come for superb and highly regarded *petatillo*, an intricate ceramic form with painted animals and flowers on a cross-hatched background. Mon–Fri 10am–7pm, Sat 9am–3pm.

Mis Amores Tonaltecas Sur 80 ☎ 333 833 3603; map p.265. A shop full of skeletons – not real ones of course, but it has all sorts of ceramics, papier-mâché and sheet-metal ones, including designs based on the works of Posada (see box, p.362), such as *La Catrina*, his famous skeleton woman with a huge floral hat. Mon–Fri & Sun 10.30am–5pm, Sat 10.30am–5.30pm.

SPECTATOR SPORTS

Bullfighting Bullfights are considered to be a sport for connoisseurs, and the cognoscenti watch the *corrida* at the city's largest bullring, the Plaza de Toros Nuevo Progreso (☎ 333 637 9982, w plazanuevoprogreso.com.mx), almost 4km northeast of the centre along Calzada Independencia. Fights occur several times in Oct, then on irregular Sundays until March (4.30pm; tickets M$150–1550).

Football Guadalajara's biggest team, FC Guadalajara (Las Chivas; w chivasdecorazon.com.mx), play their home matches at the flying-saucer-like Omnilife stadium, on the western edge of town near where Vallarta meets the Pereferico (bus #649 from Juárez with Federación). Matches are usually on Sat night or Sun afternoon. Tickets cost anything from M$120 to M$800, and can usually be bought at the gate, or in advance from Ticketmaster. The enormous Estadio Jalisco, almost opposite the bullring (*macrobús* to Monumental), is home to FC Atlas (ⓦ atlas.com.mx) – the City to Chivas' United. The stadium, formerly used by Chivas too, was a venue for matches at both the 1970 and 1986 World Cups. Tickets here are cheaper, at around M$80–M$400. Second-tier club Tecos (officially, Estudiantes de la

Universidad Autónoma de Guadalajara) have their stadium (Estadio Tres de Marzo) in Zapopan.

Rodeos Jaliscans pride themselves on their equestrian skills, notably in the regular *charreadas* (rodeos) held every Sun (from noon) at the Licenzo Charro de Jalisco, Dr Michel 577, near the Parque Agua Azul. For details call ☎ 333 619 6876 or just turn up; tickets are usually M$80.

DIRECTORY

Banks and exchange There are numerous banks with ATMs throughout the centre, including around Corona and Juárez. Virtually identical rates, faster service and longer hours are available in the *casas de cambio* around the corner of Maestranza and López Cotilla. After hours, bigger hotels will usually change money at a considerably worse rate.

Consulates Canada, World Trade Center (Torre Pacífico, 8th floor), Mariano Otero 1249 (☎ 333 671 4740); Guatemala, Mango 1440, Colonia Jardines de la Victoria (☎ 333 811 1503); South Africa, Mexicaltinzgo 1665 2nd floor, Colonia Moderna (☎ 333 825 7570); US, Progreso 175, Colonía Americana (☎ 333 268 2100).

Emergencies The general emergency number is ☎ 066.

Internet There are several internet cafés in central Guadalajara, with prices generally M$10–20/hr. Places marked on our map are at: Maestranza 175-A (closed Sun), Madero 191, López Cotilla 491, Juárez 642 and 675. Under the city council's GDL Libre scheme, there are 125 free wi-fi hot spots around town, which you'll find mapped at ⓦ vivirguadalajara.com/internet-gratis; they include Plaza de la Liberación, Plaza de Armas, Rotonda de los Jaliscenses, Parque Agua Azul, the Alameda and the Jardín de San Francisco.

Laundry The closest laundry to the centre is at Aldama 129, off Independencia in a slightly rough area a few blocks south of the Mercado Libertad (Mon–Sat 9am–7pm).

Pharmacy Farmacia Guadalajara, with several locations in the centre, including Moreno 160 near Plaza Tapatía and López Cotilla 423 at Galeana (both daily 7am–10pm).

Phones One or two of the internet places (such as the one at Maestranza 175-A) do cheap VOIP calls.

Post office Venustiano Carranza 16 at the junction with Independencia (Mon–Fri 8am–7pm, Sat 8am–3pm).

Spanish courses Guadalajara is a decent place to learn Spanish, with several schools sited close to the historic centre. One of the most popular is IMAC, Donata Guerra 180 at Madero (☎ 333 613 1080, ⓦ spanish-school.com.mx /guadalajara) with a schedule allowing short or long courses as well as classes in ceramics, guitar and flamenco, and homestay opportunities. Others worth considering are Guadalajara University's CEPE, Tomás V. Gómez 125 (☎ 333 616 4399, ⓦ cepe.udg.mx), and the Instituto Cultural Mexicano Norteamericano de Jalisco (ICMNJ), Díaz de León Sur 300 (☎ 333 825 5838, ⓦ institutocultural.com.mx).

Travel agent Mundo Joven Vallarta 2440 (☎ 333 630 9186).

Tequila

The approach to **TEQUILA**, some 50km northwest of Guadalajara, is through great fields of spiky, cactus-like blue agave. It's from these rugged plants that the quintessentially Mexican liquor has been produced since the sixteenth century, with the *indígenas* fermenting its precursor for at least 1500 years before that, a legacy which earned Tequila and its surroundings UNESCO World Heritage status in 2006. The town itself is a pretty enough little place, with its fine church and smattering of bourgeois mansions, but most tourists come to visit the distilleries.

Visiting Tequila is particularly fun during one of its **fiestas**: the town celebrates the **Día de la Santa Cruz** (May 3) with mariachi and plenty of imbibing; and **La Señora de la Salud** (Dec 8) with rodeos, cockfights, fireworks and more drinking. **World Tequila Day** (May 27) is celebrated with parades and drinking, but in Amatitán rather than Tequila itself (arguably, Amatitán was the original centre of "mescal wine" production before the arrival of the railway made Tequila its distribution centre and gave the liquor its modern name).

José Cuervo distillery

José Cuervo 35 (cnr Ramón Corona), north of the main square • Tours Mon–Fri & Sun 10am–5pm, Sat 10am–6pm; tours in English 1pm & 3pm but subject to change so check in advance • Basic tour (45min) M$105; extended tours (90min–4hr) M$155–600 • ☎ 333 134 3379 or ☎ 800 006 8630, ⓦ mundocuervo.com

Of all the distillery tours, the slickest is run by José Cuervo in their La Rojeña factory, parts of which date back to 1758. The basic tour makes a quick turn through the factory, where you can taste the raw distillate, then continues to the barrel storage area, where you can try a little of the finished product. Extended tours take in all this, give you a chance to sit down and learn how to appreciate the qualities of the various tequilas and include a margarita and a visit to the old storage cellars – it's worth the few extra pesos. At the weekend there are even more extended "VIP" tours.

Sauza distillery

Sauza Mora 80 • Tours (usually bilingual) Mon–Fri 11am, 12.30pm, 3pm & 4pm, Sat 11am & 12.30pm • M$140 (students M$70) • ☎ 333 742 4140 or ☎ 01 800 728 9287, from the US ☎ 1 866 510 2250, ✉ tourstequilasauza@beamglobal.com

Cuervo's rival proprietary firm, Sauza, offer hour-long tours at their **La Perseverancia** distillery which are a little less stage-managed than Mundo Cuervo but still informative. Their distillery is a little less central than Cuervo's, but still easy to find: to get there from the Plaza de Armas, head south for five blocks along Ramón Corona. Sauza also offer expanded tours which include their out-of-town hacienda, but you need to arrange your own transport for this.

Museo Nacional del Tequila

Ramón Corona 34 • Daily 9am–4pm • M$15

The small but proud **Museo Nacional del Tequila** is where you can learn about the history of the popular drink and its crucial role in the town's development. The museum has a fine collection of tequila bottles (both ornate and primitive), old distillery paraphernalia and agave art.

Herradura distillery

Hacienda San José del Refugio, Amatitán, 15km southeast of Tequila on the main road from Guadalajara • 90min tours Mon–Fri 9am–5pm hourly, Sat 9am, 10am, 2pm & 3pm, Sun 10am, 2pm & 3pm; tours in English by advance arrangement • M$100 (or M$150–200 with special tasting) • ☎ 01 800 710 9868, ⊕ herradura.com

For connoisseurs, the serene **Herradura distillery**, in the small town of **Amatitán**, deserves a stop. Buses between Guadalajara and Tequila will set down and pick up on the road 300m from the hacienda. Tour groups here tend to be smaller than at the proprietary distilleries in town (you may even be alone), and you get to see a distillery which uses strictly traditional methods – all of Herradura's tequilas are one hundred percent agave, and their product is considered to be among the best (the real ale of tequilas, if you like).

ARRIVAL AND INFORMATION TEQUILA

By bus Regular buses run from Guadalajara's Central Vieja (see p.266), and can also be picked up outside the Periférico Sur station, the southern terminus of Guadalajara's Tren Ligero line 1. The bus terminal in Tequila is at the eastern end of Sixto Gorjón, along which it's a 1km walk to the Plaza de Armas in the centre of town. Autotransportes Quick buses (from *Sala* B in Guadalajara's Central Vieja) go into the terminal; TequilaBus buses (from *Sala* A) stop just outside it.

Tourist office In the Presidencia Municipal, José Cuervo 25 on the Plaza de Armas (zócalo) in the centre of town (daily 9am–3.30pm; ☎ 374 742 0012).

ACCOMMODATION AND EATING

La Fonda Cholula Ramón Corona 55, southwest corner of Plaza de Armas ☎ 374 742 1079. A bright, colourful place to eat right opposite Mundo Cuervo, and indeed run by José Cuervo. They have nice shady rooftop seating and serve respectable *chiles en nogada* for M$110. Mon–Fri noon–8pm, Sat & Sun 8am–10pm.

Hostal Viajero Luís Navarro 33 ☎ 374 742 2502, ✉ hostelviajero@gmail.com. A small but bright youth hostel with a couple of dorms and three private rooms, a communal area and of course things like wi-fi and waste recycling. All in all, a friendly and fun place to stay. Breakfast included. Dorms M$120; doubles M$350

Hotel Plaza Jardín José Cuervo 13 (Plaza de Armas, south side) ☎ 374 742 0061, ✇ hotelplazajardin.com. Right on the main square, this lovely old hotel has a/c rooms, a nice rooftop terrace and its own restaurant and bar. Some of the inside rooms can be a little bit gloomy, however, and only some of the double rooms have views over the plaza. M$550

Hotel Posada del Agave Sixto Gorjón 83 ☎ 374 742

THE TEQUILA EXPRESS AND OTHER TOURS

One of the best ways to experience the Tequila region is to travel there from Guadalajara by train. This is one of only three train rides left in Mexico (the others being the longer Copper Canyon run – see p.501 – and a suburban line in Mexico City – see p.120). You have to travel as part of a tour package and it's obviously touristy, but it gives you a chance to learn something of the process and see how the agave is harvested, and includes a meal and samples.

There are two tours: the **Tequila Express** (✇ tequilaexpress.com.mx) doesn't actually take you to the town of Tequila but travels at a stately pace through blue agave fields and stops at Amatitán, home of Herradura's Hacienda San José del Refugio (see p.277), a tour of which is included. It runs at weekends and holidays. Tickets should be bought in Guadalajara a few days in advance from the Chamber of Commerce cashier department, Vallarta 4095 at Niño Obrero (☎ 333 880 9099), from their downtown office at Morelos 395 (☎ 333 614 3145) or through Ticketmaster (☎ 333 880 9099; booking fee charged).

Alternatively, José Cuervo run their own José Cuervo Express during the day at weekends, or on Friday nights. This takes you to Tequila itself, with a tour of the Cuervo distillery (see p.276), and can also be booked in Guadalajara at Vallarta 5005 (☎ 333 621 0293, ✇ josecuervoexpress .com). Most tours can be arranged by your hotel.

SMALLER DISTILLERY TOURS

Aside from the Tequila distilleries (see p.276), **tours** are also available to smaller, less well-known operations, at prices varying between M$100 and M$200, depending on what's included and how far afield. These trips can be a bit hit-or-miss, but when they're good, they can be wonderful experiences with far fewer people and a more personal touch. In Tequila itself, Jimador Tour at Albino Rojas 2, on the Plaza de Armas, offer a variety of tours. You can also go on an organized tour from Guadalajara such as the Tequila Grand Tour, bookable at their office on Morelos 231-A (☎ 333 658 2255, ✇ teqilagrandtour.mx; M$500, but sometimes with a discount if booked via tourist information booths). The tour leaves the city daily at 9.15am from Plaza de la Liberación and visits three haciendas: Cuervo, Tres Mujeres and La Cofradia.

MAKING TEQUILA

Visitors to Tequila are often surprised to hear that the town's eponymous spirit is more complex than its reputation lets on. As with alcoholic beverages considered more sophisticated, like champagne, **tequila** is subject to strictly enforced appellation rules: true tequila must be made from at least 51 percent **Weber blue agave** grown in the *Zona Protegida por la Denominación de Origen* – essentially all of Jalisco plus parts of Nayarit, Michoacán, Guanajuato and Tamaulipas. The balance can be made up with alcohol from sugar or corn, but a good tequila will be one hundred percent agave, which gives more intense and flamboyant flavours, and will be stated on the label.

The agave takes seven to ten years to reach an economically harvestable size. The plant is then killed and the spiky leaves cut off, leaving the heart, known as the **piña** for its resemblance to an oversized pineapple. On distillery tours you can see the hearts as they're unloaded from trucks and shoved into ovens, where they're baked for a day or so. On emerging from the ovens, the warm and slightly caramelized *piñas* are crushed and the sweet juice fermented, then distilled.

Tequila isn't a drink that takes well to extended **ageing**, but some time in a barrel definitely benefits the flavour and smoothness. The simplest style of tequila, known as *blanco* or *plata* (white or silver), is clear, and sits just fifteen days in stainless-steel tanks. The *reposado* (rested) spends at least two months in toasted, new white-oak barrels. The degree to which the barrels are **toasted** greatly affects the resulting flavours; a light toast gives spicy notes; a medium toast brings out vanilla and honey flavours; and a deep charring gives chocolate, smoke and roast almond overtones. If left for over a year the tequila becomes *añejo* (old), and typically takes on a darker colour. A fourth style, *joven* (young), is a mix of *blanco* with either *reposado* or *añejo*. While the nuances of tequila are slowly being explored by a select few, the benefits of oak ageing aren't appreciated by all – many still prefer the supple vegetative freshness of a good *blanco*.

0774, ✉ hotelposadadelagave@hotmail.com. Vibrant orange and lime-green decor make this quite a jolly place, though interior windows mean some of the rooms are a bit dark. All are equipped with ceiling fans and TV. <u>**M$410**</u>

Laguna de Chapala

At around 35km wide and 120km long, **Laguna de Chapala**, just over 50km south of Guadalajara, is the largest lake in Mexico. Its northern shore has long been a favourite retreat for *Tapatíos*, especially since the early years of the twentieth century when dictator Porfirio Díaz regularly spent his holidays here. Expats from north of the border, particularly Canadians, have also been appreciative of the lake scenery and even year-round temperatures. It is said that there are now around thirty thousand such people living in and around Guadalajara, a sizeable proportion of whom have settled on the lakeside – particularly in **Chapala** and in the smaller village of **Ajijic**. The same firm who run the Tequila Grand Tour (see box, p.278) also operate a day trip to Chapala and Ajijic from Guadalajara (M$350). **Peak season** is November to April, which coincides with the arrival of seasonal snowbirds.

Chapala

CHAPALA, on the northern shore of the lake, is a sleepy community with a quiet charm and relaxed pace, but it becomes positively festive on sunny weekends, when thousands come to eat, swim or take a boat ride out to one of the lake's islands. Shoreline restaurants all offer the local speciality, *pescado blanco*, famous despite its almost total lack of flavour and lake-bottom origins. Head to the left along the promenade, past streets of shuttered nineteenth-century villas, and you'll find a small **crafts market**. There's even a flat *ciclopista* (cycle path) running along the lakeside between Chapala

LAGUNA DE CHAPALA ENVIRONMENTAL PROBLEMS

The Laguna de Chapala averages only 8m deep, and during the 1980s and 1990s the **water level** dropped when the government used its feeder rivers as a freshwater supply for Guadalajara and Mexico City; the lake receded so far that shoreline property was 2km from the water's edge. Levels have now improved thanks to heavier rainfall and the work of the twenty thousand-strong group Amigos del Lago de Chapala (Ⓦamigosdelago.org), but agricultural runoff has raised **nitrate pollution** to unsustainable levels and encouraged the growth of choking water hyacinth. The *charales*, the fish for which the lake was once famed, are virtually gone.

and Ajijic for easy cycling and walking, with nice views of the lake; on a hot day it beats taking the bus.

If you're in the mood for a longer walk, you might consider heading up to the cross on the top of the hill overlooking the town: there's a path starting on López Cotilla between no. 316 and no. 318, across the street from *Hotel Candilejas* (see below).

ARRIVAL AND DEPARTURE
CHAPALA

By bus The bus station is on Madero at Miguel Martínez. Turn left at the exit and from here, the main street, Madero, stretches six blocks down to the lakeside, where Ramón Corona leads off to the left. The main square is halfway down Madero, where López Cotillo crosses it (take a left here to reach Juárez and then Zaragoza, both parallel with Madero). Hidalgo, the road to Ajijic, branches off Madero to the right just beyond the main square. Coming from

Guadalajara's Central Vieja (*Sala* A), it's best to take a *directo* service (every 30–45min, 6am–9pm; 45min) rather than the second-class bus (every 20min; 1hr 30min), which stops at every little village along the way. The last *directo* bus back to Guadalajara leaves Chapala at 7.30pm. Buses to Ajijic (15min) and San Juan Cosalá (25min) leave from the bus station every 20min, and can also be picked up along Hidalgo, as can slower local buses to the same destinations.

INFORMATION

Banks and exchange A gaggle of banks with ATMs gathers around the junction of Madero and Hidalgo, and there's a money changer at Madero 423-A.
Internet Encarnacion Rosas 8-B, just off the main square.
Laundry On the corner of López Cotilla.

Post office Hidalgo (200m down from Madero, on the left).
Telephones Caseta telefónica at Encarnacion Rosas 10, just off the main square.

ACCOMMODATION

Hotel Candilejas López Cotilla 363 (just up the hill from Madero opposite the main square) ☎376 765 2279. A simple little hotel with tiled floors and arched brick ceilings, where guests are treated like members of the family. M$450
Hotel Montecarlo Hidalgo 296 (1km west of Madero) ☎376 765 2120, Ⓦhoteles.udg.mx. A modern resort hotel by the lakeside (though fenced off from it), which offers tennis courts, a pool, lake views and airy rooms amid

grounds with grass and trees. M$1149
★**Quinta Quetzalcoatl** Zaragoza 307 ☎376 765 3653, Ⓦaccommodationslakechapala.com. The nicest option in town, where D.H. Lawrence wrote *The Plumed Serpent*. There's a wide assortment of gorgeous rooms, each with its own private terrace, set in a lovely garden with a small pool; children are not allowed, and in winter particularly, you should book well ahead. M$800

EATING

Café Paris Madero 421 ☎376 765 5353. A central café with outside tables, very popular among American expats and locals alike for good breakfasts and reasonably priced *comidas*, as well as great booths for people-watching. Daily 8am–10.30pm.
Cazadores Ramon Corona 8, at the lakeside end of Madero ☎376 765 2162. *Cazadores* has been serving hearty surf-and-turf dinners amid the faded elegance of a

grand mansion since 1956. A *filete Malinche* (steak with onion and *chile poblano* sauce) will set you back M$128, a fish fillet with trimmings M$105. Tues–Sun 1–8pm.
Chapala's Fonda Paseo de los Ausentes 621, under the portales of the main square. A good old no-nonsense Mexican diner dishing out big portions of tasty *chilaquiles* (M$30 with beans, M$50 with chicken), breakfasts, soups and *antojitos* (tacos M$36 for four). Daily 8am–6pm.

Ajijic

With its narrow cobbled streets, **AJIJIC**, 7km west of Chapala, is smaller, quieter and more self-consciously arty. It may be a wonderful place to paint or retire, with a thriving expat social and cultural life, but as a visitor you're likely to exhaust its charms in a couple of hours – long enough to wander by the lake, visit the art galleries, have a meal and perhaps check out the **Casa de Cultura**, on the north side of the plaza, which hosts musical performances and art exhibitions. The large expat community also means there are apartments and houses to rent for longer stays; check out the notice boards in shops and galleries.

ARRIVAL AND DEPARTURE
AJIJIC

By bus Slow local buses from Chapala (every 30min) will drop you in the centre, whereas larger buses (every 20min) will leave you on the Carretera Chapala, from where Colón runs six blocks southward to the lake, with the main square halfway along it.

ACCOMMODATION

Hotel Italo Guadalipe Victoria 10, two blocks east of the main square ☎376 766 2221, ⓦhotelitalo ajijic.com. Not tremendously welcoming, but a decent bet for the price, with a good Italian restaurant (see below), although the bells of the church next door ring every hour – light sleepers will want to try elsewhere. M$495

Mis Amores Hidalgo 22, one block west of the main square ☎376 766 4640, ⓦhotelmisamores.com.mx. One of the best picks in town, and Ajijic's answer to a contemporary boutique hotel, with tasteful decor, individual terraces shaded by banana trees and a warm proprietor; advance booking is advisable. Breakfast included. Rooms M$450 extra on Fri & Sat, when the breakfast improves from a continental to a slap-up "whatever you fancy". M$650

La Nueva Posada Hidalgo 22, by the lake, three blocks east of Colón ☎376 766 1444, ⓦhotelnueva posada.com. An eclectically decorated, welcoming place that feels like a grand hotel, with large rooms, lovely gardens, an excellent restaurant (see below), small pool and distant water views. Ten percent discount if you pay cash (pesos or dollars). Breakfast included. M$1200

EATING

If you're **eating** on a tight budget, head for the makeshift family-run *sopes* stands around the plaza, where you can dine heartily for M$45. Food on offer will include **hearty soups** with freshly chopped onions and cilantro, as well as *antojitos* of various sorts, and the usual hot or cold drinks.

La Casa del Cafe Colón, a block before the lake ☎376 766 2876. A delightful coffee house where you can select your own beans from a variety of Latin American origin, before kicking back in their big comfortable chairs and watching the locals and tourists stroll by on the cobbles outside. *Chilaquiles* for breakfast are particularly good, especially the chipotle variety (M$50). Wed–Sun 8am–9pm.

Hotel Italo Guadalipe Victoria 10 ☎376 766 2221, ⓦhotelitaloajijic.com. The restaurant here serves up a variety of authentic pizzas (M$70–150) and pasta dishes (M$55–80), and claims to use "original Italian ingredients". The daily specials are usually good. Daily 3–9pm.

La Nueva Posada Hidalgo 22 ☎376 766 1444, ⓦhotelnuevaposada.com. A lovely restaurant with lake views, where you can sit down to *sopa azteca* (M$70) followed by pork chops with port and cranberry sauce (M$140), or grilled salmon with Grand Marnier and balsamic glaze (M$150), all done to perfection. Daily 8am–8pm.

South towards the coast

Some of the most delightful subalpine scenery in Mexico lies southwest of Laguna de Chapala, on the road to Colima. You'll miss much of it if you stick to the speedy toll road (Hwy-54), though even that has its exciting moments as it passes the Zona de Montaña: the following places are all reached from the far slower, far more attractive, if bumpier, old road plied by second-class buses.

Tapalpa

The town of **TAPALPA**, 130km southwest of Guadalajara, makes an ideal base for a few days of relaxation amid upland pastures and pine forests. It is reached via a steep, winding road off the old highway, which climbs continuously until it crests a 2300m ridge at **El Balcón**. If you're driving, stop here to check out the view back down the valley (on a bus, it's on the left if coming up to Tapalpa) and to feel the near-constant steady breeze, a phenomenon that drew World Cup paragliding events in 2002 and 2004.

Pretty little Tapalpa, 10km further on, lies amid magnificent surroundings – ranch country and tree-clad hills that are often covered in a gentle mist. With a population of only around sixteen thousand, there's a village feel to it, especially around the plaza. Here you'll find eighteenth-century wooden-balconied houses, encircling *portales* and two impressive **churches** – the larger with an unusually plain brick interior. On the outskirts, clusters of cabañas dot the woods luring upwardly mobile *Tapatíos*, and a fair bit of desirable real estate has sprung up in recent years.

Tapalpa is on the Guadalajara weekender circuit, so try to visit midweek when its old-world charm is little affected (although hotels remain pricey). The town centres around a stunningly picturesque main square, where several old buildings have been refurbished as restaurants and hotels. The place gets very cold in winter, and even summer nights can become chilly, but people brew their own mescal, which may help warm you up.

ARRIVAL AND INFORMATION
TAPALPA

By bus Buses stop outside the ticket office at Ignacio López 10, two blocks south of the main square. If you don't coincide with a direct service, particularly to Sayula and Ciudad Guzmán, you can get a bus for 32km down to the junction (*crucero*) on the main road and pick up an onward bus there, or even hitch, but leave yourself time and only do this during daylight hours, as it's dangerous after dark.

Destinations Ciudad Guzmán (4 daily; 2hr); Guadalajara's Central Vieja (13 daily; 3hr).

Tourist information Tourist office, Hidalgo 12, on the north side of the main square (daily 9am–3pm; ☎ 343 432 0493, ⓦ tapalpaturistico.com). For independent tourist information see ⓦ turismotapalpa.com.

Banks and exchange There's a bank with ATM at Matamoros 1 in the southeast corner of the main plaza.

ACCOMMODATION

Tapalpa's general shortage of **accommodation** isn't usually a problem during the week, when there shouldn't be too many visitors, but all rooms are often taken at weekends and around the **fiesta** for the Día de la Virgen de Guadalupe (Dec 12), when the town attracts pilgrims from far and wide.

La Casa de Maty Matamoros 69, south side of main square ☎ 343 432 0189, ⓦ lacasadematy.com.mx. This is the pick of the pricier places to stay in town; its comfortable, rustic rooms, each with a fireplace, are set around a beautiful plant-filled courtyard with a fountain. M$1100

Posada La Hacienda Raúl Quintero 120 (half a block southeast of the main square) ☎ 343 432 0193. The cheapest place in town, with spacious chalet-style upstairs rooms on one side of the bougainvillea-draped patio, all doubles (room #1 has the best views), and, on the other side, bungalows with kitchenettes. Doubles M$420, bungalows M$400

Villa de San José Cerrada Ignacio López 91, one block southeast of the main square ☎ 343 432 0451. A pretty little hotel with lots of country-style charm, and rooms with warm wooden floors. M$800

WALKS AROUND TAPALPA

There's good **walking** in almost any direction from Tapalpa, with plenty of wildlife, especially birds, to spot; black vultures (urubu birds) are often seen soaring on the thermals. You can also hire horses (look for the signs) for the popular ride to the local waterfall. One especially pleasant hike is to **Las Piedrotas** (5km; around 1hr each way), which follows a decent but little-used road towards Chiquilistlán (marked as you enter Tapalpa). It passes the romantic ruins of an old water-driven paper mill, and climbs towards a gorgeous valley of pasturelands, studded with wild flowers and huge boulders. If you don't fancy walking both ways, get a taxi to drop you off (around M$80 from opposite the bus office on Ignacio López), and walk back.

EATING

Numerous **restaurants** around the main plaza serve plain country food. Look out for places selling *ponche de granada*, a local wine made from pomegranates (you can usually find it in the *mercado artesanal* west of the main square). Tapalpa is also a good place to try *queso fundido*, as the farms hereabouts produce good cheese.

Los Girasoles Obregón 110, off the southwest corner of the main square ☎ 343 432 0458. A good restaurant for treats such as chile stuffed with cheese and plantains in green coriander and *chipotle* sauce (M$75), or breast of chicken with mushrooms and brown rice (M$95). They also do their own charcuterie. Mon–Thurs 10am–9pm, Fri & Sat 9am–11pm, Sun 9am–7pm.

Paulinos Obregón 67, north side of the main square ☎ 343 432 0109. With its balcony overlooking the main

square, this is a nice spot to watch the town come awake over *huevos rancheros* (M$23), or to tuck into a T-bone for M$50. Daily except Thurs 9am–9.30pm.

La Villa Raúl Quintero 93, southeast corner of the main square ☎ 343 432 0009. This bar-restaurant with a lazy terrace on the square is an excellent place to enjoy a sundowner, but they also do food such as *sabanitas al gratin* (a slice of beef, ham and cheese; M$70), or *huevos rancheros* (M$40). Daily 9am–9pm (bar till around 11pm).

Ciudad Guzmán

The birthplace of José Clemente Orozco, **CIUDAD GUZMÁN** is a busy little town thoroughly steeped in local culture, with attractive colonnaded streets in the centre. The centre of the main plaza is a bandstand with a replica of Orozco's *Man of Fire* mural from Guadalajara (see p.259). As ever, almost everything of interest is on or around the plaza, where you'll find banks, phones and places to stay.

Museo de las Culturas de Occidente

Ángel Gonzalez 21, off Reforma, a block west of the main plaza • Tues–Sat 9.30am–6pm • M$35

The pleasant and well laid-out little town museum, the **Museo de las Culturas de Occidente** (the *occidente* in question being the west of Mexico) is really just one room, but there are some lovely clay figures and animals in the collection of local archeology.

ARRIVAL AND DEPARTURE

CIUDAD GUZMÁN

By bus Central de Autobuses is 2km west of town. Local buses (#6b and, less directly, #5a) run from outside to Reforma and the main plaza; to get back to the Central pick them up on the west side of the plaza by Portal Morelos 85 (Plaza Anita).

Destinations Colima (18 daily; 1hr); Guadalajara's Central Nueva (38 daily; 2hr); Guadalajara's Central Vieja (13 daily; 3hr 30min); Manzanillo (18 daily; 3hr); Mexico City (2 overnight; 9hr); Tapalpa (4 daily; 2hr).

ACCOMMODATION

Hotel Flamingos Federico del Toro 133, a block north of the main plaza ☎ 341 412 0203. A concrete block with large, functional rooms all with TVs, quite modern but getting a bit tatty. M$260

Hotel Zapotlán Federico del Toro 61, west side of the main plaza ☎ 341 412 0040, ✉ hotelvilladesanjose .com. The ordinary rooms are set around a beautiful

covered courtyard with palms, creepers and three tiers of cast-iron landings. Those at the top get more light, so they cost a little bit more, and the ceiling fans are quite low in some rooms, so watch your head. In the new block, behind the pool and outdoor jacuzzi, are some larger, more deluxe and considerably more expensive executive rooms, with a/c and private jacuzzis. M$400

EATING AND DRINKING

You can have an inexpensive and healthy **breakfast** with cereal and fresh juice at the stands behind the church in the main square, where you can also get soups and other simple meals. The salty local cheeses are a treat and can be bought at the daily market near the stalls.

Juanito Federico del Toro 61-A, west side of the main plaza ☎ 341 412 0039. The main dishes in this large diner aren't great bargains (steak *tampiqueña* M$145, for example), but the M$60 menu is, and it's also a good place

for breakfast. Mon–Sat 7am–10pm, Sun 8am–4pm.

Los Portales Refugio Barragán del Toscano 32, one block south of the main plaza ☎ 341 412 4073. Delicious, reasonably priced breakfasts and Mexican main dishes in a Moorish-style courtyard. Fish fillet Colima (stuffed with prawn and octopus) will set you back M$120, steak *tampiqueña* M$140. Mon–Sat 8am–10pm, Sun 8am–6pm.

Tacos Valente Federico del Toro 31-A, west side of the main plaza ☎ 341 410 6627. One of several good *taquerías* around the main plaza, with beef, pork or bean tacos at M$7.50 a go. Daily 8.15am–3.15am.

Northwestern Michoacán

From Guadalajara, the most direct route to Mexico City heads through the major junction of La Piedad and continues east towards Irapuato. If you can afford to dawdle a while, though, it's infinitely more rewarding to follow the slower, southern road through Zamora and Morelia, spending a couple of days in Uruapan and Pátzcuaro. From Uruapan, Hwy-37 slices south through the mountains to the Pacific coast at Lázaro Cárdenas (see p.219).

Uruapan

URUAPAN, they say, means "the place where flowers bloom" in the Tarascan language, though *Appleton's Guide* for 1884 tells a different story: "The word Uruapan comes from *Urani*, which means in the Tarasc language 'a chocolate cup', because the Indians in this region devote themselves to manufacture and painting of these objects." Demand for chocolate cups, presumably, has fallen since then, but whatever the truth, the modern version is certainly appropriate: Uruapan, lower (at around 1600m) and warmer than most of its neighbours, enjoys a steamy subtropical climate and is surrounded by thick forests and lush parks.

Plaza Morelos

The animated **Plaza Morelos**, a long strip of tree-shaded open space, is in every sense the heart of Uruapan. It's surrounded by everything of importance: shops, market, banks, principal churches and many of the hotels. This is the place to head first, either to find somewhere to stay or simply to get a feel for the town. The **Casa de la Cultura**, in the northwest of the plaza, undergoing reconstruction work at last check, usually hosts regular cultural events, exhibitions, concerts and dance performances.

Museo de las Cuatro Pueblos Indígenas

Plaza Morelos • Tues–Sun 9.30am–1.30pm & 3.30–6pm • Free

The town's only overt tourist attraction is **La Huatapera**, one of the oldest surviving buildings in Uruapan, which has been exquisitely restored to house the **Museo de las Cuatro Pueblos Indígenas**, a small display of arts and crafts from the state's four indigenous peoples: the Purépecha, the Nahua, the Otomí and the Mazahua. Look out for particularly fine Purépecha lacquerware gourds, and a Nahua harp with its lute-like acoustic box, as well as beaten copperware from Santa Clara del Cobre (see p.298).

The small courtyard and adjoining chapel were built by Juan de San Miguel, the Franciscan friar who founded the town itself, and were later adopted by Bishop Quiroga as a hospital and training centre. The carvings around the windows bear a marked Arab influence, as they were crafted by Christianized Moorish artisans from Spain (Mudéjares).

MICHOACÁN INFORMATION

The Michoacán state tourism department's website is ⓦ turismomichoacan.gob.mx. This chapter covers the whole of Michoacán except for the coastal region, which is covered in Chapter 8 (see p.476).

Mercado de Antojitos

Half a block north of the plaza, on the west side of the Museo de las Cuatro Pueblos Indígenas, and accessible via an alley

The **Mercado de Antojitos** is a large open **market** section, where women serve up meals for stallholders and visitors alike at a series of long, open-air tables. Here you'll find the cheapest, and very often the freshest and best, food in town – this is a great place to sample the salty regional cheese, *adobada*. The rest of the market, with herb and fruit stalls but mostly clothes, shoes and CDs, sprawls along Corregidora and Constitución.

Parque Nacional Eduardo Ruíz

Calzada de San Miguel, 1km from the plaza on the northwestern edge of downtown • Mon–Thurs 8am–6pm, Fri–Sun 8am–7pm • M$25

Comprising just fifty acres, the **Parque Nacional Eduardo Ruíz** (or Parque Nacional Barranca Cupatitzio) is far more compact than national parks you may be used to elsewhere. As much (luxuriant and tropical) city park as national, it remains one of Uruapan's proudest assets. The Río Cupatitzio flows through in a little gorge, via a series of man-made cascades and fountains. The river springs from a rock known as *La Rodilla del Diablo* ("the Devil's knee"); according to legend, water gushed forth after the Devil knelt here in submission before the unswerving Christian faith of the drought-ridden population. Alternatively, it is said that the Devil met the Virgin Mary while out strolling in the park, and dropped to his knees in respect. *Cupatitzio* means

Paricutín (45km) & Zamora (120km)

URUAPAN

4

■ ACCOMMODATION	
Casa Chikita	3
Centro	5
Continental	8
Hotel del Parque	2
Mansión del Cupatitzio	1
Posada Morelos	6
Real de Uruapan	7
Regis	4

● EATING	
Café Tradicional de Uruapan	7
La Casa	3
Cocina Económica Mary	2
Cox-Hanal	4
La Lucha	6/8
Mesón del Centro	5
La Terraza de la Trucha	1
Ventanas al Paraíso	9

La Rodilla del Diablo

Park entrance

PARQUE NACIONAL EDUARDO RUÍZ

Río Cupatitzio

Park entrance

CALZADA DE SAN MIGUEL

CALZADA SAN MIGUEL

CALZADA LA QUINTA

CALZADA JUÁREZ

JUSTO SIERRA

LERDO DE TEJADA

CULVER CITY

RAMÓN ORTIZ

PRADERA

REVOLUCIÓN

CARRILLO PUERTO

AQUILES SERDÁN

JUAN DELGADO

NERVO

JUAN AYALA

VENUSTIANO CARRANZA

HIDALGO

16 DE SEPTIEMBRE

CONSTITUCIÓN

INDEPENDENCIA

San Francisco

Mercado de Antojitos

MADERO

EMILIO CARRANZA

PLAZA MORELOS

N. ROMERO

RAMÓN ORTIZ

COLÓN

JOSÉ GARCÍA

MANUEL TREVIÑO

ARTÍCULO 123

OCAMPO

OBREGÓN

N

Museo de los Cuátro Pueblos Indígenas

MORELOS

AGUSTÍN MELGAR

20 DE NOVIEMBRE

MANUEL OCARANZA

LIBERTAD

CUPATITZIO

5 DE FEBRERO

NICOLÁS BRAVO

JUAN ALDAMA

PATIÑO

0 — 200 metres

Central de Autobuses (2km) & Pátzcuaro (65km)

La Tzaráracua & Tzararacíuta

THE DANCE OF THE LITTLE OLD MEN

The **Danza de los Viejitos**, or the **Dance of the Little Old Men**, is the most famous of Michoacán's traditional dances. It is also one of its most picturesque, with the performers (usually children), dressed in baggy white cotton and masked as old men, alternating between parodying the tottering steps of the *viejitos* they represent and breaking into complex routines. Naturally enough, there's a lot of music, too. You'll see the dance performed at festive occasions all over Michoacán, but the finest expression is at the guitar-making town of Paracho, 50km south of Zamora.

"where the waters meet", though it's invariably translated as "the river that sings" – another appropriate, if not entirely accurate, tag.

Locals come here to stroll the cobbled footpaths betweens stands of banana plants, gaze at the cascades (particularly good during or just after rain), catch trout and eat at assorted restaurants and taco stands. There are two entrances, one at the end of Independencia (take a bus along here if you don't feel like walking), and one up by the *Mansión del Cupatitzio* hotel, with a string of crafts stalls along Calzada de San Miguel between them.

La Tzaráracua

12km to the south of central Uruapan • Open access • Bus ("Tzaráracua") from the south side of the plaza at Cupatitzio (hourly)

The river crashes over the waterfall of **La Tzaráracua**, an impressive 25m plunge amid beautiful forest scenery. This is also a popular outing with locals, especially at weekends, so if you don't fancy taking the bus, you could share a taxi. If it seems too crowded here, make for the smaller falls, **Tzararacuita**, about 1km further downstream.

ARRIVAL AND DEPARTURE   URUAPAN

By plane The airport is 4km southeast of the centre, at the end of Av Latinoamericana, served by bus #66 from Hidalgo with Constitución. The only destination currently served by scheduled passenger flights from here is Tijuana (1 daily; 3hr 10min).
By bus The Central de Autobuses is 3km northeast of the centre; local buses from outside (marked "Centro") go to

Plaza Morelos in the centre of town.
Destinations Guadalajara (every 20min; 4hr 30min); Lázaro Cárdenas (33 daily; 3hr 30min); Los Reyes (19 daily; 1hr); Mexico City Pte (16 daily; 6hr); Mexico City Nte (10 daily; 6hr 30min); Morelia (every 15min; 2hr); Paracho (every 20min; 40min); Pátzcuaro (every 15min; 1hr).

INFORMATION

Banks and exchange Numerous banks with ATMs lie along Cupatitzio, a block or so south of the plaza, and there are *casas de cambio* (for US dollars only) at Portal Degollado 15 in the northeast corner of the plaza and at Carranza 14-D, just west of Juan Ayala.
Telephones There's a *caseta telefónica* at Manuel

Ocaranza 3, just south of the plaza, plus one on the west side of Plaza Morelos.
Internet The *caseta* on the west side of Plaza Morelos doubles as an internet café (daily 7am–10pm; M$15/hr). Others include Mi C@fé, Independencia 23 (daily 10am–10pm; M$15/hr).

ACCOMMODATION

★**Casa Chikita** Carranza 32-A ☎452 524 4174, ⓦ casachikita.com, ✉ reservaciones@casachikita.com. This welcoming B&B in a nineteenth-century house done out in colonial style has lovely, high-ceilinged rooms, set around an open central courtyard. Breakfast included. M$900
Centro Aldama 3 ☎452 144 0800. A family-run place with simple but clean rooms, all with bathrooms and hot water, arranged around two sunny courtyards; nothing fancy, but friendly and cheap. M$200
Continental Nicolas Bravo 34 ☎452 523 9793 or ☎01

800 714 2228. This relatively quiet hotel has a new wing with bright, modern rooms, cable TV and wi-fi, and an older wing across the street, where the rooms are slightly smaller, with only terrestrial TV, and no internet. There are also parking facilities and a restaurant. Old wing M$300, new wing M$500
Hotel del Parque Independencia 124, near the Parque Nacional ☎452 524 3845. This is the best of the cheapies: clean and friendly, with large en-suite rooms (those at the front are nicest but can be noisy), wi-fi, cable TV and parking facilities. M$250

Mansión del Cupatitzio Calzada Rodilla del Diablo 20, at the northern end of the Parque Nacional Eduardo Ruíz ☏452 523 2100 or ☏01 800 504 8793, ⓦmansiondelcupatitzio.com. Uruapan's finest hotel, with superb service, a pool, terrace restaurant and beautiful grounds full of plants and flowers. The hotel is conveniently adjacent to the entrance to the national park. Wheelchair accessible with an adapted room. M$1535

Posada Morelos Morelos 30 ☏452 523 2302. This secure, family-run hotel set around a pleasant courtyard has rooms with shared bathroom facilities for those on a budget, and slightly pricier en-suite options. Rooms adjoining the street can be noisy. M$300

Real de Uruapan Nicolas Bravo 110 ☏452 527 5900 or ☏01 800 000 7325. Nine-storey international-style hotel with carpeted rooms, each with TV and phone. The top floor is occupied by the restaurant (see below), with the standard rooms on the lower floors, superior rooms (with queen-size beds and better views, but otherwise the same) on the next few floors, and junior suites on the eighth floor. M$850

Regis Portal Carillo 12 ☏452 523 5844 (ext. 157 for reservations). Friendly place in a central location featuring characterful rooms with the accompaniment of twittering caged birds. Parking is available and some rooms overlook the plaza (though that can make them noisy). M$500

EATING

★**Café Tradicional de Uruapan** Carranza 5 ☏452 523 5680. This Uruapan classic serves great breakfasts, superb local coffee, ice cream, cakes, *antojitos*, *pozole* (M$40–73) and a decent range of herbal and fruit teas, including an intriguing piña colada. The window seating's bright and airy, the interior a bit darker. Daily 8am–11pm.

La Casa Revolución 3 ☏452 524 3611. Charming courtyard café-cum-cocktail lounge that's good for a coffee during the day or a tequila in the evening, when it becomes a bit of a hangout. Food includes cheesesteak baguettes (M$95) and wood-oven pizzas (M$80). Daily 2–11pm.

Cocina Económica Mary Independencia 63 ☏452 519 4869. A good, low-priced restaurant offering wholesome home-style cooking at low prices. They do good breakfasts, and their comidas corridas (M$56) usually have a decent choice of *guisados* (main courses), but their coffee isn't great. Mon–Sat 8am–5pm.

Cox-Hanal Carranza 31-A ☏452 524 6152. Yucatán-style *antojitos* (M$8 tacos include *cochinita pibil* and chicken *chimole*), plus ice-cold beers, all at low prices and in clean surroundings, generally getting livelier as the evening wears on. Tues–Sun 6–11pm.

La Lucha Garcia Ortiz 22 ☏452 524 0375, ⓦcafelalucha.com.mx. A small café that's been going since the Revolution, La Lucha is a big reason that Starbucks hasn't got a branch in town. There are lots of branches throughout Uruapan, but this spot is the original; still serving up great local coffee and home-made cakes the traditional way. Daily 9am–9pm.

Mesón del Centro Juan Ayala 5-A ☏452 524 0276. A homely little place decorated with photos of Michoacán attractions and regional dishes. Breakfasts and comida corridas both go for M$65 (the breaded fish fillets are usually a good choice on the latter), and they also have good desserts (cheesecake M$28), although not included in the comida corrida. Mon–Sat 8am–7pm.

La Terraza de la Trucha Calzada Rodilla del Diablo 13, by the upper entrance to the Parque Nacional Eduardo Ruíz ☏452 524 8698. Simply a delight. Enjoy trout *ceviche* (M$70), followed by grilled rainbow trout (M$84) and heavenly *aguas frescas* while surveying the park's waterfalls and giant banana trees. Daily 8am–8pm.

Ventanas al Paraíso Inside Hotel Real de Uruapan (see above) ☏452 527 5900. Top-floor restaurant with great views over the town. You can start with a corn and chile poblano soup (M$35), followed by filet Moctezuma (steak with *huitlacoche*; M$110) or prawns in garlic (M$125). Mon–Sat 2–11pm.

Paricutín

An ideal day trip from Uruapan, the "new" **volcano of Paricutín**, about 40km northwest of town, gives you an unusual taste of the surrounding countryside. On February 20, 1943, a

---

URUAPAN FIESTAS

The most exciting and interesting local fiestas are: Año Nuevo (Jan 1), when the Danza de los Viejitos (see box opposite) is performed; Palm Sunday (the week before Easter), the culmination of a week's celebration when the *indígenas* collect palms from the hills and make ornaments from the leaves; Día de María Magdalena (July 22), when there's a procession of animals through the streets; Día de San Francisco (Oct 4), one of the year's biggest saint's day celebrations; and the Feria de Aguacate (Nov/Dec), a three-week avocado fair with agricultural exhibits and artesanía displays.

Purépecha peasant working in his fields noticed the earth rumble and then smoke. The ground soon cracked and lava began to flow to the surface. Over a period of several years, it engulfed the village of Paricutín and several other hamlets, forcing the evacuation of some seven thousand inhabitants. The volcano was active for eight years, producing a cone some 400m high and devastating an area of around twenty square kilometres. Now there are vast fields of lava (mostly cooled, though there are still a few hot spots), black and powdery, cracked into harsh jags, along with the dead cone and crater. Most bizarrely, a church tower – all that remains of the buried hamlet of San Juan Parangaricutiro – pokes its head through the surface. The volcano wasn't all bad news, though: during its active life the volcano spread a fine layer of dust – effectively a fertilizer – on the fields that escaped the full lava flow, and drew tourists from around the world. It is still popular, especially on Sundays, when the upwardly mobile from Uruapan come out to play.

To see much of Paricutín you really need to set aside a day. You'll want to leave Uruapan early (say 7am or 8am) so you get as much of the hiking as possible done in the cool of the day and catch the ruined church in the morning light. It's also a good idea to take food and drink as there is very little available in Angahuan.

Angahuan

The volcano of Paricutín is visited from the small and very traditional Purépecha village of **Angahuan**, where the women still wear heavily pleated satin skirts with an embroidered apron and a shawl.

The church

On the **plaza**, the **church** warrants a second glance. Built in the sixteenth century, its doorway was carved in the largely Arab Mudéjar style by Andalusian artisans. The cross in the courtyard, on the other hand, is most definitely Mexican, complete with serpents, a skull and other pre-Hispanic motifs. In the street to the right of the church (as you look at it), across from the side gate of the courtyard, a door lintel has been turned into a kind of lava frieze of the volcano and church tower.

The Centro Turístico

Camino al Volcan Paricutín, Col Angahuan – from the plaza, head down Juárez (opposite the church) for about 200m to an ornately carved wooden house on the left (opposite no. 16); veer left here (not signposted) and head straight on for 1km • Daily, in principle open 24hr • M$10

The **Centro Turístico de Angahuan** offers superb views of the volcano from its mirador, has a small museum on the creation of the volcano and local Purépecha culture, and includes a decent restaurant.

ARRIVAL AND DEPARTURE   **PARICUTÍN**

By bus Buses leave from the Central de Autobuses in Uruapan (every 30min, 5am–8pm; 40min; M$20). They drop you on the highway by Angahuan, a 10min walk from the village's main plaza.

By car Take the main road from Uruapan to Los Reyes; the turn-off for Angahuan is well signposted.

PARICUTÍN BY HORSE

Getting off the bus in Angahuan, and in the village, and on the way to the Centro Turístico, you'll meet people offering to guide you or take you on **horseback**; it's not a bad idea to hire a **guide**, as the paths through the lava are numerous and can be difficult to follow. Prices fluctuate with demand, but you can probably expect to pay around M$400 for a guide for the day, plus another M$350 for each horse (one for the guide plus one for each tourist). A return trip to the cone of the volcano will take about eight hours, either on foot or on horseback. If you just want to see the ruined church, a couple of hours will suffice (and rates for guides and horses will be rather cheaper). The horse trail is easier than the walking trail, though it finishes at the base of the main cone, leaving you to tackle the final steep climb on your own.

ACCOMMODATION

Centro Turístico Camino al Volcan Paricutín, Col Angahuan ☎ 452 523 3934. In a beautiful location among aromatic pine trees, the Centro Turístico offers concrete cabins for four or six people, each with a bathroom and open fire, or rooms for up to three people, again with bathrooms. There's also camping. Doubles M$500, 6-bed cabins M$900, 4-bed cabins M$650, camping/person M$50

Tinganio (Tingambato)

Daily 10am–5pm • M$42 • Buses between Uruapan and Pátzcuaro (every 15min in each direction) pass right by the site; by car take the *cuota* highway from Uruapan towards Pátzcuaro then the Zirahuén exit and follow the *libre* road past Ajuno to Tingambato – it lies approximately 30km west of Pátzcuaro

The small but pretty and well-restored pre-Hispanic ruin of **TINGANIO** is roughly halfway between Uruapan and Pátzcuaro, in a town that is now called **Tingambato**. First inhabited around 450–600 AD, the site grew massively between 650 and 900 AD. Teotihuacán's influence is evident in the architecture, especially in the pyramid dominating the religious area, which overlooks a plaza with a cruciform altar. The adjacent ball-court, on the other hand, betrays Toltec influence in its design. Beyond it, a grove of avocado trees hides an unexcavated pyramid. In the residential area just to the north, a sunken plaza with two altars and five stairways, each to a separate residence, is very much in the style of Teotihuacán, but the tomb under the largest residence (which the caretaker will open on request) has a false dome suggestive of Maya influence. Surrounded by beautiful countryside, the site is best appreciated from atop the pyramid. Except on Sundays, you won't see many other visitors here.

Pátzcuaro

PÁTZCUARO is almost exactly halfway between Uruapan and Morelia, some 60km from both, yet strikingly different from either, boasting both fine colonial architecture and a rich indigenous culture. Sitting on **Lago de Pátzcuaro** (see p.294), Mexico's most beautiful lake, it hosts spectacular Day of the Dead celebrations (see box, p.296). Although the outskirts of Pátzcuaro straggle about 3km or so down to the lakeshore, the centre of town is very small, focusing on the two main squares, Plaza Vasco de Quiroga (or Plaza Grande) and Plaza Gertrudis Bocanegra (Plaza Chica).

More than anywhere else in the state, Pátzcuaro owes its position to **Bishop Vasco de Quiroga** (see box, p.291), whose affection for the area's indigenous peoples led him to settle in the Purépechan heartland on the shores of Lago de Pátzcuaro. It was he who decided, in the face of considerable opposition from the Spaniards in Morelia (then known as Valladolid), to build the cathedral here, where it would be centrally located. Although subsequent bishops moved the seat of power back to Morelia, the foundation had been laid for the community's continued success. Pátzcuaro enjoyed a building boom in the sixteenth century and has been of secondary industrial and political importance ever since. Throughout the centre are old mansions with balconies and coats of arms, barely touched since those early years. Today, quaint Pátzcuaro has developed into an upmarket and artistically inclined town with numerous boutiques. You can spend hours wandering around the beautiful – and expensive – arts, crafts and antique shops, aimed mainly at visitors from Mexico City and abroad.

Plaza Gertrudis Bocanegra and Plaza Vasco de Quiroga

Nothing much worth seeing in Pátzcuaro lies more than a few minutes' walk from **Plaza Gertrudis Bocanegra**, named after a local Independence heroine, and **Plaza Vasco de Quiroga**. The finest of Pátzcuaro's mansions are on the latter, especially the seventeenth-century **Casa del Gigante**, with its hefty pillars and crudely carved figures. Another nearby mansion is said to have been inhabited by Prince Huitzimengari, son of the last Tarascan king. Both are privately owned, however, and not open to visitors.

4

Biblioteca

Plaza Bocanegra • Mon–Fri 9am–7pm, Sat 10am–1pm • Free

There are more luxurious houses on the Plaza Bocanegra, but the most striking building is the **Biblioteca**, with its rough-hewn wooden barrel ceiling. The former sixteenth-century church of San Agustín, it has been converted into a library and decorated with **murals** by **Juan O'Gorman** depicting the history of Michoacán, notably Nuño de Guzmán burning alive the leader of the Tarascans. O'Gorman (1905–82) possessed a prodigious talent, and is one of the muralists who inherited

■ ACCOMMODATION		● EATING	
Casa del Sol	9	Don Rafa	3
La Casa Encantada	8	Doña Paca	4
Los Escudos	5	La Pacanda	5
Gran Hotel	2	El Patio	7
Hotel Posada la Basílica	1	La Pérgola	2
Hotel Posada de la Salud	3	El Primer Piso	6
Mansión Iturbe	4	La Surtidora	4
Misión San Manuel	6	Tekare	1
Posada Mandala	7		

■ DRINKING	
El Campanario	1

PÁTZCUARO

Estación, Lago de Pátzcuaro & Morelia

AVENIDA LÁZARO CÁRDENAS
ERÉNDIRA
Río Guaní
Río Guaní
DE INDUSTRIA
ÁLVARO OBREGÓN
NIÑOS HÉROES
SAN JOSÉ
TEJERÍAS
Teatro Emperador
Biblioteca
LIBERTAD
Market
PADRE LLOREDA
VOLADOR
★ Buses to Lake & Bus Station
BUENA VISTA
Templo del Santuario
PLAZA GERTRUDIS BOCANEGRA
Casa de Cambio
RAMOS
B JUÁREZ
CODALLOS
LA PAZ
AHUMADA
Basílica de Nuestra Señora de la Salud
Bank
MENDOZA
ITURBE
ENSEÑANZA ARCIGA
PLAZUELA DE LA BASÍLICA
BENIGNO SERRATO
El Humilladero (1km)
@
IBARRA
Bank
Museo de Artes y Oficios
MORELOS
ALLENDE
V QUIROGA
ALCANTARILLA
@
HIDALGO
PLAZA VASCO DE QUIROGA
MATAMOROS
Casa del Gigante
PLAZA SAN FRANCISCO
i
La Compañía
Laundry
TERÁN
PONCE DE LEÓN
ALDAMA
GUERRERO
El Sagrario
LERÍN
Templo de San Francisco
FEDERICO TENA
ROMERO
N
Templo San Juan de Dios
SAN JUAN DE DIOS
DR JOSÉ M COSS
Casa de los Once Patios
ROMERO
NAVARRETE
0   200
metres

Cerro del Calvario (1km) & Cerro del Estribo (4km)

VASCO DE QUIROGA – THE NOBLE CONQUISTADOR

When the Spaniards arrived in Michoacán in 1519, they found the region dominated by the **Purépechan** people – whom they named **Tarascans** – whose chief town, Tzintzuntzán, lay on the shores of Lago de Pátzcuaro. The Tarascan civilization, a serious rival to the Aztecs before the Conquest, had a widespread reputation for excellence in the arts, especially metalworking and feathered ornaments. Though the Tarascans submitted peaceably to the Spaniards in 1522 and their leader converted to Christianity, they did not avoid the massacres and mass torture that **Nuño de Guzmán** meted out in his attempts to fully pacify the region. Guzmán's methods were overly brutal, even by colonial standards, and an elderly Spanish nobleman-turned-priest, **Vasco de Quiroga**, was appointed bishop to the area in an attempt to restore harmony. He succeeded beyond all expectations, securing his reputation as a champion of the native peoples – a reputation that persists today. He coaxed the native population down from the mountains to which they had fled, established self-sufficient agricultural settlements and set up missions to teach practical skills as well as religion. The effects of his actions have survived in a very visible way for, despite some blurring in objects produced for the tourist trade, each village still has its own craft speciality: lacquerware in Uruapan, guitars in Paracho, copper goods in Santa Clara del Cobre, to name but a few.

Vasco de Quiroga also left behind him a deeply religious state. Michoacán was a stronghold of the reactionary **Cristero** movement, which fought a bitter war in defence of the Church after the Revolution. Perhaps, too, the ideals of Zapata and Villa had less appeal here as Quiroga's early championing of native peoples' rights against their new overlords meant that the hacienda system never entirely took over Michoacán. Unlike most of the country, the state boasted a substantial peasantry with land it could call its own, and therefore it didn't relate to calls for land and labour reform.

the mantle of Rivera and Orozco: his best-known work is the decoration of the interior of Chapultepec Castle in Mexico City (see p.95).

Basílica de Nuestra Señora de la Salud

Plazuela de la Basílica • Daily 8am–7pm, Services hourly until 5pm on Sun • Free

East of the Plaza Bocanegra, Quiroga's cathedral – the **Basílica de Nuestra Señora de la Salud**, or **Colegiata** – was intended to be Pátzcuaro's masterpiece, with space for thirty thousand worshippers. A massive structure for such a small town, it was never completed, and the existing basilica, finished in the nineteenth century, is only the nave of the original design. Even so, it is often full, for local people continue to revere Quiroga: the first chapel on the left as you walk in the main entrance is the **Mausoleo de Don Vasco**, the doors typically closed and adorned with notes of thanks for his miraculous interventions. The church also possesses a miraculous healing image of the Virgin, crafted in a traditional Tarascan method out of *pasta de caña*, a gum-like modelling paste made principally from maize. Services here are extraordinary, especially for the town's patron saint, the Virgin de la Salud, on December 8.

Museo de Artes y Oficios and around

Cnr of Alcantarilla and Enseñanza • Tues–Sun 9am–4.30pm • M$42

The **Museo de Artes y Oficios**, south of the basilica, occupies the ancient Colegio de San Nicolas. Founded by Quiroga in 1540, the college is now devoted to a superb collection of regional handicrafts: local lacquerware and pottery; copperware from Santa Clara del Cobre; and traditional masks and religious objects made from *pasta de caña*, which, apart from being easy to work with, is also very light, and hence easily carried in processions. Some of the objects on display are ancient, others the best examples of modern work, and all are set in a very beautiful building. Almost opposite, the church of **La Compañía** was built by Quiroga in 1546 and later taken over by the Jesuits.

PÁTZCUARO FIESTAS

Aside from the Day of the Dead (see box, p.296), Pátzcuaro's main fiestas are New Year (Jan 1), when the Danza de los Viejitos (Dance of the Little Old Men; see box, p.286) is performed, and La Señora de la Salud (Dec 8), a saint's day event attended by many Tarascan pilgrims. On La Señora de la Salud, you'll see worshippers in an intense, almost hypnotic fervour; the scrubby park outside the basilica becomes a fairground and there is all manner of Tarascan dances.

Casa de los Once Patios

Between Dr Coss and Lerin • Daily 10am–7pm, though individual stores may keep their own hours

The **Casa de los Once Patios** is an eighteenth-century convent converted into a crafts showhouse, full of workshops and moderate to expensive boutiques. As its name suggests, the complex is set around a series of tiny courtyards, and it's a fascinating place to stroll through even if you can't afford the goods. You can watch restored treadle looms at work, admire the intricacy with which the best lacquerware is created and wander at liberty through the warren of rooms and corridors.

El Humilladero

Nueva del Cristo, 1km from centre along Serrato • Often closed

El Humilladero ("the place of humbling") is probably the oldest church in Pátzcuaro, standing on the site where the last Tarascan king, Tanganxoan II, accepted Spanish authority – hence the humbling name. Such a tag may seem appropriate with hindsight, though a more charitable view suggests that Tanganxoan was simply hoping to save his people from the slaughter that had accompanied resistance to the Spaniards elsewhere. The church itself, pretty enough, is often closed, so there's little to see.

ARRIVAL AND INFORMATION
PÁTZCUARO

By bus to Central de Autobuses Some buses terminating in Pátzcuaro may stop at Estación (see below), but all will take you to the main Central de Autobuses, 2km south of town, and a 15min walk from the centre (cross the main road, head right and turn left down Federico Tena) or a brief bus ride (take services marked "Centro" or "Col Popular"). Buses back to the Central, can be picked up in Plaza Bocanegra or along Federico Tena. Buses for Santa Clara del Cobre start at the central but are best picked up from the main road opposite the top of Federico Tena.

Destinations Guadalajara (2 daily; 4–5hr); Mexico City Pte (10 daily; 5hr); Mexico City Nte (8 daily; 5hr 30min); Morelia (every 15min; 1hr); Quiroga (every 15min; 30min); Uruapan (every 30min; 1hr); Santa Clara del Cobre (every 5min; 20min).

By bus to Estación Through buses between Uruapan and Morelia stop at "Estación" (the old train station) by the harbour (handy for *Villa Pátzcuaro*), from where you can get a bus to the centre. Leaving town, this is also the best place to pick up buses to Uruapan and Morelia, since, in addition to the through services (every 15min), those originating at the Central also stop here.

Tourist information The tourist office is on the west side of Plaza Quiroga at Hidalgo 1 (daily 9am–8pm; ☎ 434 342 0216 ext.106).

LAKE WITH A VIEW

The best views of **Lago de Pátzcuaro** are found west along the road to the Cerro del Estribo: head out along Terán past the Templo San Francisco. It is about 1km from here to the Cerro del Calvario, a tiny hill topped by the little chapel of El Calvario. You won't be able to see much from the chapel, so take the road to the right just before you reach it and continue on along a cobbled, cypress-lined avenue. Over the subsequent 3km, you'll climb more than 200m to a viewpoint with great vistas over Lago de Pátzcuaro and Janitzio. You can get a taxi out here from town, or if you're walking and don't fancy the road, look out for a parallel horse trail on the right. From the viewpoint, 417 steps lead straight up to the summit of Cerro del Estribo (Stirrup Hill), though the views aren't especially better.

ACCOMMODATION

With a small **hostel** and an ever-expanding selection of top-end **B&Bs** and hotels, Pátzcuaro offers an excellent range of places to stay. Prices are a little higher than elsewhere in the state, but if you are prepared to pay a little more you'll get a lot more elegance. Most establishments are on one or other of the plazas, with the ritzier ones surrounding Plaza Vasco de Quiroga and a selection of simpler places around the Plaza Bocanegra. Prices generally spike at Christmas/New Year, Semana Santa and Easter. The same is true around the **Day of the Dead** (first two days of Nov), when there's little chance of getting a room unless you book at least a couple of months ahead (more like six to twelve months for some of the posher places).

Casa del Sol Michoacán 43, Col San Lazarao ☎434 342 0975, ✉casadelsolpatzcuaro@yahoo.com.mx. Homestay in a workaday *barrio* very near the bus station (instead of turning left down Federico Tena, take the next left to the top of a rise, and it's almost opposite you), where you can either rent rooms in the house, or dorm beds in a shack in the garden. It's only 10min from the centre (Michoacán is a continuation of Romero), very friendly and by far the cheapest deal in town, especially for single travellers. Dorms M$50, doubles M$200

★**La Casa Encantada** Dr Coss 15 ☎434 342 3492, US ☎+1 619 819 8398, ⌨hotelcasaencantada.com. Gorgeous and intimate American-owned B&B in the heart of town. All the rooms are different (there are even two self-catering suites), and the whole place is beautifully decorated with lovely little touches everywhere. Includes a hearty Mexican breakfast. M$944

Los Escudos Plaza Quiroga 73 ☎434 342 1290. Beautiful colonial building with good-value rooms around two flower-filled courtyards; all are carpeted and have TV, and some have fireplaces too. Ask for a room in the original hotel and not the extension next door. M$470

Gran Hotel Plaza Bocanegra 6 ☎434 342 0443 or ☎01 800 503 3090, ⌨granhotelpatzcuaro.com.mx. Smallish rooms but very homely, each with a coffee maker, not to mention TV, phone and wi-fi in a friendly hotel right on the plaza, but it's worth asking for a room with an outside window. Deals are negotiable out of season. M$450

Hacienda Mariposa km3.5 Carretera Pátzcuaro–Santa Clara del Cobre ☎443 333 0762, ⌨hacienda mariposas.com. This comfortable, upscale oasis, south of town off the Santa Clara del Cobre road, offers pony treks, ecotours and superb cuisine in serene wooded surroundings. Breakfast included. M$1200

Hotel Posada la Basílica Arciga 6, opposite the basilica ☎434 342 1108. Delightful rooms, some with fireplaces, in an eighteenth-century building with superb views of the town and a great restaurant (see p.294).

Rooms have all the expected amenities, including cable TV, phones and wi-fi. Breakfast included. M$1500

Hotel Posada de la Salud Serrato 9 ☎434 342 0058. Behind the basilica, and a short walk from the centre, this beautiful little hotel, peaceful and spotless, is in a house dating from the early nineteenth century. Some rooms have fireplaces, and there's a small garden. M$350

★**Mansión Iturbe** Plaza Quiroga 59 ☎434 342 0368, US & Canada ☎+1 866 678 6102, ⌨mansioniturbe .com. Once a muleteer's house, dating from 1790, this small luxury inn and architectural jewel is run by a mother–daughter team. There's a library, superb dining and attractive bedrooms with soaring ceilings and down duvets. Breakfast included. M$2800

Misión San Manuel Plaza Quiroga 12 ☎434 342 1050, ✉maisonmanuel5@hotmail.com. The great colonial front on this ex-convent hides a charming and beautifully maintained interior with period features (and sometimes temperamental plumbing). The rooms are spacious, and several have real fireplaces, but if you need quiet, avoid the rooms at the front, and especially those above *El Campanario*. M$413

Posada Mandala Lerin 14 ☎434 342 4176, ⌨posada mandala.com. This friendly and excellent-value guesthouse has downstairs rooms with outside bathrooms, upstairs rooms with private bathrooms (more than double the price), free tea and coffee, use of a kitchen, wi-fi, a little library and exquisite rooftop views. On Thurs–Sun it also doubles as a fantastic pizzeria, the smells emanating from which won't make it easy to stay in your room. M$200

Villa Pátzcuaro Lázaro Cárdenas, 2km north of town ☎434 342 0767, ⌨villapatzcuaro.com. Great little hotel and RV park in spacious grounds with a small pool. Rustic-style rooms (breakfast included) are tasteful, very clean and imaginatively decorated, and there are also a couple of self-contained houses for longer stays. Tent and RV campers have access to a kitchen. Frequent buses from Plaza Bocanegra pass right outside. Double M$900, house M$2500, camping/person M$70

EATING

For cheap eats try the food stalls in the **market**, which is at its most colourful and animated on Fridays. Most evenings you can also get basic food from the stalls in the Plaza Bocanegra. One feature of virtually all menus in town is *pescado blanco*, a rather flabby white fish from the lake (though usually nowadays from other lakes), and *sopa tarasca* – a tomato-based soup with chile and bits of tortilla. At the lake itself, a line of restaurants faces the landing jetty, serving *pescado blanco* for M$100–120, or whitebait-like *charales* for M$10–20.

SNACKS

La Pacanda Portal Hidalgo, Plaza Quiroga. Just a couple of wooden carts with metal tubs on ice serving superb ice cream and sorbets since 1905. Try interesting flavours like tequila (which is amazingly good), mandarin and tamarind, in portions starting at M$12. Daily 10am–8.30pm.

RESTAURANTS

★**Don Rafa** Mendoza 30 ☎ 434 342 0498. A pleasant room decorated with old photos of Pátzcuaro makes a comfortable setting for a very tasty three-course *menu del día* (M$69) or a set breakfast (M$54–70), with delicious fresh salsa on every table and attentive service. Daily 8.30am–8.30pm.

Doña Paca Plaza Quiroga 59, attached to the Mansión Iturbe hotel (see p.293) ☎ 434 342 0368. Come here for comfortable and elegant dining and a menu of reasonably priced regional dishes, including creative salads with local ingredients, *corundas* (triangular Purépechan tamales; M$45), hearty Tarascan soup (M$35–45), *churipo de carne* (beef stew with *corundas*; M$89) or fish with coriander sauce (M$105). Daily 8.30am–8.30pm.

El Patio Plaza Quiroga 19 ☎ 434 342 0484. Good coffee, reasonably priced breakfasts, *antojitos* (including local ones such as *corundas* and *huchepos*, both M$45), steaks (M$135), salads and sandwiches. You may be either reassured or put off by their statement (in English) that "Our menu is not too hot or spicy." Daily 8am–10pm.

La Pérgola Inside the Gran Hotel (see p.293) ☎ 434 342 6731. Newly renovated restaurant, where the menu changes with the seasons. It's one of the best spots in town for a hearty breakfast (M$55–85), though you can also have lunch or supper here, dining on such dishes as rainbow trout or *carne asada* (both M$90). Mon & Wed–Sun 7.30am–9pm, Tues 7.30am–9pm.

★**El Primer Piso** Plaza Quiroga 29 ☎ 434 342 0122. This gourmet place serves a mixture of regional and gourmet European flavours to create some of the finest food in town. Nicely positioned overlooking the main square, the matriarchs at the back won't rest until you're completely satisfied, with dishes like filet Roquefort (M$150) and chicken *nogoada* (M$140). Mon & Wed–Sun 2–10pm.

La Surtidora Portal Hidalgo 71, Plaza Quiroga ☎ 434 342 2835. Doubling as a liquor store, this central restaurant with all the trimmings (tablecloths, posh waiter service) does an excellent line in breakfast, lunch and supper, serving up well-presented dishes such as *sopa tarasca* (M$37) and breast of chicken stuffed with *huitlacoche* and nuts in *chile poblano* sauce (M$95). Daily 7am–10pm.

Tekare Arciga 6, inside the Hotel Posada La Basílica (see p.293) ☎ 434 342 1108. The house speciality is *kurucha urapiti* (lake fish, though not actually from Lago de Pátzcuaro nowadays; M$190), or try the chicken in peanut sauce (M$100) – a change from *mole*, though that's available too. The restaurant has great views of the town and beyond to the lake. Daily 9am–9pm.

DRINKING

El Campanario Plaza Quiroga 12. Reasonably lively bar, often with a DJ or a couple of musicians playing in the corner. The decor's a bit strange, but in a pleasing kind of way, and there's even a model of a *torero* (bullfighter) with a bull's face in a glass case on the wall. Daily 4pm–1am.

DIRECTORY

Banks and exchange There's an ATM at Plaza Quiroga 54 and one at Iturbe 43, just off Plaza Bocanegra. At the corner of Buena Vista and Ahumada there's a *casa de cambio*.

Internet Numerous places all charging around M$15/hr. Try Meg@net at Mendoza 8 and Plaza Quiroga 67.

Laundry Try the laundrette in front of the Templo San Francisco (Mon–Sat 9am–7pm).

Post office Obregón 13 (Mon–Fri 8am–4.30pm, Sat 8am–noon).

Spanish courses The Centro de Lenguas y Ecoturismo de Pátzcuaro, Navarette 50 (☎ 434 342 4764, ⊛ celep.com .mx), offers well-regarded language classes and homestays.

Telephones You can phone and fax from *casetas* on the east side of Plaza Bocanegra.

Lago de Pátzcuaro and around

Apart from the beautiful town itself, Pátzcuaro's other great attraction is **Lago de Pátzcuaro**. The lake was once a major thoroughfare, but that role has declined since the completion of roads linking the lakeside villages a few years back. Most locals now take the bus rather than paddle around the water in canoes, but there is still a fair amount of traffic and regular trips out to the closest island, **Janitzio**.

The lake's other draw is the chance to see and photograph the famous **butterfly nets** wielded by indigenous fishermen in tiny dugout canoes. It is a long time since this was considered a viable means of gaining food, but a handful of nets are maintained to catch tourists. Occasionally a group of locals lurking in readiness on the far side of Janitzio will paddle into camera range when a sufficiently large collection of money has been taken.

Finally, no visit to Pátzcuaro is complete without an excursion to the small lakeside villages, which, thanks to Vasco de Quiroga, each specialize in different **artesanía**.

The islands

From a distance, the island of **Janitzio** looks quaint, but as you get closer it appears almost squalid. With fishing becoming ever less viable and with no land flat enough for agriculture, the conical, car-free island has found itself relying increasingly on the tourism industry – you'll be besieged by souvenir hawkers from the moment you arrive. Still, it is worth the journey if only for the opportunity to spend some time on the lake and for the expansive views from the top of the island. From the dock, head straight up one of the many alleys that climb steeply between assorted **fish restaurants** (generally better away from the dock) and tacky souvenir stalls to the summit, which is crowned by an ugly 49m **statue of José María Morelos** (see box, p.303). Ascend the spiral staircase inside (daily 8am–7pm; M$10), past murals depicting Morelos' life and the struggle for Independence, to the viewpoint right by

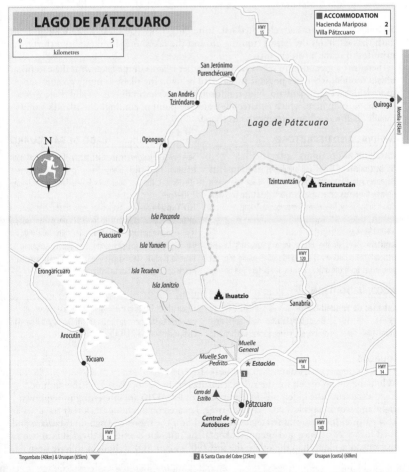

LAGO DE PÁTZCUARO

0 — 5 kilometres

■ ACCOMMODATION	
Hacienda Mariposa	2
Villa Pátzcuaro	1

4

HWY 15

San Jerónimo Purenchécuaro

San Andrés Tziróndaro

Quiroga

Lago de Pátzcuaro

Oponguo

Morelia (45km)

Tzintzuntzán ♦ **Tzintzuntzán**

N

Isla Pacanda

Puacuaro

Isla Yunuén

HWY 120

Erongaricuaro

Isla Tecuéna

Isla Janitzio

♦ **Ihuatzio**

Sanabría

Arocutín

Muelle General

Muelle San Pedrito

★ **Estación**

HWY 14

HWY 14

Tócuaro

Cerro del Estribo ▲

● **Pátzcuaro**

Central de Autobuses ★

HWY 140

HWY 14

Tingambato (40km) & Uruapan (65km) ▼   ▲ & Santa Clara del Cobre (25km) ▼   ▼ Uruapan (cuota) (60km)

THE DAY OF THE DEAD AROUND LAGO DE PÁTZCUARO

The **Day of the Dead** (Nov 1, and through the night into the next day) is celebrated in spectacular fashion throughout Mexico, but nowhere more so than on Lago de Pátzcuaro, particularly the island of **Janitzio**. On this night, the locals conduct what is an essentially private meditation, carrying offerings of fruit and flowers to the cemetery and maintaining a vigil over the graves of their ancestors until dawn, chanting by candlelight. Death is considered a continuation of life, and this is the time when the souls of *muertitos* (deceased loved ones) return to the land of the living. It's a spectacular and moving sight, especially early in the evening as indigenous people from the surrounding area converge on the island in their canoes, with a single candle burning in each bow.

Impressive and solemn though the occasion is, over the years it has become somewhat marred by its sheer press of **spectators**, both Mexican and foreign. Thousands head over to tiny Janitzio, and from around 10pm on November 1 until around 3am the following morning you can hardly move, especially in the cemetery where the vigil takes place amid a riot of marigolds and candles. If you can manage it, stay up all night and return to the cemetery around 5am when it is quiet and the first hint of dawn lightens the eastern sky. Alternatively, head to one of the other lakeside communities marking the Day of the Dead – Tzurumutaro, Ihuatzio, Cucuchucho or Tzintzuntzán. There's no guarantee of a quiet and respectful vigil, but crowds will be smaller and the cemeteries no less amazing.

an image of his upraised, clenched fist. If heights make you queasy, there's a pleasant path that encircles the island running around the lakeshore. It takes about thirty minutes to make a full circuit.

There isn't a great deal to see or do on the other islands in the lake, with the exception of **Isla Yunuén**, where it's possible to stay (see below). The island is much greener and more laid-back than Janitzio, with traditional Purepécha architecture, and there isn't a whole lot to do here, which is, after all, really the point of coming. The island's name means "half moon", in reference to its shape.

ARRIVAL AND DEPARTURE
LAGO DE PÁTZCUARO

LAGO DE PÁTZCUARO

By bus/minibus Buses and minibuses leave from Plaza Bocanegra in Pátzcuaro. Those marked "Lago" drop you right by the boats, otherwise it's a 4km (less than 1hr) walk down to the jetty; follow the "*embarcadero*" signs.

THE ISLANDS

Janitzio Fares to the island from Pátzcuaro's Muelle General (main dock area) are fixed (M$45 round trip; get your ticket from the office on the quay before you board).

Seventy-seat *lanchas* make the stately, if noisy, half-hour crossing when full (daily 7am–7pm, roughly every 20–30min). The last boat back leaves Janitzio at around 7.30–8pm.

Isla Yunuén You can get a boat from the Muelle General (main dock area) in Pátzcuaro for M$75 per person (round trip) with a minimum of three people. Failing that, it'll cost you M$200. The journey takes 1hr 40min, stopping at Janitzio. If you're staying in Yunuén, you'll have to negotiate a pick-up for your return to Pátzcuaro.

ACCOMMODATION

Cabañas de Yunuén Isla Yunuén ☎434 342 4473 or ☎434 342 1072. Beautifully rustic and absolutely immaculate wooden cabins, each with a small kitchen and TV, on a little island in the middle of the lake; very idyllic. If you want to stay here on the Day of the Dead, you'll need to book months ahead. M$400

Ihuatzio

12km north of Pátzcuaro, around 4km off the Pátzcuaro–Quiroga road • Daily 10am–6pm • M$35

While they're no match for the ruins at Tzintzuntzán (see opposite), further around Lago Pátzcuaro, the older, pre-Tarascan ruins of **IHUATZIO** are interesting in their own right and worth a peek if you have the time. Located on a remote track that traverses a cow pasture, Ihuatzio was strategically located near the shores of Lago de Pátzcuaro and used for water defence and enemy lookout. The ruins are essentially divided into two sections, one older than the other: the first (900–1200 AD) is thought to have been constructed by the Náhuatl, and the second dates from 1200–1530 AD, during the Tarascan occupation. Two 15m-high **squared-off pyramids**, once considered a sort of Plaza de Armas, are the main features of the site open to the public.

ARRIVAL AND DEPARTURE — IHUATZIO

By bus Buses to Ihuatzio leave from Plaza Bocanegra in Pátzcuaro every few minutes (M$10) during the site's opening hours. You'll be dropped at the end of a cobblestone road and will have to walk 1500m to the site's entrance. On the walk, look for three vegetated hummocks which are the unexcavated ruins of *yácatas* (see below). To continue to Tzintzuntzán, hop on one of the frequent Quiroga-bound buses or *colectivos* from the road where you were dropped off.

Tzintzuntzán

15km north of Pátzcuaro on the road to Quiroga • Daily 9am–6pm • M$52

TZINTZUNTZÁN, ancient capital of the Tarascans (aka Purépechas), was established around the end of the fourteenth century, when the capital was moved from Pátzcuaro, and by the time of the Conquest the Spaniards estimated that there were as many as forty thousand people living here, with dominion over all of what is now Michoacán and large parts of the modern states of Jalisco and Colima. Homes and markets, as well as the palaces of the rulers, lay around the raised **ceremonial centre**, but all that can be seen today is the artificial terrace that supported the great religious buildings (*yácatas*), and the partly restored ruins of these temples.

Even if you do no more than pass by on the road, you can't fail to be struck by the scale of these buildings and by their semicircular design, a startling contrast to the rigid, right-angled formality adhered to by almost every other major pre-Hispanic culture in Mexico. Climb up to the terrace and you'll find five *yácatas*, of which four have been partly rebuilt. Each was originally some 15m high, tapering in steps from a broad base to a walkway along the top less than 2m wide. Devoid of any ornamentation, the *yácatas* are in fact piles of flat rocks, held in by retaining walls and then faced in smooth, close-fitting volcanic stone. The terrace, which was originally approached up a broad ceremonial ramp or stairway on the side furthest from the water, affords magnificent views across the lake and the present-day village of Tzintzuntzán. Tzintzuntzán means "place of the hummingbirds"; you're unlikely to see one nowadays, but the theory is that there were plenty of them around until the Tarascans – who used the feathers to make ornaments – hunted them to the point of extinction. The ruins are around 1km from the village and are signposted "Zona Arqueológica" up a side road.

The village

Down in the **village**, which has a reputation for producing and selling some of the region's best ceramics, you'll find what's left of the enormous **Franciscan Monastery** founded around 1530 to convert the Tarascans. Much of this has been demolished, and the rest substantially rebuilt, but there remains a fine Baroque **Templo de San Francisco** and a huge atrium where the indigenous people would gather for sermons. Vasco de Quiroga originally intended to base his diocese here, but eventually decided that Pátzcuaro had the better location and a more constant supply of water. He did leave one unusual legacy, though: the **olive trees** planted around the monastery are probably the oldest in Mexico, since settlers were banned from cultivating olives in order to protect the farmers back in Spain. The broad, veined trunks certainly look their age, and several have just a few living branches sprouting from what look like dead trees.

ARRIVAL AND DEPARTURE — TZINTZUNTZÁN

By bus Buses to Tzintzuntzán leave from Pátzcuaro's Central de Autobuses (every 10min; 15min), but can also be picked up on the highway close to the *embarcadero*.

By colectivo You can also take a *colectivo* from Plaza Bocanegra to Ihuatzio (15min), and another from there to Tzintzuntzán (15min).

TZINTZUNTZÁN FIESTAS

Tzintzuntzán has several good **fiestas**. Carnaval here takes the form of a week-long party called La Fiesta del Señor del Rescate, celebrating a miracle in which, during a nineteenth-century measles epidemic, the sexton of the church discovered an old painting of Christ hidden away in the crypt, and made a vow that if prayers to this image would rescue the town, he would pay for a huge party in celebration; the prayers duly worked, and the party is held every year to this day. Unfortunately the miraculous image itself was destroyed by fire in 1944. Also big here is Semana Santa (the week before Easter Sunday), when the Thursday sees the ceremony of Washing the Apostles' Feet, followed on Good Friday by further scenes from Christ's Passion acted out around town.

Santa Clara del Cobre

Approximately 25km south of Pátzcuaro, via a country road over a pine-draped pass, lies **Santa Clara del Cobre**, long celebrated for the **copper crafts** on which it continues to thrive. There are no fewer than two hundred family-run studios (*talleres*) and shops, many of which line the quaint town's arcades and side streets selling everything from cheap bracelets and thimbles to hammered sinks and sparkling *carnitas* cauldrons.

Museo Nacional del Cobre

Morelos 263 at Pino Suárez • Tues–Sat 10am–3pm & 5–7pm, Sun 10am–4pm • M$60

A large amount of copper is on display at the town's **Museo del Cobre**, which exhibits a small but impressive collection of decorative and utilitarian copper crafts. Sadly, only a handful of these intricate old designs are still being incorporated into the production of modern goods.

ARRIVAL AND INFORMATION
SANTA CLARA DEL COBRE

By bus and combi Buses and *combis* (M$15) to Santa Clara from Pátzcuaro (every 5min; 20min) leave from the main road opposite the top of Federico Tena. They return to Pátzcuaro from the southwest corner of the main plaza. A taxi between Pátzcuaro and Santa Clara costs M$100.

By car Driving from Pátzcuaro, follow signs for Opopeo.

Festivals The annual Feria Nacional del Cobre (Copper Fair), combined with the Fiesta de la Virgen del Sagrario, is held in Santa Clara del Cobre from Aug 6–17. Festivities include exhibits and sales of handworked copper, as well as music and dance.

ACCOMMODATION AND EATING

Hotel Oasis Portal Allende 144, north side of main plaza ☎434 343 0040, ✉ade_zc@hotmail.com. Serviceable hotel, centrally located, with carpeted rooms, some with views over the main plaza. Rooms with mountain views are larger and cost a little bit more (though they'll take more people). M$330

El Portal Portal Matamoros 18, east side of main plaza. Serves good breakfasts (M$45–60) and *comidas corridas* (M$65–70) along with fish dishes such as lake fish done various ways (M$120), or fish soup (M$35). Daily 8.30am–10.30pm.

Morelia

The state capital, **MORELIA**, is in many ways unrepresentative of Michoacán. It looks Spanish and, despite a large indigenous population, it feels Spanish – with its broad streets lined with seventeenth-century mansions and outdoor cafés sheltered by arcaded plazas, you might easily be in Salamanca or Valladolid. Indeed, the city's name was Valladolid until 1828, when it was changed to honour local-born Independence hero José María Morelos.

City ordinances decree that all new construction must perfectly match the old, such that it preserves a remarkable unity of style. Nearly everything is built of the same faintly pinkish-grey stone (trachyte), which, being soft, is not only easily carved and embellished but weathers quickly, giving even relatively recent constructions a battered, ancient look. Best of all are the plazas dotted with little cafés where you can while away an hour or two.

Brief history

Morelia has always been a city of Spaniards. It was one of the first they founded after the Conquest – two Franciscan friars, Juan de San Miguel and Antonio de Lisboa, settled here among the native inhabitants in 1530. Ten years later, they were visited by the first viceroy of New Spain, **Antonio de Mendoza**, who was so taken by the site that he ordered a town to be built, naming it after his birthplace – Valladolid in Castile – and sending fifty Spanish families to settle it. From the beginning, there was fierce rivalry between the colonists and the older culture's town of Pátzcuaro. During the lifetime of **Vasco de Quiroga**, Pátzcuaro had the upper hand, but later the bishopric was moved here, a university founded, and by the end of the sixteenth century there was no doubt that Valladolid was predominant.

Plaza de Armas

Flanking the cathedral, the **Plaza de Armas** (or de los Martíres) is the place to sit around and revel in the city's leisurely pace – relax with a coffee and a morning paper (you can buy a few international newspapers from the stands here) in the cafés under its elegant arcaded *portales*. There are band concerts here on Sundays.

The cathedral

Madero Pte 2 • Daily 6am–8pm • Free

At the heart of the city, Morelia's massive **cathedral** boasts two soaring towers that are said to be the tallest in Mexico; they can certainly be seen from all over the city and beyond. It's an important social hub for the city's residents who are extremely proud of the beautiful building. Begun in 1640 in the relatively plain Herrerian style, the towers and dome were not completed for some hundred years, by which time the Baroque had arrived with a vengeance; nevertheless, the parts harmonize remarkably, and for all the cathedral's size and richness of decoration, perfect proportions prevent it from becoming overpowering. The interior, refitted towards the end of the nineteenth century, after most of its silver ornamentation had been removed to pay for the wars, is simple. A few early colonial religious paintings are preserved in the choir and the sacristy, and organ recitals are still held from time to time.

Museo Michoacano

On the southwestern edge of Plaza de Armas, at the corner of Allende and Abasolo • Tues–Sun 9am–4.30pm • M$42, free Sun

The **Museo Michoacano** occupies a palatial eighteenth-century mansion. Emperor Maximilian lodged here on his visits to Morelia, and it now houses a collection that reflects the state's diversity and rich history: the rooms devoted to archeology are, of course, dominated by the **Tarascan culture**, including pottery and small sculptures from Tzintzuntzán, but also display much earlier objects, notably some obsidian figurines. Out in the patio are two magnificent old carriages, while upstairs the colonial epoch is represented in a large group of religious paintings and sculptures and a collection of old books and manuscripts.

Plaza Melchor Ocampo

A smaller square, the **Plaza Melchor Ocampo**, flanks the cathedral on the other side. Facing it, the **Palacio de Gobierno** was formerly a seminary – Independence hero Morelos and his nemesis Agustín Iturbide studied here, as did Ocampo, a nineteenth-century liberal supporter of Benito Juárez. It's of interest now for Alfredo Zalce's **murals**

EATING

Café del Conservatorio	3
Café del Teatro	4
La Copa de Oro	2
Del Olmo	5
Dulces Morelianas de la Calle Real	9
Fonda Las Mercedes	6
Gaspachos la Cerrada	11
Los Mirasoles	7
San Miguelito	12
Super Cocina Las Rosas	1
El Tragadero	11
Vegetalia	10
Vegetariano Govinda's	8

ACCOMMODATION

Casino	6
Catedral	7
City Express	5
Colonial	2
Hostal San Fransiskuni	11
Hostel Allende	9
Hotel el Carmen	4
Hotel de la Soledad	1
Hotel Posada Don Vasco	10
Señorial	3
Virrey de Mendoza	8

MORELIA

adorning the stairway and upper level of the patio: practically the whole of Mexican history, and each of its heroes, is depicted.

Immediately east of the square on Madero are several **banks** that are among the most remarkable examples of active conservation you'll see anywhere: old mansions that have been refurbished in traditional style, and somehow manage to combine reasonably efficient operation with an ambience that is wholly in keeping with the setting.

Calle Nigromante and around

One block west of the Plaza de Armas, the **Colegio de San Nicolas** is part of the University of Michoacán. Founded at Pátzcuaro in 1540 by Vasco de Quiroga, and moved here in 1580, the college is the second oldest in Mexico and hence in all the Americas – it now houses administrative offices and various technical faculties. To the side, across Nigromante in what was originally the Jesuit church of **La Compañía**, is the public library, while next to this is the beautiful **Palacio Clavijero**, now converted into government offices.

Alongside the Palacio, down Gomez Farias, enclosed *portales* are home to the **Mercado de Dulces y Artesanías**, groaning with the sweets for which the city is famed, along with stalls selling leather jackets, guitars and other handicrafts, though little of much quality. At the north end of Nigromante, on another charming little plaza – the Jardín de las Rosas – you'll come across the Baroque church of **Santa Rosa** and, beside it, the **Conservatorio de las Rosas**, a music academy founded in the eighteenth century. From time to time it hosts concerts of classical music – the tourist office should have details.

Museo del Estado

Guillermo Prieto 176, near the corner of Santiago Tapia • Mon–Fri 9am–8pm, Sat & Sun 10am–6pm • Free

Inside an eighteenth-century former home, the complete furniture and fittings of a traditional *farmacia* have been reconstructed as part of the **Museo del Estado**. Somewhat incongruously, there are also prehistory and archeology collections. This is mostly minor stuff, though there are some intriguing ceramic figurines and some fine, unusual Tarascan jewellery, including gold and turquoise pieces, and necklaces strung with tiny crystal skulls. Upstairs, there's one room of colonial history and various ethnological exhibits illustrating traditional local dress and lifestyles – a butterfly fishing net from Pátzcuaro plus displays on copper working and guitar manufacture.

Casa de la Cultura and around

Casa de la Cultura, Morelos Nte • Mon–Fri 8am–9pm, Sat 10am–7pm, Sun 7am–6pm, open later if there's something special on • Free

On the north side of Plaza del Carmen, entered from Morelos, the beautiful old Convento del Carmen now houses the **Casa de la Cultura**. It's an enormous complex, worth exploring in its own right, with a theatre, café, space for temporary exhibitions and classes scattered around the former monastic buildings. International films are sometimes screened here. The collection of colonial art at the nearby **Museo de Arte Colonial**, Juárez 240 (Mon–Fri 9am–8pm, Sat & Sun 10am–6pm; free), is almost entirely regional, and not of great interest, though there is an expansive display of rather gory crucifixes.

Museo Casa de Morelos and around

Museo Casa de Morelos, Morelos Sur 323 • Tues–Sun 9am–4.45pm • M$35, free Sun

Two blocks southeast of the cathedral, the **Museo Casa de Morelos** is the relatively modest eighteenth-century house in which Independence hero José María Morelos y Pavón lived from 1801 (see box, p.303). It's now a museum devoted to his life and the War of Independence. You can see the house where the man was born, the **Casa Natal**

> **MORELIA FESTIVALS**
>
> Try to get here for the Festival Internacional de Guitarra (held in March or April, ⓦfigmorelia
> .com.mx), a fantastic gathering of musicians from around the world; Expo Feria (dates vary in
> April/May), the Michoacán Expo Fair celebrating the arts and industry of the region; Morelos'
> birthday (Sept 30), celebrated with civic events, fairs, dances and fireworks; or the Festival
> Internacional de Música (second and third week in Nov, ⓦfestivalmorelia.com.mx), an
> international festival with concerts, recitals, operas and conferences.

de Morelos, nearby at Corregidora 105, on the corner of García Obeso (Mon–Fri
8.30am–8pm, Sat 11am–7pm, Sun 8.30am–4pm; free). It now houses a library and a
few desultory domestic objects.

Iglesia de San Agustín

Garcia Obespo 162 • Daily 8am–5pm, hourly services on Sun • Free

Southwest of the cathedral is the centre's functioning church for daily worship. The
interior is equally as splendid as its larger neighbour, and it holds Mass a minimum of
four times a day, and every hour on the hour on Sundays. Look out for the black Jesus
on the left-hand side and the tasteful array of souvenirs beside the east entrance.

Casa de las Artesanías

Plaza Vallladolid • Mon–Fri 8am–4pm & 5–8pm, Sat & Sun 9am–3pm & 4–8pm • Free • ⓦ casadelasartesanias.gob.mx

Plaza Valladolid is dominated on its east side by the sixteenth-century church of **San
Francisco**. The church's former monastery, which stands next door to it, has been
turned into the **Casa de las Artesanías**, possibly the most comprehensive collection of
Michoacán's crafts anywhere. Almost all of them are for sale. The best and most
obviously commercial items are downstairs, while on the upper floor is a series of
rooms devoted to the products of particular villages, often with craftspeople
demonstrating their techniques (these are staffed by villagers and hence not always
open), and a collection of historic items which you can't buy.

The aqueduct and around

One of the most attractive parts of town to while away a few hours lies about fifteen
minutes' walk east along Madero from the cathedral, some five blocks beyond the
Baroque facade of the **Templo de las Monjas** and the adjacent Palacio Federal, to where
the old **aqueduct** leads southeastward from **Plaza Villalongin**. Built on a winding course
between 1785 and 1789, the aqueduct's 253 arches brought water into the city from
springs in the nearby hills.

Callejón de Romance

Several roads meet just south of Plaza Villalongin at the **Fuente Las Tarascas**, which
features three bare-breasted Tarascan women holding up a vast basket of fruit. East of
the fountain, Madero bears slightly left and, off to its north, just past the aqueduct, the
Callejón de Romance (Romance Lane) is a pretty, bougainvillea-draped alley of
nineteenth-century homes, which has a couple more fountains at its northern end.

Calzada Fray Antonio de San Miguel

Leading between east and southeast from Plaza Villalongin, the **Calzada Fray Antonio de
San Miguel** (named for the bishop who built the aqueduct) is a broad and shady
pedestrianized walkway that leads down to the wildly overdecorated **Sanctuario de
Guadalupe**, where market stalls, selling above all the sticky local *dulces*, set up at
weekends and during fiestas.

Avenida Acueducto

The last of the three roads east of Plaza Villalongin is Avenida Acueducto, which leads southeast, following the aqueduct. On its southern side, the **Bosque Cuauhtémoc** is a pleasant park with some beautifully laid-out flower displays, where young lovers while away the sunny afternoons together.

Museo de Arte Contemporáneo

Av Acueducto • Tues–Fri 10am–8pm, Sat & Sun 10am–6pm • Free

Avenida Acueducto passes the small **Museo de Arte Contemporáneo**, where the only permanent works on display are by local sculptor Alfredo Zalce, who died in 2003. There are always temporary exhibitions on, however, featuring modern artists from Mexico and around the world.

ARRIVAL AND DEPARTURE

MORELIA

By plane Morelia's airport, 27km northeast of town on the Zinapecuaro road (Hwy-120), has flights to a handful of US airports, as well as to Mexico City (2–5 daily; 50min) and Tijuana (1–2 daily; 3hr 15min).

By bus Morelia's modern bus station, the Central Camionera, is around 3km northwest of the centre on the city's ring road. Of the three terminal halls, *Sala* A is mostly for first-class intercity services, *Sala* B for first-class intercity and local services and *Sala* C for second-class services. To get into town, you can catch a cab (fixed-price tickets sold inside the terminal; M$35 to the cathedral) or

walk out onto the main road and wait for a Roja 1 *colectivo* (look for a white minibus with a red band) which will take you into town along Madero. To get back to the bus station, catch the same *colectivo* from along Ocampo.

Destinations Aguascalientes (8 daily; 7hr); Guadalajara (40 daily; 3hr 30min); Guanajuato (2 daily; 3hr 30min); León (hourly; 4hr); Mexico City Nte (at least 1 hourly; 4hr 30min); Mexico City Pte (at least 5 hourly; 4hr); Pátzcuaro (every 10min; 1hr); Querétaro (27 daily; 4hr); Toluca (every 30min; 4hr); Uruapan (every 30min; 2hr); Zitácuaro (every 30min; 3hr).

INFORMATION

Tourist information For information about Morelia specifically, there's a Centro de Atención al Turista at Portal Hidalgo 245, on the north side of Plaza de Armas, behind *McDonald's* (daily 9am–9pm; ☎443 312 0414 or, toll free from out of town ☎01 800 667 3542, ⓦvisitmorelia.com).

The state tourist office, for information about Michoacán more generally, is east of the centre at Tata Vasco 80 (Mon–Fri 9am–6pm, and sometimes weekends too; ☎443 317 8054, or toll free from elsewhere in the country on ☎01 800 450 2300, ⓦturismomichoacan.gob.mx).

JOSÉ MARÍA MORELOS Y PAVÓN

A student of Hidalgo, **José María Morelos** took over the leadership of the **Independence movement** after its instigators had been executed in 1811. While the cry of Independence had initially been taken up by the Mexican (Creole) bourgeoisie, smarting under the trading restrictions imposed on them by Spain, it quickly became a mass movement. Unlike the original leaders, Morelos (a *mestizo* priest born into relative poverty) was a populist and genuine reformer. Even more unlike them, he was also a political and military tactician of considerable skill, invoking the spirit of the French Revolution and calling for universal suffrage, racial equality and the break-up of the hacienda system, under which workers were tied to agricultural servitude. He was defeated and executed by Royalist armies under Agustín de Iturbide in 1815 after waging years of guerrilla warfare, a period during which Morelos had come close to taking the capital and controlling the entire country. When Independence was finally gained – by Iturbide, who had changed sides and later briefly served as emperor – it was no longer a force for change, rather a reaction to the fact that by 1820 liberal reforms were sweeping Spain itself. The causes espoused by Morelos were, however, taken up to some extent by Benito Juárez and later, with a vengeance, in the Revolution – almost a hundred years after his death.

Around Michoacán you'll see Morelos' image everywhere – notably the massive **statue** atop Isla de Janitzio (see p.295) – invariably depicted with a kind of bandana over his head. He's also pictured on the **fifty-peso note**, which features the butterfly-net fishers of Pátzcuaro, monarch butterflies and masks for the Danza de los Viejitos.

ACCOMMODATION

HOTELS

Casino Portal Hidalgo 229 ☏443 313 1328; ⓦhotelcasino.com.mx. Beautiful hotel on the Plaza de Armas set around a covered courtyard. It's in an old colonial building, and there's a great painting of the hotel around 1900 behind the reception desk, but otherwise all character has been removed to make a comfortable but generic city-centre hotel, equipped with most of the amenities you'd want, including a gym, though not a/c. Breakfast included. M$1081

Catedral Ignacio Zaragoza 37 ☏443 313 0406, ⓦhotelesmision.com.mx. Light, airy rooms with king-size beds and ceiling fans around a restaurant in a covered colonial courtyard. The hotel doubles as the Spanish consulate, and rooms with a cathedral view cost slightly more than those without. M$1094

City Express Portal Hidalgo 245, on the Plaza de Armas ☏443 310 8400, ⓦcityexpress.com.mx. Great position under the colonial arches, and very modern if rather soulless. There's free wi-fi and a gym, but only eight of its sixty rooms have outside windows. Breakfast included. M$1049

Colonial 20 de Noviembre 15 ☏443 312 1897, ⓦnovocolonial.com.mx. One of the cheaper places in the centre, in a lovely old mansion with two patios and a wide range of rooms, all with bathrooms (hot water all day), free wi-fi and its own supervised parking lot around the corner. The nicest rooms face the street. Off-season, they'll usually do you a deal. M$350

Hotel el Carmen Eduardo Ruíz 63 ☏443 312 1725, ⓦhotelelcarmenmorelia.com.mx. Friendly hotel on a pretty square, with clean rooms, mostly with TV and bathroom. The cheapest rooms are tiny and cell-like, overlooking the Plaza del Carmen. Breakfast included. M$500

★ Hotel de la Soledad Ignacio Zaragoza 90 ☏443 312 1888, ⓦhoteldelasoledad.com. This spectacular colonial building is the city's oldest inn and an absolutely gorgeous upmarket hotel. Breezy rooms, all with king-size beds, are set around a beautiful open courtyard at the front, while those round the less attractive back courtyard have been modernized with a/c, but have lost some of their character

in the process. The junior suites, on the other hand, combine the best of both worlds, with all mod cons, beautiful decor and lashings of period charm. M$1980

Hotel Posada Don Vasco Vasco de Quiroga 232 ☏443 312 1484, ⊜posada_don_vasco@hotmail.com. Far and away the best deal in this price range, in a great old colonial building, with a variety of rooms – some atmospheric, with period architecture, but others dull and modern, or small and stuffy – so it's worth having a look round before deciding. Services include cable TV, free wi-fi and free phone calls to Mexican landlines. M$320

Señorial Santiago Tapía 543 ☏443 962 9116. This shabby hotel in a run-down old colonial building is not the most salubrious place in town, but in a city where low-price accommodation is hard to find, it's perfect for hardcore budgeteers who need a really cheap place to sleep and aren't otherwise too fussy. M$100

Virrey de Mendoza Madero 310 Pte ☏443 312 0633 or ☏01 800 450 2000, US ☏+1 866 299 7492, Canada ☏+1 877 889 2161, ⓦhotelvirrey.com. Fantastic colonial grandeur: even if you can't afford to stay, it's worth dropping by to take a look or have a drink in the courtyard. The rooms aren't as impressive as the lobby, but it is a lovely spot just the same for its history, majestic public spaces and fine service. M$2200

HOSTELS

Hostel Allende Allende 843 ☏443 275 6912, ⓦhotelallendemorelia.com. Slightly institutional hotel/hostel with rooms around a leafy courtyard that's good for relaxing. Single-sex dorms are vastly outnumbered by cubicle-like private rooms, all with bathrooms. There's a small kitchen, free wi-fi and 24hr check-in. Breakfast included. Dorms M$150, doubles M$350

Hostal San Fransiskuni Alzate 302 ☏443 313 0703. A small, informal hostel in an old colonial house, equipped with pleasant four- and five-bed dorms, each with a bathroom, and a handful of private rooms with shared bathroom facilities. There's free wi-fi, and they speak English. Prices include breakfast, although you'll still find yourself hungry after the meagre offerings. Dorms M$170, doubles M$330

EATING

On a fine day it's hard to resist the temptation of the cafés and restaurants in the *portales* around the Plaza de Armas: fairly expensive for a full meal, but good for snacks or for a breakfast of coffee and *pan dulce*. As ever, the cheapest eating is at the **food market** in Plaza Capuchinas, but Morelia's big Mercado Independencia, just to its south, is on the whole a disappointment, certainly not as large or varied as you'd expect. Chief among Morelia's specialities are its **dulces**, sweets made of candied fruit or evaporated milk – cloyingly sweet to most non-Mexican tastes, they're very popular here. You can see a wide selection at the **Mercado de Dulces y Artesanías** (see p.301). Morelians also get through a lot of *rompope* (a drink that you'll find to a lesser extent all over Mexico) – again, it's very sweet, an egg concoction based on rum, milk and egg, with vanilla, cinnamon or almond flavouring.

CAFÉS

Café del Conservatorio Santiago Tapia 363 ☎ 443 312 8601. A peaceful place to enjoy a drink or a snack on the pretty Jardín de las Rosas. They also do good but rather pricey breakfasts (M$85–106), and even ice-cream sodas (M$65). Mon–Sat 8am–midnight, Sun 1–10pm.

★**Café del Teatro** upstairs in the Teatro Ocampo, on Ocampo and Prieto ☎ 443 317 3777. Overlooking Ocampo, a lush, almost baronial, interior makes this one of the most popular spots in town for good coffee and people-watching. With breakfast for M$55–75 and sweet or savoury crêpes at M$38–53, it's not as expensive as it might be. Try to get a table overlooking the street. Daily 9am–11pm.

Del Olmo Juárez 95 ☎ 443 232 0056. Sophisticated but relaxed café-bar, set around a pretty interior courtyard, with good coffee. They do breakfast deals until 1pm (M$65 for fruit, eggs al gusto, coffee and juice) and a M$70 comida corrida from then on. There's also free wi-fi. Daily 9am–11.30pm.

Dulces Morelianas de la Calle Real Madero Ote 440 ☎ 443 312 0477. Magnificent old-fashioned candy store with a café serving decadent coffees with drizzles of *cajeta*, and a wide selection of interesting confectionery prepared in traditional copper pots, including sugarless fruit sweets. The staff even sport colonial dress, and there's a small Museo del Dulces upstairs on the 4th floor (M$20). Daily 10am–7.30pm.

★**El Tragadero** Hidalgo 63 ☎ 443 313 0092. At this relaxed café-restaurant you're surrounded by old photos of Morelia. It's a good place for breakfast (M$35–60), inexpensive lunch (menu M$57) and classic Mexican creole side-dishes like pork trotters in vinegar (M$55). Favourite dishes include *filete de pescado con papas* (aka fish and chips; M$71). Daily 7.30am–11pm.

CHEAT EATS AND SNACKS

La Copa de Oro Juárez 194-B at Santiago Tapia ☎ 443 313 1049. An excellent place for fresh *jugos*, and they also do salads (M$45), baguettes (M$30) and breakfasts (M$42). Mon–Sat 7.30am–9pm, Sun 8.30am–5pm.

Gaspachos la Cerrada Hidalgo 67. Nothing like a Spanish *gazpacho*, a Morelian *gaspacho* is a finely chopped fruit salad, topped – if you like – with grated cheese and chile powder. Plenty of places around town sell it, but this

is the most renowned. A cup of *gaspacho* here will set you back M$25. Daily 9am–9pm.

Super Cocina Las Rosas Santiago Tapia at Prieto. A row of pots bubbling on the stove contain the day's dishes, which might include meatballs, or chicken breast stuffed with cheese, all for around M$50 a go. They also do breakfasts, but only with instant coffee. Note that they may close earlier if the food runs out. Daily 8.30am–5pm.

Vegetalia Allende 329-A ☎ 443 312 4615. Open-fronted and inexpensive, this vegetarian buffet eatery is a great lunch option specializing in salads (Waldorf salad M$35). The breakfasts are served until 1pm, while the buffet goes from noon until 5pm. Also has a good range of puddings. Daily 9am–6pm.

Vegetariano Govinda's Madero Ote 549 ☎ 443 313 3368. Good, inexpensive, vegetarian fare. Come for breakfast (M$42–47) or the *menu del día* (M$47–51), comprising meatless versions of Mexican staples. Or just stop by for a veggieburger (M$20). Daily 10am–6pm.

RESTAURANTS

Fonda Las Mercedes León Guzmán 47 ☎ 443 312 6113. Upscale Tarascan and Mexican dishes in a swanky setting – all white linen and big wine glasses. Expect the likes of *pechuga azteca* (chicken breast stuffed with cheese; M$155) and salmon *a la plancha* with tarragon (M$190). Mon–Sat 1.30pm–midnight, Sun 1.30–7pm.

★**Los Mirasoles** Madero 549 Pte ☎ 443 317 5775, ⓦ losmirasoles.com. Contemporary Mexican cuisine in a plush conversion of a seventeenth-century mansion – the courtyard is enchanting. There's a full range of Michoacán specialities, including trout tacos (M$59) and *chamorro* (leg of pork) in *chile* and *pulque* sauce (M$190). There's also a M$295 tasting menu. Mon–Sat 1–11.30pm, Sun 1–6pm.

San Miguelito Av Camelinas, Fraccionamiento La Loma (at the southern end of Ventura Puente, opposite the Centro de Convenciones, 2km southeast of the centre) ☎ 443 324 2300, ⓦ sanmiguelito.com.mx. Superb, unpretentious Mexican dishes such as fish cooked in a banana leaf (M$165), and you can start with a *plato mescalero* of snacks to go with mescal (M$180 including two shots). The bar is a re-created bullring. Be sure to sit in the room filled with three hundred effigies of St Anthony and say a prayer for a good spouse. Mon–Sat 2–11pm, Sun 2–5pm.

DIRECTORY

Banks and exchange There are plenty of very grand banks with ATMs along Madero Ote, plus a *casa de cambio* at Prieto 48 near the Plaza de Armas (closed Sun), and one at Tapía 79-A by *Copa de Oro*.

Internet On Line, Allende 338 (Mon–Fri 7am–10pm, Sat & Sun 9am–10pm; M$8/hr), and a nameless place at Morelos Nte 278, by Plaza del Carmen (Mon–Fri 10am–9pm; M$8/hr).

Post office Madero Ote 369 (Mon–Fri 8am–4.30pm, Sat 8am–noon).

Pharmacy Farmacias del Ahorro, Madero Pte 33, opposite the cathedral (daily 24hr).

Telephones There are a number of *casetas* dotted around town, of which the most central is at Portal Galeana 103, on Madero opposite the cathedral.

The Monarch Butterfly Sanctuary and around

120km east of Morelia • Mid-Nov to end March daily 9am–4pm • M$55 • ⓦ mariposamonarca.semarnat.gob.mx • Pick-ups from Angangueo (see p.309) in season direct to the sanctuary entrance at El Rosario (40min), and also to the highway 2km from the entrance for Sierra Chincua; if no direct transport to El Rosario, you can go via the nearby village of Ocampo, 9km down the road; in season there are also direct buses from Mexico City Pte (Autobuses Zincantepec)

Each winter more than 150 million monarch **butterflies** (see below) migrate from the northeastern US and Canada to the Oyamel fir forests in the lush mountains of Michoacán in order to reproduce. It's an amazing sight at any time, but especially in January and February when numbers peak: whole trees are smothered in monarchs, branches sagging under the weight. In the cool of the morning, they dry their wings, turning the entire landscape a rich, velvety orange, while later in the day they take to the air, millions of fluttering butterflies making more noise than you'd ever think possible. As the afternoon humidity forces them to the ground, they form a thick carpet of blazing colour. The place to see the monarchs is in the **Santuario de la Mariposa Monarca** about 120km east of Morelia, with entrances at El Rosario and Sierra Chincua, near the village of Angangueo. While the Sierra Chincua entrance is, on the face of it, less convenient, with public transport dropping you 2km short, the hike inside the sanctuary is actually less strenuous from here. There are also sections of the sanctuary across the state line in the State of Mexico, which are most easily visited from Valle de Bravo (see p.193), but can also be accessed from Zitácuaro.

Visiting the monarchs is possible on day trips from Morelia and Mexico City, but it is more satisfying to stay locally (probably in Angangueo) and visit at a more leisurely pace. It is best to go early in the morning (and preferably on weekdays, to avoid the crowds), when the butterflies are just waking up and before they fly off into the surrounding woodlands. The walk to the best of the monarch-laden trees is about 2km, mostly uphill at an altitude of almost 3000m: take it easy if you're not acclimatized.

Tour guides, who are on hand at all the various park entrances and whose services are included in the entry fee, show you around the sanctuary and give a short explanation

LIFE CYCLE AND HABITAT OF THE MONARCH BUTTERFLY

The sheer size of the congregation of monarch butterflies in the hills of Michoacán is astonishing, but not as impressive as their 4500km **migration**. In the autumn, when the weather starts to turn cold in the Great Lakes region of the US and Canada, the butterflies head south, taking just four to five weeks to make it to Michoacán. Here, in an area of less than 150 square kilometres, they find the unique microclimate a perfect place to spend the winter. The cool temperatures allow them to conserve energy, the trees provide shelter from wind and precipitation and the fog-laden air prevents them from drying out. Monarchs typically have a **life cycle** of around two to five weeks, but when they fly south they go into a phase known as "reproductive diapause", and end up living for seven months in all. The same butterflies remain in Michoacán all winter, then breed in spring in time for their caterpillars to dine on the newly emergent milkweed plants – their only food source – before returning to the US and Canada.

Around ten percent of all migrating monarchs get eaten by black-headed grosbeaks and black-backed orioles, but that offers no danger to species survival. The real threat is loss of this crucial mountain **habitat**. This was recognized as far back as 1986, when several key overwintering sites were protected from logging, but the local peasant families need the wood and they were never fully compensated for the loss of this resource. The Mexican government more than tripled the size of the reserves in 2000, but logging continued to a large enough extent that in early 2007 new president Felipe Calderón declared a "zero tolerance" policy against it, and increased policing. To learn more, check out the Monarch Watch website at ⓦ monarchwatch.org.

of the butterflies' life cycle and breeding habits. For a couple of weeks on either side of the main season, those same guides run the place unofficially, still charging the entry price and offering their services for a tip. There are fewer butterflies but it is still worth the journey any time from early November to early April, although the best time is in January or February.

Zitácuaro

Most people approaching the butterfly sanctuary change buses at **Zitácuaro**, a small town prettily scattered over low hills at around 1900m. Being a little warmer than Angangueo makes it a potential base for visiting the Butterfly Sanctuary, even though it is further away from the most popular park areas at El Rosario and Sierra Chincua. It is however closer to the less frequented, and prettier, park area at **Cerro Pelón** in the State of Mexico (see p.193), though you will need to arrange your own transport (for example through the *Hotel Rancho San Cayetano*) to go there as it is not served by public transport from Michoacán.

Zitácuaro's epicentre is the junction of Hidalgo and Revolución, around which you'll find half a dozen hotels, restaurants, cinemas, *casetas* and internet cafés. The main square, Plaza Juárez, a block south on Revolución and then a block west on Ocampo, is dominated by a statue of Benito Juárez, facing the town hall. Pleasant though it is, however, this is not a city of sights or monuments. The nearest thing to a tourist attraction is the sixteenth-century church in the neighbouring village of **San Francisco** (known locally as **San Pancho**). The village has minor movie fame as the scene of the *dénouement* in John Huston's 1948 film classic, *The Treasure of the Sierra Madre*, starring Humphrey Bogart, which was adapted from B. Traven's famous novel of the same name (see p.851).

ARRIVAL AND DEPARTURE   ZITÁCUARO

By bus The bus station is about 1km east of the centre, and is served by regular *combis* from right outside. Alternatively, you can walk to the centre, turning left along Pueblita, and then right down Hidalgo after two blocks.

Destinations Angangueo (every 15min; 50min); Mexico City Pte (every 40min; 3hr); Morelia (every 20min; 3hr); Ocampo (every 15min; 30min); Toluca (every 30min; 1hr 30min).

ACCOMMODATION

Ibarra Revolución Sur 20 ☎ 715 153 3076. There are some very cheap, cell-like rooms without bathrooms at this basic, functional hotel, next door to the *México*, but you pay M$20 to use the shared shower facilities anyway, so you may as well pay double for a larger, en-suite room. M$80

México Revolución Sur 22 ☎ 715 153 2811. A block and a half south of Revolución with Hidalgo, this refurbished hotel is one of the better choices around that

junction, with en-suite rooms, wi-fi and a downstairs restaurant. M$490

Rancho San Cayetano Carretera a Huetamo km2.3 (2km south of town) ☎ 715 153 1926, ⊕ ranchosan cayetano.com. A wonderful place, set in private woodland, with lovely scenery, attractive rooms, a pool and a good restaurant. In season, they can also advise on visits to different butterfly locations. Prices rise by M$300 on Fri and Sat. M$1475

EATING

El Centavit Hidalgo Ote 107 ☎ 715 157 5527. This is supposed to be a *taquería*, but their real speciality is iguana soup (M$75), and very tasty it is too, especially when liberally sprinkled with finely chopped onion and coriander. If you're lucky you'll get a delicious iguana egg thrown into the mix. Daily 9am–11pm.

La Trucha Alegre Revolución Nte 2 (upstairs)

☎ 715 153 9809. In this large dining room in the former Cinema Avenida, half a block north of Revolución with Hidalgo, they serve trout in 35 different guises, including stuffed or bathed in all kinds of sauces, but a simple trout *a la plancha* with *salsa verde* goes for M$85. The best tables are the small ones overlooking the street. Daily 8am–9pm.

4

JALISCO AND MICHOACÁN FIESTAS

Both Jalisco and Michoacán preserve strong native traditions and are particularly rich in fiestas: the list below is by no means exhaustive, and local tourist offices will have further details.

New Year's Day (Jan 1). Celebrated in Pátzcuaro (see p.289) and Uruapan (see p.284) with the Danza de los Viejitos (Dance of the Little Old Men; see box, p.286).

Día de los Santos Reyes (Jan 6). Twelfth Night is celebrated with many small ceremonies and dances such as Los Sonajeros (rattles), Las Pastoras (the shepherdesses) and El Baile de la Conquista (conquest). Particularly good at Los Reyes (west of Uruapan) and Cajititlán (25km south of Guadalajara).

Día de San Sebastian (Jan 20). Traditional dances in Tuxpan (30km southeast of Ciudad Guzmán).

Día de Nuestro Señor del Rescate (Feb 1). In Tzintzuntzán (see p.297), the start of a week-long fiesta founded in the sixteenth century by Vasco de Quiroga.

Carnaval (the week before Lent, variable Feb–March). Celebrated everywhere.

Festival Internacional de Guitarra (late March or early April). International Guitar Festival in Morelia (see p.298).

Palm Sunday (the Sun before Easter Sun). Palm ornament market in Uruapan (see p.284).

Semana Santa (Holy Week). Observed everywhere, but especially in Tzintzuntzán (see p.297).

Expo Feria (variable April–May). Arts and industry show in Morelia (see p.298).

Día de la Santa Cruz (May 3). Native dances in Angangueo (see opposite); mariachis and tequila in Tequila (see p.276).

Día del Señor de la Misericordia (last Sun in May). Fiesta and dances in Tuxpan (southeast of Ciudad Guzmán).

Corpus Christi (Thurs after Trinity, variable late May to early June). Traditional dances in Paracho (50km south of Zamora).

Día de San Pedro (June 29). Mariachi and dance festival in Tlaquepaque, Guadalajara (see p.255).

Día de la Preciosa Sangre de Cristo (first Sun in July). Torch-lit religious processions in Quiroga (25km northeast of Pátzcuaro).

Día de María Magdalena (July 22). Fiesta in Uruapan (see p.284) featuring a procession of animals.

Día de Santiago Apóstol (July 25). Lively celebrations and fireworks in Tuxpan (southeast of Ciudad Guzmán) and Uruapan (see p.284).

Fiesta tradicional (Aug 8). Ancient pre-Columbian fiesta in Paracho (50km south of Zamora).

Feria Nacional del Cobre (second week in Aug). National Copper Fair in Santa Clara del Cobre (see p.298), near Pátzcuaro.

Morelos' birthday (Sept 30). Celebrated in Morelia (see p.298).

Fiestas de Octubre (all month). Massive cultural festival in Guadalajara (see p.255).

Día de San Francisco (Oct 4). Saint's day celebrations in Uruapan (see p.284).

Día de la Raza (Oct 12). Uruapan (see p.284) celebrates Columbus's "discovery" of the Americas.

Día de la Virgen de Zapopan (Oct 12). Massive pilgrimage in Guadalajara (see p.255).

Festival de Coros y Danzas (Oct 24–26). Singing and dancing competitions in Uruapan (see p.284).

Día de los Muertos (Day of the Dead; Nov 2). Celebrated everywhere, but especially around Pátzcuaro (see box, p.296). Also picturesque in Zitácuaro.

Arrival of the monarch butterfly (second week of Nov). *Las monarcas* start arriving in Michoacán in big numbers around now.

Festival Internacional de Música (third week of Nov). International Music Festival in Morelia (see p.298).

Feria de Aguacate (variable Nov–Dec). Three-week avocado fair in Uruapan (see p.284).

Día de la Inmaculada Concepción (Dec 8). Celebrated in Sayula (32km north of Ciudad Guzmán on the Tapalpa road).

La Señora de la Salud (Dec 8). Pilgrimage and dances in Pátzcuaro (see p.289) and Tequila (see p.276).

Día de la Virgen de Guadalupe (Dec 12). Large celebrations in Tapalpa (see p.282).

Pastoral plays (Dec 24). Performed in Tuxpan (southeast of Ciudad Guzmán).

Angangueo

Most butterfly visitors stay at **Angangueo**, 29km north of Zitácuaro, a former mining town wedged into a valley at almost 2600m: it can be cool in the evenings. The name is Purépechas for "entrance to the cave", presumably an early reference to its mineral extraction potential. The mines have now closed, but with its terracotta-tiled roofs, winding streets and houses stacked up the hillside, it is an attractive enough place and offers the best selection of hotels and restaurants around – certainly better than Ocampo. Angangueo celebrates the Día de la Santa Cruz (May 3) with traditional dances. Most things happen on Morelos, which becomes Nacional at the point where the minor road Matamoros heads off up to the butterfly sanctuary. If you're feeling energetic, note that it's possible to walk back to Angangueo (around 2hr) downhill from the butterfly sanctuary entrance at El Rosario.

ARRIVAL AND DEPARTURE   ANGANGUEO

By bus Buses drop off at the top of the town, and then head down to the junction of Nacional and Matamoros.

Destinations Mexico City Pte (6 daily; 4hr); Ocampo (every 15min; 20min); Zitácuaro (every 15min; 50min).

ACCOMMODATION

Don Bruno Morelos 92, 1km south of the town centre ☎ 715 156 0026. The best place to stay in Angangueo by far: large, carpeted rooms (all featuring religious images) surround a lovely garden, with a good restaurant and free wi-fi. It's a bit of a climb to the bus stop, but otherwise couldn't be more convenient. M$750

Juárez Nacional 15, in the town centre ☎ 715 156 0023. A friendly place with reasonable en-suite rooms set around a flower-filled courtyard. The stationery shop next door doubles as the hotel reception. M$250

Rancho Givali El Rosario, 2km down the hill from the sanctuary entrance ☎ 715 115 5236 or (from Mexico City) ☎ 55 5239 5485 or (toll-free from elsewhere in Mexico) ☎ 01 800 087 6000. The closest accommodation to the butterfly sanctuary, right there in the woods, offering comfortable rooms, camping and a good restaurant. Double rooms have two queen-size beds, and if you want to take the chill off those winter evenings, it's worth asking for one with a fireplace. M$1289

Real Monarca Nacional 21, in the town centre ☎ 715 156 0324. Rosa Ramirez runs this very cosy posada on the main hotel street, and includes a continental breakfast with her rates. Rooms are spotless and they can organize tours of other regional sights out of season. M$280

EATING

Restaurant Los Arcos Plaza de la Constitucion 5-A ☎ 715 156 0120. The best eating place in the town centre, where you'll pay very reasonable prices for good, home-style Mexican dishes (chicken *mole*, for example, when

they have it, is M$40). The range is limited, but the food is always good, and they do great breakfasts (M$35) and *comidas corridas* (M$65). Daily 8am–7pm.

4

The Bajío

SCULPTURE AT LAS POZAS

5

The Bajío

North of Mexico City, the fertile valleys of the Bajío ("Lowlands") are sprinkled with wealthy colonial towns and rugged, dust-blown hills. This has long been the most heavily populated part of the country, providing much of the silver and grain that supported Mexico throughout the years of Spanish rule. Indeed, the legacy of Spanish architecture remains at its most impressive here, in meticulously crafted towns that – at their cores at least – have changed little over the centuries.

The Bajío grew rich on just one thing – **silver** – but in time the region also grew restive under the heavy-handed rule of Spain. The wealthy Creole (Spanish-blooded but Mexican-born) bourgeoisie were free to exploit the land and its people, but didn't control their own destinies; lucrative government posts and high positions in the Church were reserved exclusively for those actually born in Spain, while the indigenous peoples and poor *mestizos* were condemned either to landless poverty or to near-fatal labour. Unsurprisingly, then, the Bajío was ripe for revolution. This land is *La Cuna de la Independencia* (the **Cradle of Independence**), where every town seems to claim a role in the break with Spain. **Dolores Hidalgo**, in particular, is a point of pilgrimage for anyone with the least interest in Mexico's independence movement, as is, to a lesser extent, **Querétaro**, a large and booming modern city that preserves an underrated colonial quarter at its heart. Querétaro also serves as a good base for exploring the **Sierra Gorda**, particularly the concrete fantasy sculptures of **Las Pozas** near Xilitla. **Guanajuato**, quite simply one of the country's most scenic colonial towns, is close to **San Miguel de Allende**, which also has its advocates, as much for its wonderful setting as for the comforts of home, ensured by a large population of foreign artists, gringo retirees and language students. Heading north, the less-visited city of **Aguascalientes** is a real pleasure, with an appealing roster of colonial relics, art from José Posada and fabulous food. The north of the region is dominated by the colonial cities of **Zacatecas** and **San Luis Potosí** – both eponymous state capitals and oases of culture and sophistication, built largely with the bounty of the silver mines that riddle the landscape hereabouts. Approaching the Bajío from the US border, you cross several hundred kilometres of desert landscape punctuated only by the occasional ranch, or

Highlights

❶ Peña de Bernal Hike up the slopes of this stunning tower of rock, one of the world's tallest monoliths, easily accessible from the colonial city of Querétaro. **See p.322**

❷ Las Pozas Visit the surreal creation of English eccentric Edward James, a fantasy of concrete statues and structures surrounded by lush jungle. **See p.328**

❸ San Miguel de Allende Gorgeous colonial town with enticing boutique hotels and highly regarded Spanish language schools. **See p.329**

❹ Guanajuato Captivating university town set dramatically over the steep slopes of a ravine. **See p.345**

❺ Posada pilgrimage José Posada's macabre work is the pride of Aguascalientes, shown in the Museo José Guadalupe Posada and the Museo de la Muerte. **See p.362**

❻ Mercado de la Bírria The aromatic birrierías at Aguascalientes' Mercado de la Bírria are eye-popping, but slow-roasted goat is the real star. **See p.365**

❼ Zacatecas Handsome former silver-mining town located high up in the northern deserts. **See p.366**

❽ Real de Catorce Artfully restored colonial hotels, fine Italian meals and haunting desert scenery in a semi-ghost town. **See p.384**

HIGHLIGHTS ARE MARKED ON THE MAP ON PP.314–315

HIGHLIGHTS

1. Peña de Bernal
2. Las Pozas
3. San Miguel de Allende
4. Guanajuato
5. Posada pilgrimage
6. Mercado de la Bírria
7. Zacatecas
8. Real de Catorce

Saltillo — Saltillo & Monterrey

Matamoros

HWY 54

HWY 57

HWY 85

HWY 31

HWY 57

HWY 101

Río Corona

Presa de Las Adjuntas

Ciudad Victoria

...ción ...orce — Real de Catorce

8

Wadley

Matehuala

HWY 85

HWY 70

HWY 57

SAN LUIS POTOSÍ

GULF OF MEXICO

HWY 57

HWY 101

HWY 80

Ciudad Mante

San Luis Potosí

Tampico

Río Verde

HWY 70

Ciudad Valles

HWY 70

HWY 105

HWY 85

Dolores Hidalgo

HWY 57

San Luis de la Paz

Pozos

LA RESERVA DE LA BIOSFERA SIERRA GORDA

2

Xilitla

Santuario de Atotoncilo

Jalpan

Landa de Matamoros

Escondido

La ...ruta

San José Iturbide

QUERÉTARO

San Miguel de Allende

...añada ...la Virgen

3

1

Bernal

HWY 120

HWY 85

HWY 105

Ezequiel Montes

Querétaro

Tequisquiapan

HWY 45

San Juan del Río

HWY 57

HWY 85

HWY 51

Celaya

Acámbaro

Tula

Pachuca

HWY 130

Morelia

Toluca

Mexico City

5

defunct mining towns, such as the wonderfully strange semi-ghost-town of **Real de Catorce**, where decades of abandonment are gradually being reversed.

Querétaro and around

Of all the colonial cities in the Bajío, **QUERÉTARO** is perhaps the most surprising, with a tranquil historical core that boasts magnificent mansions and some of the country's finest ecclesiastical architecture. Little more than two hours from Mexico City, it's also a wealthy and booming city of over eight hundred thousand people, one of the fastest growing in the republic. Querétaro's colonial centre is particularly magical at the weekends, when festive crowds and markets throng the streets, and church bells echo across plazas linked by narrow alleys lined with restaurants and bars.

There are points of interest, too, in the surrounding hills of the Sierra Gorda, notably the small towns of **Bernal** and **Tequisquiapan**, and the much more distant charms of Edward James's jungle "sculpture garden" at **Xilitla**.

Jardín Zenéa and around

Querétaro's main plaza is the elegant **Jardín Zenéa**, with its typical triumvirate of bandstand, clipped trees and bootshines. To the west lies the commercial centre with the bulk of the chain stores, but you'll probably spend much of your time to the east among the gift shops, restaurants and bars leading to the **Plaza de la Independencia** (see p.318), or one block south to the **Plaza de la Constitución**. Formerly a market square, the latter has been transformed into an attractive modern plaza with a central fountain that mimics the domed roof of the building on its south side. Just to the north of Jardín Zenéa lies the shady **Jardín Corregidora**, with an imposing statue of La Corregidora (see box below) and several restaurants and bars where you can sit outside.

Templo de San Francisco
Jardín Zenéa • Daily 8am–9pm

The **Templo de San Francisco**, dominating the Jardín Zenéa, was one of the earliest churches founded in the city. Its eye-popping facade incorporates a dome covered in *azulejos* – coloured tiles imported from Spain around 1540 – but for the most part San Francisco was rebuilt in the seventeenth and eighteenth centuries. Take a look at the similarly opulent interior for an introduction to the city's remarkable treasure trove of religious art.

Museo Regional de Querétaro
Corregidora 3 (Jardín Zenéa) • Tues–Sun 9am–6pm • M$52 • ☎ 442 212 4888

Adjoining the Templo de San Francisco, in what used to be the Convento de San Francisco, is the **Museo Regional de Querétaro**. The building alone is reason enough to visit, though the displays inside are well worth an hour or two. Built around two large

---

LA CORREGIDORA

It was in Querétaro, meeting under the guise of literary associations, that the Mexican Independence conspirators (or "reformers") laid their earliest plans. In 1810 one of their number, María Josefa Ortiz de Domínguez, wife of the town's Corregidor (or governor – she is known as "**La Corregidora**"), was locked in her room while her husband was ordered to seek out the conspirators (though he was also sympathetic to their cause) – she managed to get a message out to Ignacio Pérez, who carried it to Independence movement leaders Allende and Hidalgo in the towns of San Miguel and Dolores, thus precipitating an unexpectedly early start to the independence struggle.

Bernal & Aeropuerto Intercontinental de Querétaro (32km)

QUERÉTARO

Central de Autobuses (6km)

Mercado Escobedo & Hospital Ángeles

Cerro de las Campanas (1km) & Museo la Magia del Pasado

5

tangerine-coloured cloisters, the museum charts the history of Querétaro state, beginning with a large section on prehistoric culture and the region's indigenous tribes. Displays upstairs focus on the spiritual history of the region under the Spanish missionaries. The final series of galleries tackles the revolutionary period, beginning with the stirrings of nationalism in the 1760s through to 1917, with artefacts, documents and detailed commentary. Precious items include the key and keyhole through which **La Corregidora** passed on her news in 1810 (see box, p.316), and the incredibly ornate table on which the **Treaty of Guadalupe Hidalgo** was signed in 1848 (ending the Mexican–American War by handing over almost half of Mexico's territory to the US). The corridor outside is lined with fifteen **Miguel Cabrera** paintings. As impressive as the museum is, you really need to read Spanish to make the most of it (no English labels).

Teatro de la República

Juárez and Ángela Peralta • Tues–Sun 10am–3pm & 5–8pm • Free • ☎ 442 212 0339

There's more to see a couple of blocks north of the Jardín Zenéa at the **Teatro de la República**. Opened in 1852, this grand theatre has played a vital role in Mexican history: a court met here to decide the fate of Emperor Maximilian in 1867, and in 1917 the Mexican Constitution was agreed upon inside. A small exhibition celebrates the latter event upstairs (above the lobby), though the main reason to walk up here is to take a peek at the theatre itself, a magnificent space with four levels of enclosed balcony seating. Today the theatre is home to the Querétaro Philharmonic Orchestra and hosts several concerts through the year – call or ask at the tourist office for the latest programme.

Plaza de la Independencia

One block east of Plaza de la Constitución and Jardín Zenéa lies the **Plaza de la Independencia**, aka Plaza de Armas, a very refined, arcaded open space and the most appealing place to eat and drink alfresco in the city (see p.323). In the middle of the plaza stands a statue of Don Juan Antonio de Urrutia y Arana, the man who built Querétaro's all-important aqueduct (see p.321), providing the city with drinking water.

Palacio de Gobierno

Plaza de la Independencia • Mon–Fri 8am–9pm, Sat 8am–6pm • Free

On the north side of Plaza de la Independencia is the Casa de la Corregidora, now the **Palacio de Gobierno**, office of the Governor of Querétaro state. It was here, on September 14, 1810, that La Corregidora was locked up (see box, p.316). The *palacio* sometimes holds special events, but there's not a great deal to see inside other than busts of La Corregidora and her husband.

Museo Casa de la Zacatecana

Independencia 59 • Tues–Sun 10am–5.30pm • M$45 • ☎ 442 224 0758, ⓦ museolazacatecana.com

One of the best museums in the city lies a block south of the Plaza de la Independencia. The **Museo Casa de la Zacatecana** is an expertly preserved

---

THE LEGEND OF THE ZACATECANA

Visit the **Museo Casa de la Zacatecana** (above) and you'll be introduced to the ghoulish legend of the woman who lived here in the seventeenth century. The story goes that the original owner – from Zacatecas – was murdered by his wife (she was rumoured to have had lovers). Soon after this the evil *zacatecana* was also stabbed to death mysteriously. Years later, human bones were dug up in the back of the house – but there were two skeletons, not one, prompting some to believe the wife had also murdered the killer she had hired to murder her husband; ghosts have been seen here ever since.

eighteenth-century mansion, incredibly evocative of the period and enhanced with English videos and English labels throughout. The rooms are filled with over six hundred pieces of art and furniture, but the real draw (for Mexican tourists, at least) is the grisly legend associated with the house (see box opposite). Less macabre highlights include the fascinating "universal history" parchment (1882) in Sala 1, with global cultures displayed like branches of a tree, and the Salon de los Cristos upstairs, containing 54 crucifixes and a Miguel Cabrera painting of the cross (1746). The Salon de los Rejoles overflows with 39 antique clocks – an interesting way to present what would otherwise be fairly dry exhibits.

Museo Nacional de Las Artes Gráficas

Pasteur 40 • Tues–Sun 10.30am–6.30pm • M$35 • ☎ 442 212 7091, ⓦ museodeartesgraficas.com

Just around the corner from the Museo Casa de la Zacatecana, the **Museo Nacional de Las Artes Gráficas** occupies the colonial mansion once owned by priest José María Sánchez and host to many of the 1810 rebel meetings. Inside, pride of place goes to the wooden **Juan Pablos** printing press, belonging to the "Gutenberg of America" who came to Mexico City from Italy in 1539. There are also special exhibits on prehistoric clay seals, prints by Manuel Manilla and José Guadalupe Posada (see p.362), and other antique printing presses.

Jardín Guerrero and around

Two blocks west of Jardín Zenéa, **Jardín Guerrero** is a far more relaxed place, with vendors dozing under trees and families enjoying the sweet snacks on offer.

Fountain of Neptune

Heading along Madero from Jardín Zenéa towards Jardín Guerrero you'll pass the famous **Fountain of Neptune** at Allende, designed by **Francisco Tresguerras** in 1797. Tresguerras (1765–1833) is rightly regarded as one of Mexico's greatest architects – he was also a sculptor, painter and poet – and was almost single-handedly responsible for developing a native Mexican architectural style diverging from (though still close to) its Spanish roots.

Templo de Santa Clara

Madero 42 • Mon–Sat 8am–2pm & 4–7pm, Sun 8am–2pm • ☎ 442 212 1777

Beside the Fountain of Neptune and backing on to the Jardín Guerrero is the deceptively simple church of **Templo de Santa Clara**, once attached to one of the country's richest monasteries, dating back to 1633. Inside it's a riot of Baroque excess, with gilded cherubs and angels swarming all over the profusely decorated *retablos* (gold-painted wooden altarpieces), created in the 1770s, virtually lining the length of the nave.

Catedral de San Felipe Neri

Madero, at Ocampo • Mon–Fri 8am–9pm, Sat 8am–6pm

Carry on west down Madero beyond Jardín Guerrero and you get to the **Catedral de San Felipe Neri**, which was completed in 1805 but only given cathedral status in 1931. The facade is a wonderful blend of pink sandstone and soaring Corinthian columns looking like carrot tops, but by Querétaro's standards, the interior is relatively plain.

Museo de la Restauración de la República

Guerrero 23 • Tues–Fri 9am–5pm, Sat & Sun 10am–5pm • Free • ☎ 442 224 3004

Aficionados of Mexican history should make time for the **Museo de la Restauración de la República**, one block north of Jardín Guerrero. An ex-Capuchin monastery founded in 1721 (though most of what you see was added in the nineteenth century), its small

5

and well-presented series of rooms and courtyards is dedicated to the history of the **French Intervention** (1863–67) and the restoration of the Republic under Benito Juárez, highlighted with period weaponry, old prints, scale models and other bits and pieces. A room is also dedicated to French-backed Emperor Maximilian himself, who was imprisoned here in 1867 before being shot – again, though, you need to read Spanish to get the most out of the museum.

Museo de la Ciudad

Guerrero 27 • Tues–Sun 11am–7pm • M$5 • ☎ 442 224 3756, ⓦ museodelaciudadqro.org

Occupying the same ex-convent premises as the Museo de la Restauración de la República, the **Museo de la Ciudad** fills a warren of rooms and galleries with temporary exhibitions, mainly contemporary installation art, painting, sculpture and photography.

Museo de Arte de Querétaro

Allende 14 • Tues–Sun 10am–6pm • M$30, free Tues • ☎ 442 212 2357, ⓦ museodeartequeretaro.com

A block south of the Jardín Guerrero lies the **Museo de Arte de Querétaro**, occupying the former Palacio Federal next to the church of **San Agustín** (another example of Baroque splendour – check out the gargoyles with water spouts on the roof). Originally an Augustinian monastery completed in 1728, the museum is one the most ornate buildings in town. In the cloister, every surface of the two storeys of portals is carved with grotesque figures, no two quite alike, and with abstract designs. The sculptures, often attributed to Tresguerras though almost certainly not by him, are full of religious symbolism, which you should try to get someone to explain to you. The large figures supporting the arches, for example, all hold their fingers in different positions: three held up to represent the Trinity, four for the Evangelists and so on. The main galleries are devoted to mediocre seventeenth-century European painting (mostly anonymous artists but some by **Miguel Cabrera**) and nineteenth-century Mexican art downstairs, along with temporary exhibition spaces usually featuring much better contemporary work.

Templo de Santa Rosa de Viterbo

Arteaga, at Montes • Daily 9am–7pm

The **Templo de Santa Rosa de Viterbo**, completed in 1752, sits a few blocks southwest of the Jardín Guerrero, but is well worth the short walk. Its magnificent interior rivals Santa Clara for richness of decoration, plastered with artwork, murals and vast gold churrigueresque *retablos*, but here there is no false modesty on the outside either. Two enormous painted flying buttresses support the octagonal cupola (remodelled by Tresguerras) and a blue-and-white-tiled dome. The tower, too, is Tresguerras' work, holding what is said to be the first four-sided public clock erected on the American continent. Inside, note the Mudéjar-style ivory pulpit and, in the sacristy, portraits of José Velázquez de Lore (who funded the church) and Sor Ana María de San Francisco y Neve (by an anonymous artist), one of the most admired religious paintings in Mexico.

Convento de la Cruz

Ejército Republicano, at Felipe Luna • Tues–Sat 9am–2pm & 4–6pm, Sun 9am–5.15pm; half-hour guided tours in English on request • Small donation requested

A short walk east from the centre lies the **Convento de la Cruz**, built on the site of the battle between the Spaniards and the Otomí and Chichimecas in 1531. According to legend, the fighting was cut short by the miraculous appearance of Spanish patron saint St James ("Santiago" in Spanish – the city's full name is Santiago de Querétaro – who coincidentally was also claimed to have helped vanquish the Moors), and a dazzling cross in the sky, which persuaded the Otomí and Chichimecas to accept defeat and become Christians.

The **Capilla del Calvarito**, next door to the monastery entrance, marks the spot where the first Mass was celebrated after the battle. The monastery itself was founded in 1683 by the Franciscans as a college (Colegio Apostólico de Propaganda Fide) and grew over the years into an important centre for the training of missionaries, with a massive library and rich collection of relics. Because of its hilltop position and hefty construction, the monastery was also frequently used as a fortress. Functioning as one of the last Spanish redoubts in the War of Independence, it was also Maximilian's headquarters for the last few weeks of his reign and he was subsequently imprisoned here to await execution (before being moved to the monastery on Guerrero; see p.319).

The monastery's greatest source of pride is the **Árbol de la Cruz**, a tree in the garden whose thorns sprout in the shape of little crosses. The tree grew, so the story goes, from a walking stick left behind by a mysterious saintly traveller who slept here one night. It certainly does produce thorns in the form of crosses, and the monks, who appear very excited by the phenomenon, point out that an additional five percent of the thorns grow with extra spikes to mark the spots where nails were driven through Christ's hands and feet; look for the framed collection in the entrance foyer.

Mausoleo de la Corregidora
Ejército Republicano • Daily 9am–5pm • Free

Come up to the Convento de la Cruz in the late afternoon, then wander 200m further east along Ejército Republicano to the **Mausoleo de la Corregidora**, where the heroine's remains (see box, p.316), along with those of her husband, are surrounded by statues of other illustrious Querétanos. Across the road the **Mirador de los Arcos** provides a spellbinding sunset view of the city's 1.3km-long **aqueduct** (Acueducto de Querétaro), a graceful series of 74 arches up to 23m high, built between 1726 and 1738 to bring water into the city from springs nearly 9km away.

Cerro de las Campañas
Tecnológico, at Hidalgo • Daily 6am–6pm • M$1 • ☎ 442 215 9031

One kilometre west of the centre via Morelos or Hidalgo, the gentle eminence of the **Cerro de las Campañas** ("Hill of Bells") commands wide, if less than scenic, views over Querétaro and its industrial outskirts. Maximilian and his two generals, Miguel Miramón and Tomás Mejía, faced the firing squad here (a small chapel, built in 1900 by Porfirio Díaz near the entrance, marks the spot). The hill is dominated by a vast stone statue of the victor of that particular war, Benito Juárez, glaring down over the town.

Museo La Magia del Pasado
Cerro de las Campanas • Tues–Sun 9am–5pm • M$30, free for kids under 15 • ☎ 442 224 0498

Beyond the statue of Benito Juárez on the Cerro de las Campañas is the mildly entertaining **Museo La Magia del Pasado**, with lots of interactive exhibits on Querétaro's history targeted primarily at kids; the main focus is the Republican attack of 1867 that led to Maximilian's capture.

ARRIVAL AND INFORMATION   QUERÉTARO

By plane Aeropuerto Intercontinental de Querétaro (☎ 442 192 5500, ⊕ aiq.com.mx) is 32km northeast of the centre on Hwy-200 to Tequisquiapan. Aeroméxico runs daily flights from Monterrey, which is much quicker than the bus, but can be expensive. There are also direct flights from Dallas and Houston in the US, and other destinations in Mexico via TAR Aerolineas and Volaris. Taxis charge around M$300–375 for the trip into town (and M$1125 to San Miguel). Hertz and Budget have rental counters at the airport.

By bus Querétaro's massive Central de Autobuses (with internet café and a 24hr left luggage (guardería)) lies 6km south of town and is one of the busiest in this part of Mexico, with three separate terminals: A for long-distance and first-class companies, and B and C for shorter runs and second-class companies (don't confuse these for salas A, B, C and D inside Terminal A). Fixed-price taxis (buy a ticket from the kiosk) run from outside all terminals (downtown is zone C; M$55), and an endless shuttle of local buses

5

(M$8.50) runs to the centre from the end of Terminal B. Buses generally don't enter the historic centre, so get off at Zaragoza, by the Alameda, and walk from there. This is also the spot to pick up services back to the bus station (#19, #25 or #36).

Note that there are six first-class buses (ETN) to San Miguel de Allende per day (M$115) beginning at 9.45am, and seven to Guanajuato (M$217) – second-class departures are a lot more frequent. You can travel to Mexico City for M$246. Destinations Aguascalientes (6 daily; 5hr); Bernal (hourly; 1hr); Dolores Hidalgo (every 40min; 2hr); Guadalajara (every 30min; 4–5hr); Guanajuato (7 daily; 2hr 30min); Jalpan (hourly; 5hr); Mexico City and Mexico City Airport (every 30min; 3–4hr); Morelia (every 30–60min; 3–4hr); San Juan del Río (every 15min; 45min); San Luis Potosí (hourly; 2hr 30min); San Miguel de Allende (every 40min; 1hr 15min); Tequisquiapan (every 30min; 1hr); Tula (9 daily; 2hr 30min); Xilitla (1 first-class daily at noon; 5–7hr; 8 second-class daily; 7hr); Zacatecas (hourly; 5hr).

Tourist office The tourist office, Pasteur Nte 4 (daily 9am–7pm; ☎442 238 5067, ⊛queretaro.travel), offers free maps and basic advice.

GETTING AROUND

By bus All city buses are M$8.50, but if the bus is part of the flashy new RedQ system (☎442 211 7000, ⊛redq.gob.mx) you'll need a pre-paid card with a minimum M$20 to board (buy them at the Casa de la Cultura or the Antigua Presidencia Municipal).

By taxi Taxis don't use meters in Querétaro so fix the price in advance (M$50–75) – the bus station should be no more than M$55 from downtown. The city is home to ride-sharing services Easy Taxi (⊛easytaxi.com) and Uber (⊛uber.com) – use of smartphones and the usual precautions apply (base fares are M$8.15, plus M$3.95/kilometre; minimum fare M$35).

ACCOMMODATION

As with most Bajío cities, there are plenty of good-value **motel** chains on the outskirts of Querétaro, but unless you are just passing through by car, or don't mind taking a lot of taxis, opt for the far more convenient options in the *centro histórico*. Querétaro now has numerous **boutique**-type places, usually conversions of old mansions. There are also several budget options and **hostels**, with dorm beds from M$130.

★**La Casa del Atrio** Allende Sur 15 ☎442 212 6314, ⊛lacasadelatrio.com. This posh B&B has garnered a loyal following, combining first-class hospitality with an art gallery; the six cosy rooms are adorned with art, rugs and murals by Claudia Ramos, with views of San Agustín church and two arches from the city aqueduct in the garden. Free wi-fi. **M$1525**

La Casa de la Marquesa Madero 41 ☎442 212 0092, ⊛hotelcasadelamarquesa.com. Enchanting hotel housed in a 1756 mansion with a gorgeous Moorish courtyard. The antique-furnished Imperial suites are magnificent, though they also have slightly less luxurious rooms in a separate building across the road. Breakfast included. Free wi-fi in public areas. **M$1525**

Centro 19 Corregidora 19, at Ángela Peralta ☎442 212 1234, ⊛centro19hotel.com. Considering the quality, location and price, this is a great option; no wonder its rooms – modern, simple but stylish – are almost always booked solid. Free wi-fi, parking and cable TV. **M$1025**

Home B&B 16 de Septiembre 104 ☎442 183 9139, ⊛queretarobandb.com. This welcoming B&B is excellent value, with ten simple, clean and cosy rooms, home-cooked gourmet breakfasts (M$105), free wi-fi and a roof terrace. **M$975**

★**Kuku Rukú** Vergara 12 ☎442 245 8777, ⊛kukuruku.mx. This hotel offers stylish double rooms and posher suites (M$1290) decked out with contemporary art, all including breakfast. Enjoy a beer on the roof deck *Terraza Beer Patio* for sunset (Wed–Sat 6pm–midnight). The hotel describes itself as "green" thanks to its use of solar power, collected rainwater and its own vegetable garden. **M$890**

Mesón Acueducto Juárez Sur 64, at Arteaga ☎442 224 1289, ⊛mesonacueductoqueretaro.com. Cheerily painted and well-cared-for budget hotel, right in the centre, with modern a/c rooms, all with cable TV. Free wi-fi on the ground floor. **M$400**

★**Villa del Villar** Vicente Guerrero Sur 33, between Pino Suárez and Arteaga ☎442 223 2330, ⊛villadelvillar.com. One of the best deals in town, with ten modern, well-equipped rooms within an enchanting sixteenth-century mansion – each one is named after a different town in Querétaro state, and features the traditional arts or crafts of that locale. Advance booking essential. Free wi-fi. **M$1355**

HOSTELS

Blue Bicycle House Ejército Republicano 15, La Pastora ☎442 455 4813, ⊛bluebicyclehouse.com. Excellent hostel with modern mixed and women's dorm (M$200) plus simple but stylish doubles with cable TV and shared bathrooms. Free wi-fi. Dorm (mixed) **M$175**; double **M$450**

Itza Hotel & Hostal Francisco Fagoaga 17, between Arteaga and Pino Suárez ☎442 212 4223, ⊛itzahostal.com.mx. Solid budget option arranged around a tranquil interior patio, with dorm beds (M$130) and cheap doubles available (some with private bathrooms). Simple breakfast included, plus use of two bikes. M$350

★**El Petate Hostel** Matamoros 20, just off Vicente Guerrero ☎442 212 7987, ⊛elpetatehostel.com. Extremely well-designed hostel in a fabulous location, with dorms decorated with cool murals and modern, comfy bunks. Also offers a variety of private rooms with single and double beds. Free wi-fi and computer use, plus bright patio with shared TV and kitchen. Dorm M$170; double M$450

EATING

There's plenty of good food in Querétaro, but try to sample a couple of **local specialities**; the hearty lentil soup (pork-broth based) laced with chunks of dried fruit (usually just called "sopa regional"), and the *enchiladas Queretanas*, tortillas fried in a chile sauce and stuffed with onions and cheese. If you want to get together something of your own, head for the **Mercado Escobedo**, sprawled across several blocks just off Calzada Zaragoza, not far from the Alameda.

CAFÉS AND SNACKS

Café del Fondo Pino Suárez 9 ☎442 212 0905. This airy multi-roomed café serves bargain breakfasts: fresh juice, good coffee (with a big coffee grinder wafting aromas over the tables), and a plate of eggs, enchiladas or hotcakes for M$45–65. There are also more substantial dishes available throughout the day. One room is often devoted to boardgames, most frequently chess, and mariachis occasionally wander in to serenade diners. Daily 8am–10pm.

El Globo Corregidora 41, at Independencia ☎442 212 8883, ⊛elglobo.com.mx. About the best *pastelería* in town (it's part of a Mexico City chain established in 1884), with lots of French pastries – croissants, pain au chocolat and so on – big sticky cakes and even their own brand of ice cream, all to take out (M$15–25). Daily 8am–9pm.

★**Tamales y Atoles Arteaga** Arteaga 48. This local secret, on a stretch of street with several tamale specialists, knocks out steaming-hot tamales as you wait: choose from regular (*salsa verde con carne* or *rajas con queso*) or *Tamales Oaxaqueños* (like *mole con pollo*) from M$15. Open daily 8–11am & 6–10pm.

Las Tortugas Andador 5 de Mayo 27 ☎442 212 9664. This venerable snack stop, decorated in bullfighting memorabilia (the original founder was a fan), has been knocking out tasty tortas (from M$22) since 1956. Crusty baps are filled with ham, cheese, chicken or mince, and enhanced by spicy salsas. Daily 9am–9pm.

RESTAURANTS

Di Vino Andador 5 de Mayo 12 ☎442 214 1273, ⊛divino.com.mx. Quality Italian restaurant and wine bar, a great place to splurge, with mains M$175–250 – superb pastas and especially fresh seafood (with over two hundred Italian wines). Top-class service and a classy atmosphere. Mon–Wed noon–11pm, Thurs–Sat noon–midnight, Sun noon–10pm.

Marrón 86 Pasteur 9, Plaza de la Independencia ☎442 214 3994. Prime real estate under the colonnades on the Plaza de Armas or in the tiny courtyard at the back. Good for pasta dishes, stuffed baguettes and salads, but the coffee is really the highlight (M$20–35). Free wi-fi. Sun–Thurs 7.30am–11pm, Fri & Sat 8am–11.30pm.

El Mesón de Corregidora Andador 16 de Septiembre 16-B (Jardín Corregidora) ☎442 212 0784. One of several decent places surrounding this attractive plaza. English menus, good-value breakfasts (from M$75) and outdoor seating, but this is primarily a place to sit, drink and watch the world go by. Daily 8am–10pm.

Restaurante 1810 Andador Libertad 65 (Plaza de la Independencia) ☎442 214 3324, ⊛restaurante1810 .com. Outstanding sidewalk restaurant that does regional specialities with a French twist. You'll have to take your chances with the live entertainment – sometimes relaxing jazz, though often cheesy crooners. Mains M$75–80. Mon–Thurs 8am–11pm, Fri & Sat 8am–midnight, Sun 8am–10pm.

★**San Miguelito** Andador 5 de Mayo 39 ☎442 224 2760, ⊛lacasona5patios.com. This unique spot has a justly earned reputation as one of the city's best restaurants, and you're guaranteed an impressive selection of delicious regional, national and international dishes in eclectic surroundings – it's set inside the courtyard of the *Casona de los Cincos Patios*. Try the chicken in chipotle sauce or one of their fine steaks. Reckon on M$300–350 for a meal. Daily 1pm–midnight.

DRINKING AND NIGHTLIFE

Evening **entertainment** tends to involve a couple of beers in one of the restaurants or an hour or two lingering in one of the cafés on the plazas – during holidays it's especially lively on Plaza de la Independencia and Jardín Zenéa, with street performers and buskers with guitars and violins, and families enjoying ice creams. For a livelier bar scene, trawl along 5 de Mayo and see where the night takes you. The bigger **clubs** are all out in the suburbs and fashions change rapidly, so ask around and follow the crowd (probably by taxi). Many have some sort of live music at weekends and charge M$50–100 to get in.

Alquimia 5 de Mayo 71 ☎442 212 1791. Sophisticated, dimly lit bodega with bottles racked up behind the bar and the doors thrown open to the street. Perfect for a quiet beer or one of their delicious cocktails. Tues–Sat 6pm–2.30am.

5

Hank's New Orleans Café & Oyster Bar Juárez Sur 7 ☎ 442 214 2620, ⓦ hanksmexico.com. The former *Harry's* bar has one of the most sought-after terraces in the city, overlooking Plaza de la Constitución (it also serves fresh seafood, Cajun and creole dishes), with a decent wine and cocktail list. Mon–Sat noon–midnight, Sun 10am–11pm.

Wicklow 5 de Mayo 86 ☎ 442 212 0947. Every aspiring international city seems to have at least one Irish pub, and Querétaro is no exception, *Wicklow's* green-washed exterior hinting at all the usual themes inside – Guinness, stews and plenty of good craic. Sun & Mon 7pm–1am, Tues–Sat 5pm–2am.

DIRECTORY

Banks and exchange There are several banks around the Jardín Zenéa that will change currency (Mon–Fri 9am–3pm), and a couple of *casas de cambio* south along Juárez.
Books and newspapers Querétaro has plenty of bookshops, but you'll be lucky to find anything in English. International weeklies can usually be found at the newspaper stands around the Jardín Zenéa and the Plaza de la Independencia. Beyond that, Sanborn's, at Constituyentes 172, 2km southeast of the centre, has a wide range of magazines.

Emergencies For general emergencies call ☎ 066; Cruz Roja ☎ 442 229 0505.
Hospital Hospital Angeles (☎ 442 192 3000, ⓦ hospitalesangeles.com/queretaro), Bernardino del Razo 21, Ensueño, is the best private hospital in the region, with English-speaking staff and 24hr facilities.
Pharmacy There are dozens of pharmacies around the centre, including the large Farmacia Guadalajara at Madero 32, just west of the Jardín Zenéa.
Post office Arteaga 5 (Mon–Fri 8am–6pm, Sat 9am–1pm).

Around Querétaro

It's worth spending a few days exploring the towns and villages of Querétaro State close to the capital, particularly the great peak at **Bernal** and the historic enclaves of **Tequisquiapan** and **San Juan del Río**.

Bernal

The pretty village of **BERNAL**, 60km east of Querétaro, hunkers under the skirts of the soaring **Peña de Bernal**, a 350m-high chunk of volcanic rock that towers over the plains. By wandering towards the peak (mototaxis are also on hand to drive you to the base) you'll soon pick up a rough but clearly marked path about two-thirds of the way to the top (the ascent takes up to an hour, half that to get down), where there's a small shrine and long views stretching out below. Only appropriately equipped rock climbers should continue up the metal rungs to the summit, passing a memorial plaque to an earlier adventurer along the way.

At weekends, half of Querétaro seems to come out here, gorging on the locally celebrated gorditas and making for a festive atmosphere, but midweek it is an altogether more peaceful place: the mountain is likely to be deserted and you'll be just about the only thing disturbing the serenity of the plaza with its charming little church (**Templo de San Sebastián**) and terracotta-washed buildings, sumptuous in the afternoon light. Be forewarned, however, that many businesses are only open at the weekends and many more shut in May.

ARRIVAL AND INFORMATION   BERNAL

By bus Flecha Amarilla provides buses every 2hr from Querétaro's bus terminal B (6.35am–7.25pm; M$40; 1hr) which drop you on the highway a 5min walk from Bernal centre; the last bus back passes at around 5pm (just flag them down).

Tourist office Try the small tourist office on Hidalgo (usually open Thurs–Tues 10am–5pm; ☎ 441 296 4126), which runs west from the plaza, though there isn't much they can tell you that you can't discover for yourself in 10min.

ACCOMMODATION AND EATING

Parador Vernal Lázaro Cárdenas 1 ☎ 441 296 4058, ⓦ paradorvernal.com.mx. If you get stuck, or just fancy a night here (not a bad thing), there are tantalizing views of the rock from the comfy rooms at *Parador Vernal*, on the

eastern edge of town. M$850
Mesón de la Roca Hidalgo 5 ☎ 441 269 4163, ⓦ mesondelaroca.com. One of the best places to eat, in a shaded courtyard, serving moderately priced and

well-presented Mexican dishes (enchiladas $117) and, for the daring, Oaxaca grasshopper tacos (M$127).

Mon–Thurs noon–8pm, Fri & Sat 10.30am–midnight, Sun 10.30am–8pm.

Tequisquiapan

Some 57km east of Querétaro, along a road lined with factories and workshops, **TEQUISQUIAPAN** ("Tequis" to locals) is a former Otomí village that developed in the Spanish colonial period primarily on account of its warm springs. Exclusive villas, all with beautifully tended walled gardens, are set around the central **Plaza Miguel Hidalgo**, itself ringed by arched *portales* on three sides and the pretty pink church of **Santa María de la Asunción** on the fourth. It is very popular with wealthy *chilangos* (residents of Mexico City) up from the capital, but has never really caught on with foreign tourists. Although perfect as a weekend escape from the city, there's little to do other than bathe in your hotel pool, dine in one of many restaurants around the plaza and nose around the boutiques, some of which are cheap, many expensive and almost all of the highest standard. Like San Juan del Río, further south, Tequisquiapan has a big **crafts market** (Mercados de Artesanías) – especially active on Sundays – one block from the main plaza.

ARRIVAL AND INFORMATION
TEQUISQUIAPAN

By bus Flecha Azul buses from Querétaro (Terminal B, every 30min; 6.30am–9pm; M$47; 1hr 15min) run direct to Tequisquiapan, and there's also a bus from San Juan del Río, 20km south (see below). From the bus station, 2km from the centre, take a local bus (M$6) or walk (20min) to the plaza.
Destinations Mexico City (every 40min; 3hr 45min); Querétaro (every 30min; 1hr); San Juan del Río (every 20min; 30min).

Tourist office Free town maps are available from the tourist office (Mon–Fri 9am–7pm, Sat & Sun 10am–8pm; ☎414 273 0295, ⓦlarutadelquesoyvino.com.mx or ⓦtequisquiapan.com.mx) on the main square (Plaza Miguel Hidalgo).

ACCOMMODATION

Hotel La Plaza Juárez 10 (Plaza Santa María) ☎414 273 0005, ⓦhotelplazatequis.com.mx. Relaxed mid-range option, with its own pool and some very attractive suites, all decked out in a vaguely Spanish colonial style. **M$850**
Hotel Rio Niños Héroes 33 ☎414 273 0015,

ⓦhotelriotx.com. One of the best hotels in town, right in the centre, with cable TV, free wi-fi, spacious gardens, palapa bar and an enticing pool. Rooms come in "classic" style (wood furniture, tapestries) or with a sleek, contemporary design. **M$1270**

EATING

Fortaleza Nicolás Bravo 8 ☎414 273 3111. This restaurant and bar, a short walk from the plaza, opened in 2013 but has swiftly garnered a loyal following with artfully prepared Mexican classics, seafood and a decent array of vegetarian dishes (mains M$100–150). Wed–Fri 1–7pm, Sat 10am–midnight, Sun 10am–7pm.
K'puchinos Restaurant y La Luna Bar Andador

Independencia 7 ☎414 273 2482, ⓦkpuchinos.com .mx. This local stalwart, right by the church, offers a tasty introduction to typical Querétaro dishes, including Tequis-style *pollo en mole* and pozoles, enchiladas Queretanas and some local artisanal cheese plates (mains M$80–150). Free wi-fi. Sister bar *La Luna* opens upstairs 7pm–2am. Sun–Thurs 8am–10pm, Fri & Sat 8am–midnight.

San Juan del Río

Though **SAN JUAN DEL RÍO**, 50km southeast of Querétaro, looks insignificant from the highway, it is in fact a major market centre and the second-largest city in the state, a popular weekend outing from both Querétaro and Mexico City. Among the

---

FESTIVALS IN TEQUIS

It is worth timing a visit to Tequisquiapan with one of the town's many **festivals**, including the **Feria del Toro de Lidia** (middle week of March), which features bullfights, and the **Feria Internacional del Queso y del Vino** (late May and early June), a major wine and cheese festival. There's plenty of free food and drink and no shortage of other entertainment, including music and dancing.

5

goods sold here are **gemstones** – mostly local opals, but also imported jewels, which are polished and set in town – as well as baskets, wine and cheese. If you're going to buy gems, be very careful: it's easy to get ripped off. Other purchases are safer, though not particularly cheap on the whole. The best-known local wine is Hidalgo, a brand sold all over the country and usually reliable. The **Mercado Reforma** and the twin central squares of the Plaza Independencia and Plaza de los Fundadores (aka Jardín Madero) are a couple of long blocks north of **Avenida Juárez**, up Hidalgo from the bus station.

Museo de la Muerte

2 de Abril 42 • Wed–Sun 10am–6pm • Free • ☎ 427 272 0884

There is more of interest a couple of blocks south of Juárez at the **Museo de la Muerte**, housed in the Neoclassical Panteón de la Santa Veracruz (used as a cemetery until 1866) on a hill overlooking town, which conveys the different ways Mexicans express their connectedness with the dead.

ARRIVAL AND INFORMATION

By bus Direct buses from Querétaro (Amealcenses from Terminal B; every 20min; around M$45) take 40min to get to San Juan del Río's bus station, a couple of km south of town. A local bus will run you up Hidalgo (M$6) and drop you on a broad section of Av Juárez, where there's a central fountain, manicured trees and an attractive arcade on one side.

Destinations Mexico City (every 15min; 3hr 15min); Querétaro (every 15min; 45min); Tequisquiapan (every 20min; 30min); Tula (9 daily; 1hr 30min).

Tourist information Visit ⓦsanjuandelrio.gob.mx for current information.

ACCOMMODATION

Layseca Juárez Ote 9 ☎427 272 0110, ⓦhotellayseca .com.mx. The best-value hotel downtown occupies an eighteenth-century colonial house with rooms decorated in period style with antiques but modern bathrooms, set around an appealing open courtyard. M$685

Portal de Reyes Juárez Pte 9 ☎427 272 5683, ⓦhotelportaldereyes.com. Another great downtown option, a short walk from the plazas, offering a bit more comfort than the *Layseca*, with satellite TV, free wi-fi, spacious modern rooms and a decent pool. M$1160

EATING

Café La Parroquia Plaza de los Fundadores 3 ☎427 272 4740. Colonial-style café with great coffee, good service and perfectly located right on the main plaza. Also serves standard Mexican dishes, including especially tasty enchiladas. Mon–Sat 8.30am–10pm.

Viva La Vida Plaza Independencia 65 ☎427 272 7000. Perched on the main plaza, this congenial place offers a wide-ranging menu of Mexican breakfasts, enchiladas, burgers, crêpes, pastas and pizzas. Sun–Thurs 8am–10pm, Fri & Sat 8am–11pm.

The Sierra Gorda and Xilitla

The hill country to the northeast of Querétaro is the **Sierra Gorda**, a remote and mountainous region where roads are winding and travel slow. Much of the area was incorporated within the **Reserva de la Biosfera Sierra Gorda** in 1997, a designation that affords its natural and historic attractions a limited amount of government protection.

Apart from the wonderful tropical fantasy world of **Las Pozas** at Xilitla, the area's main attractions are the **Sierra Gorda missions**. These five communities (each with an ornate church) were founded by Spanish Franciscan **Fray Junípero Serra** (1713–84), who spent nine years in the Sierra Gorda during the 1750s and 1760s, working with, and gaining the trust of, the indigenous people (mainly the **Pame**). Serra was canonized by Pope Francis in 2015 (becoming St Junípero Serra).

There are bus services to most places and several companies run tours, but this is an ideal region to explore by car, motorbike or even bicycle (though you'll need to be fit for the latter).

5

> ### RUTA DE LAS MISIONES (MISSION ROUTE)
> Beyond Jalpan, the other four Sierra Gorda missions are harder to visit without your own transport, but given their architectural beauty, isolation and unspoiled natural settings, well worth the effort:
>
> **San Miguel Concá** On Hwy-69 to San Ciro de Acosta, 40km north of Jalpan. The smallest of the missions, completed around 1754. Concá is a Pame word that means "with me".
>
> **Santa María de la Purísima Concepción del Agua** Built between 1760 and 1768 in Landa de Matamoros, 22km east of Jalpan on Hwy-120 towards Xilitla. The last of the missions to be built.
>
> **San Francisco de Asís de Tilaco** Best-preserved church, with a florid Baroque facade and soaring, multi-tiered tower (completed between 1754 and 1762), some 27km beyond Landa (15km east on Hwy-120, then 12km south of La Lagunita).
>
> **Nuestra Señora de la Luz de Tancoyol** (22km east of Landa along Hwy-120, then another 22km north on the signposted road to Tancoyol). The most ornate of the five missions with an incredibly intricate facade, constructed during the 1760s.

Jalpan

The main road from Querétaro towards Xilitla is Hwy-120, picked up at the small town of Ezequiel Montes. From there it twists its way through the mountains, with the only major town on route **JALPAN**, in the heart of the Sierra Gorda, 120km northeast of Querétaro. Now the largest of the mission towns and a Pueblo Mágico since 2010, it is an attractive colonial place centred on its church, **Santiago de Jalpan**. This was Serra's first mission in the area, built between 1751 and 1758, and its elaborate "Mestizo Baroque" facade became a template for the others to follow. On either side of its central stucco panel are the Virgins of Pilar and Guadalupe, the patrons of Spain and Mexico.

Museo Histórico de la Sierra Gorda
Fray Junípero Serra 1 • Tues–Sun 9am–3pm & 5–7pm • M$10 • ☎ 441 296 0165

For more background on the missions and the Pame craftsmen who built them, visit the **Museo Histórico de la Sierra Gorda** in the late sixteenth-century colonial building on the plaza (previously used as military barracks and prison), with exhibits of prints, antiques and model replicas of all the missions.

ARRIVAL AND DEPARTURE | JALPAN

By bus Jalpan bus station is 1km northeast of the centre. Primera Plus runs three first-class buses from Querétaro daily (3.5hr), at 8.10am, noon and 3.10pm. Buses return at 5am, 2pm and 5pm (M$311 one-way); the noon departure continues on to Xilitla (5–6hr; M$398 from Querétaro; M$116 from Jalpan), returning at 3pm. From Jalpan, Flecha Amarilla and Vencedor second-class services run on to Xilitla (2hr) every 30min or so from 7am–5pm (around M$70).

ACCOMMODATION

Hotel María del Carmen Independencia 8 ☎ 441 296 0328, ⊛ hotelmariadelcarmen.com. Modern hotel right on the plaza, with rooms decked out in a simple rustic style with wood-frame beds, clean tiled floors and a small pool. **M$490**

Hotel Misión Jalpán Fray Junípero Serra s/n ☎ 441 296 0445, ⊛ hotelesmision.com.mx. Next door to the museum (facing the plaza) is this inviting member of the Misión chain, a gorgeous colonial property with spectacular views of the mission church, a pool and free wi-fi. Rooms are simple but very cosy. **M$1085**

Xilitla

Travelling through the Sierra Gorda is a joy in itself, but really doesn't prepare you for the picturesque small town of **XILITLA** (pronounced Hee-leet-la), sprawled over the eastern foothills some 320km northeast of Querétaro and 55km beyond Jalpan. Hemmed in by limestone cliffs, it's set in a dramatic location, and at just 600m, it's warmer than the rest of the Bajío, with a lusher feel. There are tremendous views over the surrounding temperate rainforest, which is thick with waterfalls, birdlife and flowers, particularly wild orchids. It is

5

THE SURREAL WORLD OF EDWARD JAMES

Born in 1907 to a second-rank British aristocratic mother and American railroad millionaire father, **Edward James** may well also have been an illegitimate descendant of King Edward VII. He grew up cosseted by an Eton and Oxford education, and with no lack of money set about a life as a poet and artist. Meeting with only limited success, he turned his attentions to becoming a patron of the arts, partly in an attempt to prolong his waning marriage to a Hungarian dancer, Tilly Losch. Despite his bankrolling ballets that served as vehicles for her talent (notably those by George Balanchine's first company), she eventually left him, whereupon he retreated from London society to Europe. Here he befriended Salvador Dalí, and agreed to buy his entire output for the whole of 1938. As James increasingly aligned himself with the Surrealists, Picasso and Magritte also benefited from his patronage. Indeed, Picasso is reputed to have described James as "crazier than all the Surrealists put together. They pretend, but he is the real thing." During World War II, James moved to the US, where he partly funded LA's Watts Towers and made his first visit south of the border. After falling in love with Xilitla, he moved here in the late 1940s and experimented with growing orchids (which all died in a freak snowstorm in 1962) and running a small zoo. In his later years he was often seen with a parrot or two in tow as he went about building his concrete fantasy world. Aided by local collaborator and long-time companion **Plutarco Gastelum Esquer** and up to 150 workers, James fashioned **Las Pozas** (see below), continually revising and developing, but never really finishing anything. By the time he died in 1984, he had created 36 sculptures, spread over more than 20 acres of jungle. He left his estate to the Gastelum family, though without making any provision for the upkeep of his work.

---

a lovely place to relax, though you might devote a few minutes to admiring the beautifully preserved interior of the sixteenth-century **Ex-Convento de San Agustín**, which overlooks the central plaza, Jardín Hidalgo. The real justification for the lengthy journey to Xilitla, however, is to visit **Las Pozas**, some 2.5km east of town along a dirt road.

Museo Edward James

Ocampo 105 • Tues–Sun 10am–6pm • M$30 • ☎ 489 365 0038

Before heading out to Las Pozas, visit the **Museo Edward James**, behind the *Posada El Castillo* (it shares the space with the hotel restaurant), which showcases James's life and his work here. His handmade wooden moulds and photos of the construction are particularly worth perusing.

Las Pozas

Camino a Las Pozas • Daily 9am–6pm • M$50; tours in English M$250 • ⓦ xilitla.org • Head down Ocampo on the north side of the plaza, turn left and follow the signs. It is a pleasant walk downhill, or you can grab a taxi for around M$60

Having lived in Xilitla since 1947, English eccentric **Edward James** (see box above) spent the 1960s and 1970s creating the surreal jungle fantasy of **Las Pozas**, full of outlandish concrete statues and structures. Sprouting beside nine pools ("pozas") of a cascading jungle river, you'll find a spiral staircase that winds up until it disappears to nothing, stone hands almost 2m high, thick columns with no purpose, a mosaic snake and buildings such as the "House With Three Stories That Might be Five" and "The House Destined To Be a Cinema". Only one is in any sense liveable, a hideaway apartment four storeys up where James spent much of his time. With so little complete, there are all sorts of unprotected precipices: take care. In 2007, the Fondo Xilitla consortium bought the site for US$2.2 million (then M$24 million), with the aim of turning it into a world-class attraction; restoration has been slow since then, but check ⓦ laspozasxilitla.org.mx for the latest.

For now at least you can see everything in an hour or so, but plan to spend the better part of a day here bathing in the pools and just chilling out; the restaurant is usually open Wednesday to Sunday. You can also request a **guided tour** (in English M$250, if guide available; 1hr 15min), which can be a good way to get to grips with what's on display.

ARRIVAL AND DEPARTURE

By bus Getting to Xilitla by bus can be time-consuming – if you suffer from travel/motion sickness stock up on medication. Six twisting hours through the Sierra Gorda from Querétaro via Jalpan (Primera Plus M$398), it's more easily accessed by second-class bus from the unexciting but sizeable town of Ciudad Valles (M$112), on the highway between San Luis Potosí and Tampico, some 80km north. There are also direct services from Tampico (M$297) and San Luis Potosí (M$442). Flecha Roja, Flecha Amarilla (Jalpan and Querétaro) and Vencedor (Jalpan, Ciudad Valles and Tampico) have adjacent terminals just off the main highway on Al Centro – all a short walk from Jardín Hidalgo.

Destinations Ciudad Valles (6 daily; 2–3hr); Jalpan (9 daily; 2hr); Querétaro (8 daily; 6–7hr); San Luis Potosí (2 daily; 8–11hr); Tampico (4–5 daily; 6hr).

ACCOMMODATION AND EATING

Hotel Dolores Matamoros 211 ☎489 365 0178, ⓦhoteldoloresxilitla.com.mx. Modern and very clean budget hotel featuring elegant rooms with TV and fan, some also with a/c and fine mountain views. To get there, follow Hidalgo east from the main square for one long block, head straight across the road and down a long flight of stairs. At the bottom of the steps turn left. M$350

Hotel Hostal del Café Niños Heroes 116 ☎489 365 0018, ⓦhotelhostaldelcafe.com. Cosy option, with bright, clean rooms with rustic theme, free but slow wi-fi and a rich breakfast included. TV available in public lounge, but you'll spend more time in the lush garden or on the terrace. M$795

★**Posada El Castillo** Ocampo 105 ☎489 365 0038, ⓦlacasadelaspozas.com. The place to stay in Xilitla is *Posada El Castillo* (built by Plutarco Gastelum), in the house where James lived when he wasn't ensconced in his hut or apartment at Las Pozas. His spirit still inhabits the eight highly individual guestrooms, harmoniously blending Mexican, English and Moorish styles (fans only, no a/c). There's a lovely pool, meals are served (full breakfast is M$100) and the hosts not only speak English but also have produced a documentary on James's life and work, which they screen for guests. No credit cards. M$1100

Restaurante Cayo's Miguel Álvarez Acosta 117 ☎489 365 0044. One of several serviceable restaurants, with good basic Mexican food (try the cheese-filled *enchiladas huastecas*; or seafood soup, a speciality; mains M$75–95) and superb views across the palms. Daily 7am–midnight.

San Miguel de Allende

Set on a steep hillside overlooking the Río Laja and dominated by red rooftops and domed churches, **SAN MIGUEL DE ALLENDE** is the most hauntingly beautiful town in the Bajío. The colonial centre remains wonderfully preserved, and still serves as the spiritual centre of the Mexican community – seen at dawn, its cobbled, hilly streets are quite unlike anything else in the region. There are few major sights, but the whole town (which has been a national monument since 1926, hence no new buildings, no flashing signs and no traffic lights) is crowded with old seigniorial mansions and graceful churches.

Unsurprisingly, San Miguel's appeal has not gone unnoticed. Today it serves as a picture-perfect version of Mexico for hundreds of artists and writers, as well as flocks of foreign students drawn to the town's several language and arts schools. More visibly, it has attracted a large population of US and Canadian **expats** (mostly retirees), and property prices here are on a par with San Francisco (a *Starbucks* even graces the plaza). Though the connection goes back to the 1940s, the latest influx can in part be attributed to Tony Cohan's popular book *On Mexican Time* (published in 2000), which tells the story of a writer and his artist wife who abandon smog-ridden Los Angeles for a quieter life in San Miguel, where they restore an old house, learn the local lifestyle and are slowly seduced by the colonial city's unique charm. Now something like ten percent of the population are foreigners, some ten thousand of whom live in the vicinity more or less permanently, generally in peaceful co-existence with the locals.

For all its popularity, the town is a pleasant place to rest up in comfort for a while – assuming you have plenty of cash. The country hereabouts is still ranching territory, though even this is increasingly being taken over by tourist activities: attractions

5

0 — 100
metres

■ **ACCOMMODATION**
Belmond Casa de	
Sierra Nevada	9
Casa de la Cuesta	4
Casa Misha	8
Casa Schuck	10
La Catrina Hostel	
& Breakfast	3
Hostel Inn	2
Hotel Posada Carmina	7
Iron House Hostel	1
Matilda	11
Parador San Sebastian	5
Las Terrazas San Miguel	6

● **SHOPPING**
Ablu	5
Chocolates JOHFREJ	4
Fábrica la Aurora	1
Garrison & Garrison	2
Mixta	7
San Miguel Shoe	3
Sollano 16	6

■ **DRINKING & NIGHTLIFE**
La Azotea	8
La Coronela	4
El Gato Negro	2
El Grito	5
Hank's New Orleans Café	
& Oyster Bar	3
Limerick Pub	6
Luna Rooftop Tapas Bar	9
Mama Mia	7
Mint Club	1

● **EATING**
La Alborada	7
Apolo XI	3
Baja Fish Taquito	4
Café Oso Azul	6
Café de la Parroquia/	
La Brasserie	9
Carnitas Bautista	13
La Grotta	11
La Parada	12
El Petit Four	2
San Agustín	5
El Ten Ten Pie	10
La Ventana	8
La Virundela	1

SAN MIGUEL DE ALLENDE

N

Map labels: AV. H. COLEGIO MILITAR · CALZADA DE LA AURORA · CALZADA DE LA LUZ · Mercado de Artesanías (Sec 4) · LUCAS BALDERAS · CJON DEL PALMAR · LORETO · Mercado de Artesanías · CJON DEL PUEBLITO · RELOX · HIDALGO · ANIMAS · Templo del Oratorio de San Felipe Neri · Teatro Santa Ana · La Biblioteca · Templo de Nuestra Señora de la Salud · Mercado Ignacio Ramírez · HOMOBONO · INSURGENTES · HERNÁNDEZ MACÍAS · Templo de Santa Ana · Universidad de Leon · Laundry · PLAZA CÍVICA · COLEGIO · MESONES · APARICIO · CJON SAN DIMAS · Teatro Angela Peralta · Galería Izamal · San Francisco · QUEBRADA · Templo de la Purísima Concepción · Bellas Artes · Casa de los Perros · Presidencia Municipal · Tercer Orden · Jardín de San Francisco · La Esquina – Museo del Juguete · Casa del Mayorazgo de la Canal · Farmacia Chelo Agundis · CANAL · UMARAN · El Jardín Principal · SAN FRANCISCO · CORREO · SANTO DOMINGO · SAL. REAL A QUERETARO · ZACATEROS · Museo Histórico de San Miguel de Allende · PLAZA PRINCIPAL · CUNA DE ALLENDE · Viajes San Miguel · CHIQUITOS · JESÚS · La Parroquia de San Miguel Arcángel · CUADRANTE · HOSPICIO · DE LA GARITA · Casa del Inquisidor · ALDAMA · DIEZ DE SOLLANO DAVALOS · RECREO · Galería Nudo · Galería Casa Diana · MONTES DE OCA · BARRANCA · DEL CODO · TERRAPLEN · SUSPIROS · PLAZA DE TOROS · COR. DE LA GARZA · Farmacia Guadalajara · Taco Stands · SAN ANTONIO · PASEO DEL PARQUE · TENERIAS · HUERTAS · CHORRO · El Mirador · PIEDRAS CHINAS · Instituto Allende · ALDAMA · DIEZMO VIEJO · BAJADA DEL CHORRO · Parque Benito Juárez · Lavanderos Públicos · El Chorro · PASEO DEL CHORRO · CJON. CHORRO · Casa de la Cultura

Bus Station (2km) · & Guanajuato (90km) · & Jardín Botánico (1.5km) · Querétaro (60km)

include hot springs, a nearby golf course, horseriding at a couple of dude ranches and mountain-biking.

El Jardín Principal

Everything in San Miguel revolves around **El Jardín Principal**, the main plaza, which is within walking distance of almost everything you'll want to see – on Sundays traditional Mexican bands play live music throughout the afternoon. The plaza is dominated by its distinctive church (see below), while on the north side is a block containing the former **Presidencia Municipal**, completed in 1736, and the **Galería San Miguel** (see box, p.332). The east and west sides of the square are lined with covered *portales*, under whose arches vendors of drinks and trinkets shelter from the sun, with a row of shops behind them. Just off the plaza at Umarán 3 is the Casa del Insurgente, former home of revolutionary hero Juan de Mafuele, but better known as the **Casa de los Perros**, for its central balcony supported by little stone dogs.

La Parroquia de San Miguel Arcángel

El Jardín Principal • Daily 6am–9pm

The most famous of the city's landmarks, **La Parroquia de San Miguel Arcángel** – the parish church – takes up the south side of the Jardín Principal. This gloriously over-the-top structure, with a towering pseudo-Gothic facade bristling with turrets and spires, was built in 1880 by Zeferino Gutiérrez, a self-taught indigenous stonemason. Gutiérrez supposedly learned about architecture by studying postcards of great French cathedrals and then drew diagrams in the dust to explain to his workers what he wanted, and the church does seem to reflect the French penchant for neo-Gothic architecture at that time. Inside, the patterned tilework of the floor, the *azulejos* along the walls and the pure semicircular vaulting along the nave exhibit distinct Moorish influences. Look out for the *Cristo de la Conquista* in a side chapel to the left of the altar, a revered sixteenth-century image of Christ framed by two giant, faded murals.

Near here is the **Capilla del Santisimo**, smothered in bold, Modernist murals. Note also the small statue and shrine to San Judas Tadeo on the right side of the nave, littered with photos and votive offerings. Ex-president Anastasio Bustamante (1780–1853) spent his last days in San Miguel, and is buried in the crypt, designed by famed architect Francisco Tresguerras (usually open on Nov 2 only).

Museo Histórico de San Miguel de Allende

Allende 1 • Tues–Sun 9am–5pm • M\$47 • ☎ 415 152 2499

The Casa de Don Ignacio de Allende, at the southwest corner of the Jardín, was the birthplace of the Independence hero Miguel Allende in 1769: a plaque notes *Hic natus ubique notus* – "here was born he who is famous everywhere". The house now operates as the **Museo Histórico de San Miguel de Allende**, with artfully designed galleries chronicling the history of the town with some lovely artefacts and old documents, all with English labels. The lower floor covers the early colonial period through to the beginning of the independence movement and the arrival of Allende on the scene, following his military career from 1801. There's also a preserved *botica* (apothecary) from 1919 down here, and a reproduction of a *pulpería* (small store). Upstairs the Allende connection is explored further, with galleries dedicated to his role in the events of 1810–11, his illegitimate children, disagreements with Hidalgo and his ultimate capture and execution. The unequivocal message seems to be that Hidalgo's role in Mexican independence has been exaggerated: Allende was actually "the first to disturb America's calm".

Other rooms have been restored in period style, to reflect the lives of wealthy townsfolk in the eighteenth century, with an oratory, kitchen and various living rooms.

5

SAN MIGUEL'S TOP ART GALLERIES

San Miguel has been attracting artists since the 1930s – you'll find many of them in the Fábrica la Aurora (see p.338). Other galleries worth checking out include:

Galería Arte Contemporáneo Sollano 13 ☎415 152 5742, ⓦarte-contemporaneo.com.mx. Current and emerging Mexican talent such as abstract painter Jordi Boldó, Luis Granda and Gabriel Vergara. Wed–Sun 11am–7pm.

Galería Casa Diana Recreo 48 ☎415 152 0885, ⓦgaleriacasadiana.com. Primarily home for the work of Italian-born artist Pedro Friedeberg (his wife Diana is the gallery sub-director), including his iconic "hand chair". Mon–Sat 10am–2pm & 4–7pm.

Galería Izamal Mesones 80 ☎415 154 5409, ⓦwww.galeriaizamal.com. Features Patricia de León,

Javier García, Juan Ezcurdia, David Godinez, Javier González, Henry Vermillion and Britt Zaist. Daily 11am–3pm & 4–8pm.

Galería Nudo Recreo 36 & 10-B ☎415 115 9393, ⓦgalerianudo.com. Has shown the work of Oaxacan artist Alejandro Santiago, Nestor Quiñones and others. Mon–Sat 10am–7pm.

Galería San Miguel El Jardín Principal ☎415 152 0454. The town's first gallery, opened in 1962, remains one of the most prestigious. Mon–Fri 9am–2pm & 4–7pm, Sat 10am–2pm & 4–8pm, Sun 11am–2pm.

Casa del Mayorazgo de la Canal (Casa de Cultura Banamex)

Canal 4 • Mon–Fri 9am–6pm, Sat & Sun 10am–6pm; shop daily 10am–7pm • Free • ☎ 415 152 1004, ⓦcasasdeculturabanamex.com

Just off the plaza, the lavish **Casa del Mayorazgo de la Canal** was built for the wealthy and influential De la Canal family in the eighteenth century. Now owned by Banamex, a few rooms are open to the public for temporary art exhibitions with a Mexican theme, and there's a decent bookshop and video room. You won't see much of the interior beyond the impressive courtyard, its multi-tiered arches only hinting at the opulence further inside.

Jardín de San Francisco

A block east along San Francisco from the Jardín Principal, the quieter space of **Jardín de San Francisco** is dominated by two colonial churches. The elaborate churrigueresque facade of the **Templo de San Francisco** contrasts sharply with its Neoclassical tower (added in 1799 by Francisco Tresguerras), tiled dome and plain, but light and airy, Neoclassical interior, and overshadows the modest simplicity of its smaller neighbour, seventeenth-century **Tercer Orden**.

Plaza Cívica and around

Behind and to the north of Jardín de San Francisco, San Miguel's old market area has been refurbished to create the **Plaza Cívica**, complete with a huge equestrian statue of Allende – you'll usually see clumps of students near here, outside the Ex-Colegio de San Francisco de Salas (once a highly regarded Jesuit school), now part of the **Universidad de León**.

Templo de Nuestra Señora de la Salud

Plaza Cívica, Insurgentes s/n • Daily 6.30am–2pm & 5–9pm

Next door to the university building, the **Templo de Nuestra Señora de la Salud**, with its unusual concave churrigueresque facade topped by a scallop-shell pediment, was completed in the eighteenth century as the college chapel.

Templo del Oratorio de San Felipe Neri

Insurgentes s/n • Daily 6.30am–2pm & 5–9pm **Santa Casa de Loreto** Daily 7–9am & 6–8pm

Completed in 1712, the ornate crimson Baroque facade of the **Templo del Oratorio de San Felipe Neri** shows signs of native influence – presumably the legacy of indigenous labourers. The main interest lies inside with a series of oil paintings in the pinkish interior, among them a group of 33 around the altar and dome depicting the life of St Philip Neri, and an image to the right of the altar of the Virgen de Guadalupe attributed to Miguel Cabrera. The main altar itself is another creation of Zeferino Gutiérrez. One of the chapels inside, the gold-smothered **Santa Casa de Loreto**, is a copy of the Santa Casa di Loreto in Italy (known as the "Holy House", thought to be the actual home of Mary – miraculously transported from Nazareth), and was put up by the Conde Manuel de la Canal in 1735.

Mercado Ignacio Ramirez
Colegio • Daily 7am–8pm

The **Mercado Ignacio Ramirez** (town market) has managed to remain almost entirely traditional, with fruit, vegetables, medicinal herbs, pots and pans all on display, and little exists specifically for tourists among the cramped tables with their low canvas awnings.

Mercado de Artesanías
Balderas • Daily 10am–6.30pm

Behind the regular market along Andador Lucas Balderas lies the **Mercado de Artesanías**, crammed with the sort of handicrafts you see all over Mexico (folk art, pottery, colourful textiles, cut glass, papier-mâché and silver jewellery), though little of what's here seems especially good value. You'll find much more exciting goods in the many crafts shops around town.

La Biblioteca
Insurgentes 25 • Mon–Fri 10am–7pm, Sat 10am–2pm • Free • **House and Garden Tour** Sun noon, buy tickets from 11am • tour M$250 • **Café Santa Ana** Mon–Fri 9am–7pm, Sat 9.30am–4pm, Sun 9am–4pm • ☎ 415 152 0293, ⓦ bibliotecasma.com

From the Oratorio de San Felipe Neri you can head west along Insurgentes to **La Biblioteca**, a library that lends a substantial collection of books in English (see "Directory", p.338, for more details). They also sell a number of cheap secondhand books on Thursdays (10am–1pm). Inside the library, the *Café Santa Ana* offers a quiet space to sit down and read, while on Sundays you can join the popular two-hour **House and Garden Tour**, which takes you inside two or three historic private homes each week. You should also enquire here about the programme at the library's **Teatro Santa Ana**, which shows movies and plays.

La Esquina – Museo del Juguete Popular Mexicano
Núñez 40 • Wed–Sat 10am–6pm, Sun 11am–4pm • M$30 • ☎ 415 152 2602, ⓦ museolaesquina.org.mx

San Miguel's quirkiest museum is a short walk east of the Jardín, an unusual collection dedicated to traditional Mexican toys dubbed **La Esquina – Museo del Juguete Popular Mexicano**. The three rooms contain a variety of dolls, masks, toy instruments and rocking horses.

Bellas Artes
Hernández Macías 75 • Mon–Sat 9am–7pm, Sun 10am–2pm • Free • ☎ 415 152 0289, ⓦ elnigromante.bellasartes.gob.mx

The Centro Cultural Ignacio Ramírez "El Nigromante", more simply known as **Bellas Artes**, is just one block downhill from the Jardín. Housed in the romantic cloistered

---

SAN MIGUEL'S MURAL MASTERPIECE

Don't leave San Miguel without visiting the mesmerizing **Sala Quetzal** inside La Biblioteca (see above), all four walls smothered with exuberant murals by artist David Leonardo (born in Mexico City in 1963). Inspired by Mesoamerican art, the swirling images are a barrage of colours, peoples and symbols, depicting aspects of Mexican history. The room is open during library hours, but no photos are allowed.

5

courtyard of the 1765 **Convento de la Concepción**, it's an arts institute run by the state fine-arts organization (replacing the original school established by Felipe Cossio del Pomar here in 1938), concentrating on music and dance, but to a lesser extent teaching visual arts, too. Mexicans can take courses here for virtually nothing; foreigners pay rather more (prices vary, but reckon on around M$75 for most classes).

Around the courtyard there are various exhibitions, and several murals, including an entire room covered in vivid, abstract designs by **Davíd Alfaro Siqueiros** from the 1940s. Dedicated to the life of Ignacio Allende, the mural was left unfinished after Siqueiros fell out with the school's owner. The **Templo de la Purísima Concepción**, part of the complex, is notable mainly for its tall pink-and-yellow dome raised on a drum, said to be the work of the untrained Zeferino Gutiérrez in 1891, this time modelled on Les Invalides in Paris.

Instituto Allende

San Antonio 22 • ☎ 415 152 0190, ⓦ instituto-allende.edu.mx

In 1938 Peruvian artist Felipe Cossio del Pomar founded the Escuela Universitaria de Bellas Artes in San Miguel, an arts foundation that enjoyed an enormous boost after World War II, when returning American GIs found that their education grants could be stretched much further in Mexico; Pomar relocated the school in 1950 as today's well-respected **Instituto Allende**. A steep but pleasant walk south of the old centre, it's housed in a former 1730s hacienda of the Condes de la Canal and offers courses in all kinds of arts, from painting to sculpture to photography, in crafts like silverwork and weaving, and Spanish-language instruction at every level (see box, p.336), all within verdant, park-like grounds. There are craft shops and a café down here too, and an office dealing with long-term accommodation.

El Chorro

Ten minutes' walk south of the Jardín, shaded **Parque Benito Juárez** was created out of the fruit orchards that belonged to many of the city's old families. The homes round about are still some of the fanciest in town. From here it's an uphill stroll to **El Chorro**, the little hill whose springs supply the city with water, and the site of the settlement originally founded by Franciscan friar Juan de San Miguel in 1542. At the foot of the hill you'll find the **Lavaderos Públicos**, a series of twenty old-fashioned crimson stone tubs – some locals still occasionally do washing here.

Casa de la Cultura and El Mirador

Bajada del Chorro 4 • Mon–Fri 9am–8pm, Sat 4–8pm • ☎ 415 154 5670

From the *lavaderos* the cobbled Paseo del Chorro winds uphill past egrets nesting in trees to the old water storage building, which now serves as the **Casa de la Cultura**, another popular location for classes, events and shows. To get the best views over town, make for **El Mirador** (climb the steps behind the Casa, walk along Callejón de Chorro and turn left along Salida Real de Querétaro), the viewing point on the road to Querétaro, where there's a little belvedere, a small café and San Miguel spread out below, with the broad plain and a ridge of mountains behind.

Jardín Botánico

Paloma • Daily 9am–6pm • M$40 • ☎ 415 154 4715, ⓦ elcharco.org.mx • Follow Homobono east from the market, and continue along Cuesta de San José and Antiguo Camino a Querétaro; after 10min or so you reach signs to one of the pedestrian entrances on Paloma. Taxis are M$45

When you've had your fill of swanky cafés and artesanía shopping, consider spending a few hours at the **Jardín Botánico**, 1.5km northeast of town. Officially known as **El Charco del Ingenio**, it sprawls over the hill just behind a suburb of some of San Miguel's finest new homes. The garden itself resembles almost any patch of northern Mexico desert (it is meant to), but comes heavily planted with various types of cactus, which has made it incomparably richer botanically than the surrounding desert. Around 10km of grassy paths wind through its 220 acres, some accessible by mountain bike. If you're here around a full moon, check the website for details of the *temazcales*, ritual herb steam baths built within the garden, and open to the public (around M$250, reservations required; ☎415 154 8838).

ARRIVAL AND DEPARTURE
SAN MIGUEL DE ALLENDE

By plane San Miguel's closest major airports are at Querétaro (see p.321) or near León (see p.357), from where English-speaking Viajes San Miguel, Sollano 4 (Mon–Fri 9am–2.30pm & 4.30–7pm, Sat 10am–2pm; ☎415 152 2537, ⓦviajessanmiguel.com), runs a shuttle van (reserve in advance) meeting most flights at either airport for US$30 (M$450). BajioGo (see below) also runs a shuttle to León or Querétaro airport for US$29 (M$485); Mexico City airport is US$75 (M$1125). Taxis from Querétaro bus station or airport charge around M$500.

By bus San Miguel has frequent services to Guanajuato (first class M$130–155) and Querétaro (first class via ETN

M$115). Omnibus runs some first-class services to points north and the US border, while Primera Plus and ETN run to Mexico City (M$395). The Central de Autobuses is about 2km west of the centre at Calzada de Estación 90, from where there are taxis into the centre (M$40; fix the price first as there are no meters), and regular local buses (marked "Centro–Central"; M$6) that run into town along Canal.

Destinations Aguascalientes (2 daily; 4hr); Dolores Hidalgo (every 40min; 1hr); Guanajuato (14 daily; 1hr 30min); Mexico City (every 40min; 4hr); Querétaro (every 40min; 1hr 15min); San Luis Potosí (8 daily; 3hr).

INFORMATION

Tourist office San Miguel's helpful tourist office (Mon–Fri 9am–8pm, Sat 10am–8pm, Sun 10am–6pm; ☎415 152 0900) is on the north corner of El Jardín at no. 10. As well as the usual racks of leaflets and maps, it can provide details of local art and language courses.

Newspapers and websites For more information, pick up one of the free ad-driven booklets scattered around town, the weekly gringo newspaper *Atención San Miguel* (M$15; out Fri; ⓦatencionsanmiguel.org), or visit ⓦportalsanmiguel.com and ⓦvisitsanmiguel.travel.

TOURS AND ACTIVITIES

The tourist office can also supply lists of local guides and tour operators. Most offer walking tours of the town for M$100–150, and day trips to Dolores and Atotonilco (US$50/M$835; 6hr) and the ancient pyramids of Cañada de la Virgen (US$50/M$835; 3hr), with a minimum three people. Try BajioGo at Jesús 11 (daily 8am–8pm; ☎415 152 1999, ⓦbajiogo.com) or Viajes San Miguel (see above). For the House and Garden Tour see p.333.

Bici-Burro Hospicio 1 ☎415 152 1526, ⓦbici-burro .com. A range of van, hiking and bike tours (M$850–1500), most frequently to the Santuario de Atotonilco (38km; 5–6hr), or to Pozos (7hr).

Coyote Canyon Horseback Adventures ☎415 154 4193, ⓦcoyotecanyonadventures.com. Group and private riding trips, lessons and even moonlit excursions at a variety of levels at their ranch 16km southwest of town. All trips give a great introduction into *charro* life; they run half-day outings (US$90/M$1500) as well as full-day

(US$145/M$2420) and overnight excursions (US$195/M$3250). Other activities include hot-air ballooning (US$160/M$2670) and skydiving (US$190/M$3170).

★**Patronato Pro Niños Walking Tour** (Mon, Wed & Fri 9.45am; M$200; ☎415 152 7796, ⓦpatronatoproninos .org). Meet in the Jardín across from the Parroquia for a gentle stroll around town (2hr 30min) and a good deal of local history. All the proceeds go towards medical care for underprivileged children. Private tours at any time are M$1000 (1–4 people) and M$250 for each additional person.

ACCOMMODATION

Belmond Casa de Sierra Nevada Hospicio 42 ☎415 152 7040, ⓦbelmond.com. Luxury hotel complex with fifteen spacious rooms set in Casa del Parque, the main building, around a soothing colonial courtyard built in 1580 and lush with greenery, and four other colonial mansions. All guests have access to the hotel's refreshing pool and classy restaurant, *Andanza*. <u>M$4240</u>

★**Casa de la Cuesta** Cuesta de San José 32 ☎415 154 4324, ⓦcasadelacuesta.com. Mexican folk-art, crafts and antiques adorn this gorgeous colonial home, renovated as a boutique B&B. With just six rooms, all with fireplace and outdoor terrace, attention is personal and relaxed, and breakfast is served on the lush patio. Check out the exclusive Other Face of Mexico Gallery on site. <u>M$2475</u>

5

LEARNING SPANISH IN SAN MIGUEL

For many people, the reason to come to San Miguel is to learn Spanish. Notice boards around town advertise private lessons, but most people end up taking one of the courses run by the main **language schools**, each of which offers a range of courses taught by professional Mexican teachers. Instruction is almost entirely in Spanish, with the focus on practical usage rather than academic theory. The best known is the Instituto Allende, though the others compete admirably on both price and quality. Students usually stay with a local family (US$27–33/M$450–550/day for full board) to consolidate the instruction.

Academia Hispano Americana Mesones 4 ❶415 152 0349, ⓦahaspeakspanish.com. Respected school running four-week Spanish immersion sessions (6hr/day; US$650/M$10,840) and more relaxed semi-intensive programmes (4hr/day; US$160/M$2670 per week), plus extension courses in Mexican history, literature and folklore.

Instituto Allende Ancha de San Antonio 20 ❶415 152 0190, ⓦinstituto-allende.edu.mx. The most prestigious of the schools, the Instituto conducts university-credited four-week courses (starting the first Mon of each month), offering everything from one to four hours a day (from US$185/M$3085 for two

weeks) throughout the year at all levels. There are also intensive one-to-one classes, less demanding monthly courses and special subject courses in topics such as Mexican history, ceramics, paper-making and photography, among others.

Instituto Habla Hispana Calzada de la Luz 25 ❶415 152 1535, ⓦmexicospanish.com. Runs month-long courses for US$560 (M$9340) with around twenty contact hours per week; alternatively, you can just do a week for US$170 (M$2835). They'll also organize homestays for around US$21 a day (M$350) for a shared double, and US$26 (M$435) for a private room.

★ **Casa Misha** Callejón de Chiquitos 15 ❶415 152 0580, ⓦcasamisha.com. Another luxury boutique hotel awash with tasteful French and Mexican colonial antiques; the seven rooms come with flat-screen TVs, DVD players, MP3 hookups, wi-fi and patios that spill out onto lush gardens, but the real highlight is breakfast on the roof terrace, with sleepy San Miguel sprawled out below. M$4800

Casa Schuck Bajada de la Garita 3 ❶415 152 0657, ⓦcasaschuck.com. Splendidly styled and colourful hotel with antiques, ten amply sized rooms, a small but beautiful pool, leafy nooks and personal touches. Welcoming owners make this one of San Miguel's best bets. M$3260

Hotel Posada Carmina Cuna de Allende 7, a few metres south of the Jardín ❶415 152 0458, ⓦposadacarmina .com. Large rooms with brick floors, high ceilings and white walls are set amid yet more colonial splendour around a congenial restaurant (*La Felguera*, open till 5pm); there are cheaper, but still very comfy, remodelled rooms in an adjacent wing – all come with flat-screen satellite TVs and free wi-fi (though signal is weak beyond the courtyard). You can't beat its location, one block from the Jardín, and the staff are friendly and very helpful. M$2260

★ **Matilda** Aldama 53 ❶415 152 1015, ⓦhotel matilda.com. A slice of modern luxury amid all those colonial options in San Miguel, this flashy boutique hotel offers stylish rooms with LCD TV, iPod docks, free wi-fi and large bathrooms with double sinks, decorated with the photographs of Eduardo Zaylan. Lounge at the spa or try the gourmet restaurant, *Moxi*. M$4380

Parador San Sebastian Mesones 7 ❶415 152 7084.

Cool and tranquil, with simple rooms around a colonial courtyard. Ask for one of the larger rooms at no extra cost – a huge bargain. M$450

Las Terrazas San Miguel Santo Domingo 3 ❶415 152 5028, ⓦterrazassanmiguel.com. These four luxurious casas on the hillside, four blocks from the plaza, come with kitchen, cable TV, bathrooms, wi-fi and private terraces; breakfast and a bottle of wine on arrival are included. Fabulous option for families or groups. M$2475

HOSTELS

La Catrina Hostel & Breakfast Loreto 80 ❶415 121 4545, ⓦlacatrinahostel.com. Justly popular (reserve ahead) option with a choice of comfy dorms (M$206) and doubles, some with private bathrooms, all with a/c and cable TV. Free wi-fi throughout (plus use of computers), common room and basic breakfast included (it's M$30 for a fuller cooked breakfast). M$460

Hostel Inn Calzada de la Luz 31-A ❶415 154 6727, ⓦhostelinnmx.com. Excellent budget option a few blocks from the Jardín, with shared kitchen, free wi-fi, garden and luggage storage; choose from dorm beds (M$150), single rooms with shared bathroom (M$400) and en-suite doubles. M$460

★ **Iron House Hostel** Colegio Militar 17-D ❶415 154 6108, ⓦiron-house-hostel.blogspot.com. Small, friendly hostel about a 10min walk north of town in a quiet suburb. There are dorms, private rooms, a decent kitchen and free wi-fi. English spoken but Spanish encouraged. Dorms M$165/person, doubles M$415

EATING

Eating in San Miguel can be an expensive business; even local staples such as coffee and margaritas are likely to cost half as much again as they would in, say, Querétaro, and to find a decent supermarket or grocery store you'll have to take a taxi or bus to the outskirts. The **mercado** (see p.333) has the usual budget choices (tortas, tacos, *menudo*, *jugos* and the like), but nothing special (look for the "*fonda*" section, which has seating). Still, San Miguel's **restaurants** can be a tremendous relief for long-term travellers, with flavours you may not have tasted for weeks and a surprising array of **vegetarian** options.

Baja Fish Taquito Mesones 11 ☎415 113 6290, ⓦfacebook.com/bajafishtaquito. Small, unassuming diner with a few tables and bar stools serving authentic Ensenada-style fish (marlin) and shrimp tacos, plus tostadas, quesadillas and seafood *coctéles*. Daily 10.30am–8pm.

Café Oso Azul Zacateros 17 ☎415 154 4120, ⓦcafeosoazul.com. Contender for best coffee in town, an attractive courtyard café that roasts its own beans every few days, supplied by one of the owner's organic coffee plantations in Veracruz. Delicious, beautifully presented breakfasts from M$75. Thurs–Tues 8am–5pm.

Café de la Parroquia/La Brasserie Jesús 11 ☎415 152 3161. A great little place with seats inside or in the courtyard, justly popular with expats for breakfasts of hotcakes or yogurt and fruit (M$55–75). Good Mexican food served as well – tamales, *chilaquiles* and the like for M$90–200 – and coffee all day long. Becomes dinner spot *La Brasserie* Tues–Sat from 5pm. Tues–Sun 8am–10pm.

La Grotta Cuadrante 5 ☎415 152 4119, ⓦlagrotta .com.mx. Terrific pasta and pizza joint. Cosy room with red-washed walls and with kitchen pans hanging from the ceiling. The home-made pasta dishes (M$125) are tasty but no match for the crispy pizza (M$130–160) and calzone (M$145). Also fresh salads and a small selection of main dishes like trout and garlic prawns. Daily 2–10pm.

★**La Parada** Recreo 94 ☎415 152 0473, ⓦlaparadasma.com. This superb Peruvian restaurant has rapidly become a local institution in San Miguel, with a creative menu divided into seafood (lots of *ceviche*), soups and salads and "flavours of Peru" (slow-cooked pork sandwich, stir-fried chicken livers) sections, plus a massive pisco sour cocktail list. Wed–Sat noon–10pm, Sun & Mon

noon–9pm.

El Petit Four Mesones 99 ☎415 154 4010, ⓦelpetitfour.com. Delightful little French patisserie with a few tables where you can tuck into a pain au chocolat or a slice of *tarte aux pommes* with your espresso. Superb raspberry tarts (cakes M$15–60). Tues–Sat 9am–8pm, Sun 9am–5pm.

★**San Agustín** San Francisco 21 ☎415 154 9102. Owned by retired Argentine *telenovela* star Margarita Gralia, this tempting café is especially known for its sugary, fried *churros* eaten with hot chocolate – either sweet Spanish, semi-sweet French, or Mexican, flavoured with cinnamon (M$40). Breakfasts M$40–60. If you can, get the table with a view of Templo de San Francisco. Mon–Thurs 8am–11pm, Fri & Sat 9am–midnight.

El Ten Ten Pie Cuna de Allende 21 ☎415 152 7189. Small café with walls covered in the work of local artists, serving tasty Mexican staples (mains M$55–120) – expats like to sip drinks on the street-side patio opposite. Daily 9am–midnight.

La Ventana Sollano 11 (enter through Alborada restaurant) ☎415 154 7728. Your best bet in town for a caffeine fix, this quiet coffee shop features dark organic roasts from Chiapas and all manner of java concoctions. Drinks also available to go from a street-front window (*ventana*) for M$20–45. Daily 8am–6pm.

La Virundela Hernández Macías 48 ☎415 152 4400, ⓦwww.lavirundela.com. Some of the most succulent steaks are served in this top-notch Argentine restaurant, with meats smoked over the grill with pure mesquite hardwood embers. Also does excellent empanadas and vegetarian options. Tues & Wed 1.30–10pm, Fri & Sat 1.30–11pm, Sun noon–1pm.

STREET FOOD OF SAN MIGUEL

Looking to save money in San Miguel? Try these tasty snack options – cash only.

La Alborada Sollano 11 ☎415 154 9982. All types of *caldos* and *pozoles* (stews; chicken and pork, "red or green" style) in a small courtyard. Mon–Sat 1–10.30pm.

Apolo XI Mesones 43 ☎415 154 6252. Small shop selling cheap *carnitas* (sold by the kilo) or tortas ($22) to take away or munch on an open-air terrace upstairs. The hot and vinegary house pickles will curl your toes. Daily 9am–6pm.

★**Carnitas Bautista** Guadiana 2 (off Ancha de San Antonio) ☎415 152 6802. Be prepared for long waits at this legendary joint, where every part of the pig is roasted and served in tortillas or gorditas with fresh salsas (M$40–50). Daily 8am–3pm.

Taco stands Ancha de San Antonio and Nemesio Díez. Try the cluster of nameless stalls here for fabulous tacos (try the roasted lamb or *chicharrón* in salsa), from around 7am till early afternoon, and *barbacoa* (lunch only).

5

DRINKING AND NIGHTLIFE

BARS

La Azotea Umarán 6 ☎415 152 8265. San Miguel's hippest rooftop bar and lounge, adorned with contemporary art, drapes and comfy sofas. Pricey but exquisite margaritas. Daily 8am–1am.

La Coronela San Francisco 2 ☎415 152 5032. Dependable upmarket cantina decorated with old Mexican cinema posters, featuring two-for-one beers on Mon and Fri 4–7pm. Mon & Thurs 4pm–1am, Fri 4pm–3am, Sat 2pm–3am, Sun 2pm–1am.

El Gato Negro Mesones 12 ☎415 152 6544. Tiny and hip swinging-door cantina dating back to 1921, plastered in photos of Marilyn Monroe – plus a couple of Jim Morrison and John Lennon. The drinks are cheap, and there's no entry fee; though it looks old-fashioned, women are welcome. There's also an old-fashioned *pissoire*. Daily noon–2am.

Hank's New Orleans Café & Oyster Bar Hidalgo 12 ☎415 152 2645, �🌐hanksmexico.com. This local mini-chain restaurant has one of the most stylish bars in San Miguel (it also serves fresh seafood, Cajun and creole dishes), with a decent wine list. Mon–Sat noon–midnight, Sun 10am–11pm.

Limerick Pub Umarán 24 ☎415 154 8642. Enthusiastic Irish-themed pub, replete with pool table, dartboard, board games and Guinness, popular with locals and expats alike. It's also a fun place to watch live sports. Sun–Thurs 6.30pm–3am, Fri & Sat 6.30pm–5am.

★**Luna Rooftop Tapas Bar** (Rosewood Hotel) Nemesio Díez 11 ☎415 152 9700, �🌐rosewoodhotels .com. Enjoy fine Mexican and Spanish tapas while soaking up the most magical views of San Miguel. Great sofas and canopies to keep out the sun during the day. Daily 2pm–midnight.

Mama Mia Umarán 8 ☎415 152 2063, �🌐mamamia .com.mx. Probably the most happening nightspot in town, with restaurant (great pizza and pasta), sensational terrace bar with enthralling views over the rooftops and the adjacent after-hours *Mama's Bar*. You can count on good DJs, live bands (everything from jazz and Cuban to traditional Mexican) and live salsa on Fri and Sat nights (midnight–3am). Sun–Thurs 8am–midnight, Fri & Sat 8am–3am.

CLUBS

El Grito Umarán 15 ☎415 121 0163, �🌐elgrito.com .mx. Top club in town since 1998, and still the place to be seen for fashionable locals, if they're willing to pay; the entry fee is usually at least M$150. The cavernous interior is decked out with colonial chandeliers, stonework and sculpture, while DJs spin the usual mix of house and Latino sounds. Fri & Sat 10pm–4am.

Mint Club Mesones 99 ☎415 152 1958. San Miguel's other club attracts a glamorous crowd with a dancefloor surrounded by tables (these can be reserved). Expect to pay high prices for booze, Mexican/Latino dance music – and to dress up to get in. Fri & Sat 11pm–4am.

SHOPPING

Ablu Allende 11 ☎415 152 5870. Locally produced scented candles, bath, beauty and bodycare products. Mon–Fri 10am–2pm & 4–7pm, Sat 10am–8pm, Sun 11am–4pm.

Chocolates JOHFREJ Jesús 2A ☎415 152 3191, �🌐johfrej.com. San Miguel's artisan chocolatier since 1920. Also does scrumptious hot chocolate and home-made ice cream. Daily 10am–7pm.

★**Fábrica la Aurora** Calzada de la Aurora, via Hidalgo �🌐fabricalaaurora.com. This former cotton mill contains numerous art studios, restaurants, and shops selling home furnishings, jewellery and antiques. Mon–Sat 10am–6pm, Sun 11am–5pm.

Mixta Pila Seca 3 ☎415 152 7343, �🌐mixtasanmiguel .com. Popular store selling an eclectic mix of local, Mexican

and international products: jewellery, furniture, clothing, greeting cards and home decor. Mon–Sat 10am–7pm, Sun noon–5pm.

★**San Miguel Shoe** Relox 31 & Mesones 48 ☎415 154 4702, ⚑outersoul.com. The town's most famous shoe shops, selling a vast range of extra-comfy handmade Mexican footwear fondly known as "combat cocktail sandals". Local cobbler Santiago Gallardo Muñiz was allegedly inspired by San Miguel's unsteady cobblestones. Daily 10am–7pm.

Sollano 16 Sollano 16 ☎415 154 8872, ⚑sollano16 .com. Fashionable design store selling home furnishings, jewellery, antiques and stylish accessories. Tues–Sat 10am–6pm.

DIRECTORY

American Express Viajes Vertiz, Hidalgo 1, just north of El Jardín (Mon–Fri 9am–2pm & 4–6.30pm, Sat 10am–2pm; ☎415 152 1856, ⚑viajesvertiz.com), will hold mail, reissue stolen or lost cheques and cash them if they have enough money.

Banks and exchange Banamex, at the northwest corner

of El Jardín at Canal 4; Banorte, half a block east of Banamex at San Francisco 17; and HSBC at San Francisco 31. Most banks have ATMs.

Books The best bookshop is the US-expat-owned Garrison & Garrison at Hidalgo 26, Plaza Artesanal Bicentenaria (Mon, Wed, Fri–Sun 11am–6pm; ☎415 109 7387); it sells

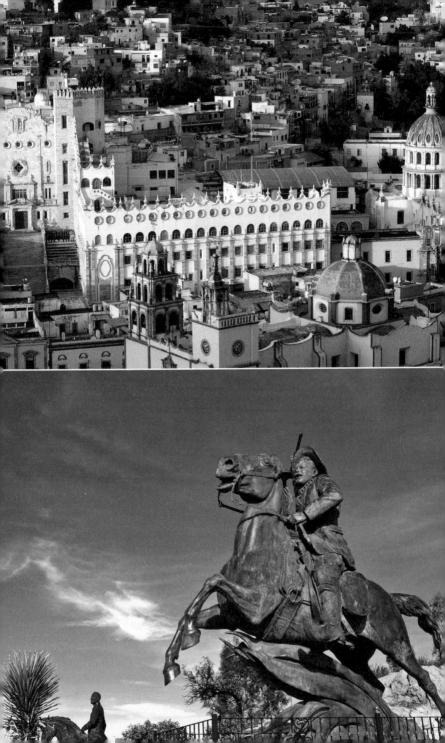

5

SAN MIGUEL'S CULTURAL CALENDAR

Like most of Mexico, Easter (Semana Santa) is the biggest celebration in San Miguel, but September is a more interesting month for visitors: on **Independence Day** (Sept 16) crowds gather to celebrate with fireworks, dances, bullfights and a rodeo. The most important town fiesta is of **San Miguel Arcángel**, two days of processions, concerts, traditional dancing, bullfights and ceremonies around September 29, St Michael's traditional feast day. The other major saint's day is the **Fiesta de San Antonio de Padua** (June 13), with a colourful parade for one of the town's patron saints, St Antony of Padua, involving a procession of garishly dressed revellers known as "Los Locos" (the Crazies).

Film and music **festivals** also pepper the year in San Miguel, kicking off with the **Guanajuato International Film Festival** (third week of July; ☎ 415 152 7264, ⓦ guanajuatofilmfestival.com), a week-long short-film festival hosted jointly by San Miguel and Guanajuato. The quarter-century-old **Festival Internacional de Música de Cámara** (Chamber Music Festival; first two weeks in Aug; ☎ 415 154 8722, ⓦ festivalsanmiguel.com) features a range of performances by internationally acclaimed musicians. The **Festival Internacional de Jazz & Blues** (last week of Nov/first week Dec; ⓦ sanmigueljazz.com.mx) includes two shows nightly by international performers at various locations in town from M$250 up. At other times, check out the programme at the **Teatro Ángela Peralta** at Mesones 82 (☎ 415 152 2200), which typically hosts ballet, theatre and occasional performances of classical music throughout the year.

a thoughtful range of new and secondhand English-language books.

Consulates US, Plaza La Luciernaga, Libramiento José Manuel Zavala 165, Colonia La Luciernaga (Mon–Thurs 9am–1pm; ☎ 415 152 2357).

Emergencies General emergencies ☎ 066; Cruz Roja ☎ 415 152 2545; police ☎ 415 152 2890.

Internet The Jardín and Biblioteca are wi-fi hot spots. Solutions at Mesones 57A charges M$15/hr (Mon–Fri 9am–6.30pm, Sat 9am–2pm).

Laundry Lavandería El Reloj at Relox 34-A charges M$18/kg (Mon–Fri 8am–8pm, Sat 8am–4pm).

Library La Biblioteca (Mon–Fri 10am–7pm, Sat 10am–2pm), Insurgentes 25, allows visitors to borrow books after obtaining a library card (two passport photocopies and M$100; check out 4 books for 15 days) and leaving a M$100 deposit.

Pharmacy Farmacia Chelo Agundis, Canal 26 (daily 10am–midnight; ☎ 415 152 1198). English spoken. Farmacia Guadalajara, at Ancha de San Antonio 13, is open 24hr.

Post office and couriers Correo 16 (Mon–Fri 8am–4pm, Sat 8am–noon). There are numerous express postal services, including DHL, at Correo 21 and opposite the post office.

Around San Miguel

One of the easiest and most enjoyable outings from San Miguel is to spend a good part of the day at one of the local **hot springs**, where the warm thermal waters are ideal for soaking your bones. There are numerous hotels and mini-resorts with geothermal pools all around the area, but the best and easiest to reach are clustered around ten minutes' drive northwest of town on the road to Dolores Hidalgo. The **Santuario de Jesús Nazareno de Atotonilco** and enigmatic **Cañada de la Virgen** are equally enticing cultural attractions, while the intriguing half-deserted settlement of **Mineral de Pozos** and historic towns of **Dolores Hidalgo** and **San José Iturbide** make easy and absorbing excursions.

La Gruta and Escondido Place

Carr San Miguel–Dolores Hidalgo, km 10 (Hwy-51) • **La Gruta** Daily 7am–5pm • M$110 (M$50 for lockers, refundable) • ☎ 415 185 2162, ⓦ lagrutaspa.com • **Escondido Place** Daily 8am–5.30pm • M$120 • ☎ 415 185 2022, ⓦ escondidoplace.com

The most popular hot spring in the San Miguel area is **La Gruta**, right by the Dolores highway, with a series of outdoor mineral pools at different temperatures all surrounded by lawns and banana trees. There's even a little grotto you can swim into, with an artificial waterfall, and a small and reasonably priced restaurant on site with snacks and fajitas. Best in the early morning – try to avoid the weekends altogether, when the pools get packed.

Around 500m before La Gruta, a side road leads just over a kilometre to **Escondido Place**, an equally appealing proposition, with small lily-filled lakes all around, outdoor pools and a series of small indoor ones linked by little tunnels and cascades. It can be quiet here midweek, but comes alive at weekends. Remember to bring towels.

| ARRIVAL AND DEPARTURE | LA GRUTA AND ESCONDIDO PLACE |

By bus Second-class buses to Dolores Hidalgo from San Miguel's bus station will drop off on the highway near both sets of pools; you can also take a "Santuario" bus from Calzada de la Luz and Relox (every hr; M$15). To get back, just flag down any bus you see.

By taxi Taxis will normally charge around M$150 each way, though locals pay half that (the spa will call a taxi for you to return).

Santuario de Jesús Nazareno de Atotonilco

C Principal, Atotonilco • Daily 9am–7pm • ☎ 415 185 2050, ⊚ santuariodeatotonilco.org

A day at the hot springs can be conveniently combined with a worthwhile outing to the "Sistine Chapel of Mexico", the **Santuario de Jesús Nazareno de Atotonilco** (easily confused with the larger Atotonilco el Grande in Jalisco state), 5km further in the same direction, then 2km down a side road. This is a dusty, rural indigenous community whose church has come to be a centre of pilgrimage for two reasons – it was founded by **Padre Felipe Neri** (constructed between 1740 and 1776), who was later canonized, and it was from here that Padre Hidalgo, marching from Dolores to San Miguel, took the banner of the Virgin of Guadalupe that became the flag of the Mexicans in the War of Independence. His comrade-in-arms Allende was married here in 1802. The six chapels of the church, liberally plastered with paintings by Baroque master **Juan Rodríguez Juárez** and murals by local artist **Miguel Antonio Martínez de Pocasangre**, are freely interspersed with poems, biblical passages and painted statues demonstrating every kind of Mexican popular art, from the naive to the highly sophisticated. The shrine was declared a UNESCO World Heritage Site in 2008.

| ARRIVAL AND DEPARTURE | SANTUARIO DE ATOTONILCO |

By bus Direct buses ("Santuario" or "Atotonilco"; M$15) leave every hour from Calzada de la Luz in San Miguel (45min) and spend ten to fifteen minutes in Atotonilco, giving you just enough time for a quick look before the run back, when you can get dropped off at the hot springs (same bus).

By taxi Taxis will charge at least M$150 one-way, M$300 return (ask the driver to wait) from San Miguel de Allende.

Cañada de la Virgen

Off Hwy-67 • Tues–Sun 10am–4pm • M$30 (no bags allowed inside the site) • ☎ 173 733 1069

The impressive ancient Mesoamerican pyramids of **Cañada de la Virgen** were opened to the public in 2011 after years of archeological excavations. Around 30km southwest of San Miguel, the intriguing site comprises seven enormous pyramidal structures associated with the Otomi of the Toltec-Chichimec culture and constructed between 540 and 1050 AD. Note that you must walk around 1.5km between the entrance and the actual site (after taking a free shuttle bus from the visitor centre). By far the easiest way to visit the pyramids is via an organized tour from San Miguel (see p.335) or with **Albert Coffee Archaeotours**, led by one of the original archeologists at the site (Tues–Sun 9am & 2pm; 4.5hr; ☎ 415 102 5583, ⊚ albertcoffeetours.com; M$750, includes all transport).

Dolores Hidalgo

Fifty kilometres or so from both Guanajuato and San Miguel de Allende, **DOLORES HIDALGO** is as ancient and as historically rich as either of its southern neighbours. This was Father Hidalgo's parish, and it was from the church in the main plaza here that the historic **Grito de la Independencia** ("Cry of Independence") was first issued in 1810 (see p.822). The town celebrates the event annually with the **Fiestas de Septiembre**, ten days of cultural and sporting events, music and fireworks, culminating with the *Grito* around dawn on the sixteenth.

5

Perhaps because of its less spectacular location or maybe because there is no university or major language school, Dolores hasn't seen a fraction of the tourist development that has overtaken other places in the Bajío (despite being named yet another Pueblo Mágico in 2002). It's a good bet, though, for a one-night stopover, and if you can't find accommodation in Guanajuato or San Miguel, this is certainly the place to head; you'll get a better room here for appreciably less. True, there is less to see, but it's an elegant little town and thoroughly Mexican.

Museo Casa de Hidalgo

Morelos 1, at Hidalgo • Tues–Sat 10am–5.45pm, Sun 10am–4.45pm • M$49 • ☎ 418 182 0171

Just a couple of blocks from the bus station as you walk along Hidalgo towards the central Plaza Principal, the **Museo Casa de Hidalgo**, Father Hidalgo's home between 1804 and 1810, was rebuilt after the Spanish destroyed it and has been converted into a museum devoted to his life, very much a point of pilgrimage for Mexicans on day trips. It's a bit heavy on written tributes from various groups to the "Father of Independence" and on copies of other correspondence he either sent or received – but it's edifying nonetheless and includes a few highlights such as his letter of excommunication from the Inquisition less than a month after the *Grito*.

Parroquia de Nuestra Señora de los Dolores

Plaza Principal • Daily 5.30am–9pm

The beautifully laid-out Plaza Principal at the heart of Dolores is dominated by the exuberant churrigueresque facade of the **Parroquia de Nuestra Señora de los Dolores**, the illustrious church where Don Miguel Hidalgo issued the *Grito* (this is where a representative of the president repeats the *Grito* every Sept 15). The church was completed in 1778, with Hidalgo assuming the position of parish priest in 1803.

Museo del Bicentenario

Plaza Principal • Tues–Sun 10am–4.45pm • M$20 • ☎ 418 182 7731

Next door to the church is the **Presidencia Municipal**, birthplace and former home of revolutionary hero Mariano Abasolo and now the **Museo del Bicentenario**. The museum chronicles the history of Dolores, primarily from the Porfirio Díaz era, with rare jewellery, old weapons, portraits and black-and-white photographs – there's even a recording of Díaz, made by Thomas Edison in 1909.

Museo de la Independencia Nacional

Zacatecas 6 • Mon–Sat 9am–4.45pm, Sun 9am–3pm • M$15, free Sun • ☎ 418 182 0193

Just off the Plaza Principal is the **Museo de la Independencia Nacional**, which served as the town jail until 1959 – Hidalgo famously freed the prison inmates here in 1810. Today, the vibrant, graphic murals inside depict significant scenes from Mexican history from the Aztec perception of the world through to the many indigenous rebellions against Spain and the life of Hidalgo.

Casa Museo José Alfredo Jiménez

Guanajuato 13 at Nuevo León • Tues–Sun 10am–5pm • M$35 • ☎ 418 154 4070

Don't leave town without paying homage to the greatest *ranchera* singer of all time at the **Casa Museo José Alfredo Jiménez**, containing a small but wonderfully presented collection of personal effects, record sleeves and biographical information. Jiménez (1926–73) was born in Dolores and is buried here, his colourful **tomb** (inside the Panteón Municipal, heading out of town on Hwy-110 to Guanajuato) topped with a giant *sarape* and sombrero.

ARRIVAL AND INFORMATION

DOLORES HIDALGO

By bus Dolores is connected to both San Miguel de Allende (45min) and Guanajuato (1hr 30min) by regular, rapid second-class buses to and from the Flecha Amarilla terminal, at Hidalgo 26 beside the river.

Destinations Guanajuato (every 20min; 1hr 15min); León (every 20min; 3hr); Mexico City (every 40min; 5–6hr); Querétaro (every 40min; 2hr 30min); San Luis de la Paz

(every 30min; 1hr 10min); San Luis Potosí (10 daily; 2hr 30min); San Miguel de Allende (every 40min; 50min).

Tourist office There's little need to visit Dolores' small tourist office (Mon–Fri 9am–5pm, Sat 10am–2pm; ☎ 418 182 1164, ⓦ dolores-hidalgo.com), Plaza Principal 11, by the church, but they can give advice on where to buy the town's famous ceramics.

ACCOMMODATION

Hotel Hidalgo Hidalgo 15 ☎ 418 182 2683, ⓦ hotel posadahidalgo.com. Comfy modern hotel located one block north of the bus station and two blocks south of the Plaza Principal, with internet, laundry and a gym on site. M$650

Posada Cocomacán Plaza Principal 4 ☎ 418 182 6086, ⓦ posadacocomacan.com.mx. Lovely colonial property dating from the 1720s, with a cool interior, cable TV and some rooms overlooking the plaza. M$650

EATING

Dolores Hidalgo is home to the country's most unusual **ice cream** flavours: Mexicans come in droves to the Plaza Principal to lick scoops of creamy alfalfa, *mole*, *cerveza*, shrimp and avocado (fortunately most vendors let you sample before you commit to a full cone). Try popular stalls *Helados Aguilar* or *Helados Josué*.

★ **Carnitas Vicente** Norte 65 ☎ 418 182 1390. This has been a Dolores tradition since 1980, a restaurant dedicated to the finest *carnitas* (spicy shredded Mexican-style pork) in the region, stuffed into gorditas or piled onto plates and served by the kilo (M$240). Daily 8am–6pm.

El Carruaje de Caudillo Plaza Principal 8 ☎ 418 182 0474. Colonial-style *El Carruaje* ("The Chariot") does a tasty *menu del día* (M$80) and weekend buffets and has live music in the evenings. House specialities include the *Molcajete*

Carruaje (grilled meats served in a pot) and chicken breast stuffed with squash blossoms. Daily 8am–11pm.

★ **DaMonica** Nayarit 67, at Sonora ☎ 418 182 4587. This top-quality Italian restaurant is gaining quite a following, with excellent service and tasty pastas (spaghetti with mussels and shrimp, gnocchi with gorgonzola), pizzas and home-made soups and breads – the owner (Monica) hails from Milan, and it shows. Mon–Sat noon–10pm.

Mineral de Pozos

San Miguel de Allende eighty years ago? That may be pushing things a bit, but **MINERAL DE POZOS** is certainly far quieter and less developed than its popular neighbour (see p.329). Once a rich and flourishing mining community, since the 1950s it's been referred to as a ghost-town, though in reality it is far from dead, having experienced a revival in the last ten years. Indeed, a San Miguel-like transformation is well under way, with foreigners buying up property, and several restaurants, attractive hotels, absorbing art galleries, shops and numerous North American artists (many of whom are part-timers) setting up shop. Around 3500 people live in the streets clustered around the white dome of **Parroquia San Pedro** and the **Jardín Principal** – in 2012 Pozos became another Pueblo Mágico, cementing its tourist potential.

Yet crumbling ruins still outnumber the development – for now at least – and the town's edges, fringed with desert, mine workings and abandoned haciendas, remain an enchanting, if potentially dangerous, place. Many tunnels are unmarked, and if you're hiking take extra care. Highlights include the ruins of the **Hacienda de Cinco Señores**, a vast abandoned mine complex, and the three distinctive sixteenth-century Jesuit smelters (*hornos*) of **Santa Brígida**. Note that Pozos lies at around 2300m above sea level, and it can get quite cold on winter nights.

ARRIVAL AND INFORMATION

MINERAL DE POZOS

By bus Travelling by bus to Pozos means changing several times, usually via Dolores Hidalgo and San Luis de la Paz; from Guanajuato it's faster to take a bus to Dolores and change there for San Luis de la Paz (1hr 10min), rather than

a direct bus to the latter. From San Miguel de Allende you'll also have to take a bus to Dolores (every 40min) and change there for San Luis de la Paz, or take an organized tour or a taxi (see p.344). Once in San Luis de la Paz; take a

5

local bus marked "Pozos" or take a taxi for around M$80 (15min). From Querétaro take a bus to San José Iturbide (M$55min) and change there.

Destinations San José Iturbide (every 30min; 40min); San Luis de la Paz (every 30min; 20min).

Cars and taxis Many travellers choose to rent cars and drive to Pozos (it's just 45min from San Miguel de Allende). Alternatively, San Miguel de Allende taxis will charge around M$800 for a round trip (up to six people); from Querétaro reckon on around M$600 one-way.

Tourist information Visit Ⓦ mineraldepozos.com for the latest information.

ACCOMMODATION

★ **Casa Mexicana** Juárez 2 on the Jardín Principal ☎ 442 293 0014, Ⓦ casamexicanahotel.com. This five-bedroom B&B boasts exquisite and individual rooms set around a blossom-filled garden, and with an on-site art gallery. Expertly prepared meals (M$100–150) are also served to non-guests, or you could just drop in for a margarita. **M$980**

El Secreto de Pozos Jardín Principal 4 ☎ 442 293 0200, Ⓦ elsecretomexico.com. Tranquil B&B with three rooms just off the plaza, all beautifully designed and blending traditional and contemporary styles; there are wood-burning fireplaces. **M$1590**

Posada de la Minas Manuel Doblado 1 ☎ 713 816 7424, Ⓦ posadadelasminas.com. A fabulous colonial mansion one block from the plaza, with six inviting rooms featuring everything from Mexican folk art to Victorian themes; internet and laundry available. **M$1990**

EATING

Caffe D'La Fama Hidalgo 1 (Jardín Principal) ☎ 468 680 1921. Atmospheric café on the main plaza (upstairs from La Fama shop), with delicious coffees, real espresso (beans sourced from Chiapas and Oaxaca) and pastries, plus salads and sandwiches. Also serves wine. Cash only.

Daily 8.30am–10pm.

La Pila Seca Aldama 8 ☎ 442 293 0020. Cheap and popular Mexican classics served in an art-smothered dining room close to the Jardín. *Enchiladas Potosinas*, *arrachera* and big breakfasts from M$50. Free wi-fi. Daily 9am–9pm.

San José Iturbide

Some 30km south of Mineral de Pozos and 55km north of Querétaro, **SAN JOSÉ ITURBIDE** is an immaculate colonial town centred on its tidy **Plaza Principal**. It's chiefly distinguished by a behemoth Neoclassical church, **Parroquia de San José**, dedicated to Agustín de Iturbide (1783–1824), an opportunist from Michoacán who started the War of Independence as a general loyal to Spain – inflicting major defeats on Morelos – only to change sides later. Having helped secure Mexico's independence without any concomitant reform, he briefly declared himself emperor in 1822 (he was executed two years later).

ARRIVAL AND DEPARTURE   SAN JOSÉ ITURBIDE

Only one first-class bus goes to/from Querétaro (M$60) and Mexico City (M$385) per day; the Central de Autobuses is at Domínguez 38, between Otoño and Gómez Pedraza, three blocks west of the Plaza Principal.

Destinations Mexico City (1 daily 6am; 4hr); Pozos (every 30min; 40min); Querétaro (first class 1 daily 6am, 2hr; second class every 15min, 2hr); San Luis de la Paz (7 daily; 1hr).

ACCOMMODATION

Hotel Los Arcos Plaza Principal 10, right by the church ☎ 419 198 0330, ✉ hotellosarcos@hotmail.com. There's little reason to stay in San José, but if you just fancy a night in a small Mexican town, then try this excellent hotel with large, modern, carpeted rooms. **M$710**

Hotel Posada Unión Callejón Olivera 10 ☎ 419 198 0071. One of the cheapest options in the centre is this convenient, comfortable but basic hotel, two blocks along Allende. **M$350**

EATING

El Diezmo Nicolás Campa 16, at Plutarco Elías calles ☎ 419 198 0645, Ⓦ eldiezmohotel.com.mx. A swish hotel with a great restaurant and wonderful views of the church. Daily 7am–10pm.

Hotel Los Arcos Plaza Principal 10 ☎ 419 198 0330. This hotel restaurant, right on the plaza, knocks out creative Mexican dishes like *nopales* paired with cheese, zesty salads and huge egg plates from M$100, and buckets of cold Corona. Mon–Sat 7am–10pm, Sun 7am–9pm.

Guanajuato and around

Shoehorned into a narrow ravine, **GUANAJUATO** was for centuries the wealthiest city in Mexico, its mines pouring out silver and gold in prodigious quantities. Today it presents an astonishing sight: upon emerging from the surrounding hills you come on the city quite suddenly, a riot of colonial architecture, tumbling down hills so steep that at times it seems the roof of one building is suspended from the floor of the last. Declared a UNESCO World Heritage Site in 1988, Guanajuato is protective of its image: there are no traffic lights or neon signs here, and the topography ensures that there's no room for new buildings. The town's pristine reputation was cemented in 2012, when **Pope Benedict XVI** chose Guanajuato (and neighbouring León) as the only stops on his Mexican visit.

Today the city of around 170,000 has plenty of life in its narrow streets, many outstanding places to eat and drink, and lots to see: churches, theatres, museums, battlefields, mines and mummified corpses, to name but a few of the city's attractions. There's an old-fashioned, backwater feel to the place, reinforced by the local students' habit of going serenading in black capes, the brass bands playing in the plazas and the city's general refusal to make any special effort to accommodate the flood of (mostly domestic) tourists.

Guanajuato's main thoroughfare is Juárez, but below this passes an underground roadway: the **Subterráneo Miguel Hidalgo**. It was built as a tunnel to take the river under the city, but the river now runs deeper below ground, and its former course, with the addition of a few exits and entrances, has proved very handy in preventing traffic from clogging up the centre entirely; more tunnels have since been added to keep the traffic flowing.

Mercado Hidalgo

Juárez, at Mendizábal • Daily 9am–9pm

Approaching the centre of Guanajuato from the west side, heading east up Juárez, the first building of note is the **Mercado Hidalgo**, a huge iron-framed construction of 1910 reminiscent of British Victorian train stations and crammed with every imaginable sort of goods (from Mexican chocolate and fresh fruit to local dolls and T-shirts). It's also a fun, cheap place to eat (see p.354).

Plaza San Roque

East of the Mercado Hidalgo, to the left and through the **Jardín de la Reforma**, with its fountain and arch, you get to the lovely, serene **Plaza San Roque**. A small, irregular, flagged space, the plaza has a distinctly medieval feel, heightened by the raised facade of the crumbling **Templo de San Roque** that towers above. It's a perfect setting for the city's annual **Festival Internacional Cervantino** (see box, p.355). The Callejón de los Olleros leads back down to Juárez, or you can cut straight through to the livelier **Plazuela San Fernando**, with its stalls and restaurants.

Callejón del Beso

Halfway along Juárez the **Plazuela de los Angeles** is little more than a slight broadening of the street, but from here steps lead up to some of Guanajuato's steepest, narrowest alleys. Just off the plazuela is the **Callejón del Beso** (20m up Callejón del Patrimonio and turn left), so-called because at only 69cm wide, it is slim enough for residents to lean out of the upper-storey balconies and exchange kisses across the street – naturally enough, there's a legend of star-crossed lovers associated with it (see box, p.346).

5

██ ACCOMMODATION	
Antiguo Vapor	4
Balcón de Cielo	11
Casa del Agua	3
La Casa del Tio	9
Casa Zuniga	12
Edelmira Hotel Boutique	6
Hostería del Frayle	10
Hotel Socavón	1
El Mesón de los Poetas	2
Mesón del Rosario	7
Quinta Las Acacias	14
San Diego	8
Villa María Cristina	13
El Zopilote Mojado Hostal	5

Parque del Cantador	

● EATING	
Café Tal	7
El Gallo Pitagórico	6
Las Mercedes	1
El Tapatío	2
Tasca de la Paz	5
Truco 7	4
La Vie en Rose	3

Plaza de la Paz

The **Plaza de la Paz** is the civic heart of Guanajuato, boasting some of its finest **colonial buildings**, notably the **Palacio Legislativo** (completed in 1900 and still in use today) and the adjacent late eighteenth-century **Casa del Conde Rul y Valenciana** (built by the owners of the richest mine in the country; Don Diego Rul was killed fighting rebels in 1814). The latter was designed by Eduardo Tresguerras, undoubtedly the finest Mexican architect of his time, and played host briefly to Baron Alexander von Humboldt in 1803, the German naturalist and writer, an event commemorated by a plaque. Today it serves as the regional courthouse. The **Casa de Gobierno** (closed to the public), a short way down towards the Jardín de la Unión (see opposite), is another fine mansion, this

---

LEGEND OF THE KISS

The legend of the Callejón del Beso is classic Romeo and Juliet: two young lovers – in this case Doña Ana and her suitor, Don Carlos – separated by mean, feuding parents. The story has a fittingly tragic ending; in a desperate bid to see his love, Don Carlos bought the house opposite Doña Ana's, across an alley so close they could hold hands. When Ana's father caught them, he was so incensed he stabbed his daughter to death at the window – poor Carlos was left kissing her lifeless hand. Today it is said that couples who kiss while standing on the third step of the Callejón del Beso are guaranteed seven years of happiness.

CENTRAL GUANAJUATO

DRINKING & NIGHTLIFE

Antik Café	1
Bar Fly	9
Bora Bora	7
La Dama de las Camelias	4
Desmond's	2
Guanajuato Grill	5
Los Lobos	6
One Bar & Lounge	3
Santo Café	8

0   100
metres

Centro Médico la Presa ▼

time with a plaque recording that Benito Juárez lived here in 1858, when Guanajuato was briefly his provisional capital.

Basílica de Nuestra Señora de Guanajuato

Plaza de la Paz • Daily 8am–9pm • **Galería Mariana** Mon & Wed–Sat 10am–6pm/Tues–Sun 11am–2pm & 4–6pm • M$20 • ☎ 473 732 0314

On the eastern side of the Plaza de la Paz stands the honey-coloured **Basílica de Nuestra Señora de Guanajuato**, a Baroque parish church that was completed in 1796 in honour of an ancient image of the Virgin, patroness of the city (aka Nuestra Señora de Guanajuato). The statue arrived in Guanajuato in 1557, a gift from Charles V and his successor Philip II, in gratitude for the wealth that was pouring from here into Spanish royal coffers. The wooden statue sits on a silver pedestal amid several paintings by Miguel Cabrera in the old baptistery, now **Galería Mariana**, with a separate entrance on the side of the basilica.

Jardín de la Unión

Just a short distance further east from Plaza de la Paz on the main street (Juárez has become Obregón at this point) is the **Jardín de la Unión**, Guanajuato's main plaza. Created in the 1860s on land once owned by the church, it's a delightful little square – or rather triangle – shaded with trees, surrounded by cafés and with a bandstand in the centre from which the town band regularly plays (usually Thurs at 6pm, Sun at noon & 7pm). This is the best time to sit and linger over a drink, enjoying the passing spectacle of the evening *paseo*.

5

LEARNING SPANISH IN GUANAJUATO

Guanajuato has become a popular place to spend a couple of weeks learning Spanish – you can opt to **stay with a local family** (typically around M$405–480 a day), sharing meals with them and getting plenty of opportunity to try out your new language skills; most schools can arrange this. Classes with up to five students usually **cost** around M$90 an hour, and a little less if you're doing more hours per day. One-to-one tuition is around M$225 an hour.

Don Quijote Guanajuato Pastita 76 ☎ 34 923 268 860, ⓦ donquijote.org. This Spanish school chain (it's based in Salamanca) has a popular operation in Guanajuato, with intensive courses from US$485 (M$8085) for one week.

Escuela Mexicana Potrero 12 ☎ 473 732 5005, ⓦ escuelamexicana.com. School in the heart of town

offering everything from one-week beginners' courses to extensive advanced classes and an array of specialist courses in such subjects as culture, literature, politics and Mexican cooking. Their intensive "Spanish for Travellers" requires four hours of coursework a day and one or two weeks' commitment; US$200–300/week (M$3335–5000), plus US$40/M$600 registration.

Templo de San Diego

Sopeña, at Jardín de la Unión • Daily 7am–6pm

Facing the Jardín de la Unión across Obregón stands the **Templo de San Diego**, inside which are several eighteenth-century oil paintings and intriguing chapels. One altar in particular (just to the left as you enter) is dedicated to the infant Jesus (Niño de la Caridad) and mawkishly filled with toys and children's tiny shoes left as offerings. The church was reconstructed around 1784 for the Franciscans in the churrigueresque style so popular at the time.

Museo Ex-Convento de Dieguino

Sopeña, at Jardín de la Unión • Daily 10am–6pm • M$12 • ☎ 473 732 5296

On the north side of Templo de San Diego a separate entrance leads down to the **Museo Ex-Convento Dieguino**, an art gallery space among the stone foundations of the church – the small display of archeological finds here, and the renovated crypt space itself, are interesting, but unless an exhibition is on show, there's not much else to see.

Teatro Juárez

Sopeña, at Jardín de la Unión • Tues–Sun 9am–1.45pm & 5–7.45pm • M$35, with camera M$30 extra

Next door to the church of San Diego is the imposing Neoclassical frontage of the **Teatro Juárez**, all Doric columns and allegorical statuary. Built at the end of the nineteenth century, it was opened in 1903 by the dictator Porfirio Díaz himself. The interior of the theatre is fabulously plush, decked out in red velvet and gilt, with chandeliers and an opulent Moorish theme throughout (the proscenium is supposed to show a panorama of Constantinople). Upstairs you can also visit the Neoclassical **Salón Tocador** (powder room, used by wealthy ladies).

Museo Iconográfico del Quijote

Manuel Doblado 1 • Tues–Sat 9.30am–6.45pm, Sun noon–6.45pm • M$30, free Tues • ☎ 473 732 3376

Beyond the Jardín, Obregón becomes Sopeña, lined with fancy boutiques, restaurants and bars as far as the pretty pink church of San Francisco, which marks the **Plaza San Francisco**. Here, too, is the **Museo Iconográfico del Quijote**, an extraordinary little collection devoted entirely to Don Quixote, testament to the influence of **Miguel de Cervantes**' seminal novel on subsequent generations of artists. The museum contains mainly paintings of the don – including some by Pedro and Rafael Coronel – but also a Dalí print, a Posada engraving of the hero as a *calavera*, an imposing sculpture by Federico Silva, murals, tapestries, sculptures, busts, miniatures, medals, plates, glassware, chess sets, playing cards, pipes and cutlery – you name it, it's here. There's also a mural-smothered shrine to the maestro himself, containing a statue of Cervantes.

Museo Olga Costa-José Chávez Morado

Pastita 158, Torre del Arco • Thurs–Sat 9.30am–4pm, Sun 10am–3pm • M$20 • ☎ 473 731 0977

The seventeenth-century Hacienda de Guadalupe is where Mexican muralist **José Chávez Morado** (1909–2002) and his German painter wife (**Olga Costa**) spent much of their married life. Morado moved out and donated the building to the city of Guanajuato on his wife's death in 1993, and today it exists as the **Museo Olga Costa-José Chávez Morado**. The house has been left largely as it was when the couple lived here, an eclectic mix of objects explained (in Spanish) by the guide: eighteenth-century majolica ceramics, seventeenth-century French chairs, Dutch porcelain, Persian wall hangings and a fine collection of ex votos. There's little of their work on show, but notice Morado's blue-and-white lamp, and his stained-glass windows – all blotches in red, yellow, blue and black – on the way up to the studio, now given over to temporary exhibitions. The museum is less than thirty minutes' walk from the Jardín de la Unión, or you can flag down any bus marked "Pastita" at the eastern end of town.

Pípila

Mirador del Cerro de San Miguel Funicular Mon–Fri 8am–9.50pm, Sat 9am–9.50pm, Sun 10am–9.50pm • M$20 each way •
Museo Pípila Daily 10am–5pm • M$10 • Bus M$6

The **Monumento al Pípila**, a bulky statue on the hillside almost directly above the Jardín de la Unión, honours local miner **Juán José Martínez**, aka "El Pípila" (see box below) – there's a small exhibit, the **Museo Pípila**, dedicated to the hero inside the monument. Built in 1939, the statue affords staggering views of Guanajuato; from the viewpoint at its base you seem to be standing directly on top of the church of San Diego, with red, blue and yellow houses spilling down the otherwise bare hills. It's an especially magical spot for the 45 minutes or so during which the sun sets behind the hills and the electric lights start to come on in town. Around you'll always find crowds of Mexican tourists trawling the food stalls here for snacks to munch while enjoying the views.

The steep climb up the hill takes about twenty minutes and ten minutes coming down. There are several possible routes up through the alleys – look for signs saying "al Pípila" – including up the Callejón del Calvario, to the right off Sopeña just beyond the Teatro Juárez; from the Plazuela San Francisco; or climbing to the left from the Callejón del Beso. The signs run out, but if you keep climbing as steeply as possible you're unlikely to get lost and the paved trail is fairly easy to follow. There's also a bus

---

EL PÍPILA

In 1810, Father Hidalgo approached Guanajuato at the head of his insurgent force – mostly peons armed with nothing more than staves and sickles. The Spanish, outnumbered but well supplied with firearms, shut themselves up in the **Alhóndiga**. The almost certainly apocryphal story goes that Hidalgo's troops could make no impact until a young miner, nicknamed **El Pípila** ("the Turkeycock"), volunteered to set fire to the wooden doors – with a slab of stone tied to his back as a shield, he managed to crawl to the gates and start them burning, dying in the effort. The rebels, their path cleared, broke in and massacred the defenders wholesale. It was a short-lived victory – Hidalgo, later forced to abandon Guanajuato, was eventually tracked down by the royalists and executed. His head and the heads of his three chief co-conspirators, Allende, Aldama and Jiménez, were suspended from the four corners of the Alhóndiga as a warning to anyone tempted to follow their example, and there they stayed for over ten years, until Mexico finally did become independent.

5

("Pípila") that takes you round the scenic Carretera Panorámica, or the **funicular**, a cliff railway that whisks you up the steep valley side from behind the church of San Diego.

Templo de La Compañía

Lascuráin de Retana, at Del Sol • Daily 7.30am–9.30pm • **Pinacoteca Virreinal** Tues–Sat 10am–5pm, Sun 10am–2pm • M$10

The **Templo de La Compañía**, a highly decorated monumental churrigueresque church, is just about all that's left of a Jesuit seminary founded in 1734; step inside to admire the unusually light interior afforded by the clear glass in the dome, added in 1884 and inspired by St Peter's in Rome. Behind the altar is a gallery or **Pinacoteca Virreinal** with a few seventeenth- to nineteenth-century religious oil paintings, mostly anonymous but including four small portraits of saints by Miguel Cabrera, and a Virgin by José de Ibarra. The Jesuit seminary was an educational establishment that eventually metamorphosed into the **Universidad Guanajuato**, now one of the most prestigious in Mexico. The current university building next door to the church is in fact quite modern – only finished in 1955 – but was designed to blend in with the town, which, for its size, it does surprisingly effectively.

Museo del Pueblo de Guanajuato

Positos 7 • Tues–Sat 10am–7pm, Sun 10am–3pm • M$20 • ☎ 473 732 2990

Next door to the Universidad Guanajuato, the **Museo del Pueblo de Guanajuato** is a collection of local art and sundry oddities, housed in the eighteenth-century home of the Marqués de San Juan de Rayas. It's an arresting building with a delightful little Baroque chapel (added in 1776), where much of the decoration has been replaced by modern murals painted by one of the standard-bearers of the Mexican muralist tradition, **José Chávez Morado** (see p.349). Look out also for paintings by **Hermenegildo Bustos** (1832–1907), one of the most influential Mexican artists of the nineteenth century.

Museo del Siglo XIX

Positos 25 • Mon–Sat 10am–6pm, Sun 10am–3pm • M$20 • ☎ 473 734 6193

Focusing on the history of Guanajuato from 1790 to 1920, the **Museo del Siglo XIX** is one of the city's newer museums, essentially a colonial mansion artfully restored and adorned with artwork from the likes of Posada, Gualdi and Felguérez, as well as old artefacts and original letters signed by Benito Juárez, Emperor Maximilian and Porfirio Díaz.

Museo Casa Diego Rivera

Positos 47 • Tues–Sat 10am–7.30pm, Sun 10am–3pm • M$20 • ☎ 473 732 1197

Guanajuato's most famous son was born here in 1886, his old home now preserved as the absorbing **Museo Casa Diego Rivera**. For most of his life Rivera, an ardent revolutionary sympathizer and Marxist (see box, p.76), went unrecognized by his conservative home town, but with international recognition of his work came this museum, in the house where he was raised until he was 6. Initially the Rivera family only occupied the lower floor, which is now furnished in nineteenth-century style, though only the beds and a cot actually belonged to them. The place is far bigger than it looks from the outside, and the extensive upper floors contain many of Rivera's works, especially early ones, in a huge variety of styles – Cubist, Pointillist, Impressionist – showing the influences he absorbed during his years in France and Spain. Although there are no major works on display, the many sketches and small paintings are well worth a look, particularly those showing his fascination with all things pre-Columbian.

Museo Regional de Guanajuato (Alhóndiga de Granaditas)

Mendizábal 6 • Tues–Sat 10am–5.30pm, Sun 10am–2.30pm • M$52, with camera M$30 extra • ☎ 473 732 1180

The Museo Regional de Guanajuato or **Alhóndiga de Granaditas**, the most important of all Guanajuato's monuments, lies west of the Museo Casa Diego Rivera, more or less above the market. Originally a granary completed in 1809, and later a prison, this was the scene of the first real battle and some of the bloodiest butchery in the War of Independence (see box, p.349).

Inside, there's a memorial hall devoted to the Martyrs of Independence and the **museum** itself, upstairs. On the staircases are **murals** by local artist José Chávez Morado (see p.349) depicting scenes from the War of Independence and the Revolution, as well as native folklore and traditions. The museum's exhibits, mostly labelled in Spanish, span local history from pre-Hispanic times to the Revolution: the most interesting sections cover the Independence battle and everyday life in the colonial period. One of the iron cages in which the rebels' heads were displayed is present, as are lots of weapons and flags and a study of Guanajuato's mining industry in the 1890s, the city's last golden age. There's also plenty of art, including a wonderful series of portraits by Hermenegildo Bustos, the celebrated artist born near León.

Museo de las Momias

Explanada del Panteón Municipal • Mon–Thurs 9am–6pm, Fri–Sun 9am–6.30pm • M$56, M$36 students (camera M$20 extra) •
☎ 473 732 0639, ⓦ momiasdeguanajuato.gob.mx • Catch buses marked "Panteón" or "Momias" (M$6) anywhere along Alonso or Juárez, or walk about 500m west of the Mercado Hidalgo, along Juárez and Tepetapa, then left onto Calzada del Panteón

Tucked away in the hills west of the Alhóndiga, the ghoulish **Museo de las Momias** contains more than a hundred mummified human corpses in glass cases, exhumed from the local public cemetery. All the bodies were originally laid out in crypts, but if after five years relatives were unable or unwilling to make the perpetuity payment, the remains were usually removed. Over time many were found to have been naturally preserved, and for years the cemetery became an unofficial tourist attraction. The damage done to the site prompted the government to step in, and now the "interesting" bodies are on display here – others, not properly mummified or too dull for public titillation, have been burned or transferred to a common grave. Some of the wasted, leathery bodies are more than a century old (including a smartly dressed mummy from the 1860s said to have been a French doctor), while others are relatively recent fatalities. The burial clothes hang off the corpses almost indecently – some are completely naked – and the labels (in English) delight in pointing out their most horrendous features: one twisted mummy, its mouth opened in a silent scream, is the "woman who was buried alive"; another, a woman who died in childbirth, is displayed beside "the smallest mummy in the world". Some of the labelling is written in the first person, adding another disturbing twist. It's all absolutely grotesque, but not without a degree of macabre fascination. At the end of the main exhibit you can exit or continue into the **Salón del Culto a la Muerte**, a house-of-horrors-style extension, with an array of holographic images, jangly motorized skeletons, a rusty old chastity belt and yet more mummies. Fans of kitsch will be delighted with the hawkers outside selling mummy models and mummy-shaped shards of rock.

Museo Ex-Hacienda de San Gabriel de Barrera

Carr Guanajuato-Marfil, km 2.5 • Daily 9am–6pm • M$25, with camera M$5 extra • ☎ 473 732 0619 • Take any bus going to Marfil (M$6), and ask to be dropped at Hotel Misión Guanajuato; Taxis charge M$40–50

If the crush of Guanajuato gets too much for you, head 2km west to the **Museo Ex-Hacienda de San Gabriel de Barrera**, once the colonial home of the wealthy Barrera family, now transformed into an alluring little museum. The seventeen beautifully restored **gardens** of the hacienda range through an eclectic selection of international

5

styles – including English, Italian, Roman, Arabic and Mexican – and make a wonderful setting for the house, which has been renovated with a colonial look. Dimly lit rooms evoke daily life among the wealthy silver barons of nineteenth-century Guanajuato and include numerous oil paintings and fine pieces of furniture dating back several centuries: simple and almost medieval on the ground floor, opulent and rich in domestic detail upstairs. It's an enlightening place to wander at your leisure and brings home the sheer wealth of colonial Guanajuato.

La Valenciana

From close by the Alhóndiga, buses labelled "Valenciana" (M$6; infrequent; taxis M$50) wind their way 4km uphill to the old silver mine shafts and stupendous church in the village of **La Valenciana**, a slice of colonial Mexico barely changed since the eighteenth century.

Templo de San Cayetano de Valenciana

Carr Guanajuato-Dolores Hidalgo, km 1.5 • Tues–Sun 9am–6pm • Free • ☎ 473 732 3596

Overlooking Guanajuato and dominating the village of La Valenciana with its elaborate facade and one completed tower is the extraordinarily sumptuous **Templo de San Cayetano de Valenciana**. Built between 1765 and 1788, it's the ultimate expression of Mexico's churrigueresque style, with a profusion of intricate adornment covering every surface – even the mortar, they say, is mixed with silver ore. Inside, notice the enormous gilded *retablos* around the main altar and in the transepts, and the delicate filigree of the roof vaulting, especially around the dome.

The church was constructed for its sponsor, the Conde de Rul y Valenciana, who also owned La Valenciana **silver mine** – for hundreds of years the richest in Mexico, tapping Guanajuato's celebrated **Veta Madre** (Mother Lode). Silver and gold are still mined around here, and exploitation continues apace with a clutch of ways to lure tourists to the associated silver shops, rock-sellers and restaurants.

Bocamina San Cayetano

Carr Guanajuato-Dolores Hidalgo • Daily 10am–6pm • M$35

Behind the Templo de San Cayetano de Valenciana, the original Mina de la Valenciana entrance now operates as the **Bocamina San Cayetano**, one of 23 interconnecting pits in the region and named after the patron saint of miners. Donning a hard hat lends some credibility to a thirty-minute tour of the upper tunnels (a steep climb 60m down), which end at a shrine to the mine's patron.

Bocamina San Ramón

Callejón de San Ramón 10 • Daily 10am–7pm • M$35 • ☎ 473 732 3551, ⓦ bocaminasanramon.com

Another Valenciana mine entrance has become the **Bocamina San Ramón**, just beyond the Templo de San Cayetano de Valenciana on the main road, which has a small museum in a lavish hacienda (once owned by one of the mine foremen), and another tour into the first section of an ancillary mine shaft (48m deep and 50m long), part of which has been converted into a bar and restaurant.

Cerro de Cubilete and the statue of Cristo Rey

The easiest way to get up here is on one of the tours advertised all around Guanajuato, though you can do the same for less than half the price by nipping out to the Central de Autobuses and picking up one of ten daily Autobuses Vasallo de Cristo, which run up there in around thirty minutes (every 1–2hr; daily 6am–6pm; M$40 return) – you can also pick up buses in Valenciana. The bus goes right to the top, waits for an hour, then returns

If you approached Guanajuato from León, you'll already have seen the huge statue of **Cristo Rey** crowning the 2661m **Cerro de Cubilete**, 20km west of the city. Variously claimed to occupy the geographical centre of the republic or just the state of Guanajuato, it seems a neat coincidence that it should be on the highest hill for many kilometres. Nevertheless, the complex of chapels and pilgrims' dormitories is without question magnificently sited, with long views across the plains. At its heart is a 20m bronze statue – erected in 1950 and ranking as the world's second-largest image of Christ, just behind Rio de Janeiro's – standing on a golden globe flanked by cherubs, one holding a crown of thorns, the other the golden crown of the "King of Kings".

ARRIVAL AND DEPARTURE
GUANAJUATO

BY PLANE

The Aeropuerto Internacional de Guanajuato (☎472 748 2120; sometimes referred to as Del Bajío International Airport, or even León airport) is actually 30km west of Guanajuato at Carr Silao-León, km 5.5 (closer to León; see p.357). Taxis operate on a very expensive fixed-rate scale of fares: direct to central Guanajuato (35–40min) should cost M$450 (central León is M$400). Heading back from central Guanajuato, you might be able get a taxi for M$400. To save money from the airport you could take a taxi to Silao for M$280 (10min), and take a bus from there to Guanajuato (M$28; 45min). In the other direction taxis from Silao to the airport should charge much less, around M$140.

VivaAerobus offers a useful no-frills service from Monterrey, while Volaris flies budget from Tijuana; Aeroméxico provides a link with Mexico City for other domestic destinations, but in all cases remember to factor in the cost of the airport taxi. Flights to various locations in the US are offered by Aeroméxico, Delta, United and American Airlines.

Destinations Chicago (1 daily; 5hr); Dallas (3 daily; 2hr); Houston (4 daily; 2hr); Los Angeles (4 weekly; 3hr); Mexico City (9 daily; 1hr); Monterrey (3–4 daily; 1hr 10min); Tijuana (2 daily; 2hr 30min).

BY BUS

The Central de Autobuses lies 6km west of the city centre. Regular local buses ("Centro–Central") shuttle into town in about 15min (M$6), usually stopping outside the Mercado Hidalgo and the Jardín de la Reforma. Taxis charge around M$40 (meters are not used).

There are relatively few first-class buses from Guanajuato direct to San Miguel de Allende (ETN runs 4 daily; 1hr 30min; M$155), but there are plenty of second-class departures; if you have problems getting anywhere else, head for León, which is on the main north–south highway and has much more frequent services. For Dolores Hidalgo (M$60), you can go to the bus terminal or go straight to the stop known as "Dos Ríos", a few blocks up the hill from the Alhóndiga in the direction of San Javier (locals should know it).

Destinations Aguascalientes (4 daily; 3hr); Dolores Hidalgo (every 30min; 1hr 30min); Guadalajara (hourly; 4hr); Lagos de Moreno (2 daily; 1hr 45min); León (hourly; 1hr); Mexico City (hourly; 5hr); Querétaro (8 daily; 2hr 30min ; San Luis Potosí (10 daily; 3hr); San Miguel de Allende (16 daily; 1hr 30min–2hr).

INFORMATION AND TOURS

Tourist information There's a basic information booth on Jardín Union (Mon–Fri 10am–7.30pm, Sat 10am–5pm, Sun 10am–2pm; ☎473 109 2104, ⓦocvguanajuato.com), where you'll find maps but not much else; there are also lots of private information booths throughout town (at Plazuela de los Angeles and Plazuela San Fernando, for example), but these primarily offer tours and hotel reservations. You might

also check out ⓦgtoexperience.mx or ⓦguanajuatocapital .com, useful websites with information on the city.

Tours Transportes Turísticos de Guanajuato, Bajos de la Basilíca 2 (daily 8.30am–9pm; ☎473 732 2134, ⓦttg .com.mx), offers a range of tours and can provide English-speaking guides. City tours start at M$150 (3.5hr), excluding entrance fees.

ACCOMMODATION

NEAR THE MERCADO HIDALGO

Antiguo Vapor Galarza 5 ☎473 732 3211, ⓦhotelavapor .com. Set in a beautifully converted eighteenth-century house, this elegant hotel has a boutique feel, combining modern luxury with exposed brick, wrought iron and wood furniture; breakfast included and free wi-fi. M$1570

Hotel Socavón Alhóndiga 41-A ☎473 732 4885. A dark tunnel opens into the sunny courtyard of this small, friendly place that's well cared for. Attractive brick-ceilinged rooms all come with TV and free wi-fi. A short walk from the centre but worth it – there's a decent Mexican restaurant (*La Fonda*

del Minero) and parking on site. M$810

Mesón del Rosario Juárez 31 ☎473 732 3284. Great location in the heart of town (midway between the mercado and jardín), set in a colonial mansion built in 1784 with small but clean rooms decked out in period style, tile-clad bathrooms, free wi-fi and local TV – good-value deals online. M$860

JARDÍN DE LA UNIÓN AND AROUND

Balcón de Cielo Carr Panorámica Pípila ☎473 732 2576. Truly spectacular location next to Pípila, high above

5

the jardín (right next to the funicular station). Free wi-fi, a lovely terrace and smallish but clean and comfy rooms. You'll need to take taxis after 9.30pm. **M$1400**

Casa del Agua Plazuela de la Compañía 4 ☎473 734 1974, ⓦhotelcasadelagua.com.mx. Elegant seventeenth-century building converted into a chic hotel on contemporary lines. There are just fifteen light and airy rooms, all very nicely appointed with spa bath, free wi-fi and cable TV. **M$1255**

La Casa del Tío Cantarranas 47 ☎473 733 9728, ⓦlacasadeltio.hostel.com. Comfortable hostel with four relatively spacious dorms (M$225) and two private rooms with bath, a small kitchen (free tea and coffee) and a charming roof terrace festooned with cacti. Free wi-fi. **M$600**

★**Casa Zuniga** Callejón de Pochote 38 ☎473 732 8546, ⓦcasazunigagto.com. Welcoming modern B&B on the slopes right next to the funicular and near the Pípila, with cosy, colonial-style rooms, free wi-fi, friendly hosts Rick and Carmen Zuniga, lip-smacking steak and eggs for breakfast and fabulous views from the terrace. Cash only. **M$1100**

★**Edelmira Hotel Boutique** Allende 7 ☎473 732 1567, ⓦedelmirahotel.com. Beautiful colonial-style property with stylish indoor pool, hot tub and spectacular rooftop terrace. Rooms feature contemporary decor with a/c, parquet floors, stone walls, free wi-fi and flat-screen TVs. **M$1540**

Hostería del Frayle Sopeña 3 ☎473 732 1179. This is the best option near the jardín, located in a lovely colonial-style building right in the heart of things with bougainvillea-draped courtyards, spacious common areas and rooms that feature artfully tiled en-suite bathrooms. Room quality varies, so look at a few first. Can be noisy, of course. Free wi-fi. **M$900**

San Diego Jardín de la Unión 1 ☎473 732 1300, ⓦhotelsandiegogto.com.mx. Fine colonial warren of a place in the very centre with tiled public areas and a variety of rooms, all with local TV only (and no a/c – some are much bigger than others so take a look before you pay. There are great plaza views from its front rooms, but overall this hotel is showing its age, and the location is its best selling point. Free wi-fi. **M$940**

El Mesón de los Poetas Positos 35 ☎473 732 0705, ⓦmesondelospoetas.com. Very comfortable rooms (with cable TV and free wi-fi), all painted in blues, yellows and reds, and lined with decorative tiles. Shady interior patios provide respite from the heat and noise of the city. Prices rise substantially from Jan to mid-March. **M$1160**

El Zopilote Mojado Hostal Mexiamora 51 ☎473 732 5311, ⓦelzopilotemojado.com. Colourful guesthouse doubling as café and arts hub, offering simple, cosy rooms with balconies and shared living room with terrace. Free wi-fi. **M$1112**

OUTSIDE THE CENTRE

Quinta Las Acacias Paseo de la Presa 168 ☎473 731 1517, ⓦquintalasacacias.com. Justly popular hotel, just outside the centre near the Presa de la Olla (lake) overlooking a shady park. Rooms feature a blend of Mexican and continental styles; four-poster beds, tiled floors and rich warm colours – the suites have jacuzzis. Free wi-fi. **M$2800**

Villa María Cristina Paseo de la Presa de la Olla 76 ☎473 731 2182, ⓦvillamariacristina.net. This opulent gem is the most luxurious (and most expensive) hotel in town (southeast of the centre on the Carr Panorámica), with just thirteen enchanting suites, featuring whirlpool tubs or steam baths and Bang & Olufsen sound systems, set in a converted colonial hacienda. Free wi-fi. **M$3640**

EATING

For a cheap meal try the **Mercado Hidalgo** and its modern annexe, the **Mercado de Gavira**, where there is tempting *birria* (goat or mutton stew), tacos and tortas – *Carnitas Latlán* is a local favourite. You'll only pay around M$35 for a filling meal, or just M$25/torta.

Café Tal Temezcuitate 4 ☎473 732 6212. Enticing if tiny café (all indoors), which roasts its own beans and consequently has some of the best coffee in town (from M$20). They also have fresh fruit and yogurt breakfasts, a variety of teas and free wi-fi. Daily 8am–midnight.

El Gallo Pitagórico Constancia 10 ☎473 732 9489. One of Guanajuato's most popular restaurants, with a predominantly Italian menu, eclectic decor and a fabulous location high on the valley slopes right behind the San Diego church (it's a steep walk). Dine on prosciutto and melon followed by a tasty *putanesca* as the sounds of the Jardín de la Unión waft up through the open windows. Around M$110 for pastas and M$120–150 for *secondis*. Daily 1–11.30pm.

Las Mercedes Arriba 6, San Javier ☎473 733 9059. One of the city's most popular restaurants is the best place for a splurge (M$600–700 per head, with wine), with just six candle-lit tables in a homely dining room and a creative menu of gourmet Mexican food. It's a little over-hyped, but with prickly-pear margaritas, *mole verde* with pistachio, duck tacos and spectacular *chile rellenos* it's certainly an experience. Reservations essential. Tues–Sat 2–10pm, Sun 2–6pm.

El Tapatío Lascuráin de Retana 20 ☎473 732 3291. This student taverna, opposite the university and always bristling with students and teachers, offers bargain *menu del día* (3 courses) for about M$65, decent cocktails and some of the best *arrachera* (steak) in town (mains $60–80). Mon–Sat 9am–9.30pm, Sun 9.30am–5pm.

Tasca de la Paz Plaza de la Paz 28 ☎473 734 2225. Smart Spanish restaurant with outdoor tables, serving European delights such as paella, chicken in white wine and *jamón serrano*. Expect to pay around M$60–85 for tapas and M$95–150 for main dishes. Comida corrida (daily 2–4pm) for M$68. Daily 8am–10pm.

Truco 7 Truco 7 ☎473 732 8374. Beautiful little old-school café with a young, convivial atmosphere, comfy chairs and art covering the walls. Great, moderately priced breakfasts, *comidas*, salads, steaks and wonderful garlic soup with an egg poached in it – there's even boiled eggs (M$12) and cornflakes (M$20). Ask for your cappuccino *sin miel* to avoid getting a dollop of corn syrup in it. Beers are just M$20. Mains average M$45–65, steaks from M$90. Cash only. Daily 8.30am–11.30pm.

★**La Vie en Rose** Cantarranas 18 ☎473 732 7556. Enticing French bakery with excellent coffee and a range of tasty pastries from almond croissants to rum chocolate cake and macarons, with views of the Jardín from the balcony. Tues–Sat 10am–10pm, Sun 11am–8pm.

DRINKING AND NIGHTLIFE

BARS

Antik Café Ayuntamiento 11 (entrance on Truco) ☎473 732 7154. Cool café with red drapes, comfy sofas and a vaguely Baroque theme; becomes a hip lounge bar at night, with live music on Fridays and a decent menu of comfort food. Cash only. Daily 10am–midnight.

Bar Fly Sóstenes Rocha 30 (on the corner) ☎473 652 1488. Tiny, sociable second-floor bar with folk, jazz or acoustic music most nights from 9pm, and seldom any entry fees; usually reverts to reggae/ska dance club later on. Daily 7pm–3am.

Bora Bora Constancia 9 ☎473 756 0571. Student favourite proudly serving ten types of *micheladas* (Mexican beer, chile salsa and lime juice) and over 25 mixed drinks. Daily 1pm–midnight.

Desmond's Positos 79 ☎473 733 2182. Intimate Irish pub and restaurant run by a long-time resident Irishman. Guinness is available, of course, and there's a different music style each evening, including Trad Irish on Wed. Mon–Sat noon–midnight.

Los Lobos Manuel Doblado 2 ☎473 732 7040. Dim and often crowded bar that resounds nightly to thumping rock classics, with pool table in the back. Cheap-ish Mexican beer. Cash only. Mon–Sat 7pm–3am.

★**One Bar & Lounge** (Hotel Boutique 1850) Jardín de la Unión 7 ☎473 732 2795. Treat yourself to a night atop one of the city's poshest hotels, with a stylish lounge bar overlooking the main plaza and hills beyond. Daily 6pm–2am.

★**Santo Café** Campanero 4 ☎473 122 2320. Reached by a small bridge over a pedestrian alley, this quiet restaurant, café and bar is a favourite of students looking to wax philosophical over a drink; there's also free wi-fi. Mon–Sat 10am–11pm, Sun 12.30–8pm.

CLUBS

★**La Dama de las Camelias** Sopeña 32, opposite Museo Iconográfico ☎473 732 7587. Great bar imaginatively decorated with evening dresses, high-heeled shoes and smashed mirror fragments. *La Dama* usually gets going around midnight, offers dancing most nights and great salsa late on Fri. Entry M$30. Mon–Sat 8pm–5am.

Guanajuato Grill Alonso 4 ☎473 597 8771. Guanajuato's most popular club tends to be packed with local youth dancing to hardcore house and techno; it's especially crammed Fri and Sat. Tues & Thurs–Sat 10pm–5am.

FESTIVE GUANAJUATO

Guanajuato's two-and-a-half-week **Festival Internacional Cervantino** (early to mid-Oct; ☎473 731 1150, ⓦfestivalcervantino.gob.mx) is the city's top fiesta, a celebration of sixteenth-century Spanish author **Miguel de Cervantes** and his most famous character, the hapless romantic, Don Quixote. The festival features performances by international and Mexican musicians, dancers, theatre groups and street-performers, and each year a different region or country is picked to be the focus. The festival has its foundations in the 1950s, when students performed **entremeses** – swashbuckling one-act plays from classical Spanish theatre – outdoors in places such as Plaza San Roque. These still take place here, and you don't need good Spanish to work out what's going on, as they're highly visual and very entertaining; some performances are free, but tickets to most plays cost around M$250–340 (ⓦticketmaster.com.mx). Guanajuato actually plays host to several boisterous **festivals**, including the **Fiestas de San Juan y Presa de la Olla** (June 24), when fireworks, fairground rides and the crowning of the "Reina de las Fiestas" (Queen of the Festivals) take place on the saint's day at the Presa de la Olla, and the **Apertura de la Presa de la Olla** (first Mon in July), the traditional opening of the dam's floodgates to sluice out and clean the city's riverbed (celebrated by local dances and serenading).

5

CALLEJÓNEADAS

An excellent way to start the evening off in Guanajuato is to follow one of the organized **callejóneadas** – walking tours that wind through the side streets and back alleys following a student minstrel group known as *estudiantinas*. *Callejóneadas* are aimed primarily at Mexicans, so without fluent Spanish and some local knowledge you'll miss most of the jokes and risqué tales, but they're great fun all the same. It is possible to buy your own beer or wine and just tag along, but for the full experience you'll need a ticket. These can be bought (for around M$120) from any of the information booths along Juárez, or from the *estudiantinas* who hang around the Jardín de la Unión from around 6.30pm. They entitle you to a *porrón* (a kind of ceramic drinking vessel), which is topped up as you promenade. In high season, there's something happening most nights of the week, but at other times of the year Tuesday, Thursday, Friday and Saturday are your best bets, and the event usually kicks off around 8.30pm.

DIRECTORY

Banks and exchange Banks can be found along Juárez: Bancomer at no. 9, Banamex on Plazuela de San Fernando and a convenient branch of Banorte between Plaza de la Paz and the Jardín de la Unión.

Emergencies Police ☎473 732 0266; Cruz Roja ☎473 732 0487.

Hospital For emergency medical attention visit Centro Médico la Presa (☎473 102 3100, ⓦwww .centromedicolapresa.mx) at Paseo de la Presa 85.

Internet Numerous places around town, especially around Plazuela Baratillo where M$10/hr is the norm (try Alfa y Omega or El Emporio). For those with laptops and PDAs, there's free wi-fi at several cafés around the Jardín de la Unión.

Laundry Lavandería del Centro, Sopeña 26 (Mon–Fri 9am–8pm, Sat 9am–4pm; ☎473 732 0680; M$20/kg).

Pharmacy Farmacia Santa Fe, Plaza de la Paz 52 (daily 9am–10pm).

Post office Ayuntamiento 25, opposite the Templo de la Compañía (Mon–Fri 8am–4.30pm, Sat 8am–noon).

León and around

Travelling north from Querétaro, most express buses bypass Guanajuato and head straight for **LEÓN**, a teeming, industrial city of 1.6 million with a long history of excellence in **leatherwork**. This tradition is reflected in the scores of shoe factories and, in the centre, hundreds of shoe shops: it's a good place to buy hand-tooled cowboy boots, jackets, belts or just about anything else made of leather, but there's little else to see.

The Zona Piel

☎477 103 9390, ⓦzonapiel.com.mx

The area around the bus station, known as the **Zona Piel**, about 3km from the city centre, has the highest concentration of leather and shoe shops, most of which have very reasonable prices, although there are also some higher-class and more expensive boutiques. If you're changing buses in León, it's well worth taking an hour to wander round the station's immediate vicinity; walk south three blocks along Hilario Medina to Plaza Piel and Plaza del Zapato (ⓦplazadelzapato.com), opposite at López Mateos Ote 1601, two malls with the best concentration of stores.

The Centro Histórico

If you have more time to explore the city, stash your bag at the bus station's guardería (M$6/day) and head for the partly pedestrianized Centro Histórico. The linked **Plaza de los Fundadores** and **Plaza de los Martíres** are spacious, tranquil and elegant, with the stately **Catedral Basílica de Nuestra Madre de la Santísima de la Luz** consecrated in 1866 (Pope Benedict XVI visited in 2012), and a typically colonial Palacio Municipal. Little else survived a disastrous flood in 1883, but the plaza is surrounded by broad boulevards lined with shops, and there is a stunning church that deserves a look, the Templo Expiatorio del Sagrado Corazón de Jesús.

Templo Expiatorio del Sagrado Corazón de Jesús

Madero 721, between 13 de Septiembre and Juan Valle • Mon–Sat 7am–2pm & 4.30–7.30pm, Sun 7am–2pm • **Crypt** Mon–Sat 10am–2pm & 5–7pm, Sun 10am–2pm • M$5

The extraordinary **Templo Expiatorio**, 500m southeast of the main plazas, is a marble and granite neo-Gothic church started in 1920 and worked on ever since (it was officially completed in 2012 for Pope Benedict's visit). The Notre Dame-like facade is particularly impressive, with its high-relief bronze doors revealing a white interior illuminated by modern stained glass. You can also visit the atmospheric crypt or *criptas* (separate entrance at the rear), a series of underground chambers where families still pay "rent" for burial spaces (their use helps fund construction).

ARRIVAL AND DEPARTURE
LEÓN

By plane The Aeropuerto Internacional de Guanajuato (☎ 472 748 2120; sometimes referred to as Del Bajío International Airport, or even León Airport) is actually closer to León than Guanajuato city. Taxis operate on a very expensive fixed-rate scale of fares: direct to central León is M$400 (see p.353 for more airport information).
By bus To get into town from the Central de Autobuses (Medina 303), walk left out of the station along Medina,

pick up a local bus marked "Centro" (M$9) headed to the right along López Mateos and get off at the "Centro Histórico" stop (heading back, take a bus marked "Central" along López Mateos). Taxis should be M$50.
Destinations Aguascalientes (hourly; 1hr); Guadalajara (hourly; 4hr); Guanajuato (constantly; 45min); Mexico City (hourly; 5hr); Querétaro (hourly; 2hr); Zacatecas (hourly; 4hr).

ACCOMMODATION

Hotel Terranova Zona Piel Salina Cruz 112 ☎ 477 763 2050, ⌨ hotelterranova.com. Best mid-range option, with simple but comfy rooms and tiled floors, free wi-fi, decent range of English-language cable TV channels and ceiling fans (a/c in executive rooms only). M$660
Hotsson Hotel López Mateos Ote 1102 ☎ 477 719 8000, ⌨ hotsson.com. Best of the López Mateos hotels, and the closest to the old centre, with a contemporary

Mexican theme, flat-screen TVs, outdoor pool and jacuzzi. M$1615
Howard Johnson Hotel Condesa Portal Bravo 14 ☎ 477 788 3929, ⌨ hjleon.com. This hotel is all about the prime location overlooking the plaza in the heart of the old town; it also offers reasonably priced four-star comforts, great views and cable TV. M$955

EATING

Don't leave León without trying its famous *guacamayas*, "invented" here in the 1950s, essentially a roll stuffed with *chicharrón* (pork rinds) and seasoned with spicy *"pico de gallo"* salsa and a dash of lime.

Guacamayas Don Diego Ignacio Altamirano 307. The most famous *guacamayas* seller in León: Don Diego's tortas are crunchy, spicy and filling (from M$15), served with fresh limes and ice-cold beer. Mon–Sat 10am–11pm.
Guacamayas de José el Soñador Américas 602, at Roma. One of the best and most traditional street sellers of *chicharrón* and *guacamayas* (from M$15), with a special spicy sauce that will knock your head off. Daily

10am–3pm.
Panteón Taurino Calz de los Héroes 404 ☎ 477 713 4969, ⌨ panteontaurino.com.mx. Slightly kitsch but incredibly fun homage to bullfighters, housed in a "museum" of *toro* paraphernalia. The *parrilladas* (grills) are great value, but everything else – Mexican dishes to pasta – is good too (mains M$100–200). Mon–Sat 1pm– midnight, Sun 1–7.30pm.

Lagos de Moreno

Just 25km northwest of León, in Jalisco state, **LAGOS DE MORENO** lies at the intersection of the old road from Mexico City to Ciudad Juárez and Hwy-80 (which runs from Guadalajara to San Luis Potosí and the northeast). Though the town has always been a major staging post, few tourists stop here now, and despite the heavy traffic rumbling around its fringes, it's a quiet and rather graceful little town, with

5

colonial streets climbing steeply from a small river to a hilltop monastery. Good bus connections make the town an absorbing day trip from Aguascalientes or even Guanajuato. Cross the bridge by the bus station and head to your left along the stream, away from the choking fumes of the main road, and it's hard to believe you're in the same place. Whether you plan to stay a couple of hours or a few days, you'll want to head for the central **Jardín de los Constituyentes.** In the streets around it is a smattering of colonial mansions and official buildings, including a forbidding-looking jail that's still in use.

Parroquia de la Asunción

Jardín de los Constituyentes • Tues–Sat 10am–1.30pm & 4.30–7.30pm, Sun 10am–1.30pm

The impressive pink stone towers of the **Parroquia de la Asunción**, completed in 1784, dominate the central square. The church is one of the finest examples of Mexican Baroque architecture, with a huge Neoclassical *retablo* and rare wooden pipe organ inside.

Teatro José Rosas Moreno

Rosas Moreno 320 • Daily 9am–6pm • Free • ☎ 474 742 3667

The **Teatro José Rosas Moreno**, on the north side of the Jardín de los Constituyentes behind the church, opened in 1907 to stage opera performances. It's worth a look for the beautiful mural on the dome depicting the Revolution and Independence, with local hero **José Rosas Moreno**, a famous writer of tales and fables, as the centrepiece.

Templo del Señor del Calvario

Constituyentes, at Escobedo • Mon & Wed–Fri noon–2pm & 4–7pm, Tues 4–7pm, Sat 10am–2pm & 5–7pm, Sun 10am–noon

Once you've seen the centre of Lagos, you might want to embark on the long climb up to the nineteenth-century **Templo del Señor del Calvario**, a hillside church ten blocks to the north designed as a mini version of St Peter's in Rome. Other than a fine sculpture, the *Señor del Calvario*, there's not much in the church itself, but it's worth the trek for the **view**, especially at sunset.

ARRIVAL AND DEPARTURE

LAGOS DE MORENO

By bus The Central de Autobuses is east of the centre at Padre Torres 380. Taxis charge M$40–50 into town.
Destinations Aguascalientes (every 30min; 1hr 30min–2hr); Guadalajara (hourly; 2–3hr); Guanajuato (roughly hourly; 1hr 30min); León (2 first-class daily, frequent second-class; 1hr); Mexico City (4 first-class daily; 5–6hr); Zacatecas (hourly; 4hr).

OUR LADY OF SAN JUAN DE LOS LAGOS

Some 45km southwest of Lagos de Moreno, on the road to Guadalajara, the old highway runs through **SAN JUAN DE LOS LAGOS**. From its outskirts, San Juan seems like any other dusty little town; in the centre, though, you'll find an enormous bus station surrounded by scores of hotels. This is thanks to **Nuestra Señora de San Juan de los Lagos**, a miraculous 38cm-tall **image of the Virgin Mary** contained in the town's vast eighteenth-century basilica, the second most important pilgrimage site in Mexico. Crafted in the early sixteenth century by the P'urhépecha of Michoacán, the statue is said to have performed its first miracle in 1623 (bringing a dead girl to life) and it's been venerated ever since. The town's busiest dates are February 2 (**Día de la Candelaria**) and December 8 (**Fiesta de la Inmaculada Concepción**), when the place is crammed with penitents, pilgrims, those seeking miraculous cures and others who are just there to enjoy the atmosphere. The celebrations build up for a couple of weeks beforehand, and spill over to several lesser events throughout the year, notably the first fortnight of August and the entire Christmas period. San Juan de los Lagos is around 122km and two hours by first-class bus (12 daily; M$213) from Guadalajara, and just one hour from Aguascalientes (10 daily; M$82).

OPPOSITE REAL DE CATORCE (P.384)>

5

Aguascalientes

The city of **AGUASCALIENTES**, 177km north of Guanajuato, is an important and booming provincial capital with some fine colonial monuments in among its newer buildings. Founded in 1575 by Spanish captain Juan de Montoro Rodríguez, Aguascalientes has mushroomed into a metropolitan area of almost one million today, with the newest development – malls, cinemas, luxury hotels – north of the centre along Hwy-45. Business travellers tend to stay up here, but if you've come to see the sights, make for the *centro histórico* instead, arranged around the **Plaza de la Patria**, with its grand cathedral, and the **Palacio de Gobierno**, with its impressive murals. A couple of engrossing **museums**, including tributes to artists José Posada and Saturnino Herrán, make the city an intriguing place to stop over for a day or two, especially when you take into account its tempting array of street **food**, particularly the sumptuous **bírria** (roast goat or mutton stew), and the city's reputation for some of the finest **fiestas** in Mexico – the **Feria de San Marcos** is the biggest, but rarely a week goes by without a celebration, or at least a band playing in one of the plazas at the weekend.

The Plaza de la Patria and around

Teatro Morelos • ☎ 449 915 1941, ⓦ vivaaguascalientes.com

The **Plaza de la Patria** is the traditional heart of Aguascalientes, an enormous area centred around the **Exedra**, an amphitheatre-shaped space for performances, overlooked by a column topped with a Mexican eagle (which symbolizes the geographical centre of Mexico). On the south side of the cathedral is the **Teatro Morelos**, built in 1882 and notable as the location for the famous convention between Zapata, Villa and Carranza in 1914, commemorated with a large plaque on the cathedral wall opposite. Call or check the city website for the current theatre programme (see p.364).

Palacio de Gobierno

Plaza de la Patria • Daily 8am–8pm • Free

An entrancing Baroque mansion, the **Palacio de Gobierno** was constructed in 1665 as a private residence (it became city hall in 1856). Built from reddish volcanic rock, it contains an arcaded courtyard with a grand central staircase, decorated with four marvellous **murals** featuring historically important *hidrocálidos* (citizens of Aguascalientes) by the Chilean artist Oswaldo Barra Cunningham, who learned his trade from Diego Rivera. The first of the murals, at the back on the ground floor, was painted in 1961, with others created in subsequent years: the most recent (from 1992) are at the front of the building.

Catedral Basílica de Nuestra Señora de la Asunción

Plaza de la Patria • Daily 7am–2pm & 4–9pm

On the other side of the plaza from the Palacio de Gobierno, the eighteenth-century **Catedral Basílica de Nuestra Señora de la Asunción** has been refurbished to reveal its full Baroque glory, in an ostentatious welter of gold, polished marble and several paintings by José de Alcíbar and Miguel Cabrera. The dome over the altar is particularly magnificent (the Virgen de la Asunción is patron of the city), but don't miss **La Capilla**

SAN MARCOS – "FESTIVAL DE MEXICO"

The nearly two-centuries-old **Feria de San Marcos** (ⓦ feriadesanmarcos.gob.mx) of Aguascalientes is famous throughout Mexico. Celebrated in the Jardín San Marcos from mid-April to mid-May, events include everything from bullfights and live music to film festivals and rides for kids (many of the events are free).

del Sagrario, to the left of it, with a captivating all-turquoise interior. Look out also for the small plaque honouring Juan de Montoro Rodríguez, city founder, whose remains are said to be buried somewhere under the floor.

Casa de la Cultura

Carranza 101 • Daily 7am–9pm • Free • ☎ 449 915 52 74

Avenida Venustiano Carranza leads west from behind the cathedral to the **Casa de la Cultura**, a delightful seventeenth-century mansion given over to music and dance classes and the occasional exhibition in the **Galería de la Ciudad** at the entrance. The notice board here is an excellent place to find out what's on around town, and in the patio there's a small café – a tranquil spot to have a drink.

Museo Regional de Historia

Carranza 118 • Tues–Sun 9am–6pm • M\$47 • ☎ 449 916 5228

A little further down Carranza from the Casa de la Cultura, the **Museo Regional de Historia** chronicles local history (Spanish captions only) in an elegant mansion built in 1901; exhibits range from a fossilized mammoth tusk and prehistoric arrowheads to Spanish colonial artefacts. Highlights include some remarkable pieces of pre-Columbian pottery and jewellery; the white shell necklace is especially striking.

■ ACCOMMODATION		● EATING		■ DRINKING & NIGHTLIFE	
Art Hotel	5	Cenaduría Farolito	4	Casa Corazón	1
Francia Aguascalientes	3	Las Costillas de Sancho	1	Merendero Kiko's	3
El Giro Hostal	2	Lechón Pascualito	7	Pub Ummagumma	2
Hotel Gya Boutique		Mercado Juárez	3	Pulquería Posada	4
Quality Inn	4	Mercado Morelos	2		
Quinta Real		Mitla Restaurante	5		
Aguascalientes	6	La Saturnina	6		

AGUASCALIENTES

6 , Central de Autobuses (2km) & ▼ Jesús Terán Peredo International Airport (Aguascalientes International Airport) (22km)

5

Jardín de San Marcos

Jardín de San Marcos Daily 6am–10.30pm • **Templo de San Marcos** Daily 7am–2pm & 4–9pm

Escape from the sun by heading west on Carranza to the shady **Jardín de San Marcos**, a lush, beautifully manicured park smothered with pink and violet bougainvillea. The park runs down to the **Templo de San Marcos**, completed in 1765 with another exuberant churrigueresque facade and dedicated to the Virgin del Carmen.

Santuario Nuestra Señora de Guadalupe

Guadalupe 213 • Daily 7am–1pm & 5–7pm

Justly regarded as one of the most beautiful churches in Mexico, the **Santuario Nuestra Señora de Guadalupe** sports an incredibly ornate Baroque facade by master architect Felipe de Ureña, credited with bringing the Spanish churrigueresque style to Mexico. The church was completed in 1789, the interior a staggering confection of intricate carvings culminating in the pink sandstone *retablo* and magnificent dome. The church is a short walk north from the Jardín de San Marcos via Nicolás Bravo.

Museo José Guadalupe Posada and around

Jardín del Encino • Tues–Sun 11am–6pm • M$10 • ☎ 449 915 4556 • To get to the Jardín del Encino, head east from the main plaza and take the first right, Díaz de León, south for about seven blocks

Though it only occupies a small building about 1km south of the centre, the **Museo José Guadalupe Posada** is one of the main reasons to visit Aguascalientes. Indeed, the town is almost a place of pilgrimage for devotees of this influential printmaker, who is best known for his political satire and criticism of the Catholic Church (see box below). The permanent exhibit here contains a well-curated collection of Posada lithographs, along with the original plates and background information in Spanish.

POSADA – THE ART OF THE MACABRE

The frequently macabre work of **José Guadalupe Posada** will be familiar even if his name is not: Diego Rivera was not so wrong when he described the prolific Posada as "so outstanding that one day even his name will be forgotten". He was born a baker's son in Aguascalientes in 1852, and was later apprenticed to a lithographer. In 1888 he moved to Mexico City, and started to create in earnest the thousands of prints for which he soon became known. He mainly worked for the editor and printer Vanegas Arroyo, and his images appeared on posters and in satirical broadsheets that flourished despite – or more likely because of – the censorship of the **Porfiriano era**. Some of Posada's work was political, attacking corrupt politicians, complacent clergy or foreign intervention, but much was simply recording the news (especially disasters, which so obsess the Mexican press to this day), lampooning popular figures or observing everyday life with a gleefully macabre eye. Later, the events and figures of the Revolution, grotesquely caricatured, came to dominate his work.

Technically, Posada moved on from lithography to **engraving** in type metal (producing the characteristic hatched effect seen in much of his work) and finally to zinc etching, an extremely rapid method involving drawing directly onto a zinc printing plate with acid-resistant ink, and then dipping it in acid until the untouched areas corrode. Although the *calaveras*, the often elegantly clad skeletons that inhabit much of his work, are his best-known creations, the Aguascalientes museum devoted to him covers the full range of his designs. They all bear a peculiar mix of Catholicism, pre-Columbian tradition, preoccupation with death and black humour that can only be Mexican – and that profoundly affected all later Mexican art. Rivera and Orozco are just two of the greats who publicly acknowledged their debt to Posada, who died in 1913.

MEXICO'S MOST MEXICAN ARTIST

A contemporary and friend of Diego Rivera, artist **Saturnino Herrán** (1887–1918) died young and never really achieved much recognition, though he has been dubbed "El más pintor de los mexicanos y más mexicano de los pintores" ("the greatest painter of the Mexicans, and the most Mexican of the painters"). Born and trained in Aguascalientes, it wasn't till his family moved to Mexico City in 1905 that he met Rivera. His breakthrough came in 1910 during the Centennial Anniversary of Mexico's Independence Day – Herrán organized an exhibition of work that incorporated indigenous Mexican as opposed to European artistic traditions, a radical idea at the time. Herrán is best known today for his naturalistic and dignified paintings of Mexican indios, but he also designed stained-glass windows, book illustrations, and, near the end of his life, murals. Visit the Museo de Aguascalientes (see p.364) to sample his work.

Templo del Señor del Encino

Jardín del Encino • Daily 7am–1pm & 5–7pm

The Museo José Guadalupe Posada occupies the former priest's house of the adjacent **Templo del Señor del Encino**, another elegant eighteenth-century church of pinkish sandstone by Francisco Bruno de Ureña, the son of Felipe de Ureña. Beyond the churrigueresque facade lies a riotously gilded interior with vast paintings depicting the Stations of the Cross, completed by Andrés Lopez and his brothers in 1796. Also here is the miraculous and much-venerated "black Christ" of Encino – also depicted in stained glass above the main door – with strangely thick, long black hair.

Museo de Arte Contemporáneo No. 8

Primo Verdad, at Morelos • Tues–Sun 11am–6pm • M$10, free Sun • ☎ 449 918 6901

A few blocks northeast of the Plaza de la Patria at the corner of Morelos and Primo Verdad, the **Museo de Arte Contemporáneo No. 8** is home to some of the most exciting and provocative art from the region, with exhibitions that change every two months. There's also a permanent collection of work by **Enrique Guzmán**, the talented but troubled painter born here in 1952, who took his own life at the age of 34.

Museo Nacional de la Muerte

Jardín del Estudiante, Rivero y Gutierrez • Tues–Sun 10am–6pm • M$20, free Sun • ☎ 449 910 7400, ⓦ museonacionaldelamuerte.uaa.mx

One block north along Morelos from the Museo de Arte Contemporáneo, in a graceful old university building next to **Templo de San Diego**, the **Museo Nacional de la Muerte** casts a morbid eye over Mexico's obsession with death rituals and images of death over the centuries, though it's not as grim as it sounds. The exhibits start with Mesoamerican traditions, with plenty of ancient statuary and a massive collection of model skulls, though these are so colourfully painted, bejewelled and stylized they seem more like kids' toys than religious totems. Labels are in Spanish only, but this is really a visual experience. The museum ends with a stylish art gallery, all red-tinted, which houses an eclectic collection of death-related art from the nineteenth century on, including work by Posada and his predecessor, **Manuel Manilla**. Afterwards, raise your spirits in the tranquil courtyard café, in the shadow of San Diego's main dome.

Templo de San Antonio

Pedro Parga at Zaragoza • Daily 7am–1pm & 5–7pm

The fabulously ornate **Templo de San Antonio** was completed around 1908 by the architect Refugio Reyes; it's an Art Nouveau gem with elements of just about every architectural style, including Russian and Arabic. Inside, murals of the miracles of San Antonio by Candelario Rivas provide a blaze of colour.

5

Museo de Aguascalientes

Zaragoza 505 • Tues–Sun 11am–6pm • M$10, Free Sun • ☎ 449 915 9043

Opposite the Templo de San Antonio is the imposing **Museo de Aguascalientes**, a bold Neoclassical palace constructed in 1903 by Refugio Reyes. This is essentially an art museum, with rooms dedicated to the block prints and paintings of **Gabriel Fernández Ledesma** (1900–83), and sculptor **Jesús F. Contreras** (1866–1902), whose sensual *Malgre Tout* (a copy of the original) and bronze friezes of Mesoamerican heroes adorn the courtyard. The main focus, however, is the naturalistic work of **Saturnino Herrán** (see box, p.363). Highlights include the baleful stare of *El Gallero*, the iconic beauty of *La Criolla del Manton*, the haunting *Vendedora de Ollas* and the vast *Labor*, with its contrasting images of motherhood and industrial workers. Herrán's large stained-glass panel, *El Hijo Prodigo*, stands in the courtyard.

Baños Termales de Ojocaliente

Tecnológico 102 • Daily 8am–8pm • M$140/hr for 1–2 people; M$170/hr for 2 adults, 2 children; massage M$250/hr • ☎ 449 979 0721 • ⓦ facebook.com/banostermalesdeojocaliente • To get there, take "Ruta 12" along López Mateos (M$6)

You'll need to travel some 4km east of the centre to experience the **hot springs** that gave Aguascalientes its name. The **Baños Termales de Ojocaliente** is really just an outdoor swimming pool complex, fed by the springs, on the road to San Luis Potosí – the private baths on site are much hotter and more atmospheric.

ARRIVAL AND INFORMATION
AGUASCALIENTES

By plane Jesús Terán Peredo International Airport (aka Aguascalientes International Airport; ☎ 449 918 2806) is 16km south of the city at Carretera Panamericana, km 22. You'll find all the major car rental firms and HSBC ATMs at the terminal. Taxis charge around M$200–225 into the centre. Interjet and Aeroméxico have connections to Mexico City, while Volaris flies to Tijuana and LA.
Destinations Dallas (2 daily; 1hr 45min); Houston (1 daily; 1hr 45min); Los Angeles (1 daily; 2hr 45min); Mexico City (7 daily; 1hr 15min); Tijuana (1 daily; 2hr 30min).
By bus The Central de Autobuses is around 2km south of the centre on the city's ring road (Av de la Convención), from where there's a frequent bus service into the Plaza de la Patria ("Centro"), at the heart of town. To get back to the bus

station from the centre, catch a bus marked "Central" from along Galeana at Insurgentes, just opposite the Plaza Patria shopping mall (all city buses charge M$6). Taxis use meters in Aguascalientes (which start at M$10.50, then M$3/km); from the bus station to Plaza Patria should only be around M$25–30, though some drivers may optimistically try and set a higher price if they can – insist on the meter.
Destinations Guadalajara (roughly hourly; 3hr); Guanajuato (2–3 daily; 3hr); León (every 30min; 2–3hr); Mexico City (hourly; 6hr); Querétaro (hourly; 6hr); San Luis Potosí (hourly; 3–4hr); Zacatecas (hourly; 2hr).
Tourist office On the ground floor of the Palacio de Gobierno (Mon–Fri 9am–8pm, Sat & Sun 10am–6pm; ☎ 449 910 0051, ⓦ vivaaguascalientes.com).

ACCOMMODATION

As with the other Bajío cities, plenty of **motel** and **hotel** chains – *One Hotels*, *Fiesta* and *Marriott* among them – have arrived on the outskirts of Aguascalientes: they're a long way from anything of interest, but they can be good value. During the *ferias* (mid-April to mid-May and the week around Nov 1), rooms are almost impossible to obtain at short notice and cost at least fifty percent more.

Art Hotel Nieto 502 ☎ 449 917 9595, ⓦ arthotel.com .mx. Bright, air-conditioned rooms with chic, contemporary decor, flat-screen TVs and free wi-fi. The roof-top *Acapella Deck* bar and lounge is a great place to relax. M$882
Francia Aguascalientes Madero 113 ☎ 449 918 7300, ⓦ hotelfranciaaguascalientes.com. This grand old dame was built in 1915 by the ubiquitous Refugio Reyes, but all its spacious, comfortable rooms have been modernized with plenty of amenities, including free wi-fi and cable TV. M$930

★ **El Giro Hostal** Allende 341 ☎ 449 917 9393, ⓦ elgirohostal.com.mx. Located next to the Plaza de Toros San Marcos, the city's only hostel is a wise choice, with friendly owners and four clean mixed dorms for 5–7 persons. You also get free wi-fi, hot water showers, tea and coffee and use of a kitchen and TV room. Dorm M$250
Hotel Gya Boutique 5 de Mayo 568 ☎ 449 915 5973, ⓦ hotelgyaboutique.com. Close to Plaza de los Mariachis, this modern business hotel features spacious rooms with polished stone floors, cable TV and free wi-fi. M$700

Quality Inn Nieto 102, on Plaza de la Patria ☎ 449 994 6670, ⓦ choicehotelsmexico.com. The former *Hotel Río Grande* has become a standard business chain hotel, offering bags of comfort in a superb location. Some rooms have views over the plaza, and all have cable TV with lots of US channels. Free wi-fi and breakfast; this is the best mid-range choice in town. **M$750**

Quinta Real Aguascalientes Aguascalientes Sur 601 ☎ 449 978 5818, ⓦ quintareal.com. Still the most luxurious hotel in the city, set in dazzling modern premises designed to look like a colonial monastery, with spacious suites and all the extras: pool, lush gardens and terrace bar. It's on the southern edge of the city – it's around 15–20min to the centre by taxi ($30). **M$1678**

EATING

Bírria (barbecued goat or mutton, shredded and served with a bowl of piquant broth, then eaten with a tortilla) and *lechón al horno* (roast pig) are specialities in Aguascalientes, along with *atole* (sweet corn- and chocolate-based drink), and desserts with guava (*guayaba*) – get a taster of the latter at *La Casa de las Guayabas* at Nieto 117, just behind the main plaza, and fine chocolate at *Xocolatl Mexica* (ⓦ xocolatlmexica.com) down the street at Nieto 115. The city has three lively markets near the centre, all excellent places to eat (see below), though **Mercado Terán** is better known for fresh fruit, piles of chiles, meat and produce – you can also check out the fresh juice stalls here.

Cenaduría Farolito Moctezuma 105, at Victoria ☎ 449 915 2404. With a great location right on the plaza, an old-world feel (it was founded in 1922), wooden tables and decent Mexican food (M$65 sets), this is a convenient option for lunch. Daily 8am–11pm.

Las Costillas de Sancho Universidad, at Sierra de Pinos ☎ 449 912 9212, ⓦ lascostillasdesancho.com.mx. For a real treat, grab a taxi and head north of the city centre to this exquisite restaurant, with a huge selection of fresh seafood, roasted meats, steaks and classic Mexican dishes (mains from M$65). The ribs (*las costillas*) are a speciality. Mon–Sat 1.30pm–2am, Sun 1.30–7pm.

Lechón Pascualito Jesús Díaz de León 101 (and a smaller branch on the other side of the street). This no-frills local shop has been knocking out *lechón* since 1956 – owners carefully roast, dice, then serve the meat in mouthwatering tacos (M$8) or tortas (M$20). Mon–Sat 9am–10pm.

★**Mercado Juárez** aka Mercado de la Bírria, Victoria and Unión. If you love street food you're in for a treat here, as this market is effectively a whole alley of cheap *bírrierias* (*bírria* stalls), with aromatic goat meat roasted right in front of you. Pick the place with the most patrons. Big

plates from M$50, small M$35. Daily 8am–8pm.

Mercado Morelos Morelos and Obregón. Giant food court loaded with tempting snack stalls; the star here is *Taquería Ruben's*, where glorious *carne asada* and *bistek* are stuffed into tortillas as you sit at the counter and spoon on the salsa (tacos M$10, burritos/enchiladas M$15–20). Daily 8am–6pm.

Mitla Restaurante Madero 222 ☎ 449 916 6157. Popular, old-fashioned Mexican restaurant that has been operating since 1938, with white-jacketed waiters serving a good selection of national and local dishes, including seafood and very reasonable comidas corridas. There's also an impressive M$85 breakfast buffet. Daily 7am–10pm.

★**La Saturnina** Carranza 110 ☎ 449 994 0449. Lovely and colourful courtyard café with a fountain, great for breakfast, buffet lunch (M$175) or just coffee and cake; try the *café de olla* (cinnamon-infused coffee), a city speciality served black in a ceramic mug, the justly lauded *chilaquiles* and local-style tacos (mains around M$90). The name is a tribute to painter Saturnino Herrán (see box, p.353) – copies of his *La criolla del mantón* adorn the walls. Mon–Sat 8am–11pm, Sun 8am–6pm.

DRINKING

Casa Corazón Carranza 124 ☎ 449 918 2404. Bar and café in an old house dating from 1870 that opens for breakfast, home-made desserts and coffee all day, but gets really busy in the evenings when it serves wine and beer. Daily 9am–2am.

Merendero Kiko's Andador Pani 132 ☎ 449 915 8129. Established in 1957 by Don Kiko himself and here since

1975, this is a multi-level sports bar with giant TV screens. Daily 1pm–2am.

Pub Ummagumma Carranza 102 ☎ 449 112 8472. Great little bar that specializes in the unlikely combo of sushi and hamburgers; live music most Wed, Fri & Sat (entry M$15–30). Cash only. Daily 6pm–2am.

BRANDY AND BURNING WATER

Hidrocálidos (citizens of Aguascalientes) love their booze. The state has been a **wine producer** since 1950, though the local brands are not always easy to find, except in the more expensive restaurants. The local **brandy** is commonly served, however: **San Marcos** is the best known, made here and sold all over the republic. You'll also come across **aguardientes** (literally "fiery waters") and **uvate**, a grape-based tipple mixed with lime juice and vodka.

5

Pulquería Posada Nieto 443. Friendly local bar, specializing in *pulque*, a milky, alcoholic tipple made from the fermented sap of the maguey plant. Daily 6pm–2am.

DIRECTORY

Banks and exchange Banamex and Bancomer are on the north side of Plaza de la Patria, both with 24hr ATMs.
Internet Try 3W inside El Parían mall (Morelos), on the upper level (Mon–Sat 9am–9pm, Sun 11am–6pm; M$12/hr).
Laundry SLYT Super Lavandería, Carranza 224 (Mon–Fri 10am–8pm, Sat & Sun 10am–4pm; M$20/kg).
Pharmacy Plenty in the centre – try Farmacia Sánchez (24hr), Madero 213, 1 block from Plaza de la Patria.
Post office The main post office (Mon–Fri 8am–6pm, Sat 9am–1pm) is at Hospitalidad 108, a block north of the plaza and reached by following Morelos and then turning right.

Zacatecas

Almost 2500m above sea level and crammed into a narrow gully between two hills, the old silver town of **ZACATECAS** is overflowing with ornate colonial architecture and intriguing museums, ranking alongside Guanajuato as the Bajío's finest destinations – the obvious wealth projected by its fine stone buildings makes this another city that seems plucked straight out of classical Spain. Zacatecas is known for its high-quality art museums and subterranean tours of the old silver mine, **Mina El Edén**, but the main highlight is the ornate **cathedral**, from which all other main sights are within walking distance. Just a few paces from the market and from the important junction of Juárez and Hidalgo, the **Jardín Independencia** is in effect the city's main plaza, where people gather in the evenings, get their shoes shined and wait for buses. West of the Jardín Independencia is the **Alameda**, a thin strip of stone benches, splashing fountains and a bandstand that makes a cool retreat from the heat of the day.

Brief history

It didn't take the conquistadors long to discover the enormous lodes of silver in the hills of Mexico's central highlands, and, after some initial skirmishes with the indigenous Zacateco, the city of Zacatecas was founded in 1546. For the next three centuries its mines disgorged fabulous wealth, enriching both the city and the Spanish Crown; in 1728 the mines here were producing one-fifth of all Mexico's silver. The end of the boom, when it came, was brought about more by the political uncertainties of the nineteenth century than by the exhaustion of the mines, some of which still operate today. Throughout nearly a century of war, Zacatecas itself became an important prize: there were major battles here in 1871, when Benito Juárez successfully put down local rebels, and in 1914 when Pancho Villa's División del Norte captured the city, completely annihilating its 12,000-strong garrison – known as the Toma de Zacatecas (Taking of Zacatecas), it was the bloodiest battle of the Revolution, with the military forces counting approximately 7,000 dead and many more civilian casualties. The loss of Zacatecas broke the back of the Huerta regime. Today Zacatecas is booming once more, its business and light industry boosted by the increasing flow of traffic between Mexico and the US.

Catedral Basílica de Zacatecas

Hidalgo 617 • Daily 7am–1pm & 4.30–9pm

Zacatecas's flamboyant **Catedral Basílica de Zacatecas** is the outstanding relic of the city's years of colonial glory: built in the pink sandstone typical of the region, it represents one of the latest, and arguably the finest, examples of Mexican Baroque architecture. It was completed in 1752, its facade carved with a wild exuberance unequalled anywhere in the country. The interior, they say, was once at least its equal

– furnished in gold and silver, with rich wall hangings and a great collection of paintings – but as everywhere, it was despoiled or the riches removed for "safekeeping", first at the time of Juárez' reforms and later during the Revolution; only the structure itself, with its bulky Doric columns and airy vaulting, remains to be admired. Look out for the chapel on the left as you enter, dedicated to local priest and martyr **San Mateo Correa Magallanes** (1866–1927), murdered during the anti-Roman Catholic persecutions of the 1920s and canonized in 2001 – his bones lie in a special glass casket.

ZACATECAS

0   100
metres

Cerro del Grillo (2690m)

Airport (27km)

Cerro de la Bufa (2650m)

Teleférico

Museo Rafael Coronel

Museo de Arte Abstracto Manuel Felguérez

Juan de Tolosa

Templo de Nuestra Señora del Patrocinio

Museo de la Toma de Zacatecas

Tirolesa 840

Observatorio Meterologico

Mina El Edén (top entrance)

La Casa Zacatecana del Mezcal

Templo de Santo Domingo

Palacio de Gobierno

Museo Pedro Coronel

Catedral Basílica

Teatro Calderón

Mercado Gonzáles Ortega

Mina El Edén (main entrance)

Museo Zacatecano

Librerías Don Quijote

Bancomer

Fuente de los Fardes

Hospital Dr. Emilio Varela Lujan

Palacio Legislativo

Ex-Templo de San Agustín

Sanborn's

Alameda

Mercado el Laberinto

Jardín Juárez

Jardín de la Madre

Templo del Sagrado Corazón

Casa de la Cultura

Farmacia Guadalajara

Jardín Independencia

Museo Francisco Goitia

Buses to Guadalupe & Centro Platero de Zacatecas

Parque Enrique Estrada

Templo de Fátima

Aqueducto del Cubo

Bus Station (3km)

Centro Platero de Zacatecas (5km) & Guadalupe (10m)

5

Palacio de Gobierno

Hidalgo 604, Plaza de Armas • Mon–Fri 8am–8pm • Free • ☎ 492 922 1211

On the east side of Plaza de Armas, next to the cathedral, the **Palacio de Gobierno** was built as the residence of the Conde Santiago de la Laguna in 1727 and subsequently bought by the state government. In keeping with local fashion, a modernist mural – completed in 1970 by Antonio Pintor Rodríguez and depicting the city's history – embellishes the staircase of the interior courtyard.

Mercado González Ortega

Hidalgo & Tacuba • Mon–Fri 9am–8pm • Free

On the south side of the cathedral, the **Mercado González Ortega** is a strikingly attractive market building, opened in 1889. It takes advantage of its sloping position to have two fronts: the upper level opening onto Hidalgo, the lower floor with entrances on Tacuba. Converted into a fancy little shopping mall, it's now filled with tourist shops and smart boutiques, as well as a superb wine store – the whole place was given a makeover in 2012. At the southern end of the mercado, broad steps help turn the little **Plaza Goytia** into a popular place for street theatre.

Templo de Santo Domingo

Plazuela de Santo Domingo • Daily 7am–1pm & 5–8.30pm

Climbing up from the west side of Plaza de Armas towards the Cerro del Grillo are streets lined with more mansions – some restored, some badly in need of work, but all deserted by the mining moguls who built them. The **Templo de Santo Domingo** stands raised on a platform above the plaza of the same name, just uphill from the Plaza de Armas – its hefty, buttressed walls a stern contrast to the lightness of the cathedral, though it was built at much the same time. The interior still gives a glimpse of the great wealth that funded its construction, with painted ceilings and ornate, gilded churrigueresque *retablos* in the side chapels.

Museo Pedro Coronel

Plazuela de Santo Domingo • Tues–Sun 10am–5pm • M$30 • ☎ 492 922 8021, ⊕ pedrocoronelbienal.com

Pedro Coronel (1923–85), older brother of Rafael Coronel (see p.370), was an artist in his own right, who managed to gather an art collection that reads like a *Who's Who* of modern but especially abstract and Catalan art. Today his collection forms the basis for the entertaining **Museo Pedro Coronel**, which occupies what was originally a seventeenth-century Jesuit monastery next to Santo Domingo church. Most of the work on display is relatively minor, but there are some real gems to look out for. You enter the complex through the nineteenth-century **library**, lined with faded tomes, and pass through a courtyard of orange trees before reaching the gallery proper on the second floor.

There are a few drawings by **Picasso** and a much larger ensemble from **Miró**, including his childlike but oddly compelling *Infancia de Ubu* series. Look out also for some typically abstract lithographs by Calder and Motherwell, and a tiny drawing by Henry Moore. Kandinsky, Braque, Chagall, Dalí, Leger and Max Ernst are all represented, and don't overlook the dark scribbles of **Jean Cocteau**, created in the 1940s.

There's also a separate room of architectural drawings by Piranesi, and engravings by Hogarth (including his famous image *Gin Lane*). Some of the peripheral galleries are also interesting, in particular the large West African and Oriental collections, the latter featuring some intriguing Japanese painted screens dating from the nineteenth century.

Museo Zacatecano

Dr Hierro 307 • Wed–Mon 10am–5pm • M$30 • ☎ 492 922 6580

Heading south along Ignacio Hierro, you'll reach the old Casa de la Moneda, Zacatecas' mint in the days when every silver-producing town in Mexico struck its own coins. This has been restored and turned into the exhaustive **Museo Zacatecano**, its vaulted halls and courtyard an evocative showcase for the region's history. More murals by Antonio Pintor Rodríguez adorn the central staircase.

Visits begin with a video presentation giving the historic overview, but as with the rest of the museum you'll need to speak Spanish to make the most of this – there are no English labels. From here a series of beautifully presented galleries, containing artefacts, video screens, rare documents, dioramas of the silver mines and examples of silverwork, takes you through the history of Zacatecas from prehistoric times. Other rooms deal with the history of the building, completed in 1799 and operating as a mint until 1842 when it was sold to an English company – examples of coins made here are displayed.

Upstairs, art takes centre stage, with galleries devoted to muralist Rodríguez, composer Manuel Ponce (born in neighbouring Fresnillo) and the painted shells of Mario Arellano Zajur. Next are a couple of hundred wonderful hand-painted *retablos* (altarpieces), depicting just about every saint, martyr and apostle going. The final galleries display two hundred Huichol embroideries that incorporate an amazing range of geometric designs, as well as maize symbols, deer and butterflies, all executed in black, red and green (for death, life and prosperity respectively).

Ex-Templo de San Agustín

Plazuela Miguel Auza, at Callejón San Agustín • Tues–Sun 10am–4.30pm • Free; admission varies for special exhibitions • ☎ 492 922 6580

The **Ex-Templo de San Agustín** has been under restoration, on and off, since the 1950s, and today its spacious, beautifully finished interior serves as an atmospheric gallery space for temporary art exhibitions, usually of a very high quality – local artists the Coronel brothers have both been featured in recent shows. The church dates back to the early sixteenth century, but after the Reform Laws it was converted into a casino and the adjoining monastery became a hotel. Don't miss the fabulously ornate Plateresque side door, a smaller version of the cathedral facade dating from the eighteenth century.

Museo de Arte Abstracto Manuel Felguérez

Colón, at Seminario • Wed–Mon 10am–5pm • M$30 • ☎ 492 924 3705

North of the centre, the **Museo de Arte Abstracto Manuel Felguérez** is an extensive modern art gallery imaginatively converted from a prison and its associated church. In

5

places the cells have been turned into mini-galleries where the intimacy of the space draws you into the works. Elsewhere several levels of cells have been ripped out to leave huge rooms with floor-to-ceiling paintings, sculptures and installations viewed from steel walkways that gradually take you higher.

Half of what's on show is by **Manuel Felguérez** (born 1928), a native of Zacatecas state and an approximate contemporary of the Coronel brothers (see p.368 & below). Within the field of abstract art he is almost as highly regarded, though it can take some effort to fully appreciate his work, particularly that of the early 1980s when he developed an obsession with male reproductive anatomy. He is perhaps most successful in his sculpture, notably the 1995 *El Arco del Día*, a huge bronze tripod that looks like it has just landed in a side chapel off the church. Nearby, his huge canvas entitled *Retablo de los Mártires* is also particularly striking. Elsewhere within the museum there is work by the Coronel brothers and several other of Felguérez' Mexican contemporaries, as well as an excellent art bookshop: almost everything is in Spanish.

Museo Rafael Coronel

Callejón de San Francisco • Thurs–Tues 10am–5pm • M$30 • ☎ 492 922 8116 • If you don't fancy the 20-minute walk from the centre, several bus routes, including #5, #8 and #9, pass close by

Pedro Coronel may have amassed a spectacular art collection, but his brother Rafael (born 1931) has a far more beautiful museum, the centrepiece of which is a huge collection of traditional masks, possibly the finest in Mexico. The wonderful **Museo Rafael Coronel** occupies the Ex-Convento de San Francisco on the north side of town. Founded in 1593 as a Franciscan mission (the facade is said to be the oldest in the city), it was rebuilt in the seventeenth century, only to begin deteriorating after the Franciscans were expelled in 1857 and finally suffer destruction during Villa's assault. The building and gardens have now been partially but beautifully restored, and the museum brilliantly integrated with the ruins.

There are more than four thousand masks on display, which makes taking it all in a bit overwhelming. The masks trace the art's development in what is now Mexico from some very ancient, pre-Columbian examples to contemporary pieces: often there are twenty or more variations on the same theme, and one little room is entirely full of the visages of Moors and Christians from the La Morisma festival (see box, p.368). As well as the masks, you can see Coronel's impressive collections of ceramics and puppets, the town's original charter granted by Philip II in 1593 and sketches and drawings connected with Coronel's wife Ruth Rivera, architect and daughter of famed muralist Diego Rivera. There's also a bookshop and a cosy café.

Museo Francisco Goitia

Enrique Estrada 102 • Tues–Sun 10am–5pm • M$30 • ☎ 492 922 0211

At the back of the Parque Enrique Estrada, in the old governor's residence, stands another local artist's museum, the **Museo Francisco Goitia**. Goitia (1882–1960) was one of Mexico's leading painters early in the twentieth century, and this enjoyable little museum houses a permanent exhibition of his work and that of more modern local artists (including Pedro Coronel), as well as hit-or-miss temporary displays and travelling art shows.

Mina El Edén

Dovalí Jaime s/n • Daily 10am–6pm; M$80; guided tour roughly every 15min, generally in Spanish, but ask if a bilingual guide is available • ☎ 492 922 3002, ⓦ minaeleden.com.mx. To reach the mine, take bus #7 from Hidalgo and Juárez to Hospital Dr Emilio Varela Lujan, or walk up Torreón, beyond the Alameda (follow the signs)

The **Mina El Edén**, or Eden Mine, is perhaps the most curious and unusual of all Zacatecas' attractions. This super-rich pit produced the silver that gave Zacatecas its immense wealth from 1586 to the 1960s. **Guided tours** (around 1hr) start at the main entrance, west of the centre, with a 500m small train ride through narrow, dark passages into the heart of the Cerro de Grillo. The first stop – where you get around fifteen minutes to wander around freely – is the well-presented **Museo de Rocas**, with displays of rocks and minerals from around the world (though mostly Mexico), including impressive geodes and fossilized ammonites and trilobites. Don't miss the stunning "Rosa del Desierto", a giant, prickly arrangement of gypsum and calcite deposits. You're then taken on a guided tour of the old mine workings – subterranean pools, chasms crossed on steel bridges and scattered machinery, all complete with colourfully lit mannequins dressed as miners and even a small shrine, the **Altar Santo Niño**.

Enthusiastic guides tell of the thousands of miners who died during the mine's four hundred years of operation. The high number of fatalities seems perfectly possible when you see level upon level of old galleries falling away for some 320m beneath you, inaccessible since the mine flooded when production stopped in 1966. The tour ends at a fountain near a lift that whisks you to the upper levels of the mine, where there's another stroll through 500m of tunnels to the upper entrance (about 200m from the cable car; see below). You can also return the way you came, or enter the mine from the upper entrance, though you may have a longer wait for a guide. It is also worth returning in the evening to *La Mina Club* (see p.374).

Cerro de la Bufa

Teleférico daily 10am–6pm • M$50 each way; Thurs–Sat also 7pm–midnight; services can be disrupted by strong winds • Taxi M$60

Zacatecas is dominated by the **Cerro de la Bufa** (2612m), with its extraordinary rock cockscomb crowning the ridge some 237m above the Plaza de Armas; at night it's illuminated, with a giant cross on top. A modern Swiss cable car connects the summit with the slopes of the **Cerro del Grillo** opposite – an exhilarating ride straight over the heart of the old town. The lower station of the **Teleférico** (cable car) is near the top entrance of Mina El Edén. It's a relatively easy climb up from the back of San Agustín (look for the signs up Callejon de Garcia Rojas, off Villalpando), or you can take bus #7 right to the door. Out from the station you pass right over the city centre – the views down on the houses are extraordinary. Most people come back the same way, but walking down the Cerro de la Bufa on the paved **Ruta del Via Crucis** is no great strain; the path ends at Altapalmira, which you can follow downhill until you see the red signs for the centre.

Templo de Nuestra Señora del Patrocinio

Explanada del Cerro de La Bufa • Daily 10am–6pm

It's a brisk uphill walk to the Plaza de la Revolución and pristine **Templo de Nuestra Señora del Patrocinio**, a chapel dating back to 1795 with an image of the Virgin said to perform healing miracles. To get there, exit the Cerro de la Bufo *teleférico* station and turn right. The main viewpoints are behind here, offering a jaw-dropping panorama of Zacatecas and its surroundings.

Museo de la Toma de Zacatecas

Explanada del Cerro de la Bufa • Daily 10am–4.30pm • M$20 • ☎ 492 922 8066

Next to the chapel on the Plaza de la Revolución, the **Museo de la Toma de Zacatecas** honours Pancho Villa's spectacular victory here in 1914, completely annihilating its twelve thousand-strong garrison – it was the bloodiest battle of the Revolution, breaking the back of the Huerta regime (see box, p.464). The museum has been given a futuristic makeover, with interactive games and exhibits sure to enthral kids, holographic images, recordings, and rare photos – some showing harrowing scenes of piled-up dead bodies – and old weapons and uniforms. There is also an exhibit

5

ZIP ZACATECAS

A more exhilarating attraction on the Cerro de la Bufa is just around the corner from Plaza de la Revolución, the museum and chapel: **Tirolesa 840**, a zip line that whips you across a gorge on the north side of the mountain (around 1km total). It's open daily 10am–6pm, with rides M$200–300. Contact ☎492 117 1530 or visit ⦿tirolesa840zacatecas.com for more information.

dedicated to Ángela Ramos aka "**Juana Gallo**" (immortalized in the eponymous 1961 Mexican movie; she is supposed to have joined the rebels at Zacatecas after her father and fiancé were murdered).

Behind the equestrian statue of Villa in the plaza outside, two paths skirt around the base of La Bufa to the **Mausoleo de los Hombres Ilustres**, where Zacatecanos who have made their mark on history have been buried since the 1940s, or at least have their memorials – unless you are a student of Mexican history, you're unlikely to have heard of any of them.

El Chico

The chapel and the museum do not sit on the actual summit of the Cerro de la Bufa: only one of the three peaks is accessible, **El Chico** (the smallest), topped by the **Observatorio Meteorologico**, another short walk uphill from behind the chapel. The observatory dates back to 1906, and though you can't go inside, the mesmerizing views are worth the climb. You might spot turkey vultures hanging out on the rocks near here.

ARRIVAL AND DEPARTURE   ZACATECAS

By plane The Aeropuerto Internacional de Zacatecas is 27km north of town; the only way to get into the centre is by taxi, which charge a fixed rate of M$400 (ask your hotel to arrange one for the trip back). Volaris links the city with Tijuana, Los Angeles and Chicago, but for other destinations you'll need to take the Aeroméxico or Interjet flight to Mexico City and transfer.
Destinations Chicago (1 daily; 4hr 25min); Los Angeles (3 weekly; 3hr); Mexico City (8 daily; 1hr 30min); Tijuana (1 daily; 2hr 30min).
By bus Zacatecas' modern Central de Autobuses is a hive of activity both day and night, 4km south of the centre (24hr guardería M$6/hr). To get into town take "Ruta 8" bus (every few min 7am–9pm; M$6.50) or a taxi – the fare should be around M$40 (no meters). If you take the bus, get off at the Jardín Independencia – it's within reasonable walking distance of most of the accommodation. To return

to the bus terminal, take "Ruta 8" (marked "Central Camionera"), which runs frequently along Villalpando and then down González Ortega.
There are frequent long-distance bus services to all parts of northern Mexico, the Bajío and Mexico City (see p.118), but if you're headed to Real de Catorce, you'll need to change at San Luis Potosí and then Matehuala: make an early start to be sure of getting there in a day. Autobuses Americanos runs daily buses direct to Laredo, El Paso and San Antonio, all in Texas.
Destinations Aguascalientes (every 30min; 2–3hr); Chihuahua (hourly; 13hr); Ciudad Juárez (hourly; 18hr); Durango (hourly; 5hr); Guadalajara (hourly; 5hr); Jerez (hourly; 1hr); León (hourly; 3–4hr); Mexico City (roughly hourly; 6–8hr); Monterrey (roughly hourly; 7–8hr); Querétaro (hourly; 6hr); San Luis Potosí (10 daily; 3–4hr); Tijuana (4 daily; 36hr).

GETTING AROUND

Once in town you should be able to get around on foot, though taxis are easy to find at the Jardín Independencia – they don't use meters, so negotiate the price in advance (M$40 should cover most destinations).

INFORMATION AND TOURS

Tourist office The tourist kiosk at Hidalgo 401 (daily 9am–9pm; ☎492 924 4047, ⦿zacatecastravel.com) can provide a smattering of leaflets and informative, friendly advice in English.
Tours Several local agencies handle general travel requirements and offer tours of the city and to surrounding attractions: try Operadora Zacatecas, Hidalgo 630 (☎492

924 0050, ⦿operadorazacatecas.com.mx), opposite the *Hotel Casa Santa Lucía*. All the bigger hotels stock leaflets detailing daily tours around the city (M$350), to Guadalupe (M$400), Jerez (M$500) and to La Quemada (M$500–600), among other destinations. Most tours require a minimum four persons.

ACCOMMODATION

Casa Torres Hotel Primero de Mayo 325 ☎ 492 925 3266, ⓦ hotelcasatorres.com. Quite unlike any other hotel in town, the rooms at this chic, modern place are tastefully decorated, with local artwork on the walls, flat-screen TVs and climate control. Standard rooms are fairly small so you may want to book a junior suite (M$1500), or even a master suite (M$1800) with balcony and cathedral views. Breakfast (included) is served in the lovely top-floor restaurant/bar. M$900

Cielito Lindo Hostal Aguascalientes 213 ☎ 492 921 1132, ⓦ cielitolindohostal.com. Beautiful old colonial property converted into a charming hotel featuring comfy dorms (M$200) with large wooden bunks, and doubles with private bathrooms, tiled floors and TVs. Free wi-fi throughout, and shared kitchen with a microwave and fridge only. Doubles M$500

Emporio Hidalgo 703 ☎ 492 925 6500, ⓦ hotel esemporio.com. Hang with Mexico's rich and famous at the city's most luxurious, opulent hotel, set in a gorgeous Baroque mansion. Rack rates are expensive, but you should get an affordable rate on the internet. The spacious rooms are decked out with modern amenities (free wi-fi, flat-screens and decent cable TV), but with a few colonial touches. You'll hear the *callejóneadas* from your room. M$1520

★**Hostel Villa Colonial** Primero de Mayo 201, at Callejón Mono Prieto ☎ 492 925 0749. A dream hostel located in the thick of it and enthusiastically run by Zacatecan locals. Comfortable four-bed dorms (M$125/person), double and twin rooms with shared bathrooms (M$250), and very cosy en-suite doubles in a separate building, some with their own kitchen. Extras include a sunny rooftop terrace, internet access, cable TV, a book exchange and a sociable atmosphere. Doubles (en suite) M$400

Hotel Casa Santa Lucía Hidalgo 717 ☎ 492 924 4900, ⓦ hotelcasasantalucia.com. Perhaps the best value of the mid-range hotels, making attractive use of its beautiful ancient structure and providing comfortable rooms with high ceilings, big tiled bathrooms, exposed stonework and simple but tasteful decor. Breakfast is included, and there's a terrace with stellar views of the cathedral and La Bufa. M$720

★**Hotel Mesón de Jobito** Jardín Juárez 143 ☎ 492 924 1722, ⓦ mesondejobito.com.mx. An entire alley off the city's most enchanting colonial square has been converted into this superb luxury hotel. Pretty, plush and private, all rooms come with a/c, and some with jacuzzis. There are two formal restaurants, and a bar with live music – just what you'd expect in a top hotel. M$1440

Hotel Santa Rita Hidalgo 507 ☎ 492 925 1194, ⓦ hotelsantarita.com. Incredibly stylish (and expensive) hotel, featuring an intelligent refit of an old colonial house, replete with contemporary art; suites come with street or patio views and terraces, free wi-fi and polished wood floors. M$1460

★**Quinta Real** Ignacio Rayón 434 ☎ 492 922 9104, ⓦ quintareal.com. Gorgeous and outrageously luxurious hotel in the shadow of the colonial aqueduct that has beautifully incorporated what was once Zacatecas' bullring. Every comfort is taken to the extreme degree (there's even a "pillow menu"), and this is certainly a place worth saving up for, not to mention one of the most distinctive properties in the Americas. M$1705

Terrasse Hotel Villalpando 209 ☎ 492 925 5315. Señora Lupita runs this centrally located, top-value guesthouse, with simple but comfy modern rooms and continental breakfast included. Advance booking crucial. M$670

EATING

For inexpensive tacos, tostadas and burgers, head away from the centre towards Ventura Sálazar, which is lined with places serving quick snacks. Other reliable hunting grounds are the compact **Mercado El Laberinto**, just north of the Jardín Independencia, and **Calle Aldama** in the mornings, for stalls selling tamales and *atoles*. While in Zacatecas, you should sample the local speciality, *asado de boda*, braised pork with chocolate and orange zest (once only served at weddings), and anything "zacatecano", usually meaning a dish smothered with poblano chiles and cream.

PICASSO AT THE ACRÓPOLIS

You might not expect to find original artwork by Picasso, Dalí and Miró in a Mexican café, but the Acrópolis in Zacatecas is a special case. Opened in 1943, its owners have assembled a formidable art collection, displayed for the pleasure of their customers; many pieces, such as those by Oaxacan painter Rufino Tamayo and zacatecano Francisco Goitia, were donated by the artists themselves (some were created specially), others donated by wealthy patrons. While sipping your coffee, try to spot *The Princess and the Herd Boy*, one of several Japanese-inspired prints by Dalí, the much-reproduced *Tres Libres* by Miró and *Lord and Girl* by Picasso, a lithograph produced in 1959. See p.374 for the café review.

5

Acrópolis Hidalgo 325, at Plazuela Candelario Huizar ☎ 492 922 1284, ⓦ acropoliszacatecas.wix .com/cafe. Established in 1943, this café serves up old-world ambience and appetizing Mexican breakfasts (M$75–95) to well-heeled zacatecanos, as well as ice cream, fruit juices, good coffee (from M$20) and standard Mexican dishes (M$75–150). English menus are available. The art collection is amazing (see box, p.373). Daily 8am–10pm.

La Cabaña Independencia 251, at Juárez ☎ 492 922 5775. Always alive with activity, this is one of the city's cheapest and most popular taco restaurants. Tasty meals served with a wide selection of salsas and beer at bargain prices in clean surroundings. Tacos are M$12–20, and a full chicken dinner costs M$120. Wonderfully fruity and thirst-quenching *aguas* are also sold to go. Try the sprightly *chía* flavour (a local herb). Daily 7am–midnight.

★ **Los Dorados de Villa** Plazuela de García 1314 ☎ 492 922 5722. Cosy little restaurant a short walk from the centre with lovely tiled walls and exotic birds. Look out for pictures of "Los Dorados", the young followers of Pancho Villa. The excellent traditional menu mostly comprises *moles* and enchiladas that keep people coming back for more. Mains average M$75–130. Reserve in advance. Mon–Sat 3pm–1am, Sun 3pm–midnight.

★ **Garufa** Jardín Juárez 135 ☎ 492 924 2910, ⓦ garufa .com.mx. Argentine restaurant chain specializing in gargantuan and super-succulent steaks imported from the pampas (M$175–250), along with much cheaper salads and pasta dishes, all of which are served in attractive rustic surroundings. Sun–Fri 1pm–midnight, Sat 1pm–1.30am.

Gorditas Doña Julia Hidalgo 409 (no phone). A one-trick pony, only serving gorditas (M$14 each) stuffed with either various cuts of meat, refried beans, shredded nopal cactus in a hot salsa or *mole* and rice, either to go or to eat in this cheerfully bright, open-fronted restaurant. Second branch at Tacuba 72. Daily 8am–10pm.

★ **La Plaza Quinta Real** Ignacio Rayón 434 ☎ 492 922 9104, ⓦ quintareal.com. Pick of the bunch for an expensive, formal meal, if only for the setting overlooking the former bullring on a series of indoor terraces. Expect to spend at least M$750/person for a full meal of nopal stuffed with shrimp, chicken in a tamarind sauce, dessert, coffee and something from the wine list – which includes a decent selection from the Valle de Guadalupe. Daily 7am–midnight.

Rostícería el Pastor Independencia 214 (no phone). The scent of wood-roasted chicken wafts to the street from this inexpensive, family-friendly joint, housed in the old Colegio de Niñas, built in 1772. M$65 buys you a 3/4 chicken dinner with all the fixings (M$55 for half a chicken). Daily 8am–8.30pm.

★ **Il San Patrizio Caffé** Hidalgo 403 ☎ 492 922 9838. The best (Illy) coffee in town, and only a little more expensive than places selling far inferior brews (M$25–40). The extra pesos are further justified by the peaceful courtyard setting, a choice of delicious cakes and a number of magazines to browse, some in English – blink and you'll miss the tiny sign, next to the tourist office. Mon–Sat 8am–10pm, Sun 10am–9pm.

DRINKING AND NIGHTLIFE

Nightlife in Zacatecas, especially while the Universidad Autónoma de Zacatecas (UAZ) is in session, is a boisterous affair, with much of the early evening action happening on the streets – there always seems to be some procession or a band playing. On Fri and Sat evenings (and sometimes Thurs and even Sun) you may well encounter a **callejóneada** (see p.356) during which musicians – usually with several big drums and a brass section – promenade around the back alleys, often with a donkey bearing carafes of tequila. Ask your hotel about buying tickets, or head to the Plaza de Armas around 9pm to catch the start.

Bar Botarel Quinta Real, Ignacio Rayón 434 ☎ 492 922 9104, ⓦ quintareal.com. Stylish cellar bar built under the seating of what used to be the bullring. Arrive soon after 6pm to get one of the intimate booths, from where you can look out at the plaza and the rest of the hotel. Prices are almost twice what you pay in other places, but nowhere else has the same sense of romance. Live music Fri and Sat until midnight. Daily 6pm–1am.

★ **Cantina Las Quince Letras** Mártires de Chicago 309 ☎ 492 922 0178. Most atmospheric bar in the city, a classic cantina with all sorts of bric-a-brac, antiques and paintings draped from the ceiling, cheap drinks and decent jukebox – live music some nights. Mon–Sat 1pm–2am.

★ **La Mina Club** Dovalí Jaime s/n, inside Mina El Edén (see p.371) ☎ 492 922 3002, ⓦ minaeleden.com.mx. Zacatecas' major club, right in the heart of the mountain and accessed on the same train used in the mine tour (see p.371). From 11pm it is pumping with Latin sounds, US and European dance tunes, but mostly cheesy electronic techno music. If you don't enjoy being trapped in an enclosed space, *La Mina* is not for you. Entry M$150 on Sat. Thurs & Fri bar only 4–10.30pm; Sat club nights 10pm–3am.

Piper's Irish Pub Allende 117 ☎ 492 921 2829. Zacatecas has its very own Irish pub, serving genuine Guinness and microbrews, but also tasty bar food like chicken wings and showing all the big sports events on TVs. Tues–Sun 11am–1am.

MEZCAL DE ZACATECAS

Mescal is a distilled, smoky-tasting spirit made from the maguey plant (a form of agave), unique to Mexico. Though most mescal is made in Oaxaca (see box, p.603), Zacatecas produces its own line of highly lauded brands. Get a decent introduction at **La Casa Zacatecana del Mezcal**, Hidalgo 729, where around twenty local mescals (including Huitzila, Antonio Aguilar, La Esclava, Hacienda de Robles and Teulito) are available to buy, taste or just drink (you can even buy miniatures for M$25).

DIRECTORY

Banks and exchange Plenty of banks are situated along Hidalgo between Juárez and Allende, all with 24hr ATMs and offering currency exchange (Mon–Fri 9am–1pm).

Books and magazines The best source of English-language magazines is Sanborn's, Hidalgo 212. It's hard to find English-language books anywhere in Zacatecas, though there are plenty of Spanish bookshops: try Librerías Don Quijote at Villalpando 601 (daily 9am–9pm), or Librería Universal at Hidalgo 109, usually open Mon–Sat 9am–9pm.

Emergencies For general emergencies call ☎ 066. Cruz Rojo (☎ 492 922 3005) handles medical emergencies.

Hospital Hospital Santa Elena (☎ 492 924 29 28) at Guerrero 143.

Laundry Fast Clean Lavandería (daily 8am–8pm), Villalpando 203, charges M$18/kg.

Pharmacy Farmacia Guadalajara at López Mateos 305 is 24hr; a more central branch is at Hidalgo and Juárez (Mon–Fri 8am–4pm, Sat 9am–1pm). Farmacias de Similares (⊛ farmaciasdesimilares.com.mx) has branches at Hidalgo 131 and Tacuba 178.

Post office Allende 111 (Mon–Fri 8am–4pm, Sat 8am–2pm).

Spanish courses Founded in 1973, Fenix Language Institute, Callejón de Montalvo 505-5A (☎ 492 922 1643, ⊛ fenixlanguageinstitute.com), has highly regarded courses for around US$150/week (M$2500) or US$20/hr (M$335) for private classes.

Around Zacatecas

It's well worth basing yourself in Zacatecas to explore the immediate surroundings, not least the silverware at the **Centro Platero de Zacatecas**, the sumptuously decorated church in **Guadalupe**, the ruins of the great desert fortress at **Quemada** and the picturesque town of **Jerez**, a pleasant day trip anytime but essential for the cowboy festival on Easter Saturday. You can venture out to any of these places independently, though several travel agents in Zacatecas offer tours (see p.372).

Centro Platero de Zacatecas

Ex-Hacienda de Bernardez, Fracc Lomas de Bernardez, Guadalupe • Mon–Fri 10am–5pm, Sat 10am–2pm • Free • ☎ 492 899 4503, ⊛ centroplaterodezacatecas.com • 5km south of central Zacatecas; "Ruta 11" from López Mateos runs to the nearest bus stop (M$6.50; 40min), where you can ask directions and walk the last km; alternatively, take a taxi to the door for M$60 (15min)

Galleries in Zacatecas sell stacks of jewellery, but prices are high. If you are serious about buying silver, or just want to see artisans at work, devote a couple of hours to visiting the **Centro Platero de Zacatecas.** Within this ex-hacienda, students and recent

LEGENDS OF QUEMADA

Though we may never know for sure, **Huichol legend** seems to support the theory that **La Quemada** was built by a local ruling class. There was an evil priest, the story runs, who lived on a rock surrounded by walls and covered with buildings, with eagles and jaguars under his command to oppress the population. The people appealed to their gods, who destroyed the priest and his followers with "great heat", warning the people not to go near the rock again. Quemada was probably destroyed by fire around 1300 AD and was never reoccupied; even today, the Huichol, in their annual pilgrimage from the Sierra Madre to collect peyote around Real de Catorce to the east, take a long detour to bypass this area.

5

graduates of the on-site silversmith school maintain a series of small workshops where you can see them creating original designs, many influenced by pre-Columbian images, or iconography associated with Zacatecas. Everything is for sale, often at very reasonable prices.

Guadalupe

Just 7km southeast of Zacatecas' centre, **Guadalupe** is a virtual suburb of the state capital these days, but it's a large, historic place in its own right, founded in 1578. The heart of town is palm-fringed **Jardín Juárez**, where you'll find the **Convento de Nuestra Señora de Guadalupe** (once the largest Franciscan monastery in the world and still home to a gaggle of monks), the town's famous Templo de Guadalupe and the top-rate Museo de Guadalupe.

Templo de Guadalupe

Jardín Juárez Oriente • Daily 7am–6pm

You can't miss the enormous bulk of the **Templo de Guadalupe** at the heart of the Convento de Nuestra Señora de Guadalupe, with its dome and asymmetric twin towers (one Baroque, the other Moorish inspired). Inside, the central **Santuario de Nuestra Señora de Guadalupe** is a confection of gold and vibrant Neoclassical decoration, while the **Capilla Oscura** (Dark Chapel) houses a venerated image of Christ, El Cristo de Acuña. To the left of the entrance is the **Capilla de Nápoles**, completed in 1849, whose mesmerizing domed interior is coated in elaborately filigreed gold leaf – sadly, this chapel is only open on special occasions.

Museo de Guadalupe

Jardín Juárez Oriente • Tues–Sun 9am–6pm • M\$52, free Sun • ☎ 492 923 2089

A flagged, tree-studded convent courtyard provides access to both the church and the **Museo de Guadalupe**, housed in the Ex-Colegio Apostólico de Propaganda Fide, founded in 1707. It's a vast and confusing warren of a place, with seemingly endless rows of cells opening off courtyards, stairways leading nowhere and kilometre-long corridors lined with portraits of monks and vast tableaux from the life of St Francis. There are guided tours in Spanish, but it's more enjoyable to wander alone, at your own pace.

Oil paintings cover every wall of the gallery's 27 rooms of rough tiled floors and whitewashed walls, mostly with a religious theme: Cristóbal de Villalpando, Antonio de Torres, Gabriel José de Ovalle, Miguel Cabrera, Luis Juárez and José de Alcívar all feature. Look particularly for the *Virgin of the Apocalypse* by Cabrera, the mid-eighteenth-century *Passion of Christ* series of oils by Zacatecan artist de Ovalle, and *La Anunciación* by Villalpando, one of Mexico's most important painters of the early eighteenth century.

ARRIVAL AND DEPARTURE   GUADALUPE

Local buses (clearly marked) from Zacatecas run out to Guadalupe every few minutes from López Mateos (M\$6; 20min) – taxis should take you for M\$60–70.

La Quemada

Carr Federal 54, km 56 • Daily 9am–6pm (last entry 4.30pm) • M\$46 **Museo de La Quemada** Tues–Sun 10am–4pm (last entry 3.30pm) • M\$20 • ☎ 492 922 5085

Surprisingly little is known about the enigmatic ruins of **LA QUEMADA**, some 52km south from Zacatecas on the road to Villanueva and Guadalajara. The scale of the complex isn't apparent until you're inside – from the road you can vaguely see signs of construction, but the whole thing, even the huge restored pyramid, blends so totally into the mountain behind as to be almost invisible. Most experts now think it developed between 400 and 1050 AD, most likely as a frontier post on the outskirts of some pre-Aztec sphere of domination – probably the **Toltecs** – charged with keeping at bay the southward depredations of the Chichimeca (over the years it has also been associated with the mythical Aztec city known as **Chicomóztoc**). Alternatively, it could simply be the work of a local ruling class, having exacted enough tribute to build themselves these palaces and needing the defences to keep their own subjects out.

In addition to the **Pirámide Votiva** (votive pyramid), you'll see the Salón de las Columnas, a large hall with eleven pillars still standing, the Juego de Pelota (ball-court), an extensive (if barely visible from the ground) system of roads heading out into the valley and many lesser, ruined structures all listed for eventual reconstruction. Much of the restoration work is based on drawings produced over the course of ten years from 1825 by a German mining engineer, Carlos de Berghes. Copies are on display in the superb **Museo de La Quemada**, at the site, which makes a masterful job of bringing the place alive with a select display of artefacts, a detailed area model and several explanatory videos (in Spanish only).

GETTING THERE	LA QUEMADA

By bus Getting to La Quemada is straightforward by public transport, with Villanueva-bound buses (around M$35) leaving every 30min or so from López Mateos in Zacatecas. They're usually happy to drop you at the start of the 2km access road (ask for "las ruinas"); the ride to this point takes about an hour, from where you've got a 30min walk to the entrance. To get back, hike to the highway and flag down the first bus you see.

By car/taxi Most visitors get to the site by car (it's a 30min drive along Hwy-54) or taxi (around M$600 round trip). Organized tours charge M$500–600/person (see p.372).

Jerez

For an enjoyable day trip from Zacatecas consider **JEREZ**, another Pueblo Mágico 57km southwest of the city, best known for being the birthplace of lauded poet **Ramón López Velarde** (1888–1921, author of *La Suave Patria*), and its particularly lively **spring festival** (see box, p.378). At other times you can simply wander the pleasant colonial centre, visiting the poet's former home, now the **Museo Casa del Ramón López Velarde** (Tues–Fri 10am–6pm, Sat 10am–3pm; M$20), at Obregón 73, the Porfiriano-era **Teatro Hinojosa** (Mon–Fri 8am–7pm, Sat & Sun 11am–5pm; free) on Jardín Hidalgo, and the attractive eighteenth-century church of **Inmaculada Concepción** (at the junction of Flores and Reloj), just south of Jardín Páez, the main plaza.

ARRIVAL AND DEPARTURE	JEREZ

By bus Buses (M$50–60) to Jerez leave hourly from Zacatecas' Central de Autobuses, and take about an hour to the bus station 1km from the centre (local "Centro" buses are M$6).

INFORMATION

Tourist office The Oficinas de Turismo is at C del Espejo 16 (Mon–Fri 8am–5pm; ☎ 494 945 5166).

San Luis Potosí

Situated to the north of the Bajío's fertile heartland, the sprawling industrial city of **SAN LUIS POTOSÍ** boasts a ravishing historic centre of colonial plazas and elegant stone buildings reminiscent of a classical Spanish town. Though a Franciscan mission was established in the area in the 1580s, San Luis was officially founded in

5

THE JEREZ SPRING FESTIVAL

If you can, time your visit to Jerez to coincide with the annual ten-day **Feria de la Primavera** (spring festival), celebrated around Easter since 1824 with *charreadas* (rodeos), bullfights, bands and much tequila drinking. The climax is the Easter Saturday procession when an effigy of Judas is burned. Festivities around the **Día de la Virgen de la Soledad** (Sept 8–15) are also worthwhile, with an opportunity to catch the Chichimecan plumes of the Danzas de los Matlachines.

1592, as a supply town for the surrounding gold and silver mines discovered that year. Today San Luis Potosí is a prosperous place of over one million *potosinos* – most of the silver is gone, but there is a considerable manufacturing base. Tucked in among the splendour are some handsome churches, notably the **Templo del Carmen**, the garish masks of the **Museo Nacional de la Máscara** and the **Museo Federico Silva**, tribute to one of Mexico's greatest sculptors.

Plaza de Armas (Jardín Hidalgo)

The grand **Plaza de Armas**, or Jardín Hidalgo, is the traditional heart of San Luis Potosí, dominated by the **Palacio de Gobierno** and the impressive bulk of the **Catedral Metropolitana**, its twin towers soaring above the square like ornate candelabras. On the east side of the plaza lies the **Palacio Municipal**, still City Hall, while the elegant **Casa de la Virreina** on the north side was once home to the Spanish viceroys – dating to 1736, it's one of the oldest buildings in the city. These days the plaza seems to host a constant stream of anti-government protests, which can make access difficult, though rarely dangerous.

Catedral Metropolitana
Plaza de Armas • Daily 7.30am–2pm & 4.30–8.30pm

Completed in 1730 and dedicated to Nuestra Señora de la Expectación, successive generations have ensured that little remains of the original **Catedral Metropolitana**. Even the Baroque towers, each a mass of twisted columns, are oddly mismatched; one tower is all grey, the other a sandy orange colour. Check out the opulent interior, decorated in the 1890s by celebrity Italian design duo Claudio Molina and Giuseppe Compiani.

Palacio de Gobierno
Plaza de Armas 11 • Mon–Fri 8am–6pm (can be closed due to special events or protests) • Free

Facing the cathedral across the Plaza de Armas is the long facade of the **Palacio de Gobierno**, with its balustraded roof. This, too, has been substantially refurbished since its completion in 1827, but at least alterations have preserved the harmony of its clean Neoclassical lines. Inside you can visit the **Sala Juárez**, a suite of rooms occupied by Benito Juárez when San Luis Potosí became his temporary capital in 1863 (head up either set of stairs and turn left). French troops supporting Emperor Maximilian soon drove him out, but Juárez returned in 1867, and in this building confirmed the death sentence passed on the hapless French puppet emperor.

FESTIVE SAN LUIS

The most entertaining San Luis fiestas are the Día de la Asunción (Assumption; Aug 15), a religious festival with traditional dances outside the cathedral that coincides with the Feria de la Uva, the city's grape festival, and the Día de San Luis Rey (Aug 25), a huge fiesta enthusiastically enjoyed by virtually the whole town – a giant procession and fireworks follow.

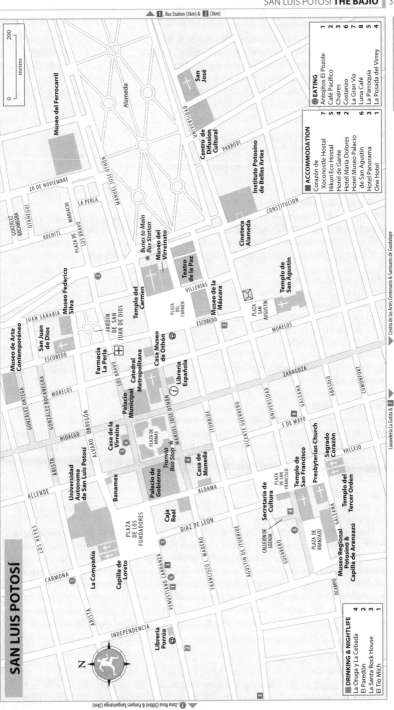

SAN LUIS POTOSÍ

▲ 1, Bus Station (3km) & 2 (3km)

▲ Airport (25km)

▲ Mercado Hidalgo (1 block)

Lavandería La Gotita & 7 ▶

Centro de las Artes Centenario & Santuario de Guadalupe ▶

● EATING

Antojitos El Pozole	7
Café Pacífico	5
Chaires	3
Costanzo	2
La Gran Vía	6
Luna Café	8
La Parroquia	5
La Posada del Virrey	4

■ ACCOMMODATION

Corazón de	7
Xoconostle Hostal	
Hikuri Eco Hostal	5
Hotel de Gante	2
Hotel María Dolores	2
Hotel Museo Palacio	6
de San Agustín	
Hotel Panorama	3
One Hotel	1

■ DRINKING & NIGHTLIFE

La Oruga y La Cebada	4
El Paredón	3
La Santa Rock House	2
El Tío Mich	1

0 — 200 metres

5

Casa Museo de Othón

Othón 225 • Tues–Fri 10am–2pm & 4–6pm, Sat & Sun 10am–2pm • M$5 • ☎ 444 812 7412

Just behind the cathedral lies the **Casa Museo de Othón**, a pretty and well-tended museum, though a rather lifeless tribute to Manuel José Othón, San Luis' most famous poet (who was born here in 1858), mainly comprising some of his manuscripts, belongings and period furniture. Othón's best-known poem is *Idilio Salvaje* ("Idyll of the Wild"), published in 1905, and hard to find in English translation.

Plaza del Carmen and around

East along Othón from Plaza de Armas lies the **Plaza del Carmen**, a much newer space created in 1973 but nevertheless ringed by historic buildings.

Templo del Carmen

Plaza del Carmen • Daily 7am–1.30pm & 4–9pm

The **Templo del Carmen** is the most beautiful and harmonious of all San Luis' churches, dating from 1764. Exuberantly decorated with a multicoloured tiled dome and elaborate Baroque facade, it has an equally flashy interior: in particular, a fantastically intricate nineteenth-century *retablo* attributed to Francisco Tresguerras.

Museo del Virreinato

Plaza del Carmen, Villerías 115 • Tues–Fri 10am–7pm, Sat 10am–9pm, Sun 10am–5pm • M$15 • ☎ 444 814 0994, Ⓦ museodelvirreinato.mx

Next door to the Templo de Carmen, housed in an eighteenth-century monastery, sits the moderately interesting **Museo del Virreinato**, a huge collection of artwork and artefacts from the Spanish colonial era. The eclectic displays include religious paintings (mostly minor work from the 1700s), ceramics, old books and heavy iron keys. There are even some creepy-looking mannequins, dressed in the various habits of the Catholic monastic orders.

Teatro de la Paz

Plaza del Carmen, Villerías 105 • Ticket office daily 10am–2pm & 4–8pm • ☎ 444 812 2698

The southeast corner of the Plaza del Carmen is dominated by the Roman-inspired bulk of the **Teatro de la Paz**, completed in 1894 under Porfirio Díaz and typical of the grandiose public buildings of that era, though its modern interior (open for performances only) fails to live up to the extravagance of the facade.

Museo Nacional de la Máscara

Plaza del Carmen, Villerías 2 • Tues–Fri 10am–6pm, Sat 10am–5pm, Sun & Mon 10am–3pm • M$20, with camera M$10 • ☎ 444 812 3025, Ⓦ museonacionaldelamascara.com

At the southern end of Plaza del Carmen you'll find the absorbing **Museo Nacional de la Máscara**, dedicated to mask art and the city's best museum. It occupies the lavish former home of local landowner Ramón Martí. Completed in 1897, it was sold to the government just six years later. The mansion is finished off like a mini-palace, with exhibits on everything from pre-Hispanic masks and jade funerary pieces to Spanish-influenced demonic masks and costumes that are still worn for fiestas and traditional dances today. The upper level contains some expertly restored period rooms and **Sala XIX**, a small collection of the decorative pieces found in homes like this in the nineteenth century.

Templo de San Agustín

Plaza San Agustín (Abasolo 650) • Mon–Sat 10am–1pm & 4–7pm, Sun open for services • ☎ 444 812 5994

One block south of the Plaza del Carmen lies another magnificent Baroque church, the **Templo de San Agustín**, built around 1700 with an extravagantly carved tower. The handsome Neoclassical interior is adorned with murals completed in the 1890s by the Italians Molina and Compiani.

Museo Federico Silva

Jardín de San Juan de Dios, Obregón 80 • Mon & Wed–Sat 10am–6pm, Sun 10am–2pm • M$30, free Sun • ☎ 444 812 3848, ⓦ museofedericosilva.org

Two blocks north of the Plaza del Carmen is the **Museo Federico Silva**, a tribute to one of Mexico's most exalted sculptors (born in Mexico City in 1923). The museum is housed in a Neoclassical school building completed in 1907, its open spaces a lovely synthesis of the classic and the contemporary, much like the works of Silva, who creates modern interpretations of Mexico's pre-Hispanic forms. His blockish volcanic stone and steel forms dominate the galleries: some are vaguely human and others geometric abstractions, but all are beautifully lit. Don't miss *Scriptum*, a huge block of stone (adorned with four simple carved circles) entirely filling a kind of crypt, below the ground floor, as if it were secreted deep within some Aztec pyramid.

Museo de Arte Contemporáneo

Morelos 235, at Ortega • Tues–Sat 10am–6pm, Sun 10am–2pm • M$20, free Sun • ☎ 444 814 4363, ⓦ macsanluispotosi.com

If the Museo Federico Silva whets your appetite for contemporary Mexican art, walk two blocks northwest to the **Museo de Arte Contemporáneo**, opened in 2010 in the handsome old post office (which dates from the 1860s). The temporary shows here feature up-and-coming local and national artists.

Plaza de los Fundadores and around

Immediately west of Plaza de Armas, the paved **Plaza de los Fundadores** is a much larger and more formal open space, commemorating the foundation of the city near this spot in 1592. The plaza is dominated by the enormous Neoclassical **Edificio Central de la Universidad**, the main state university building, and two small adjacent churches, the **Capilla de Loreto** (usually open on Sun only) and **La Compañía** (usually open daily). The fine portals of the **Ipiña Arcades** on the west side of the square continue around the corner into Avenida Venustiano Carranza.

There's more interest a block south along Aldama at Madero, where you can admire the peach-coloured Baroque facade of the **Caja Real**, the old mint dating from 1763 – one of the finest colonial mansions in San Luis. It is now owned by the university, which sometimes holds temporary exhibitions here.

Plaza and Ex-Convento de San Francisco

Templo de San Francisco Mon–Sat 10am–1pm & 4–7pm, Sun open for services

Three blocks south of Plaza de los Fundadores is the tranquil **Plaza de San Francisco**, a lovely, shaded area redolent of the city's colonial history. It's named after the sprawling Franciscan monastic complex that once stood here – most of the religious institutions that remain were once part of it. Foremost are the ochre towers of the **Templo de San Francisco**, looming over the plaza's west side, with the interior featuring a magnificent crystal chandelier in the shape of a sailing ship, hanging over the nave.

At the southern end of the plaza are two more tiny and elaborate Franciscan remnants. The **Templo de Sagrado Corazón** (which dates from 1731) and the even older and far simpler **Templo del Tercera Orden** (established in 1698) stand side by side, while the small, neo-Gothic **Iglesia Nacional Presbiteriana** (National Presbyterian Church, a later addition from 1894), terribly incongruous amid all this Baroque grandeur, faces them across Galeana.

5

Museo Regional Potosino

Plaza de Aranzazú • Tues–Sat 10am–7pm, Sun 10am–5pm • M$47, free Sun • ☎ 444 814 3572

Another remnant of the Franciscan *convento* houses the **Museo Regional Potosino**, a collection of pre-Hispanic sculpture and other archeological finds, displays of local indigenous culture and traditions and articles relating to the history of the state of San Luis Potosí. In addition to a fine cloister, there's access, upstairs, to the ornate Baroque chapel, **Capilla de Aranzazú** – said to be the only chapel in Latin America located on an upper floor – with exceedingly rich and enthusiastically restored churrigueresque decoration. You'll find the entrance to the museum behind the Templo de San Francisco at the **Plaza de Aranzazú**, another pleasant open space which hosts a small arts and crafts market on Saturdays.

Centro de las Artes and around

Calzada de Guadalupe 705 • Tues–Fri 11am–2pm & 5–8pm, Sat & Sun 11am–5pm • M$15 • ☎ 444 137 4100, ⓦ centrodelasartesslp.gob.mx

At the heart of the ambitious **Centro de las Artes** complex is the former state prison, built in the 1890s and given a stylish contemporary makeover. Temporary exhibitions here showcase local and visiting artists – check the website in advance to see if a show is taking place, otherwise it can seem rather empty. Behind the main courtyard of galleries lies the old cell block, now the **Museo del Sitio** – the cell where **Madero** was held in 1910 is preserved shrine-like, occupied now with a bust of the great man. Beyond here a series of old prison buildings has been transformed into a theatre, library and various art spaces as well as open areas sprinkled with sculptures and gardens.

The art centre is around 2km south of Plaza de Armas, a pleasant walk along pedestrianized Zaragoza and then the tree-lined walkway in the centre of the Calzada de Guadalupe (taxis should be no more than M$40). Just to the south lie the soaring 53m-high towers of **Basílica Menor del Santuario de Nuestra Señora de Guadalupe**; completed in 1800, this is the grandest church in the city.

ARRIVAL AND DEPARTURE SAN LUIS POTOSÍ

BY PLANE

Arriving at the Aeropuerto Internacional Ponciano Arriaga (25km north of downtown), taxis charge M$260 to the centre (taxis will ask for M$250–300 for the trip back); Alamo (☎ 444 818 4400), Budget (☎ 444 822 2482) and Payless (☎ 444 816 7787) all have desks at the airport, and HSBC and Bancomer have ATMs on the lower level.

Destinations Dallas (2 daily; 1hr 45min); Houston (1 daily; 1hr 45min); Mexico City (8 daily; 1hr 10min); San Antonio (1 weekly; 1hr 15min); Tijuana (1 daily; 2hr 30min).

BY BUS

Long-distance buses arrive at the main bus station (officially Terminal Terrestre Potosina or TTP), around 3km east of the centre on Hwy-57; for downtown and the Alameda, walk outside and board "Ruta 6" (M$7.60). It appears to head out of town but doubles back: get off at the former train station (now the Museo de Ferrocarril) and walk from there. To return to the bus station, pick up Ruta 6 for "Central TTP" from the northwest corner of the Alameda on Constitución. Taxis work

on a zone system from the bus station – buy a ticket before you exit the terminal. Rides into the city are M$40–60 – coming back, taxis should use the meter and should cost no more than M$40.

Buses from San Luis cover every conceivable route, with departures for Mexico City and Monterrey every few minutes, and for the US border at least hourly. Flecha Amarilla has excellent second-class services to Dolores Hidalgo, San Miguel de Allende and Guanajuato – note that there is only one first-class service to Guanajuato (via Premier Plus), at 7am (M$248). Northbound, there are frequent services to Matehuala (2hr 30min), where you change for Real de Catorce.

Destinations Aguascalientes (hourly; 2hr 30min); Dolores Hidalgo (14 daily; 2hr 30min); Guadalajara (hourly; 5–6hr); Matehuala (hourly; 2hr 30min); Mexico City (hourly; 5–6hr); Monterrey (5 daily; 6hr); Querétaro (hourly; 3hr); San Miguel de Allende (8 daily; 3hr); Tampico (4 daily; 7hr); Wadley (1 daily; 4–5hr); Zacatecas (hourly; 3hr).

GETTING AROUND

By bus Buses charge a flat M$7.60.
By taxi Taxis generally use meters that start at M$13.80

(M$16.90 at night) and go up M$4.10 every kilometre, meaning M$25–30 should be enough to cover anywhere within the centre.

On foot Though surrounded by hills, San Luis is located on a pancake-flat plateau (1860m above sea level), and the centre is easy to explore on foot.

INFORMATION

Tourist office For general information, head for the helpful state tourist office, Othón 130, just off Plaza de Armas (Mon–Fri 9am–9pm, Sat 9am–3pm; ☎ 444 812 6769, ⊛ visitasanluispotosi.com).

ACCOMMODATION

The cheapest **rooms** in central San Luis are found in the slightly run-down area north of the **Alameda**, but you'll find all the modern motel chains – offering excellent value – out along Benito Juárez (Hwy-57). These generally attract drivers passing through and business travellers, but are worth considering if you don't mind taking taxis back and forth from the centre.

Corazón de Xoconostle Hostal 5 de Mayo 1040 ☎ 444 243 9898, ⊛ corazondexoconostle.com. Excellent budget option downtown, with bright modern dorms (M$160), a women only dorm (M$180) and private doubles (with TVs), all with free wi-fi, use of computers, laundry room, shared kitchen, free coffee and basic breakfast. M$367

★**Hikuri Eco Hostal** Agustín de Iturbide 980, at Bolívar ☎ 444 814 7601, ⊛ hikuriecohostal.wix.com/hikuriecohostal. Hostel set over three floors of a beautiful old colonial building with plenty of recycled materials, a simple shared kitchen, free wi-fi, rooftop patio and super-friendly Italian/Mexican owners. There are clean, modern dorms (M$165–195) and two cosy doubles. M$415

Hotel de Gante 5 de Mayo 140 ☎ 444 812 1492, ✉ hotel_degante@hotmail.com. Central, comfortable and spacious, with cable TV but little atmosphere; superb location though, and especially good value if you can get a room overlooking Plaza de Armas. Free wi-fi. M$530

Hotel María Dolores Benito Juárez (Hwy-57), opposite the Central de Autobuses ☎ 444 822 1882. Motel set around attractive gardens studded with palms and swimming pools. Restaurants, bars and nightclubs fill ancillary buildings, and rooms, all with cable TV, free wi-fi and minibars, mostly have direct access to lawns. M$1085

Hotel Museo Palacio de San Agustín Galeana 240 at 5 de Mayo ☎ 444 144 1900, ⊛ hotelmuseopalacio desanagustin.com. It's worth visiting this jaw-dropping colonial masterpiece for a drink even if you can't afford to stay; the ornate interior and lobby, once part of a monastery, hint at the gorgeous antique-filled suites inside. Facilities include a posh spa, access to a horse and carriage, chauffeur-driven cars, free wi-fi and a golf course. M$3095

Hotel Panorama Venustiano Carranza 315, just west of Plaza Fundadores ☎ 444 812 1777, ⊛ hotel panorama.com.mx. Standard business hotel, though the rooms are fairly compact and a little overpriced; the floor-to-ceiling windows are great, but the bathrooms are tiny and some of the rooms are showing their age. You do get free wi-fi and free transport to the airport, and it's the best hotel in the centre. M$900

★**One Hotel** Benito Juárez 140, opposite the Central de Autobuses ☎ 444 100 9400, ⊛ onehotels.com. This modern chain offers superb value, with compact, minimalist rooms equipped with blond-wood furnishings, wi-fi, breakfast, flat-screen TVs and desks targeted at business travellers – cheap rates online and, mercifully, no smoking allowed anywhere in the hotel. M$945

EATING

San Luis specialities include deep-fried enchiladas and tacos or *enchiladas Potosinos* (or *Huastecas*), dripping with salsa and cheese, and *cecina*, a thin cut of marinated and dried steak. The upper-level **Mercado Hidalgo** is home to food stalls that serve them, as well as a host of regular Mexican dishes, for around M$25 or less – *Comedor Lucy* is a safe choice, but they're all pretty similar.

CENTRAL SAN LUIS

★**Antojitos El Pozole** Carmona 205, at Arista ☎ 444 814 9900, ⊛ antojitoselpozole.com. Justly popular local chain established in 1985, famous for its *pozole* (thick stew of chunky bits of chicken, corn and spices; M$72–110): order *pozole rojo* or *blanco*. The *tacos rojos* and *quesadillas de papa* are also worth trying. This branch is most central, in what feels a bit like someone's house with several small rooms. Tues–Sun noon–11.30pm.

Café Pacífico Constitución 200 ☎ 444 812 5414. Come here for a potent mix of gossip, action and basic Mexican food at moderate prices (mains M$70–150) in a diner-like setting. This very popular old-fashioned café-restaurant even has a non-smoking section; the weekend brunch buffets (9–11am) are good value. Daily 7am–midnight.

Chaires Plaza de Armas 5 ☎ 444 812 8088, ⊛ chaires .mx. Right on the plaza in part of the Casa de la Virreina, *Chaires* is alive with families, friends and canoodling couples sipping java and tucking into elaborate pastries (M$15–25). Daily 8am–10pm.

5

Costanzo Carranza 325 ☎444 812 7253 ⓦchocolates costanzo.com. Lauded confection chain since 1935, with all manner of tempting chocolates and sweet things in shiny paper. Chocolates are priced per 100g, with even the most decadent costing around M$20. Mon–Sat 10am–8.30pm, Sun 11am–7pm.

Luna Café Universidad 155 ☎444 812 4414, ⓦlunacafe.com.mx. Slightly more upscale than *Los Frailes* next door, offering gourmet coffees and cocktails from M$35. Daily 5pm–midnight.

La Parroquia Carranza 303, at Plaza Fundadores ☎444 813 0448. Comfortable middle-of-the-road diner featuring comfy booths, where crusty rolls replace the traditional stack of tortillas. Excellent breakfasts (M$80–110) and comida corrida (dishes M$75–110) – a firm favourite with local office workers. Daily 7am–midnight.

La Posada del Virrey Plaza de Armas 3 ☎444 812 3280. Housed in old Casa de la Virreina right on the main plaza, this location can't be beaten – everything graces the menu, from spaghetti to *mole poblano* (*menu del día* from M$90). Daily 7am–midnight.

LA AVENIDA

La Gran Via Carranza 560 ☎444 812 3633. Another San Luis institution, serving classic Spanish seafood and dishes such as *lechón asado* and *pollo al ajillo*. Set dinners from M$550. Mon–Sat 1pm–midnight, Sun 1–8pm.

DRINKING AND NIGHTLIFE

San Luis has a vibrant **nightlife**, with numerous **clubs** staying open until the early hours at the weekend (note that most clubs and bars are cash only). The section of Carranza (affectionately known as **La Avenida**), starting half a kilometre west of Plaza Fundadores, has traditionally been the place to go, but the smaller and more central collection of bars along Universidad, north of the Templo de San Francisco, is also a good bet. For movies, check out the wonderfully restored **Cineteca Alameda**, facing the Alameda at Constitución and Universidad (ⓦcinetecaalameda.net).

La Oruga y La Cebada Callejón de Lozada 1 ☎444 812 4508. Excellent microbrew pub ("The Caterpillar and Barley"), serving tasty pale ales and snacks. Daily 2pm–1am.

El Paredón Carranza 473 ☎444 812 5555. This themed Mexican sports bar features a huge gold statue of Pancho Villa at the door (it's named after a famous Villa victory) – a good place to get an early evening beer. Daily 6pm–2am.

La Santa Rock House Escobedo 125 ☎444 812 4533. This relaxed bar is the best place for live rock at the weekends (entry M$60), usually starting at 10pm. Most drinks cost M$20–35, though beers are often much cheaper. Mon, Thurs–Sat 9pm–4am.

El Tio Mich Carranza 1255 ☎444 481 6437. San Luis' hottest nightspot and concert hall. The meat market begins after midnight – entry fee varies. Thurs–Sat 7pm–4am, Sun 9pm–4am.

DIRECTORY

Banks and exchange There are banks with ATMs and several *casas de cambio* all around the main plazas, including Banamex at Allende and Obregón.

Books and newspapers The newsstands on Los Bravo, just off Plaza de Armas, usually have a few English-language publications, and it might be worth trying Librería Española at Manuel José Othón 170 (Mon–Sat 10am–2pm & 4–8pm), and Librería Porrúa at Carranza 410 (Mon–Fri 9am–9pm, Sat 10am–9pm, Sun 11am–8pm).

Emergencies For general emergencies dial ☎066. For medical emergencies, the most convenient clinic is Beneficencia Española, Carranza 1090 (☎444 811 5694), or just call the Cruz Roja on ☎444 815 3635.

Internet Several places, including Fox Ciberkafe at Escobedo 315 (daily 9am–9pm; M$15/hr).

Laundry Lavandería La Gotita, 5 de Mayo 870-A (☎444 814 2783), at Hernandez; M$30/load. Mon–Fri 10am–8pm, Sat 10am–3pm.

Pharmacy Farmacia La Perla, Los Bravo 240, at Escobedo (☎444 812 5922), and Farmacia Guadalajara, at Carranza 100 (24hr; ☎444 814 1955).

Post office Universidad 526 (Mon–Fri 8am–3pm).

Real de Catorce

REAL DE CATORCE is an extraordinary place. Silver mines were founded in the surrounding hills in 1772, and at the height of its production in 1898 the town had forty thousand inhabitants. But by the turn of the twentieth century mining operations had slowed, and in 1905 they ceased entirely, leaving the population to drop to virtually zero over the next fifty-odd years. For a period, a few hundred inhabitants hung on in an enclave at the centre, surrounded by derelict, roofless mansions and, further out, crumbling foundations and the odd segment of wall. Legend has it that

Real was "discovered" in the 1970s by an Italian hippy searching for peyote (which perhaps explains the town's curious Italian connection), and, particularly since the mid-1990s, an influx of artists, artesanía vendors, wealthy Mexicans and a few foreigners has given the town impetus to begin rebuilding.

The centre has been restored and reoccupied to the extent that the "ghost-town" tag is not entirely appropriate, though Real de Catorce certainly retains an air of desolation, especially in the outskirts; the occasional pick-up shoulders its way through the narrow cobbled streets, but most of the traffic is horses and donkeys. The population now stands at around 1500, the foreign contingent coexisting amiably with locals who increasingly depend on the tourist industry (it was made a Pueblo Mágico in 2001). The town has also become another popular Hollywood location, featuring in movies such as *Bandidas* (2006) and *The Mexican* (2001). There's not much in the way of sights: simply wandering around, kicking up the dust and climbing into the hills are big and worthwhile pastimes here.

REAL DE CATORCE

ACCOMMODATION

Hotel Corral del Conde	2
Hotel El Real	4
Mesón de la Abundancia	5
Mesón del Refugio	6
Real de Álamos	3
Refugio Romano	1

EATING

Al Gusto Restaurante Italiano	1
Café Azul	2
Mesón de la Abundancia	3

0   150
metres

5

> ### PEYOTE: FOOD FOR THE HUICHOL SOUL
>
> The **Wirikuta**, the flat semi-desert at the foot of the Sierra Madre Occidental near Real de Catorce (and Wadley; see p.389), was a rich source of **peyote** long before the Spanish Conquest. The Huichol people (see p.482) traditionally make a month-long, 400km annual pilgrimage here (now often shortened by truck or car) from their homelands in northeastern Nayarit to gather the precious hallucinogenic cactus (it contains psychoactive alkaloids, particularly mescaline), which they regard as essential food for the soul. After the peyote "buttons" are collected, many are dried and taken away for later use, but some are carried fresh to their sacred site, Cerro Quemada (Burnt Hill), near Real de Catorce, for ceremonies.
>
> Tales of achieving higher consciousness under the influence of peyote have long drawn foreigners, many of them converts of the books of **Carlos Castaneda** (who started writing about native Mexican shamanism in 1968). Indeed, Real de Catorce only made it onto the tourist itinerary after it became a waystation on the hippy-druggy trail in the 1970s. New Agers continue to visit, but the hills round about have been picked clean and there are fears that over-harvesting may threaten the continued Huichol tradition.

Túnel Ogarrio

Real de Catorce is built in a high mountain valley, at the end of a beautifully constructed 25km cobbled road through semi-desert dotted with agave and stunted Joshua trees. The final 2.3km is through the **Túnel Ogarrio**, opened in 1901, which is only broad enough for one vehicle at a time. As you drive through, the odd mineshaft leads off into the mountain to either side – by one there's a little shrine, the **Capilla de Nuestra Señora de los Dolores**, to miners who died at work and while building the tunnel.

Parroquia de la Purísima Concepción

Lanzagorta • Daily 7am–7pm

Real de Catorce's single main street, **Lanzagorta**, runs past the 1817 **Parroquia de la Purísima Concepción** on shaded Plaza Principal, and on down to the **Plaza Hidalgo** (aka Plaza de Armas), with its central bandstand. It's the church that attracts most Mexicans to Real, or rather the miraculous figure of St Francis of Assisi (known as Panchito, Pancho being a diminutive of Francisco) housed here. You'll soon spot the shrine by the penitents kneeling before it, but take time to head through the door to the left of the altar, where the walls are covered with hundreds of handmade *retablos* giving thanks for cures or miraculous escapes effected by the saint. They're a wonderful form of folk art, the older ones painted on tin plate, newer examples on paper or card or even photographs, depicting events that range from amazing to mundane – last-second rescues from the paths of oncoming trains, or simply the return of a stolen vehicle – all signed and dated with thanks to Panchito for his timely intervention.

Casa de Moneda (Centro Cultural Real de Catorce)

Plaza Principal • Wed–Sun 10am–7pm • M$10 • ☎ 488 887 5072

The **Casa de Moneda** is a magnificent old mansion on the other side of the plaza from the church, with two storeys on one side and three on the other, thanks to the sloping site it was built on. This is where Real's silver was minted into coin, though Emperor Maximilian closed it just fourteen months after it was completed in 1865. After a meticulous restoration it now serves as an art gallery and cultural centre, with temporary exhibitions from all over Mexico and small permanent displays on the building's role as mint, plus old photographs of the town.

Palenque de Gallos and Los Panteones

5

Palenque de Gallos Xicotencatl · Daily 9am–5pm · Free · **Los Panteones** Libertad · Daily except Tues 9am–5pm, though hours depend on the gatekeeper's mood · Free

Heading north out of town along Zaragoza, duck a few metres up Xicotencatl to the Roman-looking **Palenque de Gallos** of 1863, where cockfights were once held, then continue out along Zaragoza and Libertad to the ruinous Plaza de Toros, opposite **Los Panteones** where Real's dead lie covered by rough piles of dirt all around the decaying 1779 **Capilla de Guadalupe**. Peek inside the chapel to see its still-vibrant frescoes, which are going mouldy around the edges – just as they should be in a town like Real.

ARRIVAL AND INFORMATION

REAL DE CATORCE

By bus Most people arrive on buses from Matehuala (see below), some 60km east. The bigger buses can't get through the Ogarrio tunnel, so you'll probably have to change buses at the eastern end for the run through (if driving, you have to wait in line and pay a toll of M$20 (no toll coming back); you can park on the other side of the tunnel for M$26 during the day or M$65 for overnight). These smaller buses (free) drop you at a dusty parking lot at the tunnel's western end, from where it is a short walk down Lanzagorta to the town centre. It always pays to ask about the latest bus timetables, but there are currently departures from Matehuala (around M$80) at around 7.45am, 11.45am, 1.45pm and 5.45pm (with buses returning at similar times – you may choose to hike down to Estación Catorce and catch a bus from there: see box, p.388 for details).

Getting to Matehuala Matehuala is accessible by frequent first-class buses from Monterrey (from M$380), Saltillo (from M$265) and San Luis Potosí (from M$225). The Central de Autobus is just off Hwy-57 on Heroes Potosionos, 2km south of the centre. Buses to Catorce (30min; M$39, first class M$70) leave at around 8am, noon, 2pm and 6pm.

Destinations from Matehuala Mexico City (9 daily; 8hr); Monterrey (hourly; 3hr 15min); Real de Catorce (4 daily; 1hr 30min–2hr); Saltillo (7 daily; 3–4hr); San Luis Potosí (hourly; 2hr 30min); Wadley (4 daily; 1hr 45min).

Tourist office The tourist office (daily 10am–4pm; ☎ 488 887 5071) is in the Presidencia Municipal, Constitución 27, on Plaza Principal, but it is not always open – instead, you can get acquainted with the town by visiting private websites such as ⊚ realdecatorce.net.

ACCOMMODATION

Day and overnight visitors from San Luis Potosí and Monterrey make the town much busier at weekends, Semana Santa and Christmas, when the better hotels put up their prices by around twenty percent. The town is also packed around the **Fiesta de San Francisco de Asís**, every weekend from the second Sat in Sept to the fourth Sun in Oct and for the entire week around Oct 4. At this time buses don't run through the tunnel and you either have to walk or ride one of the numerous horse-drawn carts for a few pesos. On arrival you may be approached by villagers eager to guide you to their favoured *casa de huéspedes*. You're not obliged to accept what they show you, but chances are you'll get a plain and small but clean **room**, which at least claims to have 24hr hot water, for M$250–300: make sure there are plenty of blankets available as it can be very cold here at night. At the other end of the scale, Catorce is blessed with some wonderful hotels in converted **mansions**, often at very reasonable prices.

Hotel Corral del Conde Constitución 17 ☎ 488 887 5048, ⊚ elcorraldelconde@hotmail.com. One of the best mid-range options. Rooms in the original part of the hotel have an elegantly rustic quality with stone walls, wooden beams and ageing furniture, while a newer section across the road has more modern but equally comfortable rooms. No TVs or wi-fi. M$650

Hotel El Real Morelos 20, behind the Casa de Moneda ☎ 488 887 5058, ⊚ hotelelreal.com.mx. A charmingly converted old house with clean, airy rooms featuring native decoration, TVs (including videos and a video library), free wi-fi, fireplaces and views galore. It's reputed to be haunted. M$685

Mesón de la Abundancia Lanzagorta 11 ☎ 488 887 5044, ⊚ mesonabundancia.com. Located on the corner of Morelos, this friendly hotel was rebuilt from the 1860s ruins of the old town Treasury, and is full of masks, huge stone-built rooms with beamed ceilings, rug-covered brick floors and ancient doors with their original hefty keys. Many rooms have small balconies, and the suites (M$1350–1850) are very spacious. M$950

★ **Mesón del Refugio** Lanzagorta 55 ☎ 488 887 5068, ⊚ mesondelrefugio.net. Tastefully restored eighteenth-century mansion, completely renovated in a chic, modern style with a glass-covered courtyard and cosy rooms with free (but weak) wi-fi, satellite TV, heating, telephone, and restaurant serving breakfast. M$1320

5

Real de Álamos Constitución 21 ☎ 488 887 5009. One of the better budget hostels, just west of the Palacio Municipal, with comfortable enough concrete-walled rooms, bathrooms with hot water, magical views from the roof and low prices for singles (M$200). **M$350**

Refugio Romano Iturbide 38 ☎ 488 887 5074, ⓦ refugioromano.net. High above the town with stellar views, a lovely garden and terrace, owners Lucio and Mayra run one of the friendliest places in town. Just three stylish rooms, enhanced by home-cooked meals featuring Lucio's Italian cooking (pizza, pastas, focaccia and the like). Free wi-fi in common areas. **M$800**

EATING

Al Gusto Restaurante Italiano Lerdo de Tejada ☎ 488 887 5155. Authentic home-made Italian food (the owners Gianni and Carla Curto are Italian) with fresh pastas (try the rabbit tagliatelle), amazing salads and even vegetarian lasagne. Cash only. Mon–Sat noon–10pm.

Café Azul Lanzagorta 27, next to Mesón de la Abundancia ☎ 488 887 5131. Relaxed Swiss-run café serving the best espresso and cappuccino in town,

home-made cakes and sweet and savoury crêpes (M$25–70). Thurs–Tues 8am–5pm.

★ **Mesón de la Abundancia** Lanzagorta 11 ☎ 488 887 5044, ⓦ mesonabundancia.com. The pick of the bunch. The Mexican and Italian food is superbly cooked and presented, and worth every peso: expect to pay M$250 for a full meal including a slice of torte and espresso. Credit cards accepted. Daily 8am–9pm.

DIRECTORY

Banks Real is slowly dragging itself into the modern world and now has a single Banorte ATM, in the Presidencia

Municipal on Constitución, but bring lots of cash just in case.

HIKING AND RIDING CATORCE

Catorce's sights are soon exhausted, but you could spend days exploring the surrounding mountains, visiting ruins, or heading downhill to the *altiplano* (high plain) of the desert below. If you don't fancy the exercise, you'll see plenty of ageing US army jeeps, known here as "jeeps Willys", shuttling around the area. Negotiate the price before setting off.

HORSERIDING

One of the most relaxing ways to go is on **horseback**: horses are usually available around Plaza Hidalgo and in front of the *Mesón de la Abundancia*, from where **guides** will take you out across the hills, perhaps visiting the Huichol ceremonial site of Cerro Quemado, though this can seem unpleasantly voyeuristic if any Huichol are around. Midweek tours cost around M$100/hr; prices are higher at weekends.

SHORT HIKES

For **short hikes**, the best nearby destination is the **Pueblo Fantasmo** "Ghost Town," extensive mine ruins reached in an hour or so by following the winding track uphill, just to the left of the Ogarrio tunnel entrance as you face it.

LONG HIKES

The most rewarding unguided **longer hike** (12km one-way; 3hr down, 4hr return; 850m ascent on the way back) leads downhill on Allende from Plaza Hidalgo (with the stables on your left), then forks right after 50m and follows a 4WD track towards the trackside town of Estación Catorce. You'll soon find yourself walking among mine ruins – you'll pass a dam built to provide water and power for the mines, and the **Socavón de Purísima**, a tall chimney from one of the smelters. After about an hour you get to the small village of **Los Catorces**, and, beyond its cemetery, a second settlement known as **Santa Cruz de Carretas** (about 2hr from Real).

At this point, you've already experienced the best of the hike, but it is possible to continue to **Estación Catorce**, an hour further on. If the idea of hiking back seems too daunting, try flagging down the occasional vehicle, and be prepared to pay for your ride. Estación Catorce itself is not a place to linger, though if you get stuck, there are a couple of fleapit hotels and places to eat, located where **buses** depart, on the scruffy square by the rail tracks. Apart from local services to Wadley (at 10.30am, 4pm and perhaps a couple of others; 20min), most buses head to San Tiburcio where you can change for Saltillo and Zacatecas.

Wadley

Around 10km south of Estación Catorce (see p.388) lies **WADLEY** (or Estación Wadley, named after American railroad builder William Wadley), a small, dusty village that at first acquaintance seems even less appealing than its northern neighbour. The 1922 railway station has long been abandoned (the railway carries freight only), but Wadley has still garnered a devoted following, chiefly for its proximity to a section of desert known to the Huichol as Wirikuta (see box, p.386), renowned for its abundant **peyote** (see box, p.386; as explored in the 2008 experimental Indie flick *Wadley*).

Most people rent a room for a few days, usually with a kitchen as restaurants here are very limited: ask around and you should find somewhere for around M$200/night (or less), especially if you are staying a few days (most people end up with *Don Tomas*). Officially at least, "eating" peyote is illegal for anyone other than the Huichol, and there have been several police crackdowns in recent years.

ARRIVAL AND DEPARTURE   WADLEY

Most people visit Wadley with their own transport, or travel via Real de Catorce (see p.384), usually with a local guide or jeep driver; *colectivo* jeeps Willys depart around noon (45min) and return at 8am (M$50). Second-class buses usually run between Estación Catorce, Estación Wadley and Matehuala, but timetables often change so you must check in Real de Catorce before heading out.

Veracruz

VOLADORES DE PAPANTLA, A CULTURAL TRADITION
OF THE TOTONAC PEOPLE OF VERACRUZ

Veracruz

The central Gulf coast is among the least-visited yet most distinct areas of Mexico. From Mexico City, you descend through the southern fringes of the Sierra Madre Oriental, past the country's highest peaks, to a broad, hot and wet coastal plain. In this fertile tropical zone the earliest Mexican civilizations developed: Olmec culture dominated the southern half of the state from 1200 BC, while the civilization known as Classic Veracruz flourished between 250 and 900 AD at centres such as El Tajín. Today, Huastec and Totonac culture remains strong in the north. Cortés began his march on the Aztec capital from Veracruz, and the city remains, as it was throughout colonial history, one of the busiest ports in the country. Rich in agriculture – coffee, vanilla, tropical fruits and flowers grow everywhere – the Gulf coast is also endowed with large deposits of oil and natural gas.

The few non-Mexican tourists who find their way here are usually just passing through. In part, at least, this is because the area makes no particular effort to attract them; the **weather** can also be blamed – it rains more often and more heavily here than just about anywhere else in Mexico. Yet even in the rainy season the torrential downpours are short-lived, and within a couple of hours of the rain starting, you can be back on the streets in bright sunshine. Though there are long, windswept **beaches** all down the Atlantic coast, they are less beautiful than their Pacific or Caribbean counterparts, while the larger coastal towns are primarily commercial centres, of little interest to the visitor.

That said, domestic tourism to the area is on the rise, both to the beaches and, increasingly, for **adventure tourism** – whitewater rafting, kayaking, canyoning, climbing and more – around the eastern slopes of the **Sierra Madre** and the rivers that flow off it. **Veracruz** itself is one of the most welcoming of all Mexico's cities; too busy with its own affairs to create a separate life for visitors, the steamy tropical port draws you instead into the rhythms of its daily life, and its obsession with music. Less than an hour north lie **La Antigua** and **Villa Rica**, where Cortés established the first Spanish settlements on the American mainland, and **Cempoala**, ruined site of the first civilization he encountered. **El Tajín**, near the coast in the north of the state, is one of the most important archeological sites in the country, and **Filo Bobos**, only recently excavated, is also well worth a visit.

The colonial cities in the mountains are also delightful: **Xalapa**, seat of the Veracruz state government, is the finest, with its balmy climate, beautiful highland setting and superb anthropology museum. This area, and the high mountains around **Córdoba** and **Orizaba**, are the playground of the adrenaline tourist too. To the south, **Catemaco** is a spellbinding lake set in an extinct volcanic crater, where you can see the last remaining tract of Gulf coast **rainforest**. The area is renowned as a meeting place for native *brujos* and *curanderos*, witches and healers.

MARIMBA PLAYERS IN THE ZÓCALO, CÓRDOBA

Highlights

❶ Veracruz Salsa with divas wearing outrageous costumes at the city's exuberant Carnaval. Afterwards, or at any time of year, relax with an ice-cold mint julep and soak up the sounds of marimba in the zócalo, one of Mexico's most vibrant plazas. **See p.394**

❷ Xalapa Enjoy the café culture in this university town surrounded by coffee plantations. The Museum of Anthropology here is second only to Mexico City's. **See p.408**

❸ Whitewater rafting There are magnificent rafting opportunities, as well as other adrenaline sports, on the rivers that tumble down the tropical valleys of the Sierra Madre Oriental. Take a tour from one of the cities, or head directly to the riverside towns of Jalcomulco or Tlapacoyan. **See p.414 & p.415**

❹ El Tajín Explore the unique pyramids and ruins at this magnificent remnant of Classic Veracruz civilization; the awesome *voladores* perform their aerial dance here too. **See p.420**

❺ Catemaco Take a boat trip across this enchanting lake, surrounded by one of the last remaining tracts of jungle in central Mexico, followed by a relaxing *temazcal*, a traditional sauna, or a session with a shaman. **See p.427**

HIGHLIGHTS ARE MARKED ON THE MAP ON P.394

Veracruz

VILLA RICA DE LA VERACRUZ was the first town founded by the Spanish in Mexico, a few days after Cortés' arrival on Good Friday, 1519. Though today's city occupies the area of coast where he first came ashore, made camp and encountered Aztec emissaries, the earliest development – little more than a wooden stockade – was in fact established some way to the north (see p.416) before being moved to La Antigua (see p.416) and finally arriving at its present site in 1589. The modern city is very much the heir of the original; still the largest port on the Gulf coast, its history reflects every major event from the Conquest onwards. "Veracruz," states author Paul Theroux, "is known as the 'heroic city'. It is a poignant description: in Mexico a hero is nearly always a corpse."

Your first, and lasting, impression of Veracruz, however, will not be of its historical significance but of its present-day vitality. Its dynamic zócalo, pleasant waterfront location and relative absence of tourists make the city one of the most enjoyable places

VERACRUZ

HIGHLIGHTS
1. Veracruz
2. Xalapa
3. Whitewater rafting
4. El Tajín
5. Catemaco

in the Republic in which to sit back and observe – or join – the daily round. This is especially true in the evenings, when the tables under the *portales* of the plaza fill up and the drinking and the marimba music begin, to go on late into the evening. **Marimba** – a distinctively Latin-Caribbean sound based around a giant wooden xylophone – is *the* local sound, but at peak times there are also mariachi and *norteño* bands and individual crooners all striving to be heard over each other. When the municipal band strikes up from the middle of the square, confusion is total. Veracruz's riotous nine-day **Carnaval** celebrations (held in February) rival the best in the world, while the **Festival Internacional Afrocaribeño**, usually held in July or August, showcases dance, film, music and art from all over the Caribbean and Africa.

6

Brief history

Throughout the sixteenth and seventeenth centuries, Veracruz and the Spanish galleons that used the port were preyed on constantly by the English, Dutch and French. In the **War of Independence** the Spanish made their final stand here, holding the fortress of San Juan Ulúa for four years after the country had been lost. In **1838** the French occupied the city, in what was later dubbed "The Pastry War", demanding compensation for French property and citizens who had suffered in the years following Independence; in **1847** US troops took Veracruz, and from here marched on to capture the capital. In January **1862** the French, supported by Spanish and English forces that soon withdrew, invaded on the pretext of forcing Mexico to pay her foreign debt, but ended up staying five years and setting up the unfortunate Maximilian as emperor. Finally, in **1914**, US marines were back, occupying the city to protect American interests during the Revolution. These are the "Cuatro Veces Heroica" of the city's official title, and form the bulk of the history displayed in the museums here.

The zócalo

Fototeca de Veracruz • Tues–Sun 9am–3pm & 4–7pm • Free

The attractive **zócalo** is the heart of life in Veracruz in every sense – the place where everyone gathers, for morning coffee, lunch, afternoon strolls and at night. After dark, especially, it has an extraordinary energy, with tables set out under the *portales*, nonstop music and strolling crowds. The imposing **Catedral de Nuestra Señora de Asunción**, consecrated in 1721, dominates the square. Its most striking features are its solid, whitewashed exterior and tiled dome; inside, there's little to see other than endless restoration works. On the plaza too is the elegant **Palacio Municipal**, one of the oldest in Mexico, originally built between 1609 and 1627, though it assumed its current form in the eighteenth century. The **Fototeca de Veracruz**, alongside, hosts beautifully presented photography exhibitions.

The malecón

The harbourfront promenade, the **malecón**, begins just a couple of blocks from the zócalo, past a stupendously tacky Mercado de Artesanías. This is a worthwhile stroll at any time of day or night – evenings are particularly animated as street vendors and entertainers compete for your attention, illuminated by the twinkling lights of the ships in the port and the spotlit "dancing" fountains outside the PEMEX building. *Tranvía* city tours start from here, and *lanchas* depart for harbour jaunts (see p.399).

Castillo de San Juan de Ulúa

Northern end of the harbour • Tues–Sun 9am–4.30pm • M$52 • At weekends and in high season, *lanchas* cross the harbour to the castle (around M$35); otherwise the easiest way to get here is to take a taxi (around M$50) – you may have to queue for a ride back

The **Castillo de San Juan de Ulúa** appears impregnable when viewed from across the

6

VERACRUZ AND BOCA DEL RÌO

To Toll Highway, Xalapa & North

Castillo de San Juan de Ulúa

N

0   kilometre   1

To Toll Highway, Xalapa & North

Airport, Xalapa & Mexico City

Toll Highway, Mexico City & South

Acuario

Bus Stations

Mundo Villa Submarino

Gulf of Mexico

Isla Pajaros

Isla de Sacrificios

Playa Villa Del Mar

FOR DETAIL SEE "CENTRAL VERACRUZ" MAP

Laguna Real

Plaza Las Americas

Playa de Oro

Playa de Mocambo

Gulf of Mexico

Reserva Natural Estatal Arroyo Moreno

BOCA DEL RÌO

Río Jamapa

■ **DRINKING & NIGHTLIFE**
Classico del Puerto   2
El Muelle del Bule   1

■ **ACCOMMODATION**
Bello   1
Fiesta Americana   2
Hotel Indigo   3
Mocambo   4

● **EATING**
El Cacharrito   1
Gran Café de la Parroquia   2
Las Piragüas   4
El Recreo   3

harbour it repeatedly failed to protect. In most cases, this failure was hardly the fault of the fortress or its defenders: any sensible invader simply landed somewhere on the coast nearby, captured the city and, having cut San Juan off by land and sea, called for its surrender. Today the fortress, originally an island, now connected to the mainland by a causeway, is mostly an empty ruin of endless battlements and stairways. Apart from a small **museum**, the main attraction is the **prison** – many political prisoners died during the rule of Díaz in three dark, unpleasant cells known as El Purgatorio, La Gloria and El Infierno (Purgatory, Heaven and Hell).

6

Museo Histórico Naval

Arista 418 • Tues–Sun 10am–5pm • M$30 • Labelling in Spanish only

Fans of naval history and of model ships will enjoy the **Museo Histórico Naval**, a romp through Mexican naval history from the Olmec period to the modern day, with plenty on the various heroic defenders of the city. There's a dramatic scale model of Cortéss' battle with the Aztecs on Lago de Texcoco in 1521, and an entire room dedicated to the events of 1914, when US troops occupied Veracruz and Venustiano Carranza subsequently established his Constitutionalist government here.

Baluarte de Santiago

Francisco Canal between 16 de Septiembre & Gómez Farías • Tues–Sun 10am–4.30pm • Museum M$52 (free on Sun), fortifications free

The blackened and threatening walls of the **Baluarte de Santiago** make a bizarre sight, stranded as they are three blocks from the sea, with the cannon threatening only the passing traffic. The sole survivor of what were originally nine forts along a 2650m-long wall, the Baluarte was built in 1635 to help fend off constant attacks by pirates and buccaneers; at the time, it stood at the water's edge. The small museum inside has a few pieces of exquisite pre-Columbian gold jewellery discovered in 1976 by a local octopus fisherman. By the time the authorities got wind of his find, most of it had been melted down and sold, but what little remains is lovely.

Museo de la Ciudad

Zaragoza 397 • Tues–Sun 10am–5pm • Free

Exhibits in the **Museo de la Ciudad**, which occupies a former nineteenth-century orphanage about five blocks south of the zócalo, cover local history and folklore from the city's earliest inhabitants to the 1950s. Inevitably, given the scope of material covered, it's a potted version, and many of the exhibits go completely unexplained, but there's some beautiful Olmec and Totonac sculpture, including one giant Olmec head; thought-provoking information on Mexico's African population, much of which was concentrated in this area after the slave trade; and enlightening sections on modern society.

Cultural centres

Instituto Veracruzano de Cultura Mon–Fri 9am–8pm, Sat & Sun 10am–6pm • Free • **Las Atarazanas** J. S. Montero s/n • Daily 9am–3pm & 4–6pm • Free • **Casa Principal** Mario Molina 315 • same hours as Las Atarazanas • Free

Veracruz's municipal government sponsors numerous cultural centres across the city, chief among them the **Instituto Veracruzano de Cultura**, occupying an old convent building on Francisco Canal, at the corner of Zaragoza. As well as regularly changing art exhibitions in its galleries, other rooms off the courtyard house classes and events, and you can also pick up information about cultural happenings across the city. Just a block away, **Las Atarazanas** were colonial warehouses that once backed onto the harbour; inside are more temporary exhibition spaces. More exhibits are generally held at the **Casa Principal**, a fine, converted eighteenth-century residence.

6

Acuario and the beaches

Acuario de Veracruz • Mon–Thurs 9am–7pm, Fri–Sun 9am–7.30pm • M$120, children M$65 • ⓦ acuariodeveracruz.com

You wouldn't make a special trip to Veracruz for its **beaches**, but for an afternoon's escape to the sea, they can be very enjoyable. Strips of sand hug the coast for some 12km southeast of the centre, linked together by Bulevar María Ávila Camacho, which runs all the way to Boca del Río. For the most part this is not attractive, with concrete strip development all the way, and a six-lane highway right behind the beach, but it is where much of the city's modern life is concentrated. About halfway to Boca, Avenida Ruíz Cortines cuts inland, taking a short cut away from the beach: here is some of the city's most recent development, including vast shopping malls like the Plaza las Americas, and many of the biggest, newest hotels.

Swimmable beaches start a couple of kilometres from the centre, just beyond the Plaza Acuario shopping centre, home of the **Acuario de Veracruz**, a modern aquarium with some large ocean fish. This first section is the **Playa Villa del Mar**. The water here is not the cleanest, but it's popular with locals who frequent the many beachside palapa restaurants (for outrageously overpriced seafood), and there are boat trips to Cancuncito and the **Isla de Sacrificios**, more or less directly offshore. More attractive strands are further south, in particular in the area where Ávila Camacho and Ruíz Cortines join up again. Here **Playa Mocambo** is one of the best strips of sand, helped by the fact that the main road is for once not right alongside: there are plenty of beach bars, and a small water park with slides. It's also relatively easy to get to, as all the buses come past – get out at the *Hotel Mocambo*.

CENTRAL VERACRUZ

◼ DRINKING AND NIGHTLIFE	
Bar Palacio	1

◼ EATING	
Bola de Oro	9
El Cochinito de Oro	7
La Fonda de las Gordas	4
La Gaviota	6
Gran Café de la Parroquia	2
Gran Café del Portal	5
Nieves Güero-Güero	1
Samborcito	10
Sanborns	3
Tai Li	8

◼ SHOPPING	
Libros y Arte	3
Mercado de Artesenías	1
Popularte	2

◼ ACCOMMODATION	
Casa Blanca	7
Colonial	3
Emporio	2
Gran Hotel Diligencias	6
Holiday Inn Centro Histórico	1
Imperial	4
Mar y Tierra	9
Meson del Mar	8
Ruíz Milán	5

0   200
metres

Boca del Río

Boca del Río lends its name to the whole southern half of this coast, but it's actually a small town in its own right, ten minutes or so beyond Mocambo by bus, located, as the name suggests, at the mouth of the Río Jamapa. There are more long, grey-sand beaches here, but the main attraction is the river. A string of small restaurants lines the riverfront in town, all offering seafood at competitive prices. You can also take trips upstream: a *lancha* costs about M$300 an hour, or at busy times you should be able to join a tour for around M$50 per person.

6

ARRIVAL AND DEPARTURE

BY PLANE

Veracruz International Airport is about 10km south of the city; there are ATMs and car-rental desks. Taxis between here and the centre cost M$250; buy a ticket from the taxi desk in the terminal.

Destinations AeroMéxico (🖥 aeromexico.com), InterJet (🖥 interjet.com.mx) and Vivaaerobus (🖥 vivaaerobus.com) between them offer at least ten direct flights a day to Mexico City, and one or more a day to Cancún, Guadalajara, Monterrey and Villahermosa. International flights to Houston (daily) and Dallas (two or more weekly) are operated by United (🖥 united.com) and American Airlines (🖥 aa.com) respectively.

BY BUS

The ADO first-class bus station is about 3km from the centre at Díaz Mirón 1698, with the AU second-class terminal right behind it facing Lafragua. To reach the centre, buy a ticket for a taxi (M$30) from the booth on the south side of the first-class terminal (left as you exit). To take a local bus,

walk to the stop on Díaz Mirón to the right as you exit, and take any – most will have "Díaz Mirón" or "Centro" on the windscreen. They mostly end up on Independencia as it runs past the zócalo. Tickets can be bought downtown at the Ticket Bus booth, inside the Farmacia del Ahorro on Independencia at Mario Molina.

Destinations Cancún (3 first class daily; 20hr); Cardel (frequently, mainly second; 30min); Catemaco (12 first class daily, very frequent second; 3hr 30min); Coatzacoalcos (11 first class daily, very frequent second; 5hr 30min); Córdoba (very frequently, first & second; 1hr 45min); Mexico City (25 first class, 12 second daily; 5hr 30min); Oaxaca (5 first class, 2 second daily; 7hr); Orizaba (very frequently, first & second; 2hr 20min); Papantla (6 first class daily, 16 second; 4hr); Puebla (6 first class daily, 14 second; 3hr 30min); San Andrés Tuxtla (12 first class daily, very frequent second; 3hr); Tuxpán (15 first class daily, 16 second; 5hr 30min); Villahermosa (10 first class daily; 7hr); Xalapa (constantly first & second; 2hr).

INFORMATION AND TOURS

City tours mostly depart from the malecón, where you'll find traditional *tranvías* – buses done up to look like old trolley-cars – along with various rival tour buses. They leave every half-hour or so for a 45–60min tour of the old town (M$60, children M$40); and it's especially fun at night, when the *tranvías* are lit up.

Bus and boat tours There are also bus tours down to Boca del Río (same price) and boat trips around the harbour

(M$80; ☎ 229 935 9417, 🖥 asdic.com.mx). All of these are more frequent at weekends and in high season, and busier in the late afternoon and evening.

Harbour tour There are plenty of other opportunities to take to the water in Veracruz. Asdic, which runs the harbour tours, also offers evening sailings in its disco catamaran; and from a base on the beach by Plaza Acuario it sails around the Isla de los Sacrificios (now a nature reserve) to

---

WATERSPORTS

There's remarkably good **diving** at pretty good rates on a large number of little-visited reefs and beaches within the **Parque Nacional Sistema Arrecifal Veracruzano**. Try Mundo Submarino (☎ 229 980 6374, 🖥 mundosubmarino.com.mx), Ávila Camacho 3549; Tridente (☎ 229 260 5272, ✉ tridente_ver@hotmail.com), Ávila Camacho 353; or Scubaver (☎ 229 932 3994, 🖥 scubaver.net), Hernandez y Hernandez 563.

For more adventurous tours further afield, above all **whitewater rafting** (mostly at Jalcomulco, see box, p.414), but also canyoning, rappelling and the like, try Amphibian (Lerdo 117, in the *Hotel Colonial* ☎ 229 931 0997, 🖥 amphibianveracruz.com); Aventura Extrema (Sanchez Tagle 973 ☎ 229 202 6557, 🖥 aventuraextrema.com.mx); or Mexico Verde (☎ 01 800 362 8800, 🖥 mexicoverde.com).

6

Cancuncito, a semi-submerged sandbar in the bay where you can disembark and swim in beautifully clear seas (M$140). Banana boats and jet-skis are also available here.

GETTING AROUND

By bus Although Veracruz is a large and rambling city, the *centro histórico* is relatively small and easy to navigate – anywhere further afield can be reached by local bus from somewhere very near the zócalo. All trips within the city (and as far as Boca del Río) are M$9, including the newer, a/c express buses, often (but not always) painted yellow. Buses for the beaches (marked "Boca del Río", "Playas" or "Mocambo") pass along Zaragoza close to the zócalo. Most take the quick route via Ruíz Cortines; for the scenic route along the coastal road take buses marked "Penacho" or join the open-air tour buses from the malecón (see p.395).

By taxi Taxis are easily found on the street, charge according to a zone system and are pretty honest – trips in the centre will cost you about M$25, to the bus station M$30 and to Boca M$50. If your hotel calls for one it will be more expensive (M$50 and up), though this is generally a safer option at night.

Car rental Europcar, Hertz and Dollar have offices at the airport and in the hotel zone; Kanguro is a local operator with airport and downtown branches (ⓦkangurorental .com).

INFORMATION

Tourist information The tourist office, on the ground floor of the Palacio Municipal (daily 9am–9pm; ☎229 989 8817, ⓦdisfrutaveracruz.mx), has basic information and helpful staff on hand, though not always English-speakers.

ACCOMMODATION

There are **hotels** right next to the first-class bus station, and several very cheap and rather grim places around the back of the second-class terminal, but unless you've arrived late at night or face a very early departure, there's no point staying this far out. The other inexpensive places are mostly within a couple of blocks of the zócalo; they're nothing to write home about, and often noisy, but at least you should find a clean room with a fan. The best deals in the city are in the **mid-range**, and there are some decent hotels along the malecón within walking distance of the zócalo. If you want more luxury, head to the **beach**, where resort-style hotels form an ever-expanding hotel zone. Most of the year prices are very reasonable – and negotiable – but they double or triple for Carnaval and Semana Santa, and are also inflated at other Mexican holiday times, especially in August.

CITY CENTRE

Casa Blanca Trigueros 49 ☎229 200 4625. The pick of the budget places near the centre, with tiny but comfortable rooms facing onto a pretty tiled courtyard. Simply furnished, but clean and quiet; some rooms have a/c. M$450

Colonial Miguel Lerdo 117 ☎229 932 0193, ⓦhcolonial.com.mx. Ageing option on the zócalo, with a swimming pool, garage (extra) and a/c. Some rooms have been refurbished, including the priciest, which have great views over the square; others are in desperate need of a makeover. M$1000

Emporio Paseo del Malecón 244 ☎229 932 2222, ⓦhotelesemporio.com/veracruz. Classily modernized high-rise seafront hotel with elegant designer furnishings, three pools, gym, spa and good restaurants. Rooms ending in nine have uninterrupted sea vistas, and most have some view of the harbour. Big reductions out of season. M$2200

Gran Hotel Diligencias Independencia 1115 ☎229 923 0280, ⓦgranhoteldiligencias.com. The most modern, and best, of the hotels on the zócalo, elegantly refurbished with cable TV and wi-fi in the rooms, plus most other facilities and a pool on a terrace overlooking the action in the square. M$1400

★**Holiday Inn Centro Histórico** Morelos 225 ☎229 932 4550, ⓦholidayinn.com. Charming hotel built out of the renovated half of the nineteenth-century Faro Benito Juárez, with all the modern conveniences and a pretty pool enclosed by a courtyard embellished with elegant tiling. Look out for bargain deals online. M$1400

Imperial Miguel Lerdo 153 ☎229 955 0749, ⓦhotelimperialveracruz.com. If faded glory is your thing, you'll love the *Imperial*, an eighteenth-century building whose once magnificent public areas boast marble floors, a striking stained-glass ceiling and the first lift installed in Mexico (still going strong). Plans are in place to elevate the space from a dusty old pile into a five-star resort (the building's incredible bones will remain intact) – construction should be completed by 2016. M$900

Mar y Tierra Ávila Camacho at Figueroa ☎229 931 3866, ⓦhotelmarytierra.com. Mid-priced seafront option, a 15–20min walk from the zócalo. A/c rooms in the old section are much smaller, so it's worth the extra for a newer room: both sections have many rooms with sea views at no extra cost. M$570

Meson del Mar Ávila Esteban Morales 543 ☎229 932 5043, ⓦmesondelmar.com.mx. Beautiful eighteenth-century colonial building with high ceilings and bright guestrooms in a number of configurations (some rooms even sleep six). It's decorated with wonderfully carved wooden headboards and tiled blue birds in the bathroom. Each room is unique; ask to view one before you commit. Wi-fi in lobby only. **M$825**

Ruíz Milán Paseo del Malecón ☏229 932 6707, ⊛ruizmilan.com. Not quite as fancy as the facade and public areas might lead you to believe, this is nonetheless a comfortable, business-style hotel in a great location. Three grades of room – the best are at the front – all with a/c and cable TV, plus a small indoor pool and hot tub, and a solid restaurant serving signature Veracruz dishes. **M$800**

ACUARIO TO BOCA DEL RÍO

Bello Ruíz Cortines 258 ☏229 922 4828, ⊛hotelbello .com. The ten-storey *Bello* is among the cheaper modern options in one of the busiest restaurant and nightlife areas, hence often fully booked. There's a courtyard pool, and rooms are business-like and comfortable: those on the upper floors at the back have views to the sea, a couple of blocks away. Big low-season reductions. **M$1000**

Fiesta Americana Ávila Camacho ☏229 989 8989, ⊛fiestaamericana.com. Dominating the Playa de Oro, this massive resort has a giant pool and spacious rooms and balconies, all with sea views. One of the longest-established in the hotel zone, but still among the best, with a great beachfront position. **M$1800**

★**Hotel Indigo** Ruíz Cortines 3533 ☏229 923 5800, ⊛ihg.com. Hip, colourful, contemporary hotel. Guest-rooms have oversized all-white bedframes and furniture in shades of citrus. Updated amenities like complimentary wi-fi and iPod alarm clocks. **M$1800**

Mocambo Ruíz Cortines 4000 at Playa Mocambo ☏229 922 0200, ⊛hotelmocambo.com.mx. Grand old beachside hotel complex built in 1932 with lots of dark wood and a nautical theme. Though rather faded, it's wonderfully atmospheric – you half expect Frank Sinatra to be wandering through the lobby – and facilities include large indoor and outdoor pools, a children's play area, wi-fi and several restaurants, among which is the well-regarded, formal *La Fragata*. **M$1300**

EATING

Despite all the local specialities, it's surprisingly hard to get a decent meal in the centre, especially in the evening. The zócalo is ringed by **bars** and **cafés**, but these are really places to drink, and, though most do serve food, it's generally an overpriced afterthought. There are a number of great places serving local **coffee**. Proper restaurants, though, are relatively scarce: the area around the old market building on Landero y Coss between Serdán and Mariano Arista has a whole series of small and cheap **fish restaurants** and cooked-food stalls, almost all of them lunch time only, but most of the places that are busy in the evening are down in the hotel zone, well south of the centre.

CITY CENTRE

Bola de Oro Mario Molina 240-A. A traditional coffee shop that has had a modern makeover. They still grind and roast their own local coffee and serve it as *café lechero* (see p.402), but they also have frappes, iced cappuccinos, fruit teas, waffles and *pan dulce*. Daily 7am–10pm.

El Cochinito de Oro Zaragoza 190 at Serdán ☏229 932 3677. This friendly, no-frills eatery has been around for 75 years, offering breakfast as well as a selection of seafood dishes for no more than M$110. The menu is translated into English and there are good-value *comidas* (M$50). Mon–Thurs 7am–7pm, Fri & Sat 9am–10pm.

La Fonda de las Gordas Zamora 138 ☏229 931 4300. Handy and inexpensive fast-food style place right on the zócalo; the speciality is *gorditas rellenas*, tortilla pockets with dozens of stuffings to choose from, from just M$13.50; *pollo pibil* is particularly good. Mon–Thurs 9am–9pm, Fri–Sun 9am–10pm.

La Gaviota Trigueros 21 ☏229 932 3950. A useful address for nocturnal revellers, *La Gaviota* is open 24hr and offers a bit of everything on its extensive menu along with a well-stocked bar should you wish to keep the party going; fish or prawn main dishes for around

M$135, five-course lunch-time *comida* for M$185. All day, every day.

Gran Café del Portal Independencia 1187 at Zamora, opposite the cathedral ☏229 931 2759. A local institution, serving great coffee (roasted on the premises) and pricey food (breakfast, 7–11am, and *comidas*, 1–5pm, around M$100, main dishes M$150–200). The cavernous interior has icily effective a/c and free wi-fi; don't expect a tranquil meal if you sit outside – you'll be serenaded by the house marimba band at any time of day, and will probably draw the attention of plenty of street vendors. Daily 6am–12.30am.

Nieves Guëro-Guëro Zamora 15 at Landero y Coss. Fabulous, refreshing ice creams in tropical fruit and nut flavours; more similar to Italian *gelati* than to the creamy US variety. One of three rival operators next door to each other here (don't be swayed by the sleeker, cleaner and confusingly named Guëro-Guëra, across the street), this little window boasts the richest flavours, served in styrofoam cups. Daily till around 11pm.

Samborcito 16 de Septiembre 727 ☏229 931 4388. Large, no-nonsense local favourite with fans twirling under a palapa roof. A bit of a walk from the centre in an area that feels like a Caribbean shantytown, but worth it for the

6

COMIDA Y CERVEZA, A LA VERACRUZANA

Veracruz offers up some fabulous **food** – the state's coffee, fruit and vanilla are renowned, and the seafood is also superb. *Huachinango a la Veracruzana* (red snapper Veracruz-style) is served across the country, and is of course on every menu here; the Veracruzana sauce of tomato, chile, onions and olives can also spice up anything from steak to squid. Other local specialities include *pulpos a la marinera* (baby octopus), *arroz a la tumbada* (Veracruz-style rice, packed with seafood), *empanadas de camaron* (shrimp turnovers) and *jaiba*, a large local crab; look out too for anything made with *chile chipotle*, a hot, dark-brown chile with a very distinctive (and delicious) flavour – *chilpachole de jaiba* is a sort of crab chowder that combines the two. Sweet tamales, too, are a speciality, and to wash it all down, the brewery at Orizaba produces some of the best beers in the country. Stronger liquors include the mind-wiping *toritos*, made with fruits and blended with condensed milk and a tot of brandy.

picadas (thick tortillas with cheese), tamales and other delicious Veracruz dishes. Mon–Fri 7am–8pm, Sat & Sun 7am–9pm.

Sanborns Independencia 1069, at Miguel Lerdo ☎ 229 931 0088. The Veracruz branch of the national department store and restaurant chain. Food ranges from Mexican snacks to filet mignon, served in an a/c dining room or the cosier adjoining café. Hearty breakfasts from M$90–150. Mon–Fri 7am–11pm, Sat & Sun 7am–1am.

Tai Li Mario Molina 168, cnr Tlapacoyan; no phone. If you're looking for something different, try the extensive Chinese buffet (M$95) at *Tai Li*. They also serve a full Chinese menu. Daily 11am–9.30pm.

ACUARIO TO BOCA DEL RÍO

El Cacharrito Ruíz Cortines 15, next to Hotel Lois ☎ 229 935 7288. Formal Argentine restaurant in the hotel zone, serving fabulous steaks (M$250–400) and Argentine wines; the elegant first-floor dining room, with backlit bar and open kitchen behind glass, is an oasis of calm amid the traffic madness. With wine and three courses, it's easy to spend M$650 a head. Daily 2–11pm.

★ **Gran Café de la Parroquia** Gómez Farías 34 on the malecón ☎ 229 937 2584, and Ruíz Cortines 1815 ☎ 229 130 0200. A Veracruz institution that claims to have been going for two hundred years. *Café lechero* is the speciality – effectively a latte; you are brought a glass with black coffee, chink the glass with a spoon and another waiter arrives bearing a kettle of milk, which he adds from a great height. They serve breakfast and full meals too (around M$100 for a main). The new hotel-zone branch is equally large, and if anything even busier. Daily 7am–midnight.

Las Piragüas Riverfront boulevard at Revolución 102, Boca del Río ☎ 229 986 2889. Close to the bridge and Palacio Municipal on the Boca del Río waterfront, *Piragüas* serves excellent fish *comidas* for around M$90, or the speciality *piña* or *coco relleno de mariscos* (pineapple or coconut stuffed with seafood) at M$145. Daily all day.

El Recreo Revolución 402, Boca del Río ☎ 229 986 1145. An excellent local restaurant on the plaza in Boca del Río. Inexpensive breakfasts (around M$40), *café lechero*, handmade tortillas and gorditas, and fresh local seafood explain why this big place is always bustling. Daily 7.30am–midnight.

DRINKING AND NIGHTLIFE

An evening spent at an outdoor table under the *portales* on the **zócalo** is entertainment in itself, as mariachi, marimba and *norteño* bands compete for your attention with street vendors, fortune-tellers and uniformed nurses offering to take your blood pressure. Most evenings around 7pm the municipal band or a folkloric dance troupe strikes up from the bandstand, and local couples dance *danzón* across the square, adding to the general madness. The municipality often organizes **outdoor musical performances** elsewhere in the centre of Veracruz, too, on the otherwise quiet Plazuela de la Lagunilla, for example. **Bars** and most of the best places for **dancing**, however, are generally out of the centre, on the coast road or in the commercial strip along Ruíz Cortines. As ever, **clubs** change pretty rapidly, but many of the bigger ones are close to the junction of Ruíz Cortines and Ávila Camacho.

CITY CENTRE

Bar Palacio Miguel Lerdo on the zócalo. Along with its neighbours, *Flamingos* and *Prendes*, this is the place to take

in the zócalo action over a beer or traditional mint julep, prepared with dark rum, dry sherry, vermouth, sugar and mint. Daily 10am–late.

ACUARIO TO BOCA DEL RÍO

Classico del Puerto Ávila Camacho at Médico Militar in the hotel zone ☎ 229 130 2545. Salsa and hot Latin sounds, with a Cuban orchestra and exuberant dance shows (M$100 cover). Thurs–Sat from 10pm.

El Muelle del Bule Ávila Oviedo 101, on the waterfront ☎ 229 263 1645. Tropical themed bar-restaurant with a palapa-covered terrace overlooking the Isla de Sacrificios, lively in the evenings and at weekends. Plenty of 2-for-1 promos in the early evening, and good-value seafood at lunch time, including a weekday *comida* (M$89) and weekend buffet (M$175, Fri–Sun 2–5pm). Tues–Sun 1pm–late.

SHOPPING

6

Coffee, vanilla and cigars are the souvenirs most Mexicans take home from Veracruz, and all of these (along with necklaces and lottery tickets) will be brought to you by a string of vendors if you sit down even for a minute anywhere around the zócalo.

Libros y Arte Callejón Portal de Miranda 9, just off the zócalo beside the Fototeca. Classy bookshop that also sells a small selection of high-class artesanía and CDs of local and world music. Lots of glossy volumes on art and architecture (almost all in Spanish), plus a few guides and maps and a noticeboard of alternative events. Mon–Sat 10am–7pm.

Mercado de Artesanías Landero y Coss, cnr Paseo del Malecón. Fabulously kitsch souvenirs, shells, cheap T-shirts and almost anything else you can think of on offer at dozens of stalls. Daily 11am–7pm.

Popularte Upstairs at Mario Molina 23, cnr Landero y Coss, opposite the Mercado de Artesanías. State-run shop with high-quality (and high-priced) furniture, clothing, ceramics and jewellery. No sales pressure. Tues–Sun 10am–7pm.

DIRECTORY

Banks and exchange Branches of all the main banks, where you can change travellers' cheques and find ATM machines, are around the junction of Independencia and Benito Juárez.

Hospitals The big hospitals are mainly south of the centre towards the bus station, including Hospital General ISSSTE on Díaz Mirón (☎ 229 932 3690); Hospital Español is more central at 16 de Septiembre 955 (☎ 229 262 2300). Call ☎ 060 for an ambulance.

Internet There are a plenty of internet cafés scattered around the centre, including Copy-on, Molina 122, one at Miguel Lerdo 317 just west of 5 de Mayo, and two on Mariano Arista between Independencia and Clavijero.

Laundry Friendly, nameless lavandería at 16 de Septiembre 670, beyond Manuel Doblado (Mon–Fri 9am–7pm, Sat 9am–5pm; M$11/kg).

Left luggage Guarderías can be found in both bus stations.

Pharmacies They're everywhere. Handiest is the Farmacía del Ahorro just off the zócalo by the *Gran Café del Portal* on Independencia at Mario Molina. Farmacia ISSSTE is in the Super ISSSTE supermarket, on 16 de Septiembre between Mariano Arista and Morales.

Police ☎ 229 938 0664 or emergency ☎ 066.

Post office On the Plaza de la República (Mon–Fri 8am–7pm, Sat 9am–5pm).

Sierra Madre Oriental

If you take the direct route **from Mexico City** to Veracruz – the scenic Hwy-150 – you'll bypass every major town en route; if you're driving yourself, note that the tolls along this stretch of road are extremely high (over M$450). For those pressed for time, the fast highway is a blessing – Veracruz and the coast are very much the outstanding attractions – but the cities in the mountains merit a stop if you have room in your itinerary. Regardless of how fast you go or what form of transport you take, the journey over the **Sierra Madre Oriental** is one of the most beautiful in Mexico: as Ixtaccíhuatl gradually disappears behind you, the snow on the **Pico de Orizaba** comes into view, and the plains of corn and maguey in the west are supplanted on the eastern slopes by woods of pine and cypress, and by green fields dotted with contented cows out to pasture.

It's worth noting, however, that this is the rainiest area of the country, and while the damp brings bounties in terms of great coffee and a luxuriance of flowers, downpours can become a problem. Particularly irritating – especially in October and November – is what the locals call *chipichipi*, a persistent fine drizzle caused by warm airstreams from the Gulf hitting cooler air as they reach the eastern face of the sierra. Drivers should also watch out for the fog that frequently cloaks the higher sections of this road.

Orizaba

Midway between Puebla and Veracruz, **ORIZABA** is an industrial city and a major brewing centre: the giant Cervecería Cuauhtémoc Moctezuma produces some of the best **beer** in the republic, including globally famous brands Sol and Dos Equis – ask at the tourist office (see p.406) for details of tours. Despite the industry, the historic centre remains compact and attractive; because the old city was built up against a hill, development has spread in one direction only, so the *centro histórico* is right on the edge of town, with more modern development sprawling to the east and south. The **Parque Castillo**, with the imposing Catedral de San Miguel at Colón and Madero, marks the centre of the old town. There's not a great deal to see, but Orizaba makes an enjoyable short break or overnight stop; better yet, stay in Córdoba (see p.406), and make a day trip to see Orizaba's sights.

Palacio de Hierro

Madero Nte between Poniente 2 and 4 • Museums daily 9am–7pm • Free

The **Palacio de Hierro**, on the main square opposite the cathedral, is an extraordinary nineteenth-century iron structure, prefabricated in Belgium. It houses not only the **tourist office**, but also no fewer than seven one- or two-room **museums** – all free – including the Museo de la Cerveza (beer museum), Museo del Fútbol (soccer) and, upstairs, the Museo Raíces de Orizaba, a small collection of local archeology. Between them these won't detain you for more than forty minutes, but the building itself is well worth a look.

Cerro del Borrego

Cable-car entrance: on the riverside walk, between Poniente 5 and Colón Poniente • Mon–Fri 9am–6pm, Sat & Sun 9am–7pm • weekdays M$30, weekends M$50 • ⓦ orizaba.travel

Colón Poniente heads west from the plaza towards the looming **Cerro del Borrego**, atop which a vast Mexican flag flies and from where, if you brave the stiff climb, there are fabulous views of the city, as well as a small restaurant, tower and museum. Alternatively, you can zip up in a six-minute cable car; tickets allot you two hours at the top. Along the way, Colón crosses the **Río Orizaba**, where an attractive riverside walk winds beneath the city's many bridges, and continues past the **Palacio Municipal** before ending at the **Alameda**, a shady park beneath the Cerro.

Museo de Arte del Estado

Av Oriente 4 at C 23 Sur • Tues–Sun 9am–6pm • M$10

The 37 works by Diego Rivera housed in Orizaba's **Museo de Arte** constitute one of Mexico's finest collections of this iconic artist. Housed alongside other local art from colonial to contemporary – including many fascinating nineteenth-century portraits and local landscapes – they make this the most worthwhile visit in the city. The restored eighteenth-century Oratorio de San Felipe Neri, which houses the museum, is also an attraction in itself: unfortunately it's a long way out – over a dozen blocks east of the centre.

ARRIVAL AND INFORMATION   ORIZABA

By bus The ADO is on Av Oriente 6 near Sur 11; most second-class services also stop here or nearby. Oriente 6 is

Orizaba's main commercial street, and you'll find big business hotels and numerous restaurants here: head five

FROM TOP PICO DE ORIZABA VOLCANO (P.406); ANTHROPOLOGY MUSEUM, XALAPA (P.409); FISHING NETS ON LAKE CATEMACO (P.427)>

6

PICO DE ORIZABA

Orizaba is situated close to the foot of the loftiest peak in Mexico, the **Pico de Orizaba** (Citlaltépetl), a perfectly formed, snow-capped volcano. There is a fair amount of disagreement over its exact height – 5636m seems the most widely accepted, though locals often claim more – but there's no disputing that it's a beautiful sight and a seriously challenging climb, for experienced mountaineers only. Numerous local companies offer guides and facilities, mostly based in the village of **Tlachichuca**, which at 2600m is where the main trails begin. To get there, take a second-class bus to the small town of Serdán (2hr), where you change for Tlachichuca itself (1hr); there are also occasional buses direct from Puebla. Details of the climb (Oct–May only) can be found in R.J. Secor's *Mexico's Volcanoes*. Reliable operators include Summit Orizaba (☎245 451 5082, ⓦsummitorizaba.com) and Servimont (ⓦservimont.com .mx), both with their own accommodation in Tlachichuca.

blocks west and three north for the Parque Castillo at the heart of the old town.

Destinations Córdoba (very frequently; 45min); Mexico City (very frequently; 4hr 10min); Oaxaca (4 daily; 5hr); Puebla (very frequently; 2hr 5min); Veracruz (26 daily; 2hr 20min); Villahermosa (7 daily; 6hr 30min–9hr); Xalapa (11 daily; 4hr).

Tourist information The helpful tourist office is on the ground floor of the Palacio de Hierro (daily 9am–7pm; ☎272 728 9136, ⓦorizaba.travel).

ACCOMMODATION

Mediterraneo Av Oriente 6 505, cnr Sur 11 ☎272 724 4000. Probably the best-value hotel in this area, right next to the ADO but with well-soundproofed modern rooms, all with a/c and wi-fi. M$550

Misión Hotel Av Oriente 6 464, just up from the ADO on the opposite side of the street ☎272 724 0077, ⓦhotelesmision.com.mx. Pleasant, low-rise, business-style hotel with rooms around a tiled courtyard and good facilities including a small pool and wi-fi. Smart and comfortable. M$1100

Plaza Palacio Poniente 2 no. 2 ☎272 725 9933, ⓔhotelplazapalacio@hotmail.com. Facing the Palacio de Hierro and cathedral across a pedestrianized street, this could hardly have a better location. Rooms are simple, with fan and cable TV, but comfy and quiet. M$400

Posada del Viajero Madero Norte 242 ☎272 726 3320. Decent budget choice with clean but tiny rooms – the cell-like feel is accentuated by very high ceilings – around an internal courtyard. Just half a block from the Palacio de Hierro facing the market. M$249

EATING

There are plenty of **taco stands** in the historic centre and in the market, but surprisingly few places to sit down and eat: the bulk of those are out on Av Oriente 6 and in the more modern areas of town east of the centre. There are some great **cafés** in the centre, though. The daily Mercado Melchor Ocampo is on Madero Norte just off Parque Castillo.

La Braza Av Oriente 6 531 by the ADO ☎272 100 8885. Fast-food style grill that's always busy, day and night; grilled meats the speciality, but there's also a wide menu including breakfast, tacos and a good-value *comida*. Daily 7am–midnight.

Cafeteria Dauzon Colón Poniente 8, cnr Sur 5 ☎272 726 3619. A great café and cake shop that also serves a very good-value lunch-time *comida* (M$45) and sandwiches, to eat in or take away. Daily 8am–9pm.

Gran Cafe de Orizaba Madero Norte, cnr Poniente 2, in the Palacio de Hierro. Wonderful, old-fashioned café with original fittings and a terrace facing the cathedral. Great coffee, but little in the way of food. Daily 9am–10pm.

Mellado Colón Poniente 89, cnr Norte 3 ☎272 725 8966. Seemingly stuck in a time warp, this old-time wood-panelled café serves delicious tortas, above all, but also drinks, ice creams and other light meals. Mon–Sat 9am–5pm.

Córdoba

CÓRDOBA is a busy modern city at the centre of the area's coffee trade, built around a stunning colonial centre. Founded in 1618 by thirty Spanish families – and so also known as the "City of the Thirty Knights" – its main claim to fame is that in 1821 the last Spanish viceroy, Juan O'Donoju, signed the **Treaty of Córdoba** with General Iturbide here, formally giving Mexico independence.

The city is easy to navigate: Avenida 1 and Calle 1 intersect at the Palacio Municipal on the Plaza 21 de Mayo: avenidas run east–west, with even numbers north of the zócalo and odd numbers south. Calles run north–south, with even numbers west of the zócalo and odd numbers east.

Plaza 21 de Mayo

There's not a great deal specifically to seek out in Córdoba, where the animated zócalo, surrounded by arcaded *portales*, is the main focus. The signing of the Treaty of Córdoba took place in the Palacio de los Condes de Zevallos, now known as the **Portal de Zevallos**, on the **Plaza 21 de Mayo**; these days it's given over to handicraft shops and cafés, where you can sit and sample Córdoban coffee or julep, a rum and mint cocktail. The twin-towered **Catedral de la Inmaculada Concepción**, facing the Palacio Municipal across the plaza, is one of the most richly adorned religious buildings in the state – started in 1621, it contains a revered statue of the Virgin Mary to the right of the altar.

Museo de la Ciudad

C 3 between avenidas 3 and 5, half a block off the zócalo • Tues–Sun 9am–6pm • M$10

The exhibits in the **Museo de la Ciudad** (labelled in Spanish only) encompass some thirty centuries of local history, from Olmec and Totonac ceramics and sculpture, through Independence, to mementos of the Mexico '68 Olympics. They occupy a beautiful colonial building with gorgeous mountain views from its upper storey.

ARRIVAL AND INFORMATION CÓRDOBA

By bus The bus terminal (for first- and second-class services) is 3km south of the centre at Privada 4 between calles 39 and 41, a short taxi ride to the zócalo (buy a ticket first; M$25), or hop on a local bus marked "Centro". For Orizaba, you'll find local buses on Av 2.

Tourist information The tourist office (daily 9am–7pm; ☎ 271 717 1778, ⓦ cordoba.gob.mx) is in the Palacio Municipal.

ACCOMMODATION

Most of the big modern **hotels**, along with fast-food and fancier restaurants, are some way north of the centre on the old highway.

Bello C 5 #319 at Av 2 ☎ 271 712 8122, ⓦ hotelbello .com/cordoba. A mid-market business-style hotel with parking and a coffee shop, modern and efficient if a little characterless; a/c, cable TV and wi-fi in the rooms, some with nice mountain views. M$650

Iberia Av 2 919 ☎ 271 712 1301. Budget hotel that's much better than the exterior and location might lead you to expect. Well-kept rooms with hot water, TV and wi-fi (plus a/c for a small supplement) around a pleasant internal courtyard. M$215

★**Mansur** Av 1 301, cnr of C 3 ☎ 271 712 6000, ⓦ hotel mansur.com. Characterful central hotel with huge communal terraces overlooking the cathedral; the tempting-looking rooms at the front can be noisy. A/c, TV and wi-fi. M$500

EATING

Los 30's Av 9 2004 between calles 20 and 22 ☎ 271 712 3379. Huge and popular café in the restaurant zone near the highway. It's best known for delicious savoury crêpes, but they also serve steaks and a full Mexican-Mediterranean menu. Daily noon–midnight.

Las Delicias Av 2 307 between calles 3 and 5 ☎ 271 714 9494. Large restaurant that's a welcome escape from the raucous street in front, especially in the quieter upstairs room; a good bet for breakfast (M$75) or tasty inexpensive *comidas* (M$90). Daily 7.30am–11pm.

Mi Kasa Av 5 212-A between calles 2 and 4 ☎ 271 712 7613. For a break from Mexican food, try the sushi and other Japanese specialities at this friendly little restaurant in an area that's lively at night. Sushi roll prices range from M$55–85. Mon–Thurs & Sun 1–10pm, Fri & Sat 1–11pm.

El Patio de la Abuela C1 208, between avenidas 2 and 4 ☎ 271 712 0606. A pretty place, with a tranquil courtyard and family photos on the wall, *El Patio* serves good-value breakfasts (M$55) and traditional Mexican fare (mains from M$65). Look out for the daily special. Daily 8am–midnight.

El Tabachin Portal de Zevallos ☎ 271 712 1853. The best location in town, for an upmarket restaurant serving steaks and more traditional Mexican food, though you can also just dawdle over a drink. Alongside is the rival *Cafe La Parroquia*, equally enjoyable. Daily 8am–1am.

Xalapa and around

The capital of the state of Veracruz, **XALAPA** is a big city, remarkably attractive despite its relative modernity and traffic-laden streets. Set in countryside of sometimes breathtaking beauty, sprawling across a hillside below the volcanic peak of the **Cofre de Perote** (4282m), it enjoys views to the snowcapped Pico de Orizaba and a warm, damp climate that encourages rich, jungly vegetation. In addition to these natural advantages, Xalapa has been promoted by its civic leaders as a **cultural centre**, with a classical and traditional music festival in June, an international jazz gathering in August and a major literary festival in September, as well as many lesser events year-round. Home, too, of the **University of Veracruz** and the exceptional **Museo de Antropología**, it's a lively place, enjoyable even if you simply hang out in one of the many cafés in the centre of town, sip the locally grown coffee and watch life pass by. For adrenaline junkies and lovers of nature there's much more, though, as Xalapa is also close to numerous rivers: as they crash down from the high sierra to the coast, these create numerous spectacular **waterfalls** and some of Mexico's finest opportunities for **whitewater rafting** and kayaking.

Parque Juárez

Xalapa's appealing colonial downtown is centred on the **Parque Juárez**, its trees filled with raucous birds at dusk. There are stunning mountain views towards the Cofre de Perote from the south side of the plaza, where the land drops away steeply. The **Palacio de Gobierno**, on the east side, has interesting murals by Mexican artist Melchor Peredo.

Agorá de la Ciudad

Parque Juárez • Tues–Sun 10am–7pm • Free • ⓦ agora.xalapa.net

A cultural centre built into the southern edge of the plaza, the **Agorá de la Ciudad** attracts Xalapa's contemporary arts crowd to well-curated, revolving exhibitions and events. As well as the art spaces, there's an auditorium hosting movies and concerts, usually free of charge.

Pinacoteca Diego Rivera

Herrera 5 • Tues–Sun 10am–7pm • Free

Beneath the western edge of the Parque Juárez, the **Pinacoteca Diego Rivera** showcases some interesting temporary exhibitions in its modern galleries. Though it's named after Diego Rivera, none of his works is on display.

Museo Casa de Xalapa (MUXA)

Herrera 7 • Tues–Sun 10am–7pm • Free

The **Museo Casa de Xalapa** (MUXA) occupies a lovely eighteenth-century colonial home in whose rooms a small, modern museum of local history (lots of interactivity, but mainly in Spanish) has been installed.

Catedral Metropolitana de la Inmaculada Concepción

Enríques, cnr Revolución, on the Parque Lerdo

From the outside, the most striking thing about Xalapa's eighteenth-century **cathedral** is that it only has one tower – the other was never completed. Inside there's a richly decorated nave, a striking Calvary at the altar and a chapel dedicated to Rafael Guízar y Valencia (1878–1938), who was canonized as **St Rafael Guízar** in 2006 – the first bishop born in the Americas to receive the honour. He is most admired for resisting the state's persecution of the Church in the 1920s and 1930s, forming a "guerrilla ministry" and later becoming the bishop of Veracruz.

Museo de Antropología

Av Xalapa, about 3km north of the centre • Tues–Sun 10am–5pm • M$50, audioguide M$23 • ⓦ uv.mx/max • Bus marked "Av Xalapa" from Camacho, on the northwest corner of the Parque Juárez, or taxi (M$25).

Beyond question Xalapa's outstanding sight, the **Museo de Antropología** is a brilliant museum with arguably the best archeological collection in the country after that in Mexico City. Remarkable in both scope and quality, it makes for a wonderful introduction to the various pre-Hispanic cultures of the Gulf coast. The vast building itself is also magnificent, flowing down the hillside in a series of concrete and marble steps. Start your visit at the top of the hill, where the first halls deal with the **Olmecs**. There are several of the celebrated colossal stone heads, a vast array of other statuary and some beautiful masks; among the most impressive is the Señor de las Limas, a greenstone sculpture of a priest holding a sleeping or dead baby. Later cultures are represented mainly through their pottery – lifelike human and animal figurines especially – and there are also displays on the architecture of the major sites, including part of a reconstructed temple. Finally, with the **Totonac** and **Huastec** culture come more giant stone statues. Labels are in Spanish only, though there are a few English information sheets.

6

ARRIVAL AND DEPARTURE   XALAPA

BY PLANE

Aeromar (ⓦ aeromar.com.mx) operates two daily flights (Mon–Fri) to Mexico City from the airstrip at Lencero, just outside the city.

BY BUS

Xalapa's huge modern bus station is a couple of kilometres east of the centre on 20 de Noviembre; there are extensive facilities including ATMs, internet café and left luggage. You can get to the centre by regulated taxi, booked from a booth in the station; to catch a bus or *combi*, walk down to 20 de Noviembre and look for those marked "Centro"; going to the bus station, they're marked "CAXA" (Central de Autobuses de Xalapa).

Destinations Catemaco (4 daily; 4hr 45min); Coatzacalcos (12 daily; 6hr 30min); Mexico City (frequently, including some direct airport services; 4hr 30min); Orizaba (6 daily; 4hr); Papantla (14 daily; 4hr); Veracruz (very frequently; 1hr 45min).

INFORMATION AND TOURS

Tourist information Xalapa's tourist office occupies a kiosk under the arches of the Palacio Municipal (Mon–Sat 8am–2pm & 2.30–8.30pm; ☏ 228 842 1214, ⓦ xalapa .gob.mx).

Veraventuras Santos Degollado 81 ☏ 228 818 9579, ⓦ veraventuras.com. Rafting, zipwires, abseiling, paintballing and more from their base at the *Hotel Carrizal* near Jalcomulco. A rafting day trip costs M$830 per person, a 3-day, 2-night activity package around M$3000. See also Jalcomulco (p.414) and Tlapacoyan (p.415).

ACCOMMODATION

Casa Regia Hidalgo 12 at Canovas ☏ 228 812 0591, ⓔ posadacasaregia@hotmail.com. This brightly decorated and friendly place has peaceful, cosy rooms with TV, constant hot water and a breakfast area. Wi-fi throughout the property. M$430

Clara Luna Ávila Camacho 42 ☏ 228 167 8000, ⓦ clara lunahotel.com.mx. Comfortable four-star, international-style hotel close to the centre. Spacious rooms have a/c, wi-fi and cable TV, and there's a generous buffet breakfast included. M$1000

Hostal de la Niebla Zamora 24 ☏ 228 817 2174. Excellent, immaculate hostel with internet, simple breakfasts of bread and coffee (included), TV in the common room, wi-fi, hot water and large lockers. Dorm M$170 (student M$160). M$360

Limón Revolución 8 ☏ 228 817 2204, ⓔ hotellimon @prodigy.net.mx. One of the best budget options, close to the centre, with small, very clean rooms around a courtyard embellished with fabulous ornate tiling. Rooms have TV and 24hr hot water, and there's a laundry. M$260

Mesón del Alférez Sebastian Camacho 2 at Zaragoza ☏ 228 818 0113, ⓦ pradodelrio.com. Beautiful colonial house, once belonging to Alférez Real de Xalapa, the last Spanish viceroy of Veracruz. Each room is unique and charmingly decorated, though perhaps not great value given the simple facilities (no a/c). There's an excellent restaurant (*Hostería de la Candela*) with some vegetarian options. M$930

Posada del Caféto Canovas 8 ☏ 228 817 0023, ⓦ pradodelrio.com. Under the same management as the *Mesón del Alférez*. Rooms are set around a pretty courtyard garden; some have balconies, a couple with kitchen, all have coffee-maker, TV and wi-fi. The on-site café serves breakfast (included) and has books to read. M$690

★**Posada La Mariquinta** Alfaro 12 ☏ 228 818 1158, ⓦ www.lamariquinta.xalapa.net. Meticulously restored

---

PARKLIFE IN XALAPA

Xalapa is renowned for its **parks** and their wonderful tropical flora. A couple of fine potential picnic spots are within walking distance of the centre. The **Parque Los Tecajetes** (Tues–Sun 6am–6pm), ten minutes' walk west of the zócalo along María Ávila Camacho, is a pristine public park with lush vegetation and plenty of shaded seating areas. South of the zócalo, Herrera leads steeply down towards the **Paseo de los Lagos**, where walkways lead around a series of small, artificial lakes edged by parkland; popular with runners in the morning and strolling families later on. In the north of the city, the entrance to the woody **Parque Ecológico Macuiltépec** is close to the Anthropological Museum. At 1590m, the easily climbable Macuiltépec is the highest of the hills on which the town is built, and from its *mirador* you might catch a glimpse of the Gulf. There are panoramic views of the city even if you don't make it to the peak, and it also has a small **Museo de la Fauna** (Tues–Sun 10am–6pm; M$10) with a reptile house and aviary. Finally, on the edge of the city on the old road to Coatepec, about 3.5km from the centre, the **Jardín Botánico Francisco Clavijero** (daily 9am–5pm; M$35) boasts an impressive collection of plants native to the state.

colonial hacienda with attractive, modern rooms – starting to show their age slightly – with cable TV and phone. There is a tranquil inner garden, a common room with a vast collection of books, and an English- and French-speaking owner. More expensive extended-stay apartments are available in an adjoining concrete-and-wood extension, a fine example of modern Mexican architecture. M$660

EATING

Good **food** is abundant in Xalapa. The city is home to the **jalapeño pepper**, and there's also excellent local **coffee** (mostly grown in nearby Coatepec; see p.412), consumed in great quantities in the city's numerous **traditional cafés**. Many of these can be found along Nicolás Bravo or its continuation Primo Verdad, and there are plenty of appetizing **restaurants** and some enticing jugo and torta places in the couple of blocks between here and the zócalo.

6

Café Chiquito Nicolás Bravo 3 ☎228 812 1122. One of the largest and most distinctive cafés, with wooden tables set around a lovely colonial courtyard. There's a reasonable menu, mostly of sandwiches and *antojitos* (M$40–60), plus excellent breakfasts and *comidas* (both around M$45), along with the usual range of coffees and teas. Daily 8am–11pm.

★**Café Lindo** Primo Verdad 21 ☎228 841 9166. Traditional café with mouthwatering sandwiches in addition to Mexican-style snack foods and buffet breakfasts (M$56) and *comidas* (M$80). Lively, primarily young clientele in the large, dimly lit dining and drinking area; live music every evening from 9pm. Daily 8am–2am.

La Casona del Beaterio Zaragoza 20 ☎228 818 2119. Hundreds of old photographs adorn the walls at one of the city's best restaurants, which serves up fine, reasonably priced Mexican food and breakfasts. Bow-tied waiters scurry around a series of small courtyards. Live traditional music Wed–Sat from 9pm. Mon–Sat 8am–11pm, Sun 8am–10pm.

Don Justo South side of Parque Juárez, by the Agorá. The terrace, enjoying fabulous views south from the zócalo, is arguably the main attraction of this popular and busy meeting place. It's also an excellent modern-style café, with smoothies, frappucinos and coffees as well as panini, crêpes and cakes. Daily 9.30am–9.30pm.

★**La Fonda** Callejón del Diamante 1 ☎228 818 7282. Justifiably popular lunch-time spot (plenty of room upstairs if the street-level dining room is full) on a bustling bohemian alley. Copious and very cheap *comidas* or an à la carte choice of chicken, meat and some seafood dishes for M$60 and up. Mon–Sat 9am–5.30pm.

La Parroquia Zaragoza 18 ☎228 817 4436. Venerable fifty-year-old establishment best known for its breakfast menus starting at around M$40, but whose unpretentious and busy dining room is also open for lunch and dinner. Another, smarter, branch at María Ávila Camacho 72 (mains M$50 and above). Daily 7.30am–11pm.

La Parroquia de Veracruz Enríquez beside the Palacio Municipal. A branch of the famous Veracruz café, this new pretender has overtaken its local namesake as the smartest place to be seen downtown. A few noisy tables outside face the zócalo, but most are in the chilly, glassed-in interior: *café lechero*, breakfast and a full menu (around M$130 for a main). Expect to queue for breakfast at the weekend. Daily 7am–12.30am.

Il Postodoro Primo Verdad 11 ☎228 841 2000. The home-made pasta (from M$45) and delicious pizzas (M$75–115) are the things to go for at this welcoming Italian restaurant, with tables in a tranquil courtyard. Good wine list too. Sun–Thurs 9am–12.30am, Fri & Sat 9am–1.30am.

DRINKING AND NIGHTLIFE

Xalapa is a city of great creative energy. A number of **bars** offer live music and occasional poetry readings or theatre; downtown the place to be is the Callejón de la Perla, whose bars are packed every night. Louder **clubs** and bars tend to be further out. The giant Plaza las Américas mall on the edge of town has a good multiplex **cinema**.

La Condesa Callejón González Aparicio 4A (Callejón de la Perla) ☎228 817 4310. Bar-club that epitomizes the busy alleyway – a good place for an early evening beer, getting increasingly lively as the evening wears on and the dancefloor fills to house and dance music.

Cubanias Callejón González Aparicio 2 (Callejón de la Perla) ☎228 158 0177. Next door to La Condesa, this Cuban-themed restaurant and bar is a great late-night spot for music, mojitos and Cuba libres. Daily 5pm–1.30am.

La Opera Ruiz Cortines, cnr Cuahupopocan, about 1km west of the zócalo ☎228 812 3277. The biggest of the downtown clubs, with *banda*, Mexican and international music, theme nights and occasional live performances. Thurs–Sun from 10pm.

Teatro del Estado Ávila Camacho at Ignacio de la Llave ☎228 817 3110. For a more relaxed evening, the State Theatre hosts regular concerts by the Orquesta Sinfónica de Xalapa, dance performances by the Ballet Folklorico de Veracruz and plenty of other theatrical and musical events.

DIRECTORY

Internet Try El Sarcofago, on Allende immediately below the Agorá; Ciber 10 on Mata; or Internet Ocho, Bravo 8 opposite the *Cafe Chiquito*.

Laundry Try the laundrette at Rojano 21-A (daily 9am–8pm; M$20/kg), a block north of the post office.

Money and exchange There are plenty of banks and ATMs around the centre, including HSBC on Parque Juárez and Bancomer on Parque Lerdo.

Post office The main post office (Mon–Fri 8am–6pm, Sat 9am–2pm) is on Zamora, at Diego Leño. This is also where you'll find a Western Union office.

Coatepec

COATEPEC, less than 15km south of Xalapa, is a very popular weekend outing for folk from the city. An enjoyable little town with a beautiful setting and fine colonial architecture, it's the source of much of the coffee consumed in Xalapa – the aroma is unmistakeable as you drive in – and this, along with fresh trout (*trucha*) from the river, is the speciality at the many local cafés and restaurants. In May, the **Feria del Café** celebrates the local crop, and there's also a big celebration in September to honour the local patron saint, San Jeronimo. In addition to restaurants, you'll find a number of high-class **artesanía** outlets around the zócalo, especially in the Plazuela El Zaguán, next to Finca Andrade. It's also worth wandering into the **Casa de Cultura**, on Campillo at the corner of Cuauhtemoc, a block from the zócalo, more for the beautiful, crumbling colonial building it occupies than the occasional art or photography exhibitions housed therein.

ARRIVAL AND INFORMATION — COATEPEC

By bus Buses run regularly from Xalapa to Coatepec. Most frequent are the local services from the Terminal Excelsiór (also known as Los Sauces, after the market next to it), 2km southwest of the zócalo, though there are also second-class buses from the main terminal.

Tourist information The tourist office is in the Palacio Municipal, on the zócalo (daily 9am–7pm, ⓦ somoscoatepec.com).

ACCOMMODATION AND EATING

Thanks to all the visitors from the city, there are a number of very comfortable hotels and excellent places to eat here. Locals like the riverside **restaurants** alongside the old road from Xalapa, on the edge of town.

★**Casa Bonilla** Juárez 20 ☎228 816 0374, ⓦcasabonilla.com. Charming, traditional seafood restaurant (mains around M$150) that centres on a plant-lined courtyard filled with bright, tropical songbirds. The adjacent bar is wonderfully atmospheric, with cheeky artwork and saloon doors at the entrance. In business for more than seventy years. Daily 8am–8pm.

★**Casa Real** Zamora 58 ☎228 816 6317, ⓦcasarealdelcafe.com.mx. Very pretty, expansive property, with stylish, whitewashed buildings encircling a tiled courtyard. Continental breakfast included, and there's an on-site spa that has astonishing mountain views. M$1050

Finca Andrade Lerdo 5 on the zócalo ☎228 816 4887. An excellent, elegant restaurant (main courses M$80–100) which also serves good *cafe lechero* and *pan dulce*. There's live music Fri to Sun from around 8pm. Daily 8am–midnight.

Hostal Cafe-tal apan Aldama 51 ☎228 816 6185, ⓦelcafe-tal.com. A friendly place with basic, six-bed dorms and use of a communal kitchen, the *Hostal Cafe-tal apan* can also provide information (or check the website) about tours of their coffee plantation and museum (daily 10am–5pm, M$35), about 5km out of town on the road towards Xico and Jalcomulco. M$100

Mesón del Alférez Jiménez del Campillo 47, five blocks east of the plaza ☎228 816 6744, ⓦpradodelrio.com. Imaginatively restored colonial building with rooms off a pretty internal courtyard; some have beds on a raised gallery. Fan only – a/c is rarely needed here – and wi-fi. M$850

Posada Coatepec Hidalgo 9, cnr Aldama ☎228 816 0544, ⓦposadacoatepec.com.mx. The best-known hotel in Coatepec is still one of the most luxurious, albeit now trading on its reputation. Standard rooms are bright and cheerful, but there are also vast suites, a pool and garden. Wi-fi in common areas only. M$1400

El Tío Yeyo Santos Degollado 4, a block south of the plaza ☎228 816 3645. The best place in the centre to sample the local trout, served in at least thirty different guises (M$100–115) including with tamarind and prawn or in an almond sauce. Good steaks too (M$150) and hand-made tortillas. Daily noon–10pm.

Xico

XICO is a small colonial town, 8km south of Coatepec, whose big attraction is the spectacular **Cascada de Texolo**, to which you'll see signs on the edge of town as you enter. The falls lie 2km along a rough, cobbled road (just about driveable, or forty minutes' hot walk); beside the road along the way, coffee is grown in the shade of banana palms. If you're scared of heights, this may not be for you, as you emerge right at the top of the main 80m cascade, with only some hopelessly inadequate-looking railing to prevent you plunging over. It's a beautiful spot, though, with lots of wildlife and a couple of restaurants: the *mirador* on the far side has the best view, but it's a stiff climb up. Five minutes' walk upstream is the **Cascada la Monja**, a far smaller fall, but one where you can get very close to the bottom, and enjoy the cooling spray. Locals swim here, but it's not recommended. As a popular outing from Xalapa, Xico has a number of unexpectedly fancy restaurants. These are mostly clustered in the lower half of town towards the falls, particularly along Hidalgo, half a dozen blocks downhill from the main plaza.

6

ARRIVAL AND INFORMATION   XICO

By bus Local buses run frequently from Coatepec to Xico, as well as from the Xalapa bus terminals.

Tourist information An exceptionally helpful municipal tourist office (little English spoken) can be found on the small Plaza los Portales, on Hidalgo in the lower part of town, with plenty of information on the local area and places to stay in the surrounding countryside.

EATING

El Campanario Zaragoza 96, cnr Matamoros, near the tiny Capilla de la Santa Cruz ✆ 228 813 0675. The food in Xico is worth making a special trip for, and *El Campanario* is arguably the best place to sample it. Local fruit, nuts and vegetables feature strongly: delicious *mole de Xico* is sweeter and fruitier than classic *mole poblano*, while *sopa xonequi* is a soup made with black beans and corn dumplings, flavoured with *xonequi*, a pungent green leaf. Daily 9am–8pm.

Museo Ex Hacienda El Lencero

Carretera Xalapa–Veracruz Km 9 • Tues–Sun 10am–5pm • M$25 • If you don't have transport of your own, it's best approached by taxi (15–20min from Xalapa; M$40–50)

The **Museo Ex Hacienda El Lencero** is a colonial hacienda that was originally granted to one of Cortes' companions, Juan Lencero, and later became the property of controversial general and president Antonio López de Santa Anna (see p.823). It has been restored and furnished in its full nineteenth-century splendour, and both the grounds, with plenty of gentle walks, and the surrounding countryside are stunning. An inviting, formal restaurant occupies part of the main building.

Jalcomulco

JALCOMULCO is the prime spot in Veracruz for **whitewater rafting** and other adventure sports including kayaking, canyoning, rappelling, zipwires, horseriding and mountain biking. The village – gradually becoming something of an eco-resort, though still catatonic midweek – is about 25km southeast of Coatepec, on the banks of the Río Antigua (also known as the Río de los Pescados). Coming from Xalapa, you descend from the highlands into a steamy and impressive valley where the river runs through a series of rapids of varying intensity.

ARRIVAL AND DEPARTURE   JALCOMULCO

By bus Local buses run at least hourly throughout the day between Coatepec and Jalcomulco, terminating on the plaza, and there are half a dozen or so direct connections with Cardel and Xalapa.

6

ADVENTURE TOURISM IN JALCOMULCO

A dozen or more adventure tour **operators** have bases in and around Jalcomulco, the majority of them on the riverbank some way out of town. Most offer all-inclusive packages including accommodation, meals and activities, so there's a lot to be said for booking in advance. These are some of the best:

Aldea Ecoturismo Riverside about 3km out of town ☎ 01 800 823 5315, ⓦ aldeajalcomulco.com.mx. Accommodation is in villas sleeping four to six, and there's the usual broad range of activities, plus pool and *temazcal*. Two nights for four people from M$7200.

Ecco Sports Independencia s/n, a block from the plaza ☎ 279 832 3559, ⓦ eccosports.com. Well-run outfit offering all the usual activities, and accommodation in a comfortable hotel in town, with pool. Rafting and one night's accommodation from M$1000.

★ **Jalco Expediciones** 20 De Noviembre 17 ☎ 279 832 3687, ⓦ jalcoexpediciones.com.mx. A friendly and professional operation with a base in town so you don't necessarily have to book ahead. Wide range of activities from rafting (M$500) to zipwires (M$300) to

paintballing (M$260); M$600 for a day's activities, M$1200 two days and one night. Accommodation arranged in local hotels.

Mexico Verde Riverside about 4km out of town ☎ 01 800 362 8800, ⓦ mexicoverde.com. One of the longest-established operators, whose "eco-resort" offers accommodation in safari-style luxury tents, a *temazcal* and spa. Single activities from M$250; three days, two nights from M$2300.

Viajes de Aventura Zaragoza 54, on the plaza ☎ 01 800 841 9954, ⓦ viajesdeaventura.com.mx. Local agent who can arrange everything from zipwires to inclusive rafting packages, with a choice of camping, hostel or hotel accommodation. M$850 for a day's activities, from M$1650 for an overnight.

ACCOMMODATION AND EATING

Los Alcatraces Morelos s/n, off the main road into town ☎ 279 832 3503, ⓦ hotel-los-alcatraces.blogspot .com. Pleasant, yellow-painted, colonial-style hotel whose rooms, all with a/c and wi-fi, are arranged around a courtyard with a small pool. **M$500**

Los Cachanes Far bank of the river, between the two bridges; ☎ 279 832 3575. With a sandy (occasionally muddy) outdoor area right beside the river, *Los Cachanes* serves up great fish and seafood, including a mean *chilpachole*. Daily 9am–9pm.

Nachita II Madero s/n, on the river by the pedestrian puente colgante (suspension bridge) ☎ 279 832 3519.

Enjoying a prime riverbank location, this is the best of several restaurants with terraces overhanging the water. Good, home-cooked Mexican food. Daily 9am–8pm.

La Pizzeria 20 de Noviembre 17, close to the road bridge ☎ 279 832 3687, ⓦ jalcoexpediciones.com.mx. Run by the same people as Jalco Expediciones, this appropriately named restaurant has a great atmosphere, and a simple weekday menu of pizzas (M$50 medium, M$100 large), baguettes, garlic bread and fries; at weekends the menu expands to include pasta and Italian specials. Daily noon–10pm.

Tlapacoyan

TLAPACOYAN, some 70km north of Xalapa en route to the coast at Nautla, is another centre for rafting and river adventures, bounded to the south by the Río Bobos and to the north by the Río María de la Torre. A sizeable but unspoilt and friendly place, and a centre of citrus-fruit production, Tlapacoyan is surrounded by forested hills and pre-Columbian ruins, most important of which are the massive, little-known sites of **Filo Bobos**.

ARRIVAL AND DEPARTURE   TLAPACOYAN

By bus Tlapacoyan has regular direct connections with Xalapa, Puebla and Mexico City; for first-class services to Veracruz or Papantla, you may have to change in nearby

Martínez de la Torre. First- and second-class terminals are opposite each other, and pretty central, at Zaragoza and Ferrer: walk uphill on Ferrer then right at 5 de Mayo for the zócalo.

ACCOMMODATION AND EATING

Las Guacamayas 5 de Mayo, cnr Heroes de Tlapacoyan, on the plaza ☎ 225 315 4300. The fanciest restaurant in

town, with formal service but reasonable prices. Meat dishes for around M$80 but the speciality is seafood, especially prawns, served in a variety of guises for around M$120. Daily 9am–9pm.

Posada Oliver Cuauhtemoc 400 on the plaza ☎225 315 4212. Lovingly cared-for courtyard hotel, beautifully decorated and full of greenery, whose simple, a/c rooms are the best in town – the same management also run the nearby *Plaza*, slightly cheaper, without a/c. M$450

Filo Bobos

Work is ongoing at the **Filo Bobos** archeological project, some 15km from Tlapacoyan, where you can explore two of the several pre-Hispanic sites identified along the Río Bobos valley, **El Cuajilote** and **Vega de la Peña**. Both are worth visiting as much for the beauty of their locations, the birdlife and the serenity, as for the ruins themselves. No one yet knows for certain who occupied the Filo Bobos sites. Signs of a fertility cult suggest a **Huastec** influence, yet the other sculptures found are more Totonac in style, and the earliest buildings at El Cuajilote, which may date as far back as 1000 BC, are decidedly Olmec. Archeologists speculate that Filo Bobos was the centre of an as yet unknown Mesoamerican civilization, which provided an important trade link between the Gulf coast, its environs and the central valleys.

El Cuajilote

Daily 9am–5pm, though liable to close early • Arrange a hiking or river tour from one of the camps at El Encanto (best confirmed in advance, see box below) or local bus towards Santiago/Plan de Arroyos and walk the final 5km; signed for drivers from Tlapacoyan – 15km followed by 5km on dirt roads

El Cuajilote is an impressive site, with platforms and pyramids arranged north–south around a long, rectangular plaza measuring 31,500 square metres. A spring-fed brook snakes across the middle of the plaza. The surrounding buildings (mostly dating from 600–900 AD) appear to be a series of temples dedicated to a fertility cult: a monolithic, phallic stele more than 2m tall and oriented to the stars stands in the middle of the plaza, and at Shrine A4 more than 1500 other phallic figurines were found, though none remains at the site today.

Vega de la Peña

Daily 9am–5pm, though liable to close early • Arrange a hiking or river tour from one of the camps at El Encanto (best confirmed in advance, see box below) or drive or take a local bus to Encanto and walk the final 4km; get directions at the site for the riverside trek to Cuajilote, another 5km

Vega de la Peña covers some eight thousand square metres. There's little doubt that structures buried beneath the lush greenery here extend beyond that; some archeologists believe they may have stretched as far as Nautla. If true, this would radically alter the accepted conception of Mexican and Mesoamerican pre-Columbian history, placing the central Gulf coast in a far more prominent position than previously thought. What you see here today are small buildings, with more palatial dwellings than at El Cuajilote, and a small ball-court.

RAFTING AT TLAPACOYAN

Most of the rafting takes place near **El Encanto**, about 5km from the centre of Tlapacoyan off the Nautla road. There's a waterfall here, and spectacular river views enjoyed by a cluster of rafting camps. Good ones to try are:

Aventurec ☎225 315 4300, ⊛aventurec.com. Lots of activities including horseriding (from M$200) and kayaking as well as rafting (M$550). Accommodation in large cabins, hostel dorms or camping, and one-night packages start from around M$1400.

Filobobos Camp ☎229 202 6557, ⊛filobobos .com.mx. The largest of the operators, with a restaurant and pool plus a variety of activities in addition to rafting, including a zipwire, hiking and mountain-biking. Accommodation is in basic wooden cabins or camping. Full day of activities M$860, two-day package M$2250.

Veracruz to Papantla

Immediately north of Veracruz lie the oldest Spanish settlements in Mexico, and the sites of the indigenous towns which became Cortés' first allies. A short stretch of toll highway takes you as far as **CARDEL**, a busy little town and handy place to change buses or visit the bank, at the junction of the coastal highway and the road up to Xalapa. La Antigua lies 2km off this road. Beyond Cardel there's very little to stop for in the long coastal stretch (about 4hr on the bus) to Papantla. At **NAUTLA**, 153km from Veracruz, you pass the largest town en route to Papantla, surrounded by coconut groves, at the heart of the so-called "**Costa Esmeralda**". There are hotels, some of them pretty fancy, trailer parks and campsites all the way up here, but most are just metres from the highway, which runs close to the shore. The grey sand is frequently desolate and windswept, and it's not really a place you'd want to stay.

La Antigua

For all its antiquity, there's not a great deal to see in **LA ANTIGUA**, site of the second Spanish settlement in Mexico (it's often incorrectly described as the first – Villa Rica is further north, see opposite). It is, however, a beautiful, cobbled tropical village, just 20km north of Veracruz on the banks of the **Río La Antigua** (or Río Huitzilapan). At weekends it makes a popular excursion for Veracruzanos, who picnic by the river and swim or take boat rides.

In the semi-ruined centre of the village stand some of the oldest surviving Spanish buildings in the country: on the plaza are the **Edificio del Cabildo**, built in 1523, which housed the first *ayuntamiento* (local government) established in Mexico, and the **Casa de Cortés**, a fairly crude stone construction, which, despite the name, was probably never lived in by Cortés and is now a ruin, undergoing restoration. Nearby is the tranquil **Ermita del Rosario**, the first Christian church built in New Spain, which also dates from the early sixteenth century, though it's been altered and restored since.

On the riverbank stands a grand old tree – the **Ceiba de la Noche Feliz** – to which it is claimed that Cortés moored his ships. A pedestrian suspension bridge crosses the river near the tree, and on this stretch of the bank are *lanchas* offering river trips (from M$240) and a little row of restaurants with waterside terraces, the pick of which is *Las Maravillas*.

ARRIVAL AND DEPARTURE
LA ANTIGUA

By bus Although La Antigua does see an occasional bus, you'll find it much easier and quicker to take one heading for Cardel (about every 30min from the second-class terminal in Veracruz) and get off at the tollbooths. From here it's a 20min walk up a signed road.

Cempoala

12km north of Cardel, 4km west of Hwy-180 • Daily 9am–5pm • M$42, free Sun

The first native city visited by the conquistadors, **CEMPOALA** (or Zempoala) quickly became their ally against the Aztecs. When Cortés arrived, the city, under the leadership of Chicomacatl (dubbed the "Fat Chief" by conquistador Bernal Díaz del Castillo), had been under Aztec control for little over fifty years. Its people, who numbered some 25,000 to 30,000, had already rebelled more than once and were only too happy to stop paying their tribute once they believed that the Spaniards could protect them. This they did, although the inhabitants must have begun to have second thoughts when Cortés ordered the idols of their deities to be smashed and replaced with crosses and Christian altars.

The site

The ruins, though nowhere near as dramatic as El Tajín further north, make for an absorbing detour and take no more than an hour to explore. They date mostly from the Aztec period, and although the buildings have lost their decorative facings and thatched sanctuaries, they constitute one of the most complete surviving examples of an Aztec ceremonial centre – albeit in an atypical tropical setting and on a very small scale. The double-stairway pyramids, grouped around a central plaza, must have resembled miniature versions of those at Tenochtitlán. Apart from the main, cleared site, consisting of the **Templo Mayor**, the Gran Pirámide and the Templo de las Chimeneas, there are lesser ruins scattered throughout, and around, the modern village. Look out in particular for the circular **Templo de Ehecatl** (Temple of the Wind God) on the opposite side of the main road through the village.

6

ARRIVAL AND DEPARTURE   CEMPOALA

By bus There are a few direct second-class services between Cempoala and Veracruz, but it's generally quicker to go to Cardel and change there: local buses marked "Zempoala" leave from the bus station. Cardel has very frequent first-class services from both Veracruz and Xalapa,

and even more second class.

By taxi or tour From Cardel there are plenty of green-and-white taxis (M$70) to the site; travel agencies in Veracruz organize day trips.

Villa Rica

Around 15km north of Cardel, the sleepy village of **Villa Rica** was the first permanent Spanish settlement in New Spain. Established by Cortés in 1519, it was abandoned in 1524 for La Antigua, and only foundations remain today, close to the normally deserted beach. Just beyond, an exceptionally scenic area of steep, green hills is home to Mexico's only **nuclear plant**, on the coast at Laguna Verde.

Quiahuitzlán

Tues–Sun 9am–5pm • M$35

The ruins of **Quiahuitzlán** lie some 3km inland of Villa Rica, beneath an extraordinary looming basalt outcrop known as the Peñon de Bernal. Here the first alliance between the Totonacs and the conquistadors was made, and it's an exceptionally atmospheric and little-visited spot: utterly tranquil and with incredible views over the coast. The town was built on a series of hillside terraces – most striking today are over seventy small stone tombs, in the form of miniature temples, scattered throughout the site.

Tecolutla

A growing resort that marks the northern end of the Costa Esmeralda, where the highway finally turns inland, **TECOLUTLA** is pretty much the closest beach to Mexico City – easily accessed via the toll highway to Tuxpán – and thus can be very busy on weekends and Mexican holidays, especially Semana Santa. The rest of the time it's an enjoyably laid-back beach town with bargain accommodation, and a possible alternative base for Papantla and El Tajín. With the coast on one side and the broad Río Tecolutla on the other, the town occupies a point at the river mouth, with a lighthouse at its furthest extremity – the older and more attractive development is at this end of town.

Campamento Tortuga

Beach near the end of Niños Heroes, close to the ADO • Turtles released daily May–Nov, 7.30am–9am, centre open most days throughout the year • Free, donation or purchase required to release turtles • ☎ 766 846 0467, ⓦ vidamilenaria.org.mx

At the **Campamento Tortuga**, right in the middle of the beach, Fernando Manzano has been rescuing and releasing sea turtles for almost forty years. It has been a hugely

6

successful project, and releasing the baby turtles to find their way to the sea is both moving and fun. At the camp there are displays about turtles, and you can see the hatchlings and recovering adults.

ARRIVAL AND DEPARTURE
TECOLUTLA

By bus There are seven daily first-class buses from Tecolutla to Papantla (1hr) and Mexico City (6hr) and very frequent second-class services to Papantla via Gutiérrez Zamora, the closest point on the highway, also accessible by local bus. Change at Gutiérrez Zamora for first-class services to Veracruz (3hr 30min), Tuxpán (2hr 30min) and elsewhere.

ACCOMMODATION AND EATING

Good seafood **restaurants** line both the beach and the riverfront (where many also offer river trips, for around M$440 per boat), while every other building in town seems to offer **rooms**, with a concentration of budget places around the bus station. Beachfront properties are slightly more expensive, though out of season bargains are on offer.

Dora Emilia Hidalgo 45 ☎766 846 0185. A courtyard hotel with an exuberant paint-job, on the main street just beyond the plaza, the *Dora Emilia* has a small pool and simple, a/c rooms. M$480

Posada La Casa de las Hamacas Rafael Murillo Vidal s/n, close to the ADO ☎766 846 0168, ⍾lacasa delashamacas.com. Friendly budget place close to the Campamento Tortuga. Rooms are tiny but clean, with fans and comfy beds, and there's free wi-fi in the lobby and a small pool. M$450

Tecolutla Matamoros s/n ☎766 846 0011, ⍾hoteltecolutla.com. The original hotel here, right at the far end of town on the point by the *faro*, with slightly faded, old-fashioned rooms (not all a/c) but a fabulous position, direct access to the beach and good facilities including a large pool. M$800

Papantla and around

PAPANTLA, 227km from Veracruz, is the most attractive town on the route north, straggling over an outcrop of low, jungly hills. Even so, if it weren't for the proximity of El Tajín, few people would consider staying here. In addition to being one of the most important centres of the Mexican **vanilla** industry – the sweet, sticky odour frequently hangs over the place, and vanilla products are on sale everywhere – Papantla is also one of the last surviving strongholds of **Totonac** culture. You might see Totonacs, barefoot and in loose white robes in the markets, and can regularly witness the amazing dance-spectacle of the **Voladores de Papantla** (see box opposite).

On the edge of the zócalo, the huge **Mural Cultural Totonaca** depicts the clash between modern and traditional life, with sculpted images of Totonac gods, myths and the pyramids of El Tajín alongside oil rigs and farm machinery (the tourist office has a leaflet describing this in detail). It's best appreciated in the evening, when floodlights pick out the relief and the **zócalo** itself is wildly animated, especially at weekends, when

---

EL BAILE DE LOS NEGRITOS

Popular at festivals across the state of Veracruz, the frenetic **Baile de los Negritos** is a Totonac dance dating back to colonial times, when African slaves were imported to work on local plantations, often living and labouring alongside *indígenas*. Stories abound as to the origin of the dance: the most popular version has it that a female slave and her child escaped from a plantation near Papantla and lived in the dense jungle with local indigenous groups. After her child was poisoned by a snake bite, the mother, using African folk medicine, danced herself into a trance. The Totonacs around her found the spectacle highly amusing and, it is said, began to copy her in a spirit of mockery.

Good opportunities to see the dance are **Corpus Christi** (late May–June) in Papantla, or in Tlapacoyan (see p.414) at the **Feast of Santiago** (July 25) or the **Day of the Assumption** (Aug 15); it's frequently performed on a smaller scale at other village festivals in the area.

THE VOLADORES DE PAPANTLA

Although the full significance of the dance of the **voladores** has been lost over time, it has survived much as the earliest chroniclers reported it, largely because the Spanish thought of it as a sport rather than a pagan rite. It involves five men: a leader who provides acoustics on flute and drum, and four performers. They represent the five earthly directions – the four cardinal points and straight up, from earth to heaven. After a few preliminaries, the five climb to a small platform atop a pole, where the leader resumes playing and directs prayers for the fertility of the land in every direction. Meanwhile, the dancers tie ropes, coiled tightly around the top of the pole, to their waists and at a signal fling themselves head-first into space. As they spiral down in increasing circles the leader continues to play, and to spin, on his platform, until the four hit the ground (hopefully landing on their feet, having righted themselves at the last minute). In all, they make thirteen revolutions each, symbolizing the 52-year cycle of the **Aztec calendar**.

At **Papantla** (performances in front of the cathedral Fri, Sat & Sun 10.30am–7pm) and **El Tajín** (regular performances outside the entrance to the ruins starting at 11am), the ritual has become primarily a tourist spectacle, as the permanent metal poles attest. In local villages there is still more ceremony attached, particularly in the selection of a sufficiently tall tree to act as the pole, and its temporary erection in the place where the dance is to be performed. Note that performances are nominally free, though if you catch one of the regular shows in Papantla or El Tajín you'll be expected to make a donation.

6

there's often live music and dancing. On the terrace above the mural stands the solid **Catedral de la Asunción**, beyond which you can climb to the **Volador monument**, a giant statue affording tremendous views of the town.

ARRIVAL AND INFORMATION
PAPANTLA

By bus First-class buses use the ADO terminal on Juárez, just off the main road through town; walk uphill and you'll soon be able to see the cathedral above you, about a 10min walk (or M$20 taxi ride). The second-class terminal is much closer to the centre on 20 de Noviembre – walk steeply uphill past the Mercado Hidalgo to reach the zócalo.

Destinations First-class services to: Mexico City (8 daily; 5hr); Tuxpán (6 daily; 1hr 30min); Veracruz (6 daily; 4hr); Xalapa (11 daily; 4hr). Second class to all the above and to Poza Rica (30min); Tecolutla (1hr); and Tlapacoyan (3hr).

Tourist information There's a small tourist kiosk (Mon–Fri 8am–5pm; ⓦ papantla.mx) in the *Ayuntamiento* at Reforma 100 on the zócalo. You'll find plenty of information here, and usually an English-speaker.

ACCOMMODATION

Provincia Express Enríquez 103 on the zócalo ☎ 784 842 1645, ⓦ hotelesprovinciaexpress.infored.mx. One of a small local chain of business hotels. Recently renovated, the rooms, mainly internal, lack character but are central and quiet with a/c, cable TV and wi-fi. **M$580**

Tajín Nuñez y Domínguez 104 beside the cathedral ☎ 784 842 0121, ⓦ hoteltajin.com.mx. The town's top hotel, which isn't saying a great deal. Some rooms have good views across the city; others face only the corridor. There's a small pool which clients of the café can also use, and wi-fi. **M$600**

EATING

Papantla has an enticing spread of **local specialities** to sample, chief of which is *sacahuil* or *zacahuilt*, a giant tamale of chicken and beans, which you'll find in the markets. These are also the place to head for cheap eats: on the whole, the restaurants aren't great. There are two markets right by the zócalo: Mercado Hidalgo at the top of 20 de Noviembre, and Mercado Juárez, on the opposite (uphill) side of the *Ayuntamiento* at Reforma and 16 de Septiembre; they're basically working markets, but you can stock up here on small bottles of locally produced vanilla, and both have food stalls.

Café Catedral Below the cathedral at Nuñez y Domínguez and Curato, by Hotel Tajín. An ultra-traditional café serving little other than coffee and *pan* *dulce* (also available to take away) at old-fashioned wooden tables. Daily 8am–9pm.

Café Gourmet Volantini Reforma alongside the

Ayuntamiento. Upstairs, with a balcony in a corner of the zócalo, this modern-style café serves proper cappuccinos and a range of coffees and iced drinks to mainly youthful locals. Daily 9am–11pm.

Plaza Pardo Enríquez 105 on the zócalo ☎784 842 0059. The *Plaza Pardo* has an unbeatable position with a first-floor terrace overlooking the zócalo, though the food (mains M$80–140) doesn't always live up to the setting – probably best for breakfast (M$50–75) or an evening beer.

Daily 7.30am–11pm.

Sorrento Enríquez 105, on the zócalo ☎784 842 0067. The view and ambience at the street-level *Sorrento* are less attractive than at its neighbour, the *Plaza Pardo*, but the food is considerably tastier and the prices marginally lower. Breakfast for around M$50, daily *comida* M$55, plus a wide choice of *antojitos* and meat and fish dishes. Daily 7am–9pm.

DIRECTORY

Banks and exchange All of the major banks, where you can change travellers' cheques and find ATM machines, are on Enríquez, just off the zócalo.

Internet You'll find several internet cafés on 20 de Noviembre between the second-class bus station and the zócalo.

El Tajín

Daily 9am–5pm • M$64

With numerous substantial structures spread over an extensive site, **EL TAJÍN** is by far the most important and impressive archeological site on the Gulf coast. It divides broadly into two areas: **Tajín Viejo**, which centres on the amazing Pirámide de los Nichos, and **Tajín Chico**, a group of official residential buildings belonging to the city's ruling class built on an artificial terrace. The site **museum**, by the entrance, has a model of the site worth examining before you venture in, along with a collection of the more delicate stonework salvaged from the ruins, notably murals and columns, bits of pottery and statues – displays are primarily labelled in Spanish, but there are a few English explanations.

Brief history

The principal architecture at El Tajín dates from the Classic period (300–900 AD); the city declined in the early Post-Classic (900–1100 AD), and by the time of the Conquest it had been forgotten. Our knowledge comes entirely from archeological enquiries made since the accidental discovery of the site in 1785 – El Tajín remains one of the most enigmatic of all of Mexico's ancient cities. No one even knows who built it: some claim it was the Huastecs, others the Totonacs. Most archeologists prefer not to speculate too wildly, instead calling the civilization **Classic Veracruz**. You'll notice many of its hallmarks at El Tajín, including niches in temple walls and complex ornamental motifs known as "scrolls". Classic Veracruz influence was widespread, and is strongly felt at Teotihuacán (see p.142), to the extent that some believe that city may have been built by Veracruzanos.

Tajín Viejo

From the site entrance, a track leads through a small group of buildings to the **Plaza del Arroyo**, the city marketplace, and into the heart of **Tajín Viejo**. Around the plaza are several **ball-courts**, the most prominent of which is the South Court, or **Juego de Pelota Sur**; it looks like a wide avenue between two small pyramids. Seventeen such courts are known here, and more possibly lie unexcavated; it's thought that the game took on a greater importance here than at any other known site. The superb bas-relief sculptures that cover the walls of the South Court include portrayals of a decapitated player, and another about to be stabbed with a ritual knife by fellow players, with Death waiting to his left. Such bas-reliefs are a constant feature of the site, adorning many of the ball-courts and buildings, with more stacked in the museum.

The unique **Pirámide de los Nichos**, one of the last to be built here, is the most famous building at El Tajín, and indeed one of the most remarkable of all Mexican ruins. It rises to a height of about 20m in six receding tiers, each face punctuated with regularly

6

spaced niches; up the front a steep stairway climbs to a platform on which the temple originally stood. If you tally up the niches, including those hidden by the stairs and those, partly destroyed, around the base of the temple, there are 365 in all. Their exact purpose is unknown, but clearly they were more than mere decoration: theories include each holding some offering or sacrifice, one for each day of the year, or that they symbolized caves to the underworld – the dwellings of the earth god. Originally they were painted black, with the pyramid in red, to enhance the impression of depth. Niches are also present on other buildings at the site, some bearing the attributes of **Quetzalcoatl**, the plumed serpent, El Tajín's most depicted god.

Around the plaza in front of the pyramid stand all the other important buildings of Tajín Viejo. Opposite is **Monumento 3**, a similar pyramid without niches, and behind it **Monumento 23**, a strange steep-sided bulk, one of the last structures to be built here. To the right of the Pirámide de los Nichos, Monumento 2, a low temple, squats at the base of **Monumento 5**, a beautiful truncated pyramid with a high decorative pediment broken by a broad staircase; on the left, Monumento 4 is one of the oldest at El Tajín, and only partly restored.

Tajín Chico

From the back of Monumento 4 the path continues past the **Juego de Pelota Norte**, with its worn relief sculptures, onto the levelled terrace of **Tajín Chico**, home of the city's elite. From here, you get a great overview of Tajín Viejo. Only parts of the buildings survive, making a rather confusing whole. **Edificio C** and the adjoining **Edificio B** are the most impressive remains: Edificio C has stone friezes running around its three storeys, giving the illusion of niches. In this case, they were purely decorative, an effect that would have been heightened by a brightly coloured stucco finish. It also has the remains of a concrete roof – originally a huge single slab of poured cement, unique in ancient Mexico. **Edificio A** had a covered interior, and you can still see the entrance covered by a false arch of the type common in Maya buildings.

Estructura I (aka Edificio de las Pinturas) is distinguished by a palapa roof protecting its elaborate decoration, including relief carvings and delicately painted murals. Such luxurious decor suggests that this was probably the residence of some major political or religious

6

figure. On the hill above Tajín Chico stood the **Edificio de las Columnas**, which must have dominated the entire city. El Tajín's most famous ruler, 13 Rabbit, lived here; bas-reliefs on columns recorded his exploits, and some of these are now on show in the museum.

Gran Greca

From the terrace of Tajín Chico you can walk down the stone path to the **Gran Greca** complex, also known as Xicalcoliuhqui, whose spiral walls contain two ball-courts and more pyramids. It has been only partially cleared of jungle, but you can stroll along the walled edges to get a sense of its vast size. Built towards the end of the city's life, it is regarded as a sign of growing crisis, Tajín's rulers becoming increasingly obsessed with monumental projects in order to maintain control over a disenchanted populace.

ARRIVAL AND DEPARTURE
EL TAJÍN

BY BUS

The easiest way to get to El Tajín is from Papantla, 8km away. Local buses (M$8) take around 15min and can be picked up on Septiembre 16, behind Hotel Tajín. Note that any bus to Poza Rica will pass the ruins, though you'll have to walk 500m from the main highway. After, you can flag one down to continue northwards, connecting in the ugly oil-boom city of Poza Rica. Both buses and taxis drop you off at the collection of touristy stalls and cheap restaurants that surround the entrance, where there's also plenty of parking.

BY TAXI

Taxis to Tajín from Papantla cost around M$50.

Tuxpán

TUXPÁN (or Tuxpam) offers a far preferable overnight stay to its uglier southern neighbour, Poza Rica, on the journey up the coast to Tampico (see p.451). The town is built on the north bank of the broad Río Tuxpán, where giant tugs and half-built oil rigs lend an industrial air, and where in the evening half the town comes to stroll as the traffic rushes past them.

Museo de la Amistad México-Cuba

Obregón 1 • Daily 9am–8pm • Free • ☎ 783 840 0471 • Take one of the small boats (M$5) that shuttle across the river from in front of the Palacio Municipal; on the other side walk inland a couple of blocks and then turn right on Obregón: the museum is right at the end of the street where it hits the river

Occupying the house where Fidel Castro spent a year planning his revolutionary return to Cuba, the **Museo de la Amistad México-Cuba** is Tuxpán's only significant sight. From here, Castro, Che Guevara and eighty others sailed in December 1956 aboard the *Granma* yacht (designed for just twelve passengers), almost sinking on the way, and arrived in Cuba only to find Batista's forces waiting. The museum comprises just a couple of small rooms of photos of the revolutionaries plus assorted memorabilia, but the riverbank setting, modernist house and boat trip to get here add up to a worthwhile excursion.

Barra de Tuxpán

If you're craving a day on the sand, Tuxpán has some some long, if mediocre, beaches at **Barra de Tuxpán**, by the river mouth some 12km east of town. **Buses** (marked "Playa") run all day along riverside Bulevar Reyes Heroles, past fishing boats and tankers, and arrive twenty minutes later at a vast stretch of grey sand. There are restaurants and changing rooms here, and palapas where you can sling a hammock.

ARRIVAL AND DEPARTURE
TUXPÁN

By bus The ADO bus terminal lies on Rodríguez near the junction with Juárez, half a block from the river and some 300m east of the Palacio Municipal. Ómnibus de México (with both first- and second-class services, principally to and from the north) is further east along riverfront Reyes Heroles, beyond the huge bridge across the river. To get to the centre from either bus station, head west along the river to the Palacio Municipal and cathedral: behind these runs Juárez, and in the four blocks from here to the Parque Reforma, Tuxpán's liveliest plaza, you'll find banks, shops and most other things you might need, including the bulk of the hotels and restaurants.

Destinations From ADO: Mexico City (20 daily; 6hr); Poza Rica (very frequently; 1hr); Tampico (24 daily; 3hr); Veracruz (14 daily; 5hr 30min); Xalapa (7 daily; 6hr).

INFORMATION AND TOURS

Tourist information The helpful, well-stocked tourist office (Mon–Fri 9am–5pm, Sat 10am–2pm; ☏783 834 6407; ⓦtuxpangrandeporti.gob.mx) is in a kiosk on the forecourt of the Palacio Municipal, at Juárez 20.

Tours A wide variety of river trips, from half an hour (M$250 per boat) to a full day (M$3000), is on offer. Head for the embarcadero on the riverfront a couple of blocks west of the Palacio Municipal, or contact Turismo Negretti (☏783 835 4564, ⓦturismonegretti.mx), who can also arrange kayaking, fishing and diving.

ACCOMMODATION

Reforma Juárez 25, opposite the cathedral ☏783 834 0210, ⓦhotel-reforma.com.mx. The town's best: a traditional courtyard hotel that has been classily refurbished to provide a/c rooms with flat-screen cable TVs, wi-fi and fridges. **M$850**

Riviera Tuxpan Reyes Heroles 17-A ☏783 834 8123, ⓦbestwesterntuxpan.com. One of the few hotels in the centre with a river view, though by no means from all rooms. It's a *Best Western*, so comfortable and efficient (with wi-fi), if a little dull. **M$700**

Sara Garizurieta 44 ☏783 834 0011, ⓔhotelsara@prodigy.net.mx. Slightly worn business hotel, but good value (discounts for cash); there's a rooftop pool and it's just a couple of blocks from the ADO (head inland, then left). **M$500**

EATING

A line of stalls along one side of the Parque Reforma serves *licuados* and snacks, with tables set out on the square. There are plenty of food stalls in and around the **market** too – it's on the riverfront between Rodriguez and Pípila, opposite the ADO. Younger locals hang out along the river downstream of the centre, where there are numerous fast-food places.

Antonios Juárez 25, in the Hotel Reforma ☏783 834 0210. Excellent, somewhat formal restaurant, with linen tablecloths, good steaks and live music on Fri and Sat. There's an excellent *menu del día* for M$85. Mon–Sat 7am–11pm, Sun 7am–10pm.

El Atracadero Reyes Heroles 60, on the river about three blocks west of Parque Reforma ☏783 835 5166. Floating restaurant and bar: pricey steaks, excellent paella and great atmosphere. Daily noon–midnight.

El Mejicano Morelos 49 on Parque Reforma ☏783 834 8904. Brightly coloured, enjoyable, straightforward Mexican restaurant facing the plaza, with a wide choice of *antojitos* (from M$40), fish and meat mains (M$80–130) and a M$55 lunch-time buffet. Daily 8am–10pm.

Nuevo 303 Pípila 4, between Juárez and the river ☏783 834 2527. One of numerous places around the market, *303* is open 24hr and busy with locals for almost all of them. In an elegant, wood-panelled dining room they serve breakfasts, hamburgers and veggie options, as well as seafood dishes such as an excellent *caldo de camarón*. 24 hour.

South of Veracruz

Leaving Veracruz to the south, Hwy-180 traverses a long expanse of plain, a country of broad river deltas and salty lagoons where the river port of **Tlacotalpan** oozes elegant decay. Some 150km south of Veracruz, the volcanic hills of the **Sierra Tuxtla** are home to the townships of **Santiago Tuxtla** and **San Andrés Tuxtla**. This beautiful region of rolling green hills, known as "La Suiza Veracruzana" (the Switzerland of Veracruz, plainly named by someone who'd never been to Switzerland), makes a welcome change from the flat plains, and the cooler climate is an infinite relief. The idyllic **Laguna Catemaco**, around which the last expanse of Gulf coast **rainforest** is preserved, makes a rewarding place to break the journey south, with plenty of opportunities to explore the nearby mountains and coast. Beyond the Tuxtla mountains, low, flat, dull country leads all the way to Villahermosa (see p.697).

Historically, the region's great claim to fame is that it was the birthplace of Mexico's first civilization, the **Olmecs**. Here lies the **Volcán de San Martín**, where the Olmecs believed the earth to have been created; they built a replica "creation mountain" at their

> ### FIESTA DE LA VIRGEN DE LA CANDELARIA
>
> For ten days starting on January 31, Tlacotalpan is inundated with thousands of visitors as it celebrates its famous **Fiesta de la Virgen de la Candelaria**. Processions, bull runs, dance and music take over the town, especially for the first three days, culminating on February 2, when the image of the Virgin processes downstream accompanied by a mass of assorted riverboats.

6

city, La Venta, on the border with Tabasco (see p.706). Their second major city, at **Tres Zapotes** near Santiago Tuxtla, is now little more than a mound in a maize field. For most modern Mexicans, however, this part of southern Veracruz, especially around Lago de Catemaco, is best known as the **Tierra de los Brujos** (land of the witches/wizards).

Tlacotalpan

TLACOTALPAN is a beautiful, languid town on the north bank of the broad Río Papaloapan. An important port and railhead in the eighteenth and nineteenth centuries, it now has just six hundred permanent inhabitants, but its elegant colonial architecture has led to its being declared a UNESCO World Heritage Site. At the weekend it can be packed with locals, who come here to eat at the riverside restaurants, fish, swim or take boat rides on the river, browse the artesanía shops and hang out in the bars and cafés on the plaza. Come on a weekday afternoon and you'll find the place all but deserted.

Among Mexicans, Tlacotalpan is known as the place where musician and composer **Agustín Lara** (1900–70), whose works have been interpreted by the likes of Pavarotti, Carreras and Domingo, spent his early childhood. Two museums and a cultural centre honour the man, but unless you're a huge fan they're not worth the admission – the true pleasure here is simply to wander the streets, admiring the architecture (many of the buildings are labelled with their history) and soaking up the steamy, tropical atmosphere. On the Plaza Zaragoza are two magnificent churches and a florid, wrought-iron bandstand; Enriquez and Miguel Chazaro, parallel streets heading west from here, are lined with magnificent colonnaded houses. A market occupies a wonderful nineteenth-century building on the waterfront, just east of the centre.

Museo Salvador Ferrando
Alegre 6, on Plaza Hidalgo • Tues–Sun 10.30am–5pm • ☎ 288 884 2495 • M$20

The most enjoyable of the town's few sights is the **Museo Salvador Ferrando**. Named after one of the town's most respected painters, it's a fine old house containing an Old Curiosity Shop of paintings, antique furniture, historical artefacts and junk, around which you're given a lightning-paced tour in Spanish.

ARRIVAL AND DEPARTURE   TLACOTALPAN

By bus Tlacotalpan lies some 70km south of Veracruz, 10km inland on the winding road that heads towards Tuxtepec (and eventually Oaxaca). There are frequent buses to and from Veracruz, and there's a lot to be said for coming second class, because these will drop you right in the heart of town: the ADO terminal is a 10min walk west of the centre on the road out towards Tuxtepec.

INFORMATION

Tourist information There's a small tourist office (Mon–Fri 9am–3pm) in the Palacio Municipal, just off the Plaza Hidalgo at Alegre 6; at busy times a tourist information kiosk also operates on the waterfront Plaza Colon.

ACCOMMODATION AND EATING

Brisas del Papaloapan Rivera del Río, close to the market ☎ 288 884 2853. The riverside restaurants in Tlacotalpan are famed for their delicious, cheap seafood, and this is a typical example, with tables on a waterside terrace. Local specialities include *piripituche*, a seafood broth with crab and prawns, and *bagre*, a fish from the river. Daily noon–10pm.

Posada Don Diego Gutiérrez Zamora 5, off Carranza

near the market ☎ 288 884 3221. Small hotel with cheerful blue-and-yellow decor, whose internal a/c rooms are quiet, modern, clean and comfortable. M$380

Posada Doña Lala Carranza 11, close to river and zócalo ☎ 288 884 2580, ⓦ hoteldonalala.com.mx. The fanciest place in town, comfortable if a bit stuffy, with wi-fi, small pool and a smart restaurant serving great seafood. M$750

Reforma Carranza 2, just off the zócalo ☎ 288 884 2022, ⓦ tlaco.com.mx/hotelreforma. Good location, and a choice of basic, tile-floored rooms with fan or a/c – a couple of the latter have lovely balconies over a smaller plaza at the back. M$440

Santiago Tuxtla

6

SANTIAGO TUXTLA is the smaller of the two Tuxtlas, a quiet country town which can make for a peaceful overnight break. On the zócalo a giant **Olmec head**, 3.4m high, is proudly displayed – this is the largest ever found, and unusual also for its closed eyes, scowling mouth and simplified features.

Museo Regional Tuxteco

Ángel Carvajal, on the south side of the plaza • Tues–Fri 9am–6pm, Sat & Sun 9am–5pm • M$42

The small **Museo Regional Tuxteco** boasts an Olmec head which, by contrast to that outside on the plaza, is the smallest known; it is, however, exceptionally expressive and finely worked. The other star exhibit among a plethora of Olmec sculpture and pottery is a figure, probably an altar, known as "El Negro" – visiting celebrities and locals come here to rub their thumbs over his forehead, which reputedly provides positive energy and miraculous cures.

ARRIVAL AND DEPARTURE   SANTIAGO TUXTLA

By bus Buses stop on the main road, a short walk from the zócalo. Frequent buses pass through heading for San

Andrés (20min) and Catemaco (45min), or in the other direction to Veracruz (2hr 30min).

ACCOMMODATION

Gran Santiago Plaza 5 de Mayo, on the zócalo ☎ 294 947 0300, ⓦ hotelgransantiagoplaza.com.mx. A thoroughly incongruous, seven-storey, circular concrete construction, with business-style rooms – comfortable and efficient with wi-fi – as well as a full-size pool and coffee-shop style restaurant. M$555

Mesón de Santiago 5 de Mayo 8, in the corner of the zócalo ☎ 294 947 1670, ⓦ mesonsantiago.com.mx. A lovingly converted colonial building whose elegant rooms (with a/c and wi-fi) are set around a courtyard with a small pool. M$600

EATING

Metropoli Juárez, just off the zócalo. Bar-restaurant that's more bar than restaurant, and the centre of what local nightlife there is. Frequent live music and happy-hour offers. Tues–Sun 6pm–late.

Super La Joya Juárez, at the corner of the zócalo ☎ 294 947 0177. Supermarket and restaurant where exceptional-value, simple Mexican fare is served at tables

outside. Just M$32 for the three-course *comida*; around M$40 for breakfast. Daily 7am–11pm.

La Tamehua Ayuntamiento, cnr Iturbide, two blocks from the plaza on the road to the highway ☎ 294 114 9279. Simple, plastic-chair *taquería*, popular in the evenings with locals, serving hamburgers, tortas and grilled meats as well as tasty tacos. Daily noon–10pm.

DIRECTORY

Money and exchange There are two ATMs at the Palacio Municipal on the zócalo, and another on the main road opposite the bus station.

San Andrés Tuxtla and around

SAN ANDRÉS TUXTLA is the administrative centre of the Tuxtlas region, a substantial town with every facility you might need. Surrounded by tobacco fields, it's also home to several **cigar factories** where you can watch *puros* being hand-rolled. One such is the

6

Santa Clara cigar factory (@santaclarapuros.com) right at the heart of town, on the highway one block from the ADO bus station. The tour is fascinating and informal, and there's very little pressure to buy.

ARRIVAL AND INFORMATION   SAN ANDRÉS TUXTLA

By bus Local buses from Catemaco or Santiago will take you right into town, but the majority drop you at the top of the hill where the highway passes by; from here, Juárez leads straight down to the zócalo, a 15min walk or M$18 taxi ride. Moving on, Catemaco is around 11km east, and Santiago is 13km to the west: both are easily accessible on frequent local buses that depart in front of the giant Fenix supermarket at Pino Suárez and Constitución, two blocks east of the zócalo. There are also frequent buses to Veracruz

from the main terminal, but note that buses to Villahermosa tend to leave in the evening, getting you there in the early hours.

Destinations Catemaco (frequently; 30min); Coatzacoalcos (9 daily; 2hr 30min); Veracruz (frequently; 3hr).

Tourist information There's an exceptionally helpful tourist office in the Palacio Municipal (ask inside to find them; open office hours, but a booth is open outside on busy weekends; @descubresanandres.com).

ACCOMMODATION

Figueroa Pino Suárez 10 at Belisario Domínguez, a couple of blocks northeast of the plaza ☎294 942 0257, @hotelfigueroamexico.com. Budget hotel with a friendly welcome and lots of information and brochures on what is happening in the region, though the rooms are very basic indeed. M$300

Hotel del Parque Madero 5 on the zócalo ☎294 942 0198, @hoteldelparque.com. Big, well-run

business-style hotel with the best position in town and very well-appointed, a/c rooms with cable TV and wi-fi. M$780

Posada San Martin Juárez 304, halfway between the plaza and the bus station ☎294 942 1036. Large, attractive motel-style units, with painted wood furniture and red-tiled floors, arranged around a peaceful garden and a small pool. M$550

EATING

Montepio Allende 8 cnr Bernardo Peña, an alley off Madero by the Hotel Isabel ☎294 942 1496. Excellent steaks (M$150–170), a good wine list and a bar that welcomes women. Daily 2pm–midnight.

Palapa la Hueva Jarocha Juárez 106, a block and a half from the zócalo. Big, popular Mexican restaurant which looks like it would be more at home on the beach – with fans whirling away under a palapa roof. Seafood is the speciality, plus inexpensive grilled meat and tacos. Daily 8am–10pm.

Winni's Madero cnr 20 de Noviembre, on the zócalo ☎294 942 0110. Café-restaurant with a few outdoor tables but more in the modern, a/c interior, whose mostly glass front affords great views of the plaza action. Very busy at breakfast (M$42), but also with an extensive menu including pizzas and all the usuals (M$80–110). Daily 8am–11pm.

Market 5 de Mayo west of the zócalo. Excellent market with plenty of cheap food stalls.

Reserva de la Biosfera Los Tuxtlas

Trips into the **Reserva de la Biosfera Los Tuxtlas**, centred on the village of **Ruíz Cortines**, which preserves the primal forest around the sacred **Volcán de San Martín**, are best organized through the tourist office in San Andrés; it's not advisable to turn up unannounced. The main sights here are the **Laguna Encantada** or Enchanted Lake, so-called because its level rises in dry weather but drops when it rains, and **Yambigapan** (☎294 107 3322), a campsite with a couple of basic cabins where, by arrangement, local "pre-Hispanic" food is prepared and adventurous local tours are on offer.

Salto de Eyipantla

M$10 • Frequent local buses signed "El Salto" (M$12; 30min) run from a stop opposite the *Hotel del Parque* in San Andrés; for drivers it's well signed off the highway between San Andrés and Catemaco

The **Salto de Eyipantla**, a powerful waterfall 50m wide and 40m high, is a popular outing from San Andrés, about 12km away. Some 244 steps lead down to the base of the falls, which are pretty spectacular despite being crowded out by touristy stalls; summer weekends can see them packed with locals.

SHAMANISM, WITCHCRAFT AND WIZARDRY

Every March a gathering of *brujos* takes place on Cerro Mono Blanco (White Monkey Hill), just north of Catemaco town. Mexico has thousands of **witches**, warlocks, shamans, herbalists, seers, healers, psychics and fortune-tellers, whose belief system blends Catholicism with ancient rites and practices. The thirteen *brujos* of Catemaco, who call themselves "the Brothers", are acknowledged as the high priests of the trade.

These days, shamanism is big business in Catemaco. Many *brujos* have websites and toll-free numbers over which they sell long-distance spells, and in town you'll be pestered by their agents. By no means all of those claiming shamanistic powers are the real thing, so if you do want a consultation take advice from people locally, and be sure to know what you're getting and how much you'll be paying for it. The rituals can be fascinating – but they can also be theatrical flimflam, designed to empty your wallet rather than expand your consciousness.

Catemaco

Squatting on the western shore of the enchanting Lago de Catemaco, and by tradition a centre of native witchcraft, **CATEMACO** is a picturesque spot – perfect to break up a journey if you're heading south – with an impressive backdrop of volcanic mountains. The lake and nearby marshland and lagoons are a haven for wildlife, supporting large colonies of **water birds**, including herons, cormorants, wintering ospreys and dozens of other resident and migratory species. The town itself isn't particularly attractive, with slapdash development stretching five blocks or so back from the waterfront, but there's plenty to do on and around the lake. Veracruzanos arrive in force at weekends and holidays, when the main strip can get pretty busy; at other times the place can be dead, and many of the facilities shut.

Lago de Catemaco

A **boat trip** around the lake is one of the highlights of southern Veracruz. You're unlikely to escape the attentions of the *lancha* operators as you approach the lakefront: they all offer similar ninety-minute trips to the lake's main sights and some of its beaches (M$650 for a boatload, though bargain at quiet times; M$100 *colectivo*, in busy periods only). On the tiny **Isla de los Changos** there are stump-tailed macaques (monkeys native to Thailand), introduced here by Veracruz University in 1974 – they look bored stiff in their restricted habitat. In 1988, endangered Mexican howler monkeys were introduced to the much larger Agaltepec Island; these are far more active and aggressive. You are almost guaranteed to see a huge variety of **birds** too – herons, egrets, cormorants and shags, as well as more exotic kingfishers and ospreys.

Morelet's crocodiles, a relatively small species (up to 3m long), live in the lake too, nesting on the far bank. They're well fed and, apparently, never attack. Certainly plenty of people swim in the lake: stick to the main **beaches** and close to others if you feel uneasy. Playa Espagoya is just a short walk beyond the eastern edge of town, with Playa Hermosa and Playa Azul not much further beyond.

Iglesia de Nuestra Señora del Carmen

On the zócalo

The pretty church of **Nuestra Señora del Carmen**, with some fine stained glass, is home to a miraculous statue of the Virgin of Carmen, who is said to have appeared to a fisherman in 1714 in a narrow grotto known as El Tegal, roughly twenty minutes' walk around the lakeshore towards Playa Azulan. For Mexican Catholics the church is an important place of pilgrimage, above all around the Virgin's festival on July 15–16.

ARRIVAL AND DEPARTURE   CATEMACO

By bus The ADO first-class terminal, surely the most scenic in the country, faces the lake on the eastern edge of town, about a 5min walk from the centre. Some second-class buses also terminate at the ADO station, but most stop at

6

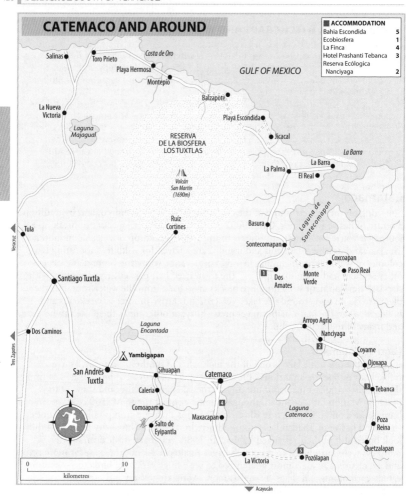

CATEMACO AND AROUND

ACCOMMODATION	
Bahia Escondida	5
Ecobiosfera	1
La Finca	4
Hotel Prashanti Tebanca	3
Reserva Ecólogica Nanciyaga	2

GULF OF MEXICO

Salinas
Toro Prieto
Costa de Oro
Playa Hermosa
Montepio
Balzapóte
La Nueva Victoria
Laguna Majagual
Playa Escondida
Jicacal
La Barra
RESERVA DE LA BIOSFERA LOS TUXTLAS
La Palma
La Barra
El Real
Volcán San Martín (1690m)
Basura
Laguna de Sontecomapan
Tula
Ruíz Cortines
Sontecomapan
Coxcoapan
Santiago Tuxtla
Dos Amates
Monte Verde
Paso Real
Dos Caminos
Laguna Encantada
Arroyo Agrio
Nanciyaga
Coyame
Yambigapan
Ojoxapa
San Andrés Tuxtla
Sihuapan
Catemaco
Tebanca
Caleria
Laguna Catemaco
Comoapam
Poza Reina
Salto de Eyipantla
Maxacapan
La Victoria
Pozólapan
Quetzalapan
N
0   10
kilometres
Acayucán

Veracruz
Tres Zapotes

the AU terminal on the main highway on the edge of town. Local buses from San Andrés Tuxtla will drop you at Lerdo and Revolución, directly inland from the ADO.

By colectivo Share-taxis to San Andrés leave from halfway up Carranza towards the main highway, near the mound known as El Cerrito. Piratas (*colectivo* pick-ups) heading to Sontecomapan and the beaches (see p.430), depart from the local bus stop at Lerdo and Revolución.

INFORMATION AND ACTIVITIES

Activities Kayaking, mountain-biking, jungle tours, shamanic spiritual cleansing, *temazcales* and more are on offer around town; some of the best activities are offered by the various lodges around the lake, especially *Nanciyaga* and *Ecobiosfera* (see p.429).

Tourist information There's a tourist office in the Palacio Municipal (Mon–Fri 9am–3pm & 6–9pm) on the main plaza, as well as a booth on the highway at the entrance to town at busy periods. ⓦ catemaco.info is a helpful local website.

ACCOMMODATION

Hotel standards in Catemaco town are not very high, though there are some great back-to-nature eco-resorts around the lake.

6

IN TOWN

Los Arcos Madero 7, between the zócalo and the lake ☎ 294 943 0003, ⊚ arcoshotel.com.mx. Pleasant, a/c rooms with TV around an attractive pool. Some of the higher rooms have lake views. Clean and well run. M$650

Juros Teresa García 14 on the lakeside very close to the centre ☎ 294 943 0084. Central, bright spot which recently underwent a snazzy refurbishment – all the rooms are brand new. The rooftop pool has stunning views of the lake. M$570

Posada Koniapan Revolución at the lakefront, on the eastern edge of town by the ADO ☎ 294 943 0063, ⊚ hotelposadakoniapan.com.mx. Gated compound with a pool and wi-fi, where the simple motel-style rooms are comfortable and those upstairs have glimpses of the lake. Breakfast included. M$550

OUT OF TOWN

Bahia Escondida On the southern lakeshore, 10km from Catemaco ☎ 294 109 3417. Basic eco-resort in idyllic spot with camping (M$50), dorms (M$70), private rooms and cabins; there's a communal kitchen, café-bar, limited electricity and friendly welcome. Room M$250, cabin M$300

Ecobiosfera Dos Amates, 10km from Catemaco on the road to Sontecomapan ☎ 294 103 3112, ⊚ ecobiosfera .blogspot.com. Fairly basic cabañas, close to nature in a stunning hillside position overlooking the lake; also

camping from M$50. They run all sorts of excellent nature and cultural tours from here, in particular into the Reserva de la Biosfera and to various waterfalls. M$300

La Finca Hwy 180 km147, on the west bank of the lake about 2km from town ☎ 294 947 9700, ⊚ lafinca.mx. The best hotel on the lake, with stunning views from almost every room, especially upstairs, a/c and wi-fi, a lovely lakeside pool and spa treatments including massage and *temazcal*. M$1600

Hotel Prashanti Tebanca On the eastern lakeshore near Tebanca, 15km from Catemaco ☎ 294 115 8886, ⊚ prashanti.com.mx. Fancier than average lakeside retreat with comfortable, though still simple, rooms and cabins, and treatments including crystal therapy, shamanic cleansing and *temazcal*. There's also a beach annexe, Prashanti Playa, at La Barra (opposite). M$1100

★Reserva Ecológica Nanciyaga On the eastern lakeshore, about 7km from Catemaco ☎ 294 943 0199, ⊚ nanciyaga.com. Simple cabañas by the lake for up to four people (no TV or phone); a great place to meet young Veracruzanos. *Nanciyaga* also offers activities to non-guests (daily 9am–2pm & 4–6pm) including *temazcal*, mud bath, shamanic cleansing, massage, guided jungle walks and kayaks, most of which are included if you're staying, and there's a restaurant with home-made bread and more. Substantial midweek discounts. M$1300

EATING

Seafood **restaurants** abound along the lakefront, most offering the local speciality, *mojarra* (small perch from the lake), best sampled when cooked *a la tachagovi* – with a delicious hot sauce. A few more modern places, serving innovations like cappuccino and pizza, are also starting to appear. At the other end of the scale, the **market**, half a block from the zócalo on Madero, has plenty of cooked-food stalls.

Casa de los Tesoros Aldama 4 Altos, overlooking the plaza ☎ 294 943 2910. Lovely café which is also an excellent artesanía store and a helpful source of local information, with free wi-fi. Good coffee, exotic teas and delicious omelettes, burgers, sandwiches, snacks and home-made cakes; they also have wine by the glass or bottle. Daily 9am–10pm.

La Casita Matamoros between Bravo and Melchor Ocampo, a few blocks north of the plaza (hard to find, so ask) ☎ 294 943 1310. Not the prettiest views, but the well-priced Mexican dishes and seafood here are perennially popular with locals. Daily 8am–8pm.

La Casona Aldama 4 ☎ 294 110 1150. Enchanting old building on the zócalo which has plenty for seafood- and

meat-lovers, served in an attractive dining room looking out onto a verdant garden or on a balcony over the zócalo. Try the *arroz a la tumbada*, lemon-scented rice with seafood (mains M$60–70). Daily 8am–9pm.

La Ceiba Paseo del Malecón, cnr Union ☎ 294 943 1377. Set under a giant ceiba tree, this popular palapa-thatched restaurant boasts great seafood dishes and postcard-perfect views of the lake. Try the locally caught *mojarra*, cooked in eight varieties. Daily 8am–8pm.

Il Fiorentino Paseo del Malecón 11, just east of the centre ☎ 294 943 2797. Italian restaurant serving decent pizza, calzone and pasta dishes, with a great location and upstairs terrace looking out over the lake. Wed & Thurs 6–11pm, Fri–Sun 11am–11pm.

DRINKING

Bossanova Paseo del Malecón 13, just east of the centre ☎ 294 109 9579. Jazz café playing some cool sounds on a lovely upstairs terrace with lake views; there are half a dozen similar lakefront terrace bars, some with late-night dancing. Daily 6pm–late.

El Cotorreo Paseo del Malecón, cnr Nicolas Bravo ☎ 294 105 4234. Fun, first-floor bar with nightly karaoke and dancing accompanied by live music on weekends. Daily 7am–3am.

Sontecomapan and the Costa de Oro

From Catemaco a paved road heads 18km to the coast and the small fishing village of **SONTECOMAPAN**. Here you can take a variety of *lancha* trips through the mangroves on the freshwater **Laguna de Sontecomapan**, which offers good **bird watching** possibilities. The most common trip is all the way to the mouth of the Laguna at **La Barra**, about 8km away (also accessible via a very rough road), where there's a lovely stretch of sand, usually deserted.

Beyond Sontecomapan a good road heads northwest along the coast for some 40km, before turning inland to rejoin the main highway beyond Santiago Tuxtla. Only one short section has been deliberately left unpaved, where it passes through the **Reserva**

6

FIESTAS IN VERACRUZ

Día de la Candelaria (Feb 2). The final day of a week-long fiesta, complete with dances, boat races and bulls let loose in the streets, in Tlacotalpan (see p.424). Colourful fiesta in Jaltipán, near Acayucán, which includes the dance of La Malinche (Cortés' Indian interpreter and mistress, who is said to have been born here).

Carnaval (the week before Lent; variable Feb–March) is celebrated all over the region, most riotously in Veracruz (see p.394).

Congreso de Brujos (first Fri in March). Shamans, witches, wizards and healers from across Mexico attend purification rituals and celebrations in and around Catemaco (see p.427), amid a festival that attracts plenty of visitors.

Fiestas de San José (March 18–19). In Naranjos, between Tuxpán and Tampico, a fiesta with many traditional dances. In Espinal, a Totonac village on the Río Tecolutla, not far from El Tajín and Papantla, you can witness the spectacular *voladores*.

Semana Santa (Holy Week, March/April). Re-creations of the Passion are widespread in this area. You can witness them in Papantla (see p.418), where you'll also see the *voladores*; in Coatzintla, a Totonac village nearby; in Cotaxtla, between Veracruz and Córdoba; and in Otatitlán. Naolinco, a beautiful village near Xalapa, stages a mock Crucifixion on Good Friday. Also celebrations in Catemaco (see p.427) and in the port of Alvarado – a ribald Fish Fiesta following the spirit of the Veracruz Carnaval.

Feria del Cafe (first two weeks of May). Coatepec (see p.412) celebrates the local crop.

Corpus Christi (variable; the Thurs after Trinity Sun). The start of a major four-day festival in Papantla (see p.418) with regular performances by the *voladores*.

Día de San Juan (June 24). Celebrated with dancing in Santiago Tuxtla (see p.425), and in Martinez de la Torre, near Tlapacoyan, where the *voladores* perform.

Día de la Virgen del Carmen (July 15–16). A massive pilgrimage to Catemaco (see p.427), accompanied by a fiesta which spills over into the following day. At the same time, Xico (see p.413) has a week-long celebration of Mary Magdalene.

Día de Santiago (July 25). Celebrated with fiestas in Santiago Tuxtla (see p.425) and Coatzintla; each lasts several days. In Tlapacoyan (see p.414) you can see the bizarre Baile de los Negritos (see box, p.418).

Day of Assumption (Aug 15). Widely celebrated, particularly in Tlapacoyan (see p.414), where you can see El Baile de los Negritos, and with a week-long festival in Tuxpán (see p.422) that includes dancing and the *voladores*.

Independence Day (Sept 15–16). Celebrated everywhere.

San Jeronimo (last week of Sept). Big celebrations in Coatepec (see p.412).

Fiesta de la Virgen del Rosario (Oct 7). In La Antigua (see p.416) the patroness of fishermen is honoured with processions of canoes on the river, while Alvarado, outside Veracruz, enjoys a fiesta filling the first two weeks of the month.

Día de los Muertos (Day of the Dead; Nov 2). Observed everywhere.

Dia del Niño Perdido (Dec 7). Huge candle-lit processions in Tuxpán (see p.422).

Día de la Virgen de Guadalupe (Dec 12). Widely observed, especially in Huatusco, Cotaxtla and Amatlán de los Reyes, near Córdoba.

Christmas (Dec 25). Celebrated everywhere. There's a very famous festival in Santiago Tuxtla (see p.425) that lasts until Twelfth Night (Jan 6).

de la Biosfera los Tuxtlas, a nature reserve most easily visited on a tour with *Ecobiosfera* (see p.429) or from San Andrés (see p.425). Some of Veracruz's most alluring and least-visited **beaches** lie off this road; most are at least a couple of kilometres away, down dirt tracks.

Montepío

At **MONTEPÍO**, 39km from Catemaco, the road finally runs right by the coast. The beach here offers warm, shallow swimming – people also swim in the nearby river – and is lined with palapa restaurants serving seafood and *cocos fríos*. At holiday times there are *lanchas* and banana-boat rides; out of season you'll find barely half a dozen people on the entire beach.

Costa de Oro

North of Montepío, the coast is being promoted as the **Costa de Oro**, though as yet there's no real development, and only the odd isolated place to stay; there are excellent beaches at Playa Hermosa and Costa de Oro, though, and a popular dive spot at Roca Partida – the split rock.

ARRIVAL AND DEPARTURE	SONTECOMAPAN AND THE COSTA DE ORO

By pirata *Colectivo* pick-ups known as *piratas* traverse the coastal road regularly; they charge about M$14 from Catemaco to Sontecomapan, M$38 to Montepío; there are also very occasional second-class buses.

By boat At Sontecomapan you can hire a *lancha* to take you to La Barra, or for a tour of the mangroves and lagoon. The journey to La Barra costs M$500 for the entire boat, including an hour or so at the beach; at busy periods you can get a *colectivo* ride for M$100.

6

The north

EL FARO DEL COMERCIO, CATHEDRAL OF
MONTERREY AND SADDLE MOUNTAIN

The north

Rich in legends of the country's revolutionary past, Mexico's north has a modern history dominated by its relationship with the United States, just across the Río Bravo. Though much of the region is harsh, barren and sparsely inhabited, far less visited than the country's tourist-saturated southern states, cross-border trade – as much about the daily movement of people as goods – means it's one of the richest and most dynamic parts of Mexico. It's not all business, though. Rugged and untamed, the north is home to deserts, mountains, seedy frontier towns and modern cities, as well as a proud and hospitable people deeply rooted in ranching culture, perhaps best symbolized by folk hero Pancho Villa (see box, p.464).

Archeological remains are also scattered throughout the north, including ancient petroglyphs and ruined Chichimec cities, all of which are thoroughly distinct from the Mesoamerican metropolises of the south. Most notable is the site of **Paquimé**, where a maze of adobe walls once housed an extensive and highly developed desert civilization.

The north promises urban appeal too. **Durango** offers a taste of colonial grandeur comparable to Mexico's heartland, while similarly attractive **Chihuahua** boasts a wealth of nineteenth-century architecture and stylish contemporary museums. The real draw, however, is **Monterrey**. Young, energetic and cosmopolitan, this modern city offers a host of cultural and artistic diversions.

Travelling overland from the south of Mexico towards the US border, there are a couple of obvious routes, with the **central corridor** via Durango and Chihuahua ending at **Ciudad Juárez** – a sprawling border town notorious for its violent drug wars. Further east, a string of smaller, calmer crossings provides rapid (and safer) access to Texas. The very shortest route north follows the **Gulf coast**. Hot, steamy and uncomfortable, this route is not especially recommended, but it is the fastest from the fine beaches and archeological ruins of Veracruz (see p.451), and, travelling by bus, avoids Mexico City.

Monterrey

The third-largest city in Mexico (with over four million in the metro area), and capital of Nuevo León, **MONTERREY** is a dynamic showcase for contemporary Mexico, though the heavy industry that made its wealth has far less importance these days – the biggest steel works closed in 1986. While the vast network of factories, the traffic, urban sprawl, pollution and ostentatious wealth that characterize the city are relatively recent developments, the older parts retain an air of colonial elegance. The city's setting, too,

Highlights

❶ **Monterrey** Art and culture reign in this bold, modern city, where superb museums and restaurants await. **See p.434**

❷ **Cabrito asado** Succulent roast goat is a speciality of Mexican cowboy country, best experienced at restaurants such as *El Rey del Cabrito* in Monterrey. **See p.445**

❸ **Valle de Parras** Explore the rambling vineyards and haciendas of North America's oldest wine-growing region, home to some eminently quaffable Cabernet Sauvignon. **See p.451**

❹ **La Tierra del Cine** Travel back to the Wild West at the John Wayne film sets at Villa del Oeste and Chupaderos. **See p.458**

❺ **Chihuahua** Lively colonial city sprinkled with grandiose nineteenth-century mansions, including the home of Pancho Villa. **See p.460**

❻ **Paquimé** The enigmatic ruins at Casas Grandes are remnants of the most significant pre-Columbian culture in northern Mexico. **See p.465**

HIGHLIGHTS ARE MARKED ON THE MAP ON P.436

is one of great natural beauty – ringed by jagged mountain peaks, the Cerro de la Silla, or "Saddle Mountain," dominates the landscape. The city in general rewards a day of wandering, but there are three places specifically worth going out of your way to visit – the old **Obispado** (bishop's palace), on a hill overlooking the centre, the giant **Cervecería Cuauhtémoc** to the north and the cluster of world-class museums around the **Macroplaza**.

Brief history

Spanish conquistador **Diego de Montemayor** founded Monterrey in 1596, at a spring close to the current location of the Museo de Historia. Steel production began in 1900, fuelling an economic boom that continues today, with Cemex (the world's third-largest cement company), FEMSA (Coca-Cola Latin America and owner of the OXXO convenience stores) and Banorte among the many companies based here – the business district of **San Pedro Garza García**, now Mexico's richest community, contains some of the highest skyscrapers outside Mexico City (on completion in 2016, the **Torre KOI** is set to become the tallest in Mexico at 276m). Once known as one of the safest cities in Mexico, Monterrey's sense of calm was rattled by **Hurricane Alex** in 2010, causing severe damage costing an estimated M$16.9 billion. That same year, conflict between the Gulf Cartel and Los Zetas (see box, p.468) began to spread to the city for the first time, culminating in a terrifying arson attack on the Casino Royale in 2011, in which more than fifty people were killed. Things have improved dramatically since that low point, and if you take the usual precautions (especially at night) you are unlikely to have any problems.

The Macroplaza and around

At the heart of Monterrey is the **Macroplaza** (officially Plaza Zaragoza, or just the "Gran Plaza"), which was created by demolishing six blocks of the city centre. It links the intensely Modernist **Palacio Municipal**, built on stilts at the southern end of the square in 1973, to the beautiful red-stone **Palacio de Gobierno** on what used to be Plaza 5 de Mayo. The result is undeniably stunning, with numerous fountains, an abundance of striking statuary, quiet gardens and shady patios, edged by the **Catedral Metropolitana**, museums and state administration buildings. You'll also see plenty of squawking red-crowned **Amazon parrots** in the trees here, the thriving descendants of escaped pet birds. There are frequent concerts, dances and other entertainments held in the park; in the evenings people gravitate here to stroll, and to admire the laser beam that flashes out from the top of the 70m-high slab of red concrete known as the **Faro del Comercio**, designed by the lauded Mexican architect Luis Barragán in 1984.

Plaza Hidalgo and Zona Rosa

West of the Macroplaza are the shops, offices and hotels of the **Zona Rosa**, beginning with little **Plaza Hidalgo** – a much more traditional, shady place, with old colonial buildings set around a statue of independence hero Miguel Hidalgo. Pedestrianized shopping streets fan out behind, crowded with window-gazing locals; Morelos and Juárez are the main thoroughfares.

Museo Metropolitano

Zaragoza, at Corregidora • Tues–Sun 10am–6pm • Free • ☎ 81 8344 2403

In between Plaza Hidalgo and the Macroplaza, in the old City Hall completed in 1887, you'll find the **Museo Metropolitano** with a small exhibit introducing the city's history, from its foundation in 1596 – labels are in Spanish only, but the lovely inner courtyard is worth a look in any case. The upstairs galleries house temporary art exhibitions.

Museo de Arte Contemporáneo (MARCO)

Zuazua, at Jardón • Tues–Sun 10am–6pm, Wed until 8pm • M$80, free Wed • ☎ 81 8262 4500, Ⓦ marco.org.mx

At the southern end of the Macroplaza lies the wonderful **Museo de Arte Contemporáneo**. Visitors are greeted by Juan Soriano's *La Paloma*, an immense sculpture of an obese bronze dove whose curvaceous lines stand in dramatic contrast to the angular terracotta lines of the museum building (designed in 1991 by one of Mexico's leading architects, **Ricardo Legorreta**). Inside, none of the floors and walls seems to intersect at the same angle. The vast, at times whimsical, open-plan interior centres on an atrium with a serene pool into which a pipe periodically gushes water: at the sound of the pump gurgling to life, you find yourself drawn to watch the ripple patterns subside.

Apart from a couple of monumental sculptures tucked away in courtyards, there is no permanent collection, but the standards maintained by the temporary exhibits are phenomenally high. A key factor in this is undoubtedly the bias towards Latin American (particularly Mexican) artists, who are currently producing some of the world's most innovative and inspiring works; the lithographs of Claudio Bravo, the feminist-influenced paintings of Paula Rego and Oaxacan print-maker Filemón Santiago have all featured in the past. The quality art bookshop and fancy *Restaurant Marco* (Mexican buffets Tues–Fri & Sun 1–4pm; M$230; ☎ 81 8262 4562) are both worth visiting (no need to pay museum admission).

Catedral Metropolitana de Nuestra Señora de Monterrey

Zuazua Sur 1100, between Abasolo and Jardón • Mon–Fri 7.30am–8pm, Sat 9am–8pm, Sun 8am–8pm • Free • ☎ 81 1158 2450

The relatively modest eighteenth-century **Catedral Metropolitana de Nuestra Señora de Monterrey** is a beautifully maintained Baroque structure with its one highly ornate multilevel tower completed in 1899. Highlights inside include the vivid murals at the altar, completed by Durango-born artist Ángel Zárraga in the 1940s. The palatial edifice just to the north of the cathedral is the **Casino Monterrey**, a posh entertainment centre for government types and strictly off-limits.

Barrio Antiguo

The oldest part of downtown survives to the east of the Macroplaza, where the **Barrio Antiguo** is populated with painted adobe houses dating from the 1890s, schools, independent galleries and, traditionally, the city's best bars and clubs. Sadly, since 2011, drug cartel violence has seen nightlife shrink in the area, and despite the improvement in security many bars have closed permanently. The Barrio Antiguo is safe during the day, but check with your hotel before you go out at night.

Museo Estatal de Culturas Populares

Abasolo 1024, at Mina • Tues–Sun 11am–6pm • Free • ☎ 81 8344 5311, ⓦ conarte.org.mx

There's usually a host of artistic goings-on at the **Museo Estatal de Culturas Populares** in the handsome Casa del Campesino (dating from 1740), where a warren of courtyards leads to small galleries showing a range of temporary art exhibitions in a variety of media. Note the bold murals smothering the entrance, created by local artist Crescenciano Garza Rivera in 1938 – the "Emiliano Zapata" auditorium to the left of the first courtyard is covered with them too.

La Casa de los Titeres

Jardón 910 • Mon–Fri 9am–1pm & 2–6pm, Sun 3–7pm • Mon–Fri M$40, Sun M$60 • ☎ 81 8343 0604, ⓦ baulteatro.com

La Casa de los Titeres is a small museum with an extensive and rather odd collection of puppets displayed behind glass. At 5pm on Sundays the owners put on a puppet show (included with admission), based on anything from *Little Red Riding Hood* to García Lorca.

Museo del Palacio

Zaragoza, at 5 de Mayo • Tues & Sun 10am–8pm, Wed–Sat 10am–6pm • Free • ☎ 81 2033 9900, ⓦ 3museos.com

At the northern end of the Macroplaza, the **Museo del Palacio** occupies the Nuevo León state government building, completed in 1908 as a magnificent example of late

Neoclassical style. The museum uses its surroundings to hypnotic effect: rooms are dimly lit and suffused with ambient music, with historic artefacts enhanced with video, images, computer screens and small, easily digested stories. The exhibits chart the history of Nuevo León, focusing on the themes of government and law – displays piece together the transition from colony to federal state, examine the evolving role of the governor over time, and end as a sort of shrine to Mexican democracy, covering the development of a Mexican constitution, elections and a free press. There are also rooms dedicated to the region's commercial development (think goats, sugar cane and oranges), and how transport and communications helped create modern Monterrey. The original *Galería de Gobernadores* is also preserved in gilded splendour – the state legislature held sessions here until 1985, when the new **Congreso del Estado** building further down the plaza took over (the governor of Nuevo León still maintains offices in the old building).

Museo de Historia Mexicana

Dr Coss Sur 445• Tues & Sun 10am–8pm, Wed–Sat 10am–6pm • M$40, free Tues & Sun; entry is free with a Museo del Noreste ticket • ☎ 81 2033 9898, ⓦ 3museos.com

The **Museo de Historia Mexicana** is another bold architectural statement with temporary and permanent displays on **Mexican national history**, with everything presented in a fairly unconventional manner. The permanent exhibits are upstairs in a vast, open-plan hall centred on the Área Tierra, a dimly lit contemplative space surrounded by faux rainforest. The rest is split into four galleries, with minimal labelling, an array of traditional costumes, interactive computer consoles and carefully selected exhibits. The highlights of the **Mexico Antiguo** section are the scale models of ancient cities such as Palenque, Monte Albán and Teotihuacán, while the **Virreinato** area covers the colonial period with a vast golden *retablo* the centrepiece (a 1960s copy of a 1670 original). The nineteenth-century and **Mexico Moderno** galleries complete the picture. This is very much an impressionistic museum – don't expect lots of dates and details – but nevertheless, if you don't read Spanish you might find the monolingual captions frustrating.

Museo del Noreste

Montemayor Sur 510 • Tues & Sun 10am–8pm, Wed–Sat 10am–6pm • M$40, free Tues & Sun; entry is free with a Museo de Historia Mexicana ticket • ☎ 81 2033 9898 • ⓦ 3museos.com

A covered walkway connects the Museo de Historia Mexicana to Monterrey's star attraction, the **Museo del Noreste**, or just MUNE. As you'd expect by now, this is not your average history museum – though it covers the **history of northeast Mexico** chronologically, from pre-colonial times through to the present, it uses a similar multimedia approach and is deeply thought-provoking. For starters, the exhibits begin with modern times and work backwards. More significantly, the "northeast" here includes the US state of Texas, and virtually every exhibit is approached through the prism of cross-border relations; the idea that the fate of both sides has been fundamentally entwined for hundreds of years makes sense, but the focus on Mexico's cultural impact on Texas, and the suggestion that it has a paramount role in its future ("by 2025 half of the Texan population will be of Mexican origin") would be viewed as highly controversial by many Americans. The museum also presents a fresh look at the much neglected indigenous tribes of the region, takes an unusually positive view of the Díaz regime and systemically lays out the tortured history of how the current US/Mexico border came to be. Labels are in Spanish and English.

Paseo Santa Lucía

Boats daily 10am–9.30pm, every 30min • M$60 round trip • ☎ 81 8126 8500

Just below the MUNE plaza lies one of the city's most impressive attractions, the **Paseo Santa Lucía**, a landscaped canal-side path replete with waterfalls, gardens and snack stalls that leads 2.5km east to the Parque Fundidora (see p.440) – it's a sweaty but tranquil thirty-minute walk, or a leisurely cruise in one of the boats that regularly plies between the two sites. Tickets are good for return trips the whole day.

DOWNTOWN MONTERREY

Río Santa Catarina

Instituto Tecnológico & Planetario Alfa

■ ACCOMMODATION		● EATING		■ DRINKING & NIGHTLIFE	
La Casa del Barrio	7	La Divina	8	Bar 1900 Gamma de	
Fastos Hotel	1	La Fonda del Rey	1	Fiesta Americana	5
Gamma de Fiesta Americana	6	Madre Oaxaca	6	Café Iguana	3
iStay Monterrey Histórico	3	Las Monjitas	2/3	McMullens	2
Quinta Real	4	El Rey del Cabrito	7	Sierra Madre Brewing Co	4
Safi Royal Luxury Towers	2	Trece Lunas	5	La Tumba	1
Yeccan Hostel	5	Vips	4		

Parque Fundidora

Fundidora, at Adolfo Prieto • Daily 6am–10pm • Free • ☎ 81 8126 8500, ⓦ parquefundidora.org • **Centro de las Artes** Tues–Sun 10am–9pm • Free • ☎ 81 8479 0015, ⓦ conarte.org.mx • **Parque Plaza Sésamo** Agrícola Ote 3700-1 • Summer and holidays daily 11am–9pm; otherwise Mon–Fri noon–8pm, Sat–Sun 11am–8pm (check website for seasonal variations) • from M$159, free for children under 90cm • ☎ 81 8354 5400, ⓦ parqueplazasesamo.com • Take Metrorrey Line 1 to Parque Fundidora (the park lies south of the station, across Madero)

Just east of the centre, at the end of Paseo Santa Lucia, **Parque Fundidora** is a surreal landscape of green parkland, industrial chimneys and former steel-processing plants, which have been converted into art halls, stadiums and museums. Get a map (free) at the park entrance, from where it's another fifteen minutes to the end of the canal and boat dock, marked by a waterfall set in a giant steel cauldron. If time is short, head straight to the **Museo del Acero Horno-3** (see opposite), but the **Centro de las Artes** is also worth a look, a series of three warehouses displaying temporary modern art exhibits. Toddlers will love the entertaining theme park honouring Sesame Street – **Parque Plaza Sésamo**.

Museo del Acero Horno-3

Parque Fundidora • Tues–Thurs 10am–6pm, Fri–Sun 11am–7pm • M$90; Paseo Cima Tues–Thurs 6–10pm, Fri–Sun 7–10pm • M$40 • ☏ 81 8126 1100, Ⓦ horno3.org

The centrepiece of the Parque Fundidora is the **Museo del Acero Horno-3**, a remarkable museum created out of the guts of a jagged steel mill. Inside are galleries tracing the history of the steel industry in Monterrey (with English labels), as well as the steel-manufacturing process itself – the highlight is the **Show del Torne**, which reproduces the dazzling (and fiery) spectacle of steel-making. You can also scale the 40m viewing platform via special iron elevators ("Paseo por la Cima"), and eat at *El Lingote* (Tues–Sun noon–midnight; ☏ 81 8126 1100, Ⓦ ellingoterestaurante.com).

El Obispado

Fray Rafael José Verger, off Padre Mier • Take the R4 bus, alighting where it turns off Padre Mier, then continue to the top of the steps at the end of Padre Mier and turn left; it's a 10min walk in all. Return to the centre using any bus heading east on Hidalgo

The elegant and beautifully renovated **Obispado**, the old bishop's palace, tops the hill to the west of downtown Monterrey like a golden temple. Its commanding position – affording magnificent views when haze and smog allow – has made it an essential target for Monterrey's many invaders. Completed in 1787, it has served as a barracks, a military hospital and a fortress: among its more dramatic exploits, the Obispado managed to hold out for two days after the rest of the city had fallen to US general Zachary Taylor in 1846.

Museo Regional de Nuevo León

Fray Rafael José Verger s/n • Tues–Sun 10am–6pm • M$52 • ☏ 81 8123 0644

After so much history elsewhere in the city, you might baulk at the **Museo Regional de Nuevo León** inside the Obispado – essentially another journey through the past of Nuevo León, with an emphasis on religious and secular art, arms from the War of Independence, revolutionary pamphlets and old carriages – but the collection has an oddly appealing charm and is evocatively set in the original stone chambers with timber ceilings. Labels are in Spanish only.

Mirador Asta Bandera

Cerro del Obispado • Daily 8.30am–10.30pm • Free • ☏ 81 8347 1533

A short, steep walk up the road behind the Obispado takes you to the top of the Cerro del Obispado and the **Mirador Asta Bandera**, a sensational viewpoint (775m) topped with a giant, 100m tall Mexican flag. Raised in 2005, the flag is the second largest in Mexico (the biggest flies in Piedras Negras on the US border, a whopping 120m tall), part of the "banderas monumentales" programme initiated by President Zedillo in 1999.

Cervecería Cuauhtémoc Moctezuma

Alfonso Reyes Nte 2202 • Tours Mon–Fri 9am–5pm, Sat 9am–2pm; tours are usually in Spanish, and you need to make a reservation if you require an English-speaking guide – reservations are recommended in any case • Free • 1hr–1hr 30min • ☏ 81 8328 5355, Ⓦ cuamoc.com **Jardín Cerveza** Daily 10am–6pm

If you like beer, head out to the massive premises of **Cervecería Cuauhtémoc Moctezuma** (Cuauhtémoc Brewery), established in 1890 and just as representative of Monterrey as any of the city's more historic sites (though it became a subsidiary of Heineken in 2010). This is where they make the wonderful Bohemia, Indio and Tecate beers you'll find throughout Mexico (as well as the rather bland Carta Blanca and export-only Sol). Free guided tours of the brewery run almost hourly throughout the day from the office next to the **Jardín Cerveza** (beer garden), 1km north of the bus station. You can claim one free glass of beer (usually Carta Blanca) here, or buy the better draught beers on offer. Note that male visitors cannot wear shorts, sandals or short-sleeved shirts, and you cannot take photos.

Museo del Vidrio

Magallanes 517, at Zaragoza • Tues–Fri & Sun 10am–6pm • M$30, free Sun • ☏ 81 8863 1052; ⊛ museodelvidrio.com • Metrorrey Line 1 to Del Golfo station (walk two blocks west and then two blocks north up Zaragoza)

For decades, glass production has been one of Monterrey's industrial strengths (for one thing, it has to provide all the beer bottles to the brewery), and to tap into the long history of Mexican glassware, pop along to the **Museo del Vidrio**. A small but select display of pieces over the centuries and a mock-up of a nineteenth-century apothecary's only act as a prelude to the attic, where modern, mostly cold-worked glass sculpture is shown to advantage; Raquel Stolarski's *Homage to Marilyn* is particularly fine.

ARRIVAL AND DEPARTURE
MONTERREY

BY PLANE
Flights arrive at Aeropuerto Internacional Mariano Escobedo (☏ 81 8345 4434), 6km or so northeast of the city, accessible by bus or taxi – taxi fares are set according to a zone system, with the centre around M$300 and San Pedro Garza García M$320 (buy a ticket at the terminal before you exit). Heading back to the airport from the centre, reckon on around M$250. Noreste (⊛ noreste.com .mx) operates buses between the airport and the Central de Autobuses (see below) every hour (daily 5am–8pm; M$65; 45min).

Aeroméxico and budget carrier Viva Aerobus make Monterrey a hub. Virtually every major destination in Mexico is fairly affordable from here if you book in advance (the list below is just a sample).

Destinations (domestic) Acapulco (4 weekly; 1hr 50min); Cancún (8 daily; 2hr 10min); Chihuahua (2 weekly; 1hr 25min); Guadalajara (5–7 daily; 1hr 25min); Los Cabos (1 daily; 1hr 50min); Mazatlán (1 daily; 1hr 25min); Mexico City (16 daily; 1hr 30min); Oaxaca (3 weekly; 1hr 50min); Puerto Vallarta (1 daily; 1hr 30min); Tampico (4 weekly; 1hr 5min); Tijuana (1 daily; 1hr 40min); Toluca (2 daily; 1hr 20min); Veracruz (1 daily; 1hr 35min).

BY BUS
Arrival Buses pull into the enormous Central de Autobuses, northwest of the centre on Colón at Amado Nervo,

complete with its own shopping centre and 24hr left luggage (guardería) on the west side (M$6/hr). To get from the bus station to the central Macroplaza, turn left on Colón to the Cuauhtémoc metro station and take Line 2, or pick up a #1, #7, #17 or #18 bus heading down Pino Suárez and get off at a suitable intersection: Ocampo, Zaragoza or Juárez, for example. You can also get just about anywhere by taxi; taxis are supposed to use meters (insist on it), with trips into the centre around M$50.

Destinations Ciudad Victoria (hourly; 4hr); Chihuahua (11 daily; 9–10hr); Durango (14 daily; 8–9hr); Guadalajara (15 daily; 12hr); Matamoros (hourly; 4hr); Matehuala (hourly; 4–5hr); Mexico City (hourly; 11–12hr); Nuevo Laredo (every 30min; 3hr); Piedras Negras (9 daily; 5–7hr); Reynosa (every 30min; 3hr); Saltillo (hourly; 1hr 30min); San Luis Potosí (hourly; 7hr); Tampico (hourly; 7–8hr); Zacatecas (hourly; 7hr–7hr 30min).

Buses to Texas Monterrey is also a good place to pick up transport into Texas: Transportes del Norte (⊛ transportesdelnorte.com.mx) has direct connections with the Greyhound system in Laredo via transfers in Nuevo Laredo (12 daily; 3hr 20min–4hr; M$386); Americanos (⊛ autobusesamericanos.com.mx) also works with Greyhound and runs buses to San Antonio via Laredo (5 daily; 7–8hr; M$755–820); and Austin (5 daily; 9hr 35min–11hr 15min; M$1265). Turimex also runs direct to San Antonio via Laredo (6hr 30min–7hr 50min; M$602).

INFORMATION

Tourist office There's usually someone who can speak English at the helpful Infotur tourist office, Washington Ote 648, inside the Antiguo Palacio Federal (daily 9am–6pm;

☏ 81 8152 3333, ⊛ nl.gob.mx). For tourist information when dialling from outside Nuevo León, call ☏ 01 800 832 2200.

GETTING AROUND

BY TAXI
The easiest way to get around Monterrey is by taxi, though traffic can be bad at the usual rush-hour times. Most taxis

you hail in the street should use meters, which start at M$8.80 – trips anywhere in the centre will rarely top M$50. Uber (⊛ uber.com) is now available in Monterrey,

OPPOSITE MUSEO DE ARTE CONTEMPORÁNEO, MONTERREY (P.437) >

with flat rates to the airport (M$300–330) and base fare of M$8.15 plus M$2.15 per minute and M$3.95 per km (minimum fare is M$35).

BY METRORREY

Though limited in scope, the fastest way to get around the city – and certainly between downtown and the bus station – is to take the clean and efficient Metrorrey light rail system, which runs on two lines: Line 1 is elevated and runs east–west above Colón (you see it as soon as you emerge from the bus station); and Line 2 runs underground from Sendero in the north of the city to the Macroplaza (at the station General I. Zaragoza), connecting with Line 1 at the Cuauhtémoc stop, right by the bus station (Line 3 is expected to open in mid-2016, running from General Anaya station on Line 2 through Barrio Antiguo). It's simple to use: tickets cost M$4.50 per journey and are available singly or as a multi-journey card (at a small saving; M$8.50 for two trips, M$16 for four) from the coin-operated ticket machines (no notes or places to change them). The system runs from around 5am until midnight, and is usually free on Sun (4.45am–midnight).

BY BUS

The streets of Monterrey are almost solid with buses, following routes that appear incomprehensible at first sight. The city authorities have tried to resolve the confusion by numbering all the stops (paradas), having the fares written on the windscreen and occasionally providing the tourist office with route plans, but it still takes a fair amount of confidence to plunge into the system. Useful MetroBús (daily 5am–midnight) routes include #1, #17 and #18, which run north–south through town and out to the northern sights – fares are M$12 within the city. Transfers to the Metrorrey system are free.

BY CAR

Car rental If you fancy renting wheels to get out to the sights immediately around Monterrey, or to explore the mountains, head to the airport or the Zona Rosa where all the main agencies have offices; Hertz is at the *Sheraton*, Hidalgo 310 (☎ 999 911 8040).

ACCOMMODATION

La Casa del Barrio Montemayor 1221 ☎ 81 8344 1800, ⊕ lacasadelbarrio.com.mx. Budget option in the heart of the Barrio Antiguo, with friendly, helpful owners who can help with all sorts of adventure tours. Dorms (four or six beds; M$190) and comfy single or double rooms, some en suite. Wi-fi and internet access, laundry and kitchen included. Doubles (per person) **M$250**

Fastos Hotel Colón Pte 956 (opposite the bus station) ☎ 81 1233 3500, ⊕ fastoshotel.com.mx. Comfortable, modern hotel with large rooms all featuring a/c and satellite TV, and internet access in the lobby. Perfect for those passing through on early/late buses. **M$600**

★**Gamma de Fiesta Americana** Ocampo Ote 443 (enter at Hidalgo and Escobedo, on Plaza Hidalgo) ☎ 81 8150 7000, ⊕ gammahoteles.com. Built as the *Gran Hotel*

Ancira in 1912 (visit the small museum in the lobby) and full of Art Nouveau elegance, including a winding marble staircase and posh restaurant replete with gilded birdcages, this old gem is still an outstanding option; now owned and operated by Fiesta Americana, it's not as modern or luxurious as the city's newer hotels, but delivers plenty of historic charm. Rooms are spacious and come with cable TV and free internet, though some are showing their age – check first. Deals on the web can make this surprisingly reasonable. **M$1590**

iStay Monterrey Histórico Morelos Pte 191 ☎ 81 8228 5100, ⊕ istay.com.mx. This centrally located member of the iStay chain offers top value for money; it's essentially a budget business hotel, with compact but modern rooms, flat-screen TVs, free wi-fi, a gym, helpful staff and a small restaurant. **M$745**

FESTIVE MONTERREY

In addition to the national and religious holidays, Monterrey has a number of exuberant local festivals.

Festibaúl Internacional de Títeres (mid-July) ⊕ baulteatro.com. This one-week puppet "festibaúl" is particularly appealing to kids, with Mexican and international puppeteers holding shows in the city.

Festival Internacional de Cine de Monterrey (end of Aug) ⊕ monterreyfilmfestival.com. The Monterrey film festival is one of Latin America's largest, showcasing the best Mexican, Latin American and international films, as well as organizing lectures and other free events.

Festival Internacional de Santa Lucía (Sept/Oct) ⊕ festivalsantalucia.gob.mx. Massive celebration of performing arts, with international dance, music and theatre.

Festival Internacional de Danza Extremadura-Lenguaje Contemporáneo (end of Oct) ⊕ danzaenmonterrey.com. Scintillating dance festival with a heavy emphasis on local and Mexican troupes (contemporary), as well as some international guests.

Quinta Real Diego Rivera 500, Valle Ote, San Pedro Garza García ☎ 81 8368 1000, ⓦ quintareal.com. Generally regarded as Monterrey's top hotel, this opulent pile is a luxurious amalgam of modern comfort and colonial style; it's a 15min ride from downtown in the hip Valle area. The spacious suites come with marble-covered bathrooms and living room; some have balconies. **M$2550**

Safi Royal Luxury Towers Pino Suárez 444 ☎ 81 8399 7000, ⓦ safihotel.com. Luxurious five-star hotel with expansive marble floors, elegant staircases and garden. The rooms are spacious, and there's a restaurant attached. **M$1425**

Yeccan Hostel Abasolo 916-A ☎ 81 8344 5265, ⓦ lamadrigueraenlinea.com (reserve at ✉ yeccan .mty@gmail.com). Spotless, trendy hostel in the Barrio Antiguo (on top of La Madriguera gallery and cultural centre), with pine-wood bed frames, two small dorms, three double rooms and shared bathrooms. Guests can use the TV room, small pool, kitchen and patio, with free wi-fi throughout. Dorm **M$210**, doubles **M$400**

EATING

Monterrey's **restaurants** cater to hearty, meat-eating *norteños*, with *cabrito al pastor* or the regional speciality *cabrito asado* (whole roast baby goat) given pride of place in window displays. In the **centre** there are dozens of places around the Macroplaza and Barrio Antiguo, all convenient for downtown hotels, but if you're prepared to drive or take taxis, the up-and-coming area known as **Zona Valle** (south of the centre in the affluent suburb of San Pedro Garza García and along Lázaro Cárdenas), and southeast Monterrey (along Garza Sada) are where you'll find the latest trendsetters and a range of international cuisines.

CENTRO

La Divina Montemayor Sur 507 ☎ 81 8040 2278, ⓦ ladivinamonterrey.com. Conveniently located close to the history museum, this traditional cantina features rustic stonewall rooms and a menu featuring tacos, stews, pastas and more substantial grilled steaks. Mariachis serenade customers in the evenings (mains M$50–80). Mon–Thurs 12.30pm–1am, Fri & Sat 12.30pm–2am.

La Fonda del Rey Matamoros Ote 816 ☎ 81 8344 9531, ⓦ fondadelrey.com. Bright and cheery cantina that serves tasty and economical Mexican staples (cactus salad, spicy enchiladas) for breakfast and lunch (M$55–65). Mon–Fri 9am–4pm.

Madre Oaxaca Jardón Ote 814 ☎ 81 8345 1459. The speciality of this beautiful restaurant is Oaxacan cooking, the most delicious of Mexico's regional cuisines. Check this place out, especially if you can't get down south (mains from M$175). Mon–Thurs 1–11pm, Fri & Sat 1pm–midnight, Sun 1–10pm.

Las Monjitas Morelos Ote 240 ☎ 81 8344 6713. Waitresses dressed as nuns dish up Mexican steaks and a selection of quality *antojitos*, including such house specialities as the *Father Chicken*, *The Sinner* and *Juan Pablo II*; the last is an artery-hardening combination of salami, pork, bacon, peppers, grilled cheese and guacamole (M$55–75). Beautiful *azulejos* on the walls and a stunningly kitsch Spanish facade make the slightly elevated prices worthwhile. Daily 10am–8pm.

★**El Rey del Cabrito** Constitución Ote 817 at Dr Coss ☎ 81 8345 3352, ⓦ elreydelcabrito.com.mx. The best place in town for *cabrito* is this slightly otherworldly restaurant, adorned with stuffed lions, an incongruous statue of Hindu elephant god Ganesha and even Egyptian hieroglyphs. The main event is sizzling, succulent baby goat meat (from M$260), and you can also try their charcoal-grilled beef – all best experienced in a group. Daily 11.30am–11pm.

Trece Lunas Abasolo 876 (next to Casa del Maiz) ☎ 81 1352 1127, ⓦ cafe13lunas.50webs.com. Hip Barrio Antiguo café serving excellent coffee, sweet and savoury crêpes, Spanish-style tortilla, club sandwiches and cannelloni salads (M$25–100) in a space decorated with murals and graffiti. Hosts tango and yoga lessons and other artsy events. Daily 8am–10pm.

Vips Hidalgo 401 ☎ 81 8343 8263, ⓦ vips.com.mx. Popular family chain restaurant (part of the Wal-Mart group), with a clean, modern interior and huge menu that includes a selection of Mexican classics, excellent soups and guacamole, pastas and decent burgers (most mains M$100–200). Get carafes of real, fresh orange, carrot and tomato juice. Sun–Thurs 7am–1am, Fri & Sat 24hr.

ZONA VALLE

El Gaucho Arroyo Seco 100 (off Garza Sada) ☎ 81 8358 4218, ⓦ restauranteelgaucho.com.mx. One of the best Valle restaurants, worth the taxi ride for the finest steaks in the city – prime slabs of Argentine beef for around M$360. Mon–Sat 12.30–11.30pm, Sun 12.30–11pm.

★**Pangea** Bosques del Valle 110-20, San Pedro Garza García ☎ 81 8356 5612, ⓦ grupopangea.com. The place for Mexican haute cuisine in Monterrey, helmed by local celebrity chef Guillermo González Beristáin: feast on roast chicken thighs stuffed with Serrano ham and goat cheese, seared sea scallops with foie gras, or rack of lamb with creamy porcini rice (mains M$310–500). Mon–Thurs 1–11pm, Fri & Sat 1pm–midnight, Sun 1–5pm.

Tacos del Julio Vasconcelos 100, at Juárez; Río Orinoco 115, Zona Valle (San Pedro Garza García) ☎ 81 8338 2033, ⓦ tacosdeljulio.com.mx. Popular Monterrey chain since 1993 that has spread north of the border thanks to its high-quality tacos and plates of five *taquitos* stuffed with all manner of tasty fillings; try the *volcanes*, with steak and cheese (M$50). Daily 6pm–6am.

7

DRINKING AND NIGHTLIFE

The traditional heart of Monterrey nightlife was the **Barrio Antiguo**, five square blocks of cobbled streets bounded by Dr Coss, Matamoros and Constitución. Since the drug cartel violence of 2011–2012 the crowds have dropped off considerably – check the latest with your hotel before going out. Alternatively, take a taxi to Zona Valle or San Pedro Garza García where the latest mega clubs and bars play host to a smart, affluent set.

CENTRO AND BARRIO ANTIGUO

Bar 1900 Gamma de Fiesta Americana Ocampo Ote 443 (enter at Hidalgo and Escobedo, on Plaza Hidalgo) ☎81 8150 7000, ⓦ gammahoteles.com. Colonial-style bar with cosy booths or bar stools, wood floors and decorated with bold Art Nouveau murals – live music most nights and a decent range of bottled beers, wines and spirits. Mon–Thurs noon–1am, Fri & Sat noon–2am.

Café Iguana Montemayor Sur 927 ☎81 8343 0822, ⓦ cafeiguana.tcom.mx. Monterrey's best rock club (though their DJs play techno and electronica most Thurs & Fri nights). Live rock bands usually perform on Sat. Entry is either free or rarely tops M$100. Thurs–Sat 9pm–3.30am.

Far West Rodeo Los Angeles 309 (off Universidad), San Nicolás de los Garza ☎81 8351 3030, ⓦ farwestrodeo .com. To remind yourself that you are still in Norteño country, make for this western-themed bar and live venue (north of the centre) – at midnight the dancefloor clears and a real rodeo kicks off. Thurs–Sun 8.30pm–4am.

McMullens Montemayor 843 ☎81 8343 7077. Not really an Irish pub, "El Mc" is a jumping bar with live bands and blend of ska, rock and indie sounds. Usually M$60 cover. Thurs 8pm–1am, Fri 8pm–2am, Sat 5pm–2am.

La Tumba Padre Mier Ote 827 ☎81 8345 6860. The main draw at this large, semi-outdoor bar is live acoustic music Thurs–Sat, and jazz on Tues. Expect to hear anything from *trova* and *son* to blues and rock. Cover varies depending on who is playing (from free to M$400). Mon–Sat 7pm–3am.

ZONA VALLE AND SAN PEDRO GARZA GARCÍA

Don Quintin Mexican Bar Garza Sada 2640 ☎81 8218 8700. Located across from the Tecnológico de Monterrey University and popular with students, this Mexican Revolution-themed bar/club features DJs, live bands and even big-screen TVs for sports. Tues–Fri 9pm–3am, Sat 3pm–4am.

Munster Public House Plaza Fiesta San Agustín, Batallón de San Patricio 1000 L-SA-8, San Pedro Garza García ☎81 8363 5284, ⓦ munsterpub.com. Monterrey's other "Irish" pub doesn't look much like an Irish pub (more like an elegant bar), but it does have over one hundred beers on offer and knocks out a respectable fish and chips. Mon–Sat 5pm–1am, Sun 1pm–midnight.

Sierra Madre Brewing Co José Vasconcelos Ote 564, San Pedro Garza García ☎81 8378 6001, ⓦ smbc.com .mx. Craft beer aficionados can indulge at the first brewpub in northern Mexico, with samplers of the local brews. Great bar food (nachos M$190, five mini burgers M$175). Also has an outpost just off the Macroplaza, on Morelos. Daily noon–1am.

DIRECTORY

Banks and exchange You can change money at any of the several *casas de cambio* on Ocampo between Zaragoza and Juárez (Mon–Fri 9am–1pm & 3–6pm, Sat 9am–12.30pm). Most banks (almost all with ATMs) are on Padre Mier, downtown.

Books Sanborn's, on Morelos near the Macroplaza (daily 7.30am–11pm), sells numerous magazines, some in English.

Consulates Australia, Parque Corporativo, Equus Torre Sur, Ricardo Margain 444, San Pedro Garza García ☎81 8158 0791; Canada, Gómez Morín 955, Suite 404, San Pedro Garza García (Mon–Fri 8.30am–1.30pm & 2.30–5pm; ☎81 8378 0240); South Africa, Díaz Ordaz 200, Colonia Santa María ☎81 8335 5949; US, Alfonso Reyes 150, Col. Valle Poniente, Santa Catarina (Mon–Fri 8am–2pm; ☎81 8047 3100, ⓦ monterrey.usconsulate.gov).

Emergencies ☎066; Ángeles Verdes (☎078); Cruz Roja (☎065); Cruz Verde (☎81 8371 5050); Police Federal de Caminos (☎81 8343 0173).

Internet As always, internet cafés open and close frequently here, though wi-fi is available in most hotels and many restaurants.

Post office In the Palacio Federal, Washington 648, at the north end of the Macroplaza (Mon–Fri 8am–4.30pm, Sat 8am–12.30pm).

Around Monterrey

Monterrey is surrounded by surprisingly wild and scenic countryside, though getting around the sights in the vicinity – the **Parque Ecológico Cola de Caballo**, for example – can be a hassle without your own vehicle. The exception is the colonial city of **Saltillo**, a worthwhile destination in its own right and easily reached by bus.

Parque Grutas de García

Carr García km 10 • Tues–Sun 9am–5pm • M$80 (includes cable car) • ☎ 81 8347 1533 • Buses run several times daily to Villa de García (1hr) from outside the Central de Autobuses, and from there you'll need to take a taxi for the remaining 9km; taxis charge around M$450–650 for the round trip (3–4hr) from downtown Monterrey

From Monterrey it's a relatively easy drive to the subterranean caverns of **Parque Grutas de García** which, despite some overdevelopment, contain an impressive array of contorted stalactites, stalagmites and an underground lake. The location is also spectacular, nestled beneath the craggy peaks of the Cerro del Fraile (1080m); guides only speak Spanish. Some 46km west of Monterrey near the village of **VILLA DE GARCÍA** (located 19km off Hwy-40), the caves are a popular outing from the city, especially at weekends, when hundreds of people can be found taking the ten-minute cable car to the main entrance (you can walk along a steep trail to the caverns instead, but the height gain is around 750m).

Parque Ecológico Cola de Caballo

Carr 20 Laguna de Sánchez km 6, La Cieneguilla • Daily 9am–6pm • M$40 • ☎ 81 8347 1533 • Taxis charge around M$650 for a round trip (3–4hr) to the park from downtown Monterrey

The trip to the **Parque Ecológico Cola de Caballo** (Horsetail Falls), 45km south of Monterrey on Hwy-85, is only really worthwhile after the rains, when the falls gush down a 25m cliff-face in scintillating fashion. The falls are a 600m hike from the car park, but you can also hire horses (M$30) or horse-drawn carriages (M$25 per person).

Santiago

Museo Histórico de Villa de Santiago Abasolo 100, at Juárez • Daily 8am–8pm • Free • ☎ 81 2285 0060

Set on the shores of the Presa Rodrigo Gómez (reservoir), **SANTIAGO** is heavily promoted as a Pueblo Mágico, with cobbled streets, a pretty 1745 church, the **Parroquia de Santiago Apóstol** and several handicraft stalls worth browsing – assuming the tour buses are not around. The region's history is chronicled in the small **Museo Histórico de Villa de Santiago**, in front of the church.

ARRIVAL AND DEPARTURE   SANTIAGO

By bus Santiago lies 35km south of Monterrey on Hwy-85. To get here by bus, take a Lineas Amarillas service from the main bus station; for Cola de Caballo you need to get off at El Cercado (M$34), just south of Santiago centre, where *camiones* (M$30) wait to take you to the falls at the junction with Hwy-20.

Saltillo

Capital of the state of Coahuila, **SALTILLO** feels far more provincial than Monterrey, despite being another large city of some seven hundred thousand. Lying just 85km to the southwest, through a high desert of yucca and Joshua trees, it's infinitely quieter than Monterrey and, at 1600m above sea level in the Sierra Madre Oriental, usually feels a little cooler.

If you read Spanish you'll get a lot out of Saltillo's surprisingly good cache of museums, but if not it's still a lovely place to stroll around, admire some beautiful buildings and soak up the colonial ambience.

Plaza de Armas and around

Mercado Juárez Plaza Acuña • Daily 7am–8pm

Two contrasting, and almost adjoining, squares grace the centre of town: the old **Plaza de Armas** is formal, tranquil, illuminated at night and sometimes hosts music performances, while **Plaza Acuña**, two blocks south, is surrounded by crowded shopping streets marking the rowdy heart of the commercial city. On the south side of

> ### AN IRISHMAN IN SALTILLO
>
> Business in Saltillo in the early twentieth century was dominated by **William Purcell** (1844–1909), a talented Irishman who left his home to seek his fortune in Texas and Mexico aged 17. When he died in San Antonio he was a millionaire, owning half a million acres of cattle ranches, cotton farms and several silver mines. In the 1890s he opened a bank in Saltillo (now a gallery, see below). You can also view the **Casa Purcell**, at Hidalgo 231, a grand English Gothic mansion built by Purcell in 1906.

Plaza Acuña, **Mercado Juárez** is a good place to browse for *sarapes* and souvenirs, and grab a cheap *caldo de res* or torta.

Catedral de Santiago

Hidalgo and Juárez, Plaza de Armas • Daily 9am–1pm & 4–7.30pm

The magnificent eighteenth-century **Catedral de Santiago** is one of the most beautiful churches in northern Mexico, with an elaborately carved churrigueresque facade and doorways, an enormous bell tower and a smaller clock tower. The spacious Neoclassical interior is relatively plain, but there are two giant gold *retablos* in the transepts, and numerous oil paintings, including an early eighteenth-century *Virgen del Carmen* by Antonio de Torres.

Museo del Palacio

Palacio del Gobierno, Hidalgo and Juárez, Plaza de Armas • Tues–Sun 10am–6pm • Free • ☎ 844 411 8529

Set inside the former Coahuila government house, completed in 1885, the stately **Museo del Palacio** contains temporary historical displays (topics have included the 1812 Constitución of Cádiz), and a permanent exhibition on the history of Coahuila.

Galería del Instituto Coahuilense de Cultura

Juárez at Hidalgo (Plaza de Armas) • Mon–Fri 9am–7pm • Free • ☎ 844 414 1781

On the south side of the Plaza de Armas the **Galería del Instituto Coahuilense de Cultura** often hosts diverting temporary exhibits by Coahuila artists, and also houses a decent Spanish bookshop and the best place for a coffee in town, *El Sorbito*.

Recinto del Patrimonio Cultural Universitario

Hidalgo 211 • Tues–Sun 10am–6pm • Free • ☎ 844 410 9705, ⊛ www.recintodelpatrimonioculturaluniversitario.uadec.mx

Just off the north side of the Plaza de Armas is Saltillo's fanciest gallery space, the **Recinto del Patrimonio Cultural Universitario**, housed in a mansion dating back to 1680. The galleries here are tastefully presented, and though the collection of eighteenth- and nineteenth-century Mexican paintings is nothing special, there are a few quality pieces, including a couple of **Miguel Cabrera** portraits. There's also work by Jose Obregón, Ignacio Rosas and a startling triptych from Saturnino Herrán (see p.363), *La Leyenda de los Volcanos*. The **Museo del Sitio** section covers the history of the building, with a section on William Purcell (see box above), a remarkable Irish merchant.

Centro Cultural Vito Alessio Robles

Hidalgo, at Aldama • Tues–Sat 10am–6pm • Free • ☎ 844 412 8645

Saltillo's oldest streets fan out from Plaza de Armas, lined with some fine colonial houses. One historical building worth seeking out is the carefully preserved **Centro Cultural Vito Alessio Robles**, the old town hall, one block north of the plaza. The walls of the courtyard and the staircase are adorned with murals completed by Elena Huerta 1973–75, depicting the history of the town from prehistoric times to the 1950s, while temporary art exhibits take up the inner galleries. There's also the small Sala Museográfica dedicated to historian **Vito Alessio Robles** (born in Saltillo in 1879), containing mementos and personal effects (his piano, uniform, photos and the like).

Museo de la Revolución Mexicana

Hidalgo Sur 167 • Tues–Sun 10am–6pm • Free • ☎ 844 410 4794

The illuminating **Museo de la Revolución Mexicana** is focused solely on the 1910 Mexican Revolution, a homage in part to local son and former president **Venustiano Carranza**, who was born in Coahuila in 1859 and studied in Saltillo. It's an impressive display, with touchscreens, videos, music and a variety of artefacts to highlight the key stages of the Revolution beginning with the Díaz regime – there's even a recording of the old dictator speaking. Francisco Madero gets his own section, as does Carranza (with photos of him in Saltillo), and the 1917 constitution is covered in some detail. Labelling is in Spanish only.

El Sarape de Saltillo

Hidalgo Sur 305 • Mon–Sat 9am–1pm & 3–7pm

Saltillo is famous for its **sarapes** (multicoloured woollen shawls), and there are several small shops where (at least on weekdays) you can watch the manufacturing process. The best is tucked at the back of the artesanía shop **El Sarape de Saltillo**. Sadly, the old ways are vanishing fast, and most now use artificial fibres and chemical dyes: many of those in the market are mass-produced in virulent clashing colours.

Museo del Sarape y Trajes Mexicanos

Allende Sur 160 • Tues–Sat 10am–6pm • Free • ☎ 844 481 6900

This eighteenth-century former home is now the **Museo del Sarape y Trajes Mexicanos**, a celebration of the city's most famous product. It's not known why sarape production blossomed here in particular from around 1750, though it's thought that the boom in sheep farming during colonial times helped, as did the migration of indigenous Tlaxcalan weavers from central Mexico. The main exhibition contains forty brightly dyed sarapes to highlight this history, and there's a showroom of traditional Mexican costumes from pre-Hispanic times.

Museo de las Aves de México

Bolívar 151, at Hidalgo • Tues–Sat 10am–6pm, Sun 11am–7pm • M$10 • ☎ 844 414 0167, ⓦ museodelasaves.org

Bird lovers should visit the **Museo de las Aves de México**, housed in what once was the Jesuit-run Colegio de San Juan, overlooking San Juan Nepomunceno church. Inside the museum you'll find five themed areas, beginning with the origins of birds and their physiology – beaks, feathers, eggs and skeletons. The birds of Mexico, from parrots to pelicans, are featured, along with a section on bird migration (the only section labelled in English) and birds from Coahuila. The main focus throughout is on a vast collection of stuffed birds, including a giant Californian condor, albatross, owls, hawks and ostrich. There's also a fun song room where the cries and tweets of various species are played.

Museo de los Presidentes Coahuilenses

Nicolás Bravo Sur 264, at Juan Antonio de la Fuente • Tues–Sun 10am–5pm • Free • ☎ 844 410 7251, ⓦ museopresidentes.mx

The compact **Museo de los Presidentes Coahuilenses** honours the five presidents of Mexico to hail from Coahuila: Venustiano Carranza (1915–20), Roque González Garza (1915), Eulalio Gutiérrez (1914–15), Francisco Madero (1911–13) and Melchor Múzquiz (1832). Each of the great men is remembered by a small exhibit containing documents, artefacts and personal effects (the first presidential sash, worn by Guadalupe Victoria, is also here), but everything is labelled in Spanish only.

Museo del Desierto

Pérez Treviño 3745, in Parque Las Maravillas • Tues–Sun 10am–5pm • M$90, children M$50 • ☎ 844 986 9000, ⓦ museodeldesierto.org

About 3km east of the centre, the impressive **Museo del Desierto** charts the development and history of deserts, displays a huge array of dinosaur and prehistoric animal fossils, and rare artefacts from Neolithic cultures in the region. Labelling is in Spanish only.

ARRIVAL AND INFORMATION

By plane Saltillo's tiny airport (Aeropuerto Internacional Plan de Guadalupe) lies 16km northeast of the city centre and serves daily Aeroméxico flights to Mexico City (3 daily; 1hr 30min). Taxis charge M$150–200 into the city.

By bus Buses (marked "Centro/Camionera" or #9; M$6) run between Saltillo's Centro de Autobuses, 3km south of the centre on Luis Echeverría, the cathedral on the Plaza de Armas and onwards a couple more stops to the Plaza Acuña, right at the heart of things (to get back, catch it on Aldama near Zaragoza). Taxis should be around M$30–40; the meter should start at M$7 and go up M$4.50 per km (as of 2015 they are legally required to use the meter, so insist on it).

Destinations Chihuahua (6 daily; 10hr); Durango (5 daily; 6–7hr); Parras (7 daily; 2hr 30min); Mexico City (every 1–2hr; 10–12hr); Monterrey (hourly; 1hr 30min); Nuevo Laredo (every 1–2hr; 4–5hr); San Luis Potosí (hourly; 5hr); Zacatecas (hourly; 4–6hr).

Tourist information Visit La Dirección de Turismo Municipal, at Morelos 137 (Mon–Fri 9am–5pm; ☎ 844 439 7195, ⓦ saltillo.gob.mx). There are usually small information booths at the bus station, and on the roads coming into town (from Monterrey, km 1.5, Gasolinera 4540; from Zacatecas, Las Teresitas 130, at Cárdenas). Check also ⓦ ocvsaltillo.com.

ACCOMMODATION

City Express Saltillo Sur Luis Echeverría 350-A ☎ 844 411 0030, ⓦ cityexpress.com.mx. Hard to beat for convenience if travelling by bus – this modern motel is right opposite the bus station. Rooms are standard business style, with internet and flat-screen TV, and breakfast is included. M$950

★ **Hotel Colonial San Miguel** General Cepeda Sur 410 ☎ 844 410 3082, ⓦ hotelcolonialsaltillo.com. Stylish rooms set in a historic building with a small pool and courtyard, blending original wood shutters and doors with contemporary furnishings, cable TV, a/c and free wi-fi. M$833

Hotel Urdiñola Victoria 211 ☎ 844 414 0940. If you want to savour some faded colonial splendour on a budget, check out this old gem, with its tiled open lobby dominated by a wide staircase flanked by suits of armour, and fountains trickling amid the greenery of the courtyard. Free (but slow) wi-fi, and basic but adequate rooms with fans only. M$630

EATING

La Canasta Carranza 2485 ☎ 844 415 8050, ⓦ restaurantelacanasta.mx. Highly acclaimed since it opened in 1965, this restaurant serves fine international and Mexican cuisine, steaks, and their specialities, *arroz huerfano* ("orphan" rice with ham, nuts and bacon; M$120) and lemon meringue pie (M$55); M$190–300 for most mains. Mon–Sat noon–midnight, Sun noon–7pm.

El Mesón Principal Carranza 4671, at Egipto ☎ 844 415 0015, ⓦ mesonprincipal.com. For high-quality sit-down meals, take a taxi out to *El Mesón Principal*, which specializes in sizzling *cabrito al pastor* (barbecued baby goat), and mouthwatering *fritada* (grilled steak platter).

Daily 8am–11pm.

Panadería Mena Pan de Pulque Madero 1326 ☎ 844 412 1671. Try Saltillo's famous *pan de pulque*, bread made of wheat, egg, cinnamon and unrefined cactus juice, at this classic bakery from 1925, three long blocks west of Carranza (two buns for M$40). Daily 9am–9pm.

Venenito Café Galería del Instituto Coahuilense de Cultura, Juárez 109 at Hidalgo (Plaza de Armas) ☎ 844 410 3066, ⓦ venenitocafe.com. For the best coffee (Oaxaca and Chiapas), frappes, cakes and panini in town (M$60), visit this cosy café in the corner of the Cultural Institute. Tues–Sun 10am–9pm.

DIRECTORY

Banks There are banks with ATMs all over the centre of town, including Banamex and HSBC, just off the plaza.

Internet Try Cyberbase at Padre Flores 159 (Mon–Sat 9.30am–10pm; M$8/hr).

Pharmacy Try the large Farmacia Guadalajara at Victoria and Purcell, overlooking the Alameda.

Post office The post office is at Guadalupe Victoria 303 (Mon–Fri 9am–4pm, Sat 9am–1pm).

Valle de Parras

Around 160km west of Saltillo, the **Valle de Parras** is the oldest **wine-growing** region in Mexico. Dismissed as poor quality for years, the region's Cabernet Sauvignons in particular, which account for around seventy percent of production, are finally garnering a following in international markets. The region is anchored by the pleasant oasis town of **PARRAS DE LA FUENTE**, a good place to base yourself.

WINES OF PARRAS

The biggest draw in the Valle de Parras is wine – most vineyards offer tours and tastings and can be visited on day trips from Parras de la Fuente.

Antigua Bodega de Perote Ramos Arizpe 131 (2km west of Parras de la Fuente) ☎ 84 2422 1698, ⍵ antiguahaciendadeperote.com. Produces fine wines as well as brandy and *sotol*, the local spirit. Runs a hotel on site (M$680); call ahead for tours and visits.

Las Bodegas de Casa Madero Carretera 102 Paila-Parras km 18.5, Hacienda San Lorenzo (8km north of Parras de la Fuente) ☎ 84 2422 0055, ⍵ madero.com.mx. This is the largest and oldest Parras wine producer, with roots going back to the Americas' first winery, established here in 1597 by the Spaniards. You can take free 30min tours of the facilities and museum, buy and taste the wine and admire the colonial Hacienda de San Lorenzo on site. Daily 8am–5.30pm.

Las Bodegas El Vesubio Madero 36, at Andrés S Viesca, Parras de la Fuente. Established by Italian Nicolás Nicolielli in 1891 in downtown Parras, this is a smaller operation. The shop is open daily. Mon–Fri 9am–1pm & 2–7pm, Sat & Sun 9am–7pm.

7

ARRIVAL AND DEPARTURE

PARRAS DE LA FUENTE

By bus Parras is around 160km from both Torreón and Saltillo in the south of Coahuila, and is served by regular second-class buses from Saltillo (2hr 30min), via Autobuses Saltillo-Parras (☎ 842 422 0870), and Monterrey (daily 10am & 6.30pm; 3hr).

ACCOMMODATION

Hostal el Farol Ramos Arizpe 301 ☎ 84 2422 1113, ⍵ hostalelfarol.com. The best place to stay in the town itself is this colonial beauty, with rustic furniture, antique bed frames, cable TV and free bottles of water. **M$930**

The coastal route

If you're determined to travel between the Yucatán, Veracruz and the US by the shortest route, avoiding Mexico City altogether, you'll need to follow the **coastal route**. North of Tuxpán (see p.422), there's plenty of sandy beachfront, but access is difficult, beaches tend to be windswept and scrubby, and much of the area is marred by oil refineries. Several small-scale resorts have been developed here (such as **La Pesca** and the villages around **Laguna Madre**), but these tend to be popular with nearby city-dwellers and have little to offer compared with the beaches further south. It's also very, very hot. Another issue is drug violence – **Tamaulipas**, the focus of the bloody conflict between the Gulf Cartel and Los Zetas, had become the most dangerous part of Mexico by 2012, and though things have improved somewhat since then (the murder rate had halved by 2014), it remains blighted by shootings and kidnapping (see box, p.468). If you have time you'd be well advised to cut inland from Tampico to **Monterrey** (see p.434), where there's plenty of metropolitan diversions and a larger choice of routes to the border.

Tampico

Some 490km north of Veracruz, on the Río Pánuco and just across the border in Tamaulipas state, **TAMPICO** is one of Mexico's busiest ports, with a population of around 860,000. It was from here that Humphrey Bogart set out to unearth *The Treasure of the Sierra Madre* in 1948, and the older parts of town still have a slightly dilapidated feel, with peeling, ramshackle clapboard houses contrasting with the affluent but characterless US mall-style development on the outskirts. However, in a bid to attract more tourists, the downtown area has been spruced up with a host of thoughtful restoration projects, and the graceful New Orleans-style cast-iron buildings add a vaguely sophisticated charm to the main plazas.

Plaza de Armas and Plaza de la Libertad

Downtown, the city's dual nature is instantly apparent. Within a hundred metres of each other are two plazas: the grandiose **Plaza de Armas** – rich and formal, it is ringed by government buildings, the impressive **Catedral Inmaculada Concepción** (built in the 1930s with money donated by American oil tycoon Edward Doheny) and the smart hotels; and the **Plaza de la Libertad**, which is raucous, rowdy – there's usually some form of music played from the bandstand each evening – and peopled by wandering vendors. Ringed by triple-decker wrought-iron verandas, it has been spruced up to form an attractive square.

Espacio Cultural Metropolitano (METRO Tampico)

Adolfo López Mateos s/n, Col Obrera • Tues–Sun 10am–6pm • ☎ 833 126 0888, ⓦ metrodetampico.com • **Museo de la Cultura Huasteca** Tues–Sun 9am–5.45pm • M$52; **Galería de Exposiciones Temporales** Sun & Tues–Fri 10am–6pm, Sat 10am–8pm • M$30, free Tues • Walk north on Olmos from Plaza de Armas till you hit the Laguna del Carpintero, then stroll (anticlockwise) around the edge till you see it (2km); or catch a "Central Camionera" bus from Olmos and ask to get off at the Parque Metropolitano; taxis should be M$40

Worth a look is the **Espacio Cultural Metropolitano** or **METRO Tampico**, home to two theatres, Teatro Metropolitano and Teatro Experimental, the highly regarded **Galería de Exposiciones Temporales**, featuring temporary art exhibits, and the **Museo de la Cultura Huasteca**, which provides an absorbing introduction to indigenous Huastec culture through original artefacts and engaging displays. **Huastec civilization** blossomed in the Postclassic era (eleventh to fifteenth centuries), before being conquered by the Aztecs and then the Spanish – today there are over 60,000 Huastec speakers, living predominantly in the Río Pánuco region.

ARRIVAL AND INFORMATION   TAMPICO

By plane Arriving at Tampico's Francisco Javier Mina airport, some 15km north of the city, you'll have to take a taxi (or pay around M$65 for a *colectivo*). The most frequent connections are to Mexico City or Monterrey.

By bus Tampico's modern Terminal Central de Autobuses (guardería 6am–midnight), Bustamante 210, is in an unattractive area some 10km north of the city. To get downtown, take a bus, a rattling *colectivo* or one of the shared *perimetral* taxis (all M$6). Buses back to the terminal leave from Plaza de Armas, at the corner of Olmos and Carranza.

Destinations Ciudad Victoria (hourly or better; 3hr); Matamoros (hourly; 7–8hr); Mexico City (every 1–2hr; 8hr); Monterrey (hourly; 7–8hr); Nuevo Laredo (2 daily; 10hr); San Luis Potosí (11 daily; 7hr); Veracruz (8 daily; 9hr).

Tourist information You'll find tourist information booths on both plazas, though these seem to be open quite irregularly. The main tourist office is northwest of the centre at Hidalgo 2703 and a real pain to get to (☎ 833 217 8940, ⓦ tampicoturismo.com).

ACCOMMODATION AND EATING

Elite Restaurante & Helados Díaz Mirón Ote 211 (near Plaza de Armas) ☎ 833 212 0364. A quiet haven in this noisy town, *Elite* does excellent ice cream, coffee, frappucinos and good Mexican staples for under M$50. Has roots in a street stall opened in 1948. Daily 7.30am–11pm.

Hotel Inglaterra Díaz Mirón 116 ☎ 833 219 2857, ⓦ hinglaterra.com.mx. On the Plaza de Armas, this is one of the most comfortable and safe central options, with compact modern rooms, a restaurant and a small pool. M$920

Impala Díaz Mirón Pte 220 ☎ 833 212 0990, ⓦ impaladetampico.com. This aged hotel has been renovated many times over the years and remains exceptionally clean, if relatively simple; the huge buffet breakfast is included (you can sometimes get a cheaper rate if you skip breakfast). M$650

Jardín Corona Hidalgo 1915, Col Smith ☎ 833 213 6710. Plush Argentine seafood and steak restaurant since 1964, worth the taxi ride for the huge plates of shrimp, crab and fresh fish, as well as fabulous *bife de chorizo*. Reckon on spending at least M$400 per head for a good meal. Live Latino sounds every Fri & Sat. Daily noon–10pm.

El Porvenir Hidalgo 1403, at Oaxaca ☎ 833 213 0568, ⓦ grupoelporvenir.com. Best seafood in the region since 1923 – come especially for the huge plates of prawn and crab, boiled, stuffed or spiced a variety of ways ("El Mercedes Benz" is fish fillet with shrimp in garlic sauce topped with clams). Daily noon–11pm.

DIRECTORY

Banks There are banks on the Plaza de Armas and all through the central area.

Post office At Madero 309, on the north side of the Plaza de la Libertad.

TAMPICO

Bus Station & Airport

Bus Station & Airport

Metro Tampico

Laguna del Carpintero

N

7

■ **ACCOMMODATION**
Hotel Inglaterra   2
Impala   1

Parque Juárez

Jardín del Arte Tampico

Parque 20-30

Parque Méndez

F. VELÁSQUEZ

Catedral Inmaculada Concepción

Banco Santander

Plaza de Armas

Templo Bethel

Palacio de Gobierno

Plaza de la Libertad

Banco Santander

Mercado Hidalgo

Río Pánuco

● **EATING**
Elite Restaurante
& Helados   3
Jardín Corona   1
El Porvenir   2

0   250
metres

The central corridor

The central corridor between Mexico City, the Bajío and the US border is one of the most well-travelled and well-served routes in the country, with fast highways and numerous bus services all the way. It's worth a diversion into **Durango**, certainly the most attractive city on route, or historic **Hidalgo del Parral**. History lovers will also enjoy **Chihuahua**, the home of Pancho Villa and a relatively affluent city that has invested a lot in its heritage, museums and art. If you have time, an excursion to the ruins at **Paquimé**, near Nuevo Casas Grandes, is worth the four-hour ride from Chihuahua – and if you have a car, there are several other enticing destinations nearby.

7

Durango

In the 1960s John Wayne came to the beautiful colonial city of **DURANGO** to make seven Westerns (among them *Chisum* and *The War Wagon*), a tradition maintained today in studios outside the city. Although the Sierra Madre still looms on the western horizon, the country around the city itself is flat; just two low hills mark it out from the plain: the **Cerro del Mercado**, a giant lump of iron ore that testifies to the area's mineral wealth, rises squat and black to the north, while to the west a climb or cable-car ride up the **Cerro de los Remedios** provides a wonderful panorama over the whole city. Durango, with its roughly 630,000 inhabitants, sits between these two hills in the Valle del Guadiana.

Catedral Basílica Menor

Negrete Pte 601 (Plaza de Armas) • **Catedral Basílica Menor** Daily 7.30am–1.30pm & 4–9pm • Free • ☎ 618 812 5077 **Museo de Arte Sacro** Tues–Fri 10am–1.30pm & 4–7pm, Sat & Sun 10am–2pm • M$15 • ☎ 618 119 6235

Almost all the monuments in downtown Durango are clustered in a few streets around the **Plaza de Armas** and the huge covered market nearby. On the plaza itself is the **Catedral Basílica Menor**, its two robust domed towers dwarfing the narrow facade. Dating back to 1695, it's a typical Mexican church: externally imposing, weighty and Baroque, with a magnificent setting overlooking the plaza, but the interior is a little disappointing – dim and uninspired by comparison. Much better is the opulent collection of religious art and historical artefacts within the cathedral's **Museo de Arte Sacro**; enter on Negrete, behind the cathedral.

Teatro Ricardo Castro

Bruno Martínez 220, at 20 de Noviembre • Daily 9am–3pm • Free • ☎ 618 811 4694

Following 20 de Noviembre down from the cathedral (stretching away to the left as you face it) brings you to the grandiose Porfiriano **Teatro Ricardo Castro**, completed in 1924, with its elegant interior of marble floors and crystal chandeliers.

Museo de Historia y Arte "El Palacio de los Gurza"

Negrete Pte 901, at Zaragoza • Tues–Fri 10am–6pm, Sat & Sun 11am–6pm • M$10 • ☎ 618 811 1720

The beautifully restored **Museo de Historia y Arte "El Palacio de los Gurza"** features innovative galleries chronicling the history of the city through ancient coins, photography, newspaper articles and contemporary art. The Porfiriana-style house mostly dates from the mid-nineteenth century, when it was owned by Antonio Gurza López, a wealthy merchant.

FERIA NACIONAL DE DURANGO

Durango's month-long **festival**, held in July, celebrates the city's foundation on July 8, 1563 by Spanish explorer Francisco de Ibarra. Festivities commence several days before and run right through till the fiesta of the Virgen del Refugio on July 22 – well worth going out of your way for, though rooms are booked solid. See ⓦ www.ferianacionaldurango.gob.mx for more information.

Airport , Central de Autobuses, Fresnillo, Zacatecas & Torreon

DURANGO

■ **ACCOMMODATION**
Casablanca	5
Durango Travellers Hostel	4
Hostal de la Monja	2
Hotel Gobernador	1
Posada San Agustín	3

● **EATING**
101 Vuelve a la Vida	1
Corleone Pizza	3
La Fogata	4
Fonda de la Tía Chona	8
Gorditas Gabino	5
Pampas Do Brasil	6
La Tostada	7
Wallander	2

7

Museo de Arqueología Ganot-Peschard

Zaragoza 315 • Tues–Fri 9am–6pm, Sat & Sun 11am–6pm • M$10 • ☎ 618 813 1047

For a glimpse into Durango's pre-Columbian past visit the **Museo de Arqueología Ganot-Peschard**, which has a fine display of prehistoric finds, fossils and ancient skulls (Spanish captions only), in a nineteenth-century edifice that once served as the state archives. The museum is named in honour of its founders and current directors, Jaime Ganot and Alejando Peschard, who uncovered numerous examples of pre-Hispanic cave art in the region in the 1970s.

Museo General Francisco Villa (Palacio de Zambrano)

5 de Febrero 97 • Tues–Fri 10am–6pm, Sat & Sun 11am–6pm • M$20 • ☎ 618 811 47 93

The elegant porticoed facade of the **Museo General Francisco Villa (Palacio de Zambrano)** dominates the north side of **Plaza IV Centenario**, one block west of Plaza de Armas. Originally the eighteenth-century mansion of Spanish mining magnate Juan José Zambrano, it was taken over by the local government after independence and became the governor's residence. Local artist Francisco Montoya de la Cruz decorated the stairwells and walls of the two-storey arcaded patio inside in 1950, with bold murals depicting the state's history. Exhibits chart the political and social history of the region since the Revolution, with special attention given to hero Pancho Villa (see box, p.464). Spanish labels only, but English-speaking guides are usually available (free).

Museo de las Culturas Populares

5 de Febrero 1107 • Tues–Fri 9am–6pm, Sat 10am–6pm, Sun noon–6pm • M$10 • ☎ 618 825 8827

A few blocks west of Plaza IV Centenario, along 5 de Febrero, lies the **Museo de las Culturas Populares**, with rooms dedicated to local, native styles of weaving, ceramics, basketware and mask making. Enthusiastic guides explain all, and there are often interesting temporary exhibitions.

Casa de Cultural Banamex (Palacio del Conde del Valle de Súchil)

5 de Febrero Ote 401, at Madero • Tues–Sat 10am–7pm, Sun 10am–6pm • Free • ☎ 618 811 7136, ⓦ casasdeculturabanamex.com

The most elaborate of Durango's Spanish-style mansions is the **Palacio del Conde del Valle de Súchil**, now reborn as the **Casa de Cultural Banamex** thanks to the Mexican banking giant. Completed in 1764 for the Conde de Súchil, former Spanish governor of Durango, its exuberantly carved columns and wealth of extravagant detail are quite undamaged by time. Inside, a series of galleries hosts temporary exhibitions from modern photography to eighteenth-century art.

Museo Regional de Durango-UJED

Victoria Sur 100, at Aquiles Serdán • Mon–Fri 8am–3pm • M$12 • ☎ 618 813 1094, ⓦ museo.ujed.mx

The stately former residence of ex-Governor Francisco Gómez Palacio, completed in 1890, is now the Universidad Juárez's **Museo Regional de Durango-UJED** or "Museo del Aguacate", after the avocado (*aguacate*) trees growing in the courtyard. It contains several absorbing galleries on local archeology and history, including special sections on Tepehuana culture, and Miguel Cabrera's cycle of ten paintings depicting the life of Mary.

Museo de Arte Guillermo Ceniceros

Independencia Nte 135 • Tues–Fri 10am–6.30pm, Sat & Sun 11am–6.30pm • Free • ☎ 618 825 0027, ⓦ guillermoceniceros.com

The legacy of whom many describe as the last great Mexican muralist is preserved at the **Museo de Arte Guillermo Ceniceros**, a vibrant showcase for local Durango artists as well Guillermo Ceniceros himself. Ceniceros was born in Durango in 1939, and later worked with muralist David Alfaro Siqueiros. The museum displays more than fifty of his works, in what was once a Carmelite convent. Other rooms house temporary exhibitions from local and national artists.

Paseo Túnel de Minería

Placita Juan Pablo II • Tues–Sun 10am–9.30pm; Legends of Durango Tues–Thurs 1pm, 6.30pm & 8pm; Fri 1pm, 6pm, 7pm & 8pm; Sat & Sun 11am, 1pm, 6pm, 7pm & 8pm • M$20 • ☎ 618 137 5361

One of Durango's biggest crowd-pleasers is the **Paseo Túnel de Minería**, commemorating the city's mining heritage but popular mainly because of the chance to shuffle through a 280m tunnel some 8m below the streets. The tunnel – enhanced with mining exhibits – links Placita Juan Pablo II, at the Arzobispado, with Plaza de Armas, and there's talk of one day extending it to Plaza IV Centenario. A melodramatic light-and-sound show (with actors) dubbed "Legends of Durango" runs several times daily (Spanish only).

Teleférico de Durango

Calle de la Cruz, between Calvario and Florida (by the central library); Remedios station on Linda Vista by Remedios church • Tues–Thurs & Sun 10am–8pm, Fri & Sat 10am–9pm • M$20 return (M$10 single); 50 percent discount for Paseo Túnel de Minería ticket holders

Durango's popular **Teleférico** (cable car) connects the Cerro del Calvario in the centre with the viewpoint on the **Cerro de los Remedios** some 750m away, topped with the Parroquia de Nuestra Señora de los Remedios and offering sensational panoramas of the city (both stations offer free wi-fi).

Parque Guadiana

Av de la Normal • Daily 24hr • Free • **Museo Bebeleche** Armando del Castillo Franco km 1.5 (Parque Sahuatoba) • Tues–Fri 9am–5pm, Sat & Sun 11am–7pm • M$50–70 (adults and children) • ☎ 618 827 2525, ⓦ bebeleche.org.mx • Take a bus marked "Remedios/Parque Guadiana" from outside the cathedral

Covering the northwestern flanks of the Cerro de los Remedios, 1km west of the city centre, the **Parque Guadiana** is a vast area of fragrant eucalyptus and shady willows, dotted with fountains and kids' playgrounds. Durango's pride and joy adjoins the park: the **Museo Bebeleche**, a lavish hands-on museum and learning centre. Youngsters will enjoy most of the interactive exhibits, though labels are in Spanish only.

ARRIVAL AND DEPARTURE   DURANGO

By plane Durango's small airport (Aeropuerto Internacional General Guadalupe Victoria) lies 15km northeast of the centre, served primarily by flights from Mexico City and Tijuana. Low-cost TAR Aerolíneas operates flights to Guadalajara, Monterrey and Puerto Vallarta. Taxis into the centre are M$180–200.

By bus Buses arrive at the Central de Autobuses or just "La Camionera" (guardería, 7am–11pm), over 4km east of downtown at Francisco Villa 102; to get to the centre, take one of the off-white buses (M$8) marked "Centro" or "ISSSTE" from

in front of the station. These will drop you right at the Plaza de Armas near the cathedral. Taxis are metered and should be around M$40–50. Note that with the completion of Puente Baluarte in 2012, the new "Carretera Interoceánica" to Mazatlán has cut travel times to the coast dramatically.

Destinations Aguascalientes (20 daily; 6hr); Chihuahua (11 daily; 8–11hr); Ciudad Juárez (at least hourly; 12–14hr); Mazatlán (11 daily; 3.5hr); Mexico City (14 daily; 11–13hr); Monterrey (5 daily; 8hr); Parral (9 daily; 6hr); Zacatecas (roughly hourly; 4–5hr).

INFORMATION

Tourist office Facing the cathedral, turn left along 20 de Noviembre (as it runs into Florida) just past Independencia to reach the second-floor tourist office (Secretaria de Turismo), Florida Pte 1106 (Mon–Fri 9am–8pm, Sat & Sun

10am–6pm; ☎ 618 811 9677, ⓦ durangoturismo.com and ⓦ durangoturistico.com). Information kiosks are normally open in Plaza de Armas (daily 9am–8pm) and the bus station (Mon–Sat 9am–9pm, Sun 9am–3pm).

ACCOMMODATION

Casablanca 20 de Noviembre Pte 811, at Zaragoza ☎ 618 811 3599, ⓦ hotelcasablancadurango.com. Big, old-fashioned colonial hotel across from the cathedral. Spacious, comfortable and reasonably good value, if unexciting. **M$700**

★ **Durango Travellers Hostel** Privada Florida 1135, Int. 5, Barrio del Calvario ☎ 618 811 3593, ⓦ durango travellershostel.com.mx. This friendly hostel helmed by

Omar and Mercedes, 10min from the plaza, is easily the best budget option in the city, with a charming rooftop terrace, shared kitchen, free wi-fi and four bright, comfy a/c dorms (for 4–5 people) and one private room (for up to 3) with shared bathroom. Dorms **M$180**, double **M$450**

Hostal de la Monja Constitución Sur 214 ☎ 618 837 1719, ⓦ hostaldelamonja.com.mx. Ignoring the international chains on the outskirts, this is the most comfortable place to stay in town, a gorgeous colonial property right on the main plaza. All rooms and suites feature polished wood floors, free wi-fi and a simple, clean style, but the cheapest rooms are small and fairly plain, given the price. M$1400

Hotel Gobernador 20 de Noviembre Ote 257 ☎ 618 813 1919, ⓦ hotelgobernador.com.mx. This luxurious monolith is surrounded by verdant gardens; the spacious rooms come with marble-clad bathrooms and wall-mounted LCD TVs, and there's a pool, gym and all the business-related extras. M$970

Posada San Agustín 20 de Noviembre Pte 906, at Hidalgo ☎ 618 837 2000, ⓦ posadasanagustin.com. Excellent mid-range option, with simple but cosy a/c rooms with cable TV, set around a courtyard in a graceful nineteenth-century building. Free wi-fi in the courtyard. M$650

EATING

101 Vuelve a la Vida Felipe Pescador, at Cuauhtémoc ☎ 618 184 1443. If you fancy seafood, it's worth hopping in a taxi (5min) for this popular, no-frills bar, serving excellent shellfish and fresh seafood platters, as well as a host of cheap beers and cocktails. Daily noon–midnight.

Corleone Pizza Constitución Nte 114, at Serdán ☎ 618 811 6900. One of the best Italian joints in the city, this buzzing family restaurant is best known for its pizzas (from M$100) and an admirable range of cocktails. Daily 1pm–midnight.

La Fogata Cuauhtémoc Sur 200, at Negrete ☎ 618 817 0347. This moderately priced, elegant restaurant is the choice of Durango's movers and shakers, serving international and Mexican food but best known for its succulent steaks. Mains M$80–160). Daily 1pm–midnight.

Fonda de la Tía Chona Nogal 110 ☎ 618 812 7748, ⓦ fondadelatiachona.com. A local dinner favourite, the rustic, antique-strewn interior is often packed with *Durangueños*. It serves excellent traditional Durango cuisine (try their *caldillo durangueño*, beef stew) at reasonable prices (M$90–160). Tues–Sat 5pm–1am, Sun 1–6pm.

Gorditas Gabino Constitución Nte 100 ☎ 618 813 0121. Bright, clean, economical restaurant serving steaks, tacos, burritos and burgers. They do a pretty decent *enchiladas rojas* for a few pesos, and the trademark gorditas (deep-fried corn meal with sausage; M$12–15) are fabulous. Daily 10am–8pm.

Pampas Do Brasil Constitución Sur 102, in the San Jorge hotel ☎ 618 827 6121, ⓦ pampasdurango.com. Fun place to stuff yourself; the menu largely comprises Brazilian cuts of juicy grilled steak and meats, in something resembling *churrascuria*-style eating. Mains M$60–150. Mon–Sat 1–11pm, Sun 1–7pm.

La Tostada Florida 1125 ☎ 618 811 4577. This pleasant, clean restaurant near the cable car is popular with the locals. It serves Mexican staples and good breakfasts too, all for under M$50. Daily 8am–3pm.

★ **Wallander** Independencia Nte 128 ☎ 618 811 7705, ⓦ wallander.com.mx. Tempting store loaded with locally made cheeses, baked goods, cookies, cakes and huge tortas for lunch (M$45–85). They also serve locally brewed Cerveza Duranguea craft beers. Mon–Sat 8.30am–9pm, Sun 9am–2.30pm.

DIRECTORY

Banks There's a convenient branch of Bancomer right by the plaza at the corner of 20 de Noviembre and Constitución, in addition to several other banks nearby.

Post office Some twelve blocks east of the cathedral, at 20 de Noviembre Ote 500-B (Mon–Fri 8am–6pm, Sat 9am–noon).

La Tierra del Cine

The region around Durango is heavily marketed to domestic tourists as the **La Tierra del Cine**, the "land of cinema", in honour of the vast number of **film** units that once came to the area to take advantage of its remarkably constant, clear, high-altitude light, its desert and mountain scenery. Westerns were the speciality, and although only half a dozen movies have been shot here in recent decades (Luc Besson's *Bandidas* in 2004 was the last major one, though the History Channel mini-series *Texas Rising* was shot here in 2014), you can still see the permanent sets at **Villa del Oeste** and **Chupaderos**.

Villa del Oeste

Carr Durango–Parral km 12 (Hwy-45) • Tues–Fri noon–7pm, Sat & Sun noon–7pm; shows 1.30, 3.30 & 5.30pm • M$25, weekends M$35; show free with park entry • ☎ 618 112 2882

Villa del Oeste (officially "Parque Temático Paseo del Viejo Oeste"), 12km north of Durango, is a kind of small theme park comprising the 100m-long street of "Bandido", which looks straight out of the Wild West until you realize the saloons and shops have been refashioned into a themed restaurant, music hall and a bar and grill. During the week it's fairly quiet, but at weekends there's a kitschy but enjoyable show featuring gun-slinging cowboys and cabaret girls.

Set Cinematográfico de Chupaderos

Carr Durango–Parral km 14 (Hwy-45) • Sat & Sun noon–7pm, shows at 2.30pm & 4.30pm • M$35 • ☎ 618 112 2882

The original Durango movie set – where films were shot starting in 1954 with Robert Wagner's *White Feather* – lies 2km north of Villa del Oeste in the dusty village of **CHUPADEROS**, preserved since 2012 as the **Set Cinematográfico de Chupaderos**. Villagers had pretty much taken over the faux Wild West main street, but thanks to government funds it now offers elaborate cowboy shows by professional actors.

ARRIVAL AND DEPARTURE   **LA TIERRA DEL CINE**

By bus The main road between Parral and Durango (Hwy-45) runs within a few hundred metres of the movie sets, so it's easy enough to get there by bus (around M$15), though flagging one down when you leave can take much longer – alternatively, you can take the special buses to both Villa del Oeste and the Set Cinematográfico de Chupaderos on Sat and Sun from Plaza de Armas in Durango (M$35, includes admission), 40min before each show.

Parral

PARRAL, or "Hidalgo del Parral" as it's officially known, is fixed in Mexican consciousness as the place where **Pancho Villa** (see box, p.464) met his demise under a spectacular hail of hot lead in 1923. The town's history goes much further than this, however, having been established in the early seventeenth century as a silver-mining centre.

Museo Francisco Villa

Gabino Barrera 13, at Juárez • Tues–Sun 10am–5pm • M$10 • ☎ 627 525 3292

The **Museo Francisco Villa**, located close to the spot where Villa's bullet-ridden vehicle came to a halt, commemorates the assassinated hero with displays of Revolution-era effects, antique weapons, a small shrine and plenty of enigmatic old photos. Every year in July, Villa's death is re-enacted here.

Mina La Prieta

Estaño 2 • Mon–Fri 10am–5pm • M$25 • ☎ 627 525 4400

The ramshackle spectre of the **Mina La Prieta**, the once great silver mine founded in 1629, overlooks Parral from a hill on the edge of town. It closed in 1975 but you can take a short tour of some of the mine workings, 40m down by elevator, left almost as they were over forty years before. At the mine head there's the **Museo Regional de Minería**, containing heaps of old mining equipment.

Palacio Alvarado

Riva Palacio 2 • Daily 10am–5pm • M$25 • ☎ 627 522 0290

Mineral profits helped build some of the town's more impressive edifices, including the **Palacio Alvarado**, an opulent 1903 mansion built for local mining magnate Don Pedro Alvarado. He was reputedly a close friend and business associate of Pancho Villa, which might explain why Villa was carried to burial in the Alvarado funerary wagon, now parked inside the building. You'll find some excellent photos that chart the town's development.

Templo de San José

Francisco Moreno Domínguez, at Plaza Principal

The town of Parral is home to several striking churches, and the **Templo de San José** on the main plaza (not to be confused with the cathedral on the Jardín Plaza de Guadalupe) is one of the oldest and most beautiful. It dates back to the 1670s, and houses the remains of the town's founder, Don Juan Rangel de Biesma.

Templo de Nuestra Señora del Rayo
Damaso Jiménez s/n, at Estanfort (just off Independencia)

Legend has it that the gorgeous plateresque **Templo de Nuestra Señora del Rayo** was constructed in the early seventeenth century by an indigenous Mexican on the proceeds of the gold mine he had discovered and worked in secret. The authorities tortured him to death in an attempt to find the mine, but its location died with him. The venerated image of the Virgin Mary inside is said to have received a scar in 1686 thanks to a miraculous lightning strike that heralded much-needed rains (thus the name "Our Lady of Lightning").

ARRIVAL AND INFORMATION   PARRAL

By bus Parral's compact colonial heart is a 20min walk from the main bus terminal (C de Lille 5) – turn left, then left again onto Independencia – or take a taxi (M$30–40). There are buses almost hourly to Durango and Chihuahua, as well as frequent services to Juárez.

Destinations Chihuahua (roughly hourly; 4hr); Durango (10 daily; 5–6hr); Guachochi (6 daily; 3hr 30min).
Tourist information The Oficina de Turismo (daily 10am–3pm; ☎ 627 525 4400) is at the Mina La Prieta (see p.459).

ACCOMMODATION

Hotel Acosta Agustín Barbachano 3 ☎ 627 522 0221. Comfortable budget option and pleasantly old-fashioned, with tiled-floor rooms that overlook the city, a rooftop terrace and 1950s atmosphere (with free wi-fi). M$350

Hotel Los Arcos Pedro de Lille 5 ☎ 627 523 0597. For a bit more comfort, only a stone's throw from the bus station, this well-maintained hotel offers rooms facing a modern, plant-filled courtyard and that come with satellite TV; there's also a decent restaurant. Free wi-fi. M$525

EATING AND DRINKING

★ **Enchiladas Doña Cuca** Del Rayo 7, at Libertad (near the river). *Doña Cuca*, "de las enchiladas", is a legendary stall that opened in 1922, making its famous enchiladas exactly the same way ever since: try the *enchiladas verdes* made with *chile pasado*, or *enchiladas rojas* with *chile California* (M$15–25). Cash only. Daily 7am–9pm.

Panificadora Parralense Ojito 13, at Del Rayo ☎ 627 523 2110. Visit this venerable bakery to try Parral's other culinary gem, *rayadas* (bread rolls baked with a hint of anise), knocked out of its ageing brick ovens. Mon–Sat 6am–10pm, Sun 6am–noon.

Chihuahua

The capital of the largest state in the republic, **CHIHUAHUA** was the favourite home of Mexican folk hero **Pancho Villa**. It's also been the scene of some crucial episodes in Mexico's history, not least the execution of **Miguel Hidalgo** (see p.462) in 1811. Today it's a sprawling, workaday city of around 900,000, but the colonial centre boasts several fine museums and is sprinkled with grandiose nineteenth-century mansions, built when silver brought wealth to the region's landowning class. This is also *vaquero* heartland, and one of the best places in the country to look for **cowboy boots**: you're spoilt for choice in the centre, especially in the blocks bounded by Calle 4, Juárez, Victoria and Ocampo. Incidentally, you're unlikely to see many of the little bug-eyed dogs here, said to have been discovered in the state in the 1850s – though in the summer months you will see over thirty multicoloured chihuahua sculptures scattered around town as part of the annual "Dog Parade".

CANDY TOWN

No one really knows why the tradition started, but Parral is lauded all over Mexico for its old-fashioned milk sweets, addictive **dulces de leche** made with coconut, apricots, pecans, peanuts, hazelnuts and pineapples. Sample the wicked treats at ★ **Dulcería La Gota de Miel**, 20 de Noviembre 51 (daily 10am–7pm; ☎ 627 522 1217), the shop founded in 1932 by Don Pablito, the acknowledged godfather of Parral's modern sweet industry.

Catedral Metropolitana

Libertad 814 (Plaza de Armas) • Tues–Sun 6am–9pm • Free • **Museo de Arte Sacro** Victoria 4 (Plaza de Armas) • Mon–Fri 10am–2pm &
4–6pm • M$18 • ☎ 614 410 38 77

Chihuahua's centre of activity is the teeming **Plaza de Armas**, where its fine **Catedral
Metropolitana** stands opposite a wonderfully camp statue of the city's founder, Don
Antonio Deza y Ulloa, in the very act of pointing to the ground, as if to say, "Right

lads, we'll build it here." The Baroque, twin-towered edifice was begun in 1725 but took more than one hundred years to complete: work well worth it, though, since the interior detail is the equal of the ornate facade. Look inside for the shrine to **Pedro Maldonado** (born here in 1892), who was beaten to death by soldiers of Mexico's anti-Catholic government in 1937. Now known as San Pedro de Jesús Maldonado Lucero, he became Chihuahua's first saint in 2000.

Museo de Arte Sacro

In a modernized crypt located beneath the cathedral (you enter the crypt via the separate entrance found on Victoria), the small **Museo de Arte Sacro** displays some fine examples of Baroque Mexican religious art which date back to the eighteenth century. Notable among the displays is a selection of sombre paintings of saints by Francisco Martínez, as well as a collection of dark and forbidding images. These depict the figure of Christ being pushed, pulled, stabbed and punched; there are also a few works by Miguel Cabrera and memorabilia from the visit of Pope John Paul II in 1990.

Museo Casa de Juárez

Juárez 321, at C 5 • Tues–Sun 9am–7pm • M$10 • ☎ 614 410 4258

Aficionados of Mexican history should visit the **Museo Casa de Juárez**, essentially a monument to **Benito Juárez** and the turbulent years of the French Intervention; forced out of Mexico City by the French, President Juárez spent three years here from 1864, when this house was the epicentre of the independent national government. Today his former offices and personal chambers have been furnished in period style, and many of his letters and personal affects are on display, including his battered horse-drawn carriage. Other rooms put the whole period in context, though you'll need to read Spanish to make the most of this.

Casa Chihuahua

Libertad 901 • Wed–Mon 10am–6pm • M$40, free Sun • ☎ 614 429 3300, ⊕ casachihuahua.org.mx

At the north end of pedestrianized Libertad you can't miss the **Casa Chihuahua**, the former Palacio Federal and now a thoroughly absorbing museum. Built in 1910, the current structure replaced the eighteenth-century Jesuit college and hospital where **Padre Miguel Hidalgo** and **Ignacio Allende**, the inspiration and early leaders of the Mexican War of Independence, were imprisoned in 1811, before being executed across the road (see below). Only one stone tower was preserved from the older structure, containing the **Calabozo de Hidalgo**, "Hidalgo's dungeon", where the rebels are said to have been held. Hidalgo's cell now forms the centrepiece of the lower-level **Museo del Sitio**, a series of multimedia exhibits charting the history of the building from the early Spanish missions to its rebirth as a museum. Upstairs, the **Museo Patrinomio** is an innovative series of galleries introducing the state of Chihuahua, divided thematically between deserts, plains and mountains, and featuring sections on art, history, traditional dress and popular culture: look out for the display on Hollywood star **Anthony Quinn**, who was born in the city in 1915, and enlightening sections on the Mormons and Mennonites.

Museo Galería de Armas and Museo de Hidalgo

Libertad, at Carranza **Museo Galería de Armas** Tues–Sun 9am–5pm • Free • **Museo de Hidalgo** Same hours • ☎ 614 410 4258

Chihuahua's **Palacio de Gobierno**, completed in 1892 on the other side of the former Jesuit college, contains two small museums worth a quick peek. The **Museo Galería de Armas** houses an assortment of weapons from the Independence struggle, including the extraordinary 3m-long "Rifle de Avancarga", while the **Museo de Hidalgo** commemorates Miguel Hidalgo himself with a replica of the sacristy in Dolores where it all began (see p.822); dioramas represent the Dolores church, the Querétaro

Conspiracy and the attack on Guanajuato (Spanish labels only). Beyond here the main courtyard is an enthralling space lined with bold **murals** of scenes from Mexico's colonial past painted by Aarón Piña Mora in the 1960s – Hidalgo and Allende were executed here in 1811, their severed heads sent for public display in Guanajuato. The site of the deed is marked with a small shrine, the **Altar de la Patria** ("the nation's altar") on the ground floor.

Plaza Mayor

North of the Palacio de Gobierno lies the modern expanse of **Plaza Mayor**, with its grand monument to freedom, the Ángel de la Libertad, erected in 2003. At the north end, the **Templo de San Francisco de Asís** is considered the oldest building in the city (dating from 1726), and though fairly plain inside has increased importance due to another Hidalgo connection. The attached Capilla de San Antonio is where the hero's headless torso was initially buried in 1811, before being exhumed and triumphantly entombed in Mexico City in 1823.

Museo Casa de Villa

C 10 no. 3010 • Tues–Sat 9am–1pm & 3–7pm, Sun 9am–5pm • M$10 • ☎ 614 416 2958 • Walk along Ocampo, or take a bus (marked "Ocampo") two blocks past the huge Iglesia del Sagrado Corazón de Jesús, then turn left along Mendez for two more blocks

Chihuahua's premier sight, the **Museo Casa de Villa**, is 2km east of the centre. This enormous mansion was built by Pancho Villa (see box, p.464) in the early twentieth century (though he only spent time here in 1914, when governor of the state) and inhabited, until her death in 1981, by Villa's "official" widow Doña Luz Corral (there were allegedly many others); it has now been taken over by the Mexican army. The collection is a fascinating mix of weapons, war plans and personal mementos, including the bullet-riddled Dodge in which Villa was assassinated in 1923. Look out for Villa's incredibly elaborate saddles and a grimly comical recruitment poster of 1915, urging "gringos" to head south and ride with Villa for "gold and glory". Quite apart from the campaign memories, the superbly preserved old bedrooms and bathrooms, richly decorated with florid murals and Spanish floor tiles, give an interesting insight into wealthy Mexican life in the early 1900s.

Centro Cultural Universitario Quinta Gameros

Paseo Bolivar 401, at C 4 • Tues–Sun 11am–2pm & 4–7pm • M$27, free Sun • ☎ 614 416 6684

The extraordinarily elaborate **Centro Cultural Universitario Quinta Gameros** was just the sort of ostentatious display of wealth that Villa and his associates were hoping to stamp out in their battle against the landed elite. The *belle époque* showcase was built for successful mine owner Don Manuel Gameros as an exact replica of a posh Parisian home – completed in 1910, just in time for the Revolution. The hapless Gameros fled the country and his mansion became the home of Venustiano Carranza (the Gameros family did reclaim the house in the 1920s before selling to the state in 1926). Today the house is fastidiously maintained by the Universidad Autónoma de Chihuahua, the interior sumptuously restored with magnificent Art Nouveau stained glass and ornate woodwork, and, curiously, scenes from *Little Red Riding Hood* painted on the children's bedroom wall.

Las Grutas de Nombre de Dios

Vialidad Sacramento, at Monte Albán • Tues–Fri 9am–4pm, Sat & Sun 10am–5pm • M$50; tours 1hr • ☎ 614 432 0518

The remarkable five-million-year-old cave system known as the **Grutas de Nombre de Dios** is just fifteen minutes' ride from downtown, accessible by guided tours only. You'll be taken through seventeen caverns on a 1.3km trail studded with astonishing features such as the "Tower of Pisa" and the "Grand Canyon", a maze of crumpled rocks and dripping stalactites. Taxis charge around M$250 with wait time.

PANCHO VILLA

Few Mexican folk heroes command so much reverence as Francisco "Pancho" Villa, the ruthless *bandito* and cattle rustler turned revolutionary, though facts about his life remain surprisingly obscure. Born in San Juan del Río, Durango, around 1878 (sources differ), to a simple peasant family, he became an outlaw while still a teenager and seems to have developed a loyal group of followers. Though he had virtually no formal education, Villa was not the average bandit; quick-witted and ambitious, in 1910 he decided to support the revolt of Francisco Madero (see p.826) against the Díaz regime. As commander of the formidable División del Norte, Villa became a key player in the **Mexican Revolution**. He became a bitter enemy of Victoriano Huerta after Madero was executed in 1913, helping to oust the dictator the following year and briefly becoming governor of Chihuahua after hard-fought victories at Chihuahua, Ciudad Juárez, Tierra Blanca and Ojinaga. When Villa fell out with the new president, Carranza, fighting continued and even spilled across the border (leading to a failed US expedition to capture the rebel). With the death of Carranza in 1920, Villa finally laid down his guns, dividing time between Hidalgo del Parral and Chihuahua. Violence continued to haunt him, however, and he was assassinated in Parral in 1923 – it was never determined who ordered the killing.

In Mexico, Villa remains a national hero, a Robin Hood-like figure who not only defeated the Mexican regime, but was also the only foreigner to attack the US (since the War of 1812) and survive. North of the border his image was enhanced by lurid US media reports – indeed, his sombrero and cartridge belts have become the stereotypical accessories of Mexican movie *banditos* ever since. Villa himself courted **Hollywood** and even starred in a film incorporating actual scenes of the Battle of Ojinaga in 1914 (portrayed by Antonio Banderas in *And Starring Pancho Villa As Himself*).

ARRIVAL AND DEPARTURE CHIHUAHUA

BY PLANE

From Chihuahua's General Roberto Fierro Villalobos International Airport (Juan Pablo II km 14; ☎ 614 420 5104), 18km southeast of the city, a fixed-fare taxi system operates – buy your voucher as you leave the terminal (around M$290 for downtown, around 30min). All the major car rental firms have desks at the airport, but there are no buses.

BY TRAIN

The Copper Canyon railway terminus (☎ 614 439 7200) is 2km southeast of the centre at Mendez and C 24; taxis are around M$50. In late 2015 a reduction in departures to alternate days was being proposed, as well as cancelling the entire schedule between Chihuahua and Creel/Divisadero (see p.500). Normally trains leave for Los Mochis at 6am (scheduled to arrive at Creel 11.47pm, Los Mochis 9.28pm).

BY BUS

The Terminal Central de Autobuses (with guardería 9am–11pm) is 10km east of the centre, near the airport on Juan Pablo II; local buses (M$10) run from right outside to and from downtown, and there are plenty of taxis, though they will insist on at least M$100. Note that most buses from Creel will drop you in the centre of town (near the plaza) before heading out to the bus terminal – check when you get on.

Destinations Ciudad Juárez (every 30min; 5–6hr); Creel (every 1–2hr; 4–5hr); Durango (10 daily; 10–12hr); Guadalajara (every 2hr; 15–16.5hr); Mexico City (every 2hr; 19–22hr); Monterrey (8 daily; 11–12hr); Nuevo Casas Grandes (11 daily; 4hr 30min); Parral (hourly; 3–5hr); Zacatecas (hourly; 12–14hr).

INFORMATION AND SERVICES

Tourist office There's a small, helpful English-speaking tourist office (Mon–Fri 9am–5pm, Sat–Sun 10am–4pm; ☎ 614 410 3596, ⊕ ah-chihuahua.com) on the ground floor of the Palacio de Gobierno (C Victoria entrance).

ACCOMMODATION

★ **Hotel Plaza Chihuahua** Cuarta (4a) 204 ☎ 614 415 1212, ⊕ www.hotelplazachihuahua.com. Bright, contemporary hotel with stylish rooms, breakfast included and free wi-fi. M$560

Jardín del Centro Victoria 818 ☎ 614 415 1832. This old hotel has lots of character, with big colonial-style rooms set around a plant-filled courtyard. The less elegant quarters

are around M$100 cheaper and a great bargain. There's a decent little restaurant attached, and free wi-fi. M$560

Posada Tierra Blanca Niños Héroes 102 ☎ 614 415 0000, ⊕ posadatierrablanca.com.mx. Spacious, motel-style place right in the heart of the city, with an open-air pool, gymnasium, on-site restaurant and bar. The a/c rooms are tidy and spacious, although not nearly as tasteful as they pretend to be. Free wi-fi. M$915

Quality Inn Victoria 409 ☎ 614 439 9000, ⊛ quality innchihuahua.com. You can't beat the location of this comfy business hotel, right on the main plaza; rooms are standard chain fare, but come with free continental breakfast, free airport, bus and train station transfers,

wi-fi and cable TV. M$1220

★ **San Felipe El Real** Allende 1055 ☎ 614 437 2037, ⊛ hotelsanfelipeelreal.com. This elegant boutique hotel is set in a gorgeous 1882 adobe mansion with six suites decked out with tasteful antiques and canopy beds, centred on a blossom-smothered courtyard. M$1245

EATING

La Calesa Juárez 3300, at Colón ☎ 614 416 0222, ⊛ lacalesa.com.mx. One of Chihuahua's fanciest restaurants, all dark wood panels, crisp linen tablecloths, sparkling wine glasses and waistcoated waiters. Northern-style steaks are the house speciality. Dine on *chiles rellenos de camarón* (chiles stuffed with prawns) or a massive plate of succulent shellfish (mains M$220–520). Bookings recommended at weekends. Daily 12.30–10pm.

Casa de los Milagros Victoria 812, opposite Hotel Reforma ☎ 614 437 0693. Casual restaurant and bar comprising a beautiful colonial courtyard with fountain, surrounded by numerous small rooms. Here, Chihuahua's well-groomed meet for margaritas, one of 25 brands of tequila, real coffee and light snacks such as *quesadilla de flor de calabaza* (squash flower), burgers and salads (M$75–150). Daily 5pm–1am.

★ **La Casona** Aldama 430, at Ocampo ☎ 614 410 0063, ⊛ casona.com.mx. If you fancy a splurge make sure you visit this sumptuous restaurant, housed inside the main courtyard of the Casa de Don Luis Terrazas, completed in 1893 for one of the state's richest landowners. Feast on fine

contemporary Mexican cuisine or Argentine steaks (mains M$195–495). Mon–Fri 8am–midnight.

★ **Chih'ua Tacos y Cortes** Universidad 2902 ☎ 614 414 0222; also at Plaza Vallarta and Plaza las Haciendas ⊛ chihuatacos.com. This much-loved local *taquería* started life in 1991 as a humble stall but has morphed into a Mexican franchise; it's worth the short taxi ride to one of its modern outlets in the city to try its huge taco plates (M$60–80) and delicious tortas. Daily 7.30am–1am.

La Doña Cocina-Café Bolivar 722, at Coronado ☎ 614 410 9025. Modern, hip coffee shop, with contemporary international cuisine, live music (jazz Fri, *trova* Sat) and happy hour Tues (6–11pm). Mon–Thurs 8am–midnight, Fri 8am–2am, Sat 8am–1am, Sun 9am–5pm.

Mi Café Victoria 1000, opposite the Hotel San Juan. Reliable American-style diner with prices and quality both a little above average. The breakfast menu is in English and Spanish and extends from *norteño* and *ranchero* dishes to hotcakes and syrup. Come here later for burgers, sandwiches and steak and seafood mains. Free wi-fi. Thurs–Tues 7.30am–10.30pm.

DRINKING

La Antigua Paz C 12 no. 2201, at Mina ☎ 614 410 1466. Lively cantina full of characters, with a history going back to 1910 (it's been in this location since 1922 and looks it) and still owned by the Carrejo family. Antiques and mementos line the walls, and there's often live music. Daily noon–1am.

Café Calicanto Bolívar 806 ☎ 614 410 8255. Popular restaurant with live Mexican folk music Fri & Sat, salsa on Thurs and a menu of meat-filled Chihuahuan specialities

for around M$80. There's also an interesting vegetarian menu, and various alcoholic coffees. Try the *beso de Santa*: coffee, milk, cognac, cinnamon and vanilla. Wed–Sat 5pm–2am.

Momposina Café Coronado 508, between C 7 and Bolívar ☎ 614 410 0975. Artsy café and bar with live music Thurs–Sun, great coffee and plenty of cakes and snacks. Mon–Thurs 4–11pm, Fri & Sat 4pm–1.30am.

DIRECTORY

Banks Most banks are centrally located, and nearly all have ATMs, with branches on Victoria and Libertad around the Plaza de Armas.

Internet You'll find a few terminals inside *Mi Café*, Victoria and C 6 (M$15/hr), and many more at Copy & Print Club at Guerrero and Ojinaga, open Mon–Sat 8am–8.30pm, Sun 10am–5.30pm (M$12/hr).

Hospital For emergency medical assistance, dial ☎ 066; Clínica del Centro at Ojinaga 816 (☎ 614 439 8100) or Hospital Cima, Hacienda del Valle 7120, Fracc Plazas las Haciendas (☎ 614 439 2862).

Police ☎ 066; tourist police ☎ 01800 201 5589.

Post office Libertad 1700, behind the church (Mon–Fri 8am–4.30pm, Sat 8am–noon).

Paquimé

Independencia 100, Casa Grandes • Tues–Sun 10am–5pm • M$62 • ☎ 636 692 4140, ⊛ centroculturalpaquime.mex.tl

The intriguing ruins of **PAQUIMÉ** are the most significant, and certainly the most thought-provoking, remains of a sophisticated civilization in northern Mexico. Originally home to an agricultural community and comprising simple adobe houses (similar to those found in Arizona and New Mexico), it became heavily influenced by Mesoamerican, probably Toltec, culture. Whether this was the result of conquest or, more likely, trade, is uncertain, but from around 1000 to 1200 AD, Paquimé flourished. **Pyramids** and **ball-courts** were constructed, and the surrounding land was irrigated by an advanced system of **canals**. At the same time local craftsmen were trading with points both south and north, producing a wide variety of elaborate ornaments and pottery. Among the finds at the site (many of them are now in the Museum of Anthropology in Mexico City) have been cages that held exotic imported birds, whose feathers were used in making ornaments; necklaces made from turquoise, semiprecious stones and shells obtained from the Sea of Cortez; and other objects of copper, bone, jade and mother-of-pearl.

Much must have been destroyed when the site was attacked, burned and abandoned around 1340 – either by a marauding nomadic tribe, such as the Apache, or in the course of a more local rebellion. Either way, Paquimé was not inhabited again, its people leaving their already depleted trade for the greater safety of the sierras. When excavation began in the late 1950s, there were only a few low hills and banks where walls had been, but by piecing together evidence archeologists have partly reconstructed the adobe houses – the largest of which have as many as fifty interconnecting rooms around an open courtyard or **ceremonial centre**. The foundations of the houses, which were originally two or three storeys high, have been reconstructed to waist height, with an occasional standing wall giving some idea of scale.

Museo de las Culturas del Norte

Independencia 100, Casas Grandes • Tues–Sun 8am–5pm • Free with main site entry

To appreciate fully the sophistication of the civilization that built Paquimé, visit the **Museo de las Culturas del Norte**, a beautifully laid-out, if thinly stocked, museum, architecturally designed to mimic the ruins of the defence towers that once stood on the site. Inside you'll find a large model of how Paquimé must have looked, interactive touch-screen consoles with commentary in Spanish and English and intelligent displays of artefacts. Modern examples of finds from the surrounding area – drums, dolls in native costume, ceramics and ceremonial masks – compete with Paquimé objects, notably striking pottery, often anthropomorphic vessels decorated in geometric patterns of red, black and brown on a white or cream background.

ARRIVAL AND DEPARTURE   PAQUIMÉ

By bus/taxi To reach the site you have to travel 260km south of Ciudad Juárez to Nuevo Casas Grandes. Travelling from Chihuahua is also an option, as buses for the four-hour journey depart regularly. Several informal shuttle-van companies also operate daily between Nuevo Casas Grandes and Phoenix and Albuquerque in the US (US$55–65/M$955–1130); try Transportes Quezada (US ☎ +1 623 937 9650) or Transportes Tarahumara (US ☎ +1 602 957 1596). Once in Nuevo Casas Grandes (buses arrive outside

the adjoining Estrella Blanca and Omnibus offices on Obregón), take one of the hourly yellow buses ("Casas Grandes/Col Juárez"; 8am–8pm) from the corner of Constitución and 16 de Septiembre to the plaza in the smaller village of Casas Grandes (about 20min; M$8), from where the site is signposted – it's a 15min walk. Taxis charge around M$100 from Nuevo Casas Grandes.
Destinations Chihuahua (hourly; 4hr 30min); Ciudad Juárez (every 1–2hr; 4hr).

ACCOMMODATION

CASAS GRANDES

If you leave Chihuahua very early you can visit Paquimé and continue to Ciudad Juárez and the US border in the same day, but if you need accommodation, there are a few inviting options in Casas Grandes.

★ **Las Guacamayas B&B** 20 de Noviembre 1101 ☎ 636 692 4144, ⓦ mataortizollas.com. Closest to the ruins, "The Macaws" offers cosy adobe rooms (in part modelled on Paquimé), wi-fi and breakfast in owner Mayté Luján's artsy

kitchen dining room, *La Tertulia*. <u>US$50 (M$870)</u>

Pueblo Viejo Courtyards Av Victoria 420 ☎ +1 915 261 0502, ✉ sm@look.net. You can stay at the *Pueblo Viejo Courtyards*, run by local fixtures Spencer and Emi MacCallum: they're artfully restored adobe houses near the main plaza, adorned with local antiques (wi-fi but no TV). One of the best houses is La Casa del Nopal, with a kitchen and a dining room, starting at just US$35/M$610 in low season (big discounts available for weekly rentals). <u>US$70 (M$1220)</u>

MORMONS IN MEXICO

George Romney (1907–95), leading Mormon, Governor of Michigan and father of 2012 presidential contender Mitt Romney, was actually born in **Colonia Dublán**, a small Mormon colony just north of Nuevo Casas Grandes. Members of **The Church of Jesus Christ of Latter-day Saints** started coming to northern Mexico in the 1880s, many to avoid prosecution for polygamy in the US. Colonia Dublán was founded in 1889, the Romneys moving here soon after, though the Mexican Revolution forced the family to flee back to the US in 1912. There's little to see in Dublán today, but **Colonia Juárez**, established in 1886 just north of Mata Ortiz (20km southwest of Casas Grandes), remains a Mormon centre, its beautiful **Colonia Juárez Chihuahua México Temple** dedicated in 1999 on a hill above town. There's also the Academia Juárez, a Mormon-owned school founded in 1897, and the Museo de Colonia Juárez chronicling the Mormon history of the region.

NUEVO CASAS GRANDES

Hotel Piñón Juárez Nte 605 ☎ 636 694 0655, ✉ motel pinon@prodigy.net.mx. If you get stuck here, aim to stay at the amicable *Hotel Piñón*, with free wi-fi, cable TV, a pool and a small museum of Paquimé clay pots. **M$520**

7

EATING AND DRINKING

CASAS GRANDES

La Finca de Don Cruz Juárez 100 (five blocks from the plaza, in the direction of Mata Ortiz) ☎ 636 692 4343. Popular with tour groups, but still serves fabulous northern Mexican cuisine. Mon–Sat noon–9pm.

El Mesón del Kiote Juárez 1201, at Ojinaga (near the PEMEX station) ☎ 636 692 4037. Offers delicious local food and freshwater fish, generous margaritas and addictive guava pie. Daily 8am–11pm.

NUEVO CASAS GRANDES

Panadería La Guadalupana Hidalgo 813 (one block behind Hotel Piñón). It's worth visiting this venerable bakery, founded over seventy years ago and serving cheap *pan dulce* baked in the traditional manner in a giant brick oven. Mon–Sat 6am–4pm.

Mata Ortiz

If you've trekked out all the way to Casas Grandes, you should also check out **MATA ORTIZ**, some 27km south of Nuevo Casas Grandes, a flourishing artisanal pottery community inhabited by artists from all over the world; it's been home to **Juan Quezada**, the godfather of rustic Mata Ortiz-style pottery, and his followers since the 1970s. It's a tranquil, appealing little village of adobe houses: soak up the atmosphere and visit any galleries you like the look of – most artists will be happy to introduce their work. Some of the best include **Jorge Quintana**'s gallery at the *Adobe Inn*, just before the train tracks (for fine pottery and Oaxaca textiles); **Juan Quezada**'s original gallery across from the old train station; and **Mauro Quezada**'s gallery (from Juan Quezada's house, take the street toward the river to the end and turn right).

ARRIVAL AND DEPARTURE   MATA ORTIZ

By taxi Taxis will take you to Mata Ortiz for M$450–600, or M$750 return from Nuevo Casas Grandes (plus M$100–120/hr waiting fee) – knock off about M$100 from Casas Grandes.

ACCOMMODATION AND EATING

Adobe Inn ☎ 636 694 6283. If you fancy staying, Jorge Quintana actually runs this comfortable inn (known locally as "the hotel"), with fifteen spacious rooms around a leafy courtyard; it also serves delicious food to non-guests (rates include three meals), but try to give them an hour's notice. **US$70 (M$1220)**

Ciudad Juárez

Sprawling **CIUDAD JUÁREZ**, just across the border from **El Paso, Texas**, is possibly Mexico's nastiest border town. Vast, dirty and riddled with visible social problems at the best of times, its spiralling drug-gang violence led to the Mexican army being deployed to patrol its bullet-spattered streets in 2008. This followed the already notorious rape and murder of over four hundred women since 1993, "las muertas de Juárez", portrayed in the depressing Jennifer Lopez movie *Bordertown* (2007) and Roberto Bolaño's seminal novel *2666*.

There's an element of paranoia to this, of course; Juárez is a city of two million people that, by and large, functions like anywhere else in Mexico, and tourists are very rarely affected by drug violence (it's also just as famous in Mexico for being the home of **Juan Gabriel**, the nation's most successful singer). The security situation has improved dramatically in recent years (murders had dropped almost 75 percent by 2014), but it's still a good idea to pass through Juárez as quickly as possible – you won't miss much. Travelling between the main transit points is perfectly safe during the day.

ARRIVAL AND DEPARTURE

CIUDAD JUÁREZ

BY PLANE
Arriving at the Aeropuerto Internacional Abraham González, 14km south of the border, you'll find ATMs and all the major car rental firms, including Budget (☎656

633 0954). Taxis into town or to the border are based on a fixed-price zone system and should be around M$250. In addition to Aeroméxico, budget carriers InterJet and Viva Aerobus operate flights to Mexico City, while Viva

---

THE MEXICAN DRUG WARS

Since 2006 the escalating **Mexican drug wars** – a violent struggle between rival cartels to control the flow of narcotics into the US, and increasingly, between these gangs and the Mexican government – has put a huge dent in the nation's tourist industry. The violence has continued to make prime-time news in the US, and has led to a stream of official travel warnings to Mexico ever since.

Mexican gangs began to take over the US cocaine trade from the Colombians in the 1990s, and were originally drawn into roughly two rival camps led by the **Gulf Cartel**, based in Matamoros, and the **Sinaloa Cartel** with its ally the **Juárez Cartel** (Gulf ally the **Tijuana Cartel** has been dramatically weakened in recent years). In 2007, however, the Juárez Cartel started a vicious turf war with the Sinaloa Cartel, for control of **Ciudad Juárez**. Drug violence and political corruption have also plagued the state of **Tamaulipas**, and to a lesser extent parts of **Veracruz**. In 2011 the attention turned to the Tamaulipas border town of **Nuevo Laredo**, and to another grisly turf war between **Los Zetas** (an especially terrifying group of former Mexican special forces soldiers) and the Gulf Cartel (until 2010 the Gulf Cartel were actually allies of the Zetas). A string of chilling crimes in 2012 included the hanging of nine bodies from a Laredo bridge and the dumping of 49 decapitated and dismembered bodies on a highway near Monterrey.

In 2006, President Felipe Calderón had ended decades of government inaction by sending federal troops to the states affected by drug violence, a policy that had led to an estimated 60,000 deaths by the end of his administration in 2012. President Peña Nieto has changed tactics slightly, focusing on reducing violence rather than head-on conflict. Zeta leader Heriberto Lazcano was killed in 2012; top Zeta bosses the Morales brothers were arrested in 2013; and Mexico's most-wanted men, Joaquín "El Chapo" Guzmán (Sinaloa Cartel), Vicente Carrillo Fuentes (Juárez Cartel) and Héctor Beltrán Leyva (Beltrán Leyva Cartel) were captured in 2014. Though Nieto's polices have so far succeeded in reducing the number of killings, the drug cartels are still very much in business. El Chapo escaped from prison in 2015, and in 2014, the Iguala mass kidnapping of 43 students by a drug gang in collusion with local police in Guerrero horrified the nation (months later it was confirmed that all 43 had been killed); the case led to national and international protests and a string of high-profile resignations and arrests.

Despite the sensational headlines, it's important to remember that most of Mexico remains peaceful. As a visitor it is extremely unlikely you'll see any sign of drug violence and there's actually little evidence that tourists are targeted by drug gangs – headlines in the media often attribute petty crime or muggings, which can happen anywhere, to drug gangs, adding to the sense of fear. It obviously makes sense to avoid the major trouble spots, however, particularly along the US border. If driving a car from the US, check the current situation with US authorities before you go (see p.60).

Aerobus also serves Monterrey, Hermosillo and Guadalajara.

BY BUS

The city's Terminal de Autobuses (☎ 656 613 6037) lies 5km from the centre at Flores and Borunda, and has services to both US and Mexican cities. To get to the border from the bus terminal, take a taxi (M$100) or any local bus marked "Centro".

Destinations Chihuahua (at least hourly; 5hr); Durango (at least hourly; 16hr); Mexico City (every 1–2hr; 24hr); Nuevo Casas Grandes (every 1–2hr; 4hr); Monterrey (11 daily; 18hr); Parral (at least hourly; 10hr); San Luis Potosí (every 1–2hr; 20hr); Zacatecas (hourly; 16hr).

US destinations International bus services are handled by Autobuses Americanos (☎ 656 610 8529, ⓦ autobuses americanos.com.mx). It runs a shuttle bus (every 1–2hr) to El Paso Greyhound Bus Station (1hr 30min; US$10–11 or M$175), and beyond: Dallas (2 daily); Los Angeles (4 daily); Phoenix (3 daily).

CROSSING THE US BORDER

Two downtown toll bridges serve one-way traffic in and out of Ciudad Juárez from neighbouring El Paso, Texas. Northbound vehicles cross the Paseo del Norte Bridge from Juárez, while southbound vehicles use the Stanton St/Lerdo Bridge (tolls: cars US$3; pedestrians US$0.50). If you're on foot you can enter on either bridge (Paseo del Norte is best); coming back, you must use the Paseo del Norte crossing (cars M$50, by foot M$8). See p.29 & p.31 for border formalities. Additionally, there are two bridges that serve two-way traffic. The Bridge of the Americas (free) lies 4km east of the city centre on the edge of the Zona Pronaf, an area of sheltered tourist development a world away from the sleazy machinations of downtown Juárez. East of here lies the Ysleta (Zaragoza) Bridge (same tolls), well connected to the main highways and good for a speedy escape. All are open 24hr.

Heading into Mexico Once across the Stanton St/Lerdo Bridge, taxis to the main Juárez bus terminal should be around M$100, or M$250 to the airport; alternatively, you can catch a local bus from the corner of Guerrero and Villa near the market for M$7.

Heading into the US Crossing the Paseo del Norte Bridge into El Paso dumps you onto Santa Fe, a shabby street of budget stores that seems like an extension of Juárez. It's a short walk straight along here to the *Camino Real* hotel (see below), or you can grab an El Paso taxi, which is metered; you should get to El Paso airport for around US$26. El Paso airport has cheaper connections to the rest of the US than Juárez airport, though you'll usually have to change planes in Houston or Phoenix. El Paso Greyhound Bus Station is at 200 W San Antonio St (☎ +1 915 532 5095).

INFORMATION

Tourist office The Ciudad Juárez tourist office is inconveniently located in the Pronaf zone at Av de las Américas 2551, just across the Bridge of the Americas (Mon–Fri 9am–5pm, Sat & Sun 10am–2pm; ☎ 656 611 3174, ⓦ visitajuarez.com).

ACCOMMODATION

None of the hotels in Ciudad Juárez is particularly good value and there's little point in **staying the night** – most business visitors stay in the comfortable chain motels on the outskirts of town (typically M$800–1200), which are little use without a car. Staying in **El Paso**, across the border, is a better idea.

Camino Real 101 South El Paso St, El Paso ☎ 915 534 3000, ⓦ caminoreal.com. The *Camino Real* is the obvious luxury option in downtown El Paso, just a short walk from the border, with plush rooms and excellent facilities. **US$97 (M$1690)**

Gardner Hotel 311 E Franklin St, El Paso ☎ 915 532 3661, ⓦ gardnerhotel.com. The most atmospheric choice in El Paso, opened in 1922 and for many years a hostel but now sporting simple doubles adorned with antique beds and furnishings. Fast and free wi-fi. Doubles US$60 (M$1045)

Hotel Colonial Abraham Lincoln 1355, Ciudad Juárez ☎ 656 613 5050, ⓦ hotelescolonial.com. The best choice close to the border is *Hotel Colonial*, in the Pronaf zone around 1km south of the Bridge of the Americas. M$550

EATING AND DRINKING

Burritos Crisóstomo Gómez Morín 8327, ⓦ burrito crisostomo.com. This legendary burrito mini-chain is a Juárez classic, and though locals complain that quality has gone down in recent years it still knocks out tasty and filling *mole* and *barbacoa* burritos made with *guisados* (stews) and freshly made flour tortillas (M$30–40). Mon–Fri 7am–6.30pm, Sat 7am–6pm, Sun 7am–4pm.

Club Kentucky Juárez 629 ☎ 656 632 6113. Still the classic place for a cold Tecate in Juárez, despite struggling with mounting losses since the downturn. Open since 1920 (the bartenders look like they've been here that long), and one of numerous Mexican cantinas to claim the invention of the margarita. Daily 11am–2am.

DIRECTORY

Banks and exchange It's easy enough to change money at *casas de cambio* and tourist shops along Juárez and 16 de Septiembre; most banks are also on 16 de Septiembre, and you'll find ATMs at nearly all of them. Most places accept US dollars, but make sure you know the current exchange rate.
Consulate US (Mon–Fri 7.30am–1pm), Paseo de la Victoria 3650, Fracc Partido Senecú ☎ 656 227 3000, ⓦ ciudadjuarez.usconsulate.gov.
Hospital For emergency medical assistance, dial ☎ 066; Star Medica, Paseo de la Victoria 4370, Partido Iglesias (☎ 656 227 5700).

Internet The public library across the border in El Paso (Mon–Thurs 10am–7pm, Fri 11am–6pm, Sat 10am–6pm, Sun noon–6pm; ☎ 915 543 5433, ⓦ elpasolibrary.org) has free internet access. Walk north past the *Camino Real* hotel for about two blocks; it's at 501 N Oregon on the corner of Franklin.
Police ☎ 066.
Post office Lerdo 205, at the corner of Peña, one block south of 16 de Septiembre (Mon–Fri 8am–5pm, Sat 9am–1pm).

The northeast border towns

Most travellers simply pass through the **northeast border towns** on their way between Texas and Mexican cities further south – the towns on the Mexican side have traditionally attracted a steady stream of day-trippers from the US for cheap bric-a-brac shopping and tasty **snacks**, though like elsewhere this trade has been severely disrupted since 2009.

The **Río Bravo**, known to Americans as the **Río Grande**, forms the border between Texas and Mexico, a distance of more than 1500km. The country through which it flows is arid semi-desert, and the towns along the lower section of the river are heavily industrialized. This is the **maquiladora** zone, where foreign-owned assembly plants produce consumer goods, most of them for export to the US.

CROSSING THE US BORDER   NORTHEAST BORDER TOWNS

Crossing the US-Mexican border can be a time-consuming affair, especially heading into the US. Canadians and US citizens require a passport to enter the US. Everyone else needs a visa or a visa-waiver (see p.31). Whichever crossing you choose, the procedures are the same, depending on what mode of transport you choose.

By bus Crossing the border by bus can save time and money, depending on your destination, though customs checks are meticulous on both sides. Heading into Mexico, there is no US immigration check, but make sure your bus driver knows if you have a foreign passport – he'll stop at the Mexican migración office so you can complete the FMM (see p.31). After that everyone gets off the bus for a thorough Mexican customs check. Heading into the US, there are no Mexican checks, but everyone gets off the bus to walk through US immigration (passport check), before a US Customs check of bags and the bus (which can take some time). Further into Texas there is likely to be a US Border Patrol check, where officers will check IDs and question everyone on the bus.

By car If driving into Mexico, remember to pull in at the migración office to get your Immigration Form (see p.31). You'll also need to get a temporary importation vehicle permit (for details see "Getting there", p.29). This must be dropped off on the Mexican side before heading back into the US. Cars also pay a toll crossing from either

side of the Río Bravo. Heading into Mexico, customs checks are often very light, whereas the queues heading back into the US can be several hours long; a US Immigration officer will check your passport at a booth (no need to leave the car), and will direct you to park if he deems a customs check necessary. If there is even a tiny hint you are carrying anything illegal, US Customs officers will literally take your car apart and have sniffer dogs all over the seats – don't expect them to clean up afterwards. You can also expect further US Border Patrol checks as you drive further into Texas, and army checkpoints on the Mexican side.

On foot Crossing the border on foot usually means a walk over a bridge traversing the Río Bravo (for a small fee), connecting with local buses or taxis on either side. Heading into Mexico, there is no US immigration and often very casual Mexican checks – remember to stop at the migración office and ask for a "multiple migration" form or "FMM" (the fee is M$350/US$20). Heading into the US, you'll have to clear US immigration (no Mexican checks), and often a full customs check of your bags.

Matamoros

Just across the Río Bravo from **Brownsville**, Texas, **MATAMOROS** is a little town with more history than the settlements strung out to its west. What began in 1774 as a cattle-ranching colony eventually became known – with the introduction of the port of Bagdad – as "La Puerta México," and in the nineteenth century Matamoros (along with Veracruz) became the main port of entry for foreign immigrants. At the turn of the nineteenth century, rail lines from both sides of the border were directed through Matamoros, and again the city found itself as the necessary link in the trade crossroads. Since the passage of **NAFTA** in 1994, Matamoros has established itself as an important point for trade, with the outskirts dominated by strip malls and factories; the **Matamoros–Brownsville Metropolitan Area** has a population of almost 1.2 million, and when restrictions on car imports were lifted in 2005 it became the used car capital of the world. Sadly, Mexico's ongoing drug wars hit Matamoros in a big way in 2015, devastating local car businesses and tourism (a feud between **Gulf Cartel** factions, nominally based here, is blamed). Though the old centre retains some provincial charm, with a slightly run-down blend of historic buildings and cheap stores, it's not advisable to visit Matamoros until the security situation stabilizes – check the latest situation online (UK foreign office at ⓦgov.uk/foreign-travel-advice, or the US at ⓦtravel.state.gov).

Plaza Hidalgo

Matamoros' busy but compact *centro histórico* is focused on spacious **Plaza Hidalgo**, dating back to the 1830s, and the humble French creole-style **Catedral de Nuestra Señora del Refugio,** more like a big church. Completed in 1833 with twin spires, its plain interior is best known today for its valuable reproduction of Michelangelo's *La Pietà*, carved from Carrera marble in Italy in 2005. On the south side of the plaza is the beautifully restored **Casino Matamorense**, completed in 1871 and used for special events.

7

THE NORTHEAST BORDER TOWNS – A ROUGH GUIDE

CIUDAD ACUÑA

The smallest of the border towns, its dusty, iconic Tex-Mex streets have proved a magnet for film-makers: Robert Rodriguez' cult Mexican thriller *El Mariachi* (1992) and its sequel, *Desperado* (1995), were shot here. Today Acuña is one of Los Zetas' primary drug smuggling gateways into the US, though it's far less violent than other towns on the border and tourists are rarely impacted. Iconic *Ma Crosby's*, a restaurant since 1925, has closed, though the *Corona Club*, the bar that opened in 1946 and featured in *Desperado*, was operating at the time of research (Hidalgo 200, ☎877 888 0922), with live country music at the weekends.

ARRIVAL AND DEPARTURE

Local buses shuttle between the border at Ciudad Acuña and the Texan town of Del Rio 5km across the Río Bravo ("Border Taxis" charge US$25/M$435), where Greyhound buses (2 daily; US$29) take 4hr 15min to reach San Antonio from the terminal at 1 N Main St. You can also take Amtrak's thrice-weekly Texas Eagle service from the same terminal (trains from Chicago to Los Angeles via St Louis, Dallas, Austin, El Paso and San Antonio). Del Rio is 246km and around 2hr 45min by car from San Antonio via Rte-90. The main Acuña bus station, at the corner of Matamoros and Ocampo, is just five blocks from the border and one from the plaza.

Destinations Monterrey (4 daily; 8hr); Piedras Negras (hourly; 1hr 30min); Saltillo (8 daily; 7hr).

PIEDRAS NEGRAS

Quaint, friendly and hassle free, with the most laid-back immigration officers you're likely to encounter anywhere in Mexico, this is the ideal border town – though it's another Los Zetas hub, violence has declined in recent years. It's also the unlikely place where nachos,

the ubiquitous Tex-Mex snack food, were "invented" in the 1940s (see box, p.474).

ARRIVAL AND DEPARTURE

Piedras Negras lies just across the Río Bravo from Eagle Pass, Texas. Once across the border, walk 200m north to the Greyhound station at 164 Jefferson St, which has two direct departures to San Antonio daily (3hr 5min; US$10–35). Eagle Pass is 229km and around 2hr 50min by car from San Antonio via Rte-57 and I-35. On the Mexican side of the border, Allende runs straight towards the Piedras bus station (☎878 782 7484) – a taxi should be around M$40. You'll find frequent first- and second-class departures to all major points south.

Destinations Ciudad Acuña (hourly; 1hr 30min); Mexico City (3 daily; 17–18hr); Monterrey (8 daily; 5–7hr); Saltillo (12 daily; 7hr).

BY PLANE

Piedras Negras airport is 9km south of the centre, and currently serves Aeromar flights to/from Mexico City. Taxis will charge at least M$200 to the border (most hotels offer free shuttles).

NUEVO LAREDO

The giant of the eastern border towns, alive with the imagery and commercialism of the frontier – which sadly includes some of the most grisly crimes committed by drug gangs such as Los Zetas (see box, p.468). Do not linger.

ARRIVAL AND DEPARTURE

If you're entering or leaving Mexico on foot, you'll take Puente Internacional No. 1; there's a small toll, payable in dollars or pesos if you're heading north, but in US currency only (US$0.75) when Mexico-bound – cars pay US$3.50. The bridge becomes the main drag, Av

Teatro de la Reforma

C 6, at Abasolo • Mon–Fri 8am–4pm • ☎ 868 812 5120

One block north of Plaza Hidalgo on Calle 6 is the historic **Teatro de la Reforma**, originally completed in 1865. In 1992 the theatre was meticulously restored to its original style at the behest of the town mayor, and now hosts drama and ballet performances and various local entertainment.

Mercado Juárez and Plaza Allende

Heading west from Teatro de la Reforma, pedestrianized **Abasolo** is the traditional shopping heart of town, with **Mercado Juárez**, between calles 9 and 10, the most interesting section – it's worth browsing the handicraft stalls inside. Two blocks south

Guerrero, on the Mexican side, but drivers can also use the nearby Puente Internacional No. 2 (same tolls), and bypass downtown. Numerous Greyhound buses (610 Salinas Av) connect Laredo, Texas, with San Antonio (2hr 50min; US$18–28). Laredo is 1248km and around 2hr 10min by car from San Antonio via I-35.

BY PLANE

Nuevo Laredo's airport (Aeropuerto Internacional Quetzalcóatl) is 6km southwest of the centre (and 12km from the border crossing) and currently serves Aeroméxico flights to/from Mexico City. Taxis charge M$200–250 to the border.

BY BUS

Nuevo Laredo's huge Central de Autobuses (24hr guardería) is around 5km south of town at Refugio Romo 4731 and Melgar, but battered city buses (marked "Puente"/"Centro") run frequently between here, the border crossings and Plaza Hidalgo (M$8); it's about a 25min journey. Buses back (marked "Carretera") leave from outside the Palacio Municipal on Camargo. Taxis should be around M$75, though drivers may ask for a lot more. More convenient is the Nueva Terminal de Autobuses (☎ 867 719 3884) at César López de Lara 3228 and Oaxaca, which is used by Autobuses del Noreste and Ómnibus de México (including Turistar Ejecutivo).

Destinations Austin (14 daily; 7hr); Chicago (2 daily; 36hr); Dallas (14 daily; 9hr); Guadalajara (5 daily; 14hr); Houston (9 daily; 7hr); Mexico City (10 daily; 15hr); Monterrey (every 30min; 3hr); Saltillo (8 daily; 4–5hr); San Antonio (hourly; 4hr); San Luis Potosí (14 daily; 12hr); Tampico (2 daily; 10hr); Zacatecas (6 daily; 8hr).

REYNOSA

A very easy border crossing with excellent transport connections. Hotels here aren't great value for your money, and, as always, it makes sense to head south as fast as possible; cartel turf wars turned especially violent here in 2015. Monterrey is only three hours by bus.

ARRIVAL AND DEPARTURE

Buses (M$8) connect the border and the centre to the Central Camionera, on Colón southeast of downtown (taxis charge around M$50). Buses to the rest of Mexico include services to Matamoros (1hr) and Ciudad Victoria (4hr 30min); Tampico (7hr) and Veracruz (16hr) on the Gulf coast; and Monterrey (3hr), Mexico City (13hr) and Zacatecas (10hr).

Crossing the Hidalgo International Bridge over the Río Bravo from McAllen, Texas (US$1 pedestrian toll, US$3 for cars), head straight on along Lerdo de Tejada, which soon becomes Zaragoza, to the Plaza Principal, about five blocks down, where you'll find a couple of banks with ATMs. From here the bus station can be reached by following Hidalgo, the pedestrianized main street, for a few blocks and then turning left into Colón. Panamericanas (⊕ panamericanas.com.mx) operates buses between Reynosa bus station and the Greyhound station in McAllen (where there are 7 daily departures to San Antonio; 4hr–4hr 50min; US$43–49), roughly every thirty minutes between 5.30am and 8.30pm (US$4.50/M$78). The 9km journey takes about 45min, including immigration. McAllen is 383km and around 3hr 40min by car from San Antonio via Rte-281 and I-37.

BY PLANE

Reynosa's airport (Aeropuerto Internacional General Lucio Blanco) is 14km southeast of the centre, and currently serves the most flights of the border towns, with regular services to Mexico City, Cancún, Poza Rica, Guadalajara and Veracruz. VivaAerobus runs a shuttle bus between the airport and the bus terminal (M$50).

7

of the mercado on Calle 10, **Plaza Allende** is the scruffy, modern counterpoint to Plaza Hidalgo, surrounded by cheap stores, bus stops and a line of tacos/torta stalls on the Calle 11 (west) side.

Museo Casamata

Santos Degollado, at Guatemala • Tues–Fri 9am–5pm, Sat & Sun 9am–2pm • Free • ☎ 868 813 5929

If you've got an hour to kill, take a taxi to the **Museo Casamata**, which houses a collection of memorabilia from the Mexican Revolution and a selection of Huastec ceramics in a fort begun in 1844 to repel invaders from north of the border. When Zachary Taylor stormed in two years later, however, the building was still unfinished.

Museo de Arte Contemporáneo de Tamaulipas (MACT)

Constitución, at C 5 • Tues–Sat 10am–6pm, Sun noon–4pm • Free • ☎ 868 813 1499

You might also check out the **Museo de Arte Contemporáneo de Tamaulipas**, an exuberant Modernist structure that shows revolving exhibitions from some of the best contemporary Mexican multimedia artists.

ARRIVAL AND DEPARTURE   MATAMOROS

TO/FROM THE US

Crossing the Puente Nuevo (24hr) between Matamoros and Brownsville incurs a toll: US$1 or M$17 for pedestrians (US$0.30 or M$5.20 coming back), and US$3.25 or M$56.50 for cars. On the Mexican side local buses (M$8) run frequently from the border along De Las Rosas and then Obregón to the centre and the Central de Autobuses (marked "Central"). Heading back, look for buses marked "Puente Internacional". Taxis at the border run on a fixed-rate system: M$60 for the bus station and M$250 for the airport.

On the US side Brownsville's Greyhound bus station (755 International Blvd) offers services to San Antonio (4 daily; US$33.50–38.50; 5hr 40min–7hr) and Houston (4 daily; US$29.50–34.50; 7hr 30min–8hr 25min). Brownsville is 445km and around 4hr by car from San Antonio via Rte-77 and I-37; it's 571km and around 5hr 20min from Houston via Rte-77 and 59.

BY BUS

The Central de Autobuses (☎ 871 812 2777; restaurant and guardería 6.30am–10.30pm) is a long way south of the centre on Canales; buses marked "Centro" (M$8) will take you towards the main plazas, while taxis will try to charge you as much as possible – M$50 should be the maximum to the plaza area, or M$60 to the border. If you're heading to the US you can take a bus straight across the border from the Central de Autobuses: Americanos runs five daily buses (US$7.50–8.50/M$130–150; 30–45min) between Matamoros and the Greyhound station in Brownsville.

Destinations Chicago (2 daily; 36hr); Ciudad Victoria (hourly; 4–5hr); Dallas (2 daily; 13hr); Houston (2 daily; 8hr); Mexico City (14hr); Monterrey (hourly; 4hr); Reynosa (every 45min; 2hr); San Antonio (4 daily; 6–7hr); Tampico (hourly; 7–8hr); Veracruz (5 daily; 16hr); Zacatecas (2 daily; 12hr).

INFORMATION

Tourist office The Matamoros tourist office (Mon–Fri 9am–6pm, Sat 9am–3pm; ☎ 868 812 0212, ⓦ visitamatamoros.com), right at the Mexican border post, is worthwhile for the latest Matamoros info, or for any destinations further south.

ACCOMMODATION

★ **Best Western Plaza Matamoros** Bravo 1421 and C 9 ☎ 868 816 1696, ⓦ bestwestern.com/mx/hotelplaza matamoros. If you're looking for a bit of comfort in the centre, this is the best choice; it's average chain hotel fare by US standards, but it's clean and safe with an airy inner atrium, and the free breakfast is good. Restaurant, parking, and rooms with a/c, free internet and cable TV. **M$890**

Ritz Matamoros 612, at C 7 ☎ 868 812 1190, ⓦ ritzhotel.org. Comfortable hotel with slightly old-fashioned rooms, but whose rates include buffet breakfast. There's a suite available for six people, plus plenty of safe parking, cable TV, and it's about M$100 cheaper at weekends. **M$600**

THE KING OF NACHOS

Contrary to popular belief, that addictive combination of crispy tortilla chips and melted cheese – a staple snack all over the US and beyond – is not traditional Mexican food. Nachos were actually dreamt up in 1943 in **Piedras Negras** by Ignacio "Nacho" Anaya, allegedly while trying to feed a group of US army wives after hours. He was forced to cook up whatever he had left in the kitchen: essentially toasted tortillas, cheese and jalapeño peppers. The idea caught on, especially in Texas, but it wasn't until the 1970s that "nachos" became popular throughout the US (it's never had quite the same appeal in Mexico). When Anaya died in 1975 a bronze plaque in his memory was erected in Piedras Negras, and the town hosts an **International Nacho Festival** around October 21 each year. The two-day event features live music, art and a goofy attempt to make the world's biggest nacho.

Sadly, the original nacho restaurant no longer exists, and the *Moderno*, where Anaya went on to work, closed in 2010.

THE NORTH'S MAJOR FIESTAS

Carnaval (week before Lent; variable Feb–March) is at its best in the Caribbean and New Orleans-like atmosphere of Tampico – also in Ciudad Victoria and Monterrey.
Birth of Benito Juárez (March 21). Ceremonies to commemorate Juárez' birth in Matamoros.
Día de Nuestra Señora del Refugio (July 4). Marked by dancing and pilgrimages in Matamoros.
Feria de la Uva (Aug 9). Exuberant festivities in Parras, between Saltillo and Torreón.
Feria de Saltillo (around Aug 13). Saltillo begins its annual festival, featuring agricultural and art exhibitions, music and dance performances, and plenty of the local *sarapes* (shawls).
Feria de Nuevo Laredo (Sept). Major festival on the border at Nuevo Laredo.
Independence Day (Sept 16). Festivities everywhere, but the biggest are in Monterrey.
Fiesta de Amistad (late Oct). Joint week-long celebrations between the border town of Ciudad Acuña and its Texan neighbour Del Rio. Bullfights, pageants and a parade, which starts in one country and ends in the other.
Día de San Martín de Porres (Nov 3). Fiesta with native dances in Tampico.
Día de la Virgen de Guadalupe (Dec 12). Big celebrations everywhere, especially in Guadalupe de Bravos; El Palmito (Durango), between Durango and Parral; Ciudad Anahuac (Nuevo León) in the north of the state; and Abasolo, near Monterrey. Monterrey itself attracts many pilgrims at this time.

7

EATING

Café Paris González 125 and C 6 ☎868 816 0316. Classic but faded old restaurant and café, serving decent coffee, main meals and even passable café-au-lait with oven-fresh rolls. Just off the main plaza. Daily 7am–10pm.

Garcia's Obregón 82 ☎868 812 3929, ⍵garcia-s.com. It doesn't get more touristy than this, but it's worth coming to the *Garcia's* complex once for the archetypal border experience, literally a few metres from the bridge to scoop up as many day-trippers as possible. You can shop, eat reasonable international dishes in the restaurant (steaks,

etc) and drink in the cabaret-like *Fiesta Bar* (which has live bands). Main dishes US$11.45–16.45 (M$200–285). Daily 8.30am–2am.

Mi Pueblito C 5 and Constitución, opposite MACT ☎868 816 0586, ⍵mi-pueblito.com. Popular family restaurant in a giant faux palapa, with big Mexican breakfasts (M$75–100) and all the classics for lunch and dinner (M$75–160) – the bar is also a good place to grab a drink, and is best known for its stock of two hundred tequilas. Sun–Thurs 7am–midnight, Fri & Sat 7am–1am.

DIRECTORY

Banks and exchange Banamex is at C7 and Moreles; there are decent currency exchange facilities in the centre: head for Banorte, on Morelos at C6.
Emergencies ☎066; Cruz Roja ☎812 0044; Federal

Police ☎817 2205; International Medical Center ☎811 0000.
Pharmacy Try Farmacia Guadalajara, González 609, at C7.
Post office Río Bravo 15 at C 11 (Mon–Fri 9am–3pm).

The northwest and Copper Canyon

"EL CHEPE" PASSENGER TRAIN

The northwest and Copper Canyon

Divided from Baja California by the Sea of Cortez, Mexico's northwest mainland is something of a bizarre – and initially uninviting – introduction to the country, despite containing one of the region's most alluring natural attractions. The Sierra Tarahumara is wonderfully wild, pristine and remote, concealing six dizzying chasms known collectively as the Barranca del Cobre (or Copper Canyon). Mexico's last surviving passenger train, nicknamed "El Chepe", steers a phenomenal course around its rim – one of the world's ultimate train rides. Other highlights include Álamos, once a silver-mining city and now a charming retreat for expats and artists, and El Fuerte, another colonial town rich in history.

Travelling in this part of Mexico can be incredibly rewarding, but beyond the coastal resorts you'll see very few tourists. At once fertile, wealthy and heavily Americanized, in parts it is also strikingly impoverished, drab and barren – drug violence in Sinaloa and Sonora has further weakened its appeal, though the risk to visitors is slight (see box, p.468). The climate's not exactly welcoming, either – summer temperatures can hit 50°C, while winter nights in the desert drop to freezing levels.

8

Yet it's this extraordinary desert scenery that grabs your attention, which, along with the huge cacti, makes for some archetypal Mexican landscapes, while the fierce sunshine makes the beach towns in this part of Mexico doubly enticing. North of Puerto Vallarta lies **San Blas**, a small, friendly town surrounded by steamy jungle and peaceful strips of sand, and the resort of **Mazatlán** with its wealth of beaches, bars and fine seafood restaurants. Heading towards the US border are the quieter beaches of **Bahía de Kino** and **San Carlos**, and the shrimping port and burgeoning resort of **Puerto Peñasco**.

Tepic

Some 170km north of Puerto Vallarta, the first place of any size is **TEPIC**, capital of the state of **Nayarit** and home to over three hundred thousand people. Founded by Hernán Cortés' brother, Francisco, in 1544, it's appealing enough in a quietly provincial way, but for most travellers it's no more than a convenient **stopover** along the route to Mazatlán, or a place to switch buses for **San Blas** (see p.482) and the coast.

Plenty of shops sell **Huichol artesanías** (see box, p.482) in Tepic, including vibrant yarn paintings and bead statues. Alternatively, you can buy them directly from Huichol artists in the **Plaza Principal**, Tepic's lush central square of fountains and gardens, overlooked by the Palacio Municipal and twin neo-Gothic towers of the Catedral de la Asunción, completed in the 1890s.

RESERVA DE LA BIOSFERA EL PINACATE

Highlights

❶ San Blas Tranquil backwater offering phenomenal bird watching, surfing and seafood, as well as a chance for some serious lounging on the beach. **See p.482**

❷ Mexcaltitán This intriguing island town claims to be the spiritual home of the Aztecs, a miniature Tenochtitlán ringed by waterways. **See p.485**

❸ Mazatlán Old-fashioned Mexican resort enriched by a spruced-up historic centre, horse-rides along the beach, zip lines in the jungle and fresh seafood. **See p.486**

❹ The Copper Canyon railway The journey through Chihuahua state's rugged canyons

offers one of the world's most gripping train experiences. **See p.501**

❺ Creel and the Sierra Tarahumara For real adventure and a window into Mexico's past, hike or bike to the waterfalls and Rarámuri villages around Creel. **See p.507**

❻ Álamos Soak up the colonial charm in this wonderfully preserved old town, with languid plazas, enticing inns and captivating desert scenery. **See p.514**

❼ Reserva de la Biósfera El Pinacate Explore this barren, moon-like reserve, a 50km-wide volcanic field of mesmerizing craters, home to all manner of wildlife. **See p.522**

HIGHLIGHTS ARE MARKED ON THE MAP ON P.480

Museo Regional de Nayarit

México Nte 91, at Zapata • Mon–Fri 9am–6pm, Sat 9am–3pm • M$47 • ☎ 311 212 1900

Worth a quick look is the small **Museo Regional de Nayarit**, housed in an adobe mansion built in 1762, south of the Plaza Principal. Inside is a small but absorbing collection of local pre-Columbian and Huichol artefacts dating back to 200 BC, and objects from the Aztatlán culture (800–1350 AD).

Museo de Los Cinco Pueblos

México Nte 105, at Zapata • Mon–Fri 9am–2pm & 4–7pm • Free • ☎ 311 212 1705

The **Museo de Los Cinco Pueblos**, housed in a former nineteenth-century hotel, contains anthropological displays, artwork, embroidery and beadwork of Nayarit's four major indigenous groups (the Coras, Huichols, Nahua, aka "mexicaneros", and Tepehuanos), as well as aspects of mestizo culture, the fifth "pueblo", recently (and controversially) added to reflect the ethnic make-up of the whole state.

Museo Amado Nervo

Zacatecas Nte 284 • Mon–Fri 9am–2pm & 4–7pm, Sat 10am–2pm • Free • ☎ 311 212 2916

The **Museo Amado Nervo** commemorates the life and works of one of Mexico's most famous poets, in the house where he was born in 1870. Inside are family photographs and some books and furniture that once belonged to Nervo. Best known for poems such as *La Raza de Bronce* (written in honour of Benito Juárez), and the heart-breaking *La Amada Inmóvil*, Nervo died in Uruguay (where he was Mexican Ambassador) in 1919.

ARRIVAL AND INFORMATION   TEPIC

By plane Tepic's airport (Aeropuerto Internacional Amado Nervo) serves Aeromar flights to Mexico City (3 daily; 1hr 55min) and Volaris flights to Tijuana (1 daily; 2hr 40min). The airport is 16km southeast of the city centre; taxis into the centre charge around M$200–250, and M$600 to San Blas; Mexcaltitán will be at least M$800.

By bus Tepic's Central Camionera lies a few kilometres east of the centre on Insurgentes Sur, but local buses (M$6) shuttle in and out from the main road outside – to reach the centre, cross the street and catch the first bus marked "Centro". Taxis should be around M$40–50. Transportes Norte de Sonora runs hourly second-class buses to San Blas

(M$56; 2hr) and Santiago Ixcuintla (M$50; 1hr 30min) till around 7.30pm.

Destinations Guadalajara (every 30min; 3hr 30min); Mazatlán (every 30min; 4hr 30min); Mexico City (4 daily; 10hr); Puerto Vallarta (hourly; 3–4hr); San Blas (hourly; 2hr); Tijuana (every 30min; 30hr).

Tourist office The main state tourism office is inconveniently located in the Ex-Convento de la Cruz, at the corner of Calz del Ejercito and México (Mon–Fri 9am–5pm; ☎ 311 214 8071, ⓦ turismonayarit.mx and ⓦ rivieranayarit .com), although the city tourist office is on the Plaza Principal (daily 9am–7pm; ☎ 311 212 8037).

ACCOMMODATION

Fray Junípero Serra Lerdo Pte 23 ☎ 311 212 2211, ⓦ frayjunipero.com.mx. A comfortable choice, right on the plaza, with modern but fairly standard business-oriented rooms and amenities (LCD TVs, free wi-fi and free parking). Breakfast adds around M$60. **M$950**

Hotel Real de Don Juan México Sur 105, at Juárez

☎ 311 216 1888, ⓦ realdedonjuan.com. Dripping with historic character, this colonial *palacio* overlooking the main plaza offers comfy, old-fashioned rooms (with cable TV and free wi-fi), a rooftop lounge and much cheaper rates online – shop around. **M$1280**

EATING AND DRINKING

Café Diligencias México Sur 29 ☎ 311 212 1535. A good place to linger over a coffee and cakes – also serves hefty Mexican lunch plates (M$75–120). Affectionately known as "café de los viejitos", this place has been open since 1968. Daily 7.30am–11pm.

Emiliano Comida y Vino Zapata Ote 91 ☎ 311 216 2010, ⓦ emilianorestaurant.com. For something smarter (though a portrait of Mexican Revolution hero Emiliano Zapata greets you at the entrance), this top-notch restaurant offers creative Mexican dining with regional

8

THE HUICHOL

The **Huichol**, or Wixárika, are the most intensely mystical of Mexico's indigenous peoples. Dwelling in isolated mountain settlements around the borders of Nayarit, Jalisco, Zacatecas and Durango, they practise an extant form of **pre-Columbian shamanism**, having accepted only token elements of Spanish Catholicism.

For the Huichol, religion and ritual are central elements of daily life. The cultivation of maize, particularly, is bound up with sacred rites and esoteric meaning. **Animism** – the belief that all objects are alive and imbued with spirit – is key to their enigmatic world-view: rocks, trees, rivers and sky all have souls and there are as many gods as there are things in the world.

Peyote, a hallucinogenic cactus, is the most important and powerful god in their vast pantheon. Gathering and ingesting this plant is a major part of the ceremonial calendar, which includes an annual cross-country pilgrimage to the sacred desert around Real de Catorce to acquire supplies (see box, p.386). Grandfather Peyote is the teacher and guardian of the Huichol. He delivers sacred visions, heals the sick and guides the community.

Huichol artesanías are particularly striking and include vivid "**yarn paintings**" that are created by pressing lengths of yarn into wax. They represent peyote visions and are filled with vibrantly rendered snakes, birds, deer and other sacred animals, as well as gourd bowls and other ritually significant objects. Circular motifs usually symbolize peyote itself, or its flower. You can buy these paintings in Tepic and elsewhere.

specialities and excellent wines from all over the country. Mains $120–200. Mon–Sat 8am–11pm.

Lonchería Flamingos Puebla 193 ☎ 311 212 1560. Not far from the plaza, this is a great spot for no-frills Mexican food, with delicious tortas, tostadas and tacos on offer (M$25–50). Thurs–Tues 10am–10.30pm.

Restaurant La Sierra Hotel Sierra de Álica, México Nte 180 ☎ 323 212 0322. This hotel restaurant is a real gem, knocking out tempting dishes such as fish *chicharrones*, steak "La Sierra" style and peanut sauce chicken from M$90. Check out the set-lunch deals. Daily 7.30am–9pm.

San Blas and around

The coastal plains of Nayarit are sultry, marshy and flat, dotted with palm trees and half-submerged under lagoons teeming with wildlife. You have to travel through this to reach **SAN BLAS**, once an important port but now an enjoyably laid-back travellers' hangout. For such a small town (with around fifteen thousand inhabitants), San Blas manages to absorb its many visitors – who come mainly in winter – without feeling overrun. During the summer it's virtually deserted, but in January and February the town is a magnet for **bird watchers**, and in February the city also hosts its biggest festival in honour of San Blas (St Blaise). Do not come here without insect repellent or you will be eaten alive: legions of ferocious sand flies (*jejénes*) plague the beaches mornings and late afternoons, and the mosquitoes descend en masse at dusk.

Las Ruinas de la Contaduría

Cerro de la Contaduría • Daily 8am–7pm • M$10 • Taxi M$30–40 (or around 30min walking from main plaza)

Beyond lying on the pristine **beaches** to the south of San Blas, **bird watching** and taking a beguiling jungle-boat trip to **La Tovara springs** (see opposite), a more focused hour can be spent at **Las Ruinas de la Contaduría**, the remains of a late eighteenth-century fort which, with the vaulted remains of a chapel, **La Iglesia de Nuestra Señora del Rosario** (1769), crown the Cerro de San Basilio near the river, 1km along Juárez towards Tepic; the ruins are said to have inspired Henry Wadsworth Longfellow's poem, *The Bells of San Blas*, though the poet never came here. From the top you get sensational views over the town to the ocean, where, according to Huichol legend, the small white island on the horizon is said to represent peyote.

La Tovara and jungle boat trips

The **lagoons and creeks** behind San Blas are unbelievably rich in **bird life** – white herons and egrets are especially prevalent. The best way to catch a glimpse is to get on one of the three-hour boat trips into the jungle, the launch negotiating channels tunnelled through dense mangrove, past sunbaking turtles. Go at dawn, before other trips have disturbed the animals; you might even glimpse a crocodile or caiman along the way. Most boats head for **La Tovara**, a cool freshwater spring that fills a beautiful clear pool perfect for swimming and pirouetting off the rope swing – if you're not put off by the presence of crocodiles, that is. Eat at the fairly pricey palapa restaurant or bring your own picnic.

Trips leave from the river bridge 1km inland from the main plaza along Juárez: get a group together for the best prices. Rates start at around M$600 for four, M$150 per extra person for three hours; it's around M$150 extra person for a side trip to the local **crocodile farm**.

Bahía de Matanchén

As well as the fine beaches right in town (**Playa El Borrego**, at the south end of C Cuauhtémoc) and on **Isla del Rey**, just offshore (M$25 by boat), there are others some 7km away around the **Bahía de Matanchén**, a vast, sweeping crescent lined entirely by fine soft sands. At the near end, the tiny community of **Matanchén** (famed for its

▲ Guadalupe Victoria

SAN BLAS

Airfield ✈

8

Topic, Bahía de Matanchén beaches & ▮

● **EATING**

Cha Cha's (aka El Cocodrilo)	1
El Delfín Garza	4
Restaurant La Isla	3
McDonald Restaurante	2

Bus Station

ℹ
✉
✕ **Palacio Municipal**
❷ ❶
@
❷
❸

Port

Boats to La Tovara

⚓
Las Ruinas de la Contaduría & La Iglesia de Nuestra Señora del Rosario

Cerro de San Basilio

San Cristóbal Estuary

❹

⊞ **Hospital**
❹ ❺
❻

Isla del Rey

PACIFIC OCEAN

N

0   100
metres

Stoner's Surf Camp ℹ
Playa El Borrego

■ **DRINKING AND NIGHTLIFE**

Mike's Place	2
San Blas Social Club	1

■ **ACCOMMODATION**

Bungalows La Quinta California	6
Casa María	3
Casa Roxanna Bungalows	4
Casa de Valorien	1
Garza Canela	5
Hotel Hacienda Flamingos	2

locally baked **banana bread**) is the launching point for the long stretch of **Playa Las Islitas** (via dirt road), which has numerous palapa restaurants on the beach that serve up grilled fish and cold beers. At the far end of the bay lies the village **Aticama** (with basic shops and places to eat), the disappointing **Playa Los Cocos**, where erosion is steadily eating away at what was once a pristine beach, and the better **Playa La Miramar** beyond. In between, acres of sand are fragmented only by flocks of pelicans and the occasional crab. There are plenty of spots where you can camp if you have the gear and lots of repellent. The waves here, which rise offshore beyond Miramar and run in, past the point, to the depths of the bay, are in the *Guinness Book of World Records* as the longest in the world: it's very rare that they are high enough for surfers to ride them all the way in, but there's plenty of lesser **surfing** potential.

ARRIVAL AND DEPARTURE
SAN BLAS AND AROUND

By bus The bus station is on Sinaloa at Canalizo at the northeast corner of the main plaza, right in the centre of town. The majority of the buses (second-class only) serving San Blas arrive from Tepic, 65km east (M$56; last bus around 7.30pm). Taxis charge around M$600 for the trip. Taxis from Puerto Vallarta airport will charge around M$3465 (it should be only M$1500 on the way back). Note that Vallarta is one hour ahead of San Blas. From Mazatlán you'll need to change at Tepic or ask to get off at the "crucero de San Blas", where you can also pick up the Tepic–San Blas buses (till around 7.30pm).

Destinations Puerto Vallarta (4 daily; 3–4hr); Tepic (hourly; 1hr–1hr 30min).

INFORMATION AND ACTIVITIES

Tourist office The tourist office (Mon–Fri 9am–3pm; 📞 323 285 0221) is located inside the Palacio Municipal on the main plaza. The best source of information, though, is 🌐 visitsanblas.com, run by local expat Pat Cordes.

Surfing Surfboards and boogie boards can be rented at Stoner's Surf Camp (🌐 stonerssurfcamp.com) at Playa El Borrego for M$50–100/hr, or M$100–200/day (lessons M$200/hr). You can also stay in basic cabins here for M$300, or camp for M$50.

GETTING AROUND

By bus The beaches of the Bahía de Matanchén can be reached by one of the buses ("El Llano") that leave around four times daily (8.30am–4.30pm) from the San Blas bus station; these go along the bay through Matanchén village (where you get off for Las Islitas (M$15); Los Cocos (M$20); and on to Santa Cruz (M$27). Coming back, just flag down the first bus. You can also take a local taxi (bargain fiercely – it should be M$100 to Los Cocos).

ACCOMMODATION

Bungalows La Quinta California Matanchén 3, Palmar de Los Cocos 📞 323 285 0310, 🌐 quintaca lifornia.weebly.com. Friendly management and bargain two-bedroom apartments set around a leafy, tranquil courtyard with cable TV and free wi-fi. Short walk from the beach, behind *El Herradero Cantina*, among the trees (take Las Islitas, off Batallón). **M$350**

Casa María Canalizo 67 📞 323 285 1057. Long-established and well-known guesthouse hosted by María and her family, with comfortable, clean rooms (with bathroom and cable TV) surrounding a courtyard filled with caged birds; shared kitchen and free washing machine. **M$400** (extra M$100 for a/c)

★**Casa Roxanna Bungalows** El Rey 1 📞 323 285 0573, 🌐 casaroxanna.com. Exceptional value with immaculate rooms and good kitchenettes, all with wi-fi, cable TV and use of pool and laundry – the pick of the self-catering apartments in town. **M$700**

Casa de Valorien Bahía de Matanchén, near Santa Cruz 📞 327 103 6876, 🌐 casavalorien.com. Excellent rental property managed by friendly hosts Janice and Valorien Harper, occupying a secluded spot on the bay with stairs down to the beach below (it's several km south of San Blas, but easy to reach by bus or taxi). Three bright and cosy rooms and fabulous meals prepared upon request. **M$1125**

Garza Canela Paredes Sur 106 (follow signs from Batallón) 📞 323 285 0112, 🌐 garzacanela.com. Luxurious a/c rooms, pool, garden and some kitchenettes. Rates include breakfast, and the poshest restaurant in town, *El Delfín*, is on site. Significant discounts during low season. **M$1090**

Hotel Hacienda Flamingos Juárez 105 📞 323 285 0485, 🌐 sanblas.com.mx. Hotel set in a gorgeous old mansion built in 1883 with a wonderful garden courtyard with pool and ping-pong table – the building has a lot more character than the rooms, which are sleek and classy but relatively standard. **M$990**

EATING

Cha Cha's (aka El Cocodrilo) Juárez 1 ☎ 323 285 004. A San Blas fixture with a great location on the plaza. Travellers and locals alike come for the excellent seafood, spaghetti and sandwiches, and to relax and drink long after the activity in the plaza has died down. Mains $75–140. Daily 8am–10pm.

★**El Delfín Garza** Canela Hotel, Paredes Sur 106. French gourmet dining in San Blas, with such delights as baked fish with pistachio, Serrano and parsley, shrimp with curry, coconut milk and coriander and chicken stuffed with cheddar, bacon and prunes. Chef Betty Vázquez was born in San Blas but attended Le Cordon Bleu in France. Mains M$190–260. Daily 8am–9pm.

Restaurant La Isla Mercado, at Paredes (two blocks from the plaza) ☎ 323 285 0407. A must, if only to admire the astonishingly kitschy decor: draped fishing nets festooned with shell pictures, shell mobiles and shell lampshades. Moderately priced meat and great seafood (M$75–160). Also known as *Chief Tony's*. Tues–Sun 2–9pm.

McDonald Restaurante Juárez 75 ☎ 323 285 0432. No relation to Ronald's place, this friendly restaurant just off the main plaza since 1952 serves excellent, good-value meals (M$60–120). Breakfasts are particularly tasty; you'll often find a crowd of expats here to enjoy them. Daily 7am–10pm.

DRINKING AND NIGHTLIFE

Mike's Place Juárez 75 (above McDonald) ☎ 323 285 0432. Quiet drinking midweek but livens up on Fri and Sat with dancing, live music and anything from Latin to classic rock. Tues–Sat 6pm–midnight (expect seasonal changes).

San Blas Social Club Batallón 35, on the Plaza Principal. Popular expat café, bar and erstwhile jazz club helmed by the amicable Agustin, with live music Fri and Sat and hearty pub food (specializing in steaks). Free wi-fi. Mid-Oct–May daily 9am–midnight.

DIRECTORY

Banks and exchange The Banamex on Juárez just east of the plaza (Mon–Fri 9am–2pm) has an ATM, but does not change foreign currency (including US$) and is plagued by long queues, poor rates and an occasional lack of funds.

Change money before you get here.
Post office A block northeast of the bus station at Sonora and Echevarría.

Santiago Ixcuintla

Centro Cultural Huichol 20 de Noviembre 452, at Constitución • Mon–Sat 9am–1pm & 4–6pm • Free • ☎ 323 235 1171

North of San Blas, off Hwy-15, is **SANTIAGO IXCUINTLA**, a market town of around seventeen thousand where the only real interest lies in the **Centro Cultural Huichol**, approximately 1.5km from the central plaza towards Mexcaltitán. This cooperative venture, founded by Huichol artist Mariano Valadez to support his people and preserve their traditions, raises money by selling quality Huichol art and offering various classes; the centre is most active between November and May.

ARRIVAL AND DEPARTURE   SANTIAGO IXCUINTLA

By bus Autotransportes Noroeste de Nayarit runs a few daily buses from Tepic (M$50; 1.5hr). *Combis* to La Batanga (for Mexcaltitán; M$25; 4 daily) depart the Santiago terminal at Juarez Ote 73, one block north of the plaza; some second-class buses also make the trip (40min). Taxis will charge M$200 return.

Mexcaltitán

Museo del Origen Porfirio Díaz 1 (Plaza Principal) • Tues–Sun 10am–2pm & 4–7pm • M$5

North of Santiago Ixcuintla, located on a lily-strewn lagoon and supporting only a few hundred habitants (mostly shrimp farmers), is the extraordinary islet of **MEXCALTITÁN**. The "House of the Mexicans" in Náhautl, the town really does look like a very tiny version of Tenochtitlán, the Aztec capital before the Spaniards arrived. Indeed, the place is one candidate for the legendary Aztec homeland Aztlán, from which the tribe set out on their exodus to the Valley of México around 1091 AD; the small **Museo del Origen** addresses that hypothesis with a collection of archeological relics. If you're in the area around the end of June you should definitely try to visit the **island fiesta**, on

8

June 28 and 29 (the feast days of Saints Peter and Paul), when there are canoe races on the lagoons and rivers; be sure to make a reservation.

ARRIVAL AND DEPARTURE — MEXCALTITÁN

By bus Mexcaltitán can only be reached from Santiago Ixcuintla (32km; see p.485). Taxis charge around M$200 (ask them to wait if you intend to do a day trip), while *combis* (M$25, 4 daily) drop you at La Batanga; the journey takes about 45min and is followed by a 15min boat ride across the lagoon (M$80 minimum for up to four, extra passengers M$20 each; M$300 for guided boat tour).

ACCOMMODATION AND EATING

Ruta Azteca Venecia s/n ☎ 323 235 6020. The single hotel in Mexcaltitán offers four scruffy bare-bones rooms near the church, with a small terrace overlooking the water. **M$250**
El Camarón Plaza Principal. There's a handful of inexpensive restaurants in Mexcaltitán, most specializing in seafood and, unsurprisingly, shrimp (you'll smell them long before you taste them). *El Camarón* is one of the more dependable places, with basic dishes for under M$100, but opening times are always subject to change. Mon–Sat noon–9pm.

Mazatlán

The languid resort of **MAZATLÁN** is far less dominated by tourism than Acapulco or Puerto Vallarta, its direct rivals, though hotels still flank its 30km of enticing sandy beaches, and activities such as horseriding and zip lines have enhanced its appeal in recent years. Yet Mazatlán's greatest pull remains its old-fashioned seaside resort atmosphere and the museums, cafés and galleries of its resurgent *centro histórico*, where much of its nineteenth-century core has been sensitively restored. Most tourists stay in the **Zona Dorada**, the "Golden Zone" along the beach, and penetrate the *centro histórico* only on brief forays, but the latter has far more character. Mazatlán actually peaked in the 1980s, and today much of the seafront looks decidedly tired, despite the steady flow of visitors. Local authorities have certainly made huge improvements in security in recent years, however, and by 2015 all the major cruise lines were once again making stops here.

Brief history

Mazatlán started life as a base for smugglers and pirates in the 1700s. An official customs office was opened here in 1828, and from then on it boomed as a respectable mining port; by 1850 the population had reached 5000 (despite a devastating cholera epidemic the year before). Mazatlán had grown into one of Mexico's most important ports by 1900, as well as a major manufacturing centre: beer producer **Cerveceria del Pacífico** was established here by German immigrants in 1900, and it remains one of the nation's most popular brands. The city was hit hard by the 1910 Revolution, however, and by the 1930s the Great Depression had killed off the local economy. After World War II Mazatlán reinvented itself as a fishing port (it still boasts the biggest canneries and shrimp fisheries in Mexico) and a tourist destination. Today it has a population of around half a million, the second-largest city in Sinaloa (after Culiacán, the capital).

THE MAZATLÁN MOSAICS

Opened in 2009, the ultra-modern **Mazatlán International Center**, Avenida del Delfín 6303 (Ⓦ mazatlaninternationalcenter.com), is best known for exhibitions and conferences, but it is also home to the world's largest mural. Sinaloa-born local artist Ernesto Ríos created the mesmerizing 25m-high three-dimensional ceramic mosaic dubbed "Sea of Cortés", which covers the whole north wall of the building and explodes with colour. The centre is studded with modern artwork inside and out, further justifying the taxi ride up here.

Zona Dorada, Nuevo Mazatlán & Aquarium ▲   Bus station ▲

CENTRO HISTÓRICO MAZATLÁN

■ ACCOMMODATION	
Best Western Hotel Posada	
Freeman Express	6
Casa Lucila Hotel Boutique	7
Hotel Lerma	2
Las 7 Maravillas	1
Melville Boutique Hotel	5
Royal Dutch Casa de	
Santa María	4
La Siesta	3

● EATING	
El Aljibe de San Pedro	8
Casa Etnika	6
Looney Bean	7
Mercado Culinario	4
Mercado Pino Suárez	1
Pastelería Panamá	2
El Shrimp Bucket	3
Topolo	5
El Túnel	9
Water's Edge	10

■ DRINKING	
Café Pacífico/	
Vintage Retro Bar	1
Edgar's Bar	2
Sky Room	3

PACIFIC OCEAN

CERRO DE LA NEVERÍA

Market

Mirador (divers)

Bahía de Olas

Playa Olas Altas

Museo Arqueológico

Museo de Arte

Courthouse

Casa Machado

Catedral de la Inmaculada Concepción

Palacio Municipal

PLAZA REPÚBLICA

Mercado Pino Suárez

Centro de las Artes

Teatro Ángela Peralta

Farmacia Guadalajara

Canal de Navegación

Isla de la Piedra

CERRO DEL VIGÍA

Ferry Terminal

Embarcadero Playa Sur

Cruise Terminal

0   500
metres

N

8

▼ Faro de Crestón

Plaza República

Mazatlán's **Plaza República** is very much the commercial heart of the city and the *centro histórico*, harbouring the cathedral, post office, dour modern government offices, main bank branches and travel agencies.

Catedral de la Inmaculada Concepción

Plaza República • Daily 6am–1pm & 4–8pm • ☏ 669 981 3352

The twin-towered **Catedral de la Inmaculada Concepción** is the only real building of note on Plaza República, completed in 1899 in an eclectic style incorporating neo-Gothic, Spanish and Romanesque elements, with a particularly grand interior and main altar.

Mercado Pino Suárez

Juárez, at Valle • Mon–Sat 6am–6pm, Sun 6am–2pm

Take time to explore the **Mercado Pino Suárez**, two blocks north of the Plaza República, a grand Art Nouveau edifice that remains exceptionally bright and clean inside. The vast iron structure was completed in 1900, and named in honour of Mexico's vice president Pino Suárez in 1915 (who had been assassinated two years earlier). You'll find the usual meat, veg and fruit stalls here, as well as souvenirs, clothes and excellent, cheap places to eat (see p.495).

Plaza Machado

Plaza Machado, a few blocks southwest of the Plaza República, is by far the most popular of the old town squares. It's surrounded by restaurants (see p.495) and fine nineteenth-century buildings, notably the **Centro Municipal de las Artes**, and the late nineteenth-century Edifico Juárez on the north side.

Teatro Ángela Peralta

Carnaval s/n · Daily 10am–5pm · M$15 · ☎ 669 982 4446, ⓦ culturamazatlan.com

Adjacent to the Centro Municipal de las Artes Teatro, the Neoclassical **Teatro Ángela Peralta** opened in 1874. The theatre is named after the "Mexican Nightingale", who died in the art centre next door in 1882 (it was a hotel at the time). In addition to seeing the opulent interior there's a small museum on the second floor and temporary art exhibitions inside.

Casa Machado

Constitución 79 · Daily 10am–6pm · M$20 · ☎ 669 982 1440

Just off Plaza Machado, the **Casa Machado** dates from 1846, with the upstairs faithfully restored to depict late nineteenth-century middle-class life in Mazatlán. The rooms, with tile and wood floors and timber beams, feature period furniture dating from 1880 to the 1910s, and there's an excellent fifteen-minute video covering the history of the city (English version available). There's also small displays dedicated to **Ángela Peralta** and the city's famous carnival, as well as the best view of Plaza Machado from the second-floor balcony.

MAZATLÁN

■ ACCOMMODATION	
Captain Moe's Bed & Breakfast	3
Crowne Plaza Resort Mazatlán	7
Emperador	1
Hotel Sands Arenas	2
Inn at Mazatlán	6
Motel Marley	5
Playa Mazatlán Beach Hotel	4

● EATING	
Los Arcos	2
Casa Loma	1
Gus y Gus	3
Pancho's	4
Tacos Escorpio by Henry	5

Museo Arqueológico

Sixto Osuna 76 • Tues–Sun 9am–6pm • M$39 • ☎ 669 981 1455

The small **Museo Arqueológico**, just a couple of blocks off Plaza Machado towards Olas Altas, is notable for having English labelling – the museum charts the pre-Hispanic cultures of Sonora state, with beautifully crafted **Aztatlán pottery** (750–1200 AD) and a collection of figurines, pots and statues, ending with the **Jorobado de la Nautical**, a strange figure of a hunchback thought to have magic powers.

Museo de Arte

Carranza at Sixto Osuna • Tues–Sat 10am–2pm & 5–8pm, Sun 10am–2pm • M$8 • ☎ 669 985 3502

Across the street from the Museo Arqueológico is the curious little **Museo de Arte**, set around a pretty courtyard and mansion built in 1898, with a permanent collection of modern Mexican paintings and sculpture from the late 1970s, and temporary exhibits of contemporary Mexican art. Exhibits rotate, but the permanent collection includes work by Sinaloan watercolour artist Edgardo Coghlan, contemporary painter Vicente Rojo, well-known abstract artist Rufino Tamayo and Oaxacan painter and sculptor Francisco Toledo.

El Acuario Mazatlán

Av de los Deportes 111 • Daily 9am–6pm • M$110, M$80 children 3–11 • ⓦ acuariomazatlan.com

The city's slightly shabby aquarium, **El Acuario Mazatlán** (just off Av del Mar halfway between the *centro histórico* and the Zona Dorada) attracts a steady stream of families and school groups for its fish tanks, seal shows and aviary (largely filled with parrots). Turtles, sharks and a variety of tropical fish (mostly but not exclusively from Mexican waters) are on show, though the labelling (Spanish only) is hit and miss. The small Museo del Mar section contains a grey-whale skeleton and various shark jaws.

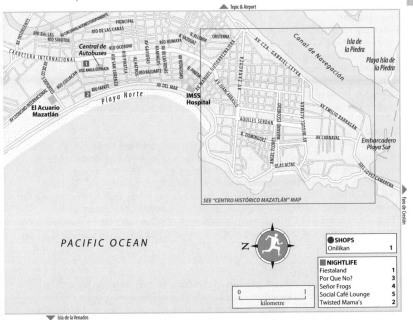

MAZATLÁN'S LONESOME TRAVELLERS

Few Mexican cities seem to celebrate their (albeit tenuous) literary connections with such pride as Mazatlán, with special plaques nailed up throughout the old town. **Herman Melville** stayed in Mazatlán for nineteen days in 1844, as a humble sailor aboard the frigate *United States*, no doubt gathering material for Moby Dick and his other subsequent novels. In 1951 beat poet **Allen Ginsberg** passed through, while **Anaïs Nin** stayed at the *Hotel Belmar* when she visited Mazatlán the same year. In her diary, Nin admires the "pink and turquoise houses, the green shutters". The following year **Jack Kerouac** spent a night and day drinking and dossing on the beach in Mazatlán, writing about his brief time here in *Lonesome Traveler* (1960): "At Mazatlan at dusk we stopped for awhile for a swim in our underwear in that magnificent surf..."

Faro de Crestón

There are scintillating **views** of Mazatlán from the top of the **Faro de Crestón**, the lighthouse at the far southern edge of the city that dates back to 1879. Taxis can take you to the foot of the hill (buses also go this far), but the only way to the top is on foot (30–45min). It's a popular hike in the mornings and late afternoons. The lighthouse itself still works and is off limits.

The beaches

Facing the Pacific on the edge of the *centro histórico*, **Playa Olas Altas** is where Mazatlán's transformation into a resort began in the 1920s, and though the faded tiles and peeling paint of the *Belmar Hotel* (which opened in 1924) are in dire need of a makeover, *Bar Belmar* and neighbouring *El Faro* (daily 7am–10pm) are still classic places for a sunset drink. The beach here is not the best place to swim – it's rather rocky and the waves tend to be powerful (*olas altas* means "high waves"). Indeed, this is a decent place to **surf** (though not for beginners) – you can rent boards at *Looney Bean* (see p.495). From Playa Olas Altas, the paved **malecón** runs for 10km to the Zona Dorada.

The Mirador

Following the seafront drive from Playa Olas Altas around the jagged coast under the Cerro de la Nevería brings you to the **Mirador** – an outcrop from which local daredevil youths or *clavadistas* plunge into the sea. At a little over 10m, it's nowhere near as spectacular as the high-diving in Acapulco, but is dangerous nonetheless. You'll see them performing whenever there are enough tourists to raise a collection, generally starting at 10am or 11am – especially during the summer and Semana Santa – and again in the late afternoon (around 5pm) when the tour buses roll through.

Zona Dorada

From the Mirador the malecón runs along the long sweep of **Playa Norte**, but it's worth skipping this and walking (or taking the bus) all the way to the **Zona Dorada**, where the first of the big hotels went up and the sands improve greatly. The beaches right in front of the hotels – known as **Playa Gaviotas** and **Playa Sábalo** further north – are clean and sheltered by little offshore islands, while further on they're wilder and emptier. Among the dozens of artesanía markets and shopping malls here, **Seashell City Museum** (daily 10am–7pm; ☎669 913 1301, ⊕seashellcitymuseum.com), at Gaviotas 407 in the heart of the Zona, stands out as the kitschiest of all – a two-storey emporium of seashells (for sale) with a "museum" upstairs of rare pieces and whale bones, and an indoor goldfish pond.

Isla de la Venados

If you fancy escaping the beach vendors of the Zona Dorada for a few hours take the boat trip to the **Isla de la Venados** (Deer Island) 2km offshore, the biggest (1.8km long) and most accessible of the three islands off Mazatlán (the other two are Isla de Pájaros and Isla de Lobos). There's a small beach and tide pools for snorkelling, and kayaking and even banana boat trips are available. Any of the tour operators in the Zona Dorada will sell tickets; boats usually depart Marina El Cid at 9.30am, returning at around 4pm (from M$400, or M$750 including food and drinks).

Playa Cerritos and Playa Bruja

If your goal is to reach a beautifully serene beach, head north to either **Playa Cerritos** or **Playa Bruja** (both accessible by bus, p.492). These are at the heart of the new mega resorts and development of **Nuevo Mazatlán**, but the beaches remain fairly free of crowds and there are plenty of restaurants and places for a post-beach drink.

Isla de la Piedra

Boat trips every 10min; daily 8am–7pm • M$30 (return) • Buses marked "Ferry" go to the end of Carnaval, from where it's a short walk to the *Embarcadero*

Just across the harbour from the *centro histórico* but a totally different world, the **Isla de la Piedra** (actually a long peninsula) offers a slice of rustic Mexico with a long, sandy beach excellent for swimming, backed by palapa restaurants and palm trees. Small motorboats shuttle back and forth from the **Embarcadero Playa Sur**, close to the ferry terminal in Mazatlán, to the dirt road just across from the Piedra beach. It is possible to sleep out or sling a hammock on the terrace of one of the small restaurants – ask the owners first. All the restaurants on the beach serve similar menus of fresh seafood and coconuts. Once a very basic community, the island is now included in many tour itineraries and can become crowded, especially on Sunday afternoons, when locals congregate for live music, dancing and kite flying.

8

ARRIVAL AND DEPARTURE   MAZATLÁN

BY PLANE

Arrival Mazatlán's General Rafael Buelna International Airport (📞 669 982 2399) is some 20km south of town (off Hwy-15), served by a system of fixed-price vans (around M$100–150/person; minimum three persons) and taxis (M$340 to the old town and most of Zona Dorada; M$380–550 for longer trips). Taxis will charge M$300–350 for the journey back from the *centro histórico*. You'll find ATMs and Budget, Hertz and Europcar car rental desks at the airport, as well as free wi-fi.

Departure Useful domestic flights include the daily Los Cabos and Puerto Vallarta connections from Aéreo Calafia (📞 669 984 4300), Aeroméxico's (📞 669 914 1111) flight to Los Mochis; Viva Aerobus (📞 81 8215 0150) to Monterrey and Mexico City and Volaris (📞 01 800 122 8000) to Tijuana. There are numerous flights to the US and Canada.

Destinations (domestic) La Paz (1 daily; 1hr 30min); Los Cabos (2 daily; 1hr 30min); Los Mochis (1 daily; 1hr); Mexico City (4 daily; 1hr 30min); Monterrey (1 weekly; 2hr 25min); Puerto Vallarta (1 daily; 1hr); Tijuana (2 daily; 2hr 30min).

BY BUS

Arrival The Central de Autobuses lies three blocks behind Playa Norte on José Ángel Espinoza, at Panuco. Taxis and *pulmonías* will charge around M$70 to the *centro histórico*, and M$70–100 to the Zona Dorada. To save money you can take a public bus (M$7–10): for the

centro histórico, turn left on Espinoza and walk one block to the main road (Av Ejercito Mexicano), and get on just about any bus heading to the right – they'll get you, by a variety of routes, to the Mercado Pino Suárez. For the Zona Dorada, walk down Espinoza in the other direction to the beach (Av de la Mar) and catch any "Sábalo" bus heading to the right.

Departure Most buses from Mazatlán are *de paso*, but with services roughly hourly north and south, you should have no problems getting a ticket. Note that with the completion of the Puente Baluarte in 2013, the new "Carretera Interoceánica" to Durango has cut travel times to the interior dramatically. There are a few direct services to Puerto Vallarta, but companies like TAP also offer more frequent services via a change in Tepic (usually the wait is 30min) – they can reserve seats all the way. For San Blas you'll need to take a bus to Tepic (M$320–350) and change. Sample fares (TAP and Omnibus): Durango (M$515), Guadalajara (M$460), Los Mochis (M$490), Mexico City (M$1055), Puerto Vallarta (M$555) and Tijuana (M$1510). Shop around, as prices do differ between companies.

Destinations Durango (12 daily; 4hr); Guadalajara (every 30min; 6–7hr); Los Mochis (every 30min; 6hr); Mexico City (5–6 daily; 14–15hr); Puerto Vallarta (5–7 daily; 7hr 30min); Tepic (every 30min; 4hr); Tijuana (every 30min; 26–28hr).

BY FERRY

Arrival Baja Ferries (☎ 669 985 0470, ⌨ bajaferries.com .mx) runs services to La Paz in Baja California (see p.565) to and from the port at Playa Sur, 1km southeast of the *centro histórico*. There are buses here (at the end of Carnaval, just outside the terminal gates), but getting an entire ferry-load of people and their baggage onto two or three of them always creates problems. Taxis (M$50–90 to the old town) are in demand, too, so try to be among the first off the boat. Heading back to port, catch any bus marked "Ferry".

Departure Information and tickets are available from Baja Ferries at the port: a basic ticket to La Paz qualifies you for a reclining seat (M$1102), while a turista-class ticket gets you a space in a four-berth cabin (M$790 extra); a small car will cost around M$2700 extra, but bicycles go free. Prices include breakfast and dinner, though the food on board isn't great; there are signs prohibiting bringing your own, though no one checks or seems to care. Travel agents in Mazatlán should also be able to arrange tickets. Destinations La Paz (4pm Mon, Wed & Fri; 12hr).

GETTING AROUND

By taxi The streets of Mazatlán are patrolled by scores of taxis (or "eco-taxis"), little open *pulmonías* (they look like souped-up golf carts but are usually modified VW Beetles) and larger pick-up trucks (*aurigas*); prices depend on your negotiation skills (and the season), but locals pay just M$80 for taxis and *aurigas*, and M$70 for *pulmonías* between Zona Dorada and the old town. *Pulmonías* and *aurigas* are not necessarily cheaper than taxis, but the latter can fit in a lot more people (it's usually M$250/hr to hire one). *Pulmonías* drivers can be hired for longer tours of the city (M$300), but tend to provide a running commentary of the locale wherever you are.

By bus Smaller city buses (daily 5.30am–10.30pm; every 15min) cost M$7–8, while the larger a/c (or "tourist") buses are M$10. There are two main tourist bus routes: Sábalo Centro (from the ferry terminal in the old town, along the seafront to Playa Bruja); and Sábalo Cocos (from Pino Suárez market to the bus station, then to the Zona Dorada and along the seafront).

By car There are dozens of car-rental outlets in Mazatlán, including: Budget, Camarón Sábalo 402 ☎ 669 913 2000; Express, Camarón Sábalo 610 ☎ 669 913 0800; and Hertz, Camarón Sábalo 314 ☎ 669 913 6060.

INFORMATION

Tourist office The Sinaloa Secretaría de Turismo office is at Av del Mar 882, on the seafront (Mon–Fri 9am–5pm; ☎ 669 981 8883), with the Asociación de Hoteles, Moteles y Empresas Turísticas de Mazatlán at Av Camarón Sábalo, Centro Comercial Las Palmas 333 (☎ 669 913 8181, ⌨ gomazatlan.com). More helpful, however, are the blue-shirted volunteers (mostly North American expats) who man stations in the old town and are a font of local

information (⌨ mazatlantouristaide.com).

Magazines and newspapers There are a couple of free English-language publications worth checking out if you're here for more than just a day: bi-monthly *Pacific Pearl* (⌨ pacificpearl.com) and *Mazatlán Interactivo* (⌨ mazatlaninteractivo.com) both contain useful information about events and attractions. See also ⌨ mazatlanlife.com.

TOURS AND ACTIVITIES

Tours and activities Any major hotel will be able to arrange tours – nature, culture or adventure – around the city and to the outlying islands or villages. Jet skis, catamarans, kayaks and boats can usually be rented on the beach with no prior arrangement.

Jah Surf School ☎ 669 149 4699, ⌨ jahsurfschool .com. Excellent English-speaking instructors offering 2hr lessons from US$50/M$870 per person (including boards).

Surfboard rentals are US$10/M$175 per hour or US$25/ M$435 per day.

Olé Tours Camarón Sábalo 7000 ☎ 669 916 6288, ⌨ oletours.com. Respected local tour agency, offering 3hr tours of the city (US$23/M$400), trips to the local baseball league games at Venados de Mazatlán (Oct–Dec 7.30pm; US$22/M$380) and tours of the surrounding villages, such as Copala, from US$55/M$955.

HUANA COA CANOPY ADVENTURE

One of the most popular day trips from Mazatlán is to the **Huana Coa Canopy Adventure** (☎ 669 990 1100, ⌨ www.huanacoa.com), a 45-minute minibus ride north in the Vinata Los Osuna, a mescal farm. Nine zip lines weave between shady huanacaxtle trees on the premises, ending with a rappel down the last one and visits to the tequila factory, founded by the Osuna family in 1876, along with free shots; the bus ride back seems much faster. Tours usually run Monday to Saturday, with pick-ups from Mazatlán at 9.30am and 11.30am. Canopy tours cost US$75/M$1305 (they also do ATV rides and horseriding).

APACHE PINE TREE ON THE RIM OF COPPER CANYON (P.500) >

Onca Explorations Río de la Plata 409, Gaviotas ☏ 669 913 4050, ⊕ oncaexplorations.com. Professional whale- (Dec–Feb only) and dolphin-watching outfit with a variety of tours from kayaking and snorkelling the islands off Mazatlán (US$65/M$1130) and dolphin adventures (US$85/M$1480) to tours of Las Labradas petroglyphs,

north of the city (US$68/M$1185).
Turtle Tours Mazatlán ☏ 669 160 9166, ⊕ turtletoursmazatlan.com. Enlightening tours of the Verde-Camacho Turtle Sanctuary (40min north of the city), where you get to help release new-born olive ridley turtles into the wild (from US$50/M$870, minimum four persons).

ACCOMMODATION

CENTRO HISTÓRICO

Best Western Hotel Posada Freeman Express Olas Altas 79 ☏ 669 985 6060, ⊕ bestwestern.com. This 1940s monolith has been given a *Best Western* makeover with modern, smart rooms with wi-fi, cable TV, a/c and free, fairly substantial buffet breakfasts – the rooftop pool is tiny but a superb place to hang out with a margarita. M$960

Casa Lucila Hotel Boutique Olas Altas 16 ☏ 669 982 1100, ⊕ casalucila.com. Fabulous place to stay, though expensive in high season; you get wonderful ocean views, a top-floor infinity pool and eight elegant rooms enhanced with flat-screen TVs, marble-clad bathrooms and jacuzzis. M$2835

Hotel Lerma Bolívar 622, between Serdán and Juárez ☏ 669 981 2436. Still the best deal in town. Sizeable, clean rooms (with fan; free wi-fi in courtyard) around a very spacious courtyard with parking (it used to be a school building), and very hospitable staff led by bilingual Carlos and Donicio Lerma. The café across the street has good, cheap breakfasts and lunches. M$220

★**Las 7 Maravillas** Las Palmas 1, at Jaboneria ☏ 669 136 0646, ⊕ las7maravillas.com. B&B in a wonderfully renovated 1950s villa helmed by Swiss expat Tatiana Genoud, with each room themed around a specific country such as Egypt and Cuba (and decked out with authentic handicrafts from that country) with views of the ocean, one block away. Rooms come with a/c, cable TV and free wi-fi, plus delicious breakfasts. Laundry M$75/kg. M$1500

★**Melville Boutique Hotel** Constitución 99 ☏ 669 982 8474, ⊕ themelville.com. This plush boutique is one of the centre's newest hotels, a gorgeous 1870s property and ex-Carmelite school blending Neoclassical architecture with a sophisticated contemporary design. There are 20 cosy suites with kitchens, a/c, cable TV and free wi-fi. M$1050

Royal Dutch Casa de Santa María Constitución 627 ☏ 669 981 4396, ⊕ royaldutchcasadesantamaria.com. Charming B&B in a colonial beauty built in 1888, with friendly and helpful Dutch management. Rates include a full breakfast, coffee and tea, as well as afternoon tea and pastries. Reserve at least two weeks in advance, as they are almost always full. M$1425

La Siesta Olas Altas 11, between Ángel Flores and Escobedo ☏ 669 981 2640, ⊕ lasiesta.com.mx. Lovely old hotel with private balconies and great sea views (worth the extra money); drawbacks are small rooms and noise from *El Shrimp Bucket* restaurant next door. M$655

NEAR THE BUS STATION

Emperador Río Panuco (opposite the bus station) ☏ 669 982 6724, ⊕ emperadorhotel@hotmail.com. Convenience and the budget price are the main attractions here, though rooms are clean and comfortable, with cable TV, free wi-fi and a/c. M$400

Hotel Sands Arenas Av del Mar 1910 ☏ 669 982 0000, ⊕ sandsarenas.com. Facing the beach, two blocks down from the bus station. Comfortable, US-style motel with pool, slide and sea views; good value off-season, when prices drop by over fifty percent. M$800

ZONA DORADA AND NUEVO MAZATLÁN

Captain Moe's Bed & Breakfast Río Bravo 403 ☏ 1866 252 6364, ⊕ captainmoes.com. Rare B&B in the Zona Dorada, three blocks from the beach, with simple but cosy rooms, all with tiled floors, fridge, free wi-fi and bathroom. You also get free access to a courtyard kitchen (self-serve breakfast included), plus laundry for M$150. M$720

★**Crowne Plaza Resort Mazatlán** Sábalo Cerritos 3110, Marina Mazatlán ☏ 669 988 0324, ⊕ crowne plaza.com/mazatlan. This M$585-million hotel was opened in 2009 by President Calderón himself, and though it's a long trek from the main part of town, the boutique suites here, dressed all in white with touches of red, remain an exceptional treat. All come with ocean views, jacuzzis and plenty of extras. M$1410

★**Inn at Mazatlán** Camarón Sábalo 6291 ☏ 669 913 5500, ⊕ innatmaz.com. This classy hotel–timeshare complex oozes chic (or at least the Mazatlán equivalent thereof). Larger apartment units with kitchens and tiled floors are excellent value for families or small groups. M$1725

Motel Marley Gaviotas 226 ☏ 669 913 5533, ⊕ travel bymexico.com/sina/marley. Just sixteen comfortable units (with cable TV, a/c and free wi-fi) in this small-scale place with a great position right on the sand, and a pool – you won't find a place on the water for much less. M$1470

Playa Mazatlán Beach Hotel Gaviotas 202 ☏ 669 989 0555, ⊕ hotelplayamazatlan.com. Vast 1950s beachside resort – if you want the full Mazatlán experience in the heart of the action, this is a solid choice, with a huge programme of activities and a great pool, though rooms are fairly standard three-star fare. M$1365

EATING

CENTRO HISTÓRICO

CAFÉS

Casa Etnika Sixto Osuna 50 ☎ 669 136 0139. Lovely courtyard café and contemporary art and crafts store serving fresh Oaxaca coffee, frappés (including decadent Oreo flavour) and piña colada smoothies (drinks from M$35–60). Mon–Sat 10am–7pm, Sun 10am–3pm.

Looney Bean Olas Altas 166-G ⓦlooneybean.com. Friendly outpost of the Californian artisan coffee chain and internet café, offering fine americanos, espressos and cappuccinos from M$25 (limited seating) – the owners are also involved in the Christian Marketplace Ministry programme in Mazatlán. Free wi-fi. Daily 7.30am–9.30pm.

★ **Mercado Culinario** Domínguez 1604, at Escobedo (one block from Plaza Machado) ☎ 669 981 1577. This trendy food hall in the historic Reynaud Building is a great place to eat or pick up fresh food for self-catering. Highlights include the coffees at Krema Café (Mon–Sat 8am–4pm), the fresh salads and sandwiches at Hector's Bistro (Mon–Sat 8am–11pm), and fresh bread and pastries from Bredhaus (Mon–Sat 8am–4pm).

RESTAURANTS

El Aljibe de San Pedro Constitución 710 ☎ 669 982 6518. Incredibly atmospheric restaurant inside a vaulted, 150-year old cistern, decorated throughout with crafts and antiques and offering a seasonal menu of Mexican dishes and fresh seafood. Cash only (around M$1000 for dinner for two, with wine). Oct–April Tues–Sat 5–10pm.

Mercado Pino Suárez Juárez and Valle. *Jugo* stalls downstairs, as well as the respected *El Tigre* seafood stall (*ceviche* M$10–15); most cafés are in the upstairs gallery overlooking Juárez, serving breakfasts and cheap *comidas* (M$35–60) – follow the crowds as always, though

Restaurante Nancy is usually a good bet. Mon–Sat 5am–7pm, Sun 5am–2pm.

Pastelería Panamá Juárez and Canizales, opposite the cathedral ☎ 669 985 1853, ⓦpanama.com.mx. Diner-style restaurant/cafeteria, good for breakfast (dishes M$80–150). You can also take away a host of delectable pastries from the bakery and eat them on the plaza. Daily 8am–10pm.

El Shrimp Bucket Olas Altas 11, between Ángel Flores and Escobedo ☎ 669 981 6350. One of the oldest and best-known restaurants in Mazatlán (since 1963). Now in bigger, plusher premises, it still has plenty of atmosphere and generous breakfast combos (M$90), marlin stew (famed hangover cure; M$85) and plenty of shrimps, served numerous different ways. Happy hour daily 4–9pm. Sun–Thurs 7am–11pm, Fri & Sat 7am–2am.

★ **Topolo** Constitución 629, at Juárez ☎ 669 136 0660, ⓦtopolomaz.com. Justly popular restaurant that offers slightly upmarket Mexican fare (like *poblano* peppers stuffed with cheese) and their home-made roasted tomato salsa (mains M$150–300) in a tranquil courtyard, while the wine bar has a happy hour 1–5pm daily – also good for mango margaritas. Tues–Sun 3–10pm (opens at noon on cruise-ship days).

El Túnel Carnaval 1207, opposite the Teatro Angela Peralta ☎ 669 910 3476. Not the best food in town these days, but still a great place for Sinaloense cuisine, patronized by locals and tourists alike since 1945 (it reopened in 2015 after a long renovation). Great Sinaloa specialities such as *asado a la plaza*, *pozole* and home-made gorditas, but no beer (although you can bring your own). Mains M$120–280. Daily 1–11pm.

★ **Water's Edge** Casa Lucila, Olas Altas 16 ☎ 669 136 0895, ⓦthewatersedgemaz.com. Romantic seaside bistro offering fine wines, artisan beers and the best ocean

8

FESTIVALS AND EVENTS IN MAZATLÁN

SEMANA SANTA

Remember to book accommodation well ahead if you are planning to be here around Semana Santa, when Mexicans descend on the city for massive celebrations (or July and Aug, when families pack the hotels and beaches).

CARNIVAL

You should also plan around the boisterous carnival held here in February, which involves a massive firework display known as the Combate Naval and is one of the world's largest, dating back to the 1840s.

FIRST FRIDAY ART WALKS

The *centro histórico* has become a magnet for Mexican and international artists in recent years; you can get a taster of the scene on the First Friday Art Walks (Nov–May 4–8pm; free; ⓦculturamazatlan.com/artwalk), held every first Friday of the month, when numerous galleries and artists (23 at last count) open their doors for self-guided tours (pick up maps at hotels or at the website).

views to accompany dishes such as red Thai curry prawns (M$185) and tequila tagliatelle with shrimp and crème fresh (M$150). Tues–Sun noon–11pm.

ZONA DORADA

Los Arcos Camarón Sábalo 1019 ☎669 913 9577, ⊛restaurantlosarcos.com. Locals flock to this relaxed modern Mexican chain restaurant, close to the beach, for some of the best seafood in the city and especially good charbroiled octopus, shrimps and fish *chicharrones* (mains from M$150). Daily noon–10pm.

★**Casa Loma** Gaviotas 104 (six blocks inland from Sábalo) ☎669 913 5398, ⊛restaurantcasaloma.com. For that perfect romantic – and expensive – evening, this secluded restaurant in a colonial setting has far more atmosphere than the big hotels. Reservations are recommended. Dishes average M$150–250. Daily 1.30–11pm.

Gus y Gus Camarón Sábalo 1730 (across from Costa De Oro hotel) ☎669 914 4501, ⊛gusygus.com. Great little open-air restaurant just off the road, serving especially good chicken fajitas, shrimp *ceviche* and marlin tacos; most main dishes run M$100–200. If you like classic rock you'll love the house band, which entertains a mostly tourist crowd nightly. Cash only. Sun–Thurs 7am–midnight, Fri & Sat 7am–2am.

Pancho's Gaviotas 408 (enter through Las Cabañas passage) ☎669 914 0911. This is another tourist favourite, with an attractive wood and tile dining room, tables overlooking the beach and excellent fresh seafood – think stuffed fish fillets, coconut shrimp and frog's legs. The zesty margaritas make it ideal for sunset drinks (mains M$90–150). Daily 7am–11pm.

PLAYA CERRITOS

Tacos Escorpio by Henry Sábalo Cerritos (parking lot of Scorpio 5 convenience store, just north of the Mayan Sea Garden Hotel) ☎669 117 9223. If you make it to the beach up here be sure to stop by this lauded taco joint, where a meal of juicy *asada* and shrimp tacos costs less than M$75 (the bean soup, chips and salsa are free). Cash only. Daily 5–11pm.

DRINKING AND NIGHTLIFE

BARS (CENTRO HISTÓRICO)

Café Pacífico/Vintage Retro Bar Constitución 505, on Plaza Machado ☎669 136 0916. Friendly bar with a selection of beers and liquors, snacks, sandwiches and coffee – the speciality is "Pacific Sunset", a rum and grenadine-based cocktail with pineapple juice. Now adorned with large TVs showing music videos from the 1980s. Wed–Sun 5pm–2am.

Edgar's Bar Serdán and Escobedo ☎669 982 7218. Dating from 1949, this venerable cantina now proclaims "Ladies welcome" in English at the door; inside it's still a slice of traditional Mazatlán, with old photos on the walls, ancient patrons, cheap beers and live music at night. Daily 9am–midnight.

★**Sky Room** Best Western Hotel Posada Freeman Express, 11/F, Olas Altas 79. Worth a visit for the spectacular views across the old town and lower Mazatlán, the cruise ships and islands, especially at night. Drinks are reasonable (happy hour 6–8pm), and you'll often have the place to yourself. Daily 8.30am–10pm.

BARS (ZONA DORADA)

Por Que No? Garzas 13 ☎669 668 2247. The old *Yoopers* location is now this popular sports bar (TV screens beam in the latest North American sports events) with superb burgers, hot dogs and cold beers. Wed–Mon 8am–1am.

SHOPPING

★**Onilikan** Gaviotas 505 ☎669 668 2370, ⊛onilikan .com. This small micro-distillery was established by Canadian investors in 2010, using a rare copper still imported from Germany. It specializes in potent liqueurs

Social Café Lounge Costa da Oro Hotel, Camarón Sábalo 710 ☎669 176 7144, ⊛socialcafelounge.com. Part coffee shop, part lounge bar, expect exceptional espresso coffee, unusual cocktails and potent margaritas. Mon–Sat 9am–10.30pm.

★**Twisted Mama's** La Laguna 500, at Garzas ☎669 129 2021. This Canadian-owned bar and restaurant has garnered a loyal following, mainly due to its party atmosphere, phenomenal margaritas – try the watermelon, mint and cucumber – and the excellent live bands (blues on Tues). The Sunday roast and fish and chips aren't bad either; and the Jell-O shots are sold for charity. Cash only. Tues–Sat 10am–11pm, Sun 9am–9pm.

CLUBS

Fiestaland Camarón Sábalo at Buelna, Zona Dorada ☎669 984 1666. This bizarre, all-white castle-like structure is a conglomeration of pricey clubs, discos and bars, of which *Valentino's* is the most popular, open from 11pm.

Señor Frogs Camarón Sábalo (next to El Cid Hotel), ☎669 985 1110, ⊛senorfrogs.com. This popular Mexican-themed bar and disco franchise has spawned, somewhat bizarrely, "official merchandise" stores all over town – the chain was actually established here in Mazatlán by Carlos Anderson back in 1970, but this branch is fairly tame these days. Daily noon–"until the last guest leaves."

and spirits made from local mango and agave (the name loosely translates as "liquor place" in Nahuatl). Mon–Fri 8.30am–5.30pm, Sat 9am–2pm.

DIRECTORY

Banks and exchange Citibank, Camarón Sábalo 424; HSBC, Camarón Sábalo 1662 (Zona Dorada) and Belizario Domínguez and Ángel Flores (*centro histórico*); and Banamex, on Juárez at Ángel Flores by the main plaza. Most places in the Zona accept US dollars though often at a poor rate, so you may want to make use of Mazatlán's numerous *casas de cambio*. Bancomer (with ATM) is at Juarez and 21 de Marzo but does not exchange cash.

Consulates Canada (consular agency only; Mon–Fri 9.30am–12.30pm), La Marina Business & Life Commercial Center, Blv Marina ☎ 669 913 7320; US (consular agency only; Mon–Fri 9am–1pm), Av Playa Gaviotas 202 (opposite *Hotel Playa Mazatlán*) ☎ 669 916 5889.

Internet In *centro histórico* try the *Looney Bean* café. You will find many internet places on Camarón Sábalo in the Zona Dorada, though most are pricey, up to four times the cost of those in the old town (M$40–80/hr). The malecón

has wi-fi, as do many restaurants.

Laundry Galerias Speed Laundry (9am–4pm), Sábalo 610, has coin-operated machines (in the arcade next to Banco Santander).

Emergencies ☎ 066.

Hospital Balboa Hospital at Sábalo 4480 has a 24hr walk-in clinic with English-speaking doctors (☎ 669 916 5533 or ☎ 669 916 7933, ⓦ hospitalbalboa.com).

Pharmacy Farmacia Guadalajara has branches at Ocampo 2 (daily 7am–10pm), 21 de Marzo 820 (24hr) and Aleman 1 at Carnaval (24hr), and also in the Zona Dorada at Sábalo1493 (24hr).

Police ☎ 060 for emergency assistance; tourist police ☎ 669 914 8444.

Post office Juárez and 21 de Marzo 1500, Plaza República (Mon–Fri 8am–6pm, Sat 9am–1pm; ☎ 669 981 2121); there's another branch at the bus station.

Northern Sinaloa

Mazatlán lies at the southern end of the vast state of **Sinaloa**, a landscape of scrubby desert and jagged mountains spilling into pristine beaches along the Sea of Cortez. The main city in northern Sinaloa is **Los Mochis**, an uninteresting destination in itself, but, as the western terminus of the **Copper Canyon railway**, an important transport hub. Many train passengers prefer to head inland to **El Fuerte**, a tranquil colonial backwater some two hours east. In recent years Sinaloa has garnered a reputation as a centre of drug cartel violence, with a subsequent drop-off in tourist numbers, but despite the scary statistics the places of interest remain safe for visitors.

Los Mochis

The modern city of **LOS MOCHIS** is a relatively new creation by Mexican standards, its origins going back to the establishment of a utopian colony on Topolobampo Bay in 1881, led by American socialist **Albert Kimsey Owen**. The colony was abandoned in the early 1900s, and Los Mochis really owes its existence to the **Sinaloa Sugar Company**, a US-owned monolith that was established by Benjamin Johnston in the 1890s (the founder and his wife are commemorated with reverential portraits in the lobby of *Hotel Santa Anita*). The city grew up around the extensive company works, and today it's a broad-streeted, prosperous, but rather dull place of 257,000 with few attractions, notable only as a major crossing point for road, rail and ferry, and above all the western terminus of the incomparable **Copper Canyon railway** (see p.501). If you're planning to take the ferry or train you'll have little choice but to stay at least one night here – don't expect much excitement. On Sundays you can check out the chaotic but fun **tianguis** (open-air market), which takes place on Zaragoza and Cuauhtémoc south of Castro. The sweltering grid of streets that makes up central Los Mochis otherwise has no real focus, but what there is of a commercial centre is on Hidalgo and Obregón, between Allende and Leyva.

Museo Regional del Valle del Fuerte

Obregón at Rosales • Mon–Sat 9am–1pm, Sun 10am–1pm • M$10 • ☎ 668 812 4692 • Librerías Educal Mon–Fri 9am–1pm & 3–7pm, Sat 10am–5pm

Facing the town's shady Plazuela 27 de Septiembre and its humble church, **Sagrado Corazón**, the **Museo Regional del Valle del Fuerte** acts as the town's equally humble

DOWNTOWN LOS MOCHIS

Tourist Office

0 — 250 metres

Estrellas del Pacifico Buses, Norte de Sonora Buses & Estrella Blanca

Transportes del Pacifico Buses

Centro Cultural

Sagrado Corazón de Jesús

Farmacia Guadalajara

JOSE MA. MORELOS

GALEANA

FCO. I. MADERO

PLAZUELA 27 DE SEPTIEMBRE

BENITO JUAREZ

PINO SUAREZ

HSBC

TIM Buses (Transports Integrados Mexicanos)

Museo Regional del Valle del Fuerte

Taxi Rank

Online Café

INDEPENDENCIA

GUADALUPE VICTORIA

Autobuses Tufesa

Banorte

Banamex

Norte de Sinaloa Buses to El Fuerte

BULEVAR ROSENDO G. CASTRO

Mercado Popular & Mercado Juárez

JUAN DE LA BARRERA

MIGUEL

HIDALGO

Mercado Municipal Independenca

VARSOVIA

JUAN ESCUTIA

AGUSTIN

MELGAR

ALVARO OBREGON

Azules del Noroeste Buses to El Fuerte

BULEVAR ROSENDO G. CASTRO

Farmacia Guadalajara

EMILIANO ZAPATA

TENOCHTITLAN

Transportes Guasave Buses

NIÑOS HEROES

Buses for Topolobampo and Playa Maviri (Mon–Sat)

Buses to Topolobampo (Sun only)

PLAZA SOLIDARIDAD

Norte de Sinaloa Buses

CUAUHTÉMOC

MARCIAL ORDOÑEZ

Palacio Municipal

CONSTITUCION

Main Bus Terminal

● EATING

La Cabaña de Doña Chayo	6/7
El Farallón	5
Pastelería y Panificadora Hong Kong	1
Patio 618	4
Restaurante España	3
Tacos a Vapor El Chavo	8
El Taquito	2

■ ACCOMMODATION

América	4
Best Western Los Mochis	2
Fénix	1
Santa Anita	3

Train Station (3km), Airport (12km), Ferry Terminal (24km) & Topolobampo (24km) ▼

TAP Bus Terminal ▼

El Fuerte, Hwy 15, Guaymas & Mazatlan ▶

main attraction. Inside are small exhibits on the history of the area, including the local **Yoreme** culture, as well as a decent bookshop.

ARRIVAL AND DEPARTURE
LOS MOCHIS

BY PLANE

Federal del Valle del Fuerte International Airport (☎ 668 818 6870) is southwest of the centre off the Topolobampo highway at km 12.5. Taxis operate on a fixed-rate system – buy a ticket at the booth before you exit the terminal. Downtown Los Mochis is M$195 (taxis charge the same coming back). Aeroméxico flies to Mexico City, Volaris flies to Tijuana and Guadalajara, while Aéreo Servicio Guerrero and Aéreo Calafia offer useful connections across to Baja California.

BY TRAIN

The train station for the Copper Canyon railway is 3km southeast of the centre; there are frequent buses (M$7) during the day (allow at least one hour), but if you're aiming to catch the 6am train, take a taxi to be safe (M$80 between the station and downtown). The *Hotel Santa Anita* lays on a minibus to the station for guests, arranged in advance (5.15am; M$50).

Schedules Only one train now makes the Copper Canyon run – in late 2015 alternate day departures were being proposed (see p.500). Trains leave for Chihuahua at 6am (scheduled to arrive at Creel 3.42pm, Chihuahua 9.35pm).

Tickets Fares for Primera are currently M$1357 to Creel and M$2482 to Chihuahua. Buy a second-class ticket if you want to save money – it's not as rough as travel agents make out. It costs M$855 to Creel and M$1564 to Chihuahua. The ticket office at the station opens at 5am for same-day sales for both trains; tickets for the Primera can also be bought the previous day at Viajes Flamingo/Balderrama Hotels & Tours (☎ 668 812 1613, ⊛ mexicoscoppercanyon.com), in the *Hotel Santa Anita* in town (see opposite), or direct from Ferrocarril Chihuahua Pacífico (☎ 614 439 7212, ⊛ chepe.com.mx).

Destinations Chihuahua (15hr); Creel (9hr 45min); El Fuerte (2hr 15min).

BY BUS

The main first-class bus station, serving Elite, Futura, Transportes Chihuahuenses and Turistar, is at Castro and Constitución 302, south of the centre, while TAP has its own terminal one block further along at Castro 620, at Domínguez. Estrella del Pacífico, Norte de Sonora and Transportes del Pacífico have terminals at Morelos 337 between Zaragoza and Leyva, while first-class Tufesa is at Zapata between Juárez and Morelos. Second-class Norte de Sinaloa is at Zaragoza and Ordonez. All of these stations are within walking distance of most downtown hotels and restaurants. Taxis will charge M$60 from bus stations for trips around the centre.

To Álamos For Álamos, take a first-class bus to Navojoa (every hr; 2hr) and change there (see p.515).

To El Fuerte Buses to El Fuerte are shared by two companies, both charging M$75 and departing roughly every hour 7.30am–8.15pm (usually with a/c but no toilets): Azules del Noreste (☎ 668 812 3491) runs from the terminal at Leyva 399, at Tenochtitlán, while Norte de Sinaloa leaves from the Terminal Independencia inside the Mercado at Independencia and Degollado (Azules also stops here). Buses marked "expresso directo" will take around 1hr 15min; others will take up to 2hr.

Other destinations Guadalajara (hourly; 13–15hr); Guaymas (every 30min; 5–6hr); Hermosillo (every 30min; 6–7hr); Mazatlán (every 30min; 6–7hr); Mexico City (hourly; 19hr); Tijuana (every 30min; 19–21hr); Topolobampo (every 15min; 40min).

BY FERRY

The La Paz (see p.565) ferry arrives at the port of Topolobampo, 24km south of Los Mochis. Local buses ply back and forth, terminating at Cuauhtémoc in Los Mochis, between Zaragoza and Prieto (Mon–Sat every 30min; 40min; M$27), and Allende between Cuauhtémoc and Tenochtitlán (Sun), or you can take a taxi (M$300). Current Baja Ferries (ⓦ bajaferries.com.mx) departures for the six-hour crossing to La Paz are Sun–Fri at 11pm; you can buy tickets as you board, but it's safest to purchase tickets and check the timetable in advance. Tickets cost M$970 for a reclining seat, an additional M$790 for a cabin and over M$2200 for a small car; they can be bought at the office at Plaza Encuentro, Centenario and Rosales (daily 9am–5pm; ☎ 668 818 6893), or at Topolobampo port (daily 9am–11pm; ☎ 668 862 1003).

INFORMATION

Tourist office The city tourist office (Mon–Fri 8am–5pm; ☎ 668 818 3992, ⓦ visitlosmochis.com.mx) is located at Allende Sur 655 (at *Hotel América*).

ACCOMMODATION

América Allende Sur 655 ☎ 668 812 5983, ⓦ los mochishotel.com. Cheerful, relatively cheap business hotel in the centre that offers excellent value (flat-screen TV and free wi-fi included). Rooms are clean and modern, with a simple, contemporary design. M$480
Best Western Los Mochis Obregón 691 ☎ 668 816 3000, ⓦ bestwestern.com. The town's best hotel is traditionally favoured by tour groups, offering smart but standard chain fare right on Plazuela 27 de Septiembre, 1km from the main bus station, with free wi-fi. M$1500
Fénix Flores 365 ☎ 668 812 2623. Decent budget option

for an overnight stay, with modern, basic but adequate rooms, cable TV, a/c and free wi-fi. M$435
Santa Anita Leyva and Hidalgo ☎ 668 818 7046, ⓦ santaanitahotel.com. This is the second luxury option in town, though it's a little old-fashioned. Rooms are still comfy and very spacious, with cable TV, free wi-fi and a mountainous breakfast buffet (extra). There's also a rather expensive restaurant, a bar and a travel agency (with buses laid on for the Copper Canyon train station). They often fill up with tour groups in the high season. M$1155

EATING

La Cabaña de Doña Chayo Obregón 99, at Allende ☎ 668 818 5498. This basic diner, established in the 1960s, specializes in tacos *carne asada* or tacos *moreno* (dried beef), with quesadilla versions of both (M$25–35); you get a lot of succulent meat for the price, but the salsas are not as fresh as on the street stalls. It also does excellent roast chicken (M$75 for half). There's a second "Centro" branch at Zaragoza and Obregón. Daily 8am–1am.
El Farallón Obregón 499, at Flores ☎ 668 812 1273, ⓦ restaurantelfarallon.com. Founded in 1961, this is still the best restaurant in Los Mochis, with an intriguing and delicious seafood menu (fish fillet cooked in numerous

ways), and *Sinaloenses* classics. Mains from around M$120–200. Daily 9am–midnight.
Pastelería y Panificadora Hong Kong Hidalgo 569, at Costilla ☎ 668 812 2737. Not a Chinese restaurant (the name is just a gimmick) but a local bakery chain selling delicious pastries, cakes and bread (doughnuts, muffins and the "ojos de buey", bright red, coconut-sprinkled cakes). Daily 5am–9pm.
★Patio 618 Canuto Ibarra 618 ☎ 668 812 4370, ⓦ patio618.mx. The top restaurant in Los Mochis is a wonderful place to spend an evening, though breakfasts are almost as exquisite (from M$85). The main menu features

8

marlin tostadas (M$115), shrimp dumplings (M$118), pastas (from M$125), burgers (M$115) and rib-eye steaks (M$300). Mon–Sat 7am–1am, Sun 8.30am–4pm.

Restaurante España Obregón 525 ☎668 812 2221, ⓦespanarestaurante.com. This reliable Mexican-Spanish restaurant has international pretensions and prices to match, though the breakfast plates are good value (from M$60), and it knocks out decent paella and buffets (M$112 Mon, $138 Tues–Sun). Mon–Sat 7am–11pm, Sun 7am–7pm.

★**Tacos a Vapor El Chavo** Cuauhtémoc and Allende ☎668 815 6816. This venerable stall has a chequered history that goes back to the early 1960s, and remains the best place to grab cheap and tasty *tacos a vapor*, smothered in rich sauce – closes by early afternoon. Five tacos plus drink M$25. Mon–Sat 8am–3pm.

El Taquito Leyva 333 at Barrera, near the Hotel Santa Anita ☎668 812 8119. No-frills canteen with formica tables, loud TVs and cheap Mexican food (burritos and other classics from M$60); though on the bland side, it's clean, safe and open 24hr.

DIRECTORY

Banks and exchange There's a Banamex with an ATM (Mon–Fri until 2pm) at the corner of Prieto and Hidalgo.

Post office Ordoñez 226, between Zaragoza and Prieto (Mon–Fri 9am–2pm & 4–6pm, Sat 9am–1pm).

The Copper Canyon

Northeast of Los Mochis, the rugged mountains of the **Sierra Tarahumara** rise from the Sinaloa coast and crumple into the southwestern part of the state of Chihuahua, encompassing the beautiful region known as the **Copper Canyon**. Confusingly, the area actually contains six rivers and over eleven major canyons – the actual **Barranca del Cobre** usually refers to the northern valley of the Río Urique. The main gorges boast depths of more than 2000m, and if you include the whole area the Grand Canyon is tiny in comparison.

Scenically, however, it's very hard to compare this region with the great canyons of the southwestern US. Part of the difficulty is in getting a true sense of its size and beauty: though the **Copper Canyon railway** cuts across some spectacular valleys, you only get a glimpse of the actual **Barranca del Cobre** once, at **Divisadero**. The train only brushes the northern edge of the Parque Nacional Barranca del Cobre, which is hard to access: there are no well-marked hiking tracks and official campsites, and serious hikers need to devote the best part of a week to their endeavours. **Creel** makes a sensible base from which to organize further exploration.

EL CHEPE TIMETABLE: PROPOSED CHANGES

At the time of research major changes were being planned for El Chepe and you should check the website/travel agents carefully for the latest. The changes are expected to be implemented by 2016, but in late 2015 nothing firm had been announced. One proposal is to only run trains daily during July, December and Easter week. For the rest of the year trains will run Chihuahua to Los Mochis on Monday, Wednesday, Friday and Sunday only; and from Los Mochis to Chihuahua on Tuesday, Thursday, Saturday and Sunday. The second proposal is **to cut some sections completely**, only running between El Fuerte and Divisadero/Creel, for example. Contact Three Amigos (see box, p.509) in Creel for the latest. Whatever the outcome, there will be just one train, with a *Primera* section and an *Económica* section tagged on the back. The official times below relate to the traditional Los Mochis to Chihuahua run and are not entirely reliable even then; trains frequently run some hours late (and rarely, if ever, on time to connect with the La Paz ferry in Los Mochis).

Los Mochis	6am	9.28pm
El Fuerte	8.19am	7.19pm
Bahuichivo	12.24pm	3.12pm
Divisadero	2.25pm	1.41pm
Creel	3.42pm	11.47pm
Cuauhtémoc	7.07pm	8.25am
Chihuahua	9.34pm	6am

Ferrocarril Chihuahua al Pacífico

The 653km, fifteen-hour train journey along the **Ferrocarril Chihuahua al Pacífico** (Copper Canyon railway), which starts on the sweaty Pacific coast at Los Mochis, fights its way up to cross the Continental Divide amid the peaks of the Sierra Madre Occidental, then drifts down across the high plains of Chihuahua, is one of the world's most extraordinary rail journeys. Mesmerizing views come thick and fast as the line hangs over the vast canyons of the **Río Urique** and its tributaries, with jagged peaks smothered in dense forest, and narrow, precipitous gorges falling away on both sides.

The route

From Los Mochis (see p.497) or El Fuerte (below), the start of the journey is an inauspicious grind across the humid coastal plain. As the line breaks into the mountains the train zigzags dizzily upwards for six hours, clinging to the canyon wall, rocketing across bridges and plunging into tunnels, only to find itself constantly just a few metres above the track it covered twenty minutes earlier. Eventually, you arrive at **Divisadero**, where there's a halt of about fifteen minutes to marvel at the view of the Copper Canyon itself. There are a couple of expensive places to stay here and a few bare-bones cheaper ones as well, but for most people it's all too rapidly back on the train, which clanks on for an hour to **Creel**, just past the halfway stage and, at 2330m, close to the highest point of the line (note, though, that after Divisadero the scenery is far less scintillating). This is the place to stop if you seriously want to explore the **Sierra Tarahumara** and the canyons.

From Creel, the train takes a further six hours to reach Chihuahua – though beautiful, it's not a truly spectacular run, and at the time of research one of the proposed El Chepe changes was to **cut this section entirely** (see p.500). In any case, there's a regular **bus** service from Creel to Chihuahua: it's cheaper than even the second-class train fare, is quicker and covers much the same ground.

INFORMATION   **FERROCARRIL CHIHUAHUA AL PACÍFICO**

The Copper Canyon line is operated by the Ferrocarril Chihuahua al Pacífico (CHP), from which the train derives its affectionate nickname, "El Chepe". There are no longer two different trains, just two classes: the first-class **Primera** section, which is primarily a tourist service, and the second-class **Económica** section, half the price but less comfortable. The *Primera* service has a/c and reserved, reclining seats – but the views are the same from either section, and if you'd rather squeeze up with the locals, you'll save a lot of cash and practise more Spanish in the second-class carriages.

8

TICKETS

Tickets for the *Económica* can only be bought from the station on the morning of departure, but *Primera* tickets can be pre-booked one week in advance either at the station (Los Mochis: Mon–Fri 5–7am & 9am–5.30pm, Sat 5–7am & 10am–12.30pm, Sun 5–7am & 8–10am; Chihuahua: Mon–Fri 5–7am & 10am–5.30pm, Sat 5–7am & 9am–12.30pm, Sun 5–7am), from travel agents (see *Hotel Santa Anita* in Los Mochis), or from Ferrocarril Mexicano direct (☎614 439 7212, ⓦchepe.com.mx). Reserve early to be sure of a first-class seat, especially from May to Sept and during Semana Santa.

Prices for the whole journey from Los Mochis to Chihuahua have risen dramatically in the past few years – to M$1564 for *Económica* and about M$2482 for *Primera* (M$1357 to

Creel). It's advisable to break up the journey, not only to get the most out of it, but also because the trip, even travelling first class, can become very tedious either side of the dramatic central section. Section costs are based on a per-kilometre rate, so you'll pay hardly any more no matter how often you break the journey.

FOOD AND DRINK

You'll save money by taking along your own food and drink; though technically you are not allowed to eat in first-class cars, snacks are generally tolerated. It's not essential in any case; meals, snacks and drinks are available on the train (though not cheaply), and throughout the journey people stand on the platforms selling tacos, *chiles rellenos*, fresh fruit, hot coffee and whatever local produce comes to hand.

El Fuerte

Founded in the sixteenth century, **EL FUERTE** is a tranquil, verdant town of handsome colonial architecture and lush mango trees. In the 1800s it became rich from mining, and was made a city in 1906; the Revolution devastated the place and it's been a backwater ever since. In 2009 the town joined Mexico's burgeoning *Pueblos Mágicos* programme, and since then the otherwise doomed-to-decay Spanish architecture near the plaza has gradually been restored. Though several boutique hotels have opened up, thanks to low tourist numbers El Fuerte has yet to see a full-scale transformation – the commercial area along Juárez remains just as scrappy as ever, the plaza relatively tourist free and most of the restored buildings are still empty. Bizarrely, recent attempts to market El Fuerte as the home of **Zorro** – the fictional character whose adventures were set in California – seem to have worked, with nightly shows at the *Posada del Hidalgo* (see p.504).

THE RARÁMURI

Even when the bare mountain peaks here are snow-covered, the climate on the Copper Canyon floor is semitropical – a fact that the indigenous **Rarámuri** (also known, incorrectly, as the Tarahumara) depend on, migrating in winter to the warmth of the deep canyons. The Rarámuri, who were driven here after the Spanish Conquest and whose population now totals some sixty thousand, live in isolated communities along the rail line and in the surrounding Sierra Tarahumara, eking out an existence from the sparse patches of cultivatable land. Although their isolation is increasingly encroached upon by commercial forestry interests, ranchers and growing numbers of travellers, they remain an independent people, close to their traditions. Despite centuries of missionary work, their religious life embraces only token aspects of Catholicism and otherwise remains true to its animist roots, their chief deities being the gods of the sun, moon and rain. Above all, the tribe is renowned for running: a common feature of local festivals is the **foot races** between villages that last at least one day and sometimes several on end, with the runners kicking a wooden ball ahead of them as they go: Norogachi is one of the best places to see this (see opposite), as is Urique, the home of the Copper Canyon Ultramarathon (see box, p.505).

Located 75km northeast of Los Mochis on the rail line, El Fuerte certainly makes a pleasant alternative start (or end) to the Copper Canyon train ride, and is a far more appealing place to stay than Los Mochis. Just make sure you take insect repellent – Fuerte's *bobos* (tiny two-winged insects more officially known as *Paraleucopis mexicana*) are a real pest in the spring.

The town centre is small and easy to navigate, being focused on the elegant *portales* of **Plaza de Armas**, with its grand **Palacio Municipal** (1907), the modest **Iglesia Sagrado de Corazón** (1745) and the fort (*fuerte*) itself, a short walk south (and clearly visible).

Museo Fuerte Mirador

5 de Mayo • Tues–Sun 9am–7pm • M$10 • ☏ 698 893 1501

El Fuerte grew up around a Spanish **fort** (from which it takes its name), completed in 1615 by steely conquistador Diego Martínez de Hurdaide to suppress the local tribes. Though the original has been lost, a reasonably authentic replica was completed in 2001 on its possible location, supplying commanding views of the streets and surrounding countryside. Inside, the **Museo Fuerte Mirador** contains an array of historical artefacts and old photos of the town (some by Ira Kneeland, a member of Kinsey's colony at Topolobampo), with mostly English labelling; old guns, an 1885 hearse and local Yoreme arts and crafts among them.

ARRIVAL AND DEPARTURE   EL FUERTE

By train The train station is a few kilometres out of town, and you'll need to arrange transport if you hope to catch the morning train to Chihuahua or Creel (8.19am) – the pricier hotels should do this for you (*Posada del Hidalgo* charges M$50), but otherwise you should scout around for a taxi near the plaza or market (around M$100). Note that there are no buses to either Creel or Chihuahua from here.

Trains to Los Mochis (*Primera* M$456) depart at 7.19pm.
By bus Buses (M$75) from Los Mochis (see p.497) arrive and depart (until 7pm) frequently at Juárez, next to the town market, near 15 de Septiembre and a short walk from Plaza de Armas.
By taxi Taxis from Los Mochis will charge around M$600 for the journey to El Fuerte, and will also negotiate return trips.

INFORMATION

Tourist information El Fuerte has no visitor centre, but the tourism department in the Palacio Municipal, on Plaza de Armas (Mon–Fri 8am–5pm; ☏ 698 893 0349,

ⓦ elfuertepueblomagico.com), usually has English-speakers if you get stuck – your hotel is likely to be more helpful, however.

ACCOMMODATION

Hotel La Choza 5 de Mayo 101 ☏ 698 893 1274, ⓦ hotellachoza.com. Charming, mid-range option, with

32 a/c rooms simply decorated with tiled floors and colourful bedspreads – you get TV, free wi-fi, a gorgeous

8

little pool and decent restaurant on site. M$850

Hotel El Fuerte Montesclaros 37 ☎698 893 0226, ⓦhotelelfuerte.com.mx. A beautiful three-hundred-year-old hacienda once owned by the wealthy Ibarra family, with exquisite rooms and a jacuzzi fed by illuminated waterfalls. Loads of colour, elegance and style make this the best luxury hotel in town. Free wi-fi, but breakfast is M$150. M$945

Posada del Hidalgo Hidalgo 101 ☎698 893 0242, ⓦhotelposadadelhidalgo.com. First-class service is provided by a small army of staff in this grand old hotel, the former 1890 home of the Almada family and self-proclaimed birthplace of Zorro. Popular with tour groups, there are spa facilities, a restaurant, pool and plenty of

quiet, leafy patios. There's also a kitsch Zorro show, nightly (included). Wi-fi is M$75/hr, and shuttles to the station are M$50. M$1415

Posada Don Porfirio Juárez 104 ☎698 893 0044. Tranquil hotel with clean, bright a/c rooms and a shady courtyard slung with hammocks. Ask the owners for a copy of *Legends of the City*, a small booklet that tells the history of El Fuerte. Free wi-fi. M$790

★**Torres del Fuerte** Robles 102 ☎698 893 1974, ⓦhotelestorres.com. Gorgeous old hotel that drips with colonial charm: lavish period rooms come with marble floors, stone sinks, rugs and Mudéjar-influenced antiques, but with modern amenities. The patio bar and gardens are a great place to relax. Free wi-fi in public areas. M$1439

EATING AND DRINKING

Mesón del General Juárez 202 (behind the plaza) ☎698 893 0260, ⓦelmesondelgeneral.com. Relatively economical option serving a range of seafood (including the prized local black bass or *lobina*) and steak dishes in a charming old courtyard and mansion built in 1860, enhanced by plants and murals. Famed for being the former home of local Revolutionary hero General Don Pablo Macías Valenzuela. Mains average M$95–200. Daily 11am–9.30pm.

Restaurant Diligencias Hotel La Choza, 5 de Mayo 101 (on the plaza) ☎698 893 1274. For a posh meal and

the best bar in town head to *La Choza*, where delectable local delicacies (including the ubiquitous *lobina* and crayfish) are served in a bright, friendly dining room. Expect to pay around M$500–600 for dinner for two. Daily 7am–11pm.

El Supremo Rosales 108 at Constitución (one block from plaza) ☎698 893 0021. For no-frills, reasonably priced home-cooked fare, visit this local diner – it looks a bit dark and dingy from the outside, but the food is good (M$60–120). Daily noon–10pm.

DIRECTORY

Banks You'll find a Banamex at Juárez 212 (Mon–Fri 9am–4pm) near the bus station, and Bancomer on Juárez and Constitución.

Internet Try Café Internet at Montesclaros (daily

8am–11pm; M$10/hr).

Post office The post office is at 5 de Mayo 95 (Mon–Fri 8am–4pm; ☎698 893 0126).

Cerocahui

The first place worth considering as a base in the mountains, travelling on the Copper Canyon railway from Los Mochis and El Fuerte, is the tiny *ejido* of **CEROCAHUI** (1525m), accessed from the train station at **Bahuichivo** (1600m). Very much in the formative stages of tourist development, with around nine hundred inhabitants, Cerocahui gives access to the **Urique** canyon system and a range of attractions including the Cerro del Gallego viewing point, hikes to Las Cascaditas (the "Little Waterfalls") and the old Sangre de Cristo gold mine. There's also the Jesuit mission of **San Francisco**, founded by Juan Maria de Salvatierra in 1694, before he moved on to Loreto (see p.559).

ARRIVAL AND DEPARTURE   CEROCAHUI

By train Cerocahui is 10km by road from Bahuichivo train station (the latter is 6.5hr and M$962 from Los Mochis). Moving on, first-class trains to Divisadero (2hr), Creel (3hr 10min) and Chihuahua (8.5hr) depart Bahuichivo at 12.20pm. If you opt to stay here your hotel will arrange a pick-up from the train station.

By bus Noroeste buses from Bahuichivo to Creel (M$210;

3.5hr) usually depart at 11am for San Rafael, but check the latest timetable with your hotel (small buses make the rougher trip between Bahuichivo and San Rafael, where you transfer to a bigger bus for the final leg to Creel). At least five buses a day connect Creel with San Rafael (via Divisadero), but the shuttle from San Rafael to Bahuichivo only departs at around 1pm.

ACCOMMODATION

Hotel Misión Plaza del Poblado (opposite the church) ☎635 456 5294, ⊛hotelmision.com. Opened in 1968, this mountain lodge offers 41 spacious rooms with old-fashioned Mexican decor, tiled bathrooms and wood stoves. Rates include lodging for two and three meals per person a day (including the hotel's famed apple pie). M$2250

★**Jade Hotel** Plaza del Poblado ☎635 456 5275, ⊛hoteljade.com.mx. Friendly owners Alberto (who speaks English) and Francia (who is an excellent cook) run this delightful budget hotel, with ten beautifully designed rooms with views over the town, and a variety of guided tours (no TV or wi-fi). Add M$150 for breakfast. M$650

San Isidro Lodge Carr Bahuichivo–Urique km 24 ☎635 456 5257, ⊛coppercanyonamigos.com. Lovely and economical accommodation can be had at this lodge run by the Muñoz family, who have ties to the local Rarámuri. The cabañas are all spacious, clean and airy with private baths. Rates include three meals a day (with real coffee) and transport from Bahuichivo station. M$1725

Wilderness Lodge at Cerocahui Carr Bahuichivo–Urique km 23 ☎635 456 4045, ⊛hotelesmargaritas .com. With just six rooms, this is an extremely romantic choice, a wooden lodge overlooking the gorge with Spanish colonial-style rooms and bathrooms. Breakfast included, and free wi-fi in public areas. M$970

Urique

The four-hour drive from Cerocahui to the bottom of the Barranca de Urique is stunning, and the town of **URIQUE** (485m) itself, at its conclusion, marks the start (or end) of the popular two-night, three-day trek to Batopilas (see p.510). The 1600 inhabitants of Urique – founded in 1724 and a former gold- and silver-mining town – survive today on their tropical fruit, corn, peanuts and coffee crops, though unofficially marijuana and poppy crops are likely the biggest earners. The main attractions here are the mesmerizing views all around, though there is also an old kiln, church, cemetery and hikes to isolated Rarámuri villages such as Guadalupe Coronado. Urique is also the home of the **Copper Canyon Ultramarathon** (see box below).

8

ARRIVAL AND DEPARTURE URIQUE

By bus Unless you take a hotel-arranged tour, reaching Urique usually involves hiring a truck at Bahuichivo train station (M$1000) or driving yourself from Creel – you'll need an SUV because the road is unpaved for much of the way. Public buses do make the trip down (for around M$150; 3.5hr) from Bahuichivo train station (usually after the last train of the day), but at the time of research the road was closed during the day (7am–7pm) for a massive road improvement project; buses have to wait till 7pm before going down, a very bumpy ride in the dark (and return before 7am).

ACCOMMODATION AND EATING

Urique contains several small, family-owned **restaurants** such as *Mama Tita's* that offer traditional Mexican dishes such as rice plates with with re-fried beans, various meats and hand-made tortillas. There are also several shops selling basic groceries.

Entre Amigos ✉threearroyos@hotmail.com, ⊛among amigos.com Legendary lodge established in 1975, with lovingly maintained dorms (M$225), camping sites (M$150), shower rooms, kitchen and organic food prepared amid hummingbird gardens and spectacular views. Guesthouse (M$750) or rooms in the main house also available. Shared toilets (outhouses). M$675

THE RUNNERS OF COPPER CANYON

Popularized by Chris McDougall's best-selling book *Born to Run* (2009), the Copper Canyon Ultramarathon or **Ultramaraton Caballo Blanco** was established in 2003 by extreme runner Micah True (his nickname was *Caballo Blanco*, or "White Horse"). True (who died in 2012) wanted to draw attention to the plight of the impoverished **Rarámuri** in the region, and the 80km race, though now open to anyone, still provides food vouchers and blankets to Rarámuri runners. In large part thanks to the book, the race has become a legend in the world of ultra-running, attracting around 100 international runners each year. Usually held in February in Urique (above), in 2015 the race was cancelled due to concerns about drug-related gang violence in the valley – check ⊛ultracb.com for the latest.

Divisadero

Around 50km northeast of Cerocahui lies **DIVISADERO**, where the train pauses for fifteen minutes for the mind-blowing "one-hundred-mile" view of the canyons – this is the closest you'll get to that Grand Canyon-like panorama, at least on the rail line. A slightly bizarre carnival atmosphere pervades when the train arrives, with Rarámuri children begging for change, mariachi singers serenading snack eaters, and trinket stalls lining the steps down to the *mirador* – below this are the depths of the **Barranca del Cobre** and, adjoining it, the **Barranca de Urique** and the **Barranca de Tararecua**. The platform at Divisadero is smothered in snack stalls, most of them selling variations of **gorditas** – absolutely scrumptious and crammed with a variety of home-made fillings, chiles, beans and cheeses (finish them before you reboard).

Parque de Aventura Barrancas del Cobre

Daily 9am–4.30pm • Cable car M$250 (every 30min; 10min each way with 20min at the *mirador*); zip line M$600 (daily 9am–1pm; 2hr); Via Ferrata (daily 9am–3pm) M$450; all three attractions M$900

Divisadero is home to the Copper Canyon's newest attraction, the government-funded **Parque de Aventura Barrancas del Cobre** – more development is likely in the coming years. The "Adventure Park" features a 2.75km **cable car** (*teleférico*) that soars over a 400m ravine to the *mirador* at the Mesa de Bacajipare. The park also includes **Via Ferrata** (featuring rappelling, walking a wire, climbing the canyon wall and swinging bridges) plus a panoramic restaurant and seven **zip lines** (450m high, with lengths ranging from 300–1200m). The new **ZipRider** attraction (basically a zip line but with a more stable chair system to sit on) is an incredible 2.8km long and costs M$1000. You can walk to the park from Divisadero station via a trail along the canyon edge (2.5km).

ARRIVAL AND DEPARTURE

DIVISADERO

By train The *Primera* service from Los Mochis to Divisadero costs M$1213 (M$716 *Económica*); from Chihuahua it's M$1349 (M$850 *Económica*). Moving on, trains depart for Creel (1hr 10min) and Chihuahua (6hr 40min) around 2.25pm. Trains depart for Los Mochis (7hr 20min) at 1.41pm.

By bus Several Noroeste buses a day ply the 44km between Divisadero and Creel (1hr; M$90), the first one passing at around 7am (from San Rafael) and last one departing at about 5pm; it's always worth checking the schedule for changes, though, so you don't get stuck.

ACCOMMODATION

If you decide to break your journey here, you'll find some stunning but pricey accommodation near the station, and more options 5km southwest near the Posada Barrancas station, which serves the sleepy village of Areponápuchi (aka "Arepo"). None of the hotels has internet or wi-fi.

Cabañas Díaz Posada Barrancas ☏635 578 3008. A congenial family-run inn with economical, cosy rooms equipped with fireplaces, and amazing home-cooked meals (from M$70) served in the Díaz family kitchen – they keep several friendly dogs, can arrange all manner of guided trips (on foot or horseback) and will drop you off in Divisadero for free. **M$790**

Divisadero Barrancas Ferrocarril Chihuahua al Pacífico km 622 ☏614 415 1199, ⓦhoteldivisadero .com. Steps away from Divisadero station, and perched right on the edge of the canyon, this hotel is a tour-group favourite featuring spacious rooms with wood-beam ceilings, most with spectacular views of the gorges – only some have balconies, though, so always ask when you make a reservation. Rates include three meals and a couple of walking tours. **M$1750**

Mansión Tarahumara Posada Barrancas ☏614 415 4721, ⓦhotelmansiontarahumara.com.mx. A rather surreal hotel resembling a fairy-tale castle (it's known as *El Castillo*); the Alpine-style cabins are clean and bright, but only the new rooms have the stunning canyon views. Breakfast included; full board available (from M$1950). **M$1270**

Hotel Mirador (Posada Barrancas) Ferrocarril Chihuahua al Pacífico km 622 ☏635 578 3020, ⓦhotelmirador.mx. Fabulous location, etched right into the canyon edge like an ancient monastery, and modern, clean rooms make this a justly popular option – each room comes with a balcony, the best feature, though there are no TVs. The set meals (included) are pretty good, usually comprising a Mexican meat dish (typically fish or pork, sometimes beef) with vegetables and rice. **M$2990**

Creel

Once nothing more than a rough-and-ready backwater, **CREEL** (2330m) has rapidly transformed into a full-blown mountain resort of ten thousand people. Indeed, Creel is yet another *Pueblo Mágico* and has seen tourism all but replace logging as its main industry; on most days (but especially Sunday) you'll be greeted by a weird juxtaposition of laid-back Western backpackers, smartly dressed locals, rich Mexican tourists in their 4WDs and ragged Rarámuri trinket sellers and their children, trying to make a buck or two. In July and August the town is invaded by Mexican tour groups – the best hotels often get completely booked up at this time. This is not to say that the town has become completely commercial; beneath the facade of development, Creel is still a rural mountain town at heart, and an ideal base from which to explore the area. Note that construction of Creel's **airport** – Aeropuerto Regional Barrancas del Cobre – was delayed in 2014 after protests by the local Rarámuri, but should be operating sometime in 2016.

Museo de la Casa de las Artesanías

Ferrocarril 178 • Mon–Sat 9am–6pm, Sun 9am–1pm • M$10 • ☎ 635 456 0080

There isn't much to do in Creel itself, other than enjoy the refreshing, pine-scented mountain air, though the **Museo de la Casa de las Artesanías** across the rail tracks from the plaza is certainly worth a visit. It contains displays on Rarámuri culture that give intriguing insights into their archaic philosophy, most notably with a series of black- and-white photos revealing their vivid ceremonial and religious life.

Artesanías Misión

Plaza Principal • Mon–Sat 10am–1pm & 3–6pm

If you're in the market for handicrafts, the Catholic mission shop **Artesanías Misión**, right on the plaza, has a host of wares including blankets, baskets, dolls, drums and violins; their products lack the vibrancy of other Mexican crafts, but make up for it with rustic charm. Profits fund the local mission hospital.

ARRIVAL AND DEPARTURE   CREEL

By train Creel is 9hr 45min from Los Mochis (*Primera* M$1357), 1hr 20min from Divisadero and around 5hr 15min from Chihuahua (M$1129), assuming trains are still running in that direction (see box, p.500).

By bus Two companies offer services to Chihuahua (around M$315) via Cuauhtémoc between 6am and 5pm, with Noroeste providing the most comfortable buses. Noroeste also runs five buses to Divisadero from 10.30am to 6.50pm (M$90), which end up at San Rafael – the 10.30am departure connects with the shuttle to Bahuichivo (M$210 from Creel). The train station and bus stops are all near the main plaza in the centre of town. The bus to Batopilas (M$600 return) usually leaves from outside Three Amigos office at Mon–Sat at 7.30am – check the current schedule in advance.

Destinations Bahuichivo via San Rafael (1 daily; 3.5hr); Batopilas (1 daily; 5.5hr; 3.5hr once road is complete); Chihuahua (14 daily; 4–5hr); Divisadero (5 daily; 1hr); Guachochi (2 daily; 3hr).

INFORMATION

Tourist information As yet, there's no official tourist office in Creel, though the small kiosk on the plaza dispenses leaflets on regional attractions. The best place to go for local information is Three Amigos (see box opposite), López Mateos 46 (daily 9am–7pm). They can supply you with maps, information and advice regarding Creel and the Copper Canyon more generally.

ACCOMMODATION

Cabañas Sierra Bonita Gran Visión s/n, about 1km out of town ☎635 456 0615, ✆sierrabonita.com.mx. Perched on a hill overlooking Creel, this four-star hotel is one of the best deals in town. Its finest rooms have a fireplace and jacuzzi – perfect for unwinding after a long, hard day of hiking. Free wi-fi in public areas. M$935

Casa Margarita's López Mateos 11 ☎635 456 0045, ✆hotelesmargaritas.com. A Creel institution and the place for travellers to meet since 1979, *Margarita's* services run the gamut from tour guides to laundry. Breakfast and supper are included. The brightly decorated traditional Mexican-style rooms come with bathrooms and free wi-fi. M$525

Complejo Eco-Turístico Arareko Carr Creel–Guachochi km 7 ☎635 456 0126, ✆sanignacioarareko.tripod.com. If you fancy staying in more natural surroundings, this Rarámuri-run accommodation agency has an office on López Mateos and rents out the basic *Cabañas Batosarachi* (M$315) and the more comfortable *Cabañas Segorachi* (M$299/person; minimum six people) around Lake Arareko, part of the San Ignacio de Arareko *ejido* (7km south of Creel on the Batopilas road). No internet access; cash only.

Hotel Los Valles Elfido Batista s/n, next to Plaza Mexicana Margarita's ☎635 456 0092, ✆hotellosvalles.com.mx. This newish motel off the main drag has eight small, clean rooms with satellite TV and free wi-fi for decent prices; one of the better bargains in town. M$570

★**The Lodge at Creel** López Mateos 61 ☎635 456 0071, US ☎+1 877 844 0409, ✆thelodgeatcreel.com. Easily the best place to stay in town, run by *Best Western* and offering cabin-style rooms with spa, sauna, jacuzzi, and full restaurant and bar (there's also *Luna Creel* on site. The wood-trimmed, rustic huts are ample and full of amenities, including coffee-makers, free wi-fi, purified water and telephones. M$1415

Plaza Mexicana Margarita's Elfido Batista, off López Mateos ☎635 456 0245, ✆hotelesmargaritas.com. The fancier sibling of *Casa Margarita's* has spacious heated rooms set around a courtyard, each decorated with murals. Popular bar on site; again the price includes breakfast and dinner. Discounts are possible in the low season, depending on demand. Free wi-fi. M$882

La Posada de Creel Ferrocarril s/n ☎635 456 0805. This backpacker-friendly hotel behind the station offers very basic rooms and dorms, though it remains one of the cheapest places to crash; breakfast included, but don't expect much. Free wi-fi in public areas. Dorm beds M$190. Shared bath M$340; en suite M$450

Villa Mexicana Creel Mountain Lodge López Mateos, on the edge of town ☎614 456 0665, ✆vmcopper canyon.com. Creel's rustic resort offers a host of facilities including a restaurant, games room and free wi-fi. Its accommodation ranges from comfy log cabins to luxury suites (rates drop by 50 percent in low season), all with satellite TVs. M$1640

EATING

Pizza del Rey López Mateos 15, on the plaza ☎635 456 0264. This small outpost of the Chihuahua chain serves reasonable enough pizzas (M$160–220 for a large one), but also popular ice creams in summer. Takeout or eat in the pleasant second-floor lodge-like dining area. Daily noon–9pm.

Restaurant Verónica López Mateos 33 ☎635 456 0631. Solid bet for all the usual Mexican classics; try their speciality, the "Norteño" – fried beef and vegetables topped with melted cheese (mains M$60–160). Free wi-fi.

Daily 7.30am–10.30pm.

Sierra Madre The Lodge at Creel, López Mateos 61 ☎653 456 0851. This hotel restaurant is best known for its decent pizzas but also does the usual range of Mexican classics (tortilla soup is a speciality) plus a tasty apple pie. Mains M$70–200. Daily 7.30am–10pm.

Tío Molcas López Mateos 35 ☎635 456 0033. Serves Mexican food but is most popular as a bar catering primarily to travellers, with a wood fire in winter. Free wi-fi. Sun–Thurs 7pm–1am, Fri & Sat 6pm–2am.

8

DIRECTORY

Bank Banco Santander at López Mateos 17 (Mon–Fri 9am–4pm) has an ATM, though it often runs out of cash.
Hospital Centro de Salud, Tarahumara 113 (☎635 456 0905).
Internet Try La Escuelita Cyber Club (daily 8am–9pm; M$15/hr), also on López Mateos.
Laundry The Lavandería Optima (Mon–Fri 9am–2pm &

3–6pm, Sat 9am–2pm) is in the two-storey house on C Villa, across the rail tracks from the plaza.
Pharmacy Farmacia Rodríguez, López Mateos 43 (Mon–Sat 9am–1pm & 3–8pm, Sun 10am–1pm).
Post office There's a post office (Mon–Fri 9am–3pm) in the Presidencia Seccional on the south side of the main plaza.

Sierra Tarahumara

Once in Creel, most travellers take the bus or continue on the Copper Canyon railway to Chihuahua (see p.460), but exploration of the **Sierra Tarahumara** around Creel is highly recommended. The rugged scenery is exceptionally wild and beautiful. If you're not up to strenuous activity, or have only limited time, an **organized tour** is the best way to see the canyons (though these normally require four to six people; see box below).

San Ignacio de Arareko

Many tours from Creel take in attractions belonging to the *ejido* (a collectively owned community) of **San Ignacio de Arareko**, a Rarámuri land-owning cooperative on the edge of town. To see them independently, follow López Mateos towards the highway, take a left onto the dirt road and continue past the cemetery and uphill into the pine forest.

A few kilometres from the *ejido* entrance (admission M$25), you'll encounter the eighteenth-century **Misión de San Ignacio** (usually locked) and a series of otherworldly rock formations, including the **Valley of the Mushrooms**, which contains surreal structures closely resembling giant toadstools, and the **Valley of the Frogs**, with its squat amphibian-like boulders. The **Valley of the Monks** lies 5km away (M$25 toll), and has tall upright stones revered by the Rarámuri as symbols of fertility. Serene **Lago de Arareko**, 7km from Creel on the main highway to Batopilas, is a beautiful spot for fishing (largemouth bass) and camping – you can stay in a cabin on the lake (see opposite) or rent a boat for M$60/hr.

Recowata hot springs

The **Recowata hot springs** (admission M$25) are 22km from Creel at the bottom of Tararecua Canyon, within biking or riding distance; follow the road to Divisadero for

---

TOURING THE SIERRA TARAHUMARA

For tours of the Sierra Tarahumara, try Three Amigos (see below) or the more popular hotels like *Casa Margarita's*. Rates should be about the same, but it's worth shopping around. Roughly speaking, a four-hour spin through the **San Ignacio** *ejido* or a two- to three-hour trip to **Cusárare** should cost M$200–400 (with a minimum four people); and a day-long trip to **Basaseachi** around M$800–1200. Find out if food is included with your tour and if there are additional costs like museum entrance or toll fees before you set out. If you don't speak Spanish, check that your guide speaks English before parting with any money.

El Aventurero Ecopaseos López Mateos ☎635 456 0558, ⌨ridemexico.com. A truly memorable way of exploring the canyons is on horseback, and if you want to be assured of animals that are cared for, speak to guide Norberto Padilla Rodríguez. Excellent, professional tours start at M$350 for a three-hour ride through the San Ignacio *ejido* (two-person minimum).
Three Amigos Canyon Expeditions López Mateos

46 ☎635 456 0546, ⌨amigos3.com. The most professional and best-equipped outfit in town. They can advise on your trip, organize a well-priced tour or rent you a well-maintained mountain bike (M$450 a day) or two-person scooter for M$885 a day. Customers also get free internet use at the shop. See also their sister operation, Amigo Trails (⌨amigotrails.com), for longer expeditions.

8

7km and look for the turning on the left. Here you can bathe in seven different concrete pools of steamy, clean, sulphurous water. Note that the steep 3km descent to (and return from) the pools can be very strenuous, and shouldn't be undertaken by the faint of heart (or when it's wet – it's a cobblestone trail). Rarámuri quad bikers are sometimes on hand to provide rides up and down (M$60 each way).

Cascada de Cusárare

Carr Creel–Guachochi km 22 • M$25

The **Cascada de Cusárare**, 30m-high falls most impressive during the rainy season (but just a trickle in April/May), lies some 22km from Creel on the Batopilas/Guachochi road, and a forty-minute walk from the highway. You can reach the falls and village by bike, or on the daily Batopilas/Guachochi buses, though you'll have a long hike back to Creel if you don't stay overnight. Hitching is a possibility, though you should exercise the usual precautions.

Cusárare

Misión de Cusárare Tues–Sun 9am–6pm • Donation suggested **Museo de Loyola** Tues–Sun 9am–6pm • M$15

The village of Cusárare itself is 3km further along the road from the Cascada de Cusárare, and contains the eighteenth-century Jesuit **Misión de Cusárare**, adorned with Rarámuri wall paintings completed in the 1970s; the mission's original art, including a set of twelve rare oil paintings by Miguel Correa (scenes from the life of Mary, painted around 1713), were painstakingly restored in the 1990s and are now housed in the **Museo de Loyola** next door.

ACCOMMODATION CUSÁRARE

Sierra Lodge ☎ 635 456 0036, ⓦ coppercanyonlodges .com. Just 2.5km along the river from the Cusárare falls, this simple but beautifully maintained lodge is a great place to relax; the log cabins are lit by kerosene lamps (no electricity, phones, TVs or internet), but the decor and comforts are luxurious. Rates include three meals and round-trip transfers from Creel train station. M$2310

Batopilas

If you want to get a true idea of the scale and beauty of the Sierra Tarahumara, consider a trip to isolated **BATOPILAS** (460m). Located 123km south of Creel, the town is more accessible now the **new road** has been opened, though the journey still takes at least four hours (at the time of research the final section of the road was still being paved, but traffic was allowed to pass). The route rises and falls through four of the sierra's six canyons before commencing a final, convoluted descent to the floor of Batopilas canyon. Founded in 1632, the town emerged as a prosperous **silver-mining** centre, with production peaking in the nineteenth century under the auspices of the American-owned Batopilas Mining Company. After the Mexican Revolution began in 1910, the town went into a permanent decline and the population plummeted. Today Batopilas is a subtropical place with a population of about 1200 – resplendent with bougainvillea, palm and citrus trees and strung along a single 2km road by the Río Batopilas, it's a world away from the fresh pine forests of Creel. Though it has garnered a reputation for drug cartel activity in recent years, tourists are never affected and the town is being spruced up in preparation for a mini-tourist boom when the road is finally complete (it was made a Pueblo Mágico in 2012).

Museo de Batopilas

Mon–Sat 11am–4pm & 5–7pm • Free

You can get a taster of the town's rich and complex past at the tiny **Museo de Batopilas**, manned by enthusiastic volunteers. The entrance looks like a mine tunnel, and inside you'll find old photos and articles from the town's glory days – estimates suggest that over three hundred mines, claims and workings have been operated in the Batopilas district since silver was first found here.

Hacienda San Miguel
Daily 8am–5pm • M$10

Just outside Batopilas you can visit the romantic ruin of **Hacienda San Miguel**, once the opulent home of Batopilas Mining Co founder (and ex-Washington D.C. governor) **Alexander Shepherd**, who washed up here in 1880. Shepherd is a fascinating and somewhat controversial figure in the US, admired for his social reforms and essentially creating modern D.C., but eventually fired for bankrupting the city. The house itself dates back to the seventeenth century and had been used by mining magnates years before Shepherd took over the place. Abandoned in the 1920s (Shepherd had died in 1902), the hacienda has been in a state of elegant decay ever since, one tower virtually engulfed by a sprawling bougainvillea. To reach the site, walk upriver for around thirty minutes, crossing the bridge when you see the ruins.

The hikes

There are several worthwhile **hikes** here, leading from Rarámuri villages as well as to abandoned mines and waterfalls. The best of these go to the "Lost Cathedral", the eighteenth-century **Misión de San Miguel de Satevó**, 8km away in a desolate landscape of cacti and dust. A longer, three-day trek leads to the town of **Urique**, and can be organized with an operator in Creel (see box, p.509).

ARRIVAL AND DEPARTURE   BATOPILAS

By bus Buses usually leave Creel six times a week from the Three Amigos office on López Mateos (Mon–Sat 7.30am; M$600 return; 5hr). Return buses leave from outside the church in Batopilas at around 5am (Mon–Sat), but always check for changes in the schedule.

INFORMATION

Tourist information There is no official tourist office in Batopilas – Three Amigos in Creel (see box, p.509) can supply you with a map and other useful information. A useful website is ⓦ visitbatopilas.com.
Banks There is no bank here, so bring enough pesos for your stay.

ACCOMMODATION

Casa Monse Plaza Principal; no phone. Run by the affable Monse family for many years, with clean, cheap hostel-like rooms in a courtyard overflowing with plants and mangos just off the plaza – best of the budget options. M$220
Hotel Juanita's Plaza Principal (next door to Casa Monse) ☏ 649 488 0043. Managed by the indomitable Juanita herself, with large, comfy rooms, a courtyard overlooking the river and many quiet enclaves in which to relax. M$400
Real de Minas Donato Guerra 1 (one block south of the plaza) ☏ 649 456 9045, ⓦ coppercanyonlodges.com. The best mid-range option, with bright, beautifully decorated rooms around a central courtyard and fountain, littered with antiques. M$1200
Riverside Lodge (two blocks north of the plaza, next to the church) ☏ 01 800 776 3942, ⓦ copper canyonlodges.com. The exquisite blue-domed *Riverside Lodge* offers luxurious accommodation, each with claw-foot bathtubs and antique beds, and even a small library, but is only open Sept to April. M$2000

EATING AND DRINKING

Restaurant Carolina Plaza de la Constitución 10 (south of the Plaza Principal) ☏ 649 456 9096. Does decent and affordable home-cooked Mexican staples for breakfast, and local specialities such as grilled trout (M$70–150). Daily 8am–8pm.

Guachochi and Cañon de la Sinforosa

About 170km to the south of Creel, **GUACHOCHI** is an unattractive ranching town of around twelve thousand that nonetheless provides access to the sierra's most remote and awe-inspiring locale, the **Cañon de la Sinforosa** (a further 18km south). Some of the hikes in Sinforosa are fairly hardcore – the canyon is 1830m deep and a trek along its length, for example, can take up to three weeks – while easier walks lead to stunning vantage points overlooking the valleys. There are also various hot springs and waterfalls in the region; the most spectacular is the **Cascada Rosalinda**, with an 80m drop. Rarámuri culture is thriving here, with **Norogachi**, 60km from Guachochi, one of the last remaining Rarámuri ceremonial centres, especially renowned for the vivid celebrations that occur during Semana Santa.

Museo Comunitario Norawa

Paseo de las Garzas s/n • Mon–Fri 8am–4pm • Free • ☎ 649 543 2145

The only real sight in Guachochi itself is the tiny **Museo Comunitario Norawa**, a sincere attempt to highlight Rarámuri history and culture (Spanish only) and to sell the work of indigenous artisans, especially local ceramics.

ARRIVAL AND DEPARTURE   GUACHOCHI

By bus Two buses connect Creel with Guachochi daily, but there are also direct buses to Chihuahua from the Estrella Blanca bus station, located in a pink building around a kilometre from the plaza, near where you'll find the Transportes Ballezanos station, which also runs several daily services to Parral.

INFORMATION AND TOURS

Information The Modulo de Información Turistica (information kiosk; Mon–Fri 9am–4pm) is located at the entrance to town next to the Museo Comunitario Norawa.
Tours If you'd like to hike in the Cañon de la Sinforosa you will need to hire a local guide in Guachochi or contact Cristina's Canyon Tours (☎ 668 818 8421, ⊛ cristinascanyontours.com).

8

ACCOMMODATION AND EATING

Doña Lucha (El Mesón) Agustín Melgar 306 ☎ 649 543 0182. A solid budget option; this is basically a small house with rooms rented out like a homestay (hot water, TV and wi-fi), with friendly owners who will pick you up from the bus station and prepare delicious home-cooked food for a few pesos. M$350
Hotel Melina Domínguez 14 ☎ 649 543 0255, ⊜ hotel_melina48@hotmail.com. Around half a kilometre from the plaza, you'll find *Hotel Melina*, with clean, comfortable rooms, satellite TV and an adjoining restaurant. M$550
Los Adobes 20 de Noviembre, at Pascual Orozco ☎ 649 543 0629. An inviting place to try the town's speciality – fresh *trucha* (trout) from the nearby Lago Las Garzas – and plenty of other tasty regional specialities (mains from M$120). Daily 10am–10pm.

DIRECTORY

Banks and exchange If you need to change money or withdraw cash, there's a branch of Scotiabank (Mon–Fri 8.30am–4pm, Sat 10am–3pm; ☎ 649 543 0006) at Francisco Villa 102 (enter at Pascual Orozco and Belisario Domínguez).

Cascada de Basaseachi

The jaw-dropping 312m **Cascada de Basaseachi** (also "Basaséachic") is the second-highest waterfall in Mexico (though the highest, Piedra Volada, a day's hike from Basaseachi, only flows during the rainy season). The falls make a long but spectacularly rewarding day's excursion – about four hours' drive to the north of Creel (163km via San Pedro), followed by two hours on foot. It's best to visit in the rainy season (mid-June to Aug), when the falls are fullest (May is the driest month). There are two viewpoints; the first is above the falls beyond the otherwise sleepy village of Basaseachi itself, while the second lies on the other side of canyon, affording the best views (trails connect both viewpoints). The falls are located within the largely unexplored **Barranca de Candameña**, the widest canyon in the region, with staggering sheer rock walls.

TOURS   BASASEACHI

Tours Public transport is very limited in this region and it's best to visit via tours arranged in Creel (see box, p.509), costing roughly M$800–1200.

Cuauhtémoc

As the Copper Canyon railway winds its way east, the pine trees, canyons and mountains of the Sierra Tarahumara gradually give way to ranching country, centred on the town of **CUAUHTÉMOC**, 70km from Creel and 130km from Chihuahua (see p.460). This is one of the chief centres for Mexican **Mennonites** (see box below). To see Mennonite cheese being made, visit *La Quesería América* (Mon–Sat 8am–6pm; ☎625 587 7249, ⓦqueseriaamerica.com) at Country Road 2-B km 7 (off Hwy-5), north of the town centre.

Museo Menonita

Álvaro Obregón (Hwy-5) km 10 • Mon–Sat 9am–6pm • M$25 • ☎625 586 1895, ⓦmuseomenonita.com • You'll need to take a taxi (around M$300 return) from the Estrella Blanca bus station at C 9 and Allende

There's not much to Cuauhtémoc itself, but if the curious Mennonite connection interests you, make a trip to the **Museo Menonita**, which displays traditional artefacts (mostly farm tools) in a replica of a typical wood-frame Mennonite home and sells Mennonite crafts, jams and the famous cheese.

ARRIVAL AND DEPARTURE
CUAUHTÉMOC

By train Assuming the Copper Canyon railway is still operating on this section (see p.500), trains normally depart Cuauhtémoc for Chihuahua at 7.07pm (M$506; 2hr 25min); the train departs for Creel (M$623; 3hr) and Los Mochis (M$1976; 12hr) at 8.25am.

By bus Buses regularly make the trip to Chihuahua (1.5hr; M$120) and Creel (3.5hr; M$195) from the Estrella Blanca terminal at C 9 and Allende and the Noroeste terminal nearby.

Sonora

North of Sinaloa, Hwy-15 slices into **Sonora**, the second-largest state in Mexico and the nation's breadbasket; note that Sonora is one hour behind Sinaloa in the summer (April–Oct). There's little to stop for on the road, though the handsome colonial town of **Álamos** is a worthy diversion, and low-key beach resorts at **San Carlos**, **Bahía de Kino** and **Puerto Peñasco** provide some relief from the scorching heat. From the coast it's a long drive through the desert to the US border at Nogales (see p.523) or the boundary with Baja California at the Colorado River – you'll also have to put your watch back an hour when you cross this state line, unless Baja California is on Daylight Saving Time (April–Oct), in which case there's no change.

THE MENNONITES

Towards the eastern end of the Copper Canyon rail line, the city of Cuauhtémoc contains Mexico's largest **Mennonite community** (around fifty thousand). You'll come across Mennonites throughout Chihuahua and Durango – the men in bib-and-tucker overalls and straw stetsons, as often as not trying to sell the tasty cheese that is their main produce, and the women, mostly silent, wrapped in long, nineteenth-century dresses with a headscarf. The Christian sect, founded in the sixteenth century by a Dutchman, Menno Simons, believe only in the Bible and their personal conscience: their refusal to do military service or take national oaths of loyalty has led to a long history of persecution; today there are famously large communities of Mennonites and their Amish cousins in Pennsylvania, US. The Mennonites arrived in Mexico in the 1920s from Manitoba, Canada, but among themselves they still speak a form of German, although so divergent as to be virtually unintelligible to a modern German-speaker. Note that the Mennonites of Cuauhtémoc are not as traditional as their American cousins these days – indeed, they own local banks, stores and restaurants.

Álamos

Another Pueblo Mágico, the enchanting town of **ÁLAMOS** offers a tranquil slice of colonial Mexico and a welcome break from the dusty cities along the main north–south highways. It's a great place to do nothing for a while: a tour of the town takes no longer than a couple of hours, and there's little else to do but soak up the languid atmosphere.

In the cooler winter months, Álamos is also a good base for exploring the fairly distinct ecosystem hereabouts; the meeting of Sonoran and Sinaloan deserts, at the foot of the Sierra Madre Occidental, has created a home for a broad range of flora and fauna. In particular, this is a **bird watching** paradise, boasting several hundred different species.

Plaza de Armas

The historic centre of Álamos is the arcaded **Plaza de Armas** and elegant **Templo de la Purísima Concepción** (daily 7am–8pm), a Baroque church dating from 1786. The **Palacio Municipal**, one block from the plaza on Juárez, is an odd but striking red-brick affair from 1899, looking a bit like a fortress, but there's not much to see inside other than the stage used during the Ortiz Tirado festival (see box opposite). From the plaza, the **Callejón del Beso** (Kissing Alley) isn't as narrow as the famous street in Guanajuato, but leads to the busy market (mostly fruit and meat), Plaza Alameda and the bus station.

Museo Costumbrista de Sonora

Guadalupe Victoria 1, Plaza de Armas • Wed–Sun 9am–6pm • M$10 • **House tour** Oct–May Sat 10am • M$175 (US$10)

On the east side of the Plaza de Armas, the mildly diverting **Museo Costumbrista de Sonora** illustrates the town's zenith through a mock-up of La Quintera silver mine, coins from the old mint and grainy photos of moustachioed workers (all in Spanish). There's also a whole shrine-like section dedicated to acclaimed singer **Dr Alfonso Ortiz Tirado**, who was born in Álamos in 1893 – his sombrero is preserved along with photos.

The museum is also the place to join the hour-long **house tour**, which visits three of the finest homes in town. Indeed, among the most appealing aspects of Álamos are these magnificent old Andalucian-style **mansions**, brooding and shuttered from the outside, but enclosing beautiful flower-filled patios.

ÁLAMOS

ACCOMMODATION

Acosta Trailer Rancho	1
Casa de María Felix	4
Casa de los Tesoros	3
Hacienda de los Santos	5
Hotel Colonial	2
Posada Tacubaya	6

EATING & DRINKING

Café Luz de Sol	3
Casa La Aduana	1
La Corregidora Bar	2
Doña Lola's	4

FESTIVAL ORTIZ TIRADO

In January, everything changes in Álamos, when thousands of people descend upon the town for the week-long **Ortiz Tirado music festival**, established in 1985 in honour of the late Dr Alfonso Ortiz Tirado (born in Álamos in 1893), sometimes referred to as the "Mexican Pavarotti". The festival includes exhibitions, dance performances, workshops, lectures, musical events and concerts from Mexico's best classical musicians and singers. Accommodation is usually booked solid at this time, so reservations are a must. See ⓦ festivalortiztirado.gob.mx.

Casa de Cultura

Loma de Guadalupe • Mon–Fri 8am–3pm • Free

Crowning the Loma de Guadalupe, the small hill behind the Plaza de Armas, the **Casa de Cultura** occupies **El Cárcel**, the old eighteenth-century stone jail (some tiny cells are still visible at the back). It houses temporary art exhibitions and holds events, but the main reason for the short climb is the stellar view of the town. Take the side street at the Palacio Municipal, turn right at the end and climb the steps up.

ARRIVAL AND INFORMATION

ÁLAMOS

By bus Álamos lies some 250km south of Guaymas, and 50km east of Navojoa, the nearest town on Hwy-15. Hourly buses (some a/c; no toilets) run back and forth to Álamos (5.30am–7.15pm; 1hr; M$35; ☎ 647 428 0096) from Navojoa, arriving at the tiny Terminal de Autobuses at Morelos 7 on Plaza Alameda. Most long-distance buses heading north or south along the Hwy-15 corridor stop at Navojoa; the TAP/Elite/Pacífico bus station is at Calzada de la Revolución (aka Sufragio Efectivo) and Allende (most of the other stations are around here). Buses to Álamos leave from the Albatros/TBC station at Guerrero and C No Reelección, four blocks away; from TAP walk up Allende to C No Reelección (three blocks) and turn right. Moving on from Navojoa, you can pick up a variety of de paso buses north or south every hour, though you won't be able to reserve tickets in advance (just turn up). Los Mochis is just two hours south (M$175).

Tourist office Victoria 5, Plaza de Armas (Mon–Fri 8am–6pm, Sat & Sun 9am–2pm; ☎ 647 428 0450, ⓦ alamosmexico.com).

ACCOMMODATION

Acosta Trailer Rancho (about 1km east of town) ☎ 647 428 0246, ✉ ranchoacosta@hotmail.com. A secluded park with camping spots (M$100) and a pool; also rents simple, clean rooms with fireplaces. To get there, follow Morelos east across the usually dry Arroyo la Aduana, then turn left at the cemetery. Oct–April. <u>M$550</u>

Casa de María Felix Galeana 41 ☎ 647 428 0929, ✉ casamariafelix@hotmail.com. This charming hotel occupies the birthplace of legendary Mexican actress María Felix (1914–2002), and features a small museum (daily 9am–noon & 3–5pm; non-guests M$15) in her honour; most of the six suites, dressed in vivid pinks, greens and indigo, come with kitchens, fireplaces, internet and jacuzzi. <u>M$930</u>

Casa de los Tesoros Obregón 10, at Gutierrez ☎ 647 428 0400, ⓦ tesoros-hotel.com. This eighteenth-century former convent now has a pool and tastefully decorated rooms, a/c for summer, fireplace for winter; there's also live music in the restaurant every night. <u>M$1200</u>

★ **Hacienda de los Santos** Molina 8 ☎ 647 428 0222, ⓦ haciendadelossantos.com. Gorgeous colonial architecture (carved out of three Spanish mansions and an eighteenth-century sugar mill), enhanced with modern amenities and antique furnishings in every room, tranquil gardens and a pool – the restaurants are also excellent. <u>M$3825</u>

Hotel Colonial Obregón 4 ☎ 647 428 1371, ⓦ alamoshotelcolonial.com. This elegant American-owned hotel occupies a mansion built in 1875, one block from the plaza, and offers ten sumptuous rooms, all decorated with antiques and furniture from around the world. There's a restaurant and a pool. <u>M$1540</u>

★ **Posada Tacubaya** Tacubaya 1 ☎ 647 428 0222, ⓦ posadatacubaya.com. This fabulous B&B is decorated by the work of local artists and warm "rustic-chic" decor. The six spacious bedrooms – with wrought-iron beds and wood-burning fireplaces – open out into blossom-filled gardens. Breakfast features mango marmalade and Chiapas coffee. <u>M$1785</u>

EATING AND DRINKING

Café Luz de Sol Obregón 3 ☎ 647 428 0466, ⓦ luzdelsolalamos.com. Take a break from Mexican food at this bright café around a courtyard, serving healthy breakfasts, salads and frappucinos. Main dishes M$75–

8

120. Free wi-fi. Tues–Sat 7.30am–6pm.

★**Casa La Aduana** La Aduana ☎ 647 404 3473. If you have transport, it's worth making reservations at this isolated restaurant and inn, 3km on a dirt road off the main Álamos highway (taxis charge M$170). Housed in a romantic adobe building dating from the 1630s, the restaurant does a superb fixed-price menu (M$170–280) of "new Sonoran cuisine" highlighting local produce: dishes like chicken in apple, *chipotle* and cream, and *shrimps al ajillo*. Wed–Sun 1–8pm.

La Corregidora Bar Juárez 6, Plaza de Armas (at Hotel Los Portales). Atmospheric old bar and the best spot to people-watch on the plaza. Has pool table, big-screen TV and karaoke. Tues–Sun 4pm–2am.

Doña Lola's Volantín, off Juárez ☎ 647 428 1109. Popular local diner, serving excellent home-cooked Mexican classics for under M$85. Connoisseurs order the *agua de cebada* (barley water), *cazuela* (beef stew) and the *molletes con carne*. Mon–Sat 7am–10pm, Sun 2–10pm.

DIRECTORY

Banks Banorte (Mon–Fri 9am–4pm) is the only bank with an ATM, across the Alameda at Madero 27.
Post office The post office (☎ 647 428 0009) is inside the Biblioteca Pública (library) on Comercio, just off

Plaza de Armas.
Internet Try Ciber Utopia at Rosales 36, just off the plaza (daily 8am–9pm; M$10/hr).

San Carlos

Around 16km west of Guaymas, the small town of **SAN CARLOS** is gradually becoming a larger resort geared towards a mainly retired North American clientele. The main activities here are **diving** and **fishing**, though the chief attraction above the water is the scenery: the resort is dominated by the barren, jagged peaks of Cerro Tatakawi, and the scorched desert landscape makes a stunning backdrop to a series of inviting bays, beaches and cobalt-blue waters. Founded only in the 1960s, San Carlos sports a seasonal population of around seven thousand. At the time of research the nearby **Delfinario Sonora** (dolphin park) was closed (or just running sea lion shows).

ARRIVAL AND GETTING AROUND

SAN CARLOS

By bus Buses (daily; every 30min 6.30am–7pm, then 8pm, 9pm & 11pm; M$12) for San Carlos leave Guaymas from C 19 by the post office, but it's easier to catch them as they head up Serdán (try the corner of C 18). It can take up to an hour to reach San Carlos. Taking a bus within San Carlos costs M$6.

By taxi Taxis charge around M$50–100 for trips in San Carlos (fix the price in advance), and around M$250 to Guaymas; from Guaymas airport (see p.519) the charge is M$300 (you can rent cars at the airport for M$700–1000/ day with Budget or Hertz).

INFORMATION AND ACTIVITIES

Tourist information The best source of information here is the Conventions and Visitors Bureau at Manlio Beltrones 19 (Mon–Fri 9am–1pm & 2–5pm, Sat 9am–2pm; ☎ 622 226 0202, �🌐 go2sancarlos.com). Also check out 🌐 sancarlosmexico.com.
Bank CI Banco (with ATM) is at Manlio Beltrones km 9.5 (next to Pemex petrol station; Mon–Fri 9am–5pm).

Gary's Dive Shop Manlio Beltrones km 10 ☎ 622 226 0049, 🌐 garysdivemexico.com. Donna and Gary Goldstein run various dive trips, starting at around M$1230 for a basic two-tank dive, and cruises around Seal Island (a sea lion colony) for M$1425. They also have a fast broadband internet connection upstairs. Daily 7am–5pm.

TRAVELLING BY CAR: THE SONORA "FREE ZONE"

If you plan to travel with a US or Canadian vehicle in Sonora north of Empalme (the area west of Hwy-15 to the coast and the border with Baja), you do not have to register and obtain a vehicle permit; Puerto Peñasco, San Carlos, Hermosillo, Kino Bay and Guaymas are all covered. The southern end of the "free zone" is at km 98 on Hwy-15, just south of Empalme. You are still required to fill in a multiple migration form or "FMM" at the US border, but for stays of no more than seven days there is no need to pay the Non-immigrant Fee. If you plan to travel beyond the Sonora "free zone", you must obtain a vehicle permit (see p.29).

ACCOMMODATION

Posada del Desierto Bajada Comodoro 195–196, Club de Yates ☎622 226 0467, ✉posadadesierto@yahoo .com. This barebones budget option near the marina offers decent value, with seven clean, a/c rooms, free wi-fi, basic kitchenettes and friendly owners – water pressure can be a problem, however. M$525

Sea of Cortez Beach Club Paseo Mar Bermejo Parcela 7 ☎622 227 0374, �🌐diamondresorts.com. There's no shortage of luxurious resorts along the shore in San Carlos, though with pool, restaurants and all the

trimmings (all rooms have patios or balconies), this oceanfront Diamond Resorts property is great value. M$1470

Totonaka RV Park Manlio Beltrones km 8 ☎622 226 0481, �🌐totonakarv.com. For something a little cheaper, aim for this RV park on the right-hand side as you enter San Carlos; it also offers free wi-fi or internet usage from its office and basic apartments (with cable TV), as well as RV (M$360 full hook-ups) and tent sites (M$210). M$540

EATING AND DRINKING

Blackie's Manlio Beltrones km 10.3 (next to PEMEX) ☎622 226 1525. Expat favourite and a good choice for dinner, with juicy steaks, seafood and the odd local dish – count on paying around M$210 for the signature rib-eye. Tues–Fri 2.30–11pm, Sat & Sun 1–11pm.

Charly's Rock Manlio Beltrones km 9 ☎622 226 0888. If you're in the mood for seafood, this restaurant serves enormous lobsters, all-you-can-eat fish and chips on Tues, and is also a good spot to have a margarita and watch the

sun go down (the view is spectacular) – service can be hit and miss, though, so be patient. Mains M$140–180. Daily 9am–9pm.

Rosa's Cantina Manlio Beltrones km 9.5 ☎622 226 1000. On the main strip, this restaurant serves fine tortas and other Mexican dishes in a Pancho Villa–themed dining room (mains M$70–150), but is especially popular for breakfast. Daily 6am–9pm.

8

Hermosillo

The thriving state capital of Sonora some 117km north of Guaymas, **HERMOSILLO** is a neat, affluent but rather odd-looking place of around 800,000, home to one of the largest Ford manufacturing plants outside the US. It's surrounded by strange rock formations and presided over, right in the centre, by the **Cerro de la Campana**, a tall outcrop crowned by radio masts and surreally illuminated at night to resemble a giant, spiral snail-shell (you can hike up or take a taxi, though sunsets can get very busy up there).

While there's little to see in the way of traditional sights, Hermosillo's laurel-lined avenues, overflowing meat markets, shops full of cowboy paraphernalia and tasty snack food make for an engaging stopover on the route north or south. Hwy-15 from Nogales (270km to the north) comes into town as Bulevar Eusebio Kino, known as Bulevar Rosales as it runs north–south through the centre of town. Virtually everything you might want to see lies to the south near Plaza Zaragoza or Serdán, the main commercial street downtown. Note that **summers** here are fierce, with temperatures often exceeding 47 °C.

Plaza Zaragoza

Palacio de Gobierno Mon–Fri 8am–8pm, Sat 8am–3pm • Free

The spacious **Plaza Zaragoza** is the venerable, shaded heart of Hermosillo and a good place to begin any wanderings around the centre. The plaza is framed by the stately **Palacio de Gobierno**, completed in 1906 and boasting a series of florid murals (painted in the 1980s) highlighting the history of Sonora, and the striking **Catedral de Nuestra Señora de la Asunción**, a grand edifice completed in 1908 but added to throughout the twentieth century.

Museo Regional de Sonora

Jesús García • Tues–Sat 10am–6pm, Sun 9am–4pm • M$47 • ☎662 217 2714

On the east side of the Cerro de la Campana you'll find the **Museo Regional de Sonora**, which houses exhibits charting the historical development of Sonora, from the conception of the Earth to the construction of *maquiladora* plants.

Museo de Arte de Sonora

Agustín Vildósola, at Cultura • Tues–Sat 10am–7pm, Sun 11am–7pm • M$30 (free on Sun) • ☎ 662 254 6397, ⓦ musasblog.mx

Hermosillo's most contemporary museum is the **Museo de Arte de Sonora** (MUSAS), a stylish art centre and gallery space for rotating contemporary art exhibitions. Past shows have featured Los Mochis-born artist Hugo Lugo, Gustavo Monroy and Helga Krebs, a German artist who settled in Hermosillo.

Museo de Culturas Populares e Indígenas de Sonora

Comonfort 22 • Tues–Fri 10am–4pm, Sat 10am–2pm • Free • ☎ 662 212 6418

Housed in a grand French-influenced mansion built for German immigrant Geo Grürinig in 1904 (who established Sonora Brewery here in the 1890s with one Dr Alberto Hoeffer, who later inherited the house), the **Museo de Culturas Populares e Indígenas de Sonora** is primarily a showcase for American artist Ethel Cook (1887–1976), whose vibrant murals based on the indigenous peoples of Sonora fill two galleries.

HERMOSILLO

● EATING	
Gordo's Hot Dogs	3
Mariachísimo	4
Sonora Steak	2
Tacos Jaas Light	1
Xochimilco	5

■ ACCOMMODATION	
Colonial Hotel	4
Hotel Suites Kino	2
Hotel Washington	1
Lucerna	3

EL CARNAVAL DE GUAYMAS

An important shrimp-fishing port on the main Hwy-15 corridor, **GUAYMAS**, around 180km north of Navojoa, claims some proud history but has little to offer visitors. Unless you're looking for somewhere to crash for one night, it's advisable to head for nearby beaches; the resort town of **San Carlos** is just a short bus ride away (see p.516). One reason to linger in Guaymas is the annual **carnival**, held here in February since 1888 and one of Mexico's best (it begins on the Thurs before Ash Wednesday and ends at the beginning of Lent). Concerts and parades are held all over town (the main location is the Plaza de los Tres Presidentes), beginning with the traditional burning an effigy of something or someone who has upset the public that year (Vicente Fox and George Bush have both featured in the past). Note that accommodation in town is booked months in advance for carnival.

ARRIVAL

Most bus companies have terminals on C 14 near C 12, a couple of blocks south of Serdán and within walking distance of the waterfront. Buses to San Carlos cost M$12. Tufesa and TAP have terminals 1km west at García López 927 and 915 respectively (near C Jaiba).

By ferry Ferries from Santa Rosalía in Baja California (see p.554) arrive at the docks 2km east of the centre, easily reached on local buses (M$7) along Serdán. The ferry from Guaymas to Santa Rosalía departs on Mon, Tues, Thurs, Fri and Sat at 8pm; the crossing takes seven hours. Always call in advance, though, as schedules often change. One-way tickets are M$885 (returns are M$1630), but you'll often get a discount on Sundays. A cabin is an additional M$985, while cars cost M$3200 (one-way). The ticket office inside the terminal is open Mon–Sat 8am–3pm (☎ 622 222 0204, ⓦ ferry santarosalia.com).

ACCOMMODATION

Armida Hotel Carr Internacional Salida al Norte s/n

☎ 622 225 2800, ⓦ hotelarmida.com.mx. If you have to stay in Guaymas, aim for this well-equipped hotel, close to the TAP and Tufesa terminals, with 124 rooms ranging from luxurious executive doubles (M$1489) to decent standards. Free wi-fi. **M$988**

Hotel del Sol García López 995 ☎ 622 224 9411, ⓔ suitesdelsol@hotmail.com. Prices here are a bit cheaper than the *Armida*, with 25 simple but adequate rooms close to the main bus terminals. Free wi-fi. **M$750**

EATING AND DRINKING

★ **Coctelería Doug Out** García López between calles 11 and 12 ☎ 622 222 2626. A no-frills food court offering excellent crab and various *ceviche, pulpo cocido* and other shellfish, all for well under M$150 (half kilo of shrimp is M$100). Cash only. Daily noon–10pm.

★ **Lonchería Doney** Serdán at C 25 ☎ 622 222 4270. A justly popular local *comedor* at the far end of Serdán, lauded for its giant *papas locas* (huge baked potatoes stuffed with meat, cheese and cream) and *tacos carne asada*. Cash only (M$50–75). Sun–Thurs 5pm–1.30am, Fri & Sat 5pm–3am.

8

HERMOSILLO

ARRIVAL AND DEPARTURE

By plane Aeropuerto Internacional General Ignacio L. Pesqueira, an important Aeroméxico hub (with flights to Mexico City, Los Angeles and numerous domestic destinations), is 10km out at Carr Bahía de Kino km 9.5. Fixed-fare taxis charge M$120–300 for most destinations in the city. *Colectivos* are just M$50–100 into the centre.

By bus The Central de Autobuses is at Luís Encinas 400, 3km east of the centre. Most intercity buses passing through Hermosillo are *de paso*, and it can be very hard to get tickets. TBC (depot left of the Central de Autobuses at Encinas 354) runs local buses to Guaymas, Navojoa and, four times daily, to

Álamos. First-class Tufesa is further west at Encinas 297. To get downtown from the bus station area, take a "Ruta 1" microbus, or a "Multirutas" town bus (all M$7) across the main road. To get back, catch a bus marked "Central Camionera" from Juárez (on east side of Jardín Juárez). Taxis charge M$70. Second-class buses to Bahía de Kino depart the terminal on Sonora between González and García.

Destinations Bahía de Kino (13 daily; 2hr); Guadalajara (every 30min; 21–23hr); Guaymas (every 30min; 2hr); Los Mochis (every 30min; 7–9hr); Mexico City (hourly; 29–33hr); Nogales (hourly; 3–4hr); Tijuana (every 30min; 12–14hr).

INFORMATION

Tourist office The Instituto Municipal de Cultura Arte y Turismo (IMCATUR) has an office at Dr Aguilar 33 (enter at Campodonico and Galeana in Col Centenario; ☎ 662 213 8638), open Mon–Fri 9am–5pm, but you'll get more from their website at ⓦ imcatur.com.mx. The helpful Oficina de

Convenciones y Visitantes has an office at Agustín de Vildósola 251, Col Emiliano Zapata (Mon–Fri 8am–5pm; ☎ 662 285 5050, ⓦ ocvhermosillo.com). Other useful websites include ⓦ gotosonora.com.

ACCOMMODATION

Nearly all the cheaper **hotels** in Hermosillo are poor value, but some very pleasant mid-range places cater to business people and the wealthy *rancheros* who come here for the markets. The most expensive hotels, such as the *Fiesta Americana* and a number of motels, are almost all in the **Zona Hotelera**, 5km northeast from the centre on Kino (Hwy-15), and only practical if you have a car.

Colonial Hotel Vado del Río 9 ☎ 662 259 0000, ⓦ hotelescolonial.com. Plush, modern motel on the southern edge of downtown, worth the extra walk if you're not driving; includes breakfast, satellite TV, internet, laundry, gym and even a small pool on site. M$850
Hotel Suites Kino Pino Suárez 151, just off Rosales near Plaza Zaragoza ☎ 662 213 3131, ⓦ hotelsuiteskino .com. Colonial-style hotel set in a nineteenth-century building with standard, motel-style rooms and all the facilities, including cable TV, free internet, coffee, parking and a pool, for low rates. M$500

Hotel Washington Noriega 68, near Guerrero ☎ 662 213 1183. Best budget option in town: ageing but good-value rooms, excellent hot showers, a very helpful staff and free coffee in the lobby. Cash only. M$300
Lucerna Paseo Río Sonora Nte 98 ☎ 662 259 5200, ⓦ hoteleslucerna.com. One of the best options if Hermosillo's selection of modern hotels and motels on the outskirts appeals, with stylish rooms, consistently high standards of service and a small pool, just south of the centre. Book ahead. M$1455

EATING

Don't leave the city without trying some of the local specialties: **hot dogs** are fabulously over the top here, wrapped in bacon and piled with all sorts of toppings – some of the best stalls are around the entrance to the Universidad de Sonora, at Luís Encinas and Rosales. Also try some of the **carne asada** – this is beef country, after all – and the **coyotas**, sweet cookies made from flour, brown sugar, molasses and milk (best sampled on the stalls along Obregón).

★ **Gordo's Hot Dogs** Olivares, at Juan Navarrete. This place is a local institution, serving the best hot dogs in town – huge, juicy, masterpieces of bacon-wrapped dogs and ground beef in a giant bun, slathered in an array of zesty condiments (M$60–85). Daily 7pm–midnight (Fri & Sat 5am).
Mariachísimo Periférico Pte 325, Col Palmar del Sol ☎ 662 218 3555. The sister restaurant of *Xochimilco* (see below), serving the same high-quality *carne asada* but with the added bonus of later opening hours and live mariachi bands (Mon–Sat 3.30pm, 10pm & midnight). Mains M$120–180. Mon–Sat noon–2am, Sun noon–7pm.
Sonora Steak Eusebio Kino 914 (Hwy-15) ☎ 662 210 0313, ⓦ sonorasteakhouse.com. Treat yourself to Sonora's pride and joy at this classic steakhouse, where staff will show you a selection of cuts before you choose the

thickness of the meat – steaks are charged by the gram. Favourite of Hermosillo's dignitaries – Sonora state governor's official residence is next door. Mains M$150–300. Mon–Sat noon–2am, Sun 1–10pm.
★ **Tacos Jaas Light** Mariscal 23 at Gómez Farías ☎ 662 214 0746, ⓦ jaaslight.com.mx. The place to gorge on prime *tacos de carne asada* (M$20–25). They have several locations, but this is the best, though it's a no-frills open-air place with plastic tables and chairs. "Light" versions, wrapped in lettuce leaves, are also available. Daily 7pm–4am.
Xochimilco Obregón 51 ☎ 662 250 4089. A Hermosillo *carne asada* favourite since 1949, serving great sit-down meals and "special plates" of charcoal-broiled beef, ribs, beans and giant tortillas (average dishes M$140–200). Daily 11am–9pm.

DIRECTORY

Banks and exchange There are numerous *casas de cambio* and banks on Serdán, and a handy Bancomer with ATM at Matamoros and Sonora, on Jardín Juárez a block from the *Monte Carlo* hotel.

Consulate US (Mon–Fri 8am–4.30pm; ☎ 662 289 3500, ⓦ hermosillo.usconsulate.gov), Monterrey 141, between Galeana and Rosales.
Post office At the corner of Serdán and Rosales.

Bahía de Kino

Boasting more than 15km of pristine Sea of Cortez coastline, 110km west of Hermosillo, **BAHÍA DE KINO** is a popular weekend escape for locals and increasingly a winter resort for North American snowbirds. For good reason; the seafront is padded with many kilometres of inviting sands, the placid waters are perfect for swimming and kayaking, the offshore islets and strange rock formations make the sunsets particularly memorable and the resort remains relatively low-key – for now. There are two settlements around the bay: the old fishing village of **Kino Viejo**, a dusty collection of corrugated-iron huts, passed over by the fruits of development, and the younger **Kino Nuevo** – an 8km strip of one-storey seafront houses, trailer parks and a handful of hotels and restaurants.

ARRIVAL AND INFORMATION   BAHÍA DE KINO

By bus Buses (M$81–92; 2hr) to Bahía de Kino leave Hermosillo from the small bus station on Sonora, a block and a half east of the *Monte Carlo* near Jardín Juárez, between Jesús García and González. There are about 12–13 a day – hourly from 5am to 1.30pm, then every two or three hours up to 7pm – with more at busy weekends; they take around two hours and end up in Kino Nuevo on Mar de Cortés, the main avenue. Once here you can ride these buses up and down the seafront for M$7 (taxis charge around M$50 for most trips in town).

ACCOMMODATION

Casablanca Inn Mar de Cortés 674 ☎ 662 242 0777, ⓦ casablancakinobay.com. Justly popular family-owned guesthouse, with clean, bright rooms (a/c and satellite TV), breakfast included (the restaurant is open all day with mains from M$50) and palapa bar (3–10pm). M$1800
Hotel Hacienda Mar de Cortés at Creta s/n ☎ 662 242 0590, ⓦ hotelhacienda.info. Friendly hotel with simple but clean rooms with tiled floor set around a small courtyard and pool (the suites are a bit more comfortable and stylish, but not much bigger). M$1200
La Playa RV & Hotel Mar de Cortés 101, at Beruit ☎ 662 242 0273. Gorgeous Mediterranean-style resort right on the beach, its rooms equipped with tiled-floor, marble-clad bathrooms, satellite TV, fridge and microwave (also offers 48 full hook-ups for RVs). M$1200

EATING AND DRINKING

Kino Bay Jorge's Restaurant Mar de Cortés and Alicantes ☎ 662 242 0049. *Jorge's* is one of a handful of places that dish up local seafood (especially lobster) just off the beach, at the northern end of Kino Nuevo. Mains M$100–180. Thurs–Tues noon–10pm.
El Pargo Rojo Mar de Cortés 1426 ☎ 662 242 0205. Head south from *Jorge's* and you'll arrive at *El Pargo Rojo*, another popular and reputable restaurant in the middle of Kino Nuevo serving decent breakfasts and seafood dishes (M$90–150). Daily 10am–9pm.

Puerto Peñasco

Not long ago, **PUERTO PEÑASCO** was little more than a tiny shrimping port on the edge of the Altar desert. Since the 1990s, though, the town has exploded into a major resort for Arizona's beach-starved masses, and it is now filled with high-rise condominiums. Travel warnings and the 2009 US recession hit Puerto Peñasco hard, but now things have settled down the development is sure to continue: a new highway along the coast (reducing driving times from California) opened in 2008, and the new Mar de Cortés International Airport was inaugurated one year later. If you like resorts, golf or just fancy a couple of days on the beach before heading into the US, "Rocky Point" (as the expat community calls it) can be lots of fun. Note that temperatures regularly top 40°C in the summer.

THE SERI

The coast around Bahía de Kino is the traditional home of the **Seri** people, once semi-nomadic hunter-gatherers who have managed to hang on to their linguistic and cultural traditions. Their former home on the offshore **Isla del Tiburón** (Shark Island) was made into a wildlife refuge in the 1960s but is still administered by the tribal government. You may come across Seri hawking traditional (and not so traditional) ironwood carvings along the beach in Kino Nuevo, though their main settlement is **Punta Chueca**, 35km north – you can buy genuine crafts here, but you'll need your own wheels to reach the settlement. The tiny **Museo de los Seris** (Wed–Sun 9am–6pm; M$10), on the plaza in the middle of Kino Nuevo, gives a little more information on Seri history.

8

Sandy Beach

From the malecón and the Old Port, the main Bulevar Juárez (Hwy-8) runs nearly parallel to the water before heading off towards Sonoyta, while the town's main attraction, **Sandy Beach**, stretches off to the northwest, an 8km strip backed by condos and resort hotels ending at **La Choya** (or Cholla Bay in English). Tides here can raise and lower sea levels by several metres, creating large numbers of tidal pools at low tide, often crammed with crabs, starfish and other marine life.

San Jorge Island

San Jorge Island, a series of iceberg-like rocks in the Sea of Cortez 45km from Puerto Peñasco, is frequented by hordes of cormorants, red-billed tropicbirds, brown pelicans and some 2500 sea lions. If they're feeling up to it, and haven't been laid low by the daytime heat, you can swim with the latter. Otherwise, there are usually numerous dolphins frolicking around. CEDO (see below) and various tour operators run trips for M$1500 (6–7hr, minimum six people).

Centro Intercultural de Estudios de Desiertos y Océanos

Las Conchas, off Blv Josefa Ortiz de Domínguez • Mon–Sat 9am–5pm, Sun 10am–2pm • Free • ☎ 638 382 0113, ⓦ cedointercultural.org

If you don't have the inclination to get in the water, you can visit the **Centro Intercultural de Estudios de Desiertos y Océanos** (CEDO), in Las Conchas residential zone 4km east of the harbour, the foremost authority on local wildlife, and currently researching the harmful effects of development on regional ecology. Inside you can check out the Gran Desierto de Altar Botanical Gardens, a 20m fin whale skeleton and the Earthship Visitors' Center (which houses various ecological exhibits). CEDO also runs various expert-led **tours** of the Estero Morúa coastal wetlands by kayak (M$750; 5hr), the Gran Desierto dunes (M$750; 5hr; Sept–May) and the Pinacate Biosphere Reserve (M$900; 6hr; Sept–May only).

Reserva de la Biósfera El Pinacate y Gran Desierto de Altar

Daily 8am–5pm • M$56 • ☎ 638 105 8030, ⓦ visitaelpinacate.org • Centro de Visitantes Schuk Toak, 7km west of Hwy-8 km 72 ☎ 638 108 0011 • La Estación Biológica, Hwy-8 km 52, Ejido Los Norteños ☎ 638 105 8016

The region's most impressive natural attraction, the **Reserva de la Biósfera El Pinacate y Gran Desierto de Altar**, lies north of Puerto Peñasco on Hwy-8. NASA used this otherworldly expanse of volcanic cinder cones and craters to train its astronauts for lunar landings. One of Pinacate's largest and most awe-inspiring craters, "**El Elegante**", is 1.6km wide and 250m deep and can be seen from space. Exhibits at the **Centro de Visitantes Schuk Toak** provide background, as well as displays of **Tohono O'odham** artefacts. No public transport runs to the reserve, so you'll have to drive or join a tour.

ARRIVAL AND DEPARTURE   PUERTO PEÑASCO

By bus The main bus stations are located on Benito Juárez (the main road into town), around 1km from the seafront; Águila (buses to Mexicali and Tijuana) is at Constitución and Juárez, while Albatros (☎ 638 388 0888) is further up at Juárez 292; the latter runs ten buses a day to Hermosillo (M$335), three to Nogales (M$292) and three to Guaymas (M$395). Several outfits also run direct minibuses to Arizona: Head Out to Rocky Point (☎ US+1 866 443 2368, ⓦ headoutto

rockypoint.com) runs buses from Phoenix (4hr) for US$100–190/M$1740–3310 return (depends on number of people).
By car Puerto Peñasco is just 100km south of the US border and around four hours' drive from Phoenix, Arizona – most visitors drive here on Hwy-8.
By taxi One of the omnipresent white taxis (locals pay around M$30–60 for a ride anywhere in town; fix the price first) should get you to wherever you need to be.

INFORMATION

Oficina de Convenciones y Visitantes de Puerto Peñasco Plaza Pelícanos, Coahuila 444, between Freemont and Víctor Estrella (Mon–Fri 9am–2pm &

4–7pm; ☎ 638 388 0444, ⓦ cometorockypoint.com). Has an ample assortment of flyers and glossy brochures. See also ⓦ puerto-penasco.com.

CROSSING THE US BORDER: NOGALES

Like most of the other US/Mexico border towns, **Nogales** is a fast-growing melange of cheap stores, *maquiladoras* (factories), street hustlers and rough bars. Crossing the border (24hr) into Mexico is straightforward; remember to have your tourist card stamped by *migración* if you're heading further south (see p.29). From here López Mateos (Hwy-15) leads south towards the main bus stations; buses to Mexico City run every hour (32–34hr) from the Central Camionera, just off the highway (Obregón 2562) about 5km south of the border; Omnibus and TAP are at Obregón 2036 (✆631 319 4154), with tickets to Hermosillo for M$220 (every 30min; 3.5hr) and Mazatlán M$945 (6 daily; 17hr); further south is the Tufesa terminal at Obregón 2030. If you plan to go to Puerto Peñasco, Albatros (✆631 319 4190) runs buses from Obregón 1945 (11am; M$292; 5hr). TBC buses to Álamos also run from here (1 daily). Taxis from the border to the bus stations are around M$100. Tufesa runs buses across the border, between Nogales bus station and Tucson, Arizona, for US$21, and Phoenix for US$40 (🖥tufesa.com.mx).

ACCOMMODATION

Peñasco del Sol Paseo las Glorias 1 ✆638 383 0300, 🖥penascodelsolhotel.com. Justly popular resort hotel, especially lively at Spring Break and holidays when this is the best place to party. The 203 handsomely furnished rooms come with plasma TVs and coffee-makers. Free wi-fi. Great deals online. M$1785

Posada La Roca Primero de Junio 2 ✆638 383 3199, 🖥hotelposadalaroca.blogspot.com. The oldest building in town (1927); room no. 10 was frequented by Al Capone during Prohibition. A great budget option with cool quarters, free wi-fi and coffee and a cosy living room. M$675

Sonoran Spa Resort Camino La Choya km 3.7 ✆US+1 888 642 3495, 🖥sonoran-spa-resort.com. One of the best luxury lodgings in Puerto Peñasco, right on Sandy Beach with three pools and all the extras; rooms are one- to three-bedroom suites with kitchens and sea views. M$1680

EATING AND DRINKING

RESTAURANTS

Aqui Es Con Flavio's Malecón Kino 10, at Primero de Junio ✆638 383 5252, 🖥en.aquiesconflavio.com. Unpretentious place right on the boardwalk, where most people come for the margaritas, frolicking pelicans and the views rather than the food. The seafood is not bad, though – groups should opt for the huge seafood combo. Mains M$140–200. Daily 8am–10pm.

La Casa del Capitán Av del Agua 1, Cerro de la Ballena ✆638 383 5698. One of the most popular restaurants in town to view the sunset (when it's always packed), with gorgeous views across the sea. There's a full international and Mexican menu. Follow Juárez to Antonio's liquor store; from there you'll see the entrance to the path leading to the top of "Whale Hill", a 15min walk. Mains M$150–250. Daily 10am–10pm.

Delfin Amigable (Friendly Dolphin) Alcantar 44 ✆638 383 2608. Local favourite with a big seafood menu and reasonable prices, enhanced with antique pictures of Mexico. Food is also served on an outdoor patio upstairs. Occasionally one of the owners will play guitar and sing to the tables. Mains average M$150–200. Daily noon–10pm.

★ **El Marlin Azul** Malecón (Old Port) ✆638 388 0056. Fabulous family-owned seafood restaurant popular with locals, specializing in flounder, shrimp tacos and marlin

(local, when they can get it fresh); try the smoked marlin, one of the town's best dishes, or the Neptune platter for two, loaded with a variety of seafood (around M$350). Noon–10pm, closed Wed.

Mary's Seafood Malecón (Old Port); no phone. Delicious and always fresh seafood on the boardwalk (with great upper deck for viewing the harbour); stand-outs include the seabass, fried shrimp and fish or beef tacos for M$25. Daily 10am–9.30pm.

BARS AND CAFÉS

JJ's Cantina 58 Seaside Av, La Choya (Cholla Bay) ✆638 383 2785, 🖥jjscantina.com. A beach bar and seafood joint that does great fish, tacos and burgers (all for less than M$100), about 20min drive from the malecón. If you don't mind the expat crowd – monthly events include chile cook-offs and "Bathtub Races" – it's an excellent place to watch the sun set over the bay. Cash only. Daily noon–midnight.

Kaffee Haus Juárez 216-B ✆638 388 1065, 🖥coffees haus.com. This friendly European-style café serves rich coffee, wonderful breakfasts and addictive pastries such as applestrudel with vanilla sauce and cherry coconut cake. Mains M$85–130. Incredibly popular, so be prepared to wait. Mon–Sat 7.30am–4pm, Sun 7.30am–2pm.

DIRECTORY

Banks There are several strung along Juárez, with ATMs; US dollars are accepted everywhere.

Post office Chiapas 1285, off Fremont (Mon–Fri 8am–3pm; ✆638 383 2350).

Baja California

SEA OF CORTES NEAR LA PAZ

9

Baja California

Graced with tantalizing desert landscapes, lush oases and rich marine life, Baja California is one of the most compelling and popular destinations in Mexico. Its human history is no less enticing, with a legacy of remote cave paintings, crumbling Spanish missions, luxury beach resorts and fabulous seafood. Yet even today, Baja maintains a palpable air of isolation from the rest of Mexico. The peninsula lies over 1300km west of Mexico City, and the sheer distances involved in traversing its length – it's over 1700km long – are not conducive to quick exploration.

One of the most magical sights in Baja is the annual **grey whale** migration from December to April; the best places to see the whales are the Laguna Ojo de Liebre, just off **Guerrero Negro**, or the lagoon near **San Ignacio**, where the town itself is an attraction in itself. The peninsula is also home to some of the most bewitching and thought-provoking **cave art** in the world – the Sierra de San Francisco, between Bahía de los Angeles and Loreto, was declared a World Heritage Site by UNESCO in 1993 because of its five hundred particularly vivid rock-art sites.

And all along the coast you'll find turquoise waters and white-sand **beaches**; most towns in Baja California Sur offer fantastic opportunities for diving, fishing and kayaking, but **Bahía Concepción**, **Loreto**, **La Paz** and the remote settlements on the **East Cape** are the standouts among them. In complete contrast, right at the end of the peninsula, the booming resort of **Los Cabos** offers its own special blend of boutique hotels, beach activities, top-notch restaurants and wild nightlife.

ESSENTIALS   BAJA CALIFORNIA

Baja information Visit ⓦ discoverbajacalifornia.com for information on the region, and especially for up-to-date travel regulations. Call ☎ 078 for visitor assistance 24hr a day.

Visas Coming from the US land border, note that all US and Canadian citizens, and foreigners who have a valid US visa, can travel as far as Ensenada without having to obtain a tourist card (FMT), provided the length of the stay does not exceed 72hr. Between 72hr and 7 days you'll need a form, but are not obliged to pay the fee. If you intend on staying for more than seven days in any region of Mexico, you are required to pay a Non-immigrant Fee (DNI) when obtaining the tourist card – if you fly in, it's included. See p.533 for crossing the border at Tijuana.

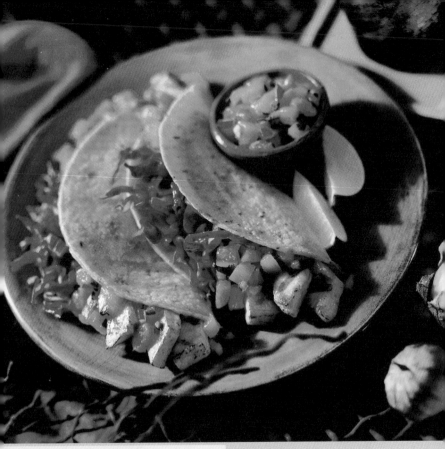

FISH TACOS

Highlights

❶ The Transpeninsular Highway One of the world's great road trips, Highway 1 runs the length of Baja California for 1711km, an enchanting drive of starry nights, vast deserts and empty beaches. **See p.529**

❷ Fish tacos The seafood in this part of Mexico is always exceptional, but the real star is the humble fish taco, found all over Baja but best experienced in Ensenada. **See p.542**

❸ Valle de Guadalupe Tour the vineyards of this rapidly maturing wine area, from giants like Vinos L.A. Cetto to boutique producers such as Casa de Piedra. **See p.543**

❹ Whale watching at Laguna San Ignacio Each winter migrating grey whales journey from

the Arctic Circle to nurse their calves in the warm waters of this pristine inlet. **See p.553**

❺ Cave art The wild, rugged mountains of Baja California protect some of the most spellbinding prehistoric cave art in the world, best explored with a local guide. **See p.557**

❻ Bahía Concepción Camp underneath a star-filled sky, lounge on gorgeous beaches and kayak alongside dolphins in serene aquamarine waters. **See p.558**

❼ La Paz All of Baja's best qualities: great restaurants, cheap rooms, vibrant street life and outdoor adventure opportunities. **See p.562**

HIGHLIGHTS ARE MARKED ON THE MAP ON P.528

THE TRANSPENINSULAR HIGHWAY (HWY-1)

The **Transpeninsular Highway** is one of North America's great road trips. Part of the thrill comes from the long spaces separating major towns, the narrow segments of highway that snake along precarious cliffs, and the animals and washouts that can block the road. But the biggest draw is the near-constant beauty of the desert, mountain, sea and ocean vistas and their illumination by brilliant blue skies and starry nights. The times below include necessary stops for petrol and army inspections; all cars and buses are searched at military checkpoints stationed between Tijuana and Ensenada (2); north of El Rosario; north of Guerrero Negro; north of San Ignacio; and north of La Paz.

Tijuana to Mexicali	1hr 50min	(198km)
Mexicali to San Felipe	2hr 15min	(195km)
San Felipe to Ensenada	3hr 10min	(245km)
Tijuana to Ensenada	55min	(109km)
Ensenada to San Quintín	3hr	(190km)
San Quintín to El Rosario	55min	(56km)
El Rosario to Cataviña	1hr 50min	(123km)
Cataviña to Parador Punta Prieta	1hr	(103km)
Parador Punta Prieta to Bahía de los Angeles	45min	(69km)
Parador Punta Prieta to Guerrero Negro	1hr 50min	(135km)
Guerrero Negro to San Ignacio	1hr 30min	(146km)
San Ignacio to Santa Rosalía	45min	(72km)
Santa Rosalía to Mulegé	40min	(62km)
Mulegé to Loreto	1hr 45min	(138km)
Loreto to Ciudad Insurgentes	1hr 20min	(141km)
Ciudad Insurgentes to La Paz	2hr 20min	(209km)
La Paz to Todos Santos	45min	(77km)
Todos Santos to Cabo San Lucas	55min	(77km)
Cabo San Lucas to San José del Cabo	25min	(32km)

PRACTICALITIES

Many Americans and Canadians take their cars to Baja; despite the scary headlines when it comes to drug violence along the US-Mexico border, this is generally easy and safe. If you intend to go on from Baja to mainland Mexico, you need to apply for a Temporary Importation of Vehicle Permit (see ⓦ banjercito.com.mx and Basics p.29). Car insurance is not mandatory but is highly recommended. There are many companies along the US-Mexico border that sell Mexican car insurance by the day, week or month (most normal US insurance policies don't provide coverage for driving in Mexico). Note also that in Tijuana, tinted windows are now banned. Other nationalities can always **rent cars** on arrival – easy enough in Los Cabos or Tijuana. See relevant sections for details.

Tijuana and around

American day-trippers have been coming to **TIJUANA**, the definitive booze-soaked border town, in significant numbers since the 1950s. Visits crashed ninety percent between 2005 and 2009 thanks to escalating drug-related violence and subsequent US travel warnings (see box, p.468), but things are much improved since then, and the main commercial drag, **Avenida Revolución**, or **La Revo**, has recovered some of its former colour. Indeed, police crackdowns have left central Tijuana safer than ever before, and drug violence rarely affects tourist areas.

Founded in 1889, Tijuana now has a population of almost two million, and despite its often shabby appearance, the region's duty-free status and its legion of **maquiladores** (assembly plants) have helped make it one of the richest cities in

San Diego

San Ysidro
Border Crossing   USA

RESTRICTED
AREA

Taxis

USA

MEXICO

AV FERNANDO SÁNCHEZ AYALA

AV ALDRETE

Footbridge   PLAZA

BAJA CALIFORNIA

AV REVOLUCIÓN

AV NEGRETE

AV PUENTE MÉXICO

CARRANZA

ARIAS BERNAL

CRISTÓBAL COLÓN

GONZÁLEZ ORTEGA

COAHUILA

AV MARTÍNEZ

Monument

AV PUENTE MÉXICO

REYES

AVENIDA

ARTÍCULO 123

Catedral Nuestra
Señora de
Guadalupe

Museo
de Cera

VÍA RÁPIDA ORIENTE

LEÓN

NOVO

GOROSTIZA

BENITO JUÁREZ (2)

Mercado
el Polo

AVENIDA CONSTITUCIÓN

AVENIDA REVOLUCIÓN

AVENIDA MADERO

URBITIA

CARRILLO PUERTO (3)

AVENIDA NIÑOS HÉROES

AVENIDA NEGRETE

AV OCAMPO

LISBOA

DÍAZ MIRÓN (4)

MUTUALISMO

Gandhi
bookshop

Centro
Cultural
Tijuana

Casa de la
Cultura de
Tijuana

EMILIANO ZAPATA (5)

ZONA
CENTRO

EL SÁNCHEZ TABOADA

VICARIO

PASEO

AV MONTE VIDEO

FLORES MAGONI (6)

GALEANA (7)

Frontón
Jai Alai

C/2 OCAMPO

LEÓN

AVENIDA DE LOS HÉROES

INDEPENDENCIA

Plaza
Fiesta

RÍO DE
JANEIRO
ROMA

RAMPA IDEPENDENCIA

AV MIGUEL HIDALGO (8)

GUADALUPE
VICTORIA

GENOVA ALLENDE

Sanborn's

Ignacio Zaragoza (9)

Mercado
Miguel
Hidalgo

Citibank

ESPAÑA
CASTELLÓN

SANTIAGO

AV INDEPENDENCIA

AV ABASOLO

DABRA AV

AV MINA

HUITZITZIL

JUAN SARABIA

C/2 QUINTANA ROO

RÍO ZUCHIATE

ZONA
RÍO

HUMBARGO

JIMÉNEZ

DOCE

RÍO COLORADO

MARIANO ARISTA

Vinos L. A.
Cetto

BOULEVARD AGUA CALIENTE

PRIMO VERDAD

CAÑÓN JHONSON NORTE

AGUSTÍN MELGAR

EMETERIO GONZÁLEZ

MANUEL NÁJERA

DURANGO

COLOMBIA

GUADALUPE VICTORIA

BLV FUNDADORES

AV AGUA CALIENTE

ABELARDO RODRÍGUEZ

LEONA VICARIO

FCO MÁRQUEZ

JESÚS NÚÑEZ

AV CUB 20-30

ESPAÑA

FRANCIA

NOVIEMBRE

SANTOS DIEGO CARO

CORONA

FRANCIA   FRANCIA

HERMOSILLO

LERDO

TAMPICO

JOHNSON SUR

PASEO CUMBRES DEL MALTRATA

Ensenada via HWY 1 free road

■ DRINKING & NIGHTLIFE	
El Dandy Del Sur	1
El Lugar del Nopal	3
La Mezcalera	2
Plaza Fiesta	5
Las Pulgas	4
La Taberna TJ	6

● EATING	
Caesar's	1
Cheripan	9
Chiki Jai	2
La Diferencia	6
Mariscos El Mazateño	3
Misión 19	5
La Querencia	8
Tacos Salceados	10
Tortas del Washmobile	4
Villa Saverios	7

0	500
metres	

Mexico. The city has developed dynamic **arts** and **culinary** scenes, with institutions like Centro Cultural Tijuana (CECUT) emerging as a breeding ground for home-grown artistic and cultural movements. In the **Zona Río**, beyond the areas where most tourists venture, you'll find sophisticated restaurants, clubs and modern concrete and glass buildings, offering the best glimpse of Tijuana's other life – one that has more in common with San Diego than the adult-themed carnival atmosphere of La Revo. And the **food** is fabulous – Tijuana excels at tasty street snacks but also boasts some of the best restaurants in Mexico.

✈ *Tijuana International Airport*

TIJUANA

■ ACCOMMODATION	
Lucerna	3
Nelson	1
Hotel Ticuán	2
Tijuana Marriott	4

Zona Centro

If you're only in town to spend a few hours, you need not wander far from the stream of bars, dance clubs and souvenir stalls on **Avenida Revolución** between calles 1a and 8a, in the **Zona Centro**. Despite a small increase in drug-related shootings between 2013 and 2014, with plenty of police around, the main drag has been generally safe since then (take the usual precautions at night). The tourist offices are here (see p.533), as is *Caesar's*, the landmark restaurant (see p.534), and a tacky wax museum, but you'll also see Tijuana's "famous" **donkeys** on street corners – painted

9

to look like zebras (seriously). Check out **Pasaje Rodríguez** (just south of Calle 3), a passage lined with murals and independent stores, for a taster of Tijuana's artsy side.

Zona Río

When the lure of cheap souvenirs and beers begins to pall, you'll do yourself a favour by heading east to the **Zona Río**; the district's backbone, Paseo de los Héroes, is Tijuana's grandest boulevard and contains the city's best restaurants, malls and cultural attractions.

Centro Cultural Tijuana

Paseo de los Héroes 9350, at Independencia • ☎ 664 687 9600, ⓦ cecut.gob.mx • **Museo El Cubo** Tues–Sun 10am–7pm • M$48 (Sun free) • **Temporary art exhibits** Tues–Sun 10am–7pm • Free • **IMAX theatre** Mon–Fri 4–9pm, Sat & Sun 11am–7pm • M$48 • **Jardín Caracol** Daily 10am–7pm • Free

The prestigious **Centro Cultural Tijuana**, or CECUT, is home to a major performance space, temporary art exhibits and an **IMAX** movie theatre – the brown globe the cinema is housed in gives the complex its nickname, "La Bola". There's also a tranquil garden dotted with replicas of Mesoamerican sculpture, a café, the absorbing **Museo de las Californias** (see below) and **Museo El Cubo**, an imaginative gallery designed by local architect Eugenio Velásquez, which houses innovative contemporary artwork.

Museo de las Californias

Paseo de los Héroes 9350, at Independencia • Tues–Sun 10am–7pm • M$27 • ☎ 664 687 9635, ⓦ cecut.gob.mx

By far the most rewarding part of the cultural centre is the **Museo de las Californias**, which chronicles the history of Baja California with scale models, old maps, artefacts and English labelling. The reproductions of cave paintings and Spanish missions are especially good, and there's information on Baja's now extinct Native American tribes such as the Guaycura. Aspects of the region's modern history – from the development of Tijuana and Mexicali to Chinese immigration and the Mexican Revolution – are covered in detail.

ARRIVAL AND DEPARTURE

TIJUANA

BY PLANE

The Aeropuerto Internacional de Tijuana (☎ 664 607 8200) is 6km east of downtown, next to the US border on the Carretera Aeropuerto (the airport now features a pedestrian skybridge across the border; see opposite). Taxi rates are tied to a seven-zone system; most places in the Zona Centro should be M$240 (or M$215 to the Zona Río). Alternatively, city buses (around M$10–12) pick up passengers in front of the terminal. Tijuana is a hub for Aeroméxico, which operates daily flights to/from eleven Mexican cities, and also serves as the base for low-cost Volaris; time-saving connections include flights to Hermosillo, La Paz, Los Mochis, Mazatlán, Puerto Vallarta, Los Cabos and Zacatecas, as well as the Aéreo Calafia flight to Loreto.

BY BUS

The large Central de Autobuses (☎ 664 621 2982), at Lázaro Cárdenas 15751, is north of the river and 6km east of the city centre. Local buses (M$10–12) marked "Centro" take 30min to get to the centre of Tijuana via C 2a; taxis should charge M$75 or US$10 (get a ticket from the booth outside). You can take hourly Greyhound services direct to the US from here (San Diego US$12.50–14.50; 1hr 10min), or numerous destinations in Mexico; buses to Ensenada (M$155) and Mexicali (M$260) are most frequent.

Destinations Ensenada (hourly; 1hr 45min); Guadalajara (every 30min; 36hr); Guerrero Negro (3–4 daily; 12hr); La Paz (3–4 daily; 24hr); Los Mochis (every 30min; 19hr); Loreto (3–4 daily; 18hr); Mexicali (every 30min; 3hr); Mexico City (hourly; 44hr).

TIJUANA WINE TASTING

If you're not planning to visit any of Mexico's wine-growing regions, stop in at **Vinos L.A. Cetto** (Mon–Sat 10am–5pm; ☎ 664 685 3031, ⓦ cettowines.com), 3km southwest of La Revo at Av Cañón Jhonson 2108. One of the largest producers in the Valle de Guadalupe (see p.543), their Tijuana outpost offers tastings (*traditionales* M$2, *reserva* M$5) and the chance to tour the packing area and underground cellars.

TIJUANA–SAN DIEGO SKYBRIDGE

A pedestrian skybridge dubbed Cross-Border Xpress (Ⓦ crossborderxpress.com) now spans the US-Mexico border at Tijuana's airport, connecting with a new passenger building on the San Diego side. At the time of writing ground transportation on the US side was still being worked out, but the link will make direct transfers between the airport and the US much faster.

BY TAXI (ROSARITO)

The easiest way to travel between Rosarito and Tijuana is to take a yellow taxi – they charge around US$25–30

(M$435–520) from the border. Tijuana airport taxis will charge at least M$550.

CROSSING THE US BORDER

Crossing the US-Mexico border at Tijuana is a simple but often time-consuming affair, given the volume of traffic. Allow more time heading into the US, especially during morning and evening rush hours, when the wait for cars and pedestrians can take up to 3hr. Both San Ysidro and Otay Mesa (around 8km east of San Ysidro) crossings are open 24hr. See p.29 & p.31 for more on border formalities. If you're planning to head straight out of Tijuana by bus, it makes more sense to take the hourly Greyhound service (see opposite) from the San Diego bus terminal at 120 West Broadway direct to Tijuana's long-distance bus station.

VIA SAN YSIDRO

On foot The San Diego Trolley (US$2.50) connects downtown San Diego to the border at San Ysidro (45min), or you can leave your car at Border Station Parking, 4570 Camino de la Plaza (US ☎ 619 428 1422; Mon–Thurs US$7/24hr, Fri–Sun US$10/24hr) in San Ysidro. Taxis from San Diego Airport to the border are around US$60 on the meter. You can just walk across the border, but remember to stop at the *migración* office and ask for a multiple migration form or "FMT" (the Non-immigrant Fee is M$330/US$20), if you intend to go further than Ensenada (these are not handed out automatically – leaving the States there is no US immigration and only very casual Mexico checks for pedestrians). Take the left-hand exit for taxis (see below), or the right-hand exit if you prefer the 20min walk to La Revo; it's a fairly well-signed route via the footbridge and along C 1a to Av Revolución. It's perfectly safe during the day, but it's best to take a taxi at night.

By car If driving across the border, remember to pull in at the *migración* office to get your Immigration Form (see p.29). Once across the border, the road splits off into a series of right-hand exits to Playas de Tijuana and the scenic toll road south to Ensenada; C 3a (Carillo Puerto), which heads downtown; and Paseo de los Héroes into Zona Río. Streets are well marked – at times half a block in advance – and blue signs on lampposts identify the distance to prominent locations. If you're taking your car off the Baja Peninsula, you'll need to get a temporary importation vehicle permit at the branch of Banjercito at the border (for details, see p.29).

Entering the US Entering the US can be extremely time-consuming at Tijuana (1–3hr), and Canadians and even US citizens now require a passport to enter. Everyone else needs a visa or a visa-waiver to enter the US (crossing the land border does not require ESTA approval, but you will need to fill in an I-94W form, and pay US$6; see p.29).

INFORMATION

Tourist offices Coming from the US, the most convenient tourist office is right at the border, at the pedestrian entry point (Mon–Sat 9am–6pm, Sun 9am–3pm; ☎ 664 683 1405). The main state-run tourist information centre is on Revolución between calles 2a and 3a (Mon–Fri 8am–8pm,

Sat & Sun 9am–1pm; ☎ 664 973 0430); there's another information booth on Revolución between calles 3a and 4a (daily 9am–6pm, closed alternate Weds; ☎ 664 685 3117). For general information call ☎ 078 or visit Ⓦ venatijuana .com.

GETTING AROUND

By bus Tijuana by bus is cheap but confusing – taxis are easier to use. The system includes larger city buses (*camiones*) and smaller minibuses or old school buses (known as *calafias*), but all of them should have the final destination on the windscreen, such as "Central Camionera" (rates range M$5–7) – just flag them down on the street. There are no route maps, however, and you'll need to speak Spanish well to use them.

By taxi The easiest and quickest way to get around is by taxi.

Cheapest are the fixed-route taxis (*los taxis de ruta*), which operate more like small minibuses. Regular cabs generally fall into two groups: the yellow *taxis amarillos*, which don't use meters and follow a fixed-rate system, and the independent *taxis libres*, which sometimes use the meter but usually set their own prices. Yellow taxis should charge M$75 from the border to Zona Río or La Revo (they'll ask for US$5), M$150 to the airport and M$120 to the bus station (check the prices on the board at the taxi rank; you can pay in US$). *Taxis*

9

libres will usually charge M$50 for trips within the centre and M$60–80 to the bus station. Uber (ⓦuber.com), the ride-sharing service, is now available in Tijuana, with rates between La Revo and the airport M$70–90, and M$65–85 between La Revo and the bus station.

By car All the major firms have desks at Tijuana airport: Budget ☎664 634 3303; Hertz ☎664 607 3950; Thrifty ☎664 683 8130.

ACCOMMODATION

Lucerna Paseo de los Héroes 10902 (Zona Río) ☎664 633 3900, ⓦhoteleslucerna.com. The six-storey main building and three annexes surround an outdoor pool with a mini waterfall. The best rooms, along with two restaurants and a bar, face this courtyard area. Every room has satellite TV, a balcony, coffee-maker, a/c and purified water. M$1665

Nelson Revolución 721, at C 1a (Zona Centro) ☎664 685 4302. Right at the top of La Revo, this stucco palace can't be beaten for location or price, but the street noise can be relentless at times. *Nelson* is one of La Revo's oldest hotels (open since 1948), so although the rooms have a/c and cable TV with a few channels, they're otherwise quite dated and worn. Free wi-fi in the lobby. M$615

★**Hotel Ticuán** 8190 C 8, at Revolución (Zona Centro) ☎664 685 8078, ⓦhotelticuan.mx. By far the best hotel in downtown Tijuana, with a convenient location just off La Revo and a 20min walk from the border. Rooms are spacious, modern and come with free wi-fi and flat-screen TVs with cable. Friendly, English-speaking staff complete the experience. M$1090

Tijuana Marriott Agua Caliente 11553 (Zona Río) ☎664 622 6600, ⓦmarriott.com. The former *Emporio* has been revamped as an upmarket *Marriott* with all the extras – wi-fi, business centre, gym and pool – though the rooms are fairly standard business hotel affairs. Free parking for guests and reasonable online rates make this a good deal. M$1900

EATING

ZONA CENTRO

★**Caesar's** Revolución 1071, between C 4 and C 5 ☎664 685 1927, ⓦcaesartijuana.com. Legend has it that Caesar Cardini first whipped up his eponymous salad in Tijuana in 1924, and this shrine to his memory still prepares the dish tableside with raw egg and garlic, Parmesan cheese, anchovies and hearts of Romaine lettuce (M$95) in an elaborate ceremony. The rest of the menu is continental-style, with pastas, steaks and the like (most mains M$235–260). Sun–Thurs noon–10pm, Fri & Sat noon–midnight.

Chiki Jai Revolución 1388, at C 7 ☎664 685 4955. Enticing Spanish Basque *taberna*, draped with bullfighting memorabilia, fading photos of Tijuana and paintings of Don Quixote. Come here for decent tapas (M$30–130), paella, sangria and *vino tinto* (M$80 for half litre). Open since 1947: the likes of Errol Flynn, Rita Hayworth and Ava Gardner once ate here. Main courses M$120–180. Sun–Fri 11am–9pm, Sat 11am–10pm.

★**Tortas del Washmobile** Agua Caliente, at Jalisco (fifteen blocks south of La Revo). This famous stall was established in 1964 next to a petrol station with a car wash (now defunct), and serves only one thing: a mouthwatering *mesquite* grilled steak sandwich marinated in a zesty sauce (*torta carne asada*). Served on *pambaso* rolls; ask for *con todo* and you'll also get heaps of guacamole and a topping of red onions, tomatoes and salsa (around M$45). Taxis should know it. Daily 8am–4pm, or until they run out of bread.

ZONA RÍO

Cheripan Escuadrón 201, no. 3151 ☎664 622 9730, ⓦcheripan.com. Argentine grill lauded for its succulent steaks (M$200–400), chops and extensive wine list, as well

as the city's best fries, coated in parsley and garlic (M$48). Mon–Wed 1–11pm, Thurs–Sat 1pm–1am, Sun 1–10pm.

La Diferencia Sánchez Taboada 10521 ☎664 634 7078, ⓦladiferencia.com. *Diferencia* has a more daring menu than most places in Tijuana, with tasty interpretations of Mexico's pre-Hispanic cuisine. Unfamiliar dishes like beef-tongue strips with chiles, the Aztec delicacy crêpes Cuitlacoche (an edible corn fungus) and prickly-pear salad are made more appealing within a romantic setting complete with a courtyard and fountain. Mains M$160–280. Mon–Sat 8am–10.30pm, Sun 8am–6pm.

Mariscos El Mazateño Calzada Tecnológico 473 at Popotla, Fracc Tomás Aquino ☎664 607 1377. Take a taxi to this iconic *taquería* for their spicy Sinaloan-style *Taco Mazatena* (*camarón enchilado* or shrimp taco), and filling smoked marlin tacos (M$17–50). Tables inside, but most locals eat standing up or crouched on the sidewalk outside. Cash only. Daily 7am–8pm.

★**Misión 19** Misión de San Javier 10643 ☎664 634 2493, ⓦmision19.com. Javier Plascencia's fashionable temple to "Baja Med" cuisine, all concrete, wood and floor-to-ceiling windows, features innovative menus fed by local wine and produce: think Peking duck with kumquat, sweet potato and blood orange sauce, risotto with beans and truffles and charred octopus with pistachio, *garbanzo* beans and smoky *habanero* sauce. Most dishes M$150–450. Mon–Thurs 1–10pm, Fri & Sat 1–11pm.

★**La Querencia** Escuadrón 201, no. 3110 ☎664 972 9935, ⓦlaquerenciatj.com. Established in 2006 by celebrity chef Miguel Guerrero, this fancy restaurant with lacquered steel dining tables and open kitchens is one of the creators of contemporary Baja Med cuisine, a blend of traditional Mexican ingredients with Mediterranean flavours. Try the *betabel* (beet) carpaccio, oyster (*ostión*) tacos or more substantial fish of the day (mains M$130–300). Mon–Thurs 1–11pm, Fri & Sat 1pm–midnight.

★**Tacos Salceados** Ermita Nte 30-A. Known locally as *La Ermita*, after the street, this knocks out the best beef tacos in the city with at least fifteen spicy salsas to choose from. Chef Javier Campos Guttiérez is also known for his gourmet creations such as smoked salmon, shrimp and strawberry, or *nopal* tacos (prickly-pear cactus). Seating is available here, but it's so popular there's almost always a wait for tables. Tacos from M$40; cash only. Wed–Mon 6pm–midnight.

Villa Saverios Sánchez Taboada and Escuadrón 201 ☎ 664 686 6442, ⊛ villasaverios.com. Set inside a marble, Tuscan-themed villa, this is another superb exponent of Baja Med cuisine, with such dishes as classic chicken cordon bleu (M$255) and "Retro" scampi, the classic dish from the 1970s (pan-seared shrimp/crab, with garlic lemon and caper cream sauce; M$285). Situated in the heart of Tijuana's Zona Gastronómica. Daily 1pm–midnight.

DRINKING AND NIGHTLIFE

Traditionally, the rowdiest action in Tijuana is along **La Revo**, where numerous pubs pump out rock music and hip-hop – aim for "La Sexta" (C 6 off Revolución) for a more contemporary cluster of bars. Most locals and visitors in the know shun La Revo in favour of the clubs and bars clustered around the shopping areas of **Zona Río**. The city has also experienced a boom in **microbreweries** in recent years, with Plaza Fiesta (see below) a good place to start.

BARS

★**El Dandy Del Sur** C 6 (Flores Magón) no. 2030, between La Revo and Madero ☎ 664 688 0052. Open since 1957 but immortalized by local techno group the Nortec Collective in 2005, this jukebox bar just off La Revo is popular with artists and plenty of locals escaping the tourist drag. The walls are decorated with mirrors and pictures of movie stars; tends to attract serious drinkers long into the early hours. Daily 6pm–5am.

La Mezcalera C 6 no. 8267 (between Revolución and Madero) ☎ 664 688 0384. Friendly bar and restaurant that looks like a shopfront, featuring, unsurprisingly, mescal, the traditional and extremely potent Mexican spirit made from the agave plant. They usually have at least six different brands of the stuff and nine different types of crema de mescal (a blend of mescal and agave syrup). Daily 5pm–2am.

★**Plaza Fiesta** Paseo de los Héroes 1001. Can't decide where to go? Locals often head here without a specific place in mind, preferring to wander between the bars and clubs until they find a scene that appeals to them. In recent years local craft microbreweries have moved in (8 at last count), with *El Tigre* (Tues–Fri 1pm–2am, Sat 10am–3am, Sun 10am–7pm) serving Lúdica Artesanal beers, *El Depa* (Wed–Sat 7pm–2am) serving Cerveza Silenus, and tap rooms for *Paralelo 28* (inside *La Plaza*; Tues–Sat 5pm–2am, Sun 1pm–midnight) and Mexicali's Cerveceria Fauna (Sun & Tues 1–10pm, Wed–Sat 1pm–2am).

★**La Taberna TJ** Fundadores 2951 ☎ 664 638 8662, ⊛ tjbeer.com. Home of *Cerveza Tijuana*, the city's acclaimed microbrewery houses a congenial pub, a few minutes' south of La Revo by taxi. Decked out with dark wood panelling and hardwood floors, the pub usually offers five or six hand-crafted Czech-style lagers and a menu of decent bar food. You can look into the brewery floor through a window, but tours must be arranged in advance. Wed 1pm–1am, Thurs–Sat 1pm–2am.

CLUBS

El Lugar del Nopal Callejón 5 de Mayo 1328 ☎ 664 685 1264, ⊛ lugardelnopal.org. This café-cum-performance space is a gathering place for Tijuana's creative class, who turn up for exhibits, screenings and live music. Wed–Sat 8am–midnight.

Las Pulgas Revolución 1127 (between C7 and C8) ☎ 664 685 9594, ⊛ laspulgas.info. Party central on La Revo, a massive club with several rooms pumping out banda, salsa, Latino pop and Norteño, with live bands often supplementing house DJs. Cover normally M$200 at weekends. Daily 9am–6am.

DIRECTORY

Banks and exchange US dollars are accepted almost everywhere in Tijuana, but you do get a slightly better return on pesos. If you're visiting no further south than Ensenada there's really no reason to change your currency – you'll lose in the exchange rate whatever savings you'd get buying in shops. If you do change it's no problem, with *casas de cambio* on virtually every corner. ATMs along Revolución dispense both dollars and pesos.

Books Sanborn's department store, at Revolución 1102 and C 8a (daily 7am–11pm; ☎ 664 688 1433), has books and magazines, some from across the border. The Gandhi bookshop at Paseo Héroes 9111, at General M. Márquez in Zona Río (daily 10am–9pm; ⊛ gandhi.com.mx), also has a good selection.

Consulates Canada, Germán Gedovius 10411, Zona Río ☎ 664 684 0461 (Mon–Fri 9.30am–12.30pm); UK, Salinas 1500 ☎ 664 686 5320; US, Paseo de las Culturas s/n, Mesa de Otay ☎ 664 622 7400, ⊛ tijuana.usconsulate.gov

(Mon–Fri 9am–2pm).
Hospital Centro Medico Excel, Paseo de los Héroes 2507 ☎ 664 634 7001.
Police If you become a victim of crime, a rip-off or simply want to make a complaint, pick up any local phone and dial ☎ 078 (foreign mobiles often cannot connect with this number). Call ☎ 066 for emergencies.
Post office Negrete and C 11a (Mon–Fri 8am–4pm, Sat & Sun 9.30am–1pm), though to send international mail you're better off crossing the border.

Rosarito

To escape the hectic pace and noise of Tijuana, head for the coastal city of **ROSARITO**, about 45 minutes' drive south on the old road to Ensenada. **Beaches** in Tijuana are invariably crowded and dirty, so Rosarito's longer and sandier beach is a good alternative and provides a more restful atmosphere during the week (the water is still chilly, however). Rosarito has been hit hard by US travel warnings since 2009 (even putting off US spring-breakers), though you'll see plenty of domestic tourists on the beach surfing or riding ATVs, horses and camels; visitors (and the city's fourteen thousand expats) rarely experience any trouble. As in Tijuana, US dollars are accepted virtually everywhere.

ARRIVAL AND DEPARTURE

ROSARITO

By bus If you're continuing south to Ensenada and beyond, you can try to pick up long-distance buses (at least hourly) at the *autopista* tollbooth 1km south of the tourist office, past the *Rosarito Beach Hotel*, but it's much easier to head back to Tijuana's main bus station (see p.532).
By car To get to Rosarito from Tijuana, drive south along either the toll (*cuota*; M$31) Hwy-1D or free (*libre*) Hwy-1 for 25km.
By taxi Taxis from the border charge US$25–30 (M$435–520). You can also take one of the cheaper *taxi de ruta* vans that leave from Madero between calles 3 and 4 (around M$20 per person); to get back, try flagging down a *taxi de ruta* on Juárez, Rosarito's main street.

INFORMATION

Rosarito Convention and Visitors' Bureau Runs three tourist information booths during US holidays and special events, the most convenient of which can be found at the Centro Comercial Oceana Plaza, Local 14, Blvd Benito Juárez 907 (Mon–Fri 9am–6pm, Sat 10am–1pm; ☎ 661 612 0396, ⊛ rosarito.org).

ACCOMMODATION

Accommodation prices are highest during Spring Break (Feb/March) and the week after Christmas, but drop considerably the rest of the year. Throughout the year it's advisable to reserve at least a week in advance if you plan on staying Fri or Sat night.

★**Casa Farolito** Bahía 299, San Antonio del Mar ☎ 664 631 3477. Charming B&B right on the beach, 5min drive or taxi ride north of town, with cosy modern rooms, LCD TVs and free wi-fi. No children under 16. **M$2230**
Los Pelicanos Ebano 113 ☎ 661 612 0445, ⊛ los

pelicanosrosarito.com. The stellar beachfront location, cheap rates and terrace bar overlooking the ocean here make up for rather lacklustre, ageing three-star rooms. **M$740**
Rosarito Beach Hotel Benito Juárez 31 ☎ 661 612 0144, US ☎ 1 800 343 8582, ⊛ rosaritobeachhotel.com.

LOBSTER TOWN

Once not much more than a dusty roadside settlement between Rosarito and Ensenada at Hwy-1 km 44, **Puerto Nuevo** is nowadays known the length of the peninsula for its near-fanatical devotion to the local speciality that bears its name: Puerto Nuevo-style grilled Pacific **lobster**. Found off the coast and throughout the rest of the Pacific Rim, these lobsters don't grow as large as their Atlantic counterparts (actually, they're giant langoustines more closely related to shrimps) and they don't have claws, but they're just as delicious.

Choosing where to sample the revered dish is made easy enough by the town's one-way street plan, which juts to the west from Hwy-1; almost every one of the thirty-odd restaurants here serves lobsters the same way, grilled and split in half with beans, rice and warm flour tortillas (M$150–300 depending on the size of the lobster). Most restaurants open 10am to 8pm on weekdays, with some open until 11pm Friday and Saturday. Cash only.

BAJA LEGENDS: HALFWAY HOUSE AND LA FONDA

Some 25km south of Rosarito, the legendary **Halfway House** ("halfway" between Tijuana and Ensenada, at Hwy-1 km 53; ☎661 614 0065; daily 9am–10pm) opened as a cantina in 1922 on a cliff overlooking the ocean. Today the old-fashioned dining room may have changed little since the 1920s, but chef Johnny's menu certainly has: think quality seafood and the infamous "golden cadillac" margaritas.

A little further south, at km 59.5 in La Misión, **La Fonda Hotel** (☎646 155 0308, ✉dmytris lafonda@gmail.com; M$1200; cash only) was established in 1962 by Eve Stocker and is now helmed by the indefatigable Dmytri and Sara (who were in legal dispute with another "La Fonda" next door at the time of research, thus the official name of "Dmytri's Original La Fonda"). The ageing, rustic Mexican inn comes with ocean views, cheap drinks and easy access to the beach (one of the best **surf breaks** in Baja). Eclectic decor, handmade furniture, a breezy deck, and a decent buffet and all-you-can drink Bloody Marys on Sunday (M$225) enhance the experience.

Legendary hotel, established in 1926 and giving the city its name; it's now a mini-village with a spa, restaurants, bars, two pools, time-share apartments, a racquetball court, craft shops, liquor stores, a history museum and an internet café. Many of the rooms have ocean views but are otherwise without charm; request an older room with garden view – they've managed to retain some character. **M$1850**

EATING

La Flor de Michoacan Benito Juárez 291 (Hwy-1) ☎661 612 1858. Founded in 1950 on the north side of town, this popular family restaurant pulls in tourists and locals alike for its piles of crispy *carnitas* (fried pork) served with rice, beans, guacamole and fresh tortillas. You'll spend around M$150/person; throw in a pitcher or two of strawberry margaritas. Mon–Fri 9am–9pm, Sat & Sun 8am–9pm.

★**Mi Casa Supper Club** Estero 54, San Antonio del Mar (off Hwy-1D) ☎661 609 3459. This wildly popular restaurant from Moroccan born chef Bo Bendana, just north of town (a short walk from *Casa Farolito*), offers a spread of exquisite fusion dishes ("Moroxican"), from the signature slow-cooked lamb with spiced prune *mole* to Moroccan-spice crusted tuna with black farfalle pasta. Tapas-style small plates from M$80–130. Thurs–Sat 5–10pm, Sun 3–8pm.

Tacos Tijuana Junior Popotla 3103, Carretera Libre

Rosarito–Ensenada (Hwy-1) km 30 ☎661 100 2598. Another local favourite, this diner-like place stands on the main road south of downtown. Try their *Plato Fiesta*, which comes with local fish, shrimp, calamari, octopus and tacos (enough for two people). Their trademark tacos are pretty good too; the *taco gobernador* is crammed with shrimp marinated in chiles and lemons (M$40–75). Daily 11am–11pm.

★**Tacos El Yaqui** La Palma 51, at Mar del Norte ☎661 612 1352. This small taco stand knocks out some of the best (and biggest) *carne asada* tacos on the coast. Tacos (flour tortillas only) with all the toppings are around M$30; you can add cheese for a couple more pesos. You'll find it one block off Juárez at the south end of town (across from Festival Plaza's parking lot). Cash only. Mon–Fri 7.30am–4pm & till 9pm Sat & Sun.

DRINKING AND NIGHTLIFE

Traditionally, Rosarito's most popular bars and clubs have been contained within what's known as the Barbachano Zone, the area between Juárez (Hwy-1) and Coronado downtown. Thanks to the drop in US visitors (especially college students), things have quietened down considerably in recent years – visit *Papas and Beer* to check out the latest situation.

Papas and Beer Coronado 400, at Eucalipto ☎664 612 0444, ⊕rosarito.papasandbeer.com. College party-goers flock to this mega club, the largest on the West Coast (with a pool, mechanical bull and volleyball court thrown in). Tacos, burritos, quesadillas, nachos and fries help soak up the Corona and tequila shots. Busy Fri & Sat but often empty on weekdays. Daily 10am–3am.

Ensenada

Perched on the edge of the Bahía de Todos Santos, 100km south of Tijuana, the attractive port of **ENSENADA** is far calmer, cheaper and smaller than its northern rival, making for an inviting pit stop and jumping-off point for the **wineries** to the east. Like

9 Tijuana, Ensenada is a relatively recent creation by Mexican standards, despite being officially "founded" (ie discovered by the Spanish) in 1542; nothing much happened until 1872, when gold was unearthed in nearby Real de Castillo. Ensenada was gradually developed as a port, the modern town effectively planned and developed by American investor George H. Sisson and the British-owned Mexican Land & Colonization Co in the 1880s. The town remained a backwater, however, with tourism and modern development only taking off in the 1950s. Note that US cruise excursions to Ensenada are booming, so be prepared for crowds on days that ships are in port (mainly during the summer months).

Downtown

Ensenada's downtown is centred on the parallel **Bulevar Lázaro Cárdenas** (the waterfront) and **Avenida López Mateos** (or C 1a, "La Primera"). On the latter you'll find scores of souvenir shops and outfits offering sport-fishing trips, as well as the bulk of the bars, hotels and restaurants. The six-block-long malecón, running along the waterfront parallel to Lázaro Cárdenas, is where the city's residents gather for sunset strolls and special events; the centrepiece is the **Plaza Ventana al Mar**, with its monumental Mexican flag visible all over town. In contrast, the real commercial heart of town is **Avenida Juárez**, five blocks north, where you'll find all the Mexican chain stores.

ENSENADA

Terminal de Autobuses

■ ACCOMMODATION	
El Cortez	3
Ensenada Backpacker	2
Estero Beach Resort	1
Hotel Coral & Marina	6
Hotel Misión	
Santa Isabel	5
San Nicolás Hotel	
& Casino	4

Parque Revolución

Bodegas de Santo Tomás

Calimex Supermarket

Chapultepec Hills

Museo de la Exaduana Marítima

Museo Histórico Regional

Taxi Rank

Mercado de Mariscos

Centro Cultural Riviera

Centro Estatal de la Artes

Museo El Caracol

All Saints Bay

Cruise ship terminal

● EATING		Manzanilla	8
Bronco's	2	Mi Kasa	6
Ceviche de		El Rey Sol	5
Guerrerense	4	Tacos Fenix	1
El Charro	3	Tacos Lucero	7

■ DRINKING & NIGHTLIFE	
Bar Andaluz	4
Cervecería Wendlandt	3
Hussong's Cantina	1
Papas & Beer	2

0 — 300 metres

Tijuana (100km) via HWY 1 Free and Toll Roads, Tecate & Valle de Guadalupe via HWY 3

Mercado de Mariscos
Malecón, at Miramar • Daily 6.30am–7pm

At the northwestern end of the malecón, the **Mercado de Mariscos** (aka Mercado Negro) contains numerous stalls selling the day's catches. The diversity of what's on display – from squirming eel and smoked fish to giant abalone – is impressive, and it's a good place to try the town's lauded **fish tacos**, which were supposedly invented in Ensenada and have been served at the market since it opened in 1958 (see p.543).

Museo Histórico Regional de Ensenada
Gastélum 56, between López Mateos (C 1) and Virgilio Uribe • Tues–Sun 9am–5pm • M$27, free Sun • ☎ 646 178 3692

For a general history of the peoples and cultures of Baja California, head over to the **Museo Histórico Regional de Ensenada**, built in 1886 as a military barracks and serving as the Ensenada jail until 1986. The old cells and rooms now act as galleries chronicling the history of the building, the town and the region with rare black-and-white photos, artefacts and displays (mostly Spanish only).

Centro Cultural Riviera de Ensenada
1421 Lázaro Cárdenas, at Club Rotario • Daily 8am–7pm • Free • ☎ 646 176 4310, ⓦ rivieradeensenada.com.mx • **Museo de Historia** Tues–Sun 9am–2pm & 3–5pm • M$20 • ☎ 646 177 0594

The Riviera del Pacífico, a former casino and hotel completed in lavish Spanish Revival style in 1930, is now the bayfront **Centro Cultural Riviera de Ensenada**. You can wander through the tranquil gardens, grab a drink at *Bar Andaluz* (see p.543), or visit the absorbing **Museo de Historia** inside. Exhibition rooms here focus on prehistoric and native cultures of Baja California, the eighteenth-century Spanish missions and the ultimate decimation of the native population through disease, all via old photos, objects and labelling in Spanish and English. The mammoth complex opposite the cultural centre is the **Caracol (Museo de Ciencas y Acuario)**, a fancy science museum showcasing the geology and environments of Baja – its opening has been delayed for years thanks to budget shortfalls, so check ⓦ caracol.org.mx for the latest news.

Museo de la Exaduana Marítima
Ryerson 99, at Ruiz • Mon–Fri 9am–4pm • Free • ☎ 646 178 2531

The tiny **Museo de la Exaduana Marítima** is located within a wooden Victorian building that was actually shipped over from England in 1887. Initially occupied by the American Co (developer of the city), it was taken over by Mexican Land & Colonization Co before becoming the customs house in 1922. Today it houses temporary exhibitions on the trade history of the region, such as artefacts recovered from the wrecks of Spanish galleons.

Bodegas de Santo Tomás
Miramar 666, between calles 6a and 7a • Daily 10am–9pm; tours daily 10am, 1pm & 3pm • M$300 for tastings and tour • ☎ 646 178 3333, ⓦ santo-tomas.com

Established in 1888, the **Bodegas de Santo Tomás**, one of the peninsula's largest and oldest wineries, offers tastings and tours of its Ensenada museum and premises. You can also visit the main **vineyard** (daily 10am–5pm; call ahead) on the site of the old Santo Tomás mission. It's the only major producer not located in the Valle de Guadalupe (see p.543) – you'll find it off Hwy-1 at km 49 (no public transport).

The beaches
Although it enjoys an enviable position on the Pacific, Ensenada lacks good **beaches**, and to find a decent stretch of sand you'll have to head about half an hour south. As in other parts of Baja it can be difficult to get to many of the best beaches without your own transport; however, you can catch a local bus from Cárdenas (every 30min; M$12)

9

to **San Miguel**, 11km north of downtown. Devotees claim San Miguel has the **best waves** in northern Baja and it's been a surf hot spot for years; huge swells barrel down a rocky headland here, and it's definitely not for beginners. It also gets very crowded, so arrive early. Taxis charge around M$150 both ways. The best **beaches** for swimming and sunbathing are at **Estero**, some 10km to the south and 2km off the main road.

La Bufadora

The most popular natural attraction in the Ensenada area, **La Bufadora** ("the snorter") is actually a blowhole, where the combined action of wind, waves and an incoming tide periodically forces a huge jet of sea water up through a vent in the roof of an undersea cavern, in ideal conditions (high tide) reaching 25–30m. Even though it's more than 20km off the main road (34km from Ensenada), and accessed by a gauntlet of souvenir stands, it's definitely worth a visit. To get there, catch a local bus at Cárdenas and Macheros labelled "Maneadero" and tell the driver you want to visit La Bufadora. Where he drops you you'll be able to catch another local bus to the blowhole at the end of Punta Banda. The whole trip should take around one hour and the buses cost around M$15 each. Taxis are open to negotiation, but tend to ask for M$600 return (or US$10 per person, minimum four), including an hour at the site.

ARRIVAL AND DEPARTURE
ENSENADA

By bus The tiny Terminal de Autobuses is at C 11a and Riveroll; there's a café and ATM but not much else. To reach the bayfront, turn right out of the station and head down Riveroll – it's a long walk with luggage (over 1km). Taxis charge around M$75; local buses are around M$12. Getting to Tijuana (M$155) is easy from here, but most of the buses to points south in Baja are *de paso* (passing through), so try to book in advance. Most buses to Tijuana make for the inconvenient central bus station, but some go direct to the airport or the border (*frontera*) – make sure you get the right one (if you're staying near La Revo in Tijuana, get the bus to the border).'Buses to Guadalajara and Mexico City

are also less frequent, and you have to change in Mexicali for most other destinations.

Destinations Guerrero Negro (6 daily; 10hr); La Paz (4 daily; 22hr); Loreto (4 daily; 16hr); Mexicali (4 daily; 4hr); San Felipe (2 daily; 4hr); Tijuana (hourly; 1hr 30min).

By car You'll pay three tolls coming south from Tijuana (total M$93) on Hwy-1D (*cuota*). Hwy-1, Hwy-1D and Hwy-3 merge into one four-lane local road that, once downtown, becomes Blvd Lázaro Cárdenas (also known as Blvd Costero) and runs along the waterfront. Entering town from the south is a bit messier. Hwy-1 enters the city as Av Reforma; to get downtown, turn left on Libramiento Sur.

INFORMATION AND ACTIVITIES

Tourist information The helpful Ensenada Visitor Information Centre (daily 8am–8pm; ☎646 178 2411, ⓦ proturismoensenada.org.mx) is at the Hwy-1 entrance into town at Lázaro Cárdenas 540 and Teniente Azueta, with a smaller booth in Plaza Cívica de la Patria, on Cárdenas at Macheros (daily Tues–Sun 10am–6pm; ☎646

178 3070). The state-run tourism centre is at the southern end of the malecón at Lázaro Cárdenas 609 and Los Rocas (Mon–Fri 8am–5pm, Sat & Sun 9am–1pm; ☎646 178 8578, ⓦ ensenadavivela.com).

Whale-watching tours From mid-December to mid-April, the California grey whale migration from the Arctic to

---

BOATS, BIKES AND THE BAJA 1000

Ensenada hosts numerous events aimed squarely at the large US encampment in town, from sporting contests to food and wine festivals. The **Newport to Ensenada Yacht Race** (ⓦ nosa .org) in April is one of the largest international regattas in the world, with yachts leaving Newport, California, on a Friday afternoon and finishing in Ensenada a day later, when the partying commences and the town gets packed. April (and September) is also when the **Rosarito–Ensenada Bike Ride** (ⓦ rosaritoensenada.com) draws thousands of cyclists here for the scenic 80km "fun ride", while off-road racing is the focus during the **Baja 500** (June) and the **Baja 1000** (Nov).

CLOCKWISE FROM TOP MISIÓN DE NUESTRA SEÑORA DE LORETO (P.559); BAHÍA CONCEPCION (P.558); VALLE DE GUADALUPE VINEYARDS (P.543) >

RUTA DEL VINO

MUSEO

SAN ANTONIO DE LAS MINAS 10 KM

EL PORVENIR 21 KM

9

the peninsula's Pacific coast can be seen on daily whale-watching tours from Ensenada, although what you'll see is nothing compared to Baja California Sur (seee box, p.551 & p.553). There are several tour companies in the harbour that offer half-day excursions for about US$30 (M$525) per person. See ⓦsergiosfishing.com.

ACCOMMODATION

If you're hoping for somewhere to **stay** at the weekend – the best time for nightlife – book ahead or arrive early; during the week there should be no problem. Though **rates** in general are high (and higher still at weekends), you'll find cheaper places on López Mateos. The best **resorts** tend to be located a long taxi ride from the centre, and are only really practical for those with cars.

CENTRO

El Cortez López Mateos 1089 ☎646 178 2306, ⓦbajainn.com. The *Baja Inn* hotels are the northern peninsula's three-star stalwarts: rather plain, but always clean and packed with basic amenities like a/c, TV, a gym and a heated pool. M$1200

Ensenada Backpacker C 2, no. 1429 (between Floresta and Guadalupe) ☎646 177 1758, ⓦensenada backpacker.com. One of the few true hostels in Baja is a great deal, with clean dorm beds from US$20-equivalent, free bus station pick-up, breakfast, wi-fi and luggage storage. Shared bathrooms. Dorms M$300

Hotel Misión Santa Isabel Lázaro Cárdenas, at Castillo 1119 ☎646 178 3616, ⓦhotelmisionsantaisabel .com. This giant 1950s hotel complex near the waterfront was given a comprehensive makeover in 2011, though the colonial-style tiled floors, domed ceilings, arched windows and tapestries remain. Free wi-fi. M$1200

San Nicolás Hotel & Casino López Mateos 1536, at Guadalupe ☎646 176 1901, ⓦsnhotelcasino.com. The closest hotel to the downtown waterfront has popular packages that include meals and deals with local aquatic outfitters. Murals by a protégé of Diego Rivera adorn many of the public spaces, and there's an Olympic-size swimming pool – the general effect is of a slightly quirky, 1970s throwback. Breakfast is always good, as are the margaritas. M$1200

OUTSIDE ENSENADA

Estero Beach Resort Lupita Novelo, off Hwy-1 around 13km south of downtown ☎646 176 6225, ⓦhotel esterobeach.com. Best-value resort in the region; some rooms are starting to show their age, but come with terracotta-tiled floors, cable TV, private patios and gardens. Most offer views across the private beach and bay. The pool, bars and restaurants are all excellent, though taxis will charge you at least US$20 (M$350) for rides into town. M$2250

Hotel Coral & Marina Hwy-1 km 103, Zona Playitas 3421 ☎646 175 0000, ⓦhotelcoral.com. This luxurious option is popular with American yachties for the excellent on-site marina facilities, and is a great choice for families or for those looking for a smart resort; standard rooms come with breezy ocean views and all the amenities, but it will cost you at least M$100 to take a taxi into town. M$1950

EATING

Bronco's López Mateos 1525 ☎646 176 4900, ⓦbroncossteakhouse.net. The five blocks that separate *Bronco's* from the heart of the tourist district will save you a good M$100 on a filet mignon (M$291). With spurs everywhere, the Wild West theme is over the top, but live bands on weekends add to the authenticity. Good-value lunch buffet Sat & Sun. Daily 8am–10.30pm.

★**Ceviche de Guerrerense** López Mateos and Alvarado ☎646 174 2114. You'll see tiny mobile seafood stalls all over Ensenada, but you should definitely try this one helmed by Doña Sabina Bandera (now a minor celebrity thanks to US TV chef Anthony Bourdain. Fresh fish, shrimp, clam, sea urchin (*erizo*), mussel tostadas and crab *ceviche* (from M$20–50), as well as sea cucumber for the more adventurous, have been served here since 1960. Go early; cash only. Wed–Mon 10am–5pm.

El Charro López Mateos 454 ☎646 178 2114. Knocking out crisp rotisserie chicken since 1956 (you'll see them roasting in the window), but also serves the full roster of classic Mexican dishes (average M$150–225; whole chicken from M$250). Tues–Sun 10am–11pm.

Manzanilla Teniente Azueta 139 ☎646 175 7073, ⓦrmanzanilla.com. This outpost of celebrity chef Benito Molina next to the port features a spacious, antique bar decorated with local art and wonderful food, from posh Spanish bar snacks like fresh sardines on toast to dinners featuring specials such as *pescado en caldo* and seafood risotto. Pricey: expect to spend over M$1000 for a meal for two. Wed–Sat 1pm–1am, Sun 1–6pm.

Mi Kaza Riveroll 87 ☎646 178 8211, ⓦmikaza restaurante.com. This cafeteria opens to a busy breakfast crowd and finishes with family dinners. In three meals you can get a broad sampling of Mexican home cooking, from *huevos con nopales* (eggs with cactus) in the morning, to chicken in *mole* at lunch and deep-fried tacos or *menudo* (stewed tripe and peppers) at dinner, all for around M$120. Daily 6.30am–10pm.

El Rey Sol López Mateos 1000 ☎646 178 1733, ⓦelreysol.com. This venerable French-style seafood restaurant was opened in 1947 (by the daughter of a

French engineer working in Santa Rosalía), and despite the hype remains an essential Ensenada experience. Stick with classics such as French onion soup (M$70), Caesar salad (M$250) and clams "El Rey Sol" (M$180). Mains range from M$120–350. Daily 7am–11pm.

★**Tacos Fenix** Espinosa at Juárez. This three-person stand operates from a sidewalk next to the former Ferretería Fenix tyre shop, from which it derives its name. The superb fish tacos are made to order with home-made batter and angel shark, and in your hands before they have

time to cool (M$15; shrimp tacos M$18). Not to be confused with the almost as good *Tacos Mi Ranchito "Fenix"* at the corner of Espinosa and C 6. Daily 7am–9pm.

Tacos Lucero Mercado Negro. The market is littered with stalls selling fish tacos, but this is one of the more dependable vendors, a small stand tucked away near the southern entrance. The fish is fresh and succulent, but the tubs of help-yourself salsas on each table really make this a stand-out option (fish tacos M$15, shrimp tacos M$20). Daily 9am–6pm.

DRINKING AND NIGHTLIFE

★**Bar Andaluz** Centro Cultural Riviera, Cárdenas at Riviera ☎ 646 176 4310. This elegant Spanish Revival bar is one of the most appealing watering holes in Baja, with tiled floors, vivid murals, a wooden bartop and sunny courtyard. One of many claimants for "home of the margarita" (David Negrete allegedly created it here in 1948, for one Margarita King Plant). Sat & Sun 10am–1am.

★**Cervecería Wendlandt** Costero 248 ☎ 664 178 2938, ⦿ wendlandt.com.mx. Like other Baja towns, Ensenada is fast developing its own craft brew scene, with local beer maker Wendlandt operating this warehouse and tap room for connoisseurs to sample its popular oatmeal stout, Vaquita Marina pale ale and excellent Perro Del Mar IPA. Tues–Sat 6pm–midnight.

Hussong's Cantina Ruiz 113 ☎ 646 178 3210, ⦿ cantinahussongs.com. Established in 1892 by German immigrant Johann Hussong and now a tourist destination with its own line in T-shirts, *Hussong's* is still an honest bar packed with locals and gringos alike. The floors are covered in sawdust, the bands are *norteña* and the drink of choice is a margarita – like other bars in the area, legend has it the tequila cocktail was actually invented here in 1941 (for one Margarita Henkel). Daily 11am–1am.

Papas & Beer López Mateos 335 at Ruiz ☎ 646 174 0145, ⦿ papasandbeer.com. It's hard to ignore the ubiquitous Baja party chain, but at least it delivers; plenty of wild boozing (M$120 margaritas), live music and themed party nights, especially during Spring Break. Daily 7am–4am.

DIRECTORY

Banks Most are on Ruiz, a few blocks north of López Mateos; with the upsurge in cruise-ship visitors, almost every business in the centre accepts US dollars.

Internet Free wireless hot spots are all over town – try

the malecón – and wi-fi is offered free in many restaurants and bars, such as *Mi Kaza* (opposite).

Post office Club Rotario and Mateos (Mon–Fri 8am–7pm, Sat 9am–1pm).

Valle de Guadalupe

The vineyards of the **Valle de Guadalupe**, just east of Ensenada, are not quite Napa Valley standard, but the region is clearly on the right track, as illustrated by growing international acclaim and the pioneering work of French-trained winemaker Hugo d'Acosta since the 1990s. Though you can show up at the major wineries without a reservation, it is best to call **vineyards** before visiting, especially if you're coming in the warmer months

BAJA WINES: FIVE OF THE BEST

Once derided for watery grapes and poor vintage, Baja wines have gathered a loyal following since the late 1990s thanks to small-production, high-quality boutique wines. These are five of the best:

Vino de Piedra, Casa de Piedra Tones of black fruit lace this blend of Tempranillo and Cabernet Sauvignon.

Viñas de Camou, Château Camou Bordeaux-style blend of Cabernet Sauvignon, Cabernet Franc and Merlot.

Cabernet Sauvignon/Merlot, Monte Xanic Smooth, dark-red wine with a peppery aroma.

Special Reserve Chardonnay, Château Camou One of the best white wines in the valley.

Gabriel, Adobe Guadalupe Another exquisite red-wine blend (55 percent Merlot), produced by Hugo d'Acosta.

9

(July–Sept). The villages of **San Antonio de las Minas** in the southwest and **Francisco Zarco** and **El Porvenir** in the northeast are the centres of the valley's production.

Museo de la Vid y el Vino

Hwy-3 km 81 (just outside Francisco Zarco) • Tues–Sun 9am–5pm • M$50 • ☏ 646 156 8165, ⓦ museodelvinobc.com

Surrounded by vineyards, the beautifully designed **Museo de la Vid y el Vino** offers an impressive introduction to the region and its history of wine-making through digital media, exhibits and displays (from giant wine barrels to antique grape presses and ancient amphorae), though not much is labelled in English. The museum staff can also help arrange tours of the valley.

Museo Comunitario Ruso

Principal 276, Francisco Zarco • Mon, Tues, Thurs & Fri 9am–5pm, Sat & Sun 9am–7pm • M$15 • ☏ 646 155 2030

Only a handful of current residents of the valley claim Russian ancestry, but you can get to grips with their legacy at **Museo Comunitario Ruso** in Francisco Zarco, which preserves a small collection of bits and pieces in a restored Russian home dating from 1905. Ask here about the **Panteón Ruso**, the old cemetery nearby, where you'll find fifteen ageing Russian tombstones.

Château Camou

Valle de Guadalupe (from Hwy-3, follow main road into Francisco Zarco, turn north after 3km) • Tours Mon–Fri 11am, 2pm & 3.30pm, Sat 11am; tastings Mon–Sat 9am–4.30pm, Sun noon–3pm • Basic tours (25–30min) from M$75 • ☏ 646 177 2221, ⓦ chateau-camou.com.mx

Two hundred acres of vineyards surround the mission-style **Château Camou**, housing a modern winery and small tasting room. From here Camou turns out thirty thousand cases of Bordeaux, Zinfandel and a dessert blend of Chardonnay, Chenin Blanc and Sauvignon Blanc. Reservations required.

Casa de Piedra

Hwy-3 km 93.5 • Tastings by appointment only (office hours 8am–4pm) • Free • ☏ 646 178 2173, ⓦ vinoscasadepiedra.com

Casa de Piedra is a boutique producer owned by Hugo d'Acosta, producing the highly respected Vino de Piedra (red) and Piedra del Sol (white); since his first harvest in 1997, Acosta's wines have achieved cult-like celebrity.

L.A. Cetto

Hwy-3 km 73.5, Francisco Zarco • Daily 10am–5pm • Tastings M$25 (M$75 for *reservas*) ☏ 646 155 2179, ⓦ cettowines.com

Although the Cetto family has been bottling wine in Baja California since 1928, they didn't set up their current operation, **L.A. Cetto**, until 1974; they're now the largest producer of table wines in Mexico, noted for their outstanding Nebbiolo, Petite Sirah, Cabernet Sauvignon and Zinfandel. For first-timers, Cetto offers a great introduction to the process through its free wine tours and tastings; it's also one of the few wineries to have food and a dining area.

Adobe Guadalupe

Parcela A-1 s/n, Col Rusa de Guadalupe (from Hwy-3, exit west at the sign to El Tigre, follow the dirt road 4km and turn north; proceed 6km past Vinos Bibayoff, then turn left at the stop sign adjacent to the Unidad Médica Familiar) • Tastings daily 8am–4pm • M$160 • ☏ 646 155 2094, ⓦ adobeguadalupe.com

Gorgeous property owned by US expats Donald and Tru Miller, doubling as an enticing bed and breakfast (see opposite) and gallery for local artist Cecilia García Amaro. Their first harvest was in 2000, with Cabernet Sauvignon, Merlot, Nebbiolo, Cabernet Franc, Tempranillo and Shiraz grown.

Vinos Bibayoff

Rancho Toro Pintos, Valle de Guadalupe (from Hwy-3, exit west at the sign to El Tigre, follow the dirt road 4km then turn north for another 5.6km) • Tours and wine tasting by appointment, Sat & Sun 10.30am–6.30pm (11am–5pm in winter) • Free • ☏ 646 176 1008

THE MILK DRINKERS

The **Molokans** (Russian for "milk drinkers") belonged to a religious sect that broke away from the Russian Orthodox Church in the seventeenth century (the name refers to their practice of drinking milk on fast days). During the early twentieth century, around two thousand Molokans emigrated to the Los Angeles area – from here a smaller colony of five hundred, led by Moses Samaduroff, split off and settled in Mexico's Guadalupe Valley in 1905. Wine was already being made here at that time (Bodegas de Santo Tomás opened in 1888; see p.539), but the Molokans – notably the Bibayoffs, who are still here – helped give the industry a boost.

The only Russian-run vineyard still open to the public, **Vinos Bibayoff** was established in 1906 and still produces five estate wines, including a Nebbiolo and Colombard. The on-site **Museo de la Familia** charts Bibayoff family history since their arrival in Mexico.

ARRIVAL AND TOURS
VALLE DE GUADALUPE

By car To reach the valley from Ensenada, leave the city along Cárdenas and follow Hwy-1 (north) through El Sauzal and exit on Hwy-3 (La Ruta del Vino) towards Tecate, just prior to the beginning of the Hwy-1D toll road north of San Miguel. The vineyards and stores begin in about 10km, near San Antonio de las Minas. With a few exceptions, the valley's vineyards are located on dirt roads that branch off a 25km stretch of the main highway. Detailed signs direct visitors how to navigate the unmarked dirt roads that link the vineyards.

Organized tours If you don't have a car you can arrange a tour from San Diego, Rosarito, Ensenada or Tijuana. Baja Viajes (w bajaviajes.com) runs popular tours from M$1200

(three vineyards and Museo de la Vid y el Vino) from Tijuana, Rosarito or Ensenada. An interesting option is Valley Girl Baja Wines (t 646 198 4024, w valleygirlbajawine.com), run by Alaska expat and local winemaker Sitara Mónica Perez, who gives fun and illuminating bespoke tours of the area (US$30/M$525–US$65/M$1135). Baja Wine Tours (t 664 625 1240, w bajawinetours.net) offers a variety of tours from Tijuana. Note also that *Hotel Coral* in Ensenada (see p.542) runs tours of the valley (US$30/M$525 per person for 5–18 passengers, or US$158/M$2750 total, for 1–4 passengers). You can also try and negotiate a half- or full-day tour with taxi drivers in Ensenada (from M$500).

ACCOMMODATION

Adobe Guadalupe Parcela A-1 s/n, Col Rusa de Guadalupe, off Hwy-3 t 646 155 2094, US t +1 949 863 9776, w adobeguadalupe.com. This romantic six-room B&B run by American ex-banker Don Miller and his wife Tru also produces wine (see opposite). Rates include breakfast for two and wine tasting (dinner is an extra M$975, lunch M$650; wine included), and you can ride

horses through the vineyards (M$1000/hr). M$3360
La Villa del Valle Hwy-3 km 89 t 646 156 8007, w lavilladelvalle.com. Another gorgeous hotel managed by Brit Phil Gregory and his wife Eileen, with six stylish rooms, a complimentary glass of wine every evening at 5.30pm (from their Vina Cava winery), outdoor pool, jacuzzi and free wi-fi. US$225 (M$3930)

EATING

Laja Hwy-3 km 83, Francisco Zarco t 646 155 2556, w lajamexico.com. Former *Daniel* and *Four Seasons* New York chef Jair Téllez, along with partner Laura Reinert, opened this prix-fixe destination (US$55–100/person) restaurant in 2001, and it continues to draw eager diners with its changing,

seasonally influenced menu – expect dishes like sea trout (*curvina*) with roasted peppers and courgettes, and oven-roasted pig with butternut squash and beets. Reservations essential. Wed–Sat 1.30–10pm (last orders 8.30pm), Sun 1.30–5.30pm; closed late Nov–early Jan.

South to La Paz

South of Ensenada, most travellers follow Hwy-1 as it shifts from suburban sprawl to farmland and then into curvy, hilly passes that eventually drop into the **Santo Tomás valley**. From here it's around 1375km to **La Paz**, a journey which can take twenty hours direct, or preferably several days, taking in the entrancing landscapes and small towns

9

along the way – you'll see far fewer tourists on this stretch of the **Transpeninsular Highway** (see box, p.529). The alternative (if you have your own transport) is to detour via Hwy-3 and Hwy-5 to **San Felipe**, then take the rugged route along the Sea of Cortez to rejoin Hwy-1 north of Guerrero Negro.

San Felipe

When the paved road to **SAN FELIPE** was completed in 1951, the tiny village was already attracting adventurous sport fishermen for its vast schools of totoaba or **totuava** (a species now fished onto the endangered list). Now a firmly established Baja fishing legend, San Felipe is no longer a frontier town; it still pulls in the fishing crowd, but also accommodates a blend of North American retirees, RV campers, spring-breakers and **off-road motorsports** enthusiasts – thousands of kilometres of trails wind their way through the surrounding desert and folded ridges of the San Pedro Martír mountains. Indeed, San Felipe's population hits around 25,000 in the winter, including some eight thousand North American residents (though tourism has certainly suffered since the 2009 recession). If fishing and biking don't appeal, San Felipe's gorgeous **beaches** and warm, emerald waters might – it's the best place to swim in northern Baja (at high tide – see box below).

ARRIVAL AND DEPARTURE   SAN FELIPE

By bus Buses from Mexicali (5 daily; 2hr 30min) and Tijuana (via Mexicali; 4 daily; 5–6hr) arrive at the bus station 1km inland on Mar de Caribe (aka Airport Rd) near the PEMEX petrol station: turn left out of the bus station and right down Manzanillo to get to Av Mar de Cortés, which runs parallel to the sea. If you're travelling on public transport, this is the end of the line – you'll

need to cut back to Tijuana or Mexicali to continue south.
By car Most visitors drive to San Felipe along Hwy-5 from Mexicali and the US border (around 2hr, depending on waits at the military checkpoints en route); fill up in Mexicali because there are no petrol stations on the way. Heading further south, see p.549.

INFORMATION AND ACTIVITIES

Tourist office The tourist office, Chetumal 101 at Mar de Cortés (Mon–Thurs 10am–4pm, Fri & Sat 10am–7pm; ☎ 646 577 1865), gives out maps and information, while the best online resource is ⓦ sanfelipe.com.mx.
San Felipe Off Road El Dorado Ranch, Hwy-5 km 176.5 (11km north of downtown) ☎ 646 577 3022, ⓦ sanfelipeoffroad.com. The place to rent dirt bikes and

ATVs (M$750/hr), take guided quad tours or buggy rides (from M$3375). Closed Tues.
Tony Reyes Sports Fishing US ☎ +1 714 538 8010, ⓦ tonyreyes.com. Fishing legend Tony Reyes pioneered six-day "midriff" boat trips (out to the area of the Sea of Cortez, rich in fish, aka "yellowtail alley") in the 1950s – his son now runs the business (trips from US$1295/M$22,600).

ACCOMMODATION

★**Casa La Vida** Misión de Santo Tomás 2738 ☎ 686 577 2807, ⓦ casalavida.com. Managed by friendly US expats 3km south of downtown (one block from the beach), these three spacious suites come with US cable TV, wi-fi and kitchens. **M$1500**
La Hacienda de la Langosta Roja Chetumal 125 ☎ 686 577 0483, ⓦ sanfelipelodging.com. The "red lobster" offers 39 simple but comfy rooms in a central part

of town, with a/c, satellite TV and free wi-fi. **M$735**
Hotel Las Palmas Mar Baltico 1101 ☎ 686 577 1382, ⓦ laspalmasanfelipe.com. Opened in 1956, this is a place with a colourful history (the restaurant is named after Sicily-born owner Alfredo Bellinghieri, the man who claims to have invented the alfredo sauce), bougainvillea-covered patios, fountains, simple but clean rooms (triples available), satellite TV and small pool. **M$750**

THE TIDES OF SAN FELIPE

The upper reaches of the Sea of Cortez experience the world's third-largest **tides** – fluctuations of 6–7m are common. You'll soon realize why tide calendars are so common in San Felipe; water that laps lazily against the beach in the morning can recede a kilometre into the hazy distance by mid-afternoon.

EATING

Not surprisingly, **seafood** is the staple diet here, with San Felipe best known for its **fish tacos** and shellfish cocktails; you'll find the best stands at an area known as Plaza Maristacos at the south end of the malecón, near the *Costa Azul Hotel* (the best stall is *Mariscos La Morena*).

Baja Mar Restaurant & Taco Factory Mar de Cortés 100 ☎ 686 577 2648. Beachfront diner and sports bar serving seafood (shrimp tacos from M$30), steaks, and classic Mexican and American dishes (with free wi-fi). Daily 10am–10pm.

Fat Boy's Pizzeria Chetumal 101, at Mar de Cortés ☎ 686 577 4092. This expat favourite knocks out decent pizza (try the chorizo), pasta and sandwiches – they also have taco Tuesdays (tacos for M$15), TV showing US sports events and punchy 64oz margaritas. Mon–Fri 10am–11pm, Sat 10am–midnight, Sun 9am–11pm.

Rice and Beans Mar de Cortés 262, between Acapulco and Zihuatanejo ☎ 686 577 1770. Sit on the veranda and soak up the sea views over breakfast, good-value fresh fish (excellent fish stew), all sorts of omelettes and stellar margaritas (mains M$75–150). Free wi-fi. Daily 7am–11pm.

La Vaquita Mar de Cortés at Puerto Peñasco ☎ 686 577 2837. Local favourite serving the best seafood in town, from *chiles habaneros* stuffed with shellfish and fresh sea bass, to seafood *molcajetes* and Orly shrimps (breaded and filled with cream cheese). Mexicali craft beers served. From M$90 per dish. Wed–Mon 1–10pm.

DRINKING

★Barefoot Bar Hotel El Cortéz, Mar de Cortés, at Isla de Cedros ☎ 686 577 1055. Classic Baja bar on the sand in front of the *Cortéz*, its wood walls adorned with signed photos of famous off-road racers and sport fishermen; there's even a stained-glass window and a dartboard. Daily 11am–2am.

Bar Miramar Mar de Cortés ☎ 686 577 1192. Francisco Arostegui's San Felipe institution has been open since 1948, an old shack with bar stools, jukebox, two pool tables, table tennis, old photos and posters peeling off the walls; watch fishing boats roll in from the seafront deck. Cash only. Wed–Mon 10am–2am.

DIRECTORY

Banks Along Cortés there's a Bancomer (at Acapulco), and a Banamex at Chetumal 42, both with ATMs (though US$ are accepted everywhere).

Hospital There is no hospital in San Felipe; if you have an accident or get sick, there is a small Centro de Salud (medical centre) in town (☎ 686 577 1521), on Mar Bermejo Sur and Ensenada, but the closest real hospitals are in Mexicali or across the US border.

Post office Mar Blanco 187, just off Chetumal, five blocks inland (Mon–Fri 8am–3pm).

South of San Felipe

South of San Felipe, most cars (and some motorbikes) can continue for around 200km (5–7hr) to rejoin Hwy-1 at **Chapula**, a once harrowing journey that is now much easier thanks to the gradual paving of the road. At the time of research the road was paved all the way to Coco's Corner – it is likely to be completed by the end of 2016. Fill up in San Felipe – there's no guarantee that you'll find petrol en route. **Puertecitos**, 85km south of San Felipe, is a small US retirement community where you'll find natural hot springs on the beach, a basic restaurant (Sat & Sun only) and a PEMEX petrol station that's usually closed. Some 60km south of Puertecitos is the turning for the Papa Fernández store and **Bahía San Luis Gonzaga**, one of the most alluring stretches of coast in Baja. Another 5km on is the Gonzaga PEMEX/Rancho Grande mini market, with a turning to *Alfonsina's* (☎ 664 648 1951, ✉ info@alfonsinasresort.mx; M$1150), where you can stay and eat. From the Gonzaga PEMEX it's 37km to isolated Coco's Corner (basic supplies), with a final 21km bone-jarring ride to Hwy-1.

Parque Nacional Sierra de San Pedro Mártir

Sierra de San Pedro Mártir • Daily 7am–8pm • M$56 per person • **Observatorio Astronómico Nacional** Daily 10am–1pm & 2–3pm by reservation only • Free • ☎ 646 174 4580, ⓦ astrossp.unam.mx

Some 130km south of Ensenada on Hwy-1, a side road at km 141 (San Telmo) heads inland towards the magnificent **Parque Nacional Sierra de San Pedro Mártir**, a tranquil

9

alpine reserve that resembles the high sierras of California. The road winds 100km up into the mountains (the park entrance is at km 84; the road is unsurfaced but in good condition beyond here), which includes the peninsula's highest peak, **Picacho del Diablo** (3095m) – where it snows in winter. As you climb, the land becomes increasingly conifer-rich, and at the end of the road (2830m) the **Observatorio Astronómico Nacional** takes advantage of the piercingly clear air – there are mesmerizing views in every direction. The new **Museo del Centro de Comunicación y Cultura** (Fri–Sun 10am–3pm; free) near the observatory offers an introduction to the indigenous history and ecology of the area. Numerous poorly defined trails wind through the park, but again, there's no public transport (or food and gas stations) and you need to be fully equipped for wilderness **camping** if you want to linger (**cabins** are also available from M$700–1700; ☎646 172 3000).

ACCOMMODATION

Rancho Meling ☎616 166 2016, ⊛ranchomeling .com. Some 50km from Hwy-1, just off the road into the park, this legendary ranch dates back to 1893, was rebuilt after being destroyed during the 1911 Revolution, and now offers an authentic taste of the Old West, with comfy cabins and rooms. Swimming, biking and horseriding are the most popular activities. <u>M$1050</u>

San Quintín

Baja's pismo clam capital, **SAN QUINTÍN** is the first town of any size south of Ensenada, and even here, though there are a couple of big hotels, most of the buildings look temporary – English colonists established the town in the 1880s, but development never really took off. Apart from a pit stop to sample the **clams**, there's no reason to stay overnight here unless you are one of the many weekend fishermen destined for the **Bahía San Quintín**, which is undeniably attractive, with five cinder-cone volcanoes as a backdrop to a series of small sandy beaches, endless fishing and superb clam digging. Fishing licences can be obtained from local tackle shops or from ⊛sportfishinginmexico.com (around US$23.20/M$405 per week). The closest beach (**Playa Santa María**) is some 20km from town (5km off Hwy-1), and there's no public transport.

ARRIVAL AND DEPARTURE   SAN QUINTÍN

By bus Buses heading north and south stop at Lázaro Cárdenas, 5km south of San Quintín, but without your own transport there's little point in getting off here.

ACCOMMODATION AND EATING

Most of the thirty million **clams** harvested in San Quintín end up north of the border, but you can sample the smoked, oversized molluscs at numerous roadside vendors in town.

Hotel Jardines Baja Lázaro Cárdenas (signposted off Hwy-1) ☎616 165 6060, ⊛hotel-jardinesbaja.com. One of the best hotels in the San Quintín area, with a variety of comfortable, modern rooms with ceiling fans, internet, lovely gardens and a great restaurant (Tues–Thurs 8am–10pm, Fri–Sun 8am–2am). <u>M$525</u>
The Old Mill Lázaro Cárdenas, off Hwy-1 (via a dirt road) ☎616 428 2779, ⊛hoteloldmill.com. Converted from the ruins of the old English mill in 1951, this hotel is another Baja classic, reopening in 2012 under new management right on the waterfront; rooms have been renovated, there's hot water and everything works. The *Molino Viejo* (daily 5.30am–10pm) restaurant next door (managed separately) has great food (including clams) and drinks. <u>M$555</u>

El Rosario

Some 60km beyond San Quintín, Hwy-1 passes through **EL ROSARIO**, the original site of the first Dominican mission in Baja, founded in 1774. Not much remains of the first mission site – since dubbed **Misión de El Rosario de Arriba** – or its 1802 replacement down river, the **Misión de El Rosario de Abajo**. Since being abandoned in 1832, the remaining adobe ruins of the latter resemble little more than melted walls. Modern El Rosario is essentially just another pit stop, comprising a petrol station, a few **motels** and a Baja culinary treasure, **Mama Espinoza's**. Beyond El Rosario, the road turns sharply inland and runs down the centre of the peninsula for some 350km to Guerrero Negro, cutting through the protected **Parque Natural del Desierto Central de Baja California**. This is where you head into Baja California proper – barren and godforsaken. For the most part the scenery is dry, brown desert, with the peninsula's low mountain spine to the left and nothing else but sand, a bizarre landscape of cactus and rocks.

ARRIVAL AND DEPARTURE

EL ROSARIO

By bus Long-distance buses will drop off and pick up passengers at the PEMEX station on demand, but moving on you won't be able to book seats in advance. Get an early start (5.30am) and pay on the first bus you see. It's about 7hr through to Tijuana (1hr to San Quintín and 3hr to Guerrero Negro).

By car If you're driving, it's absolutely essential to fill up your tank at the PEMEX station (24hr) here: there's no dependable pump until just north of the state border with Baja California Sur.

ACCOMMODATION AND EATING

Baja's Best Café Hwy-1 km 57 ☎616 159 1701. Best place for breakfast with real sausage and decent "*Starbucks*" coffee. The shrimp omelettes, tacos and burritos are made with fresh Sea of Cortez shellfish. Daily 7am–7pm.

★**Baja Cactus Motel** Hwy-1 km 55 (San Quintín–Punta Prieta) ☎616 165 8850, ⓦbajacactus.com. One of the best bargains in Baja, with plush rooms (make sure you stay in the new wing at the back), satellite TV and wi-fi access. Conveniently positioned between the PEMEX station and *Mama Espinoza's*. M$600

Mama Espinoza's Hwy-1 km 56 ☎616 165 8770, ⓦmamaespinoza.com. One of the oldest restaurants on the peninsula, with roots in the 1930s – Doña Anita "Mama" Espinoza herself (daughter of a French engineer from Santa Rosalía), though over 108 years old, was still around at the time of writing (there's even a museum in her honour). Her famous lobster burritos (M$250 for three) are rather overpriced, but everything else – beef and pork tacos and big burritos – qualifies as the best food between here and Bahía de los Ángeles. Check out the Baja 1000 and Baja 500 memorabilia on the walls. Daily 6am–10pm.

Bahía de los Ángeles

If you have your own transport, a worthy detour off Hwy-1 is **BAHÍA DE LOS ÁNGELES** (also known as L.A. Bay), a small community of fewer than one thousand on the Sea of Cortez. The town maintains an underdeveloped, frontier feeling, little changed from when Steinbeck sailed through in 1941, while the eponymous bay teems with sea life and is hemmed in by contorted mountains and lots of enticing beaches. Because of the difficulty getting supplies to the bay, lodging and food are more expensive than you'd expect, and there are no banks or ATMs, so make sure you have enough cash.

Museo de Naturaleza y Cultura

Bahía de los Ángeles • Winter daily 9am–noon & 2–4pm; summer daily 9am–noon & 3–5pm • Free • ☎200 124 9101

There's little in town other than a few hotels, cafés and fishing boats; the one exception is the small bilingual **Museo de Naturaleza y Cultura**, two blocks west of the waterfront. Its location is marked by a narrow-gauge locomotive, a relic of the gold and copper mines that first attracted Europeans to the area. Mining history and that of the local *ranchero* life is well covered, along with details of sea life in the bay.

Pinturas Rupestres de Valle Montevideo and Misión San Francisco Borja

About 13km west of Bahía de los Ángeles, signposts off Hwy-12 lead a further 11km

9

along dirt roads to the precious **Pinturas Rupestres de Valle Montevideo**, still vivid (and unprotected) rock art estimated to be ten thousand years old. A drive out here can be combined with a visit to the enigmatic ruins of the **Misión San Francisco Borja**, 20km further along the same dirt road. Built by the Jesuits in 1762 (and abandoned in 1818), much of Borja remains standing. The road can be very rough – 4WD recommended but usually not essential. Allow two hours for the drive each way.

ÁPFF – Islas del Golfo de California

Reserve office Mon–Fri 9am–2pm & 4–6pm, Sat 9am–2pm · Permits M$40/day · ☎ 200 124 9106, ⓦ conanp.gob.mx

The pristine bay itself is the star attraction at Bahía de los Ángeles, rich in marine life and studded with sixteen weathered islands, part of the **Área de Protección de Flora y Fauna Islas del Golfo de California**. Visiting or camping on them requires a permit; you can obtain one from the reserve office in town, near the *Hotel Villa Vitta*, which also can advise on boat operators and fishing guides (who typically charge M$1500/day). Highlights include the colonies of **sea lions** near **Isla Coronado**, also known as "Smith Island", and the **whale sharks** that visit the area each summer (July–Oct).

Isla Ángel de la Guarda

The largest island in the Sea of Cortez, **Isla Ángel de la Guarda** dominates the bay and is the biggest focus of Bahía de los Ángeles' leisure activities; it's the best place on the northern coast for diving and kayaking trips. Though you'll find plenty of **fishing** outfits, there aren't any other speciality operators in town, and any activity you'd like to indulge in (including **swimming with whale sharks**) is typically arranged through your campsite or motel.

ARRIVAL AND INFORMATION

BAHÍA DE LOS ÁNGELES

By car Bahía de los Ángeles is about 224km from El Rosario on Hwy-1, followed by a 66km jaunt east along well-maintained Hwy-12 from the Parador Punta Prieta junction. The town has two PEMEX petrol stations, both open daily 7am–9pm. There is no public transport to Bahía de los Ángeles. Visit ⓦ bahiadelosangeles.info for the latest information on the area.

ACCOMMODATION AND EATING

Camping is popular in Bahía de los Ángeles, with most hotels and restaurants maintaining simple sites and some free camping available along the road to Punta la Gringa, at the north end of the bay – ask in town before setting up a tent, just in case (you may have to pay a small fee). There are several cheap taco stands on the main road.

Daggett's Beach Camping & Sportfishing ☎ 200 124 9101, ⓦ campdaggetts.info. Between *Larry's* and the town, this local institution (the Daggetts are descended from an English sailor who jumped ship in the 1880s) is primarily an RV community, but they've reserved the beachfront for palapa-shaded plots (with barbecues) for campers and have cabins with one to three beds, a/c and showers. Camping M$75/person, cabins M$750

Guillermo's ☎ 200 124 9104. The best place to eat a full meal or grab a cold drink is *Guillermo's*; the fish tacos and burgers are good but the beachside location and views of the offshore islands are spectacular. Basic doubles from M$500.

Villa Bahía no tel, ⓦ villabahia.com. On the way to La Gringa (5km north of town), this laid-back complex comprises various casitas on the beach, with each unit holding at least six people, a full kitchen, and use of an outdoor communal kitchen with grills. Free satellite internet and kayaks is a nice bonus, and the whole place runs on wind and solar power. M$900

Villa Vitta Resort ☎ 200 124 9103, ☎ US +1 619 454 6108, ⓦ villavitta.com. Centrally located motel with basic but clean rooms, a pool, restaurant-bar and boat ramp. The adjoining RV park and campsite (M$150/night) has 25 spots with electrical hookups and eleven without, and showers. M$450

Guerrero Negro

Continuing south on the main highway, there's little between El Rosario and the 28th parallel, where an enormous metal monument marks the border between the states of Baja California and **Baja California Sur**; you'll have to set your watch forward an hour when you cross. **GUERRERO NEGRO**, just across the border, offers little in the way of respite from the

WHALE WATCHING FROM GUERRERO NEGRO

Whale watching is the principal reason people visit Guerrero Negro, as hordes of friendly California grey whales (up to 2000 at a time), which spend most of their lives in the icy Bering Sea around Alaska, can be observed (at remarkably close quarters) from within the nearby **Laguna Ojo de Liebre** (aka Scammon's Lagoon), thirty minutes south of town. It's a magical experience – and many visitors actually get to touch the whales, which sometimes come right up to bobbing vessels after the engines are switched off.

Organized tours (see below) begin in Guerrero, but you can also drive to the lagoon and hire a cheaper *panguero* (boat) yourself. Take Hwy-1 south for 9km and look for the sign to the **Parque Natural de la Ballena Gris**. From here it's 6km along a rough dirt road to a gate (which someone will open, but only during the whale-watching season Jan–March), and another 18km to the lagoon. You'll probably be asked to pay the park entrance fee of around M$70 (or US$4) here. Boats usually charge M$400–500 per person for 90min trips around the bay. Taxis will charge at least M$800 for the drive there and back (they wait for you at the lagoon).

Malarrimo Eco-Tours ☎ 615 157 0100, ⊛ malar rimo.com. Runs 3hr whale tours (daily 8am, noon; US$49/M$855), as well as eight-hour tours to the Sierra de San Francisco to see cave paintings (Oct–Dec; M$900) from the hotel of the same name (see below).

Also arranges local salt-mine tours for around M$150. **Mario's Tours** ☎ 615 157 1940, ⊛ mariostours.com. Whale-watching trips from Mario's cost around M$700 per person for a three-hour trip (8am and 11am), including a complimentary drink or two.

heat and aridity that has gone before (winters, however, can find the town quite chilly). Flat and dust-blown, it was only established in the 1950s as a supply centre for Exportadora de Sal, the world's largest salt manufacturer, and is surrounded by vast saltpans and drab storage warehouses. At most times of year you'll want to do little more than grab a drink and carry straight on, especially if you don't have a car – it's a dispiriting place to navigate on foot. In January and February (and, peripherally, Dec & March–April), however, Guerrero Negro is home to one of Mexico's most extraordinary natural phenomena, the congregation of scores of **grey whales** just off the coast (see box above).

ARRIVAL AND DEPARTURE
GUERRERO NEGRO

By plane The tiny airport is 6km north of town (taxis should be around M$150), with Aéreo Servicio Guerrero flying Cessna aircraft to/from Ensenada (Mon, Wed & Fri), Hermosillo (Thurs) and Guaymas (Tues, Thurs & Sat). Aéreo Calafia also serves Hermosillo/Guaymas (Mon & Sat).

By bus The Terminal de Autobuses is on Rubio, just off Zapata at the eastern end of town near Hwy-1. Buses passing through Guerrero Negro are often full; try to buy your ticket at least a day in advance.

Destinations Ensenada (6 daily; 10hr); La Paz (3–4 daily; 11–12hr); Loreto (3–4 daily; 6.5hr); Mulegé (3–4 daily; 4–5hr); San Ignacio (3–4 daily; 2hr); Tijuana (3–4 daily; 12hr).

By taxi The taxis at the stand in front of the Mercado Tianguis supermarket on Zapata adjust their rates depending on how long you'll have to wait for a bus – a ride to San Ignacio is about M$1200 per car.

ACCOMMODATION

Los Caracoles Zapata, at Calz de la República ☎ 615 157 1088, ⊛ hotelloscaracoles.com.mx. On the right as you enter Zapata, this once stellar option needs a renovation, but still offers clean rooms, satellite TV and friendly staff, as well as computers with free internet, free coffee and excellent whale-watching trips. M$750

Malarrimo Zapata, at Pipila ☎ 615 857 0250,

⊛ malarrimo.com. Another solid option, open here since 1974, with clean rooms with TV, and RV spaces (M$300) – you can also camp here for M$180. M$750

TerraSal Zapata (just off Hwy-1) ☎ 615 157 0133. Relatively new hotel with clean, large rooms with a/c, TV, free wi-fi and powerful showers, right at the entrance to town. M$550

EATING

Malarrimo Zapata, at Pipila ☎ 615 857 0250, ⊛ malarrimo.com. This hotel contains *Scavenger's Bar* (decorated with items found on windswept Malarrimo Beach) and a restaurant with excellent seafood (halibut with

crispy garlic and lunch specials from M$90), as well as decent breakfasts (lobster omelette). Daily 7.30am–10.30pm.
Mario's Hwy-1 km 217.3 ☎ 615 157 1940, ⊛ marios tours.com. On Hwy-1, just before Zapata, is this solid rustic

option for breakfast and the basics, as well as some great deals – though you'll pay up to M$600 for a dinner for two (M$255 for their steak and lobster combo). Daily 7.30am–11pm, **Santo Remedio** Carballo Félix ☎615 157 2909. The best restaurant in town can be hard to find, but is well

worth the effort (turn right at El Morro and look for the signs), with fresh, local produce (seafood, Baja beef, fruit jams and California wines) and a menu that features everything from steaks to fish tacos. Mains average M$120–180. Daily 8am–10.30pm.

San Ignacio

Leaving Guerrero Negro, Hwy-1 winds 142km inland for the hottest, driest stage of the journey, across the Desierto Vizcaíno. In the midst of this landscape, **SAN IGNACIO**'s appeal is immediate, even from a distance. Gone are the dust and concrete that define the peninsula, replaced by green palms and a cool breeze; despite being hammered by Hurricane Odile in 2014, it remains an oasis any desert traveller would hope for, and another excellent base for **whale-watching** and **cave-painting tours**. There are **no banks** in town and few places accept credit cards – it's best to come with a supply of cash.

Misión San Ignacio de Kadakaamán

Gilberto Valdivia Peña (Plaza Ecoturismo) **Museo de Pinturas Rupestres de San Ignacio** May–Oct Tues–Sat 8am–5pm; Nov–April daily 8am–5pm • Free • ☎ 615 154 0222

In town, the central **Plaza Ecoturismo**, shaded by six huge Indian laurel trees, plays hosts to concerts, festivals and children's soccer games, and is dominated by the **Misión San Ignacio de Kadakaamán** (usually open during services only). This gorgeous church was constructed from lava blocks over 1m thick, dug up from Volcan las Tres Virgenes to the east. Completed in 1786, it's probably the prettiest example of colonial architecture in the whole of Baja California, and was also one of the most successful missions, operating until 1840. The left wing of the mission now houses the tiny **Museo de Pinturas Rupestres de San Ignacio**, which contains photos and cave-art exhibits, with a focus on the nearby Sierra de San Francisco (Spanish-only captions).

ARRIVAL AND DEPARTURE
SAN IGNACIO

By bus The centre of San Ignacio lies almost 3km off the main highway, where all the buses stop. Upon arrival you may be lucky enough to pick up a taxi (M$75); otherwise it's a 30min walk down the road through the palms. Getting onward tickets can be tough: buses currently depart for Guerrero Negro (M$305; 2hr) and points north at

12.05am, 6.25am, 6.30am and 6.20pm. Buses depart for Santa Rosalía (M$160; 1hr) and points south at 11.50am, 3pm, 6.30pm and 11.30pm.
By taxi Local taxi drivers will ask for a minimum M$1500 for Guerrero Negro and M$750 for Santa Rosalía.

ACCOMMODATION

Desert Inn (on road to San Ignacio, 1.5 km off Hwy-1) ☎615 154 0300, ⬧fonaturoperadoraportuaria.gob .mx. The best place in town, a hacienda-style hotel set around a pool, with free (if sketchy) wi-fi, comfy motel chain-style rooms and TVs. Breakfast is M$120. <u>M$1200</u> **Ignacio Springs Bed and Breakfast** ☎615 154 0333, ⬧ignaciosprings.com. Camping at *Ignacio Springs Bed and Breakfast* on the northern side of Río San Ignacio is a rather bizarre but comfortable affair; the novelty here is staying in well-appointed yurts with queen-size beds, tile floors, free wi-fi, a/c and patios; some even have their own

bath. Rates include breakfast. Near the road, so can be noisy at night. Hurricane Odile devastated the site in 2014, but the Canadian owners appeared to be well on the road to recovery at the time of research. <u>M$1020</u>
Ricardo's Rice & Beans Hwy-1, San Lino ☎615 154 0283. The bus stop is actually in San Lino, a little settlement anchored by the campsite and restaurant *Ricardo's Rice & Beans*, just west of the intersection along a road parallel to the highway. There are old but clean rooms here, with hot showers, a/c and free wi-fi, and plenty of space to camp outside. <u>M$750</u>

EATING

Some of the best food in San Ignacio is cooked up in the taco stalls on the plaza; try the juicy *carne asada* tacos at *Taquería Lupita* or the frozen *raspado de tamarindo* and hot dogs at *El Capu*. Don't miss the addictive *pan de datil* (date pie) and date empanadas sold by Luz Romero from her kitchen on the edge of the plaza.

TOURS AND TRIPS FROM SAN IGNACIO

WHALE WATCHING

Although whales are most in evidence in January and February, **whale-watching** tours to the nearby **Laguna San Ignacio** (around 50km from town, on mostly paved road) are offered from December to April. If you have your own car you can cut your expenses considerably (allow 1hr to be safe). Tours arranged at the lagoon cost around M$500–600 per person; transport from San Ignacio to the lagoon can be arranged at Dago's Internet Café (☏615 154 0449) on the plaza (M$300 per person or US$120/M$2095 per van round-trip).

Antonio's Ecotours ☏615 112 5387, ⊛cabanas sanignacio.com. Charges US$55/M$960 for whale watching (lunch is M$150 extra), or US$250 (M$4360) with one night in the simple but comfy *Cabañas San Ignacio* on the lagoon (shared toilets, hot showers, free wi-fi area), with dinner and two whale excursions included.

Ecoturismo Kuyimá Morelos 23, at Hidalgo ☏615 154 0070, ⊛kuyima.com. Located opposite the church (daily Dec–April 8am–1pm & 3–8pm; May–Nov 9am–1pm), charging about US$591 (M$10,300)

all-inclusive for its four-day, three-night package, and just US$50 (M$870) for whale-watching tours only (no transport); it's an extra US$130 (M$2265) per van for day-trippers. Kuyimá also offers accommodation at the lagoon, with tents and clean palapas with solar power, plus they serve food. It's possible to visit and return in one day, but it's better to stay the night as the whales are best seen in the early morning when they venture into the shallow waters. You camp with your own equipment for just US$12 or M$210 (or rent tents for US$40/M$700).

CAVE ART

Cave-art tours from San Ignacio focus on the Sierra de San Francisco about 45km north of town, where 320 sites exist, dating back some eight thousand years; tour operators usually pass through the little town of San Francisco de la Sierra and head for the easily accessible **Cueva del Ratón**, or remoter caves such as the Cueva Pintada and Cueva de las Flechas in Cañón San Pablo, which require a minimum of two days. Ecoturismo Kuyimá (see above) offers day trips Oct–May for US$60–95 (M$1045–1655), up to US$537 (M$9185) for three days, but if you want to save some cash you can arrange a mule trip yourself in San Francisco de la Sierra (see below).

   Independent tours are possible, but you must always be accompanied by a guide (*guías arrieros*) and are required to get **INAH permission**, gained in San Ignacio from the INAH office next to the church (Mon–Sat 8am–3pm; ☏615 154 0222); the park entry fee is M$47, plus a guide fee of M$80 for Ratón and M$200 for other caves. You'll then need your own transport to get there: at km 118, 45km north of San Ignacio, you'll find a road heading east to San Francisco de la Sierra, and the first site is just over 2km further on. Once you've sorted out a guide (around M$500/day) and a mule (M$150/day), you'll be able to camp at "El Cacarizo" in the Cañón de Santa Teresa.

Ricardo's Rice and Beans Hwy-1, San Lino ☏615 154 0283. Serves traditional Mexican and seafood dishes (from M$75), not far from the bus station. Daily 7am–11pm.

Tootsie's Bar & Grill Francisco 11 at Madero ☏ 615 154

0268. Canadian expat Toni Marcer serves North American comfort food, salads, pizza and surprisingly authentic BBQ ribs on a rustic patio a block off the plaza, washed down with potent margaritas. Budget for M$600 for dinner for two, with drinks. Cash only. Mon–Sat 5–11pm.

Santa Rosalía

South of San Ignacio, Hwy-1 emerges on the east coast at **SANTA ROSALÍA**, the largest town in central Baja (with a population of around twelve thousand), and one of the most intriguing places to explore on the peninsula. Established by French miners in 1885, it has something of a transient air, and many of its buildings look strikingly un-Mexican. The streets are narrow and crowded, with the workers' houses in the valley, which feature low, angled roofs and hibiscus-flanked porches, resembling French Caribbean dwellings, and grander colonial residences for the managers lining the hill to the north.

9

Iglesia de Santa Bárbara
Obregón and Pedro Altamirano

The premier sight in Santa Rosalía is the **Iglesia de Santa Bárbara**, three blocks from Parque Morelos, a prefabricated iron church said to have been designed by Gustave Eiffel and exhibited in Paris before it was reassembled here in 1897. The rather austere interior is softened somewhat by vivid stained-glass windows reflecting its Art Nouveau style, though some experts now believe Eiffel was not the designer – just don't say that to the locals.

Museo El Boleo
Frances Altamirano, at Jean M.Cousteau • Mon–Sat 8am–3pm • M$20 • ☎ 615 152 2999

Progress up the hill from the Iglesia de Santa Bárbara and you'll see more leftovers from the mining period, culminating with the **Museo El Boleo** at the top, housed in the old mining offices. The museum outlines the history of the mine and the town through old photos and mining curios. The area around the museum is known as the **Mesa Francés**, and contains the grandest examples of the town's French architectural legacy.

ARRIVAL AND DEPARTURE
SANTA ROSALÍA

By plane Aéreo Servicio Guerrero flies to Guaymas from Santa Rosalía's tiny Palo Verde Airport, some 30km south in San Bruno; buy tickets at the office in the ferry terminal (daily 8am–1pm & 3–6pm; includes transport to airport; ☎ 615 155 1453, ⓦ asg.com.mx). Aéreo Calafia also flies to Guaymas and Hermosillo.

By bus Buses use the ferry terminal parking lot to drop off and take on passengers, with around six buses a day heading north to San Ignacio (M$135; 1hr) and Guerrero Negro (2hr 30min; M$390), but only a couple continuing to Tijuana (M$1525; 14hr); six buses head south to La Paz (M$1180; 8–9hr) via Loreto (M$360; 3hr) and Mulegé (M$115; 1hr). Taxis (☎ 615 152 0266) charge around M$50–75 to shuttle between the bus and ferry terminal and the hotels.

By ferry Ferries connect Santa Rosalía with Guaymas (see p.34), across the Sea of Cortez in the state of Sonora. The ferry terminal lies 2min walk south of centrally located Parque Morelos, on Hwy-1. One-way tickets are M$885 (returns are M$1630). A cabin is an additional M$985, while cars cost M$3200 (one-way; motorbikes M$1420). The ticket office (☎ 800 672 9053, ⓦ ferrysantarosalia .com) inside the terminal is open daily 10am–7pm. Always call in advance, though, as schedules often change.

Destinations Guaymas (departs Wed & Fri 8.30am, Sun 8pm; 9hr).

By taxi If you can't wait for a bus, you should be able to negotiate a taxi to San Ignacio or Mulegé for less than M$1000.

EL BOLEO

Legend has it that while walking in the hills around Santa Rosalía in 1868, rancher José Villavicencio chanced upon a **boleo**, a blue-green globule of rock that proved to be just a taster of a mineral vein containing more than twenty percent copper. By 1880, the wealth of the small-scale mining concessions came to the notice of the **Rothschilds**, who provided financing for the French Compagnie du Boléo (or "El Boleo") to buy mining rights and to build a massive extraction and smelting operation in 1885. Six hundred kilometres of tunnels were dug, a foundry was shipped out from Europe, and a new wharf built to transport the smelted ore north to Washington State for refining. Ships returned with lumber for the construction of a new town, laid out with houses built to a standard commensurate with their occupier's status within the company. By 1954, falling profits from the nearly spent mines forced the French to sell the pits and smelter to the Mexican government who, though the mines were eventually left idle, continued to smelt ore from the mainland until the 1990s. Starting in 2004, Canadian-listed Baja Mining Corp worked hard to reopen the mine – despite running into financing problems in 2012 (Korean Resources Corp is now the main shareholder) and damage caused by Hurricane Odile, production of copper, cobalt and zinc finally began in 2015, with the new El Boleo expected to have a minimum life of 22 years. Minera y Metalúrgica del Boleo (ⓦ mmboleo.com) has promised to work with local authorities to develop housing, infrastructure and utilities, and so far has created around 1000 new jobs in the area (with 65 percent local hires).

CLOCKWISE FROM TOP THE TRANSPENINSULAR HIGHWAY (P.529); GREY WHALE CALF, SAN IGNACIO LAGOON (P.553); CUEVA PINTADA IN THE SIERRA DE SAN FRANCISCO (P.557) >

9

ACCOMMODATION

Las Casitas Hwy-1 km 195 Santa Rosalía–Loreto ☎615 152 3023, ✉mariahsantarosalia@hotmail.com. A long walk uphill from downtown, but the panoramic views of the sea from its hillside perch make it worthwhile. The large, ceramic-tiled rooms have modern amenities (free wi-fi in common areas) and large windows overlooking the water. M$900

Hotel Francés Jean M.Cousteau 15 ☎615 152 2052. A charming colonial-style building on the hill to the north of town, beyond the museum. Built in 1920 (the original opened in 1886 but burnt down), rooms are clean and functional, but it's worth the price for a glimpse into Rosalía's French past. Free wi-fi and satellite TV, with simple breakfast included. M$850

EATING

Several inexpensive stalls are scattered along Obregón: *Super Tacos*, on Obregón just off Parque Morelos, serves tasty beef tacos for M$15, while *Tacos El Arabe*, on the south side of Parque Morelos, is noted for its similarly priced fish tacos.

El Muelle Plaza and Constitución ☎615 152 0931. Restaurant set in an old wooden building with an outdoor patio serving decent *carne asada* and *arrachera* steaks (mains M$90–160). Daily 8am–11pm.

Panadería El Boleo Obregón 30, between calles 3 and 4 ☎615 152 0310. Sadly, no French restaurants remain as a reminder of the town's beginnings. This bakery dates back to 1901 and certainly looks the part, but is definitely past its prime – the cakes are fresh enough in the morning, but the bread is nothing like the real thing. Mon–Sat 8am–7.30pm.

Terco's Pollito Obregón on Parque Morelos ☎615 152 0075. You can eat very well here, with succulent barbecue chicken and well-prepared Mexican dishes (mains M$75–100). Daily 8am–10pm.

DIRECTORY

Banks Both banks are on Obregón, and have ATMs: Bancomer (at C 5; Mon–Fri 8.30am–4pm) and Banamex (opposite; Mon–Fri 9am–4pm).

Post office The post office is on Constitución at C 2.

Mulegé

Some 60km south of Santa Rosalía lies **MULEGÉ**, a rural town on the site of one of the original Jesuit missions. Like San Ignacio, it's a real oasis: tucked into a lush valley, the town sits on the north bank of the palm-fringed Río Santa Rosalía and has clung onto its small-town atmosphere, despite a growing US expat community. The calm was shattered in 2009, when **Hurricane Jimena** caused extensive damage, and again in 2014 when **Hurricane Odile** ripped up roads and demolished houses – though the town has recovered somewhat, business has remained sluggish. Mulegé's streets branch eastward from Hwy-1 and surround both sides of the estuary, though the old centre and **Plaza Corona** lie on the north bank – base yourself here if you don't have a car.

The beaches

Outside of hurricane season the town makes a good base for the superb **beaches** strung out along the **Bahía Concepción** (see p.558). Yet again you'll miss out on the best of them without your own transport, but here hitching is at least a realistic (and safe) possibility – many visitors commute to the beaches daily, particularly during the high season (Nov to April).

Museo de Mulegé

Cananea • Mon–Fri 9am–2pm • M$10 • ☎615 153 0056

There's not a great deal to see in Mulegé itself, though the former prison has been converted into a local history museum, the **Museo de Mulegé**. Built in 1907, it was known as "prison without doors," as it allowed its inmates to work in town in the mornings and afternoons – and some were even married there. Inside you'll find information about the old mission (see opposite) and a handful of prehistoric artefacts. Perched on a hillside (walk up Zaragoza and follow the signs), it also offers decent views across Mulegé.

CAVE ART AROUND MULEGÉ

Other than as a springboard for the beaches to the south, the main reason to stop at Mulegé is to take one of the **cave-painting tours** out to the Sierra de Guadalupe. This range boasts the densest collection of rock art in Baja, as well as some of the most accessible at **La Trinidad** (29km west of town), requiring as little as five hours for the round trip (including 6.5km on foot). Getting a group together to cut costs shouldn't be a problem in high season, but you still need to shop around as the tours differ considerably. Expect to pay M$700 (US$35–45) per person or half that with your own transport. Overnight excursions are possible too, including a night at a 260-year-old ranch and two different cave locations. Head to *Las Casitas* (see below), which also acts as an informal tourist office for information on other local attractions and tours. They can connect you with Mulegé Tours, run by Salvador Castro Drew (📞615 153 0232, 🌐mulegetours .com) – Salvador grew up in the area and is one of the most knowledgeable local guides.

Misión de Santa Rosalía de Mulegé

For a short hike (20–30min) and stellar panoramas visit the **Misión de Santa Rosalía de Mulegé**. Founded by the Jesuits in 1705, the current building was completed sixty years later and sits atop a hill 3km on the other side of town – like most of the Baja missions, it was abandoned in 1828 after the indigenous population died out. The church only opens for the occasional Mass, but it's still well worth the hike up for the spectacular view from above the palms. Follow Zaragoza south underneath the highway bridge and take the dirt road on the right that climbs to the mission.

ARRIVAL AND DEPARTURE   MULEGÉ

By bus The bus stop is at the junction of Hwy-1 and Martínez, a good 10min walk southwest of the town's central Plaza Corona; to get to the plaza, follow Martínez (under the *faux* city gate), taking a right fork, and finally a second right onto Zaragoza. Taxis will charge around M$50. Mulegé does not have a ticket office, so buy your onward ticket on the bus (no reservations). Around five buses daily pass through to Guerrero Negro (4.5hr; M$595), via Santa

Rosalía (1hr; M$135). At least five buses head south to La Paz (7.5hr; M$1050) via Loreto (3.5hr; M$290), with one going on to Cabo San Lucas (M$1335).
By car There are two PEMEX stations in and around town: one in the centre on Av Martínez at Zaragoza, and another 2.5km south of town along Hwy-1.
By taxi If you can't wait for a bus, taxis will charge M$750–1000 to Santa Rosalía.

ACCOMMODATION

Casa de Huéspedes Manuelita Moctezuma s/n (left fork as you head into town from the highway) 📞615 153 0175. Slightly more comfortable than the nearby *Nachita*, but otherwise similar with basic rooms and (usually) hot showers. M$360
★**Las Casitas** Madero 50 📞615 153 0019. The former home of Mexican poet José Alán Gorosave (born here in 1920) is now the best hotel in the centre (5min from the plaza). The gift shop and restaurant give way to an orchard-like yard and dribbling fountains at the back, while the charming rooms come with TVs, ceiling fans and bathroom. M$900
Clementine's Oasis Rio Baja (off Hwy-1) 📞615 153 0319, 🌐clementinesbaja.com. Excellent option near the river, with a variety of rental properties (casitas) and smaller rooms managed by expat owners who also run a B&B in Oregon. All the rooms and houses feature modern

furnishings, free wi-fi, a/c and kitchens. Doubles M$825, Casitas M$1125
Hotel Hacienda Madero 3 (just off the plaza) 📞615 153 0021, 🌐hotelhaciendamulege.com. One of the classic Baja hotels; the front section dates back to the 1770s and it's been a hotel since the 1950s. Rooms are fading a bit, but come with Sky TV, wi-fi and a/c, and the small pool, pleasant courtyard and on-site parking make this an attractive option. Breakfast M$55. M$500
Serenidad Hwy-1 km 139 📞615 153 0530, 🌐serenidad.com.mx. Just south of town on the east side of the Transpeninsular, this comfortable hotel is another stalwart from the 1960s, though it's also starting to show its age. Look out for the summer three-night-stay specials, and the legendary Sat-night pig roast (6.30pm; M$180), a tradition since 1970. Closed Sept. M$975

EATING

Los Equipales Moctezuma (near Zaragoza) 📞615 153 0330. The best Mexican restaurant in town, offering large

steaks and seafood portions on an open second-floor terrace – a steak complete with soup, salad and potatoes costs M$130–300. Great bar for drinks also. Daily 7.30am–10.30pm.

Mago's Coffee and Sweets Martínez 7 ☎615 153 1035. No frills but cosy café selling delicious apple, cherry, cream cheese and pineapple pies, home-made ice cream plus filling breakfasts, pizza and a famed vegetarian lasagne (mains M$55). Free wi-fi for customers, plus massages for M$250. Cash only. Daily 5am–4pm.

Taquitos Mulegé Plaza Corona. The best fish and shrimp tacos in town are usually available at this stall till 1pm, or until the seafood runs out; tacos are around M$15–20. Daily 9am–1pm.

DIRECTORY

Banks Mulegé has a Bancomer (Mon–Fri 8.30am–4pm) with an ATM on Zaragoza between Martínez and Moctezuma.

Post office The small post office is at Zaragoza and Madero.

Bahía Concepción

There is good diving and fishing immediately around Mulegé, but the best beaches are between 10km and 50km south of town along the shore of **Bahía Concepción**, for once easily accessible from Hwy-1 – the drive down to Loreto along this stretch of road is truly spectacular. The bay ranges from 3km to 6.5km wide, is 48km long and is enclosed on three sides and dotted with islands. The blue-green waters, tranquil bays and white-sand beaches are spellbinding and relatively undeveloped – though you will at times find teams of RVs lining the waters – and it's a good place to break your journey for a day or so before travelling south. As far as **kayaking** goes, there are few places better than Bahía Concepción.

Playa Punta Arena

The best stretches of sand include windy **Playa Punta Arena**, signposted at Hwy-1 km 119 (17km south of Mulegé) and 3km along a dirt road, where there should be some basic palapa shelters to rent (around M$100; no facilities) – it's popular with windsurfers and kiteboarders.

Playa Santispac

Playa Santispac (km 114), some 5km further on from the Punta Arena turning, is right on the highway – despite the winter crowds of RVs, it has plenty of room to **camp** (M$100) and enough life to make staying here longer-term a realistic option (toilets, showers, basic groceries). Stop at *Ana's* (Thurs–Tues 8am–10pm, summer 2–10pm) for cheap fish tacos and potent Bloody Marys; you can also rent **kayaks** (M$250–350/day) and snorkelling gear (M$100/day).

Posada Concepción and Playa Escondida

Posada Concepción, 2km south of Santispac, shows the beginnings of Cabo-style development (see p.572), and has permanent residents (mostly retirees). If you follow the rough road to the south of Posada Concepción (at km 111), you'll pass a bend and after 1km arrive at the rather secluded **Playa Escondida**. Few trailers can make it over the hump, so the campsite is more hospitable to tent campers (M$100). It is rustic (cold showers and outhouses) and there are no services.

Playa El Coyote and Playa El Requesón

Further south there are few facilities for anything other than camping: the popular, bone-white beaches of **Playa El Coyote** (6.5km south of Santispac) and **Playa El Requesón** (a dazzling sandbar poking into the bay, 15km south of Coyote at km 92.5) are the last and the best opportunities for this (M$100 for each). Note that there's no fresh water (pit toilets and palapas only) available at either, but locals drop by in the early morning and afternoon selling everything from water to fresh shrimps.

★**Playa Frambes Lighthouse Resort** Playa Punta Arena (off Hwy-1 km 118) ⓦmulege.org. Gorgeous property 20km south of Mulegé, comprising three spacious, modern 2-bedroom cottages, a pool and a lighthouse (that you can also rent for the same price). All units are air-conditioned and powered by solar energy, and breakfast is included. US$160 (M$2790)

Posada Concepción Hwy-1 km 112 ⓦposada concepcion.net. This gated expat community offers ten RV spots with full hookups, and comfy 2-bedroom houses for nightly, weekly or monthly rental. Comes with use of the tennis court, thermal hot springs and wi-fi; kayaks are M$100 for 2 hours. Houses M$600

Loreto

Another popular escape for fishing and diving enthusiasts, **LORETO** was the site of the earliest permanent settlement in the Californias. Founded in 1697 by **Juan María Salvatierra** as the first Jesuit mission to the region, Loreto served as the administrative capital of the entire California territory until a devastating hurricane struck in 1829 and La Paz took on the role. Today Loreto is booming again; much of the centre is given over to craft shops and galleries, many selling silver, while the seafront **malecón** and central **Plaza Cívica** have been spruced up in recent years. Some 8km south of town lies the largely expat community of **Nopoló (aka Villages at Loreto Bay)**, one of the most ambitious residential developments in Mexico, and the posh *Villa del Palmar* resort. Construction has provided a massive economic boost to the entire region, but critics claim that the project threatens to overwhelm the already limited water supply and Loreto's delicate natural assets: Mexico's largest marine park, **Parque Nacional Bahía de Loreto**, lies just offshore, while the weathered landscapes of the **Sierra de la Giganta** provide a stunning backdrop.

Misión de Nuestra Señora de Loreto de Conchó

Salvatierra, at Pino Suárez • Daily 7am–8pm • Free • ☎ 613 135 0005

In downtown Loreto, Avenida Salvatierra turns into a tree-lined pedestrian mall beyond Independencia, and the few buildings of note are along this six-block-long promenade to the sea. The old mission church, the **Misión de Nuestra Señora de Loreto de Conchó**, is still standing, though heavily restored after centuries of earthquake damage. Its basic structure – solid, squat and simple – is little changed since 1752. The inscription over the door, which translates as "The head and mother church of the missions of upper and lower California", attests to its former importance, as does the richly adorned Baroque *retablo* originally transported here from Mexico City.

Museo de las Misiones

Salvatierra, between Misioneros and Pino Suárez • Tues–Sun 9am–1pm & 2–6pm • M$47 • ☎ 613 135 0441

Next door to the mission, in a former storage house and courtyard complex, stands the illuminating **Museo de las Misiones**. The museum chronicles the early conversion and colonization of Baja California and its eighteen original mission churches through a collection of religious art, weapons and tools dating from the seventeenth and eighteenth centuries.

Misión San Francisco Javier de Viggé-Biaundó

If you have a car, make time for the detour to the **Misión San Francisco Javier de Viggé-Biaundó**, 36km southwest of Loreto in the heart of the mountains. Established in 1699, it became the base of **Father Juan de Ugarte** two years later, one of the leading Jesuit pioneers in Baja. The current church, completed in 1758, is one of the most isolated and evocative on the peninsula (it was abandoned in 1817 after a devastating attack by Guaycura Indians). Mass is heard here once a month, but the church is usually open daily from around 8am to around 5pm (free entrance) – you'll find fine gilded *retablos* and a gracious statue of San Javier inside. The mission is signposted at km 118 on Hwy-1, south of

Loreto, from where a paved road snakes between vast desert mountains, dry *arroyos* and massive faces of cracked rock. Taxis will charge at least M$1200 round-trip.

Parque Nacional Bahía de Loreto

Park office Adolfo López Mateos (malecón) at Carrillo • Mon–Fri 8.30am–2pm • Park fee M$25 • ☎613 135 0477

Loreto's greatest asset is the giant body of protected waters along its eastern shore – you'll get an entrancing view of the islands from the breezy malecón. The **Parque Nacional Bahía de Loreto** was established in 1996 to protect over 2000 square kilometres of the Sea of Cortez from overfishing, and it's become another superb place for **diving** and **kayaking**. If you just want a closer look at the islands, take a tour with the Cooperativa Parque Marino, formed by 21 local fishermen (see box opposite).

ARRIVAL AND DEPARTURE

By plane Loreto International Airport is 5km south of town off Hwy-1. Aéreo Calafia offers domestic flights to Guaymas, La Paz and Tijuana, while Alaska Airlines operates flights from Los Angeles. Alamo, Hertz and Europcar have car-rental counters at the entrance and have offices downtown. There are no public buses into town: yellow *colectivo* shuttle buses wait for passengers, driving to downtown Loreto when full, and dropping off at hotels (they charge around M$120/US$7). Private taxis booked in advance with companies like Wild Loreto (see box opposite) are expensive, around US$50 (M$870) per car for four people – taxis will charge at least US$85/M$1480 for Loreto Bay. Ignore the timeshare hawkers in the terminal.

By bus Loreto's bus terminal is at Salvatierra and Paseo Pedro de Ugarte (☎613 135 0767), just in front of the baseball field. It's a hot 20min walk east along Salvatierra to the Plaza Cívica, and a further 10min in the same direction to the beach – taxis usually meet buses and charge M$85/US$5 anywhere in town. Moving on, Mulegé is M$290, Guerrero Negro M$885 and La Paz M$760.

Destinations (bus) Ensenada (3–4 daily; 15hr); Guerrero Negro (5 daily; 6–7hr); La Paz (8 daily; 5–6hr); Mulegé (7 daily; 2hr); San Ignacio (5 daily; 4hr); Santa Rosalía (7 daily; 3hr); Tijuana (3 daily; 18hr).

By taxi Taxis will ask for M$1500 to drive to Mulegé (90min), but you can usually negotiate a lower price. The taxi stand at Hidalgo near Madero serves Sitio Juárez (☎613 135 0915), while Sitio Loreto (☎613 135 0424) is usually from Juárez one block west.

TOURING LORETO BAY

Don't leave town without exploring the pristine waters and islands (there are five, including Coronados and Del Carmen, the largest) of the Parque Nacional Bahía de Loreto.

Cooperativa Parque Marino ☎613 135 1664. Tours of Isla Coronados take 5hr and cost M$1500 for a boat that can take six – you'll be able to snorkel and see a sea lion colony here. Tours of Isla Danzante take 6hr and cost M$1800 – you'll see a lot more marine life here, such as sea lions, whale sharks, dolphins, manta rays and whales. Book tours at the booth on the marina (daily 5am–9pm; Adolfo López Mateos at Carrillo).

Dolphin Dive Baja Juárez between Mateos and Davis ☎613 135 1914, ⓦdolphindivebaja.com.

Runs two-tank dive trips to Isla Coronados, Isla Del Carmen and Isla Danzante (US$135/M$2350) that include tanks, all gear, snacks, guide, boat and park fees – they also offer snorkelling off Coronado for US$70/M$1220 and PADI open-water certification for US$550/M$9585 (four days).

Wild Loreto Salvatierra ☎613 135 1493, ⓦwild loreto.com. Reputable operator running tours to Coronados (M$1290/US$74) but also San Javier (M$1130/US$65) and climbing at Tabor Canyon (M$750/US$43).

INFORMATION

Tourist office The English-speaking tourist office (Mon–Fri 8am–3pm; ☎613 135 0411) is located in the Palacio de Gobierno at Madero and Salvatierra, on the west side of the pedestrian Plaza Cívica.

Websites Helpful sites include the Loreto Hotel Association's ⓦgotoloreto.com, Baja Life Online at ⓦloreto.com and the Loreto Adventure Network at ⓦloretoadventurenetwork.com.

ACCOMMODATION

★**Las Cabañas de Loreto** Morelos (just off the malecón) ☎613 135 1105, ⓦlascabanasdeloreto.com. Justly popular spot (book ahead), with spotless, spacious cabaña studios (with a/c, wi-fi and kitchenettes), welcome fruit basket, free bikes for the ride into town, outdoor community kitchen, laundry, pool and hot tub. M$1425

★**Coco Cabañas** Davis s/n, at Constituyentes ☎613 135 1729, ⓦcococabanasloreto.com. All eight cabañas surround a patio with a lovely sunken pool and barbecue area. The rooms have kitchens and private baths (no TVs), but the real draw here is the welcoming owners Stephen and Barrett, who can set up virtually any activity and are experts on the local area. M$1335

Iguana Inn Juárez s/n, at Davis ☎613 135 1627, ⓦiguanainn.com. Another friendly bargain near the centre of town. The owners live in the front house, guests stay in the four spotless cabañas situated around a gurgling

fountain and courtyard in the back. The relatively modern rooms, with tile floors, a/c, TV and ceiling fans, have kitchenettes and private baths. M$600

La Mision Rosendo Robles, at the malecón ☎613 134 0350, ⓦlamisionloreto.com. This reconstructed behemoth has retained some of its former charm (it originally opened in 1969), and is certainly the most luxurious option on the malecón. The colonial-style rooms feature marble floors and baths, hardwood furnishings, flat-screen TVs and patios or balconies overlooking the ocean. M$2025

Posada de las Flores Salvatierra, at Madero and Plaza Cívica ☎613 135 1162, ⓦposadadelasflores.com. Alluring boutique hotel in the centre of town, set in an old building with courtyard smothered in blossoms. The theme is eighteenth-century Mexico, with rooms decked out with antiques and a wonderful rooftop pool and bar area. M$2250

EATING

Finding simple Mexican **food** is no problem at the taco stands along Hidalgo or Juárez, while the best views can be found along the malecón. The best supermarket is El Pescador, on the corner of Salvatierra and Independencia, while Mercado Juárez is just around the corner from the bus station (on Juárez). For a romantic drink, try the roof-top bar at the *Posada de las Flores* (see above).

Café Olé Madero, just off Plaza Cívica ☎613 135 0496. Popular place under a shady palapa that does good-value breakfasts (from M$65) and *antojitos* like burritos and fresh fish (mains M$55–90). Mon–Sat 7am–10pm, Sun 7am–1pm.

Medíterraneo Malecón, at Hildalgo ☎613 135 2577. Fine Italian food, posh service and fabulous second-floor

views across the sea and the islands; they also serve Mexican classics, paella, steaks and decent wines by the glass (burritos and sandwiches range from M$99–190, dinner mains from M$240). Daily 12.30–4pm & 6–10pm.

Mexico Lindo y Que Rico Hidalgo, near Colegio ☎613 135 1175. Solid choice for lunch or dinner, with a big English menu offering everything from local fish to

9

Mexican classics, all served in an enticing courtyard away from the main road – the original wrought-iron gates and well add to the sense of antiquity. Entrées M$80–250, cash only. Tues–Sun 9am–10pm.

★**Mita Gourmet** Davis 13 (Plaza Cívica) ☎613 135 2025, ⓦmitagourmet.com. Best place for a splurge in Loreto, with outdoor seating on the plaza and a menu that features fabulous salads and local fish and shrimp, cooked in a variety of ways. The clams *gratinada* (twelve clams smothered in melted mozzarella) makes a heavenly starter (mains from M$140). Wed–Mon 3–10pm.

El Rey de Taco Juárez, near Misioneros. This takeout place (there are a few seats inside) has garnered a loyal following for its fresh battered fish tacos and tacos *carne asada* (around M$30), though hours can be erratic – opens at 9am and tends to close between noon and 2pm, but days differ.

Sabor! Restaurant Just off Transpeninsular Highway (Hwy-1), near the turning to San Javier ☎613 135 0496, ⓦsaborloreto.com. Always packed, this Southwestern US and Mexican hybrid set around a small pool and garden specializes in lip-smacking wood-fired chicken, home-made breads, dishes from Jalisco and Loreto's best hamburgers. The only catch – it's on the main road just outside town, on the way to Nopoló, so you'll need to drive or take a taxi. Mains M$140–200. Wed–Sun 5–9pm.

DIRECTORY

Banks Bancomer, just across the street from the tourist office on Plaza Cívica, have the most dependable ATMs between Santa Rosalía and Ciudad Insurgentes, but the bank no longer exchanges foreign currency. Note that US dollars are increasingly accepted throughout town (credit cards are not accepted in most stores and restaurants, however).

Internet More spots in town are adding wi-fi internet access; just walk the streets with your laptop until you've picked up a signal.

Post office The post office is on Deportiva 13, just off Salvatierra on the way into town, not far from the bus terminal (Mon–Fri 8am–4.30pm, Sat 9am–1pm).

La Paz

Everyone ends up in **LA PAZ** eventually, the state capital and largest city of Baja California Sur. The outskirts may be an ugly sprawl, but the old town centre near the languid **malecón**, modernized as it is, has managed to preserve something of its sleepy provincial atmosphere. During the last week in February, La Paz livens up with its boisterous **carnival**, a plethora of colourful parades and cultural events that transform the town, while **eating** here is a real pleasure at any time. There's not much to see in the city itself, but the surrounding **beaches** are lots of fun, and a boat trip to the **Isla Espíritu Santo**, rich in marine life, should not be missed.

The malecón

The **malecón** in La Paz is one of the most attractive in Mexico; a tranquil promenade overlooking small strips of sand with ravishing views of the mountains across the bay, especially at sunset.

Museo de la Ballena

Obregón at 16 de Septiembre • Mon–Fri 9am–2pm, Sat 10am–2pm • Free, M$10 donation suggested • ☎612 348 5238

Marked by a monster 25m blue whale skeleton outside, the **Museo de la Ballena** (whale museum) reopened in these plush new premises on the malecón in 2015. Inside you'll find a large collection of whale and dolphin skeletons, educational movies and enlightening exhibits on local whales and marine life. Note that opening times and admission fees were subject to change at the time of research.

Centro Cultural La Paz

16 de Septiembre 120, at Domínguez • Mon–Fri 8am–8pm, Sat 10am–6pm • Free • ☎612 122 0065

One block from the malecón on 16 de Septiembre, the **Centro Cultural La Paz** is the most visible sign of the city's regeneration in recent years, housed in the artfully

Ferry Terminal, Pichilingue & Beaches

LA PAZ

ACCOMMODATION
El Ángel Azul 2
Casa Tuscany 6
Casa Verde Inn 7
Lorimar 7
Pension California 5
Posada de Las Flores 8
Posada Luna Sol 9
Seven Crown Hotel 4
Yeneka 1

EATING
Bismark-Cito 2
Doce Cuarenta 6
La Fuente 2
J&R Ribs Costilleria 5
Lolita Pie Boutique 4
Mc-Fisher 1
Rancho Viejo 9
Taquería Hermanos
González 8
Las Tres Vírgenes 3

DRINKING & NIGHTLIFE
Beer Box 5
Cervecería La México 4
Dubai Nightclub 3
Harker Board 1
Mezcalería La Miserable 2
Tailhunter Restaurant
& Fubar Cantina 6

SHOPS
Allende Books 3
Got Baja? Store 1
Librerías Educal 2

Central Camionera (bus terminal 1km) & Airport (12km)   Hwy 1, Los Cabos & Todos Santos

9

restored 1910 Palacio Municipal (old city hall). Inside you'll find a bookshop, courtyard café and several gallery spaces for temporary exhibitions with a Baja theme. The **Sala Codex Península** contains an absorbing display of photographs, videos and text (in English) on the history and culture of the region.

Plaza Jardín Velasco

Centro de Artes y Culturas Madero, between 5 de Mayo and Independencia • Mon–Fri 9am–8pm, Sat & Sun 9am–6pm • Free • ☎ 612 129 4176

The **Plaza Jardín Velasco** (aka Plaza Constitución), three blocks inland from the malecón on 5 de Mayo, stands as the city's tranquil but rather faded main square, presided over by the modest **Catedral de Nuestra Señora de la Paz** (daily 8am–10pm). Completed in 1865 near the site of the old mission established by Jesuit priest Jaime Bravo in 1720, it's rather plain inside by Mexican standards. On the other side of the plaza the nineteenth-century Casa de Gobierno has been converted into the **Centro de Artes y Culturas**, a small but atmospheric space for temporary local art and photography exhibitions.

Museo Regional de Antropología y Historia

Altamirano at 5 de Mayo • Daily 9am–6pm • M$39 • ☎ 612 122 0162

To get a taster of local history, visit the **Museo Regional de Antropología y Historia** (if you read Spanish – there are no English captions). The permanent exhibits begin on the first floor with geology and prehistory, with some rare arrowheads dating from 1180–1280, prehistoric skulls and some reproductions of traditional indigenous graves. The next floor features photos of Baja's mind-blowing cave paintings, while the top floor is dedicated to the development of Baja California Sur since Independence, with sections on William Walker (the US freebooter who invaded the region in 1853), the 1911 Revolution, gold, silver and copper mining in Baja, the "Loreto 70" movement and the creation of the state constitution in 1975.

The beaches

Make time for the enticing **beaches** between La Paz and the port of Pichilingue, beginning with **Playa del Tesoro** (Carr. Pichilingue km 12), and **Playa Pichilingue** itself (km 18), just beyond the ferry terminal, home to *Restaurant Playa Pichilingue* (daily 11am–9pm; ☎ 612 122 4565), offering great seafood (tacos for M$30), and loungers for M$150 per day. The most unspoiled beach is **Playa de Balandra** (km 23), a series of shallow bays, most of which are no more than waist deep (great for families and snorkelling). There are minimal vendors here and few people on weekdays – you can also rent kayaks. The biggest and busiest beach is **Playa de Tecolote** (km 24), with a real party atmosphere at the weekend – it's also the best for swimming, with views across to Isla Espíritu Santo and *El Tecolote* restaurant and bar (☎ 612 127 9494), offering seafood, drinks and boat tours (M$950).

SEA LIONS, WHALE SHARKS AND ISLA ESPÍRITU SANTO

There are plenty of opportunities for fishing, diving and **boat trips** from La Paz, but it would be a shame to leave without visiting the azure waters of uninhabited **Isla Espíritu Santo**, a short boat ride north of the city. Protected within the **Parque Nacional Archipiélago de Espíritu Santo** (including the nearby **Los Islotes**, a small group of islands that hosts a colony of **sea lions**), snorkelling trips invariably encounter dolphins, manta rays and, depending on the time of year, fin whales and whale sharks (Nov–March) – the sea lions are a sure bet and always the most entertaining. Costs vary, but average M$500–750 per person and include lunch. See p.566 for details on specific operators.

ARRIVAL AND DEPARTURE

LA PAZ

BY PLANE

The Aeropuerto Internacional Manuel Márquez de León, Ciudad Insurgentes–La Paz Hwy-1 km 10 (☎612 122 2959), is 12km southwest of the city. All the major rental car companies have desks in the airport's only terminal. Transporte Terrestre (☎612 125 1156) has a monopoly on all transport from the airport (though other firms can take you back); taxis charge around M$300 to hotels on the malecón, while shared minibus (*colectivo*) rides start around M$175 per person. As always, confirm the price before entering the taxi or shuttle. You'll pay around M$200 for the trip back to the airport by taxi. Useful budget flight connections to La Paz include Aéreo Calafia flights to Los Mochis and Mazatlán, and Volaris to Tijuana.

Destinations (domestic) Guadalajara (3 daily; 1hr 30min); Guaymas (1 daily; 40min); Los Mochis (1 daily; 55min); Mazatlán (5 weekly; 1hr 50min); Mexico City (4 daily; 2hr); Tijuana (1 daily; 2hr).

BY BUS

Most buses arrive at the Terminal Turística on the malecón at C Independencia. Buses may also pull in at the Central Camionera (main bus station) at Jalisco and Héroes de la Independencia first, but don't get off here – it's around 25 blocks from the main section of the malecón. Heading south, Ecobajatours (W ecobajatours.com) charges M$335 to Cabo, M$155 for Todos Santos, M$495 for Los Cabos airport and M$220 for Los Barriles for its minibus service (6.30am, then hourly 7–11am); Águila charges M$285 to Cabo (M$320 to San José), running every 30min or so; routes "via corta" (short) go via Todos to Cabo, while "via larga" (long) go via Los Barriles and San José. Águila/ABC Services north are far less frequent – try to buy tickets in advance. Sample fares include Loreto M$760, Santa Rosalía M$1180 and Tijuana M$2385.

Destinations Cabo San Lucas via corta (every 30min; 2hr–2hr 30min); Ensenada (3 daily; 20hr); Guerrero Negro (5 daily; 12hr); Loreto (8 daily; 5hr); Mexicali (2 daily; 28hr); Mulegé (7 daily; 7hr); San Ignacio (5 daily; 9hr); San José del Cabo via larga (6 daily; 3hr); Santa Rosalía (7 daily; 8–9hr); Tijuana (3 daily; 22hr); Todos Santos (every 30min; 1hr 15min).

BY FERRY

Baja Ferries (W bajaferries.com) connects Terminal Pichilingue, 18km north of central La Paz, with Mazatlán (see p.486) and Topolobampo (the port for Los Mochis, p.497) across the Sea of Cortez. If you have a vehicle, it's worth

checking out the alternative service provided by TMC (W ferrytmc.com), which specializes in trucks and freight but also takes cars from M$3380 to Mazatlán and M$2300 to Topolobampo. Minibuses run between Terminal Pichilingue and the Terminal Turística on the malecón (daily, 6am–6pm roughly every hr; M$61), or take a taxi (M$200), and aim to arrive at the ferry three hours in advance of the departure time.

To/from Mazatlán Ferries currently depart from La Paz at 5pm Tues, Thurs & Sun (arriving in Mazatlán at 11am); ferries depart Mazatlán 4pm Mon, Wed & Fri. One-way tickets (seat only) are M$1102; for a four-person cabin it's an additional M$790, while standard cars are an additional M$2500.

To/from Topolobampo Ferries currently make the journey to Topolobampo Mon to Fri at 2.30pm (arriving at 8.30pm), and Sat at 11pm, arriving at 6am; ferries to La Paz depart midnight Mon–Fri and 11pm Sun. One-way tickets (seat only) are M$970; for a four-person cabin it's an additional M$790, while cars are an additional M$2080.

Tickets Try to buy tickets as far ahead of time as possible, and check the website for updates to routes and schedules, as they change often and routes can close unexpectedly for months at a time. You can buy tickets with a credit card on the website, or in person at Baja Ferries downtown office at Ignacio Allende 1025 at Marcelo Rubio (Mon–Fri 8am–5pm, Sat 8am–2pm; ☎612 123 6600); the office at the terminal (☎612 125 6324) is open Mon, Wed & Fri 8am–4pm, Tues & Thurs 8am–6pm, Sat 9am–11pm and Sun 9am–5pm. Tickets can be paid for with major credit cards. Bicycles go free. Tickets for the TMC ferry must be purchased in cash or with Visa and MasterCard at its counter at Terminal Pichilingue (☎612 123 9226).

Car permits and FMM Car drivers should ensure they have a permit to drive on the mainland. This should have been obtained when crossing the border into Mexico (see p.29), but if not, take your vehicle and all relevant papers to the branch of Banjercito at the ferry terminal (daily 9am–2pm) a couple of days before you sail. If for some reason you've managed to get this far without having your multiple migration form or "FMT" stamped, you should also attend to that before sailing – there's an immigration office at 5 de Febrero between Forjadores and Durango (Mon–Fri 9am–5pm).

BY TAXI

La Paz taxis will take up to four people to Todos Santos for M$800, and Cabo San Lucas or San José del Cabo for M$1500.

GETTING AROUND

LA PAZ

By taxi/bus Getting a taxi in La Paz is never difficult; there are stands on the malecón in front of *Hotel Perla* and *Seven Crown Hotel* and on both sides of the cathedral on the plaza.

They don't use meters, but you shouldn't pay more than M$50 for most trips in the city. Local buses (including the modern Ruta de La Paz buses) charge M$10, but you are unlikely to need them.

9

By car Renting a car is a good way to see the beaches and surrounding area, with all the major chains at the airport and along the malecón: Alamo ☎ 612 122 6262; Avis ☎ 612 122 2651; Budget ☎ 612 123 1919; Europcar ☎ 612 122 3107; Fox ☎ 800 225 4369; Hertz ☎ 612 122 0919; National ☎ 612 125 6585; and Thrifty ☎ 612 125 9696. Rates start at around M$750/day with insurance for a compact car.

By bike The malecón now features a special bike lane for most of its length and renting bikes has become a popular activity for Mexican tourists. Bici-Rentals on the malecón (just south of 16 de Septiembre) rents various bikes for M$30–60/hr.

THE BEACHES

By bus Buses to the beaches leave the Terminal Turística on the malecón daily, traversing the coast to Pichilingue ferry terminal (M$61), and on to Balandra and Tecolete (M$75–80). Departures are hourly from 6am to 1pm, then 1.30pm, 3.30pm, 5pm and 6pm. The last bus back should be at 6pm, but check before you leave La Paz.

Taxis will charge around M$200 as far as Pichilingue, and at least M$250 to Balandra and Tecolete.

INFORMATION AND TOURS

Tourist information The useful tourist office (daily Mon–Fri 9am–7pm; ☎ 612 125 6844, ⓦ vivalapaz.net) is next to the Casa de Cultura at 16 de Septiembre and Domínguez. You can also visit the Got Baja? Store (☎ 612 125 5991, ⓦ gotbaja.mx) at Madero 1240, between Constitución and 5 de Mayo, for maps of the region.

Baja Diving & Service Club Cantamar Resort, Carr Pichilingue km 17 ☎ 612 122 1826, ⓦ clubcantamar .com. Offers good diving (M$2025) and snorkelling tours (M$1035), and PADI courses (from US$500/M$8715) – they'll pick you up from town.

Baja Outdoor Activities Madero, at Campeche and Tamaulipas ☎ 612 125 5636, ⓦ kayactivities.com. Kayak rental (M$525/day) and multi-day kayak expeditions to nearby islands (from US$585/M$10,200), or to the sea lion colony (shuttles US$120/M$2090). Located a 30min walk from downtown La Paz on the road to Pichilingue next to the *Hotel El Moro*.

Cortez Club La Concha Beach Resort, Carr Pichilingue km 5 ☎ 612 121 6120, ⓦ cortezclub.com. Runs beginner's through to divemaster courses for PADI dive certification (US$499–1000 or M$8700–17,435), and two-tank dives for M$2100.

Funbaja Carr Pichilingue km 6.1 (Marina Costa Baja) ☎ 612 106 7148, ⓦ funbaja.com. Runs snorkelling and scuba-diving trips, excursions to the islands, whale watching, camping, kayaking and land tours.

ACCOMMODATION

El Ángel Azul Independencia 518, at Prieto ☎ 612 125 5130, ⓦ elangelazul.com. A tastefully restored 150-year-old courthouse with sparsely furnished rooms around a garden courtyard. The nine rooms and one suite have private bathroom, a/c and free wi-fi access, with a shared lounge with cable TV and shared kitchen for guests' use. M$1200

Casa Tuscany Nicolás Bravo 110, between Mutualismo and Madero ☎ 612 128 8103, ⓦ tuscanybaja.com. The distinctive decorations that adorn the four bedrooms in this B&B come from Guatemala and Italy and all rooms have access to the rooftop terrace. There's also free wi-fi and a shared library of books and videos. M$1500

Casa Verde Inn Independencia 563, at Ramírez ☎ 612 165 5162, ⓦ casaverdeinn.com.mx. Gorgeous boutique guesthouse in the centre of town, run by friendly Italian expats Cinzia and Roberto with just three delightful rooms (all en suite with a/c) and a small pool; free wi-fi. M$1350

Lorimar Nicolás Bravo 110 ☎ 612 125 3822, ⓦ hotel lorimar.com. This small hotel two blocks from the malecón is La Paz's best budget option, especially when you factor in the helpful desk staff. Each basic but clean room has a private bath and a/c, with the larger suites (M$1050) also equipped with kitchens and TVs. M$645

Pension California Degollado 209 ☎ 612 122 2896, ⓔ pensioncalifornia@prodigy.net.mx. The very basic but bargain *Pension California* is in an old building with a courtyard just off the main shopping street. The spare, cell-like rooms all have bath and fan, and public areas include a communal kitchen, laundry and free internet. M$300

★ Posada de Las Flores Obregón 440 ☎ 612 125 5871, ⓦ posadadelasflores.com. Well-designed rooms with Mexican-colonial chic decor, plush bath products and a minibar; you'll pay more here for the boutique hotel experience than it's worth, but the location on the malecón and the view from the attached second-storey restaurant are superb. Breakfast included. M$2700

Posada Luna Sol Topete 564, between 5 de Febrero and Navarro ☎ 612 123 0559, ⓦ posadalunasol.com. The location, along a residential block west of the marina, is a bit removed from the action, but the rooms – with artisan-tiled private baths, flat-screen TVs, free wi-fi and a/c – break from the cookie-cutter hotel norm and the knowledgeable staff are excellent local resources. There's also secure, on-site parking. M$1050

Seven Crown Hotel Obregón 1710 ☎ 612 123 0559, ⓦ sevencrownhotels.com. Top location right on the malecón, with fairly simple but stylish rooms done out in minimalist furnishings and tiled floors (plus free wi-fi and satellite TV). The fourth-floor restaurant and rooftop bar have fabulous views of the bay. Parking on site. M$1245

Yeneka Madero 1520 ☎ 612 125 4688, ⓦ hotelyeneka .com. The quirkiest hotel on the peninsula is liberally sprinkled with folk art and eccentric furniture in the comfortable, clean rooms, some of which come with a/c and TV (can be noisy, however). You also get internet, laundry, complimentary coffee, continental breakfast and a free shot of tequila in the evening. M$480

EATING

Eating is a real pleasure in La Paz – the seafood, especially, is excellent. The cheapest stalls lie next to the **Mercado Francisco Madero** – look for the "Área de Comedor" facing Revolución de 1910 (at Degollado) for big plates of Mexican classics for M$50–60. Just inside the market itself you'll find *jugos* stalls where fresh juices are M$17–35.

Bismark-Cito Obregón, at Hidalgo y Costilla ☎ 612 128 9900. This enticing open-air restaurant and *taquería* since 1968 has been spruced up in recent years, with tables under a smart brick-lined palapa, waiters in white and the best lobster and tacos in town (M$22–60). Daily 10am–11pm.

Doce Cuarenta Madero 1240, between 5 de Mayo and Constitución ☎ 612 125 5991. Hip modern café (sharing a space with Got Baja?), with shaded patio, distressed wood tables and a menu that includes excellent coffee (from M$20) and a range of cakes, pastries (M$20–50) and light meals such as sandwiches (M$60–80) and quiche (M$40). Mon–Fri 7am–9.30pm, Sat 7.30am–2pm.

La Fuente Obregón, between Agustín Arriola and Lerdo de Tejeda. Always busy thanks to the scrumptious home-made ice cream on offer, from simple but tasty vanilla to delicious chocolate chip concoctions for M$30 (vaso or cup) and M$35 (cone). Daily 9am–midnight.

J&R Ribs Costilleria 5 de Mayo, at Domínguez ☎ 612 122 7977, ⓦ ribsjr.com. It might seem a little out of place here in Baja, but this tiny barbecue joint on the corner knocks out authentic, mouth-watering baby back ribs or *costillas* (full rack M$125, half M$80), with sauces allegedly based on an old Montana cowboy recipe. Mon–Thurs 1.30–10pm, Fri & Sat 1.30pm–midnight.

★ **Lolita Pie Boutique** Constitución 120 ☎ 612 129 6400. Exquisite pies with perfect, flaky crusts, from sweet creations such as lemon-lavender and grapefruit custard tart, to savoury kale and feta, turkey, and beef and Guinness pies. It also knocks out excellent quiche, scones, cookies and other baked goods. Sit at the small table inside or take away. Look for the tree with pink painted trunk. Tues–Sat 8.30am–2pm.

Mc-Fisher Morelos, between Revolución and Madero ☎ 612 122 4140. Family-run, laid-back seafood joint where plates of seafood pasta, marlin enchiladas, grilled shrimp and the exceptional yellowfin tuna run M$95–320 (the most expensive for lobster). Mon–Thurs 8.30am–11pm, Fri & Sat 8.30am–midnight, Sun 4–11pm.

★ **Rancho Viejo** Márquez de León, at Domínguez ☎ 612 128 4647. One of the most famous taco joints in La Paz, renowned for its *arrachera* (steak) taco and roast potatoes stuffed with cheese, mushroom and marinated *al pastor* (M$80–160). Also serves beer, unusually for a *taquería*. Open 24hr. There is a convenient second branch on the malecón at Obregón 460-D (daily 7am–midnight).

★ **Taquería Hermanos González** Lerdo de Tejada, at Madero. Delicious fried fish tacos (M$16), shrimp tacos (M$22) and tacos *carne asada* (M$20) are the essential eats at this popular stand (also known as "Super Tacos de Baja California"), accompanied by dollops of the help-yourself salsa and salads (extra M$10). Daily 8am–6pm.

Las Tres Vírgenes Madero 1130 ☎ 612 123 2226. Great choice for a splurge, with a romantic courtyard and posh menu of "Baja High Cuisine" featuring fine meats, seafood, poultry and exceptional dishes such as blue crab enchiladas; expect big portions. Mains M$120–300. Tues–Sun 1–11pm.

DRINKING AND NIGHTLIFE

Beer Box Independencia 201 (at Domínguez) ☎ 612 129 7299. Small hole-in-the-wall serving a huge variety of craft beers, from German wheat beers to Mexican microbrews. Mon–Wed 5–11pm, Thurs–Sat 5pm–1am.

Cervecería La México Alvaro Obregón, between 16 de Septiembre and Callejón La Paz ☎ 612 123 0697. Huge, trendy bar on the malecón, packed out with locals enjoying the litre mugs of frothy Tecate beer and live football on TV. Daily 11am–2am.

Dubai Nightclub Alvaro Obregón, at 16 de Septiembre ☎ 612 107 3793. One of several glitzy clubs along the malecón popular with a local crowd, with live Banda and Norteña as well as DJs spinning Latino pop and traditional Mexican sounds. Also shows major boxing matches, live. Thurs–Sun 10pm–4am.

Harker Board Alvaro Obregón 299, at Constitución ☎ 612 122 7661, ⓦ harkerboardco.com. This paddle-board outfit by day is a popular restaurant/bar by night, serving Baja Brewing microbrews on tap for M$40–55, Coors for M$20 and decent hamburgers and giant hot dogs (M$100) right on the waterfront. Daily 7am–2am.

Mezcaleria La Miserable 274 Domínguez, between 5 de Mayo and Constitución ☎ 612 157 3217. Superb little mescal bar with a friendly atmosphere and far more laid-back than the scene on the malecón. Try and nab one of the tables on the back patio. Mon–Sat 7pm–2am.

9

★ **Tailhunter Restaurant & Fubar Cantina** Obregón 755 ☎612 125 3311, ⓦtailhunter-international.com. Justly popular joint just north of the centre, right on the malecón, with a three-storey wooden deck, sports on TV, plenty of great home-cooked food (burgers from M$69, Baja hot dogs M$65, fish and chips M$138) and cold beers. Sun–Thurs 8am–midnight, Fri & Sat 8am–1am.

DIRECTORY

Banks Most banks and ATMs are on 16 de Septiembre near the waterfront; Banamex is at Agustín Arriola and Mutualismo, while Bancomer and HSBC are on 16 de Septiembre near Mutualismo.

Books Librerías Educal (daily 10am–8pm) on 16 de Septiembre, inside the Centro Cultural, sells some English-language magazines and books, but Allende Books, at Independencia 518 (Mon–Sat 10am–6pm; ☎612 125 9114), has the best selection of English books, maps and guides on Mexico.

Emergencies ☎066; tourist police ☎612 122 5939; Angeles Verdes (roadside assistance) ☎078; Hospital Fidepaz ☎612 124 0400.

Laundry La Paz Lava, Mutualismo 260 at Ocampo ☎612 122 3112 (daily 8am–8pm; M$18–35/load), is just behind *Seven Crown Hotel* and the malecón.

Post office Constitución, at Revolución de 1910 (Mon–Fri 8am–5pm, Sat 8am–1pm).

Los Cabos

South of La Paz, Baja California finally runs out of land where the Pacific Ocean and the Sea of Cortez come together in spectacular fashion. The ocean and sea meet at the sister towns of **Cabo San Lucas** and **San José del Cabo**, known collectively as **Los Cabos** – easily the most exclusive parcel of land in Baja. Undeniably beautiful and home to the lion's share of the peninsula's lavish resorts, golf courses and oft-photographed beaches, the area is one of the fastest-developing regions in Mexico (despite being hammered by **Hurricane Odile** in 2014), supporting a sizeable North American expat population and hordes of time-share owners.

But Los Cabos is just a tiny part of the cape. Many of its most remarkable areas still require a great deal of time and preparation to access, and many travellers rent cars to drive the **loop** north of Cabo San Lucas: via the fast Hwy-19 running straight up the Pacific coast through historic **Todos Santos**; the older Transpeninsular Highway (Hwy-1) trailing north from San José del Cabo to La Paz; and the third, most exhausting, route along the **East Cape**.

ARRIVAL AND DEPARTURE　　　　　　　　　　　　　　　　　　　　LOS CABOS

BY PLANE

Aeropuerto Internacional de Los Cabos, Hwy-1 km 43.5 (☎624 146 5111), lies 19km north of downtown San José del Cabo and a further 32km from Cabo San Lucas. Arrival at Los Cabos can be a rather confusing experience, thanks to the mobs of time-share salesmen that greet you in the terminals (who offer rides plus sales pitch). Terminal 1 handles domestic flights, while Terminal 2 (a 10–15min walk away) is for international flights. You'll find car rental desks and ATMs (Bancomer) in both terminals, plus *cambios*, but don't change money here – the exchange rates are always very poor. There is no official information desk at the airport.

Shared minibuses The most popular option is to take a shared minibus (or "shuttle bus") operated by Transportistas Josefinos (ⓦtransportistasjosefinos.com), which charges US$14 to San José (or peso-equivalent) and U$17 or peso-equivalent to Cabo San Lucas. You can usually pay for these on arrival (at the desks at the terminal) – several other companies allow you to book in advance, but shop around

(they'll often make you pay for return trips): Cabo Transfers (US☎+1877 737 2226, ⓦcabotransfers.com), Gray Line (US☎+206 331 3812, ⓦgraylineloscabos.com), Los Cabos Airport Shuttle (☎624 142 3238, ⓦloscabosairportshuttle .com), Shuttle in Cabo (☎624 146 5393, ⓦshuttleincabo .com) and Trans Baja (US☎+1877 225 2123, ⓦtransbaja .com). All these services drop passengers off at hotels.

By bus Ecobajatours (☎624 144 3066, ⓦecobajatours .com) runs small buses direct from Terminal 1 to La Paz (3–3.5hr; M$495) every hour from 12.30pm to 5.30pm; the 12.30pm and 2.30pm buses travel via Los Barriles, while the others go via Cabo San Lucas and Todos Santos (stopping at bus terminals only). You can pre-book online.

Local buses By far the cheapest option are the Ruta del Desierto (ⓦrutadeldesierto.travel) modern a/c buses that run every 10–20min between the Aguila bus station in Cabo San Lucas and the airport at Terminal 1, and the upper level (departures) of Terminal 2 (buses stop along Lázaro Cárdenas at Puerto Paraíso Mall in Cabo San Lucas, and along Hwy-1 on the edge of San José del Cabo): prices range from M$12.50 to M$26 for San José and destinations in the Corridor, to M$35 for Cabo San Lucas (allow 1hr) to/from the airport (you can save a few pesos by booking online).

Taxis Airport taxis are very expensive: fixed rates are M$590 to San José del Cabo, M$830–1070 to Cabo San Lucas and M$650–830 for Corridor resorts. Buy tickets at the dedicated taxi booth before leaving the terminal (no need to pre-book).

Destinations (domestic flights) Guadalajara (3–4 daily); Loreto (Thurs, Fri, Sat); Los Mochis (1 weekly); Mexico City (4 daily); Mazatlán (1 weekly); Monterrey (1 daily); Tijuana (2 daily); Toluca (1 daily).

BY BUS
Both San José and Cabo San Lucas have long-distance bus connections to La Paz and the rest of Baja – see individual sections for details.

GETTING AROUND

BY BUS
Travelling between Todos Santos, San José and Cabo San Lucas by bus is the cheapest option, though the bus stations are not especially convenient. See relevant sections for details.

BY CAR
Renting a car is the sensible option if you want to really explore the area and get off the beaten path. Car rental agencies have kiosks in the arrivals section of each airport terminal, and in Cabo and San José; rates start at around M$750/day, insurance included, for a compact, rising to M$2000 for a SUV. Dec and Jan is the busiest time for rentals, when SUVs and minivans usually sell out. The fastest way from the airport to Cabo San Lucas is along the 19km toll

road (M$31) that bypasses central San José (re-joining Hwy-1 at Paseo de Los Cabos); by 2016 this toll road should be extended all the way to Cabo San Lucas (45km).

Car rental agencies (airport) Alamo ☎ 624 146 1900; Avis ☎ 624 146 0201; Budget ☎ 624 146 5333; Dollar ☎ 624 146 5060; Hertz ☎ 624 146 1803; National ☎ 624 146 5021; Payless ☎ 624 105 8411; Thrifty ☎ 624 142 1671. See ⓦ cabaja.com for one-way rentals to the US border.

BY TAXI
Travelling around the area by taxi is relatively expensive unless you have a group (most taxis are minivans). You'll pay at least US$40 (or peso-equivalent) to travel between San José and Cabo San Lucas.

INFORMATION

Tourist information The Los Cabos Convention and Visitors Bureau, Carretera Transpeninsular Km 4.3, Plaza Providencia, Cabo San Lucas (office hours Mon–Fri 9am–5.30pm; ☎ 624

143 4777), runs the useful ⓦ vcabo.com and sponsors the quarterly *Los Cabos Magazine* (ⓦ loscabosguide.com), a glossy monthly usually handed out for free in Cabo.

Todos Santos

The beautifully preserved old town of **TODOS SANTOS**, located just north of the **Tropic of Cancer**, marks the halfway point between Cabo San Lucas and La Paz. Close to some fabulous beaches and home to relatively affordable boutique hotels, Todos is also a great spot for **whale watching** from the shore: sit on any of the beaches in the winter months and you are bound to see several. Recovery from **Hurricane Odile** in 2014 was relatively quick (though you may still see some evidence of the devastation), and the tiny centre is easily explored on foot, crammed with **cafés**, **art galleries** and **studios**.

Plaza Todos Santos

Palm-fringed **Plaza Todos Santos** lies in the heart of town (one block off Juárez, the main street), surrounded by the modest church (see below) and the elegant **Teatro General Manuel Márquez de León** (Mon–Fri 9am–2pm; ☎ 612 145 0225), completed in

---

WINE TASTING IN TODOS

Visit **La Bodega de Todos Santos** (☎ 612 152 0181) on Hidalgo, between Militar and Juárez, for Baja wine tastings (mostly Valle de Guadalupe, see p.543), every Monday 5–8pm. The wine shop is otherwise open Tuesday–Saturday noon–7pm, with red wine tasting (and Doña Guillermina's tamales) on Wednesdays 5–8pm. Also sells its own olive oil from the Valle de Ensenada.

9

Spanish Revival style in 1944. The theatre still hosts the local film festival (⊕ todossantoscinefest.com; Feb–March) and art festival (Feb). In a small plaza to the right of the theatre, look for the **Sun Monument**, based on the Aztec calendar and completed in 2012 with help from the Heaven and Earth Art Project.

Misión de Nuestra Señora del Pilar de la Paz
Plaza Todos Santos • Daily 7am–8pm • ☎ 612 145 0043

The squat, pale yellow **Misión de Nuestra Señora del Pilar de la Paz** was founded in 1723 as Misión de Santa Rosa, but was destroyed in the Pericú Revolt ten years later. Re-established, the name was changed after the La Paz mission was relocated here in 1748 – like many Baja missions, it was finally closed in 1840. Despite maintaining a simple, colonial-style eighteenth-century exterior, the current church was mostly rebuilt in the 1960s – the venerated image of the Virgin inside is said to date back to 1733.

Centro Cultural Profesor Nestor Agúndez Martínez
Juárez, between Obregón and Hidalgo • Mon–Fri 8am–5pm, Sat & Sun 10am–3pm • Free • ☎ 612 145 0041

The **Centro Cultural Profesor Nestor Agúndez Martínez** occupies a red-brick primary school built in 1931 (some of its original murals are still extant in the entrance). Inside are modest but absorbing collections of prehistoric tools, local art and handicrafts and a room of ageing black-and-white photos – this is more interesting than it sounds, with detailed descriptions and personal stories of the photo subjects (translated into English); look for the remarkable Don Ramón Wong, who emigrated from China in 1910, and the group photo of the "captivating women of Todos Santos".

The beaches
Playa La Poza is the first of several beaches strung out between here and Cabo San Lucas, a bumpy ten-minute ride west along any unmarked dirt road; 2km south of Todos on Hwy-19, look for the signs to **Playa Punta Lobos**, a further 2.5km west. From here, beaches line the coast for 10km south, most of them prime **surfing** country (see box opposite).

ARRIVAL AND INFORMATION   **TODOS SANTOS**

By bus With the Hwy-19 bypass completed in 2014, central Todos is now blissfully free of through traffic, though Aguila buses (with the exception of express buses) still stop at the tiny bus station at the corner of Colegio Militar and Zaragoza (facing Zaragoza, turn right to reach Juárez, the main street). Buses leave every 30min–1hr for Cabo San Lucas (6.30am–10.30pm; 1hr 15min; M$160) and La Paz (6.45am–11.15pm; 2hr; M$155). Minibuses direct to Los Cabos airport depart at 8.05am, 9.35am and 11.35am (M$320). Minibus taxis line up outside the bus

station, but the centre is easy to explore on foot.
Books and maps Librería El Tecolote (Oct–May Mon–Sat 10am–5pm, Sun 11am–3pm; reduced hours June–Sept; ☎ 612 145 0295) on Juárez at Hidalgo has a great selection of new and used English books, and sells detailed local maps. Free maps by Got Baja? (⊕ gotbaja.mx) are available all over town.
Websites Todos has no information centre but is well served by websites: try the official ⊕ todossantos.cc, and ⊕ todossantos.net blog.

TOURS AND ACTIVITIES

Todos Santos Eco Adventures ☎ 612 145 0189, ⊕ tosea.net. Arranges a vast range of activities, from horseriding (US$75/M$1305), bird watching (US$45/M$785) and nature walks through the Sierra de la Laguna

Biosphere Reserve (Nov–June 9am–3pm; US$75/M$1305), to historical tours of the town (Mon–Sat 10am–noon; US$35/M$610) and surf lessons (US$60/M$1045/hr).

ACCOMMODATION

California Juárez, between Morelos and Márquez de León ☎ 612 145 0525, ⊕ hotelcaliforniabaja.com. An evening's stay at this gem (completed in 1950) might make it worth parting with some of those pesos you've been setting aside for a rainy day. Rooms are multicultural

mestizos of Mexican and Moorish decor. There's a pool and restaurant, as well as ocean views from the top floor, though claims that this is the inspiration behind the Eagles' famous 1970s hit have long been dismissed by Don Henley and co. M$1575

María Bonita Colegio Militar, at Hidalgo ☎612 145 0289, ✉mariabonitahotel@prodigy.net.mx. Best of the budget hotels in town, with twelve simple but clean rooms with small bathrooms above a cosy café. The road can be a bit noisy, but you do get free wi-fi. **M$600**

★**Hotelito** Dom Conocido s/n Rancho de la Cachora (take C Topete off Juárez) ☎612 145 0099, ⊛the hotelito.com. Fabulous boutique hotel, with a hip contemporary Mexican style, bold colours and four individual cottages set around a central courtyard. Each comes with a terrace and seating area (with hammock), and British expat owner Jenny Armit is a font of local information. **M$1875**

Posada La Poza Domicilio Conocido, Barrio La Poza (take Olachea off Hwy-19/Degollado, south of the centre) ☎612 145 0400, ⊛lapoza.com. This tranquil boutique is justly lauded for its high quality and extra touches: binoculars and bird guide in each room, sweat lodge, saltwater swimming pool, free kayaks, bikes, fishing gear and internet. All suites have ocean or lagoon views, free wi-fi, CD players and smart furnishings – no TVs or phones, though. **M$2925**

Todos Santos Inn Legaspi 33, between Topete and Obregón ☎612 145 0040, ⊛todossantosinn.com. The most romantic historical hotel in Todos. Built in 1872 by a local sugar baron, this old hacienda contains eight elegantly decorated rooms, a lush garden patio and an enticing pool. **M$2175**

EATING

Los Adobes Hidalgo 18, between Juárez and Colegio Militar ☎612 145 0203, ⊛losadobesdetodossantos .com. Expect pricey but high-quality *alta cocina* such as hearty *sopa de mariscos*, *mole poblano* and organic *chiles rellenos*, served in a serene cactus garden dining room (mains M$150–250). Daily 11am–9pm (5pm Sun).

Café Santa Fe Centenario 4, on the plaza ☎612 145 0340, ⊛cafesantafetodossantos.com. One of the cape's best restaurants, *Santa Fe's* Northern Italian menu showcases locally grown ingredients (lobster ravioli) and a stellar wine list that combines vintages from the Valle de Guadalupe and abroad. Dinner costs about M$800 a person, and tables are set inside an 1850s hacienda or outside on the courtyard patio. Wed–Mon noon–9pm (closed Sept & Oct).

Caffé Todos Santos Centenario 33, between Obregón and Topete ☎612 145 0787. Decorated by local artists, this expat-run café with timbered-beam hall and back garden does fine breakfasts (M$100–150), coffees (from M$20), hot chocolate (M$35) and muffins (M$30). Lunch and dinner (M$100–160) are several steps above deli fare. Mon 7am–2pm, Tues–Sun 7am–9pm.

★**La Copa Cocina** Legaspi 33, at Todos Santos Inn ☎612 145 0040. Trained sushi chef Patrick Mullen helms this justly popular restaurant with an intimate courtyard, fire pit and garden. Highlights include the fresh fish tacos (M$180), the "lobster dynamite" (M$180), half a lobster stuffed with a mix of fish and crab meat, and high-quality sushi rolls (M$120–180). Thurs–Tues 5–10pm.

La Coronela Hotel California Juárez, between Morelos and Márquez de León ☎612 145 0525, ⊛hotel californiabaja.com. Touristy but still a solid bet for Mexican food – eggs Benedict with smoked marlin and cilantro hollandaise (breakfasts M$95–140) or sea bass in tamarind

---

SURF AND SWIM EL PESCADERO

Before heading further south consider stopping at **El Pescadero**, just 12km from Todos, a small dusty village close to some of the best surf breaks and beaches on the coast: **Playa San Pedrito**, a short walk from the village, and gorgeous **Playa Los Cerritos**, 1km south (look for the turn at km 65). Both beaches are good for swimming. **Mario's Surf School** (☎612 142 6156, ⊛mariosurfschool.com) rents surf boards for US$20/M$350 per day and offers lessons for US$60/M$1045 per hour at Playa Los Cerritos. Cabo San Lucas is another 60km south from Pescadero. Most buses stop at Pescadero, on Hwy-19 (every 30min or so in both directions), but you really need a car to make the most of the area.

ACCOMMODATION AND EATING

Cerritos Beach Club Playa Los Cerritos, Hwy-19 km 65 (signposted) ☎624 143 4851, ⊛cerritosbcs.com. Right on the beach, serving excellent breakfast, lunch and dinner, with live music on Sun 2–5pm (usually featuring jazz singer Daline Jones). Daily 8am–8pm.

Cerritos Surf Colony Playa Los Cerritos, Hwy-19 km 65 ☎971 544 7645 ⊛cerritossurfcolony.com. Luxurious beachfront resort with palm-roofed, solar-powered studios and villas (with kitchens), pool and bar, and free wi-fi (no TVs). **M$2985**

Pescadero Surf Camp Hwy-19 km 64 (El Pescadero) ☎612 134 0480, ⊛pescaderosurf.com. Perfectly located to make the most of the beaches and the surf, this collection of cosy palapas, each with electricity, water and bathroom, also has a pool with swim-up bar and can organize surf lessons (M$900) and board rentals (M$300/day). **M$525**, camping **M$150**

9

WHEN TO VISIT CABO

High season here, as in the rest of Baja, is November through until May, though domestic tourists also provide a mini boom July and August. January and February is the best time to see whales. Avoid Christmas and Easter (packed) and Spring Break (Feb/March) if you want to sleep; the fishing competition season in October and November can be fun but also busy. In the summer and early autumn off-season (May–June and Sept–Oct), the heat (up to 42°C) makes things less appealing (though the sea is warm; many locals swim at night). Whenever you visit, you can be assured that it rarely rains – all the fresh water comes from desalination plants.

sauce (M$265) – and tapas on a separate menu. The bar is a great place to grab a drink or sandwich (M$130–165). Sun–Thurs 7am–9pm, Fri & Sat 7am–11pm.

Miguel's Degollado (Hwy-19) and Rangel ☏ 612 145 0733. Rustic Mexican restaurant under a palapa, popular with surfers and locals for its fish tacos and superb battered *chiles rellenos* smothered in salsa (M$100). The menu also

features breakfasts (M$45–80), cheeseburgers (M$75) and ice-cold margaritas. Mon–Sat 8am–9pm.

★ **Tacos George's** Colegio Militar, between Hidalgo and Márquez de León. No-frills street canteen with a few plastic tables selling delicious fried fresh fish tacos using home-made salsas and local tortillas (tacos from M$18). Daily 9am–3pm (usually closed Thurs).

DRINKING

Kin's Martini & Mojito Lounge Zaragoza at Colegio Militar ☏ 612 145 1033. Congenial tapas and wine bar (invariably with a 1980s music soundtrack) that also serves excellent Asian fusion dishes as well as pizza, pasta and shrimp chili relleno. Mojitos made with seasonal fruits. Daily noon–late.

Shut-up Frank's Degollado (Hwy-19), betweeen Rangel and Cuauhtémoc ☏ 612 145 0707, ⓦ shutupfranks.com. The town's only sports bar and a popular hangout for US expats, with great burgers (M$90–120), draught beer (M$35), free wi-fi and some traditional Mexican food. Happy hour Mon–Fri 3–6pm. Cash only. Daily 10am–10pm.

Cabo San Lucas

Billfish capital of the world, golfing paradise, home to luxury resorts and a crazy, tequila-fuelled nightlife, **Cabo San Lucas** is hard to ignore. All around lie kilometres of gorgeous beaches set against a pristine desert hinterland, and the jagged cape which gave the town its name remains utterly entrancing – if you're looking to snorkel or dive, the allure will be even greater, with a vast range of marine life and even a friendly **sea lion** colony nearby.

True, Cabo isn't like the rest of Baja. Until the 1980s it was little more than a dusty village and tuna cannery occasionally visited by adventurous sports fishermen – Steinbeck calls it a "sad little town" in *The Log from the Sea of Cortez*. Today it can seem more like an enclave of the US than part of Mexico, with almost all aspects of civilization geared to tourism – millions of North Americans vacation here, and it's a well-established cruise port and Spring Break party town (Feb–March). Transactions are conducted in US currency and million-dollar second homes occupy the best vantage points. Yet it would be a shame for independent and budget travellers to skip Cabo – there's plenty of bargains to be had, and it's hard to resist a couple of nights of sushi, watersports or just unabashed partying.

The marina

Cabo's premier attraction is the rugged cape of **Land's End** (see p.574), though activity in the town itself is centred around the **marina** and **Puerto Paraíso** mall (shops daily 9am–9pm; ⓦ puertoparaiso.mx), which contains over two hundred stores and restaurants, and a ten-screen multiplex cinema (Cinemex; ⓦ cinemex.com). The marina is smothered in yachts and motorboats, and ringed by a pleasant **boardwalk** lined with shops, bars and hawkers touting glass-bottomed boat trips, fishing, waterskiing, scuba diving, snorkelling, paragliding or bungee jumping. Competition is fierce, prices fluctuate daily and places come and go, so shop around. Even with all this activity, you'll see plenty of pelicans and even the odd puffer fish gliding between the boats; a sea lion even makes an appearance (invariably dubbed "Paco" by the locals). The most distinctive building along the marina is the **Pabellón Cultural de la República**, a striking contemporary structure containing a theatre and open-air performance space. Next to it is the **Flea Market El Arroyo**, a lane of covered stalls selling cheap souvenirs, crafts and clothes.

Cabo Dolphins

Blvd Paseo de la Marina Lote 7-A • Daily 7am–5pm • ☏ 888 526 2238, ⓦ cabodolphins.com

Towards the southern end of the marina boardwalk, **Cabo Dolphins** offers a variety of interactive dolphin packages; the Dolphin Swim is a fifty-minute encounter (40min in water plus 10min educational presentation) for US$189 (M$3300), while other packages (US$119–159/M$2075–2775) offer less time in the water. You can also be a "trainer for a day" for US$319 (M$5565).

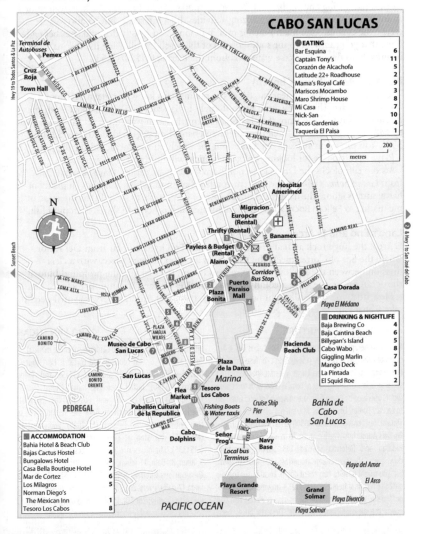

CABO SAN LUCAS

● EATING

Bar Esquina	6
Captain Tony's	11
Corazón de Alcachofa	5
Latitude 22+ Roadhouse	2
Mama's Royal Café	9
Mariscos Mocambo	3
Maro Shrimp House	8
Mi Casa	7
Nick-San	10
Tacos Gardenias	4
Taqueria El Paisa	1

0   200
metres

■ DRINKING & NIGHTLIFE

Baja Brewing Co	4
Baja Cantina Beach	6
Billygan's Island	5
Cabo Wabo	8
Giggling Marlin	7
Mango Deck	3
La Pintada	1
El Squid Roe	2

■ ACCOMMODATION

Bahia Hotel & Beach Club	2
Bajas Cactus Hostel	4
Bungalows Hotel	3
Casa Bella Boutique Hotel	7
Mar de Cortez	6
Los Milagros	5
Norman Diego's The Mexican Inn	1
Tesoro Los Cabos	8

9

Museo de Cabo San Lucas

Cabo San Lucas and Lázaro Cárdenas (on Plaza Amelia Wilkes) • Tues–Fri 10am–3pm, Sat & Sun 10am–2pm • M$15 • ☎ 624 105 0661

Facing sleepy Plaza Amelia Wilkes, the **Museo de Cabo San Lucas** occupies the old town primary school (where Baja educational pioneer Amelia Wilkes Ceseña once taught). Inside there are small rooms displaying fossils from the Sierra de la Laguna (there's also a huge whale skeleton outside), the skeleton of an ancient Pericú woman and galleries on the history, geology and biology of Cabo. Tiny **Parroquia de San Lucas**, just down Avenida Cabo San Lucas, dates back to 1746, a mission established by Jesuit priest Nicolás Tamaral.

Playa El Médano

To the east of the marina is **Playa El Médano**, Cabo's swimming-safe beach – and the place to party. The middle section is a mass of beach bars (see p.578), vendors, booming music, jet skis, parasailing and sunbathers. **Baja Watersports** (☎ 624 143 4599, ⓦ bajaswatersports .com) is one of several outfits organizing activities. It's a fun scene, but it's also easy to escape the crowds – the main beach is over 3km long, and mostly deserted at either end. Note that you can walk to the southern end of the beach by following the marina boardwalk to the end, or take water taxi from the marina (M$50/US$3).

Playa del Amor (Lovers' Beach)

The small wedge of sand near the tip of the peninsula is known as **Playa del Amor** (Lovers' Beach). The only way to reach it safely is via water taxi or tour boat from the marina or Playa El Médano: the cheapest return trip (with two hours on the beach) will be M$175 (US$10), but foreigners are often charged more (US$15–20 or M$260–350). You can swim at Playa del Amor, but the beach on the Pacific side of the point – **Playa Divorcio** – is for looking only; the **riptide** will finish off any swimmers.

A steep cliff blocks the Divorcio section from similarly precarious **Playa Solmar** (staff from *Grand Solmar* will try and prevent you from swimming here also, though plenty of hardy surfers ignore the danger). From Del Amor it's possible to swim in the direction of the marina to **Pelican Rock**, where the underwater shelf is home to shoals of tropical fish.

Land's End and El Arco

El Arco, the huge rock arch at Finisterra or **Land's End** itself, not far from Del Amor – where the Sea of Cortez meets the Pacific – is an extraordinary place, with a clear division between the shallow turquoise seawater on the east and the profound blue of the ocean out to the west; a colony of **sea lions** lives on the surrounding rocks. When it's low tide, you can walk right up to the arch from Del Amor, otherwise you'll need to take a boat trip or kayak to get close.

ARRIVAL AND DEPARTURE   CABO SAN LUCAS

By plane Aeropuerto Internacional de Los Cabos lies 43km north of Cabo San Lucas (see p.568). Don't confuse this with the grandly titled Cabo San Lucas International Airport, a small airfield 7km northwest of central Cabo with turboprop flights operated by Aéreo Calafia and Aéreo Servicio Guerrero to La Paz, Loreto, Los Mochis, Mazatlán, Puerto Vallarta and Tijuana. Taxis charge around M$300 to run into the centre.

By bus Águila buses arrive at the Terminal Central Águila at Hidalgo and Reforma (☎ 624 143 5020), 2km from downtown Cabo; taxis charge around M$160–180 into town, but you might have to flag them down. Local buses trundle past the terminal frequently (M$12) – any marked "Centro" or "Muelle" should get you to the marina (you can also flag down the air-conditioned Ruta del Desierto buses here,

which will drop you on Lázaro Cárdenas, near the marina). To La Paz the fastest route is "via corta" ("short route"; M$285–305) through Pescadero (M$115) and Todos Santos (M$130), rather than "via larga" ("long route") through San José (M$35) and Los Barriles (M$150). Destinations further north in Baja are served far less frequently. Buses to Tijuana (M$2630) and Mexicali (M$2885) will stop at Loreto (M$1045) and Mulegé (M$1335). Minibuses run direct to Los Cabos airport at 5.40am, 8.40am, 11.40am, 1.40pm, 3.40pm & 8.40pm.

Destinations Guerrero Negro (2 daily; 13.5hr); La Paz via larga (7 daily, every 2hr 5.15am–5.15pm; 3–4hr); La Paz via corta (hourly; 2hr 30min); Loreto (6 daily; 7–8hr); San José del Cabo (roughly hourly; 30–45min); Tijuana (3 daily;

27hr); Todos Santos (hourly; 1hr).

Local buses Ruta del Desierto (⊚ rutadeldesierto.travel) buses run up and down the Corridor between Cabo and San José (daily 5am–10pm; every 10–20min) for M$35 (buses continue all the way to Los Cabos airport) – flag them down on Vicario or at the bus stop on Lázaro Cárdenas (just outside Puerto Paraíso mall). It's M$12.50 to M$26 for destinations in the Corridor. Allow 30–40min to San José. Cabo Baja buses run the same route and are a little cheaper, but not as comfortable.

GETTING AROUND

By bus *Colectivo* buses trundle up and down Blvd Marina every few minutes from the Navy base at the southern end ("Muelle"), towards the bus station via Morelos, El Faro Viejo and Hidalgo (they come down Leona Vicario in the other direction). Fares are M$12.

By taxi Taxis will try to charge US dollar rates if they can, which are always higher. Trips across town cost US$8–12 (or M$140–210), the Corridor US$35 (M$610) and San José at least US$40 (or M$700); Los Cabos airport will set you back US$75 (or peso-equivalent). If you have a group, rates tend to be better (taxis are usually mini-vans).

Car rental Avis ☎ 624 143 4606; Budget ☎ 624 143 4190; Hertz ☎ 624 146 5088; National ☎ 624 143 1414; and Thrifty ☎ 624 146 5030. All are located relatively close to each other on Lázaro Cárdenas in the centre (with branches at the airport).

INFORMATION AND ACTIVITIES

INFORMATION

Tourist information Cabo has no official tourist office; the dozens of booths labelled "Tourist Information", while staffed by friendly locals, are really just places dishing out maps, drink coupons and information on tours (see also below).

TOUR OPERATORS

Andromeda Divers Playa El Médano ☎ 624 143 2765, ⊚ scubadivecabo.com. Offers local one-tank dives from US$40 (M$700), two tanks from US$66 (M$1150), PADI scuba diver courses for US$300 (M$5230) and open-water diver courses for US$430 (M$7500).

Cabo Adventures Blvd Paseo de la Marina Lote 7-A ☎ 322 226 8413, ⊚ cabo-adventures.com. The sister operation to Cabo Dolphins (see p.573) runs zip line tours into the Boca de Sierra Biosphere (US$129/M$2250), camel safaris (US$109/M$1900), snorkelling trips (US$85/M$1480) and flyboarding (where you lift into the air above the water) for US$199 (M$3470).

Cabo Expeditions Blvd Marina (Plaza de la Danza) ☎ 624 143 2700, ⊚ caboexpeditions.com.mx. Offers whale watching from US$89/M$1550, family-friendly submarine rides (US$40/M$700), parasailing (US$53/M$925), kayaking (US$74/M$1290), snorkelling (US$74/M$1290), diving Cabo Pulmo (US$189/M$3295) and city tours (US$93/M$1620).

Cabo Sky Tours ☎ 624 144 1294. Variety of sensational aerial tours (US$75/M$1305 to US$395/M$6880; 10–45min) with pilot Ernesto Magaña on ultralights (motorized handgliders). Cash only.

CABO BOAT TRIPS

Buccaneer Queen ⊚ buccaneerloscabos.com. Faithful reproduction of a Spanish galleon (aka pirate ship) that offers family-friendly cruises in local waters from US$39–69 (M$680–1200).

Cabo EcoTours (EcoCat) ☎ 624 157 4685, ⊚ cabo ecotours.com. Snorkelling and whale-watching trips (both US$49.99/M$870) on the biggest catamaran in Cabo – good for families.

Cabo Escape ☎ 624 105 0177, ⊚ caboescapetours .com. This catamaran is the preferred option for the party crowd – on the sunset cruise (US$75/M$1305) the main deck transforms into bar and club, with sounds booming across the water long after the boat docks.

CaboRey ☎ 624 143 8260, ⊚ caborey.com. Popular sunset and margarita cruises (2hr 30min) with Las Vegas-style Mexican-Argentine floor show on a huge catamaran – it seems a lot less cheesy after a few cocktails (tours from US$72/M$1250). Offers whale watching Dec–March for US$72/M$1250.

ACCOMMODATION

Most of the resorts occupy the prime real estate immediately around the marina, while downtown has a small selection of budget **accommodation**. The resorts to the east of the marina empty out onto the active Playa El Médano; those to the west have the beautiful but unswimmable Playa Solmar at their doors. Note that airbnb (⊚ airbnb.com) now offers over six hundred properties in and around Cabo, from as low as US$18 (M$315) per night.

Bahia Hotel & Beach Club El Pescador s/n ☎ 624 143 1890, ⊚ bahiacabo.mx. Funky boutique just behind Playa El Médano, with plush modern rooms featuring contemporary Mexican decor and the lauded *La Esquina* restaurant on site. M$2600

★**Bajas Cactus Hostel** Lázaro Cárdenas, between Ocampo and Matamoros ☎ 624 143 5247, ✉ bajas cactushostel@hotmail.com. Excellent budget option and

9

SAND FALLS AND NEPTUNE'S FINGER

Dive trips are big business in Cabo. Experienced **divers** shouldn't miss the rim of a marine canyon at a site known as Anegada, off Playa del Amor, where unusual conditions at 30m create the "**Sand Falls**" (famously discovered by Jacques Cousteau in the 1970s), with streams of sand starting their 2000m fall to the canyon bottom. Nearby, **Neptune's Finger** is a rock pile smothered in sea sponges, gorgonias and sea fans.

the only hostel in the centre of town, with brightly painted private rooms (shared bathrooms) and shared dorms, all with a/c and cable TV. Rates include breakfast and wi-fi. Dorms M$220; doubles M$612

★**Bungalows Hotel** Libertad, near Herrera ☎624 143 5035, ⓦthebungalowshotel.com. Perennial favourite and one of the best deals in Cabo; even the smallest rooms are cosy suites, the location is perfect (just far enough from the madness), the breakfasts are incredible, the staff are super-helpful and you get free wi-fi. M$1810

Casa Bella Boutique Hotel Hidalgo 10 (Plaza Amelia Wilkes) ☎624 143 6400, ⓦcasabellahotel.com. This handsome hacienda-style property is definitely worth a splurge, with large, clean rooms, beautiful, blossom-strewn courtyard, small pool and friendly owners in the older part of town. No TVs but free wi-fi and breakfast included. M$2386

Mar de Cortez Lázaro Cárdenas, between Guerrero and Matamoros ☎624 143 0032, ⓦmardecortez.com. Colonial-style decor in a lovely planted setting with a mix of older and modern, larger rooms around a pool; some

have terraces and all have a/c. Also has a good restaurant, free wi-fi and free parking. Closed Sept. M$960

Los Milagros Matamoros 116 ☎624 143 4566, ⓦlosmilagros.com.mx. Tasteful, studio-like rooms with high-speed internet connections, a small pool and a sun deck make this a real find, just a few blocks from the action. Reservations recommended. M$1275

★**Norman Diego's The Mexican Inn** 16 de Septiembre and Abasolo ☎624 143 4987, ⓦthe mexicaninn.com. The dirt road just outside the door gives a false impression of the comfort at this small B&B. Coffee and *postres* are served around the courtyard every morning and Mexican tile work, queen-size beds, a/c, TVs and DVD players adorn the rooms. Free wi-fi. M$850

Tesoro Los Cabos Marina s/n ☎624 173 9300, ⓦtesororesorts.com. Best all-round location if you're aiming to be in the heart of the action, with large, comfy rooms in the giant adobe-like palatial property overlooking the marina and a fabulous pool deck; the junior suites are much bigger than the standards, some with kitchens. Wi-fi is US$5/24hr (free in the hotel's Business Center). M$1650

EATING

Bar Esquina El Pescador s/n ☎624 143 1890, ⓦbahiacabo.com. This Alhambra-themed restaurant (think Moorish lamps and tiles) with lovely veranda specializes in Mexican-influenced Mediterranean flavours, using locally grown, organic produce and seafood; highlights include the short rib, blue cheese pizza and a decadent sticky toffee pudding. Mains like fish and chips from M$169; pizzas $145–198; sandwiches from M$128. The attached coffee shop (open from 7am) sells decent espresso and muffins. Daily 8am–1am.

Captain Tony's Marina 8–6 (near the Tesoro) ☎624 143 6797. Right on the water, knocking out special beer-battered fish tacos and freshly cooked catch of the day (they'll also cook yours for you). The wood-smoked pizzas are also pretty good (M$150–190). Daily 6am–10pm.

★**Corazón de Alcachofa** Pescador 4312 (Playa Médano) ☎624 143 4041, ⓦcorazondealcachofa.com. Guadalajara and West Hollywood mini-chain serving quality market-driven fresh food for menus created daily. Think chili-mango margaritas, steaks, octopus carpaccio and gorgeous desserts. Mains M$190–320 (reckon M$750 per head for a full meal). Daily 5pm–midnight.

Latitude 22+ Roadhouse Hwy-1 km 4.5 (next to Costco)

☎624 143 1516, ⓦlatno2baddays.com. Classic old Baja bar and diner, despite the incongruous location (taxis charge US$10 from downtown), draped with fishing memorabilia and offering a menu of slow-roasted prime rib, Philly cheese steak, burgers and pastas. Mains range M$75–180. Mon–Sat 8am–11pm (open Sun during US football season).

★**Mama's Royal Café** Hidalgo at Zapata ☎624 143 4290, ⓦmamasroyalcafeloscabos.com. Best known for its amazing breakfasts, especially the French toast and two-dozen *huevos* choices (M$80–125), this gringo staple is now open for lunch and dinner (sandwiches and Mexican dishes with huge salsa bar), but remains a lot cheaper and better than most of what Cabo has to offer. Daily 7am–8pm (closes at 3pm July–Oct).

Mariscos Mocambo Vicario and 20 de Noviembre ☎624 143 2122, ⓦmariscosmocambo.com.mx. This Veracruz-style seafood restaurant beneath a giant palapa is popular with locals for good reason, with fresh fish and *ceviche*, some great tequilas, fresh chocolate clams (in season), Veracruz fillets and crab dishes. Mains M$90–180. Daily noon–10pm.

Maro Shrimp House Hidalgo at Zapata ☎624 143 4966. Revived incarnation of the famed *Shrimp House* (now operated by Maro, one of the ex-employees) serving shrimp special sauce, fresh boiled shrimp by the kilo or half kilo, lobster and some Mexican plates, home-made ice cream and the famous Bulldog cocktail (comprising tequila, lemonade and beer). Most combos US$17 (M$295). Mon–Sat noon–midnight, Sun 2–10pm.

Mi Casa Cabo San Lucas (Plaza Amelia Wilkes), at Lázaro Cárdenas ⊕ 624 143 1933, ⓦ micasarestaurant .com.mx. This old Cabo joint has new Cabo prices in its otherwise low-key open-air restaurant decorated with handmade lanterns. The pan-Mexican menu – carnitas de Michoacán (pork), chicken in Oaxacan mole, Sonoran beef – runs from M$180–350 per main course. Daily 5.30–10.30pm.

Nick-San Plaza de la Danza 2, Blvd Marina ⊕ 624 143 4484, ⓦ nicksan.com. Plenty of restaurants in Baja will sell you raw fish without knowing what they're doing with

it – Nik-San is the exception (helmed by Angel Carbajal and Masayuki Niikura). In addition to the extensive selection of locally caught sushi and sashimi (sets from M$285), the Indonesian-inspired lobster soup is especially tasty. Dinner for two around M$1000. Daily 11.30am–10.30pm.

Tacos Gardenias Paseo de La Marina ⊕ 624 355 4871, ⓦ tacosgardenias.com. This justly popular taco restaurant, with an open-front, no-frills interior, has been knocking out tasty fish and shrimp tacos (M$30) and shrimp molcajete (with salsa, onion and cheese) since 1980. Daily 8am–10pm.

Taquería El Paisa Lazaro Vicario, at Alikan ⊕ 624 143 1468. This legendary taco spot offers flame-grilled steak or pork tacos topped with blackened onions making a delicious, cheap meal (M$30). You'll see several imitators with similar names all over town, but this is the original. Daily noon–1am.

THE CORRIDOR'S BEST BEACHES

The distinction between Cabo San Lucas and San José del Cabo blurs further each year as new resorts are erected along the 33km Corredor Turístico (aka Hwy-1), or just the **CORRIDOR**, separating the two towns. As a general rule, Sea of Cortez beaches may be swimmable and Pacific beaches never are, but before you **swim** or **surf** anywhere in Los Cabos, ask a local and read any posted signs. Obey any **signs** warning you off wet sand and note that beaches deemed safe one season may not be safe year-round – summer especially can be hazardous.

The good news is that every beach is free and open to the public, though getting to and from them can be a hassle without your own car. With the exception of Playa El Médano in Cabo San Lucas and Palmilla in San José, you can't comfortably reach any of the beaches on foot unless you're staying at one of the adjacent resorts. If you've got your own transport you can turn off Hwy-1 at any of the beaches and park in the sand; **local buses** (see p.575) run up and down the highway every twenty to thirty minutes between around 5am and 10pm daily (just flag them down). There are no toilets or lifeguards at the beaches, and if you want shade, food or drink, bring your own. All distances below are measured east from Cabo San Lucas towards San José del Cabo, 33km away.

Barco Varado, km 9. The remains of a Japanese trawler that sank in 1966 lie offshore here, making diving the main focus of this beach, though it's also a popular surfing spot. Take the marked dirt access road off the highway; mind the rocks on your way down.

Bahía Santa María, km 13. You can scuba and snorkel on rock reefs (rays and turtles hang out here) at both ends of this horseshoe cove, and go swimming at the protected beach in the middle. There's a secure parking lot ten minutes' walk from the beach (signposted from the highway).

Bahía Chileno, km 14.5. There are toilets here (the only beach that has them) and a dive shop that rents watersports equipment (nothing with a motor, though), making Chileno one of the easiest beaches to enjoy. Definitely the best family beach; excellent for swimming, diving and snorkelling, or just relaxing along the well-packed sand – it's also one of the few beaches with shady palm trees. Look for the signs to "Chileno Beach Club". It's popular, so go early.

Playa Palmilla, km 27. Good, safe 1.5km-long beach used by San José hotel residents needing escape from the strong riptide closer to home. Point and reef breaks when surf's up. Popular for standup paddle boarding. Access the beach by following signs to One & Only Palmilla and taking the only dirt-road cut-off to the left, about 2km from Hwy-1.

Playa Acapulquito, km 28. AKA Old Man's, this is a top surfing beach for beginners, blurring into Costa Azul. Also home to super-cool Cabo Surf.

Costa Azul, km 28.5. The region's best surfing beach is known for the Zippers and La Roca breaks during the summer (look out for rocks at low tide). Board rentals available at the car park. Swimming is possible during the late winter and early spring, but ask at Zippers beach restaurant (daily 11am–10.30pm; ⊕ 624 172 6162) before you dip in.

9

DRINKING AND NIGHTLIFE

Baja Brewing Co Marina Boardwalk, at Puerto Paraíso Mall ☏ 624 144 3805, �🌐 bajabrewingcompany.com. Baja Sur's original microbrewery comes to Cabo, serving pints such as Baja Blond and Peyote Pale Ale with live music Thurs–Sat nights after 8pm. Plenty of pub food available. There's another branch on the rooftop terrace of the Cabo Villas Beach Resort on Playa Médano. Daily 8am–midnight.

Baja Cantina Beach Playa Médano (Paseo del Pescador), �🌐 bajacantinabeachclub.com. The first beach bar on the Médano strip heading east, with shaded loungers and beach chairs serviced by a crew of cocktail-carrying staff – check the swinging chairs at the palapa bar (it's a bit posher than its neighbours). Great views, burgers and *molcajetes* (mains from M$175–280). Daily 8am–11pm (lounge to 1am Fri & Sun).

Billygan's Island Playa Médano (Paseo del Pescador) ☏ 624 143 4830. The smallest of the three central beach bar-restaurants that caters to partygoers all day, famed for its house cocktail simply dubbed "Billygan's". Breakfast, lunch and dinner are served right on the sand, and tropical drinks are poured and consumed nonstop. Daily 8am–11pm.

Cabo Wabo Vicente Guerrero, between Lázaro Cárdenas and Madero ☏ 624 163 7400, �🌐 cabowabocantina.com. Rocker Sammy Hagar (of *Van Halen* fame) opened his boisterous club in 1990 (marked by the landmark mini-lighthouse). It's still a good place to hear live music – and if you're going here over a US public holiday, perhaps you can catch Sammy himself on stage. The bar also makes a popular tequila of the same name (used on its tequila shrimp and in the signature Red Rocker cocktails), and a sensational lobster burrito. Daily

9am–2am (club daily from 8pm).

Giggling Marlin Marina s/n, at Matamoros ☏ 624 143 1182, �🌐 gigglingmarlin.com. A Cabo institution, drawing an older set than other places on the strip. Mostly a place to drink and dance to Latin standards: chances of getting out without hearing *La Bamba* are slim. Daily 8pm–2am.

Mango Deck Playa Médano (Paseo del Pescador) ☏ 624 144 4919, ⓦ mangodeckcabo.com. Sprawling complex and one of the hottest spots on the beach (especially during Spring Break, Feb–April), where local celebrity "Big Johnson" dispenses tequila shots. Bikini contests, staff shows and wet T-shirts – you get the idea. Excellent buffet Sat & Sun 8am–1pm for M$160, and live music from 7pm Tues–Sun. Daily 7am–11pm.

La Pintada Lázaro Cárdenas s/n, at 20 de Noviembre ☏ 624 105 0163, ⓦ lapintada.mx. Cabo's only microbrewery occupies large, wood-beamed premises on the otherwise uninspiring main drag; try beers such as Premium Lager and Chocolate Stout on tap (M$80), served with tasty olive and cheese breads (free), with a large range of bottled beers and excellent happy hour (two for one, daily 4–6pm and all day Wed). Decent but pricey food cooked up on a wood-fired grill (pizzas M$140; rib-eye burger M$250). Daily 1–10pm.

El Squid Roe Lázaro Cárdenas s/n, at Zaragoza ☏ 624 143 0655, ⓦ elsquidroe.com. If you just want to go nuts, this Cabo three-storey classic should be your first stop; a wild party atmosphere where table dancing is allowed. There's a full dinner menu of Tex-Mex dishes alongside cocktails such as the yard-long margarita. Daily 11am–4am.

DIRECTORY

Banks and exchange Reliable ATMs at Bancomer on Lázaro Cárdenas at Hidalgo; ATMs also line the marina boardwalk. Note that since almost every business in Cabo accepts US dollars, most banks have stopped exchanging dollars into pesos (they might change other currencies, but if you need to change money, try one of the town's several *casas de cambio*; there's one by *Giggling Marlin* (above), which offers decent rates until 11pm. Don't change at the airport, which has the worst rates. Note that if you do use US dollars to pay for things quoted in pesos, expect a very poor exchange rate (often US$1=M$10).

Consulates Canada at Plaza San Lucas, Carretera Transpeninsular km 0.5, Local 82 Col El Tezal ☏ 624 142

4262; US at Tiendas de Palmilla, Carretera Transpeninsular km 27.5, San José del Cabo ☏ 624 143 3566.

Emergencies ☏ 066; Green Angels highway help ☏ 074; Police ☏ 624 143 3997 or ☏ 624 142 0361; Federal police ☏ 088.

Hospital Hospital Amerimed (ⓦ amerimedloscabos.com) is open 24hr on Lázaro Cárdenas.

Internet You can pick up free wi-fi all over town, and most restaurants and bars now offer free wi-fi in Cabo San Lucas.

Post office On Lázaro Cárdenas, at Camino Real (Mon–Fri 8am–7pm, Sat 9am–3.30pm).

Visa extension Migración office is at Lázaro Cárdenas 1625 (to the right of Europcar). Mon–Fri 9am–4pm.

San José del Cabo

SAN JOSÉ DEL CABO, 33km northeast of Cabo San Lucas, is the older and more sedate of the two towns – if Cabo's nightlife and beach activities have little appeal, stay here instead. Founded as a mission in 1730 by Jesuits, it was abandoned after the Pericú revolt just four years later. A mix of ex-pirates, lapsed missionaries and drop-out miners

DRINKING & NIGHTLIFE
Baja Brewing Co	1
Rock & Brews	3
Shooters Sports Bar	2

ACCOMMODATION
Casa Natalia	4
El Encanto Inn	1
Hotel Posada Señor Mañana	3
Yuca Inn	2

EATING
Casa Dahlia	3
French Riviera Bakery	5
Jazmín's	2
Mi Cocina	1
Taquería El Ahorcado	8
Taquería Mexico	10
Taquería Rossy	9
Tequila	6
Tropical	4
Tropicana	7

SAN JOSÉ DEL CABO

began to repopulate the town in the early nineteenth century and turned the area into a small port and an agricultural centre. Although frequently referred to as colonial, no traces remain of San José's first settlement, and none of the buildings dates further back than the late 1880s.

Plaza Mijares

Though increasingly hemmed in by shops and resorts, sleepy **Plaza Mijares** and **Bulevar Mijares** (which now leads to the modern **Zona Hotelera** about 1km seaward) are still more or less unspoiled, though there's little to do beyond browsing the numerous

9

high-end shops, art galleries and restaurants that line the streets and shady courtyards, aimed squarely at well-heeled tourists. Dubbed the **Art District**, this part of town has been given a tasteful makeover in recent years (see Art Walk box, opposite).

The plaza's twin-towered church, **La Misión de San José del Cabo Añuití**, was built in 1932 on roughly the site of the original Jesuit foundation; though it isn't much to look at from the outside (note the tile mural on the facade depicting the murder of Father Tamaral by the Pericú), the interior offers a tranquil and cool respite from the afternoon heat. On the other side of the plaza near the giant Mexican flag, the **Jardín de los Cabeños Ilustres** proudly displays statues of the region's famous sons, including Antonio Mijares (local hero of the Mexican-American War), though non-Mexicans will have a hard time recognizing any of them.

Mercado Municipal

Between Coronado and Castro, at Ibarra • Daily 6am–4pm (*loncherías* Mon–Sat 7am–5pm, Sun 7am–3pm)

The modest town market, the **Mercado Municipal**, is a short walk from the plaza, a relatively small indoor setup with souvenir stalls, crafts, textiles and fresh veg and meat sellers. Next door is a covered annexe crammed with cheap *loncherías*.

ARRIVAL AND DEPARTURE   SAN JOSÉ DEL CABO

BY PLANE
Aeropuerto Internacional de Los Cabos lies 19km north of downtown San José del Cabo (see p.574).

BY BUS
The Terminal de Autobuses (Águila; ☎ 624 130 7339) is on Valerio González just off Hwy-1, a long, hot walk from the central Plaza Mijares. Taxis (usually waiting) will take you anywhere in town for M$70.

Departures Águila runs buses to Cabo San Lucas (30–45min; M$35) every hour or so 5.30am–9pm; the route north to La Paz (M$320) from here on Hwy-19 (via Todos Santos; M$165) is dubbed "via corta" ("short route"). Buses to La Paz via Los Barriles on Hwy-1 are "via larga" ("long route") and less frequent (6am, 8am, 10am, noon, 2pm, 4pm & 6pm). Buses to various places along the Baja Peninsula are much less frequent; Loreto is M$1080,

Mulegé M$1370 and Tijuana M$2680.

Local buses Modern Ruta del Desierto (🅦 rutadeldesierto .travel) buses run up and down the Corridor between Cabo and San José (every 10–20min) for M$35 – flag them down at the marked bus stops on Hwy-1 (Mauricio Castro). It's M$12.50–26 for destinations in the Corridor. Allow 30–40min to Cabo.

BY TAXI
You'll pay M$450 to get to Cabo San Lucas (or US$45), about M$250 to the Corridor beaches and at least M$300 (US$30) to get to the airport. Each company has its own stand; there's one on the main plaza at Zaragoza and Hidalgo, while most of the others line Mijares, but they all tend to charge the same rates. Your hotel may be able to negotiate slightly cheaper prices.

ACTIVITIES

Bajawild Hwy-1 km 28, Plaza Costa Azul 5 ☎ 624 148 2222, 🅦 bajawild.com. Arranges snorkelling and kayaking tours to Cabo Pulmo (US$140/M$2440), surfing tours (US$150/M$2615) and a range of other activities.

ACCOMMODATION

★**Casa Natalia** Mijares 4 ☎ 624 142 5100, 🅦 casa natalia.com. Gorgeous boutique hotel right on the plaza, with luxurious rooms festooned with bold, contemporary local artwork and sporting tiny, flower-draped terraces. Breakfast is delivered to your terrace, and there's a shuttle service to the beach. M$2475

El Encanto Inn Morelos 133 ☎ 624 142 0388, 🅦 elencantoinn.com. Comfortable option, just north of the plaza in the art gallery district and set inside two separate buildings, both with courtyards overflowing with blossoms and plants. Hacienda-style rooms have charm, though some are ageing a little; the pool is a great place to relax. M$1725

Hotel Posada Señor Mañana Obregón 1 ☎ 624 142 1372, 🅦 srmanana.com. Excellent budget option in the centre of town, with clean, comfy rooms, free wi-fi and a wonderful communal kitchen. M$675

Yuca Inn Obregón 1, at Plaza Mijares ☎ 624 142 0462, 🅦 yucainn.com.mx. Backpacker-friendly hostel, just off the plaza (and separate to the adjacent Señor Mañana) with a laid-back second-floor café. The free wi-fi, small pool, hammocks and common kitchen areas with lockable pantry cabinets are useful extras, and the English-speaking owner is a mine of information. Rooms are basic but adequate. M$580

ART WALK, SAN JOSÉ

Get an insider's introduction to San José's art galleries at the **Art Walk**, Thursdays 5–9pm (Nov–June only), when local galleries open their doors with special events and the odd glass of wine. There were fourteen high-quality galleries here at last count, among them the **Frank Arnold Gallery** (Ⓦfrankarnoldart.com), Comonfort 1137, home of the respected Californian artist. See Ⓦartcabo.com for more details.

EATING

Casa Dahlia Morelos, between Obregón and Zaragoza ☎624 166 0262, Ⓦcasadahlia.com. Art gallery with tranquil garden café specializing in delicious smoothies, hot chocolate, French press coffee and fish tacos among other food items. Wed–Fri evenings are movie nights (showings of old classics, with a M$300 fixed-price menu). Mon–Fri 10am–3pm & 6–9pm, Sat 10am–3pm.

French Riviera Bakery Manuel Doblado, at Miguel Hidalgo ☎624 142 3350. People keep coming to this trendy, contemporary café for coffee (cappuccino is M$47), French pastries, cakes and both savoury and sweet crêpes (M$95–200) – you can also buy baguettes and other freshly baked delights to take out. Free wi-fi. Breakfast sets from M$195–255, lunch mains M$95–160. Daily 7am–11pm.

Jazmín's Morelos, between Zaragoza and Obregón ☎624 142 1760, Ⓦjazminsrestaurant.com. The best-value traditional Mexican food in town (mains average M$170–250), in a pretty dining room decorated with brightly coloured *papel picado* (paper art) and Pancho Villa memorabilia. Also has excellent breakfasts, *and* perhaps the best *chilaquiles* on the cape. Daily 8am–midnight.

★**Mi Cocina** Mijares 4, inside Casa Natalia ☎624 142 5100. The torch-lit atmosphere is captivating, and chef Loïc Tenoux's French-influenced Mexican dishes are inspired. Charred *poblano* chiles stuffed with lamb share the menu with Baja fish and chips and seafood risotto. Dinner entrées range M$260–390; lunch (tacos, burgers and the like) is a bit cheaper (M$160–220). Wed–Mon 7.30–11am, noon–3pm & 5–10.30pm.

Taquería El Ahorcado Pescadores and Marinos ☎624 172 2093. AKA "Tacos the Hangman", this popular local stall serves juicy roasted meat, Pibil pork, quesadillas and, for the adventurous, beef tongue and even brain tacos for M$15–30. Walk to the end of Doblado, cross Hwy-1 and take the first right (on Pescador). Tues–Sun 7pm–midnight (or till he runs out).

Taquería México Valerio González, at Maestros (not far from bus station) ☎624 105 2171, Ⓦtaqueriamexico.mx. Diner with thatched palapa roof, popular as much as for its *pozole*, stuffed potatoes, fresh juices and burritos as for its beloved tacos *arrachera* and *pastor*. Try also the *taco de gobernador* (shrimp taco covered with cheese). Most mains M$60–90. Daily 11am–2am.

Taquería Rossy Hwy-1 km 33 (opposite Manuel Doblado) ☎624 142 6755. This small restaurant on the west side of Hwy-1 is the lunch spot of choice for budget travellers seeking fish tacos – worth the 20min walk from the plaza (you can also take a bus). Battered pieces of fillets, marlin, dorado and *carne asada* tacos go for M$16–34. Daily 10am–11pm.

Tequila Manuel Doblado 1011, between Mijares and Hidalgo ☎624 142 1155, Ⓦtequilarestaurant.com. The top choice in town for Mexican *alta cocina*, with a gorgeous courtyard, garden dining area and attentive waiting staff. Seafood mains range M$180–320. Cigar fans should check out the walk-in humidor. Daily 6–11pm.

★**Tropical** Plaza Mijares. Simple hole-in-the-wall selling mouth-watering ice "paletas" (lollies/popsicles) in a huge array of tropical fruit flavours (guava, pineapple, tamarind) as well as ice cream on sticks for just M$10 each. Daily 8.30am–9.30pm.

Tropicana Mijares 38 ☎624 142 1580. A colonial-style restaurant with an attractive tiled, palapa-covered sitting area on the main drag that's a popular choice for meals or afternoon drinks. Serves excellent breakfasts (M$75–120) and usual Tex-Mex fare (from M$130), often with dancers providing entertainment in the evenings (Fri features Cuban music). Daily 8am–11pm.

DRINKING AND NIGHTLIFE

Baja Brewing Co Morelos, between Obregón and Comonfort ☎624 146 9995, Ⓦbajabrewingcompany.com. Baja Sur's best microbrewery – founded by three guys from Colorado – serves its fresh beers in an open, wood-covered bar. Excellent happy hour (daily 4–8pm), and there's live music Thurs–Sat. Daily noon–1am.

Rock & Brews Plaza el Pescador, Paseo Malecón ☎624 105 2705, Ⓦrockandbrews.com. The US rock-themed franchise, owned by KISS band members, opened here in 2013, delivering its trademarked live shows (from local bands), music videos, American comfort food and decent selection of craft beers. Sun–Thurs noon–midnight, Fri & Sat noon–2am.

Shooters Sports Bar Doblado, at Mijares ☎624 146 9900, Ⓦshootersbar.com.mx. Rooftop bar with views over the town and the plaza – happy hour runs till 4pm. Also does decent bar food like chicken wings and quesadillas. Daily 9am–11pm.

9

DIRECTORY

Banks ATMs at Bancomer, on Zaragoza and Morelos (Mon–Fri 8.30am–4pm, Sat 10am–4pm), and Banamex, at Mijares and Coronado (Mon–Fri 9am–4pm, Sat 10am–2pm).
Books Librerías Educal, Doblado at Idelfonso Green (Mon–Sat 10am–7pm).
Emergencies Police ☎ 624 143 3997 or ☎ 624 142 0361; IMSS hospital ☎ 624 143 1594.
Internet Ciber Evolution, on Valerio González, just off

the beach (Mon–Fri 9am–6pm).

Mijares (Mon–Fri 8.15am–9pm, Sat 9am–3pm; M$16/hr). Free wi-fi is increasingly available in restaurants and cafés.
Laundry NM Clean Lavanderia, at Valerio González 1728, at Hidalgo (Mon–Fri 7am–5pm, Sat 8am–5pm; Sun 8am–2pm).
Pharmacy Numerous around the plaza and several on Mijares (most close for lunch).
Post office On Mijares, on the way to the hotel zone from the beach (Mon–Fri 9am–6pm).

The East Cape

The **East Cape** region features 120km of wild coastline, littered with stunningly beautiful **beaches**, especially around **Cabo Pulmo**. There is only a handful of towns and villages, with far less development than Cabo San Lucas and San José del Cabo, though thanks to a major influx of North American "snowbirds", US dollars are also widely accepted here, and English is often spoken.

Cabo Pulmo

The best of the East Cape is protected within **Cabo Pulmo National Marine Park** (𝕨 cabopulmopark.com), with pristine beaches and a rare hard coral reef just offshore. The area is anchored by the off-the-grid village of **CABO PULMO**, which has a population of around 250, basic facilities (only solar power), no paragliders and no jet skis. The beach here is rocky with strong riptides, but just fifteen minutes' drive south on a bumpy gravel road is **Playa Los Arbolites** (entry M$30), a gorgeous privately owned beach with palapas, toilets and showers, and decent snorkelling. About five minutes further south by car is **Playa Los Frailes** (free, no facilities), a picturesque cove with sensational snorkelling – it can be like swimming in a fish tank, with rays and turtles also gliding around. There's also a **sea lion colony** about 1km further along the shore, accessed by boat, kayak or by a combination of wading and swimming (strong swimmers only). Rent snorkelling gear back in Cabo Pulmo (M$150/day).

ARRIVAL AND DEPARTURE

CABO PULMO

By car/taxi There is no public transport to Cabo Pulmo. Driving, it's best to take Hwy-1 towards Los Barriles from San José, and turn off (right) where the signs says "Cabo Riveria" or "Cabo Pulmo" at km 93, before a long bridge. After the own of La Ribera the surfaced road runs out and

the last 30min is via bumpy gravel and sand track (if it's not raining heavily, normal cars can make it). Allow 2hr from Cabo San Lucas. Taxis will charge at least US$200/M$3485 each way (contact Transcabo; 𝕨 transcabo.com).

ACTIVITIES

Cabo Pulmo Dive Center Cabo Pulmo Beach Resort ☎ 624 141 0726, 𝕨 cabopulmo.com. Offers a host of dive

trips (from US$65/M$1130) and PADI courses (US$415/M$7225).

ACCOMMODATION AND EATING

Baja Bungalows 𝕨 bajabungalows.com. Huge range of affordable rooms and vacation rentals, from small bungalows to more luxurious suites and casitas (some with full kitchen), all a 3min walk from the beach (bring shampoo). Solar-powered electricity and free but slow wi-fi is available. M$1275
El Caballero Cabo Pulmo. Best place to eat Mexican food around here, and the most dependable hours, with outdoor

seating under palapas and the obligatory blaring TV. Also has a bar and sells groceries. Mains M$75–160. Daily 8am–10pm.
Cabo Pulmo Beach Resort ☎ 624 141 0726, 𝕨 cabo pulmo.com. Rustic palm-thatched bungalows just off the beach, with kitchens, solar power and a/c in the three deluxe casitas (US$119/M$2045). Doubles as the Cabo Pulmo Dive Center. M$1185

9

Los Barriles

The largest and most accessible resort town on the East Cape is **LOS BARRILES**, a **sportfishing** and **windsurfing** centre some 66km north of Los Cabos airport on Hwy-1 (beyond the turning to Cabo Pulmo). Though it gets busy in the winter, it retains a fairly laid-back scene, with low-key development along the shore. Calle Los Barriles runs down from the highway to Calle 20 de Noviembre, the main beach access road and where most of the hotels, restaurants and ATV rental shops are located. The wind, best in winter, is brilliant for experienced windsurfers (less so for beginners) and makes this a regular venue for international competitions.

ARRIVAL AND DEPARTURE   LOS BARRILES

By bus The "via larga" Águila buses between Cabo San Lucas/San José and La Paz (2hr) drop you at the intersection of the highway and Calle Los Barriles, from where there's a half-kilometre walk down to Calle 20 de Noviembre. Moving on, just flag them down at the same junction.

ACTIVITIES

Vela Windsurf Playa del Sol Hotel, Los Barriles ⓦvelawindsurf.com. The best place to rent equipment or take windsurfing lessons (M$1050/hr), operating out of the *Playa del Sol* hotel on the beach. Nov–March only.

ACCOMMODATION

East Cape RV Resort ☎624 141 0231, ⓦeastcaperv .com. Prettiest RV park on the cape, not far from the beach in the heart of town; has pool and hot tub, with wi-fi an extra M$60/day. RV lots <u>M$420</u>
Hotel Los Barriles 20 de Noviembre, north of C Los Barriles ☎624 141 0024, ⓦlosbarrileshotel.com. You'll find simple, clean and good-value lodgings at this congenial hotel, with a pool, plenty of boats for rent and all sorts of activities on offer. <u>M$975</u>
Hotel Palmas de Cortez ☎624 141 0050, ⓦvanwormerresorts.com. This plush, landmark resort dates back to 1959, right in the heart of Los Barriles, and can arrange a plethora of activities and outings for you. You can also get package deals that include all meals. <u>M$1950</u>

EATING

The choice of restaurants in Los Barriles increases every year, from no-frills *taquerías* and cafés to burger joints and gourmet restaurants, most lining 20 de Noviembre.

Caleb's Cafe 20 de Noviembre ☎612 141 0531. Small café and diner in the heart of the main drag, offering grilled fish sandwiches (M$114), fish and shrimp tacos (M$32–34), burgers (M$86) and breakfasts ranging from oatmeal (M$42) to big plates of eggs (from M$98). Tues–Sat 7.30am–3pm.

Tío Pablo's 20 de Noviembre ☎612 142 1214. This US-expat-run restaurant with a mammoth menu of delicious burgers, fish, and especially good pizzas, remains a dependable choice (mains M$80–160). Daily 11am–10pm.

Oaxaca

LOCALS RELAXING OUTSIDE SANTO DOMINGO

10

Oaxaca

The state of Oaxaca is one of the most enticing destinations in Mexico. The state capital, cosmopolitan yet utterly Mexican, encapsulates much of what the region has to offer. Here and in the surrounding countryside indigenous traditions are powerful; nowhere else in the country are the markets so infused with colour, the fiestas so exuberant, or the old languages still so widely spoken. There are traditions in the villages that long predate the Spanish Conquest; yet the city can also offer sophisticated modern dining, great places to stay and wild nightlife. The landscape, too, represents a fundamental break, as the barren deserts of the north are replaced by thickly forested hillsides, or in low-lying areas by swamp and jungle. On the Pacific coast, Puerto Escondido and Huatulco are established resorts with very different characters, while Puerto Ángel and its surrounds offer a more back-to-basics beach experience.

If you've come from Mexico City or the north, the physical differences of the region are compounded by its relative lack of development. Industry is virtually nonexistent, and while the city of Oaxaca and a few coastal hot spots have thrived on tourism, the rest of the state is woefully underdeveloped – the "Mexican economic miracle" has yet to reach the south. Indeed, the region witnessed considerable **political disturbance** in the early years of the twenty-first century, though for the moment the protests seem to have been subdued.

The city of **Oaxaca** is the region's prime destination, close enough to Mexico City to attract large numbers of tourists to its fine crafts stores, markets, seemingly constant fiestas, cobbled, gallery-lined walkways and excellent restaurants. The church of Santo Domingo here is one of the region's – and the whole of Latin America's – most magnificent examples of **Baroque** architecture, fusing Spanish and native influences to spectacular effect. And it's just one of many. Nearby, the Zapotec and Mixtec sites at **Monte Albán**, **Yagul** and **Mitla** are less well known than their ancient contemporaries in central and eastern Mexico, but every bit as important and impressive. All this is set among spectacular mountain scenery where the Sierra Madre del Sur meets the Sierra Madre de Oaxaca, the continuation of Mexico's central volcanic belt.

On the coast, west of the mountains, lie some of the emptiest and best **Pacific beaches** in Mexico. The resorts of **Puerto Escondido** and **Huatulco** are now firmly on the map, though Escondido still has the flavour of the surfer hangout in which it has its origins, while Huatulco, conceived and purpose-built as an environmentally conscious resort, can still boast some wonderful and relatively empty sands. Between the two, around **Puerto Ángel**, are several tranquil beach villages with a distinct "alternative" vibe.

ART WEAVING, OAXACA

Highlights

❶ Oaxaca Indigenous traditions fuse with colonial grandeur in one of Mexico's most hypnotic cities. **See p.590**

❷ Oaxacan food The rich *moles*, potent mescals and aromatic dishes of this exquisite regional cuisine are best experienced in Oaxaca city. **See p.602**

❸ Monte Albán A potent symbol of Zapotec power, these ruins were once an astounding ancient city with a population of over twenty thousand. **See p.605**

❹ Teotitlán del Valle Experience the rich artisan traditions of Oaxaca's Valles Centrales while shopping for iconic *tapetes* (rugs). **See p.610**

❺ Mitla The ancient Zapotec ceremonial centre with sublime greca stonework is considered to be without peer in Mexico. **See p.612**

❻ Benito Juárez Get away from it all in this quaint village named after Oaxaca's most famous son, where you can hike in gorgeous mountain surroundings. **See p.618**

❼ Puerto Escondido Ride the Mexican pipeline – or just watch – at this world-famous surfing spot. **See p.622**

❽ Mazunte See the queens of the sea, female Golfina turtles, in this tranquil oceanside town, or take a trip to the local crocodile lagoon. **See p.636**

HIGHLIGHTS ARE MARKED ON THE MAP ON PP.588–589

PUEBLA

Izúcar de Matamoros

Tehuacán

Acatlán de Osorio

Teotitlán del Camino

Lake Miguel Alemán

SIERRA MADRE DE OAXACA

Huajuapan de León

Coixtlahuaca

Santiago Apoala

Tejupan

Teposcolula

Yanhuitlan

Nochixtlán

San Martín Huamelulpan

MIXTECA

PARQUE NACIONAL BENITO JUÁREZ

Ixtlán de Juárez

Tlaxiaco

Etla

Benito Juárez

Hie El A

6

Santa A del Valle

Oaxaca

3 Monte Albán

1 **2** **4**

Teotitlán del Valle

San Antonio Arrajola

San Bartolo Coyotepec

Dainzú

Zaachila

Lambityeco

Tlacolula

Yagul

San Martín Tilcajete

Santo Tomás Jalieza

5

Mi

Ocotlán

Acapulco

VALLE DE OAXACA

HWY 131

HWY 175

SIERRA MADRE DEL SUR

Pinotepa Nacional

San José del Pacífico

HWY 200

Río Grande

Lagunas de Chacahua

Laguna Manialtepec

7

Puerto Escondido

8

Pochutla

Mazunte

San Augustinillo

Puerto Ángel

Zipolite

PACIFIC OCEAN

HIGHLIGHTS

1 Oaxaca
2 Oaxacan food
3 Monte Albán
4 Teotitlán del Valle
5 Mitla
6 Benito Juárez
7 Puerto Escondido
8 Mazunte

Oaxaca

The city of **OAXACA** sprawls across a grand expanse of deep-set valley, 1600m above sea level. Its colour, folklore, indigenous markets and magnificent colonial centre make it one of the country's most rewarding destinations even though, with a population of over 250,000, it is well on its way to becoming an industrial city. Many streets are choked and noisy and a thin veil of smog often enshrouds the valley – yet in the

10

■ ACCOMMODATION		● EATING		La Jícara	1	● SHOPPING	
Azucenas	8	La Antigua	10	La Olla	11	Amate	4
Casa Arnel	2	Biznaga	3	Pizza Nostrana	4	Arte Textil	3
Casa Cid de León	12	Café Alex	16	La Red	18	Casa de las Artesanías	
Casa de las Bugambilias	9	Casa Crespo	5	Zandunga	2	de Oaxaca	5
Casa de los Milagros	10	La Casa de la Abuela	17			Colectivo 1050°	2
Casa Oaxaca	3	Casa Oaxaca El				Instituto Oaxaqueño	
Cazomalli	3	Restaurante	9			de las Artesanías	
Las Golondrinas	5	El Catedral	15	■ DRINKING & NIGHTLIFE		(ARIPO)	1
Hostal Casa del Sótano	6	Cenadería Libres		Los Amantes	1	Mujeres Artesanías	
Hostal Don Nino	1	Tlayudas Doña Martha	14	Candela	3	de las Regiones de	
Las Mariposas	4	Cofetarika	8	Casa del Mezcal	5	Oaxaca (MARO)	6
Niut-Ja	15	La Crêpe	12	La Farola	4		
Paulina Youth Hostel	14	Los Danzantes	6	La Nueva Babel	2		
Posada del Centro	13	Le Gourmand	7				
Quinta Real Oaxaca	11	Jaguar Yu'u	13				

colonial centre the city's provincial charm is hardly affected and just about everything can be reached on foot. Simply being in Oaxaca, wandering through its streets and absorbing its life, is an experience, especially if you happen to catch the city during a **fiesta** (they happen all the time – the most important are listed on p.644). The city is an important **artistic** centre, too, with several state-run and private galleries, craft and jewellery masterclasses and regular exhibitions.

Among the highlights of any visit are the **Museo de las Culturas** and the **Museo Tamayo**, the **markets** (craft shopping in Oaxaca ranks with the best in the country) and the churches of **Santo Domingo** and **La Soledad**, along with the nearby archeological sites of **Monte Albán** and **Mitla**.

10

Brief history

Once central to the **Mixtec** and **Zapotec** civilizations, Oaxaca had a limited role during the early years of the Spanish Conquest. **Cortés**, attracted by the area's natural beauty, created the title of Marqués del Valle de Oaxaca, and until the Revolution his descendants held vast estates hereabouts. For practical purposes, though, the area was of little interest to the Spaniards, with no mineral wealth and, due to the rugged mountain terrain, no great agricultural value (though coffee was grown). This meant that the **indigenous** population was largely left to get on with life and did not have to deal with much outside influence beyond the interference of a proselytizing Church.

Nevertheless, by 1796 Oaxaca had become the third-largest city in Nueva España, thanks to the export of cochineal and, later, textile manufacturing. In the nineteenth century it produced two of Mexico's most influential statesmen: **Benito Juárez** (see box, p.594) is commemorated everywhere in Oaxaca, a privilege not shared by **Porfirio Díaz** (see p.825), the second most famous *Oaxaqueño*, whose dictatorship most people have chosen to forget. Thereafter Oaxaca was something of a political backwater until autumn 2006, when it made international headlines as striking teachers occupied the city's main plaza and clashed with riot police in a dispute that began over wages and mushroomed into protests over corruption and political cronyism; the city is perfectly safe for tourists, but occasional protests and demos rumble on to this day.

Around Plaza de la Constitución

Plaza de la Constitución, along with the adjoining **Alameda de León**, is Oaxaca's kaleidoscopic central reference point. Closed to traffic and surrounded by *portales* (arcades) sheltering languid cafés, the twin plazas offer some of the best free entertainment in the city – displays of music, song and dance, political speeches and protest marches, all overseen by a steady stream of beggars, hawkers, business people, tourists and locals. On Sundays and many weekday evenings you'll find a band playing in the centre, or else a performance or exhibition opposite the cathedral.

Museo del Palacio

Plaza de la Constitución, entry on Flores Magón · Tues–Sat 9.30am–6pm, Sun & Mon 9.30am–5pm · M$25, free Sun · ⓦ facebook.com/mupaloax

The **Museo del Palacio** occupies a substantial chunk of the Neoclassical Palacio de Gobierno, and indeed one good reason to pay the entry fee is to see the building, which has fine murals on the stairwells depicting the history of the state, and a high-tech tented roof over the courtyard. The museum itself, covering the evolution of man from the invention of fire to space travel, is modern, heavily interactive and quite impressive, albeit mainly in Spanish and largely aimed at kids. Much of the message is about biodiversity and the environment; there's a great earthquake simulator, and excellent videos on local rituals and fiestas.

10

Catedral de la Asunción

Alameda de León

Begun in 1553, the **Catedral de la Asunción** wasn't completed until the eighteenth century, thanks to several earthquakes. Since then it's been repeatedly pillaged and restored; as a result, despite a fine Baroque facade, it's far from the most exciting of Oaxaca's churches. It is impressively large though, with a heavy *coro* (choir) blocking the aisle in the heart of the church and a ring of chapels dedicated to various saints surrounding the nave. These days, most of the services are held in the Capilla del Señor del Rayo, centred on a Calvary embellished with gold votives, at the far end of the nave near the altar.

Museo de los Pintores Oaxaqueños

Independencia 607, cnr García Vigil • Tues–Sun 10am–6pm • M$20

Just across from the cathedral, the **Museo de los Pintores Oaxaqueños** occupies a beautifully renovated sixteenth-century mansion, in which it hosts temporary exhibitions of modern Oaxacan painters. The quality is usually high, and often the contemporary works are contrasted with those of earlier regional artists.

Teatro Macedonio de Alcalá

Independencia 900, cnr Armenta y López • show tickets from M$150 • ⓦ teatromacedonioalcala.org

Built in 1909 in the French style fashionable during the dictatorship of Porfirio Díaz, the **Teatro Macedonio de Alcalá** is still operating as a theatre and concert hall. It's typical of the grandiose public buildings that sprang up across Mexico in the early twentieth century – behind the *belle époque* exterior, the interior (try going to a show, or sneaking in before one, to see it) is a magnificent swathe of white marble and red plush.

Museo Textil de Oaxaca

Hidalgo 917 • Mon–Sat 10am–8pm, Sun 10am–6pm • Free, donations requested • ⓣ 951 501 1617, ⓦ museotextildeoaxaca.org.mx

The **Museo Textil de Oaxaca** is a showcase for the state's high-quality textile traditions, though it also has temporary exhibitions of textiles from all over the world. Opened in 2008, largely via funds supplied by Alfredo Harp Helú, the ex-Banamex owner turned philanthropist, the museum occupies an artfully renovated sixteenth-century convent.

Santo Domingo and around

North from the Plaza de la Constitución, Valdivieso crosses Independencia to become **Macedonio Alcalá**, the city's pedestrianized shopping street, known also as the Andador Turistico. This is the place to come for the best, and most expensive, Mexican and Oaxacan crafts: exquisitely intricate silver designs and finely executed, imaginative textiles.

Museo de Arte Contemporáneo

Alcalá 202 • Daily except Tues 10.30am–8pm • M$20 • ⓦ museomaco.com

MACO, the **Museo de Arte Contemporáneo**, is housed in a seventeenth-century building widely described as Cortés' house, though actually built after his death. Refurbished to provide expansive, modern galleries, the museum hosts temporary exhibits of national and regional contemporary art that can include anything from internationally celebrated artists like Frank Auerbach or Francis Bacon, through collections of Zapotec folk art and political caricatures, to video installations focusing on the impact of Mexican immigration to the US.

Centro Fotográfico Alvarez Bravo

Bravo 116 • Daily except Tues 9.30am–8pm • Free • ⓦ cfmab.blogspot.com

The **Centro Fotográfico Alvarez Bravo**, established by painter Francisco Toledo, has seven galleries with permanent and temporary exhibitions of historical and contemporary photographs, plus an excellent reference library.

Santo Domingo de Guzmán
Alcalá s/n • Daily 7am–1pm & 4–8pm; no sightseeing during Mass • Free

The church of **Santo Domingo de Guzmán** is one of the real highlights of Oaxaca. Consecrated in 1611, this elaborately carved and decorated extravaganza is one of the finest examples of Mexican Baroque anywhere, its external walls (10m thick in some places) solid and earthquake-proof, the interior extraordinarily rich. Parts were damaged during the Reform Wars and the Revolution – especially the chapels, pressed into service as stables – but most of the interior was restored during the 1950s.

The church drips with gold leaf throughout, beautifully set off, especially, by the afternoon light. Highlights include the great gilded main altarpiece and, on the underside of the raised choir above you as you enter, the family tree of Felix de Guzmán, father of St Dominic (the founder of the Dominican Order), in the form of a vine with leafy branches and tendrils, busts of leading Dominicans and a figure of the Virgin right at the top. Looking back from the altar, you can appreciate the relief scenes high on the walls and the biblical events depicted in the barrel roof and the ceiling of the choir, a vision of the heavenly hierarchy with gilded angels swirling in rings around God. The adjoining **Capilla de la Virgen del Rosario** (completed in 1720) is also richly painted and carved: the Virgin takes pride of place in another stunning altarpiece, all the more startlingly intense in such a relatively small space.

Museo de las Culturas de Oaxaca
Alcalá s/n • Tues–Sun 10am–6.15pm • M$64, audio guide M$50

Next to the church of Santo Domingo, the old Convento de Santo Domingo has been restored to house the absorbing **Museo de las Culturas de Oaxaca**. Construction of the vast *convento* began in 1572, and the church held its first Mass in 1608; from then until 1812 it was occupied by Dominican friars. During the Revolution, the building served as barracks for the Mexican army; the damage inflicted during this period wasn't restored until the 1990s, when the exhibits were installed.

The museum traces the history of Oaxaca in an expansive and elaborately executed labyrinth of galleries that hold displays covering everything from the pre-Hispanic period through to the present day. The archeological finds defy hyperbole, especially the true highlight here: sala 3, dedicated to the magnificent **Mixtec jewellery** discovered in Tomb 7 at Monte Albán (see p.607), including a couple of superb gold masks and armbands. This lavish treasure trove constitutes a substantial proportion of all known pre-Hispanic gold, since anything the conquistadors found they melted down. The museum also owns smaller gold pieces, as well as objects in a wide variety of precious materials – mother-of-pearl, obsidian, turquoise, amber and jade among them. The final galleries, in typically idealistic style, are dedicated to the pluralism of modern Mexico; an enlightening video shows members of each of the state's fifteen indigenous peoples speaking their own language. Signage throughout is in Spanish only, so the audio guide may be a worthwhile investment.

Jardín Etnobotánico
Entry at cnr of Reforma and Constitución • Guided visits only • Two-hour tour in English Tues, Thurs & Sat 11am M$100 • One-hour tour in Spanish Mon–Sat 10am, noon & 5pm M$50 • ⓦ jardinoaxaca.org.mx

If you visit the Museo de las Culturas de Oaxaca you'll catch tantalizing views of the mountains as well as another hidden artistic masterpiece – the cactus garden, or **Jardín Etnobotánico**. Beyond the garden's sensual appeal – it's not just an ornate collection of cacti, orchids and plumeria (frangipani), but an oasis of calm in the heart of the city – the tours are also extremely illuminating. The grounds preserve species native to Oaxaca and provide information on plants and insects, such as the *cochinilla* that dwells inside certain varieties of cactus and secretes a substance that is used to produce natural dyes for textiles.

Instituto de Artes Gráficas

Alcalá 507 • Daily 9.30am–8pm • Free • ⓦ institutodeartesgraficasdeoaxaca.blogspot.com

The **Instituto de Artes Gráficas** is one of the many cultural centres in Oaxaca state sponsored by painter Francisco Toledo. Above all there's a fabulous art library, open to the community and always busy with students, with plenty of material in English on art, archeology and literature. The institute also houses an inexpensive café in its shady courtyard and hosts temporary exhibitions and evening music recitals.

10

Museo Casa de Juárez

García Vigil 609 • Tues–Sat 10am–7pm • M$42

The **Museo Casa de Juárez**, opposite the fortress-like Templo y Convento de Carmen Alto, now mostly government offices, is where Oaxaca's most famous son, **Benito Juárez** (see box below), lived between 1818 and 1828. The house belonged to bookbinder Antonio Salanueva, who virtually adopted the young Benito after hiring him, providing him with a crucial leg-up in Mexican society. The renovated house contains a small collection of Juárez' possessions along with seminal historical documents. Wander through the kitchen, bedroom and dining area exhibits to get an idea of what life must have been like for the middle class in early nineteenth-century Oaxaca, though nothing is original to the house.

BENITO JUÁREZ

Benito Juárez ranks among Mexico's greatest national heroes. He was the towering figure of nineteenth-century Mexican politics, and his maxim – "*El respeto al derecho ajeno es la paz*" ("Respect for the rights of others is peace") – has long been a rallying cry for liberals. A **Zapotec**, he strove against nineteenth-century social prejudices and, through four terms as president, successfully reformed many of the worst remnants of Spanish colonialism, earning a reputation for honesty and fair dealing.

Juárez was born in **San Pablo Guelatao** in 1806. His parents died when he was 3, and he grew up speaking only Zapotec; at the age of 12 he was adopted by priests and moved to **Oaxaca**, where he began to study for the priesthood. Turning his talents to law, he provided his legal services to impoverished villagers free of charge, and by 1831 had earned a seat on Oaxaca's municipal council, lending his voice to a disenfranchised people. Juárez rose through the ranks of the city council to become **state governor** from 1847 to 1852, on a liberal ticket geared towards improving education and releasing the country from the economic and social stranglehold of the Church and the aristocracy. In 1853, the election of a conservative government under Santa Anna forced him into eighteen months of exile in the US.

Liberal victory in 1855 enabled Juárez to return to Mexico as minister of justice and give his name to a law abolishing special courts for the military and clergy. His support was instrumental in passing the **Ley Lerdo**, which effectively nationalized the Church's huge holdings, and bills legalizing civil marriage and guaranteeing religious freedom. In 1858, President Ignacio Comonfort was ousted by conservatives enraged by these reforms, and Juárez, as **the head of the Supreme Court**, had a legal claim to the presidency. However, he lacked the military might to hold Mexico City and retired to Veracruz, returning three years later, victorious in the War of Reform, as constitutionally elected **president**. Stymied in his attempts to reduce the power of the Church by an intractable Congress and empty coffers, Juárez suspended all national debt repayments for two years from July 1861. To protect their investments, the British, Spanish and French sent their armies in, but when it became apparent that Napoleon III had designs on the control of Mexico, the others pulled out, leaving France to install Habsburg **Archduke Maximilian** (see p.824) as puppet emperor. Juárez fled again, this time to Paso del Norte (now Ciudad Juárez) on the US border, until by 1867 he was able to return to the capital and to round up his army and execute the hapless Maximilian.

Juárez was returned as president in the 1867 elections but alienated much of his support through attempts to use Congress to amend the constitution. Nevertheless, he secured another term in the 1870 elections, spending two more years trying unsuccessfully to maintain peace before dying of a heart attack in 1872.

Arcos de Xochimilco

Four blocks north of Carmen Alto and the Casa Juárez, shadowing García Vigil, the **Arcos de Xochimilco** are remnants of the eighteenth-century aqueduct of San Felipe. The surrounding streets – increasingly gentrified and home to boutique B&Bs – make a pleasant place to stroll in relative peace, with multicoloured, low-slung, colonial-style houses surrounded by crumbling walls draped in bougainvillea, hole-in-the-wall taco joints, snoozing dogs, street lanterns and giant cacti.

El Pochote organic market

Santo Tomas Xochimilco church, north of Niños Héroes • Fri & Sat 9am–3pm

Tucked away in a churchyard, this small **organic market** features both produce and food stalls, with everything from onions or fresh goat's cheese to Italian pastries and handmade tacos. There are some great drinks stalls, too, with juice, local coffee and traditional Mexican chocolate all on offer, as well as traditional medicines and artesanías.

West of the centre

West of the plaza, the streets rapidly become busier and more traffic-choked, the shops and businesses less focused on visitors. In this direction lies one of Oaxaca's finest churches, along with a couple of interesting small museums.

Basílica Menor de Nuestra Señora de la Soledad

Jardín Socrates, between Independencia and Morelos about five blocks west of the Alameda • Daily 9am–6pm • Free • **Museum** Tues–Sun 10am–2pm & 3–7pm • Free, donation requested

The **Basílica Menor de Nuestra Señora de la Soledad**, built between 1682 and 1690, is one of Mexico's most important religious sites. It contains one of the most revered monuments in the country, a statue of the Virgen de la Soledad, Oaxaca's patron saint since 1909. The story goes that in 1620, a statue of the Virgin was mysteriously found in the backpack of a mule en route to Guatemala; some versions claim that Mary herself miraculously appeared. The basilica was constructed in her honour around the rock where this miracle is supposed to have happened (now in an iron cage on your right as you enter the church), though its wedding-cake facade is more recent. Inside, the sumptuous decoration includes a diamond-encrusted crown adorning the statue of the Virgin (a replica, since the original was stolen in the 1980s).

The church is set on a small plaza surrounded by other buildings associated with the Virgin's followers. It's a peaceful spot to watch *Oaxaqueño* life unfold over an ice cream or sorbet, both of which are sold in a beguiling variety of flavours at a cluster of stands – try *tuna* (prickly pear) and mescal in combination. The adjoining **Plaza de la Danza** is the setting of outdoor concerts, *folklórico* performances and specialist craft markets. At the back of the church courtyard the small **Museo Religioso de la Soledad** is devoted to the Virgin's followers. It's a bizarre jumble of junk and treasure – native costumes displayed on permed-blonde 1950s mannequins, *ex voto* paintings giving thanks for miracles and cures – among which the junk is generally far more interesting.

Templo de San Felipe Neri

Independencia, cnr Tinoco y Palacios • Daily 9am–6pm • Free

The church of **San Felipe Neri** is mostly Baroque, with a richly decorated proliferation of statues on its plateresque facade. It's the interior decor, though, that really makes it interesting. The church was completed in 1773 and later used as barracks during the Revolution. By the 1920s it badly needed to be repainted, which it was – in an incongruous Art Nouveau style. The building's other claim to fame is that it's the church in which Benito Juárez and Margarita Maza were married in 1843.

10

Museo Rufino Tamayo
Morelos 503 • Mon & Wed–Sat 10am–2pm & 4–7pm, Sun 10am–3pm • M$35

A private collection of pre-Hispanic artefacts gathered by the *Oaxaqueño* abstract artist Rufino Tamayo (1899–1991), the **Museo Rufino Tamayo** is set in an attractive house that dates from 1902. The displays include some truly beautiful items, especially pottery and carvings, from all over Mexico; rather than try to explain the archeological significance of its contents, the collection is deliberately laid out as an art museum, with the focus on aesthetic form. Aztec, Maya and western indigenous cultures all feature strongly, though there's surprisingly little that is Mixtec or Zapotec.

Museo Belber Jiménez
Matamoros 307 • Daily except Tues 10am–7pm • M$20 • ☎ 951 514 5095, ⓦ museobelberjimenez.org

The galleries of the **Museo Belber Jiménez** display the private collection of renowned jeweller Francisco Jiménez and wife Ellen Belber, a treasure trove that includes some magnificent gold Mixtec jewellery, colonial chains and necklaces and a fine collection of twentieth-century silver work by some of Mexico's great masters, including American expats Frederick Davis and William Spratling. There's also a selection of Oaxacan folk art, from rugs and traditional clothing to pottery and lacquer chests. Pride of place goes to the necklace given to Frida Kahlo by Diego Rivera in 1937, engraved with the word "Amor", and a woollen Mexican flag, presented to President Díaz on a visit to Oaxaca. There's also a great, if expensive, shop with high-quality crafts and jewellery including the likes of silver-chased saddles and traditional masks.

South of the Plaza de la Constitución

The **markets** are the main reason most travellers venture south of the plaza. Traditionally, **Saturday** is market day and, although nowadays the markets operate daily, it's still the day to come if you want to see the old-style *tianguis* at its best. *Indígenas* flood in from the villages in a bewildering variety of costumes, and Mixtec and Zapotec dialects replace Spanish as the *lingua franca*.

Mercado Benito Juárez
Occupying the block bordered by Las Casas, Flores Magón, Aldama and 20 de Noviembre • Daily 9am–8pm, busiest on Sat

Just one block south of the plaza, the **Mercado Benito Juárez** has something of everything: raw meat, fruit, clothes and bag stalls rub shoulders with some of the best budget places to eat in town. There are also plenty of stalls more obviously focused on tourists: mescal, local cheese and *mole* are the products of choice.

Mercado 20 de Noviembre
Occupying the block bordered by Aldama, Flores Magón, Mina and 20 de Noviembre • Daily 9am–8pm, busiest on Sat

The **Mercado 20 de Noviembre** is essentially a giant food court, a cacophony of sights, smells and tastes. Indigenous women wander labyrinthine corridors amid plumes of

---

MOLE AND CHOCOLATE

Calle Mina, south of the Mercado 20 de Noviembre, is lined with **spice** vendors selling plump bags of the chile-and-chocolate powder that makes up most Oaxacan **moles**. Cinnamon-flavoured **chocolate powder** is also available, for cooking or making into drinking chocolate. One of the best places in this area to try a mug of hot chocolate, laced with almond, cinnamon, sugar or chile and served with *pan dulce*, is *Mayordomo* (ⓦ chocolatemayordomo.com.mx), the Willy Wonka of Oaxaca; the main branch is at the corner of Mina and 20 de Noviembre. You can also buy pure cacao by the kilo and all sorts of chocolate products. Nearby *La Soledad* at Mina 212 (ⓦ chocolatedeoaxaca.com.mx) has a row of old bean-crushing machines and is drenched in the overpowering aroma of sweet cacao – choc addicts beware.

incense, inviting you to try curious Oaxacan dishes such as *chapulines* (crunchy baked grasshoppers) and *chicharrones* (crispy pork fat). An excellent place to eat, the market is lined with *comedores* serving inexpensive food, such as *chiles rellenos* and tamales. You'll also find the best **mescal** and **chocolate** stores in the surrounding streets (see boxes, p.603 & opposite).

Mercado de Artesanías

20 de Noviembre, between Mina and Zaragoza • Daily 10am–8pm, busiest on Sat

The **Mercado de Artesanías** is the place for village handicrafts, though again there's also plenty of fresh produce and flowers as well as the infamous *chapulines* (toasted grasshoppers). While many of the goods here are low in price, be warned that it's very touristy – you're harassed far more by the vendors than elsewhere and you may have to bargain fiercely to get your price. Quality is often poor, too, so always check carefully before you buy; *sarapes*, in particular, are often machine made from chemically dyed artificial fibres. You can tell real wool by plucking out a thread – artificial fibres are long, thin and shiny, woollen threads short, rough and curly. There are numerous shops around town that will give you a good idea of the potential **quality** of items you can buy in the market; see p.604 for a few of the best.

Mercado de Abastos

Periférico by the second-class bus station • Daily 7am–8pm, busiest on Sat

Biggest, busiest and arguably best of Oaxaca's markets is the sprawling **Mercado de Abastos**. This is where the serious business of buying and selling everyday goods happens; it's the place to go for fruit, vegetables, meat, herbs, spices and all manner of household goods, from traditional cooking pots to wooden utensils and furniture – you could easily spend a couple of hours lost in here, and they certainly wouldn't be wasted.

ARRIVAL AND DEPARTURE

OAXACA

BY PLANE

Oaxaca's airport (Aeropuerto Internacional Xoxocotlán), around 10km south of the city, mainly serves Mexico City; for most other destinations you'll need to change there. Transportación Terrestre Aeropuerto (☎951 514 1071) operates shared (M$60 to the centre of town) and private (from around M$285) taxis; buy your ticket at the desk. They can also bring you back to the airport; call, or visit their office at Alameda de León 1-G, opposite the cathedral (Mon–Sat 10am–2pm). Private taxis charge from M$200 for the trip (note that there are no private taxis *from* the airport, only rides headed to it). Between them Aeroméxico (ⓦaeromexico.com), Interjet (ⓦinterjet.mx) and VivaAerobus (ⓦvivaaerobus.com) operate seven to ten direct daily flights to Mexico City, with onward national and international connections; fares start at around M$1200 but increase dramatically during Mexican holiday times. VivaAerobus also flies twice a week to Monterrey, Volaris (ⓦvolaris.mx) five times weekly to Tijuana, and United (ⓦunited.com) three times a week to Houston. Aerotucán (☎951 502 0840, ⓦaerotucan.com.mx) has a daily flight to Puerto Escondido in a small plane and has in the past also offered flights to Huatulco – it only takes 30min, but at almost M$2000, it's well over ten times the cost of a bus or van.

BY BUS

Bus stations Oaxaca has two main bus stations. The first-class terminal is at Calzada Niños Héroes de Chapultepec 1036, uphill from and northeast of the centre; from here your best bet is to find a taxi (around M$40). The second-class terminal is west of the centre, off the Periférico by the Mercado de Abastos. AU and Sur second-class buses (north and west towards Mexico City and Puebla especially) stop further round the Periférico; from here cross the road. For the Pacific coast, virtually all the first-class buses take a huge detour along Hwy-190 via Salina Cruz, a 9–11hr marathon. It's much faster to take a direct minivan over the mountains (see below).

Ticketbus offices There are downtown Ticketbus offices at Valdivieso 106, half a block from the plaza, and 20 de Noviembre 103, between Hidalgo and Independencia (daily 8am–8pm; ⓦticketbus.com.mx).

Destinations Mexico City (very frequently; 6hr 30min); Pochutla (3 daily; 9hr); Puebla (frequently; 4hr 30min); Puerto Escondido (3 daily; 10hr 30min); San Cristóbal de las Casas (3 daily; 11hr); Tehuantepec (at least hourly; 4hr 30min); Veracruz (5 daily; 7hr); Villahermosa (3 daily; 12hr).

BY MINIVAN AND COLECTIVO

Much the quickest way from Oaxaca to the coast is by minivan, though the direct route across the mountains can be cramped and stomach-churning (for the steadiest ride, aim for a seat

10

close to the front). Most of the operators can be found close to the markets, south of the plaza; in the same area, particularly around the church and park of San Francisco, close to the junction of Armenta y López and La Noria, and also outside the Mercado de Abastos, you'll find terminals for *colectivo* taxis to virtually any village in central Oaxaca.

Destinations Of the minivan operators Eclipse 70 (Armenta y López 504, ☎ 951 516 1068) runs to Pochutla (for Puerto Ángel and around) almost hourly from 3.30am to 11.15pm; Atlántida (La Noria 621 at Armenta y López; ☎ 951 514 7077) has eleven daily departures to Pochutla; Servicio Express (Arista 116 and Cabrera; ☎ 951 516 4059) has around twenty departures to Puerto Escondido every day. It's about five hours to Pochutla, six to Puerto Escondido, and fares are much the same everywhere – M$170 Pochutla, M$200 Puerto Escondido.

GETTING AROUND

By bus The bus routes (M$7.50) are byzantine, and even if you manage to hop on the right one, the traffic is so slow that you could usually have strolled to your destination in half the time.

By car Alamo, 5 de Mayo 203 (☎ 951 514 8534, ⓦ alamomexico.com.mx), generally seem to have the best car rental deals; Europcar are nearby at Matamoros 101 (☎ 951 516 9305, ⓦ europcar.com.mx). Both have desks at the airport and their best prices online. You can also try locally based Only Rent a Car (☎ 951 514 0255, ⓦ onlyrentacar.com) at 5 de Mayo 215.

By taxi Taxis can usually be found on Independencia at García Vigil opposite the cathedral, or flagged down anywhere. Cabs are not metered, so fix your price first. Expect to pay M$30 around town and M$40 out to the first-class bus terminal. Note that fares go up at night (expect to pay around M$50).

By bike For bike rental try Bicicletas Pedro Martínez, hidden away inside Mesón la Brisa at Aldama 418 (☎ 951 514 5935, ⓦ bicicletaspedromartinez.com), or Zona Bici, Garcia Vigil 406 (☎ 951 516 0953, ⓦ zonabici.com.mx). Rentals start at around M$25/hr, M$70/day. See also tours, below.

On foot Walking is by far the best way to get around central Oaxaca.

INFORMATION

Tourist information The best places for tourist information are the booths at Independencia 607, inside the entrance of the Museo de los Pintores (Tues–Sun 10am–6pm) and on the plaza in front of Santo Domingo, off Alcalá (Mon–Sat 9am–6pm, Sun 10am–5pm). Staff at both are helpful and can supply maps and other handouts. You'll also find maps and leaflets at the state tourism office, Juárez 703, in the Teatro Juárez (daily 8am–8pm; ☎ 951 502 1200, ⓦ oaxaca.travel), and the municipal tourist office at Matamoros 102 (daily 8am–8pm; ☎ 951 516 8299, ⓦ ciudaddeoaxaca.org), though the latter is primarily an admin centre and you'll have to walk inside to find someone to speak to.

Oaxaca Lending Library The Oaxaca Lending Library, at Pino Suárez 519 (Mon–Fri 10am–2pm & 4–7pm, Sat 10am–1pm; ☎ 951 518 7077, ⓦ oaxlibrary.org), is a hub of local expat activity, with lectures, meetings, books and DVDs to borrow or buy, a café and a bulletin board packed with info about what's on locally. They maintain ⓦ oaxacacalendar.com, an excellent, up-to-date events listing site. There is a small membership fee to take out books.

Newspapers There are plenty of free publications on offer in cafés and tourist offices; the free monthly English-language newspaper, the *Oaxaca Times* (ⓦ oaxacatimes .com), carries topical features, events listings and apartment rentals (handy for those taking courses). The Spanish-language newspaper *Noticias* (M$10; ⓦ noticiasnet.mx) also has rental ads, and can be bought from newspaper vendors around the plaza.

Websites You can find more on Oaxaca, including accommodation listings and language courses, online at ⓦ go-oaxaca.com, ⓦ oaxacaoaxaca.com and ⓦ oaxaca-mio.com, among many others.

TOURS

Scores of operators throughout the centre offer half-day trips to **Monte Albán** and day tours of the villages of the surrounding valleys; half days start from around M$150, full days M$260. Operators include Turismo El Convento de Oaxaca, 5 de Mayo 300 in the *Quinta Real* hotel (ⓦ oaxacaexperts.com), Monte Alban Tours, Alcalá 206-F (☎ 951 520 0444), and Descubre Oaxaca, Independencia 709 (☎ 951 514 5806).

Adventure and ecotours Expediciones Sierra Norte, Bravo 210-A (☎ 951 514 8271, ⓦ sierranorte.org.mx), lead one- to five-day treks around the Pueblos Mancomunados in the Sierra Norte. Excellent Tierraventura, Abasolo 217 (☎ 951 501 1363, ⓦ tierraventura.com), have similar tours as well as others to the coast and around the central valleys. Rancho Buenavista, based in San Pedro Ixtlahuaca just outside town (☎ 901 228 2951, ⓦ ranchobuenavista.com.mx), organizes

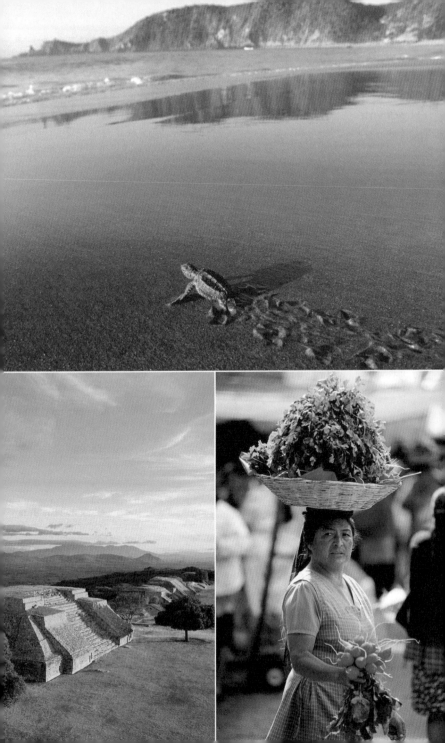

10

more adventurous hiking, mountain-biking and rock-climbing expeditions.

Bike tours Bicicletas Pedro Martínez (see p.598) runs brilliant bike tours, from half a day round the valley to a four-day off-road trip to Puerto Escondido; some of the adventure operators above also offer mountain biking.

Horseriding Horseback Mexico, Murguía 403 (☎951 199 7026, ⓦ horsebackmexico.com), offers anything from two-hour to five-day trips, starting at M$750.

ACTIVITIES

Cookery courses Cookery classes are booming in Oaxaca. *Casa Crespo* restaurant, Allende 107 (see p.602; ☎951 516 0918, ⓦ casacrespo.com), offers four-hour sessions that include shopping and sampling the produce (Tues–Sat 10am, Sun 11am; US$65). El Sabor Zapoteco (☎951 516 0918, ⓦ cookingclasseselsaborzapoteco.blogspot.com) is also excellent. It's run out of of Teotitlán del Valle, and the M$75 fee includes transportation and a market tour. Seasons of My Heart cooking school, in Rancho Aurora on the northern fringes of town (☎951 508 0469, ⓦ seasonsofmyheart.com), has a huge variety of courses and culinary tours, from half a day (US$85/US$1700) to a full week.

Charity and volunteering The Oaxaca Street Children Grassroots project (Centro de Esperanza Infantil) aims to bring a brighter future to Oaxaca's neediest children. You can contribute to their food and medical programme, or volunteer with them in Oaxaca by contacting the centre at Crespo 308 (☎951 501 1069, ⓦ oaxacastreet childrengrassroots.org). Fundación En Vía, based at the Instituto Cultural Oaxaca, Juárez 909 (☎951 515 2424, ⓦ envia.org), provides interest-free microfinance loans to local women, as well as offering free English-language classes and promoting ecotourism. They run fascinating half-day tours to local villages to meet the women they finance (M$750, all proceeds used for loans) and are in need of volunteer English teachers and tour leaders.

Spanish courses Some of the most popular language classes are offered by Amigos del Sol, Calzada San Felipe del Agua 322, meeting at Pino Suárez 802 at Llano park (☎951 520 0118, ⓦ oaxacanews.com/amigosdelsol.htm; US$168/M$2763/week, 15hr); the teachers are very friendly and student ability is properly assessed by tests on arrival. Similar services are offered at the small-scale Becari Language School, Plaza San Cristóbal, M. Bravo 210 (☎951 514 6076, ⓦ becari.com.mx; US$150/M$2467/week, 15hr). Other good schools include Instituto Cultural Oaxaca, Juárez 909 (☎951 515 3404, ⓦ icomexico.com; US$140/M$2303/week, plus registration fee, 15hr); Academia Vinigúlaza, Abasolo 503 (☎951 513 2763, ⓦ vinigulaza.com; US$135/M$2220/week, 15hr); and Oaxaca Spanish Magic, Berriozábal 200 (☎951 516 7316, ⓦ oaxacaspanishmagic.com; from M$130/M$2138/week, 15hr).

Temazcal, massage, yoga Traditional *temazcal* sauna (M$280) and massage (M$280) are offered in a peaceful garden on the outskirts of town through *Casa de las Bugambilias*, Reforma 402 (☎951 516 1165, ⓦ lasbugambilias.com; reserve at least a day in advance). Casa del Ángel, Jacobo Dalevuelta 200, between Reforma and Juárez near the Parque Juárez (☎951 518 7167, ⓦ casadelangel.com.mx), is a yoga centre and café offering a variety of activities and therapies; Sat Nam Yoga y Masajes, Callejón Boca del Monte 121 between Tinoco y Palacios and Crespo (☎951 178 9950), offers yoga, massage, reiki and more.

ACCOMMODATION

Oaxaca's cheaper **hotels** tend to be **south of Independencia**, especially around the markets where some are none too salubrious. Most of the newer and more upscale hotels can be found in the touristy zone near the **Plaza de la Constitución** and **north of Independencia**. In general, only the priciest places have a/c, though it's rarely a necessity here. **Rates** drop by ten to thirty percent outside the Christmas, Semana Santa, July and Aug high seasons.

PLAZA DE LA CONSTITUCIÓN AND SOUTH

Niut-Ja Armenta y López 609 ☎951 501 1623. Old-style, inexpensive courtyard hotel that's been revamped with some cute, artsy furnishings by its friendly young owners; the inward-facing rooms are quieter at the back. <u>M$350</u>

Paulina Youth Hostel Trujano 321 ☎951 516 2005, ⓦ paulinahostel.com. Large, efficiently run hostel which is immaculately clean and white. There are separate, large dorm rooms for men and women, clean bathrooms and some dorm-like private rooms, as well as a rooftop lounge and a small garden with fountains, but little atmosphere. Good breakfast included, but the location, on a harried street corner, isn't great. <u>M$350</u>, dorm <u>M$160</u>

Posada del Centro Independencia 403 ☎951 516 1874, ⓦ hotelposadadelcentro.com. Very friendly travellers' place with the feel of a hostel – communal areas, lots of information, wi-fi throughout – though in fact all rooms are private (some trebles and quads). They're set around a tiled courtyard; en-suite ones at the back are tranquil, shared bath ones nearer the front can have traffic noise. Shared bath <u>M$350</u>, en suite <u>M$700</u>

NORTH OF INDEPENDENCIA

Azucenas M. Aranda 203, at Matamoros ☎951 514 7918, ⓦ hotelazucenas.com. Pleasant colonial house in a quiet corner of town, with only the squeals from the school playground opposite to disturb your peace. The ten comfortable rooms come with a spread of welcoming extras: morning coffee in your room, buffet breakfast, self-serve rooftop bar (with lovely views) and wi-fi. M$775

Casa Arnel Aldama 404 ☎951 515 2856, ⊚casaarnel .com.mx. A popular, family-run place with reasonably priced rooms (with or without bath – sizes vary) around a leafy courtyard. There's a rooftop bar, where breakfast (additional cost) is served, laundry, wi-fi and a library; they also offer tours in Oaxaca and outlying areas. Newer rooms and apartments (around M$6000 a month) lie across the street. M$650

Casa Cid de León Morelos 602 ☎951 514 1893, ⊚casaciddeleon.com. With just four suites, all beautifully and idiosyncratically restored by owner, poet and artist-in-residence Leticia Rodríguez, this is one of Mexico's most memorable hotels. Each spacious room is crammed with antiques, books and trinkets – a regal, timeless aura pervades every artfully conceived nook and cranny. There is a lovely terrace where breakfast is served, and the staff are charming and efficient. Rates are halved midweek and halved again in low season. M$3000

★**Casa de las Bugambilias** Reforma 402 ☎951 516 1165, ⊚lasbugambilias.com. Peaceful and central colonial B&B with nine very individual rooms, each tastefully decorated with work by local artists. Some are a little small, but all are extremely comfortable, with some kind of outdoor area or balcony; upstairs rooms have a/c. Delicious breakfast included, and if they're full they may have rooms at sister B&B *El Secreto*. M$1050

Casa de los Milagros Matamoros 500 ☎951 501 2262, ⊚casadelosmilagros.com. Justifiably a favourite, this small, family-run, colonial hotel has just three immaculate, individually styled rooms in a dream home setting. There's a beautiful communal kitchen, a dining room and a patio – the Ángeles room even has its own "waterfall". M$1050

★**Casa Oaxaca** García Vigil 407 ☎951 514 4173, ⊚casaoaxaca.com.mx. If you are going to splurge, *Casa Oaxaca*, the personal favourite of Gabriel García Marquéz, is the place. Seven tastefully serene, spacious rooms are set around a pristine white courtyard with a tiled pool. With an emphasis on intimacy and tranquillity, the service is faultless – there's even a small library – and Oaxacan

artistry is woven through every detail. Delicious breakfast included. M$3200

Cazomalli Salto 104, cnr Aldama ☎951 513 3513, ⊚hotelcazomalli.com. Quaint little posada hidden away in an untouristy corner. The comfy rooms have carved and painted wooden furniture, and there's a gorgeous rooftop breakfast area. M$690

★**Las Golondrinas** Tinoco y Palacios 411 ☎951 514 3298, ⊚hotellasgolondrinas.com.mx. Simple but comfortable pristine rooms in an old colonial house, set around a series of flower-filled patios. Very tranquil with a distinctly local flavour. M$600

Hostal Casa del Sótano Tinoco y Palacios 414 ☎951 516 2494, ⊚hoteldelsotano.net. Classily modernized colonial mansion with pretty, brightly painted rooms with folk-art flourishes, all with a/c. Some are very small, though. There's an inviting terrace café, with views, where a basic breakfast (included) is served. M$1050

★**Hostel Don Nino** Pino Suárez 804 on Parque Juárez ☎951 518 5985, ⊚hosteldonnino.com. Stylish, well-run hostel with excellent facilities including laundry, well-equipped kitchens, wi-fi, computer terminals and several seating areas with flat-screen TVs and DVD players. Airy, well set-up dorms, plus private rooms better than at many downtown hotels; good breakfast included. M$700, four-bed dorm M$190, eight-bed dorm M$170

Las Mariposas Pino Suárez 517 ☎951 515 5854, ⊚lasmariposas.com.mx. Delightful colonial-style hotel with helpful staff and spacious rooms, some with kitchenettes and all with private bathrooms, clustered around a vibrant courtyard complete with flowers and fish-filled fountains. Very popular with long-stay Spanish students. Light breakfast and wi-fi included. M$550

Quinta Real Oaxaca 5 de Mayo 300 ☎951 516 0611, ⊚quintareal.com/oaxaca. Oaxaca's priciest hotel (lowest off-season prices start around M$2200 a night), in the beautifully converted sixteenth-century Ex-Convento de Santa Catalina. Candles light the way through flower-filled courtyards to characterful, if medievally dimensioned, rooms. If a night's stay is beyond your budget, a lingering coffee or cocktail in the courtyard is a worthy substitute. Take a tour of the hotel Wed–Fri 5pm (40min; free). M$4000

EATING

The food in Oaxaca is sensational. The cheapest places to eat are in the **markets**, especially the Mercado 20 de Noviembre (see p.596), the Mercado de Abastos (see p.597) and El Pochote organic market (see p.595). You'll also find a medley of **street stalls** dotted around the **plaza** and the surrounding streets, and on García Vigil near Carmen Alto, that serve filling staples such as *elote* (corn on the cob), tamales and *flautas* (deep-fried, rolled tortillas filled with mozzarella-like string cheese or meat). The Plaza and Alameda are also ringed by **cafés** and restaurants where you can sit outside – irresistible as ever and not as expensive as you might fear, though the food is rarely up to much – and there are plenty of simple places for everyday meals in the streets round about. Oaxaca also provides plenty of options for **vegetarians**, while at the pricier end, colonial-style and contemporary upscale restaurants offer nouvelle Mexican dishes using local herbs and produce. Virtually all the travellers' cafés and many restaurants offer free **wi-fi**.

10

LAND OF THE SEVEN MOLES – OAXACAN CUISINE

Oaxaca is known as the "land of the seven *moles*" after its most famous sauces: *mole negro* or *Oaxaqueño* (the most popular, made with chocolate, giving a distinct roasted flavour), *amarillo*, *coloradito*, *mancha manteles*, *chichilo*, *rojo* and *verde*. *Moles* are typically served with chicken or enchiladas, but you don't have to go to one of the smart restaurants serving contemporary Oaxacan cuisine to sample them: *mole negro* is often better from street or market vendors. Other specialities include **tamales**, worth trying in any form, and **chapulines**, crunchy seasoned grasshoppers. **Tlayudas**, giant crisp tortillas dressed with beans and a mild Oaxacan string cheese called **quesillo**, are staples of cafés and street stands after dark.

The place to go for exceptional home-made **ice cream** is the plaza in front of the church of La Soledad, full of rival vendors and tables where you can sit and gorge yourself while watching the world go by. Flavours are innumerable and often bizarre, including *elote* (corn), *queso*, *leche quemada* (burnt milk; even worse than it sounds), *sorbete* (cinnamon-flavoured sherbet) and exotic fruits like *mamey*, *guanabana* and *tuna* (prickly pear; a virulent purple that tastes wonderful). There are also more ordinary varieties like chocolate, strawberry and coconut. At the opposite end of town, you can sample many of these flavours at Museo de las Nieves, Alcalá 706, just up from Santo Domingo.

PLAZA DE LA CONSTITUCIÓN AND SOUTH

★**Café Alex** Díaz Ordaz 218, at Trujano ☎ 951 514 0715. Popular with locals and travellers alike, this boisterous Mexican-style diner offers excellent breakfast menus ranging from omelettes (Spanish omelette breakfast M$62), yogurt and hot cakes to refried beans, *huevos rancheros* and fresh-fruit *licuados* – it also opens early by Oaxaca standards. Mon–Sat 7am–10pm, Sun 7am–1pm.

La Casa de la Abuela Hidalgo 616 ☎ 951 516 3544. Touristy, old-fashioned and with food tailored to an American palate, but the great views over the plaza from the second floor compensate and most dishes are not that expensive (M$60–150). Mon–Sat 1–9pm, Sun 1–7pm.

La Red Las Casas 101, cnr Bustamante ☎ 951 514 6853. A bustling, no-frills seafood joint that looks a bit like a fast-food place, serving generous portions of fish (fillet M$118, whole fish M$135), soups, prawn cocktails (M$50), *ceviche* and octopus. Little atmosphere but plenty of flavour. Daily noon–9pm.

NORTH OF INDEPENDENCIA

La Antigua Reforma 401 ☎ 951 516 5761. A popular café for breakfast, with a range of American, continental and Mexican combinations plus local, organic coffee roasted on site. There's also a selection of pastries and sandwiches for a quick lunch, and a lively post-dinner scene with wine, mescal and liqueur coffees. Mon–Thurs 9am–8pm, Fri & Sat 9am–11pm.

Biznaga García Vigil 512 ☎ 951 516 1800. Elegant place popular with expats set in a lemon-walled courtyard festooned with artwork. A chalk-board outlines the daily menu, which ranges from wholesome salads and soups to *pastor*-style (tomato, oil, cilantro) fish and chicken *milanesa* filled with cheese. Service can be slow – sip an excellent margarita or Belgian beer while you wait. Main dishes around M$150, and a lunch-time menu for around M$120 which includes mescal and coffee. Mon–Sat 11am–11pm, Sun 2–8pm.

Casa Crespo Allende 107 ☎ 951 516 0918. High-concept restaurant where chef Oscar Carrizosa runs cookery courses (see p.600) and creates elaborate modern versions of traditional Oaxacan dishes. Choose from starters (from M$60) such as *memelitas* with cheese, agave worms and grasshoppers, chile stuffed with shrimp or lentil soup with plantain, pineapple and bacon, and mains (from M$170) like fish in a pumpkin seed *mole*, or turkey in *mole amarillo*, using rare varieties of chile. There's a wine list and chocolatería to match. Tues–Sun 1–11pm.

Casa Oaxaca El Restaurante Constitución 104-A ☎ 951 516 8531. The contemporary Oaxacan restaurant of the *Casa Oaxaca* hotel proved so popular that it outgrew its origins and had to move out. It still serves some of the best food in town, with starters (M$70–90) like ricotta-stuffed squash blossoms with honey and *epazote* or fish quesadillas, and mains ranging from turkey in *mole negro* (M$159) to vanilla-scented sautéed shrimp (M$210) or crispy suckling pig with *mole verde* (M$315). The gourmet menu (M$690) comes in traditional or contemporary versions. You'll need to book. Daily 1–11pm.

El Catedral García Vigil 105 ☎ 951 516 3285. Gorgeous, long-established fine-dining favourite, with tables topped by white linens and pale blue walls lit with chandeliers. There's a wonderful Sunday buffet brunch, but El Catedral is mainly favoured for dinner, with distinguished takes on Oaxacan cuisine like *mole* and contemporary dishes like roast beef seasoned with cinnamon and tamalito bean. Wed–Mon 8am–11pm.

★**Cenadería Libres Tlayudas Doña Martha** Libres 212. Incredibly popular late-night snack stop, cooking up tasty *tlayudas* (stodgy, plate-sized tortillas chargrilled and stuffed with meat, cheese and beans for M$55) to queues of hungry clubbers and taxi drivers. They're cooked over charcoal in the street, though there are tables inside in case you want to sit down to eat: you may have a long wait in the early hours. Daily 3pm–5am.

Cofetarika Alcalá 403 ☎951 278 8000. Cloistered away on the second floor of an attractive shopping complex (which also houses *Los Danzantes*; see below), the open-air *Cofetarika* peddles some of the best coffee in town, especially the cappuccinos, and offers a small but superb breakfast menu (brioche French toast, M$80). Lovely views and ambience. Mon–Sat 8am–6pm, Sun 10am–6pm.

La Crêpe Alcalá 307, upstairs ☎951 516 2200. There may not be much Oaxacan flavour to the food, but it's popular with locals, always lively and enjoys a great setting overlooking Alcalá. Vast range of sweet and savoury crêpes (M$60–85), from squash and cheese to nutella and banana, and baguettes (M$65–90), as well as fruit salads, ice creams and a range of excellent salads (from M$50). Good dessert stop-off when the music draws the pre-party crowd. Daily 9am–11pm.

Los Danzantes Alcalá 403 ☎951 501 1184. Fancy restaurant in the unlikely setting of the interior of the Plaza Comercial – in an inner courtyard where the stark modern decor is offset by ponds and water features. Good cocktails – try the mescal margarita (they produce their own excellent line of the liquor) – and imaginative dishes like mango- and mint-infused octopus, shrimp *ceviche*, barbecue chicken strips tossed with fried cactus and Oaxacan chocolate soufflé. Prices are steep by local standards, with starters around M$75 and mains M$145–245; there's a lunch-time *comida* (M$100) on Wed & Fri. Daily 1.30–11.30pm.

Le Gourmand Porfirio Díaz 410 ☎951 516 4435. Superb little New York-style deli (of all things), with home-made pickles, craft beer and ham that's cured in house. The "reuben" sandwich (with corned beef) is M$90, while bagels with all the fixings are around M$60. Mon–Sat 11am–11pm.

Jaguar Yu'u Murguía 202 ☎951 516 4238. Friendly modern café with good beverages and inexpensive snack food – sandwiches, baguettes (M$65), French toast (M$30), eggs, salads (M$40–60) – and a daily *menu del día* for M$55. Mon–Sat 8am–10pm.

La Jícara Porfirio Díaz 1105 ☎951 516 5638. Arty, sunny little café, filled with potted plants and bright flowers, that's set in a bookstore and community meeting centre. Lunch, which includes soup and salad, will set you back M$90. It's far from the centre, but great if you're near the Arcos de Xochimilco (see p.595). Mon–Wed 1–10pm, Thurs & Fri 1–11pm, Sat 1.30–11pm.

La Olla Reforma 402 ☎951 516 6668. Quaint, relaxed café/gallery with a reliable breakfast menu featuring Oaxacan specialities, enchiladas and *chilaquiles* as well as more wholesome choices. At lunch time there's an M$80 *comida* and a full menu with mains from M$60–150; an easy introduction to Oaxacan cuisine. Mon–Sat 8am–10pm.

Pizza Nostrana Alcalá 501, cnr Allende ☎951 514 0778. The best place in town for pizza (from M$90 to M$200) and well-executed pasta dishes with a vegetarian slant. The intimate, old-fashioned atmosphere and location close to Santo Domingo lend a romantic, relaxed vibe. Daily 1pm–midnight.

★**Zandunga** Garcia Vigil ☎951 516 2265. Colourful, dynamic dinner spot with a stylish clientele but an unfussy, welcoming vibe. The food is affordable and beautifully presented: splurge on oven-roasted chicken with salsa (M$180) or stay within your budget and order an excellent *platano tamale* (M$60). Great mescal list, too. Mon–Sat 2–11pm.

10

MESCAL

Mescal (or mezcal) is the *Oaxaqueño* drink of choice, sold everywhere in bottles that usually have a dead *gusano* worm (actually a type of caterpillar) in the bottom. Tradition has it that the creature lives on the cactus-like maguey plant and is there to prove that the ingredients are genuine, although these days most of the worms are farm raised. You don't have to eat the worm, though few people are in any state to notice what they're ingesting by the time they reach the bottom of the bottle. Like tequila (which is technically a type of mescal), mescal is made from the sugary heart of the agave plant, which is baked, pulverized and then distilled. Many of the best **mescal stores** can be found around the Mercado 20 de Noviembre where you can taste before you commit to buying; good brands include Los Amantes (also has a great shop, see p.604), Los Danzantes (also a restaurant, see above), Mezcal Amores and Alipús.

Several towns produce mescal, but the original is **Santiago Matatlán**, 45km from Oaxaca City near Mitla (see p.613). **Mescal tours** are advertised everywhere; one of the best guides is Canadian expat Alvin Starkman, owner of the *Casa Machaya* B&B (☎951 132 8203, ⓦoaxacadream.com). Alternatively, ask after Ulises Torrentera at Los Amantes (see above).

DRINKING AND NIGHTLIFE

If you're not content to sit around the plaza over a coffee or a beer or to while away a balmy night to the accompaniment of mariachi or brass bands, sample some of Oaxaca's handful of decent bars and clubs. Most open daily 7pm to 3am, though clubs won't get busy till after midnight and usually close between Sun and Wed. The **folk dances** at the Casa de Cantera, Federico Ortiz Armengol 104 in the north of the city (daily 8.30pm; M$185; ☎ 951 514 7585, ⓦ casadecantera.com), or Quinta Real Oaxaca (Fri 7pm; M$390 including buffet; see p.601) will at least give you a taster of the famous *guelaguetza* festival if you can't attend the real thing.

10

Los Amantes Allende 107, in Casa de Crespo ☎ 951 136 4099, ⓦ mezcalerialosamantes.blogspot.com. Tiny but trendy, hole-in-the-wall *mescalería* that frequently has them lining up outside to taste the exceptional artisan mescal in which it specializes; they also sell bottles, many sourced direct from obscure distilleries. There are a couple of other popular bars, open later, in this short stretch of Allende. Wed–Sat 5–10pm.

Candela Murguía 413 ☎ 951 514 2010. Set in a charming colonial house, *Candela* is a restaurant by day, but the place really comes alive after 11pm when the dancefloor is packed with locals and tourists coming to practise their salsa, rumba and merengue, accompanied by a live band. Try to arrive before 10pm at the weekend in order to secure a table; there are also free dance classes from 10–11pm. M$50 cover. Thurs–Sat 7pm till late.

Casa del Mezcal Flores Magón 209. Classic Mexican cantina in the market district, open since 1935, with cheap shots of mescal and a fairly liberal attitude to female patrons (though it's generally frequented by men). Pounding music and a Maya mystic theme, with murals and a carved wooden bar. Daily 3pm–late; happy hour 6–8pm.

La Farola 20 de Noviembre 3 at Las Casas. Classic cantina since 1916, with wooden tables (displaying crafts and antiquities under glass tops), friendly bar staff and two floors; come here to drink fine mescal. Daily 2pm–late.

La Nueva Babel Porfirio Díaz 224. Loungey wine bar with a Mexican kitsch theme, featuring live folk music, salsa (*son Cubano*) and poetry readings, most nights from 10pm (free). Opens as a café during the day, serving breakfast, coffee and snacks. Daily 9am–late.

SHOPPING

If it's **crafts and artesanías** you're after, you'll find dozens of high-quality shops on and around Alcalá. It's substantially cheaper, and a great deal more fun, to buy in the markets (see p.596), or even better in the villages in which the goods originate: even if that's what you intend to do, however, it's well worth checking the quality and price of the goods in the shops first.

Amate Alcalá 307 ☎ 951 516 6960. An excellent selection of new and secondhand English-language books, primarily about Mexico (including literature, travel, archeology and cooking), and magazines. Mon–Sat 10.30am–7.30pm, Sun noon–6pm.

Arte Textil Alcalá 403-2. Gorgeous, pricey textiles to covet or gift. Plush scarves, table runners, button downs and more. Daily 10am–9pm.

Casa de las Artesanías de Oaxaca Matamoros 105. A big commercial store with high-quality goods and plenty of them, from fabrics to tin, ceramics to *alebrijes*; many similar places in the vicinity. Mon–Sat 9am–8pm, Sun 10am–6pm.

Colectivo 1050° Rufino Tamayo 800 ☎ 951 132 6158, ⓦ 1050grados.com. Forged from traditional practices but shaped into contemporary styles, the pottery at this superb collective – which is devoted to preserving Oaxaca's craft and artisan culture – is well worth carting home in your suitcase. Mon–Fri 10am–5pm.

Instituto Oaxaqueño de las Artesanías (ARIPO) García Vigil 809. State-run store that feels as much like a gallery as a shop; quality and fair prices to producers are assured. Mon–Fri 9am–7pm, Sat 11am–3pm.

Mujeres Artesanías de las Regiones de Oaxaca (MARO) 5 de Mayo 204. Craft shop run by an association of local women to promote their own crafts. There's nothing very fancy but there's a lot to choose from, all very fairly priced; a great place for inexpensive souvenirs. Daily 9am–8pm.

DIRECTORY

Banks and exchange *Casas de cambio* litter the town centre and all the major banks can be found within a few blocks of the plaza. Close to the cathedral there's Santander at García Vigil, cnr Independencia, Banorte at García Vigil 103, between Morelos and Independencia, Bancomer at García Vigil and Morelos, and Banamex at Morelos and Porfirio Díaz. South of the plaza, HSBC is at Armenta y López and Guerrero, and there's another Banamex at Armenta y López and Hidalgo.

Consulates Canada, Pino Suárez 700, office 11B (☎ 951 513 3777); US, Alcalá 407, Office 20 (☎ 951 514 3054).

Emergencies Dial ☎ 060. For roadside assistance, call the Angeles Verdes on ☎ 078 or ☎ 951 516 9597.

Hospitals Aurelio Valdivieso, Porfirio Díaz 400 (☎ 951 515 1300). Clínica Hospital Carmen at Abasolo 215 (☎ 951 516 2612) has 24hr walk-in service and usually has English-speakers on hand. The vast IMSS Hospital is at Porfirio Díaz 141, north of the centre (☎ 951 515 6021).

Internet Internet cafés are abundant; most have copy and printing services, and some have long-distance call booths. Open latest is Café Internet, upstairs in the *Hostel Alcala* at Valdivieso 120 and Independencia – it closes most nights at 11pm; Inter@ctive at Alcalá 503, across from Santo Domingo, has phone services too.

Laundry Service-wash launderettes and dry cleaners are plentiful, including: Lavandería Santa Maria, Bravo 407 cnr Tinoco y Palacios (Mon–Sat 9am–8pm, Sun 9am–3pm; M$15/kg); Tintorería Antequera, Murguía 408 (Mon–Sat 8am–2pm & 4–8pm).

Post office Alameda de León 2 at Independencia (Mon–Fri 8am–7pm, Sat 8am–3pm).

Monte Albán

Daily 8am–5pm • M$64

The extraordinary city of **MONTE ALBÁN** is one of the world's great archeological treasures, legacy of the advanced Zapotec culture that dominated this part of Mexico well over a thousand years ago. Founded around 500 BC, most of the city was abandoned by 950 AD, though the Mixtecs later used it as a magnificent burial site. The main structures were cleared and restored in the 1930s; today it's the great flattened mountain top (750m by 250m), the scale of the monuments and the views over the valley that impress more than any individual aspect of the site. Sombre, grey and formal as it all appears now, in its heyday, with its roofs and sanctuaries intact, the whole place would have been brilliantly polychromed. Late afternoon, as the sun sinks into the valley, is the best time to see it.

There's a car park, restaurant and souvenir shop by the entrance, and a small **museum** in the same complex: the collection is tiny, but there are some important finds on display, including the carvings of the "dancers" (see p.606), intricate sculptures, ceramics and some gruesome mutilated skulls, presumably victims of the Zapotecs.

Brief history

It seems almost madness to have tried to build a city here, so far from the obvious livelihood of the valleys and without any natural water supply (in

MONTE ALBÁN

N

Tumba 7

Tumba 104

Museum & Ticket Office

Oaxaca (9km)

Entrance

Plataforma Norte

Juego de Pelota

Sistema IV

Edificio G

Edificio II

Los Danzantes

Edificio H

GRAN PLAZA

Edificio P

Edificio I

Palacio

Monticulo J (Observatorio)

Monticulo Q

Monticulo M

Plataforma Sur

0 — 100
metres

10

the dry season water was carried up and stored in vast urns). Yet that may have been the Zapotecs' point – to demonstrate their mastery of nature. By waging war on potential rivals, the new city soon came to dominate an area that extended well beyond the main valley – the peculiar *danzante* figures ("dancers") carved in stone that you can see at the ruins today are widely considered to be depictions of prisoners captured in battle.

By 200 AD, the population had expanded to such a degree that the Zapotecs endeavoured to level the Monte Albán spur completely to create more space, essentially forming a massive plateau. The resulting engineering project boggles the mind: without the aid of the wheel or beasts of burden, millions of tonnes of earth were shifted to build a vast, flat terrace on which the Zapotecs constructed colossal pyramids, astronomical observatories and palaces. What you see today is only the very centre of the city – its religious and political heart. On the terraced hillsides below lived a bustling population of between twenty five thousand and thirty thousand craftsmen, priests, administrators and warriors, all of whom, presumably, were supported by tribute from the valleys. It's small wonder that so top-heavy a society was easily destabilized. That said, there is still much speculation as to why the site was ultimately abandoned.

Plataforma Norte

The **Plataforma Norte**, straight ahead as you enter the site at its northeast corner, may have been the most important of all the temples at Monte Albán, although now the ceremonial buildings that line its sides are largely ruined. What survives is a broad stairway leading up from the Gran Plaza to a platform enclosing a square patio with an altar at its heart. This ceremonial centre was constructed between 400 and 750 AD, when Monte Albán was at its zenith. At the top of the stairs are the remains of a double row of six broad columns, which would originally have supported a roof to form a colonnade, dividing this plaza from the main one.

The Gran Plaza

The main path takes you south along the eastern side of the Plataforma Norte to the **Gran Plaza**, the vast, ceremonial focus of the city, surrounded by all its major buildings. As you enter you'll pass the **Juego de Pelota** (ball-court), a simple I-shaped space with no apparent goals or target rings, obviously an early example. The ball-game was used as a means to solve conflict – it is believed that the losing team was sacrificed to the gods. Otherwise, the platforms on the east side of the plaza are relatively late constructions, dating from around 500 AD onwards. Facing them from the middle of the plaza is a long tripartite building (**Edificios G**, **H** and **I**) that must have played an important role in any rites celebrated here. The central section has broad staircases by which it can be approached from east or west – the lower end temples have smaller stairways facing north and south. From here a complex of tunnels runs under the site to several of the other temples, presumably to allow the priests to emerge suddenly and miraculously in any one of them. You can see the remains of several of these tunnels among the buildings on the east side.

Monticulo J

South of the central block, **Monticulo J**, known as the observatory, stands alone in the centre of the plaza, its arrow-shaped design marking it out from its surroundings. Although the building's orientation – at 45 degrees to everything else – is almost certainly for astronomical reasons, there's no evidence that this was actually an observatory; more likely it was built (around 250 AD, but on the site of an earlier structure) to celebrate a victory in battle. The carvings and hieroglyphics on the back of the building apparently represent a list of towns captured by the Zapotecs; indeed, much of the imagery at Monte Albán points to a highly militaristic society. In the vaulted passage that runs through the heart of the building, several more panels carved in relief show *danzante* figures – these, often upside down or on their sides and in no particular order, may have been reused from an earlier building.

Plataforma Sur

The southern end of the Gran Plaza is dominated by its tallest structure, the unrestored **Plataforma Sur**, a vast square pyramid offering the best overview of the site, as well as fine panoramas of the surrounding countryside.

Monticulo M and Sistema IV

On the western side of the Gran Plaza, **Monticulo M** and **Sistema IV** are the best-preserved buildings on the site. Each consists of a rectangular platform reached by a stairway from the plaza.

Los Danzantes

The gallery and building of **Los Danzantes**, between Monticulo M and Sistema IV, are the most interesting features of Monte Albán. A low wall extending from Monticulo M to the base of the Danzantes building forms the **gallery**, originally faced all along with blocks carved in relief of "dancers". Among the oldest (dating from around 500 BC) and most puzzling features of the site, only a few of these *danzantes* remain – the originals are now preserved in the museum and what you see here are replicas. The significance of the nude male figures is disputed: many of them seem to have been cut open and may represent sacrificial victims or prisoners; another suggestion is that the entire wall was a sort of medical textbook, or that the figures are dancers, ball-players or acrobats. Whatever the truth, they show clear **Olmec** influence, and many of them have been pressed into use in later buildings throughout the site.

The outer buildings

Several lesser buildings surround the main plaza, and although they're not particularly interesting, many contain tombs in which rich treasures were discovered (as indeed did some of the main structures themselves).

Tumba 104

Tumba 104, reached by a small path behind the Plataforma Norte or from the site's main entrance, is the best preserved tomb at Monte Albán. Its vaulted burial chamber, one of several in the immediate vicinity, still preserves excellent remains of murals; polychrome frescoes vividly revealing the mystical symbolism of the Zapotec gods.

Tumba 7

Tumba 7, where the important collection of Mixtec jewellery now in the Museo de las Culturas de Oaxaca (see p.593) was found, lies a few hundred metres down the main road from the site entrance. Built underneath a small temple, it was originally constructed by the Zapotecs towards the end of Monte Albán's heyday, but was later emptied by the Mixtecs, who buried one of their own chiefs here along with his magnificent burial trove.

ARRIVAL AND DEPARTURE   **MONTE ALBÁN**

By minibus Monte Albán is 9km southwest of Oaxaca, up a steeply switchbacking road. There are two competitors for the Monte Albán run, both based on C Mina and offering similar minibus services for around M$50 return, though it's worth comparing prices. Autobuses Turísticos (☎ 951 516 6175) are at Mina 501, Lescas (☎ 951 516 0666) at the *Hotel Rivera del Ángel*, Mina 518. Each has hourly departures (every 30min high season and weekends; 30min) from 8.30am to 3.30pm, returning between noon and 5pm – you'll be allocated a fixed return time, giving three hours at the site, but it's OK to take a different bus back if there's space.

By taxi For a group of four people, it costs much the same to go by taxi (around M$100 each way), though you may have to wait for a return ride.

On foot Walking back to Oaxaca is a realistic option: more than two hours, but downhill almost all the way – get a guard or one of the kids selling "genuine antiquities" to show you the path. The route is an eye-opening experience, veering through slum dwellings that are a far cry from the comforts of much of the city below.

10

The Zapotec and Mixtec heartland

The region around Oaxaca can be divided into two parts: the **Valles Centrales**, comprising three valleys which radiate from the state capital to the south and east, towards Mitla, Ocotlán and Zaachila (collectively the Valle de Oaxaca); and the **Mixteca**, which extends northwest towards Puebla and arcs down to the Pacific coast via Tlaxiaco and Pinotepa Nacional. The Valles Centrales include the state's most famous and frequented archeological centres, craft villages and colourful markets, while the Mixteca, rich in ruined Dominican convents and ancient towns and villages, is less visited but well worth exploring.

This area saw the development of some of the most highly advanced civilizations in pre-Hispanic Mexico, most notably the Zapotecs and Mixtecs. Their craft skills – particularly Mixtec weaving, pottery and metalworking – were unrivalled, and the architecture and planning of their cities rank among ancient Mexico's greatest achievements. Traditional ways of life and indigenous languages are still vigorously preserved by Mixtec and Zapotec descendants in villages today.

GETTING AROUND   **THE ZAPOTEC AND MIXTEC HEARTLAND**

By bus/colectivo Every village in the region will have a bus service from the second-class terminal in Oaxaca; for the smaller places this may be very occasional, however, or involve a walk from the highway. In addition, *colectivo* taxis run throughout the Valles Centrales, and to bigger places further afield; their termini are in the streets around the markets in Oaxaca, in particular Bustamante, La Noria and Zaragoza around the church of San Francisco; they leave when full. While it's easy enough to get to a village, it's much harder to connect between them – you may have to

STAYING IN LOCAL COMMUNITIES AROUND OAXACA

Indigenous communities in the mountains and valleys of Oaxaca have been developing their ecotourism potential since the 1990s, when a cabins programme was established. These small, self-contained *cabañas ecoturísticas* were designed to bring income to the villages while minimizing the disruptive effects of tourism. These days many villages organize **tours** (hiking, coffee farms, biking, adventure sports and agrotourism) and some sort of "community lodging", from **homestays** to simple but comfy **cabins**, usually arranged through a local Comité de Ecoturismo. Either type of accommodation makes a convenient and economical base for exploring the villages and archeological sites of Oaxaca state. Many communities have particular **handicraft traditions**, such as carpet-weaving, wickerwork or pottery; others have museums devoted to local archeological finds and the life of the villagers.

The best place for information and reservations – ideally made a few days in advance, especially for the more accessible sites – is Oaxaca's state tourist office at Juárez 703 (see p.598); be warned that individual staff may know little about this, that their information may be out of date, and that even where they do make a reservation it may take a while to seek out the key locally when you arrive. The lending library (see p.598) is another great resource for rentals. For the Sierra Norte and the Pueblos Mancomunados contact Expediciones Sierra Norte (see p.598), which coordinates all the local community programmes in that area. For Ixtlán contact Ecoturixtlán (see p.619) directly.

Cabins usually cost M$150–500, depending on how many people are sharing, and generally have bedroom(s), fully equipped kitchen and outside shower and toilets (which can also be used by people camping in the grounds). Campers pay around M$50.

walk back to the highway to flag down onward transport, or use taxis for short hops between villages.

By car Car rental is as pricey here as anywhere in the country, but if you are planning extensive exploration of the valleys it may prove worthwhile, allowing you to trade a week of waiting for buses for a couple of days of independence; see p.598 for agents. Note that poor signposting can be frustrating, and that getting in and out of Oaxaca can be a nightmare.

Brief history

The Valles Centrales are the cradle of some of the earliest civilizations in Mexico. The story begins with the **Zapotecs**, who founded their first city – now called San José Mogoté, and little more than a collection of mounds, a few kilometres north of the state capital – some time before 1000 BC. As the city grew in wealth, trading with Pacific coastal communities, its inhabitants turned their eyes to the stars, and by 500 BC they had invented the first Mexican calendar and were using hieroglyphic writing. At this time, San José, together with smaller villages in the area, established a new administrative capital at Monte Albán, a vantage point on a mountain spur overlooking the principal Oaxaca valley (see p.605). Just like Teotihuacán, Monte Albán mysteriously began to implode from about 700 AD, and the Zapotec influence across the Valles Centrales waned. Only Yagul and Mitla, two smaller cities in the principal valley, expanded after this date, though they never reached the imperial glory of Monte Albán. As the Zapotecs disappeared, the gap they left behind was slowly filled by the **Mixtecs**, pre-Hispanic Mexico's finest craftsmen, who expanded into the southern valleys from the north to occupy the Zapotecs' magnificent cities. Influenced by the Zapotec sculptors' abstract motifs on the walls at Mitla, the Mixtecs concentrated their artistic skills on metalwork and pottery, examples of which can be seen in the state capital's museums. By the fifteenth century, the Mixtecs had become the favoured artisans to Mexico's greatest empire, their conquerors, the **Aztecs**; Bernal Díaz recounts that Moctezuma ate only from plates fashioned by Mixtec craftsmen.

Valle de Tlacolula

Hwy-190 provides access to the alluring villages of the **Valle de Tlacolula**, slicing some 45km east of Oaxaca towards **Mitla** (see p.612), before cutting south to Tehuantepec and the coast. The route is well served by *colectivos* and buses from the second-class terminal (every 30min or so), making day trips possible, even without a car. Check with the tourist office, or see the box, p.610, for which village has a market on the day you're going. If you want to explore the valley further it's a good idea to stay in one of the villages, some of which have self-catering facilities (see box opposite).

Santa María del Tule

SANTA MARÍA DEL TULE (or simply El Tule), 13km east of Oaxaca, is famous for just one thing, the giant **Árbol del Tule** in the centre of town. This mighty tree, said to be at least 1500 years old (some say two thousand), is a good 36m round (the signboard claims a girth of 58m, but this is disputed by most experts), 42m in height, and weighs in around 500 tonnes. There's a small fee to go right into the churchyard where the tree stands (M\$10; daily 8am–8pm), but you can get pretty close even without paying. The notice board gives all the vital statistics, though some of these are rather dubious: suffice to say that it must be one of the oldest living (and flourishing) objects on earth, and that it's a rare Montezuma cypress (*Taxodium mucronatum*), the national tree of Mexico. Local environmentalists claim that the Tule tree – along with other cypresses nearby – is threatened by development that has led to falling water levels; the site was added to UNESCO's World Heritage Tentative List in 2001, but has yet to be nominated.

Locals and tourists flock to visit the tree, and nearby there's a tacky souvenir market and a Mercado de Antojitos (food market), plus a string of restaurants along the main road.

10

By bus Buses (M$8) depart from Oaxaca's second-class bus station every 30min; you can save a great deal of time by flagging one down on Niños Héroes near the junction with

Blv Eduardo Vasconcelos, one block east of Oaxaca's baseball stadium (look for "Tule").

Dainzú
Daily 8am–5pm • M$35

The main allure of the ancient Zapotec site of **Dainzú** resides in its raw appeal, with few tourists or imposing facilities to detract from soulful contemplation. Just over 20km from Oaxaca on Hwy-190, Dainzú, established around 700–600 BC, stands partially excavated in a harsh landscape of cactus-covered hills around 1km south of the main road. The chief structure, **Edificio A**, is a large, rambling hillside construction set around a courtyard, with elements from several epochs. Along the far side of its base a series of *danzante* figures can be made out, similar to those at Monte Albán except that these clearly represent ball-players. Nearby is the **ball-court**, only one side of which has been reconstructed. **Edificio B** is another large and complex platform structure; its most striking feature is a tomb whose entrance is carved in the form of a jaguar.

Teotitlán del Valle

TEOTITLÁN DEL VALLE, 4km north of Hwy-190, is the most famous weaving town in Oaxaca. The rugs are the product of a cottage industry that seems to involve almost every family in town; along the road as you approach and all over the village you'll see bold-patterned and brightly coloured **rugs** and **sarapes**, some following traditional designs from Mitla, others more modern, including many based on the work of Dutch graphic artist M.C. Escher.

Even if you're not buying, poke your head into one of the compounds with rugs hanging outside. There's little hard-sell, and most weavers will be more than happy to provide a demonstration of pre-Hispanic weaving and dying techniques; traditional dyes use natural substances including indigo, pomegranate and cochineal, the latter made from a substance secreted by the cochineal beetle that, when dried, creates an inimitable blood-red colour. There's a small **Mercado de Artesanías** on the main plaza with a decent range of rugs, but quality and prices are generally better if you go direct to the producers.

Templo de la Virgen de la Natividad
On the plaza

The ancient local church, the **Templo de la Virgen de la Natividad**, is beautifully frescoed and decorated. Worship here is a fusion of Catholic and indigenous ritual, and in the

---

MARKET DAYS IN THE VILLAGES AROUND OAXACA

Despite Oaxaca's many craft stores, if it's quality you're after, or if you intend to buy in quantity, visiting the villages in which the goods originate is usually a far better, cheaper bet. Each has a different speciality (rugs in Teotitlán del Valle, or black pottery in San Bartolo Coyotepec, for example), and many have their own market each week. In the villages you'll be able to see the craftspeople in action and you may be able to have your own design made up, while a village market is an experience in itself.

Monday Miahuatlán: mescal, bread, leather. Ixtlán de Juárez: flowers, produce.
Tuesday Santa María Atzompa: pottery.
Wednesday Etla: cheese, flowers.
Thursday Zaachila: livestock, meat, nuts. Ejutla: mescal, embroidered blouses.
Friday Ocotlán: flowers, meat, pottery, textiles. San Bartolo Coyotepec: pottery.
Saturday Oaxaca: everything. Tlaxiaco: leather goods, blankets, *aguardiente* (the local firewater), baskets.
Sunday Tlacolula: mescal, ceramics, rugs, crafts.

courtyard that blend finds physical expression in the incorporation of material from the Zapotec temple that once stood here, with Mitla-style decoration. Around the back of the church you can see more substantial remains of this temple, whose base stands about 2m high.

Museo Comunitario Balaa Xtee Guech Gulal

On the plaza • Tues–Sun 10am–6pm • M$10 donation

The stated aim of the absorbing **Museo Comunitario Balaa Xtee Guech Gulal** is "to know what we were, and understand what we are". As such, the small collection covers everything from pre-Hispanic life and artefacts to information about present-day culture and carpet-weaving in the area.

10

ARRIVAL AND DEPARTURE TEOTITLÁN DEL VALLE

By bus Direct buses (M$10) run hourly throughout the day from the second-class bus station in Oaxaca. Alternatively, take any bus or *colectivo* along the highway; at the junction, *colectivo* taxis wait to cover the short run into the village (M$8).

ACCOMMODATION AND EATING

El Descanso Juárez 51, cnr Hidalgo ☏ 951 524 4152. An incongruous, hard-to-miss modern building in the centre of town houses a craft shop, carpet workshop and restaurant – they also have bungalows to rent on the edge of town. Food is simple but good, with *moles* from M$80. Restaurant daily 9am–6pm. Bungalow M$500

Tlamanalli Juárez 39. A favourite with locals as well as tour groups, *Tlamanalli* serves delicious local classics such as squash-blossom soup and stewed chicken; the menu changes daily (mains M$80–200). Tues–Sun 1–4pm.

Lambityeco

Daily 8am–5pm • M$35

Right beside the highway, the small Zapotec site of **Lambityeco**, prettily planted with agave and cactus, is easy to get to on any passing bus; you can see the whole thing in twenty minutes, but it's worth it for the exceptional carvings and stucco-work. Just two buildings of the two hundred or so that have been identified have been excavated, along with some outbuildings that include an original *temazcal*. The smaller building at the back is the **Templo de Cocijo**, extensively decorated with masks of Cocijo, Zapotec god of rain and thunder, in the form of a stylised jaguar; two stunningly preserved versions flank the tiny central patio. The larger **Palacio de los Racoqui** is thought to have been the home of several generations of an important family – perhaps the city's rulers. There are some superb friezes, including those on the lintels of two tombs, excavated where they had been buried deep inside the building, with remarkable portraits of the individuals buried there.

Tlacolula

Buses leave frequently for Tlacolula from Oaxaca's second-class bus station (M$12), and there are plenty of *colectivo* taxis too

TLACOLULA is a large and rather scruffy village, worth visiting above all on a Sunday, when it hosts one of the most important **markets** in the valley (see box opposite). The one sight is a sixteenth-century church, the **Parroquia de la Virgen de la Asunción**, whose interior is as ornate as Oaxaca's Santo Domingo, though less skilfully crafted. In the adjoining Capilla del Señor de Tlacolula, some gory carvings of martyrs include a decapitated St Paul.

Santa Ana del Valle

Take a taxi or local bus (usually every 10min) from the highway junction in Tlacolula or hike the 4km into Santa Ana

SANTA ANA DEL VALLE, 4km north of Tlacolula, is a tiny, very quiet and very traditional village with a fine selection of locally produced **rugs**. You'll see them for sale everywhere. There's a tranquil and well-managed **homestay programme** (see box, p.608) in case you want to stay; the local **baker** makes delicious bread and there's a shop where you can buy basic **provisions**. A three-hour walk, outlined on a board outside the community museum, will take you to Iki ya'a, a hilltop Zapotec site with fine views.

Museo Shan-Dany

On the plaza • Daily 10am–2pm & 3–6pm • M$10

The **Museo Shan-Dany** was the first community museum established in Mexico. Its name is Zapotec for "foot of the hill" – that is, the foot of the hill on which Iki ya'a stands – and it marks the exact spot where a couple of **tombs** were discovered in the 1950s, though they were only excavated more recently. Probably contemporary with Dainzú and Monte Albán, the Zapotec site here boasted some fine glyphs. Excavations have also been carried out beneath what are now basketball courts outside, and the pots and stones recovered there are also proudly displayed. Other exhibits (labelled in Spanish only) feature local folklore, dances, crafts and the weaving industry, and there's extensive coverage of the bloody fighting that took place here during the Revolution.

Yagul

Daily 8am–5pm • M$42

One of the least-visited archeological sites in the region, **Yagul** lies to the north of the highway at about the 35km mark – a signposted twenty-minute walk (or 1.5km drive). The large site spreads expansively across a superb defensive position, and although occupied by the Zapotecs from a fairly early date, its main features are from later on (around 900–1200 AD, after the fall of Monte Albán) and demonstrate **Mixtec** influence. On the lowest level is the **Patio de la Triple Tumba**, where the remains of four temples surround an altar and the entry to the **Triple Tomb**, whose three funereal chambers show characteristically Mixtec decoration. Immediately above the patio, you'll see a large and elegantly simple ball-court, the largest known after Chichén Itzá. Higher up, the maze-like **Palacio de los Seis Patios**, probably a residential complex, features six small courtyards surrounded by rooms and narrow passages. From here a good path leads up to a viewpoint on a mesa-like crag, with superb views over the surrounding valleys.

Mitla

Site daily 8am–5pm • M$42

The town of **MITLA** ("Place of the Dead") is a dusty and none too attractive place, which you'd visit only to see the stunning Mixtec **site** at the upper edge of town. It may not have the grandiose scale and setting of Monte Albán, but Mitla is magnificently decorated with elaborate stone mosaics that are among the finest in Mexico. You'll see these superlative bas-reliefs and geometric designs at their best if you arrive towards closing time, when the low sun throws the patterns into sharp, shadowed relief, and the bulk of the visitors have left.

Brief history

Mitla reached its apogee during the post-Classic period, when Monte Albán was in decline. Construction at the site continued until the late fifteenth century, at which point it was finally conquered by the Aztecs. The abstract designs on the buildings seem to echo patterns on surviving **Mixtec** manuscripts, and have long been viewed as purely Mixtec in style. But more recent opinion is that the buildings were constructed by **Zapotecs** and that the city was a ceremonial centre occupied by the most important Zapotec high priest. This Uija-Tao, or "great seer", was described by Alonso Canesco, a fifteenth-century Spaniard, as being "rather like our Pope", and his presence here would have made Mitla a kind of Vatican City.

Grupo de las Columnas

The **Grupo de las Columnas** is the best preserved and most impressive of the five main complexes that make up Mitla, and the obvious place to head for from the entrance.

The first large courtyard is flanked by constructions on three sides – its central **Templo de las Columnas** is magnificent, precision-engineered and quite overpowering in effect. Climbing the broad stairway and through one of three entrances in its great facade, you come to the **Salón de las Columnas**, named after the six monolithic, tapered columns of volcanic stone that supported its roof. A low, narrow passageway leads from here to a small inner patio, the **Patio de las Grecas**, lined with some of the most intricately assembled of the geometric mosaics; each of the fourteen different designs here is considered representative of the universe and the gods. Four dark rooms that open off the patio continue the mosaic theme. It is in these rooms that the Uija-Tao would have lived: if the latest theory is correct, the Zapotec architects converted the inner room of the traditional Mesoamerican temple, in which priests usually lived, into a kind of exquisitely decorated "papal flat" arranged around a private courtyard.

The second courtyard of the Columns group, adjoining the southwestern corner of the first, is similar in design though less impressive in execution. Known as the **Patio de las Tumbas**, it contains two cross-shaped tombs, long since plundered by grave-robbers. In one, the roof is supported by the **Columna de la Muerte**; legend has it that if you embrace this, the gap left between your hands tells you how long you have left to live, hand-widths being translated into years remaining (mercifully, you can no longer hug the column to test this myth).

Grupo de la Iglesia

The **Grupo de la Iglesia** is so called because the Spaniards built a church over, and from, much of it in 1590: the Templo de San Pablo Apóstol. Two of its three original courtyards survive, however, and in the smaller one the mosaic decoration bears traces of the original paint, indicating that the patterns were once picked out in white from a dark-red background.

Lesser buildings

Three other groups of buildings, which have weathered the years less well, complete the site. All of them are now in the midst of the modern town, fenced off from the surrounding houses: the **Grupo de los Adobes** can be found where you see a chapel atop a pyramid; the **Grupo del Arroyo** is near Los Adobes; and the **Grupo del Sur** lies right beside the road to the main site.

ARRIVAL AND DEPARTURE — MITLA

By bus/mototaxi/on foot Second-class buses run from Oaxaca to Mitla (1hr 30min) about every 15min throughout the day. If you don't fancy the 10–15min walk through town up to the ruins, a tricycle mototaxi will charge about M$10 to get you up there, or you can take a *colectivo* (M$20 more than the bus).

ACCOMMODATION AND EATING

Despite all the tourists, Mitla has little to offer on the food front, and few places to stay. There's one decent hotel-restaurant, but otherwise you're best off eating at one of the stalls or small *comedores* in the tacky market close to the site entrance.

Hotel Don Cenobio Juárez 3, just off the main plaza 📞 951 568 0330, 🌐 hoteldoncenobio.com. With a cheery blue-and-yellow paint job and individual, elaborately carved and painted wooden furniture in each room, the *Don Cenobio* does its best to brighten up drab Mitla. The better rooms look inward, onto a courtyard where there's a small pool. The restaurant serves all day, from breakfast (M$70) through to evening, with a rather pricey *menu turistico* (M$140) at midday. **M$725**

Santiago Matatlán

Mescal producers, from one-man artisan distilleries to large factory operations, and shops selling their products dot the countryside around Mitla. The small town of **SANTIAGO MATATLÁN**, on Hwy-190 just 6km beyond Mitla, is the traditional centre of the industry; here you can visit the ateliers in which the drink is made, enjoy free samples from the town stores and eat the maguey plant itself. Be warned that a few samples of home-made mescal can wreak havoc with your senses.

By bus/colectivo/tour Being right on the highway, Santiago Matatlán sees plenty of second-class buses from Oaxaca. However, given the fact that some of the more interesting producers are out of town, and the state you may be in, it's much easier to take a mescal tour from Oaxaca (see p.598); many will also visit Mitla and Hierve el Agua, or other villages. *Colectivos* are also available, and charge about M$20 more than the buses.

Hierve el Agua

Daily 8am–7pm • M$20

Hierve el Agua, some 25km east of Mitla, much of it on rough dirt road, is the site of a spectacular calcified rock formation that resembles a bubbling **waterfall**. As water with a very high mineral concentration bubbles out of the ground, it becomes petrified over the vertiginous cliff-tops; the resultant stalactites are a beautiful sight and the panoramas from above the pools, where there are several stalls serving tacos and other snacks, are jaw-dropping. Sadly, tourism here threatens to be more destructive than in the rest of the valley: the area can barely support the volume of visitors it receives and disputes between local villagers over how to split the proceeds sometimes close the road to the site.

By car/colectivo/tour Though you could drive (expect 30min of dirt road) or get a *colectivo* from Mitla, the tricky access makes it far easier to visit Hierve El Agua as part of an organized day trip (see p.598); most will also take in Mitla and Teotitlán del Valle, and probably a mescal distillery.

Valle de Zimatlán-Ocotlán

The **Valle de Zimatlán-Ocotlán**, almost due south of Oaxaca, doesn't have the same concentration of interesting sites as the Valle de Tlacolula, but some of the region's finest artesanía comes from these villages. You can travel around the area reasonably easily by **public transport**, or **cycling** on rented bikes from Oaxaca isn't as arduous as it might sound, especially if you are careful about the midday heat. Two major roads run in this direction: Hwy-175, the route to Pochutla and Puerto Ángel, via San Bartolo Coyotepec and Ocotlán, and Hwy-131 which eventually reaches the Pacific at Puerto Escondido, via Zaachila. With your own transport, it's easy to combine the two routes in a loop.

San Bartolo Coyotepec

Thirteen kilometres south of Oaxaca on Hwy-175, **SAN BARTOLO COYOTEPEC** is an otherwise dreary town famed for the shiny black pottery, **barro negro**, which can be found in crafts shops all around Oaxaca state, but is only made here. In 1934, one **Doña Rosa** developed a technique for adding the unique lustre to the previously ordinary pottery made in San Bartolo. The pottery may now be too weak to carry mescal to market on the back of a mule, as it did for centuries, but Doña Rosa's invention has yielded a new, purely ornamental incarnation that draws thousands of tourists every year. Her workshop (see below) still sells some of the finest quality pieces, though prices are lower elsewhere and in the little market in the centre of town, where they're prepared to haggle.

Alfarería Doña Rosa

Juárez 24 • Daily 9am–7pm • ☎ 951 551 0011

Although Doña Rosa died in the 1980s, her family still runs the biggest *alfarería* (workshop) in town, an unashamedly touristy showroom with pieces ranging from beautifully simple amphorae to ghastly clocks, and prices from M$30–3000. To find Doña Rosa from the highway, look for the street signed *alfarerías*.

Museo Estatal de Arte Popular de Oaxaca

Independencia on the south side of the plaza • Tues–Sun 10am–6pm • M$20 • ☎ 951 551 0036

The modern **Museo Estatal de Arte Popular de Oaxaca** contains an impressive display of Oaxacan folk art. There's high-quality black pottery, of course, but also interesting, often quirky, examples of all sorts of other arts and crafts from papier mâché to *alebrijes*, and a good shop too.

ARRIVAL AND DEPARTURE SAN BARTOLO COYOTEPEC

By bus/colectivo/minibus There are plenty of second-class buses along Hwy-175 that will drop you in San Bartolo, but the best way to get here is by *colectivo* from the Mercado de Abastos in Oaxaca, or minibus run by Automorsa (cnr Miguel Cabrera and Zaragoza) or Oaxaca Pacífico (Armenta y López 121).

San Martín Tilcajete

SAN MARTÍN TILCAJETE is a sleepy town, a short distance off the highway 23km from Oaxaca. The main street is lined with workshops in which the bright copal-wood figurines known as *alebrijes* are carved, painted and polished. They come in all manner of designs, from Day of the Dead skeletons to whimsical creatures, and although not as famous as those from Arrazola (see opposite), there are still plenty of attractive examples.

ARRIVAL AND DEPARTURE SAN MARTÍN TILCAJETE

By colectivo/bus *Colectivo* taxis are the most regular form of transport between Oaxaca and San Martín. The Oaxaca terminus is at Arista 107 between Cabrera and Bustamente.

EATING

Azucena Zapoteca Hwy 175 km 23.5, at the San Martín Tilcajete junction ☎ 951 524 9227. Big roadside restaurant serving up much better than expected local food at competitive prices, as far as possible home-made from local ingredients. It also has an excellent craft shop. Daily noon–8pm.

Santo Tomás Jalieza

In the tiny village of **SANTO TOMÁS JALIEZA**, the women specialize in weaving cotton on backstrap looms. An all-women's cooperative market in the centre of town sells thick woven cotton tablecloths and placemats, bags, backpacks, clothing and belts at fixed (though generally reasonable) prices.

ARRIVAL AND DEPARTURE SANTO TOMÁS JALIEZA

By colectivo *Colectivos* for Santo Tomás depart from outside the Mercado de Abastos in Oaxaca; second-class buses will drop you at the highway junction, just five minutes' walk to the market.

Ocotlán

The substantial regional centre of **OCOTLÁN**, a little over 30km from Oaxaca, is known as the birthplace of celebrated Oaxacan artist **Rodolfo Morales** (1925–2001) and for the extraordinary **clay figures** crafted here by the Aguilar sisters. The adjacent workshops of Josefina, Guillermina, Irene and Concepción, each of whom produces slightly different items in the distinctive Aguilar style originated by their mother, are on the main road into town, just past the huge *Hotel Real Ocotlán*. You can find examples of their work in Oaxaca, but a trip out here allows you to see the full range, from grotesque to amusing to religious, including figures of animals, men and buxom women at work and play, and even Nativity scenes (apparently no subject matter is off-limits), gaudily decorated in polka dots or geometric patterns. Josefina's work is especially off-the-wall, and prices are very reasonable – from M$20, to M$300 for really elaborate work. Ocotlán's Friday **market** is one of the finest in the region.

Ex-Convento de Santo Domingo de Guzmán

Zaragoza and Amador, on the zócalo • Daily 9am–6pm • M$15

The **Ex-Convento de Santo Domingo de Guzmán** is a magnificent church and monastery that was restored to much of its former glory with money from Rodolfo Morales; appropriately the paintwork and frescoes are particularly fine. Upstairs, part of the complex has been transformed into a gallery, with works by Morales himself (including his final painting, in which he foresees his death) and some brilliant examples of the Aguilar sisters' work.

ARRIVAL AND DEPARTURE

By colectivo/bus/minivan *Colectivo* taxis depart from outside the Mercado de Abastos in Oaxaca and there are second-class buses from the nearby terminal; in addition,

OCOTLÁN

Automorsa (cnr Miguel Cabrera and Zaragoza) and Oaxaca Pacífico (Armenta y López 121) run regular minivans (around M$15).

San Antonio Arrazola

SAN ANTONIO ARRAZOLA, 10km southeast of Oaxaca, 5km west of Hwy-131, is the home of the local woodcarvers and painters who produce many of the delightful boldly patterned *alebrijes*, animals made from copal wood, that you'll see for sale in Oaxaca and all over Mexico. The man responsible for transforming this local craft into an art form was Manuel Jiménez (1919–2005), still revered locally. Following on the heels of his success, entrepreneurial townspeople have created a thriving cottage industry that produces a fantastical profusion of spiky figures and polka-dot, hooped or expressionist styles, most very reasonably priced. Carvers from other villages are catching on to the popularity, but few, if any, are better than in Arrazola, where almost every home seems to contain a workshop.

ARRIVAL AND DEPARTURE

SAN ANTONIO ARRAZOLA

By colectivo/bus/bike *Colectivos* for San Antonio depart from outside the Mercado de Abastos in Oaxaca; second-class buses run from the nearby terminal. It's an easy cycle, too.

Cuilapam de Guerrero

Ex-Convento de Santiago Apóstol • Daily 9am–5pm • M$35

The village of **CUILAPAM**, 14km southeast from Oaxaca, is something of a place of pilgrimage for Mexicans, as it was here that revolutionary hero **Vicente Guerrero** was executed by firing squad in 1831. The place is entirely dominated by the vast, turreted hulk of the Dominican **Ex-Convento de Santiago Apóstol** where he was held captive and where the execution took place. Though in poor condition and with virtually no signage, it's an impressive place to wander around, with a Renaissance twin-aisled nave and largely intact vaulting; behind is the atmospheric monastery cloister, full of dark corners and hidden stairways.

ARRIVAL AND DEPARTURE

CUILAPAM DE GUERRERO

By colectivo/minibus *Colectivos* for Cuilapam can be found in Oaxaca on Bustamante, south of the markets near the church of San Francisco. Autotransportes Añasa at Bustamante 606 has minibus services.

Zaachila

ZAACHILA's Thursday **livestock market**, a huge affair that seems to take over half the town, is a thoroughly entertaining spectacle that attracts plenty of tours and visitors. At weekends a few locals visit; the rest of the time it's very quiet indeed. The one local sight is a small **zona arqueológica** (daily 9am–6pm; M$35, free on Sun) on the little hill behind the main plaza. A substantial Zapotec town is thought to have flourished here from 1200 to 1521, though it was taken over by the Mixtecs towards the end of this period; it was one of the few such cities still inhabited when the Spanish arrived.

10

Only one small pyramid has been excavated – there are far larger unexcavated mounds alongside – from which you can climb down into two opened tombs dating from the early sixteenth century. One of them, the tomb of Lord 9-Flower, probably a Mixtec priest, is lavishly decorated, with stone-carved owls guarding the entrance and two marvellous glyphs showing 9-Flower himself: richly dressed with a large headdress, carrying a bag of copal incense. A collection of treasures was buried with him, comparable to that discovered in Tomb 7 at Monte Albán and including gold, jewels, jade and turquoise masks; there are photos of these in the little site museum.

ARRIVAL AND DEPARTURE   ZAACHILA

By colectivo/minibus *Colectivos* for Zaachila can be found in Oaxaca outside the Mercado de Abastos and on Bustamante, south of the markets near the church of San Francisco. Autotransportes Añasa (Bustamante 606) has minibus services.

EATING

La Capilla Km 14 on the main road, on the edge of town ☎ 951 528 6011. A huge, open-air restaurant with a theatrical open kitchen and communal seating for hundreds, as well as more private tables under palapas dotted around the grounds. Most fun when it's busy, either on Thurs with market visitors and tour groups, or at weekends with locals; at these times mariachis and other musicians wander among the diners. The traditional Oaxacan food can tend towards mass-catering, but is generally good, if a little pricier than average – reckon on a bill upwards of M$180 per person. Daily 8am–7pm.

The Sierra Norte

North of the Oaxaca valleys the wild ranges of the **Sierra Norte** stretch for over 100km, a pristine world of pine forests, mist-cloaked mountains and rustic Zapotec villages.

The Pueblos Mancomunados

The **Pueblos Mancomunados** (literally "joint villages") occupy the southern edge of the Sierra. The landscape here is spectacular and the **biodiversity** phenomenal, with birdlife, butterflies and mammals, including ocelot, puma and jaguar – some sections of the pine forest have been classified by the World Wide Fund for Nature (WWF) as among the richest and most varied on earth. It's a rewarding place to spend a few days, enjoying nature and getting first-hand experience of rural Oaxacan life.

The hills are laced with more than 100km of signposted rural **footpaths and country roads**, suitable for hikers and mountain-bikers of all abilities, and almost every community offers simple accommodation, local guides and a roster of activities. The paths have been used for centuries by local people accustomed to sharing resources with surrounding communities, and the villages are an impressive example of social organization, with eight small towns perched on common land. One of the most enchanting hikes is along the 15km high-altitude footpath between the isolated villages of Latuvi and San Miguel Amatlán, which passes though mystical cloud forest and is believed to be part of a larger pre-Columbian route that connected the Zapotec cities in the Valles Centrales with the Gulf of Mexico – you can still see the remains of an old road along the trail (tours usually take two days to hike this route).

Benito Juárez

Perched on a ridge overlooking the Oaxaca valleys (18km north of Teotitlán) and surrounded by pine trees, the little village of **BENITO JUÁREZ** is the gateway to the Pueblos Mancomunados. Known for its spectacular sunsets – in clear weather you can see all the way to Mexico's highest mountain, Pico de Orizaba – Benito Juárez makes a good base for exploration. There's a river where you can **fish** for trout, and plenty of walking and other activities are on offer.

INFORMATION AND TOURS

Tourist information office If you prefer to travel independently, the small tourist information office (Mon–Sat 9am–5pm; ☎951 545 9994) in Benito Juárez, next to the town square, is extremely helpful. It has excellent maps which show the varying demands of each trek, and rents out reliable mountain bikes (M$120/3hr), but only with a Spanish-speaking guide (M$140/day, plus M$60 access fee). They can also help out with accommodation, and other activities such as horseriding.

THE PUEBLOS MANCOMUNADOS

Tours Don't expect one afternoon to be enough time to see this area; a visit requires forward planning and at least a couple of days to be worthwhile. Although you can travel independently, accommodation and food are best organized in advance: much the easiest, most efficient and lowest impact way to go is through one of the tour operators in Oaxaca (see p.598). Tierraventura and Expediciones Sierra Norte organize trips with guides, transport, accommodation and meals for around M$1200/day.

Ixtlán de Juárez

IXTLÁN DE JUÁREZ, a pretty Zapotec village near San Pablo Guelatao (the birthplace of Benito Juárez), 61km north of Oaxaca, is in an area of great natural beauty, and its cloud forests and pine and oak woodlands are claimed to be home to five hundred bird varieties and six thousand species of plants. Ixtlán is accessible by direct bus from Oaxaca's second-class station (2 daily; M$35), Cuenca first-class bus (M$50) or by *colectivo* (all around 2hr).

ACCOMMODATION AND TOURS

IXTLÁN DE JUÁREZ

Ecoturixtlán 16 de Septiembre, at the cnr of Revolución ☎951 553 6075. Locally run *Ecoturixtlán* organize tours (from M$300) of all the local beauty spots (Mirador del Cerro Cuachirindo, the Grutas del Arco, the Cascada del Mesofilo and the gentle woodlands of the Bosque Mesofilo), as well as the eighteenth-century village church, the Templo Santo Tomàs Apòstol. They also rent thirteen basic but comfy cabañas in the forest bordering the village, run the best local *comedor*, arrange a host of bird watching tours, rent bikes (M$30/hr) and offer ziplining (from M$15), horseriding (M$100/hr) and rappelling (M$50). Cabañas __M$550__

The Mixteca

Oaxaca's **Mixteca** region is not at first an obvious tourist destination: the pre-Hispanic sites here are far less spectacular than those in the Valles Centrales and there are no artisan centres to compare with Teotitlán or Arrazola. However, the colonial buildings are widely regarded as some of the country's most important, there's stunning mountain scenery and the low number of visitors means that you are likely to have vast crumbling monasteries and Mixtec ruins to yourself; the main appeal is their aching, faded glory and the spine-tingling sense that you're witnessing a scene that has remained relatively unchanged since before Cortés.

Broadly the region divides into two – the barren hills of the **Mixteca Baja** and the mountainous, pine-clad **Mixteca Alta**. Toll Hwy-135D, one of the country's best roads, cuts through the Baja's deforested hillsides en route from Oaxaca to Mexico City. The Mixteca Alta lies off to the south, where Hwy-125 climbs into and through the sierra before eventually descending to the Pacific coast. The **Mixteca Baja**'s highlights are three

CAPILLAS ABIERTAS

Among the most striking features of the monasteries of the Mixteca Baja are their **capillas abiertas**. These graceful open-air chapels, found only in the New World, look like unfinished, roofless churches, or cathedrals chopped in half. They face out onto huge open areas where the idea was that mass conversions of and services for indigenous people, too numerous for the church to accommodate, would take place. They are designed for congregations of thousands; the very same people whose prodigious labour produced these vast churches in the first place. Sadly, even by the time they were first completed, those populations had been decimated by disease and the demands of the Spanish overlords; the *capillas* became vast white elephants, testament to a vanished population.

vast **Dominican monasteries** – Yanhuitlán, Teposcolula and Coixtlahuaca – imposing relics of Mexico's imperial past. All three can be expertly restored and can easily be visited as a day trip from Oaxaca if you have your own transport; it's less easy if you're relying on public transport, though still possible.

Santo Domingo Yanhuitlán

Templo y Ex-Convento de Santo Domingo • Tues–Sun 9am–5pm • M$35

The first of the great Dominican establishments northwest of Oaxaca is the **Templo y Ex-Convento de Santo Domingo** at **SANTO DOMINGO YANHUITLÁN**. There was an important Mixtec city here before the Conquest, and the church, built on an enormous pre-Hispanic platform overlooking the village, was no doubt intended to remind the Mixtecs of the supremacy of the new religion. The permanent seat of the diocese of the Mixteca during the sixteenth century, the church is massive, dominating the countryside for many kilometres around, with a vaulted ceiling soaring 27m above you as you enter. The main altarpiece, dating to 1570, is the work of the Spanish artist Andrés de la Concha.

ARRIVAL AND DEPARTURE SANTO DOMINGO YANHUITLÁN

By bus There are services from Oaxaca's second-class bus station (1hr 30min), or Autotransportes de Tlaxiaco buses pass through every 30min. Their Oaxaca base is on Díaz Ordaz between Trujano and Las Casas.

By car Yanhuitlán is on Hwy-190, not far from the Nochixtlán junction of Hwy-135D.

Teposcolula

Cloister daily 9am–5pm • M$35

TEPOSCOLULA is close to the start of Hwy-125, the road that heads up to the Mixteca Alta. Here the **Ex-Convento de San Pedro y San Pablo** has one of the finest *capillas abiertas* in the Americas, completed in the 1560s. The church itself is every bit as gargantuan as the others, though its position at the heart of a reasonable-sized town perhaps makes it seem a little smaller. Notice the extraordinary scallop-shell roof of one of the chapels and, in the otherwise relatively plain interior, a huge gilded *retablo*. In the cloister are some sixteenth-century paintings, but it's the outdoor chapel that really impresses; newly restored with pristine stonework and a gilded and painted ceiling, it faces a vast field where the congregation would have gathered.

ARRIVAL AND DEPARTURE TEPOSCOLULA

By bus There are services from Oaxaca's second-class bus station (2hr), or Autotransportes de Tlaxiaco buses pass through every 30min en route to Tlaxiaco. Their Oaxaca base is on Díaz Ordaz between Trujano and Las Casas.

Coixtlahuaca

Ex-Convento de San Juan Bautista • Tues–Sun 9am–5pm • Free

COIXTLAHUACA lies just 2km east of Hwy-135D at the Coixtlahuaca exit. The small village is entirely dominated by the **Ex-Convento de San Juan Bautista**, dating from 1576 and one of the best preserved of the region's colonial structures. Newly restored to pristine perfection, it's of a size to match any European cathedral, with an elaborately carved facade and, inside, a beautiful painted ceiling and a magnificent, ceiling-height churrigueresque altarpiece. In the garden cloister there's a display on the church's restoration, and on the opposite side of the church a fine *capilla abierta*.

ARRIVAL AND DEPARTURE COIXTLAHUACA

By bus/taxi Second-class Sur buses from Oaxaca drop off at Coixtlahuaca en route to Puebla and Mexico City. If you want to head on towards Teposcolula or Yanhuitlán, there is an occasional local bus across to Tejupan, on Hwy-190, or you can get there by taxi. Alternatively, head back south to Nochixtlán and connect there.

Santiago Apoala

The rural village of **SANTIAGO APOALA** is tucked into a captivating high valley about 98km north from Oaxaca. It's a wild place, ideally located for hiking, biking and other outdoor activities involving the nearby rivers, lagoons and falls; it's hard to get to, but that ensures its continued unspoilt isolation. You're strongly advised to use a guide to explore the region, where most trails are poorly marked. Among the highlights are the **Picturas Repuestas**, five-thousand-year-old glyphs considered to be the oldest example of Mixtec art, and the hike following the Apoala River to the 60m **Cola de Serpiente** waterfall – you can swim in the pool at the bottom.

10

ARRIVAL AND TOURS
SANTIAGO APOALA

By bus The best way to reach Apoala is on a tour; alternatively, take a second-class bus or *colectivo* from Oaxaca to Nochixtlán, where a taxi or microbus (Wed & Sat 1pm, Sun noon, but check beforehand if possible) can make the remaining climb into the mountains.

By car From Nochixtlán, easily accessed on Hwy-135D, it's a further 40km to Apoala, almost all on rough dirt road.

Comité de Turismo de Santiago Apoala Pino Suárez, cnr Independencia ☎ 555 151 9154. The village ecotourism cooperative can arrange meals, accommodation, expeditions and guides (M$140/day) and provide general information; it offers basic cabañas (from around M$220) and campsites (M$40). They also rent bikes for around M$120/day. Tierraventura (see p.598) organize tours from Oaxaca, which is certainly the easiest way to come.

San Martín Huamelulpan

Museo Comunitario Hitalulu • Mon–Fri 9am–5pm • M$10 • Tlaxiaco-bound buses (see below) will drop you at the turn-off. From there you'll have to walk, hitch or hope to find a taxi for the last couple of kilometres into town

SAN MARTÍN HUAMELULPAN lies high in the pine forests of the **Mixteca Alta**, 2km up a side road off Hwy-125. This tiny mountain village has an extensive and mostly unexplored Mixtec archeological site, with two large plazas cut out of a hill, a ball-court and some temple complexes. Some of the sculptures found here have been embedded in the walls of the eighteenth-century colonial church; other artefacts from the ruins are displayed in the small **Museo Comunitario Hitalulu**, which also has information about indigenous medicines, still used by traditional healers in the local community. The surrounding countryside is picturesque, with deer and coyotes in the woodland, and a variety of unusual plants.

Tlaxiaco

TLAXIACO is traditionally the economic heart of the Mixteca; a big place, with an important **Saturday market** that attracts indigenous people from across the region – many of them in traditional dress. The town is also famed for its *pulque*, the lightly fermented drink made from cactus, best savoured at the market stalls. An attractive town square and nearby good-value hotels could serve as a base for exploring the countryside and the Mixtec and Triqui villages nearby.

ARRIVAL AND DEPARTURE
TLAXIACO

By minivan/bus Autotransportes de Tlaxiaco minivans run every 30min (M$80; 3hr) from their Oaxaca terminus on Díaz Ordaz between Trujano and Las Casas. There are also OCC first-class and Sur and Autobuses Fletes y Pasajes second-class buses. Many of these continue to Pinotepa Nacional (5–6 daily; 5hr), where you can change for Puerto Escondido and the Pacific coast.

ACCOMMODATION AND EATING

Hotel del Portal Plaza Constitución 2 ☎ 953 552 0154. This colonial mansion on the main plaza, directly opposite the market, could hardly be better located. The rooms are a little old-fashioned, but comfortable enough, especially if you get one of the pricier ones in the old building. The restaurant in the hotel courtyard is much fancier (and pricier – mains M$110–140) than you'd expect, with flowers on the table and unusual local specialities such as beef ribs with *memelitas* (bean-filled parcels) and *nopalitos* (cactus leaves) served on a sizzling plate, or *molcajete*, a stone bowl of hot stewed meat and vegetables. **M$320**

10

San José del Pacífico

The 250km journey south from Oaxaca to Pochutla and the Pacific coast via Hwy-175 is dramatic, passing through mountainous forests and descending into tropical lowlands. Around three hours' drive in this direction, perched on the side of a pine-smothered mountain with wonderful views, though often enveloped in plumes of mist, lies **SAN JOSÉ DEL PACÍFICO**. It's a great, restful place to break the journey, or to stay for a day or two if you want to enjoy the forest trails and cool mountain air (winter nights can get very chilly) before descending to the tropical lowlands of the coast. It is also known for its **mushrooms**, both culinary and hallucinogenic, and it's the latter that draw the majority of the town's visitors, many of whom make the short trip from Zipolite (see p.634), just two hours away. Mushroom season coincides with the rains, from about July to October, but they're sold preserved in honey during the rest of the year. Be warned that the mushrooms are illegal, and penalties potentially severe.

ARRIVAL AND DEPARTURE   SAN JOSÉ DEL PACÍFICO

By minivan Any minivan on the direct route between Oaxaca and Pochutla can drop you in San José del Pacífico; see p.634 for details.

ACCOMMODATION AND EATING

Cabañas/Hotel La Puesta On the main road ⊕ 951 596 7330, ⊚ sanjosedelpacifico.com. The simple wooden cabañas here offer the best accommodation in town, with incredible views over the valley. Try to get one of the cabañas furthest from the restaurant so that you get a clear view. There's also a good restaurant serving *comidas*, *dulces* and mescal. **M$300**

Rayito del Sol Main road in the centre of the village ⊕ 951 572 0111. Pleasant café and restaurant which also serves as an information centre and has cabañas. Excellent quesadillas – try the version with squash blossom – and hot chocolate to fight off the chills. All day, breakfast to dinner.

Puerto Escondido and around

Though no longer the tranquil hangout it was thirty years ago, **PUERTO ESCONDIDO** ("Hidden Port") remains an irresistible draw. With direct flights from the capital, kilometres of sandy beaches and an international surf reputation as home of the "**Mexican Pipeline**", Escondido has firmly established itself as a destination. For all the crowds, though, the place has managed to retain a languid, laid-back air; small-scale, casual and uninhibited, there is still the hint of the village it once was, and it's a world away from resorts such as Cancún. This is most evident in the early morning, when fishermen return to Playa Principal, their boats laden with marlin and red snapper. While there is a tremendous number of **hotels** to choose from, the majority tend to be small and basic, catering to long-stay travellers. Most of the visitors are young, with **surfing** high on their agendas.

Broadly speaking, Escondido can be divided into four areas. **Puerto Escondido** itself sprawls across a hill behind the bay, divided by Hwy-200 into a busy Mexican town inland, where few visitors venture except to catch a bus or visit the bank, and the tourist zone behind Playa Principal. Here the central section of the main thoroughfare,

SAFETY IN PUERTO ESCONDIDO

Despite Puerto Escondido's laid-back atmosphere, there has in the past been a problem with **muggings**, especially in La Punta and above all walking between Zicatela and town late at night. Bright new lighting has been installed in many places – try to avoid dimly lit areas and isolated beaches at night, and stick to the main road if walking back to town; better still, flag down a taxi. Take normal, sensible precautions, however, and you shouldn't have any problems.

Avenida Pérez Gasga, is known as El Adoquín – Spanish for "paving stone". Closed to traffic at 6pm, it's packed with shops, bars and restaurants. Most surfers, however, hang out not in Escondido itself but in **Zicatela**, barely 1km to the east, behind the chief surf beach, Playa Zicatela. Where once stood just a few weather-beaten huts, there's now a thriving community with dozens of hotels and increasingly sophisticated restaurants and bars. Non-surfers and surf groupies have also latched on, and Zicatela is arguably now a bigger destination than Escondido town.

For those seeking the alternative vibe that Zicatela once had, the action has moved down to **La Punta**, 3km away at the far end of Playa Zicatela. Here the sand streets, wooden shacks, camping and cabañas (though not necessarily the prices) recall a simpler era. In the other direction, west of the centre, the rapidly developing neighbourhood of **Rinconada**, with access to the calmer beaches at Puerto Ángelito and Carrizalillo, is quieter and more family oriented, with a number of lovely boutique hotels.

Zicatela hosts a huge **surf tournament** in November, and lesser ones throughout the year. The sea is warm pretty much year-round, and the summer rainy season can leave the town oppressively humid, with a vacant, lacklustre air, but this doesn't deter the hard-core surfers.

The beaches

Apart from **shopping** for international surf designs, beachwear and crafts, Escondido offers little beyond the standard **beach activities**: swimming, surfing, eating, drinking and watching beautiful sunsets, though there is a growing number of places offering classes in everything from salsa to cookery, as well as plenty of Spanish language schools.

The choice of sandy **beaches**, even within a couple of kilometres of town, is impressive. Note that wherever you are, the surf should be treated with respect – the waters along Zicatela, especially, have a lethal **undertow**. There are **lifeguards** on all the main beaches, so respect their advice.

Playa Principal

The town beach, **Playa Principal**, stretches out directly in front of town, just a step or two from the Adoquín. Frequented primarily by Mexican families, it makes for a lovely stroll after dinner, but, thanks to the number of people and the constant comings and goings of *lanchas* and fishing boats, is perhaps not the best place to swim. Come here if you want to catch a boat ride to another beach, or out to see the turtles.

Playa Marinero

Immediately east of Playa Principal, beyond the **Laguna Agua Dulce** (most of the year you can walk straight across; in wet season you may have to go round via the bridge on the main road), **Playa Marinero** is quieter and sometimes graced with gentle waves – it's a good place to bodyboard. At the far end, the rocky outcrop of El Morro divides Marinero from Zicatela.

Playa Zicatela

Playa Zicatela stretches for some 4km in all, with beach bars and palapa restaurants scattered pretty much the whole way, though with the greatest concentration at each end, at Zicatela and La Punta. One of the world's top surf beaches, Zicatela ("place of big thorns") regularly receives beach breaks of around 4m and can maintain the surf swell for days on end. This is the home of the fabled "**Mexican pipeline**" – so-called because the breaking waves curl into perfect cylinders, permitting expert surfers momentarily to ride inside the tubes. Surfboards and bodyboards can be rented from a number of places along the beach and in town, but take advice and consider your

10 Punta Colorada

strength and fitness before venturing into the water when the surf is running (you can check wave reports online at one of the internet cafés, or ask in one of the surf shops): occasionally even experienced surfers drown, despite the lifeguards patrolling the beach. La Punta generally has a much easier break. Though it can also be exceptional when the swell is up, it usually provides good, slower waves that are excellent for longboarding and for learners.

Bahía Puerto Ángelito

There are two beaches in the sheltered little bay of Puerto Ángelito, separated by a rocky outcrop; **Puerto Ángelito** itself and **Manzanillo**. They're about twenty minutes' walk from town, either by a track that leads to the left off Pérez Gasga, or direct from the highway on a road signed to Puerto Ángelito.

The water is calm and blue, the sand powdery, but both beaches, especially Ángelito which is the more sheltered and family-oriented, get very crowded. Both are surrounded by palapa restaurants with shady tables, and loungers their customers can use.

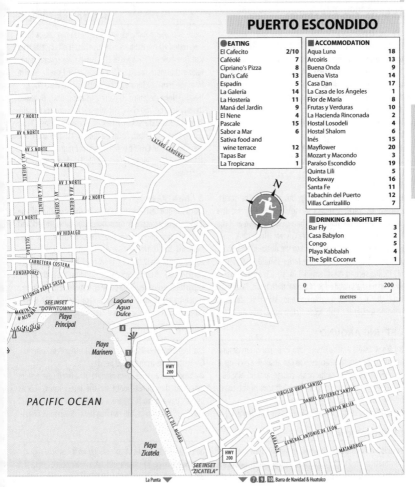

PUERTO ESCONDIDO

● EATING	
El Cafecito	2/10
Caféolé	7
Cipriano's Pizza	8
Dan's Café	13
Espadín	5
La Galería	14
La Hosteria	11
Maná del Jardín	9
El Nene	4
Pascale	15
Sabor a Mar	6
Sativa food and wine terrace	12
Tapas Bar	3
La Tropicana	1

■ ACCOMMODATION	
Aqua Luna	18
Arcoiris	13
Buena Onda	9
Buena Vista	14
Casa Dan	17
La Casa de los Ángeles	1
Flor de María	8
Frutas y Verduras	10
La Hacienda Rinconada	2
Hostal Losodeli	4
Hostal Shalom	6
Inés	15
Mayflower	20
Mozart y Macondo	3
Paraíso Escondido	19
Quinta Lili	5
Rockaway	16
Santa Fe	11
Tabachín del Puerto	12
Villas Carrizalillo	7

■ DRINKING & NIGHTLIFE	
Bar Fly	3
Casa Babylon	2
Congo	5
Playa Kabbalah	4
The Split Coconut	1

Playa Carrizalillo

The next bay, **Playa Carrizalillo**, is a spellbinding cove reached by continuing west along the same track. At the end you have to scramble down over 170 steps to reach the sand; this, and the fact that boats aren't allowed to approach, should guarantee that there won't be too many other people around. It's well worth the effort.

Playa Bacocho

Playa Bacocho is further out, following the highway towards the airport and then cutting through the hotel zone. There aren't a great number of hotels here yet, so the sand is still somewhat secluded, though swimming isn't considered safe – the beach is pounded by heavy surf and has a **strong undertow**.

Punta Colorada

Punta Colorada, a little-visited, clean beach around the point at the far end of Bacocho, is perfect for bodyboarding; you'll get tubes, and left and right breaks up to 2m high – it tends to be shallow, though.

10

ARRIVAL AND DEPARTURE

PUERTO ESCONDIDO

BY PLANE

Puerto Escondido's airport (☎ 954 582 0491), 3km north of town, sees only a couple of flights a day and has almost no facilities. Shared taxis (M$45) run into the centre; if you really want to save money, walk out to the main highway and flag down a *colectivo* for M$8. Aeromar (ⓦ aeromar.com.mx) flies at least once daily and VivaAerobus (ⓦ vivaaerobus.com) three times a week to Mexico City; fares start at just over M$2000. Aerotucán (☎ 954 582 3461, ⓦ aerotucan.com.mx) and Interjet (☎ 01 800 011 2345, ⓦ interjet.com.mx) have daily flights to Oaxaca, for around M$3000.

BY BUS

Puerto Escondido has two main bus stations. The smart, modern OCC/ADO terminal is right by El Crucero, the junction where the main road between the town and the tourist zone crosses the Carretera Costera (Hwy-200). From El Crucero it's a 5min walk down to the Adoquín and about 20min to Zicatela; taxis to the latter should cost around M$35. The second-class Terminal Turistica is on Av Oaxaca, way out on the inland edge of the modern town. Taxis from here charge M$25 downtown and M$40 to Zicatela. Heading for Oaxaca, only second-class buses take the direct

route over the mountains; the first-class ones take a huge loop round via the Isthmus, so you're better off travelling by van (see below); for Mexico City you'll save several hours taking the route via Acapulco (Turistar or Estrella Blanca from the Terminal Turistica), rather than ADO via Oaxaca.

Destinations Acapulco (6 daily 2nd class; 8hr); Huatulco (hourly 1st and 2nd class; 2hr 30min); Mexico City (3 daily 1st class, 3 2nd class; 18hr); Oaxaca (3 daily 1st class; 11hr; 2 daily 2nd class; 8hr); Pochutla (hourly 1st and 2nd class; 1hr 30min); San Cristóbal de las Casas (2 night buses daily, 1st class; 14hr); Tehuantepec (9 daily 1st class, 6 daily 2nd class; 4hr).

BY MINIVAN

Much the quickest way to Oaxaca is by minivan, though the direct route across the mountains can be cramped and stomach-churning (aim for a seat near the front). The most frequent and convenient service is with Servicio Express, based at the *Hotel Luz del Angel* on 1 Nte, cnr Av Oaxaca (☎ 954 582 0122; 7hr; M$209), with around fifteen departures every day; Villa del Mar, with fewer departures, is nearby on Hidalgo, just off Oaxaca (☎ 954 132 6182); others depart from the second-class bus station.

GETTING AROUND

By boat Take a *lancha* from Playa Principal (from around M$70) to the nearby beaches; you can arrange a pick-up at an agreed time. The same boats charge around M$500–700 (group rates are cheaper) for a full tour of the coast, beaches and local turtles.

By car For car rental, try Viajes Dimar (see box opposite) or

Los Tres Reyes (☎ 954 582 3335, ⓦ lostresreyes.com.mx). Car rental costs from M$900 per day.

By taxi Taxis around town operate on a fixed-rate system (check at the tourist booth for the latest rates). Locals usually pay around M$35 from downtown to Bacocho and M$25–35 to Zicatela. You can flag them down anywhere.

INFORMATION

Tourist information booth By far the best source of information on Puerto Escondido is the booth (Mon–Fri 10am–2pm & 4–6pm, Sat 10am–2pm; ☎ 954 582 1186) manned by the enthusiastic Gina Machorro at the western end of the Adoquín – she can help with accommodation

and tours and is a font of knowledge on the whole region.
Tourist office The main official tourist office (Mon–Fri 9am–2pm & 4–7pm; ☎ 954 582 0175) is on Hwy-200 at the western edge of town, near the turn-off to the hotel zone (near Playa Bacocho).

ACCOMMODATION

Finding somewhere to stay in Puerto Escondido shouldn't be a problem, except over Christmas, Easter and during the major surfing contests, when **prices** can rise considerably. Hotel quality is generally much lower than in Oaxaca City. Many of the hotels in town are particularly depressing; Zicatela (where most places have pools, since the sea is almost always too rough for swimming) is mostly better, while there are a few very good (but expensive) alternatives in Rinconada. Unless stated, they all have **wi-fi**. If you have a large group or intend to stay for a week or longer, consider an apartment or **villa rental**; simple studios or apartments start at around US$300/M$3900 per week and you can get a fairly luxurious beachside property from around US$1500/M$19,500 per week. For ideas, talk to Gina at the information booth on arrival (see above).

PUERTO TOWN, PLAYA PRINCIPAL AND PLAYA MARINERO

★ **Flor de María** 1a Entrada a Playa Marinero ☎ 954 582 0536, ⓦ mexonline.com/flordemaria.htm. With a perfect

location at the entry to Playa Marinero, within easy reach of Zicatela and the Adoquín, and offering great-value, laid-back comfort, this is a traveller favourite. Fan-cooled, well-kept rooms are individually decorated; some have balconies.

There's a rooftop terrace with small pool and fine views, plus a restaurant (high season only) and bar. M$800

Mayflower Andador Libertad s/n, up a flight of steps from the Adoquín ☎ 954 582 0367. Travellers love or hate this well-known place overlooking the Adoquín. Double rooms and dormitories, a bar, a communal kitchen and ample common areas foster a long-term, sociable traveller vibe – but this is definitely what the locals call "gringolandia". Some upper rooms have little balconies where you can glimpse the Pacific. Wi-fi in common areas only. Dorm M$130, private room M$400

Paraíso Escondido Unión 10 ☎ 954 582 0444, ☜ hotelpe.com. One of the longest-established hotels in the area, on the hill above the Adoquín, with stellar views and lush gardens. Tidy rooms all have balconies and are artistically decorated with kitsch mirrors, tiles and sculptures; top-floor suites have great views. There is also a central pool, bar and restaurant area. Can be a real bargain in low season. M$800

ZICATELA

Aqua Luna Vista Hermosa s/n ☎ 954 582 1505, ☜ hotelaqualuna.com. Hidden away in the backstreets, this smart, minimalist hotel's rooms range from spartan simplicity to a fully equipped luxury apartment – it's as close to a boutique hotel as you'll get in Zicatela, though still with a distinctly surfie atmosphere. Hospitably run by an Australian-Mexican couple who are knowledgeable about the area, it makes a very pleasant base. There's the added allure of a swimming pool, bar with wide-screen TV and pool table, and rooftop terrace with hot tub. Five-day minimum stay in high season. Fan room M$320, deluxe apartment M$900

Arcoiris C del Morro s/n ☎ 954 582 1494, ☜ arcoiris.mx. Rambling, yellow-painted complex with rooms on several levels; one of the better-value options if you want to be at the heart of the Zicatela surfing action. Big choice of rooms, some with fans, some a/c (about M$50 more), some with kitchenettes and large balconies with great views, along

---

ADVENTURE AND ACTIVITIES IN PUERTO ESCONDIDO

Activities and ecotourism adventures are big business in Puerto Escondido; lagoon trips, cycling, camping, rock climbing, bird watching and tours of hot springs and coffee plantations are all on offer. You can also head out onto the water in search of turtles, dolphins and even whales, or seek personal development by learning to surf, to dive, to speak Spanish or simply to unwind with yoga or massage.

TOUR AGENCIES

Viajes Dimar Pérez Gasga 905-B, Adoquín and Del Morro in Zicatela (at the Bungalows Puerta del Sol) ☎ 954 582 2305, ☜ viajesdimar.com. Helpful travel agency that can arrange almost any of the activities below, as well as tours, plane and bus tickets, and car rental.

SURFING

Central Surf Del Morro s/n at Bungalows Acuario, Zicatela ☎ 954 582 2285, ☜ centralsurfshop.com. Lessons, gear rental and a shop selling surfwear.

Oasis Surf Juárez, Rinconada ☎ 954 582 1445, ☜ oasissurffactory.com. Board manufacturer and a big surf school.

ECOTOURISM

Hidden Voyages Ecotours Based at Viajes Dimar (see above) ☜ peleewings.ca. Bird watching trips led by Canadian ornithologist Michael Malone to Laguna Manialtepec and to a coffee ranch in the hills. Dec 15–March 25 only.

Lalo Ecotours Based in the village of Las Negras, Laguna Manialtepec ☎ 954 588 9164, ☜ lalo-ecotours.com. A variety of boat, kayak and hiking tours to and around Laguna Manialtepec (see p.631), at around M$600/day; also evening tours to see the phosphorescence in the water (M$350). They also offer

bird watching tours (M$800), plus horse-riding tours to the Atotonilco hot springs (M$600).

FISHING AND BOAT TRIPS

Omar Sportfishing Playa Puerto Ángelito ☎ 954 559 4406, ☜ tomzap.com/omar.html. Captain Omar Ramírez goes after marlin and sailfish for around M$500/hr. Also dolphin and whale-watching tours.

MASSAGE, YOGA AND HEALING

Manos Curativas Las Brisas, Zicatela ☎ 954 101 3525. Yoga, massage, aromatherapy and much more – as well as surf lessons!

Temazcalli Infraganti, cnr Temazcalli, inland off Hwy-200 past Zicatela ☎ 954 582 1023, ☜ temazcalli.com. A range of therapies and treatments, from massages (M$450) to *temazcal* (M$400 for two).

SPANISH COURSES

Experiencia Andador Revolucion, off Adoquín ☎ 954 582 1818, ☜ experiencia.com. With a great base in a former hotel just off the Adoquín, Experiencia can offer excellent on-site accommodation, as well as homestays, volunteering programmes and other activities.

Oasis Language School Juárez, Rinconada ☎ 954 582 1445, ☜ oasislanguageschool.com. Private and group lessons, which can be combined with homestays or apartment rentals, or surf courses.

10

10

with luxuriant gardens, a secluded pool and a restaurant with glimpses of the ocean. M$950

Buena Vista C del Morro s/n ☏ 954 582 1474. Zicatela favourite, beloved for its great views of the surf (its elevated setting offers a great perspective on the beach, just out front), but also for its friendliness and affordability. M$300

★ **Casa Dan** Jacaranda 14 ☏ 954 582 2760, ⓦ facebook .com/hotelcasadan. Very cool place with lots of character, a short walk behind the beach. A variety of rooms is available, each with a kitchen, terrace, great views and artfully decorated bathrooms. Larger rooms are very spacious and cost-effective for groups or families; there's also a book exchange and great café (see opposite). Cabaña M$500, room M$350

Inés C del Morro s/n ☏ 954 582 0792, ⓦ hotelines.com. Excellent, sprawling place that seems to have something for everyone, from simple cabañas for four to a luxurious honeymoon suite. German-run, *Inés* has plentiful facilities for this price range, including pool, a sauna and spa, hammocks and a good dive centre. Cabaña M$450, a/c room M$880

Rockaway C del Morro s/n ☏ 855 210 5846, ⓦ hotel rockaway.com. Long-standing Zicatela haunt that recently received a souped-up redesign. Bright white rooms are clustered around a courtyard with two small swimming pools, and there's a gym (rare in these parts) and small shopping centre. M$950

Santa Fe C del Morro s/n ☏ +1 800 712 70 57, ⓦ hotel santafe.com.mx. Much the most traditional-feeling and elegant hotel in Zicatela, a beautiful, colonial-style place with waxed, red-tile floors and a range of a/c rooms with tiled bathrooms, cable TV and little balconies. There are two pools, a couple of bungalows with kitchens, and a terrace bar and restaurant overlooking the beach. M$1300

★ **Tabachín del Puerto** C del Moro s/n ☏ 954 582 1179, ⓦ tabachininfo.com.mx. Hidden away behind the *Hotel Santa Fe*, this cluster of six quirky studios, some with large, breezy balconies, is crammed with books, knick-knacks and vases that add to its comforting appeal. Substantial (and largely organic) breakfasts are included. M$975

LA PUNTA

Buena Onda Av Alejandro Cárdenas s/n, right on the beach, 1.5 blocks from the end of the road ☏ 954 582 1663, ⓔ buenaondazicatela@live.com. Cabañas as they should be, right on the beach surrounded by sand and palm trees, with cement floor, fan, bed and mosquito net, but little else. There's a communal sitting area, umbrellas and loungers on the beach and a couple of rooms and a dorm, though these are cramped and stuffy. Dorm M$100, cabaña M$250

Frutas y Verduras Av Alejandro Cárdenas s/n ☏ 954 540 1782, ⓦ frutasyverdurasmexico.com. Rooms,

camping and cabañas in a collection of palapa-roofed wooden structures. There's an observation tower, terrace with jacuzzi, communal kitchen, bar and a café-restaurant serving local produce; basic accommodation but great atmosphere. Camping M$100, cabaña M$250, room M$300

RINCONADA

La Casa de los Ángeles Zaachila 9 ☏ 954 582 0889, ⓦ casadelosangelesboutique.com. Tranquil, luxurious boutique hotel away from the action for non-surfing Escondido visitors; there are six one-bedroom suites, with kitchen, living room and terrace, hot tub and tiny outdoor gym in the garden, and rooftop palapa with telescope and barbecue. M$1300

La Hacienda Rinconada Cuilapan 15 ☏ 954 582 0279, ⓦ hotelsuiteslahacienda.com. Thanks to their gracious French owner, the six very comfortable, spacious bedrooms with kitchenettes and a/c ooze home-spun style. Outside, a colonial theme prevails, with flower-filled patios and a swimming pool surrounded by tropical foliage. A 5min walk from Playa Carrizalillo, it's not cheap, but one of the better places if you are inclined to splurge. M$1820

Hostal Losodeli 2 Nte, just off Carre Costera ☏ 954 582 4221, ⓦ hostelpuertoescondido.com. Friendly, locally run place with simple but well-set-up six-person dorms and private rooms. Communal area with cable TV, pool, hammocks, surf classes and bike rental. Dorm M$100, room M$350

Hostal Shalom Juárez 4082 ☏ 954 582 3234, ⓦ hostal shalom.com. The good news about the *Shalom* is that it has spacious grounds where you can camp, a great position just a short walk from Puerto Ángelito, a pool, communal areas with a party atmosphere, and boards and bikes to rent. The less good news is the accommodation, which is hot and cramped. Wi-fi in café only. Camping M$70, dorm M$100

Mozart y Macondo Tortugas 77 ☏ 954 104 2295, ⓦ hotelmozartymacondo.com. Suburban house whose lovingly tended rooms are full of art (available to buy). There's a two-bedroom penthouse with kitchen, and in the garden, which is the German owner's pride and joy, a breakfast area and outdoor kitchen. Carrizalillo beach is an easy walk, and guests have rights to use a nearby hotel's beach club. M$600

★ **Quinta Lili** Cangrejos 104 ☏ 555 406 4759, ⓦ quintalili.com. Delightful place, close to the beach, with neat, spacious rooms, LCD TVs, iPod docks, fans and balconies with sea views, all set in a whimsical beach house, half-palapa, half-Moorish palace. Small pool, roof terrace with jacuzzi, excellent breakfasts and helpful hosts. M$975

Villas Carrizalillo Carrizalillo 125 ☏ 954 582 1735, ⓦ villascarrizalillo.com. In a peaceful spot above the namesake beach, these discreet, spacious, individually designed villas with kitchens and stunning views are perfect for young couples and families who want a few home comforts away from the party scene. There is a great restaurant enjoying the best of the views, pool, book exchange, and bike, bodyboard and surfboard rental. **M\$1950**

EATING

It doesn't cost much to eat well in Escondido. Many of the restaurants and cafés are laid-back, low-key affairs open to cool breezes. The **seafood** is always fresh, and you can vary your diet with **vegetarian** food, excellent bread and cakes, and **international** food including Swiss, Japanese, German and Italian. For cheap snacks, it's worth strolling into the old town to the **Mercado Juárez** and the taco stalls along Oaxaca, and you can buy self-catering provisions at the Super Che supermarket near El Crucero. In Zicatela especially, plenty of restaurants double as bars as the sun goes down.

10

PUERTO TOWN, PLAYA PRINCIPAL AND PLAYA MARINERO

La Galería Adoquín ☎ 954 127 1302. One of the best Italian joints in town, with platters of home-made tortellini, spaghetti, ravioli and gnocchi as well as delicious salads and an array of pizzas, all served in a polished setting with art displayed on the walls and exposed brick. Breakfast around M\$55, pizzas M\$80–100. Daily 8am–11pm.

Pascale Andador Gloria, Playa Principal ☎ 954 582 1093. French-owned restaurant and bar right on the beach with a few more pretensions to glamour and haute cuisine than its neighbours: fresh seafood, pastas and live music on Fri evenings – main dishes M\$90–160. Tues–Sun 5.30–11pm.

Sabor a Mar Eastern end of Playa Marinero ☎ 954 102 7090. Right at the end of the beach, this relaxed open-air place serves some of the best seafood in town – fish fillets M\$95, octopus M\$150, huge prawn cocktail M\$110. Daily noon–11pm.

La Tropicana 2 Nte, just west of Av Oaxaca. Escape "gringolandia" with a stroll into town for some of the best *tacos al pastor* on the coast – add quesillo for the full special; also tortas and beans. Tues–Sun 6.30am–10.30pm.

ZICATELA

El Cafecito Del Morro s/n ☎ 954 582 0516. Justifiably long-standing favourite, best known for its substantial breakfasts, served in an open-air palapa, including the vast Gran Slams aimed at starving surfers (in various combinations of pancakes, french toast, bacon and eggs). Prices start around M\$50, but are steeper than they seem as coffee and juice are not included; there are also freshly baked pastries from their own *panadería*. The lunch-time menu has an international flavour, with burgers (M\$60–80), croissants, whole-grain sandwiches and burritos. Tasty, simple seafood dishes and other filling Mexican staples feature in the evening (M\$70–100). Daily 6am–10pm.

Cipriano's Pizza Del Morro s/n ☎ 954 582 2588. Thin, crispy, cheesy pizzas (M\$60–100), cooked in a wood-fired stone oven and served at romantic tables wedged into the sand. There's also a full Mexican menu. Daily 1pm–midnight.

Dan's Café Jacaranda 14 ☎ 954 582 2760. The restaurant at *Casa Dan* (see opposite) serves arguably the best, and best value, breakfast in Escondido. Great coffee and French toast, healthy *licuados*, and an interesting, mixed crowd. Or come at lunch time for the legendary fish tacos and cold beer. Mon–Sat 9am–5pm.

La Hostería Del Morro s/n ☎ 954 582 0005. A huge and busy Italian-themed place with wood-oven pizzas (M\$80–120) and everything from hearty breakfasts to imaginative Italian and nouvelle Mexican dishes, served with flair and a decent wine selection. Daily 7am–11pm.

Maná del Jardín Del Morro s/n, on the beach opposite Rockaway. Sometimes slow service, but the beachfront setting and great Mexican-Italian food make it worth the wait; pizzas (around M\$100), pasta (around M\$85, or M\$120 with prawns) and heavenly desserts. Daily 4.30pm–midnight.

Sativa food and wine terrace Del Morro s/n ☎ 954 107 7026. Chic bar-restaurant with an East Asian theme, reflected in dishes like prawns *sativa* (with coconut, mango and *chipotle*, M\$135) or seafood curry (M\$90); also salads and cocktails. Restaurant daily 5–11.30pm, bar till 1am (happy hour 10pm–1am).

LA PUNTA

Caféolé Av Alejandro Cárdenas s/n ☎ 954 540 1782. The café at *Frutas y Verduras* (see opposite) serves delicious, mostly organic, local produce – crêpes, omelettes and fruit and vegetable salads (all around M\$50) as well as home-made yogurt and cakes. Daily 8am–10pm.

RINCONADA

El Cafecito Juárez, between Focas and Mantarrayas ☎ 954 582 3465. Another branch of the Zicatela institution (see above). Daily 6am–10pm.

★Espadín Villas Carrizalillo, Carrizalillo 125 ☎ 954 582 0995. Fine dining in a posh palapa restaurant, with mesmerizing views of the bay – try to get a table on the edge of the terrace. The modern Mexican menu features the likes of *dorado* with pumpkin seeds (M\$175), sweet mango *mahi mahi ceviche* (M$80), chicken in *mole negro* (M$150) and spicy shrimp tacos (M$50). Also breakfast. Daily 8am–10pm.

El Nene Juárez 14. Simple but great Mexican restaurant with a few pavement tables, tasty tacos (M$40), *hamburguesas* (M$40), natural juices and the special, chile con carne (M$50). Also mains like Cajun chicken

(M$120) and the best margaritas in town (M$40). Daily 2–10pm.

Tapas Bar Juárez, between Pargos and Focas ☎ 954 582 308. Authentic, Spanish-run tapas bar with delicious, reasonably priced tapas (tortilla M$35, *camarones al ajillo* M$75) as well as main dishes for around M$100. Tues–Sun 2–10pm.

10 ## DRINKING AND NIGHTLIFE

Puerto Escondido's busiest **nightlife** scene is in Zicatela, where many of the restaurants morph into bars as the evening progresses – a couple of the longest-established bar/clubs are just off the Adoquín, though, and many of the hostels have a pretty wild party scene of their own in high season.

Bar Fly Del Morro s/n, Zicatela, upstairs from La Hostería. This eclectic lounge with a balcony overlooking the beach plays good Latin and international music and has comfy cushions for you to lie on while you sip a frosty cocktail. Daily 9pm–2am.

★ **Casa Babylon** Del Morro s/n, Zicatela, next door to the Hotel Arcoiris. Arty, friendly, late-night bar with board games, mellow music, great mojitos and a useful reference library with travel books. Daily 2pm–2am.

Congo Adoquín. Raucous, African-themed club right in the heart of town; the narrow space around the tiled bar only adds to the atmosphere, and there's a miniature terrace out back. Live salsa on Wed. Tues–Sun 8pm–late.

Playa Kabbalah Del Morro s/n, Zicatela ☎ 954 582 3887, ⊛ playakabbalah.com. Cool bar-restaurant on Playa Zicatela, with the accent firmly on drinking and dancing rather than eating. Plenty of themed parties, plus Ladies' nights Tues and Thurs with a free cocktail (10pm–midnight). Daily 10am–4am.

The Split Coconut Eastern end of Playa Marinero ☎ 954 582 0736. Favourite expat bar serving mouth-watering barbecue and burgers, with live music on Sun, good wi-fi, satellite TV showing major sports events and daily happy hour 3–5pm. The July 4 celebrations are big here. Wed–Sun 1pm–late.

DIRECTORY

Banks and exchange Inside the ADO is an ATM for Scotiabank, and there are three ATMS at the Super Che. Most banks are in town, though, including HSBC on 1 Nte just off Carr Costera (near the ADO), Bancomer at 3 Nte and 2 Pte, and Banorte on Hidalgo, just off Oaxaca.

Laundry Excellent laundry service (M$13/kg) at

Lava-Max, Pérez Gasga 405, just below Union (near *Hotel Paraíso Escondido*); Mon–Sat 9am–6pm.

Police ☎ 066 or their booth at the eastern end of the Adoquín ☎ 954 582 0721.

Post office In the old town at Oaxaca and 7A Nte (Mon–Fri 9am–4pm).

Around Puerto Escondido

All but the most hardcore surfers and sun-worshippers are going to feel the need to explore after a few days relaxing on the beach. There's a wide range of activities on offer through agencies in town (see box, p.627), many involving trips out of the city, but there are also some you can do yourself. Most obviously, these involve visiting the nearby **lagoons**, and heading out on a boat to enjoy the wildlife.

Barra de Navidad

Barra de Navidad is immediately east of Puerto Escondido, where the **Laguna Las Naranjas** at the mouth of the Río Colotepec reaches the sea. The deserted beach across the lagoon is a haven for **birdlife**, while the lagoon itself has **crocodiles** and much else to see. In the village, Galo's **Iguanario** (open daylight hours – just go in and call out; small donation) is an extraordinary place set up to preserve rare iguanas. The ramshackle complex now has several hundred of them, along with half a dozen crocodiles, snakes, birds and tortoises. Locals can take you on a 45-minute walking tour around the lagoon (around M$100), where information boards describing local wildlife have been set up; or take a *lancha* from La Ballena (see opposite).

ARRIVAL AND TOURS

By colectivo Barra de Navidad is 10min east of Puerto Escondido, off Hwy-200. Drivers should turn right immediately after the bridge that crosses the river. *Colectivos* marked "Barra" can be flagged down on the highway near El Crucero in Escondido, or behind Zicatela (M$7 per person) – more information at the tourist booth on the Adoquín (see p.626). Beyond the village of Barra the

BARRA DE NAVIDAD

dirt road splits, the left fork leading towards the mouth of the lagoon and *La Ballena* (about 1700m), the right one to Don Juan (1km); either is walkable.

Tours At *La Ballena* restaurant, you can organize a *lancha* (M$100 per person; it's also customary to tip) to take you round the lagoon.

EATING

La Ballena At the mouth of the lagoon. *La Ballena* is a community project named after the vertebrae of a stranded grey whale that are displayed here. It's a very basic place consisting of benches and an open-air kitchen, most of which is destroyed every rainy season. Oct–June only, daily 9am–4pm.

La Huerta de Don Juan y Doña Lola ☎ 954 588 3269. Local families descend at the weekend to enjoy home-cooked fish and shellfish under a huge palapa with plastic tables and chairs, set in the midst of lush coconut palms; they also have a riverside area. Daily 10am–7pm.

Laguna Manialtepec

Laguna Manialtepec, about 15km west of Puerto Escondido at km 124 on Hwy-200 to Acapulco, is cut off from the sea most of the year, forming a freshwater lake extraordinarily rich in **birdlife**. You can easily spot fifty-odd species (there are said to be 360 in total), including parrots, hawks, falcons, ospreys, kingfishers and ibises; there are also crocodiles in the water. You'll see far more if you arrive very early, around 7am, or at sunset. At night, boat tours glide over plankton that glows, as if by magic, with phosphorescence.

ARRIVAL AND TOURS

Tours The most convenient way to visit is to take an organized tour through one of the travel agencies in Puerto Escondido (see box, p.627). La Flor del Pacífico (☎ 954 588 9164), on the shore right in the village, is the local base for Lalo Ecotours (see box, p.627) and offers *lancha* trips. *La Puesta del Sol* (☎ 954 132 8294), on the lagoon 1km before the village of Las Negras, is a friendly and well-organized

LAGUNA MANIALTEPEC

restaurant right on the water; they offer *lancha* trips for around M$1000 (per boat) and kayak rental for M$150/hr.

By taxi/colectivo You can also visit independently, and if you have a group of three or more you'll save some money this way. A taxi to the lagoon will cost around M$150; a Río Grande-bound *colectivo*, from 2 Nte and 3 Pte, is just M$10.

Parque Nacional Lagunas de Chacahua

The **Parque Nacional Lagunas de Chacahua**, 75km west of Puerto Escondido, is an expansive national park incorporating some 370,000 acres of mangroves, sand dunes and forests teeming with birdlife, turtles and crocodiles. To visit independently – a great back-to-nature experience – you'll need a couple of days at least. The village of **CHACAHUA**, on the shore of the lagoon close to the magnificent ocean beach, is interesting in itself, with a small Afro-Mexican population and basic **cabañas** to rent by the water; there's also space to camp and a row of outdoor seafood restaurants where you could hang a hammock. There's good surf on the beaches and occasionally even in the lagoon; currents can be strong, though, so check where it's safe to swim.

ARRIVAL AND DEPARTURE

Tours The easy way to visit Chacahua is with a tour (see box, p.627), though a day trip may only whet your appetite. A two-hour boat tour of the lagoon will cost around M$1000 per boat. For more information check ⓦ lagunasdechacahua.com.

By taxi To get here independently from Escondido you could negotiate a cab to take you all the way to the crossing point, a 2min boat ride from Chacahua. But the

LAGUNAS DE CHACAHUA

taxi will cost at least M$800 and the road is often impassable.

By colectivo/boat *Colectivos* (every 20min; M$37) run from 2 Nte and 3 Pte to Río Grande, 50km west of Puerto Escondido on Hwy-200; then change to one of the frequent minibuses (M$12) to the port of Zapotalito. From here you can take a *lancha* to Chacahua (M$1200 for a group). *Colectivo* boats charge M$120.

10

Puerto Ángel and around

Some 65km from Puerto Escondido, at the junction of Hwy-175 from Oaxaca and coastal Hwy-200, the oppressive, shabby city of **Pochutla** is the service hub for a string of beach towns and resorts that unfurl east towards the Isthmus of Tehuantepec. **Puerto Ángel**, now firmly on the tourist radar, is a fishing village that draws budget travellers with its unpretentious, low-key vibe and picturesque setting. Seven kilometres west, the beautiful beach of **Zipolite** has gained a reputation for its liberal-minded, European-hippy vibe, while north over the headland, attractive **San Agustinillo** has a more restrained feel. Further west, **Mazunte** is the main nesting site for Golfina turtles. Rapidly developing, it has something of the feel of a junior Zipolite.

Puerto Ángel

Though it's well established as a tourist destination, **PUERTO ÁNGEL** goes about its business as a small, down-at-heel fishing port with minimum fuss. Everything remains resolutely low-key – you may very well find pigs and chickens mingling with the visitors on the streets – and locals fish off the huge concrete dock, catching yellowtail tuna and other gamefish with a simple rod and line. Though it has a gorgeous setting – around a sheltered bay ringed by mountains – the beaches are less than pristine. Small hotels, rooms and simple places to sling a hammock, however, are abundant, with some of the most promising on the road between the main village and the Playa del Panteón. If you're on a tight budget Puerto Ángel can be a fun place to spend a few days, meandering and sampling the superb local **seafood**.

The beaches

Puerto Ángel has two beaches: **Playa Principal** is right in front of the town, and **Playa del Panteón** is opposite, beyond a rocky promontory. Panteón is the cleaner of the two, reached by a steep road or a path around the base of the cliffs. Here there is some interesting snorkelling around the rocks, as well as a profusion of tenacious hawkers. By afternoon it's in the shade, so most people wander round to the town beach. With just a little more effort you can visit one of the far better beaches either side of Puerto Ángel. To the west is the more primitive **Zipolite** (see p.634), while to the east, about fifteen minutes' walk up the Pochutla road and then down a heavily rutted track to the right, is tranquil **Estacahuite**. Here you'll find three tiny, sandy coves divided by outcrops of rock. The rocks are close in, so you can't swim far, but there's wonderful **snorkelling** (beware of sharp coral and undercurrents) and rarely more than a handful of other people around.

There are other lovely beaches near Estacahuite, including idyllic **Playa del Boquilla**, where you'll find the *Hotel Bahía de la Luna* and a **restaurant**, accessible by boat from Puerto Ángel. Boquilla is signposted from the main road to Pochutla, but it's inadvisable to drive down here, as the 7km road is in a terrible state. A better idea is to arrange a boat trip in advance to both beaches, turtle-spotting along the way. You'll see plenty of **boat trips** offered, or there's **scuba diving** with Azul Profundo (☎958 584 3109), based at the *Hotel Cordelia* in Playa del Panteón.

ARRIVAL AND INFORMATION

PUERTO ÁNGEL

By pasajeras/colectivos *Pasajeras* and *colectivos* from Pochutla drop off at the junction of Vasconcelos and Uribe, the continuation of the main road into town (there's also a taxi stand here). There are occasional *colectivos* on towards Zipolite, as well as private taxis (around M$150).

Tourist information The tourist information booth is located at the pier entrance on Uribe (Mon–Fri 10am–noon & 4–8pm, Sat & Sun 10am–noon, but erratic).

ACCOMMODATION

Bahía de la Luna Playa la Boquilla ☎958 589 5020, ⓦ bahiadelaluna.com. An escape for couples happy to do without creature comforts, this jungle retreat close to beautiful Boquilla beach (wonderful snorkelling) is hard to beat. Bungalows for two to five people cling to the hillside, and a restaurant-café on the beach serves fresh fish. It also offers holistic therapy treatments, personal development workshops and yoga, and sea kayaks and scuba gear are available to rent. Taxis are around M$120 from town. **M$1450**

★ **Buena Vista** La Buena Compañia s/n, a short walk along the footpath north from Uribe, next to the Arroye River ☎ 958 584 3104, ⍟ labuenavista.com. High above town and set back from the main road, *Buena Vista* has accommodation arranged over three floors, with an ocean view from the top-floor restaurant terrace and a rooftop swimming pool. The quiet rooms may not be well equipped – not even hot water – but the Robinson Crusoe ambience is part of the appeal. **M$400**

La Cabaña Playa del Panteón ☎ 958 584 3105, ⍟ lacabanapuertoangel.com. Just metres from the beach, *La Cabaña has* spotlessly clean rooms with bathrooms, small fridge, cable TV and fans (some with a/c). There's free coffee and tea in the mornings, a tiny pool and a rooftop terrace and restaurant with spectacular views. **M$500**

Casa de Huéspedes Gundí y Tomas Uribe 2 ☎ 958 584 3068, ⍟ puertoangel-hotel.com. One of the best budget options in the village, this jungle-clad guesthouse has simple if rather worn rooms with fans, mosquito nets and random folksy flourishes. The atmosphere is very friendly – travellers exchange tales in the open-fronted lounge area and Gundí's sons, who now run the place, offer surf lessons as well as bike and motorbike rental. The restaurant serves very good food, especially the bountiful breakfasts. **M$375**

Puesta del Sol Uribe s/n ☎ 958 584 3315, ⍟ puerto angel.net/puesta_del_sol.html. A great low-priced option. Not much in the way of a view, but spotless, spacious rooms (hot water for a few pesos more) around a garden with hammocks, laundry, internet access, library, satellite TV and communal space lined with photos. **M$400**

Soraya Vasconcelos s/n ☎ 958 584 3009. A bland but efficient choice, right in the centre of town overlooking the pier. There is little character to this modern hotel – rooms are basic with frilly bedspreads, fan (some with a/c and terrace) and private bath – but it is clean and spacious and the staff are very helpful. Good sea views from the restaurant, and from a couple of the rooms. **M$675**

EATING

Beto's Uribe s/n, on the outskirts of town on the way to Zipolite. High-quality seafood at very good prices served in an unassuming, low-key setting. It becomes a lively spot for drinks later on in the evening. Daily 5–11pm.

Buena Vista La Buena Compañia s/n ☎ 958 584 3104. Romantic hotel-restaurant serving a reliable menu of Mexican and Italian classics in a lovely floral setting overlooking the bay; they also serve breakfast. Reservations recommended in high season. Daily 8–11am & 6–11pm.

Maca Uribe s/n at the bottom of the pier, no phone. Palapa-roofed open terrace beside the beach, serving good Mexican food and excellent seafood cocktails. The real attraction is the upstairs bar, though, a great place to watch the sun go down. Daily noon–midnight.

El Rincón del Mar Precariously balanced on the cliff between playas Principal and Panteón, no phone. Boasting windy views of the ocean, this locally renowned restaurant serves the best fish and seafood in the area. The thick, seared loins of tuna are mouthwatering, and the nightly specials menu features imaginative renditions of the daily catch – bonita, lobster, shrimp, snapper – all invariably delicious. Daily 4–10pm, closed in summer.

Villa Serena Florencia Uribe s/n. At its namesake hotel, this is a popular place with European and American travellers, serving hearty Italian staples such as antipasto, pasta bolognese, *arrabiata* and marinara, as well as large, leafy salads, pizzas and traditional Mexican dishes. Daily 8am–11pm.

DIRECTORY

Banks and exchange There's a Bancomer ATM (not one hundred percent reliable) on Uribe opposite the pier. Banco Azteca on Uribe (daily 9am–9pm) is more a pawn shop than a bank, but it does change money (at poor rates) and has a branch of Western Union.

Internet Gel@Net, Vasconcelos 3 (just off Uribe), is a handy internet café.

Laundry Lavandería El Ángel (M$12/kg) is on Vasconcelos high above town.

Post office The post office is on Av Principal, the main road into the centre.

Pochutla

Anyone visiting Puerto Ángel and the other beach communities along the coast almost inevitably comes through **POCHUTLA**, a scruffy city on Hwy-175, 2km north of Hwy-200. Apart from catching a bus or changing money – there are no banks at the beaches beyond Puerto Ángel – there's no reason to spend time here.

10

By bus The bus stations – second-class Estrella Blanca (☎958 584 0380) and first-class OCC (ADO; ☎958 584 0274) – are close to each other on Lázaro Cárdenas, the main street which runs through the centre of town.
Destinations Huatulco (7 daily 1st class, 3 daily 2nd class; 1hr); Oaxaca (3 daily 1st class via the Isthmus, 2 daily 2nd class; 7–9hr); Mexico City (2 daily 1st class, 2 daily 2nd class; 16hr); Puerto Escondido (hourly 1st and 2nd class; 1hr 30min); San Cristóbal (2 daily 1st class; 11hr).

By minivan The quickest and most convenient route to Oaxaca is with the many minivans that head directly there on Hwy-175, rather than the very long way round via the isthmus that most buses take. Several operators have offices on Cárdenas in the same block as the bus stations. Oaxaca Pacífico (☎958 584 0349) has three daily

departures (M$300); Eclipse at Cárdenas 85 (☎958 584 0840) and Atlantida in the nearby *Hotel Santa Cruz* (☎958 584 0116) each run vans hourly from around 4am to 10pm. For Huatulco, Transportes Rapidos de Pochutla, in the same block, have rattly vans (M$37) every 15min throughout the day.

By colectivo/pasajera "*Pasajeras*" (covered pick-up trucks) and *colectivo* taxis head frequently to Puerto Ángel, Zipolite and Mazunte; they may be waiting for passengers at the bus station, or you could just flag one down as they head along Cárdenas. Fares rarely top M$30 per person (a private taxi will be around M$150), although if you want to go further than Puerto Ángel, over to Playa del Panteón for example, make this clear as you set out or you'll be charged an outrageous amount for the last part of the journey.

ACCOMMODATION

Posada San Jose Constitución, a block from the second-class bus station ☎958 584 0153. Acceptable, inexpensive hotel if you find yourself stranded here, with

rooms around a large courtyard and an often drained pool; they claim cable TV and wi-fi too, but the claims may be as empty as the pool. **M$450**

Zipolite

While some people rave about Puerto Ángel for its laid-back lifestyle, others are ecstatic about **ZIPOLITE**, 3km north along the road. Certainly there can be few places in Mexico better for doing absolutely nothing. Everything here revolves around the beach, first discovered by hippies in the 1970s, allegedly looking for a spot to witness an eclipse. Even today the travellers' grapevine is alive with tales of widely available hallucinogens, low living costs and a liberal approach to **nudity** – rumours that are largely well founded, much to the chagrin of the locals. Certainly, nude bathing, predominantly at the western end of the beach, is sanctioned by the local military; keep cover handy for trips to the restaurants. As for drugs, grass, mushrooms and acid are just as illegal as – though more prevalent than – anywhere else in Mexico; unscrupulous dealers are not above setting people up. **Theft**, particularly along the beachfront at night, can be a problem, but seems in no way to detract from the lure of a few days of complete abandon. The village behind the main beach has a laundry and a few small shops with internet access, beach gear and other bare necessities; for anything else you'll have to head to **Pochutla**.

The beach

The origin of the name "Zipolite" is uncertain – one theory is that it comes from the Náhuatl word meaning "beach of the dead", hence the constant references to it as the "playa de los muertos". The **beach** itself is magnificent, long and gently curving, pounded by heavy surf with a **riptide** that requires some caution – drownings are depressingly common (although there are lifeguards, as well as flags denoting danger levels up and down the beach). It is divided into three segments: Roca Blanca (aka Playa Shambala) towards the western end, Playa Zipolite or simply Centro in the middle and Playa del Amor at the eastern end nearest Puerto Ángel. Palapa huts line all three, catering to visitors' basic accommodation and dining needs.

By colectivo/pasajera *Colectivos* and *pasajeras* connect Zipolite with Pochutla via Mazunte and San Agustinillo

every 20min or so, much less often via Puerto Ángel; there are also plenty of private taxis.

Boat trips All the palapas along the beachfront advertise boat trips out to sea for about M$200, where you can snorkel and sometimes spot turtles, dolphins and, if you're really lucky, whales on their way up to Baja California. Scuba diving is on offer, but the reef isn't particularly impressive here.

Yoga The Solstice Yoga Center (ⓦ solstice-mexico.com) based at *La Loma Linda* (see below) runs regular classes (M$90), as well as five-day programmes from US$750/ M$9750, including meals and accommodation.

ACCOMMODATION

Accommodation is abundant and inexpensive, but mostly pretty makeshift. At the beachfront places **hammocks** (M$65) are strung from every rafter, but it can be worth getting a room if only to have a safe place to store your gear. Most feature shared bathrooms (cold water only), mosquito nets and a working fan if you're lucky.

El Alquimista Playa Shambala ☎ 958 587 8961, ⓦ el-alquimista.com. Fourteen cosy palapas right on the beach and one of the best restaurants in town (see below), as well as bonfire parties at night. The artfully designed cabañas have private bathroom, hammocks, terrace and fan. Wi-fi. M$950

Castillo Oasis C del Amor 97 ☎ 958 106 1763, ⓦ castillo oasis.com. At the far eastern end of Zipolite beach (near Playa del Amor), with five clean, beautifully designed rooms in a leafy green oasis; all come with hammocks, and a couple have bathrooms. Wi-fi throughout. M$380

★ **Lo Cósmico** Playa Shambala, no phone ⓦ locosmico .com. One of Zipolite's best options, this idyllic hotel lies at the western end of the beach. It has beautiful cabañas, some sleeping up to six people, with views of the coast, a secluded beach out front and a restaurant (Tues–Sun 8am–4pm) serving delicious crêpes. Hammocks are also available, on a special "hammock terrace". Hammock M$60, cabaña M$175

★ **La Loma Linda** On the hillside overlooking Playa Zipolite; no phone ⓦ lalomalinda.com. Six colourful, thoughtfully designed cabañas, all with hammocks, fans, fridges, stellar views and tiled bathrooms; also a yoga centre (see above). M$800

Lyoban Hostal Eastern end of Playa Zipolite ☎ 958 584 3177, ⓦ lyoban.com.mx. Friendly hostel with space to lock luggage as well as a small pool, communal areas with bar, ping-pong and table-football, and wi-fi throughout. Hammock M$80, "rustic" cabin with shared bath M$290,

en-suite room with fan M$390

A Nice Place on the Beach Playa Shambala ☎ 958 584 3195. Eight very simple but appropriately named rooms, right next to the beach, with fans, some with private bath. There's a popular bar, too. M$300

Nude Playa Zipolite ☎ 958 584 3062, ⓦ nudezipolite .com. To the horror of some, perhaps, a vision of what Zipolite might become – elegant, modern, two-storey, white concrete cabañas on the beach, some with a/c. There's a pool, "sky-lounge" bar and wi-fi. M$1000

Posada México Playa Shambala ☎ 958 584 3194, ⓦ posadamexicozipolite.com. Among the most popular places on the beach: the ten cosy rooms (some in cute two-storey palapas) equipped with double beds, hammocks, safes and mosquito nets are a real bargain, and there's excellent Italian food and cocktails, all right on the sand. M$500

★ **Shambhala** Playa Shambala ⓦ shambhalavision .tripod.com. This long-established and slightly eccentric meditation retreat is tucked away up the side of a hill by a rocky outcrop. It boasts beautiful vistas and shares *Lo Cósmico*'s beach area, with some shabby and some nicer, new, private-bath cabañas; also dorm room and a terrace for hammocks. The area at the top of the hill behind the cabins is a meditation spot and a great place to watch the sun rise (or set) over the bay. No alcohol or drugs permitted. Dorm M$150, cabaña M$450

EATING

Zipolite is a great place for cheap, fresh food, with most of the popular **restaurants** located along the western beachfront.

3 Diciembre A block inland from the main street in the village ☎ 958 584 3157. Best known for its tasty pizzas (from M$60), *3 Diciembre* also serves vegetarian Mexican dishes, *pozole* and home-made cheesecake. Wed–Sun 7pm–2am.

★ **El Alquimista** Playa Shambala ☎ 958 587 8961. Extensive menu of international and Mexican food (mains M$60–140), with excellent seafood, chicken, steak and

wood-oven pizza, plus good coffee. What really draws the crowds, though, especially in the evenings, is the chilled-out music and the cocktails from the bar. Daily 8am–11pm.

Memo's Cafe Main road in the village, above Café Zipol. Breezy upstairs terrace where they serve juices, teas, coffee, smoothies, frappucinos, ice cream and cake, and there's free wi-fi. Daily 8am–6pm.

DRINKING AND NIGHTLIFE

La Puesta Cnr of the main road down to Playa Zipolite. This cheesy but popular open-air disco is the heart of local

nightlife, with occasional live bands and a party every night; doesn't get lively till midnight. Tues–Sat 10pm–3am.

San Agustinillo

Rounding the headland north of Zipolite you come to **SAN AGUSTINILLO**, another fine beach graced with good surfing waves. Fast developing, it has a more restrained vibe than Zipolite, with some charming and upmarket places to stay and eat. The sand is backed by restaurants, which offer space for a hammock or small rooms for rent in addition to reasonably priced, fresh seafood. *Colectivos* and *pasajeras* pass frequently along the main road, heading in one direction to Zipolite, in the other to Mazunte and Pochutla.

ACCOMMODATION AND EATING   SAN AGUSTINILLO

Cabañas Punta Placer On the beach ⓦ puntaplacer .com. Four luxurious beach-side cabins containing eight circular rooms: gorgeous all-white spaces with drape beds, bathrooms and tranquil terraces, plus fridge and wi-fi. The owners run a variety of boat trips and inland tours. M$1170

★**Posada La Termita** On the seafront ☎ 958 107 8135, ⓦ posadalatermita.com. Four rooms, all en suite

with fan and mosquito nets; the bonus here is the restaurant, with specialities from Argentina and Italy, including mouthwatering pizza. Daily 4–11pm. M$980

Un Sueño On the beach ⓦ unsueno.com. Twelve stylish, breezy cabañas with private bath at the east end of the beach. Their restaurant, *Un Secreto*, is one of the best in town, with a Mexican-Mediterranean menu. Daily 8am–11pm. M$820

Mazunte

Though it has grown in recent years, the tiny village of **MAZUNTE** remains a languid, laid-back place with a dazzling beach. It's more peaceful than Zipolite, and lacking the party vibe, though still very much with an alternative feel. The surf is less powerful here, and at the western end of the beach, beyond the rocky outcrop, there's a smaller bay where the waves are even gentler and it's safer to swim. The village's name is derived from the Náhuatl word "maxonteita", which means "please come and spawn", a reference to the **Golfina turtles** that come here to breed. Mazunte was the site of a turtle industry and abattoir that, at its most gruesome, supposedly slaughtered three thousand of the creatures a day. In 1990, the Mexican government bowed to international pressure and effectively banned the industry overnight, removing in one fell swoop the livelihood of the villagers, who then turned to slash-and-burn agriculture. Since then, Mazunte has been declared a reserve, and more sustainable, long-term ecotourism programmes have been encouraged.

Centro Mexicano de la Tortuga

Main road at the east end of the village • Wed–Sat 10am–4.30pm, Sun 10am–2.30pm • M$27 • Guided tours in Spanish every 15min • ☎ 958 584 3376, ⓦ centromexicanodelatortuga.org

The government-funded **Centro Mexicano de la Tortuga** is one of the programmes set up to create a new economy for Mazunte. It features an aquarium with some particularly large turtles and a turtle research centre; well worth the visit, especially as proceeds go towards the conservation of this majestic species.

Cosméticos Naturales

Main road through the village • Mon–Sat 9am–4pm, Sun 9am–2pm • ☎ 958 587 4860, ⓦ cosmeticosmazunte.com

Cosméticos Naturales, a cooperative of local families set up with help from companies such as The Body Shop, is another venture aiming to create a new sustainable economy. It produces and sells prettily packaged beauty products made from local ingredients and organic produce.

Punta Cometa

Don't leave Mazunte without following the trail next to the *Balamjuyuc* (see opposite), which runs past the remains of some unmarked **ruins** to **Punta Cometa**, a thirty-minute walk. This entrancing park on top of the rocky headland next to Mazunte beach is the southernmost point in Oaxaca, and has mesmerizing views at sunset. The "jacuzzi", a rocky pool that fills with foamy surf as the waves rush in, can be accessed by scrambling down the rocks at the south end of the headland – it makes a good photo but it's not safe to go in.

Playa Ventanilla

Administered by the village cooperative ☎ 958 108 7288, �🌐 laventanilla.com.mx • M$100 • **Boat rides** from M$50

The lagoon at **Playa Ventanilla**, some 2km west of Mazunte, is home to around four hundred crocodiles, as well as a rich profusion of birdlife. You can test your heart rate by going out on the water in a shallow boat to navigate among the scaly inhabitants.

10

ARRIVAL AND DEPARTURE MAZUNTE

By colectivo/pasajera Colectivos and pasajeras pass frequently along the main road, heading in one direction to San Agustinillo and Zipolite, in the other to Pochutla. If you're coming from Puerto Escondido you can save time and money by getting dropped off at San Antonio, a cluster of just a few houses and a restaurant, where you can flag down a playera or take a private taxi (M35) for the final 5km to Mazunte.

ACCOMMODATION

The palapas on the beach have **cabañas** and hammock space, along with **restaurants** serving basic breakfasts, seafood and pasta. If you are equipped and feel so inclined, you can also pitch your tent right on the beach (free).

★**Alta Mira** Up the hill above the west end of town ☎ 958 584 3104, �🌐 labuenavista.com. Smart bungalows with tiled bathrooms and jaw-dropping views from the terrace restaurant. The solar power is intermittent, but that adds to the alluring atmosphere in the evening, when candles provide the only illumination. M$650

Cabañas Balamjuyuc Signed up the hill at the west end of the beach ☎ 958 101 1808. Friendly place with impressive views of the ocean and five comfy, brightly coloured, shared-bath cabañas of varying sizes. Also has a restaurant, massage, boat trips, hammock space and fully equipped tents to rent. Hammock M$60, tent M$110, cabaña M$320

★**Casa Pan de Miel** On the hill overlooking town ☎ 958 100 4719, ⌺ casapandemiel.com. Five luxurious modern a/c suites overlooking the beach (adults only), with satellite TV, bathroom, kitchenette and wi-fi. Small pool and stellar views included. M$2100

El Copal C de Panteón s/n, above Playa Mermejita, near Punta Cometa ⌺ elcopal.com.mx. Gorgeous cluster of four palapas surrounded by palms and terraces, blending modern amenities (free wi-fi) with an ecofriendly ethos

(candles at night, cold water, dry toilets and recycling). Closed Oct. M$1450

Posada Arigalan Between San Agustinillo and Mazunte ☎ 958 108 6987, ⌺ arigalan.com. One of the best places in the area, with stunning views from its modern but charming rooms; all have private baths (most with hot water) and fan; three "suites" have a/c, king-size beds and plunge pools; there are also cabañas. Cabaña M$760, room M$1390

Posada del Arquitecto At the western end of the sandy stretch, past the rocks at the second small bay; no phone, ⌺ posadadelarquitecto.com. Eco-conscious cabañas with private bath close to the area's best swimming, with great views, café-bar, wi-fi and hammocks. Hammock M$60, cabaña M$520

Posada Ziga East end of the beach, near the turtle centre ☎ 958 583 9295, ⌺ posadaziga.com. Congenial option with a range of rooms with private bathroom and wi-fi, and services ranging from fan and mosquito net to a/c and Sky TV. There are glorious sea views from the patio restaurant, which serves decent Mexican and international food. M$400

EATING

La Dolce Vita On the main road ☎ 958 584 3464. An excellent Italian-run restaurant (they also have rooms), La Dolce Vita offers delicious wood-oven pizza, pastas with seafood (around M$110) and occasional movies in the evenings. Probably the priciest place in town, but also the best. Daily 4–11pm.

La Empanada Main road at western end of town, no phone. Popular travellers' hangout with an international menu that ranges from sushi and stir-fry to pizza and

salads – also hearty sandwiches on home-made bread and blended juices (try the delicious cucumber and lemon). Daily 10am–early hours.

Tania Main road at western end of town ☎ 958 101 8455. The gregarious Tania offers good-value meals along with tourist information; the menu includes plenty of vegetarian choices alongside the usual carnes and mariscos. Daily 9am–11pm.

Huatulco

At **HUATULCO**, some 35km from Puerto Ángel, the government began developing the latest of Mexico's purpose-built resorts in the 1980s, on a series of then-deserted bays and beaches. The intention was to construct an environmentally conscious international destination, but growth has been slower than expected, and international visitors in the minority. A safe, sanitized, manicured resort with a beautiful setting, Huatulco is certainly not at first sight the place for budget or independent travellers keen to experience the real Mexico. Nonetheless, Mexico has a way of subverting the best-laid plans, and the town of La Crucecita has its earthy side, with plenty of reasonably priced accommodation, food and drink, while the further-flung beaches, a couple protected within a national park and entirely undeveloped, are magnificent. If lying on the sand, snorkelling and tripping off to coffee plantations and attractive coves are your priorities, you could do much worse.

LA CRUCECITA

ACCOMMODATION	
Misión de los Arcos	3
Posada del Carmen	1
Posada Eden Costa	4
Posada Michelle	2

EATING	
Ay Caray	7
Casa Mayor	3
L'Échalote	4
Kristal Rose	5
Mamma Mia	1
Los Portales	2
Ve El Mar	6

DRINKING & NIGHTLIFE	
La Crema	1

La Crucecita

LA CRUCECITA is the main service centre for the resort area. Though designed to house the ten thousand locals needed to support and staff the bayside hotels, it has become a tourist centre in its own right. You won't find much to see beyond the **Parque Central** and the modern **Parroquia de Nuestra Señora de Guadalupe** (which houses a 20m mural of the Virgin of Guadalupe, said to be the world's largest), but in its thirty years of existence, Crucecita has matured well to become a friendly, functional place. You'll find the best of the budget accommodation here, along with plenty of cheap places to eat, lively bars and tacky tourist shops.

10

Santa Cruz Huatulco and the beaches

Just 2km from La Crucecita, **SANTA CRUZ HUATULCO** was conceived as the token "Mexican village", something it patently fails to be. In fact, it feels more like the Mexican section at Epcot Centre, dressed up with a marina, handicraft stalls, a few relatively inexpensive seafood restaurants and a handful of condos. Santa Cruz's **harbour**, though, is the local transport hub and its huge pier the docking point for visiting cruise ships. From here, fishing and diving trips can be organized, or you can catch one of the *lanchas* that ply the coast to the beaches and more remote bays. **Playa Santa Cruz** itself is small and overcrowded, though it does have some excellent seafood restaurants on the sand.

Playa La Entrega
Just around the bay from Santa Cruz (2.5km by road), **Playa La Entrega** is a lovely white-sand beach with trees for shade. Easy access means it's always pretty busy, predominantly with Mexican families who congregate at the numerous palapas serving fresh seafood.

Playa Maguey
A steep flight of sixty-odd steps leads down from the road to **Playa Maguey**, in the next bay west from La Entrega. Its tranquil, green-blue waters curve around jungly headlands in a sheltered bay that at quiet times feels very isolated indeed. Quiet times are rare, though, as this is another beach that can be reached by road and hence gets busy. Snorkel gear and kayaks can be rented from the restaurants and shops behind the beach, and they also offer fun tours in tiny, glass-bottomed rowing boats (M$70, including use of snorkel gear).

Playa Cacaluta
West of Bahía Maguey, the pristine sand dunes of **Playa Cacaluta** (and its neighbour Chachacual) are protected in a national park, and accessible only by boat. Cacaluta is where much of the movie *Y Tu Mamá También* was filmed, and it really is almost as magical as it appears there; at least if not too many boats are visiting.

Bahía San Agustín
There are two beaches in **Bahía San Agustín**, the westernmost extremity of Huatulco. San Agustín itself can be reached by road, though it's over 30km from Crucecita, the second half on dirt track. It's popular with Mexican holidaymakers, and has very good snorkelling, offshore reefs for diving and plenty of amenities. **La India** is the final destination of many of the boat trips from town; glorious and entirely undeveloped, it can nevertheless seem crowded when too many *lanchas* end up here at the same time.

Playa Chahué
Playa Chahué is the closest beach to Crucecita, directly south of the town. There are plenty of hotels on the boulevard behind, a couple of beach clubs (with pools) right on the water,

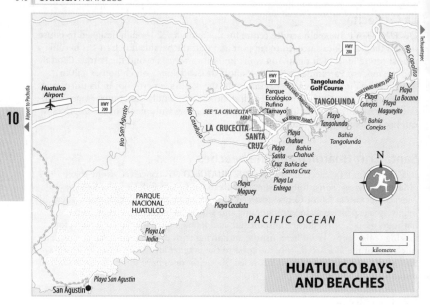

HUATULCO BAYS AND BEACHES

a marina and very fine sand. Despite all this it's little visited, probably because waves breaking right on the shore, combined with a powerful undertow, make swimming tricky.

Bahía Tangolunda

East from Chahué and Crucecita, **Bahía Tangolunda** is by far the most developed resort area, with the vast majority of Huatulco's luxury hotels along with chichi homes and an eighteen-hole golf course. The beach is fine but almost impossible to access unless you are a guest at one of the hotels, and in the restaurants you will pay upscale New York or London prices.

Bahía Conejos

The next bay east from Tangolunda, Conejos, marks the eastern edge of Huatulco. Much of the area inland has been taken over by residential development, with road access barred by security guards. However, on the far side, 500m beyond *Secrets* resort, you'll find a mosquito-ridden path through the forest that leads to **Playa Conejos** itself, a stunning crescent of sand sheltered by a thumb of land. At one end is the resort; the rest is often virtually empty, with a seasonal shack-restaurant and a few fishing boats drawn up.

ARRIVAL AND DEPARTURE

HUATULCO

BY PLANE

From Huatulco's airport, some 17km west of La Crucecita, *colectivos* offer a fixed rate of M$120 to any of the main resort centres within Huatulco (buy a ticket at the booth in the terminal); private airport taxis charge around M$500 to La Crucecita, M$1000 to Puerto Ángel, M$1800 to Puerto Escondido, though you'll pay less than half that if you walk 500m out of the terminal towards the highway and the waiting cars of Sitio Agua JE El Zapote (☎958 111 4584, ⓦtaxihuatulco.com). As for flights, there are numerous charters serving Canada and regional

Mexican airports, but scheduled services only to Mexico City (at least three daily) with Interjet (ⓦinterjet.mx), Aeroméxico (ⓦaeromexico.com), Magni Charters (ⓦmagnicharters.com) and VivaAerobus (ⓦvivaaerobus .com), and to Houston, Texas (one a week), with United (ⓦunited.com). Aerotucan (ⓦaerotucan.com.mx) offers daily flights to Oaxaca.

BY BUS

There are two bus terminals on the northern edge of La Crucecita: OCC, ADO, AU and Sur services arrive at the busy terminal on Blv Chahué at Rizcalillo; most second-class buses, including Estrella Blanca, Turistar and Transportes Rapidos de Pochutla (vans to Pochutla every 15min), have a station further out, off Blv Chahué on Av Carpinteros. For Oaxaca, it's generally quicker to go to Pochutla and catch a minibus on the direct mountain route; most buses take a long detour via the isthmus. For Mexico City, services via Acapulco, from the second-class station, are generally much quicker. From the OCC you can walk to the centre; from the second-class terminal, cross Blv Chahué and go nine blocks down Gardenia to the plaza. If you're heading straight for the beaches, take a taxi; rates are fixed and should be displayed – it's around M$30 to Santa Cruz or Chahué, M$50 to Tangolunda.

Destinations Acapulco (5 daily 2nd class; 10hr); Juchitán (10 daily 1st class, 6 daily 2nd class; 4hr); Mexico City (4 daily 1st class, 3 daily 2nd class; 16hr); Oaxaca (4 daily 1st class; 9hr; 2 daily 2nd class; 7hr); Pochutla (hourly 1st class, every 15min 2nd class; 1hr); Puerto Escondido (hourly 1st and 2nd class; 2hr 30min); San Cristóbal (2 night buses daily, 1st class; 11hr); Tehuantepec (10 daily 1st class, 6 daily 2nd class; 3hr 30min).

GETTING AROUND

By boat From the harbour at Santa Cruz you can charter a *lancha* to any of the beaches; they charge around M$1000 per boat for the furthest; the same boats offer sport fishing from M$500/hr. Also from here are tours of the seven bays with stops for swimming and snorkelling; M$230, or M$270 in a faster catamaran.

By taxi Taxis around town operate on a fixed-rate system, with the fares displayed at all the major taxi ranks. Expect to pay M$30 from Crucecita to Santa Cruz, around M$70 to Maguey or Conejos, M$170 to the airport and M$290 to San Agustín.

INFORMATION AND ACTIVITIES

Tourist information There's a helpful tourist information kiosk (Mon–Fri 9am–2pm & 4–7pm, Sat 9am–1pm) in the Parque Central in La Crucecita.

Adventure tours Booths on the Parque Central in La Crucecita and agents in most hotels offer a huge variety of adventures, from trips to the Cascada de Copalitilla to half-day quad-bike or horseriding tours (all M$480), rafting (M$390) or zipwires (M$340), along with gentler activities including massage and *temazcal*. Explora Mexico (☎958 587 2058, ⓦ explorahuatulco.com) offers more challenging rafting day trips (M$675), as well as early-morning bird watching.

Scuba diving Hurricane Divers (based at Xpert & Professional Travel at Plaza Coyula 11, behind Banamex on Santa Cruz beach ☎958 587 1107, ⓦ hurricanedivers .com) are a professional outfit offering dive trips throughout the area, along with PADI and DAN certification.

ACCOMMODATION

Budget accommodation is mostly in **La Crucecita**; the fancier resorts and hotels, at **Tangolunda** and **Playa Conejos**, are almost invariably better value if booked as part of a holiday package. Outside the high season (Dec, Semana Santa, July & Aug) prices can drop by up to fifty percent.

LA CRUCECITA AND PLAYA CHAHUÉ

Misión de los Arcos Gardenia 902 ☎958 587 0165. Friendly, Mexican/American-run colonial-style hotel just off the plaza, with bright, airy rooms with cable TV and a/c. There is a decent restaurant, free internet and discounted access to a beach club at Chahué. M$650

Posada del Carmen Palo Verde 307 ☎958 587 0593. Decent budget choice close to the heart of things, with good-sized rooms equipped with cable TV, fan and wi-fi. Not as fancy as it appears from outside. M$450

Posada Eden Costa Zapoteco 27, at Chahué, just off Blv Juárez ☎958 587 2480, ⓦ edencosta.com. Lovely mid-range option just one block from Playa Chahué, with ten rooms and four large suites, all with terraces leading out to the pool; wi-fi and continental breakfast included. Excellent on-site restaurant (see p.642). M$740

Posada Michelle Gardenia 1301, at Palo Verde ☎958 587 0535, ⓔ posadamichelle01@gmail.com. Friendly hotel with a range of very cheap singles and doubles, all with TV and wi-fi, some with a/c; some are tiny, so check rooms first. A good place to arrange tours. M$420

TANGOLUNDA AND PLAYA CONEJOS

Agua Azul La Villa Residencial Conejos ☎958 581 0265, ⓦ bbaguaazul.com. For a slice of tranquillity close to the beach, check out this Canadian-run B&B overlooking the bay. The ambience is welcoming and sociable, the hosts knowledgeable, and excellent breakfasts are served in a communal palapa dining room/lounge area. Adults only. M$1600

★**Dreams Huatulco Resort & Spa** Juárez 4 ☎958 583 0400, ⓦ dreamsresorts.com/huatulco. Best value of all the major resorts, with excellent deals online, great service and a huge roster of amenities. Modern, stylish rooms overlook the bay and come with LCD satellite TV, DVD player and balcony. M$2720

Quinta Real Juárez 2 ☎ 958 581 0428, ⓦ quintareal .com. Unabashed luxury in an exotic whitewashed property embellished with Moorish domes and curves, just off the beach. With lavish suites, a private beach club, posh restaurants and a colony of torpid iguanas in the nearby palms, you are unlikely to venture much further. M$3200

★**Villa Sol y Mar** Residencial Conejos ☎ 01 763 300 5815 (in US), ⓦ villasolymar.com. An intelligent choice for groups, a gorgeous apartment complex close to the beach with continental breakfast included; you rent one of five suites or the whole property, with fabulous views of the sunset and coast. Adults only, unless you rent the entire villa. Suites M$1850

10 EATING

Ay Caray Playa Maguey, no phone. Everyone loves this laid-back place right on the sand, overseen by the indomitable Alfredo. Especially good for fresh fish and fish tacos – fishermen can also take their catch to be cooked on site – it's also a great spot to while away the afternoon over a beer. Daily 11am–sunset.

Casa Mayor Bugambilia 601, cnr Flamboyan on the plaza, La Crucecita ☎ 958 587 1881. Café-bar on a first-floor terrace overlooking the plaza; a chilled-out spot with live music many evenings, serving coffees, baguettes, *antojitos*, hamburgers, omelettes and the like by day, cocktails at night. Fast wi-fi too. Daily 11am–1am.

★**L'Échalote** Posada Eden Costa, Zapoteco 27 at Chahué, just off Blv Juárez ☎ 958 587 2480. Exceptional restaurant featuring an eclectic menu that blends Asian, Mexican and European traditions, everything from Vietnamese dishes to Spanish classics and fabulous fondue (the owners hail from Switzerland and Laos). Mains around M$190. Tues–Sun 2–11pm.

Kristal Rose Cocotillo 218, La Crucecita ☎ 958 587 0605. Fancier-looking than most, with an icily a/c interior, *Kristal Rose* is popular with locals and tourists alike, with a warm welcome from the affable English-speaking Juan Ferra. Try the tortilla soup or anything with shrimp (the steaks are pretty average). Daily 1–11pm.

★**Mamma Mia** Gardenia, cnr Palma Real, La Crucecita ☎ 958 105 1548. Excellent pizzeria that's almost always packed with locals. In addition to good pizzas, cooked in a wood-fired oven (M$100–170), they have pasta, authentic Italian specials like baked rabbit with polenta and mushrooms, and a lunch-time *comida* for M$80. Daily 2pm–midnight.

Los Portales Bugambilia 603, on the plaza, La Crucecita ☎ 958 587 0070. Arguably the best of a number of simple Mexican restaurants on the east side of the plaza, open from breakfast (hash browns with eggs and bacon M$65) through to the early hours, with inexpensive *antojitos*, addictive nachos and cold beer plus the fancier likes of fajitas or rib-eye steak (around M$120). Daily 8.30am–12.30am.

Ve El Mar Playa Santa Cruz, close to the pier ☎ 958 587 0364. It's hard to find sand on Playa Santa Cruz not taken over by restaurant tables, so best to give in, have a drink, and enjoy the crowds, the music and the vendors. An extra plus of this waterside restaurant is that the fish and seafood are fresh, the cocktails zippy. Plain fish or prawn dishes for around M$120–160, specialities like seafood kebabs, pineapple scooped out and filled with dorado, or sweet Pacific lobster for M$270. There's even wi-fi. Daily 10am–midnight.

DRINKING AND NIGHTLIFE

La Crema Gardenia 311, La Crucecita. Quirky, crowded bar overlooking the plaza with a diverse clientele, lively rock music and tasty pizza (try the Crema Special, M$105), baked potatoes and nachos. Daily 7pm–2am.

DIRECTORY

Banks and exchange There are plenty of banks around the centre, including HSBC at the junction of Blv Chahué and Bugambilias, and Banamex at Carrizal, cnr Guamucil opposite the Plaza El Madero mall; there are also branches of Banamex and Bancomer in Santa Cruz, on the main road just past the beach, and an ATM in the OCC bus station.
Post office Blv Chahué 100, on the eastern edge of La Crucecita.

The Isthmus of Tehuantepec

The **Isthmus of Tehuantepec**, where the Pacific and the Atlantic are just 210km apart and the land never rises to more than 250m above sea level, is the narrowest strip of land in Mexico. It's a hot and steamy region, with a fascinating and unique cultural identity. The people are descendants of various indigenous groups, principally Zapotec. Historically, the Zapotec *indígenas*, especially those in the south, have been a **matriarchal** society. Though you'll still find women dominating trade in the markets (they are renowned for their tenacious, even aggressive, sales skills) while the men work in the fields, this is a tradition that is dying faster than most others in macho Mexico. Nevertheless, some elements remain: the women exude pride, many dressed in ornate hand-woven dresses and draped with gold jewellery; it's still the mother who gives away her child at a wedding (and occasionally still the eldest daughter who inherits land); and on feast days the women prove their dominance by climbing to the rooftops and throwing fruit down on the men in the *Tirada de Frutas*.

The best reason to stop in this region is if there's a **fiesta** going on, as they're among the most exciting in the country. Otherwise, you can go straight across – from Oaxaca to **Tuxtla Gutiérrez** or **San Cristóbal** in Chiapas – in a single, very long, day. Most first-class buses bypass the grimy port town of Salina Cruz, dominated by a giant oil refinery; better places to stop are Tehuantepec itself, around 250km from Oaxaca City, or nearby Juchitán.

Tehuantepec

The modest town of **TEHUANTEPEC** visibly preserves many of the isthmus's local traditions, has some of the **best fiestas** in the region and is generally a pleasant place to stop, with several inexpensive hotels. In the evening, the central plaza comes alive, with singing birds and people strolling and eating food from the stalls set up by the townswomen, some of whom still proudly wear the traditional flower-embroidered *huipil* and floor-length velvet skirt of the Zapotec. Perhaps because the town is so concentrated – a walk of ten blocks in any direction will take you out into the countryside – it's extraordinarily noisy; the din of passing buses is redoubled by the flatbed motor tricycles (*motos*) that locals use as taxis. There's a very busy **market**, just off the main plaza, which sells fruit, herbs, bread, flowers and other local produce.

Santo Domingo Cosijopí

Callejón Cosijopí, off Hidalgo • Mon–Fri 9am–2pm & 5–8pm, Sat 9am–2pm • Free

Tehuantepec's one real sight is the Dominican **church** and Ex-Convento of Rey Cosijopí. The church is an unusual double building, with a more modern Neoclassical edifice alongside the traditional conquistador-style church; the two are joined internally. The original church and monastery were founded in 1544 by Cosijopí, the last Zapotec ruler here, who formed an alliance with the Spanish against his Aztec and Mixtec rivals, and converted to Catholicism. The remains of the monastery now house the **Casa de la Cultura**, where temporary exhibitions and cultural events are held; restored in the 1980s, it has been quietly rotting ever since, though you can still make out remains of murals on the wall. It has a separate entrance; to get there head out of the church and take the first three right turns.

The ruins of Guiengola

15km north of Tehuantepec • Daily 8am–5pm • Free, though caretaker may ask for a small fee

The hilltop fortress of **Guiengola** was a Zapotec stronghold, and in 1496 its defenders successfully fought off an Aztec attempt to gain control of the area, which was never fully incorporated into their empire. It continued to be a centre of resistance during the early years of the Conquest and was a focus of indigenous revolt against Spanish rule throughout the sixteenth and seventeenth centuries.

At the site you'll see remains of pyramids and a ball-court, but the most striking feature is the massive **defensive wall**. By definition, Guiengola's superb location makes it somewhat inaccessible and it's probably best to take a **taxi**, though buses to Oaxaca do pass the turn-off to the site, 8km from Tehuantepec on Hwy-190 (look out for the "Ruinas Guiengola" sign). From here it's a hot, 7km walk uphill.

10

Juchitán

JUCHITÁN, 26km east of Tehuantepec, is a dusty commercial centre clogged with traffic and somewhat lacking in tourist infrastructure. Despite this, the city has a rich cultural life, offering glimpses into the matriarchal society the region is known for, and frequent **fiestas**, also known as **velas**, where women dress in colourful *traje* and men in formal wear for all-night marathons of music and dancing. These take place throughout the year, and in May seem to be almost daily. The residents are also known for strong political views, socialist leanings and a relatively tolerant attitude towards homosexuality; it's one of the few places in Mexico where gay men live openly, sometimes even attending *velas* in drag.

Casa de la Cultura

Belisario Domínguez cnr Colón • Mon–Fri 9am–2pm & 5–7pm, Sat 9am–1pm • Free

The **Casa de la Cultura**, beside the church of San Vicente Ferrer (which has a fine gilded altarpiece), was funded by Juchitán-born artist Francisco Toledo. Set around a courtyard whose low, wooden *portales* have a northern feel to them, it has an archeological display with pre-Hispanic stone carvings and pottery, some fine historical paintings and a roster of interesting events and temporary exhibitions.

ARRIVAL AND INFORMATION   ISTHMUS OF TEHUANTEPEC

By bus A constant stream of buses connects Tehuantepec and Juchitán. Though services in both places are broadly the same, few buses originate in Tehuantepec; if you can't find the connection you need there, it may be easier to

---

FIESTAS IN OAXACA

New Year's Day (Jan 1). Celebrated everywhere, but particularly good in Oaxaca and Mitla.

Día de San Sebastián (Jan 20). Big in Tehuantepec.

Día de la Candelaria (Feb 2). Colourful indigenous celebrations in Santa María del Tule.

Carnaval (the week before Lent; variable Feb–March). At its most frenzied in the big cities – especially Oaxaca – but also celebrated in hundreds of villages in the area.

Día de San Isidro (May 15). Peasant celebrations everywhere – famous and picturesque fiestas in Juchitán.

Día de San Juan (June 24). Falls in the midst of festivities (June 22–26) in Tehuantepec.

Fiesta de la Preciosa Sangre de Cristo (first Wed in July). Teotitlán del Valle, near Oaxaca, holds a festival with traditional dances and religious processions.

Guelaguetza (last two Mon in July). In Oaxaca, a mixture of traditional dancing and rites on the Cerro del Fortín. Highly popular; tickets for the good seats are sold at the tourist office.

Fiestas (Aug 13–16). Spectacular festivities in Juchitán (Vela de Agosto) and Tehuantepec (Fiesta del Barrio de Santa María Relatoca).

Fiesta de San Bartolomé (Aug 24). In San Bartolo Coyotepec, near Oaxaca.

Blessing of the Animals (Aug 31). In Oaxaca locals bring their beasts to the church of La Merced to be blessed.

Fiesta del Señor de la Natividad (Sept 8). In Teotitlán del Valle.

Independence Day (Sept 16). Celebrated everywhere.

Feria del Árbol (second Mon in Oct). Based around the famous tree in Santa María del Tule.

Día de los Muertos (Day of the Dead; Nov 2). Observed everywhere, with particularly strong traditions in Xoxocotlán and in Atzompa.

Día de la Inmaculada Concepción (Dec 8). Observed widely. There are traditional dances in Juquilla, not far from Puerto Escondido, and Zacatepec, on the road inland from Pinotepa Nacional.

Fiesta de la Virgen de la Soledad (Dec 18). Celebrations in Oaxaca in honour of the patroness of the state – expect fireworks, processions and music.

Fiesta de los Rabanos (Radish Festival; Dec 23). There's an exhibition of statues and scenes sculpted from radishes in Oaxaca.

Christmas Eve (Dec 24). In Oaxaca there's music, fireworks and processions before midnight Mass. *Buñuelos* – crisp pancakes that you eat before smashing the plate on which they are served – are dished up at street stalls.

head for the busier hub of Juchitán. In Tehuantepec buses stop at the OCC terminal at the northern edge of town on Hwy-185, a short moto or taxi ride (M$22) from the centre (or less than 1km walk, but that's taxing in the steamy climate). The main bus station in Juchitán is on 16 de Septiembre (which passes right through the heart of town) where it meets the highway; shared taxis to the centre wait outside and charge M$15 per person.

Destinations Acapulco (3 daily; 12hr); Coatzacoalcos (every 30min; 3hr); Mexico City (8 daily; 11hr); Oaxaca (hourly; 4hr 30min); Puerto Escondido (5 daily; 4hr); Tuxtla Gutiérrez (4 daily; 5hr); Veracruz (2 daily; 7hr 30min); Villahermosa (6 daily; 7hr).

ACCOMMODATION

TEHUANTEPEC

Hostel Emilia Ocampo 8, one block south of the plaza ☎ 971 715 0008. *Emilia* is much the most pleasant place to stay, with simple rooms with cable TV and wi-fi and a very helpful owner keen to promote local tourism through, for example, gastronomic tours of the isthmus. Fan M$270, a/c M$440

JUCHITÁN

Hotel Don Alex 16 de Septiembre 48 ☎ 971 711 1064, ⊚ hoteldonalex.com. The best of a poor crop of hotels in Juchitán, *Don Alex* is spartan but clean and comfortable; at least if you get a room in the marginally more expensive new section, where there's cable TV and a/c. Old section M$450, new section M$550

EATING AND DRINKING

Good **places to eat** are thin on the ground, especially in Tehuantepec. As ever, the best cheap eats are at market stalls. In Tehuantepec try the Mercado de Jesús on the west side of the plaza, or the steaming taco carts lining the east side of the square; and be sure to try some of the **corn bread** that local women hawk to everyone arriving on the bus. In Juchitán there are stalls set up under the *portales* of the Palacio Municipal, on the plaza.

TEHUANTEPEC

Cafetería Yizu Juárez 10, in courtyard of Hotel Donají ☎ 971 715 0064. Decent coffee, *licuados* and "*smudys*" drinks, plus breakfast and a good menu of snacks and light meals; late-night (by local standards) hangout for fashionable young *Tehuantepecos*. Daily 8am–11pm.

JUCHITÁN

Casa Grande Juárez 12 ☎ 971 711 3460. Unexpectedly elegant restaurant with leather chairs and dark-wood furnishings occupying a naturally cool internal courtyard. The food, from breakfast to dinner, is good, with an emphasis on fish and seafood (*Ensalada Casa Grande*, with prawn and pineapple, M$95; fish dishes M$145). They also have a tiny art cinema out back. Daily 7am–11pm.

Internacional 16 de Septiembre 25 ☎ 971 711 4208. Coffee-shop-style place with blissfully effective a/c, good breakfasts (M$80) and a substantial *menu del día* for M$80; also baguettes, sandwiches and *antojitos*. Daily 8am–11pm.

Chiapas and Tabasco

THE CHURCH, SAN CRISTÓBAL DE LAS CASAS

Chiapas and Tabasco

Although they're very different states – Chiapas is mountainous, and Tabasco is steamy lowlands – we group them together here because travellers will usually pass through one or both of them en route to the Yucatán. Endowed with a stunning variety of cultures, landscapes and wildlife, Chiapas has much to tempt visitors, but the biggest draw is how many indigenous traditions survive intact, as well as how much pristine wilderness exists. The state of Tabasco, by contrast, is less aesthetically attractive than its neighbour, and its rural areas see almost no tourists. But its capital, Villahermosa, is a transit hub, and archeology buffs know the region as the heartland of the Olmecs, Mexico's earliest developed civilization.

11

Chiapas was administered by the Spanish as part of Guatemala until 1824, when it seceded to join newly independent Mexico. The state is now second only to Oaxaca in Indian population: about 25 percent of its four million plus people are thought to be *indígenas*, of some fourteen ethnic groups, most of Maya origin. Tuxtla Gutiérrez is the capital, but travellers usually head straight for the colonial town of **San Cristóbal de las Casas**, tucked among the mountains in the centre of the state and surrounded by strongholds of **Tzotzil** and **Tzeltal** Maya culture. Ancient customs and religious practices carry on in these villages, yet as picturesque as life here may sometimes seem, villagers often live at the barest subsistence level, with their lands and livelihoods in precarious balance. These troubles helped fuel the 1994 **Zapatista rebellion** (see box, p.651), and although that conflict has long subsided, many of the core issues concerning land use remain unresolved. Now illegal immigration is the bigger issue, and a heavy **military** presence focuses more on the Guatemalan border and the eastern half of the state.

In Tabasco, **Villahermosa** is the vibrant, modern capital, with a wealth of parks and museums, the best of which is **Parque La Venta**, where the original massive Olmec heads are on display. In the extreme southwest, bordered by Veracruz and Chiapas, a section of Tabasco reaches into the Sierra de Chiapas up to 1000m high. Here, in a region almost never visited by outsiders, you can splash in pristine rivers in **Tapijulapa** and explore the astonishing ruins of **Malpasito**, a city of the mysterious **Zoque** culture.

Chiapas

The state of **CHIAPAS** rises from the Pacific coastal plain to the peaks of two ranges, the Sierra Madre de Chiapas and Los Altos de Chiapas. The **climate**, like the land, varies enormously. The coastal areas can be hot and muggy, while in highland towns like San Cristóbal de las Casas, nights can call for a jumper, even in August.

LAGOS DE MONTEBELLO NATIONAL PARK, CHIAPAS

Highlights

❶ Cañón del Sumidero Enjoy a boat ride through this spectacular gorge, with jungle-covered cliffs soaring 1000m up. **See p.664**

❷ San Cristóbal de las Casas The most enchanting colonial city in Chiapas, surrounded by villages rich in indigenous culture. **See p.665**

❸ Iglesia de San Juan Bautista Witness extraordinary displays of religious faith in this haunting church in the highlands village of San Juan Chamula. **See p.674**

❹ Parque Nacional Lagos de Montebello An isolated corner of Chiapas where the mountain lakes change colour in the sunlight. **See p.681**

❺ Palenque Visit the evocative ruins of one of the greatest Maya cities, then bathe in the refreshing cascades outside the town. **See p.687**

❻ Bonampak Over one thousand years old, the vivid murals here provide a startling insight into ancient Maya culture. **See p.692**

❼ Yaxchilán Perhaps the most magical of the Chiapas ruins, set deep in the forest, a boat ride away from civilization. **See p.695**

❽ Parque La Venta See the massive, Olmec-carved stone heads salvaged from the site of La Venta and now in a pretty park in Villahermosa. **See p.700**

HIGHLIGHTS ARE MARKED ON THE MAP ON P.650

Chiapas has the greatest **biological diversity** in North America. Its forests are home to howler monkeys, red macaws and jaguars. Most visitors will likely see these animals only at the **zoo** in **Tuxtla Gutiérrez**, but you can venture into the heart of the huge **Montes Azules Biosphere Reserve**, a section of the largest remaining rainforest in North America. From Ocosingo you can make forays into its heart, **Laguna Miramar**, a truly isolated wilderness destination. There's also **cloud forest** in the south of the state, protected in **El Triunfo Biosphere Reserve.** From the pretty colonial town of Comitán de Domínguez, the isolated Frontier Highway runs along the Guatemala border and past the beautiful lakes and hills of the **Parque Nacional Lagos de Montebello.**

On the east side of the mountains, at the edge of the Yucatán plain, the Classic-period Maya city of **Palenque** is one of Mexico's finest ancient sites. The limestone hills in this area are pierced by exquisite waterfalls. Palenque is the best starting point for a trip down the **Usumacinta valley**, to visit the remote ruins of **Bonampak** and **Yaxchilán**,

CHIAPAS & TABASCO

HIGHLIGHTS

1. Cañón del Sumidero
2. San Cristóbal de las Casas
3. Iglesia de San Juan Bautista
4. Parque Nacional Lagos de Montebello
5. Palenque
6. Bonampak
7. Yaxchilán
8. Parque La Venta

THE LEGACY OF THE ZAPATISTA REBELLION

On **January 1, 1994**, the day that the North American Free Trade Agreement (**NAFTA**) came into effect, several thousand lightly armed rebels calling themselves **Zapatistas** (after early twentieth-century revolutionary Emiliano Zapata) occupied San Cristóbal de las Casas, the former state capital and Chiapas' major tourist destination. The Zapatistas declared themselves staunchly anti-globalization, as well as opposed to local efforts by paramilitary groups to force indigenous people off the land. When the Mexican army recovered from its shock, it launched a violent counterattack, but international solidarity with the rebels soon forced the Mexican government to call a halt.

A ceasefire was agreed in 1995, and negotiations have continued over the years, as yet to conclude in a peace treaty. But eventually the issue of indigenous rights spread beyond the state's borders, with large-scale disturbances in Oaxaca in 2006 making Chiapas seem relatively peaceful.

Twenty years on, the word "Chiapas" is still synonymous with violent revolution, but while the Zapatistas remain nominally "at war" with the Mexican government, the struggle is now largely ideological. The organization still runs its own municipalities, "caracoles", on land seized from large landowners, and is largely left alone by the government.

Tourists have always visited Chiapas with no problems other than delays due to army (and occasional Zapatista) checkpoints. The government is hostile to foreign Zapatista sympathizers, however, as their presence is considered an illegal influence on Mexican politics – so showing obvious Zapatista support in Chiapas can potentially lead to deportation.

11

where you can cross to Guatemala by boat. This remote eastern half of Chiapas is also the home of the **Lacandón Maya**, who retreated into the forest when the Spaniards arrived, and shunned all outside contact until some fifty years ago.

The Chiapas coast

Running parallel to the coast about 20km inland, Hwy-200 provides a fast route from the Oaxaca border to Tapachula. If you're heading straight for Guatemala, this is the road to take. It traverses the steamy coastal plain of the Soconusco, once a separate province within Guatemala, but forced into union with Mexico by Santa Anna in 1842 and promptly absorbed by Chiapas. From the highway, the 2400m peaks of the Sierra Madre de Chiapas, little-visited mountains penetrated by roads only at their eastern and western extremities, are always in view. If you have your own vehicle you can explore some of the side roads leading from Hwy-200, either up into the mountains, where heavy rains give rise to dozens of rivers and waterfalls, or down to near-deserted beaches. Note, however, that the highway is two lanes each direction, often out of sight of each other; don't pull back onto the road going the wrong way – you must use the signed U-turn points.

This is a fertile agricultural area, mainly given over to coffee and bananas. Tapachula, the "capital" of the Soconusco plain, is cut off from the rest of Chiapas by the mountains, but has frequent connections to the southern border crossings into Guatemala. From Tapachula you can also take a relaxing trip up through coffee plantations to the delightful little town of Unión Juárez, the base for expeditions to Volcán Tacaná, the highest peak in Chiapas.

Tonalá

The gateway to the main beach resorts of Chiapas, the market town of **TONALÁ** is 39km from the Oaxaca state border and just off Hwy-200. With a population of some 70,000 people, it has all the basic services but not much to see. Tonalá means, quite aptly, "hot place" in Náhuatl, and you're better off pressing on to the coast, where the beachside accommodation can be more appealing.

Everything you need in Tonalá is either on the *parque central* (main plaza) – where you can start your day with a bowl of chilled *pozole* – or within a couple of blocks of it

> ## CHIAPAS ON A PLATE
>
> While the **cuisine** of Chiapas is not as famous as that of neighbouring Oaxaca, you can still eat very well while visiting the state. Dishes to look out for include *pepita con tasajo* (sliced beef marinated in chilli and herbs), tamales flavoured with local herbs like *hoja santa* and *chipilín*, pork in a *pipian* (pumpkin seed) sauce, and (in the coastal regions) dried shrimps in a tomato sauce. The city of San Cristóbal de las Casas is known for its Spanish-style cured hams and sausages, while the area around Ocosingo produces a good range of artisanal cheeses, and Chiapa de Corzo is famous for its suckling pig dishes. In terms of drinks, as well as excellent coffee from the state's highland regions, there are some more unusual beverages to sample, such as *tazcalate* (a blend of toasted corn, chocolate and cinnamon) and *pozol* (a sugary corn and chocolate drink).

11

(the market is to the south, at Matamoros). The main feature of the park is the **Estela de Tlaloc**, a large, standing stone carved by the Olmecs, depicting the rain god Tlaloc and showing the influence of Teotihuacán. The 1794 **Templo de San Francisco de Asís**, a couple of blocks northeast of the plaza, merits a quick peek for its pretty pink facade, ceiling murals and impressive gold *retablo*.

ARRIVAL AND DEPARTURE
TONALÁ

By bus All the bus companies terminate along Hidalgo, the town's main street: the main first-class companies (ADO/OCC), plus second-class Rápidos del Sur, pull in about 500m west of the plaza; all other second-class services, to the east. A taxi to the centre costs M$20–30.

Destinations ADO/OCC have first-class departures to Oaxaca (1 daily at 10.45pm; 8hr 50min); Mexico City (5 daily; 14hr–15hr 35min); Tapachula (roughly hourly; 3–4hr); and Tuxtla Gutiérrez (roughly hourly; 2hr 20min). Rápidos del Sur runs to Tapachula via all the towns on the coast highway (every 40min or so).

ACCOMMODATION AND EATING

Galilea East side of the plaza ☎ 966 663 0239. *Galilea* is well located in an attractive old building, and has basic rooms with ancient a/c units and TVs, as well as private parking. It also has a restaurant, the *Colonial*, overlooking the plaza and serving well-prepared Mexican standards. **M$600**

Grajandra Hidalgo 204 ☎ 966 663 0144, ⊚ hotel grajandra.com. Situated a couple of doors east of the bus station, the Grajandra is the most convenient place to stay in Tonalá, especially if you have to catch an early bus. It offers good value for money, with large, clean, comfortable en-suite rooms with TVs and a/c. There's also a pool. **M$750**

El Tizón Hidalgo 61 ☎ 966 102 5641. On the west side of the plaza, overlooking all the action, where the typical Mexican dishes (around M$100–150) nod to the bounty of the Pacific (only a 20min drive away): try the rich seafood soup. Daily 8am–10pm.

Puerto Arista and around

Not far from the border with Oaxaca, the first point of interest is **PUERTO ARISTA**, the only place on the Chiapas coast that even remotely resembles a resort town. Although this slightly run-down village may not be everyone's idea of a perfect beach hangout, Puerto Arista, with its kilometres of grey sand, wheeling frigate birds and crashing waves, does offer a chance to escape the unrelenting heat of the inland towns. Unless you arrive at Christmas or Semana Santa, it has a bit of a ghost-town feel, but it's a handy place to stop if you've been doing some hard travelling. The road from Tonalá dead-ends at Puerto Arista's only street, Avenida Matamoros, which locals call "el bulevar"; a landmark lighthouse, and most of the hotels, are just north. Walk a couple of kilometres northwest or southeast and you'll be on a deserted shoreline. While the waves are refreshing, be aware of the potentially dangerous **riptides** that sweep along the coast – never get out of your depth.

Boca del Cielo

You can easily get transport from Puerto Arista (or direct from Tonalá) to **Boca del Cielo**, a cluster of houses and fishing boats 15km down the coast on the landward side of Laguna La Joya, where you can board a *lancha* and speed across to a beautiful beach.

It's best at high tide, when the water comes right up to the restaurants, and at sunset. That said, without your own transport you'll need to head back well before 7pm, as it's almost impossible to find a taxi after dark. Some of the palapa restaurants will let you sling a hammock for a small fee, though be prepared for mosquitoes. The beaches along this stretch of coast are used by **turtles** for nesting: in October, the turtles lay their eggs in the sand; the next year, in June and July, the hatchlings struggle out to the sea.

ARRIVAL AND DEPARTURE · PUERTO ARISTA AND AROUND

By colectivo and combi In Tonalá, orange shared taxis (on Matamoros, between 5 de Mayo and 20 de Marzo) leave when full for Puerto Arista (22km south; 25min) and Boca del Cielo (37km). *Combis* depart one block away on Juárez between 5 de Mayo and 20 de Marzo.

By taxi Green-striped city taxis charge about M$100 to Puerto Arista.

ACCOMMODATION AND EATING

There are many **hotels** in Puerto Arista but generally few customers: you could try to bargain with a couple of the places listed here – and you can always **camp** on the beach for free. For food, a couple of dozen beachfront palapa **restaurants** near the lighthouse serve seafood, but only five or six are ever open at once; we recommend one below, but if it's closed, you can expect similar prices and menus from the others. At night, stalls sell inexpensive tacos along the main street, and there are a couple of basic restaurants for *antojitos* on the main road near the lighthouse.

José's Camping and Cabañas 1km south of Puerto Arista's main intersection and inland one block ☎994 600 9048, ⬚josescampingcabanas.com. Canadian-born José's place is the friendliest in Puerto Arista and great for budget travellers, with sturdy thatched bungalows, campsites with electricity and a flower-filled patio with hammocks and a pool. Some cabins have (clean) shared bathrooms. Cabaña M$350; camping M$50

Lizeth 300m north of Puerto Arista's main intersection, across from the lighthouse ☎994 600 9038. The most convenient place to stay in town, with cramped but clean rooms and a pool. Even though the balconies don't exactly face the beach, you can at least hear and smell the surf. Rooms have either fans or a/c. M$500

Otavento 4A Poniente 1, on the beach ☎994 600 9137. One of Puerto Arista's many palapa-roofed beachfront places, with tables so close to the surf you're better going barefoot. The seafood *cockteles* (around M$80) are huge and can't help being fresh. Daily 8am–10pm.

Playa Palo Blanco

20km south of the transit town of Pijijiapan • A *combi* from terminal in Pijijiapan (where second-class buses from Tuxtla Gutiérrez, Tapachula and Tonalá all stop), two blocks south and one east from the bus station

Around Pijijiapan, 75km from Tonalá, a series of dirt roads leads to unspoiled beaches and lagoons with opportunities for fishing, swimming or merely relaxing in the sun. The best of these is **Playa Palo Blanco**. Similar to Boca del Cielo, it's reached by launch across a narrow lagoon. Like most beaches, on Sundays, it's busy with families, who come for lunches under the large palapas between the towering palms, but during the rest of the week the incredibly broad stretch of brown sand can be deserted.

Tapachula

Some 150km northeast of Tonalá by road, in the shadow of the 4060m Volcán Tacaná, lies the busy commercial city of **TAPACHULA**. Just 16km from Guatemala, it's a border city as well as the capital of the Soconusco, with a lively cultural mix comprising immigrants from Central America as well as small German and Chinese communities. The Germans were invited to settle here by the Mexican government in the 1880s to boost the economy, establishing the state's coffee industry and leaving a legacy of fine haciendas nearby. The Chinese initially came to work on the railway, in part because the rebellious locals refused to do so; the most visible sign of their community today is the high proportion of Chinese restaurants in the city centre.

While the surrounding countryside offers some worthwhile diversions, there's not much to see in the city itself. As always, the centre of activity is the **plaza (Parque Hidalgo)**, a pleasant place to while away an evening listening to the marimba bands. Look out for vendors selling *jocotes*, so-called hog plums – they look like giant olives and are pickled in rum.

Museo Arqueológico del Soconusco

8a Av Nte 24, between 1a and 3a Pte • Tues–Sun 9am–6pm • M$39 • ☎ 962 626 4173

The main attraction in Tapachula is the **Museo Arqueológico del Soconusco**, in the former Palacio Municipal, a gold-trimmed colonial gem on the west side of the plaza. It has displays of prehistoric and Olmec finds and a decent collection of artefacts from Izapa and other local sites (explanations in Spanish only).

ARRIVAL AND DEPARTURE TAPACHULA

BY PLANE

Tapachula's airport (☎ 962 626 4189), 18km south of town, is served by regular flights to Mexico City (4 daily; 2hr), operated by Aeroméxico (ⓦ aeromexico.com) and Volaris (ⓦ volaris.com). *Colectivos* run to town; buy a ticket at the Transportes Terrestre booth just outside the arrivals hall. If you are in a group, it's cheaper to take a taxi (around M$150).

BY BUS

All the main bus stations are north of the city centre. The terminals of the various second-class companies are within walking distance of the plaza, while the first-class terminal is further out. All buses to Comitán and San Cristóbal are *via altos* and head over the mountains. All first-class and most second-class buses to Tuxtla are *via costa*, meaning they travel up the coast through Tonalá.

First-class buses OCC/ADO services (and some of the better second-class services) leave from the terminal at 17a C Ote between 1a Av and 3a Av Nte. A taxi to the centre costs about M$40; walking takes 20min or so.

Destinations Comitán (6 daily; 5hr 40min–7hr 5min); Mexico City (9 daily; 17hr 10min–19hr 15min); Oaxaca (2 daily, both at 8pm; 11hr 40min–12hr 20min); San Cristóbal (10 daily; 7hr 15min–9hr); Tonalá (roughly hourly; 3–4hr); Tuxtla Gutiérrez (roughly hourly; 4hr 30min–8hr 15min); Villahermosa (3 daily at 12.30pm, 5.30pm & 6.30pm; 11hr 10min–11hr 30min).

Second-class buses The main second-class bus operators are TRF, at the corner of 16a Av Nte and 3a C Pte, and AEXA, opposite.

CENTRAL TAPACHULA

EATING
Bambú	1
La Parrilla	2
Pronto's	3

ACCOMMODATION
Casa Mexicana	5
Fénix	4
Galerias Hotel & Arts	3
Hotel & Suites Mo Sak	1
Michell	2

TAPACHULA ORIENTATION

The town's **layout** is a little confusing, for while the streets are organized in the regular numbered grid common in Chiapas, the main plaza, Parque Hidalgo, is actually three blocks west and one block north of where Calle Central meets Avenida Central.

BY COMBI AND TAXI

The main *combi* terminals lie along 5a C Pte beyond the market, between 12a Av and 14a Av Nte. Unión y Progreso runs frequent services to Cacahoatán (every 20min or so; 30min) for Unión Juárez, as well as to the Talismán Bridge (every 3–5min; 30min) for Izapa and the Guatemalan border. Next door and opposite, respectively, Omnibus de Tapachula and Costeños de Chiapas run frequent buses to Ciudad Hidalgo (45min). On the opposite side of the plaza, Gen Paulino Navarro also offers regular *combis* to Ciudad Hidalgo (every 10min or so; 45min) from 7a C Ote and Av Central Nte. Shared taxis to Ciudad Hidalgo leave from 7a C Pte, between 2a Av and 4a Av Nte.

TO GUATEMALA

By bus Three first-class companies offer direct services to Guatemala City (around 6–8hr): Trans Galgos (3 daily at 6am, 12.15am, 11.45pm; ☎ 962 625 4588, ⓦ transgalgosinter.com.gt), Linea Dorada (1 daily at 3pm; ⓦ lineadorada.com.gt) and Tica Bus (1 daily at 7am; ☎ 962 626 2880, ⓦ ticabus.com); the latter two are a bit cheaper, though the buses aren't as nice. All run from the ADO/OCC terminal; buy tickets from a kiosk in the arrivals hall. At the border crossing at Talismán, you'll have to get off the bus for Mexican immigration, walk across the bridge, pass through Guatemalan immigration and then re-board.

Guatemalan consulate C Central Ote 42, at the junction with 5a Av Nte (Mon–Fri 10am–3pm & 4–6pm; ☎ 962 626 1525). Even if you don't need a visa, come here for free maps, brochures and other information.

INFORMATION

City tourist office On the plaza in the former Palacio Municipal (daily 9am–4pm; ☎ 962 628 7725).

Regional tourist office 2km east of the centre in Plaza Kamico on the main road to the border (Mon–Fri 8am–8pm, Sat 8am–2pm; ☎ 962 625 5409, ⓦ turismochiapas.gob.mx).

ACCOMMODATION

★**Casa Mexicana** 8a Av Sur 19 ☎ 962 626 6605, ⓦ casamexicanachiapas.com. A historic and beautifully decorated hotel arranged around a flower-laden courtyard. En suites are tastefully adorned with art and antiques, and there's also a pool and a charming restaurant with tables in the leafy courtyard garden. M$1132

Fénix 4a Av Nte 19 ☎ 962 628 9600, ⓦ fenix.com.mx. The best-value hotel in the city centre, offering large rooms with either fan or a/c (the latter are remodelled, substantially nicer and roughly double the price), and decent bathrooms. There's a cooling fountain in the courtyard plus leafy gardens complete with parrots. The place is surprisingly tranquil given the central location. M$270

Galerias Hotel & Arts 4a Av Nte 21 ☎ 962 642 7590.

A solid mid-range choice, with clean, decidedly beige en suites – all come with a/c and TVs – a decent location, and a certain artistic flair. There's also a bar on site. M$850

Hotel & Suites Mo Sak 4 Av Norte 97, between 13 and 15 west ☎ 962 626 6787, ⓦ hotelmosak.com. A good-value hotel, with spacious rooms, each with a modern bathroom, a/c and TV. If you want a kitchenette, opt for one of the kingsize rooms (M$600). M$500

Michell 5a C Pte 23-A ☎ 962 625 2640. Less than a block east of the central plaza, this hotel seems designed for the business traveller. The lobby may be cramped, but the a/c rooms and beds are big, the staff are friendly, and the price is competitive, even if it's not the most exciting place to stay. M$540

EATING

Stalls around the plaza sell local food, while 1a C Pte is lined with inexpensive **restaurants**, most with breakfast options and a comida corrida. As usual, there are budget places to eat and some fine *panaderías* around the market, beginning with the row of **juice bars** on 10a Av Nte, just west of the plaza. The row of restaurants on the south side of the plaza, under the *portales*, is a good place for drinks, while the city's liveliest clubs are clustered in the Zonas Discotecas, 2km east on C Central Ote.

Bambú 7a C Pte 23 ☎ 962 626 8622, ⓦ restaurant bambu.com.mx. The most appealing of several economical Chinese restaurants (dishes from M$30) along

this street; it also has takeaway and delivery options should the traffic fumes put you off eating in the open-fronted restaurant. Daily 10am–10pm.

11

La Parrilla 8a Av Nte 20, just south of the plaza ☎ 962 118 1428. Offers South-American-style grills as well as a delicious *taquiza mixta*, with five mouthwatering types of *supertacos*, all served in a fast-food-style diner (mains from M$50). Daily 7am–midnight.

Pronto's 1a C Pte 11 ☎ 962 626 5680. One of several good-value budget options along this street, this open-front cafeteria has hearty food like *menudo sinaloense* (a spicy tripe stew) as well as decent fried chicken (dishes around M$50–70). Daily 24hr.

DIRECTORY

Banks and exchange The main banks are one block east of the plaza, with HSBC at 1a C Pte and 2a Av Nte, but for changing cash you'll get much quicker service from Cambio de Divisas, 2a Av Nte 9, between C Central and 1a C Pte (☎ 962 625 1315; Mon–Fri 9am–5pm, Sat 9am–2pm); you can also get Guatemalan quetzales here.

Internet There are plenty of internet cafés around the city centre.

Post office The post office (Mon–Fri 9am–3pm, Sat 9am–1pm) is a long way southeast of the plaza at 1a C Ote between 7a Av Nte and 9a Av Nte.

North of Tapachula

The foothills north of Tapachula are studded with coffee plantations, established as far back as the late nineteenth century. Many of the old haciendas have been well maintained, some even by the original German families, and are an idyllic sight, tucked amid the dense forest. The peak of Volcán Tacaná, the highest in Chiapas, looms over all.

Ruta del Café

West of Tapachula • Driving from Tapachula, follow 8a C north out of town and follow signs • Taxis cost M$400–500

This winding road north and west of Tapachula passes a large number of grand old haciendas built by German coffee barons in the late nineteenth and early twentieth centuries – five are open for various tours and activities, and several provide (rather lavish) accommodation. It's a pretty but slow drive of about 40km on narrow, unpaved roads through *pequeña Alemania* – the distance and isolation make it best for an overnight trip or longer, rather than a day outing. And you'll need your own transport or a taxi to get up here – or you can arrange a tour with transport through Finca Hamburgo (see below), which has an office in Tapachula (on 9a Av Ote at 11a C Nte). Established in 1888 and still run by the same German-Mexican family, it also manages nearby Finca La Chiripa, where there are hiking trails and other outdoor activities.

ACCOMMODATION AND EATING   RUTA DEL CAFÉ

Finca Hamburgo End of the Ruta del Café ☎ 962 626 7578, ⊕ fincahamburgo.com. This grand chalet could be in the Alps – but the view down the forested mountain slope is pure Chiapas. The wood-panelled cabins here are luxurious, and the restaurant has a bit of German flair – *spätzle* (small egg noodles) with a chile kick, for instance. **M$1960**

Volcán Tacaná and around

For those travelling by bus, the route northeast of Tapachula up to **Volcán Tacaná** provides a more accessible taste of the area's coffee culture, similar to the Ruta del Café (see above) but more manageable as a day outing; the tours and lodging are also a bit more budget friendly. The road climbs up the lush green valley of the Río Suchiate, which forms the border with Guatemala. The bananas and cacao give way to coffee, and you begin to enjoy good views of two majestic **volcanoes**: Tacaná, at 4092m, the highest peak in Chiapas; and the 4220m peak of Tajumulco, the highest mountain in Guatemala (and indeed Central America).

Casa Braun

35km from Tapachula • Daily 8am–8pm • Free • ☎ 962 627 0050

As you climb into the foothills of Volcán Tacaná, the first town of interest is **Santo Domingo**, home to the wonderfully restored **Casa Braun**, a three-storey coffee-plantation house from the 1920s. Set in beautiful gardens, with balconies all around, it was the home of Enrique Braun Hansen, whose German origins are reflected in the building's architectural style – early North American meets Alpine hotel, with Art Nouveau interiors. Now part of a community-based tourism project, the house includes a restaurant, a swimming pool at the back and a coffee museum (same hours) with displays and photos charting the area's history.

Unión Juárez

Another 9km up the road, and 51km from Tapachula, the last substantial settlement on the road is **Unión Juárez**, one of the last remaining areas for the Mam people in Mexico (most of this Maya group now lives in Guatemala). Perched at 1100m on the flank of Volcán Tacaná, the community is the starting point for some of the finest hiking in southern Chiapas, passing scores of waterfalls. With a guide, you can reach the summit, where a monument symbolizes the kinship between Mexico and Guatemala. The best time to climb is the dry season between November and March, particularly December and January.

ARRIVAL AND TOURS

By bus and combi From Tapachula, take a *combi* or second-class bus to Cacahoatán (30min); bring your passport, as security checks are common near the border. From Cacahoatán, frequent buses leave from the station across the street from the Unión y Progreso terminal for both Santo Domingo (around 30min) and Unión Juárez (around 45min). Shared taxis, which are slightly faster, also wait here. Returning, buses leave Unión Juárez every

VOLCÁN TACANÁ AND AROUND

15min till 8pm; the last bus from Cacahoatán to Tapachula goes at 9pm.

Tours Fernando Valera Fuentes (☎ 962 647 2015, ✉ fernandovalerafuentes@gmail.com), an excellent Spanish-speaking guide, leads three-day trips up Tacaná for about M$750/person; the price includes government approvals and equipment. He uses the *Colonial Campestre* hotel (see below) as a headquarters.

ACCOMMODATION AND EATING

SANTO DOMINGO

Hotel Santo Domingo Opposite the entrance to Casa Braun (see opposite), around 100m along the street and just off the main road ☎ 962 627 0060. A good-value place to stay, whose ten en suites – with comfortable beds – are set around a patio garden. There's also an economical restaurant. Get off the bus at the lower end of the village, near the plaza, and you should be able to follow the signs for the "Centro Turístico" – the house is around

200m from the main road. **M$450**

UNIÓN JUÁREZ

Colonial Campestre Hidalgo 1 ☎ 962 647 2015. The economical rooms and suites here are comfortable and spacious, with private bathrooms and TV. The owner knows his coffee, having written a book about its history in the area, and his son, guide Fernando (see above), runs hikes in the surrounding mountains. **M$400**

Izapa

14km east of Tapachula • Wed–Sun 8am–5pm • Free, but the gatekeepers at each section appreciate small donations • Take any bus or *combi* to the Talismán border and ask the driver to drop you off at the signposted site

The road to the border passes straight through the archeological site of **Izapa**, an important, if little-visited, group of ruins. Besides being easy to get to, the site is large – with more than eighty temple mounds – and significant for its evidence of both the Olmec and Maya cultures. Izapa culture is seen as a transitional stage between the Olmecs and the Classic Maya period. Many of the best carved monuments have been removed to museums, but you can still see early versions of the rain god Chac and other gods, many in rather sad-looking huts surrounded by barbed wire. From its founding before 1250 BC, Izapa flourished up to and throughout the Maya pre-Classic period, until around 300 AD; most of what remains is from the later part of this period, perhaps around 200 AD.

The **northern side** of the site (left of the road as you head to the border) is the most interesting. There's a ball-court and several steles, which, though not Olmec in origin, are carved in a recognizable Olmec style. The **southern side** (Grupo A and B) is down a track about 1km back along the main road towards Tapachula. These sections are more overgrown, but you can spot altars with animal carvings – frogs, snakes and jaguars – and several unexcavated mounds.

The Guatemalan border: Talismán Bridge and Ciudad Hidalgo

Both of these southern crossing points are easy places to enter Guatemala. **Talismán Bridge** is closer to Tapachula (16km) and better for onward connections if travelling by bus, especially to Quetzaltenango and the Western Highlands. With only a few grubby hotels and unappealing *comedores*, however, the village of Talismán is not a place to linger; El Carmen, on the Guatemalan side, isn't much better.

South of Talismán Bridge, and 37km from Tapachula, the border town of **Ciudad Hidalgo** is a very busy road crossing, but useful only if you're aiming for the beaches along the Carretera al Pacífica (Pacific Highway) or the ruins at Abaj Takalik near Retalhuleu (connected to Hidalgo's Guatemalan neighbour **Tecún Umán** with regular buses).

11

ARRIVAL AND DEPARTURE   TALISMÁN BRIDGE AND CIUDAD HIDALGO

TO GUATEMALA
The two major crossings at Talismán Bridge and Ciudad Hidalgo (both are officially open 24hr, though it's generally easier to cross during the day) are usually hassle free, but things can be less predictable at several minor points of entry: Frontera Corozal, Ciudad Cuauhtémoc and El Carmen Xhan, in Chiapas, as well as El Ceibo in Tabasco. The soliciting of illegal fees sometimes still occurs at these crossings, but requesting a receipt is often a sufficient response to get them to waive the fee.

Money and exchange Changing money is best done in Tapachula, where rates are more favourable and you can check the official exchange rate beforehand.

Time Note that Mexico observes daylight-saving time, but Guatemala does not, which means that, in summer, Guatemala is one hour behind Mexico.

VIA TALISMÁN BRIDGE
To Guatemala City Buses (every 1–2hr; 5–6hr) are usually waiting, but these typically travel along the

Carretera al Pacífica via Tecún Umán (closer to Ciudad Hidalgo). The faster option is one of the international bus services from Tapachula direct to Guatemala City (see p.655).

To Quetzaltenango and the Western Highlands Take a shared taxi to Malacatán or Coatepeque and continue from there.

To Mexico Travelling into Mexico, you'll be given a tourist card at immigration; *combis* head to Tapachula, and first-class buses go from Tapachula onwards. You may have your passport checked along Hwy-200.

VIA CIUDAD HIDALGO
To Guatemala Plenty of willing locals offer to pedal you across the Puente Rodolfo Robles to Umán in Guatemala, but it's an easy walk. You have to pay a M$5 fee to cross the bridge.

To Mexico The ADO/OCC terminal is one block from immigration, where you can pick up shuttles to Tapachula every 15min (30–45min).

Tuxtla Gutiérrez and around

This city is the main gateway from central Mexico and a major transport hub. As home to over half a million, the modern, crowded capital of Chiapas does its best to deny most of the state's attraction and tradition (if you prefer a more rural setting, press on to Chiapa de Corzo or San Cristóbal de las Casas). A couple of **museums** can fill your time if you do stay here, and the city is the best base for a drive along the cliff-tops and *miradores* of the **Cañón del Sumidero** (see p.664).

The plaza and around
Museo de la Ciudad daily 9am–6pm • Free

The **plaza**, known as the Plaza Cívica, is an expanse of ostentatious marble, fountains and a statue of General Joaquín Miguel Gutiérrez Canales (1796–1838), former governor of Chiapas and campaigner for *indígena* rights. West along Avenida Central Poniente, at 2a Calle Poniente Sur, is the **Museo de la Ciudad**, with an absorbing collection of photos and items documenting the city's history, notably its role in the Mexican revolution.

CENTRAL TUXTLA GUTIÉRREZ

N

0   200 metres

● **EATING**
Café Avenida	4
Las Canteras	2
La Gran Muralla	1
El Horno Mágico	5
Naturalíssimo	3
Las Pichanchas	6

■ **ACCOMMODATION**
Casablanca	2
Fernando	3
Hostal Tres Central	4
Real Avenida	1
Regional San Marcos	5

11

Catedral de San Marcos

Av Central • Daily 6am–2pm & 4–9pm • Free

Just opposite the plaza, the whitewashed **Catedral de San Marcos** was established in the sixteenth century. Its bell tower is one of the leading local entertainments: every hour a mechanical procession of the twelve apostles goes through a complicated routine accompanied by a carillon of 48 bells.

Museo del Café

2a C Ote Nte 236, just east of the plaza • Mon–Sat 9am–5pm • M$10 • ☎ 961 611 1478, ⊛ museodelcafe.chiapas.gob.mx

In an old colonial house with a shady courtyard, this museum tells the story of coffee production in Chiapas, and Mexico generally, since its introduction as a commercial crop 160 years ago. Exhibits cover the Ruta del Café near Tapachula, plus early cultivation and processing methods – as contrasted with contemporary sustainable methods.

Parque de la Marimba

C Central Pte between 8a C Pte and 9a C Pte **Museo de la Marimba** Tues–Sun 10am–8pm • M$50

Unlike in many Mexican cities, the central plaza is not the true social centre. **Parque de la Marimba** is where evening crowds gather, often for live music, as well as to lounge in the various modern cafés around the perimeter. Real fans of marimba can visit the **Museo de la Marimba** on the corner, which highlights the history of the musical genre (displays in Spanish only).

Parque Madero

About 1km northeast of the centre **Museo Botánico** Tues–Fri 9am–3pm, Sat 9am–1pm • Free • **Museo Regional de Chiapas** Tues–Sun 9am–5pm • M$46 • **Museo de Paleontología** Tues–Fri 10am–5pm, Sat–Sun 11am–5pm • M$20

About 1km northeast of the centre, **Parque Madero** is another place where locals go to stroll in the late afternoon and evening. A promenade leads off 5a Avenida Norte Oriente, first passing the pleasant (and free to enter, being part of the park) **Jardín Botánico** and the less interesting **Museo Botánico** opposite, and on to the **Museo Regional de Chiapas**, which details the history of pre-Hispanic Chiapas and the results of the Conquest. The highlights are the intricately carved human fencers from the ruins of Chiapa de Corzo. At the end of the promenade is the city theatre and next to it the **Museo de Paleontología**, which displays local fossils, amber and the skeleton of a sabre-tooth tiger.

Zoológico Miguel Álvarez de Toro (ZOOMAT)

1a C Ote Sur, Francisco I Madero, 5km south of the centre • Tues–Sun 8.30am–5.30pm • M$30 • Bus #60, marked "Cerro Hueco" or "Zoológico", departs 1a C Ote Sur between Av 6a Sur and 7a Av Sur Ote, but can take up to 45min

If you're interested in local wildlife, it's worth heading out to the so-called **ZOOMAT (Zoológico Miguel Álvarez de Toro)**. It claims to have every species native to Chiapas, and as far as zoos go, it's not bad, with good-sized cages, natural vegetation and freshwater streams. A number of animals, including *guaqueques negros* (agoutis) – rodents about the size of a domestic cat – and large birds such as currasows and chachalacas, roam the zoo grounds. The *vivario* contains a vast collection of snakes, insects and spiders.

ARRIVAL AND DEPARTURE
TUXTLA GUTIÉRREZ

BY PLANE

Tuxtla's airport, Aeropuerto Ángel Albino Corzo, is inconveniently located 27km south of the city. All the major car rental companies and top hotels have desks in the arrivals hall, but there is nowhere to change money. There is a small Bancomer ATM tucked away in the departures hall upstairs, but this is often out of order. There's no bus to the city; buy taxi tickets at the desk in the arrivals hall (around M$250 to Tuxtla or to Chiapa de Corzo; both

35–45min). For San Cristóbal de las Casas, an ADO/OCC bus runs four times daily (1hr).

Destinations Cancún (5 weekly; 1hr 40min); Guadalajara (5 weekly; 2hr); Mexico City (10 daily; 1hr 50min); Monterrey (7 weekly; 2hr).

Airlines AeroMéxico, Belisario Dominguez 302, Plaza Bonampak (☎ 961 121 4379, ⊛ aeromexico.com); InterJet, Belisario Domínguez 1748 (☎ 800 011 2345, ⊛ interjet.com .mx).

BY BUS

First-class buses The large ADO/OCC station is on 5a Av Nte Pte, in the Plaza del Sol mall on the northwest side of town. Taxis to the centre cost around M$50. First-class buses to Villahermosa travel via the Puente Chiapas, which looks less direct but is much faster than going over the mountains. There is a TicketBus office on 2a C Pte Nte at 2a Av Pte Nte, to spare you the trip out to the station.

Destinations Cancún (6 daily; 19hr–20hr 55min); Ciudad Cuauhtémoc, for Guatemala (2 daily at 10.15am & 4.15pm; 4hr 25min–4hr 45min); Comitán, for Lagos de Montebello or the Guatemalan border (16 daily; 2hr 50min–3hr 10min); Mérida (5 daily; 13hr 25min–14hr 10min); Mexico City (11 daily; 13hr); Oaxaca (5 daily; 9hr 40min–10hr); Ocosingo (4 daily; 3hr 30min–3hr 50min); Palenque (5 daily; 6hr 10min–7hr 55min); San Cristóbal (every 30min–1hr; 1hr 10min); Tapachula (nearly every 30min; 5hr 30min–8hr); Tonalá (every 30min–1hr; 2hr 15min–4hr); Villahermosa (16 daily; 4hr 5min–5hr 15min).

Second-class buses and colectivos The main second-class terminal, the Central Camionera de Sur, is on 10a Av Sur Ote at 15a C Ote Sur. Autotransportes Tuxtla Gutiérrez (ATG) is the main company, serving San Cristóbal, Oaxaca, Villahermosa, Mérida, Palenque and Cancún. Scores of smaller companies and *colectivos* pull in here. *Colectivos* for Bochil and San Cristóbal depart from the 9a Av side. The most frequent service to San Cristóbal is with Omnibus, from a dedicated station on 4a Av Sur Oriente at 15a C Oriente Sur. For Chiapa de Corzo (30min), *colectivos* leave from the southeast corner of 1a Av Sur Ote at 5a C Ote Sur. Taxis from the Central Camionera to the centre cost around M$30.

BY CAR

For the ascent by car into the hills from Tonalá and the coast highway, a short toll highway (M$28) outside Arriaga bypasses about 20km of pretty but almost comically winding road.

11

GETTING AROUND

Car rental Try Hertz, Belisario Domínguez 1195, in the *Camino Real* hotel (☎961 617 7777, ⓦhertzmexico .com), and at the airport. Europcar (☎961 121 4922, ⓦeuropcar.com.mx) also has a central location, at Belisario Dominguez 2075, near the Walmart.

INFORMATION

Municipal tourist office at the Museo de la Marimba, Av Central Pte at 9a C (Mon–Fri 8am–8pm, Sat 8am–2pm; ☎961 612 5511). Also maintains kiosks on the plaza and at Parque Madero (both daily 10am–6pm).
Chiapas state tourist office Torre Chiapas, on Paso

Limón (daily 8am–7pm; ☎961 617 0550). Located a good way east in a high-rise. Security is tight, and parking nearly impossible, but if you need an English-speaker, it's worth a phone call.

ACCOMMODATION

Tuxtla has a reasonable selection of **places to stay**, with plenty of budget options, but they're a bit characterless, and if you arrive late in the day in busy seasons (especially Aug), you'll have to hunt for a room. Most budget hotels are on or around 2a C Nte Ote, while the city's smartest hotels – mostly chains like Marriott and Holiday Inn – are concentrated 3–4km west of the centre along Belisario Domínguez, convenient only if you have a car.

Casablanca 2a Av Nte Ote 251 ☎961 611 0305. One of the better budget options, the Casablanca has brightly painted rooms, most of them equipped with a/c and (optional) TVs, facing an inner palm-fringed garden. There's luggage storage as well. <u>M$450</u>
Fernando 2a Av Nte Ote 515 ☎961 613 1740. The best value of the options just east of the plaza, the Fernando is a modern hotel with some large, comfortable rooms, wooden furniture and TVs. Parking spaces are across the street. <u>M$550</u>
Hostal Tres Central C Central Nte 393 ☎961 611 3674, ⓦfacebook.com/trescentral. The best bet for backpackers in the city centre, this rarely full hostel has decent dorms and rooms (with either shared or private

bathrooms), a TV lounge, laundry facilities, and a terrace café. Dorm <u>M$150</u>; double <u>M$350</u>
Real Avenida Av Central Pte 1230 ☎961 612 2347, ⓦrealavenida.com.mx. Spotless and vaguely chic rooms, each with TVs, phones and wi-fi access. The only downside is the relatively long walk into the centre (though it is close to the Parque de la Marimba). <u>M$965</u>
Regional San Marcos 2a C Ote Sur 176, at 1a Av Sur Ote ☎961 613 1940. Located near the cathedral, the *Regional* underwent a renovation a few years back which has brightened things up a bit. The rooms are small, but there's a/c, plus a decent restaurant and bar. <u>M$550</u>

EATING

The centre of Tuxtla has dozens of reasonably appetizing **restaurants**, and you need never wander more than a block or so either side of Av Central to find something in every price range, including juice bars and bakeries. The very **cheapest** places are in the Mercado Díaz Ordáz, C Central Sur, between 3a and 4a Av Sur Oriente; there's also a string of pleasant, inexpensive lunch operations on 1a Av Nte, just west of C Central, with set menus for M$50 or so. Most popular for socializing and people-watching are the terrace restaurants under the arches on **Plaza San Marcos** behind the cathedral, and, for a younger scene, the cafés and bars around **Parque de la Marimba**.

Café Avenida Av Central Pte 230. An authentic Mexican coffee shop where they grind their own beans and elderly men sip black coffee (M$15–30) to a background of mariachi music and unhurried waiters. Daily 6.30am–5pm.

Las Canteras 2a Av Nte Ote, at 1a C Pte ☎ 961 611 4310. An open, airy restaurant serving traditional but refined *chiapaneco* cookery, often accompanied by live marimba music – don't expect a quiet meal here. Mains from M$100–150, and there's a good-value set lunch. Daily 10am–midnight.

La Gran Muralla 2a Av Nte Pte 334 ☎ 961 613 0899. "The Great Wall" is a passable Cantonese restaurant, for anyone needing a break from Mexican food: the range of dishes (M$60–130) is so vast, it seems to want to be Tuxtla's Chinatown all by itself. Daily noon–11pm.

★ **El Horno Mágico** C 2a Ote Nte 116, at Av Central ☎ 961 611 1553. Two French expats who know a thing or two about baking run this café, a branch of a place in San

Cristóbal de las Casas (see p.671). Pastries and breads (M$11–40) are fresh daily, along with good coffee and juices. Daily 8am–10pm.

Naturalissimo 6a C Pte Nte 124, just off Av Central Pte ☎ 961 611 0931, ⓦ naturalissimo.mx. A bright vegetarian chain restaurant that's inexpensive (about M$40–60 for most dishes), clean and modern. The daily set lunch is a particularly good deal, and there are daily specials (for example, two-for-one ice creams and pizzas on Wed). Daily 7am–10pm.

★ **Las Pichanchas** Av Central Ote 837, east of the plaza between calles 7 and 8 Ote ☎ 961 612 5351, ⓦ laspichanchas.com.mx. A bit touristy, but a great place for dinner, with marimba all evening, folk dancing (Sun 4–5pm) and excellent *chiapaneco* food all dished up in a two-storey house with a courtyard. Try the *platón de botana regional* (a selection of local cheese, sausage and more). Most dishes are M$70–100. Daily 1pm–midnight.

DIRECTORY

Banks There are plenty of banks along Av Central, with a branch of HSBC right on the plaza (C Central Nte 137). **Laundry** Lavandería Zaac, 2a Av Nte Pte 456 (closed Sun).

Post office The main post office is at 1a Av Nte Ote, near the Plaza Cívica (Mon–Fri 8.30am–4pm, Sat 8.30am–1pm).

Chiapa de Corzo and around

An elegant town of about seventy thousand, **CHIAPA DE CORZO** overlooks the **Río Grijalva**. As it's barely twenty minutes east of Tuxtla (and an easy taxi ride from the airport), it makes a scenic alternative to the big city. It's best known as the starting point for boat rides through the **Cañón del Sumidero** (see p.664), and has quite a tourist scene during Mexican holiday times. The first Spanish city in Chiapas, it was officially founded in 1528, though it had already been an important centre in pre-Classic times. A stele found here bears the oldest **Long Count date** yet discovered, corresponding to December 7, 36 BC. The ruins that remain are on private land behind the Nestlé plant, at the far end of 21 de Octubre on the edge of town (see opposite).

Fuente Colonial
Plaza Ángel Albino Corzo

The most striking feature of Chiapa de Corzo is the elaborate sixteenth-century fountain that dominates the central Plaza Ángel Albino Corzo. Built of brick in the Mudéjar style, in the shape of the Spanish crown, **Fuente Colonial** is one of the most impressive surviving early colonial monuments in Mexico. It has become a state symbol – you may recognize it from Chiapas licence plates. Just behind the fountain, the huge tree bursting from its confines is **La Pochota**, a national monument to the suffering of the *indígenas* under Spanish rule, said to have been standing here when the town was founded.

Casa Museo Ángel Albino Corzo

Northwest side of the plaza • Daily 10am–2pm & 6–9pm • Free

This museum is the former residence of the national reformer for whom the town was named. Housing an interesting jumble of period furniture and historical artefacts, it features two cannons used in the so-called Pastry War against France in 1838 (explanations in Spanish only).

Templo de Santo Domingo de Guzmán and Centro Cultural

South of the plaza • Cultural centre Tues–Sun 10am–5pm • Free

On the southern side of the plaza, *portales* (arcades) house a series of reasonably priced handicraft stores, which continue south along 5 de Febrero towards the river and the *embarcadero*. Behind the arcades is the lovely **Templo de Santo Domingo de Guzmán** and ex-convent, with a tall nave and timbered ceiling. Forming part of the complex, behind the main entrance to the church, is the **Centro Cultural**, an ambitious project that is gradually converting the old convent into a series of tasteful galleries and art studios. Upstairs on the first floor, the **Museo de Laca** (same hours) recounts the history of lacquer-making in Mexico, from pre-Hispanic times to the present, featuring various lacquered objects from gourds to pots and chests.

Chiapa de Corzo ruins

3km northeast of Chiapa de Corzo plaza • Tues–Sun 9am–5pm • Take any microbus heading east, and get off at the junction with Hidalgo and follow the signs, walking 15min to an unmarked gate; it's also possible to walk from the plaza, passing the sixteenth-century church ruin of San Sebastián

On an ancient trade route high above the Río Grijalva lie the ruins of **Chiapa de Corzo**. Having begun as a farming settlement in the early pre-Classic period (1400–850 BC), it was, by the late pre-Classic period (450 BC–250 AD), the largest centre of population in the region. The ruins are still being excavated and aren't immediately impressive. Although it is the longest continually occupied site in Chiapas, comprising some two hundred structures, what you see today are mainly low pyramids, walls and courtyards, sitting on private property split among several owners and sliced in two by the Panamerican Highway (Hwy-190).

ARRIVAL AND DEPARTURE   CHIAPA DE CORZO

By bus Long-distance buses from Tuxtla typically stop only on the main highway (about 4km north of town) on request. At peak times, you may find a *colectivo* waiting; otherwise you'll need to walk or take a private taxi (about M$40–50) to the centre.

By combi Shared vans and *colectivos* to Chiapa del Corzo from Tuxtla (southeast corner of 1a Av Sur Ote at 5a C Ote Sur) enter the town along Av Cuauhtémoc, north of the plaza, terminating near the Nestlé plant

– get off at C Mexicanidad, or where the driver says "parque", and turn right for the plaza. Heading back to Tuxtla, pick them up along the top of the plaza (Av 21 de Octubre).

By taxi If you want to carry on to San Cristóbal, the only option is to hire a taxi (about M$400–450). From Chiapa de Corzo to Tuxtla airport it's around M$250 – the same as from central Tuxtla, which makes Chiapa de Corzo a decent alternative place to stay the night before a flight.

ACCOMMODATION AND EATING

For **food**, don't miss the vendors near the **market** (southeast of the plaza), who specialize in *cochito horneado*, chile-roasted pork in a rich broth. Several **restaurants** specialize in *chiapaneco* cuisine, though they tend to be a little overpriced. The *embarcadero* along the river is a pretty spot for a drink, though nothing differentiates the somewhat pricey seafood restaurants here, and most start to wind down early.

Los Ángeles Julian Grajales 2, southeast corner of the plaza ☎ 961 616 0048, ⊛ hotel-chiapas.com. The courtyard may double as a car park, but the small rooms here are comfortable, with quiet a/c systems. The ones on the upper floor are larger, most with nice views of the

plaza. M$430

El Campanario Coronel Urbina 5, behind the municipal building east of the plaza ☎ 961 616 0390. The best dining choice in town, though there's not a great deal of competition. *El Campanario* has an inviting garden and courtyard, colourful flags hanging from the ceilings, and a menu filled with regional fare (mains around M$100–150). Daily 9am–7pm.

La Ceiba Domingo Ruíz 300, three blocks west of the plaza ☎961 616 0389, ⓦlaceibahotel.com. Probably the smartest hotel option in Chiapa de Corzo, La Ceiba has several floors enclosing a tranquil palm-filled garden, small pool and caged parrots. Rooms are simple but comfortable, with a/c and TVs. M$900

Los Corredores Madero 35, southwest corner of the plaza ☎961 616 0760. This bright place, its walls covered in portraits and pictures of market life, offers Chiapas favourites such as dried beef with a chile-laced pumpkin seed sauce (*pepita con tasajo*), plus grilled, fried or baked fish (mains around M$100). Daily 7.30am–7pm.

Cañón del Sumidero

10km north of Chiapa de Corzo • From the plaza in Tuxtla, Autobús Panorámico (Sat & Sun 9am & 1pm; 3hr 30min; M$100; minimum five passengers) runs a bus along the canyon rim; for boats, see box below

On the highway east from Chiapa de Corzo towards San Cristóbal, you catch occasional glimpses of the Río Grijalva and the lower reaches of one of Mexico's deepest canyons, with walls up to 1000m high in some places. Its rock walls are sprinkled with patches of bright green vegetation and odd rock formations, and carved out with shallow caves. A drive along the rim passes *miradores* (lookout points) that are unnervingly close to the edge – the most dramatic is at Las Coyotas. A boat ride up the river from Chiapa de Corzo (see box below) is just as awe-inspiring, snaking through the whole gorge up to the Chicoasén Dam, which forms a lake at the northern end. Along the way are several waterfalls, including the remarkable El Árbol de Navidad, where calcareous formations covered in algae resemble a Christmas tree. Crocodiles and spider monkeys can often be spotted, along with pelicans, egrets and cormorants.

The one drawback to the water-level view from the boat is the undeniable amount of rubbish in the water that collects along the stagnant edges of the canyons. It's periodically rounded up and disposed of, but it's particularly bad during the rainy season, when the water is highest. But this shouldn't deter you from seeing the greatest geological wonder in Chiapas.

Bochil and Simojovel

Just beyond Chiapa de Corzo, Hwy-195 cuts off to the north. It's an inconvenient route, as there's no continuous bus service, but for those with time and inclination, it's a part of mountainous Chiapas that's well off the tourist track. The road climbs through mountains wreathed in cloud to **BOCHIL**, some 60km from Tuxtla and a centre for the **Tzotzil Maya**.

From there, another 40km up, **SIMOJOVEL** is at the head of a spectacular valley. The pretty town is the source of most of the amber you'll find sold in local markets, and plenty of shops sell it, often for a bit less than elsewhere in the state.

ARRIVAL AND ACCOMMODATION   BOCHIL AND SIMOJOVEL

By bus and combi Second-class buses run from Tuxtla over the mountains to Pichucalco in southern Tabasco, passing through Bochil on the way. From Pichucalco, you can catch another eastbound for Teapa. From Bochil, *combis* run regularly up to Simojovel.

Posada San Pedro 1a C Pte Nte, a block from the plaza, Bochil ☎919 653 0062. One of a couple of simple places to stay, *Posada San Pedro* has a collection of basic rooms set out around a courtyard; to find it, head for Banamex at the top of the plaza and turn right. M$200

CHIAPA DE CORZO BOAT TOURS

In Chiapa de Corzo, several companies offer **boat trips** down the canyon, all for around the same price (8am–5pm; M$190–200/person). The first office you reach is Turística de Grijalva (☎961 600 6402), on the west side of the plaza. Or you can head straight south down the street to the *embarcadero*, where other companies operate. During Mexican vacation times, boats fill with the requisite ten people almost immediately, and it doesn't matter where you buy your ticket. In slower times, it's best to show up early and go from company to company to see which boat is closest to full. Tours last a couple of hours.

THE CHURCH IN THE WATER

In mid-October 2015 locals living near the Nezahualcóyotl reservoir in the far west of Chiapas reported a ghostly sight: the ruins of a sunken sixteenth-century church had emerged from the waters, which had plunged by 25m during a drought. The Temple of Santiago – also known as the Temple of Quechula – was submerged in 1966, when the Río Grijalva was dammed to generate hydroelectric power, creating a reservoir spanning almost 1000 sq km. The church had lost its roof, but its 10m walls, arches, columns and hall were all in remarkably good shape. It was built in 1564 by a group of Dominican friars led by Bartolomé de las Casas, who later became the first Bishop of Chiapas and – after initially supporting colonial policies – a fierce critic of the Spanish subjugation of Mexico's indigenous peoples. A town subsequently emerged around the Temple of Santiago, but in the 1770s a plague hit the region, and it was largely abandoned. The church, which last emerged from the waters during a drought in 2002, became something of a tourist attraction, with enterprising fishermen offering tourists impromptu boat trips out to the ruin before the water levels rose again.

El Triunfo Biosphere Reserve

Cradled within the slopes of the Sierra Madre de Chiapas, on the northern edge of the Soconusco, this dense cloud forest is a refuge for hundreds of species of birds, including the rare quetzal, the great currasow and the azure-rumped tanager, as well as (hard-to-spot) pumas, jaguars and Geoffroy's spider monkeys. Very few people come this way, so it's best to contact the reserve organization several weeks in advance to make arrangements. The jumping-off point is the town of **JALTENANGO**, also known as **Ángel Albino Corzo**, ringed with coffee plantations.

ARRIVAL AND DEPARTURE   EL TRIUNFO BIOSPHERE RESERVE

By bus Buses to Jaltenango leave Tuxtla several times a day (3–4hr) from the Cuxtepeques y Anexas station at C 10 Ote Nte and Av 3 Nte Ote.

By tour Based in Tuxtla, the Fondo de Conservación El Triunfo (**☎**961 125 1122, **ⓦ**fondoeltriunfo.org), at San Cristóbal 8, 3km northwest of the Plaza Cívica, is responsible for tourism. It runs four-day packages that include transport from Tuxtla, lodging at the simple *Campamento El Triunfo* in the mountains, a guide at the coffee *fincas* and in the wilderness, and porters, for about M$5500/person.

San Cristóbal de las Casas and around

The unofficial capital of highland Chiapas, **SAN CRISTÓBAL** – or Jovel, as many locals call it – is a major stop on the travel circuit. But the city, a clutch of tile-roofed houses huddled together in the bowl of a valley, has held up to tourism well. The modern edges of the city don't make a good first impression, but the centre has none of this unchecked development: pedestrianized central streets foster a low-key social scene, with a cosmopolitan mélange of small bars and restaurants that thrive on a certain degree of leftist-revolutionary cachet. It's also a great base for studying at one of the numerous Spanish-language schools.

San Cristóbal is also a prime base for exploring highland Chiapas, perhaps the most scenic part of Mexico. The densely forested mountains give way to dramatic gorges, jungle valleys flush with orchids, vividly coloured birds and raucous monkeys. In addition, the area's relative isolation has allowed the **indigenous population** to carry on with their lives little affected by Catholicism and modern commercialism – and this includes clothing and craft traditions as brilliantly coloured and rich as the wildlife (though older people in particular maintain a traditional aversion to photography – be sure to ask permission first, and respect the answer). Villages to the west of San Cristóbal are generally **Tzotzil**-speaking, and those to the east speak **Tzeltal**, but each village has developed its own identity in terms of costume, crafts and linguistics. Some simple words are given in the box on p.669.

11

Just 75km from Tuxtla, up the fast toll highway that breaks through the clouds into pine forests, San Cristóbal is almost 1700m higher, at 2100m. Even in August, the evenings are chilly – be prepared.

Brief history

San Cristóbal was designed as a Spanish stronghold against what was an often-hostile indigenous population – the attack here by Zapatista rebels in January 1994 (see box, p.651, for more on the Zapatistas) was only the latest in a long series of uprisings.

The colonial era

It took the Spaniards, led by conquistador Diego de Mazariegos, four years to pacify the area enough to establish a town here in 1528. The so-called Villareal de Chiapa de los Españoles was more widely known as Villaviciosa (Evil City) for the oppressive exploitation exercised by its colonists. In 1544, Bartolomé de las Casas was appointed bishop, and he promptly took an energetic stance in defence of the native population, playing a similar role to that of Bishop Vasco de Quiroga in Pátzcuaro (see box, p.291). His name is still held in something close to reverence by the local population. Throughout the colonial era,

11

SAN CRISTÓBAL DE LAS CASAS

■ DRINKING & NIGHTLIFE
Latino's	3
Makia	2
Café Bar Revolución	1

● SHOPPING
Abuelita Books	3
Librería La Pared	5
Metalistería Hermosillo	6
Museo del Ámbar	4
Sna Jolobil	1
Taller Leñateros	2

● EATING
Cacao Nativa	12
La Casa del Pan	7
Los Ches	4
El Horno Mágico	3
El Kiosco	8
Madre Tierra	13
Museo Café	2
Normita	10
Te Quiero Verde	11
Teddy's Coffee Factory	9
TierrAdentro	5
Trattoria Italiana	1
La Viña de Bacco	6

■ ACCOMMODATION
Barón de las Casas	8
Casa Margarita	7
Casa Mexicana	5
Casa Na-Bolom	4
Diego de Mazariegos	6
Fray Bartolomé de las Casas	11
La Joya Hotel	9
Rancho San Nicolás	12
Rossco Backpackers Hostel	1
Santa Clara	10
Sol y Luna	2
Villas Casa Morada	3
Villa Real II	13

San Cristóbal was the capital of Chiapas (at that time part of Guatemala), but lost this status in 1892 as a result of its continued reluctance to accept the union with Mexico.

San Cristóbal de las Casas today

Independent as the indigenous groups are, economic and social status in the mountains around the city lags far behind the rest of Mexico. This is in part due to the long duration of the *encomienda* system of forced labour, which remained in place here long after the end of Spanish colonialism. Many small villages still operate at the barest subsistence level. It's worth noting that many indigenous communities and some local transport operators refuse to observe the **time change** in summer, preferring *la hora vieja* – the old time, or, as some savvy marketers have dubbed it, "Zapatista time".

Plaza 31 de Marzo

Usually referred to simply as *el parque*, this plaza is the heart of the city, encircled by a cluster of attractive colonial mansions and the sixteenth-century **cathedral**, which boasts an ornate, pale orange facade, impressive *artesanado* ceiling and grand *retablo*. The finest of the mansions is **La Casa de las Sirenas**, now home to the *Hotel Santa Clara*, which is said to have been built by the conquistador Andrés de la Tovilla in the mid-sixteenth century and has a very elaborate doorway around the corner on Insurgentes. In the middle of the plaza there's a bandstand and a café.

Andador Eclesiástico and around

Cutting through the centre is the **Andador Eclesiástico**, a pedestrianized thoroughfare that connects the Templo del Carmen, 300m south of the plaza (on Hidalgo), to Santo Domingo, 400m to the north (on 20 de Noviembre). It's lined with touristy shops, restaurants, cafés and ice-cream parlours. The **Templo del Carmen** stands opposite the Arco del Carmen, which spans the road, and once served as the gateway to the city. Built in 1677, it shows a slight Mudéjar (Moorish) influence. The church is not particularly inspiring architecturally, but on the other side of the arch, the **Centro Cultural El Carmen** (daily 8am–8pm; free) contains a couple of galleries of contemporary painting and craftwork around gardens filled with traditional Maya plants. Considering the amount of artistic activity in and around San Cristóbal, these sights are pretty disappointing, partly due to a serious fire in 1993 that destroyed much of the city's artwork.

Templo de Santo Domingo Guzmán

20 de Noviembre, at Real de Mexicanos • Daily 7am–8pm • Free

This church is the most intrinsically interesting in San Cristóbal. Constructed between 1547 and 1551, its lovely pinkish Baroque stucco facade combines Oaxacan and Guatemalan styles. Inside, it's gilded everywhere, with a wonderfully ornate pulpit – if you see it in the evening, by the light of candles, you might well believe it's solid gold.

Museo Centro Cultural de los Altos

20 de Noviembre, at Real de Mexicanos, next to the Templo de Santo Domingo Guzmán • Tues–Sun 9am–6pm • M$52

Adjacent to the Templo de Santo Domingo, in the old convent space (look for it just to the left of the convent's main entrance, beyond Sna Jolobil; see p.673), the **Museo Centro Cultural de los Altos** has recently reopened after refurbishment. The exhibits tell the story of the city, with vivid portrayals of how the Indians fared under colonial rule.

Mercado José Castillo Tielemans

General Utrilla north of the Templo Santo Domingo • Daily 6am–6pm

San Cristóbal's daily market is an absorbing place, largely because its chaos and the crowds in its souk-like lanes contrast with the rather manicured centre, where indigenous people in traditional dress can seem a bit like part of the scenic background. Here, though, commerce is the important thing, and every villager in town for the day

11

participates – arguing over prices of fried ants, selecting the best live chickens, picking through piles of dried fish. The market is far bigger than it first appears, with sections for housewares and clothing in a network of narrow covered alleys.

Casa Na-Bolom

Vicente Guerrero 33 • **Museum** Daily 10am–6pm; tours in English at 4.30pm • M\$40, M\$50 with a tour; tickets available from gift shop opposite in Jardín de Jaguar • **Library** Daily 10am–4pm • Free

Behind Templo de Santo Domingo Guzmán, Chiapa de Corzo leads east towards the **Casa Na-Bolom**, an ethnographic museum also housing one of the best hotels in San Cristóbal and a **library** of anthropological texts. This was the home of Danish explorer and anthropologist Frans Blom, who died in 1963, and his Swiss wife, Gertrude, an anthropologist and photographer who died in 1993. Today it's renowned as a centre for the study of the region's indigenous cultures, particularly of the isolated Lacandón Maya. The centre is overseen by the Asociación Cultural Na-Bolom, which arranges some small-scale volunteer cultural and agricultural projects, though you'll need to speak Spanish to participate (see the hotel review on p.670 for contact info).

Jardín de Jaguar

Located across the road from the main complex, the gift shop-cum-ticket office in the **Jardín de Jaguar** contains a few exhibits and information boards about the various ethnic groups in Chiapas. In one corner is a replica of a traditional highlands house, made with wooden walls covered with mud and a roof thatched with grass.

The museum

The main museum occupies rooms set around a series of beautiful courtyards – it's not particularly large, and a guided tour can be illuminating, if you're able to time your visit for one. The museum exhibits discoveries from the site of **Moxviquil** (see below) and explains the history and culture of the Chiapas highlands and the Lacandón forest. There's also a collection of items belonging to Frans Blom, including the detailed maps for which he is known. After the tour, you can watch a film (mainly in English) about the life of the Bloms and the ecology, culture and politics of Chiapas.

Museo de la Medicina Maya

General Utrilla, 500m north of the centre • Mon–Fri 9am–6pm, Sat & Sun 10am–5pm • M\$20

This museum is an absorbing journey through the world of Maya medicine, complete with medicinal plants growing in the gardens and a herbal pharmacy on site to dispense remedies. You'll learn more than you ever thought to ask about Maya midwifery, and it's a great place to visit before heading out to the church at San Juan Chamula, as it explains a lot of the rituals you might see performed there.

The churches of Guadalupe and San Cristóbal

On either side of town, two churches perch on hilltop sites: **Templo de Guadalupe** to the east and **Templo de San Cristóbal** to the west. Neither offers a great deal architecturally, but the climbs are worth it for the views – San Cristóbal, especially, is at the top of a dauntingly long and steep flight of steps. It's best not to climb up to either of these relatively isolated spots after dark; there have been reports of women being harassed at San Cristóbal church.

Moxviquil

1.5km north of San Cristóbal centre via Av Yajalón • **Reserve** Tues–Sun 9am–4pm • M\$30 • **Greenhouse** Wed–Sun 9am–6pm, later in summer • Free • ☎ 967 678 5727, ⓦ moxviquil.org • Follow Av Yajalón north to the ring road (about 30min), then bear left; you will see a sign marked Reserva Ecológica; a taxi costs around M\$60

The completely deserted and ruined Maya ceremonial site of **Moxviquil** is part of a small forest reserve on the northern edge of town that makes a pleasant excursion of a

USEFUL WORDS IN TZOTZIL AND TZELTAL

	Tzotzil	Tzeltal
To ask permission	Chíkhelav	Ya shka shan
Hello	Kúshee	Bish chee
Goodbye	Batkun	Bónish
Please	Avokoluk	Há wokolook
Thank you	Kalaval	Wókolawal
Sorry/Excuse me	Tsik bunjoomul	Pasbón
Yes	Chabal	Heech
No	Moo yuk	Ho'o

few hours on foot – it's a great opportunity to explore outside town without joining a tour or getting on a bus. If you're particularly interested in the ruins, study the plans at the Casa Na-Bolom (see opposite) before you go, so you'll be able to see the logic behind the piles of rough limestone. From the entrance, a clearly marked loop trail covers about 3km in the forest, climbing fairly steeply. The ruins, such as they are, are reached via a faint spur trail (to the left if you're walking clockwise around the trail) that leads to a ridge, then a flat hilltop.

11

If you're alert during your hike, you may see wild orchids along the trail. And if you miss them, you can still see them at Orquídeas Moxviquil, the reserve's lovely orchid greenhouse and botanic gardens, at the base of the hill near the entrance. They preserve some very rare species from around Chiapas.

ARRIVAL AND DEPARTURE

SAN CRISTÓBAL DE LAS CASAS

BY BUS

First-class buses For destinations in the state and throughout the Yucatán, buses arrive at and leave from the ADO/OCC terminal, on the Carretera Panamericana (Hwy-190) on the southern edge of town (a M$30 taxi ride to the city centre). For the centre, turn right and head seven blocks north on Insurgentes to the plaza. South across the highway, AEXA runs buses to similar destinations. You can also buy first-class tickets from the TicketBus office (Mon–Sat 7am–11pm, Sun 9am–5pm; ☎ 967 678 0921) in the centre at Real de Guadalupe 14. For Villahermosa, it's usually easier to get any bus to Tuxtla and change there. Buses to the Yucatán coast go via Chetumal, where you can catch connections to Belize.

Destinations Cancún (17hr 45min–19hr 40min) via Chetumal (3 daily at 12.15pm, 3.45pm & 4pm; 12hr); Ciudad Cuauhtémoc, for Guatemala (3 daily at 11.30am, 4pm & 5.30pm; 3hr 5min–3hr 30min); Comitán (24 daily; 1hr 40min–2hr 5min); Mérida (12hr 35min) via Campeche (1 daily at 6.20pm; 10hr); Mexico City (6 daily; 13hr 45min–14hr 40min); Oaxaca (4 daily at 6.05pm, 8pm, 9pm &

10.45pm; 10hr 45min–11hr 20min); Ocosingo (10 daily; 2hr 10min); Palenque (10 daily; 4hr 50min–5hr 35min); Tapachula (9 daily; 7hr–8hr 25min); Tuxtla Gutiérrez (roughly hourly; 1hr 5min); Tuxtla Gutiérrez airport (5 daily; 1hr 5min); Villahermosa (1 daily at 10am; 6hr 30min).

Second-class buses Most stop along Hwy-190 to either side of the OCC first-class terminal, and AEXA, across the highway, runs some second-class services as well. The exception is the service for Bochil – these buses are just north of the market area.

To Guatemala Travel agency Chincultik, Real de Guadalupe 34 (☎ 967 678 0957), runs a daily bus to Guatemala City.

BY COMBI

Shared vans are a good alternative for nearby destinations such as Tuxtla Gutiérrez and Comitán – they tout for customers outside the bus stations on the main highway.

BY CAR

The toll highway to/from Tuxtla Gutiérrez costs M$48.

GETTING AROUND

By bike & moped An enjoyable way to get out to the surrounding villages is on a bike or motorbike. Los Pingüinos, Ecuador 4B (☎ 967 678 0202, ⓦ bikemexico .com/pinguinos), and Croozy, Belisario Domínguez 7 (☎ 967 683 2223), have bikes for around M$160/day. The former offers tours, while the latter also has scooters

(M$400/day) and motorbikes (M$500/day) for rent; note that they don't come with insurance, so if you get into an accident, you'll have to cover the costs.

By taxi Taxis within the centre should cost no more than M$30–40.

INFORMATION

State tourist office In the Palacio Municipal (Mon–Fri 8am–8pm, Sat 9am–8pm, Sun 9am–2pm; ☎967 678 1467, ⓦturismochiapas.gob.mx). Has free city maps, up-to-date lists of hotels, bus times and event information, but no English-speaking staff.

Municipal tourist office Next door to the state tourist office (daily 8am–8pm; ☎967 678 0665), and likewise lacks English-speakers.

Website ⓦagendasancristobal.com is a useful website on the city, with info on restaurants, bars, hotels and shops.

TOURS AND ACTIVITIES

Day tours San Cristóbal has dozens of agencies, most doing the same four standard tours: San Juan Chamula and San Lorenzo de Zinacantán; the Cañón del Sumidero; Lagos de Montebello; and Palenque and Agua Azul. Some will also arrange tours further afield to Bonampak and Yaxchilán. Nichim Tours, Hermanos Domínguez 5-A (☎967 678 3520, ⓦchiapastoursyexpediciones.com), has a broader range of tours than most; Explora, 1 de Marzo 30 (☎967 674 6660, ⓦexplorachiapas.com), specializes in trips to the Lacandón forest (see p.692), including rafting,

kayaking and caving expeditions. Alex and Raul Tours (☎967 678 3741, ⓦalexyraultours.wordpress.com) run good-value, culturally sensitive tours (M$200) to Chamula and Zinacantán; tours leave daily at 9.30am; meet at the wooden cross in front of the cathedral.

Horseriding Casa Utrilla (☎967 100 9611) runs trips to Chamula, leaving daily from the Chilam Balam bookstore, General Utrilla 3, at 9am & 12.30pm. If you phone ahead, they'll pick you up from your hotel (M$200).

ACCOMMODATION

Vast numbers of visitors and competition for business mean that San Cristóbal has some very good-value **hotels**. There are a few reliable places around the ADO/OCC terminal, but walking up Insurgentes to the plaza, you'll pass more establishments in all price ranges. Most of the best **budget options** are found in the streets east of the plaza, particularly along Real de Guadalupe and around. An ever-larger proportion of hotels here call themselves "**posadas**", and most live up to the convivial ambience this is presumably meant to convey, but it's always worth seeing your room before you pay. Even the most basic places now have hot water, though not necessarily all of the time. Nights can be pleasantly cool in summer, but cold in winter, so make sure there are enough blankets. For **longer stays**, check out the many notice boards in the bus stations, language schools and popular cafés, where you'll find rooms and even whole houses for rent.

HOTELS AND GUESTHOUSES

Barón de las Casas Belisario Domínguez 2 ☎967 678 0881, ⓔhotelbaron@hotmail.com. A well-run budget hotel with a bit of colonial charm, one block east of the plaza. The rooms here are simple, with tiled floors and spotless attached bathrooms with plenty of hot water. The owners also speak English. M$550

Casa Margarita Real de Guadalupe 34 ☎967 678 0957, ⓔhotelesmargarita@tourshotel.com.mx. Justifiably popular guesthouse with comfortable rooms set around a patio. The location couldn't be more central (though this does mean that rooms at the front can be a bit noisy). There's a slightly smarter, sister hotel, *Parador Margarita*, at Flores 39. M$950

Casa Mexicana 28 de Agosto 1 ☎967 678 0698, ⓦhotelcasamexicana.com. Charming converted colonial-era townhouse with spacious, wood-beamed en suites set around a lush garden and terrace. There's a sauna, a restaurant-bar, small gallery and a craft shop. A fine choice all round. M$1600

★**Casa Na-Bolom** Vicente Guerrero 33 ☎967 678 1421, ⓦnabolom.org. Offers very comfortable rooms with fireplaces and private bathrooms around courtyards, as well as lovely private cottages in the tranquil gardens. All are decorated with textiles, artefacts and photos taken

by the scholars who founded the place (see p.668). Rates include breakfast (with organic produce from the garden) and entry to the museum. M$1350

Diego de Mazariegos 5 de Febrero 1 ☎967 678 0833, ⓦdiegodemazariegos.com. San Cristóbal's most polished colonial hotel, set in two buildings on either side of General Utrilla. Spacious rooms – all featuring a fireplace, antique furniture and beautifully tiled bathrooms – are arranged around attractive courtyards. Book ahead, as it's often busy with tour groups. M$1500

Fray Bartolomé de las Casas Niños Héroes 2, at Insurgentes ☎967 678 0932, ⓔhotelfraybartolome @prodigy.net.mx. Split into two sections, *Fray Bartolomé de las Casas* has a charming older wing, arranged around a pretty courtyard with a central fountain. The newer section, however, is far less appealing. M$460

La Joya Hotel Madero 43A ☎967 631 4832, ⓦlajoyahotelsancristobal.com. Swish boutique hotel, bang in the centre of town, with five elegant suites decked out with working fireplaces, antiques and pieces of art; three of them have private balconies or terraces. Two-night minimum stay. Book well in advance. US$163 (M$2795)

Santa Clara Insurgentes 1, at the corner of the plaza ☎967 678 1140, ⓔhotelstaclara@hotmail.com. The spacious, plant-filled patio and lobby of this colonial mansion are adorned with period artefacts, though the rooms are a bit worn. Its heated pool is a treat, though, and big discounts are often available if you pay in cash. The hotel couldn't be more central, but this does mean noise is an issue. M$850

Sol y Luna Tonalá 27 📞 967 678 5727, 🌐 solylunainn .com. For a very private-feeling space, book one of the two large rooms at this beautifully decorated guesthouse, each with a double bed and wood-burning stove, one en suite, the other with the bathroom just outside. There's also a communal kitchen. Art and cookery classes, and horseriding trips, can be organized. US$75 (M$1285)

Villas Casa Morada Diego Dugelay 45 📞 967 674 5449, 🌐 casamorada.com.mx. A top-end hotel with ten artfully decorated, well-equipped rooms (the suites are well worth the US$20–30 extra), as well as a good restaurant-bar serving Mexican and Italian dishes (room service is available), and a garden area to relax in. US$105 (M$1800)

Villa Real II Benito Juárez 24 📞 967 678 4485. Comfortable, well-furnished, carpeted rooms all with private bathrooms, TV and access to parking. Sister hotel

Villa Real I, down the road at Juárez 8, is in a category cheaper, but much less pleasant. M$850

HOSTELS AND CAMPING

Rancho San Nicolás 2km east of the centre via Francisco León 📞 967 678 0057. The closest official campsite, open year-round and offering twenty sites, twelve with full hook-ups for RVs, as well as rustic dorm rooms in cottages and cabañas with shared toilets but plenty of hot water. Dorms M$90; cabañas M$450; camping M$65/person; RV spot M$90/person

★ **Rossco Backpackers Hostel** Real de Mexicanos 16 📞 967 674 0525, 🌐 backpackershostel.com.mx. One of the best hostels in Chiapas, with enthusiastic English-speaking owners, clean, renovated dorms (4- to 14-beds; there's a separate one for women) and private rooms. There are also free breakfasts, lockers, TV lounger and common room, daily use of a gym, Spanish lessons and a cosy campfire in the garden most evenings. Dorms M$139; doubles M$450

EATING

San Cristóbal has no lack of places to eat, with a huge variety of economical **restaurants** in the streets immediately east of the plaza, especially on Madero. Where the city really shines, however, is in lively, more international places with a bohemian feel and enticing menus with plenty of **vegetarian** options. A battery of sweets-sellers regularly sets up under the *portales* on the west side of the plaza, and a much smaller, more locally used plaza north on Belisario Domínguez often has snack carts and stands selling clove-spiked *ponche*, a warm pineapple drink that's great on a chilly night.

CAFÉS, CHEAP EATS AND SNACKS

Cacao Nativa Hidalgo 14 🌐 cacaonativa.com. A great place for a chilly evening, *Cacao Nativa* specializes in chocolate in all its forms, with the hot, drinking variety (M$26–50) a must-sample: choose from 33%, 50%, 67% and 100% cacao strengths. There's also pastries, desserts, biscuits and chocolates, if you need a further sugar hit. *Cacao Nativa* has a few other branches around town. Daily 8/9am–8/9pm.

La Casa del Pan Real de Guadalupe 55 📞 967 678 7215, 🌐 casadelpan.com. A superb range of reasonably priced vegetarian (and vegan) food and baked goods, made with local, organic ingredients. Breakfast/brunch options (M$20–60) are particularly good. It's popular with expat development workers, and there's often live music or film screenings at night. Mon–Sat 8am–10pm, Sun 9am–5pm.

El Horno Mágico General Utrilla 7, just north of the plaza 📞 967 135 8064. The facade of "the Magic Oven" may be Maya, but the goods inside testify to baking skills honed in France. There's a wonderful selection of baguettes, croissants, pains au chocolat and other pastries (M$11–40). There's another branch in Tuxtla (see p.662). Daily 8am–8.30pm.

El Kiosco In the plaza 📞 961 631 5154. In a great location under the bandstand, where you can enjoy a

coffee or alcoholic drink (beer M$25–35, cocktail M$55–75) at the outdoor tables and watch the world go by; there's often music and dancing in the evening. Daily 8am–10/11pm.

Museo Café María Adelina Flores 10 📞 762 678 7876. Attached to a small coffee museum (entry M$40), where beautiful illustrations depict the history of the coffee trade in Mexico, this café serves delicious coffee (M$15–38) and some of the best *chocolate con leche* in town. Also for sale are organic beans from a cooperative of local coffee producers (one of which you can visit – ask at the museum for information). Mon–Fri 7.30am–10.30pm, Sat 8am–9pm.

Teddy's Coffee Factory Belisario Domínguez 1 📞 967 674 0922. Superior café with a cool, modern interior and an extensive range of coffees (M$18–52), including several hard-to-find preparations (such as a Viennese-style *Einspänner*). Bagels and cupcakes are also on offer. Daily 8am–8pm.

RESTAURANTS

Los Ches Real de Guadalupe 12 📞 967 631 6386, 🌐 losches.com. Welcoming little Argentine *parrilla* (steakhouse) with images of national heroes on the walls – Maradona, Messi, Gardel, the Pope – and succulent steaks (M$185–255) and empanadas, served with a tangy

11

chimichurri dressing. Daily except Tues 1.30–11.30pm.

Madre Tierra Insurgentes 19 ☎ 967 678 4297. This joint in a colonial house has an international flavour: Mexican dishes plus home-made creative breakfasts and brunches (M$45–55), soups and salads. The late-night upstairs bar has views of ancient walls and red-tiled roofs, plus regular live music, and the bakery and deli sell whole-wheat bread and carrot cake. Café Mon–Sat 8am–8pm; bar 8pm–late.

Normita Juárez, at Flores. A great little restaurant, drawing a local crowd and serving specialities from Jalisco (try a chewy, open-face *huarache* with your choice of toppings), as well as hearty breakfasts for around M$40–50. Daily 7am–11pm.

Te Quiero Verde Niños Héroes 5 ☎ 967 678 2345. Economical vegetarian restaurant with an eclectic menu (mains M$40–62): soups and salads, pasta dishes and (vaguely) Indian-style curries, vegan brownies and fresh juices. Daily except Tues: drinks from 9am; food from 1.30–9pm.

TierrAdentro Real de Guadalupe 24 ☎ 967 674 6766. Set around a large courtyard with leather chairs and wi-fi, this meeting place and cultural centre has everything from coffee to pizzas to good-value set menus (M$47–199). The Zapatista sympathies are evident from the quotes from various revolutionaries on the walls and place mats. Daily 7.30am–11pm.

Trattoria Italiana Dr Navarro 10 ☎ 967 678 5895. Authentic, Italian-run restaurant serving delicious home-made pasta (the gnocchi is particularly good) with a range of sauces, while the chef is happy to customize to your taste. Mains M$130–190. Mon & Wed–Sat 2–10pm, Sun 2–4.30pm.

★ **La Viña de Bacco** Real de Guadalupe 7 ☎ 967 119 1985. A snug little tapas bar that looks straight out of Spain – but there's a big selection of Mexican (and international) wines by the glass, as well as platters of locally made cheeses, sausages and ham, sandwiches and tapas. You get a free bite-size *botana* with each glass (M$18–55 each). Arrive early to snare one of the few tables on the pavement. Mon–Sat 2pm–midnight.

DRINKING AND NIGHTLIFE

The major bar strips are on Real de Guadalupe and the pedestrianized street north of the plaza, but there are many smaller bar-cafés on quieter blocks throughout the centre, many with a mellow candlelit atmosphere. On a practical note, this is a rare town in Mexico where there's good wine to drink, as well as beer. Many of the city's cafés and bars host **live music** in the evenings, usually salsa or Latin pop, and only rarely impose a cover charge. *Madre Tierra* (see above) also has a bar and live music upstairs.

Latino's Madero, at Juárez ☎ 967 678 9927, **ⓦ** facebook.com/latinossc. Boisterous bar and *discoteca* playing a variety of live and recorded music, from salsa and reggae to jazz and rock, though weekends favour cumbia and merengue. Cover charges are reasonable. Mon–Sat 8pm–3am.

Makia Hidalgo, at Mazariegos ☎ 967 114 8000. Fashionable, dimly lit bar and club with a good mix of locals and travellers. But as you might expect, it's not the cheapest place, with cover charges often over M$100, and beers around M$50. Thurs–Sat 9.30pm–5am; also opens Wed & Sun during Mexican holiday periods.

Café Bar Revolución 20 de Noviembre and Flavio Paniagua ☎ 967 678 6664, **ⓦ** elrevo.com. Zapatista chic is the style at this bar on the pedestrian street. Beers from M$25, and decent bar food. Happy hour is a generous noon till 7pm, with music 8.30–10.30pm. Daily 1pm–2am.

SHOPPING

San Cristóbal is a destination for textile collectors, as every village in the area specializes in a distinctive style of weaving, embroidery and more. If you see something you like (here or in any village), you should buy it, as there's no guarantee you'll see it again in the next town. The plaza in front of Santo Domingo church, filled with **craft stalls**, is often the best place to buy souvenirs, and the **Mercado de Dulces y Artesanías** on Insurgentes is another worthwhile place to look, although traders here are less willing to bargain.

Abuelita Books Colón 2 ☎ 967 631 6720, **ⓦ** abuelitabooks.com. Excellent bookshop, with wide selection of English-language titles to buy or exchange. There's a film screening every Thursday night (7pm; M$20), and you can also pop in for a tea, coffee or brownie. Mon–Sat noon–4.30pm (though sometimes opens later).

Librería La Pared Hidalgo 13-B ☎ 967 678 6367. Another great bookshop, with one of the largest selection of new and secondhand books in English in southern Mexico; you can rent, trade or buy. Photos are also for sale. Tues–Sat 10.30am–8.30pm, Sun–Mon noon–7pm.

Metalistería Hermosillo Jardinera 12, about 2km southwest of the centre ☎ 967 678 6631. Pick up delicate handcrafted door knockers, locks or a traditional ornate cross for perching on your roof as a house blessing at this renowned metalworker's workshop. Mon–Sat 10am–2pm & 4–7pm.

Museo del Ámbar Convento de la Merced off Diego de Mazariegos ☎ 967 678 9716, **ⓦ** museodelambar.com.mx. Learn about amber at the museum adjoining this exquisite shop. Even if you don't buy here, you'll be educated for future purchases. Several other shops in town have adopted the same name; don't be deceived. Tues–Sun 10am–2pm & 4–8pm.

Sna Jolobil 20 de Noviembre ☎ 967 678 2646, ⓦ facebook.com/snajolobil. The former convento adjacent to Santo Domingo church has been converted into a craft cooperative that sells textiles and other village products. The quality is generally of a high standard, though the prices are fixed. Mon–Sat 9am–7pm.

Taller Leñateros Flavio Paniagua 54 ☎ 967 678 5174, ⓦ tallerlenateros.com. One of the more fascinating craft shops, where you can see the process of making paper by hand from banana leaves, cornstalks and bamboo, and coloured with natural dyes. The finished sheets become beautiful cards and notebooks. Mon–Fri 9am–8pm, Sat 9am–2pm.

DIRECTORY

Banks and exchange Several banks (with ATMs) are on or near the plaza; most will exchange dollars and give cash advances (generally mornings only). HSBC is at Mazariegos 6. You'll get much quicker exchange, however, at good rates from *casa de cambio* Centro Cambiario Lacantún at Real de Guadalupe 12-A (Mon–Sat 9am–2pm & 4–8pm, Sun 9am–1pm); it changes most major currencies and usually has Guatemalan quetzales.

Immigration office 2km west of the centre, at the junction of the Carretera Panamericana and Diagonal Centenario (Mon–Fri 9am–3pm; ☎ 967 678 7910).

Internet It's scarcely possible to walk a block in the centre without coming across an internet café. Typical hours are 9am–10pm; the price is usually around M$10/hr.

Laundry There are numerous laundries around the centre, most charging less than M$15/kg: try Lavandería, María Adelina Flores (closed Sun).

Post office Ignacio Allende, between Diego Mazariegos and Cuauhtémoc (Mon–Fri 8.30am–7pm, Sat 9am–1pm). In addition, most hotels have Mexipost boxes, and many of the larger ones sell stamps.

Spanish courses Centro Cultural El Puente, Real de Guadalupe 55 (☎ 967 678 3723), is the longest-established language school in San Cristóbal; it also runs courses in Maya. Instituto de Lenguas Jovel, Madero 45 (☎ 967 678 4069, ⓦ institutojovel.com), is also recommended. Both can arrange accommodation with local families.

Grutas de Rancho Nuevo

10km southeast of San Cristóbal, off the main road to Comitán • Daily 8am–5pm • M$15 • Second-class buses to Comitán stop on request; by bike, it's about a 50min ride, uphill most of the way from San Cristóbal; the spot is well signed

Some organized outings from San Cristóbal go to this enormous cavern extending deep into a mountain – but it's easy enough to go on your own as well. There's an average restaurant here for refreshment, and you can hire horses. Although the cave system is quite extensive, only 400m of pathway is open to the public.

El Arcotete

3.5km east of San Cristóbal • Follow Real de Guadalupe out of town, past the Guadalupe church, where it becomes the road to Tenejapa; about 3.5km past the church, El Arcotete is down a signed track to the right

Another popular trip from San Cristóbal, good for a few hours or so, is to **El Arcotete**, a natural limestone arch above a clean and gently flowing river. It's a nice destination if you just want to stroll out of town (or ride a bike) and see a bit of the surrounding hills. On a warm day you'll be tempted to swim, but be aware that the river, coming from below ground, is extremely chilly.

San Juan Chamula

Usually referred to as just **Chamula**, this is the closest indigenous village to San Cristóbal (10km), as well as the most frequently visited. It has a population of fifteen thousand or so, and more than ninety thousand in the surrounding municipality – despite the fact that thousands of residents have been cast out in recent decades for converting to Protestant faiths (these so-called *expulsados* create many of the crafts sold in San Cristóbal proper).

Chamula and the surrounding indigenous communities are essentially self-governing, and have their own schools, police force, and a small prison with two cells that are semi-open so as to expose the criminals to "public shame". Over the centuries, the village has been far more resistant to change than neighbouring Zinacantán, putting up fierce resistance to the Spaniards from 1524 to 1528, then acting as the centre of a rebellion described as the second "Caste War" from 1867 to 1870, inspired by the uprising in the Yucatán.

In keeping with the very traditional atmosphere in the village, photography is generally not appreciated, and it is explicitly banned inside the church.

Iglesia de San Juan Bautista

North side of the Plaza Principal • Daily 9am–7pm; **museum** daily 8am–7pm • M$20 for access to both the church and the museum • Buy tickets from the tourist office in the Palacio Municipal, on the east side of the plaza

This two-hundred-year-old church, painted a festive turquoise, is the epicentre of Tzotzil Maya religion in the area, and one of the most intensely sacred spots in Mexico. A visit can be a humbling and moving experience. The interior is glorious, the floor covered with pine needles and the light of a thousand candles casts an eerie glow. Lining the walls are statues of the saints adorned with offerings of clothes, food and mirrors (thought to aid communication with the laity), while above the altar, San Juan, patron saint of the village, takes pride of place. The customs practised inside the church incorporate aspects of Christian and Maya beliefs – each villager prays by clearing an area of pine needles and arranging a "message" in candles, and rituals frequently involve tearful chanting, singing, an array of fizzy drinks – locals believe expelling gas through burping helps to release evil spirits – and *posh*, a sugar-cane alcohol. Eggs, bones and live chickens – which are sacrificed in the church and later eaten or buried – are also used in these ceremonies.

There are no priests, Masses or marriages here, only baptisms, and the church is open 24 hours (though tourists are welcome only during daylight). It plays a central role in healing ceremonies.

Admission to the church also grants entry to the **Museo Etnográfico**, behind the Palacio Municipal. Rooms display artefacts of village life, musical instruments and costumes from Chamula and other villages.

San Lorenzo de Zinacantán

An easy 7km walk from San Juan Chamula (and 12km west of San Cristóbal), this village is more open than its neighbour. The locals here have embraced flowers as an export crop, and the steep hillsides are dotted with greenhouses. Traditional practices have not completely disappeared, and are on impressive display during fiestas. Some

AROUND SAN CRISTÓBAL

KINTA JIMULTIK IN SAN JUAN CHAMULA

During the annual Kinta Jimultik, the **carnival** (five days in Feb/March), representatives of all the villages in the area around San Cristóbal attend in traditional dress, marching in circles around Iglesia de San Juan Bautista and up to strategically placed crosses on the hillsides for the first four days. On the final day, which coincides with the last of the five ill-fated days of the Maya calendar, purification rites and fire-walking ceremonies take place in the plaza.

---

older men still wear the rose-pink and blue-green ponchos with silver threads (called *pok 'ul*), decorated with tassels and embroidered flowers, and the same colours and designs feature in the women's costumes. Tours include a visit to a typical house, where you'll see the family altar, women weaving beautiful table mats decorated with large embroidered flowers and the house fire where tortillas are prepared. You might also be invited to taste *posh*, the local spirit, made from sugar cane and sometimes flavoured with fruit or cinnamon.

Zinacantán also has a museum, the **Museo Ik'al Ojov** ("Our Great Lord"), which has displays of costumes from different social groups and a tableau of a house interior (daily 8.30am–5pm; donation requested). The museum is a short walk downhill from the main plaza (follow the signs) and the **Iglesia de San Lorenzo** (where no photography is permitted, not even in the churchyard).

Independent visitors must pay M$15 at the kiosk at the entrance to the village; this includes entrance to the church, and you will almost certainly pick up a few small children who want to lead you to craft shops. It's worth going because some also serve delicious handmade tortillas to hungry shoppers.

Comitán de Domínguez and around

The fourth-largest city in Chiapas, **COMITÁN** is 88km from San Cristóbal, southeast along the Panamerican Highway through scintillating scenery. Strategically poised on a rocky hillside, the city is surrounded by rolling farms and wild countryside in which orchids bloom. Once past the scrappier outskirts, the city has an elegant colonial core and a small but absorbing market, as well as a mellow timetable, with many businesses still observing an afternoon siesta. Travellers often pause here before heading for the border with Guatemala or deeper into the wild at the Lagos de Montebello or the Lacandón forest.

Once a major Maya population centre (the ruins of Bonampak and Yaxchilán, and even Palenque, are not far, as the parrot flies), Comitán was originally known as Balún Canán ("Nine Stars", or "Guardians"), but was renamed Comitán ("Place of Potters" in Náhuatl)

VISITING CHAMULA AND ZINACANTÁN

Almost everyone who stays in San Cristóbal visits the Tzotzil Maya villages of **San Juan Chamula** and **San Lorenzo de Zinacantán**. Both places have retained much of their unique cultural identity, including a religion that is a blend of traditional animist belief and Catholicism. The church at Chamula, in particular, is one of the most moving sights in Mexico.

It's hard not to feel a sense of intrusion in these settings, where you may be a spectator at some intense religious ritual. Though an organized tour (very easy to arrange in San Cristóbal; about M$200/person) can feel a little rushed and contrived, paradoxically it may make you feel like less of a gate-crasher – your presence in the church is made a bit more "official", and the guides can explain some of the rituals. Tours depart around 9.30am, visit both villages and return to San Cristóbal around 2pm (there is little difference between companies; see p.670).

If you do come on your own, you'll feel less conspicuous in busy tourist times (Aug primarily), when there's more of a Mexican tourist crowd, and a festive atmosphere. Inexpensive *combis* leave frequently for Chamula, Zinacantán and other villages from Edgar Robledo, just north of the market in San Cristóbal. There are no *combis* between Chamula and Zinacantán.

11

when it came under Aztec control. At 1560m, it's not as high as San Cristóbal but can still be more refreshing than the sweltering lowlands; make sure your hotel has blankets.

The plaza

Centro Cultural Rosario Castellanos • Daily 10am–7pm • Free

Comitán's spacious, manicured **plaza** is arranged on several levels around a central bandstand. The whitewashed **Palacio Municipal** dominates the north side, while the seventeenth-century **Templo de Santo Domingo**, with its partially exposed Neoclassical stone facade, is to the east. Inside is a spacious nave, timbered ceiling and marble-covered altar. On the plaza's southeast corner, the **Centro Cultural Rosario Castellanos**, named after the respected poet and author who grew up nearby, has a pretty courtyard featuring a mural depicting the city's history.

Museo de Arqueología

1a C Sur Ote, at 2a Av Ote Nte • Tues–Sun 10am–5pm • Free

Just east of the plaza, the splendid little **Museo de Arqueología** offers a chronology of local Maya sites through displays of jewellery and pottery, as well as some unsettling tooth necklaces and children's skulls deliberately deformed for ceremonial purposes.

Casa Museo Belisario Domínguez

Av Central Sur • Mon–Sat 10am–6.45pm, Sun 9am–12.45pm • M$20

One block south of the plaza, the most evocative of the city's museums is the former home of the local doctor and politician who was assassinated in 1913 for his outspoken

COMITÁN DE DOMÍNGUEZ

EATING
Acuario — 3
Los Portales del León — 1
Sanfer Coffee — 2

ACCOMMODATION
Hospedaje San Francisco — 3
Hotel del Virrey — 2
Internacional — 4
Posada Casa Lupita — 5
Posada El Castellano — 1

DRINKING & NIGHTLIFE
Jarro Café — 1

opposition to Huerta's usurpation of the presidency. Though it's packed with memorabilia (including a solemn display of the famous anti-Huerta speech that precipitated his murder), it's hard to appreciate unless you understand Spanish. Most interesting is the pharmacy, its shelves lined with diverse lotions and potions, where Domínguez would administer free treatment to the poor.

Museo de Arte Hermíla Domínguez de Castellanos

Av Central Sur at 3a C Sur • Tues–Sat 10am–6pm, Sun 9am–12.45pm • M$10

Named after the wife of Belisario Domínguez (see opposite for the Casa Museo Belisario Domínguez), this museum houses a vibrant collection of largely modern artworks by Mexican artists; several canvases by Oaxacan painter Rufino Tamayo are displayed in one room.

Templo de San José

3a Av Sur, west of Av Central • Daily 9am–8pm • Free

This twin-towered church, skirted with white and gold and featuring a blend of Gothic and Baroque architecture, is the most unusual of the city's churches. Its interior is particularly attractive, with tiled floors and stained-glass windows.

Iglesia de San Caralampio

1a Av Nte Pte, two blocks east of the plaza • Daily 9am–8pm • Free

Also worth seeking out is this Neoclassical construction from 1852, with its elaborately painted stucco facade. It is dedicated to a martyr who became an object of devotion after cholera and smallpox epidemics decimated the town in the nineteenth century. A fiesta in his name is celebrated in mid-February. Alongside the plaza at the front, Comitán's cold, potable mountain-spring water gushes from a row of fountainheads.

ARRIVAL AND DEPARTURE   COMITÁN DE DOMÍNGUEZ

By bus Buses stop along the Panamerican Highway (known as Bulevar Dr Belisario Domínguez), the wide commercial strip through town; only ADO/OCC has a terminal, between 7a and 8a Av Sur, while all others just pull in at the roadside nearby. To walk to the centre, cross the road, turn left and walk about three blocks to 1a C Sur Pte, then turn right and walk seven blocks to the plaza. A booth in the ADO/OCC terminal will call a taxi (about M$40) if required. Note that if you're headed to Ciudad Cuauhtémoc on the border, it's typically cheaper and more convenient to take a *combi*, rather than a bus.

First-class destinations Ciudad Cuauhtémoc (3 daily at 1.40pm, 5.45pm & 7.20pm; 1hr 20min); Mexico City (4 daily at 1.30pm, 3pm, 6.30pm & 8.30pm; 16hr 40min); Palenque (8hr 10min) via Ocosingo (1 daily at 2.20pm; 4hr 40min); Tapachula (5 daily; 5hr 45min); Tuxtla Gutiérrez (3hr) via San Cristóbal (roughly hourly; 2hr).

Second-class destinations Lagos de Montebello, including Laguna Bosque Azul (every 30min–1hr; 1hr),

Tziscao, Maravillas and Ixcán (every 30min; 1hr 30min–2hr); Palenque via Benemérito and San Javier (7hr), for Bonampak (hourly; 10hr).

By combi Transportes Cuxtepeques runs *combis* to Tuxtla Gutiérrez via Amatenango del Valle (5am–9pm; 1hr) and San Cristóbal from Domínguez at 2a C Sur Pte. Transportes Francisco Sarabia, at 3a Av Pte Sur 10 (between C Central Pte and 1a C Sur Pte), runs an hourly *combi* service from its ramshackle terminal to Tenam Puente (every 30min; 20min). For the Lagos de Montebello and the Frontier Highway, take one of the frequent *combis* run by Transportes Lagos de Montebello from its terminal at 2a Av Pte Sur 23, between 2a and 3a C Sur Pte. For Ciudad Cuauhtémoc, take the Alfa y Omega *combi* from Domínguez opposite 1a C Sur Pte. Transportes Tzobol runs to Amatitlán (3hr; for boats to Laguna Miramar) from its small terminal 3km from the centre along 4a Av Pte Sur, near 13a C Sur Pte, from 4am to 2pm.

INFORMATION AND TOURS

Tourist information The helpful state tourist office is on 1a Av Nte, between 2a C and 3a C (daily 8am–7.30pm; ☏ 963 632 4047). The municipal tourist office is at Av Central Nte 27, between 2a and 3a (Mon–Fri 8am–4pm, Sat 9am–2pm).

Tours Viajes Tenam, Pasaje Morales 11 (☏ 963 632 1654), can arrange domestic and international flights, as well as organize day trips to local attractions such as El Chiflón.

ACCOMMODATION

Hospedaje San Francisco 1a Av Ote Nte 13 ☎ 963 632 0194, ✉ samuel22f@prodigy.net.mx. One of the best of the budget options in town, *Hospedaje San Francisco* has tidy rooms with private bathrooms. Some of them also have TVs, and those on the front courtyard are bigger and brighter. M$350

Hotel del Virrey Av Central Nte 13 ☎ 963 632 1811. A pretty, flower-filled courtyard and a friendly staff give this attractive colonial-style hotel a welcoming feel. The rooms are bright and clean, with attached bathrooms and TVs. There's also a laundry service. M$400

Internacional Av Central Sur 16 ☎ 963 632 0110. Smart, modern hotel with a stylish edge. It's calm and cool past the wrought-iron doors. Carpeted rooms aren't large – and bathrooms are quite small – but the roomy upper lobby and communal terrace provide welcome space for relaxing. There's also a restaurant, *Girasoles*. M$1050

Posada Casa Lupita 3a C Sur Ote 22 ☎ 963 632 3362, ⊕ posadacasalupita.weebly.com. A converted home run by a friendly family, the *Lupita* has just five rooms, in various configurations, with clean bathrooms (some shared) wedged in odd corners. There's also a nice front patio covered in bougainvillea. M$240

Posada El Castellano 3a C Nte Pte 12 ☎ 963 632 3347. *Posada El Castellano* has an old-fashioned style, with an attractive courtyard with a fountain, reasonable en-suite rooms, and a decent on-site restaurant. The hotel was undergoing a renovation in 2015. M$600

EATING

Most of the best **places to eat** in Comitán are on the plaza. In the evening, for example, look for the local snack of a *cascara preparada*, a spicy vegetarian mix on a puffed rectangular tortilla the size of a roofing tile; there's usually a vendor in front of the cultural centre on the southeast corner of the plaza. The **market**, one block east of the plaza, is filled with fruit stands and ringed with some very good *comedores*. It's beautiful in its own right, with golden light casting a sepia-tone glow over the stacks of herbs and chiles in its narrow aisles.

Acuario Av Central 9, northwest corner of plaza ☎ 963 106 3729. Good-value Mexican food (M$50–110) served in clean surroundings, including tables out under the arches. Highlights include typical breakfasts like *chilaquiles* with eggs in a mild, vinegary green-chile sauce. Daily 7am–midnight.

Los Portales del León 3a Av Ote Nte, opposite the Iglesia de San Caralampio ☎ 963 632 8238, ⊕ restaurantelosportales.com. This smart cantina and grill is great for evening meals (which range from steak tartare to sea bass in a lobster sauce; around M$100–250), as well as watching the plaza action and listening to the marimba bands. Daily 7pm–midnight.

Sanfer Coffee C Central ☎ 963 106 0945. A perpetually busy café on the pedestrianized north side of the plaza, *Sanfer* offers coffee (from M$20), juices, smoothies, sandwiches and desserts. Locals crowd tables inside and out. Daily 7am–11pm.

DRINKING

Comitán is dotted with a number of lively, fairly polished **bars**. If you're in the mood for a **drink**, be sure to try *comiteco*, a rich local spirit made from agave (as tequila is) and flavoured with fruits. Most restaurants and bars serve it, even if it's not on the menu. You can buy excellent-quality bottles at Comiteco Nueve Estrellas (daily 9.30am–3pm & 5–9pm; ⊕ facebook .com/comiteco.nueveestrellas) on 1a Av Pte Sur near 2a C Sur Pte. **Free entertainment** comes in the form of live marimba, usually played in the plaza Thurs and Sun from 7pm.

Jarro Café 1a Av Pte Nte, two blocks northwest of the plaza ☎ 963 632 1170, ⊕ facebook.com/jarrocafe comitan. Styling itself as a "London pub" with a "European atmosphere", as well as a café, *Jarro Café* has something of a split personality: expect a lively atmosphere, football on TV, rock tunes and karaoke. Tues–Sun 6am–3am.

DIRECTORY

Banks and exchange Bancomer, on the plaza (Mon–Fri 8.30am–4pm), is useful for currency exchange and dollar cash advances, and also has an ATM. HSBC is at 2a C Sur Pte 7, just down from the plaza.

Consulate Guatemala, inside the complex Barrio de Guadalupe at 1a C Sur Pte 35, three blocks west of the plaza (Mon–Fri 9am–5pm; ☎ 963 632 0491).

Internet There are plenty of cyber cafés on and around the plaza.

Post office One and a half blocks south of the plaza on Av Central Sur (Mon–Fri 8am–6pm, Sat 9am–5pm, Sun 9am–1pm).

El Chiflón

40km southwest of Comitán • Daily 8.30am–5pm • M$30 • ⓦ chiflon.com.mx • From Comitán, take a Rápidos de la Angostura *combi* (every 30min, 5am–6pm) from Blv Domínguez at 1a C Sur Pte

A waterfall some 120m high is the attraction at **Centro Ecoturístico Cascadas El Chiflón**, not far from the village of Tzimol. It's a popular day outing from Comitán, as well as from San Cristóbal de las Casas. Trails run along the river, past smaller cascades with pale blue mineral-rich waters. Tour operators sometimes also call the place Cascadas Velo de Novia, or Bridal Veil Falls – this is the official name of the park entrance and ecotourism centre, with similar facilities, on the west side of the river, when you come from San Cristóbal.

ACCOMMODATION EL CHIFLÓN

Cabañas El Chiflón ⓣ 963 596 9709, ⓦ chiflon.com .mx/cabanas.html. The ecotourism group offers a dozen lovely en-suite rooms, each furnished with hand-carved wood and opening onto a long front porch ideal for watching the falls and the forest. A very good deal. M$750

Tenam Puente

14km south of Comitán, 5km off the main road • Daily 8am–5pm • M$36 • Combis run frequently from Comitán until about 6pm, from 3a Av Sur Pte, near 1a Sur Pte

This site, uncovered by Frans Blom in 1925, marks a settlement that was at its peak from 600 to 900 AD and finally abandoned around 1200 AD. The most important group of ruins, the acropolis, has three ball-courts and a 20m-high pyramid that affords magnificent views of the Comitán valley. To get to it, keep climbing the stone terraces until you reach the highest point. A path leads up past the guard's hut and into a meadow with a huge stone terrace.

Ciudad Cuauhtémoc

80km south of Comitán

A visit to the Lagos de Montebello (see p.681) is a good introduction to the landscapes of Guatemala, but if you want to see the real thing up close, it's only another 60km or so from the junction at La Trinitaria (served by plenty of passing buses) to the Mexican border post at **Ciudad Cuauhtémoc**. It's not a city at all – just a few houses, the immigration post, a restaurant and the ADO/OCC bus station; standards at the hotels here are low, so you're better off staying in Comitán, El Chiflón or around Parque Nacional Lagos de Montebello.

ARRIVAL AND DEPARTURE CIUDAD CUAUHTÉMOC

To Guatemala The Guatemalan border post is at La Mesilla, a 3km taxi ride away. As always, it's best to cross in daylight – you may not be able to get your passport stamped after 8pm. Officials at La Mesilla were once notorious for exacting illegal charges from tourists, though things are much improved. Buses to Huehuetenango (hourly; 2hr) and Quetzaltenango (hourly; 3hr 30min) wait just over the border. The money-changers will give you reasonable rates for dollars, but not as good for pesos.

To Mexico Getting into Mexico is easy: the Mexican tourist card (see p.29) will be issued free, and vans or buses will be waiting to take you to Comitán (1hr 30min).

Chinkultic

At km 31 on the Frontier Highway, at the end of a 2km track • Daily 8am–5pm • M$42 • Second-class buses from Comitán to Lagos de Montebello pass the turn

Southeast of Comitán, off the road to Lagos de Montebello, a track leads north to these Classic-period Maya ruins. Only a small portion of the site has been cleared and restored, but the setting is dramatic – worth a stop if you're travelling by car, or staying near the lakes farther down the road.

Climb the first large mound as you enter the site, and you're rewarded with a view of a small lake, with fields of maize beyond and forested mountain ridges in the background. Birds, butterflies and dragonflies abound, and small lizards dart at every step.

A ball-court and several steles have been uncovered, but the highlight is undoubtedly the view from the top of the tallest structure, **El Mirador**. Set on top of a steep hill, with rugged cliffs dropping straight down to a *cenote*, the temple occupies a commanding position; peaceful now, this was clearly an important hub in ancient times.

Parque Nacional Lagos de Montebello

50km southeast of Comitán, via the Panamerican Highway to the Frontier Highway • Daily 8am–5pm • M$30

Fifty kilometres southeast of Comitán, along the border with Guatemala, this national park is beautiful wooded country studded with more than fifty lakes, sixteen of them very large, and many edged with small restaurants providing local food and basic cabañas. The combination of forest and water is reminiscent of Scotland or Maine, with kilometres of hiking potential. For the less energetic, roadside viewpoints provide glimpses of various pools, lent different tints by natural mineral deposits and the angle of the sun. The lakes themselves are actually a series of *cenotes* (sinkholes) formed by the erosion of limestone over millions of years.

You could see quite a bit of the park in a long day trip – buses cover the route all day, with the last bus leaving the park entrance around nightfall. But to really enjoy the wilderness, and to visit the small but spectacular nearby ruins of Chinkultic (see opposite) as well, you're better off staying in or near the park.

Laguna Bosque Azul

The most easily accessible hike is at **Laguna Bosque Azul**, just past the park entrance on a 3km spur from the main highway. Most *combis* and buses come this way. This route passes a park ticket booth, then dead-ends at the lake car park. From here, you can take the dirt track a few hundred metres further to a fork. The left-hand path, signposted "Gruta San Rafael del Arco", heads into the jungle through an exquisitely forested gorge and eventually to a massive limestone arch over a river and, at the end, a cave in the cliff-face.

Laguna Tziscao

The main Frontier Highway continues deeper into the park and passes turnings for several other lakes, including **Laguna Tziscao**, 9km along. There's another park ticket booth here, and you can swim and take a tour on a wooden *balsa* (raft).

ARRIVAL AND DEPARTURE   PARQUE NACIONAL LAGOS DE MONTEBELLO

By bus Second-class buses leave Comitán (every 30min or so; 45min–1hr) for either Laguna Bosque Azul or Tziscao. Buses headed for destinations further along the Frontier Highway also pass Laguna Tziscao, among others, and will stop on request. The last bus back to Comitán leaves the park entrance at 7.30pm, but from Laguna Tziscao, the last passes at around 5pm.

By combi Transportes Lagos de Montebello depart when full from a terminal at 2a Av Pte Sur 23, between 2a and 3a C Sur Pte.

By car The main route through the park is the Carretera Fronteriza (Frontier Highway; Hwy-307), which splits from the Panamerican Highway 16km outside Comitán, at La Trinitaria. Past the park, the paved road roughly follows the Guatemalan border and runs all the way to Palenque. There are often army checkpoints – you may be asked for your passport at any time. The soldiers are invariably polite, but make sure your tourist card is valid.

ACCOMMODATION

★Museo Parador y Hotel Santa María 22km from the La Trinitaria junction, then 1.3km south on a dirt track ☎963 632 5116, ⊕paradorsantamaria.com.mx. The most comfortable of several hotels and guesthouses along the road to the park. A former hacienda, it's a lovely place, furnished with antiques and oil paintings and steeped in colonial history. There's hot water and electricity but rooms are also lit with oil lamps. A small museum (daily 9am–6pm; M$25) in the grounds is filled with religious paintings and other ecclesiastical art from the seventeenth century. US$150 (M$2570)

El Pino Felíz North side of Frontier Hwy near km 32 ☎963 131 8548. Also known as *Doña María's*, this joint has very basic rooms in wooden cabins set in a farmyard with animals ranging just outside. Baths and showers are shared (opt for the front section, to avoid always-tricky electric showerheads). The engaging host family serves home-cooked meals. Buses and *combis* will stop right outside. M$200

The Frontier Highway east

The main road continues beyond the Lagos de Montebello and through mountains with spectacular views, rushing rivers and precipitous ridgelines on its way along the Guatemalan border and north to Palenque. The largest settlement – which is not saying much – along the road is **Las Maravillas de Tenejapa**, a pretty village about two hours from Lake Tziscao.

If you drive the Frontier Highway, it's best to do it during daylight hours – there are army checkpoints and Zapatista outposts to contend with, and a chance of robberies. Benemérito, at least three hours from the Lagos de Montebello, is the closest town on the route with rudimentary services like restaurants (we can't recommend the hotels), and the only one with a Pemex station. It's possible to reach Palenque in the same day, if you leave on a very early bus, but you would have no time to stop at Bonampak and Yaxchilán. You could conceivably stay the night near either of these ruins (see p.692 & p.695), then tour them the next day, but an early start is still essential, to be sure taxis are still running from where the bus will drop you on the highway.

11

ACCOMMODATION

FRONTIER HIGHWAY

Las Guacamayas Reforma Agraria, north off the highway 20km east of Flor de Café ☎664 134 1138, ⓦlasguacamayas.mx. This remote ecotourism operation is run by the tiny village of Reforma Agraria. Tidy cabins, a restaurant and a camping area are set amid chicken runs and pastures, against a dense wall of jungle that teems with wildlife, including endangered red macaws; guides can lead you on boat trips down the Río Lacantún. Double M$1125; camping M$100

Ocosingo and around

With its streets lined with single-storey, red-tiled houses and the air thick with the scent of wood smoke, this mountain town midway between San Cristóbal and Palenque makes a good place to escape the tourist crowds. Like the other villages winding up Hwy-186 to their mountain perches, **OCOSINGO** has stayed close to its rural roots, with farmers in cowboy hats in from their ranches and local women selling *maíz* from great bubbling vats. Central to town life is the **plaza**, surrounded by *portales*, a big old country church on the east side and the modern *ayuntamiento* opposite.

ARRIVAL AND DEPARTURE

OCOSINGO

By bus Buses stop on the main road or at the small ADO/OCC terminal nearby. To get to the plaza turn right out of the terminal and walk back uphill a few blocks until you reach Av Central. Turn left and walk down to the plaza, where you'll find pretty much everything you need within a block or two. All buses are *de paso* (originating in either San Cristóbal or Palenque), so may run late, and sometimes full. Second-class service in either direction ends at 7.30pm, but first-class ADO/OCC services run after midnight.
Destinations (first class) Palenque (9 daily; 2hr 25min);
San Cristóbal de las Casas (8 daily; 2hr 15min).
By combi *Combis* stop on the main road, near the ADO/OCC terminal. Services down the road to Palenque or San Cristóbal end around 7.30pm.
By car On Hwy-186, and on Hwy-199 continuing to Palenque, cars are often stopped by locals who hold a rope across the road. It's best not to drive at night, when a lack of guardrails and the presence of pedestrians – and even the occasional report of robberies – make this a risky route.

ACCOMMODATION

Central Av Central at C Central, north side of plaza ☎919 673 0024. The neat-and-tidy rooms at Central are nicely furnished, with tiled floors and clean bathrooms. All have optional a/c (M$100); the upper rooms are the best bets, as they come with fans as well. M$400
Hospedaje Esmeralda C Central 14 ☎919 673 0014. A block north of the plaza, the basic *Esmeralda* has both decent en suites and (much poorer quality) rooms with shared bathrooms. It remains a popular travellers' meeting place, with a bright, comfortable lobby and an inexpensive restaurant with tables out on the terrace. The knowledgeable staff can arrange flights over the Toniná ruins (about M$1000 for four people, plus guide) and to Laguna Miramar (about M$2500 for four people); a day trip to Bonampak and Yaxchilán by air is around M$6500 (for four people). Restaurant Mon–Sat 7.30am–9.30pm. M$250

EATING

In the **market**, traditionally dressed indigenous women sell fruit and vegetables and locally produced cheeses, including the round and waxy *queso de bola* and the creamy and delicious *queso botanero*. To get there turn right at the church for one block, then left along C 2 Sur Ote for another four. Several other budget **places to eat** are on the square.

El Campanario Av Central Ote 2, just across from the plaza ☎ 919 673 0251. This place has pavement tables and a menu in English. The Mexican favourites (such as chicken in *mole*) aren't the same quality as in bigger towns, but the beers (around M$25) are cold and the prices fair. Daily 7am–10.30pm.

El Desván South side of the plaza ☎ 919 673 0117. This low-key joint serves simple but good Mexican fare, as well as pizzas (M$150–350). The upstairs terrace is a great perch for welcome breezes and people-watching from the late afternoon onwards. Daily 7am–11pm.

DIRECTORY

Banks and exchange There are a couple of ATMs, one at Banamex on the plaza, and another at Banco Santander opposite *Hospedaje Esmeralda* on C Central Nte.

Internet Cyber cafés include Compu Centro, near the plaza on C Central Nte.

11

Toniná

14km east of Ocosingo • **Museum and ruins** daily 8am–5pm • M$46 • *Combis* marked "Predio/Ruinas" leave from the market area; a taxi is around M$100 one-way

This Classic-period Maya site is large and impressive, especially for its massive, seven-layered central complex. Yet, as most people are rushing on to Palenque or San Cristóbal, it sees few visitors. At its height, **Toniná** was a great regional power: the city defeated Palenque and captured its ruler in 699 AD, and from then until after 900 AD, when it became the last of the great Maya centres to fall victim to whatever disaster led to them all being abandoned, it was probably the greatest power in the Usumacinta basin. It's also the place where the latest **Long Count date**, corresponding to 909 AD, was recorded, and, like all the major Maya centres, it was abandoned not long after.

The museum

At the site entrance is a good **museum**, with a helpful model of the site, as well as drawings of some of the relief carvings still in place in the buildings. It also displays some of the more fragile sculptures from the site, many of which are images of bound prisoners and of decapitation – a bit unnerving when packed together in the gallery space.

The ruins

The **ruins** themselves, a five-minute walk from the entrance (passing a small café selling locally grown macadamia nuts and coffee), are virtually all one enormous building, the **Acrópolis**, a series of seven artificial terraces built into the hillside and incorporating dozens of temples and other buildings. This is the "house of stone" that gave the site its Tzeltal name. A torch is useful to explore the labyrinthine interiors and internal staircases.

Of the remaining stucco reliefs, the finest is the enormous (16m x 4m) **Mural de las Cuatro Eras**, on the sixth platform. This remarkably well-preserved stucco codex tells the story of Maya cosmology by following the eras of the world as they were created and destroyed. The worlds are depicted as decapitated heads surrounded by flowers. A grinning, skeletal Lord of Death presents a particularly graphic image as he grasps a skinned human head. At the summit is the **Templo del Espejo Humeante** (Temple of the Smoking Mirror), built around 840 AD, and a great vantage point across the valley.

Laguna Miramar

A much more remote excursion from Ocosingo is this pristine lake in the heart of the Lacandón forest. It's part of the enchanting **Montes Azules Biosphere Reserve**, the largest surviving area of rainforest in North America. The high-canopy forest is home to abundant wildlife, including howler and spider monkeys, tapirs and jaguars, and there are rivers and caves to explore. An island in the lake has traces of a fortress, a Maya stronghold until it was finally conquered in 1559. It's best to avoid the rainy season (June–Oct).

When you arrive in Emiliano Zapata, the *ejido* near the lake's western edge that manages ecotourism here, ask for the *comisario* or *presidente*. Either will be able to organize practicalities, charged per day: expect to pay around M$250 for a guide, and M$200 for the use of canoe (highly recommended). From the village, it's a 9km hike to the lake. It costs around M$50 per person to camp or sleep in hammocks in lakeside palapas. There are a few shops and simple cafeterías in San Quintín, but supplies in Emiliano Zapata are limited, so it's best to bring your own food.

ARRIVAL AND DEPARTURE   LAGUNA MIRAMAR

You can visit Miramar on your own or on an organized tour (see box below). To travel independently takes some time and effort.

BY PLANE
Servicios Aéreos de San Cristóbal (☎963 632 4662, ⊛chiapasdesdeelcielo.com) makes the trip from Ocosingo, Comitán or Palenque in a light plane, priced at US$500 for four to five people. *Hospedaje Esmeralda* in Ocosingo (see p.682) can make arrangements. If you can't fill a plane, you can also contact the airline directly – if they have space they might let you fly one-way.

BY TRUCK AND COMBI
Most transport stops at the town (and army base) of San Quintín; from there, you need to catch a lift or walk the 2km to Emiliano Zapata.

From Ocosingo Trucks known as *tres toneladas* leave from behind the market on 3a C Sur Ote (9am–noon), running to San Quintín, the town/army base on the highway, 2km from Emiliano Zapata. It's a bone-rattling 6–7hr to cover 130km.

From Comitán First take a frequent *combi* to the small town of Las Margaritas, 16km northwest, then pick up a truck to San Quintín, about 3–4hr away. This route passes through La Realidad, a celebrated Zapatista stronghold, and may lead to extra hassle at military checkpoints in the area – check with the Comitán tourist office or *Hospedaje Esmeralda* (see p.682) before trying this.

BY BOAT
A far more exciting alternative is to come by river from the village of Amatitlán, about 15km due south of the lake. Here you can arrange a boat (around M$1800; 3hr) to take you up the winding Río Jataté to Emiliano Zapata, where you may be asked to pay another "entrance" fee, of about US$10/boat. To get to Amatitlán from Comitán, take a Transportes Tzobol *combi* (roughly 4am–2pm); the terminal is 3km south of the centre on 4a Av Pte Sur, near 13a C Sur Pte.

Palenque and around

Set in thick jungle buzzing with insects, the ancient Maya **ruins of Palenque** are some of Mexico's finest Maya sites: less crowded than Chichén Itzá, larger than Uxmal, and with the most spectacular setting. It is a relatively small site – you can see everything in a morning – but a fascinating one, strongly linked to the lost cities of Guatemala while displaying a distinctive style.

TOURS AROUND PALENQUE

Touts offer a huge variety of **tours** to local attractions in the vicinity of Palenque, above all the waterfalls at Agua Azul and Misol-Há and the ruins of Bonampak and Yaxchilán. There are also trips to Tikal in Guatemala or to Toniná, and adventure tours, including kayaking and horseriding. Prices vary according to season (and even time of day, if there's one seat left to fill) but start from around M$300 for the waterfalls, and M$700 for a day trip to Bonampak and Yaxchilán. Be sure to check what's included – entrance fees, meals and English-speaking guides most importantly. One of the more reliable agents is Viajes Na Chan Kan (☎916 345 2154, ✉chiapastour@hotmail.com or ⊛viajes.nachankan@hotmail.com), on Hidalgo at Jiménez; most hotels can also arrange tours.

■ ACCOMMODATION		● EATING	
Chan Kah	4	Café de Yara	2
Hostel Yaxkin	2	El Huachinango Feliz	3
Hotel Canek	6	Mara's	6
Hotel Maya Tulipanes	1	Maya Cañada Feliz	1
Maya Rue	3	Las Tinajas	7
Xibalba	3	Tropitacos	4/5

Nine kilometres east of the ruins, the rather helter-skelter **town of Palenque** functions as the base for exploring the ruins and the waterfalls in the nearby hills. With every facility a visitor might need, it's lively enough, but it has no real intrinsic appeal. As there are a number of excellent camping sites, cabañas and hotels near the ruins, you may prefer not to stay in town at all.

ARRIVAL AND INFORMATION

BY PLANE

Palenque's small airport (☎ 916 345 1692) is 5km northwest of town. A taxi to/from town costs a negotiable M$200. Interjet (@ interjet.com.mx) has at least two weekly flights to Mexico City (1hr 40min); Ka'an (@ kaanair.com.mx) has three to four weekly flights to Tuxtla Gutiérrez (30min).

BY BUS

Travelling on any long-distance bus (except for Lagos de Montebello vehicles), you'll arrive in Palenque town at one of two nearby terminals in the west of the town, just off the main highway. Both stations have lockers if you want to leave your stuff while you head for the ruins.

First class The new first-class ADO/OCC terminal is near the traffic circle at the intersection of Juárez and Pakalna. It's worth buying your onward ticket as soon as you know when you're leaving, because buses, particularly the first-class services, often run full.

Destinations Campeche (4 daily; 5hr–5hr 35min); Cancún (3 daily at 5.40pm, 10.30pm & 11pm; 12hr 20min–12hr 55min); Emiliano Zapata (2 daily at 8am & 9pm; 50min), for Tenosique and Guatemala; Mérida (4 daily; 7hr 40min–8hr 15min); Mexico City (2 daily, both at 7.01pm; 14hr 5min–14hr 40min); Oaxaca (1 daily at 5.30pm; 14hr

PALENQUE AND AROUND

35min); Ocosingo (6 daily; 2hr 40min); San Cristóbal (7 daily; 5hr–8hr 25min); Tuxtla Gutiérrez (6 daily; 6hr 20min–7hr 40min); Villahermosa (hourly; 2hr 30min).

Second class Auto Cardeso, Expreso Azul and others run to Cancún, Tuxtla and Villahermosa from a terminal on Juárez, a short walk from the ADO terminal. For closer destinations, Transportes Comitán Lagos de Montebello, on Velasco Suárez, just past the market, and Transportes Río Chancalá, on 5 de Mayo, run along the Frontier Highway, beginning at 3.40am. All go to Bonampak (3hr) and the turn-off (*crucero*) for Frontera Corozal (for Yaxchilán; 3hr 30min). Montebello's early-morning departures continue all the way to Comitán via Benemérito and the Lagos de Montebello. Transportes de Chamoán, on the west side of the traffic circle by the statue of the Maya head, runs regular minivans to Frontera itself; these cost a bit more, but you don't have to pay for a taxi into town.

Tourist office In the Plaza de Artesanías on Juárez at the corner of Abasolo, a block below the main plaza (Mon–Sat 9am–9pm, Sun 9am–3pm; ☎ 916 345 0356). The staff are very friendly, but the information they provide isn't always accurate. There's also a booth on the east side of the plaza (same hours). You'll generally get better information from local tour operators or at your hotel.

GETTING AROUND

By taxi/combi A taxi from the ADO/OCC bus station to the hotels on the road to the ruins should cost about M$50, but during daylight hours, it's just as easy to flag down one of the many *combis* headed for the ruins (see p.690). In town, taxis wait on the northeast corner of the plaza. They run to Agua Azul, Bonampak, Frontera, Ocosingo, Palenque ruins and around town (you can negotiate for them to wait for you while you look around).

ACCOMMODATION

Palenque has plenty of hotels on the rather noisy streets leading from the bus stations to the plaza, especially Hidalgo and 20 de Noviembre. A quieter option is the pleasant area called **La Cañada**, named for the ravine that divides it from the town centre. With brick-paved streets and soft lighting, it feels a little like a chic subdivision. It's set in a swathe of trees (birds and monkeys are audible in the morning) and is only a short walk from the action. Most hotels here are more upmarket, but there's one very good budget option. High season in the Palenque area is Mexican vacation periods – July, Aug, Christmas and Semana Santa; outside that time, rates can drop significantly.

IN TOWN

Chan Kah Juárez, at Independecia ☎916 345 0318, ⓦchan-kah.com.mx. A pretty, smart hotel in the town centre (and the only one with a lift), this comfortable spot has big rooms with a/c, many with balconies overlooking the plaza – the drawback being the noise from below, of course. M$550

Hotel Canek 20 de Noviembre 43 ☎916 345 0150, ⓔhotel-canek@hotmail.com. *Hotel Canek* is great value, and the friendly staff look after solo travellers like family. Dorm beds can be rented singly in peak times, and double rooms are huge, especially the third-floor "penthouse" with a grand view. Some have a/c, are en suite and have a street-side balcony. Meals, luggage storage and tours all available. M$450

Maya Rue C Aldama, between Juárez and 5 de Mayo ☎916 345 0743, ⓔhotelmayarue@gmail.com. The sharpest option in central Palenque: a standard urban low-rise hotel, done up with modern furnishings and oversize photographs of old Mexico. The lobby doubles as a chic coffee shop. The style compensates for the small a/c rooms and the lack of a pool or parking. M$600

LA CAÑADA

Hotel Maya Tulipanes Cañada 6 ☎916 345 0201, ⓦmayatulipanes.com.mx. A solid mid-range choice, *Hotel Maya Tulipanes* has comfortable and spacious en suites, an outdoor pool, a restaurant and even a karaoke bar. M$480

Hostel Yaxkin Hidalgo, at 5a C Pte ☎916 345 0102, ⓦhostalyaxkin.com. Welcoming hostel with ample communal areas: a nice kitchen, games, TV, and an Italian restaurant. Accommodation is more basic, in eight-bed dorms, in rustic cabañas or in private rooms with shared or attached bathrooms. Dorms M$150; doubles M$315; cabañas M$480

Xibalba Merle Green at Hidalgo ☎916 345 0411, ⓦhotelxibalba.com. Pretty, white rooms are accented with green and brown, giving a vaguely natural feel, even if they're not very large. Staff are friendly, and there's a restaurant, roof terrace and helpful travel agency. The only off note is the occasional waft of diesel from the Pemex station across the ravine. M$685

ON THE ROAD TO THE RUINS

For more isolation, opt for the places lining the road to the ruins, covering every category from luxury hotel to campsite – though the latter are becoming fewer.

Chan Kah Village Resort 3km from town, on the left ☎916 345 1100, ⓦchan-kah.com.mx. This tranquil resort, built in a patch of jungle either side of the Río Michol, has some 90 rooms and cabins (all are large, fully fitted and well spaced). The highlight is undoubtedly the stunning *cenote*-inspired swimming pool, which is shaded by coconut palms. There's also a breezy restaurant-bar on a terrace overlooking the pool, games room, and a spa. M$1450

Mayabell 6km from town and inside the park, just before the museum ☎916 341 6977, ⓦmayabell.com.mx. A favourite with backpackers and adventure-tour groups, this camping spot and trailer park has something for everyone: palapa shelters for hammocks, vehicle pads with electricity and water, and very comfortable private cabañas with hot water. The shared showers have hot water, and there's also a *temazcal* (traditional sweat lodge), spa, laundry and decent freshwater swimming pool (with occasional fish), plus frequent live music in the restaurant. Cabañas M$840; camping M$60

El Panchán 5.1km from town on the left, just before the park entrance ⓦelpanchan.com. Like a cabaña subdivision, this large swathe of forested land contains a number of separate lodging operations, divided by screens of trees and sharing a couple of restaurants and other facilities including bike rental, body piercing, travel agent and more. The vibe might be a little too nouveau-hippy for some, but most places are excellent deals. It's easy to take a *combi* here and then compare rates by walking around to the various options. *Margarita and Ed's* (☎916 348 6990, ⓦmargaritaaandedcabanas.blogspot.mx) is probably the cleanest and best value, with thatched cabins or conventional double rooms with a/c. *Jungle Palace*

(☎915 348 0520) has pleasant but tiny cabañas with shared bathrooms and terraces above the stream, plus a few en-suite versions. Avoid the places closer to the centre, near *Don Mucho* restaurant, if you want to go to bed early – there's live music and fire-spinning at night. *Margarita and Ed's* M$270; *Jungle Palace* M$150

★**Quinta Chanabnal** 2.2km from town, on the right ☎916 345 5320, ⓦquintachanabnal.com. A stunning luxury hotel with vast, ochre-toned rooms – all suites – furnished in purpose-built hardwood furniture and antique Guatemalan fabrics in a fusion of European, Far Eastern and Mexican styles. The Italian owner is an expert in Maya iconography, and modern Maya glyphs throughout the complex tell his story and that of the hotel. There's a pool, a restaurant and a small lake alive with birdlife. It's great value for the quality. US$177 (M$3035)

EATING

Food in Palenque town is fairly basic, and most restaurants serve up similar dishes, often just pasta and pizza, to customers who've really only come for the ruins. There are also several places along the road to the site – some of which cater mainly to tour groups – including a couple in *El Panchán* (see opposite). In town, bargains can be found among the set menus posted on boards outside most restaurants. **Av Juárez** also has several budget options between the bus stations and the plaza, while **Hidalgo** has more Mexican-style food. The restaurants in the La Cañada hotels are well worth a look.

IN TOWN

★**Café de Yara** Hidalgo 66, at Abasolo ☎916 345 0269. Charming café delivering proper coffee (hot, cold and alcoholic varieties are available; M$12–60), various breakfast options, and good-value set meals (M$90–140). In high season, there's often live music on Fri and Sat evenings. Daily 7am–11pm.

Mara's Juárez, at Independencia, on the plaza ☎916 345 2578. A pleasant little café from which to watch the plaza scene. The tacos are particularly good here, but you can also get sandwiches, pasta dishes, grills and so on (mains M$100–150) – as well as cold beers. Daily 7am–11pm.

Las Tinajas 20 de Noviembre, at Abasolo ☎916 345 4970. Pleasant, family-run restaurant popular for its vast menu of hearty meats, fish, chicken and pasta in addition to the usual Mexican fare. No comida corrida, but most mains are around M$115–240, and all are big enough to share. Daily 7.30am–11pm or later.

Tropitacos Juárez 49, between Allende and Abasolo ☎916 345 0818. This fast food-style joint, with two branches, diagonally opposite each other, delivers the goods at economical prices. Stick to the Mexican dishes: the tacos (M$9–19 each; five for M$40–55) are the highlights. Daily 8am–10/11pm.

LA CAÑADA

★**El Huachinango Feliz** Merle Green, at Hidalgo ☎916 345 4642. A split-level restaurant in La Cañada that serves great fish and shrimp baked in banana leaves, among other seafood. Prices are reasonable (mains M$110–140), portions are generous and the setting is pretty and quiet – a nice break from restaurants in town. Good cocktails too (M$55). Daily 8am–11pm.

Maya Cañada Feliz Merle Green, at Hidalgo ☎916 345 0216. Smarter than average restaurant in a peaceful La Cañada location: the selection of regional specialities and the fresh fish dishes are well worth a try (mains M$75–190). Daily 7am–11pm.

ON THE ROAD TO THE RUINS

Don Mucho 5.1km from town ☎916 341 8209. The social centre of *El Panchán*, serving tasty Mexican and Italian food in the evening, with live music nightly from 8pm. Great for breakfast (around M$50) or a leisurely lunch after visiting the ruins, though it can be a victim of its own success – so packed with tour groups that it can be hard to find a table. Happy hour 6–8pm. Daily 8am–2am.

DIRECTORY

Banks and exchange Several banks along Juárez have ATMs. There's also an ATM at the ADO/OCC terminal.
Internet Most hotels here have computers for guests and wi-fi, and internet cafés are plentiful. They include Ciberkonqueror, just past the post office on Independencia at Nicolas Bravo, and Ciber Vlos, on Juárez next to *Posada*

Shalom I (both around M$10/hr).
Laundry Several in town, including La Gota Azul, on Independencia between 20 de Noviembre and Corregidora.
Post office On Independencia, a block from the plaza (Mon–Fri 9am–6pm, Sat & Sun 9am–1pm).

The ruins of Palenque

9km west of Palenque town • Daily 8am–5pm, last entry 4.30pm; **museum** Tues–Sun 9am–5pm • Ruins M$64, with tickets also sold at museum after 9am; additional one-off national park entry fee M$31.50; guides M$800–1000 (for groups of up to 7; prices negotiable)

The ruins of Palenque are located in the **Parque Nacional de Palenque**, the border of which is just after *El Panchán* (see opposite). The main road first passes a well-stocked

11

artesanía shop, a café and the site museum. You can enter at the gate across the road, hiking up to the main part of the site via the waterfalls trail, but most people will press on to the main site entrance, at the top of the hill another 2km up a winding road. Near this main entrance, there's a small café and numerous souvenir stalls selling drinks, as well as toilets and some expensive lockers.

The ruins themselves bear a closer resemblance to the Maya sites of Guatemala than to those of the Yucatán, but ultimately the style here is unique – the **towered palace** and **pyramid tomb** are like nothing else, as is the abundance of reliefs and inscriptions. The setting, too, is remarkable. Surrounded by jungle-covered hills, Palenque is right at the edge of the great Yucatán plain – climb to the top of any of the structures and you look out over an endless stretch of low, pale-green flatland. If you arrive early enough in the day, the mist still clings to the treetops and the howler monkeys are roaring off in the greenery.

Brief history

Founded around 100 BC as a farming village, it was four hundred years before Palenque began to flourish, during the Classic period (300–900 AD). Towards the end of this time the city ruled over a large part of modern-day Chiapas and Tabasco, but its peak, when the population is thought to have numbered some one hundred thousand,

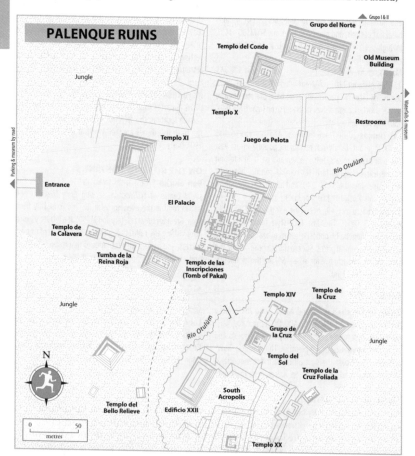

came during a relatively short period in the seventh century, under two rulers: **Hanab Pakal** (**Jaguar Shield**) and **Chan Bahlum** (**Jaguar Serpent**). Almost everything you can see (and that's only a tiny, central part of the original city) dates from this era.

The museum

Palenque's excellent **museum**, on the road 1.5km from the site entrance, will give you a good idea of the scale of Palenque, and a look at some of its treasures. Many of the glyphs and carved relief panels found at the site are on display, as are examples of the giant ceramic incense-burners in the form of gods or mythological creatures. An intricate model of El Palacio reveals how it would have appeared in the Classic period – with the tops of the buildings adorned with roofcombs.

The back wing is devoted to a replica of Pakal's sarcophagus lid from the Templo de las Inscripciones – entrance is restricted to small groups, every half hour or so. One of the most renowned iconographic monuments in the Maya world, the engraved sarcophagus lid depicts Pakal at the moment of his death, falling into Xibalba, the underworld, symbolized by a monster's jaws. Above the dead king rises the **Wakah Kan** – the World Tree and the centre of the universe – with **Itzam-Yé**, the Celestial Bird, perched on top representing the heavens. So that the deified king buried here should not be cut off from the world of the living, a psychoduct – a hollow tube in the form of a snake – runs up the side of the staircase, from the tomb to the temple.

Site entrance

As you enter the site, **El Palacio**, with its extraordinary watchtower, stands ahead of you. The path, however, leads to the right, past a row of smaller structures – one of them, the so-called **Tumba de la Reina Roja** ("Tomb of the Red Queen"), is open inside, and you can climb in to see a sarcophagus still in place.

Templo de las Inscripciones

The enormous **Templo de las Inscripciones** is an eight-step pyramid, 26m high, built up against a thickly overgrown hillside. You are not permitted to climb the pyramid, so you have to imagine the sanctuary on top, filled with stone panels carved with hieroglyphic inscriptions relating to Palenque's dynastic history. Deep inside the pyramid is the **tomb of Hanab Pakal**, or Pakal the Great (615–683 AD). Discovered in 1952, this was the first such pyramid burial found in the Americas, and is still the most important.

In 2015 a Mexican archeologist deciphered a hieroglyphic on the tomb as "The House of the Nine Sharpened Spears". Some of the smaller objects found – the skeleton and the jade death mask – are on display at the Museo Nacional de Antropología in Mexico City (see p.95), but the massive, intricately carved stone **sarcophagus** is still inside; a reproduction is in the site museum (see above).

El Palacio and around

The centrepiece of the site, **El Palacio**, is in fact a complex of buildings constructed at different times to form a rambling administrative and residential block. Its square **tower** is unique, and no one knows exactly what its purpose was – perhaps a lookout post or an astronomical observatory. Throughout you'll find delicately executed **relief carvings**, the most remarkable of which are the giant human figures on stone panels in the grassy courtyard, depicting rulers of defeated cities in poses of humiliation. An arcade overlooking the courtyard held a portrait gallery of Palenque's rulers, though many of these have been removed.

South of El Palacio and adjacent to the Templo de las Inscripciones, a small path leads to the **Templo del Bello Relieve** (**Templo del Jaguar**). More temples are being wrested from the jungle beyond, but the paths are closed, and though the path leads eventually to the *ejido* of Naranjo, you won't be permitted to pass much further into the forest without a guide. Even so, clambering around here, it's easy to believe you're

11

walking over unexcavated buildings, as the ground is very rocky and some of the stones don't look naturally formed.

The Grupo de la Cruz and around

The main path then leads across the Río Otulúm, one of several streams that cascade through the site. The Otulúm was once completely lined with stone and used as an aqueduct; the reinforcement also kept the stream from overflowing its banks and undermining the foundations of the surrounding buildings.

The path leads uphill to end in the plaza of what's called the **Grupo de la Cruz**, oddly oriented away from Palenque's more central buildings. The **Templo del Sol**, the **Templo de la Cruz** and the **Templo de la Cruz Foliada** are all tall, narrow pyramids surmounted by a small temple with an elaborate stone roofcomb. All contain carved panels representing sacred rites – the cross found here is as important an image in Maya iconography as it is in Christian, representing the meeting of the heavens and the underworld with the land of the living. On the right-hand side of the Templo de la Cruz, God L, one of the gods of the underworld, is depicted smoking tobacco – the oldest known image of someone smoking. A small path next to the Templo de la Cruz Foliada leads to the only open portion of the South Acropolis, a building with a replica relief carving, covered with elaborate glyphs and a triumphant king.

The Grupo del Norte and around

Following the Río Otulúm to the northern edge of the cleared site, you reach the lesser buildings of the **Grupo del Norte** and the **Juego de Pelota** (ball-court), on lower ground across a grassy area from El Palacio. Beyond them, two **paths** lead downhill towards the museum. One goes down some perilous stairs behind Grupo del Norte, leading to **Grupo I** and **Grupo II**, intricate complexes of interconnected rooms. The other path follows the stream as it cascades through the forest and flows over beautiful limestone curtains and terraces into a series of gorgeous pools (no swimming allowed, though). The paths join again just after a suspension bridge crossing the river; eventually the route emerges on the main road opposite the museum. If you don't want to exit here, and want to make a loop, it's best to go down via Grupo I and II – the steeper route – then make your way back up by the other, somewhat easier, trail.

ARRIVAL AND DEPARTURE   RUINS OF PALENQUE

By combi Two *combi* services, Transportes Chambalú and Transportes Pakal, run frequently (at least every 15min, 6am–6pm) from their terminals near Juárez in town, and will stop anywhere along the road to the ruins – also useful if you're staying at one of the hotels or campsites near the ruins. After 6pm, you'll either have to walk or take a taxi

(around M$70).

By car There's very limited parking space at the main entrance at the top of the hill. Even if you have your own car, you may still prefer to take a *combi*, as this enables you to exit on the downhill side of the site by the museum, and spare yourself having to hike back up to your vehicle.

Misol-Há

18km from Palenque • Daily 8am–5pm • M$30 • Second-class buses between Ocosingo and Palenque stop at the turn on request; it's a 10min walk to the falls

These smaller falls along the road to Ocosingo are a much easier day trip from Palenque than Agua Azul (see box, p.684) if travelling by public transport, and in many ways they're far more pleasant, with none of the slapdash development present at its celebrated neighbour. A 25m waterfall provides a stunning backdrop to a pool that's safe for swimming, and a fern-lined trail leads along a ledge behind the cascade – refreshing from the spray and mist even if you don't go for a dip. It's an easy 1.5km walk downhill from the road.

Organized tours often combine a visit here with Agua Azul (the bigger attraction) and Agua Clara. These latter falls are even less visited than **Misol-Há**, but aren't remarkable enough to merit a trip on your own, so we don't include them here. Also consider Welib-Ja, on the Frontier Highway (see p.692).

ACCOMMODATION AND EATING

MISOL-HÁ

Misol-Há Cabañas ☎55 5329 0995 or ☎916 345 03456, ⓦmisol-ha.com. The good-value accommodation here is a pleasant way to break up the journey if you're coming from Ocosingo by car, or if you just want to relax in the woods. Each beautiful wooden cabaña has a private bathroom and electricity, and some also have kitchens. Advance reservations are recommended, especially during Mexican holidays. **M$700**

Restaurante Misol-Ha At Misol-Há waterfalls ☎55 5151 3377, ⓦmisol-ha.com. Though it's often catering to large tour groups, this place nonetheless cranks out decent local cuisine (mains around M$100–150). The freshwater-fish *empapeladas*, baked in foil, are winners, with lime, tomatoes, onions, rice and handmade tortillas. Daily 7am–7pm.

Agua Azul

Midway between Ocosingo and Palenque, 4km north from the main road • Daily 8am–5pm • M$45 • Second-class buses between Ocosingo and Palenque stop at the turn on request; it's a 45min walk down to the falls, or around M$20 in a taxi, if one's waiting

These impressive waterfalls are worth a visit, though as a popular stop-off on the day-trip circuit, they are sometimes inundated with tourists. The main cascades lie near the car park, with several smaller but equally appealing rapids stretching for 1km up the river. The whole area is certainly picturesque, though the river near the lower falls is lined with rows of souvenir stalls and snack vendors. You could ask for lodging at the Module de Información near the car park but the cabins at **Agua Azul** are not as nice as the ones at Misol-Há (see opposite). Adjust your expectations accordingly, and it still makes for a pleasant trip.

If it's safe to walk upstream (it may not be in the rainy season), you'll come across a perilous-looking bridge over the river and eventually reach an impressive gorge where the **Río Shumulhá** explodes out of the jungle-covered mountain. At the right time of year, the river is alive with butterflies. Swimming isn't advisable: people drown here every year, and though a few signs warn of **dangerous currents**, they don't begin to mark all the perilous spots. Although you may want to get as far from the tourist scrum as possible, keep in mind that violent attacks have occurred here in the past (allegedly due to village rivalries over tourism operations). A heavy federal police guard has proved a major deterrent, but you're always safer with other people nearby.

The Usumacinta valley and the Frontier Highway

The Carretera Fronteriza (**Frontier Highway**) heads south from Palenque into the Lacandón forest and the Río Usumacinta, passing the two great Maya sites of **Bonampak** and **Yaxchilán**. The remote highway, which was paved only in 2000, to help delineate the border with Guatemala, has a reputation as a dangerous place. Although tourist convoys are no longer required, it's still not advisable to drive the road after dark: there is a risk of robbery, a lot of wildlife, and few people to help you if you break down, have an accident or encounter any trouble. Army checkpoints are common, so make sure you have your passport. If you don't visit with a group, try to pick up an information sheet on the Lacandón community from **Casa Na-Bolom** in San Cristóbal (see p.668). For a description of the road past Benemérito, see p.682.

GETTING AROUND

THE USUMACINTA VALLEY

By organized tour The easiest option, arranged in Palenque (see box, p.684). Day- or overnight-trips are options – if you stay overnight, it will be with accommodation at the Lacandón Maya community of Lacanjá Chansayab. Going with a group guarantees a place to stay and meals, both of which are harder to arrange independently.

By combi Travelling on your own, with a *combi* from Palenque (see opposite), is possible, but it's tricky to visit both sites in one day. But you do benefit from arriving at the remote

sites relatively alone, and it's substantially cheaper, although the final cost will depend on finding people to share the boat from the settlement of Frontera Corozal to Yaxchilán.

By car There is a Pemex station at Chancalá, where the Frontier Highway meets Hwy-353, and another in Benemérito, past Yaxchilán.

To Guatemala You can get a boat a short distance upstream from Frontera Corozal to Bethél across the border (see p.694).

Welib-Ja

30km southeast of Palenque, on the Frontier Highway • 8am–5pm • M$30 • All Frontier Highway *combis* (see p.682) pass here – ask to be
let off at the cascadas; start looking for a ride back by 4.30pm or so – flag down standard *combi* vans as well as pick-up trucks

These beautiful waterfalls see fewer visitors than Agua Azul or Misol-Há, and because
they're only 500m from the road they're also easier to reach by public transport. A
forest path leads alongside the river and down to the base of a towering split cascade,
close enough for the mist to spray over you. There are a few palapas for picnicking in
the shade, as well as a protected kids' swimming area, upstream from the falls.

ACCOMMODATION   WELIB-JA

A few breeze-block rooms, managed by the local *ejido*, are available for overnight stays. There's no phone, but usually one
or three staff members present. They have very basic rooms with shared toilets (you can pay extra for en suite); the price
includes access to the waterfalls. Note that walls separating rooms do not reach all the way to the top of the pitched palapa
roof, making "private" a relative term. Prices start at M$250.

Bonampak

Just outside the Montes Azules Biosphere Reserve, 2.5km from Lacanjá Chansayab village • Daily 8am–5pm • M$48 for the INAH, M$25 for
the local community

Relatively small compared with other ruined Maya cities, **Bonampak** is unique due to its
fascinating **murals**, evocative memorials to a lost civilization. Bonampak's actual buildings,
most from the eighth century, are small and not the most spectacular, but the murals
definitely make it worth the visit – there is very little like them elsewhere in the Maya
world, and even in their decayed state, the colours are vivid and the imagery memorable.

Bonampak lies in the small biosphere reserve controlled by the Lacandón on the
fringe of the much larger Montes Azules Biosphere Reserve. The site is quite isolated,
and the only facilities are toilets and a couple of huts selling crisps and carved-wood
souvenirs. The nearest settlement is the village of Lacanjá Chansayab, about 2.5km
away – basic cabañas, rented by the Lacandón people, are available here (see p.694).

Brief history

The outside world first heard of Bonampak, meaning "painted walls", in 1946, when
Charles Frey, an American who'd dodged the draft by heading to the Mexican forest
during World War II, was shown the site (but apparently not the murals) by the
Lacandón who still worshipped at the ancient temples. The first non-Maya actually to
see these murals – astonishing examples of Classic Maya art – was the American

THE LACANDÓN

You may already have encountered the impressively wild-looking **Lacandón Maya**, dressed in
simple white robes and selling exquisite (and apparently effective) bows and arrows at
Palenque. Until recently, they were the most isolated of all the Mexican Indian groups. The
ancestors of today's Lacandón are believed to have migrated to Chiapas from the Petén region
of Guatemala during the eighteenth century. Prior to that the Spanish had enslaved, killed or
relocated the original inhabitants of the forest.

The Lacandón refer to themselves as "Hach Winik" (true people). Appearances
notwithstanding, some Lacandón families are (or have been) quite wealthy, having sold timber
rights in the jungle, though most of the timber money has now gone. This change has led to a
division in their society, and most live in one of two main communities: **Lacanjá Chansayab**,
near Bonampak, a village predominantly made up of evangelical Protestants, some of whom
are keenly developing low-impact tourist facilities (see p.694); and **Nahá**, where a small group
still attempts to live a traditional life, and where it is possible to arrange stays in local homes.
The best source of information on the Lacandón in Chiapas is Casa Na-Bolom in San Cristóbal
de las Casas (see p.668), where you can find a manuscript of *Last Lords of Palenque*, by Victor
Perera and Robert Bruce. *Hach Winik*, by Didier Boremanse, is an excellent recent study of
Lacandón life and history.

photographer Giles Healey, who arrived shortly after Frey's visit, sparking a long and bitter dispute over exactly who was responsible for their discovery.

La Gran Plaza

After crossing an airstrip, you are at the northwest corner of the central plaza, 110m long and bounded by low walls that mark the edges of a former palace. In the centre of the plaza **Stele 1** shows a larger-than-life **Chaan Muan II**, the last king of Bonampak, dressed for battle – at 6m, it is one of the tallest steles in the Maya world. You'll encounter other images of him throughout the site.

The Acrópolis

Ahead of the Gran Plaza, atop several steep flights of steps, lies the **Acrópolis**. On the lower steps, more well-preserved steles show Chaan Muan with his wife, Lady Rabbit, preparing himself for blood-letting and apparently about to sacrifice a prisoner. From the highest point of the acropolis there's an impressive sense that you're surrounded by primeval forest – the Selva Lacandona – with just a small cleared space in front of you.

11

Edificio de las Pinturas

The highlight is the modest-looking **Edificio de las Pinturas**, halfway up the steps of the acropolis. Inside, in three separate chambers and on the temple walls and roof, the **Bonampak murals** depict vivid scenes of haughty Maya lords, splendidly attired in jaguar-skin robes and quetzal-plume headdresses, and equally well-dressed ladies; and bound prisoners, one with his fingernails ripped out, spurting blood. Dating to around 790 AD, these paintings show the Bonampak elite at the height of their power: unknown to them, the collapse of the Classic Maya civilization was imminent. Some details were never finished, and Bonampak was abandoned shortly after the scenes were painted.

Though you can't enter the rooms fully, the vantage point inside the doorway is more than adequate to absorb what's inside. No more than three people are permitted to enter at any one time and queues are possible, but you shouldn't have to wait long. Having said that, time and early cleaning attempts have clearly taken their toll on the murals, and apart from a few beautifully restored sections, it takes some concentration and imagination to work out what you're looking at.

The murals

In **Room 1**, an infant wrapped in white cloth (the heir apparent?) is presented to assembled nobility under the supervision of the lord of Yaxchilán, while musicians play drums, pipes and trumpets in the background. **Room 2** contains a vivid, even gruesome, exhibition of power over Bonampak's enemies: tortured prisoners lie on temple steps, while above them lords in jaguar robes are indifferent to their agony. A severed head rolls down the stairs and Chaan Muan II grasps a prisoner (who appears to be pleading for mercy) by the hair – clearly about to deal him the same fate. **Room 3** shows the price paid for victory: Chaan Muan's wife, **Lady Rabbit**, prepares to prick her tongue to let blood fall onto a paper in a pot in front of her. The smoke from burning the blood-soaked paper will carry messages to ancestor-gods. Other gorgeously dressed figures, their senses probably heightened by hallucinogenic drugs, dance on the temple steps.

ARRIVAL AND ACTIVITIES **BONAMPAK**

By combi and taxi Take a *combi* from Palenque (see p.690) to San Javier (about 3hr and 132km from Palenque) on the highway, where there's a large palapa on the right side of the road. Taxis are usually waiting to take you to the site-transport parking area, about 3km off the highway, or to the village of Lacanjá Chansayab (around M$60). From the parking area you can access the ruins only in Lacandón-run combi vans (M$70 round trip, with 1hr waiting time). Alternatively, rent a bike (M$75) to ride up to the ruins, though the business is set up another 250m past the parking area for the *combis*, and the *combi* drivers may tell you that the bikes don't exist. Note that private cars are not allowed into the Lacandón forest; you must park in the same area where taxis stop and board one of the Lacandón-run *combis*.

Hiking The cabañas operations in Lacanjá Chansayab can arrange guided walks (from around M$250–600) in the forest. Top destinations are the Cascada Ya Toch Kusam (M$35 entry), a glimmering waterfall, and the remote Lacanhá ruins. The hikes are great in the dry season (Jan to late April), but be prepared for mud at other times.

ACCOMMODATION AND EATING   LACANJÁ CHANSAYAB

Finding **accommodation** is easiest if you have a particular spot in mind – Lacanjá Chansayab is too spread out to walk around comparing options. The prices are all roughly the same – the differences come in the upkeep of the facilities. None of the ten or so operations has a phone, but there's little chance you'll wind up with nowhere to sleep.

Camping Margarito At the combi car park. The easiest, if not the best-kept, option for spending a night in the area, this place has a few simple cabins and room for tents, and also runs a restaurant with a simple menu of soups, stews and fried chicken (mains M$50–100). Prices are per person. Cabins M$100; camping M$100

Cueva del Tejón On the road to Lacanjá Chansayab ✉ cuevatejon@hotmail.com. The first place you reach en route to the village, after leaving the *combi* car park, is set by a broad section of the river. It has large concrete cabañas – with four beds in two rooms, bathrooms and power. M$400

Río Lacanjá 1km beyond the village, at the end of the road to the left of the main junction ☏ 967 631 7498, ⓦ ecochiapas.com. By far the most organized place, but booking is essential through Explora in San Cristóbal (the number listed here). It has a big restaurant (serving stews, tamales, tacos, fajitas and the like; mains M$80–150) and a good range of rooms, from basic six-bed dorms up to private cabañas with bath and riverside terrace. It also has a tiny waterfall and swimming hole, and a 45min jungle nature walk on a well-signed path (M$20 for non-guests). Dorms M$300; doubles M$600

Tucan Verde On the road to Lacanjá Chansayab ⓦ tucanverde.com. The second place along the road between the car park and the village, Tucan Verde is run by a very sweet family. It offers riverside camping, but its cabins are, sadly, a bit dilapidated now. M$400

Frontera Corozal

Fifteen kilometres beyond San Javier (the drop-off point for Bonampak) is the turn for the border village that's the gateway to **Yaxchilán**, one of the most enigmatic Maya ruins in Mexico. The ancient city can only be approached from the village by boat along the Río Usumacinta. There's not much in Frontera Corozal itself, but it is nonetheless more developed than Lacanjá Chansayab; staying here is more comfortable and a bit easier to organize, but doesn't offer the same cultural experience as the Lacandón settlement.

On the edge of town, a kiosk collects a "conservation fee" of M$15 per person. While *combis* usually bypass the main road in to pass the unremarkable centre of the village (a couple of scrappy **plazas** and a market about 400m south from the main paved road and 300m back from the river), visitors' first destination is the *embarcadero* on the banks of the Usumacinta, where you catch the boats to Yaxchilán. There's a Mexican **immigration post** (for border procedures see p.29) 200m back along the main road coming in.

Community museum

Opposite the immigration post • Daily 8am–5pm • M$20

Frontera Corozal's community **museum** showcases the history of the settlement, founded only in 1976, and the relationships between the Chol, Lacandón and Tzeltal people, local archeology (there are a few large steles) and flora and fauna. Its restaurant also has one of the few telephones in the village.

ARRIVAL AND DEPARTURE   FRONTERA COROZAL

By combi and taxi See p.690 for details on *combis* from Palenque. A few go into the village, but the majority drop you on the highway at the turn-off to Frontera (the *crucero de Corozal*); it's marked by a *comedor* and shop selling basic supplies. From here you can pick up a taxi for around M$40 for the ride 15km down the road to town.

TO GUATEMALA
Entering Guatemala from this small town is relatively easy, with plenty of *lanchas* between Frontera Corozal and Bethél, a boat ride away upstream (around M$400 1–3 people; up to M$750 for more; 30min, plus any time spent waiting for the boat to fill up). There's a Mexican immigration post 200m back along the main road into Frontera: if you're crossing

permanently to Guatemala, you should surrender your tourist card here; if you're coming back, hold on to it. Guatemalan immigration procedures can be completed in Bethél, from where buses normally depart for Flores (noon and 5pm; 5hr), mostly along dirt roads. The bus can, if you wish, be prearranged through travel agents in Palenque.

TOURS

Escudo Jaguar On the riverbank south of the boat dock ☎00502 5353 5637 (Guatemala number), ⓦescudojaguar.com. Arranges boat trips downstream from Yaxchilán to the impressive ruins of Piedras Negras on the Guatemalan bank (same day around M$4000 for one to five people; overnight around M$4600). There are rapids above the site, meaning you may well have to get out and walk along the bank at times. It's a beautiful journey, though, and well worth making if you have the time.

Siyaj Chan ☎00502 5047 5908 (Guatemala number), ⓦsiyajchan.blogspot.com. Leads hiking trips to Gruta Tzolkin, a cave deep in the forest (6hr; around M$1200).

ACCOMMODATION AND EATING

Corazón Lacandón en la Selva Main road into Frontera Corozal, 200m past turn for embarcadero, north side of street ☎00502 5203 0288 (Guatemala number), ⓔrestaurante_corazonselva@hotmail.com. A palapa-roofed, open-air operation big enough to accommodate Yaxchilán tour groups, but still informal enough to have chickens pecking around the side yard. It serves commendable Mexican foods (mains M$100 plus), such as tender *pollo en mole*, and cold beer. Daily breakfast–7pm.

Escudo Jaguar On the riverbank south of the boat dock ☎00502 5353 5637 (Guatemala number), ⓦescudojaguar.com. The longest-established place in the area, with clean-enough modern concrete-block rooms and nicer cabañas arrayed in a compound just above the water. They're the top choice for every tour group and can fill up early. There's also a restaurant. Doubles M$300; cabañas M$600; camping M$100

Nueva Alianza One block back from the river, north of the boat dock ☎00502 4638 2447 (Guatemala number), ⓦctnuevaalianza@hotmail.com, ⓦhotelnuevaalianza.com. Not as ideally situated as *Escudo Jaguar*, as it's bounded by private homes, and farther from the water, but it can be cheaper, with big group rooms in wood cabañas and camping space. Its private cabañas are nicer, and many are in an area kept intentionally dark at night. Dorms M$150; cabañas M$300; camping M$50

Yaxchilán

Daily 8am–5pm; guides through INAH office; only a few speak English; during July, Aug, Christmas and Easter, they wait at the site itself; guides and *lanchas* can also be arranged through the *Escudo Jaguar* hotel and tour operator Siyaj Chan (see above) • M$57 for the INAH, M$20 for the local community; buy your ticket in Frontera Corozal, at the INAH office by the museum; guides M$350 or so

A larger and more dramatic site than Bonampak, **Yaxchilán** was an important Classic-period centre. From around 680 to 760 AD, the city's most famous kings, Escudo Jaguar (Shield Jaguar) and his son Pájaro Jaguar IV (Bird Jaguar), led a campaign of conquest that extended Yaxchilán's sphere of influence over the other Usumacinta centres and made possible alliances with Tikal and Palenque. The buildings occupy a natural terrace above the river, with others climbing steep hills behind – a superb natural setting.

Not so many people make the trip here, which involves a ride in a narrow *lancha* with a tin roof for shade, down the broad, fast-flowing river with Mexico on one bank, Guatemala on the other. At the site, it's easy to be alone in the forest with nothing but moaning howler monkeys around you. Giant trees keep the place shady, but nonetheless the jungle heat can be palpable – bring plenty of water, as there are no services at the ruins.

Pequeña Acrópolis

From the site entrance, the main path leads straight ahead to the Gran Plaza, but if you have the energy for climbing, it's more rewarding to explore the wilder parts of the site first. Follow the branching path to the right that leads up the hillside to the **Pequeña Acrópolis**, a set of thirteen buildings. A lintel on the most prominent ruin, known as **Edificio 42**, depicts Escudo Jaguar with one of his warriors.

Templos del Sur

Walk behind Edificio 42 to find another narrow trail down through the jungle, over several unrestored mounds, until you reach a fork: to the right, the path climbs steeply once again until it reaches, in about ten minutes, Edificios 39 to 41, also called the

Templos del Sur, 90m above the river level – buildings that probably had some kind of astronomical significance. High above the main forest, this is also a good spot to look for canopy-dwelling birds like parrots, though the trees also obscure any view.

El Palacio

Retrace your steps back to the main path, and continue on until it emerges at the back of **Edificio 33**, the most famous building at the site, also known as **El Palacio**. It overlooks the main plaza from a high terrace. The lintels here are superbly preserved, and inside one of the portals is a headless statue of Pájaro Jaguar IV. In ancient times the building was a political court; more recently, it served as a religious site for the Lacandón Maya.

Gran Plaza

Descending 40m down the stairs in front of the Palacio brings you to the long **Gran Plaza**. Turn back to look up at the Palacio: with the sun shining through the building's roofcomb and tree roots cascading down the stairs, this is what you imagine a pyramid lost in the jungle should look like, especially if you've been brought up on Tintin.

To your left, just above the level of the plaza, **Edificio 23** has a few patches of coloured stucco around its doorframes – just one patch of many well-preserved paintings and relief carvings on the lintels of buildings surrounding the long green lawn. Some of the very best works were removed in the nineteenth century and are now in the British Museum in London, but the number and quality of the remaining panels are unequalled at any other Maya site in Mexico. Many of these depict rulers performing rituals.

This can also be seen on **Stele 1**, right in the middle of the plaza, near the base of the staircase. It depicts Pájaro Jaguar IV in a particularly eye-watering blood-letting ceremony, ritually perforating his penis. **Stele 3**, originally sited at Edificio 41, has survived several attempts to remove it from the site and now lies at the west side of the plaza, where it shows the transfer of power from Escudo Jaguar to Pájaro Jaguar IV.

El Laberinto

Heading back to the entrance, be sure to pass through **El Laberinto** (The Labyrinth) at the plaza's northeast corner, the most complex building on the site, where you can walk down through dim passages out onto the main path.

ARRIVAL AND DEPARTURE   **YAXCHILÁN**

By boat A number of companies offer services. Most are based at the *embarcadero* on the riverfront at Frontera Corozal, the easiest place to find other travellers to share a boat. Return fares vary with group size (M$200/passenger return; 30min, but return can take up to 1hr). To allow enough time at the site, the latest you should get on a *lancha* is 2pm. If you're headed back to Palenque or Lacanjá Chansayab the same day, you'll have to go much earlier, as the last buses and *combis* leave from in front of the *embarcadero* at 4pm. The earliest you can leave for the site in the morning is 8am, when the INAH office opens.

Tabasco

Few visitors view the state of **Tabasco** as more than a transit corridor for Palenque. Crossed by numerous slow-moving tropical rivers on their way to the Gulf, the low-lying, humid region is the homeland of the ancient **Olmec**, **Maya** and **Zoque** cultures. You can see the legendary Olmec stone heads in a beautifully done exhibition in state capital **Villahermosa**, a city otherwise often maligned for its concrete and chaos, yet boasting a historic, lively and pedestrian-friendly downtown.

Hwy-180 runs close to Tabasco's **coast**, alternating between estuaries and sand bars, salt marshes and lagoons. Though the sands are a bit insect-ridden, and the views often marred by the offshore oil industry, they do have the virtue of being frequented only by locals, if at all. Much of inland Tabasco is very flat, consisting of the flood plains of a dozen or so major rivers. **Boat trips** along the Grijalva and the Usumacinta are the best way to glimpse remote ruins and abundant birdlife. You can also travel by river into the Petén in **Guatemala**, from the far eastern corner of the state.

In the far south of the state, the foothills of the **Sierra Puana** offer a retreat from the heat and humidity. Waterfalls spill down from the mountains, and a few small spas (*balnearios*) have developed. Village tracks provide some great **hiking trails** too.

Brief history

Throughout the Maya period, Tabasco was a natural crossroads, its great rivers important trade routes to the interior. But its local Maya communities were relatively unorganized, and when **Hernán Cortés** landed at the mouth of the Río Grijalva in 1519, he easily defeated the Chontal Maya. But the town he founded, Santa María de la Victoria, was beset first by indigenous attacks and then by pirates, eventually forcing a move to the present site and a change of name to "Villahermosa de San Juan Bautista" in 1596.

Nineteenth and early twentieth centuries

For most of the colonial period, swampy Tabasco remained a relative backwater. **Independence** did little to improve matters, as local leaders fought among themselves, and it took the **French invasion** of 1862 to bring some form of unity, though Tabasco offered fierce resistance to this foreign intrusion. The industrialization of the country under dictator Porfirio Díaz passed Tabasco by, and even after the **Revolution** it was still a poor state, dependent on cacao and bananas. Though **Tomás Garrido Canabal**, Tabasco's socialist governor in the 1920s and 1930s, is still respected as a reformer whose laws regarding workers' rights and women's suffrage were decades ahead of the rest of the country, his period in office was also marked by intense **anticlericalism**. Priests were killed or driven out (a process vividly brought to life in Graham Greene's *The Power and the Glory*; he covers the aftermath in *The Lawless Roads*), all the churches were closed, and many, including the cathedral in Villahermosa, torn down.

The oil boom

The region's **oil**, discovered in the 1930s but not fully exploited until the 1970s, provided the impetus to bring Tabasco into the modern world, enabling capital to be invested in the agricultural sector and Villahermosa to be transformed into the cultural centre it is today.

Villahermosa

Huge, hot, noisy and brash as only a Mexican city can be, **VILLAHERMOSA** – or "Beautiful Town" – could at first sight hardly be less appropriately named. For travellers in this area, though, it's something of an inevitability, as a junction of road and bus routes. But it's also a distinct place, and it can grow on you. Quite apart from the

---

A TASTE OF TABASCO

The **food** of Tabasco state relies heavily on seafood and tropical fruits such as pineapple and passion fruit, which are both cultivated here, along with coffee and cacao. A freshwater fish, the skinny *pejelagarto*, is particularly prized: the green-fleshed, pike-like fish is usually barbecued and served with chile, lime and a salsa of deadly, caper-size chiles. Other typical dishes to look out for include smoked oysters, coconut tortillas, banana bread, and chirmol, a rich *mole* sauce flavoured with pumpkin seeds and local herbs that works particularly well with fish. In terms of drinks, hot (or cold) chocolate and *iliztle*, a sugar-cane alcohol flavoured with pear or peach, are popular. But note that **Tabasco Sauce** isn't actually a speciality: although Tabasco peppers are named after the state, they don't grow here, and the celebrated condiment is in fact an American product made from peppers grown in Louisiana.

sudden vistas of the Río Grijalva's broad sweep, there are attractive plazas, quiet old streets, impressive ultramodern buildings and several art galleries and museums.

Most sights are in or around the pedestrianized downtown core (called the Zona Luz), though some tourist services are 2km or so northwest, in the modern commercial centre called Tabasco 2000. Between the two areas are the spires of a half-built Gothic cathedral, begun in 1973 – a fine symbol of the city's new-old aesthetic.

CENTRAL VILLAHERMOSA

EATING
100% Natural	6
La Antigua	2
La Catedral de Sabor	5
Cockteleria El Rock and Roll	3
El Mirador	4
La Noria	1
Los Tulipanes	7

ACCOMMODATION
Marriott Villahermosa	5
Miraflores	4
Olmeca Plaza	2
Oriente	3
Plaza Independencia	8
Provincia Express	1
Quality Inn Cencali	6
Quinta Real	7

Zona Luz

The oldest part of Villahermosa can be found downtown, where vestiges of the nineteenth-century city survive on streets busy with shoppers and commerce. Many of the main shopping blocks are pedestrianized, and the buildings along them are gradually being cleaned up and restored.

Parque Juárez

Madero at Zaragoza **Centro Cultural de Villahermosa** Tues–Sun 10am–8pm • Free

At the northern end of the Zona Luz, this park is bustling in the evenings, as crowds swirl around watching the street entertainers. Facing the plaza on the east side, the futuristic glass **Centro Cultural de Villahermosa** presents changing exhibitions of art, photography and costume, as well as film screenings and concerts – stroll by and check out the schedule.

La Casa Siempreviva and around

Sáenz, at Lerdo de Tejada **Casa Museo Carlos Pellicer** Tues–Sun 9am–5pm • Free

West of the Parque Juárez, the distinctive pink and purple paint on this old mansion immediately catches the eye. One of the few fully restored houses from the early twentieth century, it has beautiful tiled floors and arched stained-glass windows. It's usually open as a gallery with a small café, and is the anchor for a bit of an arts scene in the surrounding blocks.

At the end of Lerdo de Tejada, steps lead up to a small park where budgies sing in a large cage. Around the corner on Sáenz, also look for the Casa Museo Carlos Pellicer, where the poet and anthropologist who established Parque La Venta was born. In the side streets are a number of other small art galleries.

Museo de Historia de Tabasco

27 de Febrero, at Juárez • Tues–Sun 9am–5pm • M$30

On the southern side of the Zona Luz, Tabasco's history museum provides a quirky, detailed account of the state's development. The main attraction, however, is the 1915 building itself, tiled inside and out with colourful patterns from all over Europe and the Middle East – each room is different and dazzling.

Plaza de Armas

The official centre of the city, a patch of green adjacent to a sprawling expanse of concrete, is actually less lively than the area farther north. But the grand **Palacio del Gobierno**, with its classical columns, turrets and a clock tower, sits on the north edge, and you can poke your head inside to see any art or history exhibitions.

On the south side of the park lies the pretty, white **Templo de la Concepción** – commonly called "La Conchita". The church was first built here in 1799, but this and its successor were each demolished – the present building dates only from 1945. Off the concrete side of the plaza, steps lead up to the Puente Solidaridad footbridge, and a rather bleak square tower, its observation deck erratically open to the public.

Museo Regional de Antropología Carlos Pellicer Cámara

Av Carlos Pellicer 511, on the river • Tues–Sun 9am–5pm • M$20

A fifteen-minute walk south from the Zona Luz brings you to Villahermosa's riverside cultural centre, the Centro de Investigaciones de las Culturas Olmeca y Maya, or CICOM. The centrepiece of the complex is this anthropology and archeology museum and research centre, renovated and reconfigured over the course of three years after record flooding in 2007.

The multistorey exhibition space houses thousands of artefacts grand and small. Come down here to see four fragments from the ancient hieroglyph-laden Maya

11

monument that caused all the upset about 2012. Depending on which expert you consulted, they predicted either the end of civilization or the onset of a new era in human progress. While you're down here, you can also check out the other small museums in the complex (devoted to music and contemporary art), as well as the very good restaurant (see p.703).

Parque-Museo La Venta and around

Blv Adolfo Ruíz Cortines (Hwy-180), 2km northwest of the centre • Daily 8am–4pm; sound-and-light show Tues–Sun 7pm, 8pm & 9pm • M$40; sound-and-light show M$100; buy tickets and enter at a second gate, about 250m southwest along Paseo Tabasco • Look for *combis* on Madero marked "Tabasco 2000", "Circuito 1", "Parque Linda Vista" or "Fracc Carrizal"; a taxi costs M$50 or so

A visit to this archeological park and museum 2km northwest of the centre could easily fill half a day. The most important artefacts from the Olmec site of La Venta, some 120km west of Villahermosa, were transferred here in the late 1950s, when they were threatened by Pemex oil explorations.

Just inside the entrance, a display familiarizes you with what little is known about the Olmecs, as well as the history of the discovery of La Venta. The most significant and famous items in the park are the four gigantic **basalt heads**, notable for their African-looking features. They're also extraordinary because the material from which they were hewn does not occur locally in the region, so they must have been imported from what is now Veracruz, Oaxaca or Guatemala. Additionally, there's a whole series of other Olmec stone sculptures.

To conjure a jungle setting, monkeys, agoutis (large rodents) and coatis (members of the racoon family) wander around freely, while crocodiles, jaguars and other animals from the region are displayed in sizeable enclosures. At night, there's a rather good **sound-and-light show** that involves strolling from monument to monument, dramatically illuminated amid the shadowy trees. Parque La Venta is actually set on the edge of the much larger Parque Tomás Garrido Canabal, stretching along the shore of an extensive lake, the **Laguna de Ilusiones**. There are walking trails here and boats to rent,, or you can climb the Mirador de los Águilas, a tower in the middle of the lake.

Museo de Historia Natural

Blv Adolfo Ruíz Cortínes • Tues–Sun 9am–5pm • M$20

Opposite the La Venta entrance, this small museum is a nice counterpoint to the archeology, as it focuses on the living heritage of Tabasco. Displays cover the state's geography, geology, animals and plants, focusing on the interaction between humans and the environment.

OLMEC CULTURE

Relatively little is known about the **Olmec culture**, referred to by many archeologists as the mother culture of Mesoamerica. Its legacy, which includes the Long Count calendar, glyphic writing, a rain deity and probably also the concept of zero and the ball-game, influenced all subsequent civilizations in ancient Mexico. The name Olmec comes from Nahautl (the language of the Aztecs) word "Olmecatl", meaning "rubber people"; this is a reference to the Olmecs practice of extracting latex from trees growing in the region and mixing it with the sap of local vines to produce rubber.

The fact that the Olmecs developed and flourished in the unpromising environment of the Gulf coast swamps 3200 years ago only adds to their mystery. After emerging around 1200 BC, and eventually spanning across northern Central America and much of central Mexico, the civilization began to decline around 400 BC, and over the subsequent thousand years the plains were gradually absorbed by the great Maya cities to the east, an influence most notable at **Comalcalco** (see p.707).

Yumká

Ranchería Las Barrancas, 14km from the centre, near the airport • Daily 9am–4pm • M$60, children M$30 • ☎ 993 596 6704, ⓦ yumka
.org • *Combis* leave regularly from along Amado Nervo behind the market at the top end of Constitución, and a shuttle bus (M$20) departs
from Ruíz Cortines, west of Parque La Venta, on weekends at 9am, 10.30am, noon and 1.30pm; a taxi costs around M$200–250

You probably didn't come to Mexico to see hippos, but this safari park is well managed and
fun on weekends, when it's popular with local families. It covers more than six square
kilometres, so after a guided walking tour of the Tabasco jungle, complete with monkeys,
you board a train for a tour round paddocks representing the savannahs of Africa and Asia
– elephants, rhinos, giraffes and antelopes are rarely displayed in Mexico and almost never
in such spacious surroundings. After a stop at the restaurant, you can take a boat tour of
the lagoon, where, in addition to hippos, there are good bird watching opportunities.

ARRIVAL AND DEPARTURE VILLAHERMOSA

BY PLANE

Aeropuerto Carlos A. Rovirosa (☎ 993 356 0157) is about
13km east of the centre on the main road towards
Escárcega and Palenque. No buses run to the centre; a taxi
will set you back around M$250.

Destinations Houston (1 daily; 2hr 45min); Mérida (3
daily; 1hr 30min); Mexico City (13 daily; 1hr 30min); Poza
Rica (1 daily; 1hr 40min); Veracruz (2 daily; 1hr 10min).

Airlines Aeromar, Av de los Ríos 1110, Plaza Usumacinta,
Tabasco 2000 ☎ 993 316 8510, ⓦ aeromar.com.mx;
Aeroméxico, Carlos Pellicer Cámara 511 ☎ 993 139 4541,
ⓦ aeromexico.com.

BY BUS

The bus stations are pretty close to each other northwest of
the Zona Luz. Most buses into Chiapas travel via Puente
Chiapas, which seems circuitous but knocks several hours
off the journey. For San Cristóbal de las Casas, it's often
easier to change at either Tuxtla or Palenque.

First-class buses The first-class station, with service from
ADO, OCC and TRT, is a modern building on Javier Mina. The
front of the station deals with services originating here;
tickets for *de paso* services are sold in a separate complex
behind, to the west. There's luggage storage and an
information booth, usually unstaffed. *Combis* ply the road
outside, but to get to the Zona Luz requires changing buses
at the market – it's less hassle (and less confusing) to take
a taxi (M$30–40) or walk (about 20min). To get to the
terminal from the centre, catch a *combi* from the malecón
heading for "Chedraui".

Destinations Campeche (15 daily; 5hr 35min–8hr);
Cancún (14 daily; 12hr 35min–14hr); Chetumal (6 daily;
7hr 50min); Emiliano Zapata (1–2 hourly; 2hr); Frontera
(hourly; 1hr 10min); Mérida (9 daily; 10hr 45min–11hr
55min); Mexico City (roughly hourly; 11hr); Palenque

(hourly; 2hr–2hr 30min); San Andrés Tuxtla (3 daily at
3.30am, 4am & 11am; 5hr–6hr 45min); San Cristóbal de las
Casas (1 daily at 11.40pm; 6hr 25min); Tapachula (3 daily at
4.15am, 9.40am & 6.15pm; 9hr 45min–10hr 20min);
Tenosique (10 daily; 3hr 10min–3hr 30min); Tuxtla
Gutiérrez (16 daily; 4–5hr 15min); Veracruz (roughly
hourly; 6hr 40min–9hr 35min).

Second-class buses The main second-class terminal, the
Central de Autobuses, is on Ruíz Cortines, just a few min
farther from the centre than the ADO; you'll have to walk or
take a taxi.

Destinations Tacotalpa and Coatzacoalcos, for La Venta
(every 30min; 2hr 30min); Teapa (every 30min; 1hr);
Tenosique (10 daily; 5hr).

Other terminals There's another, more dilapidated,
second-class terminal for relatively local buses near the
ADO, off Eusebio Castillo near Zozaya, with frequent buses
to Emiliano Zapata, Frontera and Paraíso, as well as
Palenque and Escárcega. Several companies run buses to
Comalcalco, the best of which is Comalli Bus, on Gil y Sáenz
above Abelardo Reyes, not far from the ADO
(4.45am–10pm; 1hr).

BY COMBI AND COLECTIVO

On Gil y Sáenz, *combis* run to Nacajuca (for Cupilco;
30min), and, just around the corner, pale yellow
colectivos go from Castellanos, just east of Gil y Sáenz.
Just to the north, off Ruíz Cortines, La Sultana runs a
comfortable service to Teapa (every 30min,
5am–10.30pm). *Colectivos* are usually faster than buses
or *combis*, and not that much more expensive. The
terminal for many other destinations is just north of the
ADO on Abelardo Reyes. The shared taxis leave when full
for Palenque, Paraíso, Frontera and Tacotalpa. You won't
have to wait long, at least in the morning.

GETTING AROUND

By taxi Villahermosa's humidity might make you consider
taking taxis more frequently – rates are around M$30
within most of the city.

By bus The local bus system comprises a confusing jumble
of *combi* minivans, with the Mercado Pino Suárez acting as
the main hub.

11

INFORMATION AND TOURS

Tourist information Despite the growth in visitor numbers in recent years, there's no handy tourist office in Villahermosa. Booths at the airport, history museum, Parque La Venta and ADO bus station can only offer leaflets, and the main state and federal office on Av de los Ríos, south of Paseo Tabasco in Tabasco 2000 (Mon–Fri 8am–6pm, Sat 8am–1pm; ☎993 310 9700 ext 5238, ⓦvisitetabasco .com), is too far away from the centre to be of much use.

Travel agents There's no shortage of travel agencies in the Zona Luz. Creatur, Paseo Tabasco 1404, on the right just beyond Ruíz Cortines (☎993 310 9900, ⓦcreaturviajes .com), is the best in the region, with multilingual staff.

Boat tours The Capitán Beuló II (ⓦolmecaexpress.com) goes on 1hr tours (Sat 12.30pm, 2.30pm, 5.30pm & 7.30pm, Sun 12.30pm, 2.30pm, 5.30pm & 7.30pm; M$180) from the west riverbank, by the cluster of bars and restaurants adjacent to the Zona Luz. Book at the *Olmeca Plaza* (see below). On the east bank of the river, across the Puente de Solidaridad, more casual pleasure boats gather at weekends.

ACCOMMODATION

Budget hotels in Villahermosa are not great value; most of the low-cost options are on Madero or Lerdo de Tejada, close to the heart of things – though none is particularly praiseworthy. A few of the top-end hotels, on the other hand, are actually well priced compared with more touristy cities, but a steady stream of Pemex employees can keep the rooms full. These pricier places are located in the Tabasco 2000 district, about 2km west of the centre along Paseo Tabasco.

Marriott Villahermosa Paseo Tabasco 1407 ☎993 310 0201, ⓦmarriott.com. One of the newer top-end hotels in the Tabasco 2000 area, the Marriott won't win any prizes for character, but it's very comfortable, well staffed and often good value, especially at weekends. US$106 (M$1590)

Miraflores Reforma 304 ☎993 358 0470, ⓦhotel miraflores.com. A bit cheaper than the *Madan*, this independent hotel has all the same amenities (parking, a lobby bar and café and lobby wi-fi), though they're not all quite as slick and new. Rooms have nice balconies, and the staff are friendly. M$870

Olmeca Plaza Madero 418 ☎1 800 201 0909, ⓦhotel olmecaplaza.com. A slick hotel with modern rooms, a great location and a swimming pool. Walk-in rates can seem a little steep, but desk clerks are often able to conjure up "promotions" if you look like you might head elsewhere. M$890

Oriente Madero 425 ☎993 312 0121, ☺hotel-oriente @hotmail.com. The best of the budget options, though a bit pricier than its neighbours – you're paying for a big tile-floor room that's actually clean, with a very firm bed and a decent bathroom. The mint-green paint job and pink staircase are a bonus. A/c rooms cost M$120 extra. M$360

Plaza Independencia Independencia 123 ☎993 312 1299, ⓦhotelesplaza.com.mx. Comfortable, well-furnished rooms and suites in a quiet area just off the Plaza de Armas. Front rooms have balconies with views over the river. Room maintenance can be a little spotty, but there's a lift, pool, good restaurant (serving Mexican standards, as well as a few local fish dishes) and bar with live music, plus secure parking. M$750

Provincia Express Lerdo de Tejada 303 ☎993 314 5376. ☺provinciaexpress09@hotmail.com. Reasonably clean and welcoming small-chain option near the malecón, with smallish rooms and bracing a/c. Ask for a room on an upper floor and east side, to get a balcony with a view of bustling Madero and the river. M$500

Quality Inn Cencali Paseo Tabasco, at Juárez ☎993 313 6611. The best-value spot in the Tabasco 2000 area. Set in quiet, luxuriant gardens on the shore of a lagoon, the *Cencali* has an inviting pool, comfortable, well-furnished rooms with a/c and suites with beautiful tiled bathrooms; upstairs rooms have balconies. Parque La Venta is a 1km walk. M$1100

Quinta Real Paseo de la Choca 1402 ☎993 310 1300, ⓦquintareal.com/villahermosa. The best of the city's luxury hotels, in grand mansion style, with vast rooms and two pools. It's 5km west from the centre, but right by the city's outer ring road, making it easily accessible for drivers, yet not too far from Parque La Venta. M$1500

EATING

The Zona Luz boasts mostly **fast food and cafés** – with a couple of exceptions noted below. On Aldama north of Lerdo de Tejada are half a dozen taco joints. As ever, the **market** – here, a vast, tidy two-storey complex trimmed with white wrought-iron trellises – is good for fruit, bread and cheap tacos. It is several blocks north of the Zona Luz on Constitución.

CAFÉS, CHEAP EATS AND SNACKS

La Antigua Lerdo de Tejada 608, on the steps by Casa de la Siempreviva ☎993 312 8472. A pleasant café for good coffee, smoothies and sandwiches, plus more substantial food including decent pasta dishes (mains M$86–190). There's often live music in the evening. Mon–

Sat 7am–8pm, Sun 1–8pm.

La Catedral de Sabor Independencia 204, adjacent to the Templo de la Concepción. Cool down with a refreshing *horchata de coco* – a Tabasco speciality (M$25 for 500ml; M$40 for a litre) – at this little pavement stand. There's also a selection of ice creams and lollies. Daily 11am–10pm.

Cockteleria El Rock and Roll Reforma 307. A bustling place with excellent seafood cocktails, *ceviche* and fish in a variety of sauces (mains M$75–180). Sadly, the rock jukebox has given way to videos on flat-screen TVs. There's slightly quieter seating upstairs. Daily 2–10pm.

RESTAURANTS

100% Natural Via 3, Local 14–17, La Hacienda, Tabasco 2000 ☎ 993 317 7604, ⊛ 100natural.com.mx. If you're staying in the Tabasco 2000 area and want to avoid US-style fast food, this Mexican chain is a good alternative, with a multinational menu and a focus on healthy eating – there are sandwiches, pasta dishes, salads and stir-fries. Great breakfasts (M$65–110) and juices too. Daily 7am–11pm.

El Mirador Madero 105 ☎ 993 314 3495. This first-floor restaurant, specializing in fish and seafood, had a slightly time-warped feel. Prices are not unreasonable – expect to pay around M$250–300/person for dinner. Mon–Sat 2–8pm, bar till 1am.

La Noria Gregorio Méndez Magaña 1008 ☎ 993 314 1659, ⊛ facebook.com/lanoriacocinaarabe. Comfortable a/c restaurant serving inexpensive Lebanese and Middle Eastern dishes like kebabs, pilafs and hummus, tastes that are rare elsewhere in the state (dishes M$35–160). Mon–Fri 10am–8pm, Sat–Sun 10am–7.30pm.

★ **Los Tulipanes** CICOM complex ☎ 993 312 9217, ⊛ facebook.com/restaurantelostulipanes. A lovely riverfront restaurant, a bit formal and unstinting on the a/c. Come here to sample delicious renditions of Tabasco cuisine: shrimp with coconut and passion-fruit salsa, fresh corn tortillas stuffed with seafood or fish soup. Dishes come in massive portions; mains M$100–220. Tues–Sat 8am–9pm (though the bar is open later), Sun 8am–6pm.

DIRECTORY

Banks and exchange Branches of all major banks, with ATMS, are at the airport and in the centre, on Madero or Juárez.

Internet One of the most centrally located is Ciber, at Aldama 526A.

Laundry Lavandería Yaveyire, corner Madero 27 de Febrero (closed Sun).

Post office The main post office is in the Zona Luz at Sáenz 131 (Mon–Fri 9am–3pm, Sat 9am–1pm).

South of Villahermosa

South of Tabasco's capital, the foothills of the Sierra de Chiapas are heavy with banana plantations, while higher up, thick forest remains and the roadside pools and wetlands are as wild as ever. The highlights of this region include numerous **caves and grottoes**, as well as several accessible spas, created by tectonic activity, in the main town of **Teapa**. From here, you can catch a series of second-class buses over the mountains, a good slow route into Chiapas.

Teapa

Fifty-nine kilometres to the south of Villahermosa, the small, friendly town of **TEAPA** is a lovely base for visiting nearby caves and hot-spring spas. The springs are sulphuric but soothing, and popular at weekends; during the week, they're often empty. We recommend one popular hotel built around them – it's also open to day visitors.

Río Puyacatengo

Walk or take the bus for Tacotalpa; taxis charge about M$25

There's swimming in the Río Teapa in town, but it's better on this larger river, 3km east. Follow signs for *balnearios* just off the road to the right of the bridge, where big natural pools form in the river and several restaurants serve food.

Grutas del Coconá

4km northeast of Teapa • Daily 9am–5pm • M$30 • Green-and-white *colectivos* run from next to the plaza in Teapa; or walk, in about 45min: from Méndez, head for the Pemex station and turn right, following the sign – when you get near the forested hills, bear left where the road divides and cross over the rail track

Eight chambers of these spectacular caves are open to tourists, as is a small museum displaying pre-Hispanic artefacts found inside. A stroll through takes about 45 minutes. The caves are surprisingly humid, and lined with oddly shaped stalactites and stalagmites.

By bus Second-class buses (every 30min; 1hr) run from Villahermosa's Central de Autobuses. They pull in at the market near the edge of town. To get to the centre, walk a couple of blocks down the hill and turn left at the green clock onto Méndez, which takes you to the plaza.

ACCOMMODATION

Los Azufrés 8km west of Teapa on Hwy-195 to Tuxtla Gutiérrez ☎ 932 327 5806; second-class buses toward Pichucalco stop here. This classy spa hotel, open to day visitors, has a huge pool and a restaurant serving local specialities, including *pejelagarto*. It also offers guided walks, bike rental and fishing. Some of the guestrooms have private thermal pools. Doubles M$600; camping M$90

Quintero Eduardo Rosario Bastar 108, Teapa ☎ 932 322 0045, ⓦ hotelquintero.com. One block away from easy swimming in the river shallows. The modern rooms have cool brick floors, a/c and TV. The restaurant serves regional *antojitos* and festive cocktails. M$400

Tapijulapa

To escape the humidity of the lowlands, head up the valley of the Río Oxolotán to the Sierra Puana, Tabasco's "hill country". This is an extraordinarily picturesque area, with quiet colonial towns set in beautiful wooded valleys, and a turquoise river laden with sulphur. The main destination is **TAPIJULAPA**, a beautiful whitewashed village with narrow cobbled streets that could, at first glance, be mistaken for a mountain town in Spain. Dubbed a Pueblo Mágico by the federal government, it's celebrated for wicker craftspeople, who have workshops all over town, and it's the starting point for a beautiful natural park. From the edge of the village, the main street, López Portillo, leads downhill to a pretty little **plaza**. At weekends, local women serve exceptionally delicious tamales and other inexpensive food in the large civic building. There were no reliable hotels at the time of research – it's best to plan on a day trip only, though you'll need to make a fairly early start.

By bus From Teapa, take a bus to Tacotalpa from the OCC terminal on Méndez (every 30min; 20min), then switch for another to Tapijulapa (hourly; 45min). The last bus back to Teapa (with connections to Villahermosa) leaves at 7pm.

Parque Natural Villa Luz

Daily 8am–5pm • Free

You probably won't make it far in Tapijulapa before you're accosted by kids offering to take you to **boats** for this natural park with its spa pools, cascades and caves. The park's outstanding feature – not least for its powerful aroma – is the stream running through it, which owes its cloudy blue-white colour to dissolved minerals, especially sulphur. Where it meets the Río Oxolotán, it breaks into dozens of cascades and semicircular pools. Thousands of butterflies settle on the riverbanks, taking nourishment from dissolved minerals, and jungle trees and creepers grow wherever they find a foothold – a truly primeval sight.

Casa Museo Tomás Garrido Canabal

1.5km outside town • Daily 8am–5pm • M$50

From the boat dock, well-signed trails (no need for a guide) lead 1.5km to the waterfalls, passing the country retreat of Canabal, the controversial former governor of Tabasco. It contains a few of his personal effects, as well as Zoque artefacts and handicrafts from the area.

Cuevas de las Sardinas Ciegas

Another path leads to the **Cuevas de las Sardinas Ciegas** – the caves of "blind sardines", sightless fish with translucent scales that have adapted to the cave's sulphur-rich waters. The gases in the cave are so powerful that it's impossible to breathe inside, but you can

peer into their precipitous entrances. In Maya cosmology the openings are believed to lead to the underworld (Xibalba). During Semana Santa, the local people catch the fish and dedicate them to the rain god, Chac. Beyond the caves are a couple of *albercas*, stream-fed **swimming pools** said to have therapeutic properties.

ARRIVAL AND DEPARTURE   PARQUE NATURAL VILLA LUZ

By boat Two companies offer boats from Tapijulapa: around M$50 return, with 2hr waiting time. The better-established operation is past the plaza: follow López Portillo till is dead-ends, then turn right to the river.

On foot It's an easy 3km (35min) walk from Tapijulapa: cross the river on the suspension bridge (to the right before you reach the plaza), head left on the concrete path, across the football field, then follow the track over the hill, keeping close to the main river.

By car The main entrance is on the main highway toward Oxolotán, a few km past the turn for Tapijulapa.

West of Villahermosa

The main attractions west of the city is a series of isolated ruins, the most famous being the Olmec site at **La Venta**, although, with the best pieces now residing in Villahermosa, the site itself is a bit empty. The little-known ancient Zoque people also flourished in this area, and the ruins at **Malpasito** reflect that unique culture.

La Venta

This small town on the border between Tabasco and Veracruz, 128km from Villahermosa, would be of little interest were it not for the nearby **archeological ruins**. The town is served by a steady stream of **buses** from Villahermosa and Coatzalcoalcos, so there's no need or real reason to stay.

The ruins

Daily 8am–5pm • M$47 • Buses from Villahermosa (every 30min 5am–9pm; 2hr 30min)

This ancient city, the name of which remains unknown, was occupied by the Olmecs between 1200 and 400 BC and is regarded as their most important centre. Most of the finest pieces found here, including the famous **basalt heads**, were transferred to Villahermosa's Parque La Venta (see p.700) in 1957 and 1958. The **museum** at the entrance to La Venta itself (800m north of the bus station) has a model of the grounds, as well as glass cases with rather confusing displays of unlabelled pottery.

The site itself retains some replicas of the sculptures and heads now displayed in Villahermosa, and a few weathered steles and monuments, but the highlight is the huge grass-covered mound, about 30m high, clearly a pyramid, with fluted sides believed to represent the ravines on the flanks of a sacred volcano. The climb up is worth the effort for the views and the breeze. Paths below take you through the jungle – fascinating for its plants and butterflies, but haunted by ferocious mosquitoes.

Malpasito and around

100km southwest of Villahermosa • Daily 8am–5pm • M$35 • To reach the area by car, exit the toll highway immediately north of the Puente Chiapas; signs point to Las Flores and Malpasito village off Hwy-187

Some 100km southwest of Villahermosa, between the borders of Veracruz and Chiapas, a narrow triangle of Tabasco thrusts into mountains known as the **Sierra Huimanguillo.** These rugged peaks are not that high, only up to 1000m, but in order to appreciate them fully, you'll need to do some hiking: not only to canyons and waterfalls, but also to the ruins of **MALPASITO**, with their astonishing **petroglyphs**.

A car, however, is necessary. Although you can get to Malpasito by bus, it arrives too late to hike up to the ruins themselves, and there is no reliable overnight accommodation in the village (though you could, in a pinch, ask in the village for Guillermo Pérez, who sometimes rents rooms).

As you're in the area, you can cool off at the **Cascadas Las Pavas**, a beautiful series of waterfalls that are set in a tranquil spot down a path through dense flowering trees, and often surrounded by butterflies. To get there from Malpasito, backtrack along the road to town, and bear left at the fork.

The archeological site

The post-Classic **Zoque** ruins are overshadowed by jagged, jungle-covered mountains, the highest point in Tabasco. Though the ruins bear a certain resemblance to Palenque, the Zoque were not a Maya group – one of the few facts known about them. On the way into the site you pass terraces and grass-covered mounds, eventually arriving at the unique **ball-court**. At the top of the stone terraces forming the south side of the court, a flight of steps leads down to a narrow room, with stone benches lining either side. Beyond this, and separate from the chamber, is a square pit more than 2m deep and 1.5m wide. This room may have been used by the ball-players to make a spectacular entrance as they emerged onto the top of the ball-court.

But the most amazing features of this site are its **petroglyphs**. More than three hundred have been discovered so far: animals, birds, houses and more, etched into the rock. One large boulder is covered in enigmatic flat-topped triangles surmounted by a square or rectangle, and shown above what look like ladders or steps – stylized houses or launching platforms for the chariots of the gods, depending on your viewpoint.

11

North to the coast

The journey from Villahermosa along **the coast**, either west to Veracruz or east to Campeche, is beautiful. The road hugs the shore, and it's never hard to find deserted beaches and lagoons. Attractive as the coastal route is, it's undeniably slow, and almost no tourists travel it, preferring the inland route to the Yucatán in order to stop by Palenque on the way. But travellers with extra time will be well rewarded by spending a day north of Villahermosa, at the ruins of **Comalcalco**. The road winds through Tabasco's **cacao plantations**, with a few minor diversions along the way.

Cupilco

Thirty kilometres out of Villahermosa, the main road passes through **CUPILCO**, notable for its roadside church, the **Templo de la Virgen de la Asunción**. Decorated in gold and blue with floral patterns, it's a beautiful example of the distinctive *tabasqueño* approach to sacred spaces.

Hacienda la Luz

In the area around Comalcalco several **cacao haciendas** have opened their doors to visitors. The first you pass, 2km before Comalcalco, is Hacienda la Luz (☎933 337 1122, ⓦhaciendalaluz.mx; tours Tues–Sun 9am, 11am, 1pm & 3pm; M$80), which makes an interesting diversion if you've got your own car – and there are plenty of chocolates on offer, if you have a sweet tooth.

Comalcalco

58km northwest of Villahermosa • Daily except Mon 8am–4pm • M$46 including museum

The Classic-period site of **COMALCALCO** is an easy, very worthwhile trip from the city. The westernmost Maya site, Comalcalco was occupied around the same time as Palenque (250–900 AD), with which it shares some features, and it may have been ruled by some of the same kings.

The area's lack of building stone forced the Chontal Maya to adopt a distinctive form of construction: kiln-fired brick. As if the bricks themselves were not sufficient to mark this site as different, the builders added mystery to technology: each brick was stamped or moulded with a geometric or representational design before firing, with the design deliberately placed facing inwards, so that it could not be seen in the finished building. Many of these astonishing designs are on display in a museum; there are also restrooms and a small café at the site.

The museum

The labels here are in Spanish only, but the marvellous work on the bricks speaks for itself. Animals depicted include crocodiles, turtles, frogs, lizards, dogs and mice, while those portraying the sculpted faces of rulers display an advanced level of artistic development. One of the most amazing figures is of a skeleton that appears to be leaping out at you from the surface of the brick.

The abundant clay that provided such a versatile medium for architects and artists here also formed the basis for many more mundane artefacts. Comalcalco means "place of the *comales*" – fired clay griddles for cooking tortillas – and these and other clay vessels have been excavated in great numbers. Some of the largest jars were used as **funerary urns** and several are on display here, including one with an intact skeleton.

The site

Though there are dozens of buildings at Comalcalco, only ten or so of the larger ones have been restored. Because the brickwork is so fragile, you're not allowed to enter or climb on many of them, but you can follow a path up to Structure 3 and around the Palacio.

Entering the site, you first come to **Temple I**, the main structure of the **North Plaza Cluster**, a tiered pyramid with a massive central stairway. Originally, the whole building (like all of the structures here) would have been covered with stucco made from oyster shells, sculpted into masks and reliefs of rulers and deities, and brightly painted. Only a few of these features remain – the exposed ones protected from further erosion by shelters, while others have deliberately been left buried.

Facing Temple I at the opposite end of the site is the **Gran Acrópolis**, a complex of buildings, some still being excavated, raised above the plaza. Here you can climb up to **El Palacio** for some excellent close-up views of the brickwork, including a series of massive brick piers and arches that once formed an enormous double corbelled vault, 80m long and over 8m wide – one of the largest enclosed spaces the Maya ever built. There's a fine stucco mask of Kinich Ahau, the Maya sun god, on **Templo VI**, and at the side of **Temple V** a small, corbel-arched room contains stucco reliefs of nine, richly dressed, half-life-size figures apparently in conversation or even argument – they may represent the **Lords of Xibalba**, the Maya underworld.

ARRIVAL AND DEPARTURE   **COMALCALCO**

By bus Comalli Bus in Villahermosa (see p.701) has services to the town of Comalcalco, on the west side of the highway (where you'll be dropped off at or near the ADO terminal) about 3km south of the ruins. There are plenty of buses back to Villahermosa (look for TRT buses, which take the fast route via Cárdenas, every 45min, or Allegro and Comalli buses, which go via Cupilco) or on to Paraíso (20min), running along the highway. From town, you can then flag down any second-class bus heading north to the ruins; ask the driver for "ruinas", or get off after 5min, when you see the sign on the right. The ruins are 1km from the highway, down a long straight paved road.

By combi From Comalcalco town, green *combis*, found outside the ADO terminal, ply the route to the ruins; some go all the way to the site, but others will drop you on the highway, 1km away.

By taxi Taxis from Comalcalco town charge around M$30–40 to the ruins.

The north coast

Passing through areas of wetland teeming with wildlife, the little-travelled **north coast** road is a treat. Mangroves and lagoons are covered with flocks of feeding water birds, and if you look hard enough you may spot the odd crocodile. However, the beaches themselves are a bit disappointing: the sand is grey-brown and, though generally clean, you've always got the oil refinery in sight to the east. There are few hotels along this stretch, but plenty of spaces for **camping** – if you can stand the swarms of mosquitoes and sandflies.

Paraíso

A weekend escape for Villahermosa residents, **PARAÍSO**, 75km away on the banks of the Río Seco, is a sleepy place, with some beaches nearby – pleasant enough if you need to wind down, and a better place to spend the night than Frontera, 77km east on the way to Campeche. The nearest beach, **Playa Limón**, where locals go for picnics on weekends, is a short *combi* or taxi ride north of Paraíso.

ARRIVAL AND GETTING AROUND   PARAÍSO

By bus Paraíso's ADO bus station is 1km south of the centre along Benito Juárez, the main road. Turn right out of the station and keep walking: eventually you'll see the town's most distinctive monument – the twin-towered colonial church – across the river up ahead. There's a daily first-class bus to Villahermosa (5pm; on the return leg the bus departs Villahermosa at 9.18am; 1hr 45min–2hr 5min).

The main second-class station, with departures for points along the coast, is north of the centre and well served by *combis*; to make the 15min walk, turn south (left) and aim for the church towers.
By combi Playa Limón is a 20min ride north of Paraíso.
By taxi Taxis to the beaches cost around M$50.

ACCOMMODATION AND EATING

Sabina Melchor Ocampo 115, east side of the plaza ☎ 933 333 2483, ⓦ hotelsabinaparaiso.com. The *Sabina* offers clean a/c en-suite rooms with TVs and drinking water. Aim for one on the second floor, where the terraces and big windows are more open to the occasional ocean-scented breezes. **M$550**

Tabasquenisimo Melchor Ocampo, east side of the plaza ☎ 933 132 3844. This restaurant has a groaning menu of seafood dishes (around M$80–160), spiked with chiles, limes and various salsas, but not so heavily that they mute the freshness of the ingredients. The *ceviche* is the best choice, and portions are plentiful. Daily 7am–10pm.

Puerto Ceiba and the coast road east

Ten kilometres east of Paraíso, the road passes through **PUERTO CEIBA** on the shores of the **Laguna de Mecoacán**. There's a *parador turístico* here offering boat trips (around M$300 for up to fourteen people) and a restaurant serving regional dishes and fish straight out of the lake. The road then crosses **Laguna Santa** to the east, and there are turn-offs for several decent beaches before it meets Hwy-180, 50km or so north of Villahermosa. The first beach is **Playa Azúl**, where you can rent boats and jet skis. **Playa Pico de Oro**, 6km or so further on, is more tranquil. If you're travelling light you could easily camp at any of these and get back to the main road in the morning.

East to the Usumacinta and Guatemala

East of Villahermosa, Hwy-186 cuts across northern Chiapas before swinging north into Campeche to Francisco Escárcega, then east again as the only road across the base of the Yucatán Peninsula. At Catazajá, in Chiapas, 110km from Villahermosa, is the junction for **Palenque**. If you've already been there and want to see Tikal in Guatemala's Petén, you can go via **Tenosique** and **La Palma**, although it's quicker and cheaper to go from Frontera Corozal (see p.694); however, if you go this way, through this odd, seldom-visited side of Tabasco, you could stop at the nearby ruins of **Pomoná**. You'll pass through the town of **Emiliano Zapata** on the way, though there's little reason to stop unless you're coming from Palenque, in which case you'll probably need to change buses here.

Tenosique

Around 220km southeast of Villahermosa, on the banks of the now placid Río Usumacinta, is the town of **TENOSIQUE**. Streets are numbered according to the Yucatán system, with even numbers running north–south, and odd numbers running east–west.

FIESTAS IN CHIAPAS AND TABASCO

The states of Chiapas and Tabasco are extremely rich in festivals. Local tourist offices should have more information on what's happening.

New Year's Day (Jan 1). San Andrés Chamula and San Juan Chamula, both near San Cristóbal, have civil ceremonies to install a new government for the year.

Día de San Sebastián (Jan 20). In Chiapa de Corzo, a large fiesta with traditional dances (including the masked *parachicos*) lasts several days, with a re-enactment on Jan 21 of a naval battle on the Río Grijalva.

Día de la Candelaria (Feb 2). Colourful celebrations at Ocosingo.

Fiesta de San Caralampio (Feb 11–20). In Comitán, celebrated with a parade to San Caralampio church, where elaborate offerings are made and dances held in the plaza outside.

Carnaval (the week before Lent; variable Feb & March). Celebrated in hundreds of villages throughout the area, but at its most frenzied in the big cities, especially Villahermosa.

Anniversary of the foundation of Chiapa de Corzo (March 1). Town fair with kiddie rides, live music and more.

Semana Santa (Holy Week). Widely observed. There are particularly big ceremonies in San Cristóbal de las Casas. Ciudad Hidalgo, at the border near Tapachula, has a major week-long market.

Feria de San Cristóbal de las Casas (April 1–7). Festival in San Cristóbal de las Casas celebrating the town's foundation.

Feria de Villahermosa (second half of April). Villahermosa hosts its annual festival, with agricultural and industrial exhibits and the election of the queen of the flowers.

Día de San Pedro (April 29). Celebrated in several villages around San Cristóbal, including Amatenango del Valle and Zinacantán.

Día de la Santa Cruz (May 3). Celebrated in San Juan Chamula and in Teapa, between Villahermosa and San Cristóbal.

Día de San Isidro (May 15). Peasant celebrations everywhere – famous and picturesque fiestas in Huistán, near San Cristóbal. There's a four-day nautical marathon from Tenosique to Villahermosa, when craft from all over the country race down 600km of the Río Usumacinta.

Día de San Antonio (June 13). Celebrated in Simojovel, near San Cristóbal, and Cárdenas (Tabasco), west of Villahermosa.

Día de San Juan (June 24). The culmination of several days' celebration in San Juan Chamula.

Día de San Cristóbal (July 17). Celebrated enthusiastically in San Cristóbal de las Casas and in nearby villages such as Tenejapa and Amatenango del Valle.

Día de Santiago (July 25). Provokes widespread celebrations, especially in San Cristóbal de las Casas.

Fiesta de Santo Domingo de Guzmán (last week of July, first week of Aug). Comitán's fair, with concerts, rodeos and more.

Fiesta de San Lorenzo (Sun nearest Aug 10). Celebrated in Zinacantán, with much music and dancing.

Día de Santa Rosa (Aug 30). Celebrated in San Juan Chamula, when the locals don traditional garb and play Tzotzil harps and instruments outside the church.

Independence Day (Sept 14–16). In Chiapas, independence celebrations are preceded by those in honour of the state's annexation to Mexico.

Día de la Virgen del Rosario (first Sun in Oct). Celebrated in San Juan Chamula and Zinacantán with Tzotzil folk music and dances. There's also a special craft market.

Día de los Muertos (Day of the Dead; Nov 1–2). The most captivating celebration of the Day of the Dead in Chiapas takes place in Comitán, where the cemeteries overflow with flowers and ornate altars.

Día de la Virgen de Guadalupe (Dec 12). An important day throughout Mexico. There are particularly good fiestas in Tuxtla Gutiérrez and San Cristóbal de las Casas.

Feria and cheese expo (Dec 17–22). Held in Pijijiapan, on the coast highway to Tapachula.

Between the main street, Calle 26 (also called Pino Suárez), which leads up to the plaza, and Calle 28, you'll find pretty much everything you need.

There's not a lot to do in Tenosique. Its main claim to fame is as the birthplace of Mexican national hero Pino Suárez (September 8, 1869). His former house is on Calle 26; it's now painted blue and white, as it's the offices of Telcel.

ARRIVAL AND DEPARTURE   TENOSIQUE

By bus Buses arrive at a small terminal close to the highway, 2.5km out of town. Inexpensive *colectivos* and shared taxis run frequently to the centre; get off when you see a large white church with red trim on the right. There are regular buses to/from Villahermosa (10 daily; 3hr 10min–3hr 30min). For the Yucatán, it's generally best to get one of the frequent buses to Emiliano Zapata (11 daily; 1hr–1hr 30min) and change there.

TO GUATEMALA
It's more convenient to enter Guatemala at the heavily policed border crossing of **El Ceibo**, 60km southeast of

Tenosique, rather than the town of La Palma, cutting travel time to Flores to around 6hr in total. Buses leave Tenosique (hourly 6am–5pm; 1hr) behind the market on the corner of C 45 and C 16, and take an hour to reach the border. From there, you can pick up a minibus to cross the new bridge to El Naranjo in Guatemala. At least eight daily buses leave for Flores (3hr). Be sure to get your passport stamped by both Mexican and Guatemalan immigration before you leave, as there is no office on the Guatemala side. There are a number of rather desperate hotels and *comedores* on El Naranjo's main road.

ACCOMMODATION AND EATING

Most of the restaurants in the centre are unimpressive and cheap, and have similar menus. A row of *comedores* lines the front of the market, off the northwest corner of the plaza. If you are going to Guatemala, stock up on provisions here.

Hacienda Tabasqueña C 26 no. 512 ☎ 934 342 2731, ⓦ hotelhaciendatabasquena.com. If you do have to stay the night in Tenosique, this mid-range place is easily the

best option, with comfortable, spacious en-suite rooms, some of which come with a/c. There's also a small café. **M$400**

DIRECTORY

Banks The banks in Tenosique aren't interested in changing money, but Bancomer on the plaza has an ATM;

for Guatemalan quetzales ask around in the shops on C 28.

Pomoná

30km west of Tenosique on Hwy-203, then 4km east • Daily except Mon 10am–5pm; **museum** daily except Mon 10am–4pm • M$46 • Taxi from Tenosique or Emiliano Zapata around M$40–60; *colectivos* also run from either town along Hwy-203, leaving you to walk the final 4km

Although this site, located in rolling countryside with views of forested hills to the south, makes a pleasant diversion, a visit is really only for the dedicated. The restored structures date from the Late Classic period; the site's largest building is a stepped pyramid with six levels. **Pomoná** was a subject of the much larger city of Piedras Negras in Guatemala, further up the valley of the Usumacinta. The small **museum** houses some interesting carved panels and steles, made even more mysterious by the omission of any explanations as to what you're seeing.

Moral-Reforma

45km north of Tenosique, near Cascadas de Reforma • Daily 8am–5pm • Free • Take a *colectivo* from Tenosique to Cascadas de Reforma, then walk 2km (some drivers may take you all the way if you ask)

Excavations at this site since 2009 have uncovered an amazing collection of stucco decoration, steles and masks. The most fragile and significant pieces are now at the archeology museum in Villahermosa (see p.700) for study and preservation, but the work has also led to the opening of two previously buried temples, with many others waiting to be rediscovered.

The Yucatán

CUADRÁNGULO DE LOS PÁJAROS, UXMAL

The Yucatán

Until the 1960s, when proper road and rail links were finally completed, the Yucatán Peninsula – the states of Campeche, Yucatán and Quintana Roo – had more contact with Europe, Cuba and the US than with central Mexico. Today, the region remains distinct, with traditional Maya life alongside massive tourist attractions such as the great ruins of Chichén Itzá and the super-resort of Cancún. Once the province of Maya rebels and palm-plantation owners, the Caribbean coast is now the so-called Riviera Maya, which includes the towns of Playa del Carmen and Tulum. But away from these big centres, especially in the south, where settlements are sparsely scattered in dense forest, there's still a distinct pioneering feel.

In northern Yucatán state, the landscape is relatively spare: shallow, rocky earth gives rise to stunted trees, and underground springs known as *cenotes* (see box, p.737) are the only source of water. Campeche state, by contrast, boasts a huge area of **tropical forest**, the Calakmul Biosphere Reserve. The entire coastline is great for spotting **wildlife** – notably turtles at the Sian Ka'an Biosphere Reserve in Quintana Roo and flocks of flamingos at Celestún and Río Lagartos in Yucatán. Along the Caribbean coast, magnificent offshore **coral growth** forms part of the world's second-largest barrier reef.

There's really only one main route around the Yucatán Peninsula; the variation comes in where you break the journey or make side trips. Whether you come from Palenque or along the coast from Villahermosa, you'll find yourself on Hwy-180, which heads up to **Campeche** then veers away from the **Gulf Coast** towards **Mérida** and east to **Valladolid** and the Caribbean coast. Near Mérida are both the excellent craft town of **Izamal** and the **Ruta Puuc**, which includes major Maya sites such as Uxmal and **Chichén Itzá**, as well as a trove of smaller, less-visited ruins. Past these, you can push on to the Caribbean beaches.

The stretch of coast between **Cancún** and **Tulum**, known as the Riviera Maya and including **Playa del Carmen** and **Isla Cozumel**, is one of Mexico's most heavily touristed areas. South of Tulum, the **Sian Ka'an Biosphere Reserve**, encompassing mangroves thick with birdlife and coral reefs offshore, briefly slows the march of progress. The coast south of the biosphere – dubbed the **Costa Maya** – is on its own development trajectory, but it's still your best bet for hammock camping. The vast, beautiful **Laguna**

12

CYCLIST IN CAMPECHE

Highlights

❶ Campeche This lovely walled city with narrow streets, pastel-coloured houses and public artworks is kept immaculate by its proud citizens. **See p.718**

❷ Mérida Although the "White City" is the largest on the peninsula – alive with music and Sunday markets – it retains a tranquil charm. **See p.725**

❸ Ruta Puuc See the distinctive sculpture at the Maya sites in this area (the largest is Uxmal), and stay in one of the quiet towns nearby. **See p.738**

❹ Izamal The best place in the Yucatán to buy craftwork and meet artisans, this little town east of Mérida is also studded with ruined pyramids. See p.747

❺ Chichén Itzá Visit the best-known of the Maya sites, with its vertiginous temple, Chac-mool figures and dramatic, snail-shaped observatory. **See p.749**

❻ Cozumel The reefs around this island, just off the coast from Playa del Carmen, are some of the best places in the world for snorkelling and scuba diving. **See p.783**

❼ Tulum The longest, finest white-sand beach on the Caribbean coast, with turquoise water and candlelit cabañas near ancient ruins, as well as the Sian Ka'an Biosphere Reserve just to the south. **See p.790**

HIGHLIGHTS ARE MARKED ON THE MAP ON PP.716–717

YUCATÁN PENINSULA

HIGHLIGHTS

1. Campeche
2. Mérida
3. Ruta Puuc
4. Izamal
5. Chichén Itzá
6. Cozumel
7. Tulum

N

GULF OF MEXICO

Sisal

RÍA CELESTÚN BIOSPHERE RESERVE

Celestún

Chunchucmil   Maxcani

Becal

Hecelchakán

HWY 180

Campeche   1

Lerma

HWY 261

Seybaplaya

Edzná

Champotón

Río Champotón

HWY 261   CAMPECHE

Isla del Carmen

HWY 180

Ciudad del Carmen

Laguna de Términos

HWY 186   Balamkú

Frontera

Francisco Escárcega

Puerto Ceiba

PANTANOS DE CENTLA BIOSPHERE RESERVE

Río Candelaria

Candelaria

HWY 186

HWY 15

Villahermosa

Río Azul

Río San Pedro

HWY 195

Palenque   Tenosique

GUATEMALA

Misol-Há

Agua Azul

de Bacalar is a crystal-clear lake that's rich in wildlife and an affordable alternative to the beaches. **Chetumal**, the state capital and a duty-free border town, is chiefly important as a gateway to and from Belize.

The road across the south of the peninsula is much less travelled. It passes through jungle territory dotted with ruins, collectively known as the **Río Bec sites**. The star is the enormous site of Calakmul, deep in the forest reserve near the Guatemalan border. From the top of its main pyramid, the tallest in the Maya world, the forest stretches to the horizon like a green sea.

Brief history

The Yucatán Peninsula is the longest continuously settled part of Mexico, with evidence of **Maya** inhabitants as early as 2500 BC. The Maya were at their cultural peak during the **Classic period** (300–900 AD), during which time they used solar, lunar and astral cycles to develop their complex and highly accurate calendar; they also had an elaborate mathematical and hieroglyphic system. Five hundred years before the Renaissance, moreover, the Maya had developed a sophisticated perspective in art. In the early ninth century AD, southern lowland cities (Tikal, in Guatemala, and Calakmul, among others) were abandoned, and northern cities such as Chichén Itzá grew. These in turn collapsed around 1200 AD, to be succeeded by Mayapán and a confederacy of other cities that probably included Tulum and Cozumel.

After the Conquest

By the time the Spanish arrived, the Maya had splintered into tribalism – although still with cities and long-distance sea trade that awed the conquistadors. The Yucatán Peninsula proved the hardest area of the country to pacify, with the Maya resisting slavery and debt peonage through constant armed rebellion. The latter half of the nineteenth century saw the **Caste Wars**, when the Maya briefly gained control of the entire peninsula. The guerrilla fighters were eventually pushed back into the wilds of southern Quintana Roo, and held out until the early twentieth century, ending their struggle with conciliation from the Mexican government. It was one of the most successful fights against colonialism in the New World.

The Yucatán today

Today, the Maya still live in the Yucatán, in many cases remarkably true to their old traditions and lifestyle. The culture and language remain a strong source of pride that sets this area apart from central Mexico.

On February 1, 2015, the state of Quintana Roo, which includes Cancún, changed time zones, swapping Central Standard Time for Eastern Standard Time. The aim was to boost tourism by creating longer, lighter evenings.

Campeche and around

Capital of the state that bears its name, beautiful **Campeche** is one of Mexico's finest colonial cities, but draws reasonably few tourists. At its heart, relatively intact, lies a historic port town still surrounded by hefty defensive **walls and fortresses**; within them, interspersed with the occasional grand Baroque church, are elegant eighteenth- and nineteenth-century houses painted in pastel shades and neatly restored. Nonetheless, the place, a UNESCO World Heritage Site, doesn't feel like an outdoor museum, with appliance stores and internet cafés occupying many of the shopfronts. Around the old **centre** are the trappings of a modern city that is once again becoming wealthy, while the **seafront**, built on reclaimed land, provides a thoroughly modern vista. Though the city is far less lively than Mérida, its immaculately preserved and tranquil streets compare favourably, and *campechanos* live up to their reputation as some of the most gracious people in Mexico.

Beyond the archeological museum in the Fuerte de San Miguel – a "must-see" – and the market, which lies just outside the wall by the Puerta de Tierra, you don't really need to venture into the modern city. Instead, one of the greatest pleasures to be had in Campeche comes from simply wandering around the old town in the early evening and on Sundays, when the central Plaza de la Independencia (which locals call the *parque principal*, or just *parque*) is closed to cars for a mellow party.

Brief history

In 1517, a crew of Spanish explorers under Francisco Hernández landed outside the Maya town of Ah Kin Pech, only to beat a hasty retreat on seeing the forces lined up to greet them. Not until 1540 did second-generation conquistador **Francisco de Montejo the Younger** found the modern town. Until the nineteenth century, Campeche was the peninsula's chief port, exporting mainly **logwood** (source of a red dye known as hematein) from local forests. It was an irresistible target for **pirates** until locals prevailed upon the Spanish authorities to fortify the city: construction of the walls, with eight massive bulwarks (*baluartes*), began in 1686 after a particularly brutal massacre. Although large sections of the walls have been replaced by a ring road, two major sections survive, along with seven of the eight *baluartes*.

Paradores de cockteleros & Fuerte de San José (3.5 km)

CENTRAL CAMPECHE

GULF OF MEXICO

12

■ ACCOMMODATION	
Castelmar	1
Hotel Socaire	3
López	4
Maya Campeche	5
Puerta Campeche	6
Regis	2

AV ADOLFO RUIZ CORTINEZ

Palacio de Gobierno Federal

TicketBus Office

16 DE SEPTIEMBRE

MIGUEL ALEMÁN

Baluarte de Santiago

CALLE 10

Best Western del Mar

American Express Buena Ventura

El Palacio Central Cultural

Hotel Baluartes

Museo de la Arquitectura Maya

Parque Principal

CALLE 8

CALLE 12

CALLE 61

AV RUIZ CORTINES

(2.5km) & Fuerte de San Miguel (4km)

PLAZA MOCH-CUOUH

Puerta del Mar

Centro Cultural Casa Seis

Playground

Palacio Legislativo

Baluarte de San Carlos

Casa de Artesanías

Templo de San José

CALLE 10

CALLE 12

Instituto Campechano

Iglesia de San Francisco

CALLE 63

CALLE 65

CALLE 14

CALLE 16

Baluarte de Santa Rosa

Laundry

CALLE 18

CALLE TALAMANTES

CALLE CENTRAL

Baluarte de San Juan

Portales de San Martín

CALLE 10

CALLE 12

CIRILCO VÁZQUEZ

La Catedral de Nuestra Señora de la Concepción

HSBC

Templo del Dulce Nombre de Jesús

Casa del Arte

CALLE 51

CALLE 53

CALLE 55

CIRCUITO BALUARTE

N

2nd-class Bus Terminal & colectivos

Baluarte de San Pedro

AV GOBERNADORES

Market

Baluarte de San Francisco

Alameda

AV REPÚBLICA

Puerta de Tierra

Sur Terminal

Baluarte de San Juan

0	200
metres	

ADO station (2km) & Airport (10km)

● EATING	
El Bastión	4
Café Frappísimo	2
Casa Vieja	6
Chocolates de la Mora	8
Luz de Luna	9
Marganzo	5
La Palapa	3
La Parroquia	7
La Pigua	1

La Catedral de Nuestra Señora de la Concepción

Plaza de la Independencia · Daily 6.45am–8pm · **Museum** 11am–5pm · Free, but M$5 donation expected

The city's most central landmark is **La Catedral de Nuestra Señora de la Concepción**, on the north side of the plaza. Founded in 1540, it's one of the oldest churches on the peninsula. The bulk of the construction, though, took place much later, and what you see now is a wedding-cake Baroque structure. Look in the adjacent museum (accessed via the cathedral) for a seventeenth-century statue of Christ, interred in a dark wood and silver catafalque, among other relics.

Centro Cultural Casa Seis

Plaza de la Independencia · Mon–Fri 8am–9pm, Sat & Sun 9am–9pm · M$20 · ☎ 981 816 1782

On the southwest side of the plaza, this cultural centre and small museum has an elegant permanent display of Baroque interiors. It also hosts art shows and performances, including musical *serenatas* most Thursdays. There's also a souvenir shop.

Museo de la Arquitectura Maya

Plaza de la Independencia · Tues–Sun 9.30am–5.30pm · M$39

On the seaward side of the plaza, the Baluarte de la Soledad, just south of the public library, houses a collection of columns, steles and other stone details helpfully arranged by regional style – Chenes, Puuc and more. Many of the carved stone pieces are accompanied by a sketch outline of the decoration – this helps train your eye to see the details. You can also climb up onto the top of the city walls.

El Palacio Centro Cultural

Plaza de la Independencia · Tues–Sun 10am–7pm · Free · ☎ 981 816 7741

Opened in 2014, **El Palacio Centro Cultural** is one for history buffs. This modern museum charts the history of the city through multimedia displays and wide-ranging exhibits, from eighteenth- and nineteenth-century costumes to replica Spanish galleons. Mostly in Spanish, but with some displays in English.

Baluarte de San Carlos

C 8 at C 65 · Museo de la Ciudad daily 8am–8pm · M$25

From the plaza, heading southwest along the line of the wall brings you to this bulwark with cannons on the battlemented roof and, underneath, the beginnings of a network of ancient tunnels that runs under much of the town. Sealed off now, the tunnels provided refuge for the populace during pirate raids, and before that were probably used by the Maya. The *baluarte* houses Campeche's **Museo de la Ciudad**, a tiny but rather lovely collection of local memorabilia that includes models of ships, with Spanish commentary.

Puerta de Tierra

C 18 at C 59 · **Ramparts and museum** Mon–Wed 8am–9pm, Thurs & Fri 8am–5pm, Sat & Sun 9am–5pm · M$15 · **Sound-and-light show** Thurs–Sat 8pm (1hr) · M$50

The second remaining chunk of city wall is on the landward side, hence the name **Puerta de Tierra**. It hosts a surprisingly dynamic and enjoyable **sound-and-light show** three times a week, starting from the Puerta de Tierra and walking along the wall in the company of the "soldiers" guarding it.

Just north along the wall, at the Baluarte de San Francisco, you can climb the ramparts and walk along the top of the walls and look over the old town on the one side and the newer, less preserved city on the other, typified by the market and the Alameda Francisco de Paula Toro, the Havana-inspired promenade next to it. Downstairs in the bulwark is a piracy museum, though it has very few physical objects, save some blunderbusses, cutlasses and crossbows: it's probably appealing for pirate obsessives only.

Fuerte de San Miguel and the Museo Arqueológico

Av Escénica, 4km south of the centre • Tues–Sun 9.30am–5.30pm • M$47 • Take a taxi (around M$40) or city bus marked "Lerma" or "Playa Bonita" along the coast road), though once you get off you'll still have a stiff climb uphill to reach the fort

On a steep hill on the southwest side of town, about 4km from the centre, the **Fuerte de San Miguel** houses Campeche's impressive archeological museum. Plaques are in Spanish only, but the beautiful relics from all over the peninsula speak for themselves. Maya artefacts from Edzná and Jaina make up much of the collection; highlights include delicate Jaina figurines, fine sculpture and pre-Hispanic gold. But the best part is the treasure from the tombs at Calakmul, including the first mummified body to be found in Mesoamerica, unearthed in 1995. The jade death masks are mesmerizing. Enjoy the view over the ramparts, too.

Fuerte de San José

C 5 at Francisco Morazán, 3.5km north of the centre • Tues–Sun 9.30am–5.30pm • M$37 • Take a taxi (around M$40) or buses marked "Morelos" or "Bellavista", starting from in front of the market

On the north side of the city, directly uphill from the *paradores de cockteleros* (see p.722), the **Fuerte de San José** faces down a giant statue of Benito Juárez on the neighbouring hill. Its museum contains armaments, scale models of the city and ships and sundry items salvaged from shipwrecks, such as centuries-old Dutch gin bottles (signage is in Spanish only). Although this museum is not as compelling as the other fort's, the view north to the green swathe of protected marshland is striking.

12

ARRIVAL AND DEPARTURE   CAMPECHE

BY PLANE

The airport (☎ 981 816 6656) is about 10km southeast of town; a taxi to the centre costs around M$100. There are a few daily flights (2hr) to Mexico City on Aeroméxico (🖥 aeromexico.com) and Interjet (🖥 interjet.com.mx).

BY BUS

Campeche has two main bus stations, one each for first- and second-class services, as well as a separate terminus for local and rural buses. The Edzná Tours travel agency on Circuito Colonias at C 8 doubles as a TicketBus office, to spare you a trek out to the first-class station.

ADO station The first-class station, called "El ADO", has ADO, OCC and some ATS services. It's about 2km from the centre on Av Central. Taxis line up outside (around M$40–50 to the centre), as do buses and *colectivos* (look for "Mercado" or "Centro"). To get back, look for "Av Central or "ADO" buses.

Destinations Cancún (6 daily; 6hr 40min–7hr 5min); Chetumal (1 daily at 2pm; 6hr 25min) via Xpujil (4hr 30min); Ciudad del Carmen (roughly hourly; 2hr 55min–3hr 40min); Francisco Escárcega (8 daily; 1hr 40min–2hr 10min); Mérida (roughly every 30min; 2hr 30min); Mérida airport (5 daily; 2hr 20min); Playa del Carmen (1 daily at

11.30pm; 8hr 35min); Veracruz (2 daily at 8.10pm & 10.20pm; 11hr 25min–12hr 55min); Villahermosa (every 1–2 hours; 5hr 55min–7hr 10min).

Second-class station The second-class terminal, with Sur and some ATS buses, is 600m northeast of the centre on Gobernadores, serving towns on Hwy-180. Walk west on Gobernadores or cross the street and take a city bus marked "Centro" or "Mercado". All head to the market, just outside the city wall on the landward side. To get back, look for "Universidad" or "Terminal Sur" buses.

Destinations Hecelchakán (every 15–30min; 45min); Francisco Escárcega (hourly; 1hr 30min); Hopelchén (18 daily; 1hr); Iturbide (9 daily, 7.45am–5.35pm; 1hr 15min); Uxmal and Santa Elena (5 daily; 2hr).

Sur Terminal A small ticket office on Av República handles Sur buses going along the coast to the south (Champotón, Seybaplaya, etc). Independent local buses stop out front, for various surrounding villages. Buses to Pich, the town nearest to Edzná, leave from here until 11.30am.

BY COLECTIVO

Colectivos for towns north and east depart from Gobernadores near the second-class station – you'll pass the marked stops where taxis wait to fill up.

GETTING AROUND

By taxi Within the city, taxis are inexpensive (generally M$30–40) but not always plentiful. Look for them at taxi stands around the centre or call ☎ 981 816 2363, ☎ 981 816 2359 or ☎ 981 816 2355.

Bike rental Buena Ventura (☎ 981 811 9191 ext 405), on

16 de Septiembre in the *Best Western Del Mar* car park, rents cruisers with baskets (M$25/hr) and leads tours around town.

Car rental Europcar, at the airport (☎ 981 823 4083, ⓦ europcar.com).

INFORMATION AND TOURS

State tourist office Plaza Moch Couoh on 16 de Septiembre opposite the Palacio Legislativo (daily 8am–4pm & 6–9pm; ☎ 981 127 3300 or ☎ 1 800 900 2267, ⓦ campeche.travel). Helpful, and there's usually someone who speaks English. It has a list of guides (speaking various languages) who lead tours of the city and archeological zones, though you might be expected to provide transport; try to make reservations a day ahead.

Campeche Tours 16 de Septiembre, in Hotel Baluartes ☎ 981 105 5747 or ☎ 981 133 2135, ⓦ campechetours .com. This agency runs a range of trips, including kayaking and fishing excursions.

City tourist office On the plaza, opposite the cathedral

(daily 8am–8pm; ☎ 981 816 1782). More convenient but less equipped than the state tourist office. Smaller information booths are at the bus stations, in the Baluarte de San Pedro and in the Casa Seis.

City tours For a concise overview of the city try the *tranvía* tour, with commentary in Spanish and English, which departs from the main plaza (hourly 9am–1pm & 5–9pm; M$100), taking a pleasant tour around neighbourhoods beyond the walls.

KankabiOK Tours C 59 no. 3-A, between C 8 and C 10 ☎ 981 811 2792, ⓦ kankabiok.com. Small agency running excursions to Edzná and Calakmul, as well as nearby *cenotes* and beaches.

ACCOMMODATION

Campeche's **hotels** are only just beginning to match tourist demand – there is an increasing number to choose from, and a couple of them are outstanding. The few decent budget options are within a few blocks of the Plaza Principal; some top-end choices are just outside the old city walls. In any case, avoid rooms overlooking the street, as Campeche's narrow lanes tend to amplify noise.

Castelmar C 61 no. 2-A, between C 8 and C 10 ☎ 981 811 1204, ⓦ castelmarhotel.com. Based in a former army barracks that dates back to 1800, this charming, colonial-style place has old floor tiles, a large courtyard and soaring ceilings. Modern touches include a small pool, a/c and satellite TV. U̲S̲$̲6̲8̲ ̲(̲M̲$̲1̲1̲6̲0̲)̲

Hotel Socaire C 55 no. 22, between C 12 and C 14 ☎ 981 811 2130, ⓦ hotelsocaire.com.mx. A justifiably popular mid-range hotel with a handful of classy rooms – each with a/c, TVs, high ceilings and nice colonial touches – as well as a lovely pool and a coffee shop. It's very good value, considering the quality. M̲$̲1̲0̲5̲0̲

López C 12 no. 189, between C 61 and C 63 ☎ 981 816 3344, ⓦ hotellopezcampeche.com.mx. A nicely renovated hotel catering mainly to Mexican business travellers (hence the free newspaper in the morning); modern a/c rooms are in a pretty Deco-era building with open halls (though the bathrooms can be a bit musty). There's a small pool. M̲$̲6̲5̲0̲

Maya Campeche C 57 no. 40, between C 14 and C 16 ☎ 981 816 8053, ⓦ mayacampechehotel.com. This small place just up from the plaza has fifteen fairly spacious rooms. Two floors open onto a slender courtyard, with a narrow shaded walkway above. All rooms have a/c, and regular promos can bring prices down by as much as M$200. M̲$̲7̲5̲0̲

★**Puerta Campeche** C 59 no. 61, between C 16 and C 18 ☎ 981 816 7508, ⓦ starwoodhotels.com. Located just inside the Puerta de Tierra, Campeche's finest hotel occupies the shell of a colonial home and warehouse. The pool winds through crumbling walls and is overlooked by a breezy terrace, a great spot for an evening drink. U̲S̲$̲2̲4̲6̲ (̲M̲$̲4̲2̲0̲5̲)̲

Regis C 12 no. 148, between C 55 and C 57 ☎ 981 816 3175. The *Hotel Regis* is a solid, if unremarkable, choice with very large rooms, all with a/c, arranged around a small patio; avoid the ones close to the neighbouring bar. M̲$̲7̲0̲0̲

EATING

Campeche is well known for good food, and restaurants abound. **Seafood**, available almost everywhere, is a good bet. For breakfast, the cafés along C 8 near the government offices offer everything from tacos to fresh juices and pastries. Later in the day, the café in the centre of the plaza serves good coffee and ice cream. Campeche's **market**, just east of the walled city, is surrounded by *comedores* offering cheap and tasty lunches. Another local favourite is the stretch of *paradores de cockteleros* on the malecón – these seafood-vending kiosks are open until around 4pm (a taxi costs about M$40 from the centre). At **night**, people snack at Portales de San Martín, just north of the walls between C 10 and C 12. Bars aren't open late, but stop by the rooftop bar at the *Puerta Campeche* hotel (Fri & Sat only) for the view.

CAFÉS, CHEAP EATS AND SNACKS

Café Frappísimo C 8 s/n ☎ 981 811 7359, ☯ facebook .com/Frappisimo. A modern, a/c coffee shop, just off the square, with well-made cappuccinos, lattes, frappuccinos and the like (M$25–52), plus tempting cakes, cookies and filled baguettes. There are also magazines, newspapers and books to flick through. Daily 8am–11pm.

Chocolates de la Mora Corner of C 59 and 10 ☎ 981 817 5658, ☯ chocolatesdelamora.com. The speciality at this delightful café is drinking chocolate spiked with cinnamon and almond, served hot or iced (M$35–50). There's also a good range of cakes, pastries, sandwiches and snacks (all M$25–65), as well as home-made chocolates. Mon–Sat 8am–11pm, Sun 9am–7pm.

Luz de Luna C 59 no. 6, between C 10 and C 12 ☎ 981 811 9624. A quirky restaurant-gallery, *Luz de Luna* offers a generous variety of Mexican favourites – from *ceviche* to fajitas (mains M$85–145). Breakfasts are particularly good and plentiful, including cinnamon-scented *cafe de olla*. Daily 7am–9pm.

La Parroquia C 55 no. 8, between C 10 and C 12 ☎ 981 816 2530. High ceilings echo with the clink of dishes at this big open-front diner. Staff can be inconsistent, as can the food, but it's inexpensive and convenient: mains cost M$60–170, while set meals are around M$70. Daily 24hr.

RESTAURANTS

El Bastión C 57, on the plaza ☎ 981 816 2128, ☯ elbastion.com.mx. The best place to eat with a plaza view (you can compare it with the old-photo wallpaper inside), though the traditional *campechano* menu (mains M$95–179) isn't quite as good as others. Daily 6.30am–midnight.

Casa Vieja C 10 no. 319, on the plaza ☎ 981 811 8016. A Cuban-owned restaurant with well-appointed balcony overlooking the main square. Food is a bit international-bland, but it's a great spot for a rum cocktail (M$40–60) or cold beer (M$35). Tues–Sat 8.30am–midnight, Sun 4pm–midnight.

Marganzo C 8 no. 267, between C 57 and C 59 ☎ 981 811 3898, ☯ marganzo.com. Touristy but still pleasant and not as expensive as it looks. The varied menu (most mains M$100–250) includes tasty crab quesadillas and generous *botanas* (bite-size snacks). Daily 7am–11pm.

La Palapa Resurgimiento, 2.5km south along the malecón from the city centre ☎ 981 815 5918. A good destination for a malecón stroll, this large bar-restaurant is right on the water. It has big seafood plates (around M$150–250), but you can also make a meal from the delicious *botanas* served with every drink. Daily 10am–8pm.

★ **La Pigua** Alemán 179-A ☎ 981 811 3365, ☯ lapigua .com.mx. Follow C 8 north to find one of the city's most legendary restaurants, a pretty, rather elegant spot with exceptionally delicious seafood, such as creamy shrimp soup and fresh fillets with garlic and herbs (mains M$160–250). Reserve for dinner. Daily 1–9pm.

DIRECTORY

American Express In the VI-PS travel agency, C 59 between Ruíz Cortines and 16 de Septiembre behind the *Best Western Del Mar* (Mon–Fri 9am–5pm, Sat 9am–1pm; ☎ 981 811 1010).

Banks and exchange HSBC, C 10 at C 55, is just off the main square and has an ATM.

Internet There are internet cafés on virtually every street in the centre of Campeche.

Laundry The most central is La Antigua at C 57, between 12 and 14.

Post office 16 de Septiembre near C 53 (Mon–Fri 8.30am–3.30pm, Sat 9am–1pm).

Edzná and the Chenes sites

Some 50km from Campeche lie the ruins of **Edzná**, surprisingly large and richly decorated, yet relatively little known to tourists. Beyond Edzná, you'll need a car to follow Hwy-261 towards the town of Hopelchén and the so-called **Chenes sites**: the ruins of Hochob and Dzibilnocac (completists can also ask for directions to El Tabasqueño and Santa Rosa Xtampak as well). They share a similar style of architecture, with colonnaded facades and monster-mouth doorways, evolved from the Río Bec further south.

Edzná

45km southeast of Campeche • Daily 8am–5pm • M$52 • **Sound-and-light show** April–Oct Thurs–Sun 8am, Nov–March 7pm (1hr) • M$120

At the height of its power, between 250 BC and 150 AD, **Edzná** was a large city, on the main route between the Maya communities of the highlands and the coast. The ruins show evidence of a complex drainage and irrigation system that probably supported a large agricultural project and more than a thousand people. Its architecture features elements of Río Bec, Classic Maya and Puuc design. The sound-and-light show is surprisingly good, and involves tramping around the site (make sure you wear insect repellent) rather than just sitting in a seat.

Templo de los Cinco Pisos

The most important structure is a stepped palace-pyramid more than 30m high. Unusually, each of the five storeys contains chambered "palace" rooms. While both solid temple pyramids and multi-storey "apartment" complexes are relatively common, it's rare to see the two combined in one building. At the front, a steep monumental staircase leads to a three-room temple, topped by a roofcomb. It's a hot climb, but the view takes in the dense greenery and the hills that mark this side of the peninsula.

As you look out over two plazas, the further of which must have been capable of holding tens of thousands of people, it is easy to imagine the power that the high priest or king commanded. Beyond lie the unexcavated remains of other large pyramids, and behind them, the vast flat expanse of the Yucatán plain. Inside the west-facing temple, a stele of the god of maize was illuminated by the sun twice a year, on the dates for the planting and harvesting of the crop.

The lesser buildings

Lesser buildings surround the ceremonial precinct. The **Nohochná** (Casa Grande, or Big House), a palace on the northwest side, is some 55m long and contains a room used as a *temazcal* (traditional sauna), with stone benches and hearths over which water could be boiled. Over in the **Pequeña Acrópolis**, the **Templo de los Mascarones** contains two eerie masks representing the sun god, rising on the east (left-hand) side and setting on the west.

Dzibilnocac

1km east of Iturbide • Daily 8am–5pm • Free

Dzibilnocac is a small site, and an easy stop if you're in a car (note that many road signs for Iturbide refer to the town as Vicente Guerrero). By bus, it's feasible, but you may feel it was not quite worth the trouble. The buildings here show the ultra-decorative facades typical of the Chenes style – its restored western temple pyramid is quite pretty.

Hochob

15km southwest of Dzibalchén (follow signs to Chencoh) • Daily 8am–5pm • M$39

Hochob features an amazing three-room temple (low and fairly small, as are most Chenes buildings), with a facade richly carved with stylized snakes and masks. The central chamber is surmounted by a crumbling roofcomb, and its decoration, with fangs, eyes and ears, creates the effect of a huge face, with the doorway as a gaping mouth.

Grutas de X'tacumbilxuna'an

3km south of Bolonchén • Daily 10am–5pm • M$50

Near Bolonchén, you'll see signs for these **caves**. Though deep and rather dramatically lit, the area you actually visit is limited, and as a result, the attraction feels a bit overpriced. But if you happen to be driving by, it's a brief scenic stop.

ARRIVAL AND DEPARTURE	EDZNÁ AND THE CHENES SITES

By bus For Edzná, Autobuses Ejidales services (30–40min) leave from in front of the Sur terminal in Campeche daily a few times in the morning, until about 11.30am, but the last bus returns at 3.45pm (confirm with the driver). For Dzibilnocac, the only other site really accessible by bus, take a second-class service from Campeche to Iturbide

(8–9 daily, 7.45am–5.35pm; 1hr 15min), from where it's a 1km walk.

By combi For Edzná, *combis* for Pich, a village 20km past the ruins, depart from in front of the Campeche market. To get back, you'll need to ask the driver to collect you at the site, or walk to Pich; go as early in the day as possible.

By car If you're driving to the Río Bec from Campeche, you can continue south from Hochob to Xpujil – it's a good back route that avoids a lot of the truck traffic that plagues Hwy-186.

By tour Organized tours from Campeche (see p.722) cover Edzná and a couple of smaller sites, and are less rushed than visiting independently on public transport.

ACCOMMODATION AND EATING

Hacienda Uayamón Carretera Uayamon–Edzná km 20, Uayamón ☎ 981 813 0530, ⓦ luxurycollection.com. Off the fast road to Edzná, this hotel was founded as a cattle ranch in the sixteenth century and later became one of the largest henequen (a type of agave used for rope-making) haciendas in the country. In addition to the luxurious rooms, many with private terrace and plunge pool, another attraction is the exuberant birdlife plus beasties like armadillos and coatis. The hacienda's restaurant is a good option for a romantic meal, or just an excuse to poke around the grounds. Call ahead for a dinner reservation. Daily 7–11pm. US$265 (M$4530)

Hwy-180 to Mérida

From Campeche north to Mérida, first-class buses take **Hwy-180**, which was once the colonial Camino Real ("Royal Road"). While the highway bypasses most of the towns along the way, second-class buses from Campeche and Mérida stop at almost all of them, and two signposted detours are especially worthwhile if you're driving. The area is a nice slice of semi-rural Maya life, with *triciclo* taxis running alongside cars, and many women wearing traditional embroidered *huipiles*.

Museo Arqueológico del Camino Real

Main plaza, Hecelchakán • Previously Tues–Sun 8.30am–5.30pm • M$35 • ☎ 981 816 9136, ⓦ inah.gob.mx • Second-class buses (every 30min–1hr; around 1hr 15min) run frequently from Campeche and Mérida

Located in the town of Hecelchakán, about 80km from Campeche, this small archeology **museum** was closed for repair at the time of research, but it's worth checking if it has reopened. It's notable for its collection of Jaina figurines, beautifully detailed clay portraits of Maya people unearthed on the Isla de Jaina, just off the coast due west of here (and unfortunately not open to visitors). Typically just 10–20cm tall, the figures have been a key to research on the everyday life of ancient Maya people: what they wore, how they altered their appearance, what they did for entertainment. The figures were placed in the graves of the people they depicted, often held in their hands or laid on their chests.

Becal

Off Hwy-180, 35km north of Hecelchakán • Second-class buses run frequently from Campeche and Mérida (see p.721)

The town of **BECAL** is synonymous with the ubiquitous Yucatecan *jipi*, or "Panama" hat (the original Panama hats actually came from Ecuador). Shops throughout town sell them, and it's interesting to see a village so consumed with a single cottage industry – a fountain made of concrete hats even graces the town square.

If you pull over, you're likely to be approached by a friendly local who will take you to a nearby hat shop, and perhaps stop at one of the town's many *cuevas*, the cool, damp cellars in which the villagers traditionally make and store the hats to keep them soft and flexible. As for the hats themselves, the best (which can be crumpled into a ball and spring back to shape) are hard to come by even here at the source; shops offer cheap and mid-range options from around M$150 to M$1200, depending on the fineness of the fibres and tightness of the weave.

Mérida

Nicknamed "La Ciudad Blanca" after its white limestone buildings (now covered in peeling layers of gem-coloured paint), the capital of Yucatán state is in every sense the leading city of the peninsula. Within its historic core, though, **MÉRIDA** retains a sense of small-town graciousness coupled with an extremely lively and sometimes avant-garde

12

cultural scene. It draws thousands of visitors, both Mexican and foreign, and has seen a rash of expat investment over the last fifteen years. Yet even as the buzz increases, the city retains its grace and manners. Every street in the centre boasts a well-maintained colonial church or museum, and the plazas throng with locals enjoying free music and other attractions. Not only can you live well here, but it's a great base for excursions to the Maya sites of Uxmal and Chichén Itzá.

Brief history

Founded in 1542, Mérida is built over, and partly from, the ruins of a Maya city known as **Tihó** or Ichcansihó. Its fortune grew as the capital for exporting **henequen**, the rope fibre that was Yucatán's "green gold".

Trade was interrupted in the spring of 1849, when, early in the Maya uprising that

SHOPPING
Casa de Artesanías	2
Librería Dante	1
La Poblana	3

ACCOMMODATION
Las Arecas	10
Casa Nico	12
Dolores Alba	13
Eclipse	7
Hacienda Xcanatun	1
Julamis	4
Luz en Yucatán	5
Merida Santiago	11
Mucuy	9
Nómadas	2
Posada Toledo	8
Santa Lucía	6
Trinidad Galería	3

DRINKING & NIGHTLIFE
El Cumbanchero	1
Los Henequenes	2
Pancho's	3
Piedra de Agua	4
La Quilla	5

EATING
Amaro	8
Bistro Cultural	4
Café Crème	1
La Chaya Maya	5
Dulcería y Sorbetería El Colón	3/11
La Habana	7
El Marlin Azul	6
La Reina Itzalana	9
Rosas and Xocolate	2
El Trapiche	10

Fiesta Americana, Clínica de Mérida & Gran Museo del Mundo Maya

(12km)

Museo de Antropología Yucatán (Palacio Cantón)

Iglesia de Santa Ana

PLAZA SANTA ANA

Market

Iglesia Santa Lucía

Parque Santa Lucía

Laundry

Teatro Peón Contreras

Universidad de Yucatán

Mexico Rent A Car

Iglesia de Jesús

Palacio de Gobierno

Parque Hidalgo

Maya Bike

Museo del Arte Popular de Yucatán

Museo de la Canción Yucateca

Parque La Mejorada

La Mejorada

Arco Dragones

Centro Olimpo de Cultura

PLAZA GRANDE

Catedral de San Ildefonso

MACAY

Palacio Municipal

Museo Casa Montejo

Arco del Puente

Parque de Santiago

Casa Catherwood &

AutoProgreso Bus Terminal

Colectivos to Progreso

Museo de la Ciudad

Mercado Lucas de Gálvez

Noreste Bus Terminal

Auto Centro Terminal

Airport (7km)

Terminal TAME

Terminal CAME

Parque San Juan

Colectivos

Arco de San Juan

CENTRAL MÉRIDA

0   200
metres

became known as the **Caste Wars**, rebel armies laid siege to Mérida. They were within a hair's breadth of capturing the city, when, legend has it, the Maya peasant fighters left the siege to plant corn. The Yucatecan elite quickly arranged a deal with the central Mexican government ceding the peninsula's independence in exchange for support against future Maya rebellions.

Mérida became an extraordinarily wealthy city, much of it poured into grandiose mansions along Paseo de Montejo. Then the henequen industry all but died around World War II, when nylon became the rope-making material of choice. But Mérida remains elegant, prosperous and intellectual, a vibrant mix of Maya, *mestizos*, Lebanese (who emigrated here in the early twentieth century) and more recent transplants from Mexico City and abroad.

Plaza Grande

Any exploration of Mérida begins naturally in this plaza, officially called the **Plaza de la Independencia**, and the largest in the city, at the intersection of calles 60, 61, 62 and 63. It's the hub of city life, particularly in the evenings, when couples meet on park benches and trios of *trovadores* wait to be hired for serenades.

Catedral de San Ildefonso

C 60 on the Plaza de la Independencia • Daily 6am–noon & 5–8pm • Free

Built in the second half of the sixteenth century, Mérida's largest **church** is in a rather severe style that veered away from earlier, more ornate Spanish styles. The building was heavily looted during the Mexican Revolution in the early twentieth century, though in a chapel to the left of the main altar, people still venerate the Cristo de las Ampollas (Christ of the Blisters), a crucifix carved from a tree in the village of Ichmul that burned for a whole night without showing the least sign of damage. Later, in 1645, the parish church at Ichmul burned down, and the crucifix survived, though blackened and blistered.

It is entirely likely that the original crucifix was also destroyed in the looting of 1915, but whether the existing statue is a reproduction is irrelevant – it remains the focal point of a local fiesta from mid-September to mid-October, when each day a different professional group, or *gremio* (taxi drivers, bakers and so on), pays its respects at the church, then parades on the plaza.

MACAY

Pasaje de la Revolución, off C 60 on the Plaza de la Independencia • Wed–Mon 10am–6pm • Free • ⓦ macay.org

Beside the cathedral, the former bishop's palace has been converted into shops, offices and the Museo de Arte Contemporáneo Ateneo de Yucatán (**MACAY**), which has the best modern art collection in southern Mexico, with permanent displays featuring the work of internationally acclaimed Yucatecan painters Fernando Castro Pacheco, Gabriel Ramírez Aznar and Fernando García Ponce.

Museo Casa Montejo

C 63 on the Plaza de la Independencia • Tues–Sat 10am–7pm, Sun 10am–2pm • **Guided tours** Tues–Sat 11am, 1pm & 5pm, Sun 11am & 1pm (1hr) • Free • ☏ 618 811 7136, ⓦ casasdeculturabanamex.com

Francisco de Montejo was the first conquistador to attempt to bring the peninsula under the control of Spain, in 1527. He failed, but his son secured the north of the peninsula in the 1540s. The father built this **palace** in 1549; it's now a Banamex office. Visitors can see the lavishly restored wood-panelled dining room, off the back right corner of the Moorish-feeling courtyard. Above a staid doorway of Classical columns, the facade is decorated in the manically ornate plateresque style (probably the first instance of it in the New World), with conquistadors depicted trampling savages underfoot.

Palacio Municipal

C 62 on the Plaza de la Independencia • Mon–Fri 9am–5pm • Free

Facing the cathedral, Mérida's **city hall** (*ayuntamiento*) is another impressive piece of sixteenth-century design, with a beautiful clock tower and a large painting upstairs that depicts the *mestizaje*, the birth of the first mixed-blood Mexican.

Palacio de Gobierno

C 61 on the Plaza de la Independencia • Daily 8am–10pm • Free

Completing the square, the nineteenth-century state government building is a must-see. On the ground floor and in the large front room upstairs, enormous, aggressively modernist murals by Fernando Castro Pacheco cover the walls. They powerfully depict the violent history of the Yucatán and the trials of its indigenous people.

North of the Plaza Grande

Most of the remaining monuments in Mérida lie north of the plaza, along the main commercial streets of Calle 60 and Paseo de Montejo. Calle 60 is a parade of historically significant buildings, and Paseo de Montejo is lined with the magnificent mansions of the henequen-rich grandees who strove to outdo one another around the end of the nineteenth century.

Museo del Arte Popular de Yucatán

C 50-A at C 57 • Tues–Sat 10am–5pm, Sun 10am–3pm • M$20

This is a small but flawless collection of Mexican **craftwork**, worth a detour if you have time and interest in the subject. It's set in an old house, with a sense of humour about the bathrooms. The gift shop is small but well stocked.

Museo de la Canción Yucateca

C 57 between C 48 and C 50 • Tues–Fri 9am–5pm, Sat & Sun 9am–3pm • M$15, free Sun • ☎ 999 923 7224

Behind the former monastery of La Mejorada, this pleasantly old-fashioned **museum** details the development of the Yucatán's traditional, painfully romantic *trova* music. It traces the diverse influences, from pre-Columbian traditions to Afro-Cuban styles, and shows off many of the classic stars. Its gift shop has plenty of CDs.

Museo de Antropología Yucatán (Palacio Cantón)

C 43 at Paseo de Montejo • Tues–Sun 8am–5pm • M$52 • ☎ 999 923 7224, 🌐 palaciocanton.inah.gob.mx • 30min walk from the plaza

The former site of the city's museum of Maya culture (now at the Gran Museo del Mundo Maya, see p.728) reopened in 2012 after renovation. As well as anthropological and other exhibits, the **museum** is worth a visit for the building itself, a Beaux Arts palace, trimmed in wrought iron and marble. It was built at the beginning of the twentieth century by Francisco Cantón Rosado, the railway tycoon, state governor and general who was a key supporter of dictator Porfirio Díaz.

Casa Catherwood

C 59 west of C 72 • Mon–Sat 9am–2pm & 5–9pm • M$50 • ☎ 999 154 5565, 🌐 casa-catherwood.com

This colonial home displays an exhibit of English artist **Frederick Catherwood**'s etchings of crumbling Maya ruins, made during his excursions with John Lloyd Stephens in the mid-1800s. The works became the illustrations for Stephens' *Incidents of Travel in Yucatán*, the first detailed English description of the ancient Maya ruins. The courtyard houses a pretty café too.

Gran Museo del Mundo Maya

C 60 Norte, 9.5km north of the centre, just inside the ring road • Mon & Wed–Sun 9am–5pm • M$150 • **Sound-and-light show**: Mon & Wed–Sun 8.30pm • Free • ☎ 999 341 0435, 🌐 granmuseodelmundomaya.com • Taxis cost about M$50

Opened in 2012 to great fanfare, the **Gran Museo del Mundo Maya** brings to life the world of the Maya, from origins to the present day, through hundreds of archeological, anthropological, ethnological and historical exhibits. The main draw is the free sound-and-light spectacle, an immersive audio-video art installation that covers Maya history and culture in grand terms.

South of the Plaza Grande

Heading south of the Plaza Grande, Mérida becomes somewhat scruffier, with the streets getting a bit more jammed with traffic and commerce, especially around the massive public market, the Mercado Lucas de Gálvez, close to which is a good museum.

Mercado Lucas de Gálvez

C 67 at C 56 • Mon–Sat 7am–late afternoon

Mérida's main **market** is in two vast joined halls, plus a clutch of stalls around the periphery, with more than two thousand vendors plying their trades. It's a wild scrum of consumer goods, from freshly hacked-up beef to hand-tooled leather belts to numerous varieties of bananas. Arrive before noon to see the most bountiful foodstuffs; **craft shops** (many in a separate wing on C 56-A at C 65) are open all day.

Museo de la Ciudad

C 56 between C 65 and C 65-A • Tues–Fri 9am–6pm, Sat & Sun 9am–2pm • Free

A nice touch of culture on the edge of the market, the grand city **museum** occupies the beautiful old central post office. The exhibits trace city history from ancient Maya times through the henequen boom. Text is in Spanish and English. There's also a gallery of local contemporary art.

12

ARRIVAL AND DEPARTURE

MÉRIDA

BY PLANE

Mérida's Manuel Crecencio Rejón airport (☎ 999 940 6090, ⦿ asur.com.mx) is 7km southwest of the centre. It has a tourist office (daily 8am–8pm), post office, long-distance phones and car-rental desks. A taxi to/from the city centre costs around M$100–140. You could also take bus #79 ("Aviación"), which goes to Parque San Juan, but the stop is a very long walk from the terminal, and it runs infrequently.

Destinations Cancún on Mayair and Hahn Air (2 daily; 1hr); Guadalajara on Volaris (1 daily; 2hr 20min); Mexico City on Aeromexico, Interjet and Volaris (16 daily; 2hr); Villahermosa on Aeroméxico, Aeromar, Hahn Air and Mayair (4 daily; 1hr 30min).

BY BUS

Mérida has two major bus stations, both on the southwest side of town, plus several smaller stations and stopping points, just about all of which are south of the plaza. In theory, they all deal with different companies and destinations, but in practice, there's a bit of overlap. In addition to the larger stations below, AutoProgreso (C 62 between C 65 and C 67) serves Progreso and nearby Dzibilchaltún, while AutoCentro (C 65 at C 48) runs an additional service to Izamal, and the only service to the ruins of Aké.

TERMINAL CAME

Located on C 70 between C 69 and C 71, for express ADO, ADO GL, ADO Platino and OCC. You'll likely arrive here if you're coming directly from Cancún, Campeche or Chichén Itzá. City buses don't head to the main plaza. A taxi costs about M$40–50, or it's a 20min walk.

Destinations Campeche (every 30min–1hr; 2hr 30min); Cancún (at least hourly; 4hr 25min); Chetumal (4 daily at 7.30am, 1pm, 6pm & 11pm; 5hr 30min–6hr); Escárcega (3 daily at 8.30am, 3pm & 9pm; 4hr 10min–4hr 40min); Mexico City (1 daily at 8.30pm; 19hr 45min); Palenque (2 daily at 8.30am & 10pm; 7hr 45min–9hr); Playa del Carmen (12 daily; 4hr 5min–5hr 25min); Tulum (4 daily at 10.40am, 12.40pm, 5.40pm & 8.15pm; 3hr 55min); Valladolid (11 daily; 2hr 15min); Villahermosa (11 daily; 8hr–9hr 5min).

TERMINAL TAME

Officially the Terminal de Segunda Clase, the TAME is across the street from the CAME, on C 69 between C 68 and C 70. ATS, Clase Europea, Mayab, Sur, TRT and some Oriente buses leave from here. Coming from Campeche, you may arrive here. There's luggage storage (at a window outside, facing the CAME entrance). City buses don't head to the main plaza. A taxi costs about M$40–50, or it's a 20min walk.

Destinations Campeche via Maxcanú, Hecelchakán and Becal (every 30min–1hr; 4hr); Cancún via Valladolid (20 daily; 4–6hr); Cancún via Felipe Carrillo Puerto (12 daily; 5–8hr); Chetumal (7–8 daily; 6hr); Chiquilá, for Holbox (1 daily at 11.30pm; 6hr); Escárcega (3 daily at 11am, 1.10pm & 3.40pm; 6hr); Felipe Carrillo Puerto (11 daily; 2hr 30min); Hopelchén via Santa Elena and Uxmal (6–7 daily; 2hr 30min); Oxkutzcab via Ticul (11 daily, 5am–9pm; 2hr); Playa del Carmen (hourly; 5–7hr); Tulum (10 daily; 5–7hr); Villahermosa via Escárcega (2 daily at 5.30am & 11am; 9hr).

FIESTA AMERICANA

Some deluxe buses (ADO, ADO GL and Platino) arrive at a car park on C 60 at Colón, just west of the Fiesta Americana, north of the centre. A taxi costs about M$30–40, or walk one block east and flag down a southbound city bus.
Destinations Cancún (8 daily; 4hr–4hr 35min); Cancún airport (3 daily at 6.15am, 9.15am & noon; 4hr); Villahermosa (2 daily at 9.30pm & 11pm; 9hr 15min).

NORESTE TERMINAL

On C 67 at C 50. Second-class buses (LUS, Noreste and Oriente) from here serve the coast and small interior towns.
Destinations Cancún via Chichén Itzá and Valladolid (15–17 daily; 4hr); Cuzamá (7 daily; 1hr 30min); Izamal (14 daily; 1hr); Maní via Acancéh and Tecoh (10 daily; 2hr); Río Lagartos (1 daily at 5.30pm; 4hr); San Crisanto (3 daily at 7am, 10.15am & 6.30pm; 1hr 45min); San Felipe (1 daily at 5.30pm; 6hr 30min); Tizimín (6 daily; 3–4hr); Tulum via Cobá (1 daily at 5.20am; 8hr).

BY COLECTIVO

Minivans often provide a more frequent service to destinations an hour or two outside the city, and to smaller villages. These, as well as small buses to Dzibilchaltún, Oxkutzcab and Ticul, congregate on Parque San Juan (C 62 at C 69). For Progreso, *colectivos* leave from the east side of C 60 between C 65 and C 67.

GETTING AROUND

By bus The city-bus system is convoluted, but in general, northbound buses run up C 56. For Paseo de Montejo, look for #17 on C 59 between C 56 and C 58, or #18 on C 56 at C 59. You can flag buses down at any corner; fares are posted on the doors.

By taxi Taxis can be hailed all around town and from ranks at Parque Hidalgo, the post office and Parque San Juan. The ones at ranks charge according to a zone system – usually M$40 around the centre, and up to M$80 to the outskirts. Cars roving the streets (signed "Radio Taxi") use meters, and are often cheaper.

Bike rental On Sun mornings for the Bici-Ruta (see p.733), bicycles are available for rent on the plaza; the rest of the week, contact Maya Byke, on C 58 between C 59 and C 57 (☎ 999 287 1795, ⓦ mayabyke.com; M$20/hr or M$100/day).

Car rental Family-run Mexico Rent a Car, at C 57-A between C 58 and C 60, has good rates with insurance (☎ 999 923 3637, ⓦ mexico-rent-acar.com). International agencies have offices in a strip on C 60 between C 55 and C 57, in the *Fiesta Americana* and at the airport.

INFORMATION AND TOURS

INFORMATION

Tourist office Teatro Peón Contreras, C 60 at C 57-A (daily 8am–8pm; ☎ 999 925 5186, ⓦ merida.gob.mx/turismo). Mérida's main tourist office is usually staffed with at least one English-speaker. Pick up a copy of the helpful *Yucatán Today* (ⓦ yucatantoday.com), in English and Spanish. Other tourist information booths are in the Palacio de Gobierno on the Plaza de la Independencia (daily 8am–8pm) and on Paseo de Montejo at Colón, just south of the *Fiesta Americana* hotel. Info kiosks staffed with tourist police (☎ 999 942 0060) are set up at the plaza.

Websites The website Yucatan Living (ⓦ yucatanliving.com) is an excellent resource, posting a weekly events calendar and commenting on local bars, restaurants and news.

CITY TOURS

Bus tours An open-sided bus tour goes further afield than you'd walk. It departs from Parque de Santa Lucía (daily 9am–8pm; M$120, children M$50; ☎ 999 927 6119, ⓦ turibus.com.mx).

Horse-drawn carriages *Calesas* are M$350 for a 45min trip around the centre and up Paseo de Montejo.

Walking and cookery tours Mérida's tourism bureau gives a free walking tour (Mon–Sat at 9.30am); reserve at the office in the Palacio de Gobierno (see p.728). You can also rent headsets for a self-guided audio tour anytime (M$80; take your passport). Chef David Sterling (ⓦ los-dos .com; 8hr) offers a range of cookery classes and food-related tours (US$185).

TOUR OPERATORS

Adventures Mexico C 10 no. 374-C, Pedregales de Tanlum (☎ 999 925 1700, ⓦ adventures-mexico.com. Does a good range of day trips to attractions around the city, as well as cookery classes and cantina tours.

Red de Ecoturismo de Yucatán (☎ 999 926 7756, ⓦ redecoturismoyucatan.blogspot.mx. A network of community eco-adventure projects, offering activities like bike trips and camping excursions.

ACCOMMODATION

Although Mérida can get crowded at peak times, you should always be able to find a good, reasonably priced **hotel** room. Unless you have a very early bus to catch, there's not much point in staying in the grimier area near the **main bus stations**, nor in the generic top-end hotels along **Paseo de Montejo**. The best options are all within a few blocks of the central plaza – which is still just a long walk or a short cab ride from the furthest transport and sights. In addition to the usual hotels, Mérida has a glut of good **B&Bs** and smaller inns in converted colonial homes.

HOTELS

Dolores Alba C 63 no. 464, between C 52 and C 54 ☎ 999 928 5650, ✆ doloresalba.com. Popular, clean mid-range place situated around two courtyards (one colonial style, and one sporting a dazzling array of mirror glass) and a large swimming pool. With parking, laundry facilities and more, you get a lot for your money, but it is on the scruffier side of the plaza. M$750

Eclipse C 57 no. 491, between C 58 and C 60 ☎ 999 923 1600, ✆ hoteleclipsemerida.com.mx. Suffering from colonial overload? This hip-and-modern hotel has spare white rooms, each with a different theme suggested with fabric accents and accessories (a lava lamp, a Warhol print, etc). A glittery-tile pool sits in the centre, and there's a small café. A/c and flat-screen TVs are part of the package. M$850

Hacienda Xcanatun 12km north of Mérida on the road to Progreso ☎ 999 930 2140, ✆ xcanatun.com. The closest hacienda to the city, this elegant eighteenth-century plantation house sits on lush grounds. Some of the luxurious suites have baths hewn from local rock. There's also a full spa and an excellent restaurant. US$310 (M$5300)

★ **Julamis** C 53 at C 54 ☎ 999 924 1818, ✆ hoteljulamis .com. Owned (and decorated) by two Cuban artists, *Julamis* is a great opportunity to stay in a colonial house for barely more than less-inspiring budget hotels. The six rooms and one suite (US$99/M$1485) all have a/c, and mix modern furnishings with soaring ceilings and old tiled floors. Perks include free beers in the in-room fridges and a plunge pool on the roof. US$69 (M$1180)

★ **Luz en Yucatán** C 55 no. 499, between C 58 and C 60 ☎ 999 924 0035, ✆ luzenyucatan.com. Delightful rambling place with fifteen rooms to suit every traveller: studios, kitchenettes, private terraces or patios (and even a whole house just down the street). Pool, kitchen, and owners who were once tour guides, so well attuned to guests' needs. The rooms are dynamically priced depending on whether you class yourself as "exceedingly", "moderately" or "not at all" financially successful. M$810

Mucuy C 57 no. 481, between C 56 and C 58 ☎ 999 928 5193. Quiet and well run, with kind staff, good-value rooms, a small pool and wi-fi in the lobby (but not, generally, in most rooms). Housekeeping isn't always as diligent as it should be, but overall it's tidy and the best of the non-hostel budget spots. A/c costs an extra M$50. M$400

Posada Toledo C 58 no. 487, at C 57 ☎ 999 923 1690, ✆ posadatoledo.com. A rambling old family compound,

ideal if you like faded elegance. Singles are a little cramped and light on character, but the high-ceiling doubles are grand (if a bit fluorescent-lit); all have beautiful tiled floors and antique furniture. M$750

Trinidad Galería C 60 no. 456, at C 51 ☎ 999 923 2463, ✆ hotelestrinidad.com. An eccentric hotel crammed full of bizarre artefacts, sculptures and paintings. Rooms upstairs are lighter and more spacious, though furnishings are a little shabby. All have cool mosaic bathrooms; some have a/c. Its sister hotel, *Trinidad* (C 62 at C 55, ☎ 999 923 2463), has some cheaper rooms with shared bathrooms and fans, and guests can use the *Galería* pool. M$450

B&BS AND GUESTHOUSES

★ **Las Arecas** C 59 no. 541, between C 66 and C 68 ☎ 999 928 3626 or ☎ 999 140 9553, ✆ lasarecas.com. A small, colonial-style guesthouse (one of the few run by a *meridano*), *Las Arecas* is a fantastic bargain. Rooms around the small garden courtyard are simply furnished, but four of the five have a/c, and there's a communal kitchen. M$525

★ **Merida Santiago** C 74-A no. 499, between C 57 and C 59-A ☎ 999 285 4447 or ☎ 999 197 6730, ✆ hotel meridasantiago.com. This colourful colonial home with six bright rooms is farther west than other options, but worth the walk for whirlpool tubs and plush beds, great breakfasts, a big pool, spa treatments, and a helpful Mexican-Dutch couple as hosts. US$106 (M$1815)

HOSTELS

Casa Nico C 63, between C 66 and C 68 ☎ 999 286 8944, ✆ hostelcasanico.com. Nominally a hostel, but the eleven simple private rooms win out here. The setting is a colonial house with a pool in the centre. Definitely the best option near the bus stations. Dorms M$100; doubles M$360

Santa Lucía C 55 no. 512, between C 62 and C 64 ☎ 999 928 9070, ✆ hostalstalucia.com. A decent back-up if *Nómadas* is full up, this hostel is set in a nice colonial house with a good location near Parque Santa Lucía with large a/c dorms, and private rooms. Dorms M$130; doubles M$350

Nómadas C 62 no. 433, at C 51 ☎ 999 924 5223, ✆ nomadastravel.com. Mérida's longest-established hostel is a smooth operation, with both mixed and single-sex dorms, space for hammocks or tent camping, and fan-only private rooms, some of which are en suite. There's even a pool, and (generally free) activities and entertainment almost nightly. Dorms M$175; doubles M$385; camping M$100

12

EATING

Good **restaurants** are plentiful in the centre of Mérida, though the best (and some of the least expensive) are often open only for lunch. At dinner, many restaurants cater largely to foreigners and are a bit overpriced; locals tend to frequent the **snack stalls** on Plaza Santa Ana (C 60 at C 47) and Parque de Santiago (C 59 between C 70 and C 72) for *panuchos*, *salbutes* and *sopa de lima*. There are also pavement cafés on **Parque Hidalgo**, along C 60 between C 61 and C 59, and a good juice bar on the southwest corner of the plaza.

CAFÉS, CHEAP EATS AND SNACKS

Bistro Cultural C 66 at C 41 ☎ 999 204 9358. Off the beaten track, but well worth the walk, this delightful French-run joint has a tranquil garden, murals on the walls, and a small, economical menu: daily specials from Europe, Mexico and further afield (M$65), plus cooling frappés and desserts like *tarte tatin* (M$40). They sometimes put on live music in the evenings. Mon–Fri 8.30am–5.30pm, Sat & Sun 8.30am–4.30pm.

Café Crème C 41 at C 60 ☎ 999 192 9565, ⓦ cafe crememerida.tumblr.com. Another French-run place, this café and patisserie with a shady patio garden has a tempting range of pastries, plus sandwiches, quiches and salads (M$50–60), as well as set meals and top-notch coffee. Mon–Fri 9am–7pm, Sat 9am–2pm.

Dulcería y Sorbetería El Colón C 61 on the central plaza ☎ 999 927 6443. A slice of old-town Mérida, with a refreshing range of fruit sorbets (from coconut to watermelon; M$40), black-and-white photos on the walls, and efficient waiters dressed in salmon-pink shirts. There's another branch on Paseo de Montejo between C 39 and C 41, near Palacio Cantón. Daily 10am–midnight.

La Habana C 62 at C 59 ☎ 999 928 4715. Mérida's older bohemian intellectual crowd doesn't come around this coffee shop so much since the national smoking ban went into effect. But the black-and-beige-clad waiters still dish out economical Mexican-style diner food (snacks from M$20), and there are excellent daily meal deals (M$59–89). It also roasts its own coffee. Daily 24hr.

★ **La Reina Itzalana** Parque de Santiago, C 59 between C 70 and C 72. This and several other basic restaurants around the same park are some of the few places near the centre to get a casual, super-cheap dinner of *panuchos*, *salbutes* and *sopa de lima* (expect to pay less than M$80 for a good meal). They're packed with local families in the evenings. Daily 8am–10pm.

RESTAURANTS

Amaro C 59 no. 507, between C 60 and C 62 ☎ 999 928 2451, ⓦ restauranteamaro.com. Set in a lovely tree-shaded courtyard with a fountain and a romantic guitarist Wed–Sat. A little overpriced (mains cost M$100–200), but

YUCATECAN CUISINE

Though it varies across the peninsula, **food** in the Yucatán has a few unifying elements, most based on **traditional Maya combinations** and accented with many earthy **spices**. Little of the food is hot, but go easy on the *salsa de chile habanero* that most restaurants have on the table. It's also called *xnipek*, Maya for "dog's nose", because the fiery chile induces a clammy sweat. The most popular dishes are:

Puchero A mutable stew that often includes chicken, beef, pork, the squash, cabbage and sweet potato in a broth seasoned with cinnamon and allspice, all garnished with radish, coriander and Seville orange.

Poc-chuc A combination of pork with tomatoes, onions and spices, widely considered the region's signature dish.

Sopa de lima Chicken broth with fragrant local citrus and tortilla chips, and the most popular appetizer or evening snack.

Pollo or cochinita pibil Chicken or suckling pig wrapped in banana leaves and cooked in a *pib*, a pit in the ground, the shredded meat then utilized in many other snacks.

Papadzules Tacos filled with hard-boiled eggs and covered in a very rich red and green pumpkin-seed sauce.

Pavo en relleno negro Turkey in a black, burnt-chile sauce.

Salbutes Crisp corn tortillas topped with shredded turkey, pickled onions, avocado and radish, ubiquitous at dinner time.

Panuchos The same as *salbutes*, with an added dab of beans.

Chaya A spinach-like green that's reputed to cure everything that ails you, often blended into a drink with pineapple.

Huevos motuleños A sweet-savoury mix of fried eggs and beans on a crisp tortilla, topped with mild salsa, ham, cheese, peas and fried banana slices.

MÉRIDA'S FREE ENTERTAINMENT

The historic centre hosts a party nearly every night of the week, all free and attended largely by locals. Many films and concerts happen at the **Centro Olimpo de Cultura**, on the northwest corner of the plaza. In addition, these are the recurring events:

Mon *Jarana* folk dances, in or in front of the Palacio Municipal on the west side of the main plaza. 9pm.

Tues Big band music, heavy on the mambo, Parque de Santiago (C 72 at C 59); *trova* at the Centro Olimpo. 8.30pm.

Wed Concert at the Centro Olimpo. 9pm.

Thurs Serenata Yucateca, traditional *trova* music, Parque Santa Lucía; classical music at the Centro Olimpo. 9pm.

Sat Noche Mexicana, music from all over Mexico, at the start of Paseo Montejo, Calle 56-A; jazz, salsa and more on the Plaza de la Independencia. 8pm.

Sun Car-free centre: in the morning (8am–noon), bicycles take over the streets for the Bici-Ruta (ⓦ merida.gob.mx/biciruta); in the afternoon and evening, the plaza is filled with music, dancing, food stalls and more. There's also an all-day flea market in the Parque Santa Lucía.

interesting veggie options, such as *crepas de chaya* (see box opposite), are novelties for non-meat-eaters tired of quesadillas. Mon–Sat 11am–2am.

★**La Chaya Maya** C 62 at C 57 ☎ 999 928 4780, ⓦ lachayamaya.com. A simple, sparkling-clean restaurant with a thorough menu of Yucatecan specialities – including *pavo en relleno negro*, *poc-chuc* and *panuchos* (see box opposite) – with handmade tortillas and lots of *chaya*, pumpkin seeds and other earthy flavours. Daily 7am–11pm.

★**El Marlin Azul** C 62, between C 57 and C 59. Long-standing local favourite for seafood, including great fish tacos and perfect fresh *ceviche* (from M$80). If there's no space in the main restaurant (under a blue awning), try the separate, smarter dining room next door to the north.

Mon–Sat 8am–4.30pm.

Rosas and Xocolate Paseo de Montejo 480, at C 41 ☎ 999 924 2992, ⓦ rosasandxocolate.com. This hip hotel restaurant is a double treat: excellent creative Mexican food (don't miss the crispy-fried octopus) plus eye candy in the form of the upper-crust *meridano* crowd. Toothsome desserts and regular live jazz performances, too. Mains from M$200. Daily 7am–11pm.

El Trapiche C 62, between C 59 and C 61 ☎ 999 928 1231. Just off the plaza, this basic, budget-friendly Yucatecan restaurant is open all day and serves everything from fresh juices for breakfast to *poc-chuc* for dinner (mains M$65–140; set lunch around M$55). Daily 8am–midnight.

DRINKING AND NIGHTLIFE

For drinks beyond the hotel bars, there are of course hard-drinking men-only **cantinas** (all over the city, including a couple on C 62, just south of the plaza), plus traditional **family bars** (*bares familiares*; look for signs saying "*100% familiar*"). These are a more mixed affair, with, yes, sometimes even kids. They're open only till about 6pm, serving beer accompanied by *botanas* – small-plate snacks delivered with each round – and often live music.

El Cumbanchero Paseo de Montejo at C 39 ☎ 999 927 3265. This small salsa bar is owned by the son of the late Rubén González, of Buena Vista Social Club. Dancing starts at dinner time with an older crowd, who then give way to younger dancers around 10pm. Tues–Sat 7pm–2am.

Los Henequenes C 56 at C 57 ☎ 999 923 6220. Despite the ubiquitous cartoonish frog logo, *Los Henequenes* is really a traditional *bar familiar*, with a local clientele, two-for-one beer specials and a stage that regularly hosts live bands. Daily 11am–7pm.

Pancho's C 59, between C 60 and C 62 ☎ 999 923 0942. A steak restaurant with a pricey haute Mexican menu, this sprawling space is better as a bar, with tasty mojitos and margaritas. Hit the happy hour (daily 6–9pm) for the best deals. Daily 6pm–2am.

Piedra de Agua C 60 no. 498, between C 59 and C 61, in the hotel of the same name ☎ 999 924 2300, ⓦ piedradeagua.com. Not a big party scene, but insiders know they can hide away in this courtyard bar and drink and talk late. The illuminated spires of the Iglesia Santa Lucia tower just beyond the ivy-covered walls. Daily 4/5pm–late.

La Quilla C 69, between C 44 and C 46 ☎ 999 576 8384. This artist-friendly café is officially an afternoon hangout but on irregular evenings (and occasional Sun afternoons) it hosts bands, DJs and films (cover M$20 or so) and stays open much later. Check the schedule, but either way, it's still a nice place for a beer. Tues–Fri 4–8pm, Sat 7pm–midnight.

12

ENTERTAINMENT

In addition to the options below, there is free music in the various **plazas** every night (see box, p.733). Or you can opt for a personal serenade at the central plaza from trios of *trovadores*, in their white shirts and trousers – M$100 gets you three songs.

Centro Cultural Universitario C 60 at C 57 ☎ 999 924 6729, ⓦ cultura.uday.mx. The Universidad de Yucatán's Ballet Folklórico puts on a colourful performance of traditional Mexican and Maya ceremonies every Fri night. It's touristy but still low-key and inexpensive. Fri 9pm.

Teatro Peón Contreras C 60 at C 57 ☎ 999 924 3843, ⓦ culturayucatan.com. Check the calendar at the city's grand old theatre, where events range from visiting pop musicians to the Yucatán symphony orchestra (the group plays alternating Fri & Sun Oct–April).

SHOPPING

In addition to hammocks (see box below), other good buys in Mérida include **clothing**, in particular men's *guayabera* shirts, which both Cubans and *meridanos* claim to have invented; Panama hats, known here as *jipis*; and embroidered *huipiles*, plus the traditional lace under-layer and checked *rebozo* shawl. Mérida's distinctive *trova* **music** is available in many gift shops on CD; it's especially cheap at the weekly serenade on Parque Santa Lucía, where vendors sell remastered classics or newer songs in the same vein. For all **crafts**, prices (and quality) in the main market are not great, unless you're an unusually skilled and determined haggler.

Casa de Artesanías C 63 two blocks west of the central plaza, in the Casa de la Cultura ☎ 999 928 6676, ⓦ artesanias.yucatan.gob.mx. This government-sponsored shop sells consistently high-quality crafts, including delicate silver filigree jewellery, at fixed prices. The clothing options are somewhat limited, however. Mon–Sat 9am–8pm, Sun 9am–2pm.

Librería Dante C 62 on the central plaza ☎ 999 928 2611, ⓦ editorialdante.com. This bookshop has predominantly Spanish-language stock, but also sells some guidebooks and maps, as well as its own line of field guides. Daily 8am–10.30pm.

La Poblana C 65 no. 492, near C 60 ☎ 999 924 0080, ⓦ hamacaslapoblana.com. More a warehouse than a shop, this place has hundreds of hammocks stacked against every wall, sold by weight; a high-quality, dense-weave *doble* weighs about 1.5kg. Mon–Sat 9am–7pm.

DIRECTORY

Banks and exchange Most banks are around C 65 between C 60 and C 64, have ATMs and are open 9am–4pm. The most centrally located is Banamex, in the entrance to the Museo Casa de Montejo on the south side of the plaza; it also has an ATM.

Consulates Opening hours are limited, so phone ahead. Belize, C 58 no. 450, at C 35 ☎ 999 928 6152, ✉ dutton @sureste.com; Cuba, C 42 no. 200, between C 1 E and C 1 D, Fracc Campestre ☎ 999 944 4216, ✉ conscuba@prodigy .net.mx; US, C 60 no. 338-K, between C 29 and C 31, Colonia Alcala Martín ☎ 999 942 5700.

Hospitals Mérida is the Yucatán's centre for medical care. Clinica de Mérida hospital, Itzáes 242 at Colón (☎ 999 942 1800, ⓦ clinicademerida.com.mx), is accustomed to dealing with foreigners.

Internet Internet cafés dot every street in central Mérida, and especially C 61 west of the plaza. There's free wi-fi in most of the city's parks.

Laundry Lavandería La Fe, C 64 between C 55 and C 57, offers an inexpensive service (Mon–Sat 8am–6pm, Sun 9am–2pm).

Post office C 53 between C 52 and C 54 (Mon–Fri 8am–4.30pm, Sat 9am–1pm). For packages, try Mayan Mail shipping service, C 58 between C 57 and C 59 (Mon–Fri 8am–8pm, Sat and Sun 9am–2pm; ☎ 999 287 1795).

BUYING A HAMMOCK

One of the most popular souvenirs of Mexico is a **hammock** – and Mérida is one of the best places in the country to buy one. If you want something you can realistically sleep in, exercise a degree of care and never buy from street vendors or even a market stall – their products are rarely good quality. Comfort is measured by the tightness of the weave and the breadth: because you're supposed to lie in a hammock diagonally to be relatively flat, the distance it stretches sideways is as crucial as the length (although obviously the woven portion of the hammock, excluding the strings at each end, should be at least as long as you are tall).

Cotton threads (*hilos de algodón*) are more comfortable and better hold their shape, but nylon is easier to wash. Sisal hammocks are generally scratchy and very poor quality – avoid them. As a guideline, a decent-size cotton hammock (*doble* at least) will set you back about M$300–400.

Gulf Coast

A wide, fast road (Hwy-261) connects Mérida with the **GULF COAST** to the north, first passing the ancient Maya complex of **Dzibilchaltún**, then arriving after 36km in the port of **Progreso**, on which *meridanos* descend en masse in summer. Due west of Mérida, the little village of **Celestún** offers a very different coastal experience from Progreso, being surrounded by a large nature reserve. In fact, most people hit the beach only after taking a boat tour around a long inlet that's home to a massive flamingo colony.

Dzibilchaltún

20km north of Mérida, east off Hwy-261 • Daily 8am–5pm; Museo del Pueblo Maya Tues–Sun 8am–4pm • M$170; guides M$200 for up to six people • *Combis* for Chablecal leave from Mérida's Parque San Juan (C 62 at C 69) and stop near the ruins; leaving, you can walk or hitch a ride to Hwy-261, where you can flag down a Progreso- or Mérida-bound bus or *combi*

The archeological importance of the ruins of the ancient city of **Dzibilchaltún** is hardly reflected in what you actually see. What it lacks in grandiosity, though, it makes up for in the small yet excellent **Museo del Pueblo Maya**, which examines the persistence of Maya culture until modern times, with exhibits on traditional crafts and religion. There's also a very pretty **cenote**, in which you can swim, and the area is part of an **eco-archeological park**, where birders can spot the rough-winged swallow and the Yucatán woodpecker. Allow about two hours to see everything.

The place was settled from 1000 BC right through to the Conquest, the longest continuous occupation of any known site. More than eight thousand structures have been mapped, but unfortunately little has survived, in particular because the ready-dressed stones were a handy building material, used in local towns and in the Mérida–Progreso road. There is very little signage at the site, so it's worth hiring a **guide** at the main entrance.

Templo de las Siete Muñecas

From the museum at the entrance, a meandering nature trail leads to the so-called Temple of the Seven Dolls. The temple was originally a simple square pyramid, subsequently built over with a more complex structure. Later still, a passageway was cut through to the original building and seven deformed clay figurines (dolls) were buried, with a tube through which their spirits were meant to commune with the priests. The structure is remarkable for being the only known Maya temple to have windows, and for having a tower in place of the usual roofcomb. On the **equinoxes**, the sun shines straight through the tower doors, in a display of ancient astronomical savvy that draws a crowd of tourists.

Cenote Xlacah

One of the ancient causeways that linked the city's major points runs straight from the temple to another cluster of ruins. The centre of the grassy field is dominated by the shell of a Franciscan chapel. A little further west, **Cenote Xlacah** not only provided the ancient city with water, but also held ritual importance for the Maya. More than six thousand offerings – including human remains – have been discovered in its deeper end. It's also home to several types of fish, including the Yucatán tetra, a type of sardine found only in the peninsula.

Progreso

First impressions of **PROGRESO** – a working port with a 6km-long concrete pier – can be uninspiring, especially at the end of a summer weekend when crowds of day-trippers have pulled out, leaving beer bottles and food wrappers in their wake. But if you're craving a beach, the long, broad one here makes a pleasant enough day out from Mérida. If you're here in the winter, the beach will be empty, except perhaps for a few intrepid tourists from one of the cruise ships that dock here occasionally. The towns of **Yucalpetén**, **Chelem** and **Chuburná** – respectively fifteen, twenty and thirty minutes from Progreso – are much quieter, especially in the low season. Further west, though, the road is impassable, and it's not worth making a detour back to the coast at **Sisal**, Mérida's chief port in colonial times – it's now practically deserted.

Progreso itself is a small place, and it's not difficult to find your way around. Calle 80 is the main street, running north–south and dead-ending at the beach. Here you'll find the market (the fruit and veg vendors are usually shut by 2pm), along with a few banks with ATMs, and a couple of internet cafés.

ARRIVAL AND INFORMATION   PROGRESO

By bus Frequent departures from Mérida's AutoProgreso depot (see p.729), arriving in Progreso's station on C 29 at C 82, four blocks south of the water. Returning to Mérida, you can catch the bus, or a *combi*, from C 80 at C 31 near the post office, on the north side of Progreso's Parque Central. Leaving on summer Sun evenings, with the rest of the weekend crowds, you'll have a very long wait for a seat.

Tourist information The tourist office is in the Casa de la Cultura on C 80 at C 27 (Mon–Fri 8am–2pm, Sat 8am–1pm; ☎ 969 935 0104), but it has only a free map and a few flyers.

ACCOMMODATION AND EATING

Hotels in town range from very seedy to somewhat overpriced, but Progreso is a popular family destination, so many have large rooms ideal for groups. The high season is July, Aug and Semana Santa; outside of that, prices drop considerably. You can also often find good house-rental deals for this stretch of coast on ⓦ vrbo.com and similar sites. For cheap comidas corridas, the town's small market, on C 80 at C 27, has several good stalls; also try the area around the plaza at C 80 and C 31.

Casa Aliso B&B C 21 no. 84, between C 50 and C 52 ☎ 969 935 2391, ⓦ freewebs.com/casaalisobb. With only two rooms, this small-scale operation requires booking ahead. It has a prime location just off the beach but several blocks from the malecón party scene. One of the rooms is more like an apartment, though both are the same price. **US$75 (M$1285)**

Eladio's Malecón at C 80 ☎ 969 935 5670. A lively, fairly slick bar-restaurant on the beach, where you can easily make a meal of the tasty *botanas* that come free with beers; mains are about M$120–180. Daily 11am–9pm.

Playa Linda C 76, between 19 and 21 ☎ 969 103 9214, ⓦ playalindayucatan.com. Located right on the seafront, a few steps away from the beach, this neat and tidy hotel has bright rooms and larger suites with balconies and kitchenettes (M$900); all types of rooms have TVs and a/c. **M$600**

East of Progreso

It's best to have a car to explore this direction, as the pleasures come more from poking along the ever-narrowing road rather than heading for a particular destination. Chicxulub Puerto is notorious as the spot where a meteor crashed some 65 million years ago, one of the most significant events in the history of the earth (see box, p.737); there's now a very good seafood restaurant. Alongside Hwy-27 at the Uaymitún inlet (around km 15), there's a free viewing platform (*mirador turístico*) for spotting flocks of flamingos; go in late afternoon, but before the 6pm closing time (7pm in summer). The road continues to **Telchac Puerto**, a laid-back seaside village popular in the summer with escapees from Mérida, then another 9km to **San Crisanto**, where a village organization leads **mangrove tours**. In the village of Santa Clara, the beach is tranquil and the seafood fresh.

Finally, at the end of the coast road is **Bocas de Dzilam**, a state nature reserve in the Parque Natural San Felipe comprising freshwater springs on the seabed. The water's minerals nourish turtles, tortoises, crocodiles and dozens of bird species.

ARRIVAL AND TOURS   EAST OF PROGRESO

By bus Buses from Progreso do come out this way, but infrequently. You can get a more direct bus to Dzilam de Bravo from Mérida from the Noreste terminal (4 daily at 5am, 7.15am, 2pm & 8pm; 1hr 30min).

San Crisanto cooperative Just south of the crossroad, San Crisanto ☎ 991 959 7205, ⓦ sancrisanto.org. The

12

CHICXULUB AND CENOTES

Some 65 million years ago the Chicxulub asteroid struck the Yucatán Peninsula – near the town of the same name (see opposite) – an event that is considered to have contributed to the extinction of the dinosaurs. The strike also caused large sections of the region's limestone bedrock to collapse, in turn forming thousands of *cenotes* (sinkholes).

The region's network of *cenotes* – which are generally filled with fresh water – was crucial for the Maya civilization that dominated the Yucatán Peninsula before the arrival of the Spanish conquistadors in the 1500s. These flooded subterranean chambers were vital sources of potable water in an area short on rivers and lakes, and towns, villages and ceremonial sites often sprung up around them. They were also considered sacred gateways to the Maya underworld, known as Xibalba ("the place of fear"). At Cenote Sagrado at Chichén Itzá (see p.752), for example, the Maya threw statues, pottery, incense, textiles, jade, gold and human sacrifices into the water as offerings to the gods of the underworld. The few human sacrifices who survived the ordeal, incidentally, were considered to have spoken with the gods, and have developed prophetic powers.

Today the region's *cenotes* – some of them have been turned into theme parks, others remain blissfully undeveloped – are perhaps the most memorable places for a swim, snorkel or dive in the Yucatán. Two of the most spectacular are Cenote X'Keken and Cenote Samula (see p.756), just outside the city of Valladolid.

village leads trips through the mangroves in small rowing boats (M$50 per person; 1hr 30min) – great for birding, and you end at a *cenote* for a swim. Look for the office south of the main road, near the baseball field.

Sayachuleb cooperative One block east from the north edge of the square, Dzilam de Bravo ☎ 991 912 2520. Runs tours (around M$1000 for up to five people; 5hr) to the Bocas de Dzilam.

ACCOMMODATION AND EATING

You can easily cover this area as a day drive; if you get stuck overnight, the hotel options are limited. On the other hand, you can eat quite well and inexpensively out this way.

Moctezuma Off the northeast corner of the plaza in Chicxulub Puerto ☎ 969 934 0403. Also known as "*Los Barriles*", a reference to the giant wood barrels that form its front entrance, this long-running seafood restaurant is a traditional favourite for a lazy lunch of fried fish and other

delights (from M$60). Daily 11am–7pm.

San Crisanto Cooperative Just south of the crossroad, San Crisanto ☎ 991 959 7205, ⓦ sancrisanto.org. The same group that runs mangrove tours in this town (see opposite) also rents out large, clean and fairly basic cabañas that can sleep up to six people (just about). **M$850**

Celestún

Were it not for its amazing flamingo-filled lagoon, **Celestún,** 93km west of Mérida, would be little more than a one-boat fishing village. It's literally the end of the road, dead-straight for most of the drive through the forest, until you emerge and cross a bridge to the end of a sandbar on the northwest coast of the peninsula. The town has grown a tiny bit in the twenty-first century (with an ATM and a petrol station, finally), but still has a castaway feel; it's busy only on occasional Sundays and during Mexican holidays.

The beach is wide, and the sea is cloudy yet clean – but it's the birds in the 600-square-kilometre Ría Celestún Biosphere Reserve here that are the real draw. A typical boat tour takes in the flamingos, most numerous from November to May, when blue-winged teal and shovellers also migrate. Dedicated birders can hire a skilled guide, or, if you are looking for something more active, there is the option to bike and canoe through the mangroves.

ARRIVAL AND DEPARTURE

CELESTÚN

By bus Departures from Mérida's Noreste terminal (13 daily; 2hr).

By car If you're driving from Mérida and don't want to

backtrack, take the small road south via Chunchucmil; it was redone in 2012, and makes a nice loop.

SEEING CELESTÚN'S FLAMINGOS

The primary **boat tour** goes from the large, palapa-roofed *parador turístico*, off the north side of the main road into town, just past the bridge (ask the bus driver to drop you here, as it's a 20min walk back from the main square, or M$30–40 in a *triciclo* taxi). The basic one-hour tour (M$200) stops at the flamingo feeding grounds and a freshwater spring amid mangroves. The two-hour trip (M$300) also visits a "petrified forest", really a spooky swath of salt-choked trees. Guides (a negotiable M$400/hr) are definitely recommended – all speak English and can identify most of the birds you'll see. You may be approached by unlicensed captains outside the *parador*; they will offer a competitive price, but their deep-keel boats are not designed for the inlet, and some passengers have found themselves pushing their craft out of the mud.

For extended **bird watching** tours, look for Alberto Rodriguez Pisté, a fluent English-speaker and longtime birder; he's one of the expert guides at the *parador turístico*. If he's not there, he can usually be found at *Restaurant Celestún*, on the waterfront.

A few other ecotourism operations have opened in recent years. The best organized is Manglares de Dzinitún (☎999 232 5915 or ☎988 967 6130), off the main road a bit west of the *parador turístico*, and south about 1km. It offers kayak and canoe trips for M$300–400, as well as birding trips and night tours to spot nocturnal fauna.

ACCOMMODATION AND EATING

For cheap home cooking, visit the *loncherías* by the small market (just off the inland side of the plaza). There's also a bakery on the plaza, and a bar-restaurant that's open in the evening; the seafood places on the beach are generally open for lunch only.

Casa de Celeste Vida C 12 no. 49-E ⓦhotelcelestevida .com. Good if you want to settle in for a while, this restored house, 1km north of town on the beach road, has three rooms with kitchens. Fishing trips, bikes and kayaks are all available, as are discounted weekly accommodation rates. US$95 (M$1625)

Manglares de Dzinitún 1km south of the main highway, just west of the parador turístico ☎999 232 5915, ✉dzinitun@gmail.com. This bare-bones ecotourism place has a solar-powered cabaña and camping space (they'll supply the tent). It's a great wild location next to the mangroves, but pack some DEET-heavy insect spray. Cabaña US$30 (M$515); camping US$10 (M$170)

María del Carmen C 12 no. 111, at C 15 ☎988 916 2170, ✉mcrodriguez@hotmail.com. An adequate choice for accommodation on the beach, *María del Carmen* has rooms with balconies overlooking the water; a/c costs a little extra. Very popular during Mexican holiday times, so you'll need to book ahead. M$350

La Palapa C 12 ☎999 916 2083. Of several seafood restaurants along the beach, this one is the biggest and unfortunately the priciest, but it's also generally more reliable than others in the centre. Expect to pay around M$150–200 for dinner. Daily 11am–7pm.

Xixim 10km north of town ☎988 916 2100, ⓦhotelxixim.com. Operating primarily on wind and solar power, this remote and lovely eco-resort has stylish cabañas with outdoor showers, plus a good restaurant. The real treat, though, is the utterly wild beach. A number of tours are on offer. US$207 (M$3540)

South and east of Mérida

South of Mérida are two scenic routes, steeped in Maya and colonial history: both are best experienced in a car, though you can get to a couple of major attractions by bus. East of the city, by car or bus, lies the *pueblo mágico* ("magic village" – an official Mexican government designation) of Izamal, which is exceptionally scenic and rich in tradition. Taken as a whole, this area represents the essence of Maya rural life, the heart of the Yucatán, in dozens of villages linked by narrow roads through dense forest. Life is slower here, often conducted by bicycle – stay alert while driving.

Ruta Puuc

About 80km south of Mérida in the Puuc hills lies a group of important and well-restored archeological sites, linked along a road commonly called the **Ruta Puuc**. The chief attraction is **Uxmal**, second only to Chichén Itzá in tourist appeal, as well as in its

TRANSPORT ON THE RUTA PUUC

Because the sites on the Ruta Puuc are far apart, and on a road poorly served by buses, it's best to rent a car in Mérida. You can drive through in a day, but if you spend the night mid-route, you can explore the key sites and take in the Ruta de Conventos as well. The Ruta Puuc bus from Mérida was not running at the time of research, but scores of Mérida travel agencies offer Puuc-route **trips** that include meals and a guide, from around M$500 per person.

size and historical significance. From Uxmal, Hwy-261 continues on to the lesser site of **Kabáh**; shortly after that, bearing east on a smaller side road, you pass **Sayil** and **Labná**. From Labná you can continue to the farming town of **Oxkutzcab**, on the road between Muna and Felipe Carrillo Puerto, and head back to Mérida via **Ticul** and Muna. Or you can follow the longer **Ruta de los Conventos** (see p.745) back.

The distinctive **Puuc sites** clearly evolved from themes in the Río Bec and Chenes regions: you'll see the same gaping monster mouths and facades decorated in mosaic-like Xs and checkerboards. In both cases, though, the techniques reflect a new strategy of **mass production** – the mask-covered front of the Codz Poop at Kabáh, for instance, is dotted with hundreds of consistently round carved eyes. A new core-and-veneer style of construction, rather than stone blocks stacked with mortar, yielded sounder buildings with a smoother appearance.

Uxmal

Hwy-261 • Daily 8am–5pm • M$234 • **Sound-and-light show** Winter 7pm, summer 8pm • M$78, or included in price of day entrance ticket • **Guides** About M$550 for a small group • **Parking** M$22

Meaning "thrice-built", the UNESCO World Heritage Site of **Uxmal** (pronounced OOSH-mal) represents the finest achievement of the Puuc-region Maya culture before it fell into its ultimate decline near 1000 AD. Its spectacular buildings are encrusted all over with elaborate, and sometimes grisly, decoration. Uxmal is potentially more rewarding than a visit to Chichén Itzá, as the crowds can be a bit lighter, the decorative detail is fascinating, and you can still climb one of the pyramids. If you arrive close to opening time (the drive from Mérida takes about an hour), you can see the major buildings in a couple of hours and leave before the buses start rolling in. There's a pay car park at the entrance to the site, where the visitor centre includes a small museum, bookshop with guides to the site, crafts store, snack bar and ATM.

The main restored buildings are set out on a roughly north–south axis in a large cleared site; the alignment of individual buildings often has astrological significance. As in all Maya sites in the Yucatán, the face of **Chac**, the rain god, is everywhere. Chac must have been more crucial in this region than almost anywhere, for Uxmal and the other Puuc sites have no *cenotes* or other natural sources of water, relying instead on *chultunob*, jug-shaped underground cisterns, to collect and store rainwater (most have been filled in, to prevent mosquitoes breeding, but Kabáh has an extant one).

Brief history

Little is known of the city's history, but the chief monuments, which marked its peaks of power and population, were erected around 900 AD. Sometime after that, the city began to decline, and by 1200 Uxmal and the other Puuc sites, together with Chichén Itzá, were all but abandoned. Political infighting, ecological problems and loss of trade with Tula, near Mexico City, may have played a part. Later, the **Xiu dynasty** settled at Uxmal, making it one of the central pillars of the League of Mayapán (see p.746), but a 1441 rebellion put an end to centralized Maya authority.

Pirámide del Adivino

Entering the site, you first see the most remarkable of all Mexican pyramids, the so-called **Pyramid of the Magician**, soaring at a startling angle from its uniquely oval

12

base. The legend of the pyramid's creation tells that an old sorceress, who lived in a hut where the pyramid now stands, hatched a dwarf son from an egg and encouraged him to challenge the king to a series of tests – all of which the dwarf won, thanks to a little magic. Finally the king challenged him to build a pyramid overnight. The dwarf succeeded, and became ruler of Uxmal.

Archeological evidence is a bit less magical, showing at least five stages of construction – six if you count the modern restoration, which may not correspond to any of its earlier incarnations. At the base of the rear (east) stairway, a tunnel reveals **Templo III**, one of the earlier levels. Walk around to the west face of the pyramid into the **Cuadrángulo de los Pájaros** (named for the macaws that stud the roofline of the building on the west side) to admire the even steeper stairway that runs down either side of a second, earlier sanctuary in a different style. Known as the **Edificio Chenes** (or Templo IV), as it reflects the architecture of the Chenes region (see p.723), the building's entire front forms a giant mask of Chac. At the bottom of the west face, divided by the stairway, is the very first stage of construction.

Cuadrángulo de las Monjas

Behind the pyramid, the **Nunnery Quadrangle** is a beautiful complex enclosing a plaza. The Spanish gave it this name, but it wasn't a convent; theories range from a military academy to a sort of earthly paradise, where intended sacrificial victims would spend their final months in debauchery. The four buildings, probably constructed between 895 and 906 AD, are each set on a slightly different level, possibly representing the four main levels of the Maya universe. The facade of each is decorated with complex reliefs, and the quadrangle itself is a slightly irregular shape, apparently to align with Venus.

Maya architectural skills are at their finest here, as the false vaults of the interiors are taken about as wide as they can go without collapsing (wooden crossbeams provided further support), and the frontages are slightly bowed in order to maintain a proper horizontal perspective. The **north building**, probably also the oldest, has a strip of plain stone facade (from which doors lead into vaulted chambers) surmounted by a slightly raised panel of mosaics, featuring geometric patterns and human and animal figures, with representations of Maya huts above the doorways. The **west building**, which has been heavily reconstructed, boasts even more varied themes, and the whole of its ornamentation is surrounded by a coiling, feathered rattlesnake with the face of a warrior emerging from its jaws. The **east building** mirrors the west one in its proportions; its snake decorations, however, run in long horizontal bars.

An arched passageway through the middle of the **south building**, the lowest of the four, is directly aligned with the **ball-court** (ham-fistedly rebuilt with cement) outside.

Casa de las Tortugas

Today a path leads between the ruined side walls of the ball-court and up onto the levelled terrace on which stands the **Casa de las Tortugas** (House of the Turtles). This very simple, elegant building, named after the stone turtles carved around the cornice, demonstrates another constant theme of Puuc architecture: stone facades carved to resemble rows of narrow columns. These, marked with bands of masonry, probably represent the Maya huts still in use today, with walls of bamboo or saplings lashed together.

Palacio del Gobernador

Adjacent to the Casa de las Tortugas, the **Governor's Palace** marks the finest achievement at Uxmal. Arriving at the then virtually unknown site in June 1840, explorer and writer John L. Stephens did not doubt its significance. "If it stood this day on its grand artificial terrace in Hyde Park or the Garden of the Tuileries," he wrote, "it would form a new order...not unworthy to stand side by side with the remains of the Egyptian, Grecian and Roman art."

The palace faces east, away from the buildings around it, probably for astronomical reasons – its central doorway aligns with the column of the altar outside and the point where Venus rises. The use of light and shade on the long, low facade lends a remarkable harmony, as do the strong diagonals that run through its broad band of mosaic decorations. Close up, the mosaic features masks of Chac alternating with grid-and-key patterns and highly stylized snakes. The patterns vary in depth, lending a fascinating texture to the facade.

Grupo Sur

Behind the palace, you can climb the rebuilt staircase of the **Gran Pirámide** to see the temple on top, decorated with macaws and more masks of Chac – some of these have even smaller carved faces set inside their mouths. **El Palomar** was originally part of a quadrangle like that of the Nunnery, but the only building to retain any form is this, topped with the great latticed roofcomb that gives it its name: it looks somewhat like a dovecote.

Beyond, the scrub forest is the perfect place to spot some of the Yucatán's more distinctive birds, such as the turquoise-browed motmot with its pendulum-like tail, particularly along the path that runs off the south side of the Palacio del

Gobernador. The trail leads to an odd display of small **stone phalluses**, protected by a thatch roof – collected from all over the site, they're evidence of a fertility cult centred on Uxmal (they're also worked into the back of the building on the west side of the Nunnery Quadrangle).

ARRIVAL AND DEPARTURE UXMAL

By bus Buses (5 daily; 1hr) run direct from Mérida, and any bus heading down the main road towards Hopelchén will drop you a short walk from the entrance. Note that no buses run back to Mérida after the hour-long sound-and-light show.

ACCOMMODATION AND EATING

Several **hotels** are close to the site, but none in the budget category. All are subject to sudden arrivals of huge tour groups, which can make the quality of service and food erratic, but you may be able to negotiate a good deal when they're not full. A short drive away, however, are good budget options in Santa Elena (see below), as well as the ultra-deluxe *Hacienda Temozón* (see box opposite).

The Lodge at Uxmal Adjacent to the Uxmal site entrance ☎ 998 877 2495, ⓦ mayaland.com. Spacious and filled with greenery, if a bit overpriced. Its breezy restaurant and bar, *La Palapa*, is a convenient spot for a cool drink. The same management runs *Hacienda Uxmal*, on the highway opposite the turn to the site; the rooms have more colonial grandeur, for similar rates. **US$208 (M$3550)**

Choco-Story México (Ecomuseo del Cacao)

Ruta Puuc, a 5min walk north of Uxmal • Daily 9am–7.30pm • M$120 • ☎ 999 121 8839, ⓦ choco-storymexico.com

Choco-Story México (also known as **Ecomuseo del Cacao**) produces and celebrates the main ingredient in quality chocolate. The Belgian owner, who also operates chocolate shops in Mérida, is working with a Maya collective to re-establish cacao production in the region. The museum explores the sacred significance of the cacao bean to the Maya and shows sustainable production methods. And don't miss the tastings, of course, of chocolate in both liquid and solid forms.

Santa Elena

16km south of Uxmal, and just 7km from Kabáh, **SANTA ELENA** is worth visiting mainly for the magnificent view from its large hilltop **church**, visible for many kilometres around. Beside the church is a morbidly interesting small **museum** (daily 8am–6pm; free) with displays on local funerary practices, including the two-hundred-year-old mummified remains of four children discovered under the church floor in 1980. Just outside town, where Hwy-261 bypasses the centre, are several exceptionally pleasant places to stay; buses can drop you next to them on request.

ACCOMMODATION AND EATING SANTA ELENA

El Chac Mool Hwy-261 ☎ 985 978 5117. The only restaurant not affiliated with a hotel around the ruins, *El Chac Mool* does decent local food (M$80–170), cheaper than the other options, although it closes a bit early. Daily 9am–8/9pm.

Flycatcher Inn Off Hwy-261 by the Santa Elena turn ☎ 997 978 5350, ⓦ flycatcherinn.com. The first accommodation you reach when coming from Uxmal, a B&B with seven rooms and a separate guest cottage, all decorated with local craftwork and furnished with comfy beds. It's about a 5min walk south from the main square, or buses from Mérida will drop you on the highway very nearby. **US$60 (M$1025)**

★ **The Pickled Onion** Hwy-261, east of the Santa Elena turn ☎ 997 111 7922, ⓦ thepickledonionyucatan.com. British expat Valerie Pickle rents a handful of Maya-style cabañas in all sizes, with bigger ones great for families. There's also a large pool. Her restaurant (mains around M$120–160) has a mostly international menu but also does excellent versions of local dishes; picnic lunches and children's meals are available. Summer 7.30am–9.15pm, winter 7.30am–8.30pm. **US$45 (M$770)**

Sacbe Bungalows Hwy-261, Santa Elena ☎ 997 978 5158, ⓦ sacbebungalows.com.mx. A hospitable Mexican–French couple offer basic but spotless bungalow rooms, all with porches, dotted about spacious grounds; there's also a cottage that sleeps up to five people (US$81). Meals are available. **US$43 (M$735)**

HACIENDA HOPPING

Along the Ruta Puuc are numerous ruined henequen plantations, in various states of repair. *Yaxcopoil* and *Ochil* lie right beside the road, so it's easy enough to be dropped here if travelling by bus, and flag down the next bus or *colectivo* to continue to Uxmal or Mérida (though check the schedule before you leave, as buses aren't terribly frequent).

Hacienda Ochil 40km south of Mérida, just west of Hwy-261 ☎999 924 7465, ⍟haciendaochil .com. This attractively refurbished hacienda operates as a good Yucatecan restaurant (mains around M$120–180), a small museum and some excellent handicraft workshops, plus a small land-art work in a *cenote* by James Turrell. The entry fee of M$20 is waived if you're eating at the restaurant. Daily 10am–6pm.

Hacienda Temozón 35km south of Mérida, about 8km east off Hwy-261 ☎999 923 8089, ⍟hacienda temozon.com. One of the peninsula's best hotels – lavish rooms, a swish restaurant with an international menu, an opulent spa and a delightful swimming pool. Breakfast is not too expensive, so if you're doing the route by car, it can be a treat to start your day here. US$200 (M$3420)

Hacienda Yaxcopoil On the edge of Yaxcopoil village ☎999 900 1193, ⍟yaxcopoil.com. One of the closest haciendas to Mérida, and also one of the most dramatic. At its height, it employed four hundred people, but now the main house stands in a state of picturesque disrepair – peeling walls, sagging ceilings, rooms full of mildewed tablecloths and faded pictures. It also has wonderful (and less decrepit) accommodation in an adjacent guesthouse: a huge, high-ceilinged room with two double beds, as well as a stand-alone casita. A restaurant on the grounds serves Yucatecan breakfast and dinner. Mains average M$50, and kids eat free. Mon–Sat 8am–6pm, Sun 9am–5pm. US$80 (M$1370)

Ticul

12

Located 80km south of Mérida on Hwy-184, **TICUL** is another good base for exploring the Puuc region, though not especially scenic. Historically an important centre of Maya shamanism, it's also a shoe-manufacturing town, full of shops stocked with wildly impractical sparkly sandals. It's well served by **buses** to and from Mérida and with services to Cancún and the east coast. The centre of town is around the junction of calles 25 and 26, with a large plaza to either side, plus a massive church and several hotels; the market, locally noted for great tortas at night, is to the west on Calle 23 between calles 28 and 30.

ARRIVAL AND DEPARTURE   TICUL

By bus Buses from Mérida and elsewhere use a station directly behind the church at the corner of C 24 and C 25-A. Destinations Caribbean coast via Felipe Carrillo Puerto (17 daily; 4hr 20min); Chetumal (6 daily; 6hr).
By colectivo *Colectivos* for Mérida, as well as Santa Elena,

Oxkutzcab and surrounding villages, set off when they're full from various points in the immediate vicinity of the bus station: for Mérida near the corner of C 24 and C 25, other destinations mainly from C 25-A alongside the church.

ACCOMMODATION

Plaza C 23 no. 201, between C 26 and C 26-A ☎997 972 0484, ⍟hotelplazayucatan.com. The smartest option in town, *Hotel Plaza* has all the amenities, if no particular style. As you'd expect, the en-suite rooms all come with TVs, telephones and a/c. There's a decent restaurant, and staff can organize guides and tours. M$500
Posada Jardín C 27 no. 216, between C 28 and C 30 ☎997 972 0401, ⍟posadajardin.com. For a little greenery, head away from the centre to *Posada Jardín*,

which has four excellent-value cabins with separate sleeping and sitting areas, set in a bright garden with a small, sometimes murky, pool. All rooms have fridges, but a/c and breakfast cost extra. M$400
Sierra Sosa C 26 no. 199-A, between C 23 and C 21 ☎997 972 0008. The simplest of the hotels in town, *Sierra Sosa* has basic, rather cramped rooms with shower and fan, with the option of a/c and TVs. Opt for one of the most spacious rooms, upstairs. M$250

EATING

Los Almendros C Principal, heading out of town towards Oxkutzcab ☎997 972 0021, ⍟restaurante

losalmendros.com.mx. Ticul's best-known restaurant is the original location of what is now a small chain and claims to have invented the classic Yucatecan dish of *poc-chuc* (see box, p.732). Unfortunately that's no guarantee you'll get a great meal, but it's worth a try. The big building has a pool for diners, and it's packed with families at weekends. Daily 10am–9pm.

La Carmelita C 23 at C 26 ☎ 997 972 0515. In the centre of town, just off the plaza, this casual restaurant serves up an inexpensive set meal, as well as other à la carte dishes (M\$50–180): the seafood options are particularly good. Daily 9.30am–6.30pm.

Kabáh

Hwy-261 east of Uxmal • Daily 8am–5pm • M\$47

This site lies on both sides of the highway some 25km from Uxmal. Much of Kabáh ("Mighty Hand") remains unexcavated, but the one great building, the **Codz Poop**, or Palace of Masks, lies not far off the highway. The facade of this amazing structure is covered all over, in ludicrous profusion, with goggle-eyed, trunk-nosed masks of Chac – to get into the doorways, you need to tread over the mask's noses. Even in its present state, with most of the curved noses broken off, this remains one of the strangest and most striking of all Maya buildings, decorated so obsessively, intricately and repetitively that it seems the product of an insane mind. At the front of the building is a rare working *chultun* (cistern), with a concave stone floor gathering water into the underground chamber.

On the other side of the road is an unusual circular **pyramid** – now simply a green conical mound that, once you spot it, is so large you can't believe you missed it. Just beyond, a sort of triumphal arch marks the point where an ancient 30km causeway, or *sacbé*, from Uxmal, entered the city.

Sayil

Ruta Puuc, 5km east of the junction with Hwy-261 • Daily 8am–5pm • M\$47

A sober, restrained contrast to the excesses of Kabáh, **Sayil** was once one of the most densely populated areas in the Puuc region, home to an estimated seventeen thousand people from 700 AD to 1000 AD. It is dominated by one major structure, the 80m-long **Gran Palacio** (Great Palace), built with three storeys, each smaller than the one below. Although several large masks of Chac adorn a frieze around the top of the middle level, the decoration mostly takes the form of stone pillaring that mimics the look of bamboo poles – seen more extensively here than at any other Puuc site. The interiors of the middle level, too, are lighter and airier than usual, thanks to the use of broad openings, their lintels supported on fat columns.

Few other structures have been cleared, and those that have been are widely scattered in the forest – a walk to these remote spots is a long, hot one, but it gives you a better sense of the scale of the old city, as well as a chance to view wildlife such as hummingbirds. From the Gran Palacio a path leads through the forest to the small temple of **El Mirador**, and in the other direction to a stele, carved with a phallic figure and now protected under a thatched roof. The path (in fact, a former ceremonial *sacbé*) carries on to the **Palacio Sur**, a large, little-restored structure with another characteristic bamboo facade.

Xlapak

Ruta Puuc km 10 • Daily 8am–5pm • Free

The minor road continues from Sayil past the smallest and least-visited of the Puuc sites. If you have the time, stop to see the one restored building, a small, elegant palace with huge Chac masks above its doorways and geometric patterns on the facades.

Labná

Ruta Puuc, 3km east of Xlapak • Daily 8am–5pm • M\$47

This ancient city was historically far smaller and less important than Sayil, but it is in many ways a more impressive site. There has been more excavation here, so the main buildings can all be seen as part of a harmonious whole. The **Palacio**, near the entrance, bears traces of sculptures including the inevitable Chac, and a crocodile-snake figure with a human face emerging from its mouth – thought to symbolize a god emerging from the jaws of the underworld. Remnants of a *sacbé* lead from here to the **Arco de Labná**. Originally part of a complex linking two great squares, like the Nunnery at Uxmal, it now stands alone, richly decorated on both sides: on the east with geometric patterns, on the west (the back) with these and niches in the form of Maya huts or temples. Nearby is **El Mirador**, a barely restored temple mound topped by the well-preserved remains of a tall roofcomb. An inner passageway at one time led to the site's principal temple.

Grutas de Loltún

Ruta Puuc, south of the junction with Hwy-18 • Daily 8am–5pm • M$115 • From Oxkutzcab, take a *colectivo* or truck from C 51 next to the market; getting back may require a wait, as trucks are full of workers and produce; a taxi from town is approximately M$60–80

Located just before you reach Oxkutzcab on the road from Labná, these are the most impressive **caves** in the Yucatán. The two-hour tour (for which you can request an English-speaking guide) concentrates on strange rock formations and patterns in giant stalactites and stalagmites. At the entrance, a huge bas-relief Maya warrior guards the opening to the underworld, and throughout are traces of ancient paintings and carvings on the walls. The surrounding jungle is visible through the collapsed floor of the last gallery, and 10m-long tree roots find an anchor on the cavern floor.

Oxkutzcab

From Labná, you can head back to Mérida on the fast Hwy-18 (look for signs just north of the Grutas de Loltún), or you can stop off in the village of **OXKUTZCAB**, at the heart of Yucatán's citrus orchards. If you visit early in the morning, you'll see its huge daily **market** at the centre of town, at the junction of calles 50 and 51.

12

ARRIVAL AND DEPARTURE   OXKUTZCAB

By bus Buses to Mérida via Ticul (hourly; 2hr) depart from the Noreste bus station at the corner of C 56 and C 51.

By colectivo Shared vans come and go from beside the market on C 51.

ACCOMMODATION

★**Hotel Puuc** C 55 at C 44, on the way out of town towards Labná ☎ 997 975 0103, ⟲ hotelpuuc.com.mx. The best accommodation option in town, with a sand-coloured, fortress-like exterior, *Hotel Puuc* is a good-value place, with bright, clean rooms (a/c costs M$50 extra) and a pool. The only drawback is the less than central location, which is awkward if you don't have your own wheels. **M$420**

Ruta de los Conventos

From Mérida by car, the easiest route out is C 69 east to the *periférico* (ring road), then following signs to Mayapán. This takes you to Hwy-18, with the towns all well signposted and only a short way from the new road. Second-class buses to Maní stop at all the smaller towns en route, and can be flagged down on the highway.

The "Convent Route" – Hwy-18 from Oxcutzcab to Mérida – is a natural extension of the Ruta Puuc, or an easy day outing from Mérida on its own. Every town along the route has an immense fortress church, but the historic highlights are **Maní** and the late Maya site of **Mayapán**. The **churches** date mainly from the seventeenth century or even earlier, as the Spanish were trying to establish their control. They were built so huge partly to impress, as a sign of the domination of Christianity over traditional gods, and partly as fortresses and places of refuge in times of trouble.

Maní

12km north of Oxkutzcab • Regular buses from Mérida's Noreste terminal (C 67 at C 50) until about 8pm

This small town was founded by the Xiu after they abandoned Uxmal, and it was the largest city encountered by the Spanish in the Yucatán, though almost no trace now survives. Avoiding a major confrontation, Maní's ruler, Ah Kukum Xiu, converted to Christianity and became an ally of the Spanish. In 1548 one of the earliest and largest **Franciscan monasteries** in the Yucatán was founded here. This still stands, surrounded now by Maya huts, and just about the only evidence of Maní's past glories is the ancient stones used in its construction and in walls around the town. In front of the church, in 1562, Bishop Diego de Landa held his infamous auto-da-fé, in which he burned the city's records (because they "contained nothing in which there was not to be seen the superstitions and lies of the devil"), destroying virtually all original Maya literature.

Mayapán

Hwy-18, halfway between Maní and Mérida • Daily 8am–5pm • M$39 • Buses from the Noreste terminal to Maní (see p.745) stop at the ruins on request

The ruins of the most powerful city in the Yucatán from the thirteenth to the fifteenth centuries sit right beside the road. It was a huge population centre by the standards of the day, with some fifteen thousand people living on a site covering five square kilometres, in which traces of more than four thousand buildings have been found.

What can be seen today is less than grand – the buildings were crude and small by Maya standards, at best poor copies of what had gone before, and only a few have been restored (a visit doesn't take long). The Mayapán society was initially dismissed as decadent and failing, but a case can be made for the fact that it was merely a changing one. As the priests no longer dominated here, what grew instead was a more genuinely urban society: highly militaristic, no doubt, but also far more centralized and more reliant on trade than previous Maya culture.

Brief history

According to Maya chronicles, Mayapán, Chichén Itzá and Uxmal formed the **League of Mayapán**, which exercised control over the entire peninsula from around 987 to 1185. It broke up when Mayapán's **Cocom** dynasty attacked the already declining Chichén Itzá and took control of the peninsula. The archeological evidence, however, suggests Mayapán was not founded until 1263, after the fall of Chichén Itzá.

Either way, hegemony was maintained until 1441, when Ah Xupan, a Xiu leader from Uxmal, overthrew the Cocom and destroyed their city. But this led to factionalism, which aided the Spanish Conquest considerably.

Acancéh

Maya pyramid Daily 8am–5pm • M$39

A mix of Maya, modern and colonial architecture, the town of Acancéh (pronounced "ah-kan-KAY") encapsulates Yucatecan history. At the central plaza, beside the sixteenth-century church, is a large Maya pyramid plus two smaller ones, all surrounded by everyday life. At the top of the large pyramid are four huge stucco masks, some of the finest of their kind.

The ancient Maya Palacio de los Estucos is about four blocks away, behind the market (get directions from the booth at the main pyramid). The stucco decoration on the long, low building is far from complete, but there are plenty of easily identifiable figures, animals and glyphs.

Los Tres Cenotes

Village of Chunkanán, south of Cuzamá • Daily 8am–5pm • M$300/truk (up to 4 passengers; the last one departs around 3.30pm) • LUS buses (15 daily; 1hr 30min) and minibuses (2hr) depart from Mérida's Noreste terminal and Parque San Juan respectively for Cuzamá; from here take a tricicilo to Chunkanán (around M$30); combis also run from Acancéh

The trip to three cavernous **cenotes** is less a detour off the convent route than a separate day outing, as it typically takes at least six hours, including the drive from the main highway to the village of Chunkanán, followed by a 45-minute ride on a *truk* (or *carrito*), a rickety, horse-drawn carriage down old narrow-gauge rail lines. But the reward is great scenery, refreshing swims and a taste of bygone hacienda history. You'll want to bring swimming gear, towels and perhaps a picnic, as locals do on weekends.

The process of hiring a *truk* is slightly complicated by a business rivalry. Coming from

Cuzamá, east of Acancéh, you first reach a large parking area off the right side of the road, signed as Los Tres Cenotes. This is an upstart organization, run by people from Cuzamá and greatly resented by the people of Chunkanán – another 2km south on a narrow road – who have no other income in their village. If you press on less than 1km down the road, you will find the original operation, in front of a multi-storey palapa restaurant. If you're in a taxi or *triciclo* from Cuzamá, you'll get steered to the first, Cuzamá-run *truk* stop; if you want to go to Chunkanán without raising a fuss, you can always say you're headed for the restaurant.

ACCOMMODATION AND EATING

★**El Dzapakal** Main road, Chunkanán ☎999 564 2435. El Dzapakal is a superb restaurant serving up hearty Yucatecan food (avoid the so-so international dishes), beautifully presented and very reasonably priced (most mains M$60–120). Daily 10am–6.30pm.

El Príncipe Tutul-Xiu C 26 between C 25 and C 27, Maní ☎997 978 4257, ⓦrestaurantes-elprincipetutul-xiu.blogspot.co.uk. Méridans often come down to Maní on day trips to dine at this festive palapa-roofed restaurant that has been serving Yucatecan standards (from M$60) for more than thirty years. It can be an absolute zoo on

RUTA DE LOS CONVENTOS

Sundays, but the food is always delicious. There are other branches in Mérida and Oxkutzcab. Daily 11am–7pm.

Sac-Nicté Chunkanán ☎999 923 7598, mobile ☎044 999 189 3133, ⓦmayanvillagerental.com. An authentically Maya-style compound (which can accommodate up to six people), where one small palapa hut houses two hammocks (with mosquito nets), another has a toilet and bathtub and another has a kitchen and extra hammock. At the back is a pool, and there are good-value weekly rates too. M$1000

Aké

12

Midway between Izamal and Mérida on the back road via Cacalchén • Daily 8am–5pm • M$39 • From Mérida or Izamal AutoCentro buses pass the ruins (6 daily; 45min); last bus to Mérida is around 8pm, but confirm before setting off; by car turn south in Euan, or take the direct road from Hwy-180, opposite Tahmek

On the scenic, slow route from Mérida, dense with Maya towns, these **ruins** are partially integrated into an inhabited village and working henequen plantation. Aké was probably in alliance with the old city of Izamal, as it is linked by one of the peninsula's largest *sacbeob* (Maya roads). The most impressive building is the **Edificio de las Pilastras**, a large platform topped with more than twenty stone pillars. The Maya rubble intermingles with San Lorenzo de Aké, a fine neo-French henequen **hacienda** from the late nineteenth century. You're welcome to wander through the antique-looking machinery to see the fibre-making process.

Izamal

This excellent regional crafts centre is easy enough to visit from Mérida on a day trip, but don't leave before sunset, when the place takes on a perfect golden glow, thanks to the striking ochre-yellow that covers all of the buildings. If you prefer the country to the city, **Izamal** can also be a good alternative to Mérida as a base for sightseeing. In this case, though, it's nice to have a car, as Izamal is served only by second-class buses.

Convento de San Antonio de Padua

Central plaza • **Convent** Daily 8am–9.30pm • Free • **Sound-and-light show** Mon–Sat 8.30pm • M$90 • **Museum** Tues–Sat 10am–1pm & 3–6pm, Sun 9am–4pm • M$5

In 1552 Fray Diego de Landa (later responsible for a vicious Inquisition and auto-da-fé in Maní) lopped the top off a pyramid and began building this grand convent, which now anchors Izamal's two adjacent main plazas. The porticoed atrium occupies some 24,000 square metres. When the complex was completed in 1561, de Landa consecrated it with one of two statues of the Virgin that he had brought from Guatemala.

Several years later, when church leaders from Valladolid attempted to claim the statue, it is said to have become impossibly heavy, and they were forced to leave it in

A CRAFT TOUR OF IZAMAL

A free map, available from most hotels and businesses, identifies the workshops of wood-carvers, papier-mâché artists and other artisans around Izamal – they're all well marked and easily reached by bike, available from the craft museum. Be sure to visit Don Esteban, on Calle 26 at Calle 45, whose jewellery made from henequen spines is striking and modern, and whose effusive character is memorable. Agustín Colli, on Calle 19 between calles 24 and 26, makes double-weave hammocks that are positively luxurious (and well worth the M$800 or so).

For a broader selection of craftwork, visit Hecho a Mano on the south side of the convent plaza. This particularly good craft and folk-art shop is stocked with everything from Mexican wrestling masks to Huichol yarn paintings from Nayarit, as well as excellent photography by the owner; note that the hours (Tues–Sat 10am–2pm & 4–7pm) can be erratic.

Izamal. A cult developed and she is now the official patroness of the Yucatán; on a visit to the town in 1993, Pope John Paul II gave her a silver crown. During the **fiesta** dedicated to the Virgin on December 8, penitents climb the monastery's staircase on their knees, and worshippers sing in the church the entire night before.

The statue is on view in the *camarín*, a chapel around the back of the main altar. Next to the chapel, the **Museo Santuario de Nuestra Señora** shows many elaborate gowns that have clothed the statue. In the evenings, a **sound-and-light show** is projected on the front facade of the main church.

Kinich Kakmó

C 27 between C 28 and C 26 • Daily 8am–8pm • Free

Izamal was formerly an important religious centre for the Maya, where they worshipped **Itzamná**, mythical founder of the ancient city and one of the gods of creation, at a series of huge pyramid-temples. Most of these are now no more than low mounds in the surrounding country, but several survive in the town itself, and are fascinating to see right in the middle of the residential grid; some businesses on the plaza have pyramids literally in their backyards. Kinich Kakmó is the largest pile, dedicated to the sun god and now partly restored. It's just a couple of blocks north of the two adjacent central plazas.

Centro Cultural y Artesanal

C 31 on the plaza • Tues–Sat 10am–8pm, Sun 10am–5pm • M$20 • ☎ 988 954 1020

This museum showcases choice pieces of craftwork from all over Mexico, with a wing devoted to Yucatecan specialities. It houses a nice shop, a small café (peek behind to see some pyramid remnants) and a quiet, perfumed back room where you can get a foot massage.

ARRIVAL AND INFORMATION   IZAMAL

By bus All buses arrive at a small station one block west of the main plaza. For Mérida-bound services, Oriente is preferable to Centro because you arrive closer to the town centre.

Destinations Cancún (hourly; 4hr; slightly faster Oriente service 3 daily, via Tizimín); Valladolid (hourly; 1hr); Mérida (roughly every 30min; 1–2hr).

By car From Mérida, it's easiest to go via Tixkokob or Motul. Coming from the west on Hwy-180 *libre*, go to Kantunil then turn north by following signs for the *cuota* to Cancún, then make an awkward U-turn. From the westbound *cuota*, look for a direct right turn off the highway immediately before km 68. If you miss the turn (easy to do), you can continue to Hoctún, then backtrack.

Tourist office North plaza (daily 9am–9pm; ☎ 988 954 0009).

GETTING AROUND

By horse-drawn carriage Horse-drawn carriages lined up around the plaza will take you for a pleasant *paseo* around the town (20min; M$100).

By bike Rent a bicycle (around M$100/day) from the Centro Cultural y Artesanal on the plaza.

ACCOMMODATION

Macan Ché B&B C 22, between C 33 and C 35 ☎ 988 954 0287, ⓦmacanche.com. This B&B has an assortment of comfortable cottages (a/c costs US$10 extra) tucked among rambling gardens taking up nearly a whole block east of the plaza; rates include breakfast, and other meals are available as well. **M$720**

Rinconada del Convento C 33 no. 294, at C 28 ☎ 988 954 0151, ⓦhotelizamal.com. On the south side of the convent, *Rinconada* has eleven a/c rooms with shiny tile floors, mission-style furniture and plenty of natural light through large windows and patio doors. There's a pool in a tiered garden-courtyard. **M$705**

San Miguel Arcangel C 31-A no. 308, between C 30 and C 30-A, on the plaza ☎ 988 954 0109, ⓦsan miguelhotel.com.mx. An airy two-storey hotel just across from the convent. Rooms are clean and bright and have a/c, while the upper ones along the front have balconies (for M$100 more) that afford close-up views of the plaza action. For less noise, ask for a room off the courtyard, where you'll have a view of one of Izamal's ruined pyramids. Communal facilities include a hot tub. **M$750**

EATING

Los Arcos C 28, on the north plaza. Of the handful of evening snack operations under the *portales* that edge the north plaza, this one's notable for its breakfast options, enormous tortas and delicious fresh fruit drinks (M$25–40). Daily 8am–10pm.

Kinich C 27, between C 28 and C30 ☎ 988 954 0489. This palapa-roofed place is a good traditional restaurant, even if it is a top tour-group destination. Women pat tortillas by hand, and the Yucatecan dishes like *sopa de lima* and *poc-chuc* are reasonably priced (around M$80–160). Daily 8am–10pm.

El Toro C 33 no. 303-G, at C 30 ☎ 988 954 1169. Just south of the convent, this small family-owned place is open for dinner, with a hearty Yucatecan menu of dishes (from M$40) like *chaya* tamales and *queso relleno*. Mon–Thurs & Sun 8am–11pm, Fri & Sat 8am–1am.

DIRECTORY

Banks and exchange On the north plaza, C 31 at C 28, you'll find a Banorte bank with ATM; there's another ATM at the Super Willy's grocery, just off the main plaza.

Internet An internet café is on C 32 just south of the bus station.

Laundry A laundry is on C 30 two blocks north of the north plaza.

Post office On the main plaza (Mon–Fri 8am–2.30pm).

12

Chichén Itzá and around

The most famous, the most extensively restored and by far the most visited of all Maya sites, **Chichén Itzá** lies conveniently along the main highway from Mérida to Cancún, a little more than 200km from the Caribbean coast. To do the ruins justice and to see them when they're not entirely thronged with tourists, an overnight stop is well worth considering – either at the site itself or, less extravagantly, in the rather dreary village of **Pisté**, about 3km west. The village exists almost entirely to provide visitors with accommodation so they can get an early start. Larger **Valladolid**, to the east, is a better option as a base, as it's both convenient and inexpensive, and has some general city life.

The ruins

Hwy-180 *libre*, just east of Pisté • Daily: winter 8am–5pm; summer 8am–6pm, last entry an hour earlier • **Sound-and-light-show** (in Spanish) Nightly winter 7pm, summer 8pm • M$193 • **Visitor centre** Daily 8am–10pm • M$220 in total, comprising two tickets (for two separate site management bodies) • **Guide** (2hr) M$750 • **Horseriding trips** cost around US$50/M$855 and are bookable at *Hotel Mayaland*

The main entry to the site is on the west side. A huge visitor centre houses a museum, restaurant, ATM and shops selling souvenirs, film, maps and guides. You can also get in at the smaller eastern gate by the *Hotel Mayaland*. Either way, you'll want to go in at opening time, as tour buses from Cancún and Mérida start arriving around 10.30am. Allow about three hours to see the site, and if crowds are light, start with the iconic buildings in the Itzá-era Chichén Nuevo (New Chichén) on the north side, then retreat to the Terminal Classic (Chichén Viejo) to the south, where fewer visitors go.

Brief history

Though in most minds Chichén Itzá represents the Maya, it is in fact the site's divergence from Maya tradition that makes it archeologically intriguing. Experts are fairly certain that the city was established around 300 AD, and began to flourish in the Terminal Classic period (between 800 and 925 AD). The rest of its history, however, and the roots of the **Itzá clan** that consolidated power in the peninsula here after 925

CHICHÉN ITZÁ

HWY 180

0   100
metres

Cenote Sagrado

CHICHÉN
NUEVO

Sacbé

N

Piste, Cuota entrance & Mérida

Grutas de Balankanché & Valladolid

12

Hwy-180 & Piste

Templo Norte

Gran
Juego de
Pelota

Parking

Tzompantli

Plataforma
de Venus

Plataforma de
Águilas y
Jaguares

Templo de
los Jaguares

Templo de los
Guerreros

Visitors centre
& main entrance

El Castillo

Grupo de las
Mil Columnas

Juego de Pelota

El Osario

Plataforma
de las Tumbas

Juego de Pelota

Casa de los
Metates

Temazcalli

Templo del
Venado

Mercado

East entrance

Cenote
Xtoloc

Hotel Mayaland

Casa
Colorada

CHICHÉN
VIEJO

2

El
Caracol

Templo de los
Tableros

Edificio de
las Monjas

Akab Dzib

La Iglesia

3

Annexe

■ ACCOMMODATION	
Dolores Alba	1
Hacienda Chichén	2
Villa Arqueológica Chichén Itzá	3

Hwy-180

AD, remain in dispute. Much of the evidence at the site – an emphasis on human sacrifice, the presence of a huge ball-court and the glorification of military activity – points to a strong influence from central Mexico. For decades researchers guessed this was the result of the city's defeat by the Toltecs, a theory reinforced by the resemblance of the Templo de los Guerreros to the colonnade at Tula, near Mexico City, along with Toltec-style pottery remains and numerous depictions of the Toltec god-king, the feathered serpent Quetzalcoatl (Kukulcán to the Maya).

Work since the 1980s, however, supports a theory that the Itzá people were not Toltec invaders, but fellow Maya who had migrated from the south, which would explain why their subjects referred to them in texts as "foreigners". The Toltec artefacts, this view holds, arrived in central Yucatán via the Itzás' chief trading partners, the **Chontal Maya**, who maintained allegiances with Toltecs of central Mexico and Oaxaca.

Chichén Nuevo

The main path leads directly to **El Castillo** (also called the Pyramid of Kukulcán), the structure that sits alone in the centre of a great grassy plaza. It is a simple, relatively unadorned square building, with a monumental stairway ascending each face (though only two are restored), rising in nine receding terraces to a temple at the top. The simplicity is deceptive, however, as the building is in fact the **Maya calendar** rendered in stone: each staircase has 91 steps, which, added to the single step at the main entrance to the temple, amounts to 365; other numbers relevant to the calendar recur throughout the construction. Most remarkably, near sunset on the spring and autumn equinoxes, the great serpents' heads at the foot of the main staircase are joined to their tails (at the top of the building) by an undulating body of shadow – an event that lasts just a few hours and draws spectators, and awed worshippers, by the thousands. The effect is re-created nightly in the sound-and-light show.

Inside El Castillo, where visitors cannot enter, an earlier pyramid survives almost intact, and in the temple's inner sanctuary, archeologists discovered one of the greatest treasures at the site: an altar, or perhaps a throne, in the form of a jaguar, painted bright red and inset with jade "spots" and eyes.

The "Toltec" plaza

El Castillo marks one edge of a **plaza** that formed the focus of Chichén Nuevo, and in addition to a *sacbé* leading to **Cenote Sagrado**, all its most important buildings are here, many displaying a strong Toltec influence in their structure and decoration. The **Templo de los Guerreros** (Temple of the Warriors), lined on two sides by the **Grupo de las Mil Columnas** (Group of the Thousand Columns), forms the eastern edge of the plaza. These are the structures that most recall the great Toltec site of Tula, both in design and in detail – in particular the colonnaded courtyard (which would have been roofed with some form of thatch) and the use of Atlantean columns representing battle-dressed warriors, their arms raised above their heads.

The temple is richly decorated on its north and south sides with carvings and sculptures of jaguars and eagles devouring human hearts, feathered serpents, warriors and, the one undeniably Maya feature, masks of the rain god Chac, with his curling snout. On top (now visible only at a distance, as you can no longer climb the structure) are two superb examples of figures called **Chac-mools**, once thought to be introduced by the Toltecs: offerings were placed on the stomachs of these reclining figures, which are thought to represent either the messengers who would take the sacrifice to the gods or perhaps the divinities themselves.

The "thousand" columns alongside originally formed a square, on the far side of which is the building known as the **Mercado**, although there's no evidence that this actually was a marketplace. Near here, too, is a small, dilapidated ball-court.

North of El Castillo is the **Plataforma de Venus**, a raised block with a stairway up each side guarded by feathered serpents. Here, rites associated with Quetzalcoatl when he took

12

the form of Venus, the morning star, would have been carried out. Slightly smaller, but otherwise identical in design, the adjacent **Plataforma de Águilas y Jaguares** features reliefs of eagles and jaguars holding human hearts. Human sacrifices may have been carried out here, judging by the proximity of a third platform, the **Tzompantli**, where victims' heads likely hung on display. This is carved on every side with grotesque grinning stone skulls.

Gran Juego de Pelota

Chichén Itzá's ball-court, on the west side of the plaza, is the largest known in existence, with walls some 90m long. Its design is a capital "I" surrounded by temples, with the goals, or target rings, halfway along each side. Along the bottom of each side runs a sloping **panel** decorated with scenes of the game. Although the rules and full significance of the game remain a mystery, it was clearly not a Saturday-afternoon kick-about in the park; for more on the game's significance, see p.606.

On the panel, the players are shown proceeding from either side towards a central circle, the symbol of death. One player, just right of the centre (whether it's the winning or losing captain is up for debate), has been decapitated, while another holds his head and a ritual knife. Along the top runs the stone body of a snake, whose heads stick out at either end. The court is subject to a whispering-gallery effect, which enables you to be heard clearly at the far end of the court, and to hear what's going on there.

Templo de los Jaguares

This temple overlooks the playing area from the east side. At the bottom – effectively the outer wall of the ball-court – is a little portico supported by two pillars, between which a stone jaguar stands sentinel. The outer wall panels, the left and the right of the interior space, are carved with the images of Pawahtuns, the gods who supported the sky and who are thought to be the patrons of the Itzá people. Inside are some worn but elaborate relief carvings of the Itzá ancestors inserted in the Maya creation myth – a powerful demonstration of their entitlement to rule.

Cenote Sagrado

The city's largest *cenote* lies at the end of the *sacbé* that leads about 300m off the north side of the plaza. It's an almost perfectly round hole in the limestone bedrock, some 60m in diameter and more than 30m deep, the bottom third full of water. It was thanks to this natural well (and perhaps another in the southern half of the site) that the city could survive at all, and it gives Chichén Itzá its name (literally "at the edge of the well of the Itzá"). The well was regarded as a portal to the underworld, called Xibalba, and the Maya threw in offerings such as statues, jade and engraved metal discs (a few of them gold), as well as human sacrifices – all of them boys, recent research has shown. The Maya thought that any boy who managed to survive the ordeal had communed with the gods.

Chichén Viejo

The **southern half of the site** is the most sacred part for contemporary Maya, though the buildings here are not in such good condition. They were built for the most part prior to 925 AD, in the architectural styles used in the Puuc and Chenes regions.

El Osario

A path leads from the south side of El Castillo to the major structures, passing first the pyramid **El Osario** (the Ossuary; also called the High Priest's Grave), the only building in this section that shows Toltec-style detail. Externally it is very similar to El Castillo, but inside a series of **tombs** was discovered. A shaft, first explored at the end of the nineteenth century, drops down from the top through five crypts, in each of which was found a skeleton and a trap door leading to the next. The fifth is at ground level, but here too was a trap door, and steps cut through the rock to a sixth chamber that opens onto a huge underground cavern: the burial place of the high priest.

El Caracol

Follow the main path and you arrive at **El Caracol** (the Snail, for its shape; also called the Observatory), a circular, domed tower standing on two rectangular platforms and looking remarkably like a modern-day observatory. The roof has slits aligned with various points of astronomical significance. Four doors at the cardinal points lead into the tower and a circular chamber. A spiral staircase leads to the upper level, where observations were made.

Las Monjas

Immediately to the south of El Caracol, the so-called **Monjas** (Nunnery) palace complex shows several stages of construction. Part of the facade was blasted away in the nineteenth century, but it is nonetheless a building of grand proportions. Its **annexe**, on the east end, has an elaborate facade in the Chenes style, covered in small heads of Chac that combine to make one giant mask, with the door as a mouth. By contrast, **La Iglesia**, a small building standing beside the convent, is a clear demonstration of Puuc design, its low band of unadorned masonry around the bottom surmounted by an elaborate mosaic frieze and roofcomb. Masks of Chac again predominate, but above the doorway are also figures of the four mythological creatures that held up the sky – a snail, a turtle, an armadillo and a crab.

Beyond Las Monjas

A path leads, in about ten minutes, to a further group of ruins that are among the oldest on the site, although they are unrestored; this is a good area for bird watching, with few people around to disturb the wildlife. Just east of Las Monjas is the **Akab Dzib**, a relatively plain block of palace rooms that takes its name ("Obscure Writings") from undeciphered hieroglyphs found inside. Red palm prints – frequently found in Maya buildings – adorn the walls of some of the chambers. Backtrack along the main path to the building opposite El Osario, the **Plataforma de las Tumbas**, a funerary structure topped with small columns; behind it is a jungle path that heads back to the main east–west road via the site's other water source, Cenote Xtoloc.

Grutas de Balankanché

Hwy-180, 1.6km east of the *Dolores Alba* hotel (see p.754) • **Tours** (in English) Daily 9.30am, 11am, 12.30pm & 4pm • M$113 • Second-class buses and *colectivos* between Valladolid and Mérida can drop you at *las grutas*; a taxi from Pisté costs about M$60–80

These damp caverns are a refreshingly cool way to pass an hour. They were reopened in 1959, when a sealed passageway was discovered, revealing a path to an underground altar to Chac, the rain god. Tours with taped commentary lead past an underground pool, stalagmites and stalactites to a huge rock formation that resembles a *ceiba*, the Maya tree of life. Around its base lie many of the original Maya offerings, such as clay pots in the shapes of gods' faces.

Cenote Yokdzonot

Hwy-180, 14km west of Pisté • Daily 9am–6pm • M$61 • Any of the second-class buses along Hwy-180 *libre* stop on request at the town plaza; the *cenote* is about 350m south; a taxi costs around M$350, factoring in waiting time

The village of Yokdzonot is known for its well-kept *cenote*. It has excellent facilities, with good showers and toilets, plus a restaurant and camping facilities. Life jackets and snorkel gear are available, and you can take a bike tour to another nearby *cenote*.

ARRIVAL AND DEPARTURE · CHICHÉN ITZÁ AND AROUND

Arriving at Chichén Itzá, Hwy-180 *libre* curves around the site to the north, making an arc that merges with the site access road (the original highway straight through) at both ends.

THE RUINS

By bus First-class buses from all the peninsula's major towns and cities stop in the site parking lot.

Destinations Cancún (roughly hourly; 4hr), with the

4.30pm ADO express bus (3hr); Playa del Carmen (2 daily at 7.35am & 4.30pm; 3hr 20min–3hr 50min); Tulum (2 daily at 7.35am & 4.30pm; 2hr 20min–2hr 50min), with the first bus stopping at Cobá (2hr 10min); Valladolid (at least hourly; 40–55min).

PISTÉ

By bus There are two bus stations, one at each end of town. You can buy tickets for any service at either station, but first-class buses stop only at the east end.
Destinations All destinations are the same as at the ruins, plus Mérida on second class (14 daily; 3hr).

ACCOMMODATION AND EATING

Visitors to Chichén Itzá have a choice of staying in more expensive **hotels** immediately **east of the ruins** (all but one are on the short east-side access road off Hwy-180 *libre*, signposted "Zona Hotelera"), or cheaper ones along the main street in the town of **Pisté**, west of the site. In Pisté, most hotels are on the main road, between the village and the ruins, so it's easy to shop around – though quality can be low and occupancy high. Though the town is short on good places to eat, there is a row of *loncherías* at the west end of town, facing the plaza – they serve comida corrida for about M$50, and are also open in the evenings, with lighter meals.

NEAR THE RUINS

Dolores Alba Hwy-180 libre km 122, 2km east of Chichén Itzá east entrance ☎999 928 5650, ⍟dolores alba.com. The best-value hotel near the ruins, with clean, colourful rooms (though rather tiny, spare bathrooms), a good restaurant and two swimming pools. Transport is provided to the site, but not back. The restaurant is good and affordable, and diners can use the pool. Across the road, you may notice the appealing-looking Parque Ikkil, but it is a massive package-tour-with-buffet juggernaut, not really even worth entering for its *cenote*. Daily noon–2pm & 7–10pm. M$900

★ **Hacienda Chichén** Off Hwy-180 libre, near the east entrance to the ruins ☎985 920 8407, ⍟hacienda chichen.com. Of the two luxury choices at the ruins (*Mayaland* is the other), this place has a more old-colonial, Mexican feel: the hacienda it is based on dates back to 1523. Some rooms are in cottages that housed Carnegie Institution archeologists in the 1920s. There's also a spa. US$213 (M$3640)

Villa Arqueológica Chichén Itzá Off Hwy-180 libre, near the east entrance to the ruins ☎985 851 0187, ⍟villasmex.com. Not as lavish as its neighbours, but comfortable enough, and handy for the site. The snug, thick-walled rooms (each with a double bed and a single bed) and suites are set round a patio enclosing a pool and cocktail bar. US$69 (M$1180)

PISTÉ

Felix Inn Hwy-180 libre, midway through town ☎999 851 0033, ✉hotelfelixinnchichenitza@hotmail.com.

A sensible and sunny alternative to the hotels by the ruins. Clean-enough a/c rooms are laid out around a garden and pool, plus a restaurant and an internet café with sometimes-iffy connections. Rooms are shielded from highway noise by the lobby. M$650

Las Mestizas Hwy-180 libre, midway through Pisté ☎999 851 0069. One of the more welcoming places in Pisté, this is a palapa-roofed setup with a similar menu to its neighbours; the best options are probably the regional dishes (M$50–180), such as the refreshing *sopa de lima*. Mon–Sat 8am–10pm.

Pirámide Inn Hwy-180 libre at the west end of town, next to the bus station ☎985 851 0115, ⍟chichen .com. Good rates, a pool and vintage Sixties style, but it's all fairly dilapidated. Recommendable only for its location very close to the ruins, and the fact that you can camp in the big gardens (bring your own tent). Doubles M$500; camping (per person) M$50

Posada Olalde On C 6, off Hwy-180 libre; turn south across from Posada Carrousel ☎985 851 0086, ✉volalde_ucan@hotmail.com. This is one of the quieter spots in town, as it's off the main road. Palapa-roofed cabañas with fans crowd the tiny yard behind the main house, but they're a fresher alternative to the tired rooms in the older complex behind. M$350

Restaurante San Antonio Hwy-180 libre, opposite the east-end bus station in Pisté. Compared with the massive buffet restaurants nearby, this basic lunch spot (dishes M$40–120) is easy to overlook. However, it serves a daily stew special, has nice outdoor seating and is less of a tourist scrum than many of its neighbours. Daily noon–3pm.

Valladolid and around

Yucatán state's second city, **VALLADOLID** is around 40km east of Chichén Itzá, still close enough to beat the crowds to the site on an early bus, and of interest in its own right. Although it took a severe bashing in the nineteenth-century Caste Wars, it has retained a strong colonial feel and exudes the unpretentious attitude of a rural capital, catering to the farmers and ranchers who live nearby, and the village women who come here to sell their hand-embroidered *huipiles* and other crafts. It's also an excellent place to eat, with traditional Yucatecan food still flourishing.

The heart of the city is the *parque principal*, the main plaza at the intersection of calles 39 and 40, where the two white towers of the eighteenth-century Catedral de San Gervasio rise gracefully over the south side. It's the place to be at dusk, when the curving love seats are filled with chatting couples and the bubbling fountain, topped with a statue of a woman in a traditional Yucatecan *huipil*, is lit from below. During the day, you can walk upstairs in the city hall (*ayuntamiento*; on the southeast corner) to see murals and photos of Valladolid's history, including a wall of portraits of city leaders.

Casa de los Venados

C 40 no. 204, just off the plaza • **Tours** Daily 10am (in English and Spanish) • M$70 • ☎ 985 856 2289, ✉ javenator1@gmail.com, ⓦ casadelosvenados.com

This private home, a beautifully renovated seventeenth-century mansion, contains a truly dazzling collection (over 3000-strong) of modern Mexican folk art, shown by house-proud owners, an American couple, who are delighted to answer questions. Pre-arrange a visit by email, ideally, or drop by at 10am, the default tour time. The entry fee supports local charities.

Iglesia de San Bernardino de Siena

Parque de San Bernardino, 1km southwest of the plaza via C 41-A • **Church** Mon & Wed–Sun 9am–8pm; Mass daily 6pm • Free • **Museum** Mon–Sat 9am–6pm • M$30

Franciscan missionaries began work on this sturdy **church** shortly after the Spanish established Valladolid as an outpost in 1545. In 1848 Maya rebels sacked it; despite this, a fine Baroque altarpiece from the eighteenth century remains, as do some striking seventeenth-century paintings on the side walls.

The monastery on the north side is now a museum, where you can see weapons that were dredged up from the on-site *cenote*, and other relics from the revolution. You can also see the beautiful structure that houses the water wheel over the *cenote*, and the sprawling gardens where the self-sufficient monks grew their own food.

Cenote Zací

On the block formed by C 34, C 36, C 37 and C 39 • Daily 8am–6pm • M$25

This *cenote* was the water source for the former Maya stronghold of Zací ("white hawk"), from where the fierce Cupul clan fought against the first conquistadors. Broad stairs lead down into a huge cavern where the air is cool, and light reflects off the green water. It's also home to lots of catfish. Swimming is permitted, but not encouraged – there are no changing rooms, though you could tidy up in the open-air restaurant at the top, so long as you order something.

12 Cenotes X'keken and Samula

7km west of Valladolid on Hwy-180 *libre* • **Cenote X'keken** Daily 8am–6pm • M$65 • **Cenote Samula** Daily 8am–6pm • M$65 • *Colectivos* run to the village of Dzitnup from outside the *María Guadalupe* hotel on C 44 (see opposite); or cycle on a paved bike path starting from C 49 west of San Bernardino; or take a taxi (around M$250 return with waiting time)

Perhaps the most photogenic swimming hole in the Yucatán, the remarkable **Cenote X'keken** is also called Dzitnup like the nearby village. Visitors descend through a tunnel into a huge vaulted cave, where a nearly circular pool of crystal-clear turquoise water glows under a shaft of light from an opening in the ceiling. A swim in the ice-cold water is an invigorating experience. A short walk away, in the same complex, at the even more impressive (thanks to spooky natural lighting) **Cenote Samula**, the roots of a huge tree stretch down towards the pool. Facilities include changing rooms, souvenir stalls, life jackets (to rent) and a restaurant. Not to be missed.

ARRIVAL AND DEPARTURE   VALLADOLID

By bus Valladolid's main bus station is on C 39 at C 46, a block and a half west of the main plaza. Additionally, AutoCentro buses serve Izamal (15 daily; 1hr) from the old Oriente terminal west of the centre, C 37 at C 54.
Destinations Cancún (1–2 hourly; 2hr 15min–4hr 20min); Chetumal (4 daily at 5.25am, 7.30am, 2.25pm & 8.30pm; 5hr 20min), via Carrillo Puerto and Bacalar; Chichén Itzá (hourly; 40min); Izamal (2 daily at 12.45pm & 3.50pm; 3hr); Mérida (12 daily; 2hr 10min), plus numerous second-class services; Playa del Carmen (13 daily; 2hr 30min–3hr 10min); Tizimín (4 daily at 8.49am, 12.24pm, 7.24pm &

9.30pm; 50min–1hr); Tulum via Cobá (11 daily; 1hr 30min–2hr 10min).
By colectivo Shared vans and taxis are convenient for nearby towns and sights, such as Tizimín, Ek-Balam and Dzitnup. Most depart from marked points along C 44 just west of the plaza, though the Ek-Balam service seems to shift around. For Chichén Itzá, Servicio Plus vans leave from C 39 between C 44 and C 46; these can be faster than buses in the morning, and much cheaper. They also serve X'keken and Samula, with departures at 8am from the same spot.

GETTING AROUND

By bike With its small scale and light traffic, Valladolid is a good place to get around by bike; you can also reach nearby

cenotes via bike paths. Rent (for M$90/day) from MexiGO Tours, which offers a self-guided bike tour (see p.757).

INFORMATION AND TOURS

Tourist office On the southeast corner of the main plaza, by the *ayuntamiento* (Mon–Fri 9am–9pm, Sat 9am–8pm, Sun 9am–7pm; ☎ 985 856 2529, ⓦ valladolid.com.mx). It has plenty of information, including free maps, but is erratically staffed.

Tours MexiGO Tours (C 43 no. 204-C, between C 40 and C 42 ☎ 985 856 0777, ⓦ mexigotours.com) runs trips to Río Lagartos and other nearby attractions, as well as bike trips (self-guided is an option) to local houses and *cenotes*.

ACCOMMODATION

Valladolid's budget hotels are good, and higher-end places are excellent value. Also note that the *Genesis Retreat* (see p.759) is less than half an hour away.

La Aurora C 42 at C 35 ☎ 985 856 1219, � la.aurora .hotel@hotmail.com. Great mix of old colonial style and new features: sparkling rooms around a central courtyard and pool but retaining the building's old tile floors. For quiet, though, request a room away from the street, where traffic noise hammers off the stone pavements. M$720

★**La Candelaria** Parque la Candelaria, C 35 between C 44 and C 42 ☎ 985 856 2267, ⓦ hostelvalladolidyucatan .com. The excellent local hostel, facing one of the city's loveliest squares, has spotless dorms and private rooms, plus a garden, laundry facilities, an outdoor kitchen and low-cost bike rental. Dorms M$155; doubles M$380

★**Casa Hamaca** C 49 no. 202-A, at C 40 on the southwest corner of Parque San Juan ☎ 985 856 5287, ⓦ casahamaca.com. Set in a garden packed with fruit trees, this charming B&B has eight expansive rooms in a big two-storey building. There's also a pool, and the expert owner can arrange massages, spa treatments and nature tours. M$1120

María Guadalupe C 44 no. 198, between C 39 and C 41 ☎ 985 856 2068, ⓦ hotelmariaguadalupe.com. The best of Valladolid's cheapies, *María Guadalupe* has

well-kept rooms featuring private baths and optional a/c in a small two-storey 1960s building. *Colectivos* for *cenotes* X'keken and Samula leave from outside. M$500

El Mesón del Marqués C 39 no. 203, on the main plaza ☎ 985 856 2073, ⓦ mesondelmarques.com. Lovely hotel that started in a mansion, then expanded into neighbouring buildings. It's where most tour groups stay, but the quality is high. It has a wonderful palm-fringed pool, and one of the best restaurants in town (see below). M$850

Tunich-Beh C 41-A, between C 46 and C 48 ☎ 985 856 2222, ⓦ tunichbeh.com. En route to the Iglesia de San Bernardino, on one of the city's prettiest streets, and well worth the walk out of the centre. Spacious and clean rooms are well off the street, set behind a car park and palapa-covered walkway, in a verdant courtyard next to a clean pool. M$850

Zací C 44 no. 191, between C 37 and C 39 ☎ 985 856 2167, ⓦ hotelzaci.com.mx. A pleasant, modern, three-storey hotel with a quiet courtyard and pool, all of which make it exceptionally good value. The big rooms have a fan, or – for a few dollars more – a/c and TV. M$595

EATING

Whatever your budget, you'll eat well in Valladolid – all of the restaurants recommended here could be considered "author picks". The city market, the Mercado Municipal, is on C 32 between C 35 and C 37 and ringed with snack stands. For nightlife, there's not much beyond people-watching on the plaza, where there's usually some live music on Sun.

El Bazar Northeast corner of the main plaza. A sort of semi-open-air food court with an excellent selection of inexpensive, busy *loncherías* and pizzerias. Most of the stands are open at lunch, but a few also serve breakfast, and some serve lighter meals (M$35–60). Generally daily 8am–10pm.

★**Casa Italia** Parque Candelaria, C 35 no. 202-J, between C 42 and C 44 ☎ 985 856 5539, ⓦ casaitalia .com. Sweet, family-owned Italian restaurant that's both delicious and inexpensive (pizzas M$125–150, pastas M$65–85). It draws local families as well as tourists, and there are seats outside on the city's prettiest small plaza. Tues–Sat 7–11pm.

Conato 1910 C 40, between C 45 and C 47 ☎ 985 108 2003. A few rooms in an old house, furnished with antique

oddities and vinyl booths. The food is eclectic, beautifully presented and home-made (most mains M$80–150), and includes a few sweets such as a rich coconut pudding. It's a family place, but still has a special atmosphere. Mon–Sat 7–10.30pm.

Hostería El Marqués C 39 no. 203, in El Mesón del Marqués ☎ 985 856 2073, ⓦ mesondelmarques.com. Valladolid's best (and quite reasonably priced) restaurant is set in an interior courtyard on the main plaza. Don't be put off if you see it packed with a tour group – the excellent menu (mains M$80–250) features Yucatecan classics such as *sopa de lima* and *poc-chuc*, along with city specialities like *escabeche de Valladolid* (chicken in a spicy vinegar broth). Daily 8am–10.30pm.

12

★**Squimz** C 39 no. 219, between C 44 and C 46 ☎ 999 856 4156, ⓦ squimz.com.mx. A cute, somewhat stylish restaurant-café: pastries and coffee up front, full dinners at the back. The core of the menu is Yucatecan, but often presented in a creative, lighter way (mains M$77–125). Daily 7am–10pm.

Zací C 36, between C 37 and C 39 ☎ 985 856 0721, ⓦ cenotezaci.com.mx. The restaurant at the *cenote* of the same name is reasonably priced (mains M$85–120) and features some hearty regional food, such as ultra-smoky *longaniza* sausage, and handmade tortillas. The setting is cool and shady. Daily noon–6pm.

DIRECTORY

Banks and exchange There are numerous banks in the city centre. Bancomer, next door to the post office on the plaza, changes travellers' cheques and has an ATM.

Internet There are several internet cafés in the centre, including the Ladatel *caseta* on the plaza.

Laundry Lavanderia Daniela at C 41-A, on the way to the Iglesia de San Bernardino de Siena.

Post office On the plaza, C 40 near the corner of C 39 (Mon–Fri 9am–3pm).

North of Valladolid

From Valladolid, most traffic heads straight east to the Caribbean beaches. The north, however, is less explored and makes a nice detour for wildlife: flamingo colonies at Río Lagartos are the main draw. You can also visit the small but flawless Maya site of Ek-Balam.

Ek-Balam

20km north of Valladolid, then 7km east • Daily 8am–5pm • M$130; given the rich detail at the site, it's worth hiring a guide for about M$350 for a small group; Juan Canul, who has worked on many excavations, is recommended (ask for him at the ticket desk); he speaks Spanish and English

Notable for the high quality and unique details of its fantastically preserved stucco sculpture, **Ek-Balam** is nonetheless rarely crowded. The compact site, enclosed by a series of defensive walls, is really only the ceremonial centre; the entire city, which was occupied from the pre-Classic period through to the Spanish Conquest, spreads out over a very wide area, punctuated by *sacbeob* leading out in all directions.

The entrance is along one of these ancient roads, leading through a freestanding four-sided arch. Beyond are two identical temples, called **Las Gemelas** (the Twins), and a long **ball-court**.

El Acrópolis

The principal building, on the far side of the plaza, is the massive **Acrópolis**, the stones along its 200m-long base adorned with bas-reliefs. Thatched awnings at the top protect the site's finest treasure, an elaborate stucco frieze fully uncovered only recently; 85 percent of what you see is original plaster from the ninth century that didn't even require retouching once the dirt was brushed away.

A staircase leads up the centre of the building. On the first level, two doorways flanking the steps display near-matching designs of twisted serpents and tongues; in the right-hand carving, the snake's tongue is emblazoned with a glyph thought to represent the city. Just below the summit, a **Chenes-style doorway** in the form of a giant gaping mouth is studded with protruding teeth. This is the **entrance to the tomb** of Ukit-Kan-Lek-Tok, Ek-Balam's king in the mid-ninth century. The lower jaw forms the floor, while skulls, lilies, fish and other symbols of the underworld carved below reinforce its function as a tomb gateway. Back on the ground, in the plaza, an exceptionally well-preserved **stele** depicts a king receiving the objects of power from Ukit-Kan-Lek-Tok, the smaller seated figure at the top of the stele.

Cenote Xcanché

Daily 9am–5pm • M$64 • ☎ 985 100 9815, ⓦ cenotexcanche.com.mx

In the parking area at the Ek-Balam site, you'll find someone selling tickets to a seemingly bottomless pool that's a 2km walk from the ruins. You can rent a bike to ride there, and try other activities such as rappelling and kayaking at the *cenote*. There's a small restaurant too.

12

By colectivo The village and ruins are easily reached from Valladolid in a *colectivo*, departing from C 44 just west of the plaza.

By taxi A round-trip taxi from Valladolid costs about M$300 with waiting time.

ACCOMMODATION AND EATING

★ **Genesis Retreat** East of the village plaza ☎ 985 852 7980, ⊛ genesisretreat.com. Not far from the ruins, this beautiful ecolodge has a big garden and a bio-filtered pool. Guests can take tours around the village and in the nearby forest. The vegetarian café makes a great stop after the ruins, with organic, local produce. Some taxi drivers may attempt to take you to another, less savoury, lodge around the corner – *Genesis* has a doghouse labelled "Concierge" out front. En-suite rooms cost around M$200 extra; the treehouse-style "Birdhouse" room is a fun option for children. Daily 1–3pm. M$579

Tizimín

Travelling by bus from Valladolid north to Río Lagartos, you have to transfer in **TIZIMÍN**, the unofficial capital of Yucatán's cattle country, 51km from Valladolid. It's pleasant enough, but travellers rarely come this way, even though it is a handy transport hub for northeastern Yucatán (you can go straight from here to Mérida or Cancún, for instance). One seasonal draw is the Feria de los Tres Reyes, which takes place during Epiphany in early January. The fair's festivities draw both Catholic pilgrims and cowboys (who show off their barbecue skills). The rest of the year, it's worth arranging your schedule to pass through Tizimín at lunch time, for a meal at one of the region's best restaurants.

By bus Two bus stations are around the corner from each other at C 46 and C 47, about at 10min walk northeast of the main plaza.
Destinations Cancún (6 daily; 4hr–4hr 10min); Chiquilá for Holbox (3 daily at 7.30am, 1.30pm & 4.30pm; 3hr); Mérida (5 daily; 3hr); Río Lagartos (12 daily; 1hr–2hr); San Felipe (7 daily; 1hr–1hr 30min).

ACCOMMODATION AND EATING

Hotel San Carlos C 54 no. 407, between C 51 and C 53 ☎ 986 863 2094, ⊛ hotelsancarlostizimin.com. There's no real reason to stay the night in Tizimín, but if you do want to, *Hotel San Carlos* is one of the better options in town, with tidy en-suite rooms with a/c and TVs. M$450

★ **Tres Reyes** C 52 at C 53 ☎ 986 863 2106. A great restaurant with hand-patted, chewy tortillas, black-as-ink beans and succulent meats – the soul of Yucatecan cooking (dishes M$60–220). It's on the plaza, a 10min walk from the two bus stations. Daily 8am–11pm.

Río Lagartos

This village 100km north of Valladolid is set on a small spit, surrounded on three sides by water and protected from the open sea by a barrier island. The resulting shallow inlet is inhabited much of the year by tens of thousands of **pink flamingos**, among nearly four hundred bird species in the **Río Lagartos Biosphere Reserve**. Though there's not much in the town itself, the flamingos alone make a visit worthwhile; the best time of year to see them is the spring nesting season, from April to July. There is no bank or ATM in town, so plan accordingly.

FLAMINGO TOURS IN RÍO LAGARTOS

As soon as you arrive at the bus station or get out of your car, you'll be approached about boat tours to see the flamingos. Several experienced **guides** operate in town: ask for Ismael Navarro and Elmer Canul of Río Lagartos Expeditions (☎ 986 862 0452, ⊛ riolagartosexpeditions.com) at the *Restaurante Isla Contoy*, on the waterfront on the west side. They run **boats** to visit the many feeding sites; a two-hour tour usually costs about M$1350 for a maximum of six people and includes a swim; a three-hour trip (M$1785) includes a "spa treatment" at some mud flats. The agency also offers fishing, snorkelling, crocodile-spotting and sunset trips.

By bus The station is on C 19 just east of the main north–south street through town. There's a return service from Tizimín (12 daily; 1–2hr), but the last bus back there (for connections to Mérida or Cancún) departs around 5.15pm.

By combi Ask around the bus station area for shared taxis – they often depart at more convenient times.

ACCOMMODATION

Diego y Matilde's Posada C 19 no. 134 ☎986 100 8390, ⊛riolagartosnaturetours.com. A 5min walk from the waterfront, this four-room inn is run by the people behind Río Lagartos Expeditions (see box, p.759); the rooms are comfortable and come with a/c, TVs and a light breakfast in the morning. M$600

Hotel Villa de Pescadores End of C 14, on the waterfront ☎986 862 0020, ⊛hotelriolagartos.com .mx. An appealing hotel, right on the water, with spick and span rooms with a/c and TVs; some have tiny balconies with views over the inlet. There's a restaurant onsite, and staff can arrange tours. M$860

San Felipe

If it's beaches you're after, head to this tidy town, where an offshore spit is lined with white sand. The town, which is also a popular destination for sport-fishing, is 12km west of Río Lagartos; many of the buses from Tizimín to Río Lagartos come out here as well.

The beach

Boats (M$20/person) depart from the east end of the malecón, where you can also buy tickets for various bird watching and nature tours (from M$300 for up to five people).

At Mexican holiday times – notably July, August and Semana Santa – the beach is crowded; the rest of the year, though, it's quite deserted, and you can set up camp here. If you do, be sure to bring protection against mosquitoes.

By bus From Tizimín, there are several daily buses (7 daily; 20min) to San Felipe; the last one back leaves around 5.45pm.

ACCOMMODATION

San Felipe de Jesús C 9, between C 14 and C 16 ☎986 862 2027, ⊜hotelsf@hotmail.com. San Felipe's one hotel is average at best (nearby Río Lagartos has better options; see p.759), but it has a decent restaurant and the views across the water are undoubtedly beautiful. Daily noon–2pm & 7–9pm. M$650

Isla Holbox

Near the northeastern corner of the Yucatán, **HOLBOX** (pronounced "ol-BOSH") has just one small sand-street village of about two thousand people, wooden houses and virtually no cars. It's technically not an island, but a very long peninsula – but you still must cross by ferry from the village of Chiquilá. The gulf waters here do not have the same glittering clarity as the Caribbean (nor the vibrant reefs), but they're warm and clean, and Isla Holbox is rapidly becoming the trendiest coastal destination in the region.

Development is of course marching on, but fishing remains the main industry and much of the area remains wild and harbours all manner of birds, including flamingos. From May to mid-September, visitors come to see the huge and rare whale sharks (see box, p.762) that congregate just off the cape; on the hour-long boat ride to see and swim with them, you may also see dolphins, rays and flying fish.

One spot of trouble in paradise: truly fearsome mosquitoes during the wet season. And after the bustle of whale-shark season, the island basically shuts down for the rest of September and October – it can feel a bit dreary at this time.

By bus There are daily buses from Cancún to Chiquilá (4.30am, 6am, 8am, 12.30pm, 1.30pm & 2.15pm; returning 5.30am, 7.30am & 1.30pm; services drop off a bit during the winter; 3hr 30min–4hr). Buses leave Mérida (1

ACTIVITIES ON ISLA HOLBOX

For whale sharks, Monkeys (☎ 984 875 2442, ⍟ holboxmonkeys.com) is one of the most established tour operators, though every hotel and guesthouse can arrange the trip. The price is typically the same with every company (about M$1800–2500/person, including lunch and snorkel gear; 5–6hr), but may change from season to season. For **fishing**, try Holbox Tarpon Club (☎ 984 875 2103, ⍟ holboxtarponclub.com; 8hr fishing trip US$850/M$14,540). *Posada Mawimbi* (see opposite) runs **snorkelling** excursions – though there is not so much to see underwater here– as well as kayaking. Kitesurfing lessons/equipment rental and horseriding trips are available at *Casa las Tortugas* (see below). In 2015 a conservation project, Crocodile Quay, was being put together, the intention being to run kayak trips to see the crocodiles and turtles in the mangroves towards the north of Holbox.

daily at 11.30pm; 6hr) and Valladolid (1 daily at 3am; 3hr) in the middle of the night and arrive in time for the 6am ferry. If you'd rather go during the day, there are three buses, though you'll have to transfer in Tizimín. You can also take any second-class bus along Hwy-180 *libre* and get off at the tiny town of El Ideal; from there, you can take a taxi north to Chiquilá for about M$400–500, or transfer to the bus coming from Cancún.

By car Turn north off Hwy-180 *libre* (there's no exit off the toll highway) at the tiny town of El Ideal. Secure parking is available near the ferry pier in Chiquilá (set the price before you leave – usually around M$50 for any portion of a day).

By ferry There are numerous ferries (11 daily, fewer during the winter; 15–30min; M$80). If you're with a group or arrive between departures, you might want to hire a private boat (about M$600). But don't miss the last ferry: Chiquilá is not a place to get stranded. There's a restaurant, basic hotel, store and petrol station, but little else.

GETTING AROUND

For orientation, you'll usually receive a map on the ferry, though street names are seldom used.

By pedicab When you arrive, you'll be greeted by *triciclo* or golf-cart taxis, which can spare you the 10min trek to the plaza, straight ahead from the ferry dock; the maximum charge is around M$80, to the very furthest hotels.

By golf cart The popular alternative to cars, which are rare. They're available to rent (around M$150/hr or M$1000/24hr) from several outlets near the *parque*, including Monkeys (see box above).

By bike You can also get around by bike, from many of the same golf-cart-rental agencies (around M$100/24hr), though they aren't always maintained very well.

INFORMATION

Services On the modest main square, called the *parque*, you'll find a post office, money-exchange desk and a couple of (unreliable) ATMs – always bring extra cash. Internet access is also a bit patchy.

Websites ⍟ holboxisland.com and ⍟ en-holbox.com are both useful, and ⍟ ipaffestival.com has info on the International Public Art Festival, which is held in April.

ACCOMMODATION

Small-scale hotel development stretches east of town for a couple of kilometres. In early summer and before Christmas, rates for some of the upmarket rooms can fall by almost half; July and August, however, can be priced nearly as high as Christmas and Easter weeks. The beachfront hotels are all mid-range to luxury, but there are a few decent cheaper options away from the water. Locals have successfully contested plans for large-scale resorts in the past, but pressure from hoteliers remains.

Casa Barbara Tiburón Ballena, between the pier and the plaza ☎ 984 875 2302, ⍟ holboxcollection.com /hotels/casabarbara_holbox-hotel.php. You're away from the beach here (about a 10min walk), but also away from the town hubbub. The a/c rooms are clean and spacious and set along a deep courtyard with a pool. **M$1050**

Casa Takywara Tiburón off Coldwell, west of the plaza ☎ 984 875 2352, ⍟ takywara.com. A bit of a hike west, but right on the beach and away from party noise. The Colombian owner uses the hotel income to fund her pet project, the island's only animal refuge (injured pelicans, stray raccoons, even a crocodile have a home here – securely fenced and away from guests). There are six rooms in total, including one cabaña on the water; all have kitchenettes. **US$165 (M$2820)**; cabaña **US$198 (M$3385)**

Casa las Tortugas On the beach two blocks east of the plaza ☎ 984 875 2129, ⍟ holboxcasalastortugas.com. Italian-run *Casa las Tortugas* has a great little collection of round, two-storey, a/c cabañas, beautifully decorated and tucked among dense greenery. Staff can organize yoga, horseriding and kiteboarding, among other activities. There are plans for a patisserie too. US$140 (M$2395)

Ida y Vuelta Escobedo, east of the plaza, behind Xaloc ☎ 998 875 2358, ⓦ holboxhostel.com. A friendly hostel just a couple of blocks off the beach, with screened shelters for tents or hammocks as well as a few beds, clean bathrooms and a shared kitchen. The Swiss-Italian owner also has a tour company that can arrange fishing, snorkelling and of course whale-shark trips. Dorms M$165; cabaña M$410; camping (per person) M$120; hammock (per person) M$165

Posada Mawimbi On the beach two blocks east of the plaza ☎ 984 875 2003, ⓦ mawimbi.net. *Posada Mawimbi* has a similar set-up to *Casa las Tortugas* in terms of layout, but the rates are slightly lower. All rooms have a/c, but if you like a breeze it's worth paying US$30 extra for an upstairs room with a balcony. US$128 (M$2190)

★**Tribu** Coldwell, three blocks west of the plaza ☎ 984 875 2507, ⓦ tribuhostel.com. One of the best hostels in the Yucatán, located just a half-block from the beach, and notable for its extremely helpful staff and back to basics, natural aesthetic. The complex, which includes a big kitchen, a bar and a movie room, was mostly hand-built by the owners. Tidy and simple private rooms might even convert non-hostel fans. Dorms US$11.50 (M$195.50); doubles US$40 (M$685)

EATING

Dining options on Holbox generally consist of Mexican, Italian and seafood, though the range of choices is rapidly expanding. Restaurants are all very casual, and this can extend to opening hours as well – they vary greatly depending on the season.

Buena Vista Juárez at Coldwell ☎ 984 875 2102. A very simple family-run fish restaurant, half a block back from the beach, *Buena Vista* specializes in seafood (mains M$90–260). Fried whole fish – plucked straight from the water that day – is the thing to order. Daily 10.30am–10.30pm.

La Chaya Coldwell near Palomino, close to the beach. This open-air restaurant is a great way to start a day in paradise, with ample and inexpensive breakfasts (around M$80–100) and very good juices and smoothies (if you're on a health kick try the spinach-like *chaya* flavour). Friendly staff can spread cheer even if it's drizzling. Daily 7am–late evening.

La Conquista Juárez at Coldwell, one block north off the northwest corner of the plaza. This screened-in wooden hut is a typical local place, and one of the best places to eat if you're on a tight budget – you'd be hard-pushed to spend more than M$100 on a meal. There are great empanadas (M$20–30) and daily seafood specials. Daily 11am–8pm.

★**Los Pelones** West side of the plaza ☎ 984 120 9685. Authentic, handmade Italian food cooked by a friendly couple. There are familiar pasta dishes such as ravioli with blue cheese and walnuts (all pasta is home-made, and perfectly delicious), but also farther-reaching creations like fresh fish in a champagne and garlic sauce (mains M$130–250). Great cocktails, too. Daily 5pm–late.

DRINKING AND NIGHTLIFE

Don't expect much in the way of nightlife on Holbox; locals generally lounge around on the plaza.

Carioca's On the beach, two blocks east of the plaza. If you want a drink, you'll probably wind up here – it's one of the few nightlife options in town. And it's worth coming earlier for the "suxi" (pronounce it Maya-style) and other creative blends of Japanese, Mexican and Italian cuisines (the *ceviche* is particularly good). Daily 5pm–late.

La Colibri Southwest corner of the plaza ☎ 984 875 2162. This little wooden house, painted with flowers, is enticing – it's a nice place to start the morning with a big fruit juice (M$30–50), or end the day with a (more expensive) frozen margarita. There's a food menu too, but you're better off eating elsewhere. Daily 8am–10pm.

Cancún and around

Independent travellers often find the glitz of Mexico's mammoth resort city, **CANCÚN**, off-putting and its beachfront pleasures brash and expensive. Certainly, for anyone who has been out in the rest of the Yucatán or is eager to get there, all the concrete can be a downer. But a night spent here on the way in or out doesn't have to be wasted, so long as you appreciate the city as an energetic, successful frontier experiment, rather than lament its lack of history. A closer look reveals hidden beach bars and inexpensive taco stands frequented by *cancunenses* who are friendly and proud of their city's prosperity.

Brief history

If nothing else, Cancún is proof of the government's remarkable ability to get things done in a hurry – so long as the will exists. In the late 1960s, the Mexican government decided to develop a new resort area to diversify the economy. Computers crunched weather data, and surveyors scouted the country's natural attractions to identify a 25km-long barrier island just off the northern Caribbean coast as the ideal combination of beautiful beaches, sparse population and accessible position. Construction began in 1970, and when the first hotel opened in 1974, it relied on a generator for electricity and trucked-in water.

Cancún today

In the twenty-first century, the city has struggled to shed its reputation for tacky fun (Spring Break happens only a month a year, after all), but it has successfully courted Mexican tourists. It faced a serious crisis after Hurricane Wilma severely eroded the beach in 2005, but restoration schemes finally seem to have taken hold.

DOWNTOWN CANCÚN

ACCOMMODATION	
Alux	3
Hostel Quetzal	7
Ibis Cancún Centro	8
Kin Mayab	5
Mallorca	6
Mundo Joven	2
Las Palmas	1
El Rey del Caribe	4

EATING	
100% Natural	4
Los Bisquets Obregón	1
Checándole	3
Pescaditos	5
Ty-Coz	2

DRINKING AND NIGHTLIFE	
El Camarote	1
El Pabilo	2

PRICES ON THE CARIBBEAN COAST

Because Cancún, Cozumel and other destinations along Quintana Roo's coast (including Isla Holbox) cater largely to foreign tourists, local businesses often quote prices in US dollars, and peg them to the exchange rate. In this Guide we list prices in pesos, except when a business quotes a price solely in US dollars. For easier comparison, the peso equivalent at the time of research follows in brackets (for hotels) or after a forward slash – it's meant as a guideline only.

Downtown Cancún

There's little in the way of sights in **downtown Cancún**, though it is a pleasant place to stroll in the evenings. Both the sociable **Parque de las Palapas** and **mercados 23 and 28** are good places to browse for a souvenir or get something to eat.

Parque de las Palapas

This large "park" – really, a large concrete **plaza** – at the heart of Cancún's downtown is the city's social centre. It's liveliest on Sundays, when the bandstand hosts some kind of music or entertainment, and most evenings, families come here to socialize. Craft stands are set up on one side, and on the other is a row of excellent food stalls, open every night. Smaller parks in the neighbourhood host craft or art shows.

Markets

For a sense of the city's hum away from the tourist trade, head for **Mercado 23**, north of the bus station off Avenida Tulum at Cedro. The market is a small maze of stalls with the flavour of a village market, complete with butchers, herbalists and vegetable sellers. The bigger **Mercado 28**, west on Avenida Sunyaxchén, was formerly the main general market, but now stocks primarily tourist tat; its restaurants are quite good, though.

12

Zona Hotelera

Most visitors head straight for the overdeveloped *zona hotelera* and its myriad resorts, restaurants, bars and **beaches**. Each of the latter is popular with a different crowd: among the best are **Playa Las Perlas**, **Playa Caracol** and **Playa Delfines**.

Beaches

Paseo Kukulcán

The public beaches on the north coast of the *zona hotelera* face a bay, so the water is calm and often shallow. Playa Las Perlas (km 2.5) is small and has a playground for kids and palapas for shade. Playa Tortugas (km 6) has several good bars and more casual restaurants, while Playa Caracol (km 8.5) is the prettiest of the bay beaches, with plenty of palm trees; official entrance is by the Xcaret bus stop, but it's easier to walk through *Kinha Villas* hotel (which has a nice simple bar).

CANCÚN ORIENTATION

The city has two separate parts: the *centro* (downtown) on the mainland and the *zona hotelera*, or hotel zone, a narrow barrier island shaped like a "7" that holds a long strip of hotels, malls, restaurants and other tourist facilities. The island is connected to the mainland at each end by causeways enclosing a huge lagoon. Paseo Kukulcán runs the length of *zona hotelera*, from the airport up to Punta Cancún (where the road splits around the convention centre and a warren of bars) and back onto the mainland. Street addresses in the beach zone are all kilometre markers on Paseo Kukulcán. The count starts on the north end, near downtown. It's not an exact science: two sets of markers exist, and are out of sync by about half a kilometre, so addresses are guidelines at best.

On the east coast, the beaches have more surf and occasionally dangerous currents. Delfines (km 17.5) is by far the most scenic because it doesn't have hotels behind it, and even when it's packed with locals at weekends, there's still plenty of room.

El Rey

Paseo Kukulcán km 18 • Daily 8am–5pm • M$47

This small **Maya ruin** overlooks the Nichupté Lagoon. It's the largest Maya site in Cancún, though that's not saying a lot. The buildings are on the small side, built during the empire's decline in the late Post-Classic period, contemporary with those on Cozumel and at Tulum. There's very little information available to explain them, but the area is peaceful and good for spotting birds and iguanas.

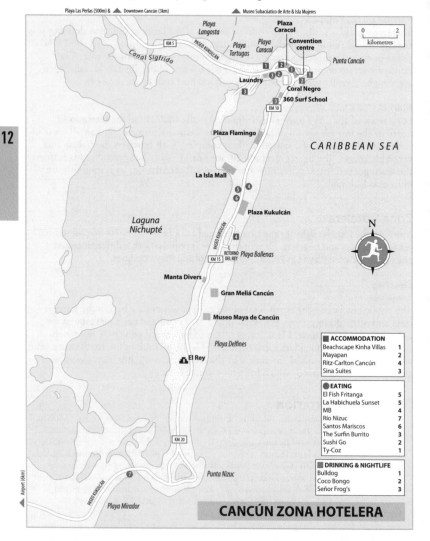

ACCOMMODATION
Beachscape Kinha Villas	1
Mayapan	2
Ritz-Carlton Cancún	4
Sina Suites	3

EATING
El Fish Fritanga	5
La Habichuela Sunset	5
MB	4
Río Nizuc	7
Santos Mariscos	6
The Surfin Burrito	3
Sushi Go	2
Ty-Coz	1

DRINKING & NIGHTLIFE
Bulldog	1
Coco Bongo	2
Señor Frog's	3

CANCÚN ZONA HOTELERA

UNDERWATER ART

Cancún may not have any museums on land, but under the waves are more than four hundred sculptures. This underwater sculpture park, the **Museo Subacuático de Arte** (MUSA; ☎ 998 887 5501, ⓦ musacancun.com), is the work of English artist Jason deCaires Taylor. The concrete casts are largely based on real Mexicans, and some create surreal scenarios, such as a bureaucrat's office on the sea floor. The aim of the ever-expanding museum is to draw visitors away from stressed reefs, while also giving coral a new place to grow. Though the first works were installed only in 2009, some of the figures are sprouting colourful buds and attracting other sea life.

A few of the works are in shallow water (4–10m), so snorkellers can drift above them. But the MUSA is really better visited as a **dive excursion** (see box, p.768): with a full scuba kit, you can submerge and look the strikingly realistic portraits in the eye. There are also glass-bottom boat and parasailing trips (see the website for more info).

Museo Maya de Cancún

Paseo Kukulcán km 16.5 • Tues-Sun 9am–6pm, last entry 5.30pm • M$64 • ☎ 998 885 3842

This long-overdue **museum** provides a rare dose of culture in Cancún. The space displays hundreds of small finds from ruins along the coast like Tulum, including Maya jewellery, burial masks, weapons, ceramics and the 10,000-year-old La Mujer de las Palmas ("The Woman of the Palms"), whose remains were found in a *cenote* in 2002. It also hosts occasional travelling shows from the national archeology trove in Mexico City. The site also contains the modest San Miguelito ruins (entry included in the museum admission fee), which include a small pyramid.

ARRIVAL AND DEPARTURE

CANCÚN

12

BY PLANE

Charter flights from Europe and South America, along with direct scheduled flights from dozens of cities in Mexico, the Caribbean and North and Central America, land at Cancún International Airport (ⓦ cancun-airport.com), 20km south of the centre. Most international flights arrive at terminal 3; domestic flights and some charter flights come into terminal 2; the recently renovated terminal 1 is mainly served by charter and low-cost flights. The terminals have currency exchange desks and ATMs.

Buses run from the terminals (every 30min, 9.20am–12.30am; 25min; M$64) to the bus station downtown; look for the ADO desk after customs. There's also a bus directly to Playa del Carmen (every 45min, 9.30am–11.50pm; 1hr; M$156), stopping at Puerto Morelos on request. Shared vans take you to any part of the *zona hotelera* for a fixed price (around US$18–20/M$305–340 per person; buy tickets at the respective desks outside customs. Taxis cost around US$40–50/M$685–855 to anywhere in the *zona hotelera* or downtown. Returning to the airport, a taxi costs about M$400 from the *zona hotelera*, a bit less from downtown.

Destinations Aguascalientes (3 weekly; 2hr 40min); Bogotá (4 daily; 3hr 25min); Guadalajara (3–5 daily; 2hr 45min); Havana (1–2 daily; 1hr 20min); León (4 weekly; 2hr 35min); Mérida (2 daily; 1hr); Mexico City (up to 39 daily; 2hr 30min); Monterrey (6–10 daily; 2hr 25min); Panama City (6 daily; 2hr 35min); Puebla (1 daily; 2hr 15min); San Salvador (1 daily; 1hr 35min); Tuxtla Gutiérrez

(1 daily; 1hr 35min); Veracruz (1–3 daily; 1hr 45min); Villahermosa (6 weekly; 1hr 30min).

BY BUS

Arriving by bus, you'll pull in at the city's main station at the corner of Tulum and Uxmal downtown; it has luggage storage (daily 6am–9.30pm). The bus to Playa del Carmen and Puerto Morelos has its own lane and ticket desk. You can walk to most downtown hotels, or take a city bus to *zona hotelera* options.

Destinations Campeche (11 daily; 6hr 35min–7hr 50min); Chetumal (every 30min–1hr; 5hr 35min–6hr 50min) and second class (roughly hourly; 7hr); Chiquilá, for Holbox (6 daily; fewer in the winter; 3hr 30min–4hr); Izamal (second class only (14 daily; 4hr); Mahahual (1 daily at 6.45am, plus more in summer; 4hr 35min); Mérida (every 30min–1hr; 4hr-4hr 15min); Palenque (4 daily at 3.45pm, 5.35pm, 6.30pm & 8.30pm; 12hr 30min–13hr 45min); Tizimín (6 daily; 4hr 5min); Playa del Carmen via Puerto Morelos (every 15min; 1hr); Tulum (every 30min–1hr; 2hr 20min–2hr 30min); Valladolid (1–2 hourly; 2hr–3hr 30min); Villahermosa (17 daily; 12hr 45min–15hr 10min).

BY CAR

Heading west by car to Valladolid, Chichén Itzá and Mérida, you have a choice between the speed-bump-filled free road (*libre*) or the fast toll highway (*cuota*). From the bus station, drive north on Tulum about 1km, then turn left onto López Portillo; after a few kilometres you can get on the toll road. There's another entrance to the *cuota* only off Hwy-307, 1.5km south of the airport. You pay in advance, at the booths on the highway, for the sections you intend to travel along.

Car rental International groups at the airport, most hotels and various locations downtown. A local option is Speed Car Rental, Uxmal 22 (☏ 998 845 1373, ⓦ car rentalspeed.com).

BY COLECTIVO

Often more efficient (and slightly cheaper) than the bus, these shared vans run between Cancún and Playa del Carmen whenever they're full (a matter of minutes at peak times). The most comfortable, run by Playa Express, depart from the bus station parking lot. Across Av Tulum are other, slightly more cramped, vans, to either Puerto Morelos or Playa del Carmen.

GETTING AROUND

By bus To get to and around the *zona hotelera*, city buses marked "R-1 – Hoteles" run along Tulum every few minutes; several others run from different parts of downtown, all likewise marked "Hoteles". For the ferry to Isla Mujeres, buses marked "Juárez" run north on Tulum, but these are not so frequent, so look for *colectivos* as well.

By car A car isn't necessary within the city, but it's not a liability either, as parking is not too difficult.

By colectivo You'll need these shared minivans for getting to Gran Puerto (for the Isla Mujeres ferry) from the bus station. They're marked "Pto Juárez" or "Punta Sam"

and stop in front of the *McDonald's* on Tulum.

By taxi Taxis are plentiful and can be hailed almost anywhere. Fares are based on a zone system, and you should agree on the fare before getting in. Big hotels have sample rates posted, which reflect a small surcharge to what you'd pay from the street. The trip between downtown and the *zona hotelera* costs around M$200.

By bike Numerous places rent out bikes (around M$100/ day); not quite all of the *zona hotelera* has a proper bike lane or pavement, though, so proceed with caution.

INFORMATION AND TOURS

12

Tourist information The city does not have a walk-in tourist office, but maps and brochures are available at every hotel. Kiosks advertising "tourist info" are usually selling timeshares or excursions.

Tours Most hotels in the *zona hotelera* have in-house agencies

that can arrange standard day trips to the chief Maya sites. For more variety, EcoColors (Camarón 32, SM 27, north and west of Mercado 28; ☏ 998 884 3667, ⓦ ecotravelmexico.com), runs single- and multi-day kayaking, birding, whale- and shark-watching or cycling tours.

WATERSPORTS IN CANCÚN

SNORKELLING

Most **snorkelling** in Cancún is at Punta Nizuc, at the far southern point of the peninsula, but its coral has been damaged by crowds – you're much better off making the short trip down the coast to the great reef at Puerto Morelos. In Cancún, operators spice up the ho-hum local snorkelling with a so-called jungle tour, which entails riding two-passenger speedboats through lagoon mangroves, then out to the reef. A trip can be arranged at most hotels and many marinas along the lagoon, for about M$700–900 per person.

Another popular snorkelling trip, only in the summer, is to see the whale sharks near Isla Holbox (see box, p.762). It's a long boat ride, but well worth it. Trips are cheaper from Isla Mujeres (see p.771), but you can arrange through your Cancún hotel for a surcharge.

DIVING

Other reefs off Cancún's coast make good beginner **diving**, with easy access and little current, as does the Museo Subacuático de Arte (see box, p.767). Contact Manta Divers (Paseo Kukulcán km 16; ☏ 998 849 4050, ⓦ mantadivers.com); open-water certification is around US$389/M$6650.

KITEBOARDING

Ikarus (☏ 984 803 3490, ⓦ kiteboardmexico.com), based in Playa del Carmen (see p.780), gives classes from US$95/hr (M$1625) on a remote beach north of Cancún.

SURFING

360 Surf School (☏ 998 241 6443, ⓦ 360surfschoolcancun.com) offers private and group classes from US$90/90min (M$1540), with a guarantee you'll be able to stand on the board; equipment is also available to rent from US$35/day (M$600). Sign up at the office on Paseo Kukulcán km 9.5 in the *zona hotelera*.

ACCOMMODATION

Cancún has a dizzying number of hotels. **Downtown**, on or near Av Tulum, holds the only hope of a true budget room, as hostels have proliferated. In the **zona hotelera**, you can stay on the lagoon side for less than in the glittering beachfront palaces – but on the beach, last-minute or low-season online deals can be impressive. Try "opaque" booking sites like ⑩ hotwire.com, where you reserve without knowing the name of the hotel – you can't go wrong with any four- or five-star property.

HOTELS

DOWNTOWN

Alux Uxmal 21 ☎ 998 884 0662, ⑩ hotelalux.com.mx; map p.764. *Alux* has unremarkable but perfectly functional rooms: although they are a bit dim, they do come with a/c and TVs. The hotel's main appeal is the short walk to the bus station. US$33 (M$565)

Ibis Cancún Centro Tulum s/n at Nichupte ☎ 998 272 8500, ⑩ ibis.com; map p.764. This sizeable outpost of the international chain is a good-value, if unexciting, choice: clean, comfortable rooms (with a/c and TVs), professional staff, and a reasonable on-site restaurant. M$730

Kin Mayab Tulum 75 at Uxmal ☎ 998 884 2999, ⑩ hotelkinmayab.com; map p.764. This centrally located hotel is clean and secure, with the most comfortable rooms and best pool in its price range (book ahead). Request the back section, by the pool and away from the street noise. M$925

Mallorca Gladiolas 11 ☎ 998 884 4285, ⑩ mallorca hotelandsuites.com; map p.764. Located just off Parque de las Palapas, this mid-range hotel offers excellent value in downtown. Bathrooms are a bit small, but rooms come with fridges and have nice colonial style, with lots of hand-carved wood details. US$100 (M$1700)

El Rey del Caribe Uxmal 24 at Nader ☎ 998 884 2028, ⑩ reycaribe.com; map p.764. Sunny yellow rooms with kitchenettes, plus a pool, spa services and generous breakfast at this casual hotel that feels like it should be on a beach in Tulum. One of the few places in Cancún with a real ecofriendly sensibility. US$70 (M$1195)

ZONA HOTELERA

★**Beachscape Kinha Villas** Paseo Kukulcán km 8.5 ☎ 998 891 5400, ⑩ beachscape.com.mx; map p.766. No frills, but in the best possible way: big, clean rooms with two double beds, as well as family-friendly suites. Every room has a terrace or balcony, and the beach is deep and palm-shaded – the best on the bay side. The handy location is within walking distance of Punta Cancún. US$159 (M$2720)

Ritz-Carlton Cancún Retorno del Rey 36, near Paseo Kukulcán km 14 ☎ 998 881 0808, ⑩ ritzcarlton.com/cancun; map p.766. The last word in luxury in Cancún: all chandeliers, oil paintings, and deep carpeting, plus impeccable service. While high-season rates are predictably high, the *Ritz-Carlton* is a great example of Cancún's off-season value, when prices can drop by as much as fifty percent. US$429 (M$7335)

Sina Suites Quetzal 33 ☎ 998 883 1017, ⑩ suitessinacancun.com; map p.766. Personable staff preside over comfy rooms and suites with TVs and quiet a/c systems; the suites have either one or two bedrooms, a sofa bed in the living room and a full kitchen and dining room. There's a huge pool, and the sundeck overlooks the lagoon. US$72 (M$1230)

HOSTELS

DOWNTOWN

Hostel Quetzal Orquideas 10 ☎ 998 883 9821, ⑩ quetzal-hostel.com; map p.764. Super-friendly guesthouse-hostel with arty style, starting with cool graffiti at the front. Private rooms, with private outdoor space, will please even people who normally avoid hostels. The dorms (which include a women-only one) also have nice big windows, and there's a/c everywhere. Rates include both breakfast and an exceptionally good dinner. Dorms M$250; doubles M$450

Mundo Joven Uxmal 25 ☎ 998 898 2104, ⑩ mundo jovenhostels.com; map p.764. Cancún's official Hostelling International hostel is nicely designed, and its all-white decor looks crisp, not dingy. There's a/c everywhere, and both single-sex and mixed dorms, as well as private rooms. The hot tub on the roof says it all, though – this is a party place, for better or worse. Dorms M$230; doubles M$575

Las Palmas Palmera 43 ☎ 998 884 2513, ⑩ laspalmashotel.com.mx; map p.764. This adequate family operation caters as much to Mexican workers as to backpackers, so there's less of the typical hostel party atmosphere. The real draw: the cheapest a/c beds in town, in big single-sex dorms, and a few huge private rooms. Dorms M$120; doubles M$360

ZONA HOTELERA

Mayapan Paseo Kukulcán km 8.5, west end of Plaza Maya Fair ☎ 998 883 3227, ⑩ hostalmayapan.com; map p.766. The only hostel in the *zona hotelera*, with a great central location. However, there are a few drawbacks: pricey private rooms, no common hangout space and a weird setting in a spooky wing of an abandoned mall. Dorms M$280; doubles M$1050

12

EATING

In downtown Cancún, the most popular eating places line Tulum and its side streets. For **budget food**, follow the locals for lunch at the downtown markets: **Mercado 23** and **Mercado 28** (see p.765). At night, excellent food stalls at **Parque de las Palapas** serve open-face *huaraches* and quesadillas with an array of toppings; they're open until about 11pm. Many of the restaurants in the **zona hotelera** are a rip-off, but the exceptions recommended here are solidly delicious.

CAFÉS, CHEAP EATS AND SNACKS

DOWNTOWN

100% Natural Sunyaxchén 26 at Yaxchilán ☎998 884 0102, ⓦ100natural.com.mx; map p.764. Largely vegetarian and decidedly wholesome, with veggie burgers and granola, as well as fresh-tasting Mexican dishes. Breakfasts (M$65–110) are especially nice, with lots of interesting juice combos. Daily 7am–11pm.

Los Bisquets Obregón Nader 9 ☎998 887 6877, ⓦbisquetsobregon.com. map p.764. Part of a national chain, this bustling diner serves excellent *café con leche* (M$25) and Mexican pastries in the morning – just pick from the platter the waiter brings around. Daily 7.30am–midnight.

Pescaditos Yaxchilán at Gladiolas; map p.764. A bit of the beach downtown: light reggae vibe, with fantastic lightly battered fish and shrimp for a song (around M$50 for a generous basket), deadly shrimp-stuffed *chiles rellenos*, and good *ceviches*. Daily noon–10pm.

Ty-Coz Tulum, behind Comercial Mexicana ☎998 884 6060; map p.764. This French sandwich shop is a treat. The specialities are stacked baguettes (M$18–75), but *Ty-Coz* is also good for breakfast, with buttery pastries and strong coffee. There are a few other "Express" branches in and around the *zona hotelera*, including at km 9, near the Chedraui supermarket. Mon–Sat 8am–10pm.

ZONA HOTELERA

★**El Fish Fritanga** Paseo Kukulcán km 12.5 ☎998 840 6216, ⓦelfishfritanga.com; map p.766. Hidden behind a *Domino's*, this lagoon-side seafood specialist is inexpensive, laid-back and frequented by residents – there's even a bit of beach, so you can stick your feet in the sand while you eat. The menu ranges from *ceviche* to lobster tails in a garlic butter sauce (most mains M$100–250). Daily 11am–11pm.

The Surfin Burrito Paseo Kukulcán km 8 ☎998 883 0083, ⓦfacebook.com/TheSurfinBurrito; map p.766. This hidden gem, on a nondescript parade of shops and eateries, serves up Californian-style burritos, plus tacos, ice cream, well-mixed margaritas, and cold beer (expect to eat and drink for under M$100). Delivery available. Daily 24hr.

Sushi Go Paseo Kukulcán km 8 ☎998 883 0808, ⓦsushigo.com.mx; map p.766. Close to *The Surfin Burrito*, this is a good, low-key spot for fresh sushi (M$80–115), as well as rice and noodle dishes, tempura, *teppanyaki* and soups. There are a couple of other branches in town, and they will also deliver to your hotel. Daily 1–11pm.

RESTAURANTS

DOWNTOWN

Checándole Xpuhil 6 ☎998 884 5621; map p.764. A buzzing, popular restaurant that has been around since the earliest days, with a breezy terrace and a selection of satisfying and fresh-tasting Mexican classics (around M$70–100) like enchiladas; the set lunch is M$60. Mon–Sat noon–8pm.

ZONA HOTELERA

La Habichuela Sunset Paseo Kukulcán km 12.6 ☎998 840 6280, ⓦlahabichuela.com; map p.766. The hotel zone outpost of a classic downtown restaurant is pricey for its Caribbean-ish food (mains M$238–625), but a great spot for a sunset drink, with windows overlooking the lagoon. There's a cultural show on Wed and Fri (8pm). Daily 12.30–11pm.

MB Paseo Kukulcán km 12.5, in Live Aqua ☎998 881 7600, ⓦliveaqua.com; map p.766. No sea view, but one of Cancún's best hotel restaurants. Miami chef Michelle Bernstein mixes Latin, Spanish and even Asian flavours in a stylish but not-too-formal atmosphere. There's a small but good wine list, too. Expect to pay M$350 or more per person. Daily 6–11pm.

Río Nizuc Off Paseo Kukulcán near km 22; map p.766. Few tourists find this seafood spot (dishes from M$100) tucked amid the mangroves at the south end of the hotel zone. *Ceviche* and *tikin-xic* fish are popular with locals, who crowd in at weekends. Look for the turn just west of Puente Nizúc. Daily 11am–6pm.

★**Santos Mariscos** Paseo Kukulcán km 12.5 ☎998 840 6300; map p.766. A cool seafood joint just south of *El Fish Fritanga* that serves West-coast-style seafood (wedges of crispy *jicama* topped with shrimp, for instance) at very reasonable prices (around M$200–250 per person). Mon–Thurs & Sun noon–11pm, Fri & Sat noon–midnight.

DRINKING AND NIGHTLIFE

Cancún's goal is to entertain millions of visitors each year, with the **zona hotelera**'s array of huge dance clubs, theme bars and top-volume everything (most clustered around Punta Cancún and rolling from about 10pm till the wee hours). **Downtown** offers a mellower scene: people often dance on weekend evenings at the Parque de las Palapas to traditional

Mexican music, and the stretch of Yaxchilán north of Sunyaxchén is a popular local nightlife area, with terrace restaurant-bars and karaoke open till 3am or 4am, all punctuated by roving *trovadores*.

BARS AND LIVE MUSIC
DOWNTOWN

El Camarote Uxmal 26, in the Plaza Kokai hotel ☎ 998 193 3170, ⓦ hotel-plaza-kokai-cancun.com; map p.764. Ignore the sports bar outside; in the small theatre inside, *El Camarote*, Yucatecan crooners perform romantic classics for an older crowd. Cover charges from M$50. Thurs–Sat 10.30pm–late.

El Pabilo Yaxchilán 31, in the Xbalamqué hotel ☎ 998 892 4553, ⓦ facebook.com/ElPabilo; map p.764. Mellow coffee shop with good cappuccino, espresso and snacks. Live guitar music or readings at night, sometimes out on the roadside terrace. A bulletin board has notices of art openings, concerts and the like. Mon 4–11pm, Tues–Sun 6pm–midnight.

ZONA HOTELERA

Señor Frog's Paseo Kukulcán km 9.5 ☎ 998 883 1092, ⓦ senorfrogscancun.com; map p.766. Practically synonymous with Cancún, *Frog's* is the first stop off the plane for the Spring Break hordes – think foam parties, karaoke nights, and so on. Go for live reggae or just as an anthropological experience. Definitely don't go for the food. Daily noon–3am.

CLUBS
ZONA HOTELERA

Bulldog Paseo Kukulcán km 9.5, south end of Krystal hotel ☎ 998 848 9850, ⓦ bulldogcafe.com; map p.766. A mega-club in Punta Cancún, notable because, outside of high Spring Break season, it's frequented more by local kids, with hip-hop and *rock en español* on the speakers, and the occasional touring band. Daily 10pm–dawn.

Coco Bongo Paseo Kukulcán km 9.5, in the Forum by the Sea shopping centre ☎ 998 883 5061, ⓦ cocobongo .com.mx; map p.766. *Coco Bongo* remains the epitome of the Cancún nightclub experience, and what all other mega-clubs imitate. The night warms up with a floor show involving acrobats, Beatles and Lady Gaga impersonators and roving candid cameras zooming in on the shapeliest customers. Music, once it really gets started, is of the broadest, most crowd-pleasing variety. Cover with open bar: Mon–Wed US$65/M$1110, Thurs–Sun US$75/M$1280. Daily 10am–3.30am.

DIRECTORY

Banks and exchange Most banks (usually Mon–Fri 9.30am–3pm, Sat 9.30am–1pm) are along Tulum between Uxmal and Cobá and in the biggest shopping malls – Kukulcán, Plaza Caracol – in the *zona hotelera*. The HSBC, Tulum 192, stays open until 7pm on weekdays.

Consulates Canada, Centro Empresarial, Paseo Kukulcán km 12 ☎ 998 883 3360; Cuba, Pecari 17 SM 20 ☎ 998 884 3423; South Africa, Granada 30, SM 2A ☎ 998 884 9513; UK, Paseo Kukulcán km 13.5, at the *Royal Sands* ☎ 998 881 0184; US, Torre La Europea, Paseo Kukulcán km 13, Torre La Europea ☎ 998 883 0272.

Hospital The largest hospital close to the *zona hotelera* is AmeriMed, on Bonampak at Nichupté, behind Plaza las

Américas (☎ 998 881 3400 or ☎ 881 3434 for emergencies, ⓦ amerimedcancun.com).

Internet Immediately across from the bus station and northwest on Uxmal are several internet cafés; some are *casetas* as well. In the *zona hotelera*, web access is significantly more expensive, but every hotel, and virtually every bar and restaurant, offers wi-fi.

Laundry Lavandería Las Palmas, on Uxmal just west of the bus station (open daily). In the *zona hotelera*, try Lumi Express at Paseo Kukulcán km 9.5 (closed Sun), next to The Surfin Burrito.

Post office Sunyaxchén at Xel-Ha (Mon–Fri 8am–6pm, Sat 9am–1pm).

Isla Mujeres

Just a few kilometres off the coast of Mexico, in the startlingly clear Caribbean, little **ISLA MUJERES** is substantially mellower than Cancún, drawing people for long stays despite (or because of) the lack of tourist attractions. The 8km-long patch of land is now substantially built up – it's no desert island – yet retains a certain air of bohemian languor in its narrow streets lined with colourful wooden houses. It's a respite for anyone who has been slogging across Mexico, as well as a pleasant place to start your trip in Mexico (the whole trip from Cancún airport takes under two hours).

The attractions are simple: beach and sea – plus the fun of zipping around the island, on the lone perimeter road, by bike, moped or golf cart, to more sea, more beaches and the tiny Maya temple that the conquistadors chanced upon, once full of female figures, which gave the place its name.

Playa Norte

Northern end of the island • Free

The most popular **beach**, just five minutes' walk from the town plaza, is **Playa Norte** – curving up and around the northern tip of the island, but protected from the open sea by a promontory on which stands a large resort. Aim to be under the palms here by late afternoon, as it's one of the few places along Mexico's east coast where you can enjoy a glowing sunset over the water. After dark, the palapa-roofed bars become the island's mellow nightlife centre.

ISLA MUJERES

Playa Norte

CALLE ZAZIL-HA

CALLE CARLOS LAZO

Cementerio Municipal

CALLE MATEOS

Artesanías Glenssy

Laundry

CALLE JUÁREZ

AVENIDA HIDALGO

CALLE GUERRERO

Market

Loncherías

AVENIDA RUEDA MEDINA

CALLE MATAMOROS

CARIBBEAN SEA

CALLE ABASOLO

Captain Tony García

Enrique's Unique Dives

CALLE MADERO

Cooperativo de Lancheros dock

CALLE MORELOS

Banamex

PLAZA

Magaña pier

HSBC

Ultramar pier

CALLE BRAVO

CALLE ALLENDE

Isla Contoy

Downtown Cancún (Gran Puerto & Puerto Juárez)

Cancún Zona Hotelera

N

● EATING	
Barlito	5
Caffe Italia	2
La Cazuela M&J	3
Cocktelería Picus	6
La Lomita	7
El Poc-Chuc	4
Qubano	1
El Varadero	8

■ ACCOMMODATION	
Carmelina	7
Casa El Pío	9
Casa Sirena	8
Francis Arlene	6
El Marcianito	5
María del Pilar	4
Na Balam	2
Nautibeach Condos	1
Poc-Na	3

0	200
metres	

, Turtle Farm, Hacienda Mundaca & beach clubs, Garrafón Park & Templo de Ixchel

12

ISLA MUJERES BEACH CLUBS

Aside from the broad expanse of Playa Norte, the island has a few other stretches of sand with lounge chairs and restaurants – they're not dramatically more beautiful than Playa Norte, but they are a very good excuse for a golf-cart outing and a nice lunch.

Capitán Dulche Southwest coast ☎ 998 849 7589, ⓦ capitandulche.mx. This sprawling place has beautiful grounds and good food (though it's fairly pricey; mains from M$120). There's a small maritime museum, open occasionally for guided tours (M$65), and intriguing art scattered around. Daily 10am–6pm.

Garrafón de Castilla Southern end of the island ☎ 998 877 0107. This basic beach club adjacent to Garrafón Park is set around a small protected bay where you can spot a few colourful fish. There's not a lot of actual sandy beach, but different levels and areas for lounging. Food is reasonably priced, after an entry fee of M$50. Daily 9am–5pm.

Playa Lancheros Mid-island, just south of the roundabout. This small, palm-fringed beach is virtually deserted except at lunch time, when the good, very simple restaurant fires up the grill for *tikin-xic* fish. It's been in operation for decades and is one of the best places to sample this Maya beach classic. Daily 11am–6pm.

Hacienda Mundaca
Mid-island, at the roundabout • Daily 9am–4pm • M$35

About halfway down the length of the island lurk the barely visible remains of the **Hacienda Mundaca**, to which scores of romantic pirate legends are attached. Only one small house has been pieced together, with a few photos of old-time Isla Mujeres inside. There's also a somewhat random display of a traditional Maya hut. The best spot is the suitably gothic-feeling garden at the back of the property – where insect repellent is a must. In front of the entrance, outside the hacienda grounds (so no need to pay hacienda admission), the island's cultural directorate manages a few galleries with photos of the island, local art projects, crafts (sometimes including someone demonstrating hammock-weaving) and more.

12

Turtle Farm
Sac Bajo road • Daily 9am–5pm • M$35

Heading north from the mid-island roundabout, the road up the Sac Bajo Peninsula leads to a government-run **turtle farm** and research centre, which breeds endangered sea turtles for release in the wild. It also rescues threatened nests and keeps them buried in the sand on the grounds until they hatch. The entrance fee helps fund the preservation project.

Garrafón Park
Southwestern tip of the island • Daily 10am–5pm • US$89–199, depending on what package of activities you go for • ☎ 866 393 5158, ⓦ garrafon.com

The longest stretch of reef on Isla Mujeres is mostly dead, and now enclosed in **Garrafón Park**, a slick operation with a zipline, kayaking and other mild thrills. But it's grossly overpriced and usually crowded with day-trippers from Cancún. The penny-pinchers' alternative is *Garrafón de Castilla* beach club next door (see box above); better, though, to go on a trip with the *lancheros* (see box, p.774).

Templo de Ixchel
Southern tip of the island • Daily 9am–6.30pm • M$30 (or free with Garrafón ticket)

This isn't much of a **ruin** (the fertility figures the Spaniards spotted here have been removed), and the walk to it has been tarted up with some now-rusty modern sculptures, to justify the admission price. But it is situated on low rocky cliffs where the waves crash dramatically. As the easternmost point of Mexico, it's where islanders come on New Year's Day to watch the sun rise.

By passenger ferry Passenger ferries arrive at Isla Mujeres town at two adjacent piers; the car ferry comes in further south. From the piers, it's about a 20min walk to the opposite side of the island and the most distant hotels. Two companies, Ultramar (ⓦgranpuerto.com .mx) and Magaña, run passenger ferries from Cancún to Isla Mujeres. Ultramar boats (M$73) leave from Gran Puerto (every 30min, 5am–12.30pm; 20min) at the end of Av López Portillo, and Magaña boats (M$70) depart from Puerto Juárez, 250m north (hourly, at 10min after the hour, and at 40min after the hour going the other way; 20min). Ultramar boats are nicer, but Magaña is handy if you're in a hurry and have just missed an

Ultramar departure. Some boats also run from Playa Tortugas in the *zona hotelera*.

Transport to the ferry In Cancún, buses ("R-1 – Pto Juárez") that go this far north are not common; also look for *combis* (marked "*Juárez*"), which stop in front of the *McDonald's* on Tulum, across from the bus station. A taxi from the bus station costs around M$80; it's M$200 from the *zona hotelera*.

By car ferry There's also a car ferry (M$250 per car with one driver, M$30 per extra person; 4–7 daily; 45min), but you don't need a vehicle, as the island is quite small and has plenty of bicycles and mopeds for rent. The boat leaves from Punta Sam, 6km north of Puerto Juárez.

GETTING AROUND

By bus Every 30min from Rueda Medina in the main town down to the southern end of the island.

By moped or golf cart The best way of getting around the small island is by moped (around M$250–300/24hr) or golf cart (around US$60/24hr). Virtually every other shop rents out both forms of transport for approximately the same rates.

By taxi Rates are posted at the stand between the ferry piers, starting at around M$40 for hotels in the main town and running up to M$90 to the south end of the island.

By bike Many places rent out bikes (around M$100–150/ day). You should be in decent shape to make a full island loop – there are a couple of hills, and usually a headwind coming back north.

INFORMATION

Tourist office On Medina just northwest of the passenger ferry piers (Mon–Fri 8am–8pm, Sat & Sun 9am–2pm;

ⓣ998 877 0307). You can pick up leaflets and maps.

ACCOMMODATION

Isla Mujeres has a few solid budget places to stay, though they fill up quickly in the high season – advance reservations are recommended. Most of the reasonably priced options are on the northwestern edge of the island; some of the less expensive waterfront views are on the northeastern side, where the sea is generally too rough for swimming.

ACTIVITIES ON ISLA MUJERES

There are several **dive shops** on the island – recommended is Enrique's Unique Dives (Medina 1, by the Pemex station; ⓣ998 145 3594, ⓦdivingislamujeres.com), which offers a range of trips, including some to the MUSA (see box, p.767), as well as the "Cave of the Sleeping Sharks", where tiger, bull, grey reef, lemon and nurse sharks are regularly encountered. You can also take **snorkelling** trips with a couple of *lancheros* cooperatives, which are set up on the piers, and cost around US$25–30/M$425–515 for two hours.

In recent years, the *lancheros* have also begun offering tours to see the **whale sharks** that gather off the coast from (roughly) mid-May to mid-September (a trip more commonly taken from Isla Holbox; see box, p.762), with prices around M$1700. While every shop touts the trip, only a small number of boats have the permit. Boats usually leave at 7.30–8am, and the trip to the sharks takes a couple of hours; there's lunch and reef snorkelling on the way back.

If it's not whale-shark season, the next-best outing is to the bird sanctuary of **Isla Contoy**, 30km north. Designated a national park in 1961, the small island is home to some 150 bird species, including large colonies of pelicans, cormorants and frigates. You can go with the *lancheros* cooperative, or with Captain Tony García (Matamoros 7; ⓣ998 877 0229, ⓔcaptaintony@hotmail.com); both come highly recommended by island regulars. Tours last from 9am till 3pm or so and include a basic breakfast, grilled fish for lunch, soft drinks and snorkel gear for about US$1200/M$20,520 per person.

HOTELS AND SELF-CATERING

Carmelina Guerrero 4 ☎998 877 0006, ✉hota carmelina@hotmail.com. The rooms at this motel-style budget operation, trimmed in lavender paint, are a steal, considering they have a/c and a fridge. However, the singles can be dismally small. **M$400**

Casa El Pío Hidalgo 3, at Bravo, no phone, ⓦcasaelpio .com. The five rooms at this stylish hotel get booked up fast. All have one bed, plus a separate living room with a daybed. The owners' colour-saturated photos decorate the white walls, and the minimalist-cool wood furniture is made on the island. Three-night minimum; no Sun check-ins. **US$80 (M$1365)**

Casa Sirena Hidalgo between Bravo and Allende, no phone, ⓦcasasirenamexico.com. Very nicely redone home that has kept some old details, such as tiled floors, and added modern bathrooms and a breezy roof terrace. Breakfasts are lavish, happy hour on the roof deck is legendary and there are even two small pools. Three-night minimum in winter, two in summer; advance reservations required. **US$149 (M$2550)**

Francis Arlene Guerrero 7, at Abasolo ☎998 877 0310, ⓦfrancisarlene.com. A small family-owned hotel with well-tended courtyards, a big roof terrace and clean, brightly painted – if rather twee – rooms with plenty of comforts (though a/c costs an additional US$10/M$170). **US$60 (M$1025)**

El Marcianito Abasolo 10 ☎998 877 0111, ⓦmarcianito.islamujeres.biz. This budget hotel is a good-value option: the simple but clean rooms come with fans and well-maintained private bathrooms; the breezier, a/c ones on the upper floors cost M$230 more. **M$550**

María del Pilar Abasolo 15 ☎998 877 0071, ⓦmariadelpilar.hostel.com. Under renovation at the time of research, the four rooms on the upper floor of this basic little hotel are supplied with a shared outdoor kitchen – they're spartan and cool, with screen doors (but no windows). Two suites at the back share another kitchen, and the front room has its own porch. A/c costs extra. **M$500**

Na Balam Zazil Ha 118 ☎998 881 4770, ⓦnabalam .com. Overlooking Playa Norte, *Na Balam* is a good, upper mid-range all-rounder: spacious rooms and suites, a lush garden, spa facilities, pool, hot tub, restaurant-bar, and an on-site yoga school (see p.776). **US$175 (M$2990)**

Nautibeach Condos Playa Norte ☎998 877 0606, ⓦnautibeach.com. A good option for families or groups, *Nautibeach* has enormous two-bedroom apartments, each with a balcony or veranda, in a modest, well-maintained complex facing the beach. **US$130 (M$2225)**

HOSTELS

Poc-Na Matamoros at Carlos Lazo ☎998 877 0090, ⓦpocna.com. This compound sleeps 150, but it's split into many smaller rooms that feel a bit cosier. Facilities can be less than spotless and there's no guest kitchen, but it opens directly onto a broad beach (great for camping) on the windy side. There's an on-site dive centre. Dorms **M$145**; doubles **M$350**; camping **M$100**

12

EATING

The area along and around Hidalgo between Morelos and Abasolo is lined with **restaurants** and **bars**. For inexpensive, basic Mexican food and great fruit salads, head for the few **loncherías** on Guerrero between Mateos and Matamoros, opposite *Las Palmas* hotel. In the adjoining public market, you can get inexpensive juices and produce. There's a supermarket on the plaza.

★**Barlito** Marina Paraiso Hotel, Rueda Medina, around 1.5km south of the centre ☎998 229 0042, ⓦmarinaparaiso-islamujeres.com. Huge and mouth-watering bagels, hot sandwiches and burgers (M$95–155) are the speciality at this café-restaurant. Good breakfast options are available too, including home-made cinnamon rolls (M$45). Daily 8am–9.30pm.

Caffe Italia Matamoros at Guerrero. This brightly painted Italian restaurant serves reliable pasta (M$90–160), pizzas (M$90–190) and panini (M$70–100) as well as cold beers (M$30–40). There's a selection of secondhand books on the far wall. Daily 8am–11.30pm.

La Cazuela M&J Abasolo at Guerrero ☎998 884 0407, ⓦlacazuelamj.com. This casual café serves inexpensive (mostly Mexican) breakfasts. Its speciality is egg dishes baked in small casseroles (*cazuelas*), for M$85–105. Big glasses of green *chaya* juice are another healthy option.

Tues–Sun 7am–2pm.

Cocktelería Picus Rueda Medina, just north of the ferry piers. One of several similar joints, this small beachfront hut with plastic chairs in the sand serves fresh and inexpensive *ceviche* (M$130–150) and shrimp cocktails (M$50–150). Daily noon–8.30pm.

La Lomita Juárez 25-B, two blocks southeast of the plaza ☎998 826 6335. Locals line up for a helping of the chef-owner's daily special, anything from bean soup and *chiles rellenos* to pan-fried fish with salsa verde. Hearty home cooking (mains M$80–190) that's worth the hike up the small hill two blocks south of the plaza. Daily 9am–11pm.

El Poc-Chuc Abasolo at Juárez. This bargain *lonchería* with red vinyl tablecloths and a giant mural of Chichén Itzá is handily also open for dinner (although not all of the big meals are available at night). Fish soup and crispy *panuchos* are two reliable offerings (dishes cost from M$30). Daily 8am–10pm.

Qubano Hidalgo, between Mateos and Matamoros ☎ 998 214 2118, ⓦ facebook.com/QubanoIsla. There's a great range of bulging sandwiches (M$99–130) at *Qubano*: If you're struggling to choose, go for the signature chicken *tostón*, a messy delight between two slabs of crispy-fried plantain slices. Mon–Sat noon–10pm.

El Varadero West coast, adjacent to Puerto Isla Mujeres ☎ 998 877 1600. This super-casual Cuban restaurant, drawing a predominantly local crowd, is nestled among palm trees a little way out of town. Garlicky pork and refreshing mojitos are the specialities (cocktails M$40–60). Tues–Sun 1.30–9pm.

DIRECTORY

Banks and exchange HSBC, on Rueda Medina opposite the ferry docks, has an ATM; Banamex is on Morelos at Juárez.

Books *Caffe Italia* (see p.775) sells secondhand books in several languages.

Internet There are numerous internet cafés in the centre of town.

Laundry The cheapest laundry is Lavandería Mis Dos Angelitos, Guerrero at Mateos (closed Sun).

Post office Guerrero at Mateos (Mon–Thurs 9am–5.30pm).

Yoga Vastu School of Yoga (ⓦ vastuyoga.com) offers daily yoga classes at the *Na Balam* hotel (see p.775).

Puerto Morelos

The quietest town in the Riviera Maya, **PUERTO MORELOS**, is actually the closest to Cancún, just fifteen minutes from the airport by taxi or bus. With a working fishing fleet, it's unpretentious and calm, drawing visitors for long stays – but although it's not ritzy, even the cheapest hotels might be over budget for some. The **Mesoamerican Barrier Reef** begins here, just 600m offshore, and it's in very good shape due to efforts of the townspeople to protect it. It's a great, uncrowded place to get your scuba certification.

There are two parts to PoMo, as it is sometimes referred to: the beach town 2km from Hwy-307, with a small traditional plaza and church; and the rapidly growing *zona urbana* (or *colonia*) on the inland side of the highway. Most visitors will spend all their time in the beach town.

Jungle Market

C 2, *zona urbana* • **Market** Winter only, Sun 10.30am–3/4pm • Free • **Spa** Tues–Sat by appointment • Massages from US$70/M$1200/hr • ☎ 998 208 9148

If you're in town on a Sunday, don't miss the "**jungle market**", where a women's cooperative sells their wares, which include great food as well as handicrafts. There's also some dancing. It's a touristy event, but all low-pressure, local-run fun, and a good excuse to explore the inland side of town. The same group of women runs a very affordable spa in the same spot year-round.

CENOTES NEAR PUERTO MORELOS

The so-called Ruta de los Cenotes is a road that runs inland from Puerto Morelos, passing several swimming holes and **caves** (all open daily 10am–5pm). Look for the turn inland just south of the main Puerto Morelos intersection, marked by a large cement arch. Taxis from Puerto Morelos cost about M$200–250 one-way; a round trip depends on waiting time. Dive shops in Puerto Morelos (see p.777) also run snorkelling and diving trips out here.

Several spots are for group tours from Cancún, but a couple are open for independent travellers. The best is **Cenote Las Mojarras** (☎ 998 147 0168, ⓦ facebook.com/ParqueCenote LasMojarras; M$250), at km 12.5, a big open pool with a zipline. Entry fees can be lower if you're only staying a couple of hours, but with nature trails, lunch cooked over a wood fire and an enthusiastic manager who knows everything about the local plants, you can spend all day here. Several kilometres further is **Siete Bocas** (M$100), a water-filled cave with seven points of entry, best for divers, as there's not much natural light. At km 17.5, **Verde Lucero** (M$60) is a pretty, rustic-feeling pool with only basic facilities – some bathrooms and basic snacks.

Jardín Botánico Dr Alfredo Barrera Marín

East side Hwy-307, south of town • Nov–April daily 8am–4pm, May–Oct Mon–Sat 9am–5pm • M$150 • ☎ 988 206 9233

These rambling **botanical gardens** provide a good overview of the Yucatán's flora. A 3km path leads through medicinal plants, ferns, palms, some tumbledown Maya ruins and a mock-up *chiclero* camp, where you can see how the sap of the *zapote* (sapodilla) tree is tapped before being used in the production of gum.

ARRIVAL AND INFORMATION

By bus Buses between Cancún and Playa del Carmen stop on Hwy-307 at the town's main intersection on request (every 15min; 30min). They also leave directly from Cancún's airport (every 45min; 30min). Taxis wait on the east side of the highway to take you the 2km into the beach town (around M$30–40 to the plaza). If you're leaving on the airport bus, buy your ticket at least one day in advance, to make sure the bus stops and has a seat for you. If you're just hopping to central Cancún or Playa del Carmen, it's easier to flag down a *colectivo* van.

PUERTO MORELOS

Banks and exchange A few ATMs are scattered around the plaza, but there is no actual bank. Avoid the generic machines not run by a specific bank, as their fees are extortionate. A couple of *cambios* can be found on the plaza.

Internet There is an internet café on the southwest corner of the plaza, next to the Oxxo shop. There's free wi-fi around the plaza, provided by the cable company.

Laundry Lavaplus, on Niños Héroes, one block north of the plaza.

TOURS AND ACTIVITIES

Cooking classes The Little Mexican Cooking School, on Rojo Gómez two blocks north of the plaza (☎ 998 251 8060, ⓦ the littlemexicancookingschool.com), runs half-day cooking classes for US$128/M$2190 in a sunny kitchen with an enthusiastic Mexican-Canadian chef. The school also has a small shop that sells cooking tools and locally produced foods.

Diving Long-established Almost Heaven Adventures (Rojo Gómez, one block north of the plaza; mobile ☎ 998 846 8009, ⓦ almostheavenadventures.com) offers certification courses for US$350/M$5985 and one- and two-tank dives for US$50–90/M$855–1540, as well as diving tours to

inland *cenotes* for US$140/M$2400.

Snorkelling You can go with Almost Heaven (which does night trips as well), or with any of the boats at the two piers in town, for around US$30/M$510 per person. Note that a couple of booths on the plaza are actually selling timeshares, but might try to reel you in by offering a snorkelling trip. Regardless, although you could swim to the reef, regulations require you to go with a guide.

Day tours Ecab Explorer (☎ 998 123 5062, ⓦ ecabexplorer .com) runs day trips to Chichén Itzá, Tulum, Cobá, Ek-Balam, and more.

ACCOMMODATION

Most people stay in rental properties – Alma Libre bookshop (see p.778) has nice ones – so the hotel scene is fairly limited.

Acamaya Reef Park On the beach, 5km north of town ☎ 987 871 0131, ⓦ acamayareef.com. Located a 40min walk from town (turn near the entrance to the Crococun zoo), this is a little slice of the good old-fashioned beach life, holding out between the resorts. It's the only place in the area you can camp. Or opt for a thatched-roof cabaña, all but one of which are en suite. Cabañas US$48 (M$820); camping per person US$15 (M$255)

Amar Inn On the seafront, 500m north of the main plaza ☎ 998 871 0026, ❸ amar_inn@hotmail.com. This bohemian, family-run hotel just off the beach has seven large rooms and three cabañas (fan only); some have high ceilings, loft beds and kitchenettes. A delicious Mexican breakfast is included. Cabañas M$1400; doubles M$1100

Casa Cacahuate C 2 in the zona urbana ☎ 998 208 9148, ⓦ mayaecho.com. With two spacious guestrooms, the "Peanut House" is a great chance to be in the forest in relative comfort, as well as to interact with the non-touristy side of Puerto Morelos. It's also a handy place for solo

travellers to get acclimatized, under the wing of hostess Sandra Dayton, a long-time Mexico resident (who also runs the Jungle Market; see opposite). US$55 (M$940)

Posada Amor Av Rojo Gómez, just south of the plaza ☎ 998 871 0033, ⓦ posada-amor.wix.com/puertom. One of the longest-established hotels in town, *Posada Amor* is well run and clean. Some of the quirky, individually decorated rooms (with either fans or a/c) are the least expensive around. A decent alternative if *Posada El Moro* is full, though try to get a room away from the bar. Puerto Morelos' low-key nightlife centres around the bar at *Posada Amor* and another next door. M$550

★ **Posada El Moro** Rojo Gómez 17, just north of the plaza ☎ 987 871 0159, ⓦ posadaelmoro.com. Sunny, spacious rooms with choice of fan or a/c (US$10/M$170 extra). Suites have kitchens, and the weekly rates are a steal. Inside is a pretty little garden and even a small pool. DIY continental breakfast included. US$79 (M$1350)

12

EATING

For a town of its size, Puerto Morelos has a disproportionately large number of great **places to eat**, offering a mix of local cuisine and flavours brought in by various expats. Most places are on the plaza, where everyone seems to convene at night. Also look out for informal eateries run out of people's front yards.

Café d'Amancia Southwest corner of the plaza ☎ 998 206 9242, ⓦ facebook.com/CafeDeAmancia. Come here for deadly strong coffee and a breakfast bagel or lunch-time sandwich (M$50–80), plus a great vantage point for watching the action on the square. Mon & Wed–Sun 7am–3pm & 6–10pm.

La Casa del Pescador North side of the plaza ☎ 998 251 4813. This restaurant, run by the fishermen's cooperative (located up the green spiral staircase), is simple and great value – a good place for lunch, or for dinner, when *La Playita* is shut. Fish fillets from around M$120. Daily 10am–10pm.

Al Chimichurri Rojo Gómez, south of the plaza ☎ 998 192 1129. If you've overdosed on seafood, follow the smell of sizzling steak to this expert Uruguayan restaurant, where you can stock up on meat, empanadas, hearty lasagne and *dulce de leche* crêpes (most mains M$150–250). It also serves breakfast and lunch at an adjacent café. Service, however, can be slow. Tues–Sun 8am–10pm.

Govinda's Niños Héroes, three blocks north of the plaza ☎ 998 230 5573. This small barely-a-restaurant in the front of a yoga studio serves a set menu of vegetarian Indian food that's delicious and excellent value (around M$60). Go early, as it can run out. Mon–Fri noon–4pm.

Lonchería Mimi Niños Héroes, north of the plaza. Look for the pale-green facade on this tidy *cocina económica*, where a team of women cooks up daily specials (M$40–80) in a spotless open kitchen. Go early, as food tends to run out – and the handful of tables fills up fast. Daily 8am–2pm.

★**La Playita** Melgar, half a block north of the plaza. This casual spot on the beach is where the town fishermen kick back and enjoy the fresh catch of the day, sold by the kilo and perfectly fried. A whole *pescado frito* for two and a few beers will set you back about M$300. Daily noon–10pm.

SHOPPING

Alma Libre On the plaza, south side ☎ 998 252 2207, ⓦ almalibrebooks.com. Probably Mexico's most extensive secondhand English-language bookshop, the Canadian-run *Alma Libre* has some twenty thousand volumes to choose from, including many on the area's natural and archeological attractions. They also stock some good-quality souvenirs. Oct–May Mon–Sat 10am–6pm, Sun 4–9pm.

Hunab-Ku Artesanía Two blocks south of the plaza on Rojo Gómez. Reasonably priced craftwork in a little "Maya mini-mall" where you can often see the artisans at work. As a bonus, crocodiles hang out in the swamp just behind. Daily 9am–5pm.

Playa del Carmen and around

Once a soporific fishing village where travellers camped out en route to Isla Cozumel, **PLAYA DEL CARMEN** (often called simply "Playa") is now a hot spot with pretensions of being the next Miami Beach – and, from a local perspective, a goldmine of employment in construction. Mexico City's elite pop in, as do day-trippers from Cancún and passengers from cruise ships docked on Cozumel. As a result, the town's main centre of activity, Avenida 5 (also called **La Quinta**), a long, pedestrianized strip one block back from the sea, is often packed to capacity with tourists rapidly emptying their wallets in pavement cafés, souvenir outlets and designer-clothes shops.

Nonetheless, the low-rise development and numerous European-owned businesses make it seem, at least on the quieter north side, relatively cosmopolitan and calm (certainly when compared to Cancún). The **nightlife** in particular has a hip edge, but as the town has grown, it has become tougher on budget travellers.

Playa's **main beach** has suffered some erosion and looks thin in some stretches. More serious beach-goers head to the area north of Constituyentes, called **Playa Norte**, where the deep, silky sand drops into waist-high green water with mid-size swells. A couple of beach clubs (see p.782) form the major social scene here.

12

CENTRAL PLAYA DEL CARMEN

■ ACCOMMODATION	
3B	9
El Acuario	6
Alux	1
Casa de las Flores	4
Casa Tucan	5
Jungla Caribe	3
One	2
Paraíso Azul	7
Vive la Vida	8

● EATING	
100% Natural	7
Los Aguachiles	2
Babe's	8
Café Veracruz	11
Casa Mediterranea	10
La Cueva del Chango	1
La Floresta	13
El Fogón	3/9
Karma Bagels	6
Nativo	5
La Tarraya	12
Yaxché	4

■ DRINKING & NIGHTLIFE	
Alux	10
Caiman	3
Canibal Royal	1
Diablito Cha Cha Cha	5
Fusion	8
Kitxen	4
Mamita's Beach Club	2
Ranita	7
La Santanera	6
El Tigre	9

ARRIVAL AND DEPARTURE

By bus Most visitors arrive on short-haul buses at the central bus station, sometimes referred to as the *terminal turística*, on Av 5 at Juárez, the main street from the highway to the beach. There are luggage storage facilities upstairs at the bus station. Another station, on Av 20 between C 12 and C 12, handles longer-haul trips on ADO; you can buy tickets at either station. From both, a taxi to the hotels furthest north should be no more than M$40–50. From Cancún airport, buses run to Playa (every 45min; 1hr). Numerous private minibus operators will take you directly to your hotel (about US$32/M$550 per person), or you can take a taxi (around US$90/M$1540).

Destinations Cancún (every 15min; 1hr 15min); Cancún airport (every 45min; 1hr 5min); Chetumal (every 30min–1hr; 4–5hr 20min) via Tulum (1hr); Chichén Itzá (2 daily at 7.30am & 8am; 3hr 40min–4hr); Cobá (10 daily; 1hr 45min–2hr); Mérida (16 daily; 4hr 50min–5hr 40min); Palenque (5 daily; 11hr 10min–12hr 40min); San Cristóbal de las Casas (5 daily; 16hr 5min–18hr 5min); Valladolid (18 daily; 2hr 40min–3hr 20min); Villahermosa (7 daily; 12hr 5min–14hr).

By car Driving into or through Playa can be a bit of a chore, due to the traffic. Easing things slightly is an express overpass on Hwy-307 with several well-signed off-ramps onto Playa's major east–west arteries. If you need to head north or south in town, it can make sense to head toward Hwy-307 and use the overpass.

By colectivo To reach smaller towns or beaches just north and south of Playa, *colectivos* are the easiest option: the Cancún service departs frequently from Juárez just west of the main bus station, and vans heading south to Tulum leave from C 2 between Av 10 and Av 15.

By taxi Private taxis can take you anywhere you need to go along the coast – they're more expensive than *colectivos*, but far cheaper than any tour company, even when you pay for waiting time.

GETTING AROUND

By car All the large car-rental companies have outlets in Playa – most are situated on the main coastal highway at the turn-off into town or in Plaza Marina near the Cozumel ferry pier at C 1 Sur.

By taxi You can hire taxis from stands on Av 5, or flag one down on the trafficked streets.

By bike The central area of town is walkable, but as Av 5 extends ever northward, it can be nice to ride a bicycle to the farthest points; a bike path runs along Av 10. For rentals contact Holabike (w holabike.com); book in advance and they'll deliver your wheels to your hotel (M$450/day; helmets M$15/day).

INFORMATION AND ACTIVITIES

Tourist information Tourist info kiosks, on Juárez near Av 15 and on the main plaza (daily 9am–9pm; t 984 873 2804, e turismo@solidaridad.gob.mx), have bilingual staff who do their best to answer any enquiries. w rivieramaya .mx and w playa.info are useful websites.

Kiteboarding Ikarus, Av 5 at C 20 (t 984 803 3490, w kiteboardmexico.com; 3hr group lesson US$195/M$3335).

Scuba diving and snorkelling Tank-Ha, C 10 between Av 5 and Av 10 (t 984 873 0302, w tankha.com), offers PADI certification courses, one- and two-tank dives (US$45–65) and snorkelling trips (US$65–85/M$1110–1450).

ACCOMMODATION

Hotel prices are inflated in Playa, especially along Av 5 and the beach. These more central hotels are also noisy, due to general party ruckus (south of C 26 or so) or construction (on the ever-expanding north side). Heading inland a bit, to Av 15 and beyond, gets you both a better rate and a better night's sleep. High season in Playa includes July and Aug, when Europeans come, as well as mid-Dec to April.

HOTELS

★ **El Acuario** Av 25, between C 2 and C 4 t 984 873 2133, w elacuariohotel.com.mx. A great example of the deals you can get by heading away from the beach, *El Acuario* has big rooms, all with a terrace or balcony, and some with kitchenettes, clustered around a central pool and garden (which also features a tortoise enclosure). Nice touches include free coffee and beach towels, plus a book exchange. Good online offers. US$75 (M$1275)

Alux C 14, between Av 10 and Av 15 t 984 803 2482, w hotelalux.com. *Alux* is a little frumpy, like its downtown Cancún counterpart (see p.769), and marketing is not its strong suit, with a barely legible sign out front. But on the whole it's a good deal; rooms have a/c and the more expensive options have kitchenettes. M$600

Casa de las Flores Av 20, between C 4 and C 6 t 984 873 2898, w hotelcasadelasflores.com. A charming place to stay, with spacious and stylish en-suite rooms overlooking the lush garden (all have a/c; rooms with TVs and fridges cost an extra US$10/M$170). There's a nice pool, and bikes are available to rent (US$15/M$255 per day). US$95 (M$1620)

Casa Tucan C 4, between Av 10 and Av 15 t 984 873 0283, w casatucan.de. A Playa institution, retaining a hippy atmosphere. Rooms can be a bit dark and musty – and you'll either love the elaborate murals or hate them. But with perks like laundry service, a big swimming pool, and great coffee at the restaurant, it's hard to beat the price. Rooms come with a/c and there are also cabañas with fans. Book ahead. Cabañas US$50 (M$850); doubles US$80 (M$1365)

Jungla Caribe Av 5 at C 8 ☎ 984 873 0650, ⓦ jungla -caribe.com. On a prime corner on La Quinta, this quirky hotel has a courtyard that's so overgrown you can hardly see the pool. Stairs trimmed in black-and-white tiles ascend like an M.C. Escher etching to rooms with a similar black-and-white (and somehow Eighties-looking) style. A/c can be noisy (as can the street), but the little balconies are fun for people-watching. US$86 (M$1465)

One Av 25, between C 12 and C 12 bis ☎ 984 877 3060, ⓦ onehotels.com. This large, rather generic business traveller-style chain hotel is near the long-distance bus depot. Ordinarily it wouldn't be worth recommending, but in Playa del Carmen, it represents a rare spot of mid-range value. M$800

Paraíso Azul C 2, between Av 10 and Av 15 ☎ 964 873 0054, ⓦ casadegopala.com. Convenient for the bus station and the *colectivo* stands, *Paraíso* aims to live up to its name with a lush palm- and banana-laden courtyard that helps mute the bustle of its central location. The second-floor terrace is inviting, the rooms are big and clean, and there's an unusually deep pool on the roof terrace, where the owner teaches scuba diving. US$75 (M$1275)

HOSTELS

3B Av 10 at C 1 ☎ 984 147 1207, ⓦ hostel3b.com. A self-described "party hostel", *3B* has a rooftop bar, modern kitchen, positively chic bathrooms and furniture, and professional staff. Despite its "boutique" aspirations, it's still very much a hostel, convenient for buses, *colectivos* and the Cozumel ferry. Dorms M$220; doubles M$700

Vive la Vida C 2, between Av 25 and Av 30 ☎ 984 109 2457, ⓦ hostelvivelavida.com. A rare good hostel in Playa, this one is clean, well designed and well managed by an enthusiastic young staff. There's a pool in the smallish courtyard, and a stocked communal kitchen. Dorms M$160; doubles M$450

EATING

12

Playa del Carmen is heaving with **restaurants** of every kind, and even the traditional Mexican places stay open late. **Av 5** is lined with tables – but if you're on a **budget** you'll need to search out where locals go: try the taco carts on Juárez close to the beach (breakfast and lunch only), stalls on Av 10 at C 6 (open at night) and various restaurants on Av 30. There's a **supermarket** on Av 30 at C 20, and the smaller DAC store, half a block north, has great produce. One warning: the turnover in restaurants in Playa is so high as to make a guidebook writer despair – half these places may have closed by the time you go; the good news is that new places will have opened.

CAFÉS, CHEAP EATS AND SNACKS

100% Natural Av 5, between C 10 and C 12 ☎ 998 885 2904, ⓦ 100natural.com.mx. This link in a mini-chain serves fresh, healthy versions of Mexican food (lots of it vegetarian), fresh fruit juices and great breakfasts (M$65– 110 for the latter). A good alternative to *La Cueva del Chango* (see below), in a more central location. Daily 7am–11pm.

★ **Los Aguachiles** C 34 at Av 25 ☎ 984 142 7380, ⓦ los aguachiles.mx. An array of salsas arrives at your table along with the menu at this open-air seafood-snack place, and the challenge is not ordering too many dishes as an excuse to use them all. Even a simple *aguachido* (a tostada piled high with fish, cabbage and herbs) is a substantial snack here (around M$40–50). Daily noon–10pm.

Café Veracruz C 2, between Av 20 and Av 25. No-nonsense café – or rather counter – with just one item on the menu: flavoursome black coffee (M$15) made from freshly roasted, organic beans (which are also for sale) from Veracruz. Ideal if you're waiting for a *colectivo* to Tulum or Cancún. Daily 8/9am–6/7pm.

★ **La Cueva del Chango** C 38, between Av 5 and the beach ☎ 984 876 2537, ⓦ lacuevadelchango.com. This garden restaurant is a local favourite, especially for long, late breakfasts. The menu includes tasty empanadas and crêpes, house-roasted coffee, and inventive main meals (M$160–215). Mon–Sat 8am–11pm, Sun 8am–2pm.

★ **La Floresta** West side of Hwy-307, just north of Av Juárez ☎ 984 803 3885. This big palapa next to the highway is a road-tripper's delight, serving overstuffed *tacos de camarón*, the perfect marriage of batter-fried shrimp, mayo and chunky tomato salsa. Should you need variety, seafood cocktails and *ceviches* are available, too (dishes from M$15). Daily 8.30am–6pm.

Karma Bagels Corner of La Quinta and Constituyentes ☎ 984 803 2192, ⓦ karmabagels.com. Playa outpost of a small Mexican chain, with a simple menu featuring several differtent types of bagels and an even greater array of meat, fish, cheese and veggie fillings (M$90–110), plus fresh salads. Daily 8am–10pm.

Nativo Av 30, between Constituyentes and C 20 ☎ 984 873 0758, ⓦ facebook.com/NativoRestaurants. Delicious fresh-fruit smoothies and Mexican food like tortas (M$65–80) and tacos (M$60–85), across the street from the similarly excellent DAC market. Daily 7am–midnight.

RESTAURANTS

Babe's C 10, between Av 5 and Av 10 ☎ 984 879 3569, ⓦ babesnoodlesandbar.com. This cheerful, Swedish-owned Thai noodle house – which also serves a fine Cuban mojito – typifies Playa's international hodgepodge. Dishes like pad thai start at M$90 for a huge portion. Tues–Sun 4pm–midnight.

★**Casa Mediterranea** Av 5, between C 6 and C 8 ☎ 984 806 4679. Tucked inside the Jardín del Marieta, amid art galleries, this modest little trattoria (there are only about six seats) serves delicious fresh pasta, such as fettuccine with shrimp and squash (M$175–350). Daily 2–11pm.

El Fogón Av 30 at C 6 bis. Follow your nose to the meat-covered grill at this basic, brightly lit taco joint that's generally mobbed with locals. No booze is served, but you can wash down all the meat with a big selection of *aguas frescas*, all for less than M$100 per person. There's another branch on Av 30 near C 28. Daily 8am–10pm.

La Tarraya On the beach at C 2 ☎ 984 873 2040. This local institution has been open for more than thirty years, well before Playa was a gleam in a developer's eye. It still serves standard beach food (most mains M$70–100) like *ceviche* and *pescado frito* with plenty of cold beer. Daily noon–9pm.

Yaxché Corner of La Quinta and C 22 Nte ☎ 984 873 3011, ⓦ mayacuisine.com. This elegant restaurant (pronounced "jag-SHAY") specializes in traditional Maya cuisine (mains M$105–375). The menu features dishes like chicken in a sour orange and chipotle sauce, slow-cooked suckling pig, and *tikin xic*, a marinated fish fillet cooked in a banana leaf. Daily 8.30am–10.30pm.

DRINKING AND NIGHTLIFE

At night, La Quinta becomes one long street party, and you can find any sort of music in the array of bars, though most people will wind up around the lively intersection with C 12. If you're looking for a mellower atmosphere, head north of C 16, even as far up as C 40. Happy-hour specials can ease you into the night without depleting funds too rapidly.

BARS

Alux Juárez, 400m west of Hwy-307 ☎ 984 803 2936, ⓦ aluxrestaurant.com. It's expensive and a trek from the main drag (tell the cab driver "ah-LOOSH"), but how often do you get to party in a technicolor-lit cave? Opens early for drinks, followed by dinner (overpriced, but fine; mains M$150–380); a DJ or a floor show of belly dancers and jazz musicians gets started around 10pm. Usually no cover charge. Daily 5.30pm–late.

Caiman C 24, between Av 5 and Av 10 ☎ 984 803 5250. A welcome change of pace from the often brash Playa bar scene, *Caiman* is a low-key joint with a friendly crowd of locals and expats. Cold beers cost M$30–50. Daily 11am–midnight.

Diablito Cha Cha Cha C 12 at Av 1 ☎ 984 803 5250. Mexico-goes-rockabilly is the loose theme at this retro-cool open-air lounge. Fuel up on Mexi-Asian snacks (tempura red snapper, spicy hand rolls, and so on), or just go straight for the tequila-mango cocktails (around M$100). Daily 6pm–late.

Fusion C 6 at the beach ☎ 984 873 0373. This mellow beach bar, with tables in the sand and the glow of kerosene lamps, is a great slice of old-fashioned, pre-club-scene Playa. There's live music most nights, and a strong drinks menu (beer M$15–45, cocktails M$100–120). Daily 9am–late.

Kitxen Av 5, between Av Constituyentes and C 20 ☎ 984 879 4749, ⓦ facebook.com/Kitxen. This cool bar-restaurant is owned by a member of legendary Mexican rock group Los Jaguares, so live bands often accompany good bar-snack food and drinks. Daily 5pm–2am.

Ranita C 10, between Av 5 and Av 10 ☎ 984 873 0389, ⓦ ranancasada.com/bar-ranita.html. A crew of regulars – mostly expats – hang out around the horseshoe-shaped bar. Unless there's a live band wedged into the small space, it's a mellow scene and a welcome break from other high-volume places. Sun–Thurs 1pm–2am, Fri–Sat 1pm–3am.

El Tigre Av 10, between C 2 and C 4. Good local spot for beers (around M$20–40), *ceviche* and ridiculously generous *botanas*. Women will probably feel more comfortable accompanied by a man; the billiards area upstairs is men only. Daily 11am–5pm.

BEACH CLUBS

Canibal Royal C 48 at the beach ☎ 984 803 4506. Your long walk to the farthest north beach is rewarded with a 1950s Brazilian lounge vibe, creative food and delectable eye candy, in the form of all the Mexico City hipsters who hang out here. Daily 11am–7pm.

Mamita's Beach Club C 28 at the beach ☎ 984 803 2867, ⓦ mamitasbeachclub.com. Of the two clubs at Playa Norte (*Kool* is the other), this one is marginally nicer and has better food. It has plenty of room to spread out and a hip but not overbearing party atmosphere. Chairs and umbrellas are for rent, or you can spread a towel at the water's edge and still get waiter service for drinks; the food is good (if a tad pricey). Daily 10am–7pm.

CLUBS

La Santanera C 12, between Av 5 and Av 10 ☎ 984 803 5250, ⓦ facebook.com/LaSantanera. Super-stylish club with a comfortable, breezy lounge area, diverse music and good strong drinks. The scantily clad party crowd – equal parts visitors and residents – usually staggers out just before dawn. Wed–Sat 10pm–6am.

DIRECTORY

Banks and exchange HSBC, Juárez between Av 10 and Av 15 (Mon–Fri 9am–7pm); Bancomer, Juárez between Av 25 and Av 30 (Mon–Fri 9am–4pm). Both have ATMs.

Consulates Canada, Av 10 at C 1, Plaza Paraíso ☎ 984 803 2411; US, C 1 Sur between Av 15 and Av 20 ☎ 984 873 0303.

Internet The streets off Av 5 hold numerous internet cafés; La Tabería on C 4 between Av 5 and Av 10 doubles as a *caseta*.

Laundry Lavanderías are scattered every other block on the side streets. Try Gigalav, on C 2 between Av 10 and Av 15 (daily 8am–9pm; M$15/kg).

Post office Av 20 at C 2 (Mon–Fri 8am–2pm); geared to dealing with tourists.

Isla Cozumel

A 40km-long island directly off the coast from Playa del Carmen, **ISLA COZUMEL** is known to package tourists as a cruise-ship port: nearly every day, up to ten liners, each with several thousand passengers, dock at one of the island's three dedicated piers, all just south of the only town, **San Miguel**. But Cozumel's other major attraction provides the perfect escape from the crowds: the reefs that dazzled Jacques Cousteau in the early 1960s are some of the finest in this hemisphere. Even if you don't dive, there's a certain appeal in wandering the relaxed inland blocks of San Miguel, away from the piers, spotting Maya ruins and birds (the Maya called the island cuzamil – "land of the swallows") in the dense forests and being the only person on the windswept eastern beaches.

San Miguel

Along the malecón (Av Rafael Melgar), downtown **SAN MIGUEL** caters to cruise-shippers with restaurants, souvenir shops, tour agencies and jewellery stores. There are typically fewer boats in port at weekends, and on Sunday evenings, *cozumeleños* come out to the main plaza for live music.

12

Museo de la Isla de Cozumel

Av Melgar between Av 4 and Av 6 • Mon–Sat 9am–4pm • US$4 • ☎ 987 872 0093, Ⓦ cozumelparks.com

This attractive museum has small displays of the flora, fauna and marine life of the island, as well as a good collection of Maya artefacts and old photos. It occasionally hosts live music and theatre events – check what's on with the tourist office.

The southwest coast

Aside from a small public beach on the north side of San Miguel (at C 16) and a small strip north of town, all the beach action is south of town on the Carretera Costera Poniente. Beach clubs typically charge about M$50 for beers, and seafood mains for M$150–250; you're expected to buy a nominal amount.

Parque Chankanaab

Southwest coast, 8km south of San Miguel • Mon–Sat 8am–4pm • Adults US$21, children aged 3–11 US$14 • ☎ 987 872 0093, Ⓦ cozumelparks.com

Tourists are usually steered right to the **Parque Chankanaab**. It's a lovely lagoon, but overdeveloped, with mini-golf, dolphin pens, botanical gardens and kayak tours. You'll probably want to skip it unless you have kids, who will like the calm water.

El Cedral

A large arch on the inland side of the road at km 17.5 marks the turn for the village of **El Cedral**, founded in 1847 and now primarily a vacation spot for San Miguel's better-off residents. There's no reason to drive up except in late April and early May, when the village hosts the ten-day-long Fiesta de la Santa Cruz, a huge fair with bullfights, prize-winning livestock and dancing.

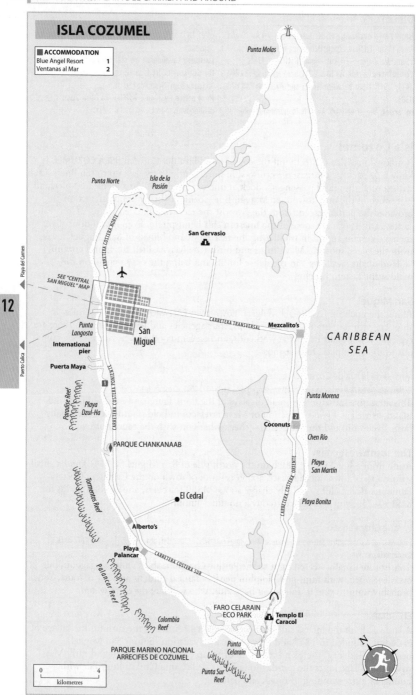

ISLA COZUMEL

■ ACCOMMODATION
Blue Angel Resort	**1**
Ventanas al Mar	**2**

Punta Molas

Punta Norte

Isla de la Pasión

San Gervasio

CARRETERA COSTERA NORTE

SEE "CENTRAL SAN MIGUEL" MAP

12

Playa del Carmen

Puerto Calica

Punta Langosta

International pier

Puerta Maya

San Miguel

CARRETERA TRANSVERSAL

Mezcalito's

CARIBBEAN SEA

Paradise Reef

Playa Dzul-Ha

CARRETERA COSTERA PONIENTE

1

Punta Morena

2

Coconuts

Chen Río

PARQUE CHANKANAAB

Playa San Martín

Tormentos Reef

El Cedral

Playa Bonita

CARRETERA COSTERA ORIENTE

Alberto's

Playa Palancar

CARRETERA COSTERA SUR

Palancar Reef

Colombia Reef

FARO CELARAIN ECO PARK

Templo El Caracol

Punta Celarain

PARQUE MARINO NACIONAL ARRECIFES DE COZUMEL

Punta Sur Reef

0	4

kilometres

N

REEF ETIQUETTE

Coral reefs are among the richest and most complex ecosystems on earth, but they are also very fragile. The colonies grow at a rate of only around 5cm per year, so they must be treated with care and respect if they are not to be damaged beyond repair. Follow these **simple rules** – and advise your guide to do so as well – while you are snorkelling, diving or in a boat.

Use only biodegradable sunscreen in reef areas; oils in standard formulas stifle coral growth.

Never touch or stand on corals, as the living polyps are easily damaged. Also avoid disturbing the sand around them, as it can smother them.

Don't remove anything from the reef.

Don't anchor boats on the reef; use permanently secured buoys instead.

Check where you are allowed to go fishing.

Review your diving skills before you head out.

Alberto's

Southwest coast, km 17.5 • Daily 10am–11pm • ☎ 987 869 1228

Immediately opposite the turn for El Cedral, this is the most rustic of the **beach clubs** on the west coast, with a great beach and snorkelling. There's nothing but a small, very good restaurant, boasting fish fresh-caught with its own boats. Snorkel trips to the best reefs run from here. The boat ride is shorter (and cheaper) from Playa Palancar (see below), but the beach there can be a party scene, while *tranquilo* is the watchword at Alberto's.

Playa Palancar

Southwest coast, km 19 • Daily 9am–6pm; dive shop closed Sun • Snorkel tours around M$400 • ☎ 987 118 5154

The last **beach** on the western shore is pretty, centred around a restaurant that serves good *tikin-xic*, and there's a dive shop where you can arrange a boat ride (2hr) out to Palancar Gardens just offshore. With parasailing, wave-runners and kayaks on offer, it's good for active beach-goers; others might find it a bit noisy.

Faro Celarain Eco Park

Southern tip of the island • Mon–Sat 9am–4pm; **museum of navigation** daily 10am–4pm (same ticket) • Adults US$14, kids 3–11 US$8 • ☎ 987 872 0093, ⓦ cozumelparks.com

The southernmost point of the island is a protected reserve for diverse wildlife, the **Faro Celarain Eco Park** (also called Parque Punta Sur). The site contains several lovely beaches, where you can hang out in a hammock, take a kayak tour around the lagoon or snorkel out and possibly spot some hawksbill turtles. This is also a prime spot for **bird watching**, as the mangroves host both migratory and endemic species, including the widespread Cozumel vireo and the Cozumel thrasher, once thought to be extinct. On the way in, you pass the tiny **Templo El Caracol**, which may have been built by the Maya as a lighthouse, though it's awfully squat. When the wind is right, it whistles through the shells embedded in its walls. You can climb to the top of the Punta Celarain **lighthouse** for amazing views over the coast, or visit the adjacent **museum of navigation** in the former lightkeeper's house.

Within the park, a bus transports visitors between various sites (or you can rent bicycles), including viewing towers over a network of lagoons and a beach restaurant serving good fried fish.

San Gervasio

6km north of the Carretera Transversal • Daily 8am–3.45pm • US$9.50 • ☎ 987 872 0093, ⓦ cozumelparks.com

Midway across the island, **San Gervasio** is the only excavated Maya site on Cozumel (the main ancient city, part of a major sea-trade network in the pre-Conquest era, was covered by a US air base, now the airport). With several small temples connected by *sacbeob*, or long white roads, it was one of the many independent city-states that survived the fall of Chichén Itzá, flourishing between 1200 AD and 1650 AD. It was

12

also one of the most important Mesoamerican centres of pilgrimage for Ixchel, the goddess of fertility and weaving – though it's not particularly impressive now. As part of a larger nature reserve, however, the site is worth a visit for the numerous birds and butterflies you can spot early in the morning or late in the day.

The east coast

Cozumel's rugged, windy eastern shore remains undeveloped because it faces the open sea and is usually too rough for swimming. The Carretera Costera Oriente runs 20km south to Punta Sur, passing many tantalizing empty **beaches** (swim only where you see others, and be wary of currents) and the occasional beach hut serving margaritas, but only until sundown because there's no electricity. Punta Morena occasionally draws surfers, and the beach at Chen Río has two protected coves where you can swim or snorkel, plus a very good restaurant (*El Galeón*). Playa San Martín, just south, is usually best for swimming.

CENTRAL SAN MIGUEL

ACCOMMODATION	
Aguilar	6
Amaranto	8
Las Anclas	7
La Casona Real	4
Flamingo	1
Hostelito	3
Pepita	5
Tamarindo B&B	

EATING	
La Candela	1
Casa Denis	5
Le Chef	9
Chilangos	8
Conchita del Caribe	11
Corazón Contento	3
Nacho Crazy Boy	4
New Especias	7
Panadería Cozumeleña	6
Restaurant del Museo	2
Rock'n Java	10

DRINKING & NIGHTLIFE	
Kelley's	2
La Morena	3
Tiki-Tok	1

UNDERWATER IN COZUMEL

DIVING

Some of the top **dive spots** are Colombia Deep and Punta Sur, directly south from the marshes on the southern tip, but the latter has strong currents. There are dozens of **dive shops** in town – Deep Blue (Salas at Av 10; ☎ 987 872 5653, ⊚ deepbluecozumel.com) is one of the best, offering tailor-made small-group tours; a two-tank dive costs US$76–80/ M$1295–1360, depending on the size of the group. For certification courses, Caribbean Divers (Av 5 at C 3; ☎ 987 872 1145) comes recommended, as does Blue Magic Scuba (C 4 no. 71; ☎ 987 872 6143, ⊚ bluemagicscuba.com).

SNORKELLING

As soon as you get off the ferry, you'll be offered trips. Short tours (1–2hr), priced at around US$40/M$680, go to nearby reefs such as Villa Blanca, which are fine but not spectacular. The best destinations are Palancar Shallows and Colombia Shallows; they're off the southwest coast, so better visited from Playa Palancar's beach club (see p.785). There's also **walk-in snorkelling** – the good sites closest to San Miguel are Villa Blanca Shallows (Carretera Sur km 3.5), near the *Sunset Grill*, and Paradise Shallows – turn off near Carretera Sur km 5, then turn right at the marina.

ARRIVAL AND DEPARTURE ISLA COZUMEL

By plane From the airport, where there's an ATM, a *combi* van service makes the short trip into town (about M$60). Destinations include Cancún (on Mayair; 4–5 daily; 20min).

By bus You can buy tickets for onward mainland travel at the ADO office on Av 10 at C 2.

By passenger ferry The passenger ferry dock is in the centre of San Miguel, with the plaza directly across the street. Two passenger ferry companies, Mexico Waterjets (⊚ mexicowaterjets.com) and Ultramar (⊚ granpuerto .com.mx), depart from the pier at C 1 Sur in Playa del Carmen, for San Miguel in Cozumel (roughly hourly, 6am–11pm). The price is the same (M$163), and the boats are roughly equivalent as well, so just pick whichever is departing soonest – and buy only a one-way ticket, so you have the same freedom on the return trip. Returning to Playa, the ferries depart Cozumel hourly (5am–10pm), though this can change according to the season.

By car ferry Transbordadores del Caribe (☎ 987 872 7688, ⊚ transcaribe.net) operates a car ferry (Mon–Sat 4 daily, Sun 2 daily; 1hr 15min) to Cozumel from Puerto Calica (also called Punta Venado), 7km south of Playa del Carmen. At M$817 per car and M$67 per passenger, it's worthwhile only if you'll be staying on the island more than a few days. If you opt not to take your car, the closest parking to the ferry terminal in Playa del Carmen is the secure car park behind the main bus station.

GETTING AROUND

By bus Buses run around town, but the only one you might use is the hourly one to the beaches and hotels just north and south of town. Look for the northbound bus on Av 10; the southbound, on Av 15. But note that the majority that go by are for other routes within San Miguel. To get outside town, you'll have to book a tour, take a taxi or rent a vehicle.

By car Numerous local *rentadoras* in the town centre have similar prices (around M$800–1000/day), and haggling often doesn't get you much; you can often do better booking with a chain online.

By taxi If you have substantial luggage, you'll want a taxi for any hotel east of Av 10. They're plentiful and operate on a zone system.

By bike Cycling is only really feasible in town and to the beaches to the north or south as far as Parque Chankanaab, where there's a separate track. Sombrero Rentals (☎ 987 857 0085, ⊚ sombrerorentals.com) has well-maintained mountain bikes and beach cruisers for about US$15/M$255 per day; they'll deliver to your hotel.

By moped Fun on a clear day, but opt for a car if there's any sign of rain. In addition to the discomfort, roads are very slick when wet. Sombrero Rentals (see above) has them (around US$50/M$850 per day).

INFORMATION

Tourist office The island tourist office (Mon–Sat 8.30am–5pm; ☎ 987 872 7585) is in the complex on the east side of the plaza, up the escalators.

Website ⊚ cozumel.travel is a useful source of information.

12

ACCOMMODATION

The **hotels** in Cozumel are divided into two categories: resorts (most all-inclusive) strung out along the coast on either side of San Miguel, and more affordable places in the town centre – though none of these, even the lone **hostel**, is very cheap. Along the beach, the hotels to the north require a taxi ride into town, while a few to the south are within walking distance from the action. At the town hotels, sea views are overrated, as they usually come with traffic noise from the malecón (San Miguel's seaside promenade) below.

SAN MIGUEL

Aguilar C 3 Sur 98 at Av 5 Sur ☎ 987 872 0307, ⓦ hotelaguilar.com; map p.786. A reasonable low-cost option, *Hotel Aguilar* has clean, tile-floor rooms with no shortage of plastic flowers; all have a/c and fridges. There's a small pool on site, and car rental is available. M$595

Amaranto C 5 no. 321, between Av 15 and Av 20 ☎ 987 564 4262, ⓦ amarantobedandbreakfast.com; map p.786. Winding staircases and curving walls distinguish these three fanciful stucco palapas and two apartments stacked in a tile-trimmed tower. Rooms – all with fridge and microwave, some with a/c – are clustered around a cosy courtyard and small pool. US$62 (M$1055)

Las Anclas Av 5 Sur 325 ☎ 987 872 5476, ⓦ hotelvillalasanclas.com; map p.786. A cluster of two-storey suites with kitchenettes; each sleeps up to four, with a queen-size bed upstairs and two day-beds downstairs (though the latter are best for kids). A lush central garden makes the place feel homely. US$125 (M$2130)

La Casona Real Juárez at Av 25 ☎ 987 872 5471, ⓦ hotel-la-casona-real-cozumel.com; map p.786. So long as you love orange and yellow (the wall colours of choice) and you can forgive exposed and questionably joined pipes in the bathrooms, you'll appreciate the excellent value at this modern hotel with a/c and a courtyard pool. US$119 (M$2025)

Flamingo C 6, between Melgar and Av 5 ☎ 987 872 1264, ⓦ hotelflamingo.com; map p.786. Popular with the scuba set, with a roof terrace and a bar (noise alert: occasional live salsa bands). "Courtyard" rooms aren't as breezy as the larger "superior" ones, but all have a nice modern style, and the full inclusive breakfast is very good. US$90 (M$1530)

Hostelito Av 10 no. 42, between Juárez and C 2 ☎ 987 869 8157, ⓦ hostelcozumel.com; map p.786. A fine hostel, with six-bed dorms (including one with a/c) and private a/c rooms, as well as a convenient location, a small book exchange, a roof terrace and luggage storage. Dorms M$180; doubles M$550

Pepita Av 15 Sur 120, at C 1 Sur ☎ 987 872 0098, ⓦ hotelpepitacozumel.com; map p.786. One of the oldest hotels in town, and also one of the best kept, with clean, simple tiled-floor rooms with a/c, fridges and TVs. Amenities include a pretty courtyard and free coffee in the morning. M$550

Tamarindo B&B C 4 no. 421, between Av 20 and Av 25 ☎ 987 872 6190, ⓦ tamarindocozumel.com; map p.786. At this French-owned B&B, rooms have cosy nooks and whimsical touches. A full breakfast is included, and the owner's excellent cooking and island expertise put guests at ease. A/c rooms and apartments cost US$10–30/M$170–510 extra. US$59 (M$1005)

OUTSIDE SAN MIGUEL

Blue Angel Resort Carretera Costera Sur km 2.2 ☎ 987 872 7258, ⓦ blueangelresort.com; map p.784. Close to town, and with an excellent dive shop and shallow-dive training both in the pool and right off the hotel's small beach. All rooms have sea views and private balconies. US$118 (M$2010)

Ventanas al Mar On the east coast, 5km south of Mezcalito's beach bar and the intersection with the Carretera Transversal ☎ 984 267 2237, ⓦ ventanas almar.com; map p.784. This hotel – the only one on the east coast – runs entirely on wind power. The giant rooms and the two-storey suites, which sleep four, have basic kitchenettes, as well as terraces overlooking the crashing surf. Bring groceries if you plan to stay a while. Two-night minimum stay. US$135 (M$2300)

EATING

A good number of San Miguel's **restaurants** are pasta-and-steak tourist traps catering to a dull palate, but tucked in the backstreets are a surprising number of small family-run operations. The cheapest snacks of all can be had through the afternoon at the city market, on Salas between Av 20 and Av 25.

CAFÉS, CHEAP EATS AND SNACKS

Chilangos Av 30, between C 3 and Morelos; map p.786. At this tiny family-operated place, design your own quesadilla or *huarache* by pointing at the ingredients on display in a small glass case – lots of veggies, among other things. Then the masters behind the counter assemble a great, reasonably priced meal (around M$50–70). Daily 7–11pm/midnight.

Corazón Contento C 2 at Av 10 ☎ 987 876 1526; map p.786. At this very welcoming operation near the plaza, the coffee is atypically strong and delicious, and the breakfasts – which range from fruit salads to French toast – are good value (from M$70). Daily 7am–10pm.

Nacho Crazy Boy Av 20, between C 1 and Juárez; map p.786. The eponymous Nacho operates a battery of blenders and squeezers in front of his house, to create inexpensive and delicious juice drinks (M$30–60). Opening hours can be a bit erratic. Daily 8am–11pm.

Panadería Cozumeleña C 3 at Av 10; map p.786. Stop by this sweet-smelling bakery (entrance on C 3) to pick up a pastry (M$10–40) to go, or, for a more leisurely light breakfast, settle in at the adjacent coffee shop, a neighbourhood hangout (entrance on the corner). Daily 7am–10pm.

Restaurant del Museo Melgar, between C 4 and C 6, at the Museo de la Isla de Cozumel ☎ 987 872 0838; map p.786. Enjoy a quiet breakfast (M$40–100), lunch or dinner on the balcony of the museum with a view of the sea. The food – from *huevos rancheros* to club sandwiches – is fresh and filling. Mon–Sat 7am–11pm.

RESTAURANTS

La Candela Av 5 at C 6 Nte ☎ 987 878 4472; map p.786. Home-cooked breakfast and lunch, with a half-Cuban twist (black beans and rice, mojitos). The "fish Candela" (in a tomatillo cream sauce) is just one of many tasty house dishes (around M$150). Nice breezy terrace seating at the back. Mon–Sat 8am–6pm.

Casa Denis C 1, between Av 5 and Av 10 ☎ 987 872 0067, ⓦ casadenis.com; map p.786. A little wood-frame house, this is the best bet for eating near the plaza, even if some of the bigger meals can be a little bland. Best to stick with a beer and some snacks (M$30–80) and watch the action from your pavement table. Daily 8am–10pm.

★ **Le Chef** Av 5 at C 5 Sur ☎ 987 878 4391, ⓦ facebook.com/LeChefCozumel; map p.786. A charming little spot (also known as *Le Bistrot*) where the chef-owner devises new specials every day, such as various pizzas and creative sandwiches (lobster and bacon is the house speciality). Expect to pay around M$150 for a meal and a drink. Mon–Sat noon–11pm.

Conchita del Caribe Av 65, between C 13 and C 15 ☎ 987 872 5888, ⓦ laconchitadelcaribe.mx; map p.786. This locally famous informal seafood spot (dishes from M$60) is worth the cab ride deep into town. The generous portions of *ceviche* are particularly good, and on Sundays you can get paella. Daily 11.30am–7.30pm.

New Especias C 3 Sur at Av 5 ☎ 987 876 1558, ⓦ facebook.com/NewEspecias; map p.786. A good-value restaurant specializing in Italian food, from bruschetta and gnocchi to thin-crust pizzas, seafood and steaks (mains around M$140–200). The menu also features a few more unusual dishes, such as sweet Nutella pizzas and barbecued lion fish (an invasive species that threatens Cozumel's reefs). Mon–Sat 6–11.30pm.

Rock'n Java Melgar 602, between C 7 and Quintana Roo (C 11) ☎ 987 872 4405, ⓦ rocknjavacozumel.com; map p.786. At this American-owned seafront diner, healthy sandwiches, salads and veggie chile are balanced out by hearty burgers and fantastically rich and delicious desserts (like double fudge brownies). Mains M$90–140. Mon–Fri 7am–10pm, Sat 7am–2pm.

DRINKING AND NIGHTLIFE

Kelley's Av 10, between Salas and C 1 Sur ☎ 987 117 9224, ⓦ facebook.com/KelleysBarCozumel; map p.786. Big open-air sports bar with a pool table and live music on weekends – you might see your diving instructor or tour guide there off-hours. Tasty American food during the day (steaks around M$200). Daily noon–11pm.

La Morena Av 10, between C 3 and C 5; map p.786. A restaurant with a back garden serving earthy Yucatecan food, and also a great place to hang out in the afternoon,

when beers cost around M$30 and you can fill up on the *botanas* served with each round. Daily 11am–11pm.

Tiki-Tok Melgar, between C 2 and C 4 ☎ 987 869 8189, ⓦ facebook.com/TikTokcCozumel; map p.786. This second-floor bar doles out the umbrella drinks, and the party gets started earlier than most, as this is one of the few bars in town with a sunset view over the water. There's live salsa music (dance classes Fri night) later on. Daily 7am–5am.

DIRECTORY

Banks and exchange HSBC (Mon–Fri 9am–7pm) is on Av 5 at C 1 Sur.

Internet Scarce in the centre of town, but more numerous around the public market.

Laundry There are two *lavanderías* on Quintana Roo (C 11) just east of Melgar.

Medical care Hyperbaric chamber and clinic on C 5

between Melgar and Av 5 (☎ 987 872 5050, ⓦ cozumelhyperbaricchamber.com). 24hr Centro de Salud, on Av 20 at C 11 (☎ 987 872 0140). Most doctors are accustomed to dealing with English-speaking patients and those with diving-related issues.

Post office Melgar at C 7 Sur (Mon–Fri 9am–4pm, Sat 9am–1pm).

South to Tulum

Much of the seafront **south of Playa del Carmen** has been developed into resorts or condominium villages, and their access gates line the east side of Hwy-307, leaving little or no access to the sea for non-guests. There are just a couple of good beach spots, but on the inland side, you'll find some good **cenotes**.

Xcaret

6km south of Playa del Carmen • Daily 8.30am–9.30pm • M$1475 (a bit cheaper if you book online) • ☎ 984 206 0038, ⓦ xcaret.com • Second-class buses stop on request; dedicated ADO bus from Playa del Carmen runs 3 times every morning; taxi from Playa around M$200

The attraction you see billboards for everywhere is actually a surprisingly pleasant theme park: **Xcaret** offers all the Yucatán's attractions in one handy place, with a museum, a tropical aquarium, a "Maya village", a beach, some small authentic ruins, pools and more than a kilometre of subterranean rivers down which you can swim, snorkel or float. Neighbouring Xplor (ⓦ xplor.travel) is dedicated to ziplines and other outdoor adventure – but it's very expensive for what it is.

Río Secreto

6km south of Playa del Carmen, opposite Xcaret • Tours daily at 9am, 10am, noon, 1pm & 2pm • US$79/M$1345 • ☎ 888 844 5010, ⓦ riosecretomexico.com • Second-class buses stop on request; a taxi from Playa del Carmen costs around M$200

This tour through a water-filled cave is a slick operation, but an undeniably cool one. You don a wetsuit to clamber over rocks and swim through sparkling-clear rivers, and the only light comes from your own headlamp. It's a good adventure, but still doable for kids or not-so-strong swimmers. It's also a good activity for a rainy day.

Xcacel

Hwy-307, just south of km 247 • Daily 8am–6pm • M$20

A few kilometres south of Akumal and immediately south of Chemuyil, **Xcacel** is a **sea-turtle** research station and pristine beach with good waves for body-surfing. Visitors are welcome, and there are basic toilets and a shower. Ticket-sellers will check that you're using only biodegradable sunscreen. It's only 500m from the highway – handy if you're coming by bus or *combi*.

Parque Xel-Há

Hwy-307, 13km north of Tulum • **Park** Daily 8.30am–6pm • US$89/M$1515 (a bit cheaper if you book online) including all food and drink • ☎ 984 206 0038, ⓦ xelha.com • **Ruins** Daily 8am–5pm • M$47

Despite a sky-high entrance fee and a theme-park feel, this **natural water park** is a highlight of this coast, especially if you have children. If you spend a full day, it can seem pretty good value. Built around a system of lagoons, inlets and caves, it's a beautiful place with rope swings, snorkelling, cliff jumping and a lazy tube float. Across the highway, not to be confused with the water park, is a set of small **Maya ruins** with some notable paintings of birds, and miniature temples like those at Tulum.

Hidden Worlds

Hwy-307, 14km north of Tulum • **Tours** Daily 9am–dark • Snorkelling around US$35/M$595; diving around US$130/M$2215 for two tanks • **Dos Ojos** Daily 8am–6pm • M$100 • ☎ 984 877 8535

This park area encompasses some exceptionally beautiful *cenotes* and caverns. Guided group snorkelling and diving trips run several times a day, with options for ziplines and the like. You can also visit glimmering **Dos Ojos** *cenote* on your own, for a fee paid at a separate entrance just to the north on Hwy-307, though it is also a popular place to dive.

Tulum and around

To visitors, **TULUM** can mean several things. First, it's one of the most picturesque of all the ancient Maya sites, poised on 15m-high cliffs above the impossibly turquoise Caribbean. Tulum also refers to a stretch of broad, white beach, dotted with lodging options that range from bare-bones to ultra-swank; many of them, as well as many super-casual beach bars, still show their backpacker-friendly roots in style, if not in price. Finally, it's a booming town (often called **Tulum Pueblo** to distinguish it from the beach) that has evolved from roadside waystation to real population centre, where visitors can arrange tours into the Sian Ka'an Biosphere Reserve (see p.798), among other things.

Long considered the hippest coastal destination in the region – a title Isla Holbox is now vying for (see p.760) – Tulum is rapidly developing: there's even a *Starbucks* now. Despite this, it remains a wonderful place to visit.

Tulum ruins

Hwy-307 • Daily 8am–5pm, last entry 4.30pm • M$64 • Parking on the main highway; tickets sold at the site entrance, about 1km east; a shuttle (M$20) runs between the parking area and the ruins; you can also approach from the south, parking at the dead-end of the beach road and walking in

On a sunny day, with the turquoise sea glittering behind the weather-beaten grey stones, your first glimpse of the **Tulum ruins** can be breathtaking, despite the small scale of its buildings, all clustered in a compact mass. When the Spaniards first set eyes on the place in 1518, they considered it as large and beautiful as Seville. They were, perhaps, misled by their dreams of El Dorado and the brightly painted facades of the buildings, for architecturally Tulum is no match for the great Maya cities. Mostly built after 1200, the structures seem a bit haphazard because walls flare outward and doorways taper in – not the effect of time, but an intentional design, and one echoed in other post-Classic sites along the coast like El Rey in Cancún and San Gervasio on Cozumel.

The site itself takes only an hour or so to see, though you may want to allow time to **swim** at the tiny, perfect beach that punctuates the cliffs (see p.793). Arrive in the early morning or late afternoon to avoid the worst crowds. You walk in through a breach in the wall that surrounded the city on three sides; the fourth faced the sea. The first building past the entrance is the **Casa del Noroeste**, one of the many small-scale buildings which typify the site, with their slanty walls and narrow windows. Closer to the sea sits the **Casa del Cenote**, a square structure straddling what was once a water-filled cave, the source of life for the settlement. On the bluff above and to the right are the **Templos Miniaturas**, several small-scale temples, complete with tiny lintels and mouldings, which were probably used as shrines.

Templo del Díos Descendente

Skirt the small beach to reach the **Templo del Díos Descendente**. The small, upside-down winged figure depicted above the temple's narrow entrance appears all

AROUND TULUM

Cenotes, Cobá & Valladolid   Playa del Carmen & Cancún

Kitesurfing Extreme Control

Tulum ruins

HWY 307

SEE "TULUM RUINS" MAP

Acuatic Tulum

El Paraíso Beach Club

SEE TULUM TOWN MAP

Felipe Carrillo Puerto & Chetumal

CARIBBEAN SEA

0   1
kilometre

● EATING

El Capitán	2
Hartwood	7
Hechizo	6
Mateo's	3
Qué Fresco	4
El Tábano	5
Urge Taquito	1

■ ACCOMMODATION

Cabañas Copal	4
Cabañas Zazil-Kin	3
Dos Ceibas	7
Hostal Chalupa	1
Nueva Vida de Ramiro	6
Teetotum	2
Zamas	5

■ DRINKING & NIGHTLIFE

Mezzanine	2
La Vita è Bella	1
La Zebra	3

Cenote

Sian Ka'an Biosphere Reserve & Punta Allen

12

CARIBBEAN SEA — TULUM RUINS

Templos Miniaturas

Templo del Díos del Viento

Beach

Entrance

Casa del Cenote

Casa del Noroeste

Plataformas

Entrance

Wall

Torre de Guardia

Ticket Booth

El Castillo

Templo del Díos Descendente

Gran Palacio

Plataformas

Casa de Chultun

Templo del Mar

Templo de la Estela

Templo de las Pinturas

Exit

Wall

Torre de Guardia

0 — 50 metres

Beach road & Sian Ka'an Biosphere Reserve

Visitors centre, Hwy-307 (1km) & Tulum town (2km)

over the city, but in only a handful of places elsewhere in the Maya world. It may represent the setting sun, or the bee god, as honey was one of the Maya's most important exports.

El Castillo

Immediately adjacent to the Templo del Díos Descendente, the **Castillo**, on the highest part of the site, commands fine views in every direction – but to protect the worn stones, visitors may now only look up at the building from the base of the hill. The pyramid may have served not just as a temple, but also as a lighthouse. Even without a light, it would have been an important landmark for mariners.

Templo de las Pinturas and around

Away from the sea, a cluster of buildings is arranged on a city-like grid, with the chief structures set on stone platforms along parallel streets. Of these, the **Templo de las Pinturas** (Temple of the Paintings) is intriguing: the intricate carvings on its exterior slowly reveal themselves as you look closely. The corners form glowering masks trimmed with feather headdresses, and the "descending god" can be spotted in one niche. Unfortunately, you can no longer view this section of the temple, as it's closed off (it is actually on the *exterior* of an older, smaller temple, which has been preserved by the surrounding gallery), but one remarkable scene, created at a later date than the others, shows the rain god Chac seated on a four-legged animal – likely inspired by the conquistadors on horseback.

> ### TULUM ORIENTATION
>
> Coming into the Tulum area on **Hwy-307** from the north, you arrive first at the well-marked pedestrian and bus entrances to the **ruins** – the site itself is on the water, 1km east. There's a long-haul bus stop here, so you don't have to double back from town.
>
> Another kilometre or so south is a traffic light marking the main intersection. A left turn here leads, in about 3km, to the **beach**, where accommodation is strung along a narrow but paved road running north–south along the water. To the north (left from the junction) are a few hotels, the better publicly accessible beaches and, after 2km, a back entrance to the ruins. To the south (right from the junction), hotels dot 7km of road, up to the border of the Sian Ka'an Biosphere Reserve.
>
> Back on Hwy-307 (here called **Av Tulum**), the centre of town is just a little further south.

The best view of the whole site is from the cliff edges to the south of the Castillo. A small trail leads along the edge, delivering a great perspective on the sea and the ruins, then loops down through the greenery.

Tulum beach

Tulum town is generally empty of visitors by day because they've all decamped to the **beach**, the longest, most impeccable stretch of sand outside Cancún. The easiest access is at one of the beach clubs, where you pay for lounge chairs and drinks; far south, especially in the **biosphere reserve**, there's easier free access. The most popular clubs are walking distance from the ruins, making it easy to sightsee, then grab lunch and a spot in the sun. *El Paraiso Beach Club*, about 500m south of the ruins' back entrance, has a generous stretch of sand, often with bands, beach soccer and volleyball. The designated public beach close to the ruins is Playa Maya, a little south of El Paraiso; local fishermen's co-ops here offer snorkel tours and fishing trips. And just south of that is *El Mariachi Beach Club*, more of a locals' hangout, where you can get super-fresh *ceviche*.

ARRIVAL AND DEPARTURE   TULUM

By plane Airport shuttle Tucan Kin (☎ 984 134 7535, ⊕ tucankin.com) runs both from, and to, Cancún airport, dropping at all hotels; shared service from US$24/M$410 per person.

By bus The bus station is near the southern end of Tulum Pueblo; during the high season it's worth booking your seat in advance.

Destinations Cancún (every 30min; 2hr 20min–3hr); Chetumal via Felipe Carrillo Puerto and Bacalar (hourly; 3hr 15min–4hr 10min); Chichén Itzá (3 daily at 8.36am, 9am &

2.45pm; 2hr 30min–2hr 50min); Cobá (10 daily; 40min–1hr); Mahahual (1 daily at 9am; 2hr 20min); Mérida (7 daily; 3hr 50min–4hr); Playa del Carmen (every 30min; 1hr); San Cristóbal de las Casas (5 daily; 15hr 5min–16hr 35min) via Palenque (11hr); Valladolid (roughly hourly; 1hr 40min–2hr 10min).

By colectivo *Colectivos* gather almost next door to the bus station. Passenger vans run very frequently to Playa del Carmen and every hour or so to Felipe Carrillo Puerto, stopping anywhere in between on request.

GETTING AROUND

By car To rent a car for a day outing, try Hertz (⊕ hertz .com) on Av Tulum.

By taxi The main taxi office is on the west side of Av Tulum between Centauro and Orión; most prices are shown on a board outside (M$50–100 to beach hotels). Tulum's taxi drivers have a reputation for denying the

existence of hotels that don't pay them commission; if you have planned on a particular hotel, insist on being taken there.

By bike Many hostels and hotels offer bikes to rent (or even free for guests), as do most travel agencies.

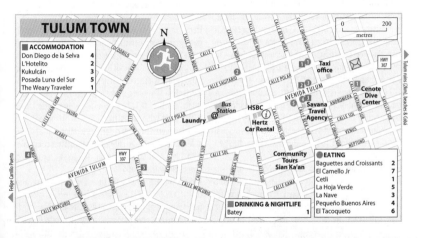

TULUM TOWN

ACCOMMODATION
Don Diego de la Selva   4
L'Hotelito   2
Kukulcán   3
Posada Luna del Sur   5
The Weary Traveler   1

DRINKING & NIGHTLIFE
Batey   1

EATING
Baguettes and Croissants   2
El Camello Jr   7
Cetli   1
La Hoja Verde   5
La Nave   3
Pequeño Buenos Aires   4
El Tacoqueto   6

INFORMATION, TOURS AND ACTIVITIES

INFORMATION

Tourist information Info kiosk with erratic hours on Av Tulum at Osiris, just north of HSBC. The *Weary Traveler* hostel (see opposite) usually has good free maps.

TOUR OPERATORS

Community Tours Sian Ka'an Osiris and Sol de Oriente ☏ 984 871 2202. The best tours of Sian Ka'an Biosphere Reserve, run by Centro Ecológico Sian Ka'an. Birding, sunset (with cheese and wine), kayaking and fishing are among the trips on offer.

Savana Travel Agency Av Tulum, between Orion and

Beta Sur ☏ 984 142 2422, ⓦ tulumtravelandtours.com. A full-service travel agency for flights and car rental, as well as local tours.

ACTIVITIES

Diving Reefs off the coast are fine but not lush – *cenote* diving is the real attraction in this area. Acuatic Tulum are reliable operators, on the beach at *Cabañas Zazil-Kin* and just off Hwy-307 on the road to the beach (☏ 984 871 2508, ⓦ acuatictulum.com.mx).

Kitesurfing Extreme Control at Caleta Tankha, north of the ruins (☏ 984 745 4555, ⓦ extremecontrol.net).

ACCOMMODATION

Basic sand-floor cabañas **on the beach** made Tulum famous with hippy backpackers, but they're in short supply now, as more comfortable (and much more expensive) places have sprung up. In fact, you may want to stay in **town** if you arrive late, have a limited amount of time (and money) or just prefer hot water round-the-clock: most hotels on the **beach road** have power only in the evenings (though this is changing), drawing on solar panels, windmills and (less ecofriendly) diesel generators. Depending on your point of view, the candle-lit ambience is rustic charm or expensive primitivism, and the thatched palapa roofs on cabañas can be a liability in the rain. As in Playa del Carmen, most hotels also charge high-season rates in the European holiday period of July and Aug. Addresses for the beach hotels are given in terms of distance from the junction with the highway access road. In addition to those listed below, *Las Ranitas*, which was closed for renovation at the time of research but is due to reopen in early 2016, is worth a look (ⓦ lasranitashotel.com).

HOTELS, B&BS AND CABAÑAS

ON THE BEACH

Cabañas Copal 700m south of the junction ☏ 1 800 681 9537 in Mexico, ☏ 01 866 471 3472 in the US, ⓦ ecotulum.com/cabanascopal.html; map p.791. The round, cement-floor cabañas are quite crowded together, but they're relatively well priced. There's electricity only in public areas but plenty of hot water, and a clothing-optional beach. Good spa on site. US$110 (M$1880)

Cabañas Zazil-Kin 2.4km north of the junction ☏ 984 124 0082, ⓦ zazilkintulum.com; map p.791. Although we've heard reports of theft, this is probably still the best value of the remaining backpacker-friendly operations, with a lively bar scene. Of the basic, concrete-floor cabañas (cold water only), a couple have private bath; a dozen rooms in a new block have a/c. It's perennially popular – so reserve or arrive early, as rooms go fast. US$53 (M$905)

Dos Ceibas 5.5km south of the junction ☏ 984 877 6024, ⓦ dosceibas.com; map p.791. Colourful, spacious cabañas in front of a turtle-hatching beach. Solar power and recycling mean that *Dos Ceibas'* "eco" label is more convincing than most; yoga and meditation classes offered. The cheapest cabaña has a bathroom outside. US$100 (M$1700)

Nueva Vida de Ramiro 4.5km south of the junction ☏ 984 877 8512, ⓦ tulumnv.com; map p.791. Peaceful, quirky eco-hotel powered entirely by wind turbines. Attractive wood cabins on stilts and cement cabins with big tiled bathrooms are built over and around untamed

greenery. The restaurant serves tasty seafood. With several suites and whole houses, it's a good choice for families and groups. US$115 (M$1960)

Zamas 1.3km south of the junction ☏ 984 877 8523, ⓦ zamas.com; map p.791. Enormous, comfortable rooms and bathrooms, some right on one of the prettiest stretches of beach in Tulum. Hot water and electricity are plentiful, but the style remains bohemian. Good restaurant (see p.796) too. US$160 (M$2730)

IN TOWN

Don Diego de la Selva West side of Hwy-307, south of town ☏ 984 114 9744, ⓦ dtulum.com; map p.793. French-owned hideaway just out of town, with a pool, tranquil garden, Gallic-influenced restaurant and big, white rooms with terraces; choice of fan or a/c. Guests can use facilities at beachfront sister hotel, *Don Diego de la Playa* (which is also recommended). US$75 (M$1280)

L'Hotelito West side of Av Tulum between Beta and Orión ☏ 984 136 1240, ⓦ hotelitotulum.com; map p.793. Good-value Italian-run hotel with palapa roofs and a garden courtyard, quiet despite its location in the middle of town. Rooms have an old-fashioned, comfy feel: upstairs with high ceilings and fan or, for US$11 extra, a/c; downstairs with a/c. US$60 (M$1020)

Kukulcán East side of Av Tulum between Beta and Orión ☏ 984 871 2112 ✉ nios_67@hotmail.com; map p.793. This basic budget hotel has faded but clean tiled-floor rooms that open onto small garden spaces at the back

CENOTES NEAR TULUM

The area north and west of Tulum has one of the largest concentrations of **cenotes** on the peninsula, including **Ox Bel Ha**, which at almost 170km is the longest water-filled cave system in the world. Many of these freshwater sinkholes are accessible from Hwy-307 or off the road to Cobá. Some, like Hidden Worlds (see p.790), have been developed as adventure centres, and the guides and marked trails at these places can help put first-time visitors at ease in dark water and tight spaces. But it's also worth visiting one of the less developed alternatives, such as **Gran Cenote**, 4km up the road to Cobá from Tulum (8am–6pm; M$120), where the only service is snorkel-gear rental. Either way, you can float above stalagmites and other rock formations – all the fun of cave exploration, with none of the scrabbling around. Zacil-Há, 4km further (M$80), is a local hangout and a great beginner pool, as you can see the sandy bottom.

Divers must have open-water certification for **cavern diving** (in which you explore within the reach of daylight), but **cave diving** (in which you venture into closed passageways and halls) requires rigorous training. One of the best cave-diving specialists in the area is Aquatech Divers at *Villas de Rosa* (☎984 875 9020, ⓦcenotes.com; *cenote* dives from US$95/M$1620) at Aventuras beach.

Local development may threaten *cenotes* in the long run, but clumsy visitors can do more damage in the short term. All the same rules for reef preservation (see box, p.785) apply here; and be very careful climbing in and out of the water – use the paths and ladders provided.

– a nice patch of green in town. All rooms have ceiling fans, and some also have a/c. M$650

Posada Luna del Sur Luna Sur 5 ☎984 871 2984, ⓦposadalunadelsur.com; map p.793. This *posada* has exceptionally comfortable, tranquil rooms set around a small garden, with welcoming and helpful staff to create an intimate B&B atmosphere. No children under the age of 15 are allowed, and there's no breakfast during the low season. US$150 (M$2555)

Teetotum On the road to the beach, 200m from Hwy-307 ☎984 745 8827, ⓦteetotumhotel.com; map p.791. Four sharply designed rooms with iPod docks, a/c and mod furniture – though it's overpriced, and housekeeping, and service in general, needs sharpening up. There's a plunge pool and a café-bar, and the location on the road to the beach hits a sweet spot: quiet, but walking distance to town and an easy bike ride (on free bicycles) to the water. US$135 (M$2300)

HOSTELS
IN TOWN

Hostal Chalupa On the road to the beach, 50m from Hwy-307 ☎984 871 2116; map p.791. Excellent hostel with rooftop bar and small pool; dorm beds are in three- or four-bed dorms, all a/c and en suite. Two private rooms, sleeping up to four people, are available too. Vegetarian kitchen. Dorms M$230; private rooms M$685

The Weary Traveler Av Tulum, just south of the bus station ☎984 871 2390, ⓦwearytravelerhostel.com; map p.793. The best-known and most convenient hostel in town; basic, large dorms as well as private rooms, some of which are en suite. Very party-centric and not always the cleanest, but a great meeting place. Don't expect service: it's DIY from check-in to breakfast in the communal kitchen. There's a shuttle to the beach. Dorms M$150; doubles M$400

EATING

Because the accommodation in Tulum is spread over 10km and the town is so far from the beach, almost every hotel has its own restaurant and bar. Guests tend to stick to their own hotels, but a few **places to eat** along the beach road merit a special trip. In town, a number of inexpensive **cafés** serve comida corrida and rotisserie chicken, and there's an increasing number of cheerful, mid-range places run by European expats.

CAFÉS, CHEAP EATS AND SNACKS
IN TOWN

Baguettes and Croissants Pte at Alfa ☎984 141 7600; map p.793. Good-value bakery café, a short walk off the main drag, serving sandwiches and filled baguettes (from M$25), cakes, pastries, light meals and decent coffee. Useful for picnics or bus journeys. Daily 7am–9pm.

El Camello Jr East side of Hwy-307 at the south edge of town; map p.793. Unpretentious, plastic-table-and-chair place, but the crowds will tell you the seafood is excellent

and cheap – from the *ceviche* to whole fried fish (mains M$110–200). It's typically closed Wed in low season. Mon–Sat 9am–9pm.

La Hoja Verde Beta, just off Av Tulum ☎984 000 0000; map p.793. This vegetarian/vegan restaurant, opposite the meat-focused *Pequeño Buenos Aires* (see p.796), offers a pleasing change of pace, with tasty ratatouille, falafel, quinoa risotto and curries (mains M$95–105), plus great juices and smoothies. Tues–Sun 2–10pm.

La Nave North side of Av Tulum between Orión and

Beta ☏ 984 871 2592; map p.793. A busy hangout with fresh-fruit breakfasts, inexpensive pizza from a wood-fired oven (M$110–200) and Italian staples like pasta, gnocchi and *saltimbocca*. Daily 8am–11pm.

El Tacoqueto East side of Av Tulum at C Acuario; map p.793. A dependable *lonchería* with gut-busting daily specials (feel free to poke your head in the kitchen to see what looks good) for about M$60, or delicious hot-off-the-grill tacos for even less. Daily 8am–9pm.

★**Urge Taquito** West side of Hwy-307, one block north of the traffic lights ☏ 984 100 0118; map p.791. Humble roadside place specializing in (grilled or fried) tacos filled with fish or shrimp (around M$30), which you can dress up with fixings from the salsa bar or the epic condiments rack. Not to be missed. Mon–Sat noon–5pm.

RESTAURANTS

IN TOWN

El Capitán On the road to the beach, 200m from Hwy-307 ☏ 984 116 3967, ⊕ restaurant-elcapitan.com; map p.793. Vast portions of high-quality, keenly-priced fish, seafood and Mexican classics are served up at this friendly restaurant: the *ceviche* is particularly good (mains M$80–230). The mosquitos, however, are ferocious, so bring repellent. Daily 8am–10.30pm.

★**Cetli** Polar at Orión ☏ 984 108 0681; map p.793. Chef-owner Claudia trained in Mexico City's premier culinary academy; at her casual restaurant, try refined versions of Mexican classics (mains about M$200), such as chicken stuffed with *chaya* (similar to spinach) with a cactus fruit jelly. Mon, Tues & Thurs–Sun 5–10pm.

Pequeño Buenos Aires East side of Av Tulum at Beta ☏ 984 871 2708; map p.793. Giant Argentine steaks and *parrilladas* (huge mixed grills; M$590–1190 for two people to share), washed down with some excellent wines from an extensive list (by Tulum standards). The hamburger, using top-quality beef, is great value. Daily noon–10.30pm.

ON THE BEACH

Hartwood 7.6km south of the junction, on the beach road ⊕ hartwoodtulum.com; map p.791. The menu at this jungle-side restaurant, run by a New Yorker who aims to have a zero-carbon impact, changes daily, uses local (and often unusual) produce, and is cooked entirely on a wood fire. Expect modern, international dishes (around M$150–400) like slow-braised pork ribs, tangy lime tart and cinnamon-spiked plantains. Wed–Sun 6–10/11pm.

Hechizo 7.5km south of the junction, on the beach road ☏ 984 879 5020, ⊕ hechizotulum.com; map p.791. This gem of a restaurant is owned by a former *Ritz-Carlton* chef and features a short, sophisticated international menu (mains M$250–370; daily 5-course prix fixe M$740) that changes frequently. Email to reserve one of the eight tables. Mon–Sat 7–10.30pm in the high season; private parties only in the low season.

Mateo's 1.3km south of the junction, on the beach road across from Zamas ☏ 984 179 4160, ⊕ mateos mexicangrill.us; map p.791. Very popular Tex-Mex-style roadside diner with burgers, tacos, fajitas, coconut shrimp and the like (mains M$125–320). Service may be slow, as almost everything is cooked on a single oil-drum barbecue. Daily 11am–late.

Qué Fresco 1.2km south of the junction, on the beach road, at Zamas ☏ 984 877 8523, ⊕ zamas.com; map p.791. Very popular mid-range restaurant with fresh salads, pastas, pizzas, and some of the healthier Mexican dishes (mains M$110–230). Its beachside setting makes it a great way to start the day, too. Daily 8am–10.30pm.

El Tábano 2.3km south of the junction, inland side of the beach road ☏ 984 134 8725, ⊕ eltabanorestaurant .com; map p.791. As an open-air operation in an area without utilities, every day at this creative Mexican place starts with spanking-fresh seafood and produce – nothing from the freezer here (most mains M$125–250). The setting means mosquitoes, though, so bring repellent. Daily 8.30am–9.30pm.

DRINKING AND NIGHTLIFE

You'll have to ask around about nightlife as there's no single place where people reliably congregate, though *El Paraíso Beach Club* often has a party around the full moon.

IN TOWN

Batey Centauro, just off Tulum; map p.793. An old VW Beetle out front has been converted into a sugar-cane press at this hip bar, which specializes in mojitos (try the ginger flavour; M$40–60) and is a great spot for a sundowner. There's often live music and DJs, and a selection of tapas is on offer. Mon–Sat 4/5pm–1/2am.

ON THE BEACH

Mezzanine 800m north of the junction, on the beach road ☏ 984 131 1596, ⊕ mezzaninetulum.com; map p.791. This cool bar-lounge does excellent cocktails and Thai food (mains M$135–425); it's the only place on the beach where you can regularly find a dance scene in high season, every Fri. (Annoyingly, though, non-guests can't rent loungers/umbrellas.) Daily 8am–10/11pm.

La Vita è Bella 1.6km north of the junction, on the beach road ☏ 984 151 4723; map p.791. Reasonably priced sandwiches and wood-oven pizzas (M$130–230) are served until 11pm; a cocktail bar opens at 9.30pm, and a European party crowd often gets dancing later under the big palapa. Non-guests can rent loungers/umbrellas, if there's space (M$100). Daily 8am–11pm.

La Zebra 4.6km south of the junction, on the beach road ☎984 115 4728, ⍵lazebratulum.com; map p.791. Live music from Thurs right through the weekend, with a Sun salsa party that draws both tourists and residents, starting with free classes at 6pm (coinciding with happy hour). There's a huge selection of tequilas, and the restaurant's Mexican food (dishes from M$85) is good as well. Daily noon–late.

DIRECTORY

Banks and exchange HSBC, with an ATM, is in the middle of town, on the east side of Tulum between Osiris and Alfa; there are other ATMs at the bus station and nearby on the west side of Av Tulum.

Internet Plenty of places offer internet access, and most hotels have wi-fi. Reliable downtown places include Riviera Movil, just south of the ADO.

Laundry Several in town, including Lavandería Cheemil-Po, Av Tulum, just south of the bus station.

Post office West side of Av Tulum between Satélite and Centauro (Mon–Sat noon–3pm).

Cobá

45km northwest of Tulum • Daily 8am–6pm • M$64

A wide highway cuts through the jungle inland from Tulum, leading to the ancient city of **COBÁ** (and the tiny Maya village next to it). It's a fascinating and increasingly popular site. The clusters of buildings are spread out over several kilometres, so the area can absorb lots of visitors without feeling crowded, and you can ramble through the forest in peace, looking out for toucans, egrets, coatis and myriad tropical butterflies, including the giant iridescent blue morpho. A visit here requires at least a couple of hours; renting a **bicycle** just inside the site entrance is highly recommended. Although the ruins aren't as well restored as those at Tulum, their scale is more impressive, and the dense greenery and wildlife make a good counterpoint to the coast.

Ceramic studies indicate that the city was occupied from about 100 AD up until the arrival of the Spaniards – the site is even mentioned in the *Chilam Balam* of Chumayel, a book of Maya prophecy and lore written down in the eighteenth century, well after the city was abandoned. The city's zenith was in the Late Classic, around 800 AD, when its wealth grew from links with the cities of **Petén**, in lowland Mexico and Guatemala. These cities influenced Cobá's architecture and use of steles, typically seen only in the southern Maya regions. Cobá also prospered later through its connections with coastal cities such as Tulum, and several structures reflect the style found at those sites.

Nohoch Mul

The centrepiece of the site is the giant pyramid **Nohoch Mul**, taller than El Castillo at Chichén Itzá and, in its narrow and precipitous stairway, resembling the pyramid at Tikal in Guatemala; at the top, a small temple, similar to structures at Tulum, dates from around 1200. The view takes in nearby lakes, as well as the jungle stretching uninterrupted to the horizon.

Grupo Macanxoc

If you're feeling intrepid, head 1km down a shady *sacbé* to **Grupo Macanxoc**, a cluster of some twenty steles, most carved during the seventh century AD. Stele 1 shows part of the Maya creation myth and the oldest date recorded in the Maya Long Count calendar system, which tracks the days since the moment of creation. Other steles depict a high number of women, suggesting that Cobá may have had female rulers.

Cobá cenotes

6km south of Cobá • M$55 each • Buy tickets and arrange a taxi (around M$300, inclusive) at the entrance to the Cobá parking area; by car, buy tickets at the first *cenote*

After visiting the ruins, or as a separate excursion, you can make a trip to a group of **cenotes** outside the village of Cobá. The first you reach, Choo-Ha, is the least good for swimming, though its stalactites are impressive. The second, Tankah-Ha, is the most spectacular, a grand subterranean dome. Multún-Ha is deeper, and no natural light penetrates.

ARRIVAL AND DEPARTURE COBÁ

By bus Numerous buses (10 daily; 40min–1hr 10min) run to Cobá from Tulum; the first one leaves Tulum at 7.17am. Confusingly, there are generally fewer buses heading in the opposite direction.

By taxi A taxi from Tulum to Cobá costs about M$400–450 each way.

ACCOMMODATION AND EATING

Hotelito Sac-bé On the south side of the main street through the village ☎ 984 206 7140. Leagues better than the other budget options in town, *Hotelito Sac-bé* has a handful of clean rooms offering various amenities (some have a/c). The restaurant here serves an excellent, generous inclusive breakfast. M$450

La Pirámide Facing the lake. The best of the big restaurants that ring the parking lot by the site entrance, this is a casual, open-sided place dishing up all the usual Yucatecan specialities (around M$120–180). Daily 7.30am–9pm.

Reserva de Monos Arañas de Punta Laguna

Highway to Nuevo X-Can, 18km northeast of Cobá roundabout • Guides available from 6am or so • M$50/person, plus around M$300 for a guide for a group of up to ten people • No buses come this way; arrange a taxi or tour in Tulum

This small forest reserve protects one of the northernmost populations of **spider monkeys**. From the entrance kiosk, you're required to hike with a guide to where the monkeys usually congregate. There's no guarantee you'll see them, but they're at their liveliest in the early morning and after about 3.30pm. You can also rent canoes at the lake here.

Sian Ka'an Biosphere Reserve

SIAN KA'AN means "the place where the sky is born" in Maya, which seems appropriate when you experience the sunrise in this beautiful part of the peninsula. Created by presidential decree in 1986 and made a UNESCO World Heritage Site in 1987, the biosphere reserve is a sparsely populated region sprawling along the coast south of Tulum. One of the largest protected areas in Mexico, it covers 1.3 million acres. Most of the thousand or so permanent residents are fishermen and subsistence farmers gathered in the village of **Punta Allen**. Most visitors enter at the north border, from Tulum, on day trips; only a few hardier travellers press on to Punta Allen and stay for a stretch.

The reserve contains all three of the principal ecosystems found in the Yucatán Peninsula and the Caribbean: the area is approximately one-third **tropical forest**, one-third fresh- and saltwater **marshes** and **mangroves**, and one-third **marine** environment, including a section of the Mesoamerican Barrier Reef. All five species of Mexican **wild cat**, including jaguars, live in the forest, along with spider and howler monkeys, tapir and deer. More than three hundred species of **birds** have been recorded. The Caribbean beaches provide nesting grounds for four endangered **marine turtle** species, while extremely rare West Indian **manatees** have been seen in the inlets. Morelet's and mangrove **crocodiles** lurk in the lagoons.

Punta Allen

Right at the tip of a narrow spit of land, with a lighthouse guarding the northern entrance to the **Bahía de la Ascensión**, the remote fishing village of **PUNTA ALLEN** is not the kind of place you stumble across by accident – it really is the end of the road, with no mobile signal, no ATMs and limited internet access. Bonefish and tarpon in the bay

CLOCKWISE FROM TOP HACIENDA YAXCOPOIL (BOX, P.743); CONVENTO DE SAN ANTONIO DE PADUA (P.747); CHICHÉN ITZÁ (P.749) >

are a draw for active travellers; layabouts come for hammock-lounging. The beach isn't great for swimming, though, as there's lots of sea grass, and, depending on the currents, a bit of rubbish.

Chunyaxché

Hwy-307, 20km south of Tulum • Daily 8am–5pm • M$39; boardwalk M$40; 2hr boat tours around M$350/person • Second-class buses or *colectivos* from Tulum to Chetumal stop on request; it's easier to return to Tulum than to continue south, as *colectivos* are often full

The little-visited ruins of **Chunyaxché** – also known as **Muyil**, for the nearby village – lie on the north border of the Sian Ka'an Biosphere. Despite the size of the site – probably the largest on the Quintana Roo coast – and its proximity to Hwy-307, you're likely to have the place to yourself, as few people travel further south than Tulum.

Muyil was occupied from the pre-Classic period until after the arrival of the Spanish, after which its people probably fell victim to European diseases. Most of the buildings you see today date from the post-Classic period, between 1200 and 1500. The tops of the tallest structures, just visible from the road, rise 17m from the forest floor. There are more than one hundred mounds and temples, none of them completely clear of vegetation, and it's easy to wander around and find buildings buried in the jungle, but climbing them is forbidden.

The centre of the site is connected by a *sacbé* to the small **Muyil lagoon** 500m away. This is joined to the large Chunyaxché lagoon and ultimately to the sea at **Boca Paila** by an amazing **canalized river** – the route used by ancient Maya traders. Wildlife scatters as you follow the boardwalk that leads through the mangroves to the lagoon. At the end of the path, you might find someone offering a boat tour down the canals and past less-explored Maya sites – but it's not a reliable way to enter the reserve.

ARRIVAL AND DEPARTURE	SIAN KA'AN BIOSPHERE RESERVE

By car The road south from Tulum has helped maintain Punta Allen's special quality: it's famously rutted and flooded – and often impassable – in the rainy season, and can still be slow going during the dry months, typically requiring at least 3hr for the 50km drive. Think twice about coming down here in a rental car, especially if there's any chance of rain; even if you can get through, you may be trapped if there's a storm. There are perpetual rumours the road will be paved, but this is unlikely due to reserve regulations. There's an alternative, very bumpy route from the highway south of Chunyaxché (see above) and in to Vigia Chico, where you can catch the launch that meets the

TOURING THE SIAN KA'AN BIOSPHERE

You can enter the biosphere unaccompanied (M$25), on the road south from Tulum's beach hotels, but you will benefit far more from an organized tour, easily arranged in Tulum. One of the best operators is **Community Tours Sian Ka'an** (☎984 871 2202, ⓦsiankaantours.org), part of a non-profit group called Centro Ecológico de Sian Ka'an (CESIAK), which funds its research and educational programmes with a couple of tours. One heads off by day through the ancient Maya canals that crisscross the marshy areas here, while another is a late-afternoon excursion that takes in sunset inside the reserve; both cost around US$80/M$1360. Half-day kayaking and fly-fishing excursions are available too, as are trips looking at the process behind making traditional Maya-style chewing gum. These are great trips around the fringes of the reserve's vast open spaces, with excellent opportunities for bird watching. You can reserve a spot at the office in Tulum (see p.794).

If you really want to go it alone, you can stop and swim at deserted beaches almost anywhere along the way, and there's a visitor centre about 9km inside the reserve where you can rent kayaks, follow nature trails and arrange boat trips around the lagoons (from around M$1500–2000/boat).

In Punta Allen, hotels can arrange fishing tours, as can the local tourism co-op, for around M$3500 for the day (per boat); book at the office signed "tourist info", beside the beach as you enter the village. The co-op can also arrange nature tours of the Sian Ka'an lagoons.

Punta Allen *colectivo*.

By colectivo A *colectivo* (daily at 2pm; around 3hr) runs from next to the taxi syndicate in Tulum (call ☎ 984 879 8040 in the morning to reserve a seat). Another goes from Felipe Carrillo Puerto (see p.802; daily at 6am; around 3hr)

via an even more bone-rattling route to Vigia Chico (also called El Playón), where launches cross the bay to the village. From Punta Allen, the *colectivo* for Tulum leaves at 6am, and the launch for the Carrillo Puerto service goes at 7am (reserve your seat beforehand at Tienda Caamal).

ACCOMMODATION AND EATING

Although there are many enticing stretches of sand along the road from Tulum, biosphere regulations prohibit camping to control erosion – which is not to say it's not done, unfortunately. All hotels in the area have their own restaurants, and independent restaurants are very few. A truck travels the peninsula on Wed and Sat, selling fresh items you can't get in the Punta Allen tiendas; it arrives in the afternoon or evening, depending on road conditions.

★**Boca Paila** Camps Carretera Tulum–Boca Paila, 8.5km inside the biosphere ☎ 984 871 2499, ⓦ siankaan.org. This rustic but comfortable operation, run by Centro Ecológico de Sian Ka'an, is a cluster of "tent cabins" set among the trees in a prime location near the beach. It's rigorously ecofriendly: guests share bathrooms (with composting toilets), but there is hot water, thanks to solar and wind power. The staff are very well informed about the reserve, and the inexpensive restaurant is great at sunset for its view across the jungle. US$80 (M$1360)

Cuzan Guesthouse South end, Punta Allen ☎ 983 834 0358, ⓦ flyfishmx.com. The longest-established place in town, with a wide variety of cabañas and palapas, as well as a restaurant and bar. The focus is firmly on fishing here, and there is a range of packages on offer. US$50 (M$850)

Posada Sirena Northern end, Punta Allen ☎ 984 877 8521, ⓦ casasirena.com. Entering Punta Allen from the north, past the naval station on the right and beached boats on the left, the first and cheapest of the accommodation options is the bohemian *Posada Sirena*, with four cabañas and an owner with tales to tell. US$38 (M$650)

Serenidad Shardon Southern end, Punta Allen ☎ 984 876 1827, ⓦ shardon.com. South of *Cuzan*, *Serenidad Shardon* has the most comfortable beach houses, as well as dorm beds and space for camping (which is permitted in the grounds here) with the option of renting tents and all the gear inside, all with access to showers and a communal kitchen. Dorms M$300, cabañas US$150, camping M$50

Tulum to Chetumal

The road from Tulum to Chetumal skirts the Sian Ka'an Biosphere Reserve and heads into the Maya heartland, past the ruins of Chunyaxché and on to **Felipe Carrillo Puerto**, the capital of Maya resistance. Closer to Chetumal is **Laguna de Bacalar**, as scenic as any Caribbean beach.

Felipe Carrillo Puerto

The slow-paced agricultural town of **FELIPE CARRILLO PUERTO** doesn't look like much on the surface, and few people make a special trip here, except perhaps to catch a *colectivo* to Punta Allen (as an alternative to the one from Tulum). But if you're driving, it's an interesting short stop, being an important cultural and spiritual centre for the modern Maya, following its role as capital of the independent "Zona Maya" during the nineteenth-century Caste Wars (when it was called **Chan Santa Cruz**). In the 1850s, rebels from the north gathered forces here and took guidance and inspiration from a miraculous talking cross that told them to fight on against their oppressors.

You can still visit the **Santuario de la Cruz Parlante**, built on the site of the talking cross (its remnants have been moved to a smaller town nearby). To reach it, turn west off the main street (C 70 or Av Juárez) at the Pemex; the complex is at Calle 62. Back on the plaza, the Franciscan-style **Iglesia de Balam Na** was in fact built by the rebel Maya as a temple – using the slave labour of captured white fighters, no less; it was consecrated as a Catholic church only in 1948.

ARRIVAL AND INFORMATION   FELIPE CARRILLO PUERTO

By bus The station is on the plaza at the corner of C 65 and C 66, a couple of blocks west of the highway. Buses

between Tulum and Chetumal stop here, as do buses from Mérida via Ticul.

By colectivo *Colectivos* from Tulum (1hr) stop on Hwy-307 at C 73, one block north of the main traffic circle, and a few blocks northeast of the plaza. The *colectivo* to Punta Allen (2 daily at 9am & 3pm; 3hr) leaves from the first block east out of the main traffic circle.

Tourist information The small tourist office, on C 70 at C 59 (Mon–Fri 9am–4pm; ☏ 983 267 1452), has information on surrounding Maya villages. Or stop in at Xiimbal Tours, on the plaza at C 65 (☏ 983 834 1073).

ACCOMMODATION AND EATING

Hotel Turquesa Maya On the main road, at C 56 ☏ 983 834 1218, ⚑ hotelturquesamaya.com. If you need to stay a night, this is the best option in town, a solid mid-range hotel that does the simple things well: comfy, well-equipped en suites, a good restaurant, and efficient staff. **US$57 (M$970)**

Costa Maya and Bacalar

The beaches that line the 250km of coast between the southern edge of the Sian Ka'an reserve and the Belizean border may not be as picture-perfect as those in Tulum – they're often shaded with pines, not palms – but they are beautiful in their sheer emptiness. Despite development pressure in the form of a cruise-ship pier, the **COSTA MAYA**, as the area is known, still has a very end-of-the-world feel. The two towns in the area, **Mahahual** and the smaller **Xcalak**, were hit hard by Hurricane Dean in 2007. Mahahual was rebuilt, but Xcalak is still quite battered. Beachcombers typically stay around Mahahual; divers and anglers head south to Xcalak.

Inland from the coast is the surprise respite of **Laguna de Bacalar**, every bit as clear and beautiful as the Caribbean and harbouring its own special wildlife. Like the Costa Maya, its shores are a respite from development up the coast.

Mahahual

Puerto Costa Maya, where the cruise ships dock, is out of sight north of **MAHAHUAL** (60km east of Hwy-307), but its influence is felt on cruise-ship days, when the village springs to life with souvenir stands and jet-ski rentals along the slick seafront promenade, an extremely miniature version of Playa del Carmen. It's a surreal juxtaposition with the rest of the ramshackle town. To avoid any crowds and capture the real Robinson Crusoe vibe, just head down the bumpy dirt beach road south of town.

ARRIVAL AND INFORMATION

MAHAHUAL

By bus Mahahual is linked to Cancún (1 daily at 6.45am, returning at 5pm; 4hr 20min–4hr 35min) and Chetumal (2 daily at 6.30am & 3.30pm, returning at 5.40am & 4.10pm; 2hr 30min) by daily buses. Additional buses may run at weekends and peak Mexican holiday times. Given the limited direct services, consider taking a bus to Limones (2 daily at 6.30am &

DIVING ON THE COSTA MAYA

The **Banco Chinchorro**, declared a biosphere reserve in 2003, lies 35km off the coast. The lush coral atoll, littered with shipwrecks, is the main draw for divers visiting the Costa Maya, and it can be reached from either Mahahual or Xcalak – though not all shops have a licence to visit. Dreamtime Dive Centre, about a kilometre south of town on the coast road (☏ 983 124 0235, ⚑ dreamtimediving.com; single-tank dives from US$55/M$935; full-day trips from US$160/M$2725), is a reliable place with regular trips; Gypsea Divers, on the malecón at Nacional beach club (☏ 983 130 3714, ⚑ gypseadivers.com; as well as diving, from US$65/M$1105, offers snorkelling trips, from US$25/M$425), also comes highly recommended.

In Xcalak, Diving XTC (☏ 983 831 0461, ⚑ xtcdivecenter.com) has a Chinchorro licence. The reefs closer to the shore here are lovely too; it also runs snorkelling (from US$40/M$680) and fishing (from US$249/M$4240) trips, and offers open-water certification courses (from US$529/M$9010).

3.30pm, returning at 7.15am & 5.45pm; 55min), at the junction on Hwy-307, then a taxi to the coast (see below).

By car There's a Pemex station on the main road just outside Mahahual, the only fuel locally. Be prepared for a roadblock and thorough car inspection on the main road leaving Mahahual.

By taxi You can get a taxi from Limones for about M$400–600, depending on your bargaining skills and final destination. In Mahahual, local taxis hang out at the corner of Sierra, just beyond the bus station; it's around M$70–80 to the beach hotels.

Money It's wise to bring plenty of cash: there are at least three ATMs (at V@mos internet, the Pemex station and *Hotel Luna de Plata*), but they are frequently out of order.

ACCOMMODATION

We give addresses for places in town below, though the only street signs are on the malecón; Huachinango is the main street south through town. Virtually everything is here or on the malecón. Many places have higher rates at weekends, when it's a popular escape for Chetumal residents.

Almaplena Eco Resort and Beach Club Coast road south at km 12.5 ☎ 983 137 5070, ⊛ almaplena beachresort.com. At the higher end of lodging options, but done right, with a commitment to the "eco" in its name and sparkling rooms with handmade Argentine furniture and tapestries from Chiapas. To avoid the long haul on the rutted beach road, take the paved inland road toward Xcalak, then cut toward the coast road and turn north. US$115 (M$1960)

Balamku Coast road south at km 5.5 ☎ 983 839 5332, ⊛ balamku.com. Serious ecofriendly outlook, recycling grey water, generating solar power and keeping natural landscaping around its attractive white stucco, thatch-roofed cottages. Wi-fi access and kayaks are included. US$113 (M$1925)

Las Cabañas del Doctor Coast road immediately south of town ☎ 983 832 2102, ⊛ lascabanasdeldoctor .com. Across the road from the beach and in easy walking distance of the centre, this place has economical cabañas (with private bathrooms) and camping spots. Kayaks and snorkelling gear are available to rent. Cabañas US$30 (M$510); camping US$7 (M$120)

Kohunbeach Coast road south at km 7 ☎ 983 700 2820, ⊛ kohunbeach.com. A good budget option with a handful of clean and roomy palapa-roofed cabañas (each with a shady terrace and hammock) so close to the surf you're nearly in the Caribbean. Kayaks and bikes are available to rent. M$700

★**Maya Luna** Coast road south at km 4.5 ☎ 983 836 0905, ⊛ hotelmayaluna.com. Idyllic bungalows right on the beach (no a/c, but breezy enough), with private roof terraces for stargazing, plus a couple of smaller apartments. The restaurant serves Dutch/Indonesian/Mexican fusion food, and rates include an excellent breakfast. Primarily solar-powered. M$1200

★**Mayan Beach Garden** Placer, on the coast 20km north of Mahahual ☎ 983 132 2603, ⊛ mayan beachgarden.com. A real getaway: a beautiful spot on a relatively empty beach, with lovely, well-equipped palapa-roof rooms. Some units have kitchens and a/c. Use of kayaks and snorkel gear is included; excellent meals are available too. US$96 (M$1635)

Posada Pachamama Huachinango between Martillo and Coronado ☎ 983 134 3049, ⊛ posada pachamama.net. Run by friendly Italian owners, *Posada Pachamama* has a selection of very comfortable rooms with a/c (though no real views), a café, and access to the beach club next door. Staff can organize tours and activities. M$1200

EATING

Fernando's 100% Agave Malecón between Sierra and Chema ☎ 983 112 2724. This sand-floored, palapa-roofed place is the best in town for simple Mexican meals (around M$80–180), and just about every visitor and local hangs out at the bar here in the early evening. The "100%" may refer to owner Fernando's hospitality. Tues–Sun noon–9/10pm.

★**Travel in'** Coast road south at km 6 ☎ 983 110 9496, ⊛ travel-in.com.mx. A popular meeting place for the local expat community with great food from an eclectic menu (like shrimp curry and pork *shawarma*; M$40–200), home-made pitta bread and frequent theme nights – tapas on Wed, for example, and regular fondue sessions. There's also an attached guesthouse. Tues–Sat 5.30–9pm (plus Mon Christmas to Easter).

Xcalak

It's hard to believe **Xcalak** was once the largest town in Quintana Roo: today it's a desolate village that still hasn't recovered from being flattened by a hurricane. Forty kilometres south of Mahahual, it can only be reached by a paved but potholed road that runs inland. The main reason to visit is its superb **snorkelling**, **diving** and **fishing**;

it has no real beaches. Phone service remains patchy, so some companies conduct much of their business by email; see the websites ⓦxcalak.info and ⓦxcalak-info.com for more information.

ARRIVAL AND DEPARTURE   XCALAK

By bus Caribe buses depart Chetumal daily (around 6am and 4pm; 5hr). Return journeys from Xcalak go at around 5am and 2pm; schedules are prone to change, so check before setting off. From anywhere on Hwy-307, you can connect with the Caribe bus at the town of Limones (7.30am and 5.30pm), where most first-class services on the main highway should stop.

By car Xcalak is 40km south of Mahahual, but the coast road is impassable. You must take a narrow road, paved but potholed, that turns south off the highway just before you reach Mahahual. The only petrol is in Mahahual.

ACCOMMODATION AND EATING

Costa de Cocos Coast road north of town, no phone, ⓦcostadecocos.com. A long-established, laid-back fly-fishing and diving centre with its own boats and dive instructor, plus good snorkelling off the dock. Accommodation is in old-fashioned wooden cabañas and there's also a popular restaurant. US$90 (M$1535)

Tierra Maya North of town ☏983 839 8012, ⓦtierramaya.net. This welcoming guesthouse is a short drive north of town, and unlike other places around Xcalak, it has a bit of a sandy beach. All the rooms have fans, and most face the water. There's a good restaurant, too. US$90 (M$1535)

Laguna de Bacalar

12

Inland from the Costa Maya and some 35km north of Chetumal, the gorgeous **Laguna de Bacalar** stretches along the east side of Hwy-307. If you haven't checked a map, it's easy to mistake it for the Caribbean, glinting through the trees in flashes of colour from palest aqua to deep indigo. About 45km long and 1km wide, it's the secondlargest lake in Mexico (after Laguna de Chapala, south of Guadalajara), but still attracts only a small number of Mexican tourists and a small expat community with a bent for ecology and yoga. The birdlife here is exceptionally vibrant.

The small town on the edge of the lake, **BACALAR**, was once a key point on the pre-Columbian trade route, and unexcavated **Maya remains** surround the lake. The *Chilam Balam* of Chumayel, one of the Maya's sacred books, mentions it as the first settlement of the Itzá, the tribe that occupied Chichén Itzá.

Museo de San Felipe

Bacalar plaza • Tues–Thurs & Sun 9am–7pm, Fri & Sat 9am–8pm • M$60

Bacalar's juicy history is detailed in this small but interesting **museum**, set in a restored fort built by the Spanish in 1730 for protection against pirates from what's now Belize, and later used as a Maya stronghold in the Caste Wars. The fort is just off the plaza, the centre of Bacalar town, about 1.2km from the highway, where the bus stops.

Balneario Municipal

Lakeshore just downhill from the Fuerte de San Felipe, Bacalar • Daily 10am–6pm • M$10

The liveliest and most scenic of the **swimming** spots on the lake, this town-run "beach" has changing rooms, a reasonably priced restaurant and other facilities. The water is shallow, with a white-sand bottom – easy for kids to frolic in.

Cenote Azul

Southern end of the lake, a few kilometres south of Bacalar on the lakeshore drive • Daily 9am–6pm • Free • A taxi from Bacalar costs about M$50

A distinct attraction from the lake itself, this "bottomless" *cenote* is an enormous inky-blue hole in the ground, with invigorating cold water. Around the edge is a restaurant that features live musicians at weekends, when it's a destination for Mexican families – this is the only time the place is busy with swimmers and dive-bombing teens.

By bus Second-class buses (every 1–3 hours; 30–40min) northbound from Chetumal stop at Av 5, off the plaza; southbound services stop on Av 7, a block uphill. Some first-class buses will drop you off on the highway.
Information ⓦ bacalarmosaico.com is a useful website.

Tours Active Nature (☎ mobile 983 120 5742, ⓦ activenaturebacalar.com), based at *Villas Ecotucan*, does 2hr jungle walks (M$160) or lake trips (in kayaks or Hawaiian-style outrigger canoes; from M$530), as well as multi-day kayak camping trips (from M$1800).

ACCOMMODATION

Casita Carolina In Bacalar, south of the fort on the lakeshore drive ☎ 983 834 2334, ⓦ casitacarolina .com. A pleasant guesthouse with seven rooms as well as accommodation in two parked RV trailers (named "Boler" and "Scamp") in a spacious back garden that stretches almost to the shore. There's a pool, and kayaks are available to rent. Doubles M$400; trailers M$300

Laguna Azul At the northern tip of the lake, mobile ☎ 983 114 7002, ⓦ hotellagunaazul.com. A remote location, but wonderfully welcoming, with a great little restaurant and bar. Choose from sturdy en-suite cabañas, camping spaces or RV sites, and rent a kayak to explore the lake. Cabañas M$500; camping/RV sites (per person) M$75

Laguna Bacalar South of Bacalar, on the lake ☎ 983 834 2206, ⓦ hotellagunabacalar.com. Wonderfully kitsch and comfortable, this old-style Mexican resort is decorated with seashell-encrusted countertops and plaster pillars galore. There's a pool that's also open to anyone dining at the restaurant. A taxi here from the plaza costs about M$50. M$1100

Villas Ecotucan Hwy-307, 5km north of Bacalar ☎ 983 120 5743, ⓦ villasecotucan.info. Large cabañas on attractively landscaped grounds between the lake and acres of untouched forest. You can also visit just for a swim, and to climb the observation tower; there's a small fee to use both. *Colectivos* and second-class buses can drop you on the highway near the entrance. Doubles M$950; camping M$75

EATING AND DRINKING

Gaia Av 3, just off the southeast corner of the plaza, Bacalar ☎ 983 834 2963. *Gaia* is an excellent vegetarian restaurant (dishes M$40–140) serving fine breakfasts and a good-value *comida* – even staunch carnivores will be able to find something to their tastes. Tues–Sun 8am–4pm (but hours can vary).

Orizaba Av 7, one block off the northwest corner of the plaza, Bacalar ☎ 983 834 2069. This popular, low-key place has a loyal local following. It serves up satisfying but inexpensive Mexican classics (M$70–120), as well as a good-value daily set meal. Daily 8am–4pm.

12

Chetumal and around

If you're heading south to Belize, you can't avoid the capital of Quintana Roo, **CHETUMAL**, 1.5km from the border. The neighbouring country's influence is reflected in everything from people's quirky English names to the clapboard houses. Many of these old wooden cottages were wiped out by Hurricane Janet in 1955, however, and Chetumal was rebuilt in concrete. The city is bustling but largely oblivious to tourists, which can be refreshing after the hedonism of the Riviera Maya. But you must have a particular love for border towns to appreciate the place as a destination. It does make a decent one-day stop for resting and restocking, as everything (except car rental) is relatively cheap. Nightlife is pretty tame, but on weekend evenings the plaza by the malecón has food stalls, and residents flock to the bar-restaurants strung along the seafront east of here.

Museo de la Cultura Maya

Niños Héroes at the northern edge of the centre • Tues–Thurs & Sun 9am–7pm, Fri & Sat 9am–6pm • M$62

Architecturally spectacular, this **museum** is in desperate need of refurbishment, as many of its interactive features only work sporadically. Nonetheless, the full-scale replica of the mural-filled room at Bonampak is great, especially if you'll be headed to those Chiapas ruins. An auditorium, meanwhile, hosts film screenings and free modern art displays. On the street in front, the *Alegoría del Mestizaje* sculpture is one of the most striking depictions of the popular theme of the intermingling of Spanish and indigenous cultures, showing modern Mexico born of a conquistador and a Maya woman.

Museo de la Ciudad

Niños Héroes at Chapultepec • Tues–Sun 9am–7pm • M$15

If you have a nostalgic streak, the city museum, with its romantic memorabilia of Chetumal's swashbuckling days, is a better use of your sightseeing time than

CHETUMAL

EATING	
Las Arracheras de Don José	4
El Emporio	5
Marisquería Mi Viejo	2
Los Milagros	3
Pantoja	1

ACCOMMODATION	
Arges	5
Capital Plaza Hotel	2
Los Cocos	4
Juliet	3
Ucúm	1

the Maya museum. It's next to the **Centro Cultural de las Bellas Artes**, a striking 1936 neo-Maya-style compound, where there's usually live music on weekend evenings.

Maqueta Payo Obispo

C 22 de Enero near Av Reforma • Tues–Sat 9am–3pm, Sun 9am–2pm • Free

A Caribbean house contains this scale model of Chetumal as it looked in the 1920s, hand-carved by a resident with the perfectly *chetumaleño* name of Luís Reinhardt McLiberty. The small adjacent **museum** tells the story of the lighthouse barge *Chetumal*, with which the Mexican army helped establish the town and the country's border with British Honduras.

ARRIVAL AND DEPARTURE · CHETUMAL

By plane The airport, with services to Mexico City (1 or 2 daily with Interjet; 1hr 50min), is 2km west of town.

By bus Chetumal's main bus station is on the north side of town, a short taxi ride (around M$30) from the centre. A bus ticket office in town, on Belice at Colón, handles long-haul services. A few second-class buses, including Mayab services to Cancún, actually depart from the dusty yard adjacent to this office – it's worth checking here for service before heading out to the main station.

Destinations Cancún (every 30min; 5hr 20min–6hr 25min), most via Tulum (3hr 5min–3hr 50min) and Playa del Carmen (4hr 10min–5hr); Escárcega (8 daily; 4hr) via Xpujil (2hr), for the Río Bec; Mahahual (2 daily at 5.40am, 6am, 4pm & 4.10pm, with additional services in Aug; 2hr 30min), some services continuing to Xcalak (4hr 30min); Mérida (4 daily first class at 7.30am, 1.30pm, 5pm & 11.30pm; 5hr 30min–6hr 5min) and second-class Clase Europea and Mayab (10 daily; 6hr 30min); San Cristóbal de las Casas (7 daily; 11hr 55min–12hr 40min), some via Palenque (7hr); Villahermosa (3 daily at 1.05am, 10.40pm & 11.15pm; 8hr 15min–8hr 50min).

By car Continental (☎983 832 2411, ⓦcontinentalcar .com.mx), in the lobby of the *Capital Plaza Hotel* (see p.808), or Europcar, Niños Héroes 129, opposite *Los Cocos* (☎983 833 9959), and at the airport (☎983 107 9008, ⓦeuropcar.com.mx).

By combi The Terminal de Combis on Hidalgo at Primo de Verdad. Services include Bacalar (every 30min; 45min) and Nicolás Bravo (4 daily; 1hr 15min), for the nearest Río Bec sites.

TO BELIZE

Entry requirements Citizens of the UK, US, Canada, Australia and New Zealand do not need a visa to enter Belize. If you are planning to return to Mexico, make sure to keep your tourist card, or you will have to purchase another.

By bus Buses run frequently between Chetumal and Corozal (1hr), the closest town across the border. You must get off the bus and walk over the bridge at Subteniente López, 8km west of Chetumal. The cheapest, very rattle-trap buses leave from the mercado nuevo, 1km north of the centre on Calzada Veracruz (roughly 4am–5pm; more frequently in the morning). A few of these continue to Orange Walk (2hr 30min) and Belize City (5hr). First-class services – a bit more comfortable – run by Linea Dorada, San Juan and Premier Lines depart from the main bus station (5 daily; 3hr to Belize City), as do at least two buses a day to Flores in Guatemala (for Tikal, via Belize), one or more in the early morning (6am) and another at lunch time (12.45pm).

By water taxi From the *Muelle Fiscal* on the downtown waterfront, San Pedro Water Taxi (☎+501 226 2194 in Belize, ⓦsanpedrowatertaxi.com) runs services (daily 3pm) to San Pedro on Ambergris Caye (US$60/M$1020) and Caye Caulker (US$65/M$1105), as does San Pedro Belize Express (☎983 839 2324, ⓦbelizewatertaxi.com; 3–4 weekly at 3.30pm; full schedule online; US$55/M$935). Buy tickets at the dock, from travel agents in town or via the companies' websites.

By car Cars rented in Mexico cannot generally be driven into Belize.

INFORMATION AND TOURS

Tourist information The main tourist office, on 5 de Mayo at Carmen Ochoa de Merino (Mon–Fri 9am–5pm; ☎983 832 2031), is friendly enough but not particularly knowledgeable. There are also information kiosks at the bus station and on the malecón at Hidalgo.

ACCOMMODATION

Arges Lázaro Cardenas 212, between Niños Héroes and Juárez ☎983 832 9525, ⓦhotelarges.com. The Lebanese-Yucatecan owner of this place is determined to make this blocky, Soviet-inspired hotel more appealing, with big, clean rooms at reasonable prices, a pool and free parking. __M$550__

12

Capital Plaza Hotel Niños Héroes 171 ☎01 800 1717, ⓦcapitalplaza.mx. A centrally located, mid-range hotel, *Capital Plaza* has comfortable (if bland) en suites, plus numerous facilities including a restaurant, a swimming pool, a gym, car rental (Continental; see p.807) and an in-house travel agency. **M$1100**

Los Cocos Niños Héroes 134 ☎01 800 719 5840, ⓦhotelloscocos.com.mx. The pick of the downtown deluxe hotels with large, comfortable rooms (the "premier" category is worth the upgrade; M$1100), a pool and a sprawling terrace bar and restaurant. Also has some very pleasant suites. **M$800**

Juliet Efraín Aguilar 171 ☎983 129 1871, ⓦhoteljulietchetumal.com. On a pedestrian walkway just off Niños Héroes, close to the old market, *Hotel Juliet* has clean all-white rooms with TVs, and fans or a/c. Bland, but comfortable enough. **M$550**

Ucúm Gandhi 167 ☎983 832 0711, ⓦhotel ucumchetumal.com. One of the better deals in town, though it looks unpromising from the motel-like front section (where a few bargain rooms are just M$250, but dim and noisy). Rooms in the back building, however, by the huge pool, are brighter and quieter, and have a choice of a/c or fan. **M$400**

EATING

The intersection of Niños Héroes and Obregón has the highest concentration of **restaurants**, while the stalls at the "old market", south of the Museo de la Cultura Maya, have good, inexpensive lunches.

Las Arracheras de Don José Blv Bahía, between Cozumel and Josefa Ortíz ☎983 832 8895, ⓦfacebook.com/ArracherasDonJose. The speciality of this sprawling terrace restaurant, very popular on weekend nights, is meat tacos of every kind (fill up for around M$120), served with an array of fresh salsas. You can also get good-value steaks, stuffed baked potatoes and pastas. Daily 11am–10pm.

El Emporio Merino, just east of Reforma ☎983 832 0601. An excellent Uruguayan restaurant in a historic wooden house – steaks (M$200 plus) are served with lashings of garlicky *chimichurri*, the empanadas make a tasty starter (for those with big appetites), and there's a good selection of South American wines. Follow the smell of grilled meat. Daily 1–11.30pm.

Marisquería Mi Viejo Av Belice 166 ☎983 833 1737.

This *bar familiar*, with a crooner onstage backed by a tired keyboard player, may not seem promising at first glance. But the food (M$110–220) is a lot livelier: try the *sopa de mariscos*, which brims with purple squid tentacles and shrimp, or the *ceviche*. Daily 11am–5pm.

Los Milagros Zaragoza, between Niños Héroes and 5 de Mayo ☎983 832 4433. Enjoy a tasty, inexpensive breakfast (M$30–70) at this little pavement café, busy day and night, with a real air of a locals-in-the-know hangout. Daily Mon–Sat 8am–9pm, Sun 8am–1pm.

Pantoja Gandhi at Av 16 de Septiembre ☎983 832 3958. With a good comida corrida and hearty dishes like *mondongo* (tripe), *chilaquiles* and hefty tortas, this is a popular spot for a morning or midday meal (M$40–80). Mon–Sat 8am–2pm.

DIRECTORY

Banks and exchange Banks with ATMs cluster at the junction of Juárez and Obregón.

Consulates Belize, Genova 369 (Mon–Fri 9am–noon; ☎983 285 3511).

Internet Plenty of options, including Arba, with branches in the old market and opposite, on Aguilar.

Post office Plutarco Elias calles at 5 de Mayo (Mon–Fri 8am–6pm, Sat & Sun 9am–12.30pm).

Calderitas

Frequent buses depart Chetumal from Cristóbal Colón west of Niños Héroes, behind the Museo de la Cultura Maya, but do not go on to Oxtankah

At weekends, Chetumal descends en masse on the small seaside resort of **Calderitas**, just 6km north around the bay. You can hire a boat at *El Rincón de las Tortugas* bar (☎983 834 4220) for various day outings: to the beaches on the nearby empty island of Tamalcab (around M$500 for 6–8 people); a tour around the bay to look for manatees (around M$1800; 3hr); or to several other nature spots.

Oxtankah

7km north of Calderitas • Daily 8am–5pm • M$47 • Taxi from Chetumal, about M$300 with waiting time

Established in the Classic period (200–600 AD), the ancient city of **Oxtankah** is more interesting for its recent history. It's allegedly the site of the first *mestizaje*, where shipwrecked conquistador Gonzalo Guerrero married into a Maya family and fathered mixed-race children – the origin story of modern Yucatán, and Mexico. What remains are the ruins of several buildings around two squares, with an architectural style similar to that of the Petén region in Guatemala, and a chapel built by the Spanish. It's a peaceful wooded place, with trees and other flora neatly labelled.

Río Bec sites

West of Chetumal, along the border with Guatemala, lie the little-visited but dramatic **RÍO BEC** sites, many tucked in dense jungle that harbours diverse birds and beasts, especially in the Calakmul Biosphere Reserve, around the ruins of the same name. The area was once heavily populated by lowland Maya, and linked with the site of Tikal in Guatemala. The largest ruins here, with their long, low buildings, dramatic towers (really elongated, stylized pyramids) and intricate carvings, are easily as impressive as Chichén Itzá, heightened by the jungle setting. The area is accessible either from Campeche or from Chetumal, and you'll need to have a car or hire a taxi to see many of these sites – but this means you'll see few other tourists.

The largest town in the area is **Francisco Escárcega** (usually just called Escárcega), far to the west in Campeche state. It's a major bus hub, but somewhat dusty and unwelcoming, so most visitors to the sites use the much smaller village of **Xpujil**, on the border of Campeche and Quintana Roo, as a base for visiting the area. It's a one-street town straddling Hwy-186, with basic hotels and restaurants, as well as taxi drivers prepared to shuttle visitors around. If you're in your own car, note that there's a gas station just east of town.

12

Xpujil

Hwy-186 in Xpujil, 250m west of the bus station • Daily 8am–5pm • M$47

The most accessible of the Río Bec sites, **Xpuhil** is also the smallest. Dating from between 500 and 750 AD, it is in excellent condition, and it has three striking ersatz pyramids, which have almost vertical and purely decorative stairways.

VISITING THE RÍO BEC SITES

The typical strategy for visiting this string of ruins is to spend the night in **Xpujil**, hire an early-morning taxi to visit **Calakmul** and **Balamkú**, and return to Xpujil to see the ruins in town in the late afternoon. You can then take a late bus to Chetumal or Campeche. If you have the time, though, it will be a more rewarding and relaxing visit if you take at least two days and allow yourself to see more. Renting a car in Campeche or Chetumal affords the most flexibility, but taking **taxis** can cost about the same amount, leaving you the option of continuing on a loop route rather than returning your car.

Using Xpujil as a base, taxis can be arranged through the hotels, though you'll usually get a slightly cheaper rate if you deal directly with the drivers gathered at the crossroads in town. Rates vary depending on both the number of people and your bargaining skills, but reckon on paying around M$900–1600 to go to Calakmul and Balamkú or to Kohunlich and Dzibanché, half that for Chicanná, Becán and Xpujil, including waiting time.

If you're not in a hurry, it's also possible to start off sightseeing from Chetumal by taking a *combi* to the town of **Nicolás Bravo**, hiring a taxi from there to visit Dzibanché and Kohunlich, and then flagging down a second-class bus to Xpujil.

Alternatively, there are organized **tours** to Calakmul from Campeche (see p.722); if your Spanish is up to it, go with the experienced (but not very bilingual) team at Servidores Turísticos de Calakmul (☎983 871 6064), which runs the unofficial tourist office in Xpujil and a campsite in the biosphere reserve. Tours may costs more, but a good guide can really make the area come alive, as many of the sites have little or no signage.

Becán

Off Hwy-186, 6km west of Xpujil then 500m north • Daily 8am–5pm • M$52

Unique among Maya sites, the city of **Becán** is entirely surrounded by a dry moat, 16m wide and 5m deep. Along with the wall on its edge, it forms one of the oldest known defensive systems in Mexico. This has led some to believe that Becán, rather than present-day Flores in Guatemala, was the site of Tayasal, an early capital of the Itzá, who later ruled at Chichén Itzá. First occupied in 600 BC, Becán reached its peak between 600 and 1000 AD. Unlike the sites in northern Yucatán, many of the buildings here seem to have been residential rather than ceremonial. In fact, the tightly packed structures – with rooms stacked up and linked by internal staircases – create a strong sense of urbanism, akin to modern apartment blocks.

Chicanná

Off Hwy-186, 2km west of Becán and just south • Daily 8am–5pm • M$47

The buildings at **Chicanná** are the precursors of the Chenes style, with their elaborate decoration and repetitive masks of Chac. The gaping, square-carved doorway at the impressive Structure II gives the site its name ("House of the Serpent Mouth"). The rest of the building is covered in smaller masks of hook-nosed Chac, made up of intricately carved mosaic pieces of limestone, many still painted with red stucco, in a style that was developed in this area and the adjacent Chenes cities, then picked up and refined by later builders in the Puuc region to the north.

Balamkú

Off Hwy-186, 5km west of the turn-off to Calakmul • Daily 8am–5pm • M$39

This main draw at **Balamkú** is the elaborate, beautifully preserved 17m-long stucco frieze. It's inside the site's central palace; ask the caretaker to let you in. The embellished wall, crawling with toads, crocodiles and jaguars, seems to undulate in the dim light, and the rolling eyes of the red-painted monster masks, though smaller than those at Kohunlich (see opposite), are perhaps more alarming here.

Hormiguero

22km south of Xpujil • Daily 8am–5pm • Free • Taxi about M$250–300 round trip with waiting time

The small site of **Hormiguero** is accessible only by a bumpy, forty-minute ride, and a visit takes the same amount of time. But the decoration and the wild jungle setting make it a particularly transporting one. Excellently preserved carved monster mouths from the Late Classic era adorn the two excavated buildings, which are topped with impossibly steep towers. Keep your eyes on the forest floor here as you explore – Hormiguero has its name ("anthill") for good reason.

Río Bec

Off Hwy-186, 10km east of Xpujil and south of the *ejido* of 20 de Noviembre

The scattered buildings of the city of **Río Bec** are usually closed to visitors, though some years it opens for a few months in the spring. If you do visit, you will see the most extreme example of the Río Bec false-pyramid style: as at Xpujil, the "steps" on the twin towers were never meant to be climbed – the risers actually angle outward. Ask at the tourist office in Xpujil about arranging an expedition on horseback.

12

Calakmul

Off Hwy-186, down a signposted road midway between Escárcega and Xpujil · Daily 8am–5pm · M$52, plus M$54 per person for the reserve

The ruined Maya city of **Calakmul** is one of the best places for contemplating the culture's architectural legacy. The complex is only partially restored and a long drive south of Hwy-186, but its location in the heart of the jungle and its sheer size are awe-inspiring. Probably the biggest archeological area in Mesoamerica, Calakmul has nearly seven thousand buildings in the central area alone and more steles and pyramids than any other site; the great pyramid here is the largest Maya construction in existence, with a base covering almost five acres.

The view of the rainforest from the top is stunning, and on a clear day you can even glimpse the tip of the Danta pyramid at El Mirador in Guatemala. Arrive early (the gate to the biosphere on Hwy-186 opens at 7am) to look for **wildlife** such as wild turkeys, peccaries, toucans and jaguars. Even if you don't spot anything, you'll likely hear booming howler monkeys and raucous frogs. Plan to spend about four hours exploring the site – longer if you're a Maya-phile. Bring snacks and water, as there's no vending at the ruins.

Brief history

During the Classic period, the city had a population of about two hundred thousand and was the regional capital. A *sacbé* (Maya road) running between Calakmul and El Mirador (another leads on to Tikal) confirms that these cities were in regular communication. Calakmul reached its zenith between 500 and 850 AD but, along with most other cities in the area, it was abandoned by about 900 AD. Excavations begun in the 1980s have so far uncovered only a fraction of the buildings, the rest being earthen mounds. Some of Calakmul's treasures are on display in the archeological museum at Campeche (see p.721), including two hauntingly beautiful jade masks. Another mask was found in a tomb in the main pyramid in 1998.

Kohunlich

Off Hwy-186, about 60km west of Chetumal, then 9km south from the village of Francisco Villa · Daily 8am–5pm · M$62

If you stop for only one ancient site in the Río Bec area, make it **Kohunlich**. The ruins, seldom visited by anyone other than enormous butterflies and wild parrots, are beautifully situated, peering out above the treetops. The buildings date from the late pre-Classic to the Classic periods (100–900 AD) and the majority are in the Río Bec architectural style. Foliage has reclaimed most of them, except for the **Templo de los Mascarones**, which is named after the five 2m-high stucco masks that decorate its facade. Disturbing enough now, these wide-eyed, open-mouthed images of the sun god, Kinich Ahau, once stared out from a background of smooth, bright-red-painted stucco. Also look for an elite residential area called the **27 Escalones**, worth the detour to see the great views over the jungle canopy from the cliff edge on which it is built (prime real estate was just as valuable 1400 years ago, it seems).

Kinichná and Dzibanché

North off Hwy-186 81km west of Chetumal · Daily 8am–5pm · M$52

Set in a drier area sparsely populated with trees, these two neighbouring ruins are on a smaller scale than Kohunlich but still merit a visit. **Kinichná**'s hulking pyramid, built in metre-high stones layer upon layer by successive leaders, barely clears the trees, but you can look over the surrounding terrain (and spot a glimpse of the rather squat **Dzibanché**), now broken into farmland.

ARRIVAL AND DEPARTURE

BY BUS

XPUJIL

From the bus stop in Xpujil, ADO (2 daily) and Mayab (4 daily) buses run to Chetumal, plus at least four more second-class services, a couple of which continue all the way to Cancún. To Escárcega, there are around fourteen departures, many continuing to Villahermosa. Second-class buses run north out of town, past the Chenes sites towards Hopelchén; most continue to Campeche, though some head to Mérida via the Ruta Puuc.

ESCÁRCEGA

The ADO first-class bus station is at the west end of town, at

RÍO BEC SITES

the junction of Hwy-261 and Hwy-186; from there, it's 1.5km to the east end and the Sur second-class bus station, which you might use for more frequent services to Xpujil (you can buy tickets for all services at ADO).

Destinations from ADO Campeche (11 daily; 1hr 50min–2hr 25min); Chetumal (11 daily; 3hr 35min–4hr 30min); Mérida (7 daily; 4hr 40min); Palenque (6 daily; 2hr 50min–3hr 25min); San Cristóbal de las Casas (5 daily; 8hr 5min–11hr); Xpujil (4 daily at 12.16am, 4.20pm, 8.10pm & 10.46pm; 2hr 15min–2hr 30min).

BY CAR

If you're driving from Mérida or Campeche, the back route

FIESTAS IN THE YUCATÁN

A highlight of village festivals in the area is the massive bullrings, elaborate hand-built structures made entirely of saplings. Expect plenty of fireworks and *jaranas*, one of the traditional Maya dances. Carnaval, the week before Lent, is colourfully celebrated in Mérida and on Cozumel and Isla Mujeres. For events in smaller villages, ask at the Yucatán state tourism office in Mérida, which maintains a full list, or check the weekly events bulletin at ⓦ yucatanliving.com, which often mentions nearby fiestas.

Fiesta de los Tres Reyes (Jan 1–6). In the cattle town of Tizimín (Yucatán); expect steak.
Día de la Candelaria (Feb 2). Candlemas: candlelight processions at Tecoh and Kantunil (Yucatán). The week prior is a fiesta in Valladolid (Yucatán).
Equinox (March 21). Huge gathering for the serpent shadow at Chichén Itzá.
Semana Santa (Holy Week, beginning Palm Sunday, variable March–April). Passion plays in Mérida, Acanceh and Maní (Yucatán).
Fiestas de Santa Cruz (end of April). Two-week fair in Cozumel's El Cedral (Quintana Roo), ending on or near May 3.
Fiesta de la Cruz Parlante (May 12–18). Chancah Veracruz (Quintana Roo), near Felipe Carrillo Puerto, celebrates the Talking Cross of the Caste Wars.
Feria del Jipi (May 20). In Becal (Campeche), celebration of the Panama hat.
Torneo de Pesca (last weekend in May). Fishing tournament and party in Puerto Morelos.
Día de la Chispa (June 4). In Valladolid (Yucatán), re-enactment of the battle that sparked the 1910 Revolution.
Fiesta de San Pedro y San Pablo (June 26–30). On Cozumel and in Panaba (Yucatán).
Fiesta de Nuestra Señora del Carmen (July 15–30). Ciudad del Carmen (Campeche) and Motul (Yucatán).
Chac ceremony (dates variable). In Edzná (Yucatán), to encourage the spring rains.
Feria (Aug 10–16). Town celebration in Oxcutzcab (Yucatán).
Feria de San Román (Sept 14–30). Campeche's city festival.
Gremios (mid-Sept to mid-Oct). Pilgrimages and processions to Mérida's main church.
Equinox (Sept 21). Another serpent spectacle at Chichén Itzá (see March).
Día de San Miguel (Sept 29). Cozumel's main town festival.
El Cristo de Sitilpech (Oct 18–28). The miraculous Black Christ is paraded from Sitilpech (Yucatán) to neighbouring Izamal, where there's ten days of celebration.
Feria del Estado de Yucatán (first three weeks of Nov). At fairgrounds south of Mérida.
Feria de Motul (Nov 4–11). Festival in Motul (Yucatán) with bullfights.
Día de la Inmaculada Concepcíon (Dec 8). Widely celebrated, especially in Izamal, where crowds gather to sing the entire night before.
Día de la Virgen de Guadalupe (Dec 12). Celebrated everywhere; roads are filled in the days prior with church groups running relays.
Christmas Fiesta (Dec 25–Jan 6). In Temax (Yucatán), featuring the procession of Las Pastorelas, in which images of the Holy Family are carried from house to house.

via Hopelchén and Hwy-269, arriving in Xpujil from the north, is a good road, narrow but usually empty. Expect a police checkpoint at the border between Yucatán and Campeche states.

INFORMATION AND TOURS

Tourist information At the east end of Xpujil, about 2km from the crossroads, ecotourism group Servidores Turísticos Calakmul runs an unofficial info office (Tues–Sun 9am–1pm & 4–7.30pm; ☎983 871 6064, ⓦecoturismocalakmul.com). The group can also arrange day tours and ecotourism activities, such as camping and biking, though staff primarily speak Spanish.

ACCOMMODATION AND EATING

XPUJIL

Calakmul About 500m west of the bus station, Xpujil ☎983 871 6029. Of the two main places to stay in Xpujil (the other is the *Mirador Maya*, another 500m west), this one is marginally preferable, with tidy cabins with a/c and TVs. The perfectly functional restaurant stays open a little later than most things in town. M$590

CHICANNÁ

Chicanná Ecovillage Resort Hwy-186, across the highway from the Chicanná site ☎981 811 9192, ⓦchicannaecovillageresort.com. The most comfortable rooms (in cute thatched-roof bungalows) in the area – though the "eco" label isn't really accurate. If you're breaking a sweat sightseeing, you can also stop by here for a drink at the restaurant and a dip in the pool. US$77 (M$1310)

CALAKMUL

Rio Bec Dreams Hwy-186 km 142, west of Calakmul turn ⓦriobecdreams.com. A smaller lodging option, as well as a great travellers' resource: the owners are archeology buffs who can advise on the latest site openings and arrange good tours. The restaurant, with its varied (non-Mexican) menu, is open to all. Rooms include en-suite cabañas (quieter, as they're away from the road) or wood "jungalows" on stilts with shared toilets. Cabañas M$1250; jungalows M$1050

Yaax' Che Calakmul reserve road km 7 ☎983 871 6064, ⓦecoturismocalakmul.com. Servidores Turísticos Calakmul, an excellent ecotourism organization, maintains this campsite with basic cabañas and space for tents. It also rents gear and will point you to nature trails within the reserve. You can try stopping in for a meal, but as the kitchen uses all local products, it may not have provisions on hand in slow seasons. Cabañas M$500; camping M$200

KOHUNLICH

Explorean Km 6.5, a 40min drive from Chetumal ☎01 443 310 8137 (US), ⓦfiestamericana.com/explorean. The most luxurious hotel in the region, by some distance, *Explorean* provides accommodation in delightful bungalows, plus a well-equipped spa and a lovely pool. A wide range of tours is on offer, and rates are all-inclusive. US$366 (M$6235)

ESCÁRCEGA

Hotel Real Primaveras C 55 s/n ☎982 824 0810, ⓦrealprimaveras.com. If you're stuck overnight in Escárcega, this is a solid mid-range choice. All the en suites here are bright and well equipped (a/c, TVs, etc), and there's a café and small terrace. M$690

La Teja Southwest across the traffic circle from the ADO station. For a bite to eat in Escárcega, this is one of the nicer options, and convenient for the bus station. All the usual Mexican and Yucatecan dishes (from M$40) are on offer, with fresh juices too. Daily 24hr.

12

PANCHO VILLA, EMILIANO ZAPATA AND
THE REVOLUTIONARIES, 1915

Contexts

History

The modern, independent nation of Mexico has existed since 1821, yet its people are descended from civilizations that date back thousands of years. Our knowledge of these peoples is largely taken from histories recorded long after the events or from archeological conjecture, as the Spanish did their best to erase all traces of the extraordinary societies that preceded them.

Early civilizations

The first signs of settled habitation in Mexico – the cultivation of corn, followed by the emergence of crude pottery, stone tools and even some trade – come from the **Archaic** period, around 8000 to 2000 BC. The first established civilization did not appear until the **pre-Classic** or **Formative** era (2000 BC to 250 AD) with the rise of the Olmecs.

The Olmecs (1500–400 BC)

Still the least understood of all the ancient societies, the **Olmecs** thrived in the low-lying coastal jungles of Tabasco and Veracruz. Many of their political, cultural, artistic and architectural innovations can be observed in later Mesoamerican cultures (including **ritual blood-letting** and the **ball game**, and possibly even writing and the Long Count calendar). What you see of them in the museums today is a magnificent artistic style, exemplified in their sculpture and famous colossal basalt heads. These, with their puzzling "baby-faced" features, were carved from monolithic blocks and somehow transported over 90km from the quarries to their final settings – proof in itself of a hierarchical society commanding a sizeable workforce. By the end of the pre-Classic period, the Olmec civilization was already in decline – **La Venta**, the most important cultural centre, seems to have been abandoned around 400 BC, and the other towns followed over the next few hundred years.

Classic civilizations

As the Olmec weakened, new civilizations grew in strength and numbers, establishing cities throughout central Mexico. These sites, such as **Monte Albán** (500 BC–750 AD) near Oaxaca, were obviously influenced by the earlier Olmec. To the north, in the Valley of México, **Tlatilco** (1200–200 BC) hoarded Olmec objects, suggesting significant contact with Monte Albán – at least through trade. Meanwhile, there were hints of bigger things to come: **Cuicuilco** (700 BC–150 AD, now in the capital's suburbs) was an important city until it was buried by a volcanic eruption around the beginning of the first century AD; at the same time, the first major buildings of the city of Teotihuacán were being constructed.

8000–2000 BC	2000 BC–250 AD	250–900 AD
Archaic period.	Pre-Classic period. Rise and dominance of the Olmecs.	Classic period. Teotihuacán dominates central Mexico. Maya cities flourish in the highlands of Guatemala and Honduras, as well as the Mexican Yucatán.

Teotihuacán (100 BC–600 AD)

Teotihuacán, the first truly urban Mesoamerican society, dominated central Mexico at the beginning of the **Classic** period (250–900 AD). Its architectural and religious influences reached as far south as the Maya heartland of Guatemala. Even today, the ruins of the city, with the great Pyramids of the Sun and Moon, are an impressive testimony to the civilization's strength. Very little is known about Teotihuacán (even the name was coined later by the Aztecs – it means "the place where men became gods"), but what is certain is that the city's period of dominance ended between 500 and 600 AD, and that within a century it had been abandoned altogether. Mysteriously, several societies throughout Mesoamerica, particularly the Maya, seem to have been disrupted at around the same time.

Other important centres grew up on the Gulf coast at **El Tajín** (600–1200 AD), part of the **Classic Veracruz culture**, and in the **Zapotec** areas around Monte Albán – but were followed by rapid decline. There are numerous theories to account for this, but none is entirely convincing, although the fall of Teotihuacán must have affected its trading partners throughout Mexico. In all likelihood, once started, the disasters – probably provoked by some sort of agricultural failure or ecological disaster – led to a loss of faith in rulers and perhaps even rebellion, and had a knock-on effect.

The Maya

The best known and most romanticized of the classic civilizations is the **Maya**, in part because of the wealth of architectural remains and carvings they left behind in ancient cities throughout modern Mexico, Guatemala and Honduras. The great Maya centres to the south survived longer than Teotihuacán, but by around 800 AD had also been abandoned in what has become one of history's greatest unsolved mysteries. In the Yucatán the Maya fared rather better, their cities revived from about 900 by an injection of ideas from central Mexico and, archeologists now propose, new leaders from the south. The famous structures at **Chichén Itzá** mostly date from this later phase, around 900 to 1100 AD.

THE WORLD TREE – PRE-COLUMBIAN BELIEF

The great **Mesoamerican civilizations** comprised some of the purest theocracies the world has known. Every aspect of life was a part of a cosmic interplay between the material world and the dreamlike spirit world, home to a pantheon of gods and the souls of dead ancestors. The priests and kings who governed Mesoamerica had privileged access to this realm, communicating with its denizens while in a state of trance, predicting the effect of the spiritual on the material from the motion of the stars, and maintaining the balance between the two worlds, thus avoiding misfortune or disaster. Every part of life was sacred, as were the days of the week and the cardinal points with their associated deities and spiritual properties. Every event, from the planting of crops to the waging of war, had to occur at the correct spiritual time.

One stele at the Olmec site of La Venta depicts what is thought to be the first representation of the **World Tree**, a symbol of the "axis mundi" at the centre of the Mesoamerican universe: its roots in the earth, its branches in the heavens, linking the underworld with the earth and sky. In contemporary Mexico, Day of the Dead celebrations have their roots in this shamanic conception of the universe, as do the rituals of modern Mexican witchcraft. The best modern examples, though, are the belief systems of the tribes of northern Mexico, such as the Yaqui (whose shamanic traditions have been immortalized by Carlos Castaneda) or the Huichol.

900–1520 AD	1325	1519	1521
Post-Classic period. Toltecs make their capital at Tula.	Foundation of Aztec capital of Tenochtitlán.	Cortés lands in present-day Veracruz.	Tenochtitlán falls to the Spanish and their Tlaxcalan allies; Cortés personally tortures and kills Cuauhtémoc, the last emperor, in 1525.

THE LONG COUNT CALENDAR

The Mesoamericans believed that the relationship between the spirit and material worlds was recorded in the stars. For both the Maya and Aztecs, the stars were embodiments of gods and the constellations re-enactments of cosmic events. This preoccupation led to the invention of the **calendar**, probably by the Zapotecs of Monte Albán around 600 BC. By the time of the Classic Maya (250–900 AD), a 260-day calendar had become the fundamental map of the relationship between the spirit and material worlds, and the highest tool of prediction and divination outside the trance state itself. Every number and day had its own significance; each of the twenty day names was connected with a specific god and a particular direction, passing in a continuous anticlockwise path from one day to the next until a cycle of time was completed. This calendar was used alongside a 365-day calendar, roughly matching the solar year, but lacking the leap days necessary to give it real accuracy. This was divided into eighteen groups of twenty days plus an unlucky additional five days. Each twenty-day grouping and each solar year also had a supernatural patron. When the two calendars were set in motion and were running concurrently, it took exactly 52 years for the cycle to repeat. In addition to these two calendars, the pre-Classic Maya developed what is known as the **Long Count**, recording the total number of days elapsed since a mythological date when the first great cycle began (August 11, 3114 BC, to be exact). For Mesoamerican civilizations, the ending of one cycle and the beginning of another heralded apocalypse and, afterwards, a new age and a reassertion of the ordered world from the disordered and demonic; one symbol of this new age was the construction of new temples over the old every 52 years. The Maya Long Count ended on **December 23, 2012**; many believed that this date would herald the end of the world.

The post-Classic era and the Toltecs

The start of the **post-Classic** era (900–1520 AD) saw the beginning of a series of invasions from the north that must have exacerbated any existing problems. Wandering tribes would arrive in the fertile Valley of México, like what they saw, build a city adopting many of the styles and religions of their predecessors in the area, enjoy a brief period of dominance and be subdued in turn by a new wave of invaders, or **Chichimeca**. All such marauding tribes were known as Chichimea, which implies barbarian (even if many of them were at least semi-civilized before they arrived), and all claimed to have set out on their journeys from the legendary seven caves of Chicomoztoc. Of the many people who founded cities in the valley in this bellicose era, two names stand out – the Toltecs and the Aztecs.

The **Toltec** people, who dominated the central valleys around 950–1150 AD, were among the first to arrive – indeed, some say that it was a direct attack by them that destroyed Teotihuacán. Later, they assumed a mythical significance for the Aztecs, who regarded them as the founders of every art and science and claimed direct descent from Toltec blood. In fact, it appears that the Toltecs borrowed most of their ideas from Teotihuacán.

Nevertheless, there were developments under the Toltecs. In particular, the cult of **Quetzalcoatl** assumed new importance: at **Tula**, the Toltec capital, the god is depicted everywhere, perhaps embodied as a king or dynasty of kings, and it was from here that he was driven out by the evil god Texcatlipoca. (The prediction of his return was later to have fatal consequences for the Aztecs.) The structure of Toltec society was at least as militaristic as it was religious, and human sacrifice was practised on a far larger scale than had previously been recorded.

1524	1546	1550–90	1551–1687	1683
First Franciscan monks arrive.	The Spanish discover silver in the Zacatecas region.	Chichimeca War.	Spanish conquest of Yucatán.	Jesuit priest Eusebio Kino founds Misión San Bruno in Baja California.

The Aztecs (1325–1521 AD)

When the **Aztecs** arrived in central Mexico around the end of the twelfth century they found numerous small city-states, with none in a position of dominance. They spent some years scavenging and raiding until about 1325 – when legend has it that they saw the prophesied sign (an eagle perched on a cactus devouring a snake) telling them to build their own city.

The new city, **Tenochtitlán**, was to become the heart of the most formidable of all Mexican empires, but its birth was not easy. The chosen setting, an island in a lake (now Mexico City), was hardly promising, and the city was at first a subject of its neighbours. The Aztecs overcame the lack of arable land by growing crops on floating reed islands that they fashioned in the lake. This agricultural success led to self-sufficiency and a burgeoning population. They became the most powerful civilization in the valley, and around 1428 formed the so-called Triple Alliance with neighbouring Texcoco and Tlacopán, establishing the **Aztec empire**. The empire's achievements were remarkable – in less than a hundred years the Aztecs came to control and to demand labour tribute and taxes from the whole of central and southern Mexico. Tenochtitlán grew huge – the invading Spanish could not believe its size and grandeur – but even as it expanded, the gods continued to demand more war: to suppress rebellious subjects, and to capture fresh victims for the constant rituals of human sacrifice.

Meanwhile, other societies had continued much as they had before the Aztec rise. In present-day Oaxaca, the Zapotecs were subjected to invasions by **Mixtecs** from the mountains. By war and alliance the Mixtecs came eventually to dominate this region – developing the trades of the potter and goldsmith as never before – and fell to the Aztecs only in the last years before the Spanish Conquest. In the Yucatán, the **Maya** were never conquered, but their civilization was in decline and any form of central authority had broken down into city-states. Nevertheless, they carried on trade all around the coasts, and Christopher Columbus himself (though he never got to Mexico) encountered a heavily laden boat of Maya traders, plying the sea between Honduras and the Yucatán. On the Gulf coast Aztec supremacy was total by the time the Spanish arrived, but they were still struggling to subdue the west.

THE GODS RETURN?

The legend goes that a great Toltec prince **Topiltzin Quetzalcoatl**, renowned for his wisdom and holiness and founder of the great city of Tula, decided to make an end to human sacrifice and attempted to convince the inhabitants of Tula to give it up. He was unsuccessful, however, as the shamanic god, Tezcatlipoca, tricked the Toltecs and forced Topiltzin Quetzalcoatl into exile. Topiltzin Quetzalcoatl built a raft and left "for the east" from the Gulf coast, promising to return one day to banish false rulers and reinstate a higher order, where human sacrifice would play no part. It is a well-known irony that Cortés landed on the Gulf coast, whence Topiltzin Quetzalcoatl was said to have left, at the time predicted for his return. But did this really lead to the fall of the Aztec empire? Probably not – most modern scholars claim that the story of Moctezuma believing Cortés to be the returning Quetzalcoatl actually developed after the Spanish Conquest.

1697	1767	1810	1815
Juan María Salvatierra founds the Loreto Jesuit mission in Baja.	Jesuits expelled from Mexico.	Hidalgo proclaims Mexican Independence at the Grito de Dolores. He is executed in 1811.	Execution of rebel leader José María Morelos.

The Spanish Conquest

Perhaps the most driven, ruthless and most spectacularly successful conquistador of all time, **Hernán Cortés** (1485–1547) was born in Medellín, Spain, to a family of lower nobility. He arrived in the New World in 1504, a colonist in Hispaniola, but soon earned his military stripes as a soldier in Cuba; it was from the latter that he launched the expedition that landed on the Mexican coast near modern Veracruz in the spring of 1519. With him were just 550 men, a few horses, dogs and a cannon; yet less than three years later the Spaniards had defeated the Aztecs and effectively established control over most of Mexico. Several factors enabled them to do so. First was Cortés himself: he burned the expedition's boats within days of their arrival, so that there was literally no turning back. In addition, his men had little to lose and much to gain, and their metal weapons and armour were greatly superior to anything the Aztecs had (although many Spaniards adopted Aztec-style padded cotton, which was warmer, lighter and almost as protective). Their gunpowder and cannon could also wreak havoc on opposing armies, both physically and psychologically. The horses and attack dogs, too, terrified the Aztecs. None of these, though, in the end counted a fraction as much as Cortés' ability to form alliances with tribes who were chaffing under Aztec subjugation and whose numbers eventually swelled his armies tenfold.

Moctezuma

Moctezuma, the Aztec leader, could certainly have destroyed the Spanish before they left their first camp, since his spies had brought news of their arrival almost immediately. Instead he sent a delegation bearing gifts of gold and jewels, which he hoped would persuade them to leave in peace. This served only to inflame the greed of the Spanish. By all accounts Moctezuma was a morose, moody and indecisive man, but his failure to act against Cortés had deeper roots: he was heavily influenced by religious omens, and the arrival of Cortés coincided with the predicted date for the return of **Quetzalcoatl**. The invaders were fair-skinned and bearded, as was Quetzalcoatl, and they had come from the east, where the deity had vanished (though we'll never really know what Moctezuma really believed; see box opposite). Although he put obstacles in their way, even persuading his allies to fight them, when the Spanish finally reached Tenochtitlán in November 1519, Moctezuma welcomed them as his guests. They promptly repaid his hospitality by taking him prisoner within his own palace.

The Pánfilo de Narváez expedition

This first phase of the Conquest, during which Spanish troops skirmished with a number of other Indian tribes and made allies of many – most significantly the **Tlaxcalans** – lasted for about a year. In April 1520 news came of a second Spanish expedition, led by **Pánfilo de Narváez** (1478–1528), who was under orders from the governor of Cuba to capture Cortés and take him back (Cortés' mission had always been unofficial, and many others hoped to seize the wealth of Mexico for themselves). Again, though, Cortés proved the more decisive commander – he marched back east, surprised Narváez by night, took him prisoner and persuaded most of his troops to switch allegiance.

Noche Triste

Meanwhile, the Spaniards left behind in Tenochtitlán had finally provoked their hosts beyond endurance by killing a group of Aztec priests during a religious ceremony, and

1821	1824	1833	1836
Independence achieved; Agustin de Iturbide declares himself emperor.	Iturbide executed; Mexican republic founded under President Guadalupe Victoria.	Santa Anna becomes president.	Texas declares independence – battles of the Alamo and San Jacinto.

were under siege in their quarters. Cortés, with his reinforcements, fought his way back into the city on June 24, only to find himself trapped as well. On June 27, Moctezuma (still a prisoner) was killed – stoned to death by his own people while attempting to appeal for peace according to the Spanish, though rumour has it that he was garrotted by Cortés himself. Finally Cortés decided to break out on the night of June 30 – still commemorated as **Noche Triste** – when the Spanish lost over half their number on the causeways across the lake. Most of them were so weighed down with gold and booty that they were barely able to move, let alone swim in the places where the bridges had been destroyed.

The fall of Tenochtitlán

Once more, though, the Aztecs failed to follow up their advantage, and the Spanish survivors managed to reach their allies in Tlaxcala, where they regrouped. The final assault on Tenochtitlán began in January 1521, with more supplies and fresh troops, tens of thousands of whom were Tlaxcalans and other Indians. The city, besieged, was also ravaged by an epidemic of smallpox, among whose victims was Moctezuma's successor, Cuitláhuac. The Aztecs held out for several more months under **Cuauhtémoc** – in Mexican eyes the only hero of this long episode – but on August 13, 1521, Tenochtitlán finally fell to the Spanish. Although much of the country remained to be pacified, the defeat of the Aztec capital made it inevitable that it would be.

Spanish colonial rule (1521–1810)

By dint of his success, Cortés was appointed governor of this new territory, although in practice he was watched over by minders from Spain and never had much real freedom of action (he was to die a wealthy but embittered man back in Spain in 1547). In 1535 **Nueva España** (New Spain) was formally established. There followed nearly three centuries of direct Spanish rule, under a succession of 61 viceroys responsible to the Spanish king. By the end of the sixteenth century the entire country had effectively been subjugated, its boundaries stretched by exploration from Panama to the western states of the current US (although the area from Guatemala south, including the Mexican state of Chiapas, was administered by the Audiencia of Guatemala from 1543).

THE DESTRUCTION OF NATIVE MEXICO

When the Spaniards arrived, the **native population** of central Mexico was at least 25 million; by the beginning of the nineteenth century the total population of Nueva España was just six million, at most half of these were pure-blooded natives. Some had been killed in battle, a few as a result of ill-treatment or simply from being left without homes or land to live on, but the vast majority died as a result of **successive epidemics** of European diseases (mainly smallpox, influenza and hepatitis) to which the New World had no natural immunity. The few survivors found the burden of labour placed on them ever-increasing as their numbers dwindled – for certainly no European came to Mexico to do manual work – and became more and more like slaves. Today the government counts just under ten million Mexicans as indigenous (around ten percent of the population), mostly living in the central and southern states. They remain some of the poorest people in the country.

1846	1848	1852–55	1858–61
Mexican-American War begins.	Treaty of Guadalupe Hidalgo: half of Mexican territory ceded to US.	Santa Anna returns to power.	Reform Wars between liberals under Benito Juárez and Church-backed conservatives.

The first tasks, in the Spanish mind, were reconstruction, pacification and conversion. At first there was quite remarkable progress: hundreds of towns were laid out according to a plan drawn up in Spain, with a plaza surrounded by a grid of streets. Thousands of churches were built (by 1800, the count reached twelve thousand), often in areas that had been sacred to the Indians, or on top of their pyramids; mass conversions were the order of the day. In a sense the indigenous peoples were used to all this – the Aztecs and their predecessors had behaved in a similar manner – but they had never experienced a slavery like that which was to follow.

The Church, which at first championed indigenous rights and attempted to record native legends and histories and educate the children, grew more and more concerned with money. Any attempt to treat the Indians as human was, in any case, violently opposed by Spanish landowners, to whom they were rather less than machines (in fact, cheaper than machinery, and therefore more expendable). By the end of the colonial era, the Church owned more than half of all the land and wealth in the country, yet most native villages would be lucky to see a priest once a year.

In a sense Mexico was a wealthy nation – certainly the richest of the Spanish colonies – but its riches were confined to the local elite and the nobility in Spain. No local trade or agriculture that would compete with Spain was allowed, so the cultivation of vines or the production of silk was banned; heavy taxes on other products – coffee, sugar, tobacco, cochineal, silver and other metals – went directly to Spain or to still poorer colonies. Since the Flota de Indias (the Spanish treasure fleet) sailed between Veracruz and Spain just once a year and was even then subject to the vagaries of piracy, this was a considerable handicap.

Even among the wealthy Spanish-descended landowners there was growing **resentment**, fuelled by the status of those among them born in Mexico: only *peninsulares* or "**gachupines**", Spaniards born in Spain, could hold high office in the government or Church. Of the six million people in Mexico in 1800, only forty thousand were *gachupines* – the rest were **criollos** (creoles, born in Mexico of Spanish blood) who were generally educated, wealthy and aristocratic, and **mestizos** (of mixed race) who dominated the lower ranks of the Church, army and civil service, or lived as anything from shopkeepers and small ranchers to bandits and beggars.

The struggle for independence

By the beginning of the nineteenth century Spain's status as a world power was in severe decline. At the same time, new political ideas were transforming the world; although the works of such political philosophers as Rousseau, Voltaire and Paine were banned in Mexico, the opening of the ports in 1796 made it inevitable that their ideas would spread. Literary societies set up to discuss these books quickly became centres of **political dissent**.

The spark, though, came when the French invaded Spain in 1808, and Napoleon placed his brother Joseph on the throne. Colonies throughout Latin America refused to recognize the Bonaparte regime. In Mexico, the *gachupine* rulers proclaimed their loyalty to Ferdinand VII (the deposed king) and hoped to carry on much as before, but creole discontent was not so easily assuaged. The literary societies continued to meet, and from one, in Querétaro, emerged the first leaders of the Independence movement: **Father Miguel Hidalgo y Costilla** (1753–1811), a creole priest, and **Ignacio Allende** (1769–1811), a disaffected junior army officer.

1861	1861–67	1863	1867
Juárez triumphant; suspends payment of foreign debt. France, Spain and Britain send naval expeditions.	French Intervention.	French take Mexico City. Maximilian becomes emperor.	Juárez defeats Maximilian, restores the Republic.

The Grito de Dolores

When their plans for a coup were discovered, the conspirators were forced into premature action, with Hidalgo issuing the famous *Grito de Dolores* (culminating in the rallying cry, *Méxicanos, viva México!*) from his parish church in Dolores on September 16, 1810 – the day is still celebrated as **Independence Day**. The mob of Indians and *mestizos* who gathered behind the banner swiftly took the towns of San Miguel, Guanajuato and others to the north of the capital, but their behaviour – seizing land and property, slaughtering the Spaniards – horrified the wealthy creoles who had initially supported them. In spring 1811, Hidalgo's army, huge but undisciplined, moved on the capital, but at the crucial moment Hidalgo threw away a clear chance to overpower the royalist army. Instead he chose to retreat, and his forces broke up as quickly as they had assembled. Within months, Hidalgo, Allende and the other ringleaders had been captured and executed.

The rise and fall of José María Morelos

By this time most creoles had rejoined the ranks of the royalists. However, many *mestizos* and much of the indigenous population remained in a state of revolt, with a new leader in the *mestizo* priest **José María Morelos** (1765–1815). Morelos was not only a far better tactician than Hidalgo – instituting a highly successful series of guerrilla campaigns – he was also a genuine radical. By 1813 he controlled virtually the entire country, with the exception of the capital and the route from there to Veracruz, and at the **Congress of Chilpancingo** he declared the abolition of slavery and the equality of the races. The royalists, however, fought back with a series of crushing victories. Morelos was executed in 1815, and his forces, led by **Vicente Guerrero** (1782–1831), were reduced to carrying out the occasional minor raid.

Independence

Ironically, it was the introduction of liberal reforms in Spain, of just the type feared by the Mexican ruling classes, which finally brought about **Mexican Independence**. Worried that such reforms might spread across the Atlantic, many creoles pre-empted a true revolution by assuming a "revolutionary" guise themselves. In 1820, **Agustín de Iturbide** (1783–1824), a royalist general but himself a *mestizo*, threw in his lot with Guerrero; in 1821, he proposed the **Iguala Plan** to the Spanish authorities, who were hardly in a position to fight, and Mexico was granted independence. With self-determination, though, came none of the changes which had been fought over for so long – the Church retained its power, and one set of rulers had simply been changed for another, local, set.

The first republic

In 1822, Iturbide proclaimed himself emperor; a year later, deserted by many of his former allies, he was forced to abdicate and go into exile, and a year after that, attempting to return to the country, he was arrested and executed by firing squad. In 1824 the country was officially proclaimed the **United Mexican States**, a **federal republic**.

It was the first of many such events in a century which must rank among the most confused – and disastrous – in any nation's history. Not only had Independence brought no real social change, it had left the new nation with virtually no chance of successful government: the power of the Church and of the army was far greater than

1876	1882	1886	1910
Porfirio Díaz accedes to power.	Influential writer and thinker José Vasconcelos born in Oaxaca.	Diego Rivera born in Guanajuato.	Francisco Madero stands for election, sparking the Revolution.

that of the supposed rulers; there was no basis on which to create a viable economy; and if the state hadn't already been bankrupted by the Independence struggle, it was to be cleaned out time and again by the demands of war and internal disruption. There were no fewer than 56 governments in the next forty years. In what approaches farce, the name of former Spanish soldier **General Antonio López de Santa Anna** (1794–1876) stands out as the most bizarre figure of all – the man became president or dictator on eleven separate occasions and masterminded the loss of more than half of Mexico's territory.

The era of Santa Anna

Under the auspices of the 1824 constitution the country was divided into thirteen states and **Guadalupe Victoria** (1786–1843), a former guerrilla general, elected its first president. He lasted three years, something of a record. In 1829, the Spanish attempted a rather half-hearted **invasion**, easily defeated, after which they accepted the fact of Mexican independence. In 1833, Santa Anna was elected president (officially) for the first time, the fifth man to hold the post thus far.

In 1836, a rather more serious chain of events was set in motion when Texas (Mexican territory but largely inhabited by migrants from the US) declared its independence. Santa Anna commanded a punitive expedition that besieged **the Alamo** in the famous incident in which Jim Bowie and Davy Crockett, along with 150 other defenders, lost their lives. Santa Anna himself, though, was promptly defeated and captured at the subsequent battle of **San Jacinto**, and rather than face execution he signed a paper accepting **Texan independence**.

Mexican-American War (1846–48)

In 1845, the **US annexed Texas**, and although the Mexicans at first hoped to negotiate a settlement, the redefinition of Texas to include most of Arizona, New Mexico and California made yet another war almost inevitable. In 1846, clashes between Mexican troops and US cavalry in these western zones led to the declaration of the **Mexican-American War**. Following defeats for the Mexicans at Palo Alto and Resaca, three small US armies invaded from the north. At the same time General Winfield Scott took Veracruz after a long bombardment, and commenced his march on the capital. Santa Anna was roundly defeated several times, and in September 1847, after legendary resistance by the Niños Héroes (cadets at the military academy), Mexico City itself was captured. In 1848, by the **Treaty of Guadalupe Hidalgo**, the US paid $15 million for Texas, New Mexico, Arizona and California, along with parts of Colorado and Utah; in 1854, the present borders were established when Santa Anna sold a further strip down to the Río Grande for $10 million under the **Gadsden Purchase**.

THE PASTRY WAR

One of the most bizarre episodes in Mexican history began in 1838, when a French pastry chef claimed that his *patisserie* in Mexico City had been looted during the lawless disorder of the previous decade. With an eye on huge debts owed France by Mexico, French king Louis Philippe happily followed up the claim; when compensation was not forthcoming the French invaded **Veracruz**. The "**Pastry War**" lasted about four months, during which Santa Anna lost a leg, and ended with President Bustamante promising to pay the French 600,000 pesos.

1911	1913	1917	1919–20
Madero wins election; Díaz flees into exile.	Madero murdered; Huerta becomes president.	Mexican Constitution adopted; Carranza becomes president.	Zapata and Carranza assassinated.

La Reforma

Mexico finally saw the back of Santa Anna when, in 1855, he left for exile (he would return to die in Mexico in 1876), but the country's troubles were by no means at an end. A new generation had grown up, knowing only an independent Mexico in permanent turmoil and espousing once more the liberal ideals of Morelos. Above all, this generation saw its enemy as **the Church**: immense, self-serving and far wealthier than any legitimate government, it had further sullied its reputation by refusing to provide funds for the American war. Its position enshrined in the constitution, it was an extraordinarily reactionary institution, bleeding the peasantry for the most basic of sacraments (few could afford official marriage, or burial) and failing to provide the few services with which it was charged. All education was in Church schools, which for 95 percent of the population meant no education at all.

The rise of Benito Juárez

Benito Juárez (1806–72), a Zapotec Indian from Oaxaca who had been adopted and educated by a priest and trained as a lawyer, led this liberal movement (La Reforma) through several years of civil war. When the **liberals** first came to power following Santa Anna's exile they began relatively mild attempts at **reform**: permitting secular education, liberating the press, attempting to distance the Church from government and instituting a new democratic constitution. The Church responded by threatening to excommunicate anyone cooperating with the government. In 1858, there was a conservative coup leading to the **War of Reform** for the next three years, **internal strife** on an unprecedented scale. With each new battle the liberals proclaimed more drastic reforms, churches were sacked and priests shot, while the conservatives responded by executing anyone suspected of liberal tendencies. In 1861, Juárez emerged triumphant, at least temporarily. Church property was confiscated, monasteries closed, weddings and burials became civil affairs and set fees were established for the services of a priest. It wasn't until 1867 that most of these **Reform Laws** were fully enacted, but the conservatives had one more card to play.

The French Intervention (1861–67)

At the end of the civil war, with the government bankrupt, Juárez had suspended payment of all foreign debts, and in 1861 a joint British, Spanish and French expedition occupied Veracruz to demand compensation. It rapidly became clear, however, that the French were after more than mere financial recompense. Britain and Spain withdrew their forces, and Napoleon III ordered his troops to advance on Mexico City. Supported by Mexican conservatives, the aim was to place **Maximilian** (1832–67), a Habsburg archduke, on the throne as emperor.

Despite a major defeat at **Puebla** on May 5, 1862 (now the **Cinco de Mayo** holiday), the French sent for reinforcements and occupied Mexico City in 1863. The new emperor arrived the following year. In many ways, Maximilian was a pathetic figure. He came to Mexico with almost no knowledge of its internal feuds (having gleaned most of his information from a book on court etiquette), and expecting a victorious welcome. A liberal at heart – he refused to repeal any of Juárez' reforms – he promptly lost the support of even the small group of conservatives who had initially welcomed him. While his good intentions seem undeniable, few believe that he would have been capable of putting them into practice even in the best of circumstances. And these were hardly ideal

1920	1923	1924–28	1926–29
Álvaro Obregón becomes president.	Pancho Villa assassinated.	Presidency of Plutarco Elías Calles.	The Cristero War.

times. With Union victory in the **US Civil War**, the authorities there threw their weight behind Juárez, providing him with arms and threatening to invade unless the French withdrew (on the basis of the Monroe doctrine: America for the Americans). Napoleon III, already worried by the growing power of Bismarck's Prussia back home, had little choice but to comply. After 1866 Maximilian's position was hopeless. He stayed at the head of his vastly outnumbered troops to the end – May 15, 1867 – when he was defeated and captured at **Querétaro**. A month later, he faced the firing squad.

The restoration of the Republic

Juárez reassumed power in 1867, managing this time to ride through the worst of the inevitable bankruptcy. The first steps towards **economic reconstruction** were taken, with the completion of a railway from Veracruz to the capital, encouragement of industry and the development of a public education programme. Juárez died in office in 1872, having been re-elected in 1871, and was succeeded by his vice-president, **Sebastián Lerdo de Tejada** (1823–89), who continued on the same road, though with few new ideas.

The Porfiriato (1876–1910)

Tejada was neither particularly popular nor spectacularly successful, but he did see out his term of office. However, there were several Indian **revolts** during his rule and a number of plots against him, the most serious of them led by a new radical liberal, **Porfirio Díaz** (1830–1915). Díaz had been a notably able military officer under Juárez, but in 1876, despite the re-election of Tejada, he assumed the presidency himself then consolidated power to effectively become **dictator** for the next 34 years. At first his platform was a radical one – including full implementation of the Reform Laws and a decree of no re-election to any political office – but this was soon dropped in favour of a brutal policy of **modernization**. Díaz did actually stand down at the end of his first term in 1880, but he continued to rule through a puppet president, Manuel González, and in 1884 resumed the presidency for an unbroken stretch until 1911.

In many ways the **achievements** of his dictatorship were remarkable: some 16,000km of railway were built, industry boomed, telephones and telegraph were installed and major towns, reached at last by reasonable roads, entered the modern era. In the countryside, Díaz established a police force – the notorious *rurales* – which stamped out much of the banditry that had plagued the nation. Almost every city in Mexico seems to have a grandiose theatre and elegant public buildings from this era. But the costs were high: rapid development was achieved basically by handing over the country to **foreign investors**, who owned the majority of the oil, mining rights, railways and other natural resources. At the same time, there was a policy of massive land expropriation, in which formerly communal village holdings were handed over to foreigners or simply grabbed by corrupt officials.

Agriculture, meanwhile, was ignored entirely. The owners of vast haciendas could make more than enough money by relying on the forced labour of a landless peasantry, and had no interest in efficiency or production for domestic consumption. By 1900 the whole of Mexico was owned by some three to four percent of its population. Without land of their own, peasants had no choice but to work on haciendas or in forests, where their serfdom was ensured by wages so low that they were permanently in debt to their employers. The rich became very rich indeed, while the poor had lower incomes and

1929	1934–40	1935	1938
PRI founded (initially known as the PRD or Party of the Democratic Revolution).	Lázaro Cárdenas president.	Diego Rivera completes mural cycle at National Palace.	Oil companies nationalized into PEMEX.

fewer prospects than they had a century earlier. The press was censored, education strictly controlled and **corruption** rife.

The Mexican Revolution (1910–21)

By the onset of the **twentieth century**, Díaz was old and beginning to lose his grip on reality. While he had every intention of continuing in power until his death, a real middle-class opposition began to develop, concerned above all by the racist policies of their government (which favoured foreign investors above native ones) and by the lack of opportunity for themselves – the young educated classes.

Phase 1: Francisco Madero

In 1910 **Francisco Madero** (1873–1913) stood against Díaz in the presidential election. The dictator responded by imprisoning his opponent and declaring himself victor. Madero, however, escaped to Texas, where he proclaimed himself president, and called on the nation to support him.

This was an entirely opportunist move, for at the time there were no revolutionary forces, but several small bands immediately took up arms. Most important were those in the northern state of Chihuahua, where **Pancho Villa** (see box, p.464) and **Pascual Orozco** (1882–1915) won several minor battles, and in the southwest, where **Emiliano Zapata** (see box opposite) began to arm indigenous guerrilla forces. In May 1911, Orozco captured the major border town of Ciudad Juárez, and his success was rapidly followed by a string of Revolutionary victories. By the end of the month, hoping to preserve the system, if not his own role in it, Porfirio Díaz had fled into exile (he died in Paris in 1915). On October 2, 1911, Madero was formally declared president. He freed the press, encouraged the formation of unions and introduced genuine **democracy**, but failed to do anything about the condition of the peasantry or the redistribution of land.

Phase 2: Victoriano Huerta

Madero was immediately faced by a more dangerous enemy: US business interests. **Henry Lane Wilson**, US ambassador, began openly plotting with **Victoriano Huerta** (1850–1916), a government general, and **Felix Díaz**, a nephew of the dictator, who was held in prison. Fighting broke out between supporters of Díaz and those of Madero, while Huerta refused to commit his troops to either side. When he did, in 1913, it was to proclaim himself president. Madero was shot in suspicious circumstances (few doubt an assassination sanctioned by Huerta), and opponents on the right, including Díaz, were either imprisoned or exiled. The new government was promptly recognized by the US and most other foreign powers, but not by Madero's former supporters within the country.

Phase 3: Constitution versus Convention

Villa and Zapata immediately took up arms against Huerta, and in the north Villa was joined by **Alvaro Obregón** (1880–1928), governor of Sonora, and **Venustiano Carranza** (1859–1920), governor of Coahuila. Carranza was appointed head of the **Constitutionalist** forces, though he was always to be deeply suspicious of Villa, despite Villa's constant protestations of loyalty. At first the Revolutionaries made little headway – Carranza couldn't even control his own state – although Obregón and Villa did enjoy

1940	1942–45	1943	1950
Leon Trotsky murdered in Mexico City.	Mexico sides with the Allies in World War II.	Football (soccer) becomes professional sport in Mexico.	Octavio Paz publishes *The Labyrinth of Solitude*.

some success raiding south from Chihuahua and Sonora. Almost immediately the new US president, **Woodrow Wilson**, withdrew his support from Huerta and, infuriated by his refusal to resign, began supplying arms to the Revolution.

In 1914, the Constitutionalists began to move south, and in April of that year **US troops occupied Veracruz** in their support (though neither side was exactly happy about the foreign presence). Huerta, now cut off from almost every source of money or supplies, fled the country in July (he was to die in a US jail), and in August Obregón occupied the capital, proclaiming Carranza president.

Renewed fighting broke out straight away, this time between Carranza and Obregón, the Constitutionalists, on one side, and the rest of the Revolutionary leaders on the other, the so-called **Conventionalists** whose sole point of agreement was that Carranza should not lead them. The three years of fighting that followed were the most bitter and chaotic yet, with petty chiefs in every part of the country proclaiming provisional governments, joining each other in factions and then splitting again, and the entire country in a state of anarchy. Each army issued its own money, and each forced any able-bodied men it came across to join it. It was reckoned that about nine hundred thousand people were killed between 1910 and 1921, out of a total population of fifteen million.

Gradually, however, Obregón and Carranza gained ground – Obregón defeated Villa several times in 1915, and Villa withdrew to carry out raids into the US, in the hopes of provoking an invasion (which he nearly did: US troops led by General "Black Jack" Pershing pursued him across the border but were never able to catch up, and withdrew following defeat in a skirmish with Carranza's troops). Zapata, meanwhile, had some conspicuous successes – and occupied Mexico City for much of 1915 – but his troops tended to disappear back to their villages after each victory. In 1919, he was tricked into a meeting with one of Carranza's generals and assassinated. Villa retired to a hacienda in his home state and was murdered in 1923.

The Mexican Constitution of 1917

Meanwhile, Carranza continued to claim the presidency, and in 1917 he set up a constitutional **congress** to ratify his position. The document it produced – the present **Mexican Constitution** – included most of the Revolutionary demands, among them workers' rights, a mandatory eight-hour working day, national ownership of all mineral rights and the distribution of large landholdings and formerly communal properties to

---

¡TIERRA Y LIBERTAD!

Emiliano Zapata (1879–1919), born into a peasant family in Morelos, was perhaps the one true revolutionary in the whole long conflict of the Mexican Revolution. In 1911 he fell out with Madero over land reform, supporting instead the radical Plan de Ayala which called for massive land redistribution. He fought bitterly against Huerta, but tried to stay neutral during the Villa/Carranza conflict that followed; Carranza's general Pablo González eventually attacked Zapata's stronghold in the south, ambushing and killing the rebel leader in 1919. Zapata's battle cry of "**¡Tierra y libertad!**" ("Land and liberty!") and his insistence that "it is better to die on your feet than live on your knees" still make him a revered figure among the peasants – and revolutionaries of the namesake EZLN – of the present day.

1954	1957	1962	1968
Women given right to vote in Mexico. Death of painter Frida Kahlo.	Death of famed muralist Diego Rivera.	Carlos Fuentes publishes *The Death of Artemio Cruz*.	Mexico City hosts Olympic Games; Tlatelolco massacre.

the peasantry. Carranza was formally elected in May 1917 and proceeded to make no attempt to carry out any of its stipulations, certainly not with regard to land rights.

Final phase: the end of Revolution

In 1920, Carranza was forced to step down by Obregón, and was shot while attempting to reach Veracruz (though some suggest he killed himself). The inauguration of Obregón as President is generally regarded as the end of the core period of Revolution.

Obregón, at least, was well intentioned – but his efforts at land reform were again stymied by fear of US reaction: in return for American support, he agreed not to expropriate land. In 1924, **Plutarco Elías Calles** (1877–1945) succeeded him and initiated some real progress towards the ideals of the Revolutionary constitution. Large public-works schemes began – roads, irrigation systems, village schools – and about eight million acres of land were given back to the villages as communal holdings. At the same time, Calles instituted a policy of virulent **anticlericalism**, closing churches and monasteries and forcing priests to flee the country or go underground.

These moves provoked the last throes of a backlash, as the **Cristero War** (1926–29) in defence of the Church, a bitter conflict that claimed some ninety thousand lives. Isolated incidents of vicious banditry and occasional full-scale warfare continued until 1935, eventually burning themselves out as the stability of the new regime became obvious, and religious controls were relaxed. In 1928, Obregón was re-elected, but was assassinated three weeks later in protest at the breach of the "no reelección" clause of the constitution. He was followed by **Portes Gil**, **Ortíz Rubio** and then **Abelardo Rodríguez**, who were all controlled behind the scenes by Calles and his political allies, who steered national politics to the right in the bleak years of the 1930s Depression.

The road to modern Mexico

By 1934 Mexico enjoyed a limited degree of peace. A new culture had emerged – most boldly reflected in the great murals of **Diego Rivera** and **José Clemente Orozco** that began to adorn public buildings throughout the country – in which native heroes like Hidalgo, Morelos, Juárez and Madero replaced European ideals.

The government of Lázaro Cárdenas (1934–40)

With the election of **Lázaro Cárdenas** (1895–1970) in 1934, such doubts were finally laid to rest. As the spokesman of a younger generation, Cárdenas expelled Calles and his supporters from the country, simultaneously renaming the broad-based party that Calles had set up the **PRI** (Party of the Institutional Revolution); it was to stay in power

---

THE TLATELOLCO MASSACRE

Embarrassed by protests of around ten thousand pro-democracy students in Mexico City, just days before Mexico was to host the Olympic Games of 1968, the PRI government ordered a heavy-handed crackdown that soon got out of control; in the chaos that followed at least forty students were killed – exact numbers are still disputed (estimates range from thirty to three hundred). Indeed, the **Tlatelolco massacre** remains a controversial issue, with former President Luis Echeverria arrested on charges of genocide in 2006 (the case was dismissed in 2009).

1970	**1985**	**1990**	**1992**
Mexico hosts FIFA World Cup; it hosts a second time in 1986.	Mexico City earthquake kills at least ten thousand people.	Octavio Paz first Mexican to win Nobel Prize for Literature.	*Like Water for Chocolate* becomes highest-grossing Spanish-language film of all time.

for the rest of the century. Cárdenas set about an unprecedented programme of reform, redistributing land on a huge scale (170,000 square kilometres during his six-year term), creating peasant and worker organizations to represent their interests at national level and incorporating them into the governing party. He also relaxed controls on the Church to appease internal and international opposition.

In 1938, Cárdenas nationalized the **oil companies**, an act which has proved one of the most significant in shaping modern Mexico and bringing about its industrialization. For a time it seemed as if yet more foreign intervention might follow, but a boycott of Mexican oil by the major consumers crumbled with the onset of **World War II**, and was followed by a massive influx of money and a huge boost for Mexican industry as a result of the war. By the time he stood down in 1940, Cárdenas could claim to be the first president in modern Mexican history to have served his full six-year term in peace, and to have handed over to his successor without trouble.

PRI rule and the Mexican Economic Miracle (1940–70)

Over the next thirty years or so, massive oil income continued to stimulate industry, and the PRI maintained a masterly control of all aspects of public life. Though it was an accepted fact that governments would line their own pockets first – a practice which allegedly reached its height under **José López Portillo** (1976–82) – the unrelenting populism of the PRI, its massive powers of patronage and, above all, its highly visible and undoubted progress maintained it in power with amazingly little dissent.

This is not to say there were no problems. The year 1959 saw the repression of a national railway strike during which ten thousand workers lost their jobs and their leaders were jailed, and in **1968**, hundreds of students were massacred in Mexico City (see box opposite). The PRI was still very much in control, though, and snuffed out these movements by the mid-1970s.

Economic crisis (1970–94)

By the 1980s the PRI was losing its populist touch. The years between 1970 and 1982, later dubbed the "**Docena Trágica**" (tragic dozen), saw rapid growth based on booming oil prices. But this growth was accompanied by inflation and devaluation of the peso; vast sums were misappropriated, corruption flourished as never before, and by 1982 Mexico had run up a foreign debt of almost US$100 billion, borrowed against future oil earnings. When the 1980s bubble burst and the price of oil collapsed, the government of **Miguel de la Madrid** (1982–88) found itself faced with an unprecedented economic crisis on a national and international scale. A US-educated financier, he adopted **austerity measures** imposed by the World Bank that produced massive unemployment and drastically reduced standards of living (the average wage-earner lost fifty percent of his or her purchasing power).

The movement against the PRI was accelerated in 1985, when a huge **earthquake** (8.1 on the Richter scale) hit the capital. The quake revealed widespread corruption – many of the buildings that collapsed were government-owned and turned out to have been constructed using inferior materials. The country became increasingly polarized: in the relatively wealthy, US-influenced north, the right-wing **PAN** (National Action Party) won a string of minor elections, while in the south opposition was far more radical and left-wing: a socialist/peasant alliance held power for a while in Juchitán (Oaxaca) before being ousted by strong-arm tactics.

1994	1995	1998
NAFTA comes into force; Zapatista uprising in Chiapas; Mexican peso crisis or the "Tequila crisis", caused by the sudden devaluation of the Mexican peso.	Colima-Jalisco earthquake kills at least 49 people.	Death of Octavio Paz in Mexico City.

In this climate, the **1988 election** was tainted by allegations of fraud. Predictably, the PRI candidate, **Carlos Salinas de Gortari**, was declared the comfortable winner. It is widely believed, however, that **Cuauhtémoc Cárdenas**, son of the much-loved Lázaro, actually gained the majority of the votes, having split from the PRI and succeeded in uniting the Mexican left for the first time since the Revolution.

By 1993, nearly forty million Mexicans were living below the official **poverty** line (about half the population), while 24 were listed in the Forbes list of the five hundred wealthiest men in the world, most grown rich on privatized utilities. To boost foreign investment, Salinas expanded the "**maquiladora**" programme, which allowed foreign companies to set up assembly plants along the US-Mexican border while enjoying substantial tax concessions. He also pushed through the North American Free Trade Agreement (**NAFTA; TLC** in Spanish) in 1994, which created a free market between Canada, the US and Mexico. None of this was popular, especially among those on the left, but perhaps the most important change from a domestic point of view was the amendment of Article 27 of the constitution. This article had been written to protect communal village landholdings, known as **ejidos**; under Salinas, their status shifted from state property to private property, allowing them to be sold.

The Chiapas uprising (1994–97)

On New Year's Day 1994, NAFTA took effect and at the same time an armed guerrilla movement known as the **Zapatista Army of National Liberation** (EZLN) took control of San Cristóbal de las Casas and four other municipalities in the state of Chiapas. The guerrillas were mainly indigenous villagers, and their action took the country almost entirely by surprise; they demanded an end to the feudal system of land tenure in Chiapas, free elections, the repeal of NAFTA and the restoration of Article 27 of the constitution. The government reacted with a predictable use of force, committing numerous human-rights abuses along the way, including the bombing of civilians and the torture and murder of prisoners, particularly in the town of Ocosingo.

In the subsequent **negotiations** the main spokesman for the Zapatistas was **Subcomandante Marcos**. The balaclava-clad, pipe-smoking guerrilla became a cult hero, his speeches and communiqués full of literary allusions and passionate rhetoric (he was later exposed as, allegedly, Rafael Guillén, a philosophy professor from Mexico City, though this did little to dent his popularity). Negotiations ended in March, when an accord was drawn together.

In June 1994, the EZLN finally rejected the accord, and in July a leftist candidate for the governorship of Chiapas, **Amado Avendaño Figueroa**, met with a suspicious "accident" when a truck with no numberplates collided with his car, killing three passengers; Avendaño lost an eye. In national elections in August the PRI triumphed, helped by an electorate that had been shaken by the uprising. **Ernesto Zedillo** was declared president in what appeared a relatively clean election, the party also sweeping up most senate and governorship posts that were on offer.

In **Chiapas**, however, where the PRI also claimed to have won the governorship, Avendaño declared himself "rebel governor" after denouncing the elections as fraudulent. By this point Chiapas was essentially in a state of **civil war**. Ranchers and landowners organized paramilitary **death squads** to counter a mobilized peasantry. Land seizures and roadblocks were met with assassinations and intimidation, and a build-up of federal troops

2000	**2001**	**2006**
PAN candidate Vicente Fox Quesada elected president; end of PRI hegemony.	Release of acclaimed movie *Y Tu Mamá También*, nominated for Best Original Screenplay at the 2002 Academy Awards.	Felipe Calderón, controversially elected president, institutes a fierce campaign against the drug cartels.

in the state only made things worse. On January 8, 1995, Zedillo attended the swearing-in of the PRI governor of Chiapas. Ten days later, the EZLN deployed its forces, breaking the army cordon surrounding its positions and moving into 38 municipalities (it had previously been confined to four). The government briefly launched an offensive against the EZLN, resulting in thousands of peasants, terrified by the army and by right-wing landowners' paramilitary groups, becoming internal refugees.

New negotiations eventually resulted in the **San Andrés Accords on Rights and Indigenous Cultures** (named after the village near San Cristóbal where the talks took place), signed in February 1996. The accords guaranteed indigenous representation in national and state legislatures, but to this day they have not been fully implemented. For a while relations between the Zapatistas and the government hit a new low, while the remorseless increase of the military presence on the Zapatistas' perimeter appeared to give the paramilitary groups even greater freedom to operate. This culminated in the December 1997 **Acteal Massacre**: 45 displaced Tzotzil Indians, 36 of them women and children, were murdered at a prayer meeting by forces linked to PRI officials.

Mexico today

Despite the crisis in Chiapas, Mexico's **political reforms** continued, with limits on campaign spending and the establishment of a federal electoral body in 1996 – the economy started to grow again that year (after another financial collapse, the "Tequila Crisis" of 1994), and has continued to expand ever since. But the biggest change of all came on July 2, 2000, when **Vicente Fox Quesada**, the PAN candidate, was voted in as president. It was a landmark event: not only was he the first opposition candidate ever to have been democratically placed in power, it was also the first peaceful transition between opposing governments since Independence. Most remarkably, though, it was the end of seven decades of PRI rule – the world's longest-lasting one-party dynasty, surpassing even the Soviet Communist party.

In spite of his political shortcomings, Fox for the most part retained his popularity, and set the stage well for the July 2006 election – which, in many ways, was even more crucial than the previous one, as it would either prove the PAN victory a fluke or help consolidate the party's power.

President Felipe Calderón (2006–12)

In 2006 PAN candidate **Felipe Calderón Hinojosa** replaced Fox as president after one of the most controversial elections in modern Mexican history. Calderón won by the slimmest of margins (0.56 percent or 233,831 votes), and his opponent, PRD-candidate **Andrés Manuel López Obrador** (the popular leftist former mayor of Mexico City) never really accepted the result, even when the Federal Electoral Tribunal ruled that his accusations of vote tampering were not sufficient to call a new vote count. The numbers told the story of a divided Mexico – every state north of the capital (for the most part, the wealthier part of the country) supported Calderón, while Obrador took all of the poor, southern states with large indigenous populations. The only exception in the south was Yucatán state, not coincidentally home to a substantial upper class.

Despite relative stability and continuing economic growth, the nation continued to face huge **challenges**. The outbreak of **swine flu** in 2009 did nothing to help tourism or the

2009	**2009**	**2010**
President Calderón sends five thousand Mexican Army troops to patrol the streets of Ciudad Juárez as a result of the drug wars.	Swine Flu (H1N1) epidemic hits Mexico; 398 people die.	Carlos Slim Helú, born in Mexico City, becomes richest man in the world (worth US$71 billion).

country's international image, while Mexico's relationship with the US, if better than it sometimes has been, remained problematic – the 592km **border fence** proposed by President Bush in 2006 was a rather brutal symbol of how intractable the debate over **illegal immigration** had become (Calderón passed a bill actually decriminalizing undocumented immigration into Mexico in 2008). On the plus side, Calderón's move towards **universal healthcare** coverage was one of his most popular policies, and he continued expanding the highway network and building new universities.

The Mexican drug war

Drugs, however, have dominated the headlines. Calderón was determined to face the problem head-on, and committed 45,000 army personnel, as well as five thousand *federales*, to what can only be described as a war against the cartels that control the transportation of cocaine, heroin, ecstasy and marijuana through Mexico into the US (see box, p.468). Assessing Calderón's success is difficult and highly controversial; many drug lords were killed or imprisoned, and security in some cities certainly improved. On the other hand, the biggest players remain very much in business and the steady stream of gruesome murders continues. Critics argue that the Calderón campaign simply intensified the violence, jeopardizing foreign investment and tourism in Mexico.

The 2012 Presidential election: the return of the PRI

In a typically dramatic 2012 Presidential election, the PRD candidate was once again Andrés Manuel López Obrador, with PAN nominee Josefina Vázquez Mota hoping to become the first female president of Mexico. Yet both were trumped by **Enrique Peña Nieto**, the enigmatic former PRI governor of the State of Mexico who collected 39.1 percent of the vote (Obrador came second with 32.43 percent). Unsurprisingly, Obrador once again demanded a full recount, and once again he was disappointed: the Federal Electoral Institute confirmed Nieto as President-elect. With accusations of PRI voter fraud widespread, protests continued throughout the summer of 2012, but Peña Nieto officially assumed office in December – the next election will be in 2018.

The Peña Nieto presidency (2012–)

President Nieto has had some success reducing drug cartel violence since 2012; Zeta leader Heriberto Lazcano was killed in 2012; top Zeta bosses the Morales brothers were arrested in 2013; and Mexico's most-wanted man, **Joaquín "El Chapo" Guzmán** (Sinaloa Cartel), plus Vicente Carrillo Fuentes (Juárez Cartel) and Héctor Beltrán Leyva (Beltrán Leyva Cartel) were captured in 2014. Nevertheless, the **Iguala mass kidnapping** of September 2014, when 43 students from Ayotzinapa were abducted and later murdered by a drug gang in collusion with local police in Guerrero horrified the nation; the case led to national and international protests and a string of high-profile resignations and arrests. And in 2015, after barely a year in Mexico's top prison, **El Chapo escaped** yet again in what was a massive embarrassment for the Nieto administration.

Despite these setbacks Mexico's economy has continued to grow under Peña Nieto, with huge investments in the car manufacturing industry, inflation and interest rates at record lows and continued increase in GDP. Huge inequalities of wealth remain, however, between the north and south, and between the city and rural populations. Relations with the US remain strained, if cordial, with drugs and **border security** still the major points of contention.

2012	2014	2014
Enrique Peña Nieto wins the presidency, heralding the return to power for the PRI. Death of writer Carlos Fuentes.	Hurricane Odile devastates Baja California.	"El Chapo" Guzmán, leader of the Sinaloa Cartel and Mexico's most-wanted man, is captured; he escapes prison in 2015 before being recaptured in January 2016.

Environment and wildlife

Mexico is one of the world's most biologically diverse countries, with the second-highest number of mammal species for its size (about five hundred), more than a thousand species of birds, at least thirty thousand species of higher plants (including half of the world's pines) and more reptile species (seven hundred) than anywhere else on the globe. Many of these are endemic, and this diversity, combined with the country's vast size (1,960,000 square kilometres) and tremendous range of natural environments, makes Mexico an ideal location for the visiting naturalist, irrespective of expertise.

Unfortunately, much of Mexico's natural beauty is under threat either from direct hunting or from the indirect effects of **deforestation** and **commercialization**. Not only is it extremely irresponsible to buy, even as souvenirs, items that involve wild animals in their production, but it is also generally **illegal** to bring them back to the UK or the US. This applies specifically to: tortoiseshell; black coral; various species of butterfly, mussels and snails; stuffed baby crocodiles; cat skins; and turtle shells. Trade in living animals, including tortoises, iguanas and parrots (often sold as nestlings), is also illegal, as is the uprooting of cacti.

Mexican flora

The influence of long-term **deforestation** for charcoal or slash-and-burn agriculture has substantially denuded large areas of Mexico. Today the northern mountains contain tracts of conifer, cedar and oak, especially around Durango, where the largest **pine forest** reserves are found. At lower altitudes, grass-covered **savannahs** are interrupted by the occasional palm or palmetto tree, and the riverbanks are graced with poplar and willow. **Tropical rainforests**, which border the Gulf of Mexico, form a band that extends southwards from Tampico across the base of the Yucatán Peninsula and northern Oaxaca. They contain mahogany, cedar, rosewood, ebony and logwood. **Seasonal tropical forest** and **dry scrub** cover the remaining areas of the Gulf coast and the lowlands of the Pacific coast. One particularly notable tree is a single **ahuehuete** (Montezuma cypress) in the state of Oaxaca, which measures 36m around; it's alleged to be at least 1200 years old. Extensive **mangrove forests** once lined much of the Gulf coast and the Caribbean, and grew along sheltered reaches of the Pacific shore, but tourism along the coasts has eaten away at the swamps – a short-sighted move, as runoff from the trees' root systems nourishes the coral reefs that draw tourists.

The tropical forests provide supplies of both **chocolate** (from the cacao trees of Chiapas) and **vanilla**. Also harvested are **chicle**, from the latex of the **sapodilla** tree, used in the preparation of chewing gum, and **wild rubber** and **sarsaparilla**. The pharmaceutical industry makes use of **digitalis** from wild **foxgloves** and various **barks** used in the preparation of purges and disinfectants. One medicinal plant unique to Mexico is **Discorea composita**, which is harvested in Veracruz, Oaxaca, Tabasco and Chiapas, and is used in the preparation of a vegetable hormone that forms an essential ingredient of the contraceptive pill.

The deserts

The flatter lands of the north, the north Pacific and portions of central Mexico are characterized by dry scrub and grassland – better known as the **Sonoran** and **Chihuahuan deserts**, though they are hardly the empty sands that the term "desert" conjures. The most conspicuous vegetation here is the **cactus**. Various species adorn these flatlands: the **saguaro** is a giant, tree-like growth which can exceed 15m in height, whereas the columns of the **cereus** cactus stand in lines, not dissimilar to fence posts, and can reach 8m. Another notable variety is the **prickly pear** (*nopal*), which produces a fruit (*tuna*) that can be eaten raw or used in the production of sweets. Other harvested varieties include the pulpy-leaved **maguey cactus** (a member of the agave family), whose fermented juice forms the basis of tequila, mescal and *pulque*, and **henequen** (another agave), which was once grown extensively on the Yucatán Peninsula and used in the production of rope. The temperate grasslands are composed primarily of clumped bunch grass and wiry, unpalatable **curly mesquite**. Low-lying shrubs found among these grassy expanses include spindly ocotillo, **creosote** bush and palm-like **yucca**, with **mesquite** and **acacia bushes** in the more sheltered, damper areas.

Flowers

Flowers are commonplace throughout Mexico and form an integral part of day-to-day life. Once, **frangipani** and **magnolia** were considered to be of such value that they were reserved for the Aztec nobility. Today the blue blossoms of **jacaranda** trees and purple and red **bougainvillea** still adorn the walls of cities and towns during the spring and summer. Even the harsh arid deserts of the north are carpeted with wild flowers during the brief spring that follows the occasional rains; the cacti blooms are particularly vivid. Many of these floral species are indigenous to Mexico, including **cosmos**, **snapdragons**, **marigolds** and **dahlias**. In the wetter areas, several species of **wild orchid** are endemic, while more than eight hundred other species have been classified from the forests of Chiapas alone.

Insects

Insect life is abundant throughout Mexico, but numbers and diversity reach their peak in the tropical rainforests. For the most part, insect life makes itself known through the variety of bites and sores incurred while wandering through these areas: **mosquitoes** are a particular pest, with malaria still a risk in some areas. Openings in the tree canopy also attract a variety of colourful **butterflies**, **gnats** and **locusts**. The **garrapata** is a particularly tenacious tick found everywhere livestock exists, and readily attaches itself to human hosts. A range of **scorpions**, whose sting can vary from extremely painful to definitively lethal, is found throughout the country.

In the forests, long columns of **leafcutter ants** crisscross the floor in their search for tasty bits of fungus on tree bark, and surrounding tree trunks provide ideal shelter for large nests of **termites**. Carnivorous **army ants** also sweep through in waves, devouring grasshoppers and other pests but leaving greenery untouched. One species of ant, local to Tlaxcala, provides for seasonal labour twice each year: first, during the egg stage, when it is harvested for a highly prized form of caviar, and secondly during the grub stage, when it is an equally loved food source. The most spectacular insect migration can be seen in winter in eastern Michoacán, where thousands of **monarch butterflies** hatch from their larval forms en masse, providing a blaze of colour and movement (see p.306).

Fish, reptiles and amphibians

The diversity of Mexican inland and coastal habitats has enabled large numbers of both marine and freshwater species to survive. Among the freshwater species, **rainbow** and **brook trout**, **silversides** and **catfish** are particularly abundant (as are European **carp** in certain areas, where it has been introduced). The most highly regarded is a species of **whitefish** found in Laguna de Chapala and Lago de Pátzcuaro.

Offshore, Mexican waters contain over one hundred marine species of significance, including varieties of tropical and temperate climates, coastal and deep waters, surface and ground feeders and sedentary and migratory lifestyles. Among the most prevalent are **goliath grouper** (which can grow up to 5m), **swordfish, snapper, king mackerel, snook, tuna, mullet** and **anchovy. Shrimp, crayfish** and **spiny lobster** are also important commercial species. The marine fishing grounds on the Pacific coast are at their best off the coast of Baja California, where the warmer southern waters merge with subarctic currents from the north. Similarly, deep ocean beds and coastal irregularities provide rewarding fishing in the waters of the Campeche bank in the Gulf of Mexico.

The lower river courses that flow through the southern forests are frequented by **iguanas, crocodiles** and their close relative, the **caiman. Lizards** range from tiny nocturnal lizards along the Gulf coast to **tropical iguanas**, which can reach up to 2m in length. **Marine turtles**, including the loggerhead, green, hawksbill and leatherback, are still found on both the Atlantic and Pacific coasts, though several species are endangered. Hunting of both adults and eggs is now illegal, and a number of official and unofficial turtle sanctuaries have been established, with positive results. Several kinds of **rattlesnake** are common in the deserts of northern Mexico, and further south the rainforests hold a substantial variety of other snakes, including the **boa constrictor, fer-de-lance, bushmaster** and the small **coral snake**. Amphibian life includes salamanders, several types of **frog** and one marine toad that measures up to 20cm in length.

Birds

More than five hundred species of tropical birds live in the rainforests and cloud forests of southern Mexico alone. Among these are resplendent **macaws, parrots** and **parakeets**, which make a colourful display as they fly among the dense tree canopy. The cereal-eating habits of the parrot family have not endeared them to local farmers, and for this reason (and their continuing capture for sale as pets) their numbers have been seriously depleted in recent times. Big-billed **toucans** perch on lower branches and a few larger game birds, such as **curassow, crested guan, chachalaca** and **ocellated turkey**, can be seen on the ground, amid the dense vegetation.

Particularly rare are the brilliantly coloured **trogons**, including the dazzling **quetzal**, which inhabits the cloud forests of the Sierra Madre de Chiapas (in El Triunfo Reserve). The ancient Maya coveted its long, emerald-green tail feathers, which were used in priestly headdresses; its current status is severely endangered. The drier tropical deciduous forests of northern Yucatán to the east, the Pacific coastal lowlands and the interior lowlands provide an ideal habitat for several predatory birds including **owls** and **hawks**. The most familiar large birds of Mexico, however, are the carrion-eating **black** and **turkey vultures** – locally *zopilote* – often seen soaring in large groups. The Yucatán is also one of the last remaining strongholds of the small **Mexican eagle**, which features in the country's national symbol.

Large numbers of coastal lagoons provide both feeding and breeding grounds for a wide variety of aquatic birds – some of them winter visitors from the north – including **ducks, herons** and **grebes**. Foremost among these are the substantial flocks of graceful **flamingos** which can be seen at selected sites along the western and northern coasts of the Yucatán Peninsula. In the north of Mexico, where the harsher and drier environment is less attractive, outlying towns and villages form a sanctuary for a variety of **doves** and **pigeons**, and the areas with denser cover have small numbers of **quail** and **pheasant**. Any water feature in these drier zones, as well as wetland areas further south, provides attractive migration stopover sites for North American species, including **warblers, wildfowl** and **waders**.

Mammals

Zoologists divide the animals of the Americas into two categories: the **Nearctic** region of the mid-latitudes, in which the native animals are of North American affinity, and the **Neotropical** region of the lower latitudes, in which the fauna is linked to that of

South America. The Isthmus of Tehuantepec marks the border between these two regions, serving as a barrier to many larger mammalian species.

The Nearctic region is predominantly composed of open steppe and desert areas and higher-altitude oak and pine forests. Relatively few large mammals inhabit the highland forests, although one widespread species is the **white-tailed deer**, which is still hunted as a source of food. The northern parts of the Sierra Madre Occidental mark the southernmost extent of several typically North American mammals, such as **mountain sheep** and **black** and **brown bears**, though the latter are near extinction. Bears live in the Cumbres de Monterrey National Park, and wild horned **sheep** can be seen at the San Pedro Mártir National Park in Baja California. Other mammals include **deer**, **puma**, **lynx**, **marten**, **grey fox**, **mule sheep**, **porcupine**, **skunk**, **badger**, **rabbit** and **squirrel**. A large array of smaller **rodents**, and their natural predators, the **coyote** and the **kit fox**, are also widespread throughout the forests. Nowadays the extensive grassland plains are frequented only by sporadic herds of white-tailed deer; the days of the pronghorn and even the bison have long passed under the burden of overhunting. Within the desert scrub, the **peccary** is still widely hunted, and rodents, as ever, are in abundance, forming an ample food supply for the resident **bobcats**, **ocelots** and even the occasional **jaguar** – more commonly associated with the country's jungle regions, but also at home in the drier areas and known to roam across the US–Mexico border.

Baja California forms an outstanding wildlife sanctuary for marine mammals, harbouring nearly forty percent of the world's species. Isla Guadalupe is one of the few remaining breeding sites of the endangered **elephant seal**, and the only known mating and nursery sites of the **grey whale** are around Guerrero Negro.

Although some southern species (notably the opossum and armadillo) have succeeded in breaching the Tehuantepec line, and now thrive in northern Mexico and the southern US, on the whole the **Neotropical** region holds a very different collection of mammals. The relationship between these species and the lush vegetation of the tropical rainforest and the highland cloud forests is particularly apparent. Many species are arboreal, living in the tree canopies: these include **spider** and **howler monkeys**, **opossums**, **tropical squirrels**, the racoon-like **coati** and the gentle **kinkajou**.

Because of the paucity of grass on the shaded forest floors, ground-dwelling mammals are relatively scarce. The largest is the **tapir**, a distant relative of the horse, with a prehensile snout, and usually found near water. Two species of wild pig, wander the forest floors seeking their preferred foods (roots, palm nuts and even snakes), and there's also the smaller **brocket deer**. The **agouti** and the spotted **cavy** are large rodents living along the streams and riverbanks. These are hunted by large cats, including the **jaguar**, **puma** and **ocelot**.

The drier tropical and subtropical forests of northern Yucatán, the Pacific coastal lowlands and the interior basins produce a more varied ground cover of shrubs and grasses, which supply food for the **white-tailed deer** and abundant small rodents, including the spiny tree **rat** and the **paca**, which in turn provide food for a variety of predators such as the **coyote**, **margay** and **jaguarundi**. Other large mammals which can still be found in small numbers are **anteaters**, **opossums** and **armadillos**. The reefs and lagoons which run along the Quintana Roo coast have small colonies of the **manatee**, or sea cow, a docile creature which feeds on sea grass.

Wildlife sites

It would be almost impossible to compile a comprehensive list of sites of wildlife interest in Mexico, particularly as so much can be seen all over the country. The following is a selection of some of the outstanding areas, particularly ones that are easily accessible or close to major tourist centres. The few zoos that exist in Mexico are generally depressing places, but there is one outstanding exception – the conservation-oriented **Zoológico Miguel Álvarez de Toro** in Tuxtla Gutiérrez (see p.660).

GREY WHALE MIGRATION AND BREEDING

Each year the **grey whale migration** attracts an estimated 250,000 visitors to Baja California. The whales' **migratory route** runs the length of the Pacific seaboard, from Baja to the Bering Sea and back; this is a round trip of some 20,000km – the longest recorded migration undertaken by any mammal. The whales spend the summer months feeding on the abundant krill in the Arctic and building up body reserves for the long journey south to the breeding lagoons. The migration begins as the days shorten and the pack ice thickens, with the majority of the whales arriving in January and February, though they can be observed here from December to April.

Nowadays human interest in the whales is purely voyeuristic, though times have not always been so peaceful; less than 150 years ago, the secret breeding grounds of the whales were discovered by **Charles Melville Scammon**. The Laguna Ojo de Liebre (renamed in recent times after the infamous whaler) was rapidly emptied of almost all of these magnificent beasts, and it wasn't until the establishment of **Scammon's Bay** as the world's first whale sanctuary in 1972 that their numbers began to rebound. The population in the area is currently estimated at about twenty thousand – a dramatic recovery in a relatively short time span. The protected area now includes nearby San Ignacio Lagoon, forming an all-embracing national park, the **Biosfera El Vizcaíno**. San Ignacio Lagoon presents a daunting entrance of pounding surf and treacherous shoals, but inside its calmer waters flatten and spread inland for 15km towards the distant volcanic peaks of the Santa Clara mountains. Accessible points for land-based observation lie further north in the Parque Natural de Ballena Gris ("Grey Whale Natural Park").

Baja California

The peninsula of **Baja California** is a unique part of the Mexican landmass. Its coastline provides sanctuary for a wide variety of marine mammals, including the major wildlife attraction of the area, the migratory **grey whale**. The lagoons where these whales gather can also offer views of other whales, including blue, humpback, fin, minke, sperm and orca (killer whales). Dolphins, sea lions and a variety of sea birds (pelicans, ospreys, plovers and sanderlings) inhabit the lagoons too. The sparse vegetation provides roosting sites for jaegers (skuas) and peregrines, and coyotes may occasionally be seen wandering the shores.

Offshore, several small islands with protected status have been colonized by highly diverse animal communities. Furthest north is the island of **Todos Santos**, where the sandy beaches, festooned with the remnants of shellfish, are used as occasional sunning spots by the resident harbour seals. The atmosphere is ripe with an uncommon blend of guano, kelp and Californian sagebrush. The Pacific swell frequently disturbs the resting cormorants, which bask in the hot sunshine, and the skies are filled with wheeling western gulls.

Further south lies the island of **San Benito**, just northeast of the much larger Isla Cedros. San Benito provides ideal nesting grounds for migrating ospreys, which travel south from the US. The hillsides are covered by tall agave (century plants) whose brief, once-in-a-lifetime blooms add an attractive splash of colour to the slopes. These towering succulents produce a broad rosette of golden florets, which are a welcome supply of nectar for resident hummingbirds, and ravens soar above, searching for carrion. Along with Isla Cedros and the distant **Isla Guadalupe** (now a biological reserve), the island also provides a winter home to thousands of elephant seals, now happily recovering after years of overhunting. The large adult males arrive in December, and the pebbly coves are soon crammed with the noisy and chaotic colony of mothers, calves and bachelor bulls, all ruled by one dominant bull (or beach master) which can weigh up to two tonnes. The males make a terrifying spectacle as, with necks raised and heads thrown back, they echo their noisy threats to any would-be rivals.

The interior of the peninsula also has several areas of wildlife interest, many of which are now protected as nature reserves. Most significant are the national parks of the **Sierra San Pedro Mártir** and the **Desierto Central**. Here the chaparral-covered hills cede to Jeffrey pine forests and high meadows, interspersed with granite *picachos* (peaks) and volcanic mesas. The **Parque Nacional Constitución de 1857** is another green oasis in the arid lowlands, where the coniferous woodlands form a picturesque border to the central **Laguna Hanson**. These sierras are renowned for the numerous palm-filled canyons which cut deep into the eastern escarpment; they make spectacular hiking areas with their miniature waterfalls, ancient petroglyphs, caves, hot springs and groves of fan palms.

Durango

Durango lies within a dry, hilly area where the intermittent oak and pine woodland is surrounded by large expanses of low-lying scrub. These areas are frequented by large numbers of birds, whose presence is an extension of their North American range. Typical species include red-tailed hawk, American kestrel and mockingbird. The denser, wooded areas provide the necessary cover for several more secretive varieties such as Mexican jay, acorn woodpecker, hepatic grosbeak and the diminutive Mexican chickadee. This is also an occasional haunt of the mountain lion (or puma) and the coyote. In the dry scrub, scorpions abound. Other nearby sites worthy of investigation include **El Salto** and **El Palmito**.

The Teacapán estuary

South of Mazatlán on the Pacific coast, the **Teacapán estuary** is an extensive area of sands with marshy margins: ideal feeding grounds for a variety of waders and wildfowl, including marbled godwit, greater yellowlegs and willet. Large numbers of herons and egrets feed in the shallow waters (including little green and Louisiana heron and snowy and cattle egret), while further out to sea passage birds include laughing gull, gull-billed tern and olivaceous cormorant. Most spectacular of all are the magnificent, aptly named frigate birds, which make a dramatic sight as they skim over the water's surface in their search for fish, with their long wings (sometimes more than 2m across), forked tails and hooked bills.

The rocks offshore provide a breeding site for both brown- and blue-footed boobies, and the pools at the northern end of the town, behind the large hotels, have some interesting water birds, including jacana, ruddy duck and canvasback.

San Blas

Immediately around **San Blas** are lagoons with wildlife very similar to that found in the estuary near Mazatlán; boat tours from San Blas take you out to see herons and egrets, with the possibility of seeing a caiman being the big attraction. Deeper in the wetlands the landscape forms areas of thicker scrub and at higher altitudes dense forest. In the lower-lying scrub, it is possible to see the purplish-backed jay, Gila woodpecker and tropical kingbird, while the skies above have the patrolling white-tailed kite. At higher altitudes, birdlife includes the San Blas jay, white-crowned parrot and cinnamon hummingbird. The town provides sufficient scraps for scavengers such as black and grey hawks and various rodents.

Veracruz and the Gulf coast

The eastern coastline of Mexico has attractions of its own, and none is more rewarding than the final remaining tract of rainforest on the Mexican **Gulf coast**, southeast of **Veracruz**. The vegetation is lush, the tended citrus orchards yielding to rolling tropical forest, with its dense growth of ficus, mango and banana trees and the occasional coconut palm. These trees provide cover for a colourful underlying carpet, including orchids, lemon trees, camellias, fragrant cuatismilla and gardenias. The roadsides are lined with banks of hibiscus, oleander and the pretty, white-flowered shrub known locally as *cruz de Malta*. At the centre of the whole area, **Lago de Catemaco** is outstandingly beautiful.

The surrounding forest has suffered much in recent times, and many of the larger mammals that once resided in this region are no longer to be found. One sanctuary which remains amid this destruction is the ecological research station of **Los Tuxtlas**. Although the institute's holding is fairly small, it adjoins a much larger state-owned reserve of some

WILDLIFE AT CHICHÉN ITZÁ

When visiting the famed Maya site at **Chichén Itzá**, save a little time at the end of the day for an exploration of the forested areas which lie to the south of the "Nunnery". The drier climate and lower altitude in this part of the peninsula encourage a sparser vegetation, where the oaks and pines are less obvious. The colours among the greenness come from a variety of splendid flowers, such as the multicoloured bougainvillea, the aromatic frangipani and the blue and mauve blooms of the jacaranda tree. Occasional splashes are added by the red bracts of the poinsettia and the brilliant yellows of golden cups. The resident birds appear oblivious to the tourists, and in the quieter areas to the south and southwest of the main site, the abundant birdlife includes the plain chachalaca, ferruginous pygmy owl, cinnamon hummingbird, turquoise-browed motmot and numerous brilliant vireos, orioles and tanagers.

25,000 acres on the flank of the **San Martín volcano**. Despite problems of poaching and woodcutting, the area has the last remaining populations of brocket deer, black howler monkey, ocelot, jaguarundi, kinkajou and coati. It also boasts 92 species of reptile, fifty amphibians, thousands of insects and over three hundred species of birds. With patience, it is possible to see such outstanding avian varieties as the keel-billed toucan, black-shouldered kite, gold-crowned warbler, red-throated ant tanager, plain-breasted brush finch, red-lored parrot, ivory-billed woodpecker and the magnificent white hawk.

The Chiapas uplands and Palenque

In the **Chiapas uplands**, the absence of climatic moderation and coastal breezes creates dense, lush vegetation that makes it truly worthy of the name of tropical rainforest. The **Sierra Madre de Chiapas** is of particular interest, particularly the Pacific slopes at altitudes between 1500m and 2500m, as these are the last sanctuary of the endangered horned guan and azure-rumped tanager, and even the quetzal. **El Triunfo Reserve**, at 1800m in the very southeastern corner of the country, less than 50km from the Guatemalan border, makes an excellent base camp for exploration of the area. The cloud forest here is dense, and the tall epiphyte-laden trees grow in profusion on the slopes and in the valleys, in the humid conditions which occur after the morning fogs have risen (generally by early afternoon).

Another area of interest in eastern Chiapas is the **Parque Nacional Lagos de Montebello**, where more determined bird watchers may be rewarded with views of the azure-hooded jay and the barred parakeet. Human encroachment has substantially reduced the population of large mammals in the area, but small numbers of howler monkey, tapir and jaguar (known locally as *el tigre*) are a reminder of bygone days. Another speciality of the region is a vivid and diminutive tree frog, whose precise camouflage ensures that it is more often heard than seen.

At the archeological site of **Palenque** you're back among the tourists (and the howler monkeys), but the birding is unrivalled, and local species include the chestnut-headed oropendola, scaled ant pitta, white-whiskered puffbird, slaty-tailed trogon and masked tanager. In the area of marshland around the nearby **Río Usumacinta**, pinnated bittern, everglade kite and the rare lesser yellow-headed vulture have all been recorded.

The Yucatán Peninsula

The vegetation of the **Yucatán Peninsula** is influenced by its low relief and the ameliorating effects of its extensive coastline, which bring regular and fairly reliable rain along with year-round high temperatures. In the north it's predominantly dry scrub and bush, although large areas have been cleared for the cultivation of crops such as citrus fruits and henequen. To the south is lusher tropical and subtropical forest, where the effects of agriculture are less obvious and the dense forest of acacia, albizia, gumbo limbo and *ceiba* is in parts almost impenetrable. These form an ideal shelter for scattered populations of both white-tailed and brocket deer.

> ## SIAN KA'AN BIOSPHERE RESERVE
>
> The real highlight of the Yucatán Peninsula's protected areas is the magnificent **Sian Ka'an Biosphere Reserve**, which includes coral reef, mangroves, fresh- and salt-water wetlands and littoral forest – possibly the widest range of flora and fauna in Mexico. See p.798 for more.

The **birdlife** on the peninsula is particularly outstanding. The abundant and spectacular birds which fill the treetops include squirrel cuckoo, citreoline trogon and Aztec parakeet, while circling in the skies above are the resident birds of prey such as the bat falcon, snail kite and the ever-present black and turkey vultures (these can be distinguished, even at great heights, as the wings of the latter are clearly divided into two bands – the darker primaries and the lighter secondaries being quite distinct). It is also possible to see all three species of Mexican toucan: collared aracari, emerald toucanet and the spectacular keel-billed. The denser areas of forest also hold small remnants of the original black howler and spider monkey populations.

The village of **Cobá** borders a lake with extensive reed margins along its eastern edge, which attracts a variety of water birds. Typical visitors, either migratory or resident, include the grebe, the elusive spotted rail, ruddy crake, northern jacana and the occasional anhinga – a cormorant-like bird which captures fish by spearing them with its dagger-like bill. The reed beds provide cover for several more-secretive species, including mangrove vireo, ringed kingfisher and blue-winged warbler, as well as several varieties of hirundine such as mangrove swallow and grey-breasted martin. The lake is also home to a variety of turtles and large numbers of Morelet's crocodiles.

Cancún, Cozumel and the Caribbean coast

Even the mega-resort of **Cancún** has wildlife-spotting possibilities: the lagoons that line the outskirts have a variety of birds (such as great-tailed grackle and melodious blackbird). These wetlands form an ideal breeding ground for a number of brilliantly coloured dragonflies and damselflies.

More importantly, the longest **barrier reef** in the Americas begins just south of the city, off the coast of **Puerto Morelos**, where the scuba diving and snorkelling are stunning. Formed by the limey skeletons of dozens of species of coral, the reefs show spectacular diversity, with varieties such as star, lettuce, gorgonian, elkhorn and staghorn. The reefs provide food and shelter for more than four hundred species of fish, including several varieties of parrotfish, butterfly fish, beau gregories, rock beauties and porkfish; the blaze of colour is unforgettable. The coral also provides protection for other residents including spiny lobster, sea urchins, crabs and tentacled anemones.

Natural parks and nature reserves worthy of special mention include **Celestún**, on the west coast, and **Río Lagartos**, to the north. Both have spectacular flocks of migratory flamingos, which winter here in the milder climate. The **Isla Contoy** bird sanctuary off the northeastern tip of the peninsula is a worthwhile and popular day trip from Cancún, and **Isla Holbox**, off the north coast, is the closest point to an annual gathering of more than one hundred whale sharks. The largest **botanic garden** in Mexico is near Puerto Morelos.

Playa del Carmen is frequented by various wetland species including American wigeon, and the ferry trip to **Cozumel** island produces sightings of sea birds such as royal and Caspian terns, black skimmer, frigate birds and Mexican sheartails. On Cozumel, the most rewarding sites are a couple of kilometres inland on the main road that runs across the island. The sparse woodland and hedgerows provide shelter for many typical endemics, such as Caribbean dove, lesser nighthawk, Yucatán and Cozumel vireo, the splendid bananaquit and a variety of tanagers. Elusive species which require more patient exploration (best through the mangroves which lie 3km north of **San Miguel** along the coast road) are the mangrove cuckoo, yellow-lored parrot, Caribbean ealania and Yucatán flycatcher. Cozumel, though, is better known for the **coral reefs** that ring the island, some of Mexico's finest.

Music

Mexico has an enormous and vibrant music scene which made world headlines in the 1950s when the **golden age** of cinema immortalized songs like "*Bésame Mucho*" and artists like **Pedro Infante**. While Cuban and Brazilian music rode the crest of the world music boom in the late 1980s, however, Mexico largely missed out – with notable exceptions like Lila Downs and Los de Abajo.

Son

Son is the music of the Mexican fiesta, the heart of a rural culture that stubbornly survives throughout the country. *Son* is where the story of Mexican music begins: the style that celebrated independence from Spain at the beginning of the nineteenth century and is still, today, a source of regional pride and identity. Although *son* survives on the margins of urban culture, more adventurous rock groups like **Café Tacuba** and divas like **Eugenia León** and **Lila Downs** have taken versions of this music to the big stage.

Like much of Latin American music, *son* is the bastard child of indigenous, Spanish and African parents. It is what musicologists call a "super-genre", meaning that there are eight or nine different styles of *son* that vary from region to region. In general, this is the music of country dances that begin at dusk – at the end of a celebration for a saint's day or a wedding – and last through the night. It is music to be enjoyed rather than listened to passively; the public adds a line of percussion with their **zapateado** foot-stamp dancing, and the musicians respond to their calls and comments with verses that are improvised on the spot. *Son* is played mainly by string bands but in some regions – especially in indigenous towns and villages – also by brass bands of twenty or thirty musicians. The different styles of *son* feature *copla* verses that are witty, sexual, poetic and proud.

Son Jaliscience and mariachi

Probably best known outside Mexico are the **sones** from Jalisco, the west-coast state that is the home of the **mariachi**. The latter became nationally and internationally popular in the 1950s, a time when regional music was recorded by major labels. A few of these treasures can be found in markets, although the original country sound – played on a couple of violins and guitars and sometimes a harp – almost disappeared when Rubén Fuentes rewrote the **son jaliscience** repertoire for radio and cinema, introducing slick violin sections, trumpets and the portable bass known as the *guitarrón*. These groups, made up of twelve or even sixteen musicians, spectacularly dressed in tight trousers and large hats, played their show-business versions of the traditional repertoire ("*Son de la Negra*" and "*El Cihualteco*" are two classics) as well as a simpler accompaniment for the *ranchera* stars of the day. To hear the original *son jalisciense*, look out for Vol 1 of *The Anthology of Mexican Sones* and also for the CD by **Mariachi Reyes del Aserradero**, a post-Fuentes group that is still very much in touch with local tastes.

The stars of big-time mariachi music are **Vicente Fernández** and, for the past twenty years or so, his son **Alejandro**, a mega-star who has taken the music so far down the commercial path that all that is really left are the lines of silver buckles down the trouser legs and some of the instrumentation. Look out too for **Aida Cuevas** (the "Queen of Ranchera") and younger stars **Pedro Fernández** and **Pepe Aguilar**; television has stripped away the original intensity of the music but the singing is still spectacular and the mariachi will always be a strong symbol of the Mexican passion to party.

Every year there is an enormous **mariachi congress** in Guadalajara (capital of Jalisco) where hundreds of bands gather from all over Mexico and the world – especially from Japan and the US, where there are countless mariachis of different genders and musical abilities. Many Mexican towns and cities still have a central square where the mariachis meet to offer their music on a nightly basis. Most famous of these is **Plaza Garibaldi** in

INDIGENOUS SON

Although *son* is basically *mestizo* music, several **indigenous cultures** play *sones* to accompany their ritual dances. These are generally purely instrumental and are slower and more melancholy than those from other regions. Exceptions are the *sones* from Purépecha and Zapotec communities which are beautiful, bilingual songs that have been widely covered by urban stars. **Sones abajeños** are the frenetic party music of the Purépecha of Michoacán, played on guitars, violins and a double bass. Between the *abajeños*, the same musicians sing the hauntingly beautiful *pirecua* love songs, with words exclusively in Purépecha. Outstanding Purépecha *son* bands include **Atardecer** (Sunset), from the lake village of Jarácuaro, and **Erandi** (Dawn). This region is probably more famous for the dances that accompany the local *sones*; there is the athletic "Dance of the Old Men" and the slow, incredibly beautiful dances of the *cúrpites* in which small, subtle steps are taken by elaborately costumed dancers. There is nothing folkloric about this tradition, which remains an important part of Purépecha fiestas. In the southern state of Oaxaca, the vibrant Zapotec culture has produced some of the country's great love songs and inspired mainstream Mexican romantic singers along the way. Sung in both Zapotec and Spanish, the **sones istmeños**, from the Tehuantepec Isthmus, are played to a slower, more melancholy 3/4 rhythm and boast some great solo passages on the *requinto* guitar. These *sones* can be accompanied by small guitar bands or by brass bands made up of at least eighteen musicians. Again, this is the music of fiestas and, to some extent, of cantinas.

Mexico City, where hundreds of musicians serenade young girls and old ladies under the stars while hustlers bring in business for the many bars and food stalls that line the plaza. Mexicans come here at all hours of the day and night to hire bands for private parties; this is the real business for the mariachis since it is much better paid than playing to tourists.

Son Jarocho

After the *sones* from Jalisco, **son jarocho** from Veracruz is probably the best-known style. Many Jarocho musicians like **Andrés Huesca**, **Nicolás Sosa** and **Lino Chávez** tasted the big time in Mexico City before returning to the main square of Veracruz. Today, there is a new interest in *son jarocho*, especially in the country style from the south of the state, where there are some three hundred bands – many of them including fifth- or sixth-generation country musicians – playing a fairly traditional repertoire at local fiestas and on the national and international circuit.

The story of this huge revival of interest in *son jarocho* goes back to 1977 when a young *jarocho* from Tres Zapotes, a small town in southern Veracruz, emigrated to Mexico City and asked himself why the *peña* folk-clubs were full of urban musicians in ponchos playing Bolivian and Chilean music. Where was Mexican music and specifically the *son jarocho* that he had danced to as a child? **Gilberto Gutiérrez** formed a band called **Mono Blanco**, recording with some of the most outstanding musicians from southern Veracruz, setting up workshops, making records and giving countless concerts all over Mexico and the US and to some extent in Europe as well. His younger brother Ramón formed his own band, **Son de Madera**, also enormously successful on the roots circuit, and this helped to revive the *fandango* tradition of dancing within the same communities that had originally produced the music. Today, there is a huge following for *son jarocho* in Mexico City and musicians are fusing it with new and old styles so that now it's common to hear a *jarocho* band opening for a rock band or featuring in a programme of classical music.

Further north, in the port of Veracruz, the style of *son jarocho* that had made it to the big screen in the 1950s is still alive and kicking, although the worldwide success of the late harpist **Graciana Silva**, "La Negra Graciana" (she died in 2013), has not been repeated by other bands. Graciana's style, like that of Nicolás Sosa and the legendary Lino Chávez, was faster than the *jaranero* style of the southern bands, and there was more African influence in the mix, whereas the *jaranero* bands (others include **Los Utrera** and **Los Cojolites**) reveal a gentle melancholy, associated with a more indigenous culture.

For *son jarocho* fans the *jaranero* festival held on February 2 in Tlacotalpan (see box, p.424) is a must: a huge fiesta dedicated to the Virgin of the Candelaria with a stage for *jaraneros* on which professional, amateur, local and foreign musicians have an open microphone in a party atmosphere.

Son Huasteco

A third style that is less well known internationally, but which has a very passionate following in Mexico, is **son huasteco**, from the Huasteca region in central and northern Mexico. The line-up, in contrast with the two previous styles, is always the same: a violin, a *huapanguera* guitar and the smaller, higher pitched *jarana* guitar. These three instruments, aided by the falsetto voice of at least one of the trio, creates a music that is surprisingly complete and which has a capacity to move audiences from a frightening melancholy, through to humour and to great joy. For the past twenty years at least, the most important trio has been **Los Camperos de Valles**, led by the singer **Marcos Hernández** whose falsetto can be heard on Vol III of the *Anthology of Sones* CD set, in a recording that was made just before he formed Los Camperos. "*El San Lorenzo*", played by Los Camperos Huastecos, features Marcos' angelic falsetto as it sounded when he was 17. Today – over forty years later – it is still worth taking a ten-hour bus journey from Mexico City to Ciudad Valles to hear Marcos, accompanied by Gregorio Solano on *jarana* and the outstanding violin of newcomer Camilo Ramírez.

Son huasteco is enjoying a huge revival which is almost completely driven by local tastes. There are hundreds of trios playing in the states of Hidalgo, Tamaulipas and San Luis Potosí, as well as many more who have emigrated to Mexico City. They have recorded countless CDs, some of which have local DJ-style introductions with synthesizers and extra-echo, but, when the intro fades out, you are left with a perfect performance of the violin and two guitars playing the old repertoire. Apart from Los Camperos, look out for CDs by **Real Hidalguense** or the other classic trio **Armonía Huasteca**. There are many events in Mexico City and all over the Huasteca where it's possible to dance all night long to the *son* of different trios, but these are not usually announced beyond the local community so it can be hard to identify them. In February and April there are big local **festivals** in San Joaquín de los Minerales which are highly recommended. For the less adventurous, the Museo de Culturas Populares in Mexico City sometimes presents good trios from all over the Huasteca.

Other sones

Seldom heard in the city but enormously popular back home in the villages of the Sierra Gorda, the **arribeño style** is the most poetic form of *son*. Here, the *trovador* – who seems to be the natural successor of the medieval troubadour – is a country poet, often with no formal education, who composes verses about local heroes, the planets, the earth and the continuing struggles for land. Usually two *trovadores*, both playing the *huapanguera* guitar and each accompanied by two violins and the small *vihuela* guitar, confront each other on makeshift wooden platforms that are erected on two sides of the village square. The poets enter into musical combat, improvising verses which are interspersed with *zapateado* dancing. Each year on December 31, the greatest living *trovador*, **Guillermo Velázquez**, organizes a festival in his village, paying homage to the old musicians before starting a *topada* musical combat that lasts all night. Guillermo is an outstanding musician with a sharp wit that he uses to satirize the political situation and, in the sense of bringing a political message to deep-roots traditional music, he is unique in Mexico.

Based in the Mexican west, in the Tierra Caliente (hot lands) of the Río Balsas basin, the **son guerrerense** has a tradition of exceptional violinists, exemplified by **Juan Reynoso**, who died in 2007 at the age of 95. Reynoso became the unwitting guru of a generation of Mexico City and US musicians who would travel to Guerrero and sit at his feet, learning to play his own compositions as well as the traditional repertoire. As an old man, Reynoso toured the West Coast of the United States, participating in fiddlers' festivals. In his own region he is remembered by the name given to him by a local poet: "The Paganini of the Hotlands".

Further west, in a region where the heat is so intense that it's known as "Hell's Waiting Room", **sones de arpa grande** (*sones* of the big harp) are one of Mexico's best-kept musical secrets. These bands – made up of a big harp, one or two violins and

ON RECORD

Mexican music is widely available online: try Amazon or Smithsonian Folkways (Ⓦfolkways .si.edu). A small selection from this enormous world of musical styles includes the following:

COMPILATIONS

★**Anthology of Mexican Sones** (Discos Corasón, Mexico). The definitive survey of Mexican traditional music, featuring wonderful recordings of rural bands. Excellent accompanying notes plus lyrics.

Beso Asesino (Discos Corasón, Mexico). Traditional *trova* from the Yucatán and from Santiago de Cuba. An excellent celebration of the shared roots of the *bolero*.

Mexico – Fiestas of Chiapas & Oaxaca (Nonesuch Explorer, US). Recordings from village festivities in southern Mexico. Marimba *conjuntos*, brass bands, some eccentric ensembles and great fireworks on the opening track.

The Rough Guide to the Music of Mexico (World Music Network, UK). This set examines a wide variety of both traditional and contemporary music, including *rancheras, corridos, boleros,* indie rock and various stylistic fusions.

La Tortuga (Discos Corasón, Mexico). A heartfelt collection of the Zapotec *sones istmeños* from southwest Oaxaca; this repertoire has been successfully mined by urban artists but here it is in the original form.

SONES AND MARIACHI

★**Los Camperos de Valles** *La Pasión*. The definitive CD by the definitive Huastecan *son* band and the last recording by violinist Heliodoro Copado who was the inspiration for the current generation of *soneros*.

Conjunto Alma Jarocha *Sones Jarochos*. First in a series of regional Mexican releases, featuring *sones* from Veracruz with harps and *jarana* guitars.

Juan Reynoso *El Paganini de la Tierra Caliente*. A cult recording in Mexico which led the great country violinist to gain national and international fame. Other CDs and DVDs followed, but this is considered the best.

Mariachi Coculense de Cirilo Marmolejo *Mexico's Pioneer Mariachis Vol 1*. Wonderful archive recordings from the 1920s and 1930s of one of the seminal groups.

Mariachi Reyes del Aserradero *Sones from Jalisco*. An excellent mariachi band from Jalisco state play the original *sones* from the region where mariachi was born.

Mariachi Vargas *20 Exitos*. Highly polished, big-band style mariachi from Silvestre Vargas (died in 1985), who managed to stay at the top of his field for over fifty years.

★**Mono Blanco** *El Mundo se va a Acabar*. The most ambitious record from the band that led the revival of *son jarocho* in Mexico; although less traditional than their usual style, this is stunning.

RANCHERA AND NORTEÑO

Banda del Recodo *Nuestra Historia*. This enormously popular collective releases hit CDs rather than classics, so possibly the best introduction is this 2003 release that brings together material from their long history.

★**Chavela Vargas** *Noche Bohemia*. There was a flood of CDs after Chavela's return to the music scene in the late 1980s (she died in 2012), but nothing rivals this early recording with the legendary guitarist, Antonio Bribiesca.

★**Flaco Jiménez** *Ay Te Dejo en San Antonio y Más*. The best of Flaco's many recordings; he's a huge name in the Tex-Mex world north of the border.

José Alfredo Jiménez *Homenaje a José Alfredo Jiménez*. Jiménez was the king of *ranchera* and an icon in Mexico: his classic repertoire of songs tells of the perfidy of women and the healing qualities of tequila. He may have created some of the worst clichés about machismo, but his music is irresistible.

two guitars – don't thrive as they used to, but great harpists, like **Juan Pérez Morfín** and his band **Alma de Apatzingán**, can still be tracked down in the region. In the brothels of Apatzingán and in the region's country fairs, the sound boxes of the big harps are beaten in counter-rhythm by one of the band members or by a fan who pays for the privilege. The harpist, meanwhile, must hold onto the melody with *jananeo* vocals that

Linda Ronstadt *Canciones de Mi Padre* and *Más Canciones*. *Ranchera* classics sung very convincingly by the Mexican-American vocalist, accompanied by Mariachi Vargas.

Los Lobos *La Pistola y El Corazón*. The East LA band's brilliant 1988 tribute to their Mexican roots, with David Hidalgo pumping the accordion on their blend of *conjunto* and rock and roll.

Los Tigres del Norte *Corridos Prohibidos*. A collection of *corridos* about Mexican low life and heroism from one of the best *norteño* groups.

TROPICAL AND MÚSICA ROMÁNTICA

★**Agustín Lara** *Agustín Lara*. The legendary *bolero* singer and composer of classics such as "*Rival*" and "*Noche de Ronda*". There are countless recordings by him and the myriad of artists who have dedicated covers of his *boleros* to him (including Plácido Domingo and Pedro Vargas).

Armando Manzanero *20 Éxitos Originales*. A key figure for Cuban artists like Omara Portuondo, this Yucatecan pianist modernized the *bolero* and, now in his 80s, is still a huge figure who moves comfortably between the commercial and the alternative. Various artists (Tania Libertad and Alejandro Sanz are just two) queue up to sing duets with him. His voice isn't great but his songs are classics and this is a typical, very polished, selection of re-mastered classics.

Guty Cárdenas *100 Años del Ruiseñor Yucateco*. A collection of *trova yucateca* and other genres in the voice and guitar of a man who was an enormous star in the early years of recorded sound but who was assassinated in 1932. The tracks have been masterfully restored and are accompanied by a documentary.

Sonora Dinamita *Mi Cucu*. Mexican *cumbia* performed by a breakaway group of artists who took the name of the Colombian originals. Their lyrics, full of double entendres, are performed with a zest that has brought huge success in Mexico.

Toña La Negra *Antología*. A well-kept secret outside Mexico – where she was an enormous star in the 1950s – this *bolero* singer from Veracruz reveals how close Mexico is to Cuba (and vice versa). She died in 1982.

ROCK AND POP

★**Café Tacuba** *Re*. The second CD in a long list of successes from a band that has been at the top of the Mexican rock scene for more than twenty years, this is a highly recommended classic; try also *Cuatro Caminos* and *Sino*.

Eugenia León *Pasional*. One of the best releases by this great singer who has been much more successful on stage than on record. This 2007 CD celebrates the mature voice of a woman who has a powerful, emotional presence and has been at the top of the loosely named "Latin American song" tradition for over 25 years.

Julieta Venegas *Sí*. The 2003 record that firmly established Julieta as a major figure on the pop-rock scene. There is something very attractive about her funky innocence which saves her from a closer association with mainstream pop. Her 2007 release *Limón y Sal* won the Grammy for best Latin pop album.

★**Lila Downs** *La Sandunga*. Not the most recent but an excellent CD by this singer, who presents Mexican *sones* and *boleros* to a wider audience.

★**Maná** *Drama y Luz*. Considered the pioneers of the "Rock en Espanol" movement, this album garnered the old-timers a justly deserved Latin Grammy in 2011.

Molotov¿ *Dónde Jugarán las Niñas?* This aggressive, political hip-hop album was banned in Mexico for obscenity (and possible use of an underage model on its cover). Needless to say, it was a mammoth hit, and the band's "*Gimme Tha Power*" perfectly captures a moment in Mexican youth culture. Their songs about migrant workers, corruption and minibus drivers are contemporary classics.

Nortec Collective *Tijuana Sessions Vol 3*. More so than Vol 1 (which errs on the side of generic techno), this album shows off the funky potential of remixing blaring Mexican horns for the dancefloor.

can sound something like a shout from the soul. Concerts are often organized by stable-owners who pride themselves on their **dancing horses**: *conjunto* music is also popular in this region, but the horses only dance to the big harp music, and they do so on wooden platforms, beating out the rhythm and counter-rhythm with their hooves.

Tropical

Mexico has had a very close musical relationship with Cuba and Colombia since the earliest days of the recording industry, and music that is born in one of the three countries tends to have a rebirth in another. It was in Mexico that **Damasio Pérez Prado** "discovered" the **mambo**; Cuban chanteuse **Celia Cruz** lived here, as did **Bienvenido Granda**, **Beny Moré**, **Rubén González**, **Enrique Jorrín** and **Miguel Matamoros** among others. All the different styles of upbeat and romantic music that these gods produced tend to be known in Mexico as **música tropical** and they are still much consumed, although the younger generation prefer **reggaetón**: a Latin (mainly Puerto Rican) version of hip-hop blaring from bars and radio all over the country.

Trova yucateca, a local style from the Yucatán, was present at the birth of the **bolero** in Santiago de Cuba and this romantic repertoire has a long history of coming and going between the two countries. This is hardly surprising, since Mérida, the sleepy capital of Yucatán state, is geographically (and in some ways culturally) closer to Havana than to Mexico City. In the 1950s, trios like **Los Panchos** took the Cuban *bolero* and the Yucatecan *trova* and established the formula of a *requinto* guitar, two Spanish guitars and the harmony of three voices.

Such trios were enormously popular throughout the second half of the twentieth century and, although they are few and far between in Mexico City today, at least ten trios gather every night in the main square of Mérida to offer their local repertoire, performed in the style of Los Panchos, while in the theatres and clubs, there is a series of excellent groups that are fusing *trova* with Cuban *son* and other styles. **Yahal Kaab** offers an almost perfect contemporary fusion of the Yucatán and Cuba while the younger, more commercial group **Los Juglares** have a spectacular energy and stage presence. For people who (understandably) fall in love with the music, look for CDs by the grandfather of this style, **Guty Cárdenas**, who died in 1932 at the age of 27 but whose magic is still very much alive. **Armando Manzanero** was a *trovador* who emigrated to Mexico City in the 1970s and developed a new *bolero* style which has made him a favourite, not just in Mexico but all over Latin America and especially in Cuba.

Danzón and cumbia

Like the *bolero*, **danzón** is originally Cuban, but the Mexican version, which is always instrumental and more formal than the original, filled oversized dance halls in Mexico City for more than half a century. It is still danced under the stars in the main square of Veracruz and behind the Ciudadela market in Mexico City: bastions of elderly couples who are masters of elegance and style and who won't let their age get in the way of a subtle sensuality that is…irresistible.

It is a similar story with the **cumbia**, a commercial style that was born in Colombia and became enormously popular in Mexico in the 1970s, when **Sonora Dinamita** came, saw and conquered, and then fractured into several different groups, each with the same name.

Norteño

From Mexico's northern border came **norteño**, known in the US as **Tejano** or just Tex-Mex, traditional music that broke into the mainstream and became enormously popular in the early 1990s. This achievement is associated, above all, with **Los Tigres del Norte**, a band who had a mammoth hit with their 1988 Grammy winner "*Gracias América sin Fronteras*". *Norteño*, the preferred style for accompanying the *corrido* ballads that are also played on the Pacific coast and in Morelos in central Mexico, has a history that long predates its commercial breakthrough. The late 1920s were the golden age of the **corrido**, when songs of the recent Revolution were recorded in San Antonio, Texas, and distributed on both sides of the border. The accordion, which had arrived with German immigrants in the late nineteenth century, was introduced into the originally guitar-based groups by **Narciso Martínez** and **Santiago Jiménez** (father of the famous Flaco) in the 1930s, and the sound that they developed became the essence of *corrido* ensembles on both sides of the border.

Along with the **accordion** came the polka, and by the 1950s this had blended with the traditional duet-singing of northern Mexico and with salon dances like the waltz, mazurka and the *chotis* (the central European *schottische* that travelled to Spain and France before arriving in northern Mexico) to produce the definitive *norteño* style. The accordion pepped up the songs with lead runs and flourishes between the verses, but the *conjuntos norteños* needed to round out their sound to keep up with the big bands and so added bass and rolling drums – the basis of today's **conjuntos**.

The *corrido* ballads tell of anti-heroes: small-time drug runners, illegal immigrants, a thief with one blond eyebrow who defied the law. *Norteño* reflects the mood of a country that generally considers the government to be big-time thieves and hence has a certain respect for everyday people with the courage to stand up to a crooked system. Groups like Los Tigres del Norte and **Los Cadetes del Norte** take stories from the local papers and convert them into ballads that usually begin "Voy a cantarles un corrido" ("I'm going to sing you a *corrido*") before launching into a gruesome tale sung in a deadpan style as if it were nothing to go to a local dance and get yourself killed.

Los Tigres are still the superstars of *norteño*, on both sides of the border. Quite early in their career, the band modified the traditional line-up by adding a sax and mixed the familiar rhythms with *cumbias*; however, their nasal singing style and the combination of instruments identifies the music very clearly as *norteño*. The likes of **Ramón Ayala** continue to play the *norteño* repertoire and **Los Tucanes de Tijuana** get themselves into trouble with their narco-*corridos*, but most of the original bands have moved into the *conjunto* mould, playing romantic music as well as upbeat songs that combine elements of *música tropical* and *norteño*. Today the lines are very blurred between *conjuntos*, *norteño*, *banda* and a new favourite: the **duranguense**, which has its own, very popular dance and a range of artists such as **El As de la Sierra**, **K-Paz de la Sierra** and **AK7**, whose names confirm their origins in the narco-dominated mountain towns of the north.

The Banda boom

The enormous success of Los Tigres del Norte and their updated *norteño* sound resulted in a phenomenon that changed the face of Mexican music in the mid-1990s: **banda** music. This is a fusion of the *norteño* style with the brass bands that have played at village fiestas all over the country for the last century. There are now hundreds of *bandas* in Mexico – ranging in size from eight to twenty musicians – all playing brass and percussion, with just an occasional guitar. Their repertoire includes *norteño* polkas, *ranchera* ballads, *cumbia*, merengue and salsa. The most exciting of these groups is a fiery orchestra from Mazatlán, the **Banda El Recodo**. This is not a new band; indeed, its former leader, **Don Cruz Lizárraga**, had been in the business for half a century, starting out in a traditional *tambora* marching band (the *tambora* is the huge, carried side drum). However, Don Cruz had always had an eye for musical fashions, adapting his material to merengue, *ranchera* or whatever anyone wanted to hear. His great *banda* hit was a version of Cuban bandleader Beny Moré's classic "*La Culebra*". Other big-name bands include **Banda Limón** and the extravagant **Banda Cuisillos** that have been known to dress up in feathers and perform a neo-Aztec ritual before launching into the *banda* repertoire.

The *banda* boom dominated the national airwaves in the 1990s, and the genre remains incredibly popular. Outside the big cities, it is still the *bandas* that fill the stadiums and village halls, and it's their names you'll see painted in enormous multicoloured letters on patches of white wall along the roads. The craze brought with it a series of new dances, too, particularly the *quebradita* – a gymnastic, very intimate combination of *lambada*, polka and even a little bit of swing and hip-hop, which is danced with particular skill in points north of Guadalajara. Despite its enormous following outside the capital, *banda* music is considered very unsophisticated by the urban elite. It exists as a parallel musical culture that has created its own aesthetics in terms of the slightly off-the-note vocal style developed by singers like Mazatlán-based **Julio Preciado**, cultivating the image of the Mexican macho in tight leather pants and a black cowboy hat with lines of ladies screaming at their feet.

Divas and Música Ranchera

Don't expect **women** in Mexico to take the macho culture sitting down. There is a very long and glorious tradition of female **divas** who share less in terms of their musical styles and more in terms of their fierce independence, and the confidence to take on different influences and make them their own.

A forerunner who has inspired many of the later divas was **Lucha Reyes**, the remarkable singer of the **ranchera** repertoire which took the bucolic, upbeat *sones* and – in the flood of nostalgia that accompanied the growth of the cities in the 1940s – converted them into a sad lament for a lost way of life in which the woman was always the downfall and tequila the remedy. It was a man, **José Alfredo Jimenez**, who converted this music – so much more simple than the complex *sones* – into an art form. He composed songs like "*El Rey*" in which he sings of a man who has no money, no throne, nobody to maintain him and yet, despite that, he continues to be the king.

A close friend of José Alfredo's, **Chavela Vargas** was a remarkable figure in the 1950s. In a conservative, Catholic culture, she was proud to be gay, and she sang José Alfredo's songs in bars and nightclubs, changing the words so that she could lament and celebrate the love of a woman. Chavela retired early but, after giving up alcohol, she returned to professional life in the late 1980s and was serenaded by Pedro Almodovar, among others. She played at the Olympia in Paris, recording with the elite of Spanish superstars, and then returned to Mexico, the home she had adopted after leaving Costa Rica as a young girl. At the age of 90 Chavela recorded one final CD, *Por mi Culpa!*, before passing away in 2012.

One composer favoured by Chavela was **Agustín Lara**, "El Flaco de Oro", who fused the spirit of *ranchera* music with the Cuban *bolero*, creating a style that remains enormously popular in Mexico and all over Latin America, where it coexists alongside the Cuban *boleros*. "*El rival*", "*Amor de mis amores*" and "*Mujer*" are among the many classics that have survived for more than fifty years. Each generation of mainstream Mexican artists reinvents Lara for its own glory, and the countless CDs dedicated to his memory now include several recorded by flamenco singers from Andalucía.

Possibly the greatest contemporary diva is **Eugenia León**, who typifies the style with an exquisite voice that brought her fame first as a protest singer in the 1970s, later singing *ranchera boleros*, *norteño* and songs that were composed especially for her by writers like the late Marcial Alejandro. Despite her repute and more than thirty years at the top, she remains remarkably natural and is a generous artist who now spends much of her time promoting the talents of other musicians through her TV interviews and documentaries.

Mexican pop and "Latin Alternative"

Latin pop music has traditionally been dominated by Colombian, Puerto Rican and American Latino performers, but Mexico has its own extremely influential scene. Since the 1990s the biggest name has been **Thalía**, the singer/dancer/actress and "Queen of Latin Pop" from Mexico City who has sold over 40 million records – she's also one of only a few Mexican artists to have recorded albums in English (the eponymous *Thalía* in 2003). Thalía's contemporary, singer **Paulina Rubio** has been almost as successful (with over 20 million records sold) and has also recorded in English (*Border Girl* in 2002) – both stars have millions of fans across the US border. Similarly iconic singers include rock-pop superstar **Alejandra Guzmán**, **Ana Gabriel** (another performer who often switches genres) and **Gloria Trevi**, who lives across the border in McAllen, Texas. On the men's side is crooner **Luis Miguel** (actually born in Puerto Rico) and **Marco Antonio Solís**, a multi-Grammy award winner, both dominating charts since the 1990s. Younger stars include Madrid-born **Belinda Peregrín**, the "Princess of Latin Pop", whose debut album *Belinda* (2003) was a massive hit. Her most recent release, *Catarsis* (2013), reached number two on the US Latin pop chart.

Lila Downs, who enjoys tremendous success both in Mexico and beyond, has remained largely apart from mainstream pop, using her admirable voice to project her own versions of music from Veracruz; *boleros, ranchera* classics in the style of Lucha Reyes and, more recently, a repertoire that is very much her own (sometimes dubbed "**Latin Alternative**"). The daughter of a US filmmaker and a Mixtec mother from Oaxaca, she has carved an important place for herself on both sides of the border. With her neo-Frida Kahlo image, Lila has a tremendous stage presence and she was confirmed as a major international artist with her performance at the 2003 Oscar ceremonies.

In the wake of Lila come **Julieta Venegas** from Tijuana, whose platinum-selling CDs are favourites on the pop-rock circuit, but whose natural style and quirky innocence separate her from media-born artists, and two new names who have a fierce independence that distinguishes them from the mainstream. **Ximena Sariñana** and **Natalia Lafourcade** are both younger, feisty singers who move in and out of the pop-rock world, according to their different moods.

Rock en Español

One reason that traditional forms such as *son* flourished in Mexico is that the country was closed to **rock** music until the late 1980s, when the government finally lifted import regulations and laws banning rock concerts. These had been in place since the 1971 Arándaro festival, dubbed the "Mexican Woodstock", scandalized the nation and effectively drove the country's rock music culture underground. When the borders opened in 1990, international rock music flooded the local market and Mexican rock began to flourish. The boom began in Mexico City, with middle-class rockers like **Los Caifanes** playing to middle-class audiences who knew about the outside scene because they, or their parents, travelled regularly to Europe and the US. Ironically, the Caifanes' massive hit was a 1988 cover of a traditional Cuban *son*, "*La Negra Tomasa*", which appealed to a public that understood *son* and salsa better than the British punk referenced in other songs. A little later, the eclectic **Café Tacuba** began to reach a bigger audience, with an interest, to some extent, in exploring Mexican roots and reinterpreting Mexican *son* in their own way. Then came **Maldita Vecindad** from Mexico City and **Maná**, from Guadalajara, and Mexican rock – now rather slickly produced – entered the superstar level.

In the late 1990s, the scene began to splinter into subcultures. The industrial town of Monterrey, home to a prestigious university and a lot of English-speaking, US-oriented youth, was a seemingly bottomless well of talent that drew comparisons to Seattle in the grunge years. Funky mix-masters **Plastilina Mosh**, ska band **El Gran Silencio** and **Control Machete**'s hip-hop went from here to Latin MTV. In Tijuana, meanwhile, **Nortec Collective** helped create an international club scene with its remixes of classic *norteño* sounds with techno beats. In Mexico City **ska** became immensely popular alongside **hip-hop**, with excellent bands such as **Molotov** making piercing social commentary in their songs about politics, corruption and what it feels like to live on the wrong side of the US border.

The music section was originally written by Mary Farquharson. Mary is co-founder of Discos Corason (⦿ corason .com) and was one of the original founders of World Circuit. She has lived in Mexico since 1987.

Books

Mexico has attracted more than its fair share of famous foreign writers, and has inspired a vast literature and several classics. Until very recently, however, Mexican writers had received little attention outside the country. Books with a ★ symbol are highly recommended.

IMPRESSIONS OF MEXICO

Jeff Biggers *In the Sierra Madre*. Biggers juxtaposes the history of the Copper Canyon region – with all its indigenous tribes and foreign treasure-hunters – with his present-day experiences living there amid the Rarámuri, the drug-runners and other colourful characters. Really lively story-telling from someone with an obvious love of the place.

Tony Cohan *Mexican Days: Journeys into the Heart of Mexico*. Cohan, an American novelist, relocated to San Miguel de Allende in the 1980s; this is a travelogue of his explorations into small towns after some twenty years in Mexico – a perspective that's both respectful and informed.

Carl Franz, Lorena Havens and Steve Rogers *The People's Guide to Mexico*. Not a guidebook as such: more a series of anecdotes and words of advice for staying out of trouble and heading off the beaten track. Perennially popular with old hippies of all ages (2012 saw the publication of the fourteenth edition), and deservedly so.

Richard Grant *God's Middle Finger: Into the Lawless Heart of the Sierra Madre* (published in the UK as *Bandit Roads: Into the Lawless Heart of Mexico*). A British journalist's adventures as he finds himself caught up in the north-east's drug wars post-2000 and barely escapes with his life; a thoroughly entertaining read.

★ **Graham Greene** *The Lawless Roads*. In the late 1930s Greene was sent to Mexico to investigate the effects of the persecution of the Catholic Church. The result (see also his novel, opposite) was this classic account of his travels in a very bizarre era of modern Mexican history.

D.H. Lawrence *Mornings in Mexico*. A very slim volume, half of which is devoted to the Hopi Indians of New Mexico, this is an uncharacteristically cheerful account of Lawrence's stay in southern Mexico, and beautifully written – although his characterizations of native culture will likely strike modern readers as condescending.

John Lloyd Stephens *Incidents of Travel in Central America, Chiapas, and Yucatán*. Stephens was a classic nineteenth-century traveller. Acting as American ambassador to Central America, he indulged his own enthusiasm for archeology. His journals, full of superb Victorian pomposity punctuated with sudden waves of enthusiasm, make great reading, especially as companions to the great Maya ruins, many of which he helped uncover. The best editions include the fantastic original illustrations by Frederick Catherwood; you won't have trouble finding inexpensive paperback versions in Mexico, and it's available for free on Kindle.

John Steinbeck *Log from the Sea of Cortez*. The record of Steinbeck's jaunt around Baja California by boat in 1940, part travelogue, part marine-life guide; you'll find it far more amusing than Steinbeck's often bleak novels.

John Kenneth Turner *Barbarous Mexico*. Turner was a journalist, and this account of his travels through nineteenth-century Mexico exposing the conditions of workers in the plantations of the Yucatán, serialized in US newspapers, did much to discredit the regime of Porfirio Díaz.

Ronald Wright *Time Among the Maya*. A vivid and sympathetic account of travels from Belize through Guatemala, Chiapas and Yucatán in the 1990s, meeting the Maya of today and exploring their obsession with time. The level of detail makes this a complex read – best for readers with a specific interest in ancient Maya culture.

MEXICAN FICTION

Mariano Azuela *The Underdogs*. The first novel of the Revolution (finished in 1915), *The Underdogs* is told through the eyes of a group of peasants who form a semi-regular Revolutionary armed band; it relates their escapades, progress and eventual betrayal and massacre. Initially fighting for land and liberty, they end up caught in an uncontrollable cycle of violence and descend into brutal nihilism.

Carmen Boullosa *The Miracle Worker*. One of Mexico's best contemporary writers, Boullosa focuses on traditional Mexican themes, often borrowing characters from history and myth. *The Miracle Worker* explores Mexican attitudes to Catholicism through the eyes of a messianic healer and her followers. The story can be seen as a parable about the Mexican political system, where ordinary Mexicans petition a distant government for favours, which are granted or refused in seemingly arbitrary decisions. You may be able to find Boullosa's novel *Leaving Tabasco* (2002) more readily; it's not as strong a work, but an interesting vision of small-town life (and trauma) through the eyes of a child.

María Amparo Escandón *Gonzalez & Daughter Trucking Co.* A story within a story, told with gusto by an inmate at a women's prison in Mexicali – borderline pulp, with cliffhangers and campy drama, but heartwarming and funny in its treatment of loyalty and freedom. Escandón's earlier work, *Esperanza's Box of Saints*, is a charming, quick-read tale of female emancipation.

★ **Laura Esquivel** *Like Water for Chocolate*. Adapted to film, Esquivel's novel proved a huge hit in Mexico and abroad. The book is even better: funny, sexy, sentimental (schmaltzy, even), it deals with the star-crossed romance of Tita, whose lover marries her sister. Using the magic of the kitchen, she sets out to seduce him back. The book is written in monthly episodes, each of which is prefaced with a traditional Mexican recipe. The author's 2006 novel, *Malinche*, is not nearly as successful, but presents a sympathetic version of Cortés' courtesan and translator, whose name is synonymous with "traitor" in Mexico.

★ **Carlos Fuentes** *The Death of Artemio Cruz* and *The Old Gringo*. Fuentes is by far the best-known Mexican writer outside Mexico, influenced by Mariano Azuela and Juan Rulfo, and an early exponent of magical realism. In *The Death of Artemio Cruz*, the hero, a rich and powerful man on his deathbed, looks back over his life and loves, from an idealist youth in the Revolution through disillusion to corruption and power. *The Old Gringo* takes place during the Revolution, imagining that vanished American writer Ambrose Bierce has joined Pancho Villa's army; it's shorter, but no less carefully crafted. These are the classics, but Fuentes was a prolific writer and you'll find plenty of others if these pique your interest.

Mónica Lavín (ed) *Points of Departure*. A collection of short stories from some of the country's most respected contemporary writers – the selection is a little uneven, but

it may be interesting and refreshing to read stories that *don't* involve magical realism.

★ **Octavio Paz** (ed) *Mexican Poetry*. Edited by Paz (perhaps the leading man of letters of Mexico's post-Revolutionary era) and translated by Samuel Beckett, this is as good a taste as you could hope for of modern Mexican poets. Some of Paz's own poetry is also available in translation.

Elena Poniatowska *Here's to You, Jesúsa!* One of Mexico's best-known essayists and journalists lightly fictionalizes the life story of her cleaning lady to create a lively "autobiography" covering her marriage, involvement in the Revolution and the postwar period. Some of Poniatowska's other excellent works available in English include *Massacre in Mexico*, a collage of testimonies of those present at the 1968 massacre of students in Tlatelolco, and *Tinisima*, a portrait of Communist organizer and photographer Tina Modotti.

Juan Rulfo *Pedro Páramo*. First published in 1955, this is widely regarded as the greatest Mexican novel of the twentieth century and a precursor of magical realism. The living and spirit worlds mesh when, at the behest of his dying mother, the narrator visits the deserted village haunted by the memory of his brutal father, Pedro Páramo. Dark, but ultimately very rewarding. Rulfo's short-story collection, *The Burning Plain and Other Stories*, was rated by Gabriel García Márquez as the best in Latin America.

Ignacio Solares *Yankee Invasion*. An account of the 1847 US capture of Mexico City from the perspective of an ageing journalist, looking back at his youthful involvement. A sometimes uneasy mix of romance, psychology and history, but ultimately an enjoyable read. Solares is one of Mexico's leading men of letters.

FOREIGN FICTION

There are hundreds of novels by non-Mexicans set in Mexico, all too many in the sex-and-shopping genre. Apart from those below, others to look out for include a whole clutch of modern Americans, especially **Jack Kerouac**'s *Desolation Angels* and several of Richard Brautigan's novels. And of course there's **Carlos Castaneda**'s *Don Juan* series – a search for enlightenment through *peyote*.

Graham Greene *The Power and the Glory*. Inspired by his investigative travels, this story of a doomed whisky priest, on the run from the authorities, makes a great yarn and a wonderful movie.

D.H. Lawrence *The Plumed Serpent*. One of Lawrence's own favourites, the novel reflects his intense dislike of the country that followed on from the brief honeymoon period of *Mornings in Mexico* (see opposite). Fans of his heavy spiritualism will love it.

Haniel Long *The Marvellous Adventure of Cabeza de Vaca*. Two short stories in one volume – the first the account of a shipwrecked conquistador's journey across the new continent, the second the thoughts and hopes of Malinche, Cortés' interpreter.

★ **Malcolm Lowry** *Under the Volcano*. A classic since its publication, Lowry's account of the last day in the life of

the British consul in Cuernavaca – passed in a mescal-induced haze – is totally brilliant. His *Dark as the Grave Wherein My Friend Is Laid* is also based on his Mexican experiences.

★ **B. Traven** various works. In the 1920s and 1930s, the mysterious Traven – whose true identity is itself the subject of a series of books – wrote a series of compelling novels set in Mexico. Among the best-known are *Treasure of the Sierra Madre* (later a film starring Humphrey Bogart) and *The Death Ship*, but of more interest if you're travelling are such works as *The Bridge in the Jungle* and the other six books in the *Jungle* series: *Government*, *The Carreta*, *March to the Monteria*, *Trozas*, *The Rebellion of the Hanged* and *General from the Jungle*. These latter all deal with the state of the peasantry and the growth of revolutionary feeling in the last years of the Díaz dictatorship.

HISTORY

Bartolome de Las Casas *A Short Account of the Destruction of the Indies*. The counterpoint to Díaz and Cortés, with Las Casas leaving no doubt that the conquest of Mexico was a bloody, gruesome affair.

Inga Clendinnen *Ambivalent Conquests: Maya and Spaniard in Yucatán 1517 to 1570*. A product of meticulous research that documents the methods and consequences of the Spanish Conquest of the Yucatán. The ambivalence in the title reflects doubts about the effectiveness of the Conquest in subjugating the Maya, and the book provides insights into the rebellions that followed: more than three hundred years later, the Maya rose in revolt during the Caste Wars, and almost succeeded in driving out their white overlords. Later editions also comment briefly on the 1994 Chiapas uprising.

Hernán Cortés *Letters from Mexico*. The thoughts and impressions of the conquistador, at first hand. Less exciting than Díaz, though.

★ **Bernal Díaz** *The Conquest of New Spain*. This abridged version is still the best available of Díaz's classic *Historia Verdadera de la Conquista de la Nueva España*. Díaz, having been on two earlier expeditions to Mexico, accompanied Cortés throughout his campaign of conquest, and this magnificent eyewitness account makes compelling reading.

Adolfo Gilly *The Mexican Revolution*. Considered the classic work on the Revolution, this was written in Mexico City's notorious Lecumberri jail (Gilly was later granted an absolute pardon). Heavy-going and highly theoretical, though.

John Mason Hart *Empire & Revolution: The Americans in Mexico since the Civil War*. A fascinating study of the relationship between the US and Mexico, and in particular US imperialist aspirations and involvement in Mexican financial affairs. Hart's *Revolutionary Mexico* is a detailed history of the Mexican Revolution following the same theme of US involvement. Both are serious works of history, heavy-going in parts.

Enrique Krauze *Mexico: Biography of Power*. First published in Spanish, this sprawling history covers most of the nineteenth and twentieth centuries – the biography format makes it very readable, and easier to dip into if you can't weather all 896 pages. Street names and public holidays will make a lot more sense, at the very least.

Greg Niemann *Baja Legends*. Essential reading for travellers to Baja California, a detailed compendium of all the crazy characters, historical events and places that make it such a magical destination.

★ **Richard and Rosalind Perry** *Maya Missions*. One in a series of expertly written guides to the sometimes overlooked treasures of Mexico's colonial religious architecture. *More Maya Missions* covers Chiapas. Both are illustrated by the authors' simple but beautiful drawings. These specialist offerings, ideal for travellers who want more information than most guidebooks can provide, are not widely available, though you can sometimes find them in tourist bookshops in the areas they cover (and online).

John Reed *Insurgent Mexico*. This collection of his reportage of the Mexican Revolution was put together by Reed himself. He spent several months in 1913 and 1914 with various generals of the Revolution – especially Villa – and the book contains great descriptions of them, their men and the mood of the times.

★ **Nelson Reed** *The Caste War of the Yucatan*. Reed's book is the authority on this tumultuous and defining era in Yucatán history, with great detail on the Talking Cross movement. A must-read for anyone intrigued by this period.

★ **Jasper Ridley** *Maximilian & Juárez*. This comprehensive, highly readable account of one of "the great tragicomedies of the nineteenth century" charts the attempt by Napoleon III to establish Archduke Maximilian as the emperor of Mexico. The colourful narrative brings to life an unmitigated political disaster with huge consequences, including the execution of Maximilian, the insanity of his wife Carlota and the emergence of the US as a world power.

Hugh Thomas *Conquest: Montezuma, Cortés, and the Fall of Old Mexico* (published in the UK as *The Conquest of Mexico*). A brilliant narrative history of the Conquest by the British historian previously best known for his history of the Spanish Civil War. A massive work of real scholarship and importance – much of the archive material was unearthed only in the 1980s and 1990s – but also humorous and readable, with appendices on everything from Aztec beliefs, history and genealogy to Cortés' wives and lovers.

ANCIENT MEXICO

Warwick Bray *Everyday Life of the Aztecs*. An informative volume about Aztec warfare, music, games, folklore, religious ritual, social organization, economic and political systems and agricultural practice. Although the book is now showing its age, and some of its conclusions are a bit dubious, its attractive comprehensiveness more than makes up for this. An excellent general introduction.

Inga Clendinnen *Aztecs: An Interpretation*. A social history of the Aztec empire that seeks to explain the importance – and acceptance – of human sacrifice and other rituals. Fascinating, though best to know something about the Aztecs before you start.

Michael D. Coe *The Maya*. The best available general introduction to the Maya: concise, clear and comprehensive. Coe has also written several weightier, academic volumes. His *Breaking the Maya Code*, a history of the decipherment of the Maya glyphs, owes much to the fact that Coe was present at many of the most important meetings leading to the breakthrough that demonstrated how the glyphs actually did reproduce Maya speech. It is a beautifully written, ripping yarn, though the attacks on Eric Thompson become a bit wearisome. In *Mexico: From the Olmecs to the Aztecs*, co-authored with Rex Koontz, he introduces Mexico's other early cultures.

★**Nigel Davies** *The Ancient Kingdoms of Mexico*. Although no single text covers all the ancient cultures, this comes pretty close, covering the central areas from the Olmecs through Teotihuacán and the Toltecs to the Aztec empire. An excellent mix of historical, archeological, social and artistic information, but it doesn't cover the Maya. Davies is also the author of several more-detailed academic works on the Aztecs and Toltecs, including *The Aztecs, A History*.

Munro S. Edmonson (trans.) *Heaven Born Merida and Its Destiny: The Book of Chilam Balam of Chumayel*. The *Chilam Balam* is a recollection of Maya history and myth, compiled by the Maya over centuries; this version was written in Maya in Latin script in the eighteenth century. Although the style is not easy, it's one of the few keys into the Maya view of the world.

Diego de Landa *Yucatán Before and After the Conquest*. A translation by William Gates of the work written in 1566 as *Relación de las Cosas de Yucatán*. De Landa's destruction of almost all original Maya books as "works of the devil" leaves his own account as the chief source on Maya life and society in the immediate post-Conquest period. Written during his imprisonment in Spain on charges of cruelty to the Indians, the book provides a fascinating wealth of detail. Various other translations are widely available in Mexico.

Simon Martin and Nikolai Grube *Chronicle of the Maya Kings and Queens*. A more graphic approach to Maya history, replete with photo illustrations, timelines, hieroglyphics and the like, making the complex dynasties a little easier to grasp.

★**Mary Ellen Miller and Karl Taube** *An Illustrated Dictionary of the Gods and Symbols of Ancient Mexico and the Maya*. A superb modern reference on ancient Mesoamerica, written by two leading scholars. Taube's *Aztec and Maya Myths* is perfect as a short, accessible introduction to Mesoamerican mythology.

Chris Morton and Ceri Louise Thomas *The Mystery of the Crystal Skulls*. Intriguing, if somewhat sensationalist, investigation into an ancient Amerindian legend that tells of a number of life-size crystal skulls said to contain vital information about the destiny of mankind. Following the discovery that such a skull actually exists, film-makers Morton and Thomas set off on a journey through Mexico and Central America, meeting experts in Maya culture, archeologists and modern-day shamans and reaching their own conclusions.

Linda Schele, David Freidel et al. *A Forest of Kings: The Untold Story of the Ancient Maya*. The authors, at the forefront of the "new archeology", have been personally responsible for decoding many Maya glyphs, revolutionizing and popularizing this field. Although their populist writing style is controversial, it has also inspired a devoted following. They have shown that, far from being governed by peaceful astronomer-priests, the ancient Maya were ruled by hereditary kings, lived in populous, aggressive city-states and engaged in a continuous entanglement of alliances and war. The story continues in *The Blood of Kings*, by Linda Schele and Mary Ellen Miller.

Robert Sharer *The Ancient Maya*. The classic, comprehensive (and weighty) account of Maya civilization, now in its sixth edition. Required reading for archeologists, it also provides a fascinating reference for the non-expert.

Popol Vuh The Quiché Maya bible, a fascinating creation myth, is available in two main translations (many others can also be found): the classic version by Dennis Tedlock is arguably still the most readable; Allen J Christenson's two-volume approach gives a literal translation as well. The Maya obsession with time can be well appreciated here, where dates are recorded with painstaking precision.

Ptolemy Tompkins *This Tree Grows Out of Hell*. An interesting attempt to piece together the mystery of Mesoamerican religion, synthesizing and making readable many of the late twentieth-century findings in the area. The latter half of the book is a thoroughly unconvincing apology for the brutality of the Aztecs.

Richard F. Townsend *The Aztecs*. Companion in the series to Coe's *Maya* book (see opposite), this attempts to be an introduction to all aspects of Aztec history and culture, but if you haven't done some prior reading, the details of names and battles may be overwhelming. That said, it's a comprehensive reference, updated in a third edition (2009).

SOCIETY, POLITICS AND CULTURE

Taisha Abelar *The Sorcerer's Crossing*. The extraordinary true story of an American woman who joins an all-female group of sorcerers in Mexico and undergoes a rigorous physical and mental training process, designed to enable her to breach the limits of ordinary perception.

★**Jorge G. Castaneda** *Manana Forever? Mexico and the Mexicans*. Fabulous exposé of Mexican culture by a former foreign minister, tackling the thorny issue of why Mexico's soccer team has fared so poorly, as well as meatier subjects such as Mexico's relationship with the US.

Clare Ferguson *Flavours of Mexico*. All the classics are here: tortillas, enchiladas, empanadas, *flautas* and tamales, along with party-food suggestions and a few vegetarian recipes. A colourful and straightforward cookbook that will inspire you to keep feasting on Mexican cuisine once back home.

Hayden Herrera *Frida: A Biography of Frida Kahlo.* This mesmerizing biography brings to life a woman of extreme magnetism and originality. Starting with her childhood in Mexico City, the account describes the crippling accident she had as a teenager that left her in chronic pain, her tempestuous marriage to Diego Rivera and the various men with whom she had affairs, including, most notoriously, Leon Trotsky. The book contains numerous colour reproductions of her paintings.

Diana Kennedy *From My Mexican Kitchen: Techniques and Ingredients.* Kennedy was a pioneer in bringing the multifaceted cuisine of Mexico to the attention of Americans, when she published her first cookbook in 1972. This book is a good starting point for anyone new to Mexican cooking. Her many other titles are good too: look out for *My Mexico: A Culinary Odyssey with More Than 300 Recipes*, which has a great travelogue element.

Patrick Marnham *Dreaming with His Eyes Open: A Life of Diego Rivera.* A gripping account of the extraordinary life of the great Mexican muralist in which truths are revealed and myths are unravelled.

★ **Susanna Palazuelos** *Mexico: The Beautiful Cookbook.* Recipes from Mexico's most popular celebrity chef, the Acapulco-based Palazuelos, translated into English. Blends the traditional with contemporary, as well as more unusual regional dishes from all over the country.

Octavio Paz *The Labyrinth of Solitude.* An acclaimed series of philosophical essays exploring the social and political state of modern Mexico. Paz, who died in 1998, won the Nobel Prize for literature in 1990 and was universally regarded as the country's leading poet and philosopher (see p.851).

★ **John Ross** *Rebellion from the Roots.* A fascinating early account of the build-up to and first months of the 1994 Zapatista rebellion, and still the definitive book on the subject. Ross's reporting style provides a detailed and informative background, showing the uprising was no surprise to the Mexican army. His *Zapatistas: Making Another World Possible: Chronicles of Resistance 2000–2006* updated the ongoing saga.

WILDLIFE AND ENVIRONMENT

★ **Les Beletsky** *Travellers' Wildlife Guides Southern Mexico.* An excellent, if rather bulky, field guide, with colour plates of not just birds but also reptiles and mammals found through the Yucatán, Oaxaca and Chiapas.

★ **Steve Howell and Sophie Webb** *A Guide to the Birds of Mexico and Northern Central America.* A tremendous work, the result of years of research, this is the definitive book on the region's birds. Essential for all serious birders, though a bit hefty to use in the field. Howell's *Where to Watch Birds in Mexico* details more than a hundred sites.

Paul Humann and Ned DeLoach *Snorkeling Guide to Marine Life: Florida, Caribbean, Bahamas.* A handy, spiral-bound field guide to corals, fish, plants and other underwater life off the Caribbean coast. The same authors have individual titles on *Reef Fish Identification*, *Reef Creature Identification* and *Reef Coral Identification* for the same area, and a separate *Reef Fish Identification* title for the Pacific coast.

Victoria Schlesinger *Animals and Plants of the Ancient Maya: A Guide.* Examines the cultural significance of more than a hundred species in the ancient Maya world.

Language

Once you get into it, Spanish is a straightforward language, and in Mexico people are eager to understand and to help even the most faltering attempt. English is widely spoken, especially in heavily visited areas, but you'll get a far better reception if you at least try to communicate with people in their own tongue. You'll be helped by the fact that Mexicans speak relatively slowly, at least compared with Spaniards.

Rules of pronunciation

Relative to English, the rules of pronunciation are clear-cut and, once you get to know them, strictly observed. Unless there's an accent, words ending in d, l, r and z are stressed on the last syllable, all others on the second last. All vowels are pure and short.

A is between the A sound of "back" and that of "father".

E as in "get"

I as in "police"

O as in "hot"

U as in "rule"

C is spoken like S before E and I, hard otherwise: cerca is pronounced "SER-ka".

G is a guttural H sound (a little softer than the ch in "loch") before E or I, a hard G elsewhere: gigante becomes "hi-GAN-te".

H is always silent.

J is the same sound as a guttural G: jamón is pronounced "ham-ON".

LL sounds like an English Y: tortilla is pronounced "tor-TEE-ya".

N is as in English unless it has a tilde (accent) over it, when it becomes NY: mañana sounds like "ma-NYA-na".

QU is pronounced like an English K.

R is rolled; RR, doubly so.

V sounds more like B, vino becoming "BEE-no".

X has an S sound before consonants; between vowels in place names, it has an H sound, like México ("MEH-hee-ko") or Oaxaca ("wa-HA-ka"). In many place names from indigenous languages, the X is pronounced as S – as in Xochimilco ("so-chee-MIL-co"); in Maya, however, X sounds like SH – Xel-Ha is pronounced "shel-ha".

Z is the same as a soft C, so cerveza becomes "ser-VAY-sa".

Useful words and phrases

Although we've listed a few essential words and phrases here, if you're travelling for any length of time some kind of dictionary or phrasebook is obviously a worthwhile investment: the *Rough Guide to Mexican Spanish* is the best practical guide, correct and colloquial, and will have you speaking the language faster than any other phrasebook. One of the best small Latin American Spanish dictionaries is the University of Chicago version (Pocket Books), widely available in Mexico, although the Langenscheidt pocket dictionary is also handy because its yellow plastic cover holds up well. If you're using an older dictionary, bear in mind that CH, LL and Ñ are traditionally counted as separate letters and are listed after the Cs, Ls and Ns respectively; most current dictionaries, however, follow more familiar alphabetizing procedures, though Ñ retains its own section.

BASICS

Yes, No	Sí, No	**With, Without**	Con, Sin
Open, Closed	Abierto/a, Cerrado/a	**What?, How much?**	¿Qué?, ¿Cuánto?
Please, Thank you	Por favor, Gracias	**Good, Bad**	Buen(o)/a, Mal(o)/a
Push, Pull	Empujar, Tirar	**Here, There**	Aquí or Acá, Allí or Allá
Where?, When?	¿Dónde?, ¿Cuándo?	**Big, Small**	Gran(de), Pequeño/a

This, That	Éste, Eso	Today, Tomorrow	Hoy, Mañana
More, Less	Más, Menos	Yesterday	Ayer
Cheap, Expensive	Barato/a, Caro/a	Now, Later	Ahora, Más tarde

GREETINGS AND PLEASANTRIES

Hello, Goodbye	¡Hola!, Adiós	I am English	Soy inglés(a)
Good morning	Buenos días	...American*	...americano(a)
Good afternoon/night	Buenas tardes/noches	...Australian	...australiano(a)
How do you do?	¿Qué tal?	...Canadian	...canadiense(a)
See you later	Hasta luego	...Irish	...irlandés(a)
Sorry	Lo siento/disculpeme	...Scottish	...escosés(a)
Excuse me	Con permiso/perdón	...Welsh	...galés(a)
How are you?	¿Cómo está (usted)?	...New Zealander	...neozelandés(a)
Not at all/You're welcome	De nada/por nada		
I (don't) understand	(No) Entiendo		
Do you speak English?	¿Habla (usted) inglés?	*Mexicans are from the Americas too, so describing
I (don't) speak Spanish	(No) Hablo español	yourself as American can occasionally cause offence.
What (did you say)?	¿Mande?	Another option is "estadounidense" (or, more simply,
My name is...	Me llamo...	"de Los Estados Unidos", from the United States) if
What's your name?	¿Cómo se llama usted?	you are a US American.

NEEDS: HOTELS, TRANSPORT AND DIRECTIONS

I want...	Quiero...	How do I get to...?	¿Por dónde se va a...?
I'd like...please	Quisiera...por favor	Left, right, straight on	Izquierda, derecha,
Do you know...?	¿Sabe...?		derecho
I don't know	No sé	This way, that way	Por acá, por allá
There is...	(¿)Hay...(?) (Is there...?)	Where is...?	¿Dónde está...?
Give me...	Deme... (one like that)	...the bus station	...la camionera central
	(uno así)	...the nearest bank	...el banco más cercano
Do you have...?	¿Tiene...?	...the ATM	...el cajero automático
...the time	...la hora	...the post office	...el correo (la oficina
...a room	...un cuarto		de correos)
...with two beds/	...con dos camas/	...the toilet	...el baño/sanitario
...double bed	...cama matrimonial	Where does the bus	¿De dónde sale el autobús
It's for one person	Es para una persona	to...leave from?	para...?
(two people)	(dos personas)	Is this the train for	¿Es éste el tren para
...for one night	...para una noche	Chihuahua?	Chihuahua?
(one week)	(una semana)	I'd like a (return)	Quisiera un boleto (de
It's fine, how much is it?	¿Está bien, cuánto es?	ticket to...	ida y vuelta) para...
It's too expensive	Es demasiado caro	What time does it leave	¿A qué hora sale
Don't you have	¿No tiene algo más	(arrive in...)?	(llega en...)?
anything cheaper?	barato?	What is there to eat?	¿Qué hay para comer?
Can one...?	¿Se puede...?	What's that?	¿Qué es eso?
...camp (near) here?	¿...acampar (cerca de)	What's this called in	¿Cómo se llama éste
	aquí?	Spanish?	en español?
Is there a hotel nearby?	¿Hay un hotel cerca de		
	aquí?		

NUMBERS AND DAYS

1	un/uno/una	6	seis
2	dos	7	siete
3	tres	8	ocho
4	cuatro	9	nueve
5	cinco	10	diez

11	once	500	quinientos
12	doce	700	setecientos
13	trece	1000	mil
14	catorce	2000	dos mil
15	quince		
16	dieciséis	first	primero/a
17	diecisiete	second	segundo/a
20	veinte	third	tercero/a
21	veintiuno	fifth	quinto/a
30	treinta	tenth	decimo/a
40	cuarenta		
50	cincuenta	Monday	Lunes
60	sesenta	Tuesday	Martes
70	setenta	Wednesday	Miércoles
80	ochenta	Thursday	Jueves
90	noventa	Friday	Viernes
100	cien(to)	Saturday	Sábado
101	ciento uno	Sunday	Domingo
200	doscientos		

Food and drink terms

ON THE TABLE

Azúcar	Sugar	Pimienta	Pepper
Cuchara	Spoon	Queso	Cheese
Cuchillo	Knife	Sal	Salt
Cuenta	Bill/check	Salsa	Sauce
Mantequilla	Butter	Servilleta	Napkin
Pan	Bread	Tenedor	Fork

COOKING TERMS

A la parilla	Grilled over charcoal	Con mole	In a thick, rich sauce of chiles, nuts, spices and chocolate
A la plancha	Grilled on a hot plate		
A la tampiqueña	Strips of grilled meat served with guacamole	Empanizado/a	Breaded
A la veracruzana	Stewed with tomatoes, onions, olives and chile	En mojo de ajo	Fried with slow-cooked garlic
Al horno/horneado	Baked	Frito	Fried
Asado/a	Broiled	Poco hecho/a punto/bien cocido	Rare/medium/ well done
Barbacoa/pibil	Wrapped in banana leaves and steamed/ baked in a pit		

BREAKFAST

Huevos…	Eggs…	…rancheros	…fried, on a tortilla, smothered in a red chile sauce
…a la Mexicana	…scrambled with tomato, onion and chile		
…con jamón	…with ham	…revueltos	…scrambled
…con tocino	…with bacon	…tibios	…lightly boiled
…motuleños	…fried, served on a tortilla with beans, ham and cheese	Pan dulce	Pastries

SOUPS (SOPAS) AND STARTERS

Caldo	Broth (with bits in)	Sopa...	Soup...
Ceviche	Raw fish pieces, marinated in lime juice	...de fideos	...with noodles
		...de lentejas	...with lentils
Entremeses	Hors d'oeuvres	...de verduras	...with vegetables

TORTILLA AND CORN DISHES (ANTOJITOS)

Burritos	Wheat-flour tortillas, rolled and filled	Queso fundido	Melted cheese, served with tortillas and salsa
Chilaquiles	Tortilla chips stewed with meat and tomato sauce	Sincronizadas	Tortillas with melted cheese and ham
Enchiladas	Rolled-up tacos, covered in chile sauce and baked	Sopes	Bite-size tostadas
		Tacos	Soft corn tortillas with filling
Enchiladas suizas	As above, with green chile and cheese	Tacos al pastor	With spicy pork
		Tacos dorados	Deep-fried tacos
Flautas	Small, filled, fried tortillas	Tamales	Corn husk or banana-leaf packets of steamed corn-meal dough with a savoury or sweet filling
Gorditas	Small, fat, stuffed corn tortillas		
Machaca	Shredded dried meat scrambled with eggs	Tlacoyo	Fat tortilla stuffed with beans
Molletes	Split roll with beans and melted cheese	Torta	Filled bread roll, often toasted like a panino
Quesadillas	Toasted or fried tortillas topped with cheese	Tostadas	Flat crisp tortillas piled with meat and salad

FISH AND SEAFOOD (PESCADOS Y MARISCOS)

Anchoas	Anchovies	Langosta	Rock lobster
Atún	Tuna	Merluza	Hake
Cabrilla/Corvina	Sea bass	Ostión	Oyster
Calamares	Squid	Pez espada	Swordfish
Camarones	Prawns	Pulpo	Octopus
Cangrejo	Crab	Robalo	Bass
Caracol	Conch	Sardinas	Sardines
Filete entero	Whole, filleted fish	Trucha	Trout
Huachinango	Red snapper		

MEAT (CARNE) AND POULTRY (AVES)

Alambre	Kebab	Chuleta	Chop (usually pork)
Albóndigas	Meatballs	Conejo	Rabbit
Arrachera	Skirt steak	Cordero	Lamb
Barbacoa	Barbecued meat	Costilla	Rib
Bistec	Steak	Filete	Tenderloin/fillet
Cabrito	Kid	Guisado	Stew
Carne (de res)	Beef	Hígado	Liver
Carne adobado	Barbecued/spicily stewed meat	Lomo	Loin (of pork)
		Milanesa	Breaded escalope
Carnitas	Pork cooked with garlic until crispy	Pato	Duck
		Pavo/Guajolote	Turkey
Cerdo	Pork	Pechuga	Breast
Chivo	Goat	Pierna	Leg
Chorizo	Spicy sausage	Pollo	Chicken

Salchicha	Sausage	Ternera	Veal
Salpicón	Shredded meat with vinegar	Tripa/Callos	Tripe
		Venado	Venison

VEGETABLES (VERDURAS)

Aguacate	Avocado	Frijoles	Beans
Betabel	Beetroot (often as a juice)	Huitlacoche	Corn fungus, "Mexican truffles"
Calabacita	Courgette (zucchini)		
Calabaza	Squash	Jitomate	Tomato
Cebolla	Onion	Lechuga	Lettuce
Champiñones/hongos	Mushrooms	Lentejas	Lentils
Chícharos	Peas	Nopales	Prickly pear fronds
Col	Cabbage	Papas	Potatoes
Elote	Corn on the cob	Pepino	Cucumber
Espáragos	Asparagus	Rajas	Strips of mild green poblano pepper
Espinacas	Spinach		
Flor de calabaza	Squash blossoms	Zanahoria	Carrot

FRUITS (FRUTA) AND JUICE (JUGO)

Albaricoque/chabacano	Apricot	Melón	Melon
Cherimoya	Custard apple (sweetsop)	Naranja	Orange
Ciruela	Plum	Papaya	Papaya
Coco	Coconut	Piña	Pineapple
Durazno	Peach	Pitahaya	Dragonfruit, a type of cactus fruit
Frambuesa	Raspberry		
Fresa	Strawberry	Plátano	Banana/plantain
Guanábana	Soursop	Sandía	Watermelon
Guayaba	Guava	Toronja	Grapefruit
Higo	Fig	Tuna	Prickly pear fruit
Limón	Lime	Uva	Grape
Mamey	Large fruit with sweet pink flesh	Zapote	Sapodilla, fruit of the chicle tree

SWEETS (DULCES)

Ate	Quince paste	Ensalada de frutas	Fruit salad
Cajeta...	Caramel confection often served with...	Flan	Crème caramel
		Helado	Ice cream
...crepas	...pancakes	Nieve	Sorbet
...churros	...cinnamon fritters		

Glossary

Ahorita diminutive of ahora (now) meaning "right now" – but seldom applied as literally as a visitor might expect.

Alameda city park or promenade; large plaza.

Ayuntamiento town hall/government.

Aztec the empire that dominated the central valleys of Mexico from the thirteenth century until defeated by Cortés.

Barrio area within a town or city; suburb.

Camino blanco unpaved rural road, so called because it is paved with limestone gravel.

Camioneta small truck or van.

Cantina bar, traditionally men-only, but increasingly open to women.

Cenote underground water source in the Yucatán, a natural sinkhole in the limestone surface.

Chac Maya god of rain.

Chac-mool recumbent statue, possibly a sacrificial figure or messenger to the gods.

Comal large, round flat plate made of clay or metal used for cooking tortillas.

Comedor cheap restaurant, literally dining room; also called a cocina económica.

Convento either convent or monastery.

CTM central union organization.

Cuauhtémoc the last Aztec leader, commander of the final resistance to Cortés, and a national hero.

Descompuesto out of order.

Don/Doña courtesy titles (sir/madam), mostly used in letters or for professional people or the boss.

Ejido communal farmland.

Enramadas palapa-covered restaurants.

EPR Ejército Popular Revolucionario, the Popular Revolutionary Army. Guerrilla group, not allied to the Zapatistas; their first appearance was in Guerrero in 1996.

EZLN Ejército Zapatista de Liberación Nacional, the Zapatista Army of National Liberation.

Feria fair (market).

Finca ranch or plantation.

FONART government agency to promote crafts.

Fonda simple restaurant or boarding house.

FONATUR government tourism agency.

Fray Spanish word for friar.

Gringo not necessarily insulting, though it does imply North American – said to come from invading US troops, either because they wore green coats or because they sang "Green grow the rushes oh!..."

Guayabera embroidered Cuban-style shirt, usually for men.

Güera/o blonde – very frequently used description of Westerners, especially shouted after women in the street; again, not usually intended as an insult.

Hacendado plantation owner.

Hacienda plantation estate or the big house on it.

Henequen a variety of agave cactus grown mainly in Yucatán, the fibres of which are used to make rope.

Huipil Maya women's embroidered white smock dress or blouse, worn over a white petticoat, usually with a small checkered scarf.

Huitzilopochtli Aztec god of war.

I.V.A. fifteen percent value-added tax (VAT).

Kukulkán Maya name for Quetzalcoatl, the plumed serpent god.

Ladino as applied to people, means Spanish-influenced as opposed to Indian; determined entirely by clothing (and culture) rather than physical race.

Licenciado a common title, literally meaning "graduate" or "licensed"; abbreviated Lic.

Malecón seafront promenade.

Malinche Cortés' Indian interpreter and mistress, a symbol of treachery.

Mariachi quintessentially Mexican music, with lots of brass and sentimental lyrics.

Marimba xylophone-like musical instrument, also used of the bands based around it; derives from northern Mexico.

Maya people who inhabited Honduras, Belize, Guatemala and southeastern Mexico from earliest times, and still do.

Mestizo mixed race, of Indian and Spanish descent.

Metate flat stone for grinding corn; used with a mano, a grinding stone.

Milpa a small subsistence farm plot, usually tended with slash-and-burn agricultural practices.

Mirador lookout point.

Mixtec people from the mountains of Oaxaca.

Moctezuma Montezuma, the leader of the Aztec empire when the Spanish arrived in Mexico.

Muelle jetty or dock.

NAFTA the North American Free Trade Agreement including Mexico, the US and Canada; see also TLC below.

Nahuatl ancient Aztec language, still the most common after Spanish.

Norteño literally northern – style of food and music.

Palacio mansion, but not necessarily royal.

Palacio de Gobierno headquarters of state/federal authorities.

Palacio municipal headquarters of local government.

Palapa palm thatch. Used to describe any thatched/palm-roofed hut.

Palenque cockpit (for cockfights).

PAN Partido de Acción Nacional (National Action Party), conservative party that first took power when Vicente Fox became president in 2000.

Paseo a broad avenue, but also the ritual evening walk around the plaza.

PEMEX the Mexican national oil company.

Planta baja ground floor – abbreviated PB in lifts.

Porfiriato the three decades of Porfirio Díaz's dictatorship.

PRD Partido Revolucionario Democrático (Party of the Democratic Revolution), the left-wing opposition formed and led by Cuauhtémoc Cárdenas.

PRI Partido Revolucionario Institucional (Party of the Institutional Revolution), the ruling party for eighty years, until the PAN upset in 2000.

PT Partido del Trabajo (Workers' Party), small party but with opposition seats in Congress.

PVEM Partido Verde Ecologista de México (Green Party), small opposition party.

Quetzalcoatl the plumed serpent, most powerful, enigmatic and widespread of all ancient Mexican gods.

Romería procession.

Sacbé ancient Maya road, paved with limestone; plural sacbeob.

Stele freestanding carved monument; plural steles.

Tenochtitlán the Aztec capital, on the site of Mexico City.

Teotihuacán ancient city north of the capital – the first major urban power of central Mexico.

Tianguis Nahuatl word for market, still used of particularly varied marketplaces.

Tlaloc Toltec/Aztec rain god.

TLC Tratado de Libre Comercio, the Spanish name for NAFTA (see opposite).

Toltec tribe which controlled central Mexico between Teotihuacán and the Aztecs.

Tope speed-bump or other barrier on rural roads for slowing traffic.

Trova romantic Yucatecan song style popular in the early twentieth century, still played by trovadores.

Tula the Toltec capital.

Tzompantli Aztec skull rack or "wall of skulls".

Virreinal from the period of the Spanish viceroys – ie colonial.

Wetback derogatory term for illegal Mexican (or any Hispanic) in the US; mojado ("wet") is the Spanish slang term, without the negative connotations.

Zapotec tribe which controlled the Oaxaca region to about 700 AD.

Zócalo the main plaza of any town.

Small print and index

A ROUGH GUIDE TO ROUGH GUIDES

Published in 1982, the first Rough Guide – to Greece – was a student scheme that became a publishing phenomenon. Mark Ellingham, a recent graduate in English from Bristol University, had been travelling in Greece the previous summer and couldn't find the right guidebook. With a small group of friends he wrote his own guide, combining a highly contemporary, journalistic style with a thoroughly practical approach to travellers' needs.

The immediate success of the book spawned a series that rapidly covered dozens of destinations. And, in addition to impecunious backpackers, Rough Guides soon acquired a much broader readership that relished the guides' wit and inquisitiveness as much as their enthusiastic, critical approach and value-for-money ethos.

These days, Rough Guides include recommendations from budget to luxury and cover more than 120 destinations around the globe, as well as producing an ever-growing range of ebooks.

Visit **roughguides.com** to find all our latest books, read articles, get inspired and share travel tips.

Rough Guide credits

Editors: Greg Dickinson, Brendon Griffin, Rebecca Hallett
Layout: Pradeep Thapliyal
Cartography: Rajesh Mishra
Picture editor: Aude Vauconsant
Proofreader: Jan McCann
Managing editor: Mani Ramaswamy
Assistant editor: Payal Sharotri

Production: Jimmy Lao
Cover photo research: Aude Vauconsant
Editorial assistant: Freya Godfrey
Senior pre-press designer: Dan May
Programme manager: Gareth Lowe
Publishing director: Georgina Dee

Publishing information

This tenth edition published June 2016 by
Rough Guides Ltd,
80 Strand, London WC2R 0RL
11, Community Centre, Panchsheel Park,
New Delhi 110017, India
Distributed by Penguin Random House
Penguin Books Ltd, 80 Strand, London WC2R 0RL
Penguin Group (USA), 345 Hudson Street, NY 10014, USA
Penguin Group (Australia), 250 Camberwell Road,
Camberwell, Victoria 3124, Australia
Penguin Group (NZ), 67 Apollo Drive, Mairangi Bay,
Auckland 1310, New Zealand
Penguin Group (South Africa), Block D, Rosebank Office
Park, 181 Jan Smuts Avenue, Parktown North, Gauteng,
South Africa 2193
Rough Guides is represented in Canada by DK Canada, 320
Front Street West, Suite 1400, Toronto, Ontario M5V 3B6
Printed in Singapore
© Rough Guides, 2016
Maps © Rough Guides

880pp includes index
A catalogue record for this book is available from the
British Library
ISBN: 978-0-24123-993-3
The publishers and authors have done their best to
ensure the accuracy and currency of all the information in
The Rough Guide to Mexico, however, they can accept
no responsibility for any loss, injury, or inconvenience
sustained by any traveller as a result of information or
advice contained in the guide.
1 3 5 7 9 8 6 4 2

MIX
Paper from
responsible sources
FSC™ C018179
www.fsc.org

Help us update

We've gone to a lot of effort to ensure that the tenth
edition of **The Rough Guide to Mexico** is accurate and up-
to-date. However, things change – places get "discovered",
opening hours are notoriously fickle, restaurants and
rooms raise prices or lower standards. If you feel we've got
it wrong or left something out, we'd like to know, and if
you can remember the address, the price, the hours, the
phone number, so much the better.

Please send your comments with the subject line
"Rough Guide Mexico Update" to mail@uk.roughguides
.com. We'll credit all contributions and send a copy of the
next edition (or any other Rough Guide if you prefer) for
the very best emails.
Find more travel information, connect with fellow
travellers and plan your trip on ⓦroughguides.com.

ABOUT THE AUTHORS

Alasdair Baverstock is an award-winning foreign correspondent based in Mexico City. He has also updated the Rough Guides to *Central America on a Budget* and *South America on a Budget*.

Sarah Hull has been a contributor to Rough Guides since 2005, writing about New England, Canada, New York City, Miami and the American South. Her love for Mexico began with a long-ago visit to the blue house in Coyoacán and shows no sign of diminishing, especially if she's sifting through an Oaxacan marketplace. When she's not on the road, she's in New York Supreme Court reporting on corporate shenanigans and celebrity lawsuits.

Stephen Keeling first travelled around Mexico by bus in 1991 and has been covering the country for Rough Guides since 2006. He worked as a financial journalist for seven years before writing his first travel guide, and has written books on Spain, Puerto Rico, New York, New England, Florida, Canada, Taiwan and Tuscany. He lives in New York City.

Shafik Meghji first visited Mexico in 1999. A south London-based travel writer and journalist, he has worked on over 25 Rough Guides and writes regularly for publications around the world. Shafik is a fellow of the Royal Geographical Society, a member of the British Guild of Travel Writers and a trustee of the Latin America Bureau. Follow his travels at ⓦshafikmeghji.com, ⓤunmappedroutes.com or ⓣtwitter.com/ShafikMeghji.

Acknowledgements

Alasdair Baverstock: To my wife Oriana

Sarah Hull: Sarah Hull would like to thank Stephen Keeling for being the best kind of friend: wise, sympathetic and hilarious. Endless gratitude and a big shout-out goes to Lourdes Moreno at the state tourism office in Oaxaca, and to the unbeatable Gina Machorro, patron saint of Puerto Escondido. Saul Orocio, a true friend, was generous with mescal and introduced me to the Oaxacan countryside. Greg Dickinson was a terrific editor: thoughtful, patient and kind. Finally, thanks to Janon Fisher, for keeping the light on, being a constant beam of support and generally improving everything with his restorative sense of humour.

Stephen Keeling: Constancia Wu and Sunshine & Chloe Fisher for good times in Baja; Rebecca at Amigo Trails; fellow authors Alasdair Baverstock, Sarah Hull and Shafik Meghji; Greg Dickinson and Andy Turner in London for all their hard work and editing; and lastly to Tiffany Wu, whose love and support made this possible.

Shafik Meghji: Thanks to the many readers, travellers and locals who helped out along the way. A special muchas gracias must go to: Andy Turner, Greg Dickinson and Rebecca Hallett at Rough Guides HQ; MaryAnne Nelson of Journey Latin America for her help with logistics; Jean, Nizar and Nina Meghji; and Sioned Jones for her companionship in the Yucatán.

Readers' updates

Thanks to all the readers who have taken the time to write in with comments and suggestions (and apologies if we've inadvertently omitted or misspelt anyone's name):

Elena; Carl Brandt; Linda Kruusmägi; Hagan Neurath; Pat Rourke; Ellen Rowland and Helen Ward.

Photo credits

All photos © Rough Guides except the following:
(Key: t-top; c-centre; b-bottom; l-left; r-right)

Index

Maps are marked in grey

Map symbols

The symbols below are used on maps throughout the book

✈ Airport	⬩ Place of interest	〰 Mountain range	▦ Building
★ Bus stop	♟ Museum	▲ Mountain peak	⬛ Church
🅿 Parking	🏮 Lighthouse	◠ Cave	⚓ Church (regional)
✉ Post office	〰 Viewpont	~ Swamps	▭ Market
ⓘ Information office	⊙ Statue	∧∧ Hot spring pool	◯ Stadium
🕐 Telephone	🏛 Waterfall	/Ⅱ\ Volcano	▭ Park
@ Internet access	)(Bridge	ⅢⅢ// Hill	▭ Beach
⛽ Petrol station	⚙ Ruins	🪨 Cliff	⊞ Cemetery
⊞ Hospital	⊤ Fountain	～～ Reef	
Ⓜ Metro	Ⓑ Metrobus		

Listings key

◼ Accommodation	
● Eating	
◼ Drinking and nightlife	
● Shopping	

"WHAT CAN I CONFESS? I'M ASHLAR. I'M TALTOS.

It's centuries since I've seen one single member of my own species. Oh, there have been others. I've heard of them, chased after them, and in some instances almost found them. Mark, I say almost. But not in centuries have I touched my own flesh and blood, as humans are so fond of saying. Never in all this time. . . ."

When Ashlar learns that another Taltos has been seen, he is suddenly propelled into the haunting world of the Mayfair family, the New Orleans dynasty of witches forever besieged by ghosts, spirits, and their own dizzying powers. For Ashlar knows this powerful clan is intimately linked to the heritage of the Taltos.

In a swirling universe filled with death and life, corruption and innocence, this mesmerizing novel takes us on a wondrous journey back through the centuries to a civilization half human, of wholly mysterious origin, at odds with mortality and immortality, justice and guilt. It is an enchanted, hypnotic world that could come only from the imagination of Anne Rice. . . .

"SIMPLY IRRESISTIBLE . . . (An) alluring supernatural romance."
—*Chicago Sun-Times*

TALTOS

LIVES OF THE
MAYFAIR WITCHES

Anne Rice

BALLANTINE BOOKS · NEW YORK

A Ballantine Book
Published by The Random House Publishing Group
Copyright © 1994 by Anne O'Brien Rice
Excerpt from *Servant of the Bones* copyright © 1996 by Anne O'Brien Rice

Published in the United States by Ballantine Books, an imprint of The Random House Publishing Group, a division of Random House, Inc., New York, and simultaneously in Canada by Random House of Canada Limited, Toronto.

BALLANTINE and colophon are registered trademarks of Random House, Inc.

ISBN 978-0-345-40431-2

This edition published by arrangement with Alfred A. Knopf, a division of Random House, Inc.

Printed in the United States of America

www.ballantinebooks.com

First Ballantine Books Trade Edition: September 1995
First Ballantine Books International Mass Market Edition:
        November 1995
First Ballantine Books Domestic Mass Market Edition: May 1996

OPM   29   28   27   26   25   24

THE GARDEN OF LOVE

I went to the Garden of Love,
And saw what I never had seen:
A Chapel was built in the midst,
Where I used to play on the green.

And the gates of this Chapel were shut,
And Thou shalt not. writ over the door;
So I turn'd to the Garden of Love,
That so many sweet flowers bore.

And I saw it was filled with graves,
And tomb-stones where flowers should be:
And Priests in black gowns, were walking their rounds,
And binding with briars, my joys & desires.

From *Songs of Experience*,
William Blake

TALTOS

One

IT HAD SNOWED all day. As the darkness fell, very close and quickly, he stood at the window looking down on the tiny figures in Central Park. A perfect circle of light fell on the snow beneath each lamp. Skaters moved on the frozen lake, though he could not make them out in detail. And cars pushed sluggishly over the dark roads.

To his right and his left, the skyscrapers of midtown crowded near him. But nothing came between him and the park, except, that is, for a jungle of lower buildings, rooftops with gardens, and great black hulking pieces of equipment, and sometimes even pointed roofs.

He loved this view; it always surprised him when others found it so unusual, when a workman coming to fix an office machine would volunteer that he'd never seen New York like this before. Sad that there was no marble tower for everyone; that there was no series of towers, to which all the people could go, to look out at varying heights.

Make a note: Build a series of towers which have no function except to be parks in the sky for the people. Use all the beautiful marbles which you so love. Maybe he would do that this year. Very likely, he would do it. And the libraries. He wanted to establish more of these, and that would mean some travel. But he would do all this, yes, and soon. After all, the parks were almost completed now, and the little schools had been opened in seven cities. The carousels had been opened in twenty different places. Granted, the animals were synthetic, but each was a meticulous and

1

indestructible reproduction of a famous European hand-carved masterpiece. People loved the carousels. But it was a time for a spate of new plans. The winter had caught him dreaming. . . .

In the last century, he had put into material form a hundred such ideas. And this year's little triumphs had their comforting charm. He had made an antique carousel within this building, all of the original old horses, lions, and such that had provided molds for his replicas. The museum of classic automobiles now filled one level of the basement. The public flocked to see the Model Ts, the Stutz Bearcats, the MG-TDs with their wire wheels.

And of course there were the doll museums—in large, well-lighted rooms on two floors above the lobby—the company showcase, filled with the dolls he'd collected from all parts of the world. And the private museum, open only now and then, including the dolls which he himself had personally cherished.

Now and then he slipped downstairs to watch the people, to walk through the crowds, never unnoticed, but at least unknown.

A creature seven feet in height can't avoid the eyes of people. That had been true forever. But a rather amusing thing had happened in the last two hundred years. Human beings had gotten taller! And now, miracle of miracles, even at his height, he did not stand out so very much. People gave him a second glance, of course, but they weren't frightened of him anymore.

Indeed, occasionally a human male came into the building who was in fact taller than he was. Of course the staff would alert him. They thought it one of his little quirks that he wanted such people reported to him. They found it amusing. He didn't mind. He liked to see people smile and laugh.

"Mr. Ash, there's a tall one down here. Camera five."

He'd turn to the bank of small glowing screens, and quickly catch sight of the individual. Only human. He usually knew for certain right away. Once in a great while, he wasn't sure of it. And he went down in the silent, speeding

2

elevator, and walked near the person long enough to ascertain from a score of details that this was only a man.

Other dreams: small play buildings for children, made exquisitely out of space-age plastics with rich and intricate detail. He saw small cathedrals, castles, palaces—perfect replicas of the larger architectural treasures—produced with lightning speed, and "cost effective," as the board would put it. There would be numerous sizes, from dwellings for dolls to houses which children could enter themselves. And carousel horses for sale, made of wood resin, which almost anyone could afford. Hundreds could be given to schools, hospitals, other such institutions. Then there was the ongoing obsession—truly beautiful dolls for poor children, dolls that would not break, and could be cleaned with ease—but that he had been working on, more or less, since the new century dawned.

For the last five years he had produced cheaper and cheaper dolls, dolls superior to those before them, dolls of new chemical materials, dolls that were durable and lovable; yet still they cost too much for poor children. This year he would try something entirely different. . . . He had plans on the drawing board, a couple of promising prototypes. Perhaps . . .

He felt a consoling warmth steal through him as he thought of these many projects, for they would take him hundreds of years. Long ago, in ancient times as they called them, he had dreamed of monuments. Great circles of stone for all to see, a dance of giants in the high grass of the plain. Even modest towers had obsessed him for decades, and once the lettering of beautiful books had taken all his joy for centuries.

But in these playthings of the modern world, these dolls, these tiny images of people, not children really, for dolls never really did look like children, he had found a strange and challenging obsession.

Monuments were for those who traveled to see them. The dolls and toys he refined and manufactured reached every country on the globe. Indeed, machines had made all sorts of new and beautiful objects available for people of all nations—the rich, the impoverished, those in need of com-

3

fort, or sustenance and shelter, those kept in sanitariums and asylums which they could never leave.

His company had been his redemption; even his wildest and most daring ideas had been put into successful production. Indeed, he did not understand why other toy companies made so few innovations, why cookie-cutter dolls with vapid faces lined the shelves of emporiums, why the ease of manufacture had not produced a wilderness of originality and invention. Unlike his joyless colleagues, with each of his triumphs he had taken greater risks.

It didn't make him happy to drive others out of the market. No, competition was still something he could only grasp intellectually. His secret belief was that the number of potential buyers in today's world was unlimited. There was room for anyone marketing anything of worth. And within these walls, within this soaring and dangerous tower of steel and glass, he enjoyed his triumphs in a state of pure bliss which he could share with no one else.

No one else. Only the dolls could share it. The dolls who stood on the glass shelves against the walls of colored marble, the dolls who stood on pedestals in the corners, the dolls who clustered together on his broad wooden desk. His Bru, his princess, his French beauty, a century old; she was his most enduring witness. Not a day passed that he didn't go down to the second floor of the building and visit the Bru—a bisque darling of impeccable standards, three feet tall, her mohair curls intact, her painted face a masterpiece, her torso and wooden legs as perfect now as they were when the French company had manufactured her for the Paris market over one hundred years ago.

That had been her allure, that she was a thing for hundreds of children to enjoy; a pinnacle had been reached in her, of craft and mass production. Even her factory clothes of silk represented that special achievement. Not for one, but for many.

There had been years when, wandering the world, he had carried her with him, taking her out of the suitcase at times just to look into her glass eyes, just to tell her his thoughts, his feelings, his dreams. In the night, in squalid lonely rooms, he had seen the light glint in her ever-watchful eyes.

4

And now she was housed in glass, and thousands saw her yearly, and all the other antique Bru dolls now clustered around her. Sometimes he wanted to sneak her upstairs, put her on a bedroom shelf. Who would care? Who would dare say anything? Wealth surrounds one with a blessed silence, he thought. People think before they speak. They feel they have to. He could talk to the doll again if he wanted to. In the museum, he was silent when they met, the glass of the case separating them. Patiently she waited to be reclaimed, the humble inspiration for his empire.

Of course this company of his, this enterprise of his, as it was so often called by papers and magazines, was predicated on the development of an industrial and mechanical matrix which had existed now for only three hundred years. What if war were to destroy it? But dolls and toys gave him such sweet happiness that he imagined he would never hereafter be without them. Even if war reduced the world to rubble, he would make little figures of wood or clay and paint them himself.

Sometimes he saw himself this way, alone in the ruins. He saw New York as it might have appeared in a science-fiction movie, dead and silent and filled with overturned columns and broken pediments and shattered glass. He saw himself sitting on a broken stone stairway, making a doll from sticks and tying it together with bits of cloth which he took quietly and respectfully from a dead woman's silk dress.

But who would have imagined that such things would have caught his fancy? That wandering a century ago through a wintry street in Paris, he would turn and gaze into a shop window, into the glass eyes of his Bru, and fall passionately in love?

Of course, his breed had always been known for its capacity to play, to cherish, to enjoy. Perhaps it was not at all surprising. Though studying a breed, when you were one of the only surviving specimens of it, was a tricky situation, especially for one who could not love medical philosophy or terminology, whose memory was good but far from preternatural, whose sense of the past was often deliberately relinquished to a "childlike" immersion in the present, and

5

a general fear of thinking in terms of millennia or eons or whatever people wanted to call the great spans of time which he himself had witnessed, lived through, struggled to endure, and finally cheerfully forgotten in this great enterprise suited to his few and special talents.

Nevertheless, he did study his own breed, making and recording meticulous notes on himself. And he was not good at predicting the future, or so he felt.

A low hum came to his ears. He knew it was the coils beneath the marble floor, gently heating the room around him. He fancied he could feel the heat, coming up through his shoes. It was never chilly or smotheringly hot in his tower. The coils took care of him. If only such comfort could belong to the entire world outside. If only all could know abundant food, warmth. His company sent millions in aid to those who lived in deserts and jungles across the seas, but he was never really sure who received what, who benefited.

In the first days of motion pictures, and later television, he had thought war would end. Hunger would end. People could not bear to see it on the screen before them. How foolish a thought. There seemed to be more war and more hunger now than ever. On every continent, tribe fought tribe. Millions starved. So much to be done. Why make such careful choices? Why not do everything?

The snow had begun again, with flakes so tiny he could barely see them. They appeared to melt when they hit the dark streets below. But those streets were some sixty floors down. He couldn't be certain. Half-melted snow was piled in the gutters and on the nearby roofs. In a little while, things would be freshly white again, perhaps, and in this sealed and warm room, one could imagine the entire city dead and ruined, as if by pestilence which did not crumble buildings but killed the warm-blooded beings which lived within them, like termites in wooden walls.

The sky was black. That was the one thing he did not like about snow. You lost the sky when you had it. And he did so love the skies over New York City, the full panoramic skies which the people in the streets never really saw.

"Towers, build them towers," he said. "Make a big mu-

6

seum high up in the sky with terraces around it. Bring them up in glass elevators, heavenward to see . . ."

Towers for pleasure among all these towers that men had built for commerce and gain.

A thought took him suddenly, an old thought, really, that often came to him and prodded him to meditate and perhaps even to surmise. The first writings in all the world had been commercial lists of goods bought and sold. This was what was in the cuneiform tablets found at Jericho, inventories. . . . The same had been true at Mycenea.

No one had thought it important then to write down his or her ideas or thoughts. Buildings had been wholly different. The grandest were houses of worship—temples or great mud-brick ziggurats, faced in limestone, which men had climbed to sacrifice to the gods. The circle of sarsens on the Salisbury Plain.

Now, seven thousand years later, the greatest buildings were commercial buildings. They were inscribed with the names of banks or great corporations, or immense private companies such as his own. From his window he could see these names burning in bright, coarse block letters, through the snowy sky, through the dark that wasn't really dark.

As for temples and places of worship, they were relics or almost nought. Somewhere down there he could pick out the steeples of St. Patrick's if he tried. But it was a shrine now to the past more than a vibrant center of communal religious spirit, and it looked quaint, reaching to the skies amid the tall, indifferent glass buildings around it. It was majestic only from the streets.

The scribes of Jericho would have understood this shift, he thought. On the other hand, perhaps they would not. He barely understood it himself, yet the implications seemed mammoth and more wonderful than human beings knew. This commerce, this endless multiplicity of beautiful and useful things, could save the world, ultimately, if only . . . Planned obsolesence, mass destruction of last year's goods, the rush to antiquate or render irrelevent others' designs, it was the result of a tragic lack of vision. Only the most limited implications of the marketplace theory were to blame for it. The real revolution came not in the cycle of make

7

and destroy, but in a great inventive and endless expansion. Old dichotomies had to fall. In his darling Bru, and her factory-assembled parts, in the pocket calculators carried by millions on the streets, in the light beautiful stroke of rolling-ball pens, in five-dollar Bibles, and in toys, beautiful toys sold on drugstore shelves for pennies—there lay salvation.

It seemed he could get his mind around it, he could penetrate it, make tight, easily explainable theories, if only—

"Mr. Ash." It was a soft voice that interrupted him. Nothing more was required. He'd trained them all. Don't make a sound with the door. Speak quietly. I'll hear you.

And this voice came from Remmick, who was gentle by nature, an Englishman (with a little Celtic blood, though Remmick didn't know it), a manservant who had been indispensable in this last decade, though the time would soon come when, for security's sake, Remmick must be sent away.

"Mr. Ash, the young woman's here."

"Thank you, Remmick," he said in a voice that was even softer than that of his servant. In the dark window glass, if he let himself, he could see Remmick's reflection—a comely man, with small, very brilliant blue eyes. They were too close together, these eyes. But the face was not unattractive, and it wore always a look of such quiet and nondramatic devotion that he had grown to love it, to love Remmick himself.

There were lots of dolls in the world with eyes too close together—in particular, the French dolls made years ago by Jumeau, and Schmitt and Sons, and Huret, and Petit and Demontier—with moon faces, and glittering glass eyes crowding their little porcelain noses, with mouths so tiny they seemed at first glance to be tiny buds, or bee stings. Everybody loved these dolls. The bee-sting queens.

When you loved dolls and studied them, you started to love all kinds of people too, because you saw the virtue in their expressions, how carefully they had been sculpted, the parts contrived to create the triumph of this or that remarkable face. Sometimes he walked through Manhattan, deliberately seeing every face as made, no nose, no ear, no wrinkle accidental.

"She's having some tea, sir. She was terribly cold when she arrived."

"We didn't send a car for her, Remmick?"

"Yes, sir, but she's cold nevertheless. It's very cold out-side, sir."

"But it's warm in the museum, surely. You took her there, didn't you?"

"Sir, she came up directly. She is so excited, you under-stand."

He turned, throwing one bright gleam of a smile (or so he hoped it was) on Remmick and then waving him away with the smallest gesture that the man could see. He walked to the doors of the adjoining office, across the floor of Carrara marble, and looked beyond that room, to yet another, also paved, as were all his rooms, in shining marble, where the young woman sat alone at the desk. He could see her profile. He could see that she was anxious. He could see that she wanted the tea, but then she didn't. She didn't know what to do with her hands.

"Sir, your hair. Will you allow me?" Remmick touched his arm.

"Must we?"

"Yes, sir, we really ought to." Remmick had his soft little brush out, the kind that men used because they could not be seen using the same kind of brush as women, and reaching up, Remmick brought it quickly and firmly through his hair, hair that ought to be trimmed and cut, Remmick had said, hair that fell sloppily and defiantly over his collar.

Remmick stood back, rocking on the balls of his feet.

"Now you look splendid, Mr. Ash," he said with raised eyebrows. "Even if it is a bit long."

He made a soft chuckle.

"You're afraid I'll frighten her, aren't you?" he asked, teasingly, affectionately. "Surely you don't really care what she thinks."

"Sir, I care that you look your best always, for your own benefit."

"Of course you do," he said quietly. "I love you for it."

9

He walked towards the young woman, and as he drew closer, he made a polite and decent amount of noise. Slowly she turned her head; she looked up; she saw him, and there came the inevitable shock.

He extended his arms as he approached.

She rose, beaming, and she clasped his hands. Warm, firm grip. She looked at his hands, at the fingers, and at the palms.

"I surprise you, Miss Paget?" he asked, offering her his most gracious smile. "My hair has been groomed for your approval. Do I look so very bad?"

"Mr. Ash, you look fabulous," she said quickly. She had a crisp California-style voice. "I didn't expect that ... I didn't expect that you would be so tall. Of course, everyone said you were. . . ."

"And do I look like a kindly man, Miss Paget? They say this of me too." He spoke slowly. Often Americans could not understand his "British accent."

"Oh, yes, Mr. Ash," she said. "Very kindly. And your hair is so nice and long. I love your hair, Mr. Ash."

This was really very gratifying, very amusing. He hoped that Remmick was listening. But wealth makes people withhold judgment on what you have done, it makes them search for the good in your choices, your style. It brings out not the obsequious but the more thoughtful side of humans. At least sometimes . . .

She was plainly telling the truth. Her eyes feasted on him and he loved it. He gave her hands a tender squeeze and then he let them go.

As he moved around the desk, she took her seat again, eyes still locked upon him. Her own face was narrow and deeply lined for one so young. Her eyes were bluish violet. She was beautiful in her own way—ashen-haired, disheveled yet graceful, in exquisitely crushed old clothes.

Yes, don't throw them away, save them from the thrift-shop rack, reinvent them with nothing more than a few stitches and an iron; the destiny of manufactured things lies in durability and changing contexts, crushed silk beneath fluorescent light, elegant tatters with buttons of plastic in colors never achieved within geological strata, with stock-

10

ings of such strong nylon they could have been made into braided rope of incalculable strength if only people didn't rip them off and toss them into wastebaskets. So many things to do, ways to see . . . If he had the contents of every wastebasket in Manhattan, he could make another billion just from what he would find there.

"I admire your work, Miss Paget," he said. "It's a pleasure to meet you at last." He gestured to the top of the desk. It was littered with large color photographs of her dolls.

Was it possible she hadn't noticed these? She seemed overcome with pleasure, her cheeks reddening. Perhaps she was even a little infatuated with his style and manner, he wasn't sure. He did tend to infatuate people, sometimes without trying to do it.

"Mr. Ash," she said. "This is one of the most important days of my life." She said it as if trying to realize it, and then she became silently flustered, perhaps because she thought she had said too much in saying what really mattered.

He let his smile brighten, and dipped his head slightly, as he often did—a trait people remarked on—so that he appeared to be looking up at her for a moment, though he was much taller than she.

"I want your dolls, Miss Paget," he said. "All of them. I'm very pleased with what you've done. You've worked so well in all the new materials. Your dolls aren't like anyone else's. That's what I want."

She was smiling in spite of herself. It was always a thrilling moment, this, for them and for him. He loved making her happy!

"Have my lawyers presented everything? Are you quite sure of the terms?"

"Yes, Mr. Ash. I understand everything. I accept your offer, completely. This is my dream."

She said the last word with gentle emphasis. And this time she did not falter or blush.

"Miss Paget, you need someone to bargain for you!" he scolded. "But if I've ever cheated anyone, I don't remem-

11

ber it, and I would honestly like to be reminded so that I could correct what I've done."

"I'm yours, Mr. Ash," she said. Her eyes had brightened, but they were not filling with tears. "The terms are generous. The materials are dazzling. The methods . . ." She gave a little shake of her head. "Well, I don't really understand the mass-production methods, but I know your dolls. I've been hanging around in the stores, just looking at everything marketed by Ashlar. I know this is simply going to be great."

Like so many, she had made her dolls in her kitchen, then in a garage workroom, firing the clay in a kiln she could barely afford. She had haunted flea markets for her fabrics. She had taken her inspiration from figures in motion pictures and in novels. Her works had been "one of a kind" and "limited edition," the sort of thing they liked in the exclusive doll shops and galleries. She had won awards, both large and small.

But her molds could be used now for something utterly different—half a million beautiful renditions of one doll, and another and another, out of a vinyl so skillfully worked that it would look as lovely as porcelain, with eyes painted as brilliantly as if they were real glass.

"But what about the names, Miss Paget? Why won't you choose the dolls' names?"

"The dolls have never had names for me, Mr. Ash," she said. "And the names you chose are fine."

"You know you'll be rich soon, Miss Paget."

"So they tell me," she said. She seemed suddenly vulnerable, indeed fragile.

"But you have to keep your appointments with us, you have to approve each step. It won't take so much time, really. . . ."

"I'm going to love it. Mr. Ash, I want to make—"

"I want to see anything that you make, immediately. You'll call us."

"Yes."

"But don't be sure you will enjoy the process here. As you have observed, manufacture is not the same thing as crafting or creating. Well, it is. But seldom do people see

12

it that way. Artists don't always see mass production as an ally."

He did not have to explain his old reasoning, that he did not care for the one-of-a-kinds and the limited editions, that he cared only for dolls that could belong to everyone. And he would take these molds of hers, and he would produce dolls from them year after year, varying them only when there seemed a reason to do it.

Everyone knew this about him now—that he had no interest in elitist values or ideas.

"Any questions about our contracts, Miss Paget? Don't hesitate to put these questions directly to me."

"Mr. Ash, I've signed your contracts!" She gave another little riff of laughter, distinctly careless and young.

"I'm so glad, Miss Paget," he said. "Prepare to be famous." He brought up his hands and folded them on the desk. Naturally, she was looking at them; she was wondering at their immense size.

"Mr. Ash, I know you're busy. Our appointment's for fifteen minutes."

He nodded as if to say, This is not important, go on.

"Let me ask you. Why do you like my dolls? I mean, really, Mr. Ash. I mean—"

He thought for a moment. "Of course there's a stock answer," he said, "which is wholly true. That your dolls are original, as you've said. But what I like, Miss Paget, is that your dolls are all smiling broadly. Their eyes are crinkled; their faces are in motion. They have shining teeth. You can almost hear them laugh."

"That was the risk, Mr. Ash." Suddenly she herself laughed, and looked for one second as happy as her creations.

"I know, Miss Paget. Are you perhaps going to make me some very sad children now?"

"I don't know if I can."

"Make what you want. I'm behind you. Don't make sad children. Too many other artists do that well."

He started to rise, slowly, the signal of dismissal, and he wasn't surprised when she rushed to her feet.

"Thank you, Mr. Ash," she said again, reaching for his

hand—his huge, long-fingered hand. "I can't tell you how much . . ."

"You don't have to."

He let her take his hand. Sometimes people didn't want to touch him a second time. Sometimes they knew he wasn't a human. Never repelled by his face, it seemed, they were often repelled by his big feet and hands. Or, deep in their subconscious, they realized his neck was just a little too long, his ears too narrow. Humans are skilled at recognizing their own kind, tribe, clan, family. A great part of the human brain is organized around merely recognizing and remembering types of faces.

But she was not repelled, merely young and overwhelmed, and anxious over simple transitions.

"And by the way, Mr. Ash, if you don't mind my saying it, the white streaks in your hair are very becoming. I hope you don't ever color them out. White hair is always becoming on a young man."

"Now, what made you say that, Miss Paget?"

She flushed once more, but then gave in to laughter. "I don't know," she admitted. "It's just that the hair is so white, and you're so young. I didn't expect you to be so young. That's what is so surprising—" She broke off, unsure; he had best release her before she tumbled too quickly into her own imagined failures.

"Thank you, Miss Paget," he said. "You've been very kind. I've enjoyed talking with you." Reassurance, blunt and memorable. "I hope to see you again very soon. I hope you'll be happy."

Remmick had come to spirit the young woman away. She said something else hastily, thanks, avowals of inspiration and determination to please the whole world. Words to that sweet effect. He gave her one final sober smile as she went out and the bronze doors were shut behind her.

When she got home, of course, she would drag out her magazines. She would do addition on her fingers, maybe even with a calculator. She would realize he couldn't be young, not by anyone's count. She'd conclude he was past forty, and carefully fighting fifty. That was safe enough.

But how must he deal with this in the long run, for the

14

long run was always his problem? Here was a life he loved, but he would have to make adjustments. Oh, he couldn't think of something so awful just now. What if the white hair really began to flourish? That would help, wouldn't it? But what did it really mean, the white hair? What did it reveal? He was too content to think of it. Too content to court cold fear.

Once again he turned to the windows, and to the falling snow. He could see Central Park as clearly from this office as from the others. He put his hand on the glass. Very cold.

The skating lake was deserted now. The snow had covered the park, and the roof just below him; and he noticed another curious sight which always made him give a little laugh.

It was the swimming pool on top of the Parker Meridien Hotel. Snow fell steadily on the transparent glass roof while, beneath it, a man was swimming back and forth in the brightly illuminated green water, and this was some fifty floors perhaps above the street.

"Now that is wealth and that is power," he mused quietly to himself. "To swim in the sky in a storm." Build swimming pools in the sky, another worthy project.

"Mr. Ash," said Remmick.

"Yes, my dear boy," he said absently, watching the long strokes of the swimmer, seeing clearly now that it was an elderly and very thin man. Such a figure would have been the victim of starvation in times past. But this was a physically fit individual—he could see it—a businessman, perhaps, snared by economic circumstances in the bitter winter of New York, swimming back and forth in deliciously heated and safely sanitized water.

"Phone call for you, sir."

"I don't think so, Remmick. I'm tired. It's the snow. It makes me want to curl up in bed and go to sleep. I want to go to bed now, Remmick. I want some hot chocolate and then to sleep and sleep."

"Mr. Ash, the man said you would want to speak to him, that I was to tell you . . ."

"They all say that, Remmick," he answered.

"Samuel, sir. He said to tell you that name."

15

"Samuel!"

He turned from the window, and looked at the manservant, at his placid face. There was no judgment or opinion in his expression. Only devotion and quiet acceptance.

"He said to come to you directly, Mr. Ash, that it was the custom when he called. I took the chance that he—"

"You did right. You can leave me alone for a little while now."

He took his chair at the desk.

As the doors closed, he picked up the receiver, and pressed the tiny red button.

"Samuel!" he whispered.

"Ashlar," came the answer, clear as if his friend were truly at his ear. "You've kept me waiting fifteen minutes. How important you've become."

"Samuel, where are you? Are you in New York?"

"Certainly not," came the reply. "I'm in Donnelaith, Ash. I'm at the Inn."

"Phones in the glen." It was a low murmur. The voice was coming all the way from Scotland . . . from the glen.

"Yes, old friend, phones in the glen, and other things as well. A Taltos came here, Ash. I saw him. A full Taltos."

"Wait a minute. It sounded as if you said—"

"I did say this. Don't get too excited about it, Ash. He's dead. He was an infant, blundering. It's a long story. There's a gypsy involved in it, a very clever gypsy named Yuri, from the Talamasca. The gypsy would be dead right now if it weren't for me."

"Are you sure the Taltos is dead?"

"The gypsy told me. Ash, the Talamasca is in a dark time. Something tragic has happened with the Order. They'll kill this gypsy soon, perhaps, but he's determined to go back to the Motherhouse. You must come as soon as you can."

"Samuel, I'll meet you in Edinburgh tomorrow."

"No, London. Go directly to London. I promised the gypsy. But come quickly, Ash. If his brothers in London catch sight of him, he'll be dead."

"Samuel, this can't be a correct story. The Talamasca

16

wouldn't do such things to anyone, let alone its own people. Are you sure this gypsy is saying true things?"

"Ash, it has to do with this Taltos. Can you leave now?"

"Yes."

"You won't fail me?"

"No."

"Then there's one more thing I must tell you right now.
You'll see it in the papers in London as soon as you land.
They've been digging here in Donnelaith, in the ruins of
the cathedral."

"I know this, Samuel. You and I have talked about this
before."

"Ash, they dug up the grave of St. Ashlar. They found
the name engraved in the stone. You'll see it in the papers,
Ashlar. Scholars are here from Edinburgh. Ash, there are
witches involved in this tale. But the gypsy will tell you.
People are watching me. I have to go."

"Samuel, people are always watching you, wait—"

"Your hair, Ash. I saw you in a magazine. Are those
white streaks in your hair? Never mind."

"Yes, my hair *is* turning white. But it's happening slowly.
I haven't aged otherwise. There are no real shocks for you,
except the hair."

"You'll live till the end of the world, Ash, and be the one
to make it crumble."

"No!"

"Claridge's in London. We are leaving now ourselves.
That's a hotel where a man can make a big oak fire in the
grate, and sleep in a big old cozy bedroom full of chintz
and hunter-green velvet. I'll be waiting for you there. And
Ash. Pay the hotel, will you? I've been out here in the glen
for two years."

Samuel rang off.

"Maddening," he whispered. He laid down the phone.

For long moments he looked at the bronze doors.

He didn't blink or focus when the doors opened. He
scarcely saw the blurred figure who came into the room. He
was not thinking, he was merely repeating the words
Taltos and *Talamasca* inside his head.

When he did look up, he saw only Remmick pouring

17

chocolate from a small, heavy silver pitcher into a pretty china cup. The steam rose in Remmick's patient and slightly weary face. Gray hair, now that was gray hair, an entire head of it. I do not have so much gray hair.

Indeed, he had only the two streaks flowing back from his temples, and a bit of white in his sideburns, as they were called. And yes, just a tiny touch of white in the dark hair of his chest. Fearfully he looked down at his wrist. There were white hairs there, mingled with the dark hair that had covered his arms now for so many years.

Taltos! Talamasca. The world will crumble. . . .

"Was it the right thing, sir, the phone call?" asked Remmick, in that wonderful, near-inaudible British murmur that his employer loved. Lots of people would have called it a mumble. And we are going now to England, we are going back among all the agreeable, gentle people. . . . England, the land of the bitter cold, seen from the coast of the lost land, a mystery of winter forests and snow-capped mountains.

"Yes, indeed, it was the right thing, Remmick. Always come to me directly when it's Samuel. I have to go to London, right now."

"Then I have to hurry, sir. La Guardia's been closed all day. It's going to be very difficult—"

"Hurry, then, please, don't say anything further."

He sipped the chocolate. Nothing tasted richer to him, sweeter, or better, except perhaps unadulterated fresh milk.

"Another Taltos," he whispered aloud. He set down the cup. "Dark time in the Talamasca." This he wasn't sure he believed.

Remmick was gone. The doors had closed, the beautiful bronze gleaming as if it were hot. There was a trail of light across the marble floor from the light embedded in the ceiling, rather like the moon on the sea.

"Another Taltos, and it was male."

There were so many thoughts racing through his head, such a clatter of emotion! For a moment he thought he'd give way to tears. But no. It was anger that he felt, anger that once again he had been teased by this bit of news, that his heart was beating, that he was flying over the sea to

18

learn more about another Taltos, who was already dead—a male.

And the Talamasca—so they had come into a dark time, had they? Well, wasn't it inevitable? And what must he do about it? Must he be drawn into all this once more? Centuries ago, he had knocked on their doors. But who among them knew this now?

Their scholars he knew by face and name, only because he feared them enough to keep track of them. Over the years, they had never stopped coming to the glen. . . . Someone knew something, but nothing ever really changed.

Why did he feel he owed them some protective intervention now? Because they had once opened their doors, they had listened, they had begged him to remain, they hadn't laughed at his tales, they'd promised to keep his secret. And like him, the Talamasca was old. Old as the trees in the great forests.

How long ago had it been? Before the London house, long before, when the old palazzo in Rome had been lighted still with candles. No records, they had promised. No records, in exchange for all he had told . . . which was to remain impersonal, anonymous, a source of legend and fact, of bits and pieces of knowledge from ages past. Exhausted, he had slept beneath that roof; they had comforted him. But in the final analysis they were ordinary men, possessed of an extraordinary interest perhaps, but ordinary, short-lived, awestruck by him, scholars, alchemists, collectors.

Whatever the case, it was no good to have them in a dark time, to use Samuel's words, not with all they knew and kept within their archives. Not good. And for some strange reason his heart went out to this gypsy in the glen. And his curiosity burned as fierce as ever regarding the Taltos, the witches.

Dear God, the very thought of witches.

When Remmick came back, he had the fur-lined coat over his arm.

"Cold enough for this, sir," he said, as he put it over the boss's shoulders. "And you looked chilled, sir, already."

"It's nothing," he replied. "Don't come down with me.

There's something you must do. Send money to Claridge's in London. It's for a man named Samuel. The management will have no trouble identifying Samuel. He is a dwarf and he is a hunchback and he has very red hair, and a very wrinkled face. You must arrange everything so that this little man has exactly what he wants. Oh, and there is someone with him. A gypsy. I have no idea what this means."

"Yes, sir. The surname, sir?"

"I don't know what it is, Remmick," he answered, rising to go, and pulling the fur-lined cape closer under his neck. "I've known Samuel for so long."

He was in the elevator before he realized that this last statement was absurd. He said too many things of late that were absurd. The other day Remmick had said how much he loved the marble in all these rooms, and he had answered, "Yes, I loved marble from the first time I ever saw it," and that had sounded absurd.

The wind howled in the elevator shaft as the cab descended at astonishing speed. It was a sound heard only in winter, and a sound which frightened Remmick, though he himself rather liked it, or thought it amusing at the very least.

When he reached the underground garage the car was waiting, giving off a great flood of noise and white smoke. His suitcases were being loaded. There stood his night pilot, Jacob, and the nameless copilot, and the pale, straw-colored young driver who was always on duty at this hour, the one who rarely ever spoke.

"You're sure you want to make this trip, tonight, sir?" asked Jacob.

"Is nobody flying?" he asked. He stopped, eyebrows raised, hand on the door. Warm air came from the inside of the car.

"No, sir, there are people flying."

"Then we're going to fly, Jacob. If you're frightened, you don't have to come."

"Where you go, I go, sir."

"Thank you, Jacob. You once assured me that we fly safely above the weather now, and with far greater security than a commercial jet."

"Yes, I did do that, sir, didn't I?"

He sat back on the black leather seat and stretched out his long legs, planting his feet on the seat opposite, which no man of normal height could have done in this long stretch limousine. The driver was comfortably shut away behind glass, and the others followed in the car behind him. His bodyguards were in the car ahead.

The big limousine rushed up the ramp, taking the curbs with perilous but exciting speed, and then out the gaping mouth of the garage into the enchanting white storm. Thank God the beggars had been rescued from the streets. But he had forgotten to ask about the beggars. Surely some of them had been brought into his lobby and given warm drink and cots upon which to sleep.

They crossed Fifth Avenue and sped towards the river. The storm was a soundless torrent of lovely tiny flakes. They melted as they struck the dark windows and the wet sidewalks. They came down through the dark faceless buildings as if into a deep mountain pass.

Taltos.

For a moment the joy went out of his world—the joy of his accomplishments, and his dreams. In his mind's eye he saw the pretty young woman, the dollmaker from California, in her crushed violet silk dress. He saw her in his mind dead on a bed, with blood all around her, making her dress dark.

Of course it wouldn't happen. He never let it happen anymore, hadn't in so long he could scarce remember what it was like to wrap his arms around a soft female body, scarce remember the taste of the milk from a mother's breast.

But he thought of the bed, and the blood, and the girl dead and cold, and her eyelids turning blue, as well as the flesh beneath her fingernails, and finally even her face. He pictured this because if he didn't, he would picture too many other things. The sting of this kept him chastened, kept him within bounds.

"Oh, what does it matter? Male. And dead."

Only now did he realize that he would see Samuel! He and Samuel would be together. Now that was something that flooded him with happiness, or would if he let it. And he had become a master of letting the floods of happiness come when they would.

He hadn't seen Samuel in five years, or was it more? He had to think. Of course they had talked on the phone. As the wires and phones themselves improved, they had talked often. But he hadn't actually seen Samuel.

In those days there had only been a little white in his hair. God, was it growing so fast? But of course Samuel had seen the few white hairs and remarked on it. And Ash had said, "It will go away."

For one moment the veil lifted, the great protective shield which so often saved him from unendurable pain.

He saw the glen, the smoke rising; he heard the awful ring and clatter of swords, saw the figures rushing towards the forest. Smoke rising from the brochs and from the wheel houses ... Impossible that it could have happened!

The weapons changed; the rules changed. But massacres were otherwise the same. He had lived on this continent now some seventy-five years, returning to it always within a month or two of leaving, for many reasons, and no small part of it was that he did not want to be near the flames, the smoke, the agony and terrible ruin of war.

The memory of the glen wasn't leaving him. Other memories were connected—of green fields, wildflowers, hundreds upon hundreds of tiny blue wildflowers. On the river he rode in a small wooden craft, and the soldiers stood on the high battlements; ah, what these creatures did, piling one rock upon another to make great mountains of their own! But what were his own monuments, the great sarsens which hundreds dragged across the plain to make the circle?

The cave, he saw that too again, as if a dozen vivid photographs were shuffled suddenly before him, and one moment he was running down the cliff, slipping, nearly falling, and at another Samuel stood there, saying,

"Let's leave here, Ash. Why do you come here? What is there to see or to learn?"

He saw the Taltos with the white hair.

"The wise ones, the good ones, the knowing ones," they had called them. They had not said "old." It would never have been a word they would have used in those times, when the springs of the island were warm, and the fruit fell from the trees. Even when they'd come to the glen, they had never said the word "old," but everyone knew they had lived the longest. Those with the white hair knew the longest stories. . . .

"Go up now and listen to the story."

On the island, you could pick which of the white-haired ones you wanted, because they themselves would not choose, and you sat there listening to the chosen one sing, or talk, or say the verses, telling the deepest things that he could remember. There had been a white-haired woman who sang in a high, sweet voice, her eyes always fixed on the sea. And he had loved to listen to her.

And how long, he thought, how many decades would it be before his own hair was completely white?

Why, it might be very soon, for all he knew. Time itself had meant nothing then. And the white-haired females were so few, because the birthing made them wither young. No one talked about that either, but everybody knew it.

The white-haired males had been vigorous, amorous, prodigious eaters, and ready makers of predictions. But the white-haired woman had been frail. That is what birth had done to her.

Awful to remember these things, so suddenly, so clearly. Was there perhaps another magic secret to the white hair? That it made you remember from the beginning? No, it wasn't that, it was only that in all the years of never knowing how long, he had imagined that he would greet death with both arms, and now he did not feel that way.

His car had crossed the river, and was speeding towards the airport. It was big and heavy and hugged the slippery asphalt. It held steady against the beating wind.

On the memories tumbled. He'd been old when the horsemen had ridden down upon the plain. He'd been old when he saw the Romans on the battlements of the Antonine Wall, when he'd looked down from Columba's door on the high cliffs of Iona.

Wars. Why did they never go out of his memory, but wait there in all their full glory, right along with the sweet recollections of those he'd loved, of the dancing in the glen, of the music? The riders coming down upon the grassland, a dark mass spreading out as if it were ink upon a peaceful painting, and then the low roar just reaching their ears, and the sight of the smoke rising in endless clouds from their horses.

He awoke with a start.

The little phone was ringing for him. He grasped it hard and pulled it from its black hook.

"Mr. Ash?"

"Yes, Remmick?"

"I thought you'd like to know, sir. At Claridge's, they are familiar with your friend Samuel. They have arranged his usual suite for him, second floor, corner, with the fireplace. They are waiting for you. And, Mr. Ash, they don't know his surname either. Seems he doesn't use it."

"Thank you, Remmick. Say a little prayer. The weather's very volatile and dangerous, I think."

He hung up before Remmick could begin the conventional warnings. Should never have said such a thing, he thought.

But that was really amazing—their knowing Samuel at Claridge's. Imagine their having gotten used to Samuel. The last time Ash had seen Samuel, Samuel's red hair had been matted and shaggy, and his face so deeply wrinkled that his eyes were no longer fully visible, but flashed now and then in random light, like broken amber in the soft, mottled flesh. In those days Samuel had dressed in rags and carried his pistol in his belt, rather like a little pirate, and people had veered out of his path on the street.

"They're all afraid of me, I can't remain here. Look at them, they're more afraid in these times than long ago."

And now they were used to him in Claridge's! Was he having his suits made for him on Savile Row? Did his dirty leather shoes not have holes? Had he forsaken his gun?

The car stopped, and he had to force the door open, his driver rushing to help him, as the snow swept against him in the wind.

Nevertheless, the snow was so pretty, and so clean before it struck the ground. He stood up, feeling a stiffness in his

24

limbs for a moment, and then he put his hand up to keep the soft, moist flakes from striking his eyes.

"It's not so bad, really, sir," said Jacob. "We can get out of here in less than an hour. You should board immediately, sir, if you please."

"Yes, thank you, Jacob," he said. He stopped. The snow was falling all over his dark coat. He could feel it melting in his hair. Nevertheless, he reached into his pocket, felt for the small toy, the rocking horse, yes, it was there.

"This is for your son, Jacob," he said. "I promised him."

"Mr. Ash, for you to remember something like that on a night like this."

"Nonsense, Jacob. I'll bet your son remembers."

It was embarrassingly insignificant, this little toy of wood; he wished now that it were something infinitely better. He would make a note—something better for Jacob's son.

Taking big steps, he walked too fast for the driver to follow. He was too tall for the umbrella anyway. It was just a gesture, the man rushing beside him, umbrella in hand, for him to take it if he wanted it, which he never did.

He boarded the warm, close, and always frightening jet plane.

"I have your music, Mr. Ash."

He knew this young woman, but he couldn't remember her name. She was one of the best of the night secretaries. She'd been with him on the last trip to Brazil. He had meant to remember her. Shameful not to have her name on the very tip of his tongue.

"Evie, isn't it?" he asked, smiling, begging forgiveness with a little bit of a frown.

"No, sir, Leslie," she said, forgiving him instantly.

If she'd been a doll, she would have been bisque, no doubt of it, face underpainted with a soft rose blush to cheeks and lips, eyes deliberately small, but dark and deeply focused. Timidly she waited.

As he took his seat, the great leather chair made especially for him, longer than the others, she put the engraved program in his hand.

There were the usual selections—Beethoven, Brahms,

Shostakovich. Ah, here was the composition he had requested—the Verdi *Requiem*. But he couldn't listen to it now. If he slipped himself into those dark chords and dark voices, the memories would close in.

He put his head back, ignoring the winter spectacle outside the little window. "Sleep, you fool," he said without moving his lips.

But he knew he wouldn't. He would think about Samuel and the things Samuel had said, over and over, until they saw one another again. He would remember the smell of the Talamasca house, and how much the scholars had looked like clerics, and a human hand with a quill pen, writing in great curled letters. "Anonymous. Legends of the lost land. Of Stonehenge."

"Just want to be quiet, sir?" asked the young Leslie.

"No, Shostakovich, the Fifth Symphony. It will make me cry, but you must ignore me. I'm hungry. I want cheese and milk."

"Yes, sir, everything's ready." She began to speak the names of the cheeses, those fancy triple creams that they ordered for him from France and Italy and God only knows where else. He nodded, accepting, waiting for the rush of the music, the divinely piercing quality of this engulfing electronic system, which would make him forget the snow outside, and the fact that they would soon be over the great ocean, pushing steadily towards England, towards the plain, towards Donnelaith, and towards heartbreak.

TWO

AFTER THE FIRST day, Rowan didn't talk. She spent her time out under the oak, in a white wicker chair, her feet propped on a pillow, or sometimes merely resting on the grass. She stared at the sky, eyes moving as if there were a procession of clouds above, and not the clear spring blue, and the bits of white fleece that blew silently across it.

She looked at the wall, or the flowers, or the yew trees. She never looked down at the ground.

Perhaps she'd forgotten that the double grave was right beneath her feet. The grass was growing over it, quick and wild, as it always does in spring in Louisiana. There had been rain aplenty to help it, and sometimes the glory of the sun and rain at the same time.

She ate her meals—approximately a fourth to one-half of what they gave her. Or so Michael said. She didn't look hungry. But she was pale, still, and her hands, when she did move them, would shake.

All the family came to see her. Groups came across the lawn, standing back as if they might hurt her. They said their hellos, they asked about her health. They told her she looked beautiful. That was true. Then they gave up and they went away.

Mona watched all this.

At night Rowan slept, Michael said, as if she were exhausted, as if she'd been hard at work. She bathed alone, though this scared him. But she always locked the bathroom door, and if he tried to stay inside with her, she

27

merely sat there on the chair, looking off, doing nothing. He had to leave before she'd get up. Then he'd hear the lock turn.

She listened when people spoke, at least in the beginning. And now and then when Michael pleaded with her to speak, she clasped his hand warmly as if comforting him, or pleading with him to be patient. This was sad to watch.

Michael was the only one she touched, or acknowledged, though often this little gesture was made without a change in her remote expression or even a movement of her gray eyes.

Her hair was growing full again. It was even a little yellow from her sitting in the sun. When she'd been in the coma, it had been the color of driftwood, the kind you can see on the muddy riverbanks. Now it looked alive, though if memory served Mona correctly, hair was dead, wasn't it? Already dead by the time you brushed it, curled it, did stuff to it.

Every morning Rowan rose of her own accord. She would walk slowly down the stairs, holding the railing to the left, and leaning on her cane with the right hand, placing it firmly on each tread. She didn't seem to care if Michael helped her. If Mona took her arm, it didn't matter.

Now and then Rowan stopped at her dresser before she went down, and put on a bit of lipstick.

Mona always noticed. Sometimes Mona was waiting for Rowan in the hallway, and she saw Rowan do this. Very significant.

Michael always remarked on it too. Rowan wore nightgowns and negligees, depending upon the weather. Aunt Bea kept buying them and Michael would wash them, because Rowan only wore new clothes after they had been washed, or so he had remembered, and he laid them out for her on the bed.

No, this was no catatonic stupor, Mona figured. And the doctors had confirmed it, though they could not say what was wrong with her. The one time one of them, an idiot Michael had said, stuck a pin in her hand, Rowan quietly withdrew the hand and covered it with her other one. And

Michael went into a rage. But Rowan didn't look at the guy or say a word.

"I wish I'd been here for that," said Mona.

Of course Mona had known he was telling the truth. Let the doctors speculate and stick pins in people. Maybe when they went back to the hospital, they stuck pins in a doll of Rowan—voodoo acupuncture. Mona wouldn't have been surprised.

What *did* Rowan feel? What did she remember? Nobody was sure anymore. They had only Michael's word that she had awakened from the coma fully aware, that she had spoken with him for hours after, that she knew everything that had happened, that in the coma she had heard and understood. Something terrible on the day of her awakening, *another one*. And the two buried together beneath the oak.

"I never should have let her do it," Michael had said to Mona a hundred times. "The smell that came out of that hole, the sight of what was left . . . I should have taken care of things."

And what had the other one looked like, and who had carried it down, and tell me all the things that Rowan said—Mona had asked him these questions too often.

"I washed the mud from her hands," Michael had told Aaron and Mona. "She kept looking at it. I guess a doctor doesn't want her hands to be soiled. Think about it, how often a surgeon washes her hands. She asked me how I was, she wanted . . ." And there he had choked up, both times that he told this story. "She wanted to take my pulse. She was worried about *me*."

Wish to God I had seen it, what they buried! Wish to God she had spoken to me!

It was the strangest thing—to be rich now, the designee at thirteen, to have a driver and a car (vulgate translation: flashy black stretch limo with disc, tape player, color TV, and lots of room for ice and Diet Coke), and money in her purse all the time, like twenty-dollar bills, no less, and heaps of new clothes, and people patching up the old house on St. Charles and Amelia, catching her on the fly with swatches of "raw silk" or handpainted "wall coverings."

29

And to want *this*, to want to know, to want to be part of, to want to understand the secrets of this woman and this man, this house that would one day come to her. A ghost is dead beneath the tree. A legend lies under the spring rains. And in its arm, *another one*. It was like turning away from the sure, bright glitter of gold, to take dark trinkets of inestimable power from a small hiding place. Ah, this is magic. Not even her own mother's death had so distracted Mona.

Mona talked to Rowan. A lot.

She came on the property with her own key, the heiress and all that. And because Michael said she could. And Michael, no longer looking at her with lust in the eye, had practically adopted her.

She went back to the rear garden, crossed the lawn, skirting the grave if she remembered, and sometimes she didn't, and then she sat at the wicker table and said, "Rowan, good morning." And then talked and talked.

She told Rowan all about the development of Mayfair Medical, that they had chosen a site, that they had agreed upon a great geothermal system for the heating and cooling, that plans were being drawn. "Your dream is coming into being," she told Rowan. "The Mayfair family knows this city as well as anybody. We don't need feasibility studies and things like that. We're making the hospital happen as you wanted it."

No response from Rowan. Did she even care anymore about the great medical complex that would revolutionize the relationship between patients and their attending families, in which teams of caretakers would assist even the anonymous patients?

"I found your notes," said Mona. "I mean, they weren't locked up. They didn't look private."

No answer. The giant black limbs of the oak moved just a little. The banana leaves fluttered against the brick wall.

"I myself have stood outside Touro Infirmary, asking people what they wanted in an ideal hospital, you know, talking to people for hours."

Nothing.

"My Aunt Evelyn is in Touro," Mona said quietly.

"She's had a stroke. They ought to bring her home, but I don't think she knows the difference." Mona would cry if she talked about Ancient Evelyn. She'd cry if she talked about Yuri. She didn't. She didn't say that Yuri had not written or called for three weeks now. She didn't say that she, Mona, was in love, and with a dark, charming, British-mannered man of mystery who was more than twice her age.

She'd explained all that several days ago to Rowan—the way that Yuri had come from London to help Aaron Lightner. She'd explained that Yuri had been a gypsy and he understood things that Mona understood. She even described how they'd met together in her bedroom the night before Yuri went away. "I worry all the time about him," she had said.

Rowan had never looked at her.

What could she say now? That last night, she had some terrible dream about Yuri that she couldn't remember.

"Of course, he's a grown man," she said. "I mean he's past thirty and all, and he knows how to take care of himself, but the thought that somebody in the Talamasca might hurt him." Oh, stop this!

Maybe this was all wrong. It was too easy to dump all these words on a person who couldn't or wouldn't answer.

But Mona could swear there was a vague acknowledgment in Rowan that Mona was there. Maybe it was only that Rowan didn't look annoyed, or sealed off.

Mona didn't sense displeasure.

Her eyes swept Rowan's face. Rowan's expression was so serious. Had to be a mind in there, just had to be. Why, she looked twenty million times better than she had looked in the coma. And look, she'd buttoned her negligee. Michael swore he didn't do those things for her. She'd buttoned three buttons. Yesterday it had only been one.

But Mona knew that despair can fill up a mind so completely that trying to read its thoughts is like trying to read through thick smoke. Was it despair that had settled on Rowan?

Mary Jane Mayfair had come this last weekend, the mad country girl from Fontevrault. Wanderer, buccaneer, seer, and genius, to hear her tell it, and part old lady and part fun-loving girl, at the ripe old age of nineteen and a half. A fearsome, powerful witch, so she described herself.

"Rowan's just fine," Mary Jane had declared after staring and squinting at Rowan, and then pushing her own cowboy hat off her head so it laid against the back of her neck. "Yep, just brace yourself. She's taking her time, but this lady here knows what's happening."

"Who *is* this nut case?" Mona had demanded, though she'd felt a wild compassion for the child actually, never mind that she was six years older than Mona. This was a noble savage decked out in a Wal-Mart denim skirt no longer than the middle of her thighs, and a cheap white blouse that was much too tight across her egregious breasts, and even missing a crucial button. Severely deprived, and playing it off beautifully.

Of course, Mona had known who Mary Jane was. Mary Jane Mayfair actually lived in the ruins of Fontevrault Plantation, in the Bayou Country. This was the legendary land of poachers who killed beautiful white-necked herons just for their meat, alligators that could overturn your boat and eat your child, and crazy Mayfairs who'd never made it to New Orleans and the wooden steps of the famous New Orleans Fontevrault outpost, otherwise known as the house on St. Charles and Amelia.

Mona was actually dying to see this place, Fontevrault, that stood still with its six columns up and six columns down, even though the first floor was flooded with three feet of water. Seeing the legendary Mary Jane was the next best thing, the cousin only recently returned from "away" who tethered her pirogue to the newel post, and paddled across a stagnant pool of treacherous slime to get to the pickup truck she drove into town for her groceries.

Everybody was talking about Mary Jane Mayfair. And because Mona was thirteen, and the heiress now, and the only legacy-connected person who would talk to people or acknowledge their presence, everybody thought Mona would find it especially interesting to speak about a teen-aged hick cousin who was "brilliant" and "psychic" and wandered about the way Mona did, on her own.

Nineteen and a half. Until Mona laid eyes on this brilliant bit of work, she had not considered someone of that age a true teenager.

Mary Jane was just about the most interesting discovery they had made since they'd started rounding up everyone for genetic testing of the entire Mayfair family. It was bound to happen, finding a throwback like Mary Jane. Mona wondered what else might crawl out of the swamps soon.

But imagine a flooded plantation house of Greek Revival grandeur, gradually sinking into the duckweed, with globs of plaster falling off "with a splash" into the murky waters. Imagine fish swimming through the stairway balusters.

"What if that house falls on her?" Bea had asked. "The house is *in* the water. She can't stay there. This girl must be brought here to New Orleans."

"Swamp water, Bea," Celia had said. "Swamp water, remember. It's not a lake or the Gulf Stream. And besides, if this child does not have sense to get out of there and take the old woman to safety—"

The old woman.

Mona had all of this fresh in her memory this last weekend when Mary Jane had walked into the backyard and plunged into the little crowd that surrounded the silent Rowan as if it were a picnic.

"I knew about y'all," Mary Jane had declared. She'd addressed her words to Michael too, who stood by Rowan's chair as if posing for an elegant family portrait. And how Michael's eyes had locked onto her.

"I come over here sometimes and look at you," said Mary Jane. "Yeah, I do. I came the day of the wedding. You know, when you married her?" She pointed to Michael, then to Rowan. "I stood over there, 'cross the street, and looked at your party?"

Her sentences kept going up on the end, though they weren't questions, as though she was always asking for a nod or a word of agreement.

"You should have come inside," Michael had said kindly, hanging on every syllable the girl spouted. The trouble with Michael was that he did have a weakness for pubescent

33

pulchritude. His tryst with Mona had been no freak of nature or twist of witchcraft. And Mary Jane Mayfair was as succulent a little swamp hen as Mona had ever beheld. Even wore her bright yellow hair in braids over the top of her head, and filthy white patent leather shoes with straps, like a little kid. The fact that her skin was dark, sort of olive and possibly tanned, made the girl look something like a human palomino.

"What did the tests say on you?" Mona had asked. "That's what you're doing here, isn't it? They tested you?"

"I don't know," said the genius, the mighty powerful swamp witch. "They're so mixed up over there, wonder they got anything right. First they called me Florence Mayfair and then Ducky Mayfair, finally I says, 'Look, I'm Mary Jane Mayfair, looky there, right there, on that form you got in front of you.'"

"Well, that's not very good," Celia had muttered.

"But they said I was fine and go home and they'd tell me if anything was wrong with me. Look, I figure I've probably got witch genes coming out the kazoo, I expect to blow the top off the graph, you know? And, boy, I have never seen so many Mayfairs as I saw in that building."

"We own the building," said Mona.

"And every one of them I could recognize on sight, every single person. I never made a mistake. There was one infidel in there, one outcast, you know, or no, it was a halfbreed type, that's what it was, ever notice that there are all these Mayfair types? I mean there are a whole bunch that have no chins and have kind of pretty noses that dip down just a little right here and eyes that tilt at the outside. And then there's a bunch that look like you," she said to Michael, "yeah, just like you, real Irish with bushy brows and curly hair and big crazy Irish eyes."

"But, honey," Michael had protested in vain, "I'm not a Mayfair."

"—and the ones with the red hair like her, only she's just about the most pretty one I've seen. You must be Mona. You have the gleam and glow of somebody who's just come into tons of money."

"Mary Jane, darling," said Celia, unable to follow up

34

with an intelligent bit of advice or a meaningless little question.

"Well, what does it feel like to be so rich?" Mary Jane asked, big, quivering eyes fastened still to Mona. "I mean really deep in here." She pounded her cheap little gaping blouse with a knotted fist, squinting up her eyes again, and bending forward so that the well between her breasts was plainly visible even to someone as short as Mona. "Never mind, I know I'm not supposed to ask that sort of question. I came over here to see her, you know, because Paige and Beatrice told me to do it."

"Why did they do that?" asked Mona.

"Hush up, dear," said Beatrice. "Mary Jane is a Mayfair's Mayfair. Darling Mary Jane, you ought to bring your grandmother up here immediately. I'm serious, child. We want you to come. We have an entire list of addresses, both temporary and permanent."

"I know what she means," Celia had said. She'd been sitting beside Rowan, and was the only one bold enough to wipe Rowan's face now and then with a white handkerchief. "I mean about the Mayfairs with no chins. She means Polly. Polly has an implant. She wasn't born with that chin."

"Well, if she has an implant," declared Beatrice, "then Polly has a visible chin, doesn't she?"

"Yeah, but she's got the slanty eyes and the tipped nose," said Mary Jane.

"Exactly," said Celia.

"You all afraid of the extra genes?" Mary Jane had thrown her voice out like a lasso, catching everybody's attention. "You, Mona, you afraid?"

"I don't know," said Mona, who was in fact not afraid.

"Of course, it's nothing that's even remotely likely to happen!" Bea said. "The genes. It's purely theoretical, of course. Do we have to talk about this?" Beatrice threw a meaningful look at Rowan.

Rowan had stared, as she always did, at the wall, maybe at the sunshine on the bricks, who could possibly know?

Mary Jane had plunged ahead. "I don't think anything that wild will ever happen to this family again. I think the moment for that kind of witchcraft is past, and another eon of new witchcraft—"

"Darling, we really don't take this entire witchcraft thing too seriously," said Bea.

"You know the family history?" Celia had asked gravely.

"Know it? I know things about it you don't know. I know things my granny told me, that she heard from Old Tobias, I know things that are written on the walls in that house, still. When I was a little child, I sat on Ancient Evelyn's knee. Ancient Evelyn told me all kinds of things that I remember. Just one afternoon, that's all it took."

"But the file on our family, the file by the Talamasca . . ." Celia had pressed. "They did give it to you at the clinic?"

"Oh, yeah, Bea and Paige brought that stuff to me," said Mary Jane. "Look here." She pointed to the Band-Aid on her arm that was just like the Band-Aid on her knee. "This is where they stuck me! Took enough blood to sacrifice to the devil. I understand the entire situation. Some of us have a whole string of extra genes. You breed two close kins with the double dose of double helix, and wham, you've got a Taltos. Maybe! Maybe! After all, think about it, how many cousins have married and married, and it never happened, did it, till . . . Look, we shouldn't talk about it in front of her, you're right."

Michael had given a weary little smile of gratitude.

Mary Jane again squinted at Rowan. Mary Jane blew a big bubble with her gum, sucked it in, and popped it.

Mona laughed. "Now that's some trick," she said. "I could never do that."

"Oh, well, that might be a blessing," said Bea.

"But you did read the file," Celia had pressed. "It's very important that you know everything."

"Oh, yeah, I read every word of it," Mary Jane had confessed, "even the ones I had to look up." She slapped her slender, tanned little thigh and shrieked with laughter. "Y'all talking about giving me things. Help me get some education, that's about the only thing I could really use. You know, the worst thing that ever happened to me was my mama taking me out of school. 'Course, I didn't want to go to school then. I had much more fun in the public library, but—"

"I think you're right about the extra genes," Mona said. And right about needing the education.

Many, many of the family had the extra chromosomes which could make monsters, but none had ever been born to the clan, no matter what the coupling, until this terrible time.

And what of the ghost this monster had been for so long, a phantom to drive young women mad, to keep First Street under a cloud of thorns and gloom? There was something poetic about the strange bodies lying right here, beneath the oak, under the very grass where Mary Jane stood in her short denim skirt with her flesh-colored Band-Aid on her little knee, and her hands on her little hips, and her little filthy white patent leather buckle shoe rolled to one side and smeared with fresh mud—with her little dirty sock half down in her heel.

Maybe Bayou witches are just plain dumb, Mona thought. They can stand over the graves of monsters and never know it. Of course, none of the other witches in this family knew it either. Only the woman who won't talk, and Michael, the big hunk of Celtic muscle and charm standing beside Rowan.

"You and I are second cousins," Mary Jane had said to Mona, renewing her approach. "Isn't that something? You weren't born when I came to Ancient Evelyn's house and ate her homemade ice cream."

"I don't recall Ancient Evelyn ever making homemade ice cream."

"Darlin', she made the best homemade ice cream that I ever tasted. My mama brought me into New Orleans to—"

"You've got the wrong person," said Mona. Maybe this girl was an impostor. Maybe she wasn't even a Mayfair. No, no such luck on that. And there was something about her eyes that reminded Mona a little of Ancient Evelyn.

"No, I got the right person," Mary Jane had insisted. "But we didn't really come on account of the ice cream. Let me see your hands. Your hands are normal."

"So what?"

"Mona, be nice, dear," said Beatrice. "Your cousin is just sort of outspoken."

"Well, see these hands?" said Mary Jane. "I had a sixth finger when I was little, on both hands? Not a real finger? You know? I mean just a little one. And that's why my mother brought me to see Ancient Evelyn, because Ancient Evelyn has just such a finger herself."

"Don't you think I know that?" asked Mona. "I grew up with Ancient Evelyn."

"I know you did. I know all about you. Just cool off, honey. I'm not trying to be rude, it's just I am a Mayfair, same as you, and I'll pit my genes against your genes anytime."

"Who told you all about me?" Mona asked.

"Mona," said Michael softly.

"How come I never met you before?" said Mona. "I'm a Fontevrault Mayfair. Your second cousin, as you just said. And how come you talk like you're from Mississippi when you say you lived all that time in California?"

"Oh, listen, there's a story to it," said Mary Jane. "I've done my time in Mississippi, believe you me, couldn't have been any worse on Parchman Farm." It had been impossible to crack the kid's patience. She had shrugged. "You got any iced tea?"

"'Course we do, dear, I'm so sorry." Off Beatrice had gone to get it. Celia had shaken her head with shame. Even Mona had felt negligent, and Michael had quickly apologized.

"No, I'll git it myself, tell me where it is," Mary Jane had cried.

But Bea had disappeared already, conveniently enough. Mary Jane popped her gum again, and then again in a whole side-mouth series of little pops.

"Awesome," said Mona.

"Like I said, there's a story to it all. I could tell you some terrible things about my time in Florida. Yeah, I been there, and in Alabama for a while, too. I had to sort of work my way back down here."

"No lie," said Mona.

"Mona, don't be sarcastic."

38

"I seen you before," Mary Jane had said, going on as if nothing at all had happened. "I remembered you when you and Gifford Mayfair came out to L.A. to go to Hawaii. That's the first time I was ever in an airport. You were sleeping right there by the table, stretched out on two chairs, under Gifford's coat, and Gifford Mayfair bought us the best meal???"

Don't describe it, Mona had thought. But Mona did have some hazy memory of that trip, and waking up with a crick in her neck in the Los Angeles airport, known by the snappy name of LAX, and Gifford saying to Alicia that they had to bring "Mary Jane" back home someday.

Only thing, Mona had no memory of any other little girl there. So this was Mary Jane. And now she was back home. Gifford must be working miracles from heaven.

Bea had returned with the iced tea. "Here it is, precious, lots of lemon and sugar, the way you like it, isn't that right? Yes, darling."

"I don't remember seeing you at Michael and Rowan's wedding," said Mona.

"That's 'cause I never came in," said Mary Jane, who took the iced tea from Bea as soon as it entered the nearest orbit, and drank half of it, slurping it and wiping it off her chin with the back of her hand. Chipped nail polish, but what a gorgeous shade of crape myrtle purple.

"I told you to come," said Bea. "I called you. I left a message for you three times at the drugstore."

"I know you did, Aunt Beatrice, ain't nobody who could say that you didn't do your level best to get us to that wedding. But, Aunt Beatrice, I didn't have shoes! I didn't have a dress? I didn't have a hat? See these shoes? I found these shoes. These are the first shoes that are not tennis shoes that I have worn in a decade! Besides, I could see perfect from across the street. And hear the music. That was fine music you had at your wedding, Michael Curry. Are you sure you aren't a Mayfair? You look like a Mayfair to me; I could make let's say seven different points about your appearance that's Mayfair."

"Thank you, sweetheart. I'm not a Mayfair."

"Oh, you are in your heart," said Celia.

"Well, of course," said Michael, never taking his eyes off the girl even once, no matter who spoke to him. And what do men see when they look at bundles of charm like this?

"You know when we were little," Mary Jane had gone on, "we didn't have anything out there, we just had an oil lamp and a cooler with some ice in it and a lot of mosquito netting hung all over the porch and Granny would light the lamp every evening and . . ."

"You didn't have electricity?" Michael had asked. "How long ago was this? How long ago could it have been?"

"Michael, you've never been in the Bayou Country," said Celia. And Bea gave a knowing nod.

"Michael Curry, we were squatters, that's what we were," said Mary Jane. "We were just hiding out in Fontevrault. Aunt Beatrice could tell you. Sheriff would come to throw us out periodically. We'd pack and he'd take us into Napoleonville and then we would go back and he'd give up on us, and we'd be in peace for a while, till some goody-two-shoes passed by in a boat, some game warden, somebody like that, and called in on us. We had bees, you know, on the porch for honey? We could fish right off the back steps? We had fruit trees all around the landing then, before the wisteria got them like a giant boa constrictor, you know, and blackberries? Why, I'd just pick all I wanted right there where the road forks. We had everything. Besides, now I *have* electricity! I hooked it up myself from the highway, and I did the same thing with the cable TV."

"You really did that?" asked Mona.

"Honey, that's against the law," said Bea.

"I certainly did. My life's far too interesting for me to ever tell lies about it. Besides, I've got more courage than imagination, that's always been the case." She drank the iced tea with another noisy slurp, spilling more of it. "God, that's good. That's so sweet. That's artificial sweetener, isn't it?"

"I'm afraid so," said Bea, staring at her in mingled horror and embarrassment. And to think she had said "sugar." And Bea did hate people who ate and drank sloppily.

"Now, just think of it," said Mary Jane, wiping the back of her hand across her mouth and then wiping her hand on

40

her denim skirt. "I'm tasting something now that is fifty times sweeter than anything anybody ever tasted on earth until this very time. That's why I've bought stock in artificial sweetener."

"You've bought what?" asked Mona.

"Oh, yeah. I have my own broker, honey, discount broker but that's the best kind, since I do the picking most of the time anyway. He's in Baton Rouge. I've got twenty-five thousand dollars sunk in the stock market. And when I make it rich, I'm draining and raising Fontevrault. I'm bringing it all back, every peg and board! You wait and see. You're looking at a future member of the Fortune Five Hundred."

Maybe there was something to this dingbat, Mona had thought. "How did you get twenty-five thousand dollars?"

"You could be killed, fiddling with electricity," declared Celia.

"Earned every penny of it on the way home, and that took a year, and don't ask me how I did it. I had a couple of things going for me, I did. But that's a story, now, really."

"You could be electrocuted," said Celia. "Hooking up your own wires."

"Darling, you are not in the witness box," said Bea anxiously.

"Look, Mary Jane," said Michael, "if you need anything like that, I'll come down there and hook it up for you. I mean it. You just tell me when, I'll be there."

Twenty-five thousand dollars?

Mona's eyes had drifted to Rowan. Rowan was frowning just a little at the flowers, as if the flowers were talking to her in a quiet and secret tongue.

There followed a colorful description from Mary Jane of climbing swamp cypresses, of knowing just what electric wires to touch and not to touch, of purloined work gloves and boots. Maybe this girl was some kind of genius.

"What other stocks do you own?" asked Mona.

"What do you care at your age about the stock market?" asked Mary Jane with blithering ignorance.

"Good heavens, Mary Jane," Mona had said, trying to

sound as much as she could like Beatrice, "I've always had a great obsession with the stock market. Business to me is an art. Everyone knows that about me. I plan someday to run my own mutual fund. I assume you know the term, mutual fund?"

"Well, sure I do," said Mary Jane, laughing at herself in an utterly agreeable and forgiving manner.

"I have, in the last few weeks, already completely designed my own portfolio," Mona said, and then she'd broken off, feeling dumb for having been baited like that by someone who probably was not even listening to her. Derision from the firm of Mayfair and Mayfair was one thing—and it would not last long—but from this girl it was another.

But the girl had really looked at her, and stopped just using her for a sounding board, while taking little peeping glances in between her own hasty words.

"Is that so?" asked Mary Jane. "Well, let me ask you something now. What about this Shopper's Channel on TV? I think this is going to go over like crazy? You know? I've put ten grand in the Shopper's Channel. You know what happened?"

"The stock's nearly doubled in the last four months," said Mona.

"You got it, that's right, now how did you know that? Well, you're some strange kid, aren't you now? And I thought you were one of those uptown girls, with that ribbon in your hair, you know, that you always wore, and going to Sacred Heart, you know? And I figured you wouldn't even talk to me."

A little pain had flared in Mona at that moment, pain and pity for this girl, for anybody who felt that cast out, that snubbed. Mona had never in her life suffered that lack of confidence. And this girl was interesting, putting it all together on her own, with far less nuts and bolts than Mona had.

"Hold it, please, darlings, let's not talk Wall Street," said Beatrice. "Mary Jane, how is Granny? You haven't told us a word. And it's four o'clock, and you have to leave soon if you're going to drive all the way back—"

"Oh, Granny's fine, Aunt Beatrice," said Mary Jane, but she had been looking straight at Mona. "Now, you know what happened to Granny after Mama came and got me and took me away to Los Angeles? I was six years old then, you know. Did you hear this story?"

"Yeah," said Mona.

Everybody had. Beatrice was still embarrassed about it. Celia stared at the girl as though she were a giant mosquito. Only Michael seemed uninformed.

What had happened was this: Mary Jane's grandmother, Dolly Jean Mayfair, had been slapped in the parish home after her daughter left with six-year-old Mary Jane. Dolly Jean was supposed to have died last year and been buried in the family tomb. And the funeral had been a big affair, only because when somebody called New Orleans, all the Mayfairs drove out there to Napoleonville, and beat their chests in grief and regret that they had let this old woman, poor Dolly Jean, die in a parish home. Most of them had never heard of her.

Indeed, none of them had really known Dolly Jean. Or at least they had not known her as an old lady. Lauren and Celia had seen her many times when they were all little girls, of course.

Ancient Evelyn had known Dolly Jean, but Ancient Evelyn had never left Amelia Street to ride to a country funeral, and no one had even thought of asking her about it.

Well, when Mary Jane hit town a year ago, and heard the story of her grandmother dying and being buried, she'd scoffed at it, even laughing in Bea's face.

"Hell, she's not dead," Mary Jane had said. "She came to me in a dream and said, 'Mary Jane, come get me. I want to go home.' Now I'm going back to Napoleonville, and you have to tell me where that parish home is."

For Michael's benefit, she had now repeated the entire tale, and the look of astonishment on Michael's face was becoming unintentionally comic.

"How come Dolly Jean didn't tell you in the dream where the home was?" Mona had asked.

Beatrice had shot her a disapproving look.

"Well, she didn't, that's a fact. And that's a good point,

43

too. I have a whole theory about apparitions and why they, you know, get so mixed up."

"We all do," said Mona.

"Mona, tone it down," said Michael.

Just as if I'm his daughter now, thought Mona indignantly. And he still hasn't taken his eyes off Mary Jane. But it had been said affectionately.

"Honey, what happened?" Michael had pushed.

"Well, an old lady like that," Mary Jane had resumed, "she doesn't always know where she is, even in a dream, but she knew where she was from! This is exactly what happened. I walked into the door of that old folks' home, and there, slap-bang in the middle of the recreation room, or whatever they called it, was my grandmother and she looked up at me, right at me, and after all those years she said, 'Where you been, Mary Jane? Take me home, *chère*, I'm tired of waiting.'"

They had buried the wrong person from the old folks' home.

The real Granny Dolly Jean Mayfair had been alive, receiving but never laying eyes upon a welfare check every month with somebody else's name on it. A royal inquisition had taken place to prove it, and then Granny Mayfair and Mary Jane Mayfair had gone back to live in the ruins of the plantation house, and a team of Mayfairs had provided them with the basic necessities, and Mary Jane had stood outside, shooting her pistol at soft-drink bottles and saying that they'd be just fine, they could take care of themselves. She had some bucks she'd made on the road, she was kind of a nut about doing things her own way, no thank you kindly.

"So they let the old lady live with you in this flooded house?" Michael had asked so innocently.

"Honey, after what they did to her in the old folks' home out there, mixing her up with some other woman and putting her name on a slab and all, what the hell are they going to say to me about her living with me? And Cousin Ryan? Cousin Ryan of Mayfair and Mayfair? You know? He went down there and tore that town apart!"

"Yeah," said Michael. "I bet he did."

"It was all our fault," said Celia. "We should have kept track of these people."

"Are you sure you didn't grow up in Mississippi and maybe even Texas?" Mona had asked. "You sound like an amalgam of the whole South."

"What is an amalgam? See, that is where you have the advantage. You're educated. I'm self-educated. There's a world of difference between us. There are words that I don't dare pronounce and I can't read the symbols in the dictionary."

"Do you want to go to school, Mary Jane?" Michael had been getting more and more involved by the second, his intoxicatingly innocent blue eyes making a head-to-toe sweep about every four and one-half seconds. He was far too clever to linger on the kid's breasts and hips, or even her round little head, not that it had been undersized, just sort of dainty. That's how she'd seemed, finally, ignorant, crazy, brilliant, a mess, and somehow dainty.

"Yes, sir, I do," said Mary Jane. "When I'm rich I'll have a private tutor like Mona here is gettin' now that she's the designee and all, you know, some really smart guy that tells you the name of every tree you pass, and who was president ten years after the Civil War, and how many Indians there were at Bull Run, and what *is* Einstein's Theory of Relativity."

"How old are you?" Michael had asked.

"Nineteen and a half, big boy," Mary Jane had declared, biting her shiny white teeth into her lower lip, lifting one eyebrow and winking.

"This story about your granny, you're serious, this really happened? You picked up your granny and . . ."

"Darling, it all happened," said Celia, "exactly as the girl says. I think we should go inside. I think we're upsetting Rowan."

"I don't know," said Michael. "Maybe she's listening. I don't want to move. Mary Jane, you can care for this old lady all by yourself?"

Beatrice and Celia had immediately looked anxious. If Gifford had still been alive, and there, she too would have

45

looked anxious. "Leaving that old woman out there!" as Celia had said so often of late.

And they had promised Gifford, hadn't they, that they would take care of it? Mona remembered that. Gifford had been in one of her hopeless states of worry about relatives far and wide, and Celia had said, "We'll drive out and check on her."

"Yes, sir, Mr. Curry, it all happened, and I took Granny home with me, and don't you know that the sleeping porch upstairs was just exactly the way we'd left it? Why, after thirteen years, the radio was still there, and the mosquito netting and the ice chest."

"In the swamps?" Mona had demanded. "Wait a minute."

"That's right, honey, that's exactly right."

"It's true," Beatrice had confessed dismally. "Of course, we got them fresh linen, new things. We wanted to put them in a hotel or a house or . . ."

"Well, naturally," said Celia. "I'm afraid this story almost made the papers. Darling, is your granny alone out there right now?"

"No, ma'am, she's with Benjy. Benjy's from the trappers live out that way—real crazy people, you know??? The kind that live in those shacks all made out of pieces of tin, and windows from salvage and even cardboard? I pay him below minimum wage to watch Granny and to cover the phones, but I don't take out any deductions."

"So what?" said Mona. "He's an independent contractor."

"You sure are smart," said Mary Jane. "Don't you think I know that? I was actually biting my lip on another little tidbit right at that point, you know??? That Benjy, bless his heart, has already discovered how to make some easy money in the French Quarter down here, you know?? Peddling nothing but what God give him."

"Oh my Lord," said Celia.

Michael laughed. "How old is Benjy?" he asked.

"Twelve years old this September," said Mary Jane. "He's all right. His big dream is to be a drug dealer in New

46

York, and my big dream for him is to go to Tulane and become a medical doctor."

"But what do you mean, cover the phones?" asked Mona. "How many phones have you got? What are you actually doing down there?"

"Well, I had to spring for some money for the phones, that was an absolute necessity, and I've been calling my broker, naturally enough. Who else? And then there's another line that Granny can talk on to my mother, you know, my mother is never getting out of that hospital in Mexico."

"What hospital in Mexico?" asked Bea, utterly aghast. "Mary Jane, you told me two weeks ago how your mother died in California."

"I was trying to be polite, you know, save everybody the grief and the trouble."

"But what about the funeral?" Michael had asked, drawing close enough most likely to sneak a look down Mary Jane's tightly laced junk polyester blouse. "The old lady. Who *did* they bury?"

"Darlin', that's the worst part of it. Nobody ever found out!" said Mary Jane. "Don't worry about my mother, Aunt Bea, she thinks she's on the astral plane already. She might *be* on the astral plane for all I know. Besides, her kidneys are shot."

"Now, that's not exactly true about the woman in the grave," said Celia. "They believe it was . . ."

"Believe?" asked Michael.

Maybe big breasts are markers of power, Mona had thought as she watched the girl bend nearly double and laugh and laugh as she pointed at Michael.

"Look, that's all very sad about the woman in the wrong grave," said Beatrice. "But, Mary Jane, you have to tell me how to reach your mother!"

"Hey, you don't have a sixth finger," said Mona.

"Not now, precious," said Mary Jane. "My mother had some doctor in Los Angeles chop it off. That's what I was going to tell you. They did the same thing to—"

"Enough of this talk, really," said Celia. "I'm so worried for Rowan!"

"Oh, I didn't know," said Mary Jane. "I mean—"

"Same thing to whom?" asked Mona.

"Now that's another thing. When do you say 'whom' instead of 'who,' exactly?"

"I don't think you're at that stage yet," Mona had replied. "There are a lot of other basic things. . . ."

"Enough, ladies and gentlemen!" Bea had declared. "Mary Jane, I'm going to call your mother."

"You're going to be so sorry, Aunt Bea. You know what kind a' doctor cut off my sixth finger in L.A.? It was a voodoo witch doctor from Haiti, and he did it on the kitchen table."

"But can't they dig up the wrong woman and find out once and for all who she was?" Michael asked.

"Well, they have a very good suspicion, but . . ." Celia had started.

"But what?" Michael had asked.

"Oh, it has to do with welfare checks," Beatrice had declared, "and that's none of our business. Michael, please forget about that dead woman!"

How *could* Rowan just ignore these proceedings? And here he was, calling Mary Jane by name, doing everything but eating Mary Jane up with a spoon. If this didn't snap Rowan to, then a tornado wouldn't do it.

"Well, Michael Curry, come to find out they'd been calling that dead lady Dolly Jean for some time before she passed on. Wasn't anybody in that place with a lick a' sense, if you ask me. I think one night they just started putting Granny in the wrong bed, and what do you know, the old lady in Granny's bed died, and there you have it. They buried some poor old stranger in the Mayfair grave!"

At that point Mary Jane had flashed her eyes on Rowan.

"She's listening!" Mary Jane had cried. "Yes, she is, swear to God. She's listening."

If it was true, no one else could see it or sense it. Rowan had remained oblivious to the eyes turning to her. Michael had flushed as though hurt by the kid's outburst. And Celia had studied Rowan, doubting, and grim.

"There's nothing wrong with her," Mary Jane had declared. "She'll snap right out of it, you watch. People like her, they talk when they want to. I can be like that."

Mona had wanted to say, Why don't you start now?

But in truth, she had wanted to believe that Mary Jane was right. This girl might just be some powerful witch after all, Mona had figured. If Mary Jane wasn't, she would still make it, somehow or other.

"Don't you worry none now about Granny," she said as she was "fixin' to go." She'd smiled and slapped her naked brown thigh. "Let me tell you something, it may have turned out for the best."

"Good Lord, how?" Bea had asked.

"Well, in all those years in that home, you know, they said she never said much of anything, just sort of talked to herself and acted like people were there who weren't and all that, and well now?? She knows who she is, you know??? She talks to me and she watches the soaps, and never misses 'Jeopardy' or 'Wheel of Fortune'?? I think it was all that commotion as well as anything else, and coming back to Fontevrault and finding things up in the attic? Did you know she could climb those steps?? Listen, she's fine, don't you worry about her, I'm getting cheese and graham crackers for her when I get home, and her and me will watch the late show, or the country-western channel, she likes that too, you know, 'Achy Breaky Heart' and all that stuff. Why, she can sing those songs. Never you mind. She's terrific."

"Yes, precious, but really . . ."

Mona had even sort of liked her for five minutes, a kid who could take care of an old woman like that, making it up every day with Band-Aids and hot wires.

Mona had walked out to the front with her, and watched her hop in her pickup truck, which had bare springs sticking out of the passenger seat, and roar off in a cloud of blue exhaust.

"We've got to take care of her," Bea had said. "We've got to sit down and talk about the Mary Jane situation very soon."

True, Mona had agreed. The Mary Jane Situation was a good label for it.

And though this girl clearly had evinced no remarkable powers on the spot, there was something exciting about her.

49

Mary Jane was spunky and there was something irresistible about the idea of showering her with Mayfair money and benefits, and trying to improve her. Why couldn't she come in and study with this tutor who was going to free Mona from the boredom of regular school forever? Beatrice had been chomping at the bit to buy Mary Jane some clothes before she left town, and no doubt had been sending her the crème de la crème of once-worn hand-me-downs.

And there was one other little secret reason why Mona liked Mary Jane, a reason which nobody would ever understand. Mary Jane had been wearing a cowboy hat. It was small and made of straw, and she'd let it fall down behind her shoulders on its strings, but it had been there for two minutes when she first walked up. And she'd popped it back on her head before she pulled hard on the stick shift of that old truck and rushed off, waving at everybody.

A cowboy hat. It had always been Mona's dream to wear a cowboy hat, especially when she was really rich and in control of things, and flying about the world in her own plane. Mona had for years pictured herself as a mogul in a cowboy hat, entering factories and banks and ... well, Mary Jane Mayfair did have a cowboy hat. And with her braids on top of her head, and her slick, tight denim skirt, there was something all together about her. She had, in spite of everything, a sort of deliberate and successful style. Even her chipped and peeling purple fingernail polish had been part of it, giving her a kind of earthy seductiveness.

Well, it wouldn't be hard to verify that, would it?

"And those eyes, Mona," Beatrice had said as they walked back into the garden. "The child is adorable! Did you look at her? I don't know how I could ever ... And her mother, her mother, oh, that girl always was insane, nobody should have ever let her run away with that baby. But there had been such bad blood between us and those Fontevrault Mayfairs."

"You can't take care of all of them, Bea," Mona had reassured her, "any more than Gifford could." But they would, of course. And if Celia and Beatrice didn't, well, Mona would. That had been one of the keenest revelations of that afternoon, that Mona was now part of the team; she wasn't going to let that kid not fulfill her dreams, not while she had breath in her little thirteen-year-old body.

"She's a sweet thing in her own way," Celia had admitted.

"Yeah, and that Band-Aid on her knee," Michael had muttered under his breath, not thinking. "What a girl. I believe what she said about Rowan."

"So do I," said Beatrice. "Only . . ."

"Only what?" Michael had asked desperately.

"Only what if she never makes up her mind to speak again!"

"Beatrice, shame on you," Celia had said, glancing pointedly at Michael.

"You think that Band-Aid's sexy, Michael?" Mona had asked.

"Well, er, yeah, actually. Everything about that girl was sexy, I guess. What does it matter to me?" He'd seemed sincere enough, and sincerely exhausted. He'd wanted to get back to Rowan. He'd been sitting with Rowan and reading a book, by himself, when they'd all come together.

For a while after that afternoon, Mona could have sworn, Rowan looked different, that her eyes were tighter now and then, and sometimes more open, as though she were posing a question to herself. Maybe Mary Jane's big gush of words had been good for Rowan. Maybe they ought to ask Mary Jane back, or maybe she'd just come back. Mona had found herself actually looking forward to it, or maybe just asking the new driver to fire up the monstrous stretch limo, pack the leather pockets with ice and drinks, and drive down there to that flooded house. You could do that when you had your own car. Hell, Mona had not gotten used to any of this.

For two or three days Rowan had seemed better, showing that little frown more and more, which was, after all, a facial expression.

But now? On this quiet, lonely, sticky sunny afternoon?

Mona thought that Rowan had slipped back. Even the heat did not touch her. She sat in the humid air, and the droplets of sweat appeared on her brow, with no Celia to boldly wipe them away, but Rowan didn't move to wipe them herself.

"Please, Rowan, talk to us," Mona said now in her frank, almost brash girlish voice. "I don't want to be the designee of the legacy! I don't even want to be the heiress if you don't approve of it." She leaned on her elbow, her red hair making a veil between her and the iron gates to the front garden. Felt more private. "Come on, Rowan. You know what Mary Jane Mayfair said. You're in there. Come on. Mary Jane said you could hear us."

Mona reached up for her own hair ribbon, to adjust it, to make her head stop itching. There was no hair ribbon. She hadn't worn her bow since her mother died. It was a little pearl-studded barrette, holding a clump of her hair too tight. Hell with it. She loosened it and let her hair slip down.

"Look, Rowan, if you want me to go, give me a sign. You know, like just do something weird. And I'll be out of here that quick."

Rowan was staring at the brick wall. She was staring at the bacon-'n'-eggs lantana—the wildly grown hedge of little brown and orange flowers. Or maybe she was just staring at the bricks.

Mona gave a sigh, a pretty spoiled and petulant thing to do, really. But then she had tried everything except throwing a tantrum. Maybe that's what somebody ought to do!

Only it can't be me, she thought dismally.

She got up, went to the wall, pulled off two sprigs of the lantana and brought them back, and put them before Rowan like an offering to a goddess who sits beneath an oak listening to people's prayers.

"I love you, Rowan," she said. "I need you."

For one moment her eyes misted. The burning green of the garden seemed to fold into one great veil. Her head throbbed slightly, and she felt some tightening in her throat and then a release that was worse than crying, some dim and terrible acknowledgment of all the terrible things that had come to pass.

This woman was wounded, perhaps beyond repair. And she, Mona, was the heiress who could bear a child now, and must indeed try to bear one, so that the great Mayfair

52

fortune could be passed on. This woman, what would she do now? She could no longer be a doctor, that was almost certain; she seemed to care for nothing and no one.

And suddenly Mona felt as awkward and unloved and as unwelcome as she ever had in her life. She ought to get out of here. It was shameful that she had stayed so many days at this table, begging for forgiveness for once lusting after Michael, begging for forgiveness for being young and rich and able someday to have children, for having survived when both her mother, Alicia, and her Aunt Gifford, two women she loved and hated and needed, had died.

Self-centered! What the hell. "I didn't mean it with Michael," she said aloud to Rowan. "No, don't go into that again!"

No change. Rowan's gray eyes were focused, not dreaming. Her hands lay in her lap in the most natural little heap. Wedding ring so thin and spare it made her hands look like those of a nun.

Mona wanted to reach for one of her hands, but she didn't dare. It was one thing to talk for half an hour, but she couldn't touch Rowan, she couldn't force a physical contact. She didn't dare even to lift Rowan's hand and put the lantana in it. That was too intimate to do to her in her silence.

"Well, I don't touch you, you know. I don't take your hand, or feel it or try to learn something from it. I don't touch you or kiss you because if I was like you, I think I'd hate it if some freckle-faced, red-haired kid came around and did that to me."

Red hair, freckles, what had that to do with it, except to say, Yes, I slept with your husband, but you're the mysterious one, the powerful one, the woman, the one he loves and has always loved. I was nothing. I was just a kid who tricked him into bed. And wasn't as careful that night as I should have been. Wasn't careful at all, in fact. But not to worry, I've never been what anyone would call regular. He looked at me the way he looked later at that kid, Mary Jane. Lust, that was all. Lust and nothing more. And my period will finally come, like it always does, and my doctor will give me yet another lecture.

53

Mona gathered up the little sprigs of lantana there on the table, next to the china cup, and she walked away.

For the first time, as she looked up at the clouds moving over the chimneys of the main house, she realized it was a beautiful day.

Michael was in the kitchen, fixing the juices, or "brewing the concoction" as they had come to call it—papaya juice, coconut, grapefruit, orange. There was lots of undefinable slop and pulp all over.

It occurred to her, though she tried not to process the thought, that he looked healthier and handsomer with every passing day. He'd been working out upstairs. The doctors encouraged him. He must have gained fifteen good pounds since Rowan had woken up and climbed out of bed.

"She *does* like it," he said now, as if they'd been discussing this concoction all along. "I know she does. Bea said something about its being too acid. There's no evidence she finds it too acid." He shrugged. "I don't know," he said.

"I think," said Mona, "that she stopped talking because of me."

Mona stared at him, and then the tears came, wet and frightening. She didn't want to break down. She didn't want to make such a demand or display. But she was miserable. What the hell did she want from Rowan? She scarcely knew Rowan. It was as if she needed to be mothered by the designee of the legacy who had lost her power to carry on the line.

"No, honey," he said with the softest, most comforting smile.

"Michael, it's because I told her about us," she said. "I didn't mean to. It was the first morning I spoke to her. All this time, I've been scared to tell you. I thought she was just being quiet. I didn't . . . I don't . . . She never spoke after that, Michael. It's true, isn't it? It was after I came."

"Honey chile, don't torture yourself," he said, wiping up some of the sticky gunk from the counter. He was patient, reassuring, but he was too tired for all this, and Mona was ashamed. "She'd stopped talking the day before, Mona. I told you that. Pay attention." He gave her a little smile to mock himself. "I just didn't realize it then, that she'd quit talking." He stirred the juice again. "Well, now comes the big decision. Egg or no egg."

"Egg! You can't put an egg in fruit juice."

"Sure I can. Honey, you've never lived in Northern California, have you? This is a first-rate health-food special. And she needs the protein. But a raw egg can give you salmonella. Old problem. The family is split right down the middle on the subject of the raw egg. I should have asked Mary Jane her opinion last Sunday."

"Mary Jane!" Mona shook her head. "Damn the family," she said.

"I don't know about that," said Michael. "Beatrice thinks raw eggs are dangerous, and she has a point. On the other hand, when I was in high school, playing football, I used to pop a raw egg into a milkshake every morning. But Celia says . . ."

"Lord deliver me," said Mona, imitating Celia perfectly. "What does Aunt Celia know about raw eggs?"

She was so sick of the family discussing Rowan's tiny likes and dislikes, and Rowan's blood count, and Rowan's color, that if she found herself in one more pointless, ineffectual, and tiresome discussion, she would start screaming to be let out.

Maybe she had just had too much of it all, from the day they'd told her she was the heiress—too many people giving her advice, or asking after her as though *she* were the invalid. She'd written mock headlines on her computer:

GIRL KNOCKED ON HEAD BY WHOLE LOAD OF MONEY. Or, WAIF CHILD INHERITS BILLIONS AS LAWYERS FRET.

Naaah, you wouldn't "fret" in a headline today. But she liked the word.

She felt so terrible suddenly as she stood here in the kitchen that the tears spilled out of her eyes like they would from a baby, and her shoulders began to shake.

"Look, honey, she stopped the day before, I told you," he said. "I can tell you the last thing she said. We were sitting right there at the table. She'd been drinking coffee. She'd said she was dying for a cup of New Orleans coffee. And I'd made her a whole pot. It was about twenty-two hours from the time she woke up, and she hadn't slept at all.

Maybe that was the problem. We kept talking. She needed her rest. She said, 'Michael, I want to go outside. No, stay, Michael. I want to be alone for a while.' "

"You're sure that was the last thing she said?"

"Absolutely. I wanted to call everyone, tell them she was all right. Maybe *I* scared her! I'm the one, making that suggestion. And after that, I was leading her around, and she wasn't saying anything, and that's the way it's been since then."

He picked up what appeared to be a raw egg. He cracked it suddenly on the edge of the plastic blender and then pulled open the two halves of shell to let loose the icky white and yolk.

"I don't think you hurt her at all, Mona. I really, really doubt you did. I wish you hadn't told her. If you must know, I could have done without your telling her that I committed statutory rape on the living room couch with her cousin." He shrugged. "Women do that, you know. They tell afterwards." He gave her a bright reproving look, the sunlight glinting in his eyes. "We can't tell, but they can tell. But the point is, I doubt she even heard you. I don't think . . . she gives a damn." His voice trailed off.

The glass was foamy and faintly disgusting-looking.

"I'm sorry, Michael."

"Honey, don't—"

"No, I mean I'm okay. She's not okay. But I'm okay. You want me to take that stuff to her? It's gross, Michael, I mean gross. Like it is absolutely disgusting!"

Mona looked at the froth, the unearthly color.

"Gotta blend it," he said. He put the square rubber cap on the container, and pressed the button. Then came the ghastly sound of the blades turning as the liquid jumped inside.

Maybe it was better if you didn't *know* about the egg.

"Well, I put lots of broccoli juice in it this time," he said.

"Oh God, no wonder she won't drink it. Broccoli juice! Are you trying to kill her?"

"Oh, she'll drink it. She always drinks it. She drinks anything I put before her. I'm just thinking about what's in it. Now listen to me. If she wasn't listening when you made your confession, I'm not sure it came as a surprise. All that time she was in the coma, she heard things. She told me. She heard things people said when I was nowhere about. Of course, nobody knew about you and me and our little, you know, criminal activity."

"Michael, for chrissakes, if there is a crime of statutory rape in this state, you'd have to get a lawyer to look it up to be sure. The age of consent between cousins is probably ten, and there may even be a special law on the books lowering the age to eight for Mayfairs."

"Don't kid yourself, sweetheart," he said, shaking his head in obvious disapproval. "But what I was saying is, she heard the things you and I said to each other when we sat by the bed. We're talking about witches, Mona." He fell into his thoughts, staring off, brooding almost, looking intensely handsome, beefcake and sensitive.

"You know, Mona, it's nothing anybody said." He looked up at her. He was sad now, and it was very real, the way it is when a man of his age gets sad, and she found herself just a little frightened. "Mona, it was everything that happened to her. It was . . . perhaps the last thing that happened. . . ."

Mona nodded. She tried to picture it again, the way he'd so briefly described it. The gun, the shot, the body falling. The terrible secret of the milk.

"You haven't told anyone, have you?" he said in a serious whisper. God help her if she had, she thought, she would have died at this moment, the way he was looking at her.

"No, and I never will," she said. "I know when to tell and when not to tell, but . . ."

He shook his head. "She wouldn't let me touch the body. She insisted on carrying it down herself, and she could hardly walk. Long as I live, I'm not going to get that sight out of my mind, ever. All the rest of it—I don't know. I can take it in stride, but something about the mother dragging the body of the daughter . . ."

"Did you think of it that way, like it was her daughter?"

He didn't answer. He just continued to look off, and gradually the hurt and trouble slipped away from his face, and he chewed his lip for a second, and then almost smiled.

"Never tell anyone that part," he whispered. "Never, never, never. No one needs to know. But someday, perhaps, she'll want to talk about it. Perhaps it's that, more than anything else, that's made her silent."

"Don't ever worry that I'll tell," she said. "I'm not a child, Michael."

"I know, honey, believe me, I know," he said with just the warmest little spark of good humor.

Then he was really gone again, forgetting her, forgetting them, and the huge glass of gunk, as he stared off. And for one second he looked as if he was giving up all hope, as if he was in a total despair beyond the reach of anyone, even maybe Rowan.

"Michael, for the love of God, she will be all right. If that's what it is, she'll get better."

He didn't answer right away, then he sort of murmured the words:

"She sits in that very place, not over the grave, but right beside it," he said. His voice had gotten thick.

He was going to cry, and Mona wouldn't be able to stand it. She wanted with all her heart to go to him and put her arms around him. But this would have been for her, not him.

She realized suddenly that he was smiling—for her sake, of course—and now he gave her a little philosophical shrug. "Your life will be filled with good things, for the demons are slain," he said, "and you will inherit Eden." His smile grew broader and so genuinely kind. "And she and I, we will take that guilt to our graves of whatever we did and didn't do, or had to do, or failed to do for each other."

He sighed, and he leaned on his folded arms over the counter. He looked out into the sunshine, into the gently moving yard, full of rattling green leaves and spring.

It seemed he had come to a natural finish.

And he was his old self again, philosophical but undefeated.

Finally he stood upright and picked up the glass and wiped it with an old white napkin.

"Ah, that's one thing," he said, "that is really nice about being rich."

"What?"

"Having a linen napkin," he said, "anytime you want it. And having linen handkerchiefs. Celia and Bea always have their linen handkerchiefs. My dad would never use a paper handkerchief. Hmmm. I haven't thought about that in a long time."

He winked at her. She couldn't stop herself from smiling. What a dope. But who the hell else could play off a wink like that with her? Nobody.

"You haven't heard from Yuri, have you?" he asked.

"I would have told you," she said dismally. It was agony to hear Yuri's name.

"Have you told Aaron that you haven't heard from him?"

"A hundred times, and three times this morning. Aaron hasn't heard anything, either. He's worried. But he's not going back to Europe, no matter what happens. He'll live out his days with us right here. He says to remember that Yuri is incredibly clever, like all the investigators of the Talamasca."

"You do think something has happened?"

"I don't know," she said dully. "Maybe he just forgot about me." It was too dreadful to contemplate. It couldn't have been that way. But one had to face things, didn't one? And Yuri was a man of the world.

Michael looked down into the drink. Maybe he would have the brains to see it was flat-out undrinkable. Instead he picked up a spoon and started to stir it.

"You know, Michael, that just may shock her out of her trance," Mona said. "I mean, while she's drinking it, right at that very moment, when half the glass is sliding down her throat, just tell her in a clear voice what's in it."

He chuckled, his deep-chested, fabulous chuckle. He picked up the jug of slop and poured a full, egregious glass of it.

"Come on, come out there with me. Come and see her."

Mona hesitated. "Michael, I don't want her to see both of us together, you know, standing side by side."

"Use a little of your own witchcraft, honey. She knows I am her slave till the day I die."

His expression changed again, very slowly. He was looking at her in a calm but almost cold fashion. And again there came over her a sense of how bereft he really was.

"Yeah, bereft," he said, and there was something almost mean in his smile. He didn't say anything more. He picked up the glass and went out the door.

"Let's go talk to the lady," he said over his shoulder. "Let's go read her mind together. Two heads, you know, and all that. Maybe we should do it again, Mona, on the grass, you know, you and me, and maybe she'd wake up."

Mona was shocked. Did he mean that? No, that wasn't the question. The question was, How could he say that?

She didn't answer him, but she knew what he felt. Or at least she thought she did. On some level she knew she couldn't really know, that things were painful for a man of his age in a different way from what they were for a young girl. She knew this in spite of so many people having told her this, more or less. It was a matter not of humility but logic.

She followed him out onto the flagstones and along the pool and then into the rear gates. His jeans were so tight, she could hardly stand it. His natural walk was a seductive swagger. *This is nice, think sexy thoughts! No way!* And his polo shirt wasn't exactly loose-fitting either. She loved the way it moved over his shoulders and back.

Can't stop it. She wished he hadn't made that bitter little joke. Do it on the grass! An awful restlessness took hold of her. Men were always complaining about how the sight of sexy women aroused them. Well, with her it was words as well as images. His tight jeans, and the sharp images that had invaded her mind after what he'd said.

Rowan was seated at the table, the way she'd been when Mona left her; the lantana was still there, the sprigs scattered a little, as if the wind had stirred them with one finger and then let them alone.

Rowan was frowning slightly, as if weighing something in her mind. Now that was always a good sign, Mona thought, but she would get Michael's hopes up if she talked about it. Rowan didn't seem to know that they were there. She was still looking at the distant flowers, at the wall.

Michael bent to kiss her on the cheek. He set the glass on the table. There was no change in her, except the breeze caught a few strands of hair. Then he reached down and he lifted her right hand and he placed her fingers around the glass.

"Drink it, honey," he said. He used the same tone he'd used to Mona, brusque and warm. Honey, honey, honey means Mona, Rowan, or Mary Jane, or any female being perhaps.

Would "honey" have been appropriate for the dead thing, buried in the hole with its father? Christ, if she had only laid eyes on one of them, for just a precious second! Yeah, and every Mayfair woman who laid eyes on him during his little rampage had paid with her life for it. Except Rowan. . . .

Whoa! Rowan was lifting the glass. Mona watched with a fearful fascination as she drank without ever moving her eyes from the distant flowers. She did blink naturally and slowly as she swallowed, but that was all. And the frown remained. Small. Thoughtful.

Michael stood watching her, hands in his pockets, and then he did a surprising thing. He talked about her to Mona, as if Rowan couldn't hear. This was the first time.

"When the doctor spoke to her, when he told her she should go in for tests, she just got up and walked off. It was like a person on a park bench in a big city. You'd think someone had sat down beside her, maybe too close to her. She was isolated like that, all alone."

He collected the glass. It looked more disgusting than ever. But to tell the truth, Rowan looked like she would have drunk anything that he'd put in her hand.

Nothing registered on Rowan's face.

"I could take her to the hospital for the tests, of course. She might go along. She's done everything else I've wanted her to do."

"Why don't you?" asked Mona.

"Because when she gets up in the morning she puts on her nightgown and her robe. I've laid out real clothes for her. She doesn't touch them. That's my cue. She wants to be in her nightgown and her robe. She wants to be home."

He was angry suddenly. His cheeks were red, and there was a frank twisting to his lips that said it all.

"The tests can't help her anyway," he continued. "All these vitamins, that's the treatment. The tests would only tell us things. Maybe it's none of our business now. The drink helps her."

His voice was tightening. He was getting angrier and angrier as he looked at Rowan. He stopped speaking.

He bent down suddenly and set the glass on the table, and laid his hands flat on either side of it. He was trying to look Rowan in the eye. He drew close to her face, but there was no change in her.

"Rowan, please," he whispered. "Come back!"

"Michael, don't!"

"Why not, Mona? Rowan, I need you now. I need you!" He banged the table hard with both hands. Rowan flinched, but did not otherwise change. "Rowan!" he shouted. He reached out for her as if he was going to take her by the shoulders and shake her, but he didn't.

He snatched up the glass and turned and walked away.

Mona stood still, waiting, too shocked to speak. But it was like everything he did. It had been the good-hearted thing to do. It had been rough, though, and sort of terrible to watch.

Mona didn't come away just yet. Slowly she sat down in the chair at the table, across from Rowan, the same place she'd taken every day.

Very slowly, Mona grew calm again. She wasn't sure why she stayed here, except it seemed the loyal thing to do. Perhaps she didn't want to appear to be Michael's ally. Her guilt just hung all over her all the time these days.

Rowan did look beautiful, if you stopped thinking about the fact that she didn't talk. Her hair was growing long, almost to her shoulders. Beautiful and absent. Gone.

"Well, you know," Mona said, "I'll probably keep coming until you give me a sign. I know that doesn't absolve me, or make it okay to be the pest of a shocked and mute person. But when you're mute like this, you sort of force people to act, to make choices, to decide. I mean, people can't just let you alone. It's not possible. It's not really kind."

She let out her breath, and felt herself relax all over.

"I'm too young to know certain things," she said. "I mean, I'm not going to sit here and tell you I understand what happened to you. That would be too stupid." She looked at Rowan; the eyes looked green now, as if picking up the tint of the bright spring lawn.

"But I . . . ah . . . care about what's happening to everybody, well, almost everybody. I know things. I know more than anybody except Michael or Aaron. Do you remember Aaron?"

That was a dumb question. Of course Rowan remembered Aaron, if she remembered anything at all.

"Well, what I meant to say was, there's this man, Yuri. I told you about him. I don't think you ever saw him. In fact, I'm sure you didn't. Well, he's gone, very gone, as it stands now, and I'm worried, and Aaron's worried, too. It's like things are at a standstill now, with you here in the garden like this, and the truth is, things never stand still—"

She broke off. This was worse than the other approach. There was no way to tell if this woman was suffering. Mona sighed, trying to be quiet about it. She put her elbows on the table. Slowly she looked up. She could have sworn that Rowan had been looking at her, and had only just looked away.

"Rowan, it's not over," she whispered again. Then she looked off, through the iron gates, and beyond the pool and down the middle of the front lawn. The crape myrtle was coming into bloom. It had been mere sticks when Yuri left.

She and he had stood out there whispering together, and he had said, "Look, whatever happens in Europe, Mona, I am coming back here to you."

Rowan *was* looking at her. Rowan was staring into her eyes.

She was too amazed to speak or move. And she was frightened to do either, frightened that Rowan would look away. She wanted to believe this was good, this was ratification and redemption. She had caught Rowan's attention, even if she had been a hopeless brat.

Gradually Rowan's preoccupied expression seemed to fade as Mona stared at her. And Rowan's face became eloquent and unmistakably sad.

"What's the matter, Rowan?" Mona whispered.

Rowan made a little sound, as if she were clearing her throat.

"It's not Yuri," Rowan whispered. And then her frown tightened, and her eyes darkened, but she didn't drift away.

"What is it, Rowan?" Mona asked her. "Rowan, what did you say about Yuri?"

It appeared for all the world as if Rowan thought she was still speaking to Mona, and didn't know that nothing was coming out.

"Rowan," Mona whispered. "Tell me. Rowan—" Mona's words stopped. She'd lost the nerve, suddenly, to speak her heart.

Rowan's eyes were still fixed on her. Rowan lifted her right hand and ran her fingers back through her pale ashen hair. Natural, normal, but the eyes were not normal. They were struggling. . . .

A sound distracted Mona—men talking, Michael and someone else. And then the sudden, alarming sound of a woman crying or laughing. For one second, Mona couldn't tell which.

She turned and stared through the gates, across the glaring pool. Her Aunt Beatrice was coming towards her, almost running along the flagstone edge of the water, one hand to her mouth and the other groping as if she were going to fall on her face. She was the one who was crying, and it was most certainly crying. Bea's hair was falling loose from her invariably neat twist on the back of her head. Her silk dress was blotched and wet.

Michael and a man in ominous plain dark clothes followed quickly, talking together as they did.

Great choked sobs were coming from Beatrice. Her heels sank into the soft lawn, but on she came.

"Bea, what is it?" Mona rose to her feet. So did Rowan. Rowan stared at the approaching figure, and as Beatrice rushed across the grass, turning her ankle and righting herself immediately, it was to Rowan that she reached out.

"They did it, Rowan," said Bea, gasping for breath. "They killed him. The car came up over the curb. They killed him. I saw it with my own eyes!"

Mona reached out to support Beatrice, and suddenly her aunt had put her left arm around Mona and was near crushing her with kisses while the other hand still groped for Rowan, and Rowan reached to take it and clasp it in both of hers.

"Bea, who did they kill, who?" Mona cried. "You don't mean Aaron."

"Yes," Bea answered, nodding frantically, her voice now dry and barely audible. She continued to nod, as Mona and Rowan closed against her. "Aaron," she said. "They killed him. I saw it. The car jumped the curb on St. Charles Avenue. I told him I'd drive him over here. He said no, he wanted to walk. The car deliberately hit him, I saw it. It ran over him three times!"

As Michael, too, put his arms around her, Bea slumped as if she would faint, and let herself fall to the ground. Michael collected her and held her and she sank, crying, against his chest. Her hair fell in her eyes, and her hands were still reaching, trembling, like birds that couldn't light.

The man in the ominous clothes was a policeman—Mona saw the gun and the shoulder holster—a Chinese American, with a tender and emotional face.

"I'm so sorry," he said with a distinct New Orleans accent. Mona had never heard such an accent from such a Chinese face.

"They killed him?" Mona asked in a whisper, looking from the policeman to Michael, who was slowly soothing Bea with kisses and a gentle hand that straightened her hair. In all her life Mona had never seen Bea cry like this, and for one moment two thoughts collided in her: Yuri must be dead already; and Aaron had been murdered, and this meant perhaps that they were all in danger. And this was terrible, unspeakably terrible above all for Bea.

Rowan spoke calmly to the policeman, though her voice was hoarse and small in the confusion, in the clattering of emotion.

"I want to see the body," said Rowan. "Can you take me

65

to it? I'm a doctor. I have to see it. It will take me only a moment to dress."

Was there time for Michael to be amazed, for Mona to be flabbergasted? Oh, but it made sense, didn't it? Horrible Mary Jane had said, "She's listening. She'll talk when she's ready."

And thank God she had not sat still and silent through this moment! Thank God that she couldn't or didn't have to, and was with them now.

Never mind how fragile she looked, and how hoarse and unnatural her voice sounded. Her eyes were clear as she looked at Mona, ignoring the policeman's solicitous answer that perhaps it was better she did not see the body, the accident having been what it was.

"Bea needs Michael," said Rowan. She reached out and clasped Mona's wrist. Her hand was cool and firm. "I need you now. Will you go with me?"

"Yes," said Mona. "Oh yes."

Three

H E HAD PROMISED the little man he would enter the hotel moments after. "You come with me," Samuel had said, "and everyone will see you. Now keep the sunglasses on your face."

Yuri had nodded. He didn't mind sitting in the car for the moment, watching people walk past the elegant front doors of Claridge's. Nothing had comforted him so much since he'd left the glen of Donnelaith as the city of London.

Even the long drive south with Samuel, tunneling through the night on freeways that might have been anywhere in the world, had unnerved him.

As for the glen, it was vivid in his memory and thoroughly gruesome. What had made him think it was wise to go there alone—to seek at the very roots for some knowledge of the Little People and the Taltos? Of course he had found exactly what he wanted. And been shot in the shoulder by a .38-caliber bullet in the process.

The bullet had been an appalling shock. He'd never been wounded before in such a fashion. But the truly unnerving revelation had been the Little People.

Slumped in the back of the Rolls, he suffered again a vivid memory of that sight—the night with its heavy rolling clouds and haunting moon, the mountain path wildly overgrown, and the eerie sound of the drums and the horns rising against the cliffs.

Only when he had seen the little men in their circle had he realized they were singing. Only then had he heard their baritone chants, their words thoroughly unrecognizable to him.

He wasn't sure he had believed in them until then—

Round in the circle they went, stunted, humpbacked, lifting their short knees, rocking back and forth, giving forth rhythmic bursts in the chants, some drinking from mugs, others from bottles. They wore their gunbelts over their shoulders. They fired their pistols into the great windy night with the riotous hilarity of savages. The guns did not roar. Rather they went off in tight bursts, like firecrackers. Worse, by far, were the drums, the awful pounding drums, and the few pipes whining and struggling with their gloomy melody.

When the bullet struck him, he thought it had come from one of them—a sentry perhaps. He had been wrong.

Three weeks had passed before he'd left the glen.

Now Claridge's. Now the chance to call New Orleans, to speak to Aaron, to speak with Mona, to explain why for so long he'd been silent.

As for the risk of London, as for the proximity of the Talamasca Motherhouse and those who were trying to kill him, he felt infinitely safer here than he had in the glen only moments before the bullet had knocked him on his face.

Time to go upstairs. To see this mysterious friend of Samuel's, who had already arrived, and who had not been described or explained to Yuri. Time to do what the little man wanted because the little man had saved Yuri's life, nursed him back to health, and wanted him to meet this friend who had, in this great drama, some mammoth significance.

Yuri climbed out of the car, the genial British doorman quickly coming to his assistance.

His shoulder ached; there was a sharp pain. When would he learn not to use his right arm! Maddening.

The cold air was fierce but momentary. He went directly into the lobby of the hotel—so vast, yet warm. He took the great curving staircase to his right.

The soft strains of a string quartet came from the nearby bar. The air was still all around him. The hotel calmed him and made him feel safe. It also made him feel happy.

What a wonder it was that all of these polite Englishmen—the doorman, the bellhops, the kindly gentleman coming down the stairs past him—took no visible notice of his dirty sweater or his soiled black pants. Too polite, he mused.

He walked along the second floor until he came to the door of the corner suite, which the little man had described to him, and finding the door open, he entered a small, inviting alcove rather like that of a gracious home, and which looked into a large parlor, dowdy yet luxurious as the little man had said it would be.

The little man was on his knees, piling wood into the fireplace. He had taken off his tweed jacket, and the white shirt pulled painfully over his stunted arms and hump.

"There, there, come in here, Yuri," he said, without so much as looking up.

Yuri stepped into the doorway. The other man was there.

And this man was as strange to behold as the little man, but in an entirely different fashion. He was outrageously tall, though not impossibly so. He had pale white skin and dark, rather natural-looking hair. The hair was long and free and out of keeping with the man's fine black wool suit and the dull sheen of the expensive white shirt that he wore, and his dark red tie. He looked decidedly romantic. But what did this mean? Yuri wasn't sure. Yet it was the word that came to his mind. The man did not look decisively athletic—he was not one of those freakish sports giants who excel in televised Olympic games or on noisy basketball courts—rather he looked romantic.

Yuri met the man's gaze with no trouble. There was nothing menacing in this extraordinary and rather formal figure. Indeed, his face was smooth and young, almost pretty for a man, with its long, thick eyelashes and full, gently shaped androgynous lips—and not intimidating. Only the white in his hair gave him an air of authority, which he clearly did not regularly enforce. His eyes were hazel and rather large, and they looked at Yuri wonderingly. It was altogether an impressive figure, except for the hands. The hands were a little too big, and there was an abnormality about the fingers, though Yuri wasn't sure what it was. Spidery thin they were, maybe that was the sum of it.

"You're the gypsy," said the man in a low, pleasing voice that was almost a little sensual and very unlike the caustic baritone of the dwarf.

"Come inside, sit down," said the dwarf impatiently. He had now lighted the fire and was fanning it with the bellows. "I sent for something to eat, but I want you to go into the bedroom when they bring it, I don't want you seen."

"Thank you," said Yuri quietly. He realized suddenly that he'd failed to remove his dark glasses. How bright the room was suddenly, even with its deep green velvet furniture and old-fashioned flowered curtains. An agreeable room, with the imprint of people upon it.

Claridge's. He knew the hotels of the world, but he had never known Claridge's. He had never lodged in London except at the Motherhouse, to which he could not go now.

"You're wounded, my friend told me," said the tall man, approaching him and looking down at him in such a kindly way that the man's height aroused no instinctive fear. The spidery hands were raised and extended as if, in order to see Yuri's face, the man had to frame it.

"I'm all right. It was a bullet, but your friend removed it. I would be dead if it wasn't for your friend."

"So he's told me. Do you know who I am?"

"No, I don't."

"Do you know what a Taltos is? That is what I am."

Yuri said nothing. He had no more suspected this than he had suspected that the Little People really existed. Taltos has meant Lasher—killer, monster, menace. He was too shocked to speak. He merely stared at the man's face, thinking that the man looked to be no more and no less, except for the hands, than a giant human.

"For the love of God, Ash," said the dwarf, "have some guile for once." He brushed off his pants. The fire was vigorous and splendid. He seated himself in a soft, rather shapeless chair that looked extremely comfortable. His feet didn't touch the ground.

It was impossible to read his deeply wrinkled face. Was he really so cross? The folds of flesh destroyed all expression. Indeed, the voice alone carried everything with the little man, who only occasionally made bright wide eyes as he spoke. His red hair was the appropriate cliché for his impatience and his temper. He drummed his short fingers on the cloth arms of the chair.

Yuri walked to the couch and took a stiff place at the very end of it, conscious that the tall one had gone to the mantel and was looking down at the fire. Yuri did not mean to stare rudely at this creature.

"A Taltos," said Yuri. His voice sounded acceptably calm. "A Taltos. Why do you want to talk to me? Why do you want to help me? Who are you, and why have you come here?"

"You saw the other one?" the tall man asked, turning and looking at Yuri with eyes that were almost shy in their openness, but not quite. This man might have been knock-dead beautiful if it hadn't been for the hands. The knuckles looked like knots.

"No, I never saw him," said Yuri.

"But you know for certain he is dead?"

"Yes, I know that for certain," said Yuri. The giant and the dwarf. He was not going to laugh at this, but it was horribly amusing. This creature's abnormalities made him pleasing to look at. And the little man's abnormalities made him seem dangerous and wicked. And it was all an act of nature, was it? It was somewhat beyond the scope of the range of accidents in which Yuri believed.

"Did this Taltos have a mate?" asked the tall one. "I mean another Taltos, a female?"

"No, his mate was a woman named Rowan Mayfair. I told your friend about her. She was his mother, and his lover. She is what we call a witch in the Talamasca."

"Aye," said the little man, "and what we would call a witch as well. There are many powerful witches in this tale, Ashlar. There is a brood of witches. You have to let the man tell his story."

"Ashlar, that's your full name?" asked Yuri. It had been a jolt.

For hours before he'd left New Orleans, he had listened to Aaron summarize the tale of Lasher, the demon from the glen. St. Ashlar—that name had been spoken over and over again. St. Ashlar.

"Yes," said the tall one. "But Ash is the single-syllable version, which I heartily prefer. I don't mean to be impolite, but I so prefer the simple name Ash that often I don't answer to the other." This was said firmly but with courtesy.

The dwarf laughed. "I call him by his full name to make him strong and attentive," he said.

The tall one ignored this. He warmed his hands over the fire; with fingers splayed apart, they looked diseased.

"You're in pain, aren't you?" the man said, turning away from the fire.

"Yes. Excuse me, please, that I show it. The wound's in my shoulder, in such a place that every little movement pulls it. Will you forgive me that I slouch back on this sofa, and try to remain like this, looking lazy? My mind is racing. Will you tell me who you are?"

"I've done that, have I not?" asked the tall one. "You speak. What happened to you?"

"Yuri, I told you," said the dwarf, with rather good-natured impatience, "that this is my oldest confidant and friend in the world. I told you that he knew the Talamasca. That he knows more about it than any living being. Please trust him. Tell him what he wants to know."

"I trust you," said Yuri. "But to what purpose do I tell you my business, or of my adventures? What will you do with this knowledge?"

"Help you, of course," said the tall one slowly, with a gentle nod of his head. "Samuel says the men in the Talamasca are trying to kill you. This is hard for me to accept. I have always, in my own way, loved the Order of the Talamasca. I protect myself from it, as I do from anything which would constrict me in any way. But the men of the Talamasca have seldom been my enemies . . . at least not for very long. Who tried to hurt you? Are you sure these evil people came from the Order itself?"

"No, I'm not sure," said Yuri. "This is what happened, more or less. When I was an orphan boy, the Talamasca took me in. Aaron Lightner was the man who did it. Samuel knows who this man is."

"So do I," said the tall one.

"All my adult life I've served the Order, in a traveling capacity mostly, often performing tasks which I myself don't fully understand. Apparently, unbeknownst to me, my vows rested upon a loyalty to Aaron Lightner. When he went to New Orleans to investigate a family of witches, things somehow went wrong. This family was the Mayfair family, this family of witches. I read their history in old records of the Order before these records were closed to me. It was from Rowan Mayfair that the Taltos was born."

"Who or what was the father?" asked the tall one.

"It was a man."

"A mortal man. You're certain of this?"

"Without question, but there were other considerations. This family had been haunted for many, many generations by a spirit, both evil and good. This spirit took hold of the infant inside Rowan Mayfair, took possession of it and assisted its unusual birth. The Taltos, springing up full-grown from this woman, possessed the soul of the haunting spirit complete and entire. They called this creature Lasher in the family. I've never known any other name for him. Now this creature is dead, as I've told you."

The tall man was frankly amazed. He gave a little sympathetic shake of his head. He walked to the nearby armchair and sat down, turning politely towards Yuri, and crossing his long legs and ankles very much as Yuri had done. He sat very straight, as though never ashamed or uneasy about his height.

"From two witches!" said the tall one in a whisper.

"Absolutely," said Yuri.

"You say absolutely," said the tall one. "What can this mean?"

"There is genetic evidence, an abundance of it. The Talamasca has this evidence. The witch family carries an extraordinary set of genes within its various lines. Genes of the Taltos, which under the ordinary circumstances are never switched on by nature, but which in this case—either through witchcraft or possession—did indeed do their work to make the Taltos come into the world."

The tall man smiled. It surprised Yuri, because the smile

73

so fired the face with expression and affection and simple delight.

"You speak like all the men from the Talamasca," said the tall one. "You speak like a priest in Rome. You speak as if you weren't born in these times."

"Well, I was educated on their documents in Latin," said Yuri. "Their story of this creature, Lasher, it went back to the sixteen hundreds. I read all of it, along with the story of this family—its rise to great wealth and power, its secret doings with this spirit, Lasher. And I have of course read a hundred such files."

"Have you?"

"Not stories of the Taltos," said Yuri, "if that's what you mean. I never heard the word until I was in New Orleans—until two members of the Order were killed there, trying to free this Taltos, Lasher, from the man who killed him. But I cannot tell that tale."

"Why? I want to know who killed him."

"When I know you better, when you've matched my confessions with your own."

"What can I confess? I'm Ashlar. I'm a Taltos. It's centuries since I've seen one single other member of my own species. Oh, there have been others. I've heard tell of them, chased after them, and in some instances almost found them. Mark, I say almost. But not in centuries have I touched my own flesh and blood, as humans are so fond of saying. Never in all this time."

"You're very old, that's what you're telling me. Our lifespan is nothing compared to yours."

"Well, apparently not," said the man. "I must be old. I have this white hair now, as you see. But then how am I to know how old I am, and what my decline may be, and how long it will take in human years? When I lived in happiness among my own, I was too young to learn what I would need for this long, lonely voyage. And God did not gift me with a supernatural memory. Like an ordinary man, I remember some things with haunting clarity; others are completely erased."

"The Talamasca knows about you?" asked Yuri. "It's crucial that you tell me. The Talamasca was my vocation."

"Explain how this changed."

"As I told you, Aaron Lightner went to New Orleans. Aaron is an expert on witches. We study witches."

"Understood," said the dwarf. "Get on with it."

"Hush, Samuel, mind your manners," said the tall one softly but seriously.

"Don't be an imbecile, Ash, this gypsy is falling in love with you!"

The Taltos was shocked and outraged. The anger flared in him beautifully and fully, and then he shook his head and folded his arms as if he knew how to deal with such anger.

As for Yuri, he was again stunned. It seemed the way of the world now—outrageous shocks and revelations. He was stunned and hurt because he had in some way warmed to this being far beyond the ways in which he'd warmed to the little man, which were, in the main, more intellectual.

He looked away, humiliated. He had no time now to tell the story of his own life—how he had fallen so totally under the dominance of Aaron Lightner, and the force and power which strong men often exerted over him. He wanted to say this was not erotic. But it was erotic, insofar as anything and everything is.

The Taltos was staring coldly at the little man.

Yuri resumed his story.

"Aaron Lightner went to help the Mayfair witches in their endless battles with the spirit Lasher. Aaron Lightner never knew whence this spirit came, or what it really was. That a witch had called it up in Donnelaith in the year 1665—that was known, but not much else about it.

"After the creature was made flesh, after it had caused the deaths of too many witches for me to count—only after all this did Aaron Lightner see the creature and learn from its own lips that it was the Taltos, and that it had lived in a body before, in the time of King Henry, meeting its death in Donnelaith, the glen which it haunted until the witch called it up.

"These things are not in any Talamasca file known to me. Scarcely three weeks have passed since the creature was slaughtered. But these things may be in secret files known to someone. Once the Talamasca learnt that Lasher had been reincarnated, or whatever in the name of God we should call it, they moved in on him and sought to remove him for their own purposes. They may have coldly and deliberately taken several lives in the process. I don't know. I know that Aaron had no part in their schemes, and felt betrayed by them. That is why I'm asking you: Do they know about you? Are you part of the Talamasca knowledge, because if you are, it is highly occult knowledge."

"Yes and no," said the tall one. "You don't tell lies at all, do you?"

"Ash, try not to say strange things," grumbled the dwarf. He too had sat back, letting his short, stumpy legs stretch out perfectly straight. He had knitted his fingers on his tweed vest, and his shirt was open at the neck. A bit of light flashed in his hooded eyes.

"I was merely remarking on it, Samuel. Have some patience." The tall man sighed. "Try not to say such strange things yourself." He looked a little annoyed and then his eyes returned to Yuri.

"Let me answer your question, Yuri," he said. The way he had spoken the name was warm and casual. "Men in the Talamasca today probably know nothing of me. It would take a genius to unearth what tales of us are told in Talamasca archives, if indeed such documents still exist. I never fully understood the status or the significance of this knowledge—the Order's files, as they call them now. I read some manuscript once, centuries ago, and laughed and laughed at the words in it. But in those times all written language seemed naive and touching to me. Some of it still does."

To Yuri, this was a fascinating point. The dwarf had been right, of course; he was falling under the sway of this being, he had lost his healthy reluctance to trust, but that was what this sort of love was about, wasn't it? Divesting oneself so totally of the customary feelings of alienation and distrust that the subsequent acceptance was intellectually orgasmic.

"What sort of language doesn't make you laugh?" asked Yuri.

"Modern slang," said the tall one. "Realism in fiction,

76

and journalism which is filled with colloquialisms. It often lacks naiveté completely. It has lost all formality, and instead abides by an intense compression. When people write now, it is sometimes like the screech of a whistle compared to the songs they used to sing."

Yuri laughed. "I think you're right," he said. "Not so the documents of the Talamasca, however."

"No. As I was explaining, they are melodic and amusing."

"But then there are documents and documents. So you don't think they know about you now."

"I'm fairly certain they don't know about me, and as you tell your tale, it becomes very clear that they cannot possibly know about me. But go on. What happened to this Taltos?"

"They tried to take him away, and they died in the process. The man who killed the Taltos killed these men from the Talamasca. Before they died, however, when these men were seeking to take the Taltos into their custody, you might say, they indicated that they had a female Taltos, that they had for centuries sought to bring the male and the female together. They indicated it was the avowed purpose of the Order. The clandestine and occult purpose, I should say. This was demoralizing to Aaron Lightner."

"I can see why."

Yuri went on.

"The Taltos, Lasher, he seemed unsurprised by all this; he seemed to have figured it out. Even in his earlier incarnation, the Talamasca had tried to take him out of Donnelaith, perhaps to mate him with the female. But he didn't trust them and he didn't go with them. He was a priest in those days. He was believed to be a saint."

"St. Ashlar," said the dwarf more soberly, the voice seeming to rumble not from the wrinkles of his face but from his heavy trunk. "St. Ashlar, who always comes again."

The tall one bowed his head slightly, his deep hazel eyes moving slowly back and forth across the carpet, almost as if he were reading the rich Oriental design. He looked up

77

at Yuri, head bowed, so that his dark brows shadowed his eyes.

"St. Ashlar," he said in a sad voice.

"Are you this man?"

"I'm no saint, Yuri. Do you mind that I call you by name? Let's not speak of saints, if you please. . . ."

"Oh, please do call me Yuri. And I will call you Ash? But the point is, are you this same individual? This one they called the saint? You speak of centuries! And we sit here in this parlor, and the fire crackles, and the waiter taps at the door now with our refreshments. You must tell me. I can't protect myself from my own brothers in the Talamasca if you don't tell me and help me to understand what's going on."

Samuel slipped off the chair and proceeded towards the alcove. "Go into the bedroom, please, Yuri. Out of sight now." He swaggered as he went past Yuri.

Yuri rose, the shoulder hurting him acutely for a moment, and he walked into the bedroom, closing the door behind him. He found himself in a shadowy stillness, with soft, loose curtains filtering the subdued morning light. He picked up the telephone; quickly he punched the direct-dial number, followed by the country code for the United States.

Then he hesitated, feeling wholly unable to tell the protective lies that he would have to tell to Mona, eager to speak to Aaron and tell him what he knew, and half afraid he would be momentarily stopped from calling anyone.

Several times on the drive down from Scotland, he had found himself at public phones, experiencing the same dilemma, when the dwarf had commanded him to get in the car now.

What to tell his little love? How much to tell Aaron in the few moments he might have to speak with him?

In haste, he punched in the area code for New Orleans, and the number of the Mayfair house on St. Charles and Amelia, and he waited, a little worried suddenly that it might be the very middle of the night in America, and then realizing suddenly that indeed it was.

Rude and terrible mistake, whatever the circumstances.

78

Someone had answered. It was a voice he knew but could not place.

"I'm calling from England. I'm so sorry. I'm trying to reach Mona Mayfair," he said. "I hope I haven't waked the house."

"Yuri?" asked the woman.

"Yes!" he confessed without obvious surprise that this woman had recognized his voice.

"Yuri, Aaron Lightner's dead," said the woman. "This is Celia, Beatrice's cousin. Mona's cousin. Everybody's cousin. Aaron's been killed."

There was a long pause in which Yuri did nothing. He didn't think or visualize anything or rush to any conclusion. His body was caught in a cold, terrible fear—fear of the implications of these words, that he would never, never see Aaron again, that they would never speak to each other, that he and Aaron—that Aaron was forever gone.

When he tried to move his lips, he found trouble. He did some senseless and stupid little thing with his hand, pinching the telephone cord.

"I'm sorry, Yuri. We've been worried about you. Mona's been very worried. Where are you? Can you call Michael Curry? I can give you the number."

"I'm all right," Yuri answered softly. "I have that number."

"That's where Mona is now, Yuri. Up at the other house. They will want to know where you are and how you are, and how to reach you immediately."

"But Aaron . . ." he said, pleadingly, unable to say more. His voice sounded puny to him, barely escaping the burden of the tremendous emotions that even clouded his vision and his equilibrium, his entire sense of who he was. "Aaron . . ."

"He was run over, deliberately, by a man in a car. He was walking down from the Pontchartrain Hotel, where he'd just left Beatrice with Mary Jane Mayfair. They were putting Mary Jane Mayfair up at the hotel. Beatrice was just about to go into the lobby of the hotel when she heard the noise. She and Mary Jane witnessed what happened. Aaron was run over by the car several times."

"Then it *was* murder," said Yuri.

"Absolutely. They caught the man who did it. A drifter. He was hired, but he doesn't know the identity of the man who hired him. He got five thousand dollars in cash for killing Aaron. He'd been trying to do it for a week. He'd spent half the money."

Yuri wanted to put down the phone. It seemed utterly impossible to continue. He ran his tongue along his upper lip and then firmly forced himself to speak. "Celia, please tell Mona Mayfair this for me, and Michael Curry too—that I am in England, I am safe. I will soon be in touch. I am being very careful. I send my sympathy to Beatrice Mayfair. I send to all . . . my love."

"I'll tell them."

He laid down the phone. If she said something more, he didn't hear it. It was silent now. And the soft pastel colors of the bedroom lulled him for a moment. The light filled the mirror softly and beautifully. All the fragrances of the room were clean.

Alienation, a lack of trust either in happiness or in others. Rome. Aaron coming. Aaron erased from life—not from the past, but utterly from the present and from the future.

He didn't know how long he stood there.

It began to seem that he had been planted by the dressing table for a long, long time. He knew that Ash, the tall one, had come into the room, but not to detach Yuri from the telephone.

And some deep, awful grief in Yuri was touched suddenly, disastrously perhaps, by the warm, sympathetic voice of this man.

"Why are you crying, Yuri?"

It was said with the purity of a child.

"Aaron Lightner's dead," said Yuri. "I never called to tell him they'd tried to kill me. I should have told him. I should have warned him—"

It was the slightly abrasive voice of Samuel that reached him from the door.

"He knew, Yuri. He knew. You told me how he warned you not to come back here, how he said they'd come for him at any time."

"Ah, but I . . ."

"Don't hold on to it with guilt, my young friend," said Ash.

Yuri felt the big, spidery hands close tenderly on his shoulders.

"Aaron . . . Aaron was my father," Yuri said in a monotone. "Aaron was my brother. Aaron was my friend." Inside him the grief and the guilt boiled and the stark, awful terror of death became unendurable. It doesn't seem possible that this man is gone, totally gone from life, but it will begin to seem more and more possible, and then real, and then absolute.

Yuri might as well have been a boy again, in his mother's village in Yugoslavia, standing by her dead body on the bed. That had been the last time he'd known such pain as this; he couldn't bear it. He clenched his teeth, fearing that in an unmanly way he would cry out or even roar.

"The Talamasca killed him," said Yuri. "Who else would have done it? Lasher—the Taltos—is dead. He didn't do it. Lay all the murders upon them. The Taltos killed the women, but he did not kill the men. The Talamasca did it."

"Was it Aaron who killed the Taltos?" asked Ash. "Was he the father?"

"No. But he did love a woman there, and now perhaps her life too has been destroyed."

He wanted to lock himself in the bathroom. He had no clear image of what he meant to do. Sit on the marble floor, perhaps, with his knees up, and weep.

But neither of these two strange individuals would hear of it. In concern and alarm, they drew him back into the living room of the suite, and seated him on the sofa, the tall one being most careful not to hurt his shoulder, the little man rushing to prepare some hot tea. And bring him cakes and cookies on a plate. A feeble meal, but a particularly enticing one.

It seemed to Yuri that the fire was burning too fast. His pulse had quickened. Indeed, he felt himself breaking out in a sweat. He took off the heavy sweater, pulling it roughly over his neck, causing intense pain in his shoulder before he realized what he was doing, and before he realized he had nothing on under his sweater and was now sitting here bare-chested, with the sweater in his hands. He sat back and hugged the sweater, uncomfortable to be so uncovered.

He heard a little sound. The little man had brought him a white shirt, still wrapped around laundry cardboard. Yuri took it, opened it, unbuttoned it, and slipped it on. It was absurdly too big for him. It must have belonged to Ash. But he rolled up the sleeves and buttoned several of the buttons and was grateful to be concealed once more. It felt comforting, like a great pajama shirt. The sweater lay on the carpet. He could see the grass in it, the twigs and bits of soil clinging to it.

"And I thought I was so noble," he said, "not calling him, not worrying him, letting the wound heal and getting back on my feet before I reported in, to confirm to him that I was well."

"Why would the Talamasca kill Aaron Lightner?" asked Ash. He had retreated to his chair and was sitting with his hands clasped between his knees. Again, he was ramrod straight and unlikely and very handsome.

Good Lord, it was as if Yuri had been knocked unconscious, and was seeing all of this again for the first time. He noticed the simple black watchband around Ash's wrist, and the gold watch itself, with digital numbers. He saw the red-haired hunchback standing at the window, which he had opened a crack now that the fire was positively roaring. He felt the ice blade of the wind cleave through the room. He saw the fire arch its back and hiss.

"Yuri, why?" asked Ash.

"I can't answer. I had hoped somehow we were mistaken, that they hadn't had such a heavy hand in all this, that they hadn't killed innocent men. That it was a fanciful lie or something, that they had the female that they had always wanted. I couldn't think of such a tawdry purpose. Oh, I don't mean to offend you—"

"—of course not."

"I mean, I had thought their aims so lofty, their whole evolution so remarkably pure—an order of scholars who record and study, but never interfere selfishly in what they observe; students of the supernatural. I think I've been a fool! They killed Aaron because he knew about all this. And that's why they must kill me. They must let the Order sink back into its routines, undisturbed by all this. They must be watching at the Motherhouse. They must be anxious to prevent me entering it at all costs. They must have the phones covered. I couldn't call there or Amsterdam or Rome if I wanted to. They'd intercept any fax that I sent. They'll never let down this guard, or stop looking for me, till I'm dead.

"Then who will there be to go after them? To tell the others? To reveal the awful secret to the brothers and sisters that this Order is evil ... that the old maxims of the Catholic Church perhaps have always been true. What is supernatural and not of God is evil. To find the male Taltos! To bring him together with the female ..."

He looked up. Ash's face was sad. Samuel, leaning against the closed window, appeared, for all the fleshy folds of his face, sad and concerned as well. Calm yourself, he thought, make your words count. Do not lapse into hysteria.

He went on. "You speak of centuries, Ash," he said, "the way others speak of years. Then the female within the Talamasca might have lived for centuries. This might have been the only purpose always. Out of dark times, a web spun that is so evil and so perverse that modern men and women can't even conceive of it! It's too simple, all of these stupid men and women watching out for one single being—a Taltos, a creature that can breed with its mate so fast and so successfully that its kind would quickly overtake the world. I wonder what makes them so sure of themselves, the invisible and anonymous and secretive Elders of the Order, so sure that they themselves are not being—"

He paused. It had never occurred to him. Of course. Had he ever been in a room with a sentient being who wasn't human? Now he was, and who was to say how many such species lived in our comfortable little world, walking about, passing for human while servicing their own agenda in every respect? Taltos. Vampire. The aged dwarf, with his own clock and his own grudges and stories.

How quiet they both were. Had there been an unspoken decision to let him rave?

"You know what I would like to do?" Yuri asked.

"What?" asked Ash.

"Go to the Amsterdam Motherhouse and kill them, the Elders. But that's just it, I don't think I can find them. I don't think they are in the Amsterdam Motherhouse, or that they ever have been. I don't know who or what they are. Samuel, I want to take the car now. I have to go home here in London. I have to see the brothers and the sisters."

"No," said Samuel. "They'll kill you."

"They can't all be in it. That's my last hope; we are all dupes of a few. Now, please, I want to take the car outside London to the Motherhouse. I want to walk inside quickly, before anyone is the wiser, and grab hold of the brothers and sisters, and make them listen. Look, I have to do this! I have to warn them. Why, Aaron's dead!"

He stopped. He realized he'd been frightening them, these two strange friends. The little man had his arms folded again, grotesquely, because they were so short and his chest was so big. The folded flesh of his forehead had descended in a frown. Ash merely watched him, not frowning, but visibly worrying.

"What do you care, either one of you!" said Yuri suddenly. "You saved my life when I was shot in the mountains. But nobody asked you to do this. Why? What am I to you?"

A little noise came from Samuel, as if to say, This is not worth an answer. Ash answered, however, in a tender voice.

"Maybe we are gypsies, too, Yuri," he said.

Yuri didn't answer, but he did not believe in the sentiments this man was describing. He didn't believe in anything, except that Aaron was dead. He pictured Mona, his little red-haired witch. He saw her, her remarkable little face and her great veil of red hair. He saw her eyes. But he could feel nothing for her. He wished with all his heart that she were here.

"Nothing, I have nothing," he whispered.

"Yuri," said Ash. "Please mark what I tell you. The Talamasca was not founded to search for the Taltos. This you can believe on my word. And though I know nothing of the Elders of the Order in this day and age, I have

84

known them in the past; and no, Yuri, they were not Taltos then and I cannot believe they are Taltos now. What would they be, Yuri, females of our species?"

The voice went on unhurried and tender still, but profoundly forceful.

"A female Taltos is as willful and childlike as a male," said Ash. "A female would have gone at once to this creature, Lasher. A female, living only among females, could not have been prevented from doing it. Why send mortal men to capture such a prize and such a foe? Oh, I know to you I don't seem formidable, but you might be very surprised by my tales. Take comfort: your brothers and your sisters are not dupes of the Order itself. But I believe that you have hit upon the truth in your considerations. It is not the Elders who subverted the avowed purpose of the Talamasca, so that they might capture this creature, Lasher. It was some other small coterie of members who have discovered the secrets of the old breed."

Ash stopped. It was as if the air had been emptied of music suddenly. Ash was still regarding Yuri with patient, simple eyes.

"You have to be right," said Yuri softly. "I can't bear it if you are not."

"We have it in our power to discover the truth," said Ash. "The three of us together. And frankly, though I cared for you immediately upon meeting you, and would help because you are a fellow creature, and because my heart is tender to you in general, I must help you for another reason. I can remember when there was no Talamasca. I can remember when it was one man. I can remember when its catacombs enclosed a library no bigger than this room. I can remember when it became two members, and then three, and later five, and then it was ten. I can remember all these things, and those who came together to found it, I knew them and I loved them. And of course my own secret, my own story, is hidden somewhere in their records, these records being translated into modern tongues, and stored electronically."

"What he's saying," said Samuel, harshly but slowly for all his annoyance, "is that we don't want the Talamasca to be subverted. We don't want its nature to change. The Talamasca knows too much about us for such a thing to be tolerated. It knows too much about too many things. With me, it's no matter of loyalty, really. It's a matter of wanting to be left alone."

"I do speak of loyalty," said Ash. "I speak of love and of gratitude. I speak of many things."

"Yes, I see it now," said Yuri. He could feel himself growing tired—the inevitable finish to emotional tumult, the inevitable rescue, the leaden, defeated need for sleep.

"If they knew about me," said Ash in a low voice, "this little group would come for me as surely as they came for this creature, Lasher." He made a little accepting gesture. "Human beings have done this before. Any great library of secrets is dangerous. Any cache of secrets can be stolen."

Yuri had started to cry. He didn't make a sound. The tears never spilled. His eyes filled with water. He stared at the cup of tea. He'd never drunk it, and now it was cold. He took the linen napkin, unfolded it, and wiped his eyes. It was too rough, but he didn't care. He was hungry for the sweets on the plate, but didn't want to eat them. After a death, it seemed not proper to eat them.

Ash went on: "I don't want to be the guardian angel of the Talamasca," he said. "I never wanted this. But there have been times in the past when the Order has been threatened. I will not, if I can prevent it, see the Order hurt or destroyed."

"There are many reasons, Yuri," said Samuel, "why a little band of Talamasca renegades might try to trap this Lasher. Think what a trophy he would be. They are human beings perhaps who would capture a Taltos for no earthly reason. They are not men of science or magic or religion. They are not even scholars. But they would have this rare and indescribable creature; they would have it to look upon, to talk to, to examine and to know, and to breed under their watchful eyes, of course, inevitably."

"They would have it to chop it to pieces, perhaps," said Ash. "Lamentably, they would have it to stick it with needles and see if it screamed."

"Yes, it makes such good sense," said Yuri. "A plot from

outside. Renegades or outsiders. I'm tired. I need to sleep in a bed. I don't know why I said such terrible things to you both."

"I do," said the dwarf. "Your friend's dead. I wasn't there to save *him*."

"The man who tried to kill you," Ash said, "did you kill him?"

Samuel gave the answer. "No, *I* killed him. Not on purpose, really. It was either knock him off the cliff or let him fire another shot at the gypsy. I must confess I did it rather for the hell of it, as Yuri and I hadn't yet exchanged a single word. Here was this man aiming a gun at another man. The dead man's body is in the glen. You want to find it? It's a good chance the Little People left it right where it fell."

"Ah, it was like that," said Ash.

Yuri said nothing. Vaguely he knew that he should have found this body. He should have examined it, taken its identifying papers. But that really had not been feasible, given his wound and the awesome terrain. There seemed something just about the body being lost forever in the wilderness of Donnelaith, and about the Little People letting the body rot.

The Little People.

Even as he had fallen, his eyes had been on the spectacle of the tiny men, down in the little pocket of grass far below him, dancing like many twisted modern Rumplestiltskins. The light of the torches had been the last thing he saw before he lost consciousness.

When he'd opened his eyes to see Samuel, his savior, with the gunbelt and pistol, and a face so haggard and old that it seemed a tangle of tree roots, he had thought, They've come to kill me. But I've seen them. I wish I could tell Aaron. The Little People. I've seen them. . . .

"It's a group from outside the Talamasca," said Ash, waking him abruptly from the unwelcome spell, pulling him back into this little circle. "Not from within."

Taltos, thought Yuri, and now I have seen the Taltos. I am in a room with this creature who is the Taltos.

Had the honor of the Order been unblemished, had the

87

pain in his shoulder not been reminding him every moment of the shabby violence and treachery which had engulfed his life, how momentous it would have been to see the Taltos. But then this was the price of such visions, was it not? They always carried a price, Aaron had told him once. And now he could never, never discuss this with Aaron.

Samuel spoke next, a little caustic. "How do you know it's not a group from within the Talamasca?"

He looked nothing now like he had that night, in his ragged jerkin and breeches. Sitting by the fire, he had looked like a ghastly toad as he counted his bullets and filled the empty spaces in his belt and drank his whiskey and offered it over and over to Yuri. That was the drunkest Yuri had ever been. But it was medicinal, wasn't it?

"Rumplestiltskin," Yuri had said. And the little man had said, "You can call me that if you like. I've been called worse. But my name is Samuel."

"What language are they singing in?" *When will they stop with the singing, with the drums!*

"Our language. Be quiet now. It's hard for me to count."

Now the little man was cradled comfortably by the civilized chair, and swaddled in civilized garments, staring eagerly at the miraculous willowy giant, Ash, who took his time to answer.

"Yes," said Yuri, more to snap himself out of it than anything else. "What makes you think it's a group from outside?" Forget the chill and the darkness and the drums—the infuriating pain of the bullet.

"It's too clumsy," said Ash. "The bullet from a gun. The car jumping the curb and striking Aaron Lightner. There are many easy ways to kill people so that others hardly notice at all. Scholars always know this; they have learnt from studying witches and wizards and other princes of *maleficia*. No. They would not go into the glen stalking a man as if he were game. It is not possible."

"Ash, the gun is now the weapon of the glen," said Samuel derisively. "Why shouldn't wizards use guns if Little People use them?"

"It's the toy of the glen, Samuel," said Ash calmly. "And you know it. The men of the Talamasca are not monsters who are hunted and spied upon and must retreat from the world into a wilderness and, when sighted, strike fear in men's hearts." He went on with his reasoning. "It is not from within the Elders of the Talamasca that this menace has arisen. It is the worst nuisance imaginable—some small group of people from outside, who happened upon certain information and chose to believe it. Books, computer disks. Who knows? Perhaps these secrets were even sold to them by servants. . . ."

"Then we must seem like children to them," said Yuri. "Like monks and nuns, computerizing all our records, our files, gathering old secrets into computer banks."

"Who was the witch who fathered the Taltos? Who killed him?" demanded Ash suddenly. "You told me you'd tell me if I were to tell things to you. What more can I give you? I've been more than forthcoming. Who is this witch that can father a Taltos?"

"Michael Curry is his name," said Yuri. "And they'll probably try to kill him too."

"No, that wouldn't do for them, would it?" Ash said. "On the contrary, they will strive to strike the match again. The witch Rowan . . ."

"She can no longer bear," said Yuri. "But there are others, a family of others, and there is one so powerful that even—"

Yuri's head felt heavy. He raised his right hand and pressed it to his forehead, disappointed that his hand was so warm. Leaning forward made him feel sick. Slowly he eased back, trying not to pull or flick his shoulder, and then he closed his eyes. He reached into his pants pocket and pulled out his little wallet and opened it.

He slipped out of hiding the little school picture of Mona, very vividly colored; his darling with her smile, her even white teeth, her heap of coarse and beautiful red hair. Childwitch, beloved witch, but witch without question.

Yuri wiped his eyes again, and his lips. His hand was trembling so badly that Mona's lovely face was out of focus.

He saw the long, thin fingers of Ash touch the edges of the photograph. The Taltos was standing over him, one long arm behind him, braced against the back of the sofa, while with the other hand he steadied the picture and studied it in silence.

"From the same line as the Mother?" said Ash softly.

Suddenly Yuri pulled in the photograph and crushed it flat to his chest. He pitched forward, sick again, the pain in his shoulder immediately paralyzing him.

Ash politely withdrew and went to the mantel. The fire had gone down somewhat. Ash stood with his hands on the mantel shelf. His back was very straight, his bearing almost military, his full dark hair curling against his collar, completely covering his neck. From this vantage point, Yuri could see no white in his hair, only the deep dark locks, brownish black.

"So they'll try to get her," said Ash, with his back turned still, raising his voice as needed. "Or they will try to get her or some other witch in this family."

"Yes," said Yuri. He was dazed, yet maddened. How could he have thought that he did not love her? How could she have been so distant from him so suddenly? "They'll try to get her. Oh, my God, but we've given them an advantage," he said, only just realizing it, and realizing it completely. "Good God, we have played into their hands. Computers! Records! It's just what happened with the Order!"

He stood up. The shoulder was throbbing. He didn't care. He was still holding the picture, tight, under the cover of his palm, and pressed to the shirt.

"How so, played into their hands?" asked Ash, turning, the firelight flashing up on his face so that his eyes looked almost as green as Mona's and his tie looked like a deep stain of blood.

"The genetic testing!" Yuri said. "The whole family is going through the testing, so as never to match again a witch to a witch that might make the Taltos. Don't you see? There are records being compiled, genetic, genealogical, medical. It will be in these records who is a powerful witch and who is not. Dear God, they will know whom to single out. They'll know better than the foolish Taltos! They'll have a weapon in this knowledge he never had. Oh, he tried

90

to mate with so many of them. He killed them. Each died without giving him what he wanted—the female child. But . . ."

"May I see the picture of the young red-haired witch again?" Ash asked timidly.

"No," said Yuri. "You may not."

The blood was throbbing in his face. He felt a wetness on his shoulder. He had torn the wound. He had a fever.

"You may not," he said again, staring at Ash.

Ash said nothing.

"Please don't ask me," Yuri said. "I need you, I need you very much to help me, but don't ask me to see her face, not now."

The two looked at each other. Then Ash nodded.

"Very well," he said. "Of course, I won't ask to see it. But to love a witch that strong is very dangerous. You know this, don't you?"

Yuri didn't answer. For one moment he knew everything—that Aaron was dead, that Mona might soon come to harm, that almost all that he had ever loved or cherished had been taken from him, almost all, that only a scant hope of happiness or satisfaction or joy remained to him, and that he was too weak and tired and hurt to think anymore, that he had to lie in the bed in the next room, which he had not even dared to glance at, the first bed he had seen in all this time since the bullet hit him and nearly killed him. He knew that never, never, should he have shown Mona's picture to this being who stood looking at him with deceptive softness and seemingly sublime patience. He knew that he, Yuri, might suddenly drop where he stood.

"Come on, Yuri," said Samuel to him with gruff gentleness, coming towards him with the usual swaggering walk. The thick, gnarled hand was reaching out for his. "I want you to go to bed now, Yuri. Sleep now. We'll be here with some hot supper for you when you wake up."

He let himself be led towards the door. Yet something stopped him, caused him to resist the little man, who was as strong as any full-sized man Yuri had ever known. Yuri found himself looking back at the tall one by the mantel.

Then he went into the bedroom and, to his own surprise, fell dazed upon the bed. The little man pulled off his shoes. "I'm sorry," said Yuri.

"It's no bother," said the little man. "Shall I cover you?"

"No, it's warm in here, and it's safe."

He heard the door close, but he didn't open his eyes. He was already sliding away from here, away from everything, and in a spike of dream reality which caught him and shocked him awake, he saw Mona sitting on the side of her bed and telling him to come. The hair between her legs was red, but darker than the hair of her head.

He opened his eyes. For a moment he was only aware of a close darkness, a disturbing absence of light that ought to be there. Then gradually he realized Ash was standing beside him, and looking down at him. In instinctive fear and revulsion, Yuri lay still, not moving, eyes fixed forward on the wool of Ash's long coat.

"I won't take the picture while you sleep," said Ash in a whisper. "Don't worry. I came to tell you that I must go north tonight, and visit the glen. I'll come back tomorrow and must find you here when I come."

"I haven't been very clever, have I?" asked Yuri. "Showing you her picture. I was a fool."

He was still staring at the dark wool. Then, right before his face, he saw the white fingers of Ash's right hand. Slowly he turned and looked up, and the nearness of the man's large face horrified him, but he made no sound. He merely peered up into the eyes that were fixed on him with a glassy curiosity, and then looked at the voluptuous mouth.

"I think I'm going mad now," said Yuri.

"No, you are not," said Ash, "but you must begin to be clever from now on. Sleep. Don't fear me. And remain here safe with Samuel until I return."

Four

THE MORGUE WAS small, filthy, made of little rooms with old white tile on the walls and on the floor, and rusted drains and creaking iron tables.

Only in New Orleans, she thought, could it be like this. Only here would they let a thirteen-year-old girl step up to the body and see it and start to cry.

"Go out, Mona," she said. "Let me examine Aaron."

Her legs were shaky, her hands worse. It was like the old joke: you sit there palsied and twisting and someone says, "What do you do for a living?" and you say, "I'm a ba-ba-ba-rain surgeon!"

She steadied herself with her left hand and lifted the bloody sheet. The car had not hurt his face; it was Aaron.

This was not the place to pay him reverence, to remember his multiple kindnesses and his vain attempts to help her. One image perhaps flared brightly enough to obscure the dirt, the stench, the ignominy of the once-dignified body in a heap on the soiled table.

Aaron Lightner at the funeral of her mother; Aaron Lightner taking her arm and helping her to move through the crowd of utter strangers who were her kin, to approach her mother's coffin; Aaron knowing that that was exactly what Rowan wanted to do, and had to do—look upon the lovely rouged and perfumed body of Deirdre Mayfair.

No cosmetic had touched this man who lay here beyond distinction and in profound indifference, his white hair lustrous as it had always been, the badge of wisdom side by side with uncommon vitality. His pale eyes were unclosed, yet unmistakably dead. His mouth had relaxed perhaps into its more familiar and agreeable shape, evidence of a life lived with amazingly little bitterness, rage, or sinister humor.

She laid her hand on his forehead, and she moved his head just a little to one side and then back again. She figured the time of death at less than two hours ago.

The chest was crushed. Blood soaked the shirt and the coat. No doubt the lungs had instantly collapsed, and even before that, the heart might have been ruptured.

Gently she touched his lips, prying them apart as if she were a lover teasing him, preparing to kiss him, she thought. Her eyes were moist, and the feeling of sadness was so deep suddenly that scents of Deirdre's funeral returned, the engulfing presence of perfumed white flowers. His mouth was full of blood.

She looked at the eyes, which did not look back at her. *Know you, love you!* She bent close. Yes, he had died instantly. He had died from the heart, not the brain. She smoothed his lids closed and let her fingers rest there.

Who in this dungeon would do a proper autopsy? Look at the stains on the wall. Smell the stench from the drawers.

She lifted the sheet back farther, and then ripped it aside, clumsily or impatiently, she wasn't sure which. The right leg was crushed. Obviously the lower portion and the foot had been detached and put back into the wool trouser. The right hand had only three fingers. The other two had been severed brutally and totally. Had someone collected the fingers?

There was a grinding sound. It was the Chinese detective coming into the room, the sound of dirt under his shoe making that awful noise against the tile.

"You all right, Doctor?"

"Yes," she said. "I'm almost finished." She went round to the other side. She laid her hand on Aaron's head, and on his neck, and she stood quiet, thinking, listening, feeling.

It had been the car accident, plain and savage. If he had suffered, no image of it hovered near him now. If he had struggled not to die, that too would be unknown forever. Beatrice had seen him try to dodge the car, or so she thought. Mary Jane Mayfair had reported, "He tried to get out of the way. He just couldn't."

Finally she drew back. She had to wash her hands, but where? She went to the sink, turned on the ancient faucet, and let the water flood over her fingers. Then she turned off the faucet and she shoved her hands in the pockets of her cotton coat, and she walked past the cop and back out into the small anteroom before the drawers of unclaimed corpses.

Michael was there, cigarette in hand, collar open, looking utterly wasted by grief and the burden of comfort.

"You want to see him?" she asked. Her throat still hurt, but this was of no importance to her whatsoever. "His face is all right. Don't look at anything else."

"I don't think so," said Michael. "I never was in this position before. If you say he's dead and the car hit him and there's nothing for me to learn, I don't want to see him."

"I understand."

"The smell's making me sick. It made Mona sick."

"There was a time when I was used to it," she said.

He drew close to her, gathering the back of her neck in his large, roughened hand, and then kissing her clumsily, wholly unlike the sweet and apologetic way he had kissed her all during her weeks of silence. He shuddered all over, and she opened her lips and kissed him back, and crushed him with her arms, or at least made an attempt to do so.

"I have to get out of here," he said.

She drew back only a step, and glanced into the other room, at the bloody heap. The Chinese cop had restored the covering sheet, out of respect perhaps, or procedure.

Michael stared at the drawers lining the opposite wall. Bodies inside made the abominable smell. She looked. There was one drawer partly open, perhaps because it couldn't be closed, and she could see the evidence of two bodies inside, the brown head of one facing up, and the molding pink feet of another lying directly on top of the first. There was green mold on the face, too. But the horror was not the mold; it was the two stacked together. The unclaimed dead, as intimate in their own way as lovers.

"I can't . . ." said Michael.

"I know, come on," she said.

By the time they climbed into the car, Mona had stopped crying. She sat staring out the window, so deep in thought she forbade any talk, any distraction. Now and then she turned and threw a glance at Rowan. Rowan met the glance and felt the strength of it, and the warmth. In three weeks of listening to this child pour out her heart—a lovely load of poetry which often became simply sound to Rowan in her somnambulant state—Rowan had come to love Mona completely.

Heiress, the one who will bear the child that will carry on the legacy. Child with a womb inside her, and the passions of an experienced woman. Child who had held Michael in her arms, who in her exuberance and ignorance had feared not at all for his battered heart, or that he might die at the pinnacle of passion. He hadn't died. He'd climbed out of invalidism and readied himself for the homecoming of his wife! And now the guilt lay on Mona, far too intoxicating, confusing all the mighty doses which she had had to swallow.

No one spoke as the car moved on.

Rowan sat next to Michael, in a little heap against him, resisting the urge to sleep, to sink back, to be lost again in thoughts that flowed with all the steadiness and imperturbability of a river, thoughts like the thoughts that had gently overlaid her for weeks, thoughts through which words and deeds had broken so slowly and so gently that they had hardly reached her at all. Voices speaking to you over the muffling rush of water.

She knew what she meant to do. It was going to be another terrible, terrible blow for Michael.

They found the house alive. Guards surrounded it once again. That was no surprise to any of them. And Rowan required no explanations. No one knew who had hired the man to run down Aaron Lightner.

Celia had come and had taken Bea in hand, letting her "cry it out" in Aaron's regular guest room on the second floor. Ryan Mayfair was in attendance, the man always prepared for court or church in his suit and tie, speaking cautiously of what the family must do now.

They were all looking at Rowan, of course. She had seen these faces at her bedside. She had seen them pass before her during her long hours in the garden.

She felt uncomfortable in the dress that Mona had helped her choose, because she could not remember ever seeing it before. But it didn't matter nearly as much as food. She was ravenously hungry, and they had laid out a full Mayfair-style buffet in the dining room.

Michael filled a plate for her before the others could do it. She sat at the head of the dining table and she ate, and she watched the others moving here and there in little groups. She drank a glass of ice water greedily. They were leaving her alone, out of respect or out of helplessness. What could they say to her? For the most part, they knew very little of what had actually taken place. They would never understand her abduction, as they called it, her captivity and the assaults that had been made upon her. What good people they were. They genuinely cared, but there was nothing they could do now, except leave her alone.

Mona stood next to her. Mona bent and kissed her cheek, doing this very slowly, so that at any time, Rowan might have stopped her. Rowan didn't. On the contrary, she took Mona's wrist, pulled her close, and kissed her back, loving the soft baby feel of her skin, thinking only in passing how Michael must have enjoyed this skin, to see, to touch, to penetrate.

"I'm going upstairs to sack out," Mona said. "I'll be there if you want me."

"I do want you," she said, but she said it in a low voice so that Michael perhaps wouldn't notice it. Michael was at her right, devouring a plate of food and a can of cold beer.

"Yeah, okay," said Mona. "I'll just be lying down." There was a look of dread in her face, weariness and sadness and dread.

"We need each other now," Rowan said, speaking the words as low as she could. The child's eyes fixed on her, and they merely looked at each other.

Mona nodded, then left, without even a quick farewell to Michael.

The awkwardness of the guilty, Rowan thought.

Someone in the front room laughed suddenly. It seemed that no matter what happened, the Mayfairs always laughed. When she had been dying upstairs, and Michael had been crying by her bed, there had been people in the house laughing. She remembered thinking about it, thinking about both sounds in a detached way, without alarm, without response. Drifting. The truth is, laughter always sounds more perfect than weeping. Laughter flows in a violent riff and is effortlessly melodic. Weeping is often fought, choked, half strangled, or surrendered to with humiliation.

Michael finished off the roast beef and the rice and gravy. He took down the last of the beer. Someone came quickly to put another can by his plate, and he picked this up and drank half of it immediately.

"This is good for your heart?" she murmured. He didn't respond.

She looked at her plate. She had finished her portion as well. Downright gluttonous.

Rice and gravy. New Orleans food. It occurred to her that she ought to tell him that during all these weeks she had loved it that he had given her food with his own hands. But what was the use of saying something like that to him?

That he loved her was as much a miracle as anything that had happened to her, as anything that had happened in this house to anyone. And it had all happened in this house, she mused, when you got right down to it. She felt rooted here, connected in some way she had never felt anywhere else—not even on the *Sweet Christine*, bravely plowing through the Golden Gate. She felt the strong certainty that this was her home, would never stop being that, and staring at the plate, she remembered that day when Michael and she had walked about the house together, when they'd opened the pantry and found all this old china, this precious china, and the silver.

And yet all of this might perish, might be blown away from her and from everyone else, by a tempest of hot breath, breath from the mouth of hell. What had her new friend, Mona Mayfair, said to her only hours ago? "Rowan, it's not finished."

No, not finished. And Aaron? Had they even called the Motherhouse to let his oldest friends there know what had happened to him, or was he to be buried among new friends and conjugal kindred?

The lamps burned brightly on the mantel.

It was not yet dark outside. Through the cherry laurels, she could see the sky was the legendary purple. The murals gave off their reassuring colors to the twilight in the room, and in the magnificent oaks, the oaks that could comfort you even when no human being could, the cicadas had begun to sing, and the warm spring air rolled through the room, from windows that were open everywhere around them—here, and in the parlor, and perhaps in the back to the great unused pool, windows open to the garden graveyard where the bodies lay—the bodies of her only children.

Michael drank the last of the second beer, and gave the can the usual squeeze, and then laid it down neatly, as if the big table demanded such propriety. He didn't look at her. He stared out at the laurels brushing the colonnettes of the porch, brushing the glass of the upper windows. Maybe he was looking at the purple sky. Maybe he was listening to the commotion of the starlings that swooped down at this hour in great flocks to devour the cicadas. It was all death, that dance, the cicadas swarming from tree to tree, and the flocks of birds crisscrossing the evening sky, just death, just one species eating another.

"That's all it is, my dear," she had said on the day of her awakening, her nightgown covered with mud, her hands covered with mud, her bare feet in the wet mud on the side of the new grave. "That's all it is, Emaleth. A matter of survival, my daughter."

Part of her wanted to return to the graves and the garden, to the iron table beneath the tree, to the *danse macabre* of the winged creatures high above, making the bold purple night throb with incidental and gorgeous song. Part of her didn't dare. If she walked out of here and went back to that table, she might open her eyes to discover that a night had passed away, perhaps more. . . . Something as wretched and ugly as the death of Aaron would catch her again unawares and say to her, "Wake, they need you. You know what you must do." Had Aaron been there himself for a split second, disembodied and merciful, whispering it in her ear? No, it had been nothing so clear or personal.

She looked at her husband. The man slouching in the chair, crushing the hapless beer can into something round and almost flat, his eyes still settled on the windows.

He was both wondrous and dreadful—indescribably attractive to her. And the awful, shameful truth was that his bitterness and suffering had made him more attractive; it had tarnished him rather marvelously. He didn't look so innocent now, so unlike the man he really was inside. No, the inside had seeped through the handsome skin and changed the texture of him all over. It had lent a slight ferocity to his face, as well as many soft and ever-shifting shadows.

Saddened colors. He had told her something once about saddened colors, in the bright newlywed time before they knew their child was a goblin. He had said that when they painted houses in the Victorian times they used "saddened" colors. This meant darkening the colors somewhat; this meant somber, muted, complex. Victorian houses all over America had been painted in that way. That's what he'd said. And he had loved all that, those brownish reds and olive greens and steel grays, but here one had to think of another word for the ashen twilight and the deep green gloom, the shades of darkness that hovered about the violet house with its bright painted shutters.

She was thinking now. Was he "saddened"? Was that what had happened to him? Or did she have to find another word for the darker yet bolder look in his eye, for the manner in which his face yielded so little now, at first glance, yet was not for a moment mean or ugly.

He looked at her, eyes shifting and striking her like lights. Snap. Blue and the smile almost there. Do it again, she thought as he looked away. Make those eyes at me. Make them large and blue and really dazzling for a moment. Was it a handicap to have such eyes?

She reached out and touched the shadowy beard on his face, on his chin. She felt it all over his neck, and then she

100

felt his fine black hair, and all the new coarser gray hair, and she sank her fingers into the curls.

He stared forward as if he were shocked, and then very cautiously he turned his eyes, without much turning his head, and looked at her.

She withdrew her hand, rising at the same time, and he stood up with her.

There was almost a throb in his hand as he held her arm. As he moved the chair back and out of her way, she let herself brush fully against him.

Up the stairs they went quietly.

The bedroom was as it had been all this time, very serene and overly warm, perhaps, with the bed never made but only neatly turned down so that she could at any moment sink back into it.

She shut the door and bolted it. He was already taking off his coat. She opened her blouse, pulling it out of the skirt with one hand and peeling it off and dropping it to the floor.

"The operation they did," he said. "I thought perhaps . . ."

"No, I'm healed. I want to do it."

He came forward and kissed her on the cheek, turning her head as he did it. She felt the blazing roughness of the beard, the coarseness of his hands, pulling a little hard on her hair as he bent her head back. She reached out and pulled at his shirt.

"Take it off," she said.

When she unzipped the skirt, it dropped to her feet. How thin she was. But she didn't care about herself or want to see herself. She wanted to see him. He was stripped now, and hard. She reached out and caught the black curling hair on his chest, and pinched his nipples.

"Ah, that's too hard," he whispered. He drew her against him, pushing her breasts right into the hair. Her hand came up, between his legs, finding him hard and ready.

She tugged on him as she climbed up on the bed, moving across it on her knees and then falling down on the cool cotton sheet and feeling his weight come down clumsily on top of her. God, these big bones crushing her again, this swarm of hair against us, this scent of sweet flesh and vintage perfume, this scratching, pushing, divine roughness.

"Do it, do it fast," she said. "We'll go slowly the second time. Do it, fill me up," she said.

But he needed no goading words.

"Do it hard!" she whispered between her teeth.

The cock entered her, its size shocking her, hurting her, bruising her. The pain was gorgeous, exquisite, perfect. She clenched the cock as best she could, the muscles weak and aching and not under her command—her wounded body betraying her.

Didn't matter. He battered her hard, and she came, giving no cue of cries or sighs. She was thoughtless, red-faced, hands flung out, and then tightening on him with all her might, on the very pain itself, as he drove into her repeatedly and then spent in great jerking motions that seemed to lift him off her and then abandon him to fall into her arms, wet and familiar and loved, desperately loved. Michael.

He rolled off. He wouldn't be able to do it so soon again. That was to be expected. His face was wet, the hair stuck to his forehead. She lay still in the cooling air of the room, uncovered and watching the slow movement of the fan blades near the ceiling.

The movement was so slow. Perhaps it was hypnotizing her. Be quiet, she said to her body, her loins, her inner self. She half dreamed, in fear, revisiting the moments in Lasher's arms and, mercifully, found them wanting. The savage, lustful god, yes, he might have seemed that; but this had been a man, and a brutal man with an immense and loving heart. It was so divinely rough, so divinely crude, so utterly blinding and bruising and simple.

He climbed out of the bed. She was certain he would sleep, and she herself knew she couldn't do it.

But he was up and dressing himself again, dragging clean clothes from the rods in the bathroom closet. He had his back to her, and when he turned around, the light from the bathroom shone on his face.

"Why did you do it!" he said. "Why did you leave with him!" It came like a roar.

"Shhhhh!" She sat up and put her finger to her lips.

"Don't bring them all. Don't make them come. Hate me if you will . . ."

"Hate you? God, how can you say that to me? Day in and day out, I've told you that I love you!" He came towards the bed, and put his hands firmly on the footboard. He glowered over her, horrifically beautiful in his rage. "How could you leave me like that!" He whispered the cry. "How!"

He came round the side, and suddenly grabbed her by her naked arms, fingers hurting her skin unbearably.

"Don't do it!" she screamed back, struggling to keep her voice low, knowing how ugly it was, how filled with panic. "Don't hit me, I warn you. That's what he did, that's what he did over and over and over again. I'll kill you if you hit me!"

She pulled loose and rolled to the side, tumbling off the bed and pushing into the bathroom, where the cold marble tile burned her naked feet.

Kill him! Goddamn it, if you don't stop yourself you will, you will, with your power you'll kill Michael!

How many times had she tried it with Lasher, spitting it at him, the puny hatred, kill him, kill him, kill him, and he had only laughed. Well, this man would die if she struck with her invisible rage. He would die as surely as the others she had killed—the filthy, appalling murders that had shaped her life, brought her to this very house, this moment.

Terror. The stillness, the quietness of the room. She turned slowly and looked through the door and she saw him standing beside the bed, merely watching her.

"I ought to be afraid of you," he said. "But I'm not. I'm only afraid of one thing. That you don't love me."

"Oh, but I do," she said. "And I always did. Always."

His shoulders sagged for a minute, just a minute, and then he turned away from her. He was so hurt, but he would never again have the vulnerable look he had had before. He would never again have the pure gentleness.

There was a chair by the window to the porch, and he appeared to find it blindly and choose it indifferently as he sat down, still turned away from her.

And I'm about to hurt you again, she thought.

She wanted to go to him, to talk to him, to hold him again. To talk the way they had that first day after she'd come to herself, and buried her only daughter—the only daughter she'd ever have—beneath the oak. She wanted to open now with the kindling excitement she'd felt then, the utter love, thoughtless and rushed and without the slightest caution.

But it seemed as beyond reach now as words had been so soon after that.

She lifted her hands and ran them back hard through her hair. Then, rather mechanically, she reached for the taps in the shower.

With the water flooding down, she could think, perhaps clearly, for the first time. The noise was sweet and the hot water was luscious.

There seemed an impossible wealth of dresses to choose from. Absolutely confounding that there were so many in the closets. Finally she found a pair of soft wool pants, old pants she'd had eons ago in San Francisco, and she put those on, and on top a loose and deceptively heavy cotton sweater.

It was plenty cool enough now for the spring night. And it felt good to be dressed again in the clothes she herself had loved. Who, she wondered, could have bought all these pretty dresses?

She brushed her hair, and closed her eyes, and thought. "You are going to lose him, and with reason, if you do not talk to him now, if you do not once again explain, if you do not struggle against your own instinctive fear of words, and go to him."

She laid down the brush. He was standing in the doorway. She'd never shut the door all this while, and when she looked up at him, the peaceful, accepting look on his face was a great relief to her. She almost cried. But that would have been ludicrously selfish.

"I love you, Michael," she said. "I could shout it from the rooftops. I never stopped loving you. It was vanity and it was hubris; and the silence, the silence was the failure of a soul to heal and strengthen itself, or maybe just the necessary retreat that the soul sought as if it were some selfish organism."

He listened intently, frowning slightly, face calm but never innocent the way it had been before. The eyes were huge and glistening but hard and shadowed with sadness.

"I don't know how I could have hurt you just now, Rowan," he said. "I really don't. I just don't."

"Michael, no . . ."

"No, let me say it. I know what happened to you. I know what he did. I know. And I don't know how I could have blamed you, been angry with you, hurt you like that, I don't know!"

"Michael, I know," she said. "Don't. Don't, or you'll make me cry."

"Rowan, I destroyed him," he said. He had dropped his voice to a whisper the way so many people did when they spoke of death. "I destroyed him and it's not enough! I . . . I . . ."

"No, don't speak anymore. Forgive me, Michael, forgive me for your sake and my sake. Forgive me." She leant forward and kissed him, took the breath out of him deliberately so it would remain wordless. And this time when he folded her into his arms, it was full of the old kindness, the old cherishing warmth, the great protective sweetness that made her feel safe, safe as it had when they'd first made love.

There must have been something more lovely than falling in his arms like this, more lovely than merely being close to him. But she couldn't think what it was now—certainly not the violence of passion. That was there, obviously, to be enjoyed again and again, but this was the thing she'd never known with any other being on earth, this!

Finally he drew back, taking her two hands together and kissing them, and then flashing her that bright boyish smile again, precisely the one she thought sure she'd never receive again, ever. And then he winked and he said, his voice breaking:

"You really do still love me, baby."

"Yes," she said. "I learned how once, apparently, and it will have to be forever. Come with me, come outside, come

105

out under the oak. I want to be near them for a while. I don't know why. You and I, we are the only ones who know that they're there together."

They slipped down the back stairs, through the kitchen. The guard by the pool merely nodded to them. The yard was dark as they found the iron table. She flung herself at him, and he steadied her. Yes, for this little while and then you'll hate me again, she thought.

Yes, you'll despise me. She kissed his hair, his cheek, she rubbed her forehead back and forth across his sharp beard. She felt his soft responsive sighs, thick and heavy and from the chest.

You'll despise me, she thought. But who else can go after the men who killed Aaron?

Five

THE PLANE LANDED in Edinburgh's airport at 11:00 p.m. Ash was dozing with his face against the window. He saw the headlamps of the cars moving steadily towards him, both black, both German—sedans that would take him and his little entourage over the narrow roads to Donnelaith. It was no longer a trek one had to make on horseback. Ash was glad of it, not because he had not loved those journeys through the dangerous mountains, but because he wanted to reach the glen itself with no delay.

Modern life has made all impatient, he thought quietly. How many times in his long life had he set out for Donnelaith, determined to visit the place of his most tragic losses and reexamine his destiny again? Sometimes it had taken him years to make his way to England and then north to the Highlands. Other times it had been a matter of months.

Now it was something accomplished in a matter of hours. And he was glad of it. For the going there had never been the difficult or the cathartic part. Rather it was the visit itself.

He stood up now as this tentative young girl, Leslie, who had flown with him from America, brought his coat and a folded blanket and a pillow as well.

"Sleepy, my dearest?" he asked her, with gentle reproach. Servants in America baffled him. They did the strangest things. He would not have been surprised if she had changed into a nightgown.

107

"For *you*, Mr. Ash. The drive is almost two hours. I thought you might want it."

He smiled as he walked past her. What must it be like for her, he wondered. The nocturnal trips to far-flung places? Scotland must seem like any other place to which he had at times dragged her or his other attendants. No one could guess what this meant to him.

As he stepped out onto the metal stairway, the wind caught him by surprise. It was colder here even than it had been in London. Indeed, his journey had taken him from one circle of frost to another and then another. And with childish eagerness and shallow regret, he longed for the warmth of the London hotel. He thought of the gypsy sleeping so beautifully against the pillow, lean and dark-skinned, with a cruel mouth and jet black eyebrows and lashes that curled upwards like those of a child.

He covered his eyes with the back of his hand and hurried down the metal steps and into the car.

Why did children have such big eyelashes? Why did they lose them later on? Did they need this extra protection? And how was it with the Taltos? He could not remember anything that he had ever known, per se, to be childhood. Surely for the Taltos there was such a period.

"Lost knowledge . . ." Those words had been given to him so often; he could not remember a time when he didn't know them.

This was an agony, really, this return, this refusal to move forward without a bitter consultation with his full soul.

Soul. You have no soul, or so they've told you.

Through the dim glass he watched young Leslie slip into the passenger seat in front of him. He was relieved that he had the rear compartment entirely to himself—that two cars had been found to carry him and his little entourage northward. It would have been unendurable now to sit close to a human, to hear human chatter, to smell a robust female human, so sweet and so young.

Scotland. Smell the forests; smell the sea in the wind.

The car moved away smoothly. An experienced driver. He was thankful. He could not have been tossed and

108

pushed from side to side clear to Donnelaith. For a moment he saw the glaring reflection of the lights behind him, the bodyguards following as they always did.

A terrible premonition gripped him. Why put himself through this ordeal? Why go to Donnelaith? Why climb the mountain and visit these shrines of his past again? He closed his eyes and saw for a second the brilliant red hair of the little witch whom Yuri loved as foolishly as a boy. He saw her hard green eyes looking back at him out of the picture, mocking her little-girl hair with its bright colored ribbon. Yuri, you are a fool.

The car gained speed.

He could not see anything through the darkly tinted glass. Lamentable. Downright maddening. In the States, his own cars had untinted windows. Privacy had never been a concern to him. But to see the world in its natural colors, that was something he needed the way he needed air and water.

Ah, but maybe he would sleep a little, and without dreams.

A voice startled him—the young woman's, coming from the overhead speaker.

"Mr. Ash, I've called the Inn; they're prepared for our arrival. Do you want to stop for anything now?"

"No, I want only to get there, Leslie. Snuggle with the blanket and the pillow. It is a long way."

He closed his eyes. But sleep didn't come to him. This was one of those journeys when he would feel every minute, and every bump in the road.

So why not think of the gypsy again—his thin, dark face, the flash of his teeth against his lip, so white and perfect, the teeth of modern men. Rich gypsy, perhaps. Rich witch, that had come plain to him in the conversation. In his mind's eye he reached for the button of her white blouse in the photograph. He pulled it open to see her breasts. He gave them pink nipples, and he touched the blue veins beneath the skin which had to be there. He sighed and let a low whistle come from his teeth and turned his head to the side.

The desire was so painful that he forced it back, let it go. Then he saw the gypsy again. He saw his long dark arm

109

thrown up over the pillow. He smelled again the woods and the vale clinging to the gypsy. "Yuri," he whispered in his fantasy, and he turned the young man over and bent to kiss his mouth.

This too was a fiery furnace. He sat up and forward and put his elbows on his knees and his face in his hands.

"Music, Ash," he said quietly, and then, settling back once more, his head against the window, his eyes large and struggling to see through the horrid dark glass, he began to sing to himself in a wee voice, a tiny falsetto, a song no one might understand but Samuel, and even Samuel might not know for sure.

It was 2:00 a.m. when he told the driver to stop. He could not continue. Beyond the dark glass lurked all the world that he had come here to see. He could wait no longer.

"We're almost there, sir."

"I know we are. You'll find the town only a few miles ahead. You're to go there directly. Settle into the Inn and wait for me. Now call the guards in the car behind us. Tell them to follow you in. I must be alone now here."

He didn't wait for the inevitable arguments or protests.

He stepped out of the car, slamming the door before the driver could come to his assistance, and with a little good-will wave of his hand, he walked fast over the edge of the road and into the deep, cold forest.

The wind was not strong now. The moon, snared in clouds, gave an intermittent and filmy light. He found himself enveloped by the scents of the Scotch pines, the dark cold earth beneath his feet, the brave blades of early spring grass crushed beneath his shoe, the faint scent of new flowers.

The barks of the trees felt good beneath his fingers.

For a long time he moved on and on, in the dark, sometimes stumbling, sometimes catching hold of a thick tree trunk to steady himself. He didn't stop to catch his breath. He knew this slope. He knew the stars above, even though the clouds tried to obscure them.

Indeed, the starry heavens brought him a strange, painful

110

emotion. When at last he stopped, it was upon a high crest. His long legs ached a little, as legs should perhaps. But being in this sacred place, this place which meant more to him than any other bit of land in the world, he could remember a time when his limbs would not have ached, when he could have hurried up the hill in big, loping steps.

No matter. What was a little pain? It gave him an insight into the pain of others. And humans suffered such terrible pain. Think of the gypsy asleep in his warm bed, dreaming of his witch. And pain was pain, whether physical or mental. Not the wisest of men or women or Taltos would ever know which was worse—the pain of the heart or the pain of the flesh.

At last he turned and sought even higher ground, climbing steadily up the slope even when it seemed impossibly steep, often reaching for a grip upon branches and firm rock to help himself.

The wind came up, but not strongly. His hands and feet were cold, but it was not a coldness he couldn't endure. Indeed, coldness had always refreshed him.

And indeed, thanks to Remmick he had his fur-collared coat; thanks to himself he had his warm wool clothes; thanks to heaven, perhaps, the pain in his legs grew no worse, only a little more annoying.

The ground crumbled a little. He could have fallen here, but the trees were like tall balusters keeping him safe, letting him go on and on rapidly.

At last he turned and found the path he had known would be here, winding up between two gently rising slopes where the trees were old, untouched, perhaps spared by all intruders for centuries.

The path descended into a small vale covered with sharp stones that hurt his feet, and made him more than once lose his balance. Then up again he went, thinking the slope quite impossible except for the fact that he'd climbed it before and he knew that his will would overcome the evidence of his senses.

At last he emerged into a small clearing, eyes fixed on the distant overhanging peak. The trees were so close he could not easily find the path now, or any simple footing.

111

He moved on, crushing the smaller shrubbery as he went. And as he turned now to his right, he saw far below, beyond a great deep crevasse, the waters of the loch shining with the pale illumination of the moon, and farther still the high, skeletal ruins of a cathedral.

His breath went out of him. He had not known they had rebuilt so much. As he fixed his eyes on the scheme below, he made out the entire cross pattern of the church, or so it seemed, and a multitude of squat tents and buildings, and a few flickering lights that were no more than pinpoints. He rested against the rock, safely nestled, peeping, as it were, on this world, without any danger of tumbling and falling down to it.

He knew what that was, to fall and to fall, to reach and cry out and be unable to stop the fall, his helpless body gaining weight and speed with every few feet of bruising terrain beneath him.

His coat was torn. His shoes were wet from the snow.

For a moment all the smells of this land engulfed him and overpowered him so that he felt an erotic pleasure moving through him, gripping his loins and sending the coarse ripples of pleasure over his entire skin.

He closed his eyes and let the soft, harmless wind stroke his face, let it chill his fingers.

It's near, it's very near. All you have to do is walk on and up, and turn there before the gray boulder you can see right now under the naked moon. In a moment the clouds may again cover the light, but it will be no less easy for you.

A distant sound touched his ears. For a moment he thought perhaps he was imagining it. But there it was, the low beat of the drums, and the thin flat whine of the pipes, somber and without any rhythm or melody he could discern, which drew from him a sudden panic and then a low, pumping anxiety. The sounds grew stronger, or rather he allowed himself to hear them more truly. The wind rose, then died away; the drums came strong from the slopes below, the pipes whining on, and again he sought to find the pattern and, finding none, ground his teeth and pressed the

112

heel of his palm to his right ear to shut the sound off finally.

The cave. Go on. Go up and go into it. Turn your back on the drums. What are the drums to you? If they knew you were here, would they play a true song to draw you in? Are the songs even known to them anymore?

He pushed up and on, and coming round the boulder, he felt the cold surface of the rock with both hands. Twenty feet ahead, perhaps more, lay the mouth of the cave, overgrown, concealed perhaps from any other climber. But he knew the random formations of stone above it. He walked higher, with one steep, heavy step after another. The wind whistled here among the pines. He pushed at the heavy overgrowth, letting the small branches scratch at his hands and face. He didn't care. At last he stepped into the blackness itself. And slumped, breathing heavily against the wall, and closing his eyes again.

No sound came to him from the depths. Only the wind sang as before, mercifully obscuring the distant drums if, indeed, they still made their awful ugly mayhem.

"I am here," he whispered. And the silence leapt back from him, curling perhaps into the very depths of the cave. Yet nothing gave an answer. Dare he say her name?

He took a timid step and then another. He moved on, with both hands upon the close walls, his hair brushing the roof overhead, until the passage broadened and the very echo of his footfalls told him that the roof was rising above him to a new height. He could see nothing.

For one moment fear touched him. Perhaps he had been walking with his eyes closed; he didn't know. Perhaps he had been letting his hands and ears guide him. And now, as he opened his eyes, as he sought to draw the light into them, there was only the blackness. He might have fallen, he was so afraid. A deep sense told him he was not alone. But he refused to run, refused to scramble out like some frightened bird, awkward, humiliated, perhaps even injuring himself in his haste.

He held fast. The darkness had no variation in it. The soft sound of his breath seemed to move out forever and ever.

113

"I'm here," he whispered. "I've come again." The words drifted away from him into nothingness. "Oh, please, once more, for mercy's sake ..." he whispered.

Silence answered him.

Even in this cold, he was sweating. He felt sweat on his back under his shirt, and around his waist, beneath the leather belt that tightened around his wool pants. He felt the wetness like something greasy and filthy on his forehead.

"Why have I come?" he asked, and this time his voice was small and distant. Then he raised it as loud as he could. "In the hope that you would take my hand again, here, as you did before, and give me solace!" The swollen words, dying away, left him shaken.

What collected in this place was no tender apparition, but the memories of the glen which would never leave him. The battle, the smoke. He heard the cries! He heard her voice again from the very flames:

". . . cursed, Ashlar!" The heat and the anger struck his soul as it had struck his eardrums. He felt for a moment the old terror, and the old conviction.

". . . may the world around you crumble before your suffering is ended."

Silence.

He had to go back, he had to find the closer passage now. He would fall if he remained here, unable to see, unable to do anything but remember. In a panic, he pivoted and rushed forward, until he did feel the stone walls, harsh and closing in on him.

When at last he saw the stars, he breathed a sigh so deep that the tears threatened to come. He stood still, his hand over his heart, and the sound of the drums rose, perhaps because the wind had again died away, and there was nothing to prevent it from coming closer. A cadence had begun, quick and playful and then slow again, like the drums that beat for an execution.

"No, get away from me!" he whispered. He had to escape from this place. Somehow his fame and fortune had to assist him now to escape. He couldn't be stranded on this high peak, faced with the horror of the drums, with the pipes that now played a distinct and menacing melody.

How could he have been so foolish as to come? And the cave lived and breathed just over his shoulder.

Help me. Where were those who obeyed his every command? He had been a fool to separate himself from them and climb to this terrible place alone. His pain was so sharp that he made a soft sound, like a child crying.

Down he went. He didn't care if he stumbled, or if his coat was torn, or if his hair was here and there caught. He ripped it loose and went on, the rocks beneath his feet hurting him but not stopping him.

The drums were louder. He must pass close by. He must hear these pipes and their nasal pulsing song, both ugly and irresistible. No, don't listen. Stop your ears. On down he climbed, and even though he had clamped his hands to his head, he could hear the pipes, and the grim old cadence, slow and monotonous and pounding suddenly as if it came from inside his brain, as if it were emanating from his very bones, as if he were in the midst of it.

He broke into a run, falling once and ripping the fine cloth of his pants, and pitching forward another time to hurt his hands on the rocks and the torn bushes. But on he went, until quite suddenly the drums surrounded him. The pipes surrounded him. The piercing song ensnared him as if in loops of rope, and he turned round and round, unable to escape, and opening his eyes, saw through the thick forest the light of torches.

They did not know he was there. They had not caught his scent or heard him. Perhaps the wind had been on his side, and was with him now. He held to the trunks of two small pines as if they were the bars of a prison, and he looked down into the dark little space in which they played, dancing in their small and ludicrous circle. How clumsy they were. How horrid to him.

The drums and the pipes were a hideous din. He couldn't move. He could only watch as they jumped and pivoted and rocked back and forth, and one small creature, with long, shaggy gray hair, moved into the circle and threw up his small, misshapen arms, calling out above the howl of the music in the ancient tongue:

"O gods, have mercy. Have mercy upon your lost children."

Look, see, he told himself, though the music would not let him articulate these syllables even inside his imagination. Look, see, do not be lost in the song. See what rags they wear now, see the gunbelts over their shoulders. See the pistols in their hands, and now, now they draw their guns to shoot, and tiny flames burst from the barrels! The night cracks with guns! The torches nearly die in the wind, then bloom again like ghastly flowers.

He could smell burning flesh, but this was not real; it was only memory. He could hear screams.

"Curse you, Ashlar!"

And hymns, oh yes, hymns, and anthems in the new tongue, the Romans' tongue, and that stench, that stench of flesh consumed!

A loud sharp cry ripped through the din; the music came to a halt. Only one drum sounded perhaps two more dull notes.

He realized it had been his cry, and that they had heard him. Run, but why run? For what? Where? You don't need to run any longer. You are not of this place anymore! No one can make you be of it.

He watched in cold silence, his heart racing, as the little circle of men grew together, torches blazing very close to one another, and the small mob moved slowly towards him.

"Taltos!" They had caught his scent! The group scattered with wild cries, and then drew close to make one small body again.

"Taltos!" cried a rough voice. The torches moved closer and closer.

Now he could see their faces distinctly as they ranged about him, peering up, holding the torches high, the flames making ugly shadows on their eyes and their cheeks and their little mouths. And the smell, the smell of the burning flesh, it came from their torches!

"God, what have you done!" he hissed, making his two hands into fists. "Have you dipped them in the fat of an unbaptized child?"

There came a shriek of wild laughter, and then another,

116

and finally a whole crackling wall of noise going up around him to enclose him.

He turned round and round.

"Despicable!" he hissed again, so angry that he cared nothing for his own dignity, or the inevitable distortions of his face.

"Taltos," said one who drew near. "Taltos."

Look at them, see what they are. He held his fists even tighter, prepared to fend them off, to beat them, and lift them and hurl them to right and left, if needs be.

"Aye, Aiken Drumm!" he cried, recognizing the old man, the gray beard dripping to the earth like soiled moss. "And Robin and Rogart, I see you."

"Aye, Ashlar!"

"Yes, and Fyne and Urgart; I see you, Rannoch!" And only now did he realize it. There were no women at all left among them! All the faces staring back at him were those of men, and men he'd known always, and there were no hags, no hags screaming with their arms outstretched. There were no more women among them!

He began to laugh. Was this absolutely true? Yes, it was! He walked forward, reaching out, and forcing them backwards. Urgart swung the torch near him, to hurt him or better illuminate him.

"Aaaahhh, Urgart!" he cried, and reached out, ignoring the flame, as if to grab the little man's throat and lift him.

With guttural cries they scattered, wild, in the darkness. Men, only men. Men, and no more than fourteen now at most. Only men. Oh, why in hell hadn't Samuel told him?

He sank down, slowly, to his knees. He laughed. And he let himself keel over and land upon the forest floor, so that he could see straight up through the lacy branches of the pines, the stars spread out gloriously above the fleece of the clouds, and the moon sailing gently northward.

But he should have known. He should have calculated. He should have known when last he'd come, and the women had been old and diseased, and thrown stones at him and rushed up to scream in his ears. He had smelled death all around him. He smelled it now, but it was not the blood smell of women. It was the dry, acid smell of men.

117

He turned over and let his face rest right against the earth. His eyes closed again. He could hear them scurrying around him.

"Where is Samuel?" one of them asked.

"Tell Samuel to come back."

"Why are you here? Are you free of the curse?"

"Don't speak to me of the curse!" he cried out. He sat up, the spell broken. "Don't speak to me, you filth." And this time he did catch hold, not of a little man, but of his torch, and holding the flaming brand close, he did catch the unmistakable smell of human fat burning. He threw it away in disgust.

"Damn you to hell, you cursed plague!" he cried.

One of them pinched his leg. A stone cut his cheek, but not deeply. Sticks were hurled at him.

"Where is Samuel?"

"Did Samuel send you here?"

And then the loud cackle of Aiken Drumm, riding over all. "We had a tasty gypsy for our supper, we did, till Samuel took him to Ashlar!"

"Where's our gypsy?" screamed Urgart.

Laughter. Shouts and cries of derision; guffaws and curses now. "May the devil take you home piece by piece!" cried Urgart. The drums had begun again. They were beating them with their fists, and a wild series of notes burst from the pipes.

"And you, all of you into hell," cried Ash. "Why don't I send you now?"

He turned and ran again, not sure at first of his direction. But the ascent had been steady and that was his best guide, and in the crunching of his feet, and in the crackling of the brush, and in the air rushing past him, he was safe from their drums, their pipes, their jeers.

Very soon he could no longer hear their music or their voices. Finally he knew he was alone.

Panting, chest hurting him, legs aching and feet sore, he walked slowly until, after a very long time, he came to the road, and stepped out upon the asphalt as if from a dream, and stood again in the world he knew, empty and cold and

118

silent as it was. Stars filled every quadrant of the heavens. The moon drew her veil and then lowered it again, and the soft breeze made the pines shiver ever so slightly, and the wind swept down as if urging him onward.

When he reached the Inn, Leslie, his little assistant, was waiting up for him. With a small cry of shock, she greeted him and quickly took the torn coat from him. She held his hand as they climbed the stairs.

"Oh, so warm," he said, "so very warm."

"Yes, sir, and the milk." There stood the tall glass by the bed. He drank it down. She was loosening the buttons of his shirt.

"Thank you, my dear, my little dear," he said.

"Sleep, Mr. Ash," she said.

He fell heavily on the bed, and felt the big feather comforter come down upon him, the pillow plumping beneath his cheek, the entire bed sweet and soft as it caught him and turned him in the first circle of sleep and drew him downward.

The glen, my glen, the loch, my loch, my land.

Betrayer of your own people.

In the morning he ate a quick breakfast in his room, as his staff prepared for an immediate return. No, he would not go down to see the Cathedral this time, he said. And yes, he had read the articles in the papers. St. Ashlar, yes, he had heard that tale, too. And the young Leslie was so puzzled.

"You mean, sir, that's not why we came here, to see the shrine of the saint?"

He only shrugged. "We'll be back someday, my dear."

Another time perhaps they would take that little walk.

By noon he had landed in London.

Samuel was waiting for him beside the car. He was cleanly attired in his tweed suit, with a fresh, stiff white shirt and tie, and looked the diminutive gentleman. Even his red hair was combed decently, and his face had the respectable look of an English bulldog.

"You left the gypsy alone?"

"He left while I slept," Samuel confessed. "I didn't hear him go out. He's gotten clean away. He left no message."

Ash thought for a long moment. "Probably just as well," he said. "Why didn't you tell me that the women were gone?"

"Fool. I wouldn't have let you go if there had been any women. You should have known. You don't think. You don't count the years. You don't use reason. You play with your toys and your money and all your fine things, and you forget. You forget and that's why you're happy."

The car carried them away from the airport and towards the city.

"Will you go home to your playground in the sky?" Samuel asked.

"No. You know I won't. I have to find the gypsy," he said. "I have to discover the secret in the Talamasca."

"And the witch?"

"Yes." Ash smiled and turned to Samuel. "I have to find the witch, too, perhaps. At least to touch her red hair, to kiss her white skin, to drink the scent of her."

"And—?"

"How will I know, little man?"

"Oh, you know. You know you do."

"Then let me in peace. For if it's to be, my days are finally numbered."

Six

IT WAS EIGHT o'clock when Mona opened her eyes. She heard the clock strike the hour, slowly, in deep, rich tones. But it was another sound that had awakened her, the sharp ring of a phone. It must have been coming from the library, she reasoned, and it was too far away from her and had been ringing far too long for her to answer it. She turned over, nestling into the big velvet couch with its many loose pillows, and stared out the windows into the garden, which was flooded with the morning sun.

The sun was coming in the windows, actually, and making the floor amber and beautiful to look at right before the side porch.

The phone had stopped. Surely one of the new staff around here had answered it—Cullen, the new driver, or Yancy, the young boy about the house who was always up, they said, by 6:00 a.m. Or maybe even old Eugenia, who stared so solemnly at Mona now, every time their paths crossed.

Mona had fallen asleep here last night, in her new silk dress, right on the very couch of sin where she and Michael had done it together, and though she had tried her best to dream of Yuri—Yuri, who had called, leaving a message with Celia that indeed he was all right, and he would be in touch very soon with all of them—she had found herself thinking about Michael, thinking about those three tumbles, and how they'd been, very forbidden and perhaps the best erotic fling she'd scored so far.

121

It was not that Yuri had not been marvelous, the lover of her dreams. But the two had been so careful with each other; it had been lovemaking, yes, but in the safest way imaginable. And it had left Mona wishing that she had been more forthcoming on that last night about her usual rampant desires.

Rampant. She really loved that word. It suited her. "You are running rampant." That was the kind of thing Celia or Lily would say to her. And she would say, "I treasure the compliment, but I do get the point."

God, if only she'd talked to Yuri herself. Celia had told him to call First Street. Why hadn't he done it? She'd never know.

Even Uncle Ryan had been irritated. "We need to talk to this man. We need to talk to him about Aaron."

And that was the really sad part, that it was Celia who'd told Yuri, and maybe nobody else in the world knew what Aaron had meant to Yuri, except Mona, in whom he'd confided, preferring to talk than to make love on their one and only stolen night. Where was he now? How was he? In those few hours of passionate exchange, he'd proven intensely emotional, black eyes glittering as he'd told her in stripped-down language—the very beautiful English of those for whom it is a second tongue—the key events of his tragic but amazingly successful life.

"You just can't tell a gypsy something like that, that his oldest friend's been run over by some maniac."

Then it hit her. The phone had been ringing. Perhaps that had been Yuri, and no one in this place could find her. No one had seen her come in here last night and collapse on the couch.

Of course, she'd been utterly captivated by Rowan, and had been since the first moment yesterday afternoon when Rowan had climbed to her feet and begun to speak. Why had Rowan asked her to stay here? What did Rowan have to say to her, to her alone, and in private? What was really on Rowan's mind?

Rowan was OK, that was certain. All afternoon long and into the evening, Mona had watched her gain strength.

Rowan had shown no signs of lapsing back into the silence that had imprisoned her for three weeks. On the contrary, she had taken easy command of the house, coming down alone late last night, after Michael had gone to sleep, to comfort Beatrice and persuade her to go up to bed in Aaron's old room. Beatrice had been leery of subjecting herself to "Aaron's things," only to confess finally that curling up in his bed, here in the guest bedroom, was exactly what she wanted to do.

"She'll smell the scent of Aaron all around her," Rowan had said to Ryan, almost absently, "and she'll feel safe."

That wasn't a normal comment, Mona had thought, but surely that was the trick of seeking your mate's bed after a death, and people had talked about that cure for grief being very good. Ryan had been so concerned about Bea, so concerned for everyone. But in Rowan's presence he had had the air of a general, all seriousness and capability, in the presence of the Chief of Staff.

Rowan had taken Ryan into the library, and for two hours, the door open for anyone who cared to stand in it or listen at it, they'd discussed everything from the plans for Mayfair Medical to various details about the house. Rowan wanted to see Michael's medical records. Yes, he seemed as sound now as he had been the day she met him. But she needed the records, and Michael, not wanting to argue, had referred her to Ryan.

"But what about your own recovery? They want you to go for tests, you know," Ryan had been saying as Mona came in for a final good-night.

Yuri had left his message at Amelia Street just before midnight, and Mona had experienced enough hate, love, grief, passion, regret, longing, and excruciating suspense to finally wear her out.

"I don't have time to take these tests," Rowan had been saying. "There are much more important things. For instance, what was found in Houston when you opened the room where Lasher had been keeping me?"

At that point Rowan had stopped because she'd seen Mona.

She'd risen to her feet as if she were greeting some important adult. Her eyes were brilliant now, and not so much cold anymore as serious, a real important distinction.

"I don't mean to disturb you," Mona had said. "I don't want to go home to Amelia," she'd said sleepily. "I was wondering if I could stay here—"

"I wish you would stay," said Rowan without hesitation. "I've kept you waiting for hours."

"Yes and no," said Mona, who would rather have been here than home.

"It's unforgivable," said Rowan. "Can we talk in the morning?"

"Yeah, sure," Mona had said, with an exhausted shrug. She's talking to me like I'm a grown woman, thought Mona, which is more than anybody else around here ever does.

"You *are* a woman, Mona Mayfair," Rowan had said, with a sudden, deeply personal smile. She'd immediately sat down again and resumed her conversation with Ryan.

"There should have been papers there, in my room in Houston, reams of scribbled writing. This was his writing, genealogies he had made before his memory deteriorated. . . ."

Boy, Mona had thought, stepping away about as slowly as she could—she's talking to Ryan of all people about Lasher, and Ryan still can't say that name, and now Ryan has to deal with hard evidence of what he still won't accept. Papers, genealogies, things written by the monster who killed his wife, Gifford.

But what Mona had realized in a flash was that she wasn't necessarily going to be shut out of all this. Rowan had just spoken to her again as if she were important. Everything was changed. And if Mona asked Rowan tomorrow or the day after what those papers were—Lasher's scribblings—Rowan might even tell her.

Incredible to have seen Rowan's smile, to have seen the mask of cold power broken, to have seen the gray eyes crinkle and glisten for an instant, to have heard the deep chocolate voice take on that extra little warmth that a smile can give it—amazing.

Mona had finally hurried out of sight. Quit while you're ahead. You're too sleepy to be eavesdropping, anyway.

The last thing she'd heard was Ryan saying in a strained voice that everything from Houston had been examined and cataloged.

Mona could still remember when all of those things had reached Mayfair and Mayfair. She could still remember that scent of him that came from the boxes. She could still—occasionally—catch that scent in the living room, but it was almost gone now.

She had flopped on the living room couch, too tired to think about it all just now.

All the others had left by that time. Lily was sleeping upstairs near Beatrice. Michael's Aunt Vivian had moved back to her own apartment on St. Charles Avenue.

The living room had been empty, the breeze floating in through the windows to the side porch. A guard had been walking back and forth out there, so Mona had figured, I don't have to close those windows, and facedown on the couch she had crashed, thinking Yuri, then Michael, and pushing her face into the velvet and going sound asleep.

They said when you grew older you couldn't sleep that way. Well, Mona was ready for it. That sort of blotto sleep always made her feel cheated, as if she'd checked out on the universe for a span of time that she herself could not control.

But at four o'clock she'd awakened, unsure of why.

The floor-length windows had been open still, and the guard was out there smoking a cigarette.

Sleepily she'd listened to the sounds of the night, the birds crying in the dark trees, the distant roar of a train along the waterfront, the sound of water splashing as in a fountain or a pool.

She must have listened for half an hour before the sound of the water began to prey on her. There was no fountain. Someone was swimming in the pool.

Half expecting to see some delicious ghost—poor Stella, for instance, or God only knew what other apparition—Mona had slipped out in her bare feet and crossed the lawn.

The guard was nowhere in sight now, but that didn't mean much on a property of this size.

Someone had been swimming steadily back and forth across the pool.

Through the gardenia bushes, Mona had seen that it was Rowan, naked, and moving with incredible speed through lap after lap. Rowan took her breaths regularly, head to the side, the way professional swimmers do it, or the way that athletic doctors do it, who want to work the body and condition it, and maybe even heal it and bring it back into prime form.

No time to disturb her, Mona had thought, still sleepy, longing for the couch again, in fact, so sluggish she might have fallen down on the cool grass. Something about the scene had disturbed her, however; maybe that Rowan was nude, or that she swam so rapidly and so steadily; or maybe just that the guard was around and might be a peeping Tom in the bushes right now, which Mona didn't like.

Whatever, Rowan had known all about the guards on the property. She'd spent an hour with Ryan on that subject alone.

Mona had gone back to sleep.

Now, as she woke, it was Rowan she thought of, even before invoking the face of Yuri, or feeling routinely and religiously guilty about Michael, or at once reminding herself, rather like giving her own arm a cruel pinch, that Gifford and her mother were both dead.

She stared at the sunlight bathing the floor and the gold damask chair nearest the window. Maybe that was what this was all about. The lights had gone dim for Mona when Alicia and Gifford died, there was no doubt of it. And now, just because this woman was interested in her, this mysterious woman who meant so much to her for countless reasons, the lights were bright again.

Aaron's death was terrible, but she could handle it. In fact, what she felt more than anything else was the same selfish excitement she'd known yesterday at Rowan's first expression of interest, at her first confidential and respectful glance.

Probably wants to ask me if I want to go to boarding

school, Mona thought. High heels lying there. She couldn't put those on again. But it was nice to walk on the bare boards at First Street. They were always polished now, with the new staff. Yancy, the houseman, buffed them for hours. Even old Eugenia had been working more and grumbling less.

Mona rose, straightened out the silk dress which was perhaps ruined now, she wasn't really sure. She walked over to the garden window and let the sun flood over her, warm and fresh, the air full of humidity and sweetness from the garden—all the things she usually took for granted, but which at First Street seemed doubly wonderful, and worth a moment's meditation before rushing headlong into the day.

Protein, complex carbos, vitamin C. She was famished. Last night there had been the usual groaning sideboard, with all the family coming to put their arms around Beatrice, but Mona had forgotten to eat.

"No wonder you woke up in the night, you idiot." When she failed to eat, she invariably had a headache. Now she thought again, suddenly, of Rowan swimming alone, and the thought disturbed her again—the nudity, the strange disregard for the hour and the presence of the guards. Hell, you idiot, she's from California. They do stuff like that out there night and day.

She stretched, spread her legs apart, touched her toes with her hands, and then leaned backwards, shaking her hair from side to side till it felt loose and cool again, and then she walked out of the room and back the long corridor, through the dining room and into the kitchen.

Eggs, orange juice, Michael's concoction. Maybe there was a goodly supply.

The smell of fresh coffee surprised her. Immediately she took a black china mug from the cupboard and lifted the pot. Very black, espresso, Michael's kind of coffee, the kind he'd loved in San Francisco. But she realized this wasn't what she wanted at all. She craved something cool and good. Orange juice. Michael always had bottles of it, mixed and ready, in the refrigerator. She filled another cup with

127

orange juice, and carefully capped the jug to keep all the vitamins from dying in the air.

Suddenly she realized she wasn't alone.

Rowan was sitting at the kitchen table, watching her. Rowan was smoking a cigarette which she tapped now above a fine china saucer with flowers along the edge. She wore a black silk suit and pearl earrings, and there was a little string of pearls around her neck, too. It was one of those suits with a long curvaceous jacket, double-breasted and fully buttoned, with no blouse or shirt beneath it, only bare flesh to a discreet cleft.

"I didn't see you," Mona confessed.

Rowan nodded. "Do you know who bought these clothes for me?" The voice was as chocolaty and smooth as it had been last night, after all the soreness had gone away.

"Probably the same person who bought this dress for me," said Mona. "Beatrice. My closets are bulging with stuff from Beatrice. And it's all silk."

"So are my closets," said Rowan, and there came again that bright smile.

Rowan's hair was brushed back from her face, but otherwise natural, curling loosely just above her collar; her eyelashes looked very dark and distinct, and she wore a pale violet-pink lipstick that carefully outlined a rather beautifully shaped mouth.

"You're really OK, aren't you?" asked Mona.

"Sit down here, will you?" said Rowan. She gestured to the chair at the other end of the table.

Mona obeyed.

An expensive fragrance emanated from Rowan, rather like citrus and rain.

The black silk suit was really terrific; in the days before the wedding, Rowan had never been seen in anything so deliberately sensual. Bea had a way of sneaking into people's closets and checking their sizes, not just by label but with a tape measure, and then dressing them up the way that she, Beatrice, thought they ought to look.

Well, with Rowan she'd done well.

And I've destroyed this blue dress, thought Mona. Just

not ready for this kind of thing. Or those high heels she'd kicked off on the living room floor.

Rowan lowered her head as she crushed out her cigarette. A deep forward curl of ash-blond hair fell into the hollow of her cheek. Her face looked lean and awesomely dramatic. It was as if sickness and sorrow had given her the very gauntness for which starlets and models starve themselves to death.

For this sort of beauty, Mona was no contender. It was red hair and curves with her, and always would be. If you didn't like it, you wouldn't like Mona.

Rowan gave a soft laugh.

"How long have you been doing it?" asked Mona, taking a deep gulp of her coffee. It had just reached the right temperature. Delicious. In two minutes it would be too cold to drink. "Reading my mind, I mean. It's not consistent, is it?"

Rowan was caught off guard, but seemed faintly amused. "No, it's not consistent at all. I'd say it happens in flashes when you're sort of preoccupied, kind of slipping into your own reflections. It's like you suddenly strike a match."

"Yeah, I like that. I know what you're saying." Mona took a deep swallow of the orange juice, thinking how good it was, and how cold. For a moment her head hurt from the cold. She tried not to stare worshipfully at Rowan. This was like having a crush on a teacher, something that Mona had never known.

"When you look at me," said Rowan, "I can't read anything. Maybe it's your green eyes blinding me. Don't forget about them when you're making your tally. Perfect skin, red hair to die for, long and outrageously thick, and enormous green eyes. Then there's the mouth, and the body. No, I think your view of yourself is slightly blurred right now. Perhaps it's only that you're more interested in other things—the legacy, what happened to Aaron, when will Yuri come back?"

Clever words came to Mona's mind and faded away instantly. She had never in her life lingered before a mirror more than necessary. She had not looked in one this morning at all.

"Look, I don't have much time," Rowan said. She

129

clasped her hands on the table. "I need to talk to you straight."

"Yes, do it," said Mona. "Please."

"I understand completely about your being the heiress. There is no malice between you and me. You're the finest conceivable choice. I knew this myself in my own instinctive fashion as soon as I came to grasp what had been done. But Ryan cleared up the matter completely. The tests and the profile are complete. You are the gifted daughter. You have the intelligence, the stability, the toughness. You have the perfect health. Oh, the extra chromosomes are there, all right, but they've been there in Mayfair women and men for centuries. There's no reason to expect that anything like what happened on Christmas will ever happen again."

"Yeah, that's what I figure," said Mona. "Besides, I don't have to marry anyone with the extra string, do I? I'm not in love with a member of the family. Oh, I know that's bound to change, you're thinking, but I mean at present there isn't any kind of childhood-sweetheart syndrome with someone loaded with deadly genes."

Rowan thought about this and then she nodded. She looked down into her coffee cup, then lifted it and took the last swallow and set the cup a little to the side.

"I don't hold any malice against you for what happened with Michael. You must understand that too."

"It's hard to believe. Because I think what I did was so wrong."

"Thoughtless perhaps, but not wrong. Besides, I think I understand just what happened. Michael doesn't talk about it. I'm not referring to the seduction anyway. I'm talking about the effect."

"If I did cure him, then I won't go to hell after all," said Mona. She pressed her lips together in a sad smile. There was more than a trace of guilt and self-loathing in her voice and face, and she knew it. But she was so relieved now, she couldn't put that part into words.

"You cured him, and perhaps you were meant to do this. Someday maybe we can talk together about the dreams you had, and the Victrola that materialized in the living room."

"Then Michael told you."

"No, you told me. All the times you thought about it out there, remembering the waltz from *La Traviata*, and the ghost of Julien telling you to do it. But this isn't important to me. It's only important that you not worry about my hating you anymore. You have to be strong to be the heiress, especially the way things are now. You can't be worried about the wrong things."

"Yes, you're right. You really don't hold it against me. I know you don't."

"You could have known sooner," said Rowan. "You're stronger than I am, you know. Reading people's thoughts and emotions, it's almost a trick. I always hated it when I was a child. It frightened me. It frightens lots of gifted children. But later on, I learned to use it in a subtle, almost subconscious way. Wait a beat after someone speaks to you, especially if the words are confusing. Wait a beat and you'll know what the person feels."

"You're right, it's like that, I've tried it."

"It gets better and stronger. I would think that knowing what you know—about everything—it would be easier for you. I was supposed to be disgustingly normal, an honors student with a passion for science, growing up with all the luxuries of a well-to-do only child. You know what you are."

She paused. She drew a cigarette out of the pack lying on the table. "You don't mind, do you?" she asked.

"No, not at all," said Mona. "I like the smell of cigarettes, always have."

But she stopped. She slipped the cigarette back in the pack. She laid the lighter beside it.

Then she looked at Mona, and her face seemed incidentally hard suddenly, as though she'd fallen deep in thought and forgotten to conceal her strong inner self.

The look was so cold and so quietly fierce that it made her seem sexless to Mona. It might be a man looking at her, this person with the gray eyes and the dark straight eyebrows and the soft blond hair. It might have been an angel. Surely, it was a beautiful woman. Mona was far too intrigued and excited by all this to let her eyes be forced away.

Almost at once the expression did soften, deliberately perhaps.

"I'm going to Europe," said Rowan. "I'm leaving in a little while."

"Why? Where are you going?" demanded Mona. "Does Michael know this?"

"No," she said. "And when he finds out, he'll be hurt again."

"Rowan, you can't do that to him, wait a second. Why are you going?"

"Because I have to. I'm the only one who can figure out this little mystery about the Talamasca. I'm the only one who can find out why Aaron died like he did."

"But Michael, you've got to take Michael with you, you've got to let him help. You leave him again, Rowan, and it's going to take more than a nubile thirteen-year-old to save his ego and whatever manhood he's got left."

Rowan listened to this, thoughtfully.

Mona instantly regretted what she'd said, then instantly thought she hadn't said it strongly enough.

"It's going to hurt," said Rowan.

"Oh, you're kidding yourself," said Mona. "Maybe he won't be waiting around here when you get back."

"Look, what would you do if you were me?" Rowan asked.

It took a second for this question to sink in. Mona took another big drink of the orange juice and then pushed the glass to the side. "You're really asking me?"

"There's no one I'd rather ask."

"Take him with you to Europe. Why not? What's he staying here for?"

"There are things," she said. "He's the only one who understands the kind of danger directed against the family. And there's the question of his own safety, but then I don't know just how critical that is."

"His safety? If the Talamasca guys want to hit him, they know where to find him if he just hangs around this house. Besides, Rowan, what about your own safety? You know more about all this than anyone except Michael. Don't you

132

need him with you? You're really prepared to go over there alone?"

"I wouldn't be alone, I'd be with Yuri."

"Yuri?"

"He called again this morning, only a little while ago."

"Why didn't you tell me?"

"I'm telling you now," Rowan said coolly. "He had only a few minutes. He was in a pay booth in London. I persuaded him to meet me at Gatwick. I have only a few hours before I leave."

"You should have called me, Rowan, you should have . . ."

"Hold it, Mona. Yuri's purpose in calling was to warn you to stay close to your family and remain under guard. That's what's important here. He thinks there are people who may try to get hold of you, Mona. He was very serious. He wouldn't explain any more. He said things about the genetic testing, people accessing the records, figuring out that you were the most powerful witch in the clan."

"Yeah, well, I probably am. I figured that out a long time ago, but, Rowan, if they are after witches, why aren't they after you?"

"Because I can't give birth ever again, Mona. But you can. Yuri thinks they may want Michael also. Michael fathered Lasher. These evil people, whoever they are, will try to bring you together. I think Yuri's wrong."

"Why?"

"Mating two witches? Expecting the extra genes to throw a Taltos? It's as unlikely now as it ever was. You might say that breeding two witches is the long way of doing it. According to our records, the one and only successful attempt took three hundred years. There was intervention and purpose in that one success. I gave it my assistance at a crucial moment. Maybe it could not have happened without that."

"And Yuri thinks they'd try to force Michael and me to do that?"

All this while Rowan's gray eyes were fixed on her, scanning her, weighing her response to every word.

"I don't agree with him," said Rowan. "I think the villains of the piece killed Aaron to cover their tracks. That's why they've also tried to kill Yuri. That's why they may be arranging some sort of accidental death for me. On the other hand . . ."

"Then you are in danger! And what happened to Yuri? When did it happen, where?"

"This is my simple point," Rowan said. "We don't know the limits of the danger for anyone who's in any way involved. We can't know because we don't really know the motives of the killers. Yuri's theory, that they won't give up until they've bred a Taltos, is obviously the most pessimistic and the most inclusive. And that's what we should go with. You and Michael both have to be protected. And Michael is the only one in the family, really, who knows why. It's imperative you remain within the house."

"So you're leaving us together here? All cozy and comfortable under your own roof? Rowan, I want to say something to you that takes a lot of nerve."

"You shouldn't have any problem," said Rowan simply.

"You're underestimating Michael. You're selling him short in every respect. He's not going to go for this. And if you leave him without telling him, he's not likely to hang around and play the assigned role. If he does, what do you think the man in him is going to want? And if he does want to do it—sleep with me, that is—what do you think I am? Rowan, you're arranging all this as if we were pawns you're moving on a chessboard. Rowan, we're not."

Rowan didn't answer. After a little pause, she smiled.

"You know, Mona, I wish I could take you with me," she said. "I wish you'd come."

"I will! Take me and Michael! The three of us should go."

"The family would never tolerate such a betrayal on my part," said Rowan. "And I couldn't do it to you myself."

"That's crazy, Rowan. Why are we having this conversation? Why are you asking me things like what I think about what's going on?"

"There are too many reasons, Mona, why you have to stay here with Michael."

"And what if we do get in the sack together?"

"That's up to you."

"Terrific, punch him out, and expect me to comfort him but not to—"

Absently, Rowan slipped out a cigarette, then stopped exactly as she had before, gave a little sigh, and pushed it back in the pack.

"I don't care if you smoke," said Mona. "I don't do it, due to my superior intelligence, but—"

"You'll care very soon."

"What do you mean by that?"

"Don't you know?"

Mona was flabbergasted. She didn't answer. "You're saying . . . oh God, I should have known."

She sat back. Still, there had been so many near misses in the past. She was always on the phone to her gynecologist. "I think I did it this time."

"It's no near miss," said Rowan. "Is it Yuri's child?"

"No," Mona answered. "That's impossible. Sir Galahad was too careful. I mean, that is flatly impossible."

"It's Michael's child."

"Yes. But are you certain I am pregnant? I mean, this was only a month ago, and . . ."

"Yes," said Rowan. "The witch and the doctor know the same thing."

"So this could be the Taltos," said Mona.

"Do you want a reason to get rid of it?"

"No, absolutely not. There's nothing on earth that's going to make me get rid of it."

"You're certain?"

"How certain do I have to be?" Mona asked. "Rowan, this is a Catholic family. We don't do away with babies. Besides, I wouldn't do away with this baby no matter who the father was. And if it's Michael's, that's all the more reason for everybody to be happy, because Michael's part of the family! You really don't know us so well, Rowan. You're not getting it, even now. If it's Michael's baby . . . if it's really there, that is . . ."

"Please finish."

"Why don't you finish for me?"

"No, I would like to hear you say it, if you don't mind."

"If it's Michael's, then Michael would be the father of the next generation that will inherit this house."

"Yes."

"And if the baby were a girl, I could designate it as the one to inherit everything, and . . . you and Michael could be its godparents and we could stand at the baptismal font together. We could stand there and then Michael would have a baby, and I'd have a father who I wanted for the baby that everyone will trust and love."

"I knew you would paint a more colorful description than I would," said Rowan softly, a little sadly. "That went beyond my expectations. You're right. There are still things about this family I have to learn."

"Color in St. Alphonsus Church, where Stella and Antha and Deirdre were baptized. And I think . . . I think they baptized you over there too."

"That they've never told me."

"Seems I heard it. Seems like something they would do."

"There's no chance that you might decide to get rid of it."

"You gotta be kidding! I want it. I'd want any baby of my own, be serious. Look, I'm going to be so rich I can buy anything in the world, but there's no substitute in existence for my own baby. I can make that happen only one way. Oh, if you knew the family more, if you hadn't spent your life out there in California, you'd understand it's not even a question, unless, of course . . . But even then . . ."

"Even then?"

"Let's worry about that when it happens. There must be indications, all kinds of little signs, if it's abnormal."

"Perhaps so. Perhaps not. When I carried Lasher, there were no signs until the moment came."

Mona wanted to respond, to say something, but she was too deep in her thoughts. Her own child. Her own child, and nobody, I mean nobody, was going to shove her around anymore. Her own child, and she would have passed over into adulthood regardless of age. Her own child. Suddenly she didn't think thoughts so much as she saw things. She saw a cradle. She saw a baby, a real live little baby, and she saw herself holding the emerald necklace and then she put the necklace around the baby's neck.

"What about Yuri?" asked Rowan. "Will he understand about this?"

Mona wanted to say yes. The truth was she didn't know. She thought of Yuri, quickly, sort of completely. He was sitting on the side of the bed that last night, and saying to her, "There are all sorts of very important reasons why you must marry among your people." She didn't want to think that she was thirteen and fickle. She realized suddenly that Yuri's understanding about the baby was the least of her worries, the very least.

Why, she hadn't even found out yet how they tried to kill Yuri. She hadn't even asked if he was hurt.

"An attempt was made to shoot him," said Rowan, "and the attempt failed. Unfortunately the assassin was killed by the person who foiled him. And the body won't be easy to find. We won't try to find the body anyway. We have a different plan."

"Listen, Rowan, whatever your plan, you've got to tell Michael all this. You can't just leave."

"I know."

"Why aren't you scared that these bad guys will kill you and Yuri both?"

"I have a few weapons that are strictly my own. Yuri knows the Motherhouse completely. I think I can get into it. I can reach one of the very old members, one of the most trusted and revered. I need perhaps fifteen minutes with him to know whether this evil springs from the Order collectively, or from a small group."

"Can't be one person, Rowan. Too many people are dead."

"You're right, and three of their soldiers are dead. But it could be a very small group within the Order, or outsiders who have a connection within."

"You think you can get to the bad guys themselves?"

"Yes."

"Use me for bait!"

"And the child inside you too? If it is Michael's—"

"It is."

"Then they might want that more than they want you. Look, I don't want to speculate. I don't want to think of witches as some sort of rare commodity to those who know how to use them, of women in the family falling victim to a new species of mad scientist. I've had enough of mad science. I've had enough of monsters. I only want to end this. But you can't go. And neither can Michael. You have to be here."

Rowan pulled back the black silk of her jacket sleeve and looked at a small gold watch. Mona had never seen her wear this watch. Probably Beatrice had bought it too. It was delicate, the kind of watch women wore when Beatrice was a girl.

"I'm going to go upstairs and talk to my husband," said Rowan.

"Thank God," said Mona. "I'm going with you."

"No, please."

"I'm sorry. I'm going."

"For what reason?"

"To make sure you tell him everything that you should."

"All right, then let's go together. Maybe you're one jump ahead of me. You're going to give him the reason to cooperate. But let me ask you one more time, Jezebel. Are you sure this child is his?"

"It was Michael. I can tell you when it probably happened. It happened after Gifford's funeral. I took advantage of him again. I didn't think about precautions any more than I had the first time. Gifford was dead and I was possessed of the devil, I swear it. It was right after that that somebody tried to get in the library window and I smelled that scent."

Rowan said nothing.

"It was the man, wasn't it? He'd come for me after he'd been with my mother. Must have been that way. When he tried to get in, it woke me up. And then I went to her and she was already dead."

"Was it strong, the scent?"

"Very. Sometimes I can still smell it in the living room here, and upstairs in the bedroom. Can't you?"

Rowan didn't reply.

138

"I want you to do something just because I ask you," Rowan said.

"What's that?"

"Don't tell Michael about the baby until the usual tests have been done. There is someone you can confide in, isn't there, someone who can be like a mother? There must be."

"Don't worry about it," said Mona. "I have my secret gynecologist, I'm thirteen."

"Of course," said Rowan. "Look, whatever happens, I'm going to be back here before you have to tell anyone at all."

"Yeah, I hope so. Wouldn't that be something, if you could finish it that quick? But what if you never come back and Michael and I never know what happened to you or to Yuri?"

Rowan thought about this, apparently, and then she merely shrugged. "I'll come back," she said. "One more caution, if you don't mind."

"Hit me with it."

"If you do tell Michael about this baby, and then decide to get rid of it later, that will kill him. Twice before, this has been promised to him and taken away. If there's any doubt, any whatever, don't tell him till that doubt is resolved."

"I can't wait to tell him. I can get my doctor to see me this afternoon. I'll tell her I'm having a nervous breakdown and I'm on my way over. She's used to this stuff with me. When the tests come back okay, nothing's going to keep me from telling him. And nothing, I mean nothing, is going to keep a baby of mine from being born."

She was about to get up when she realized what she'd said, and that Rowan would never face this particular dilemma again. But Rowan seemed not at all offended by her words, and certainly not hurt. Her face was very quiet. She was looking at the cigarettes.

"Get out of here so I can smoke in peace, will you?" Rowan asked, smiling. "And then we'll wake up Michael. I have an hour and a half to make the plane."

"Rowan, I . . . I'm still sorry about doing it with him. I just can't be sorry about the child."

"Neither can I," said Rowan. "If he comes out of this with a child of his own, and a mother who'll let him love it, well, maybe he'll find a way to forgive everything as the years pass. Just remember. I'm still his wife, Jezebel. You've got the emerald and the baby. But Michael is still mine."

"Got it," said Mona. "I really like you, Rowan. I really, really like you. That's aside from loving you because you're my cousin and we're Mayfairs. If I wasn't pregnant I'd make you take me with you, for your sake and Yuri's and everybody else's."

"And how would you make me take you, Mona?"

"What were your words? Secret weapons of my own."

They looked at one another, and then slowly Rowan nodded and smiled.

Seven

THE HILL WAS muddy and cold, but never had Marklin made this slippery climb, either in winter or summer, when he had not loved it—to stand on Wearyall Hill beside the Holy Thorn and look down upon the quaint and picturesque town of Glastonbury. The country round was always green, even in winter, but now it had the new intense color of spring.

Marklin was twenty-three, and very fair, with blond hair and pale blue eyes, and thin clear skin that chilled easily. He wore a raincoat with a wool lining, and a pair of leather gloves, and a small wool cap on his head that fitted well and kept him warmer than one might expect from such a little article of clothing.

He'd been eighteen when Stuart had brought them here—he and Tommy both eager students, in love with Oxford, in love with Stuart and eager for every word that dropped from Stuart's lips.

All during their Oxford days, they had honored this place with regular visitations. They'd taken small, cozy little rooms at the George and Pilgrims Hotel, and walked High Street together perusing the bookshops and the stores that sold crystals and the Tarot, whispering to each other of their secret research, their keen scientific approach to things which others held to be purely mythological. The local believers, called variously the hippies of yore or the New Age fanatics, or the bohemians and artists who always seek the charm and tranquillity of such a place, held no charm for them.

They were for decoding the past, rapidly, with all the tools at their command. And Stuart, their instructor in ancient tongues, had been their priest, their magical connection to a true sanctuary—the library and the archives of the Talamasca.

Last year, after the discovery of Tessa, it had been on Glastonbury Tor that Stuart had told them, "In you two, I have found everything I ever sought in a scholar, a pupil, or a novice. You are the first to whom I truly want to give all I know."

That had seemed a supreme honor to Marklin—something finer than any honors awarded him at Eton or Oxford, or anywhere in the wide world where his studies had carried him later on.

It had been a greater moment even than being accepted into the Order. And now, in retrospect, he knew that that acceptance had meant something only because it had meant everything to Stuart, who had lived all his life as a member of the Talamasca, and would soon die, as he so often said, within its walls.

Stuart was now eighty-seven, and perhaps one of the oldest active men alive in the Talamasca, if one could call tutoring in language an activity of the Talamasca, for it was more the special passion of Stuart's retirement. The talk of death was neither romantic nor melodramatic. And nothing really had changed Stuart's matter-of-fact attitude to what lay ahead.

"A man of my age with his wits about him? If he isn't brave in the face of death, if he isn't curious, and rather eager to see what happens, well, then, he's wasted his life. He's a damned fool."

Even the discovery of Tessa had not infected Stuart with any last-ditch desperation to lengthen the time remaining to him. His devotion to Tessa, his belief in her, encompassed nothing so petty. Marklin feared Stuart's death far more than Stuart did. And Marklin knew now that he had overplayed his hand with Stuart, and that he must woo him back to the moment of commitment. To lose Stuart to death

142

was inevitable; to lose Stuart before that time was unthinkable.

"You stand on the sacred ground of Glastonbury," Stuart had told them that day, when it all began. "Who is buried within this tor? Arthur himself, or only the nameless Celts who left us their coins, their weapons, the boats with which they traveled the seas that once made of this the isle of Avalon? We'll never know. But there are secrets which we can know, and the implications of these secrets are so vast, so revolutionary, and so unprecedented that they are worth our allegiance to the Order, they are worth any sacrifice we must make. If this is not so, then we are liars."

That Stuart now threatened to abandon Marklin and Tommy, that he had turned against them in his anger and revulsion, was something Marklin could have avoided. It had not been necessary to reveal every part of their plan to Stuart. And Marklin realized this now, that his refusal to assume full leadership himself had caused the rift. Stuart had Tessa. . . . Stuart had made his wishes clear. But Stuart should never have been told what had really happened. That had been the error, and Marklin had only his own immaturity to blame, that he had loved Stuart so much he had felt compelled to tell Stuart everything.

He would get Stuart back. Stuart had agreed to come today. He was no doubt already here, visiting Chalice Well as he always did before coming to Wearyall Hill and leading them up on the tor itself. Marklin knew how much Stuart loved him. This breach would be repaired with an appeal from the soul, with poetry and with honest fervor.

That his own life would be long, that this was only the first of his dark adventures, Marklin had no doubt. His would be the keys to the tabernacle, the map to the treasure, the formula for the magic potion. He was utterly certain of it. But for this first plan to end in defeat would be a moral disaster. He would go on, of course, but his youth had been a chain of unbroken successes, and this too must succeed so that his ascent would lose no momentum.

I must win, I must always win. I must never attempt anything that I cannot do with utter success. This had always been Marklin's personal vow. He had never failed to keep it.

As for Tommy, Tommy was faithful to the vows the three had taken, faithful to the concept and the person of Tessa. There was no worry with Tommy. Deeply involved in his computer research, his precise chronologies and charts, Tommy was in no danger of disaffection for the very reasons that made him valuable; he was not the one to see the whole scheme, or to question the validity of it.

In a very basic sense, Tommy never changed.

Tommy was the same now as the boy whom Marklin had come to love in childhood—collector, collator, an archive unto himself, an appreciator and an investigator. Tommy without Marklin had never existed, as far as Marklin knew. They had first laid eyes upon each other at the age of twelve, in boarding school in America. Tommy's room had been filled with fossils, maps, animal bones, computer equipment of the most esoteric sort, and a vast collection of paperback science fiction.

Marklin had often thought that he must have seemed to Tommy to be one of the characters in those fantastic novels—Marklin himself hated fiction—and that Tommy had gone from an outsider to a featured player in a science fiction drama upon meeting Marklin. Tommy's loyalty had never, for even one moment, been in question. Indeed, during the years when Marklin had wanted his freedom, Tommy had been too close, always on hand, always at Marklin's service. Marklin had invented tasks for his friend, simply to give himself space to breathe. Tommy had never been unhappy.

Marklin was getting cold, but he didn't mind it.

Glastonbury would never be anything for him but a sacred place, though he believed almost nothing, literally, that was connected with it.

He would, each time he came to Wearyall Hill, with the private devotion of a monk, envision the noble Joseph of Arimathea planting his staff upon this spot. It did not matter to him that the present Holy Thorn had been grown from a scion of the ancient tree, now gone, any more than other specific detail mattered. He could in these places feel an excitement appropriate to his purpose, a religious renewal as it were, which strengthened him and sent him back into the world more ruthless than ever.

Ruthlessness. That was what was needed now, and Stuart had failed to see it.

Yes, things had gone dreadfully wrong, no doubt of it. Men had been sacrificed whose innocence and substance surely demanded a greater justice. But this was not entirely Marklin's fault. And the lesson to learn was that ultimately none of it mattered.

The time has come for me to instruct my teacher, Marklin thought.

Miles from the Motherhouse, in this open place, our meeting safely explained by our own customs of so many years, we will come together again as one. Nothing has been lost. Stuart must be given moral permission to profit by what has happened.

Tommy had arrived.

Tommy was always the second. Marklin watched Tommy's antique roadster slowing as it came down High Street. He watched as it found a parking place, and as Tommy shut the door, failing to lock it as always, and started his climb up the hill.

What if Stuart failed to show? What if he was nowhere near? What if he had truly abandoned his followers? Impossible.

Stuart was at the well. He drank from it when he came, he would drink from it before he left. His pilgrimages here were as rigid as those of an ancient Druid or Christian monk. From shrine to shrine to shrine traveled Stuart.

Such habits of his teacher had always aroused a tenderness in Marklin, as had Stuart's words. Stuart had "consecrated" them to a dark life of penetrating "the mystique and the myth, in order to lay hands upon the horror and the beauty at the core."

It seemed tolerable poetry both then and now. Only Stuart had to be reminded of it, Stuart had to be convinced in metaphors and lofty sentiments.

Tommy had almost reached the tree. He took his last steps carefully, for it was easy to lose one's footing in the

145

slippery mud, and fall. Marklin had done it once, years ago, when they'd first begun their pilgrimages. This had meant a night at the George and Pilgrims Hotel while his clothes were thoroughly cleaned.

Not bad that it had happened; it had been a marvelous evening. Stuart had stayed down with him. They'd spent the night talking together, even though Marklin had been confined to a borrowed robe and slippers and a small, charming bedchamber, and both had longed in vain to climb the tor in the midnight, and commune with the spirit of the sleeping king.

Of course, Marklin had never for a moment in his life believed that King Arthur slept beneath Glastonbury Tor. If he had believed it, he would have taken a shovel and started digging.

Stuart had come late in life to his conviction that myth was only interesting when a truth lay behind it, and that one could find that truth, and even the physical evidence of it.

Scholars, thought Marklin, theirs is an inevitable flaw; words and deeds become the same to them. That was at the very basis of the confusion now. Stuart, at eighty-seven years of age, had had perhaps his first excursion into reality.

Reality and blood were intermingled.

Tommy at last took his place at Marklin's side. He blew on his cold fingers and then reached into his pockets for his gloves—a classic Tommy routine, to have walked up the hill without them, to have forgotten his gloves were even there until he saw Marklin's leather gloves, the very ones he'd long ago given Marklin.

"Where is Stuart?" Tommy asked. "Yes, gloves." He stared at Marklin, eyes enormous through his round, thick, rimless glasses, red hair clipped neatly short so that he might have been a lawyer or a banker. "Gloves, yes. Where is he?"

Marklin had been about to say that Stuart had not come, when in fact he saw Stuart beginning the very last leg of the ascent from his car, which he had brought as close as permissible up Wearyall Hill. Unlike Stuart to have done this.

But Stuart seemed otherwise unchanged—tall, narrow in his familiar greatcoat, with the cashmere scarf around his neck and streaming out behind him in the wind, his gaunt face looking as if it were carved out of wood. His gray hair resembled, as always, a jay's crest. It seemed in this last decade he had scarcely changed at all.

He looked right at Marklin as he drew near. And Marklin realized that he himself was trembling. Tommy stepped aside. Stuart stopped some six feet from both of them, his hands clenched, his thin face anguished as he confronted the two young men.

"You killed Aaron!" Stuart cried. "You, both of you. You killed Aaron. How in the name of God could you have done such a thing?"

Marklin was speechless, all his confidence and plans deserting him suddenly. He tried to stop the tremor in his hands. He knew if he spoke his voice would be frail and without any authority. He could not bear for Stuart to be angry, or disappointed in any way.

"Dear God, what have you done, both of you!" Stuart ranted. "And what have I done that I set this scheme into motion? Dear God, the blame is mine!"

Marklin swallowed, but kept his silence.

"You, Tommy, how could you have been a party to this!" Stuart continued. "And Mark. Mark, you, the very author of all of it."

"Stuart, you must hear me out!" Marklin declared before he could stop himself.

"Hear you out?" Stuart drew closer, his hands shoved into his coat pockets. "Hear you out, should I? Let me ask you a question, my brilliant young friend, my finest, my bravest hope! What's to stop you now from killing me, as you've done with Aaron and Yuri Stefano?"

"Stuart, it was for you that I did it," Marklin insisted. "If you would only listen, you'll understand. These are but flowers of the seeds you planted when we began this together. Aaron had to be silenced. That he had not reported back, that he had not come home to the Motherhouse itself, was pure luck, Stuart! He might have any day, and Yuri Stefano would also have come. His visit to Donnelaith was a fluke. He might have come straight home from the airport."

"You speak of circumstance, you speak of detail!" Stuart said, taking yet another step towards them.

Tommy stood quiet, seemingly emotionless, his red hair tousled by the wind, eyes squinting behind his glasses. He watched Stuart steadily, his shoulder very close to Marklin's arm.

Stuart was beside himself.

"You speak of expediency, but you don't speak of life and death, my pupil," he insisted. "How could you do it! How could you bring an end to Aaron's life!"

And here Stuart's voice failed him, and the grief displayed itself, monstrous as the rage. "I would destroy you, Mark, if I could," said Stuart. "But I cannot do such things, and that is perhaps why I did not think that you could! But you've amazed me, Mark."

"Stuart, it was worth any sacrifice. What is sacrifice if it is not moral sacrifice!"

This horrified Stuart, but what else could Marklin do, other than take the plunge? Tommy really ought to say something, he thought, but he knew that when Tommy spoke, he would stand firm.

"I put an end to those who could have stopped us," said Mark. "That is all there is to it, Stuart. You grieve for Aaron because you knew him."

"Don't be a fool," said Stuart bitterly. "I grieve for innocent blood shed, I grieve for monstrous stupidity! Oh yes, that is what it was. Do you think the death of such a man will go unavenged within the Order? You think you know the Talamasca, you think with your shrewd young mind you could size it up in a matter of a few years. But all you've done is to learn its organizational weaknesses. You could live all your life in the Talamasca and not know the Talamasca. Aaron was my brother! It was my brother you killed! You have failed me, Mark. You have failed Tommy. You have failed yourself! You have failed Tessa."

"No," Mark said, "you don't speak the truth, and you know it. Look at me, Stuart, look into my eyes. You left it to me to bring Lasher here, you left it to me to step out of the library and plot everything. And to Tommy as well. Do you think this could have been orchestrated without us?"

"You miss a crucial point, don't you, Mark?" Stuart asked. "You failed. You did not rescue the Taltos and bring him here! Your soldiers were fools, and so it must be said of the general."

"Stuart, have patience with us," said Tommy. It was his usual matter-of-fact tone. "I knew the first day we spoke that this couldn't be accomplished without someone paying for it with his life."

"You never spoke such words to me, Tommy."

"Let me remind you," Tommy said in the same monotone manner, "you said that we were to render Yuri and Aaron powerless to interfere, and erase all evidence that the Taltos itself had been born into the Mayfair family. Now, how was this to be done except in the ways that we did it? Stuart, we have nothing to be ashamed of in our actions. What we seek makes these things utterly insignificant."

Marklin tried desperately to conceal his sigh of relief.

Stuart looked from Tommy to Marklin and then back again, and then out over the pale landscape of gently rolling green hills, and then up to the peak of Glastonbury Tor. He turned his back on them to face the tor, and he hung his head as if communing with some personal deity.

Marklin drew close, and he placed his hands very tentatively on Stuart's shoulders. He was far taller now than Stuart, and Stuart in old age had lost some of his earlier height. Marklin drew close to his ear.

"Stuart, the die was cast when we got rid of the scientist. There was no turning back. And the doctor . . ."

"No," said Stuart, shaking his head with dramatic emphasis. His eyes were narrow and fixed on the tor. "These deaths could have been blamed on the Taltos himself, don't you see? That was the beauty of it. The Taltos canceled the deaths of the two men who could have only misused the revelation granted to them!"

"Stuart," said Mark, very aware that Stuart had not sought to free himself from his light embrace. "You must understand that Aaron became the enemy of us when he became the official enemy of the Talamasca."

"Enemy? Aaron was never an enemy of the Talamasca! Your bogus excommunication broke his heart."

"Stuart," Marklin pleaded, "I can see now in retrospect that the excommunication was a mistake, but it has been our only mistake."

"There was no choice in the matter of the excommunication," said Tommy flatly. "It was either that or risk discovery at every turn. I did what I had to do, and I made it damned convincing. I could not have kept up a bogus correspondence between the Elders and Aaron. That would have been too much."

"I admit," said Marklin, "it was a mistake. Only loyalty to the Order might have kept Aaron quiet about the various things he'd seen and come to suspect. If we made an error, Stuart, the three of us made it together. We shouldn't have alienated him and Yuri Stefano. We should have tightened our hold, played our game better."

"The web was too intricate as it was," said Stuart. "I warn you, both of you. Tommy, come here. I warn you both! Do not strike against the Mayfair family. You have done enough. You have destroyed a man who was finer than any other I ever knew, and you did it for so small a gain that heaven will take its vengeance on you. But do not, for whatever remains to us now, strike against the family!"

"I think we already have," said Tommy in his usual practical voice. "Aaron Lightner had recently married Beatrice Mayfair. Besides, he had become so close to Michael Curry—indeed, to all of the clan—that the marriage was hardly required to cement the relationship. But there was a marriage, and to the Mayfairs marriage is a sacred bond, as we know. He had become one of them."

"Pray you're wrong," said Stuart. "Pray to heaven you're wrong. Risk the ire of the Mayfair witches, and God himself couldn't help you."

"Stuart, let us look at what must be done now," said Marklin. "Let's leave the hill and go down to the hotel."

"Never. Where others can hear our words? Never."

"Stuart, take us to Tessa. Let us discuss it there," pressed Marklin.

It was the key moment. Marklin knew it. He wished now

150

that he had not said Tessa's name, not yet. He wished he had not played to this climax.

Stuart was eyeing both of them with the same deliberate condemnation and disgust. Tommy stood solidly, gloved hands clasped in front of him. The stiff collar of his coat rose to hide his mouth, and thereby leave nothing to scrutiny but his level, untroubled gaze.

Marklin himself was close to tears, or so he imagined. Marklin had actually never wept even once in his life that he could remember.

"Perhaps this is not the time to see her," Marklin said, hastening to repair the damage.

"Perhaps you should never see her again," said Stuart, voice small for the first time, eyes large and speculating.

"You don't mean what you say," said Mark.

"If I take you to Tessa, what's to stop you from doing away with me?"

"Oh, Stuart, you hurt us both; how can you ask this of us? We aren't without principle. We're simply dedicated to a common goal. Aaron had to die. So did Yuri. Yuri was never really one of the Order. Yuri left so easily and so quickly!"

"Yes, and neither of you were ever members either, were you?" Stuart asked. His manner was changing, hardening.

"We are dedicated to you and always have been," said Marklin. "Stuart, we waste our valuable time. Keep Tessa to yourself if you will. You will not shake my faith in her, or Tommy's. And we will move towards our goal. We cannot do otherwise."

"And what now is the goal?" Stuart demanded. "Lasher is gone now, as if he'd never existed! Or do you doubt the word of a man who would follow Yuri doggedly over land and sea only to finally shoot him?"

"Lasher is beyond destiny now," said Tommy. "I think we are all in agreement on that. What Lanzing saw couldn't be interpreted any other way. But Tessa is in your hands, as real as she was the day you discovered her."

Stuart shook his head. "Tessa is real, and Tessa is alone as she has always been alone. And the union shall not take

151

place, and my eyes will close without ever seeing the miracle."

"Stuart, it is still possible," said Marklin. "The family, the Mayfair witches."

"Yes," cried Stuart, his voice out of control, "and strike them and they will destroy you. You have forgotten the very first warning I ever gave you. The Mayfair witches win over those who would hurt them. They always have! If not as individuals, they win as a family!"

They stood quiet for a moment.

"Destroy *you*, Stuart?" Tommy asked. "Why not the three of us, Stuart?"

Stuart was in despair. His white hair, blown back and forth by the wind, resembled the unkempt hair of a drunkard. He looked down at the earth beneath his feet, his hooked nose glistening as though it were nothing now but polished cartilage. An eagle of a man, yes, but not an elderly one, never that.

Marklin feared for him in the wind. Stuart's eyes were red and tearing. Marklin could see the map of blue veins spreading up from his temples. Stuart was trembling in every limb.

"Yes, you're right, Tommy," said Stuart. "The Mayfairs will destroy all of us. Why would they not?" He looked up and straight at Marklin. "And what is the greatest loss to me? Is it Aaron? Is it the marriage itself, of male and female Taltos? Is it the chain of memory we hoped to discover link by link to its earliest source? Or is it that you are damned now, both of you, for what you've done? And I have lost you. Let the Mayfairs come to destroy the three of us, yes, it will be justice."

"No, I don't want this justice," said Tommy. "Stuart, you can't turn on us."

"No, that you can't do," said Marklin. "You cannot call a defeat for us. The witches can bear the Taltos again."

"Three hundred years hence?" asked Stuart. "Or tomorrow?"

"Listen to me, sir, I beg you," said Marklin. "The spirit of Lasher possessed knowledge of what he had been, and what he could be, and what happened to the genes of

Rowan Mayfair and Michael Curry happened under the spirit's knowing vigilance and to fulfill his purpose.

"But *we* have that knowledge now—of what a Taltos is, and perhaps was, and what can make it. And Stuart, *so do the witches!* For the first time, the witches know the destiny of the giant helix. And their knowing is as powerful as Lasher's knowing."

Stuart had no answer for this. Clearly he had not thought of it. He looked at Marklin a long time. Then he asked, "You believe this?"

"Their awareness is even more powerful, perhaps," said Tommy. "The telekinetic assistance that can be rendered by the witches themselves in the event of a birth can't be underestimated."

"Ever the scientist," said Marklin with a triumphant smile. The tide was changing. He could feel it, see it in Stuart's eyes.

"And one must remember," said Tommy, "that the spirit was addled and blundering. The witches are leagues from that, even at their most naive and ineffectual."

"That is a guess, Tommy."

"Stuart," Marklin pleaded. "We have come too far!"

"To put it another way," said Tommy, "our accomplishments here are by no means negligible. We verified the incarnation of the Taltos, and if we could get our hands on any notes written by Aaron before his death, we might verify what all suspect, that it was not incarnation but reincarnation."

"I know what we've done," said Stuart. "The good, the bad. You needn't make your summation for me, Tommy."

"Only to clarify," said Tommy. "And we have witches who know not only the old secrets now in abstract, but who believe in the physical miracle itself. We could not possibly have more interesting opportunities."

"Stuart, trust us again," said Marklin.

Stuart looked at Tommy and then back at Marklin. Marklin saw the old spark, the love.

"Stuart," he went on, "the killing is done. It's finished. Our other unwitting assistants can be phased out without their ever knowing the grand design."

"And Lanzing? He must know everything."

"He was a hireling, Stuart," said Marklin. "He never understood what he saw. Besides, he too is dead."

"We didn't kill him, Stuart," said Tommy, in an almost casual manner. "They found part of his remains at the foot of Donnelaith Crag. His gun had been fired twice."

"Part of his remains?" asked Stuart.

Tommy shrugged. "They said he'd been a meal for wild animals."

"But you can't be sure, then, that he killed Yuri."

"Yuri has never returned to the hotel," said Tommy. "His belongings are still unclaimed. Yuri is dead, Stuart. The two bullets were for Yuri. How Lanzing fell, or why, or if some animal attacked, those things we can't know. But Yuri Stefano is, for our purposes, gone."

"Don't you see, Stuart?" said Marklin. "Except for the escape of the Taltos, everything has worked perfectly. And we can withdraw now, and focus upon the Mayfair witches. We don't need anything further from the Order. If the interception is ever uncovered, no one will ever be able to trace it to us."

"You don't fear the Elders, do you?"

"There is no reason to fear the Elders," said Tommy. "The intercept continues to work perfectly. It always has."

"Stuart, we've learned from our errors," said Marklin. "But perhaps things have happened for a purpose. I don't mean in the sentimental sense. But look at the overall picture. All the right people are dead."

"Don't talk so crudely to me of your methods, either of you. What about our Superior General?"

Tommy shrugged. "Marcus knows nothing. Except that he will very soon be able to retire with a small fortune. He'll never put all the pieces together afterwards. No one will be able to. That's the beauty of the entire plan."

"We need a few more weeks at most," said Marklin. "Just to protect ourselves."

"I'm not so sure," said Tommy. "The smart thing may be to remove the intercepts now. We know everything the Talamasca knows about the Mayfair family."

"Don't be so hasty, so confident!" said Stuart. "What

154

happens when your phony communications are finally discovered?"

"You mean *our* phony communications?" asked Tommy. "At the very worst, there'll be a little confusion, perhaps even an investigation. But no one could trace the letters or the interception itself to us. That's why it's very important that we remain loyal novices, that we do nothing now to arouse suspicion."

Tommy glanced at Marklin. It was working. Stuart's manner had changed. Stuart was giving the orders again . . . almost.

"This is all electronic," said Tommy. "There is no hard evidence of anything anywhere, except a few piles of paper in my flat in Regent's Park. Only you and Mark and I know where those papers are."

"Stuart, we need your guidance now!" said Marklin. "We go into the most exciting phase yet."

"Silence," said Stuart. "Let me look at you both, let me take your measure."

"Please do it, Stuart," said Marklin, "and find us brave and young, yes, young and stupid, perhaps, but brave and committed."

"What Mark means," said Tommy, "is that our position now is better than we could possibly have expected. Lanzing shot Yuri, then fell, fatally injuring himself. Stolov and Norgan are gone. They were never anything but a nuisance, and they knew too much. The men hired to kill the others don't know us. And we are here, where we began, at Glastonbury."

"And Tessa is in your hands, unknown to anyone but the three of us."

"Eloquence," said Stuart almost in a whisper. "That's what you give me now, eloquence."

"Poetry is truth, Stuart," said Marklin. "It is the highest truth, and eloquence is its attribute."

There was a pause. Marklin had to get Stuart down from this hill. Protectively, he put his arm around Stuart, and to his great relief, Stuart allowed this.

"Let's go down, Stuart," said Marklin. "Let's have our supper now. We're cold, we're hungry."

"If we had it to do over again," said Tommy, "we'd do it better. We didn't have to take those lives. It might have been more of a challenge, you know, to accomplish our purpose without really hurting anyone."

Stuart seemed lost in thought, only glancing at Tommy absently. The wind rose again, cuttingly, and Marklin shivered. If he was this cold, what must Stuart be feeling? They must go down to the hotel. They must break bread together.

"We are not ourselves, you know, Stuart," Marklin said. He was looking down at the town, and conscious that both of the others were staring at him. "When gathered together, we make a person whom none of us knows well enough, perhaps, a fourth entity which we should give a name, because he is more than our collective selves. Perhaps we must better learn to control him. But destroy him now? No, that we cannot do, Stuart. If we do, we all betray each other. It's a hard truth to face, but the death of Aaron means nothing."

He had played his final card. He had said the finest and the worst things that he'd had to say, here in the chill wind, and without real forethought, with only his instinct to guide him. Finally he looked at his teacher and at his friend, and saw that both had been impressed by these words, perhaps even more than he could have hoped.

"Yes, it was this fourth entity, as you call him, who killed my friend," said Stuart quietly. "You are right about that. And we know that the power, the future of this fourth entity, is unimaginable."

"Yes, exactly," said Tommy in a flat murmur.

"But the death of Aaron is a terrible, terrible thing! You will never, either of you, ever speak to me of it again, and never, never will you speak of it lightly to anyone."

"Agreed," said Tommy.

"My innocent friend," said Stuart, "who sought only to help the Mayfair family."

"No one in the Talamasca is really innocent," Tommy said.

Stuart appeared startled, at first enraged and then caught by this simple statement.

"What do you mean by this?"

"I mean that one cannot expect to possess knowledge which does not change one. Once one knows, then one is acting upon that knowledge, whether it is to withhold the knowledge from those who would also be changed, or to give it to them. Aaron knew this. The Talamasca is evil by nature; that's the price it pays for its libraries and inventories and computer records. Rather like God, wouldn't you say, who knows that some of his creatures will suffer and some will triumph, but does not tell his creatures what he knows? The Talamasca is more evil even than the Supreme Being, but the Talamasca creates nothing."

So very right, thought Marklin, though he could not have said such a thing aloud to Stuart, for fear of what Stuart would say in return.

"Perhaps you're right," said Stuart under his breath. He sounded defeated, or desperate for some tolerable point of view.

"It's a sterile priesthood," said Tommy, the voice once again devoid of all feeling. He gave his heavy glasses a shove with one finger. "The altars are barren; the statues are stored away. The scholars study for study's sake."

"Don't say any more."

"Let me talk of us, then," said Tommy, "that we are not sterile, and we will see the sacred union come about, and we will hear the voices of memory."

"Yes," said Marklin, unable to assume such a cold voice. "Yes, we are the real priests now! True mediators between the earth and the forces of the unknown. We possess the words and the power."

Another silence had fallen.

Could Marklin ever get them off this hill? He had won. They were together again, and he longed for the warmth of the George and Pilgrims. He longed for the taste of hot soup and ale, and the light of the fire. He longed to celebrate. He was wildly excited again.

"And Tessa?" asked Tommy. "How is it with Tessa?"

"The same," said Stuart.

"Does she know that the male Taltos is dead?"

"She never knew he was alive," said Stuart.

"Ah."

157

"Come on, teacher," said Marklin. "Let's go down now, to the hotel. Let's dine together."

"Yes," said Tommy, "we're all too cold now to speak anymore."

They began the descent, both Tommy and Marklin steadying Stuart in the slippery mud. When they had reached Stuart's car, they opted for the drive rather than the long walk.

"This is all very good," said Stuart, giving over the car keys to Marklin. "But I will visit Chalice Well as always before we go."

"What for?" asked Marklin, making his words quiet, and respectful, and seemingly expressive of the love he felt for Stuart. "Will you wash your hands in Chalice Well to cleanse the blood off them? The water is already bloody itself, teacher."

Stuart gave a little bitter laugh.

"Ah, but that is the blood of Christ, isn't it?" Stuart said.

"It's the blood of conviction," said Marklin. "We'll go to the well after dinner, and just before dark. I promise you that."

They drove down the hill together.

Eight

MICHAEL TOLD CLEM he wanted to leave by the front gate. He'd bring the suitcases out. There were only two of them—Rowan's and his. This was no vacation that required trunks and garment bags.

He looked at his diary before he closed it. There was a long statement there of his philosophy, written on Mardi Gras night, before he had ever dreamed that he would be awakened later by a plaintive gramophone song or by the vision of Mona dancing like a nymph in her white night-gown. Bow in hair, fresh and fragrant as warm bread, fresh milk, strawberries.

No, can't think any more about Mona just now. Wait for the phone call in London.

Besides, it was the passage he wanted to read:

And I suppose I do believe, in the final analysis, that a peace of mind can be obtained in the face of the worst horrors and the worst losses. It can be obtained by faith in change and in will and in accident; and by faith in ourselves, that we will do the right thing, more often than not, in the face of adversity.

Six weeks had passed since that night, when, in illness and in grief, he'd written those sentiments. He'd been a prisoner of this house then, and up until this very moment.

He closed the diary. He slipped it into his leather bag, tucked the bag under his arm, and picked up the suitcases.

159

He went down the stairs, a bit nervous since neither hand was free to reach for the rail, reminding himself that he would suffer no dizzy spell now, or any other form of weakness.

And if he was wrong about that, well, then he would die in action.

Rowan stood on the porch talking to Ryan, and Mona was there, with tears in her eyes, peering up at him with renewed devotion. She looked as delectable in silk as in anything else; and when he looked at her now, he saw what Rowan had seen, saw it as he had once been the first to see it in Rowan—the new swell of the breasts, the higher color of the cheeks, and a brilliance in Mona's eyes, as well as a slightly different rhythm to her subtlest movements.

My child.

He'd believe it when she confirmed it. He'd worry about monsters and genes when he had to. He'd dream of a son or a daughter in his arms when there was a real chance of it.

Clem took the suitcases quickly, and carried them out the open gate. Michael liked this new driver so much better than the last, liked his good humor and his matter-of-fact ways. He made Michael think of musicians he'd known.

The trunk of the car was shut. Ryan kissed Rowan on both cheeks. Only now did Michael pick up Ryan's voice.

". . . anything further that you can tell me."

"Only that this situation won't last long. But don't for a moment think it's safe to let the guards go. And don't let Mona out alone under any circumstances."

"Chain me to the walls," said Mona with a shrug. "They would have done it to Ophelia if she hadn't drowned in the stream."

"Who?" asked Ryan. "Mona, so far I have taken this whole thing very well indeed, considering the fact that you are thirteen years old and—"

"Chill, Ryan," she said. "Nobody's taking it better than I am."

She smiled in spite of herself. Ryan stood baffled, staring at her.

This was the moment, Michael figured. He couldn't endure a long Mayfair goodbye. And Ryan was confused enough.

"Ryan, I'll be in touch with you as soon as possible," he said. "We'll see Aaron's people. Learn what we can. Come home."

"Now, can you tell me *exactly* where you're going?"

"No, can't do it," said Rowan. She had turned and was headed right out of the gate.

Mona suddenly clattered down the steps after her. "Hey, Rowan!" she said, and Mona flung her arms around Rowan's neck and kissed her.

For one moment Michael was terrified that Rowan would not respond, that she'd stand like a statue beneath the oaks, neither acknowledging this sudden desperate hug, nor trying to free herself from it. But something entirely different happened. Rowan held Mona tight, kissing Mona's cheek and then smoothing her hair, and even laying her hand on Mona's forehead.

"You're going to be all right," Rowan said. "But do everything that I've told you to do."

Ryan followed Michael down the steps.

"I don't know what to say except good luck," Ryan said. "I wish you could tell me more about all this, what you're *really* doing."

"Tell Bea we had to go," said Michael. "I wouldn't tell the others any more than you have to."

Ryan nodded, obviously full of suspicion and concern, but basically stymied.

Rowan was already in the car. Michael slipped in beside her. In seconds they were sliding away beneath the lowering tree branches, and Mona and Ryan made a little picture, standing together in the gate, both waving, Mona's hair like a starburst, and Ryan clearly baffled as ever and highly uncertain.

"Seems he's doomed," said Rowan, "to run things for a coterie who will never tell him anything that's really happening."

"We tried once," said Michael. "You should have been there. He doesn't want to know. And he will do exactly what you tell him. Mona? Will she? I have no idea. But he will."

"You're still angry."

"No," he said. "I stopped being angry when you gave in."

But this wasn't true. He was still hurt to the quick that she had planned to leave without him, that she had seen him not as a companion on this trip, but as some keeper of the house, and of the baby inside Mona.

Well, hurt wasn't anger, was it?

She'd turned away. She was looking forward, and so he felt maybe it was safe to look at her. She was too thin still, far too thin, but her face had never been more lovely to him. The black suit she wore, the pearls, the high heels—all of it had given her a deceptively wicked glamour. But she had not needed these things. Her beauty lay in her purity—in the bones of her face, in the dark straight eyebrows that so vividly determined her expression, and in her soft long mouth which he wanted to kiss now with a brutal male desire to waken her, part her lips, make her soften all over in his arms again, have her.

That was the only way, ever, to have her.

She lifted her hand and pressed the button for the leather privacy panel to go up behind the driver. Then she turned to Michael.

"I was wrong," she said, without rancor or pleading. "You loved Aaron. You love me. You love Mona. I was wrong."

"You don't have to go into this," he answered. It was hard for him to look her in the eye, but he was determined to do it, to calm himself inside, to stop being hurt or mad or whatever this was right now.

"But there's something you have to understand," she said. "I don't plan to be kind and law-abiding with these people who killed Aaron. I don't intend to answer to anyone about what I do—even to you, Michael."

He laughed. He looked into her large, cold gray eyes. He wondered if this was what her patients had seen as they looked up, right before the anesthesia began to work on them.

"I know that, honey," he said. "When we get there, when we meet Yuri, I want to know, that's all, what he knows. I want to be there with you both. I'm not claiming to have your capabilities, or your nerve. But I want to be there."

She nodded.

"Who knows, Rowan?" he asked. "Maybe you'll find a purpose for me." The wrath had come out. It was too late now to draw back in. He knew that his face had gone red. He looked away from her.

When she spoke this time, it was a secret voice he'd never heard her use except with him, and in the past months it had gained a new depth of feeling.

"Michael, I love you. But I know you're a good man. I'm no longer a good woman."

"Rowan, you don't mean that."

"Oh yes, I do. I've been with the goblins, Michael. I've been down into the inner circle."

"And you've come back," he said, looking at her again, trying to put the lid on these feelings that were about to explode out of him. "You're Rowan again, and you're here, and there are things to live for other than vengeance."

That was it, wasn't it? He had not roused her from her waking sleep. It had been Aaron's death that had done the trick, bringing her back to all of them.

If he didn't think of something else quick, he was going to lose his temper again, the hurt was so intense, it was so out of his control.

"Michael, I love you," she said. "I love you very much. And I know what you've suffered. Don't think I don't know, Michael."

He nodded. He'd give her that much, but maybe he was lying to both of them.

"But don't think you know what it's like to be the person I am. I was there at the birth, I was the mother. I was the cause, you might say, I was the crucial instrument. And I paid for that. I paid and I paid and I paid. And I'm not the same now. I love you as I always did, my love for you was never in question. But I'm not the same and I can't be the same, and I knew it when I was sitting out there in the garden, unable to answer your questions or look at you or put my arms around you. I knew it. And yet I loved you, and I love you now. Can you follow what I'm saying?"

Again he nodded.

"You want to hurt me, and I know you do," she said.

"No, not hurt you. Not that. Not hurt you, just . . . just . . . rip your little silk skirt off, perhaps, and tear off that blazer that's been so skillfully painted on and make you know I'm here, I'm Michael! That's shameful, isn't it? It's disgusting, isn't it? That I want to have you the only way I can, because you shut me out, you left me, you . . ."

He stopped. This had sometimes happened to him before, that in the midst of cresting anger, he had seen the futility of what he was doing and saying. He had seen the emptiness of anger itself, and realized in a moment of utter practicality that he could not continue like this, that if he did, nothing would be accomplished except his own misery.

He sat still and he felt the anger leave him. He felt his body grow relaxed and almost tired. He sat back against the back of the seat. And then he looked at her again.

She'd never turned away. She looked neither frightened nor sad. He wondered if, in her secret heart, she was bored and wishing him safe at home as she plotted the next steps she would take.

Clear away these thoughts, man, because if you don't, you can't love her again, ever.

And he did love her. There wasn't any doubt suddenly. He loved her strength, he loved her coldness. That's how it had been in her house on Tiburon, when they'd made it beneath the bare beam roof, when they had talked and talked, with no possible inkling of how they had, all their lives, been moving towards one another.

He reached out and touched her cheek, very aware that her expression hadn't changed, that she seemed as totally in control as she ever had.

"I do love you!" he whispered.

"I know," she said.

He laughed under his breath.

"You do?" he asked. He felt himself smile, and it felt good. He laughed silently and shook his head. "You know it!" he said.

164

"Yes," she said with a little nod. "I'm afraid for you, always have been. It's not because you aren't strong, aren't capable, aren't everything you ought to be. I'm afraid because there's a power in me that you don't have, and there's a power in these others—these enemies of ours who killed Aaron—a power that comes from a total lack of scruples." She flicked a bit of dust off the tight little skirt. When she sighed, the soft sound of it seemed to fill up the car, rather like her perfume.

She lowered her head, a small gesture that made her hair go very soft and longish around her face. And as she looked up, her brows seemed especially long and her eyes both pretty and mysterious.

"Call it witch power, if you will. Maybe it's as simple as that. Maybe it's in the genes. Maybe it's a physical capability to do things that normal people can't do."

"Then I have it," he said.

"No. Coincidentally, perhaps, you have the long helix," she said.

"Coincidentally, like hell," he said. "He chose me for you, Rowan. Lasher did that. Years ago when I was a kid and I stopped at the gate of that house, he chose me. Why do you think he did that? Not because he ever thought I'd be a good man and destroy his hard-won flesh, no, that wasn't it. It was for the witch in me, Rowan. We come from the same Celtic root. You know we do. And I'm the worker's son and so I don't know my story. But it goes back to the same beginnings as yours. The power's there. It was there in my hands when I could read the past and the future in people's touch. It was there when I heard the music played by a ghost especially to lead me to Mona."

She gave a small frown, and her eyes grew small for one tiny instant and then large again and wondering.

"I didn't use that power to bring Lasher down," he said. "I was too scared to use it. I used my strength as a man, and the simple tools, as Julien had told me I would. But the power's there. It has to be. And if that's what it takes for you to love me, I mean really love me, then I can reach down inside me and find out just what that power can do. That has always been my option."

165

"My innocent Michael," she said, but it had the tone of a query rather than a declaration.

He shook his head. He leant forward and kissed her. It was not the best thing to do, perhaps, but he couldn't stop himself. He held her by the shoulders, and he did press her back against the seat and cover her mouth with his mouth. He felt her instant response, the way her body was united at once in passion, arms sliding up around his back, mouth kissing him back, back arching as if she would press her entire self against him.

When he let her go, it was only because he had to.

The car was moving swiftly along the freeway. The airport loomed ahead. And there was no time now for the passion he felt, for the consummation of anger and hurt and love that he needed so desperately.

This time it was she who reached out for him, who clasped his head in her hands, and kissed him.

"Michael, my love," she said, "my one and only love."

"I'm with you, darling," he said. "And don't ever try to change it. What we have to do—for Aaron, for Mona, for the baby, for the family, for God knows what—we do together."

It wasn't until they were over the Atlantic that he tried to sleep. They'd eaten their gluttonous fill, and drunk a little too much, and talked for an hour about Aaron. Now the cabin was dark and silent, and they bundled beneath a loose half-dozen blankets.

They needed sleep, he figured. Aaron would advise them to sleep now, wouldn't he?

They'd land in London after eight hours, and it would be early morning there, though it was really night to their bodies, and there would be Yuri, eager to hear and entitled to hear how Aaron had died. Pain. Grief. The inevitable.

He was slipping off, not certain whether he was going right straight into a nightmare or into something as bright and meaningless as a bad cartoon, when he felt her touch his arm.

He let his head roll on the leather seat as he turned to her. She lay back beside him, hand clasping his hand.

"If we see this through," she whispered, "if you don't back off from what I do, if I don't shut you . . ."

"Yes . . ."

"Then nothing will ever come between us. Nobody ever will. And anything you might have with a girl bride will be forfeit."

"I want no girl brides," he said. "I never did. I didn't dream of other women while you were gone from me. I love Mona in my own way, and always will, but that's part of who we are, all of us. I love her and I want the child. I want the child so much I don't even want to talk about it. It's too soon. I'm too desperate. But I want only you, and that's been true since the first day I was with you."

She closed her eyes, her hand still warm and tight on his arm, and then it slipped away rather naturally, as if she'd gone to sleep. Her face looked serene and utterly perfect.

"You know, I've taken life," he said in a whisper. But he wasn't sure she was awake still. "I've taken life three times, and I've walked away from those deeds without regret. That changes anyone."

No answer from her lips.

"I can do it again," he said, "if I have to."

Her lips moved.

"I know that you can," she said softly, not opening her eyes, still lying there as if in deep sleep. "But you see, I'm going to do it whether I have to or not. I have been mortally offended."

She drew in close and kissed him again.

"We're not going to make it to London," he said.

"We're the only ones in the entire first-class cabin," she said, raising her eyebrows, and then kissing him again. "I was once riding on a plane when a certain sort of love was made known to me. It was Lasher's first kiss, you might say. It had a wild, electric quality to it. But I want your arms. I want your cock. I want your body! I can't wait until London. Give it to me."

Enough said, he thought. Thank God she'd opened the blazer, or he might have torn the buttons in proverbial romantic fashion.

Nine

IT WAS NOT SO changed. It stood in its forest or park, without locked gates or dogs to protect it, a great manor house of fine arched windows and myriad chimneys, luxuriously large and luxuriously well cared for. One could imagine those times, looking at it. Their brutality and darkness, their particular fire—all this drew breath and hissed in the empty night.

Only the cars lining the gravel drive, the cars parked in the open garages in long rows, betrayed the modern age. Even the wires and cables ran underground.

He walked through the trees, and then up close to the foundations and along the stones, searching for the doors he remembered. He wore no suit or coat now, but only simple clothes, long workman's pants of brown corduroy and a thick sweater made from wool, the favorite of seamen.

The house seemed to grow to immense size as he approached it. Sprinkled throughout were weak and lonely lights, but lights nevertheless. Scholars in their cells.

Through a series of small barred windows he saw a cellar kitchen. Two lady cooks in white were setting aside the kneaded bread to let it rise. And white flour covered their hands and the pale wood of the counter. The smell of coffee came up to him from this room—very rich and fresh. There had been a door ... a door for deliveries and such. He walked along, out of the helpful illumination of the windows, feeling the stone wall with his hands, and then coming to a door, though it was one that had not been lately used, and it seemed quite impassable.

It was worth a try. And he had come equipped. Perhaps it was not wired with alarms as any door of his own would have been. Indeed, it looked neglected and forlorn and when he studied it, he saw that it had no lock at all, but merely old hinges, very rusted, and a simple latch.

To his amazement, it opened to his touch, and made a yawning creak that startled him and unnerved him. There was a stone passage and a small stairway leading upwards. Fresh foot tracks on the stairs. A gush of warm and faintly stale air, the indoor air of winter.

He entered and pushed the door closed. A light leaked down the stairs from above, illuminating a carefully written sign that said DO NOT LEAVE THIS DOOR OPEN.

Obediently, he made sure that it was shut and then turned and made his way upwards, emerging into a large, darkly paneled corridor.

This was the hall he remembered. He walked along, not trying to hide the sound of his tennis shoes or to conceal himself in the shadows. Here was the formal library he remembered—not the deep archive of priceless and crumbling records, but the daily reading room, with long oak tables and comfortable chairs, and heaps of magazines from throughout the world, and a dead fireplace, still warm beneath his foot, with a few scattered embers still glowing among its charred logs and ashes.

He had thought the room was empty, but on closer inspection he saw an old man dozing in a chair, a heavyset individual with a bald head and small glasses on the end of his nose, a handsome robe over his shirt and trousers.

It would not do to begin here. An alarm could be too easily sounded. He backed out of the room, careful to be silent this time and feeling lucky that he had not waked this man, and then he went on to a large stairway.

Bedchambers began on the third floor in olden times. Would it be the same now? He went all the way up. It was certainly likely.

When he reached the end of the corridor on the third

floor, he turned down another small hall and spied light beneath a door, and decided upon that as his beginning.

Without knocking, he turned the knob and let himself into a small but elegant bedroom. The sole occupant was a woman with gray hair, who looked up from her desk with obvious but fearless amazement.

This was just what he had hoped for. He approached the desk.

There was a book open there under her left hand, and with her right she'd been underlining words in it.

It was Boethius. *De topicis differentiis.* And she had underlined the sentence, "Syllogism is discourse in which, when certain things have been laid down and agreed to, something other than the things agreed to must result by means of the things agreed to."

He laughed. "Excuse me," he said to the woman.

She was looking up at him, and had not moved at all since he entered.

"It's true but it's funny, isn't it? I had forgotten."

"Who are you?" she asked.

The gravel in her voice, the age of it perhaps, startled him. Her gray hair was heavy and worn in an old-fashioned bun on the back of her head rather than the sexless bob of the present fashion.

"I'm being rude, I know," he said. "I always know when I'm being rude, and I beg your pardon."

"Who are you?" she asked again in almost precisely the same tone of voice as before, except that she put a space after each word for emphasis.

"*What* am I?" he asked. "That's the more important question. Do you know what I am?"

"No," she said. "Should I?"

"I don't know. Look at my hands. See how long and thin they are."

"Delicate," she said in the same gravelly voice, her eyes moving only very quickly to his hands and then back to his face. "Why have you come in here?"

"My methods are those of a child," he said. "That is my only way of operating."

"So?"

"Did you know that Aaron Lightner was dead?"

She held his gaze for a moment and then slipped back in her chair, her right hand releasing the green marker. She looked away. It was a dreadful revelation to her.

"Who told you?" she asked. "Does everyone know?"

"Apparently not," he said.

"I knew he wouldn't come back," she said. She pursed her mouth so that the heavy lines above her lips were very defined and dark for a moment. "Why have you come here to tell me this?"

"To see what you would say. To know whether or not you had a hand in killing him."

"What?"

"You heard what I said, did you not?"

"Killing him?" She rose slowly from her chair and gave him a cruel look, especially now that she realized how very tall he was. She looked to the door—indeed, she seemed about ready to move towards it—but he lifted his hand, gently, asking for her patience.

She weighed this gesture.

"You're saying Aaron was killed by someone?" she asked. Her brows grew heavy and wrinkled over the silver frames of her glasses.

"Yes. Killed. Deliberately run over by a car. Dead."

The woman closed her eyes this time, as if, unable to leave, she would allow herself to feel this appropriately. She looked straight ahead, dully, with no thought of him standing there, apparently, and then she looked up.

"The Mayfair witches!" she said in a harsh, deep whisper. "God, why did he go there?"

"I don't think it was the witches who did it," he said.

"Then who?"

"Someone from here, from the Order."

"You don't mean what you're saying! You don't know what you're saying. No one of us would do such a thing."

"Indeed I do know what I'm saying," he said. "Yuri, the gypsy, said it was one of you, and Yuri wouldn't lie in such a matter. Yuri tells no lies as far as I can tell, none whatsoever."

"Yuri. You've seen Yuri. You know where he is?"

"Don't you?"

"No. One night he left, that's all anyone knows. Where is he?"

"He is safe, though only by accident. The same villains who killed Aaron have tried to kill him. They had to."

"Why?"

"You're innocent of all this?" He was satisfied.

"Yes! Wait, where are you going?"

"Out, to find the killers. Show me the way to the Superior General. I used to know the way, but things change. I must see him."

She didn't wait to be asked twice. She sped past him and beckoned for him to follow. Her thick heels made a loud sound on the polished floor as she marched down the corridor, her gray head bowed, and her hands swinging naturally at her sides.

It seemed forever that they walked, until they had reached the very opposite end of the main corridor. The double doors. He remembered them. Only in former times they had not been cleaned and polished to such a luster. They'd been layered with old oil.

She pounded on the door. She might wake the entire house. But he knew no other way to do this.

When the door opened, she went inside, and then turned very pointedly to reveal to the man within that she was with another.

The man within looked out warily, and when he saw Ash, his face was transformed from amazement to shock and immediate secrecy.

"You know what I am, don't you?" said Ash softly.

He quickly forced his way into the room and closed the doors behind him. It was a large office with an adjoining bedroom. Things were vaguely messy, lamps scattered and dim, fireplace empty.

The woman was watching him with the same ferocious look. The man had backed up as if to get clear of something dangerous.

"Yes, you know," said Ash. "And you know that they killed Aaron Lightner."

The man was not surprised, only deeply alarmed. He was

172

large and heavily built, but in good health, and he had the air of an outraged general who knows that he is in danger. He did not even try to pretend to be surprised. The woman saw it.

"I didn't know they were going to do it. They said you were dead, you'd been destroyed."

"I?"

The man backed up. The man was now in terror. "I was not the one who gave the order to kill Aaron. I don't even know the purpose of the order, or why they wanted you here. I know next to nothing."

"What does all this mean, Anton?" the woman asked. "Who is this person?"

"Person. Person. What an inappropriate word," said the man called Anton. "You're looking at something that . . ."

"Tell me what part you played in it," Ash said.

"None!" he said. "I'm the Superior General here. I was sent here to see that the wishes of the Elders were carried out."

"Regardless of what those wishes were?"

"Who are you to question me?"

"Did you tell your men to bring the Taltos back to you?"

"Yes, but that's what the Elders told me to do!" said the man. "What are you accusing me of? What have I done that you should come here, demanding answers of me? The Elders picked those men, not I." The man took a deep breath, all the while studying Ash, studying the small details of his body. "Don't you realize my position?" the man asked. "If Aaron Lightner's been harmed, don't you realize it's the will of the Elders?"

"You accept this. Does anyone else?"

"No one else knows, and no one is meant to know," said the man indignantly.

The woman let out a small gasp. Perhaps she hoped that Aaron was not dead after all. Now she knew.

"I have to tell the Elders you're here," said the man. "I must report your appearance at once."

"How will you do that?"

The man gestured to the fax machine on the desk. The office was large. Ash had scarcely noticed. The fax was a plain-paper fax, replete with many glowing lights and trays for paper. The desk was full of drawers. Probably one of these harbored a gun.

"I'm to notify them immediately," said the man. "You'll have to excuse me now."

"I don't think so," said Ash. "You are corrupt. You are no good. I can see this. You sent men from the Order to do harm."

"I was told by the Elders."

"Told? Or paid?"

The man was silent. In a panic he looked to the woman. "Call for help," he said. He looked at Ash. "I said they were to bring you back. What happened was not my doing. The Elders said I was to come here and do what I had to do, at all costs."

Once again, the woman was visibly shocked. "Anton," she said in a whisper. She didn't move to pick up the phone.

"I give you one final chance," said Ash, "to tell me something that will prevent me from killing you." This was a lie. He realized it as soon as the words were out of his mouth, but on the other hand, perhaps the man would say something.

"How dare you!" said the man. "I have but to raise my voice and help will come to me."

"Then do it!" said Ash. "These walls are thick. But you should try it."

"Vera, call for help!" he cried.

"How much did they pay you?" asked Ash.

"You know *nothing* about it."

"Ah, but I do. You know what I am, but very little else. Your conscience is decrepit and useless. And you're afraid of me. And you lie. Yes, you lie. In all probability you were very easy to corrupt. You were offered advancement and money, and so you cooperated with something you knew to be evil."

He looked at the woman, who was plainly horrified.

"This has happened before in your Order," he said.

"Get out of here!" said the man. He cried out for help,

his voice sounding very big in the closed room. He cried again, louder.

"I intend to kill you," said Ash.

The woman cried, "Wait." She had her hands out. "You can't do things this way. There's no need. If some deliberate harm came to Aaron, then we must call the Council immediately. The house is filled this time of year with senior members. Call the Council now. I'll go with you."

"You can call them when I am gone. You are innocent. I don't intend to kill you. But you, Anton, your cooperation was necessary for what took place. You were bought, why don't you admit this to me? Who bought you? Your orders did not come from the Elders."

"Yes, they did."

The man tried to dart away. Ash reached out, easily catching hold of the man due to the uncommon length of his arms, and he wrapped his fingers very tightly around the man's throat, more tightly perhaps than a human being could have done. He began to squeeze the life out of the man, doing it as rapidly as he could, hoping his strength was sufficient to break the man's neck, but it wasn't.

The woman had backed away. She'd snatched up the telephone and was now speaking into it frantically. The man's face was red, eyes bulging. As he lost consciousness, Ash squeezed tighter and tighter until he was very sure the man was dead, and would not rise from the floor gasping for breath, as it sometimes happened. He let the man drop.

The woman dropped the telephone receiver.

"Tell me what happened!" she cried. It was almost a scream. "Tell me. what happened to Aaron! Who are you?"

Ash could hear people running in the hallway.

"Quickly, I need the number through which I can reach the Elders."

"I can't give you that," she said. "That's known only to us."

"Madam, don't be foolish. I have just killed this man. Do as I ask you."

She didn't move.

"Do it for Aaron," he said, "and for Yuri Stefano."

She stared at the desk, her hand rising to her lips, and

then she snatched up a pen, wrote something fast on a piece of white paper, and thrust it towards him.

There was a pounding on the double doors.

He looked at the woman. There was no time to talk further.

He turned and opened the doors, to face a large group of men and women who had only just come to a halt, to range round him and look at him.

Here were some who were old and others quite young, five women, four men, and a boy very tall, but still almost beardless. The old gentleman from the library stood among them.

He closed the doors behind him, hoping to delay the woman.

"Do you—any of you—know who I am?" Ash asked. Quickly he looked from face to face, eyes darting back and forth until he was certain he had memorized the features of each person. "Do you know what I am? Answer me, please, if you know."

Not a single one gave him anything but a puzzled expression. He could hear the lady crying inside the room, a thick, heavy sobbing rather like her speaking voice, roughened with age.

Alarm was now spreading through the group. Another young man had arrived.

"We have to go in," said one of the women. "We have to see what's happened inside."

"But do you know me? You!" Ash spoke to the latecomer now. "Do you know what I am and why I might have come here?"

None of them did. None of them knew anything. Yet they were people of the Order, scholars all, not a service person among them. Men and women in the prime of life.

The woman in the room behind him tugged at the knobs of the doors, then flung them open. Ash stepped to the side.

"Aaron Lightner's dead!" she cried. "Aaron's been murdered."

There were gasps, small cries of dismay and surprise. But all around, there was innocence. The old man from the library looked mortally wounded by this news. Innocent.

It was time to get away.

Ash pushed through the loose gathering quickly and decisively and made for the stairs, going down two by two before anyone followed. The woman screamed for them to stop him, to not let him escape. But he had too good a head start, and his legs were so much longer than theirs.

He reached the side exit before his pursuers found the top of the little stairway.

He went out into the night and walked fast across the wet grass, and then, glancing back, began to run. He ran until he had reached the iron fence, which he easily vaulted, and then he walked up to his car and made a hasty gesture for his driver to open the door for him and then take off out of here.

He sat back as the car moved faster and faster on the open highway.

He read the fax number written by the woman on a piece of paper. It was a number outside of England, and if memory served him right, it was in Amsterdam.

He pulled loose the phone hooked beside him on the wall of the car, and he punched in the number for the long-distance operator.

Yes, Amsterdam.

He memorized the number, or tried to, at least, and then he folded the paper and put it into his pocket.

When he returned to the hotel, he wrote down the fax number, ordered supper, then bathed at once, and watched patiently as the hotel waiters laid out for him a large meal on a linen-draped table. His assistants, including the pretty young Leslie, stood anxiously by.

"You're to find me another place of residence as soon as it's daybreak," he told Leslie. "A hotel as fine as this one, but something much larger. I need an office and several lines. Come back for me only when everything is arranged."

The young Leslie seemed overjoyed to be so commissioned and empowered, and off she went with the others in tow. He dismissed the waiters, and began to consume the meal of sumptuous pasta in cream sauce, lots of cold milk, and the meat of a lobster, which he did not like, but which was, nevertheless, white.

Afterwards he lay on the sofa, quietly listening to the crackling of the fire and hoping perhaps for a gentle rainfall.

He also hoped that Yuri would return. It wasn't likely. But he had insisted they remain here at Claridge's on the chance that Yuri would trust them again.

At last Samuel came in, so drunk that he staggered. His tweed jacket was slung over his shoulder, and his white shirt was rumpled. Only now did Ash see that the shirt was specially made, as the suit had been, to fit Samuel's grotesque body.

Samuel lay down by the fire, awkward as a whale. Ash got up, gathered some soft pillows from the couch, and put them beneath Samuel's head. The dwarf opened his eyes, wider than usual, it seemed. His breath was fragrant from drink. His breath came in snorts, but none of this repelled Ash, who had always loved Samuel.

On the contrary, he might have argued to anyone in the world that Samuel had a rocklike, carven beauty, but what would have been the use?

"Did you find Yuri?" Samuel asked.

"No," said Ash, who remained down on one knee, so that he could speak to Samuel almost in a whisper. "I didn't look for him, Samuel. Where would I begin in all of London?"

"Aye, there is no beginning and no end," said Samuel with a deep and forlorn sigh. "I looked wherever I went. Pub to pub to pub. I fear he'll try to go back. They'll try to kill him."

"He has many allies now," said Ash. "And one of his enemies is dead. The entire Order has been alerted. This must be good for Yuri. I have killed their Superior General."

"Why in the name of God did you do that?" Samuel forced himself up on his elbow and struggled to gain an upright position, but Ash had finally to help him.

Samuel sat there with his knees bent, scowling at Ash.

"Well, I did it because the man was corrupt and a liar. There cannot be corruption in the Talamasca that isn't dangerous. And he knew what I was. He believed me to be Lasher. He pleaded the Elders as his cause when I threatened his life. No loyal member would have mentioned the Elders to anyone outside, or said things that were so defensive and obvious."

"And you killed him."

"With my hands, the way I always do. It was quick. He didn't suffer much, and I saw many others. None of them knew what I was. So what can one say? The corruption is near the top, perhaps at the very top, and has not by any means penetrated to the rank and file. If it has, it has penetrated in some confused form. They do not know a Taltos when they see one, even when given ample opportunity to study the specimen."

"Specimen," said Samuel. "I want to go back to the glen."

"Don't you want to help me, so that the glen remains safe, so that your revolting little friends can dance and play the pipes, and kill unsuspecting humans and boil the fat from their bones in cauldrons?"

"You have a cruel tongue."

"Do I? Perhaps so."

"What will we do now?"

"I don't know the next step. If Yuri hasn't returned by morning, I suppose that we should leave here."

"But I like Claridge's," Samuel grumbled. He keeled over, eyes closing the moment he hit the pillow.

"Samuel, refresh my memory," Ash said.

"About what?"

"What is a syllogism?"

Samuel laughed. "Refresh your memory? You never knew what a syllogism was. What do you know about philosophy?"

"Too much," said Ash. He tried to remember it himself. All men are beasts. Beasts are savage. Therefore all men are savage.

He went into the bedroom and lay down on the bed.

For one moment, he saw again the pretty-haired witch, Yuri's beloved. He imagined that her naked breasts were

179

pressed gently against his face, and that her hair covered them both like a great mantle.

Then he was fast asleep. He dreamed he was walking through the doll museum in his building. The marble tile had just been polished, and he could see all the many colors, and how colors changed depending upon what color was right beside them. All the dolls in their glass cases began to sing—the modern, the antique, the grotesque, the beautiful. The French dolls danced, and swung their little bell-shaped dresses as they did so, their round little faces full of glee, and the magnificent Bru dolls, his queens, his most treasured queens, sang high soprano, their paperweight eyes glistening in the fluorescent lights. Never had he heard such music. He was so happy.

Make dolls that can sing, he thought in his dream, dolls that can really sing—not like the old ones that were bad mechanical toys, but dolls with electronic voices that will sing forever. And when the world ends, the dolls will still sing in the ruins.

Ten

"THERE'S NO QUESTION," said Dr. Salter. She set down the manila folder on the edge of the desk. "But it didn't happen six weeks ago."

"Why do you say that?" said Mona. She hated this little examining room because it didn't have any windows. Made her feel she was going to smother.

"Because you're almost three months along, that's why." The doctor approached the table. "Here, you want to feel it yourself? Give me your hand."

Mona let the doctor lift her wrist and then place her hand on her own belly.

"Press hard. You feel that? That's the baby. Why do you think you're wearing that loose thing? You can't stand anything tight against your waist, now, can you?"

"Look, my aunt bought me these clothes. They were hanging there, or it was hanging there." What was it, damn it, oh yeah, linen, black for funerals, or for looking nifty with fancy high-heeled black-and-white string shoes. "I can't be that pregnant," said Mona. "That's just not possible."

"Go home and check your computer log, Mona. You are."

Mona sat up, and jumped down from the table, smoothing down the black skirt and quickly slipping into the fancy shoes. No need to lace or unlace, though if Aunt Gifford had seen her stuffing her foot like that into an expensive shoe, she would have screamed.

181

"I gotta go," she said. "I'm expected at a funeral."

"Not that poor man who married your cousin, the one killed by the car?"

"Yep, that poor man. Listen, Annelle. Can we do one of those tests where you see the fetus?"

"Yes, and it will confirm exactly what I've been telling you—that you're twelve weeks along. Now listen, you have to take all the supplements I'm giving you. A thirteen-year-old body is not ready to have a baby."

"Okay, I want to make an appointment for that test where we look at it." Mona started for the door, and had her hand on the knob when she stopped. "On second thought," she said, "I'd rather not."

"What's the matter?"

"I don't know. Let's just leave it alone in there for a while. Tests can be scary, can't they?"

"My God, you're turning white."

"No, I'm not, I'm just going to faint like women in the movies."

She went out, passing through the small, carpeted outer office, and out the door, though the doctor was calling to her. The door swished shut heavily, and she hurried through the glass-enclosed lobby.

The car was waiting at the curb. Ryan stood beside it, arms folded. Dressed in dark blue for the funeral, he looked almost the same as always, except that his eyes were watery now, and he was plainly very tired. He opened the door for her.

"Well, what did Dr. Salter say?" he asked. He turned to look at her, up and down and with care.

She really wished everybody would stop looking at her.

"I'm pregnant all right," said Mona. "Everything's OK. Let's get out of here."

"We're going. Are you unhappy? Perhaps this has all begun to sink in."

"Of course I'm not unhappy. Why would I be unhappy? I'm thinking about Aaron. Has Michael or Rowan called?"

"No, not yet. They're probably asleep right now. What's the matter, Mona?"

"Ryan, chill, OK? People keep asking me what's the

182

matter. Nothing's the matter. Things are just happening . . . awfully fast."

"You have a very uncharacteristic look on your face," said Ryan. "You look frightened."

"Naw, just wondering what it's going to be like. My own child. You did tell everybody, didn't you? No sermons or lectures."

"It wasn't necessary," he said. "You're the designee. No one is going to say anything to you. If anyone were likely, it would be me. But I can't bring myself to make the requisite speeches, to issue the usual warnings and reservations."

"Good," she said.

"We've lost so many, and this is a brand-new life, and I see it rather like a flame, and I keep wanting to cup my hands around it and protect it."

"You're flipping out, Ryan. You're really tired. You need to rest for a while."

"Do you want to tell me now?"

"Tell you what?"

"The identity of the father, Mona. You do plan to tell us, don't you? Is it your cousin David?"

"No, it's not David. Forget about David."

"Yuri?"

"What is this? Twenty questions? I know who the father is, if that's what you're wondering, but I don't want to talk about it now. And the identity of the father can be confirmed as soon as the baby's born."

"Before then."

"I don't want any needles going into this baby! I don't want any threat to it. I told you I know who the father is. I'll tell you when it's . . . when I think it's time."

"It's Michael Curry, isn't it?"

She turned and glared at him. Too late now to field the question. He had seen it in her face. And he looked so exhausted, so without the usual backbone. He was like a man on strong medicine, a little punchy, and more open than usual. Good thing they were in the limo, and he wasn't driving. He would go straight into a fence.

"Gifford told me," he said, speaking slowly, in the same

183

druggy fashion. He looked out the window. They were driving slowly down St. Charles Avenue, the prettiest stretch of newer mansions and very old trees.

"Come again?" she asked. "Gifford told you? Ryan, are you OK?" What would happen to this family if Ryan went off his rocker? She had enough to worry about as it was. "Ryan, answer me."

"It was a dream I had last night," he said, turning to her finally. "Gifford said the father was Michael Curry."

"Was Gifford happy or sad?"

"Happy or sad." He pondered. "Actually, I don't remember."

"Oh, so that's great," said Mona. "Even now that she's dead, no one is paying attention to what she says. She comes in a dream, and you don't even pay attention."

This startled him, but only a little. He took no offense, as far as she could tell. When he looked at her, his eyes were remote and very peaceful.

"It was a nice dream, a good dream. We were together."

"What did she look like?" There was really something wrong with him. I'm alone, she thought. Aaron's been murdered. Bea needs our sympathy; Rowan and Michael haven't called in yet, we're all scared, and now Ryan is drifting, and maybe, just maybe, that is all for the best.

"What did Gifford look like?" she asked again.

"Pretty, the way she always looked. She always looked the same to me, you know, whether she was twenty-five or thirty-five, or fifteen even. She was my Gifford."

"What was she doing?"

"Why do you want to know?"

"I believe in dreams. Ryan, please tell me. Think back—was Gifford doing anything?"

He shrugged, and gave a little smile. "She was digging a hole, actually. I think it was under a tree. I believe it was Deirdre's oak. Yes, that's what it was, and the dirt was piled high all around her."

For a moment Mona didn't answer. She was so shaken she didn't trust her voice.

He drifted away again, looking out the window, as if he'd already forgotten they were talking.

184

She felt a pain in her head, very sharp, through both temples. Maybe the movement of the car was making her sick. That happened when you were pregnant, even if the baby was normal.

"Uncle Ryan, I can't go to Aaron's funeral," she said suddenly. "The car is making me feel sick. I want to go, but I can't. I have to go home. I know it sounds stupid and self-centered, but . . ."

"I'll take you right home," he said gallantly. He reached up and pressed the intercom. "Clem, take Mona to First Street." He shut off the intercom. "You did mean First Street, didn't you?"

"Yeah, I certainly did," said Mona. She had promised Rowan and Michael she would move in immediately, and she had. Besides, it was more home than Amelia Street, with her mother gone, and her father dead drunk now, only getting up occasionally at night to look for his bottles or his cigarettes, or his dead wife.

"I'm going to call Shelby to stay with you," said Ryan. "If Beatrice didn't need me, I'd stay with you myself."

He was very concerned. This certainly was a whole new ball game. He was positively doting on her, the way he used to do when she was very little, and Gifford would dress her in lace and ribbons. She should have known he would react like this. He loved babies. He loved children. They all did.

And I'm not a child anymore to them, not at all.

"No, I don't need Shelby," she said. "I mean, I want to be alone. Just alone up there, with only Eugenia. I'll be all right. I'll take a nap. That's a beautiful room up there, to nap in. I've never been there alone before. I have to think and sort of feel things. And besides, the fences are being patrolled by a force equivalent to the French Foreign Legion. Nobody's going to get in there."

"You don't mind being in the house itself alone?"

Obviously he was not thinking of intruders, but old stories, stories that had always excited her in the past. They now seemed remote, romantic.

"No, why should I?" she said impatiently.

"Mona, you are some young woman," he said, and he

smiled in a way that she'd seldom seen him smile. Perhaps it took exhaustion and grief to bring him to the point where something so spontaneous could happen with him. "You're not afraid of the baby, and not afraid of the house."

"Ryan, I was never afraid of the house. Never. And as for the baby, the baby's making me sick right now. I'm going to throw up."

"But you're afraid of something, Mona," he said sincerely.

She had to make this good. She couldn't go on like this, with these questions. She turned to him and put her right hand on his knee.

"Uncle Ryan, I'm thirteen. I have to think, that's all. There's nothing wrong with me, and I don't know what scared or frightened means, except for what I have read of those words in the dictionary, OK? Worry about Bea. Worry about who killed Aaron. That's something to worry about."

"OK, Mona dear," he said with another smile.

"You miss Gifford."

"You didn't think I would?" He looked out the window again, not waiting for an answer. "Now, Aaron is with Gifford, isn't he?"

Mona shook her head. He was really bad off. Pierce and Shelby must know how their father needed them.

They had just turned the corner of First Street.

"You have to tell me the minute that Rowan or Michael calls," Mona said. She gathered her handbag and prepared to jump out. "And ... and kiss Bea for me ... and ... Aaron."

"I will," he said. "You're sure you can stay here alone? What if Eugenia isn't here?"

"That would be too much to hope for," she said over her shoulder. Two young uniformed guards were at the gate, and one of them had just unlocked it for her. She gave him a nod as she passed.

When she reached the front door, she put her key into the lock, and was inside within seconds. The door closed as always with a deep, muffled, heavy sound, and she collapsed against it with her eyes shut.

Twelve weeks, that was flat-out impossible! This baby

186

had started when she slept with Michael the second time. She knew it! She knew it as surely as she knew anything else. Besides, there just wasn't anybody between Christmas and Mardi Gras! No, twelve weeks was out of the question!

Crisis! Think.

She headed for the library. They had brought her computer over last night and she'd set it up, creating a small station to the right of the big mahogany desk. She flopped in the chair now, and at once booted the system.

Quickly she opened a file: / WS / MONA / SECRET / Pediatric.

"Questions that must be asked," she wrote. "How fast did Rowan's pregnancy progress? Were there signs of accelerated development? Was she unusually sick? No one knows these answers because no one knew at that time that Rowan was pregnant. Did Rowan appear pregnant? Rowan must still know the chronology of events. Rowan can clarify everything, and wash away these stupid fears. And of course there was the second pregnancy, the one no one else knows about, except Rowan and Michael and me. Do you dare ask Rowan about this second . . ."

Stupid fears. She stopped. She sat back and rested her hand on her belly. She didn't press down to feel the hard little lump that Dr. Salter had let her feel. She simply opened her fingers and clasped her belly loosely, realizing that it was altogether bigger than it had ever been.

"My baby," she whispered. She closed her eyes. "Julien, help me, please."

But she felt no answer coming to her. That was all past.

She wanted so to talk to Ancient Evelyn, but Ancient Evelyn was still recovering from the stroke. She was surrounded by nurses and equipment in her bedroom at Amelia Street. She probably didn't even know that they'd brought her home from the hospital at all. It would be too maddening to sit there babbling out her heart to Ancient Evelyn and then realize that Ancient Evelyn couldn't understand a word she said.

No one, there is no one. Gifford!

She went to the window, the very one that had been opened that day so mysteriously, perhaps by Lasher, she'd

187

never know. She peered out through the green wooden shutters. Guards on the corner. A guard across the street.

She left the library, walking slowly, falling into a dragging rhythm almost, though she didn't know why, except that she was looking at everything that she passed, and when she stepped out into the garden, it seemed gloriously green and crowded to her, with the spring azaleas almost ready to bloom, and the ginger lilies laden with buds, and the crape myrtles filled with tiny new leaves, making them enormous and dense.

All the bare spaces of winter had been closed. The warmth had unlocked everything, and even the air breathed a sigh of relief.

She stood at the back garden gate, looking at Deirdre's oak, and the table where Rowan had sat, and the fresh green grass growing there, brighter and more truly green than the grass around it.

"Gifford?" she whispered. "Aunt Gifford." But she knew she didn't want a ghost to answer her.

She was actually afraid of a revelation, a vision, a horrible dilemma. She placed her hand on her belly again and just let it stay there, warm, tight.

"The ghosts are gone," she said. She realized she was talking to the baby as well as herself. "That's finished. We aren't going to need those things, you and I. No, never. They've gone to slay the dragon, and once the dragon's dead, the future's ours—yours and mine—and you'll never even have to know all that happened before, not till you're grown and very bright. I wish I knew what sex you were. I wish I knew the color of your hair—that is, if you have any. I should give you a name. Yes, a name."

She broke off this little monologue.

She had the feeling someone had spoken to her— somebody very close had whispered something—just a tiny fragment of a sentence—and it was gone, and she couldn't catch it now. She even turned around, spooked suddenly. But of course no one was near her. The guards were around the periphery. Those were their instructions, unless they heard an alarm sound in the house.

She slumped against the iron post of the gate. Her eyes

moved over the grass again and up over the thick black arms of the oak. The new leaves burst forth in brilliant mint-green clusters. The old leaves looked dusty and dark and ready perhaps to dry up and drop away. The oaks of New Orleans were never really barren, thank heaven. But in spring they were reborn.

She turned around and looked to her right, towards the very front of the property. Flash of a blue shirt beyond the front fence. It was more quiet than she'd ever known it to be. Possibly even Eugenia had gone to Aaron's funeral. She hoped so.

"No ghosts, no spirits," she said. "No whispers from Aunt Gifford." Did she really want there to be any? Suddenly, for the first time in her life, she wasn't so sure. The whole prospect of ghosts and spooks confused her.

Must be the baby, she thought, and one of those mysterious mental changes that comes over you, even this early, guiding you to a sedentary, unquestioning existence. Spirits were not the thing, now. The baby was everything. She'd read plenty on these physical and mental changes last night in her new books on pregnancy, and she had plenty more to read.

The breeze stole through the shrubbery as it always had, grabbing loose petals and leaves and little blossoms here and there, and tumbling them across the purple flags, then dying away to nothing. A slow warmth rose from the ground.

She turned and walked back inside, and through the empty house to the library.

She sat down at the computer and began to write.

"You would not be human if you did not have these doubts and suspicions. How can you not wonder whether or not the baby is all right, under these circumstances? Undoubtedly, this fear has some hormonal origin, and it is a survival mechanism. But you are not a mindless incubator. Your brain, though flooded with new chemicals and combinations of chemicals, is still your brain. Look at the facts.

"Lasher guided the earlier disaster from the beginning. Without the intervention of Lasher, Rowan might have had a completely healthy and beautiful . . ."

She stopped. But what did that mean, Lasher's intervention?

The phone rang, startling her, even hurting her a little. She reached for it hastily, not wanting it to ring again.

"Mona here, start talking," she said.

There was a laugh on the other end. "That's a hell of a way to answer, kid."

"Michael! Thank God. I *am* pregnant, Dr. Salter says there is absolutely no doubt."

She heard him sigh. "We love you, sweetheart," he said. "Where are you?"

"We're in some frightfully expensive hotel in a French-style suite full of fruitwood chairs standing on tiptoe. Yuri is well, and Rowan is examining this gunshot wound of his. It's become infected. I want you to wait on talking to Yuri. He's overexcited, and talking out of his head a little, but otherwise OK."

"Yeah, sure. I don't want to tell him now about this baby."

"No, that wouldn't be good at all."

"Give me your number."

He gave her the number.

"Honey, are you okay?"

Here we go again, even he can tell that you're worried about it. And he knows why you might be worried. But don't say anything! No, not one word. Something inside her closed up, fearful suddenly of Michael, the very person she'd wanted so to talk to, the very person, along with Rowan, whom she'd felt she could trust.

Play this carefully.

"Yeah, I'm fine, Michael. Ryan's office has your number?"

"We're not going to disappear, honey."

She realized she was staring at the screen, at the questions she had so intelligently and logically listed:

How fast did Rowan's pregnancy progress? Were there signs of accelerated development?

Michael would know these answers. No, don't let on.

"I'm going to go, honey. I'll call you later. We all love you."

" 'Bye, Michael."

She hung up the phone.

She sat quiet for a long time, then began to type rapidly:

"It is too early to ask them stupid questions about this baby, too early to have fears which may affect your health and your peace of mind, too early to worry Rowan and Michael, who have on their minds much more important things. . . ."

She broke off.

There had been a whisper near her! It was like somebody right next to her. She looked around and then rose and walked across the room, looking back at it to make certain of what she already knew. There had been no one there, no wispy spooks, no shadows even. Her fluorescent desk lamp had taken care of that.

Guards outside on Chestnut? Maybe. But how could she hear them whispering through eighteen inches of solid brick?

Minutes ticked past.

Was she afraid to move? This is crazy, Mona Mayfair. Who do you think it is? Gifford, or your own mother? Oncle Julien come again? Doesn't he deserve a rest now? Maybe this goddamned house was just plain haunted, and always had been, by all kinds of spirits, like the ghost of the upstairs maid from 1859 or that of a coachman who fell to his death tragically from the roof in 1872. Could be. The family didn't write down everything that happened. She started to laugh.

Proletarian ghosts in the Mayfair house on First Street? Ghosts who weren't blood kin? Boy, what a scandal! Nah, there weren't any ghosts here at all.

She looked at the gilt frame of the mirror, the dark brown marble mantel, the shelves of old decaying books. A calm descended on her, kind of comfortable and nice. She loved this place best of all, she thought, and there wasn't any spirit gramophone playing, and no faces in the mirror. You belong here. You're safe. You're home.

"Yes, you and me, kid," she said, talking to the baby again. "This is our house now, with Michael and with

191

Rowan. And I promise you, I will come up with an interesting name."

She sat down again, and began to type as fast as before:

"Nerves on edge. Imagining things. Eat protein, vitamin C for nerves and for general overall condition. Hearing voices whispering in my ear, sounds like . . . sounds like, unsure, but think it sounds like someone singing or even humming! Kind of maddening. Could be a ghost or a deficiency in vitamin B.

"Aaron's funeral is presently under way. This no doubt contributes to overall jumpiness."

Eleven

"**Y**OU'RE CERTAIN THIS was a Taltos?" Rowan asked. She had put away the bandages and the antiseptic, and washed her hands. She stood in the bathroom door of the suite, watching Yuri as he walked back and forth, a dark, gangly, and unpredictable figure against the carefully fringed silks and abundant ormolu of the room.

"Oh God, you don't believe me. It was a Taltos."

"This could have been a human who had a reason for deceiving you," she said. "The height alone does not necessarily mean—"

"No, no, no," Yuri said, in the same crazed and manic tone in which he'd been talking since he'd found them at the airport. "It wasn't human. It was . . . it was beautiful and hideous. Its knuckles were enormous, and its fingers, they were so long. The face could have been human, certainly. Very, very handsome man, yes. But this was Ashlar, Rowan, the very one. Michael, tell her the story. St. Ashlar, from the oldest church in Donnelaith. Tell her. Oh, if only I had Aaron's notes. I know he made them. He wrote down the story. Even though we were excommunicated by the Order, he wouldn't have failed to write everything down."

"He did make notes, son, and we have them," said Michael. "And I've told her everything I know as well."

Michael had already explained this twice, if Rowan wasn't mistaken. The endless repetition and circumlocutions of the day had worn on her. She was badly jet-lagged. Her entire constitution had been aged and weakened, she knew that now, if there had ever been any real hope to the contrary. Thank God she had slept on the plane.

Michael sat against the arm of the fancy French couch, with his socked feet crossed on the gold pillows. He had taken off his jacket, and his chest, in the turtleneck sweater, looked massive, as though it housed a heart that would beat triumphantly for another fifty years. He shot a secretive, commiserating glance at Rowan.

Thank God you are here, she thought. Thank God. Michael's calm voice and manner were beyond reassuring. She could not imagine herself here without him.

Another Taltos. Another one of them! God, what secrets does this world harbor, what monsters are camouflaged amid its forests, its big cities, its wilderness, its seas? Her mind played tricks on her. She could not clearly picture Lasher. The figure was all out of proportion. His strength seemed supernatural. That was not accurate. These creatures were not all-powerful. She tried to banish these jarring memories, of Lasher's fingers bruising her arms, and the back of his hand striking her so hard that she lost consciousness. She could feel that moment of disconnection, and the moment of awakening, when, stunned, she'd found herself trying to crawl, for safety, under the bed. But she had to snap out of this, had to concentrate and make Yuri concentrate.

"Yuri," she said in her most quiet and unobtrusive authoritarian manner, "describe the Little People again. Are you certain—"

"The Little People are a wild race," said Yuri, words coming in a rush as he pivoted, hands out, as if to hold a magic glass in which he saw the images of all that he described. "They're doomed, said Samuel. They have no women anymore. They have no future. They will die out, unless a female Taltos comes among them, unless some female of their kind is found in some other remote part of Europe or the British Isles. And this happens. Mark my words, it happens. Samuel told me. Or a witch, don't you see? A witch? The wise women in those parts never go near the glen. The tourists and the archaeologists go and come in groups and by day."

194

They had been over this, but Rowan had begun to realize that each time he told it, he added something, threw in some new and possibly important detail.

"Of course, Samuel told me all this when he thought I was going to die in that cave. When the fever broke, he was as surprised as I was. And then Ash. Ash has no duplicity in him whatsoever. You cannot imagine the candor or simplicity of this being. Man, I want to say man. Why not man, as long as you remember that he is a Taltos? No human could be so direct, unless he was an idiot. And Ash is not an idiot."

"Then he wasn't lying when he told you he wanted to help you," said Rowan, watching him keenly.

"No, he wasn't lying. And he wants to protect the Talamasca, why I can't tell you. It all has to do with the past, and perhaps the archives, the secrets, though what is really in those archives nobody knows now. Oh, if I could only trust that the Elders were not part of it. But a witch, don't you see, a witch of Mona's power is simply too valuable to Ash and to Samuel. I should never, never have told them about Mona. Oh, I was a fool to tell them all about the family. But you see, this Samuel, he saved my life."

"But did this Taltos say he had no mate?" asked Michael. "If 'mate' is the proper word?"

"That was plainly obvious. He came here because Samuel told him that a Taltos—Lasher, with you, Rowan!—had appeared at Donnelaith. Ash came immediately from someplace far off, I don't know where. Ash is rich. He has bodyguards, attendants, he travels in a little motorcade, so Samuel tells me. Samuel talks too freely, really, for his own good."

"But he didn't mention a female Taltos?"

"No. Both of them gave me the distinct impression that they did not know of the existence of a female Taltos! Rowan, don't you see, the Little People are dying, and the Taltos is damned near extinct. God, Ash could be the only one living, now that Lasher is gone. Imagine it! You see what Mona means to these two?"

"All right, you want my opinion?" asked Michael. He reached for the coffeepot on the tray beside him and refilled his cup, holding it like a mug, without the saucer. "We've done all we can about Ashlar and Samuel." He looked at Rowan as he spoke. "There is a one-in-ten chance, perhaps, that we can locate them at Claridge's even—"

"No, you must not approach them," said Yuri. "You must not even let them know that you are here. Especially not you."

"Yeah, I understand," said Michael, nodding, "but—"

"No, you don't understand," said Yuri, "or you don't believe me. Michael, these creatures can tell a witch when they see it, male or female. They know. They do not require modern medical tests to know that you have the chromosomes which are so precious to them. They know you, by scent perhaps, and surely by sight."

Michael gave a little shrug, as if to say he was reserving judgment, but he wouldn't push this now.

"Okay, so I don't go over there to Claridge's right now. But it's awfully hard not to do that, Yuri. I mean, you're saying that Ash and Samuel are only five minutes away from this hotel."

"God, I hope they are gone. And I hope they are not gone to New Orleans. Why did I tell them? Why was I not more clever? Why was I so foolish in my gratitude and in my fear?"

"Stop blaming yourself for this," said Rowan.

"The guards are quadrupled in New Orleans," said Michael. His relaxed posture hadn't changed. "Let's just leave the subject of Ashlar and Samuel for a moment, and go back to the Talamasca. Now, we were making a list of the oldest members in London, ones who could either be trusted or must surely have smelled a rat."

Yuri sighed. He was very near to a small satin chair by the window, one dressed in the same high-pitched moiré as the draperies, so that it was scarcely visible at all. He flopped down on the edge of it, putting his hands over his mouth. He let out his breath again slowly. His hair was rumpled.

"Okay," said Yuri. "The Talamasca, my refuge, my life. Ah, the Talamasca." He counted now upon his right fingers. "We had Milling, he's bedridden, there's no way to get to him. I don't want to call him and agitate him. Then there was ... there was ..."

"Joan Cross," said Michael. He picked up the yellow pad from the coffee table. "Yeah, Joan Cross. Seventy-five years old, invalid. Wheelchair. Declined to be appointed Superior General due to crippling arthritis."

"Not the devil himself could subvert Joan Cross," said Yuri, words tumbling faster than ever. "But Joan is too self-absorbed. She spends all her time in the archives. She wouldn't notice now if the members were running around naked."

"Then the next one, Timothy Hollingshed," said Michael, reading it from the pad.

"Yes, Timothy, if only I knew him better. No, the one we should select is Stuart Gordon. Did I say Stuart Gordon? I said Stuart Gordon before, didn't I?"

"No, you didn't, but it's quite all right to say it now," said Rowan. "Why Stuart Gordon?"

"He's eighty-seven and he still teaches, at least within the Order itself. Stuart Gordon's closest friend was Aaron! Stuart Gordon may know all about the Mayfair witches. Why, he almost certainly knows! I remember him telling me once in passing, last year it was, that Aaron had been near to the family too long. I swear on my soul that nothing could corrupt Stuart Gordon. He's the man we should take into our confidence."

"Or at least draw out," said Rowan under her breath.

"You have another name here," said Michael. "Antoinette Campbell."

"She's younger, much younger. But if Antoinette is corrupt, then so is God. But Stuart—if there is anyone on that list who may be an Elder, and we never know who they are, you see, it would be Stuart Gordon! That's our man."

"We'll save the other names. We shouldn't contact more than one of these people at a time."

"So what do you lose by contacting Gordon now by telephone?" asked Michael.

"He lets them know he's alive," said Rowan. "But perhaps that's inevitable." She was watching Yuri. How would he ever handle a key phone conversation with anyone in

197

this state? Indeed, the sweat had broken out on him again. He was shaking. She'd gotten him clean clothes, but they were already soaked with sweat.

"Yes, it's inevitable," said Yuri, "but if they don't know where I am, there's no danger. I can get more out of Stuart in five minutes than anyone else I can think of, even my old friend Baron in Amsterdam. Let me make this call."

"But we cannot forget," said Rowan, "that he may be in on the conspiracy. It may be the entire Order. It may be all of the Elders."

"He would rather die than hurt the Talamasca. He has a pair of brilliant novices who might even help us. Tommy Monohan, he's some sort of computer genius. He might be of great assistance in tracing down the corruption. And then there's the other one, the blond one, the pretty one, he has a strange name, Marklin, that's it, Marklin George. But Stuart must judge this situation."

"And we are not to trust Stuart until we know that we can."

"But how will we know?" Yuri looked at Rowan.

"There are ways to know," she said. "You're not going to call from here. And when you do, I want you to say certain things. You cannot open up to this man, you understand, no matter how much you trust him."

"Tell me what to say," said Yuri. "But you realize Stuart may not talk to me. No one may talk to me. I am excommunicated, remember? Unless, of course, I appeal to him as Aaron's friend. That's the key with Stuart! He loved Aaron so much."

"Okay, the phone call is a crucial step," said Michael, "we've got that. Now the Motherhouse, can you draw a plan of the house, or give me the info and I'll draw the plan for your approval? What do you think?"

"Yes, that is an excellent idea," said Rowan. "Draw a plan. Show us the location of the archives, the vaults, the exits, everything."

Yuri was on his feet again, as though someone had shoved him forward. He was looking around.

"Where is the paper? Where is the pencil?"

Michael picked up the phone and asked for the front desk.

"We'll get those things," said Rowan. She took Yuri's hands. They were moist and shaking still. His black eyes were frenzied, darting from object to object. He did not want to look at her. "Take it easy," she said, gripping his hands firmly, thinking *Calm*, and drawing closer, until he had to look right into her eyes.

"I am rational, Rowan," he said. "Believe me. I am only . . . only fearing for Mona. I made a hideous blunder. But how often does one meet such beings? I never laid eyes on Lasher, not for one moment, I was not there when he told his tale to Michael and to Aaron. I never saw him! But I saw these two, and not in some cloud of vapor! They were with me as you are with me, they were in a room!"

"I know," she said. "But it's not your fault, all this, that you told them about the family. You must let this go. Think about the Order. What else can you tell us? What about the Superior General?"

"Something's wrong with him. I don't trust him. He is too new. Oh, if you could have seen this creature Ash, you would not have believed your eyes."

"Why not, Yuri?" she asked.

"Ah, yes. Yes, you saw the other one. You knew the other one."

"Yes, in every sense. What makes you certain this one is older, that he's not trying to confuse you with those easy statements he made?"

"Hair. In his hair, two white streaks. Means age. I could tell it."

"White streaks," she said. This was new information. How much more could Yuri spill if they continued to question him? She lifted her hands to her head, as if to say, Where were these streaks of white hair?

"No, here, from the temples, the graying pattern of humans. These streaks alarmed Samuel as soon as he saw them. The face? The face is that of a man of thirty. Rowan, the lifespan of these beings is unknown. Samuel described Lasher as a newborn."

"That's what he was," said Rowan. She realized suddenly that Michael was watching her. He'd gotten to his feet and was standing near the door, arms folded.

She turned to face him. She blotted all thought of Lasher from her mind.

"There is no one who can help us with this, is there?" Michael said. He was speaking only to her.

"No one," she said. "Haven't you known that all along?"

He didn't answer, but she knew what he was thinking. It was as if he wanted her to know. He was thinking that Yuri was cracking. Yuri had to be protected now. And they had counted more upon Yuri, for judgment, direction, help.

The bell sounded. Michael searched in his pocket and drew out some pound notes as he went to the door.

How extraordinary, she thought, that he remembers such things, that he keeps everything going. But she had to get a grip on herself. Lasher's fingers biting into her arm. Her entire body convulsed suddenly and she reached for the place where he'd hurt her again and again and again. Heed your own advice, Doctor. Be calm.

"Now, Yuri, you have to sit down and draw pictures," said Michael. He had the paper and the pencils.

"What if Stuart doesn't know that Aaron is dead?" asked Yuri. "I don't want to be the one to tell him this. God, they must know. They know, don't they, Rowan?"

"Pay attention," said Rowan gently. "I've explained to you before. Ryan's office did not call the Talamasca. I insisted that they wait. The excommunication gave me my excuse. I wanted time. Now we can use their ignorance to our advantage. We have to plan to have this telephone conversation."

"There's a good-sized desk in the other room," said Michael. "This little Louis Quinze thing will fall apart if we try to use it."

She smiled. He'd said he loved French furniture, but everything in this room seemed to be prancing. The gilded moldings were bubbling up and down the paneled walls as if they were made of neon lights. Hotel rooms, she had been in so many of them. All she could think of when she'd arrived was, Where are the doors, where are the phones, does the bathroom have a window for possible es-

cape? Another flash of Lasher's hand closing on her arm.
She flinched. Michael was watching her.

Yuri was staring off. He hadn't seen her shut her eyes,
and then struggle to catch her breath.

"They know," Yuri said. "Their newspaper clippers will
have seen it in the New Orleans papers. Mayfair. They
will have seen it, and faxed the clippings home. They
know everything," he said. "Absolutely everything. All my
life is in their files."

"All the more reason," said Michael, "to set to work
now."

Rowan stood still. *He's gone, he's dead, he can't hurt
you. You saw his remains, you saw them covered with earth
when you put Emaleth with him. You saw.* She had folded
her arms and she was rubbing her elbows. Michael was
speaking to her, but she hadn't caught the words.

She looked at Michael.

"I have to see this Taltos," she said. "If he exists, I have
to see him."

"It's too dangerous," said Yuri.

"No, it isn't. I have a small plan. It will take us only so
far, but it is a plan. You said that Stuart Gordon was Aaron's friend?"

"Yes, for years they worked together. You want us to
take Stuart into our confidence? You want to trust Ash that
he has told us the truth?"

"You said that Aaron had never heard the word 'Taltos'
until it came from Lasher's lips?"

"That's correct," said Michael.

"You can't contact those two, you can't do it!" said Yuri
frantically.

"Michael, the drawing can wait. I have to call Claridge's."

"No!" cried Yuri.

"I'm not a fool," she said with a small smile. "Under
what name are these odd-sized persons registered?"

"I don't know."

"Describe them," said Michael. "Say the name Samuel.
Yuri said everyone knew him, they treated him as if he

201

were a jolly little Father Christmas. The sooner we make this call the better. They could have already left."

"Aaron never knew what a Taltos was, he never read anything or heard anything—"

"That's right," said Yuri. "Rowan, what are you thinking?"

"All right. I make my call first," said Rowan. "Then you make yours. We should go now."

"Don't you want to tell me what you mean to do?" asked Michael.

"Let's see if we can reach these two. It falls apart if we can't reach them, and we're back to the starting line. Let's go."

"I don't have to draw pictures?" asked Yuri. "You said something about pictures."

"Not now, get your jacket, come on," said Michael. But Yuri looked as helpless and confused as he had all morning. Michael took the jacket off the chair and put it over Yuri's shoulders. He looked at Rowan.

Her heart was pounding. *Taltos.* Got to make this call.

Twelve

MARKLIN HAD NEVER seen the house in such an uproar. This was a test of his talent to dissemble to the max. The council room was crowded with members, but the meeting had not been called to order. No one noticed him as he passed in the corridor. The noise was deafening under the arched wooden ceilings. But this commotion was a blessing. No one seemed to care about one novice and his reactions, or what he did or where he went.

They had not even awakened him to let him know what was happening. He'd stumbled onto all of this when he'd finally opened his door and discovered several members "patrolling" the hallway. He and Tommy had scarcely exchanged words.

But by now Tommy had reached Regent's Park and disconnected the fax interception. All physical evidence of the false communications was being destroyed.

And where was Stuart? Not in the library, not in the parlors, not in the chapel praying for his beloved Aaron, not in the council room, either.

Stuart could not break under this pressure! And if he was gone, if he was gone to be with Tessa . . . But no, he would not have fled. Stuart was with them again. Stuart was their leader, and it was three against the world.

The big case clock in the hallway said 11:00 a.m., the face of the bronze moon smiling above the ornate numerals. In the noise, the chimes were nearly inaudible. When would they begin formal deliberations?

Did he dare to go up to Stuart's room? But wouldn't that be natural for him? Stuart was his tutor within the Order. Wouldn't that be the right thing to do? And what if Stuart was in panic again, crumbling, questioning everything? What if Stuart turned on him again, as he had on Wearyall Hill, and he did not have Tommy to help him bring Stuart back?

Something had just happened. He could hear it in the council room. He took a few steps, until he found himself in the north door. Members were taking their seats around the huge oak table. And there was Stuart, Stuart looking straight at him—a sharp-beaked bird with small, round blue eyes, in the usual somber, almost clerical clothes.

Dear God, Stuart stood beside the empty chair of the Superior General. He had his hand on the back of the chair. They were all looking at Stuart. They had appointed Stuart to take over! Of course.

Marklin reached to cover his imprudent but inevitable smile with a curled hand and a muffled cough. Too perfect, he thought, it's as though the powers that be were on our side. After all, it might have been Elvera, or Joan Cross. It might have been old Whitfield. But it was Stuart! Brilliant! Aaron's oldest friend.

"Come inside, all of you, be seated, please," said Stuart. He was extremely nervous, Marklin could see it. "You must forgive me," said Stuart, forcing a polite smile which was certainly not required and was hardly appropriate. *Dear God, he's not going to be able to pull this off!* "I have not quite recovered yet from my shock. But you know I've been appointed to take over. We're waiting at this very moment for communication from the Elders."

"Surely they've answered, Stuart," said Elvera. Surrounded by cronies, she had been the star all morning, the witness to Anton Marcus's murder, the one who had conversed with the mysterious man who had entered the building and asked strange questions of those he encountered, and then coldly and methodically strangled Marcus to death.

"There is no answer yet, Elvera," said Stuart patiently.

"Sit down there, all of you over there. It's time for this meeting to begin."

At last the room fell silent. The giant table was surrounded by curious faces. Dora Fairchild had been crying, and looked it. So had Manfield Cotter. So had others whom Marklin didn't even know. All friends of Aaron Lightner, or worshipers, to be more correct.

No one here had really known Marcus. His death had horrified everyone, of course. But grief was not a problem there.

"Stuart, has the Mayfair family answered?" came another question. "Do we have any more information about what happened to Aaron?"

"Patience, all of you. I will post the information as soon as it's received. What we know now is that something has gone terribly wrong within this house. Intruders have come and gone. Perhaps there have been other breaches of security. We do not know if all these events are connected."

"Stuart," said Elvera, raising her voice shrilly. "This man asked me if I knew that Aaron was dead! He walked into my room and started talking about Aaron!"

"Of course it's connected," said Joan Cross. Joan had been in a wheelchair for a year now; she looked impossibly frail, even her short white hair was thinning, but her voice was impatient and domineering as it had always been. "Stuart, our first priority is to determine the identity of this killer. We have the authorities telling us the fingerprints are untraceable. But we know that this man might have come from the Mayfair family. They do not."

"Yes . . . all connected somehow, doesn't it seem?" Stuart was actually stammering. "But we have no further indication. That is what I meant." Suddenly his deep-set eyes fixed upon Marklin, who sat almost at the far end of the table, looking calmly at him.

"Gentlemen, to tell you the truth," said Stuart, tearing his eyes away and searching the faces around him, "I'm completely inadequate to take Anton's place. I think . . . I think I should pass the scepter to Joan, if it's all right with the entire assembly. I can't continue!"

Stuart, how could you! Marklin stared at the table, trying to conceal his disappointment just the way he'd tried moments ago to conceal his triumphant smile. You're in the driver's seat, he thought bitterly, but you can't handle it. You're stepping down when you are needed to block the very communication that will hasten things. You are a fool.

"I have no alternative!" said Stuart loudly, as if he were speaking only to his novice. "Gentlemen, I'm too ... I'm too upset over Aaron's death to be of use."

Interesting statement, wise statement, thought Marklin. Stuart had always taught them, if you have some secret you must keep from the psychics around you, think something close to the truth.

Stuart had risen. He was giving the chair to Joan Cross. There were cries of "Aye!" and approval coming from all sides. Even Elvera was nodding. Young Crawford, one of Joan's pupils, was maneuvering her wheelchair into position at the head of the table. Stuart stood back, near the wall. Stuart was going to try to slip out!

Not without me, thought Marklin, but how could he leave now? Stuart wasn't going to get away from him, he wasn't going to get a chance to flee to that secret place where he kept Tessa. No, that was not going to happen.

Once again, there was a hubbub. One of the old men was complaining that in this emergency the Elders present should identify themselves. Someone else had told the old man to be silent, not to mention such a thing again.

Stuart was gone! Quickly, Marklin slipped out of the chair and hurried through the north doorway. He could see Stuart leagues ahead of him, it seemed, moving towards the Superior General's office. Marklin didn't dare call out. There were two younger members with Stuart—Ansling and Perry, both secretarial assistants. They had been a threat to the operation since the beginning, though neither had had the wits to realize that anything had been wrong.

Suddenly the trio disappeared through the double doors and closed them. Marklin stood alone in the empty hall.

A gavel sounded in the council room, or something very like it. Marklin stared at the doors. On what pretext could he enter? To offer his help, his condolences? Everyone knew he was devoted to Stuart. Good God, what should he do under normal circumstances, if he wasn't ... Don't think about it, don't ever clearly dwell upon it, not here, not within these halls.

He glanced at his watch. What were they doing? If Stuart had resigned the position, why was he in that office at all? Perhaps the fax was feeding out a message from the Elders. Tommy had had time to stop the interception. Or perhaps Tommy had written the communication that might be coming in.

At last he couldn't stand it any longer. He marched forward, rapped on the doors, and opened them without waiting for permission.

The two young men were alone in the office, Perry seated at Marcus's desk, talking on the telephone, and Ansling hovering above him, obviously trying to follow the call. The fax was silent. The doors to Anton's bedroom were closed.

"Where is Stuart?" Marklin asked loudly and directly, though both men gestured for him to be silent.

"Where are you now, Yuri?" said Perry into the receiver. *Yuri!*

"You shouldn't be here," said Ansling. "Everyone should be in the council room!"

"Yes, yes ..." Perry was saying, clearly humoring the man on the other end of the line.

"Where is Stuart?" demanded Marklin.

"I can't tell you."

"You will tell me!" said Marklin.

"That's Yuri Stefano on the phone," said Ansling, obviously very ambivalent about what he was revealing, glancing anxiously now from Perry to Marklin. "Stuart's gone to meet him. He told Stuart that he had to come alone."

"Where? How did he leave?"

"Well, down the Superior General's private stairs, I imagine," said Ansling. "How should I know?"

"Shut up, both of you!" said Perry. "Ah, God, he's just rung off!" He slammed down the receiver. "Marklin, get out of here."

"Don't speak to me in that tone, you idiot," said Marklin furiously. "Stuart's my tutor. What private stairs?"

He went right past them, ignoring their indignant and imperious voices, moving through the bedroom and then seeing the perfect cutout of a doorway in the paneling, the unmarked door itself pushed only a few inches ajar. He shoved it back. There was the stairway! Damn!

"Where's he gone to meet Yuri?" he shouted to Ansling, who had only just entered the room.

"Get away from that passage," Perry said. "Get out of this bedroom now. You don't belong in the Superior General's bedroom."

"What's the matter with you, Marklin!" said Ansling. "The last thing we need now is insubordination. Go back to the council room at once."

"I asked you a question. I want to know where my tutor has gone."

"He didn't tell us, and if you'd shut up and stayed out of this, I might have gotten it out of Yuri Stefano myself."

Marklin stared at the two angry, frightened young men. Idiots, he thought, idiots. I hope they blame you and your sniveling, subservient kind for everything. I hope they expel you. He turned and went down the hidden stairs.

A long, narrow passage wound round the corner before leading to a small door. It opened directly to the park, as he knew it would. He had never even noticed this door! There were so many. A few scattered stepping-stones led off across the lawn in the direction, more or less, of the garage.

He broke into a run, but he knew it was useless. When he reached the cars, the attendant was on his feet.

"They've asked everyone to stay in, sir, until the meeting's over."

"Stuart Gordon. Did he take a staff car?"

"No, sir, his own, sir. But his orders were that no one else should leave without express permission, sir, that's what he said."

"I'm sure!" said Marklin furiously. He went directly to his own Rolls, and slammed the door on the attendant who had followed him. He hit thirty before he reached the gates.

On the highway he quickly accelerated to sixty, then seventy, eighty. But Stuart was long gone. And he could not know whether Stuart had even taken the highway—whether it was to Tessa or to Yuri that Stuart had gone. And since he had no idea whatsoever where Tessa was, or Yuri, he was following nothing and no one!

"Tommy, I need you," he said aloud. He reached for the car phone and, with his thumb, punched in the number of the secret digs in Regent's Park.

No answer.

Tommy might have already disconnected everything. Oh, why hadn't they made a plan to meet in London? Surely Tommy would realize the error. Surely Tommy would wait there.

The loud screech of a horn startled him. He slammed down the phone. He had to pay attention to what he was doing. He floored the accelerator and passed the truck in front of him, pushing the Rolls to its top speed.

Thirteen

I**T WAS AN** apartment in Belgravia, not far from Bucking-
ham Palace, and expertly fitted with everything he required. Georgian furnishings surrounded him, a great deal
of fine new white marble, and soft shades of peach, lemon,
oyster white. A staff of expert clerks had been retained to
do his bidding, stringently efficient-looking men and
women who set to work immediately preparing the fax machine for him, the computer, the phones.

He saw that the near-unconscious Samuel was put to bed
properly in the largest of the bedrooms, and then he took
possession of the office, seating himself at the desk to read
through the papers quickly, and absorb whatever he could
of the story of the murder outside London, the man who
had been strangled by a mysterious intruder with very large
hands.

The articles made no mention of his height. Curious. Had
the Talamasca decided to keep this secret, and if so, why?

"Surely Yuri has seen this," he thought, "if Yuri is functioning at all normally." But then, how could he know
whether or not Yuri was?

Messages were already coming in from New York.

Yes, these were things he had to attend to. He couldn't
pretend even for one day, really, that the company could
run without him.

The young Leslie, who apparently never slept, looked radiant as she waited upon him, receiving yet another few
pages from a clerk, and placing them to one side.

"Your lines are connected, sir," she said. "Anything else?"

"Dearest," he said, "see that a great roast is prepared in the kitchen for Samuel. He'll be a bear when he opens his eyes."

He was already punching in the direct line to Remmick in New York as he continued speaking to her.

"See to it that my car and driver are ready for me whenever I need them. Fill the refrigerators with fresh milk, and buy some cheeses for me, soft double- and triple-cream cheeses. All manner of the best Camembert and Brie that you can find. But you must send out for all this. I need you here. Tell me immediately if Claridge's calls with a message, and if you don't hear from them, call every hour on the hour, you understand?"

"Yes, Mr. Ash!" she said zealously, and at once began to scribble everything on a notebook which she held two inches from her eyes.

In a twinkling, she had vanished.

But he was to see her rushing about with marvelous energy every time he glanced up.

It was three o'clock when she came to the desk, with all the enthusiasm of a schoolgirl.

"Claridge's, sir, they want to talk to you personally. Line two."

"Excuse me," he said, pleased to see that she at once backed away.

He picked up the lighted line.

"Yes, this is Ashlar, you are calling me from Claridge's?"

"No. This is Rowan Mayfair. I got your number from Claridge's about five minutes ago. They said you'd left this morning. Yuri is with me. He's afraid of you, but I have to talk to you. I have to see you. Do you recognize my name?"

"Absolutely, Rowan Mayfair," he said softly. "Will you tell me where I can meet you, please? Yuri is unharmed?"

"First tell me why you're willing to meet me. What precisely do you want?"

"The Talamasca is full of treachery," he said. "Last night

211

I murdered their Superior General." No response from her. "The man was part of the conspiracy. The conspiracy is connected with the Mayfair family. I want to restore order to the Talamasca so that it will go on being the Talamasca, and also because I vowed once that I would always look out for the Talamasca. Rowan Mayfair, do you know Yuri is in danger? That this conspiracy is a threat to his life?"

Silence on the other end of the line.

"I haven't lost you, have I?" he asked.

"No. I was just thinking about the sound of your voice."

"The Taltos you bore did not live past infancy. His soul had not been at peace before he was born. You cannot think of me in those terms, Rowan Mayfair, even if my voice reminds you of him."

"How did you kill the Superior General?"

"I strangled him. I did it as mercifully as I could. There was a purpose to what I did. I wanted to expose the conspiracy to the entire Order, so that the innocent might know, as well as the guilty. However, I do not think the problem involves the whole Order, only a few." Silence. "Please let me come to you. I will come alone if you like. We can meet in a crowded place. Perhaps you know you've reached me in Belgravia. Tell me where you are."

"Yuri is meeting with a member of the Talamasca right now. I can't leave him."

"You must tell me where this meeting is taking place." Quickly he stood up and motioned to the doorway. The clerk appeared immediately. "I need my driver!" he whispered. "Now!" He lifted the mouthpiece again. "Rowan Mayfair, this meeting could be dangerous to Yuri. It could be a very, very bad mistake."

"But that man too is coming alone," said Rowan. "And we will see him before he sees us. His name is Stuart Gordon. Does that name mean anything to you?"

"I have heard the name. The man is very old, that's all I can tell you."

Silence. "Do you know anything else about him, anything that would make it likely that he would know about you?"

"No, nothing," he said. "Stuart Gordon and other members of the Talamasca do go from time to time to the glen of Donnelaith. But they have never seen me there. Or anywhere. They have never laid eyes upon me."

"Donnelaith? You're sure it was Gordon?"

"Yes. I am very sure. Gordon used to appear there often. The Little People have told me. The Little People steal things from the scholars during the night. They take their knapsacks, or whatever they can snatch in a moment. I know the name Stuart Gordon. The Little People are careful not to kill the scholars from the Talamasca. It makes trouble to kill them. They don't kill the people of the countryside, either. But they kill other people who wander in with binoculars and rifles. They tell me who comes to the glen."

Silence.

"Please trust me," said Ash. "This man I killed, Anton Marcus, he was corrupt and unscrupulous. I never do these things on impulse. Please accept my word that I am not a danger to you, Rowan Mayfair. I must talk to you. If you will not let me come—"

"Can you find the corner of Brook Street and Spelling?"

"I know where it is," he said. "Are you there now?"

"Yes, more or less. Go to the bookshop. It's the only bookshop on the corner. I'll see you when you arrive there, and I'll come to you. Oh, and do hurry. Stuart Gordon should be here soon."

She rang off.

He hurried down the two flights of steps, Leslie following, asking all the requisite questions: Did he want his guards? Should she go along?

"No, dear, stay here," he said. "Brook and Spelling, just up from Claridge's," he told the driver. "Do not follow me, Leslie." He climbed into the back of the car.

He did not know whether he should take the car to the very meeting place. Surely Rowan Mayfair would see it and memorize its license, if such a thing was even necessary with a Rolls-Royce stretch limousine. But why should he worry? What had he to fear from Rowan Mayfair? What had she to gain from hurting him?

It seemed he was missing something, something extremely important, some probability that would make itself

213

known to him only with pondering and time. But this line of thinking made his head ache. He was far too eager to see this witch. He would go the way of the child.

The limousine bumped and shoved its way through the busy London traffic, arriving at the destination, two busy shopping streets, in less than twelve minutes. "Please stay here, near at hand," he said to the driver. "Keep your eyes on me, and come to me if I call you. You understand?"

"Yes, Mr. Ash."

Fancy shops dominated the corner of Brook and Spelling. Ash got out, stretched his legs for a moment, walked slowly to the edge of the corner, and scanned the crowd, ignoring the inevitable gawkers and the few persons who made loud, good-natured remarks to him about his height.

There was the bookshop, catercorner from him. Very fancy, with polished wood window frames and brass fixtures. It was open, but there was no one standing outside.

He crossed the intersection boldly, walking against the traffic, infuriating a couple of drivers, but he reached the other corner, naturally, unharmed.

There was a small crowd inside the bookshop. None of them witches. But she had said that she would see him and that she would meet him here.

He turned around. His driver was holding the position, in spite of the traffic going around him, with all the arrogance of a chauffeur at the wheel of a monstrous limousine. That was good.

Quickly, Ash surveyed the shops on Brook to his left, and then, looking across, down the length of Spelling, taking the shops and the passersby one by one.

Against the crowded window of a dress shop stood a man and woman. Michael Curry and Rowan Mayfair. It had to be.

His heart quite literally stood still.

Witches. Both of them.

Both of them were looking at him, and they had witches' eyes, and they gave off that very faint sheen that witches always possessed in his eyes.

He marveled. What was it that made the sheen? When he touched them, if he did indeed do that, they would be

214

warmer than other humans, and if he put his ear to their heads, he would hear a low, organic sound that he could not detect in other mammals or people who were not witches. Though occasionally, very occasionally, he had heard this soft, whispering murmur from the body of a living dog.

Good God in heaven, what witches! It had been so long since he had seen witches of this power, and he had never seen witches with more. He didn't move. He merely looked at them, and tried to pull loose from their staring eyes. No easy thing. He wondered if they could tell it. He remained composed.

The man, Michael Curry, was Celtic to the core. He might have been from Ireland, and not America. There was nothing about him that was not Irish, from his curly black hair to his blazing blue eyes and the wool hunting jacket, which he wore for fashion, obviously, and his soft flannel pants. He was a big man, a strong man.

The father of the Taltos, and its murderer! He remembered it with a dull shock. Father . . . killer.

And the woman?

She was very thin and extremely beautiful, though in a completely modern way. Her hair was simple, yet lustrous and alluring, around her narrow face. Her clothes, too, were seductive, calculatedly skimpy, indeed almost flamboyantly erotic. Her eyes were far more frightening than those of the man.

Indeed, she possessed the eyes of a man. It was as though that part of her face had been removed from a male human and put there, above the soft, long, womanish mouth. But he often saw this seriousness, this aggressiveness, in modern females. It's just that this was, well, a witch.

Both were enthralled.

They did not speak to each other, or move. But they were together, one figure slightly overlapping the other. The wind didn't carry their scent to him. It was blowing in the other direction, which meant, strictly speaking, that they ought to catch his.

The woman suddenly broke the stillness, but only with the slight movement of her lips. She had whispered something to her companion. But he remained silent, studying Ash as before.

Ash relaxed all over. He let his hands hang naturally at his sides, which he seldom did, due to the length of his arms. But they must see he concealed nothing. He walked back across Brook Street, very slowly, giving them time to run if they wanted it, though he prayed to God they would not.

He moved towards them slowly on Spelling. They did not move. Suddenly one of the pedestrians bumped him accidentally and dropped an entire paper sack of small items to the pavement with a crash. The sack broke. The items were scattered.

"Now of all times," he thought, but quickly he smiled, and dropped down on one knee and began to pick up everything for the poor individual. "I'm so very sorry," he said.

It was an elderly woman, who gave him a cheery laugh now, and told him that he was too tall to bend down to do such things as this.

"I don't mind at all. It was my fault," he said, shrugging. He was close enough to the witches, perhaps, for them to hear him, but he could not show fear.

The woman had a large canvas bag over her arm. Finally he had gathered up all of the little bundles and deposited them in the canvas bag. And away she went, waving to him as he waved cordially and respectfully to her.

The witches hadn't moved. He knew it. He could feel them watching him. He could feel the same power which caused the sheen to them in his vision, perhaps the same energy. He didn't know. There was now at most twenty feet between them.

He turned his head and looked at them. He had his back to the traffic, and he could see them clearly in front of the plate-glass window full of dresses. How fearsome they both looked. The light emanating from Rowan had become a very subtle glow in his eyes, and now he did smell her—bloodless. A witch who could not bear. The scent of the man was strong, and the face was more terrible, filled with suspicion and perhaps even wrath.

216

It chilled him, the way they looked at him. But everyone cannot love you, he thought with a small smile. Not even all witches can love you. That is far too much to ask. The important thing was that they had not run away.

Again, he started to walk towards them. But Rowan Mayfair startled him. She gestured with a pointing finger, and a hand held close to her breast, for him to look across the street.

Perhaps this is a trick. They mean to kill me, he thought. The idea amused him, but only partially. He looked as she had directed. He saw a coffee shop opposite. And the gypsy was just emerging, with an elderly man at his side. Yuri looked ill, worse than ever, and his haphazard jeans and shirt were far too light for the chilly air.

Yuri saw Ash at once. He stepped clear of the busy entrance. He stared at Ash madly, or so it seemed. Poor soul, he is crazy, thought Ash, truly. The elderly man was talking very intently to Yuri, and did not seem to notice that Yuri was looking away.

This elderly man. It had to be Stuart Gordon! He wore the somber, old-fashioned clothes of the Talamasca, wing-tip shoes and very narrow lapels, and the vest to match his coat. Almost precious. Yes, it was Gordon, surely, or another member of the Talamasca. There could be no mistake.

How Gordon pleaded with Yuri, how distraught he seemed. And Yuri stood not one foot from this man. This man could at any moment kill Yuri in any of a half-dozen secret ways.

Ash started across the street, dodging one car and forcing another to a hasty and noisy stop.

Suddenly, Stuart Gordon realized that Yuri was being distracted. Stuart Gordon was annoyed. He wanted to see what distracted Yuri. He turned just as Ash bore down upon him, reaching the curb, and reaching out to grab Stuart Gordon's arm.

The recognition was indisputable. He knows what I am, thought Ash, and his heart sank slightly for this man. This man, this friend of Aaron Lightner, was guilty. Yes, without question, the man knew him, and gazed up into his face with mingled horror and a deep secretive recognition.

217

"You know me," said Ash.

"You killed our Superior General," said the man, but this he had latched upon in desperation. The confusion and recognition went far beyond anything which had happened only last night. Gordon went into a panic and began to claw at Ash's fingers. "Yuri, stop him, stop him."

"Liar," said Ash, "look at me. You know full well what I am. You know about me. I know you do, don't lie to me, guilty man."

They had become a spectacle. People were cutting out into the street to get around them. Others had stopped to watch.

"Get your hands off me now!" said Stuart Gordon furiously, teeth clenched, face coloring.

"Just like the other," said Ash. "Did you kill your friend Aaron Lightner? What about Yuri? You sent the man who shot him in the glen."

"I know only what I was told about these things this morning!" said Stuart Gordon. "You must release me."

"Must I?" said Ash. "I'm going to kill you."

The witches were beside him. He glanced to his right and saw Rowan Mayfair at his elbow. Michael Curry stood right beside her, eyes full of venom as before.

The sight of the witches struck new terror in Gordon.

Holding tight to Gordon, Ash glanced to the corner and quickly raised his left hand for his driver. The man was out of the car, and had been watching the whole proceedings. He slid behind the wheel at once, and the car was turning to come down the street.

"Yuri! You're not going to let him do this to me, are you?" Gordon demanded. Desperate, brilliant, counterfeit indignation.

"Did you kill Aaron?" Yuri asked. This one was almost insane now, and Rowan Mayfair moved to restrain him as he pressed in on Gordon. Gordon began to writhe in courageous fury, scratching again at Ash's fingers.

The long Rolls-Royce jolted to a halt beside Ash. The driver stepped out immediately.

"Can I help you, Mr. Ash?"

"Mr. Ash," said the terrified Gordon, who stopped his vain struggling. "What sort of name is 'Mr. Ash'?"

"Sir, there's a policeman coming," said the driver. "Tell me what you want me to do."

"Let's get out of here, please," said Rowan Mayfair.

"Yes, all of us, come." Ash turned and dragged Stuart, stumbling, off the sidewalk.

As soon as the back door of the car was open, he flung the helpless Gordon into the backseat. He slipped in beside him, forcing him to the far side. Michael Curry had slipped in the front, beside the driver, and Rowan climbed in now across Ash, her skin burning him as it touched his leg, and took the jumpseat opposite, as Yuri collapsed beside her. The car lurched, then took off.

"Where shall I take you, sir?" the driver called out. The glass panel was sliding down. Now it had vanished into the back of the front seat and Michael Curry had turned and was peering past Yuri, right into Ash's eyes.

These witches, their eyes, thought Ash desperately.

"Just get out of here," said Ash to the driver.

Gordon reached for the door handle.

"Lock the doors," said Ash, but he didn't wait for the familiar electronic click. He clamped his right hand on Gordon's right arm.

"Let go of me, you bastard!" declared Gordon, with low, thundering authority.

"You want to tell me the truth now?" asked Ash. "I'm going to kill you the way I killed your henchman Marcus. What can you tell me that will prevent me from doing it?"

"How dare you, how can you . . ." Stuart Gordon began again.

"Stop lying," said Rowan Mayfair. "You're guilty, and you didn't accomplish this alone. Look at me."

"I will not!" said Gordon. "The Mayfair witches," he said bitterly, all but spitting out the words. "And this thing, this thing you've conjured from the swamps, this Lasher, is it your avenger, your Golem?"

The man was suffering exquisitely. His face was white with shock. But he was far from defeated.

219

"All right," said Ash quietly. "I'm going to kill you, and the witches can't stop me. Do not think that they can."

"No, you won't!" said Gordon, turning so that he might face Ash as well as Rowan Mayfair, his head back against the upholstered corner of the car.

"And why is that?" asked Ash gently.

"Because I have the female!" whispered Gordon.

Silence.

Only the sounds of traffic around them as the car moved speedily and belligerently ahead.

Ash looked at Rowan Mayfair. Then at Michael Curry, peering back at him from the front seat. And finally at Yuri, across from him, who seemed unable to think or to speak. Ash let his eyes return to Gordon.

"I've always had the female," said Gordon, in a small, heartfelt, yet sardonic voice. "I did this for Tessa. I did it to bring the male to Tessa. That was my purpose. Now let go of me, or you will never lay eyes on Tessa, any of you. Especially not you, Lasher, or Mr. Ash, whoever you may be. Whatever you call yourself! Or am I tragically mistaken, and do you have a harem of your own?"

Ash opened his fingers, stretching them, letting them frighten Gordon, and then withdrawing them and laying his hand in his lap.

Gordon's eyes were red and teary. Still stiff with outrage, he pulled out a huge, rumpled handkerchief and blew his tender-looking beak of a nose.

"No," said Ash quietly. "I'm going to kill you now, I think."

"No! You'll never see Tessa!" snapped Gordon.

Ash leaned over him, very close to him. "Then take me to her, please, immediately, or I *will* strangle you now."

Gordon was silent, but only for a moment.

"Tell your driver to go south," he said. "Out of London, towards Brighton. We're not going to Brighton, but that will do for now. It's an hour and a half."

"Then we have time to talk, don't we?" asked the witch, Rowan. Her voice was deep, almost husky. She made a dazzle in Ash's vision, glinting slightly in the dark car. Her breasts were small but beautifully shaped beneath the black silk lapels of the deep-cut jacket. "Tell me how you could do it," she said to Gordon. "Kill Aaron. You're a man like Aaron, yourself."

"I didn't do it," said Gordon bitterly. "I didn't want it done. It was a stupid, stupid, and vicious thing to do. And it happened before I could stop it. Same with Yuri and the gun. I had nothing to do with it. Yuri, in the coffee shop, when I told you I was concerned for your life, I meant it. There are some things which are simply beyond my control."

"I want you to tell us everything now," said Michael Curry. He looked at Ash as he spoke. "We really can't restrain our friend here. And we wouldn't even if we could."

"I'm not telling you anything more," said Gordon.

"That's foolish," said Rowan.

"No, it isn't," said Gordon. "It's the only move I have. Tell you what I know before you reach Tessa, and when you have her, you'll do away with me at once."

"I'll probably do it anyway," said Ash. "You are buying a few hours of life."

"Not so quick. There are many things I can tell you. You have no idea. You'll need much more than a few hours."

Ash didn't reply.

Gordon's shoulders slumped. He took a deep breath, eyeing his captors one by one again, and then returning to Ash. Ash had drawn back until he too was in the corner. He did not wish to be near this human, this feisty and vicious human whom he knew that he would eventually kill.

He looked at his two witches. Rowan Mayfair sat with her hand on her knee, much as Ash did, and she raised her fingers now in a rolling gesture, begging him, perhaps, to be patient.

The snap of a lighter startled Ash.

"Mind if I smoke, Mr. Ash, in your fancy car?" asked Michael Curry from the front seat. His head was already bowed over the cigarette and the tiny flame.

"Please, do what you wish," said Ash with a cordial smile.

To his amazement, Michael Curry smiled back at him.

"There's whiskey in this car," said Ash. "There is ice and water. Would any of you care for a drink?"

"Yeah," said Michael Curry with a little sigh, exhaling the cigarette. "But in the name of virtue, I'll wait till after six."

And this witch can father the Taltos, Ash thought, studying Michael Curry's profile and his slightly crude but charmingly proportioned features. His voice had a lust in it that surely extended to many things, thought Ash. Look at the way he is watching the buildings as we pass them. He misses nothing.

Rowan Mayfair continued to look only at Ash.

They had just left the city proper.

"This is the right way," said Gordon, in a thick voice. "Keep going until I tell you."

The old man looked away as if he were merely checking their position, but then his forehead struck the window hard, and he began to weep.

No one spoke. Ash merely looked at his witches. Then he thought of the photograph of the red-haired one, and when he let his eyes drift to Yuri, who sat directly opposite, beside Rowan, he saw that Yuri's eyes were closed. He had curled up against the side of the car, his head turned away from them, and he too was shedding tears, without making much of a sound.

Ash leant forward to lay a comforting hand on Yuri's leg.

Fourteen

IT WAS ONE o'clock, perhaps, when Mona woke up in the upstairs front bedroom, her eyes turned towards the oaks outside the window. Their branches were filled with bright Resurrection ferns, once again green from the recent spring rain.

"Phone for you," said Eugenia.

Mona almost said, God, I'm glad someone's here. But she didn't like admitting to anyone that she'd been spooked in the famous house earlier, and that her dreams had been deeply disturbing to her.

Eugenia looked askance at Mona's big, billowy white cotton shirt. So what was wrong? It was loungewear, wasn't it? In the catalogs, they called them Poets' Shirts.

"Oughtn't be sleepin' in your pretty clothes!" declared Eugenia. "And look at those beautiful big sleeves all rumpled, and that lace, that delicate lace."

If only she could say *Buzz off*. "Eugenia, it's meant to be rumpled."

There was a tall glass of milk, frosty, luscious looking, in Eugenia's hand. And in the other, an apple on a small white plate.

"Who's this from?" asked Mona, "the Evil Queen?"

Of course, Eugenia didn't know what she was talking about, but it didn't matter. Eugenia pointed to the phone again. Mona was about to pick up the phone when her mind, veering back to the dream, discovered the dream was gone. Like a veil snatched away, it left nothing but a faint memory of texture and color. And the very strange certainty that she must name her daughter Morrigan, a name she'd never heard before.

"And what if you're a boy?" she asked.

She picked up the receiver.

It was Ryan. The funeral was over, and the Mayfair crowd was arriving at Bea's house. Lily was going to stay there for a few days, and so would Shelby and Aunt Vivian. Cecilia was uptown, seeing to Ancient Evelyn, and was doing well.

"Could you offer some old-fashioned First Street hospitality to Mary Jane Mayfair for a while?" asked Ryan. "I can't take her down to Fontevrault till tomorrow. And besides, I think it would be good if you got to know her. And naturally, she's half in love with First and Chestnut and wants to ask you a thousand questions."

"Bring her over," said Mona. The milk tasted good! It was just about the coldest milk she'd ever tasted, which killed all the ickiness of it, which she had never much liked. "I'd welcome her company," she went on. "This place is spooky, you are right."

Instantly she wished she hadn't admitted it, that she, Mona Mayfair, had been spooked in the great house.

But Ryan was off on the track of duty and organization and simply continued to explain that Granny Mayfair, down at Fontevrault, was being cared for by the little boy from Napoleonville, and that this was a good opportunity to persuade Mary Jane to get out of that ruin, and to move to town.

"This girl needs the family. But she doesn't need any more of this grief and misery just now. Her first real visit has for obvious reasons been a disaster. She's in shell shock from the accident. You know she saw the entire accident. I want to get her out of here—"

"Well, sure, but she'll feel closer to everybody afterwards," said Mona with a shrug. She took a big, wet, crunchy bite of the apple. God, was she hungry. "Ryan, have you ever heard of the name Morrigan?"

"I don't think so."

"There's never been a Morrigan Mayfair?"

"Not that I remember. It's an old English name, isn't it?"

"Hmmm. Think it's pretty?"

"But what if the baby is a boy, Mona?"

"It's not, I know," she said. And then caught herself. How in the world could she know? It was the dream, wasn't it, and it also must have been wishful thinking, the desire to have a girl child and bring her up free and strong, the way girls were almost never brought up.

Ryan promised to be there within ten minutes.

Mona sat against the pillows, looking out again at the Resurrection ferns and the bits and pieces of blue sky beyond. The house was silent all around her, Eugenia having disappeared. She crossed her bare legs, the shirt easily covering her knees with its thick lace hem. The sleeves were horribly rumpled, true, but so what? They were sleeves fit for a pirate. Who could keep anything like that neat? Did pirates? Pirates must have gone about rumpled. And Beatrice had bought so many of these things! It was supposed to be "youthful," Mona suspected. Well, it was pretty. Even had pearl buttons. Made her feel like a . . . a little mother!

She laughed. Boy, this apple was good.

Mary Jane Mayfair. In a way, this was the only person in the family that Mona could possibly get excited about seeing, and on the other hand, what if Mary Jane started saying all kinds of wild and witchy things? What if she started running off at the mouth irresponsibly? Mona wouldn't be able to handle it.

She took another bite of the apple. This will help with vitamin deficiencies, she thought, but she needed the supplements Annelle Salter had prescribed for her. She drank the rest of the milk in one Olympian gulp.

"What about 'Ophelia'?" she said aloud. Would that be right, to name a girl child after poor mad Ophelia, who had drowned herself after Hamlet's rejection? Probably not. Ophelia's my secret name, she thought, and you're going to be called Morrigan.

A great sense of well-being came over her. Morrigan. She closed her eyes and smelled the water, heard the waves crashing on the rocks.

A sound woke her, abruptly. She'd been asleep and she didn't know how long. Ryan was standing beside the bed, and Mary Jane Mayfair was with him.

"Oh, I'm sorry," said Mona, swinging her legs over the side of the bed and coming round to greet them. Ryan was already backing out of the room.

"I presume you know," he said, "that Michael and Rowan are in London. Michael said he would call you." Then he was off, headed down the stairs.

Here stood Mary Jane.

What a change from the afternoon she'd come sprouting diagnoses of Rowan. But one had to remember, thought Mona, that those diagnoses had been correct.

Mary Jane's yellow hair was hanging loose and splendid, like flax, over her shoulders, and her big breasts were poking against the tight fit of a white lace dress. There was a little mud, from the cemetery, probably, on her beige high-heeled shoes. She had a tiny, mythical Southern waist.

"Hey there, Mona, I hope this doesn't hang you up, my being here," she said, immediately grabbing Mona's right hand and pumping it furiously, her blue eyes glittering as she looked down at Mona from her seemingly lofty height of about five foot eight inches in the heels. "Listen, I can cut out of here any time you don't want me. I'm no stranger to hitchhiking, I can tell you. I'll get to Fontevrault just fine. Hey, lookie, we're both wearing white lace, and don't you have on the most darlin' little smock? Hey, that's just adorable, you look like a white lace bell with red hair. Hey, can I go out there on the front porch?"

"Yeah, sure, I'm glad to have you here," said Mona. Her hand had been sticky from the apple, but Mary Jane hadn't noticed.

Mary Jane was walking past her.

"You have to push up that window," said Mona, "then duck. But this is really not a dress, it's some kind of shirt or something." She liked the way it floated around her. And she loved the way that Mary Jane's skirts flared from that tiny waist.

Well, this was no time to be thinking about waists, was it?

She followed Mary Jane outside. Fresh air. River breeze.

"Later on, I can show you my computer and my stock-market picks. I've got a mutual fund I've been managing for six months, and it's making millions. Too bad I couldn't afford to actually buy any of the picks."

"I hear you, darlin'," said Mary Jane. She put her hands on the front porch railing and looked down into the street. "This is some mansion," she said. "Yeah, it sure is."

"Uncle Ryan points out that it is not a mansion, it is a town house, actually," said Mona.

"Well, it's some town house."

"Yeah, and some town."

Mary Jane laughed, bending her whole body backwards, and then she turned to look at Mona, who had barely stepped out on the porch.

She looked Mona up and down suddenly, as if something had made an impression on her, and then she froze, looking into Mona's eyes.

"What is it?" asked Mona.

"You're pregnant," said Mary Jane.

"Oh, you're just saying that because of this shirt or smock or whatever."

"No, you're pregnant."

"Well, yeah," said Mona. "Sure am." This girl's country voice was infectious. Mona cleared her throat. "I mean, everybody knows. Didn't they tell you? It's going to be a girl."

"You think so?" Something was making Mary Jane extremely uneasy. By all rights, she should have enjoyed descending upon Mona and making all kinds of predictions about the baby. Isn't that what self-proclaimed witches did?

"You get your test results back?" asked Mona. "You have the giant helix?" It was lovely up here in the treetops. Made her want to go down into the garden.

Mary Jane was actually squinting at her, and then her face relaxed a little, the tan skin without a single blemish and the yellow hair resting on her shoulders, full but sleek.

"Yeah, I have the genes all right," said Mary Jane. "You do too, don't you?"

Mona nodded. "Did they tell you anything else?"

"That it probably wouldn't matter, I'd have healthy children, everybody always did in the family, 'cept for one incident about which nobody is willing to talk."

"Hmmmmm," said Mona. "I'm still hungry. Let's go downstairs."

"Yeah, well, I could eat a tree!"

Mary Jane seemed normal enough by the time they reached the kitchen, chattering about every picture and every item of furniture she saw. Seemed she'd never been *in* the house before.

"How unspeakably rude that we didn't invite you," said Mona. "No, I mean it. We weren't thinking. Everybody was worried about Rowan that afternoon."

"I don't expect fancy invitations from anybody," said Mary Jane. "But this place is beautiful! Look at these paintings on the walls."

Mona couldn't help but take pride in it, the way Michael had refurbished it, and it occurred to her suddenly, as it had upwards of fifty million times in the last week, that this house would someday be hers. Seemed it already was. But she mustn't presume on that, now that Rowan was OK again.

Was Rowan ever going to be really OK? A flash of memory came back to her, Rowan in that sleek black silk suit, sitting there, looking at her, with the straight dark eyebrows and the big, hard, polished gray eyes.

That Michael was the father of her baby, that *she* was pregnant with a baby, that this connected her to both of them—these things suddenly jarred her.

Mary Jane lifted one of the curtains in the dining room. "Lace," she said in a whisper. "Just the finest, isn't it? Everything here is the best of its kind."

"Well, I guess that's true," said Mona.

"And you, too," said Mary Jane, "you look like some kind of princess, all dressed in lace. Why, we're both dressed in lace. I just love it."

228

"Thanks," said Mona, a little flustered. "But why would somebody as pretty as you notice somebody like me?"

"Don't be crazy," said Mary Jane, sweeping past her into the kitchen, hips swinging gracefully, high heels clicking grandly. "You're just a gorgeous girl. I'm pretty. I know I am. But I like to look at other girls who are pretty, always have."

They sat together at the glass table. Mary Jane examined the plates that Eugenia set out for them, holding hers up to the light.

"Now this is real bone china," she said. "We got some of this at Fontevrault."

"Really, you still have those sorts of things down there?"

"Darlin', you'd be amazed what's in that attic. Why, there's silver and china and old curtains and boxes of photographs. You should see all that. That attic's real dry and warm too. Sealed tight up there. Barbara Ann used to live up there. You know who she was?"

"Yeah, Ancient Evelyn's mother. And my great-great-grandmother."

"Mine too!" declared Mary Jane triumphantly. "Isn't that something."

"Yep, sure is. Part of the entire Mayfair experience. And you should look at the family trees where it gets all criss-crossed, like if I were to marry Pierce for instance, with whom I share not only that great-great-grandmother, but also a great-grandfather, who also pops up . . . damn, it's the hardest thing to keep track of. There comes a point in the life of every Mayfair when you spend about a year drawing family trees everywhere, trying just to keep it clear in your mind who is sitting next to you at the family picnic, know what I mean?"

Mary Jane nodded, eyebrows raised, lips curled in a smile. She wore a kind of smoky violet lipstick, to die for. My God, I am a woman now, Mona thought. I can wear all that junk, if I want to.

"Oh, you can borry all my things, if you want," said Mary Jane. "I've got an overnight case??? You know??? Just full of cosmetics that Aunt Bea bought for me, and all of them from Saks Fifth Avenue, and Bergdorf Goodman in New York."

"Well, that's very sweet of you." *Mind reader, be careful.*

Eugenia had taken some veal out of the refrigerator, little tender cuts for scallopini, which Michael had set aside for Rowan. She was frying these now, the way Michael had taught her, with sliced mushrooms and onions, already prepared, from a little plastic sack.

"God, that smells good, doesn't it?" said Mary Jane. "I didn't mean to read your mind, just happens."

"I don't care about that, it doesn't matter. As long as we both know it's very hit-and-miss, and easy to misunderstand."

"Oh, absolutely," said Mary Jane.

Then she looked at Mona again, the way she had looked at her upstairs. They were sitting opposite each other, just the way that Mona and Rowan sat, only Mona was in Rowan's place now, and Mary Jane was in Mona's. Mary Jane had been looking at her silver fork, and suddenly she just stopped moving and narrowed her eyes again and looked at Mona.

"What's the matter?" asked Mona. "You're looking at me like something's the matter."

"Everybody just looks at you when you're pregnant, they always do, soon as they know."

"I know that," said Mona. "But there's something different in the way you're looking at me. Other people are giving me swoony, loving looks, and looks of approbation, but you—"

"What's approbation?"

"Approval," said Mona.

"I got to get an education," said Mary Jane, shaking her head. She set the fork down. "What is this silver pattern?"

"Sir Christopher," said Mona.

"You think it's too late for me to ever be a truly educated person?"

"No," said Mona, "you're too smart to let a late start discourage you. Besides, you're already educated. You're just educated in a different way. I've never been the places you've been. I've never had the responsibility."

230

"Yeah, well, I didn't always want that myself. You know, I killed a man? I pushed him off a fire escape in San Francisco and he fell four stories into an alley and cracked open his head."

"Why did you do it?"

"He was trying to hurt me. He'd shot me up with heroin and he was giving it to me and telling me that him and me were going to be lovers together. He was a goddamned pimp. I pushed him off the fire escape."

"Did anyone come after you?"

"No," said Mary Jane, shaking her head. "I never told that story to anybody else in this family."

"I won't either," said Mona. "But that kind of strength isn't unusual in this family. How many girls, do you think, had been turned out by this pimp? That's the phrase for it, isn't it?"

Eugenia was serving them and ignoring them. The veal did look OK, well browned and juicy, with a light wine sauce.

Mary Jane nodded. "Lots of girls. Idiots," she said.

Eugenia had set down a cold salad of potatoes and peas, another Michael Curry gentleman's special, tossed in oil and garlic. Eugenia plopped a big spoon of it on Mary Jane's plate.

"Do we have any more milk?" asked Mona. "What are you drinking, Mary Jane?"

"Coca-Cola, please, Eugenia, if you don't mind, but then I can certainly get up and get it myself."

Eugenia was outraged at the suggestion, especially coming from an unknown cousin who was obviously a perfect rube. She brought the can and the glass of ice.

"Eat, Mona Mayfair!" Eugenia said. She poured the milk from the carton. "Come on now."

The meat tasted awful to Mona. She couldn't figure why. She loved this kind of food. As soon as it had been set before her, it had begun to disgust her. Probably just the usual bout of sickness, she thought, and that proves I'm on schedule. Annelle had said it would happen at just about six weeks. That is, before she'd declared the baby was a three-month-old monster.

231

Mona bowed her head. Little wisps of that last dream were catching hold of her, very tenacious and full of associations that were just moving away from her at jet speed as soon as she tried to catch them, and hold them, and open up the dream itself.

She sat back. She drank the milk slowly. "Just leave the carton," she said to Eugenia, who hovered over her, wrinkled and solemn, glaring at her, and at her untouched plate.

"She'll eat what she needs to eat, won't she?" asked Mary Jane, helpfully. Sweet kid. She was already gobbling her veal, and noisily stabbing every bit of mushroom and onion she could find with her fork.

Eugenia finally ambled off.

"Here, you want this?" said Mona. "Take it." She pushed the plate towards Mary Jane. "I never touched it."

"You sure you don't want it?"

"It's making me sick." She poured herself another glass of milk. "Well, I was never much of a milk lover, you know, probably because the refrigerator in our house never kept it cold. But that's changing. Everything's changing."

"Oh yeah, like what?" Mary Jane asked, rather wide-eyed. She chugalugged her entire Coke. "Can I get up and get another one?"

"Yes," said Mona.

She watched Mary Jane as she bounced towards the refrigerator. Her dress had just enough flare to remind you of a little girl's. Her legs looked beautifully muscled, thanks to the high heels, though they had looked beautifully muscled the other day when she'd been wearing flat shoes.

She flopped back down and started devouring Mona's offering.

Eugenia poked her head in the door from the butler's pantry.

"Mona Mayfair, you didn't eat nothin'. You live on potato chips and junk!"

"Get out of here!" Mona said firmly. Eugenia vanished.

"But she's trying to be maternal and all," said Mary Jane. "Why did you yell at her?"

"I don't want anybody to be maternal with me. And besides, she's not. She's a pest. She thinks . . . she thinks I'm

232

a bad person. It's too long to explain. She's always scolding me about something."

"Yeah, well, when the father of the baby is Michael Curry's age, you know, people are either going to blame him or you."

"How did you know that?"

Mary Jane stopped gobbling, and looked at Mona.

"Well, it is him, isn't it? I kinda figured you were sweet on him, first time I come here. I didn't mean to make you mad. I thought you were happy about it. I keep getting this vibe that you're really happy that he's the father."

"I'm not sure."

"Oh, it's him," said Mary Jane. She jabbed the fork through the last piece of veal, picked it up, and stuffed it in her mouth and chewed it lustily, her smooth brown cheeks working furiously without so much as a line or a wrinkle or any real distortion. This was one beautiful girl. "I know," she said, as soon as she had swallowed a wad of chewed meat big enough to catch in her windpipe and choke her to death.

"Look," said Mona. "This is something I haven't told anybody yet, and . . ."

"Everybody knows it," said Mary Jane. "Bea knows it. Bea told me. You know what's going to save Bea? That woman is going to get over her grief for Aaron on account of one simple reason. She never stops worrying about everybody else. She's real worried about you and Michael Curry, because he's got the genes, as everybody knows, and he's Rowan's husband. But she says that gypsy you fell in love with is just all wrong for you. He belongs with another kind of woman, somebody wild and homeless and without a family, like himself."

"She said all that?"

Mary Jane nodded. Suddenly she spied the plate of bread which Eugenia had set out for them, slices of plain white bread.

Mona didn't consider bread like that fit for consumption. She only ate French bread, or rolls, or something properly prepared to accompany a meal. Sliced bread! Sliced *white* bread!

Mary Jane grabbed the top slice, mushed it together, and started sopping up veal juice.

"Yeah, she said all that," said Mary Jane. "She told Aunt Viv and she told Polly and Anne Marie. Didn't seem to know that I was listening. But I mean, this is what is going to save her, that she's got so much on her mind about the family, like coming down to Fontevrault and making me leave."

"How could they all know this about me and Michael?"

Mary Jane shrugged. "You're asking me? Darlin', this is a family of witches, you're supposed to know that better than I do. Any number of ways they could have found out. But, come to think of it, Ancient Evelyn spilled the beans to Viv, if I am not mistaken. Something about you and Michael being here alone?"

"Yeah," said Mona with a sigh. "So big deal. I don't have to tell them. So much for that." But if they started being mean to Michael, if they started treating him any differently, if they started . . .

"Oh, I don't think you have to worry about that, like I said, when it's a man that age and a girl your age, they blame one or the other, and I think they blame you. I mean, not in a mean way or anything, they just say things like, 'Whatever Mona wants, Mona gets,' and 'Poor Michael,' and you know, stuff like, 'Well, if it got him up off that bed and to feeling better, maybe Mona's got the healing gift.' "

"Terrific," said Mona. "Actually, that's exactly the way I feel myself."

"You know, you're tough," said Mary Jane.

The veal juice was gone. Mary Jane ate the next slice of bread plain. She closed her eyes in a deliberate smile of satiation. Her lashes were all smoky and slightly violet, rather like her lipstick actually, very subtle however, and glamorous and beautiful. She had a damned near perfect face.

"Now I know who you look like!" cried Mona. "You look like Ancient Evelyn, I mean in her pictures when she was a girl."

"Well, that makes sense, now doesn't it?" said Mary Jane, "being's we're come down from Barbara Ann."

Mona poured the last of the milk into her glass. It was

234

still wonderfully cold. Maybe she and this baby could live on milk alone, she wasn't sure.

"What do you mean, I'm tough?" asked Mona. "What did you mean by that?"

"I mean you don't get insulted easily. Most of the time, if I talk like this, you know, completely open-like, with no secrets, like really trying to get to know somebody??? You know??? I offend that person."

"Small wonder," said Mona, "but you don't offend me."

Mary Jane stared hungrily at the last thin, forlorn slice of white bread.

"You can have it," said Mona.

"You sure?"

"Positive."

Mary Jane grabbed it, tore the middle out of it, and started rolling the soft bread into a ball. "Boy, I love it this way," she said. "When I was little??? You know??? I used to take a whole loaf, and roll it all into balls!"

"What about the crust?"

"Rolled it into balls," she said, shaking her head with nostalgic wonder. "Everything into balls."

"Wow," said Mona flatly. "You know, you really are fascinating, you're the most challenging combination of the mundane and mysterious that I've ever run across."

"There you go, showing off," said Mary Jane, "but I know you don't mean any harm, you're just teasing me, aren't you? Did you know that if mundane started with a *b*, I'd know what it meant?"

"Really? Why?"

"Because I'm up to *b* in my vocabulary studies," said Mary Jane. "I've been working on my education in several different ways, I'd like to know what you think about it. See, what I do is, I get a big-print dictionary??? You know???? The kind for old ladies with bad eyes??? And I cut out the *b* words, which gives me some familiarity with them right there, you know, cutting out each one with the definition, and then I throw all the little balls of paper . . . oops, there we go again," she laughed. "Balls, more balls."

"So I notice," said Mona. "We little girls are just all obsessed with them, aren't we?"

Mary Jane positively howled with laughter.

"This is better than I expected," said Mona. "The girls at school appreciate my humor, but almost no one in the family laughs at my jokes."

"Your jokes are real funny," said Mary Jane. "That's because you're a genius. I figure there are two kinds, ones with a sense of humor and those without it."

"But what about all the *b* words, cut out, and rolled into balls?"

"Well, I put them in a hat, you know??? Just like names for a raffle."

"Yeah."

"And then I pick them out one at a time. If it's some word nobody ever uses, you know, like *batrachian*?? I just throw it away. But if it's a good word like *beatitude*—'a state of utmost bliss'???? Well, I memorize it right on the spot."

"Hmmm, that sounds like a fairly good method. Guess you're more likely to remember words that you like."

"Oh yeah, but really, I remember almost everything, you know?? Being as smart as I am?" Mary Jane popped the bread ball into her mouth and started pulverizing the frame of crust.

"Even the meaning of *batrachian*?" asked Mona.

" 'A tailless leaping amphibian,' " Mary Jane answered. She nibbled on the crust ball.

"Hey, listen, Mary Jane," said Mona, "there's plenty of bread in this house. You can have all you want. There's a loaf right over there on the counter. I'll get it for you."

"Sit down! You're pregnant, I'll git it!" Mary Jane declared. She jumped up, reached for the bread, caught it by its plastic wrapping, and brought it down on the table.

"How about butter? You want some butter? It's right here."

"No, I've conditioned myself to eat it without butter, to save money, and I don't want to go back to butter, because then I'll miss the butter and the bread won't taste so good." She tore a slice out of the plastic, and scrunched up the middle of it.

"The thing is," said Mary Jane, "I will forget *batrachian* if I don't use it, but *beatitude* I will use, and not forget."

"Gotcha. Why were you looking at me in that way?"

Mary Jane didn't answer. She licked her lips, tore loose some fragments of soft bread, and ate them. "All this time, you remembered that we were talking about that, didn't you?"

"Yes."

"What do you think about your baby?" asked Mary Jane, and this time she looked worried and protective, sort of, or at least sensitive to what Mona felt.

"Something might be wrong with it."

"Yeah." Mary Jane nodded. "That's what I figure."

"It's not going to be some giant," said Mona quickly, though with each word, she found it more difficult to continue. "It's not some monster or whatever. But maybe there's just something wrong with it, the genes make some combination and . . . something could be wrong."

She took a deep breath. This might be the worst mental pain she'd ever felt. All her life she'd worried about things—her mother, her father, Ancient Evelyn, people she loved. And she'd known grief aplenty, especially of late. But this worrying about the baby was wholly different; it aroused a fear so deep in her that it was agony. She found she'd put her hand on her belly again. "Morrigan," she whispered.

Something stirred inside her, and she looked down by moving her eyes instead of her head.

"What's wrong?" asked Mary Jane.

"I'm worrying too much. Isn't it normal to think that something's wrong with your baby?"

"Yeah, it's normal," said Mary Jane. "But this family has got lots of people with the giant helix, and they haven't had horrible deformed little babies, have they? I mean, you know, what's the track record of all this giant-helix breeding?"

Mona hadn't answered. She was thinking, What difference does it make? If this baby's not right, if this baby's . . . She realized she was looking off through the greenery outside. It was still early afternoon. She thought of Aaron in the drawerlike crypt at the mausoleum, lying one shelf up from Gifford. Wax dummies of people, pumped with fluid. Not Aaron, not Gifford. Why would Gifford be digging a hole in a dream?

A wild thought came to her, dangerous and sacrilegious, but not really so surprising. Michael was gone. Rowan was gone. Tonight she could go out there into the garden alone, when no one was awake on the property, and she could dig up the remains of those two that lay beneath the oak; she could see for herself what was there.

Only trouble was, she was frightened to do it. She had seen plenty of scenes in horror movies over the years in which people did that sort of thing, traipsed off to the graveyard to dig up a vampire, or went at midnight to discover just who was in what grave. She had never believed those scenes, especially if the person did it by herself or himself. It was just too frightening. To dig up a body, you had to have a lot more balls than Mona had.

She looked at Mary Jane. Mary Jane had finished her feast of bread, apparently, and she just sat there, arms folded, looking steadily at Mona in a manner that was slightly unnerving, Mary Jane's eyes having taken on that dreamy luster that eyes have when the mind has drifted, a look that wasn't vacant but deceptively seriously focused.

"Mary Jane?" she said.

She expected to see the girl startle, and wake up, so to speak, and immediately volunteer what she had been thinking. But nothing like that happened. Mary Jane just kept looking at her in exactly the same fashion, and she said:

"Yes, Mona?" without a single change in her face.

Mona stood up. She went towards Mary Jane, and stood right beside her, looking down at her, and Mary Jane continued to look at her with the same large and frightening eyes.

"Touch this baby, here, touch it, don't be shy. Tell me what you feel."

Mary Jane turned the gaze on Mona's belly, and she reached out very slowly, as if she was going to do what Mona had asked her to do, and then suddenly she jerked her hand back. She rose from the chair, moving away from Mona. She looked worried.

"I don't think we should do it. Let's not do witchcraft with this baby. You and I are young witches," she said. "You know, we really are. What if witchcraft can, you know??? Have an effect on it???"

Mona sighed. Suddenly she didn't want to talk about this anymore; the feeling of fear was too draining and too damned painful, and there had been quite enough.

The only person in the world who could answer her questions was Rowan, and she was going to have to ask them, sooner or later, because she could feel this baby now, and that was flat-out impossible, really, to feel a baby moving like this, just this tiny, tiny movement, even, when a baby was only six or even ten or even twelve weeks.

"Mary Jane, I have to be alone right now," she said. "I'm not being rude. It's just this baby has me worried. That is the simple truth."

"You sure are sweet to explain this to me. You go right ahead. I'm going upstairs if it's okay. Ryan??? He put my suitcase in Aunt Viv's room, you know??? I'm going to be in there."

"You can use my computer if you want," said Mona. She turned her back to Mary Jane and looked out again in the garden. "It's in the library, there are plenty of open programs. It boots right to WordStar, but you can go to Windows or Lotus 1-2-3 simply enough."

"Yeah, I know how to do that, you take it easy, Mona Mayfair, you call me if you need me."

"Yeah, I will. I . . ." She turned around. "I really like having you here, Mary Jane," she said. "There's no telling when Rowan or Michael will come back."

What if they never came back? The fear was growing, including all things at random that came into her mind. Nonsense. They were coming back. But of course they had gone to look for people who might very well want to hurt them. . . .

"Don't you worry now, darlin'," said Mary Jane.

"Yeah," said Mona again, pushing open the door.

She wandered out on the flagstones and off towards the

back garden. It was still early and the sun was high and falling down on the lawn beneath the oak, as it would be, really, until late in the day. Best, warmest time in the back garden.

She walked out on the grass. This had to be where they were buried. Michael had added earth to this place, and the newest, tenderest grass grew here.

She went down on her knees, and stretched out on the earth, not caring that it was getting on her beautiful white shirt. There were so many of them. That's what it meant to be rich, and she was already feeling it, having so many of everything, and not having to wear shoes with holes. She pressed her cheek to the cool mud and grass, and her billowing right sleeve was like a big white parachute fallen beside her from heaven. She closed her eyes.

Morrigan, Morrigan, Morrigan ... The boats came across the sea, torches lifted. But the rocks looked so dangerous. Morrigan, Morrigan, Morrigan ... Yeah, this was the dream! The flight from the island to the north coast. The rocks were the danger, and the monsters of the deep who lived in the lochs.

She heard the sound of someone digging. She was wide awake and staring across the grass at the distant ginger lilies, at the azaleas.

No one was digging. Imagination. You want to dig them up, you little witch, she said to herself. She had to admit it was fun playing little witches with Mary Jane Mayfair. Yeah, glad she'd come. Have some more bread.

Her eyes slid closed. A beautiful thing happened. The sun struck her eyelids, as if some big branch or cloud had just freed it, and the light made the darkness brilliant orange, and she felt the warmth creeping all over her. Inside her, in the belly that she could still sleep on, the thing stirred again. *My baby.*

Someone was singing the nursery rhyme again. Why, that must be the oldest nursery rhyme in the world. That was Old English, or was it Latin?

Pay attention, said Mona. I want to teach you how to use a computer before you are four years old, and I want you to realize that there's nothing stopping you from being anything you ever want to be, you're listening?

The baby laughed and laughed. She turned somersaults and stretched her tiny arms and hands and laughed and laughed. It looked like a tiny "tailless leaping amphibian." Mona couldn't stop laughing either. "That's what you are!" she said to the baby.

And then the voice of Mary Jane said—in a pure dream now, and on some level Mona knew it, yes, because Mary Jane was all dressed up like Ancient Evelyn, in old lady clothes, a gabardine dress and string shoes, this was definitely a dream—the voice of Mary Jane said, "There's more to it than that, darlin'. You better make up your mind real soon."

Fifteen

"**L**OOK, FORGET WHAT you did, bolting," said Tommy. They were driving back to the Motherhouse, because Tommy insisted. "We have to behave as if we are guilty of nothing. All the evidence is gone now, the route destroyed. They can't trace any phone to any other phone. But we have to go back there and we have to behave as if nothing's happened, and we have to show our concern over the death of Marcus, that's all."

"I'll tell them I was so worried about Stuart," said Marklin.

"Yes, that's exactly what you should tell them. You were worried about Stuart. Stuart was under such a terrible strain."

"Maybe they didn't even notice, I mean, maybe the older ones took no notice that I was even gone."

"And you didn't find Stuart, and now you've come back home. Got it? You have come back home."

"And then what?"

"That depends on them," said Tommy. "Regardless of what happens, we must remain there so as not to arouse suspicion. Our attitude is simply, 'What has happened? Won't anyone explain?'"

Marklin nodded. "But where is Stuart?" he asked. He chanced a glance at Tommy. Tommy was as calm as he'd been at Glastonbury, when Marklin would have fallen on his knees before Stuart and begged him to come back.

"He's gone to meet Yuri, that's all. Stuart isn't under suspicion, Mark. You're the one who may be under suspicion because of the way you bolted. Now get a grip, old man, we have to play this well."

"For how long?"

"How should I know?" asked Tommy, same calm voice. "At least until we have some natural reason to leave again. Then we go back to my place in Regent's Park and we decide. Is the game up? What do we have to lose by remaining in the Order? What do we have to gain?"

"But who was it that killed Aaron?"

Tommy shook his head. He was watching the road now, as if Marklin needed a pilot. And Marklin wasn't so sure that he didn't. If he hadn't known this route by heart, he wasn't sure he could have made it.

"I'm not sure we should go back there," said Marklin.

"That's foolish. They haven't an inkling of what really happened."

"How do you know?" asked Marklin. "My God, Yuri could have told them! Tommy, will you use your head? Perhaps it's not a healthy sign to be so calm in the face of this. Stuart went to see Yuri, and Yuri may be at the Motherhouse himself by now."

"You don't think Stuart had the sense to tell Yuri to stay away? That there was some sort of conspiracy, and that Stuart didn't know the extent of it?"

"I think you would have the sense to do that, and perhaps I would, but I don't know about Stuart."

"And so what if Yuri is there? They know about the conspiracy, they just don't know about us! Stuart wouldn't tell Yuri about us, no matter what happened. You're the one who's not thinking. What does Yuri have to tell? He'll fill them in on whatever happened in New Orleans, and if that goes into the records . . . You know, I think I'm going to regret that I destroyed the intercept."

"I don't regret it!" said Marklin. He was becoming irritated by Tommy's businesslike manner, his absurd optimism.

"You're afraid you can't pull it off, aren't you?" asked Tommy. "You're afraid you'll crack like Stuart. But, Marklin, you have to realize Stuart has been in the

243

Talamasca all his life. What is the Talamasca to you or to me?" Tommy gave a little flat laugh. "Boy, they made a mistake with us, didn't they, brother?"

"No, they didn't," said Marklin. "Stuart knew just what he was doing, that we'd have the nerve to carry out schemes that he could never realize. Stuart didn't make a mistake. The mistake was that somebody killed Anton Marcus."

"And neither of us stayed around long enough to find out about this person, this crime, this fortuitous incident. You do realize it's fortuitous, don't you?"

"Of course I do. We're rid of Marcus. That's that. But what happened at the moment of the murder? Elvera talked to the killer. The killer said things about Aaron."

"Wouldn't it be simply marvelous if the intruder was one of the Mayfair family? A top-notch witch? I tell you, I want to read that whole file on the Mayfair witches from cover to cover. I want to know everything about those people! I was thinking. There must be some way to lay claim to Aaron's papers. You know Aaron. He wrote down everything. He must have left cartons of papers. They must be in New Orleans."

"You're moving too far ahead! Tommy, Yuri may be there. Stuart may have cracked. They may know everything."

"I doubt it seriously," said Tommy, with an air of one who wants to meditate on more important things. "Marklin, the turn!"

Marklin had almost missed it, and when he swerved, it was into the path of another car, but the car gave way, and Marklin raced forward. Within seconds he was away from the highway and going down the country road. He relaxed, realizing only then that he had braced himself so hard for an accident that his jaw was aching from the clenching of his teeth.

Tommy was glaring at him.

"Look, ease up on me!" Marklin said suddenly, feeling the heat behind his eyes which always meant that he was perfectly furious, and had not completely realized it. "I'm not the problem here, Tommy. They are! Now back off. We play it naturally. We both know what to do."

Tommy turned his head slowly as they went through the front gates of the park.

"Everybody in the Order must be here. I've never seen this many cars," said Marklin.

"We'll be lucky," said Tommy, "if they haven't commandeered our quarters for some deaf and blind octogenarian from Rome or Amsterdam."

"I hope they have. It's a perfect excuse to turn everything over to the old guard and very considerately clear out."

Marklin brought the car to a halt, several yards from the busy attendant who was directing the car in front of them to a parking spot quite far away, on the other side of the hedge. In all these years, Marklin had never seen cars packed side by side on the other side of the hedge.

He got out, and tossed the keys to the attendant. "Will you park, please, Harry?" he said. He peeled off several pound notes, a bribe sufficient to waive all objections to this breach of custom, and headed towards the front doors of the house.

"Why in the hell did you do that?" Tommy said, catching up with him. "Try to follow the rules, will you? Fade into the woodwork. Say nothing. Do nothing to attract attention, are we agreed?"

"You're too nervous yourself," said Marklin crossly.

The front doors stood open. The hall was choked with men and women, thick with cigar smoke, and positively roaring with voices. It had the air of a crowded wake or intermission at the theatre.

Marklin stopped. Every instinct in him told him not to go in. And all his life he had believed in his instincts, as surely as he believed in his intelligence.

"Come on, man," said Tommy, between his teeth. He urged Marklin forward.

"Oh, hello," said a bright-faced old gentleman who turned to greet them. "And who are you?"

"Novices," said Marklin. "Tommy Monohan and Marklin George. Are novices allowed to come in?"

"Of course, of course," said the man, stepping aside. The crowd pressed in behind him, faces turning towards him and then away indifferently. A woman was whispering to a man on the other side of the doorway, and when her eyes met Marklin's, she made a small noise of surprise and distress.

"This is all wrong," said Marklin under his breath.

"You should all be here, of course," the jolly man was saying, "all the young ones should be here. When something like this happens, everyone is called home."

"Why, I wonder," said Tommy. "Nobody liked Anton."

"Shut up," said Marklin. "It's quite remarkable, isn't it, the way that people—you and I for instance—respond to stress."

"No, unfortunately, it's not remarkable at all."

They edged their way through the press. Strange faces to the right and left. People everywhere were drinking wine and beer. He could hear French, Italian, even people speaking Dutch.

There sat Joan Cross, in the first of the formal parlors, surrounded by faces unknown to Marklin, but all of them in serious conversation.

No Stuart.

"You see?" said Tommy, whispering in his ear. "They're doing what comes naturally after someone dies—gathering, talking, as if it were a party. Now that's what we have to do. What comes naturally. You understand?"

Marklin nodded, but he didn't like it, no, not at all. He glanced back once, trying to find the door, but the door had been closed, apparently, and the crowd blocked his view in any event. He could see nothing. Indeed, it struck him as strange that there were so many foreign faces, and he wanted to say something to Tommy, but Tommy had moved away.

Tommy was chatting with Elvera, nodding as Elvera explained something to him. She looked as dowdy as ever, with her dark gray hair knotted at the nape of her neck, and her rimless glasses halfway down her nose. Enzo stood beside her, that devious-looking Italian. Where the hell was his twin?

How dreadful to spend one's life in this place, he thought. Did he dare to ask about Stuart? Certainly he didn't dare to ask about Yuri, though of course he knew. Ansling and Perry had told him about Yuri's call. Oh God, what was he to do? And where were Ansling and Perry?

Galton Penn, one of the other novices, was pushing his way towards Marklin.

"Hey, there, Mark. What do you think of all this?"

"Well, I don't know that people are talking about it here," said Marklin. "But then I haven't really listened."

"Let's talk about it now, man, before they forbid all conversation on the subject. You know the Order. They haven't a clue as to who killed Marcus. Not a clue. You know what we're all thinking? There's something they don't want us to know."

"Like what?"

"That it was some supernatural agency, what else? Elvera saw something that horrified her. Something bad happened. You know, Mark, I'm very sorry for Marcus and all, but this is the most exciting thing that's ever happened since I was received."

"Yes, I know what you mean," Mark answered. "Haven't seen Stuart, have you?"

"No, not at all, not since this morning, when he declined to take charge. Were you here when that happened?"

"No. I mean yes," said Mark. "I was wondering if he went out or what."

Galton shook his head. "You hungry? I am. Let's get some chow."

This was going to be rough, very rough. But if the only people who spoke to him were bright-faced imbeciles like Galton, he would do just fine, just fine indeed.

Sixteen

THEY'D BEEN ON the road over an hour, and it was almost dark, the sky clabbering with silvery clouds, and a drowsy look coming over the great expanses of rolling hills and bright green farmland, neatly cut into patterns as if the landscape were covered with a great patchwork quilt.

They made a pit stop in a little one-street village with several black and white half-timbered houses and a small, overgrown cemetery. The pub was more than inviting. It even had the proverbial dart board and a couple of men playing darts, and the smell of the beer was wonderful.

But this was hardly the time to stop for a drink, thought Michael.

He stepped outside, lit a fresh cigarette, and watched with quiet fascination the formal gentleness with which Ash guided his prisoner into the pub and inevitably towards the bathroom.

Across the street, Yuri stood at a phone booth, talking rapidly, having made his connection to the Motherhouse, apparently, and Rowan stood beside him, arms folded, watching the sky or something in it, Michael couldn't be sure which. Yuri was upset again, wringing his right hand as he held the receiver with the left, nodding over and over again. It was plain that Rowan was listening to his words.

Michael leaned back against the plaster wall, and drew in on the smoke. It always amazed him how tiring it was to simply ride in a car.

Even this journey, with its agonizing suspense, was no

different ultimately, and now that darkness had closed off the lovely countryside, he would grow more sleepy, he figured, no matter what was yet to come.

When Ash and his prisoner emerged from the pub, Gordon looked resentful and desperate. But obviously he'd been unable to solicit help, or had not dared to try.

Yuri hung up the phone. It was his turn to disappear into the pub now; he was still anxious, if not crazed. Rowan had been watching him attentively during the drive, that is, when she was not riveted to Ash.

Michael watched Ash as he returned Gordon to the backseat. He didn't try to disguise the fact that he was staring. That seemed unnecessarily cumbersome. The thing about the tall man was this: he did not in any way appear hideous, as Yuri had averred. The beauty was there, and rather spectacular, but the hideousness? Michael couldn't see it. He saw only a graceful frame, and easy, efficient movements that indicated both alertness and strength. The man's reflexes were amazing. He'd proved that when Stuart Gordon had reached again for the lock of the door when they were stopped at a crossroads about a half hour back.

The man's soft black hair reminded him all too much of Lasher; too silky, too fine, too much body to it, he didn't know for certain. The white streaks added a kind of high luster to the whole figure. The face was far too big-boned to be feminine in any conventional sense, but it was delicate, the long nose redeemed perhaps by the fact that the eyes were so large and set so wide apart. The skin was mature skin and not baby-fine. But the real allure of the man was mixed up with his voice and his eyes. His voice could have talked you into anything, Michael thought, and the eyes were highly persuasive as well.

Both bordered on a childlike simplicity, but were not ultimately simple. The effect? The man seemed some sort of angelic being, infinitely wise and patient and yet resolved, without question, to murder Stuart Gordon exactly as he had said that he would.

Of course, Michael wasn't assuming anything about the age of this creature. It was pretty hard not to think he was human, just different, unaccountably strange. Of course,

249

Michael knew he wasn't. He knew it by a hundred little details—the size of Ash's knuckles, the curious way he widened his eyes now and then so that he looked awestruck, and above all perhaps by the absolute perfection of his mouth and teeth. The mouth was baby-soft, impossible for a man with that skin, really, or at least highly improbable, and the teeth were as white as some sort of flashing advertisement that had been shamelessly retouched.

Michael didn't for a moment believe this creature was ancient, or that he was the great Saint Ashlar of the Donnelaith legends, the ancient king who had converted to Christianity in the last days of the Roman Empire in Britain, and allowed his pagan spouse, Janet, to be burnt at the stake.

But the grim tale he had believed when Julien had told it to him. And this was one of the many Ashlars, no doubt—one of the mighty Taltos from the glen—a being of the very same ilk as the one that Michael had slaughtered.

These things were not disputed by any part of his mind.

He had experienced too much for him to doubt. It was only that he couldn't believe the tall, beautiful man was that old St. Ashlar himself. Perhaps he just didn't want it to be so, for very good reasons that made sense within these elaborate frameworks which he'd now totally accepted.

Yes, you are living now with a whole series of completely new realities, he thought. Maybe this is why you're taking it all calmly. You've seen a ghost; you've listened to him; you know he was there. He told you things you could have never manufactured or imagined. And you've seen Lasher and you've heard his long plea for sympathy, and that was also something completely unimaginable for you, something filled with new information and strange details that you can still remember with puzzlement, now that the misery you were feeling when Lasher told it is over, and Lasher lies buried under the tree.

Oh yeah, don't forget, the burying of the body, dropping the head down in the hole beside it, and then finding the emerald, picking it up, and holding it in the dark while the decapitated body lay down there in the wet earth, ready to be covered up.

Perhaps you can become accustomed to anything, he figured. And he wondered if that was what had happened to Stuart Gordon. He had no doubt that Stuart Gordon was guilty, dreadfully and inexcusably guilty of everything. Yuri had no doubt. But how had the man managed to betray his values?

Michael had to admit he himself had always had a susceptibility to this very kind of Celtic darkness and mystery. His very love of Christmas had its roots in some irrational longing for rituals born in these isles, perhaps. And the tiny Christmas ornaments he had so lovingly collected over the years were all in some way emblematic of old Celtic gods, and a worship overlaid on pagan secrets.

His love of the houses he'd restored had brought him at times as close to this atmosphere of old secrets, old designs, and a dormant knowledge to be revealed as one could ever get in America.

He realized he understood Stuart Gordon in a way. And very soon the figure of Tessa would explain Gordon's sacrifices and terrible mistakes, very clearly.

Whatever, Michael had been through so much that his calm now was only inevitable.

Yes, you've been through these things, and you've been used by them and battered by them, and now you stand here, by the village pub in this small, picture-postcard village, with its gently sloping stone street, and you think about all this without emotion—that you are with something that is not human, but is as intelligent as any human, and is soon to meet a female of its kind, an event of such enormous significance that no one really wants to touch upon it, perhaps only out of respect for the man who is supposed to die.

It's hard to ride in a car for an hour with a man who is supposed to die.

He'd finished the cigarette. Yuri had just come out of the pub. They were ready to push off.

"You did reach the Motherhouse?" Michael asked quickly.

"Yes, and I reached more than one person. I made four different calls and reached four different individuals. If these four, my oldest and closest friends, are part of it, then I despair."

Michael gave Yuri's thin shoulder a squeeze. He followed Yuri to the car.

Another thought came to him, that he wasn't going to think about Rowan and her reactions to the Taltos any more now than he had all the way down here, when a deep, instinctive possessiveness had almost caused him to demand that they stop the car, that Yuri climb in the front, so that he could sit by his wife.

No, he wasn't going to give in to this. He couldn't any way in the world know what Rowan was thinking or feeling as she looked at this strange creature. A witch he might be, by genetic profile, and perhaps by some peculiar heritage of which he knew nothing. But he wasn't a mind reader. And he had been aware from the very first moments of their encounter with Ashlar that Rowan would probably not be harmed by making love to this strange creature, because now that she could not have children, she could not suffer the sort of terrible hemorrhage which had brought down Lasher's Mayfair victims one by one.

As for Ash, if he was lusting after Rowan, he was keeping it a gentlemanly secret, but then the creature was driving towards a female of his species, who was perhaps one of the last female Taltos in the world.

And then there's the immediate consideration, isn't there, he thought as he slipped into the passenger seat and firmly shut the door. Are you going to stand by and let this giant of a man murder Stuart Gordon? You know perfectly well you can't do that. You can't watch somebody be murdered. That's impossible. The only time you've ever done it, it happened so quick, with the crack of the gun, that you scarcely had time to breathe.

Of course, you have killed three people yourself. And this misguided bastard, this crazed man who claims to have a goddess under lock and key, has killed Aaron.

They were leaving the little village, which had all but disappeared into the gathering shadows. How tender, how manageable, how tame this landscape. At any other time he would have asked them to stop so that they could walk for a while along the road.

When he turned to the side, he was surprised to discover that Rowan had been watching him. That she was sitting to the side herself and had brought her leg up on the seat right behind him, apparently so that she could look at him. Of course her half-naked legs looked glorious, but so what? She had pulled her skirt down properly. It was no more than a fashionable flash of nylon-covered thigh.

He stretched out his arm along the old leather upholstery, and he laid his left hand on her shoulder, which she allowed, quietly looking at him with her immense and secretive gray eyes, and giving him something far more intimate than a smile.

He had avoided her the entire time they were in the village, and now he wondered why he had done that. Why? On impulse, he decided to do something rude and vulgar.

He leaned over, reaching out to cup the back of her head with his hand, and he kissed her quickly, and then settled back. She could have avoided it, but she didn't. And when her lips had touched him, he had felt a sharp little pain inside, that now began to glow and to increase in intensity. *Love you! Dear God, give it a chance again!*

And no sooner had that reprimand come into his mind than he realized he wasn't talking to her at all; he was talking to himself *about* her.

He settled back, looking out the windshield, watching the dark sky thicken and lose the last of its porcelain luster, and leaning his head to the side, he closed his eyes.

There was nothing stopping Rowan from falling madly in love with this being who could not wring monstrous babies from her, nothing but her marriage vows and her will.

And Michael realized he was not sure of either one. Perhaps he would never be sure again.

Within twenty minutes the light was gone. Their headlights forged through the darkness, and this might have been any highway, anywhere in the world.

Finally Gordon spoke up. The next road right, and left on the one immediately following.

The car turned off into the weald, into the high dark

253

trees, a mixture of beech and oak it seemed, with even some light flowering fruit trees that he could not clearly see. The blossoms looked pink here and there in the head-lights.

The second side road was unpaved. The woods grew thicker. Maybe this was the remnant of an ancient forest, the kind of grand, Druid-infested woods that had once covered all of England and Scotland, possibly all of Europe, the kind of forest that Julius Caesar had cleared away with ruthless conviction so that the gods of his enemies would either flee or die.

The moon was fairly bright. He could see a little bridge now as they drew closer, and then came another turn, and they were driving along the borders of a small and peaceful lake. Far across the water stood a tower, perhaps a Norman keep. It was a sight so romantic that surely the poets of the last century had gone mad for the place, he thought. Perhaps they had even built it, and it was one of those beautiful shams which were thrown up everywhere as the recent love for the Gothic transformed architecture and style worldwide.

But as they drew closer, as they swung round and came near to the tower, Michael saw it more clearly. And realized that it was a rounded Norman tower, rather large, with perhaps three stories rising to its battlements. The windows were lighted. The lower portion of the building was shrouded by trees.

Yes, that was exactly what it was, a Norman tower—he had seen many in his student years, wandering the tourists' roads over all England. Perhaps on some summer sabbatical which he could no longer remember he had even seen this one.

It didn't seem so. The lake, the giant tree to the left, all of this was too nearly perfect. Now he could see the foundations of a larger structure, wandering away in crumbling lumps and pieces, worn down by rain and wind, no doubt, and further blurred by mounds of wild ivy.

They drove through a thick copse of young oaks, losing track of the building altogether, and then emerged, surprisingly close to it, and Michael could see a couple of cars parked in front of it, and two tiny electric lights flanking a very large door.

All very civilized, it seemed, livable. But how marvelously preserved it was, unmarred by any visible modern addition. Ivy crawled over the rounded and mortared stone, up above the simple arch of the doorway.

No one spoke.

The driver stopped the car finally, in a small graveled clearing.

Michael at once got out and looked around. He could see a lush and wild English garden spreading towards the lake and towards the forest, banks of flowers just coming into bloom. He knew their dim shapes, but they had closed up in the darkness, and who knew what glory would be all around when the sun rose?

Were they going to be here when the sun rose?

An enormous larch tree stood between them and the tower, a tree that was surely one of the oldest Michael had ever seen.

He walked towards its venerable trunk, realizing that he was walking away from his wife. But he couldn't do otherwise.

And when he finally stood under the tree's great spreading branches, he looked up at the façade of the tower, and saw a lone figure in the third window. Small head and shoulders. A woman, her hair loose or covered with a veil, he couldn't be certain.

For one moment the entire scene overwhelmed him—the dreamy white clouds, the high light of the moon, the tower itself in all its rough grandeur.

Though he could hear the crunch of the others coming, he didn't step out of the way, or move at all. He wanted to stand here, to see this—this serene lake to his right, water interrupted and framed now by the delicate fruit trees with their pale, fluttering flowers. Japanese plum, most likely, the very kind of tree that bloomed all over Berkeley, California, in the springtime, sometimes making the very light in the small streets a rosy pink.

He wanted to remember all this. He wanted never to forget it. Perhaps he was still weakened by jet lag, maybe even going predictably crazy like Yuri. He didn't know. But this, this was some image that spoke of the entire venture, of its horrors and revelations—the high tower and the promise of a princess within it.

The driver had switched off the headlamps. The others were walking past him. Rowan stood at his side. He looked one more time across the lake and then at the enormous figure of Ash walking in front of him, Ash's hand still clamped to Stuart Gordon, and Stuart Gordon walking as if he would soon collapse—an elderly gray-haired man, the tendons of his thin neck looking woefully vulnerable as he moved into the light of the doorway.

Yes, this was the quintessential moment, he thought, and it hit him rather like somebody slamming him with a boxing glove, that a female Taltos lived in this tower, like Rapunzel, and that Ash was going to kill the man he was guiding towards the door.

Maybe the memory of this moment—these images, this soft chilly night—maybe this was all he would salvage from this experience. It was a very real possibility.

Ash wrested the key with a firm but slow gesture from Stuart Gordon, and slipped the key into a large iron lock. The door opened with modern efficiency and they entered a lower hall, electrically heated and filled with large, comfortable furnishings, massive Renaissance Revival pieces with bulbous but beautifully carved legs, claws for feet, and tapestried fabrics, worn but still very pretty, and genuinely old.

Medieval paintings hung on the walls, many with the high imperishable gloss of true egg tempera. A suit of armor stood, covered with dust. And other treasures were heaped here and there in careless luxury. This was the den of a poetic man, a man in love with England's past, and perhaps fatally alienated from the present.

A staircase came down into the room, on their left, following the curve of the wall as it descended. Light shone down from the room above and, for all Michael knew, from the room above that.

Ash let go of Stuart Gordon. He went to the foot of the

stairs. He laid his right hand on the crude newel post and began to go up.

Rowan followed him immediately.

Stuart Gordon seemed not to realize that he was free.

"Don't hurt her," he cried suddenly, viciously, as though it was the only thing he could think of to say. "Don't touch her without her permission!" he pleaded. The voice, issuing from the skeletal old face, seemed the last reservoir of his masculine power. "You hurt my treasure!" he said.

Ash stopped, looking at Gordon thoughtfully, and then again he started to climb.

They all followed, finally even Gordon, who pushed past Michael rudely, and then shoved Yuri out of his way. He caught up with Ash at the head of the stairway and disappeared out of Michael's sight.

When they finally reached the top, they found themselves in another large room as simple as the one below it, its walls the walls of the tower, except for two small rooms, skillfully built of old wood, and roofed over—bathrooms perhaps, closets, Michael couldn't tell. They seemed to melt back into the stone behind them. The great room had its share of soft couches and sagging old chairs, scattered standup lamps with parchment shades making distinct islands in the darkness, but the center was wonderfully bare. And a single real iron chandelier, a circle of melting candles, revealing a great pool of polished floor beneath it.

It took a moment for Michael to realize the room held another partially concealed figure. Yuri was already looking at this figure.

Across the circle from them, at the far end of the diameter, so to speak, sat a very tall woman at a stool, apparently working on a loom. One small gooseneck lamp illuminated her hands, but not her face. A small bit of her tapestry was revealed, and Michael could see that it was very intricate and full of muted color.

Ash stood stock-still, staring at her. The woman stared back. It was the long-haired woman Michael had seen at the window.

The others made no move. Gordon rushed towards her.

"Tessa," he said, "Tessa, I'm here, my darling." The

257

voice was speaking in a realm of its own, the others forgotten.

The woman rose, towering over the frail figure of Gordon as he embraced her. She yielded with a sweet, delicate sigh, her hands rising to gently touch Gordon's thin shoulders. In spite of her height, she was so slight of build that she seemed the weaker one. With his arms around her, he brought her forward into the brighter light, into the circle.

There was something grim in Rowan's expression. Yuri was enthralled. Ash's face was unreadable. He merely watched as the woman came closer and closer and now stood beneath the chandelier, the light gleaming on the top of her head and on her forehead.

Perhaps on account of her sex, the woman's height seemed truly monstrous.

Her face was perfectly round, flawless, rather like that of Ash, but not so long or deeply defined. Her mouth was tender and tiny, and her eyes, though big, were timid and without unusual color. Blue eyes, however, kind, and fringed, like those of Ash, with long, luxuriant lashes. A great mane of white hair grew back from her forehead, falling about her almost magically. It seemed motionless and soft, more a cloud than a mane, perhaps, and so fine that the light made the mass of it appear faintly transparent.

She wore a violet dress, beautifully smocked just beneath her breasts. The sleeves were gorgeously old-fashioned, gathered around the small of her upper arms and then ballooning to the cuffs that fitted tightly at the wrists.

Dim thoughts of Rapunzel came to Michael—or more truly of every speck of romance that he had ever read—a realm of fairy queens and princes of unambiguous power. As the woman drew near to Ash, Michael couldn't help but see that her skin was so pale it was almost white. A swan of a princess she seemed, her cheeks firm and her mouth glistening slightly, and her lashes very vivid around her glowing blue eyes.

She frowned, which made a single pucker in her forehead, and seemed like a baby about to bawl.

"Taltos," she whispered. But this was said without the slightest alarm. Indeed, she looked almost sad.

258

Yuri let out a tiny, faint gasp.

Gordon was transformed with astonishment, as if nothing had actually prepared him for this meeting to take place. He seemed for a moment almost young, eyes fired with love and with rapture.

"This is your female?" asked Ash softly. He was gazing at her, even smiling slightly, but he had not moved to greet her or touch her outstretched hand. He spoke slowly.

"This is the female for whom you murdered Aaron Lightner, for whom you tried to kill Yuri, the female to whom you would have brought the male Taltos at any cost?"

"What are you saying!" said Gordon in a timorous voice. "You dare to hurt her, either with words or actions, I'll kill you."

"I don't think so," said Ash. "My dearest," he said to the woman, "can you understand me?"

"Yes," she said softly, in a tiny bell of a voice. She shrugged and threw up her hands, almost in the manner of an ecstatic saint. "Taltos," she said, and gave a small sad shake of her head, and frowned again with almost dreamy distress.

Had the doomed Emaleth been so fair and feminine?

With a shock, Michael saw Emaleth's face collapse as the bullets struck it, saw the body fall over backwards! Was this why Rowan was crying, or was she merely tired and wondering, eyes watering slightly as she watched Ash looking down at the woman and the woman looking up. What must this be for her?

"Beautiful Tessa," Ash said with a slight rise of his eyebrows.

"What's wrong?" asked Gordon. "Something is wrong—for both of you. Tell me what's wrong." He moved closer, but stopped, obviously not willing to step between them. His voice was rich and sorrowful now. It had the quality of an orator, or of someone who knew how to affect his listeners. "Oh, God in heaven, this is not what I imagined—to meet here in this place, surrounded by those who can't truly grasp the meaning."

But he was too full of emotion for there to be any arti-

259

fice in what he was saying or doing at all. His gestures were no longer hysterical. They were tragic.

Ash stood as still as ever, smiling at Tessa very deliberately, and then nodding with pleasure as her little mouth opened and expanded, and her cheeks grew small and plump with her own smile.

"You're very beautiful," Ash whispered, and then he raised his hand to his lips, and kissed his fingers and gently placed this kiss on her cheek.

She sighed, stretching her long neck and letting her hair tumble down her back, and then she reached out for him, and he took her in his arms. He kissed her, but there was no passion in it. Michael could see it.

Gordon came between them, circling Tessa's waist with his left hand and gently drawing her back.

"Not here, I beg you. Oh, please, not as if it were in a common brothel."

He let go of Tessa and approached Ash, hands clasped as if praying, peering up without fear now, caught in something more crucial to him even than his own survival.

"What is the place for the wedding of the Taltos?" he said reverently, voice rich and imploring. "What is the holiest place in England, where St. Michael's line runs over the crest of the hill, and the ruined tower of the ancient Church of St. Michael is a sentinel still?"

Ash regarded him almost sadly, composed, merely listening, as the impassioned voice continued.

"Let me take you there, both of you, let me see the wedding of the Taltos on Glastonbury Tor!" His voice dropped low and the words came evenly, almost slowly. "If I see this, if I see the miracle of the birth there on the sacred mountain, in the place where Christ himself came to England—where old gods have fallen and new gods risen, where blood was shed in the defense of the sacred—if I see this, the birth of the offspring, full-grown and reaching out to embrace its parents, the very symbol of life itself, then it doesn't matter whether I go on living, or whether I die."

His hands had risen as if he held the sacred concept in them, and his voice had lost all its hysteria, and his eyes even were clear and almost soft.

260

Yuri watched with obvious suspicion.

Ash was the picture of patience, but for the first time Michael saw a deeper and darker emotion behind Ash's eyes and even his smile.

"Then," said Gordon, "I will have seen the thing that I was born to see. I will have witnessed the miracle of which poets sing and old men dream. A miracle as great as any ever made known to me from the time my eyes could see to read, and my ears could hear the tales told to me, and my tongue could form words that would express the strongest inclinations of my heart.

"Grant me these last precious moments, the time to travel there. It's not far. Scarcely a quarter of an hour from here—a mere few minutes for us all. And on Glastonbury Tor, I will give her over to you, as a father would a daughter, my treasure, my beloved Tessa, to do what you both desire."

He stopped, looking to Ash desperately still, and deeply saddened, as if behind these words were some complete acceptance of his own death.

He took no notice of Yuri's plain though silent contempt.

Michael was marveling at the transformation in the old man, the sheer conviction.

"Glastonbury," Stuart whispered. "I beg you. Not here." And finally, he shook his head. "Not here," he whispered, and then fell silent.

Ash's face did not change. And then, very gently, as if breaking a terrible secret to a tender heart, one for which he had compassion, he said:

"There can be no union, there can be no offspring." He took his time with the words. "She is old, your beautiful treasure. She is barren. Her fount is dried."

"Old!" Stuart was baffled, disbelieving. "Old!" he whispered. "Why, you're mad, how can you say this?" He turned helplessly to Tessa, who watched him without pain or disappointment.

"You're mad," said Stuart again, his voice rising. "Look at her!" he cried out. "Look at her face, her form. She's magnificent. I've brought you together with a spouse of such beauty that you should fall to your knees and give me

261

your thanks!" Suddenly he was stricken, disbelieving and yet slowly being crushed.

"Her face will be that way, perhaps, the day she dies," Ash said with his characteristic mildness. "I have never seen the face of a Taltos that was different. But her hair is white, completely white, not a single live strand remains in it. No scent comes from her. Ask her. Humans have used her again and again. Or perhaps she has wandered longer even than I. Her womb is dead within her. Her fount is dried."

Gordon gave no further protest. He had clapped his hands over his lips, the little steeple of his fingers collapsed to shut in his pain.

The woman looked a little puzzled, but only vaguely disturbed. She stepped forward and put her long, slender arm lightly around the shivering Gordon, and addressed her words very distinctly to Ash.

"You judge me for what men have done to me, that they used me in every village and every town I entered, that over the years they made the blood flow again and again, until there was no more?"

"No, I don't judge you," Ash said earnestly and with great concern. "I don't judge you, Tessa. Truly I do not."

"Ah!" Once again she smiled, brightly, almost brilliantly, as if this was a reason to be supremely happy.

She looked at Michael suddenly, and then at the shadowy figure of Rowan near the stairway. Her expression was eager and loving.

"I'm saved from these horrors here," she said. "I'm loved in chastity by Stuart. This is my refuge." She stretched out her hands to Ash. "Won't you stay with me, talk to me?" She tugged him towards the center of the room. "Won't you dance with me? I hear music when I look into your eyes."

She drew Ash closer. She said with deep, true feeling, "I'm so glad you've come."

Only now did she look at Gordon, who had slipped away, forehead furrowed, fingers still pressed to his lips, stepping backwards and finding a heavy old wooden chair. He sank down on it, and rested his head against the hard planks that made up the back of it, and turned wearily to the side. The spirit had gone out of him. It seemed his very life was leaving him.

"Dance with me," said Tessa. "All of you, don't you want to dance?" She flung out her arms and threw back her head and shook out her hair, which did indeed look like the lifeless white hair of the very very old.

She turned round and round until her long, full, violet skirts swung out around her, making a bell, and she was dancing on tiptoe with small slippered feet.

Michael couldn't take his eyes off her, off the subtle swaying movements with which she made a great circle, leading with her right foot, and then bringing the other closer to it, as though it were a ritual dance.

As for Gordon, it was too painful even to look at him, and this disappointment seemed far more important to him than his life. Indeed, it was as if the fatal blow had already been struck.

Ash, too, stared rapt at Tessa—touched perhaps, worried certainly, and maybe even miserable.

"You lie," Stuart said. But it was a desperate, broken murmur. "You're telling a terrible and abominable lie."

Ash didn't bother to answer him. He smiled and nodded at Tessa.

"Stuart, my music. Please play my music. Play my music for . . . for Ash!" She gave Ash a great bow and another smile, and he too bowed and reached out to take her hands.

The figure in the chair was incapable of movement, and, once again in a murmur, he said, "It's not true," but he didn't believe his own denial.

Tessa had begun to hum a song, turning again in a circle.

"Play the music, Stuart, play it."

"I'll play it for you," said Michael in a low voice. He turned, looking for some possible source, hoping against hope it wasn't an instrument, a harp, a fiddle, something that required a player, because if it was, then he could not rise to the moment.

He felt heartbroken himself, impossibly sad, unable to enjoy the great relief he ought to have been feeling. And for one moment his eyes moved over Rowan, and she too seemed lost in sadness, veiled in it, her hands clasped, her body very upright against the stair railing, her eyes following the dancing figure who had begun to hum a distinct melody, something that Michael knew and loved.

Michael discovered the machines—modern stereo components, designed to look almost mystically technical, with hundreds of tiny digital screens, and buttons, and wires snaking in all directions to speakers hung at random intervals along the wall.

He bent down, tried to read the name of the tape inside the player.

"It's what she wants," said Stuart, staring still at the woman. "Just start it. She plays it all the time. It is her music."

"Dance with us," said Tessa. "Don't you want to dance with us?" She moved towards Ash, and this time he could not resist. He caught her hands, and then embraced her as a man might embrace a woman for a waltz, in the modern intimate position.

Michael pressed the button.

The music began low, the throb of bass strings plucked slowly—flowing out of the many speakers; then came trumpets, smooth and lustrous, over the shimmering tones of a harpsichord, descending in the same melodic line of notes and now taking the lead, so that the strings followed.

At once Ash guided his partner into wide graceful steps, and a gentle circle.

This was Pachelbel's Canon, Michael knew it at once, played as he'd never heard it, in a masterly rendition, with the full brass perhaps intended by the composer.

Had there ever been a more plaintive piece of music, anything more frankly abandoned to romance? The music swelled, transcending the constraints of the baroque, trumpets, strings, harpsichord now singing their overlapping melodies with a heartrending richness so that the music seemed both timeless and utterly from the heart.

It swept the couple along, their heads bending gently, their wide steps graceful and slow and in perfect time with the instruments. Ash was smiling now, as fully and completely as Tessa. And as the pace quickened, as the trumpets began to delicately trill the notes, with perfect control, as all voices blended magnificently in the most jubilant moments of the composition, faster and faster they danced, Ash swinging Tessa along almost playfully, into bolder and bolder circles. Her skirts flared freely, her small feet turned with perfect grace, heels clicking faintly on the wood, her smile ever more radiant.

Another sound was not blended into the dance—for the canon, when played like this, was surely a dance—and slowly Michael realized it was the sound of Ash singing. There were no words, only a lovely openmouthed humming, to which Tessa quickly added her own, and their faultless voices rose above the dark lustrous trumpets, effortlessly traveling the crescendos, and now, as they turned faster, their backs very straight, they almost laughed in what seemed pure bliss.

Rowan's eyes had filled with tears as she watched them—the tall, regal man and the lithesome, graceful fairyqueen, and so had the eyes of the old man, who clung to the arm of his chair as if he were very close to the limit of his resources.

Yuri seemed torn inside, as if he would lose control finally. But he remained motionless, leaning against the wall, merely watching.

Ash's eyes were now playful, yet adoring, as he rocked his head and swayed more freely, and moved even more quickly.

On and on they danced, spinning along the edge of the pool of light, into shadow and out of it, serenading one another. Tessa's face was ecstatic as that of a little girl whose greatest wish has been granted her.

It seemed to Michael that they should withdraw—Rowan, Yuri, and he—and leave them to their poignant and gentle union. Perhaps it was the only embrace they'd ever really know with each other. And they seemed now to have forgotten their watchers, and whatever lay ahead of them.

But he couldn't go. No one moved to go, and on and on the dance went until the rhythm slowed, until the instruments played more softly, warning that they would soon take their leave, and the overlapping lines of the canon blending in one last full-throated voice and then slacking, drawing away, the trumpet giving forth a final mournful note, and then silence.

The couple stopped in the very center of the floor, the light spilling down over their faces and their shimmering hair.

Michael rested against the stones, unable to move, only watching them.

Music like that could hurt you. It gave you back your disappointment, and your emptiness. It said, *Life can be this. Remember this.*

Silence.

Ash lifted the hands of the fairyqueen, looking at them carefully as he did so. Then he kissed her upturned palms and he let her go. And she stood staring at him, as if in love, perhaps not with him, perhaps with the music and the dance and the light, with everything.

He led her back to her loom, gently urging her to sit again on her stool, and then he turned her head so that her eyes fell on her old task, and as she peered at the tapestry, she seemed to forget that he was there. Her fingers reached for the threads, and began immediately to work.

Ash drew back, careful not to make a sound, and then he turned and looked at Stuart Gordon.

No plea or protest came from the old man, fallen to one side in the chair, his eyes moving without urgency from Ash to Tessa and then to Ash again.

The awful moment had come, perhaps. Michael didn't know. But surely some story, some long explanation, some desperate narrative would forestall it. Gordon had to try. Somebody had to try. Something had to happen to save this miserable human being; simply because he was that, something had to prevent this imminent execution.

"I want the names of the others," said Ash in the usual mild fashion. "I want to know who your cohorts were, both within and outside the Order."

Stuart took his time in answering. He didn't move, or look away from Ash. "No," he said finally. "Those names I will never give you."

It sounded as final as anything Michael had ever heard.

266

And the man, in his pain, seemed beyond any form of persuasion.

Ash began to walk calmly towards Gordon.

"Wait," said Michael. "Please, Ash, wait."

Ash stopped, politely looking to Michael.

"What is it, Michael?" he asked, as if he could not possibly presume to know.

"Ash, let him tell us what he knows," Michael said. "Let him give us his story!"

Seventeen

EVERYTHING WAS CHANGED. Everything was easier. She lay in Morrigan's arms and Morrigan lay in hers and—

It was evening when she opened her eyes.

What a great dream that had been. It was as if Gifford and Alicia and Ancient Evelyn had been with her, and there was no death and no suffering, and they had been together, dancing even, yes, dancing, in a circle.

She felt so good! Let it fade; the feeling remained with her. The sky was Michael's violet.

And there was Mary Jane standing over her, looking so goddamned cute with her flaxen yellow hair.

"You're Alice in Wonderland," said Mona, "that's who you are. I should nickname you Alice."

Going to be perfect, I promise you.

"I cooked the supper," said Mary Jane. "I told Eugenia to take the night off, hope you don't mind, when I saw that pantry I went crazy."

" 'Course I don't mind," said Mona. "Help me up, you're a real cousin."

She jumped up refreshed, feeling so light and free, like the baby tumbling inside, the baby with its long red hair swishing in the fluid, like a teeny rubbery doll with the teensiest little knobby knees. . . .

"I cooked yams, rice, and baked oysters in cheese, and broiled chicken with butter and tarragon."

"Wherever did you learn to cook like that?" asked Mona. Then she stopped and threw her arms around Mary Jane.

"There's nobody like us, is there? I mean, you know your blood, don't you?"

Mary Jane beamed at her. "Yeah, it's just wonderful. I love you, Mona Mayfair."

"Oh, I'm so glad to hear it," said Mona.

They had reached the kitchen doors, and Mona peered inside.

"God, you did cook a big supper."

"You better believe it," said Mary Jane proudly, again displaying her perfect white teeth. "I could cook when I was six years old. My mama was living with this chef then?? You know?? And then later on, I worked in a fancy restaurant in Jackson, Mississippi. Jackson's the capital, remember? This was a place where the senators ate. And I told them, 'You want me to work here, then you let me watch when the cook's doing things, you let me learn what I can.' What do you want to drink?"

"Milk, I'm starving for it," said Mona. "Don't run inside yet. Look, it's the magic time of twilight. This is Michael's favorite time."

If only she could remember in the dream who had been with her. Only the feeling of love lingered, utterly comforting love.

For a moment she worried fiercely for Rowan and Michael. How would they ever solve the mystery of who killed Aaron? But together they could probably defeat anybody, that is, if they really cooperated, and Yuri, well, Yuri's destiny had never been meant to involve itself with hers.

Everybody would understand when the time came.

The flowers had begun to glow. It was as if the garden were singing. She slumped against the door frame, humming with the flowers, humming as if the song were being made known to her by some remote part of her memory where beautiful and delicate things were never forgotten, but only securely stored. She could smell some perfume in the air—ah, it was the sweet olive trees!

"Honey, let's eat now," said Mary Jane.

"Very well, very well!" Mona sighed, threw up her arms and said farewell to the night, and then went inside.

She drifted into the kitchen, as if in a delicious trance, and sat down at the lavish table that Mary Jane had set for them. She'd taken out the Royal Antoinette china, the most delicate pattern of all, with fluted and gilded edges to the plates and saucers. Clever girl, such a wonderful clever girl. How unboring of her to have found the very best china by instinct. This cousin opened up a whole vista of possibilities, but how adventuresome was she, really? And how naive of Ryan to have dropped her off here, and left the two of them alone!

"I never saw china like that," Mary Jane was saying, bubbling away. "It's just like it's made of stiff starch cloth. How do they do it?" Mary Jane had just come back with a carton of milk and a box of powdered chocolate.

"Don't put that poison in the milk, please," said Mona, as she snatched the carton, tore it open, and filled her glass.

"I mean, how can they make china that's not flat, I don't get it, unless the china's soft like dough before they bake it, but even then—"

"Haven't the faintest idea," said Mona, "but I have always adored this pattern. Doesn't look good in the dining room. It's overshadowed by the murals. But looks absolutely splendid on this kitchen table, and how smart of you to have found the Battenburg lace table mats. I'm starving again, and we just had lunch. This is glorious, let's pig out now."

"We didn't just have lunch, and you didn't eat a thing," said Mary Jane. "I was scared to death you might mind me touching these things, but then I thought, 'If Mona Mayfair minds, I'll just slap-bang put them all away, like I found them.' "

"My darling, the house is ours for now," said Mona triumphantly.

God, the milk was good. She'd splashed it on the table, but it was so good, so good, so good.

Drink more of it.

"I am, I'm drinking it," she said.

"You're telling me," said Mary Jane, sitting down beside her. All the serving bowls were full of delectable and scrumptious things.

Mona heaped the steaming rice on her plate. Forget the gravy. This was wonderful. She began to eat it, not waiting for Mary Jane to serve herself, who was too busy dropping spoon after spoon of dirty chocolate powder into her own milk.

"Hope you don't mind. I just love chocolate. I can't live for too long without chocolate. There was a time when I made chocolate sandwiches, you know???? You know how to do that? You slap a couple Hershey bars between white bread, and you put sliced bananas and sugar too, and I'm telling you, that's delicious."

"Oh, I understand, might feel the same way if I wasn't pregnant. I once devoured an entire box of chocolate-covered cherries." Mona ate one big forkful of the rice after another. No chocolate could equal this. The chocolate-covered cherries had faded to an idea. And now the funniest thing. The white bread. It looked good too. "You know, I think I need complex carbohydrates," she said. "That's what my baby is telling me."

Laughing, or was it singing?

No problem; this was all so simple, so natural; she felt in harmony with the whole world, and it wouldn't be difficult to bring Michael and Rowan in harmony also. She sat back. A vision had taken hold of her, a vision of the sky speckled with all the visible stars. The sky was arched overhead, black and pure and cold, and people were singing, and the stars were magnificent, simply magnificent.

"What's that song you're humming?" asked Mary Jane.

"Shhh, hear that?"

Ryan had just come in. She could hear his voice in the dining room. He was talking to Eugenia. How marvelous to see Ryan. But he sure as hell wasn't taking Mary Jane out of here.

As soon as he stepped in the kitchen, Mona felt so sorry for him with his tired expression. He was still wearing his somber funeral suit. Ought to wear seersucker, the way the other men did this time of year. She loved the men in their seersucker suits in summer, and she loved the old ones who still wore the straw hats.

271

"Ryan, come join us," she said, chewing another huge mouthful of rice. "Mary Jane's cooked a feast."

"Just you sit right down here," said Mary Jane, hopping to her feet, "and I'll serve your plate, Cousin Ryan."

"No, I can't, dear," he said, being punctiliously polite to Mary Jane, because she was the country cousin. "I'm rushing. But thank you."

"Ryan is always rushing," said Mona. "Ryan, before you go, take a little walk outside, it's simply beautiful. Look at the sky, listen to the birds. And if you haven't smelled the sweet olives, it's time to do it now!"

"Mona, you're stuffing yourself with that rice. Is this going to be that kind of pregnancy?"

She tried not to go into spasms of laughter.

"Ryan, sit down, have a glass of wine," she said. "Where's Eugenia? Eugenia! Don't we have some wine?"

"I don't care for any wine, Mona, thank you." He made a dismissing gesture to Eugenia, who appeared for one moment in the lighted door, gnarled, angry, disapproving, and then slipped away.

Ryan looked so handsome in spite of his obvious crossness—a man who'd been polished all over with a big rag. She started to laugh again. Time for a gulp of milk, no, drink the whole glass. Rice and milk. No wonder people from Texas ate these two things together.

"Cousin Ryan, won't take a second—" said Mary Jane. "Just you let me fill you a plate."

"No, Mary Jane, thank you. Mona, there's something I have to tell you."

"Right now, during dinner? Oh, well, shoot. How bad can it be?" Mona poured some more milk from the carton, slopping a bit on the glass table. "After everything that's already happened? You know, the problem with this family is entrenched conservatism. I wonder if that is redundant. What do you think?"

"Miss Piggy," said Ryan dourly, "I am talking to you."

Mona went into hysterics. So did Mary Jane.

"I think I got a job as a cook," said Mary Jane, "and all I did to that rice was throw in some butter and garlic."

"It's the butter!" declared Mona, pointing at Mary Jane.

"Where's the butter? That's the secret, slop butter on everything." She picked up a slice of ordinarily pukey white bread, and carved out a glomp of oozy warm butter slowly melting on the saucer.

Ryan was looking at his watch, the infallible signal that he would remain in this spot no more than four more minutes. And God bless us all, he had not said one word about taking Mary Jane away.

"What is it, big boy?" asked Mona. "Hit me with it. I can take it."

"I don't know if you can," he said in a low voice.

That sent her into another reel of laughter. Or maybe it was the blank expression on Ryan's face. Mary Jane couldn't stop giggling. She stood beside Ryan, with her hand over her mouth.

"Mona, I'm off," he said, "but there are several boxes of papers up in the master bedroom. These are things that Rowan wanted, writings that came out of her last room in Houston." He gave a pointed look to Mary Jane, as if to say, She is not to know about all that.

"Oh yeah, writings," said Mona. "I heard you talking about it last night. You know, I heard a funny story, Ryan, that when Daphne du Maurier, you know who she was?"

"Yes, Mona."

"Well, when she was writing *Rebecca*, it began as an experiment to see how long she could go on without naming her first-person narrator. Michael told me this. It's true. And you know by the end of the book the experiment didn't matter. But you never do know the name of Maxim de Winter's second wife in that novel, or in the movie. Did you see the movie?"

"What's the point?"

"Well, you're like that yourself, Ryan, you're going to go to the grave without ever saying Lasher's name." Again, she broke into laughter.

Mary Jane laughed and laughed as though she knew everything.

There is nothing funnier than someone laughing at a joke, except for someone who does not even crack a smile and stares at you with a face full of outrage.

"Don't touch the boxes," said Ryan solemnly. "They belong to Rowan! But there is something I must tell you, about Michael, something I found in a genealogy in those papers. Mary Jane, please do sit down and eat your supper."

Mary Jane sat down.

"Right, genealogies," said Mona. "Wow, maybe Lasher knew things we didn't know. Mary Jane, genealogy is not a special interest with this family, it's a full-time obsession. Ryan, your four minutes are nearly up."

"What four minutes?"

She was laughing again. He had to leave. She was going to get sick, laughing like this.

"I know what you're gonna say," said Mary Jane, who jumped up again out of her chair, as though for truly serious conversations she had to be standing. "You're going to say Michael Curry is a Mayfair. I told you!"

All the vitality drained out of Ryan's face.

Mona drank down the fourth glass of milk. She had finished her rice, and lifting the serving bowl, she tipped it and let a new little mountain of soft, steaming rice grains fall on her plate.

"Ryan, stop staring at me," she said. "What is it about Michael? Is Mary Jane right? Mary Jane said Michael was a Mayfair the first time she met him."

"He is," declared Mary Jane. "I saw the resemblance right away, and you know who he looks like? He looks like that opera singer."

"What opera singer?" asked Ryan.

"Yeah, what opera singer?"

"Tyrone MacNamara, the one that Beatrice has pictures of, you know????? Those engravings on her wall???? Julien's father???? Well, Ryan, he must be your great-grandfather. I saw a passel a' cousins at the genealogical laboratory looked like that, Irish as can be, you never noticed? Of course you didn't, but then y'all have got Irish blood, French blood—"

"And Dutch blood," said Ryan in a terse, uncomfortable little voice. He looked at Mona, and then back at Mary Jane. "I have to go."

"Wait a second, is that it?" Mona demanded. She gulped

down her mouthful of rice, took another drink of milk. "Is that what you were going to tell me? Michael is a May-fair?"

"There is a mention," Ryan said, "in those papers, that apparently pertains to Michael, explicitly."

"God damn, you don't mean it," said Mona.

"You all are sooooo divinely inbred!" said Mary Jane. "It's like royalty. And here sits the Czarina herself!"

"I'm afraid you're right," said Ryan. "Mona, have you taken any medicine?"

"Certainly not, would I do that to my daughter?"

"Well, I have no choice but to go," he said. "Do try to behave yourselves. Remember the house is surrounded by guards. I don't want you going out, and please don't devil Eugenia!"

"Shucks," said Mona. "Don't leave. You're the life of the party. What do you mean 'devil Eugenia'?"

"When you've returned to your senses," said Ryan, "would you please call me? And what if this child is a boy? Certainly you aren't going to risk his life with one of those tests to determine gender."

"He's not a boy, silly," said Mona. "She's a girl and I've already named her Morrigan. I'll call you. Okay? Okay."

And away he went, hurrying in his own special quiet way of hurrying. Kind of like the way nuns hurry, or doctors. With a minimum of sound and fuss.

"Don't touch those papers," he called out from the butler's pantry.

Mona relaxed, took a deep breath. That was the last adult scheduled to be looking in on them, as far as she knew.

And what was this about Michael? "God, you think it's true? Hey, Mary Jane, when we're finished, let's go up and look at those papers."

"Oh, Mona, I don't know, he just said those were Rowan's papers, didn't he just say that? 'Don't touch those papers.' Mona, have some cream gravy. Don't you want the chicken? That's the best chicken I ever fixed."

"Cream gravy! You didn't say it was cream gravy. Morrigan doesn't want meat. Doesn't like meat. Look, I

275

have a right to look at those papers. If *he* wrote things, if *he* left anything in writing."

"Who's *he*?"

"Lasher. You know who he is. Don't tell me your Granny didn't tell you."

"She told me, all right, you believe in him?"

"Believe in him, dollface, he almost attacked me. I almost became a statistic like my mother and Aunt Gifford and all those other poor dead Mayfair women. Of course I believe in him, why he's . . ." She caught herself pointing to the garden, in the direction of the tree. No, don't tell her that, she'd sworn to Michael, never tell anyone, buried out there, and the other one, the innocent one, Emaleth, the one that had to die, though she'd never done anything to anyone ever.

Not you, Morrigan, don't you worry, baby girl!

"Long story, no time for it," she said to Mary Jane.

"I know who Lasher is," said Mary Jane. "I know what happened. Granny told me. The others didn't come right out and say he was killing the women. They just said Granny and I had to come to New Orleans and stay with everybody else. Well, you know? We didn't do it and nothing happened to us!"

She shrugged and shook her head.

"That could have been a terrible mistake," said Mona. The cream gravy tasted wonderful with the rice. Why all this white food, Morrigan?

The trees were filled with apples, and their meat was white, and the tubers and roots we pulled from the earth were white and it was paradise. Oh, but look at the stars. Was the unspoiled world really unspoiled, or were the everyday menaces of nature so terrible that everything was just as ruined then as it was now? If you live in fear, what does it matter. . . .

"What's the matter, Mona?" said Mary Jane. "Hey, snap out of it."

"Oh, nothing, actually," said Mona. "I just had a flash of the dream I had out there in the garden. I was having a hell of a conversation with somebody. You know, Mary Jane, people have to be educated to understand one another. Like

276

right now, you and I, we are educating each other to understand each other, you get what I mean?"

"Oh yeah, exactly, and then you can pick up your phone and call me down at Fontevrault and say, 'Mary Jane, I need you!' and I'd just leap up and get in the pickup and take off and be at your side."

"Yes, that's it, exactly, you know I really, really meant it, you'd know all kinds of things about me, and I'd know all kinds of things about you. It was the happiest dream I ever had. It was such a . . . such a happy dream. We were all dancing. A bonfire that big would normally scare me. But in the dream I was free, just perfectly free. I didn't care about anything. We need another apple. The invaders didn't invent death. That's a preposterous notion, but one can see why everybody thought that they had . . . well, sort of, everything depends on perspective, and if you have no sure concept of time, if you don't see the basic relevance of time, and of course hunter-gatherer people did and so did agricultural people, but perhaps those in tropical paradises don't ever develop that kind of relationship because for them there are no cycles. The needle's stuck on heaven. You know what I mean?"

"What *are* you talking about?"

"Well, pay attention, Mary Jane! And you'll know! It was that way in the dream, the invaders had invented death. No, I see now, what they had invented was *killing*. That's a different thing."

"There's a bowl full of apples over there, you want me to get you an apple?"

"Right, later. I want to go upstairs to Rowan's room."

"Well, lemme finish my meal," pleaded Mary Jane. "Don't go without me. Matter of fact, I don't know if we have any right to go up there at all."

"Rowan won't mind, Michael might mind. But you know???" said Mona, imitating Mary Jane. "It doesn't matter???"

Mary Jane nearly fell out of the chair laughing. "You are the worst child," she said. "Come on. Chicken's always better cold, anyway."

And the meat from the sea was white, the meat of the

shrimps and the fishes, and of the oysters and the mussels. Pure white. The eggs of gulls were beautiful, because they were all white outside, and when you broke them open one great golden eye stared at you, floating in the clearest fluid.

"Mona?"

She stood still in the door to the butler's pantry. She closed her eyes. She felt Mary Jane grip her hand.

"No," she said with a sigh, "it's gone again." Her hand moved to her belly. She spread her fingers out over the rounded swelling, feeling the tiny movements within. Beautiful Morrigan. Hair as red as my hair. *Is your hair so very red, Mama?*

"Can't you see me?"

In Mary Jane's eyes I see you.

"Hey, Mona, I'm going to get you a chair!"

"No, no, I'm okay." She opened her eyes. A lovely surge of energy shot through her. She stretched out her arms and ran, through the pantry and the dining room and down the long hall, and then up the stairway.

"Come on, let's go!" she was shouting.

It felt so good to run. That's one of the things she missed from childhood, and she hadn't even known it, just running, running all the way down St. Charles Avenue as fast as she could with her arms out. Running upstairs two at a time. Running around the block just to see if you could do it without stopping, without fainting, without having to throw up.

Mary Jane came pounding after her.

The door to the bedroom was closed. Good old Ryan. Probably locked it.

But no. When she opened it, the room was dark. She found the light switch, and the overhead chandelier went on, pouring a bright light over the smooth bed, the dressing table, the boxes.

"What's that smell?" asked Mary Jane.

"You smell it, don't you?"

"Sure do."

"It's Lasher's smell," she whispered.

"You mean it?"

278

"Yes," said Mona. There was the pile of brown cardboard boxes. "What's it like to you, the smell?"

"Hmmmm, it's good. Kind of makes you want butterscotch or chocolate or cinnamon, or something like that. Wooof. Where's it coming from? But you know what?"

"What?" asked Mona, circling the pile of boxes.

"People have died in this room."

"No kidding. Mary Jane, anybody could have told you that."

"What do you mean? About Mary Beth Mayfair, and Deirdre and all that. I heard all that when Rowan was sick in here, and Beatrice called down to get Granny and me to come to New Orleans. Granny told me. But somebody else died in here, somebody that smelled sort of like him. You smell it? You smell the three smells? The one smell is the smell of him. The other smell is the smell of the other one. And the third smell is the smell of death itself."

Mona stood very still, trying to catch it, but for her the fragrances must have been mingled. With a sharp, nearly exquisite pain, she thought of what Michael had described to her, the thin girl that was not a girl, not human. Emaleth. The bullet exploded in her ears. She covered them.

"What's the matter, Mona Mayfair?"

"Dear God, where did it happen?" Mona asked, still holding tight to her ears and squinching her eyes shut, and then opening them only to look at Mary Jane, standing against the lamp, a shadowy figure, her eyes big and brilliantly blue.

Mary Jane looked around, mostly with her eyes, though she did turn her head a little, and then she began to walk along the bed. Her head looked very round and small beneath her soft, flattened hair. She moved to the far side of the bed, and stopped. Her voice was very deep when she spoke.

"Right here. Somebody died right here. Somebody who smelled like him, but wasn't him."

There was a scream in Mona's ears, so loud, so violent it was ten times as terrible as the imagined gunshot. She clutched her belly. *Stop it, Morrigan, stop it. I promise you . . .*

279

"Goodness, Mona, you going to be sick?"

"No, absolutely not!" Mona shuddered all over. She began to hum a little song, not even asking herself what it was, just something pretty, something perhaps that she made up.

She turned and looked at the heap of irresistible boxes.

"It's on the boxes, too," said Mona. "You smell it real strong here? From him. You know, I have never gotten another single member of this family to admit that they could smell that smell."

"Well, it's just all over the place," said Mary Jane. She stood at Mona's side, annoyingly taller, and with more pointed breasts. "It's more all over these boxes, too, you're right. But look, all these boxes are taped up."

"Yes, and marked in neat black felt-tip pen, by Ryan, and this one, conveniently enough, says, 'Writings, Anonymous.' " She gave a soft laugh, nothing as giddy as before. "Poor Ryan. 'Writings, Anonymous.' Sounds like a psychology support group for books who don't know their authors."

Mary Jane laughed.

Mona was delighted, and broke into giggles. She went round the boxes, and eased down on her knees, careful not to shake the baby. The baby was still crying. The baby was flip-flopping like crazy. It was the smell, wasn't it? As much as all the foolish talk and imagining and picturing. She hummed to the baby . . . then sang softly:

" 'Bring flowers of the fairest, bring flowers of the rarest, from garden and woodland and hillside and dale!' " It was the gayest, sweetest hymn she knew, one that Gifford had taught her to sing, the hymn from the Maytime. " 'Our full hearts are swelling, our glad voices telling the tale of the loveliest rose of the dale!' "

"Why, Mona Mayfair, you've got a voice."

"Every Mayfair has a voice, Mary Jane. But really I haven't. Not like my mother did, or Gifford. You should have heard them. They were real sopranos. My voice is low."

She hummed the tune now without the words, picturing the forests, and the green land, and flowers. " 'Oh, Mary, we crown thee with blossoms today, queen of the angels, queen of the May. Oh, Mary, we crown thee with blossoms today. . . .' "

She rocked on her knees, her hand on her belly, the baby rocking gently with the music, her red hair all around her now, looking magnificent in the water of the womb, as if it were orange ink dropped into water, billowing out, that weightless, that translucent, that beautiful. Such tiny feet and tiny fingers. *What color are your eyes, Morrigan?*

I can't see my eyes, Mama, I can see only what you see, Mama.

"Hey, wake up, I'm scared you're gonna fall."

"Oh yes. I'm glad you called me back, Mary Jane, you did right to call me back, but I pray to heaven and the Blessed Mary Ever Virgin that this baby has green eyes like mine. What do you think?"

"Couldn't be a better color!" Mary Jane declared.

Mona laid her hands on the cardboard box in front of her. This was the right one. It reeked of him. Had he written these sheets in his own blood? And to think his body was down there. I ought to dig up that body. I mean, everything is changed now, Rowan and Michael are going to have to accept that, either that or I'm simply not going to tell them, I mean, this is an entirely new development and this one concerns *me*.

"What bodies are we going to dig up?" asked Mary Jane with a puckered frown.

"Oh, stop reading my mind! Don't be a Mayfair bitch, be a Mayfair witch. Help me with this box."

Mona ripped at the tape with her fingernails and pried back the cardboard.

"Mona, I don't know, this is somebody else's stuff."

"Yessssss," said Mona. "But this somebody else is part of my heritage, this somebody else has her own branch on this tree, and up through the tree from its roots runs this potent fluid, our lifeblood, and he was part of it, he lived in it, you might say, yes, ancient, and long-lived and forever, sort of like trees. Mary Jane, you know trees are the longest-lived things on earth?"

"Yeah, I know that," she said. "There's trees down near

Fontevrault that are so big???? I mean there's cypress trees down there with knees sticking up out of the water?"

"Shhhh," said Mona. She had pushed back all the brown wrapping—this thing was packed like it had to carry the Marie Antoinette china all the way to Iceland—and she saw the first page of a loose stack covered in a thin plastic, and bound with a thick rubber band. Scrawl, all right, spidery scrawl, with great long *l*'s and *t*'s and *y*'s, and little vowels that were in some cases no more than dots. But she could read it.

She made her hand a claw and tore the plastic.

"Mona Mayfair!"

"Guts, girl!" said Mona. "There's a purpose to what I do. Will you be my ally and confidante, or do you wish, right now, to abandon me? The cable TV in this house gets every channel, you can go to your room, and watch TV, if you don't want to be with me, or take a swim outside, or pick flowers, or dig for bodies under the tree—"

"I want to be your ally and confidante."

"Put your hand on this, then, country cousin. You feel anything?"

"Oooooh!"

"He wrote it. You are looking at the writing of a certified nonhuman! Behold."

Mary Jane was kneeling beside her. She had her fingertips on the page. Her shoulders were hunched, her flaxen hair hanging down on both sides of her face, spectacular as a wig. Her white eyebrows caught the light against her bronzed forehead, and you could practically see every hair. What was she thinking, feeling, seeing? What was the meaning of the look in her eyes? This kid is not stupid, I'll say that for her, she's not stupid. Trouble is . . .

"I'm so sleepy," Mona said suddenly, realizing it as soon as she said it. She put her hand to her forehead. "I wonder if Ophelia went to sleep before she drowned."

"Ophelia? You mean Hamlet's Ophelia?"

"Oh, you know what I mean," she said. "That's just great. You know, Mary Jane, I just love you."

She looked at Mary Jane. Yes, this was the Ultimate Cousin, the Cousin who could be a Great Friend, the

Cousin who could know everything that Mona knew. And nobody, really, nobody knew everything that Mona knew.

"But I'm so drowsy." She let herself fall gently to the floor, stretching out her legs and then her arms until she lay flat, looking up at the bright, pretty chandelier. "Mary Jane, would you go through that box? If I know Cousin Ryan, and I do, the genealogy is marked."

"Yeah," said Mary Jane.

How refreshing that she had stopped arguing.

"No, I'm not arguing, I figure we've gone this far, and beings this is the writing of a certified nonhuman being, beings we've gone this far . . . well, the point is, I can put it all back when we're through."

"Precisely," said Mona, laying her cheek against the cool floor. The smell was very strong in the floorboards! "And beings," she said, imitating Mary Jane, but without malice, no, no malice whatsoever, "and beings that knowledge is precious, one has to get it where one can."

Wow, the most incredible thing had happened. She'd closed her eyes and the hymn was singing itself. All she had to do was listen. She wasn't pushing these words out, these notes, it was just unfolding, like she was in one of those brain experiments where they zap part of your brain with an electrode and wham, you see visions, or you smell the creek on the hill behind your house when you were a little kid!

"That's what both of us have to realize, that witchcraft is an immense science," she said drowsily, talking easily over the pretty hymn, since it sang itself now. "That it is alchemy and chemistry and brain science, and that those things collected make up magic, pure lovely magic. We haven't lost our magic in the age of science. We have discovered a whole new bunch of secrets. We're going to win."

"Win?"

Oh Mary we crown thee with blossoms today, queen of the angels, queen of the May, oh Mary we crown thee . . . "Are you reading the pages, Mary Jane?"

"Well, hey, lookie, he has a whole folder here of Xerox

283

copies. 'Inventory in Progress: Relevant Pages, incomplete genealogy.' "

Mona rolled over on her back again. For a moment she didn't know where they were. Rowan's room. There were tiny prisms in the crystal baubles above. The chandelier that Mary Beth had hung there, the one from France, or had it been Julien? Julien, where are you? Julien, how did you let this happen to me?

But the ghosts don't answer unless they want to, unless they have a reason of their own.

"Well, I'm reading this here incomplete genealogy."

"You got it?"

"Yeah, the original and a Xerox. Everything here is in duplicate. Original and Xerox. Little packets like. What he's got circled here is Michael Curry, all right, and then all this stuff about Julien sleeping with some Irish girl, and that girl giving up her baby to Margaret's Orphanage, and then becoming a Sister of Mercy, Sister Bridget Marie, and the baby girl, the one in the orphanage, marrying a fireman named Curry, and him having a son, and then him, something, Michael! Right here."

Mona laughed and laughed. "Oncle Julien was a lion," she said. "You know what male lions do, when they come to a new pride? They kill all the young, so that the females go into heat at once, and then they sire as many young as they can. It's the survival of the genes. Oncle Julien knew. He was just improving the population."

"Yeah, well, from what I heard, he was pretty picky about who got to survive. Granny told me he shot our great-great-great-grandfather."

"I'm not sure that's the right number of 'greats.' What else do all those papers say?"

"Well, sugar plum, to tell you the truth, I couldn't have made this out if somebody hadn't marked it. There's just all kinds of things here. You know what this is like? It's like the writing that people do when they're high on drugs and they think they're being brilliant and the next day, lo and behold, they look at the tablets and see they've written little bitty jagged lines, like the lines, you know??? That make up an electrocardiogram?"

"Don't tell me you've been a nurse?"

"Yeah, for a while, but that was at this crazy commune where they made us all take an enema every day to get rid of the impurities in our system."

Mona started to laugh again, a lovely sleepy laugh. "I don't think a commune of the Twelve Apostles could have made me do that," she said.

This chandelier was damned near spectacular. That she had lived this long without lying on the floor and looking up at one of these things was just inexcusable. The hymn was still going, only this time, miracle of miracles, it was being played on some instrument, like a harp perhaps, and each note merged with the next note. She could almost not feel the floor under her, when she concentrated on the music and on the lights above.

"You didn't stay in that commune, did you?" she asked drowsily. "That sounds horrible."

"Sure didn't. I made my mother leave. I said, lookie, you leave with me or I cut out of here on my own. And as I was about twelve years old at the time, she wasn't about to let that happen. Lookie, here's Michael Curry's name again. He drew a circle around it."

"Lasher did? Or Ryan?"

"You got me. This is the Xerox, I can't tell. No, I see, the circle's drawn on the Xerox. Must have been Ryan, and this says something about 'waerloga.' Well, you know??? That probably means 'warlock.' "

"Right you are," said Mona. "That's Old English. I have at one time or another looked up the derivation of every single word that pertains to witches and witchcraft."

"Yeah, so have I. Warlock, right you are. Or it means, don't tell me, it means somebody who knows the truth all the time, right?"

"And to think it was Oncle Julien who wanted me to do this, that's the puzzle, but then a ghost knows his own business and Oncle Julien maybe didn't know. The dead don't know everything. The evil people do, whether they're dead or alive, or at least they know enough to tangle us up in such a web we can never escape. But Julien didn't know that Michael was his descendant. I know he didn't. He wouldn't have told me to come."

"To come where, Mona?"

"To this house on Mardi Gras night, to sleep with Michael, to make this baby that only Michael and I could have made, or maybe you too could have made it with Michael, perhaps, because you can smell that smell coming up out of these boxes, that smell of him?"

"Yeah, maybe I could, Mona. You never know."

"Right, sweets, you never know. But I got him first. I got Michael while the door was open before Rowan came home. Just slipped through the cracks, and wham! This baby, this marvelous little baby."

Mona turned over and lifted her head, resting her chin on her hands, elbows on the carpet.

"Mary Jane, you have to know everything."

"Yeah, I do," said Mary Jane. "I want to. I'm kind of worried about you."

"Me? Don't worry. I couldn't be better. I'm thirsty for some more milk, but otherwise, I'm fine. Look, I can still lie on my belly, well, actually no." She sat up. "That wasn't so comfortable, guess I have to kiss that goodbye for a while, you know, sleeping on your stomach?"

Mary Jane's brows had gone together in a very serious expression. She looked so cute! No wonder men were so damned patronizing to women. Did Mona look cute this way?

"Little witches!" said Mona in a hissing whisper, and she made her fingers flutter beside her hair.

Mary Jane laughed. "Yeah, little witches," she said. "So it was the ghost of Oncle Julien told you to come up here and sleep with Michael, and Rowan was nowhere around."

"Exactly, nowhere around. And Oncle Julien had more than a heavy hand in it, I tell you. The thing is, I fear he has gone to heaven and left us to our own devices, but then that is fine. I wouldn't want to have to explain this to him."

"Why wouldn't you?"

"It's a new phase, Mary Jane. You might say it's witch-craft in our generation. It's got nothing to do with Julien or

Michael or Rowan and the way that they would have solved things. It's something else altogether."

"Yeah, I see."

"You do, don't you?"

"Yep. You're really sleepy. I'm going to go get you some milk."

"Oh, that would be divine."

"You just lie down and go on to sleep, darlin'. Your eyes look really bad. Can you see me at all?"

"Sure, I can, but you're right. I'm just going to sleep right here. And, Mary Jane, take advantage of the situation."

"Oh, you're too young for that, Mona."

"No, silly, I didn't mean that," said Mona, laughing. "Besides, if I'm not too young for men, I'm not too young for girls either. As a matter of fact, I'm curious about doing it with a girl, or a woman perhaps, a beautiful woman like Rowan. But what I meant was, the boxes are opened. Take advantage of that fact, and read what you can out of them."

"Yeah, maybe I'll do that. I can't really read his handwriting, but I can read hers. And she's got stuff here."

"Yeah, read it. If you're going to help me, you have to read it. And down in the library, Mary Jane, the file on the Mayfair witches. I know you said you read it, but did you really read it?"

"You know, Mona? I'm not sure I really did."

Mona turned over on her side, and closed her eyes.

And as for you, Morrigan, let's go back, way, way back, none of this foolishness about invaders and Roman soldiers, way back to the plain, and tell me how it all began. Who is the dark-haired one that everyone so loves? "Good-night, Mary Jane."

"Listen, before you fly away here, darlin', who would you say is your very best trusted next of kin?"

Mona laughed. She almost forgot the question, then woke with a start.

"Aaah, you are, Mary Jane."

"Not Rowan and Michael?"

"Absolutely not. They must now be perceived as the enemy. But there are things I have to ask Rowan, I have to know from her, but she doesn't have to know what's going on with me. I have to think out the purpose for my questions. As for Gifford and Alicia, they're dead, and Ancient Evelyn is too sick, and Ryan is too dumb. And Jenn and Shelby are too innocent. And Pierce and Clancy are simply hopeless, and why ruin normal life for them? Have you ever put much of a premium on normal life?"

"Never."

"I guess I'm depending upon you, then, Mary Jane. 'Bye now, Mary Jane."

"Then what you're saying is, you don't want me to call Rowan or Michael in London and ask their advice."

"Good heavens, no." Six circles had formed, and the dance was beginning. She didn't want to miss it. "You mustn't do that, Mary Jane. You absolutely mustn't. Promise me you won't, Mary Jane. Besides, it's the middle of the night in London and we don't know what they're doing, do we? God help them. God help Yuri."

Mona *was* floating away. Ophelia, with the flowers in her hair, moving steadily downstream. The branches of the trees came down to stroke her face, to touch the water. No, she was dancing in the circle, and the dark-haired one was standing in the very center and trying to tell them, but everyone was laughing and laughing. They loved him, but they knew he had a habit of going on and on, with such foolish worries. . . .

"Well, I am worried about you, Mona, I should tell you . . ."

Mary Jane's voice was very far away. Flowers, bouquets of flowers. That explains everything, why I have dreamed gardens all my life, and drawn pictures of gardens with crayons. Why are you always drawing gardens, Mona, Sister Louise asked me. I love gardens, and First Street's garden was so ruined until they cleared it and changed it, and now, all clipped and kept, it harbors the worst secret of all.

No, Mother, don't . . .

No, the flowers, the circles, *you talk!* This dream was going to be as good as the last one.

"Mona?"

"Let me go, Mary Jane."

Mona could barely hear her; besides, it didn't make any difference what she said.

And that was a good thing, too, because this was what came out of Mary Jane's mouth, far, far away . . . before Mona and Morrigan began to sing.

". . . you know, Mona Mayfair, I hate to tell you this, but that baby's grown since you went to sleep out by the tree!"

Eighteen

"**I** THINK WE should leave now," said Marklin.
He lay on Tommy's bed, his head resting on his clasped hands, studying over and over the knots in the wood of the bed's coffered canopy.

Tommy sat at the desk, feet crossed on the black leather ottoman. This room was larger than Marklin's, with a southern exposure, but he had never resented it. He had loved his own room. Well, he was ready now to get out of it. He had packed everything of importance in one suitcase, and hidden it under his own bed.

"Call it a premonition. I don't want to stay here," he said. "There's no reason to stay longer."

"You're being fatalistic and a bit silly," said Tommy.

"Look, you've wiped the computers. Stuart's quarters are absolutely impenetrable, unless we want to risk breaking in the doors, and I don't like being under a curfew."

"The curfew is for everyone, may I remind you, and if we were to leave now, we wouldn't make it to the door without a dozen questions. Besides, to walk out before the memorial service would be blatantly disrespectful."

"Tommy, I can't endure some tenebrious ceremony in the small hours of the morning, with a lot of preposterous speeches about Anton and Aaron. I want to go now. Customs; rituals. These people are fools, Tommy. It's too late to be anything but frank. There are back stairs; there are side stairs. I'm for leaving here immediately. I have things on my mind. I have work to do."

"I want to do what they asked us to do," said Tommy, "which is what I intend to do. Observe the curfew they have asked us to observe. And go down when the bell is sounded. Now, please, Marklin, if you have nothing insightful or helpful to say, be quiet, will you?"

"Why should I be quiet? Why do you want to stay here?"

"All right, if you must know, we may have a chance during the memorial, or whatever it is, to find out where Stuart is keeping Tessa."

"How could we find out that?"

"Stuart's not a rich man, Marklin. He's bound to have a home somewhere, a place we've never seen, some ancestral manse or something. Now, if we play our cards right, we can ask a few questions about this subject, out of concern, of course, for Stuart. Have you got a better idea?"

"Tommy, I don't think Stuart would hide Tessa in a place that was known to be his home. He's a coward, perhaps, a melodramatic lunatic even, but he's not stupid. We are not going to find Stuart. And we are not going to find Tessa."

"Then what do we do?" asked Tommy. "Abandon everything? With what we know?"

"No. We leave here. We go back to Regent's Park. And we think. We think about something far more important to us now than anything the Talamasca can offer."

"Which is?"

"We think, Tommy, about the Mayfair witches. We go over Aaron's last fax to the Elders. And we study the File, we study it closely for every clue as to which of the clan is most useful for our purposes."

"You're going too fast," said Tommy. "What do you mean to do? Kidnap a couple of Americans?"

"We can't discuss it here. We can't plan anything. Look, I'll wait till the damned ceremony starts, but then I'm leaving. I'm stepping out at the first opportunity. You can come later if you like."

"Don't be stupid," said Tommy. "I don't have a car. I have to go with you. And what if Stuart's at the ceremony? Have you thought of that?"

"Stuart's not coming back here. He has better sense.

Now, listen, Tommy. This is my final decision. I'll stay for the beginning of the ceremony, I'll pay my respects, chat with a few of the members, that sort of thing. And then I'm out of here! And on, on to my rendezvous with the Mayfair witches, Stuart and Tessa be damned."

"All right, I'll go with you."

"That's better. That's intelligent. That's my practical Tommy."

"Get some sleep then. They didn't say when they'd call us. And you're the one who's going to drive."

Nineteen

THE TOPMOST ROOM of the tower. Yuri sat at the round table, looking down into the cup of steaming Chinese tea before him.

The condemned man himself had made the tea. Yuri didn't want to touch it.

All his life in the Talamasca, he had known Stuart Gordon. He had dined countless times with Gordon and Aaron. They had strolled the gardens together, gone to the retreats in Rome together. Aaron had talked so freely with Gordon. The Mayfair witches and the Mayfair witches and the Mayfair witches. And now it was Gordon.

Betrayed him.

Why didn't Ash kill him now? What could the man give that would not be contaminated, not perverted by his madness? It was almost a certainty that his helpers had been Marklin George and Tommy Monohan. But the Order would discover the truth on that score. Yuri had reached the Motherhouse from the phone booth in the village, and the mere sound of Elvera's voice had brought him to tears. Elvera was faithful. Elvera was good. Yuri knew that the great chasm that had opened between him and the Talamasca had already begun to close. If Ash was right, that the conspiracy had been small, and indeed that seemed to be the case—that the Elders were not involved—then Yuri must be patient. He must listen to Stuart Gordon. Because Yuri had to take back to the Talamasca whatever he learned tonight.

Patience. Aaron would want it thus. Aaron would want the story known, and recorded for others to know. And Michael and Rowan, were they not entitled to the facts? And then there was Ash, the mysterious Ash. Ash had uncovered Gordon's treachery. If Ash had not appeared in Spelling Street, Yuri would have accepted Gordon's pretense of innocence, and the few foolish lies Gordon had told while they sat in the café.

What went on in Ash's mind? He was overwhelming, just as Yuri had told them. Now they knew. They saw for themselves his remarkable face, the calm, loving eyes. But they mustn't forget that he was a menace to Mona, to any of the Mayfair family—

Yuri forced himself to stop thinking about this. They needed Ash too much just now. Ash had somehow become the commander of this operation. What would happen if Ash withdrew and left them with Gordon? They couldn't kill Gordon. They couldn't even scare him, at least Yuri didn't think so. It was impossible to gauge how much Rowan and Michael hated Gordon. Unreadable. Witches. He could see that now.

Ash sat on the other side of the circle, his monstrous hands clasped on the edge of the old, unfinished wood, watching Gordon, who sat to his right. He did hate Gordon, and Yuri saw it by the absence of something in Ash's face, the absence of compassion, perhaps? The absence of the tenderness which Ash showed to everyone, absolutely everyone else.

Rowan Mayfair and Michael Curry sat on either side of Yuri, thank God. He could not have endured to be close to Gordon. Michael was the wrathful one, the suspicious one. Rowan was taken with Ash. Yuri had known she would be. But Michael was taken with no one just yet.

Yuri could not touch this cup. It might as well have been filled with the man's urine.

"Out of the jungles of India," said Stuart, sipping his own tea, in which he had poured a large slug of whiskey. "I don't know where. I don't know India. I know only that the natives said she'd been there forever, wandering from village to village, and that she'd come to them before the war, and that she spoke English and that she didn't grow

294

old, and the women of the village had become frightened of her."

The whiskey bottle stood in the middle of the table. Michael Curry wanted it, but perhaps he could not touch the refreshments offered by Gordon either. Rowan Mayfair sat with her arms folded. Michael Curry had his elbows on the table. He was closer to Stuart, obviously trying to figure him out.

"I think it was a photograph, her undoing. Someone had taken a picture of the entire village, together. Some intrepid soul with a tripod and a wind-up camera. And she had been in that picture. It was one of the young men who uncovered it among his grandmother's possessions when the grandmother died. An educated man. A man I'd taught at Oxford."

"And he knew about the Talamasca."

"Yes, I didn't talk much to my students about the Order, except for those who seemed as if they might want to . . ."

"Like those boys," said Yuri.

He watched the light jump in Stuart's eye, as if the lamp nearby had jumped, and not Stuart.

"Yes, well, those boys."

"What boys?" asked Rowan.

"Marklin George and Tommy Monohan," said Yuri.

Stuart's face was rigid. He lifted the mug of tea with both hands and drank deeply.

The whiskey smelled medicinal and sickening.

"Were they the ones who helped you with this?" asked Yuri. "The computer genius and the Latin scholar?"

"It was my doing," said Stuart, without looking at Yuri. He was not looking at any of them. "Do you want to hear what I have to say, or not?"

"They helped you," said Yuri.

"I have nothing to say on the subject of my accomplices," Gordon said, looking coldly at Yuri now, and then back again into empty space, or the shadows along the walls.

"It was the two young ones," said Yuri, though Michael was gesturing to him to hold back. "What about Joan Cross, or Elvera Fleming, or Timothy Hollingshed?"

Stuart made an impatient and disgusted gesture at the mention of these names, hardly realizing how this might be interpreted in relation to the boys.

"Joan Cross doesn't have a romantic bone in her body," Stuart said suddenly, "and Timothy Hollingshed has always been overrated due simply to his aristocratic background. Elvera Fleming is an old fool! Don't ask me these questions anymore. I won't be made to speak of my accomplices. I won't be made to betray them. I'll die with that secret, be assured."

"So this friend," said Ash, his expression patient but surprisingly cold, "this young man in India, he wrote to you, Mr. Gordon."

"Called me, as a matter of fact, told me he had a mystery for me. He said he could get her to England, if I'd take over once she arrived. He said that she couldn't really fend for herself. She seemed mad, and then not mad. No one could quite analyze her. She spoke of times unknown to the people around her. And when he'd made inquiries, with a view to sending her home, he found she was a legend in that part of India. I have a record of it all. I have our letters. They are all here. There are copies in the Motherhouse as well. But the originals are here. Everything I value is in this tower."

"You knew what she was when you saw her?"

"No. It was extraordinary. I found myself enchanted by her. Some selfish instinct dominated my actions. I brought her here. I didn't want to take her to the Motherhouse. It was most peculiar. I couldn't have told anyone what I was doing or why, except for the obvious fact that I was so charmed by her. I had only lately inherited this tower from my mother's brother, an antiquarian who had been my family mentor. It seemed the perfect place.

"The first week, I scarcely left at all. I had never been in the company of such a person as Tessa. There was a gaiety and simplicity in her which gave me inexpressible happiness."

"Yes, I'm sure," said Ash softly, with a trace of a smile. "Please go on with your story."

"I fell in love with her." He paused, eyebrows raised, as

if amazed by his own words. He seemed excited by the revelation. "I fell completely in love with her."

"And you kept her here?" asked Yuri.

"Yes, she's been here ever since. She never goes out. She's afraid of people. It's only when I've been here a long while that she'll talk, and then she tells her amazing tales.

"She's seldom coherent, or I should say chronological. The little stories always make sense. I have hundreds of recordings of her talking, lists of Old English words and Latin words which she has used.

"You see, what became clear to me almost immediately was that she was speaking of two different lives, a very long one which she was living now, and a life she'd lived before."

"Two lives? Then you mean, simply, reincarnation."

"After a long while, she explained," said Gordon. He was now so passionately involved in his tale, he seemed to have forgotten the danger to him. "She said that all her kind had two lives, sometimes more," he went on. "That you were born knowing all you needed to know to survive, but then gradually an earlier life came back to you, and bits and pieces of others. And it was the memory of this earlier life that kept you from going mad among human beings."

"You had realized," asked Rowan, "by this time, that she wasn't human. She would have fooled me."

"No. Not at all. I thought she was human. Of course, there were strange characteristics to her—her translucent skin, her tremendous height, and her unusual hands. But I didn't think, 'No, this being isn't human.'

"It was she who said that she wasn't human. She said it more than once. Her people lived before humans. They had lived thousands of years in peace on islands in the northern seas. These islands were warmed by volcanic springs from the depths, by geysers of steam, and pleasant lakes.

"And this she knew, not because she herself had lived at that time, but because others she had known in her first lifetime could remember a former life in this paradise, and that was how her people knew their history, through the inevitable and always singular remembrance of earlier lives.

"Don't you see? It was incredible, the idea that everyone

would come into this world with some distinct and valuable historical memories! It meant that the race knew more of itself than humans could possibly know. It knew of earlier ages from, so to speak, firsthand experience!"

"And if you bred Tessa to another of her race," said Rowan, "you would have a child who could remember an earlier life—and then perhaps another child and another life remembered."

"Exactly! The chain of memory would be established, and who knows how far back it would go, for each one, remembering some earlier existence, remembering the tales of those he had known and loved in that time who remembered having lived before!"

Ash listened to all this without comment, or any perceptible change of emotion. None of it seemed to surprise him or offend him. Yuri almost smiled. It was the same simplicity he'd observed in Ash at Claridge's, when they had first spoken.

"Someone else might have dismissed Tessa's claims," said Gordon, "but I recognized the Gaelic words she used, the bits of Old English, the Latin, and when she wrote down the runic script, I could read it! I knew she told the truth."

"And this you kept to yourself," said Rowan, neutrally, as if merely trying to quell Gordon's annoying emotion and get back on track.

"Yes! I did. I almost told Aaron about it. The more Tessa talked, the more she spoke of the Highlands, of early Celtic rituals and customs, of Celtic saints even, and the Celtic church.

"You do know that our church in England then was Celtic or Briton or whatever you want to call it, founded by the Apostles themselves, who had come from Jerusalem to Glastonbury. We had no connection with Rome. It was Pope Gregory and his henchman, St. Augustine, who thrust the Roman church on Britain."

"Yes, but then you did not tell Aaron Lightner?" asked Ash, raising his voice just slightly. "You were saying . . . ?"

"Aaron had already gone to America. He had gone there to make contact once more with the Mayfair witches, and

298

to pursue other paths in psychic investigation. It was no time to question Aaron about his early research. And then, of course, I had done something wrong. I had taken a woman entrusted to me as a member of the Order, and I had kept her for myself, almost a prisoner. Of course, there has never been anything stopping Tessa from leaving, nothing but her own fear. But I had closeted this woman away. I had told the Order nothing about it."

"But how did you make the connection?" asked Ash. "Between Tessa and the Mayfair witches?"

"Oh, it wasn't that difficult at all. One thing followed upon another. As I said, Tessa's speech was full of references to archaic Highland customs. She spoke over and over of the circles of stones built by her people and later used by the Christians for bizarre rituals to which their priests could never put a stop.

"You know our mythology, surely all of you, some of you. The ancient myths of Britain are full of mythic giants. Our stories say the giants built the circles, and so did Tessa. Our giants lingered long after their time in the dark and remote places, in the caves by the sea, in the caves of the Highlands. Well, Tessa's giants, hunted from the earth, almost annihilated, also survived in secret places! And when they did dare to appear among human beings, they incited both worship and fear. It was the same, she said, with the Little Folk, whose origins had been forgotten. They were revered on the one hand, and feared on the other. And often the early Christians of Scotland would dance and sing within the circle of stones, knowing that the giants had once done this—indeed, had built the circles for that purpose—and they would, by their music, lure the giants from hiding, so that the giants came down to join the dance, at which point these Christians would slaughter them to satisfy the priests, but not before using them to satisfy old gods."

"How do you mean, 'using them'?" asked Rowan.

Gordon's eyes glazed slightly, and his voice dropped to a soft, nearly pleasant tone, as if the mere mention of these things could not but evoke a sense of wonder.

"Witchcraft, that is what we are talking about—early,

299

blood-drenched witchcraft, in which superstition, under the yoke of Christianity, reached back into a pagan past for magic, to do *maleficia*, or to gain power, or only to witness a dark secret rite which thrilled them as criminal acts have always thrilled humankind. I longed to corroborate Tessa's stories.

"Without confiding in anyone, I went to the very cellars of the Motherhouse, the places where the oldest unexamined material on British folklore had been stored. These were manuscripts that had been deemed 'fanciful' and 'irrelevant' by the scholars, like Aaron, who had spent years translating old documents. This material did not exist in our modern inventory or our modern computer banks. One had to touch the crumbling pages with one's own hand.

"Oh, what I found! Crumbling quartos and books of beautifully illustrated parchment, the works of Irish monks and the Benedictines and the Cistercians, complaining of the mad superstition of the common people, and filled with tales of these giants and these Little Folk, and how the common people persisted in believing in them, in luring them out, in using them in various ways.

"And right there, mixed in with these ranting condemnations, were tales of giant saints! Giant knights and kings!

"Here, at Glastonbury, only a little way from where we sit now, a giant of seven feet was unearthed in former times, and declared to be King Arthur. What was this but one of Tessa's giants, I ask you? Such creatures have been found all over Britain.

"Oh, a thousand times I was tempted to call Aaron. How Aaron would have loved these stories, especially those which had come directly from the Highlands and its haunted lochs and glens.

"But there was only one person in this world in whom I could confide. And that was Tessa.

"And as I brought home my carefully excavated stories, Tessa recognized these rituals, these patterns—indeed, the names of saints and kings. Of course, Tessa didn't speak with sophisticated words. It came in fragments from her, how her people had become a sacred quarry, and could save themselves from torture and death only by rising to power and gaining sway over the Christians, or by fleeing deeper and deeper into the great forests which still covered the mountains in those years, and into the caves and the secret valleys where they struggled to live in peace."

"And this you never told Aaron," said Yuri.

Gordon ignored the words. He continued:

"Then, in a painful voice, Tessa confessed to me that she had once suffered horribly at the hands of Christian peasants, who had imprisoned her and forced her to receive man after man from all the villages round. The hope was that she would give birth to another giant like herself, a giant who would spring from the womb, speaking, knowing, and growing to maturity within hours—a creature which the villagers might then have killed before her eyes!

"It had become a religion to them, don't you see? Catch the Taltos, breed it, sacrifice the offspring. And Christmas, that time of ancient pagan rituals, had become their favorite period for the sacred game. From this hideous captivity Tessa had finally escaped, having never given birth to the sacrificial creature, and only suffering a flow of blood from the seed of each human man."

He stopped, his brows knit. His face became sad, and he looked at Ash.

"This is what hurt my Tessa? This is what dried the fount?" It wasn't so much a question as a confirmation of what had been revealed earlier, only Ash, feeling no need, apparently, to confirm it, did not speak.

Gordon shuddered.

"She spoke of horrible things!" he said. "She talked of the males lured down into the circles, and of the village maidens offered to them; but if the giant was not born to such a maiden, death would surely result. And when enough maidens had died that the people doubted the power of this male giant, he was then burnt as the sacrifice. Indeed, he was always burnt, whatever the outcome, or whether or not he had fathered a sacrificial offspring, because the males were so greatly feared."

"So they didn't fear the women," said Rowan. "Because the women didn't bring death to the human men who lay with them."

"Exactly," said Gordon. "However!" He held up his finger with a little delighted smile. "However! It did now and then happen, yes! That the male giant or the female giant did parent, as it were, the magical child of its own race. And there would be this newborn giant for all to behold.

"No time was more propitious for such a union than Christmas, December Twenty-fifth, the feast of the old solar god! And it was said then—when a giant was born—that the heavens had once again copulated with the earth, and out of the union had come a great magic, as had happened at the First Creation; and only after great feasting, and singing of the Christmas songs, was the sacrifice carried out in Christ's name. Now and then a giant fathered or mothered many such off-spring, and Taltos mated with Taltos, and the fires of sacrifice filled the glens, the smoke rising to heaven, bringing an early spring and warm winds and good rains, and making the crops grow."

Gordon broke off, turning enthusiastically to Ash. "You must know all of this. You yourself could give us links in the chain of memory. Surely you too have lived an earlier life. You could tell us things which no human can ever discover in any other way. You can tell them with clarity and power, for you're strong, and not addled, like my poor Tessa! You can give us this gift."

Ash said nothing. But his face had darkened, and Gordon seemed not at all aware of it.

He's a fool, thought Yuri. Perhaps that is what great schemes of violence always require—a romantic fool.

Gordon turned to the others, even to Yuri, to whom he appealed now. "Don't you understand? Surely you understand now what such possibilities meant to me?"

"What I know," said Yuri, "is that you didn't tell Aaron. And you didn't tell the Elders, either, did you? The Elders never knew. Your brothers and sisters never knew!"

"I told you. I could trust no one with my discoveries, and frankly, I would not. They were mine. Besides, what would our beloved Elders have said, if 'said' is even appropriate for their endless silent communications! A fax would have come through directing me to bring Tessa to the Motherhouse at once, and to— No, this discovery was mine by right. I had found Tessa."

"No, you lie to yourself and everyone else," said Yuri. "Everything that you are is because of the Talamasca."

"That's a contemptible thought! Have I given the Talamasca nothing? Besides, it was never my idea to hurt our own members! The doctors involved, yes, I agreed to this, though again I would never have proposed it."

"You did kill Dr. Samuel Larkin?" asked Rowan in her low, expressionless voice, probing but not meaning to alarm him.

"Larkin, Larkin ... Oh, I don't know. I get confused. You see, my helpers had some very different notions from mine, about what was required to keep the whole thing secret. You might say I went along with the more daring aspects of the plan. In truth, I can't imagine simply killing another human being."

He glared at Ash, accusingly.

"And your helpers, their names?" asked Michael. His tone was not unlike Rowan's, low-key, entirely pragmatic. "The men in New Orleans, Norgan and Stolov, you invited those men to share these secrets?"

"No, of course not," declared Gordon. "They weren't really members, any more than Yuri here was a member. They were merely investigators for us, couriers, that kind of thing. But by that time it had ... it had gotten out of hand, perhaps. I can't say. I only know my friends, my confidants, they felt they could control those men with secrets and money. That's what it's always about, corruption— secrets and money. But let's get away from all that. What matters here is the discovery itself. That is what is pure and what redeems everything."

"It redeems nothing!" said Yuri. "For gain you took your knowledge! A common traitor, looting the archives for personal gain."

"Nothing could be farther from the truth," declared Gordon.

"Yuri, let him go on," said Michael quietly.

Gordon calmed himself with remarkable will, appealing to Yuri again in a manner that infuriated Yuri.

"How can you think that my goals were other than spiritual?" asked Gordon. "I, who have grown up in the shadow of Glastonbury Tor, who all his life has been devoted to esoteric knowledge, only for the light it brings into our souls?"

"It was spiritual gain, perhaps," said Yuri, "but it was gain, personal gain. And that is your crime."

"You try my patience," said Gordon. "Perhaps you should be sent from this room. Perhaps I should say nothing more. . . ."

"Tell your story," said Ash calmly. "I'm growing impatient."

Gordon stopped, gazed at the table, one eyebrow raised, as if to say he need not settle for this ultimatum.

He looked at Ash coldly.

"How did you make the connection?" asked Rowan. "Between all of this and the Mayfair witches?"

"I saw a connection at once. It had to do with the circle of stones. I had always known the original tale of Suzanne, the first Mayfair, the witch of the Highlands who had called up a devil in the circle of stones. And I had read Peter van Abel's description of that ghost and how it pursued him, and taunted him, and evinced a will far stronger than any human haunt.

"The account of Peter van Abel was the first record of the Mayfair witches which Aaron translated, and it was to me, naturally, that he came with many questions about the old Latin. Aaron was always coming to me in those days for assistance."

"How unfortunate for him," said Yuri.

"Naturally it occurred to me, what if this Lasher were the soul of another species of being seeking to reincarnate? How well it fitted the whole mystery! And Aaron had only lately written from America that the Mayfair family faced its darkest hour when the ghost who would be made flesh was threatening to come through.

"Was this the soul of a giant wanting its second life? At last my discoveries had become too momentous. I had to share them. I had to bring into this those I trusted."

"But not Stolov and Norgan."

"No! My friends . . . my friends were of an entirely different ilk. But you're confusing me. Stolov and Norgan weren't involved then. No. Let me continue."

"But they were in the Talamasca, these friends," said Rowan.

"I will tell you nothing of them except that they were . . . they were young men in whom I believed."

"You brought these friends here, to the tower?"

"Indeed not," said Stuart. "I'm not that much of a fool. Tessa I revealed to them, but in a spot chosen by me for the purpose, in the ruin of Glastonbury Abbey, on the very spot where the skeleton of the seven-foot giant had been unearthed, only to be later reinterred.

"It was a sentimental thing, my taking her there, to stand over the grave of one of her own. And there I allowed her to be worshiped by those whom I trusted to help with my work. They had no idea that her permanent abode was less than a mile away. They were never to know.

"But they were dedicated and enterprising. They suggested the very first scientific tests. They helped me obtain with a syringe the first blood from Tessa, which was sent to various laboratories for anonymous analysis. And then we had the first firm proof that Tessa was not human! Enzymes, chromosomes, it was all quite beyond me. But they understood it."

"They were doctors?" Rowan asked.

"No. Only very brilliant young men." A shadow passed over his face, and he glanced viciously at Yuri.

Yes, your acolytes, Yuri thought. But he said nothing. If he interrupted again, it would be to kill Gordon.

"Everything was so different at that point! There were no plots to have people killed. But then, so much more was to happen."

"Go on," said Michael.

"My next step was obvious! To return to the cellars, to all the abandoned folklore, and research only those saints of exceedingly great size. And what should I come upon but a pile of hagiography—manuscripts saved from destruction at the time of Henry VIII's ghastly suppression of the mon-

305

asteries, and dumped in our archives along with thousands of other such texts.

"And ... And among these treasures was a carton marked by some long-dead secretary or clerk: 'Lives of the Scottish Saints.' And the hastily scribbled subtitle: 'Giants'!

"At once I happened upon a later copy of an early work by a monk at Lindisfarne, writing in the 700s, who told the tale of St. Ashlar, a saint of such magic and power that he had appeared among the Highlanders in two different and separate eras, having been returned by God to earth, as was the Prophet Isaiah, and who was destined, according to legend, to return again and again."

Yuri looked at Ash, but Ash said nothing. Yuri couldn't even remember whether Gordon had ever understood Ash's name. But Gordon was already staring at Ash, and then said quickly:

"Could this be the very personage for whom you were named? Could it be that you know of this saint yourself, through your remembrances or those you heard from others, assuming you have known others like yourself?" Gordon's eyes blazed.

Ash didn't answer. The silence this time was stony. Something changed again in Ash's face. Was it pure hatred that he felt for Gordon?

Gordon at once resumed his account, his shoulders hunched and his hands working now in his excitement.

"I was overcome with enthusiasm when I read that St. Ashlar had been a giant of a being, standing perhaps seven feet tall, that St. Ashlar had come from a pagan race whom he himself had helped to exterminate—"

"Get on with it," said Ash softly. "How did you connect this with the Mayfair witches? How did men come to die as the result?"

"All right," said Gordon patiently, "but you will perhaps grant this dying man one request."

"Perhaps not," said Ash. "But what is it?"

"You will tell me whether or not these tales are actually known to you, whether you yourself have remembrances of these early times?"

Ash made a gesture that Gordon should continue.

"Ah, you are cruel, my friend," said Gordon.

Ash was becoming deeply angry. It was plain to see. His full black hair and smooth, almost innocent mouth rendered his expression all the more menacing. He was like an angel gathering its anger. He did not respond to Gordon's words.

"You brought home these tales to Tessa?" asked Rowan.

"Yes," said Gordon, ripping his eyes off Ash finally and looking to her. A little false smile came over his mouth as he continued—as if to say, Now we will answer the question of the pretty lady in the first row.

"I did bring the tale home to Tessa; over supper, as always, I told her of my reading. And the history of this very saint, she knew! Ashlar, one of her own people, and a great leader, a king among them, who had converted to Christianity, betraying his own kind. I was triumphant. Now I had this name to track through history.

"And the following morning I was back at the archives and hard at work. And then, and then . . . came my momentous discovery, that for which other scholars of the Talamasca would give their eyeteeth, if only they knew."

He paused, glancing from one face to another, and even to Yuri finally, his smile full of pride.

"This was a book, a codex of vellum, such as I had never seen in my long life of scholarship! And never dreamed that I would see 'St. Ashlar,' that was the name carved on the cover of the wood box which contained it. 'St. Ashlar.' That was the name of the saint that leapt from the dust and the shadows as I went along the shelves with my electric torch."

Another pause.

"And beneath that name," said Gordon, again looking from one to the other to enlarge the drama. "Beneath, in runic script, were the words, 'History of the Taltos of Britain!' and in Latin: 'Giants in the Earth!' As Tessa was to confirm for me that very night with a simple nod of her head, I had hit upon the crucial word itself.

"Taltos. 'That is what we are,' she said.

"At once I left the tower. I drove back to the Motherhouse. I went down into the cellar. Other records I had always examined within the house, in the libraries or

307

wherever I chose. When has such scholarship ever attracted anyone's notice? But *this* I had to possess."

He rose, resting his knuckles on the table. He looked at Ash, as if Ash would move to stop him. Ash's face was dark, and some imperceptible change had rendered it utterly cold.

Gordon drew back, turned, and then went directly to a big carved cabinet against the wall, and took out of it a large rectangular box.

Ash had watched him calmly, not anticipating an attempt at escape, or confident that he could catch Gordon if Gordon had run for the stairway.

And now Ash stared at the box as Gordon set it down before them. It seemed something was building in Ash, something that might explode.

Good God, the document is genuine, thought Yuri.

"See," Gordon said, his fingers resting on the oiled wood as if on the sacred. "St. Ashlar," he said. And again he translated the rest.

"And what do you think is in this box, all of you? What would you guess?"

"Get on with it, please, Gordon," said Michael, throwing a pointed glance at Ash.

"I shall!" Gordon declared in a whisper, and then, opening the box, he drew out a huge book with stiff leather covers, and laid it down in front of him, as he pushed the box aside.

At once he opened the cover and revealed the title page on the vellum, beautifully illustrated in crimson and gold and royal blue. Tiny miniatures speckled the Latin text. He turned the page carefully. Yuri saw more gorgeous writing and more fine, tiny illustrations whose beauty could only be studied by someone looking through a glass.

"Behold, for you have never in your life seen such a document. For it was written by the saint himself.

"It is the history of the Taltos from their earliest beginnings; the history of a race annihilated; and his own confession that he himself—priest, miracle worker, saint if you will—is not human, but one of the lost giants. It is his plea, to Saint Columba himself, the great missionary to the Picts, abbot and founder of the Celtic monastery on Iona, to believe that the Taltos are not monsters, but beings with immortal souls, creatures made by God, who can share in Christ's grace—it is too magnificent!"

Suddenly Ash rose to his feet, and snatched the book away from Gordon, tearing it loose from Gordon's very hands.

Gordon stood frozen by his chair, Ash standing over him.

The others rose slowly to their feet. When a man is this angry, one must respect his anger, or at least acknowledge it, thought Yuri. They stood quietly gazing up at him as he continued to glare at Gordon as if he would kill the man now.

To see the mild face of Ash disfigured with rage was a terrible thing to behold. This is what angels look like, thought Yuri, when they come with their flaming swords.

Gordon was slowly yielding from outrage to plain terror.

When Ash finally began to speak, it was in a soft whisper, the voice of his former gentleness, yet loud enough for all of them to hear:

"How dare you take this into your possession?" The voice rose in its anger. "You are a thief as well as a killer! You dare!"

"And you would take it from me?" demanded Gordon with blazing eyes. He threw his anger in the face of Ash's anger. "You would take it from me as you will take my life? Who are you to take it? Do you know what I know of your own people?"

"I wrote it!" declared Ashlar, his face now flushed with his rage. "It's mine, this book!" he whispered, as if he didn't dare to speak aloud. "I inscribed every word," he said. "I painted every picture. It was for Columba that I did this, yes! And it is mine!" He stepped back, clutching the book against his chest. He trembled and blinked his eyes for a moment and then spoke again in his soft voice: "And all your talk," he said, "of your research, of remembered lives, of . . . chains of memory!"

The silence quivered with his anger.

Gordon shook his head. "You're an impostor," he said. No one spoke.

Gordon remained firm, his face almost comic in its insolence. "Taltos, yes," he said, "St. Ashlar, never! Your age would be beyond calculation!"

No one spoke. No one moved. Rowan's eyes were searching Ash's face. Michael watched all, it seemed, as Yuri did.

Ash gave a deep sigh. He bowed his head slightly, still holding tight to the book. His fingers relaxed ever so slightly around the edges of it.

"And what do you think," he asked sadly, "is the age of that pathetic creature who sits at her loom below?"

"But it was of the remembered life that she spoke, and other remembered lives related to her in her—"

"Oh, stop it, you miserable old fool!" Ash pleaded softly. His breath came haltingly, and then at last the fire started to drain from his face.

"And this you kept from Aaron Lightner," he said. "This you kept from the greatest scholars of your Order, for you and your young friends to weave a filthy plot to steal the Taltos! You are no more than the peasants of the Highlands, the ignorant, brutish savages that lured the Taltos into the circle to kill him. It was the Sacred Hunt all over again."

"No, never to kill!" cried Gordon. "Never to kill. To see the coupling! To bring Lasher and Tessa together on Glastonbury Tor!" He began to weep, choking, gasping, his voice half strangled as he went on. "To see the race rise again on the sacred mountain where Christ himself stood to propagate the religion that changed the whole world! It was not to kill, never to kill, but to bring back to life! It's these witches who have killed, these here who destroyed the Taltos as if he were nothing but a freak of nature! Destroyed him, coldly and ruthlessly, and without a care for what he was, or might become! They did it, not I!"

Ash shook his head. He clutched the book ever more tightly.

"No, you did it," said Ash. "If only you had told your tale to Aaron Lightner, if only you had given him your precious knowledge!"

"Aaron would never have cooperated!" Gordon cried. "I could never have made such a plan. We were too old, both

310

of us. But those who had the youth, the courage, the vision—they sought to bring the Taltos safely together!"

Again Ash sighed. He waited, measuring his breaths. Then again he looked at Gordon.

"How did you learn of the Mayfair Taltos?" Ash demanded. "What was the final connection? I want to know. And answer me now or I will rip your head from your shoulders and place it in the lap of your beloved Tessa. Her stricken face will be the very last thing you see before the brain inside sputters and dies."

"Aaron," said Gordon. "It was Aaron himself." He was trembling, perhaps on the verge of blacking out. He backed up, eyes darting from right to left. He stared at the cabinet from which he'd taken the book.

"His reports from America," said Gordon, moving closer to the cabinet. "The Council was convened. The information was of critical importance. A monstrous child had been born to the Mayfair witch, Rowan. It had happened on Christmas Eve. A child that had grown within hours perhaps to the size of a man. Members throughout the world were given the description of this being. It was a Taltos, I knew it! And only I knew."

"You evil man," whispered Michael. "You evil little man."

"You call me that! You, who destroyed Lasher! Who killed the mystery as if he were a pedestrian criminal to be dispatched by you to hell in a barroom brawl?"

"You and the others," said Rowan quickly. "You did this on your own."

"I've told you we did." He took another step towards the cabinet. "Look, I won't tell you who the others were, I told you."

"I mean the Elders weren't any part of it," said Rowan.

"The excommunications," said Gordon, "were bogus. We created an intercept. I didn't do it. I don't even understand. But it was created, and we let through only those letters to and from the Elders that did not pertain to this case. We substituted our own exchanges for those between Aaron or Yuri and the Elders, and those from the Elders to them. It wasn't difficult—the Elders, with their penchant for secrecy

311

and simplicity, had left themselves wide open for such a trick."

"Thank you for telling us this," said Rowan gravely. "Perhaps Aaron suspected it."

Yuri could scarcely bear the kindness with which she was speaking to the villain, giving him comfort, when he should have been strangled then and there.

Then she said, "What else can we get out of him?" She looked at Ash. "I think we're finished with him."

Gordon understood what was happening. She was giving Ash permission to kill him. Yuri watched as, slowly, Ash set down the precious book again and turned to face Gordon, his hands free now to carry out the sentence which he himself had imposed.

"You know nothing," Gordon declared suddenly. "Tessa's words, her history, the tapes I made. Only I know where they are."

Ash merely stared at him. His eyes had grown narrow, and his eyebrows came together now in a scowl.

Gordon turned, looking to the left and the right.

"Here!" he cried. "I have another important thing which I shall voluntarily show you."

He dashed to the cabinet again, and when he spun around, he held a gun in both hands, pointing it at Ash, and then at Yuri, and then at Rowan and Michael.

"You can die by this," said Gordon. "Witches, Taltos, all of you! One bullet from this through your heart, and you are as dead as any man!"

"You can't shoot all of us," said Yuri, moving around the edge of the table.

"Don't you dare, or I will shoot!" Gordon screamed.

It was Ash who made the swift move to close the gap between himself and the man. But Gordon turned to face him again, and cocked the gun. Ash didn't stop, but the gun didn't go off, either.

With a grimace, Gordon brought the gun close to his own chest, his shoulders suddenly hunched, the other hand opening and closing. "God in heaven!" he gasped. The gun fell to the floor, clattering on the bare boards.

"You," he said, glaring at Rowan. "You, witch, Mayfair

312

witch!" he cried. "I knew it would be you. I told them. I knew it—" Bent near double, he shut his eyes, and collapsed against the cabinet. It seemed he would fall forward, but then he slipped to the floor. With his right hand he pushed vainly at the floorboards, as if trying to lift himself. Then his body went entirely limp, and his eyelids slid down halfway over his eyes, giving them the dull look of the dead.

He lay there, with only the most haphazard and tawdry air of finality.

Rowan stood as before, without a single outward sign that she had caused it. But she had, Yuri knew, and he could see that Michael knew. He could see it in the way that Michael looked at her—without condemnation, but with a quiet awe. Then a sigh came out of Michael. He took his handkerchief out of his pocket and mopped his face with it.

He turned his back on the dead man, shaking his head, and he moved away, into the shadows, near to the window.

Rowan merely stood there, her arms folded now, her eyes fixed on Gordon's.

Perhaps, thought Yuri, she sees something that we don't see. She senses something we can't sense.

But it really didn't matter. The bastard was dead. And for the first time, Yuri could breathe. He could express a long sigh of relief, so different from the mournful whisper of sound that had just come from Michael.

He is dead, Aaron. He is dead. And the Elders were not part of it. And they will find out, they will surely find out, who his helpers were, if they were those proud young novices.

It seemed a foregone conclusion to Yuri that those young men—Marklin George and Tommy Monohan—were guilty. Indeed, the whole scheme seemed the work of the young, rash and ruthless and full of waste—and perhaps it had been truly beyond the old man's imagining.

No one moved. No one spoke. They all stood there, paying some sort of dark homage to the dead body, perhaps. Yuri wanted to feel relief, but he felt none.

Then Ash went to Rowan, very deliberately and formally,

and touching her arms lightly with his long fingers, he bent to kiss her on both cheeks. She looked up, into his eyes, as if she'd been dreaming. Hers was the unhappiest expression Yuri had ever seen.

Ash withdrew and then turned to Yuri. He waited, without speaking. They were all waiting. What was there to say? What must happen now?

Yuri tried to plan, but it was quite impossible.

"Will you go home now, to the Order?" Ash finally asked.

"Yes," said Yuri with a quick nod. "I'll go home to the Order!" He whispered, "I've already alerted them to everything. I called them from the village."

"I saw you," said Ash.

"I spoke with Elvera and with Joan Cross. I have no doubt it was George and Monohan who helped him, but they'll find out."

"And Tessa," said Ash with a little sigh. "Can you take Tessa under your roof?"

"You would let me do it?" Yuri asked. "Of course we would take her. We would shelter her and care for her forever. But you would let this happen?"

"What other place is safe for her?" said Ash, rather frankly sad now, and weary. "She does not have long to live. Her skin is as thin as the vellum pages of my book. She will probably die very soon. But how soon, I have no idea. I don't know how long any of us have to live. We died so often by violence. In the very early days, we believed that was the only way that people died. Natural death, we didn't know what it—"

He broke off, scowling, dark eyebrows beautifully curved beneath the scowl and along the ridge over the end of the large eyes.

"But you take her," he resumed. "You'll be kind to her."

"Ash," said Rowan softly. "You will give them incontrovertible evidence of the Taltos! Why would you do such a thing?"

"That's the best thing that could happen," said Michael. His vehemence caught Yuri off guard. "Do it, do it for Aaron's sake," said Michael. "Take her there, to the Elders.

You've done your best to blow the lid off the whole conspiracy. Give them the precious information!"

"And if we're wrong," said Rowan, "if it was not a mere handful of men ..." She hesitated, looking down at the small, desolate dead body of Gordon. "Then what do they have?"

"Nothing," said Ash softly. "A creature who will die soon, and become once again legend, no matter how many scientific tests are taken with her gentle forbearance, no matter how many photographs or tapes are made. Take her there, Yuri, I ask you. Make her known to the Council. Make her known to everyone. Destroy the secrecy so cruelly used by Gordon and his friends."

"And Samuel?" asked Yuri. "Samuel saved my life. What will Samuel do when he discovers they have her in their very possession?"

Ash pondered, eyebrows rising very gracefully, face softened with thought, and very much the way it had been when Yuri first saw it, the countenance of a large, loving man, perhaps more human than humans, he would never know.

Such a lovely thought, suddenly, that he who lives forever becomes ever more compassionate. But it wasn't true. This being had taken life, and would have killed Gordon if Rowan hadn't somehow forced Gordon's heart to come to a fatal stop. This being might move heaven and earth to get to Mona, Mona the witch, who could make another Taltos.

How in God's name was he to protect Mona?

It was too confusing suddenly, too overwhelming. Of course he would take Tessa with him; he would call them now and beg them to come, and they would, and he would be home again, and he would talk to the Elders once more, and they would be his guardians and his friends. They would help him know what to do. They would take the decisions from his shoulders.

"And I will protect Mona," said Rowan quietly.

He was startled. The gifted witch had been reading his thoughts. How much could she read in all their hearts and souls? How much could the Taltos beguile her and fool her?

"I am no enemy to Mona Mayfair," said Ash, apparently catching on easily. "You have been wrong on this from the beginning. I would not endanger the life of a child. I would force myself upon no woman. You have worries enough. Leave Mona Mayfair to these two witches who love her and will take care of her. Leave the family to them. That is what the Elders will tell you, no doubt, when you do reach them. Let the family heal the family. Let the Order cleanse itself."

Yuri wanted to answer. But he didn't know what to say. *I want this so much to be true?*

Suddenly Ash came towards him, and covered Yuri's face gently in kisses. Yuri looked up, overcome with love, and then, clamping his hand behind Ash's neck, he put his lips to Ash's mouth.

The kiss was firm and chaste.

Somewhere in the back of his mind were Samuel's careless words, that he had fallen in love with Ash. He didn't care. That was the thing about trust. Trust brought such a relief to one, such a lovely feeling of being connected, and that is how you let down your guard, and you can be destroyed.

"I'll take the body now," Ash said. "I'll put it somewhere where men aren't likely to find it."

"No," said Yuri. He was looking right into Ash's large, calm eyes. "I've already spoken to the Motherhouse, as I said. When you're a few miles away, call them. Here, I'll get the number for you. Tell them to come here. We will take care of the body of Stuart Gordon, along with everything else."

He moved away from Ash and stood at the foot of the crumpled body. How puny in death Gordon looked, Gordon the scholar whom everyone had so admired, the friend of Aaron, and the mentor to the boys. Yuri bent down, and without disturbing anything else about the body, slipped his hand in the inside pocket of Gordon's jacket, and found there the inevitable stash of small white cards.

"Here, this is the number of the Motherhouse," he said to Ash as he righted himself, and put a single card in Ash's hand. He looked back at the body. "There's nothing to connect anyone to this dead man," he said. And, realizing it suddenly, the wonderful truth of it, he almost laughed.

"How marvelous," he announced. "He is simply dead, with no mark on him of violence. Yes, call the number and they will come. They'll take us all home."

He turned and looked at Rowan and Michael. "I'll contact you soon."

Rowan's face was sad and unreadable. Michael was plainly anxious.

"And if you don't," said Michael, "then we'll know that we were wrong."

Yuri smiled and shook his head. "I understand now, I understand how it could happen; I see the weaknesses, the charm." He looked about the tower room. Part of him hated it so much; part of him saw it as a sanctuary to deadly romanticism; part of him could not endure the thought of waiting for rescue. But he was too tired, really, to think of anything else, or to do it in any other way.

"I'll go talk to Tessa," said Rowan. "I'll explain that Stuart is very very ill, and that you're going to stay with her until help comes."

"Oh, that would be too good of you," said Yuri. And then, for the first time, he felt his full exhaustion. He sat down on the chair at the table.

His eyes fell on the book or codex, as Stuart had called it so properly or so pedantically, he wasn't sure which.

He saw the long fingers of Ash close on either side of it, picking it up. And then Ash held it again to his chest.

"How can I reach you?" Yuri asked him.

"You can't," said Ash. "But in the days that follow, I promise, I will contact you."

"Please don't forget your promise," said Yuri wearily.

"I must warn you about something," said Ash softly, thoughtfully, holding the book as if it were some sort of sacred shield. "In the months and years to come," he continued, "you may see my likeness here and there, in the normal course of your life, as you happen to pick up a newspaper or a magazine. Don't ever try to come to me. Don't ever try to call me. I am well guarded in ways you cannot dream of. You will not succeed in reaching me. Tell the same to your Order. I will never acknowledge, to any one of them, the things I've told you. And for the love of God, please warn them not to go to the glen. The Little People are dying out, but until they do, they can be most dangerous. Warn them all: stay away from the glen."

"Then you are saying that I can tell them what I've seen."

"Yes, you'll have to do that, you'll have to be utterly open with them. Otherwise you can't go home."

Yuri looked up at Rowan and then at Michael. They drew close, one on either side of him. He felt Rowan's hand touch his face as she kissed him. He felt Michael's hand on his arm.

He didn't say anything. He couldn't. He had no more words. Perhaps he had no more tears.

But the joy in him was so alien to his expectations, it was so wondrous that he longed to tell them, to let them know. The Order would come to get him. The disastrous treachery was finished. They were coming, his brothers and sisters, and he could lay bare the horrors and the mysteries he'd seen.

He didn't look up as they left him. He heard them descending the winding staircase. He heard the distant sound of the front door. He also heard soft voices just beneath him.

Slowly he climbed to his feet. He went down the steps to the second floor.

Beside the loom, in the shadows, Tessa stood like a great sapling, her hands pressed together, nodding her head as Rowan spoke too softly for Yuri to hear. Then Rowan gave the woman her kisses of parting, and quickly walked towards the stairs.

"Goodbye, Yuri," she said gently as she passed him, and she turned with her hand on the rail. "Yuri, tell them everything. Make sure the file on the Mayfair witches is finished, just as it should be."

"Everything?" he asked.

"Why not?" she asked with a strange smile. And then she disappeared.

Quickly he looked to Tessa. He'd forgotten about Tessa

for those few moments. And Tessa was bound to be miserable when she saw Stuart. Dear God, how would he stop her from going upstairs?

But Tessa was at her loom again, or her tapestry frame, perhaps that's what it was, and she was sewing and singing a little to herself, or making of her normal respiration a little song.

He drew close to her, afraid of disturbing her.

"I know," she said now, looking up at him, smiling sweetly and brightly, with a round and radiant face. "Stuart's died now, and gone, perhaps to heaven."

"She told you?"

"Yes, she did."

Yuri looked out the window. He did not know what he actually saw in the darkness. Was it the gleaming water of the lake? He couldn't tell.

But then, without mistake, he saw the headlights of a car moving away. Through the dark pockets of forest, the lights flashed and then the car disappeared.

For a moment he felt deserted, and horribly exposed. But they would make the call for him, of course they would. They were probably making the call right now. Then there would be no record on the phone here, connecting those who were to come, and those with whom he and the woman would go.

Suddenly he was so tired. Where was the bed in this place? He wanted to ask, but he didn't. He stood merely watching her at her sewing, listening to her humming, and when finally she looked up, she smiled again.

"Oh, I knew it was coming," she said. "I knew it every time I looked at him. I've never known it to fail with your kind. Sooner or later, you all grow weak and small and you die. It took me years to realize it, to realize that no one escaped it. And Stuart, poor dear, he was so very weak, I knew the death would come for him at any time."

Yuri said nothing. He felt a powerful aversion to her, so powerful that he struggled with all his being to disguise it, lest she feel some chill, lest she be hurt. Dimly he thought of his Mona; he saw her aflame with human life, fragrant and warm and continuously surprising. He wondered, did the Taltos see humans that way? Rougher? Wilder? Were we coarse animals to them, animals perhaps of volatile and dangerous charm? Rather like lions and tigers are to us?

Mona. In his mind, he caught a handful of Mona's hair. He saw her turn to look at him, green eyes, lips smiling, words coming rapidly with a lovely American vulgarity and charm.

He felt more certain than ever that he would never see Mona again.

He knew that that was what was meant for her, that her family enfold her, that someone of her own mettle, within her own clan, should be her inevitable love.

"Let's not go upstairs," Tessa said now in a confidential whisper. "Let's let Stuart be dead by himself. It's all right, don't you think? After they're dead, I don't think they mind what you do."

Slowly Yuri nodded, and looked back out into the secretive night beyond the glass.

Twenty

S HE STOOD IN the dark kitchen, deliciously full. All the
milk was gone, every single drop of it, and the cream
cheese, and the cottage cheese, and butter too. That's what
you call a clean sweep. Oops, forgot something, thin slices
of yellow processed cheese, gag me with a spoon, full of
chemicals and dye. Ugh, yuk. She chewed them up, gone,
thank you.

"You know, darling, if you had turned out to be an
idiot . . ." she said.

*That was never a possibility, Mother, I am you and I am
Michael. And in a very real way, I am everyone who has
been speaking to you from the beginning, and I am Mary
Jane.*

She burst into laughter, all alone, in the dark kitchen,
leaning against the refrigerator. What about ice cream! Shit,
she almost forgot!

"Well, honey, you drew a good hand," she said. "You
couldn't have drawn better. And am I to presume you did
not miss a single syllable. . . ."

Häagen-Dazs vanilla! Pints! Pints!

"Mona Mayfair!"

Who was that calling? Eugenia? Don't want to talk to
her. Don't want her to disturb me or Mary Jane.

Mary Jane was still in the library, with the papers she'd
sneaked out of Michael's desk, or was it Rowan's, now that
Rowan was back in circulation? Never mind, it was all
kinds of medical stuff and lawyer business, and papers re-

lating to things that had happened only three weeks ago. Mary Jane, once introduced to the various files and histories, had proved insatiable. The history of the family was now her ice cream, so to speak.

"Now, the question is, do we share *this* ice cream with Mary Jane, in cousinly fashion, or do we gobble it?"

Gobble it.

It was time to tell Mary Jane! The time had come. When she'd passed the door just a few minutes ago, before the final raid on the kitchen, Mary Jane had been mumbling things about those dead doctors, God help them, Dr. Larkin and the one out in California, and the chemical autopsies on the dead women. The key thing was to remember to put that stuff back so that neither Rowan nor Michael was unduly alarmed. After all, these things were not being done casually, there was a purpose, Mary Jane was the one upon whom she had fully to depend!

"Mona Mayfair."

It was Eugenia calling, what a nuisance. "Mona Mayfair, it's Rowan Mayfair on the phone, all the way from England, calling you!"

Scold, scold. What she needed was a tablespoon for this ice cream, even if she had almost finished the entire pint. There was one more pint to go.

Now, whose were those little feet coming tippy-tap in the dark, someone running through the dining room? Morrigan clicked her tiny tongue in time with the tippy-tapping.

"Why, it's my beloved cousin, Mary Jane Mayfair."

"Shhhh." Mary Jane put a finger to her lips. "She's looking for you. She's got Rowan on the phone. Rowan wants to talk to you, she said for us to wake you up."

"Pick it up in the library and take the message, I can't risk talking to her. You've got to fool her. Tell her we're fine, I'm in the bathtub or something, and ask about everybody. Like how's Yuri and how's Michael and is she all right?"

"Got it." And off went the teeny tiny feet, tippy-tapping on the floor.

She scraped up the last of that pint and threw the container in the sink. What a messy kitchen! And all my life

I have been so neat, and now look, I'm corrupted by money. She tore open the next pint.

Once again came the magic feet. Mary Jane, ripping into the butler's pantry, and flying around the edge of the door, with her corn-yellow hair and her long thin brown legs, and her teensy waist and her white lace skirts swinging like a bell.

"Mona!" she said in a whisper.

"Yeah!" Mona whispered back. What the hell. She ate another big spoon of the ice cream.

"Yes, but Rowan said she had momentous news for us," said Mary Jane, very obviously aware of the import of this message. "That she would tell us all when she saw us, but that right now she had something she had to do. Same for Michael. Yuri's okay."

"You did a splendid job. What about the guards outside?"

"She said to keep them, not to change anything. Said she'd already called Ryan and told him. Said for you to stay inside and rest, and do whatever your doctor tells you."

"Practical woman, intelligent woman. Hmmmmm . . ." Well, this second carton was empty already. Enough is enough. She started to shiver all over. So coooold! Why hadn't she gotten rid of those guards?

Mary Jane reached out and rubbed Mona's arms. "You okay, darlin'?" Then Mary Jane's eyes dropped to Mona's stomach and her face went blank with fear. She lowered her right hand, wanting to touch Mona's stomach, but she didn't dare.

"Listen, it's time to tell you everything," said Mona. "To give you your choice right now. I was going to lead you into it step by step, but that's not fair and it's not necessary. I can do what I have to do, even if you don't want to help me, and maybe you'd be better off not helping. Either we go now and you help me, or I go alone."

"Go where?"

"That's just it. We're clearing out of here, right now. Guards or no guards. You can drive, can't you?"

She pushed past Mary Jane and into the butler's pantry. She opened the key cabinet. Look for the Lincoln insignia. The limo was a Lincoln, wasn't it? When Ryan had bought it for her, he'd said she should never be in a limousine that was not black and was not a Lincoln. Sure enough, there were the keys! Michael had his keys and the keys to Rowan's Mercedes, but the keys to the limo were right here, where Clem was supposed to leave them.

"Well, sure, I can drive," said Mary Jane, "but whose car are we taking?"

"Mine. The limousine. Only we're not taking the driver with it. You ready? We're counting on the driver being fast asleep out back. Now, what do we need?"

"You're supposed to tell me everything, and give me my choice."

Mona stopped. They were both in the shadows. The house was dark all around them, light pouring in from the garden, from the big zone of blue illumination that was the pool. Mary Jane's eyes were huge and round, making her nose look tiny and her cheeks very smooth. Tendrils of her hair moved behind her shoulders, but mostly it was corn silk. The light struck the cleft of her breasts.

"Why don't *you* tell *me*?" said Mona.

"OK," said Mary Jane. "You're going to have it, no matter what it is."

"Right you are."

"And you're not lettin' Rowan and Michael kill it, no matter what it is."

"Right you are!"

"And the best place for us to go is where nobody will be able to find us."

"Right you are!"

"Only the only place I know is Fontevrault. And if we cut loose every skiff at the landing, the only way they can get out there into the basin after us is to bring in their own boat, if they even think of coming down that way."

"Oh, Mary Jane, you genius! Right you are!"

Mama, I love you, Mama.

And I love you too, my little Morrigan. Trust in me. Trust in Mary Jane.

"Hey, don't faint on me! Lissen, I'm going to go get pillows, blankets, stuff like that. You got any cash?"

"Heaps, twenty-dollar bills in the drawer by the bed."

"You sit down, come in here with me, and sit down." Mary Jane led her through the kitchen and to the table. "Put your head down."

"Mary Jane, don't freak out on me, don't, no matter what it looks like."

"Just you rest till I come back."

And away went the clicky high heels, running through the house.

The song started again, so sweet, so pretty, the song of flowers and the glen.

Stop, Morrigan.

Talk to me, Mother, and Oncle Julien brought you here to sleep with my father, but he didn't know what would happen, but you understand, Mother, you said you understood, that the giant helix was in this case not allied to any ancient evil, but was purely an expression of a genetic potential in you and in Father that had always been there. . . .

Mona tried to answer, but it wasn't necessary, the voice went on and on, singsong and soft and very rapid.

Hey, slow down. You sound like a bumblebee when you do that.

". . . immense responsibility, to survive and to give birth, and to love me, Mother, don't forget to love me, I need you, your love, above all things, without which I may lose in my frailty the very will to live. . . ."

They were all gathered together in the stone circle, shivering, crying, the tall dark-haired one had come, trying to quiet them. They drew in close to the fire.

"But why? Why do they want to kill us?"

And Ashlar said, "It is their way. They are warlike people. They kill those who are not of their clan. It is as important as eating or drinking or making love is to us. They feast on death."

"Look," she said aloud. The kitchen door had just slammed. Be quiet, Mary Jane! Don't bring Eugenia down here. But we've got to be scientific about this, I should have been recording all this on the computer, typing it in as I see it, but it's almost impossible to accurately record when surrendering to a trance. When we reach Fontevrault,

325

we will have Mary Jane's computer. Mary Jane, the god-send.

Mary Jane had come back, shutting the kitchen door quietly this time, thank heaven.

"That is what the others have to understand," said Mona, "that this is not from hell, but from God. Lasher was from hell, one could say that, you know, speaking metaphysically or metaphorically, I mean religiously or poetically, but when a creature is born this way of two human beings, both of whom contain a mysterious genome, then it's from God. Who else but God? Emaleth was the child of rape, but not this child. Well, at least the mother wasn't the one who got raped."

"Shhh, let's us get out of here. I told the guards that I'd seen somebody funny out front, and that I was driving you up to your house to get you some clothes and then to the doctor. Come on!"

"Mary Jane, you are a genius."

But when she stood up, the world swam. "Holy God."

"I have you, now you hold on to me. Are you in pain?"

"Well, no more than anybody would be, with a nuclear explosion going on in her womb. Let's get out of here!"

They crept out down the alley, Mary Jane steadying her when she needed it, but she was doing all right hanging on to the gate and to the fence, and then they were in the carport. And there was the big sleek limousine, and bless her heart, Mary Jane had started the engine, and the door was open. Here we go.

"Morrigan, stop singing! I have to think, tell her about the gate-opener. You have to press the little magic twanger."

"I know that! Get in."

Roar of the engine, and the rusty, creaky sound of the gate rolling back.

"You know, Mona, I've got to ask you something. I've got to. What if this thing can't be born without your dying?"

"Shhhh, bite your tongue, cousin! Rowan didn't die, did she, and she gave birth to one and the other! I'm not dying. Morrigan won't let me."

No, Mother, I love you. I need you, Mother. Don't talk of dying. When you talk of death, I can smell death.

"Shhhhhh. Mary Jane, is the best place Fontevrault? You're sure? Have we considered all the possibilities, perhaps a motel somewhere . . ."

"Lissen, Granny's there, and Granny can be completely trusted, and that little boy staying with her will light out of there soon as I give him one of these twenty-dollar bills."

"But he can't leave his boat at the landing, not for someone else to—"

"No, he won't do that, honey, don't be silly, he'll take his pirogue up home to his place! He doesn't come by the landing. He lives up near town. Now just you sit back and rest. We've got a stash of things at Fontevrault. We have the attic, all dry and warm."

"Oh yes, that would be wonderful."

"And when the sun comes up in the morning, it will come into all the attic windows. . . ."

Mary Jane hit the brakes. They were already at Jackson Avenue.

"Sorry, honey, this car is so powerful."

"You're having trouble? God, I never sat up here before, with the whole damned stretch behind me. This is weird, like driving a plane."

"No, I'm not having trouble!" Mary Jane took the turn onto St. Charles. " 'Cept with these creepy drunken New Orleans drivers. It's midnight, you know. But this is a cinch to drive, actually, especially if you've driven an eighteen-wheeler, which I certainly have."

"And where the hell did you do that, Mary Jane?"

"Arizona, honey, had to do it, had to steal the truck, but that's another story."

Morrigan was calling her, singing again, but in that rapid humming voice. Singing to herself, perhaps.

I can't wait to see you, to hold you! I love you more for what you are! Oh, this is destiny, Morrigan, this eclipses everything, the whole world of bassinets and rattles and happy fathers, well, he will be happy eventually, when he comes to understand that the terms now have changed utterly. . . .

327

The world spun. The cold wind swept down over the plain. They were dancing in spite of it, trying desperately to keep warm. Why had the warmth deserted them? Where was their homeland?

Ashlar said, "This is our homeland now. We must learn the cold as well as we learned the warmth."

Don't let them kill me, Mama.

Morrigan lay cramped, filling the bubble of fluid, her hair falling around her and under her, her knees pressed against her eyes.

"Honey, what makes you think anyone will hurt you?"

I think it because you think it, Mama. I know what you know.

"You're talking to that baby?"

"I am, and it's answering me."

Her eyes were closing when they hit the freeway.

"Just you sleep now, darlin'. We're burning up the miles, honey, this thing does ninety and you can't even feel it."

"Don't get a ticket."

"Honey, don't you think a witch like me can handle a policeman? They never finish writing the ticket!"

Mona laughed. Things couldn't have worked out better. Really, they couldn't have.

And the best was yet to come.

Twenty-one

THE BELL TOLLING ...

He was not really dreaming; he was planning. But when he did this on the edge of sleep, Marklin saw images vividly, saw possibilities that he could not see any other way.

They would go to America. They would take with them every scrap of valuable information which they had amassed. To hell with Stuart and with Tessa. Stuart had deserted them. Stuart had disappointed them for the last time. They would carry with them the memory of Stuart, Stuart's belief and conviction, Stuart's reverence for the mystery. But that would be all of Stuart that they would ever need.

They would set up some small apartment in New Orleans, and begin their systematic watch of the Mayfair witches. This might take years. But both of them had money. Marklin had real money, and Tommy had the unreal kind that expressed itself in multimillions. Tommy had paid for everything so far. But Marklin could support himself, no problem. And the families could chew on some excuse about an informal sabbatical. Perhaps they would even enroll in courses at the nearby university. Didn't matter.

When they had their sights on the Mayfairs, the fun would begin again.

The bell, dear God, that bell ...

Mayfair witches. He wished he were in Regent's Park now, with the entire file. All those pictures, Aaron's last reports, still in Xerox typescript. Michael Curry. Read Aaron's copious notes on Michael Curry. This was the man who could father the monster. This was the man whom Lasher had chosen in childhood. Aaron's reports, hasty, excited, full of concern finally, had been clear on that point.

Was it possible for an ordinary man to learn a witch's powers? Oh, if only it were a matter of mere diabolic pact! What if a transfusion of the witch's blood could give him the telepathic abilities? Sheer nonsense, more than likely. But think of the power of the two of them—Rowan Mayfair, the doctor and the witch; Michael Curry, who had fathered the beautiful beast.

Who had called it the beautiful beast? Was that Stuart? Where the hell was Stuart? Damn you, Stuart. You ran like a ruptured duck. You left us, Stuart, without so much as a phone call, a hasty word of parting, a hint of where and when we might meet.

Go on without Stuart. And speaking of Aaron, how could they get his papers from this new wife in America?

Well, everything rested upon one thing. They had to leave here with an unblemished reputation. They had to ask for a leave of absence, without arousing the least suspicion.

With a start, he opened his eyes. Had to get out of here. Didn't want to spend another minute. But there was the bell. It had to be the signal for the memorials. Listen to it, tolling, an awful, nerve-racking sound.

"Wake up, Tommy," he said.

Tommy was slumped over in the chair by the desk, snoring, a tiny bit of drool on his chin. His heavy tortoiseshell glasses had reached the very tip of his rounded nose.

"Tommy, it's the bell."

Marklin sat up, straightened his clothes as best he could. He climbed off the bed.

He shook Tommy by the shoulder.

For one moment Tommy had that baffled, annoyed look of the just-awakened, and then the common sense returned.

"Yes, the bell," he said calmly. He ran his hands over his sloppy red hair. "At last, the bell."

They took turns washing their faces. Marklin took a bit of Kleenex, smeared it with Tommy's toothpaste, and cleaned his teeth by hand. He needed to shave, but there was no time for it. They'd go to Regent's Park, get everything, and leave for America on the first flight out.

"Leave of absence, hell," he said now. "I'm for leaving, just going. I don't want to go back to my own room to pack. I'm for heading out of here immediately. The hell with the ceremony."

"Don't be so foolish," Tommy murmured. "We'll say what we have to say. And we'll learn what we can learn. And then we'll leave at the appropriate and less conspicuous time."

Damn!

A knock sounded at the door.

"We're coming!" Tommy said, with a little raising of his eyebrows. He straightened his tweed jacket. He looked both mussed and hot.

Marklin's own wool blazer was badly rumpled. And he'd lost his tie. Well, the shirt looked all right with the sweater. Would have to do, wouldn't it? The tie was in the car, perhaps. He'd ripped it off when he was driving away the first time. He should never, never have come back.

"Three minutes," came the voice through the door. One of the old ones. The place was going to be choked with them.

"You know," said Marklin, "none of this was bearable even when I thought of myself as a dedicated novice. Now I find it simply outrageous. Being awakened at four in the morning . . . Good God, it's actually five . . . for a mourning ceremony. It's as stupid as those modern-day Druids, dressed up in sheets, who carry on at Stonehenge on the summer solstice, or whenever the hell they do it. I may let you say the appropriate words for us. I may wait in the car."

"The hell you will," said Tommy. He took several swipes at his dry hair with the comb. Useless.

They went out of the room together, Tommy stopping to lock the door. The hall was predictably cold.

"Well, you can do that if you wish," said Marklin, "but I'm not coming back up to this floor. They can have whatever I've left in my room."

331

"That would be perfectly stupid. You'll pack as if you were leaving for normal reasons. Why the hell not?"

"I can't stay here, I tell you."

"And what if you've overlooked something in your room, something that would blow the lid off the entire affair?"

"I haven't. I know I haven't."

The corridors and the staircase were empty. Possibly they were the last of the novices to hear the bell.

A soft whisper of voices rose from the first floor. As they came to the foot of the steps, Marklin saw it was worse than he could have imagined.

Look at the candles everywhere. Everyone, absolutely everyone, dressed in black! All the electric lights had been put out. A sickening gush of warm air surrounded them. Both fires were blazing. Good heavens! And they had draped every window in the house with crepe.

"Oh, this is too rich!" Tommy whispered. "Why didn't someone tell us to dress?"

"It's positively nauseating," said Marklin. "Look, I'm giving it five minutes."

"Don't be a blasted fool," said Tommy. "Where are the other novices? I see old people, everywhere, old people."

There must have been a hundred in small groups, or simply standing alone against the dark oak-paneled walls. Gray hair everywhere. Well, surely the younger members were here somewhere.

"Come on," said Tommy, pinching Marklin's arm and pushing him into the hall.

A great supper was spread on the banquet table.

"Good Lord, it's a goddamned feast," Marklin said. It made him sick to look at it—roast lamb and beef, and bowls of steaming potatoes, and piles of shiny plates, and silver forks. "Yes, they're eating, they're actually eating!" he whispered to Tommy.

A whole string of elderly men and women were quietly and slowly filling their plates. Joan Cross was there in her wheelchair. Joan had been crying. And there was the formidable Timothy Hollingshed, wearing his innumerable titles on his face as he always did, arrogant bastard, and not a penny to his name.

Elvera passed through the crowd with a decanter of red wine. The glasses stood on the sideboard. Now that is something I can use, thought Marklin, I can use that wine.

A sudden thought came to him of being free from here, on the plane to America, relaxed, his shoes kicked off, the stewardess plying him with liquor and delicious food. Only a matter of hours.

The bell was still tolling. How long was that going to go on? Several men near him were speaking Italian, all of them on the short side. There were the old grumbly British ones, the friends of Aaron's, most of them now retired. And there was a young woman—well, at least she seemed young. Black hair and heavily made-up eyes. Yes, when you looked you saw they were senior members, but not merely the decrepit class. There stood Bryan Holloway, from Amsterdam. And there, those anemic and pop-eyed male twins who worked out of Rome.

No one was really looking at anyone, though people did talk to each other. Indeed, the air was solemn but convivial. From all around came soft murmurs of Aaron this, and Aaron that . . . always loved Aaron, adored Aaron. Seems they had forgotten Marcus entirely, and well they should, thought Marklin, if only they knew how cheaply Marcus had been bought out.

"Have some wine, please, gentlemen," said Elvera softly. She gestured to the rows and rows of crystal glasses. Old stemware. All the old finery. Look at the antique silver forks with their deep encrustations. Look at the old dishes, dragged from some vault somewhere perhaps, to be loaded with fudge and iced cakes.

"No, thank you," said Tommy, tersely. "Can't eat with a plate and a glass in my hands."

Someone laughed in the low roar of whispers and murmurs. Another voice rose above the others. Joan Cross sat solitary in the midst of the gathering, her forehead resting in her hand.

"But who are we mourning?" asked Marklin in a whisper. "Is it Marcus or Aaron?" He had to say something.

The candles made an irritating glare, for all the swimming darkness around him. He blinked. He had always loved this scent of pure wax, but this was overpowering, absurd.

Blake and Talmage were talking together rather heatedly in the corner. Hollingshed joined them. As far as Marklin knew, they were in their late fifties. Where were the other novices? No other novices. Not even Ansling and Perry, the officious little monsters. What does your instinct tell you? Something is wrong, very wrong.

Marklin went after Elvera, quickly catching her elbow.

"Are we supposed to be here?"

"Yes, of course you are," said Elvera.

"We're not dressed."

"Doesn't matter. Here, do have a drink." This time she put the glass in his hand. He set down his plate on the edge of the long table. Probably a breach of etiquette, nobody else had done it. And, God, look at this spread. There was a great roasted boar's head, with the apple in its mouth, and the suckling pig surrounded by fruit on its steaming silver platter. The mingled fragrances of the meat were delicious, he had to admit it. He was getting hungry! How absurd.

Elvera was gone, but Nathan Harberson was very close to him, looking down at him from his lofty mossback height.

"Does the Order always do this?" Marklin asked. "Throw a banquet when someone dies?"

"We have our rituals," said Nathan Harberson in an almost sad voice. "We are an old, old order. We take our vows seriously."

"Yes, very seriously," said one of the pop-eyed twins from Rome. This one was Enzo, wasn't it? Or was it Rodolpho? Marklin couldn't remember. His eyes made you think of fish, too large for expression, indicative only of illness, and to think it had struck both of them. And when the twins both smiled as they were doing now, they looked rather hideous. Their faces were wrinkled, thin. But there was supposed to be some crucial difference between them. What was it? Marklin could not recall.

"There are certain basic principles," said Nathan

334

Harberson, his velvety baritone voice growing a little louder, a little more confident, perhaps.

"And certain things," said Enzo, the twin, "are beyond question with us."

Timothy Hollingshed had drawn near and was looking down his aquiline nose at Marklin, as he always did. His hair was white and thick, like Aaron's had been. Marklin didn't like the look of him. It was like looking at a cruel version of Aaron, much taller, more ostentatiously elegant. God, look at the man's rings. Positively vulgar, and every one was supposed to have its history, replete with tales of battle, treachery, vengeance. When can we leave here? When will all this end?

"Yes, we hold certain things sacred," Timothy was saying, "just as if we were a small nation unto ourselves."

Elvera had returned. "Yes, it isn't merely a matter of tradition."

"No," said a tall, dark-haired man with ink-black eyes and a bronzed face. "It's a matter of a deep moral commitment, of loyalty."

"And of reverence," said Enzo. "Don't forget reverence."

"A consensus," said Elvera, looking straight at him. But then they were *all* looking at him. "On what is of value, and how it must be protected at all costs."

More people had pressed into the room, senior members only. A predictable increase in soft chatter. Someone laughing again. Didn't people have the sense not to laugh?

There is something just flat-out wrong with this, that we're the only novices, thought Marklin. And where was Tommy? Suddenly in a panic, he realized he had lost sight of Tommy. No, there he was, eating grapes from the table like some sort of Roman plutocrat. Ought to have the decency not to do that.

Marklin gave a quick, uneasy nod to those clustered around him and pushed through a tight press of men and women, and, nearly tripping over someone's foot, landed finally at Tommy's side.

"What the hell's the matter with you?" Tommy demanded. He was looking at the ceiling. "For God's sake, relax. We'll be on the plane in a few hours. Then we'll be in . . ."

"Shhh, don't say anything," said Marklin, conscious that his voice was no longer normal, no longer under his control. If he had ever been this apprehensive in his life, he didn't remember it.

For the first time he saw that the black cloth had been draped everywhere along the walls. The two clocks of the great hall were covered! And the mirrors, the mirrors were veiled in black. He found these things totally unnerving. He had never seen such old-fashioned funeral trappings. When people in his family had died, they'd been cremated. Someone called you later to tell you that it had been done. That was precisely what had happened with his parents. He'd been at school, lying on his bed, reading Ian Fleming, when the call came, and he had only nodded and gone on reading. *And now you've inherited everything, absolutely everything.*

Suddenly he was thoroughly sick from the candles. He could see the candelabra everywhere, such costly silver. Some of them were even encrusted with jewels. God, how much money did this Order have stashed away in its cellars and its vaults? A small nation indeed. But then it was all the fault of fools like Stuart, who had long ago willed his entire fortune to the Order, and must surely have changed that will, all things considered, of course.

All things. Tessa. The plan. Where was Stuart now—with Tessa?

The talk grew louder and louder. There was the tinkling of glasses. Elvera came again and poured more wine into his glass.

"Drink up, Mark," she said.

"Do behave, Mark," whispered Tommy, unpleasantly close to his face.

Marklin turned. This wasn't his religion. This wasn't his custom, to stand about feasting and drinking in black clothes at dawn!

"I'm going now!" he suddenly declared. His voice seemed to explode from his mouth and echo throughout the room!

336

Everybody else had gone silent.

For one second, in the ringing stillness, he almost gave in to a scream. The desire to scream was more pure in him than ever in childhood. To scream in panic, in horror. He didn't know which.

Tommy pinched his arm, and pointed.

The double doors to the dining hall had been opened. Ah, so that was the reason for the silence. Dear God, had they brought the remains of Aaron home?

The candles, the crepe—it was the very same in the dining hall, another cavern of grimness. He was determined not to enter, but before he could act upon this decision, the crowd moved him slowly and solemnly towards the open doorway. He and Tommy were being almost carried along.

Don't want to see any more, want to leave here . . .

The press loosened as they passed through the doors. Men and women were filing around the long table. Someone *was* laid out on the table. God, not Aaron! Can't look at Aaron. *And they know you can't look at him, don't they? They are waiting for you to panic, and for Aaron's wounds to bleed!*

Horrible, stupid. He clutched Tommy's arm again, and heard Tommy's correction. "Do be still!"

At last they had come to the edge of the grand old table. This was a man in a dusty wool jacket, with mud on his shoes. Look, mud. This was no corpse properly laid out.

"This is ludicrous," said Tommy under his breath.

"What sort of funeral is this!" he heard himself say aloud.

Slowly he leant over so that he could see the dead face that was turned away from him. Stuart. Stuart Gordon, dead and lying on this table—Stuart's impossibly thin face, with its bird-beak of a nose, and his lifeless blue eyes. Dear God, they had not even closed his eyes! Were they all insane?

He backed away awkwardly, colliding with Tommy, feeling his heel on Tommy's toe, and then the swift removal of Tommy's foot. All thought seemed beyond him. A dread took hold of him totally. Stuart is dead, Stuart is dead, Stuart is dead.

Tommy was staring at the body. Did he know it was Stuart?

"What is the meaning of this?" Tommy asked, his voice low and full of wrath. "What's happened to Stuart. . . ." But the words had little conviction. His voice, always a monotone, was now weak with shock.

The others drew in all around them, pressing them right against the table. Stuart's limp left hand lay right near them.

"For the love of heaven," said Tommy angrily. "Someone close his eyes."

From one end of the table to the other, the members surrounded it, a phalanx of mourners in black. Or were they mourners? Even Joan Cross was there, at the head of the table, arms resting on the arms of her wheelchair, her reddened eyes fixed upon them!

No one spoke. No one moved. The first stage of silence had been the absence of speech. This was the second stage, the absence of movement, with members so still he could not even hear anyone draw breath.

"What's happened to him!" demanded Tommy.

Still no one answered. Marklin could not fix his gaze on anything; he kept looking at the small dead skull, with its thin covering of white hair. *Did you kill yourself, you fool, you crazed fool? Is that what you did? At the first chance of discovery?*

And suddenly, very suddenly, he realized that all the others were not looking at Stuart, they were looking at Tommy and at him.

He felt a pain in his chest as though someone had begun to press on his breastbone with impossibly strong hands.

He turned, desperately searching the faces around him—Enzo, Harberson, Elvera, and the others, staring at him with malign expressions, Elvera herself staring straight up into his eyes. And right beside him, Timothy Hollingshed, staring coldly down at him.

Only Tommy did not stare at him. Tommy stared across the table, and when Marklin looked to see what had so distracted him, what had made him oblivious to the perfect horror of all this, he saw that Yuri Stefano, clothed in proper funereal black, was standing only a few feet away.

338

Yuri! Yuri was here, and had been here all along! Had Yuri killed Stuart? Why in the name of God hadn't Stuart been clever, why hadn't he known how to deflect Yuri? The whole point of the intercept, of the bogus excommunication, was that Yuri would never, never be able to reach the Motherhouse again. And that idiot Lanzing, to have let Yuri escape from the glen.

"No," said Elvera, "the bullet found its mark. But it wasn't fatal. And he's come home."

"You were Gordon's accomplices," said Hollingshed disdainfully. "Both of you. And you and only you are left."

"His accomplices," said Yuri from the other side of the table. "His bright ones, his geniuses."

"No!" said Marklin. "This is not true! Who is accusing us?"

"Stuart accused you," said Harberson. "The papers scattered all through his tower house accused you, his diary accused you, his poetry accused you, Tessa accused you."

Tessa!

"How dare you enter his house!" thundered Tommy, red with rage as he glared about him.

"You don't have Tessa, I don't believe you!" Marklin screamed. "Where is Tessa? It was all for Tessa!" And then, realizing his terrible error, he realized in full what he already knew.

Oh, why hadn't he listened to his instinct! His instinct had told him to leave, and now his instinct told him, without question—*It is too late*.

"I'm a British citizen," said Tommy under his breath. "I won't be detained here for any sort of vigilante court."

At once the crowd shifted and moved against them, pushing them slowly from the head of the table, towards the foot. Hands had taken hold of Marklin's arms. That unspeakable Hollingshed had hold of him. He heard Tommy protest once more, "Let me go," but it was now utterly impossible. They were being pressed into the corridor and down it, the soft thudding of feet on the waxed boards echoing up beneath the wooden arches. It was a mob which had caught him, a mob from which he couldn't conceivably escape.

With a loud metallic shuffle and crack, the doors of the old elevator were thrown back. Marklin was shoved inside, turning frantically, a claustrophobia gripping him that again pushed him to scream.

But the doors were sliding shut. He and Tommy stood pressed against each other, surrounded by Harberson, Enzo, Elvera, the dark-haired tall one, and Hollingshed and several other men, strong men.

The elevator was clattering and wobbling its way down. Into the cellars.

"What are you going to do to us?" he demanded suddenly.

"I insist upon being taken to the main floor again," said Tommy disdainfully. "I insist upon immediate release."

"There are certain crimes we find unspeakable," said Elvera softly, her eyes fixed on Tommy now, thank heaven. "Certain things which, as an order, we cannot possibly forgive or forget."

"Which means what, I'd like to know!" said Tommy.

The heavy old elevator stopped with a shattering jolt. Then it was out into the passage, the hands hurting Marklin's arms.

They were being taken along some unknown route in the cellars, down a corridor supported with crude wooden beams, rather like a mineshaft. The smell of the earth was around them. All the others were beside them or behind them now. They could see two doors at the end of this passage, large wooden doors inset beneath a low arch, and bolted shut.

"You think you can detain me here against my will?" said Tommy. "I'm a British citizen."

"You killed Aaron Lightner," said Harberson.

"You killed others in our name," said Enzo. And there was his brother beside him, repeating in a maddening echo the very same words.

"You besmirched us in the eyes of others," said Hollingshed. "You did unspeakable evil in our name!"

"I confess to nothing," said Tommy.

"We don't require you to confess," said Elvera.

"We don't require anything of you," said Enzo.

"Aaron died believing your lies!" said Hollingshed.

"God damn it, I will not stand for this!" roared Tommy.

But Marklin could not bring himself to be indignant, outraged, whatever it was he ought to be, that they were holding him prisoner, forcing him now towards the doors.

"Wait a minute, wait, please, don't. Wait," he stammered. He begged. "Did Stuart kill himself? What happened to Stuart? If Stuart were here, he would exonerate us, you can't really think that someone of Stuart's years . . ."

"Save your lies for God," said Elvera softly. "All night long we've examined the evidence. We've spoken with your white-haired goddess. Unburden your soul of the truth to us, if you wish, but don't bother us with your lies."

The figures closed ranks tightly against them. They were being moved closer and closer to this chamber or room or dungeon, perhaps, Marklin couldn't know.

"Stop!" he cried suddenly. "In the name of God! Stop! There are things you don't know about Tessa, things you simply don't understand."

"Don't cater to them, you idiot!" snarled Tommy. "Do you think my father won't be asking questions! I'm not a bloody orphan! I have a huge family. Do you think—"

A strong arm gripped Marklin about the waist. Another was clamped around his neck. The doors were being opened inward. Out of the corner of his eye, he saw Tommy struggling, knee bent, foot kicking at the men behind him.

An icy gust of air rose from the open doors. Blackness. I cannot be locked in blackness. I cannot!

And finally he screamed. He couldn't hold it back any longer. He screamed, the terrible cry begun before he was pushed forward, before he felt himself topple from the threshold, before he realized he was plunging down and down into the blackness, into the nothingness, that Tommy was falling with him, cursing them, threatening them, or so it seemed. It was quite impossible to know. His scream was echoing too loudly off the stone walls.

He'd struck the ground. The blackness was outside him and also within. Then the awakening to pain throughout his limbs. He lay among hard and jagged things, cutting things.

Dear God! And when he sat upright, his hand fell on objects which crumbled and broke and gave off a dull ashen smell.

He squinted in the single shaft of light that fell down upon him, and looking upwards, he realized with horror that it came from the door through which he'd fallen, over the heads and shoulders of the figures who filled it in black silhouette.

"No, you can't do it!" he screamed, scrambling forward in the darkness, and then, without compass points or touchstones of any kind, climbing to his feet.

He couldn't see their darkened faces; he couldn't make out even the shapes of their heads. He'd fallen many feet, many, perhaps thirty feet, even. He didn't know.

"Stop it, you can't keep us here, you can't put us here!" he roared, raising his hands to them, imploring them. But the figures had stepped back out of the lighted opening, and with horror he heard a familiar sound. It was the hinges creaking as the light died, and the doors were closed.

"Tommy, Tommy, where are you?" he cried desperately. The echo frightened him. It was locked in with him. It had nowhere to go but up against him, against his ears. He reached out, patting the floor, touching these soft, broken, crumbling things, and suddenly he felt something wet and warm!

"Tommy!" he cried with relief. He could feel Tommy's lips, his nose, his eyes. "Tommy!"

Then, in a split second, longer in duration, perhaps, than all his life, he understood everything. Tommy was dead. He'd died in the fall. And they had not cared that he might. And they were never coming back for Marklin, never. Had the law, with its comforts and its sanctions, been a possibility, they would not have thrown either one of them from such a height. And now Tommy was dead. He was alone in this place, in the dark, beside his dead friend, clinging to him now, and the other things, the things round which his fingers curled, were bones.

"No, you can't do it, you can't countenance such a thing!" His voice rose again in a scream. "Let me out of here! Let me out!" Back came the echo, as if these cries

342

were streamers rising and then tumbling back down upon him. "Let me out!" His cries ceased to be words. His cries grew softer and more full of agony. And their terrible sound gave him a strange comfort. And he knew it was the last and only comfort he'd ever know.

He lay still, finally. Beside Tommy, fingers locked around Tommy's arm. Perhaps Tommy wasn't dead. Tommy would wake up, and they would search this place together. Perhaps that's what they were supposed to do. There was a way out, and the others meant for him to find it; they meant him to walk through the valley of death to find it, but they didn't mean to kill him, not his brothers and sisters in the Order, not Elvera, dear Elvera, and Harberson and Enzo, and his old teacher Clermont. No, they were incapable of such things!

At last he turned over and climbed to his knees, but when he tried to rise to his feet, his left ankle gave out from under him in a flash of pain.

"Well, I can crawl, damn it!" he whispered. "I can crawl!" He screamed the words. And crawl he did, pushing the bones away from him, the debris, the crumbled rock or bone or whatever it was. Don't think about it. Don't think about rats, either. Don't think!

His head was suddenly struck, or so it seemed, by a wall.

Within sixty seconds he had traveled along that wall, and along another and another, and finally another. The room was no more than a shaft, it was so small.

Oh, well, don't have to worry about getting out, it seems, not till I feel better and I can stand up and look for some other opening, something other than a passage, a window perhaps. After all, there's air, fresh air.

Just rest awhile, he thought, snuggling close to Tommy again, and pressing his forehead against Tommy's sleeve, rest and think what to do. It is absolutely out of the question that you could die like this, you, this young, die like this, in this dungeon, thrown here by a pack of evil old priests and nuns, impossible. . . . Yes, rest, don't confront the entire issue, just yet. Rest . . .

He was drifting. How stupid of Tommy to have utterly alienated his stepmother, to have told her he wanted no fur-

ther contact. Why it would be six months, a year even . . .
No, the bank would be looking for them, Tommy's bank,
his bank, when he didn't draw his quarterly check, and
when was that? No, this couldn't be their final decision, to
bury them alive in this awful place!

He was startled wide awake by a strange noise.

Again came the noise, and then again. He knew what
that was, but he couldn't identify it. Damn, in utter darkness, he could not identify even the direction. He must listen. There was a series of sounds, actually, picture it, try to
picture it, and then he did.

Bricks being fitted into place, and mortar troweled over
them. Bricks and mortar, high above.

"But that's absurd, absolutely absurd. It's medieval, it's
utterly outrageous. Tommy, wake up. Tommy!" He would
have screamed again, but it was too humiliating, that those
bastards up there would hear him, that they'd hear him
roaring as they bricked up the bloody door.

Softly, he cried against Tommy's arm. No, this was temporary, a contrivance to make them miserable, contrite, before turning them over to the authorities. They didn't mean
for them to remain here, *to die here*! It was some sort of
ritual punishment and only meant to frighten him. But of
course, the awful part was that Tommy was dead! But still,
he'd be glad to say that this had been an accident. When
they came, he'd be entirely cooperative. The point was to
get out! That's what he'd wanted to do all along, get out!

I can't die like this, it's unthinkable that I should die like
this, it's impossible, all my life forfeit, my dreams taken
from me, the greatness I only glimpsed with Stuart and
with Tessa . . .

Somewhere in the back of his mind, he knew there were
awful flaws in his logic, fatal flaws, but he continued, con-
structing the future, their coming, telling him they had only
meant to scare him, and that it had been an accident, Tommy's dying, they hadn't known the drop was so dangerous,
foolish of them, murderous, vengeful liars and fools. The
thing was to be ready, to be calm, to sleep perhaps, sleep,
listening to the sounds of the brick and the mortar. No,
these sounds have stopped. The door is sealed, perhaps, but

that doesn't matter. There have to be other ways into this dungeon, and other ways out. Later he'd find them.

For now, best to cling to Tommy, just to snuggle close to him and wait till the initial panic was gone, and he could think what to do next.

Oh, how foolish of him to have forgotten Tommy's lighter. Tommy never smoked any more than he did, but Tommy always carried that fancy lighter, and would snap it for pretty girls lifting cigarettes to their lips.

He felt in Tommy's pockets, pants, no, jacket, yes. He had it, the little gold lighter. Pray it had fluid or a cartridge of butane, or whatever the hell made it burn.

He sat up slowly, hurting the palm of his left hand on something rough. He snapped the light. The little flame sputtered and then grew long. The illumination swelled around him, revealing the small chamber, cut deep, deep into the earth.

And the jagged things, the crumbling things, were bones, human bones. There lay a skull beside him, sockets staring at him, and there another, oh God! Bones so old, some had turned to ashes, bones! And Tommy's dead, staring face, red blood drying on the side of his mouth and on his neck, where it had run down into his collar. And before him and beside him and behind him, bones!

He dropped the lighter, his hands flying to his head, his eyes closing, his mouth opening in an uncontrollable and deafening scream. There was nothing but the sound and the darkness, the sound emptying from him, carrying all his fear and his horror heavenward, and he knew in his soul he would be all right, he would be all right, if only he did not stop screaming, but let the scream pour forth from him, louder and louder, and forever, without cease.

Twenty-two

A PLANE RARELY ever fully insulated you. Even in this plane, so lavishly upholstered, with its deep chairs and large table, you knew you were in a plane. You knew you were thirty-eight thousand feet over the Atlantic, and you could feel the small ups and downs as the plane rode the wind, rather like a great vessel rides the sea.

They sat in the three chairs grouped around the table. At the three points of an invisible equilateral triangle. One chair had been specially made for Ash, that was obvious, and he'd been standing by that chair when he had gestured for Rowan and Michael to take the other two.

Other chairs, along the windowed walls of the cabin, were empty, big upturned gloved hands waiting to hold you firm and tight. One of them was larger than the others. For Ash, no doubt.

The colors were caramel, gold. Everything streamlined and near perfect. The young American woman who had served the drinks, perfect. The music, for the little while it had played, Vivaldi, perfect.

Samuel, the astonishing little man, slept in a rear cabin, curled up in bed, holding tight to the bottle he'd brought from the flat in Belgravia, and demanding a bulldog which Ash's servants had not procured for him. "You said, Ash, that I was to have anything I wanted. I heard you tell them. Well, I wanted a bulldog! And I want a bulldog now."

Rowan lay back in the chair, holding the backs of her arms.

346

She didn't know how long it had been since she'd slept. Sometime before they reached New York, she'd have to sleep. Right now she was curiously electrified, staring at the two men opposite her—at Michael, who smoked his little stub of a cigarette, holding it in two fingers, the red brand of the lighted end facing inwards.

And Ash, in another one of those long, full-cut, double-breasted silk coats, all the rage, with sleeves turned up carelessly, white shirt cuffs adorned with gold and stone cuff links that made her think of opals, though she realized she was not much of an expert on precious or semiprecious stones or anything of that sort. Opals. His eyes had a rather opalescent quality, or so she had thought several times. His pants were loose, rather like pajamas, but that too was fashionable. He had brought up his foot, disrespectfully, on the edge of the leather, his leather, and on his right wrist he wore a thin gold bracelet without any obvious use, a thin band of metal, glittering and looking maddeningly sexual to her, though why she couldn't explain.

He lifted his hand, ran it back through his dark hair, running the little finger through the white streak as if he didn't want to forget it, leave it out, but collect it with all the other dark waves. It made his face come alive for her again, just this little movement, and the way his eyes scanned the room and then stopped on her.

She herself hardly noticed what she'd taken hastily from her suitcase. Something red, something soft, something loose and short that barely touched her knees. Michael had put the pearls around her neck, a small, neat necklace. It had surprised her. She'd been so dazed then.

Ash's servants had packed up everything else.

"I didn't know whether or not you wanted us to get Samuel a bulldog," the young one, Leslie, had said several times, very distressed that she'd displeased the boss.

"It doesn't matter," Ash had said finally, hearing her, perhaps for the first time. "In New York we will get Samuel bulldogs. He can keep his bulldogs in the garden on the roof. Do you know, Leslie, there are dogs who live on the rooftops of New York who have never, never been to the street below?"

347

What must she think he is? Rowan had wondered. What do they all think he is? Is it to his advantage that he is blindingly rich? Or blindingly handsome?

"But I wanted a bulldog tonight," the little man had fussed until he'd passed out again, "and I want it now."

The little man had on first sight terrified Rowan. What was that, witch genes? Witch knowledge? Or was it the physician in her, horrified by the folds of flesh slowly covering his entire face? He was like a great variegated and living piece of stone. What if a surgeon's scalpel removed those folds, revealing eyes, a full, correctly shaped mouth, the bones under the cheeks, the chin? What would his life become?

"Mayfair witches," he'd said when he saw them, Rowan and Michael.

"Does everyone in this part of the world know us?" Michael had asked testily. "And does our reputation always go before us? When I get home, I mean to read up on witchcraft, to study it in earnest."

"Very good idea," Ash had said. "With your powers, you can do many things."

Michael had laughed. They liked each other, these two. She could see it. They shared certain attitudes. Yuri had been so frenzied, shattered, so young.

All the way back from the grim confrontation at Stuart Gordon's tower, Michael had told them the long story related to him by Lasher, of a life lived in the 1500s, and of Lasher's strange account of earlier memories, of his sense that he had lived even before that. There had been nothing clinical in the telling—rather a ragged outpouring of the tale which he and Aaron alone had known. He had told it once before to Rowan, yes, and she remembered it more as a series of images and catastrophes than words.

To have heard it again in the black limousine, flying over the miles towards London, was to see it again and in greater detail. Lasher the priest, Lasher the saint, Lasher the martyr, and then, a hundred years later, the beginning of Lasher the witch's familiar, the invisible voice in the dark, a force of wind lashing the fields of wheat, and the leaves from the trees.

"Voice from the glen," the little man had said in London, jabbing his thumb to point at Michael.

Was it? She wondered. She knew the glen, she would never forget it, forget being Lasher's prisoner, being dragged up through the ruins of the castle, never forget the moments when Lasher had "recalled" everything, when the new flesh had reclaimed his mind and severed it from whatever true knowledge a ghost can possess.

Michael had never been there. Maybe someday they would, together, visit that place.

Ash had told Samuel to go to sleep as they drove for the airport. The little man had drunk another pint of whiskey, with a lot of grunting and groaning and occasional belching, and had been comatose when carried onto the plane.

Now they were flying over the Arctic.

She closed and opened her eyes. The cabin shimmered.

"I would never hurt this child Mona," said Ash suddenly, startling her, waking her more fully. He was watching Michael with quiet eyes.

Michael took a final drag off the stubby little cigarette, and crushed it out in the big glass tray so that it became a hideous little worm. His fingers looked large, powerful, dusted with dark hair.

"I know you wouldn't," said Michael. "But I don't understand it all. How can I? Yuri was so frightened."

"That was my fault. Stupidity. This is why we have to talk to each other, we three. There are other reasons as well."

"But why trust us?" asked Michael. "Why befriend us at all? You're a busy man, some sort of billionaire, obviously."

"Ah, well, we have that in common then, too, don't we?" said Ash, earnestly.

Rowan smiled.

It was a fascinating study in contrasts, the deep-voiced man with the flashing blue eyes and the dark, almost bushy eyebrows; and the tall one, so beguilingly slender, with graceful movements of the wrist that made you almost dizzy. Two exquisite brands of masculinity, both bound up with perfect proportions and fierce personality, and both men—as big men often do—seemed to luxuriate in a great self-confidence and inner calm.

She looked at the ceiling. In her exhaustion, things were distorted. Her eyes were dry and she would have to sleep soon, simply have to, but she couldn't now. Not now.

Ash spoke again.

"You have a tale to tell which no one can hear but me," said Ash. "And I want to hear it. And I have a tale to tell that I will tell only to you. Is it that you don't want my confidence? That you don't want my friendship or ever, possibly, my love?"

Michael considered this. "I think I want all that, since you ask," said Michael, with a little shrug and laugh. "Since you ask."

"Gotcha," said Ash softly.

Michael laughed again, just a low little rumble. "But you know, don't you, that I killed Lasher? Yuri told you this. You hold this against me, that I killed one of you?"

"He was not one of me," said Ash, smiling kindly. The light glinted on the white streak coming from his left temple. A man of thirty, perhaps, with elegant gray streaks, a sort of boy genius of the corporate world, he must have seemed, prematurely rich, prematurely gray. Centuries old, infinitely patient.

It gave her a small warm burst of pride, suddenly, that she had killed Gordon. Not him.

She had done it. It was the first time in all her sad life that she had enjoyed using the power, condemning a man to death with her will, destroying the tissues inside him, and she had confirmed what she had always suspected, that if she really wanted to do it, if she really cooperated with it, rather than fighting this power, it could work awfully fast.

"I want to tell you things," Ash said. "I want you to know them, the story of what happened and how we came to the glen. Not now, we're all too tired, surely. But I want to tell you."

"Yeah," said Michael, "and I want to know." He was reaching into his pocket, pulling the pack halfway up and then shaking loose the cigarette. "I want to know all about you, of course. I want to study the book, if you still mean to let us do that, see the book."

"All that is possible," said Ash, with an easy gesture, one hand resting on his knee. "You are a veritable tribe of witches. We are close, you and I. Oh, it isn't terribly complicated, really. I have learned to live with a profound loneliness. I forget about it for years and years. Then it surfaces, the desire to be placed in context by somebody else. The desire to be known, understood, evaluated morally by a sophisticated mind. That was always the lure of the Talamasca, from the beginning, that I could go there and confide in my scholars, that we would talk late into the night. It's lured many another secretive nonhuman. I'm not the only one."

"Well, that's what all of us need, isn't it?" asked Michael, glancing at Rowan. There passed another one of those silent, secret moments, rather like an invisible kiss.

She nodded.

"Yes," Ash agreed. "Human beings very seldom survive without that kind of exchange, communication. Love. And our breed was such a loving breed. It took so long for us to come to understand aggression. We always seem like children when humans first meet us, but we're not children. It's a different kind of mildness. There's a stubbornness in it, a desire to be gratified at once, and for things to remain simple."

He fell silent. Then he asked, very sincerely, "What really troubles you? Why did you both hesitate when I asked you to come with me to New York? What went through your minds?"

"Killing Lasher," said Michael. "It was a matter of survival with me, no more, no less. There was one witness, one man present who could understand and forgive, if a forgiving witness is required. And that man's dead."

"Aaron."

"Yeah, he wanted to take Lasher, but he understood why I didn't let him. And those other two men, well, that, we could say, was self-defense. . . ."

"And you suffer over these deaths," said Ash gently.

"Lasher, that was the deliberate murder," said Michael, as if he were speaking to himself. "The thing had hurt my

351

wife; it had taken my child somehow, taken my child. Though what that child would have been, who can say? There are so many questions, so many possibilities. And it had preyed upon the women. Killed them, in its drive to propagate. It could no more live with us than could some plague or insect. Coexistence was unthinkable, and then there was—to use your word—the context, the way it had presented itself from the beginning, in ghostly form, the way it had . . . used me from the start."

"Of course I understand you," Ash said. "Were I you, I would have killed him too."

"Would you?" asked Michael. "Or would you have spared him because he was one of the very few of your kind left on the earth? You would have had to feel that, a species loyalty."

"No," said Ashlar. "I don't think you understand me, I mean in a very basic way. I have spent my life proving to myself that I am as good as human. Remember. To Pope Gregory himself I once made the case that we had souls. I am no friend to a migrant soul with a thirst for power, an aged soul that had usurped a new body. This arouses no such loyalty in me."

Michael nodded as if to say *I see*.

"To have spoken with Lasher," said Ash, "to have talked about his remembrances, that might have given me considerable pause. But no, I would have felt no loyalty to him. The one thing that the Christians and the Romans never believed was that murder is murder, whether it is a human murder or a murder of one of us. But I believe it. I have lived too long to hold foolish beliefs that humans aren't worthy of compassion, that they are 'other.' We are all connected; everything is connected. How and why, I couldn't tell you. But it's true. And Lasher had murdered to reach his ends, and if this one evil could be stamped out forever, only this one . . ." He shrugged and his smile came back, a little bitter perhaps, or only sweet and sad. "I always thought, imagined, dreamed, perhaps, that if we did come back, if we had again our chance on the face of the earth, we could stamp out that one crime."

Michael smiled. "You don't think that now."

"No," said Ash, "but there are reasons for not thinking about such possibilities. You'll understand when we can sit down and talk together in my rooms in New York."

"I hated Lasher," said Michael. "He was vicious and he had vicious habits. He laughed at us. Fatal error, perhaps. I'm not entirely certain. I also believed that others wanted me to kill him, others both alive and dead. Do you believe in destiny?"

"I don't know."

"What do you mean, you don't know?"

"I was told centuries ago that to be the lone survivor of my people was my destiny. It's happened. But does that mean it was really destiny? I was cunning; I had survived winters and battles and unspeakable tribulations. So I continued to survive. Destiny, or survival? I don't know. But whatever the case, this creature was your enemy. Why do you need my forgiveness now for what you did?"

"That isn't really the worry," said Rowan. She spoke before Michael could answer. She remained curled in the chair, head to one side against the leather. She could see both of them comfortably, and they were both looking at her. "At least I don't think it's Michael's worry."

He didn't interrupt her.

"His worry," she said, "is something that I've done, which he himself could not do."

Ash waited, just as Michael waited.

"I killed another Taltos, a female," Rowan said.

"A female?" Ash asked softly. "A true female Taltos?"

"Yes, a true female, my own daughter by Lasher. I killed her. I shot her. I killed her as soon as I realized what she was and who she was, and that she was there, with me. I killed her. I feared her as much as I'd feared him."

Ash appeared fascinated, but in no way disturbed.

"I feared a match of male and female," said Rowan. "I feared the cruel predictions he'd made and the dark future he'd described, and I feared that somewhere out there, among the other Mayfairs, he'd fathered a male, and the male would find her and they would breed. That would have been his victory. In spite of all I suffered and what Michael had suffered, and all the Mayfair witches, from the

353

beginning, for this ... this coupling, this triumph of the Taltos."

Ash nodded.

"My daughter had come to me in love," said Rowan.

"Yes," Ash whispered, obviously eager for her to go on.

"I shot my own daughter," she said. "I shot my own lonely and unprotected girl. And she'd cured me, she'd come to me with her milk and given me this and healed me of the trauma of her birth.

"That's what worries me and what worries Michael, that you should know this, that you'll discover it, that you, who want to be close to us, will be horrified when you discover that a female might have been within your grasp if I hadn't snuffed out her life."

Ash had leant forward in the chair, his elbows resting on his knee, one finger curled beneath his soft lower lip, pressing into it. His eyebrows were raised, coming together in a frown only slightly, as he peered into her face.

"What would you have done?" Rowan asked. "If you had discovered her, my Emaleth?"

"This was her name!" he whispered, amazed.

"The name her father gave her. Her father had forced me and forced me, though the miscarriages were killing me. And finally, for some reason, this one, Emaleth, was strong enough to be born."

Ash sighed. He sat back again, putting his arm on the edge of the leather arm of the chair, and he studied her, but he seemed neither devastated nor angry. But then, how could one know?

For one split second, it seemed madness to have told him, to have told him here, of all places, on his own plane, flying silently through the sky. But then it seemed simply inevitable, something that had to be done, if anything was to progress, if anything was to come of their knowing each other, if love was in fact already growing between them out of what they'd already witnessed and heard.

"Would you have wanted her?" Rowan asked. "Would you have, perhaps, moved heaven and earth to get to her, to save her, to take her away safely, and father the tribe again?"

Michael was afraid for her, she could see it in his eyes. And she realized as she looked at both of them that she wasn't really saying all this just for them. She was talking for her own sake, the mother who had shot the daughter, pulled the trigger. She flinched suddenly, eyes shut tight, shuddering, her shoulders rising, and then sitting back in the chair, head to one side. She'd heard the body drop on the floor, she'd seen the face collapse before that, she'd tasted the milk, the thick sweet milk, almost like a white syrup, so good to her.

"Rowan," said Ash gently, "Rowan, Rowan, don't suffer these things again on my account."

"But you would have moved heaven and earth to get to her," Rowan said. "It's why you came to England when Samuel called you, when he told you Yuri's story. You came because a Taltos had been seen in Donnelaith."

Slowly Ash nodded. "I can't answer your question. I don't know the answer. Yes, I would have come, yes. But tried to take her away? I don't know."

"Oh, come now, how could you not want it?"

"You mean how could I not want to make the tribe again?"

"Yes."

He shook his head and looked down, thoughtfully, the finger curled beneath his lip again, elbow on the arm of the chair.

"What strange witches you are, both of you," he whispered.

"How so?" asked Michael.

Ash rose to his feet suddenly, his head almost touching the top of the cabin. He stretched and then turned his back, walking a few steps, head bowed, before he turned around.

"Listen, we cannot answer each other's questions this way," he said. "But what I can tell you now is I am glad the female is dead. I am glad it's dead!" He shook his head, and placed his hand on the sloped back of the chair. He was looking off, hair falling down over his eyes, rather wild now, so that he looked especially gaunt and dramatic, and rather like a magician, perhaps. "So help me, God," he said. "I'm relieved, I'm relieved that you tell me in the same breath it was there and that it is no more."

Michael nodded. "I think I'm beginning to see."

"Do you?" asked Ash.

"We can't share this earth, can we, the two tribes so apparently similar and so utterly unalike?"

"No, we can't share it," Ash said, shaking his head with emphasis. "What race can live with any other? What religion with any other? War is worldwide; and the wars are tribal, no matter what men say they are! They are tribal, and they are wars of extermination, whether it be the Arabs against the Kurds, or the Turks and the Europeans, or the Russian fighting the Oriental. It's never going to stop. People dream that it will, but it can't, as long as there are people. But of course, if my kind came again, and if the humans of the earth were exterminated, well, then, my people could live in peace, but then, doesn't every tribe believe this of itself?"

Michael shook his head. "It doesn't have to be strife," he said. "It is conceivable that all tribes stop fighting each other."

"Conceivable, yes, but not possible."

"One breed doesn't have to reign over another," insisted Michael. "One breed doesn't even have to know about the other."

"You mean that we should live in secret?" Ash asked. "Do you know how quickly our population doubles itself and then triples and then quadruples? Do you know how strong we are? You can't know how it was, you have never seen the Taltos born knowing, you've never seen it grow to its full height in those first few minutes or hours or days or however long it takes; you've never seen it."

"I've seen it," said Rowan. "I've seen it twice."

"And what do you say? What would come of my wanting a female? Of grieving for your lost Emaleth and seeking to find a replacement for her? Of troubling your innocent Mona with the seed that might make the Taltos or might make her die?"

"I can tell you this," said Rowan, taking a deep breath. "At the moment I shot Emaleth, at that moment there

356

wasn't the slightest doubt in my mind that she was a threat to my breed, and that she had to die."

Ash smiled; he nodded. "And you were right."

They were all silent. Then Michael spoke.

"You have our worst secret now," he said.

"Yes, you have it," said Rowan softly.

"And I wonder," said Michael, "if we have yours."

"You will," said Ash. "We should sleep now, all of us. My eyes hurt me. And the corporation waits with a hundred small tasks which only I can perform. You sleep now, and in New York I'll tell you everything. And you will have all my secrets, from the worst to the least."

Twenty-three

"**M**ONA, WAKE UP."

She heard the swamp before she actually saw it. She heard the bullfrogs crying, and the night birds, and the sound of water all around her, murky, still, yet still moving somewhere, in a rusted pipe perhaps, or against the side of a skiff, she didn't know. They had stopped. This must be the landing.

The dream had been the strangest yet. She had had to pass an examination, and she that passed would rule the world, so Mona had to answer every question. From every field the questions had come, on science, mathematics, history, the computer she so loved, the stocks and bonds, the meaning of life, and that had been the hardest part, because she'd felt so alive that she could not begin to justify it. *You know, you just know that it is magnificent to be alive.* Had she scored the perfect one hundred percent? Would she rule the world?

"Wake up, Mona!" Mary Jane whispered.

Mary Jane couldn't see that Mona's eyes were open. Mona was looking through the glass window at the swamp, at the ragged, tilting trees, sickly and strung with moss, at the vines snarled like ropes around the huge old cypresses. Out there in the light of the moon she could see patches of water through the covering of still duckweed, and the knees of the cypress trees, so many dangerous spikes sticking up all around the thick trunks of the old trees. And black things, little black things flying in the night. Could be roaches, but don't think about it!

Her back ached. As she tried to sit forward, she felt heavy and achy all over, and wanting more milk. They'd stopped twice for milk, and she wanted more. They had cartons and cartons in the ice chest, best to get to the house. Then drink it.

"Come on, honey, you get out and wait for me right here, and I'm going to hide this car where nobody's likely to see it."

"Hide this car, this enormous car?"

Mary Jane opened the door and helped her out, and then stood back, obviously horrified again looking at her, and trying not to show it. The light came from inside the car on Mary Jane's face.

"Lord, Mona Mayfair, what if you die?"

Mona grasped Mary Jane's wrist as she stood up, her feet squarely planted on the soft earth thick with dredged white shells, glowing beneath her. There went the pier, out into the dark.

"Stop saying that, Mary Jane, but I'll give you something to think about, just in case it happens," said Mona. She tried to lift the sack of groceries from the floor, but she could not bend down that far.

Mary Jane had just lighted the lantern. She turned around and the light went up into her eyes, making her ghastly. It shone on the weathered shack behind her and on the few feet of dilapidated pier, and on the tendrils of moss that hung down from the dead-looking branches right above her.

God, there were so many flying things in the dark.

"Mona Mayfair, your cheekbones are sticking right out of your face!" said Mary Jane. "I swear to God, I can see your teeth through the skin around your mouth."

"Oh, stop it, you're being crazy. It's the light. You look like a ghost yourself." Whoa, she felt horrible. Weak, and full of aching. Even her feet ached.

"And you wouldn't believe the color of your skin, my God, you look like somebody sunk in a bath of milk of magnesia."

"I'm okay. I can't lift this stuff."

359

"I'll get it, you rest there against that tree, that's the tree I told you about, the cypress tree, oldest one in these parts, you see this was the pond out here, the little pond???? You know??? Where the family would go rowing??? Here, take the lantern, the handle doesn't get hot."

"It looks dangerous. In the western movies, they are always throwing a lantern like that into the barn where the hero has been trapped by the bad guys. It breaks and sets the barn on fire every time. I don't like it."

"Well, nobody's going to do that out here," shouted Mary Jane over her shoulder, as she moved one sack after another, plunking them down on the shells. "And there isn't any hay, besides, and if there was, it would be soggy."

The headlights of the car bored into the swamp, deep into the endless forest of trunks, thick and thin, and the wild broken palmetto and jagged banana. The water breathed and sighed and trickled again, for all its stagnant stench and motionlessness.

"Jesus Christ, this is a wild place," Mona whispered, but in a way she loved it. She loved even the coolness of the air here, languid and soft, not moving with a breeze, but nevertheless stirred, perhaps by the water.

Mary Jane let the heavy ice chest drop.

"No, lookie, get over to one side, and when I get in the car and turn it around like to go back out, you look yonder where the light shines and you'll see Fontevrault!"

The door slammed, the tires churned the gravel.

The big car backed up to the right, and the beams slid over the spindly phantom trees, and lo and behold, lo and behold, she saw it—enormous, and listing horribly in the light, its attic gable windows flashing and winking out as the car made its circle.

The night went dark, but what she had seen remained, a great black hulk against the sky, impossible. The house was falling.

She almost screamed, though why she wasn't certain. They couldn't be going to that house, not a house leaning like that, a crippled house. A house underwater was one thing, but a house like that? But even as the car drove away, with a small, healthy blast of white smoke, she saw that there were lights in this impossible ruin. She could see through the upstairs fanlight in the center of the porch, way back, deep inside, lights. And when the last sound of the car was gone, she thought for a moment that she heard something like the playing of a radio.

The lantern was bright enough, but this was country dark, pitch black. There was nothing but the lantern and that dim, glowing coal of light inside the collapsing mansion.

Dear God, Mary Jane doesn't realize this damned place has keeled over in her absence! We've got to get Granny out, assuming that Granny has not already been unceremoniously dumped into the drink! And what drink, what slime! The smell was the greenest smell she had ever smelled, oh, but when she looked up, the sky was that glowing pink that it can be in the Louisiana night, and the disappearing trees stuck their futile little branches out to connect with each other, and the moss became translucent, veils and veils of moss. The birds, listen to the birds crying. The very topmost branches were thin and covered over with webs, silvery webs, were they spiders or silkworms?

"I do see the charm of this place," she said. "If only that house wasn't about to topple."

Mama.

I'm here, Morrigan.

There was a sound on the road behind her. Christ, Mary Jane was running towards her, all alone in the dark. The least she could do was turn around and hold up the lantern. Her back ached now almost unbearably, and she wasn't even lifting anything or trying to reach anything, just holding up this awfully heavy lantern.

And is this theory of evolution supposed to account for absolutely every species on the planet at this time? I mean, there is no secondary theory, perhaps, of spontaneous development?

She shook herself awake all over. Besides, she didn't know the answer to that question. Truth was, evolution had never seemed logical to her. *Science has reached a point where once again various kinds of beliefs, once condemned as metaphysical, are now entirely possible.*

Mary Jane came right out of the blackness, running like a little girl, clasping her high-heeled shoes together in the fingers of her right hand. When she got to Mona, she stopped, bent over double, and caught her breath and then looked at Mona.

"Jesus Christ, Mona Mayfair," she said with anxious gasps, her pretty face gleaming with a thin polish of sweat, "I've got to get you to that house pronto."

"Your panty hose are split to pieces."

"Well, I should hope so," said Mary Jane. "I hate them." She picked up the ice chest and started running down the pier. "Come on, Mona, hurry it up. You're going to die on me right here."

"Will you stop that? The baby can hear you!"

There was a loud noise, a splash. Mary Jane had heaved the ice chest into the boat. So that meant there *was* a boat. Mona tried to hurry across the creaky, splintery boards, but each step was excruciating for her. Then, quite suddenly, she felt the real thing, had to be. A pain like a whip wrapping around her back and her waist, or what was left of her waist. She stopped, biting down hard not to shout.

Mary Jane was running back to the boat already with her second load.

"I want to help," said Mona, but she could barely get out the last word. She walked slowly to the edge of the pier, thinking she was glad she had on her flat slippers, though she couldn't really remember thinking to put them on, and then she saw the wide shallow pirogue as Mary Jane put in the last of the sacks, and all the tumbling pillows and blankets.

"Now gimme that lantern and you stay right there till I back her up."

"Mary Jane, I'm kind of, well, sort of, scared of the water? I mean I feel real clumsy, Mary Jane, I don't know if I should climb into the boat."

The pain flashed again. *Mama, I love you, I'm afraid.*

"Well, don't be afraid, shut up!" said Mona.

"What did you say?" asked Mary Jane.

Mary Jane jumped in the big metal pirogue, grabbed the long stick that was somehow anchored to the side, and then

362

backed up the boat with some quick dipping pushes. The lantern stood at the very front, like there was a little bench or something especially for it. All the stuff was behind her.

"Come on now, honey, just step into it, quick-like, yeah, that's right, both feet."

"Oh God, we're going to drown."

"Now, darlin', that's plain silly, this water isn't six feet deep here! We'll get filthy, but we won't drown."

"I could easily drown in six feet of water," said Mona. "And the house, Mary Jane, look at the house."

"What about it?"

The world mercifully ceased to rock and roll. Mona was hurting Mary Jane's hand, probably. And now Mary Jane had to let go. Okay, easy! Mary Jane had both hands on the pole, and they were moving away from the pier.

"But, Mary Jane, look, Mary Jane," said Mona.

"Yeah, that's it, honey, we don't go but fifty feet, you just stand still, real still. This is a big, steady pirogue. Nothing's going to make it tip. You can kneel down if you want, or even sit down, but at this point I would not recommend the bother."

"The house, Mary Jane, the house, it's tilted to one side."

"Darlin', it's been like that for fifty years."

"I knew you'd say that. But what if it sinks, Mary Jane! God, I can't stand the sight of it! It's horrible, something that big tilting like that, it's like . . ."

Another flash of pain, small and mean and deep, for all its quickness.

"Well, stop looking at it!" Mary Jane said. "You will not believe this, but I myself, with a compass and a piece of glass, have actually measured the angle of the tilt, and it is less than five degrees. It's just all the columns make those vertical lines and look like they're about to fall over."

She lifted the pole, and the flat-bottomed boat slipped forward fast on its own momentum. The dreamy night closed all around them, leafy and soft, vines trailing down from the boughs of a listing tree that looked as if it might fall too.

Mary Jane dug the pole in again and shoved hard, sending the boat flying towards the immense shadow looming over them.

"Oh my God, is that the front door?"

"Well, it's off the hinges now, if that's what you mean, but that's where we're headed. Honey, I'm going to take you right up to the staircase inside. We're going to tie this boat right there like always."

They had reached the porch. Mona put her hands over her mouth, wanting to cover her eyes, but knowing she'd fall if she did. She stared straight up at the wild vines tangled above them. Everywhere she looked she saw thorns. Must have been roses once, and maybe would be again. And there, look, blossoms glowing in the dark, that was wisteria. She loved wisteria.

Why don't the big columns just fall, and had she ever seen columns so wide? God, she'd never, when looking at all those sketches, ever dreamed the house was on this scale, yes, it was, absolutely Greek Revival grandeur. But then she'd never actually known anyone who really lived here, at least not a person who could remember.

The beading of the porch ceiling was rotted out, and a hideous dark hole gaped above that could just harbor a giant python, or what about a whole nest of roaches? Maybe the frogs ate the roaches. The frogs were singing and singing, a lovely sound, very strong and loud compared to the more gentle sound of garden cicadas.

"Mary Jane, there are no roaches here, are there?"

"Roaches! Darlin', there are moccasins out here, and cottonmouth snakes, and alligators now, lots of them. My cats eat the roaches."

They slid through the front door, and suddenly the hallway opened up, enormous, filled with the fragrance of the wet soaked plaster and the glue from the peeling wallpaper, and the wood itself, perhaps, oh, there were too many smells of rot and the swamp, and living things, and the rippling water which cast its eerie light all over the walls and the ceiling, ripples upon ripples of light, you could get drugged by it.

Suddenly she pictured Ophelia floating away on her stream, with the flowers in her hair.

But look. You could see through the big doors into a ruined parlor and, where the light danced on the wall there, the sodden remnant of a drapery, so dark now from the water it had drunk up that the color was no longer visible. Paper hung down in loose garlands from the ceiling.

The little boat struck the stairs with a bump. Mona reached out and grabbed the railing, sure it would wobble and fall, but it didn't. And a good thing, too, because another pain came round her middle and bit deep into her back. She had to hold her breath.

"Mary Jane, we've got to hurry."

"You're telling me. Mona Mayfair, I'm so scared right now."

"Don't be. Be brave. Morrigan needs you."

"Morrigan!"

The light of the lantern shivered and moved up to the high second-floor ceiling. The wallpaper was covered with little bouquets, faded now so that only the white sketch of the bouquet remained, glowing in the dark. Great holes gaped in the plaster, but she could not see anything through them.

"The walls are brick, don't you worry about a thing, every single wall, inside, out, brick, just like First Street." Mary Jane was tying up the boat. Apparently they were beached on an actual step. They were steady now. Mona clung to the railing, as fearful of getting out as of staying in the little boat.

"Go on upstairs, I'll bring the junk. Go up and straight back and say hello to Granny. Don't worry about your shoes, I got plenty of dry shoes. I'll bring everything."

Cautiously, moaning a little, she reached over, took hold of the rail with both hands, and stepped up out of the boat, hoisting herself awkwardly until she found herself standing securely on the tread, with dry stairway ahead of her.

If it hadn't been tilting, it would have felt perfectly secure, she thought. And quite suddenly she stood there, one hand on the railing, one on the soft, spongy plaster to her left, and looking up, she felt the house around her, felt its rot, its strength, its obdurate refusal to fall down into the devouring water.

It was a massive and sturdy thing, giving in only slowly, perhaps stopped at this pitch forever. But when she thought of the muck, she didn't know why they weren't both sucked right down now, like bad guys on the run in motion-picture quicksand.

"Go on up," said Mary Jane, who had already hurled one sack up on the step above Mona. Crash, bang, slam. The girl was really moving.

Mona began to walk. Yes, firm, and amazingly dry by the time she reached the very top, dry as if the sun of the spring day had been fiercely hot, trapped in here, and bleaching the boards, look, yes, bleaching it as surely as if it were driftwood.

At last she stood on the second floor, estimating the angle to be less than five degrees, but that was plenty enough to drive you mad, and then she narrowed her eyes the better to see to the very end of the hallway. Another grand and lovely door with sidelights and fanlight, and electric bulbs strung on crisscrossing wire, hanging from the ceiling. Mosquito netting. Was that it? Lots and lots of it, and the soft electric light, nice and steady, shining through it.

She took several steps, clinging to the wall still, which did indeed feel hard and dry now, and then she heard a soft little laugh coming from the end of the hall, and as Mary Jane came up with the lantern in hand and set it down beside her sack at the top of the stairs, Mona saw a child standing in the far doorway.

It was a boy, very dark-skinned, with big inky eyes and soft black hair and a face like a small Hindu saint, peering out at her.

"Hey, you, Benjy, come help me here with all this. You gotta help me!" shouted Mary Jane.

The boy sauntered forward, and he wasn't so little as he came closer. He was maybe almost as tall as Mona, which wasn't saying much, of course, since Mona hadn't broken five feet two yet, and might never.

He was one of those beautiful children with a great mysterious mingling of blood—African, Indian, Spanish, French, probably Mayfair. Mona wanted to touch him, touch his cheek and see if his skin really felt the way it

366

looked, like very, very fine tanned leather. Something Mary Jane had said came back to her, about him selling himself downtown, and in a little burst of mysterious light, she saw purple-papered rooms, fringed lampshades, decadent gentlemen like Oncle Julien in white suits, and of all things, herself in the brass bed with this adorable boy!

Craziness. The pain stopped her again. She could have dropped in her tracks. But quite deliberately she picked up one foot and then the other. There were the cats, all right, good Lord, witches' cats, big, long-tailed, furry, demon-eyed cats. There must have been five of them, darting along the walls.

The beautiful boy with the gleaming black hair carried two sacks of groceries down the hall ahead of her. It was even sort of clean here, as if he'd swept and mopped.

Her shoes were sopping wet. She was going to go down.

"That you, Mary Jane? Benjy, is that my girl? Mary Jane!"

"Coming, Granny, I'm coming, what are you doing, Granny?"

Mary Jane ran past her, holding the ice chest awkwardly, with her elbows flying out and her long flaxen hair swaying.

"Hey, there, Granny!" She disappeared around the bend. "What you doing now?"

"Eating graham crackers and cheese, you want some?"

"No, not now, gimme a kiss, TV broken?"

"No, honey, just got sick of it. Benjy's been writing down my songs as I sing them. Benjy."

"Listen, Granny, I got to go, I got Mona Mayfair with me. I've got to take her up to the attic where it's really warm and dry."

"Yes, oh yes, please," Mona whispered. She leant against the walls which tilted away from her. Why, you could lie right on a tilted wall like this, almost. Her feet throbbed, and the pain came again.

Mama, I am coming.

Hold on, sweetheart, one more flight of steps to climb.

"You bring Mona Mayfair in here, you bring her."

"No, Granny, not now!" Mary Jane came flying out of

the room, big white skirts hitting the doorjamb, arms out to reach for Mona.

"Right on up, honey, right straight, come on around now."

There was a rustling and a clatter, and just as Mary Jane turned Mona around and pointed her to the foot of the next stairs, Mona saw a tiny little woman come scuttling out of the back room, gray hair in long loose braids with ribbons on the end of them. She had a face like wrinkled cloth, with amazing jet black eyes, crinkled with seeming good humor.

"Got to hurry," Mona said, moving as quickly as she could along the railing. "I'm getting sick from the tilt."

"You're sick from the baby!"

"You go on ahead, and turn on those lights," shouted the old woman, clamping one amazingly strong and dry little hand to Mona's arm. "Why the hell didn't you tell me this child was pregnant. God, this is Alicia's girl, like to died when they cut off that sixth finger."

"What? From me, you mean?" Mona turned to look into the little wrinkled face with the small lips pressed tight together as the woman nodded.

"You mean I had a sixth finger?" asked Mona.

"Sure did, honey, and you almost went to heaven when they put you under. Nobody ever told you that tale, about the nurse giving you the shot twice? About your heart nearly stopping dead, and how Evelyn came and saved you!"

Benjy rushed by, headed up the stairs, his bare feet sounding dusty on the bare wood.

"No, nobody ever told me! Oh God, the sixth finger."

"But don't you see, that will help!" declared Mary Jane. They were headed up now, and it only looked like one hundred steps to the light up there, and the thin figure of Benjy, who, having lighted the lights, was now making his slow, languid descent, though Mary Jane was already hollering at him.

Granny had stopped at the foot of the steps. Her white nightgown touched the soiled floor. Her black eyes were calculating, taking Mona's measure. A Mayfair, all right, thought Mona.

"Get the blankets, the pillows, all that," said Mary Jane. "Hurry up. And the milk, Benjy, get the milk."

"Well, now, just wait a minute," Granny shouted. "This girl looks like she doesn't have time to be spending the night in that attic. She ought to go to the hospital right now. Where's the truck? Your truck at the landing?"

"Never mind that, she's going to have the baby here," said Mary Jane.

"Mary Jane!" roared Granny. "God damn it, I can't climb these steps on account of my hip."

"Just go back to bed, Granny. Make Benjy hurry with that stuff. Benjy, I'm not going to pay you!!!!"

They continued up the attic steps, the air getting warmer as they ascended.

It was a huge space.

Same crisscross of electric lights she'd seen below, and look at the steamer trunks and the wardrobes tucked into every gable. Every gable except for one, which held the bed deep inside, and next to it, an oil lamp.

The bed was huge, built out of those dark, plain posts they used so much in the country, the canopy gone, and only the netting stretched over the top, veil after veil. The netting veiled the entrance to the gable. Mary Jane lifted it as Mona fell forward on the softest mattress.

Oh, it was all dry! It was. The feather comforter went *poof* all around her. Pillows and pillows. And the oil lamp, though it was treacherously close, made it into a little tent of sorts around her.

"Benjy! Get that ice chest now."

"*Chère,* I just carry that ice chest to the back porch," the boy said, or something like it, the accent clearly Cajun. Didn't sound like the old woman at all. She just sounds like one of us, thought Mona, a little different maybe. . . .

"Well, just go git it," Mary Jane said.

The netting caught all the golden light, and made a beautiful solitary place of this big soft bed. Nice place to die, maybe better than in the stream with the flowers.

The pain came again, but this time she was so much

more comfortable. What were you supposed to do? She'd read about it. Suck in your breath or something? She couldn't remember. That was one subject she had not thoroughly researched. Jesus Christ, this was almost about to happen.

She grabbed Mary Jane's hand. Mary Jane lay beside her, looking down into her face, wiping her forehead now with something soft and white, softer than a handkerchief.

"Yes, darlin', I'm here, and it's getting bigger and bigger, Mona, it's just not, it's . . ."

"It will be born," Mona whispered. "It's mine. It will be born, but if I die, you have to do it for me, you and Morrigan together."

"What!"

"Make a bier of flowers for me—"

"Make a what?"

"Hush up, I'm telling you something that really matters."

"Mary Jane!" Granny roared from the foot of the steps. "You come down here and help Benjy carry me up now, girl!"

"Make a raft, a raft, all full of flowers, you know," Mona said. "Wisteria, roses, all those things growing outside, swamp irises . . ."

"Yeah, yeah, and then what!"

"Only make it fragile, real fragile, so that as I float away on it, it will slowly fall apart in the current, and I'll go down into the water . . . like Ophelia!"

"Yeah, okay, anything you say! Mona, I am scared now. I am really scared."

"Then be a witch, 'cause there's no changing anybody's mind now, is there?"

Something broke! Just as if a hole had been poked through it. Christ, was she dead inside?

No, Mother, but I am coming. Please be ready to take my hand. I need you.

Mary Jane had drawn up on her knees, her hands slapped to the sides of her face.

"In the name of God!"

"Help it! Mary Jane! Help it!" screamed Mona.

Mary Jane shut her eyes tight and laid her hands on the

mountain of Mona's belly. The pain blinded Mona. She tried to see, to see the light in the netting, and to see Mary Jane's squeezed-shut eyes, and feel her hands, and hear her whispering, but she couldn't. She was falling. Down through the swamp trees with her hands up, trying to catch the branches.

"Granny, come help!" screamed Mary Jane.

And there came the rapid patter of the old woman's feet!

"Benjy, get out!" the old woman screamed. "Go back downstairs, out, you hear me?"

Down, down through the swamps, the pain getting tighter and tighter. Jesus Christ, no wonder women hate this! No joke. This is horrible. God help me!

"Lord, Jesus Christ, Mary Jane," Granny cried. "It's a walking baby!"

"Granny, help me, take her hand, take it. Granny, you know what she is?"

"A walking baby, child. I've heard of them all my life, but never seen one. Jesus, child. When a walking baby was born out there in the swamps, to Ida Bell Mayfair, when I was a child, they said it stood taller than its mother as soon as it came walking out, and Grandpère Tobias went down there and chopped it up with an ax while the mother was laying there in the bed, screaming! Haven't you never heard of the walking babies, child? In Santo Domingo they burned them!"

"No, not this baby!" wailed Mona. She groped in the dark, trying to open her eyes. Dear God, the pain. And suddenly a small slippery hand caught hers. *Don't die, Mama.*

"Oh, Hail Mary, full of grace," said Granny, and Mary Jane started the same prayer, only one line behind her, as if it were a reel. "Blessed art thou among women, and blessed is . . ."

"Look at me, Mama!" The whisper was right by her ear. "Look at me! Mama, I need you, help me, make me grow big, big, big."

"Grow big!" cried the women, but their voices were a long way off. "Grow big! Hail Mary, full of grace, help her grow big."

Mona laughed! That's right, Mother of God, help my walking baby!

But she was falling down through the trees forever, and quite suddenly someone grabbed both her hands, yes, and she looked up through the sparkling green light and she saw her own face above her! Her very own face, pale and with the same freckles and the same green eyes, and the red hair tumbling down. Was it her own self, reaching down to stop her fall, to save her? That was her own smile!

"No, Mama, it's me." Both hands clasped her hands. "Look at me. It's Morrigan."

Slowly she opened her eyes. She gasped, trying to breathe, breathe against the weight, trying to lift her head, reach for her beautiful red hair, raise up high enough just to . . . just to hold her face, hold it, and . . . kiss her.

Twenty-four

IT WAS SNOWING when she awoke. She was in a long cotton gown they'd given her, something very thick for the New York winters, and the bedroom was very white and quiet. Michael slept soundly against the pillow.

Ash worked below in his office, or so he had told her that he would. Or maybe he had finished his tasks and gone to sleep as well.

She could hear nothing in this marble room, in the silent, snowy sky above New York. She stood at the window, looking out at the gray heavens, and at the ways the flakes became visible, emerging distinct and small to fall heavily on the roofs around her, and on the sill of the window, and even in soft graceful gusts against the glass.

She had slept six hours. That was enough.

She dressed as quietly as possible, putting on a simple black dress from her suitcase, another new and expensive garment chosen by another woman, and perhaps more extravagant than anything she might have bought for herself. Pearls and pearls. Shoes that laced above the instep, but with dangerously high heels. Black stockings. A touch of makeup.

And then she walked through the silent corridors. Press the button marked *M*, they had said, and you will see the dolls.

The dolls. What did she know of dolls? In childhood they had been her secret love, one which she had always been ashamed to confess to Ellie and Graham, or even to her friends. She had asked for chemistry sets at Christmastime, or a new tennis racket, or new stereo components for her room.

Wind howled in the elevator shaft as if it were a chimney. She liked the sound.

The elevator doors slid open, revealing a cab of wood paneling and ornate mirrors, which she scarcely recalled from this morning, when they'd arrived just before dawn. They had left at dawn. They had arrived at dawn. Six hours had been given back to them. It was evening for her body and she felt it, alert, ready for the night.

Down she went, in mechanical silence, listening to the howling, thinking how utterly ghostly it was, and wondering if Ash liked it too.

There must have been dolls in the beginning, dolls she didn't remember. Doesn't everybody buy them for girls? Perhaps not. Perhaps her loving foster mother had known of the witches' dolls in the trunk in the attic, made of real hair and real bone. Maybe she had known that there was one doll for every Mayfair witch of past years. Maybe dolls gave Ellie the shivers. And there are people who are, regardless of background, taste, or religious beliefs, simply afraid of dolls.

Was she afraid of dolls?

The doors opened. Her eyes fell on glass cases, brass fittings, the same pristine and shining marble floors. A brass plaque on the wall said simply, THE PRIVATE COLLECTION.

She stepped out, letting the door rush closed behind her, realizing that she stood in a vast, brilliantly lighted room.

Dolls. Everywhere she looked, she saw their staring glass eyes, their flawless faces, their mouths half open with a look of frank and tender awe.

In a huge glass case right before her stood a doll of some three feet in height, made of bisque, with long mohair tresses and a dress of finely tailored faded silk. This was a French beauty from the year 1888, made by Casimir Bru, said the little card beneath it, greatest dollmaker perhaps in the world.

The doll was startling, whether one liked it or not. The

blue eyes were thick and filled with light and perfectly almond-shaped. The porcelain hands of pale pink were so finely wrought they seemed about to move. But it was the doll's face, of course, her expression, that so captivated Rowan. The exquisitely painted eyebrows were ever so slightly different, giving movement to its gaze. Curious and innocent and thoughtful it looked.

It was a nonpareil of its kind, one couldn't doubt it. And whether or not she'd ever wanted dolls, she felt a desire to touch this one now, to feel its round and brightly rouged cheeks, to kiss, perhaps, its slightly parted red lips, to touch with the tip of her right finger the subtly shaped breasts pressed so erotically beneath its tight bodice. Its golden hair had thinned with the ages, obviously. And its fancy little leather shoes were worn and cracked. But the effect remained timeless, irresistible, "a joy forever." She wished she could open the case and hold it in her arms.

She saw herself rocking it, rather like a newborn, and singing to it, though it was no infant. It was just a little girl. Little blue beads hung from its perfectly fashioned ears. A necklace hung about its neck, fancy, a woman's perhaps. Indeed, when one considered all the aspects of it, it was no child at all, really, but a sensual little woman of extraordinary freshness, perhaps a dangerous and clever coquette.

A little card explained its special features, that it was so very large, that it wore its original garments, that it was perfect, that it had been the first doll ever purchased by Ash Templeton. And no further identification for Ash Templeton was given or apparently required.

The first doll. And he had told her briefly, when he explained about the museum, that he had seen it when it was new in the window of a Paris shop.

No wonder it had caught his eye and his heart. No wonder he had lugged it with him for a century; no wonder he'd founded his enormous company as some sort of tribute to it, to bring, as he had said, "its grace and beauty to everyone in new form."

There was nothing trivial about it, and something sweetly mysterious. Puzzled, yes, quizzical, reflective, a doll with things on her mind.

In seeing this, I understand all of it, she thought.

She moved on, through the other displays. She saw other French treasures, the work of Jumeau and Steiner and others whose names she'd never remember, and hundreds upon hundreds of little French girlies with round moonlike faces and tiny red mouths and the same almond eyes. "Oh, what innocents you are," she whispered. And here came the fashion dolls, in their bustles and exquisite hats.

She could have spent hours wandering here. There was infinitely more to see than she had imagined. And the quiet was so enticing, the vision outside the windows of the unceasing snow.

But she was not alone.

Through several banks of glass, she saw that Ash had joined her, and had been watching her, perhaps for some time. The glass faintly distorted his expression. When he moved, she was glad.

He came towards her, making no sound at all on the marble, and she saw that he held the beautiful Bru in his hands.

"Here, you may hold it," he said.

"It's fragile," she whispered.

"It's a doll," he said.

It evoked the strongest feeling, just cupping its head in the palm of her left hand. There came a little delicate sound from its earrings, tinkling against the porcelain neck. Its hair was soft, yet brittle, and the stitching of the wig was visible in many spots.

Ah, but she loved its tiny fingers. She loved its lace stockings and its silk petticoats, very old, very faded, apt to tear at her touch.

Ash stood very still, looking down at her, face rested, almost annoyingly handsome, streaked hair brushed to a luster, hands a little steeple beneath his lips. His suit was white silk today, very baggy, fashionable, probably Italian, she honestly didn't know. The shirt was black silk, and the tie white. Rather like a decorative rendition of a gangster, a tall, willowy man of mystery, with enormous gold cuff links, and preposterously beautiful black-and-white wing-tip shoes.

"What does the doll make you feel?" he asked innocently, as if he really wanted to know.

"It has virtue to it," she whispered, frightened of her voice being louder than his. She placed it in his hands.

"Virtue," he repeated. He turned the doll and looked at her, and made a few very quick and natural gestures of grooming her, moving her hair, adjusting the ruffles of her dress. And then he lifted her and tenderly kissed her and lowered her slowly, gazing down at her again. "Virtue," he said. He looked at Rowan. "But what does it make you feel?"

"Sad," she said, and turned away, placing her hand on the case beside her, looking at the German doll, infinitely more natural, sitting inside in a small wooden chair. MEIN LEIBLING, said the card. She was far less decorative and overdone. She was not the coquette of anyone's imagination, yet she was radiant, and as perfect as the Bru in her own way.

"Sad?" he asked.

"Sad for a kind of femininity that I've lost or never had. I don't regret it, but the feeling is sadness, sadness for something perhaps I dreamed about when I was young. I don't know."

And then, looking at him again, she said, "I can have no more children. And my children were monsters to me. And my children are buried together beneath a tree."

He nodded. His face was very eloquent of sympathy, so he said not a word.

There were other things she wanted to say—that she had not guessed there was such craft or beauty in the realm of dolls, that she had not guessed they could be so interesting to look at, or that they were so different, one from the other, that they had such a frank and simple charm.

But beneath these thoughts, running deep in the coldest place in her heart, she was thinking, Their beauty is sad beauty, and I don't know why, and so is yours.

She felt suddenly that if he were to kiss her now, if he were so inclined, she would yield very easily, that her love for Michael wouldn't stop her from yielding, and she hoped and prayed that there was no such thought in his mind.

Indeed, she wasn't going to allow time for it. She folded her arms and walked past him into a new and unexplored area, where the German dolls ruled. Here were laughing and pouting children, homely little girls in cotton frocks. But she didn't see the exhibits now. She couldn't stop thinking that he was just behind her, watching her. She could feel his observation, hear the faint sound of his breath.

Finally, she looked back. His eyes surprised her. They were too charged with emotion, too full of obvious conflict, and very little if any struggle to hide it from her.

If you do this, Rowan, she thought, you will lose Michael forever. And slowly she lowered her gaze and walked softly, slowly away.

"It's a magical place," she said over her shoulder. "But I'm so eager to talk to you, to hear your story, I could savor it more truly at another time."

"Yes, of course, and Michael's awake now, and Michael should be almost finished with breakfast. Why don't we go up? I am ready for the agony. I am ready for the strange pleasure of recounting it all."

She watched as he set the big French doll back in her glass cabinet. And once again his thin fingers made quick, busy gestures to groom her hair and her skirts. Then he pressed a kiss to his fingers and gave this to the doll. And he shut the glass and turned the small golden key, which he then put away.

"You are my friends," he said, turning to face Rowan. He reached past her and pressed the button for the tower. "I think I am coming to love you. A dangerous thing."

"I don't want it to be dangerous," she said. "I'm too deep under your spell to want our knowledge of each other to wound or disappoint. But tell me, as to the present state of things, do you love us *both*?"

"Oh yes," he said, "or I would beg you on bended knee to let me make love to you." His voice fell to a whisper. "I would follow you to the ends of the earth."

She turned away, stepping into the elevator, her face hot and her mind swimming for the moment. She saw one grand flash of the dolls in their finery before the doors slid shut.

"I'm sorry that I told you this," he whispered timidly. "It was a dishonest thing to do, to tell you and to deny it, it was wrong."

She nodded. "I forgive you," she whispered. "I'm too . . . too flattered. Isn't that the right word?"

"No, 'intrigued' is the word you want," he said. "Or 'tantalized,' but you're not really flattered. And you love him so wholeheartedly that I feel the fire of it when I'm with you. I want it. I want your light to shine on me. I should never have said those words."

She didn't answer. If she'd thought of an answer, she might have said it, but nothing really came to her mind. Except that she couldn't imagine being severed from Ash right now, and she didn't think that Michael could, either. In a way, it seemed that Michael needed Ash more than she did, though Michael and she had not had a moment, really, to talk of these things.

When the doors opened, she found herself in a large living room, with the floor tiled in rose- and cream-colored marbles, with the same kind of large, snug leather furnishings that had been on the plane. These chairs were softer, larger, yet remarkably similar, as if designed for comfort.

And once again, they gathered around a table, only this time it was very low, and set out with a dozen or more little offerings of cheeses and nuts and fruits and breads that they might eat as the hours passed.

A tall, cold glass of water was all she required just now.

Michael, his horn-rimmed glasses on, and wearing a battered tweed Norfolk jacket, sat bent over the day's *New York Times*.

Only when they were both seated did he tear himself away, fold the paper neatly, and put it to the side.

She didn't want him to take off the glasses. They were too appealing to her. And it struck her, suddenly, making her smile, that she rather liked having these two men with her, one on either side.

Vague fantasies of a ménage à trois flitted through her mind, but such things, as far as she knew, never really worked, and she could not imagine Michael either tolerating it or participating in it in any way. Sweeter, really, to think of things precisely the way they were.

You have another chance with Michael, she thought. You know you do, no matter what he may think. Don't throw away the only love that's ever really mattered to you. Be old enough and patient enough for kinds of love, seasons of it, be quiet in your soul so that when happiness comes again, if it ever does, you will know.

Michael had put away his glasses. He'd sat back, his ankle on his knee.

Ash had also relaxed into his chair.

We are the triangle, she thought, and I am the only one with bare knees, and feet tucked to the side as if I have something to conceal.

That made her laugh. The smell of the coffee distracted her. She realized the pot and cup were right in front of her, easy to reach.

But Ash reached to pour for her before she could do it, and he put the cup in her hand. He sat at her right, closer to her than he'd been in the plane. They were all closer. And it was the equilateral triangle again.

"Let me just talk to you," Ash said suddenly. He'd made his fingers into the little steeple again and was pushing at his lower lip. There came the tiny scowl to the very inside tips of his eyebrows, and then it melted, and the voice went on, a bit sad. "This is hard for me, very hard, but I want to do it."

"I realized that," said Michael. "But why do you want to do it? Oh, I'm dying to hear your story, but why is it worth the pain?"

He thought for a moment, and Rowan could hardly bear to see the tiny signs of stress in his hands and his face.

"Because I want you to love me," Ash said softly.

Once again, she was speechless, and faintly miserable.

But Michael just smiled in his usual frank fashion and said, "Then tell us everything, Ash. Just . . . shoot."

Ash laughed at once. And then they all fell silent, but it was an easy silence.

And he began.

Twenty-five

A LL TALTOS ARE born knowing things—facts of history, whole legends, certain songs—the necessity for certain rituals, the language of the mother, and the languages spoken around her, the basic knowledge of the mother, and probably the mother's finer knowledge as well.

Indeed, these basic endowments are rather like an uncharted vein of gold in a mountain. No Taltos knows how much can be drawn from this residual memory. With effort, amazing things can be discovered within one's own mind. Some Taltos even know how to find their way home to Donnelaith, though why no one knows. Some are drawn to the far northern coast of Unst, the northernmost island of Britain, to look out over Burrafirth at the lighthouse of Muckle Flugga, searching for the lost land of our birth.

The explanation for this lies in the chemistry of the brain. It's bound to be disappointingly simple, but we won't understand it until we know precisely why salmon return to the river of their birth to spawn, or why a certain species of butterfly finds its way to one tiny area of forest when it comes time to breed.

We have superior hearing; loud noises hurt us. Music can actually paralyze us. We must be very, very careful of music. We know other Taltos instantly by scent or sight; we know witches when we see them, and the presence of witches is always overwhelming. A witch is that human which cannot—by the Taltos—be ignored.

But I'll come to more of these things as the story goes

on. I want to say now, however, that we do *not*, as far as I know, have two lives, as Stuart Gordon thought, though this might have been a mistaken and oft-repeated belief about us among humans for some time. When we explore our deepest racial memories, when we go bravely into the past, we soon come to realize these cannot be the memories of one particular soul.

Your Lasher was a soul who had lived before, yes. A restless soul refusing to accept death, and making a tragic, blundering reentry into life, for which others paid the price.

By the time of King Henry and Queen Anne, the Taltos was a mere legend in the Highlands. Lasher did not know how to probe the memories with which he was born; his mother had been merely human, and he set his mind upon becoming a human, as many a Taltos has done.

I want to say that, for me, actual life began when we were still a people of the lost land, and Britain was the land of winter. And we knew about the land of winter, but we never went there, because our island was always warm. My constitutional memories were all of that land. They were filled with sunlight, and without consequence, and they have faded under the weight of events since, under the sheer weight of my long life and my reflections.

The lost land was in the northern sea, within very dim sight of the coast of Unst, as I've indicated, in a place where the Gulf Stream of that time apparently made the seas fairly temperate as they struck our shores.

But the sheltered land in which we actually developed was, I believe now when I remember it, nothing less than the giant crater of an immense volcano, miles and miles in width, presenting itself as a great fertile valley surrounded by ominous yet beautiful cliffs, a tropical valley with innumerable geysers and warm springs rising bubbling from the earth, to make small streams and finally great clear and beautiful pools. The air was moist always, the trees that grew about our little lakes and riverets immense, the ferns also of gigantic size, and the fruit of all kinds and colors—mangos, pears, melons of all sizes—always abundant, and the cliffs hung with vines of wild berry and grape, and the grass forever thick and green.

The best fruit was pears, which are nearly white. The best food from the sea was the oyster, the mussel, the limpet, and these were white too. There was a breadfruit that was white once you peeled it. There was milk from the goats, if you could catch them, but it wasn't as good as milk from your mother or the other women who would let those they loved have their milk.

Scarcely ever did the winds come into the valley, sealed off as it was, except for two or three passes, from the coasts. The coasts were dangerous, for though the water was warmer than on the coast of Britain, it was nevertheless cold, and the winds violent, and one could be swept away. Indeed, if a Taltos wanted to die, which I was told did happen, that Taltos would go out and walk into the sea.

I think, though I'll never know, that ours *was* an island, very large, yet an island. It was the custom of some very white-haired ones to walk completely around it, along the beaches, and I was told that this trek took many many days.

Fire we had always known, because there were places up in the mountains where fire breathed right out of the earth. Hot earth itself, molten lava, came in a tiny trickle from some of these places, running down to the sea.

We had always known how to get fire, keep it alive, feed it, and make it last. We used fire to light up the longer nights of winter, though we had no name for it, and it wasn't cold. We used fire occasionally to cook big feasts, but most of the time this wasn't necessary. We used fire in the circle sometimes when the birth was happening. We danced around fire, and sometimes played with it. I never beheld a hurtful incident in which any of us was injured by fire.

How far the winds of the earth can carry seeds, birds, twigs, branches, uprooted trees, I have no idea, but that which loved heat thrived in this land, and this is where we began.

Now and then, someone among us told of visiting the islands of Britain—known now as the Shetlands or the Orkneys—or even the coast of Scotland. The islands of winter, that's what we called them, or, more literally, the islands of the bitter cold. This was always an exciting tale.

Sometimes a Taltos was washed out, and somehow managed to swim to the land of winter, and make a raft there for the return home.

There were Taltos who went to sea deliberately to seek adventure, in hollow log boats, and if they did not drown, they would often come home, half dead from the cold, and never travel to the land of winter again.

Everybody knew there were beasts in that land, covered with fur, that would kill you if they could. And so we had a thousand legends and ideas and wrong notions and songs about the snows of winter, and the bears of the forests, and ice that floated in great masses in the lochs.

Once in a very great while, a Taltos would commit a crime. He or she would couple without permission and make a new Taltos that was not, for one reason or another, welcome. Or someone would willfully injure another, and that one would die. It was very rare. I only heard of it. I never saw it. But those outcasts were taken to Britain in the large boats, and left there to die.

We did not know the actual cycle of the seasons, by the way, for to us even the summer in Scotland felt fatally cold. We reckoned time in moons only, and we did not have a concept, as I recall, of a year.

Of course there was a legend you will hear all over the planet, of a time before the moon.

And that was the legendary time before time, or so we thought, but no one actually remembered it.

I can't tell you how long I lived in this land before it was destroyed. I knew the powerful scent of the Taltos in that land, but it was as natural as air. Only later did it become distinct, to mark the difference between Taltos and human.

I remember the First Day, as do all Taltos. I was born, my mother loved me, I stayed for hours with my mother and father, talking, and then I went up to the high cliffs just below the lip of the crater, where the white-haired ones sat, who talked and talked. I nursed from my mother for years and years. It was known that the milk would dry if a woman didn't let others drink from her breasts, and not come again till she gave birth. Women didn't want ever for the milk to dry, and they loved having the men nurse from them; it gave them divine pleasure, the sucking, the stimulation, and it was a common custom to lie with a woman and let the suckling, in one form or another, be the extent of the love. The semen of the Taltos was white, of course, like the semen of human beings.

Women, of course, nursed from women, and teased men that their nipples had no milk. But then our semen was thought to be like milk, not as tasty but in its own way just as nourishing and good.

One game was for the males to find a female alone, pounce upon her, and drink her milk, until others heard her protests and came and drove us away. But no one would have thought of making another Taltos with that woman! And if she really didn't want us sucking her milk, well, within a reasonable amount of time we stopped.

The women would every now and then gang up on other women also. And beauty had much to do with the allure of those who were sought for this kind of pleasure; personality was always mixed with it; we had distinct personalities, though everyone was pretty much always in a good mood.

There were customs. But I don't remember laws.

Death came to Taltos through accidents. And as Taltos are playful by nature, indeed physically rough and reckless, many Taltos were always dying of accidents, of having slipped from a cliff or choked on a peach pit, or being attacked by a wild rodent, which attack then caused bleeding which could not be stopped. Taltos rarely if ever broke their bones when they were young. But once a Taltos's skin had lost its baby softness and there were perhaps a few white hairs in his head, well, then he could be killed by falling from the cliffs. And it was during those years, I think, that most Taltos died. We were a people of the white-haired, and the blond, the red, and the black-haired. We didn't have many people of the mixed hair, and of course the young greatly outnumbered the old.

Sometimes a pestilence came over the valley that greatly diminished our numbers, and the stories of the pestilence were the saddest that we were ever told.

But I still don't know what the pestilence *was*. Those which kill humans do not apparently kill us.

I could "remember" pestilence, and nursing sick ones. I was born knowing how to get fire and carry it safely back to the valley. I knew how to make fire so that I did not have to go to get it, though getting it from someone else was the easiest way. I was born knowing how to cook mussels and limpets with fire. I knew how to make black paste for painting from ashes of fire.

But to return to the subject of death, there was no murder. The idea that one Taltos had the power to kill another was not generally believed. Indeed, if you did quarrel and push someone off a cliff, and that person fell and died, it was still an "accident." You hadn't really done it, though others might condemn you for your appalling carelessness and even send you away.

The white-haired ones who liked to tell tales had been alive the longest, certainly, but no one thought of them as old. And if they lay down one night and failed to wake in the morning, it was assumed they had died of a blow from an accident that had not been observed. The white-haired ones often had very thin skin, so thin you could almost see the blood running under it; and often they had lost their scent. But other than that, we didn't know age in any particular.

To be old was just to know the longest and the best stories, to have stories to relate from Taltos who were gone.

Tales were told in loose verses, or were sung as songs, or sometimes merely poured forth in a rush, with lavish images and rhythms and little bits and pieces of melody and much laughter. Telling, telling was joyful; telling was glorious; telling was the spiritual side of life.

The material side of life? I'm not sure there was one, in the strict sense. There was no ownership, except perhaps of musical instruments or pigments for painting, but even these were fairly liberally shared. Everything was easy.

Now and then a whale would be washed ashore, and when the meat had rotted, we would take the bones and make things of them, but to us, these were toys. Digging in the sand was fun, digging loose rocks to make them tumble downhill was fun. Even carving little shapes and circles into the bone with a sharp stone or another bone—this was fun.

But telling, ah, that took respectable talent, and true remembering, and remembering not only in one's own head, but remembering what other people had remembered and told as well.

You see what I am driving at. Our assumptions about life and death were founded upon these special conditions and notions. Obedience was natural to Taltos. To be agreeable was apparently natural. Seldom was there a rebel or a visionary, until the human blood became mixed with ours.

There were very few white-haired women, perhaps one to every twenty men. And these women were much sought after, for their fount was dried, like that of Tessa, and they wouldn't birth when they gave themselves to the men.

But in the main, childbirth killed the women, though we never said so at the time. It weakened women, and if a woman did not die by the fourth or fifth birth, she would almost always fall asleep later and die. Many women did not care to give birth at all, or would do it only once.

Birth always followed the true coupling of a pair of true Taltos. It was only later, when we mingled with humans, that women were worn out, like Tessa, by having bled again and again. But the Taltos descended from human origins have many traits entirely peculiar to them which I will recount in time. And who knows but that Tessa didn't have offspring? It is entirely possible, as you know.

Generally, birth was something that a woman did want to do. But not for a long time after she was born. Men wanted to do it all the time, because they enjoyed it. But no one who thought of coupling did not know that a child would be born from it, as tall as his own mother, or taller, and so no one thought to do it just for fun.

Just for fun was woman making love to woman in many ways, and man making love to man; or man finding a white-haired beauty who was free now for pleasure. Or one male being approached by several young virgins, all eager to bear his child. Fun was occasionally finding the woman who could bear six and seven children without injury. Or the young woman who, for reasons no one knew, could not bear at all. Nursing from the breasts of women was exquisite pleasure; to gather in groups to do this was splendid, the woman who gave her breasts often going into a sensuous trance. Indeed, women could derive complete pleasure in this way, reaching satisfaction with scarcely any other contact at all.

I don't remember rape; I don't remember execution; I don't remember grudges that lasted very long.

I remember pleading and arguments and much talk, and even some quarreling over mates, but always it was in the realm of songs or words.

I do not remember bad tempers or cruelty. I do not remember uneducated souls. That is, all were born knowing some concept of gentleness, goodness, the value of happiness, and a strong love of pleasure and a desire for others to share that pleasure, for the pleasure of the tribe to be assured.

Men would fall deeply in love with women, and vice versa. They would talk for days and nights; then finally the decision would be made to couple. Or argument would prevent this from ever taking place.

More women were born than men. Or so it was said. But no one really counted. I think more women were born, and that they died much more easily; and I think this is one reason the men felt so utterly tender to the women, because they knew the women were likely to die. The women passed on the strength of their bodies; simple women were cherished because they were gay all the time, and glad to be living and not afraid of giving birth. In sum, the women were more childlike, but the men were simple too.

Deaths by accident were invariably followed by a ceremonial coupling and a replacement of the dead one; and times of pestilence gave way to times of rampant and orgiastic mating, as the tribe sought to repopulate the land.

There was no want. The land never became crowded. Never did people quarrel over fruit or eggs or milk animals. There was too much of everything. It was too warm and lovely, and there were too many pleasant things to do.

It was paradise, it was Eden, it was the golden time that all peoples speak of, a time before the gods became angry, a time before Adam ate the fatal apple, a time of bliss and plenty. The only point is, I remember it. I was there.

I do not remember any concept of laws.

I remember rituals—dances, songs, forming the circles, and each circle moving in the opposite direction from the one inside it, and I remember the men and the women who could play pipes and drums, and even stringed harps that were small and sometimes made of shells. I remember a band of us carrying torches along the most treacherous cliffs, just to see if we could do it and not fall.

I remember painting, that those who liked to do it did it on the cliffs, and in the caves that surrounded the valley, and that sometimes we would go on a day's journey to visit all the caves.

It was unseemly to paint too much at any one given time; each artist mixed his or her own colors from earth, or from her blood, or from the blood of a poor fallen mountain goat or sheep, and from other natural things.

At several intervals I remember the whole tribe coming together to make circle after circle after circle. It is conceivable the whole population was then gathered. Nobody knew.

At other times we gathered in small, single circles and made the chain of memory as we knew it—not what Stuart Gordon has described to you.

One would call out, "Who remembers from long, long ago?" And someone would venture, telling a tale of white-haired ones long gone, whom he had heard tell when he was newborn. Those tales he would relate now, offering them as the oldest, until someone raised his voice and told tales that he could place before those.

Others would then volunteer their earliest recollections; people would argue with or add to or expand the stories of others. Many sequences of events would be put together and fully described.

That was a fascinating thing—a sequence, a long period of events linked by one man's vision or attitude. That was special. That was our finest mental achievement, perhaps, other than pure music and dance.

These sequences were never terribly eventful. What inter-

389

ested us was humor or a small departure from the norm, and of course beautiful things. We loved to talk of beautiful things. If a woman was born with red hair, we thought it a magnificent thing.

If a man stood taller than the others, this was a magnificent thing. If a woman was gifted with the harp, this was a magnificent thing. Terrible accidents were very, very briefly remembered. There were some stories of visionaries—those who claimed to hear voices and to know the future—but that was very infrequent. There were tales of the whole life of a musician or an artist, or of a red-haired woman, or of a boatbuilder who had risked his life to sail to Britain and had come home to tell the tale. There were tales of beautiful men and women who had never coupled, and they were much celebrated and sought after, though as soon as they did couple, they lost this charm.

The memory games were most often played in the long days—that is, those days on which there was scarcely three hours of darkness. Now, we had some sense of seasons based on light and dark, but it had never become terribly important because nothing much changed in our lives from the long days of summer to the shorter days of winter. So we didn't think in terms of seasons. We didn't keep track of light and dark. We frolicked more on the longer days, but other than that, we didn't much notice. The darkest days were as warm as the longest for us; things grew in profusion. Our geysers never ceased to be warm.

But this chain of memory, this ritual telling and recounting, it is important to me now for what it later became. After we migrated to the land of bitter cold, this was our way of knowing ourselves and who we had been. This was crucial when we struggled to survive in the Highlands. We, who had no writing of any kind, held all our knowledge in this way.

But then? In the lost land? It seemed like a pastime. A great game.

The most serious thing that happened was birth. Not death—which was frequent, haphazard, and generally deemed to be sad but meaningless—but the birth of a new person.

Anyone who did not take this seriously was considered to be a fool.

For the coupling to happen, the guardians of the woman had to consent that she could do it, and the men had to agree that they would give permission to the particular man.

It was known always that the children resembled the parents, that they grew up at once, possessing characters of one or the other, or both. And so the men would argue vehemently against a male of poor physique seeking to couple, though everyone was entitled by custom to do it at least once.

As for the woman, the question was, did she understand how hard it might be to bear the child? She would have pain, her body would be greatly weakened, she might even bleed afterwards, she might even die when the child came out of her, or die later on.

It was also deemed that some physical combinations were better than others. In fact, this was the cause of what we might have called our disputes. They were never bloody, but they could be very noisy, with Taltos shouting finally, and some foot-stomping, and so forth and so on. Taltos loved to outshout each other, or to rail at one another in a great, speedy buzz of language until the other was exhausted and couldn't think.

And very, very seldom, there was one prime male or female considered to be so perfect of limb and fair of face, so tall, so well proportioned, that coupling with him or her to produce a beautiful offspring was a great honor; and this did lead to contests and games. Indeed, there was a whole realm of these.

But those are the only painful or difficult things I remember, and I won't tell of them now. Maybe because the only time I knew desperation was in these games. Also, we lost those rituals when we traveled to the land of bitter winter. We had too many real sorrows to contend with from then on.

When the couple had finally obtained permission—I remember once having to beg permission of twenty different people, and having to argue and wait for days on end—the tribe would gather, forming the circle, and then another and another, quite far back, until people felt it was no fun anymore because it was too far away to see.

The drums and the dancing would begin. If it was night, the torches would appear. And the couple would embrace and play lovingly with each other for as long as they could before the final moment had to come. This was a slow feast. To go on for an hour, that was lovely, to go on for two hours was sublime. Many could not go on more than half an hour. Whatever, when the consummation came, it too held the couple for an amazing period of time. How long? I don't know. More, I think, than humans or Taltos born of humans could endure. Perhaps an hour, perhaps more.

When at last the couple fell back away from each other, it was because the new Taltos was about to be born. The mother would swell painfully. The father would then help to take the long, ungainly child out of the mother and to warm it with his hands, and to give it to its mother's breasts.

All drew in to watch this miracle, for the child, commencing as a being of perhaps twenty-four to thirty-six inches, very slender and delicate, and apt to be damaged if not carefully handled, began to elongate and enlarge at once. And over the next fifteen minutes or less, it would often grow to full and majestic height. Its hair would pour down, and its fingers stretch, and the tender bones of its body, so flexible and strong, would make the big frame. The head would grow to three times its birth size.

The mother lay as dead after, sleeping the mother's thin sleep. But the offspring lay with her, talking to her, and the mother sometimes never really slipped into dreams, but talked and sang to the young one, though she was always groggy and often humorous, and she would draw from the young one the first memories, so that the young one wouldn't forget.

We do forget.

We are very capable of forgetting. And to tell is to memorize, or to imprint. To tell is to strike out against the awful loneliness of forgetting, the awful ignorance of it, the sadness. Or so we thought.

This offspring, whether male or female, and most often it was female, caused great joy. It meant more to us than the birth of a single being. It meant the life of the tribe was good; the life of the tribe would go on.

Of course, we never doubted it would, but there were always some legends that at times it had not, that at times women had coupled and runtish offspring had been born to them, or nothing, and that the tribe had dwindled to a very few. Pestilence now and then sterilized the women, and sometimes the men too.

The offspring was much loved and cared for by both parents, though if it was a daughter, it might be taken away after a while to a place where only women lived. In general, the offspring was the bond of love between the man and the woman. They did not seek to love each other in any other or private way. Childbearing being what it was, we had no concept of marriage or monogamy, or of remaining with one woman. On the contrary, it seemed a frustrating, dangerous, and foolish thing to do.

It did sometimes happen. I'm sure it did. A man and a woman loved each other so much that they would not be parted. But I don't remember it happening myself. Nothing stood between one seeing any woman or any man, and love and friendship were not romantic; they were pure.

There are many things more about this life I could describe—the various kinds of songs we sang, the nature of arguments, for there were structures to them, the types of logic that held currency with us, which you would probably find preposterous, and the types of awful errors and blunders young Taltos inevitably made. There were small mammalian animals—very like monkeys—on the island, but we never thought of hunting them or cooking them or eating them. Such an idea would have been vulgar beyond tolerance.

I could describe also the kinds of dwellings we built, for they were many, and the scant ornaments we wore—we did not like clothing or need it or want to keep something so dirty next to our skin—I could describe our boats and how bad they were, and a thousand such things.

There were times when some of us crept to the place

where the women lived, just to see them in each other's arms, making love. Then the women would discover us and insist that we go away. There were places in the cliffs, grottoes, caves, small alcoves near bubbling springs, which had become veritable shrines for making love, for both men and men, and women and women.

There was never boredom in this paradise. There were too many things to do. One could romp for hours on the seashore, swim even, if one dared. One could gather eggs, fruit, dance, sing. The painters and the musicians were the most industrious, I imagine, and then there were the boat-builders and the hut builders too.

There was great room for cleverness. I was thought to be very clever. I discerned patterns in things which others did not notice, that certain mussels in the warm pools grew faster when the sun shone on the pools, and that some mushrooms thrived best in the dark days, and I liked to invent systems—such as simple lifts of vines and twig baskets, by which fruit could be sent down from the tops of trees.

But as much as people admired me for this, they also laughed at it. It really wasn't necessary to do things like this, it was supposed.

Drudgery was unheard of. Each day dawned with its myriad possibilities. No one doubted the perfect goodness of pleasure.

Pain was bad.

That is why the birth aroused such reverence and such caution in all of us, for it involved pain for the woman. And understand, the woman Taltos was no slave of the man. She was often as strong as the male, arms just as long, and just as limber. The hormones in her formed a totally different chemistry.

And the birth, involving both pleasure and pain, was the most significant mystery of our lives. Actually, it was the only significant mystery of our lives.

You have now what I wanted you to know. Ours was a world of harmony and true happiness, it was a world of one great mystery and many small, wondrous things.

It was paradise, and there was never a Taltos born, no

matter how much human blood ran in his veins from whatever corrupt lineage, who did not remember the lost land, and the time of harmony. Not a single one.

Lasher most surely remembered it. Emaleth most surely remembered it.

The story of paradise is in our blood. We see it, we hear the songs of its birds, and we feel the warmth of the volcanic spring. We taste the fruit; we hear the singing; we can raise our voices and make the singing. And so we know, we know what humans only believe, that paradise can come again.

Before we move on to the cataclysm and the land of winter, let me add one thing.

I do believe there were bad ones among us, those who did violence. I think there were. There were those who killed perhaps, and those who were killed. I'm sure it must have been that way. It had to be. But no one wanted to talk about it! They would leave such things out of the tales! So we had no history of bloody incidents, rapes, conquests of one group of men by another. And a great horror of violence prevailed.

How justice was meted out, I don't know. We didn't have leaders in the strict sense, so much as we had collections of wise ones, people who drew together out of presence and formed a loose elite, so to speak, to whom one might appeal.

Another reason I believe that violence must have happened was that we had definite concepts of the Good God and the Evil One. Of course the Good God was he or she (this divinity was not divided) who had given us the land and our sustenance and our pleasures; and the Evil One had made the terrible land of bitter cold. The Evil One delighted in accidents which killed Taltos; and now and then the Evil One got into a Taltos, but that was really rare!

If there were myths and tales to this vague religion, I never heard them told. Our worship was never one of blood sacrifice or appeasement. We celebrated the Good God in songs and verses, and in the circle dances always. When we danced, when we made the child, we were close to the Good God.

Many of these old songs come back to me all the time.

Now and then I go down in the early evening, and I walk through the streets of New York, solitary, amid the crowds, and I sing all of these songs that I can then remember, and the feeling of the lost land returns to me, the sound of the drums and the pipes, and the vision of men and women dancing in the circle. You can do that in New York, no one pays any attention to you. It's really amusing to me.

Sometimes others in New York who are singing to themselves, or mumbling loudly, or chattering, will come near to me, chatter at me, or sing towards me, and then drift off. In other words, I am accepted by the crazies of New York. And though we are all alone, we have each other for those few moments. The twilight world of the city.

Afterwards, I go out in my car and give coats and wool scarves to those who don't have them. Sometimes I send Remmick, my servant, to do this. Sometimes we bring in the street people to sleep in the lobby, to feed them and bed them down. But then one will fight with another, perhaps even knife another, and out they all must go, into the snow again.

Ah, but that brings me to one other pitfall of our life in the lost land. How could I have forgotten? There were always those Taltos who were caught in music and couldn't get out. They could be caught by the music of others, so that others had to be made to stop the music in order to release them. They could be caught in their own song, and truly sing until they fell dead. They could dance until they fell dead.

I often fell into great spells of singing and dancing and rhyming, but I always woke out of it, or the music came to a ceremonial finish, or I grew weary perhaps, or lost the rhythm. Whatever, I was never in any danger of death. Many did as I did. But there were always deaths in this manner.

Everyone felt that the Taltos who died dancing or singing had gone to the Good God.

But nobody talked much about it. Death just wasn't a fit subject for Taltos. All unpleasant things were forgotten. That was one of our basic ideals.

I'd been alive a long time by the time of the cataclysm.

But I don't know how to measure. Let me estimate twenty or thirty years.

The cataclysm was entirely a thing of nature. Later, men told tales of Roman soldiers or the Picts driving us from our island. No such thing happened at all. In the lost land, we never laid eyes on human beings. We knew no other people. We knew only ourselves.

A great upheaval of the earth caused our land to tremble and begin to break apart. It started with vague rumblings, and clouds of smoke covering the sky. The geysers began to scald our people. The pools were so hot we couldn't drink from them. The land moved and groaned both day and night.

Many Taltos were dying. The fish in the pools were dead, and the birds had fled the cliffs. Men and women went in all directions seeking a place that was not turbulent, but they did not find it, and some came running back.

At last, after countless deaths, all the tribe built rafts, boats, dugouts, whatever they could, to make the journey to the land of bitter cold. There was no choice for us. Our land grew more tumultuous and treacherous with every day.

I don't know how many remained. I don't know how many got away. All day and all night, people built boats and went into the sea. The wise ones helped the foolish ones—that was really the way we divided old from young—and on about the tenth day, as I would calculate it now, I sailed with two of my daughters, two men whom I loved, and one woman.

And it is really in the land of winter, on the afternoon that I saw my homeland sink into the sea, on that afternoon, that the history of my people really began.

Then began their trials and their tribulations, their real suffering, and their first concept of valor and sacrifice. There began all the things human beings hold sacred, which can only come from difficulty, struggle, and the growing idealization of bliss and perfection, which can only flourish in the mind when paradise is utterly lost.

It was from a high cliff that I saw the great cataclysm reach its conclusion; it was from that height that I saw the land break into pieces and sink into the sea. It was from there that I saw the tiny figures of Taltos drowning in that sea. It was from there that I saw the giant waves wash the foot of the cliffs and the hills, and crash into the hidden valleys, and flood the forests.

The Evil One has triumphed, said those who were with me. And for the first time the songs we sang and the tales we recited became a true lament.

It must have been late summer when we fled to the land of bitter cold. It was truly cold. The water striking the shores was cold enough to knock a Taltos unconscious. We learned immediately that it would never be warm.

But the full breath of winter was something of which we had not truly dreamed. Most of the Taltos who escaped the lost land died the first winter. Some who remained bred furiously to reestablish the tribe. And as we had no real idea that winter was going to come again, many more died the following winter, too.

Probably we caught on to the cycle of the seasons by the third or fourth year.

But those first years were times of rampant superstition, endless chattering and reasoning as to why we had been cast out of the lost land, and why the snow and wind came to kill us, and whether or not the Good God had turned against us.

My penchant for observation and making things elevated me to the undisputed leader. But the entire tribe was learning rapidly about such things as the warm carcasses of dead bears and other large animals, and then the good warmth from their furry skins. Holes were warmer obviously than caves, and with the horns of a dead antelope we could dig deep underground homes for ourselves, and roof them over with tree trunks and stones.

We knew how to make fire, and very soon got good at it, because we didn't find any fire to be had for nothing, simply breathing out of the rock. Different Taltos at different times developed similar kinds of wheels, and crude wagons were soon fashioned to carry our food, and those who were sick.

Gradually, those of us who had survived all the winters of the land of bitter cold began to learn very valuable things which had to be taught to the young. Paying attention mattered for the first time. Nursing had become a means of survival. All women gave birth at least once, to make up for the appalling rate of death.

If life had not been so hard, this would have been seen perhaps as a time of great creative pleasure. I could list the various discoveries that were made.

Suffice it to say we were hunter-gatherers of a very primitive sort, though we did not eat the meat of animals unless we were really starving, and that we progressed erratically in a completely different fashion from human beings.

Our large brains, our enhanced verbal capacity, the strange marriage in each of us of instinct and intelligence—all this made us both more clever and more clumsy, more insightful and more foolish in many respects.

Of course, quarrels broke out among us, as the result of scarcity or questions of judgment—whether to go this way or that to seek game. Groups broke off from the main group and went their own way.

I had by this time become accustomed to being the leader, and did not frankly trust anybody else to do it. I was known simply by name, Ashlar, as no titles were required among us, and I exerted tremendous influence over the others, and lived in terror of their getting lost, being eaten by wild animals, or fighting each other in harmful ways. Battles, quarrels, they were now daily occurrences.

But with each passing winter we had greater and greater skills. And as we followed the game south, or moved in that direction simply by instinct or by accident, I don't know, we came into warmer lands of fairly extended summer, and our true reverence for, and reliance upon, the seasons began.

We began to ride the wild horses for fun. It was great sport to us. But we didn't think that horses could really be tamed. We did all right with the oxen to pull our carts, which, in the beginning, of course, we had pulled ourselves.

Out of this came our most intense religious period. I invoked the name of the Good God every time chaos came upon us, striving to put our lives back in order. Executions took place sometimes twice a year.

There's so much I could write or say about those centuries. But in a very real sense they constitute a unique time—between the lost land and the coming of human beings—and much of what was deduced, surmised, learned, memorized, was shattered, so to speak, when the humans came.

It is enough to say that we became a highly developed people, worshiping the Good God largely through banquets and dances as we had always done. We still played the game of memory, and still kept to our strict rules of conduct, though now men "remembered" at birth how to be violent, to fight, to excel, and to compete, and women were born remembering fear.

And certain strange events had had an incredible impact upon us, far greater than anyone realized at the time.

Other men and women were afoot in Britain. We heard of them from other Taltos—and that they were loathsome and as mean as animals. The Taltos had slaughtered them in self-defense. But the strange people, who were not Taltos, had left behind pots made of brittle earth, painted with pretty pictures, and weapons made of magical stone. They had also left behind curious little creatures like monkeys, though hairless and very helpless, who might be their young.

This settled the question that they were bestial, for in our minds only the beasts had helpless little young. And even the young of the beasts weren't as helpless as these little creatures.

But Taltos took mercy on them; they nourished them on milk and kept them, and finally, having heard so much about them, we bought about five of these little creatures, who by that time were no longer crying all the time, and actually knew how to walk.

These creatures didn't live long. What, thirty-five years, perhaps, but during that time they changed dramatically; they went from little wriggling pink things to tall, strong beings, only to become wizened, withered old things. Purely animal, that was our conjecture, and I don't think we treated these primitive primates any better than they might have treated dogs.

They were not quick-witted, they didn't understand our very rapid speech; indeed, it was quite a discovery that they could understand if we spoke slowly, but they had no words, apparently, of their own.

Indeed, they were born stupid, we thought, with less innate knowledge than the bird or the fox; and though they gained greater reasoning power, they always remained fairly weak, small, and covered with hideous hair.

When a male of our kind mated with a female of them, the female bled and died. The men made our women bleed. They were crude and clumsy, besides.

Over the centuries we came upon such creatures more than once, or bought them from other Taltos, but we never saw them in any organized force of their own. We supposed them to be harmless. We had no name for them, really. They taught us nothing, and they made us cry with frustration when they couldn't learn anything from us.

How sad this is, we thought, that these big animals look so much like Taltos, even walking upright and having no tails, but they have no minds.

Meanwhile, our laws had become very strict. Execution was the ultimate punishment for disobedience. It had become a ritual, though never a celebrated one, in which the offending Taltos was quickly dispatched with deliberate and severe blows to the skull.

Now, the skull of a Taltos stays resilient long after other bones in his body have become hard. But the skull can be crushed easily, if one knows how to do it, and we had—unfortunately—learned.

But death still horrified us. Murder was a very infrequent crime. The death penalty was for those who threatened the entire community. Birth was still our central sacred ceremony, and when we found good places to settle, which argued for permanence, we frequently selected places for our religious circle dancing, and we laid out stones to mark these places, sometimes very, very large stones, in which we took pride.

Ah, the circles of stones! We became, though we never thought of it that way, the people of the stone circles all over the land.

When we were forced to a new territory—either by starvation or because another band of Taltos was coming towards
us whom none of us liked, and with whom no one wanted
to live in close quarters—we got in the custom of making a
new circle at once. Indeed, the diameter of our circle and the
weight of its stones became a claim upon a certain area, and
the sight of a very large circle built by others was a sign to
us that this was their land and we should move on.

Anybody foolish enough to disregard a sacred circle?
Well, they would be given no peace and quiet till they decamped. Of course, it was scarcity that imposed these rules
often. A great plain could support very few hunters, really.
Good spots on lakes and rivers and on the coast were better, but no place was paradise, no place was the endless
fountain of warmth and plenty that had been the lost land.

Claims of sacred protection were asserted against invaders or squatters. And I remember myself carving a figure of
the Good God, as I perceived God—with both breasts and
a penis—upon an immense stone in one of these circles, a
plea to other Taltos that they must respect our holy circle
and therefore our land.

When there was a true battle, born of personality and
misunderstanding, and rank greed for a particular portion
of the earth, the invaders would knock down the stones of
those who lived there, and make a new circle entirely of
their own.

To be driven out was exhausting, but in a new home the
desire to build a larger, more imposing circle burnt hot. We
would find stones, we vowed, so large that no one could
ever dislodge them, or would ever try.

Our circles spoke of our ambition and our simplicity—of
the joy of the dance and our willingness to fight and die for
the territory of the tribe.

Our basic values, though unchanged since the days of the
lost land, had hardened somewhat around certain rituals. It
was mandatory for all to attend the birth of a new Taltos.
It was the law that no woman could give birth more than
twice. It was the law that reverence and sensuality attend
these births; indeed, a great sexual euphoria was often sustained.

The new Taltos was seen as an omen; if not perfect of limb and form, beautiful to behold, and full sized, a terrible fear came over the land. The perfect newborn was the blessing of the Good God as before, but you see, our beliefs had darkened; and as they darkened, as we drew all the wrong conclusions from purely natural events, so did our obsession with the great circles darken, our belief in them as pleasing to the Good God, and as morally essential for the tribe.

At last came the year when we settled on the plain.

This was in the south of Britain, now known as Salisbury, where the climate was beautiful to us, and the best we had ever been able to find. The time? Before the coming of human beings.

We knew by then that the winter would always be with us; we did not think it possible to escape the winter anywhere in the world. If you think about this, it's a perfectly logical assumption. Alas! The summers were longest and sweetest in this part of Britain, I knew this firsthand now, and the forests were thick and full of deer, and the sea was not far away.

Herds of wild antelope wandered the plain.

Here we decided that we would build our permanent home.

The idea of moving all the time, to avoid arguments or to chase the food supply, had long since lost its appeal. We had become, to some extent, a people of settlements. The search was on among all our peoples for permanent refuge and a permanent place to perform the sacred singing, the sacred memory game, and the sacred dance, and of course the ritual of the birth.

We had deeply resented our last invasion, and had only left after endless argument (Taltos always try words first), some pushing and shoving, and finally a lot of ultimatums, such as "All right, if you are determined to crowd these woods, then we shall leave them!"

We held ourselves to be vastly superior to the other tribes for any number of reasons, and certainly because we had so many who had lived in the lost land, and many, many still with white hair. We were in many respects the most clearly organized group, and we had the most customs. Some of us had horses now, and could manage to ride them. Our caravan was comprised of many wagons. And we had good-sized herds and flocks of sheep, goats, and a form of wild cattle that no longer exists.

Others poked fun at us, especially for riding horses, off which we fell repeatedly, but in general other Taltos held us in awe, and came running to us for help in bad times.

Now, upon the Salisbury Plain, determining that it would be ours forever, we chose to make the greatest circle of stones ever seen in the world.

By this time, too, we knew that the very making of the circle united the tribe, organized it, kept it from mischief, and made the dances all the more joyous, as stone after stone was added, and the circle grew ever more impressive to behold.

This great undertaking, the building of the biggest circle in the world, shaped several centuries of our existence, and pushed us forward rapidly in terms of inventiveness and organization. The search for the sarsens, or the sandstone, as it is now called, the means of bringing the boulders back, of dressing them and erecting them, and finally laying in place the lintels—this consumed us; it became a justification for life itself.

The concept of fun and play was almost gone from us now. We were survivors of the bitter cold. The dance had been sanctified. Everything had been sanctified. Yet this was a great and thrilling time.

Those who would share our life joined us, and we grew to such a number that we could resist invasion; indeed, the very first monstrous stone of our great plan inspired such inspiration that other Taltos came to worship, to join our circle or to watch it, rather than to steal part of the plain.

The building of the circle became the backdrop against which our development took place.

During these centuries our life reached its highest peak. We built our encampments all over the plain, in easy walking distance of our great circle, and gathered our animals into small stockades. We planted the elderberry and the blackthorn around our encampments, and these encampments became forts.

We arranged for the orderly burial of the dead; indeed, we built some graves beneath the ground during this time. Indeed, all the consequences of permanent settlement played themselves out. We did not begin to make pottery, but we bought a great deal of it from other Taltos who claimed to have bought it from the short-lived hairy people who came to the coast in boats made of animal skin.

Soon tribes came from all over Britain to make the living circle of the dance within our standing stones.

The circles became great winding processions. It was deemed to be good luck to give birth within our circle. And much trade and prosperity came our way.

Meanwhile, other large circles were being erected in our land. Vast, marvelous circles, but none, absolutely none, to rival our own. Indeed, sometime during this productive and wondrous era, it became known that ours was indeed the circle of circles; people did not seek to rival it, but rather only to see it, to dance in it, to join the procession weaving in and out of the various doorways formed by the lintels and the standing stones.

To travel to another circle, to dance with the tribe there, became a regular event. At such gatherings we learnt much from each other, and celebrated great chains of memory, swapping tales and reinforcing the details of the most cherished stories, and correcting the legends of the lost land.

We would go in bands to see the circle which is now called Avebury, or to see other circles farther south, near Stuart Gordon's beloved Glastonbury Tor. We went north to worship at others.

But all the while, ours was the most magnificent, and when Ashlar and his people came to visit the circle of another tribe, it was considered to be a great honor, and we were asked for advice, and begged to remain, and given fine gifts.

Of course, you know that our circle became Stonehenge. Because it and many others of our sacred rings are standing even today. But let me explain what may be obvious only to scholars of Stonehenge. We did not build the whole thing that is there now, or is believed to have been there at one time.

We built only two circles of sarsens, quarried in other areas, including the distant Marlborough Downs, but mainly at Amesbury, which is very near to Stonehenge. The inner circle had ten standing stones, and the outer thirty. And the placing of the lintels atop these stones was a matter of great debate. From the beginning, we opted for the lintels. But I never much appreciated them. I had dreamed of a circle of stones to imitate a circle of men and women. Each stone was to be roughly twice the size of a Taltos, and as wide as a Taltos is tall. That was my vision.

But to others of the tribe, the lintels gave the impression of shelter, reminding them of the great volcanic cone which had once protected the tropical valley of the lost land.

It was later peoples who built the circle of blue stones, and many other formations at Stonehenge. At one time, all of our beloved open-air temple was enclosed into some sort of wooden edifice by savage human tribes. And I do not care to think of the bloody rites practiced there. But this was not our doing.

As to the emblems carved upon the sarsens, we used only one, upon a central stone which is long gone. It was a symbol of the Good God with breasts and phallus, and it was deeply etched within reach of a Taltos, so that he or she might trace it in the dark by touch.

Later, human beings put other carvings upon the sarsens, just as they put Stonehenge to other use.

But I can tell you that no one—Taltos, human, or other species—has ever happened upon our great circle who did not to some extent respect it or come to feel the presence of the sacred when within it. Long before it was ever completed, it became a place of inspiration, and it has been one ever since.

In this monument you have the essence of our people. It is the only great monument we were ever to build.

But to fully appreciate what we were, remember, we retained our values. We deplored death and did not celebrate it. We made no blood sacrifice. We did not see war as glorious so much as chaotic and unpleasant. And the high expression of our art was the singing and dancing circles assembled in and around Stonehenge.

At their greatest height, our birth festivals and festivals of memory or music would include thousands of Taltos, come from far and wide. It was impossible to count the circles formed, or to measure the widest of them. It is impossible to say how many hours and days these rituals went on.

Imagine it, if you will, the vast snowy plain, the clear blue sky, smoke rising from the encampments and the huts built near to the stone circle, for warmth and food and drink. See the Taltos, men and women all, and of my height, with hair long, often to the waist or even to the ankles, wearing carefully sewn skins and furs and high boots of leather, and linking hands to form these beautiful, simple configurations as the voices rose in song.

Ivy leaves, mistletoe, holly, whatever was green in winter, we wore in our hair, and brought with us, and laid upon the ground. The branches of the pine or whatever tree did not lose their leaves.

And in summer we brought flowers aplenty; and indeed, deputations were kept going all day and night into the woodlands to find flowers and fresh green boughs.

The singing and the music alone were magnificent. One did not tear oneself from the circles easily. Indeed, some people never left of their own accord, and small fires were made within the margins between moving lines of dancers, for warmth. Some danced and sang and embraced others until they fell down in a faint or dead.

In the beginning we had no one presiding, but that changed. I was called upon to go into the center, to strike the strings of the harp, to begin the dance. And after I had spent many hours there, another came to stand in my place, and later another and another, each new singer or musician making a music which the others imitated, taking the new song out from small circle to big circle, like the ripples in a pond from a falling stone.

At times, many great fires were constructed beforehand, one in the center and others at various points, so that the dancers would pass near to them often as they followed the circular path.

The birth of the Taltos in our circle was for the newborn an event unrivaled even in the lost land. For there the circles had been voluntary and spontaneous and small. But here the new creature opened its eyes upon an enormous tribe of its own kind, and heard a chorus like that of angels, and dwelt within that circle, being suckled and stroked and comforted for the first days and nights of life.

Of course, we were changing. As our innate knowledge changed, we changed. That is, what we learned changed the genetic makeup of the newborn.

Those born in the time of the circles had a stronger sense of the sacred than we old ones did, and were frankly not so given to rampant humor or irony or suspicion as we were. Those born in the time of the circles were more aggressive, and could murder when they had to, without giving way to tears.

Had you asked me then, I would have said our kind would rule forever. Had you said, "Ah, but men will come who will slaughter people for fun, who will rape and burn and lay waste simply because it is what they do for a living," I would not have believed it. I would have said, "Oh, but we'll talk to them, we'll tell all our stories and memories and ask them to tell theirs, and they'll start dancing and singing, and they'll stop fighting or wanting things they shouldn't have."

When human beings did come down on us, we assumed, of course, that they would be simple little hairy people, of the gentle ilk of the amiable, grunting little traders who sometimes came to the coast in boats of skin to sell us goods and then went away.

We heard tales of raids and massacres but we could not believe these. After all, why would anyone do such things?

And then we were amazed to discover that the human beings coming into Britain had smooth skin like ours, and that their magic stone had been hammered into shields and helmets and swords, that they had brought their own trained horses with them by the hundreds, and on horseback they rode us down, burning our camps, piercing our bodies with spears, or chopping off our heads.

They stole our women and raped them until they died of the bleeding. They stole our men and sought to enslave them, and laughed at them and ridiculed them, and in some instances drove them mad.

At first their raids were very infrequent. The warriors came by sea, and descended upon us by night from the forests. We thought each raid was the last.

Often we fought them off. We were not by nature as fierce as they, by any means, but we could defend ourselves, and great circles were convened to discuss their metal weapons and how we might make our own. Indeed, we imprisoned a number of human beings, invaders all, to try to pry the knowledge from them. We discovered that when we slept with their women, whether willing or unwilling, they died. And the men had a deep, inveterate hatred of our softness. They called us "the fools of the circle," or "the simple people of the stones."

The illusion that we could hold out against these people crumbled almost in the space of one season. We only learned later that we'd been saved from earlier annihilation by one simple fact: we didn't have much that these people wanted. Principally, they wanted our women for pleasure, and some of the finer gifts which pilgrims had brought to the circle shrine.

But other tribes of Taltos were flocking onto the plain. They'd been driven from their homes along the coast by the human invaders, who inspired in them only deathly fear. Their mounts gave these human beings a fanatical sense of power. Humans enjoyed these invasions. Massacre was sport to them.

We fortified our camps for the winter. Those who had come to join us replaced many of the fighting men we had lost.

Then the snow came; we had plenty to eat, and we had peace. Maybe the invaders didn't like the snow. We didn't know. There were so many of us gathered together, and we had lifted from the dead so many spears and swords, that we felt safe.

It was time for the winter birth circle to be convened, and it was most important, as so many had been killed in the last year. Not only must we make new Taltos for our villages; we had to make them to send to other villages where the inhabitants had been burnt out.

Many had come from far and wide for the winter birth circle, and we heard more and more tales of slaughter and woe.

However, we were many. And it was our sacred time.

We formed the circles, we lit the sacred fires; it was time to declare to the Good God that we believed the summer would come again, to make birth happen now as an affirmation of that faith, and an affirmation that the Good God wanted us to survive.

We had had perhaps two days of singing and dancing and birthing, of feasting and drinking, when the tribes of human beings descended on the plain.

We heard the enormous rumble of the horses before we saw them; it was a roar like the sound of the crumbling of the lost land. Horsemen came from all sides to attack us; the great sarsens of the circles were splashed with our blood.

Many Taltos, drunk on music and erotic play, never put up any resistance at all. Those of us who ran to the camps put up a great fight.

But when the smoke had cleared, when the horsemen were gone, when our women had been taken by the hundreds in our own wagons, when every encampment had been burnt to the ground, we were only a handful, and we had had enough of war.

Indeed, the horrors we'd seen we never wanted to witness again. The newborns of our tribe had all been slain, to the last one. They had blundered into death in the first days of their lives. Few women remained to us, and some had given birth too many times in the past.

By the second nightfall after the massacre, our scouts came back to tell us what we had feared was true: the warriors had set up their camps in the forest. They were building permanent dwellings; indeed, there was talk of their villages dotting the southern landscape.

We had to go north.

We had to return to the hidden valleys of the Highlands, or places too inaccessible for these cruel invaders. Our journey was a long one, lasting the rest of the winter, in which birth and death became daily occurrences, and more than once we were attacked by small bands of humans, and more than once we spied upon their settlements and learned of their lives.

We massacred more than one band of the enemy. Twice we raided lowland forts to rescue our men and women, whose singing we could hear from great distances.

And by the time we discovered the high valley of Donnelaith, it was spring, the snow was melting, the rich forest was green again, the loch was no longer frozen, and we soon found ourselves in a hideaway accessible to the outside world only by a winding river whose route was so circuitous that the loch itself could not be seen from the sea. Indeed, the great cove through which a seafarer enters it appears to all eyes as a cave.

Understand, the loch in later times became a port. Men did much by that time to open it to the sea.

But in those times we found ourselves hidden and safe at last.

We had many rescued Taltos with us. And the stories they told! The human beings had discovered the miracle of birth with us! They were spellbound by the magic of it; they had tortured the Taltos women and men mercilessly, trying to force them to do it, and then had screamed in delight and thrilling fear when the new Taltos appeared. They had worried some of these women to death. But many of our kind had resisted, refusing to be so violated; some women had found ways to take their own lives. Many had been killed for struggling, for attacking every human who came near them, and finally for trying repeatedly to escape.

When humans discovered that the newborns could breed immediately, they forced them to do it, and the newborns, muddled and frightened, did not know what to do but comply. The humans knew the power of music over the Taltos, and how to use it. The humans thought the Taltos sentimental and cowardly, though what the words were for it then, I don't now know.

In sum, a deep hatred grew between us and the warriors. We thought them animals, of course, animals that could talk and make things, perfect horrors, actually, aberrations that might destroy all beautiful life. And they thought us amusing and relatively harmless monsters! For it soon became apparent that the wide world was filled with people of their height or even smaller, who bred and lived as they did, and not with people like us.

From our raids we had gathered many objects which these people had brought from far and wide. The slaves repeated tales of great kingdoms with walls about them, of palaces in lands of desert sand and jungle, of warring tribes and of great congregations of people in encampments of such size that one could not imagine it. And these encampments had names.

All of these people, as far as we knew, bred in the human way. All had tiny, helpless babies. All brought them up half-savage and half-intelligent. All were aggressive, liked to war, liked to kill. Indeed, it was perfectly obvious to me that the most aggressive among them were the survivors, and they had weeded out over the centuries anyone who was not aggressive. So they had had a hand in making themselves what they were.

Our early days in the glen of Donnelaith—and let me say here that *we* gave it that name—were days of intense pondering and discussion, of building the finest circle that we could, and of consecration and prayer.

We celebrated the birth of numerous new Taltos, and these we schooled vigorously for the ordeals that lay ahead. We buried many who died of old wounds, and some women who died from childbearing, as always happens, and we buried others who, having been driven from the plain of Salisbury, simply did not want to live.

It was the worst time of suffering for my people, even worse than the massacre itself had been. I saw strong Taltos, white-haired ones, great singers, abandon themselves completely to their music, and fall at last without breath into the high grass.

Finally, when a new council had been appointed, of new-borns and wiser Taltos, of the white-haired and of those who wanted to do something about all this, we came to the one very logical position.

Can you guess what it was?

We realized that humans had to be annihilated. If they weren't, their warring ways would destroy all that had been given us by the Good God. They were burning up life with their cavalry and their torches and swords. We had to stamp them out.

As for the prospect that they existed all over distant lands in great numbers, well, we bred much faster than they did—was that not so? We could replace our slain very quickly. They took years to replace a fallen warrior. Surely we could outnumber them as we fought against them, if only . . . if only we had the stomach for the fight.

Within a week, after endless argument, it was decided that we did not have the stomach for the fight. Some of us could do it; we were so angry and full of hate and irony now that we could ride down upon them and hack them to pieces. But in the main, Taltos simply could not kill in this way; they could not match the malicious lust of humans for killing. And we knew it. Humans would win by sheer meanness and cruelty in the end.

Of course, since that time, and possibly a thousand times before it, a people has been annihilated because it lacked aggression; it could not match the cruelty of another tribe or clan or nation or race.

The one real difference in our case was that we knew it. Whereas the Incas were slaughtered in ignorance by the Spanish, we understood much more of what was involved.

Of course, we were certain of our superiority to humans; we were baffled that they didn't appreciate our singing and stories; we did not believe that they knew what they were doing when they struck us down.

And realizing that we really couldn't match them in combat, we assumed that we could reason with them, we could teach them, we could show them how much more pleasant and agreeable life was if one did not kill.

Of course, we had only just begun to understand them.

413

By the end of that year, we had ventured out of the glen to take a few human prisoners, and from these we learned that things were far more hopeless than we thought. Killing lay at the very basis of their religion; it was their sacred act!

For their gods they killed, sacrificing hundreds of their own kind at their rituals. Indeed, death was the very focus of their lives!

We were overcome with horror.

We determined that life would exist for us within the glen. As for other Taltos tribes, we feared the worst for them. In our little forays to find human slaves, we had seen more than one village burnt out, more than one field of wasting, sinewy Taltos bones being scattered by the winter wind.

As the years passed, we remained secure in the glen, venturing out only with the greatest care. Our bravest scouts traveled as far as they dared.

By the end of the decade, we knew that no Taltos settlements remained in our part of Britain. All the old circles were now abandoned! And we also came to find out from the few prisoners we took—which was not easy—that we were hunted now, and very much in demand to be sacrificed to the humans' gods.

Indeed, massacres had become a thing of the past. Taltos were hunted strictly for capture, and only killed if they refused to breed.

It had been discovered that their seed brought death to human women, and on that account the males were kept in unbearable bondage, laden with metal chains.

Within the next century the invaders conquered the earth!

Many of the scouts who went out to seek other Taltos, and bring them into the glen, simply never came back. But there were always young ones who wanted to go, who had to see life beyond the mountains, who had to go down to the loch and travel to the sea.

As the memories were passed on in our blood, our young Taltos became even more warlike. They wanted to slaughter a human! Or so they thought.

Those wanderers who did return, and frequently with at

least a couple of human prisoners, confirmed our most terrible fears. From one end of Britain to the other, the Taltos was dying out. Indeed, in most places it was no more than legend, and certain towns, for the new settlements were nothing less than that, would pay a fortune for a Taltos, but men no longer hunted for them, and some did not believe anymore that there had ever been such strange beasts.

Those who were caught were wild.

Wild? we asked. What in the name of God is a wild Taltos?

Well, we were soon told.

In numerous encampments, when it came time for sacrifice to the gods, the chosen women, often fanatically eager for it, were brought to embrace a prisoner Taltos, to arouse his passion, and then to die by his seed. Dozens of women met their deaths in this fashion, precisely as human men were being drowned in cauldrons, or decapitated, or burnt in horrid wicker cages for the gods of the human tribes.

But over the years some of these women had not died. Some of them had left the sacred altar alive. And a few of these, within a matter of weeks, had given birth!

A Taltos came out of their bodies, a wild seed of our kind. This Taltos invariably killed its human mother, not meaning to, of course, but because she could not survive the birth of such a creature. But this didn't always happen. And if the mother lived long enough to give her offspring milk, which she had aplenty, this Taltos would grow, within the customary time of three hours, to full size.

In some villages this was counted as a great omen of good fortune. In others it was disaster. Human beings could not agree. But the name of the game had become to get a pair of such human-mothered Taltos and to make them breed more Taltos, and to keep a stock of these prisoners, to make them dance, to make them sing, to make them give birth.

Wild Taltos.

There was another way that wild Taltos could be born. A human man now and then made one grow in the body of a Taltos woman! This poor prisoner, being kept for pleasure, did not suspect at first that she had conceived. Within

415

weeks her child was born to her, growing to full height as she knew it would, only to be taken from her and imprisoned, or put to some grisly use.

And who were the mortals who could breed with Taltos in this way? What characterized them? In the very beginning we did not know; we could not perceive any visible signs. But later, as more and more mixture occurred, it became clear to us that a certain kind of human was more prone than any other, either to conceive or to father the Taltos, and that was a human of great spiritual gifts, a human who could see into people's hearts, or tell the future, or lay healing hands upon others. These humans to our eyes became quite detectable and finally unmistakable.

But this took centuries to develop. Blood was passed back and forth.

Wild Taltos escaped their captors. Human women swelling monstrous with Taltos fled to the glen in hope of shelter. Of course we took them in.

We learned from these human mothers.

Whereas our young were born within hours, their young took a fortnight to a month, depending upon whether or not the mother knew of the child's existence. Indeed, if the mother knew and was to address the child, quiet its fears, and sing to it, the growth was greatly accelerated. Hybrid Taltos were born knowing things their human ancestors had known! In other words, our laws of genetic inheritance embraced the acquired knowledge of the human species.

Of course, we had no such language then to discuss these things. We only knew that a hybrid might know how to sing human songs in human tongues, or to make boots such as we had never seen, very skillfully, from leather.

In this way, all manner of human knowledge passed into our people.

But those wild ones, born in captivity, were always full of the Taltos memories too, and conceived a hatred for their human tyrants. They broke for freedom as soon as they could. To the woods they fled, and to the north, possibly to the lost land. Some unfortunates, we learned later, went home to the great plain and, finding no refuge, survived hand-to-mouth in the nearby forest, or were captured and killed.

Some of these wild Taltos inevitably bred with each other. As fugitives they found one another; or within captivity they were bred. They could always breed with the pure Taltos prisoner, giving birth in the pure way, immediately; and so a fragile race of Taltos was hanging on in the wilderness of Britain, a desperate minority of outcasts, incessantly searching for their ancestors and for the paradise of their memories, and carrying in their veins human blood.

Much, much human blood came into the wild Taltos during these centuries. And the wild Taltos developed beliefs and habits of their own. They lived in the green treetops, often painting themselves entirely green for camouflage, making the paint of several natural pigments, and clothing themselves when they could in ivy and leaves.

And it was these, or so it was claimed, who somehow created the Little People.

Indeed, the Little People may have always lived in the shadows and hidden places. We had glimpsed them surely in our early years, and during the time of our rule of Britain, they had kept themselves entirely away from us. They were but a kind of monster in our legends. We scarcely noticed them any more than hairy human beings.

But now tales came to our ears that they had begun with the spawning of Taltos and human—that when the conception occurred but the development failed, a hunchbacked dwarf was born, rather than the wiry and graceful Taltos.

Was this so? Or did they spring from the same root as we did? Were we cousins of each other in some time before the lost land, when perhaps we had mingled in some earlier paradise? The time before the moon? Was that the time of our branching off, one tribe from the other?

We didn't know. But at the times of hybrids, and experiments of this sort, of wild Taltos seeking to discover what they could or could not do, or who could breed with whom, we did learn that these horrid little monsters, these malicious, mischievous, and strange Little People, could breed with us. Indeed, if they could seduce one of us into coupling with them, man or woman, the offspring was more often than not a Taltos.

A compatible race? An evolutionary experiment closely related to us?

Again, we were never to know.

But the legend spread, and the Little People preyed upon us as viciously as human beings. They set traps for us; they tried to lure us with music; they did not come in warrior bands; they were sneaks, and they tried to entrance us with spells which they could cast by the powers of their minds. They wanted to make the Taltos. They dreamed of becoming a race of giants, as they called us. And when they caught our women, they coupled with them until they died; and when they caught our men, they were as cruel to them to make them breed as humans.

Over the centuries the mythology grew; the Little People had once been as we were, tall and fair. They had once had our advantages. But demons had made them what they were, cast them out, made them suffer. They were as long-lived as we were. Their monstrous little offspring were born as quickly and as fully developed proportionately as ours were.

But we feared them, we hated them, we did not want to be used by them, and we came to believe the stories that our children could be like them if not given milk, if not loved.

And the truth, whatever it was, if anyone ever knew, was buried in folklore.

In the glen the Little People still hang on; there are few natives of Britain who do not know of them. They go by countless names, lumped with other creatures of myth—the fairies, the Sluagh, the Ganfers, the leprechauns, the elves.

They are dying out now in Donnelaith, for a great many reasons. But they live in other dark, secret places still. They steal human women now and then to breed, but they are no more successful with humans than we are. They long for a witch—a mortal with the extra sense, the type that, with one of them, often conceives or fathers the Taltos. And when they find such creatures, they can be ruthless.

Never believe that they won't hurt you in the glen, or in

other glens and remote woods and valleys. They would do it. And they would kill you and burn the fat of your bodies on their torches for the sheer joy of it.

But this is not their story.

Another tale can be told of them, by Samuel, perhaps, should he ever be moved to tell it. But then Samuel has a tale all his own of his wanderings away from the Little People, and that would make a better adventure, I think, than their history.

Let me return to the wild Taltos now, the hybrids who carried the human genes. Banding together outside the glen, whenever possible, they exchanged the memories, the tales, and formed their own tiny settlements.

And periodically we went in search of them and brought them home. They bred with us; they gave us offspring; we gave them counsel and knowledge.

And surprisingly enough, they never stayed! They would come to the glen from time to time to rest, but they had to return to the wild world, where they shot arrows at humans, and fled through the forests laughing afterwards, believing themselves to be the very magical creatures, sought for sacrifice, which humans believed them to be.

And the great tragedy, of course, of their desire to wander is that inevitably they carried the secret of the glen to the human world.

Simpletons, that is what we are in a true sense. Simpletons, that we did not see that such a thing would have to happen, that these wild ones, when finally captured, would tell tales of our glen, sometimes to threaten their enemies with the prospect of vengeance from a secret nation, or out of sheer naiveté, or, that the tale having been told to other wild Taltos who had never seen us, would be passed on by them.

Can you see what happened? The legend of the glen, of the tall people who gave birth to children who could walk and speak at birth, began to spread. Knowledge of us was general throughout Britain. We fell into legend with the Little People. And with other strange creatures whom humans seldom saw, but would have given anything to capture.

And so the life we'd built in Donnelaith, a life of great

stone towers or brochs, from which we hoped someday to successfully defend ourselves against invasions, of the old rituals carefully preserved and carried out, of the memories treasured, and of our values, our belief in love and birth above all things held sacred—that life was in mortal danger from those who would hunt for monsters for any reason, from those who only wanted to "see with their own eyes."

Another development took place. As I said earlier, there were always those born in the glen who wanted to leave. It was deeply impressed upon them that they must remember the way home. They must look at the stars and never forget the various patterns that could guide them home. And this became a part of innate knowledge very rapidly because we deliberately cultivated it, and this cultivation worked. In fact, it worked amazingly well, opening up to us all kinds of new possibilities. We could program into the innate knowledge all manner of practical things. We put it to the test by questioning the offspring. It was quite astonishing. They knew the map of Britain as we knew it and preserved it (highly inaccurate), they knew how to make weapons, they knew the importance of secrecy, they knew the fear and hatred of human beings and how best to avoid them or triumph over them. They knew the Art of the Tongue.

Now, the Art of the Tongue, as we called it, was something we never thought of until the humans came. But it was essentially talking and reasoning with people, which we did with each other all the time. Now, basically we speak among ourselves much, much faster than humans, sometimes. Not always. Just sometimes. It sounds to humans like a whistling or a humming, or even a buzzing. But we can talk more in human rhythm, and we had learned how to speak to humans on their level, that is, to confuse them and entangle them in logic, to fascinate them and to influence them somewhat.

Obviously this Art of the Tongue wasn't saving us from extinction.

But it could save a lone Taltos discovered by a pair of humans in the forest, or a Taltos man taken prisoner by a small human clan with no ties to the warrior people who had invaded the land.

Anyone venturing out must know the Art of the Tongue, of speaking slowly to humans, on their level, and doing it in a convincing way. And inevitably some of those who left decided to settle outside.

They built their brochs, that is, our style of tower, of dry stone without mortar, and lived in wild and isolated places, passing for humans to those new peoples who happened to pass their home.

It was a sort of clan existence that developed defensively, and in scattered locales.

But inevitably these Taltos would reveal their nature to humans, or humans would war on them, or someone would learn of the magical Taltos birth, and again talk of us, talk of the glen, would circulate among hostile men.

I myself, having ever been inventive and forward-looking and refusing to give up, ever—even when the whole lost land was exploding, I did not give up—more or less thought ours was a lost cause. We could, for the present, defend the glen, that was true, when outsiders did occasionally break in on us, but we were essentially trapped!

But the question of those who passed for human, those who lived among human beings, pretending to be an old tribe or clan—that fascinated me. That got me to thinking. . . . What if we were to do this? What if, instead of shutting human beings out, we slowly let them in, leading them to believe that we were a human tribe too, and we lived in their midst, keeping our birth rituals secret from them?

Meantime great changes in the outside world held a great fascination for us. We wanted to speak to travelers, to learn.

And so, finally, we devised a dangerous subterfuge. . . .

Twenty-six

"**Y**URI STEFANO HERE. Can I help you?"

"Can you help me! God, it's good to hear your voice," said Michael. "We've been separated less than forty-eight hours, but the Atlantic Ocean is between us!"

"Michael. Thank God you called me. I didn't know where to reach you. You're still with Ash, aren't you?"

"Yes, and we will be for another two days, I think. I'll tell you all about it, but how are things with you?"

"It's over, Michael. It's over. All the evil is gone, and the Talamasca is itself again. This morning I received my first communication from the Elders. We're taking serious measures to see that this sort of interception can never happen again. I have my work cut out for me, writing my reports. The new Superior General has recommended that I rest, but that's impossible."

"But you have to rest some of the time, Yuri. You know you do. We all do."

"I sleep for four hours. Then I get up. I think about what happened. I write. I write for maybe four, five hours. Then I sleep again. At mealtimes they come and get me. They make me go downstairs. It's nice. It's nice to be back with them. But what about you, Michael?"

"Yuri, I love this man. I love Ash the way I loved Aaron. I've been listening to him talk for hours. It's no secret, what he's telling us, of course, but he won't let us record any of it. He says that we should take away only what we naturally remember. Yuri, I don't think this man will ever hurt us or anyone connected with us. I'm sure of it. You know, it's one of those situations. I've put my trust in him. And if he does come to hurt us, for any reason, well, that's going to be what happens."

"I understand. And Rowan? How is she?"

"I think she loves him too. I know she does. But how much and in what way, well, that's her story. I never could speak for Rowan. We're going to stay here, as I said, for another two days, maybe more, then we have to go back down south. We're a little worried about Mona."

"Why?"

"It's nothing terrible. She's run off with her cousin Mary Jane Mayfair—this is a young woman you've not had the pleasure of meeting—and they're a bit too young to be running around without any parental supervision."

"Michael, I've written a letter to Mona. I had to write it. You know, before I left New Orleans, I pledged my heart to Mona. But Mona is too young for such a pledge, and now that I am home, back with the Order, I realize more than ever how unsuited I am to court Mona. I've sent my letter to the Amelia Street address, but I fear that Mona will, for a little while at least, be angry with me."

"Yuri, Mona has other things on her mind right now. This is probably the best decision you could have made. We forget that Mona is thirteen. Everybody forgets it. And certainly Mona forgets it. But you've done the right thing. Besides, she can contact you if she wants to, can't she?"

"Yes, I am here. I am safe. I am home."

"And Tessa?"

"Well, they took her away, Michael. That's the Talamasca for you. I'm sure that's what happened to her. She was surrounded by a very courtly group of companions and invited to go with them, probably to Amsterdam. I kissed her goodbye before she left. There was some talk of a nice place for her where she could rest, and where all her memories and stories would be recorded. No one seems to know how to calculate her age. No one knows if what Ash has said is true, that she will die soon."

"But she's happy, and the Talamasca has taken care of her."

"Yes, absolutely. Of course, if she ever wants to leave, she can leave. That's our way. But I don't think Tessa thinks in those terms. I think she drifted for years—how many years, no one knows—from one protector to another. She didn't grieve too long for Gordon, by the way. She says that she doesn't care to dwell on unpleasant things."

Michael laughed. "I understand. Believe me. Look, I've got to go back now. We're having some supper together, and then Ash is going to go on with his story. It's beautiful here where we are. Snowing and cold, but beautiful. Everything that surrounds Ash reflects his personality. It's always that way. The buildings we choose for ourselves, they're always reflections of us. This place is filled with colored marble and with paintings, and with . . . with things that interest him. I don't suppose I should talk about it much. He does want his privacy, to be left in peace after we leave him."

"I know. I understand. Listen, Michael, when you see Mona, you must tell her something for me . . . that . . . you must tell her that I . . ."

"She'll understand, Yuri. Mona has other things on her mind right now. It's an exciting time for her. The family wants her to leave Sacred Heart, to start studying with private tutors. Her IQ is off the charts, just as she always said it was. And she is the heir to the Mayfair legacy. I think for the next few years Mona will be spending a lot of time with Rowan and with me, studying, traveling, getting sort of the ideal education for a lady of what . . . how shall I say, great expectations. I'm going to go now. I'll call you again from New Orleans."

"Please do this, please. I love both of you. I love . . . the three of you. Will you tell the others for me, Ash and Rowan?"

"Yes. By the way, those cohorts, those helpers of Gordon?"

"It's all finished. They're gone, and they can never hurt the Order again. I'll talk to you soon, Michael."

"Goodbye, Yuri."

Twenty-seven

EVERYBODY ALWAYS TOLD him the Fontevrault Mayfairs were crazy. "That's why they come to you, Dr. Jack." Every single one of them was mad, said the town, even the rich kin in New Orleans.

But did he have to find it out for himself on an afternoon like this, when it was as dark as night, and half the streets in town were flooded out?

And bringing out a little newborn baby in such a storm, wrapped up in smelly little blankets and lying in a plastic ice chest, no less! And Mary Jane Mayfair expecting him just to make out the birth certificate right there in his office.

He'd demanded to see the mother!

Of course, if he'd known she was going to drive this limousine like this over these shell roads, right through this storm, and that he'd end up holding this baby in his arms, he would have insisted on following her in his pickup.

When she'd pointed to the limousine, he'd thought the woman had a driver. And this was a brand-new car, too, twenty-five feet long if it was a foot, with a moon roof and tinted glass, a compact disc player, and a goddamned telephone. And this teen Amazon queen at the wheel—in her dirty white lace dress, with mud spattered on her bare legs and her sandals.

"And you mean to tell me," he shouted over the rain, "that with a big car like this, you couldn't have brought this baby's mother to the hospital?"

The baby looked fine enough, thank God for that, about

425

a month premature, he figured, and undernourished, of course! But otherwise okay and sleeping right now, deep in the ice chest with all the stinky little blankets around it, as he held the thing on his knees. Why, these blankets actually reeked of whiskey.

"Good heavens, Mary Jane Mayfair, slow down!" he said finally. The branches were making a racket on the top of the car. He flinched as the clumps of wet leaves slapped right against the windshield. He could hardly stand it, the way she ran right over the ruts! "You're going to wake the baby."

"That baby's just fine, Doctor," said Mary Jane, letting her skirt fall all the way back down her thighs to her panties. This was a notorious young woman, nobody had to tell him that. He'd been pretty damn sure this was her baby and she was going to make up some cock-and-bull story about its having been left on the doorstep. But no, there was a mother out there in those swamps, praise God. He was going to put this in his memoirs.

"We're almost there," Mary Jane called out, half smashing a thicket of bamboo on their left, and rolling right on past it. "Now, you got to carry the baby in the boat, all right, Doctor?"

"What boat!" he shouted. But he knew damn good and well what boat. Everybody had told him about this old house, that he ought to drive out to Fontevrault Landing just to see it. You could hardly believe it was standing, the way the west side had sunk, and to think this clan insisted upon living there! Mary Jane Mayfair had been slowly cleaning out the local Wal-Mart for the last six months, fixing the place up for herself and her grandmother. Everybody knew about it when Mary Jane came to town in her white shorts and T-shirts.

She was a pretty girl, though, he had to give her that much, even with that cowboy hat. She had the most high-slung and pointed pair of breasts he'd ever seen, and a mouth the color of bubble gum.

"Hey, you didn't give this baby whiskey to keep it quiet, did you?" he demanded. The little tucker was just snoring away, blowing a big bubble with its tiny little pink lips.

Poor child, to grow up in this place. And she hadn't let him even examine this baby, saying Granny had done all that! Granny, indeed!

The limousine had come to a halt. The rain was teeming. He could scarcely see what looked like a house up ahead, and the great fan leaves of a green palmetto. But those were electric lights burning up there, thank God for that. Somebody'd told him they didn't have any lights out here.

"I'll come round for you with the umbrella," she said, slamming the door behind her before he could say they should wait till the rain slacked off, and then his door flew open and he had no choice but to pick up this ice chest like a cradle.

"Here, put the towel over it, little guy will get wet!" Mary Jane said. "Now run for the boat."

"I will walk, thank you," he said. "If you'll just kindly lead the way, Miss Mayfair!"

"Don't let him fall."

"I beg your pardon! I delivered babies in Picayune, Mississippi, for thirty-eight years before I ever came down to this godforsaken country."

And just why did I come? he thought to himself as he had a thousand times, especially when his new little wife, Eileen, born and raised in Napoleonville, wasn't around to remind him.

Lord in heaven, it was a great big heavy aluminum pirogue, and it didn't have a motor! But there was the house, all right, the entire thing the color of driftwood, with the purple wisteria completely wrapped around the capitals of those upstairs columns, and making its way for the balusters. At least the tangle of trees was so thick in this part of the jungle that he was almost dry for a moment. A tunnel of green went up to the tilting front porch. Lights on upstairs, well, that was a relief. If he had had to see his way around this place by kerosene lamp, he would have gone crazy. Maybe he was already going crazy, crossing this stretch of duckweed slop with this crazy young woman, and the place about to sink any minute.

"That's what's going to happen," Eileen had said. "One morning we'll drive by there, and there won't be any house, whole thing, lock, stock, and barrel, will have sunk into the swamp, you mark my words, it's a sin, anybody living like that."

Carrying the ice chest and its quiet little contents with one hand, he managed to get into the shallow boat, thrilled to discover that it was full of about two inches of water. "This is going to sink, you should have emptied it out." His shoes filled up to the ankles immediately. Why had he agreed to come out here? And Eileen would have to know every last detail.

"It's not going to sink, this is a sissy rain," said Mary Jane Mayfair, shoving on her long pole. "Now hang on, please, and don't let the baby get wet."

The girl was past all patience. Where he came from, nobody talked to a doctor like that! The baby was just fine under the towels, and pissing up a storm for a newborn.

Lo and behold, they were gliding right over the front porch of this dilapidated wreck and into the open doorway.

"My God, this is like a cave!" he declared. "How in the world did a woman give birth in this place? Will you look at that. There are books in there on the top shelf of that bookcase, right above the water."

"Well, nobody was here when the water came in," said Mary Jane, straining as she pushed on the pole.

He could hear the *thonk-thonk* of it hitting the floor-boards beneath them.

"And I guess lots of things are still floating around in the parlor. Besides, Mona Mayfair didn't have her baby down here, she had it upstairs. Women don't have their babies in the front room, even if it isn't underwater."

The boat collided with the steps, tossing him violently to the left, so that he had to grab the slimy wet banister. He leapt out, immediately stamping both his feet to make sure the steps weren't going to sink under him.

A warm flood of light came from upstairs, and he could hear, over the hiss and roar of the rain, another sound, very fast, *clickety, clickety, clickety.* He knew that sound. And with it, a woman's voice humming. Kind of pretty.

"Why doesn't this stairway just float loose from the wall?" he asked. He started up, the ice-chest cradle beginning to feel like a sack of rocks to him. "Why doesn't this whole place just disintegrate?"

"Well, in a way, I guess it is," said Mary Jane, "only it's taking a couple hundred years, you know???" She went thumping up the steps in front of him, pushing right in his way as she hit the second-floor hall, and then turning around and saying, "You come with me, we got to go up to the attic."

But where was that *clickety, clickety, clickety* coming from? He could hear somebody humming, too. But she didn't even give him a chance to look around, rushing him to the attic steps.

And then he saw old Granny Mayfair at the very top in her flowered flannel gown, waving her little hand at him.

"Hey, there, Dr. Jack. How's my handsome boy? Come give me a kiss. Surely am glad to see you."

"Glad to see you too, Grandma," he said coming up, though Mary Jane once again shoved right past him, with the firm admonition that he was to hold tight to the baby. Four more steps and he'd be glad to set this bundle down. How come he was the one who'd wound up carrying it, anyway?

At last he reached the warm, dry air of the attic, the little old lady standing on tiptoe to press her lips to his cheeks. He did love Grandma Mayfair, he had to admit that much.

"How you doing, Grandma, you taking all your pills?" he asked.

Mary Jane picked up the ice chest as soon as he set it down, and ran off with it. This wasn't such a bad place, this attic; it was strung with electric lights, and clean clothes hanging on the lines with wooden clothespins. Lots of comfortable old furniture scattered around, and it didn't smell too much like mold; on the contrary, it smelled like flowers.

"What is that 'clickety-clickety' sound I'm hearing on the second floor down there?" he asked as Grandma Mayfair took his arm.

"You just come in here, Dr. Jack, and do what you got to do, and then you fill out that baby's birth certificate. We don't want any problems with the registration of this baby's birth, did I ever tell you about the problems when I didn't register Yancy Mayfair for two months after he was born, and you wouldn't believe the trouble I got into with the city hall and them telling me that . . ."

"And you delivered this little tyke, did you, Granny?" he asked, patting her hand. His nurses had warned him the first time she came in that it was best not to wait till she finished her stories, because she didn't. She'd been at his office the second day he opened up, saying none of the other doctors in this town were ever going to touch her again. Now that was a story!

"Sure did, Doctor."

"The mama's over there," said Mary Jane, pointing to the side gable of the attic, all draped in unbleached mosquito netting as if it were a tent with its peaked roof, and the distant glowing rectangle of the rain-flooded window at the end of it.

Almost pretty, the way it looked. There was an oil lamp burning inside, he could smell it, and see the warm glow in the smoky glass shade. The bed was big, piled with quilts and coverlets. It made him sad, suddenly, to think of his own grandmother years and years ago, and beds like that, so heavy with quilts you couldn't move your toes, and how warm it had been underneath on cold mornings in Carriere, Mississippi.

He lifted the long, thin veils and lowered his head just a little as he stepped under the spine of the gable. The cypress boards were bare here, and dark brownish red and clean. Not a leak anywhere, though the rainy window sent a wash of rippling light over everything.

The red-haired girl lay snug in the bed, half asleep, her eyes sunken and the skin around them frighteningly dark, her lips cracked as she took her breaths with obvious effort.

"This young woman should be in a hospital."

"She's worn out, Doctor, you would be too," said Mary Jane, with her smart tongue. "Why don't you get this over with, so she can get some rest now?"

At least the bed was clean, cleaner than that makeshift bassinet. The girl lay nestled in fresh sheets, and wearing a fancy white shirt trimmed in old-fashioned lace, with little pearl buttons. Her hair was just about the reddest he'd ever seen, and long and full and brushed out on the pillow. The baby's might be red like that someday, but right now it was a bit paler.

And speaking of the baby, it was making a sound at last in its little ice-chest bed, thank God. He was beginning to worry about it. Granny Mayfair snatched it up into her arms, and he could tell from the way she lifted it that the baby was in fine hands, though who wanted to think of a woman that age in charge of everything? Look at this girl in the bed. She wasn't even as old as Mary Jane.

He drew closer, went down with effort on his knees, since there was nothing else to do, and he laid his hand on the mother's forehead. Slowly her eyes opened, and surprised him with their deep green color. This was a child herself, should never have had a baby!

"You all right, honey?" he asked.

"Yes, Doctor," she said in a bright, clear voice. "Would you fill out the papers, please, for my baby?"

"You know perfectly well that you should—"

"Doctor, the baby's born," she said. She wasn't from around here. "I'm not bleeding anymore. I'm not going anywhere. As a matter of fact, I am fine, better than I expected."

The flesh beneath her fingernails was nice and pink. Her pulse was normal. Her breasts were huge. And there was a big jug of milk, only half drunk, by the bed. Well, that was good for her.

Intelligent girl, sure of herself, and well bred, he thought, not country.

"You two leave us alone now," he said to Mary Jane and the old woman, who hovered right at his shoulders like two giant angels, the little baby whining just a little, like it had just discovered again that it was alive and wasn't sure it liked it. "Go over there so I can examine this child, and make sure she's not hemorrhaging."

"Doctor, I took care of that child," said Granny gently. "Now do you think I would let her lie there if she was hemorrhaging?" But she went away, bouncing the baby in her arms, pretty vigorously, he thought, for a newborn.

He thought sure the little mother was going to put up a fuss, too, but she didn't.

There was nothing to do but hold this oil lamp himself, if he wanted to make sure everything was all right. This was hardly going to be a thorough examination.

She sat up against the pillows, her red hair mussed and tangled around her white face, and let him turn back the thick layer of covers. Everything nice and clean, he had to hand it to them. She was immaculate, as though she'd soaked in the tub, if such a thing was possible, and they had laid a layer of white towels beneath her. Hardly any discharge at all now. But she was the mother, all right. Badly bruised from the birth. Her white nightgown was spotless.

Why in the world didn't they clean up the little one like that, for God's sake? Three women, and they didn't want to play dolls enough to change that baby's blankets?

"Just lie back now, honey," he said to the mother. "The baby didn't tear you, I can see that, but it would have been a damned sight easier for you if it had. Next time, how about trying the hospital?"

"Sure, why not?" she said in a drowsy voice, and then gave him just a little bit of a laugh. "I'll be all right." Very ladylike. She'd never be a child again now, he thought, pint-sized though she was, and just wait till this story got around town, though he wasn't about to tell Eileen one word of it.

"I told you she was fine, didn't I?" asked Granny, pushing aside the netting now, the baby crying a little against her shoulder. The mother didn't even look at the baby.

Probably had enough of it for the moment, he thought. Probably resting while she could.

"All right, all right," he said, smoothing the cover back. "But if she starts to bleed, if she starts running a fever, you get her down into that limousine of yours and get her into Napoleonville! You go straight on in to the hospital."

"Sure thing, Dr. Jack, glad you could come," said Mary Jane. And she took his hand and led him out of the little tent enclosure, away from the bed.

"Thank you, Doctor," said the red-haired girl, softly. "Will you write it all out, please? The date of birth and all, and let them sign it as witnesses?"

"Got a wooden table for you to write on right here," said Mary Jane. She pointed to a small makeshift desk of two pine boards laid over two stacks of old wooden Coke bottle crates. It had been a long time since he'd seen Coke crates like that, the kind they used to use for the little bottles that used to cost a nickel. Figured she could probably sell them at a flea market these days to a collector. Lots of things around here she could sell. He spied the old gas sconce on the wall just above him.

It broke his back to lean over and write like this, but it wasn't worth complaining about. He took out his pen. Mary Jane reached up and tipped the naked light bulb towards him.

There came that sound from downstairs, *clickety-clickety-clickety*. And then a whirring sound. He knew those noises.

"What is that sound?" he asked. "Now let's see here, mother's name, please?"

"Mona Mayfair."

"Father's name?"

"Michael Curry."

"Lawfully wedded husband and wife."

"No. Just skip that sort of thing, would you?"

He shook his head. "Born last night, you said?"

"Ten minutes after two this morning. Delivered by Dolly Jean Mayfair and Mary Jane Mayfair. Fontevrault. You know how to spell it?"

He nodded. "Baby's name?"

"Morrigan Mayfair."

"Morrigan, never heard of the name Morrigan. That a saint's name, Morrigan?"

"Spell it for him, Mary Jane," the mother said, her voice very low, from inside the enclosure. "Two *r*'s, Doctor."

"I can spell it, honey," he said. He sang out the letters for her final approval.

"Now, I didn't get a weight. . . ."

"Eight pounds nine ounces," said Granny, who was walking the baby back and forth, patting it as it lay on her shoulder. "I weighed it on the kitchen scale. Height, regular!"

He shook his head again. He quickly filled in the rest,

433

made a hasty copy on the second form. What was the point of saying anything further to them?

A glimmer of lightning flashed in all the gables, north and south and east and west, and then left the big room in a cozy, shadowy darkness. The rain teemed softly on the roof.

"Okay, I'm leaving you this copy," he said, putting the certificate in Mary Jane's hand, "and I'm taking this one to mail it into the parish from my office. In a couple of weeks you'll get the official registration of your baby. Now, you should go ahead and try to nurse that child a little, you don't have any milk yet, but what you have is colostrum and that . . ."

"I told her all that, Dr. Jack," said Granny. "She'll nurse the baby soon as you leave, she's a shy little thing."

"Come on, Doctor," said Mary Jane, "I'll drive you back."

"Damn, I wish there was another way to get home from here," he said.

"Well, if I had a broom, we'd fly, now, wouldn't we?" asked Mary Jane, gesturing for him to come on as she started her thin-legged march to the stairway, loose sandals clopping on the boards.

The mother laughed softly to herself, a girl's giggle. She looked downright normal for a moment, with a bit of rosy color in her cheeks. Those breasts were about to burst. He hoped that baby wasn't a snooty little taster and lip-smacker. When you got right down to it, it was impossible to tell which of these young women was the prettiest.

He lifted the netting and stepped up again to the bed. The water was oozing out of his shoes, just look at it, but what could he do about it? It was running down the inside of his shirt, too.

"You feel all right, don't you, honey?" he asked.

"Yes, I do," she said. She had the jug of milk in her arms. She'd been drinking it in big gulps. Well, why not? But she sure as hell didn't need it. She threw him a bright schoolgirl smile, just about the brightest he'd ever seen, showing a row of white teeth, and just a sprinkle of freckles on her nose. Yes, pint-sized, but just about the prettiest red-head he'd ever laid eyes on.

"Come on, Doctor," Mary Jane positively shouted at him. "Mona's got to get her rest, and that baby's going to start yowling. 'Bye now, Morrigan, 'bye, Mona, 'bye, Granny."

Then Mary Jane was dragging him right through the attic, only stopping to slap on her cowboy hat, which she had apparently taken off when they'd come in. Water poured off the brim of it.

"Hush, now, hush," said Granny to the baby. "Mary Jane, you hurry now. This baby's getting fussy."

He was about to say they ought to put that baby in its mother's arms, but Mary Jane would have pushed him down the steps if he hadn't gone. She was all but chasing him, sticking her little breasts against his back. Breasts, breasts, breasts. Thank God his field was geriatrics, he could never have taken all this, teenage mothers in flimsy shirts, girls talking at you with both nipples, damned outrageous, that's what it was.

"Doctor, I'm going to pay you five hundred dollars for this visit," she said in his ear, touching it with her bubble-gum lips, "because I know what it means to come out on an afternoon like this, and you are such a nice, agreeable . . ."

"Yeah, and when will I see that money, Mary Jane Mayfair?" he asked, just cranky enough to speak his mind after all this. Girls her age. And just what was she likely to do if he turned around and decided to cop a feel of what was in that lace dress that she had just so obligingly mashed up against him? He ought to bill her for a new pair of shoes, he thought, just look at these shoes, and she could get those rich relatives in New Orleans to pay for it.

Oh, now wait a minute now. If that little girl upstairs was one of those rich Mayfairs come down here to—

"Now don't you worry about a thing," Mary Jane sang out, "you didn't deliver the package, you just signed for it."

"What are you talking about?"

"And now we have to get back in that boat!"

She hurried on to the head of the lower steps, and he

sloshed and padded right behind her. Well, the house didn't tilt that much, he figured, once you were inside of it. *Clickety, clickety, clickety*, there it was again. Guess you could get used to a tilted house, but the very idea of living in a place that was half flooded was perfectly—

The lightning let go with a flash like midday, and the hall came to life, wallpaper, ceilings, and transoms above the doors, and the old chandelier dripping dead cords from two sockets.

That's what it was! A computer. He'd seen her in the split second of white light—in the back room—a very tall woman bent over the machine, fingers flying as she typed, hair red as the mother up in the bed, and twice as long, and a song coming from her as she worked, as if she was mumbling aloud whatever she was composing on the keyboard.

The darkness closed down around her and her glowing screen and a gooseneck lamp making a puddle of yellow light on her fluttering fingers.

Clickety, clickety, clickety!

Then the thunder went off with the loudest boom he'd ever heard, rattling every piece of glass left in the house. Mary Jane's hands flew to her ears. The tall young thing at the computer screamed and jumped up out of her chair, and the lights in the house went out, complete and entire, pitching them all into deep, dull afternoon gloom that might as well have been evening.

The tall beauty was screaming her head off. She was taller than he was!

"Shhhh, shhhh, Morrigan, stop!" shouted Mary Jane, running towards her. "It's just the lightning knocked out the power! It will go back on again!"

"But it's dead, it's gone dead!" the young girl cried, and then, turning, she looked down and saw Dr. Jack, and for one moment he thought he was losing his faculties. It was the mother's head he saw way up there on this girl's neck, same freckles, red hair, white teeth, green eyes. Good grief, like somebody had just pulled it right off the mother and plunked it down on this creature's neck, and look at the size of this beanpole! They couldn't be twins, these two. He himself was five foot ten, and this long, tall drink of water was at least a foot taller than that. She wasn't wearing anything but a big white shirt, just like the mother, and her soft white legs just went on forever and ever. Must have been sisters. Had to be.

"Whoa!" she said, staring down at him and then marching towards him, bare feet on the bare wood, though Mary Jane tried to stop her.

"Now you go back and sit down," said Mary Jane, "the lights will be on in a jiffy."

"You're a man," said the tall young woman, who was really a girl, no older than the pint-sized mother in the bed, or Mary Jane herself. She stood right in front of the doctor, scowling at him with red eyebrows, her green eyes bigger than those of the little one upstairs, with big curling lashes. "You are a man, aren't you?"

"I told you, this is the doctor," said Mary Jane, "come to fill out the birth certificate for the baby. Now, Dr. Jack, this is Morrigan, this is the baby's aunt, now Morrigan, this is Dr. Jack, sit down now, Morrigan! Let this doctor get about his business. Let's go, Doctor."

"Don't get so theatrical, Mary Jane," declared the beanpole girl, with a great spreading smile. She rubbed her long, silky-looking white hands together. Her voice sounded exactly like that of the little mother upstairs. Same well-bred voice. "You have to forgive me, Dr. Jack, my manners aren't what they should be yet, I'm still a little rough all over at the edges, trying to ingest a little more information, perhaps, than God ever intended for anyone of my ilk, but then we have so many different problems which we have to solve, for example, now that we have the birth certificate, we do have that, do we not, Mary Jane, that is what you were trying to make plain to me when I so rudely interrupted you, was it not, what about the baptism of this baby, for if memory serves me right, the legacy makes quite a point of the matter that the baby must be baptized Catholic. Indeed, it seems to me that in some of these documents which I've just accessed and only skimmed, that baptism is a more important point actually than legal registration."

"What *are* you talking about?" asked Dr. Jack. "And where in God's name did they vaccinate you, RCA Victor?"

437

She let out a pretty peal of laughter, clapping both of her hands together, very loudly, her red hair rippling and shaking out from her shoulders as she shook her head.

"Doctor, what are *you* talking about!" she said. "How old are you? You're a fairly good-sized man, aren't you, let me see, I estimate you are sixty-seven years old, am I right? May I see your glasses?"

She snatched them off his nose before he could protest, peering through them into his face. He was flabbergasted; he was also sixty-eight. She became a fragrant blur before his naked eyes.

"Oh, now this is major, really, look at this," she said. And quickly put the glasses back on the bridge of his nose with perfect aim, flaring into detail again, with plump little cheeks and a cupid's bow of a mouth just about as perfect as he'd ever seen. "Yes, it makes everything just a fraction bigger, doesn't it, and to think this is but one of the more common everyday inventions I'm likely to encounter within the first few hours of life, eyeglasses, spectacles, am I correct? Eyeglasses, microwave oven, clip-on earrings, telephone, NEC MultiSync 5D computer monitor. It would seem to me that later on, at a time of reflection on all that's taken place, one ought to be able to discern a certain poetry in the list of those objects which were encountered first, especially if we are right that nothing in life is purely random, that things only have the appearance from different vantage points of being random and that ultimately as we better calibrate all our tools of observation, we'll come to understand that even the inventions encountered on two stories of an abandoned and distressed house, do cluster together to form a statement about the occupants that is far more profound than anyone would suppose at first thought. What do *you* think!"

Now it was his turn to let out the peal of laughter. He slapped his leg. "Honey, I don't know what I think about that, but I sure do like the style with which you say it!" he declared. "What did you say your name was, you're the one that baby's named after, Morrigan, don't tell me you're a Mayfair, too."

438

"Oh yes, sir, absolutely, Morrigan Mayfair!" she said, throwing up her arms like a cheerleader.

There was a glimmer, then a faint purring sound, and on came the lights, and the computer behind them in the room began to make its grinding, winding, start-up noises.

"Ooops, there we go!" she said, red hair flying about her shoulders. "Back on line with Mayfair and Mayfair, until such time as Mother Nature sees fit to humble all of us, regardless of how well we are equipped, configured, programmed, and installed. In other words, until lightning strikes again!"

She dashed to the chair before the desk, took up her place before the screen, and began typing again, just as if she'd completely forgotten he was standing there.

Granny shouted from upstairs, "Mary Jane, go on, this baby's hungry!"

Mary Jane pulled on his sleeve.

"Now wait just a minute," he said. But he had lost the amazing young woman, totally and completely, he realized that, just as he realized that she was purely naked under the white shirt, and that the light of her gooseneck lamp was shining right on her breast and her flat belly and her naked thighs. Didn't look like she had any panties on, either. And those long bare feet, what big bare feet. Was it safe to be typing on a computer in a lightning storm in your bare feet? Her red hair just flooded down to the seat of the chair.

Granny shouted from above.

"Mary Jane, you got to get this baby back by five o'clock!"

"I'm going, I'm going, Dr. Jack, come on!"

" 'Bye there, Dr. Jack!" shouted the beanpole beauty, suddenly waving at him with her right hand, which was at the end of an amazingly long arm, without even taking her eyes off the computer.

Mary Jane rushed past him and jumped in the boat. "You coming or not?" she said. "I'm pulling out, I got things to do, you want to be stuck here?"

"Get that baby *where* by five o'clock?" he demanded, coming to his senses, and thinking about what that old woman had just said. "You're not taking that baby out again to be baptized!"

"Hurry up, Mary Jane!"

"Anchors aweigh!" Mary Jane screamed, pushing the pole at the steps.

"Wait a minute!"

He took the leap, splashing into the pirogue as it rocked against the balusters and then the wall. "All right, all right. Just slow down, will you? Get me to the landing without dumping me into the swamp, would you do that, please?"

Clickety, clickety, clickety.

The rain had slacked up a bit, praise God. And a little bit of sun was even breaking through the heavy gray clouds just enough to shine on the drops!

"Now, here, Doctor, you take this," said Mary Jane, as he climbed into the car. It was a fat envelope just full of bills, and, he saw by the way she ruffled them with her thumb, all new twenties. He eyeballed that to be a thousand. She slammed the door and ran around to the other side.

"Now that's just too much money, Mary Jane," he said, but he was thinking Weed Eater, lawn mower, brand-new electric shrub clippers, *and* Sony color TV, and there wasn't a reason in the world to declare this on his taxes.

"Oh, shut up, you keep it!" she said. "Coming out on a day like this, you earned it." There went her skirt, back down to her thighs. But she couldn't hold a candle to that flaming darling upstairs, and what would it be like to get his hands on something like that, just for five minutes, something that young and that sleek and fresh and that beautiful, with those long long legs! Hush now, you old fool, you're going to give yourself a heart attack.

Mary Jane threw the car into reverse, wheels whirring in the wet shells of the road, and then made a dangerous one-hundred-eighty-degree turn and headed off over the familiar potholes.

He looked back at the house one more time, the big hulk of rotting columns and wood towering over the cypresses, with the duckweed muck lapping at its half-sunk windows, and then at the road ahead. Boy, he was glad to get out of here.

And when he got home and his little wife Eileen said, "What all did you see out there at Fontevrault, Jack?" what was he going to tell her? Not about the three prettiest young women he'd ever seen under one roof, that's for sure. And not about this wad of twenty-dollar bills in his pocket, either.

Twenty-eight

WE INVENTED A human identity for ourselves.

We "became" an ancient tribe called the Picts, tall because we came from the northern countries where men grow tall, and we were eager to live in peace with those who would not disturb us.

Of course, we had to go about this very gradually. Word went out before we did. There was a waiting period at first, during which no strangers were admitted to the glen; then occasional travelers were let through, and from these we gleaned valuable knowledge. Then we ventured out, declaring ourselves to be the Picts and offering enlightened friendship to those whom we encountered.

Over time, in spite of the legend of the Taltos, which was always around, and gained some new impetus every time some poor Taltos was captured, we succeeded with this ruse. And our security improved not through battlements, but through our slow integration with human beings.

We were the proud and reclusive Clan of Donnelaith, but others would receive hospitality at our brochs. We did not speak of our gods much. We did not encourage questions about our private ways or our children.

But we lived as noblemen; we held the concepts of honor, and pride in our homeland.

It began to work rather beautifully. And with the doors of the glen open finally, new learning came to us for the first time directly from outside elements. We quickly learned to sew, to weave, and weaving proved a trap for the obsessive

Taltos. Men, women, all of us would weave. We would weave for days and nights on end. We could not stop ourselves.

The only remedy was to pull away and turn to some other new craft and master it. Working with metals. We learned this. And though we never did more than forge a few coins and make arrowheads, we nevertheless went mad for a while with it.

Writing also had come to us. Other peoples had come to the shores of Britain, and unlike the uncouth warriors who had destroyed our world of the plain, these people wrote things on stone, on tablets, and on sheepskin especially worked by them to be permanent and beautiful to see and touch.

The writing on these stones, tablets, and scrolls of vellum was Greek and Latin! And we learnt it from our slaves as soon as the first marvelous connection between symbol and word was made. And then later from the traveling scholars who came into the valley.

Indeed, it became an obsession to many of us, myself in particular, and we read and wrote incessantly, translating our own tongue, which is far older than any in Britain, into written words. We made a script called Ogham, and it formed our secret writings. You can see this script on many a stone in the north of Scotland, but no one today can decipher it.

Our culture, the name we took, that of the Pictish people, and our art and our writing continue in modern times to be a complete mystery. You'll see the reason for that soon—for the loss of the Pict culture.

As a practical point, I wonder sometimes what became of those dictionaries which I so laboriously completed, working months on end without stopping except to collapse for a few hours of sleep or to send out for food.

They were hidden away in the souterrains or earth houses which we built beneath the floor of the glen, the ultimate hiding place in case humans ever swept down on us again. Also hidden were many of the manuscripts in Greek and Latin from which I studied in those early days.

Another great trap for us, something which could entrance us, was mathematics, and some of the books that came into our possession were concerned with theorems of geometry which set us talking for days and days, and drawing triangles in the mud.

The point is that these were exciting times for us. The subterfuge gave us a perfect access to new developments. And though we had all the time to watch and chastise the foolish young Taltos that they weren't to confide in the newcomers or fall in love with their men and women, we generally came to know much of the Romans who had come into Britain, and to realize that these Romans had punished the Celtic barbarians who had inflicted such atrocities on us.

Indeed, these Romans put no faith in the local superstitions about the Taltos. They spoke of a civilized world, vast and full of great cities.

But we feared the Romans as well. For though they built magnificent buildings, the likes of which we'd never seen, they were more skilled at war than the others. We heard lots of stories of their victories. Indeed, they had refined the art of war and made it even more successful at destroying lives. We kept to the remote glen. We never wanted to meet them in battle.

More and more traders brought their books to us, their scrolls of vellum, and I read avidly their philosophers, their playwrights, their poets, their satirists, and their rhetoricians.

Of course, no one of us could grasp the actual quality of their lives, the ambience, to use the modern word, their national soul, their character. But we were learning. We knew now that all men were not barbarians. Indeed, this was the very word the Romans used for the tribes that were filling Britain from all sides, tribes which they had come here to subdue in the name of a mighty empire.

The Romans, by the way, never did reach our glen, though for two hundred years they campaigned in Britain. The Roman Tacitus wrote the story of Agricola's early campaign which reached Scotland. In the next century the Antonine Wall was built, a marvel to the barbarian tribes who resisted Rome, and very near it for forty-five miles the

444

Military Way, a great road on which not only the soldiers passed, but traders bringing all manner of goods from the sea, and tantalizing evidence of other civilizations.

Finally the Roman Emperor himself, Septimus Severus, came to Britain to subdue the Scottish tribes, but even he never penetrated our strongholds.

For many years after that the Romans remained, providing much strange booty for our little nation.

By the time they withdrew from those lands, and gave them up to the barbarians at last, we were no longer really a hidden people. Hundreds of human beings had settled in our valley, paying homage to us as the lords, building their smaller brochs around our larger ones, and seeing us as a great, mysterious, but altogether human family of rulers.

It was not easy always to maintain this ruse. But nowhere was the life of the times more suited to it. Other clans were springing up in their remote strongholds. We were not a country of cities, but of small feudal holdings. Though our height and our refusal to intermarry were deemed unusual, we were in every other way completely acceptable.

Of course the key was never, never to let the outsiders see the birth ritual. And in this the Little People, needing our protection from time to time, became our sentries.

When we chose to make the circle amid the stones, all lesser clans of Donnelaith were told that our priests could only preside over our family rites in the strictest privacy.

And as we grew bolder, we let the others come, but only in far-reaching outer circles. Never could they see what the priests did in the very heart of the assembly. Never did they see the birth. They imagined it was only some vague worship of sky and sun and wind and moon and stars. And so they called us a family of magicians.

Of course, all this depended upon considerable peaceful cooperation with those who lived in the glen, and this remained stable for centuries.

In sum, we passed for people, in the midst of people. And other Taltos partook of our subterfuge, declaring themselves Picts, learning our writing and taking it, with our styles of building and ornament, to their strongholds. All

Taltos who truly wanted to survive lived in this way, fooling human beings.

Only the wild Taltos continued to flash about in the forests, risking everything. But even they knew the Ogham script and our many symbols.

For example, if a lone Taltos lived in the forest, he might carve a symbol on a tree to let other Taltos know that he was there, a symbol without meaning for human beings. One Taltos seeing another in an inn might approach and offer him some gift, which was in fact a brooch or pin with our emblems.

A fine example of this is the bronze pin with a human face, discovered many centuries later by modern peoples in Sutherland. Humans do not realize, when they write about this pin, that it is a picture of an infant Taltos emerging from the womb, its head huge, its small arms still folded, though ready to unfold and grow, rather like the wings of a new butterfly.

Other symbols we carved into rock, at the mouths of caves or upon our sacred stones, represented fanciful conceptions of the animals of the lost land of tropical abundance. Others had purely personal meanings. Pictures of us as fierce warriors were deceptive, and skillfully made to actually show people meeting in peace, or so we imagined.

The art of the Picts is the common name given to all of this. And that tribe has become the great mystery of Britain.

What was our worst fear? The worst threat, so to speak? Enough time had passed that we did not fear human beings who really knew anything about us. But the Little People knew and the Little People longed to breed with us, and though they needed us, to protect them, they still occasionally caused us trouble.

But the true threats to our peace came from witches. Witches—those singular humans who caught our scents, and could somehow breed with us, or were the descendants of those who had bred with us. For the witches—who were always very rare, of course—passed on, from mother to daughter and father to son, the legends of our kind, and the lovely, mad notion that if they could ever couple with us, they could make monsters of size and beauty who might never die. And other fanciful propositions inevitably grew up around this idea—that if they drank the blood of the Taltos, the witches could become immortal. That if they killed us, with the proper words and the proper curses, they could take our power.

And the most awful aspect of all this, the only real, true part of it, was that the witches could often tell on sight we were not mere tall humans, but real Taltos.

We kept them out of the glen. And when traveling abroad, we took great pains to avoid the village witch, or the sorcerer who lived in the wood. But they of course had reason to fear us too, for we too knew them infallibly on sight and, being very clever and very rich, we could make plenty of trouble for them.

But when a witch was about, it was a dangerous game. And all that was required to make it worse was one clever or ambitious witch determined to find the true Taltos of the Highlands among the tall clans that dwelt there.

And now and then there was the worst challenge, a powerful spellbinding witch capable of luring Taltos out of their dwellings, of wrapping them up in charms and music, and drawing them to her rituals.

Occasionally there would be talk of a Taltos found elsewhere. There would be talk of hybrid births; there would be whispers of witches and Little People and magic.

By and large, we were safe in our strongholds.

The glen of Donnelaith was now known to the world. And as the other tribes squabbled with one another, our valley was left in peace, not because people feared that monsters dwelt there, but only because it was the stronghold of respectable noblemen.

It was in those years a grand life, but a life with a lie at its core. And many a young Taltos could not endure it. Off he would go into the world, and never return. And sometimes hybrid Taltos came to us who knew nothing of who or what had made them.

Very gradually, over time, a rather foolish thing happened. Some of us even intermarried with human beings.

It would happen in this way. One of our men would go on a long pilgrimage, perhaps, and come upon a lone witch in a dark wood with whom he fell in love, a witch who could bear his offspring without difficulty. He would love this witch; she would love him; and being a ragged poor creature, she would throw herself upon his mercy. He would bring her home; she might at some point in the distant future bear him another child before she died. And some of these hybrids married other hybrids.

Sometimes, too, a beautiful female Taltos would fall in love with a human man, and forsake everything for him. They might be together for years before she would bear, but then a hybrid would be born, and this would unite the little family even more closely, for the father saw his likeness in the child, and laid claim to its loyalty, and it of course was a Taltos.

So that is how the human blood in us was increased. And how our blood came into the human Clan of Donnelaith that eventually survived us.

Let me pass over in silence the sadness we often felt, the emotions we evinced at our secret rituals. Let me not try to describe our long conversations, pondering the meaning of this world, and why we had to live among humans. You are both outcasts now. You know it. And if God is merciful and you really don't, well, then, you can still imagine it.

What is left of the glen today?

Where are the countless brochs and wheelhouses which we built? Where are our stones with their curious writing and strange serpentine figures? What became of the Pictish rulers of that time, who sat so tall on their horses, and impressed the Romans so much with their gentle manner?

As you know, what is left at Donnelaith is this: a quaint inn, a ruined castle, an immense excavation that is slowly revealing a giant cathedral, tales of witchcraft and woe, of earls who died untimely deaths, and of a strange family, gone through Europe to America, carrying with them an evil strain in the blood, a potential to give birth to babies or monsters, an evil strain evidenced by the glow of witches' gifts, a family wooed for that blood and those gifts by Lasher—a wily and unforgiving ghost of one of *our* people.

How were the Picts of Donnelaith destroyed? Why did

they fall as surely as the people of the lost land and the people of the plain? What happened to them?

It was not the Britons, the Angles, or the Scots who conquered us. It was not the Saxons or the Irish, or the German tribes who invaded the island. They were far too busy destroying each other.

On the contrary, we were destroyed by men as gentle as ourselves, with rules as strict as our own, and dreams as lovely as our dreams. The leader they followed, the god they worshiped, the savior in whom they believed was the Lord Jesus Christ. He was our undoing.

It was Christ himself who brought an end to five hundred years of prosperity. It was his gentle Irish monks who brought about our downfall.

Can you see how it might happen?

Can you see how vulnerable we were, we, who in the solitude of our stone towers would play at weaving and writing like little children, who would hum or sing all day long for the love of it? We, who believed in love and in the Good God, and refused to hold death sacrosanct?

What was the pure message of the early Christians? Of both the Roman monks and the Celtic monks who came to our shores to preach the new religion? What is the pure message, even today, of those cults which would consecrate themselves anew to Christ and his teachings?

Love, the very thing we believed in!

Forgiveness, the very thing we thought practical. Humility, the virtue we believed, even in our pride, to be far more noble than the raging hubris of those who warred endlessly upon others. Goodness of heart, kindness, the joy of the just—our old values. And what did the Christians condemn? The flesh, the very thing that had always been our downfall! The sins of the flesh, which had caused us to become monsters in the eyes of humans, copulating in great ceremonial circles and bringing forth full-grown offspring.

Oh, we were ripe for it. Oh, it was made for us!

And the trick, the sublime trick, was that at its core Christianity not only embraced all this, but managed somehow to sacralize death and at the same time redeem that sacralization.

Follow my logic. Christ's death had not come in battle, the death of the warrior with the sword in his hand; it had been a humble sacrifice, an execution which could not be avenged, a total surrender on the part of the Godman to save his human children! But it was death, and it was everything!

Oh, it was magnificent! No other religion could have had a chance with us. We detested pantheons of barbarian gods. We laughed at the gods of the Greeks and Romans. The gods of Sumer or India we would have found just as alien and distasteful. But this Christ, why, my God, he was the ideal of every Taltos!

And though he had not sprung full-grown from his mother's womb, he had nevertheless been born of a virgin, which was just as miraculous! Indeed, the birth of Christ was just as important as his submissive crucifixion! It was our way, it was the triumph of our way! It was the God to whom we could give ourselves without reservation!

Lastly, let me add the *pièce de résistance*. These Christians, too, had been once hunted and persecuted and threatened with annihilation. Diocletian, the Roman emperor, had subjected them to these things. And refugees came seeking shelter in our glen. We gave it to them.

And the Christians won our hearts. When we spoke to them, we came to believe that possibly the world was changing. We believed that a new age had dawned and that our elevation and restoration were now at least conceivable.

The final seduction was simple.

A lone monk came into the glen for refuge. He had been chased thither by ragged wandering pagans and begged shelter. Of course we would never refuse such a person, and I brought him into my own broch and into my own chambers, to pick his brains about the outside world, as I hadn't ventured out in a while.

This was the mid-sixth century after Christ, though I didn't know it. If you would picture us then, see men and women in long, rather simple robes trimmed in fur, embroidered with gold and jewels; see the men with their hair trimmed above the shoulders. Their belts are thick, and their swords are always near at hand. The women cover their hair with silk veils beneath simple gold tiaras. See our towers very bare, yet warm and snug, and filled with skins and comfortable chairs, and raging fires to keep us warm. See us as tall, of course, all of us tall.

And see me in my broch alone with this little yellow-haired monk in brown robes, eagerly accepting the good wine I offered him.

He carried with him a great bundle which he was eager to preserve, he said, and first off, he begged me that I give him a guard to escort him home to the island of Iona in safety.

There had been three in his party originally, but brigands had murdered the other two, and now he was wretchedly alone, dependent upon the goodwill of others, and must get his precious bundle to Iona, or lose something more valuable than his own life.

I promised to see that he reached Iona safely. Then he introduced himself as Brother Ninian, named for the earlier saint, Bishop Ninian, who had converted many pagans at his chapel or monastery, or whatever it was, at Whittern. This bishop had already converted a few wild Taltos.

Young Ninian, a very personable and beautiful Irish Celt, then laid out his invaluable bundle and revealed its contents.

Now, I had seen many books in my time, Roman scrolls and the codex, which was now the popular form. I knew Latin. I knew Greek. I had even seen some very small books called *cathachs* which Christians wore as talismans when they rode into battle. I had been intrigued by the few fragments of Christian writing I had beheld, but I was in no way prepared for the treasure which Ninian revealed to me.

It was a magnificent altar book that he carried with him, a great illustrated and decorated account of the Four Gospels. Its front cover was decorated with gold and jewels, it was bound in silk, and its pages were painted with spectacular little pictures.

At once I fell on this book and virtually devoured it. I began to read the Latin aloud, and though there were some irregularities in it, in the main I understood it, and began to run with the story like someone possessed—nothing very extraordinary, of course, for a Taltos. It felt like singing.

But as I turned the vellum pages, I marveled not only at the tale which was being told to me, but also at the incredible drawings of fanciful beasts and of little figures. It was an art which I loved truly, from having done my own similar form of it.

Indeed, it was very like much art of that time in the islands. Later ages would say it was crude, but then come to love the complexity and ingenuity of it.

Now, to understand the effect of the gospels themselves, you have to remind yourself of how very different they were from any literature which had come before them. I didn't include the Torah of the Hebrews, because I didn't know it, but the gospels are even different from that.

They were different from everything! First off, they concerned this one man, Jesus, and how he had taught love and peace and been hounded, persecuted, tormented, and then crucified. A confounding story! I couldn't help but wonder what the Greeks and the Romans thought of it. And the man had been a humble person, with only the most tenuous of connections to ancient kings, that was obvious. Unlike any god of whom I'd ever heard, this Jesus had told his followers all sorts of things which they had been charged to write down and teach to all nations.

To be born again in spirit was the essence of the religion. To become simple, humble, meek, loving, that was the gist of it.

Now step back a moment and see the whole picture. Not only was this god amazing and this story amazing; the whole question of the relationship of the tale to writing was amazing.

As you can tell from this narrative, the one thing we had once shared with our barbarian neighbors was that we distrusted writing. Memory was sacred to us, and we thought that writing was not good for it. We knew how to read and write. But we still distrusted it. And here was this humble god who quoted from the sacred book of the Hebrews, connected himself with its innumerable prophecies concerning a messiah, and then charged his followers to *write about him*.

But long before I'd finished the last gospel, pacing, reading aloud, holding the big altar book in two arms, with fingers curled over the tops of the pages, I came to love this Jesus for the strange things that he said, the way he contradicted himself, and his patience with those who killed him. As for his resurrection, my first conclusion was that he was as long-lived as were we—the Taltos. And that he had put one over on his followers because they were mere humans.

We had to do such tricks all the time, to assume different identities when speaking to human neighbors, so that they would become confused and fail to realize that we were living for centuries.

But I soon realized through Ninian's zealous instructions—and he was a joyful and ecstatic monk—that Christ had in fact risen from the dead. And truly ascended into heaven.

I saw in something of a mystical flash the whole picture—this god of love, martyred for love, and the radical nature of his message. In a mad way, the thing gripped me because it was so utterly unbelievable. Indeed, the entire combination of elements was cumbersome and preposterous.

And another fact—all Christians believed the world would end soon. And apparently—this emerged slowly from my conversations with Ninian—they always had! But preparing for this end of the world was also the essence of the religion. And the fact that the world hadn't ended yet discouraged nobody.

Ninian spoke feverishly of the growth of the church since Christ's time, some five hundred years before, of how Joseph of Arimathea, his dear friend, and Mary Magdalene, who had bathed his feet and dried them with her own hair, had come to England in the southern part, and founded a church on a sacred hill in Somerset. The chalice from Christ's last supper had been brought to that spot, and indeed a great spring flowed bloodred year-round from the magic presence of Christ's blood having been poured into it. And the staff of Joseph, having been put into the ground of Wearyall Hill, had grown into a hawthorn which had never ceased to flower.

I wanted to go there at once, to see the sacred place where Our Lord's own disciples had set foot on our own island.

"Oh, but please," cried Ninian, "my good-hearted Ashlar, you've promised to take me home to my monastery on Iona."

There the abbot, Father Columba, was expecting him. Many books such as this were being made in monasteries all over the world, and this copy was most important for study at Iona.

I had to meet this Columba. He sounded as strange as Jesus Christ! Perhaps you know the story. Michael, probably you know it.

This is how Ninian described Columba. Columba was born of a rich family, and might have in the scheme of things become King of Tara. Instead he became a priest and founded many Christian monasteries. But then he got into a battle with Finnian, another holy man, over whether or not he, Columba, had had a right to make a copy of the Psalter of St. Jerome, another holy book, which Finnian had brought to Ireland. A quarrel over the possession of the book? The right to copy?

It had led to blows. Three thousand men had died as a result of this dispute, and Columba had been blamed for it. He had accepted this judgment, and off he had gone to Iona, very near our coast, in order to convert *us*, the Picts, to Christianity. It was his plan to save three thousand pagan souls to exactly make up for the three thousand men who had died as the result of his quarrel.

I forget who got the copy of the Psalter.

But Columba was now at Iona and, from there, was sending missionaries everywhere. Beautiful books such as this were being made in these Christian compounds, and all were invited into this new faith. Indeed, Christ's church was for the salvation of everyone!

And it soon became clear that though Columba and many missionary priests and monks like him had been kings or persons of royal blood, the rule of the monasteries was extraordinarily severe, demanding constant mortification of the flesh and self-sacrifice.

For example, if a monk spilled milk while helping to serve at community meals, he must go into the chapel during the singing of Psalms and lie on his face, prostrate, until twelve of them had been completely finished. Monks were beaten when they broke their vows of silence. Yet nothing could restrain the rich and powerful of the earth from flocking into these monasteries.

I was dumbfounded. How could a priest who believed in Christ get into a war in which three thousand died! Why would the sons of kings submit to being lashed for common offenses? But, ah, it had a simple potency to it, a captivating logic.

I set out with Ninian and two of my recent sons to go to Iona. Of course we kept up our masquerade as human beings. Ninian thought we were human beings.

But as soon as I arrived at Iona, I became further spellbound by the monastery itself and the personality of Columba.

It was a magnificent island, forested and green, with splendid views from its cliffs, where the openness and cleanness of the sea brought peace to the soul immediately.

In fact, a wondrous calm descended upon me. It was as if I had found again the lost land, only now the dominant themes were penance and austerity. But the harmony was there, the faith in the sheer goodness of existence.

Now the monastery was Celtic, and not at all like the Benedictine monasteries which later covered Europe. It was made of a great circular enclosure—the vallum, as it was called—which suggested a fort, and the monks lived in small, simple huts, some no more than ten feet wide inside. The church itself was not grand, but a humble wooden structure.

But never was a complex of buildings more in keeping with its natural setting. It was a place to listen quietly to the birds, to walk, to think, to pray, to talk with the enchanting and friendly and truly gracious Columba. This man had royal blood; I had long been a king. Ours was the north country of Ireland and Scotland; we knew each other; and something in me touched the saint as well—the sincerity of the Taltos, the foolish way of coming directly to the point, an easy outpouring of enthusiasm.

Columba soon convinced me that the harsh monastic life and the mortification of the flesh were the keys to the love which Christianity demanded of a man. This love was not a sensual thing. This love was spiritually elevated beyond expression through the body.

He longed to convert my entire tribe, or my clan. He longed to see me an ordained priest among my people.

"But you don't know what you're saying," I said. And then, binding him under the seal of the confessional—that is, to eternal confidentiality—I told him the tale of my long life, of our secret and miraculous way of giving birth, of how it seemed that many of us seemed capable of living an endless life of eternal youth, unless accident or disaster or some specific pestilence destroyed us.

Some things I did not tell. I did not tell that I had once been the leader of the great circle dances at Stonehenge.

But all the rest I told, even of the lost land, and how we had lived in our glen for so many hundreds of years, passing from secrecy to a masquerade as human beings.

All this he listened to with great fascination. Then he said an amazing thing. "Can you prove these things to me?"

I realized that I could not. The only way any Taltos can prove he is a Taltos is by coupling with another and producing the offspring.

"No," I said, "but look well at us. Look at our height."

This he dismissed; there were tall men in the world. "People have for years known of your clan; you are King Ashlar of Donnelaith, and they know you are a good ruler. If you believe these things about yourself, it is because the devil has put them into your imagination. Forget them. Proceed to do what God wants you to do."

"Ask Ninian, the whole tribe is of this height."

But he'd heard of that, very tall Picts in the Highlands. It seems my own ruse was working!

"Ashlar," he said, "I've no doubt of your goodness. Once

456

again, I counsel you to disregard these illusions as coming from the devil."

Finally I agreed, for one reason. I felt that it made no difference whether he believed me or not about my past. What mattered was that he had recognized a soul in me.

Michael, you know that this was a great point in Lasher's tale—that, alive in the time of Henry, he wanted to believe that he had a soul, that he would not accept that he could not be a priest of God the same as a human.

I know this awful dilemma. All who are outsiders in their own way know it. Whether we talk of legitimacy, of a soul, of citizenship, or of brotherhood or sisterhood, it is all the same, we long to be seen as true individuals, as inherently valuable inside as any other.

This I longed for too, and I made the terrible error of accepting Columba's advice. I forgot what I knew to be true.

There on Iona, I was received into the Christian faith. I was baptized, and so were my sons. Another baptism was to follow, but for me and my sons it was only ceremonial. On that island, removed from the mists of the Highlands, we became Christian Taltos.

I spent many days at the monastery. I read all the books that were in it; I was charmed by the pictures, and very soon took to making copies of them. With official permission, of course. I copied a psalter, then a gospel, amazing the monks with my typical Taltos obsessive behavior. I drew strange beasts in brilliant colors by the hour. I made the priests laugh sometimes with bits of poetry I copied out. I pleased them with my good Greek and Latin.

What community had ever been more like the Taltos? Monk children is what they seemed, surrendering the entire concept of sophisticated adulthood to serve the abbot as their lord, and thereby serve their Lord Himself, the Crucified Christ who had died for them.

These were happy, happy days.

Gradually I began to see what many a heathen prince had come to see in Christianity: absolute redemption of everything! All my suffering made sense in light of the woes of the world and Christ's mission to save us from sin. All the disasters I'd witnessed had done nothing but improve my soul and school it for this moment. My monstrousness, indeed the monstrousness of all the Taltos, would be accepted by this church, surely, for all were welcome into it, regardless of race, it was an utterly open faith, and we could submit as well as any human being to the baptism of water and the spirit, to the vows of poverty, chastity, obedience.

The stringent rules, which bound even laymen to purity and restraint, would help us to control our terrible urge to procreate, our terrible weaknesses for dance and for music. And the music we would not lose; we would, within the constraints of the monastic life—which for me at this point was synonymous with the Christian life—sing our greatest and most joyful songs ever!

In sum, if this church accepted us, if it embraced us, all our past and future sufferings would have meaning. Our true loving nature would be allowed to flower. No subterfuge would be required any longer. The church would not let the old rituals be forced upon us. And those who dreaded the birthing now, as I did, out of age and experience and seeing so many young die, could consecrate themselves to God in chastity.

It was perfect!

At once, with a small escort of monks, I returned to the glen of Donnelaith and drew all my people together. We must pledge our allegiance to Christ, I told them, and I told them why, in long rippling speeches, not too fast for my human companions to understand, talking passionately of the peace and harmony that would be restored to us.

I also spoke of the Christian belief in the end of the world. Very soon all this horror would be over! And then I spoke of heaven, which I imagined to be like the lost land, except that no one would want to make love, everyone would be singing with the choirs of angels.

We must all now confess our sins and prepare to be baptized. For a thousand years I had been the leader, and all must follow me. What greater guidance could I give my people?

I stood back at the end of this speech. The monks were overcome with emotion. So were the hundreds of Taltos gathered in the glen around me.

At once began the heated discussions for which we were known—all in the human Art of the Tongue—the endless debates and telling of little tales and relating of this to that, and drawing memories into it where they seemed to pertain, and beneath it all the great theme: we could embrace Christ. He was the Good God! He was our God. The souls of the others were as open to Christ as was my soul.

A great many at once declared their faith. Others spent the afternoon, the evening, and the night examining the books I'd brought back, arguing somewhat about the things they'd heard, and there were some very fretful whispers about its being contrary to our nature to be chaste, absolutely contrary, and that we could never live with marriage.

Meantime I went out to the human beings of Donnelaith and preached this great conversion to them as well, and the monks followed me. We called all the clans of the valley together.

And in our great gathering ground, amid the stones, hundreds declared their desire to come to Christ, and indeed, some of the humans confessed they had already converted, maintaining it as a secret for their own protection.

I was very struck by this, particularly when I found that some human families had been Christian for three generations. "How very like us you are," I thought, "but you don't know it."

It seemed then that all were on the verge of conversion. En masse, we begged the priests to begin the baptisms and the blessings.

But one of the great women of our tribe, Janet, as we had come to call her, a name very current then, raised her voice to speak out against me.

Janet too had been born in the lost land, which she mentioned now quite openly before the human beings. Of course they didn't know what she meant. But we did. And she reminded me that she had no white streaks in her hair, either. In other words, we were wise and young, both of us, the perfect combination.

I had had one son by Janet, and truly loved her. I had spent many, many nights at play in her bed, not daring to have coitus, of course, but nursing from her rounded little breasts, and exchanging all kinds of other clever embraces that gave us exquisite pleasure.

I loved Janet. But there had never been any doubt in my mind that Janet was fierce in her own beliefs.

Now she stepped forth and condemned the new religion as a pack of lies. She pointed out all its weaknesses in terms of logic and consistency. She laughed at it. She told many stories which made Christians look like braggarts and idiots. The story of the gospel she declared unintelligible.

The tribe was immediately split. So loud was the talk that I could not even tell how many were for Janet's point of view or against it. Violent verbal quarrels ensued. Once again we undertook our marathon debates, which no human being could watch without realizing our differences.

The monks withdrew to our sacred circle. There they consecrated the earth to Christ, and prayed for us. They did not fully understand yet how different we were, but they knew we were not like other people.

At last a great schism occurred. One third of the Taltos refused utterly to be converted, and threatened battle with the others if we tried to make the glen a haven of Christianity. Some evinced a great fear of Christianity and the strife it would cause among others. Others simply did not like it, and wanted to keep to our own ways and not live in austerity and penance.

The majority wanted to convert, and we did not wish to give up our homes—that is, to leave the glen and go elsewhere. To me, such a possibility was unthinkable. I was the ruler here.

And like many a pagan king, I expected my people to follow me absolutely in my conversion.

The verbal battles progressed to physical pushing and shoving and threats, and I saw within an hour that the entire future of the valley was threatened.

But the end of the world was coming. Christ had known this and come to prepare us. The enemies of Christ's church were the enemies of Christ!

Bloody skirmishes were being fought in the grasslands of the glen. Fires broke out.

Accusations were flung out. Humans who had always

460

seemed loyal suddenly turned on Taltos and accused them of wretched perversity, of having no lawful marriage, no visible children, and of being wicked magicians.

Others declared that they had long suspected the Taltos of evil things, and now was the time to have it out. Where did we keep our young? Why did no one ever see any children among us?

A few crazed individuals, for reasons of their own, shouted the truth. A human who had mothered two Taltos pointed at her Taltos husband and told all the world what he was, and that if we were to sleep with human women we would soon annihilate them.

The frenzied zealots, of whom I was the most outspoken one, declared that these things no longer mattered. We, the Taltos, had been welcomed into the church by Christ and Father Columba. We would give up the old licentious habits, we would live as Christ would have us live.

There followed more confusion. Blows were struck. Screams rang out.

Now I saw how three thousand people could die in an argument over the right to copy a book! Now I perceived everything.

But too late. The battle had already commenced. All rushed to their brochs to take up arms and to defend their positions. Armed men poured out of doors, attacking their neighbors.

The horror of war, the horror I had sought to hide from all these years in Donnelaith, was now upon us. It had come through my conversion.

I stood confounded, my sword in my hand, hardly knowing what to make of it. But the monks came to me. "Ashlar, lead them to Christ," they said, and I became as many a zealot king before me. I led my converts against their brothers and sisters.

But the real horror was yet to come.

When the battle was over, the Christians still stood in the majority, and I saw, though it did not register very clearly yet, that most of them were human. The majority of the Taltos elite, never very numerous anyway, thanks to our rigid control, had been slaughtered. And only a band of some *fifty of us* remained, the oldest, the wisest, in some ways the most dedicated, and we were all still convinced of our conversion.

But what were we to do with the few humans and Taltos who had not come over to us, who had not been killed only because the killing had stopped before everyone was dead? Now gathered from the battlefield, wounded, limping, these rebels, with Janet as their leader, cursed us. They would not be driven from the glen, they declared, they would die where they stood in opposition to us.

"You, Ashlar, look at what you've done," Janet declared. "Look, everywhere on the bodies of your brothers and sisters, men and women who have lived since the time before the circles! You have brought about their death!"

But no sooner had she laid on me this terrible judgment than the zealous human converts began to demand: "How could you have lived since the time before the circles? What were you, if you were not human beings?"

At last one of the boldest of these men, one who had been a secret Christian for years, came up and slit open my robe with his sword, and I, baffled as Taltos often are by violence, found myself standing naked in the circle.

I saw the reason. They would see what we were, if our tall bodies were the bodies of men. Well, let them see, I announced. I stepped out of the fallen robe. I laid my hand upon my testicles in the ancient fashion, to swear an oath— that is, testify—and I swore that I would serve Christ as well as any human.

But the tide had turned. The other Christian Taltos were losing their nerve. The sight of the slaughter had been appalling to them. They had begun to weep, and to forget the Art of the Tongue, and to talk in the high, rapid speech of our kind, which quickly terrified the humans.

I raised my voice, demanding silence, and demanding allegiance. I had put back on my slashed robe, for all that it mattered. And I walked back and forth in the circle, angry, using the Art of the Tongue as well as I'd ever used it.

What would Christ say to us on account of what we had done? What was the crime here, that we were a strange tribe? Or that we had murdered our own in this dispute?

I wept with great gestures and tore my hair, and the others wept with me.

But the monks were now filled with fear, and the human Christians were filled with fear. What they had suspected all their lives in the glen was almost revealed to them. Once again the questions flew. Our children, where were they?

At last another Taltos male, whom I greatly loved, stepped forward and declared that from this moment forth he was, in the name of Christ and Virgin, celibate. Other Taltos made the same pledge, women and men both.

"Whatever we were," the Taltos women declared, "does not matter now, for we will become the Brides of Christ and make our own monastery here in the spirit of Iona."

Great cries rang out, of joy and agreement, and those humans who had always loved us, who loved me as their king, rallied quickly around us.

But the danger hung in the air. At any moment the bloody swords might clash again, and I knew it.

"Quickly, all of you, pledge yourself to Christ," I declared, seeing in this Taltos vow of celibacy our only chance for survival.

Janet cried out for me to cease with this unnatural and evil plan. And then, in a great volley of words, rushing sometimes too fast and sometimes too slow, she spoke of our ways, of our offspring, our sensuous rites, our long history, everything that I was now prepared to sacrifice.

It was the fatal mistake.

At once the human converts descended upon her and bound her hand and foot, as those who sought to defend her were cut down. Some of the converted Taltos tried to flee, and they were immediately cut down, and another vicious battle broke out, in which cottages and huts were set aflame and people ran hither and thither in panic, screaming for God to help us. "Kill all the monsters," was the cry.

One of the monks declared it was the end of the world. Several of the Taltos did also. They dropped to their knees. Humans, seeing those Taltos in that submissive posture, at once killed those whom they did not know, or feared or disliked, sparing only those few who were beloved of everyone.

Only I and a handful were left—those who had been most active in the leadership of the tribe, and had magnetic personalities. We fought off the few who had the stamina to attack us, subduing others with mere ferocious looks or vociferous condemnations.

And at last—when the frenzy had peaked, and men fell under the burden of their swords, and others screamed and wept over the slain, only five of us remained—Taltos dedicated to Christ—and all those who would not accept Christ, except for Janet, had been annihilated.

The monks called for order.

"Speak to your people, Ashlar. Speak or all is lost. There will be no Donnelaith, and you know it."

"Yes, speak," said the other Taltos, "and say nothing that will frighten anyone. Be clever, Ashlar."

I was weeping so hard this task seemed utterly beyond me. Everywhere I looked I saw the dead, hundreds born since the circle of the plain, dead and gone now, into eternity, and perhaps into the flames of hell without Christ's mercy.

I fell to my knees. I wept until I had no more tears, and when I stopped, the valley was still.

"You are our king," said the human beings. "Tell us that you are no devil, Ashlar, and we will believe you."

The other Taltos with me were desperately afraid. Their fate hung now with mine. But they were those most known to the human population and most revered. We did have a chance, that is, if I did not despair and seal the fate of all of us.

But what was left of my people? What? And what had I brought into my valley?

The monks came close. "Ashlar, God tries those whom He loves," they said. And they meant it. Their eyes were filled with sadness too. "God tests those whom he would make saints," they said, and heedless of what others might think of our monstrousness, our sinfulness, they threw their arms around me, and stood firm against the rest, risking their own safety.

Now Janet, held tight by her captors, spoke:

"Ashlar, you are the betrayer of your people. You have brought death to your own in the name of a foreign god. You have destroyed the Clan of Donnelaith, which has lived in this glen since time immemorial."

"Stop the witch!" someone cried.

"Burn her," said another. And another and another.

And even as she continued to speak, there was whispering, and those going to prepare a stake in the stone circle.

All this I saw from the corner of my eye, and so did she, and still she kept her courage.

"I curse you, Ashlar. I curse you in the eyes of the Good God."

I couldn't speak, and yet I knew that I had to. I had to speak to save myself, the monks, my followers. I had to speak if I was to stop the death of Janet.

Wood had been dragged to the stake. Coal was being thrown down. Humans, some of whom had always feared Janet and every female Taltos whom they could not have, had brought torches.

"Speak," whispered Ninian beside me. "For Christ, Ashlar."

I closed my eyes, I prayed, I made the Sign of the Cross, and then I made my plea to all to listen.

"I see before me a chalice," I declared, speaking softly but loud enough for all to hear. "I see the Chalice of Christ's blood which Joseph of Arimathea brought to England. I see the blood of Christ emptied into the Well; I see the water run red, and I know its meaning.

"The blood of Christ is our sacrament and our nourishment. It shall forever replace the cursed milk we sought from our women in lust; it shall be our new sustenance and our portion.

"And in this awful slaughter today, may Christ receive our first great act of self-sacrifice. For we loathe this killing. We loathe it and we always have. And we do it only to the enemies of Christ, that His kingdom may come on earth, that he may rule forever."

It was the Art of the Tongue as best I knew it, and it was said with eloquence and tears, and it left the entire mob of human and Taltos alike cheering and praising Christ and throwing their swords to the ground and tearing off their finery, their bracelets, their rings, and declaring themselves to be born again.

And at that moment, as they had come from my lips, I knew these words were lies. This religion was a deceiving thing, and the body and blood of Christ could kill as surely as poison.

But we were saved, we who stood there exposed as monsters. The crowd no longer wanted our death. We were safe—all except for Janet.

They dragged her now to the stake, and though I protested, weeping and begging, the priests said no, that Janet must die, that she might die as a lesson to all those who would refuse Christ.

The fire was lighted.

I threw myself to the ground. I couldn't bear it. Then, leaping up, I ran at the slowly gathering blaze, only to be pulled back and held against my will.

"Ashlar, your people need you!"

"Ashlar, set an example!"

Janet fixed her eyes on me. The fire licked at her rose-colored gown, at her long yellow hair. She blinked to clear her eyes of the rising smoke, and then she cried out to me:

"Cursed, Ashlar, cursed for all time. May death elude you forever. May you wander—loveless, childless—your people gone, until our miraculous birth is your only dream in your isolation. I curse you, Ashlar. May the world around you crumble before your suffering is ended."

The flames leapt up, obscuring her fair face, and a low roar came from the rapidly burning timbers. And then came her voice again, louder, full of agony and full of courage.

"A curse on Donnelaith, a curse on its people forever! A curse on the Clan of Donnelaith. A curse on Ashlar's people."

Something writhed within the flames. I did not know if it was Janet in her final pain, or some trick of light and shadow and flickering.

I had fallen to my knees. I couldn't stop the tears and I couldn't look away. It was as if I had to go as far as I could

466

with her into her pain, and I prayed to Christ, "She knows not what she says, take her to heaven. For her kindnesses to others, for her goodness to her people, take her to heaven."

The flames leapt heavenward, and then at once began to die away, revealing the stake, the smoldering heap of wood and burnt flesh and bone that had been this gracious creature, older and wiser than I was.

The glen was still. Nothing remained of my people now but five males who vowed to be celibate Christians.

Lives that had existed for centuries had been snuffed out. Torn limbs, severed heads, and mutilated bodies lay everywhere.

The human Christians wept. We wept.

A curse on Donnelaith, she had said. A curse. But, Janet, my darling Janet, I prayed, what more can happen to us!

I collapsed on the ground.

At that moment I wanted no more of life. I wanted no more of suffering or death, or of the best of intentions resulting in abominable ruin.

But the monks came to me, lifting me to my feet. My followers called to me. I was to come, they said, to behold a miracle that had happened before the ruined and burnt-out tower that had once been the home of Janet and those closest to her.

Dragged there, dazed, unable to speak, I was gradually made to understand that an old spring, long dried, had come to life, clear water bubbling up from the earth once again, and cutting its path through the old dried bed, between hillocks and the roots of the trees and into a great drift of wildflowers.

A miracle!

A miracle. I pondered. Should I point out that that stream had come and gone a number of times in the century? That the flowers were blooming yesterday and the day before because the earth there was already damp, presaging the little fount which had now at last broken through the surface again?

Or should I say:

"A miracle."

I said, "A sign from God."

"Kneel, all," cried Ninian. "Bathe in this holy water. Bathe away the blood of those who wouldn't accept God's grace and have gone now to eternal perdition."

Janet burning in hell forever, the pyre that will never go out, the voice that will curse me still crying . . .

I shuddered and all but fainted again, but I fell on my knees.

In my soul, I knew that this new faith must sweep me up, it must consume my whole life, or I was lost forever!

I had no more hope, no more dreams; I had no more words, and no more thirst for anything! This had to save me, or I should die in this very spot now, by sheer will, never speaking or moving or taking nourishment again until death stole over me.

I felt the cold water slapped against my face. I felt it running down into my robes. The others had gathered. They too were bathing. The monks had begun to sing the ethereal psalms which I had heard on Iona. My people, the humans of Donnelaith crying and sad, and eager for the same grand redemption, took up the song, in the old-fashioned way, singing the lines right after the monks, until voices everywhere were raised in praise of God.

We were all baptized in the Name of the Father, and of the Son, and of the Holy Ghost.

The Clan of Donnelaith was Christian thereafter. All human save for five Taltos.

Before the following morning a few more Taltos were discovered, mostly very young women who had been shielding two almost newborn males in their house, from which they had seen the whole tragedy, including Janet's execution. They were six altogether.

The Christian humans brought them to me. They would not speak, either to accept or deny Christ, but looked at me in terror. What should we do?

"Let them go, if they will," I said. "Let them flee the valley."

No one had the stomach for any more blood or death. And their youth and their simplicity and their innocence made a shield around them. As soon as the new converts stepped back, these Taltos fled, with nothing but the clothes on their backs, right into the forest.

In the days that followed, we five males who were left did win the entire goodwill of the people. In the fervor of their new religion, they praised us that we had brought Christ to them, and honored us for our vows of celibacy. The monks prepared us with instructions day and night to accept Holy Orders. We pored over our holy books. We prayed constantly.

Work was begun upon the church, a mighty Roman-style building of dry stone, with rounded arch windows and a long nave.

And I myself led a procession through the old circle, at which we effaced any symbols from olden times, and carved into the rocks new emblems, from the Altar Book of the Gospels.

These were the fish, which stood for Christ, the dove, which stood for the Apostle John, the lion for Mark, the ox for Luke, and the man for Matthew. And in a little Taltos fury we carved other biblical scenes into the flatter stones, and moved into the cemetery, putting crosses upon the old graves, in the style of the crosses of the book, very ornate and ornamented.

It was a brief interlude in which something returned of the old fervor that had once taken hold of all of us on the Salisbury Plain. But we were only five now, and not an entire tribe, five who had renounced their own nature to please God and the human Christians, five who had been cast in the role of saints in order not to be massacred.

But a dark terror lurked inside me and in the others. How long would this uneasy truce last? Would not the slightest sin topple us from our pedestals?

Even as I prayed to God to help me, to forgive me for all my errors, to bind me to him as a good priest, I knew that we five could not remain in Donnelaith much longer.

And I could not endure it myself! Even at my prayers, and during the singing of psalms with the monks, I heard Janet's curse in my ears, I saw my people covered in blood. Christ, give me faith, I prayed, yet in my secret heart I did not believe that the only path for my kind was one of such

469

renunciation and chastity. How could it be? Did God mean for us to die out?

This was not self-sacrifice, it was a form of utter denial. For Christ, we had become no one!

Yet the love of Christ burned hot in me. It burned desperately. And a very strong personal sense of my Savior developed in me as it has in Christians always. Night after night in my meditations I envisioned the Chalice of Christ, the holy hill on which Joseph's hawthorn bloomed, the blood in the water of Chalice Well. I made a vow to go in pilgrimage to Glastonbury.

There were rumblings from outside the glen. Men had heard of the Holy Battle of Donnelaith, as it had come to be called. They had heard of the tall celibate priests with strange powers. Monks had written to other monks, passing on the story.

The legends of the Taltos came alive. Others who had lived as Picts in small communities had now to flee their homes as their pagan neighbors taunted and threatened them, and as Christians came to plead with them to renounce their wicked ways and become "holy fathers."

Wild Taltos were found in the forest; there were rumors of the magic birth having been witnessed in this or that town. And the witches were on the prowl, boasting that they could make us reveal ourselves, and render us powerless.

Other Taltos, richly dressed and armed to the teeth, and now exposed for what they were, came in heavily defended groups to the glen and cursed me for what I had done.

Their women, beautifully clothed, and guarded on all sides, spoke of Janet's curse, having heard whispers of this, no doubt from the Taltos who had fled Donnelaith, and demanded that I repeat the curse to all, and hear their judgments.

I refused. I said nothing.

Then, to my horror, these Taltos repeated the entire curse to me, for indeed they already knew it.

"Cursed, Ashlar, cursed for all time. May death elude you forever. May you wander—loveless, childless—your people gone, until our miraculous birth is your only dream

470

in your isolation. ... May the world around you crumble before your suffering is ended."

It had become a poem to them which they could recite, and they spat at my feet when they were finished.

"Ashlar, how could you forget the lost land?" the women demanded. "How could you forget the circle of Salisbury Plain?"

These brave few walked amid the ruins of the old brochs; the human Christians of Donnelaith looked on them with cold eyes and fear, and sighed with relief when they took their final leave of the valley.

Over the months that followed, some Taltos came who had accepted Christ and wanted to become priests. We welcomed them.

All over northern Britain, the quiet time for my people had ended.

The race of the Picts was fast disappearing. Those who knew the Ogham script wrote terrible curses on me, or they carved into walls and stones their newfound Christian beliefs with fervor.

An exposed Taltos might save himself by becoming a priest or a monk, a transformation which not only appeased the populace but greatly exhilarated it. Villages wanted a Taltos priest; Christians of other tribes begged for a celibate Taltos to come and say the special Mass for them. But any Taltos who did not play this game, who did not renounce his pagan ways, who did not claim the protection of God, was fair game for anyone.

Meantime, in a great ceremony, some five of us, and four who had come later, accepted Holy Orders. Two female Taltos who had come into the glen became nuns in our community, and dedicated themselves to caring for the weak and the sick. I was made Father Abbot of the monks of Donnelaith, with authority over the glen and even the surrounding communities.

Our fame grew.

There were times when we had to barricade ourselves in our new monastery to escape the pilgrims who came "to see what a Taltos was" and to lay hands on us. Word got around that we could "cure" and "work miracles."

Day after day, I was urged by my flock to go to the sacred spring, and bless the pilgrims there who had come to drink the holy water.

Janet's broch had been torn down. The stones from her home, and what metal could be melted down from her plate and few bracelets and rings, were put into the building of the new church. And a cross was erected at the holy stream, inscribed with Latin words to celebrate the burning of Janet and the subsequent miracle.

I could barely look at this. Is this charity? Is this love? But it was more than plain that for the enemies of Christ, justice could be as bitter as God chose to make it.

But was all this God's plan?

My people destroyed, our remnants turned into sacred animals? I pleaded with our monks from Iona to discourage all those beliefs! "We are not a magical priesthood!" I declared. "These people are on the verge of declaring that we have magical powers!"

But to my utter horror the monks said that it was God's will.

"Don't you see, Ashlar?" said Ninian. "This is why God preserved your people, for this special priesthood."

But all that I had envisioned had been laid waste. The Taltos had not been redeemed, they had not discovered a way to live on the earth at peace with men.

The church began to grow in fame, the Christian community became enormous. And I feared the whims of those who worshiped us.

At last I set aside each day an hour or two when my door was locked and no one might speak to me. And in the privacy of my cell, I began a great illustrated book, using all the skill I had acquired from my teacher on Iona.

Done in the style of the Four Gospels, it was to be, complete with golden letters on every page, and tiny pictures to illustrate it, the story of my people.

My book.

It was the book which Stuart Gordon found in the crypts of the Talamasca.

For Father Columba, I wrote every word, lavishing on it my greatest gift for verse, for song, for prayer, as I described the lost land, our wanderings to the southern plain, the building of our great Stonehenge. In Latin, I told all I knew of our struggles in the world of men, of how we'd suffered and learned to survive, and how at last my tribe and clan had come to this—five priests amid a sea of humans, worshiped for powers we did not possess, exiles without a name, a nation, or a god of our own, struggling to beg salvation from the god of a people who feared us.

"Read my words here, Father," I wrote, "you who would not listen to them when I tried to speak them. See them here inscribed in the language of Jerome, of Augustine, of Pope Gregory. And know that I tell the truth and long to enter God's church as what I truly am. For how else will I ever enter the Kingdom of Heaven?"

Finally my task was complete.

I sat back, staring at the cover to which I myself had affixed the jewels, at the binding which I myself had fashioned from silk, at letters which I myself had written.

At once I sent for Father Ninian, and laid the book before him. I sat very still as Ninian examined the work.

I was too proud of what I'd done, too certain now that somehow our history would find some redeeming context in the vast libraries of church doctrine and history. "Whatever else happens," I thought, "I have told the truth. I have told how it was, and what Janet chose to die for."

Nothing could have prepared me for the expression on Ninian's face when he closed the volume.

For a long moment he said nothing, and then he began to laugh and laugh.

"Ashlar," he said, "have you lost your mind, that you would expect me to take this to Father Columba!"

I was stunned. In a small voice I said, "I've given it all my effort."

"Ashlar," he said, "this is the finest book of its kind I've ever beheld; the illustrations are perfectly executed, the text written in flawless Latin, replete with a hundred touching phrases. It is inconceivable that a man could have created this thing in less than three to four years, in the solitude of the scriptorium at Iona, and to think that you have done it here within the space of a year is nothing short of miraculous."

"Yes?"

"But the contents, Ashlar! This is blasphemy. In the Latin of Scripture, and in the style of an Altar Book, you have written mad pagan verses and tales full of lust and monstrousness! Ashlar, this is the proper form for Gospels of the Lord, and psalters! Whatever possessed you to write your frivolous stories of magic in this manner?"

"So that Father Columba would see these words and realize they were true!" I declared.

But I had already seen his point. My defense meant nothing.

Then, seeing me so crushed, he sat back and folded his hands and looked at me.

"From the first day I came into your house," he said, "I knew your simplicity and your goodness. Only you could have made such a foolish blunder. Put it aside; put your entire history aside once and for all! Devote your extraordinary talent to the proper subjects."

For a day and a night I thought on it.

Wrapping my book carefully, I gave it again to Ninian.

"I am your abbot here at Donnelaith," I said, "by solemn appointment. Well, this is the last order I shall ever give you. Take this book to Father Columba as I've told you. And tell him for me that I have chosen to go away on a pilgrimage. I don't know how long I will be gone, or where. As you can see from this book, my life has already spanned many lifetimes. I may never lay eyes on him again, or on you, but I must go. I must see the world. And whether I shall ever return to this place or to Our Lord, only He knows."

Ninian tried to protest. But I was adamant. He knew that he had to make a journey home to Iona soon anyway, and so he gave in to me, warning me that I did not have Columba's permission to go away, but realizing that I did not care about this.

At last he set out with the book, and a strong guard of some five human beings.

I never saw that book again until Stuart Gordon laid it out on the table in his tower at Somerset.

Whether it ever reached Iona I don't know.

My suspicion is that it did, and it may have remained at Iona for many years, until all those who knew what it was, or knew who'd written it or why it was there, were long gone.

I was never to know whether Father Columba read it or not. The very night after Ninian went on his way, I resolved to leave Donnelaith forever.

I called the Taltos priests together into the church and bade them lock the doors. The humans could think what they liked, and indeed this did make them naturally restless and suspicious.

I told my priests that I was leaving.

I told them that I was afraid.

"I do not know if I have done right. I believe, but I do not know," I said. "And I fear the human beings around us. I fear that any moment they might turn on us. Should a storm come, should a plague sweep through the land, should a terrible illness strike the children of the more powerful families—any of these disasters could provoke a rebellion against us.

"These are not our people! And I have been a fool to believe that we could ever live in peace with them.

"Each of you, do what you will, but my advice to you as Ashlar, your leader since the time we left the lost land, is go away from here. Seek absolution at some distant monastery, where your nature is not known, and ask permission to practice your vows in peace there. But leave this valley.

"I myself shall go on a pilgrimage. First to Glastonbury, to the well there where Joseph of Arimathea poured the blood of Christ into the water. I will pray there for guidance. Then I will go to Rome, and then perhaps, I do not know, to Constantinople to see the holy icons there which are said to contain the very face of our Christ by magic. And then to Jerusalem to see the mountain where Christ died for us. I herewith renounce my vow of obedience to Father Columba."

There was a great outcry, and much weeping, but I stood

firm. It was a very characteristic Taltos way of ending things.

"If I am wrong, may Christ lead me back to his fold. May he forgive me. Or . . . may I go to hell," I said with a shrug. "I'm leaving."

I went to prepare for my journey. . . .

Before these parting words to my flock, I had taken all of my personal possessions out of my tower, including all my books, my writings, my letters from Father Columba, and everything of any importance to me, and I had hidden these in two of the souterrains I had built centuries ago. Then I took the last of my fine clothes, having given up all else for vestments and for the church, and I dressed in a green wool tunic, long and thick and trimmed in black fur, and put around it my only remaining girdle of fine leather and gold, strapped on my broadsword with its jeweled scabbard, placed on my head an old hood of fur, and a bronze helmet of venerable age. And thus garbed as a nobleman, a poor one perhaps, I rode out, with my possessions in a small sack, to leave the glen.

This was nothing as ornate and heavy as my kingly raiment had been, and nothing as humble as a priest's robes. Merely good clothing for travel.

I rode for perhaps an hour through the forest, following old trails known only to those who had hunted here.

Up and up I went along the heavily wooded slopes towards a secret pass that led to the high road.

It was late afternoon, but I knew I would reach the road before nightfall. There would be a full moon, and I meant to travel until I was too tired to go further.

It was dark in these dense woods, so dark, I think, that people of this day and age cannot quite imagine it. This was a time before the great forests of Britain had been destroyed, and the trees here were thick and ancient.

It was our belief that these trees were the only living things that were older than us in the whole world—for nothing we had ever beheld lived as long as trees or Taltos. We loved the forest and we had never feared it.

But I had not been in the darkest forest for very long when I heard the voices of the Little People.

I heard their hisses and whispers and laughter.

Samuel had not been born in that time, so he was not there, but Aiken Drumm and others alive today were among these that called, "Ashlar, the fool of the Christians, you've betrayed your people." Or, "Ashlar, come with us, make a new race of giants and we shall rule the world," and other such things. Aiken Drumm I have always hated. He was very young then, and his face was not so gnarled that one couldn't see his eyes. And as he rushed through the undergrowth, shaking his fist at me, his face was full of malevolence.

"Ashlar, you leave the glen now after destroying everything! May Janet's curse be upon you!"

Finally they all fell back and away for a simple reason. I was coming close to a cave on the mountainside, about which I had—for simple reasons—entirely forgotten.

Without even thinking, I'd chosen the path that ancient tribes had taken to worship there. In the time when the Taltos lived on the Salisbury Plain, these tribes had filled this cave with skulls, and later peoples revered it as a place of dark worship.

In recent centuries the peasants had sworn that a door was open inside this cave by which one might hear the voices of hell, or the singing of heaven.

Spirits had been seen in the nearby wood, and witches sometimes braved our wrath to come here. Though there had been times when we rode up the hills in fearsome bands to drive them out, we had not in the last two hundred years much bothered with them.

I myself had only been up this way a couple of times in all my life, but I had no fear of the cave at all. And when I saw that the Little People were afraid, I was relieved to be rid of them.

However, as my horse followed the old trail closer and closer to the cave, I saw flickering lights playing in the thick darkness. I came to see there was a crude dwelling in the mountainside, made out of a cave itself perhaps, and covered over with stones, leaving only a small door and a

477

window, and a hole higher up through which the smoke passed.

The light flickered through the cracks and crevices of the crude wall.

And there, many feet above, was the path to the great cave, a yawning mouth altogether hidden now by pine and oak and yew trees.

I wanted to keep clear of the little house as soon as I saw it. Anyone who would live in the vicinity of this cave had to be trouble.

The cave itself vaguely intrigued me. Believing in Christ, though I had disobeyed my abbot, I did not fear pagan gods. I did not believe in them. But I was leaving my home. I might not ever come back. And I wondered if I should not visit the cave, perhaps even rest there a while, hidden, and safe from the Little People.

Twenty-nine

"**N**OW LISTEN TO me, both of you," she said without taking her eyes off the road. "This is the point where I am going to take over. I've thought this over since I was born, and I know exactly what we need to do. Is Granny asleep back there?"

"Sound asleep," said Mary Jane from the jump seat, where she was stretched out sideways, so she could see Morrigan behind the wheel.

"What do you mean," asked Mona, "that you are going to take over?"

"Just exactly this," said Morrigan, both her hands together at the top of the wheel, gripping it easily on account of the fact that they had been going ninety miles an hour for quite some time now, and no cop, obviously, was going to stop them. "I've been listening to you argue and argue, and you're stuck on things that are utterly beside the point, sort of moral technicalities."

Morrigan's hair was tangled and falling all over her shoulders and her arms, a brighter red, as far as Mona could tell, but in the same family as her own hair. And the uncanny resemblance between their faces was enough to completely unnerve Mona if she let herself stare too long at Morrigan. As for the voice, well, the big danger was obvious. Morrigan could pretend to be Mona on the phone. She had done it with ease when Uncle Ryan had finally called Fontevrault. What a hilarious conversation that had been! Ryan had asked "Mona" very tactfully if she was taking amphetamines, and reminded her gently that anything ingested might hurt the baby. But the point was, Uncle Ryan had never guessed that the fast-talking and inquisitive female on the other end of the line was not Mona.

They were all dressed in their Easter Sunday best, as Mary Jane had called it earlier, including Morrigan, whom they had outfitted in the fashionable shops of Napoleonville. The white cotton shirtwaist dress would have been ankle length on Mona or even Mary Jane. On Morrigan it came to the knee; the waste was cinched really tight, and the plain V neck, the symbol of matronly good sense, became against her fairly well-developed breasts a plunging neckline. It was the old story; put a plain, simple dress on a flamboyantly beautiful girl, and it becomes more eye-catching than gold foil or sable. Shoes had been no problem, once they had faced that she was a size ten. One size larger and they would have had to put her in men's lace-ups. As it was, she had stiletto heels and had danced around the car in them for fifteen minutes, before Mona and Mary Jane had laid firm hands on her, told her to shut up, don't move, and get in. Then she had demanded to drive. Well, it wasn't the first time. . . .

Granny, in Wal-Mart's best cotton knit pantsuit, slept beneath her baby-blue thermal blanket. The sky was blue, the clouds magnificently white. Mona wasn't sick anymore at all, thank God, just weak. Dismally weak.

They were now one half hour from New Orleans.

"Like what moral technicality?" asked Mary Jane. "This is a question of safety, you know, and what do you mean, 'take over'?"

"Well, I'm talking about something inevitable," said Morrigan, "but let me break it to you in stages."

Mona laughed.

"Ah, you see, Mother is smart enough to know, of course, to see the future as a witch might, I suppose, but you, Mary Jane, persist in being a cross between a disapproving aunt and the devil's advocate."

"You sure you know the meaning of all those words?"

"My dear, I have imbibed the entire contents of two dictionaries. I know all the words my mother knew before I

480

was born, and a great many my father knew. How else would I know what a socket wrench is, and why the trunk of this car contains an entire set of them?

"Now back to the crisis of the moment: Where do we go, which house? And all of that nonsense?"

Immediately she answered her own questions.

"Well, my thinking is that whose house we go to is not all that fired important. Amelia Street would be a bad idea, simply because it is loaded with other people, as you have thrice described, and though it may be Mother's house in a sense, it truly belongs to Ancient Evelyn. Fontevrault is too far away. We are not going back, I don't care what happens! An apartment is a hideout which I cannot, in my anticipatory anxiety, abide! I will not choose some small impersonal lodgings obtained under false pretenses. I cannot live in boxes. First Street does belong to Michael and Rowan, that's true, but Michael is my father! What we need is at First Street. I need Mona's computer, her records, the papers Lasher scribbled out, any notes my father has made in his copy of his famous Talamasca file, everything which is presently in that house, and to which Mona has acknowledged access. Well, not Lasher's scribblings, but again, that is a technicality. I claim the rights of breed to take those notes. And I do not have a single scruple about reading Michael's diary if I do find it. Now don't start screaming, both of you!"

"Well, just slow down for one thing!" shouted Mary Jane. "And I get a creepy feeling in my bones from the way you say those words, 'take over.'"

"And let's think this out a little further," said Mona.

"You have reminded each other enough in my presence that the name of the game is survival," Morrigan replied. "I need this knowledge—diaries, files, records—for survival. And First Street is empty now, we know that, and we can make our preparations in peace for Michael and Rowan's homecoming. So I will make the decision here and now that that is where we go, at least until Michael and Rowan have returned and we have apprised them of the situation. If my father then wishes to banish me from the house, we seek an appropriate dwelling, or put into operation Mother's plan to obtain funds for the complete restoration of Fontevrault. Now, do you have all this in your memories?"

"There are guns in that house," said Mary Jane, "she has told you that. Guns upstairs, downstairs. These people are going to be scared of you. This is their house. They're going to start screaming! Don't you understand? They think that Taltos are evil beings, evil! Trying to take over the world!"

"I am a Mayfair!" declared Morrigan. "I am the daughter of my father and my mother. And the hell with guns. They are not going to aim a gun at me. That's perfectly absurd, and you are forgetting that they are not expecting me to be there at all, and will be utterly unprepared when you search them for guns, as if they would be carrying guns at all, and furthermore you will be there, both of you, to protect me, and speak for me, and to issue dire warnings that they are not to harm me, and please remember for more than five consecutive minutes at a stretch that I have a tongue in my mouth with which to protect myself, that nothing in this situation is analogous to any that existed before, and that it is best to settle in there, where I can examine everything I should examine, including this famous Victrola, and the backyard—there you go, stop screaming, both of you!"

"Just don't dig up the bodies!" Mona cried.

"Right, leave those bodies under the tree!" declared Mary Jane.

"Absolutely, I will. I shall. I told you. No digging up bodies. Bad, bad idea. Morrigan is sorry. Morrigan won't do it. Morrigan has promised Mona and Mary Jane. No time for bodies! Besides, what are these bodies to me?" Morrigan shook her head, making her red hair tumble and tangle and then giving it a vigorous and determined toss. "I am the child of Michael Curry and Mona Mayfair. And that is what matters, isn't it?"

"We're scared, that's all!" Mary Jane declared. "Now, if we turn around right now, and we go back to Fontevrault—"

"No. Not without the appropriate pumps, scaffolding, jacks, and lumber to straighten out that house. I shall have a sentimental attachment to it all of my life, of course, but at this time I simply cannot remain there! I am dying to see the world, don't both of you understand, the world is not Wal-Mart and Napoleonville and the latest issues of *Time*, *Newsweek*, and *The New Yorker*. I cannot remain waiting any longer. Besides, for all you know, they are home now, Rowan and Michael, and I am for an immediate confrontation. No doubt they will make the records available to me, even if in their secret hearts they have opted for extermination."

"They're not home," said Mona. "Ryan said two more days."

"Well, then, what are you all so afraid about?"

"I don't know," cried Mona.

"Then First Street it is, and I don't want to hear another word about it. There is a guest room, is there not? I'll stay in there. And I want all this squabbling to stop. We can then obtain a secure home base of our own at our leisure. Besides, I want to see this house, I want to see the house the witches built. Do not either of you understand the degree to which my being and my fate are connected to this house, this house designed to perpetuate the line with the giant helix? Why, if we strip away most of the clouding sentiment, it is perfectly obvious that Stella, Antha, and Deirdre died so that I might have life, and the bumbling literalist dreams of this evil spirit, Lasher, have resulted in an incarnation he could never foresee, but which is now my destiny. I am tenacious of life, I am tenacious of position!"

"Okay," Mona said, "but you have to be quiet, and you have to not speak to the guards, and you cannot answer the phone again!"

"Yeah, the way you grab for a phone when it rings," said Mary Jane, "any phone at all, is just downright loco."

Morrigan gave a shrug. "What you fail to realize is that each day achieves for me an enormous series of developments. I am not the girl I was two days ago!" She flinched suddenly, and gave a little groan.

"What's the matter, what's wrong?" asked Mona.

"The memories, the way they come. Mother, turn on the tape recorder, will you? You know, it's the strangest thing, the way some of them fade, and some of them don't and it's as if they are memories from lots and lots of people, people like me, I mean. I see Ashlar through everybody's eyes. . . . The glen is the same glen in the Talamasca file, I know it. Donnelaith. I can hear Ashlar say it."

"Speak loud," said Mary Jane, "so I can hear you."

"This is about the stones again, we're not in the glen yet, we're near the river, and the men are dragging the stones out onto the rolling logs. I tell you that there are no accidents in this world, nature is sufficiently random and lush for things to happen almost inevitably. This may not make sense at first, but what I am saying is this—that out of all the chaos and pain of resistant and defiant witches has come the moment when this family must become a family of humans and Taltos. The strangest feelings come over me. I have to go there, to see that place. And the glen. The circle is smaller, but it's ours too, Ashlar has consecrated both circles, and the stars overhead are in the winter configuration. Ashlar wants the dark woods to shelter us, to lie between us and the hostile world. I am tired. Sleepy."

"Don't let go of the wheel," said Mary Jane. "Describe this man, Ashlar, again. Is he always the same, I mean, in both circles and both times?"

"I think I'm going to cry. I keep hearing the music. We have to dance when we get there."

"Where?"

"First Street, anywhere. The glen. The plain. We have to dance in a circle. I'll show you, I'll sing the songs. You know? Something terrible has happened more than once, to my people! Death and suffering, they have become the norm. Only the very skilled avoid them; the very skilled see human beings for what they are. The rest of us are blinded."

"Is he the only one with a name?"

"No, just the one whose name everyone knows, everyone. Like a magnet drawing everyone's emotions. I don't want to . . ."

"Take it easy," said Mona. "When we get there you can write it all out again, you can have peace and quiet, two whole days before they come."

"And who will I be by that time?"

"I know who you are," said Mona. "I knew who you were when you were in me. You're me and Michael, and something else, something powerful and wondrous, and part of all the other witches, too."

"Talk, honey," said Mary Jane. "Tell us, tell us about him and everybody making the little chalk dolls. I want to hear about that, burying the dolls at the foot of the stones. You remember what you said?"

"I think I do. They were dolls with breasts and penises."

"Well, you never mentioned that before."

"They were sacred dolls. But there must be a purpose to this, a redemption for this pain, I . . . I want the memories to let go, but not before I take everything of value from them. Mary Jane, would you please, honeybunch, grab a Kleenex there and wipe my eyes? I am saying this for the record, pay attention. This is stream of consciousness. We are taking the long stone to the plain. Everybody is going to dance and sing around it for a long time, before they begin to make the scaffolding out of logs by which we'll make it stand upright. Everyone has been carving their dolls. You can't tell the difference, each doll looks somehow like every one of them. I am sleepy. I'm hungry too. I want to dance. Ashlar is calling everyone to attention."

"Fifteen more minutes and we pull in the back gate," said Mary Jane. "So just keep your teary little peepers open."

"Don't say a word to the guards," said Mona. "I'll handle them. What else do you remember? They're bringing the stone to the plain. What's the name of the plain? Say it in their language."

"Ashlar calls it simply 'the flat land' and 'the safe land' or 'the grass land.' To say it right I have to speak it very, very fast, to you it will sound like whistling. But everyone knows those stones. I know everyone does. My father knows them, has seen them. God, do you suppose there is another of me anywhere in this whole world? Don't you think there has to be? Another me besides those buried under the tree? I can't be the only one alive!"

"Settle down, honey," said Mary Jane. "There's a lot of time to find out."

"We are your family," said Mona. "Remember that. Whatever else you are, you are Morrigan Mayfair, designated by me to be heir to the legacy, and we have a birth certificate, a baptismal certificate, and fifteen Polaroid photographs with my solemn word on a sticker label pasted to the back of each of them."

"Somehow or other that sounds insufficient," said Morrigan, crying now, making a pout like a baby, the tears making her blink. "Hopelessly contrived, possibly legally irrelevant." The car moved on, in its own lane, but they had come into Metairie, the traffic was getting heavy. "Perhaps a videotape is required, what do you think, Mother? But nothing in the end will suffice, will it, but love? Why do we speak of legal things at all?"

"Because they're important."

"But, Mother, if they don't love—"

"Morrigan, we'll do a videotape at First Street, soon as we get there. And you will have your love, mark my words. I'll get it for you. I won't let anything go wrong this time."

"What makes you think that, given all your reservations and fears, and desires to hide from prying eyes?"

"I love you. That's why I think it."

The tears were springing from Morrigan's eyes as if from a rainspout. Mona could hardly bear it.

"They will not have to use a gun, if they don't love me," Morrigan said.

Unspeakable pain, my child, this.

"Like hell," said Mona, trying to sound very calm, very controlled, very much the woman. "Our love is enough, and you know it! If you have to forget them, you do it. We are enough, don't you dare say we're not, not enough for now, you hear me?" She stared at this graceful gazelle, who was driving and crying at the same time, passing every laggard in her path. *This is my daughter.* Mine has always been monstrous ambition, monstrous intelligence, monstrous courage, and now a monstrous daughter. But what *is* her nature, besides brilliant, impulsive, loving, enthusiastic, super-sensitive to hurts and slights, and given to torrents of fancy and ecstasy? What *will* she do? What does it mean to remember ancient things? Does it mean you possess them

486

and know from them? What *can* come of this? You know, I don't really care, she thought. I mean not now, not when it's beginning, not when it's so exciting.

She saw her tall girl struck, the body crumple, her own hands out to shield her, taking the head to her breast. *Don't you dare hurt her.*

It was all so different now.

"All right, all right," Mary Jane interjected. "Lemme drive, this is really getting crowded."

"You are out of your mind, Mary Jane," cried Morrigan, shifting forward in the seat and pressing on the accelerator to pass the car threatening on the left. She lifted her chin, and took a swat at her tears with the back of her hand. "I am steering this car home. I wouldn't miss this for anything!"

Thirty

WHAT WAS IT like in the cave, I wondered. The voices of hell I had no desire to hear, but what about the singing of heaven?

I thought it over, and then decided to pass by. I had a long journey ahead of me. It was too early for rest. I wanted to be away from here.

I was about to set off and go around this part of the slope, when a voice called to me.

It was a woman's voice, very soft and seemingly without a source, and I heard it say:

"Ashlar, I've been waiting for you."

I turned, looking this way and that. The darkness was unnerving. The Little People, I thought, one of their women, determined to seduce me. Again I determined to be on my way, but the call came again, soft as a kiss:

"Ashlar, King of Donnelaith, I am waiting for you."

I looked at the little hovel, with its lights flickering in the dimness, and there I saw a woman standing. Her hair was red, and her skin very pale. She was human, and a witch, and she carried the very faint scent of a witch, which could mean, but might not, that she had the blood of the Taltos in her.

I should have gone on. I knew it. Witches were always trouble. But this woman was very beautiful and in the shadows my eyes played tricks on me, so that she looked somewhat like our lost Janet.

As she came towards me, I saw that she had Janet's

severe green eyes and straight nose, and a mouth that might have been carved from marble. She had the same small and very round breasts, and a long graceful neck. Add to this her beautiful red hair, which has ever been a lure and a delight to the Taltos.

"What do you want of me?" I said.

"Come lie with me," she said. "Come into my house. I invite you."

"You're a fool," I said. "You know what I am. I lie with you and you'll die."

"No," she said. "Not I." And she laughed, as so many witches had before her. "I shall bear the giant by you."

I shook my head. "Go your way, and be thankful I'm not easily tempted. You're beautiful. Another Taltos might help himself. Who is there to protect you?"

"Come," she said. "Come into my house." She drew closer, and in the few feeble rays of light that broke through the branches, the long, very golden light of the last of the day, I saw her beautiful white teeth, and how her breasts looked beneath her fine lace blouse, and above her painfully tight leather girdle.

Well, it wouldn't hurt just to lie with her, just to put my lips on her breasts, I thought. But then. She is a witch. Why do I allow myself to even think of this?

"Ashlar," she said, "we all know your tale. We know you are the king who betrayed your kind. Don't you want to ask the spirits of the cave how you might be forgiven?"

"Forgiven? Only Christ can forgive me my sins, child," I said. "I'm going."

"What power has Christ to change the curse that Janet has laid upon you?"

"Don't taunt me anymore," I said. I wanted her. And the angrier I became, the less I cared about her.

"Come with me," she said. "Drink the brew that I have by the fire, and then go into the cave, and you will see the spirits who know all things, King Ashlar."

She came up to the horse, and laid her hand on mine, and I felt the desire rising in me. She had a witch's penetrating eyes; and the soul of Janet seemed to look out of them.

489

I had not even made up my mind when she'd helped me from my horse, and we were walking together through the thick bracken and elderberry.

The little hut was a rank and frightening place! It had no windows. Above the fire, a kettle hung on a long skewer. But the bed was clean, and laid with skillfully embroidered linen.

"Fit for a king," she said.

I looked about, and I saw a dark open doorway opposite that by which we'd come in.

"That is the secret way to the cave," she said. She kissed my hand suddenly, and pulling me down onto the bed, she went to the kettle and filled a crude earthen cup with the broth inside it.

"Drink it, Your Majesty," she said. "And the spirits of the cave will see you and hear you."

Or I will see them and hear them, I thought, for God only knows what she had put in it—the herbs and oils which made witches mad, and likely to dance like Taltos under the moon. I knew their tricks.

"Drink, it's sweet," she said.

"Yes," I replied. "I can smell the honey."

And while I was looking into the cup and resolving not to take a drop, I saw her smile, and as I smiled back, I realized I was lifting the cup, and suddenly I drank a deep swallow of it. I closed my eyes.

"What if?" I whispered. "What if there *is* magic in it?" I was faintly amused and already dreaming.

"Now lie with me," she said.

"For your sake, no," I replied, but she was taking off my sword and I let her do it. Getting up long enough only to bolt her door, I fell back on the bed and pushed her down beneath me. I dragged her blouse loose from her breasts, and thought I would weep at the mere sight of them. Ah, the Taltos milk, how I wanted it. She was not a mother, this witch, she would have no milk, Taltos or human. But the breasts, the sweet breasts, how I wanted to suckle them, to bite the nipples and pull at them, and lick at them with my tongue.

Well, that won't do her any harm, I thought, and when

490

she is moist and hot with desire, I'll place my fingers between her hidden hairy lips and make her shiver.

At once I began to suckle her. I began to kiss her and nuzzle against her. Her skin was firm and young and smelled young. And I loved the sound of her soft sighs, and the way her white belly felt to my cheek, and the way her nether hair looked, when I pulled down her skirt, and found it red, like the hair of her head, flaming and softly curly.

"Beautiful, beautiful witch," I whispered.

"Take me, King Ashlar," she said.

I sucked hard on her breast, letting my cock suffer, thinking, no, I will not kill her. She is a fool, but she does not deserve to die for it. But she pulled my cock between her legs, she pressed its tip against her hair, and quite suddenly, as many a male has done, I decided that if she really wanted it so, I would do as she asked of me.

I came in her hard, with as little care as I would have had for a Taltos, riding her, and loving it. She flushed and wept and cried out to spirits whose names I didn't know.

Immediately it was over. Sleepily she looked at me from the pillow, a triumphant smile on her lips. "Drink," she said, "and go into the cave." And she closed her eyes to sleep.

I downed the rest of the cup. Why not? I had gone this far. What if there was something in that remote darkness, one last secret my own land of Donnelaith had to give me? God knew the future held trials, pain, and probably disillusionment.

I climbed off the bed, put my sword back on, buckling everything properly so that I was ready should I meet with trouble, and then, taking a crude lump of wax with a wick, which she kept at hand, I lighted the wick, and I entered the cave by this secret doorway.

I went up and up in the darkness, feeling my way along the earthen wall, and finally I came to a cool and open place, and from there, very far off, I could see a bit of light stealing in from the outside world. I was above the cave's main entrance.

I went on up. The light went before me. With a start, I

came to a halt. I saw skulls gazing back at me. Rows and rows of skulls! Some of them so old they were no more than powder.

This had been a burial place, I reasoned, of those people that save only the heads of the dead, and believe that the spirits will talk through those heads, if properly addressed.

I told myself not to be foolishly frightened. At the same time I felt curiously weakened.

"It is the broth you drank," I whispered. "Sit down and rest."

And I did, leaning against the wall to my left, and looking into the big chamber, with its many masks of death grinning back at me.

The crude candle rolled out of my hand, but did not go out. It came to rest in the mud, and when I tried to reach for it, I couldn't.

Then slowly I looked up and I saw my lost Janet.

She was coming towards me through the chamber of the skulls, moving slowly, as if she were not real, but a figure in a dream.

"But I am awake," I said aloud.

I saw her nod, and smile. She stepped before the feeble little candle.

She wore the same rose-colored robe that she had the day they had burnt her, and then I saw to my horror that the silk had been eaten away by fire, and that her white skin showed through the jagged tears in it. And her long blond hair, it was burnt off and blackened on the ends, and ashes smudged her cheeks and her bare feet and her hands. Yet she was there, alive, and near to me.

"What is it, Janet?" I said. "What would you say to me now?"

"Ah, but what do you say to me, my beloved King? I followed you from the great circle in the southland up to Donnelaith and you destroyed me."

"Don't curse me, fair spirit," I said. I climbed to my knees. "Give me that which will help all of us! I sought the path of love. It was the path to ruin."

A change came over her face, a look of puzzlement and then awareness.

492

She lost her simple smile, and taking my hand, she spoke these words as if they were our secret.

"Would you find another paradise, my lord?" she asked. "Would you build another monument such as you left on the plain for all time? Or would you rather find a dance so simple and full of grace that all the peoples of the world could do it?"

"The dance, Janet, I would. And ours would be one great living circle."

"And would you make a song so sweet that no man or woman of any breed could ever resist it?"

"Yes," I said. "And sing we would, forever."

Her face brightened and her lips parted. And with a look of faint amazement, she spoke again.

"Then take the curse I give you."

I began to cry.

She gestured for me to be still, but with patience. Then she spoke this poem or song in the soft, rapid voice of the Taltos:

> *Your quest is doomed, your path is long,*
> *Your winter just beginning.*
> *These bitter times shall fade to myth*
> *And memory lose its meaning*
> *But when at last her arms you see,*
> *Outstretched in bold forgiveness,*
> *Shrink not from what the earth would do*
> *When rain and winds do till it.*
> *The seed shall sprout, the leaves unfurl,*
> *The boughs shall give forth blossoms,*
> *That once the nettles tried to kill, and*
> *Strong men sought to trample.*
> *The dance, the circle, and the song,*
> *Shall be the key to heaven,*
> *As ways that once the mighty scorned*
> *Shall be their final blessing.*

The cave grew dim, the little candle was dying, and with a subtle farewell gesture of her hand, she smiled again, and disappeared completely.

It seemed the words she'd spoken were carved in my mind as if engraved on the flat stones of the circle. And I saw them, and fixed them for all time, even as the last reverberation of her voice left me.

The cave was dark. I cried out, and groped in vain for the candle. But quickly climbing to my feet, I saw that my beacon was the fire burning in the little hut far back down the tunnel by which I'd entered.

Wiping at my eyes, overcome with love for Janet and a terrible confusion of sweetness and pain, I hurried into the small warm room and saw the red-haired witch there, on her pillow.

For one moment it was Janet! And not this gentle spirit who had just looked at me with loving eyes, and spoken verses that promised some remission.

It was the burnt one, the suffering and dying woman, her hair full of small flames, her bones smoldering. In agony she arched her back and tried to reach for me. And as I cried out and reached to snatch her from her own flames, it was the witch again, the red-haired one who had brought me into her bed and given me the potion.

Dead, white, quiet forever in death, the blood staining her gathered skirts, her little hut a tomb, her fire a vigil light.

I made the Sign of the Cross.

I ran out of the place.

But nowhere in the dark wood could I find my horse, and within moments I heard the laughter of the Little People.

I was at my wits' end, frightened by the vision, uttering prayers and curses. Fiercely I turned on them, challenging them to come out, to fight, and was in a moment surrounded. With my sword I struck down two and put the others to flight, but not before they had torn and dragged from me my green tunic, ripped away my leather girdle, and stolen my few belongings. My horse, too, they had taken.

A vagabond with nothing left to me but a sword, I did not go after them.

I made for the high road by instinct, and by the stars,

which a Taltos can always do, and as the moon rose, I was walking south away from my homeland.

I didn't look back on Donnelaith.

I did go on to the summerland, as it was called, to Glastonbury, and I did stand on the sacred hill where Joseph had planted the hawthorn. I washed my hands in Chalice Well. I drank from it. I crossed Europe to find Pope Gregory in the ruins of Rome, I did go on to Byzantium, and finally to the Holy Land.

But long before my journey took me even to Pope Gregory's palace amid the squalid ruins of Rome's great pagan monuments, my quest had changed, really. I was not a priest anymore. I was a wanderer, a seeker, a scholar.

I could tell you a thousand stories of those times, including the tale of how I finally came to know the Fathers of the Talamasca. But I cannot claim to know their history. I know of them what you know, and what has been confirmed now that Gordon and his cohorts have been discovered.

In Europe I saw Taltos now and then, both women and men. I thought that I always would. That it would always be a simple thing, sooner or later, to find one of my own kind and to talk for the night by a friendly fire of the lost land, of the plain, of the things we all remembered.

There is one last bit of intelligence I wish to communicate to you.

In the year 1228, I finally returned to Donnelaith. It had been too long since I had laid eyes on a single Taltos. I was beginning to feel a fear on this account, and Janet's curse and her poetry were ever in my mind.

I came as a lone Scotsman wandering through the land, eager to talk to the bards of the Highlands about their old stories and legends.

My heart broke when I saw that the old Saxon church was gone and a great cathedral now stood upon the very spot, at the entrance of a great market town.

I had hoped to see the old church. But who could not be impressed by this mighty structure, and the great glowering castle of the Earls of Donnelaith that guarded the whole valley?

Bending my back, and pulling my hood up high to disguise my height, I leaned on my cane as I went down to give thanks that my tower still stood in the glen, along with many of the stone towers built by my people.

I cried tears of gratitude again when I discovered the circle of stones, far from the ramparts, standing as it always had in the high grass, imperishable emblems of the dancers who had once gathered there.

The great shock came, however, when I entered the cathedral and, dipping my hand into the water fount, looked up to see the stained-glass window of St. Ashlar.

There was the very image of myself in the glass, clothed in a priest's robes, with long flowing hair such as I had worn in those days, and peering down at my own true self with dark eyes so like my own they frightened me. Stunned, I read the prayer inscribed in Latin.

> *St. Ashlar Beloved of Christ*
> *And the Holy Virgin Mary*
> *Who will come again*
>
> *Heal the sick*
> *Comfort the afflicted*
> *Ease the pangs*
> *Of those who must die*
>
> *Save us*
> *From everlasting darkness*
> *Drive out the demons from the valley.*
> *Be our guide*
> *Into the Light.*

For a long time I was overcome with tears. I could not understand how this could have happened. Remembering to play the cripple still, I went to the high altar to say my prayers, and then to the tavern.

There I paid the bard to play all the old songs he knew, and none of them were familiar to me. The Pict language had died out. No one knew the writing on the crosses in the churchyard.

But this saint, what could the man tell me about him, I asked.

Was I truly Scots, the bard asked.

Had I never heard of the great pagan King Ashlar of the Picts, who had converted this entire valley to Christianity?

Had I never heard of the magic spring through which he worked his miracles? I had only to go down the hill to see it.

Ashlar the Great had built the first Christian church on this spot, in the year 586, and then set out for Rome on his first pilgrimage, being murdered by brigands before he had even left the valley.

Within the shrine his holy relics lay, the remnants of his bloody cloak, his leather belt, his crucifix, and a letter to the saint himself from none other than St. Columba. In the scriptorium I might see a psalter which Ashlar himself had written in the style of the great monastery at Iona.

"Ah, I understand it all," I said. "But what is the meaning of this strange prayer, and the words 'who will come again'?"

"Ah, that, well now, that's a story. Go to Mass tomorrow morning and look well at the priest who celebrates. You will see a young man of immense height, almost as tall as yourself, and such men are not so uncommon here. But this one is Ashlar come again, they say, and they tell the most fantastic story of his birth, how he came from his mother speaking and singing, and ready to serve God, seeing visions of the Great Saint and the Holy Battle of Donnelaith and the pagan witch Janet burnt up in the fire as the town converted in spite of her."

"This is true?" I asked, in quiet awe.

How could it be? A wild Taltos, born to humans who had no idea they carried the seed in their blood? No. It could not have been. What humans could make the Taltos together? It must have been a hybrid, sired by some mysterious giant who had come in the night and coupled with a woman cursed with the witches' gifts, leaving her with his monster offspring.

"It has happened three times before in our history," said the bard. "Sometimes the mother does not even know she's with child, other times she is in her third or her fourth month. No one knows when the creature inside her shall start to grow and become the image of the saint, come again to his people."

"And who were the fathers of these children?"

"Upstanding men of the Clan of Donnelaith, that's who they were, for St. Ashlar was the founder of their family. But you know there are so many strange tales in these woods. Each clan has its secrets. We're not to speak of it here, but now and then such a giant child is born who knows nothing of the Saint. I have seen one of these with my own eyes, standing a head taller than his father moments after he left his mother to die at the hearthside. A frantic thing, crying in fear, and possessed of no visions from God, but wailing for the pagan circle of stones! Poor soul. They called it a witch, a monster. And do you know what they do with such creatures?"

"They burn them."

"Yes," came his answer. "It's a terrible thing to see. Especially if the poor creature is a woman. For then she is judged to be the devil's child, without trial, for she cannot possibly be Ashlar. But these are the Highlands, and our ways have always been very mysterious."

"Have you yourself ever laid eyes on the female thing?" I asked.

"No," he said. "Never. But there are some who say they have known those who have seen it. There is talk among the sorcerers, and those who cling to the pagan ways. People dream that they will bring the female and the male together. But we should not speak of these things. We suffer those witches to live because now and then they can cure. But no one believes their stories, or thinks them proper for the ears of Christian people."

"Ah, yes," I said. "I can well imagine." I thanked him.

I did not wait for morning Mass to see the strange, tall priest.

I caught his scent as soon as I approached the rectory, and when he came to the door, having caught mine, we stood staring at one another. I rose to my full height, and of course he had done nothing to disguise his own. We merely stood there, facing one another.

In him I saw the old gentleness, the eyes almost timid, and the lips soft, and the skin as fresh and free of blemish as that of a baby. Had he really been born of two human beings, two powerful witches perhaps? Did he believe his destiny?

Born remembering, yes, born knowing, yes, and thank God for him it had been the right time that he remembered—and the right battle, and the right place. And now he followed the old profession they had marked for us hundreds of years ago.

He came towards me. He wanted to speak. Perhaps he could not believe his eyes, that he was looking upon one exactly like him.

"Father," I asked in Latin, so that he was most likely to answer, "was it really from a human mother and father you came?"

"How else?" he asked, quite clearly terrified. "Go if you will to my parents themselves. Ask them." He grew pale, and was trembling.

"Father," I said, "where is your like among women?"

"There is no such thing!" he declared. But now he could scarcely keep himself from running away from me. "Brother, where have you come from?" he asked. "Here, seek God's forgiveness for your sins, whatever they are."

"You have never seen a woman of our kind?"

He shook his head. "Brother, I am the chosen of God," he explained. "The chosen of St. Ashlar." He bowed his head, humbly, and I saw a blush come to his cheeks, for obviously he'd committed a sin of pride in announcing this.

"Farewell, then," I said. And I left him.

I left the town and I went again to the stones; I sang an old song, letting myself rock back and forth in the wind, and then I made for the forest.

Dawn was just rising behind me when I climbed the wooded hills to find the old cave. It was a desolate spot, dark as it had been five hundred years before, with no sign now of the witch's hovel.

In the early light, cold and bitter as that of a winter's eve, I heard a voice call me.

"Ashlar!"

I turned around and I looked at the dark woods.

"Ashlar the cursed, I see you!"

"It's you, Aiken Drumm," I cried. And then I heard his mean laughter. Ah, the Little People were there, garbed in green so that they would blend with the leaves and the bracken. I saw their cruel little faces.

"There's no tall woman here for you, Ashlar," cried Aiken Drumm. "Nor will there ever be. No men of your ilk but a mewling priest born of witches, who falls to his knees when he hears our pipes. Here! Come. Take a little bride, a sweet morsel of wrinkled flesh, and see what you beget! And be grateful for what God gives you."

They had begun to beat their drums. I heard the whining of their song, discordant, ghastly, yet strangely familiar. Then came the pipes. It was the old songs we had sung, the songs we taught them!

"Who knows, Ashlar the cursed?" he cried out. "But your daughter by one of us this morn might be a female! Come with us; we have wee women aplenty to amuse you. Think, a daughter, Your Royal Majesty! And once again the tall people would rule the hills!"

I turned and ran through the trees, not stopping till I had cleared the pass and come once more to the high road.

Of course Aiken Drumm spoke the truth. I had found no female of my kind in all of Scotland. And that was what I'd come to seek.

And what I would seek for another millennium.

I did not believe then, on that cold morning, that I would never lay eyes again upon a young or fertile female Taltos. Oh, how many times in the early centuries had I seen my female counterparts and turned away from them. Cautious, withdrawn, I would not have fathered a young Taltos to suffer the confusion of this strange world for all the sweet embraces of the lost land.

And now where were they, these fragrant darlings?

The old, the white of hair, the sweet of breath, the scentless, these I had seen many a time and would see again—creatures wild and lost, or wrapped in a sorceress's dreams, they had given me only chaste kisses.

In dark city streets once I caught the powerful scent, only to be maddened, unable ever to find the soft folds of hot and secret flesh from which it emanated.

Many a human witch I've lured to bed, sometimes warning her of the dangers of my embrace, and sometimes not, when I believed her strong, and able to bear my offspring.

Across the world I've gone, by every means, to track the mysterious ageless woman of remarkable height, with memories of long ago, who greets men who come to her with sweet smiles and never bears their children.

She is human or she is not there at all.

I had come too late, or to the wrong place, or plague took the beauty many years ago. War laid waste that town. Or no one knows the story.

Would it always be so?

Tales abound of giants in the earth, of the tall, the fair, the gifted.

Surely they are not all gone! What became of those who fled the glen? Are no wild female Taltos born into the world of human parents?

Surely somewhere, in the deep forest of Scotland or the jungles of Peru, or the snowy wastes of Russia, there lives a family of Taltos, a clan, in its warm and well-defended tower. The woman and the man have their books, their memories to share, their games to play, their bed in which to kiss and play, though the act of coitus must, as always, be approached with reverence.

My people can't be gone.

The world is huge. The world is endless. Surely I am not the last. Surely that has not been the meaning of Janet's terrible words, that I should wander through time, mateless forever.

Now you know my story.

I could tell many tales. I could tell of my journeys through many lands, my years in various occupations; I could tell of the few male Taltos I met over the years, of the stories I heard of our lost people who had once lived in this or that fabled village.

The story you tell is the story you choose to tell.

And this is the story we share, Rowan and Michael.

501

You know now how the clan of Donnelaith came into being. You know how the blood of the Taltos came to be in the blood of humans. You know the tale of the first woman ever burnt in the beautiful valley. And the sad account of the place to which the Taltos brought such misery, not once, but again and again, if all our stories are history.

Janet, Lasher, Suzanne, her descendants, even to Emaleth.

And you see now that when you raised your gun, when you lifted it, Rowan, and you fired the shots that brought down this child, the girl who had given you her milk, it was no small act of which you need ever be ashamed, but destiny.

You have saved us both. You have saved us all perhaps. You have saved me from the most terrible dilemma I could ever know, and one which I may be not meant to know.

Whatever the case, don't weep for Emaleth. Don't weep for a race of strange, soft-eyed people, long ago driven from the earth by a stronger species. This is the way of the earth, and we are both of it.

What other strange, unnamed creatures live within the cities and jungles of our planet? I have glimpsed many things. I have heard many stories. The rain and wind till the earth, to use Janet's words. What next shall spring from some hidden garden?

Could we now live together, the Taltos, the human, in the same world? How would such be possible? This is a world where human races battle endlessly, where people of one faith still slaughter people of another. Religious wars rage from Sri Lanka to Bosnia, from Jerusalem to American cities and towns where Christians still, in the name of Jesus Christ, bring death in his name to their enemies, to their own, even to little children.

Tribe, race, clan, family.

Deep within us all are the seeds of hate for what is different. We do not have to be taught these things. We have to be taught *not* to give in to them! They are in our blood; but in our minds is the charity and the love to overcome them.

And how would my gentle people fare today, if they did come back, as foolish now as they were then, unable to meet the ferocity of men, yet frightening even the most innocent humans with their bold eroticism? Would we choose tropical islands on which to play our sensuous games, to do our dances and fall into our spells of dancing and singing?

Or would ours be a realm of electronic pastimes, of computers, films, games of virtual reality, or sublime mathematical puzzles—studies suited to our minds, with their love of detail and their inability to sustain irrational states such as wrath or hatred? Would we fall in love with quantum physics the way we once fell in love with weaving? I can see our kind, up night and day, tracing the paths of particles through magnetic fields on computer screens! Who knows what advances we might make, given those toys to preoccupy us?

My brain is twice the size of the human brain. I do not age by any known clock. My capacity to learn modern science and modern medicine cannot be imagined.

And what if there rose among us but one ambitious male or female, one Lasher, if you will, who would the supremacy of the race restore, what then might happen? Within the space of one night, a pair of Taltos could breed a battalion of adults, ready to invade the citadels of human power, ready to destroy the weapons which humans know how to use so much better, ready to take the food, the drink, the resources of this brimming world, and deny it to those less gentle, less kind, less patient, in retribution for their eons of bloody dominance.

Of course, I do not wish to learn these things.

I have not spent my centuries studying the physical world. Or the uses of power. But when I choose to score some victory for myself—this company you see around you—the world falls back from me as if its obstacles were made of paper. My empire, my world—it is made of toys and money. But how much more easily it could be made of medicines to quiet the human male, to dilute the testosterone in his veins, and silence his battle cries forever.

And imagine, if you will, a Taltos with true zeal. Not a dreamer who has spent his brief years in misted lands nourished on pagan poetry, but a visionary who, true to the very principles of Christ, decided that violence should be annihilated, that peace on earth was worth any sacrifice.

Imagine the legions of newborns who could be committed to this cause, the armies bred to preach love in every hamlet and vale and stamp out those, quite literally, who spoke against it.

What am I finally? A repository for genes that *could* make the world crumble? And what are you, my Mayfair witches—have you carried those same genes down through the centuries so that we may finally end the Kingdom of Christ with our sons and our daughters?

The Bible names this one, does it not? The beast, the demon, the Antichrist.

Who has the courage for such glory? Foolish old poets who live in towers still, and dream of rituals on Glastonbury Tor to make the world new again.

And even for that mad old man, that doddering fool, was murder not the first requisite of his vision?

I have shed blood. It is on my hands now for vengeance's sake, a pathetic way to heal a wound, but one to which we turn again and again in our wretchedness. The Talamasca is whole again. Not worth the price, but done. And our secrets are safe for the present.

We are friends, you and I, I pray, and we will never hurt each other. I can reach for your hands in the dark. You can call out to me, and I'll answer.

But what if something *new* could happen? Something wholly new? I think I see it, I think I imagine. . . . But then it escapes me.

I don't have *the answer*.

I know I shall never trouble your red-haired witch, Mona. I shall never trouble any of your powerful women. Many centuries have passed since lust or hope has tricked me into that adventure.

I am alone, and if I am cursed, I've forgotten it.

I like my empire of small, beautiful things. I like the playthings that I offer to the world. The dolls of a thousand faces are my children.

In a small way they are my dance, my circle, my song. Emblems of eternal play, the work perhaps of heaven.

Thirty-one

AND THE DREAM repeats itself. She climbs out of bed, runs down the stairs. "Emaleth!" The shovel is under the tree. Who would ever bother to move it?

She digs and digs, and there is her girl, with the long slack hair and the big blue eyes.

"Mother!"

"Come on, my darling."

They're down in the hole together. Rowan holds her, rocking her. "Oh, I'm so sorry I killed you."

"It's all right, Mother dear," she says.

"It was a war," Michael says. "And in a war, people are killed, and then afterwards . . ."

She woke, gasping.

The room was quiet beneath a faint drone of heat from the small vents along the floor. Michael slept beside her, his knuckles touching her hip as she sat there, hands clasped to her mouth, looking down at him.

No, don't wake him. Don't put him through the misery again. But she knew.

When all the talk was over and done with, when they'd had their dinner and their long walk through the snowy streets, when they'd talked till dawn and breakfasted and talked some more and vowed their eternal friendship, she knew. She should never never have killed her girl. There was no reason for it.

How could that doe-eyed creature, who had comforted her so, in that kindly voice, milk spilling from her breasts, hhhmmm, the taste of the milk, how could that trembling creature have hurt anyone?

What logic had made her lift the gun, what logic had made her pull the trigger? Child of rape, child of aberration, child of nightmare. But child still. . . .

She climbed out of the bed, finding her slippers in the dark, and reaching for a long white negligee on the chair, another one of these strange garments which filled her suitcase, full of the perfume of another woman.

Killed her, killed her, killed her, this tender and trusting thing, full of knowledge of long-ago lands, of valley and glen and plains and who knew what mysteries? Her comfort in the dark, when she'd been tied to the bed. *My Emaleth.*

A pale white window was hung in the darkness at the far end of the hallway, a great rectangle of glowing night sky, light spilling on the long path of colored marble.

To that light she moved, the negligee ballooning out, her feet making a soft skittering tap on the floor, her hand out for the button of the elevator.

Take me down, down, down to the dolls. Take me out of here. If I look from that window, I'll jump. I'll open the glass, and I'll look out over the endless lights of the largest city in the world, and I'll climb up and put my arms out, and then I'll drop down into the ice-cold darkness.

Down, down, down with you, my daughter.

All the images of his tale went through her mind, the sonorous timbre of his voice, his gentle eyes as he spoke. And she is now debris beneath the roots of the oak, something erased from the world without a jot of ink upon a piece of paper, without a hymn sung.

The doors closed. The wind sounded in the shaft, that faint whistling, like wind in mountains perhaps, and as the cab descended, a howling as if she were in a giant chimney. She wanted to crumple and fall on the floor, to go limp without will or purpose or fight anymore, just to sink into the darkness.

No more words to say, no more thoughts. No more to know or to learn. I should have taken her hand, I should

506

have held her. So easy it would have been to keep her, tender, against my breasts, my darling, my Emaleth.

And all those dreams that sent you out the door with him—of cells within cells the like of which no human had ever seen, of secrets gleaned from every layer and fiber gently plied from willing hands, willing arms, willing lips pressed to sterile glass, and droplets of blood given with the smallest frown, of fluids and maps and schemes and X rays made without a pinch of hurt, all to tell a new tale, a new miracle, a new beginning—all that, with her, would have been possible! A drowsy feminine thing that would not have hurt any mortal being, so easy to control, so easy to care for.

The doors opened. The dolls have been waiting. The gold light of the city comes through a hundred high windows, caught and suspended in squares and rectangles of gleaming glass, and the dolls, the dolls wait and watch with hands uplifted. Tiny mouths ever on the verge of greeting. Little fingers hovering in the stillness.

Silently she walked through the dolls, corridor after corridor of dolls, eyes like pitch-black holes in space, or gleaming buttons in a glint of light. Dolls are quiet; dolls are patient; dolls are attentive.

We've come back to the Bru, the queen of the dolls, the big cold bisque princess with her almond eyes and her cheeks so rosy and round, her eyebrows caught forever in that quizzical look, trying vainly to understand what? The endless parade of all these moving beings who look at her?

Come to life. Just for a moment come to life. Be mine. Be warm. Be alive.

Out from under the tree in the dark, walk again as if death were a part of the tale you could have erased, as if those fatal moments could be omitted forever. No stumbling in this wilderness. No false steps.

Hold you in my arms.

Her hands were splayed out on the cold glass of the case. Her forehead pressed against it. The light made two crescent moons in her eyes. The long mohair tresses lay flat and heavy against the silk of her dress, as if they were

507

moist with the dampness of the earth, the dampness of the grave perhaps.

Where was the key? Had he worn it on a chain around his neck? She couldn't remember. She longed to open the door, to take the doll in her arms. To hold it tight for one moment against her breast.

What happens when grief is this mad, when grief has blotted out all other thoughts, feelings, hopes, dreams, wonder?

Finally exhaustion comes. The body says return to sleep, lie down now to rest, not torment. Nothing's changed. The dolls stare as the dolls will always stare. And the earth eats at what is buried inside of it as it always has. But a kind weariness overtakes the soul, and it seems possible, just possible, to wait to weep, to wait to suffer, to wait to die and lie down with them, to have it finished, because only then is all guilt gone, washed away, when you are as dead as they are.

He was there. He was standing before the glass. You couldn't mistake him for anyone else. There is no one else that tall, and even if it weren't for that, she knew his face too well now, the line of his profile.

He'd heard her in the dark, walking back down the corridor. But he didn't move. He was just leaning there against the window frame and watching the light gather outside, watching the blackness fade and turn to milk and the stars dissolve as though melted in it.

What did he think? That she'd come to seek him out?

She felt shattered inside, weak. Unable to reason what to do, needing perhaps to walk across the floor, to stand beside him and look down on the smoky gloom of early roofs and towers, on lights twinkling along hazy streets, and smoke rising and curling from a hundred stacks and chimneys.

She did this. She stood beside him.

"We love each other now," he said. "Don't we?"

His face was so sad. It hurt her. It was a fresh hurt, touching her right in the midst of the old pain, something immediate that could bring the tears where before there had only been something as black and empty as horror.

"Yes, we do, we love each other," she said. "With our whole hearts."

"And we will have that," he said. "Won't we?"

"Yes, always. For as long as we live. We are friends and we will always be, and nothing, nothing will ever break the promises between us."

"And I'll know you're there, it's as simple as that."

"And when you don't want to be alone anymore, come. Come and be with us."

He turned for the first time, as if he had not really wanted to look at her. The sky was paling so fast, the room just filling up and opening wide, and his face was weary and only slightly less than perfect.

One kiss, one chaste and silent kiss, and no more, just a tight clasp of fingers.

And then she was gone, drowsy, aching, glad of the day spilling down over the soft bed. Now I can sleep, daylight at last, now I can sleep, tumbling under the soft covers, next to Michael again.

Thirty-two

IT WAS TOO cold to be out, but winter would not let go its hold upon New York. And if the little man wanted to meet at the Trattoria, so be it.

Ash didn't mind the walk. He did not want to be alone in his lonely tower rooms, and he was fairly certain that Samuel was on his way, and could not be persuaded to return.

He enjoyed the crowds on Seventh Avenue rushing in the early dusk, bright shop windows full of lavishly colored Oriental porcelains, ornate clocks, bronze statues, and rugs of wool and silk—all the gift merchandise sold in this part of midtown. Couples were hurrying to dinner so that they might make the curtain at Carnegie Hall for a young violinist who was causing a worldwide sensation. Lines at the ticket office were long. The fancy boutiques had not yet closed; and though the snow fell in tiny little flakes, it could not possibly cover either asphalt or sidewalks due to the continuous thunder of human feet.

No, this is not a bad time to be walking. This is a bad time for trying to forget that you have just embraced your friends, Michael and Rowan, for the last time until you hear from them.

Of course they don't know that that is the rule of the game, the gesture his heart and his pride would require, but more than likely, they would not have been surprised. They had spent four days, all told, with him. And he was as unsure of their love now as he had been the very first moment in London when he had laid eyes on them.

No, he did not want to be alone. Only problem was, he should have dressed for anonymity and the freezing wind, but he had dressed for neither. People stared at a seven-foot-tall man with dark wavy hair who wore a violet silk blazer in such weather. And the scarf was yellow. How mad of him to have thrown on these decidedly private-realm clothes and then rushed out into the street wearing them.

But he had changed before Remmick gave him the news: Samuel had packed and gone; Samuel would meet him at the Trattoria. Samuel had left behind the bulldog, that it might be his New York dog, if Ash didn't mind. (Why would Ash mind a dog that both drooled and snored, but then Remmick and the young Leslie undoubtedly would be the ones to endure the brunt of this. The young Leslie was now a permanent fixture in the tower offices and rooms, much to her glee.) Samuel would get another dog in and for England.

The Trattoria was already packed, he could see this through the glass, patrons shoulder to shoulder along its winding bar and at its innumerable little tables.

But there was Samuel, as promised, puffing on a small damp cigarette (he murdered them the way Michael did), and drinking whiskey from a heavy little glass, and watching for him.

Ash tapped on the window.

The little man took him in, head to toe, and shook his head. The little man himself was spruce in his new style, tweed with waistcoat, brand-new shirt, shoes shined like mirrors. There was even a pair of brown leather gloves lying like two ghost hands, all collapsed and mashed, on the table.

It was impossible to know what feelings were concealed behind the folds and wrinkles of Samuel's flesh, but the neatness and style of the overall figure argued for something other than the bleary, drunken, grumbling melodrama of the last forty-eight hours.

That Michael had found Samuel so amusing was a blessing. Indeed, one night they had drunk each other under the

511

table, telling jokes, while Rowan and Ash had only smiled indulgently, to be left at last with the awful tension of knowing that if they went to bed more would be lost than gained—unless Ash thought of himself, and only himself entirely.

Not in Ash's nature.

"Not in my nature to be alone, either," he thought. There was a leather portmanteau beside Samuel's glass. Leaving.

Ash pushed very gently past those entering and exiting, giving a little nod and a point of the finger to Samuel to let the harried doorman know he was expected.

The cold died away at once, and with the loud crash of voices and pots and pans, dishes and shuffling feet, there came the warm air like a fluid oozing around him. Inevitably heads turned, but the marvelous thing about any restaurant crowd in New York was that table partners were twice as animated as anywhere else, and always so seriously focused on each other. All meetings seemed crucial; courses devoured in a rush; faces evincing infatuation, if not with one's partner, then certainly with the evening's ever-quickening momentum.

Surely they saw the tall man in the outrageous violet silk take the chair opposite the smallest man in the place, a chunky little fellow in heavy clothes, but they saw it out of the corner of the eye, or with a movement of the neck swift enough to injure the spinal cord, and they did not miss a beat of their own conversations. The table was right before the front glass, but then people on the streets were even more skilled at secret observation than the people in the warm safety zone of the restaurant.

"Go ahead and say it," said Ash under his breath. "You are leaving, you are going back to England."

"You knew I would. I don't want to be over here. I always think it's going to be wonderful and then I get tired, and I have to go home. I have to go back to the glen, before those fools from the Talamasca start invading it."

"They won't do that," Ash said. "I hoped you'd stay for a little while." He marveled at the control he managed to maintain over his own voice. "That we'd talk about things . . ."

"You cried when you said goodbye to your human friends, didn't you?"

"Now, why do you ask me that?" said Ash. "You are determined that we part with cross words?"

"Why did you trust them, the two witches? Here, the waiter's talking to you. Eat something."

Ash pointed to something on the menu, the standard pasta he always ordered in such places, and waited for the man to disappear before resuming.

"If you hadn't been drunk, Samuel, if you hadn't seen everything through a tiresome haze, you would know the answer to that question."

"Mayfair witches. I know what they are. Yuri told me all about them. Yuri talked in a fever a lot of the time. Ash, don't be stupid again. Don't expect these people to love you."

"Your words don't make sense," said Ash. "They never did. They're just a sort of noise I've grown used to hearing when I'm in your presence."

The waiter set down the mineral water, the milk, the glasses.

"You're out of sorts, Ash," said Samuel, gesturing for another glass of whiskey, and it was pure whiskey, Ash could tell by the smell. "And it's not my fault." Samuel slumped back in the chair. "Look, my friend, I'm only trying to warn you. Let me put it this way, if you prefer. Don't love those two."

"You know, if you insist upon this lecture, I just may lose my temper."

The little man laughed outright. It was a low, rumbly laugh, but the folds over his eyes even showed his sudden bemusement.

"Now that might keep me in New York another hour or two," he said, "if I thought I was really going to see that."

Ash didn't respond. It was too terribly important not to say anything he didn't mean, not now, not to Samuel, not to anyone. He had believed that all his long life, but periodically he was brutally reminded of it.

After a moment, he said:

"And who should I love?" It was said with only the softest note of reproach. "I'll be glad when you're gone. I mean . . . I mean I'll be glad when this unpleasant conversation is over."

"Ash, you should never have drawn so close to them, never told them all you did. And then the gypsy, letting him just go back to the Talamasca."

"Yuri? And what did you want me to do? How could I stop Yuri from going back to the Talamasca?"

"You could have lured him to New York, put him to work for you some way. He was a man with a broken life; but you sent him home to write volumes on what happened. Hell, he could have been your companion."

"That was not right for him. He had to go home."

"Of course it was right. And he was right for you—an outcast, a gypsy, the son of a whore."

"Please don't make your speech as offensive and vulgar as you possibly can. You frighten me. Look, it was Yuri's choice. If he had not wanted to go back, he would have said so. His life was the Order. He had to go back, at least to heal all the wounds. And after that? He wouldn't have been happy here in my world. Dolls are pure magic to those who love them and understand them. To others they are less than toys. Yuri is a man of coarse spiritual distinctions, not subtle ones."

"That sounds good," said Samuel, "but it's stupid." He watched the waiter set the fresh drink before him. "Your world is full of things that Yuri might have done. You could have turned him loose to build more parks, plant more trees, all these grandiose schemes of yours. What were you telling your witches, that you were going to build parks in the sky so that everyone could see what you see from your marble chambers? You could have kept that kid busy all his life, and you would have had his companionship—"

"I wish you would stop. This didn't happen. It simply did not happen."

"But what happened is that you want the friendship of those witches, a man and woman married to each other with a great clan around them, people who are *a priori* committed to a family way of living that is intensely human—"

"What can I do to make you stop?"

"Nothing. Drink the milk. I know you want it. You're ashamed to drink it in front of me, afraid I might say something like 'Ashlar, drink your milk!' "

"Which you now have, even though I have not touched the milk, you realize."

"Ahh, this is the point. You love those two, the witches. And it is incumbent upon those two—as I see it—to forget all this, this nightmare of Taltos, and the glen, and murdering little fools who infiltrated the Talamasca. It is essential to the sanity of that man and woman that they go home and build the life the Mayfair family expects them to build. And I hate it when you love those who will only turn their backs on you, and those two have to do it."

Ash didn't answer.

"They are surrounded by hundreds of people for whom they must make this part of their lives a lie," Samuel continued to expostulate. "They will want to forget you exist; they will not want the great realm of their day-to-day life lost in the glare of your presence."

"I see."

"I don't like it when you suffer."

"Is that so?"

"Yes! I like to open magazines and newspapers and read about your little corporate triumphs, and see your smiling face above flippant little lists of the world's ten most eccentric billionaires, or New York's most eligible bachelors. And now I know you will break your heart wondering if these witches are your true friends, if you can call them when your heart aches, if you can depend on them for the knowledge of yourself that every being requires—".

"Stay, please, Samuel."

This put a silence to the lecture. The little man sighed. He drank some of the fresh drink, about half, and licked his heavy crooked lower lip with an amazingly pink tongue.

"Hell, Ash, I don't want to."

"I came when you called me, Samuel."

"You regret that now?"

"I don't think in that way. Besides, how could I regret it?"

"Forget it all, Ash. Seriously, forget it. Forget a Taltos came to the glen. Forget you know these witches. Forget you need anyone to love you for what you are. That's impossible. I'm afraid. I'm afraid of what you will do now. The pattern's all too familiar."

"What pattern is that?" asked Ash quietly.

"You'll destroy all this, the company, the corporation, the Toys Without Limit or Dolls for the Millions, whatever it's called. You'll sink into apathy. You'll just let it go. You'll walk out and far away, and the things you've built and the things you've made will just slowly fall apart without you. You've done it before. And then you'll be lost, just the way I'm lost, and some cold winter evening, and why you always choose the dead of winter I don't know, you'll come to the glen again looking for me."

"This is more important to me, Samuel," he said. "It's important for many reasons."

"Parks, trees, gardens, children," sang the little man.

Ash didn't reply.

"Think about all those who depend on you, Ash," said Samuel, continuing the same sermon for the same congregation. "Think of all these people who make and sell and buy and love the things you manufacture. That can substitute for sanity, I think, having other warm beings of intellect and feeling dependent upon us. You think I'm right?"

"It doesn't substitute for sanity, Samuel," said Ash. "It substitutes for happiness."

"All right, that's fine then. But don't wait for your witches to come to you again, and for God's sake never seek them on their own turf. You'll see fear in their eyes if they ever see you standing in their garden."

"You're so sure of all this."

"Yes, I'm sure. Ash, you told them everything. Why did you do that? Perhaps if you had not, they wouldn't fear you."

"You don't know what you're saying."

"And Yuri and the Talamasca, how they will plague you now."

"They will not."

"But those witches, they are not your friends."

516

"So you keep saying."

"I know they are not. I know their curiosity and awe will soon change to fear. Ash, it's an old cliché, they're only human."

Ash bowed his head and looked away, out the window at the blowing snow, at shoulders hunkered against the wind.

"Ashlar, I know," Samuel said, "because I am an outcast. And you are an outcast. And look out there at the multitudes of humans passing on the street, and think how each one condemns so many others as outcast, as 'other,' as not human. We are monsters, my friend. That's what we'll always be. It's their day. That we're alive at all is enough to worry about." He downed the rest of the drink.

"And so you go home to your friends in the glen."

"I hate them, and you know it. But the glen we won't have for long. I go back for sentimental reasons. Oh, it's not just the Talamasca, and that sixteen genteel scholars will come with tape recorders, begging me to recite all I know over lunch at the Inn. It's all those archaeologists digging up St. Ashlar's Cathedral. The modern world has found the place. And why? Because of your damned witches."

"You can't lay that on me or on them, and you know it."

"Eventually we'll have to find some more remote place, some other curse or legend to protect us. But they're not my friends, don't think they are. They don't."

Ash only nodded.

Food had come, a large salad for the little man, the pasta for Ash. The wine was being poured in the glasses. It smelled like something gone utterly wrong.

"I'm too drunk to eat," Samuel said.

"I understand if you go," Ash said softly. "That is, if you're bound to go, then perhaps you should do it."

They sat in silence for a moment. Then the little man lifted his fork and began to devour the salad, shoveling it into his mouth, as bits and pieces fell to the plate despite his most diligent efforts. Loudly he scraped up every last bit of olive, cheese, and lettuce on the plate, and then drank a big gulp of the mineral water.

"Now I can drink some more," he said.

Ash made a sound that would have been a laugh if he had not been so sad.

Samuel slid off the chair and onto his feet. He picked up the leather portmanteau. He sauntered over to Ash, and crooked his arm around Ash's neck. Ash kissed his cheek quickly, faintly repelled by the leathery texture of the skin, but determined at all costs to hide it.

"Will you come back soon?" Ash asked.

"No. But we'll see each other," said Samuel. "Take care of my dog. His feelings are hurt very easily."

"I'll remember that."

"And pitch yourself into your work!"

"Anything else?"

"I love you."

And with that Samuel pushed and swaggered his way through the press of those being seated and those rising to go, and all the backs and elbows clumped against him. He went out the front door and along the front window. The snow was already catching in his hair and on his bushy eyebrows, and making dark wet spots on his shoulders.

He lifted his hand in farewell, and then he passed out of the frame, and the crowd became the crowd again.

Ash lifted the glass of milk and slowly drank all of it. Then he put some bills beneath his plate, stared at the food as if telling it goodbye, and went out himself, walking into the wind on Seventh Avenue.

When he reached his bedroom high above the streets, Remmick was waiting for him.

"You're cold, sir, much too cold."

"Am I?" Ash murmured. Patiently he let Remmick take away the silk blazer and the outrageous scarf. He put on the flannel smoking jacket of satin-lined wool, and taking the towel Remmick gave to him, he wiped the dampness from his hair and his face.

"Sit down, sir, let me take off your wet shoes."

"If you say so." The chair felt so soft, he could not imagine climbing out of it later on to go to bed. And all the rooms are empty. Rowan and Michael are gone. We will not be walking downtown tonight, talking eagerly together.

"Your friends arrived safely in New Orleans, sir,"

518

Remmick said, peeling off the wet socks, and then quickly putting on fresh dry socks so deftly that his fingers barely grazed Ash's flesh. "The call came right after you left for dinner. The plane is on its way back. It should be landing in about twenty minutes."

Ash nodded. The leather slippers were lined with fur. He did not know whether they were old or new. He couldn't remember. Suddenly all the little details seemed to have fled. His mind was horrifyingly empty and still; and he felt the loneliness and the stillness of the rooms completely.

Remmick moved at the closet doors like a ghost.

We hire those who are unobtrusive, Ash thought, and then they can't comfort us; what we tolerate cannot save us.

"Where's the young Leslie, Remmick? Is she about?"

"Yes, sir, with a million questions, it seems. But you look so very tired."

"Send her in. I need to work. I need to have my mind on something."

He walked down the corridor, and into the first of his offices, the private office, the one where papers were stacked here and there, and a file cabinet stood open, the one no one was allowed to clean, the one that was insufferably cluttered.

Leslie appeared within seconds, face brimming with excitement, dedication, devotion, and inexhaustible energy. "Mr. Ash, there's the International Doll Expo next week, and a woman from Japan just called, said you definitely wanted to see her work, you told her so yourself last time you were in Tokyo, and there were about twenty different appointments missed while you were gone, I've got the entire list. . . ."

"Sit down, then, and we'll get to it."

He took his position behind the desk, making a small note that the clock said 6:45 p.m., and that he would not look at it, not even steal a glance, until he was certain that the time would be past midnight.

"Leslie, put all that aside. Here are some ideas. I want you to number them. The order is not important. What's important is that you give me the whole list every day, without fail, with notes on the progress we've made regard-

519

ing each and every idea, and a large mark of 'no progress' on those I allow to remain inactive."

"Yes, sir."

"Singing dolls. Perfect first a quartet, four dolls that sing in harmony."

"Oh, that's a wonderful idea, Mr. Ash."

"Prototypes should reflect some aim at being cost-effective; however, that is not the most important point. The dolls must sound good and sing even after they are hurled to the floor."

"Yes, sir . . . 'hurled to the floor.' "

"And a tower museum. I want a list of the top twenty-five available penthouses in midtown, purchase price, lease price, every pertinent detail. I want a museum in the sky so that people can go out and look at the view on a glass-enclosed gallery. . . ."

"And what will the museum hold, sir, dolls?"

"Dolls on a certain theme. The exact same assignment is to be given to two thousand doll artists. Make your interpretation in three connected figures of the Family of Humankind. No, four figures. One can be a child. Yes, the description will be exact, I need to be reminded. . . . For now, get the best building."

"Yes, sir, got it, yes," she said, engraving her pad with the fine-point pen.

"And on the singing dolls, everyone should be advised that eventually there will be an entire choir. A child or a doll collector could conceivably over the years acquire the entire choir, or chorus, or whatever name is best, you know, you follow me?"

"Yes, sir . . ."

"And I don't want to see any mechanical plans; this is electronic, computer chip, state of the art, and there should be . . . there should be some way for the voice of one doll to work some responsive change in the voice of another. But those are details. Write it up. . . ."

"Materials, sir? Porcelain?"

"No, not porcelain. Never. I don't want them to break. Remember, they should not break, ever."

"Sorry, sir."

"And I'll design the faces. I need pictures, pictures from all over, I want everyone's work. If there is an old woman in a village in the Pyrenees making dolls, I want to see pictures. And India, why do we have no dolls from India? Do you know how often I have asked this question? Why don't I get answers? Write this memo to the vice presidents, to the marketing people, post it! India. Who are the art-doll makers of India? I think I will go to India, yes, find a time for me to go. I'll find the people who are making dolls if no one else has the sense. . . ."

The snow had begun to fall heavily outside, very white near the glass.

All the rest was once again blackness. Tiny random sounds came from the streets below, or was it from the pipes, or the snow falling on the roof above, or just the glass and steel of the building breathing as inevitably as wood breathes, the building, for all its dozens of stories, swaying ever so slightly in the wind, like a giant tree in the forest?

On and on he talked, watching her fierce little hand move with the fine-point pen. About the replicas of monuments, the small plastic version of Chartres Cathedral which the children could enter. The importance of scale, ratios. And what if there were a park with a great circle of stones there?

"Oh, and yes, a special assignment, something I want you to do tomorrow perhaps, or the day after. No, later. You do this. You're to go down to the Private Museum. . . ."

"Yes, sir."

"The Bru, are you familiar with the Bru, the big French doll? My princess."

"*The* Bru, sir, yes sir, oh, that doll."

"Bru Jne 14; thirty-six inches in height; wig, shoes, dress, slip, et cetera, all original. Exhibit Number One."

"Yes, sir, I know exactly."

"She's to be packed by you, and no one else, with appropriate assistance, and then properly insured, and see to that yourself, and then shipped . . . shipped to . . ." But to whom? Was it presumptuous to send it directly to the unborn child? No, it should go to Rowan Mayfair, shouldn't

521

it? Of course it should. And for Michael, some other memento, just as precious in its own way, something carefully crafted of wood, one of the very, very old toys, the knight on its horse, yes, all made of wood, that one, with the original paint clinging to it . . .

But no, that was not the right gift, not for Michael. There was one gift, one precious gift, something as fine as the Bru, and something he wanted to put in Michael's hands.

He rose from the desk, bidding the young Leslie to keep her chair, and moved across the spacious sitting area and down the hall to his bedroom.

He had placed it beneath the bed, the simple signal to Remmick that it was precious and must not be touched by the most well-meaning of servants. He dropped to his knees, felt for it, then slipped it out, the light blazing beautiful on the jeweled cover.

The moment of long ago was right there, the pain, the humiliation, Ninian laughing at him, telling him what a terrible blasphemy he had done, to put their tale into sacred style with sacred language.

For a long moment he sat, cross-legged, shoulder against the side of the bed. He held the book. Yes, for Michael. Michael, the boy who loved books. Michael. Michael would never be able to read it perhaps; it did not matter. Michael would keep it and it was rather like giving it to Rowan, too. She would understand that.

When he came back into the inner office, he had the book wrapped in a large white towel.

"This, this book, for Michael Curry, and the Bru for Rowan Mayfair."

"*The* Bru, sir, the princess?"

"Yes. That one. The packing is terribly important. I may want you to take these gifts down yourself. The fact that the Bru might break, it's unthinkable. Neither present must be lost. Now let's get on to other things. Send out for food if you're hungry. I have a memo here that the Prima Ballerina is out of stock worldwide. Tell me this is a lie."

"It isn't."

"Take dictation. This is the first of seven faxes pertaining to the Prima Ballerina. . . ."

And on they went down the list, and when he did finally look at the clock again, with any serious intent, it was well past midnight. Indeed, the hour had dwindled to one. The snow still fell. Little Leslie's face had turned the color of paper. He was tired enough to sleep.

He fell into the large soft empty bed, vaguely conscious that the young Leslie was still hovering about, asking questions he could no longer hear that well. Extending her invitation.

"Good night, darling," he said.

Remmick opened the window just a little bit, the way he'd been instructed to, and the wind made a fierce howl that blotted out all sounds, all time, any conceivable lesser noise rising up the narrow margins between the dark and mournful buildings. A bit of icy air touched his cheek, making the warmth of the heavy covers all the more delicious.

Don't dream of witches; don't think of their red hair; don't think of Rowan in your arms. Don't think of Michael with the book in his hands, cherishing it as no one else ever did, except those evil brethren who betrayed Lightner. Don't think of the three of you sitting together at their hearth; don't go back to the glen, not now, not for a long long time; don't walk among circles of stone; don't visit caves; don't succumb to the temptation of mortal beauties who may die at your touch. . . . Don't call them, don't beg to hear a coldness, estrangement, evasion in their voices.

And by the time the door was closed, he was slumbering.

The Bru. The street in Paris; the woman in the store; the doll in its box; the big paperweight eyes looking up at him. The sudden thought beneath the streetlamp that a point had come in history where money could make possible all manner of miracles, that the pursuit of money even for one single individual could have great spiritual repercussions for thousands. . . . That in a realm of manufacture and mass production, the acquisition of wealth could be utterly creative.

In a shop on Fifth Avenue only steps from his door, he had stopped to look at The Book of Kells, the perfect reproduction which anyone could own now, and leaf through and love, the precious book that had taken so many to create at Iona.

"For the Man Who Loves Books" is what he would write on the card to Michael. He saw Michael smiling at him, hands in his pockets, just the way Samuel shoved his hands in his pockets. Michael asleep on the floor, and Samuel standing over him, saying drunkenly, "Why didn't God make me into this?" It had been too sad for laughing. And that strange statement Michael had made, as they stood near the fence in Washington Square, all of them so cold, why do people do these things, stand outdoors in snow, and Michael had said, "I always believed in the normal. I thought being poor was abnormal. I thought when you could choose what you wanted, that was normal." Snow, traffic, the night prowlers of the village, Michael's eyes when he looked at Rowan. And she remote, quiet, the words for her so much harder than for him.

This isn't a dream. This is worry, this is going back over it, and making it come to life again, and holding tight. What's it like when they lie together? Is her face a sculpture of ice? Is he the satyr of the wood? Witch touching witch; witch upon witch . . .

Will the Bru see these things from a marble mantel?

"Something about the way you held it." That's all he would write on the card to Rowan. And there would be the blue-eyed Bru staring up from the tissue, make the tissue the color of her eyes, remember to tell Leslie.

And it would be Rowan's decision, and Michael's decision, whether or not to keep those cherished gifts close, as he had done, decade after decade, like idols with which one prays, or to pass them on to Michael and Mona's baby. And maybe the big paperweight eyes of the gorgeous Bru Jne 14 would gaze upon that little child, and would they see the witches' blood as he might if ever, if ever he dared to journey there, some time after the baby had come into this world, as they say—if he dared, just to spy upon them all— The Family of Witch Kind—from the fabled garden where once the ghost of Lasher walked, and his remains were committed to the earth—from that garden which could hide another phantom, could it not, peering through a small, unnoticed winter window.

Thirty-three

PIERCE HAD COLLECTED them from the airport, far too polite to inquire about the owner of the plane, or where they had been, and only too eager to take them to the site of the new medical center.

It was so warm as to be stifling, Michael thought. My kind of town. So glad to be back, and yet so utterly uncertain of anything—whether grass will continue to grow, whether Rowan will become warm and trusting again in his arms, whether he could stay away from the tall man in New York with whom he had known the most extraordinary friendship.

And the past; the past was not fun anymore and never would be, but something inherited with its burdens, its curses, its secrets.

Take your eyes off the bodies of the dead; forget the old man crumpling to the floor; and Aaron, where has Aaron gone? Did his spirit rise into the light, were all things clear finally, and forgiven? To forgive is such a gift to us.

They got out at the edge of the huge rectangle of churned earth. Signs read MAYFAIR MEDICAL with a dozen names and dates. And something too small for his aging eyes to read. He wondered if they'd stop being so blue when they couldn't really see anymore. Did that happen? Or would he have that last claim to fame even when he couldn't see the girls giving him a second look, or Rowan melting slightly, lips curled at the edges.

He tried to focus on the construction site, to realize what

his mind told him, that the progress had been amazing, that some hundred men were working out here in these four blocks, that Mayfair Medical had truly begun.

Were those tears in Rowan's eyes? Yes, the smooth lady with the bobbed hair and the slim tailored suit of supple cloth was crying silently. He moved closer, what the hell was all this distance about, all this respecting of one another's privacy, feelings? He hugged her tight and, finding the softest part of her neck, placed his kisses there, until he felt her rustling against him, bending slightly, and a nice quiver running through her hands as she clasped his head, and said:

"You went on with it, all of you. I could never have expected such a thing." Her eyes moved to Pierce, shy Pierce, who was blushing now under these compliments.

"It's a dream you gave to us, Rowan. And now it's our dream too, and since all our dreams are coming true—since you're here and with us again—well, this one also will be realized."

"Now that's a lawyerly speech, with pacing and just enough force," Michael said. Was he jealous of this young kid? Women did tend to dote when their eyes fell upon Pierce Mayfair. If only Mona could see it, see perhaps that he was the one for her, especially now that in the wake of Gifford's death, her son had drifted away from his fiancée, Clancy. More and more Pierce came to sit some distance from Mona and stare. Yeah, maybe a little interest in Mona was brewing. . . .

Michael reached for Rowan's cheek. "Kiss me."

"This is a vulgar display," she purred, "and you know it. All those workmen are staring at us."

"I hope so," he said.

"Let's go home," she whispered.

"Pierce, how's Mona, you've got an update?" Michael asked. They climbed into the car. He had forgotten what it meant to ride in normal automobiles, live in normal houses, have normal dreams. Ash's voice sang to him in his sleep. He heard the musical whisper in his ear even now. And would they ever truly see Ash again? Or would Ash vanish behind all those bronze doors, shutting them out, insulated by his company, his billions, remembering them only perhaps with occasional notes, though they might call, come to New York, press his bell in the very dead of night. "I need you!"

"Ah, Mona, yes," said Pierce. "Well, she's acting strange. When Dad talks to her, she sounds like she's high as a kite. But she's okay. She's hanging around with Mary Jane. And yesterday a team started work on Fontevrault."

"Oh, I'm so glad to hear that," Michael said. "So they're going to save that place."

"Well, it had to be done, obviously, since neither Mary Jane nor Dolly Jean will stand to see it demolished. Oh, I think Dolly Jean is with them too. Now Dolly Jean looks like a withered apple, but they say she is very quick."

"I'm glad she's there," he said. "I like old people." Rowan laughed softly, resting her head on his shoulder. "Maybe we'll ask Aunt Viv to come over," he said. "And how is Bea? What is happening with Bea?"

"Well, now," said Pierce with a little tilt of his head. "Ancient Evelyn has worked the miracle there, simply by coming home from the hospital and needing care, and guess who has dashed up to Amelia to feed her soft-boiled eggs and make her talk, and make her grip tight with both hands? Dad says it's the perfect antidote for grief. I wonder if Mother's spirit isn't there."

"All the news is good news now," Rowan said with a wan smile, her voice deep as always. "And the girls will be in the house, and the silence will have to wait, and the spirits recede into the walls."

"You think they're still there?" Pierce asked with touching innocence.

God bless the Mayfairs who have never seen, and don't really believe.

"No, son," Michael said. "It's just a big beautiful house, and it's waiting for us, and for . . . new generations to come."

"For Mayfairs yet unborn," whispered Rowan.

They had just turned onto St. Charles Avenue, the heavenly corridor of green, oaks in blinding spring leaf, sun mellow, traffic slow, flash of one lovely house after another.

My town, home, everything all right, Rowan's hand in mine.

"Ah, and Amelia Street, look," he said.

How dapper the Mayfair house looked in the San Francisco style, with its fresh coat of peach with white trim and green shutters. And all the weeds gone. He almost wanted to stop, to see Evelyn and Bea, but he knew he had to see Mona first, he had to see the mother and child rolled into one. And he had to be with his wife, talking quietly in the big bedroom upstairs, about all that had happened, the tales they'd heard, the strange things they'd seen and might never tell anyone . . . except Mona.

And tomorrow he would go out to the mausoleum where Aaron was buried, and he'd do the Irish trick of just talking to Aaron, out loud, as if Aaron were answering, and if anybody didn't like it, well, they could just get out of there, couldn't they? All his family had always done that, his father going out to St. Joseph's Cemetery and talking to his grandmother and grandfather any time he felt like it. And Uncle Shamus when he was so sick, saying to his wife, "You can still talk to me after I'm gone. The only difference is I won't be answering you."

Once again the light changed, darkening, and the trees expanded, crowding out the sky and breaking it into tiny glowing fragments. The Garden District. First Street. And wonder of wonders, the house on the corner of Chestnut, amid its spring banana trees and ferns, and azaleas in bloom, waiting for them.

"Pierce, you must come in."

"No, they're waiting for me downtown. You rest. Call us when you need us." He had already slipped out to lend a manly hand as Rowan climbed from the car. And then his key was in the gate, and he was waving goodbye to them.

A uniformed guard walked along the side fence, disappearing discreetly around the end of the house.

The silence was healed, the car slipping off in light and shadow, noiseless, removed, the dying afternoon burnished and warm and without the slightest resistance. The scent of the sweet olive hung over the whole yard. And tonight he'd smell the jasmine again.

Ash had said that fragrance was the sharpest trigger of memory, a transport into forgotten worlds. And he had been so right, and what did it do to you, to be taken away from all the fragrances you needed to breathe?

He opened the front door for his wife, and felt a sudden impulse to carry her over the threshold. Hell, why not!

She gave a little unrestrained cry of delight, clutching his neck as he scooped her up.

The thing about gestures like this was not to drop the lady in question.

"And now, my dear, we are home," he growled against her soft neck again, forcing her head back as he kissed her beneath her chin, "and the smell of the sweet olive gives way to Eugenia's ever-present wax, and the scent of the old wood, and something musty and expensive and delicious to breathe."

"Amen," she said.

As he went to put her down, she clung to him for a moment. Ah, that was nice! And his aging, battered heart had not begun to pound. She would hear it, wouldn't she, with a doctor's ear? No, he stood hale and quiet, holding her against him, smelling her clean soft hair, and gazing down the polished hall, past the great soaring white doorway, at the distant murals of the dining room, touched still by the afternoon sun. Home. Here. Now, as it has never, never been for either of us.

At last she slipped from him, landing on her feet. The tiniest frown came to her forehead. "Oh, it's nothing," she said. "Only certain memories will die hard, you know. But then I think of Ash, and that is something to contemplate rather than all the sad things."

He wanted to answer, he wanted to say something about his own love for Ash, and something else, something else that was almost torturing him. It would be better to leave it alone, that's what others would advise, if ever he asked them. But he couldn't. He looked into her eyes, opening his own very wide, perhaps wide enough to look angry when he didn't mean to at all.

"Rowan, my love," he said. "I know you could have stayed with him. I know you made a choice."

"You're my man," she said with a soft explosion of breath, "my man, Michael."

Nice to carry her up the stairs, but he'd never make it, not all twenty-nine steps, and where were the young ladies, and Granny, the resurrected one? No, they could not shut themselves away now, unless by some luck the entire tribe had gone out for an early dinner.

Closing his eyes, he kissed her again. Nobody could stop him from doing that at least a dozen times. Kiss. And when he looked up again, he saw the red-haired beauty at the end of the hall, two in fact, one very, very tall, and that mischievous Mary Jane, blond braids on top of her head again, three of the most gorgeous necks in the universe, young girls like that are swans. But who was this new beauty who stood incredibly tall, and looked, why, she looked exactly like Mona!

Rowan turned, staring back down the hall.

The Three Graces, they were, against the dining room door, and Mona's face seemed to occupy two different places. This wasn't resemblance, it was duplication, and why did they stand so still, all of them in their cotton dresses, merely staring as if from a painting?

He heard Rowan gasp. He saw Mona break into a run, and then rush towards him across the polished floor.

"No, you can't do anything. You can't. You have to listen."

"Dear God," Rowan said, her weight falling heavily against him, her body shaking.

"She's my child," Mona said. "My child and Michael's, and you won't hurt her."

Suddenly it struck him, as things often do, in a rush of different stages, all clattering together to take his breath away. The baby is this young woman. The giant helix produced this. This is a Taltos as surely as Ash is a Taltos, as surely as those two under the tree are Taltos. Rowan is going to faint, she is going to go down, and the pain in my chest is killing me.

He clutched for the newel post.

"Tell me now, neither of you will hurt her."

"Hurt her? How could I do that?" Michael said.

And then Rowan began to cry, blubbering hopelessly against her clasped hands. "Oh God."

The tall girl had taken a shaky step and then another. And now would that helpless voice come out, the child voice he'd heard from the other before the shot was fired? He felt dizzy. The sun was dying as if on cue, the house returning to its natural darkness.

"Michael, sit down, sit down there on the step," said Mona.

"Dear God, he's sick," said Mary Jane.

And Rowan, snapping to, wrapped her long wet fingers around his neck.

And the tall one said:

"Well, I know this is a dreadful shock for you both, and Mother and Mary Jane have worried for days, but I myself am relieved to see you at last, and force a decision as to whether I can remain beneath this roof, as they say, your child as well as Mona's child. As you can see here, she has placed the emerald around my neck, but I bow to your decision."

Rowan was speechless. So was he. It would have been Mona's voice except it sounded older, and a little less strong, as though chastened already by the world.

He looked up to see her standing there, big spill of vivid red locks, woman's breasts and long curved legs, and her eyes, her eyes like green fire.

"Father," she whispered, dropping to her knees. Her long fingers shot out and clasped his face.

He closed his eyes.

"Rowan," she said. "Love me, please, and then maybe he will."

Rowan cried, her fingers tightening on his neck. His heart was thudding in his ears, thudding as if it were growing bigger and bigger.

"Morrigan is my name," she said.

"She's mine, my child," Mona said, "and yours, Michael."

"And I think it's time that you let me speak," said Morrigan, "that I take the burden of decision from both of you."

"Honey, slow down," he said. He blinked his eyes slowly, trying to clear his vision.

But something had disturbed this long nymph. Something had made her draw back her hands and then sniff at her fingers. Her eyes flashed to Rowan and then to him. She rose, rushing close to Rowan, before Rowan could possibly move away, sniffing at Rowan's cheeks, and then standing back.

"What is that scent?" she said. "What is it! I know that scent!"

"Listen to me," Rowan said. "We'll talk. That's what you said. Now come." She moved forward, releasing him to die of a heart attack entirely by himself, and she put her arms around the girl's waist, the girl staring down at her with comically frightened eyes.

"The scent's all over you."

"What do you think it is?" Mona asked. "What could it be?"

"A male," the girl whispered. "They've been with him, these two."

"No, he's dead," said Mona, "you're picking it up again from the floorboards, from the walls."

"Oh no," she whispered. "This is a living male." Suddenly she grabbed Rowan by the shoulders. Mona and Mary Jane sped to her side, gently tugging her arms away. Michael was on his feet. God, the creature was the same height as he was. Mona's face, but not Mona, no, not Mona at all.

"The smell is driving me mad," she whispered. "You keep this secret from me? Why?"

"Give them time to explain," Mona pleaded. "Morrigan, stop it, listen to me." And then she had the girl's hands in hers, holding them tight. And Mary Jane was standing on tiptoe.

"Now just you simmer down, long tall Sally, and let them tell us the scoop."

"You don't understand," Morrigan said, voice suddenly thick and tears gathering in her huge green eyes, as she looked again to Michael, to Rowan. "There's a male, don't you see? There's a male of me! Mother, you can smell the scent. Mother, tell the truth!" It was a scream. "Mother, please, I can't stand it!" And her sobs came like something tumbling downstairs, her face clenched in pain, her tall angular body wobbling, and bending gently as she let the other two embrace her and keep her from falling.

"Let us take her now," said Mary Jane.

"Just don't do anything, you have to swear," Mona pleaded.

"And we'll meet and we'll talk, and we'll . . ."

"Tell me," the stricken girl whispered. "Tell me, *where is he?*"

Rowan pushed Michael towards the elevator, pulling open the old wooden door. "Get in."

And the last thing he saw, as he leaned against the back wall of the elevator, was those pretty cotton dresses, as the three of them fled up the stairs together.

He lay on the bed.

"Now, don't think of it now. Don't think," Rowan said.

The wet rag felt exactly like a wet rag. He didn't like it.

"I'm not going to die," he said quietly. And what an effort, the words. Was it defeat again, was it a great ghastly defeat, and the scaffolding of the normal world buckling beneath its weight, and the future forecast once more in the colors of death and Lent, or was it something that they could embrace and contain, something that they could somehow accept without the mind shattering?

"What do we do?" she whispered.

"You are asking me this, you? What do we do?" He rolled over on his side. The pain was a little less. He was sweating all over and despised it, the feel of it, the inevitable smell. And where were they, the three beauties? "I don't know what we do," he answered.

She sat still on the side of the bed, her shoulders slightly hunched, her hair falling down against her cheek, her eyes gazing off.

"Will *he* know what to do?" Michael asked.

Her head turned as if pulled sharply by a string.

"*Him?* You can't tell him. You can't expect him to learn something like that and not . . . not go as crazy as she's

534

gone. Do you want that to happen? Do you want him to come? Nobody and nothing will stand between them."

"And what happens then?" he asked, trying to make his voice sound strong, firm, when the firmest thing he knew to do was to ask questions.

"What happens! I don't know. I don't know any more than you do! Dear God, there are two of them and they are alive and they're not ... they're not ..."

"What?"

"Not some evil that stole its way in, some lying, deceiving thing that nourished alienation, madness. They're not that."

"Keep talking," he said. "Keep saying those things. Not evil."

"No, not evil, only another form of natural." She stared off, her voice dropping low, her hand resting warmly on his arm.

If only he wasn't so tired. And Mona, Mona for how long had she been alone with this creature, this firstborn thing, this long-necked heron of a girl with Mona's features stamped on her face. And Mary Jane, the two witches together.

And all the time they had been so dedicated to their tasks, to save Yuri, to weed out the traitors, to comfort Ash, the tall being who was no one's enemy and never had been and never would be.

"What can we do?" she whispered. "What right have we to do anything?"

He turned his head, trying to see her clearly. He sat up, slowly, feeling the bite beneath his ribs, small now, unimportant. He wondered vaguely how long one could hang on with a heart that winced so quickly, so easily. Hell, not easily. It had taken Morrigan, hadn't it? His daughter, Morrigan. His daughter crying somewhere in the house with her childmother, Mona.

"Rowan," he said. "Rowan, what if this *is* Lasher's triumph? What if this was the plan all along?"

"How can we know that?" she whispered. Her fingers had gone to her lips, the sure sign that she was in mental pain and trying to think her way through it. "I can't kill again!" she said, so soft it was like a sigh.

"No, no . . . not that, no, I don't mean that. I can't do that! I . . ."

"I know. You didn't kill Emaleth. I did."

"That's not what we have to think about now. What we have to think about is—do we handle this alone? Do we try? Do we bring together others?"

"As if she were an invading organism," Rowan murmured, eyes wide, "and the other cells came to surround her, contain her."

"They can do that without hurting her." He was so tired, and almost sick. In a minute he was going to throw up. But he couldn't leave her now, he refused to be ignominiously sick. "Rowan, the family, the family first, all the family."

"Frightened people. No. Not Pierce and Ryan and Bea and Lauren . . ."

"Not alone, Rowan. We can't make the right choices alone, and the girls, the girls are swept off their feet, the girls are walking the dark paths of magic and transformation, she belongs to the girls."

"I know," Rowan sighed. "The way that he once belonged to me, the spirit who came to me, full of lies. Oh, I wish in some horrible, cowardly way . . ."

"What?"

She shook her head.

There was a sound at the door. It popped a few inches, then rode back. Mona stood there, her face faintly streaked from crying too, her eyes full of weariness.

"You won't hurt her."

"No," he said. "When did it happen?"

"Just a few days ago. Listen, you've got to come. We've got to talk. She can't run away. She can't survive out there on her own. She thinks she can, but she can't. I'm not asking you to tell her if there's really a male somewhere, just come, accept my child, listen."

"We will," said Rowan.

Mona nodded.

"You're not well, you need to rest," said Rowan.

"It was the birth, but I'm all right. She needs the milk all the time."

"Then she won't run away," said Rowan.

"Perhaps not," said Mona. "Do you see, both of you?"

"That you love her? Yes," said Rowan. "I see."

Mona slowly nodded her head. "Come down. In an hour. I think by then she'll be all right. We bought her lots of pretty dresses. She likes those. She insists we dress up too. Maybe I'll brush her hair back and put a ribbon in it the way I used to do in mine. She's smart. She's very smart and she sees . . ."

"Sees what?"

Mona hesitated. And then her answer came, small and without conviction. "She sees the future."

The door closed.

He realized he was looking at the pale rectangular panes of the window. The light was waning fast, the twilight of spring so quick. The cicadas had begun outside. Did she hear all that? Did it comfort her? Where was she now, this, his daughter?

He groped for the lamp.

"No, don't," Rowan said. She was a silhouette now, a line of gleaming light defining her profile. The room closed and then grew vast in the darkness. "I want to think. I want to think out loud in the darkness."

"Yes, I understand," he said.

She turned, and very slowly, with highly effective movements, she slipped the pillows behind him so that he could lean back, and hating himself, he let her do it. He rested, he pulled a deep breath of air into his lungs. The window was glazed and white. And when the trees moved, it was like the darkness outside trying to peer in. It was like the trees listening.

Rowan talked:

"I tell myself we all run the risk of horror; any child can be a monster, a bringer of death. What would you do if it were a baby, a tiny pink thing like they ought to be, and a witch came and laid her hands on it and said, 'It will grow up to wage war, it will grow up to make bombs, it will grow up to sacrifice the lives of thousands, millions.'

Would you choke it? I mean if you really believed? Or would you say 'No'?"

"I'm thinking," he said. "I'm thinking of things that make a kind of sense, that she's newborn, that she must listen, that those who surround her have to be teachers, and as the years pass, as she grows older, then . . ."

"And what if Ash were to die without ever knowing?" Rowan asked. "Do you remember his words? What was it, Michael? 'The dance, the circle, and the song . . .' Or do you believe the prediction in the cave? If you do believe it, and I don't know that I do, but if you do, what then? We spend our lives keeping them apart?"

The room was completely dark. Pale white streaks of light fell tentatively across the ceiling. The furnishings, the fireplace, the walls themselves had disappeared. And the trees outside still held their color, their detail, because the streetlights were shining up at them.

The sky was the leftover sky—and the color of rosy flesh, as sometimes happens.

"We'll go down," he said. "And then we'll listen. And then perhaps, perhaps, we'll call the entire family! Tell them all to come, come as they did when you were lying in this bed, when we thought you were going to die—all of them. We need them. Lauren and Paige and Ryan, yes, Ryan, and Pierce and Ancient Evelyn."

"Perhaps," she said. "Know what will happen? They will look at her, in her undeniable innocence and youth, and then they'll look to us, wondering, 'Is it true, is it so?' and begging for us to choose some path."

He slid gently off the bed, fearing nausea, making his way through the dark easily from bedpost to bedpost and then into the narrow white marble bathroom. A memory came back—the first time they had come into this part of the house, he and the Rowan he meant to marry. And there had been small bits of a broken statue lying here, on the white tiles that now appeared in the soft, colorless drench of the light. The Virgin's veiled head, snapped unevenly at the neck; one small plaster hand. What had it been, an omen?

Dear God, if Ash found her, and she found him! Dear God, but that is their decision, is it not?

"It's out of our hands," Rowan whispered from the dark.

He leaned over the basin, turned on the tap, washed his face with the cold water. For a while it ran almost warm through the pipes, and then it came from the deep earth and it was really cold. At last he dried off, patting his skin with a little mercy for once, and then he laid aside the towel. He slipped out of his jacket, stiff crumpled shirt with the stench of sweat all over it now. He wiped himself dry, and took the recommended spray can from the shelf to kill his scent. He wondered if Ash could have done that, killed the scent cold so that they wouldn't have picked it up from farewell kisses he'd given them both.

And in ancient times, could the human female pick up the scent of the human male coming through the forest? Why have we lost that gift? Because the scent is no longer the predictor of danger. The scent is no longer a reliable indicator of any threat. For Aaron, the hired killer and the stranger were one and the same. What had scent to do with two tons of metal crushing Aaron against the wall?

He pulled on a fresh shirt, and a light sweatshirt over that. Cover it all up.

"Shall we go down now?" He snapped off the light, and searched the darkness. He thought he saw the outline of her bowed head. He thought he saw a glimmer of the deep burgundy of her coat, and then he did see the white blaze of her blouse as she turned, so Southern the way she was dressed, so finished.

"Let's go," she said, in the deep, commanding voice that made him think of butterscotch and sleeping with her. "I want to talk to her."

The library. They were gathered already.

As he came in the door, he saw that Morrigan herself sat at the desk, regal in white Victorian lace with high neck and fancy cuffs and a cameo at her throat, a flood of taffeta skirt showing behind the mahogany. Mona's twin. And Mona, in softer, more careless lace, curled in the big chair, the way she'd been that day when he had appealed to Ryan

539

and Pierce to help him find Rowan. Mona, needing a mother herself and certainly a father.

Mary Jane held down the other corner, picture perfect in pink. Our witches come in pastels, he thought. And Granny. He had not realized she was there, at the corner of the sofa, until he saw her tiny wrinkled face, her playful little black eyes, and a crinkled smile on her lips.

"There they are!" she said with great flair, stretching out her arms to him. "And you a Mayfair too, out of Julien, think of it. I would have known." He bent to be kissed, to smell the sweet powder rising from her quilted robe, the prerogative of the very old, to go about clothed for bed perpetually. "Come here to me, Rowan Mayfair," she said. "Let me tell you about your mother. Your mother cried when she gave you up. Everyone knew. She cried and turned her head away when they took you from her arms, and never was the same again, ever."

Rowan clasped the small dry hands, and she too bent to receive the kiss. "Dolly Jean," she said. "You were there when Morrigan was born?" She cast her eye on Morrigan. She had not had the nerve yet to take a good look at her.

"Sure, I was," said Dolly Jean. "I knew she was a walking baby before she ever stuck her foot out of the womb. I knew! And remember, whatever you say, whatever you think, this is a Mayfair, this girl. If we've the stomach for Julien and his murdering ways, we've the stomach for a wild thing with a long neck and an Alice-in-Wonderland face! You listen now. Maybe this is a voice you've never heard before."

He smiled. Well, it was damned good that she was there, that she had taken it so in her stride, and it made him want to reach for the phone now, and begin the calls that would bring all Mayfairs together. Instead he merely sat facing the desk. And Rowan took the chair beside him.

All looked at the ravishing red-haired thing that suddenly laid her head against the high back of her chair, and curled her long white hands around its arms, breasts pushing through her stiff starched lace, waist so frail he wanted to put his hands around it.

"I'm your daughter, Michael."

"Tell me more, Morrigan. Tell me what the future holds. Tell me what you want from us, and what we should expect from you."

"Oh, I'm so glad to hear you say those words. Do you hear that?" She looked back and forth at the others and then at Rowan. "Because I've been telling them that is what was bound to happen. I have to forecast. I have to speak. I have to declare."

"Then go ahead, my dear," he said. And quite suddenly he couldn't see her as monstrous at all; he could only see her as alive, as human, as tender and fragile as all of those in this room, even himself, the one who could kill the others with his bare hands if he wanted to. And Rowan, who could kill any human with her mind. But not this creature.

"I want teachers," she said, "not the confines of a school, but tutors, with Mother and with Mary Jane, I want to be educated, to learn everything in the world, I want the solitude and protection in which to do this, with assurances that I will not be cast out, that I am one of you, that someday ..." Here she stopped as if a switch had been thrown. "Someday I shall be the heiress as my mother has planned for me, and after me, another from her line who is human perhaps ... if you ... if the male ... if the scent ..."

"Play it off, Morrigan," said Mary Jane.

"Just keep talking," said the little mother.

"I want those things which a special child would ask, of searing intelligence and insatiable hungers, but one which is reasonable and lovable, yes, surely, one whom it is possible to love and educate and thereby control."

"This is what you want?" Michael asked. "You want parents."

"Yes, the old ones to tell their tales to me, the way it was once for us."

"Yes," said Rowan firmly. "And then you will accept our protection, which means our authority and our guidance, that you're our newborn girl."

"Yes."

"And that we will care for you."

"Yes!" She rose slightly in the chair, and then stopped,

clutching both sides of the big desk, her arms like long, slender bones that should have supported wings. "Yes. I am a Mayfair. Say this with me. I am one of you. And one day, one day perhaps, by a human man, I'll conceive, and others like me will be born, from witches' blood as I was born, that I have this right to exist, to be happy, to know, to flourish. . . . God, you still have that scent. I can't bear the scent. You have to tell me the truth."

"And what if we do?" asked Rowan. "And what if we say that you must stay here, that you are far too young and innocent to meet this male, that we will set the time for a meeting . . ."

"What if we promise," said Michael, "that we will tell him? And that you can know where he is, but only if you promise . . ."

"I swear," she cried. "I'll swear anything."

"Is it that strong?" Mona whispered.

"Mother, they're frightening me."

"You have them in the palm of your hand," said the diminutive Mona nestled in the leather chair, cheeks wasted, skin pale. "They cannot harm anything that explains itself so well. You're as human as they are, don't you see? They see. Play it off. Continue."

"Give me my place," she said, her eyes growing wide and seeming to catch fire as they had when she'd cried. "Let me be what I am. Let me couple if I will. Let me be one of you."

"You can't go to him. You can't couple," said Rowan. "Not yet, not until your mind is capable of making that decision."

"You make me mad!" she cried, drawing back.

"Morrigan, knock it off," said Mona.

"You just simmer down," said Mary Jane, climbing to her feet and moving cautiously behind the desk until she could put her hands on Morrigan's shoulders.

"Tell them about the memories," said Mona. "How we taped them all. And the things you want to see."

She was trying to pick up the thread again, to prevent a flood of tears or screams, he didn't know which.

542

"To go to Donnelaith," Morrigan said in a shaky voice, "to find the plain."

"You remember those things?"

"Yes, and all of us together in the circle. I remember. I remember. I reach out for their hands. Help me!" Her voice rose again. But she had clapped her hand over her mouth, and when she cried now it was muffled.

Michael stood up and came round, gently nudging Mary Jane out of the way.

"You have my love," he said in her ear. "You hear me? You have it. You have my love and the authority that goes along with it."

"Oh, thank God." She leant her head against him, just the way Rowan did it now and then, and she cried.

He stroked her soft hair, softer, silkier than Mona's. He thought of the brief union on the sofa, on the library floor, and this, this frail and unpredictable thing.

"I know you," she whispered, rubbing her forehead against his chest. "I know your scent too, and the things you've seen, I know the smell of the wind on Liberty Street, and the way the house looked when you first walked in, and how you changed it. I know different kinds of wood, and different tools, and what it's like to rub tung oil into the grain for a long, long time, the sound of the cloth on the wood. And I know when you drowned, when you were so cold, you got warm, you saw witches' ghosts. Those are the worst kind, the strongest kind, except maybe for the ghost of a Taltos. Witches and Taltos, you must have some of us inside you, waiting to come out, to be reborn, to make a race again. Oh, the dead know everything. I don't know why they don't talk. Why doesn't he come to me, or any of them? They just dance in my memories and say those things that mattered to them then. Father, Father, I love you."

"I love you too," he whispered, his hand closing tightly on her head. He felt himself tremble.

"And you know," she said, looking up at him, tears draining from her eyes in stains down her white cheeks. "You know, Father, that one day I shall take over completely."

543

"And why is that?" he asked calmly, with a tight grip on his voice, on his face.

"Because it has to be," she said in the same sincere, heated whisper. "I learn so quickly, I'm so strong, I know so much already. And when they come from my womb, and they will come, like I came from Mother and from you, they will have this strength, this knowledge, memories of both ways, the human, the Taltos. We have learned the ambition from you. And the humans will flee from us when they know. They will flee, and the world will . . . the world will *crumble*. Don't you think, Father?"

He was shivering inside. He heard Ash's voice. He looked at Rowan, whose face remained still, impassive.

"To live together, that was our vow," he said. He bent, his lips just touching Morrigan's forehead. Smell of baby skin, fresh and sweet. "Those are the dreams of the young, to rule, to dominate all. And the tyrants of history were those who never grew up," he said. "But you will grow. You will have all the knowledge that all of us can give you."

"Boy, this sure is going to be something," Mary Jane said, folding her arms.

He stared at her, shocked rudely by her words, and the little laugh that came out of her as she shook her head. He looked at Rowan, whose eyes were once again reddened and sad as she turned her head slightly to the side, gazing at the strange daughter, and then at Mona. And only in Mona's face did he see not wonder and shock, but fear, a calculated, controlled fear.

"The Mayfairs are my kind now, too," Morrigan whispered. "A family of walking babies, don't you see? And the powerful ones should be brought together. Computer files must be scanned; all those with the double helix made to couple at once; until the numerical score has been evened, at least, at least, and then we will be side by side. . . . Mother, I must work now. I must get into the Mayfair computer again."

"Simmer down," said Mary Jane.

"What do you think and feel?" Morrigan demanded, staring directly at Rowan.

"You have to learn our ways, and maybe you'll discover someday that they are your ways too. No one is made to couple in our world. Numerical scores are not our forte. But you'll see. We'll teach you, and you will teach us."

"And you won't hurt me."

"We can't. We wouldn't," Rowan said. "We don't want to."

"And the male. This male who left his scent all over you. Is he alone too?"

Rowan hesitated, then nodded.

Morrigan looked up into Michael's eyes.

"All alone like me?"

"More alone," Michael said. "You have us, your family."

She rose to her feet, hair flying out, making several quick pirouettes as she crossed the room, the taffeta skirts rustling, reflecting the light in fluid racing flashes.

"I can wait. I can wait for him. I can wait. Only tell him, please. I leave it to you, I leave it to the tribe. Come, Dolly Jean, come, Mona, it's time to dance. Mary Jane, do you want to? Rowan and Michael, I want to dance."

She lifted her arms, turning round and round, head falling back, hair hanging long and low. She hummed a song, something soft, something Michael knew he had heard before, something perhaps that Tessa had sung, Tessa, closeted away to die without ever seeing this child? Or Ash, had he hummed this song, Ash, who would never never forgive them if they kept this secret from him, the world-weary wanderer.

She dropped to her knees beside Rowan. The two young women stiffened, but Mona motioned that Mary Jane was to wait.

Rowan did nothing. She was hugging her knees with her clasped hands. She did not move as the lithe, silent figure drew very close, as Morrigan sniffed at her cheeks, her neck, her hair. Then slowly Rowan turned, staring into her face.

Not human, no, dear God, not at all. What is she?

Calm and collected, Rowan gave no sign that she might be thinking the very same thing. But surely she sensed something like danger.

545

"I can wait," Morrigan said softly. "Write it in stone, his name, where he is. Carve it in the trunk of the funeral oak. Write it somewhere. Keep it from me, but keep it, keep it until a time comes. I can wait."

Then she drew back and, making those same pirouettes, left the room, humming to herself, the humming higher and higher until it became like a whistle.

They sat in silence. Suddenly Dolly Jean said, "Oh!" She had fallen asleep, and now she was awake. "Well, what happened?" she asked.

"I don't know," Rowan said.

She looked at Mona, and Mona looked at her, and something silent passed between them.

"Well, I better go watch her," said Mary Jane, hurrying out of the room. "Before she goes and jumps in the swimming pool again with all her clothes, or lies down on the grass back there, trying to smell those two dead bodies."

Mona sighed.

"So what does the mother have to say to the father?" Michael asked.

Mona thought for a long moment. "Watch. Watch and wait." She looked at Rowan. "I know now why you did what you did."

"You do?" Rowan whispered.

"Yeah," Mona said. "Yeah, I know." Slowly she climbed to her feet. She was leaving the room, when suddenly she turned. "I didn't mean . . . I didn't mean it was all right to hurt her."

"We know that it's not all right," said Michael. "And she's my child too, remember."

Mona looked up at him, torn, helpless, as if there were a thousand things she wanted to say, to ask, to explain. And then she only shook her head and, turning her back on them, moved towards the door quietly. At the very last, she looked back, her face a radiant burst of light, of feeling. The little girl with the woman's body beneath her fussy dress. And my sin has done this, my sin has unleashed this thing, as if from the heart and mind of Mona herself, he thought.

"I smell it too, the scent," said Mona. "A living male.

Can't you wash it off? Scrub it off with soap. Then maybe, maybe she'll calm down, she'll stop thinking about it and talking about it, she'll be all right. In the night, she may come into your room, you may wake up with her bending over you. She won't hurt you. In a way you've got the upper hand."

"How so?" Michael asked.

"If she doesn't do everything we say, you'll never tell her about the male. It's simple."

"Yes, it's a means of control," said Rowan.

"There are other means. She suffers so."

"You're tired, honey," said Michael. "You should rest."

"Oh, we will, in each other's arms. It's only when you wake and you see her sniffing at the clothes, don't be frightened. It can look kind of terrible."

"Yes," said Rowan. "We will all be prepared."

"But who is he?" Mona asked.

Rowan turned, as if to make sure she had heard this question right.

Dolly Jean, her head bowed, gave a sudden startling snore.

"Who is the male?" asked Mona, insistent, her eyes suddenly half-mast with exhaustion and slightly haunted.

"And if I tell you," said Rowan, "then you must keep it from her. Let us be the strong ones on that score. Trust us."

"Mother!" Morrigan called. A waltz had begun, Richard Strauss, strings, one of those lovely bland records that you can listen to for the rest of your life. He wanted to see them dancing, but in a way he didn't.

"Do the guards know she's not to go out?" Michael asked.

"Well, not really," Mona said. "You know, it would be easier if you told them to go away. She . . . she upsets them. I can control her more easily if they're gone. She won't run away, not from her mother."

"Yes," Rowan said. "We'll dismiss them."

Michael was unsure.

But then he nodded. "We are in this . . . together."

The voice of Morrigan called out again. The music surged. Mona slowly turned and left them.

Late in the night, he could hear them laughing still, and the music now and then, or was it a dream of Stuart Gordon's tower? Then the keys of the computer tapping away, and that laughter, and the soft rumble of their running feet on the stairs. And the sound of mingled voices, young and high and very sweet, singing that song.

Why try to sleep, but then he was gone, too tired, too needy of rest and of escape, too hungry for the simplicity of cotton sheets, and Rowan's warm body against his. Pray, pray for her. Pray for Mona. Pray for them. . . .

"Our Father, Who art in Heaven, hallowed be Thy name, Thy kingdom come—"

His eyes opened wide. "Thy kingdom come. No." The feeling of sudden distress was too vast, yet elusive. He was too tired. "Thy kingdom come." He couldn't think it out. He turned over and buried his face in the crook of Rowan's warm neck and shoulder.

"Love you," she whispered, a murmured prayer out of the depths of sleep, perhaps, more comforting than his prayer had been.

Thirty-four

THE CLEAN MONOTONY of snow, of meetings without end, of phone calls, of the sheets of faxes full of statistics, summaries, of the business of life which he himself had made, reaching for the gold and dreams.

At midday he put his head down on the desk. It had been a full five days since Michael and Rowan had gone home, and they had not called him, or written even a note. And now he wondered if his gifts had somehow made them sad or been the wrong thing, or if they were blotting him out the way he tried to blot out the memory of Tessa, of Gordon dead on the floor, of Yuri stammering and wringing his hands, of cold winter in the glen, and the jeers of Aiken Drumm.

What do we seek? What do we need? How can we know what will make us happy? It was a simple thing to pick up the phone, to call Rowan or Michael, to ask if they were all right, if they had recovered from their journey.

And what if their voices were brittle and indifferent, and he was left with the instrument in his hand, and the wire gone dead after careless farewells? No, that would have been worse than nothing.

Or more truly, it was not what he wanted.

Just go there. Just see them. Without lifting his head, he pressed the button. Prepare the plane. Fly away from the city of bitter cold, to the lost land of love. Just look at them, see their house with its warm lights, see through the windows they so lovingly described, and go away without a sound, without begging for their eyes to meet yours. Just look at them.

There will be a comfort in that.

Once all dwellings were small and shut up, windowless, fortified. And you couldn't see the beings within. But now it was different. One could gaze upon a perfect life as if peering at a painting. Sheer glass was enough to shut one out, and demarcate the secret turf of each one's love. But the gods were kind, and you could peep inside. You could see those you missed.

It will be enough. Do it. And they'd never know. He wouldn't frighten them.

The car was ready. Remmick had sent the bags down. "Must be good to be going south, sir," he said.

"Yes, to summerland," he replied.

"That's what Somerset means, sir, in England."

"Yes, I know," he said. "I'll see you soon. Keep my rooms warm. Call me at once if . . . Well, don't hesitate if there is anything."

A speaking twilight, a city so wooded still that the creatures of the air sang the songs of dusk. He slipped out of the car blocks from the house. He knew the way. He had checked his map, and now he walked past the iron picket fences, and vines of florid pink trumpet flower. Windows were already full of light, yet the sky stretched radiant and warm in all directions. Listen to the cicadas' song, and are those starlings who swoop down as if to plant a kiss, when it is simply to devour?

He walked faster and faster, marveling at the uneven sidewalks, the buckling flags, the moss-covered bricks, so many many beautiful things to touch and to see. And at last he came to their corner.

There stood the house where a Taltos had been born. Grand for these times, with its stucco walls made to look like stone, and chimneys rising high into the clouds.

His heart beat too fast. His witches.

Not to disturb. Not to beg. Merely to see. Forgive me that I walk along the fence, under the bending boughs of these flowered trees, that here suddenly in this deserted street, I climb the fence and slip down into the moist shrubbery.

No guards around this place. Does that mean you trust me, that I would never come, in stealth, unbidden, unexpected? I don't come to steal. I come only to take what anyone can have. A look from afar, we take nothing from those who are watched.

Take care. Keep to the hedges and the tall shiny leafed trees swaying in the wind. Ah, the sky is like the moist soft sky of England, so near, so full of color!

And this, was it the crape myrtle tree, beneath which their Lasher had stood, frightening a small boy, beckoning Michael to the gate, Michael a witch child whom a ghost could spot, passing in the real world through zones of enchantment.

He let his fingers touch the waxy bark. The grass was deep beneath his feet. The fragrance of flowers and green things, of living things and breathing soil, was everywhere. A heavenly place.

Slowly he turned and looked at the house. At the iron lace porches stacked one upon the other. And that had been Julien's room up there, where the vines groped with helpless tendrils in the empty air. And there, beyond that screen, the living room.

Where are you? Dare I come just a little closer? But to be discovered now would be so tragic, when the evening is descending in this raiment of violet, and the flowers glow in their beds, and once again the cicadas sing.

Lights went on in the house. Behind lace curtains. Illuminating paintings on the walls. Was it so simple that, veiled in the dark, he could draw near to those windows?

The murals of Riverbend, wasn't that what Michael had described, and might they be gathering this soon for their meal? He walked as lightly as he could across the grass. Did he look like a thief? Rosebushes shielded him from those behind the glass.

So many. Women old and young, and men in suits, and voices raised in controversy. This was not my dream. This was not my hope. But, eyes fastened to the portal, he couldn't step away. Just give me one glimpse of my witches.

And there Michael was, like the direct answer to his prayer, gesticulating in a little fury it seemed, with others who pointed their fingers and talked, and then all on cue sat down, and the servants glided through the room. He could smell the soup, the meat. Alien food.

Ah, his Rowan, coming into the room, and insisting upon something as she looked at the others, as she argued, as she made the men again take their seats. A white napkin had dropped to the floor. The murals blazed with perfect summer skies. If only he could have moved closer.

But he could see her clearly and him too, and hear the noises of spoons against plates. Scent of meat, of humans, scent of . . . ?

That had to be his error! But the scent was so sharp and old and tyrannical that it took hold and the moment slipped right out of his hands. *Scent of the female!*

And just when he was telling himself again, It cannot be, when he was searching for the little red-haired witch, there came into the room the Taltos.

He closed his eyes. He listened to his heart. He breathed her scent as it emanated through brick walls, out of seams and cracks around glass, seeping from God knows where, to stir the organ between his legs, to make him stand back, breathless, wanting to flee, and absolutely immovable.

Female. Taltos. There. And her red hair all aflame beneath the chandelier and the arms out as she spoke, rapid, anxious. He could hear the bare high notes of her voice. And, oh, the look on her face, her newborn face, her arms so delicate in her sheer dress of Point d'Esprit and her sex, deep underneath, pulsing with the scent, a flower opening in darkness and alone, the scent penetrating to his brain.

My God, and they have kept this from him! Rowan! Michael!

She is there, and they have not told him, and would that he never knew. His friends, you *witches*!

Coldly, shivering, maddened by the scent and drugged, he watched them through the glass. Humankind, not his kind, shutting him out, and the lovely princess standing there, and was she crying out, was she ranting, were those tears in her eyes? Oh, splendid, beautiful creature.

He moved out from behind the shrubbery, not by will but by simple allowance. Behind the slim wooden post he stood, and now he could hear her plaintive cries.

"It was on the doll, the same scent! You threw away the wrapping, but I smelled it on the doll. I smell it in this house!" Bitterly she wailed.

Oh, newborn baby.

And who was this august council that would not answer her plea? Michael gestured for calm. Rowan bowed her head. One of the other men had risen to his feet.

"I'll break the doll if you don't tell me!" she screamed.

"No, you won't do that," Rowan cried out, and now it was she who rushed to the girl. "You won't, you won't, Michael, get the Bru, stop her!"

"Morrigan, Morrigan . . ."

And she, crying so softly and the scent gathering and moving on the air.

And I loved you, thought Ash, and I thought for a little while I would be one of you. Anguish. He wept. Samuel had been so right. And there, behind these thin panes . . . "Do I weep, do I go?" he whispered. "Do I smash the glass? Do I confront you with your own deceptive silence, that you did not tell me this! That you did not! That you did not!

"Oh, we weep like children!"

And he wept as she wept. Didn't they understand? She had picked up his scent from those gifts, dear God, what agony for her, poor newborn!

She lifted her head. The men gathering around her could not make her sit down. What had caught her eye? What made her look to the window? She couldn't see him beyond the self-contained glare of the light.

He stepped backwards into the grass. The scent, yes, catch the scent, my dear, my darling newborn woman, and closing his eyes, he staggered backwards.

She had pressed herself to the very glass. Her hands spread out on the panes. She knew he was there! She'd caught it.

What were prophecies, what were plans, what was reason, when for eternity he had seen her ilk only in his dreams, or old and withered and mindless as Tessa had been, when she was hot and young, and searching for him.

He heard the glass break. He heard her cry, and watched in stunned, overwhelmed silence as she ran towards him.

"Ashlar!" she cried in that thin high voice, and then her words came in the rush that only he could hear, singing of the circle, the memories, singing of him.

Rowan had come to the edge of the porch. Michael was there.

But that was gone, and with it all its obligations.

Across the wet grass she came.

She flew into his arms, her red hair wrapping round him. Bits and pieces of shining glass fell from her. He held her against him, her breasts, her warm beating breasts, his hand slipping up beneath her skirts to touch the warmth of her sex, the living fold, wet and heated for him, as she moaned and licked at his tears.

"Ashlar, Ashlar!"

"You know my name!" he whispered, kissing her roughly. How could he not tear loose her clothes here and now?

She was no one that he had ever known or remembered. She was not Janet who had died in the flames. She did not need to be. She was herself, his kind, his pleading, begging love.

And look how still they stood, watching him, his witches. Others had come to the porch, witches all! Look at them! Not lifting a finger to come between them, to part him from the precious female that had fled to his arms, Michael's face wondering, and Rowan's, what was it, what did he see in the light, was it resignation?

He wanted to say, I am sorry. I must take her. You know this. I am sorry. I did not come to take her away. I did not come to judge and then steal. I did not come to discover and then withhold my love.

She was eating him with her kisses, and her breasts, her tender full breasts. But who had come now, rushing out across the flags, was it the red-haired witch, Mona?

554

"Morrigan!"

"I am gone now, Mother, I am gone." She sang the words so fast, how could they understand? But it was enough for him. He lifted her, and just as he began to run, he saw Michael's hand raised in farewell, the sharp simple gesture which gives permission to go, and all good speed, and he saw his beautiful Rowan nod her head. The little witch Mona only screamed!

He hurried with his beauty through the darkness, her long light limbs nothing to him as he ran, across the dark stretch of grass, along stone paths, through yet another dark and fragrant garden. Moist and thick as the ancient forests.

"It's you, it's you. Oh, and the scent on the gifts, it drove me mad."

On the top of the wall he placed her, vaulting it and gathering her up again in the dark, empty street. He could scarcely bear this. Catching her hair in a great handful, he tugged her head back, lips moving down her throat.

"Ashlar, not here!" she cried, though she was soft and submissive in his arms. "In the glen, Ashlar, in the glen, in the circle at Donnelaith. It stands still, I know it, I see it."

Yes, yes, he didn't know how, in the long hours of the transatlantic flight, bundled with her in the dark, he would endure. But he mustn't hurt her tender nipples, he mustn't break her fragile glowing skin.

Clasping her hand, he ran, bringing her with great youthful strides alongside him.

Yes, the glen.

"My darling," he whispered. He took one glance back at the house, rising so darkly and solidly there, as if full of secrets, of witches, of magic. Where the Bru watches all. Where the book resides. "My bride," he said, crushing her to his chest. "My baby bride."

Her feet rang out on the stones, and then he swept her up again, running faster than they could run together.

Janet's voice came to him from the cave. Old poetry, mixed with fear and remorse, skulls gleaming in the dark.

And memory is no longer the goad, no longer the thought, no longer the mind making order of all that ponderous weight of our lives, failures, blunders, moments of

555

exquisite loss, humiliation—our long lives. No, memory was something as soft and natural as the dark trees rising over their heads, as the purple sky in its last valiant light, in the woodland purr of the evening all around them.

Inside the car, he took her in his lap, tore open her dress, grabbed her hair, and rubbed it to his lips, his eyes. She hummed, she cried.

"The glen," she whispered, her face reddened, eyes glistening.

"Before morning comes here, it will be morning there, and we will be in those stones," he said. "We will lie in that grass, and the sun will rise on us, inseparable."

"I knew it, I knew . . ." she whispered in his ear. His mouth closed on her nipple, sucking the sweet nectar of flesh alone, moaning as he burrowed against her.

And the dark car sped out of the multishaded gloom, leaving behind the somber corner and its regal house, the great leafy branches holding darkness like ripe fruit beneath the violet sky, the car a projectile destined for the green heart of the world, carrying them inside it, the two, male and female, together.

2:30 a.m. July 10, 1993

From Anne Rice's

SERVANT
of the
BONES

available in mass market paperback . . .

"I DIDN'T REMEMBER JERUSALEM," he said. "I wasn't born there. My mother was carried off as a child by Nebuchadnezzar along with our whole family, and our tribe, and I was born a Hebrew in Babylon, in a rich house—full of aunts and uncles and cousins—rich merchants, scribes, sometime prophets, and occasional dancers and singers and pages at court.

"Of course," he smiled. "Every day of my life, I wept for Jerusalem." He smiled. "I sang the song: 'If I forget thee, O Jerusalem, may my right hand wither.' And at night prayers we begged the Lord to return us to our land, and at morning prayers as well.

"But what I'm trying to say is that Babylon was my whole life. At twenty, when my life came to its first—shall we say—great tragedy, I knew the songs and gods of Babylon as well as I knew my Hebrew and the Psalms of David that I copied daily, or the book of Samuel, or whatever other texts we were constantly studying as a family.

"It was a grand life. But before I describe myself further, my circumstances, so to speak, let me just talk of Babylon.

"Let me sing the song of Babylon in a strange land. I am not pleasing in the eyes of the Lord or I wouldn't be here, so I think now I can sing the songs I want, what do you think?"

"I want to hear it," I said gravely. "Shape it the way you would. Let the words spill. You don't want to be careful

559

with your language, do you? Are you talking to the Lord God now, or are you simply telling your tale?"

"Good question. I'm talking to you so that you will tell the story for me in my words. Yes. I'll rave and cry and blaspheme when I want. I'll let my words come in a torrent. They always did, you know. Keeping Azriel quiet was a family obsession."

This was the first time I'd seen Azriel really laugh, and it was a light heartfelt laugh that came up as easily as breath, nothing strangled or self-conscious in it.

He studied me.

"My laugh surprises you, Jonathan?" he asked. "Don't you know laughter is one of the common traits of ghosts, spirits and even powerful spirits like me? Have you been through the scholarly accounts? Ghosts are famous for laughing. Saints laugh. Angels laugh. Laughter is the sound of heaven, I think. I believe. I don't know."

"Maybe you feel close to heaven when you laugh," I said.

"Maybe so," he said. His large cherubic mouth was really beautiful. Had it been small it would have given him a baby face. But it wasn't small, and with his thick black eyebrows and the large quick eyes, he looked pretty remarkable.

He seemed to be taking my measure again too, as if he had some capacity to read my thoughts. "My scholar," he said to me, "I've read all your books. Your students love you, don't they? But the old Hasidim are shocked by your biblical studies, I suppose."

"They ignore me. I don't exist for the Hasidim," I said, "but for what it's worth my mother was a Hasid, and so maybe I'll have a little understanding of things that will help us."

I knew now that I liked him, whatever he had done, liked him for himself in a way—young man of twenty, as he said, and though I was still fairly stunned from the fever, from his appearance, from his tricks, I was actually getting used to him.

He waited a few minutes, obviously ruminating, then began to talk:

"Babylon," he said. "Babylon! Give the name of any city which echoes as loud and as long as Babylon. Not even Rome, I tell you. And in those days there was no Rome. The center of the world was Babylon. Babylon had been built by the gods as their gate. Babylon had been the great city of Hammurabi. The ships of Egypt, the Peoples of the Sea, the people of Dilmun, came to the docks of Babylon. I was a happy child of Babylon.

"I've seen what stands today, in Iraq, going there myself to see the walls restored by the tyrant Saddam Hussein. I've seen the mounds of sand that dot the desert, all of this covering old cities and towns that were Assyrian, Babylonian, Judean.

"And I've walked into the museum in Berlin to weep at the sight of what your archaeologist, Koldewey, has recreated of the mighty Ishtar Gate and the Processional Way.

"Oh, my friend, what it was to walk on that street! What it was to look up at those walls of gleaming glazed blue brick, what it was to pass the golden dragons of Marduk.

"But even if you walked the length and breadth of the old Processional Way, you would have only a taste of what was Babylon. All our streets were straight, many paved in limestone and red breccia. We lived as if in a place made of semiprecious stones. Think of an entire city glazed and enameled in the finest colors, think of gardens everywhere.

"The god Marduk built Babylon with his own hands, they told us, and we believed it. Early on I fell in with Babylonian ways, and you know everybody had a god, a personal god he prayed to, and beseeched for this and that, and I chose Marduk. Marduk himself was my personal god.

"You can imagine the uproar when I walked in the house with a small pure-gold statue of Marduk, talking to it, the way the Babylonians did. But then my father just laughed. Typical of my father, my beautiful and innocent father.

"And throwing back his head, he sang in his beautiful voice, 'Yahweh is your God, the God of your Father, your Father's Father, the God of Abraham, Isaac, and Jacob.'

"To which one of my somber uncles popped up at once, 'And what is that idol in his hands!'

"'A toy!' said my father. 'Let him play with it. Azriel,

when you get sick of all this superstitious Babylonian stuff, break the statue. Or sell it. You cannot break our god, for our god is not in gold or precious metal. He has no temple. He is above such things.'

"I nodded, went into my room, which was large and full of silken pillows and curtains, for reasons I'll get to later, and I lay down and I started just, you know, calling on Marduk to be my guardian.

"In this day and age, Americans do it with a guardian angel. I don't know how many Babylonians took it all that seriously either, the Babylonian personal god. You know the old saying, 'If you plan ahead a god goes with you.' Well, what does that mean?"

"The Babylonians," I said, "they were a practical people rather than superstitious, weren't they?"

"Jonathan, they were exactly like Americans today. I have never seen a people so like the ancient Sumerians and Babylonians as the Americans of today.

"Commerce was everything, but everybody went about consulting astrologers, talking about magic, and trying to drive out evil spirits. People had families, ate, drank, tried to achieve success in every way possible, yet carried on all the time about luck. Now Americans don't talk about demons, no, but they rattle on about 'negative thinking' and 'self-destructive ideas' and 'bad self-image.' It was a lot the same, Babylon and America, a lot the same.

"I would say that here in America I have found the nearest thing to Babylon in the good sense that I have ever found. We were not slaves to our gods! We were not slaves to each other.

"What was I saying? Marduk, my personal god. I prayed to him all the time. I made offerings, you know, little bits of incense when nobody was watching; I poured out a little honey and wine for him in the shrine I made for him in the deep brick wall of my bedroom. Nobody paid much attention.

"But then Marduk began to answer me and talk to me. I'm not sure when Marduk first started answering me. I think I was still fairly young. I would say something idly to him, 'Look, my little brothers are running rampant and my

562

father just laughs as though he were one of them and I have to do everything here!' and Marduk would laugh. As I said spirits laugh. Then he'd say some gentle thing like 'You know your father. He will do what you tell him, Big Brother.' His voice was soft, a man's voice. He didn't start actually speaking questions in my ear till I was about nine and some of these were simply little riddles and jokes and teasing about Yahweh. . . .

"He never got tired of teasing me about Yahweh, the god who preferred to live in a tent, and couldn't manage to lead his people out of a little bitty desert for over forty years. He made me laugh. And though I tried to be most respectful, I became more and more familiar with him, and even a little smart mouthed and ill behaved.

" 'Why don't you go tell all this nonsense to Yahweh Himself since you are a god?' I asked him. 'Invite him to come down to your fabulous temple all full of cedars from Lebanon and gold.' And Marduk would fire off with 'What? Talk to your god? Nobody can look at the face of your god and live! What do you want to happen to me? What if he turns into a pillar of fire like he did when he brought you out of Egypt . . . ho, ho, ho . . . and smashes my temple and I end up being carried around in a tent!'

"I didn't truly think about it till I was perhaps eight years old. That was when I first came to know that not everybody heard from his or her personal god, and also I had learnt this: I didn't have to talk to Marduk to start him off talking to me. He could begin the conversation and sometimes at the most awkward moments. He also had bright ideas in his head. 'Let's go down into the potters' district, or let's go to the marketplace,' and we would."

"Azriel, let me stop you," I said. "When all this happened, you spoke to the little statue of Marduk or you carried it with you?"

"No, not at all, your personal god was always with you, you know. The idol at home, well, it received the incense, yes, I guess you could say that the god came down into it then to smell the incense. But no, Marduk was just there."

THE WITCHING HOUR

by Anne Rice

~3

On the lonely veranda of a faded New Orleans mansion, a mute and fragile woman sits rocking. *The Witching Hour* begins. . .a story of a great dynasty of witches spanning four centuries, of a family given to poetry and incest, to murder and philosophy, a family that over the ages is itself haunted by a powerful, dangerous and seductive being. . .

Published by The Random House Publishing Group.
Available at bookstores everywhere.

THE MUMMY

by Anne Rice

Dr. Ramsey, an expert Egyptologist and socialite in turn of the century London, hides a secret. He is really the great Ramses of Egypt's glorious past, doomed forever to wander the earth for drinking the elixir of life. His passion to quell hungers that can never be satisfied grows more intense, and searing memories of his last reawakening at the behest of Cleopatra burn in his immortal soul. These very emotions will drive Ramsey to commit an act of unspeakable horror to fulfill a great love undiminished by the centuries. . .

Published by The Random House
Publishing Group.
Available at bookstores everywhere.

Look for
Anne Rice's mesmerizing saga:

SERVANT OF THE BONES

Anne Rice takes us now into the world of Isaiah and Jeremiah, and the destruction of Solomon's temple, to tell the story of Azriel, Servant of the Bones.

He is ghost, genii, demon, angel—pure spirit made visible. He pours his heart out to us as he journeys from an ancient Babylon of royal plottings and religious upheavals to the Europe of the Black Death and to the modern world. There he finds himself, amidst the towers of Manhattan, in confrontation with his own human origins and the dark forces that have sought to condemn him to a life of evil and destruction.

Published by The Random House
Publishing Group.

Also available as a Random House
Large Print Edition.